SerboCroatian-English Colloquial Dictionary

An Exercise in Cross-cultural Cognitive Linguistics

Danko Šipka

SerboCroatian-English Colloquial Dictionary

All inquiries should be directed to:
Dunwoody Press, 6564 Loisdale Ct., Suite 800
Springfield, VA 22150, USA

ISBN: 1-881265-71-4
Library of Congress Catalog Card Number: 00-104526
Printed and bound in the United States of America

SerboCroatian-English Colloquial Dictionary

An Exercise in Cross-cultural Cognitive Linguistics

Danko Šipka

2000
Dunwoody Press

Acknowledgments

I wish to thank the following who have helped in production of this dictionary by contributing their time and expertise:

Wayles Browne, who has read the first, second, and third drafts, provided useful comments and corrected my non-native English.

Tom Creamer, who has read portions of the preliminary draft, the entire first, second, third and final drafts, helped format the text, contributed valuable lexicographic comments and corrected my non-native English.

Pavle Ćosić, who has read the preliminary list and appended it with new entries and senses, supplied the etymologies for a number of entries, and provided a number of comments on the first draft.

Siniša Gligić, who has recorded several tapes which are included in the corpus.

Paul Hackett, who has supplied the font used in the dictionary.

Marti Hawkins, who has read the introductory text as well as portions of the second draft and provided useful comments.

Jack Jones, who has read the introductory text and provided valuable comments.

Dušan-Vladislav Pažđerski-Pavlović, who has recorded several tapes which are included in the corpus.

Aung Kyaw Oo, who has formatted the dictionary.

Stephen Poulos, who made possible numerous automatic replacements and corrections.

"Viper-Man" (also known as David, Bill, Bob, Joker, Loser, Tony's Uncle, Uncle Pedro's ex brother-in-law, copulating linguist's next-door neighbor, and Steven Harrell), who has served as a consultant on American English slang.

Rajna Dragičević, Vladimir Šipka, and Marinko Zekić, each of whom appended numerous entries and their meanings.

Linnea Hasegawa, who has read the final draft and suggested useful comments.

Last but not least, I would like to thank my wife Ljiljana and my children Olja and Igor for their continuous support during this project.

Table of Contents

KENT

Fellow, I know thee.

OSWALD:

What dost thou know me for?

KENT

A knave; a rascal; an eater of broken meats; a
base, proud, shallow, beggarly, three-suited,
hundred-pound, filthy, worsted-stocking knave; a
lily-livered, action-taking knave, a whoreson,
glass-gazing, super-serviceable finical rogue;
one-trunk-inheriting slave; one that wouldst be a
bawd, in way of good service, and art nothing but
the composition of a knave, beggar, coward, pandar,
and the son and heir of a mongrel bitch: one whom I
will beat into clamorous whining, if thou deniest
the least syllable of thy addition.

King Lear, II, 2

Nota Bene: Serbo-Croatian, like all languages, has a colloquial or sub-language which is well known to and widely used by native speakers but is less often seen in print. Within this colloquial language is a considerable corpus of “off-color” speech which very seldom appears in print and is rarely documented at all. This off-color corpus is rich in obscene and abusive terminology, including bitter racial and ethnic slurs and quite imaginative sexual and scatological imagery. Such language is widely used in the Serbo-Croatian speaking nations of the country formerly known as Yugoslavia, often quite casually, often with extreme malice, and as elaborate invective such as that in the passage from the work of William Shakespeare cited on the opposite page. Dunwoody Press and the author undertook the compilation of this book in response to the need to document the Serbo-Croatian colloquial corpus. Some users may find certain terms and their English translations offensive, but the author and his editors have endeavored to reflect and document a part of the language which has heretofore not been adequately treated. If we have done this adequately, we will have fulfilled our role as linguists and lexicographers.

1. Colloquial Serbo-Croatian

1.1 Defining Colloquial

The notion of the colloquialness is an elusive one. It is an example of what Lipka (1992) calls a 'notational term', the definition of which depends not only on content, but also on the approach used. The description of colloquial lexicon as used in this dictionary is shown in Figure 1.

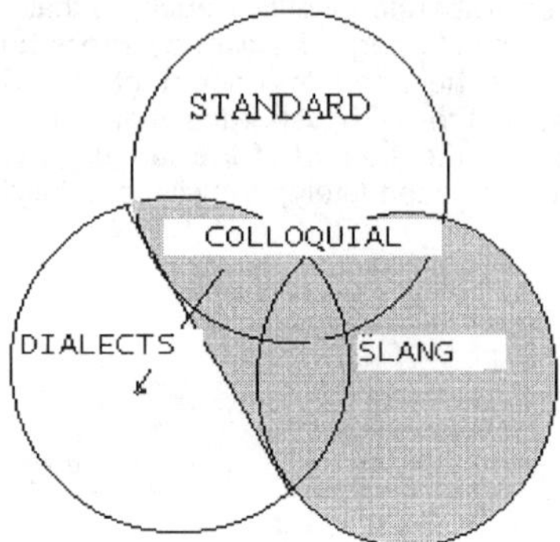

Figure 1: Spheres of the Colloquial

For our purposes "colloquial" includes:

1. slang words,
2. words that belong to one or more of the standard languages, but are more a part of spoken style than written style,
3. words from dialects, if they are known and used over a sufficiently wide area so that an outsider might actually encounter them (not just in a few villages).

Thus, all these components are informal and spoken.

The following two quotations from AHD (1992:s.v.) express other possible terms which can be used to refer to this field or its subfields.

> **non·stan·dard** [...] ***Usage Note:*** The term *nonstandard* was introduced by linguists and lexicographers to describe usages and language varieties that had previously been labeled with terms such as *vulgar* and *illiterate. Nonstandard* is not simply a euphemism but reflects the empirical discovery that the varieties used by low-prestige groups have rich and systematic grammatical structures and that their stigmatization more often reflects a judgment about their speakers rather than any inherent deficiencies in logic or expressive power. Note, however, that the use of nonstandard forms is not necessarily restricted to the communities with which they are associated in the public mind. Many educated speakers freely use forms such as *can't hardly* or *ain't I* to set a popular or informal tone. Some dictionaries use the term *substandard* to describe forms, such as *ain't,* associated with uneducated speech, while reserving *nonstandard* for forms such as *irregardless,* which are common in writing but are still regarded by many as uneducated. But *substandard* is itself susceptible of disparaging interpretation, and most linguists and lexicographers now use only *nonstandard,* the practice followed in this dictionary.

> **di·a·lect** [...] ***Synonyms:*** *dialect, vernacular, jargon, cant, argot, lingo, patois.* These nouns denote forms of language that vary from the standard. *Dialect* applies to the vocabulary, grammar, and pronunciation characteristic of a specific geographic area or locality. The *vernacular* is the everyday language spoken by a people as distinguished from the literary language. *Jargon* is the specialized language used by a social or occupational group but not understood by the general public. *Cant* now usually refers to the specialized vocabulary of a group or trade and is often marked by the use of stock phrases. *Argot* applies especially to the language of the underworld or, by extension, to that of any specific group. *Lingo* is applied, often humorously or

contemptuously, to language that is unfamiliar or so specialized that it is difficult to understand. *Patois* refers especially to a regional dialect without a literary tradition or to a creole.

The term *colloquial* used here is a compromise between scholarly rigor on the one hand, and a term with which a potential user would be familiar, on the other hand.

Relations between standard and colloquial lexemes are not merely ones of neighboring and exclusion as might appear at first glance. As can be seen from Table 1, some Serbo-Croatian colloquialisms have the same pronunciation as standard lexemes, while other colloquialisms have the same meaning as their corresponding standard lexemes.

	Standard		*Colloquial*	
Level	*Phonological*	*Semantic*	*Phonological*	*Semantic*
1.	s(j)ekira	'axe'	sikira	'axe'
2.	kuća	'house'	ćaku	'house'
3.	l(j)etovalište	'summer vacation resort'	l(j)etovalište	'prison'
4.	zujati	'buzz'	zujati	'have fun'

Table 1

In examples 1. and 2. above the substandard lexemes have identical semantic units with their standard counterparts, while their phonological units have been transformed. In examples 3. and 4., however, the phonological units are identical and the semantic ones are transformed. In both cases the substandard lexemes are based directly on the existence of their standard counterparts.

It is therefore important to stress the links between the standard and colloquial forms of Serbo-Croatian. The sphere of colloquial hinges on the sphere of the standard speech.

1.2 Serbo-Croatian: Its Colloquial and Standard Forms

There are at least three different standard forms of Serbo-Croatian, distinguished ethnically or geographically: 1. Serbian, spoken by Serbs (8 million), 2. Croatian, spoken by Croats (4.5 million), 3. Bosnian Muslim, spoken by Bosnian Muslims (2 million). The vast majority of Montenegrins (600,000) speak the Serbian standard, but recently there have been attempts to create Montenegrin, as a fourth standard within Serbo-Croatian. These standards are in official use in the countries and territories where their respective ethnic groups constitute the majority. Serbian is thus the official standard of the Federal Republic of Yugoslavia and of the Republic of Srpska (a part of Bosnia-Herzegovina). Croatian is the official standard of Croatia and the regions of the Muslim-Croat Federation (a part of Bosnia-Herzegovina) with a Croatian majority. And finally Bosnian Muslim is the official standard of the regions of the Muslim-Croat Federation with a Bosnian Muslim majority. These standards share grammatical structures (with some minor exceptions) while exhibiting lexical differences.

A map of the region and its ethnic composition in the year 1991 is presented in Figure 2a. The distribution of ethnic groups in the region has been substantially changed by the policies of ethnic cleansing, and the present-day distribution is approximately as presented in Figure 2b.

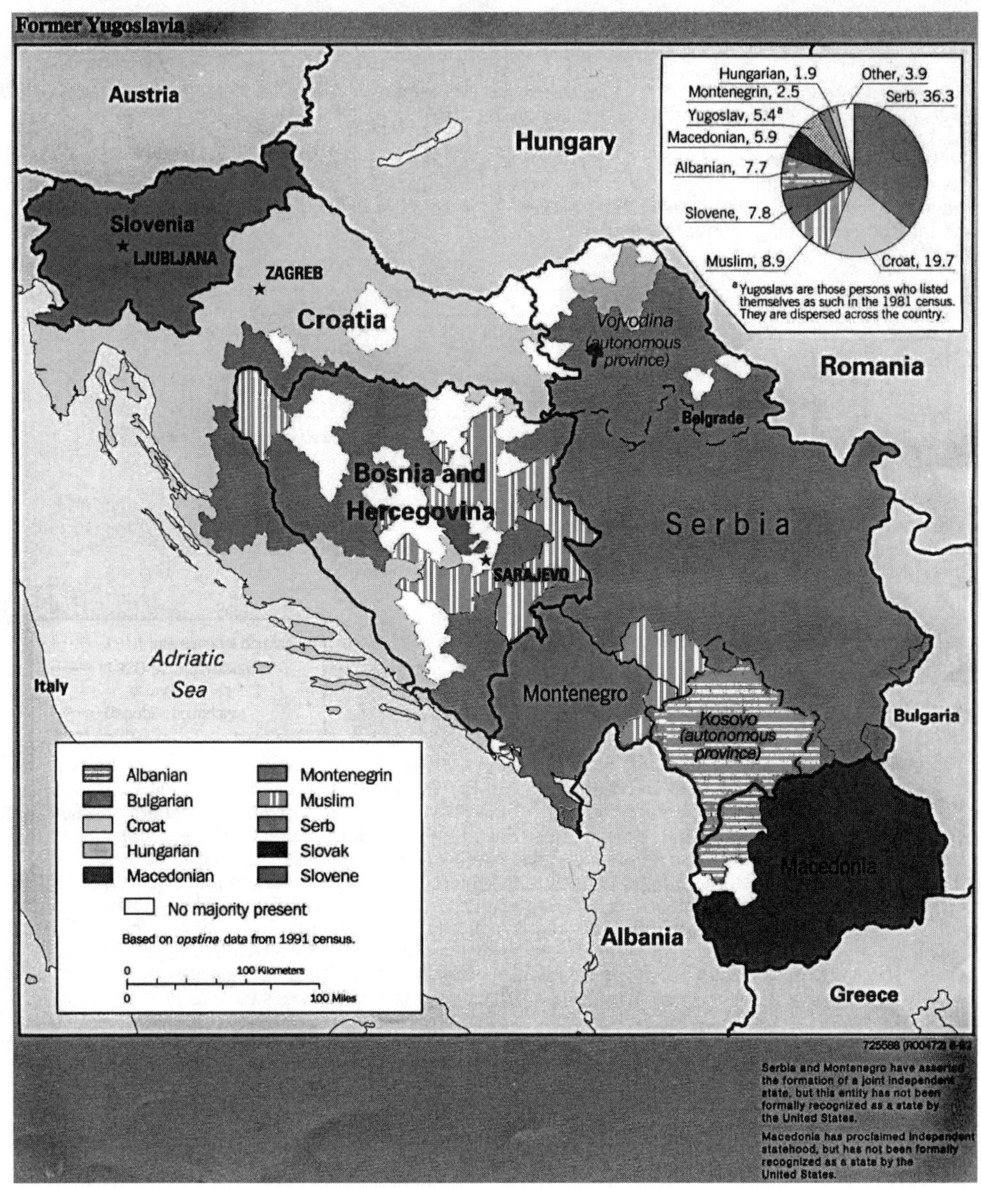

Figure 2a: Ethnic Distribution in pre-1990 Yugoslavia

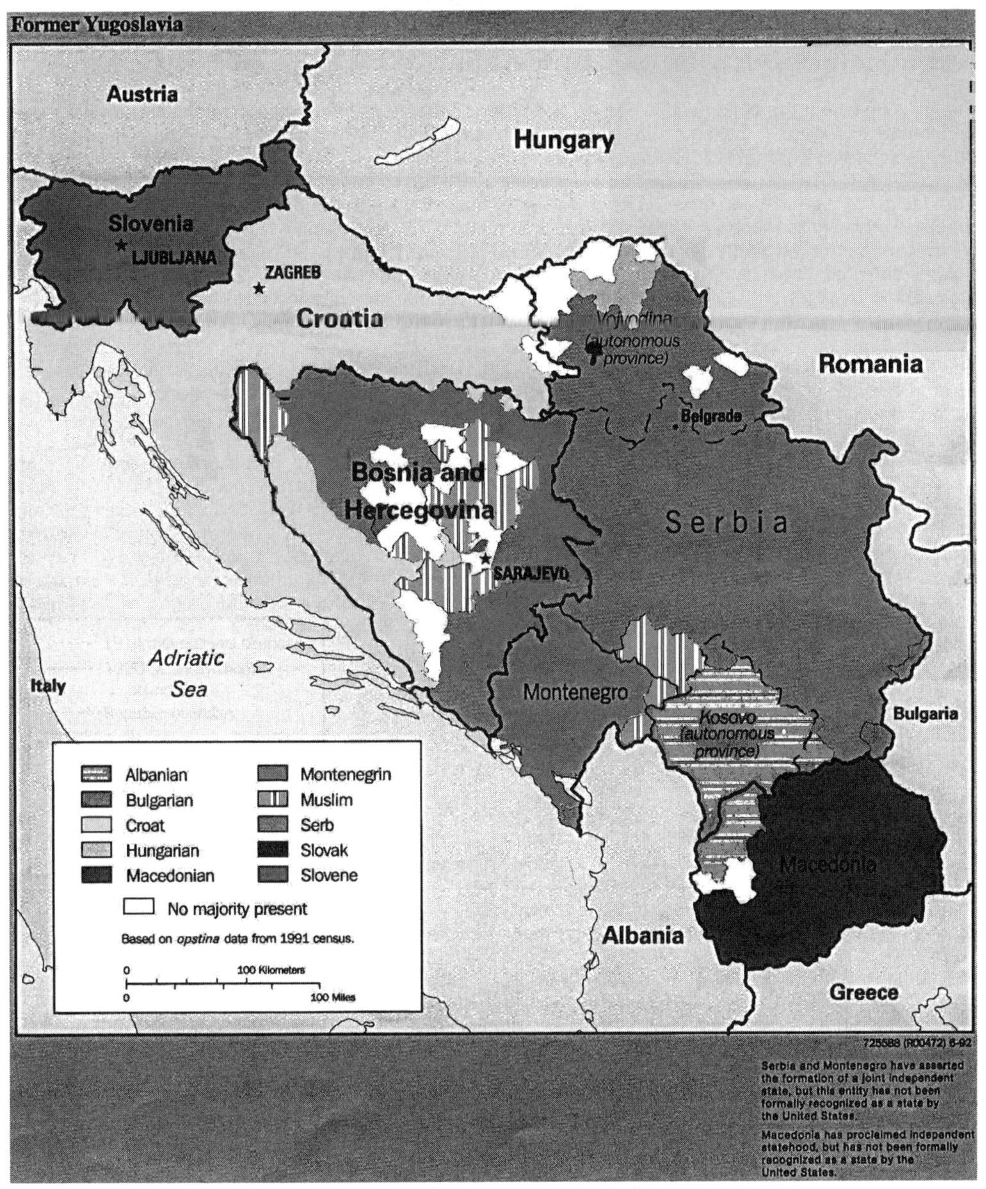

Figure 2b: Ethnic Distribution in the Former Yugoslavia as of 1996

Because of these national standards, some linguists deny the existence of Serbo-Croatian per se, claiming that each of these standards represents a distinct Slavic language (see Okuka, 1998, Bugarski and Hawkesworth, 1992 for more information).

The division within the colloquial field is an even more intricate one. In addition to the three categories mentioned in Figure 1 (colloquial in its narrower sense, dialects, and slang) and ethnic background, other factors also contribute to diversity in this field.

The factor of ethnicity is often interwoven with that of territory. Some lexemes are thus used exclusively by Serbs (such as *bùva* 'lie', 'false information', 'joke'), others used only by the speakers of Serbo-Croatian in Serbia (for example *bïoskop* 'cinema'). Others are used by inhabitants of Bosnia (like *bölan* 'intensifier used to address a single male in direct informal communication'), notwithstanding their ethnic background. These territorial boundaries are not always consistent with either dialectal or administrative borders, but more frequently reflect historic and/or cultural circles and influences.

The colloquial lexicon is also divided along the lines of different social and professional groups, such as drug addicts, criminals, students, etc. Each of these groups constitutes a subculture of its own, with its own specific beliefs and values.

There is no one-to-one correspondence between the three ethnic standards and colloquial forms used by Serbs, Croats and Bosnian Muslims. On the one hand, two urban vernaculars within the same ethnic group might be mutually unintelligible (as Croatian vernaculars of Split and Zagreb can be), and on the other hand, one urban vernacular can be shared by people with different ethnic affiliation (as was the case in the pre-1990 Sarajevo). Thus, according to *Playboy* (1999) a policeman is *drot, pajkan, rijamu, rora* in Zagreb and *murjak, pandur, tovarić* in Split. In contrast, all ethnic groups in Sarajevo use the word *drot* to refer to a police officer. Furthermore, even if a colloquial lexeme is ethnically marked, it frequently represents a tendency to more frequent usage within one ethnic group rather than an either/or situation.

Even though colloquial forms differ from the standard ones primarily in the lexicon, there are also certain differing colloquial grammatical features which will be discussed in the next section.

1.3 Grammatical Features of Colloquial Serbo-Croatian

Varieties of colloquial Serbo-Croatian differ from their standards to a greater or lesser degree. While the most common features are listed below, one should also consult the relevant literature (such as Peco, 1970; Ivić, 1958; Polovina, 1989) for a comprehensive account of possible differences.

Phonological differences can be found in both inventory and distribution. Varieties of colloquial Serbo-Croatian exhibit the following significant differences from the standards.

Phonemic inventories (standard forms are given in parentheses):

a. additional phonemes, which cannot be found in the standards: *ś, ź, dz, ∂* (schwa or semivowel as pronounced in English 'Columbus' [k∂l∂mb∂s]), as in *śes* (sjesti 'sit'), *źenica* (zjenica, 'pupil of the eye'), *dzvono* (zvono 'bell'), *s∂s* (sa 'with'), most of which are limited to one dialectal territory,
b. absence of phonemes which exist in the standards: *h, f* as in *aljina* (haljina 'female dress'), *vabrika* (fabrika 'factory'),
c. neutralization of certain oppositions which exist in the standards, for example the opposition: *č:ć, dž:đ*, as in *ćesto* (često 'frequently'), ćega (čega 'what' in genitive case), *hođa* (hodža 'imam'), *đamija* (džamija 'mosque'),
d. the existence of diphthongs where the standards have simple vowels, for example: *uon* 'he' instead of standard *on,*
e. different acoustic values, especially of the vowels, for example a very narrow or very wide *e* sound, as opposed to the neutral *e* in the standards.

The differences in phonemic inventories are not evenly distributed throughout the Serbo-Croatian language area. For example, additional phonemes, such as *ś, ź* are restricted to some Montenegrin and Herzegovian dialects, and *č/ć* neutralization is more likely to occur with Bosnian Muslims and Croats than with Serbs.

Distribution of the phonemes:

a. vowel *i* in the context where the standards have e, je or ije (ikavian reflex of the old-Slavonic vowel jat'), for example: *pisma* (pesma, pjesma 'song'), *mliko* (mleko, mlijeko 'milk'),

b. loss of a vowel, mostly after the stress, for example: *stànca (stànica 'station, stop'), stòlca (stòlica 'chair'), četr̃nēst* (četr̃naēst 'fourteen'), *sràt (sràti 'defecate'),*
c. vowel contractions: *išo (išao 'went'), debo (debeo 'obese'),*
d. consonant cluster reductions: *varedni (vanredni 'extraordinary'), masan (mastan 'fat'),*
e. secondary consonant next to another consonant: *oktombar (oktobar 'October'), vazna (vaza 'vase'), cvikcangle (cvikcange 'cutting pliers'),*
f. secondary consonant between two vowels: *radijo (radio 'worked'), nosijo (nosio 'carried'),*
g. doubling of a consonant: *jedannes (jedanaest 'eleven'),*
h. phonemic permutations: *infrakt (infarkt 'heart attack').*

In addition to these differences, syllabic permutations are frequently encountered, such as: *diora (radio 'worked'), tisra (srati 'defecate').* These syllabic permutations initially were meant to produce a secret language. Now they are somewhat of a language game, where one moves the first syllable to the end of the word, thus, for example: *sra-ti* → *ti-sra.* There is also a more complex and not so widely distributed form of this game, where in addition to the permutation the prefix jo- and the suffix -nj are attached, for example *doktor* → *ktordo* → *jo-ktordo-nj* → *joktordonj* 'doctor'.

There are also considerable differences in the accent system (for example, dynamic stress as opposed to tonal accent in the standards) and in the placement of accent (stress on the final syllable, which cannot be found in the standards).

Morphological differences vary from a typologically different inflection system to a minor difference in certain endings. Thus Southern Serbian dialects have analytic declension (prepositions instead of endings, for example: dialectal: *na brat*, standard: *bratu* 'to brother'), and prefixal comparative (as opposed to the suffixal one in the standards, for example: dialectal: *brz-pobrz* 'fast-faster', standard: *brz:brži* 'fast-faster'). Numerous other urban vernaculars and dialects exhibit the following differences in relation to the standard (standard forms are given in brackets):

a. absence of a form which exists in the standard (e.g. aorist and imperfect tenses, as in imperfect *radijah* 'I have been working', aorist *uradih* 'I have completed my work'),
b. presence of a form which does not exist in the standard (e.g. narrative imperative, as in *Mi udri po njima* 'We attacked them'),
c. *ije*-pronominal and adjectival endings, e.g.: *tije (tih 'that', genitive plural, ovije (ovih 'this', genitive plural), dobrije (dobrih 'good', genitive),*
d. indeclinable adjectives, e.g.: *bomba* 'excellent', *puška* 'excellent', *super* 'excellent',
e. *t/ć*-infinitive, e.g.: *nosit (nositi 'carry'), radit (raditi 'work'), doć (doći 'to arrive'),*
f. *o/a*-masculine singular past participle, e.g.: *došo (došao 'came'), doša (došao 'came'), reko (rekao 'told'), reka (rekao 'told'),*
g. *l*-masculine singular past participle, e.g.: došal *(došao 'came'), nosil (nosio 'carried').*

Syntactic differences range from specific uses of particular forms to unique verb governing patterns, for example:

a. *za* + infinitive instead of za + deverbal noun: *za pojest (za jelo 'for eating'), za popit (za piće 'for drinking'),*
b. narrative imperative instead of the perfect tense: *on udri po nama (on je udario po nama 'he started to hit us'),*
c. *za* + genitive instead of *za* + accusative: *za puta (za put 'for the trip'), za čega (za šta 'for what'),*
d. *sa sve* + instrumental instead of *sa* + instrumental: *sa sve decom (sa decom 'with children').*

Similar to phonological differences, morphological and syntactic markers of substandard forms are not evenly distributed throughout the entire area. For example, the a-past participle is found mostly along the Adriatic coastline, the *sa sve* + instrumental construction is found mostly in Serbia.

1.4 Colloquial Serbo-Croatian and Its Cultures

Urban versus rural, ethnic, regional, and social are the main cultural divisions within colloquial Serbo-Croatian.

The division between urban and rural cultures differentiates slang from dialects. Urban culture is innovative and heterogeneous, while rural culture remains traditional and monolithic. This is mirrored in the language so that the dialectal lexicon comes mostly from the common Slavic heritage and borrowings from those languages which had historical ties with Serbo-Croatian. It remains almost free from semantic extensions. In slang, on the other hand, one can observe abundant semantic extensions.

Ethnic boundaries coincide with those of religion. Serbs are Orthodox Christians, Croats are Catholic, and Bosnian Muslims are followers of Islam. These three religions represent at the same time three cultural spheres in the region. In language this means that certain notions either will be present or absent. Bosnian Muslims have several derogatory names for pigs, because their religion requires that they avoid pork in their diet, which is not the case with Serbs and Croats. The cultural sphere also determines the languages from which the borrowings come. Bosnian Muslims thus use more Turkish loanwords than Serbs or Croats.

Regional differentiation divides the area of colloquial Serbo-Croatian into the following broadly defined regions:

1. Mediterranean, along the Adriatic coast,
2. Dinaric, in the Dinaric mountains in the center, with its subregions
    2a. Bosnian (in Bosnia),
    2b. Montenegrin (in Montenegro),
3. Kajkavian, in the north west,
4. Serbian Ekavian, in the east with its subsets,
    4a. southern Serbian,
    4b. Vojvodinian in the North.

Each of these regions has both different dialectal features (Kajkavian and Southern Serbian being most distant from the standard) and different sources of borrowing (the Mediterranean region has a high proportion of borrowings from Italian, and the Dinaric region has numerous Turkish loanwords).

Finally, slang is divided into several spheres, which broadly overlap with social groups and/or areas of interest. With respect to their relevance in the lexicon, the following categories can be identified:

a. alcohol,
b. automotive,
c. crafts,
d. crime,
e. features and characteristics,
f. gambling,
g. media,
h. military,
i. music,
j. narcotic drugs,
k. politics,
l. school,
m. sexual and digestive organs and activities,
n. sports,
o. university.

1.5 Lexical Fields and Relationships Within Colloquial Serbo-Croatian

Based on the analysis above, one can build a network of lexical fields within colloquial Serbo-Croatian as presented in Figure 3:

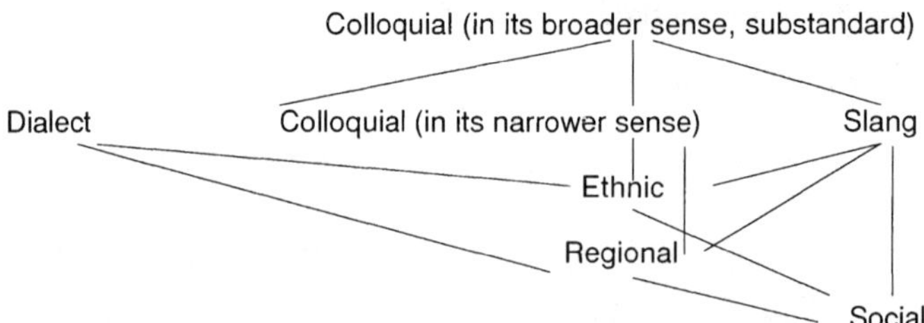

Figure 3: Relations between Colloquial Lexical Fields

A lexeme can thus be marked by a category of social stratification, ethnic and regional factors all at the same time.

The distribution of lexical fields in the data of this dictionary is presented in Tables 2a and 2b.

Domain	Count	Percent
Colloquial	4870	19.96
Colloquial and Dialectal	349	1.43
Colloquial and Slang	14	0.06
Dialectal	388	1.59
Dialectal and Colloquial	171	0.7
Slang	18612	76.27
Total	*24404*	*100.01*

Table 2a: Distribution of Lexical Fields in the One-Word Lexical Units

Domain	Count	Percent
Colloquial	1751	36.43
Colloquial and Dialectal	80	1.66
Dialectal	465	9.67
Dialectal and Colloquial	32	0.67
Slang	2479	51.57
Total	*4807*	*100.00*

Table 2b: Distribution of Lexical Fields in the Multi-Word Lexical Units

A more elaborate count for these fields is provided in section 2.8.

Synonymy is the most prominent of all lexical relations in this lexicon. Table 3 shows the number of synonyms for the concepts, which have fifty or more synonyms in their respective nests. The fact that these concepts have a large number of synonyms is a window into the conceptual world of the speakers who use them. For example, the abundance of the synonym nest of synonyms for male homosexuals paired with the sparseness of the lexemes denoting female counterparts points both to intolerance toward sexual minorities and to the inequality of women. The dominance of the nest for sexual intercourse, paired with the high frequency of synonyms for other activities related to it, point to an exaggerated interest in sex.

Synonym nest	Number of synonyms
moderate curse	940
strong curse	571
engage in sexual intercourse with (of a male)	484
weak curse	372
stupid or mentally deficient person	256
penis	227
beat up	205
female	201
lie	186
vagina	178
cheat, swindle	176
male homosexual, gay	169
talk persistently and meaninglessly, blabber, chatter	167
prostitute, hooker	160
sexual intercourse	151
policeman, cop	150
very strong curse	138
hit, punch	137
die, kick the bucket	132
sleep, nap	125
steal, swipe	121
run away, flee	109

engage in sexual intercourse with	105
buttocks, butt	103
get drunk	102
fight, fist fight	99
trick, cheat, swindle	94
prison	90
inhabitant of the countryside, hick, bumpkin	86
excellent, awesome	84
drink (alcohol)	82
loose woman	82
spend one's time in useless activities, fool around, mess around	80
troublemaker, rowdy, ruffian	78
prolonged and meaningless talk, blabber, chatter	69
senior citizen	69
alcoholic, drunk	67
informer, stoolie, snitch	65
worthless or despicable person	63
cheating, swindling	61
engage in fellatio	61
masturbate	58
money	58
walk	58
insane, nuts	57
look, watch, scope out	57
urinate	57
boring person, bore	55
male sexual partner (of a female)	55
coward, chicken	52
destroy, ruin	50

Table 3: Synonym Nests

The list of all nests for one-word entries is provided in section 4.2 (English-SerboCroatian Index).

One should stress that there is a wide range of differences between these Serbo-Croatian cultures and their English equivalents. The differences range from the emphasis on ethnicity in the Serbo-Croatian cultures (as opposed to race and geography in English) to the existence of a more sizable and varied field of obscenities and curses in Serbo-Croatian than in English. The task of bridging these two worlds is therefore considerably more intricate than in a general dictionary.

1.6 Polysemic Structures

One of the most prominent features of substandard lexemes is the abundance of semantic extensions, most notably the metaphoric ones.

The semantic extensions identified in the dictionary point to the three relevant distinctions given in Table 4:

1.	substandard-internal	standard→substandard
2.	semantic-internal	phonetic→semantic
3.	culture-bound	more general

Table 4: Types of Semantic Extensions

Line 1, Table 4 indicates that a substandard semantic extension can have its source domain in substandard or in standard lexicon. The first can be seen in *mundaroš* 'cheater, swindler' with its destination domain 'smuggler' (both meanings are substandard) or *eki* 'pragmatic operator used to express surprise' and 'question tag' (both meanings are substandard). The second situation can be illustrated by: *devojka* 'young female' (standard) and 'prostitute' (substandard) or standard *taster* 'key' (e.g. on a keyboard) and substandard 'informer'.

The first part of line 2, Table 4 has been thoroughly discussed by linguists. For example, the metaphor *Udaljeno mesto je kao rupa* 'Remote place is like a hole' in an internal semantic extension *rupa* 'hole' - 'remote place, hellhole' or *Riđi ljudi izgledaju kao mrkva* 'Redheads look like carrots' is behind the extension *mrkva* 'carrot' and 'redhead'. The second value is seldom mentioned in literature. This concept applies to the partial similarity of forms which triggers semantic extension. Thus, substandard Serbo-Croatian has a series of lexemes to denote a homosexual with the following source domains: *pedala 'pedal', pedikir 'pedicure', pešak 'pedestrian', peškir 'towel', Peđa 'proper name', Pežo 'Peugeot, make of car'.* The only link between these meanings and 'male homosexual' is that they are phonologically similar to *peder,* the most common substandard word for a male homosexual.

Finally, the extension can be culture-bound or more general as indicated in line 3. Table 5 provides several examples of culture-bound metaphoric extensions:

	lexeme	***source domain***	***link***	***target domain***
1.	*krmak*	'boar' (the animal)	a non Muslim is like a boar	'non-Muslim'
2.	*leš*	'corpse'	a senior citizen is already a corpse	'senior citizen'
3.	*pop*	'priest'	a homosexual is like a priest (no wife)	'homosexual'
4.	*dijete*	'child'	a female child is just a child, i.e. not the (male) child one wishes to have	'female child'

Table 5: Culture-Bound Extensions

Example 1 is determined by one's religious/ethnic affiliation (Bosnian Muslim) and certain religious practices. Example 2 is determined by one's membership in an age group. Example 3 is determined by the Catholic religion (celibacy is compulsory for Catholic priests). Example 4 is determined by sexism.

On the other hand: *rasturiti* 'destroy' which extends into 'win' or *plakati* 'cry', which extends into 'complain' has a much wider cross-cultural distribution for the simple fact that they are based on certain (almost) universal cognitive and affective faculties of the human species.

The (sub)cultural characteristics which determine any particular semantic extension can be very intricate and non-transparent for those outside that (sub)cultural milieu. The lexeme *fataljist* 'person who cleans parks' is determined by the following linguistic facts: a. The existence of a substandard verb *fatati* 'to catch'; b. the existence of the noun *list* 'leaf'; c. the existence of a stereotype that an Albanian accent turns *l* into *lj*, which changes *list* into *ljist*; and d. the existence of the noun *fatalist* 'fatalist'. In addition, there is a common perception that Albanians (therefore c. above) performed such jobs in the former Yugoslavia. The lexeme *fatalist* is changed into 'Albanian' *fataljist*, re-segmented into: *fata-ljist* 'catches leaves' but still remains present (a person with the social-economic status of a garbage man is perceived as a fatalist). The dictionary corpus contains numerous examples of similar intricate networks.

The data further shows that there are three typical organizations of semantic structures, understood as Weberian ideal types (i.e. an ideal notion which does not necessarily appear in that form in each of its concrete instances):

1. radial (Figure 4)
2. linear (Figure 5)
3. network (Figure 6)

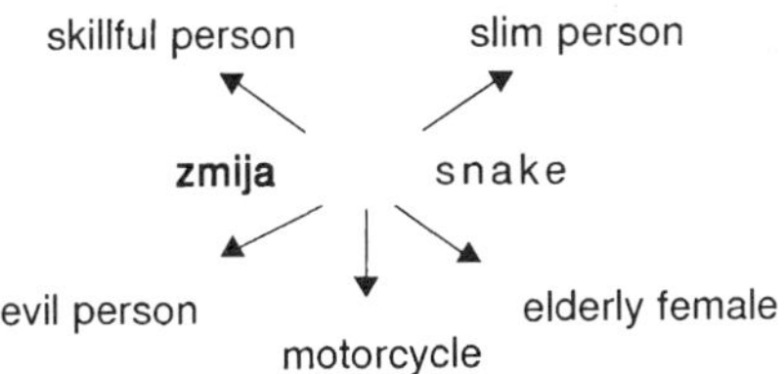

Figure 4: Radial Extension

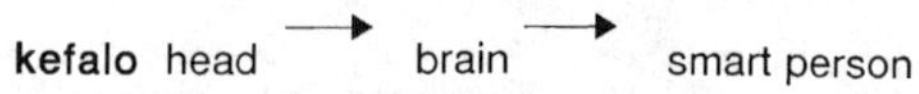

Figure 5: Linear Extension

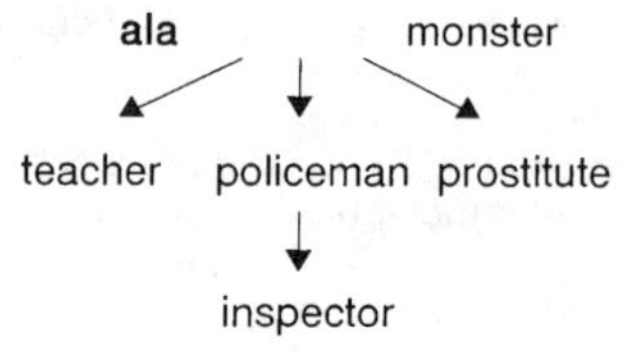

Figure 6: Network Extension

In the first example (Figure 4), the lexeme *zmija* in its literal meaning 'snake', is the source for all of the other extensions: A skillful person will get through everything just like a snake, a slim person looks like a snake... All metaphoric extensions spread radially from this source. Where there are only two meanings (i.e. the case of branching), they can be viewed as a special case of the radial category. In the second example (Figure 5), the semantic structure develops in a linear manner: from *kefalo* 'head' to 'brain' (the brain is in the head) and from this meaning develops 'smart person' (who 'has brains'). Finally, the third example (Figure 6) combines both previously mentioned principles. From *ala* 'monster' we have radial development into 'teacher' (a monster to students), 'policeman' (a monster to criminals) and finally 'prostitute' (as ugly as a monster). At the same time there is a linear development 'monster'→'policeman'→'inspector', just as in the example from Figure 5.

Each of these three models has a standard-substandard version, where the source belongs to the standard lexicon; and an internal substandard version, where both meanings belong to the substandard lexicon. If we compare the following two examples from Table 6 we can see both standard-substandard (lexeme 1) and internal substandard situations (lexeme 2).

Lexeme	*Standard*	*Substandard*	*Substandard*
1. KELERABA	kohlrabi ->	inhabitant of the countryside ->	mentally deficient person
2. KEFALO	head ->	mind ->	smart person
Lexeme	*Substandard*	*Substandard*	*Substandard*

Table 6: Standard and Substandard in Semantic Extensions

The most frequent instances of semantic extensions include:

1. All females are desirous of sex
2. All females are prostitutes
3. Elderly people are already dead
4. A female is equal to her vagina
5. A handicapped person is stupid
6. Inhabitants of the countryside are mentally deficient
7. Male homosexuals are ridiculous and unfriendly
8. Outgroup members are lower beings
9. Sexual intercourse is an act of violence with a male in the active role

Therefore the verbs 'chop', 'drill', 'gnaw', 'hit', 'kick', 'nail', 'poke', 'prick', 'stab', 'slaughter', 'tear apart', are all used to designate sexual intercourse.

Again, the nature and frequency of these extensions offers an insight into the conceptions rooted in different Serbo-Croatian cultures. The most salient features mirrored in the language are the lack of tolerance for anything beyond traditional patriarchal patterns of behavior and beliefs, and strong male chauvinism.

1.7 The Origin of Colloquial Serbo-Croatian

Colloquial Serbo-Croatian evolves mostly from semantic extensions. All other factors (derivation, transformations of form, borrowing) contributed to the formation of this lexicon to a lesser degree. For example, the non-modified loan-words constitute less than 8% of the total lexicon.

The following table represents the proportion of the factors mentioned above for each meaning in the main dictionary text:

Factor	Count	Percent
Semantic Extension	10420	42.70%
Modification	1993	8.17%
Word Formation	1332	5.46%
Word Formation, Semantic Extension	4196	17.19%
Word Formation, Modification	21	0.09%
Modification, Word Formation	11	0.05%
Modification, Semantic Extension	984	4.03%
Word Formation, Modification, Semantic Extension	32	0.13%
Semantic Extension, Modification	3	0.01%
Semantic Extension, Word Formation	1	0.00%
Word Formation, Semantic Extension, Modification	4	0.02%
Modification, Word Formation, Semantic Extension	5	0.02%
Lack of any Modification, Word Formation, or Extension	5402	22.14%
Total	24404	100.00%

Table 7: Factors in the Origin of the One-Word Lexical Items

The proportion of main sources from which the meanings have been borrowed is given in Table 8.

Origin	Count	Percent
Common Slavic inheritance in Serbo-Croatian	13369	54.79
German	2195	9.00
Near Eastern	1941	7.95
Arbitrarily Invented or Unclear	1689	6.91
Latin	796	3.26
English	681	2.79
Greek	668	2.74
Italian	663	2.72
French	617	2.53
Gypsy	385	1.58
Slavic onomastic item	260	1.07
[. . .]	[. . .]	[. . .]
Total (106 sources)	24404	100.00

Table 8: Sources of Borrowing of the One-Word Lexical Items

Other sources of borrowing are below the 1%. It is important to stress the dominance of Slavic vocabulary and also the rather high appearance of Gypsy lexical elements, much higher than in the standards.

As far as English borrowings are concerned both semantic and formal modifications exhibit considerable differences when compared with the situation in the general lexicon (see Filipović, 1990 for a comprehensive account of the English loanwords in standard Serbian/Croatian).

The following processes are characteristic for the substandard adaptation of the borrowings as opposed to the standard one:

1. Clippings, as in: *čiketina* 'chicken meat' (chick/en/+/pil/etina 'chicken'),

2. re-semantizations, as in *antifriz* 'bad hair day', where *antifriz* 'antifreeze' has been re-semantized into: *anti-* 'anti' and *friz/ura/* 'hairstyle', *dizajn* 'stealing', where *dizajn* 'design' has been re-semantized to coincide with the root of the verb *dizati* 'lift', and in slang 'steal',
3. intentional creation of ambiguity, as in: *Dragiša* '24-hour food and variety store', where the English word *drugstore* (*dragstor* in Serbo-Croatian) has been modified to coincide with the proper name *Dragiša*.
4. Creative use of metaphors, as in *džuboks* 'prostitute' derived from 'jukebox' using the insertion of coins into a jukebox as the basis for this metaphorical extension,
5. modifications by methods specific for substandard usage, as in *arba* 'bar' (modified from 'bar' by permutation and vowel insertion),
6. extensive use of borrowed suffixes, as in: *bediška* 'bad feeling' (English bad with the Gypsy suffix -*iška*), *filmadžija* 'film maker' (English film with the Turkish suffix -*džija*),
7. influence of the Anglo-Saxon popular culture, media in particular, as in *Bond* 'very important and influential person' (after movie character James Bond), *čita* 'ugly person' (after Tarzan's ape).

The presence of English loanwords in slang confirms the general trend of the use of language in this sphere. It is active and creative since various modifications of both form and meaning have been performed more frequently and with a wider spectrum of modifying mechanisms than in the standards.

2. Dictionary Structure

2.1 Methodology

The methodological framework used in this dictionary can be described as cross-cultural cognitive linguistics. The following concepts are of particular importance:

1. The concept that "The conventional meaning of a lexical item must be equated with the entire network, not with any single node." Langacker (1991:3),
2. the binary (phonological-semantic) model of symbolic units, as presented in Langacker (1991),
3. the role of metaphor in language, as presented in Lakoff and Johnson (1980),
4. the concept that "In natural language meaning consists in human interpretation of the world. It is subjective, it is anthropocentric, it reflects predominant cultural concerns and culture-specific modes of social interaction as much as any objective features of the world 'as such'", Wierzbicka (1988:2).

The above four concepts have shaped the microstructure of this dictionary. Thus a notation to register the network of semantic, mostly metaphorical, extensions has been devised. The field with literal translation of the meaning was introduced to bridge the gap between the cultures of Serbo-Croatian and those of the English language. Finally, all alternations of the phonological side of linguistic signs have been marked.

In presenting items with semantic extensions source senses precede their metaphorical extensions even if the extensions are more frequent. This strategy was recently advocated by van der Meer (1999).

2.2 Scope, Sources, Inclusion Criteria, Size

The scope of this dictionary is colloquial Serbo-Croatian as defined in 1.1 above. The dictionary contains over 23,800 entries, with over 19,300 one-word and over 4,500 multi-word lexical items.
As has been argued, the colloquial field is a very elusive one. In order to make the dictionary as representative as possible, triangulation has been used as a principal strategy in gathering materials for this dictionary. Therefore the field is approached from several different perspectives and the sources used represent qualitatively different categories which complement each other. The following sources have been used:

a. dictionaries and word lists (slang, dialects, obscene words, thematic lists, etc.),
b. papers and monographs about colloquial language,
c. works of literature (drama in particular) in which colloquial language has been used,
d. popular music lyrics,
e. newspapers in which colloquial language is used,
f. recordings of informal spoken language from electronic and printed media,

g. colloquial language in the movies,
h. recordings of spontaneous speech in informal situations,
i. surveys and interviews of native speakers,
j. consultations with colleagues involved in similar projects.

A full list of sources used in this dictionary is provided in section 2.9.1.

The policy was to include only those examples from the sources listed above. It was not possible to include all phonetically changed forms. One should therefore be aware that practically any lexeme listed in the dictionary can also be found in a form which has the features described in 1.3. Thus the infinitive of any verb listed in the dictionary with its *-ti* or *-ći* (*raditi, doći*) ending can also occur in its shorter form ending in *-t* or *-ć* (*radit, doć*) respectively.

Several additional issues relating to inclusion criteria should be highlighted here. First, onomastic material is included only if it is connected with the colloquial milieu either through the denotative side (e.g., denoting popular bars or promenades) or through the effect pertinent to that milieu (e.g. by being obscene). Second, the status of some entries labeled as Bosnian Muslim (such as *hudovica* 'widow', *hastal* 'table, desk') is at present unclear. These entries have been a part of colloquial speech for years but there have recently been attempts to introduce them into standard Bosnian Muslim. Such entries have been included simply because most speakers of Serbo-Croatian accept them as colloquial. Third, a rather liberal policy in including multi-word lexical items has been applied. One of the most prominent features of the colloquial sphere is its dynamic development, which makes the difference between lexicalized items and collocations rather fuzzy. The author's main strategy was to include those items that are either fully lexicalized or on their way to being lexicalized. Although the author has excluded those multi-lingual items with obvious collocational or occasional status (such as *Klinci koncertiraju* 'Children are engaging in an orgy', lit. 'Kids are playing a concert'), the dictionary still contains a number of items which might be interpreted as non-lexicalized in a different approach. One should mention curses in this respect. Curses are not only an inextricable element of the colloquial discourse but they also offer a kind of window into the culture. Although in Serbo-Croatian one can curse practically anything, certain entities such as mother, sister, father, and God occur in these curses most frequently, which in turn points to predominant values in the culture. It is important to note that there is no shock value in cursing someone or something that is not dear to the person intended to be hurt or insulted by the curse.

2.3 Macrostructure

The main body of the dictionary is a list of entries alphabetized according to the Latin Serbo-Croatian alphabet in the following order:

ə A B C Č Ć D DŽ Đ DZ E F G H I J K L LJ M N NJ O P R S Š Ś T U V Z Ž Ź

The letters ə, DZ, Ś, Ź are not part of the standard alphabet but are needed for some colloquial items.

Multiword lexical units are included in the entries of their respective heads, and also as separate alphabetically ordered units if they are not adjacent to their headword. The head of the multiword lexical unit is typically a 'trajector' (the most prominent element in the scene construal, as defined in cognitive linguistics) or any most prominent element of the phrase. This vastly overlaps with the traditional distinction of heads versus complements or modifiers in a phrase.

Appendix

An English-SerboCroatian index for one-word entries is included.

2.4 Microstructure

Each entry in the main body consists of:

1. Headword with marked stress,
2. part of speech and inflectional tag,
3. alternative form(s) of the headword with the part-of-speech and inflectional tag(s) (where applicable), with two consecutive slashes denoting an alternative part-of-speech and inflectional tag(s) of the same headword,
4. definition in Standard English,

5. nonstandard English equivalent (where applicable, only in those cases in which the definition does not suffice to fully convey the Serbo-Croatian meaning),
6. regional label (when applicable),
7. domain label,
8. attitude label (when applicable),
9. etymological labels,
10. literal meaning, given only in the cases in which the meaning is the source domain for metaphorical extensions, such as 'balvan' lit. log -> moron,
11. form in standard language, used only in the case in which colloquial form is a transformation of the form in standard language, as in: standard 'bicikl' -> coll. 'baciklo',
12. example and translation - given only when the definition is not sufficient to determine the meaning,
14. cross-referencing, used in the case of alternative forms which could not be treated within one entry.

Multiword units in this list have the following structure:

1. Multiword lexical unit,
2. grammar label,
3. equivalent(s),
4. regional, domain, and attitude labels (see above),
5. examples and their translations, where applicable.

If the keyword of a multiword lexical unit is standard i.e. not treated in this dictionary per se, the phrase *See the following* is used after the keyword.

Each entry in the index consists of:

1. English definition,
2. all Serbo-Croatian one-word equivalents.

Numbering

In order to represent the dynamism of semantic extensions in the dictionary, the following notation has been used to represent coordination (two or more meanings representing independent extensions from one or more source domains) and subordination (one meaning as an extension from another):

Notation	Level, relation
1. 2. 3...	first, coordination
a.b.c...	first, subordination
i. ii. iii...	second, coordination
aa. bb. cc...	second, subordination
x. xx. xxx...	third, coordination
aaa.bbb.ccc...	third, subordination

Table 9: Hierarchy of the Numbering

If we take a look at the following lexical items, three relations of subordination can be identified:

aplauz 'applause' (source meaning belongs to the standard lexicon)
|
a. 'slap' (one slaps with his/her palm)
|
b. 'punch, hit' (slapping is a kind of hitting)
|
c. 'fight' (many punches and hits make a fight)

whereas in the following case the two meanings are coordinated. Both meanings are derived from a cult comic book, *Alan Ford*, but the first has to do with an old automobile owned by one of the characters and the second with a crossword puzzle on the cover of this comic book. This example also shows us that source meaning does not have to be explicit.

fordaljka ' ' *(source meaning is in the network of knowledge)*
/ \
1. 'old automobile' 2. 'very difficult problem'

It is a matter of course that these two relations can be combined, as they are in the following entry:

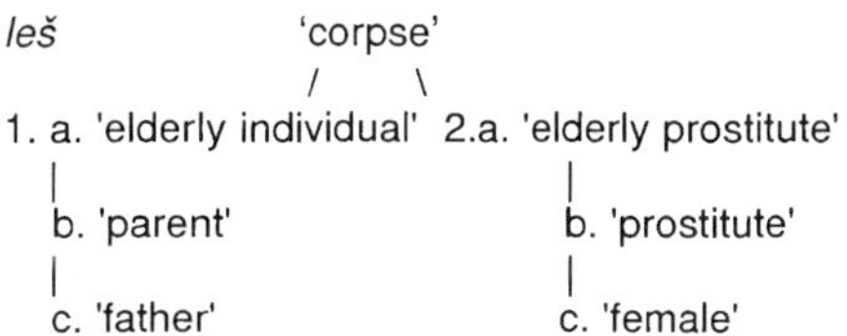

with the following extensions:

An elderly individual is already a corpse (0->1a)
A parent is an elderly individual (1a->1b)
A father is a parent (1b->1c)
An elderly prostitute is as ugly as a corpse (0->2a)
An elderly prostitute is a kind of prostitute (2a->2b)
Females are prostitutes (2b->2c)

The treatment of polysemy can mirror the three basic models of semantic extensions (radial, linear, and network). At the same time, the treatment of polysemy can help the user to recognize further extensions, while predicting extensions not listed in the dictionary.

A particular challenge in this dictionary was to establish exact English slang equivalents. Due to the simple fact that the two cultural and language systems differ significantly and that Serbo-Croatian is more abundant than English in its repertoire of obscenities and curses, numerous Serbo-Croatian entries are assigned the same English equivalent.

2.5 Labels Used in the Dictionary

Part-of-speech and inflectional tags used in the main dictionary text:

Explanations

A. Open-set inflected parts of speech

Nouns
Each noun tag consists of a genitive singular ending and the gender tag (masc. - masculine, fem. - feminine, neut. - neuter). Plural-only nouns have 'pl.' right after their gender tag (masc. pl., fem. pl., neut. pl.). Masculine nouns have the following additional tag elements: +ov, +ev (extended plural), -in (reduced plural), acc.=gen. (the accusative is equal to the genitive). In addition, accent shift and irregular morphofonemic alternations are indicated using the following abbreviations: dat. = the dative case, acc. = the accusative, voc. = the vocative, ins. = the instrumental, loc. = the locative. Syllabic permutations are indicated by perm.

Adjectives
Each adjective tag consists of the ending in feminine and neuter genders and the tag 'adj.'

Adverbs are marked by 'adv.'

Verbs
Each verb tag consists of the ending in the first person singular and the third person plural present tense and of the part which shows its features. The verb government and aspect features are marked as follows:
biasp. = biaspectual
perf. = perfective
imperf. = imperfective
intrans. = intransitive

B. Closed-set partially inflected parts of speech

Pronouns are marked by 'pron.'
Numerals are marked by 'num.'

Uninflected parts of speech

Prepositions. Case(s) abbreviations are used: acc. - accusative, dat. - dative, gen. - genitive, ins. - instrumental, loc. - locative
Conjunctions 'conj.'
Particles 'part.'
Exclamations 'excl.'

Idiom structure labels used in the Idioms section

AdjP	Adjective phrase
AdvP	Adverb phrase
c.conj.	Complex conjunction
ExcP	Exclamation phrase
LSF	Lexical-syntactic frame
NP	Noun phrase
NumP	Numeral phrase
PartP	Particle phrase
PP	Preposition phrase
ProP	Pronoun phrase
S	Sentence
vb.	Verb (in any form)
VP	Verb phrase

Etymological labels (used exclusively in the main dictionary text)

Explanations

Items from the list of etymological labels are combined if a loanword is a hybrid (Gre-Lat, for example). The last four items (given in boldface) are attached to the labels to denote an onomastic lexical unit or to denote changes in form and/or meaning. The sign * can be followed by a number in superscript to mark the number of semantic extensions, for example $^{*1,\ *2,\ *3,}$ etc.

Etymological labels

Abb	Abbreviation
Alb	Albanian
Aram	Aramaic
bn	Brand name
Cze	Czech
Dut	Dutch
Eng	English
Fin	Finnish
Fre	French
Ger	German
Gre	Greek
GreMod	Modern Greek
Gyp	Gypsy
Heb	Hebrew
Hun	Hungarian
Ind	Indonesian
Ita	Italian
Jap	Japanese
Lat	Latin
Malay	Malay
NE	Near Eastern (Turkish, Arabic, Persian)
Pol	Polish
Poly	Polynesian
Port	Portuguese
Rum	Rumanian
Rus	Russian
Slav	Slavic
Sans	Sanskrit
Slo	Slovenian
Spa	Spanish
O	Onomastic Item, i.e. Proper Name
✐	Transformation of the form
*1, *2, *3, etc.	Number of semantic extensions
❖	Word-formation

Domain labels

These labels can be combined using the - sign (e.g. dia-col). In all these combinations, the more prominent part is listed prior to the less prominent one. If, for example, a lexeme is more dialectal than colloquial it will be listed as dia-col. If, on the other hand, a lexeme is more colloquial than dialectal, it will be listed as col-dia.

col	colloquial
dia	dialectal
sl	general slang
sl-arch	archaic slang
sl-auto	automotive slang
sl-crafts	craftmanship slang
sl-crime	criminal slang
sl-drink	drinking slang
sl-drugs	drug slang
sl-fea	slang pertaining to various features and characteristics
sl-gamble	gambling slang
sl-media	media slang
sl-mil	military slang
sl-music	musical slang
sl-polit	political slang
sl-sex	the slang of sexual and digestive organs and activities
sl-sports	sports slang
sl-sstu	the slang of school students
sl-stu	the slang of college and university students

Ethnic and regional labels

This set of labels is used to indicate that a lexeme or its meaning has a feature specific to one ethnic group or to one region. This does not mean that it cannot be used in other ethnic groups or regions.

Bos	Bosnian
BosM	Bosnian Muslim
Cro	Croatian
Din	Dinaric
Gast	Yugoslav Guest workers in Germany
Kajk	Kajkavian (Northwestern Croatian)
Med	Mediterranean
Mont	Montenegrin
SSer	Southern Serbian
Ser	Serbian
SerE	Serbian Ekavian
Vojv	Vojvodinian

Attitude labels

These labels can be combined using the - sign (e.g. Der-Obs) and the principles explained in the section about domain labels. These labels are intended to indicate illocutory and perlocutory force of lexical items. Some of those labels are additionally specified in the definitions. Thus for each offensive curse the definition states if it is a weak, moderate, strong, or very strong curse. Although one can have well-founded arguments against such a scale, the opinion of the author is that it gives an idea about the strength of the curse. The following attitude labels have been used:

Abbreviation	Attitude Label	Explanation
App	Appreciative	Items intended to express admiration, approval, etc.
Der	Derogatory or depreciative	Items intended to express depreciaton, negative opinion, to diminish
Fac	Facetious	Items with humorous intentions and effects
Fam	Familiar, intimate	Items intended to express close emotional relationship with a person or an object
Iro	Ironic	Items intended to express irony, sarcasm, etc.
Obs	Obscene	Items involving lexemes related to sexual and/or digestive activities
Off	Offensive	Items intended to offend one's interlocutor or a third person

Obviously, this is merely an indication of the potential of the items in their absolute position. Their actual attitudinal value and corresponding locutory force will depend on the setting of the concrete speech act in which they have been used.

2.6 Sample Dictionary Entries

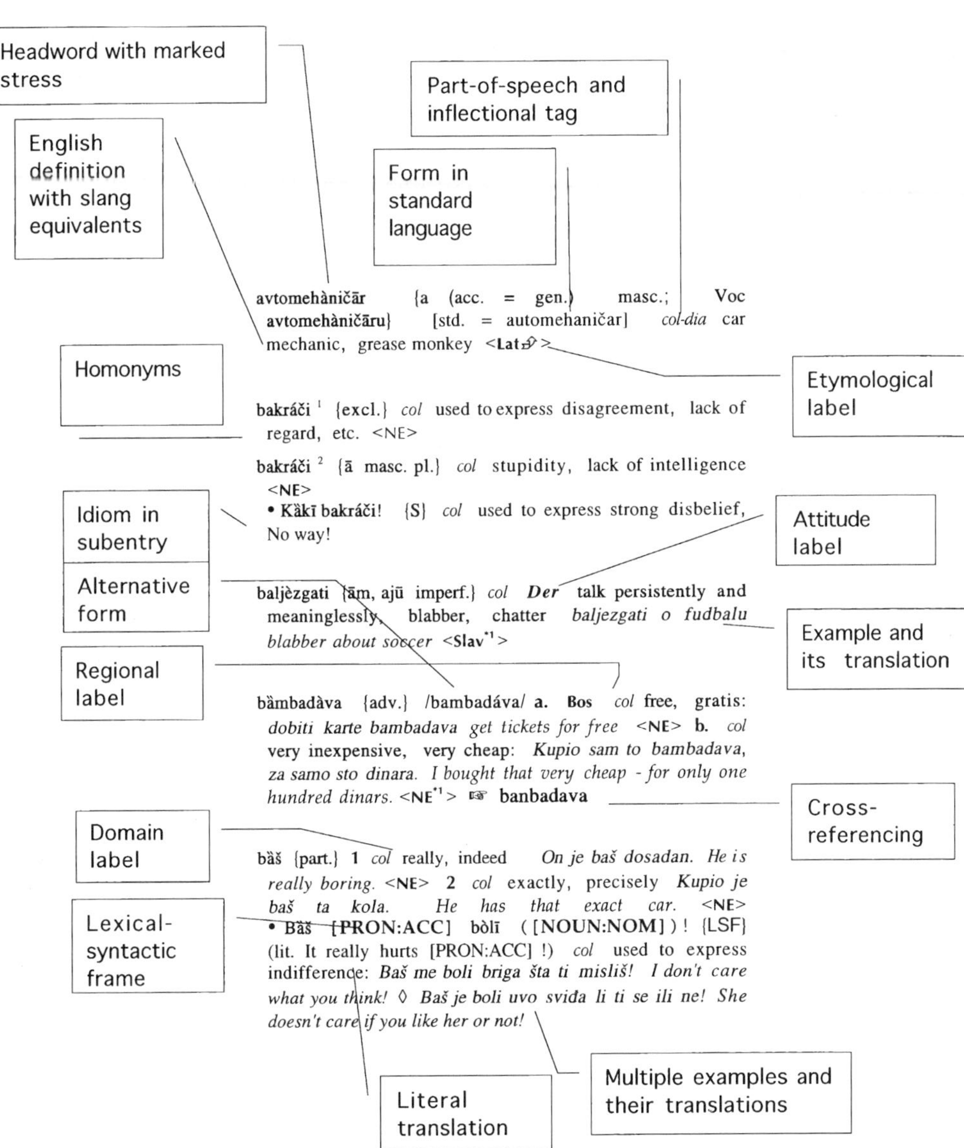

2.7 Dictionary Statistics

2.7.1.1 Domains for each meaning of the one-word lexical items

Domain	Count	Percent
Colloquial	4870	19.96
Colloquial, Dialectal	349	1.43
Colloquial, Slang	14	0.06
Dialectal	388	1.59
Dialectal, Colloquial	171	0.70
Slang, General	6938	28.43
Slang, Archaic	334	1.37
Slang, Automotive	304	1.25
Slang, Colloquial	18	0.07
Slang, Crafts	163	0.67
Slang, Crime	1172	4.80
Slang, Dialectal	3	0.01
Slang, Drinking	690	2.83
Slang, Drugs	399	1.63
Slang, Features	4583	18.78
Slang, Features, Dialectal	2	0.01
Slang, Gambling	163	0.67
Slang, Media	20	0.08
Slang, Military	113	0.46
Slang, Music	124	0.51
Slang, Politics	72	0.30
Slang, Sex	3025	12.40
Slang, Sports	230	0.94
Slang, University Students	191	0.78
Slang, School Students	68	0.28
Total	24404	100.01

2.7.1.2 Domains for each meaning of the multi-word lexical items

Domain	Count	Percent
Colloquial	1751	36.43
Colloquial, Dialectal	80	1.66
Dialectal	465	9.67
Dialectal, Colloquial	32	0.67
Slang, General	1005	20.91
Slang, Archaic	11	0.23
Slang, Automotive	17	0.35
Slang, Crafts	1	0.02
Slang, Crime	126	2.62
Slang, Drinking	69	1.44
Slang, Drugs	33	0.69
Slang, Features	668	13.90
Slang, Gambling	30	0.62
Slang, Media	3	0.06
Slang, Military	23	0.48
Slang, Music	2	0.04
Slang, Politics	8	0.17
Slang, Sex	416	8.65
Slang, Sports	20	0.42
Slang, School Students	39	0.81

Sl, School Students and Criminals	1	0.02
Slang, University students	7	0.15
Total	*4807*	*100.01*

2.7.2.1 Parts-of-speech for each meaning of the one-word lexical items

Part-of-Speech	Count	Percent
Exclamation	1098	4.50%
Particle	114	0.46%
Noun	14912	61.11%
Verb	6482	26.56%
Adjective	1275	5.22%
Conjunction	16	0.07%
Preposition	6	0.02%
Adverb	428	1.75%
Numeral	28	0.11%
Pronoun	42	0.17%
Determiner	2	0.00%
Total	*24404*	*99.97%*

2.7.2.2 Phrase structures for each meaning of the multi-word lexical items

Phrase Structure	Count	Percent
Adjective Phrase	135	2.81
Adverb Phrase	38	0.79
Complex Conjunction	2	0.04
Conjunction Phrase	1	0.02
Exclamation Phrase	30	0.62
Lexical-Syntactic Frame	123	2.56
Noun Phrase	823	17.12
Numeral Phrase	11	0.23
Particle Phrase	1	0.02
Prepositional Phrase	266	5.53
Pronoun Phrase	6	0.12
Sentence	1741	36.22
Complex Verb	3	0.06
Verb Phrase	1627	33.85
Total	*4807*	*99.99*

2.7.3.1 Regional and ethnic distribution for each meaning of the one-word lexical units

Ethnic Group/Region	Count	Percent
Dinaric	77	0.32
Bosnian Muslim	269	1.10
Mediterranean	113	0.46
Croatian	179	0.73
Serbian	85	0.35
Vojvodinain	14	0.06
Bosnian	55	0.23
Guest Workers	9	0.04
Serbian Ekavian	353	1.45
Southern Serbian	34	0.14
Montenegrin	13	0.05
Kajkavian	37	0.15
Non-Stratified	23166	94.93
Total	*24404*	*100.01*

2.7.3.2 Regional and ethnic distribution for each meaning of the multi-word lexical units

Ethnic Group/Region	Count	Percent
Serbian Ekavian	280	5.82
Bosnian	10	0.21
Mediterranean	6	0.12
Bosnian Muslim	9	0.19
Serbian	22	0.46
Dinaric	4	0.08
Southern Serbian	139	2.89
Croatian	57	1.19
Vojvodinian	3	0.06
Kajkavian	2	0.04
Non-Stratified	4275	88.93
Total	*4807*	*99.99*

2.7.4.1 Attitude distribution for each marked meaning of the one-word lexical units

Attitude	Count	Percent
Derogatory	839	3.44
Appreciative	190	0.78
Familiar	167	0.68
Offensive	123	0.50
Facetious	886	3.63
Derogatory and Facetious	21	0.09
Obscene	1676	6.87
Facetious and Obscene	461	1.89
Ironic and Derogatory	1	0.00
Ironic	47	0.19
Obscene and Facetious	15	0.06
Facetious and Derogatory	6	0.02
Derogatory and Obscene	167	0.68
Appreciative and Facetious	3	0.01
Facetious and Appreciative	17	0.07
Obscene and Familiar	1	0.00
Obscene and Derogatory	12	0.05
Facetious and Offensive	1	0.00
Derogatory, Facetious, and Obscene	1	0.00
Familiar and Obscene	3	0.01
Appreciative and Obscene	5	0.02
Facetious, Obsene, and Derogatory	2	0.01
Facetious, Appreciative, and Obscene	1	0.00
Offensive and Obscene	1	0.00
Facetious, Derogatory, and Obscene	2	0.01
Facetious and Familiar	1	0.00
Ironic and Facetious	1	0.00
Unmarked	19754	80.95
Total	*24404*	*99.96*

2.7.4.2 Attitude distribution for each marked meaning of the multi-word lexical units

Attitude	Count	Percent
Facetious	395	8.22%
Appreciative	34	0.71%
Derogatory or Depreciative	51	1.06%
Derogatory and Obscene	26	0.54%
Obscene	442	9.19%

Ironic	24	0.50%
Familiar	10	0.21%
Offensive	1204	25.05%
Obscene and Derogatory	2	0.04%
Offensive and Facetious	21	0.44%
Facetious and Obscene	126	2.62%
Obscene and Facetious	10	0.21%
Facetious and Offensive	2	0.04%
Facetious and Derogatory	7	0.15%
Facetious and Ironic	1	0.02%
Derogatory and Facetious	6	0.12%
Appreciative and Obscene	2	0.04%
Unmarked	2444	50.84%
Total	*4807*	*100.00%*

2.8 Sources and References

2.8.1 Corpus materials, dictionary sources:

PPJ - Prilozi proučavanju jezika
SDZ - Srpski dijalektološki zbornik
BDZ - Bosansko-hercegovački dijalektološki zbornik

A conversation with a Bosnian Serb (recorded by Siniša Gligić).
A corpus of Dušan Kovačević's dramas available on the Internet at www.yurope.org.
Agatonović, Slavica, et al. *Serbian - Swedish Slang dictionary* (electronic document, used with permission of the authors).
Andrić, Dragoslav. *Dvosmerni rečnik srpskog žargona i žargonu srodnih reči i izraza*, BIGZ, 1976.
Anić, Vladimir. *Rječnik hrvatskoga jezika*, Novi Liber, Zagreb, 1994
Ćosić, Pavle. Various articles about Belgrade slang, files obtained in electronic form from the author.
Audicija theater show (recorded by Siniša Gligić).
Baotić, Josip. "Registar leksema obuhvaćenih upitnikom za ispitivanje bosansko-hercegovačkih govora", BDZ 2, p. 313-347.
Bogdanović, Nedeljko. "Leksika", u: *Govor Bučuma i Belog Potoka*, SDZ 25, p. 139-168.
Budzinska, Sybilla. *Internet list of onomatopoeia and interjections* (available at ftp://main.amu.edu.pl/pub/Serbo-Croat).
Colloquial rock tape and BB Show tape (recorded by Dušan-Vladislav Pažđerski-Pavlović).
Ćupić, Drago i Željko. "Rečnik govora Zagarača", SDZ, vol. 44, SANU, Beograd 1997.
Dadić, Ivan. *Božje ogledalo. banatski muški humor*, Den Satelit, Pančevo, 1996.
Danko Šipka's collection of lexemes related to alcohol.
Danko Šipka's list of Serbo-Croatian car mechanic terms.
Danko Šipka's own recordings and competence.
Database of lexemes characteristic for colloquial Bosnian, predominantly from Škaljić, Abdulah *Turcizmi u srpskohrvatskom jeziku*, Svjetlost, Sarajevo, 1989.
Dešić, Milorad. "Tekstovi", u: *Zapadnobosanski ijekavski govori*, SDZ 21, p. 312-316.
Dinić, Jakša. "Rečnik timočkog govora" (drugi dodatak), SDZ, vol. 38, SANU, Beograd 1992, p. 381-586.
Dinić, Jakša. "Rečnik timočkog govora", SDZ 34, p. 7-336.
Doslovno naraslo. A list of literal English translations of some Serbo-Croatian phrases posted on the discussion group ST-L (st-l@main.amu.edu.pl) on September 29, 1999.
Dragičević, Milan. "Tekstovi" in: *Govor ličkih jekavaca*, SDZ 32, p. 204-225.
Đukanović, Petar. "Leksika" in: *Govor Dragačeva*, SDZ, vol. 41, SANU, Beograd, 1995, p. 177-220.
Đukanović, Petar. "Leksika" in: *Govor slela Gornje Caparde*, SDZ 29, p. 266-285.
Đurović, Radoslav. "Prelazni govori južne Bosne i visoke Hercegovine", SDZ, vol. 38, p. 9-378.
Feral Tribune Weekly, January 6, 1997.
Gajdzinski, Michal. *Internet list of sport terminology* (available at: ftp://main.amu.edu.pl/pub/Serbo-Croat).
Galetin, Gordana. "Iz leksičke problematike Severne Šajkaške", PPJ 16, p. 59-92.
Gerzić, Borivoj. *Rečnik anglo-američkog slenga (i vulgarnog jezika)*, Istar, Beograd, 1997.
Grković, Jasmina. "Prilog poznavanju dijalekatske leksike Šumadije", PPJ 18, p. 125-153.
Grković, Milica. "Dijalekatski tekstovi sa Kopaonika", PPJ 7, p. 157-166.

Index Radio Theater Internet corpus from several radio shows available at http://www.yurope.com.
Kašić, Zorka. "Iz leksike" in: *Govor Konavala*, SDZ, vol. 41, SANU, Beograd 1995 p. 352-371.
Keno, Rejmon. *Stilske vežbe*, Nolit, Beograd, 1964 (translation by Danilo Kiš).
Klajić, Bratoljub Veliki rječnik stranih riječi i izraza, Zora, Zagreb, 1974.
Klajn, Ivan. "Leksika", in: M. Radovanović *Srpski jezik na kraju veka*, SANU, Beograd 1996, p. 159-170.
Klajn, Ivan. *Rečnik novih reči*, Matica srpska, Novi Sad, 1992.
Lalević, M.S. *Sinonimi i srodne reči srpskohrvatskog jezika*, Leksikografski zavod Sveznanje, Beograd, 1974.
Maksić, Mirjana. "Prilog proučavanju leksike Srema", PPJ 16, p. 93-122.
Malbaša, Zdravko. "Iz leksike sela Donjih Ramića kod Ključa u Bosanskoj Krajini", PPJ 12, p. 95-117.
Marković, Blagoje B. "Iz leksike i frazeologije. "društvenih" igara Vračana", PPJ 11, p. 163-177.
Marković, Miodrag. "Rečnik narodnog govora u Crnoj Gori", SDZ 32, p. 243-500.
Matešić, Josip Frazeološki rječnik hrvatskoga ili srpskoga jezika, IRO Školska knjiga, Zagreb, 1982.
Mihajlović, Velimir. "Prilog rečniku srpskohrvatskih geografskih termina", PPJ 6, p. 153-182.
Miletić, Branko. "Registar", in: *Crmnički govor*, SDZ 9, p. 621-650.
Milovanović, Emilija. "Prilog poznavanju leksike Zlatibora", PPJ19, p. 15-70.
Minimax talk show , August 1998 (recorded by Siniša Gligić).
Mitrović, Brana. *Rečnik leskovačkog govora*, Leskovac, 1984.
Moerk, Henning. *Serbo-Croatian literature corpus* (almost 4Mb of texts available at www.yurope.com).
Nikolić, Berislav. "Napomene iz sintakse i leksike" in: B. Nikolić Kolubarski govor, SDZ,vol 18, p. 58-67.
Nikolić, Berislav M.. "Leksika" u: Mačvanski govor, SDZ 16, p. 285-298.
Nikolić, Miroslav B.. "Reči kojih nema u Vukovom Rječniku i druge interesantne reči in: M. Nikolić Govor sela Gorobilja", SDZ, vol. 19, p. 706-711.
Pavle Ćosić. Confirmations and new lexical entries (he confirmed each entry in A-Pa, and only appended new meanings and entires in Pb-Z).
Pavlović, Milivoj. "Registar", u: Govor Sretečke župe, SDZ 8, p. 295-347.
Peco, Asim. *Pregled dijalekata srpskohrvatskog jezika*, Naučna knjiga, Beograd,1989.
Peić, Marko and Grgo Bačlija. Rečnik bačkih Bunjevaca, Matica srpska, Novi Sad, 19.
Pešikan, Mitar. "Registar i akcenatski rečnik" in: *Starocrnogorski srednjokatunski i lješanski govori*, SDZ 15, p. 217-294.
Petrović, Dragoljub. "Tekstovi", in: *O govoru Zmijanja*, Matica srpska, Novi Sad, 1973, p. 194-202.
Radić, Prvoslav. "Crtice o govoru sela Mrče u kuršumlijskom kraju", SDZ, vol. 36, p. 47-63.
Rečnik vojvođanskog žargona (available at: http://151.200.15.145/novisad/recnik/index.html).
Remetić, Slobodan. "Registar reči" u: Govori centralne Šumadije, SDZ 31, p. 507-546.
Sabljak, Tomislav Šatra, Globus, Zagreb, 1981.
Savić, Svenka and Vesna Polovina. *Razgovorni srpskohrvatski jezik*, Filozofski fakultet, Novi Sad, 1989.
SII Electronic corpus from the discussion group (sii@calstatela.edu) (almost 4Mb of text).
Simić, Radoje. "Tuđice" in: *Levački govor*, SDZ, vol. 19, p. 508-513.
Stanić, Milija. *Uskočki rečnik*, Naučna knjiga, Beograd, 1990-91.
Stijović, Rada. "Iz leksike Vasojevića", SDZ, vol. 36, p. 126-379.
Subotić, Jelisaveta. "Nazivi za stoku, opremu i stočarske proizvode u govoru Krivošija", PPJ 8, p. 145-160.
Šipka, Danko. *Opscene reči u srpskom jeziku*, CPL - Prometej, Beograd, 1999.
Šokica, Slavica. "O značenju konverzacionih partikula u telefonskoj komunikaciji", PPJ 23, p. 189-210.
Tešić, Milosav. "Rečnik" in: *Govor Lještanskog*, SDZ, vol. 22, p. 259-297.
Telephone teasing tape (recorded by Siniša Gligić).
Top lista nadrealista radio show 1989 (recorded by Siniša Gligić).
Top lista nadrealista radio show 1993. (recorded by Siniša Gligić).
Top lista nadrealista radio show, the mid-eighties (recorded by Siniša Gligić).
Ugrešić, Dubravka et. al The Lexicon of Yu-mythology (http://home.wxs.nl/sima/home.html).
Untitled article about Croatian slang, *Playboy* (Croatian edition), January 1999, p. 99-105.
Vlajković, Dragoljub. "Rečnik. "frajerskih" (šatrovačkih) reči", in: Prilozi proučavanju jezika 2, p. 89-98.
Vujović, Luka. "Osvrt na rječnik mrkovićkog dijalekta" in: L. Vujović Mrkovićki dijalekt, SDZ, vol. 18, p. 353-356.
Vuković, Cvijetin. *Jež u strnjištu, Erotske i druge različne pjesme iz Bosne*, Zajednica književnih klubova Srbije, 1982.
Yugoslav Drama Corpus (over 1Mb of texts from the Internet available at http://www.knjizevnarec.yu).
Yugoslav movies corpus (twenty movies have been watched and colloquial lexical items have been noted).
Zabranjeno pušenje (lyrics from all their albums).
Zlatković, Dragoljub. "Frazeologija omalovažavanja u pirotskom govoru", SDZ, vol. 36, p.429-740.

2.8.2 Sources for Etymologies

Broz, Ivan and Franjo Iveković. *Rječnik hrvatskoga jezika*, Zagreb, 1901.
Karadžić, Vuk Stefanović. *Srpski rječnik*, Vienna, 1818.
Klajić, Bratoljub. *Veliki rječnik stranih riječi i izraza*, Zora, Zagreb, 1974.
Mićunović, Ljubo. *Rječnik stranih riječi i izraza*, Novi Sad, 1988.
Moskovljević, Miloš. *Rečnik savremenog srpskohrvatskog jezika*, Beograd, 1968.
MS(MH). *Rečnik srpskohrvatskoga književnog jezika*, Novi Sad (Zagreb), 1967-76.
SANU. *Rečnik srpskohrvatskog književnog i narodnog jezika*, 1959-.
Skok, Petar. *Etimologijski rječnik hrvatskoga ili srpskoga jezika*, Zagreb 1971-74 .
Stanić, Milija. *Uskočki rečnik*, Beograd, 1990.
Škaljić, Abdulah. *Turcizmi u srpskohrvatskom jeziku*, Sarajevo, 1989.
Uhlik, Rade. "Ciganizmi u šatrovačkom argou i sličnim govorima", Glasnik Zemaljskog muzeja u Sarajevu, nova serija, tom IX, s. 5-31.
Uhlik, Rade. *Sprskohrvatsko-romsko-engleski rječnik*, Svjetlost, Sarajevo, 1983.
Vujaklija, Milan. *Leksikon stranih reči i izraza*, Beograd, 1991.

2.8.3 General Sources on Colloquial Serbo-Croatian

-, Untitled article about Croatian slang, *Playboy* (Croatian edition), January 1999, p. 99-105.
-,. "Zlikovački rječnik" in: *Kriminalna taktika*, Zagreb, 1943.
-, *Šatrovački žargon*, newsletter of the Ministry of Interior of the Socialist Republic of Croatia, s.a..
Alimpić, Dušan *Policiski rečnik*, vol. I-III, Beograd, 1924.
Andrić, Dragoslav *Dvosmerni rečnik srpskog žargona i žargonu srodnih reči i izraza*, BIGZ, 1976.
Antonić, Ivana. "Govorni jezik u radio prenosu fudbalske utakmice", *PPJ*, Novi Sad, 21, 131-141, 1985.
Bauer, I. *Observations on the Syntax of the Zagreb Kajkavian Dialect*, unpublished Master's thesis, The Pennsylvania State University, University Park, PA, 42pp.
Benson, Morton. "Yugoslav Culture and the Lexicon", *Folia Slavica* 8, 1, 53-62.
Berisavljević, S *Razgovor doktora I pacijenta*, Filozofski fakultet, Novi Sad, unpublished B.A. paper, 1989.
Bovan, Vladimir. "Tajni jezici radnika Sredske i Sirinića", *Glasnik Muzeja Kosova*, vol. XI, 1971-72.
Bugarski, Ranko. "O urbanom idiomu", in *Jezik u savremenoj komunikaciji*, Belgrade, Cetar za marksizam, p. 221-222.
Đorđević, Tihomir. "Beleške o tajnim jezicima /u Aleksincu/", *Karadžić* II, 1900, 156-164.
Đorđević, Dušan. "Frajerski govor u opštoj problematici govora", *Psihološki bilten*, number 1'3, 1960.
Gačić, J.. "Romanski elementi u splitskom čakavskom govoru", *Čakavska rič*, 1, 3-54; 2, 107-155, 1979.
Gavran, Ignacije. *Bludna psovka*, Sarajevo, 1962.
Hamm, Josip. "Dvije tri o govoru zagrebačkih srednjoškolaca" in: *Nastavni vjesnik*, Zagreb, vol. 48, nr 4, January-February 1939-40.
Hinrichs, Uwe and Ljiljana Hinrichs *Serbische Umgangssprache*, Harrasowitz, 1995.
Hudolin, Vladimir. "Ovisnički žargon", in the book: Christiane F. *Mi djeca s kolodvora ZOO*, Zagreb, 1980.
Jović, Dušan. "Književni jezik i urbani idiom", *Jezik u savaremenoj komunikaciji*, Beograd, Univerzitet, Centar za marksizam, 24'52, 1982.
Jutronić-Tihomirović, Dunja. "Language change in an urban setting", in: Radovanović, M. (ed.) *Yugoslav General Linguistics*, John Benjamins, 145-162..
Jutronić-Tihomirović, Dunja. "Morfološke promjene u splitskom dijalektu", *Filologija*, Zagreb, 14, 153-160.
Jutronić-Tihomirović, Dunja. "Standard Language and Dialects in Contact", in: Bugarski, R. and C. Hawkesworth *Language Planning in Yugoslavia*, Slavica Publishers, 1992, p. 200-211.
Kalogjera, Damir. "Attitudes towards Serbo-Croatian language varieties", *Intenational Journal of the Sociology of Language*, 52, 93-111.
Komlenović, Veljko. "Šatrovački žargon", *Naša praksa*, nr 4, 1961.
Kuzmanović, Mladen. "Kreativnost žargonske tvorbe", *Umjetnost riječi*, nr. 1-2, 1970.
Kuzmanović, Mladen. "Vidni kut žargona", *15 dana*, nr 2, 1970.
Ladan, Tomislav. "Zabrane i riječi", *Kritika*, nr. 9, 1969.
Lepojević, Spasoje. "Nadopuna šatrovačkog rečnika", in: *Bilten Odelenja za kriminalističku službu DSUP-a FNRJ*, nr 3-4, 1953.
Levinger, Jasna. *Konverzacioni čin kao vid verbalne komunikacije*, Filozofski fakultet u Zagrebu, Zagreb, doktorska disertacija, 1988.
Magner, Thomas. "A Century of the Niš Dialect", *Language and Literary Theory, Papers in Slavic Philology*, 5, eds. B.A. Stolz, I.R. Titunik, and Lj. Doležel, Ann Arbor, Michigan, 133-145.

Magner, Thomas. *A Zagreb Kajkavian Dialect*, Penn State Studies, 18, 1966.
Magner, Thomas. "City Dialects in Yugoslavia", *American Contributions to the Eighth International Congress of Slavists*, vol. 1, ed. H. Birnbaum, Columbus, Ohio, p. 465-82.
Magner, Thomas. "Diglossia in Split", *Folia Slavica*, 1, 3, 400-436.
Magner, Thomas F. "Urban Vernaculars and the Standard Language in Yugoslavia", in: Bugarski, R. and C. Hawkesworth *Language Planning in Yugoslavia*, Slavica Publishers, 1992, p. 189-199.
Magner, Thomas. "The Dialect of Split. A preliminary Sketch", *Xenia Slavica*, eds. R. Lenček and B.O.Unbegaun, The Hague, 384-91.
Magner, Thomas "Yugoslav City Dialects: In Search of a Methodology", *Zbornik radova Katedre za anglistiku*, eds. S. Dekanić-Janoški and M. Jovanović, Niš, vol. 3, p. 39-44.
Majetić, Miljenko. "Frajerština i književnost", *Ogledalo*, November, 1958.
Milićević, Milan Đ. *Dr Vatroslav Jagić u Srbiji I Soviji*, Beograd 1895 (contains a list of slang words).
Peco, Asim. "Govorna i pisana riječ danas", *Izraz*, Sarajevo, 18/8-9, p. 773-782.
Petković, Živko D. *Jezik naših šatrovaca* (sa rečnikom šatrovačkih reči), Beograd, 1928.
Polovina, Vesna. "Gramatika govornog jezika", in: *Gramatika u nastavi maternjeg i stranih jezika*, Beograd, Društvo za primenjenu lingvistiku Srbije, 1984, p. 83-93.
Polovina, Vesna. "Opšte karakteristike razgovornog jezika i mogućnosti njihove primene u nastavi srpskohrvatskog jezika strancima", *Živi jezici*, Beograd, 1989.
Polovina, Vesna. "Specifičnosti kolokacija u razgovornom engleskom i srpskohrvatskom jeziku", in: *Zborink radova instituta za strane jezike i književnosti*, Filozofski fakultet, Novi Sad, 8, p.179-196, 1987.
Popović, Ljubomir. "Kasarnski argo", *Književnost i jezik*, nr. 1, 1970.
Sabljak, Tomislav. "Život i smrt šatre", *Večernji list*, 14.VIII. 1974.
Sabljak, Tomislav. "Ne samo jezik. "podzemlja"", *Vjesnik*, 16.IX 1969.
Sabljak, Tomislav "Opaske o šatrovačkom", *Književnik*, number 14, 1960.
Sabljak, Tomislav. "Predgovor" in: *Rječnik šatrovačkog govora*, Globus, Zagreb, 1981, p. 5-21.
Sabljak, Tomislav. "Sjaj i bijeda šatrovačkog", *Oko*, 27.VI.1973.
Sabljak, Tomislav. "Šatra ispod šatora - jezik distanciranja", *Vjesnik*, 8.VIII.1976.
Savić, Svenka and Vesna Polovina *Razgovorni srpskohrvatski jezik*, Novi Sad, 1989.
Savić, Svenka. "Govoru prenosu fudbalske utakmice preko radija i televizije", *Godišnjak Saveza društava za primenjenu lingvistiku Jugoslavije*, Beograd, p. 143-154, 1985.
Savić, Svenka. *Narativi kod dece*, Filozofski fakultet, Institut za južnoslovenske jezike, Beograd, 1985.
Simić, Ilija. A list of slang words published in the journal *Delo*, Belgrade IV-IV, 1969 and II, 1970.
Simić, Ilija. "Šatrovački govor", *Jugoslovenska revija za kriminologiju I krivično pravo*, nr. 4, 1970.
Stojčić, Đoko. *Sjaj razgovora - leksikon srpskih narodnih izreka*, Beograd, 1994.
Škiljan, Dubravko. *Jezik svakodnevice*, Novi Sad, Književna zajednica, 1988.
Šoljan, Antun and Ivan Slamnig. "O šatrovačkom", *Krugovi*, nr. I, 1955.
Tešić, Đorđe. "Prilog proučavanju šatrovačkog govora", *Glasnik etnografskog muzeja u Beogradu*, nr. 17, 1954.
Todorović, Miroljub. *Gejak glanca guljarke*, Prosveta, Beograd, 1974.
Trojanović, Sima. A paper in *Južnoslovenski filolog*, nr. 5, Belgrade 1925-26 (contains a list of archaic slang words).
Uhlik, Rade. "Ciganizmi u šatrovačkom argou i u sličnim govorima", *Glasnik Zemaljskog muzeja u Sarajevu*, vol. 9, 1954.
Vlajković, Dragoslav. "Rečnik. "frajerskih" (šatrovačkih) reči i izraza", *PPJ*, Novi Sad, nr 2, 1966.
Vodinelić, Vlado. "Šatrovački žargon", in: *Bilten Odelenja za kriminalističku službu DSUP-a FNRJ*, nr. 1-2, 1953.
Zečević, Vesna. "Status. "grešaka" u usmenoj komunikaciji na standardnom jeziku", *Govor*, Zagreb, nr. VI/1, p. 53-64.
Zorić, Vukašin. "Taj čudni, posebni jezik - ta šatra", *Vjesnik* 10. XII 1972.
Žic-Fuchs, Milena. "Osnovna obilježja oslovljavanja u Zagrebu", *SOL*, Zagreb, 3/2, 27-28, 1988.

2.8.4 References

AHD (1992) *The American Heritage Dictionary of the English Language, Third Edition*, Houghton Mifflin Company.
Bugarski, Ranko and Celia Hawkesworth. (1992) *Language Planning in Yugoslavia*, Slavica.
Filipović, Rudolf. (1990) *Anglicizmi u hrvatskom ili srpskom jeziku*, JAZU, Zagreb.
Ivić, Pavle. (1958) *Die serbokroatischen Dialekte: ihre Struktur und Entwicklung, vol. 1: Allgemeines und die štokavische Dialektgruppe*, Mouton.
Lakoff, George and Mark Johnson (1980) *Metaphors We Live By*, U. of Chicago Press.
Langacker, Ronald W. (1991) *Concept, Image, and Symbol. The Cognitive Basis of Grammar*, Mouton de Gruyter.
Lipka, Leonhard. (1992) *An Outline of English Lexicology*, Max Niemeyer.

Meer van der, Geart (1999) "Metaphors and Dictionaries: The Morass of Meaning or How to Get Two Ideas for One", *International Journal of Lexicography*, Vol. 12, No. 3, p. 195-208.
Okuka, Miloš. (1998) *Eine Sprache Viele Erben*, Wieser Verlag.
Peco, Asim. (1970) *Pregled dijalekata srpskohrvatskog jezika*, Naučna knjiga.
Pike, Keneth Lee. (1996) *Talk, Thought, and Thing*, SIL.
Polovina, Vesna. "Opšte osobine srpskohrvatskog razgovornog jezika", in: Savić, S. and V. Polovina *Razgovorni srpskohrvatski jezik*, Filozofski fakultet u Novom Sadu.
Wierzbicka, Anna. (1988) *The Semantics of Grammar*, John Benjamins.
Wierzbicka, Anna. (1992) *Semantics, culture and cognition: universal human concepts in culture-specific configurations*, Mouton de Gruyter.

3. List of symbols and abbreviations used in this dictionary

✎	transformation of the form
❖	word formation
^{*1}, ^{*2}, ^{*3}, etc.	number of semantic extensions
+ov/+ev	extended plural
abb.	abbreviation
adj.	adjective
adjp.	adjective phrase
adv.	adverb
advp.	adverb phrase
Alb.	Albanian
Aram.	Aramaic
biasp.	biaspectual verb
bn.	brand name
Bos.	Bosnian
BosM.	Bosnian Muslim
c.conj.	complex conjunction
colloq.	colloquial
conj.	conjunction
Cro.	Croatian
Cze.	Czech
dat.	dative
dial.	dialectal
Din.	Dinaric
Dut.	Dutch
Eng.	English
excl.	exclamation
exclp.	exclamatory phrase
fem.	feminine
Fin.	Finnish
Fre.	French
Gast.	Yugoslav guest workers in Germany
gen.	genitive
Ger.	German
Gre.	Greek
GreMod.	Modern Greek
Gyp.	Gypsy
Heb.	Hebrew
Hun.	Hungarian
imperf.	imperfective
-in	reduced plural
Ind.	Indonesian
ins.	instrumental
intr.	intransitive
irreg.	irregular
Ita.	Italian
Jpn.	Japanese
Kajk.	Kajkavian (Northwestern Croatian)
Lat.	Latin
loc.	locative
LSF	lexical-syntactic frame
Malay	Malay

masc. masculine
Med. Mediterranean
Mont. Montenegrin
NE. Near Eastern (Turkish, Arabic, Persian)
neut. neuter
NP noun phrase
num. numeral
NumP numeral phrase
part. particle
PartP particle phrase
perf. perfective
perm. syllabic permutation
pl. plural
O onomastic item, i.e. proper name
Pol. Polish
Poly. Polynesian
Port. Portuguese
pp. prepositional phrase
pron. pronoun
PronP pronoun phrase
Rum. Rumanian
Rus. Russian
S sentence
Sans. Sanskrit
Ser. Serbian
SerE. Serbian Ekavian
sl. general slang
Sla. Serbo-Croatian common-Slavic inheritance
sl-arch. archaic slang
sl-auto. automotive slang
sl-crafts. craftmanship slang
sl-crime. criminal slang
sl-drink. drinking slang
sl-drugs. drug slang
sl-fea. slang pertaining to various features and characteristics
sl-gamble. gambling slang
sl-media. media slang
sl-mil. military slang
sl-music. musical slang
sl-polit. political slang
sl-sex. the slang of sexual and digestive organs and activities
sl-sports. sports slang
sl-sstu. the slang of elementary, middle, and high school students
sl-stu. the slang of college and university students
Slo. Slovenian
Spa. Spanish
SSer. Southern Serbian
vb. verb (in any form)
voc. vocative
Vojv. Vojvodinian
VP verb phrase

The Dictionary

Aa

a [1] {excl.} **1** *col* used to express satisfaction, surprise, delight, dislike, pain, etc., ah, aah <Slav> **2** *col* the sound made by a newborn, goo-goo

a [2] {part.} *col* intensifying particle, ah: *A šta uradi! Ah, look what have you done!* <Slav>

- **A na**[ADJ/NOUN/PRON:ACC]! {LSF} (lit. And to [ADJ/NOUN/PRON:ACC]!) *col* ***Obs*** used to express disappointment, anger, etc., Damn it!: *Nikad nećemo uspjeti! A na goli! We'll never make it! Damn it!*
- **A** [NOUN:GEN]! {LSF} *col* used to stress the intensity of a feature or event: *A b(u)dale! What a fool!* ◊ *A belaja! What a problem!*
- **A u** [NOUN:ACC]! {LSF} (lit. And to [NOUN: ACC]!) *col* ***Obs*** used to express disappointment, anger, etc.: *A u pizdu materinu! Neću više da radim! Damn it! I don't wanna work any more!*

Â [3] {masc.} (lit. clipping of Akademija 'Academy') Ser *sl* name for Arts Academy Club (Belgrade, Serbia) <Abb ☞>

A jâ [PRON:DAT] (jèbēm) ([ADV]) (i) [NOUN:ACC] /rep/(i [NOUN:ACC])! {LSF} (lit. And I fuck [ADV] *both* [NOUN] (and [NOUN]) to [PRON:ACC]) *col* ***Off*** used in response to another curse: *A ja ti jebem i ženu i dete! Fuck you too!* ☞ **jebati**

a kȍnto [NP:GEN] {c.conj} (lit. on account of [NP:GEN]) *col* regarding, with regard to: *Rekao mi je nešto a konto tebe. He told me something regarding you.* ☞ **konto**

a-hâ {excl.} *col* used to express surprise (usu. when one remembers something), a ha, oh: *A-ha, sad znam ko je to uradio. Oh, now I know who did it.* <Slav>

ȁ-nu {excl.} *col* used to emphasize a directive: *A-nu, podigni to! Well, pick it up!* <Slav> ☞ **anu, anute**

áaa {excl.} /áaaa excl./ **1** *col* used to express approval or appreciation: *Aaa, to je prava supa. Well now, this is what I call good soup.* <Slav> **2** *col* used to express surprise, wow <Slav>

àbər {masc.} [std. = aber] **1** SSer *dia* news (in general) <NE> **2** SSer *dia* message <NE> ☞ **aber, haber**

àba {ē fem.} **a.** *dia* aba (a kind of thick woolen fabric used for clothing, usu. homemade) <NE> **b.** *sl* clothing, garment <NE[*1]>

ȁbānje {a neut.} [std. = habanje] *col* abrasion <Slav☞>

àbart {a masc.} *sl-auto* auto with high performance engine, souped up car <BN>

àbartovān {a, o adj.} *sl-auto* high performance (of cars), souped up <BN✤>

àbartovati {tujēm, tujū biasp.} *sl-auto* tune an engine for high performance (usu. of an automobile), soup up a car <BN✤>

abasàmis {a (acc. = gen.) masc.} *sl-sstu* conductor (on a train, bus, or streetcar)

àbaša {ē fem.} *sl-sex* brothel, whorehouse <Ita[*1]>

abàžur {abažúra (acc. = gen.) masc.; Voc ȁbažūru} (lit. lampshade) **1** *sl-fea* ***Der*** naive male <Fre[*1]> **2** *sl-fea* ***Fac*** boyfriend <Fre[*1]> **3** *sl-fea* ***Fac*** male protector (usu. in relation to a female) <Fre[*1]>

ABD [ā-bê-dê] {part.} (lit. abbreviated from Ako Bog da 'if God allows') *col* used to indicate lack of control over events, God willing: *Stiću ABD sutra. God willing, I will arrive tomorrow.* <Abb>

abderíćanin {a (acc. = gen.) -in (rd. pl.) masc.} *sl-fea* ***Der*** stupid or mentally deficient person <Gre>

àbdika {ē fem.; Dat àbdiki} **a.** *sl* poison, venom <Gre[*1]> **b.** *sl-fea* evil person <Gre[*2]>

ȁber {a masc.} **a.** Din *col* news (in general) <NE> **b.i.** Din *dia* message <NE[*1]> **ii.** Din *dia* interest in something <NE[*1]> **iii.** Din *dia* testament, will <NE[*1]> ☞ **abər, haber**

àbīb {abíba (acc. = gen.) masc.; Voc ȁbībe} *sl-fea* ***Der*** naive male <NE>

ȁbić {a masc.} [std. = abortus] *sl-sex* ***Obs*** abortion (of a fetus) <Lat☞✤>

ablatírati {làtīrām, latírajū biasp. intr.} *sl-stu* be destroyed, be ruined: *Totalno je ablatirao od kockanja. Gambling has completely ruined him.* <Lat[*1]>

ablènder {a (acc. = gen.) masc.} /àblender /a (acc. = gen.) masc./ (lit. light switch) *sl-fea* ***Fac-Off*** bald male <Ger[*1]>

àblendovati {dujēm, dujū biasp.} **a.** *col* dim headlights <Ger> **b.** *sl* look back at somebody: *Ona koka ti ablenduje. That babe is checking you out.* <Ger[*1]>

abmarkírati {màrkīrām, markírajū biasp. intr.} (lit. mark down) *sl* disappear, evaporate, vanish: *Abmarkirala je taman kad sam mislio da sam je uhvatio. Just when I thought I'd found her, she disappeared.* <Ger[*1]>

abmarkírati se {màrkīrām, markírajū biasp. intr.} *col* step back, make way: *Abmarkiraj se da prođem! Step back and let me through!* <**Ger***1>

abonȅntica {ē fem.} (lit. subscriber) *sl-sex* ***Fac-Obs*** long-term female sexual partner (of a male) <**Fre***1>

abonȅntkinja {ē fem.} (lit. subscriber) **1** *sl-sex* ***Fac*** long-term female sexual partner (of a male) <**Fre***1> **2** *sl-sex* ***Fac*** loose woman <**Fre***1>

Abortàna {ē fem.} (lit. abortion place) *sl* ***Fac*** motel where spouse-cheaters meet, no-tell motel <**Lat**❖>

abòrtīrān {a, o adj.} (lit. aborted) *sl-fea* ***Off*** short (in height, of a person) <**Lat***1>

abortírati {abòrtīrām, abortírajū biasp.} (lit. abort *a fetus*) **1** *sl* ***Fac*** take out, remove, get rid of: *Abortirao sam stara kola. I've gotten rid of my old car.* <**Lat***1> **2** *sl* ***Fac*** cut off, chop off: *Abortiraj vrh, pa će jelka stati u stan. Cut off the tip, and the Christmas tree will fit into your apartment.* <**Lat***1>

abortȉška {ē fem.; Dạt abortȉški} *sl-sex* ***Obs*** abortion (of a fetus) <**Lat**❖>

àbortovānā {ē fem. (adj. decl.)} (lit. the one who has aborted a baby) *sl* female who has had an abortion or miscarriage <**Lat***1>

abòrtus {adj.} /àbortus/ (lit. abortion) *sl-fea* ***Off*** pertaining to a physically or psychologically underdeveloped person <**Lat***1>

- **kokòšjī abòrtus** {NP} (lit. hen's abortion) *sl-drink* brandy-and-coke

àbronoša {ē masc.} *sl-fea* extremely talkative person, chatterbox

abulȁnta {ē fem.} [std. = ambùlanta] *dia-col* outpatient department (of a hospital) <**Lat**✍>

ȁc {excl.} **1** *col* used to lure a goat <**Slav**> **2** *col* used when giving something and then pulling it back in a taunting fashion: *Evo ti knjiga, ac! Here's the book!* <**Slav**>

âčenā strȁnka {NP} (lit. the side which is fucked) **SSer** *dia* ***Obs*** person who gets the short end: *Ispao je ačena stranka u poslu s Čečencima. He got the short end on the deal with the Chechens.* ☞ **stranka**

áčiti se {âčīm, čē imperf. intr.} **a.** *col* ***Der*** grimace, make faces (to entertain others) <**NE**> **b.** *col* ***Der*** clown around <**NE***1>

àdam {a (acc. = gen.) masc.} (lit. Adam) *sl-sstu* ***Fac*** failing grade <**Heb***1>

ádet {a masc.} **Din** *col* custom, habit: *U nas je taki adet da se nosi kahva u posjetu. We have a custom of bringing coffee when visiting other people.* <**NE**>

àdijo {excl.} Med *col-dia* used to take leave of somebody informally, bye-bye, adieu <**Ita**> ☞ **adio, adios**

àdio {excl.} Med *col-dia* used to take leave of somebody informally, bye-bye, adieu <**Ita**> ☞ **adijo, adios**

adȉos {excl.} *sl* used to take leave of somebody informally, bye-bye, adios <**Spa**> ☞ **adio, adijo**

- **adȉos grȉngos** {ExcP} *sl-crime* ***Fac*** prison

[ADJ] kòlikō je tėžak {AdjP} (lit. as [ADJ] as heavy) *col* used to denote a high intensity (usu. of a negative personality trait): *On je pokvaren koliko je težak. He is big time sly.* ☞ **težak**

[ADJ/PPRON] mȁslo {LSF} (lit. [ADJ] butter) used to signal someone's fault: *Ta krađa je njegovo maslo. He had his fingers in that theft.* ☞ **maslo**

[ADJ/PPRON] pòsla {NP} (lit. [ADJ] business) *col* ***Off*** used to denote a negative feature specific to a given group, [ADJ/PPRON] dirty business: *Njihova posla će ih odvesti u zatvor. Their dirty business will land them in prison.* ☞ **posla**

àdrapovac {àdrapōvca (acc. = gen.) masc.; Voc àdrapōvče} *sl* ***Der*** homeless person, bum <**Ger**❖>

adrèsa {ē fem.} (lit. address) *sl-crime* ***Fac*** occasion ripe for stealing: *Imaš adresu kod onih što su otišli na ljetovanje. Those people are away on vacation - it's a good chance to rob their home.* <**Lat**>

- **krȋvā adrèsa** {NP} (lit. wrong address) *col* failure

àduak {àduāka masc.} *sl-crime* bumping into and picking somebody's pockets: *Danas sam napravio tri aduaka. Today I bumped into three people and picked their pockets.*

àdūt {adúta masc.} (lit. trump, trump-card) **1** *sl-sstu* ***Fac*** failing grade <**Fre***1> **2** Obs *sl-sex* ***Fac*** penis <**Fre***1>

àdverbovati {bujēm, bujū biasp. intr.} *sl* practice law <**Lat**❖*1>

advòkāt *See the following*

- **dȓvenī advòkāt** {NP} (lit. wooden attorney) *col* person who always stands up for others (e.g. in disputes or before authorities)

àđār {ađára (acc. = gen.) masc.; Voc àđāre} **Din** *dia-col* hero

àē {excl.} *col* used to express satisfaction, surprise, delight, dislike, pain, etc., ah, aah <**Slav**>

aékati {àēkām, aékājū imperf. intr.} *col* keep pronouncing 'ae' to express satisfaction, surprise, delight, dislike, pain, etc. <**Slav**❖> ☞ **ae**

aéknuti {àēknēm, nū perf. intr.} *col* pronounce 'ae' to express satisfaction, surprise, delight, dislike, pain, etc. <Slav⁘> ☞ **ae**

ȁerodrom {a masc.} (lit. airport) *sl-drugs* gathering place for drug addicts <Gre*1>

• **àerodrom za mȕhe** {NP} (lit. airport for flies) *sl-fea* ***Fac*** bald head

afèrim {excl.} **Din** *col* ***App*** used to express appreciation, way to go, good show <NE> ☞ **averım**

afganistánac {nca (acc. = gen.) masc.; Voc afganīsānče} *sl-drugs* Afghani hash <Slav⁘>

àfīnger {a masc.} (lit. hanger) *sl* ***Der-Fac*** slender female <Ger*1>

Afrikánac {nca (acc. = gen.) masc.; Voc Ȁfrikānče} (lit. African) *sl* ***Off*** Gypsy (male) <Slav*1>

àga {ē masc.} (lit. agha, landowner in Ottoman Empire) *sl-col* ***Fac*** boss <NE*1>

ȁgbaba {ē masc.} *sl-sex* ***Obs*** male who engages in sexual intercourse with elderly females <Slav✍>

àgiš {a (acc. = gen.) masc.} *sl-crime* detective <Lat⁘>

àgiša {ē masc.} **a.** *sl-crime* detective <Lat⁘> **b.** *sl-crime* policeman, cop <Lat⁘*1>

agitȉška {ē fem.; Dat agìtiški} **a.** *sl-polit* political agitation <Lat⁘> **b.** *sl-polit* urging, pressing <Lat⁘*1>

agresívac {vca (acc. = gen.) masc.; Voc ȁgresīvče} *col* aggressive person, bully <Lat⁘>

ȁh {excl.} *col* used to express satisfaction, surprise, delight, dislike, pain, etc., ah <Slav>

ȁhā [1] {excl.} /ahâ excl./ **1** *col* used to express satisfaction, surprise, delight, dislike, pain, etc., ah, oh, ugh <Slav> **2** *col* used to maintain the channel of communication by signaling attention, uh-huh, right <Slav>

ahȁ [2] {excl.} *col* used to express that something important, usu. dangerous or illegal, is observed, aha <Slav>

ahâ [3] {excl.} *col* used to indicate that the import of what was said has been grasped, uh-huh, got it <Slav>

ahàluk {a masc.} BosM *dia-col* pronouncing 'aha' when grasping the import of conversation <Slav-NE⁘> ☞ **ahȁ**

ȁhat {a (acc. = gen.) masc.} [std. = at] BosM *col* horse (the animal) <NE✍>

ȁhbāb {ahbába (acc. = gen.) masc.; Voc ȁhbābe, ȁhbābu} BosM *col* close friend, good buddy <NE>

ahíret {a masc.} BosM *col* afterlife <NE>

ahíretskī {ā, ō adj.} BosM *col* pertaining to the afterlife <NE>

àhlak {a masc.} **BosM** *col-dia* ***App*** good behavior, moral behavior: *Njemu je ahlak uvijek bio najpreči. Good behavior was always the most important thing to him.* <NE>

ȁi {excl.} **a.** *col* used to express surprise, astonishment, etc., hey <Slav> **b.** *col* used to express grief, pain, astonishment, etc., oh, woe <Slav*1>

ȁih {excl.} *col* used to express surprise, astonishment, etc., hey <Slav>

ȁiii {excl.} *col* used to express astonishment, etc., hey <Slav>

àir {a masc.} **Din** *dia* profit, gain: *Od tog prljavog posla nema aira. One cannot profit from that dirty business.* <NE> ☞ **hair**

àj {excl.} [std. = hajde] **1** *col* used in direct informal communication with a person to urge him/her to do something, do it, why don't you, go ahead: *Aj kupi novine! Why don't you buy the newspaper?* <Slav> **2** *col* used in direct informal communication with a person to urge him/her to move, come on: *Aj sa mnom, idemo odavde! Come on, let's get out of here!* <Slav> **3** *col* used to express pain or astonishment, ah <Slav> ☞ **ajd, ajde, hajd, hajde**

• **Àj ćȁo!** {ExcP} *col* used as an informal farewell (usu. by younger people), See ya!

• **àj dòbro** {ExcP} *col* used to express a hesitant approval, well, OK: *A: Hoćeš li sa mnom u kino? B: Aj dobro. A: Will you go to the movies with me? B: Well, OK.*

• **Àj u[NP]!** {LSF} (lit. Go to [NP]) *col* ***Off*** used as an angry response to disliked action or words, Damn you!: *Aj u kurac krasni! Neću da to radim! Damn you! I won't do it!*

• **Àj vâmo!** {ExcP} *col* used to make one's interlocutor get to the place where one is located, Get over here!

• **Àj zdrȁvo!** {ExcP} *col* ***Fam*** used as an informal farewell, See ya!

ȁjāj {excl.} *col* used to express grief, pain, despair, etc., oh, ow <Slav>

ȁjaō {excl.} *col* used to express grief, pain, despair, etc., oh, ow <Slav>

ȁjaoh {excl.} *col* used to express grief, pain, despair, etc., oh, ow <Slav>

ȁjati {ām, ajū imperf. intr.} *dia* wander, roam <Slav✍>

àjd {excl.} [std. = hajde] **1** *col* used in direct informal communication with another person to encourage him/her to act <Slav> **2** *col* used in direct informal communication with another person to encourage him/her to move <Slav> ☞ **aj, ajde, hajd, hajde**

• **Àjd niz mòjēga!** {S} (lit. Go down my prick!) *col Off* used as an angry response to disliked action or words, Damn you!

• **Àjd u[NP:ACC]!** {LSF} (lit. Go to [NP:NOM]!) *col Off* used as an angry response to disliked action or words, Damn you!: *Neću to da radim! Ajd u kurac! I'm not gonna do that! Fuck you!*

• **Àjd uz mòjēga!** {S} (lit. Go up my prick!) *col Off* used as an angry response to disliked action or words, Damn you!

• **Àjd zdrȁvo!** {ExcP} *col* used as an informal farewell, See ya!

ȁjdē [1] {part.} /ȁjde part./ *col* question tag: *A: Bio sam u Beogradu. B: Ajde? A: I've been to Belgrade. B: No kidding?* <Slav>

àjde [2] {excl.} [std. = hajde] **1** *col* used in direct informal communication with another person to encourage him/her to act <Slav> **2** *col* used in direct informal communication with another person to encourage him/her to move on <Slav> ☞ **aj, ajd, hajd, hajde**

• **àjde dȅ** {ExcP} *col* phrase used to indicate the minimal expected action: *Da se javio da neće doći, ajde de! At least he should have called to say he wasn't coming!*

• **Àjde natȑči pȁ ću te jèbati!** {S} (lit. Run over here and I will fuck you!) *col Off* used as a threat, I'm gonna beat the shit out of you!

• **Àjde u[NP:ACC]!** {LSF} (lit. Go to [NP:ACC]!) *col Off* used as an angry response to disliked action or words, Fuck you!: *Ajde u kurac! Neću da to radim! Fuck you! I won't do it!*

àjdūk {ajdúka (acc. = gen.) masc.; Voc ȁjdūče} [std. = hajduk] **a.** *col* Serbian guerilla fighter during the Ottoman Empire <Slav> **b.i.** *col App* courageous person <Slav*1> **ii.** *col Der* troublemaker, rowdy, ruffian <Slav*1>

àjdukovati {kujēm, kujū imperf.} [std. = hajdukovati] *col* act as a Serbian guerilla fighter in the Ottoman Empire <Slav>

ȁjfōr {a masc.} âjfor/ /IFOR/ *col* IFOR (Implementation Forces for Dayton Peace Agreement in Bosnia in the 1990s) <EngO*1>

ȁjhāj {excl.} *col* used to express joy, satisfaction, etc., yes <Slav>

àjkula {ē fem.} (lit. shark) **1** *sl Der* big-boned female, whale <Ger*1> **2** *sl-sex App* sexually aroused female, hot chick <Ger*1> **3** *sl-auto* big Citroen (make of car) <Ger*1>

àjkuna {ē fem.} BosM *dia* female <NE> ☞ **hajkuna**

àjlučār {a (acc. = gen.) masc.} //ajlukčára (acc. = gen.) masc/ **a.** BosM *dia* mercenary <NE> **b.** BosM *dia* monthly wage earner <NE*1> ☞ **ajlugdžija**

ajlùgdžija {ē masc.} **a.** BosM *dia* mercenary <NE> **b.** BosM *dia* monthly wage earner <NE*1> ☞ **ajlučar**

àjmana {ē fem.} *dia Der* careless person <NE>

àjmo {excl.} [std. = hajdemo] *col* used to stimulate to a common action: *Ajmo u kino! Let's go to the movies!* <Slav> ☞ **hajmo**

àjncelafale {ea masc.} /ajncelȁfale /ea masc./ *sl-crime* walk in the prison courtyard <Ger>

àjnpren-čórba {ē fem.} *col* simple soup with flour only <Ger-NE>

ȁjnšlājg {a masc.} *sl-auto* turn e.g. wide turns of a truck) <Ger>

àjnšprel-dízna {ē fem.} *sl-auto* injection nozzle <Ger>

àjnštancovati {cujēm, cujū imperf. intr.} *sl* stand in one place for a long time (usu. while waiting for someone) <Ger>

ȁjōj {excl.} *col* used to express pain, grief, despair, oh, ow <Slav>

ȁjs {excl.} *dia-col* used to urge an ox to move on <Slav>

ȁjskānje {a neut.} *col* pronouncing 'ajs' to urge an ox to move on <Slav> ☞ **ajs**

ȁjskati {ām, ajū imperf. intr.} *col* keep pronouncing 'ajs' to urge an ox to move on <Slav> ☞ **ajs**

ȁjsnuti [1] {nēm, nū perf. intr.} *col* pronounce 'ajs' to urge an ox to move on <Slav> ☞ **ajs**

ȁjsnuti [2] {nēm, nū perf.} **a.** *sl* hit, punch: *Ajsnuo ga je u bradu da mu je potekla krv. He hit him on the chin and he bled.* <Slav> **b.** *sl-sex* engage in sexual intercourse with (of a male), bang <Slav*1>

ȁjsovānje {a neut.} *sl-sex* anal sexual intercourse <Slav❖*1>

ȁjsovati {sujēm, sujū imperf.} *sl-sex* engage in anal sexual intercourse with (of a male) <Slav❖*1>

àjte {excl.} [std. = hajdete] **1** *col* used in direct informal communication with several persons or formal communication with a person to encourage them to act or move: *Ajte sad uradite zadaću! Now do your homework!* <Slav> **2** *col* used in direct informal communication with several persons or formal communication with a person to encourage them to act or move: *Ajte sa mnom! Come on, let's go!* <Slav> ☞ **hajte**

ak {c.} [std. = ako] *col* if <Slav☞>

akadèmija *See the following*

• **Sȅmenārskā akadèmija - Ȍdsēk za leblèbije** {NP} (lit. Chick-pea Department of the Seed Academy) **SerE** *sl-fea* ***Fac*** substandard vocational school

ȁkānje {a neut.} **1** *sl-sex* ***Obs*** sexual intercourse <**Slav***1> **2** *sl* ***Der*** annoying, bothering <**Slav***1>

ȁkati {ām, ajū imperf.} **1** *sl-sex* ***Obs*** engage in sexual intercourse with (of a male) <**Slav***1> **2a.** *sl* ***Der*** annoy, bother, pester <**Slav***1> **b.** *sl* ***Der*** destroy, ruin <**Slav***2>

ȁkati se {ām, ajū imperf. intr.} **1** *sl-sex* ***Obs*** engage in sexual intercourse with <**NE***1> **2** *sl-sex* spend one's time in useless activities, fool around, mess around <**NE***1>

àkcija {ē fem.} **a.** *col* event <**Lat**> **b.i.** *sl-crime* car theft <**Lat***1> **ii.** *sl-drugs* dealing drugs <**Lat***1>

Ȁknēm ti ga! {S} (lit. I bang it to you!) SSer *dia* ***Off*** used as a moderate curse, Fuck you! ☞ **aknuti**

ȁknuti {nēm, nū perf.} **1a.** *sl* beat up <**Slav***1> **b.i.** *sl-sex* ***Obs*** engage in sexual intercourse with (of a male) <**Slav***2> **ii.** *sl-crime* steal, swipe <**Slav***2> **2** *sl* throw away, toss out <**Slav***1>

• **Ȁknēm ti ga!** {S} (lit. I bang it to you!) SSer *dia* ***Off*** used as a moderate curse, Fuck you!

ȁko {excl.} *col* used to express indifference and lack of control: *A: On će se obogatiti na naš račun. B: Ako. A: He will get rich at our expense. B: So be it.* <**Slav**>

• **ako Bôg dâ** {S} (lit. If God allows) *col* used to express lack of control over events, God willing: *Stići ću, ako Bog da, u četvrtak. God willing, I'll be there on Thursday.*

• **Ako[PRON:DAT] (jâ) (zà tō) (ne) [VERB:PRES] ([NP:ACC])!** {LSF} (lit. If I *[NOT]*[VERB] ([NP:ACC])) *col* ***Off*** used as a threat in response to an undesired action: *Ako ti pokažem! Nećeš me više zajebavati! I'm gonna show you! You won't mess with me any more!*

ȁkobōgda {excl.} (lit. if God allows) [std. = ako bog da] *col* used to express one's uncertainty and lack of control over events, God willing <**Slav**✍>

akȍnto {gen.} *col* about, concerning: *Nisam ništa rekao akonto njegovih grešaka. I didn't say anything about his mistakes.* <**Ita**>

àkrap {a (acc. = gen.) masc.} (lit. scorpion) *sl* ***Der*** unattractive person <**NE***1>

àkrep {a masc.} (lit. scorpion) **a.** *sl-fea* ***Der*** unattractive person <**NE***1> **b.** *sl-fea* ***Der*** slender female <**NE***2>

akròbat {a (acc. = gen.) masc.} (lit. acrobat) *sl* ***App*** skillful and adept male <**Gre***1>

akròbata {ē masc.} (lit. acrobat) *sl* ***App*** skillful and adept male <**Gre***1>

ȁksa {ē fem.} *sl-auto* axle <**Ger**>

ȁksav {a, o adj.} *sl* ***Der*** lame (limping) <**Ger**✣*1>

ȁksavica {ē fem.} *sl* leg (human) <**Ger**✣*1>

aksávko {a masc.} *sl-fea* ***Der*** lame male <**Lat**✣>

ȁkšam {a masc.} BosM *col* sunset, evening <**NE**>

akšȁmlučār {a (acc. = gen.) masc.} **BosM** *col* evening drinker, person who prefers to drink alcohol in the evening <**NE**>

akšȁmlučārskī {ā, ō adj.} BosM *col* pertaining to one who prefers to drink alcohol in the evening <**NE**>

akšȁmlučiti {čīm, čē imperf. intr.} BosM *col* drink alcohol in the evening <**NE**>

akšȁmluk {a masc.} BosM *col* drinking (alcohol) in the evening <**NE**>

àkšēnka {ē fem.} *sl-auto* axle <**Ger**>

ȁktalica {ē fem.} *sl* eye (sight organ) <**Lat***1>

ȁktati {ām, ajū biasp.} **a.** *sl* look, watch, scope out <**Lat***1> **b.i.** *sl* observe (somebody or something) <**Lat***2> **ii.** *sl* contemplate, think <**Lat***2>

ȁktēr {aktéra masc.; Voc ȁktēru} (lit. actor) *sl-crime* pistol, revolver <**Lat***1>

aktívac {vca (acc. = gen.) masc.; Voc àktīvče} (lit. activist) *sl-sex* ***Obs*** male homosexual who takes the active role <**Lat**✣*1>

aktìvist {a (acc. = gen.) masc.} (lit. activist) *sl-sex* ***Obs-Fac*** male homosexual who takes the active role <**Lat**✣*1>

aktìvista {ē masc.} (lit. activist) *sl-sex* ***Obs*** male homosexual who takes the active role <**Lat**✣*1>

àktn-tàška {ē fem.; Dat àktn-tàški} *col* briefcase <**Lat**> ☞ **aktn-tašna, aktovka**

àktn-tàšna {ē fem.} *col* briefcase <**Lat**> ☞ **aktn-taška, aktovka**

ȁktōvka {ē fem.; Dat ȁktovki} *col* briefcase <**Lat**> ☞ **aktn-taška, aktn-tašna**

akumulâtor {a masc.} (lit. car battery) *sl* ***Fac*** stomach, belly, gut <**Lat***1>

• **tùrskī akumulâtor** {NP} (lit. Turkish battery) *sl-fea* person who thinks slowly, dim bulb

akùstičan {čna, čno adj.} (lit. acoustic) **a.** *sl* empty (room, hall, etc.) <**Gre***1> **b.** *sl* boring, uninteresting <**Gre***2>

akušírānje {a neut.} (lit. obstetrics) *sl* ***Iro*** beating up <Fre*1>

akušírati {kùšīrām, kušírajū imperf.} (lit. give obstetric help) *sl* ***Iro*** beat up <Fre*1>

akvârīj {rīja masc.} (lit. aquarium) **a.** *sl* ***Fac*** bar with large windows <Lat*1> **b.** Cro *sl* ***Fac*** name of a bar at Ilica and Marinkovićeva streets in Zagreb, Croatia <Lat*1>

akvârijum {a masc.} (lit. aquarium) **1a.** *sl* ***Fac*** bar with large windows <Lat*1> **b.i.** *sl* ***Fac*** name of a bar with large windows at the Albania building in Belgrade, Serbia <Lat*2> **ii.** *sl* ***Fac*** name of a department store in the Beograđanka high-rise in Belgrade, Serbia <Lat*2> **3** *sl* ***Fac*** place swarming with females <Lat*1>

ȁkvla {àkavla masc.; perm} //ē fem./ [std. = vlak] Cro *sl* train <Slav✍>

al {part.} [std. = ali] *col* intensifying particle <Slav✍>
- **Àl si me[VERB:PRES]!** {LSF} (lit. Did you [VERB: PRES]!) *col* used to refer to that an action has achieved its intended effect: *Al si me prepo! You really scared me!*
- **Al ȕ kūrcu!** {S} (lit. But in *your* prick!) *col* ***Obs*** used as a strong negative response, no way, never
- **Al u pánjevima!** {S} (lit. But in the tree-stumps!) *col* ***Iro*** used as a strong negative response, no way, never
- **Al[VERB]!** {LSF} *col* ***App*** used to refer to the high intensity of action: *Al vozi. How well he drives!*

ȁla [1] {ē fem.} (lit. dragon) **1a.** *sl-crime* ***Der*** policeman, cop <NE*1> **b.i.** *sl-crime* ***Der*** spy, spook <NE*2> **ii.** *sl-crime* ***Der*** police investigator <NE*2> **2** *sl-sstu* ***Der*** strict teacher <NE*1> **3** *sl-sex* ***Der*** prostitute, hooker <NE*1>

àlā [2] {excl.} **1** *col* used to express surprise, admiration, etc., wow: *Ala! Kakvo iznenađenje! Wow! What a surprise!* <Slav> **2** *col* used to make somebody go away <Slav> ☞ **alaj**

àlā [3] {part.} *col* intensifying particle, wow: *Ala je dobar! Wow! He sure is good!* <Slav> ☞ **alaj**

alabânda {excl.} Med *dia* used in folk songs without any semantic content <Ita>

aladùmati {ām, ajū imperf.} *sl* contemplate, think: *Aladumam već dvije sedmice da li da kupim taj auto. I have been considering buying that car for two weeks now.* <Rus✍>

àlāj [1] {excl.} *col* used to express surprise, ah <Slav> ☞ ala

àlāj [2] {part.} *col* intensifying particle: *Alaj ste se brzo vratili! Gosh, how fast you got back!* <Slav> ☞ **ala**

àlāj-bàrjāk {a masc.} BosM *dia* regimental colors <NE>

àlājbeg {a (acc. = gen.) masc.; Voc àlājbeže} BosM *dia* military commander (esp. in Ottoman times) <NE>

àlājbegov {a, o adj.} BosM *dia* military commander's (esp. in Ottoman times) <NE>

àlāl [1] {alála masc.} **Din** *col* forgiveness <NE*1> ☞ **halal**

àlāl [2] {part.} **Din** *col* intensifying particle: *Alal su nas prešli. They really made fools of us.* <NE*1>
- **Àlāl([PRON:DAT]) [NOUN:NOM]!** {LSF} *col* ***App*** used to express approval, appreciation, etc.: *Odlično urađeno! Alal vera! Excellent job! Good for you!* ◊ *Super ručak! Alal ti ćufte! Super dinner! Good for you!* ◊ *Kako ova riba peva! Alal joj ripče! She's an awesome singer! Good for her!*

aláliti {àlālīm, lē biasp.} **Din** *col* forgive, pardon <NE*1> ☞ **halaliti**

alàmunja {ē fem.} *col* ***Fam*** irresponsible person <Slav>

alàpača {ē fem.} *sl-fea* ***Off*** extremely talkative female, chatterbox <NE*1>

alásiti se {àlāsīm, sē imperf. intr.} *sl* get rid of, do away with: *Alasio sam se svog svojeg smeća. I've gotten rid of all my junk.* <Hun*1>

àlat [1] {a (acc. = gen.) masc.} Bos *dia* bay (horse) <NE>

àlāt [2] {aláta masc.} (lit. tools) *sl-sex* ***Fac-Obs*** penis, tool <NE*1>

alàtljikār {a (acc. = gen.) masc.; Voc alàtljikāru} (lit. the one who has the tools) *sl-sex* ***Fac-App-Obs*** sexually potent male <NE✣*1>

ȁlav {a, o adj.} **Din** *col* ***Der*** greedy (food, money, etc.): *On je toliko alav da počije jesti prije nego što drugi sjednu za sto. He is so greedy that he starts eating before others even reach the table.* <NE>

ȁlavac {lāvca (acc. = gen.) masc.} *col* ***Der*** greedy male (for food, money, etc.) <NE✣*1>

alàvānta {ē fem.} **a.** *sl* street fight: *Izgubio je oko u jednoj od alavanti. He lost his eye in one of his street fights.* <NE> **b.** *sl* mess, disorder, disturbance: *Djeca su napravila toliku alavantu da sam poludjela. The kids made such a mess that I went nuts.* <NE>

alavèrtisati se {išēm, išū imperf. intr.} *sl* succeed, separate, part from: *Alavertisao se od roditelja prošle godine. He split from his parents last year.* <Fre*1>

ȁlavica {ē fem.} *col* ***Der*** greedy female (for food, money, etc.) <NE✣*1>

alavȋja {ē fem.} **Med** *col* good luck, lucky strike, run of luck: *Imala je alaviju na ruletu, pa je dobila tri hiljade maraka. She had a run of luck at the roulette and won three thousand German marks.* <**Ita**>

àlbaksa {ē fem.} *sl-auto* half axle <**Ger**>

albȁšča {ē fem.} /àlbašča /e fem./ **a.** **BosM** *dia* flower garden <**NE**> **b.** **BosM** *dia* ornamental coin (usu. worn as a part of a folk costume) <**NE**[*1]>

ȁlčak {a (acc. = gen.) masc.} **Din** *col-dia* ***Fam*** joker, trickster, rascal <**NE**>

aldùmāš {aldumáša masc.; Voc ȁldumāšu} **a.** *sl* drinking (alcohol) <**Hun-NE**> **b.i.** *sl* party (social gathering) <**Hun-NE**[*1]> **ii.** *sl* celebration <**Hun-NE**>

ȁle {excl.} *col* used to signal assurance <**Slav**>

âle {eta neut.} *sl-crime* ***Der*** policeman, cop <**NE**☝>

aléja *See the following*

- **aléja ìslūženih** {NP} (lit. boulevard of the used up ones) *sl* ***Fac*** cemetery

alelúja {excl.} *col* used to express praise or joy (usu. religious), hallelujah <**Heb**>

Alemànja {ē fem.} *sl* Germany <**Fre**>

ȁlhos {a (acc. = gen.) masc.} *sl-drink* alcoholic, drunk <**NE**☝>

Àlibaba *See the following*

- **Àlibaba i četrdèsēt hajdúkā** {NP} (lit. Alibaba and the forty thieves *some classes in the former Yugoslavia have forty students*) *sl-sstu* ***Fac*** teacher with his/her students

aligâtor {a (acc. = gen.) masc.; Voc aligâtoru} (lit. alligator) *sl-fea* ***Der*** unattractive male, dog <**Spa**[*1]>

aligâtorica {ē fem.} (lit. she-alligator) Cro *sl-fea* ***Der*** unattractive female, dog <**Spa**❖[*1]>

aligâtōrka {ē fem.; Dat aligâtōrki} (lit. she-alligator) *sl-fea* ***Der*** unattractive female, dog <**Spa**❖[*1]>

alijánović {a (acc. = gen.) masc.} *sl-crime* ***Der*** detective <**NE**❖[*1]>

àlijeriti {rīm, rē imperf. intr.} *sl-dia* sneak, attempt not to be observed: *Šta mi alijeriš iza kuće? Why are you sneaking behind my house?* <**Slav**>

alìluj {excl.} *col* used to express praise or joy (usu. religious), hallelujah <**Heb**>

alilúja {excl.} *col* used to express praise or joy (usu. in religious contexts), hallelujah <**Heb**>

ȁlk {a +ov (ext. pl) masc.; Nom Pl àlkovi} *sl-drink* alcoholic beverage <**NE**☝>

àlka {ē fem.; Dat àlki} (lit. door knocker) **1a.** *sl-sex* ***Obs*** anus, asshole <**NE**[*1]> **b.** *sl-sex* ***Obs*** buttocks, butt <**NE**[*2]> **2a.** *sl* ***Fac*** finger ring <**NE**[*1]> **b.** *sl* hole, opening <**NE**[*2]> **c.** *sl* ***Fac*** wedding ring <**NE**[*2]> **3** *sl-crime* ***Der*** spy, spook <**NE**[*1]>

alkárēnje {a neut.} *sl-sex* ***Obs*** male homosexual intercourse <**NE**[*1]>

àlkica {ē fem.} **1a.** *sl-sex* ***Obs*** anus, asshole <**NE**❖[*1]> **b.** *sl-sex* ***Obs*** buttocks, butt <**NE**❖[*2]> **2** *sl* fruit <**NE**❖[*3]> **3** *sl-crime* undercover agent <**NE**[*1]>

ȁlkić {a (acc. = gen.) masc.} *sl-drink* ***Fam*** alcoholic, drunk <**NE**❖☝>

ȁlko {a masc.} *sl-drink* drinking (alcohol) <**NE**☝>

ȁlko-trȉp {a +ov (ext. pl) masc.; Nom Pl ȁlko-trìpovi} *sl-drink* drinking bout <**NE-Eng**[*1]>

alkohòlisānje {a neut.} *sl-drink* drinking (alcohol) <**NE**❖>

alkokòličār {a (acc. = gen.) masc.} [std. = alkoholičar] *sl-drink* ***Fac*** alcoholic, drunk <**NE**❖☝>

ȁlkos {a (acc. = gen.) masc.} /ȁlkos/ *sl-drink* alcoholic, drunk <**NE**☝> ☞ **alkoholičar**

Àllah *See the following*

- **Ȁllāhu drâgī!** {S} (lit. Dear God!) BosM *col* used to express astonishment, etc., Good God!

ȁlō {excl.} /alô excl./ **1** *col* used to open telephonic conversation or maintain the channel of communication, hello <**Eng**> **2** *col* used to address a male in direct informal communication, hey <**Eng**[*1]> ☞ **halo**

àlōv {excl.} *col* used to urge somebody to do something <**Fre**>

alternatívac {vca (acc. = gen.) masc.} (lit. the alternative one, used initially for environmentalists and other alternative political parties) **1** *col* alternative politician (outside mainstream politics) <**Lat**❖> **2** *col* healer, one who practices non-conventional medicine <**Lat**❖> **3** *col* alternative artist (in general) <**Lat**❖> **4** *col* bohemian, one who lives unconventionally <**Lat**❖>

ȁljav {a, o adj.} **a.** *col* ***Der*** untidy, messy: *On je toliko aljav da mu se ne vidi pod u spavaćoj sobi. He is so untidy that you can't see the floor of his bedroom.* <**Slav**> **b.** *col* ***Der*** messy, disorderly: *Mrzim aljkavu kuhinju. I hate a messy kitchen.* <**Slav**[*1]>

àljina {ē fem.} [std. = haljina] *col-dia* dress (female garment) <**Slav**☝> ☞ **aljna**

ȁljkav {a, o adj.} *sl-fea* ***Der*** careless <**Hun**>

ȁljkavac {vca (acc. = gen.) masc.} *sl-fea* ***Der*** careless, irresponsible, and sloppy male <Hun❖>

ȁljkavica {ē fem.} *sl-fea* ***Der*** careless, irresponsible, and sloppy female <Hun❖>

aljkàvuša {ē fem.} *sl-fea* ***Der*** careless, irresponsible, and sloppy female <Hun❖>

ȁljna {ē fem.} [std. = haljina] *col-dia* dress (female garment) <Slav✍> ☞ **aljina**

ȁma {excl.} *col* used to express difference of opinion, but: *Ama nije to taj čovjek o kome sam pričala! But that is not the man I was telling you about!* <Slav>

amàkluk {a masc.} BosM *col-dia* lack of intelligence, stupidity <NE>

àmāl {amála masc.; Voc. ȁmālu} *col* porter <NE> ☞ **hamal**

amàluk {a masc.} BosM *col-dia* stupidity, lack of intelligence <NE>

àmān[1] {excl.} Din *col* used to express surprise, astonishment, etc., oh, God: *Aman, šta je ovo! Oh, God, what is this!* <NE>

amȁn[2] *See the following*

- **amȁn járabi** {ExcP} **BosM** *col* used to express astonishment, usu. about something undesirable, Oh God!: *Aman jarabi kolko su ljudi poubijali. Oh God, how many people have they killed.*

àmān-zàmān {excl.} *col* used to express surprise, astonishment, etc., oh, God: *Aman-zaman! Ko je to uradio? God! Who did this!* <NE>

amánet {a masc.} **1** Din *col* testament, will <NE> **2** Din *col* heritage, inheritance <NE>

amánetnī {ā, ō adj.} Din *col* pertaining to testament, will <NE>

ambálaža {ē fem.} (lit. wrapping) **a.** *sl-col* ***Fac*** clothing, garment <Fre[*1]> **b.** *sl* ***Fac*** sweatshirt <Fra[*2]>

ȁmbār {a masc.} (lit. barn) **1** *sl-crime* ***Fac*** pocket (on a coat, trousers, etc.) <NE[*1]> **2** *sl-auto* ***Fac*** garage <NE[*1]>

ambasáda {ē fem.} (lit. embassy) **1** *sl* ***Fac*** apartment <Fre[*1]> **2** *sl* ***Iro*** prison, the big house <Fra[*1]>

àmbisati se {išēm, išū imperf. intr.} *sl* decay, rot <Gre[*1]>

àmbulja {ē fem.} **a.** *sl* unattractive clothing <Gre[*1]> **b.** *sl* winter coat <Gre[*2]>

améba {ē fem.} (lit. amoeba) *sl-fea* ***Der*** coward, chicken <Gre[*1]>

ámen {excl.} (lit. amen) Cro *col* used to signal approval (usu. religious), amen <Heb>

Ȁmer {a (acc. = gen.) masc.; Voc Ȁmeru} *col* American (person) <SlavO✍>

Amerȉgos {a (acc. = gen.) masc.} (lit. American) *sl* ***Fac*** American (person) <SpaO❖[*1]>

Amèrika {ē fem.} **1** *sl-crime* ***App*** occasion ripe for stealing <Slav> **2** *sl* ***App*** something very good <Slav> **3** *sl* rich person <Slav>

Amerikánac {nca (acc. = gen.) masc.; Voc Ȁmerikānče} **1** *sl-crime* ***Iro*** watch smuggler who pretends to be an American (person) <SlavO> **2** *sl-sports* ***App*** nicely shaped glass marble (the toy) <SlavO>

amerikáner {a (acc. = gen.) masc.} (lit. American) **1** *sl-crafts* monkey wrench <GerO[*1]> **2** *sl* a mixture of soda water and mineral water <GerO[*1]>

amerȉkanke {ī fem. pl.} (lit. Americans) *sl-crime* handcuffs, cuffs <SlavO❖[*1]>

Amèrka {ē fem.} [std. = Amerika] *col* America <Slav✍>

ȁmf {a +ov (ext. pl) masc.; Nom Pl àmfovi} *sl-drugs* amphetamine, benny <Lat✍>

ȁmfī {īja masc.} *sl-drugs* amphetamine, benny <Lat✍>

àmfībija {ē fem.} (lit. amphibian) *sl-sex* ***Fac-Obs*** bisexual, AC/DC <Gre[*1]>

ȁmfić {a masc.} *sl-drugs* amphetamine, benny <Lat✍>

ȁmfora {ē fem.} (lit. amphora) **1** *sl* ***Der*** senior citizen: *U taj restoran dolaze samo amfore. Only old timers go to that restaurant.* <Gre[*1]> **2** *sl-sex* ***Obs*** lover (female) <Gre[*1]>

àmidža {ē masc.; Voc àmidža} BosM *col* uncle (father's brother) <NE>

àmidžić {a (acc. = gen.) masc.} BosM *col* cousin (paternal) <NE>

àmidžīnica {ē fem.} BosM *col* aunt (wife of father's brother) <NE>

ámin {excl.} Ser *col* used to signal approval (usu. religious), amen <Heb>

áminovati {nujēm, nujū imperf.} **Ser** *col* approve, confirm, sanction: *Šef je aminovao njegov projekt. The boss approved his project.* <Heb❖>

àmōrka {ē fem.; Voc àmōrki} *sl-sex* lover (female) <Lat❖>

amortȉzēr {tizéra masc.} (lit. shock absorber) *sl-sex* ***Fac-Obs*** female breast, tit <Lat❖[*1]>

ȁmp {a +ov (ext. pl) masc.; Nom Pl àmpovi} *sl-drugs* ampoule of methedrine <**Lat**✐>

amputírati {pùtīrām, putírajū perf.} (lit. amputate) *sl* ***Fac*** get rid of: *Amputirao sam stari auto. I've gotten rid of my old car.* <**Lat**[*1]>

àmrēl {amréla masc.} *col* umbrella <**Ita**>

amréla {ē fem.} *col* umbrella <**Ita**>

amza {ē masc.} *sl* ***Der*** lazy or shiftless person, bum, good for nothing <**NE**[*1]>

ân [1] {a +ov (ext. pl) masc.; Nom Pl ánovi} [std. = han] **Din** *col-dia* low-class tavern or inn (esp. in Ottoman times) <**NE**✐>

an [2] *See the following*

- **an trčân** {PP} (lit. en running) *sl* ***Fac*** en passant

Ȁna *See the following*

- **svêtā Ȁna** {NP} (lit. St. Ann) *sl-sex* female who frequently engages in fellatio

ánalica {ē fem.} *sl-arch* fruit

analìtičār [1] {a (acc. = gen.) masc.} (lit. analyst) *sl-sex* ***Obs*** male who engages in anal sexual intercourse <**Lat**⁘[*1]>

analìtičār [2] {a masc.} (lit. analyst) *sl-sex* ***Obs*** anus, asshole <**Lat**⁘[*1]>

analìtičārka {ē fem.; Dat analìtičārki} (lit. analyst) **1** *sl-sex* ***Fac-Obs*** female who enjoys anal sexual intercourse <**Lat**⁘[*1]> **2** *sl-sex* ***Obs*** anus, asshole <**Lat**⁘[*1]>

ȁnamo {adv.} [std. = onamo] *dia-col* there: *Moja je kuća anamo iza brda. My house is there behind the hill.* <**Slav**>

anatèmate {excl.} *col-dia* ***Off*** used to cast spell on somebody <**Gre**>

anàtomke {ī fem. pl.} (lit. anatomic trousers) *sl-col* ***Fac*** tight trousers <**Gre**>

ȁnda {ànada masc.; perm} [std. = dan] *sl* day <**Slav**✐>

andarmólja {ē fem.} **a.** *col* trifle, thing of little importance or value: *Kupio je neke andramolje za osamsto kuna. He bought some trifles for eight hundred kunas.* <**GreMod**> **b.** *sl-sex* intrauterine device, IUD <**GreMod**[*1]> ☞ **andrmolj, andrmolja**

ȁndergrâund {a masc.} (lit. underground) **a.** *sl* underground (organization) <**Eng**> **b.i.** *sl* basement <**Eng**[*2]> **ii.** *sl-drugs* shelter for drug addicts <**Eng**[*1]> **iii.** *sl-media* underground movie or music <**Eng**[*1]>

àndrak [1] {a (acc. = gen.) masc.} *col-dia* devil <**NE**>

àndrak [2] {a masc.} **1** *col-dia* trouble, problem: *Imao je neki andrak sa poreznicima. He had some problems with the IRS.* <**NE**> **2** *col-dia* bush, shrub <**NE**>

- **Kòjī ti je àndrāk?** {S} (lit. What kind of devil is it to you?) *dia* used to express negative attitude toward one's interlocutor, What the devil is wrong with you?

andrèsa {ē fem.} [std. = adresa] *dia-col* address (mail, etc.) <**Fre**✐>

andresírati {drèsīrām, dresírajū biasp.} [std. = adresirati] *dia-col* address (mail, etc.) <**Fre**✐>

andr̀mōlj {drmólja masc.} *col* thing of little importance or value, trifle <**GreMod**[*1]> ☞ **andramolja, andrmolja**

andrmólja {ē fem.} *col* thing of little importance or value, trifle <**GreMod**> ☞ **andramolja, andrmolj**

àndžār {andžára masc.} *dia* dagger (esp. one used as a weapon) <**NE**> ☞ **handžar**

anđèlčić {a (acc. = gen.) masc.} (lit. little angel) *sl-crime* ***Iro*** policeman, cop <**Gre**⁘[*1]>

ânđeō {ela (acc. = gen.) masc.} (lit. angel) *sl-crime* ***Iro*** policeman, cop <**Gre**[*1]>

- **plâvī ânđeō** {NP} (lit. blue angel) *sl-crime* policeman, cop, man in blue

ânđeoskī prâh {NP} (lit. angel dust) *sl-drugs* phencyclidine, angel dust ☞ **prah**

ánež {a masc.} *sl-arch* food <**NE**[*1]>

ȁniti {nīm, nē imperf.} *sl-arch* eat, devour: *Anio je kokice. He was feeding his face with popcorn.* <**Slav**✐>

ànlaser {a masc.} *sl-auto* starter <**Ger**>

ànlaserovānje {a neut.} (lit. car ignition) *sl* initial flirting <**Ger**⁘[*1]>

ànlasovānje {a neut.} (lit. car ignition) *sl* ***Fac*** initial flirting <**Ger**⁘[*1]>

ȁnsta {ànasta masc.; perm} //e masc// *sl* apartment <**Slav**✐>

ànšpric-dízna {ē fem.} *sl-auto* injection nozzle <**Ger**>

anténa {ē fem.} (lit. antenna) **1** *sl-fea* ***Fac*** tall person: *udariti po anteni* box on the ear <**Lat**[*1]> **2** *sl* ***Fac*** ear <**Lat**[*1]>

antibiòtik {a masc.} (lit. antibiotic) *sl* ***Fac*** bus (usu. in public transportation) <**Gre**[*1]>

àntifrīz {a masc.} (lit. antifreeze) *sl* ***Fac*** bad hair day: *doći u školu s antifrizom come to school on a bad hair day* <**Eng**[*1]>

antìkvār {tikvára (acc. = gen.) masc.} (lit. antiquarian) *sl-sex* ***Obs*** male who engages in sexual intercourse with elderly females <**Lat**[*1]>

antìkvārnjāk {a masc.} *col-sl* antique store <Lat✣*1>

antilòpa {ē masc.} (lit. antelope) *col-sl* ***App*** fast runner, antelope, gazelle <Gre*1>

antiprồtīvan {vna, vno adj.} [std. = protivan] *col* opposing, having objections to: *biti antiprotivan svakom prijedlogu oppose each and every suggestion* <Lat-Slav✣>

ȁnu {excl.} **1** *col* used to draw attention<Slav> **2** *col* used to emphasize a directive: *Anu, podigni to! Well, pick it up!* <Slav> ☞ **a-nu, anute**

ȁnute {excl.} *col* used to emphasize a directive: *Anute, podigni to! Well, pick it up!* <Slav> ☞ **a-nu, anu**

ànjesti {njēm, njū perf. irreg.} *sl-arch* baptize (into a church)

ànjesti se {njēm, njū perf. irreg.} *sl* be baptized (into a church)

ánjež {a masc.} *sl-arch* food <NE*1>

ànzac {a masc.} *sl-auto* cylinder casing <Ger>

ȁo {excl.} *col* used to express satisfaction, surprise, delight, dislike, pain, etc., ah <Slav>

ȁoh {excl.} *col* used to express surprise, amazement, etc., ah <Slav>

ȁoj {excl.} *col* used to express grief, pain, astonishment, etc., oh, woe <Slav>

ȁokle {adv.} [std. = odakle] *col-dia* from where: *Aokle je ovaj došo? Where did this guy come from?* <Slav☞>

ȁp [1] {excl.} *col* the sound made by swallowing, gulp <Slav>

ȁp [2] {a +ov (ext. pl) masc.; Nom Pl àpovi} (lit. up) *sl-drugs* onset of drug effect <Eng*1>

ápa [1] {ē fem.} *col* ***Fam*** food <Rum*1> ☞ **hapa**

ȁpa [2] {ē masc.} *sl-dia* ***Fam*** father, daddy <Hun>

àpan {a masc.} *sl-crime* ***Der*** petty thief <Slav✣> ☞ **apisati, hapati**

apanírānje {a neut.} (lit. appanage) *sl* assistance, help: *tražiti nečije apaniranje ask for others' help* <Fre*1>

apàrāt {paráta masc.} (lit. gadget) *sl-auto* ***Fac*** car, wheels <Lat*1>

àpāš {apáša (acc. = gen.) masc.; Voc ȁpāšu} *sl-crime* ***Der*** cheater, swindler <Fre>

apatéka {ē fem.; Dat apatéki} [std. = apoteka] *dia-col* drugstore, pharmacy <Gre☞>

apcìgati {ām, ajū biasp.} *sl-sex* ***Obs*** masturbate, beat off <Ger*1>

• **apcìgati maslikána** {VP} (lit. shake the monkey) *sl-sex* ***Obs*** masturbate, spank the monkey

aperácija {ē fem.} [std. = operacija] *col-dia* surgery <Lat☞>

apetìtis {a masc.} [std. = apetit] *sl-col* appetite: *izgubiti apetitis za ribu lose one's appetite for fish* <Lat✣>

• **apetìtis razvalìtis** {NP} (lit. smashing appetite) *sl* ***Fac*** strong appetite

àpisati {išēm, išū imperf.} **a.** *sl-crime* steal, swipe: *apisati novčanike swipe wallets* <Slav> **b.** *sl* take, get hold of, pick <Slav*1> **c.** *sl* eat, devour <Slav*2> ☞ **hapati, apan**

ȁpiti {pīm, pē perf.} **a.** *sl-crime* steal, swipe: *apiti tašnu swipe a purse* <NE> **b.** *sl* take, get hold of, pick <NE*1> **c.** *sl* eat, devour <NE*2>

aplàuz {a masc.} /àplauz /a masc./ (lit. applause) **a.** *sl* ***Fac*** slap, smack: *Dobio je aplauz kad je probo da je poljubi. He got a slap when he tried to kiss her.* <Lat*1> **b.** *sl* ***Fac*** hit, punch <Lat*2> **c.** *sl* ***Fac*** fight (e.g. fist fight) <Lat*3>

• **aplàuz preko tàmburē** {NP} (lit. applause on one's tamburica - mandolin-like folk instrument) *sl* ***Fac*** slap, smack

àpljara {ē fem.} *sl-sex* ***Obs*** prostitute, hooker <Slav☞*1>

ȁpnuti {nēm, nū perf.} **a.** *sl-crime* steal, swipe: *apnuti sat swipe a wristwatch* <NE*1> **b.** *sl* take, get hold of, pick <NE*1> **c.** *sl* eat, devour

ȁpos {a masc.} *sl-drugs* drugstore, pharmacy <Gre☞>

àpostōlka {ē fem.; Dat àpostōlki} (lit. apostolic sandal) *col* sandal (shoe), Jesus boot <Gre✣*1>

ȁpoznāt {a, o adj.} *sl* unknown: *apoznata osoba unknown person* <Slav✣>

ȁprijātan {tna, tno adj.} *sl-fea* unpleasant: *aprijatna situacija unpleasant situation* <Slav☞>

aprìlīlī {excl.} *col* used after a joke or trick is played on April Fools' day, April fool! <Lat✣*1>

aproksimâlis {a masc.} *sl* going insane, freaking out <Lat✣*1>

ȁps {a +ev (ext. pl) masc.; Nom Pl àpsevi} *col* prison <Gre☞> ☞ **apsa**

ȁpsa {ē fem.} *col* prison <Gre☞> ☞ **aps**

apsalȕtno {adv.} [std. = apsolutno] *col-dia* absolutely, totally, completely: *On je apsalunto lud. He is completely nuts.* <Lat*1>

apsàna {ē fem.} *sl-crime* prison <Gre>

ȁpsić {a (acc. = gen.) masc.} /àpsīć/ [std. = apsolvent] *sl-stu* graduating university student <Lat✍>

àpsik {adj.} *sl* ***App*** good, neat: *apsik tene neat sneakers* <NE[*1]>

apsìkulja {ē fem.} *sl-sex* ***App*** attractive female <NE✣[*1]>

ȁpsiti {sīm, sē imperf.} [std. = hapsiti] *col* put under arrest <Gre✍>

• **ȁpsiti brìgu** {VP} (lit. arrest one's worries) *sl-drink* ***Fac*** drink alcohol to forget one's troubles, drown one's worries

ȁpsnuti {nēm, nū perf.} *sl-crime* steal, swipe <Gre✍[*1]>

apsolȕtan {tna, tno adj.} *sl-col* ***App*** excellent, superb, awesome: *apsolutan auto awesome car* <Lat[*1]>

apsolvírati {sòlvīrām, solvírajū perf.} (lit. absolve) *sl-stu* ***Fac*** cease bothering, stop disturbing: *Apsolvirao je Marka. He has eased up and stopped bothering Marko.* <Lat[*1]>

arábatija {ē fem.} *col* very old or malfunctioning car or device <NE> ☞ **harabatija**

àrāč {aráča masc.} (lit. historical tax collected in the Ottoman Empire *usu. forcibly*) [std. = harač] *dia* ***Fac*** tax <NE✍[*1]> ☞ **harač**

aràčlija {ē fem.} (lit. tax collector in the Ottoman Empire, who usu. used force) [std. = haračlija] *dia-col* robber, thief <NE✍[*1]> ☞ **haračlija**

àrambaša {ē masc.} **a.** *col* rebel leader: *Njegov arambaša mi je razbio prozor. His brat broke my window.* <NE✍> **b.i.** *col* problem child, brat <NE✍[*1]> **ii.** *col* violent person, bully: *Treba zvati policiju da uhapsi tog arambašu. One should call the police to arrest that bully.* <NE✍[*1]> ☞ **harambaša**

àrap {a (acc. = gen.) masc.} (lit. Arab) **1** *sl* boy, kid: *njeni arapi her friends* <Slav[*1]> **2** *sl* friend (male) <Slav[*1]> **3** *sl* stranger (male): *Tu je neki arap za tebe. Some stranger is here for you.* <Slav[*1]>

ȁrati {ām, ajū imperf.} *dia* loot, pillage: *Vojnici araju po selu. The soldiers are looting the village.* <NE[*1]> ☞ **harati**

ȁrba {àraba masc.; perm} /e fem./ [std. = bar] *sl-drink* late-night bar <Eng✍>

àrbajt {a masc.} **1** **Gast** *sl-col* work, labor: *Pritiso me arbajt. I am overwhelmed with this work.* <Ger> **2** **Gast** *sl-col* job: *Ima arbajt u pilani. He has a gig in the sawmill.* <Ger>

àrbajtovati {tujēm, tujū imperf.} Gast *sl-col* work hard (at manual labor) <Ger>

Arbànas {a (acc. = gen.) masc.} *col* ***Off*** Albanian (person) <Slav>

arbànaškī {ā, ō adj.} *col* ***Off*** Albanian (pertaining to a person or nation) <Slav>

ârčiti {čīm, čē imperf.} **a.** *col* spend, squander: *arčiti imanje spend, lose one's property* <NE✍> **b.** *sl-sex* engage in sexual intercourse with (of a male)

àrdija {ē fem.} **1** *sl-gamble* clandestine gambling place <NE[*1]> **2** *sl-sex* clandestine place intended for sexual intercourse <NE[*1]>

ardìjān {dijána masc.} *sl-arch* wine <NE>

àrdžija {ē fem.} *sl-fea* stubborn person, pigheaded person <NE>

ȁre {excl.} *sl* used to signal presence: *A: Gdje je cuga? B: Are! A: Where's the booze? B: Here!*

àrgat {a (acc. = gen.) masc.} *col-dia* ***Der*** manual laborer <NE>

àrgatovati {tujēm, tujū imperf.} *col-dia* ***Der*** work hard (at manual labor) <NE>

Argentíner {a (acc. = gen.) masc.} *sl-polit* political emigrant to Argentina <Ger>

àrgō {òa masc.} (lit. argot) *sl-sex* ***Obs*** loose woman, slut <Fre[*1]>

arhìvār {hivára (acc. = gen.) masc.; Voc ȁrhivāru} (lit. archivist) *sl-fea* elderly male <Gre[*1]>

ârija {ē fem.} Med *dia* air <Ita>

arìvati {ām, ajū perf.} Med *dia-col* arrive, come: *arivati u Veneciju arrive in Venice* <Ita>

àrka {ē fem.; Dat àrki} *dia* back (of a person) <NE>

• **Àrka tèbi**! {S} (lit. Back side to you!) *sl* ***Off*** used as an angry response to disliked action or words, Kiss my ass!

àrkan {a masc.} *sl-sex* ***Obs*** penis, dick, prick <Lat[*1]>

arkàna {ē fem.} *sl-sex* ***Obs*** penis, dick, prick <Lat[*1]>

àrlati {ām, ajū imperf.} **a.** *sl* talk: *arlati uz kafu talk over coffee* <NE[*1]> **b.** *sl-fea* talk persistently and meaninglessly, blabber, chatter: *Maja po cijeli dan arla. Maya blabbers all day long.* <NE[*2]>

arlaúkati {làučēm, učū imperf.} *col-sl* scream in pain, fear, or outrage <NE>

arlaúknuti {nēm, nū perf.} **a.** *col-sl* scream in pain, fear, or outrage <NE> **b.** *sl* ***Fac*** die, kick the bucket <NE[*1]>

àrlija {ē fem.} *dia* stubborn person, pigheaded person <NE>

armáda [1] {ē fem.} *sl-mil* military (armed forces in general) <Spa> ☞ **armata**

Armáda [2] {ē fem.} *col* Rijeka soccer team fan club from Rijeka, Croatia <Spa[*1]>

armáta {ē fem.} *sl-mil* military (armed forces in general) <Spa[*1]> ☞ **armada**

àrmija *See the following*
• **za kìnēskū àrmiju** {PP} (lit. for Chinese army) *col* too much, overwhelming

armònika {ē fem.} [std. = harmonika] *col-dia* accordion, squeeze box <Gre*✐> ☞ **ramunika**

armonìkāš {āša (acc. = gen.) masc.} [std. = harmonikaš] *col-dia* accordion player <Gre❖✐>

Arnàut {a (acc. = gen.) masc.} *col-dia* ***Off*** Albanian (person) <NE>

arnàutskī {ā, ō adj.} *col-dia* ***Off*** Albanian (pertaining to a person or nation) <NE>

àrniška {ē fem.; Dat àrniški} *sl* egg <Gyp>

ȁrstva {àristva fem.; perm} /ē fem./ [std. = stvar] *sl* thing, object <Slav✐>

àrtān {artána masc.} *sl-drugs* a brand name of prescription drug used by drug addicts to produce a narcotic effect <BN>

artičòka {ē fem. & masc.; Dat artičòki} /artičóka/ (lit. artichoke) *sl-fea* snob <Fre[*1]>

àrtija {ē fem.} [std. = hartija] SerE *col-dia* paper (e.g. sheets of paper): *artija za pisanje writing paper* <Gre✐>

artiljèrija {ē fem.} (lit. artillery) *sl-drugs* ***Fac*** drug paraphernalia <Fre[*1]>

ȁrto {excl.} *dia-col* used to urge on a horse <Slav>

ȁs {a (acc. = gen.) +ov (ext. pl) masc.; àsovi} (lit. ace *card marked with number one*) **1** *sl-sstu* failing grade <Lat[*1]> **2** Cro *sl* streetcar line number one in Zagreb, Croatia <Lat[*1]>

ȁsba {àsaba masc.; perm} /ē fem./ [std. = bas] *sl-music* bass (musical instrument or tone) <Ita✐>

àsfalterica {ē fem.} (lit. the one from the asphalt) *sl-sex* prostitute, streetwalker <Gre❖[*1]> ☞ **asfalterka, asfaltuša**

asfàltērka {ē fem.; Dat asfàltērki} (lit. the one from the asphalt) *sl-sex* prostitute, streetwalker <Gre❖[*1]> ☞ **asfalterica, asfaltuša**

asfaltírati {fàltīrām, faltírajū biasp.} (lit. asphalt) *sl* ***Fac*** knock down, floor <Gre❖[*1]>

àsfaltnī pût {NP} (lit. pavement road) *sl-sex* ***Fac*** overly stiff hymen ☞ **put**

asfàltuša {ē fem.} (lit. the one from the asphalt) *sl-sex* prostitute, streetwalker <Gre❖[*1]> ☞ **asfalterica, asfalterka**

àskara {ē fem.} (lit. military in the Ottoman Empire) *sl-mil* military (armed forces in general) <NE✐[*1]>

àsker {a (acc. = gen.) masc.} (lit. soldier in the Ottoman Empire) *sl-mil* soldier <NE[*1]>

askèrija {ē fem.} (lit. military in the Ottoman Empire) *sl-mil* military (armed forces in general) <NE[*1]>

askèrōl {keróla masc.} (lit. fluid used to clean weapons) *sl-mil* ***Fac*** coffee with milk <BN>

àsna {ē fem.} **Din** *col-dia* profit, gain: *Imaju veliku asnu od pekare. They've been making a great profit from their bakery.* <NE> ☞ **hasna**

aspìrīn {pirína masc.} (lit. aspirin) *sl-drugs* ***Fac*** drugstore, pharmacy <BN>

aspiríni {ā masc. pl.} (lit. aspirins) *sl-drugs* ***Fac*** narcotic drug, dope <BN>

àstāl {astála (acc. = gen.) masc.} *col-dia* table, desk <Hun> ☞ **hastal**

astrònom {a (acc. = gen.) masc.} (lit. astronomer) *sl* person wearing eyeglasses, four-eyes <Gre[*1]>

àsvalt {a masc.} [std. = asfalt] *col* asphalt <Gre✐>

ȁš {part.} *sl-arch* negative particle, no: *nemati aš problema have no problems whatsoever* <NE>

ȁša {adj.} *sl-arch* big, awesome: *aša auto awesome car* <NE>

ȁšati {ām, ajū imperf.} *sl-arch* lie <NE[*1]>

ȁšav {a, o adj.} *sl-fea* ***Der*** insane, nuts <NE>

àščija {ē masc.; Voc àščija} /àšćija /e masc./ **1 BosM** *dia-col* cook in a Turkish-style restaurant <NE> **2 BosM** *dia-col* owner of a Turkish-style restaurant <NE>

àščījskī {a, o adj.} /àšćīskī /a, o adj./ **1 BosM** *dia-col* pertaining to a Turkish-style restaurant <NE> **2 BosM** *dia-col* pertaining to a soup kitchen <NE>

àščīnica {ē fem.} /àšćinica/ /àšćīnca /e fem./ / e fem./ **1 BosM** *dia-col* Turkish-style restaurant <NE> **2 BosM** *dia-col* soup kitchen <NE>

ašćáre {adv.} BosM *dia-col* intentionally, on purpose <NE>

ašìgdžija {ē masc.} **a.** BosM *dia* gallant <NE> **b.** BosM *dia* suitor <NE[*1]>

àšik {a masc.} BosM *dia* love <NE>

ašìkluk {a masc.} BosM *dia* flirting <NE>

àšikovati {kujēm, kujū biasp. intr.} **a.** **Bos** *col-dia* flirt: *Meho ašikuje sa Suadom. Meho is flirting with Suada.* <NE> **b.i.** Bos *col-dia* be in love <NE*1> **ii.aa.** Bos *sl* look, watch, scope out <NE*1> **bb.** Bos *sl* make preparations for an action of some kind: *ašikujem put u Ameriku I am working on my trip to the States* <NE*2>

ȁšōv {a (acc. = gen.) masc.} /ȁšov/ (lit. spade) **a.** *sl* unattractive female <Hun*1> **b.** *sl* low-class prostitute <Hun*2>

ȁštro {a neut.} [std. = šatrovački] *sl* slang <NE✍>

ȁt {a +ov (ext. pl) masc.; Nom Pl àtovi} *dia* horse (the animal) <NE>

Ȁtamān {a (acc. = gen.) masc.} *sl* ***Fac*** boss <Rus*1>

aterírati {tèrīrām, terírajū biasp. intr.} (lit. land *of a space ship*) **a.** *sl-col* arrive, come: *aterirati u školu arrive at school* <Fre*1> **b.i.** *sl* cease an action: *Brbljao je ali je brzo aterirao. He was babbling but soon stopped.* <Fre*2> **ii.** *sl* start flirting: *aterirati na Mariju start flirting with Mary* <Fre*2>

atmosféra {ē fem.} (lit. atmosphere) *sl* head <Gre*1>

atòmnjāk {tomnjáka masc.} (lit. the atomic one) *sl* sauerkraut <Gre*1>

ȁu {excl.} *col* used to express surprise, astonishment, etc., ah, wow <Slav>

àubakse {ē fem.} *sl-sex* ***Obs*** buttocks, butt <Ger*1>

ȁuer {a masc.} (lit. hour) *sl* hour <Eng>

ȁuf {excl.} *col* used to express surprise, astonishment, etc., ah <Slav>

àufīnger {a masc.} **a.** *col* hanger (for clothes) <Ger> **b.** *col* ***Fac-Der*** slender female <Ger*1>

àufīngerka {ē fem.; Dat àufingerki} (lit. the one who looks like a hanger) *sl* slender female <Ger⁘*1>

ȁuh {excl.} *col* used to express surprise, astonishment, etc., ah <Slav>

àuspuf {a masc.} *sl-auto* exhaust pipe, tail pipe <Ger>

àuspūh {auspúha masc.} **a.** *sl-auto* exhaust pipe, tail pipe <Ger> **b.** *sl-sex* ***Fac*** buttocks, tail, butt <Ger*1>

ȁut [1] {a masc.} (lit. out) **1** *sl-drugs* missing one's vein <Eng*1> **2** *sl-fea* going insane, freaking out <Eng*1>
• **u ȁutu** {PP} (lit. in out) **a.** *sl-fea* expelled: *On je bio u autu iz Amerike. He was expelled from the United States.* **b.** *sl-fea* suspended, on ice

ȁut [2] {adj.} **a.** *sl* out, eliminated: *Mi smo aut sa Svjetskog prvenstva. We are out of the World Cup Championship.* <Eng> **b.** *sl* old-fashioned, passé: *Taj vic je aut. That joke is passé.* <Eng*1>

àutīć {autíća masc.} (lit. small car) *col* ***App*** car, auto <Lat⁘>

àuto {a neut.} *col* car, auto <Lat✍>
• v.d.[vê-dê] **àuto** {NP} (lit. deputy car) *sl-auto* ***Fac*** Trabant (make of simple East German car)

àutolakìrērka {ē fem.} (lit. car-body sprayer) *sl-fea* ***Fac*** female with nail polish <Lat-Ger⁘*1>

automàtičār {a (acc. = gen.) masc.; Voc automàtičār} (lit. expert on automation) **1** *sl-sex* ***Fac*** male habitually on the lookout for females <Lat⁘*1> **2** *sl-sex* ***Fac*** boring sexual partner <Lat⁘*1>

àutostráda {ē fem.} (lit. highway) *sl-sstu* ***Fac*** corridor, hall <Ita*1>

àutotàbanić {a masc.} (lit. foot-car) *sl* ***Fac*** walking <Lat-NE⁘*1>

ȁutsajd {a masc.} (lit. outside) *sl* being absent: *Josip je danas autsajd. Josip is out today.* <Eng*1>

ȁuuu {excl.} *col* used to express surprise, astonishment, etc., wow <Slav>

ȁv {excl.} *col* the sound made by a dog, arf <Slav>

àva {ē fem.} *col-dia* air: *Idi napolje da udahneš avu! Get out and get some fresh air!* <NE> ☞ **hava**

àvāj {excl.} *col* used to express grief, despair, etc., oh, alas: *Avaj, to neće pomoći! Alas, that will not help!* <Slav>

àvanzovati {zujēm, zujū biasp. intr.} *col* get a promotion <Fre*1>

àvaz [1] {a masc.} **Din** *col-dia* voice <NE>

àvaz [2] {a (acc. = gen.) masc.} **Din** *sl-crime* informer, stoolie, snitch <NE*1>

Àvēnija {ē fem.} (lit. avenue) **Cro** *sl-sex* name of a place where prostitutes gather in Zagreb, Croatia near the train station <Fre>
• **àvēnija ȍčāja** {NP} (lit. avenue of despair) **Cro** *sl-sex* ***Fac-Der*** name of a place where prostitutes gather in Zagreb, Croatia near the train station

ȁver {a (acc. = gen.) masc.; Voc ȁveru} **a.** *col* friend (male) <Hebr✍> **b.i.** *sl-crime* accomplice <Hebr✍*1> **ii.** *sl-crime* ***Iro*** informer, stoolie, snitch <Hebr✍*1> **iii.aa.** *sl-crime* ***Iro*** policeman, cop <NE✍*1> **bb.** *sl-crime* ***Iro*** police investigator <NE✍*2> **cc.** *sl* ***Iro*** spy, spook <NE✍*1> **iv.** *sl-sstu* ***Iro*** failing grade <NE✍*1> ☞ **haver**

avèrim {excl.} Din *col-dia* ***App*** used to express appreciation, congratulate, etc. <NE> ☞ **aferim**

avètānje {a neut.} *col* prolonged and meaningless talk, blabber, chatter <NE❖*1>

ávetast {a, o adj.} (lit. ghostly) *sl-fea* careless, irresponsible, shiftless: *Ona je avetasta, nikad ništa ne radi. She is irresponsible. She is never at work.* <NE❖*1>

avètati {ām, ajū imperf.} *col* talk persistently and meaninglessly, blabber, chatter <NE❖*1>

avétinja {ē fem.} /avètinja/ (lit. ghost) **1** *col* evil female, witch <NE❖*1> **2** *col* stupid or mentally deficient person: *Ona avetinja ne zna da koristi kompjuter. That idiot doesn't know how to use a computer.* <NE*1> **3** *col* unattractive person <NE*1>

ávetnīk {a (acc. = gen.) masc.} (lit. ghost) *col* stupid or mentally deficient male <NE❖*1>

àvgān {avgána masc.} (lit. Afghan) *sl-drugs* Afghani hash <Slav*1> ☞ **avganistanac, afganistanac**

avganistánac {nca masc.} (lit. Afghan) *sl-drugs* Afghani hash <Slav*1> ☞ **avgan, afganistanac**

avijàtičār {a (acc. = gen.) masc.} (lit. flier) **1** *sl-fea* handsome male, hunk <Lat❖*1> **2** *sl-crime* fugitive, runaway: *Policija je uhvatila nekog avijatičara. The police have captured a fugitive.* <Lat❖*1>

avijàtika {ē fem.} *sl-sstu* ***Fac*** cutting classes, skipping classes <Lat❖*1>

avijàtiko {a masc.} *sl-sstu* ***Fac*** male student who cuts classes <Lat❖*1>

avìjōn {vijóna masc.} [std. = avion] *col* airplane <Fre✍>

avìōn {vióna (acc. = gen.) masc.; Voc ȁviōne} (lit. plane) **a.** *sl-sex* ***App*** attractive female <Fre*1> **b.** *sl-fea* ***Der*** obese female <Fre*2>

aviònče {eta neut.} (lit. small airplane) *sl-sstu* ***Fac*** failing grade <Fre❖*1>

aviōnka {ē fem.} (lit. she-plane) **a.** *sl-sex* ***App*** attractive female <Fre❖*1> **b.** ***Der*** obese female

àviška {ē fem.; Dat àviški} *sl* adventure <Fre✍❖>

avlijáner {a (acc. = gen.) masc.} (lit. the one from the yard) *sl* ***Fac*** crossbreed dog, mutt, mongrel <NE❖*1>

Avnoslâvija {ē fem.} (lit. AVNOJ - abbreviation for Antifašističko vijeće narodnog oslobođenja, communist body which formed the second Yugoslavia X -slavija - second part from Yugoslavia) *col* ***Fac*** the second Yugoslavia (1945-1990) <Slav❖>

ȁvrlj-bȁvrlj {adv.} *col* here and there, all over: *Ona se mota avrlj-bavrlj. She's been sneaking here and there.* <Slav>

àvte {excl.} *dia-col* ***Der*** used to make somebody go away, beat it, scram <Slav> ☞ **avtos**

àvto {a neut.} [std. = auto] *col-dia* car, auto <Lat✍>

avtomehàničār {a (acc. = gen.) masc.; Voc avtomehàničāru} [std. = automehaničar] *col-dia* car mechanic, grease monkey <Lat✍>

avtomehàničārskī {ā, ō adj.} [std. = automehaničarski] *col-dia* car-mechanic <Lat✍>

ȁvtos {excl.} /ȁvtos excl./ *sl* ***Der*** used to make somebody go away <Gre*1>

àvtuga {ē fem.; Dat àvtugi} *sl-arch* hay <Gre>

Azúri {ā masc. pl.} *sl-sports* players on an Italian national team (e.g. soccer, basketball) <Ita>

aždàha {ē fem.; Dat aždàhi} (lit. dragon) [std. = aždaja] **a.** BosM *col* dragon <NE> **b.** BosM *col-sla* unattractive female, dog: *Nije mi jasno zašto se oženio tom aždajom. I don't understand why he married that dog.* <NE*1>

aždàja {ē fem.} (lit. dragon) **1** *sl-col* ***Der*** unattractive female, dog <NE*1> **2** *sl-sstu* ***Der*** strict teacher: *Aždaja me izbacila s matiša. That strict teacher threw me out of the math class.* <NE*1> **3a.** *sl-crime* ***Der*** policeman, cop <NE*1> **b.** *sl* ***Der*** spy, spook <NE*2>

ȁždìti {dīm, dē imperf.} *sl* eat, devour <Slav✍>

Bb

bâ {excl.} **1** *col* used to address one or more persons in direct informal communication <Slav> **2** *col* the sound made by a sheep, baa <Slav> **3** *col* used to express surprise, astonishment, etc., oh <Slav> ☞ **bolan, bona, boni**

bába [1] {ē masc.} Vojv *col* ***Fam*** father, daddy <NE>

bȁba [2] {ē fem.} **a.** *col* elderly female <Slav*1> **b.** *sl-sstu* ***Der*** teacher <Slav*2>

- **bȁba séra** {NP} (lit. shit granny) *sl* ***Fac*** female bathroom attendant
- **bȁba srȁlja** {NP} (lit. shit granny) *sl* ***Fac*** female bathroom attendant

bábac {pca (acc. = gen.) masc.} **a.** *col* ***Der*** senior citizen <**Slav**> **b.** *sl-sex* attractive elderly female <**Slav**[*1]>

bằbāč {a (acc. = gen.) masc.} *sl* troublemaker, rowdy, ruffian <**Slav**⁘[*1]>

bằbāj {a (acc. = gen.) masc.} *sl-crime* policeman, cop <**Slav**⁘[*1]>

babajága {ē fem.; Dat babajági} *col* witch (the Serbo-Croatian equivalent of bogeyman) <**Slav**>

babaróga {ē fem.; Dat babarógi} *col* witch (the Serbo-Croatian equivalent of bogeyman) <**Slav**>

babarúga {ē fem.; Dat babarúgi} *col* witch (the Serbo-Croatian equivalent of bogeyman) <**Slav**>

bằbini jàrčevi {NP} (lit. old lady's goats) *col* hail ☞ jarac

bằbini kȕrčevi {NP} (lit. old lady's pricks) *sl* ***Obs*** hail ☞ kurac

bábo {ē masc.} /bábo /a masc./ **a.** **BosM** *col-dia* ***Fam*** father, daddy <**NE**> **b.i.** *sl-crime* ***Iro*** investigating judge, magistrate <**NE**[*1]> **ii.** *sl-crime* ***Iro*** prison administrator <**NE**[*1]>

babojébac {pca (acc. = gen.) masc.} (lit. old women's fucker) *sl-sex* ***Obs-Fac*** male who engages in sexual intercourse with elderly females <**Slav**⁘>

bằbos {a (acc. = gen.) masc.} *sl-fea* ***Der-Fac*** senior citizen <**Slav**✍>

bàbula {ē fem.} *col* ***Der*** senior citizen <**Slav**[*1]>

bàbule {eta masc.} *col* ***Der*** senior citizen <**Slav**[*1]>

bàbura {ē fem.} **a.** *col* a kind of round pepper <**Slav**> **b.** *col* nose <**Slav**[*1]>

babùrina {ē fem.} **a.** *sl-fea* elderly female <**Slav**⁘> **b.i.** *sl-fea* ***Der*** hated elderly female <**Slav**⁘[*1]> **ii.** *sl-fea* ***Der*** unattractive elderly female, hag <**Slav**⁘[*1]> **iii.** *sl-sex* attractive elderly female <**Slav**⁘[*1]>

babùskara {ē fem.} **a.** *sl-fea* elderly female <**Slav**⁘> **b.i.** *sl-fea* ***Der*** hated elderly female <**Slav**⁘[*1]> **ii.** *sl-fea* ***Der*** unattractive elderly female, hag <**Slav**⁘[*1]> **c.** *sl-sex* attractive elderly female <**Slav**[*2]>

babùskera {ē fem.} **a.** *sl-fea* elderly female <**Slav**⁘> **b.i.** *sl-fea* ***Der*** hated elderly female <**Slav**⁘[*1]> **ii.** *sl-fea* ***Der*** unattractive elderly female, hag <**Slav**⁘[*1]> **iii.** *sl-sex* attractive elderly female <**Slav**⁘[*1]>

bàcāč {bacáča masc.} (lit. thrower, grenade launcher) *sl-sex* ***Fac-Obs*** female breast, tit <**Slav**[*1]>

- **bàcāč plằmena** {NP} (lit. flame thrower) *sl-gamble* ***Fac*** gambler
- **rùčni bàcāč** {NP} (lit. hand thrower) **1** *sl-mil* mortar **2** *sl-mil* bazooka

bacàkati {ām, ajū imperf.} (lit. throw around) **1** *col* joke around <**Slav**[*1]> **2** *col* cheat, swindle: *Bacakali su ga kad su mu naplatili dvaes banke za jednu kartu. They were cheating him when they charged him twenty bucks for one ticket.* <**Slav**[*1]>

bacàkati se {ām, ajū imperf. intr.} (lit. throw around) *col* strive, try hard: *Bacakali se za povišicu try hard to get a raise* <**Slav**[*1]>

bàcānje *See the following*

- **bàcānje plằmena** {NP} (lit. flame throwing) *sl-gamble* ***Fac*** gambling
- **bàcānje u brázdu** {NP} (lit. throwing into the furrow) *sl-sex* ***Fac-Obs*** cunnilingus

bàcati *See the following*

- **bàcati divljáke** {VP} (lit. throw savages) *sl-crime* resell, fence
- **bàcati dȑvlje i kàmēnje** {VP} (lit. throw logs and stones) *col* attack verbally, denounce: *Bacali su na njega drvlje i kamenje kad je u svoju firmu uveo promjene. They denounced him when he introduced the changes to his business.*
- **bàcati fárove** {VP} (lit. throw the headlights) *sl* ***Fac*** look, watch, scope out: *Ona riba ti baca farove. That chick is checking you out.*
- **bàcati fólove** {VP} (lit. throw tricks) *sl* lie: *Bacala je folove da će glumiti u pozorištu. She lied that she was going to act in the theater.*
- **bàcati gôvna** {VP} (lit. throw shit) *sl* ***Der-Obs*** talk persistently and meaninglessly, blabber, chatter: *bacati govna o politici blabber about politics*
- **bàcati kípce** {VP} (lit. throw cards) *sl-gamble* play cards
- **bàcati klâmfe** {VP} (lit. throw cramp-irons) *sl* ***Fac*** flirt: *bacati klamfe dobroj koki flirt with a hot chick*
- **bàcati kȕke** {VP} (lit. throw the hooks) *sl* ***Fac*** look, watch, scope out: *Bacao je kuke kroz prozor da vidi rulju prije nego što je ušao. He looked through the window to check out the crowd before going in.*
- **bàcati lȋre** {VP} (lit. throw lies) **a.** *sl* trick, cheat, swindle: *bacati lire naivcu cheat a naive guy* **b.** *sl* flirt: *bacati lire frstaku flirt with a cutie*
- **bàcati lȋtre** {VP} (lit. throw liters) *sl* trick, cheat, swindle: *bacati litre naivki trick a naive chick*
- **bàcati lồptice** {VP} (lit. throw small balls) **a.** *sl* trick, cheat, swindle: *bacati loptice roditeljima trick one's parents* **b.i.** *sl* flirt: *bacati loptice konobarici flirt with a waitress* **ii.** *sl* spread the news: *bacati loptice da je pala vlada spread news that the government has*

resigned

• **bàcati mâlōg u nèsvēst** {VP} (lit. throw the small one into an unconscious state) SerE *sl-sex* ***Fac-Obs*** masturbate, beat off

• **bàcati mâlōg u nèsvjēst** {VP} (lit. throw the small one into an unconscious state) *sl-sex* ***Fac-Obs*** masturbate, beat off

• **bàcati ȍkoslave** {VP} (lit. throw eyes) *sl* ***Fac*** look, watch, scope out: *bacati okoslave na komšinicu prije iznajmljivanja stana check out the neighbor before renting an apartment*

• **bàcati pijèsak u ȍči** {VP} (lit. throw sand into the eyes) **a.** *sl* trick, cheat, swindle: *bacati pijesak u oči nastavnicima bamboozle one's teachers* **b.** *sl* lie: *Dosta si mi bacao pijesak u oči, više ti ništa ne vjerujem. You lied to me enough, I don't believe you anymore.*

• **bàcati pȉkule u ȍči** {VP} (lit. throw pebbles in the eyes) *sl* trick, cheat, swindle: *bacati pikule u oči šefu cheat one's boss*

• **bàcati pràšinu u ȍči** {VP} (lit. throw dust in the eyes) **a.** *sl* trick, cheat, swindle: *bacati prašinu u oči poreznicima cheat the IRS* **b.** *sl* lie: *Ne bacaj mi prašinu u oči, nego reci istinu! Don't lie to me, just tell the truth!*

• **bàcati róvce na [NOUN/PRONOUN:ACC]** {VP} *sl* be interested in [NOUN/PRONOUN:ACC]: *Uposlednje vreme bacam rovce na Svetlanu. I have been interested in Svetlana lately.*

• **bàcati u kljûn** {VP} (lit. throw into one's beak) *sl* ***Fac*** eat, wolf: *bacati u kljun jedan hamburger za drugim wolf down one hamburger after another*

• **bàcati u záhod** {VP} (lit. throw in the toilet) *sl* ***Fac*** eat, wolf: *U tom bircu dobro se baca u zahod. In that bar one can eat well.*

• **bàcati ȕši** {VP} (lit. throw one's ears) *sl* ***Fac*** listen: *bacati uši na predavanje listen to a lecture*

bàcati se {ām, ajū imperf. intr.} (lit. throw oneself) **a.** *col* be interested in something, be keen on: *baca se na lovu she is keen on getting a better paying job* <**Slav**[*1]> **b.** *col* flirt: *bacati se na dobru ribu flirt with a hot chick* <**Slav**[*1]>

• **bàcati se pod ìglu** {VP} (lit. throw oneself under the needle) *sl-drugs* ***Fac*** take narcotic drugs intravenously, mainline, shoot up

bacìklo {a neut.} [std. = bicikl] *col-dia* bicycle, bike <**Lat-Gre**>

báciti *See the following*

• **báciti bùvu** {VP} (lit. throw a flea) *col* spread rumors: *baciti buvu da će da poskupi šećer spread rumors that sugar will get more expensive*

• **báciti ga u nèsvēst** {VP} (lit. throw it into an unconscious state) *sl-sex* ***Fac-Obs*** masturbate, beat off

• **báciti kádar** {VP} (lit. throw a sequence of a movie) *sl* ***Fac*** take a look: *Bacio je kadar na restoran prije nego što je rezervisao sto. He took a look at the restaurant before making reservations.*

• **báciti kàšiku u gôvna** {VP} (lit. throw one's spoon into shit) *sl* ***Fac-Obs*** die, kick the bucket: *baciti kašiku u govna od starosti die from old age*

• **báciti kàšiku u pèkmez** {VP} (lit. throw one's spoon into jam) *sl* ***Fac*** die, kick the bucket: *Bacio je kašiku u pekmez u januaru. He kicked the bucket in January.*

• **báciti kȍplje u tȑnje** {VP} (lit. throw one's spear into the thorns) *sl* ***Fac*** die, kick the bucket: *Bacićeš koplje u trnje ako nastaviš da pušiš. You will kick the bucket if you continue to smoke.*

• **báciti lȉru** {VP} (lit. throw a lie) **a.** *sl* trick, cheat, swindle: *baciti liru naivcu trick a naive dude* **b.i.** *sl* lie: *baciti liru o odlasku u vojsku lie about joining the military* **ii.** *sl* flirt: *baciti liru komšinici flirt with one's neighbor* **iii.** *sl* beg, ask for money

• **báciti lȕk** {VP} (lit. throw a look) *sl* take a look: *Bacio sam luk na sat i shvatio da je kasno. I took a look at my watch and realized that it was late.*

• **báciti ȍko** {VP} (lit. throw one's eye) **a.** *col* take a look: *baciti oko na fotografiju take a look at a photograph* **b.** *col* be interested in something, be keen on: *Bacio je oko na to auto. He was interested in that car.*

• **báciti péglu** {VP} (lit. throw the iron) *sl* ***Fac*** vomit, throw up, puke

• **báciti pod nȁmeštāj** {VP} (lit. throw under the furiniture) *sl* knock down, floor: *Udario ga je tako jako da ga je bacio pod nameštaj. He punched him so hard he knocked him down.*

• **báciti pùšlek** {VP} *sl* vomit, throw up, puke

• **báciti sìdro** {VP} (lit. throw the anchor) **a.** *col* stay for a while, spend some time: *Bacio sam sidro u Njujorku. I stayed in New York for a while* **b.** *sl* stop (when driving, etc.): *Baci sidro tamo! Stop over there!*

• **báciti šmȋnku** {VP} (lit. throw some makeup) **a.** *sl* ***Der*** be conceited, be stuck-up: *Nemoj da mi bacíš šminku na žurci! Don't be stuck-up at the party!* **b.** *sl* be superior: *Bacila je šminku u plivanju na bazenu. She is the best swimmer at the pool.*

• **báciti štánglu u ústa** {VP} (lit. throw a stick into one's mouth) *sl-drugs* ***Fac*** smoke a strong drug

• **báciti u neznánje** {VP} (lit. throw into ignorance) *sl* ***Fac*** confuse, mix up: *Bacili su me u neznanje kad su pustili pogrešan film. They confused me when they put on the wrong movie.*

• **báciti u pjȇnu** {VP} (lit. throw into the foam) *sl* make agitated, get into a lather: *Njegovo osorno ponašanje bacilo me u pjenu. His rude behavior got me into a* *lather.*

• **báciti u sèvdāh** {VP} (lit. throw into yearning for love) Bos *col* make happy: *Njegovo pjevanje bacilo me u sevdah. His singing made me happy.*

• **báciti u trȍšak** {VP} (lit. throw into cost) *col* cost considerable amount of money: *Novi namještaj bacio me u trošak. The new furniture was very expensive.*

• **báciti ȕdicu** {VP} (lit. throw a fishing hook) **a.** *col* lure: *baciti udicu na soma lure catfish* **b.** *sl* be interested in something, be keen on: *baciti udicu na novu ribu u kancelariji be interested in the new girl in the office*

• **báciti ȕši** {VP} (lit. throw one's ears) *sl* listen: *baciti uši na radio program listen to a radio program*

• **báciti vàlter** {VP} (lit. throw a lie) *sl* trick, cheat, swindle: *baciti valter starcima trick one's parents*

• **báciti vȕnu** {VP} (lit. throw some wool) *sl* ***Fac*** frighten, scare: *baciti vunu učenicima frighten one's students*

báciti se *See the following*

• **báciti se na kȍp** {VP} (lit. throw oneself to digging) *sl* ***Fac*** start working: *Bacio se na kop u sedam ujutro. He started to work at seven a.m.*

bàculja {ē fem.} (lit. thrower) *sl* coffee <Slav*1>

bȁčiti {čīm, čē perf.} [std. = baciti] *dia-col* throw away, toss out: *bačiti loptu throw a ball* <Slav⚘>

• **bȁčiti u sèvdāh** {VP} (lit. throw into yearning for love) *col* make happy: *Baklave su me bačile u sevdah. Baklawa cake had made me happy.*

bȁčka {ē fem.; Dat bȁčki} *sl-arch* cow <Slav>

bȁčva {ē fem.} (lit. barrel) **1** *sl* apartment <Slav*1> **2** *col-sl* ***Der*** obese person <Slav*1>

bȁčvār {a (acc. = gen.) masc.} (lit. barrel maker) *sl-drink* waiter <Slav✣*1>

Bàćuška [1] {ē fem.; Dat Bàćuški} *col* the Soviet Union <Rus*1>

Bàćuška [2] {ē masc.; Dat Bàćuški} *col* Russian (person) <Rus*1>

bàdati {ām, ajū imperf.} *sl* bathe <Ger>

bàdati se {ām, ajū imperf. intr.} *sl* bathe <Ger>

badàva {adv.} /bàdava adv./ **a.** *col* free, gratis <NE> **b.** *col* in vain, for nothing: *Sad je to što radiš sve badava kad ionako ne možemo na put. Now all your efforts are for nothing when we cannot travel anyway.* <NE*1> ☞ badavad

badàvad {adv.} **a.** *col* free, gratis: *piće badavad drinks for free* <NE> **b.** *col* in vain, for nothing: *Badavad pokušava da nauči kineski. He is trying in vain to learn Chinese.* <NE*1> ☞ badava

badavàdžija {ē masc.} *col* ***Der*** lazy or shiftless person, bum, good for nothing <NE>

badavàdžisati {išēm, išū imperf. intr.} *sl-fea* spend one's time in useless activities, fool around, mess around <NE✣>

bádža {ē masc.} **1** *col* male, guy <NE*1> **2** *sl* short person <NE*1> **3** *sl* gentleman <NE*1> **4** *sl-sex* brothel client <NE*1>

bága {ē fem.; Dat bági} *sl-crime* bullet or knife wound <NE*1>

bagađóra {ē fem.} *sl-sex* ***Obs*** penis, dick, prick <NE*1>

bagatèla [1] {ē fem.} *col* very inexpensive merchandise <Ita>

bagatèla [2] {adj.} /bagatȅla, bagàtela/ *col* inexpensive, cheap: *kupiti bagatela kola buy an inexpensive car* <Ita>

bagatèla [3] {adv.} /bagatȅla, bagàtela/ *col* inexpensively, cheaply: *nabaviti bagatela buy inexpensively* <Ita>

bȁgatēlan {lna, lno adj.} *col* very inexpensive, bargain <Ita>

Bágeri {gērā masc. pl.} (lit. bulldozers: these lakes were dug by bulldozers) Cro *sl* name for Jarun lakes (Zagreb, Croatia) <Ger*1>

bagèrist {a (acc. = gen.) masc.} (lit. bulldozer driver) *sl-sex* ***Fac*** male who engages in sexual intercourse with elderly females <Dut✣*1>

baglàma {ē fem.} Din *col* door hinge <NE>

bȁgman {a (acc. = gen.) masc.} (lit. bag man) *sl-drugs* drug dealer, pusher <Eng*1>

bàgōv {bagòva masc.} *sl* cigarette, smoke <Hun*1>

bȁgra {ē fem.} **a.** *col* ***Der*** worthless or despicable group of persons, scum <NE> **b.** *sl* people <NE*1>

bȁh {excl.} *col* used to express surprise, astonishment, etc., oh: *Bah! Kakav je to odvratan miris? Oh! What is that awful smell?* <Slav>

bahána {ē fem.} /bahȁna /e fem./ [std. = banana] *sl* banana <Port>

bàhara {ē fem.} **1** *sl-crime* prison <Slav⚘> **2** Cro *sl* name for Patria Movie Theater (formerly called Triglav, Zagreb, Croatia) <Slav⚘>

bàhnuti {bȃhnēm, bȃhnū perf. intr.} [std. = banuti] BosM *col-dia* arrive unexpectedly, appear out of nowhere, pop in: *Bahnuo je u dva sata u noći. He popped in at two a.m.* <Slav⚘>

bahùljati {ām, ajū imperf. intr.} [std. = bauljati] BosM *col* creep (of a lizard, child, etc.) <Slav✍>

bȁir {a masc.} *dia* slope of a hill <NE>

bâj {excl.} *col* used to take leave of somebody informally, bye <Eng>

bâj-bâj {excl.} *col* used to take leave of somebody informally, bye-bye <Eng>

bája[1] {ē masc.} /bȁja /e masc./ **a.** *col* ***Fam*** one's older brother. <Slav> **b.i.** *col* ***Fam*** friend (male) <Slav[*1]> **ii.** *col-dia* I (when a male refers to himself): *Baja će kupiti novi auto. I will buy a new car* <Slav[*1]> **c.i.** *sl-crime* hardened criminal <Slav[*1]> **ii.** *sl-fea* kind male, nice guy <Slav[*1]>

bȁja[2] {ē masc.; Voc bȁja} /bȁja /e masc./ **a.** *col* ***Fam*** one's older brother <Slav> **b.i.** *col* ***Fam*** friend (male) <Slav[*1]> **ii.** *col-dia* I (when a male refers to himself): *Baja je kupio auto. I bought a car.* <Slav[*1]> **c.i.** *sl-crime* hardened criminal <Slav[*1]> **ii.** *sl-fea* kind male, nice guy <Slav[*1]>

bȁja[3] {excl.} *col* ***Fam*** used to address a male in direct informal communication, buddy <Slav>

bajadéra {ē fem.} (lit. a kind of candy produced by Kraš factory, Zagreb, Croatia) *sl-sex* ***Obs*** female who frequently engages in fellatio <Por[*1]>

bajági {part.} *col* pretending, as if: *On bajagi spava. He pretends to be sleeping.* <NE> ☞ **kobajagi**

bȁjalica {ē fem.} /bájalica/ *col* fortune-teller <Slav>

bȁjalija {ē fem.} *sl-arch* pitcher (container for liquids) <NE>

bâjan {jna, jno adj.} *col* nice, cool: *bajna haljina cool dress* <Slav>

bàjat {a, o adj.} **Din** *col* stale (usu. food, esp. bread) <NE>

bȁjati {ām, ajū imperf.} /bájati/ (lit. cast spells) **a.** *col* lie <Slav[*1]> **b.** *col* trick, cheat, swindle <Slav[*2]>

bajbèlide {adj.} *sl-fea* obese, fat <Slav✍>

bàjbočiti {čīm, čē imperf.} *col* be in prison <Ger⁘✍>

bàjbok {a masc.} *col* prison <Ger✍>

bajbokàna {ē fem.} *col* prison <Ger⁘✍>

bàjbuk {a masc.} *col* prison <Ger✍>

bȁjc {a +ev (ext. pl) masc.; Nom Pl bàjčevi} *col-sl* bike, bicycle <Eng✍>

bȁjk {a +ov (ext. pl) masc.; Nom Pl bàjkovi} *col-sl* bike, bicycle <Eng>

bâjka {ē fem.} (lit. fairy tale) *col* lie <Slav[*1]>

bajònēt {jonéta masc.} (lit. bayonet) *sl-sex* ***Fac-Obs*** penis, dick, prick <Fre[*1]>

bàjrāk {bajráka masc.} [std. = barjak] BosM *col* flag <NE✍>

bȁjs {a +ev (ext. pl) masc.; Nom Pl bàjsevi} **1** *col* bike, bicycle <Eng✍> **2** *col* bass (musical instrument or tone) <Ita✍>

bȁjsati {ām, ajū imperf.} *sl-sex* ***Obs*** engage in sexual intercourse with (of a male) <Ita⁘[*1]>

bâjta {ē fem.} (lit. shack) *sl-drink* low-class bar, dive <Ita[*1]>

bȁka {excl.} *col* used when passing something to somebody, here you go <NE>

bákac {kca (acc. = gen.) masc.} **a.** *sl* grandfather, grandpa <Slav⁘> **b.** *sl-fea* senior citizen <Slav⁘[*1]>

bakàlār {kalára (acc. = gen.) masc.} (lit. cod) *sl-fea* slender male <Ita[*1]>

bàkālnica {ē fem.} **Din** *col* grocery store <NE>

bakàluk {a masc.} **Din** *col* shopping (i.e. the goods one has bought) <NE>

bàkāndža {ē fem.} *col* hard-soled shoe <Hun>

bàkćati se {bȁkćēm, kćū imperf. intr.} *col* bother with, waste time over: *bakćati se s pokvarenim kolima bother with a broken car* <NE> ☞ **baktati se**

bȁke {bèkē fem.; perm} [std. = keba] *sl* knife <Ita✍[*1]>

bȁki[1] {īja (acc. = gen.) masc.} *col* ***Fam*** brother <Slav>

bȁki[2] {excl.} *col* ***Fam*** used to address a male in direct informal communication, brother <Slav>

bakráči[1] {excl.} *col* used to express disagreement, lack of regard, etc. <NE>

bakráči[2] {ā masc. pl.} *col* stupidity, lack of intelligence <NE>

- **Kȁkī bakráči!** {S} *col* used to express strong disbelief, No way!

bȁks {a masc.} *sl-col* dollar, buck <Eng>

bàksara {ē fem.} *sl-crime* prison <NE⁘[*1]>

bȁksi {īja masc.} *sl* dollar, buck <Eng⁘>

bàktati se {bȁkćēm, kćū imperf. intr.} /bȁktati se/ *col* bother with, waste time over: *baktati se s pisanjem glupog izvještaja waste one's time on a stupid report* <NE> ☞ **bakćati se**

bȁku {bȅku fem.; perm} *sl* ***Fam*** grandmother, grandma <**Slav☝**>

bàkūt {bakúta (acc. = gen.) masc.} *sl-col* senior citizen <**Slav❖**>

bàkuta {ē fem.} **a.** *sl* grandmother, grandma <**Slav❖**> **b.** *sl-fea* ***Der*** elderly female <**Slav❖**[*1]>

bakùtān {kutána (acc. = gen.) masc.} **a.** *sl* grandmother, grandma <**Slav❖**> **b.** *sl* ***Der*** senior citizen <**Slav❖**[*1]>

bakutáner {a (acc. = gen.) masc.} **a.** *sl* grandmother, grandma <**Slav❖**> **b.** ***Der*** senior citizen <**Slav❖**[*1]>

bâl *See the following*

- **bâl vampírā** {NP} (lit. vampires' ball, party) *sl-sstu* ***Fac*** school board meeting

bȁla {ē fem.} *col* nasal mucus, snot <**Slav**>

balàban {a (acc. = gen.) masc.} (lit. bear) *col-dia* ***Der*** stupid or mentally deficient person <**NE**[*1]>

balabȕćkati {ām, ajū imperf.} **1** *sl* hesitate, stall: *Nemoj da balabućkaš, nego uradi zadaću. Don't hesitate, just do your homework.* <**Slav❖**> **2** *sl* trick, cheat, swindle: *Balabućkali su ga oko troškova. They cheated them on the price.* <**Slav❖**>

baláda *See the following*

- **na kràju baládē** {PP} (lit. at the end of the ballad) *col* in the end

baladírati {làdīrām, ladírajū imperf.} (lit. play a ballad) *sl* lie: *baladirati o ocjenama lie about one's grades* <**Fre**[*1]>

balalàjder {a (acc. = gen.) masc.} *sl* ***Der*** young and immature male <**Slav❖**[*1]>

balalàjdērka {ē fem.; Dat balalàjderki} *sl* ***Der*** young and immature female <**Slav❖**[*1]>

bȁlav {a, o adj.} **a.** *col* covered with mucus, snotty <**Slav**> **b.** *col* ***Off*** young <**Slav**[*1]>

bȁlavac {lāvca (acc. = gen.) masc.} (lit. the snotty one) *col* ***Off*** young and immature male <**Slav**[*1]>

balavànder {a (acc. = gen.) masc.} (lit. the snotty one) *sl* ***Der*** young and immature male <**Slav❖**[*1]>

balavànderka {ē fem.; Dat balavànderki} (lit. the snotty one) *sl* ***Der*** young and immature female <**Slav❖**[*1]>

bȁlavī krètēn {NP} (lit. the snotty cretin) *sl-sex* ***Fac-Obs*** penis, dick, prick ☞ **kreten**

bȁlavī lùdāk {NP} (lit. the snotty fool) *sl-sex* ***Fac-Obs*** penis, dick, prick ☞ **ludak**

bȁlavica {ē fem.} (lit. the snotty one) *col* ***Off*** young and immature female <**Slav**[*1]>

baláviti {bȁlāvīm, vē imperf.} **a.** *col* release mucus involuntarily. <**Slav**> **b.i.** *sl* cry, shed tears, weep: *Balavila je tokom cijelog filma. She was crying all during the movie.* <**Slav**[*1]> **ii.** *sl* talk persistently and meaninglessly, blabber, chatter: *Nepodnošljivo je balavio, pa sam izašao. He was blabbering unbearably, so I left.* <**Slav**[*1]>

balávko {a masc.} (lit. the snotty one) **1** *sl-sex* ***Obs*** penis, dick, prick <**Slav**[*1]> **2** *sl-fea* ***Der*** child, kid <**Slav**[*1]>

balávljēnje {a neut.} **a.** *col* releasing mucus <**Slav**> **b.i.** *sl* crying: *balavljenje zbog propuštenih šansi crying over missed opportunities* <**Slav**[*1]> **b.ii.** *sl* meaningless talk, blabber: *balavljenje o politici blabber about politics* <**Slav**[*1]>

balavnȉška {ē fem.; Dat balavnȉški} **1** *sl-crime* policeman, cop <**Gyp**> **2** *sl* gentleman <**Gyp**>

balàvurda {ē fem.} *col* ***Der*** youth <**Slav❖**[*1]>

balavȕrdija {ē fem.} *col* ***Der*** youth <**Slav❖**[*1]>

bȁlčak *See the following*

- **do bȁlčaka** {PP} (lit. to the sword-hilt) *col* completely, totally, to the hilt: *napiti se do balčaka get completely drunk*

bàldisati {išēm, išū imperf. intr.} **1** *sl-fea* be in a difficult situation: *baldisati zbog dugova be in a difficult situation over one's debts* **2** *sl-fea* be worn out, be exhausted: *baldisati od vežbanja be exhausted from exercising*

bâle [1] {eta masc.} **a.** *sl-col* ***Fam*** brother <**Slav**> **b.** *sl-col* ***Fam*** friend (male) <**Slav**[*1]>

bâle [2] {excl.} *sl-col* ***Fam*** used to address a male in direct informal communication, brother <**Slav**>

balègānje {a neut.} (lit. shitting) *sl* prolonged and meaningless talk, blabber, chatter: *baleganje o poslednjoj modi blabber about the latest fashion* <**Slav**[*1]>

balègara {ē fem.} (lit. shit-brandy) *col* low-quality brandy <**Slav❖**[*1]>

balègati {ām, ajū imperf.} (lit. shit) *col* ***Der*** talk persistently and meaninglessly, blabber, chatter: *balegati o predsjedničkim izborima blabber about the presidential elections* <**Slav❖**[*1]>

balètān {letána (acc. = gen.) masc.} (lit. ballet dancer) *sl* ***App-Fac*** skillful and adept male <**Ita❖**[*1]>

bȁlfica {ē fem.} *sl-sports* ***Fam*** soccer <**Eng-Ger☝**>

bàlija {ē masc.} *sl-fea* ***Off*** Bosnian Muslim (male) <**NE**[*1]>

bàlījskī {ā, ō adj.} *sl-fea* ***Off*** Bosnian Muslim (pertaining to a person or nation) <NE❖*1> ☞ **baliski, balinski**

balìnkuša {ē fem.} *sl-fea* ***Off*** Bosnian Muslim (female) <NE*1>

bàlīnskī {ā, ō adj.} *sl-fea* ***Off*** Bosnian Muslim (pertaining to a person or nation) <NE❖*1> ☞ **balijski, baliski**

bàlīskī {ā, ō adj.} *sl-fea* ***Off*** Bosnian Muslim (pertaining to a person or nation) <NE❖*1> ☞ **balijski, balinski**

bȁliti {līm, lē imperf.} **a.** *col* release mucus <Slav> **b.** *col* cry, shed tears, weep: *baliti na ljubavnom filmu cry during a chick flick* <Slav*1>

bàlkōn {balkóna masc.} (lit. balcony) *sl-sex* ***Fac-Obs*** female breast, tit <Ita*1>

bálo [1] {a (acc. = gen.) masc.; Voc bâlo} /bálo /e masc./ **a.** *col* ***Der*** person with mucus on his/her face <Slav*1> **b.** *col* ***Der*** young and immature male

bálo [2] {a masc.} /bálo /e masc./ *sl* lie: *Ta njegova priča je balo. That story of his is a lie.* <Slav*1>

bàlōn [1] {balóna (acc. = gen.) masc.} (lit. balloon) *col* boaster, braggart, blowhard <Fre*1>

bàlōn [2] {balóna masc.} (lit. balloon) **1** *sl-sex* ***Fac-Obs*** female breast, tit <Fre*1> **2** *col* false news <Fre*1>

bálonja {ē masc.} **a.** *col* person with mucus on his/her face <Slav> **b.** *col* ***Der*** young and immature male <Slav*1>

bàlsamovān {a, o adj.} (lit. embalmed) Ser *sl-drink* ***Fac*** drunk, pickled <Gre❖*1>

bàlsamovānje {a neut.} (lit. embalming) *sl-drink* ***Fac*** drinking (alcohol) <Gre❖*1>

bàlsamovati {mujēm, mujū biasp.} (lit. embalm) *sl-drink* ***Fac*** drink (alcohol): *balzamovati pivu drink beer* <Gre❖*1>

bàlsamovati se {mujēm, mujū biasp. intr.} (lit. embalm oneself) *sl-drink* ***Fac*** get drunk, get pickled: *balzamovati se votkom get pickled on vodka* <Gre*1>

bàltazār {a (acc. = gen.) masc.} (lit. Balthazar) *sl-sex* ***Obs*** penis, dick, prick <HebO*1>

bàltija {ē fem.} *sl-arch* axe <NE>

bàlūn {balúna masc.} Med *sl-sports* ball (esp. soccer ball) <Ita*1>

bàlvan [1] {a (acc. = gen.) masc.} (lit. log) **1** *col* ***Der*** inhabitant of the countryside, hick, bumpkin <Slav*1> **2** *col* ***Der*** stupid or mentally deficient person <Slav*1> **3** *col* troublemaker, rowdy, ruffian <Slav*1>

bàlvan [2] {a masc.} (lit. log) **1** *sl-sex* ***Obs*** penis, dick, prick <Slav*1> **2** *sl-crime* juvenile detention center, juvie <Slav*1>

bàlvan-revolúcija {ē fem.} *col* ***Der-Fac*** Serbian rebellion in Kraina (a province of Croatia) in the early 1990s <Slav-Lat❖*1>

bàlvani {bȁlvānā masc. pl.} (lit. logs) **1** *sl-crime* prison <Slav*1> **2** *sl* strong legs <Slav*1>

bàljaz {a masc.} *sl* mouth <Slav*1>

bȁljēnje {a neut.} **a.** *col* releasing mucus <Slav> **b.** *col* crying <Slav*1>

baljèzgānje {a neut.} *col* ***Der*** prolonged and meaningless talk, blabber, chatter: *baljezganje o politici blabber about politics* <Slav*1>

baljèzgati {ām, ajū imperf.} *col* ***Der*** talk persistently and meaninglessly, blabber, chatter: *baljezgati o fudbalu blabber about soccer* <Slav*1>

bàljoz {a masc.} *sl-arch* mouth <Slav*1>

baljùško {adj.} *sl-arch* multicolored <Slav*1>

balzàmīrān {a, o adj.} (lit. embalmed) Cro *sl-drink* ***Fac*** drunk, pickled <Gre❖*1>

bȁm {excl.} *col* the sound made by an explosion, bang <Slav>

bȁmbadàva {adv.} /bambadáva/ **a.** Bos *col* free, gratis: *dobiti karte bambadava get tickets for free* <NE> **b.** *col* very inexpensive, very cheap: *Kupio sam to bambadava, za samo sto dinara. I bought that very cheap - for only one hundred dinars.* <NE*1> ☞ **banbadava**

bȁmbàška {adv.} Bos *col* separately, individually, each on their own: *Njih dvoje žive bambaška. Both of them live alone.* <NE>

bambr̀ljati {ām, ajū imperf.} *sl-fea* ***Der*** touch or play with, fiddle with, fool with: *Ne bambrljaj taj televizor, pokvarićeš ga. Don't fiddle with that TV, you will break it.* <Slav✍>

bàmbus [1] {a masc.} (lit. bamboo) **1** *sl-sex* ***Obs*** penis, dick, prick <Malay*1> **2** *sl-drink* wine with juice or cola <Malay*1>

bàmbus [2] {a (acc. = gen.) masc.} (lit. bamboo) **1** *sl-fea* ***Der*** senior citizen <Malay*1> **2** *sl-fea* ***Der*** little boy, sprout <Malay*1>

bân [1] {excl.} Bos *col* used to address a male in direct informal communication, hey <Slav> ☞ **bolan, ba**

bân [2] {a (acc. = gen.) +ov (ext. pl) masc.; Nom Pl bánovi} (lit. historically, viceroy in Croatia, also pre-WWII provincial governor) *sl* ***Fac*** boss: *ban preduzeća boss of the company* <Slav*1>

bȁnak {nka masc.} **1** *dia* bench <Ita> **2** *col-sl* ten paras; a ten-para coin <Ita*1> **3** *col-sl* ten dinars; a ten-dinar coin <Ita*1>

bȁnalica {ē fem.} **a.** *sl* hand <Slav> **b.** *sl* arm <Slav*1>

banána {ē fem.} (lit. banana) **1** *sl-auto* clamp (the tool) <Por*1> **2** *sl-sports* blocked shot (in basketball) <Por*1> **3** *sl-sex* penis <Por*1> **4** *sl-fea* ***Off*** African American (male) <Por*1>

banána repùblika {NP} (lit. banana republic) *sl-media* ***Der*** country dominated by a foreign power ☞ **republika**

banànāš {nanáša (acc. = gen.) masc.} (lit. the one who eats bananas) **a.** *sl* monkey, ape <Por⁘*1> **b.** *sl-fea* ***Der*** stupid or mentally deficient person, one who is "bananas" <Por⁘*2>

banàndžija {ē masc.} (lit. the one who eats bananas) **a.** *sl* monkey, ape <Por⁘*1> **b.** *sl-fea* ***Der*** stupid or mentally deficient person, one who is "bananas" <Por⁘*2>

bȁnbadàva {adv.} /banbadáva/ Bos *col* free, gratis: *dobiti rakiju banbadava get some brandy for free* <NE> ☞ **bambadava**

bȃnčiti {čīm, čē imperf. intr.} *col* party (engage in social gathering) <Slav*1>

bànčura {ē fem.} *sl* ten dinars; a ten-dinar bill <Ita⁘*1>

bȃnda {ē fem.} /bánda/ **1** *dia* side or edge of something <Ita> **2a.** *col* gang (criminal group) <Ita*1> **b.** *col* ***Der*** worthless or despicable person, bum <Ita*2>

bàndara {ē fem.} *sl* leg (human) <Ita⁘*1>

bàndāž {bandáža masc.} *sl-auto* patch (used to repair hoses) <Fre>

bandàžīrān {a, o adj.} *sl* dressed formally, dressed up: *Na konferenciji su svi bili bandažirani. Everybody was dressed up at the conference.* <Fre*1>

• **brȍdo bandàžīrān** {NP} (lit. bandaged well) *sl* dressed formally, dressed up

bandéra {ē fem.} (lit. lamppost) **1** *sl-fea* tall person <Ita*1> **2** *sl-sstu* failing grade <Ita*1>

bàndīt {bandíta (acc. = gen.) masc.; Voc bȁndīte} (lit. bandit) **a.** *sl* musician <Lat*1> **b.** *sl* jazz musician <Lat*2>

bandòglav {a, o adj.} *col* stubborn, pigheaded: *Savetovao sam ga da ne ide na put, ali on je bio bandoglav. I advised him not to take that trip, but he was pigheaded.* <Slav*1>

bandòglavac {lāvca (acc. = gen.) masc.} *col* stubborn person, pigheaded person <Slav>

bándža {ē fem.} *sl* punch in the head

bȁnež {a masc.} **1** *sl* store <Slav*1> **2** *sl* work, labor <Slav*1>

bàngalo {a neut.} *sl* bag <Gyp⁘*1>

bȁngav {a, o adj.} **a.** *col* ***Der*** lame (limping) <Gyp> **b.** *sl-fea* ***Der*** superficial <Gyp*1> **c.** *sl-fea* insane, nuts <Gyp*1>

bangéja[1] {ē masc.} *sl-fea* ***Der*** lame person <Gyp⁘*1>

bangéja[2] {adj.} *sl-fea* ***Der*** lame (limping) <Gyp⁘*1>

bȁngja {adj.} *sl-fea* ***Der*** lame (limping) <Gyp✍>

Bȁngkok {a masc.} (lit. Bangkok) Ser *sl* Belgrade (Yugoslavia) <Slav*1>

bángo {a masc.} *sl-fea* ***Der*** lame person <Gyp⁘*1>

bȁniti {nīm, nē imperf.} **a.** *sl-arch* work, labor: *Danas banim do tri. I work until three p.m. today.* <Slav> **b.** *sl-arch* build, construct, erect: *baniti kuću build a house* <Slav*1>

bȁnk {a +ov (ext. pl) masc.; Nom Pl bànkovi} *sl-crafts* work bench <Ita*1>

bȁnka {ē fem.; Dat bànki} /bànka, bánka /e fem./ **1** *sl* ten currency units; a ten-unit bill <Ita*1> **2** *sl* hundred currency units; a hundred-unit bill <Ita*1> **3** *sl* thousand currency units; a thousand-unit bill, a grand <Ita*1> **4** *sl-mil* ten days of military service <Ita*2> **5** *sl* ten years <Ita*2> **6** *sl-sex* vagina <Ita*1>

• **čȉje trȋ bȁnke** {S} (lit. whose thirty bucks) *sl* used in the middle of the conversation to confuse one's interlocutor, what: *A: I tako sam ja pošao... B: Čije tri banke? A: So I went to... B: What?*

• **dvȇ bȁnke kȉlo** {NP} (lit. twenty dinars for two pounds) *sl* ***Fac*** of very low quality, lousy: *cene dve banke kilo rock bottom prices*

• **ko šȇst bȁnki u sitnìni** {PP} (lit. like sixty dinars in metal) *sl-fea* obese and unattractive, fat and ugly

bȁnkār {bankára (acc. = gen.) masc.} /bànkār /a (acc. = gen.) masc./ *sl-gamble* banker <Ita*1>

bànkara {ē fem.} *sl* female <Ita⁘*1>

bȃnke {ī fem. pl.} *sl* Ray Ban sunglasses <BN✍>

bȁnkīr {bankíra (acc. = gen.) masc.} (lit. banker) *sl-crime* reseller of stolen merchandise <Ita⁘*1>

Bȁnkok {a masc.} (lit. Bangkok) Ser *sl* Belgrade (Yugoslavia) <Slav*1>

bánōf {a masc.} Gast *col* train station <Ger>

bantùstān {tustána masc.} *col* country established by a foreign force <**Slav**[*1]>

bànuti {bȁnēm, bȁnū perf. intr.} *col* arrive unexpectedly, appear out of nowhere, pop in: *banuti nepozvan pop in uninvited* <**Slav**> ☞ **bahnuti**

bȁnja[1] {excl.} (lit. bath) *col* ***App*** used to express satisfaction, approval, etc. <**Ita**>

bȁnja[2] {ē fem.} /bánja /e fem./ (lit. bath) **1** *sl-sex* ***Obs*** urine, piss <**Ita**[*1]> **2a.** *sl* ***App*** something excellent: *Taj hotel je banja. That hotel is excellent.* <**Ita**[*1]> **b.** *sl-crime* ***Iro*** prison <**Ita**[*2]> **c.** *sl-thie* ***Iro*** strict prison <**Ita**[*2]>
- **Matàruškā Bȁnja** {NP} (lit. Mataruška Banja, a spa in Serbia *the initial character sequence is the same as in mat 'checkmate'*) *sl-sports* checkmate

bȁnjati se {ām, ajū imperf. intr.} (lit. bathe) **1** *sl* swim <**Ita**[*1]> **2** *sl* feel hot (temperature): *banjati se na suncu feel hot in the sun* <**Ita**[*1]>

banjáža {ē fem.} **a.** *col* bath <**Fre**> **b.** *sl-sports* swimming <**Fre**[*1]>

bànjeje {njaje neut.; perm} [std. = jebanje] *sl-sex* ***Obs*** sexual intercourse <**Slav**⇪>

bànzāč {banzáča (acc. = gen.) masc.; Voc bȁnzāču} *sl-fea* loafer, idler <**Jap**⁘[*1]>

bànzōv {banzòva (acc. = gen.) masc.} *sl-fea* loafer, idler <**Jap**⁘[*1]>

bȁp {excl.} *col* the sound made by a mild collision, bap <**Slav**>

bapírati {bàpīrām, bapírajū biasp.} (lit. bop) *sl-music* play a musical instrument <**Eng**[*1]>

bàpist {a (acc. = gen.) masc.} (lit. bopper) *sl-music* musician <**Eng**[*1]>

bȁpnuti {nēm, nū perf. intr.} **1** *sl* arrive unexpectedly, appear out of nowhere, pop in: *bapnuti u ranu zoru pop in at dawn* <**Slav**[*1]> **2** *sl-sex* have sexual intercourse with <**Slav**[*1]>
- **bȁpnuti šȁrana** {VP} (lit. hit the carp) *sl-sex* ***Fac-Obs*** engage in sexual intercourse with (of a male)

bâr *See the following*
- **cȅker bâr** {NP} (lit. shopping-bag bar) Cro *sl* ***Fac*** name of a bar near a market place in Zagreb, Croatia
- **ćȅlavac bâr** {NP} (lit. bald man's bar) *sl-drink* ***Fac*** name of a bar frequented by retirees in Zagreb, Croatia
- **kokošínjac bâr** {NP} (lit. hen-house bar) *sl-drink* Neboder bar, Zagreb, Croatia
- **sȉflis bâr** {NP} (lit. syphilis bar) Cro *sl-drink* name for Tingl-Tangl bar in Zagreb, Croatia

Bȁr dân! {NP} (lit. Good day!) *col* ***Fam*** used as an informal greeting, What's up! ☞ **dan**

Bȁra[1] {ē fem.} (lit. pond) *sl* Sava (river, former Yugoslavia) <**Slav**[*1]>

bȁra[2] {ē fem.} (lit. pond) **1** *col-sl* ***Fac*** ocean <**Slav**[*1]> **2** *col-sl* ***Fac*** sea <**Slav**[*1]> **3** *sl-crime* border (between countries) <**Slav**[*1]>

baràba {ē fem. & masc.} *col* ***Der*** worthless or despicable person <**Heb**[*1]>
- **Baràbo jèdna!** {NP} *col* ***Off*** used as a moderate curse, Fuck you!

barabȁr[1] {adj.} **Din** *col* equal: *On je barabar s Ivanom po snazi. He is equal to Ivan in strength.* <**NE**>

barabȁr[2] {adv.} **a. Din** *col* equally <**NE**> **b. Din** *col* side by side, jointly <**NE**>

baràbīn {a, o adj.} *col* ***Der*** pertaining to a despicable or worthless person <**Heb**[*1]>

baràbōv {a, o adj.} *col* ***Der*** pertaining to a despicable or worthless person <**Heb**[*1]>

baràčit {a masc.} *sl-crime* manhunt

baràka {ē fem.} (lit. shack) Cro *sl* name of a dance club on Trnjanska cesta, Zagreb, Croatia <**Spa**[*1]>

baràlisati {išēm, išū imperf.} *sl* smoke (tobacco) <**Gyp**>

baràpče {eta neut.} *col* ***Der*** young and despicable or worthless person <**Heb**[*1]>

baràpština {ē fem. & masc.} *col* ***Der*** worthless or despicable person <**Heb**[*1]>

baràtati {ām, ajū imperf.} *col* manipulate (an instrument, vehicle): *Mali dobro barata s kompjuterom. The kid is good with computers.* <**Ita**>

bârba {ē masc.} /ē masc./ **Med** *col* used to address or refer to an older male (esp. by children), mister, sir <**Ita**[*1]>

bȁrbar {a (acc. = gen.) masc.} (lit. Barbarian) Cro *sl-fea* ***Der*** unattractive male, dog <**Gre**[*1]>

bárbekju {ua masc.} *col* charcoal barbecue (cooking device) <**Eng**>

Bàrbika {ē fem.; Dat Bàrbiki} (lit. Barbie doll) *sl-sex* ***App*** attractive female, doll <**BN**[*1]>

bárbikju {ua masc.} *col* charcoal barbecue (cooking device) <**Eng**>

bȁrdo {brȁdo, brȍdo adj.; perm} *sl* good, neat <**Slav**⇪>

Bȁre {Bârā fem. pl.} (lit. name for Sarajevo's main cemetery) **Bos** *sl* death: *Ne ginu mu Bare. His death is certain.* <**Slav**[*1]>

bȁri {bȅri fem.; perm} (lit. fish) [std. = riba] **1** *sl-sex* female, chick <Slav✍> **2** *sl-sex* male looking for a loose woman, guy on the make <Slav✍*1>

Bȁrica {ē fem.} /Bȁrica/ (lit. Barica 'woman's name' X *kono*barica 'waitress') [std. = konobarica] *sl-drink* waitress <Slav✍>

barȉlček {a masc.} (lit. small barrel) *sl-sex* ***Fac-Obs*** tight vagina <Ita✤*1>

bàriška {ē fem.; Dat bàriški} *sl-drink* late-night bar <Eng✤*1>

barìtān {baritána (acc. = gen.) masc.; Voc bȃritāne} *sl-crime* policeman, cop <Gre✤*1>

báriti {bȃrīm, rē imperf.} (lit. cook) **1a.** *col* persuade, convince: *Mala ga bari da joj kupi bicikl. The kid is persuading him to buy her a bike.* <Slav*1> **b.** *col* seduce: *bariti ribu score with a chick* <Slav*2> **2** *sl-drink* drink (alcohol): *bariti lozu drink grape brandy* <Slav*1>

báriti se {bȃrīm, rē imperf. intr. } (lit. cook oneself) **a.** *sl* feel hot (temperature), bake: *bariti se na suncu feel hot in the sun* <Slav*1> **b.** *sl-drink* get drunk, get toasted: *bariti se vinom get toasted on wine* <Slav*2>

bàrjāk {barjáka masc.} **a.** BosM *col* flag <NE> **b.i.** *sl* credit, loan <NE*1> **ii.** *sl-sex* ***Fac-Obs*** penis, dick, prick <NE*1>

- **na bàrjāk** {PP} (lit. to a flag) *col* on credit: *kupiti kola na barjak buy a car on credit*

bȃrka {ē fem.; Dat bȃrki} (lit. boat) **a.** *sl-crime* wallet <Ita*1> **b.** *sl* suitcase <Ita*2>

bȁrkati {ām, ajū imperf.} *col* touch, put one's hands onto, mess with: *Ne barkaj mi knjige! Don't mess with my books!* <Slav>

bàrkist {a (acc. = gen.) masc.} *sl-crime* pickpocket <Ita✤*1> ☞ **barka**

bàrkonj {a (acc. = gen.) masc.; perm} [std. = konobar] *sl-drink* waiter <Slav✍>

barlȉjānje {a neut.} *sl-fea* ***Der*** prolonged and meaningless talk, blabber, chatter: *barlijanje o vremenu blabber about the weather* <Slav*1>

barlȉjati {ām, ajū imperf.} **a.** *sl-fea* ***Der*** talk persistently and meaninglessly, blabber, chatter: *barlijati o politici blabber about politics* <Slav*1> **b.** *sl-fea* ***Der*** talk, have a conversation: *Barlijali smo preko telefona. We spoke over the phone.* <Slav*2>

bȁro[1] {excl.} *sl* used to signal agreement, okay: *A: Idemo li na plažu? B: Baro! A: Are we gonna hit the beach? B: Okay!* <Ita✍*1>

bȁro[2] {bero fem.; perm} /bàro/ [std. = roba] *sl* merchandise <Ita✍>

- **bȁro kòja zvòni i pȁda u ȁktalice** {NP} (lit. the merchandise which rings and falls into arms) *sl-crime* excellent merchandise
- **bȁro za valjážu** {NP} (lit. the merchandise for rolling) *sl-crime* merchandise which sells well
- **vȁtrenā bȁro** {NP} (lit. sizzling hot merchandise) *sl-crime* merchandise which can cause problems to its possessor

bàrōn {baróna (acc. = gen.) masc.} (lit. baron, i.e. baron Mȕnchhausen) *sl* liar <Ita*1>

baròniјe {nījā fem. pl.} (lit. the baron stuff i.e. baron Mȕnchhausen) lies, made-up events <Ita✤*1>

baronírati {rònīrām, ronírajū biasp.} (lit. act like a baron i.e. Mȕnchhausen) *sl* lie <Ita✤*1>

baròniѕati {išēm, išū imperf.} (lit. act like a baron i.e. Mȕnchhausen) **a.** **Ser** *sl* ***Fac*** lie: *baronisati o knjigama boast about one's books* <Ita✤*1> **b.i.** Ser *sl* ***Fac*** boast, brag <Ita✤*2> **ii.** Ser *sl* ***Fac*** be conceited, be stuck up, put on airs <Ita✤*3>

bàrtati {ām, ajū imperf.} *sl* carry, have along: *bartati pištolj pack a pistol* <Slav*1>

bàrtol {a (acc. = gen.) masc.} (lit. Bart) *sl-sex* ***Obs*** penis, dick, prick <Heb*1>

barùnica {ē fem.} (lit. baroness) Cro *sl-sex* ***Off*** male homosexual, gay <Ita✤*1>

barùnisati {išēm, išū biasp.} (lit. act like a baron, i.e. Mȕnchhausen) *sl* ***Fac*** lie <Ita✤*1>

barúniti {bàrūnīm, nē imperf.} *sl-crime* ***Fac*** hide from a manhunt, be on the lamb <Ger✤*1>

bàrunja {ē fem.} *sl-crime* prison <Ger✤*1>

barutàna {ē fem.} (lit. gunpowder storage) **1** *sl* ***Fac*** dangerous place, powder keg <NE*1> **2** *sl-fea* ***Fac*** senior citizen <NE*1>

bȁs {a +ov (ext. pl) masc.; Nom Pl bàsovi} *col* bus <Eng>

bȁsamak {mka masc.} BosM *col* stair <NE>

bȁsniti {nīm, nē perf.} *sl-sex* ***Obs*** engage in sexual intercourse with (of a male) <NE*1>

bȁsta {excl.} *col* used to stop action, basta <Ita>

bastȉlja {ē fem.} (lit. bastille) **1** *sl-sstu* ***Fac*** school <Fre*1> **2** **Ser** *sl-polit* ***Fac*** any institution affiliated with the regime in Serbia in the 1990s <Fre*1>

bȁš {part.} **1** *col* really, indeed: *On je baš dosadan. He is really boring.* <NE> **2** *col* exactly, precisely: *Kupio je baš ta kola. He has that exact car.* <NE>

• **Bȁš[PRON:ACC] bȍlī ([NOUN:NOM])!** {LSF} (lit. It really hurts [PRON:ACC]!) *col* used to express indifference: *Baš me boli briga šta ti misliš! I don't care what you think!* ◊ *Baš je boli uvo sviđa li ti se ili ne! She doesn't care if you like her or not!*

• **Bȁš[PRON:ACC] brȉga!** {LSF} (lit. This trouble really hurts [PRON:ACC]!) *col* used to express indifference: *Baš me briga hoćeš li doći ili ne! I don't care if you come or not!*

• **Bȁš[PRON:ACC] zàbolī!** {LSF} (lit. It really hurts [PRON:ACC]!) *col* used to express indifference: *Baš ga zaboli hoćeš li crći ili preživjeti! He doesn't care if you live or die!*

• **Bȁš si [NOUN:NOM]!** {LSF} (lit. You are really a [NOUN:NOM]!) *col* ***Off*** used as a moderate reprimand, usu. in response to a refusal: *Baš si peder! Nećeš ni da pričaš sa mnom! You're mean! You won't even talk to me!*

bàšaliti {līm, lē imperf.} *sl* beat up <NE❖*1>

bàšanica {ē fem.} *sl* fight (e.g. fist fight) <NE❖*1>

bȁšča {ē fem.} BosM *col* garden (vegetable, flower, etc.) <NE>

bȁščica {ē fem.} BosM *col* small garden (vegetable, flower, etc.) <NE❖>

bȁšća {ē masc.} **a.** BosM *col-sl* garden (vegetable, flower, etc.) <NE> **b.** BosM *sl* village <NE*1> ☞ **bašča**

bašibòzuk {a masc.} (lit. soldier, rowdy) **Din** *sl* nonsense: *To da će za Novu godinu biti raspad sistema je bašibozuk. The story that there will be a total collapse of the system is nonsense.* <NE*1>

bàška [1] {part.} **Din** *col* not to mention: *On je prevarant, a baška to što krade. He's a cheat, not to mention a thief.* <NE>

bàška [2] {adv.} **Din** *col* apart, separately, individually: *Njih dvojica su putovali baška. The two of them travelled separately.* ◊ *Ona živi baška od roditelja. She lives apart from her parents.* <NE>

bȁšnuti {nēm, nū perf.} *sl* cut with knife, slice (e.g. a tomato, potato) <Slav>

bàšta [1] {ē fem.} *sl* fight (e.g. fist fight) <Ita>

bášta [2] {ē masc.} (lit. garden) **1a.** *sl-crime* person from whom it is easy to steal, easy mark <NE*1> **b.** *sl-fea* naive person <NE*1> **2** *sl* father, daddy <Slav>

baštánac {nca masc.} **a.** *sl* bat, stick, rod <Ita❖> **b.** *sl* fight (e.g. fist fight)

baštànija {ē fem.} *sl* fight (e.g. fist fight) <Ita❖>

bàštānje {a neut.} **a.** *sl* beating up <Ita❖> **b.** *sl* fighting <Ita❖*1>

bàštati {ām, ajū imperf.} *sl* beat up <Ita>

bàštati se {ām, ajū imperf. intr.} *sl* fight (e.g. fist fight): *Dva tipa se baštaju iza ugla. Two guys are fighting around the corner.* <Ita*1>

bàšter {a (acc. = gen.) masc.; Voc bàšteru} *sl* troublemaker, rowdy, ruffian <Ita❖*1>

baštòvān {tována (acc. = gen.) masc.} (lit. gardener) **1** *sl* ***Der*** stupid or mentally deficient person <NE❖*1> **2** *sl* ***Fac*** lame male <NE❖*1>

baštovàndžika {ē fem. & masc.; Dat baštovàndžiki} (lit. gardener) **1** *sl* ***Der*** stupid or mentally deficient person <NE❖*1> **2** *sl* ***Fac*** lame person <NE❖*1>

bàštrac {a (acc. = gen.) masc.; Voc bàštrače} *sl-sex* ***Off*** male homosexual, gay <Ita❖*1>

bàštrāč {baštráča (acc. = gen.) masc.} *sl-sex* ***Off*** male homosexual, gay <Ita❖*1>

bàštrānje {a neut.} **a.** *col* pushing, showing: *baštranje na ulazu u lift pushing at the elevator entrance* <Ita*1> **b.** *col* elbowing, maneuvering: *baštranje da se dobije povišica elbowing for a raise* <Ita*1>

bàštūnka {ē fem.} *sl* rifle <Ita❖*1>

baštúnjac {njca masc.} *sl-arch* tree <Ita❖*1>

bȁtāk {a masc.} /bȁtk /tka masc./ (lit. chicken leg quarter) **1a.** *sl-sex* leg (of a female) <Slav*1> **b.** *sl-sex* ***App*** attractive female <Slav*2> **2** *sl-sex* ***Obs*** penis, dick, prick <Slav*1>

bàtalica {ē fem.} *sl-arch* tree <Slav*1>

batáliti {bàtālīm, lē perf.} *col* leave without finishing, lose interest in, drop: *bataliti učenje španskog drop learning Spanish* <NE> ☞ **zabataliti**

bàtan {a (acc. = gen.) masc.} **a.** *col* ***Fam*** brother <Slav> **b.** *col* ***Fam*** friend (male) <Slav*1>

bȁte {eta masc.} SSer *dia-col* ***Fam*** brother <Slav>

bàtērija {ē fem.} /batèrija e, fem./ *sl-auto* car battery <Fre>

• **na bàtērije i na strúju** {PP} (lit. plug and battery powered) *sl-sex* ***Fac*** bisexual, AC/DC

bȁti {bêm, bû biasp.} [std. = jebati] *sl-sex* ***Obs*** engage in sexual intercourse with (of a male) <Slav✍>

• **Bêm[PRON:ACC] u [NP:ACC]!** {LSF} (lit. I screw [PRON:ACC] in *your* [NOUN:NOM]!) *col* ***Off*** used as a moderate curse or threat, Fuck you!: *Bem te u leđa! Ja ne idem! Screw you! I'm not going!*

• **Bêm[PRON:DAT] [NP:ACC]!** {LSF} (lit. I screw [PRON:ACC] [NOUN:NOM]!) *col* ***Off*** used as a moderate curse or threat, Fuck you!: *Bem ti Boga! Ne zovi me opet! Fuck you! Don't call me again!*

bàtije {bèmjē, būjē biasp.; perm} [std. = jebati] *sl-sex* ***Obs*** engage in sexual intercourse with (of a male) <**Slav**✍>

bàtina {ē fem.} (lit. bat, stick) **1** *sl-sex* ***Obs*** penis, dick, prick <**Slav**[*1]> **2a.** *sl-fea* ***Der*** insane person, nut case <**Slav**[*1]> **b.** *sl-fea* ***Der*** stupid or mentally deficient person <**Slav**[*1]> **3** *sl-fea* very important or influential person, big shot <**Slav**[*1]>

batínac {nca masc.} *sl* bat, stick, rod <**Slav**✣>

bàtine {bàtīnā masc. pl.} (lit. thrashing) *sl-drugs* marijuana, pot, grass <**Slav**[*1]>

bȁtje {bȅmjē, bȕjē biasp.; perm} /bàtje/ [std. = jebati] *sl-sex* ***Obs*** engage in sexual intercourse with (of a male) <**Slav**✍>

bâto[1] {excl.} (lit. bro) *col* used to address a male in direct informal communication, bro <**Slav**>

báto[2] {ē masc.} **a.** *col* ***Fam*** brother <**Slav**> **b.i.** *sl-sex* ***Fam-Obs*** penis, dick, prick <**Slav**[*1]> **ii.** *sl* ***App*** muscular male <**Slav**[*1]>

bȁtre {bȅtrē fem.; perm} /bàtre/ [std. = treba] *sl* female <**Slav**✍[*1]>

batȑgača {ē fem.} *sl-drink* strong plum brandy <**Slav**[*1]>

batȑgati se {ām, ajū imperf. intr.} *col* put up resistance: *batrgati se prilikom hapšenja give resistance during the arrest* <**Slav**>

bàtunjac {njca masc.} *sl* bat, stick, rod <**Slav**✣>

bȁu {excl.} *col* used to scare somebody (esp. young children), boo <**Slav**> ☞ **bau-bau**

bȁu-bȁu {excl.} *col* used to scare somebody (esp. young children), boo <**Slav**> ☞ **bau**

baùljati {ām, ajū imperf.} *col* crawl, creep: *Gušteri mi baurljaju po sobi. Lizards are crawling around in my room.* <**Slav**>

bȁviti se *See the following*

• **bȁviti se literatúrōm**{VP} (lit. study literature) *sl-drink* ***Fac*** drink (alcohol): *Bavili smo se literaturom do tri ujutro. We were boozing until three am.*

bȁvlju {bàviljū perf.; perm} /bàvlju/ [std. = ljubav] *sl* love (in general) <**Slav**✍>

bavȑljanje {a neut.} *col* prolonged and meaningless talk, blabber, chatter: *bavrljanje o politici blabber about politics* <**Slav**>

bavȑljati {ām, ajū imperf.} *col* talk persistently and meaninglessly, blabber, chatter: *bavrljati o politici blabber about politics* <**Slav**>

bȃz {a +ev (ext. pl) masc.; Nom Pl bázevi} *col* unpleasant odor, stench <**Slav**> ☞ **bazd**

báza {ē fem.} (lit. base) **1** *col* gathering place (for a group of people) <**Gre**[*1]> **2** *sl* female

bàzāč {bazáča (acc. = gen.) masc.; Voc bȁzāču} *sl* walker (person) <**Gre**✣[*1]>

bázalo {a neut.} *sl-fea* ***Der*** lazy or shiftless person, bum, good for nothing <**Slav**✣>

bázānje {a neut.} *col* wandering, roaming <**Gre**✣[*1]>

bazárēnje {a neut.} (lit. bazaar spree) *col* shopping <**NE**✣[*1]>

bázati {bâzām, bázajū imperf. intr.} *col* wander, roam: *bazati po cijelom gradu wander throughout the city* <**Gre**✣[*1]>

bâzd {a +ov (ext. pl) masc.; Nom Pl bázdovi} *col* unpleasant odor, stench <**Slav**> ☞ **baz**

bàzdeti {dīm, dē imperf.} /bázdeti/ **SerE** *col* smell, stink: *Smeće već bazdi, treba ga izbaciti. The garbage stinks, somebody should take it out.* <**Slav**>

bàzditi {dīm, dē imperf.} /bázditi/ **a.** *col* smell, stink: *Ova svlačionica bazdi. This locker room reeks.* <**Slav**> **b.** *sl* be boring: *Nemoj da sjedamo za njegov sto, on bazdi. Let's not sit at his table, he is boring.* <**Slav**[*1]>

bȅ {excl.} SSer *col* used in direct informal communication with a person, hey <**NE**> ☞ **ba, bre**

Bê-Hâ[1] {fem.} *col* Bosnia and Herzegovina <**Abb**[*1]>

bê-hâ[2] {adj.} *col* Bosnian <**Abb**[*1]>

bebèrōn {beróna (acc. = gen.) masc.} *sl* baby, newborn <**Eng**✣>

bebijáner {a (acc. = gen.) masc.} *sl* baby, newborn <**Eng**✣>

bebìrōn {biróna (acc. = gen.) masc.} **1** *sl* baby, newborn <**Eng**✣> **2** *sl* fruit juice <**Eng**✣[*1]>

becìklo {a neut.} [std. = bicikl] *col-dia* bicycle, bike <**Lat-Gre**✍>

béčiti se {bêčīm, čē imperf. intr.} **1** *col* stare at, be fixated on: *bečiti se na gole žene stare at the naked women* <Slav> **2** *col* grimace, make faces to entertain or mock: *bečiti se na nastavnika make faces at the teacher* <Slav>

béčkā škôla {NP} (lit. Vienna school) **a.** *col* elegance **b.** *col* very elegant person ☞ **škola**

béčkā škôla ìsturenō odelénje Nîš {NP} (lit. Vienna school branch office in Niš *a city in Southern Serbia*) SerE *col* ***Fac*** provincial snob: *Mića misli da je prefinjen a u stvari je bečka škola istureno odelenje Niš. Miça thinks he is sophisticated, but he's just a provincial snob.* ☞ **škola**

bȅčke {ī fem. pl.} *sl* trousers, pants <Slav[*1]>

bèćār {bećára (acc. = gen.) masc.} **a.** *col* lazy or shiftless person, bum, good for nothing <NE[*1]> **b.** *col* alcoholic, drunk <NE[*2]>

bȅd {a +ov (ext. pl) masc.; Nom Pl bèdovi} **1** *sl* unpleasant feeling: *bed od lošeg vina hangover from the bad wine* <Eng> **2** *sl* unfavorable situation: *Ako ne završim posao na vreme, biću u bedu. I will be in a bind if I don't finish this job on time.* <Eng>

bȅd blû bôjsi {NP} (lit. bad blue boys) *sl-sports* fans of Dinamo (in the 1990s "Croatia", a soccer team from Zagreb, Croatia) ☞ **bojs**

bȅd trȉp {NP} (lit. bad trip) *sl-drugs* unpleasant effect of narcotic drugs, bad trip ☞ **trip**

bèdāk [1] {bedáka (acc. = gen.) masc.} Cro *col-dia* stupid or mentally deficient person <Slav>

bèdāk [2] {bedáka masc.} **a.** *sl* pessimism <Slav[*1]> **b.i.** *sl* condition of being broke (financially): *Bedak je jer je prockao platu. He is broke 'cause he gambled his paycheck away.* <Slav[*2]> **ii.** *sl* hard times <Slav[*2]>

bȅdast {a, o adj.} Cro *col-dia* ***Der*** insane, nuts <Slav>

bedastòća {ē fem.} Cro *col* stupidity, lack of intelligence <Slav>

bedèvija {ē fem.} **1** *dia* young mare <NE> **2a.** *dia* big-boned mare <NE> **b.** *sl* big-boned female <NE[*1]>

bèdiška {ē fem.; Dat bèdiški} **1** *sl* unpleasant feeling <Eng✣> **2** *sl* unfavorable situation <Eng✣>

begènisati {išēm, išū imperf.} **1** Din *col* wish, hope for: *Begenišem onaj auto odavno. I've had my eye on that car for a long time.* <NE> **2** Din *col* reserve, book: *Begeniso dva litra loze kod komšije. I reserved two liters of grape brandy at my neighbors.* <NE>

Bègiš {a masc.} Ser *sl* ***Fam*** name for Belgrade (Yugoslavia) <Slav✍>

Bêhâ [1] {fem.} *col* Bosnia and Herzegovina: *Ona je iz Beha. She is from Bosnia and Herzegovina.* <Slav✍>

bêhâ [2] {adj.} *col* Bosnian: *beha pasoš Bosnian passport* <Slav✍>

bèhūt {behúta masc.} Bos *col* loss of consciousness <NE>

bêjbī {excl.} (lit. baby) *col* ***Fam*** used to address a female in direct informal communication, dear <Eng>

bêk {excl.} *col* the sound made by a sheep, baa <Slav>

bȅka {ē fem.; Dat bȅki} *col* bleating (of sheep), baaing <Slav>

bèkan {a (acc. = gen.) masc.} *col* ***Fam*** lamb (the animal) <Slav>

békānje {a neut.} *col* bleating (of sheep), baaing <Slav>

békati {bêčēm, bêčū imperf.} *col* bleat (of sheep), baa <Slav>

bȅkav {a, o adj.} (lit. bleating) *col* stuttering <Slav[*1]>

békavac {kāvca (acc. = gen.) masc.} (lit. the bleating one) *col* stutterer <Slav[*1]>

békavica {ē fem.} (lit. the bleating one) *col* sheep (the animal) <Slav>

bȅkavo {adv.} (lit. bleating) *col* in a stuttering manner: *govoriti bekavo speak in a stuttering manner* <Slav[*1]>

bekéljiti se {bèkēljīm, ljē imperf. intr. } *col* grimace, make faces to entertain or mock: *Đaci se bekelje na nastavnika na času. Students are making faces at their teacher during class.* <Slav>

bekendírati {kèndīrām, kendírajū biasp.} **a.** *sl* hit, punch: *Bekendirao ga je u oko. He hit him in the eye.* <Eng[*1]> **b.** *sl* beat up: *Bekendirali su ga da se nije mogo dići. They beat him up so bad he couldn't get up.* <Eng[*2]>

bekètānje {a neut.} *col* bleating (of goat), baaing <Slav>

bekètati {ām, ajū imperf.} *col* bleat (of goat), baa <Slav>

bȅkgrâund {a masc.} *col* background, the ground or scenery behind something <Eng>

béknuti {bêknēm, bêknū perf. intr.} **a.** *col* bleat (of sheep), baa: *Da nisi beknuo! You are not supposed to say a word!* <Slav> **b.** *col* tell, say (usu. in the negative) <Slav[*1]>

bèkrija {ē masc.} **a.** *col* lazy or shiftless person, bum, good for nothing <NE> **b.** *col* alcoholic, drunk <NE[*1]>

bekr̀jati {ām, ajū imperf. intr.} *col* party (engage in social gathering): *Bekrijali su do dva u noći. They partied until two am.* <NE>

bêlā {ē fem. (adj. decl.)} SerE *sl-drink* brandy <Slav[*1]>

bêlā kȑvnā zŕnca {NP} (lit. white blood cells) SerE *sl-sex* ***Fac-Obs*** sperm ☞ **zrnce**

bêlā tȁčka {NP} (lit. the white spot) SerE *sl-sports* penalty kick (in soccer) ☞ **tačka**

bêlā tèhnika {NP} (lit. white technology) SerE *col* kitchen appliances ☞ **tehnika**

bélac [1] {lca (acc. = gen.) masc.} SerE *sl* doctor, doc <Slav[*1]>

bélac [2] {lca masc.} **1** SerE *sl* dinar (Yugoslav currency unit) <Slav[*1]> **2** *sl* finger <Slav[*1]>

bèlāč {beláča masc.} SerE *sl-arch* lime (calcium oxide) <Slav[*1]>

bèlača {ē fem.} SerE *sl-drink* brandy <Slav[*1]>

bèlāj {a masc.} **a.** Bos *col* trouble, problem: *Ako ne platiš račune, biće belaj. If you don't pay these bills, you'll be in trouble.* <NE> **b.** Bos *col* mess, disorder, disturbance: *Vidi kakav su belaj ostavili iza sebe. Look what a mess they left behind.* <NE[*1]>

belégija {ē fem.} *col* polishing machine <NE>

belengùzac {sca (acc. = gen.) masc.} (lit. the one with a white ass) SerE *col* ***Obs*** a kind of songbird <Slav>

bèli {part.} BosM *col* used as a strong affirmative response, of course, yeah, you bet: *A: Ideš li na utakmicu? B: Beli! A: Are you going to the ball game? B: You bet!* <NE>

bêlī bùbrezi {NP} (lit. white kidneys) SerE *sl-sex* ***Fac*** testicles ☞ **bubreg**

Bêlī màrdelj {NP} (lit. white prison) **1** SerE *sl* countryside, province **2** *sl* Belgrad (Yugoslavia) ☞ **mardelj**

bêlka {ē fem.; Dat bêlki} (lit. the white one) SerE *col* one dinar; a one-dinar coin <Slav[*1]>

Belmȍndo nȁočāri {NP} (lit. Belmondo: French actor popular in the 1970s eyeglasses) *sl* ***Fac*** black eye, shiner ☞ **naočari**

belnèguza {ē fem.} (lit. the one with white ass) SerE *col* ***Obs*** a kind of songbird <Slav>

bélo [1] {adv.} /bêlo adv./ SerE *col* dull, uninterested: *Ona je gledala belo kad sam joj rekao o njemu. She gave me an uninterested look when I told her about him.* <Slav[*1]>

bêlō [2] {ōg neut.} /bélo/ SerE *sl-drugs* heroin, horse, smack <Slav[*1]>

beločaràpāš {rapáša (acc. = gen.) masc.; beločȁrapāšu} (lit. the one who wears white socks) **1** SerE *sl-sex* ***Off*** male homosexual, gay <Slav✤[*1]> **2** SerE *sl-fea* ***Der*** inhabitant of the countryside, hick, bumpkin <Slav✤[*1]>

Bêlōga ti bȍga! {S} (lit. *I screw* your white God!) SerE *col* ***Off*** used as a moderate curse or threat, Fuck you! ☞ **bog**

bȅlogūz [1] {a masc.} SerE *col* ***Fac-Obs*** person with white buttocks <Slav>

bȅloguz [2] {a, o adj.} /belòguz /a, o adj./ *col* pertaining to a person with white buttocks <Slav[*1]>

belòguza {ē fem. (adj. decl.)} (lit. the one with white buttocks) SerE *col* ***Obs*** a kind of songbird <Slav>

belosvètskī {a, o adj.} (lit. white world's) SerE *col* ***Iro-Der*** cosmopolitan: *Njujork je veoma kosmopolitsko mesto. New York is a very cosmopolitan city.* <Slav[*1]>

béljiti {ljīm, ljē imperf.} *col* stare at, be fixated on: *beljiti u dobru ribu stare at a hot chick* <Slav>

béljiti se {ljīm, ljē imperf. intr. } *col* stare at, be fixated on: *beljiti se u nova kola stare at a new car* <Slav>

Bêm [PRON:ACC] u [NP:ACC]! {LSF} (lit. I screw [PRON: ACC] in *your* [NOUN:NOM]!) *col* ***Off*** used as a moderate curse or threat, Screw you! ☞ **bati**

Bêm [PRON:DAT] [NP:ACC]! {LSF} (lit. I screw [PRON: ACC] [NOUN:NOM]!) *col* ***Off*** used as a moderate offense or threat, Screw [PRON:ACC]! ☞ **bati**

bȅmbāč {a (acc. = gen.) masc.} *sl-auto* BMW (make of car), Bemmer <BN>

Bȅn *See the following*

- **Bȉg Bȅn** {NP} (lit. Big Ben) Cro *sl* name of a dance club on Bogovićeva street in Zagreb, Croatia

bȅna {ē fem.} *sl-fea* ***Der*** stupid or mentally deficient person <NE>

bȅnas {asta, asto adj.} *col-dia* ***Der*** insane, nuts <NE✍> ☞ **benast, benav**

bȅnast {a, o adj.} *col* ***Der*** insane, nuts <NE> ☞ **benas, benav**

bȅnav {a, o adj.} *col* ***Der*** insane, nuts <NE> ☞ **benas, benast**

benáviti {bènāvīm, vē imperf.} (lit. be insane) **a.** *sl-fea* ***Der*** talk persistently and meaninglessly, blabber, chatter: *benaviti o nevažnim stvarima blabber about some unimportant things* <NE✤> **b.** talk, have a conversation: *benaviti preko telefona talk over the phone* <NE✤[*1]>

benáviti se {bènāvīm, vē imperf. intr.} *sl-fea* grimace, make faces to entertain or mock <**Slav**[*1]>

benávljenje {a neut.} (lit. being insane) *sl-fea* ***Der*** prolonged and meaningless talk, blabber, chatter: *benavljenje o poslednjoj modi blabber about the latest fashions* <**NE**❖>

bènćta {ē fem.} *sl-auto* BMW (make of car), Bemmer <**BN**>

bȅnd {a +ov (ext. pl) masc.; Nom Pl bèndovi} *col* band (usu. rock music) <**Eng**>

bèndati {ām, ajū imperf.} **Bos** *col* have respect for: *Hamo ne benda nikoga. Hamo don't have any respect for anybody.* <**NE**>

bèndiks {a masc.} *sl-auto* cogwheel <**BN**>

béndža {ē masc.} **1 SerE** *sl-auto* BMW (make of car), Bemmer <**BN**✍> **2 SerE** *sl-drugs* Benzedrine, benny <**BN**✍>

bendžèluk {a masc.} *col-dia* low-quality hard liquor, rot gut <**NE**>

béndžo {a masc.} /béndžo /e masc./ *sl-auto* BMW (make of car), Bemmer <**BN**✍>

benđóla {ē fem.} *sl-auto* BMW (make of car), Bemmer <**BN**>

bȅnešiti {šīm, šē imperf.} (lit. from the name: Marijan Beneš, a Yugoslav boxer popular in the 1970s) *sl* beat up: *Benešila su ga tri tipa, pa je skoro rikno. Three guys trashed him so bad that he almost kicked the bucket.* <**SlavO**❖[*1]>

benètānje {a neut.} (lit. being insane) *sl* prolonged and meaningless talk, blabber, chatter: *Dosadilo mi je njeno benetanje. I am bored with her blabber.* <**NE**[*1]>

benètati {ām, ajū imperf.} (lit. be insane) *sl* talk persistently and meaninglessly, blabber, chatter: *benetati s prijateljicama blabber with friends* <**NE**[*1]>

bèntānje {a neut.} (lit. being insane) *sl* prolonged and meaningless talk, blabber, chatter: *bentanje o tuđim kućama blabber about others' houses* <**NE**❖[*1]>

bêntati {ām, ajū imperf.} (lit. be insane) *sl* talk persistently and meaninglessly, blabber, chatter: *bentati o modi blabber about the latest fashions* <**NE**[*1]>

bèpče {eta neut.} Ser *col* ***Fam*** baby, newborn <**Eng**❖>

bèrba {ē fem.} (lit. harvest) **1** *sl-crime* ***Fac*** robbery <**Slav**[*1]> **2** *sl-crime* ***Iro*** conviction (for a crime) <**Slav**[*1]>

berbijáner {a masc.} *sl* fruit juice <**Slav-Ger**❖[*1]>

bèretka {ē fem.; Dat bèretki} (lit. beret esp. as worn by young females in the 1950s) *sl* very young female, little girl <**Fre**[*1]>

- **zèlenā bèretka** {NP} (lit. green beret) *sl-mil* Bosnian Muslim soldier

berìćet {a masc.} **Din** *sl* profit, gain <**NE**>

berìćetan {tna, tno adj.} /bèrićetan /tna, tno adj./ **a. Din** *col* ***App*** fruitful, bountiful: *berićetan službeni put fruitful business trip* <**NE**> **b. Din** *col* ***App*** profitable: *berićetna finansijska operacija profitable financial operation* <**NE**[*1]>

berìćetno {adv.} /bèrićetno adv./ **a. Din** *col* ***App*** fruitfully: *raditi berićetno work fruitfully* <**NE**> **b. Din** *col* ***App*** profitably: *proći berićetno get profit* <**NE**[*1]>

bernardínac {nca (acc. = gen.) masc.} (lit. St. Bernard dog) **a.** *sl-fea* ***Der-Fac*** inhabitant of the countryside, hick, bumpkin <**GerO**[*1]> **b.** *sl-fea* ***Der*** stupid or mentally deficient person <**GerO**[*2]>

bésan {sna, sno adj.} (lit. rabid) **1** SerE *col* furious, livid <**Slav**[*1]> **2** SerE *col* excellent, awesome <**Slav**[*1]>

- **bésan ko lèptir** {AdjP} (lit. as angry as a butterfly) **SerE** *sl* ***Fac*** intensely agitated, mad as a hatter: *biti besan ko leptir zbog prekovremenog rada be very mad about having to work overtime*
- **bésan ko óvca** {AdjP} (lit. as angry as a sheep) **SerE** *sl* ***Fac*** intensely agitated, mad as a hatter: *Bio sam besan ko ovca posle sastanka. I was very mad after the meeting.*
- **bésan ko pȕška** {AdjP} (lit. as angry as a gun) **SerE** *col* intensely agitated, mad as a hatter: *biti besan ko puška zbog dečijih loših ocena be very mad about the kids' poor grades*
- **bésan ko rȉs** {AdjP} (lit. as angry as a lynx) **SerE** *col* intensely agitated, mad as a hatter: *Novi trener je besan ko ris zbog poraza. The new coach is very mad about losing.*

bèskućnīk {a (acc. = gen.) masc.} (lit. homeless person) *sl-crime* ***Fac*** night-shift policeman <**Slav**[*1]>

bèskūrčević {a (acc. = gen.) masc.} (lit. the one without a prick) *col-dia* ***Obs*** unmanly husband (in all aspects of life) <**Slav**❖[*1]>

bèstija {ē fem.} **a.** *col* beast (the animal) <**Lat**> **b.** *sl-fea* ***Der*** stupid or mentally deficient person <**Lat**[*1]>

bȅstraga {excl.} *col* used to express anger, hell <**Slav**>

- **bȅstrāga[PRON:DAT] gláva** {LSF} (lit. let [PPRON:NOM] head be lost without any traces) *col* ***Der*** used to express disapproval, disgust, etc.: *Bestraga mu glava! The hell with him!*

bestrágija {ē fem.} *col* a place of extreme wretchedness or squalor, hellhole <**Slav**[*1]>

béše {part.} /bèše part./ **SerE** *col* used to express uncertainty: *To mi je beše rekao Pera. I think that was what Pera told me.* ◊ *Jel ti ono beše Markov sin? Aren't you Marko's son?* <**Slav**>

bèštija {ē fem.} **a.** *col* beast (the animal) <**Lat**> **b.** *col* ***Der*** evil person, beast <**Lat**[*1]>

bètōn [1] {betóna (acc. = gen.) masc.} (lit. concrete) **1** *sl-fea* ***Der*** stupid or mentally deficient person <**Fre**[*1]> **2** *sl-polit* ***Der*** dyed in the wood communist <**Fre**[*1]>

bètōn [2] {betóna masc.} (lit. concrete) **1** *sl-crime* prison <**Fre**[*1]> **2** *sl-drink* shot and beer, boilermaker <**Fre**[*1]> **3a.** *sl-gamble* two aces with two kings (in poker) <**Fre**[*1]> **b.** *sl-gamb* cautious gambling <**Fre**[*2]>

betònīrān {a, o adj.} (lit. set in concrete) **1** *sl-fea* ***Der*** insane, nuts <**Fre**⁘[*1]> **2** *sl-drink* ***Fac*** drunk, plastered <**Fre**⁘[*1]>

betonírati {tònīrām, tonírajū biasp.} (lit. set in concrete) **1a.** *sl-drink* drink boilermakers <**Fre**⁘[*1]> **b.** *sl-drink* get very drunk, get plastered <**Fre**⁘[*2]> **2** *sl* beat up <**Fre**⁘[*1]>

betonírati se {tònīrām, tonírajū biasp. intr.} (lit. set oneself in concrete) *sl-drink* get very drunk, get plastered <**Fre**[*1]>

bez fárōvā {PP} (lit. without headlights) *sl-fea* ***Fac*** blind (of a person) ☞ **farovi**

bez kȍske {PP} (lit. without a bone) *sl-sports* swish (basketball shot that does not touch the rim) ☞ **koska**

bez pedigrȅa {PP} (lit. without a pedigree) **a.** *sl-crime* ***Fac*** of suspicious origin **b.** *sl-crime* ***Fac*** stolen, swiped ☞ **pedigre**

bez šprȉcē {PP} (lit. without a syringe) *sl-sex* ***Fac*** without any venereal diseases (usu. of a prostitute) ☞ **šprica**

bez vȅzē {PP} (lit. without a connection) **a.** *col* evil, mean: *frajer bez veze mean dude* **b.i.** *col* stupid, clueless: *bez veze knjiga stupid book* **ii.** *col* nothing special, no big deal: *A: Kako je bilo? B: Bilo je bez veze. A: How was it? B: It was no big deal.* ☞ **veza**

bezbèli {part.} /bèzbeli part./ **BosM** *col* used as a strong affirmative response, of course, yeah, you bet: *Bezbeli da ću kupiti ta jeftina kola. Of course I will buy that cheap car.* <**NE**>

bèzē {excl.} [std. = bez veze] *col* used to express indifference, nothing special, no big deal: *A: Kakva je ta plaža? B: Beze. A: What is that beach like? B: No big deal.* <**Slav**✍>

bèzec {excl.} *sl* used to signal occupancy, this one's taken (e.g. a seat) <**Ger**>

bèzecovati {cujēm, cujū imperf.} *col* occupy, reserve: *bezecovati sto u ćošku reserve a corner table* <**Ger**>

bezìstān {a masc.} BosM *col* bazaar, indoor market place <**NE**>

bezìsten {a masc.} BosM *col* bazaar, indoor market place <**NE**>

bèzjājnīk {a (acc. = gen.) masc.} (lit. the one without balls) *sl-fea* ***Der-Obs*** impotent male <**Slav**⁘[*1]>

bȅzjak {a (acc. = gen.) masc.} **a.** *sl-fea* ***Der*** stupid or mentally deficient person <**Slav**[*1]> **b.** *sl-fea* ***Der*** insane person, nut case <**Slav**[*2]>

bèzjebica {ē fem.} (lit. fucklessness) *sl-sex* ***Obs*** period without sexual intercourse <**Slav**⁘>

bèzvezan {zna, zno adj.} (lit. without connection) **a.** *col* bad, of low quality: *bezvezna pjesma bad song* <**Slav**⁘[*1]> **b.i.** *sl* unintelligent, stupid, dumb: *bezvezan učenik stupid student* <**Slav**⁘[*1]> **ii.** *sl* insane, nuts: *bezvezan komšija insane neighbor* <**Slav**⁘[*1]> **iii.** *col* unknown: *bezvezan slikar unknown painter* <**Slav**[*1]> **iv.** *col* unimportant <**Slav**[*1]>

bèzveze {adv.} /bezvèze/ (lit. without connection) *col* worthless: *Kupila je neki bezveze kasetaš. She's bought a worthless boombox.* <**Slav**⁘[*1]>

bezvèzist {a (acc. = gen.) masc.} (lit. the one without connections) *sl-fea* ***Der*** stupid or mentally deficient person <**Slav**⁘[*1]>

bezvèznjāk {veznjáka (acc. = gen.) masc.} (lit. the one without connections) **a.** *col* ***Der*** average person <**Slav**⁘[*1]> **b.** *col* ***Der*** clumsy male, klutz: *Taj bezveznjaković ne zna ni da zaveže cipele. That klutz doesn't even know how to tie his shoelaces.* <**Slav**⁘[*2]>

bezveznjáković {njákovića (acc. = gen.) masc.} (lit. the one without connections) *col* ***Der*** clumsy male, klutz <**Slav**⁘[*1]>

bezveznjákovićka {a (acc. = gen.) masc.} (lit. the one without connections) *col* ***Der*** clumsy female, klutz <**Slav**⁘[*1]>

bèzvzē {excl.} (lit. without connection) [std. = bez veze] *col* used to signal indifference, nothing special, no big deal <**Slav**✍>

bêž {excl.} SerE *col* used to make somebody go away: *Bež, eto policije! Beat it, the heat is on!* <**Slav**✍>

bežȁnija {ē fem.} SerE *col* flight, running away <**Slav**>

bèzzē {excl.} (lit. without connections) [std. = bez veze] *col* used to signal indifference, nothing special, no big deal <Slav✍>

bìber 1 {a masc.} (lit. pepper) *col* small bit, small amount <NE*1>

• **ko bìber po pìlavu** {NP} (lit. like pepper over pilaf) BosM *col* favorably

• **bìber po pìlavu** {NP} (lit. pepper over pilaf) BosM *col* favorable event

bìber 2 {adj.} (lit. pepper) *col* tiny, minute (of a person, object, etc.) <NE*1>

bìber-štrȕc {a +ov (ext. pl) masc.; Nom Pl bìber-štrùcovi} *col* leap frog (the game) <NE❖*1>

bíbice {bīcā fem. pl.} *sl-gamble* dice <NE*1>

bìblija {ē fem.} (lit. Bible) **1** *col* ***Fac*** senior citizen <Gre*1> **2** *col* law <Gre*1>

bȉbliōzan {zna, zno adj.} (lit. Biblical) *col* ***Fac*** very old <Gre❖*1>

bìbliš {a masc.} [std. = biblioteka] *sl-stu* library <Gre✍>

bîc {a +ev (ext. pl) masc.; Nom Pl bícevi} [std. = bicikl] *col* bike, bicycle <Lat-Gre✍>

bicìkl {a masc.} (lit. bicycle) *sl-mil* setting fire to someone's toes, giving someone a hotfoot <Lat*1>

bicíkla {ē fem.} [std. = bicikl] *col-dia* bike, bicycle <Lat-Gre✍>

bicìklista {ē masc.} (lit. cyclist *male*) **a.** *sl-fea* naive male: *Tog biciklistu svako može prevariti. Anybody can cheat that chump.* <Lat❖*1> **b.** *sl-fea* ***Der*** ingratiator (male), brownnoser, ass kisser <Lat❖*2>

bicìklistkinja {ē fem.} (lit. cyclist *female*) **a.** *sl-sex* ***Fac*** prostitute, hooker <Lat❖*1> **b.** *sl-sex* ***Fac*** loose woman <Lat❖*2>

bicìklo {a neut.} [std. = bicikl] *col* bike, bicycle <Lat-Gre✍>

bìciš {a masc.} [std. = bicikl] *col* bike, bicycle <Lat-Gre✍❖>

bìciška {ē fem.; Dat bìciški} [std. = bicikl] *col* bike, bicycle <Lat-Gre✍❖>

bȉckalica {ē fem.} *sl-auto* stroboscope <Ger❖*1>

bȉcnuti {nēm, nū perf.} **a.** *sl* hit, punch <Slav*1> **b.** *sl-sex* ***Obs*** engage in sexual intercourse with (of a male), bang <Slav*2>

bíčak {čka masc.} *sl-arch* knife <NE✍>

bičànica {ē fem.} *sl-arch* razor <NE❖>

• **šúmnā bičànica** {NP} *sl-arch* saber, sword

Bȉće kȉšē! {S} (lit. The rain is coming!) *sl-crime* used to refer to the approach of a dangerous situation ☞ **kiša**

Bȉće sránja! {S} (lit. Shit will happen!) *sl-crime* used to refer to the approach of a dangerous situation ☞ **sranje**

bȉćkati {ām, ajū imperf.} *sl-arch* choose, select: *Bićkaj nešto da idemo kući! Choose something so we can go home!* <Slav>

bȉdnuti {nēm, nū imperf.} [std. = biti] *dia-col* be <Slav✍>

bídža {ē fem. & masc.} *col* stubborn male, pigheaded guy: *Taj bidža nikoga ne sluša. That pigheaded guy doesn't listen to anybody.* <NE*1>

bìfēj {biféja masc.} [std. = bife] *col* bar (drinking place) <Fre✍>

bȉfić {a masc.} *sl-drink* bar (drinking place) <Fre❖>

bȉflant {a (acc. = gen.) masc.} *sl-stu* ***Der*** student who learns mechanically <Ger>

bȉflati {ām, ajū imperf.} *sl-stu* ***Der*** learn mechanically <Ger>

Bȉg Bȅn {NP} (lit. Big Ben) Cro *sl* name of a dance club on Bogovićeva street in Zagreb, Croatia ☞ **Ben**

Bȉgāč {a masc.} Cro *sl* name of a dance club on Bogović's street in Zagreb, Croatia <Eng❖*1>

bihuzúriti {hùzūrīm, rē perf.} **BosM** *col* annoy, bother, pester: *Ne bihuzuri me tim glupim pitanjima! Don't bother me with those dumb questions!* <NE*1>

Bijȁfra 1 {ē fem.} (lit. Biafra: a breakaway province of Nigeria) **Cro** *sl* former student dormitory on Tvrtko street in Zagreb, Croatia <SlavO*1>

bijȁfra 2 {ē fem.} (lit. Biafra: a breakaway province of Nigeria) *sl-fea* extremely slender person, walking skeleton <SlavO*1>

bìjaro {bìjēro fem.; perm} [std. = robija] **a.** *sl-crime* prison <Slav✍> **b.** *sl-crime* term in prison <Slav✍*1>

bijèlā múrja {NP} (lit. white cops) *sl-crime* bribed police officers, cops on the take ☞ **murija**

bìjēlā tèhnika {NP} (lit. white technology) *col* kitchen appliances ☞ **tehnika**

bijèlī đȁvō {NP} (lit. white devil) *sl-sstu* ***Fac*** high-school principal ☞ **đavo**

bijèlī jȅlēn {NP} (lit. white deer) *sl-sex* ***Fac*** male homosexual, gay ☞ **jelen**

bijèlī kàdilāk {NP} (lit. white Cadillac) *sl-drugs* phencyclidine ☞ **kadilak**

bijésan {sna, sno adj.} **a.** *col* ***Der*** insane, nuts <Slav*1> **b.** *col* ***App*** excellent, awesome: *Dobili su neka bijesna kola. They've got an awesome car.* <Slav*2>

- **bijésan ko lèptīr** {AdjP} (lit. as angry as a butterfly) *sl* ***Fac*** intensely agitated, mad as a hatter: *biti bijesan ko leptir zbog izgubljene utakmice be very mad about a lost ball game*
- **bijésan ko óvca** {AdjP} (lit. as angry as a sheep) *sl* ***Fac*** intensely agitated, mad as a hatter: *Zorica je bijesna ko ovca jer je mama nije pustila u kino. Zorica is very mad about her mom not letting her go to the movies.*
- **bijésan ko pȕška** {AdjP} (lit. as angry as a rifle) *col* intensely agitated, mad as a hatter: *Ne prilazi mu sada, bijesan je ko puška. Do not approach him now, he is very mad.*
- **bijésan ko rȉs** {AdjP} (lit. as angry as a lynx) *col* intensely agitated, mad as a hatter: *Šef je bio bijesan ko ris. The boss was very mad.*

bijèsnā trúba {NP} (lit. rabid trumpet) *sl* female ☞ **truba**

bijèsnē glíste {NP} (lit. rabid worms) *col* exaggerated requests, whims ☞ **gliste**

bȉjus {a masc.} [std. = bioskop] SerE *sl* movie house, theater <Gre✍>

bîk [1] {a +ov (ext. pl) masc.; Nom Pl bíkovi} (lit. bull) [std. = bioskop] SerE *sl* movie house, theater <Gre✍>

bȉk [2] {a (acc. = gen.) +ov (ext. pl) masc.; Nom Pl bìkovi} /bîk/ (lit. bull) **a.** *col* muscular male <Slav*1> **b.** *col* stupid or mentally deficient person <Slav*2>

- **bîk kòjī sèdī** {NP} (lit. a sitting bull) SerE *sl* ***Fac*** father
- **bîk kòjī sjèdī** {NP} (lit. a sitting bull) *sl-sex* ***Fac*** slowly erectable penis

bȉks [1] {a (acc. = gen.) +ev (ext. pl) masc.; Nom Pl bìksevi} *sl-sports* body builder (male) <Eng✍>

bȉks [2] {a +ev (ext. pl) masc.; Nom Pl bìksevi} **1a.** *sl* main thing, most important thing: *Biks je da se dobije dozvola za rad. The main thing is to get a work permit.* <Ger✍*1> **b.** *sl* main idea: *Biks je da se kupi velika količina akcija. The main idea is to buy a great quantity of shares.* <Ger✍*2> **c.** *sl* finding, discovery <Ger✍*3> **d.i.** *sl* example <Ger✍*4> **ii.aa.** *sl* trick, joke <Ger✍*4> **bb.** *sl* lie <Ger✍*5> **cc.** *sl* anecdote <Ger✍*6> **2** *sl* skillfulness <Ger✍*1>

bìksna {ē fem.} *sl-crafts* rivet <Ger>

bȉla {part.} BosM *col* indeed, really: *On je bila profesor. He is really a professor.* <NE✍> ☞ **bilaj, bilahi, bilaj**

Bíla je pȕška. {S} (lit. There was a gun.) *sl-crime* used to refer to a dangerous situation in the past ☞ **puška**

bȉlāh {part.} BosM *col* indeed, really <NE> ☞ **bila, bilahi, bilaj**

bȉlāhī {part.} BosM *col* indeed, really <NE> ☞ **bila, bilah, bilaj**

bìlaj {part.} BosM *col* indeed, really <NE✍> ☞ **bila, bilah, bilahi**

bìldati {ām, ajū imperf.} /bȉldati/ *sl-sports* practice body building <Eng❖>

bìlder {a (acc. = gen.) masc.} **a.** *sl-sports* body builder (male) <Eng❖> **b.** *sl* muscular male <Eng❖*1>

bilderàna {ē fem.} *sl-sports* ***Fac*** gym <Eng❖*1>

bìlderka {ē fem.; Dat bìlderki} *sl-sports* body builder (female) <Eng❖>

bȉldovati {dujēm, dujū imperf.} Ser *sl-sports* practice body building <Eng❖>

bȉle {eta neut.} *sl-drugs* low-quality hashish <Slav*1>

bȋlī {ōg (acc. = gen.) masc.} (lit. the white one: the players in the white jerseys) [std. = bijeli] Med *col* player or fan of Hajduk (a soccer team from Split, Croatia) <Slav✍>

bilìjār *See the following*

- **džèpnī bilìjār** {NP} (lit. pocket pool) *sl-sex* ***Fac*** playing with one's testicles through one's pocket, pocket pool

bilìjara {ē fem.} *sl-gamble* card gambling <Fre*1>

bìlmez {a (acc. = gen.) masc.} **a.** *sl-fea* ***Der*** stupid or mentally deficient person <NE> **b.** *sl-fea* ***Der*** clumsy person, klutz <NE*1>

bîlja {ē fem.} *sl-fea* ***Der*** stupid or mentally deficient person <Slav❖*1>

biljáriti {bìljārīm, rē imperf.} (lit. collect plants) **1** *sl-sex* ***Obs*** masturbate, beat off <Slav*1> **2** *sl-gamble* play cards <Slav*1>

bìljārskā kúgla {NP} (lit. billiard ball) *sl-fea* ***Fac*** bald male ☞ **kugla**

bìljčica {ē fem.} /bîljčica/ (lit. small plant) *sl-sex* ***Off*** male homosexual, gay <Slav*1>

bîlje {a neut. pl.} (lit. plants, herbs) *sl-drugs* low-quality hashish <Slav*1>

• egzòtičnō bîlje {NP} (lit. exotic herbs) **a.** *sl-fea* ***Fac*** superficial person **b.** *sl-fea* ***Fac*** snob

biljètić {a masc.} *col-dia* entrance ticket or fare: *autobuski biljetić bus fare* <**Fre**❖>

bîljka {ē fem.} (lit. plant) **1** *sl-drugs* ***Der*** low-quality hashish <**Slav***1> 2 *sl-fea* ***Der*** stupid or mentally deficient person <**Slav***1> 3 *sl-fea* ***Der*** quadriplegic <**Slav***1>

bȉm-bȁm {excl.} *col* the repeated sound made by a small bell, ding-ding <**Slav**>

bímbo {ē masc.} *sl-sex* ***Obs*** penis, dick, prick <**NE***1>

bína {ē fem.} (lit. stage) *sl* hotel <**Ger***1>

bȉonja {ē fem.} /biònja/ [std. = bioskop] SerE *sl* movie house, theater <**Gre**✍>

bioskopìjān {jána masc.} [std. = bioskop] SerE *sl* movie house, theater <**Gre**✍>

bioskopijáner {a masc.} [std. = bioskop] SerE *sl* movie house, theater <**Gre**✍>

bioskopijánović {a masc.} [std. = bioskop] SerE *sl* movie house, theater <**Gre**✍>

bȉpovati {pujēm, pujū imperf. intr.} (lit. BIP: abbreviation for Beogradska industrija piva 'Belgrade Beer Industry') SerE *sl* drink beer <**BN**❖*1>

bîr {excl.} *col* used to lure a turkey or goose <**Slav**>

bȉra {ē fem.} *sl-drink* beer <**Ita**>

bȉrc {a +ev (ext. pl) masc.; Nom Pl bìrcevi} *col* bar (drinking place) <**Ger**✍>

bìrcuz {a masc.} *col* bar (drinking place) <**Ger**✍>

bȉri {excl.} *col* used to lure a turkey or goose <**Slav**>

bȉrić {a masc.} *sl-drink* ***Fam*** beer <**Ita**❖>

birìćet {a masc.} **a. Din** *col* crops: *imati izdašan birićet have bountiful crops* <**NE**> **b. Din** *col* good luck, lucky strike, run of luck: *Imao sam birićet na tom poslu. I had good luck on that job.* <**NE***1> ☞ **berićet**

birìćetan {tna, tno adj.} **a. Din** *col* ***App*** fruitful, bountiful: *birićetna žetva bountiful harvest* <**NE**> **b. Din** *col* ***App*** profitable: *birićetan poso profitable job* <**NE***1> ☞ **berićetan**

bȉrt {a +ov (ext. pl) masc.; Nom Pl bìrtovi} *col* bar (drinking place) <**Ger**✍>

bȉrtāš {birtáša (acc. = gen.) masc.; Voc bȉrtāšu} /bìrtāš/ **1** *col* bartender <**Ger**❖> 2 *col* barkeep, bar-owner (male) <**Ger**❖>

birtàšica {ē fem.} **1** *col* barmaid <**Ger**❖> 2 *col* barkeep, bar-owner (female) <**Ger**❖>

bìrtija {ē fem.} *col* bar (drinking place) <**Ger**✍>

bìrtījskī {ā, ō adj.} *col* pertaining to a bar, tavern (usu. low-class) <**Ger**❖>

bȉs [1] {excl.} *col* used to encourage an additional performance, encore <**Lat**>

bȉs [2] {a +ev (ext. pl) masc.; Nom Pl bìsevi} [std. = bioskop] SerE *sl* movie house, theater <**Gre**✍>

bìser [1] {a masc.} (lit. pearl) **a.** *col* ***App*** good idea <**Slav***1> **b.** *col* ***Iro*** stupid idea <**Slav***2> **c.** *col* slip of tongue <**Slav***3>

bìser [2] {a (acc. = gen.) masc.} (lit. pearl) *sl-fea* ***Iro*** stupid or mentally deficient person <**Slav***1>

bìsērka {ē fem.} *sl-arch* church <**Rum**>

bisérko {a masc.} (lit. male with pearls) *sl-fea* ***Iro*** stupid or mentally deficient person <**Slav***1>

bìskis {a masc.} [std. = bioskop] SerE *sl* movie house, theater <**Gre**✍>

bìskiš {a masc.} [std. = bioskop] SerE *sl* movie house, theater <**Gre**✍>

bismìlāh {excl.} /bismìllāh excl./ **BosM** *col* used to support important thoughts or actions by giving them a religous approval, in the name of God: *Mi ćemo, bismillah, pobijediti ćaure. In the name of God, we will defeat the infidels.* <**NE**> ☞ **bismilaj**

bismìlāj {excl.} /bismȉllāj excl./ **BosM** *col* used to support important thoughts or actions by giving them a religous approval, in the name of God <**NE**✍> ☞ **bismilah**

bȉstar {tra, tro adj.} (lit. clear, bright) *col* ***App*** intelligent, smart, bright: *bistar učenik smart student* <**Slav***1>

• **bȉstar ko bóza** {AdjP} (lit. as clear as wheat juice) *col* ***Fac*** very stupid

bìstērna {ē fem.} Med *dia* cistern <**Slav**>

bìstijērna {ē fem.} Med *dia* cistern <**Slav**>

bȉstrica {ē fem.} **a.** *col* swift mountain river or spring <**Slav**❖> **b.** smart person: *On je prava bistrica, ima sve petice. He's a brain, he's got straight As.* <**Slav**❖*1>

bíša {ē masc.} **1** *sl-arch* wolf (the animal) <**Slav***1> 2 SerE *sl* movie house, theater <**Gre***1>

bȉšop {a (acc. = gen.) masc.} (lit. bishop) *sl-fea* liar <**Eng***1>

Bȉt će kȉšē! {S} (lit. The rain is coming!) *sl-crime* used to refer to the approach of a dangerous situation ☞ **kiša**

bȉti [1] {bȉnēm, bȉnēš imperf.} [std. = biti, budem, budeš...] *col-dia* be (in any of its Serbo-Croatian meanings used in forms different from the standard): *Nemoj da bineš neposlušan. Don't be disobedient.* ◊ *Zapaliću kad binem vani. I'll smoke when I get outside.* <Slav>

bȉti [2] {bȕdnēm, bȕdnēš imperf.} [std. = biti, budem, budeš...] *col-dia* be (in any of its Serbo-Croatian meanings used in forms different from the standard): *Pitajte nekoga za put kad budnete tamo. Ask somebody for the directions.* ◊ *Sve ćeš razumjeti kad budneš u mojim godinama. You'll understand everything when you get to be my age.* <Slav>

• **bȉti ȁutsajd** {VP} (lit. be outside) *sl-drugs* go insane, freak out

• **bȉti bìsēran** {VP} (lit. be full of pearls) *sl* act violently

• **bȉti cŕnac** {S} (lit. be an African American) *sl-crime* ***Fac*** be a long-term prisoner

• **bȉti cŕnac** {S} (lit. be an African American) *sl-crime* ***Fac*** be a long-term prisoner

• **bȉti dúžan jèdan mȓz** {VP} (lit. owe one hating) *sl* ***Fac*** hate, despise

• **bȉti frȉgīdan** {VP} (lit. be frigid) *sl* be indifferent toward, be uninterested in: *biti frigidan za košarku be uninterested in basketball*

• **bȉti gênije za**[NP:ACC] {LSF} (lit. be a genius for [NP:ACC]) 1 *col* like [NP:ACC] very much, be mad about [NP:ACC]: *Ja sam genije za sarmu. I am mad about cabbage rolls.* 2 *col* ***App*** be a very talented [NOUN:ACC]-er, be one hell of a [NOUN:ACC]-er: *Moj Miško je genije za fudbal. My Mike is one hell of a soccer player.*

• **bȉti grîz** {VP} (lit. be a bite) *sl* be fit, be in top physical and psychological shape: *Svakodnevno vežbam pa sam griz. I exercise on a daily basis, so I'm fit.*

• **bȉti grȍbār** {S} (lit. be an undertaker) *sl-crime* ***Fac*** be a convicted murderer

• **bȉti grȍbār** {S} (lit. be an undertaker) *sl-crime* ***Fac*** be a convicted murderer

• **bȉti inteligèntan** {VP} (lit. be intelligent) *sl* ***Fac*** earn: *Danas sam inteligentan dvije banke. Today I earned twenty dinars.*

• **bȉti iz Kóteža** {VP} (lit. be from Kotež: a small town in Serbia) *sl-fea* ***Der*** be a provincial, be parochial

• **bȉti kvȉt** {VP} (lit. be over) *col* be even with, be quits with

• **bȉti lȅgālan** {VP} (lit. be legal) *sl-sex* ***Fac-Obs*** readily engage in sexual intercourse (usu. of women)

• **bȉti na féderima** {VP} (lit. be on springs) *sl-sstu* be at school

• **bȉti na kònju** {VP} (lit. be on a horse) *col* ***App*** be in a favorable position, be in the saddle: *Ako dobijem povišicu, biću na konju. If I get that raise, I will be in the saddle.*

• **bȉti na pèvānju** {VP} (lit. be at the singing lesson) SerE *sl-crime* ***Fac*** be interrogated by a police inspector

• **bȉti na prijèstolju** {VP} (lit. be on the throne) *sl* be very important or influential, be a bigshot

• **bȉti naívac** {VP} (lit. be a naive painter) **a.** *sl-fea* be naive: *On je naivac, svako može da ga prevari. He's naive, anybody can cheat him.* **b.i.** *sl-fea* be in love: *Naivac je otkako je sreo Mirnu. He has been in love from the moment he met Mirna.* **ii.** *sl-fea* be unskilled

• **bȉti obèsāćen** {VP} (lit. be watchless, i.e. deprived of one's watch) *sl* ***Fac*** be without a watch

• **bȉti obèspōjmljen** {VP} (lit. be idealess, i.e. deprived of any concepts) *sl* ***Fac*** be unaware of, be clueless

• **bȉti pȍslān na konzervatôrij** {VP} (lit. be sent to a conservatory) *sl-crime* ***Iro*** be sent to prison

• **bȉti pun ȉkrē** {VP} (lit. be full of roe) *sl-sex* ***Fac*** be without sex for a while

• **bȉti sa Dìvčibārā** {VP} (lit. be from Divčibare *a small town in Serbia*) *sl-fea* ***Der*** be provincial, be parochial

• **bȉti slȉčan ko jáje góvnu** {VP} (lit. be similar as an egg to a piece of shit) *sl* ***Iro*** be completely different, be poles apart

• **bȉti u ȁutu** {VP} (lit. be out of bounds) *sl* be in a difficult situation

• **bȉti u bȕli** {VP} (lit. be in a hole) *sl-gamble* lose, be in the hole

• **bȉti u čàbru** {VP} (lit. be in a barell) *sl* be in a difficult situation, be over a barrel

• **bȉti u dubiózi** {VP} (lit. be dubious) *sl-gamble* lose

• **bȉti u fazónu** {VP} (lit. be in style) *sl* feel well

• **bȉti u fôrmi** {VP} (lit. be in form) *col* be fit, be in top physical and psychological shape

• **bȉti u fȑci** {VP} *col* be busy, be occupied

• **bȉti u frìku** {VP} (lit. be in freak) *sl* get frightened, get scared

• **bȉti u gȑču** {VP} (lit. have cramps) *col* be tense

• **bȉti u hóru** {VP} (lit. be in a choir) *sl-crime* ***Fac*** inform the police, sing

• **bȉti u lòšēm fazónu** {VP} (lit. be in a bad style) *sl* be blue, feel bad, be in a funk

• **bȉti u nìskōm stàrtu** {VP} (lit. be in a low start) *sl* ***Fac*** be ready for action

• **bȉti u ȍfsājdu** {VP} (lit. be off-side) 1 *sl-drink* be drunk 2 be sick

• **bȉti u**[POSS PRON:LOC] **fazónu** {LSF} (lit. be in [PPRON] style) *sl* ***App*** used to refer to agreement, satisfaction, etc.: *On je u mom fazonu. (lit. He is in my* *style.) I agree with him.*

• **bȉti u pȑvōm lícu** {VP} (lit. be in the first person) *sl* ***Fac*** be conscious

• **bȉti u štósu** {VP} (lit. be in the trick) *sl* be fit, be in shape

• **bȉti u tȉptop fôrmi** {VP} (lit. be in tip-top form) *col* be in the best physical and psychological form, be in tip-top form

• **bȉti unútra** {VP} (lit. be inside) *sl* be lost, unable to find one's way

• **bȉti vêzān ko créva** {VP} (lit. be tied like intestines) SerE *sl-fea* ***Fac*** be overly introverted

• **bȉti za pêt** {S} (lit. deserve a grade A) *sl* ***App*** be likable

• **bȉti zasèčen cirkulárom** {VP} (lit. be cut by a circular saw) *sl-crime* ***Fac*** have a police record

• **bȉti žîvī tèlefōn** {S} (lit. be a live telephone) *sl-fea* re-tell everything

• **Ìmā fórē**. {S} *col* used to express that plenty of time is available, No rush.

• **Ìmā kȁdē**. {S} *dia* used to indicate that plenty of time is available, No rush.

• **Jèsi dȍbar?** {VP} (lit. Are you good?) *col* used as an informal greeting, How are you doing?

• **nè biti ni rôd ni pomòzibôg** {VP} (lit. be neither a relative nor God with you) *col* be totally unrelated: *On mi nije ni rod ni pomozibog. I'm not related to him at all.*

• **nè biti nȍrmālan** {VP} (lit. be abnormal) *sl-fea* be insane, be nuts

• **nè biti pri čȉstōj svésti** {VP} (lit. lack clear consciousness) SerE *col* be insane, be nuts

• **nè biti sâm** {VP} (lit. be with somebody) *sl-fea* be insane, be nuts

• **nè biti sâm** {VP} (lit. not be alone) *sl-fea* be insane, be nuts

• **nè biti zdrȁv** {VP} (lit. be unhealthy) *col* be insane, be nuts

• **nȇā problémā** {VP} (lit. no problems) *sl* used to refer to approval, consent, etc., no problem, no big deal: *A: Hvala! B: Nea problema. A: Thanks! B: No big deal.*

• **nêmā grȅškē** {VP} (lit. no mistake) *col* used to indicate that a problem can be solved, no problem, no big deal: *Nema greške za parkiranje. Parking is no big deal.*

• **nêmā hljȅba** {VP} (lit. no bread) *col* used to refer to the futility of all efforts, it's no use

• **nêmā šȃnsē** {VP} (lit. no chance) *col* used as a strong negative response, no way, never

• **nêmā šansónē** {VP} (lit. no chanson) *sl* used as a strong negative response, no way, never

• **nêmā tèōrijē** {VP} (lit. no theory) *col* used as a strong negative response, no way, never

• **nêmā tȉjē pârā** {VP} (lit. no money like that) *dia* used to indicate that something is priceless, money cannot buy it

• **nêmā vȅzē** {VP} (lit. no connection) *col* used to refer to irrelevance of something, doesn't matter

• **nêmā zímē** {VP} (lit. no winter) *col* used to indicate that a problem can be solved, no problem, no big deal

• **Nêmā žíva ròba.** {S} (lit. Not a live slave is here.) *sl* used to indicate that a place is empty, Nobody there.

• **nìje mi nȕmera** {VP} (lit. not my number) *sl* used to express dissatisfaction, not my style, not for me

• **nìje nȁpēto** {VP} (lit. it is not tense) *sl* boredom

• **nìje nȍrmālno** {VP} (lit. it is not normal) *col* used to refer to something unusual: *Kakva dobra kolica, nije normalno! What a cool car, I can't believe it!*

• **nìje ròdilo** {VP} (lit. no yields) *sl* used to refer to one's shortage of something

• **Nìje šèćer ȕ vodu!** {S} (lit. Sugar did not get into the water!) *col-dia* used to indicate that ample time is available

• **Nìje ti ćâle staklorézac!** {S} (lit. Your father is not a glass cutter!) **SerE** *sl* used to express that somebody is blocking one's view, You make a better door than a window!

• **Nìje ti stâri stȁklār!** {S} (lit. Your old man is not a glass cutter!) *sl* used to express that somebody is blocking one's view, You make a better door than a window!

• **nísam frȁjer** {VP} (lit. I am not a dude) *sl* used to refer to one's knowledge of the dangers in a situation, I'm not that stupid

• **Nísam vèslo sȉsaō!** {S} (lit. I didn't suck an oar!) *sl* used to refer to one's knowledge of a situation, I am not a fool!

• **Nísam vèslo sȉsō!** {S} (lit. I didn't suck an oar!) *sl* used to refer to one's knowledge of a situation, I am not a fool!

• **Nísi ni zà kurac!** {S} (lit. You are not even for a prick!) *sl* ***Off*** used as a moderate curse, Screw you!

bȉti[3] {ijēm, ijū imperf.} *sl-sports* beat, defeat <**Slav**>

• **bȉti po ȕšima** {VP} (lit. box on one's ears) *col* force, coerce: *Ko te bio po ušima da to radiš? Who forced you to do that?*

bȉtić {a masc.} *sl-music* beat music (the style) <**Eng**⁘>

bȉtlis {a (acc. = gen.) masc.} (lit. the Beatles) *sl-fea* male with long hair, long hair <**EngO**✐[*1]>

bȉtls {a (acc. = gen.) masc.} (lit. the Beatles) *sl-fea* male with long hair, long hair <**EngO**[*1]>

bitùmen {ē fem.} (lit. bitumen, bitumenous earth) *sl-sex* ***Fac*** prostitute, hooker <**Lat**[*1]>

bívā {part.} *col* particle used to express uncertainty, I think, if I am not mistaken: *To mi je biva rekao on. I think that's what he told me.* <Slav>

bȉvkati {ām, ajū imperf. intr.} *col* live from day to day <Slav>

bivòlčina {ē masc.} (lit. big buffalo) *col* extremely strong male, bull, ox <Slav[*1]>

bȋvšī {ā, ō adj.} (lit. former) **a.** *col* dead <Slav[*1]> **b.** *col* sick, ill: *Mirko je bivši, pa nije došao u školu. Mirko is sick, so he didn't come to school.* <Slav[*2]>

bȉz {a +ev (ext. pl) masc.; Nom Pl bìzevi} *sl-drugs* drug paraphernalia <Eng✍>

bìzgōv {bizgòva (acc. = gen.) masc.} **1a.** *sl-fea* ***Der*** stupid or mentally deficient person: *Taj bizgov ne zna da parkira kola. That moron doesn't know how to park.* <Slav> **b.** *sl-fea* ***Der*** clumsy male, klutz <Slav[*1]> **2** *sl-fea* troublemaker, rowdy, ruffian <Slav>

bȉznis {a masc.} /bìznis/ *col* business (any kind of) <Eng>

bìzōn {bizóna (acc. = gen.) masc.} (lit. bison) *sl-fea* ***Fac*** senior citizen, old goat <Lat[*1]>

bjȁži {excl.} used to make somebody go away, beat it

bjelènguza {ē fem.} (lit. the one with white buttocks) *col* ***Obs*** a kind of songbird <Slav⁘[*1]>

bjeločàrapić {a (acc. = gen.) masc.} (lit. the one with white socks) *sl-fea* ***Fac*** inhabitant of the countryside, hick, bumpkin <Slav⁘[*1]>

bjȅlogūz [1] {a masc.} *col* ***Obs*** male with white buttocks <Slav⁘>

bjelòguz [2] {a, o adj.} *col* ***Obs*** having white buttocks <Slav⁘>

bjelòguzā {ē fem. (adj. decl.)} (lit. the one with white buttocks) *col* ***Obs*** a kind of songbird <Slav⁘[*1]>

bjêž {excl.} /bjȇž/ *col* used to make somebody go away, beat it <Slav>

bježànija {ē fem.} *col* running away, fleeing <Slav>

blâ-blâ [1] {neut.} (lit. blah-blah) *col* prolonged and meaningless talk, blabber, chatter <Slav>

blâ-blâ [2] {excl.} *col* the sound made by meaningless and prolonged talk, blah-blah <Slav>

blâg {a +ov (ext. pl) masc.; Nom Pl blágovi} *sl-arch* sugar <Slav[*1]>

blȁga {ē fem.; Dat blȁgi} *sl-arch* muddy terrain <Slav[*1]>

blȁgo *See the following*

- **blȁgo mȅni** {AdvP} (lit. good for me) **a.** *col* used to stimulate a group of people or a person to act: *Ajde, blago meni, donesi rakiju! Bring the brandy if you will!* **b.** *col* used to emphasize one's point: *On će, blago meni, vrlo loše završiti. I'd say that he will end up in big trouble.*
- **blȁgo[PRON:DAT]** {LSF} *col* ***App*** used to express envious adoration: *Blago njemu! Lucky him!*

blȁgoslōv *See the following*

- **Kûrčīn blȁgoslōv!** {S} (lit. Prick's blessing!) *dia* ***Obs*** used to express lack of interest, Fuck it!

blagovaóna {ē fem.} (lit. dining room) *sl-crime* ***Iro*** courthouse <Slav[*1]>

blȁgovest *See the following*

- **Blȁgovēsti ti tvòji!** {S} (lit. *I fuck* your good news!) SSer *dia* ***Off*** used as a weak curse, Damn you!

blȁjbinger {a masc.} *sl* simple but effective solution <Ger[*1]>

blȁjštānga {ē fem.; Dat blȁjštāngi} *sl-auto* connecting rod <Ger>

blȁjzna {ē fem.} *sl-sex* ***Obs*** penis, dick, prick <Ger[*1]>

blȁm {a +ov (ext. pl) masc.; Nom Pl blàmovi} /blâm/ *col* shame, disgrace, scandal: *Imala je blam zbog loših ocena. Her bad grades brought her disgrace.* <Fre[*1]>

blamírati se {blàmīrām, blamíraju imperf. intr.} *sl* make a fool of oneself: *Napila se, pa se blamirala. She got drunk and made a fool of herself.* <Fre>

blȁnjati {ām, ajū imperf.} (lit. smoothe with a plane) *sl-sex* ***Obs*** engage in sexual intercourse with (of a male) <Slav[*1]>

blȁto *See the following*

- **ko blȁta** {PP} (lit. as many as mud) *col* in large quantities, very many

blȁtobrān [1] {a (acc. = gen.) masc.} (lit. fender) *sl-auto* body man, mechanic <Slav[*1]>

blȁtobrān [2] {a masc.} (lit. fender) *sl-auto* ***Fac*** ear <Slav[*1]>

blȁvorēnje {a neut.} *sl-fea* ***Der*** prolonged and meaningless talk, blabber, chatter <Slav[*1]>

blȁvoriti {rīm, rē imperf.} *sl-fea* ***Der*** talk persistently and meaninglessly, blabber, chatter <Slav[*1]>

blȁziš {adj.} *sl* unintelligent, stupid, dumb <Fre[*1]>

blebètalo {a neut.} *col* ***Der*** extremely talkative person, chatterbox <Slav>

blebètānje {a neut.} *col* ***Der*** prolonged and meaningless talk, blabber, chatter <**Slav**>

blebètati {blèbećēm, ećū imperf.} *col* ***Der*** talk persistently and meaninglessly, blabber, chatter <**Slav**>

bléćak {ćka (acc. = gen.) masc.} (lit. the baa one) *col* ***Der*** stupid or mentally deficient person

blêd {bléda, blédo adj.} (lit. pale) **SerE** *col* weak, lacking strength or excellence: *Njegova uloga u sinoćnjoj predstavi bila je bleda. His role in last night's performance was weak.* <**Slav**>

• **blêd kao kȑpa** {AdjP} (lit. as pale as a rag) SerE *sl-fea* pale as a sheet

blȅf {blèfa +ov (ext. pl) masc.; Nom Pl blèfovi} *col* bluff, pretend <**Eng**>

blȅfati {ām, ajū biasp.} *col* bluff, pretend <**Eng**>

blȅfer {a (acc. = gen.) masc.} /blȅfer/ **a.** *col* bluffer <**Eng**> **b.** *sl-drink* alcoholic, drunk <**Eng**[*1]>

blȅferi {fērā masc. pl.} *sl* trousers, pants <**Eng**[*1]>

blefírānje {a neut.} *col* bluffing <**Eng**>

blefírati {lèfīrām, lefírajū imperf.} *col* bluff, pretend <**Eng**>

bléjānje {a neut.} **a.** *col* bleating (of sheep), baaing <**Slav**> **b.** *col* staring <**Slav**[*1]>

bléjati[1] {jīm, jē imperf. intr.} **a.** *col* bleat (of sheep), baa <**Slav**> **b.** *col* stare at in astonishment, exaggerated interest or absent-mindedness <**Slav**[*1]> **c.** *sl-fea* spend one's time in useless activities, fool around, mess around <**Slav**[*2]>

bléjati[2] {jīm, jē imperf.} *sl-drink* drink (alcohol): *blejati pivo drink beer* <**Slav**> *sl*

blȅjav {a, o adj.} *col* pertaining to the bleating of sheep <**Slav**>

blejìkuša {ē fem.} *dia* sheep (the animal) <**Slav**>

bléjiti {jīm, jē perf.} *col* stare at, be fixated on <**Slav**>

blêk {a +ov (ext. pl) masc.; Nom Pl blékovi} *col* bleating (of sheep), baaing <**Slav**>

blȅka {ē fem.; Dat blȅki} **1** *col* bleating (of sheep), baaing <**Slav**> **2** *sl* stupid or mentally deficient person <**Slav**>

blèkača {ē fem.} *dia* sheep (the animal) <**Slav**>

blȅkēt {a (acc. = gen.) masc.} *sl* deaf-and-dumb person <**Slav**>

blénta {ē fem. & masc.} SerE *col* ***Der*** stupid or mentally deficient person <**Slav**>

blêntav {a, o adj.} *col* insane, nuts <**NE**[*1]>

blénto {a masc.} /blénto /e masc./ *col* stupid or mentally deficient person <**Slav**>

blȅnuti {nēm, nū perf. intr.} *col* stare at in astonishment, exaggerated interest or absent-mindedness <**Slav**>

• **blȅnuti kao tèle u šarèna vráta** {VP} (lit. stare like a calf at a multicolored door) *col* ***Der*** stare at in astonishment or absent-mindedness

blȅsa {ē fem.} **a.** *col* ***Der*** stupid or mentally deficient person <**Slav**> **b.** *col* ***Der*** insane person, nut case <**Slav**[*1]>

blèsan {a (acc. = gen.) masc.} **a.** *col* ***Der*** stupid or mentally deficient person <**Slav**> **b.** *col* ***Der*** insane person, nut case <**Slav**[*1]>

blȅsav {a, o adj.} *col* ***Der*** insane, nuts <**Slav**>

blèsimetar {tra masc.} (lit. facetious name for a non-existing machine meant to measure stupidity) *col* ***Fac*** gadget (any device considered to be unnecessary or of low quality): *Marko je kupio neki blesimetar. Marko has bought some stupid gadget.* <**Slav-Gre**> ☞ **blesometar**

blȅska {ē fem. & masc.; Dat blȅski} *sl* stupid or mentally deficient person <**Slav** ❖>

bléso {a masc.; Voc blêso} /bléso /e masc./ *col* stupid or mentally deficient male <**Slav**>

blèsometar {tra masc.} (lit. facetious name for a non-existing machine meant to measure stupidity) *col* ***Fac*** gadget (any device considered to be unnecessary or of low quality) <**Slav-Gre**> ☞ **blesimetar**

blȉcānje {a neut.} (lit. flashing) *sl* cheating (usu. by a waiter), ripping off <**Ger**[*1]>

blȉcati {ām, ajū perf.} (lit. flash) *sl* cheat, swindle <**Ger**[*1]>

blȉcnuti {nēm, nū perf.} (lit. flash) *sl* cheat, swindle <**Ger**[*1]>

blȉjēd {blijéda, blijédo adj.} (lit. pale) *sl-fea* low-quality <**Slav**>

• **blȉjēd kao kȑpa** {AdjP} (lit. as pale as a rag) *col* pale as a sheet

blȉnd {adv.} (lit. blind) *col* haphazardly, by pure luck: *Osvojio sam karte blind. I won those tickets by pure luck.* <**Ger**[*1]>

• **na blȉnd** {PP} (lit. on blind) *col* haphazardly, by pure luck

blìnder {a (acc. = gen.) masc.; Voc blìnderu} (lit. blind person) *sl-crime* person who steals without discriminating either victims or objects stolen <**Ger**[*1]>

blìstati {ām, ajū imperf. intr.} (lit. shine) *col* be proud of, beam with pride <Slav[*1]>

• **blìstati ko lȉpa** {VP} (lit. shine like a linden-tree) *sl* ***Fac*** dress formally, dress up: *blistati ko lipa za prijem dress up for the reception*

blȉstav *See the following*

• **blȉstav ko lȉpa** {AdjP} (lit. as shiny as a linden-tree) **1** *sl* ***Fac*** dressed formally, dressed up: *Bila blistava ko lipa za intervju. She was dressed formally for the interview.* **2a.** *sl* ***Fac*** very successful: *Ove godine bio sam blistav ko lipa. I was very successful this year.* **b.** *sl* ***Fac*** smart

blìtvāš {blitváša masc.} (lit. the Swiss-chard one *the vegetable is widespread in Dalmatia*) *sl* ***Der-Fac*** Dalmatian (inhabitant of Dalmatia, Croatia) <Slav⁘[*1]>

blȉzanac {zānca (acc. = gen.) masc.; Voc blȉzānče} (lit. twin) *sl-sstu* lowest passing grade <Slav[*1]>

blízo {adv.} [std. = blizu] *col-dia* near, close by: *Njegova kuća je blizo. His house is close by.* <Slav✍>

blíža {ē fem.} (lit. the close one) *sl-gamble* a kind of coin-throwing game where one tries to place coins as close to a wall or a line as possible, pitching pennies, lagging <Slav>

blòkēj {blokéja (acc. = gen.) masc.; Voc blòkēju} *sl* child from high-rise building <Fre⁘[*1]>

blòkīrān {a, o adj.} *col* blocked, prevented <Fre[*1]>

blokírānje {a neut.} *col* blocking, preventing <Fre[*1]>

blokírati {blòkīrām, blokírajū biasp.} *col* block, prevent: *blokirati protivnika da dođe do lopte prevent one's adversary from getting to the ball* <Fre[*1]>

blômba {ē fem.} [std. = plomba] **a.** *col* filling (e.g. in a tooth) <Fre✍[*1]> **b.** *sl-sex* virgin <Fre✍[*2]>

blûdnica {ē fem.} /blúdnica/ (lit. harlot: This high-register word when used in slang creates a facetious effect based on inappropriate mixing of registers) *sl-sex* ***Fac*** prostitute, hooker <Slav[*1]>

blȕhī {īja masc.} *sl-sex* bra <Ger✍>

bljȁk {excl.} *col* used to express disgust, yuck <Slav>

bljȁncati {ām, ajū imperf.} *sl* slurp <Slav>

bljezgáriti {bljèzgārīm, rē imperf.} *col* ***Der*** talk persistently and meaninglessly, blabber, chatter <Slav>

bljȕcoš {a (acc. = gen.) masc.} *sl-fea* ***Der*** worthless or despicable person <Slav[*1]>

bljȕtav {a, o adj.} **a.** *sl-fea* tasteless, gross: *bljutavo jelo tasteless food* <Slav> **b.** *sl-fea* unattractive, ugly: *bljutava riba unattractive chick* <Slav[*1]>

bljȕva {ē fem.} (lit. vomiting) *sl-drink* alcoholic beverage <Slav[*1]>

bljùvati {bljȕjēm, bljȕjū biasp.} (lit. vomit) *sl-fea* ***Der*** talk persistently and meaninglessly, blabber, chatter <Slav[*1]>

bljuvoȉzazōvan {a, o adj.} (lit. emetic) *sl* unattractive, ugly <Slav[*1]>

bljùvotina {ē fem.} (lit. vomit) **a.** *sl-fea* banal talk: *bljuvotina o modi banal talk about fashion* <Slav[*1]> **b.** *sl-fea* hurtful statement, caustic remark: *razvesti se zbog bljuvotina divorce over a hurtful statement* <Slav[*2]> **c.** *sl* lie <Slav[*3]>

bljúzga {ē fem.; Dat bljȕzgi} **a.** *sl* slush, sleet: *Njegova bljuzga me zapanjuje. His stupidity astonishes me.* <Slav> **b.** *sl-fea* stupidity, lack of intelligence <Slav[*1]>

bljȕzgavica {ē fem.} **a.** *sl* slush, sleet <Slav> **b.** *sl-fea* stupidity, lack of intelligence <Slav[*1]>

bóba {ē fem.} **a.** *col* berry (in general) <Slav> **b.** *col* small quantity of something <Slav[*1]>

• **Bóba je fȁlila.** {S} (lit. A berry was missing.) *col* used to refer to a situation which was potentially very dangerous: *Boba je falila da ne poginemo. It was really close and we almost got killed.*

• **u bóbu** {PP} (lit. in berry) *col* exactly, precisely

bòban {a (acc. = gen.) masc.} *sl-fea* stupid or mentally deficient person <Slav[*1]>

bȍbī {īja (acc. = gen.) masc.} /bȍbi/ (lit. bobby: British policeman) *sl-crime* policeman, cop <Eng>

bóbica {ē fem.} (lit. small berry) *sl-drink* one-deciliter bottle of alcoholic beverage <Slav[*1]>

bobína {ē fem.} *sl-auto* ignition coil <Fre>

bȍc {excl.} *col* the sound made by pricking <Slav>

bóca {ē fem.} (lit. the pricking one) **1** *sl-crime* knife <Slav[*1]> **2** *sl-drugs* syringe, needle <Slav[*1]>

bocijáner {a (acc. = gen.) masc.} [std. = boca] *sl-drink* bottle <Ita✍>

bȍcka {ē fem.; Dat bȍcki} *sl-crime* knife <Slav[*1]>

bȍckānje {a neut.} (lit. pricking) **1** *col* teasing <Slav[*1]> **2** *sl-sex* engaging in sexual intercourse with <Slav[*1]> **3** *sl-drugs* intravenous drug use, mainlining <Slav[*1]>

bȍckati {ām, ajū imperf.} (lit. prick) *col* tease <Slav[*1]>

bȍckati se {ām, ajū imperf. intr.} (lit. prick oneself) *sl-drugs* take narcotic drugs intravenously, mainline, shoot up <Slav[*1]>

bȍčka {ē fem.; Dat bȍčki} *sl-arch* cow <Slav[*1]>

bòčkan {a (acc. = gen.) masc.} *sl-arch* ox (the animal) <Slav*1>

bòdača {ē fem.} *sl-arch* sewing needle <Slav*1>

bòdāljka {ē fem.; Dat bòdāljki} (lit. stabber) *sl-arch* sewing needle <Slav*1>

bòdēnje {a neut.} (lit. stabbing) *sl-sex* ***Obs*** sexual intercourse <Slav*1>

bȍdī-bìlder {a (acc. = gen.) masc.} *col* body builder (male) <Eng>

bȍdī-bìldīng {a masc.} *col* body building <Eng>

bódlja {ē fem.} (lit. thorn) *sl-arch* sewing needle <Slav*1>

bòdul {a (acc. = gen.) masc.} *col* inhabitant of Croatian islands <Ita>

bófl [1] {a +ov (ext. pl) masc.} *col* low-quality merchandise, junk: *Jeftino je kupila neki bofl. She bought some inexpensive junk.* <Ger*1>

bófl [2] {adj.} *col* bad (usu. in reference to merchandise), junk: *bofl roba junk merchandise* <Ger*1>

Bôg {Bȍga +ov (ext. pl) masc.; Nom Pl bògovi} /bôg /a +ov (ext. pl) masc./ (lit. God) **1** *col* ***App*** very important or influential person, big shot <Slav*1> **2** *col* ***App*** likable person <Slav*1>

• **Bêlōga ti bȍga!** {S} (lit. *I screw* your white God!) SerE *col* ***Off*** used as a moderate curse or threat, Fuck you!

• **bôg bògōvā** {NP} (lit. the God of all Gods, lord of lords) *col* ***App*** excellent, awesome: *Njegova kuća je bog bogova. His house is awesome.*

• **bôg i bàtina** {NP} (lit. God and the stick) *col* ***App*** very important or influential person, big shot

• **Bôg[PRON:ACC] jȅbō, dà [PRON:ACC] jȅbō!** {LSF} (lit. I hope God fucks [PRON:ACC], that God really fucks [PRON:ACC]!) *col* ***Off*** used as a moderate curse or threat, Fuck you!

• **Bôg si òvē hȅftē!** {S} (lit. You are the God of this week!) Bos *col* ***App*** used to express appreciation, You're the one!

• **Bôg te!** {S} (lit. I hope God *punishes* you!) *col* ***Obs*** used to express astonishment, It is unbelievable!

• **Bôg te jȅbō!** {S} (lit. I hope that God fucks you!) *col* ***Obs*** used to express astonishment, It is unfuckingbelievable!

• **Bôg te mȁzno!** {S} (lit. I hope that God takes you!) *col* used to express astonishment, Unbelievable!

• **Bôg te mȁzo!** {S} (lit. I hope that God takes you!) *col* used to express astonishment, Unbelievable!

• **Bôg te pîtā** {S} (lit. God is asking you) *col* used to refer to uncertainty, God knows: *On se bavi Bog te pita čim. God knows what he does (for a living).*

• **Bôg te pȍpišō!** {S} (lit. I hope that God pisses on you!) *sl* ***Fac-Off*** used to express astonishment, It is unbelievable!

• **Bôg te vȉdeō!** {S} (lit. I hope that God sees you!) *col* used to express astonishment, Unbelievable!

• **Bôg te vȉdeō!** {S} (lit. Let God see you!) SerE *col* used to express astonishment

• **Bȍga li[PRON:DAT] mȉlosnōg!** {LSF} (lit. *I fuck* [PPRON] merciful God!) *col* ***Off*** used as a moderate curse or threat, Fuck you!

• **Bȍga li [PRON:DAT] [POSSPRON:ACC] jèbēm!** {LSF} (lit. I do fuck [PPRON] God!) *col* ***Off*** used as a moderate curse or threat, Fuck you!

• **Bȍga mu pòljūbim.** {S} (lit. I am to kiss his God.) *col* used to emphasize a portion of discourse: *Boga mu poljubim zašto ne radiš. Well then, why don't you get to work.*

• **Bȍga pîtāj** {S} (lit. ask God) *col* used to refer to uncertainty, God knows

• **Bȍga[PRON:DAT] jèbēm!** {LSF} (lit. I fuck [PPRON:NOM] God!) *col* ***Off*** used as a moderate curse or threat, Fuck you!

• **Bȍga[PRON:DAT] nèbeskōg jèbēm!** {LSF} (lit. I fuck [PPRON] heavenly God) *col* ***Off*** used as a moderate curse or threat, Fuck you!

• **Bȍga[PRON:DAT][POSPRON:ACC]!** {LSF} (lit. *I fuck* [PPRON] God!) *col* ***Off*** used as a moderate curse or threat, Fuck you!

• **Bȍga ti!** {S} (lit. *I fuck* your God!) *col* used to express astonishment, Unbelievable!

• **Bȍga ti?** {S} (lit. Do you swear to God?) *col* used as a question tag, Really?

• **bȍgu iza jájā**{NP} (lit. behind God's balls) *sl* ***Fac-Obs*** far away, utterly remote

• **bȍgu iza kȉčmē** {NP} (lit. behind God's spine) *sl* ***Fac*** far away, utterly remote

• **bȍgu iza kȗrca** {NP} (lit. behind God's prick) *col* ***Fac*** far away, utterly remote

• **bȍgu iza lèđā** {NP} (lit. behind God's back) *col* far away, utterly remote

• **bȍgu iza múdā** {NP} (lit. behind God's balls) *sl* ***Fac*** far away, utterly remote

• **bȍgu iza nȍgū** {NP} (lit. behind God's feet) *col* ***Fac*** far away, utterly remote

• **bȍže drâgī** {NP} (lit. dear God) *col* used to express amazement, astonishment, dear God, good God

• **dâj bȍže** {ExcP} (lit. God give) *col* used to express lack of control over events, God willing

• **dȍ Boga** {PP} (lit. to God) *col* really, very (usu. in a negative context): *On je do Boga uobražen. He is really stuck-up.*

• **gdȅ je Bôg rȅkō lȁku nôć** {S} (lit. where God said: "Good night") SerE *col* used to refer to a very remote place, hellhole: *On živi gde je Bog rekao laku noć. He lives in a hellhole.*

• **gdjȅ je Bôg rȅkō lȁku nôć** {S} (lit. where God said: "Good night") *col* used to refer to a very remote place, hellhole: *Žive gde je Bog rekao laku noć. They live in a hellhole.*

• **kao bôg** {PP} (lit. like a God) *col* ***App*** excellent, awesome: *stančuga kao bog awesome nest*

• **ko bôg** {PP} (lit. like a God) *col* ***App*** excellent, awesome: *supa ko bog awesome soup*

• **ko nè dāj Bȍže** {PP} (lit. like God save us from that) *sl-fea* ***Der*** extremely unattractive, ugly as sin

• **Trî ti bȍga jèbēm!** {S} (lit. I fuck your three gods!) SSer *dia* ***Off*** used as a moderate curse, Fuck you!

• **Trȉsta li ti bȍga jèbēm!** {S} (lit. I fuck your three hundred gods!) SSer *dia* ***Off*** used as a moderate curse, Fuck you!

bȍgam {part.} [std. = Boga mi] **1** *col* indeed, really <Slav✍> 2 used to emphasize one's own point, I swear to God! ☞ **bogami, bogomi, bogumi**

bȍgami {part.} (lit. *I swear* to God) [std. = Boga mi] **1** *col* indeed, really: *On je bogami sve bolji i bolji. He is indeed getting better and better.* <Slav✍> 2 *col* used to emphasize one's own point, I swear to God!: *Sutra će, bogami, padati kiša. I say it will rain tomorrow.* <Slav✍> ☞ **bogam, bogomi, bogumi**

bôgbògōva {excl.} (lit. the God of all gods) [std. = Bog bogova] *col* ***App*** excellent, awesome <Slav✍>

bôgdaj {excl.} (lit. God willing) [std. = Bože daj] *col-dia* used to express good intentions or wishes, good luck <Slav✍> ☞ **bogdo**

bôgdo {excl.} (lit. God willing) [std. = Bog dao] *col* used to express good intentions or wishes, good luck <Slav✍> ☞ **bogdaj**

bógec *See the following*

• **dìvljī bógec** {NP} (lit. wild poor guy) Kajk *sl* child born out of wedlock, bastard

bógīn {a, o adj.} *col* in a difficult situation: *Ako ne završiš projekt na vrijeme, bićeš bogin. If you do not finish that project on time, you will be in a difficult situation.* <Slav[*1]>

bòginja {ē fem.} (lit. Goddess) *col* ***App*** popular and beloved female, goddess <Slav[*1]>

bògme {part.} *col* used to emphasize one's own point, I swear to God!: *Noćas će bogme kiša I swear, it will rain tonight.* <Slav✍>

bôgnsȅk {a masc.} *sl-crafts* saw (the tool) <Ger[*1]>

bȍgoljūb {a (acc. = gen.) masc.} (lit. God lover) *sl* ***Fac*** senior citizen <Slav⁘[*1]>

bȍgomi {part.} [std. = Boga mi] Mont *col-dia* used to emphasize one's own point, I swear to God! <Slav✍> ☞ **bogam, bogami, bogumi**

bogòmolja *See the following*

• **Bogòmolju ti jȅbēm!** {S} (lit. I fuck your place of worship!) *col* ***Off*** used as a moderate curse or threat, Fuck you!

Bogoròdica *See the following*

• **Bogoròdicu ti jèbēm!** {S} (lit. I fuck your Holy Mother!) *col* ***Off*** used as a moderate curse or threat, Fuck you!

bògovskī {ā, ō adj.} /bogòvskī/ (lit. divine) *col* ***App*** excellent, awesome <Slav[*1]>

bȍgu iza jájā {NP} (lit. behind God's balls) *sl* ***Fac-Obs*** far away, utterly remote ☞ **Bog**

bȍgu iza kîčmē {NP} (lit. behind God's spine) *sl* ***Fac*** far away, utterly remote ☞ **Bog**

bȍgu iza kûrca {NP} (lit. behind God's prick) *col* ***Fac*** far away, utterly remote ☞ **Bog**

bȍgu iza lèđā {NP} (lit. behind God's back) *col* far away, utterly remote ☞ **Bog**

bȍgu iza múdā {NP} (lit. behind God's balls) *sl* ***Fac*** far away, utterly remote ☞ **Bog**

bȍgu iza nȍgū {NP} (lit. behind God's feet) *col* ***Fac*** far away, utterly remote ☞ **Bog**

bȍgumi {part.} (lit. *I swear* to my God) [std. = Boga mi] Mont *col-dia* used to emphasize one's own point, I swear to God! <Slav✍> ☞ **bogam, bogami, bogomi**

bôgznā {part.} [std. = Bog zna] *col* used to express uncertainty, God only knows: *To je stiglo bogzna odakle. That came from God only knows where.* <Slav✍>

bòing {a masc.} (lit. Boeing) *sl-sex* ***App*** very attractive female, hot number <BN>

• **bòing 707**[**bòing sȅdamsto sȅdam**] {NP} (lit. Boeing 707) *sl-fea* ***App*** very attractive female, hot number

bojàdisati {išēm, išū imperf.} *col* paint (wall, ceiling, etc.) <NE>

bȍjalija {ē fem.} *sl-arch* jug <NE[*1]>

bòjati se *See the following*

• **Bòjīm se (tȍgā) kao pízda kȉšē!** {S} (lit. I fear that like a cunt fears rain!) *col* ***Obs-Fac*** used to refer to absence of any danger

bôjs {a (acc. = gen.) masc.} *sl* boy, kid <Eng✍>

• **bȅd blû bôjsi** {NP} (lit. bad blue boys) *sl-sports* fans of Dinamo (in the 1990s called "Croatia", a soccer team from Zagreb, Croatia)

bȍk {a +ov (ext. pl) masc.; Nom Pl bòkovi} (lit. hip) *sl-drugs* pleasant feeling induced by narcotic drugs, high <Slav[*1]>

bokȁčo {a masc.} (lit. Boccaccio *Italian writer*) *sl* weak male, wimp <Slav[*1]>

bokàlić {a masc.} *col* small glass jug <Ita⁘>

bokalȉška {adj.} *sl-fea* hungry <Gyp>

bòkār {bokára masc.} *sl-arch* bread <Hun[*1]>

bòkče {eta neut.} *sl-arch* child, kid <Slav⁘[*1]>

• **Bòkče ti bògovo!** {S} (lit. *I screw* your God's little God!) *col* ***Off*** used as a moderate curse or threat, Fuck you!

• **Bòkče ti jèbēm!** {S} (lit. I screw your little God!) *col* ***Off*** used as a moderate curse or threat, Fuck you!

• **dȉvljē bòkče** {NP} (lit. poor little wild guy) *sl* child born out of wedlock, bastard

• **Mȉlō li ti bòkče jèbēm!** {S} (lit. I fuck your dear little God!) **SerE** *dia* ***Off*** used as a moderate curse or threat, Fuck you!

bȍkor {a masc.} *sl-arch* bread <Hun[*1]>

bȍks {a +ov (ext. pl) masc.; Nom Pl bòksovi} (lit. box) *col* carton of cigarettes <Eng[*1]>

bȍks-ȍfis {a masc.} *sl-media* box office <Eng>

bòkser {a masc.} *sl-crime* brass knuckles <Eng[*1]>

bokserȉška {ē masc.; Dat bokserȉški} /bokserȉška/ *sl-crime* brass knuckles <Eng⁘[*1]>

bôl {a +ov (ext. pl) masc.; Nom Pl bólovi} *sl-drugs* pleasant feeling induced by narcotic drugs, high <Slav[*1]>

bȍlan {excl.} (lit. ill, sick) **Bos** *col* used to address a male in direct informal communication, hey <Slav[*1]> ☞ ba, bre

bòlcn {a +ov (ext. pl) masc.} *sl-crafts* shaft (e.g. of an engine) <Ger[*1]>

bòlcna {ē fem.} *sl-crafts* shaft (e.g. of an engine) <Ger[*1]>

Bòlē [PRON:ACC] [NOUN:NOM]. {LSF} (lit. My [NOUN] is hurting me.) **Ser** *dia* used to express indifference: *Bole me tuki oćeš li ostati ili otići! I don't give a damn if you stay or leave!* ☞ **boleti**

bȍlēs {lesti fem.} *col-dia* illness <Slav✍>

• **Bȍles ti jèbēm!** {S} (lit. I fuck your sickness!) *col* ***Off*** used as a moderate curse or threat, Fuck you!

bȍlesnā žlézda {NP} (lit. sick gland) SerE *sl-sex* ***Fac*** large female breast ☞ **žlezda**

bolèsnica {ē fem.} (lit. patient) *sl-fea* ***Der*** insane female, nut case <Slav[*1]>

bolèsnīk {lesníka (acc. = gen.) masc.} (lit. patient) **a.** *sl-fea* ***Der*** strange person, weirdo <Slav[*1]> **b.** *sl-fea* ***Der*** insane person, nut case: *Tog bolesnika treba poslati u ludnicu. That nut case should be sent to a mental institution.* <Slav[*2]> **c.** *sl-fea* ***Der*** stupid or mentally deficient person <Slav[*3]>

bȍlest *See the following*

• **kokȍšjā bȍlēst** {NP} (lit. hen's disease) *sl-sex* anal sexual intercourse

bȍlestan {sna, sno adj.} (lit. sick) *col* ***Der*** insane, nuts <Slav[*1]>

bolȅšljiv {a, o adj.} *col* sickly <Slav⁘>

boléština {ē fem.} *col* sickness <Slav⁘>

bòleti, bòljeti *See the following*

• **Bòlē me múda!** {S} (lit. My balls are hurting me!) *col* ***Obs*** used to express indifference

• **Bòlē[PRON:ACC] [NOUN:NOM].** {LSF} (lit. My [NOUN] is hurting me.) **Ser** *dia* used to express indifference: *Bole me tuki oćeš li ostati ili otići! I don't give a damn if you stay or leave!*

• **bòlī gláva** {VP} (lit. you have a headache from that) *col* used to express high quality of an object, it blows your mind: *Kakva im je kuća - boli glava! What a house they have, it blows your mind!*

• **bòlī[PRON:ACC] [NOUN:NOM] (zà to)!** {LSF} (lit. [PPRON:NOM] [NOUN:NOM] is hurting [PRON:ACC]) *col* used to express indifference: *Boli me kurac za tvoje probleme. I don't give a shit about your problems.* ◊ *Boli ga dupe za to što govoriš. He doesn't give a shit about what you say.*

bòlīd {bolída (acc. = gen.) masc.} *sl* ***Der*** stupid or mentally deficient person <Gre[*1]>

bòliti {bòlīm, bòlē imperf. intr.} [std. = boleti, boljeti] *col* hurt, feel pains <Slav✍>

bólnica [1] {ē fem.} (lit. hospital) *sl-crime* ***Iro*** prison <Slav[*1]>

bólnica [2] {adj.} (lit. hospital) *sl* ill, sick: *Jovan je bolnica. Jovan is sick.* <Slav[*1]>

bȍlovānje {a neut.} (lit. sick leave - a common practice in the former Yugoslavia is to obtain a certificate for sick leave from a physician and use that time for a vacation) *sl* ***Fac*** vacation <Slav[*1]>

bolùckati {ām, ajū imperf.} *col* have a slight ache: *Bolucka me glava. I have a slight headache* <Slav>

bòluk {a masc.} *sl-arch* fish <NE*1>

bȍljē *See the following*

• **Jè l ti dànas bȍljē?** {S} (lit. Are you feeling better today?) *sl* ***Fac*** used as an informal greeting, Hi! How goes it?

bȍljēt {i fem.} *sl-sex* ***Obs*** penis, dick, prick <Slav*1>

boljítak {tka masc.} *col* improvement <Slav*1>

bômba [1] {adj.} (lit. bomb) *col* ***App*** excellent, awesome: *bomba film awesome movie* <Ita*1>

bômba [2] {ē fem.} (lit. bomb) **1** *sl-drink* ***App*** brandy: *piti bombu drink brandy* <Slav*1> **2** *sl-sex* ***App*** attractive female, bombshell <Slav*1> **3a.** *sl-media* revelation, bombshell: *bomba o ljubavnoj aferi predsjednika bombshell about president's love affair* <Slav*1> **b.** *sl-media* false news <Slav*2> **c.** *sl* lie <Slav*3>

bombàrdēr {bardéra (acc. = gen.) masc.} (lit. bombardier) *sl* troublemaker, rowdy, ruffian <Ita*1>

bòmbāš {bombáša (acc. = gen.) masc.; Voc bȍmbāšu} (lit. bomber) **1** *sl-fea* liar <Ita✣*1> **2** *sl-crime* pickpocket <Ita✣*1>

bombášiti {bòmbāšīm, šē imperf.} (lit. bomb) *sl* lie <Ita✣*1>

bòmbati {ām, ajū imperf.} (lit. bomb) *sl* spread rumors: *bombati o napadu spread rumors about a strike* <Ita*1>

bòmbe {eta masc.} *sl-drugs* strong heroin <Eng*1>

bòmbica {ē fem.} (lit. small bomb) *sl-drink* miniature (small bottle of alcoholic beverage) <Ita✣*1>

bombína {ē fem.} [std. = bobina] *sl-auto* ignition coil <Fre✍>

bòme {part.} **1** *col* used as a strong affirmative response, of course, yeah, you bet <Slav> **2** *col* intensifying particle, really, indeed: *On će bome pobijediti. He will really win.* <Slav>

bôn {a +ov (ext. pl) masc.; Nom Pl bónovi} (lit. coupon, stamp e.g. a food stamp) **1** *sl* ten dinars; a ten-dinar bill <Fre*1> **2** *sl* thousand dinars; a thousand-dinar bill, grand <Fre*1>

• **prólaznī bôn** {NP} (lit. transient coupon) *sl-stu* temporary food coupon (for use in a cafeteria)

bóna {excl.} *col* used to address a female in direct informal communication, hey, yo <Slav*1> ☞ **bolan**

bonavèna {ē fem.} (lit. Bonavena: actor known for his wide shoulders) *sl-arch* type of wide-shouldered jacket <ItaO*1>

bônba {ē fem.} [std. = bomba] *col-dia* bomb <Ita✍>

bònbōn {a masc.} /bonbôn /a masc./ (lit. candy) **1** *sl-drugs* narcotic drug, dope <Fre*1> **2** *sl* pork rind <Fre*1>

bonbòndžija {ē masc.} (lit. candy lover) *sl-drink* alcoholic, drunk <Fre✣*1> ☞ **bonbonđija**

bonbònđija {ē masc.} (lit. candy lover) *sl-drink* alcoholic, drunk <Fre✣*1> ☞ **bonbodžija**

bonbònisānje {a neut.} (lit. eating candies) *sl-drink* drinking (alcohol) <Fre✣*1>

bonbònisati {išēm, išū imperf.} (lit. eat candies) *sl-drink* drink (alcohol) <Fre✣*1>

Bȍnd {a (acc. = gen.) masc.} (lit. Bond: British movie character) **1** *sl* boss <EngO*1> **2** *sl* very important or influential person, big shot <EngO*1>

bóni {excl.} **Bos** *col* used to address several persons in direct informal communication, you guys, you folks: *Šta to boni radite? Hey you guys, what's up?* <Slav*1>

bonìta {ē fem.} *sl-drugs* milk sugar used as a substitute for heroin <Spa*1>

bȍnkāč {a masc.} *sl* candy <Fre✣*1>

bórac {rca (acc. = gen.) masc.} (lit. fighter) **1** *sl* friend (esp. from the military), buddy <Slav*1> **2** *sl-sex* ***Fac*** person who engages in sexual intercourse <Slav*1> **3** *sl* ***Fac-Der*** quarrelsome female <Slav*1>

• **stârī bórac** {NP} (lit. old fighter) *sl-mil* conscript with short time before his discharge, short timer

bȍrami {excl.} (lit. *I swear* to a pine) [std. = Boga mi] *dia* used to express assurance, I swear to God! <Slav✍>

bòrba {ē fem.} /bórba/ (lit. battle, fight) *sl-crime* police <Slav*1>

bòrbāš {borbáša (acc. = gen.) masc.; Voc bȍrbāšu} (lit. fighter) *sl-crime* lookout (accomplice) <Slav*1>

bȍrčula {ē masc.} **1** *sl* troublemaker, rowdy, ruffian <NE*1> **2** *sl* stubborn person, pigheaded person <NE*1>

bórder {a (acc. = gen.) masc.} *sl-crime* policeman, cop <Eng*1>

bòrdō {adj.} (lit. burgundy: the color of the jerseys) *sl-sports* pertaining to the soccer team "Sarajevo" from Sarajevo, Bosnia <Fre*1>

Bòrdžija {ē masc.} (lit. Borgia: surname of Italian Renaissance family known for numerous intrigues) *sl* insinuator: *Ta Bordžija mu je namestila igranku. That insinuator witch got him mixed up in an intrigue.* <ItaO*1>

bórer {a masc.} **a.** *sl-crafts* drill (tool) <Ger> **b.** *sl-sex* ***Fac-Obs*** penis, dick, prick <Ger*1>

bóro *See the following*

• **mâlī bóro** {NP} (lit. little Boro) *sl* Marlboro (cigarette brand)

borosána {ē fem.} *col* female orthopedic shoe <BN>

bȍrovati {rujēm, rujū biasp.} **a.** *sl-crafts* drill (using tools) <Ger> **b.** *sl-sex* ***Fac-Obs*** engage in sexual intercourse with (of a male), drill <Ger*1>

bòrovica {ē fem.} *col* pine brandy <Slav>

bòrovice {vīcā fem. pl.} *sl* cemetery <Slav*1>

Borsalîno {a (acc. = gen.) masc.} *sl* Italian (person) <BN*1>

bȍs[1] {a +ov (ext. pl) masc.; Nom Pl bòsovi} *col-sl* boss <Eng>

bôs[2] *See the following*

• **bôs po glávi** {AdjP} (lit. barefoot at his head) *sl-fea* ***Fac*** bald

Bosančȅros {a (acc. = gen.) masc.} /Bosančêros/ *col* ***Der*** Bosnian (person) <Slav✍>

Bȍsnatrans {a masc.} (lit. Bosnatrans: name of a coach company from Bosnia) *sl* ***Fac*** Bosnians <BN*1>

bosòglav {a, o adj.} (lit. bare-headed) *sl-fea* ***Fac*** bald <Slav⁘*1>

bȍsti {bòdēm, bòdū imperf. irreg.} (lit. poke, prick, stab) *sl-sex* ***Obs*** engage in sexual intercourse with (of a male), poke <Slav*1>

bȍšča {ē fem.} BosM *col* veil <NE>

boščàluk {a masc.} BosM *col* wedding present <NE>

bȍškāč {a (acc. = gen.) masc.} **a.** *sl-arch* male, guy <Slav*1> **b.** *sl-arch* worker (usu. manual): *boškač iz fabrike factory worker* <Slav*2> **c.** *sl-arch* bricklayer: *boškači na građevini bricklayers at the construction site* <Slav*3> ☞ **boškać**

bȍškāć {a (acc. = gen.) masc.} **a.** *sl-arch* male, guy <Slav*1> **b.** *sl-arch* worker (usu. manual) <Slav*2> **c.** *sl-arch* bricklayer <Slav*3> ☞ **boškač**

Bȍško {a (acc. = gen.) masc.} (lit. Boško: insane Yugoslav movie character) *sl* stupid or mentally deficient person <SlavO*1>

bòtača {ē fem.} *sl-arch* earth, soil <Alb>

bóza[1] {ē fem.} (lit. beverage from corn) *sl-media* ***Der*** low-quality movie <NE*1>

bóza[2] {adj.} (lit. beverage from corn) *col* ***Der*** worthless: *boza ideje worthless ideas* <NE*1>

bȍže drâgī {NP} (lit. dear God) *col* used to express amazement, astonishment, dear God, good God ☞ **Bog**

Bòžić *See the following*

• **Bòžić ti jèbēm!** {S} (lit. I fuck your Christmas!) *col* ***Off*** used as a moderate curse or threat, Fuck you!

Bòžidār {a (acc. = gen.) masc.} **1** *sl* lover (male) <SlavO*1> **2** *sl* young male, boy, kid <SlavO*1>

bȍžje {excl.} (lit. divine) *col* ***App*** excellent, awesome <Slav*1>

Bȍžjū ti kȕvaricu! {S} (lit. *I screw* your God's cook!) *col* ***Off-Fac*** used as a moderate curse or threat, Fuck you! ☞ **kuvarica**

Bȍžjū ti nèdelju! {S} (lit. *I fuck* your God's Sunday!) *col* ***Off*** used as a moderate curse or threat ☞ **nedjelja**

bȓ {excl.} /bȓr excl./ *col* used to express discomfort (usu. from being cold), brr <Slav>

brȁbonjac {njca masc.} (lit. sheep excrement) *sl* ***Fac*** small tie knot <Slav*1>

brȁbonjak {njka masc.} (lit. sheep excrement) *sl* ***Fac*** small tie knot <Slav*1>

bràcika {excl.} (lit. baby brother) *col* ***Fam*** used to address a male in direct informal communication, brother <Slav✍*1>

bráco[1] {ē masc.} **a.** *col* ***Fam*** baby brother <Slav> **b.** *col* young boy <Slav*1>

brâco[2] {excl.} *col* ***Fam*** used to address a male in direct informal communication, brother <Slav✍*1>

brâčni pâr {NP} (lit. spouses) *sl-sex* ***Fac*** testicles ☞ **par**

brȁća *See the following*

• **brȁća Bájić** {NP} (lit. Bajić brothers: popular country music performers in the 1970s) *sl-crime* ***Fac*** police patrol

brȁćo {excl.} *col* ***Fam*** used to address several persons in direct informal communication, you all, you guys: *Nemojte se, braćo, svađati! Yo guys, stop quarreling!* <Slav*1>

bráda[1] {ē fem.} (lit. beard) *sl* broom <Slav*1>

bráda[2] {ē masc.} (lit. beard) *col* bearded male <Slav*1>

brájko *See the following*

• **môj brâjko** {NP} (lit. my bro) *col* used to address a male in an intimate manner, buddy, pal,

Brakolómac {mca masc.} (lit. marriage wrecker) *sl Fac* motel where spouse-cheaters meet, no-tell motel <Slav[*1]>

brána {ē fem.} (lit. dam) *sl-sex Obs* vagina, cunt <Slav[*1]>

bràniti *See the following*

- **bràniti bòje (klûba)** {VP} (lit. defend the colors of the *club*) *col* play for: *Marković brani boje Partizana. Markoviç plays for Partizan, Belgrade.*

brânka {ē fem.} *Med sl-sports* goal (in soccer, water polo, etc.) <Cze>

brȁo {excl.} [std. = bravo] *col App* used to express approval, bravo <Ita✍> ☞ **bravo, bravos**

bràstvo {a neut.} [std. = bratstvo] *col* brotherhood <Slav✍>

brȁšnjevača {ē fem.} *col* flour brandy <Slav>

brȁt {a (acc. = gen.) masc.} (lit. brother) **1** *sl* I (when a male refers to himself): *Brat je sredio stvar. I have arranged it.* <Slav[*1]> **2** *sl* male, guy <Slav[*1]>

- **brȁte mȉlī** {NP} *col* used to address a male in an intimate manner, buddy, pal,
- **mȍkrī brȁt** {NP} (lit. wet brother) *sl-drink* alcoholic, drunk
- **tȍplī brȁt** {NP} (lit. warm brother) *sl-sex Der* male homosexual, gay
- **vînskī brȁt** {NP} (lit. wine brother) *sl-drink* alcoholic, drunk

brȁte {excl.} *col Fam* used to address a male in direct informal communication, hey: *Pusti ga, brate! Hey, leave him alone!* <Slav[*1]> ☞ **braćo**

brȁti *See the following*

- **brȁti ljùšture** {VP} (lit. pick up shells) *sl* earn (money)

bràtija {ē fem.} (lit. fraternity) *col Der-Fac* company (group of people) <Slav>

bratùčed {a (acc. = gen.) masc.} *col* nephew (one's brother's son) <Slav>

brȁva [1] {adj.} (lit. lock) *sl* closed: *brava restoran closed restaurant* <Slav[*1]>

brȁva [2] {ē fem.} (lit. lock) **1** *sl-sex Obs* buttocks, butt <Slav[*1]> **2** *sl-crime* imprisonment <Slav[*1]>

- **iza brȁvē** {PP} (lit. behind the lock) *col* in prison, behind the bars, locked up

brȁvār *See the following*

- **nòćnī brȁvār** {NP} (lit. nighttime locksmith) *sl-crime Fac* burglar

brȁvo {excl.} /brâvo/ *col* used to express approval, bravo <Ita> ☞ **brao, bravos**

brȁvos {excl.} [std. = bravo] *sl* used to express approval, bravo <Ita✍> ☞ **brao, bravo**

brázda {ē fem.} (lit. furrow) *sl-sex Obs* vagina, cunt <Slav[*1]>

bȑb {excl.} *col* the sound made by an explosion, boom <Slav>

bȑbljati {ām, ajū imperf.} *col* talk persistently and meaninglessly, blabber, chatter <Slav[*1]>

- **bȑbljati kao stârā bȁba** {VP} (lit. blabber like an old woman) *col Der* talk persistently and meaninglessly, blabber, chatter

bȑbljivac [1] {ljīvca (acc. = gen.) masc.} *col Der* talkative male, chatterbox <Slav>

bȑbljivac [2] {ljīvca masc.} (lit. chatterbox) *sl Fac* radio <Slav[*1]>

bȑbot {a masc.} *col* gurgle (creek, etc.) <Slav>

brbòtānje {a neut.} *col* gurgle (creek, etc.) <Slav>

brbòtati {br̀boćēm, oćū imperf. intr.} *col* gurgle (creek, etc.) <Slav>

brbòtav {a, o adj.} *col* gurgling (of creek, spring, etc.) <Slav>

brbùkānje {a neut.} *col* gurgling (of creek, spring, etc.) <Slav>

brbùkati {ām, ajū imperf.} *col* gurgle (creek, etc.) <Slav>

brbùtati {br̀bućēm, ućū imperf.} *col* gurgle (creek, etc.) <Slav>

bȑč {a +ev (ext. pl) masc.; Nom Pl bȑčevi} *col* splash <Slav>

bȑč-brč {excl.} *col* the repeated sound made by splashing, splash-splash <Slav>

bȑčak {čka masc.} *col* splash <Slav>

bȑčkānje {a neut.} *col* splashing <Slav>

bȑčkati {ām, ajū imperf.} *col* splash: *brčkati vodu u kadi splash water in a bathtub* <Slav>

bȑčkati se {ām, ajū imperf. intr.} *col* bathe <Slav>

bȑčkavica {ē fem.} *col* muddy terrain <Slav>

bȑčkotina {ē fem.} *sl* tasteless food <Slav>

bȑđanin {a (acc. = gen.) -in (reduced plural) masc.} (lit. highlander) *col Der* inhabitant of the countryside, hick, bumpkin <Slav>

brȅ {excl.} Ser *col* used to address one or more persons in direct informal communication with various additional meanings ranging from disapproval to familiarity, etc., hey you, man; the hell, damn it; for heaven's sake, wow: *Ko si bre ti da mi pričaš! Who the hell are you to tell me!* ◊ *Slušaj bre ovamo! For heaven's sake, please pay attention!* <NE> ☞ ba, bolan

bregáda {ē fem.} [std. = brigada] *col* brigade (military) <Fre✍>

brȅmz-pedála {ē fem.} *sl-auto* brake <Ger>

brȅmza {ē fem.} *sl-auto* brake <Ger>

brȅmze {a fem. pl.} *sl* green peas <Ger[*1]>

brȅnovati {nujēm, nujū imperf.} **a.** *col* respect, obey: *Taj razbojnik ne brenuje nikoga. That rascal doesn't respect anybody.* <Ger[*1]> **b.** *col* appreciate, enjoy, like: *brenovati nečiji rad appreciate somebody's work* <Ger[*2]> **c.** *col* worry about: *brenovati ispite worry about exams* <Ger[*3]>

brȅnta {ē fem.} *sl-sex* pregnant female <Ita[*1]>

brèntača {ē fem.} *sl* big belly <Ita[*1]>

brȅskovača {ē fem.} *col* peach brandy <Slav>

Brȅšč {a +ev (ext. pl) masc.} Cro *sl* name of a dance club on Brešč street in Zagreb, Croatia <SlavO>

brez {gen.} [std. = bez] *dia-col* without: *rezervar brez benzina gas tank without gasoline* <Slav✍>

brezòbrazan {zna, zno adj.} [std. = bezobrazan] *dia-col* impudent, insolent: *brezobrazan balavac impudent youngster* <Slav✍>

brezobràzluk {a masc.} [std. = bezobrazluk] *dia-col* instance of impudence, insolence <Slav✍>

brezòbraznica {ē fem.} [std. = bezobraznik] *dia-col* impudent or insolent female <Slav✍>

brezòbraznīk {a (acc. = gen.) masc.} [std. = bezobraznik] *dia-col* impudent or insolent male <Slav✍>

bríca [1] {ē fem.} (lit. razor) *sl-sex* ***Obs*** vagina, cunt <Slav[*1]>

bríca [2] {ē masc.} SerE *col* barber <Slav>

bríco {a masc.} *col* barber <Slav>

brȉdžer {a (acc. = gen.) masc.} *sl-gamble* bridge player <Eng✣>

brȉga *See the following*

• **Brȉga[PRON:GEN/ACC]** (za [NP:ACC])! {LSF} (lit. It is worry to [PRON:ACC] *for PRON:ACC]*) *col* used to indicate indifference, [PRON:NOM] [NOT] care (for [NP: ACC])!: *Briga me za njega. I don't care for him.* ◊ *Briga nje za ocjene. She doesn't care for her grades.*

brȉfovati {fujēm, fujū imperf.} *col* brief <Eng>

brȉjati {jēm, jū imperf.} (lit. shave) **a.** *sl-crime* pick pockets <Slav[*1]> **b.** *sl-crime* rob, fleece, rip off <Slav[*2]>

• **brȉjati mȕstera** {VP} (lit. shave a dude) *sl-crime* rob, fleece, rip off

brȉjati se *See the following*

• **brȉjati se jèzikom** {VP} (lit. shave with one's tongue) *sl-fea* ***Fac*** be outspoken, have a sharp tongue

• **brȉjati se peškírom** {VP} (lit. shave with one's towel) *sl-fea* ***Fac*** be a clean shaver

brȉk {brȉka +ov (ext. pl) masc.; Nom Pl brȉkovi} *sl-drugs* one kilogram of marijuana, brick <Eng[*1]>

brȋs [1] {excl.} (lit. swipe) *col* used to make somebody go away, beat it <Slav✍[*1]>

brȋs [2] {a +ev (ext. pl) masc.; Nom Pl brísevi} *col* the act of running away from <Slav✍[*1]>

brȉsānje {a neut.} *col* the act of running away from <Slav[*1]>

brȉsati {išēm, išū imperf. intr.} *sl* run away, flee: *brisati iz kasarne run away from the barracks* <Slav[*1]>

brisavȅla {ē fem.} *sl* the act of running away <Slav✍[*1]>

brísnuti {brȋsnēm, nū perf. intr.} *sl* run away, flee: *brisnuti iz zatvora escape from prison* <Slav[*1]>

brȉš {excl.} (lit. swipe) [std. = briši] *sl* used to make somebody go away, beat it <Slav✍[*1]>

brȉši {excl.} (lit. swipe) *col* used to make somebody go away, beat it <Slav[*1]>

brȉś {excl.} (lit. swipe) [std. = briši] *sl* used to make somebody go away, beat it <Slav✍[*1]>

Británac {nca (acc. = gen.) masc.} (lit. the Britisher) **Cro** *sl* name for Britanski trg (a square in Zagreb, Croatia) <Slav[*1]>

brȉtva [1] {excl.} (lit. razor) *sl* used to make somebody go away, beat it <Slav[*1]>

brȉtva [2] {adv.} (lit. razor) *sl* ***App*** excellent, sharp, awesome <Slav[*1]>

brȉtva [3] {ē fem.} (lit. razor) **1** *sl* the act of running away: *britva pred policijom running away from the police* <Slav[*1]> **2** *sl* national border: *preći britvu cross the border* <Slav[*1]> **3** ***App*** smart person, sharp cookie: *Taj student je britva. That student is a sharp cookie.* <Slav[*1]>

brȉtva [4] {adj.} (lit. razor) **1** *sl* ***App*** smart, sharp: *britva dete smart child* <Slav[*1]> **2** *sl* ***App*** excellent, sharp, awesome: *britva žurka awesome party* <Slav[*1]>

brȉza {ē fem.} *sl-arch* cheese <Rum[*1]>

Brìžitkino kòleno {NP} (lit. Brigitte Bardot's knee: French actress popular in the 1970s) **SerE** *sl-fea* ***Fac*** bald head ☞ **koleno**

bȓk {a +ov (ext. pl) masc.; Nom Pl bȓkovi} (lit. mustache) *sl* loan, credit <Slav*1>
• **bȓkovi ko dvádeset do pêt** {NP} (lit. mustaches like twenty minutes to five o'clock) *sl-fea* ***Fac*** Fu Manchu mustache
• **na bȓk** {PP} (lit. on a mustache) *sl* on credit: *kupiti kola na brk buy a car on credit*

bŕkati {bȑkām, bŕkajū imperf.} **a.** *col* confuse, mix up: *brkati dvije potpuno različite stvari confuse two completely different issues* <Slav> **b.** *sl* stir: *brkati piće stir a drink* <Slav*1>

bŕknuti {bȑknēm, bŕknū perf.} (lit. confuse) **1** *sl* take <Slav*1> **2** *sl* hit, punch <Slav*1>

bŕko {a masc.} (lit. male with mustache) *sl-crime* prison administrator <Slav*1>

bŕlog {a masc.} (lit. lair) **1** *sl* apartment <Slav*1> **2** *sl-crime* hideout <Slav*1>

bŕlja {ē fem.} **1** *col* weak brandy <Slav> **2** *col* untidy female, slob <Slav>

bŕljati [1] {bȑljām, bŕljajū imperf.} (lit. make a mess) *col* destroy, ruin: *brljati planove ruin the plans* <Slav>

bŕljati [2] {bȑljām, bŕljajū imperf. intr.} (lit. make a mess) **a.** *col* make a mistake, screw up: *brljati u godišnjem izvještaju make mistakes in the annual report* <Slav> **b.** *col* work poorly <Slav>

brljáviti {bȑljāvīm, vē imperf. intr.} (lit. make a mess) **1a.** *col* make a mistake, screw up <Slav*1> **b.** *col* work poorly <Slav*2> **2** *col* talk persistently and meaninglessly, blabber, chatter <Slav*1> **3** *col* go insane, freak out <Slav>

bȑljos {a (acc. = gen.) masc.} *sl* garbage man <Slav✣>

bȑnjica {ē fem.} (lit. muzzle) **1** *sl* ***Der*** mouth, muzzle, face <Slav*1> **2** *dia* ear-ring <Slav*1>

bȑnza {ē fem.} *sl-arch* cheese <Rum>

brȍć {a +ev (ext. pl) masc.; Nom Pl bròćevi} *sl* stupidity, lack of intelligence <Slav>

brôd {a +ov (ext. pl) masc.; Nom Pl bròdovi} (lit. ship) *sl-crime* suitcase (construed as an object of stealing) <Slav*1>

brȍdo {adv.; perm} /bròdo/ [std. = dobro] *sl* well: *voziti brodo drive well* <Slav⇗>

brȍdo bandàžīrān {NP} (lit. bandaged well) *sl* dressed formally, dressed up ☞ **bandažiran**

brôjnīk {a (acc. = gen.) masc.} (lit. numerator) *sl-crime* ***Fac*** policeman, cop <Slav*1>

brȍš {a +ev (ext. pl) masc.; Nom Pl bròševi} (lit. brooch) *sl* female from a blue-collar family <Fre*1>

bȓr {excl.} /bȓrr excl./ *col* used to express discomfort (usu. from being cold), brr <Slav>

bŕstiti *See the following*
• **bŕstiti trávu** {VP} (lit. graze on grass) *sl* joke with, make a fool of

brȕca {ē fem.} (lit. pubic hair) *sl-sex* ***Obs*** vagina, cunt <Slav*1>

brȕjān {a (acc. = gen.) masc.} (lit. the one who has just started to grow his pubic hairs) *sl* rookie <Slav*1>

brújati {jīm, jē perf. intr.} *col* hum, hiss <Slav>

brȕka {ē fem.} *col* shame, disgrace, scandal: *Pukla je bruka zbog njenih ljubavnih afera. Her love affairs have brought her disgrace.* <Slav>
• **brȕka i sramòta** {NP} (lit. shame and disgrace) *col* shame, disgrace, scandal: *Njegovo učešće u ovom ratu je prava bruka i sramota za sve nas. His participation in this war is a real disgrace for all of us.*

brȕkati {ām, ajū imperf.} *col* shame on, ashame, bring disgrace: *Nemoj da me brukaš lošim ocjenama. Do not let your bad grades bring us disgrace.* <Slav>

brúnda {ē fem.} *sl* head <Slav>

brûshàlter {a masc.} *col* bra <Ger>

bȑvnār *See the following*
• **lìvanjskī bȑvnār** {NP} (lit. lumber jack from Livno: a city in Bosnia) *sl* left pocket

bȑzac [1] {brzàca (acc. = gen.) masc.} *col* fast runner, speedster <Slav>

bȑzac [2] {brzàca masc.} (lit. the quick one) **1** *sl* telephone, phone <Slav*1> **2** *sl* fast train, express train <Slav*1>
• **na bȑzac** {PP} (lit. on a quickie) *col* quickly
• **na brzàca** {PP} (lit. on a quickie) *col* quickly

bȑzāk {brzáka masc.} (lit. rushing) **1** *sl* fast train, express train <Slav*1> **2** *sl-sex* quick sexual intercourse, quickie <Slav*1>
• **na brzáka** {PP} (lit. on a quickie) *col* quickly

bȑzalica {ē fem.} **1** *col* effective reply: *spustiti nekome brzalicu give somebody an effective reply* <Slav*1> **2** *col* occasional joke: *Pustio je brzalicu o direktoru. He had an occasional joke about the boss.* <Slav*1> **3** *col* tongue twister <Slav*1>

bȑzati {ām, ajū imperf.} (lit. rush) *sl-sex* ***Obs*** engage in quick sexual intercourse with, have a quickie <Slav*1>

bȑzovōzno {adv.} (lit. quick riding) *col* quickly <**Slav**✣>

bȕ {excl.} *col* the sound made by an explosion, boom <**Slav**>

bȕah {excl.} /buàh/ *col* used to express sorrow or dismay, woe <**Slav**>

bȕav {a, o adj.} *sl* obese, fat <**Slav**[*1]>

bȕb {excl.} *col* the sound made by an explosion, bang <**Slav**>

bȕba {ē fem.} (lit. bug) **1** *col* a defect in the code or routine of a computer program, bug <**Slav**[*1]> **2** *sl-auto* Volkswagen (make of car), bug, beetle <**Slav**[*1]> **3** *sl-sex* female <**Slav**[*1]>
• **lênjā bȕba** {NP} (lit. lazy bug) SerE *sl-fea* lazy or shiftless person, bum, good for nothing

búbalica {ē fem. & masc.} *col* ***Der*** person who studies mechanically <**Slav**>

búbalo {a neut.} *col* ***Der*** person who studies mechanically <**Slav**>

bubamára {ē fem.} (lit. ladybug) *sl-sports* soccer ball <**Slav**[*1]>

bùbant {a (acc. = gen.) masc.} *col* ***Der*** person who studies mechanically <**Slav**>

bûbanj {bnja masc.} (lit. drum) *sl-crime* prison <**Slav**[*1]>
• **u bûbnju** {PP} (lit. in a drum) *sl-crime* in custody waiting to be convicted

Bûbanj pòtok {NP} (lit. Drum creek) *sl-crime* ***Fac*** prison ☞ **potok**

búbanje {a neut.} (lit. drumming) *col* ***Der*** mechanical studying <**Slav**>

bȕbastī {ōg masc.} *sl-fea* obese male <**Slav**[*1]>

bubašvàbista {ē masc.} (lit. the roach one X švaba 'German, Kraut' in that many German tourist used to get a tan while on their vacation along the Adriatic coast) *sl-fea* sunburned person <**Slav**✍[*1]>

búbati {bûbām, búbajū imperf.} (lit. drum) **1a.** *sl-sstu* study mechanically: *bubati za ispit cram for an exam* <**Slav**[*1]> **b.** *sl-fea* talk persistently and meaninglessly, blabber, chatter<**Slav**[*2]> **2** *sl* eat in great quantities, pig out: *bubati piletinu pig out on the chicken* <**Slav**[*1]>

bubètānje {a neut.} (lit. drum) *sl-fea* ***Der*** prolonged and meaningless talk, blabber, chatter <**Slav**[*1]>

bubètati {ām, ajū imperf.} (lit. drum) *sl-fea* ***Der*** talk persistently and meaninglessly, blabber, chatter <**Slav**[*1]>

bȕbī-bubī {masc.} *sl-sstu* ***Der*** A-student, student who makes As <**Slav**[*1]>

bȕbica {ē fem.} (lit. small bug) *sl* very young female, little girl <**Slav**[*1]>

bùbini {a, o adj.} *sl* sick, ill <**Slav**✍[*1]>

bȕbiti {bīm, bē perf. intr.} (lit. bang) *col* arrive unexpectedly, appear out of nowhere, pop in <**Slav**[*1]>

bùbnā tȕpičnica {NP} (lit. the place of grinding and preaching) *sl-sstu* ***Fac*** school ☞ **tupičnica**

bȕbnūt {a, o adj.} (lit. banged) *col* ***Der*** insane, bonkers <**Slav**[*1]>

bȕbnuti {nēm, nū perf.} (lit. bang) *col* say something unintelligent, blurt out: *bubnuti tešku glupost blurt out something very stupid* <**Slav**[*1]>

bȕbnuti {nēm, nū perf. intr.} (lit. bang) *col* arrive unexpectedly, appear out of nowhere, pop in: *bubnuti u ponoć pop in unexpectedly at midnight* <**Slav**[*1]>

bùbnjača {ē fem.} (lit. banger) *sl-sex* ***Obs*** vagina, cunt <**Slav**[*1]>

bùbnjār {bubnjára (acc. = gen.) masc.} (lit. drummer) *sl-fea* ***Der-Fac*** extremely talkative person, chatterbox <**Slav**[*1]>

bȕbos {a (acc. = gen.) masc.} **a.** *sl* bug (insect) <**Slav**✍> **b.** *sl* roach (insect) <**Slav**✍>

bùbreg {a masc.} (lit. kidney) **1** *sl* brain <**NE**[*1]> **2** *sl* money belt <**NE**[*1]>
• **bêlī bùbrezi** {NP} (lit. white kidneys) SerE *sl-sex* ***Fac*** testicles
• **kao bùbreg u lòju** {AdvP} (lit. like a kidney in fat) *col* excellently (usu. in reference to one's lifestyle): *živjeti kao bubreg u loju live high on the hog*

bùbrežnjāk {a masc.} (lit. meat around kidneys) *col* wrap or band worn around body to protect kidneys from cold <**NE**[*1]>

bubuléja {ē masc.} (lit. Bubuleja: uneducated and rude Yugoslav TV series character) *sl* troublemaker, rowdy, ruffian <**SlavO**[*1]>

bubùljōn {buljóna masc.} *sl* pimple <**Slav**[*1]>

búca {ē fem. & masc.} *sl-fea* ***Fam*** obese person <**Slav**[*1]>

búcati {bûcām, búcajū imperf.} *col* rip, tear apart <**Slav**>

bùcina {ē fem.} *sl* old trousers <**Slav**>

búciti se {bûcīm, bûce imperf. intr.} *sl-fea* gain weight <**Slav**✣[*1]>

bȕcko {a masc.} *sl-fea* ***Fam*** obese person <**Slav**[*1]>

bȕcmas {sta, sto adj.} [std. = bucmast] *col* obese, fat <**Slav**✍>

bȕcnuti se {nēm, nū perf. intr.} *col* gain weight <Slav>

búco {ē masc.} /búco /a masc./ *sl-fea* ***Fam*** obese person <Slav[*1]>

bȕć {excl.} *col* the sound made by splashing, splash <Slav>

bȕća {ē masc.} *sl* head <Slav[*1]>

bȕćkurīš {a masc.} /bućkùrīš/ *col* low-quality food, slop <Slav>

bȕda [1] {ē fem.} *sl* loss, detriment: *U budi sam dvije milje marona od kockanja. I lost two thousand German marks gambling.* <Ger[*1]>

bȕda [2] {ē fem. & masc.} *sl-fea* stupid or mentally deficient person <NE✍[*1]>

budàla {ē fem.} **a.** *col* stupid or mentally deficient person <NE> **b.** *sl* head <NE[*1]>

budàlastōst {i fem.} *col* stupidity, lack of intelligence <NE✣>

budàlāš {daláša (acc. = gen.) masc.} (lit. insane male) *sl-sex* ***Fac-Obs*** penis, dick, prick <NE✣>

budaláština {ē fem.} *col* stupidity, lack of intelligence <NE✣>

budàlčina {ē fem.} *col* stupid or mentally deficient person <NE✣>

budàliti {līm, lē imperf. intr.} *col* go insane, freak out: *budaliti od puno posla go nuts from being overworked* <NE✣>

bùdūćī intelektuálac {NP} (lit. future intellectual) *sl-sstu* ***Fac*** elite high-school student ☞ **intelektualac**

búdža {ē masc.} **a.** *col* stick, bat <NE[*1]> **b.i.** *sl-sex* ***Obs*** penis, dick, prick <NE[*1]> **ii.** *col* very important or influential person, bigshot: *Bio je predsjednik i nekoliko drugih budža. The president was there with several other bigshots.* <NE[*1]>

bùdžāk {budžáka masc.} *col* corner (in a house) <NE>

bùdžātor {a (acc. = gen.) masc.} **a.** *sl-fea* person who makes noise <NE✣[*1]> **b.** *sl-fea* troublemaker, rowdy, ruffian <NE✣[*2]>

búdžiti {džīm, džē imperf. intr.} **1** *sl* boast, brag <NE✣[*1]> **2** *sl* upgrade: *budžiti kompjuter upgrade a computer* <NE✣[*1]> **3** *sl* exaggerate: *budžiti priču exaggerate a story* <NE✣[*1]>

búdžiti se {džīm, džē imperf. intr.} *sl* be conceited, be stuck-up <NE✣[*1]>

budžóbus {a masc.} (lit. bigshot bus) *sl-auto* ***Fac*** Mercedes (make of car) <NE-Eng>

budžòvān {džována (acc. = gen.) masc.} *col* very important or influential person, bigshot <NE✣[*1]>

búđa {ē fem.} *sl-crime* hiding place (for things) <Slav>

buđèlār {đelára masc.} *col* wallet <Lat[*1]>

buđóla {ē fem.} (lit. a sort of sausage) *sl-sex* ***Fac-Obs*** penis, dick, prick <Ita[*1]>

bùfalo {a masc.} (lit. buffalo) *sl* shoe <Eng[*1]>
• **klȍkovačkī bùfalo** {NP} *sl-fea* ***Fac*** high-quality shoe

bȕftati {ām, ajū imperf.} *sl* beat up: *Buftali su ga neki silosi. Some bullies have beat him up.* <Slav[*1]>

bugàčica {ē fem.} (lit. blatter) **1** *sl-crime* informer, stoolie, snitch <Slav[*1]> **2** *sl* sanitary napkin <Slav[*1]>

Bȕgar {a (acc. = gen.) masc.} (lit. Bulgarian: they are known for their rose gardeners) *sl* gardener <Slav[*1]>

bugárac {rca masc.} *sl* dancing <Slav[*1]>

bȕgarēnje {a neut.} *sl-fea* prolonged and meaningless talk, blabber, chatter <Slav[*1]>

Bȕgari {gārā masc. pl.} (lit. Bulgarians) *sl* small yellow coins of any currency (pennies) <Slav[*1]>

bȕgarin {a (acc. = gen.) -in (rd. pl.) masc.} *sl* pirated CD (produced in Bulgaria) <SlavO[*1]>

búger {a masc.} **1a.** *sl-sstu* failing grade <Fre[*1]> **b.** *sl-sstu* grade D <Fre[*1]> **2 Ser** *sl* streetcar line number two in Belgrade, Serbia <Fre[*1]>

bugojánac {nca (acc. = gen.) masc.} (lit. man from Bugojno, a small town in Bosnia) *sl* naive inhabitant of the countryside <Slav[*1]>

bùha {ē fem.; Dat bùhi} (lit. flea) *sl-auto* Vespa (model of motorcycle) <Slav[*1]>

buhalètka {ē fem.; Dat buhalètki} (lit. bookkeeper) **1** *sl-sex* ***App*** muscular female <Ger[*1]> **2** *sl-sex* ***App*** female with large breasts and buttocks <Ger[*1]>

bùhara {ē fem.} *sl-crime* prison <Slav[*1]>

bùhtl {a masc.} (lit. doughnut) *sl-sex* ***Obs*** vagina, jelly roll <Ger[*1]>

bújati {jīm, jē imperf. intr.} *col* ***Fam*** sleep, nap <Slav>

búji-báji {perf.} *col* ***Fam*** sleep, nap <Slav>

bújiti {jīm, jē imperf. intr.} *col* ***Fam*** sleep, nap <Slav>

bújkiti {kīm, kē imperf. intr.} *col* ***Fam*** sleep, nap <Slav>

bùjrum {excl.} **1 BosM** *col* used to express approval: *A: Mogu li doći? B: Bujrum! A: Can I come? B: Please do!* <NE> **2** BosM *col* used when offering food, help yourself, dig in <NE>

bukágije {gījā fem. pl.} *sl-crime* handcuffs, cuffs <NE*1>

bùkar {a masc.} *sl-arch* bread <Slav*1>

bùkarenje {a neut.} *sl-sex* ***Obs*** sexual intercourse <Slav*1>

bȕke *See the following*

- **bȕke kâljskō** {NP} *sl-arch* oats

bùkēt {bukéta masc.} (lit. bouquet) *sl* ***Fac*** female <Fre*1>

bukètāš {ketáša masc.} *sl-arch* cornbread <Fre*1>

bùklija {ē fem.} *sl-arch* head <NE*1>

bùkljāf {bukljáfa masc.} *sl-crime* hiding place <Slav✍>

bȕksa {ē fem.} *sl-crime* prison <Ger*1>

bùksara {ē fem.} *sl-crime* prison <Ger⁘*1>

bukùrija {ē fem.} *dia-col* church <NE*1>

bukùrlija {ē fem.} *sl-arch* church <NE*1>

- **zȍtskā bukùrlija** {NP} *sl-arch* mosque

bȕkva {ē fem.} (lit. beech) **1** *col* ***Der*** stupid or mentally deficient person <Slav*1> **2** *sl* mosque <Slav*1>

bùkvan {a (acc. = gen.) masc.} (lit. the beech-tree one) *col* ***Der*** stupid or mentally deficient person <Slav*1>

bȕkvār {adj.} *sl-fea* simple, easy: *bukvar ispit simple exam* <Slav*1>

bȕkvica {ē fem.} **1** *col* reproach, scold: *bukvica zbog nepristojnog ponašanja reprimand for indecent behavior* <Slav*1> **2** *sl-mil* military ID: *izgubiti bukvicu lose one's military ID* <Slav*1>

bȕla {ē fem.} **1a.** *sl-gamble* gambling loss: *bula od dvije hiljade zelembaća gambling loss of two grand* <NE*1> **b.** *sl* trouble, problem <NE*1> **2** *col* ***Der*** Muslim female <NE*1>

búlac {lca masc.} *sl* train <NE⁘*1>

bulahȅtka {ē fem.; Dat bulahȅtki} *sl-sex* ***App*** attractive female <NE⁘*1>

bulájko {a masc.} *sl-sex* ***Off*** male homosexual, gay <NE*1>

bulázniti {bùlāznīm, nē imperf.} *col* ***Der*** talk persistently and meaninglessly, blabber, chatter <Slav*1>

bulážēnje {a neut.} *col* ***Der*** prolonged and meaningless talk, blabber, chatter <Slav*1>

bulážnjēnje {a neut.} *col* ***Der*** prolonged and meaningless talk, blabber, chatter <Slav*1>

bùldožder {a (acc. = gen.) masc.} (lit. bulldozer) *sl-sex* ***Fac*** male sexual partner (of a female) <Eng*1>

bulèvar *See the following*

- **bulèvār ȍpruženīh** {NP} (lit. boulevard of the stretched-out ones) *sl* ***Fac*** cemetery
- **bulèvār pȕdlīcā** {NP} (lit. poodle's boulevard) *sl-sex* ***Fac*** name of a place in Zagreb, Croatia where homosexuals are known to gather
- **bulèvār sprȕženīh** {NP} (lit. boulevard of the stretched-out ones) *sl* ***Fac*** cemetery

bùluk {a masc.} *sl-arch* ***Der-Fac*** fish <NE*1>

bulùmēnta {ē fem.} /bulumȅnta, e fem./ BosM *col* crowd, mob <NE*1>

bûlj {a +ev (ext. pl) masc.; Nom Pl búljevi} *sl-sex* ***Obs*** buttocks, butt <Gyp✍>

búlja [1] {ē fem.} **1a.** *sl-sex* ***Obs*** buttocks, butt <Gyp> **b.i.** *sl* ***Obs*** head <Gyp*1> **ii.** *sl* ***Obs*** female <Gyp*1> **2** *sl* ***Der*** wide-eyed female <Slav>

- **Búlja gȁće žvâćē.** {S} (lit. Your ass is chewing the pants.) *sl* ***Fac-Obs*** state of intense fear in dangerous situations: *Evo drotova. Bulja gaće žvaće? The cops are coming. Scared shitless, huh?*

búlja [2] {ē masc.} **a.** *sl-fea* short-sighted male <Slav*1> **b.** *sl-fea* wide-eyed male <Slav*1>

bùljāf {buljáfa masc.} *sl-sex* ***Obs*** buttocks, butt <Gyp⁘*1>

buljáfer {a masc.} *sl-sex* ***Obs*** buttocks, butt <Gyp⁘*1>

bùljāk {buljáka masc.} *sl* head <Gyp⁘*1>

buljáker {a masc.} *sl-sex* ***Obs*** buttocks, butt <Gyp⁘*1>

buljàkser {a masc.} *sl-sex* ***Obs*** buttocks, butt <Gyp-Slav.⁘*1>

buljànder {a masc.} *sl-sex* ***Obs*** buttocks, butt <Gyp⁘*1>

buljànfer {a masc.} *sl-sex* ***Obs*** buttocks, butt <Gyp⁘*1>

bùljara {ē fem.} *sl-sex* ***Obs*** large buttocks <Gyp⁘*1>

buljáriti {bùljārīm, rē imperf.} *sl* stare at, be fixated at <Slav⁘*1>

buljàsker {a masc.} *sl-sex* ***Obs*** buttocks, butt <Gyp✍>

bùljāš {buljáša (acc. = gen.) masc.; Voc bȕljāšu} *sl-sex* ***Off*** male homosexual, gay <Gyp⁘*1>

bȕljav {a, o adj.} *sl* bald <Slav⁘*1>

buljèskara {ē fem.} *sl-sex* ***Obs*** large buttocks <Gyp⁘*1>

bùljilo {a neut.} *sl* door window <Slav⁘*1>

bùljina {ē fem.} *sl-sex* ***Obs*** buttocks, butt <Gyp⁘*1>

búljiti {ljīm, ljē imperf. intr.} *col* stare at, be fixated on: *buljiti u prazan kompjuterski ekran stare at a blank computer screen* <Slav>

bùljkāf {buljkáfa masc.} **1a.** *sl-sex* ***Obs*** buttocks, butt <**Gyp❖**[*1]> **b.i.** *sl-crime* ***Obs*** hideout: *Tu imam buljkaf za lovu. Here's where I stash my money.* <**Gyp❖**[*1]> **ii.** *sl-sex* ***Obs*** place intended for sexual intercourse <**Gyp❖**[*1]> **iii.** *sl-gamble* place intended for gambling, gambling den <**Gyp❖**[*1]>

búljko {a masc.} *sl-fea* ***Der*** cross-eyed person <**Slav❖**>

bȕljobrīs {a masc.} (lit. asswipe) *sl* ***Fac*** bathroom tissue, ass wipe <**Gyp-Slav❖**[*1]>

buljóka {ē fem.; Dat buljóki} *col* ***Der*** big-eyed person <**Slav❖**[*1]>

bùljōn {buljóna masc.} *sl-sex* ***Obs*** buttocks, butt <**Gyp❖**[*1]>

bȕljos {a masc.} *sl-sex* ***Obs*** buttocks, butt <**Gyp☞**>

buljòsava {ē fem.} *sl-sex* ***Obs*** buttocks, butt <**Gyp❖**[*1]>

bȕljoš {a masc.} *sl-sex* ***Obs*** buttocks, butt <**Gyp❖**[*1]>

buljouvlàčilac {čioca (acc. = gen.) masc.} (lit. butt intruder) *sl* ***Der-Fac*** ingratiator (male), brownnoser, ass kisser <**Gyp-Slav❖**[*1]>

buljouvlàkāč {lakáča (acc. = gen.) masc.} (lit. butt intruder) *sl* ***Der-Obs*** ingratiator (male), brownnoser, ass kisser <**Gyp-Slav❖**[*1]>

bȕljūk {a masc.} **a.** *col* crowd, mob <**NE**> **b.** *col* multitude: *buljuk djece whole bunch of kids* <**NE**[*1]>

bȕm [1] {excl.} *col* the sound made by an explosion, boom <**Slav**>

bȕm [2] {a +ov (ext. pl) masc.; Nom Pl bùmovi} (lit. boom) *col* time of prosperity, boom <**Eng**>

- **bȕm bȁm** {ExcP} *col* the sound of a bell, ding-dong
- **bȕm bȕm** {ExcP} *col* the sound made by artillery fire, bang -bang

bȕm-bȁm {excl.} *col* the sound of a bell, ding-dong <**Slav**>

bumȁška {ē fem.; Dat bumȁški} **1** *col* ID (separate document which every adult citizen of the former Yugoslavia had to carry on their person) <**Rus**[*1]> **2** *col* thousand dinars; a thousand-dinar bill, grand <**Rus**[*1]> **3** *col* ten dinars; a ten-dinar bill <**Rus**[*1]>

bȕmbār {a (acc. = gen.) masc.} (lit. bumblebee) **1** *sl-crime* ***Fac*** policeman, cop <**Slav**[*1]> **2** *sl* ***Fac*** brother <**Slav**[*1]>

bunàcānje {a neut.} *sl* ***Der*** prolonged and meaningless talk, blabber, chatter <**Slav**[*1]>

bunàcati {ām, ajū imperf.} *sl* ***Der*** talk persistently and meaninglessly, blabber, chatter <**Slav**[*1]>

bùnār {bunára masc.} /bȕnār/ (lit. water well) **1** *sl-crime* pocket (on a coat, trousers, etc.): *maznuti šlajpek iz bunara swipe a wallet from a pocket* <**Slav**[*1]> **2** *sl* boot <**Slav**[*1]>

bunàrati {ām, ajū imperf.} (lit. dig a well) *sl-fea* ***Der*** talk persistently and meaninglessly, blabber, chatter <**Slav**[*1]>

bunàrče {eta neut.} (lit. small well) *sl-crime* safe <**Slav**[*1]>

bunàrdžija {ē masc.} (lit. well digger) *sl-crime* pickpocket <**Slav**[*1]>

bunárēnje {a neut.} (lit. digging wells) **1** *sl* ***Der*** prolonged and meaningless talk, blabber, chatter <**Slav**[*1]> **2** *sl-crime* picking pockets <**Slav**[*1]>

bunàrisati {išēm, išū imperf.} (lit. dig a well) **1** *sl-crime* steal, swipe: *bunarisati barke swipe wallets* <**Slav**[*1]> **2** *sl* joke <**Slav**[*1]>

bunáriti {bùnārīm, rē imperf.} (lit. dig a well) *sl-crime* pick pockets <**Slav**[*1]>

bùnāroš {a (acc. = gen.) masc.} (lit. well digger) *sl* pickpocket <**Slav**[*1]>

bùncānje {a neut.} *sl-fea* ***Der*** prolonged and meaningless talk, blabber, chatter <**Slav**[*1]>

bùncati {ām, ajū imperf.} *sl-fea* talk persistently and meaninglessly, blabber, chatter <**Slav**[*1]>

bùncek {a (acc. = gen.) masc.} (lit. pork leg quarter) *sl-fea* ***Fac*** obese female, porker <**Slav**[*1]>

bûnda {ē fem.} (lit. fur coat) *sl-sex* ***Fac-Obs*** pubic hair, fur <**Slav**[*1]>

bùndara {ē fem.} *sl* fur <**Slav☞**>

bùndeva {ē fem.} (lit. pumpkin) *sl* ***Fac*** head, pumpkin <**Slav**[*1]>

bùnker {a masc.} (lit. bunker) **1** *sl-drink* late-night bar <**Ger**[*1]> **2** *sl-sex* clandestine brothel <**Ger**[*1]> **3** *sl-crime* illegal distillery, still <**Ger**[*1]> **4** *sl-media* place where movies prohibited by censorship are stored <**Ger**[*1]> **5** *sl-sports* defensive soccer <**Ger**[*1]>

bunkerírati se {kèrīrām, kerírajū biasp. intr.} (lit. bunker oneself, hide in the bunker) *sl* hide from publicity, lay low <**Ger❖**[*1]>

bunkèrisati {išēm, išū imperf.} (lit. bunker, hide in the bunker) Ser *col* hide from publicity, lay low <**Ger❖**[*1]>

bunkèrisati se {išēm, išū imperf. intr.} (lit. bunker oneself) *sl* ***Fac*** hide from publicity, lay low <**Ger❖**[*1]>

bùnket {a (acc. = gen.) masc.} *sl* miser, tightwad, skinflint

bȕnt {a +ov (ext. pl) masc.; Nom Pl bùntovi} *sl* necktie <**Ger**[*1]>

bùnjalo {a neut.} /búnjalo/ *sl-fea* homeless person, bum <Slav>

bȕp {excl.} *col* the sound made by a hit or strike, bang, bop <Slav[*1]>

bȕra {ē fem.} (lit. north wind on Croatian coastline) *sl* female <Slav[*1]>

bùrāg {burága masc.} (lit. first stomach of ruminant) *sl* stomach, belly, gut <Rum[*1]>

burànija {ē fem.} [std. = boranija] **a.** *col-dia* string beans <Slav✍> **b.i.** *col-dia* ***Der*** unimportant person, nobody, nothing: *On je buranija, ne treba ga se bojati. You don't have to fear him, he's small potatoes.* <Slav✍[*1]> **ii.** *col-dia* ***Der*** worthless object <Slav✍[*1]>

bùrat {a masc.} *sl* stomach, belly, gut <Ita[*1]>

bȕrāz [1] {a (acc. = gen.) masc.} **a.** Bos *col* ***Fam*** brother <NE> **b.** Bos *col* ***Fam*** friend (male) <NE[*1]>

buráz [2] {excl.} (lit. my brother) *col* ***Fam*** used to address a male in direct informal communication, yo, my brother, my friend <NE[*1]> ☞ **burazere, brate**

burázer {a (acc. = gen.) masc.} **a.** Bos *col* ***Fam*** brother <NE> **b.** Bos *col* ***Fam*** friend (male) <NE[*1]>

burázeru {excl.} (lit. my brother) *col* ***Fam*** used to address a male in direct informal communication, yo, my brother, my friend <NE[*1]> ☞ **burazere, brate**

bùrdelj {a masc.} (lit. bordello) *sl-crime* ***Fac*** prison <Ita[*1]>

bȕre {eta neut.} (lit. barrel) *sl* ***Fac*** home <Slav[*1]>

bùrgija {ē fem.} (lit. drill *tool*) **1** *sl-sex* ***Fac-Obs*** penis, dick, prick , drill <NE[*1]> **2** *col* joke: *burgija o Bosancima Bosnian joke* <NE[*1]>

burgìjati {ām, ajū imperf.} (lit. drill) *sl-sex* engage in sexual intercourse with (of a male), drill <NE[*1]>

bùrljati {ām, ajū imperf.} *sl-fea* talk persistently and meaninglessly, blabber, chatter

burmànisati se {išēm, išū aiv+v} (lit. put a 'burma' /wedding ring) on) *sl* ***Fac*** get married, get hitched <NE❖[*1]>

bȕrza {ē fem.} *sl-drink* ***Fac*** bar (drinking place) <Ita[*1]>

bùržūj {buržúja (acc. = gen.) masc.} (lit. bourgeois) *sl* ***Der*** affluent male, moneybags <Fre[*1]>

buržùjčina {ē masc.} (lit. big bourgeois) *sl* ***Der*** very affluent male <Fre[*1]>

bȕs {a +ev (ext. pl) masc.; Nom Pl bùsevi} *col* bus <Eng>

bùsanja {ē fem.} *sl* bus <Eng✍>

bȕsēn {sena (acc. = gen.) masc.} (lit. turf, sod) *sl-fea* hairy male, hairy ape <Slav[*1]>

busogrȕdadžija {ē masc.} (lit. boaster) *sl-fea* stupid or mentally deficient person <Slav❖[*1]>

búša {ē fem.} *sl* stomach, belly, gut <Slav>

búšan {šna, šno adj.} **a.** *col* flat (e.g. tire) <Slav> **b.** *sl* clumsy, klutzy: *bušan fudbaler klutzy soccer player* <Slav[*1]>

bȗšnī {ōg (acc. = gen.) masc.} (lit. the one with a hole in it) *sl-sports* incompetent goalie (soccer, etc.) <Slav[*1]>

bùšotina {ē fem.} (lit. bore hole) *sl-sex* ***Der-Obs*** loose woman, slut <Slav[*1]>

bȕštra {ē fem.} *sl* Bosnian Muslim (female) <Slav[*1]>

bùštura {ē fem.} *sl* Bosnian Muslim (female) <Slav[*1]>

bùšturica {ē fem.} *sl* young Bosnian Muslim (female) <Slav[*1]>

bȕt {a +ov (ext. pl) masc.; Nom Pl bùtevi} (lit. thigh) **1** *sl* bundle of money <Slav[*1]> **2** *sl-sex* leg (human) <Slav[*1]>

bȕta {ē fem.} *sl-sex* ***Obs*** buttocks, butt <Slav[*1]>

bùtelja {ē fem.} Med *col* bottle <Ita>

bùter {a masc.} /bȕter/ (lit. butter) *sl-sex* ***App*** attractive female <Ger[*1]>

bùtevi {tēvā masc. pl.} (lit. thighs) *sl-sex* attractive legs (of a female) <Slav[*1]>

bùtīga {ē fem.; Dat bùtīgi} Med *col* store <Ita>

bȕtka {ē fem.; Dat bȕtki} *sl* thigh <Slav[*1]>

bȕtnuti {nēm, nū perf.} /bȕtnuti/ (lit. thigh) *sl-sex* ***Obs*** engage in sexual intercourse with (of a male) <Slav[*1]>

• **Bȕtnēm ti ga!** {S} (lit. I thigh it to you!) SSer *dia* ***Off*** used as a moderate curse or threat, Up yours!

bȕtra {ē fem.; perm} [std. = treba] *sl* female

bȗu {excl.} *col* used to scare one's interlocutor, boo <Slav>

bùva {ē fem.} (lit. flea) **a.** Ser *col* lie: *To da on ima dobre ocene je buva. That he has good grades is a lie.* <Slav[*1]> **b.** Ser *col* false information, rumor: *Pustio je buvu da je opljačkana banka. He was spreading rumors that the bank has been robbed.* <Slav[*1]> **c.** Ser *col* joke <Slav[*1]>

• **kȕćnā bùva** {NP} (lit. house flea) Ser *sl* housekeeper, maid

bùvara {ē fem.} (lit. flea place) **1** Ser *col* prison <Slav[*1]> **2** Ser *sl* movie house, theater <Slav[*1]>

buvárēnje {a neut.} (lit. acting like a flea) **1** Ser *sl* kissing: *buvarenje u parku kissing in the park* <Slav[*1]>

2 Ser *sl-fea* prolonged and meaningless talk, blabber, chatter: *buvarenje o stripovima blabber about comic books* <**Slav**[*1]>

buváriti {bùvārīm, rē imperf.} (lit. act like a flea) **1** Ser *sl-fea* ***Der*** talk persistently and meaninglessly, blabber, chatter <**Slav**[*1]> **2** Ser *sl* spread new slang words: *On je mnogo buvario na žurci. He spread many new slang words at the party.* <**Slav**[*1]>

bùvātor {a (acc. = gen.) masc.} Ser *sl-fea* liar <**Slav**[*1]>

bùvljā pìjaca {NP} (lit. flea market) *sl-sstu* ***Fac*** high-school students on break between classes ☞ pijaca

bùvljāk {buvljáka masc.} *col* flea market <**Slav**[*1]>

bȕvos {a (acc. = gen.) masc.} Ser *sl* flea (the insect) <**Slav**☝>

buvoskùpljāč {kupljáča (acc. = gen.) masc.} (lit. flea collector) Ser *sl* dog, flea bag <**Slav**⁘[*1]>

bûz {a +ov (ext. pl) masc.; Nom Pl búzovi} *sl-drink* alcoholic beverage <**Eng**>

búzda {ē fem. & masc.} (lit. mace) **1** *sl-fea* ***Der*** stupid or mentally deficient person <**NE**☝[*1]> **2** *sl-sex* attractive female <**NE**☝[*1]>

buzdòhān[1] {dohána (acc. = gen.) masc.} (lit. mace) BosM *col* ***Der*** stupid or mentally deficient person <**NE**[*1]>

buzdòhān[2] {dohána masc.} [std. = buzdovan] BosM *col* mace (medieval weapon) <**NE**☝>

buzdòvān[1] {dována (acc. = gen.) masc.} (lit. mace) *sl-fea* ***Der*** stupid or mentally deficient person <**NE**[*1]>

buzdòvān[2] {dována masc.} (lit. mace) *sl-sex* ***Fac-Obs*** penis, dick, prick <**NE**[*1]>

bȕzer {a (acc. = gen.) masc.} *sl-sex* ***Off*** male homosexual who takes the passive role, femme <**Ita**[*1]>

buzerȁnt {a (acc. = gen.) masc.} /buzèrant/ *sl-sex* ***Off*** male homosexual who takes the passive role, femme <**Ita**[*1]>

bȕzić {a (acc. = gen.) masc.} *sl-sex* ***Off*** male homosexual, gay <**Ita**[*1]>

bùzićār {a (acc. = gen.) masc.} *sl-sex* ***Off*** male homosexual, gay <**Ita**⁘[*1]>

buzorȁnt {a (acc. = gen.) masc.} /buzòrant/ *sl-sex* ***Off*** male homosexual, gay <**Ita**⁘[*1]>

buzurȁnt {a (acc. = gen.) masc.} /buzùrant/ *sl-sex* ***Off*** male homosexual, gay <**Ita**⁘[*1]>

bzȉkati {ām, ajū imperf.} *col* buzz (usu. of flies) <**Slav**>

Cc

cáca {ē fem.} *sl* female <**Slav**[*1]>

càcoriti {rīm, rē imperf.} (lit. cock-a-doodle-do) *sl-fea* ***Der*** talk persistently and meaninglessly, blabber, chatter <**Slav**[*1]>

cȁfa {cȇfa fem.; perm} //e fem./ *sl* face (human) <**Ita**☝>

càfuta {ē fem.} **1** *sl-sex* prostitute, hooker <**Ita**[*1]> **2** *sl* trick, prank <**Ita**[*1]>

cáger {a masc.} *sl-crafts* indicator (on a machine, gadget, etc.) <**Ger**>

càglja {ē fem.} *dia* linen bag <**Slav**>

cája {ē masc.} *sl-crime* policeman, cop <**Gre**☝>

cájac {jca (acc. = gen.) masc.} *sl-crime* policeman, cop <**Gre**☝>

câjka {ē fem.; Dat câjki} **1** *sl-crime* policeman, cop <**Gre**☝⁘> **2** *sl* female <**Slav**⁘[*1]>

càjkan {a (acc. = gen.) masc.} *sl-crime* policeman, cop <**Gre**☝⁘>

cȁjkoš {a (acc. = gen.) masc.} *sl-crime* policeman, cop <**Gre**☝⁘>

cájo {ē masc.} /cájo /a masc./ *sl-crime* policeman, cop <**Gre**☝>

càjper {a masc.} **1** *sl-sstu* poke, prod, or pinch on the buttocks, goose <**Ger**[*1]> **2** *sl-sstu* failing grade <**Ger**[*1]>

cȁjt {a +ov (ext. pl) masc.; Nom Pl càjtovi} *col* time (in general): *Sad nemam cajta za ćaskanje. I don't have time for small talk now.* <**Ger**>

càjtnot {a masc.} *col* lack of time <**Ger**>

cȁk {excl.} /cȁka excl./ *col* the sound made by metal objects, clang <**Slav**>

cȁk-cȁk {excl.} /cȁka excl./ **1** *col* the repeated sound made by metal objects, clang-clang <**Slav**> **2** *col* the sound made by a clock, tick-tock <**Slav**>

cáka {ē fem.; Dat cáki} **a.** *col* trick, joke <**Ger**> **b.** *col* solution, answer to the problem: *U čemu je caka? What's the solution?* <**Ger**[*2]>

cȁka-cȁka {excl.} *col* the repeated sound made by metal objects, clang-clang <**Slav**>

càkan {a, o adj.} *col* handsome, cute <**Slav**[*1]>

càkāroš {a (acc. = gen.) masc.} *sl-fea* joke teller <Ger❖[*1]>

cȁkat {a masc.} *col* ping (sharp metal sound) <Slav>

càkliti se {līm, lē imperf. intr.} /cȁkliti se/ *col* shine (reflect light) <Slav>

càklo {a neut.} *col-dia* glass (in general) <Slav>

cȁknuti [1] {nēm, nū perf.} *col* kick, strike: *caknuti fudbal kick a soccer ball* <Slav❖>

cȁknuti [2] {nēm, nū perf. intr.} *col* ping (produce a sharp metal sound) <Slav❖>

cȁkum-pȁkum {adj.} *col* very tidy, tip-top: *Kuća joj je cakum-pakum. Her house is very tidy.* <Ger✍>

cȁkūnt {a, o adj.} *col* ***App*** excellent, awesome <Ger✍[*1]>

cálac {lca (acc. = gen.) masc.} *sl-fea* inhabitant of the countryside, hick, bumpkin <Slav[*1]>

calapȑdati {ām, ajū imperf.} *sl-fea* talk persistently and meaninglessly, blabber, chatter <Slav[*1]>

cȁlnuti {nēm, nū perf.} *sl* pay (bills, etc.): *calnuti tri milje za kola pay three thousand dollars for a car* <Ger❖>

càltati {ām, ajū biasp.} *sl* pay (bills, etc.): *caltati za struju pay one's electricity bill* <Ger❖>

cȁn {excl.} *col* the sound made by a small bell, ding <Slav>

cȁn-cȁn {excl.} *col* the repeated sound made by a small bell, ding-ding <Slav>

cána {ē fem.} **a.** *sl-sex* ***Obs*** vagina, cunt <Slav[*1]> **b.** *sl* ***Obs*** female, cunt <Slav[*2]>

cangàrānje {a neut.} *col* ringing (bell, etc.) <Slav❖>

cangàrati {ām, ajū imperf.} *col* ring (a bell, etc.) <Slav❖>

cánge {ī fem. pl.} *sl-crafts* pliers <Ger>

cángle {ī fem. pl.} *sl-crafts* pliers <Ger✍>

cánta {ē fem.} **a.** *sl* leather bag <Slav[*1]> **b.** *sl-sex* ***Obs*** vagina, cunt <Slav[*2]>

cȁnjati {ām, ajū imperf.} *sl* have, possess: *canjati auto have a car* <Slav[*1]>

cȁnjati se {ām, ajū imperf. intr.} *sl* behave: *Dobro se canjajte, djeco! Children, behave!* <Slav[*1]>

cȁnjkati {ām, ajū imperf.} *col* ring (a bell, etc.) <Slav>

cȁp {excl.} *col* the sound made by taking away, snatch <Slav>

cȁpi {cȇpi fem.; perm} /càpi/ [std. = pica] **a.** *sl-sex* ***Obs*** vagina, cunt <Slav✍> **b.** *sl* ***Obs*** female, cunt <Slav✍[*1]>

cȁpka {ē fem.; Dat cȁpki} *sl-sex* leg (of a female) <Slav[*1]>

cȁpkānje {a neut.} *col* taking away, snatching <Slav❖>

cȁpkati {ām, ajū imperf.} *col* drip <Slav❖>

cȁpnuti [1] {nēm, nū perf.} *sl-crime* steal, swipe <Slav❖>

cȁpnuti [2] {nēm, nū perf. intr.} **1** *sl* ***Fac*** die, kick the bucket <Slav❖[*1]> **2** *col* drip <Slav❖[*1]>

cȁr {càra (acc. = gen.) +ev (ext. pl) masc.; Nom Pl càrevi} (lit. emperor) **1** *col* friend (male) <Lat[*1]> **2** *col* good and loved male, nice guy <Lat[*1]>

cára {ē fem.} [std. = čarapa] *sl* sock, stocking <NE✍>

cârda {ē fem.} **a.** *sl* home <Hun✍[*1]> **b.** *sl-drink* bar (drinking place): *carda za kamiondžije trucker's bar* <Hun✍[*1]>

cȁre {excl.} (lit. my czar) *col* ***Fam*** used to address a male in direct informal communication, my man <Lat[*1]>

cȁrica {ē fem.} (lit. Czarina) *col* nice woman, friendly female <Lat[*1]>

cârka {ē fem.; Dat cárki} *sl-gamble* gambling <Slav>

cáva {ē fem. & masc.} **1a.** *sl-fea* inhabitant of the countryside, hick, bumpkin <Slav[*1]> **b.** *sl-fea* naive male: *Onom cavi svako može da digne lovu. Anybody can take money from that rube.* <Slav[*2]> **2a.** *sl-fea* attractive female <Slav[*1]> **b.** *sl* loose woman <Slav[*2]> **c.** *sl* female <Slav[*3]>

cȅc {excl.} *col* the sound made by a small explosion, bang <Slav>

cȅca {ē fem.} *sl-sex* ***Obs*** female breast, tit <Ger✍>

cècil {a masc.} *sl-drink* mark on a shot glass showing one deciliter <Lat[*1]>

cedíliti {cèdīlīm, lē imperf.} *sl-drink* drink (alcohol) <Lat[*1]>

céditi {cêdīm, dē perf.} (lit. squeeze) SerE *sl-fea* annoy, bother, pester <Slav[*1]>

cȅdulja {ē fem.} /cèdulja/ **a.** *col* piece of paper, scrap of paper <Ita> **b.** *col* document (in general) <Ita[*1]>

cedùljče {eta neut.} *col* small piece of paper <Ita[*1]>

cêđ {i fem.} SerE *sl-fea* ***Der*** boring person, bore <Slav[*1]>

céger {a masc.} *col* shopping bag <Ger>

cȅglja {ē fem.} *sl* wrapper, bag <Ger✍>

cȅhmâjstor {a (acc. = gen.) masc.} *col* person who pays the check in a restaurant, host <Ger❖>

cèhulja {ē fem.} *sl* female who abuses males <Ger❖[*1]>

céja {ē fem.} [std. = centar] *sl* downtown <Lat✍>

cȅker {a masc.} *col* shopping bag <Ger>

cëker bâr {NP} (lit. shopping-bag bar) Cro *sl Fac* name of a bar near a market place in Zagreb, Croatia ☞ bar

cëler {a masc.} *sl-crafts* odometer (or any other counter on a mechanism) <Ger>

celívati {cèlīvām, celívajū perf.} (lit. kiss) **SerE** *sl Iro* hit, punch: *Neki pijanac celiva ljude na ulici. Some drunk is hitting people on the street.* <Slav[*1]>

cêlka {ē fem.; Dat cêlki} (lit. the whole one) SerE *sl-sex Fac* virgin <Slav[*1]>

cëlorouk {a (acc. = gen.) masc.} *sl-fea* slender female <Slav✐[*1]>

cëlrouk {a (acc. = gen.) masc.} *sl-fea* slender female <Slav✐[*1]>

cèment [1] {a (acc. = gen.) masc.} (lit. cement) *sl-fea Der* stupid or mentally deficient person <Lat[*1]>

cèment [2] {a masc.} (lit. cement) **1** *sl-drugs* Centedrine <Lat[*1]> **2** mashed potatoes <Lat[*1]>

cementírati {mèntīrām, mentírajū biasp.} (lit. cement) *sl* stand still <Lat✣[*1]>

cêndrati {ām, ajū biasp.} *col Der* cry, shed tears, weep <Slav[*1]>

céner {a masc.} **a.** *col* ten <Ger> **b.** *col* ten units (of any currency) <Ger[*1]> **c.** *col* one hundred dinars; a hundred-dinar bill <Ger[*2]>

céniti {cênīm, nē imperf.} (lit. appreciate) **a. SerE** *col* appreciate, enjoy, like: *ceniti dobru knjigu like good literature* <Slav[*1]> **b.** SerE *col* estimate, guess: *Cenim da si autentični srpski rodoljub. I assume you're a real Serbian patriot.* ◊ *Cenimo da će nas to koštati dvadeset hiljada maraka. We estimate the costs at twenty thousand German marks.* <Slav[*1]>

cênrād {a masc.} *sl-crafts* cogwheel <Ger>

cënt [1] {a (acc. = gen.) +ov (ext. pl) masc.; Nom Pl cèntovi} *sl* pickpocket who has been caught <Lat[*1]>

cënt [2] {a masc.} *sl-drugs* Centedrine <Lat[*1]>

cèntipleh {a masc.} *sl-crafts* gap measuring plates <Ger>

centírati {cèntīrām, centírajū biasp.} *sl-crime* notice a pickpocket at work <Lat✣[*1]>

centrála {ē fem.} (lit. the headquarters) **a.** *sl-sex Fac* buttocks, butt <Lat[*1]> **b.** *sl-sex Fac* anus <Lat[*2]>

Cëp {a +ov (ext. pl) masc.; Nom Pl Cèpovi} Ser *sl* name for Cepelin discotheque (in Belgrade, Serbia) <GerO✐[*1]>

cépāljka {ē fem.} (lit. chopper) SerE *sl-sex* prostitute, hooker <Slav[*1]>

cêpān {a, o adj.} (lit. chopped) SerE *sl-drink* drunk, hammered, smashed <Slav[*1]>

cepànica {ē fem.} (lit. log) **a. SerE** *sl-fea Der* stupid or mentally deficient person <Slav[*1]> **b. SerE** *sl-drink Der* alcoholic, drunk <Slav[*2]>

cépānje {a neut.} (lit. chopping) **1 SerE** *sl-crime* court session <Slav[*1]> **2 SerE** *sl-sex* sexual intercourse <Slav[*1]> **3** SerE *sl-drink* drinking (alcohol) <Slav[*1]>

cèpārnica {ē fem.} (lit. chopping place) **1 SerE** *sl-sex* brothel, whorehouse <Slav[*1]> **2 SerE** *sl-drink* bar (drinking place) <Slav[*1]>

cèpārnīk {a masc.} (lit. chopping place) SerE *sl-crime Fac* court of law <Slav[*1]>

cèpāroš {a (acc. = gen.) masc.} (lit. chopper) SerE *sl-sports Fac* aggressive soccer player <Slav[*1]>

cépati {cêpām, cépajū imperf.} (lit. chop) **1** SerE *sl* work <Slav[*1]> **2** SerE *sl-drink* drink (alcohol) <Slav[*1]>

- **cépati cirádu** {VP} (lit. cut the tarpaulin) **1 SerE** *sl-fea Fac* talk persistently and meaninglessly, blabber, chatter **2** SerE *sl-fea Fac* spend one's time in useless activities, fool around, mess around
- **cépati ìglu** {VP} (lit. cut the needle) **SerE** *sl-drugs Fac* take narcotic drugs intravenously, mainline, shoot up
- **cépati kao lûd** {VP} (lit. cut like crazy) SerE *sl-stu Fac* do well on an exam
- **Kòliko cêpāš?** {S} (lit. How much do you cut?) **SerE** *sl* used in bargaining (e.g. in a market, bazaar, etc.), How much?

cépati se {cêpām, cépajū imperf. intr.} (lit. chop oneself) **1 SerE** *sl-sex* fight (e.g. fist fight): *Dve bande se cepaju iza ćoška. Two gangs are fighting around the corner.* <Slav[*1]> **2** SerE *sl-sex Obs* engage in sexual intercourse <Slav[*1]>

- **cépati se ko šìfōnskē gàće** {VP} (lit. tear apart like a pair of chiffon panties) **SerE** *sl Fac* find something highly humorous
- **cépati se u venu** {VP} (lit. cut oneself in the vein) **SerE** *sl-drugs* take narcotic drugs intravenously, mainline, shoot up

cepáža {ē fem.} (lit. chopping) **1** SerE *sl* fight (e.g. fist fight) <Slav[*1]> **2** SerE *sl-music* rock music <Slav[*1]>

cëpēt {a masc.} *col* chattering (of the teeth, when feeling cold) <Slav>

cèpidlačkī {ā, ō adj.} /cepìdljačkī/ SerE *col* hairsplitting, nitpicking <Slav>

cèpidlaka {ē fem.; Dat cèpidlaki} /cepìdlaka/ SerE *col* hairsplitter, nit picker <Slav>

cépiti {cêpīm, pē imperf.} (lit. immunize) *sl-drink* ***Fac*** drink (alcohol) <Slav*1>

cȅpnuti {nēm, nū perf.} (lit. chop) **1 SerE** *sl-sex* ***Obs*** engage in sexual intercourse with (of a male) <Slav*1> **2** *sl* overcharge, rip off <Slav*1>

cepodȉpāč {a (acc. = gen.) masc.} SerE *sl* ***Fac*** supervisor (on public transportation) <Slav❖*1>

cèpteti {tīm, tē imperf. intr.} **SerE** *col* shake (usu. in outrage), boil: *Cepteo je kad je čuo da neće dobiti povišicu. He boiled when he heard that he won't get a raise.* <Slav>

cèpulja {ē fem.} (lit. chopper) SerE *sl-sex* ***Fac*** prostitute, hooker <Slav*1>

cepùrija {ē fem.} (lit. chopping) **SerE** *col* ridiculous thing, absurd event: *To što se desilo u Skupštini je najobičnija cepurija. What happened in Parliament was really an absurd event.* <Slav❖*1>

cêr {a +ev (ext. pl) masc.; Nom Pl cérevi} /cêr /a +ov (ext. pl) masc/ *sl* grin <Slav>

ceráda {ē fem.} *col* tarpaulin <Ita>

cȅrēk {a masc.} *col* loud laugh <Slav>

cerèkānje {a neut.} *col* loud laughing <Slav>

cerèkati se {ām, ajū imperf. intr.} **a.** *col* grin <Slav> **b.** *col* laugh aloud <Slav>

cȅstār {a (acc. = gen.) masc.} (lit. road worker) *sl-fea* troublemaker, rowdy, ruffian <Slav*1>

cȅstolīz {a (acc. = gen.) masc.} (lit. road licker) *sl* ***Fac*** street cleaner, street sweeper <Slav❖*1>

cêvčēnje {a neut.} (lit. working with a tube) **a. SerE** *sl-drink* drinking (alcohol) <Slav*1> **b. SerE** *sl-drink* sipping (alcohol) <Slav*2>

cêvčiti {čīm, čē imperf. intr.} (lit. work with a tube) SerE *sl-drink* drink (alcohol) <Slav*1>

cêvka {ē fem.; Dat cêvki} (lit. small tube) **1** SerE *sl-crime* rifle <Slav*1> **2** SerE *sl-sex* ***Fac*** virgin <Slav*1>

cevrljúgnuti {vȑljūgnēm, nū perf.} *sl-sex* ***Obs*** engage in sexual intercourse with (of a male) <Slav>

Cȅzār {a masc.} /Cêzar/ (lit. Caesar X centralni zatvor 'central prison') *sl-crime* central prison <Lat*1>

cȉ {excl.} *col* the sound made by a small bird, tweet <Slav>

cȉbati {ām, ajū imperf.; perm} [std. = bacati] *sl* throw away, toss out <Slav✍>

cȉbos {a (acc. = gen.) masc.} *sl-sports* player or fan of Cibona (a basketball team from Zagreb, Croatia) <BN✍>

Cȉbosi {bōsā masc. pl.} *sl-sports* players for Cibona (a basketball team from Zagreb, Croatia) <BN✍>

cȉc {excl.} *col* used to lure a cat <Slav>

cȉc-mȉc {neut.} *col* hesitation: *Nemoj ti cic-mic, nego počni da radiš! Start working without any further hesitation!* <Slav>

cȉca {ē fem.} /cíca/ **a.** *sl-sex* ***Obs*** female breast, tit <Ger> **b.** *sl* ***Obs*** female <Ger*1>

cícānje {a neut.} **1** *sl-drink* drinking (alcohol) <Slav*1> **2** *col* tuning, adjusting, fixing <Slav*1>

cícati {cîcām, cícajū imperf.} **1** *sl-drink* drink (alcohol): *cicati konjak drink cognac* <Slav*1> **2** *col* tune, adjust, fix: *cicati radio stanicu tune to a radio station* <Slav*1>

cìcija {ē fem.} *col* ***Der*** miser, tightwad, skinflint <NE>

cicìjāš {cijáša (acc. = gen.) masc.} *col* ***Der*** miser, tightwad, skinflint <NE❖>

cicijášiti {cìjāšīm, šē imperf.} *col* ***Der*** be miserly, be a tightwad, be a skinflint <NE❖>

cȉcko {a masc.} *sl-fea* ***Der*** coward, chicken <Ger❖*1>

cìncȅker {a masc.} (lit. tit bag) *sl-sex* ***Fac*** bra <Ger❖>

cìcntréger {a masc.} (lit. tit carrier) *sl-sex* ***Fac*** bra <Ger❖>

cȉcoš {a (acc. = gen.) masc.} *sl-fea* ***Der*** miser, tightwad, skinflint <NE✍>

cìculja {ē masc.} *sl-fea* ***Der*** miser, tightwad, skinflint <NE✍>

cȉcvara {ē fem.} *col* a kind of mush made of cheese, fat and corn flour <Slav>

• **Cȉcvaru ti dètīnju!** {S} (lit. *I screw* your kid's mush!) SerE *dia* ***Off*** used as a weak threat, Screw you!

• **Cȉcvaru ti jèbēm!** {S} (lit. I screw your mush!) *dia* ***Off*** used as a weak threat, Screw you!

cìcvariti {rīm, rē imperf.} *col-dia* waste one's time on unimportant things, fool or mess around: *Neka banda se cicvari ispred pozorišta. Some punks are just fooling around in front of the theater.* <Slav❖>

Cȉcvaru ti dètīnju! {S} (lit. *I fuck* your kid's mush!) SerE *dia* ***Off*** used as a mild threat, Fuck you! ☞ **cicvara**

Cicvaru ti jebem! {S} (lit. *I fuck* your mush made of cheese, fat and corn flour!) *dia* ***Off*** used as a mild threat, Fuck you! ☞ **cicvara**

cìčati {čīm, čē imperf.} /cíčati/ **a.** *col* scream in pain, fear, or outrage <Slav> **b.** *col* beep (alarm, etc.) <Slav*1>

cìčiti {čīm, čē imperf.} /cíčiti/ **a.** *col* scream in pain, fear, or outrage <Slav> **b.** *col* beep (alarm, etc.) <Slav[*1]>

cìferblat {a masc.} (lit. dial:- on a watch or clock) *sl* face (human) <Ger[*1]>

cìferšlus {a (acc. = gen.) masc.} (lit. zipper) *sl-sex* ***Fac*** virgin <Ger[*1]>

cifilìnder {a masc.} *sl-sex* syphilis, the pox <Lat✍>

cȉfra {ō fem.} (lit. digit) *sl* money <NE[*1]>

cíga {ē masc.; Dat cígi} SerE *col* ***Off*** Gypsy (male) <Slav✍>

cȉganin {a (acc. = gen.) -in (rd. pl.) masc.} (lit. Gypsy) **1** *sl-sports* ***Off*** fan of Crvena Zvezda (a soccer team in Belgrade, Serbia) <Slav[*1]> **2** *sl-fea* ***Off*** dirty and untidy person, slob, pig <Slav[*1]>

cigára {ē fem.} (lit. cigar) **a.** *col* cigarette, smoke <Spa[*1]> **b.** *sl-sex* ***Fac-Obs*** penis, dick, prick <Spa[*1]>

cigarèta {ē fem.} (lit. cigarette) *sl-sex* ***Fac*** boy's penis <Spa>

• **čȅškē cigarète** {NP} (lit. Czech cigarettes X češati se 'scratch', 'get for free from others') *sl* ***Fac*** cigarettes obtained from others, bummed cigarettes

cigarȉlos {a masc.} (lit. cigarillos) *sl* cigarette, smoke <Spa>

cigàršpic {a masc.} *col* cigarette holder <Spa-Ger>

cígla {ē fem.} (lit. brick) **a.** *sl* ten thousand dinars; a ten-thousand dinar bill <Ger[*1]> **b.** *sl* million dinars or units of any other currency; a million-dinar bill <Ger[*2]>

ciglírati {ām, ajū biasp.} (lit. brick) *sl* hit, punch: *ciglirati u facu hit in the face* <Ger⁘[*1]>

cȉglja {ē fem.} *sl* bread <Ger[*1]>

cígo {ē masc.} *col* ***Off*** Gypsy (male) <Slav>

cigòjner {a (acc. = gen.) masc.} *sl-fea* ***Off*** Gypsy (male) <Ger>

cȉgos {a masc.} *sl* cigarette, smoke <Spa✍>

cȋgoš {a (acc. = gen.) masc.} *sl-fea* ***Off*** Gypsy (male) <Slav✍>

cigùljati {ām, ajū imperf.} *sl-fea* ***Der*** talk persistently and meaninglessly, blabber, chatter <Slav[*1]>

cȉh {excl.} *col* the sound made by sneezing, achoo <Slav>

cȉhā {excl.} *col* the sound made by sneezing, achoo <Slav>

cȉja {ē fem.} (lit. *poli*cija 'police' X cija 'CIA') **1** *sl-crime* the police <Eng[*1]> **2** *sl-crime* spy, spook <Eng[*1]>

cȉjēv *See the following*

• **tòpovskā cȉjēv** {NP} (lit. cannon barrel) *sl-sex* ***Fac-Obs*** anus, asshole

cȉjēvi {cijévī fem. pl.} (lit. tubes) *sl* trousers, pants <Slav>

cȉju {excl.} *col* the sound made by a small bird, tweet <Slav>

cȉjūk {a masc.} *col* the sound made by a small bird, tweet <Slav>

cijùkānje {a neut.} **a.** *col* the sound made by a small bird, tweet <Slav> **b.** *col* screaming in pain, fear, or outrage <Slav[*1]>

cijùkati {ām, ajū imperf.} **a.** *col* tweet, produce the sound of a small bird <Slav> **b.** *col* scream in pain, fear, or outrage <Slav[*1]>

cijùkav {a, o adj.} *col* tweety (sound made by a small bird) <Slav>

cȉk [1] {excl.} *col* the sound made by a small bird, tweet <Slav>

cȋk [2] {a +ov (ext. pl) masc.; Nom Pl cíkovi} **a.** *col* the sound made by a small bird, tweet <Slav> **b.** scream in pain, fear, or outrage <Slav[*1]>

cȉka {ē fem.; Dat cȉki} **1** *col* louse (the insect) <Slav> **2a.** *col* the sound made by a small bird, tweet <Slav> **b.** *col* screaming in pain, fear, or outrage <Slav[*1]>

cȉkālj {a masc.} *col-dia* burr, burdock <Slav⁘[*1]>

cíkati {cȋčēm, cȋču imperf.} *col* scream in pain, fear, or outrage <Slav>

cȉkav {a, o adj.} **a.** *col* the sound made by a small bird, tweet <Slav> **b.** *col* screaming in pain, fear, or outrage <Slav>

cȉkavica {ē fem.} *col* robin <Slav>

cikètān {ciketána (acc. = gen.) masc.} **a.** *sl-fea* average male: *On je običan ciketan, ne treba ga slušati. He is just an average man, you don't have to listen to him.* <Slav[*1]> **b.** *sl-fea* boring male, bore <Slav[*2]>

cȉkica {ē fem.} *sl-sex* female breast <Ger⁘>

cȉkić {a masc.} *sl-fea* tidy and orderly male, neatnik <Slav[*1]>

cikìljav {a, o adj.} **a.** *col* tweety (sound made by a small bird) <Slav> **b.** *col* squeaking <Slav[*1]>

cȉkla {ē fem.} (lit. red beets) *sl-sex* ***Fac*** menstruation, period <Slav[*1]>

cìkljevina {ē fem.} **a.** *col* the sound made by a small bird, tweet <Slav> **b.** *col* scream in pain, fear, or outrage <Slav[*1]>

cîknūt {a, o adj.} **a.** *sl* half-dead <Slav> **b.** *sl-fea* ill, sick <Slav[*1]>

cíknuti {cîknēm, nū perf. intr.} **a.** *col* scream in pain, fear, or outrage <Slav[*1]> **b.** *sl* die, kick the bucket <Slav[*2]>

cȉkot {a masc.} *col* noise <Slav>

cȉktāj {a masc.} **a.** *col* squeak <Slav> **b.** *col* scream in pain, fear, or outrage <Slav[*1]>

cìktānje {a neut.} **a.** *col* screaming in pain, fear, or outrage <Slav> **b.** *col* noise <Slav[*1]>

cȉkūt {a masc.} *col* sharp sound (e.g. of a steam whistle) <Slav>

cîle *See the following*

• **cîle mîle** {NP} *col* being soft, abstaining from enforcing discipline or principles: *Nemoj ti s njim cile mile, nego mu naredi da iznese đubre. Don't be soft on him, just tell him to take the garbage out.*

cîle-mîle {adv.} *col* softly: *Nemoj ti s njim cile-mile, nego mu naredi da to uradi! Don't go softly on him, just tell him to do it!* <Slav❖>

cilemilezírānje {a neut.} *sl* ***Der*** ingratiate, brownnose, kiss ass <Slav❖[*1]>

cilemilezírati {lèzīrām, lezírajū imperf. intr.} *sl* ***Der*** ingratiate, brownnose, kiss ass <Slav❖[*1]>

cilemizírānje {a neut.} *sl* ***Der*** ingratiate, brownnose, kiss ass <Slav❖>

cȉlīk {a masc.} **a.** *col* screaming in pain, fear, or outrage <Slav> **b.** *col* beeping (alarm, etc.) <Slav[*1]>

cilíkānje {a neut.} **a.** *col* screaming in pain, fear, or outrage <Slav> **b.** *col* beeping (alarm, etc.) <Slav[*1]>

cilíkati {ām, ajū imperf. intr.} /cìlīčēm, čū imperf. intr./ **a.** *col* scream in pain, fear, or outrage <Slav> **b.** *col* beep (alarm, etc.) <Slav[*1]>

cilìnkānje {a neut.} **a.** *col* screaming in pain, fear, or outrage <Slav> **b.** *col* beeping (alarm, etc.) <Slav[*1]>

cilìnkati {ām, ajū imperf. intr.} **a.** *col* scream in pain, fear, or outrage <Slav> **b.** *col* beep (alarm, etc.) <Slav[*1]>

cîljka {ē fem.; Dat cíljki} *sl* eye (sight organ) <Slav❖[*1]>

cȉmāj {excl.} (lit. pull) *sl* used to make somebody go away, beat it <Ita[*1]>

cȉmati {ām, ajū imperf.} **a.** *col* pull, tug <Ita> **b.i.** *sl-drink* drink (alcohol) <Ita[*1]> **ii.** *sl-fea* bother, disturb <Ita[*1]>

• **cȉmati pljúgu** {VP} (lit. keep pulling a cigarette) *sl* smoke (tobacco)

cìmenat {nta masc.} [std. = cement] *col* cement <Lat☞>

cìment {nta masc.} [std. = cement] *col* cement <Lat☞>

cȉmēnta {ē fem.} [std. = cement] *col* cement <Lat☞>

cȉmer {a (acc. = gen.) masc.} /címer, cìmer /a (acc. = gen.) masc./ *col* roommate (male) <Ger☞>

cȉmērka {ē fem.; Dat cìmērki} /címerka, cìmerka /e fem./ *col* roommate (female) <Ger☞>

cȉmnuti {nēm, nū imperf.} *sl-drink* drink (alcohol) <Ita[*1]>

cȉn {excl.} **1** *col* the sound made by a small bell, ding <Slav> **2** *col* the sound made by a small bird, tweet <Slav>

cȉn-cȁn {excl.} **1** *col* the repeated sound made by a small bell, ding-ding <Slav> **2** *col* the sound made by a small bird, tweet <Slav>

cincàkati {ām, ajū imperf. intr.} *col* ring (a bell, etc.) <Slav❖>

cȉncarin {a (acc. = gen.) -in (rd. pl.) masc.} *sl-fea* ***Der*** miser, tightwad, skinflint <SlavO[*1]>

cȉncer {a (acc. = gen.) masc.} *sl-fea* miser, tightwad, skinflint <SlavO☞[*1]>

cȉnci-lȉnci-dvójka-Dòrćol {excl.} (lit. ding dong number two, Dorćol: a neighborhood in Belgrade, Serbia) *sl* ***Off*** used to express the feeling of not being threatened by one's interlocutor <Slav>

cincìkati {ām, ajū imperf. intr.} *col* ring (a bell, etc.) <Slav>

cȉncoš {a (acc. = gen.) masc.} *col* ***Der*** miser, tightwad, skinflint <NE☞>

cinculírānje {a neut.} **1a.** *sl* making a fool of **b.** *sl* false incrimination, frame: *cinculiranje Obrada da je krao framing Obrad for stealing* **2** *sl* hesitating

cinculírati {cùlīrām, culírajū imperf. intr.} **1** *sl* spend one's time in useless activities, fool around, mess around: *cinculirati ispred bioskopa fool around in front of the movie house* **2** *sl* cheat, swindle: *Cinculirao me za cenu polovnih kola. He cheated me on the price of the used car.*

cindàrati {ām, ajū imperf. intr.} *col-dia* sing monotonously and in one voice, drone <Slav[*1]>

cìngara {ē fem.} *dia* cow bell <Gre[*1]>

cȉtba {cȉmba, cȅba perf.; perm} [std. = baciti] *sl* throw away, toss out <**Slav**✍>

cȉtra {ē fem.} *sl* louse (the insect) <**Ita**>

cìtrīrati {ām, ajū biasp.} *sl* lie <**Ita**>

cìvare {a fem. pl.} *col* litter (used on construction sites) <**Ita**>

cìvīlka {ē fem.} (lit. civilization) *sl-mil* civilian clothing one buys right before one leaves the military, civies <**Lat**⁘*1>

cìvīl {civíla (acc. = gen.) masc.} (lit. civilian) *sl-crime* undercover policeman, plainclothes cop <**Lat***1>

civilizácija {ē fem.} (lit. civilization) *sl-mil* civilian clothing one buys right before one leaves the military, civies <**Lat***1>

civìlnjāk {vilnjáka (acc. = gen.) masc.} (lit. civilian) *sl-crime* undercover policeman, plainclothes cop <**Lat***1>

cîvka {ē fem.; Dat cîvki} *sl-arch* louse (the insect) <**Slav***1>

cjéditi {cjêdīm, dē imperf.} (lit. squeeze) *sl* ***Fac*** cry, shed tears, weep <**Slav***1>

cjèpāljka {ē fem.; Dat cjèpāljki} (lit. chopper) *sl-sex* ***Fac*** prostitute, hooker <**Slav***1>

cjepànica {ē fem.} (lit. log) **a.** *sl-fea* ***Der*** stupid or mentally deficient person <**Slav***1> **b.** *sl-drink* alcoholic, drunk <**Slav***2>

cjépānje {a neut.} (lit. chopping) **a.** *sl* fight (e.g. fist fight) <**Slav***1> **a.** *sl-sports* aggressive play (e.g. in soccer) <**Slav***2>

cjèpārnik {a masc.} (lit. chopping place) *sl-crime* ***Fac*** court of law <**Slav***1>

cjèpāroš {a (acc. = gen.) masc.} (lit. chopper) *sl-sports* ***Fac*** aggressive soccer player <**Slav***1>

cjépati {ām, ajū imperf.} (lit. chop) **1** *sl* beat up <**Slav***1> **2** *sl* overcharge, rip off: *Cjepali su ga godinama u tom restoranu, ali on je stalno išao tamo. They have been ripping him off at that restaurant for years, but he keeps going there.* <**Slav***1>

cjepáža {ē fem.} (lit. chopping) **1** *sl* fight (e.g. fist fight) <**Slav***1> **2** *sl-music* loud rock music <**Slav***1>

ckȁmnā {ē fem. (adj. decl.)} *sl-arch* louse (the insect) <**Slav**>

ckȁmnī {ā, ō adj.} **a.** *sl-arch* unattractive, ugly: *ckamna koka ugly chick* <**Slav**> **b.** *sl-arch* worthless: *ckamni kompjuter worthless computer* <**Slav**>

ckȁmnī [1] {ckemni fem.; perm} *sl-crime* prison <**Slav**>

ckȁmnī [2] {ija (acc. = gen.) masc.} *sl-arch* goat (the animal) <**Slav**>

ckȁmnī ćêm {NP} *sl-arch* wolf ☞ ćem

ckȁmnjāk {a (acc. = gen.) masc.} *sl-arch* devil <**Slav**>
• **ckȁmnjāk od žáre** {NP} *sl-arch* ash (from a cigarette, etc.)

ckȉvalo {a neut.} *sl-arch* eye (sight organ) <**Slav**>

cknȕti {nēm, nū perf.} **a.** *col* bang (loud and abrupt sound) <**Slav**> **b.** *col* crush, break, squish <**Slav***1>

ckȕljān {a masc.} *sl-sex* bathroom <**Slav***1>

cmákati {cmâkām, cmákajū imperf.} // cmâčēm, čū imperf./ *col* kiss loudly and conspicuously <**Slav**>

cmákati se {cmâkām, cmákajū imperf. intr.} // cmâčēm, čū imperf. intr./ *col* kiss loudly and conspicuously <**Slav**⁘>

cmȁknuti {nēm, nū perf.} *col* kiss <**Slav**>

cmìljati {ām, ajū imperf.} *sl* ***Der*** talk persistently and meaninglessly, blabber, chatter <**Slav**⁘*1>

cmȉzdra {ē fem.} (lit. one who cries) *col* ***Der*** weak and cowardish person, crybaby <**Slav**>

cmȉzdravac {vca (acc. = gen.) masc.} (lit. one who cries) *sl-fea* weak and cowardish male, crybaby <**Slav**⁘*1>

cmȉzdravica {ē fem.} (lit. one who cries) *sl-fea* weak and cowardish female, crybaby <**Slav**⁘*1>

cmizdrávko {a (acc. = gen.) masc.} (lit. one who cries) *col* ***Der*** weak and cowardish male, crybaby <**Slav**⁘>

cmȉzdriti {rīm, rē imperf. intr.} *col* cry, shed tears, weep <**Slav**>

cmȍk [1] {excl.} *col* the sound of a loud kiss <**Slav**>

cmȍk [2] {a +ov (ext. pl) masc.; Nom Pl cmòkovi} *col* loud kiss <**Slav**>

cmòkac {kca masc.} *col* loud kiss <**Slav**>

cmókānje {a neut.} *col* kissing <**Slav**>

cmókati {cmôkām, cmókajū imperf.} *col* kiss <**Slav**>

cmȍknuti {nēm, nū perf. intr.} **1** *col* click (produce a short, sharp, non-resonant sound) <**Slav**> **2** *col* kiss <**Slav**>

cmokòtānje {a neut.} *col* kissing <**Slav**>

cmokòtati {cmòkoćem, ću imperf.} *col* kiss <**Slav**>

cmòktati {ām, ajū imperf.} *col* kiss <**Slav**>

cmólja {ē masc.} **a.** **SerE** *col* untidy male, slob: *On je takav cmolja da nikad ne čisti gajbu. He's such a slob, he never cleans his place.* <**Slav**[*1]> **b.** SerE *col* clumsy male, klutz <**Slav**[*2]> **c.** SerE *col* average male <**Slav**[*3]>

cmóljiti {cmôljīm, ljē imperf.} **1** *col* cry, shed tears, weep <**Slav**> **2** *col* kiss <**Slav**>

cȍbri {cȅbri (acc. = gen.) masc.; perm} [std. = brico] *sl* barber <**Slav**✍>

cȍca {ē fem.} *sl-sex* female sexual partner (of a male) <**Slav**[*1]>

cȍcnuti {nēm, nū perf.} **1** *sl-sstu* get a failing grade, flunk <**Slav**> **2** *sl-stu* fail an exam (flunk) <**Slav**>

cȍkiti {kīm, kē perf.} *col* kiss <**Slav**>

cȍknuti {nēm, nū perf.} **1** *col* pronounce 'ccc' to express disbelief <**Slav**> **2** *col* kiss <**Slav**> ☞ ccc

cȍkot {a masc.} *col* the sound of a clock, tick-tock <**Slav**>

còktati {cȍkćēm, ćū perf.} /cȍktati/ *col* pronounce 'ccc' to express disbelief <**Slav**> ☞ ccc

còkula {ē fem.} /cȍkula/ **a.** *col* hard-soled shoe <**Ita**> **b.** *col* shoe <**Ita**[*1]>

còlāš {colášа masc.} *sl* customs officer <**Ger**⁘>

cólati {côlām, cólajū biasp.} *sl* pay (bills, etc.) <**Ger**✍>

cȍlovati {lujēm, lujū biasp.} *sl* pay (bills, etc.) <**Ger**✍>

còlštok {a masc.} *sl-crafts* tape measure <**Ger**>

cȍprati {ām, ajū imperf.} *col* cast a spell on <**Ger**✍>

cóto {a masc.} /cóto /e masc./ *sl-fea* lame male <**Ita**>

crapàjce {i fem. pl.} *sl-arch* scissors

cȑcoljak {ljka (acc. = gen.) masc.} *col* short person <**Slav**>

cȑcvoljak {ljka (acc. = gen.) masc.} *col* short person <**Slav**>

cȑći {cȑknēm, cȑknū, ȑk, ȑk perf. irreg.} (lit. die) **a.** *col* be broken, malfunction, die: *Crko mi je televizor. My TV died.* <**Slav**[*1]> **b.** *col* be tired (from work, sports, etc.): *Baš sam završio posao i crko sam. I just finished working and I'm pooped.*

• **cȑći na ȍsećāj** {VP} (lit. die at one's feeling) **SerE** *sl-fea* ***Fac*** be careless: *Otkako je došao u Beograd, crkao je na osećaj. He is careless since he moved to Belgrade.*

• **Cȑkō dàbōgdā!** {S} (lit. I hope God makes you dead!) *col* used to express negative attitude and unfavorable wishes toward, Drop dead!

crèvār {crevára (acc. = gen.) masc.} (lit. the one with intestines) *sl-music* accordion player <**Slav**>

crèvara {ē fem.} (lit. the one with intestines) *sl-sex* ***Fac-Obs*** buttocks, butt <**Slav**>

crévce {eta neut.} (lit. small intestine) **1** **SerE** *sl-sex* ***Obs-Fac*** vagina <**Slav**[*1]> **2** **SerE** *sl-fea* ***Der*** average person <**Slav**[*1]> **3** SerE *sl-fea* ***Der*** short person <**Slav**[*1]>

• **U crévce te jèbēm!** {S} (lit. I screw you in your small intestine!) **SerE** *dia* ***Off*** used as a weak curse, Screw you!

crévo {a neut.} (lit. intestine) **a.** SerE *sl-sex* ***Obs-Fac*** penis <**Slav**> **b.** SerE *sl-sex* ***Obs-Fac*** limp penis <**Slav**>

• **U crévo te jèbēm!** {S} (lit. I screw you in your intestine!) **SerE** *dia* ***Off*** used as a weak curse, Screw you!

crevokȅnjastī {ōg (acc. = gen.) masc.} (lit. intestine-shitty) SerE *sl-fea* ***Der*** obese male <**Slav**>

crijévo {a neut.} (lit. intestine) *sl-music* ***Fac*** accordion, squeeze box <**Slav**>

cȑkaō {kla, klo adj.} (lit. died) **1** *col* broken, malfunctioning, dead: *crkao kompjuter dead computer* <**Slav**[*1]> **2** *col* very tired, dead tired <**Slav**[*1]>

crkávati {cȑkāvām, crkávajū imperf. intr.} **a.** *col* die, kick the bucket <**Slav**> **b.** *sl-gamble* lose money: *Svake noći crkavao je u kockarnici. Each night he was loosing money in gambling.* <**Slav**[*1]>

• **crkávati od glâdi** {VP} (lit. die from starvation) *col* be very hungry, be starved: *crkavati od gladi zbog nedostatka prihoda starve from the lack of income*

• **crkávati od smêha** {VP} (lit. die from laughing) SerE *col* find something highly humorous

• **crkávati ȍd smijēha** {VP} (lit. die from laughing) *col* find something highly humorous

cȑkavci {vācā masc. pl.} (lit. the dying ones) *sl* parents, old folks <**Slav**[*1]>

cȑkavica {ē fem.} **a.** *col* ***Der*** petty cash, chump change, peanuts: *Neću više da radim za ovu crkavicu. I don't want to work for chump change anymore.* <**Slav**[*1]> **b.** *col* ***Der*** low income <**Slav**[*2]>

cȑknuti {nēm, nū perf. intr.} **a.** *col* die, kick the bucket <**Slav**[*1]> **b.** *col* get tired, exhausted (from work, sports, etc.): *crknuti posle dugog radnog dana get tired after a long day at work* <**Slav**[*2]>

• **da mi cȑknē mȁčka ako lȁžēm** {S} (lit. let my cat die if I'm lying to you) *col* ***Fac*** used to emphasize the truth of what has been said, If I'm lying, I'm dying!

cȑkō {kla, klo adj.} (lit. dead) **1** *sl-fea* broken, malfunctioning, dead <**Slav**[*1]> **2** *sl-fea* very tired, dead tired <**Slav**[*1]>

cȕgeher {a masc.} (lit. accessories) **1** *sl-drink* alcoholic beverage <**Ger**[*1]> **2** *sl* party (social gathering) <**Ger**[*1]>

cȕger [1] {a (acc. = gen.) masc.} *sl-drink* alcoholic, drunk <**Ger**>

cȕger [2] {a masc.} **1** *sl* one hundred dinars; a hundred-dinar bill <**Ger**> **2** *sl-sports* speed chess tournament <**Ger**>

cugèrāš {geráša (acc. = gen.) masc.} **1** *sl-drink* alcoholic, drunk <**Ger**✤> **2** *sl-sports* speed chess player <**Ger**✤>

cȕgerica {ē fem.} *sl-sports* a game of speed chess <**Ger**>

cugèrisati {išēm, išū imperf. intr.} *sl-sports* play speed chess <**Ger**✤>

cȕglati {ām, ajū biasp.} **a.** *sl* carry, bear: *cuglati ruksak carry a backpack* <**Ger**[*1]> **b.** *sl* work, labor: *cuglati u fabrici work in a factory* <**Ger**[*2]>

cȕgnuti {nēm, nū perf.} *sl-drink* drink (alcohol) <**Ger**>

cȕgos {a (acc. = gen.) masc.} *sl-drink* alcoholic, drunk <**Ger**✤>

cȕgoš {a (acc. = gen.) masc.} *sl-drink* alcoholic, drunk <**Ger**✤>

cȕhnuti {nēm, nū perf.} *col* stink intensely, stink to high Heaven <**Slav**✤[*1]>

cûjka {ē fem.; Dat cûjki} **a.** *sl-drink* low-proof plum brandy <**Rum**[*1]> **b.** *sl-drink* brandy <**Rum**[*2]>

cȕkar [1] {kra masc.} Med *col-dia* sugar <**Ita**[*1]>

cȕkar [2] {a (acc. = gen.) masc.} *col* horse (the animal) <**Ger**>

cukàrče {eta neut.} *sl-arch* colt (young horse) <**Slav**✤[*1]>

cukàrica {ē fem.} *sl-arch* mare <**Slav**>

cȕker {kra masc.} *col-dia* sugar <**Ita**[*1]>

cúko {ē masc.} *col* ***Fam*** dog (the animal), doggie

cȕnuti {nēm, nū perf. intr.} *sl* drink (alcohol) <**Slav**>

cȕnjati[1] {ām, ajū imperf.} /cúnjati /cûnjām, cúnjajū imperf./ **1** *sl-arch* search, look for: *cunjati cvike search for one's eyeglasses* <**Slav**> **2** *sl-arch* throw away, toss out: *cunjati stare stvari kroz prozor throw out junk* <**Slav**>

cúnjati [2] {ām, ajū imperf. intr.} *col* spend one's time in useless activities, fool around, mess around <**Slav**>

cȕpa {ē fem.} *sl* female <**Slav**✍[*1]>

cȕpī {fem.; perm} /cùpi ija masc./ **a.** *sl-sex* ***Obs*** vagina, cunt <**Slav**✍> **b.** *sl* ***Obs*** female, cunt <**Slav**✍> ☞ **capi, pica**

cùpina {ē fem.; perm} [std. = pica] *sl* mouth <**Slav**✤[*1]>

cupìnati {ām, ajū imperf. intr.} *sl* yawn <**Slav**✤[*1]>

cùplīnger {a (acc. = gen.) masc.} *sl-sex* procurer, pimp <**Slav**✍-**Ger**[*1]>

cùprīnger {a (acc. = gen.) masc.} *sl-sex* procurer, pimp <**Slav**✍-**Ger**[*1]>

cȕra {ē fem.} **1** *col* female <**Slav**> **2** *sl-arch* water <**Slav**>

cúrac {rca (acc. = gen.) masc.} **a.** *col-dia* boy, kid <**Slav**> **b.** *col-dia* male, guy <**Slav**[*1]>

cùrān {curána (acc. = gen.) masc.} *col-dia* boy, kid <**Slav**>

cȕrica {ē fem.} *col* small female child, little girl <**Slav**>

curȉk {excl.} *col* used to make a horse or ox back up, back <**Ger**>

curíknuti se {cùrīknēm, nū perf. intr.} *col* return, get back: *curiknuti se iz inostranstva get back from abroad* <**Ger**>

cúriti {rīm, rē imperf. intr.} (lit. leak) *col* walk <**Slav**[*1]>

cûrka {ē fem.; Dat cûrki} **1** *sl-arch* candle <**Slav**[*1]> **2** *sl* ***Fac*** menstruation, period <**Slav**[*1]>

cȕrkati {ām, ajū imperf.} (lit. drip) *sl-crime* steal, swipe <**Slav**[*1]>

cȕrskī {ā, ō adj.} *col-dia* girl's <**Slav**>

cȕvaks {a masc.} *sl-crime* transport of new prisoners: *Danas u pet stiže cuvaks. A transport of new prisoners will be here at five o'clock.* <**Ger**[*1]>

cv [cê-vê] {vȇa masc.; perm} [std. = WC [vê-cê]] *sl-sex* toilet <**Abb**✍>

cvàjcvrkovati {ujēm, ujū imperf.} *sl-sex* ***Obs*** engage in sexual intercourse with (of a male)

cvàjter {a masc.} (lit. the second one) *sl-sex* ***Obs*** anus, asshole <**Ger**[*1]>

cvàjterica {ē fem.} (lit. the second one) *sl-sex* female sexual partner of a married male <**Ger**✤[*1]>

cvànciger {a masc.} (lit. the twentieth) **1** *sl-sex* ***Obs-Fac*** large penis <**Ger**[*1]> **2** *sl-crime* ***Obs-Fac*** handcuffs, cuffs <**Ger**[*1]>

cvàncik {a masc.} (lit. twenty) *sl* petty cash, chump change, peanuts <**Ger**>

cvánja {ē fem.} *sl-sstu* lowest passing grade <**Ger**✍>

cvànjek {njka masc.} Cro *col-dia* egg <**Slav**>

cvȁsti {vàtēm, vàtū imperf. irreg.} (lit. blossom) **1** *sl* be excited: *cvatu zbog odlaska na more they are excited about going to the seashore* <**Slav**[*1]> **2** *sl* be happy: *cvasti zbog povišice be happy about the raise* <**Slav**[*1]>

cvéba {ē fem.} (lit. raisin) **1** *sl-sex* ***Obs-Fac*** vagina <Ger*1> **2** *sl* news (in general) <Ger*1>

cvètati {ām, ajū imperf. intr.} (lit. blossom) SerE *sl* earn money <Slav*1>

cvètīć {cvetíća (acc. = gen.) masc.} (lit. small flower) SerE *sl* young female, girl <Slav*1>

cvétnica {ē fem.} (lit. the flowery one) SerE *sl-arch* week <Slav>

cvíčak {čka masc.} (lit. the second one) Cro *sl* streetcar line number two in Zagreb, Croatia <Ger✍>

cvȉjēt *See the following*

• **cvȉjēt hȑvātskōg národa** {NP} (lit. the flower of the Croatian nation) *col* ***Off*** Bosnian Muslim (male)

• **mȍdrī cvȉjēt** {NP} (lit. blue flower) *sl-sex* ***Fac-Obs*** buttocks, butt

cvȉk-cvȉk {excl.} *sl* used after making one's interlocutor scared <Ger✍>

cvíka {ē fem.; Dat cvíki} **1** *sl* fear: *Bila mu je cvika da će ga ćopit drotovi. He had fear that the heat was going to get him.* <Ger> **2** *sl-sstu* failing grade <Ger>

cvȉkalo {a neut.} *sl* eye (sight organ) <Ger⁘*1>

cvìkāroš {a (acc. = gen.) masc.} *sl-fea* ***Der*** coward, chicken <Ger⁘*1>

cvȉkati {ām, ajū imperf. intr.} *sl* get frightened, get scared <Ger>

cvȉkato {a (acc. = gen.) masc.} *sl* ***Der*** coward, chicken <Ger⁘>

cvìkātor {a (acc. = gen.) masc.} *sl* ***Der*** coward, chicken <Ger⁘*1>

cvȉkcánge {i fem. pl.} *sl-crafts* cutting pliers <Ger>

cvȉkcángle {i fem. pl.} *sl-crafts* cutting pliers <Ger✍>

cvȉker {a (acc. = gen.) masc.} (lit. eyeglasses) *sl-sstu* ***Fac*** professor, high-school teacher (male), prof <Ger*1>

cvikèrāš {keráša (acc. = gen.) masc.; Voc cvȉkerāšu} *sl-fea* ***Der*** male with eyeglasses, four-eyes <Ger⁘>

cvikeràšica {ē fem.} *sl-fea* ***Der*** female with eyeglasses, four-eyes <Ger⁘>

cvìkeri {cvȉkērā masc. pl.} *sl* eyeglasses <Ger>

cvìkerica {ē fem.} **1** *sl-fea* female with eyeglasses, four-eyes <Ger⁘> **2** *sl-sex* ***App*** adequate female sexual partner (of a male) <Ger⁘>

cvȉkos {a (acc. = gen.) masc.} *sl-fea* ***Der*** coward, chicken <Ger✍>

cvȉkoš {a masc.} *sl-fea* ***Der*** coward, chicken <Ger✍>

cvíliti {līm, lē imperf.} (lit. squeal) **a.** *col* cry, shed tears, weep <Slav> **b.i.** *col* ***Der*** complain, bitch: *Stalno cvili da nemamo love. She keeps bitching that we don't have any money.* <Slav*1> **ii.** *col* cry, shed tears, weep <Slav*1>

cvȉške {i fem.} *sl* sunglasses <Ger✍>

cvȋt {a +ov (ext. pl) masc.; Nom Pl cvȉtovi} [std. = cvet, cvijet] Cro *dia* flower <Slav✍>

cvȍcati {ām, ajū imperf. intr.} **1** *col* preach, give lectures to: *Cvoca mu što ne traži više novca. She is getting on his case for not asking for more money.* <Slav*1> **2** *col* reproach, scold <Slav*1>

cvȍk [1] {excl.} *col* the sound made by chatter <Slav>

cvȍk [2] {a +ov (ext. pl) masc.; Nom Pl cvòkovi} **1** *col* fear <Slav*1> **2** *sl-sstu* failing grade <Slav*1>

cvȍkānje {a neut.} *sl-fea* ***Der*** prolonged and meaningless talk, blabber, chatter <Slav⁘*1>

cvȍkati {ām, ajū imperf.} **1** *sl-fea* ***Der*** talk persistently and meaninglessly, blabber, chatter <Slav⁘*1> **2** *sl-fea* ***Der*** kiss <Slav⁘*1>

cvȍker {a masc.} **1** *sl* fear <Ger*1> **2** *sl-sstu* failing grade <Ger*1>

cvòkōt {a masc.} **1** *sl* talk persistently and meaninglessly, blabber, chatter <Slav⁘*1> **2** *sl* kissing <Slav⁘*1>

cvokòtānje {a neut.} *sl-fea* prolonged and meaningless talk, blabber, chatter <Slav*1>

cvokòtati {ām, ajū imperf.} *sl* chatter (of the teeth) <Slav>

cvokòtav {a, o adj.} *col* chattering (of the teeth) <Slav>

cvȍkotno {adv.} (lit. chattering) *sl* cold: *Napolju je cvokotno. It's cold outside.* <Slav⁘*1>

cvȍktānje {a neut.} *col* chattering (of the teeth) <Slav*1>

cvȍktati {ām, ajū imperf. intr.} *col* chatter (of the teeth) <Slav>

cvónja {ē fem.} (lit. two) *sl-sstu* lowest passing grade <Ger✍>

cvónjak {njka masc.} (lit. two) *col* petty cash, chump change, peanuts <Ger✍>

cvȓ {excl.} *col* the sound made by a bird, chrip <Slav>

cvȓc {excl.} **1** *col* used to express disbelief <Slav*1> **2** *col* used to express indifference, who cares <Slav*1>

• **cvȓc Milòjka** {NP} (lit. sizzle Milojka: female proper name) **1** *sl* ***Der*** used to express disbelief, don't give me that shit **2** *sl* used to express negative attitude toward, that's worth shit

čaršijáner {a (acc. = gen.) masc.} *sl-fea* crude and ill-mannered male, Neanderthal <NE❖>

čaršijánerka {ē fem.; Dat čaršijánerki} *sl-fea* crude and ill-mannered female, Neanderthal <NE❖>

čȁruga {ē masc.; Dat čȁrugi} **a.** *sl-fea* troublemaker, rowdy, ruffian <NE[*1]> **b.** *sl-crime* thief <NE[*2]>

čȁrup {a masc.} *sl-arch* opanak (a kind of peasant shoe) <NE>

čȁs *See the following*

• **čȁs pȍsla** {NP} (lit. a moment of work) *col* very quickly: *skuvati ručak čas posla whip up something to eat*

čȁsnā *See the following*

• **čȁsnā piònīrska** {AdjP} (lit. pioneer's word of honor) SerE *col* used to emphasize the truth of what has been said, I swear!

čȁsnā rêč {NP} (lit. a word of honor) SerE *col* used to emphasize the truth of what has been said, I swear! ☞ reč

čȁsnā séka {NP} (lit. nun) *sl-sex* ***Fac*** prostitute, hooker ☞ seka

čȁsnā sèstra {NP} (lit. nun) *sl-sex* ***Fac*** prostitute, hooker ☞ sestra

čâst *See the following*

• **čâsti mi** {NP} (lit. *I swear* on my honor) *col* used to emphasize the truth of what has been said, I swear!

• **svȁkā čâst** {NP} (lit. every honor *to you*) *col* used to express appreciation, good for you

• **svȁkā[PRON:DAT] čâst** {LSF} (lit. every honor to [PRON:ACC]) *col* used to express appreciation: *Svaka ti čast! Good for you!*

čȁtr̄lj {a (acc. = gen.) masc.} *sl* priest <NE☝>

čatȑljān {trljána (acc. = gen.) masc.} *sl* priest <NE☝>

čáva {ē masc.} *sl-fea* ***Der*** stupid or mentally deficient person <NE☝>

čâvka {ē fem.; Dat čâvki} (lit. crow) **a.** *sl-sex* ***Fac*** prostitute, hooker <Slav> **b.** *sl* ***Der*** female <Slav[*1]>

čȁvlik {excl.} **a.** *col* the sound made by a smallish explosion, bang <Slav> **b.** *col* the sound made by spanking, spank <Slav[*1]>

čavȑkān {vrkána masc.} *dia* nail (fastening device) <Ita☝>

čavȑljati {ām, ajū imperf.} *col* talk persistently on trivial topics <Slav[*1]>

čȁzben {a, o adj.} *col-dia* ***App*** honorable <Slav>

ččȅ {ēa neut.} *sl* female

čȅče {eta neut.} *sl-arch* female

čéda {ē masc.} SerE *sl-fea* ***Der*** inhabitant of the countryside, hick, bumpkin <Slav[*1]>

čédo {ē masc.} /čédo a, m/ *col* ***Off*** Serb (person) <Slav[*1]>

čègā [1] {pron.} [std. = šta] *col-dia* what (in any of its Serbo-Croatian meanings used in forms different from the standard): *Za čega ti je to? What do you need that for?* <Slav☝>

čéga [2] {ē fem.} *sl* certificate, diploma <NE☝>

čȅgović {a (acc. = gen.) masc.} /čegȍvić /a (acc. = gen.) masc/ Mont *col-dia* ***App*** male from a respected family <Slav>

čȅgovićka {ē fem.; Dat čȅgovićki} Mont *col-dia* ***App*** female from a respected family <Slav>

čegȑtati {ām, ajū imperf.} *sl-fea* ***Der*** talk persistently and meaninglessly, blabber, chatter <Slav[*1]>

Čȅh *See the following*

• **pȉjanī Čȅh** {AdjP} (lit. drunk Czech) *sl* streetcar line

čȅhla {čȁhla fem. pl.; perm} [std. = hlače] *sl* trousers, pants <Slav☝>

čȅk {excl.} [std. = čekaj] *col* used to ask for a pause, hold on, hang on <Slav☝>

čȅka {excl.} [std. = čekaj] *col* used to ask for a pause, hold on, hang on <Slav☝>

čȅkati *See the following*

• **čȅkati da pȁdnu óvnova múda** {VP} (lit. wait for the ram's balls to fall down) *sl* ***Fac-Obs*** spend one's time in useless activities, fool around, mess around

• **čȅkati lȉmūn** {VP} (lit. wait for lemon) *sl* spend one's time in useless activities, fool around, mess around

• **čȅkati lòpatu** {VP} (lit. wait for a shovel) *sl* ***Iro*** suffer from tuberculosis, have TB

čekìćānje {a neut.} *sl* ***Fac*** waiting for a long time <Slav☝-NE>

čekìćati {ām, ajū imperf.} *sl* ***Fac*** wait for a long time <Slav☝-NE>

čȅkinjo {a masc.} *sl-fea* bearded male <Slav☝>

čȅkinjos {a (acc. = gen.) masc.} *sl-fea* hairy male <Slav☝>

čekírati {čȅkīrām, čekírajū biasp.} **a.** *col* check, make sure <Eng❖> **b.** *sl* notice, observe: *Čekirao sam da nemam benzina. I noticed that I was out of gas.* <Eng❖[*1]>

čȅkmeče {eta neut.} **a.** *col-dia* box <NE> **b.** *col-dia* drawer <NE[*1]>

čȅlēnka {ē fem.} *col* head <NE>

čeličàna {ē fem.} (lit. steel works) **1** *sl-fea* ***Fac*** muscular male <NE*1> **2** *sl-fea* ***Fac*** muscularity <NE*1>

čèlikovac {vca (acc. = gen.) masc.} *col* fan or player for Čelik (a soccer team in Zenica, Bosnia) <NE❖*1>

čèlista {ē masc.} (lit. cello player) *sl-sex* ***Fac*** male homosexual, gay <Ita❖*1>

čèlo {a neut.} (lit. forehead) *sl* head <Slav*1>

čȅljād {i fem.} *col* one's wife and children <Slav>

čȅnč {a +ev (ext. pl) masc.; Nom Pl čènčevi} *sl* exchange (of money, goods, etc.) <Eng✍>

čȅnčati {ām, ajū biasp.} *sl* exchange (money, goods, etc.) <Eng❖✍>

čȅp [1] {a (acc. = gen.) +ov (ext. pl) masc.; Nom Pl čèpovi} (lit. cork) *sl-fea* ***Fac*** ingratiator (male), brownnoser, ass kisser <Slav*1>

čȅp [2] {a +ov (ext. pl) masc.; Nom Pl čèpovi} (lit. cork) *sl* tooth <Slav*1>

čépa {ē fem.} **1** *sl-sex* loose woman <Slav*1> **2** *sl-fea* coward, chicken <Slav*1>

čèpina {ē fem.} (lit. big cork) *sl* tooth <Slav*1>

čépiti se {čēpīm, pē imperf. intr.} (lit. squat, crouch) *sl* ingratiate, brownnose, kiss ass <Slav*1>

čèpulja {ē fem.} (lit. squatter) *sl-fea* ingratiator (male), brownnoser, ass kisser <Slav*1>

čèrečēnje {a neut.} (lit. cutting in quarters) *sl-sex* ***Obs*** sexual intercourse <NE*1>

čèrečiti {čīm, čē imperf.} (lit. cut in quarters) *sl-sex* ***Obs*** engage in sexual intercourse with (of a male) <NE*1>

čerùpati se {pām, pajū sē imperf. intr.} *sl* ***Fac*** take one's dress off, strip <Slav*1>

čèsov {pron.} [std. = čiji] *dia* whose (in any of its Serbo-Croatian meanings used in forms different from the standard): *Česova je to kuća? Whose house is that?* <Slav✍>

čèstitār {a (acc. = gen.) masc.} (lit. the honorable one) *sl-sex* ***Fac*** male homosexual, gay <Slav*1>

čȅšalj [1] {šlja (acc. = gen.) masc.} (lit. the one who produces combs) *sl-fea* ***Fac*** person who abuses others (usu. financially), parasite, leech <Slav*1>

čȅšalj [2] {šlja masc.} (lit. comb) *sl-crafts* gap measuring plates <Slav*1>

čȅšāljka {ē fem.} (lit. the one who works with combs) *sl-sex* ***Fac*** prostitute, hooker <Slav*1>

čèšānje {a neut.} (lit. combing) *col* living at another's expense, leeching off somebody <Slav*1>

čèšāroš {a (acc. = gen.) masc.} (lit. the one who uses combs) *sl-fea* person who lives at another's expense, leech <Slav❖*1>

čèšati se {čȇšēm, šū imperf. intr.} (lit. comb) **a.** *sl* live at another's expense, leech off somebody: *češati se o rođake live on relatives' expenses* <Slav*1> **b.** *sl* beg, ask for money <Slav*1>

čèšātor {a (acc. = gen.) masc.} (lit. the one who scratches) *sl-fea* person who abuses others (usu. financially), parasite, leech <Slav*1>

čèšātorka {ē fem.; Dat čèšatōrki} (lit. scratcher) *sl-sex* ***Fac*** prostitute, hooker <Slav*1>

čèšire *See the following*

- **Čèšire ti jèbēm!** {S} *col* ***Off*** used as a moderate curse, Fuck you!

čȅškē cigarète {NP} (lit. Czech cigarettes X češati se 'scratch', 'get for free from others') *sl* ***Fac*** cigarettes obtained from others without paying for them, bummed cigarettes ☞ **cigareta**

čèšljānje {a neut.} (lit. combing) **1** *col* living at another's expense, leeching off somebody <Slav*1> **2** *col* police interrogation <Slav*1>

čèšljārka {ē fem.} (lit. comb lady) *sl-sex* ***Fac*** prostitute, hooker <Slav*1>

čèšljati {ām, ajū imperf.} (lit. comb) **1** *sl-sex* ***Obs*** engage in sexual intercourse with (of a male) <Slav*1> **2** *sl-sports* ***Fac*** defeat, outplay: *Zvezda je češljala Vojvodinu celo drugo poluvreme. Zvezda outplayed Vojvodina throughout the second half.* <Slav*1>

- **čèšljati kârte** {VP} (lit. comb cards) *sl-gamble* ***Fac*** play cards
- **čèšljati zûbe na rázdjeljak** {VP} (lit. comb teeth in a parting) SerE *sl-fea* ***Fac*** have gaps in one's teeth

češljùgār {ljugára masc.} (lit. goldfinch) [std. = češalj] *sl* comb <Slav*1>

čèšnjāk [1] {češnjáka (acc. = gen.) masc.; Voc čèšnjāče} (lit. garlic) *sl-fea* ***Fac*** senior citizen <Slav*1>

čèšnjāk [2] {češnjáka masc.} (lit. garlic) *sl-sex* ***Obs-Fac*** penis <Slav*1>

čȅta *See the following*

- **za célu čȅtu** {PP} (lit. for the whole company) SerE *col* too much, overwhelming
- **za cijélu čȅtu** {PP} (lit. for the whole company) *col* too much, overwhelming

čkȁmni {īja masc.} *sl-arch* prison <Slav*1>

čkȁpi {čkēpi fem.; perm} **/čkàpi/ a.** *sl-sex* ***Obs*** vagina, cunt <Slav✍> **b.** *sl* ***Obs*** female, cunt <Slav✍*1> ☞ **pička**

čkávac {vca (acc. = gen.) masc.} **a.** *sl* male, guy <Slav*1> **b.** *sl* gentleman <Slav*1>

čkàvela {ē masc.} *sl* male, guy <Slav*1>

čkembíći {bíćā masc. pl.} *col* tripe <NE✍>

čkȉcapi {čkȉcepi fem.; perm} (lit. small cunt) *sl-sex* ***Obs*** attractive female <Slav✍>

čkȉde {masc. pl.; perm} [std. = dečki] *sl* boys <Slav✍>

čkȉljavac {ljāvca (acc. = gen.) masc.} *sl-arch* dog (the animal) <Slav*1>

čkȉljnuti {nēm, nū perf.} *col* look, watch, scope out <Slav*1>

čkòjači {jāčā masc. pl.} SSer *sl-arch* cart (e.g. oxcart) <Slav*1>

čkȍjalica {ē fem.} *sl* leg (human) <Slav*1>

čkòjiti {jīm, jē imperf.} **a.** *sl* walk <Slav*1> **b.** *sl* run away, flee

čkôjka {ē fem.; Dat čkôjki} *sl* leg (human) <Slav*1>

čkòliti {līm, lē imperf. intr.} *sl* keep one's mouth shut <Slav*1>

čkȍriti {rīm, rē imperf. intr.} *sl* walk <Slav*1>

čkôrka {ē fem.; Dat čkórki} *sl* leg (human) <Slav*1>

čkùljān {kuljána masc.} *sl-sex* ***Fac*** bathroom <Slav*1>

čkȕljati {čkȕljām, ljajū imperf.} *sl-sex* ***Obs*** defecate, shit <Slav*1>

čkȕljiti {ljīm, ljē imperf.} *sl* ***Obs*** defecate, shit <Slav*1>

čmȁki {čmēki fem.; perm} **/čmàki/** [std. = kičma] *sl* backbone <Slav✍>

čmára {ē fem.} (lit. the one with an asshole) *sl-sex* ***Obs*** buttocks, butt <Slav⁘>

čmàrisati {išēm, išū imperf.} (lit. asshole) *sl-fea* ***Der-Obs*** ingratiate, brownnose, kiss ass <Slav⁘*1>

čmárko {a masc.; Voc čmârko} (lit. the one with an asshole) *sl-fea* ***Der-Obs*** ingratiator (male), brownnoser, ass kisser <Slav⁘>

čmáronja {ē masc.} (lit. the one with an asshole) *sl-fea* ***Der-Obs*** ingratiator (male), brownnoser, ass kisser <Slav⁘>

čmávalo {a neut.} *col* sleepy person, sleepy head <Slav⁘>

čmávati {čmâvām, čmávajū imperf. intr.} *sl* sleep, nap <Slav⁘>

čmčić {a masc.} *sl-arch* egg <Slav>

čmúrati se {čmûrām, čmúrajū imperf. intr.} *sl-fea* ***Der*** ingratiate, brownnose, kiss ass: *Ona se svaki dan čmura novom šefu. She brownnoses the new boss every day.* <Slav⁘✍>

čȍban {a (acc. = gen.) masc.} **a.** *col* shepherd <NE> **b.** *col* ***Der*** inhabitant of the countryside, hick, bumpkin <NE*1>

čȍbanin {a (acc. = gen.) -in (rd. pl.) masc.} **a.** *col* shepherd <NE> **b.** *col* inhabitant of the countryside, hick, bumpkin <NE*1>

čȍče {excl.} [std. = čov(j)eče] Mont *col-dia* used to address a male in direct informal communication, man <Slav✍>

čȍek {a (acc. = gen.) masc.} [std. = čov(j)ek] **a.** *col* male, guy <Slav✍> **b.** *col* husband <Slav✍*1>

čȍha {ē fem.; Dat čȍhi} *sl* fight (e.g. fist fight) <NE*1>

čȍhānje {a neut.} *sl* fight (e.g. fist fight) <NE*1>

čȍhati {ām, ajū imperf.} *sl* beat up <NE*1>

čòjāk {a (acc. = gen.) masc.} [std. = čov(j)ek] *col-dia* male, guy <Slav✍>

čȍjek {a (acc. = gen.) masc.} [std. = čov(j)ek] **a.** *col-dia* male, guy <Slav✍> **b.** *col-dia* husband <Slav✍*1>

čȍk [1] {čòka masc.} *sl-auto* choke <Eng>

čôk [2] {a (acc. = gen.) masc.} [std. = čov(j)ek] *dia* male, guy <Slav✍>

čȍkānj {a masc.} *sl-drink* cone-shaped container used to drink hard liquor <NE>

čȍkī {īja (acc. = gen.) masc.} *sl-fea* ***Der*** person with seeing difficulties <NE✍>

čókljo {ē masc.} *sl-fea* ***Der*** slender boy <NE*1>

čokoláda {ē fem.} (lit. chocolate) *sl-fea* ***Off*** African American (person) <Spa*1>

čȍkolādnī {ōg (acc. = gen.) masc.} (lit. the chocolate one) *sl-fea* ***Off*** African American (male) <Spa*1>

čȍkolādnī vȉc {NP} (lit. chocolate joke) *sl-polit* ***Fac*** dangerous political joke ☞ **vic**

čȍmati se {ām, ajū biasp. intr.} *sl* scratch oneself <NE*1>

čȍmbe {eta masc.} **a.** *sl-crime* informer, stoolie, snitch **b.** *sl-fea* unfriendly person

čónta {ē fem.} **a.** *sl* head <Slav*1> **b.** *sl* female <Slav*1>

čȍntara {ē fem.} *sl* head <Slav⁘*1>

čȍntāš {a (acc. = gen.) masc.} *sl-fea* person with a large head <Slav❖[*1]>

čòpeti {pīm, pē imperf.} *sl-crime* steal, swipe <Slav[*1]>

čȍporac {rca (acc. = gen.) masc.} (lit. the one from the pack, herd) *sl-fea* moderately strong male <Slav❖>

čȍporatīvno {adv.} (lit. in a pack, herd) *sl* collectively <Slav❖>

čórba {ō fem.} /čòrba /e fem./ **a.** *col* soup <NE> **b.** *sl-auto* gasoline <NE[*1]>
- **čórbinē čórbē čórba** {NP} (lit. soup's soup's soup) **a.** *col* unrelated event **b.** *col* information acquired indirectly: *To što si čuo o otpuštanju radnika je čorbine čorbe čorba. What you heard about them firing workers is third-hand information.*

čòrbavina {ē fem.} *sl* ***Fac*** coffee <NE❖>

čòrbovina {ē fem.} *sl* ***Fac*** coffee <NE❖>

čòrbovinja {ē fem.} *sl* ***Fac*** coffee <NE❖>

čòreti {rīm, rē imperf.} *sl-crime* steal, swipe <NE❖[*1]>

čòsik {a masc.} *sl-gamble* interrupted game <NE[*1]>

čȍveče {excl.} SerE *col* used to address a male in direct informal communication, man <Slav>

čȍvek {a (acc. = gen.) masc.} /čòvek/ SerE *col* husband <Slav[*1]>

čȍvik {a (acc. = gen.) masc.} [std. = čov(j)ek] Med *dia* male, guy <Slav✍>

čȑčkati {ām, ajū imperf.} *col* write, scribble <Slav>

čȑk {a masc.} *col* the sound made by a small bird, tweet <Slav>

čȑvenā {ē fem. (adj. decl.)} (lit. the red one: the color of the bill) *col* ten dinars; a ten-dinar bill <Pol✍[*1]>

čȕ {excl.} [std. = čuj] *col* used to express surprise, disbelief, etc., oh <Slav✍>

čȕbe {excl.} *sl* used to make somebody go away <Slav>

čȕbica {ē fem.} *sl-sex* ***Obs*** small vagina <Slav[*1]>

čúčānje {a neut.} (lit. crouching) *sl* waiting for a long time <Slav[*1]>

čúčati {čīm, čē imperf. intr.} (lit. crouch) **1** *col* wait for, expect: *Trebala je doći u tri, a ja sam čučao do četri. She was going to come at three o'clock and I waited until four.* <Slav[*1]> **2** *sl* be suitable, fit: *Dobro joj čuči novi friz. That new hairstyle really suits her.* <Slav[*1]>

čúčavac {čāvca (acc. = gen.) masc.} /čȕčavac/ **1** *sl* beans <Slav❖> **2** *col* toilet <Slav❖>

čȕčehla {čȕčihla fem. pl.} *sl* trousers, pants <Slav✍>

čȕčko {a masc.} *sl-fea* moderately strong male <Slav❖[*1]>

čȕdo {a neut.} [std. = miracle] *sl-fea* ***App*** extraordinary high-quality item <Slav[*1]>

čȕgati {ām, ajū imperf.} *sl-drink* drink (alcohol) <Ger✍>

čûj [1] {excl.} (lit. listen) *col* used to draw attention: *Čuj, on je doktor. He is a doctor, you know.* <Slav[*1]>

čûj [2] {excl.} (lit. listen) *col* used to express amazement, disbelief, etc. <Slav[*1]>

čȕk {excl.} *col* the sound made by knocking, knock <Slav>

čȕka {ē fem.; Dat čȕki} (lit. knocker) **a.** *sl* watch, clock <Slav[*1]> **b.i.** *sl* hour <Slav[*2]> **ii.** *sl* heart <Slav[*2]>

čúkac {kca (acc. = gen.) masc.} *sl-crime* guard, watchman <Slav✍>

čùkāč {čukáča (acc. = gen.) masc.} (lit. knocker) **1** *sl* watch, clock <Slav❖> **2** *sl* troublemaker, rowdy, ruffian <Slav❖>
- **Dȉmče čùkāč** {NP} (lit. Dimče, proper name, knocker) *sl-fea* ***Fac*** troublemaker, rowdy, ruffian

čȕkadžija {ē masc.} **1** *sl* watchmaker <Slav❖> **2** *sl-fea* ***Der*** stupid or mentally deficient person <Slav❖>

čùkalac {kaoca masc.} (lit. knocker) *sl* watch, clock <Slav❖>

čùkalec {lca masc.} (lit. knocker) *col* watch, clock <Slav❖>

čȕkalica {ē fem.} (lit. knocker) *sl-crafts* hammer (the tool) <Slav❖>

čȕkalo {a neut.} (lit. knocker) **1** *sl-sex* ***Obs*** penis, dick, prick <Slav[*1]> **2** *sl-crime* pistol, revolver <Slav[*1]>

čȕkalj {klja masc.} *sl* concept, idea <Slav[*1]>

čȕkam [1] {imperf.} SSer *dia* knock (on a door, etc.) <Slav>

čȕkam [2] {excl.} *sl* used to express extreme dissatisfaction <Slav>

Čȕkām dòbro! {S} (lit. I knock well!) SSer *dia* ***Obs*** used to express lack of interest in, Fuck it! ☞ **čukati**

čukánjac {njca masc.} *sl-auto* minor car crash, fender bender <Slav❖>

čȕkānje {a neut.} *sl-sex* ***Obs*** sexual intercourse <Slav❖[*1]>

čùkara {ē fem.} **1** *sl-sex* ***Fac*** prostitute, hooker <Slav[*1]> **2** *sl-crafts* watchmaker's <Slav[*1]>

čukárac {rca masc.} **1** *sl* watch, clock <Slav❖[*1]> **2** *sl* heart <Slav❖[*1]>

ćálo {ē masc.} *sl-fea* ***Der*** stupid or mentally deficient person <Slav[*1]>

ćȁlōv {ćalòva (acc. = gen.) masc.; Voc ćàlove} *sl-fea* ***Der*** stupid or mentally deficient person <Slav❖[*1]>

ćȁo {excl.} **1** *col* used to greet informally on arrival, ciao, hi <Ita> **2** *col* used to take leave of somebody informally, ciao, bye <Ita>

ćȁos {excl.} **1** *sl* used to greet informally on arrival, ciao, hi <Ita✍> **2** *sl* used to take leave of somebody informally, ciao, bye <Ita✍>

ćȁp {excl.} *col* the sound made by taking objects, whoosh <Ita>

ćapírati {ćàpīrām, ćapírajū imperf.} *sl-crime* steal, swipe <Ita❖>

ćȁpiti {pīm, pē perf.} **a.** *col* grab, snatch <Ita> **b.** *sl-crime* steal, swipe <Ita[*1]>

ćaplàisānje {a neut.} *sl-sex* ***Obs*** sexual foreplay, petting, feeling up <Slav>

ćapr̀dānje {a neut.} *col* prolonged and meaningless talk, blabber, chatter <Slav❖>

ćapr̀dati {ām, ajū imperf. intr.} *sl* talk persistently and meaninglessly, blabber, chatter <Slav❖>

ćȁrke {ī fem. pl.} *sl-gamble* dice <NE❖>

ćàršija {ē fem.} BosM *col* city <NE✍> ☞ **čaršija**

ćása {ē fem.} *col* bowl (food container) <NE>

ćȁskati {ām, ajū imperf.} *col* chat <Slav>

ćȁur {a (acc. = gen.) masc.} BosM *col* ***Der*** non-Muslim <NE>

ćȁurin {a (acc. = gen.) -in (rd. pl.) masc.} BosM *col* ***Der*** non-Muslim <NE>

ćàvāp {ćavápa masc.} [std. = ćevap] **a.** *sl-sex* ***Fac-Obs*** penis, dick, prick <NE✍[*1]> **b.** *sl-sex* ***Fac-Der-Obs*** small penis <NE✍[*2]>

ćȅbovānje {a neut.} (lit. blanketing) *sl-crime-sl-mil* covering with a blanket and beating up <NE❖[*1]>

ćȅbovati {bujēm, bujū biasp.} (lit. blanket) *sl-crime-sl-mil* cover with a blanket and beat up <NE❖[*1]>

ćéđo {ē masc.} **a.** *col* ***Off*** Serbian fighter (male) <Slav✍[*1]> **b.** *col* ***Off*** Serb (person) <Slav✍[*2]>

ćȅf {a +ov (ext. pl) masc.; Nom Pl ćèfovi} *col* whim, pleasure, fancy <NE>

ćeflèisān {a, o adj.} *sl-drink* slightly drunk, tipsy <NE>

ćȅga {ćȃgā fem. pl.; perm} [std. = gaće] *sl* underpants, underwear <Slav✍>

ćehlìbār {libára masc.} [std. = ćilibar] BosM *col* amber <NE>

ćȅja {excl.} *col* used to urge cattle on <Slav>

ćȅjf {a +ov (ext. pl) masc.; Nom Pl ćéjfovi} *col* whim, pleasure, fancy <NE>

ćêjfiti {fīm, fē imperf. intr.} *col* enjoy, like <NE❖>

ćȅla {ē fem.} *sl-crime* prison cell <NE✍>

ćélac {lca (acc. = gen.) masc.} *sl* male, guy <NE❖>

ćȅlav {a, o adj.} (lit. bald) **1** *sl* ***Fac*** out of money, broke <NE> **2** *sl* holy <NE>

ćȅlavac {lāvca masc.} *sl-drugs* ***Fac*** minimal dose of a drug <NE❖[*1]>

ćȅlavac bâr {NP} (lit. bald man's bar) *sl-drink* ***Fac*** name of a bar frequented by retirees in Zagreb, Croatia ☞ **bar**

ćèlče {eta neut.} *sl-arch* dog (the animal) <NE❖[*1]>

ćȅle kúla {NP} (lit. A tower the Turks built from the skulls of their enemies during their rule in the Balkans) *sl-drink* ***Fac*** name of a bar frequented by retirees in Zagreb, Croatia ☞ **kula**

ćȅle-kúla {ē fem.} (lit. A tower the Turks built from the skulls of their enemies during their rule in the Balkans) *sl-drink* name of a bar frequented by retirees in Zagreb, Croatia <NE[*1]>

ćȅlica {ē fem.} **1** *sl-crime* prison cell <Lat❖> **2** *sl-crime* solitary prison cell <Lat❖>

ćèlija {ē fem.} (lit. cell) *sl* ***Iro*** hotel room <Lat>

ćêlka {ē fem.; Dat ćêlki} (lit. the bald one) **1** *sl* loose woman <NE❖[*1]> **2** *sl* prison cell <Gre❖>

ćélo {ē masc.} /ćélo, a masc./ (lit. the bald one) **a.** *sl-fea* bald male <NE> **b.** *sl-crime* recidivist <NE>

ćêm {a (acc. = gen.) +ov (ext. pl) masc.; Nom Pl ćémovi} *sl-arch* dog (the animal) <NE[*1]>

- **ckȁmnī ćêm** {NP} *sl-arch* wolf (the animal)

ćèmče {eta neut.} *sl-arch* puppy <NE❖[*1]>

ćȅmica {ē fem.} **a.** *sl-arch* she-wolf <NE❖[*1]> **b.** *sl-arch* bitch (female dog) <NE❖[*2]>

- **ćȅmica ckȁmnā** {NP} *sl-arch* she-wolf

ćémka {ē fem.} *sl-arch* evil female, bitch <NE❖[*1]>

ćènef {a masc.} *col* toilet <NE>

ćènīf {ćenífa masc.} *col* toilet <NE>

ćenífa {ē fem.} *col* toilet <NE>

ćȅpī {ćȃpi neut.; perm} /ćèpi/ [std. = piće] *sl-drink* drink (alcohol) <Slav✍>

ćéra[1] {ē fem.} *col* house, home <Gyp>

ćéra[2] {ē fem.} *col* ***Fam*** daughter <Slav✍> *sl*
- **Ćéru li ti mȉlū tvòju!** {S} (lit. *I fuck* your dear daughter!) *col* ***Off*** used as a strong curse, Fuck you!

ćérka *See the following*
- **Ćȅrke ti ga!** {S} (lit. *I fuck* your daughter!) SSer *dia* ***Off*** used as a strong curse, Fuck you!

Ćéru li ti mȉlū tvòju! {S} (lit. *I fuck* your dear daughter!) *col* ***Off*** used as a strong curse, Fuck you! ☞ **ćera**

ćȅsa {ē fem.} *sl-sports* ball <NE[*1]>

ćȅti {òću, òćē imperf.} [std. = ht(j)eti] *col-dia* want, wish (in all its meanings in the form different from the standard): *Oće da idu. They wanna go.* <Slav✍>

ćȅtnīk {a (acc. = gen.) masc.} [std. = četnik] **a.** *col* ***Off*** Serbian fighter <Slav✍[*1]> **b.** *col* ***Off*** Serb (person): *One ćetnike ne mogu očima. I hate these Serbs' guts.* <Slav✍[*2]>

ćéto {ē masc.} *col* ***Off*** Serb (person) <Slav✍[*1]>

ćȅvāp {ćevápa masc.} **a.** *sl-sex* ***Fac-Obs*** penis, dick, prick <NE✍[*1]> **b.** *sl-sex* ***Fac-Der-Obs*** small penis <NE✍[*2]>

ćevàpčić {a masc.} /ćevàpčīć /a masc./ (lit. meat ball) **1** *sl-fea* small finger <NE[*1]> **2** *sl-sex* ***Fac-Obs*** small penis <NE[*1]>

ćȅvka {ē fem.; Dat ćȅvki} *sl-arch* bitch (female dog) <Slav[*1]>

ćȅvnuti {nēm, nū perf.} *sl-drink* sip (alcohol) <Slav[*1]>

ćȉber {a neut.} *sl* match (lighting device) <NE[*1]>

ćȉbra {ē fem.} *sl* match (lighting device) <NE[*1]>

ćȉbre {eta neut.} *sl* match (lighting device) <NE[*1]>

ćífo {ē masc.} *col* ***Off*** Jew <NE>

ćȉfut {a (acc. = gen.) masc.} *col* ***Off*** Jew <NE>

ćȉku {adv.; perm} [std. = kući] *sl* home <Slav✍>

ćȉlim {a masc.} (lit. carpet) *sl-drugs* short hashish pipe <NE[*1]>

ćinífa {ē fem.} *sl* toilet <NE>

ćíra {ē masc.} SerE *col* narrow-gauge train <SlavO[*1]> ☞ **ćiro**

ćirìlica {ē fem.} (lit. Cyrillic letters) Fac *sl-music* country or folk music <Gre[*1]>

ćȉrisān {a, o adj.} *sl-drink* drunk <Slav[*1]>

ćȉrisānje {a neut.} *sl-drink* drinking (alcohol) <Slav[*1]>

ćȉrisati {išēm, išū imperf.} *sl-drink* drink (alcohol) <Slav[*1]>

ćíro {a masc.} **1** *col* narrow-gauge train <SlavO[*1]> **2** *col* bus <SlavO[*1]> ☞ **ćira**

ćȉtāb {ćitába masc.} **a.** BosM *col* book <NE> **b.** BosM *col* Muslim religious book (in general) <NE[*1]>

ćȉtāp {ćitápa masc.} **a.** BosM *col* book <NE> **b.** BosM Muslim religious book (in general) <NE[*1]>

ćȉverica {ē fem.} *col* head <Ita>

číza {ē fem.} **a.** Bos *col* line (thin continuous mark) <NE> **b.** Bos *col* stereo set <NE[*1]>
- **číza blíza** {NP} (lit. line close) **Bos** *sl* game of throwing coins where competitors attempt to place it as close to a line or wall as possible, pitching pennies

ćnȅf {a masc.} *sl* bathroom <NE>

ćȍeće {excl.} BosM *col* used to address a male in direct informal communication, man <Slav✍>

ćȍf {a +ov (ext. pl) masc.; Nom Pl ćȍfovi} [std. = fićo] *sl-auto* Zastava 750 (make of car) <BN✍>

ćȍkavac {kávca masc.} *sl-arch* egg <Slav[*1]>

ćȍkle {eta neut.} *sl-crafts* hammer (the tool) <Slav✣[*1]>

ćónta {ē fem.} *sl* head <Slav>

ćȍpav {a, o adj.} *sl-fea* lame (limping) <NE>

ćȍpavā nòga {NP} (lit. lame leg) *sl-drink* name of a night club in Zagreb, Croatia called Corson ☞ **noga**

ćopávānje {a neut.} **a.** *sl* catching, grasping <Slav[*1]> **b.** *sl-crime* theft <Slav[*2]>

ćopávati {ćȍpāvām, ćopávajū imperf. intr.} **a.** *sl* catch, grab: *ćopavati leptirove catch butterflies* <Slav[*1]> **b.** *sl-crime* steal, swipe <Slav[*2]>
- **ćopávati prȅko tanjúra** {VP} (lit. steal over the plate) Cro *sl-crime* break in through the balcony

ćȍpavī {ōg (acc. = gen.) masc.} *sl-fea* lame male <NE>

ćȍpić {a (acc. = gen.) masc.} (lit. the last name of the popular children's writer Branko ćopić X ćopiti 'steal, lift') *sl-crime* thief, sticky fingers <SlavO[*1]>

Ćȍpila [PRON:ACC] šíza. {LSF} (lit. Madness has caught [PRON:ACC].) *sl* used to indicate someone's insanity, [PRON:NOM] is going nuts.: *Ćopila ga šiza. He is going nuts.* ☞ **ćopiti**

ćȍpisati {išēm, išū biasp.} *sl-crime* steal, swipe <Slav[*1]>

ćȍpiti {pīm, pē perf.} **a.** *sl* grab, snatch <Slav[*1]> **b.** *sl-crime* steal, swipe <Slav[*2]>

Da [PRON:DAT] jèbēm mâjku mȉlū. {LSF} (lit. I fuck [PPRON] dear mother to [PRON:ACC].) *col* ***Off*** used as a threat of physical violence: *Da ti jebem majku milu! Neću to da radim! Fuck you! I'm not gonna do it!* ☞ **jebati**

da pròstē [NP:NOM] (lit. may [NP:NOM] forgive me) used to introduce an obscene element of discourse ☞ **prostiti**

da pròstī [NP:NOM] (lit. may [NP:NOM] forgive me) used to introduce an obscene element of discourse, pardon my French ☞ **prostiti**

da pròstīš {S} (lit. forgive me) *col* used to introduce an obscene element of discourse, pardon my French ☞ **prostiti**

dà sam jâ s tȍbōm {S} (lit. If I were with you) *col* used to introduce a piece of advice, if I were you: *Da sam ja s tobom, ne bih putovao po ovom vremenu. If I were you, I would not travel in weather like this.* ☞ **ja**

dà se smȓznēš {VP} (lit. it makes you freeze) *col* very frightening, very scary: *Film je bio da se smrzneš. The movie was very frightening.* ☞ **smrznuti se**

Dà ti jèbēm bȍga Ȉsusa! {S} (lit. Let me fuck your God Jesus!) *col* ***Off*** used as a moderate curse, Fuck you! ☞ **jebati**

Dà ti jèbēm mȁmicu mȓtvū! {S} (lit. Let me fuck your little dead mother!) *col* ***Off*** used as a strong curse, Fuck you! ☞ **jebati**

dà ti pȁmēt stȁnē {S} (lit. so that your mind stops working) *col* used to indicate the unusual feature of an object or event, mind boggling: *Kakva dobra kola, da ti pamet stane. What a car, that's unbelievable.* ☞ **pamet**

Dà ti sèstricu na tràvicu! {S} (lit. Let me *screw* your little sister on the grass!) SSer *dia* ***Off-Fac*** used as a weak curse, Screw you! ☞ **sestrica**

Dà ti sèstricu u vodènicu! {S} (lit. Let me *screw* your little sister in a watermill!) SSer *dia* ***Off-Fac*** used as a weak curse, Screw you! ☞ **sestrica**

Da vȉdīmo čȉja mâjka cȓnū vȕnu préde! {S} (lit. Let us see whose mother combs black wool!) *col* used as a threat, Let 's see who's gonna pay for this! ☞ **videti**

dàbōgda {excl.} *col* used to express the hope that something will happen: *Dabogda dobio tu stipendiju! I hope you get that scholarship!* <Slav✣>
• **Dàbōgdā cȓkō!** {S} (lit. I hope God makes you dead!) *col* used to express a negative wish, Drop dead!
• **Dàbōgdā[VERB:PAST PARTICIPLE]!** {S} (lit. I hope that [VERB]!) *col* used to express a wish: *Dabogda se odselio! I hope that you move out!*

dabògme {part.} *col* used as a strong affirmative response, of course, yeah, you bet <Slav> ☞ **dabome**

dabòme {part.} *col* used as a strong affirmative response, of course, yeah, you bet <Slav✣> ☞ **dabogme**

dàcka {ē fem.; Dat dàcki} (lit. plank) *sl-sex* ***Fac-App*** flat-breasted female <Slav✍*1>

dȁd {a +ov (ext. pl) masc.; Nom Pl dàdovi} *sl* cigarette butt

dáda[1] {ē fem.} /dàda fem./ **1** SSer *col-dia* ***Fam*** mother, mom <NE*1> **2** SSer *col-dia* sister, sis <NE*1>
• **Dàdu li ti!** {S} (lit. *I fuck* your mother!) SSer *dia* ***Off*** used as a strong curse, Fuck you!
• **Dàdu li ti tvòju!** {S} (lit. I fuck your mother!) SSer *dia* ***Off*** used as a strong curse, Fuck you!
• **Dàdu ti mȉlosnū!** {S} (lit. *I fuck* your dear mother!) SSer *dia* ***Off*** used as a strong curse, Fuck you!
• **Dàde ti tvòje!** {S} (lit. I fuck your mother!) SSer *dia* ***Off*** used as a strong curse, Fuck you!
• **Dàde ti tvòje kȓvavō!** {S} (lit. I fuck your bloody mother!) SSer *dia* ***Off*** used as a strong curse, Fuck you!

dádica {ē fem.} /dàdica /e fem./ SSer *col-dia* ***Fam*** mother, mom <NE✣>
• **Dàdicu ti mȉlū!** {S} (lit. I fuck your dear little mother!) SSer *dia* ***Off*** used as a strong curse, Fuck you!

dáda[2] {ē fem.} (lit. gives-gives) *col-dia* ***Fac*** loose woman <Slav*1>

dádo {adj.} *sl-fea* ***Der*** unintelligent, stupid, dumb <Fre*1>

Dàdu li ti! {S} (lit. *I fuck* your mother!) SSer *dia* ***Off*** used as a strong curse, Fuck you! ☞ **dada**

Dàdu li ti tvòju! {S} (lit. *I fuck* your mother!) SSer *dia* ***Off*** used as a strong curse, Fuck you! ☞ **dada**

Dàdu ti mȉlosnū! {S} (lit. *I fuck* your dear mother!) SSer *dia* ***Off*** used as a strong curse, Fuck you! ☞ **dada**

dàidža {ē masc.} BosM *col* uncle (mother's brother or mother's sister's husband) <NE>

dàidžić {a (acc. = gen.) masc.} BosM *col* cousin (mother's brother's or mother's sister's son) <NE✣>

dàidžīnica {ē fem.} BosM *col* aunt (mother's sister or mother's brother's wife) <NE✣>

dâj {excl.} **1** *col* used to stimulate somebody to do something: *Daj uradi zadaću. Why don't you do your homework.* <Slav> **2** *col* used to express disbelief: *A: On je osvojio prventstvo. B: Daj! A: He won the championship. B: No way!* <Slav>

dâj bȍže {ExcP} (lit. God give) *col* used to express lack of control over events ☞ bog

dâjde {excl.} [std. = daj] *col-dia* used to stimulate somebody to pass something <Slav>

dàjdža {ē masc.} BosM *col* uncle (mother's brother or mother's sister's husband) <NE>

dȁjk {a (acc. = gen.) +ov (ext. pl) masc.; Nom Pl dȁjkovi} *sl-ser* lesbian <Eng>

dâjka {ē fem.; Dat dâjki} **1** SSer *col-dia* mother <NE⁘*1> **2** SSer *col-dia* sister <NE⁘*1>
- **Dȁjku li ti!** {S} (lit. *I fuck* your mother!) SSer *dia* ***Off*** used as a strong curse, Fuck you!

dâjna {excl.} *col* used to take leave of somebody informally <Slav>

dàkako {part.} /dakàko/ *col* used as a strong affirmative response, of course, yeah, you bet <Slav>

dàklem {part.} [std. = dakle] *col-dia* particle used to sum up a point and: *Daklem, oni će ići u instranstvo? So then, they are going abroad?* <Slav✍>

daktilògraf {a (acc. = gen.) masc.} (lit. typist) *sl-crime* ***Fac*** informer, stoolie, snitch <Gre*1>

dàlabu {dàlebu masc.; perm} *sl-fea* ***Der*** stupid or mentally deficient person <NE✍>

dalèko *See the following*
- **dalèko je sûnce** {S} (lit. the sun is far away) *sl-sstu* ***Fac*** the end of the school year
- **dalèko[PRON:DAT] lêpā kȕća** {AdvP} (lit. let [PPRON] pretty house be far away) SerE *col* used to express a negative attitude toward: *Daleko mu lepa kuća! Don't mess with him!*

dalekòzor {a masc.} (lit. binoculars) *sl* eyeglasses <Slav*1>

dȁlga {excl.} *sl* used to make somebody go away, beat it <NE*1>

dalmatàjner {a (acc. = gen.) masc.} *sl* ***Der*** Dalmatian (inhabitant of Dalmatia, Croatia) <Ger*1>

Dȁlmoš {a (acc. = gen.) masc.} /Dâlmoš/ *col* ***Der*** Dalmatian (inhabitant of Dalmatia, Croatia) <SlavO⁘>

dàljāš {daljáša (acc. = gen.) masc.; Voc dȁljāšu} *sl-sports* long jumper <Slav>

Dȁm {Dàma +ov (ext. pl) masc.} *sl* Amsterdam (Holland) <HolO✍>

dáma {ē fem.} (lit. lady, which is number thirteen in some card games) *sl* bus line number thirteen in Belgrade, Serbia <Fre*1>
- **dvòrskā dáma** {NP} (lit. court lady) *sl-sex* ***Fac*** male homosexual

dȁmfati {ām, ajū imperf. intr.} (lit. puff) **a.** *sl* break wind, fart <Ger*1> **b.** *sl* smell, stink <Ger*2>

dâmnjī {ā, ē adj.} *col-dia* old <Slav✍>

dȁn [1] {excl.} **1** *col* the sound made by a bell, ding <Slav> **2** *col* the sound made by an explosion, bang <Slav>

dân [2] *See the following*
- **Bàr dân!** {NP} (lit. Good day!) *col* ***Fam*** used as an informal greeting, What's up!
- **Dân ti tvôj!** {S} (lit. *I screw* your day!) *col* ***Off*** used as a weak curse, Screw you!
- **za dȍbar dân** {PP} (lit. for a good day) *col* used to indicate that something has been performed without any hesitation, just that easy, just like that

dàndara {ē fem.} *sl* slap, smack <Gyp*1>

dàndara {ē fem. & masc.} **1** *sl-fea* ***Der*** irresponsible person: *Nemoj da on vozi, on je dandara. Don't let him drive, he is irresponsible.* <Gyp*1> **2** *sl-fea* ***Der*** troublemaker, rowdy, ruffian <Gyp*2>

dàndiška {ē fem.; Dat dàndiški} *sl* tooth <Gyp>

dȁnfa {ē fem.} *sl-sex* ***Obs*** vagina, cunt <Ger*1>

dȁnfati {ām, ajū biasp.} **1** *sl* bother, disturb: *Danfala me dva sata. She bothered me for two hours.* <Ger*1> **2** *sl* betray, turn in to authorities: *Danfala ga, pa su saznali gdje se krije. She betrayed him, so they found his hideout.* <Ger*1>

dȁnga {ē fem.; Dat dȁngi} /dánga /e fem./ *sl* slap, smack <NE*1>

dàngānje {a neut.} *sl* fight (e.g. fist fight) <NE⁘*1>

dȁngla {ē fem.} /dánga /e fem./ *sl* slap, smack <NE*1>

dànguba {ē fem. & masc.} *sl-fea* loafer, idler <Slav⁘>

Dànica {ē fem.} *sl* name of a swimming pool on Daničićeva street in Zagreb, Croatia <SlavO*1>

Dȁnkinja {ē fem.} /Dânkinja/ (lit. Danish female) *sl-sex* ***Fac*** loose woman <SlavO*1>

dȁr-mâr {a masc.} /dâr-mâr, dàrmār/ **1** *col* fight (e.g. fist fight) <NE*1> **2** *col* mess, disorder, disturbance <NE*1>

dàre {fem.} *col-dia* mother <NE⁘>
- **Dàre ti ga tȕrīm!** {S} (lit. I stick it to your mother!) SSer *dia* ***Off*** used as a moderate curse, Fuck you!

darèžljīvka {ē fem.} (lit. the one who likes to give) *sl-sex* ***Fac*** loose woman <Slav*1>

dèfus {a masc.} *sl-fea* ***Der*** stupid or mentally deficient person <Lat✍>

dègēn {degéna (acc. = gen.) masc.} (lit. the degenerate one) **a.** *sl-fea* ***Der*** stupid or mentally deficient person <Lat[*1]> **b.** *sl-fea* ***Der*** insane person, nut case <Lat[*2]>

degènečiti {čīm, čē imperf.} *col* beat up <NE>

degènek {a (acc. = gen.) masc.} *dia* big-boned male <NE[*1]>

degènek {a masc.} **a.** *col-dia* bat, stick, rod <NE> **b.** *col-dia* beating up: *Ako ne vratiš pare, ne gine ti degenek. If you don't return that money, you gonna be trashed.* <NE[*1]>

degenèrik [1] {adj.} (lit. degenerate) **a.** *sl-fea* ***Der*** unconventional, weird: *Ona nosi divlje šešire da bi bila degenerik. She wears weird hats just to be unconventional.* <Lat[*1]> **b.** *sl-fea* ***Der*** unattractive, ugly: *degenerik riba ugly chick* <Lat[*2]>

degenèrik [2] {a masc.} **a.** *sl-fea* ***Der*** stupid or mentally deficient person <Lat> **b.** *sl-fea* ***Der*** male who behaves unconventionally, weirdo <Lat[*1]>

déka [1] {ē masc.; Dat déki} *col* ***Fam*** grandfather, grandpa <Slav>

dȅka [2] {ē fem.; Dat dȅki} *col* decagram (10 grams) <Gre✍>

dèkān {dekána (acc. = gen.) masc.} (lit. the dean) *sl-sex* ***Fac-App*** seven-inch long penis <Lat[*1]>

dèken {excl.} *sl-crime* used to warn and command hiding of some object (usu. from the police), hide it <Ger>

dȅkica {ē masc.} *sl-drugs* dezoxine <Lat✣✍>

dekíka {ē fem.; Dat dekíki} BosM *col* minute (unit of time) <NE>

dekintácija {ē fem.} *sl* being broke, being out of money <Alb✣>

dekìntīrān {a, o adj.} *sl* broke (financially) <Alb✣>

dekívānje {a neut.} *sl* fight (e.g. fist fight) <Ger✣[*1]>

dèkl {a +ov (ext. pl) masc.} *sl-crafts* cover, lid <Ger>

dèkla {ē fem.} *sl-crafts* cover, lid <Ger✣>

dèklica {ē fem.} *sl-crafts* cover, lid <Ger✣>

dȅkmantl {a masc.} (lit. overcoat) *sl-fea* cover, lid <Ger[*1]>

dèkna {ē fem.} *sl-crafts* cover, lid <Ger✣>

deknlàntl {a masc.} *sl* shade (of a tree, etc.) <Ger>

dȅknuti {nēm, nū perf.} **a.** *sl* hide, cover up <Ger> **b.** *sl-crime* kill, murder <Ger[*1]>

dekoltê {ea masc.} (lit. décolletage, neckline) *sl-fea* bald male <Fre[*1]>

dekòltirān {a, o adj.} *sl-fea* bald <Fre[*1]>

dekorácija {ē fem.} (lit. decoration) *sl* medal, decoration <Lat[*1]>

dȅkoratīvan {vna, vno adj.} (lit. decorative) *sl* beautiful <Lat[*1]>

dȅkoratīvan švȁler {NP} (lit. decorative lover) *sl-fea* male who just walks with females to be seen with them ☞ švaler

dȅkovānje {a neut.} **1** *sl* hiding <Ger✣> **2** *sl* protecting <Ger✣>

dȅkovati {kujēm, kujū imperf.} **a.** *sl* cover up, hide: *dekovati pištolj cover up a gun* <Ger> **b.** *sl-crime* cover for one's accomplice <Ger[*1]>

dȅkovati se {kujēm, kujū imperf. intr.} *sl* hide (usu. from the police): *dekovati se na selu hide in the countryside* <Ger>

dȅkrati {ām, ajū imperf.; perm} /dèkrati/ [std. = krasti] *sl-crime* steal, swipe <Slav✍>

dèkrēt {dekréta (acc. = gen.) masc.; Voc dȅkrēte} (lit. decree X a contamination from de*te* 'child' and kret(en) 'cretin') **a.** *sl-fea* ***Fac-App*** foolish child <Slav-Fre> **b.** *sl-fea* ***Fac-Der*** stupid or mentally deficient person <Slav-Fre[*1]>

dȅks {a +ev (ext. pl) masc.; Nom Pl dèksevi} [std. = deksedrin] *sl-drugs* dexedrine <Lat✍>

dèkster {a masc.} *sl-crime* detective <Lat✍>

dekurácija {ē fem.} (lit. decockation; 'dekoracija' has been altered to include the root of the word kurac 'penis') [std. = dekoracija] *sl* ***Fac-Obs*** decoration <Lat✍>

dèkūt {dekúta (acc. = gen.) masc.} *sl-fea* senior citizen <Slav✍>

dekúta {ē masc.} *sl* grandfather, grandpa <Slav✍>

dekùtān {a (acc. = gen.) masc.} *sl-fea* senior citizen <Slav✍>

dekutáner {a (acc. = gen.) masc.} *sl* grandfather, grandpa <Slav✍>

dȅla {excl.} *col* used to urge somebody to act, do it <Slav[*1]>

delánac {nca (acc. = gen.) masc.} Cro *sl-drink* doctored wine, wine diluted with water <Slav[*1]>

dȅlati {ām, ajū imperf.} [std. = raditi] **1** **Cro** *col-dia* do, create: *delati nered create a mess* <Slav> **2** *col-dia*

work, labor: *delati u birtiji work in a bar* <Slav>
• **dèlati kȕhinju** {VP} (lit. make a kitchen) **a.** Kajk *sl* lie **b.** Cro *sl* cheat, swindle

delègāt {legáta (acc. = gen.) masc.} (lit. delegate) **1** *sl-sex* ***Fac*** penis <Lat[*1]> **2** *sl* ***Fac*** guest worker

dèlija {ē masc.} **a.** *sl-fea* handsome male, hunk <NE[*1]> **b.** *sl-sports* fan of Crvena Zvezda (a soccer team in Belgrade, Serbia) <NE[*2]>

delikvèncija {ē fem.} [std. = delinkvencija] *col* delinquency <Lat☞>

delȉričār {a (acc. = gen.) masc.} *sl-drink* incurable alcoholic, hopeless drunk <Lat⁘>

delírko {a masc.} *sl-drink* alcoholic, drunk <Lat☞>

dèlisati {išēm, išū imperf.} **1** *sl* give, pass: *delisati cigare pass the smokes* <Gyp[*1]> **2** *sl-gamble* deal (playing cards) <Gyp[*2]>

déliti *See the following*
• **déliti aplàuze** {VP} (lit. distribute applauses) SerE *sl* ***Fac*** slap, smack

dèlkati {ām, ajū perf.} SerE *sl-gamble* deal (playing cards) <Slav☞>

dȅlkos {a, o adj.} *sl-crime* criminal <Slav[*1]>

dȅlnuti {nēm, nū perf.} SerE *sl-gamble* deal (playing cards) <Slav⁘>

deltòid {a masc.} *sl-sex* ***Fac-Obs*** female breast, tit <Gre[*1]>

dèljāk {deljáka masc.} **a.** SerE *sl* halves, splitting costs <Slav⁘> **b.** SerE *sl* sharing <Slav⁘[*1]>

dȅljati {ām, ajū imperf.} (lit. carve) *sl* beat up <Slav[*1]>

dèmbel {a (acc. = gen.) masc.} *sl-fea* lazy or shiftless person, bum, good for nothing <NE[*1]>

dembèlisānje {a neut.} *sl-fea* doing nothing, fooling around <NE⁘[*1]>

dȅme {eta neut.} *sl* a bundle of money

dȅmfati {ām, ajū imperf.} *sl* hide, cover up: *demfati ukradenu robu cover up stolen merchandise* <Ger[*1]>

demìdžana {ē fem.} Med *col-dia* glass container for liquids, demijohn <Ita>

dèmija[1] {ē fem.} *sl-stu* academy <Gre☞>

Dèmija[2] {ē fem.} (lit. *aka*demija 'academy') *sl-stu* the Arts Academy Club in Belgrade, Serbia <Gre☞>

demìjuna {ē fem.} Med *col-dia* glass container for liquids, demijohn <Ita>

demoìćìku {excl.; perm} [std. = idemo kući] *sl* used to stimulate common departure from a certain place, let's go home <Slav☞>

demòlīrān {a, o adj.} (lit. destroyed) *sl-fea* unattractive, ugly: *demoliran auto ugly car* <Lat[*1]>

demòntīrān {a, o adj.} (lit. disassembled) *sl-fea* unattractive, ugly: *demontiran tip ugly guy* <Lat[*1]>

dȅn {masc.} [std. = dan] *dia* day <Slav☞>

dèndī {īja (acc. = gen.) masc.} *col* dandy, fop <Eng>

dèndiš {a masc.} *sl* modern and popular place, hip place <Eng⁘>

dèneska {adv.} *dia-col* today <Mac>

dènim {a masc.} *col* denim <Eng>

dènjāk {denjáka masc.} *sl* wrap, bundle <Slav[*1]>

dèponovati {nujēm, nujū perf.} (lit. dump) *sl* dump one's boyfriend or girlfriend <Lat>

dȅpre {ea (acc. = gen.) masc.; perm} /dèpre/ [std. = peder] *sl-sex* ***Der*** male homosexual, gay <Gre☞>

dêr {part.} *col* intensifying particle: *Kupi der novine! Buy the newspaper, will you!* <Slav[*1]>

deràčina {ē fem.} (lit. screaming) *col* noise <Slav⁘[*1]>

dèrape {ea (acc. = gen.) masc.; perm} [std. = peder] *sl-sex* ***Der*** male homosexual, gay <Gre☞>

dèrati {dȇrēm, rū imperf.} (lit. tear apart) **1** *sl-sex* engage in intensive sexual intercourse with (of a male) <Slav[*1]> 2 *sl* overcharge, rip off: *derati mušterije rip off customers* <Slav[*1]> 3 *sl-gamble* defeat in gambling or any kind of competition <Slav[*1]>
• **dèrati ȁkse do plȉnarē** {VP} (lit. tear axles to the gas works) *sl* walk a lot
• **dèrati vrȇću** {VP} (lit. tear a bag) *sl-crime* pick pockets

dèrati se {rēm, rū imperf. intr.} (lit. tear oneself apart) *sl-sex* engage in sexual intercourse with <Slav[*1]>

dèrigūz {a masc.} (lit. ass tearer) *dia* ***Obs*** thorny field <Slav[*1]>

Dèrigūz {a masc.} (lit. ass tearer) *dia* ***Obs*** name of a field in Lika, Croatia <Slav[*1]>

dȅrīšte {a neut.} (lit. screamer) *col* ***Der*** child, kid <Slav[*1]>

derìvāt {adj.} (lit. derivate) *sl-fea* beaten up <Lat[*1]>

dèrle {eta neut.} **a.** *col* spoiled child, brat <Slav[*1]> **b.** child, kid <Slav[*2]>

• **kako mu se dĩgnē** {AdvP} (lit. as it lifts to him) *col Obs* whenever he wants

Dígo {ē masc.} /Dígo /a masc./ *sl-fea* ***Fac*** Italian (person), Dago <Ita❖[*1]>

Dìgol {a (acc. = gen.) masc.} /dìgol /a (acc. = gen.) masc./ *sl* ***Fac*** Italian (person), Dago <Ita❖[*1]>

dîhãnje {a neut.} [std. = disanje] *col* breathing <Slav✍>

dîhati {dîhãm, dîhajū imperf.} [std. = disati] *col* breathe <Slav✍>

dìhtũng {a masc.} **a.** *sl-crafts* gasket <Ger> **b.** *sl-crafts* idea, thought <Ger[*1]>

dijabóla {ē fem. & masc.} *sl-fea* stupid or mentally deficient person

dĩjãč {a masc.} *dia* photographic slide <Fre❖>

dijalogizírati {gìzīrām, gizírajū imperf.} (lit. dialogue) *sl-gamble* play cards <Gre[*1]>

dijòptrije {dijȍptrījā fem. pl.} (lit. diopter) *sl* eyeglasses <Gre[*]✍>

dìkan {a (acc. = gen.) masc.} (lit. Dikan: a popular comic book character) *sl-sex* ***Obs*** penis, dick, prick <SlavO[*1]>

dìklãš {a (acc. = gen.) masc.} *sl-crime* white-slaver, one who is engaged in white-slave trafficking

dìkljati {ãm, ajū imperf.} *sl* search, look for <Slav[*1]>

dĩksī {ija (acc. = gen.) masc.} (lit. Dixie) **1** *sl-sstu* principal <Eng✍> **2** *sl* director, boss, manager <Eng✍>

dîl {a +ov (ext. pl) masc.; Nom Pl dîlovi} **a.** *sl* deal, business <Eng> **b.** *sl* share, split <Eng[*1]>

diláber [1] {a (acc. = gen.) masc.} **a.** *sl-fea* ***Der*** stupid or mentally deficient person <NE> **b.** *sl-fea* insane person, nut case <NE>

diláber [2] {a masc.} *sl* brilliantine (hairdressing cream) <NE[*1]>

dilâjla {ē fem. & masc.} *sl-fea* ***Der*** stupid or mentally deficient person <Fre✍[*1]>

dĩlati {ãm, ajū biasp.} *sl-drugs* deal narcotic drugs, be a pusher <Eng>

dìlber {a (acc. = gen.) masc.} (lit. lover) *sl-fea* ***Der*** stupid or mentally deficient person <NE[*1]>

dilbèruša {ē fem.} *sl-fea* ***Der*** foolish female <NE[*1]>

dìldik {a (acc. = gen.) masc.} *sl-fea* ***Der*** stupid or mentally deficient person <Fre✍>

dìldika {ē fem. & masc.; Dat dìldiki} **a.** *sl-fea* ***Der*** stupid or mentally deficient person <Fre✍> **b.** *sl-fea* ***Der*** insane person, nut case <Fre✍[*1]>

dilèa {ē masc.} *sl-fea* ***Der*** stupid or mentally deficient person <Fre✍>

diléja {ē fem. & masc.} **a.** *sl-fea* ***Der*** stupid or mentally deficient person <Fre✍> **b.** *sl-fea* naive male <Fre✍[*1]>

dilèjisãnje {a neut.} *sl* ***Der*** insanity, craziness <Fre✍[*1]>

dĩler {a (acc. = gen.) masc.} **a.** *sl-drugs* drug dealer, pusher <Eng> **b.** *sl* dealer (e.g. car dealer) <Eng>

diletȁnt {a (acc. = gen.) masc.} **a.** *sl-fea* ***Der*** stupid or mentally deficient person <Fre[*1]> **b.** *sl-fea* naive male <Fre[*2]>

dĩlfa {ē masc.} *sl* director, boss, manager <Lat✍>

Dìlinger {a (acc. = gen.) masc.} (lit. *John* Dillinger) *sl-crime* troublemaker, rowdy, ruffian <EngO[*1]>

diližȁnsa {ē fem.} (lit. coach) *sl-drugs* drug session <Fre[*1]>

dìlkan {a (acc. = gen.) masc.} **a.** *sl-fea* ***Der*** stupid or mentally deficient person <Fre✍[*1]> **b.** *sl-fea* ***Der*** insane person, nut case <Fre✍[*2]>

dìlkan klûb {NP} (lit. mad man's club) *sl* ***Fac*** mental institution, madhouse ☞ **klub**

dilkàna {ē fem.} *sl* psychiatric hospital <Fre✍[*1]>

dilkànica {ē fem.} *sl* psychiatric hospital <Fre✍[*1]>

dilkániti {dìlkānīm, nē imperf. intr.} **1** *sl* fight (e.g. fist fight): *dilkaniti u bircuzu fight in a bar* <Fre✍[*1]> **2** *sl* go insane, freak out: *dilkaniti od previše posla freak out from being overworked*

dìlkãrnica {ē fem.} *sl* psychiatric hospital <Fre✍[*1]>

dìlkãš {a (acc. = gen.) masc.} *sl-sex* procurer, pimp <Fre✍[*1]>

dĩlke [1] {ea (acc. = gen.) masc.} //eta masc./ *sl-fea* ***Der*** stupid or mentally deficient person <Fre✍[*1]>

dĩlke [2] {adj.} *sl-fea* ***Der*** insane, nuts <Fre✍[*1]>

dĩlkoš {a (acc. = gen.) masc.} *sl-fea* stupid or mentally deficient person <Fre✍[*1]>

dĩlnica {ē fem.} *sl-crime* prison solitary <Fre✍[*1]>

dĩlovati {lujēm, lujū imperf.} /dîlovati/ **1** *sl-drugs* deal narcotic drugs, be a pusher <Eng> **2** *sl-crime* resell, fence <Eng>

dĩm [1] {excl.} (lit. smoke) *sl* used to make somebody go away <Slav[*1]>

dȉm [2] {a +ov (ext. pl) masc.; Nom Pl dìmovi} (lit. smoke) **1** *sl-drink* whiskey <**Slav**[*1]> **2** *sl-crime* escape, getaway: *dim iz ćorke escape from the slammer* <**Slav**[*1]>

• **pı́cīn dȉm** {NP} (lit. cunt's smoke) *sl* ***Obs*** unimportant issue or object: *Taj ispit, to je bio picin dim! That exam, that was fucking nothing!*

• **pȉčkīn dȉm**{NP} (lit. cunt's smoke) *col* ***Obs*** unimportant issue or object: *Akra je pičkin dim za Bagdad. Accra is fucking nothing in comparison with Baghdad.*

• **pízdīn dȉm** {NP} (lit. cunt's smoke) **a.** *col* ***Obs*** unimportant person, nobody, nothing **b.** *col* ***Obs*** worthless object, junk: *Sva ta politika, to je pizdin dim! All that politics, it's just fucking nothing!*

dȉmac {mca masc.} *sl* cigarette smoke <**Slav**❖>

dìmara {ē fem.} *sl* cigarette, smoke <**Slav**❖>

dìmbōn {dimbóna (acc. = gen.) masc.} *sl-fea* stupid or mentally deficient person <**Fre**✍[*1]>

Dȉmče čùkāč {NP} (lit. Dimče, proper name knocker) *sl-fea* ***Fac*** troublemaker, rowdy, ruffian ☞ **čukač**

dimidȕs {adv.} *sl* completely, totally <**NE**✍>

dimírati {dìmīrām, dimírajū imperf. intr.} (lit. smoke) *sl-crime* run away, flee <**Slav**❖[*1]>

dìmisati {išēm, išū imperf. intr.} (lit. smoke) *sl-crime* run away, flee <**Slav**❖[*1]>

dȉmiti {mīm, mē imperf. intr.} **a.** *sl* smoke (tobacco) <**Slav**> **b.** *sl-crime* run away, flee <**Slav**[*1]>

Dimìtrije {a (acc. = gen.) masc.} *sl-fea* stupid or mentally deficient person <**GreO**>

dȉmnica {ē fem.} (lit. smoking place) *sl* name of a restaurant at the main train station in Zagreb, Croatia <**Slav**❖[*1]>

dȉmnīčār {a (acc. = gen.) masc.} (lit. chimney sweeper) *sl-fea* liar <**Slav**[*1]>

dȉmnjačār {a (acc. = gen.) masc.} (lit. chimney sweeper) *sl* ***Off*** African American (male) <**Slav**[*1]>

dȉmnjāk {a masc.} (lit. funnel, chimney) *sl* cigarette, smoke <**Slav**[*1]>

dȋn {a +ov (ext. pl) masc.; Nom Pl dínovi} BosM *col* faith, religion <**NE**>

• **Dína mi imána!** {S} (lit. *I swear* to my faith) **BosM** *col* used to emphasize the truth of what has been said, I swear!

dȋn-dȍn {a masc.} *col* bell <**Slav**[*1]>

dȋn-dȕšman {a (acc. = gen.) masc.} BosM *col* archenemy <**NE**>

dȋn-dȕšmanin {a (acc. = gen.) -in (rd. pl.) masc.} BosM *col* archenemy <**NE**>

dináma {ē fem.} [std. = dinamo] *col* dynamo <**Gre**>

dinàmit {a masc.} (lit. dynamite) *sl* beans <**Gre**[*1]>

dȉnamovac {vca (acc. = gen.) masc.} *col* fan or player for Dinamo (in the 1990s called Croatia, a soccer team from Zagreb, Croatia) <**Gre**[*1]>

dȋnārskī tȋp {NP} (lit. dinar type) *sl-fea* ***Fac*** person with large income (in any business) ☞ **tip**

díndža {ē fem.} **1** *sl* effective move <**NE**[*1]> **2** *sl* dinar (Yugoslav currency unit) <**NE**[*1]>

dȉndžī {īja masc.} *sl* dinar (Yugoslav currency unit) <**NE**[*1]>

diòptrija {ē fem.} (lit. diopters) *sl-sex* ***Fac-Obs*** volume of female breast <**Gre**[*1]>

diòptrije {diōptrījā fem. pl.} (lit. diopters) *sl* eyeglasses <**Gre**[*1]>

dìora {dījara masc.; perm} [std. = radio] *sl* radio <**Lat**✍>

dȉpiti {pīm, pē imperf.} *sl-crime* steal, swipe <**Slav**✍[*1]> ☞ **zdipiti**

dìplāš {dipláša (acc. = gen.) masc.; Voc dȉplāšu} *col* diple (double flute, a traditional musical instrument) player <**Gre**>

dȉpliti {līm, lē imperf.} *col* play the diple (double flute, a traditional musical instrument) <**Gre**>

diplomírati {lòmīrām, lomírajū biasp.} (lit. graduate) *sl* ***Fac*** get married, get hitched <**Gre**[*1]>

dȉpovati {pujēm, pujū imperf. intr.} *sl-drugs* take (usu. narcotic drugs), do <**Eng**>

dírati *See the following*

• **nè dírājte mi ravnìcu** {VP} (lit. don't touch my flatlands) *sl-sex* ***Fac*** small female breast

dìreks {a (acc. = gen.) masc.} [std. = direktor] *sl-sstu* principal <**Lat**✍>

dìrekt {adv.} [std. = direktno] *col* directly, straight: *Vozi direkt do prvog semafora! Drive straight to the first lights!* <**Lat**✍>

dìrīnčiti {čīm, čē imperf.} *col* work hard (at manual labor) <**NE**>

dìrīndžiti {džīm, dže imperf.} *col* work hard (at manual labor) <**NE**>

dȉrke {ī fem. pl.} *sl-auto* races (usu. auto or motorcycle) <**Slav**✍[*1]>

dȉzati {ižēm, ižū imperf.} (lit. lift up) *sl-drugs* begin to take effect (of narcotic drugs) <Slav*1>

- **dȉzati pȁre** {VP} (lit. lift up money) *sl* earn amply
- **dȉzati vȁtru** {VP} (lit. lift up fire) **a.** *col* argue, quarrel **b.** *col* make noise
- **Dȉži dȕpe**! {S} (lit. Lift up your ass!) *col* ***Off*** used to make somebody move, Move your ass!

dízel {a masc.} *col* diesel fuel <GerO>

dizèlāš {zelāša (acc. = gen.) masc.; Voc dìzelāšu} (lit. Diesel engine) **1** *sl-auto* car with diesel engine, diesel <GerO⁘> **2a.** *sl-fea* troublemaker, rowdy, ruffian <GerO⁘*1> **b.** *sl-fea* inhabitant of the countryside, hick, bumpkin <GerO⁘*2>

dízēlka {ē fem.; Dat dízēlki} *col* diesel engine (usu. of a train) <GerO>

dízna {ē fem.} *col* nozzle <Ger☞>

dizúljak {ljka masc.} *sl* elevator <Slav⁘>

djèčijā rȁdōst {NP} (lit. children's joy) *sl-mil* bread spread with marmalade ☞ **radost**

djèčjī grȍb {NP} (lit. child's grave) *sl* ***Fac*** large shoe ☞ **grob**

djȅditi {dīm, dē imperf. intr.} *sl-fea* cry, shed tears, weep <Slav*1>

djèvōjka {ē fem.} **a.** *sl* girlfriend <Slav> **b.** *sl-sex* prostitute, hooker <Slav*1>

djȕtić {a masc.} /djùtīć/ *col* duty free shop <Eng⁘>

dlȁčica *See the following*

- **stȋdnā dlȁčica** {NP} (lit. shame hair) *sl-sex* pubic hair

dlȁka {ē fem.; Dat dlȁki} (lit. hair) *sl-fea* bald head <Slav*1>

- **dlȁka, dlȁka, pa pàuza** {NP} (lit. hair, hair, and then a break) *sl-fea* ***Fac*** very sparse hair
- **dlȁka je fȁlila** {S} (lit. only a hair was missing) *col* used to refer to a dangerous situation in the past: *Dlaka je falila da nas ne uhapse. It was really close. We could have been arrested.*
- **u dlȁku** {PP} (lit. in a hair) *col* exactly, precisely
- **za dlȁku** {AdjP} (lit. for a hair) *col* closely

dlȁkār {a (acc. = gen.) masc.} /dlàkār/ (lit. hairy person) *sl-sex* ***Fac-App*** male homosexual, gay <Slav⁘*1>

dlȁkārskī {ōg masc.} (lit. hairy) *sl* slang <Slav*1>

dlȁkavica {ē fem.} (lit. hairy thing) *sl-sex* ***Obs*** vagina, cunt <Slav*1>

dlȁn {dlàna +ov (ext. pl) masc.; Nom Pl dlànovi} (lit. palm) *sl* slap, smack <Slav*1>

dlànovac {vca masc.} **a.** *sl* slap, smack <Slav⁘> **b.** *sl* punch in the head <Slav⁘*1>

dnêvnē lȁži {NP} (lit. daily lies) *sl* ***Fac*** newspaper ☞ **laž**

do bȁlčaka {PP} (lit. to the sword-hilt) *col* completely, totally, to the hilt: *napiti se do balčaka get completely drunk* ☞ **balčak**

dȍ Boga {PP} (lit. to God) *col* really, very (usu. in the negative): *On je do Boga uobražen. He is really stuck-up.* ☞ **Bog**

do dàskē {PP} (lit. to the plank) **1** *col* to full volume: *odvrnuti radio do daske turn the radio all the way up* **2** totally, completely, fully **3** until the end ☞ **daska**

do Džȁja {AdjP} (lit. to Džajić: Yugoslav soccer legend) *sl* fully, to the hilt: *dati gas do Džaja put the pedal to the metal* ☞ **Džaja**

do Džȁjića {AdjP} (lit. to Džajić: Yugoslav soccer legend) *sl* fully, to the hilt: *napiti se do Džaja be completely drunk* ☞ **Džajić**

do jájā {PP} (lit. to the balls) *sl* ***Obs*** excellent, awesome ☞ **jaja**

Do jájā! {PP} (lit. To the balls!) **1** *sl* ***Der*** used to express anger **2** *sl* ***App*** used to express satisfaction, Great! ☞ **jaja**

do kȍskē {PP} (lit. to the bone) *col* completely, totally, to the bone ☞ **koska**

do krâjnīkā {PP} (lit. to the tonsils) *sl* ***Fac*** completely, totally ☞ **krajnik**

Dò kūrca! {PP} (lit. To the prick!) *sl* ***Obs*** used to express anger, Fuck it! ☞ **kurac**

Dò mōga! {PP} (lit. To mine! *i.e. my penis*) *sl* ***Obs*** used to express anger, Fuck it! ☞ **moj**

Do mòjēga! {PP} (lit. To mine! *i.e. my penis*) *sl* ***Obs*** used to express anger, Fuck it! ☞ **moj**

do sȓži {PP} (lit. to the bone marrow) *col* completely, totally: *pokvaren do srži completely ill-natured* ☞ **srž**

doahtánja {excl.} *sl* ***Fac*** used to take leave of somebody informally, bye-bye

dòakati {ām, ajū perf. intr.} *col* outwit, outsmart <NE⁘*1>

dȍbar [1] {bra, bro adj.} (lit. good) *sl* referring to the one who has earned some money: *Dobar sam dva soma. I'm two grand ahead.* <Slav*1>

dȍbar [2] {bra, bro, bolji adj.} *sl-fea* strong, muscular <Slav*1>

- **dȍbar kô blȁto** {AdjP} (lit. as good as mud) *sl-fea*

Fac very nice and very good person

- **dȍbar kô hlȅb** {AdjP} (lit. as good as bread) SerE *col* ***App*** very nice and very good person
- **dȍbar kô hljȅb** {AdjP} (lit. as good as bread) *col* ***App*** very nice and very good person
- **dȍbar ko krȗ** {AdjP} (lit. as good as bread) *col* ***App*** very nice and very good person
- **dȍbar ko krȗh** {AdjP} (lit. as good as bread) *col* ***App*** very nice and very good person
- **dȍbar ko ljȅb** {AdjP} (lit. as good as bread) *col* ***App*** very nice and very good person
- **dȍbar ko pánja** {AdjP} (lit. as good as bread) *sl-fea* ***App*** very nice and very good person
- **dȍbar ko zdrâvlje** {AdjP} (lit. as good as health) *sl-fea* ***App*** very nice and very good person
- **dȍbar[PRON:DAT] [BE] [onaj:NOM] [NOUN: NOM]** {LSF} *col* ***App*** used to express appreciation: *Dobar ti je onaj auto! Your car is really awesome!*
- **dȍbar si mi** {AdjP} *col* used to express appreciation, way to go
- **Kòlikō je dȍbar?** {S} (lit. How good is he?) *sl* used to inquire about the financial state of a third party, How much money does he have?

dȍbar kòmād {NP} (lit. a good piece) *sl-sex* ***App*** good-looking person ☞ **komad**

dobàrtati {ām, ajū perf. intr.} *sl-arch* bring along: *dobartati kasetaš bring a boombox along* <**Slav**✎[*1]>

dobaùljati {ām, ajū imperf.} *col* crawl to (usu. of an infant) <**Slav**>

dòbeg {a (acc. = gen.) masc.} (lit. one who has ran to) SerE *col* refugee <**Slav**[*1]>

Dòbil je òrlova mùda s màčevima! {S} (lit. He has gotten a pair of eagle's balls with swords!) **SSer** *dia* ***Fac-Obs*** used to refer to a negative outcome for the third person male, He got fucking nothing! ☞ **dobiti**

dȍbiti {dȍbijēm, dȍbijū perf.} (lit. get, receive) **1** *sl-fea* be beaten up <**Slav**[*1]> **2** *sl-sex* have one's period <**Slav**[*1]>

dòbiti *See the following*

- **Dòbiće kȕrac!** {S} (lit. He will get a prick!) *sl* ***Obs*** used to refer to a negative outcome for the third person, He will get fucking nothing!
- **Dòbil je òrlova mùda s màčevima!** {S} (lit. He has gotten a pair of eagle's balls with swords!) **SSer** *dia* ***Fac-Obs*** used to refer to a negative outcome for the third person male, He got fucking nothing!
- **dòbiti bébu** {VP} (lit. have a baby) *sl-sex* ***Fac*** suffer from gonorrhea, have the clap
- **dòbiti cȓvenī kàrtōn** {VP} (lit. get a red card) *col* be thrown out, be fired: *dobiti crveni karton na poslu be fired from one's job*
- **dòbiti dèbelī pȍklōn** {Vp} (lit. get a fat present) *sl-sex* ***Fac*** suffer from syphilis, get the pox
- **dòbiti dlȁn** {VP} (lit. get a palm) *sl* ***Fac*** be slapped
- **dòbiti dȓšku na stomáku** {VP} (lit. get a handle on one's stomach) *sl* ***Fac*** get married, get hitched
- **dòbiti gâs** {VP} (lit. get gas) *sl-drink* continue to drink
- **dòbiti ȉšijās trȅpavīcā** {VP} (lit. get lumbago of the eyelashes) *sl* ***Fac*** stare at, be fixated on
- **dòbiti káru na žáru** {S} (lit. get a roasted prick) *col* ***Obs*** get nothing, come up empty
- **dòbiti míndžu na pìrindžu** {S} (lit. get a cunt with rice) *col* ***Obs*** get nothing, come up empty
- **dòbiti kórpu** {VP} (lit. get a basket) **a.** *sl* be dumped by one's boyfriend or girlfriend **b.** *sl* be refused, be denied, be turned down
- **dòbiti kȓpu** {VP} (lit. get a rag) *sl* be dumped by one's girlfriend
- **dòbiti kȕrac** {VP} (lit. get a prick) *sl* ***Obs*** get nothing, come up empty
- **dòbiti máru** {VP} (lit. get a beating) *sl* be beaten up
- **dòbiti nȍge** {VP} (lit. get legs) *sl-crime* ***Fac*** be stolen, grow legs
- **dòbiti nȍgu** {VP} (lit. get a leg) **1** *col* be fired **2** *col* be dumped by one's boyfriend or girlfriend **3** *col* be thrown out: *dobiti nogu iz resortana be thrown out of a restaurant*
- **dòbiti òspice od** {VP} (lit. get the pox from) *sl* ***Fac*** be disturbed by, be bothered by
- **dòbiti pedálu** {VP} (lit. get a pedal) *sl* ***Fac*** be thrown out, get the boot
- **dòbiti plâvu štráftu oko vrâta** {VP} (lit. get a blue line around one's neck) *sl* ***Fac*** be bothered, be disturbed
- **dòbiti po nòsu** {VP} (lit. get on one's nose) *col* get beaten up
- **dòbiti po pȉčki** {VP} (lit. get on one's cunt) *col* get beaten up
- **dòbiti po ùšima** {VP} (lit. get on one's ears) *col* get beaten up
- **dòbiti šípak** {VP} (lit. get a wild rose bud) *col* get nothing, come up empty
- **dòbiti šȕt-kàrtōn** {VP} (lit. get a kick-card) *sl* be thrown out, get the boot: *dobiti šut karton sa zabave be thrown out from a party*
- **dòbiti šȕt-kártu** {VP} (lit. get a kick-card) *sl* be thrown out, get the boot
- **dòbiti žȗlj** {VP} (lit. get a blister) *sl-sex* ***Fac*** get pregnant, get knocked up
- **dòbiti žȗtī kàrtōn** {VP} (lit. get a yellow card) *col* be warned

dòbjeg {a (acc. = gen.) masc.} (lit. one who has run to) *col* refugee <Slav*1>

dòbro[1] {part.} 1 *col* used to change the topic of conversation, well, ok: *Dobro, šta sad da radim? Well, what should we do now?* <Slav> 2 *col* particle used to express affirmation or approbation in response to adjacent statement or sequence, good, fine, well <Slav> 3 *col* particle used to express active listening, uh-huh, ok, gotcha <Slav>

dòbro[2] {adv.} *col* much, very: *On je dobro bolestan. He is very sick.* <Slav*1>

dòbro párče {NP} (lit. good piece) *sl-sex* ***App*** attractive person ☞ **parče**

Dòbro sȁšīto! {S} (lit. Well sewed!) *sl* used to express satisfaction, appreciation, etc., Everything's fine! ☞ **sašiti**

dobrotánović {a (acc. = gen.) masc.} *sl-fea* ***App*** good and loved male <Slav❖>

dȍbrovōljnī óvan {NP} (lit. voluntary ram) *sl-fea* ***Fac*** person susceptible to deception, easy mark ☞ **ovan**

dóca {ē masc.} SerE *sl* ***Fam*** doctor, doc <Lat✍>

docìpljati {ām, ajū imperf. intr.} *sl-arch* bring <Hun❖✍*1>

dòckan {adv.} *col* late: *Već je dockan. It's getting late.* <Slav>

dòcnijē {adv.} *col* later: *Doći ću docnije, sad sam zauzet. I'll come later, now I'm busy.* <Slav>

dòcniti {nīm, nē imperf.} *col* be late: *docniti na sastanak be late to a meeting* <Slav>

dočèkuša {ē fem.} 1a. *sl* female who stands at the entrance to greet visitors (usu. to one's own home) <Slav❖> b. *sl* female who approaches males (usu. offering sexual favors to them) <Slav❖> 2 *col* first coffee served to one's guests <Slav❖>

dȍčkati {ām, ajū perf.} *sl* bring along <Slav>

dočkòjati {ām, ajū perf.} *sl* bring along <Slav>

Dóće Cíca na kolíca! {S} (lit. A kitten will come to the carriage!) *col* used when somebody refuses to offer his/her help, You will need me one day! ☞ **doći**

Dóće máca na vratánca! {S} (lit. A kitten will come to the small door!) *col* used when somebody refuses to offer his/her help, You will need me one day! ☞ **doći**

dòćerati {ām, ajū perf.} [std. = dotjerati, doterati] *dia-col* drive to <Slav✍>

• **dòćerati càra do dȕvāra** {VP} (lit. bring an emperor to the wall) *col-dia* bring to final consequences

dôći {ođem, ođu, ođ, oš perf. irreg.} /dóći/ *col* cost <Slav*1>

• **Dóće Cíca na kolíca!** {S} (lit. A kitten will come to the carriage!) *col* used when somebody refuses to offer his/her help, You will need me one day!

• **Dóće máca na vratánca!** {S} (lit. A kitten will come to the small door!) *col* used when somebody refuses to offer his/her help, You will need me one day!

• **dóći do** {VP} (lit. come to) *col* get, obtain: *doći do kafe get some coffee*

• **dóći do cîlja** {VP} (lit. come to the finish) *col* achieve, fulfill one's goals: *Dugo je radio dok nije došao do cilja. He worked a lot until he fulfilled his goals.*

• **dóći gláve** {VP} (lit. cost one's head) *col* ruin

• **dóći kô šȁka na ȍko** {VP} (lit. be convenient like a fist in one's eye) *sl* ***Fac*** be highly inappropriate: *Takvo odgovaranje šefu došlo je ko šaka na oko. Talking back to the boss that way was highly inappropriate.*

• **dóći nȁ noge** {VP} (lit. come to one's legs) *col* obey: *doći roditeljima na noge obey one's parents*

• **dóći nȁ rūke** {VP} (lit. come to one's arms) *col* be beaten up

• **dóći na rȕkomēt** {VP} (lit. come to one's handball) *sl* ***Fac*** be beaten up

• **dóći na sȉcer** {VP} (lit. come to certainty) *sl* take revenge

• **dôći na svòje** {VP} *col* profit from the final outcome of a situation

• **dóći na zȉcer** {VP} (lit. come to certainty) *sl* take revenge

• **dóći[PRON/NOUN:DAT] iz dȕpeta u glâvu** {VP} (lit. come [PRON/NOUN:ACC] from one's ass to one's head) *col* ***Obs*** understand, realize: *Dugo nije htio da me sluša, ali mu je na kraju došlo iz dupeta u glavu da sam u pravu. He didn't want to listen to me for a long time, but he finally realized that I was right.*

• **dóći preko gláve** {VP} (lit. come over one's head) *col* have enough of, be sick and tired of

• **dóći sèbi** {VP} (lit. come to oneself) *col* recover, get better: *Jedva je došao sebi od sinoćnje pijanke. He had major difficulties to recover from last night's party.*

• **dóći šâka** {VP} (lit. come to one's hands) *sl* beat up

• **Dȍšla Cíca na kolíca!** {S} (lit. Cica came to the carriage!) *col* used in response to a person who previously refused to offer help, Now you need something from me!

• **Dȍšla máca na vratánca!** {S} (lit. A kitten came to the small door!) *col* used in response to a person who previously refused to offer help, Now you need something from me!

dòdati *See the following*

• **dòdati gâs** {VP} (lit. press the accelerator) *sl-drink* ***Fac*** continue to drink

dodìjati {jēm, jū imperf.} *col* have enough of, be sick and tired of: *Dodijale su mi Markove gluposti. I had enough of Marko's nonsense.* <**Slav**>

dodúšē {part.} **1** *col* particle used to signal a contradiction between two parts of a discourse or to amend previous information, well: *On je stalno s djecom. Doduše, on ne radi. He is with the kids all the time. Well, but he doesn't work.* <**Slav**> **2** *col* as a matter of fact: *Ona je doduše u Italiji. As a matter of fact, she is in Italy.* <**Slav**>

dȍđavola {excl.} **/dòđavola/** *col* used to express anger, hell <**Slav**>

dôđoš {a (acc. = gen.) masc.} (lit. one who came) **a.** *col* ***Der*** newcomer <**Slav**❖> **b.** *col* ***Der*** snob: *Taj dođoš ima punu kuću kičeraja. That snob has a house full of kitschy things.* <**Slav**❖[*1]>

dȍdž {a +ev (ext. pl) masc.; Nom Pl dòdževi} (abbreviation from domaća obična **dđukela** *common domestic mongrel*) *sl-fea* ***Fac*** mixed breed dog, mutt, mongrel <**Abb**>

dofúrati {dòfūrām, dofúrajū perf. intr.} *col* arrive, come: *dofurati na sastanak come to a meeting* <**Ger**❖>

dofúrati se {ām, ajū perf. intr.} *col* arrive, come <**Ger**❖>

dofurijánović {a masc.} *sl* arrival <**Ger**❖>

dògaćnica {ē fem.} (lit. next to the underpants) **1** *sl* ***Fac*** trousers, pants <**Slav**❖> **2** ***Fac*** skirt <**Slav**❖>

dògambati {ām, ajū perf. intr.} *sl* arrive, come <**Ita**❖>

dogambávānje {a neut.} *sl* arrival <**Ita**❖>

dogégati se {dògēgām, dogégajū perf. intr.} *col* arrive with difficulty <**Slav**>

dogíbati {dògībām, dogíbajū perf. intr.} *sl* arrive, come <**Slav**[*1]>

dogìljati {ām, ajū perf. intr.} *sl* arrive, come <**Gyp**>

dògljati [1] {ām, ajū perf.} *sl* add <**Gyp**>

dògljati [2] {ām, ajū perf. intr.} *sl* arrive, come <**Gyp**>

dògnjati {ām, ajū perf. intr.} *sl* arrive, come <**Slav**>

dògod {adv.} [std. = dok god] *col* as long as <**Slav**✍>

dogodóvština {ē fem.} *col* adventure: *Kad nas je seljak zaganjo sa sjekirom, to je bila prava dogodovština. When the peasant started to run after us with an axe, now that was a real adventure.* <**Slav**>

dogòrjeti *See the following*

• **Dogòrjelo[PRON:DAT] do nokátā.** {LSF} (lit. It has burned up to one's fingernails.) **a.** *col* used to indicate a difficult situation, [PRON:NOM] [BE] in a very difficult situation: *Dogorjelo joj do nokata. She is in a very difficult situation.* **b.** *col* used to refer to the state of having had enough of something

dogòvoreno {excl.} *col* used to signal approval, readiness, etc., deal, agreed <**Slav**>

dogúliti {dògūlīm, dògūlē imperf.} *sl-fea* be boring <**Slav**[*1]>

dogurívati {gùrujēm, gùrujū imperf. intr.} *sl* arrive, come <**Slav**>

dòhajbati {ām, ajū perf. intr.} *sl* arrive, come <**Ger**❖>

dòhakati {ām, ajū perf. intr.} *col* outwit, outsmart <**NE**❖[*1]>

Dòjčland {a masc.} *sl* Germany <**Ger**>

dȍjčmàrka {ē fem.; Dat dȍjčmàrki} *sl* German mark <**Ger**✍>

dòjčura {ē fem.} *sl-sex* ***Obs*** large-breasted female <**Slav**✍[*1]>

dojèbati {dòjebēm, bū imperf.} *sl-sex* ***Obs*** end sexual intercourse <**Slav**>

dòjiti *See the following*

• **dòjiti frȁjera** {VP} (lit. milk a guy) *sl-sex* ***Fac-Obs*** engage in fellatio

dòjkara {ē fem.} *sl-sex* ***Obs*** large-breasted female <**Slav**✍[*1]>

dȍk {a (acc. = gen.) +ov (ext. pl) masc.; Nom Pl dòkovi} *sl* doctor, doc <**Eng**>

dok kâžēš kȅks {S} (lit. before you say "biscuit") *col* right away, before you can say "boo" ☞ **kazati**

dok kâžēš brȉtva {S} (lit. before you say "razor") *col* right away, before you can say "boo" ☞ **kazati**

dok nè kāžēš brȉtva {S} (lit. before you don't say "razor") *col* right away, before you can say "boo" ☞ **kazati**

dok nè kāžēš kȅks {S} (lit. before you don't say "biscuit") *col* right away, before you can say "boo" ☞ **kazati**

dok si rèkaō brȉtva {S} (lit. before you said "razor") *col* right away, before you can say "boo" ☞ **reći**

dok si rèkō brȉtva {S} (lit. before you said "razor") *col* right away, before you can say "boo" ☞ **reći**

dok si rèkō kȅks {S} (lit. before you said "biscuit") *col* right away, before you can say "boo" ☞ **reći**

dòkačiti {čīm, čē perf.} **1** *col* hit, punch <**Slav**> **2** *col* mention, hit on <**Slav**>

dòkan {a masc.} *sl-sex* ***Obs*** penis, dick, prick <**Lat**✍[*1]>

dòkl īnčiti {čīm, čē perf.} *col* be boring <Slav>

dòklēn {adv.} [std. = dokle] *dia-col* where to, where do you want to go: *Doklen ide ovaj voz? Where is this train going to?* <Slav✍>

dokolènica {ē fem.} (lit. knee sock) SerE *sl-fea* short female <Slav>

dokolèničārka {ē fem.; Dat dokolèničārki} (lit. the one in knee socks) 1 SerE *sl* passionate female dancer (one who makes exaggerated moves while dancing) <Slav[*1]> 2 SerE *sl* very young female, little girl <Slav[*1]>

dòkon {a, o adj.} *col* without any duties: *Ona je dokona, pa stalno piše po Internetu. She is without any duties, so she keeps posting on the Internet.* <Slav>

dòkonōst {i fem.} *col* free time <Slav❖>

dȍktoš {a (acc. = gen.) masc.} *sl* doctor, doc <Lat✍>

dȍktūr {a (acc. = gen.) masc.} Med *col-dia* doctor, doc <Lat✍>

dòkūčiti {čīm, čē perf.} *col* reach, bring an object closer to oneself: *dokučiti cigare reach for the smokes* <Slav>

dokurcàna {ē fem.} (lit. next to penis) 1 *sl* ***Obs*** loss, detriment: *Imali smo dokurcanu s benerficijama u ovom novom poslu. We lost some benefits with this new job.* <Slav❖[*1]> 2 *sl* ***Obs*** suffering <Slav❖[*1]>

dòkūrčiti {čīm, čē perf.} *sl* ***Obs*** be boring <Slav❖[*1]>

• **Dòkurčilo[PRON:DAT]!** {LSF} *sl* ***Obs*** used to express extreme dissatisfaction, [PRON:NOM] [BE] fucking sick and tired of all this!: *Dokurčilo mi! I am fucking sick and tired of all this!*

• **Dòkūrčilo[PRON:DAT] je svȅ!** {LSF} *sl* ***Obs*** used to express extreme dissatisfaction, [PRON:NOM] [BE] fucking sick and tired of all this!: *Dokurčilo mi je sve! I am fucking sick and tired of all this!*

dòkuriti {rīm, rē perf. intr.} *sl* arrive quickly <Slav[*1]>

dòlāp {dolápa masc.} *sl* escalator <NE[*1]>

dȍlār *See the following*

• **pròbūšenī dȍlār** {NP} (lit. drilled dollar) *sl-sex* ***Obs*** former virgin

doları̏ška {ē fem.; Dat doları̏ški} /doları̏ška/ *sl* US dollar, buck <Eng✍>

dolčevı̏ta {ē fem.} *col* turtleneck shirt <Ita[*1]>

dȍle {adv.} (lit. downstairs) Gast *col* in one's home country <Slav[*1]>

dolepȑšati {ām, ajū perf. intr.} (lit. fly to) *col* arrive, come <Slav[*1]>

dȍlga {ē fem.; Dat dȍlgi} *sl* daily wage

dòlibaša {ē fem.} *col-dia* person in charge of distributing hard liquor at parties <Slav-NE❖>

dolı̀na *See the following*

• **Dolı̀na Slònōvā** {NP} (lit. Elephant Valley) *sl* ***Fac*** name for New Belgrade (Yugoslavia)

dolôres {a masc.} *sl* US dollar, buck <Eng✍>

dȍm *See the following*

• **KP[kâ-pê] dȍm** {NP} *sl-crime* juvenile detention center, juvie

dòmāćī {ā, ē adj.} (lit. domestic) *col* home-made: *domaća rakija home-made brandy* <Slav[*1]>

domàćica {ē fem.} (lit. housewife) 1 *sl-drugs* ***Fac*** marijuana, pot, grass <Slav[*1]> 2 *sl-music* ***Fac*** music from one's own country <Slav[*1]>

• **Domàćicu ti jèbēm!** {S} (lit. I screw your housewife!) *col* ***Off*** used as a weak curse, Screw you!

domàzet {a (acc. = gen.) masc.} *col* ***Der*** male who lives with his in-laws <Slav>

domı̀nati {ām, ajū imperf.} *sl* eat greedily, wolf, stuff one's face <Ita[*1]>

dòmindžos {a masc.} (lit. next to vagina) *sl* ***Fac*** mini-skirt <Gyp❖[*1]>

dòmindžos-sȕknja {ē fem.} (lit. next-to-vagina skirt) *sl* ***Fac*** mini-skirt <Gyp-Slav❖[*1]> ☞ suknja

dòminđos {a masc.} (lit. next to vagina) *sl* ***Fac*** mini-skirt <Gyp❖[*1]>

dòminđos-sȕknja {ē fem.} (lit. next-to-vagina skirt) *sl* ***Fac*** mini-skirt <Gyp-Slav❖[*1]> ☞ suknja

dȍmine {ā fem. pl.} (lit. domino) *sl* teeth <Lat[*1]>

dȍmino {a masc.} (lit. domino) *sl* tooth <Lat[*1]>

dòmlāznjāk {a (acc. = gen.) masc.} (lit. next to the jet of water) *col* ***Fac*** street cleaner, street sweeper <Slav❖[*1]>

dòmovina {ē fem.} (lit. home country) *sl* ***Fac*** stomach, belly, gut <Slav[*1]>

domunđávati se {mùnđāvām, munđávajū imperf. intr.} *sl-fea* conspire, plot <Slav❖[*1]>

dòmuz {a (acc. = gen.) masc.} (lit. pig) BosM *col* ***Off*** non-Muslim <NE[*1]>

dȍn {dòna (acc. = gen.) +ov (ext. pl) masc.; Nom Pl dònovi} *sl-fea* stupid or mentally deficient person

dȍnje {num.; perm} *sl* one <Slav✍>

dȍnje vidíkovac {NP} (lit. one promenade deck) *sl* one example: *Daj mi donje vidikovac toga. Give me one example of that.* ☞ vidikovac

dôp {a +ov (ext. pl) masc.; Nom Pl dòpovi} **/dôp/ a.** *sl-drugs* narcotic drug, dope <Eng> **b.** *sl-drugs* heroin, horse, smack <Eng*1>

dopèrjati {ām, ajū perf. intr.} (lit. feather to) *col* arrive, come <Slav*1>

dopíliti {līm, lē perf.} (lit. finish sawing) *sl-fea* be boring <Slav*1> *Dopilio mi je ovaj posao I am sick and tired of this job.*

dopízdeti {dòpīzdīm, dē perf. intr.} (lit. cunt to) **1** *sl-fea* ***Obs*** be boring: *Dopizdio mi je Marko. I find Marko very boring.* <Slav*1> **2** *sl-fea* ***Obs*** have enough of, be sick and tired of <Slav*1> *Sve mi je dopizdilo. I am sick and tired of everything.* ☞ **dopižđeti, dopizditi**

dopízditi {dòpīzdīm, dē perf. intr.} (lit. cunt to) **1** *sl-fea* ***Obs*** be boring: *Dopizdio mi je Marko. I find Marko very boring.* <Slav*1> **2** *sl-fea* ***Obs*** have enough of, be sick and tired of <Slav*1> *Sve mi je dopizdilo. I am sick and tired of everything.* ☞ **dopižđeti, dopizdeti**

dopížđeti {dòpīzdīm, dē perf. intr.} (lit. cunt to) **1** *sl-fea-dia* ***Obs*** be boring <Slav*1> **2** *sl-fea-dia* have enough of, be sick and tired of <Slav*1> ☞ **dopizdeti, dopizditi**

dòplaziti {zīm, zē perf. intr.} (lit. crawl to) *sl* arrive, come <Slav*1>

dòpuzati {ām, ajū perf. intr.} (lit. crawl to) *sl* arrive, come <Slav*1>

dòrat {a (acc. = gen.) masc.} (lit. black horse) *sl-fea* stupid or mentally deficient person <NE*1>

dorìvati se {ām, ajū imperf. intr.} *sl* arrive, come <Ita❖>

dósa {ē fem.} **a.** *sl* piglet <Slav*1> **b.** *sl* pig (the animal) <Slav❖*2>

dosađínstvo {a neut.} (lit. boring thing) **1** *sl* housekeeping <Slav✍> **2** *sl-sstu* course, class <Slav✍>

dosánac {nca (acc. = gen.) masc.} *sl* boar (the animal) <Slav❖*1>

dòsānče {eta neut.} **a.** *sl* piglet <Slav❖*1> **b.** *sl* pig (the animal) <Slav❖*2>

dòsānka {ē fem.} **a.** *sl* piglet <Slav❖*1> **b.** *sl* pig (the animal) <Slav❖*2>

dòsinac {nca (acc. = gen.) masc.} *sl* boar (the animal) <Slav❖*1>

dòsprintati {ām, ajū perf.} (lit. sprint to) *sl* arrive quickly <Eng❖>

dȍsta {excl.} *col* used to mark an end of one's own words: *Dosta! Neću više da pričam o tome! That's it! I don't wanna talk about that anymore!* <Slav>

dostàvljāč {tavljáča (acc. = gen.) masc.} (lit. courier) *sl-crime* ***Der*** informer, stoolie, snitch <Slav*1>

dòšājbati {ām, ajū perf. intr.} *sl* arrive, come <Ger❖>

došétati *See the following*

- **došétati ȕho[PRON/NOUN:DAT]** {VP} (lit. walk one's ear [PRON/NOUN:ACC]) *sl* ***Fac*** listen to: *došetati uho profesoru listen to the professor*
- **došétati ȕvo[PRON/NOUN:DAT]** {VP} (lit. walk one's ear [PRON/NOUN:ACC]) **Ser** *sl* ***Fac*** listen to: *došetati uvo majci listen to one's mother*

Dòšla Cíca na kolíca! {S} (lit. Cica came to the carriage!) *col* used in response to a person who previously refused to offer help, Now you need something from me! ☞ **doći**

Dòšla máca na vratánca! {S} (lit. A kitten came to the small door!) *col* used in response to a person who previously refused to offer help, Now you need something from me! ☞ **doći**

dòšlepati {ām, ajū perf. intr.} *sl* arrive, come <Ger❖*1>

dóšlo {a masc.} **//ē masc./** (lit. the one who came) *sl-fea* ***Der*** newcomer <Slav*1>

dòšljār {došljára (acc. = gen.) masc.} *sl-fea* stranger (male) <Slav❖>

dòšprintati {ām, ajū perf. intr.} *sl* arrive quickly <Eng❖>

dòštartati {ām, ajū perf. intr.} *sl* arrive quickly <Ger❖*1>

- **dòštartati u sìtnōj kȓpi** {VP} (lit. arrive wearing some small rags) *sl* arrive in one's underwear (e.g. at a party)

dotepénac {nca (acc. = gen.) masc.} *sl-fea* ***Der*** newcomer <Slav*1>

dòterati càra do dȕvāra {VP} (lit. bring the emperor to the wall) SerE *col* corner somebody ☞ **doterati**

dòterati *See the following*

- **dòterati càra do dȕvāra** {VP} (lit. bring the emperor to the wall) SerE *col* corner somebody

dòtičnā {ē fem. (adj. decl.)} *col* person in question (female) <Slav*1>

dòtičnī {ā, ō adj.} *col* person in question (male) <Slav*1>

dòtjerati *See the following*

- **dòtjerati càra do dȕvāra** {VP} (lit. bring the emperor to the wall) *col* corner somebody

dȍtka {ē fem.; Dat dȍtki} *sl-sex* ***Obs*** vagina, cunt <Slav>

dòtle bi i óvca naùčila da ȉgrā mícē s brȁbōnjcima {S} (lit. by that time even a sheep would learn to play checkers with its shit) *sl* ***Fac*** used to indicate impatience, that something takes too long ☞ **naučiti**

dòtrajān {a, o adj.} *col* used (not new) <**Slav**[*1]>

dòtūći {dotúčem, túku, dòtuk, dòtuk perf. irreg.} (lit. finish beating up) *col* ruin somebody (emotionally or financially): *Dotukla ga je vest o smrti oca. The news about his father's death finished him.* <**Slav**[*1]>

dòtūr {a (acc. = gen.) masc.} Med *dia* doctor, doc <**Lat**✍>

dòturiti {rīm, rē perf.} *col* supply in a clandestine manner, give on the sly <**Slav**>

dôup {a +ov (ext. pl) masc.; Nom Pl dóupovi} **a.** *sl-drugs* narcotic drug, dope <**Eng**> **b.** *sl-drugs* heroin, horse, smack <**Eng**[*1]>

dȍvečē {adv.} *col-dia* in the evening <**Slav**>

doviđénce {excl.} *col* ***Fam*** used to take leave of somebody informally, bye-bye <**Slav**✍>

doviđénja {excl.} *col* used to take leave of somebody, bye-bye <**Slav**⁘>

- **Doviđénja, prȉjātno!** {ExcP} (lit. Bye, have a nice time!) *col* used to mark the end of the discourse, That's all!

dòvući {dovúčem, vúku, dòvuk, dòvuk perf. irreg.} (lit. drag) *col* bring: *Dovuko je dva prijatelja na zabavu. He brought two of his friends to the party.* <**Slav**[*1]>

dòzlaboga {adv.} *col* very: *Marija je dozlaboga ozbiljna oko svog posla. Mary is very serious about her work.* <**Slav**[*1]>

dozlogŕditi {lògr̄dīm, dē imperf.} *col* have enough of, be sick and tired of: *Dozlogrdila mi je ova muzika. I had enough of this music.* <**Slav**[*1]>

drâč {a +ev (ext. pl) masc.; Nom Pl dràčevi} *sl* flowers <**Slav**[*1]>

drȁča {ē fem.} *col* thorny plant <**Slav**>

drádža {ē fem.} *sl* 24-hour convenience store <**Eng**✍>

dragȉčka {excl.} *col* good news <**Slav**[*1]>

dràgiša {ē masc.} *sl* 24-hour convenience store <**Eng**✍>

drágović *See the following*

- **drágoviću môj** {NP} (lit. my dear) *col* used as an intensifier in direct informal communication

drágoviću {excl.} (lit. my dear) *col* used to address a male in direct informal communication <**Slav**[*1]>

dràgstor {a masc.} *col* 24-hour convenience store <**Eng**[*1]>

dràjfer {a (acc. = gen.) masc.} *sl-sex* ***Der*** male homosexual, gay <**Ger**[*1]>

drȁjfnuti {nēm, nū perf.} *sl* hit, punch <**Ger**[*1]>

drȁjfovati {fujēm, fujū imperf.} *sl-crime* feel a thief stealing one's wallet <**Ger**[*1]>

dràjvati {ām, ajū biasp.} *sl-auto* drive (a vehicle) <**Eng**>

drajvírati {ràjvīrām, rajvírajū imperf. intr.} *sl-auto* drive (a vehicle) <**Eng**>

dràkula {ē fem. & masc.} /dràkula/ (lit. Dracula) *sl-fea* unattractive person <**RumO**[*1]>

dràkulić {a (acc. = gen.) masc.} /dràkulić/ (lit. Dracula's son) *sl-fea* unattractive male <**RumO**⁘[*1]>

dràkulīn čȁj {NP} (lit. Dracula's tea) *sl-sex* ***Fac*** menstruation, period ☞ **čaj**

Dràkulović {a (acc. = gen.) masc.} (lit. Dracula's son) *sl-fea* unattractive male, dog <**RumO**⁘[*1]>

dràkūt {drakúta (acc. = gen.) masc.} (lit. Dracula) *sl-fea* unattractive person <**RumO**✍>

drâle {eta neut.} (lit. Dracula) *sl-fea* unattractive male, dog <**RumO**✍>

drȁm {a (acc. = gen.) +ov (ext. pl) masc.; Nom Pl dràmovi} *col* small quantity of something <**NE**[*1]>

drȁmati {ām, ajū biasp.} *sl-music* drums <**Eng**>

drȁmer {a (acc. = gen.) masc.} /dràmer/ **1** *sl-music* drummer <**Eng**> **2** *sl* alarmist (male) <**Gre**[*1]>

drȁmeri {a masc. pl.} /dràmeri/ *sl-music* drums <**Eng**>

dramȉli dȕpeta {NP} (lit. having a small ass) *sl-fea* ***Obs*** miserly, stingy ☞ **dupe**

drȁmiti {mīm, mē imperf.} (lit. dramatize) **1** *sl-fea* panic, freak out: *Ne drami, nije ništa strašno! Don't panic, it's not that bad!* <**Gre**[*1]> **2** *sl-fea* boast, brag <**Gre**[*1]>

drȁmiti se {mīm, mē imperf. intr.} *sl* pretend <**Gre**⁘[*1]>

dramòser {a masc.} *col* miser, tightwad, skinflint <**NE-Slav.**[*1]>

drangùlija {ē fem.} **1** *col* detail <**NE**[*1]> **2** *col* gadget <**NE**[*1]>

drangùlije {a fem. pl.} *col* items of no value or importance <**NE**[*1]>

drapačóza {ē fem.} *sl-sex* ***Fac*** elderly prostitute <**Slav**✍>

drápati {drâpām, drápajū imperf.} (lit. tear) **1** *sl-sex* ***Obs*** engage in sexual intercourse with (of a male) <**Slav**[*1]> **2** *sl-crime* ***Der*** steal, swipe <**Slav**[*1]>

drápati se {drâpām, drápajū imperf. intr.} **1** *sl-sex* have sexual foreplay, pet, feel up: *drapati se s frajerom feel* *up one's boyfriend* <**Slav**[*1]> 2 *sl-auto* drive fast, speed: *drapati se na autoputu speed on a highway* <**Slav**[*1]>

dràpavac {vca masc.} (lit. scratcher) *sl* finger <**Slav**[*1]>

dràpiti {pīm, pē imperf.} *sl* eat, devour <**Slav**[*1]>

dràplja {ē fem.} *sl-fea* ***Der*** senior citizen <**Slav**[*1]>

dràmer {a (acc. = gen.) masc.} *sl-music* drummer <**Eng**✍>

dráža {ē fem.} (lit. drugstore X Draža, man's name) *sl* 24-hour convenience store <**Eng**✍>

Dràžen {a masc.} (lit. a proper name) *sl-sex* ***Obs*** clitoris <**SlavO**[*1]>

drébank {a masc.} *sl-crafts* lathe <**Ger**>

dréčati {čīm, čē imperf. intr.} *col* scream in pain, fear, or outrage <**Slav**>

drèk [1] {a +ov (ext. pl) masc.; Nom Pl drèkovi} **a.** Cro *col* excrement <**Ger**> **b.** Cro *col* ***Der*** dirty object <**Ger**[*1]>
- **drèk na šìbici** {NP} (lit. shit on a match) **1** *sl* ***Der-Obs*** worthless object, shit **2** *sl* ***Der-Obs*** low-quality object

drèk [2] {a +ov (ext. pl) (acc. = gen.) masc.; Nom Pl drèkovi} **Cro** *col* ***Der*** worthless or despicable person: *Taj drek me opet izradio. That scum has cheated me again.* <**Ger**>

drèka {ē fem.; Dat drèki} *col* noise <**Slav**>

drékalica {ē fem.} *sl-crime* policeman, cop <**Slav**❖>

drékniti {drêknēm, drêknū perf.} *col* scream in pain, fear, or outrage <**Slav**✍>

dréknuti {drêknēm, drêknū perf. intr.} *col* scream in pain, fear, or outrage <**Slav**>

drémati *See the following*
- **Drème ko bîvā na mòkar kùrac!** {S} (lit. He sleeps as if being on a wet cock!) **SSer** *dia* ***Obs*** used to express negative attitude toward, Fuck him!

drêmka {ē fem.} SerE *col* sleeping <**Slav**❖>

drenòvān {nována (acc. = gen.) masc.} *sl* archbishop <**Slav**[*1]>

drèsīrān {a, o adj.} *sl* well-dressed <**Eng**>

dréšiti {drêšīm, šē imperf.} SerE *col* untie <**Slav**[*1]>
- **dréšiti kèsu** {VP} (lit. open one's bag) SerE *col* give money, open one's wallet

drèto {adv.} **Med** *col-dia* directly, straight: *voziti dreto do prvog križanja pa skreni lijevo drive straight to the first intersection and turn left* <**Ita**>

dréždati {dīm, dē imperf. intr.} *col* wait for a long time <**Slav**>

drìblati *See the following*
- **Kȍ te drìblā!** {S} (lit. Who is dribbling you?) *sl* ***Off*** used as a weak curse, Screw you!

drìblovati {lujēm, lujū imperf.} (lit. dribble) **a.** *sl* lie: *driblovati o putu u Španiju lie about a trip to Spain* <**Eng**[*1]> **b.** *sl* cheat, swindle <**Eng**[*2]>

drìbljati {ām, ajū imperf.} **a.** *sl-sports* dribble (e.g. in basketball) <**Eng**✍[*1]> **b.** *sl-fea* cheat, swindle <**Eng**✍[*1]>

drìbljer {a (acc. = gen.) masc.} **a.** *col* dribbler (e.g. in basketball) <**Eng**✍> **b.** *sl* cheater, swindler <**Eng**✍[*1]>

drijéšiti {šīm, šē imperf.} *col* untie <**Slav**>

drîncati {ām, ajū imperf. intr.} *col* sleep, nap <**Ger**>

drìnk {a +ov (ext. pl) masc.; Nom Pl drìnkovi} **a.** *sl-drink* drinking (alcohol) <**Eng**> **b.** *sl-drink* alcoholic beverage <**Eng**[*1]>
- **zèsta drìnk** {NP} *sl-drink* drink (alcohol)

drìnkati {ām, ajū biasp.} *sl-drink* drink (alcohol) <**Eng**>

drìnker {a (acc. = gen.) masc.} *sl-drink* alcoholic, drunk <**Eng**>

drìnkī {adj.} *sl-drink* drunk <**Eng**>

drìnkovati {kujēm, kujū imperf. intr.} *sl-drink* drink (alcohol) <**Eng**>

drípac {pca (acc. = gen.) masc.} **a.** *col* joker, trickster, rascal <**Slav**[*1]> **b.** *col* troublemaker, rowdy, ruffian <**Slav**[*2]>

drìskati {ām, ajū biasp.} **a.** *sl-sex* ***Obs*** defecate, shit <**Slav**[*1]> **b.** *sl-sex* ***Der*** talk persistently and meaninglessly, blabber, chatter <**Slav**[*2]>

drìstati {ām, ajū biasp.} *sl-sex* ***Obs*** defecate, shit <**Slav**[*1]>

drìto {adv.} *col-dia* directly, straight <**Ita**>

dȑkadžija {ē masc.} **a.** *sl-sex* ***Obs-Der*** masturbator (male) <**Slav**> **b.** *sl-fea* ***Obs-Der*** worthless or despicable person <**Slav**[*1]>
- **Dȑkadžijo jèdan!** {S} (lit. You jackoff!) *sl* ***Off*** used as a moderate curse

dȑkadžījka {ē fem.} **a.** *sl-sex* ***Obs-Der*** masturbator (female) <**Slav**> **b.** *sl-fea* ***Obs-Der*** worthless or despicable female, bitch <**Slav**[*1]>

Dȑkāj - mȁži líce! {S} (lit. Jack off and then put it on your face!) *sl* ***Obs*** used to silence one's interlocutor, Shut up! ☞ **drkati**

dȑkalica {ē fem.} **1** *dia* ***Obs*** trifle, thing of little importance or value <**Slav**> **2** *dia* ***Obs*** futile discussion: *Od te drkalice niko nema koristi. That futile discussion is of no use at all.* <**Slav**>

dȑkānje {a neut.} **a.** *sl-sex* ***Obs*** masturbation <Slav> **b.** *sl-fea* ***Obs*** prolonged and meaningless talk, blabber, chatter <Slav[*1]>
• **dȑkānje kȗrca** {NP} (lit. jacking off) *sl* ***Obs*** prolonged and meaningless talk, blabber, chatter

dȑkāroš {a (acc. = gen.) masc.} *sl-fea* ***Der-Obs*** worthless or despicable person <Slav[*1]>

dȑkati {ām, ajū imperf.} **a.** *sl-sex* ***Obs*** masturbate, beat off <Slav> **b.** *sl-fea* ***Obs*** talk persistently and meaninglessly, blabber, chatter <Slav[*1]>
• **Dȑkāj - mȁži líce!** {S} (lit. Jack off and then put it on your face!) *sl* ***Obs*** used to silence one's interlocutor, Shut up!

dȑkati se {ām, ajū imperf. intr.} **a.** *sl-sex* ***Obs*** masturbate, beat off <Slav> **b.** *sl-fea* ***Obs*** be angry <Slav[*1]> **c.** *sl* attack, strike <Slav[*2]>

dȑkelja {ē masc.} *sl-fea* boring person, bore <Slav❖[*1]>

drkȅljisati {išēm, išū imperf.} **a.** *sl-sex* ***Obs*** masturbate, beat off <Slav❖> **b.** *sl-fea* ***Obs*** talk persistently and meaninglessly, blabber, chatter <Slav❖[*1]>

dȑkezina {ē fem.} *sl-sex* ***Der-Obs*** masturbator (male) <Slav❖[*1]>

dȑklje {eta neut.} *sl-fea* senior citizen <Slav[*1]>

dȑknūt {a, o adj.} *sl-fea* ***Der*** insane, nuts <Slav❖[*1]>

dȑknuti {nēm, nū perf.} **a.** *sl-sex* ***Obs*** engage in sexual intercourse with (of a male) <Slav[*1]> **b.** *sl* hit, punch: *drknuti u njokalicu hit in the face* <Slav[*2]>

dȑknuti se {nēm, nū perf. intr.} *sl-fea* be conceited, be stuck-up <Slav❖[*1]>

dȑkopīš {a masc.} (lit. masturbator who pisses) *sl-fea* bad joke <Slav✍[*1]>

dȑkoš {a (acc. = gen.) masc.} *sl-sex* ***Der-Obs*** masturbator (male) <Slav❖>

dȑkotina {ē fem.} **1** *sl-fea* unattractively dressed female <Slav❖[*1]> **2** *sl-fea* stupid or mentally deficient person <Slav❖[*1]>

dȑkšezina {ē fem.} *sl-sex* ***Der-Obs*** masturbator (male) <Slav❖[*1]>

dȑktati {tīm, tē imperf.} [std. = drhtati] *col-dia* shiver from cold or fright <Slav✍>

dȑkūn {drkúna (acc. = gen.) masc.} *sl-fea* boaster, braggart, blowhard <Slav✍[*1]>

drkȕnica {ē fem.} *sl-fea* conceited female <Slav✍[*1]>

drkúniti se {nīm, nē aiv} *sl-fea* be conceited, be stuck-up <Slav✍[*1]>

drkȕnjača {ē fem.} *sl-fea* conceited female <Slav✍[*1]>

dȑljav {a, o adj.} *col* with untidy clothing <Slav>

dȑm-zvȑc {excl.} *col* nonsense <Slav[*1]>

dȑmadžija {ē masc.} (lit. shaker) **a.** *sl-sex* ***Der-Obs*** masturbator (male) <Slav❖[*1]> **b.** *sl-fea* extremely talkative male, chatterbox <Slav❖[*1]>

dȑmāljka {ē fem.; Dat dȑmāljki} (lit. female shaker) *sl-sex* ***Fac*** loose woman <Slav❖[*1]>

dȑmānje {a neut.} (lit. shaking) **1** *sl-sex* ***Obs*** masturbating <Slav[*1]> **2** *sl-drink* drinking <Slav[*1]>

dȑmāroš {a masc.} (lit. shaker) *sl-fea* very important or influential person, big shot <Slav[*1]>

dȑmati {ām, ajū imperf.} (lit. shake) **1** *sl-sex* ***Obs*** masturbate, beat off <Slav[*1]> **2** *sl-drink* drink (alcohol) <Slav[*1]>
• **dȑmati fȁks** {VP} (lit. shake the university) *sl-stu* ***Fac*** study
• **dȑmati na trapézu** {VP} (lit. shake on a trapeze) *sl-crime* ***Fac*** steal through windows

dȑmati se {ām, ajū imperf. intr.} (lit. shake oneself) *sl* dance <Slav[*1]>

dȑmātor {a (acc. = gen.) masc.} (lit. shaker) **1** *sl-sex* ***Der-Obs*** masturbator (male) <Slav[*1]> **2** *col* dictator <Slav[*1]>

drmáža {ē fem.} (lit. shaking) **1** *sl* dancing <Slav-Fre[*1]> **2** *sl-drink* drinking (alcohol) <Slav-Fra[*1]>

dȑmbati {ām, ajū imperf.} *col* work hard: *drmbati u rudniku uglja work hard in a coal mine* <Slav[*1]>
• **dȑmbati fȁk** {VP} (lit. shake the university) *sl-stu* ***Fac*** study

dȑmež {a masc.} *sl* dancing <Slav[*1]>

dȑmnūt {a, o adj.} (lit. shaken) *sl-fea* ***Der*** insane, nuts <Slav[*1]>

dȑmnuti {nēm, nū perf.} (lit. shake) **a.** *sl-crime* steal, swipe <Slav[*1]> **b.** *sl* get rich quickly <Slav[*2]>
• **dȑmnuti aplȁuz** {VP} (lit. shake applause) **a.** *sl* ***Fac*** slap, smack **b.** *sl* ***Fac*** hit, punch

dȑmpuc {a (acc. = gen.) masc.} **1** *sl-fea* obese boy <Slav[*1]> **2** *sl-fea* energetic boy <Slav[*1]>

dȑmulja {ē fem.} (lit. female shaker) *sl* female <Slav❖[*1]>

drmȕsati {ām, ajū imperf.} (lit. shake mildly) *col* shake (an object, person, etc.) <Slav>

dȑn-zvȑc {excl.} *col* nonsense <Slav[*1]>

dȑncati {ām, ajū imperf. intr.} *sl* sleep, nap <Slav>

dȑnda {ē fem.} **a.** *sl* roaring (engine, etc. <Slav> **b.** *sl* wreck <Slav[*1]>

dȑndalo {a neut.} *dia* wool comb <Slav>

drndàljka {ē fem.; Dat dȑndāljki} *sl* female <Slav[*1]>

dȑndānje {a neut.} *sl-fea* prolonged and meaningless talk, blabber, chatter <Slav[*1]>

dr̀ndara [1] {ē fem.} *sl-sex* ***Obs*** buttocks, butt <Slav>

dr̀ndara [2] {ē fem. & masc.} **1** *sl-fea* irresponsible person: *Ne dajte mu kola, on je drndara. Don't give him the car, he is irresponsible.* <Slav[*1]> **2** *sl-fea* troublemaker, rowdy, ruffian <Slav[*1]>

dr̀ndāš {drndáša (acc. = gen.) masc.; Voc dȑndāšu} *sl-fea* extremely talkative male, chatterbox <Slav[*1]>

dȑndati {ām, ajū imperf.} **a.** *dia* comb wool <Slav> **b.** *col* make noise <Slav[*1]> **c.** *col* talk persistently and meaninglessly, blabber, chatter <Slav[*2]>
- **Kȍ te dȑndā!** {S} (lit. Who is shaking you?) *sl* ***Off*** used as a weak curse, Screw you!

dȑndav {a, o adj.} *col* roaring engine, etc.) <Slav[*1]>

dr̀ndos {a (acc. = gen.) masc.} *sl-fea* extremely talkative male, chatterbox <Slav✍[*1]>

dr̀ndoš {a (acc. = gen.) masc.} *sl-fea* extremely talkative male, chatterbox <Slav✍[*1]>

dr̀ndōv {drndòva (acc. = gen.) masc.} *sl-fea* stupid or mentally deficient person <Slav❖[*1]>

drndòvčina {ē fem.} *sl-fea* stupid or mentally deficient person <Slav❖[*1]>

dr̀ndulja {ē fem.} **a.** *sl-sex* ***Obs*** buttocks, butt <Slav❖[*1]> **b.** *sl* ***Obs*** female <Slav❖[*2]>

dȑnka {ē fem.; Dat dȑnki} *sl-music* country or folk music <Slav[*1]>

dȑnka-dȑnka {dȑnka-dȑnkē fem.; Dat dȑnka-dȑnki} *sl-music* country or folk music <Slav[*1]>

dròbara {ē fem.} *sl-sex* ***Obs*** buttocks, butt <Slav[*1]>

dròbilica {ē fem.} (lit. smasher) *sl* ***Fac*** mouth <Slav[*1]>

dròbiti {bīm, bē imperf.} (lit. crush) **1** *sl* lie <Slav[*1]> **2** *sl-fea* talk persistently and meaninglessly, blabber, chatter <Slav[*1]>

dróca {ē fem.} **a.** *sl-sex* ***Obs*** prostitute, hooker <Slav❖[*1]> **b.** *sl-sex* ***Obs*** loose woman, slut <Slav❖[*1]>

drȍcica {ē fem.} /drócica/ *sl* female <Slav❖[*1]>

dròcika {ē fem.; Dat dròciki} *sl-sex* ***Obs*** prostitute, hooker <Slav❖[*1]>

drȍcka {ē fem.; Dat drȍcki} *sl-sex* ***Obs*** prostitute, hooker <Slav❖[*1]>

drȍcnuti {nēm, nū perf.} *sl-stu* fail an exam (flunk) <Slav❖[*1]>

dròculja {ē fem.} *sl-sex* ***Obs*** prostitute, hooker <Slav❖[*1]>

dròćkāš {droćkáša (acc. = gen.) masc.; Voc drȍćkášu} **a.** *sl-sex* ***Obs*** male who breaks wind while defecating <Slav❖[*1]> **b.** *sl-fea* ***Der-Obs*** extremely talkative male, chatterbox <Slav❖[*2]>

drȍćkati {ām, ajū imperf. intr.} **a.** *sl-sex* ***Obs*** break wind while defecating <Slav[*1]> **b.** *sl-fea* ***Der-Obs*** talk persistently and meaninglessly, blabber, chatter <Slav[*2]>

drȍćnuti {nēm, nū perf. intr.} **a.** *sl-sex* ***Obs*** break wind while defecating <Slav[*1]> **b.** *sl-fea* ***Obs*** defecate quickly <Slav[*2]>

dróga {ē fem.; Dat drógi} (lit. drug) **a.** *sl-drink* alcoholic beverage <Fre[*1]> **b.** *sl-drink* brandy <Fre[*2]>
- **pod drógōm** {PP} (lit. under drugs) *sl-drink* drunk

drògāroš {a masc.} *sl-drugs* drug addict, junkie <Fre-Slav.>

drȍgati {ām, ajū imperf.} (lit. take drugs) *sl* smoke (tobacco) <Fre[*1]>

dróge {ā fem. pl.} (lit. drugs) *sl-drugs* LSD, acid <Fre[*1]>

drȍger {a (acc. = gen.) masc.} **a.** *sl-drugs* drug addict, junkie <Fre> **b.** *sl-drink* alcoholic, drunk <Fre[*1]>

drogèrāš {geráša masc.} *sl-drugs* drug addict, junkie <Fre❖>

drȍgī {īja (acc. = gen.) masc.} *sl-drugs* drug addict, junkie <Fre✍>

drògīrān {a, o adj.} (lit. on drugs) *sl-drink* ***Fac*** drunk <Fre[*1]>

drògīrānī màjmun {NP} (lit. stoned monkey) *sl-sports* ***Der*** incompetent goalie (soccer, etc.) ☞ **majmun**

drogirànt {a (acc. = gen.) masc.} *sl-drugs* drug addict, junkie <Fre❖>

drogírānje {a neut.} (lit. taking drugs) *sl-drink* drinking (alcohol) <Fre[*1]>

drogírati se {ām, ajū imperf. intr.} (lit. take drugs) *sl-drink* drink (alcohol) <Fre❖[*1]>

drȍgomān {a (acc. = gen.) masc.} *sl-drugs* drug addict, junkie <Fre-Eng>

drȍgomānka {ē fem.; Dat drȍgomānki} *sl-drugs* drug addict, junkie <Fre-Eng❖>

drȍgos {a (acc. = gen.) masc.} *sl-drugs* drug addict, junkie <Fre✍>

drȍgoš {a (acc. = gen.) masc.} *sl-drugs* drug addict, junkie <Fre⁘>

dròkljača {ē fem.} *sl-fea* unattractive female, dog <Slav*1>

drȍknuti {nēm, nū perf.} *sl-stu* fail an exam (flunk) <Slav*1>

drȍksa {ē fem.} *sl-sex* ***Obs*** prostitute, hooker <Slav*1>

drȍlja {ē fem.} **a.** *sl-sex* ***Obs*** prostitute, hooker <Slav*1> **b.** *sl-sex* ***Obs*** loose woman, slut <Slav*2>

drȍljār {a masc.} *sl* US dollar, buck <Slav*1>

dròmbulja {ē fem.} *sl-sex* ***Obs*** prostitute, hooker <Hun*1>

dròmfulja {ē fem.} *sl-sex* ***Obs*** prostitute, hooker <Hun*1>

drȍncānje {a neut.} *col* objecting, criticism, bitching <Slav*1>

drȍncati {ām, ajū imperf.} /drôncati/ *col* object, criticize <Slav*1>

drònfulja {ē fem.} *sl-sex* ***Obs*** prostitute, hooker <Hun*1>

drónja {ē fem.} *sl-sex* ***Obs*** prostitute, hooker <Slav*1>

drónjak {njka masc.} (lit. rag) **a.** *col* used and dirty clothing <Slav> **b.** *sl* coat (outer garment) <Slav*1>

drȍnjav {a, o adj.} *sl-fea* dressed in used and dirty clothing <Slav>

drȍnjavac {vca masc.} *sl* used clothing store <Slav*1>

drònjčina {ē masc.} *sl-fea* poor person <Slav⁘*1>

drònjguz {a (acc. = gen.) masc.} *sl-fea* ***Fac-Obs*** spoiled child, brat <Slav⁘*1>

drȍplja {ē fem.} *sl-sex* ***Obs*** prostitute, hooker <Slav*1>

dròpljača {ē fem.} *sl-sex* ***Obs*** prostitute, hooker <Slav⁘*1>

drȍpljār {a (acc. = gen.) masc.} *sl* beggar <Slav*1>

drȍt {a (acc. = gen.) +ov (ext. pl) masc.; Nom Pl dròtovi} *sl-crime* policeman, cop <Ger*1>

drȍtār {a (acc. = gen.) masc.} *sl-crime* policeman, cop <Ger⁘*1>

drȍter {a (acc. = gen.) masc.} *sl-crime* policeman, cop <Ger⁘*1>

dròver {a (acc. = gen.) masc.} *sl-crime* policeman, cop <Ger⁘*1>

dȓp {a +ov (ext. pl) masc.; Nom Pl dŕpovi} *sl-crime* theft, swiping <Slav⁘>

dŕpalica {ē fem.} *sl* hand <Slav⁘*1>

dŕpānje {a neut.} **1** *sl-sex* ***Obs*** sexual foreplay, petting, feeling up <Slav*1> **2** *sl-crime* ***Der*** theft, swiping <Slav*1>

drpárēnje {a neut.} *sl-crime* theft, swiping <Slav*1>

drpáriti {dȑpārīm, rē imperf.} *sl-crime* steal, swipe <Slav*1>

dȑpārnica {ē fem.} *sl-crime* self-service store <Slav⁘*1>

dȑpāroš {a (acc. = gen.) masc.} *sl-crime* thief, sticky fingers <Slav⁘*1>

dŕpati {ām, ajū imperf.} **1** *sl-sex* ***Obs*** engage in sexual foreplay, pet, feel up <Slav*1> **2** *sl-crime* ***Der*** steal, swipe <Slav*1>

dȓpavac {vca masc.} *sl-crime* finger <Slav⁘*1>

drpáža {ē fem.} **1** *sl-sex* ***Obs*** sexual foreplay, petting, feeling up <Slav-Fre*1> **2** *sl-crime* ***Der*** theft <Slav-Fre*1>

dŕpež [1] {a masc.} *sl-crime* theft, swipe <Slav*1>

dŕpež [2] {a (acc. = gen.) masc.} *sl-crime* thief, sticky fingers <Slav*1>

dȑpisānje {a neut.} *sl-crime* theft, swipe <Slav*1>

dȑpisati {išēm, išū imperf.} *sl-crime* steal, swipe <Slav*1>

dȓpiti {pīm, pē perf.} *sl-crime* steal, swipe <Slav*1>

dȓpljen {a, o adj.} **1** *sl-crime* stolen, hot <Slav*1> **2** *sl-crime* arrested <Slav*1>

dȓpnuti {nēm, nū perf.} **a.** *sl* take <Slav*1> **b.** *sl-crime* steal, swipe <Slav*2>

dȓška *See the following*
- **dȓška od stomáka** {NP} (lit. stomach handle) *sl-sex* ***Fac*** penis

dȓtle {eta masc.} *sl-fea* senior citizen <Slav*1>

drûg ȍrgān {NP} (lit. comrade organ) *sl-crime* ***Fac-Der*** policeman, cop ☞ **organ**

drûg Trèmens {NP} (lit. comrade tremens) *sl-drink* ***Fac*** alcoholic, drunk ☞ **Tremens**

drùgār [1] {drugára (acc. = gen.) masc.} *col* friend (male) <Slav>

drùgār [2] {excl.} *col* ***Fam*** used to address a male in direct informal communication, pal, buddy <Slav>

drugárac {rca masc.} *col* social gathering (usu. in the evening) <Slav⁘*1>

drȕgi pádež {NP} (lit. the second case) *col* another issue, another kettle of fish ☞ **padež**

drȕgī pâr čȁrāpā {NP} (lit. another pair of stockings) *col* another issue, another kettle of fish ☞ **čarapa**

drȕk {a +ov (ext. pl) masc.; Nom Pl drùkovi} (lit. printing) *sl-crime* informing the police or other authorities, snitching, squealing <Ger*1>

drȕka-drȕka {drȕka-drȕkē fem.; Dat drȕka-drȕki} *sl-fea* ***Fac-App*** country or folk music <Slav[*1]>

drȕkati {ām, ajū imperf.} (lit. print) **a.** *sl-crime* inform the police or other authorities, snitch, squeal <Ger[*1]> **b.** *sl-sports* cheer for, root for <Ger[*1]>

drùkātor {a (acc. = gen.) masc.} (lit. printer) *sl-crime* ***Der*** informer, stoolie, snitch <Ger[*1]>

drȕkčē {adv.} [std. = drukčije] *col-dia* differently <Slav[*1]>

drȕkčī {a, e adj.} [std. = drukčiji] *col-dia* different <Slav✍>

drȕker {a (acc. = gen.) masc.} (lit. printer) *sl-crime* ***Der*** informer, stoolie, snitch <Ger[*1]>

drȕklāger {a masc.} *sl-crafts* pressure bearing <Ger>

drȕknuti {nēm, nū perf.} (lit. print) *sl-crime* inform the police or other authorities, snitch, squeal <Ger[*1]>

drȕkovati {kujēm, kujū imperf.} (lit. print) *sl-crime* inform the police or other authorities, snitch, squeal <Ger[*1]>

drȕks {a +ev (ext. pl) masc.; Nom Pl drȕksevi} [std. = drug] *sl* ***Fac*** comrade (communist party official) <Slav✍>

drȕkšē {adv.} [std. = drukčije] *col-dia* differently <Slav✍>

drȕkšī {a, e adj.} [std. = drukčiji] *col-dia* different <Slav✍>

drȕm {excl.} (lit. road) *sl* used to make somebody go away, hit the road, beat it <NE[*1]>

drȕmskā lepòtica {NP} (lit. road beauty) SerE *sl-sports* ***Fac-Der*** incompetent player (soccer, etc.) ☞ **lepotica**

drúsla {ē fem.} *sl* female <Slav[*1]>

drúsnjača {ē fem.} *sl-fea* obese female <Slav[*1]>

drùškan {a (acc. = gen.) masc.} *sl* ***Fam*** friend (male) <Slav[*1]>

drȕštvenē ìgre {NP} (lit. social games) **1** *sl-gamble* ***Fac*** gambling **2** *sl-sex* ***Fac-Obs*** sexual intercourse ☞ **igra**

drùžina {ē fem.} *sl-fea* gang, group of one's close friends <Slav[*1]>

drváriti {dr̀vārīm, rē imperf.} **a.** *sl* enjoy, like <Slav[*1]> **b.** *sl-drink* drink (alcohol) <Slav[*2]>

dr̀vārnica {ē fem.} (lit. wood storage) *sl-fea* slender female <Slav[*1]>

dȑven {a, o adj.} (lit. wooden) **a.** *sl-fea* stiff <Slav[*1]> **b.** *sl-fea* clumsy, klutzy <Slav[*2]>

dȑvenā Màrija {NP} (lit. wooden Mary) *sl-fea* clumsy person, klutz: *Tako je drven da mu sve ispada iz ruku. He is so klutzy that he drops everything.* ☞ **Marija**

dȑvenī advòkāt {NP} (lit. wooden attorney) *col* one who always stands up for others (e.g. in disputes or before authorities) ☞ **advokat**

dŕviti {vīm, vē imperf.} (lit. wood) **1** *sl-sex* ***Obs*** masturbate, beat off <Slav[*1]> **2** *sl-fea* ***Der*** preach, give lectures to <Slav[*1]>

dŕviti se {vīm, ve imperf. intr.} (lit. wood oneself) *col* be conceited, be stuck-up: *Drvi se jer mu je stari političar. He's stuck-up because his dad is a politician.* <Slav[*1]>

drvljànīk {drvljaníka masc.} *dia* logs <Slav>

dȑvo {eta neut.} (lit. wood) **1** *sl* match (lighting device) <Slav[*1]> **2** *sl-fea* insensitive male, cold dude <Slav[*1]>

dȑž {excl.} [std. = drži] *col* used when passing something, here <Slav✍>

Dȑž mu, nànče, glàvče! {S} (lit. Grandmother, grab his head!) SSer *dia* ***Obs*** used to express negative attitude toward ☞ **držati**

Dȑž mu, nàne, glàvu! {S} (lit. Grandmother grab, his head!) SSer *dia* ***Obs*** used to express negative attitude toward ☞ **držati**

Dȑž se! {S} (lit. Hold yourself!) *col* ***Fam*** used as an informal farewell, Take care of yourself! ☞ **držati se**

dȑž-nèdāj {adv.} (lit. grab it, don't give it) *col* used to refer to a hectic or dangerous situation: *Bilo je drž-nedaj. It was dangerous.* ☞ **drži-nedaj**

dȑžati *See the following*

- **Dȑž se!** {S} (lit. Hold yourself!) *col* ***Fam*** used as an informal farewell, Take care of yourself!
- **Dȑžī se kô kȕrac u làšči vȍdu!** {S} (lit. He acts like a prick in water!) SSer *dia* ***Obs*** used to express negative attitude toward
- **Dȑž mu, nànče, glàvče!** {S} (lit. Grandmother, grab his head!) SSer *dia* ***Obs*** used to express negative attitude toward
- **Dȑž mu, nàne, glàvu!** {S} (lit. Grandmother, grab his head!) SSer *dia* ***Obs*** used to express negative attitude toward
- **dȑžati bánku** {VP} *sl-gamble* keep the bank
- **dȑžati dò sebe** {VP} (lit. respect oneself) *sl* ***Fac*** be conceited, be stuck-up
- **dȑžati fȉge** {VP} (lit. hold some figs) *col* keep one's fingers crossed for somebody or something
- **dȑžati pálčeve** {VP} (lit. hold thumbs) *col* keep one's fingers crossed for somebody or something
- **dȑžati svéću** {VP} (lit. hold a candle) SerE *col* voyeur
- **dȑžati svijéću** {VP} (lit. hold a candle) *col* voyeur
- **dȑžati štángu** {VP} (lit. hold a rod) *sl* support, back (person, plan, etc.)

• **dȑži vȍdu dok mâjstori ȍdu** {S} (lit. hold the water until the repairmen leave) *col* they fixed it so that it will not last long

dȑžāvnā tàmbura {NP} (lit. government tamburica - mandolin-like folk instrument) *sl-crime* ***Fac*** prison ☞ **tambura**

Dȑžī se kô kȕrac u làšči vȍdu! {S} (lit. He acts like a prick in water!) {S} *dia* ***Obs*** used to express negative attitude toward ☞ **držati se**

dȑži-nèdāj {adv.} (lit. grab it, don't give it) *col* used to refer to a hectic or dangerous situation: *Bilo je drž-nedaj. It was dangerous.* ☞ **drž-nedaj**

dȕ {excl.} *col* the sound made by a gun, bang <Slav>

Dúba {ē fem.} *sl* Dubrovnik (a city in Croatia) <Slav✍>

dúbak {pka masc.} *col* stroller (for children) <Slav>

dùbara {ē fem.} **a.** *sl-sex* ***Obs*** buttocks, butt <Slav⁘> **b.** *sl-sex* ***Obs*** anus, asshole <Slav⁘[*1]>

Dubijána {ē fem.} *sl* Dubrovnik (a city in Croatia) <Slav✍>

dubióza {ē fem.} *sl* problem, trouble <Lat[*1]>

dȕbiōzan {zna, zno adj.} (lit. dubious) **a.** *col* stupid or mentally deficient <Lat[*1]> **b.** *col* meaningless: *dubiozan plan meaningless plan* <Lat[*2]>

dúbiti {bīm, bē imperf. intr.} *col* stand on one's head <Slav[*1]>

• **dúbiti na glávi** {VP} (lit. stand on one's head) *sl* spend one's time in useless activities, fool around, mess around

dȕckī {ija masc.} **a.** *sl-sex* ***Obs*** buttocks, butt <Slav[*1]> **b.** *sl-sex* ***Obs*** anus, asshole <Slav[*2]>

dùćān {dućána masc.} **a.** *col* store <NE> **b.** *col* zipper, fly <NE[*1]>

dȕd {dùda +ov (ext. pl) masc.; Nom Pl dùdovi} (lit. mulberry) *sl* cigarette butt <Slav[*1]>

dȕda [1] {ē fem.} (lit. pacifier) **1** *sl-sex* ***Fac-Obs*** penis, dick, prick <Slav[*1]> **2** *sl-sex* ***Obs*** female breast, tit <Slav[*1]>

Dȕda [2] {ē fem.} *sl* name of a restaurant on Margaretska street, Zagreb, Croatia <Slav✍>

dùdek {a (acc. = gen.) masc.} **1** *sl-fea* stupid or mentally deficient person <Slav⁘> **2** *sl-sex* male homosexual, gay <Slav⁘>

Dùdlāj ga! {S} (lit. Suck it!) *sl* ***Obs*** used as a moderate offense, Suck my dick! ☞ **dudlati**

dùdlānje {a neut.} (lit. sucking pacifier) *sl-sex* ***Obs*** fellatio <Slav[*1]>

dudlàšica {ē fem.} (lit. pacifier sucker) *sl-sex* ***Obs*** female who frequently engages in fellatio <Slav[*1]>

dȕdlati {ām, ajū imperf.} (lit. suck pacifier) **1** *sl-sex* ***Obs*** engage in fellatio <Slav[*1]> **2** *sl-sex* ***Obs*** engage in cunnilingus <Slav[*1]>

• **Dùdlāj ga!** {S} *sl* ***Obs*** used as a moderate curse, Suck my prick!

• **dùdlati kȕrac** {VP} (lit. suck prick) *col* ***Obs*** engage in fellatio

dȕdlo gòlo {NP} (lit. suck naked) *sl-sex* ***Fac*** male homosexual, gay ☞ **golo**

dȕdloje {a (acc. = gen.) masc.} (lit. pacifier sucker) *sl-sex* ***Fac-Obs*** male homosexual, gay <Slav[*1]>

dùdljānje {a neut.} *sl-sex* ***Obs*** cunnilingus <Slav✍>

dȕdnūt {a, o adj.} **1** *sl-fea* lame (limping) <Slav[*1]> **2** *sl-fea* cross-eyed <Slav[*2]>

dȕdos {a (acc. = gen.) masc.} *sl-fea* stupid or mentally deficient person <Slav[*1]>

dûdoš {a (acc. = gen.) masc.} *sl-fea* ***Der*** stupid or mentally deficient person <NE>

dȕdovānje {a neut.} *sl* standing in one place for a long period of time (usu. while waiting for someone) <Slav[*1]>

dȕdovati {dujēm, dujū imperf.} *sl* stand in one place for a long time (usu. while waiting for someone) <Slav[*1]>

dùduk {a (acc. = gen.) masc.} **a.** *sl-fea* stupid or mentally deficient person <NE[*1]> **b.** *sl-fea* stupid or mentally deficient <NE[*2]>

duèliti {līm, lē imperf. intr.} *sl* be friends <Fre⁘[*1]>

dȕfter {a (acc. = gen.) masc.} *sl-fea* street child <Ger[*1]>

dúga {ē fem.; Dat dúgi} **1** *sl* ticket, fare <Slav[*1]> **2** *sl-gamble* playing card <Slav[*1]>

dugàna {ē fem.} *sl-crime* name of a prison in Stara Gradiška, Croatia <Slav[*1]>

dugànija {ē fem.} *sl-gamble* card playing <Slav⁘[*1]>

dȕganje {a neut.} *sl-gamble* the act of playing cards <Slav⁘[*1]>

• **dȕganje u rȉbu** {NP} (lit. playing cards for fish) *sl-gamble* gambling

dùgār {a (acc. = gen.) masc.} *sl* conductor (on a train, bus, or streetcar) <Slav⁘[*1]>

dugárēnje {a neut.} *sl-crime* the act of reselling tickets illegally, scalping tickets <Slav⁘[*1]>

dugáriti {dùgārīm, rē imperf.} **1** *sl-crime* resell tickets illegally, scalp tickets <Slav❖*1> **2** *sl-gamble* play cards <Slav❖*1>
• **dugáriti za lóvu** {VP} (lit. play cards for money) *sl-gamble* gamble
• **dùgati kèrpo** {VP} (lit. play poker) *sl-gamble* play poker

dȕgati se {ām, ajū biasp. intr.} *sl-gamble* gamble <Slav❖*1>

dùgme {eta neut.} (lit. button) *sl-sex* buttocks, butt <NE*1>

Dugmíći {ā masc. pl.} *sl-music* name for Bijelo dugme (a very popular rock band in the former Yugoslavia during the 1970s and 1980s) <NE❖*1>

dugolásec {sca (acc. = gen.) masc.} Cro *sl-music* hairy musician <Slav*1>

dugotàlāsan {adj.} (lit. long wave) *sl-fea* slow in understanding <Slav*1>

dugòvratī {ōg (acc. = gen.) masc.} (lit. the one with long neck) *sl-sex* ***Fac-Obs*** penis, dick, prick <Slav*1>

dȕh {a (acc. = gen.) +ov (ext. pl) masc.; Nom Pl dùhovi} (lit. ghost) *sl-drugs* LSD, acid <Slav*1>

dúhānje {a neut.} BosM *col* blowing (wind, etc.) <Slav>

dúhati {dûšēm, dûšū imperf. intr.} BosM *col* blow (wind, etc.) <Slav>

dúja {ē fem.} /dȕja/ *sl* the streetcar line number two in Zagreb, Croatia <Ita✍>

dújo {ē masc.} *sl-gamble* good playing card <Slav>

dùkat {a masc.} *col* buttocks, butt <Slav>

dȕks {a +ev (ext. pl) masc.; Nom Pl dùksevi} *col* thick sweatshirt <Ger✍*1>

dȕks-màjica {ē fem.} *col* thick sweatshirt <Ger✍*1>

dȕkserica {ē fem.} /dùkserica/ *col* thick sweatshirt <Ger✍*1>

dùlavka {ē fem.} *sl-sex* ***Obs*** buttocks, butt <NE*1>

dùlum {a masc.} Bos *col* dunum (surface measure of approx. 100 square yards) <NE>

duljìna {ē fem.} *sl* dress <Slav*1>

duljìne {ljínā fem. pl.} *sl* clothing <Slav*1>

dúljiti {dûljīm, ljē perf.} (lit. make it longer) **1** *sl-sports* win at marbles <Slav*1> **2** *sl-fea* talk persistently and meaninglessly, blabber, chatter <Slav*1>

dȕm {excl.} *col* the sound made by an explosion, bang <Slav>

dȕmānje {a neut.} *sl* thinking, pondering <Rus>

dȕmati {ām, ajū imperf.} *sl* think, ponder <Rus>

dumbàrānje {a neut.} **1** *sl* lying <Slav*1> **2** *sl-fea* prolonged and meaningless talk, blabber, chatter <Slav*1>

dumbàrati {ām, ajū imperf.} **1** *sl* lie <Slav*1> **2** *sl-fea* talk persistently and meaninglessly, blabber, chatter <Slav*1>

dumbarȅska {ē fem.; Dat dumbarȅski} *sl* fun <Slav❖*1>

dùmbāroš {a (acc. = gen.) masc.} *sl-crime* pickpocket <Slav❖*1>

dumbèrāš {beráša (acc. = gen.) masc.} *sl-crime* burglar

dumbòrāš {boráša (acc. = gen.) masc.} *sl-crime* pickpocket <Slav❖*1>

dȕmer {a (acc. = gen.) masc.} *sl* thinker <Rus❖>

dumèrāš {meráša (acc. = gen.) masc.} *sl-crime* pickpocket <Rus❖*1>

dùmina {ē fem.} *sl* lie <Rus❖*1>
• **u dùmini** {PP} **a.** *sl* as if **b.** *sl* never

dumírati {dùmīrām, dumírajū biasp.} *sl* lie <Rus❖*1>

dunàjeger {a (acc. = gen.) masc.} *sl* person who lives off of others' successes <Ger*1>

dùnđer {a (acc. = gen.) masc.} *sl-crafts* construction worker <NE*1>

dùnđerskī {ā, ō adj.} *sl-crafts* construction workers' <NE*1>

Dúni mi u múda! {S} (lit. Blow my balls!) *col* ***Off*** used as a moderate curse, Blow me! ☞ **dunuti**

dunìjati {ām, ajū imperf.} *sl-sex* ***Obs*** engage in sexual intercourse with (of a male) <NE*1>

dùnlop {a (acc. = gen.) masc.} *sl-fea* obese male <BN*1>

dȕnst {a +ev (ext. pl) masc.; Nom Pl dùnstevi} *sl* understanding, realizing <Ger*1>

dȕnster {a masc.} /dùnster/ *sl-fea* ignorant person, dunce <Ger❖*1>

dûnūt {a, o adj.} (lit. blown) *sl-fea* ***Der*** insane, nuts <Slav*1>

dúnuti {dûnēm, nū perf.} (lit. blow) **1** *sl* leave hastily, split <Slav*1> **2** *sl* hit, punch <Slav*1>
• **Dúni mi u múda!** {S} (lit. Blow my balls!) *col* ***Off*** used as a moderate curse, Blow me!
• **dúnuti fóru** {VP} (lit. blow a trick) *sl* trick, cheat, swindle
• **dúnuti u kàpislu** {VP} (lit. blow into the detonator) *sl* calm down, cool off

dúpac {pca (acc. = gen.) masc.} *sl-sex* ***Fac-Obs*** male with large buttocks <Slav❖>

dȕpe {eta neut.} *col* buttocks, butt <Slav>
• **dramȉli dȕpeta** {NP} (lit. having a small ass) *sl-fea* ***Obs*** miserly, stingy
• **Dȕpe gȍvnavō!** {S} (lit. Your ass is full of shit!) *col* ***Off*** used as a moderate curse, You are full of shit!
• **ko iz dȕpeta** {PP} (lit. as if it comes from the ass) *col* ***Der-Obs*** worthless, worth shit
• **ù dupe na vášar** {PP} (lit. to the ass to a fair) *col* nowhere
• **Ù dupe te jèbēm!** {S} (lit. I fuck you in your ass!) *col* ***Off*** used as a moderate curse, Up yours!
• **Ù dupe te pȑtenō jèbēm!** {S} (lit. I fuck you in your linen ass!) *dia* ***Off*** used as a moderate curse, Up yours!
• **Ù dupe te šȕgavō jèbēm!** {S} (lit. I fuck you in your mangy ass!) *dia-col* ***Off*** used as a moderate curse, Up yours!

dȕpe-gláva {ē fem.} (lit. buttocks - head) **1** *sl-fea* egotist <Slav> **2** *sl-sex* sexual intercourse with simultaneous mutual oral stimulation, 69 <Slav>

dupedávac {vca (acc. = gen.) masc.} (lit. the one who gives his buttocks) *sl-sex* ***Fac-Obs*** male homosexual, gay <Slav❖[*1]>

dupelízac {sca (acc. = gen.) masc.} (lit. the one who licks buttocks) *sl-fea* ***Der-Obs*** ingratiator (male), brownnoser, ass kisser <Slav❖[*1]>

dupénce {eta neut.} *sl-fea* small buttocks <Slav❖>
• **U dupénce te jèbēm!** {S} (lit. I fuck you in your small ass!) *dia-col* ***Off*** used as a moderate curse, Up yours!

dùpēnda {ē fem.} *sl-sex* ***Obs*** person with large buttocks <Slav❖>

dupepévac {vca (acc. = gen.) masc.} (lit. buttocks singer) **1** SerE *sl-fea* extremely talkative person, chatterbox <Slav❖[*1]> **2** *sl-fea* slender male <Slav❖[*1]>

dupeprának {nca (acc. = gen.) masc.} *sl-fea* weak male, wimp <Slav❖[*1]>

dȕper {a (acc. = gen.) masc.} *sl-fea* ***Der-Obs*** ingratiator (male), brownnoser, ass kisser <Slav❖[*1]>

dùpeška {ē fem.; Dat dùpeški} **1** *sl-sex* ***Obs*** large buttocks <Slav❖> **2** *sl-sex* ***Obs*** female with large buttocks <Slav❖[*1]>

dupèško {a masc.} **a.** *sl-fea* male with large buttocks <Slav❖> **b.** *sl-fea* greedy male (for food, money, etc.) <Slav❖[*1]>

dupètara {ē fem.} *sl-sex* ***Obs*** female with large buttocks <Slav❖>

dupetárović {a (acc. = gen.) masc.} *sl-sex* ***Obs*** male with large buttocks <Slav❖>

dupètāš {petáša (acc. = gen.) masc.} *sl-sex* ***Fac-Obs*** male homosexual, gay <Slav❖[*1]>

dupètati se {ām, ajū imperf. intr.} (lit. use one's ass) **1** *sl-fea* boast, brag: *dupetati se zbog dobrih ocjena boast over good grades* <Slav❖[*1]> **2** *sl-fea* talk persistently and meaninglessly, blabber, chatter <Slav❖[*1]>

dùpetina {ē fem.} **a.** *sl-sex* ***Obs*** large buttocks <Slav❖> **b.** *sl-sex* ***Obs*** female with large buttocks <Slav❖[*1]>

dȕpetrōn {a masc.} (lit. ass throne) *sl* ***Fac-Obs*** chair <Slav-Gre❖[*1]>

dupévac {vca (acc. = gen.) masc.} (lit. ass-singer) SerE *sl-sex* ***Fac-Obs*** stupid or mentally deficient person <Slav[*1]>

dùpinger {era masc.} *sl-sex* ***Obs*** buttocks, butt <Slav✍>

dùpke pȕn {AdjP} *col* completely filled with, jam packed ☞ **pun**

dùplā nȕla {NP} (lit. double zero) *sl-sex* ***Fac-Obs*** buttocks, butt ☞ **nula**

dùplī [1] {ā, ō adj.} *col* double (of double size or quantity) <Lat>

dùplī [2] {ōg (acc. = gen.) masc.} *sl-sex* ***Der*** bisexual, AC/DC <Lat>

duplikànt {a (acc. = gen.) masc.} *sl-fea* person who is both a factory worker and a farmer <Lat❖[*1]>

duplikànt {a (acc. = gen.) masc.} *sl-fea* person who is both a factory worker and a farmer <Lat>

duplìkāt {likáta (acc. = gen.) masc.} *sl-fea* person who is both a factory worker and a farmer <Lat[*1]>

dȕplo {adv.} (lit. doubly) *col* insincerely <Lat>

dùplō gòlo {AdjP} (lit. double naked) *col* double zero domino

dùplōnka {ē fem.; Dat dùplōnki} (lit. the double) **a.** *sl-sex* ***Der*** bisexual, AC/DC <Lat❖[*1]> **b.** *sl-sex* ***Der*** male homosexual, gay <Lat❖[*2]>

dùpljāk [1] {dupljáka (acc. = gen.) masc.; Voc dȕpljāče} *sl-fea* duplicitous person <Lat❖>

dùpljāk [2] {dupljáka masc.} **1** *sl-drink* double (shot of alcohol) <Lat❖[*1]> **2** *sl* double coffee <Lat❖[*1]> **3** *sl-crime* faked merchandise <Lat❖[*1]>

dupodèrānje {a neut.} (lit. tearing apart one's ass) *sl-fea* prolonged and meaningless talk, diarrhea of the mouth <Slav❖[*1]>

dupodèrati {pòderēm, rajū imperf.} (lit. tear apart one's ass) *sl-fea* talk persistently and meaninglessly, blabber, chatter <Slav❖[*1]>

dupodèrina {ē fem.} (lit. ass tearing) *sl* unpleasant fact <Slav❖[*1]>

dupojébac {pca (acc. = gen.) masc.} (lit. ass fucker) *sl-sex* ***Fac-Obs*** male homosexual, gay <Slav❖[*1]>

dûr {excl.} *col* used to calm down a horse <Slav>

dûr-mâr {a +ev (ext. pl) masc.; Nom Pl dûr-márevi} *sl* fight (e.g. fist fight) <Slav-Gyp[*1]>

dȕra {excl.} *col* used to calm down a horse <Slav>

dùrača {ē fem.} *sl* leg (human) <Ita[*1]>

dùrbīn {dirbína masc.} (lit. binoculars) *sl* eyeglasses <NE[*1]>

durbíni {ā masc. pl.} (lit. binoculars) *sl* eyeglasses <NE[*1]>

dùrdur {a masc.} /dûr-dûr/ **1** *col* the sound made by a turkey, gobble <Slav[*1]> **2** *sl-sports* ball game similar to soccer in which one is not supposed to score a goal but rather to avoid scoring it <Slav[*1]>

dȕre *See the following*

• **u dȕre** {PP} (lit. in order) *sl* affirmative response, ok, no problem

dúrēnje {a neut.} *sl* laughter <Slav[*1]>

durgárac {rca masc.} *sl* party (social gathering) <Slav✍>

durgùzica {ē fem.} *sl* trouble, problem <Slav>

dùrkan {a masc.} *sl-crime* house with two entrances <Slav[*1]>

dȕrmiti {mīm, mē imperf.} *sl* sleep, nap <Ita✍>

dȕrnuti {nēm, nū perf.} *sl* hit, punch

dùrpan {a (acc. = gen.) masc.; perm} //dùrapan (acc. = gen.) masc./ *sl-crime* policeman, cop <Slav✍>

dȕršlāg {a masc.} *sl-crafts* punch (the tool) <Ger>

dȕs {adj.} *sl-fea* unable to serve in the military for any reason <NE[*1]>

dȕs tàbani {NP} *col* flat feet ☞ **taban**

dȕse {eta neut.} *sl-gamble* successful gambling

dȕst {a masc.} *sl-drugs* cocaine, coke <Eng>

dustabànlija {ē masc.} *sl-fea* person with flat feet <NE[*1]>

dúša {ē fem.} (lit. soul) *sl-sex* ***Obs*** buttocks, butt <Slav[*1]>

• **dúša**[PRON:DAT] je [VERB:INF] {LSF} (lit. it is [PPRON] soul) *col* used to indicate someone's strong affinity toward something, [PRON:NOM] likes to [VERB:INF] more than anything else: *Duša mu je igrati lopte. He likes to play soccer more than anything else.*

• **dúše mi** {NP} (lit. I swear to my soul) *col* used to emphasize the truth of what has been said, I swear!: *Ja sam, duše mi, bio u Bagdadu. I swear I was in Baghdad.*

• **ko dúša** {PP} (lit. like soul) *col* very good (of a person)

dȕšak {ška masc.} *col* period in which one holds one's breath <Slav>

dȕškati {ām, ajū imperf. intr.} *sl* take a rest, take a break, relax <Slav[*1]>

Dȕškec {a masc.} *sl* name for Dušanovac (a neighborhood in Belgrade) <SlavO✍>

Dȕško {a masc.} *sl* name for Dušanovac (a neighborhood in Belgrade) <SlavO✍>

dȕšmanin {a (acc. = gen.) -in (rd. pl.) masc.} *col* enemy <NE>

• **pȉčkīn dȕšmanin** {NP} (lit. cunt's enemy) *sl-sex* ***Fac-Obs*** highly potent male, stud

dúšo [1] {dušòa masc.} *sl-fea* stupid or mentally deficient person <Slav[*1]>

dûšo [2] {excl.} (lit. my soul) *col* ***Fam*** used to address a person in an intimate manner, my dear <Slav[*1]>

dȕšodājnā {ē fem. (adj. decl.)} (lit. the soul-giving one) *sl-sex* ***Fac-Obs*** loose woman, slut <Slav❖>

dušogúbac {pca (acc. = gen.) masc.} (lit. soul killer) **a.** *sl-fea* troublemaker, rowdy, ruffian: *Prebio ga neki dušogubac. Some troublemaker has beaten him up.* <Slav❖[*1]> **b.** *sl-crime* criminal <Slav❖[*2]>

Dûvā prȍmaja iz tvòjīh vráta! {S} (lit. I can feel a draft from your door!) *sl* ***Fac*** used to express negative opinion or attitude, That's nonsense! ☞ **duvati**

dùvāč {a (acc. = gen.) masc.} (lit. blower) *sl-drugs* person who smokes hashish <Slav[*1]>

dȕvadžija {ē fem.} (lit. blower) *sl-fea* boaster, braggart, blowhard <Slav-NE❖[*1]>

Dûvāj ga! {S} (lit. Blow it!) *sl* ***Off*** used in angry dismissal, Get lost! ☞ **duvati**

dùvān {duvána masc.} *sl* cigarette, smoke <NE[*1]>

duvànder {a (acc. = gen.) masc.} (lit. blower) **a.** *sl-fea* boaster, braggart, blowhard <Slav❖[*1]> **b.** *sl-fea* conceited male: *On je duvander, niko neće da ima s njim posla. He is conceited and nobody wants to deal with him.* <Slav❖[*1]>

duvániti {dùvānīm, nē imperf.} **1** *sl* give cigarettes <NE❖> **2** *sl* smoke (tobacco) <NE❖>

dúvānje {a neut.} **1a.** *sl-drugs* smoking (hashish or marijuana) <Slav⁘> **b.** *sl-drugs* hashish or marijuana <Slav⁘[*1]> 2 *sl-drugs* sniffing glue <Slav⁘>

dùvanjskī {ā, ō adj.} *sl* right (as contrasted to left) <SlavO[*1]>

dúvati {dûvām, dúvajū imperf.} (lit. blow) **a.** *sl* smoke (tobacco) <Slav[*1]> **b.** *sl-fea* smoke drugs <Slav[*2]>

• **Dûvā prȍmaja iz tvòjīh vráta!** {S} (lit. I can feel a draft from your door!) *sl* ***Fac*** used to express negative opinion or attitude, That's nonsense!

• **Dûvāj ga!** {S} (lit. Blow it!) *sl* ***Off*** used in angry dismissal, Get lost!

• **dúvati da se ne ùgāsī** {VP} (lit. blow to prevent extinguishing) *sl* ***Fac*** smoke (tobacco)

• **Mȍgu da mi dúvajū!** {S} (lit. They can blow me!) *col* ***Obs*** used to express the state of not being threatened

dûvka {ē fem.; Dat dúvki} **a.** *sl-drugs* smoking (hashish or marijuana) <Slav⁘> **b.** *sl-drugs* hashish or marijuana <Slav⁘[*1]>

dúza {ē fem.} *sl-sex* ***Obs*** small buttocks <Slav✍>

dȕzdibidȕs {adj.} Bos *sl* ***App*** excellent, awesome: *duzdibidus stančuga awesome apartment* <NE[*1]>

dȕzdibidȕs {adv.} /dùzdibidus/ **a.** *sl* completely, totally: *Napio se i duzdibidus usro dernek. He was drunk and completely ruined the party.* <NE> **b.** *sl* superb, awesome <NE[*1]>

dvâ *See the following*

• **dvâ sa dvâ** {NumP} (lit. two by two) **a.** *sl-fea* very big **b.** *sl-fea* ***Iro*** very small, minute

dvâ kéca {NP} (lit. two aces) *sl* the number eleven trolley bus line in Belgrade, Serbia ☞ **kec**

dvâ mȅtra ispod krèča {NP} (lit. two meters under the lime) *sl-fea* ***Fac*** very senile person ☞ **metar**

dvâ štápa u dvê tȉkve{NP} (lit. two sticks in two pumpkins) *sl-fea* ***Fac*** having skinny legs ☞ **štap**

dvàes {num.} [std. = dvadeset] *col* twenty <Slav✍>

dvàjes {num.} [std. = dvadeset] *col* twenty <Slav>

dvánajs {num.} [std. = dvanaest] *col* twelve <Slav✍>

dvánēs {num.} [std. = dvanaest] *col* twelve <Slav✍>

dvánest {num.} [std. = dvanaest] *col* twelve <Slav✍>

dvê bànke kȉlo {NP} (lit. twenty dinars for two pounds) SerE *sl* ***Fac*** of very low quality, lousy: *cene dve banke kilo rock bottom prices* ☞ **banka**

dvȅsta *See the following*

• **dvȅsta iz mȅsta** {NumP} (lit. two hundred kilometers from the start) SerE *col* abruptly, forcefully

dvjȅsta *See the following*

• **dvjȅsta iz mjȅsta**{NumP} (lit. two hundred kilometers from the start) *col* abruptly, forcefully

dvòbanka {ē fem.; Dat dvòbanki} *sl* bus line number twenty in Belgrade, Serbia <Slav-Ita[*1]>

dvòcēvka {ē fem.; Dat dvòcēvki} SerE *col* double-barrelled gun <Slav>

dvòcjēvka {ē fem.; Dat dvòcjēvki} **a.** *col* double-barrelled gun <Slav> **b.i.** *sl-sex* female who simultaneously engages in sexual intercourse with two males <Slav[*1]> **ii.** *sl-sex* bisexual, AC/DC <Slav[*1]>

dvòglāvka {ē fem.} *sl* two dinars; a two-dinar coin <Slav[*1]>

dvȍglēd {a masc.} /dvògled/ *sl* eyeglasses <Slav✍[*1]>

dvògrbā déva {NP} (lit. a two-humped camel) *sl-drink* ***Fac*** alcoholic, drunk ☞ **deva**

dvȍguza {ē fem.} (lit. the two-assed one) *sl-drink* two-liter bottle (usu. of wine) <Slav[*1]>

dvójka [1] {ē fem.} *col* lowest passing grade <Slav>

dvójka [2] {excl.} *sl* used to make somebody go away, beat it <Slav[*1]>

• **Dvójka si!** {S} (lit. You are number two!) *sl-mil* used in angry dismissal, Get lost!

• **Dvójka ti je!** {S} (lit. Here is number two to you!) *sl-mil* used in angry dismissal, Get lost!

dvójkīn krûg {NP} (lit. the circle made by the streetcar number two) Ser *sl* downtown Belgrade ☞ **krug**

dvojkírati {dvòjkīrām, dvojkírajū perf.} (lit. two *originally military command dva 'two', i.e. soldier is dismissed*) *sl* send away, dismiss <Slav⁘[*1]>

dvònožac {šca (acc. = gen.) masc.} (lit. the two-legged one) *sl* courier <Slav>

dvorhàna {ē fem.} [std. = dvorana] BosM *col* auditorium <Slav-NE>

dvòrskā dáma {NP} (lit. court lady) *sl-sex* ***Fac*** male homosexual, gay ☞ **dama**

dvòrskā lȕda {NP} (lit. court fool) *sl-sex* ***Fac-Obs*** penis, dick, prick ☞ **luda**

dvosòbnjāk {sobnjáka masc.} *col* one-bedroom apartment <Slav⁘>

dvȍtko {a neut.} *sl* station, stop (bus, train, streetcar, etc.)

dvotȍčkāš {a masc.} (lit. two-wheeler) *sl* ***Fac*** bicycle, bike <Slav[*1]>

DŽdž

dž {adv.} *sl* free, gratis <NE✍>

džə {adv.} **a.** *sl* free, gratis <NE✍> **b.** *sl* very inexpensive, bargain: *Ta haljina je džə! That dress is a bargain!* <NE✍>
- **za džə** {PP} *sl* free, gratis

džȁ {excl.} *col* used to frighten one's interlocutor, boo
- **džȁ ili bȕ** {ExcP} *col* used to refer to willingness to act notwithstanding the consequences, whatever happens: *Otići ću na ljetovanje, pa dža ili bu! I will go on vacation whatever happens!*
- **pa džȁ ili bȕ** {ExcP} (lit. either dža or bu) *col* used to refer to willingness to act notwithstanding the consequences, whatever happens

džȁb-džabàluk {adv.} *col* very inexpensive, bargain <NE>

džȁb-džȁbē {adv.} **a.** *col* absolutely free <NE> **b.** *col* very inexpensive, bargain: *U toj prodavnici sve je džab-džabe. Everything is a bargain in that store.* <NE[*1]>

džȁba {adv.} **a.** *col* free, gratis <NE> **b.** *col* in vain, for nothing <NE[*1]>

džàbāk {adv.} **a.** *sl* very inexpensive, bargain: *Kola su bila džabak. The car was a bargain.* <NE> **b.** *sl* in vain, for nothing <NE[*1]>

džabáka {adv.} *sl* free, gratis <NE✍>

džabalək {masc.} SSer *dia* very inexpensive item or service <NE✍>

džabalèbār {lebára (acc. = gen.) masc.; Voc džabalēbāru} SerE *col-dia* loafer, idler <NE-Slav⁘>

džabalebárēnje {a neut.} SerE *col-dia* spend one's time in useless activities, fool around, mess around <NE-Slav>

džabalebáriti {rīm, rē imperf. intr.} **SerE** *col-dia* spend one's time in useless activities, fool around, mess around <NE-Slav⁘>

džabalèbāroš {a (acc. = gen.) masc.} SerE *sl-fea* person who spends time in useless activities <NE-Slav⁘>

džabalèbisānje {a neut.} **SerE** *col* spending one's time in useless activities, fooling around, messing around <NE-Slav⁘>

džabalèbisati {išēm, išū imperf.} **SerE** *col-dia* spend one's time in useless activities, fool around, mess around <NE-Slav>

džabalèbović {a (acc. = gen.) masc.} **SerE** *col-dia* person who spends time in useless activities, slacker <NE-Slav[*1]>

džabalèskū {adv.} **a.** *sl* free, gratis <NE-Rum✍> **b.** *sl* very inexpensive, bargain <NE-Rum✍[*1]>

džabàli {adv.} Bos *col* free, gratis <NE>

džabàlučina {ē fem.} **Din** *sl* free items or services <NE✍>

džabàlučiti {čīm, čē imperf. intr.} *col* spend one's time in useless activities, fool around, mess around <NE⁘[*1]>

džabàluk {a masc.} *col* very inexpensive item or service <NE>

džȁbē {adv.} **a.** **Din** *col* free, gratis <NE> **b.** *col* in vain, for nothing <NE[*1]>

džȁbrāk {džabráka (acc. = gen.) masc.} *sl-fea* ***Der*** worthless or despicable person <NE[*1]>

džáda [1] {excl.} (lit. road) *sl* used to make somebody go away, hit the road <NE[*1]>

džáda [2] {ē fem.} **Din** *col* road <NE>

džàdati {ām, ajū imperf.} *sl* run <NE⁘[*1]>

džàdisati {išēm, išū perf.} *sl* run away, flee <NE⁘[*1]>

džȁdnuti {nēm, nū perf. intr.} *sl* run away, flee <NE⁘[*1]>

džáfer {a (acc. = gen.) masc.} *sl-fea* extraordinary male <NE[*1]>

džȁftara {ē fem.} *col* extremely talkative female, chatterbox <Gyp[*1]>

džága {ē fem.; Dat džági} *sl-crafts* saw (the tool) <Ger[*1]> ☞ **žaga**

Džȁja *See the following*
- **do Džȁja** {AdjP} (lit. to Džajić *Yugoslav soccer legend*) *sl* fully, to the hilt: *dati gas do Džaja put the pedal to the metal*

Džȁjić *See the following*
- **do Džȁjića** {AdjP} (lit. to Džajić *Yugoslav soccer legend*) *sl* fully, to the hilt: *napiti se do Džajića be completely drunk*

džȁka {ē fem.; Dat džȁki} *col* noise <NE>

džȁkati {ām, ajū imperf.} **a.** *col* make noise <NE> **b.** *sl* reproach, scold: *džakati zbog izgubljenog ključa reprimand over losing a key* <NE[*1]>

Džamahȋrija [1] {ē fem.} *col* ***Fac*** Bosnia and Herzegovina <NE[*1]>

džamahîrija[2] {ē fem.} *col* Islamic country <NE>

džȁmbās {a (acc. = gen.) masc.} **a.** *col* troublemaker, rowdy, ruffian <NE[*1]> **b.** *col* irresponsible person: *Ne dajte tom džambasu da vozi! Don't let that irresponsible person drive!* <NE[*2]>

džȁmbo {adj.} *sl-fea* large <Eng[*1]>

džȁmin {džemīn fem.} perm} *sl-sex* ***Obs*** vagina, cunt <Gyp✍> ☞ **mindža**

džȁmiti {mīm, mē imperf. intr.} *sl* smoke (tobacco) <NE[*1]>

džȁmpȁp {a masc.} (lit. jump up) *sl-drugs* good feeling induced by narcotic drug effect, high <Eng>

džȁmuga {ē fem.; Dat džȁmugi} *sl-fea* African American (male) <Slav✍[*1]>

džȃn {masc.} SSer *dia* soul <NE>

- **Džȁn ti jèbēm!** {S} (lit. I fuck your soul!) SSer *dia* ***Off*** used as a moderate curse, Fuck you!

džána {ē fem.} /dȁna/ **a.** *sl-sex* ***Obs*** hymen <NE[*1]> **b.** *sl-sex* ***Obs*** virgin <NE[*2]>

- **džána polòvača** {NP} (lit. half hymen) *sl-sex* ***Fac-Obs*** stiff hymen

džȁndār {a (acc. = gen.) masc.} *sl-crime* policeman, cop <Fre✍>

džȁnfer {a masc.} **a.** *sl-sex* ***Obs*** hymen <NE⁘[*1]> **b.** *sl-sex* ***Obs*** virgin <NE⁘[*2]>

džȁnferica {ē fem.} *sl-sex* ***Obs*** virgin <NE⁘[*1]>

džangrìzati {ām, ajū imperf.} *col* annoy, bother, pester <NE>

džangrìzav {a, o adj.} *sl-fea* quarreling <NE⁘[*1]>

džȁnifer {a masc.} **a.** *sl-sex* ***Obs*** hymen <NE✍[*1]> **b.** *sl-sex* ***Obs*** virgin <NE✍[*1]> **c.** *sl-sex* virginity <NE✍[*2]>

džȁnisānje {a neut.} *sl* observing, looking <Gyp⁘[*1]>

džȁnisati {išēm, išū biasp.} *sl* understand, realize <Gyp[*1]>

džániti {nīm, nē biasp.} **a.** *sl* understand, realize <Gyp[*1]> **b.** *sl* like, appreciate: *džaniti narodnjake like country music* <Gyp[*2]>

džȁnk {a +ov (ext. pl) masc.; Nom Pl džȁnkovi} (lit. junk) *sl-drugs* narcotic drug, dope <Eng>

džȁnkī {ija (acc. = gen.) masc.} /džȁnki/ *sl-drugs* drug addict, junkie <Eng>

džanjávati {džȁnjāvām, vajū imperf.} *sl-crime* sell (exchange merchandise for money) <NE⁘[*1]>

džápati se {džȃpām, džápajū imperf. intr.} *col* fight (e.g. fist fight) <NE[*1]>

džárati {džȃrām, džárajū imperf.} **1** *sl-sex* engage in sexual intercourse with (of a male) <NE[*1]> **2** *sl* annoy, bother, pester: *Ne džaraj me dok radim! Don't disturb me while I'm working!* <NE[*1]> **3** *sl* touch <NE[*1]>

džȁrkati {ām, ajū imperf. intr.} *col* touch <NE[*1]>

džavr̀ljati {ām, ajū imperf.} *col* talk persistently and meaninglessly, blabber, chatter <Slav[*1]>

džbûn {a +ov (ext. pl) masc.; Nom Pl džbȗnovi} **a.** *col* bush, shrub <Slav> **b.** *sl-sex* female pubic hairs, bush <Slav[*1]>

džȁdráknuti {drâknēm, drâknū perf.} *col* look, watch, scope out <Slav>

džebàna {ē fem.} *col* ammunition, ammo <NE>

džèbrak {džebráka (acc. = gen.) masc.} *sl-fea* rude male <Cze[*1]>

džédžānje {a neut.} *sl* standing in one place for a long period of time (usu. while waiting for someone) <NE[*1]>

džédžati {džȇdžām, džédžajū imperf.} *sl* stand for a long time <NE[*1]>

džéđiti {đīm, đē imperf. intr.} *sl* stand in one place for a long time (usu. while waiting for someone) <NE[*1]>

Džȅf {a (acc. = gen.) +ov (ext. pl) masc.; Nom Pl Džȅfovi} *sl-fea* stupid or mentally deficient person <EngO[*1]>

džȅga {ē fem.; Dat džȅgi} **1** *sl-drugs* drug session <NE[*1]> **2** *sl-drugs* money <NE[*1]>

džehènnem {a masc.} BosM *col* hell (religion) <NE>

Džȅk {a (acc. = gen.) +ov (ext. pl) masc.; Nom Pl Džȅkovi} **1** *sl-fea* dandy, fop <EngO[*1]> **2** *sl* boy, kid <EngO[*1]>

džekírati {džȅkīrām, džekírajū imperf. intr.} *sl-fea* boast, brag <EngO⁘[*1]>

džekírati se {džȅkīrām, rajū imperf. intr.} *sl-fea* boast, brag <Eng⁘[*1]>

Džȅksōn {a masc.} (lit. Jackson) *sl* name of a dance club at Jakšić dance school in Zagreb, Croatia <EngO[*1]>

džèlāt {dželáta (acc. = gen.) masc.} (lit. executioner, hangman) *sl* ***Fac*** butcher (literally) <NE[*1]>

džèmāt {džemáta masc.} **a.** BosM *col* community <NE> **b.** BosM *col* Muslim religious community <NE[*1]>

džȅmper {a masc.} (lit. sweater) *sl* ***Fac*** straight jacket <Eng[*1]>

džempèrāš {peráša (acc. = gen.) masc.; Voc džȅmperāšu} (lit. one who wears sweaters) *col* habitual casual dresser <Eng❖>

džemperȉška {ē fem.; Dat džemperȉški} /džemperȉška/ *sl* sweater <Eng✍>

dženáza {ē fem.} BosM *col* funeral <NE> ☞ **đenaza**

džènet {a masc.} /džènnet /a masc./ BosM *col* heaven (religion) <NE>

dženga {ē fem.; Dat džȅngi} *sl* money <NE[*1]>

džènifer {a masc.} *sl-sex* ***Obs*** virginity <EngO[*1]>

džȅp {džèpa +ov (ext. pl) masc.; Nom Pl džèpovi} (lit. pocket) *sl-crime* pocket picking <NE>

džepárēnje {a neut.} *sl-crime* pocket picking <NE❖>
- **džepárēnje šlȉcēvā** {NP} (lit. stealing from zippers) *sl-sex* ***Fac*** working as a prostitute

džepáriti {džèpārīm, rē imperf.} *sl-crime* pick pockets <NE❖>

džèpāroš {a (acc. = gen.) masc.} *col* pickpocket <NE❖>

džèpiner {a masc.} *sl-crime* pocket (on a coat, trousers, etc.) <NE✍>

džȅpka {ē fem.; Dat džȅpki} *sl-crime* pocket picking <NE❖>

džèpnī bilȉjār {NP} (lit. pocket pool) *sl-sex* ***Fac*** playing with one's testicles through one's pocket, pocket pool ☞ **bilijar**

džèpnō izdánje {NP} (lit. pocket edition) *sl-fea* ***Fac*** short female ☞ **izdanje**

džèpnjāk {džepnjáka masc.} 1 *col* pocketbook <NE❖> 2 *col* pocket watch <NE❖>

džȅpos {a (acc. = gen.) masc.} *sl-crime* pickpocket <NE❖>

džèrima *See the following*
- **Džèrimu ti jèbēm!** {S} (lit. I screw your fine!) *dia* ***Off*** used as a weak curse, Screw you!

džéva {ē fem.} **a.** *col* mess, disorder, disturbance: *Digla se dževa oko para. There was a disturbance over money.* <NE> **b.** *col* noise <NE>

džèvātor {a (acc. = gen.) masc.} **a.** *col* loud and angry person <NE❖> **b.** *col* person who makes noise <NE❖[*1]>

džȅzerica {ē fem.} *sl-music* jazz music <Eng❖>

džȉber {a masc.} /džíber/ **a.** *sl-drink* brandy drinker <NE❖> **b.** *sl-fea* inhabitant of the countryside, hick, bumpkin <NE❖[*1]>

džibèrisati se {išēm, išū imperf. intr.} *sl-fea* be conceited, be stuck-up <NE[*1]>

džȉberskī {ā, ō adj.} *sl-drink* alcoholic, drunk <NE❖>

džȉbra {ē fem.} **a.** *sl-drink* low-quality brandy <NE❖> **b.** *sl* bad merchandise, junk <NE❖[*1]>

džȉbriti *See the following*
- **džȉbriti mašínu** {VP} *sl-auto* speed (auto, etc.)

džȉbronja {ē masc.} **a.** *sl-drink* brandy drinker <NE❖> **b.** *sl-fea* snob <NE❖[*1]>

džídža {ē fem.} **a.** **Din** *col* small decorative element (e.g. on garment) <NE> **b.** **Din** *col* trifle, thing of little importance or value <NE[*1]>

džídža-bídža {ē fem.} **a.** **Din** *col* small decorative element (e.g. on garment) <NE> **b.** **Din** *col* trifle, thing of little importance or value <NE>

džídžati {džȉdžām, džídžajū imperf.} **a.** *col* decorate (a person, house, etc.) <NE> **b.** *col* collect (e.g. stamps) <NE[*1]>

džidžibúdžiti {džīm, džē imperf.} *sl-sex* ***Obs*** engage in sexual intercourse with (of a male) <NE✍>

džȉga {ē fem.; Dat džȉgi} *sl-gamble* loss, detriment <NE[*1]>

džȉgera {ē fem.} [std. = džigerica] *col* liver (the organ) <NE✍>

džȉgerica *See the following*
- **U džȉgerice ti ga kȍknēm!** {S} (lit. I bang it in your liver!) **SSer** *dia* ***Off*** used as a weak curse, Screw you!

džigèrisati {išēm, išū imperf.} *sl-fea* act as a troublemaker <NE❖[*1]>

džigèrisati se {išēm, išū imperf. intr.} *sl* act like a coward <NE❖[*1]>

džigérnjača *See the following*
- **stô grâmā džigérnjačē** {NumP} (lit. hundred grams of liver) *sl* hit in the plexus

džȉglja {ē fem.} *sl-fea* slender female <NE[*1]>

džȉgljast {a, o adj.} *col* tall and slender (of a person) <Slav>

džȉhādovac {vca (acc. = gen.) masc.} (lit. jihad fighter) *col* ***Der*** Bosnian Muslim (male) <NE❖[*1]>

džȉhādskī {ā, ō adj.} (lit. jihad) *col* ***Der*** Bosnian Muslim (pertaining to a person or nation) <NE❖>

džilítnuti {džȉlītnēm, nū perf. intr.} *sl* kick, strike <NE❖[*1]>

Džȉm {a (acc. = gen.) +ov (ext. pl) masc.; Nom Pl Džȉmovi} (lit. Jim) **a.** *sl-fea* stupid or mentally deficient person <EngO[*1]> **b.** clumsy person, klutz

džindōv {džindòva (acc. = gen.) masc.} *sl-sex* ***Obs*** penis, dick, prick <NE❖[*1]>

džȉndžati {ām, ajū imperf.} *sl-sex* ***Obs*** engage in sexual intercourse with (of a male) <NE☞>

džȉndžōv {a (acc. = gen.) masc.} *sl-fea* stupid or mentally deficient person <NE❖*1>

džȉnfis {a masc.} *sl-sex* agreement to have group sexual intercourse with <Eng*1>

džȉngiskān {a (acc. = gen.) masc.} *sl-sex* penis <NEO*1>

džȋnserıce {rica fem. pl.} *col* jeans <Eng [illegible]

džȉv-džȉv {excl.} *col* the sound made by a sparrow, tweet <Slav>

džȉvdža {ē masc.} *col* sparrow <Slav❖>

džnjávati {džnjâvām, džnjávajū imperf.} *sl-crime* sell (exchange merchandise for money) <NE*1>

džófa {ē fem.} *sl* sleep, nap <NE*1>

džȍfra {ē fem.} *sl* sleep, nap <NE*1>

džȍgara {ē fem.} *sl-sex* ***Fac*** prostitute, hooker <NE*1>

džȍint {a masc.} *sl-drugs* marijuana cigarette, joint <Eng>

džȍjnt {a +ov (ext. pl) masc.; Nom Pl džȍjntovi} *sl-drugs* marijuana cigarette, joint <Eng>

džȍka {ē fem.; Dat džȍki} *sl* jacket <NE*1>

džókānje {a neut.} *sl-drink* drinking (alcohol) <NE*1>

džókati {džôkām, džókajū imperf.} *sl-drink* drink (alcohol) <NE❖*1>

džȍker {a (acc. = gen.) masc.} (lit. joker) **a.** *sl* wildcard person <Eng*1> **b.** *sl* person with dark complexion <Eng*2>

džȍmba {ē fem.} /džómba/ **a.** *sl* bump (usu. in road) <NE> **b.i.** *sl-fea* muscular female <NE*1> **ii.** *sl-mil* old soldier <NE*1>

džȍmbe {eta neut.} **a.** *sl* bump (usu. in road) <NE> **b.i.** *sl-fea* muscular female <NE*1> **ii.** *sl-mil* old soldier <NE*1>

• **stárā džȍmba** {NP} (lit. old bump) *sl-mil* old soldier

džȍna {ē masc.} *sl-sex* ***Obs*** penis, dick, prick <NE*1>

džȍndra {ē fem.} **a.** *sl-fea* homeless person, bum <NE*1> **b.** *sl-fea* unattractive person <NE*1>

Džȍnī {īja masc.} **a.** *sl-sex* penis <SlavO*1> **b.** *sl-drugs* needle <SlavO*1>

• **Džȍnī Šètāč** {NP} *sl-drink* ***Fac*** Johnny Walker (a brand of whiskey)

džónjānje {a neut.} **a.** *sl* sleeping <NE*1> **b.** *sl* standing in one place for a long period of time (usu. while waiting for someone) <NE*1>

džȍnjāroš {a (acc. = gen.) masc.} *sl* male waiting for his date to arrive <NE❖*1>

džónjati {džônjām, džónjajū biasp.} **1** *sl* wander, roam <NE*1> **2a.** *sl* sleep, nap: *džonjati popodne take an afternoon nap* <NE*1> **b.** *sl* stand for a long time

Džȍrdžika {ē masc.; Dat Džȍrdžiki} (lit. Georgie *after a hospital on George Washington street in Belgrade, Serbia*) Ser *sl-sex* ***Fac*** venereal disease hospital <EngO*1>

džȍvān {džována (acc. = gen.) masc.} **a.** *sl-fea* inhabitant of the countryside, hick, bumpkin <NE*1> **b.** *sl-fea* snob <NE*1>

džȍzeri {zērā masc. pl.} *sl* eyeglasses <NE❖>

džȍzluci {džȍzlūkā masc. pl.} *col* eyeglasses <NE>

džȑker {a (acc. = gen.) masc.} (lit. jerker) *sl-fea* worthless or despicable person <Eng>

džȕba {ē fem.} *sl* garbage <NE☞>

džȕbār {a (acc. = gen.) masc.} *sl* garbage man <NE☞>

džȕber {a (acc. = gen.) masc.} *sl* garbage man <NE☞>

džùboks {a masc.} (lit. jukebox) *sl-sex* ***Fac*** prostitute, hooker <Eng☞>

džȕbos {a (acc. = gen.) masc.} **a.** *sl* garbage man <NE☞> **b.** *sl* unattractive person <NE☞*1>

džȕdža {ē fem. & masc.} **a.** *sl-fea* inhabitant of the countryside, hick, bumpkin <NE> **b.** *sl-fea* snob <NE*1>

džudžȍvān {džována (acc. = gen.) masc.} **a.** *sl-fea* inhabitant of the countryside, hick, bumpkin <NE❖> **b.** *sl-fea* snob <NE❖*1>

džudžovànder {a (acc. = gen.) masc.} **a.** *sl-fea* inhabitant of the countryside, hick, bumpkin <NE❖> **b.** *sl-fea* worthless or despicable person, bum <NE❖*1>

džȕka {ē masc.; Dat džȕki} *sl-arch* horse (the animal) <NE>

džúkac {kca (acc. = gen.) masc.} **a.** *col* mixed breed dog, mutt, mongrel <Gyp❖> **b.** *col* dog of any breed <Gyp❖*1> **c.** *sl-fea* inhabitant of the countryside, hick, bumpkin <Gyp❖*2>

džùkela {ē fem. & masc.} **a.** *col* ***Der*** mixed breed dog, mutt, mongrel <Gyp> **b.** *sl-fea* ***Der*** inhabitant of the countryside, hick, bumpkin <Gyp*1> **c.** *sl-fea* ***Der*** worthless or despicable person, bum <Gyp*2>

džukèljisati {šēm, šū imperf.} *sl-sex* ***Fac-Obs*** engage in sexual intercourse with (of a male) <Gyp❖*1>

džȕklja {ē fem. & masc.} **a.** *sl-sex* ***Der*** prostitute, hooker <Gyp*1> **b.** *sl-fea* ***Der*** unattractive person <Gyp*3>

džȕkljavac {vca (acc. = gen.) masc.} *sl* dog (the animal) <**Gyp**[*]❖>

džùkser {a (acc. = gen.) masc.} **a.** *sl-fea* inhabitant of the countryside, hick, bumpkin <**Gyp**✍❖[*1]> **b.** *sl-fea* snob <**Gyp**✍❖[*2]>

džùlōv {džulòva (acc. = gen.) masc.} **a.** *sl-fea* stupid or mentally deficient person <**NE**❖[*1]> **b.** *sl-fea* lazy or shiftless person, bum, good for nothing <**NE**❖[*2]>

džȕmbus {a masc.} *col* mess, disorder, disturbance: *Njegova soba je džumbus. His room is a mess.* <**NE**[*1]>

džùmina {ē fem.} **a.** *sl-sex* ***Obs*** vagina, cunt <**Gyp**✍> **b.** *sl* ***Obs*** female, cunt <**Gyp**✍[*1]>

džùngla {ē fem.} **1** *sl-fea* long hair <**Eng**[*1]> **2** *sl-fea* city <**Eng**[*1]>

džȕra {ē fem.} *sl-arch* water

džȗrka {ē fem.; Dat džȗrki} *sl-arch* candle <**NE**[*1]>

džvȁnjkānje {a neut.} *sl-fea* prolonged and meaningless talk, blabber, chatter <**Slav**✍[*1]>

džvȁnjkati {ām, ajū imperf. intr.} **a.** *sl* preach, give lectures to <**Slav**✍[*1]> **b.** *sl* reproach, scold: *džvanjkati zbog izgubljene utakmice reproach over a lost game* <**Slav**✍[*2]>

Đđ

đȁ {excl.} *col* used to urge a horse to move on <**Slav**>

đabàskati {ām, ajū imperf.} *sl-crime* resell, fence <**Slav**[*1]>

đȁbē {adv.} **1** **BosM** *col* free, gratis <**NE**✍> **2** **BosM** *col* in vain, for nothing: *Đabe to radiš. You are doing this in vain.* <**NE**✍> ☞ **džaba, džabe**

đáda [1] {excl.} (lit. road) BosM *sl* ***Der*** used to make somebody go away, hit the road <**NE**✍[*1]>

đáda [2] {ē fem.} **a.** BosM *col* road <**NE**✍> **b.** BosM *col* escape, flee <**NE**✍[*1]>

đȁkati {ām, ajū imperf.} *col* talk, have a conversation <**Gre**❖>

đȁker {a (acc. = gen.) masc.} *sl-sstu* school student <**Gre**❖>

đȁkomo {a masc.} *sl-sstu* school student <**Gre**✍>

đálac {lca (acc. = gen.) masc.} *sl-arch* child, kid

đalafȕsnuti {nēm, nū perf.} *sl-sex* engage in sexual intercourse with (of a male)

đâle {eta neut.} *sl-arch* child, kid <**Slav**[*1]>

đȁlisati {išēm, išū imperf.} *sl-crime* run away, flee <**Slav**[*1]>

đȁlnuti {nēm, nū perf. intr.} *sl-crime* run away, flee <**Slav**[*1]>

đȁmiti {mīm, mē imperf.} *sl* smoke (tobacco) <**NE**[*1]>

đána {ē fem.} **a.** *sl-sex* ***Obs*** hymen <**Ger**[*1]> **b.** *sl-sex* ***Obs*** virgin <**Ger**[*2]>
- **đána polòvača** {NP} (lit. half hymen) *sl-sex* ***Obs*** stiff hymen

đànel {a masc.} *sl* look, glimpse <**Gyp**[*1]>

đȁnf {a (acc. = gen.) +ov (ext. pl) masc.; Nom Pl đànfovi} **a.** *sl-sex* ***Obs*** virgin <**Ger**❖[*1]> **b.** **Cro** *sl-drink* ***Obs*** name of a bar at Nikola Tesla street in Zagreb, Croatia <**Ger**❖[*2]>

đȁnfa {ē fem.} **a.** *sl-sex* ***Obs*** vagina, cunt <**Ger**❖[*1]> **b.** *sl-sex* ***Obs*** virgin <**Ger**❖[*2]>

đȁnferica {ē fem.} **a.** *sl-sex* ***Obs*** virgin <**Ger**❖[*1]> **b.** *sl-sex* ***Obs*** female <**Ger**❖[*2]>

đànisānje {a neut.} *sl* looking, watching, scoping out <**Gyp**>

đànisati {išēm, išū imperf.} **a.** *sl* look, observe: *đanisati na ulicu šta se dešava watch on the street what's happening* <**Gyp**> **b.** *sl* know, have knowledge of: *đanisati matiš know math* <**Gyp**[*1]>

đániti {nīm, nē imperf.} **/đȁniti/** *sl* look, watch, scope out <**Gyp**>

đȁnkati {ām, ajū imperf.} *sl* look, watch, scope out <**Gyp**>

đȁnkī {īja (acc. = gen.) masc.} **/đànki/** *sl-drugs* drug addict, junkie <**Eng**>

đankóza {ē fem.} *sl-drugs* drug addict, junkie <**Eng**❖>

đàpan {a (acc. = gen.) masc.} *sl-crime* ***Der*** thief, sticky fingers <**Slav**[*1]>

đȁra {excl.} *col* the sound made by machine gun, rat-a-tat-tat <**Slav**>

Đȁrma {Đàrama (acc. = gen.) masc.; perm} [std. = Mađar] *sl-fea* Hungarian (person) <**Hun**✍>

đȁur {a (acc. = gen.) masc.} BosM *col* non-Muslim <**NE**>

đȁurin {a (acc. = gen.) -in (rd. pl.) masc.} BosM *col* non-Muslim <**NE**>

đàvlac {a (acc. = gen.) masc.} *sl-arch* child, kid <**Slav**[*1]>

đàvlāš {đavláša (acc. = gen.) masc.; Voc đàvlāšu} *sl-arch* male, guy <Slav❖[*1]>

đàvle {eta neut.} *sl-arch* child, kid <Slav❖[*1]>

đàvō {vola (acc. = gen.) masc.} (lit. devil) **1** *sl* boss <Gre[*1]> **2** *sl* spoiled child, brat: *Njihov sin je pravi đavo. Their son is a real brat.* <Gre[*1]>

• **bijèlī đàvō** {NP} (lit. white devil) *sl-sstu* ***Fac*** high-school principal

• **Đàvo[PRON:ACC] ȍdneō!** {LSF} (lit. Let the devil take [PRON:ACC]!) **SerE** *col* ***Der*** used to express negative attitude toward: *Đavo je odneo! The hell with her!*

• **kòjī[PRON:DAT] je đàvō** {LSF} (lit. what kind of devil is it with [PRON:ACC]) *col* used to express negative attitude toward one's interlocutor, what's wrong with [PRON: ACC]: *koji ti je đavo what's wrong with you*

đàvol {ā (acc. = gen.) masc.} [std. = đavo] *col* devil <Gre✍>

đȅ {adv.} [std. = gd(j)e] *col-dia* where <Slav✍>

• **đȅ li** {ProP} Bos *col* who knows where

• **Đȅ si?** {AdvP} (lit. Where are you?) **Bos** *col* ***Fam*** used as an informal greeting, What's up!: *Đe si jarane! What's up buddy!*

• **Đȅ si ba?** {S} (lit. Where are you, man?) Bos *col* ***Fam*** used as an informal greeting, What's up!

• **Đȅ si ti vôjsku slúžio?** {S} (lit. Where did you serve in the military?) **Din** *sl* ***Fac*** used to express impatience, Where have you been up to now?

đećárac {rca (acc. = gen.) masc.} (lit. the one who is beslobbered) *col* youngster, kid <Slav[*1]>

đȅd {a +ov (ext. pl) masc.; Nom Pl dèdovi} [std. = d(j)ed(a)] *col-dia* grandfather, grandpa <Slav✍>

đèđe {adv.} [std. = gd(j)egd(j)e] *col-dia* here and there, all over: *Điđe se još mogu naći dobri konji. You can still find good horses here and there.* <Slav✍>

đèkad {adv.} [std. = gd(j)ekad] *col-dia* from time to time: *Đekad zapalim cigaru. I smoke from time to time.* <Slav✍>

đèko {pron.} [std. = gd(j)eko] *col-dia* one or another <Slav✍>

đȅl {excl.} *dia* used to urge somebody to approach, come here <Slav>

đȅla {excl.} *dia* used to urge somebody to approach, come here <Slav>

đélac {lca (acc. = gen.) masc.} *sl-arch* boy, kid <Slav[*1]>

đelàrče {eta neut.} *sl-arch* child, kid <Slav❖[*1]>

đêm {a (acc. = gen.) +ov (ext. pl) masc.; Nom Pl đèmovi} *sl-arch* dog (the animal) <NE[*1]>

đèmāt {đemáta masc.} **a.** BosM *col* community <NE> **b.** BosM *col* Muslim religious community <NE[*1]>

đenáza {ē fem.} BosM *col* funeral <NE> ☞ **dženaza**

đȅne-đȅne {adv.} **1** *sl* used to refer to the regular state of affairs (usu. in response to the question Kako si? 'How are you?'), so-so <NE> **2** *sl* here and there, every now and then: *Viđamo se đene-đene. We've been seeing each other every now and then.* <NE>

đenèrāl {nerála (acc. = gen.) masc.} [std. = general] Ser *sl-mil* general <Lat✍>

đȅnge {ī fem. pl.} *sl-crime* money <NE[*1]>

đêngi {đȅnāgā fem. pl.} *sl* money <NE[*1]>

đènisati {išēm, išū imperf.} *sl* look, watch, scope out <NE[*1]>

đȅnt {a (acc. = gen.) +ov (ext. pl) masc.; Nom Pl đèntovi} *sl* elegant male <Ita✍>

đèrček {excl.} *col-dia* used to express joy, oh yeah <NE>

đȅriti {rīm, rē imperf.} *sl* look, watch, scope out <NE[*1]>

đȅś {adv.} [std. = Gd(j)e ćeš?] Bos *col* where to, where do you want to go <Slav✍>

đȅt {a (acc. = gen.) +ov (ext. pl) masc.; Nom Pl đètovi} [std. = d(j)ed] *dia* grandfather, grandpa <Slav✍>

đéte {eta neut.} [std. = d(ij)ete] **a.** *dia* child, kid <Slav✍> **b.** *dia* daughter <Slav✍[*1]>

đȅtić {a (acc. = gen.) masc.} [std. = d(j)etić] **a.** Mont *col* child, kid <Slav✍> **b.** Montenegrin (person) <Slav✍[*1]>

đèvče {eta neut.} *sl-arch* dog (the animal) <Slav[*1]>

đȅver {a (acc. = gen.) masc.} [std. = d(j)ever] *col-dia* brother-in-law <Slav◊✍>

đevòjčica {ē fem.} [std. = d(j)evojčica] *dia* female child, girl <Slav✍>

đèvōjka {ē fem.} [std. = d(j)evojka] *dia* young female, girl <Slav✍>

đèvrek {a masc.} (lit. round oriental pastry) *sl-auto* ***Fac*** steering wheel <NE>

đî {excl.} *col* used to urge a horse to go ahead or go at a faster pace, giddyup <Slav>

đî-đî [1] {ija (acc. = gen.) masc.} (lit. giddyup-giddyup) *col* ***Fam*** horse (the animal) <Slav[*1]>

đî-đî [2] {ija masc.} (lit. giddyup-giddyup) *col* ***Fam*** riding (horseback) <Slav[*1]>

đìdati {đīdām, ajū imperf.} *sl* cheat in marbles <NE[*1]>

đìhā {excl.} *col* used to urge a horse to go ahead or go at a faster pace, giddyup <Slav>

đìja {excl.} *col* used to urge a horse to go ahead or go at a faster pace, giddyup <Slav>
- **đìja, đìja svè čètiri krúte** {S} (lit. go, go all four legs are stiff *from a popular children's verse*) *sl* used to refer to disbelief, just promises

đìjo {excl.} *col* used to urge a horse to go ahead or go at a faster pace, giddyup <Slav>

đijòtāljka {ē fem.} *dia* horse whip <Slav❖>

đìjotka {ē fem.; Dat đìjotki} *dia* horse whip <Slav❖>

đìk {excl.} **1** *col* used when jumping, hop <Slav> **2** *col* the sound made by a small bird, tweet <Slav>

đìkan {a masc.} *sl-drink* denatured alcohol <Slav[*1]>

đìkavac {kāvca masc.} *col* tweeting bird <Slav❖[*1]>

đìlda {ē fem.} *sl* pre-WW II Yugoslavia

đìlkoš {a (acc. = gen.) masc.} **/đìlkoš/ a.** *sl-fea* ***Der*** worthless or despicable person <Hun[*1]> **b.** *sl-fea* homeless person, bum <Hun[*1]>

đìmnā {ē fem.} *sl-sstu* high school <Gre✍>

đìnđuha {ē fem.; Dat đìnđuhi} **a.** BosM *col* inexpensive jewelry <NE> **b.** BosM *col* trifle, thing of little importance or value <NE> ☞ **đinđuva**

đìnđuva {ē fem.} **a.** *col* inexpensive jewelry <NE> **b.** *col* trifle, thing of little importance or value <NE[*1]> ☞ **đinđuha**

đìo {excl.} *col* used to hurry up a horse, giddyup <Slav>

đìp {excl.} *col* used when jumping, hop <Slav>

đìpac {excl.} *col* used when jumping, hop <Slav>

đípati {đîpām, đípajū imperf.} *col* jump <Slav❖>

đìpati se {ām, ajū imperf. intr.} *col* jump <Slav[*1]>

đìpiti {pīm, pē perf.} **a.** *col* jump <Slav❖> **b.** *col* beat energetically (as of heart), beat like crazy <Slav❖[*1]>

đìr {a +ev (ext. pl) masc.; Nom Pl đírevi} **a.** *sl* circle <Ita> **b.** *sl* turn (e.g. when riding a bicycle) <Ita[*1]>

đìrati {ām, ajū imperf.} *sl* walk or drive in circles <Ita❖>

đirávati {đìrāvām, đirávajū imperf.} Med *dia* walk or drive in circles <Ita❖>

đìsiti {sīm, sē perf.} *sl* jump abruptly, leap <Slav[*1]>

đìtra {ē fem.} [std. = gitara] *sl-music* guitar <Gre✍>

đìtrati {ām, ajū biasp. intr.} *sl-music* play guitar <Gre❖✍>

đìv-đìv {excl.} *col* the sound made by a sparrow, tweet <Slav>

đìvrati *See the following*
- **đìvrati mašínu** {VP} *sl-auto* speed (auto, etc.)

đógo {a masc.} Bos *col-dia* horse (the animal) <NE✍>

đóka {ē masc.; Dat đóki} (lit. George) SerE *sl-sex* ***Obs*** penis, dick, prick <GreO✍>
- **Đóka bez ȍka** {NP} (lit. one-eyed George) SerE *sl-sex* ***Obs-Fac*** penis, dick

đòkan {a (acc. = gen.) masc.} (lit. George) *sl-sex* ***Obs*** penis, dick, prick <GreO[*1]>

đȍkica {ē masc.} (lit. George) **1** *sl-sex* ***Obs*** penis, dick, prick <GreO[*1]> **2** *sl* boy, kid <GreO[*1]>

đóko {ē masc.} (lit. George) *sl-sex* ***Obs*** penis, dick, prick <GreO[*1]>

đôle {eta neut.} (lit. George) *sl-sex* ***Obs*** penis, dick, prick <GreO[*1]>

đȍlī {īja (acc. = gen.) masc.} *sl-crime* skillful criminal <Eng[*1]>

đȍmka {ē fem.; Dat đómki} *sl-arch* cornbread <Slav✍>

đȍn {a +ov (ext. pl) masc.; Nom Pl đȍnovi} (lit. shoe sole) **1** *sl-stu* crib sheet, cheat sheet <NE[*1]> **2** *sl* indecent action <NE[*1]>

đòniti {nīm, nē imperf.} *sl-stu* prepare crib-sheets for an exam <NE❖[*1]>

đȍnka {ē fem.; Dat đónki} *sl-arch* cornbread <Slav>

đónjati {đônjām, đónjajū biasp.} *sl* sleep, nap <NE✍>

đôr {a +ov (ext. pl) masc.; Nom Pl đórevi} *sl* exchange (goods, money, etc.) <NE[*1]>
- **đôr za kȋntu** {NP} (lit. exchange for money) *sl* sell (exchange merchandise for money)

đóra {ē fem.} *col* exchange (goods, money, etc.) <NE>

đórānje {ē fem.} *col* exchange (goods, money, etc.) <NE>

đórati {đôrām, đórajū biasp.} *col* exchange (goods, money, etc.) <NE>

đórati se {đôrām, đórajū biasp. intr.} *col* exchange (goods, money, etc.) <NE>

Đôrđe {eta neut.} (lit. George) *sl* thousand dinars; a thousand-dinar bill, grand <GreO[*1]>

đòrđić {a masc.} *sl-crime* detective <GreO[*1]>

đòrđija {ē fem.} *sl* ten dinars; a ten-dinar bill <GreO[*1]>

đòrđika {ē fem.; Dat đòrđiki} (lit. Georgie *after a hospital on George Washington street in Belgrade, Serbia*) *sl-sex* venereal disease hospital <EngO☞*1>

đòrzluci {đòrzlūkā masc. pl.} *sl* eyeglasses <NE☞>

đȍzle {i fem. pl.} *sl* eyeglasses <NE☞>

đòzluci {đȍzlūkā masc. pl.} *sl* eyeglasses <NE>

đòzluk {a (acc. = gen.) masc.} *sl-fea* person who wears eyeglasses, four-eyes <NE*1>

đòzluk {a masc.} Bos *col* eyeglasses <NE>

đȕbos {a (acc. = gen.) masc.} *sl* garbage man <NE☞>

đȕbre {eta neut.} (lit. trash) **1** *sl-fea* ***Der*** worthless or despicable person <NE*1> **2** *sl-sex* anus <NE*1>
- **Đȕbre jèdno!** {S} (lit. You piece of garbage!) *col* ***Off*** used as a moderate curse
- **Đȕbre màtorō!** {S} (lit. You old piece of garbage!) *col* ***Off*** used as a moderate curse
- **Đȕbre pòkvārenō!** {S} (lit. You piece of rotten garbage!) *col* ***Off*** used as a moderate curse

đȕbrēnje {a neut.} (lit. fertilizing) *sl-fea* prolonged and meaningless talk, blabber, chatter <NE>

đubretárac {rca masc.} *col* short coat with elongated wooden buttons <NE❖*1>

đubrijéra {ē fem.} *col* garbage can <NE❖*1>

đȕbriti {rīm, rē imperf.} (lit. fertilize) **a.** *sl-sex* ***Fac-Obs*** defecate <NE*1> **b.** *sl-fea* talk persistently and meaninglessly, blabber, chatter <NE*2>
- **đȕbriti njȉvu** {VP} (lit. fertilize one's acre) *sl-sex* ***Fac*** defecate at one's own home

đȕka {ē fem.; Dat đȕki} *sl-sex* old prostitute <SlavO*1>

đúkac {kca (acc. = gen.) masc.} *col* dog (the animal) <NE☞>

đȕklija {ē fem.} *sl-crime* police dog <NE❖>

đȕkser {a (acc. = gen.) masc.} *sl-fea* inhabitant of the countryside, hick, bumpkin <NE☞*1>

đȕla {ē fem.} **a.** *sl* knife <NE*1> **b.** *sl* dagger (esp. one used as a weapon) <NE*2>

đùlāvka {ē fem.} *sl-sex* ***Obs*** buttocks, butt <NE*1>

đúle {eta neut.} (lit. cannonball) **1** *dia* shell, bomb <NE*1> **2** *sl-fea* obese male <NE*1>

đȗn {a masc.} *sl-arch* day <NE>

đunìjati {ām, ajū imperf.} *sl-sex* ***Obs*** engage in sexual intercourse with (of a male) <NE❖*1>

đȗrač {a masc.} *sl* thousand dinars; a thousand-dinar bill, a grand <SlavO*1>

đȗrać {a (acc. = gen.) masc.} *sl* thousand dinars; a thousand-dinar bill, grand <GreO*1>

đȗrđa {ē fem.} **1** *sl* thousand dinars; a thousand-dinar bill, a grand <GreO*1> **2** *sl* ten dinars; a ten-dinar bill <GreO*1>

đȗrka {ē fem.; Dat đȗrki} *sl-arch* candle <NE*1>

đùrōv {a masc.} *sl-arch* tobacco <NE*1>

đùrōvnīk {a masc.} *sl-arch* tobacco <NE*1>

đȕs {a +ev (ext. pl) masc.; Nom Pl đùsevi} *col* juice <Eng>

đȕska {ē fem.; Dat đȕski} *sl* dance <Slav*1>

đȕskati {ām, ajū imperf.} *sl* dance <Slav*1>

đȕskavac {vca masc.} **a.** *sl* dance <Slav❖*1> **b.** *sl* dance floor <Slav❖*1>

đȕšiti {šīm, še imperf.} *sl* look, watch, scope out <NE*1>

đȕtka {ē fem.; Dat đȕtki} *sl-crime* prison <Ita☞*1>

đȕturē {adv.} /đùture/ *col* together, collectively: *Razred ide u kino đuture. The class is going to the movies together.* <NE>

đutùrum {a (acc. = gen.) masc.} *sl-fea* senior citizen <NE>

đȕva {ē fem.} *sl-fea* affluent senior citizen <NE☞>

đuvègija {ē fem.} **a.** *col* boyfriend <NE*1> **b.** *sl-fea* obese female <NE*2>

đuvèglija {ē masc.} *col* boyfriend <NE*1>

đuzbekàna {ē fem.} *sl-crime* prison <NE>

đùzel {adj.} BosM *sl-fea* wonderful, beautiful: *đuzel hanuma beautiful woman* <NE>

đùzle {ī fem. pl.} *sl* eyeglasses <NE>

DZdz

dzȁdz {excl.} *col* used to frighten one's interlocutor, boo <Slav>

dzȉljati {ām, ajū imperf.} *sl* look, watch, scope out <Slav☞>

dzîljka {ē fem.} *sl* eye (sight organ) <Slav☞>

dzîljke {ī fem. pl.} *sl* eyeglasses <Slav☞>

dzìndzōv {dzindzòva (acc. = gen.) masc.} **a.** *sl-fea* stupid or mentally deficient person <**Slav**✍> **b.** *sl-fea* ill-behaved youngster, brat

dzôr {a masc.} *dia* force, power, strength <**NE**✍>

dzȕra {ē fem.} *sl-arch* water <**Slav** ✍>

dzvȅr {a (acc. = gen.) masc.} SSer *dia* beast <**Slav**✍>

dzvȅzda {e fem.} SSer *dia* star (celestial body) <**Slav** ✍>

dzvȍno {a neut.} SSer *dia* bell <**Slav**✍>

Ee

ê [1] {excl.} **1** *col* used to draw attention in direct informal communication, hey <**Slav**> **2** *col* used to express disagreement <**Slav**>

ê [2] {part.} **1** *col* used to change the topic of conversation, well, ok: *E, to je vrlo dobro. Well, that's very good.* <**Slav**> **2** *col* stutter word, uh <**Slav**>

E jèbi ga! {S} (lit. Well, fuck it!) *col* ***Obs*** used to express dissatisfaction and lack of control over events, Fuck it! ☞ **jebati**

E, jèsi kȕrac! {S} (lit. Yeah, you are my prick!) *col* ***Obs*** used as a strong negative response, no way, never ☞ **kurac**

E u pízdu mȁterinu! {S} (lit. Well, into *your* mother's cunt!) *col* ***Obs*** used to express dissatisfaction and lack of control over events, Fuck it! ☞ **pizda**

eberȇčkē *See the following*

- **eberȇčke ebertȕte** {NP} *sl* a kind of children's game in which they choose a person to do something

Èdipe {excl.} (lit. Oedipus) **1** *sl* used to express impossibility of an event, don't even think about it <**GreO**[*1]> **2** *sl* used to express negative opinion, nonsense <**GreO**[*1]>

èdnōm {adv.} [std. = jednom] *dia-col* once <**Slav** ✍>

êee [1] {excl.} *col* used to express various emotions, such as satisfaction, surprise, delight, dislike, or pain, oh, well: *Eee, sad mogu da se odmorim. Well, now I can get some rest.* <**Slav**>

êee [2] {part.} *col* used to change the topic of conversation, well, ok: *Eeee, neće moći tako. Well, that will be impossible.* <**Slav**>

eéhaa {excl.} *col-dia* used to stop a horse, whoa <**Slav**>

ȅf {a +ov (ext. pl) masc.; Nom Pl èfovi} *sl-sex* venereal disease department (of a hospital) <**Abb**[*1]>

efèndi {adj.} BosM *col* used to address a male in direct informal communication, mister, sir <**NE**>

efèndija {ē fem.} BosM *col* gentleman <**NE**❖>

efendínīca {ē fem.} BosM *col* lady, woman <**NE**❖>

ȅfše {èfaše masc.; perm} [std. = šef] *sl* boss <**Ger**✍>

egalìzīrka {ē fem.} *col* levelling <**Fre**❖>

ègede {ea masc.} *sl-crime* prison <**NE**[*1]>

èglen {a masc.} BosM *col* conversation, talk <**NE**>

eglènisānje {a neut.} BosM *col* talking, chatting <**NE**❖>

eglènisati {išēm, išū biasp.} **a.** **BosM** *col* talk, have a conversation: *Eglenisati uz kahvu. Chat over coffee.* <**NE**> **b.** *sl-fea* persistent and meaningless talk, blabber <**NE**[*1]>

egzòtičnō bîlje {NP} (lit. exotic herbs) **a.** *sl-fea* ***Fac*** superficial person **b.** *sl-fea* ***Fac*** snob ☞ **bilje**

egzòtika {ē fem.} (lit. exotics) *sl* extraordinary matter <**Gre**[*1]>

ȅh {excl.} *col* used to express different emotions ranging from satisfaction to grief, ah, oh <**Slav**>

êhā {excl.} *col-dia* used to stop a horse, whoa <**Slav**>

ȅhe {excl.} *col* used to draw attention in direct informal communication, hey <**Slav**>

ȅhe-hē {excl.} *col* used to express surprise, astonishment, etc. <**Slav**>

ȅhēj {excl.} *col* used to draw attention in direct informal communication, hey <**Slav**>

ȅhkati {ām, ajū imperf.} *col* keep pronouncing 'eh' to express different emotions ranging from satisfaction to grief <**Slav**>

êj {part.} *col* used to draw attention in direct informal communication, hey <**Slav**>

éja {excl.} *col-dia* used to stop a horse, whoa <**Slav**>

ȅjkānje {a neut.} *col* pronouncing 'ej' to draw attention <**Slav**>

ȅjkati {ām, ajū perf. intr.} *col* keep pronouncing 'ej' to draw attention <**Slav**>

ȅjs {excl.} *col-dia* used to urge an ox to move on <**Slav**>

èjvalā {excl.} BosM *col* used to express appreciation, good for you <**NE**>

èki {excl.} *sl* used to express surprise, disbelief, etc., no kidding <**Gyp**[*1]> ☞ **ekši**

ekípa {ē fem.} (lit. crew) **a.** *sl* company (group of people) <Fre[*1]> **b.** *sl-crime* gang, group of one's close friends <Fre[*2]>

ekmèčija {ē masc.} BosM *col* baker <NE>

èkrān {ekrána masc.} (lit. screen) *sl-sex* ***Fac-Obs*** buttocks, butt <Fre>

ekráni {ā masc. pl.} (lit. screens) *sl* eyeglasses <Fre[*1]>

ȅks [1] {adj.} *col* ex, former: *eks Jugoslavija former Yugoslavia* <Lat>

ȅks [2] {a masc.} [std. = ekstazi] *sl-drugs* ecstasy (narcotic drug) <Eng✍>

ekscènder {dra masc.} *sl-crafts* eccentric point (e.g. on a shaft) <Lat>

èkscesnuti {nēm, nū perf. intr.} *sl* make a mistake, screw up <Lat⁘[*1]>

èkser {a masc.} (lit. nail *fastening device*) *sl-drugs* ecstasy (narcotic drug) <NE[*1]>

• **za èksere** {PP} (lit. for the nails) *sl-fea* without being properly paid

èkspres [1] {adj.} *col* express, quick: *ekspres pošilja express mail* <Lat>

èkspres [2] {adv.} *col* express, quickly: *To će biti gotovo ekspres. That will be finished quickly.* <Lat>

• **pȍnī èkspres** {NP} (lit. pony express) Cro *sl* streetcar line number two in Zagreb, Croatia

èkspres lònac {NP} (lit. express pot) *col* pressure cooker ☞ **lonac**

èkspresan {sna, sno adj.} *col* express, quick <Lat>

ekstáza {ē fem.} *sl-drugs* ecstasy (narcotic drug) <Gre[*1]>

ȅkstazī {īja masc.} *sl-drugs* ecstasy (narcotic drug) <Eng>

ȅkstra [1] {adv.} (lit. extra) *col* extra, additionally: *Dobio je radio ekstra kad je kupio televizor. He got a radio extra when he bought a tv set.* <Lat>

ȅkstra [2] {adj.} /èkstra/ (lit. extra) *col* superb, awesome <Lat>

èkstrēm {ekstréma (acc. = gen.) masc.} *sl-fea* extremist <Lat✍>

èkši {excl.} *sl* used to express surprise, disbelief, etc., no kidding <Gyp[*1]> ☞ **eki**

el {c.} [std. = je li] **1** *dia* if: *Oš pivu el vino? Would you like a beer or some wine?* <Slav✍> **2** *dia* or <Slav✍>

ȅlā {excl.} *col* used to urge somebody to act, do it <Gre>

ȅlāj {excl.} *col* used to urge somebody to act, do it <Gre>

eldorâdo {a neut.} (lit. El Dorado) **1** *sl-sports* a series of weak adversaries (e.g. in a tournament) <Spa[*1]> **2** *sl-crime* convenient place for stealing <Spa[*1]>

èleg {adj.} *sl-fea* elegant <Lat>

elegàntno pòpunjen {AdjP} (lit. elegantly stuffed) *col* ***Iro*** obese, fat ☞ **popunjen**

elèktričār {a (acc. = gen.) masc.} (lit. electrician) *sl-music* rock or pop musician <Gre[*1]>

èlem {part.} *col* particle used to sum up previous facts. *Elem, on je našao posao. He finally found a job.* <NE>

eliminâtor {a (acc. = gen.) masc.} *sl-crime* eliminator <Lat[*1]>

èlkānta {ē fem.} *sl-crafts* oil can <Ger>

ȅlovac {ȅlōvca (acc. = gen.) masc.} (lit. the L one: student drivers' cars are marked with a letter L) *sl-auto* student driver <Abb>

èlpūmpa {ē fem.} *sl-auto* oil pump <Ger>

em *See the following*

• **em ... em** {c.conj} *col* paired coordinate conjunction and intensifier, both ... and: *On je pravi razbojnik. Em pije, em puši. He's a real rascal. He both drinks and smokes.*

èma-èsesa {ē fem.} *col* a kind of jump-rope played by girls with an elastic band <EngO✍[*1]>

emajlírati {emàjlīrām, emajlírajū biasp. intr.} *sl* e-mail somebody <Eng✍>

emancìpicovan {a, o adj.} (lit. emancicunted *emancipovan 'emancipated' X pica 'cunt'*) *sl-fea* ***Fac-Obs*** emancipated: *emancipicovana žena emancipated woman* <Lat✍>

ȅmbriōn {a (acc. = gen.) masc.} /embrìōn/ (lit. embryo) *sl* baby, newborn <Gre[*1]>

ȅmentāler {a (acc. = gen.) masc.} (lit. Emmenthaler *a kind of cheese*) *sl-fea* blond male <Ger[*1]>

emȉgos {a (acc. = gen.) masc.} *sl* emigrant <Lat✍>

emigrȁnt {a (acc. = gen.) masc.} (lit. emigrant) *sl-fea* person who wants to push into a group of people without being invited <Lat[*1]>

emotívac {vca (acc. = gen.) masc.} *col* emotional person <Lat⁘>

èmsel {a (acc. = gen.) masc.} *sl-drugs* morphine

ȅnac {nca masc.} /énac/ *sl-sports* hand ball (in soccer) <Eng✍>

enciklopêdija *See the following*
- **žívā enciklopêdija** {NP} (lit. living encyclopedia) *col* omniscient person, walking encyclopedia

endeâzija {ē fem.} *col* Independent State of Croatia (Croatian Nazi state during WWII) <Abb⁘>

endèhāški {ā, ō adj.} *col* pertaining to the Independent State of Croatia (Croatian nazi state during WWII) <Abb⁘>

ènē {excl.} [std. = eno] *dia* look, watch, scope out: *Ene Marka! Here comes Marko!* <Slav✍>

Ènglēskinja {ē fem.} *sl-sstu* English teacher (female) <SlavO[*1]>

Ènglēz {Engléza (acc. = gen.) masc.; Voc Ȅnglēzu} *sl-sstu* English teacher (male) <SlavO[*1]>

englézer {a masc.} *sl-fea* dandy, fop <Gre[*1]>

ȅno {excl.} *col* used to point to something, there <Slav>
- **ȅno[NOUN:GEN]** {LSF} *col* used to point to an object or person: *Eno Marka! There comes Marko!* ◊ *Eno mora! There's the sea!*

ȅntī {ōg (acc. = gen.) masc.} *col* any in a series of numbers, nth <Abb[*1]>

Entìtēt {a masc.} (lit. entity) *col* Republic of Serbska (so called by the Bosnian Muslims) <Lat[*1]>

Ènverić {a masc.} (lit. small Enver *Hoxha, former Albanian dictator*) *sl-drink* Albanian cognac <NEO[*1]>

ȅo {excl.} [std. = evo] *col* here: *Eo ti novine. Here, take the newspaper.* <Slav✍>

epìtēt {pitéta masc.} *col* ***Iro*** offense, epithet: *Niko ne treba da je suočen s takvim epitetima. No one should have to put up with such insults.* <Gre[*1]>

Éra {ē masc.} **1** **SerE** *col* Herzegovinian (inhabitant of the Southern part of Bosnia and Herzegovina) <Slav> **2** **SerE** *col* inhabitant of Užice (a city in Serbia) <Slav>

erbéjac {jca masc.} (abbreviation from ručni bacač, lit. 'hand thrower') *sl-mil* bazooka ☞ **ručni bacač**

ȅrcavā {ē fem. (adj. decl.)} *sl-fea* noble or aristocratic female <Ger[*1]>

Èrcegovac {vca (acc. = gen.) masc.} [std. = Hercegovac] *col* Herzegovinian (inhabitant of the Southern part of Bosnia and Herzegovina) <SlavO>

èrćava {ē fem.} *sl* lady, woman <Ger✍>

ergȅla {ē fem.} /ergèla/ (lit. horse-farm) **1** *sl* plenty of money, stack of cash <NE[*1]> **2** *sl* females dated by a single male <NE[*1]>

érić [1] {a (acc. = gen.) masc.} *sl-arch* God <Slav[*1]>

érić [2] {a masc.} **1** *sl-arch* the Sun <Slav[*1]> **2** *sl-arch* sky <Slav[*1]>

ȅrlav {a, o adj.} *sl-fea* unintelligent, stupid, dumb <Slav[*1]>

Éro {ē masc.} **1** *col* Herzegovinian (inhabitant of the Southern part of Bosnia and Herzegovina) <Slav> **2** *col* inhabitant of Užice (a city in Serbia) <Slav>

ȅros {a masc.} (lit. erotica) **a.** *sl-sex* ***Fac*** lust, sexual urge <Gre> **b.** *sl-sex* ***Fac*** sexual foreplay, petting, feeling up <Gre[*1]>

ȅscājg {a masc.} *col* cutlery <Ger>

esdeȅsovac {vca (acc. = gen.) masc.} *sl-polit* member of the SDS (Srpska demokratska stranka 'Serbian Democratic Party', a Serbian party in Bosnia) <Abb⁘>

esdepȅovac {vca (acc. = gen.) masc.} *sl-polit* member of the SDP (Socijaldemokratska partija 'Social Democratic Party', a party in Croatia) <Abb⁘>

esembê {adj.} (abbreviated from SMB [esembe], sivomaslinasta boja 'grayish green color') *sl-mil* army green, olive drab <Abb>

esembȅovac {vca (acc. = gen.) masc.} (lit. the army green one) *sl-mil* soldier: *U bircu su bila dva esembeovca. There were two soldiers in the bar.* <Abb⁘>

èsid {a masc.} **a.** *sl-drugs* LSD, acid <Eng[*1]> **b.** *sl-drugs* heroin, horse, smack <Eng[*2]>

eskàrōl {karóla masc.} *sl-mil* ***Fac*** coffee with milk <BN>

èsker {a masc.} [std. = ekser] *col* nail (fastening device) <NE✍>

Èskīm {Eskíma (acc. = gen.) masc.; Voc Ȅskīme} (lit. Eskimo) *sl-fea* phlegmatic male <SlavO[*1]>

Eskímac {mca (acc. = gen.) masc.} (lit. Eskimo) *sl-fea* phlegmatic male <SlavO⁘[*1]>

eskimírati {kìmīrām, kimírajū biasp.} (lit. Eskimo) *sl-fea* be frigid sexually <SlavO⁘[*1]>

Èskīmka {ē fem.; Dat Èskīmki} (lit. Eskimo) **a.** *sl-fea* phlegmatic female <SlavO⁘[*1]> **b.** *sl-sex* sexually frigid female <SlavO⁘[*1]>

eskivâtor {a (acc. = gen.) masc.} *sl-fea* person who avoids his/her duties, shirker <Fre⁘[*1]>

eskiváža {ē fem.} *col* avoiding <Fre>

eskivírati {kìvīrām, kivírajū perf.} **a.** *sl* avoid work, shirk work <Fre⁘[*1]> **b.** *sl-drugs* take money without giving narcotic drugs in return <Fre⁘[*1]>

eskuváža {ē fem.} *sl* avoiding <Fre☞>

Ȅspa {ē fem.} Cro *sl* name for hotel Esplanade in Zagreb, Croatia <BN☞>

espeȅsovac {vca (acc. = gen.) masc.} *sl-polit* member of the SPS (Socijaldemokratska partija Srbije 'Social Democratic Party of Serbia', a party in Serbia) <Abb⁘>

Ȅspić {a masc.} Cro *sl* the hotel Esplanade in Zagreb, Croatia <BN⁘☞>

ȅškula {excl.} *sl* used to express approval, good intentions, etc., cheers <NE[*1]>

etikȇcija {ē fem.} (lit. etiquette) [std. = etiketa] *sl* price tag <Fre☞>

ȅto {excl.} **1** *col* used when pointing to or passing something: *Eto ti makaze. Here, the scissors.* <Slav> **2** *col* used to mark the end of a significant point: *Eto, tako su oni uspjeli da pobjegnu iz Sarajeva. And that's it. That's how they managed to escape from Sarajevo.* <Slav>

- **ȅto[NOUN:GEN]** {LSF} *col* used to point to an object or person: *Eto Marka! Here comes Marko!*
- **ȅto ti** {ExcP} *col* used to sum up one's point, That's how it is!

ȅvalā {excl.} BosM *col* used to express appreciation, good for you <NE>

ȅvalāj {excl.} BosM *col **App*** used to express appreciation, good for you <NE>

èvē {excl.} [std. = evo] *dia-col* here <Slav☞>

- **Èvē[PRON:DAT] ga!** {LSF} *dia **Off*** used as a moderate offense usu. in negative response, Fuck [PRON: ACC]!: *Eve ti ga! Nikad nisam rekao da si lažov! Fuck you! I never called you a liar!*

ȅvo {excl.} **1** *col* used when pointing to or passing something <Slav> **2** *col* used to heighten attention to what follows conversationally, so, well <Slav>

- **ȅvo[NOUN:GEN]** {LSF} *col* used to point to an object or person, Here comes [NOUN]!: *Evo Marka! Here comes Marko!*
- **ȅvo ovàkō** {ExcP} *col* used to introduce a new topic, Listen up now!
- **Ȅvo[PRON:DAT] múda od šàrana!** {LSF} (lit. Here are some carp's balls for [PRON:ACC]!) *dia **Off-Fac*** used as a mild offense, Screw [PRON:ACC]!: *Evo ti muda od šarana! Fuck you!*
- **Ȅvo ti ga!** {S} (lit. Here is it to you!) *col **Off*** used as a moderate curse, Fuck you!
- **Ȅvo ti ga nȁ!** {S} (lit. Here, take it!) **1** *col **Off*** used as a moderate curse usu. in negative response, Fuck you! **2** *col **Off*** used to refer to the impossibility of an event: *Evo ti ga na što ćeš ići na ljetovanje. No way that you're gonna go on summer vacation.*
- **Ȅvo ti ga újka!** {S} (lit. Here is your uncle!) SerE *col **Off*** used as a weak curse: *Evo ti ga ujka ako ne podnosiš šale! Screw you if you can't take a joke!*
- **Ȅvo ti glàvica pa prȍšētaj** {S} (lit. Here is a head for you to walk!) *sl* used to make somebody go away, Leave me alone, will you!
- **Ȅvo ti kȕrac!** {S} (lit. Here is a prick for you!) **a.** *col **Off*** used as a moderate curse: *Evo ti kurac, nikad to nisam rekao! Fuck you, I never said that!* **b.** *col **Off*** used to express the improbability of an event: *Evo ti kurac što ćeš me pobijediti. No way that you're gonna beat me.*
- **Ȅvo ti kȕrac u ústa jȍš!** {S} (lit. Here is a prick into your mouth in addition to that!) *col **Off*** used as a strong curse: *Evo ti kurac u usta još, ti si idiot! Fuck you, you're an idiot!*
- **Ȅvo ti šípak!** {S} (lit. Here is a wild rose bud for you!) **1** *col* used in angry dismissal, Beat it! **2** *col* used as a strong negative response, No way!
- **Ȅvo vam ga újac, nȁ!** {S} (lit. Here is an uncle for you, here!) *dia **Off*** used as a mild threat to a group of people: *Evo vam ga ujac, na, vaš tim nema šanse! Screw you, your team doesn't have a chance!*

ȅvtin {a, o adj.} [std. = jeftin] *col-dia* inexpensive, cheap: *evtine jabuke cheap apples* <Slav☞>

ȅx {adj.} *col* ex, former: *ex Jugoslavija former Yugoslavia* <Lat>

Ff

fȁca {ē fem.} **a.** *sl* face (human) <Ita> **b.** *sl* male, guy: *faca s pištoljem guy with a gun* <Ita[*1]>

- **fȁca s plȁca** {NP} (lit. face from the square) *sl* person from Trešnjevka square in Zagreb, Croatia
- **gràdskā fȁca** {NP} (lit. urban face) *sl-fea* male popular in town
- **slȍbodnā fȁca** {NP} (lit. free face) *sl-fea* insane person, nut case
- **vážna fȁca ko trȍjānskī kȍnj** {NP} (lit. face as important as the Trojan horse) *sl-fea* conceited male

fȁcan {a (acc. = gen.) masc.} *sl* male, guy <Ita⁘[*1]>

facírati {fȁcīrām, facírajū imperf.} **a.** *sl* cheat, swindle: *facirati naivca cheat a naive guy* <Ita⁘[*1]> **b.** *sl* make jokes with <Ita⁘[*2]>

faćaljīst {a (acc. = gen.) masc.} (lit. leaf-catcher X fatalist) *sl* person who picks up leaves and garbage in parks <**Lat**✎>

fàćkalica {ē fem.} (lit. the catching one) **1** *sl-sex* ***Fac*** prostitute, hooker <**Slav**[*1]> **2a.** *sl* trap, catch **b.** *sl-fea* person who abuses others (usu. financially), parasite, leech: *Ta faćkalica mu je isisala posljednje pare. That leech has taken the last money he had.*

faćkáriti {fàćkārīm, rē imperf.} *sl-sex* look for clients (of prostitutes) <**Slav**❖[*1]>

fàćkāroš {a (acc. = gen.) masc.} *sl-fea* person who likes to pet females <**Slav**[*1]>

fàćkati {ām, ajū imperf.} **a.** *col* catch <**Slav**> **b.i.** *sl-sex* look for clients (of prostitutes) <**Slav**[*1]> **ii.** *sl-sex* engage in sexual foreplay, pet, feel up <**Slav**[*1]>

fàćok {a (acc. = gen.) masc.} **a.** *sl-arch* son <**Slav**[*1]> **b.** *sl-arch* stepchild <**Slav**[*2]>

fàf {a masc.} *sl-sex* ***Obs*** fellatio <**Slav**[*1]>

fafàčica {ē fem.} *sl-sex* ***Obs*** female who frequently engages in fellatio <**Slav**❖[*1]>

fàfānje {a neut.} *sl-sex* ***Obs*** fellatio <**Slav**[*1]>

fàfati {ām, ajū imperf.} *sl-sex* ***Obs*** engage in fellatio <**Slav**[*1]>

fàfer {a masc.} *sl-sex* ***Der-Obs*** male homosexual, gay <**Slav**❖[*1]>

fafùnjati {ām, ajū biasp.} *sl* cry, shed tears, weep <**Slav**❖[*1]>

fàhman {a (acc. = gen.) masc.} *sl-fea* ***App*** skillful person: *Hamo je pravi fahman, sve zna popraviti. Hamo is really skillful, he can repair everything.* <**Ger**[*1]>

fahríja {ē fem.} BosM *col* a kind of Bosnian Muslim heroic song <**NE**[*1]>

fâjčiti {čīm, čē imperf.} **1** *sl-sex* ***Obs*** engage in sexual intercourse with (of a male) <**Ger**[*1]> **2** *sl-sex* ***Obs*** engage in fellatio <**Ger**[*1]>

fàjda {ē fem.} *col* profit, gain <**NE**>

fàjdica {ē fem.} *col* small profit, peanuts: *Imao sam neku fajdicu od tog posla. I only made a small profit from that job.* <**NE**❖>

fàjercāg {a masc.} **a.** *col* lighter <**Ger**> **b.** *sl* face (human) <**Ger**[*1]>

fàjercajg {a masc.} **a.** *col* lighter <**Ger**> **b.** *sl* face (human) <**Ger**[*1]>

fàjfa {ē fem.} (lit. pipe) **1** *sl-music* saxophone, sax <**Ger**[*1]> **2** *sl-sex* penis <**Ger**[*1]>

fàjfati {ām, ajū imperf.} **a.** *sl* smoke (tobacco) <**Ger**[*1]> **b.** *sl-sex* engage in fellatio <**Ger**[*2]> **c.** *sl-sex* engage in cunnilingus <**Ger**[*3]>

fàjn [1] {adj.} *sl* superb, awesome <**Ger**>

fàjn [2] {adv.} *col* superb, awesome <**Ger**>

fàjronat [1] {excl.} *sl-drink* used to express the closing time of a bar, last call <**Ger**>

fàjronat [2] {nta masc.} *sl-drink* closing time, last call <**Ger**>

fàjront [1] {excl.} *sl-drink* closing time, last call <**Ger**>

fàjront [2] {a masc.} *sl-drink* closing time, last call <**Ger**>

fàjt {a +ov (ext. pl) masc.; Nom Pl fàjtovi} *sl* fight (e.g. fist fight) <**Eng**>

fâjta {ē fem.} **1** *sl* relatives <**Hun**> **2** *sl* sort, kind of: *To je loša fajta jabuka. That's a bad kind of apples.* <**Hun**>

fàjtara {ē fem.} (lit. fighter) *sl-fea* person who frequently and gladly engages in fights <**Eng**❖>

fàjter {a (acc. = gen.) masc.} (lit. fighter) **a.** *col* fighter <**Eng**> **b.** *sl-fea* smart male <**Eng**[*1]>

fàk [1] {a +ov (ext. pl) masc.; Nom Pl fàkovi} [std. = fakultet] *sl-stu* university <**Lat**✎>

fàk [2] {excl.} (lit. fuck) *sl* used to express extreme disgust <**Eng**[*1]>

fàkat [1] {adv.} *col* really, indeed: *On je fakat otišo u zatvor. He really went to jail.* <**Lat**[*1]>

fàkat [2] {kta masc.} *col* truth <**Lat**[*1]>

fàkati {ām, ajū imperf.} *sl-sex* ***Obs*** engage in sexual intercourse with (of a male) <**Eng**>

fàkīn {fakína (acc. = gen.) masc.} *sl-fea* ***Der*** worthless or despicable person <**Ita**>

fakináža {ē fem.} *sl-fea* the condition of being a despicable or worthless person <**Ita**>

fàkiš {a masc.} [std. = fakultet] *sl-stu* university <**Lat**✎>

fàks {fàksa +ev (ext. pl) masc.; Nom Pl fàksevi} **1** *col* fax <**Eng**> **2** *sl-stu* university <**Lat**✎>

fakultètlija {ē masc.} *sl-fea* person with university degree <**Lat-NE**❖>

fála {excl.} [std. = hvala] *col* used to express gratitude, thanks <**Slav**✎>

• **fála Bȍgu** {NP} *col* used to express gratitude, thank God: *Stigli smo kući bezbjedno, hvala Bogu! We arrived home safely, thank God!*

fàlat {a masc.} Vojv *col* piece, chunk <**Hun**>

falàtati {ām, ajū imperf.} Vojv *col* cut into pieces, slices (e.g. bread, sausage, etc.) <**Hun**>

fȁlc {a masc.} *sl-crafts* croze <**Ger**[*1]>

fȁlce {eta masc.} *sl-sex* ***Obs*** penis, dick, prick <**Ger**[*1]>

Fȁlī [PRON:DAT] dȁska u glávi. {LSF} (lit. [PRON:NOM] is missing a plank in [PPRON] head.) *col* ***Fac*** used to express negative attitude toward: *Fali im daska u glavi. They have a screw loose.* ☞ **faliti**

fȁličan {čna, čno adj.} **a.** *col* incomplete <**Ger**❖> **b.** *sl-fea* slightly insane, nutty <**Ger**❖[*1]>

fȁlīnka {ē fem.; Dat fȁlīnki} *col* error, mistake <**Ger**❖>

fȁliti [1] {līm, lē imperf.} *col* miss, long for, be without: *Fali mi Mira. I miss Mira.* <**Ger**>
• **Fȁlī[PRON:DAT] dȁska u glávi.** {LSF} (lit. [PRON: NOM] is missing a plank in [PPRON] head.) *col* ***Fac*** used to express negative attitude toward, [PRON:NOM] [Be] nuts.: *Fali im daska u glavi. They are nuts.*

fȁliti [2] {līm, lē perf. intr.} *col* make a mistake, screw up: *faliti na ispitu make a mistake on an exam* <**Ger**[*1]>

fáliti se {fâlīm, lē imperf. intr.} [std. = hvaliti se] *col* boast, brag <**Slav**✍>

fȁlkōn {a masc.} *sl-sex* ***Obs*** penis, dick, prick <**Lat**[*1]>

falsifȉkāt {fikáta (acc. = gen.) masc.} (lit. forgery) *sl-crime* prisoner at the prison in Turopolje, Croatia <**Lat**[*1]>

fȁlš [1] {adj.} *col* false <**Ger**>

fȁlš [2] {adv.} (lit. false) *col* insincerely <**Ger**[*1]>

fȁlšara {ē fem.} *sl-crime* counterfeit ticket <**Ger**❖[*1]>

fȁlšārka {ē fem.; Dat fȁlšārki} *sl-crime* counterfeit ticket <**Ger**❖[*1]>

falšírati {fȁlšīrām, falšírajū imperf.} *sl-music* sing out of tune <**Ger**❖[*1]>

fáma {ē fem.} **1** *sl* fight (e.g. fist fight) <**Lat**[*1]> **2** *sl* mess, disorder, disturbance: *Nastala je fama na policijskoj stanici. There was a disturbance at the police station.* <**Lat**[*1]>

fȁmeja {ē fem.} Med *dia-col* family <**Ita**>

fȁmfulja {ē fem.} *sl* mouth, muzzle, face <**Slav**✍[*1]>

fȁmīlija {ē fem.} *col* family <**Ger**>

fȁmōzan {zna, zno adj.} **a.** *col* famous <**Lat**> **b.** *sl-fea* dependable: *Ona je famozna, ne treba se bojati za njen rad. She is dependable, one does not have to worry about her work.* <**Lat**[*1]> **c.** *sl-fea* excellent <**Lat**[*2]> **d.** *sl-fea* infamous, notorious <**Lat**[*3]>

fȁn {a +ov (ext. pl) masc.; Nom Pl fȁnovi} **a.** *sl* fun <**Eng**> **b.** *sl-drugs* measure for opium <**Eng**>

fȁnđosati {ām, ajū imperf.} *sl-auto* speed (auto, etc.) <**SpaO**[*1]>

fȁnfara {ē fem.} *sl* head <**Fre**>

fȁnfrlja {ē fem.} *sl* mouth, muzzle, face <**Slav**[*1]>

fȁnfulja {ē fem.} **a.** *sl-sex* ***Obs*** vagina, cunt <**Slav**[*1]> **b.** *sl-sex* ***Der*** prostitute, hooker

fanfuljȁgis {a (acc. = gen.) masc.} *sl* changeable mind <**Slav**✍[*1]>

fȁntara {ē fem.} *sl* head <**Lat**>

fantȁstičan {čna, čno adj.} *col* ***App*** excellent, awesome <**Gre**>

fȁntōm {fantóma (acc. = gen.) masc.} (lit. phantom) *sl-sex* rapist <**Gre**[*1]>

fȁnjati {ām, ajū imperf.} **a.** *sl* catch, grab <**Ita**[*1]> **b.** *sl* engage in sexual intercourse with (of a male) <**Ita**[*2]>

fȁr {a +ov (ext. pl) masc.; Nom Pl fárovi} *sl* eye (sight organ) <**Gre**[*1]>

fȁraga {ē fem.; Dat fȁragi} *sl* person who destroys escalators out of sheer boredom

farȁun {a (acc. = gen.) masc.} *sl-fea* ***Der*** worthless or despicable person <**NE**✍>

fȁrba {ē fem.} **a.** *col* paint (wall, ceiling, etc.) <**Ger**> **b.** *sl* lie: *farba o putu u Ameriku lie about the trip to America* <**Ger**[*1]>

fȁrbānje {a neut.} /fȁrbānje /a neut./ **a.** *col* painting <**Ger**❖> **b.** *sl* cheating, swindling: *farbanje roditelja cheating one's parents* <**Ger**❖[*1]>

fȁrbati {ām, ajū imperf.} /fȁrbati /am, aju imperf./ **a.** *col* paint (wall, ceiling, etc.)<**Ger**> **b.** *sl* lie: *farbati roditelje lie to one's parents* <**Ger**[*1]> **c.** *sl* cheat, swindle <**Ger**[*2]>
• **fȁrbati zrâk** {VP} (lit. paint the air) *sl-sex* ***Fac*** break wind, fart

fȁrisati {išēm, išū imperf.} *sl* estimate, guess: *farisati veličinu sobe estimate the size of a room* <**Gre**❖[*1]>

fȁrkānje {a neut.} *sl* looking, watching, scoping out <**Gre**❖[*1]>

fȁrkati {ām, ajū imperf.} *sl* watch, look, observe: *farkati kroz prozor look through the window* <**Gre**❖[*1]>

fȁrmerice {a fem. pl.} *col* blue jeans <**Eng**❖[*1]>

fȁrmērke {ī fem. pl.} *col* blue jeans <**Eng**❖[*1]>

fȁrmosi {mōsā masc. pl.} *sl* blue jeans <**Eng**>

fáronja {ē masc.} *sl* franc (French currency unit) <Fre✍>

fárovi {rōvā masc. pl.} /fârovi/ *sl* eyes <Gre❖[*1]>
• **bez fárōvā** {PP} (lit. without headlights) *sl-fea* ***Fac*** blind (of a person)

Fáruk {a (acc. = gen.) masc.} *sl-sex* passionate male sexual partner <NEO[*1]>

fȁs *See the following*
• **u fȁsu** {PP} *sl* used as a strong affirmative response, sure

fasáda {ē fem.} **1** *sl* face (human): <Fre[*1]> **2** *sl* object used as a hideout: *Korpa za smeće mi je bila fasada. The garbage bin was my hideout.* <Fre[*1]>

fasáda-mȉnjāk {minjáka masc.} *sl* mini-skirt <Fre-Lat❖[*1]>

fȁsadeks {a masc.} *sl* deceptive face <Fre✍>

fasȁdēr {sadéra (acc. = gen.) masc.} *sl-fea* boy who manages to do nothing more than to walk with his girlfriend <Fre❖[*1]>

fȁsovati {sujēm, sujū perf.} *col* be beaten up: *Fasovo je od dvojice silosa. He was beaten up by two rowdies.* <Ger❖[*1]>

fȁstica {ē fem.} *sl-music* fast melody <Eng❖>

fȁsūng {a masc.} *sl* face (human) <Ger[*1]>

fȁsūnga {ē fem.; Dat fȁsungi} *col* food ration <Ger[*1]>

fȁšer {a (acc. = gen.) masc.} *sl* fascist <Lat✍>

fašírati {fȁšīrām, ajū biasp.} (lit. stuff) **1** *sl* beat up severely: *Faširа ga neki rmpalija. Some troublemaker beat him up severely.* <Fre[*1]> **2** *sl-fea* bother, disturb: *Faširao je šefa za povišicu. He pestered the boss for a raise.* <Fre[*1]>

fȁta {ē fem.} *col-dia* cotton <NE✍>

Fáta {ē fem.} (lit. Fata is a proper name of a joke character) *col* ***Fac*** Bosnian Muslim (female) <NEO[*1]>

fȁtalo {a neut.} (lit. catching device) [std. = hvatalo] *sl* ***Fac*** hand <Slav✍>

fataljȉst {a (acc. = gen.) masc.} (lit. leaf-catcher X fatalist) *sl* ***Fac*** person who picks up leaves and garbage in parks <Lat✍>

fȁtāljka {ē fem.} (lit. catcher) *sl-sex* ***Fac*** prostitute, hooker <Slav>

fȁtati {ām, ajū imperf.} [std. = hvatati] **a.** *col-dia* catch, grab <Slav✍> **b.** *sl-sex* engage in sexual foreplay, pet, feel up: *fatati ribu feel up a chick* <Slav✍[*1]>
• **fȁtati ȁvu** {VP} (lit. catch the air) *sl* ***Fac*** spend one's time in useless activities, fool around, mess around
• **fȁtati zjȁle** {VP} *sl* spend one's time in useless activities, fool around, mess around

fȁtati se {ām, ajū imperf. intr.} [std. = hvatati se] **a.** *col* stick to something <Slav✍> **b.** *sl-sex* engage in sexual foreplay, pet, feel up <Slav✍[*1]>
• **fȁtati se nȍgē** {VP} (lit. catch one's foot) *sl* run away, flee, beat feet

fȁzān {fazána (acc. = gen.) masc.} (lit. pheasant) **1** *sl-mil* rookie soldier, first month soldier <NE[*1]> **2** *sl-fea* dandy, fop <NE[*1]>

fȁzōn {fazóna masc.} **1a.** *col* trick, joke <Fre[*1]> **b.** *col* joke <Fre[*2]> **2a.** *sl* style of behavior <Fre[*1]> **b.i.** *sl* appearance <Fre[*2]> **ii.** *sl* style, kind: *Koji fazon muzike voliš? What kind of music do you like?* <Fre[*2]>
• **iz fȁzōna** {PP} (lit. for a trick) *col* for fun
• **ȕ tomē je fȁzōn** {S} (lit. that's where the trick is) *col* used to sum up one's point, That's how it is!

fazóna {ē fem.} **a.** *col* manner: <Fre> **b.** *col* sort, kind of *pogrešna fazona cipela wrong kind of shoes* <Fre[*1]>

fazònēr {zonéra (acc. = gen.) masc.} **a.** *sl-fea* ***App*** skillful person <Fre[*1]> **b.** *sl-fea* joke teller <Fre[*2]>

fazonírānje {a neut.} *sl* dressing formally, dressing up <Fre[*1]>

fazonírati {fazònīrām, ajū imperf.} *sl-sex* ***Obs*** engage in sexual intercourse with (of a male) <Fre[*1]>

febètār {betára (acc. = gen.) masc.; Voc fȇbetāru} *sl-fea* ***Der*** coward, chicken <Ita[*1]>

fèbruār {a (acc. = gen.) masc.} (lit. February) *sl-fea* stupid or mentally deficient person <Lat[*1]>

féder {a (acc. = gen.) masc.} **a.** *col* spring (mechanical part) <Ger> **b.** *sl-sex* male homosexual, gay <Ger[*1]>
• **špìrāl féder** {NP} (lit. spiral spring) *sl-crafts* spiral spring

féder-rȉnga {ē fem.; Dat féder-rȉngi} *sl-crafts* spring ring <Ger>

féder-šâjba {ē fem.} *sl-crafts* spring washer <Ger>

féder-šȁjbna {ē fem.} *sl-crafts* spring washer <Ger>

federácija [1] {ē fem.} *sl-auto* shock absorption system <Ger[*1]>

Federácija [2] {ē fem.} *col* Croat-Muslim Federation (in Bosnia) <Lat[*1]>

fèderālnī {ā, ō adj.} *col* related to the Croat-Muslim Federation (in Bosnia) <Lat❖[*1]>

federírati {dèrīrām, derírajū biasp.} *sl-auto* absorb shocks <Ger❖>

fédervajs {a masc.} *sl-crafts* talc <**Ger**>

fefèrōnka {ē fem.; Dat fefèrōnki} (lit. hot pepper) *sl-sex* ***Fac*** passionate female, hot female <**Ger**[*1]>

fèktāroš {a (acc. = gen.) masc.} *sl-fea* ***Der*** worthless or despicable person <**Hun**❖[*1]>

fèktati {ām, ajū imperf.} *sl* beg, ask for money <**Hun**❖[*1]>

féla {ē fem.} **a.** *col* sort, kind of: *fela psa breed of dog* <**Hun**> **b.** *sl* female <**Hun**[*1]>

felàcati {ām, ajū biasp.} *sl* zig-zag <**Hun**[*1]>

fèler {a masc.} *col* mistake, error <**Ger**[*1]>

fèlga {ē fem.; Dat fèlgi} *sl-auto* wheel rim <**Ger**>

fèlna {ē fem.} *sl-auto* wheel rim <**Ger**✍>

fèlšati {ām, ajū imperf. intr.} *sl-fea* go astray (usu. of a ball) <**Ger**>

félja {ē fem.} *sl* female <**Lat**✍>

fèmisānje {a neut.} **a.** *col* pretending <**Lat**[*1]> **b.** *col* insincere excuse <**Lat**[*2]>

fèmisati se {išēm, išū imperf. intr.} *col* hesitate, be shy: *femisati se pred nepoznatima be shy around strangers* <**Lat**[*1]> ☞ **femkati se**

fèmka {ē fem.; Dat fèmki} **a.** *sl-fea* feminized male <**Lat**❖> **b.** *sl-fea* weak person, wimp <**Lat**❖[*1]>

fèmkānje {a neut.} *col* lame excuse <**Lat**❖[*1]>

fèmkati se {ām, ajū imperf. intr.} *col* hesitate, be shy: *Femka se da pita za povišicu. She is hesitant to ask for a raise.* <**Lat**❖[*1]> ☞ **femisati se**

fència {ē fem.} *sl* lamp <**NE**✍>

fèndža {ē fem.} *sl* money <**NE**✍[*1]>

fènđa {ē fem.} *sl* lamp <**NE**✍>

fenírati {fènīrām, fenírajū imperf.} *sl-crafts* style hair with a blow drier <**Ger**❖>

fènomenālan {lna, lno adj.} /fenomenâlan/ *col* superb, awesome <**Gre**[*1]>

fènomenālno {adv.} /fenomenâlno adv./ *col* superb, awesome <**Gre**[*1]>

fènsī {adj.} *sl-fea* fancy <**Eng**>

fènjer {a (acc. = gen.) masc.} (lit. lantern) **a.** *sl-drink* alcoholic, drunk <**NE**[*1]> **b.** *sl-fea* eye (sight organ) <**NE**[*1]>

fenjèrāš {njeráša (acc. = gen.) masc.; Voc fènjerāšu} (lit. lantern carrier) *col* last place finisher (in any competition) <**NE**❖[*1]>

fenjèrdžija {ē masc.} (lit. lantern carrier) *sl-sports* last place finisher (in any competition) <**NE**[*1]>

fèrāl {ferála masc.} Med *dia-col* lamp <**Ita**>

fèrcandrgovati {gujēm, gujū perf.} *sl* falsely incriminate, frame <**Ger**✍>

fercèrati {ām, ajū imperf. intr.} *col* blink <**Ger**✍[*1]>

fèrgajn {a (acc. = gen.) masc.} **a.** *sl* male, guy <**Ger**✍> **b.** boy, kiddo <**Ger**✍[*1]>

fergázer {a masc.} *sl-auto* carburetor <**Ger**[*1]>

férići {rīćā masc. pl.} *sl-sstu* vacation <**Lat**✍>

ferkìćati {ām, ajū imperf.} *sl* sell (exchange merchandise for money)

fèrku {adj.; perm} (lit. suitcase) [std. = kufer] *sl* difficult: *ferku situacija difficult situation* <**Ger**✍[*1]>

fèrmāj {excl.} *dia-col* used to silence one's interlocutor, Shut up! <**Ita**[*1]>

fèrmati {ām, ajū imperf.} **1a.** *col* respect, obey: *fermati roditelje respect one's parents* <**NE**> **b.** *col* appreciate, enjoy, like <**NE**[*1]> **2** Med *dia-col* stop <**Ita**[*1]>

fèršati {ām, ajū biasp.} **a.** *sl* zig-zag <**Ger**[*1]> **b.** *sl* cheat, swindle <**Ger**[*1]>

fertàjler {a masc.} *sl-auto* distributor head <**Ger**>

fertùtma {ē fem.} *col* mess, disorder, disturbance <**NE**>

fèsko {a (acc. = gen.) masc.} *sl-sex* ***Der*** male homosexual, gay <**Gre**✍>

fèstica {ē fem.} *sl-music* music festival <**Lat**>

fèstira {ē fem.} *sl-music* music festival <**Lat**✍>

fèstivāl {festivála masc.} (lit. festival) *sl* lament <**Lat**[*1]>

fèško {a (acc. = gen.) masc.} *sl-sex* ***Der*** male homosexual, gay <**Gre**✍>

fèšta {ē fem.} *col* party (social gathering) <**Ita**>

fèta {ē fem.} *sl* piece, chunk <**Gre**[*1]>

fètī {ija (acc. = gen.) masc.} *sl-fea* obese male <**Eng**❖>

fètiti {tīm, tē biasp.} *sl-crime* steal, swipe <**Ger**[*1]>

fètva {ē fem.} BosM *col* judgement <**NE**>

fiaška {ē fem.; Dat fiaški} *sl-sex* prostitute, hooker

fíca {ē fem.} *sl* coffee <**NE**✍>

fić {a masc.} *sl-crime* policeman, cop <**Hun**✍[*1]>

fíća {ē masc.} SerE *sl-auto* Fiat 750 (make of car) <**BN**✍>

fićātor {a (acc. = gen.) masc.} *sl-crime* policeman, cop <**Hun**✍[*1]>

fićfìrić {a (acc. = gen.) masc.} *sl-fea* dandy, fop <**Hun**>

fìćka {fìćaka masc.; perm} //e fem./ [std. = kafić] *sl-drink* cafe <**Fre** ✍>

fíćo {ē masc.} *sl-auto* Zastava 750 (make of car) <**BN**✍>

fìćok {a masc.} *sl-drink* shot glass <**Slav**[*1]>

fìćūk {a masc.} *col* whistle <**Slav**[*1]>

fićùkānje {a neut.} *col* whistling <**Slav**[*1]>

fićùkati {ām, ajū imperf.} *col* whistle <**Slav**[*1]>

fìfa {ē fem.} *sl-sex* prostitute, hooker <**Slav**[*1]>

fifì {īja (acc. = gen.) masc.} *sl-sex* ***Fac*** male homosexual, gay <**FreO**[*1]>

fìfica {ē fem.} *sl-sex* prostitute, hooker <**FreO**[*1]>

fifik {a masc.} *sl-fea* ***App*** skillful person <**Ger**✍[*1]>

fìftāč {a masc.} *sl-drink* wine with water <**Eng**⁘[*1]>

fifti-fifti {adv.} *col* fifty-fifty, halfs: *podeliti plen fifti-fifti split the loot fifty-fifty* <**Eng**>

fiftić {a masc.} *sl-drink* a drink made of one half wine and one half water <**Eng**✍[*1]>

fìga {ē fem.; Dat fìgi} **a.** *dia* fig <**Ita**> **b.** *sl-sex* vagina <**Ita**[*1]>

figúra {ē fem.} *sl-auto* Fiat 750 (make of car) <**Lat**[*1]>
• **markȁntna figúra** {NP} (lit. remarkable figure) *sl-fea* person who earns his/her salary in German marks

Fijáker {a masc.} (lit. chariot, coach X Fiijanova 'the street name') **Cro** *sl* name of a dance club in Fijanova street in Zagreb, Croatia <**Fre**⁘[*1]>
• **tàbanovića fijáker** {NP} (lit. foot cart) *col* walking

fijóka {ē fem.} (lit. drawer) *sl-crime* prison <**Hun**[*1]>

fìjūk {a masc.} **a.** *col* wham (e.g. of a door slammed shut) <**Slav**> **b.** *col* blow (wind, etc.) <**Slav**[*1]>

fijùkānje {a neut.} **a.** *sl* whamming (e.g. of a door slammed shut) <**Slav**> **b.** *col* blowing (wind, etc.) <**Slav**[*1]>

fijùkati {ām, ajū imperf.} **a.** *col* wham (e.g. of a door slammed shut) <**Slav**> **b.** *col* blow (wind, etc.) <**Slav**[*1]>

fijùkav {a, o adj.} *col* blowing (wind, etc.) <**Slav**>

fijúknuti {nēm, nū perf.} **a.b.** *col* wham (e.g. of a door slammed shut): *fijuknuti vrata slam the door shut* <**Slav**> **b.** *col* blow (wind, etc.) <**Slav**[*1]> **c.** *sl* die, kick the bucket <**Slav**[*2]>

fik {excl.} *col* the sound made by cutting with scissors, snip <**Slav**>

fìknuti {nēm, nū perf.} **a.** *col* rip off: *fiknuti mušteriju rip off a customer* <**Slav**⁘> **b.** *col* throw away, toss out: *fiknuti stare cipele throw away the old shoes* <**Slav**⁘[*1]>

fìks {a +ev (ext. pl) masc.; Nom Pl fiksevi} **1** *sl-drugs* intravenous intake of narcotic drugs, mainlining, shooting up <**Eng**> **2** *sl-drugs* narcotic drug, dope <**Eng**>

fìks idéja {NP} *col* idee fixe, delusion ☞ **ideja**

fiksac {a (acc. = gen.) masc.} *sl-drugs* drug addict, junkie <**Eng**⁘>

fiksácija {ē fem.} (lit. fixation) *sl-fea* person in love <**Lat**[*1]>

fìksāć {a (acc. = gen.) masc.} *sl-drugs* drug addict, junkie <**Eng**⁘>

fìksānje {a neut.} *sl-drugs* intravenous intake of narcotic drugs, mainlining, shooting up <**Eng**⁘>

fìksati {ām, ajū imperf. intr.} *sl-drugs* take narcotic drugs intravenously, mainline, shoot up <**Eng**>

fìksati se {ām, ajū imperf. intr.} *sl-drugs* take narcotic drugs intravenously, mainline, shoot up <**Eng**⁘>

fìkser {a (acc. = gen.) masc.} *sl-drugs* drug addict, junkie <**Eng**⁘>

fiksírati {fiksīrām, fiksírajū biasp. intr.} (lit. fix) *col* stare at, be fixated on <**Lat**[*1]>

fiksòtis {a masc.} *sl-drugs* intake of narcotic drugs, doing drugs <**Eng**✍>

fìksovati {sujēm, sujū sē imperf. intr.} (lit. fix) *sl-drugs* take narcotic drugs, do drugs <**Eng**⁘>

fíkus {a (acc. = gen.) masc.} (lit. fig-tree) *sl-auto* Fiat 750 (make of car) <**Lat**[*1]>

fìlac {ioca masc.} *sl* pen (for writing) <**Gre**[*1]>

filadèlfija [1] {ē fem.} (lit. Philadelphia) *sl-fea* ***App*** skillful person <**EngO**[*1]>

filadèlfija [2] {adv.} (lit. Philadelphia) *sl* superb, big time: *igrati filadelfija fudbal play big time soccer* <**EngO**[*1]>

filadèlfija [3] {adj.} (lit. Philadelphia) *sl* superb, awesome: *filadelfija šulja awesome shirt* <**EngO**[*1]>

filatèlija {ē fem.} (lit. philately 'marka' in Serbo-Croatian means both 'post stamp' and 'German mark') *sl* Germany <**Gre**[*1]>

filatèlist {a (acc. = gen.) masc.} (lit. philatelist 'marka' in Serbo-Croatian means both 'post stamp' and 'German mark') *sl* person who saves or who is in possession of German marks <**Gre**[*1]>

filatèlista {ē masc.} (lit. philatelist 'marka' in Serbo-Croatian means both 'post stamp' and 'German mark') *sl* person who saves or who is in possession of German marks <Gre[*1]>

filcírati {filcīrām, filcírajū biasp.} *sl* stare at, be fixated on: *filcirati dobru ribu stare at a hot chick* <Ger[*1]>

fìlcmâjstor {a (acc. = gen.) masc.} *sl-sex* ***Fac*** adequate male sexual partner <Ger[*1]>

fìlcovānje {a neut.} *sl-sex* ***Obs*** sexual foreplay, petting, feeling up <Ger⁘[*1]>

fìlcovati {cujēm, cujū imperf.} *sl-sex* ***Obs*** engage in sexual foreplay, pet, feel up <Ger⁘[*1]>

fìldžān {fildžána masc.} **a. Bos** *col* small Near Eastern-style coffee cup <NE> **b. Bos** *sl* eye (sight organ): *plavi fildžani blue eyes* <NE[*1]>

fìldžān-líga {ē fem.; Dat fildžān-lígi} Bos *sl-sports* minor leagues, bush leagues <NE-Spa[*1]>

filèksīr {fileksíra (acc. = gen.) masc.} *sl-crime* burglar

fìlić {a masc.} *sl-drink* doctored wine, wine diluted with water <Eng[*1]>

fìlip {a (acc. = gen.) masc.} (lit. Philip) *sl-auto* Fiat 750 (make of car) <GreO[*1]>

fìlm {a +ov (ext. pl) masc.; Nom Pl filmovi} (lit. film, movie) *sl-drugs* drug-induced hallucination <Eng[*1]>
• **Tâj fìlm nêćeš glèdati!** {S} (lit. You will not see that movie!) *col* used to express the improbability of an event, No way!

fìlmadžija {ē fem.} *sl-media* cineaste, film maker <Eng⁘>

filmāš {filmáša (acc. = gen.) masc.; Voc filmāšu} *sl-media* cineaste, film maker <Eng⁘>

fìlmčina {ē fem.} **1** *col* bad movie: *Nisam više mogao da gledam tu filmčinu. I could not watch that bad movie any more.* <Eng⁘> **2** *col* excellent movie <Eng⁘>

fìlmčuga {ē fem.; Dat filmčugi} *sl* excellent movie <Eng⁘>

filòksera {ē fem.} **a.** *sl-fea* intruder <Gre[*1]> **b.** *sl-fea* boring person, bore <Gre[*2]>

fìlop {a (acc. = gen.) masc.} *sl-auto* Fiat 750 (make of car) <BN>

fìlovati {lujēm, lujū imperf.} (lit. stuff) **1** *sl* decorate: *filovati stančugu decorate an apartment* <Ger[*1]> **2** *sl* lie <Ger[*1]>

fìlter [1] {a masc.} [std. = filtar] *col* filter (in general) <Lat✍>
• **u fìlterima** {PP} (lit. in the filters) *sl* never

fìlter [2] {adj.} (lit. filter) *sl-fea* smart <Lat[*1]>

fìn {a, o adj.} *col* nice, cute (object or person): *fina tašna nice handbag* ◊ *fin frajer cute guy* <Ger>

Fínac {nca (acc. = gen.) masc.} (lit. Finn *male*) *sl-fea* nice and kind male <SlavO[*1]>

fìnger {a masc.} **1** *sl-drugs* narcotic drugs hidden in one's anus <Eng[*1]> **2** *sl-auto* finger on the distributor head (auto body) <Eng[*1]>

Fínkinja {ē fem.} (lit. Finn *female*) *sl-fea* nice and kind female <SlavO[*1]>

fìno {adv.} *col* fine, nicely (e.g. dressed) <Ger>

finòća {ē fem.} *col* niceness, kindness <Ger⁘>

Fînskā *See the following*
• **iz Fînskē** {PP} (lit. from Finland *also: fin 'nice'*) *sl-fea* ***Fac*** kind, nice (of a person)
• **kò da je iz Fînskē** {PP} (lit. as if he is from Finland, also related to the adjective fin 'nice') *sl-fea* ***Fac*** very kind

fînskī {ā, ō adj.} (lit. Finnish) *sl-fea* nice, kind <SlavO[*1]>

fìnta {ē fem.} **a.** *col* trick, joke <Ita> **b.** *col* joke <Ita[*1]>

fìnjāk {a masc.} *sl-fea* ***App*** decent behavior <Ger⁘>
• **na finjáka** {PP} (lit. on niceness) *sl* nicely

fìrānga {ē fem.; Dat firāngi} *col-dia* window blinds <Ger>

Firàun {a (acc. = gen.) masc.} **a.** *col* ***Off*** Gypsy (male) <NE[*1]> **b.** *col* ***Der*** lazy or shiftless person, bum, good for nothing <NE[*2]>

fìrcānje {a neut.} *sl-sex* ***Obs*** sexual intercourse <Hun⁘[*1]>

fìrcati se {ām, ajū imperf. intr.} *sl-sex* ***Obs*** engage in sexual intercourse with <Hun⁘[*1]>

fìrciger {a (acc. = gen.) masc.} **1** *sl-fea* forty-year-old male <Ger[*1]> **2** *sl-fea* young rascal <Ger[*1]>

fìrcigerica {ē fem.} *sl-fea* forty-year-old female <Ger[*1]>

fírer {a (acc. = gen.) masc.} (lit. Fuehrer, from German word for leader, esp. used in reference to Adolf Hitler) *sl-crime* jailer <Ger[*1]>

Fìrga {ē masc.; Dat Fìrgi} *sl* ***Off*** Gypsy (male) <NE⁘[*1]>

Fìrgoš {a (acc. = gen.) masc.} *sl* ***Off*** Gypsy (male) <NE⁘[*1]>

fìrlī {ija (acc. = gen.) masc.} **1** *sl-crime* person who resells stolen watches **2** *sl-crime* person who sells fake gold rings

fȉrma [1] {ē fem.} (lit. company) *sl* reputation (usu. good) <**Ger**[*1]>

fȉrma [2] *See the following*

• **jáka fȉrma** {NP} (lit. strong firm) *col* ***Iro*** nothing special, no big deal: *Taj auto auto je jaka firma. That car is nothing special.*

fȉrnajs {a masc.} *col* varnish <**Ger**>

fȉrnajz {a masc.} *col* varnish <**Ger**>

fíro {ē masc.} *sl-music* musician <**Ger**✤>

fìrovati {rujēm, rujū imperf.} *sl* take somebody along (e.g. to a party) <**Ger**✤>

fȉs {excl.} *col* the sound made by slapping, slap <**Slav**>

fȉskac {excl.} *col* the sound made by slapping, slap <**Slav**>

fìstati {ām, ajū imperf.} *sl-drink* drink (alcohol)

fȉšbajn {a (acc. = gen.) masc.} **a.** *sl-sex* ***Fac*** male homosexual, gay <**Ger**[*1]> **b.** *sl-fea* elegant male: *Taj fišbajn uvek nosi Armanijeva odela. That elegant male always wears Armani suits.* <**Ger**[*2]>

fìšek {a masc.} **a.** *col* cone (usu. made of paper and used by street merchants to package seeds or roasted chestnuts): *fišek marona a cone of chestnuts* <**NE**> **b.** *sl-crime* bullet <**NE**[*1]>

fìškāl {āla (acc. = gen.) masc.} *col-dia* ***Der*** lawyer, attorney <**Lat**>

fȉštiti {tīm, tē imperf.} *sl-sex* ***Obs*** engage in sexual intercourse with (of a male)

fȉt {a masc.} **a.** *col* feet <**Eng**> **b.** *sl-drugs* drug paraphernalia: *Našli su mu fit u gajbi. They found drug paraphernalia at his place.* <**Eng**[*1]>

fitȋlj [1] {fitílja masc.} (lit. fuse) **a.** *sl* mind <**NE**[*1]> **b.** *sl-fea* skillfulness <**NE**[*2]>

fitȋlj [2] {fitílja (acc. = gen.) masc.} **1** *sl-fea* person who is likely to be beaten <**NE**[*1]> **2** *sl-fea* dying person <**NE**[*1]>

fitiljȉška {ē fem.; Dat fitiljȉški} /fitiljìška/ *sl-fea* person who is likely to be beaten <**NE**✤> *sl-fea* dying person <**NE**✤[*1]>

fitíljiti {līm, lē imperf.} *sl-fea* annoy, bother, pester <**NE**✤[*1]>

fíza {ē fem.} **a.** *sl-sstu* physics (as a school course) <**Gre**✍> **b.** *sl-sstu* physics teacher <**Gre**✍[*1]>

fȉzbajn {a (acc. = gen.) masc.} *sl-sex* ***Fac*** male homosexual, gay <**Ger**[*1]>

fizìčār {a (acc. = gen.) masc.} **1** *sl-fea* manual laborer <**Gre**✤[*1]> **2** *sl-sstu* physics teacher (male) <**Gre**✤[*1]>

fizikálac {a (acc. = gen.) masc.} *sl-fea* manual laborer <**Gre**✤[*1]>

fizikàlisati {išēm, išū imperf.} *sl-fea* do manual labor <**Gre**✤[*1]>

fizikáner {a (acc. = gen.) masc.} *sl-fea* manual laborer <**Gre**✤[*1]>

fȉzikos {a (acc. = gen.) masc.} **1** *sl-sstu* physics teacher (male) <**Gre**✍[*1]> **2** *sl-fea* manual laborer <**Gre**✍[*1]>

fȉzikus {a (acc. = gen.) masc.} *sl-fea* manual laborer <**Gre**✍[*1]>

fizioterapèut {a (acc. = gen.) masc.} *sl-fea* ***Fac*** boring person, bore <**Gre**[*1]>

fȉzis {a masc.} *sl-sstu* physics (as a school course) <**Gre**✍>

fȉzos {a (acc. = gen.) masc.} *sl-fea* manual laborer <**Gre**✍[*1]>

fȉžbajn {a (acc. = gen.) masc.} **a.** *sl-fea* dandy, fop <**Ger**[*1]> **b.** *sl-fea* student from a blue-collar family <**Ger**[*2]>

fjȁka {ē fem.; Dat fjȁki} **Med** *col* laziness, a fit of laziness: *O fjake se ni moga pokrenit. He could not move out of sheer laziness.* <**Ita**>

flȁhcānge {i fem. pl.; Dat flȁhcāngi} *sl-crafts* flat pliers <**Ger**>

flȁhcāngle {i fem. pl.} *sl-crafts* flat pliers <**Ger**>

flájer {a masc.} /flâjer/ *sl* flyer, leaflet <**Eng**>

flȁm {a +ov (ext. pl) masc.; Nom Pl flàmovi} *sl* stomach, belly, gut <**Slav**[*1]>

flândra {ē fem.} *sl-sex* ***Der*** old prostitute <**DutO**✍[*1]>

flȁnka {ē fem.; Dat flȁnki} **a.** *sl* side, flank <**Ger**> **b.** *sl* hip <**Ger**[*1]>

flȁntati {ām, ajū biasp.} *sl* lie <**Fre**[*1]>

flȁster {a (acc. = gen.) masc.} (lit. bandage) **a.** *sl* spy, spook <**Gre-Ger**[*1]> **b.** *sl* intruder <**Gre-Ger**[*2]>

flasterírati *See the following*

• **flasterírati njȕpavce** {VP} (lit. put a bandage on one's eaters) Cro *sl* ***Fac*** cure one's toothache

flastèrisati se {išēm, išū imperf. intr.} *sl* engage in a fight (fists, etc.) <**Ger**[*1]>

flȁša *See the following*

• **U pívskū flȁšu!** {S} (lit. To beer bottle!) *col-dia* used to express lack of control over events, Damn it!

flášīrāno sránje {NP} (lit. bottled shit) *sl* ***Fac-Obs*** diarrhea, runs, trots ☞ **sranje**

flȁšovati {šujēm, šujū imperf.} (lit. bottle) *sl* hit with a bottle (e.g. in a street fight) <**Ger**✤>

flàuta {ē fem.} (lit. flute) *sl* ***Fac*** nose <**Ita**[*1]>

flaùtati {ām, ajū imperf.} (lit. play a flute) *sl-sex* ***Fac-Obs*** engage in fellatio <**Ita**❖[*1]>

flègma {ē fem.} *sl-fea* phlegmatic person <**Gre**[*1]>

flȅka {ē fem.; Dat flȅki} **a.** *col* stain <**Ger**> **b.** *sl-drink* hangover: *imati fleku od sinoćnje pijanke have a hangover from last night's party* <**Ger**[*1]>

flèkati se {ām, ajū imperf. intr.} **a.** *col* stain oneself <**Ger**> **b.** *sl-sex* engage in sexual intercourse with <**Ger**[*1]>

flènter {a (acc. = gen.) masc.} *sl-fea* ***Der*** worthless or despicable person <**Ger**[*1]>

flȅrt {a +ov (ext. pl) masc.; Nom Pl flèrtovi} *col* flirt <**Eng**>

flȅrtovānje {a neut.} *col* flirting <**Eng**>

flȅrtovati {tujēm, tujū imperf. intr.} *col* flirt <**Eng**>

flȅš {a +ev (ext. pl) masc.; Nom Pl flèševi} *sl-drugs* flash (effect of narcotic drugs) <**Eng**>

flȅš-bȅk {a +ov (ext. pl) masc.; Nom Pl flȅš-bèkovi} *sl-drugs* flashback <**Eng**>

flȉcka {ē fem.; Dat flȉcki} *sl-sex* prostitute, hooker <**Ger**[*1]>

flȉćka {ē fem.; Dat flȉćki} *sl-sex* prostitute, hooker <**Ger**[*1]>

flȉćkica {ē fem.} **a.** *sl-sex* prostitute, hooker <**Ger**❖[*1]> **b.** *sl-sex* loose woman

flȉkati {ičem, iču imperf.} *sl* beat up <**Ger**[*1]>

flȉknuti {nēm, nū perf.} **a.** *sl* hit, punch <**Ger**[*1]> **b.** *sl* beat up

flȉnt {adj.} *sl-crime* killing <**Ger**[*1]>

flȉnta {ē fem.} **a.** *sl-sex* prostitute, hooker <**Ger**[*1]> **b.** *sl-sex* old prostitute <**Ger**[*2]>

flȉp {a +ov (ext. pl) masc.; Nom Pl flìpovi} *sl* ***Der*** insanity, craziness <**Eng**[*1]>

flȉper {a (acc. = gen.) masc.} (lit. pinball machine) *sl-fea* ***Der*** insane person, nut case <**Eng**[*1]>

flȉper {a masc.} (lit. pinball machine) *sl* ***Der*** insanity, craziness <**Eng**[*1]>

flȉpnuti {nēm, nū perf. intr.} *sl-fea* become insane, flip out, go nuts <**Eng**[*1]>

flȉt {a (acc. = gen.) +ov (ext. pl) masc.; Nom Pl flìtovi} **a.** *sl-fea* good-looking male, hunk <**BN**❖[*1]> **b.** *sl-fea* muscular male

flôjsa {ē fem.} *sl-sex* ***Der*** prostitute, hooker <**Ger**☞[*1]>

flóka {ē masc.; Dat flóki} *sl-sstu* marker (writing device) <**BN**☞>

flòkiš {a masc.} *sl-sstu* marker (writing device) <**BN**☞>

flȍks {a +ev (ext. pl) masc.; Nom Pl flòksevi} *sl-sstu* marker (writing device) <**BN**☞>

flòmīć {flomíća masc.} *sl-sstu* marker (writing device) <**BN**☞>

flônda {ē fem.} *sl-sex* ***Obs*** vagina, cunt <**DutO**☞[*1]>

flôndra {ē fem.} *sl-sex* ***Der*** old prostitute <**DutO**☞[*1]>

flôndža {ē fem.} *sl-sex* ***Obs*** vagina, cunt <**DutO**☞[*1]>

flônđa {ē fem.} *sl-sex* ***Obs*** vagina, cunt <**DutO**☞[*1]>

flóra {ē fem.} *sl-fea* hair on the head <**Lat**[*1]>

Floramî {fem.} *sl-sex* ***Fac*** male homosexual, gay <**FreO**>
- **Mâlā Floramî** {NP} (lit. Little Florami, a ballet character) *sl-sex* male homosexual

flȍrijān {jna, jno adj.} *sl-fea* naive male <**Lat**[*1]>

fl ûndra {ē fem.} *sl-fea* old prostitute <**DutO**[*1]>

flûndra {ē fem.} *sl-sex* ***Der*** old prostitute <**DutO**☞[*1]>

fljakafljóca {ē fem.} *sl-sex* ***Der*** prostitute

fljȁs {excl.} *col* the sound made by spalshing, splash <**Slav**>

fljȁsnuti {nēm, nū perf.} *col* splash <**Slav**>

fljȁška {ē fem.; Dat fljȁški} **a.** *sl-sex* prostitute, hooker **b.** *sl* female

fljéjiti {jīm, jē imperf.} *sl* sleep, nap

fljȉs {excl.} *col* the sound made by spanking, spank <**Slav**>

fljȉsnuti {nēm, nū perf.} *col* spank <**Slav**>

fljȕs {excl.} *col* the sound made by splashing, splash <**Slav**>

fljȕsnuti {nēm, nū perf.} *col* splash <**Slav**>

fljȕzgati {ām, ajū imperf.} *sl-sex* ***Obs*** engage in sexual intercourse with (of a male) <**Slav**❖>

fȍjerbah {a masc.} *sl* lighter <**Ger**[*1]>

fòjnikina {ē masc.} *sl-fea* ***Der*** insane female, nut case

fȍka {ē fem.; Dat fȍki} (lit. seal, the animal) **1** *sl-sex* ***Obs*** vagina, cunt <**Gre**[*1]> **2** *sl* sailor <**Gre**[*1]>

fȍks *See the following*
- **tvèntī sȅnčerī fȍks** {NP} (lit. Twentieth Century Fox) *sl-fea* cross-eyed person

fôl [1] {part.} *col* used to express uncertainty: *Oni fol rade. They sort of work.* <**Ita**[*1]>

fôl [2] {a +ov (ext. pl) masc.; Nom Pl fólovi} *col* cheating, swindling <**Ita**[*1]>

• dìvljī fôl {NP} (lit. wild trick) *sl* unsuccessful lie
• Kàkvi su to fólovi? {S} (lit. What kind of tricks are those?) *col* used to ask for additional information
• na fôl {PP} (lit. on trick) *col* using mischief
• strȍg fôl {NP} (lit. strict joke) **a.** *sl-fea* successful trick **b.** perfect lie
• u fôl {PP} (lit. in the trick) *sl* as if
• ù tomē je fôl {S} (lit. that's where the trick is) *col* used to sum up one's point, That's how it is!

fôl[3] {adj.} *col* fraudulent, counterfeit: *fol karte counterfeit tickets* <Ita*1>

fôl[4] {adv.} *col* insincerely: *govoriti fol speak insincerely* <Ita*1>

fȍlcić {a masc.} *sl-auto* Volkswagen (make of car) <BN☞>

fȍlcika {ē fem.; Dat fȍlciki} *sl-auto* Volkswagen (make of car) <BN☞>

fôle {i fem.} *sl* money <Ita✤*1>

fȍler {a (acc. = gen.) masc.} **a.** *sl-fea* liar <Ita✤> **b.** *sl-fea* person who is broke (financially): *Od tog posla postao je foler. He went broke in that business.* <Ita✤*1>

folijánac {nca masc.} *sl-crime* avoiding the law <Ita*1>

folijánović {a (acc. = gen.) masc.} *sl-fea* liar <Ita✤>

folijȁnt {a (acc. = gen.) masc.} *sl-fea* crook, thief <Ita✤>

fȍlina {ē fem.} **a.** *sl* trick, joke <Ita✤> **b.** *sl* cheating, swindling <Ita*1>

folìnjati {ām, ajū imperf.} **a.** *sl* lie <Ita✤> **b.** *sl* talk, have a conversation: *folinjati tri sata na telefon talk on the phone for three hours* <Ita✤*1>
• folìnjati u ťȉriti {VP} *sl* read a book

folirȁncija {ē fem.} **a.** *col* cheating, swindling: *folirancija klijenata cheating one's clients* <Ita> **b.** *col* pretending: *njena folirancija da je plemkinja her pretending to be an aristocrat* <Ita*1>

folirȁnt {a (acc. = gen.) masc.} **a.** *sl-crime* cheater, swindler <Ita✤> **b.** *sl-crime* confederate in shell game <Ita✤*1>

folírānje {a neut.} **a.** *sl* cheating, swindling <Ita✤> **b.** *sl* lying <Ita✤*1>

folírati {fòlīrām, folírajū imperf.} **a.** *sl* cheat, swindle <Ita✤> **b.** *sl-drugs* take narcotics drugs for recreational purposes <Ita✤*1>

folírati se {fòlīrām, folírajū imperf. intr.} **a.** *col* be conceited, be stuck-up <Ita✤> **b.** *col* impersonate somebody else, be a con artist: *Folira se da je stranac. This con man pretends to be a foreigner.* <Ita✤*1>

fȍlk[1] {a +ov (ext. pl) masc.; Nom Pl fȍlkovi} *sl-music* folk or country music <Eng>

fȍlk[2] {adj.} *sl-music* folk (pertaining to the style of music) <Eng>

fȍlks-vagína {ē fem.} (lit. folksvagen, Volkswagen X 'folk vagina') *sl-sex* ***Fac*** prostitute, hooker <BN☞*1>

fȍlksić {a masc.} *sl-auto* Volkswagen (make of car) <BN☞>

folksvagína {ē fem.} (lit. folksvagen, Volkswagen X folk vagina) **1** *sl-sex* ***Fac*** prostitute, hooker <BN☞*1> 2 *sl-auto* ***Fac*** Volkswagen (make of car) <BN☞>

fȍluška {ē fem.; Dat fȍluški} *sl* trick, joke <Ita✤>

fȍnd *See the following*
• cȓnī fȍnd {NP} (lit. black reserve) *col* money hidden and kept for emergency situations or clandestine activities, slush fund

fȍntele {ea masc.; perm} *sl* telephone, phone <Gre☞>

fóra[1] {excl.} *sl* used to express disbelief <Ger>

fóra[2] {ē fem.} **1** *sl* very important or influential person, bigshot <Ger*1> 2 *sl* trick, joke <Ger*1> *sl*
• fóra s môra i Zlàtibōra {NP} (lit. joke from the seashore and from Zlatibor, a mountain in Serbia) *sl* ***Fac*** cheap trick, uninteresting joke
• Kàkve su to fóre? {S} (lit. What kind of tricks are those?) *col* used to ask for additional information
• Kȍjē su to fóre? {S} (lit. What kind of tricks are those?) *col* used to ask for additional information
• Na kȍjū fóru? {PP} (lit. On which trick?) *sl* used to ask for additional information
• trúba fóra {NP} (lit. trumpet trick) *sl* cheating, swindling
• trȕlā fóra {NP} (lit. rotten trick) *sl* cheating, swindling
• ù tomē je fóra {S} (lit. that's where the trick is) *col* used to sum up one's point, That's how it is!

fȍrdāljka {ē fem.; Dat fȍrdāljki} (lit. After Alan Ford, a cult comic book from the former Yugoslavia with a difficult cross-word puzzle on its cover and a character who drove an old car) **1** *sl-auto* old car, wreck <BN☞> 2 *sl* unsolvable problem: *Buba u tom programu je fordaljka. The bug in that program is an unsolvable problem.*

fȍrka {ē fem.; Dat fȍrki} *sl* win, gain <Ger☞>

forlírānje {a neut.} *sl* cheating, swindling <Ita☞>

fȍrpās[1] {excl.} *col* no problem, no big deal <Fre*1>

fòrpās [2] {adj.} **a.** *sl* bad, malfunctioning: *forpas auto malfunctioning car* <**Fre***1> **b.** *sl* worthless: *forpas ideja worthless idea* <**Fre***1>

fòrpās [3] {a (acc. = gen.) masc.} *sl* clumsy male, klutz <**Fre***1>

fòrpās [4] {a masc.} *sl* very difficult situation <**Fre***1>
• **príma fòrpās** {NP} (lit. superb trick) *sl-fea* unimportant person, nobody, nothing

forsírati {ām, ajū biasp.} *col* insist <**Fre***1>
• **forsírati pòtok** {VP} (lit. force a creek) *sl-sex* ***Fac-Obs*** urinate

fòrtati {ām, ajū imperf.} **a.** *col* torture <**Ger***1> **b.** *col* lie <**Ger***1>

fòsīl {fosìla (acc. = gen.) masc.; Voc fòsīle} **a.** *sl-fea* senior citizen <**Lat**> **b.** *sl* parent

fòsna {ē fem.} *sl-fea* slender person

fóta {ē fem.} *sl* a kind of token in a children's game where the person with the token has to do something (usu. sensitive or unpleasant) <**Ger**>

fotèljēr {teljéra (acc. = gen.) masc.} (lit. the one from the armchair) *sl-fea* very important or influential person, big shot <**Fre***1>

fòtić {a masc.} *sl* photographic camera <**Gre***1>

fòtka {ē fem.; Dat fòtki} *sl* photo <**Gre**⁘>

fòto-safârī {īja masc.} (lit. photo safari) *sl-sex* ***Fac*** voyeurism <**Gre-NE***1>

fòto-šòk {a masc.} (lit. photo shock) *sl-sstu* failing grade <**Gre-Eng***1>

fòtos {a masc.} *col* photo <**Gre**⁘>

fráca {ē masc.} *sl* male, guy <**Ger***1>

fràj {adv.} *col* free, gratis <**Ger**>

fràjer {a (acc. = gen.) masc.} **a.** *sl* male, guy <**Ger**> **b.** *sl* boyfriend <**Ger***1>
• **Fràjeri šìštē.** {S} (lit. The guys are hissing.) *sl* used to refer to the spread of sensitive information or rumors
• **pòkopān fràjer** {NP} (lit. buried guy) *sl-fea* ruined male (e.g. financially)
• **tuturùtū fràjer** {NP} (lit. toot guy) **a.** *sl-fea* clumsy person, klutz **b.** *sl-fea* loser

fràjerica {ē fem.} **a.** *sl* female <**Ger**⁘> **b.** *sl* lolita <**Ger**⁘*1>

frajèrisānje {a neut.} **a.** *sl* spending one's time in useless activities, fooling around, messing around <**Ger**⁘> **b.** *sl* prolonged and meaningless talk, blabber, chatter: *frajerisanje o politici blabber about politics* <**Ger**⁘*1> **c.** *sl* boasting, bragging <**Ger**⁘*2>

frajèrisati {išēm, išū imperf.} **a.** *sl* spend one's time in useless activities, fool around, mess around <**Ger**⁘> **b.** *sl* talk persistently and meaninglessly, blabber, chatter: *frajerisati o fudbalu blabber about soccer* <**Ger**⁘*1>

fràjērka {ē fem.; Dat fràjerki} **a.** *sl* female <**Ger**⁘> **b.** *sl-fea* stupid or mentally deficient person <**Ger**⁘*1>

fràjkan {a (acc. = gen.) masc.} *sl* male, guy <**Ger**⁘>

frâjla {ē fem.} **a.** *col* female <**Ger**> **b.** *sl-fea* elderly female <**Ger***1>

frâjlica {ē fem.} *sl-sex* ***Der*** young female with loose morals, jailbait <**Ger**⁘>

fràjština {ē fem.} *sl* something available for free, freebie <**Ger**⁘>

frakafljòca {ē fem.} *sl-sex* ***Der*** prostitute, hooker

frakàfulja {ē fem.} *sl-sex* ***Der*** prostitute, hooker

fràkcionā destilácija {NP} (lit. fractional distillation) *sl* ***Fac*** beating up ☞ **destilacija**

frakfljóca {ē fem.} *sl-sex* ***Der*** prostitute, hooker

fràkfulja {ē fem.} *sl-sex* ***Der*** prostitute, hooker <◊✍>

framàzōn {mazóna (acc. = gen.) masc.} *sl-crime* skillful criminal <**Fre***1>

fràncek {a (acc. = gen.) masc.} Cro *sl* Frenchman <**SlavO**>

fràncūskī ključ {NP} (lit. monkey wrench) *sl-sex* ***Fac*** penis ☞ **ključ**

Fràncūz {Francúza (acc. = gen.) masc.} (lit. Frenchman) *sl-fea* ***Der*** worthless or despicable person <**SlavO**>

fràncūz {francúza masc.} (lit. Frenchman) **1** *sl-crafts* monkey wrench <**SlavO***1> **2** *sl-sex* gonorrhea, the clap <**SlavO***1>

francùzica {ē fem.} (lit. the French one) *col* beret <**SlavO**⁘>

francùzice {cūzīcā fem. pl.} (lit. the French ones) *sl* very tight panties <**SlavO**⁘*1>

francùzljiv {a, o adj.} *sl* French <**SlavO**✍>

Frànkenštajn {a (acc. = gen.) masc.} (lit. Frankenstein) *sl-fea* unattractive male, Frankenstein <**GerO***1>

Frànkfurt *See the following*
• **Frànkfurt na Mâjci**{NP} (lit. Frankfurt on the mother) *sl* ***Fac*** Frankfurt am Main (city, Germany)

frànkopān {a (acc. = gen.) masc.} (lit. Frankopan: a Croatian aristocrat family) Cro *sl* money <**SlavO***1>

fránja {ē masc.} *sl* franc (French currency unit) <SlavO*1>

frȃs {a +ev (ext. pl) masc.; Nom Pl frásevi} *col* state of shock <Ger>

frasírati se {ãm, ajū perf. intr.} *sl* be in a state of shock <Ger❖>

fȑc {excl.} *col* the short sound made by metal objects, ping <Slav>

fȑcãngla {ē fem.} *sl* used in general reference: *kupiti frcangle buy just anything* <Ger✍>

fȑcãngle {excl.} *sl* used as a strong negative response, no way, never <Ger✍>

frcóka {ē fem.; Dat frcóki} *sl-fea* very young female, little girl <Slav❖>

frcòkla {excl.} *sl* used as a strong negative response, no way, never

frcòkla {ē fem.} *sl* slang word

fȑč {a +ev (ext. pl) masc.; Nom Pl fȑčevi} *sl* lock (of hair)

fȑčalija {ē fem.} *sl-arch* bearded male <Slav*1>

fȑčen {a, o adj.} *sl-fea* old <Slav*1>

fȑčule {eta neut.} *sl-arch* beans <Slav*1>

frȅmt {a +ov (ext. pl) masc.; Nom Pl frèmtovi} *sl* vacation <Ger>

frȅnd {a (acc. = gen.) +ov (ext. pl) masc.; Nom Pl frèndovi} **a.** *sl* friend (male) <Eng> **b.** *sl* roommate (male) <Eng*1>

frȅndāć {a (acc. = gen.) masc.} **a.** *sl* friend (male) <Eng❖> **b.** *sl* roommate (male) <Eng❖*1>

frȅndica {ē fem.} **a.** *sl* friend (female) <Eng❖*1> **b.** *sl* roommate (female) <Eng❖*1>

frȅndić {a (acc. = gen.) masc.} *sl* friend (male) <Eng❖*1>

frȅnk {a (acc. = gen.) masc.} (lit. Frank: proper name) *sl* male, guy <EngO*1>

frȅnta {ē fem.} *sl* wandering, roaming <Ger>

frȅntāč {a (acc. = gen.) masc.} **a.** *sl* friend (male) <Eng✍> **b.** *sl* roommate (male) <Eng✍*1>

frènter {a (acc. = gen.) masc.} *sl* homeless person, bum <Ger*1>

frèšak {ška, ško adj.} Med *col-dia* fresh: *freška riba fresh fish* <Ita>

Frézer {a (acc. = gen.) masc.} (lit. the American boxer Joe Fraser X German fressen 'devour', 'grind', etc.) **a.** *sl-sex* male sexual partner (of a female) <Ger*-EngO*1> **b.** *sl-sex* ***App*** very potent male <Ger*-EngO*2>

frézer {a masc.} *sl-crafts* grinding machine <Ger>

frȅzovānje {a neut.} *sl-crafts* polishing <Ger❖>

fȑfljãnje {a neut.} **a.** *sl-fea* speaking with difficulties, stuttering due to physiological reasons <Slav❖> **b.** *sl-fea* prolonged and meaningless talk, blabber, chatter <Slav❖*1>

fȑfljati {ãm, ajū imperf.} **a.** *sl-fea* speak with difficulties, stutter due to physiological reasons <Slav❖> **b.** *sl-fea* talk persistently and meaninglessly, blabber, chatter <Slav❖*1>

frfȍkljica {ē fem.} *sl* invented word, word which does not exist <Slav>

fȑga {ē fem.; Dat fȑgi} *sl-sex* ***Obs*** vagina, cunt <Slav*1>

fȑgati {ãm, ajū imperf.} Med *col* fry <Ita>

fȑgīdno {adv.} *sl* cold: *Napolju je frigidno. It's cold outside.* <Lat*1>

frìgita {ē fem.} *sl-sex* ***Der*** sexually frigid female <Lat✍>

frȉgos {a masc.} **1** *sl* fridge, refrigerator <Lat✍*1> **2** *sl-sex* sexually frigid female <Lat✍*1>

frȉk [1] {a (acc. = gen.) +ov (ext. pl) masc.; Nom Pl frìkovi} **a.** *sl-fea* weak person, wimp <Eng*1> **b.** *sl-fea* clumsy male, klutz <Eng*2>

frȉk [2] {a +ov (ext. pl) masc.; Nom Pl frìkovi} *sl* fear: *frik od letenja fear of flying* <Eng>

frȋkaut {a masc.} *sl-fea* going insane, freaking out <Eng>

frikòvit {a, o adj.} *sl-fea* scary <Eng❖*1>

frìkulja {ē fem.} **a.** *sl-fea* weak person <Eng❖> **b.** *sl-fea* snob <Eng❖*1>

frȉškić {a masc.} *sl* new newspaper <Ger❖>

frȋz {a +ev (ext. pl) masc.; Nom Pl frízevi} *col* haircut <Fre✍>

frizèrāj {zerája masc.} *col* hairdresser's <Ger>

frìzērka {ē fem.; Dat frìzērki} (lit. hairdresser) *sl-sex* loose woman <Fre❖>

frizírati {frìzīrām, frizírajū biasp.} *sl-auto* tune or rebuild an engine for maximum performance, soup up a car <Fre❖*1>

• **frizírati mòtōr** {VP} (lit. hairstyle the engine) *sl-auto* tune or rebuild an engine for maximum performance, soup up a car

frȋzmȁher {a masc.} *sl* razor <Fre-Ger*1>

frižìdēr {frižidéra masc.} (lit. fridge) **1** *sl-crime* prison <Fre*1> **2** *sl-auto* Fiat (make of car) <Fre*1>

frižìdērka {ē fem.; Dat frižìdērki} (lit. she-fridge) *sl-sex* ***Fac-App*** frigid female <Fre❖*1>

fr̂k {excl.} *col* the sound made by rapid movement, whoosh <Slav>

fr̂ka {ē fem.} **1a.** *sl* mess, disorder, disturbance <NE*1> **b.** *sl* panic, freak out <NE*2> **c.** *sl* rush, hurry <NE*3> **d.** *sl* fight (e.g. fist fight) <NE*4> **e.** *sl* fear <NE*5> **2** *sl* buttocks, butt <NE*1>

- **gènerālnā fr̂ka** {NP} (lit. general nervousness) *sl* danger, dangerous situation

fr̂kāroš {a masc.} *sl-fea* alarmist (male) <NE❖*1>

fŕkati *See the following*

- **fŕkati stàklēnkama**{VP} (lit. swing one's glass things) *sl* ***Fac*** turn one's eyes to express disdain

fr̂kātor {a (acc. = gen.) masc.} **a.** *sl-fea* person who makes noise <NE❖*1> **b.** *sl-fea* alarmist (male) <NE❖*1>

frkávati {fr̂kāvām, frkávajū biasp.} *sl* sell (exchange merchandise for money): *frkavati satove sell watches* <NE❖*1>

fr̂kēt {frkéta masc.} *col* opposite side (knitting) <Ger>

frkìćati {ām, ajū biasp.} *sl* sell (exchange merchandise for money): *frkićati jabuke sell apples* <NE❖*1>

fr̂kisati {išēm, išū imperf.} **a.** *sl* panic, freak out: *frkisati na ispitu panic at an exam* <NE❖*1> **b.** *sl* make noise: *Oni vrata pored su frkisali do ponoći. The neighbor next door made noise until midnight.*

fr̂knuti {nēm, nū perf.} **1** *sl* take <NE❖*1> **2** *sl* grab, snatch <NE❖*1>

frkolévati {kòlēvām, kolévajū biasp.} *sl-crime* resell, fence <NE*1>

fŕlja {ē fem.} *sl* female <Slav*1>

frljácnuti {fr̂ljācnēm, nū perf.} *col* throw away, toss out <Slav✍*1>

frljáknuti {fr̂ljaknēm, nū perf.} *col* throw away, toss out <Slav✍*1>

fŕljānje {a neut.} **a.** *sl* throwing away, tossing out <Slav> **b.** *sl-fea* prolonged and meaningless talk, blabber, chatter <Slav*1>

fr̂ljati {ām, ajū imperf.} *sl-fea* talk persistently and meaninglessly, blabber, chatter <Slav*1>

fr̂ljati se {ām, ajū imperf. intr.} **/**fŕljati se**/** **1** *sl-fea* boast, brag: *frljati se dobrim ocenama boast about good grades* <Slav*1> **2** *sl-fea* make a mistake, screw up: *frljati se na poslu make mistakes at work* <Slav*1> **3** *sl* misuse: *frljati se službenim kolima misuse a company car* <Slav*1> **4** *sl* engage in sexual intercourse with <Slav*1>

fr̂ljka {ē fem.} *sl-fea* boasting, bragging <Slav*1>

fr̂ljnuti {nēm, nū perf.} **a.** *sl* throw away, toss out <Slav> **b.** *sl-sex* engage in sexual intercourse with (of a male) <Slav*1>

fŕljo {ē masc.} **/**fr̂ljo /a masc.**/** *sl-sex* syphilis with symptoms appearing on one's face <Slav>

frljóka {ē fem.; Dat frljóki} *sl-sports* eccentric (not perfectly round) soccer ball <Slav>

frljóknuti {fr̂ljōknēm, nū perf.} *sl* throw away, toss out <Slav>

fr̂ndati {ām, ajū imperf.} *sl-sex* ***Obs*** engage in sexual intercourse with <Slav*1>

fr̂nditi {dīm, dē imperf.} *sl-sex* ***Obs*** engage in sexual intercourse with (of a male) <Slav*1>

fr̂ntulja {ē fem.} *sl-sex* ***Der*** prostitute, hooker

fŕnja {ē masc.} *sl* marble (the toy) <Slav*1>

fŕnjo {ē masc.} **/**fr̂njo /a masc.**/** **a.** *sl-sex* syphilis, the pox <Slav*1> **b.** *sl-fea* pockmarked face <Slav*2>

frnjóka {ē fem.; Dat frnjóki} **a.** *sl* face (human) <Slav*1> **b.** *sl* nose <Slav*2>

frnjókalica {ē fem.} **a.** *sl* face (human) <Slav*1> **b.** *sl* mouth <Slav*2>

frnjókica {ē fem.} *sl* face (human) <Slav*1>

fr̂r {excl.} *col* used to express disgust, phew <Slav>

fr̂skānje {a neut.} **1a.** *col* hiss (snake, gas, etc.) <Slav> **b.** *col* lisping <Slav*1> **2** *col* pinging, making a sharp metallic sound <Slav>

fr̂skati {ām, ajū imperf. intr.} **1a.** *col* hiss (snake, gas, etc.) <Slav> **b.** *col* lisp, mispronounce dental consonants due to physiological reasons <Slav*1> **2** *col* ping (produce sharp metal sound) <Slav>

fr̂snuti {nēm, nū perf.} *col* ping (produce a sharp metal sound) <Slav>

fr̂stāk {frstáka (acc. = gen.) masc.; Voc fr̂stāče} *sl-fea* highly attractive male, hunk <Eng❖*1>

fr̂stuša {ē fem.} *sl-fea* highly attractive female <Eng❖*1>

fr̂škati {ām, ajū imperf.} *sl* squeak <Slav*1>

fr̂štati {ām, ajū imperf.} *sl* squeak <Slav*1>

frtàjler {a masc.} *sl-auto* distributor head <Ger✍>

frtālj {frtálja masc.} **a.** *col* one fourth, quarter <Ger> **b.** *sl-drugs* quarter of a cc (measure for narcotic drugs) <Ger[*1]>

frtùtma {ē fem.} *col* mess, disorder, disturbance <NE>

frùla {ē fem.} (lit. folk flute) **1** *sl-music* clarinet <Slav[*1]> 2 *sl* nose <Slav[*1]>

frùla-pantalóne {a fem. pl.} (lit. small folk flutes) *sl-fea* tight trousers <Slav-Fre[*1]>

frùlati [1] {ām, ajū biasp.} (lit. play folk flute) *sl* cheat, swindle: *frulati naivca swindle a naive guy* <Slav⁘[*1]>

frùlati [2] {ām, ajū biasp. intr.} (lit. play folk flute) *sl* wait: *frulati dva sata wait for two hours* <Slav⁘[*1]>

frùle {a fem. pl.} (lit. folk flutes) *sl* tight trousers <Slav[*1]>

frùlice {a fem. pl.} (lit. small folk flutes) *sl* tight trousers <Slav[*1]>

frustrírati {frùstrīrām, frustrírajū perf.} (lit. frustrate) *sl* provoke, incite <Lat[*1]>

frùštuk {a masc.} Vojv *col-dia* breakfast <Ger>

ftàknuti {nēm, nū perf.} Kajk *sl-sex* ***Obs*** engage in sexual intercourse with (of a male) <Slav✍>

ftèrati {ām, ajū imperf.} Kajk *sl-sex* ***Obs*** engage in sexual intercourse with (of a male) <Slav✍>

fȕ {excl.} *col* used to express disgust, phew <Slav>

fȕati {ām, ajū imperf.} *sl* run away, flee

fúca {ē fem.} **1** *sl-sex* ***Der*** prostitute, hooker <Slav[*1]> 2 *sl-sports* ***Fam*** soccer <Eng✍>

fȕč {excl.} *col* it's gone <Ger>

fȕć {excl.} *col* it's gone <Ger>

Fȕćkā mi se! {S} (lit. I feel like whistling!) *sl* used to express indifference ☞ **fućkati**

fȕćkāj! {excl.} *col* used to make somebody go away <Slav>

fȕćkalica {ē fem.} *col* whistle <Slav>

fȕćkānje {a neut.} *col* whistling <Slav>

fȕćkati {ām, ajū imperf.} *col* whistle <Slav>
- **Fȕćkā mi se!** {S} (lit. I feel like whistling!) *sl* used to express indifference

fȕćnuti {nēm, nū perf.} *col* whistle (produce the sound) <Slav>
- **Fȕćnēm ti ga!** {S} (lit. I whistle it to you!) *sl* ***Off-Fac*** used as a moderate curse

fudžijàma {ē fem.} *sl-sex* ***Fac-Obs*** vagina, cunt <JapO[*1]>

fȕfa {ē fem.} /fùfa/ **a.** *sl-sex* ***Der*** prostitute, hooker <Ita[*1]> **b.** *sl-sex* ***Der*** loose woman <Ita[*2]>

fȕfica {ē fem.} **a.** *sl-sex* ***Der*** prostitute, hooker <Ita⁘[*1]> **b.** *sl-sex* ***Der*** loose woman <Ita⁘[*1]>

fȕfika {ē fem.; Dat fùfiki} *sl-sex* ***Der*** prostitute, hooker <Ita⁘[*1]>

fȕfka {ē fem.; Dat fȕfki} *sl* fear

fȕfljati {ām, ajū imperf. intr.} *sl-fea* talk persistently and meaninglessly, blabber, chatter

fȕga {ē fem.; Dat fȕgi} **a.** *sl-sex* ***Der*** prostitute, hooker **b.** *sl-sex* ***Der*** loose woman

fȕj {excl.} *col* used to express disgust, phew <Slav>

fȕk [1] {excl.} *col* the sound made by an abrupt movement, wham <Slav[*1]>

fȕk [2] {a +ov (ext. pl) masc.; Nom Pl fùkovi} **a.** *sl-sex* ***Obs*** sexual intercourse <Ger> **b.** *sl-crime* prison <Ger[*1]>

fȕk-féder {a masc.} (lit. fuck spring) **a.** *sl-sex* intrauterine device, IUD <Eng-Ger[*1]> **b.** *sl* key ring <Eng-Ger[*2]>

fȕka {ē fem.; Dat fȕki} **1** *col* whistling <Slav> 2 *sl-sex* prostitute, hooker <Ger>

fȕkāč {fukáča (acc. = gen.) masc.} /fȕkač/ *sl-fea* male sexual partner (of a female) <Ger⁘>

fȕkalo {a neut.} *sl-fea* penis <Ger⁘[*1]>

fukánac {nca masc.} *sl-sex* ***Obs*** sexual intercourse <Ger⁘>

fȕkānje {a neut.} *sl-sex* ***Obs*** sexual intercourse <Ger⁘>

fukaóna {ē fem.} *sl-sex* ***Obs*** place intended for sexual intercourse <Ger⁘>

fukàra [1] {ē fem.} **1** *sl-fea* poor person <NE⁘> 2 *sl-sex* prostitute, hooker <Ger⁘>

fùkara [2] {ē fem.} *sl-sex* ***Fac-Obs*** prostitute, hooker <Ger⁘>

fȕkati {ām, ajū imperf.} *sl-sex* ***Obs*** engage in sexual intercourse with (of a male) <Ger⁘>

fúkcija {ē fem.} [std. = funkcija] *col* position, duty one performs <Lat✍>

fȕkī {īja (acc. = gen.) masc.} *sl-sex* ***Fac-Obs*** prostitute, hooker <Ger⁘>

fȕkica {ē fem.} **1** *sl-sex* ***Obs*** vagina, cunt <Ger⁘> 2 *sl-sex* ***Obs*** prostitute, hooker <Ger⁘>

fȕkić {a (acc. = gen.) masc.} **a.** *sl* boy, kid <Ger⁘[*1]> **b.** *sl* teenager (male) <Ger⁘[*2]>

fȕknuti {nēm, nū perf.} *col* slam (a door, etc.) <Slav>

fȕkodrōm {a masc.} **a.** *sl-sex* ***Fac-Obs*** room intended for sexual intercourse <Ger-Gre[*1]> **b.** *sl* ***Fac-Obs*** king-size bed <Ger*Gre[*2]>

fȕkos {ē fem.} *sl-sex* ***Fac-Obs*** prostitute, hooker <Ger⁘>

fukòura {ē fem.} *sl-sex* ***Obs*** prostitute, hooker <Ger☞>

fȕksa {ē fem.} **a.** *sl-sex* ***Der*** prostitute, hooker <Ger> **b.** *sl-fea* ***Der*** selfish person <Ger*1>

fȕl {adj.} *sl* full, packed: *Kafić je super, ali je uvek ful. That cafe is super, but it's always packed.* <Eng>

fulágerka {ē fem.; Dat fulágerki} **a.** *sl-sex* ***Der*** loose woman <Ger*1> **b.** *sl* ***Der*** female <Ger*2>

fȕlati {ām, ajū biasp.} /fùlati/ *sl* miss, fail to hit <Ita*1>

fȕlja {ē fem.} *sl* head

fȕljiti se {ljīm, ljē imperf. intr.} **1** *sl* get angry <Fre☞*1> **2** *sl* break wind silently, fart silently

fȕma {ē fem.} *sl* cigarette, smoke <Ita❖>

fȕmati {ām, ajū biasp.} /fùmati/ **a.** *sl* smoke (tobacco) <Ita> **b.** *sl-sex* engage in fellatio <Ita*1>

fȕndača {ē fem.} *sl-fea* unattractive elderly female, hag <Ita*1>

fȕndati {ām, ajū imperf.} /fùndati/ **a.** *sl-sex* ***Obs*** engage in sexual intercourse with (of a male) <Ita*1> **b.** *sl* ***Obs*** fill, stuff: *fundati sarmu stuff cabbage rolls* <Ita*1>

fȕndra {ē fem.} **1** *sl* female <Ita*1> **2** *sl* lazy or shiftless person, bum, good for nothing <Ita*1>

fȕnfa {ē fem.} /fùnfa/ *sl-sex* ***Der*** prostitute, hooker <Ita*1>

funkcionànisati {išēm, išū imperf.} (lit. functurbate *funkcionisati 'function' X onanisati 'masturbate'*) [std. = funkcionisati] *sl* ***Fac*** function, operate: *Sistem ne funkcionaniše dobro. The system does not operate well.* <Lat-Gre☞>

fùnkīn {funkína (acc. = gen.) masc.} *sl* female

fȕntiti {tīm, tē imperf.} *sl-sex* ***Obs*** engage in sexual intercourse with (of a male)

fùnjara [1] {ē fem.} **1a.** *sl-sex* ***Der*** prostitute, hooker <NE*1> **b.** *sl-fea* ***Der*** unpleasant female, bitch <NE*2> **2** *sl-fea* ***Der*** evil, bad, mean person <NE*1>

fȕnjara [2] {ē fem. & masc.} *sl-fea* ***Der*** worthless or despicable person <NE>

fúnjati {fûnjām, fúnjajū biasp.} *sl-fea* talk persistently and meaninglessly, blabber, chatter

fȗr {a +ev (ext. pl) masc.; Nom Pl fúrevi} *sl-sex* prostitute, hooker <Ger*1>

fúra {ē fem.} *sl* promenade <Ger*1>

• **na fúri** {PP} (lit. on the line) *sl-sex* on the street (of prostitutes)

fúralica {ē fem.} *sl* enjoying <Ger❖>

fúrānje {a neut.} **a.** *sl* speeding (auto, etc.) <Ger> **b.** *sl* dating somebody <Ger*1>

fúrati {fûrām, fúrajū imperf. intr.} **a.** *sl* speed (auto, etc.) <Ger*1> **b.** *sl* date, go out with <Ger*2>

• **fúrati àlbānskē svjèćice** {VP} (lit. keep Albanian plugs) *sl-fea* ***Fac*** understand slowly and with difficulty

• **fúrati bȍjler** {VP} (lit. keep a water heater) *sl-fea* ***Fac*** have a sizable belly

• **fúrati dȓvo** {VP} (lit. keep a tree) *sl-fea* ***Fac*** be blind

• **fúrati dugàčak fìtīlj** {VP} (lit. keep a long fuse) *sl-fea* ***Fac*** understand slowly

• **fúrati fàzōn** {VP} (lit. keep a trick) *sl* ***Fac*** be fit, be in shape

• **fúrati fazóne** {VP} (lit. keep tricks) **a.** *sl* be fit, be in shape **b.** *sl* be happy

• **fúrati fìlm** {VP} (lit. keep a movie) *sl-drugs* hallucinate

• **fúrati jebáča i jebíča** {VP} (lit. keep fucker and fucker) *sl-sex* ***Obs*** have one boyfriend in Belgrade, Serbia and another in Zagreb, Croatia

• **fúrati kljûč od lúdnicē** {VP} (lit. keep a key to the psychiatric hospital) *sl* ***Fac*** pretend to be insane

• **fúrati kravàtu** {VP} (lit. keep a tie) *sl* ***Fac*** date an older male

• **fúrati nȁ veliko** {VP} (lit. keep a big business) *sl* have great fun, have a blast

• **fúrati p. p.** {VP} *sl-sex* suffer from syphilis, have the pox

• **fúrati slȁdolēd** {VP} (lit. keep ice cream) *sl-fea* ***Fac*** have a sizable belly

• **fúrati spȍmenīk** {VP} (lit. keep a monument) *sl-fea* ***Fac*** have a sizable belly

• **fúrati svôj fazón** {VP} (lit. drive one's own trick) *col* live one's own lifestyle: *Ona fura svoj fazon i nije je briga šta govore drugi. She's been living her lifestyle and she doesn't care what others have to say.*

• **fúrati svôj fìlm** {VP} (lit. keep one's own movie) *sl* live one's own lifestyle: *furati svoj film bez obzira na sve live one's own lifestyle no matter what*

• **fúrati šȁnt** {VP} (lit. keep whispering) *sl* have social or professional connections

• **fúrati túbicu** {VP} (lit. keep a tube) *sl-fea* ***Fac*** have a sizable belly

• **fúrati vèlikū màrku** {VP} (lit. keep a big brand name) *sl-fea* be very ambitious

• **fúrati vèlikū ȍcenu** {VP} (lit. keep a high score) SerE *sl-fea* be very ambitious

fúrati se {fûrām, fúrajū imperf.} **a.** *sl* live, exist <Ger> **b.** *sl* be interested in something, be keen on <Ger*1>

fùrdačiti {čīm, čē imperf.} *sl* destroy, ruin <NE❖>

fȕrešt {a (acc. = gen.) masc.} Med *col* tourist <**Ita**>

furijáda {ē fem.} *sl-crime* prison term <**Ger✣**>

furijandžȅlī {īja masc.} **a.** *sl* running away, fleeing <**Ger☞**> **b.** *sl* dating <**Ger☞*1**>

furijanđȅlī {īja masc.} **a.** *sl* running away, fleeing <**Ger☞**> **b.** *sl* dating somebody <**Ger☞*1**>

furijanȅlī {īja (acc. = gen.) masc.} *sl* escape, flee <**Ger☞**>

furijánović {a masc.} **a.** *sl* escape, flee <**Ger☞**> **b.** *sl* dating somebody <**Ger☞*1**>

fȕriti {rīm, rē imperf.} *col* eat, devour <**NE*1**>

fȕriti se {rīm, rē imperf. intr.} **a.** *sl* get angry <**NE*1**> **b.** *sl* be offended: *furiti se na kritiku be offended by criticism* <**NE*2**>

fȕrka {ē fem.} **1** *sl* lifestyle <**Ger✣*1**> **2** *sl* walking <**Ger✣*1**>

fȕrnuti [1] {nēm, nū perf. intr.} *sl* run away, flee <**Ger✣*1**>

fȕrnuti [2] {nēm, nū perf.} **a.** *sl* stick in, insert: *furnuti ključ u bravu stick a key into a keyhole* <**Ger✣*1**> **b.** *sl* push, shove <**Ger✣*2**>

fȕrnjāk {furnjáka masc.} *sl* wagon <**Ger✣**>

fȕrt {adv.} Cro *col* constantly: *On furtom dosađuje. He constantly bothers me.* <**Ger**>

fȕrtom {adv.} *sl-fea* right away, now: *Idi furtom donesi novine. Go and bring the newspaper right away.* <**Ger**>

fȕrtum {adv.} Vojv *dia-col* really, indeed: *Moj komšija je bio furtum pijan. My neighbor was really drunk.* <**Ger**>

fȕruna {ē fem.} **a.** *col* stove <**NE**> **b.** *sl* ***Fac*** beach <**NE*1**>

fȕska {ē fem.; Dat fȕski} *col* slap, smack <**Slav*1**>

fȕš {fȕša masc.} Cro *col* work done outside regular working hours, moonlighting

fúšer {a (acc. = gen.) masc.} **/fȕšer/** **a.** *col* incompetent laborer <**Ger**> **b.** *col* superficial person <**Ger*1**>

fušȅrāj {fušerája masc.} *col* incompetently or superficially performed job <**Ger**>

fušȅrisati {išēm, išū imperf. intr.} *col* work superficially <**Ger✣**>

fúšeriti {rīm, rē imperf. intr.} *col* work superficially <**Ger✣**>

fúšerka {ē fem.; Dat fúšerki} **/fȕšer/** **a.** *col* incompetent female laborer <**Ger**> **b.** *col* superficial female <**Ger*1**>

fȕtati {ām, ajū imperf.} *sl-sex* ***Obs*** engage in sexual intercourse with (of a male) <**Eng✣*1**>

fȕtić {a masc.} *sl-sports* soccer <**Eng☞**>

fȕtiti {tīm, tē perf.} **a.** *sl* hit, punch: *futiti kamenom u glavu hit with a stone in the head* <**Eng✣*1**> **b.** *sl* beat up

fȕtiti se {tīm, tē imperf. intr.} *sl* engage in a fight (fists, etc.) <**Eng*1**>

fȕtrānje {a neut.} *sl* cheating, swindling <**Ger*1**>

fȕtrati {ām, ajū biasp.} **a.** *sl* cheat, swindle <**Ger*1**> **b.** *sl* lie <**Ger*2**>

futróla {ē fem.} *col* glove <**Ger**>

fȕzbāl {a masc.} [std. = futbal] *sl-sports* soccer <**Ger**>

Gg

g *See the following*

- **plâvi g** [gê] {NP} (lit. blue g) *sl-crime* policeman, cop, man in blue

gâ {excl.} *col* the sound made by a goose, honk <**Slav**>

gâ-gâ {excl.} *col* the sound made by a newborn, goo-goo <**Slav**>

gâbor {a (acc. = gen.) masc.} **a.** *sl-fea* unattractive person <**SlavO*1**> **b.** *sl-sex* prostitute, hooker **c.** *sl* female

gácānje {a neut.} (lit. stepping over) *sl-sex* ***Fac-Obs*** sexual intercourse <**Slav*1**>

gácati {gâcām, gácajū imperf.} (lit. step over) *sl-sex* ***Fac-Obs*** engage in sexual intercourse with (of a male) <**Slav*1**>

gaćȁrica {ē fem.} *sl* pipe (smoking) <**Slav*1**>

gȁće *See the following*

- **ko tésne gȁće** {PP} (lit. like a tight pair of panties) SerE *sl-fea* very boring

gaćerónci {rônācā masc. pl.} *sl* underpants, underwear <**Slav☞**>

gaćeróne {ā fem. pl.} **a.** *sl* underpants, underwear <**Slav☞**> **b.** *sl* trousers, pants <**Slav☞*1**>

gȁd {a +ov (ext. pl) masc.; Nom Pl gàdovi} *sl-fea* ***Der*** worthless or despicable person <**Slav*1**>

gadȁrija {ē fem.} *col* ***Der*** disliked action or situation <**Slav✣**>

gàdnjāk {gadnjáka (acc. = gen.) masc.; Voc gȁdnjāče} *sl-fea* dangerous male, one who acts violently <Slav✤>

gȁdro {gȅdro fem.; perm} /gàdro/ *sl-drugs* narcotic drug, dope <Fre✍>

gàdulja {ē fem.} *sl-fea* ***Der*** dirty and untidy female, slob <Slav✤*1>

gàdura {ē fem.} *sl-fea* ***Der*** dirty and untidy female, slob <Slav✤*1>

gáđānje {a neut.} (lit. shooting, hitting) *sl-sex* ***Fac-Obs*** sexual intercourse, banging <Slav*1>

gáđati {gâđām, gáđajū imperf.} (lit. shoot, hit) *sl-sex* ***Fac*** engage in sexual intercourse with (of a male), bang <Slav*1>

- **gáđati krȍz noge** {VP} (lit. shoot through the legs) *sl-sex* ***Fac*** engage in cunnilingus
- **gáđati mȅtrima i kàmēnjem** {VP} (lit. throw meters and stones) *sl-crime* ***Fac-Iro*** convict to a long prison term

gáđati se {gâđām, gáđajū imperf. intr.} (lit. hit oneself) *sl-drugs* take narcotic drugs, do drugs <Slav*1>

- **gáđati se epitétima** {VP} (lit. throw epithets) *col* curse
- **gáđati se pádežima** {VP} (lit. throw cases) *col* speak ungrammatically

gȁf {gàfa +ov (ext. pl) masc.; Nom Pl gàfovi} **a.** *col* mistake, error (usu. in social relations) <Fre> **b.** *col* good joke <Fre*1>

gȁfer {a (acc. = gen.) masc.} *sl-fea* clumsy male, klutz <Fre✤>

gafírati se {gàfīrām, rajū imperf. intr.} *sl* make a fool of oneself <Fre✤>

gàgul {a (acc. = gen.) masc.} *sl-arch* devil

gâj {a +ev (ext. pl) masc.; Nom Pl gájevi} (lit. grove) *col* garden <Slav*1>

gâjba {ē fem.} /gȁjba /e fem./ (lit. crate) **1** *sl* apartment: *gajba na trećem spratu a pad on the fourth floor* <Ita*1> **2** *sl* room <Ita*1> **3** *sl-crime* prison <Ita*1> **4** *sl-sport* goal (in soccer, water polo, etc.): *zabiti gajbu score a goal*

gàjbica {ē fem.} (lit. small crate) **1** *sl* efficiency, studio (apartment) <Ita✤*1> **2** *sl* small room <Ita✤*1>

gajbijána {ē fem.} **1** *sl* apartment <Ita✍*1> **2** *sl* room <Ita✍*1>

gajbijàšica {ē fem.} **1** *sl* apartment <Ita✍*1> **2** *sl* room <Ita✍*1>

gàjger {a (acc. = gen.) masc.} *sl-crime* ***Der*** informer, stoolie, snitch <Ger*1>

gajgerírati {gèrīrām, gerírajū biasp.} **1** *sl-crime* inform the police or other authorities, snitch, squeal <Ger✤*1> **2** *sl* walk for a long time <Ger✤*1>

gájiti {jīm, jē imperf.} (lit. raise) **a.** *col* have, possess <Slav*1> **b.i.** *col* keep <Slav*2> **ii.** *col* love <Slav*2>

- **gájiti frȁjera** {VP} (lit. raise a dude) *sl* date, go out with
- **gájiti ȉrvāse** {VP} (lit. raise reindeer) *sl-fea* be senile

gȁjnc {adv.} *col* completely, totally: *Kupio je gajnc nov auto. He bought a brand new car.* <Ger> ☞ **ganc, ganjc**

gájtan {a masc.} *col* cable, wire <NE>

gájtaniti {nīm, nē imperf.} **a.** *col* whip <NE✤*1> **b.** *col* beat <NE✤*2> **c.** *sl-sex* engage in sexual intercourse with (of a male) <NE✤*2>

gàjtarēnje {a neut.} *sl-sex* ***Obs*** sexual intercourse <NE✤*1>

gȁla [1] {adv.} *col* ***App*** excellent, big time: *gala se naigrati play big time* <Spa>

gȁla [2] {adj.} *col* ***App*** excellent, awesome: *gala haljina awesome dress* <Spa>

gàlāh {galáha (acc. = gen.) masc.} *sl-arch* priest

gàlant {adv.} *col* elegantly <Spa>

galapâgos {a (acc. = gen.) masc.} *sl-fea* senile person <SpaO*1>

gàlban {a masc.} *sl-arch* gold coin <Rum✍*1>

gȁlofāk {a (acc. = gen.) masc.} (lit. Galofak: brandname for pig feed) *sl-fea* obese person <BN*1>

gȁlofaks {a (acc. = gen.) masc.} (lit. Galofak: brandname for pig feed) *sl-fea* very young female, little girl <BN*1>

gàlop {a masc.} (lit. gallop) **a.** *sl* fast run <Fre*1> **b.** *sl* dance <Fre*2>

galòpēr {lopéra (acc. = gen.) masc.} (lit. galloper) *sl-fea* millionaire <Fre✤*1>

galopírati {lòpīrām, lopírajū imperf.} (lit. gallop) **a.** *sl-fea* run fast <Fre✤*1> **b.** *sl* talk loud: *Toliko je galopirao da su se djeca probudila. He talked so loudly that the children woke up.* <Fre✤*1>

gàlzīn {galzína masc.} *sl-arch* gold coin

gȁmād {i fem.} **a.** *col* ***Der*** insects <Slav> **b.** *col* immoral group of persons <Slav*1>

gȁmba {ē fem.} *sl* leg (human) <Ita>
• **gȁmbu u gȍvnaru** {NP} (lit. leg in the ass) *sl* ***Obs*** kick in the buttocks

gàmbati {ām, ajū imperf.} **a.** *sl* walk <Ita❖> **b.** *sl* run <Ita❖[*1]> **c.** *sl* learn, study: *gambati matiš study math* <Ita❖[*2]>

gàmbātor {a masc.} *sl* running away, fleeing <Ita❖>

gȁmbavica {ē fem.} *sl* leg (of a female) <Ita❖>

gȁmbica {ē fem.} *sl* leg (of a female) <Ita❖>

gàmen {a (acc. = gen.) masc.} **a.** *sl-fea* dandy, fop <Fre> **b.** *sl-fea* lazy or shiftless person, bum, good for nothing <Fre[*1]>

gȁn {a +ov (ext. pl) masc.; Nom Pl gànovi} **a.** *sl-drugs* gun pistol <Eng> **b.** *sl-drugs* needle <Eng[*1]>

gȁnc {adv.} *col* totally, completely, fully <Ger> ☞ gajnc, ganjc

Gȁnci {īja (acc. = gen.) masc.; perm} **/Gànci /Gànaci** (acc. = gen.) masc.**/** [std. = Ciganin] *sl* ***Off*** Gypsy (male) <SlavO✍>

Gàncimetar {tra (acc. = gen.) masc.; perm} [std. = Ciganin] *sl* ***Off*** Gypsy (male) <SlavO✍>

gânča {ē masc.} **a.** *sl-fea* loafer, idler **b.** *sl-fea* lazy or shiftless person, bum, good for nothing **c.** *sl-fea* liar **d.** *sl-crime* thief

gàndža {ē fem.} *sl-drugs* hashish, hash <Hind>

gàner {a (acc. = gen.) masc.} *sl-fea* troublemaker, rowdy, ruffian <Eng[*1]>

gȁniti {nīm, nē imperf.} *sl* lie <NE[*1]>

gȁnk {a +ov (ext. pl) masc.; Nom Pl gànkovi} *sl-drugs* morphine

gȁno {geno fem.; perm} **/gàno/** *sl* leg (human) <Slav✍>

gȁnu {ua masc.; perm} **/gànu/** *sl* leg (human) <Slav✍>

gánjalo {a neut.} (lit. chaser) *sl-sex* ***Fac*** male homosexual, gay <Slav[*1]>

gánjati {ām, ajū imperf.} (lit. chase) *col* deal with, arrange, take care of (usu. with authorities of some kind): *Već preko dva mjeseca ganjam dozvolu za uvoz kola. I have been trying to get this car import permit for more than two months.* <Slav[*1]>

gȁnjc {adv.} *col* very <Ger> ☞ gajnc, ganc

gȁper {a (acc. = gen.) masc.} *sl-drugs* addict in need of narcotic drugs, junkie needing a fix <Eng>

gȁra {ē fem.} **1** *sl-fea* brunette <Slav[*1]> **2** *sl-crime* pistol, revolver <Slav[*1]> **3** *sl* coffee <Slav[*1]>

garàbīn {garabína masc.} *sl-crime* gun pistol <Fre✍>

gàraci {gàreci fem.; perm} *sl* cigarette, smoke <Spa✍>

garagâbor {a (acc. = gen.) masc.} *sl-crime* very unattractive female, real dog <SlavO[*1]>

gàragan {a (acc. = gen.) masc.} *sl-fea* male with dark complexion <Slav❖✍>

garàvān {raváṇa (acc. = gen.) masc.} (lit. the sooty one) *sl-fea* ***Off*** Gypsy (male) <Slav❖>

gȁravica {ē fem.} (lit. the sooty one) *sl* ***Fac*** coffee <Slav❖>

garáža {ē fem.} (lit. garage) *sl-crime* hiding place for stolen goods, stash <Fre[*1]>

gàrdiš {a masc.} *sl* clothing, garment <Fre✍[*1]>

gàrdos {a masc.} *sl* clothing, garment <Fre✍[*1]>

gargâbor {a (acc. = gen.) masc.} *sl-crime* very unattractive female, real dog

Garȉnča *See the following*
• **Garȉnča na kvàdrāt** {NP} (lit. Garincha, a popular soccer player for Brazil, to the second power) *sl-fea* ***Fac*** in love

gȁriti {rīm, rē imperf.} **/gáriti/** *sl* hurry up, rush <Slav[*1]>

gȁrka {ē fem.; Dat gȁrki} **1** *sl* leg (human) <Slav✍[*1]> **2** *sl* cigarette, smoke <Slav✍[*1]>

garnȉzōn {a masc.} *sl-sstu* high school <Fre[*1]>

gȁrsić {a masc.} *sl* efficiency, studio (apartment) <Fre❖>

gâs *See the following*
• **pod gâsom** {PP} (lit. under gas) *sl-drink* drunk, gassed

gastarbàjter {a (acc. = gen.) masc.} *col* guest worker <Ger>

gastarbàjterka {ē fem.; Dat gastarbàjterki} *col* guest worker <Ger❖>

gastarbàjterskī {ā, ō adj.} *col* guest worker's <Ger>

gastarbàjterstvo {a neut.} *col* status of a guest worker <Ger❖>

gȁster {gàstera (acc. = gen.) masc.} *sl* guest worker <Ger✍>

gȁstić {a (acc. = gen.) masc.} *sl* guest worker <Ger✍>

gȁstos {a (acc. = gen.) masc.} **/gâstos/** *sl* guest worker <Ger✍>

gȁta {ē fem.} *sl-sex* ***Obs*** penis, dick, prick <Slav✍[*1]>

gatárēnje {a masc.} *sl-sex* ***Obs*** sexual intercourse <Slav✍[*1]>

gàtila {žȇmla, žȗla imperf.; perm} [std. = lagati] *sl* lie <Slav✍>

gàvan {a (acc. = gen.) masc.} *sl-fea* very important or influential person, big shot <SlavO*1>

gȁvrān {a (acc. = gen.) masc.} (lit. raven) *sl-crime* policeman, cop <Slav*1>

gavrànčina {ē fem.} (lit. big raven) *sl-sex* ***Obs*** vagina, cunt <Slav✤*1>

gȁzalica {ē fem.} (lit. stepper) *sl* leg (human) <Slav✤>

gȁzalo {a neut.} (lit. stepper) *sl* leg (human) <Slav✤>

gȁzda {ē masc.} **1** *col* boss <Hun> **2** *col* landlord <Hun> **3** *sl-crime* gang leader <Hun> **4** *sl* leader <Hun>

gȁzdarica {ē fem.} **1** *col* boss <Hun✤> **2** *col* landlady <Hun✤>

gȁziti {zīm, zē imperf.} (lit. squish by stepping on) **1** *sl* speed, step on the gas <Slav*1> **2** *sl* date <Slav*1> **3a.** *sl* beat up: *Gaze ga tri silosa. Three troublemakers are beating him up.* <Slav*1> **b.i.** *sl-sex* engage in sexual intercourse with (of a male) <Slav*2> **ii.** *sl* defeat <Slav*2>

- **gȁziti lȅptīr-mášnu** {VP} (lit. step on a bow-tie) *sl-fea* ***Fac*** turn one's back on somebody
- **gȁziti po gànglijama** {VP} (lit. step on one's ganglia) *sl-fea* ***Fac*** get on one's nerves
- **gȁziti po vȉjugama** {VP} (lit. step on one's convolutions) *sl-fea* ***Fac*** get on one's nerves
- **gȁziti štȁke** {VP} (lit. step on the crutches) *sl-fea* ***Fac*** limp

gáža {ē fem.} **a.** *sl* job, gig <Fre> **b.** *sl-music* contract for a band <Fre*1> **c.** *sl* money <Fre*1>

- **mòrskā gáža** {NP} (lit. seashore gig) *sl-music* summer job for an orchestra

gdȅ {part.} (lit. where) **SerE** *col* particle used to express disbelief: *A: Ona je pobegla u Mađarsku. B: Gde! A: She ran away to Hungary. B: No way!* <Slav*1>

- **Gdȅ si?** {S} (lit. Where are you?) **SerE** *col* used as a greeting in direct informal communication with one person, How are you!

gdȅ je Bôg rȅkō lȁku nôć {S} (lit. where God said: "Good night") **SerE** *col* used to refer to a place of extreme wretchedness or squalor, hellhole: *Odrastao je gde je Bog rekao laku noć pa nije ni čudo što je takav razbojnik. He was raised in a hellhole, no wonder he's such a hooligan.* ☞ Bog

Gdȅ su ti ȉrvāsi? {S} (lit. Where are your reindeer?) **SerE** *sl-fea* ***Fac*** used to express astonishment, Did you loose your mind? Are you nuts? ☞ **irvas**

gdjȅ je Bôg rȅkō lȁku nôć {S} (lit. where God said: "Good night") *col* used to refer to a place of extreme wretchedness or squalor, hellhole: *Odrastao je gdje je Bog reko laku noć, pa nije ni čudo što je takav razbojnik. He was raised in a hellhole, no wonder he's such a hooligan.* ☞ Bog

geȁčina {ē masc.} *sl-fea* inhabitant of the countryside, hick, bumpkin <NE✤>

gȅāk {a (acc. = gen.) masc.} /gèāk/ **a.** *sl-fea* inhabitant of the countryside, hick, bumpkin <NE*1> **b.** *sl-fea* lazy or shiftless person, bum, good for nothing

geàkinja {ē fem.} *sl-fea* inhabitant of the countryside, hick, bumpkin <NE✤>

gȅba {ē fem.} *sl* teeth <Ger✍>

gȅbis {a masc.} *sl* tooth <Ger>

gedóre {a fem. pl.} *sl-crafts* wrench set <BN*1>

gédža {ē masc.} **a.** *sl-fea* inhabitant of the countryside, hick, bumpkin <NE*1> **b.i.** *sl-fea* stupid or mentally deficient person <NE*2> **ii.** *sl-fea* Serbian from Serbia proper <NE*2>

gédžānje {a neut.} **1** *sl* fight (e.g. fist fight) <NE*1> **2** *sl* something important <NE*1>

gédžo {ē masc.} /gédžo /a masc./ **a.** *sl-fea* inhabitant of the countryside, hick, bumpkin <NE*1> **b.i.** *sl-fea* stupid or mentally deficient person <NE*2> **ii.** *sl-fea* Serbian from Serbia proper <NE*2>

gedžòvān {džována masc.} **a.** *sl-fea* inhabitant of the countryside, hick, bumpkin <NE*1> **b.i.** *sl-fea* stupid or mentally deficient person <NE*2> **ii.** *sl-fea* Serbian from Serbia proper <NE*2>

géđa {ē masc.} *sl-fea* inhabitant of the countryside, hick, bumpkin <NE✍*1>

gêee {excl.} *col* used to express surprise, whoa <Slav>

gégati {gêgām, gégajū imperf. intr.} *col* walk <Slav*1>

gégati se {gêgām, gégajū imperf. intr.} *col* limp <Slav*1>

gȅgav {a, o adj.} *col* lame (limping) <Slav*1>

gȅgavac {vca (acc. = gen.) masc.} *sl-fea* beggar who pretends to limp <Slav*1>

gȅgavačkī {ōg masc.} *sl* slang <Slav*1>

gȅgavskī {ōg masc.} *sl* slang <Slav*1>

gȅgeš {a masc.} *sl* throat <Slav✍>

gègiš {a masc.} *sl-sstu* geography (as a science course) <Gre✍>

gȅgula {ē masc.} *sl-fea* inhabitant of the countryside, hick, bumpkin <NE*1>

geguláner {a (acc. = gen.) masc.} *sl-fea* inhabitant of the countryside, hick, bumpkin <NE*1>

gȅha {ē fem.; Dat gȅhi} *sl* teeth

gehȁjz {a masc.} *sl-crafts* housing <Ger>

gêj {a +ev (ext. pl) masc.; Nom Pl géjevi} (lit. gey) *sl-sex* ***Der*** male homosexual, gay <Eng>

gêjša {ē fem.} (lit. geisha) *sl-sex* ***Fac*** obese male homosexual <Jap*1>

géknuti {gêknēm, nū perf.} **a.** *sl* hit, punch <Slav*1> **b.** *sl* go insane, freak out <Slav*2>

gèleng {a masc.} *sl-crafts* joint (a part of a mechanism) <Ger>

gelȉpter {a (acc. = gen.) masc.} *sl-fea* troublemaker, rowdy, ruffian <Ger>

gèljati {ām, ajū imperf.} *sl* limp

gȅm {gèma +ov (ext. pl) masc.; Nom Pl gèmovi} *sl-drink* wine with water <Ger✍>

gènditi {dīm, dē imperf. intr.} *sl* cry in grief

gȅnđiti {đīm, đē imperf. intr.} *sl* cry in grief

gène [1] {excl.} /gêne/ *sl-mil* my generation <Lat✍>

gène [2] {eta masc.} /gêne/ *sl-mil* general <Lat✍>

genèrāl {nerála (acc. = gen.) masc.} (lit. general) *sl-crime* prison administrator <Lat*1>

Generȁlić {a (acc. = gen.) masc.} (lit. *Ivan* Generalić, a well-known folk painter) *sl-fea* naive male, sucker <SlavO*1>

genèrālka {ē fem.} **1** *sl-media* dress rehearsal <Lat❖> **2** *sl-crafts* complete overhaul <Lat❖>

gȅnerālnā fȑka {NP} (lit. general nervousness) *sl* danger, dangerous situation of any kind ☞ **frka**

gȅnerālnā vráta {NP} (lit. general door) *sl* danger, dangerous situation of any kind ☞ **vrata**

gènga {ē fem.; Dat gȅngi} *sl* money

- **rȍđenā gènga** {NP} (lit. own money) *sl* money earned at one's work

gèngāš {gengáša (acc. = gen.) masc.} **1** *sl-crime* pickpocket <Eng❖*1> **2** *sl-crime* person who illegally exchanges money <Eng❖*1>

genijálac {lca (acc. = gen.) masc.} **a.** *sl-fea* genius <Lat❖> **b.** *sl-fea* highly humorous person, laugh, scream <Lat❖*1>

genijálština {adj.} (lit. genius) *sl* highly humorous <Lat❖>

gèniš {adj.} [std. = genijalan] *sl-fea* witty <Lat✍>

genitálac {lca (acc. = gen.) masc.} *sl-fea* genius <Lat❖✍>

gènter {a (acc. = gen.) masc.} *sl-crime* detective <Lat✍>

génja {ē masc.} **a.** *sl* gentleman <Eng✍> **b.** *sl* boss <Eng✍*1>

génjo {excl.} *sl-mil* my generation <Lat✍>

geògraf {a (acc. = gen.) masc.} *sl-fea* elderly male <Gre*1>

geògrafskī pójam {NP} (lit. geographical concept) **a.** *sl-fea* ***Fac*** boring person, bore **b.** *sl-fea* ***Fac*** unimportant person, nobody, nothing ☞ **pojam**

gȅpa {ē fem.} *sl-crime* theft, swipe <Slav✍*1>

gȅpār {a (acc. = gen.) masc.} /gèpār/ *sl-crime* thief, sticky fingers <Slav✍*1>

gȅpavac {vca (acc. = gen.) masc.} *sl-crime* thief, sticky fingers <Slav❖✍*1>

gȅpavac {vca masc.} **a.** *sl* finger <Slav❖✍*1> **b.** *sl* hand **c.** *sl* arm

gȅpavica {ē fem.} **a.** *sl* hand <Slav❖✍*1> **b.** *sl* arm

Gêpê {ea neut.} (abbreviation GP i.e. Gradski podrum 'City cellar') *sl-drink* name for Gradski podrum restaurant in Zagreb, Croatia <Abb>

gèpek {a masc.} **a.** *col* trunk (of a car) <Ger> **b.** *sl-sex* buttocks, butt <Ger*1>

gȅpiti {pīm, pē perf.} *sl-crime* steal, swipe <Slav❖✍*1>

gȅposlāv {a (acc. = gen.) masc.} /gèposlav/ *sl-crime* pickpocket <Slav❖✍*1>

Gȅrkos {a (acc. = gen.) masc.} *sl* Greek (person) <SlavO✍>

gèrla {ē fem.} **a.** *sl-sex* prostitute, hooker <Eng> **b.** *sl* female

Germánac {nca (acc. = gen.) masc.} *sl* German (person), Kraut <SlavO>

gêro {excl.} *sl-mil* used to emphasize a close relationship with a person from the same generation, my generation <Lat✍>

géša {ē masc.} **1** *sl-fea* genius <Lat✍> **2** *sl-mil* general <Lat✍>

getríba {ē fem.} *sl-auto* gearbox <Ger>

getríbe {ā fem. pl.} (lit. gearboxes) *sl* attractive leg (of a female) <Ger>

gevéra {ē fem.} (lit. firearms) **a.** *sl* trick, joke <**Ger**[*1]> **b.** *sl* joke

gìbak {pka, pko adj.} *sl* witty <**Slav**[*1]>

gíbalica {ē fem.} *sl* fun <**Slav**[*1]>

gíbānje {a neut.} *sl* walking <**Slav**[*1]>

gíbati {ām, ajū imperf. intr.} *sl* walk <**Slav**[*1]>

gíbati se {ām, ajū imperf. intr.} *sl* walk <**Slav**[*1]>

gìbōn {gibóna (acc. = gen.) masc.} *sl-fea* unattractive male, dog <**Ind**[*1]>

gȉc {excl.} *col* used to lure a pig <**Slav**>

gíca {ē m fem.} (lit. pig) *sl-fea* obese person, porker <**Slav**[*1]>

gìcīnka {ē fem.; Dat gìcīnki} *sl-fea* female who peeps, peeper <**Slav**⁘[*1]>

gíciti {cīm, cē imperf.} *sl* peep, look at others <**Slav**[*1]>

gȉcka {ē fem. & masc.; Dat gȉcki} *sl-fea* senior citizen <**Slav**⁘[*1]>

gȉcle {eta masc.} *sl-fea* elderly male <**Slav**✍[*1]>

gíco {ē masc.} (lit. pig) *sl-fea* obese person, porker <**Slav**[*1]>

gȉdru {num.; perm} /gìdru/ [std. = drugi] *sl* second <**Slav**✍>

gȉftānje {a neut.} (lit. poisoning) *sl* anger <**Ger**[*1]>

gȉftati se {ām, ajū biasp. intr.} (lit. poison) *sl* get angry <**Ger**[*1]>

gȉgantostrȁka {ē masc.; Dat gȉgantostrȁki} **a.** *sl-fea* stubborn male, pigheaded guy <**Lat-Slav.**[*1]> **b.** *sl-fea* conceited male <**Lat-Slav**[*2]>

gilènder {a masc.} **a.** *sl-fea* inhabitant of the countryside, hick, bumpkin <**Ger**[*1]> **b.** *sl-fea* stupid or mentally deficient person <**Ger**[*2]>

gȉlja [1] {ē fem.} /gílja/ **a.** *sl* shoe <**Gyp**⁘[*1]> **b.** *sl* foot <**Gyp**⁘[*2]>

gílja [2] {ē fem.} *sl* shoe <**Gyp**>

gȉljāč {goljáča (acc. = gen.) masc.} *sl* worker <**Gyp**⁘>

gȉljalica {ē fem.} /gíljalica/ *sl* shoe <**Gyp**⁘>

gȉljār {giljára masc.} *sl* shoe <**Gyp**⁘>

gȉljara {ē fem.} *sl* shoe <**Gyp**⁘>

gȉljarica {ē fem.} **a.** *sl* shoe <**Gyp**⁘> **b.i.** *sl* leg (human) <**Gyp**⁘[*1]> **ii.** *sl* street <**Gyp**⁘[*1]>

gȉljārka {ē fem.; Dat gȉljārki} **a.** *sl* shoe <**Gyp**⁘> **b.** *sl* leg (human) <**Gyp**⁘[*1]>

giljàrōn {ljaróna masc.} **a.** *sl* shoe <**Gyp**⁘> **b.** *sl* leg (human) <**Gyp**⁘[*1]>

gȉljati {ām, ajū imperf.} /gíljati/ **a.** *sl* walk <**Gyp**⁘> **b.i.** *sl* work, labor <**Gyp**⁘[*1]> **ii.** *sl* vegetate, barely live (socially or financially) <**Gyp**⁘[*1]> **iii.** *sl* step over <**Fre**⁘[*1]>

• **gȉljati u kùtiju** {VP} (lit. run into a box) *sl* ***Fac*** take an elevator

giljáviti {gìljāvīm, gìljāvē imperf.} **a.** *sl* walk; *giljaviti u centar go downtown* <**Gyp**⁘> **b.** *sl* walk slowly, amble <**Gyp**⁘[*1]>

gìljer {a (acc. = gen.) masc.} **a.** *sl-crime* escape, flee <**Gyp**⁘> **b.** *sl-crime* fugitive, runaway <**Gyp**⁘[*1]>

gȉljka {ē fem.; Dat gíljki} *sl* shoe <**Gyp**⁘>

gȉljos {a (acc. = gen.) masc.} *sl* worker <**Gyp**✍>

gȉljotina {ē fem.} *sl* marriage <**Fre**[*1]>

gȉljotrēs {a (acc. = gen.) masc.} *sl* worker <**Gyp-Slav.**[*1]>

giljòvān {ljována (acc. = gen.) masc.} *sl* worker <**Gyp**⁘>

gȉmna {ē fem.} *sl-sstu* high school <**Gre**✍>

ginekòlog *See the following*

• **mùškī ginekòlog** {NP} (lit. male gynecologist) *sl-sex* ***Fac*** male homosexual, gay

gìngibas {a masc.} *sl-sex* ***Fac-Obs*** penis, dick, prick

gȉnuti {nēm, nū imperf.} *sl-fea* strive, try hard <**Slav**[*1]>

• **nè gìnē[PRON:DAT]** ([NOUN:NOM]) {LSF} (lit. [NOUN:NOM] doesn't die to [PRON:ACC]) *col* used to refer to inevitability of an event: *Ne gine ti zatvor. You cannot avoid going to jail.*

gȉrica {ē fem.} (lit. picarel, a small sea fish) **1** *sl-fea* ***Der*** coward, chicken <**Lat**[*1]> **2** *sl-fea* ***Fac*** Dalmatian (inhabitant of Dalmatia, Croatia) <**Ita**[*1]> **3** *sl* ten dinars; a ten-dinar bill <**Ita**[*1]>

gȉstro [1] {adj.; perm} (lit. strict) [std. = strogi] **a.** *sl* real <**Slav**[*1]> **b.** *sl* not real, fake <**Slav**[*2]>

gȉstro [2] {adv.; perm} [std. = strogi] **a.** *sl-fea* sort of: *Danas sam gistro radio. I sort of worked today.* <**Slav**✍> **b.** *sl-fea* used to refer to something which one does not consider to be true: *On je gistro bolestan, a ja ga videla kako igra fudbal. They say that he is sick, but I saw him playing soccer.* <**Slav**✍>

gȉt {a masc.} [std. = kit] *col* putty <**Ger**✍>

gitára {ē fem.} (lit. guitar) *sl-mil* setting fire to someone's fingers <**Gre**[*1]>

gitáre {a fem. pl.} *sl-crime* prison bars <**Gre**[*1]>

gȉtovānje {a neut.} [std. = kitovanje] *col* puttying <Ger❖✍>

glàbati {ām, ajū imperf.} *sl* bite (a bone, etc.)

glâd {i fem.} *sl* being broke (financially) <Slav*1>

gladijâtor {a (acc. = gen.) masc.} (lit. gladiator) *sl-sex* ***Fac*** masturbator (male) <Lat*1>

gladiòla {ē fem.} /gladióla/ *sl-sex* ***Obs*** buttocks, butt <Lat*1>

glȁditi {dīm, dē imperf.} **1** *sl* ***Der*** ingratiate, brownnose, kiss ass <Slav*1> **2** *sl* request <Slav*1> **3** *sl* beat up <Slav*1>

- **glȁditi dàske** {VP} (lit. smoothe the planks) *sl-fea* ***Fac*** be a regular (e.g. in a bar)

glâdnā gȍdina {NP} (lit. a hungry year) **a.** *col* long period of time **b.** *sl-sex* ***Fac*** longer period without sexual intercourse ☞ **godina**

glȁfōr {a (acc. = gen.) masc.} **1** *sl-fea* boss <Slav-Ger✍> **2** *sl-fea* very important or influential person, big shot <Slav-Ger✍*1>

glágol {a masc.} (lit. verb) **a.** *sl-sex* ***Obs*** sexual intercourse <Slav*1> **b.** *sl* curse, profanity <Slav*2>

glâj {excl.} [std. = gledaj] *col* used to attract attention of a person in direct informal communication: *Glaj, ptica! Look, a bird!* <Slav✍>

glȁnc {a +ev (ext. pl) masc.; Nom Pl glȁncevi} *col* shine (on any polished object) <Ger>

glâncati {ām, ajū imperf.} /glȁncati/ **a.** *col* polish, shine <Ger❖> **b.** *sl-sex* ***Fac-Obs*** engage in sexual intercourse with (of a male) <Ger❖*1>

- **glâncati kȉtu** {VP} (lit. polish one's prick) *sl-sex* ***Fac*** masturbate, beat off

glȁncerica {ē fem.} (lit. polishing lady) *sl-sex* ***Fac*** lesbian <Ger❖>

glàntāš {lantáša masc.} *sl* hat

glȁsnī {ōg (acc. = gen.) masc.} (lit. the loud one) *sl-crime* ***Der*** informer, stoolie, snitch <Slav*1>

glȁt {adv.} *col* easily: *pobijediti glat win easily* <Ger*1>

glàtkī {ā, ō adj.} (lit. smooth) *sl-fea* bald <Ger*1>

glȁtko {adv.} (lit. smoothly) *col* easily: *glatko osvojiti prvo mjesto win first place easily* <Ger*1>

gláva {ē fem.} (lit. head) **1** *sl* dinar (Yugoslav currency unit) <Slav*1> **2** *sl* hundred dinars; a hundred-dinar bill <Slav*1> **3** *sl* ten paras; a ten-para coin <Slav*1> **4** *sl* ten dinars; a ten-dinar coin <Slav*1> **5** *sl* heads (of a coin) <Slav*1> **6** *sl* hat <Slav*1> **7** *sl* cap, hat <Slav*1> **8** *sl* general <Slav*1> **9** *sl* hundred German marks

- **kȉselā gláva** {NP} (lit. sour head) *sl-drugs* notorious drug addict
- **lêpā gláva** {NP} (lit. cute head) *sl-crime* name of a prison in Lepoglava, Croatia (Croatia)
- **ni za žívu glâvu** {PP} (lit. not even for a live head) *col* used as a strong negative response, no way, under no circumstances,
- **od glávē do pétē** {PP} (lit. from head to heel) *col* from head to toe, completely
- **šést glávā** {NP} (lit. six heads) *sl-gamble* gambling success
- **U glâvu te jèbēm!** {S} (lit. I fuck you in your head!) *dia-col* ***Off*** used as a moderate curse
- **ùsijanā gláva** {NP} (lit. a glowing head) *sl-fea* quick-tempered or impetuous person, hothead
- **zȁ glāvu** {PP} (lit. for head) *col* urgently

glavàljica {ē fem.} *sl* leg (human) <Slav*1>

glavarskā radiónica {NP} (lit. headman's workshop) *sl-fea* ***Fac*** mental institution, madhouse ☞ **radionica**

glàvat {a, o adj.} (lit. large-headed) *sl* violent <Slav*1>

glàvati {ām, ajū biasp.} (lit. head) **a.** *sl* walk <Slav*1> **b.** *sl* go, be directed to <Slav*2>

glàvica {ē fem.} (lit. small head) *sl* one dinar; a one-dinar coin <Slav*1>

- **U glàvicu te jèbēm!** {S} (lit. I screw you in your small head!) *dia-col* ***Off*** used as a weak curse

glàvīć {lavíća masc.} (lit. glans *of the penis*) *sl-sex* ***Fac-Obs*** male homosexual, gay <Slav*1>

glavìnjati {ām, ajū imperf.} (lit. head) *col* be in a hurry <Slav*1>

glàvir {a masc.} *sl* head <Slav✍>

glàvka {ē fem.} (lit. small head) *sl* one dinar; a one-dinar coin <Slav*1>

glàvnā mȑtvāčnica {NP} (lit. main morgue) *sl-fea* ***Fac*** name for Petrinjska street prison, Zagreb, Croatia ☞ **mrtvačnica**

glàvnī [1] {ā, ō adj.} (lit. the main one) *col* very important or very influential <Slav*1>

glàvnī [2] {ōg (acc. = gen.) masc.} (lit. the main one) **1** *sl-fea* person with a large head <Slav*1> **2** *sl-crime* gang leader <Slav*1> **3** *sl-fea* rich male <Slav*1> **4** *sl-fea* skillful male <Slav*1>

glȁvnīk {a masc.} *sl* day <Slav❖*1>

Glàvnjača {ē fem.} *sl-crime* prison <Slav❖*1>

glavòbolja {ē fem.} (lit. headache) **a.** *sl* ***Fac*** wife <**Slav***1> **a.** *sl* ***Fac*** female <**Slav***2>

glávonja {ē masc.} (lit. large-headed person) **1a.** *sl-fea* smart person, brain: *Taj glavonja zna da riješi svaki zadatak. That brain can solve any math problem.* <**Slav***1> **b.** *sl-fea* very important or influential person, big shot <**Slav***2> **c.** *sl-fea* politician <**Slav***3> **d.** *sl-polit* dictator <**Slav***4> 2 *sl* dad <**Slav***1> 3 *sl-sex* penis

glȁvoseča {ē fem. & masc.} /glavóseča/ (lit. decapitation) SerE *sl-fea* humpbacked person <**Slav***1>

glȁvudža {ē fem.} (lit. head of an animal) *sl* head <**Slav***1>

glȁvūrda {ē fem.} (lit. large head of a human or animal) *col* head <**Slav***1>

glȁvuša {ē fem.} (lit. head of an animal) *col* head <**Slav***1>

glazbènjāk {benjáka masc.} Cro *sl* music shool <**Slav***1>

glȅ {excl.} *col* used to attract attention in direct informal communication, look, watch <**Slav**>

glèdāljka {ē fem.; Dat glèdāljki} *sl* eye (sight organ) <**Slav**✤*1>

glȅdati {ām, ajū imperf. intr.} (lit. look) *col* try, strive for: *Gledam da uzmem godišnji u julu. I am trying to get my vacation in July.* <**Slav***1>
• **glȅdati bélo** {VP} (lit. look white) SerE *sl-fea* stare, glare at in surprise, gawk
• **glȅdati bijèlo** {VP} (lit. look white) *sl-fea* stare, glare at in surprise, gawk
• **glȅdati u nȕlu** {VP} (lit. look at a zero) *sl-fea* ***Fac*** be blind
• **kò da glȅdām** {PP} (lit. as if I have been watching it) *col* I can tell that

glédīti {dīm, dē imperf.} [std. = gledati] *dia-col* look, watch, scope out <**Slav**✍>

glȅnār {a masc.} *col* coal <**NE***1>

glènder {a (acc. = gen.) masc.} *sl-fea* inhabitant of the countryside, hick, bumpkin <**NE***1>

glênđer {a (acc. = gen.) masc.} *sl-fea* inhabitant of the countryside, hick, bumpkin <**NE***1>

glîb {a +ov (ext. pl) masc.; Nom Pl glíbovi} *col* mud <**Slav**>

Glinènjāk {nenjáka masc.} *sl-crime* name of a juvenile detention center in Glina, Croatia <**SlavO***1> ☞ **Glinica**

Glȉnica {ē fem.} *sl-crime* name of a juvenile detention center in Glina, Croatia <**SlavO***1> ☞ **Glinenjak**

glȉpši {ija masc.; perm} **a.** *sl* mirror <**Ger**✍> **b.** *sl-fea* slender person <**Ger**✍*1>

glísta {ē fem.} (lit. worm) **1** *sl-fea* slender person <**Slav***1> **2** *sl-sex* penis <**Slav***1>
• **bijèsnē glíste** {NP} (lit. rabid worms) *col* exaggerated requests, whims

glístiti {tīm, tē imperf. intr.} *sl* recover, get better <**Slav***1>

glístiti se {tīm, tē imperf. intr.} *sl-fea* hesitate, stall <**Slav**✤*1>

glȉtā {part.} *col* used as a strong affirmative response, of course, yeah, you bet: *A: Hoćemo li na utakmicu? B: Glita! A: Are we going to the ball game? B: You bet!*

glô {glȍa masc.} *sl-drink* drink (alcohol) <**Slav**>

glô-glô {glȍa masc.} *sl-drink* alcoholic beverage <**Slav***1>

glòba {ē fem.} (lit. fine, ticket, e.g., speeding ticket) *sl* ***Fac*** cab, taxi <**Slav***1>

glòbār {globára (acc. = gen.) masc.; Voc glȍbāru} *sl* person who abuses others (usu. financially), parasite, leech <**Slav**✤*1>

glóbus {a masc.} (lit. globe) **a.** *sl-fea* bald head <**Lat***1> **b.** *sl-fea* skinhead (a person with shaved head) <**Lat***2>

glȍckati {ām, ajū perf. intr.} (lit. bite) *sl-sex* ***Fac-Obs*** engage in fellatio <**Slav**✍*1>

glȍcnuti {nēm, nū perf.} (lit. bite) *sl-sex* ***Fac-Obs*** engage in fellatio <**Slav**✍*1>

glȏd {a +ov (ext. pl) masc.; Nom Pl glódovi} *sl-sex* ***Obs*** sexual intercourse <**Slav**✤*1>

glòdalica {ē fem.} (lit. gnawer) *sl* female <**Slav**✤*1>

glòdāljka {ē fem.; Dat glòdāljki} (lit. gnawer) *sl* teeth <**Slav***1>

glȍdār {a (acc. = gen.) masc.} (lit. rodent) **1a.** *sl-crime* policeman, cop <**Slav***1> **b.** *sl-crime* police investigator <**Slav***2> **c.** *sl-crime* undercover agent <**Slav***2> **2** *sl-fea* loafer, idler <**Slav***1>

glȍdārka {ē fem.} (lit. rodent) **a.** *sl-sex* ***Fac*** prostitute, hooker <**Slav***1> **b.i.** *sl* female who financially abuses males **ii.** *sl-fea* unattractive female, dog

glòdati {ođēm, ođū imperf.} (lit. gnaw) *sl-sex* ***Obs*** engage in sexual intercourse with (of a male) <**Slav***1>
• **glòdati dàsku** {VP} (lit. bite a plank) *sl-sex* ***Fac*** engage in cunnilingus
• **glòdati kȏst** {VP} (lit. bite a bone) *sl-sex* ***Fac*** engage in fellatio

glȍdavac {vca (acc. = gen.) masc.} (lit. rodent) *sl* tooth <**Slav***1>

glȍđati {đēm, đū imperf.} (lit. bite) *sl-sex* ***Fac-Obs*** engage in fellatio <Slav✍[*1]>

glògotānje {a neut.} /glogòtānje/ *col* gurgle (creek, etc.) <Slav>

glȍmot {a masc.} *col* noise <Slav>

glomòtati {ām, ajū imperf.} *col* make noise <Slav>

glòmtati {ām, ajū imperf.} *col* make noise <Slav>

glȏnđa {ē fem.} **a.** *sl-sex* ***Obs*** vagina, cunt **b.** *sl* ***Obs*** female, cunt

GLP [gê-ȅl-pê] {masc.} (abbreviation of gala ludi provod: super crazy fun) *sl* party (social gathering) <Abb>

glùbara {ē fem.} **a.** *sl-crime* prison **b.** *sl-crime* name of a juvenile detention center in Lepoglava, Croatia

gluháriti {glùhārīm, rē imperf. intr.} *sl* spend one's time in useless activities, fool around, mess around <Slav[*1]>

glûho *See the following*

• **glûho bílo** {AdvP} (lit. let it be deaf) **BosM** *col* used to refer to an undesired event: *Da nas, gluho bilo, ne napadnu. God save us from their attack.*

glúma {ē fem.} (lit. acting) **1** *sl* laughter <Slav[*1]> **2** *sl* funeral <Slav[*1]>

glúmac {mca (acc. = gen.) masc.} (lit. actor) *sl-crime* criminal who is good at pretending to be innocent <Slav[*1]>

glumàtati {ām, ajū imperf.} *col* act poorly (e.g. in a movie, theater play) <Slav[*1]>

glúmiti {mīm, mē imperf.} (lit. act) **a.** *col* pretend <Slav[*1]> **b.** *col* lie <Slav[*2]> **c.** *sl-fea* be conceited, be stuck-up <Slav[*3]> **d.** *sl-fea* boast, brag: *glumiti o velikoj plati boast about a high income* <Slav[*4]>

• **glúmiti pȁvijāna** {VP} (lit. play the baboon) *sl-fea* ***Fac*** pretend to be insane

• **glúmiti Tàrzana** {VP} (lit. play the Tarzan) *sl-fea* ***Fac*** be conceited, be stuck-up

glûp *See the following*

• **glûp kao ćùskija** {AdjP} (lit. as stupid as a crowbar) *col* ***Der*** extremely stupid, dumb as a brick

• **glûp kao gùzica** {AdjP} (lit. as stupid as somebody's ass) *col* ***Der-Obs*** extremely stupid, dumb as a brick

• **glûp kao kȕrac** {AdjP} (lit. as stupid as a prick) *sl-fea* ***Der*** extremely stupid, dumb as a brick

• **glûp ko ćùskija** {AdjP} (lit. as stupid as a bar) *col* ***Der*** extremely stupid, dumb as a brick

• **glûp ko dȕpe** {AdjP} (lit. as stupid as somebody's ass) *col* ***Der*** extremely stupid, dumb as a brick

• **glûp ko klȁda** {AdjP} (lit. as stupid as a log) *col* ***Der*** extremely stupid, dumb as a brick

• **glûp ko kȍnj** {AdjP} (lit. as stupid as a horse) *col* ***Der*** extremely stupid, dumb as a brick

• **glûp ko kȕrac** {AdjP} (lit. as stupid as a prick) *col* ***Der*** extremely stupid, dumb as a brick

• **glûp ko nôć** {AdjP} (lit. as stupid as the night) *col* ***Der*** extremely stupid, dumb as a brick

• **glûp ko nòga** {AdjP} (lit. as stupid as a leg) *sl-fea* ***Der*** extremely stupid, dumb as a brick

• **glûp ko tȍp** {AdjP} (lit. as stupid as a cannon) *col* ***Der*** extremely stupid, dumb as a brick

• **Glûp si ko môj kȕrac!** {S} (lit. You are as stupid as my prick!) *col* ***Off*** used as a moderate curse, You're dumb as a brick!

glùpača {ē fem.} *col* stupid or mentally deficient female <Slav>

glùpāk {glupáka (acc. = gen.) masc.} *col* stupid or mentally deficient male <Slav>

glùpan {a (acc. = gen.) masc.} *col* stupid or mentally deficient male <Slav>

glupànder {a (acc. = gen.) masc.} *sl-fea* stupid or mentally deficient person <Slav✍>

glupàntrop {a (acc. = gen.) masc.} *sl-fea* stupid or mentally deficient person <Slav✍>

glȕpav {a, o adj.} **a.** *col* stupid or mentally deficient <Slav> **b.** *col* meaningless: *glupav predlog meaningless proposal* <Slav[*1]>

glùpērda {ē fem.} *col* stupid or mentally deficient person <Slav✍>

glupírānje {a neut.} *col* making a fool of oneself <Slav⁘>

glupírati se {glùpīrām, ajū imperf. intr.} *col* make a fool of oneself <Slav>

glùpsan {a (acc. = gen.) masc.} *sl-fea* stupid or mentally deficient person <Slav✍>

glùpson {a (acc. = gen.) masc.} *sl-fea* stupid or mentally deficient person <Slav✍>

glùpuša {ē fem.} *sl-fea* mentally deficient female <Slav✍>

glûv *See the following*

• **glûv tâjm in d mûn** {NP} *sl-fea* spending one's time in useless activities, fooling around, messing around

glúvac {vca (acc. = gen.) masc.} **a.** *sl-fea* loafer, idler <Slav[*1]> **b.i.** *sl-fea* unemployed person: *Bio sam tri meseca gluvac, ali sam prošle sedmice našao posao. I was unemployed for three months, but last week I found a job.* <Slav[*2]> **ii.** *sl-fea* worthless or despicable person, bum <Slav[*2]>

glùvāć {gluváća (acc. = gen.) masc.} *sl-fea* deaf person <Slav*1>

glùvara {ē fem.} **a.** *sl-fea* deaf person <Slav*1> **b.** *sl-fea* deaf senior citizen <Slav*2>

gluvárenje {a neut.} *col* spending one's time in useless activities, fooling around, messing around <Slav*1>

gluváriti {glùvārīm, rē imperf. intr.} *col* spend one's time in useless activities, fool around, mess around: *gluvariti na ulici fool around on the street* <Slav*1>

glûvka {ē fem.} *sl* spending one's time in useless activities, fooling around, messing around <Slav*1>

gljâjka {ē fem.; Dat gljâjki} *sl* shoe <Gyp⁘*1>

gljàka 1 {excl.} *sl* used to make somebody go away <Gyp⁘*1>

gljàka 2 {ē fem.; Dat gljàki} **a.** *sl* shoe <Gyp⁘*1> **b.** *sl* leg (human) <Gyp⁘*2>

gljànuti {nēm, nū perf.} *sl* run away, flee <Gyp⁘*1>

gljàra {ē fem.} *sl* shoe <Gyp⁘*1>

gljárak {rka masc.} *sl* shoe <Gyp⁘*1>

gljârka {ē fem.; Dat gljârki} **a.** *sl* shoe <Gyp⁘*1> **b.** *sl* leg (human) <Gyp⁘*2>

gljárnica {ē fem.} **a.** *sl* shoe <Gyp⁘*1> **b.** *sl* peasant shoe <Gyp⁘*2>

gljârnīk {a masc.} *sl* road <Gyp⁘*1>

gljàti {gljâm, gljàjū imperf.} **a.** *sl* walk <Gyp⁘*1> **b.** *sl* run away, flee <Gyp⁘*2>

gljàva *See the following*
- **stȅreo gljàva** {NP} (lit. stereo shoe) *sl-fea* high-quality shoe

gljàvati {ām, ajū imperf.} *sl* walk <Gyp⁘*1>

gljàvica {ē fem.} *sl* leg (human) <Gyp⁘*1>
- **stȅreo gljàvica** {NP} (lit. stereo little shoe) *sl-fea* high-quality shoe

gljȉvica {ē fem.} (lit. small mushroom) *sl* teenager <Slav*1>

gmâz {a +ov (ext. pl) (acc. = gen.) masc.; Nom Pl gmázovi} (lit. reptile) *sl-fea* ***Der*** ingratiator (male), brownnoser, ass kisser <Slav*1>

gmȉza {ē fem.} (lit. reptile) *sl-fea* ***Der*** ingratiator (male), brownnoser, ass kisser <Slav*1>

gmȉzavac {vca (acc. = gen.) masc.} (lit. reptile) *sl-fea* ***Der*** ingratiator (male), brownnoser, ass kisser <Slav*1>

gnâs {a +ov (ext. pl) masc.; Nom Pl gnásovi} *sl-drugs* hashish, hash

gnézdo {a neut.} (lit. nest) SerE *sl* apartment <Slav*1>

gnójac {jca masc.} *sl-sex* gonorrhea, the clap <Slav*1>

gnȍjīvo *See the following*
- **ùmjetnō gnȍjīvo** {NP} (lit. artificial fertilizer) Cro *sl-drugs* drug addict, junkie

gnjàti {ām, ajū imperf.} *sl* run away, flee

gnjàvātor {a (acc. = gen.) masc.} *sl-fea* boring person, bore <Slav⁘*1>

gnjaváža {ē fem.} *sl* boring or unpleasant matter, hassle <Slav⁘>

gnjávež {a masc.} **a.** *sl* boredom <Slav⁘> **b.** *sl* inconvenience, boring or unpleasant matter: *gnjavež s popravkom kola inconvenience of one's car in the shop* <Slav⁘*1> **c.** *sl-fea* boring person, bore <Slav⁘*2>

gnjáviti {gnjâvīm, vē imperf.} **a.** *sl* bother, disturb <Slav> **b.** *sl* do something very slowly <Slav*1> **c.** *sl* hesitate, stall <Slav*2>

gnjéčiti {gnjêčīm, čē imperf.} (lit. squeeze) **a.** *sl* beat up <Slav*1> **b.** *sl-sex* engage in sexual intercourse with (of a male) <Slav*2>

gnjȉda {ē fem.} (lit. nit) **a.** *sl-fea* ***Der*** worthless or despicable person, bum <Slav*1> **b.** *sl-fea* ***Der*** ingratiator (male), brownnoser, ass kisser <Slav*2>

gnjúrac {rca (acc. = gen.) masc.} (lit. diver) *sl-sex* ***Fac*** breaking wind, farting <Slav*1>

gnjȕriti {rīm, rē imperf.} (lit. dive) *sl* work <Slav*1>

gô {gola masc.} *sl-sports* goal (in soccer, water polo, etc.) <Eng☞>
- **gô ko pìštōlj** {AdjP} (lit. naked like a gun) *col* very poor

gòblēn *See the following*
- **ko gòblēn** {PP} (lit. like a Gobelin tapestry) *sl-fea* boring

gȍdina *See the following*
- **glâdnā gȍdina** {NP} (lit. a hungry year) **a.** *col* long period of time **b.** *sl-sex* ***Fac*** longer period without sexual intercourse
- **sûšnā gȍdina** {NP} (lit. dry year) *sl-fea* a year when one cannot go to the seashore for a vacation

gȍdīšće {a neut.} [std. = godina] Med *dia* year <Slav☞>

gòdišnjāk 1 {a masc.} /godȉšnjāk/ *sl* vacation <Slav*1>

gòdišnjāk[2] {a (acc. = gen.) masc.} /godìšnjāk /godišnjāka (acc. = gen.) masc./ *sl-mil* soldier who serves only one year <Slav*1>

gòdišnjī {ēg masc.} *col* vacation <Slav✎>

godrìna {ē fem.} *sl* satisfaction <Slav✎>

gôj {a (acc. = gen.) +ev (ext. pl) masc.; Nom Pl gójevi} *sl* Gentile, Goy <Heb>

gója {ē masc.} *sl* Gentile, Goy <Heb>

gòjiti {jīm, jē imperf.} *dia-col* raise, bring up <Slav*1>

gòjzerica {ē fem.} **a.** *col* hard-soled shoe <Ger> **b.** *sl-auto* Renault 4 (make of car) <Ger*1>

gȍlā {ē fem. (adj. decl.)} (lit. naked) *col* nudist beach <Slav*1>

Gȍlā gôvna! {NP} (lit. naked shit) *col* ***Der*** used to express dissatisfaction, Shit! ☞ **govno**

gòlāć {goláća masc.} (lit. the naked one) **a.** *col* nudist <Slav*1> **b.** *sl-sstu* school student

golánfer {a (acc. = gen.) masc.} **a.** *sl-fea* ***Der*** worthless or despicable person <NE*1> **b.** *sl-sex* male homosexual, gay <NE*2>

gôld {a +ov (ext. pl) masc.; Nom Pl góldovi} (lit. gold) *sl* money <Ger>

gȍldāć {a masc.} *sl-fea* something or someone excellent: *Taj frajer je goldać, treba svakako da ga zaposliš. That guy is excellent, you should definitely hire him.* <Ger*1>

gòlēmča {ē masc.} **a.** *col* gentleman <Slav*1> **b.** *col* boss <Slav*2>

gòlēmša {ē masc.} **a.** *col* gentleman <Slav*1> **b.** *col* boss <Slav*2>

gòlgolj {a masc.} *col* gurgle (creek, etc.) <Slav>

golgòljiti {ljīm, ljē perf.} *col* gurgle (creek, etc.) <Slav>

gòlgot {a masc.} *col* gurgle (creek, etc.) <Slav>

golgòtati {gòlgoćēm, ćū imperf.} *col* gurgle (creek, etc.) <Slav>

golijána {ē fem.} *sl* nudist beach <Slav✎>

gȍlō {ōg neut.} (lit. naked) *sl* beans (served without meat) <Slav*1>

• **dȕdlo gòlo** {NP} (lit. suck naked) *sl-sex* ***Fac*** male homosexual

• **dùplō gòlo** {AdjP} (lit. double naked) *col* double empty domino

gològuz {a (acc. = gen.) masc.} (lit. the bare-assed one) *sl-fea* poor male <Slav>

gològuz {a, o adj.} (lit. bare-assed) **a.** *col* naked <Slav*1> **b.** *col* poor <Slav*2>

Gològuzā {ē fem.} (lit. the bare-assed one) *dia* ***Fac*** place name in Srem, Serbia <Slav*1>

gològuza {ē fem.} (lit. the bare-assed one) **1** *dia* weed (the plant) <Slav*1> **2** *dia* poor female <Slav*1>

gològuzas {a, o adj.} (lit. bare-assed) *dia* naked <Slav*1>

gològuzast {a, o adj.} (lit. bare-assed) *dia* naked <Slav*1>

gologùzica {ē fem. & masc.} (lit. naked ass) *dia* poorly dressed person <Slav*1>

gologùzīle {a masc.} (lit. the one with naked ass) *dia* naked male <Slav>

gȍlokūr {a masc.} /golòkūr/ (lit. the one with the naked prick) *dia* poor male <Slav*1>

gȍlokūr {a, o adj.} /golòkūr/ (lit. with the naked prick) **a.** *dia* naked (of a male) <Slav*1> **b.i.** *dia* poor (of a male) <Slav*2> **ii.** *dia* weary (of a male) <Slav*2>

golokùrīle {a (acc. = gen.) masc.} (lit. the one with the naked prick) *dia* poor male <Slav*1>

golòmud {a, o adj.} (lit. with naked balls) **a.** *dia* naked (of a male) <Slav*1> **b.** *dia* poor (of a male) <Slav*2>

golopíca {ē fem.} (lit. the one with naked cunt) **a.** *sl-sex* ***Obs*** provocatively dressed female <Slav*1> **b.** *sl-fea* ***Obs*** evil female, bitch <Slav*2>

golopìčast {a, o adj.} /golòpičast/ (lit. with naked cunt) *sl-fea* naked (of a female) <Slav*1>

golopȉčka {ē fem.; Dat gȍlopički} /golòpička/ (lit. naked cunt) *sl-sex* ***Obs*** provocatively dressed female <Slav*1>

golopízda {ē fem.} (lit. naked cunt) **a.** *sl-sex* ***Obs*** provocatively dressed female <Slav*1> **b.** *sl-fea* ***Obs*** evil female, bitch <Slav*2>

golopìzdalo {a neut.} (lit. the one with naked cunt) **a.** *sl-sex* ***Obs*** poor female <Slav*1> **b.** *sl-fea* ***Obs*** homeless person, bum <Slav*2>

golopìzduša {ē fem.} (lit. the one with naked cunt) *sl-fea* poor female <Slav⁘*1>

golòtinja {ē fem.} *col* nakedness <Slav>

golòtrbas {sta, sto adj.} (lit. with naked belly) *dia* naked <Slav*1>

gȍlūb {a (acc. = gen.) masc.} (lit. pigeon) **1a.** *sl* male, guy <Slav*1> **b.** *sl* lover (male) <Slav*2> **2** *sl* breaking wind, farting <Slav*1> **3** *sl-polit* moderate politician, dove <Slav*1>

golùbārnīk {a masc.} (lit. pigeon coop) **1** *sl* mouth <Slav*1> **2** *sl* nicely furnished room <Slav*1> **3** *sl* studio (painter's etc.) <Slav*1> **4** *sl* weekend house <Slav*1>

golùbica {ē fem.} (lit. dove) *sl* thousand dinars; a thousand-dinar bill, a grand <Slav*1>

golùbinjāk {a masc.} (lit. pigeon coop) *sl* one-room attic apartment <Slav*1>

gȍlūbovo {a neut.} *sl-arch* wheat <Slav*1>

gȍljāhan {hna, hno adj.} [std. = go(l)] BosM *col* naked <Slav✍>

Gòljāk {Goljáka masc.} (lit. the naked one) *sl-crime* name for Goli island prison (Croatia, where the former communist regime detained its political enemies) <SlavO✤>

gôlje {a neut.} *sl* cold temperature <Slav>

gòmila {ē fem.} (lit. pile) *sl* crowd, mob <Slav*1>

gòndola {ē fem.} /gôndola/ **a.** *sl* shoe <Ita*1> **b.** *sl* old shoe <Ita*2>

gôndža {ē fem.} *sl-sex* ***Obs*** vagina, cunt

gonétati {gònētām, gonétajū imperf.} *col* tell fortunes <Slav>

gȍng {a +ov (ext. pl) masc.; Nom Pl gòngovi} *sl-drugs* opium pipe <Malay>

Gòni mi se ù kurac! {S} (lit. Go to my prick!) *col* ***Off*** used in angry dismissal, Fuck off! ☞ **goniti**

Gòni se! {S} *col* ***Off*** used in angry dismissal, Beat it! ☞ **goniti**

Gòni se u pízdu màterinu! {S} (lit. Go to your mother's cunt!) *col* ***Off*** used in angry dismissal, Fuck off! ☞ **goniti**

Gòni se u trî pízde màterine! {S} (lit. Go to three mother's cunts!) *col* ***Off*** used in angry dismissal, Fuck off! ☞ **goniti**

gònīč *See the following*

- **gònīč ȉrvāsā** {NP} (lit. reindeer farmer) *sl-fea* ***Fac*** senile person

gòniti {gȍnīm, gȍnē perf.} **a.** *col-dia* drive (e.g. animals to pasture) <Slav*1> **b.** *col-dia* drive (a vehicle) <Slav*2>

- **Gòni mi se ù kurac!** {S} (lit. Go to my prick!) *col* ***Off*** used in angry dismissal, Fuck off!
- **Gòni se!** {S} *col* ***Off*** used in angry dismissal, Beat it!
- **Gòni se u pízdu màterinu!** {S} (lit. Go to your mother's cunt!) *col* ***Off*** used in angry dismissal, Fuck off!
- **Gòni se u trî pízde màterine!** {S} (lit. Go to three mother's cunts!) *col* ***Off*** used in angry dismissal, Fuck off!
- **Gònite se u trî màterine** [NOUN:VOC]! {LSF} (lit. Go to your three mother's *cunts* you [NOUN:NOM]!) *col* ***Off*** used in angry dismissal of a group of people: *Gònite se u trî màterine pederi! Fuck you faggots!*

gonoréja {ē fem.} (lit. gonorrhea) *sl-fea* unattractive female <Gre*1>

gȍre {adv.} (lit. above) *col* abroad, overseas <Slav*1>

gòrēnje {a neut.} (lit. burning) *sl* laughter <Slav*1>

gorîkā {adv.} [std. = gore] *dia* above, upstairs: *Šime je gorika na tavanu. Šime is upstairs in the attic.* <Slav✍>

gorȉla {ē fem.} /gorȉla/ (lit. gorilla) **a.** *col* lifeguard <Gre*1> **b.** *col* muscular male

gòripetlja {ē fem.} *sl-arch* pepper <Slav✤*1>

gȍrīvo *See the following*

- **pod gȍrīvom** {PP} (lit. under fuel) *sl-drink* drunk, tanked

gòrkīć {gorkíća masc.} *sl* bitter coffee <Slav*1>

gòrnjāk [1] {gornjáka (acc. = gen.) masc.} (lit. the upper one) *sl* husband <Slav✤>

gòrnjāk [2] {gornjáka masc.} (lit. the upper one) *col* jeans jacket <Slav✤>

gorògan {a (acc. = gen.) masc.} *sl-fea* big-boned male <Slav✍*1>

gòrštāk {gorštáka (acc. = gen.) masc.} (lit. highlander) *col* inhabitant of the countryside, hick, bumpkin <Slav✤*1>

gȍsn {excl.} *col* used to address a male in direct informal communication, mister, sir <Slav✍> ☞ **gospodine**

gȍsn {a (acc. = gen.) masc.} *col* used to address a male in direct informal communication, mister, sir <Slav✍> ☞ **gospodin**

góspa {ē fem.} *col* lady, woman <Slav*1>

- **mâlā góspa** {NP} (lit. little Virgin Mary) **1** *sl-sex* ***Fac*** virgin **2** Cro *sl-fea* female from Zagorje, Croatia
- **vȅlikā góspa** {NP} (lit. Assumption, 'Great Lady') **1** *sl-sex* virgin **2** Cro *sl-fea* female from Split, Croatia

gȍspođica {ē fem.} (lit. miss) *sl-sex* ***Fac*** male homosexual, gay <Slav*1>

gȍspoja [1] {excl.} [std. = gospođo] *dia-col* used to address a female politely in direct formal communication, ma'am <Slav✍>

gȍspoja [2] {ē fem.} [std. = gospođa] *dia-col* lady, woman <Slav✍>

gȍspojica {ē fem.} [std. = gospođica] *dia-col* missy <Slav✍>

gôst {gȍsta (acc. = gen.) masc.; N.Pl. gȍsti} (lit. guest) *sl-fea* ***Der*** informer, stoolie, snitch <Slav*1>

gòtiv màrdelj {NP} *sl-fea* fair ☞ **mardelj**

gotívac {vca (acc. = gen.) masc.} **1a.** *sl-fea* handsome male, hunk <Ger❖*1> **b.** *sl-fea* dandy, fop **c.** *sl-fea* rich male: *gotivac težak petsto hiljada marona rich male with five hundred thousand German marks* **2a.** *sl* intimate friend **b.i.** *sl-thie* pickpocket: *uhapšen gotivac arrested pickpocket* **ii.** *sl-fea* good and loved male

gȍtīvan {vna, vno adj.} **a.** *sl* ***App*** excellent, awesome <Ger❖*1> **b.i.** *sl* ***App*** affluent **ii.** *sl* ***App*** fast

gotȉvica {ē fem.} *sl-drink* brandy <Ger❖*1>

gotíviti {gòtīvīm, vē imperf.} **1a.** *sl* seduce <Ger❖*1> **b.** *sl* treat well **2a.** *sl* appreciate, enjoy, like: *gotiviti dobru mjuzu appreciate good music* **b.** *sl* like **3** *sl* persuade, convince **4** *sl-thie* steal from, rip off **5** *sl* have, possess

• **gotíviti šarȅnicu** {VP} (lit. pet a multi-colored stuff) *sl* write a letter to: *gotiviti šarenicu devojci write a letter to a girlfriend*

gȍtīvno {adv.} *sl* ***App*** excellent, awesome <Ger❖*1>

gȍtivnō ȍko {NP} (lit. nice eye) *sl* clock, watch ☞ **oko**

gotȉvnjāk {tivnjáka (acc. = gen.) masc.} **a.** *sl-fea* dandy, fop <Ger❖*1> **b.** *sl-fea* handsome male, hunk

gotòviti {vīm, vē imperf.} *col* be fond of, like: *gotoviti pivo like beer* <Slav*1>

gȍtvan {vna, vno adj.} *sl* ***App*** excellent, awesome <Ger❖✍*1>

govánce {eta neut.} (lit. small piece of shit) *sl-sex* ***Obs*** small excrement <Slav>

gòvedo {a neut.} (lit. head of cattle) **1** *sl-fea* ***Der*** worthless or despicable person <Slav*1> **2** *sl-sex* ***Der*** male looking for a loose woman, guy on the make <Slav*1>

gòveđā nòga {NP} (lit. beef leg) *sl-sex* ***Fac*** penis ☞ **noga**

gôvna {gȍvāna neut. pl.} (lit. shit) *sl* ***Obs*** phone <Slav*1>

Gôvna i kȕčine! {S} (lit. shit and tow) *sl* ***Obs*** used to express dissatisfaction, Shit! ☞ **govno**

gȍvnāć [1] {a (acc. = gen.) masc.} (lit. shitter) *sl-fea* ***Der-Obs*** worthless or despicable person, shithead <Slav❖*1>

gȍvnāć [2] {a masc.} (lit. crapper) *sl-sex* ***Obs*** bathroom, crapper <Slav❖*1>

gȍvnād {i fem.} (lit. shit) *sl-fea* worthless or despicable person <Slav*1>

govnàdija {ē fem.} (lit. shitters) *sl-fea* worthless or despicable persons, scum <Slav❖*1>

gȍvnānje {a masc.} (lit. shitting) *sl-fea* prolonged and meaningless talk, diarrhea of the mouth <Slav❖*1>

gȍvnār {a (acc. = gen.) masc.} /gòvnār/ (lit. shitter) **a.** *sl-fea* ***Der-Obs*** worthless or despicable person, scum, shithead: *S tim govnarom neću da imam posla. I don't want to mess with that scum.* <Slav*1> **b.i.** *sl-fea* ***Der-Obs*** parent <Slav*2> **ii.** *sl-fea* ***Der-Obs*** child, kid <Slav*2>

• **Gȍvnaru jèdan!** {S} (lit. You shitter!) *col* ***Off*** used as a moderate curse, You shithead!

gòvnara {ē fem.} (lit. shitter) **1** *sl-sex* ***Obs*** buttocks, butt <Slav*1> **2** *sl-sex* ***Obs*** bathroom, crapper <Slav*1> **3** *sl* ***Obs*** mouth <Slav*1> **4** *sl-drink* ***Obs-Der*** low-quality brandy <Slav*1>

govnàrčina {ē fem.} (lit. big shit) *sl-fea* ***Der-Obs*** worthless or despicable person <Slav❖*1>

govnàrija {excl.} (lit. Shit) *sl* used to express extreme dissatisfaction <Slav❖*1>

govnàrija {ē fem.} **a.** *sl-sex* ***Obs*** excrement, shit <Slav❖> **b.i.** *sl* ***Obs*** worthless or despicable persons <Slav❖*1> **ii.** *sl* ***Obs*** difficult situation, deep shit <Slav❖*1>

gòvnārka {ē fem.; Dat gòvnārki} (lit. shitter) *sl-fea* ***Der-Obs*** worthless or despicable female <Slav❖*1>

gòvnati {ām, ajū imperf.} (lit. shit) *sl-fea* talk persistently and meaninglessly, bullshit <Slav❖*1>

gȍvnav {a, o adj.} *sl-sex* ***Der-Obs*** defecated on, shitty <Slav❖*1>

gȍvnen {a, o adj.} **a.** *sl-sex* ***Der-Obs*** defecated on, shitty <Slav❖> **b.** *sl-fea* ***Der-Obs*** worthless, worth shit <Slav❖*1>

gòvniti {nīm, nē perf.} *sl-sex* ***Obs*** defecate, shit <Slav❖>

góvno [1] {excl.} *sl-sex* ***Obs*** used to express extreme dissatisfaction <Slav>

góvno [2] {a neut.} /góvno /eta neut./ **a.** *sl-sex* ***Obs*** excrement, shit <Slav> **b.** *sl-fea* ***Obs*** coward, chicken <Slav*1> **c.** *sl-fea* worthless or despicable person, shithead <Slav*2>

• **Gȍlā gôvna!** {NP} (lit. naked shit) *col* ***Der*** used to express dissatisfaction, Shit!

• **Gôvna i kȕčine!** {S} (lit. shit and tow) *sl* ***Obs*** used to express dissatisfaction, Shit!

• **Góvno jèdno!** {S} (lit. You piece of shit!) *col* ***Off*** used as a moderate curse, You piece of shit!

• **Góvno mi se zalèdilo!** {S} (lit. My shit has frozen!) *sl-fea* ***Fac-Obs*** used to refer to a dangerous situation in the past, I was scared shitless!

• **Góvno mu krénulo niz bùtinu!** {S} (lit. My shit went down the leg of my trousers!) *sl-fea* ***Fac*** used to refer to a dangerous situation in the past, He was scared shitless.

• **góvno od čovèka** {NP} (lit. a shit of a man) SerE *sl-fea* ***Off*** despicable or mean person, shithead

• **góvno od čȍvjeka** {NP} (lit. a shit of a man) *sl-fea* ***Off*** despicable or mean person, shithead

• **Góvno[PRON:DAT] se formíralo!** {LSF} (lit. [PPRON] shit has formed itself) *sl-fea* ***Fac*** used to refer to a dangerous situation in the past, [PRON:NOM] is scared shitless!: *Govno mu se formiralo! He was scared shitless!*

• **ko pìjanačkō góvno** {PP} (lit. like a drunk's shit) *sl-fea* ***Der-Obs*** of unpleasant odor, stinking

govnòćera {ē fem. & masc.} (lit. shit-driver) **a.** *dia* ***Der-Obs*** worthless or despicable person, shithead <Slav❖[*1]> **b.** *dia* ***Der-Obs*** poor person <Slav❖[*2]>

govnoglávac {vca (acc. = gen.) masc.} (lit. shithead) *sl-fea* ***Der-Obs*** worthless or despicable person, shithead <Slav❖[*1]>

govnogrízac {sca (acc. = gen.) masc.} (lit. shit-biter) *sl-fea* worthless or despicable person, shithead <Slav❖[*1]>

gȍvnojēd {a (acc. = gen.) masc.} (lit. shit-eater) **a.** *sl-fea* ***Der-Obs*** worthless or despicable person <Slav❖[*1]> **b.** *sl-fea* obese male <Slav❖[*2]>

gȍvnokljūn {a (acc. = gen.) masc.} (lit. shit pecker) *sl-fea* ***Der-Obs*** worthless or despicable person, shithead <Slav❖[*1]>

gȍvnonoša {ē masc.} /govnònoša/ (lit. shit carrier) *sl-fea* ***Der-Obs*** worthless or despicable person, shithead <Slav❖[*1]>

góvnonja {ē fem. & masc.} (lit. shitter) *sl-fea* ***Der-Obs*** worthless or despicable person, shithead <Slav❖[*1]>

gȍvnovālj {a (acc. = gen.) masc.} (lit. dung roller) **a.** *sl-fea* ***Obs*** scarab, dung beetle <Slav❖[*1]> **b.** *dia* ***Obs*** worthless or despicable person, shithead <Slav❖[*2]>

gôvnović {a (acc. = gen.) masc.} (lit. McShit) *sl-fea* ***Der-Fac-Obs*** worthless or despicable person, shithead <Slav❖[*1]>

gòvnulja {ē fem.} (lit. shitter) *sl-fea* ***Der-Obs*** evil female, bitch <Slav❖[*1]>

gòvnuša {ē fem.} (lit. shitter) *sl-fea* ***Der-Obs*** evil female, bitch <Slav❖[*1]>

gòvnjāk {govnjáka masc.} (lit. shitter) *sl-fea* ***Der-Obs*** worthless or despicable person, shithead <Slav❖[*1]>

gȍvo {a neut.} *sl-drugs* hashish, hash <Slav❖[*1]>

govòriti *See the following*

• **govòriti mòrskī** {VP} (lit. speak a seashore language) *sl-sex* ***Fac*** strip off a girl's panties

• **govòriti tȅčno** {VP} (lit. speak fluently) *sl-fea* ***Fac*** spit while talking

gòzba *See the following*

• **gòzba zvȅrī** {NP} (lit. the feast of the beasts) *sl-sstu* ***Fac*** school board meeting

gȓ {excl.} *col* the sound made by an angry dog, grr <Slav>

grȁba {ē fem.} *sl-sex* ***Obs*** vagina, cunt <Ger[*1]>

• **mòntēr grâbā**{NP} (lit. cunt assembler) *sl-sex* ***Fac-Obs*** gynecologist's dispensary

gràbljati {ām, ajū biasp.} (lit. rake) *sl-crime* steal, swipe <Slav[*1]>

grȁblje {a fem. pl.} (lit. rake) *sl* ***Fac*** comb <Slav[*1]>

gràbsti {bēm, bū perf. irreg.} *sl-arch* wrest from <Slav[*1]>

gràbulja {ē fem.} (lit. rake) **a.** *sl* hand <Slav[*1]> **b.** *sl* arm <Slav[*2]>

grabùljati {ām, ajū imperf.} (lit. rake) *sl* search, look for <Slav[*1]>

gràdele {grȁdēlā fem. pl.} Med *col-dia* barbecue, grill <Ita>

Gradijáner {a masc.} *sl-crime* name of a prison in Stara Gradiška, Croatia <SlavO✍>

grádnja *See the following*

• **dìvljā grádnja** {NP} (lit. wild building) *col* building erected without the proper paperwork

gràdskā fàca {NP} (lit. urban face) *sl-fea* male who is popular in the town ☞ **faca**

gràdskō mljekárstvo {NP} (lit. city's dairy company) *sl-sex* ***Fac*** large breasts ☞ **mljekarstvo**

grádža {ē masc.} *sl* turntable <Gre✍>

građevínac {nca (acc. = gen.) masc.} **1** *sl-stu* civil engineering student <Slav> **2a.** *col* construction worker <Slav> **b.** *sl-fea* elderly male <Slav[*1]>

grȁfičār {a (acc. = gen.) masc.} **a.** *sl-fea* inhabitant of the countryside, hick, bumpkin <Gre[*1]> **b.** *sl-fea* naive male <Gre[*2]>

grafijáner {a (acc. = gen.) masc.} *sl-stu* student from a blue-collar family <Gre✍[*1]>

gr̀àfikos {a (acc. = gen.) masc.} **a.** *sl-fea* inhabitant of the countryside, hick, bumpkin <**Gre**☞[*1]> **b.** *sl-fea* lazy or shiftless person, bum, good for nothing <**Gre**☞[*2]>

grȁfos {a (acc. = gen.) masc.} **a.** *sl-fea* inhabitant of the countryside, hick, bumpkin <**Gre**☞> **b.i.** *sl-fea* naive male <**Gre**☞[*2]> **ii.** *sl-fea* student from a blue-collar family <**Gre**☞[*2]>

grȁh {a +ov (ext. pl) masc.; Nom Pl gràhovi} (lit. beans) *sl-mil* ammunition, ammo <**Slav**[*1]>

grȁha {ē fem.; Dat grȁhi} **1** *sl-sex* ***Obs*** vagina, cunt <**Slav**[*1]> **2** *sl-sports* name for Trešnjevka soccer field in Zagreb, Croatia <**Slav**[*1]>

grȁhlje {a fem. pl.} *sl* comb <**Slav**☞>

grája {ē fem.} *col* noise <**Slav**>

grâk {a +ov (ext. pl) masc.; Nom Pl grákovi} *col* caw (of a crow) <**Slav**>

grȁka {ē fem.; Dat grȁki} *col* caw (of a crow) <**Slav**>

grȁkāt {a masc.} *col* caw (of a crow) <**Slav**>

grákati {grâčēm, grâčū imperf.} *col* caw (of a crow) <**Slav**>

gráknuti {grâknēm, grâknū perf.} *col* caw (of a crow) <**Slav**>

gràktānje {a neut.} **a.** *col* cawing (of a crow) <**Slav**> **b.** *col* making noise <**Slav**[*1]>

gràktati {grȁkćem, grȁkću imperf.} **/**gràktati**/** **a.** *col* caw (of a crow) <**Slav**> **b.** *col* make noise <**Slav**[*1]>

grȁktav {a, o adj.} *col* cawing (of a crow) <**Slav**>

grȁmfić {a masc.} *sl* turntable <**Gre**☞>

grȁmofōn {a (acc. = gen.) masc.} (lit. phonograph) *sl-fea* ***Der*** boaster, braggart, blowhard <**Gre**[*1]>

grána {ē fem.} (lit. grana 'branch of a tree' X granica 'border') *sl* border (between countries) <**Slav**[*1]>

grànap {a masc.} *col* grocery store <**Abb**>

grȁndić {a masc.} *sl* large silver coin <**Fre**[*1]>

grándža {ē fem.} *sl* turntable <**Gre**☞>

grànīčārka {ē fem.; Dat grànīčārki} (lit. border guard) *sl-sex* ***Fac*** menstruating female <**Slav**[*1]>

grànit {ē fem.} (lit. granite) **a.** *sl-sex* ***Fac*** prostitute, hooker <**Lat**[*1]> **b.** *sl-sex* ***Fac*** loose woman <**Lat**[*2]>

gràpiška {ē fem.; Dat gràpiški} *sl* shoe <**Slav**☞[*1]>

gràpsiti {sīm, sē imperf.} *sl* take, get hold of, pick: *grapsiti jabuke pick some apples* <**Slav**☞[*1]>

gràpsti {gràbem, gràbu perf. irreg.} *sl-arch* wrest from <**Slav**[*1]>

grâs {a +ov (ext. pl) masc.; Nom Pl grásovi} **a.** *sl* grass (the plant) <**Eng**> **b.** *sl-drugs* marijuana, pot, grass <**Eng**[*1]>

gràstano {a neut.} *sl* clock, watch

grášak {ška masc.} (lit. green peas) *sl-mil* ammunition, ammo <**Slav**[*1]>

gràtati *See the following*

gràtati pízdu {VP} (lit. scratch one's cunt) *sl-fea* ***Obs*** lose time in useless activities, goof around

gȑba {ē fem.} (lit. hump) *sl-fea* senior citizen <**Slav**[*1]>

gȑbača {ē fem.} (lit. hump) *col* back (of a person) <**Slav**>

gȑbav {a, o adj.} (lit. hump-backed) **1a.** *col* faulty <**Slav**[*1]> **b.** *col* guilty: *grbav za krađu guilty of theft* <**Slav**[*2]> **2** *col* old <**Slav**[*1]>

gȑč {a +ev (ext. pl) masc.; Nom Pl gȑčevi} (lit. cramp) **1** *sl* fear <**Slav**[*1]> **2** *sl* joke: *grč o plavušama dumb blonde joke* <**Slav**[*1]> **3** *sl* love whisper <**Slav**[*1]>

gȑčiti se {čīm, čē imperf. intr.} (lit. contract oneself) **a.** *sl-fea* have a hard time, experience difficulties <**Slav**[*1]> **b.** *sl-fea* get scared, get frightened <**Slav**[*2]>

Gȑčkā {ē fem. (adj. decl.)} (lit. Greece) *sl-fea* ***Der-Fac*** coward, chicken <**SlavO**[*1]>

gȓd {gŕda, gŕdo adj.} *col* unattractive, ugly <**Slav**>
• **gȓd ko lópov** {AdjP} (lit. as ugly as a thief) *sl-fea* ***Der*** extremely unattractive, ugly as sin

gȓdan {dna, dno adj.} (lit. awesome) **a.** *col* unattractive, ugly <**Slav**[*1]> **b.** *col* poor <**Slav**[*2]>

gŕditi {gȓdīm, gȓdē imperf.} *col* castigate <**Slav**[*1]>

gȓdno {adv.} (lit. awesome) *col* very: *Grdno sam se prevario. I was very wrong.* <**Slav**[*1]>

grdòba {ē fem.} **a.** *col* unattractive person <**Slav**> **b.** *col* something unattractive <**Slav**[*1]>

grdòsija {ē fem.} *sl-fea* big-boned person <**Slav**>

gȑđa {ē fem. & masc.} *sl-fea* unattractive person <**Slav**>

gréba {ē fem.} (lit. scratching) **1** *sl* financial abuse <**Slav**[*1]> **2** *sl* female <**Slav**[*1]> **3** *sl* scratch-off lottery <**Slav**[*1]>

grèbāč {grebáča (acc. = gen.) masc.} (lit. scratcher) *sl* tomcat <**Slav**⁘[*1]>

grèbāljka {ē fem.} (lit. scratcher) *sl-sex* ***Fac*** prostitute, hooker <**Slav**[*1]>

grȅbān {a (acc. = gen.) masc.} (lit. scratcher) *sl* tomcat <Slav⁘*1>

grȅbānje {a neut.} (lit. scratching) *col* living at another's expense, leeching off somebody <Slav*1>

grȅbāroš {a (acc. = gen.) masc.} (lit. scratcher) **a.** *col* person who borrows frequently <Slav⁘*1> **b.** *col* person who abuses others (usu. financially), parasite, leech <Slav⁘*2>

grèbati {bēm, bū imperf.} (lit. scratch) **a.** *col* search, look for <Slav*1> **b.** *col* beat up <Slav*2> **c.** *sl-sex* engage in sexual intercourse with (of a male) <Slav*3>

grèbati se {bēm, bū imperf. intr.} (lit. scratch oneself) **a.** *col* abuse financially, rip off <Slav*1> **b.i.** *col* take cigarettes from the others, bum smokes <Slav*2> **ii.** *col* have one's check paid by others <Slav*2>

• **grèbati se o vòla** {VP} (lit. scratch at an ox) *sl-crime* pick pockets

grèbātor {a (acc. = gen.) masc.} (lit. scratcher) *col* male who abuses others (usu. financially), parasite, leech <Slav⁘*2>

• **grèbātori vjȅšaju žnábl** {VP} (lit. the scratchers are hanging their mouths) *sl* used to refer to the absence of the will to give a tip

grèbātorka {ē fem.; Dat grèbātorki} (lit. scratcher) *col* female who abuses others (usu. financially), parasite, leech <Slav⁘*2>

grebènār {benára (acc. = gen.) masc.} *dia-col* barber <Slav>

grèbulje {grèbūljā fem. pl.} *dia* rake (the tool) <Slav>

Grȅbza {ē fem.; perm} [std. = Zagreb] *sl* name for Zagreb, Croatia <Slav✍>

gréda {ē fem.} (lit. beam) **a.** *sl* problem, trouble: *U čemu je greda? What's the problem?* <Slav> **b.** *sl* thing, object <Slav>

• **U čèmu je gréda?** {S} (lit. In what is the beam?) *col-dia* used to ask for additional information, What's up?

Grȅgor {a masc.} (lit. Gregory) *sl-sex* ***Obs*** clitoris <GreO*1>

grȅjati *See the following*

• **grȅjati ćóše** {VP} (lit. heat a corner) SerE *sl-fea* ***Fac*** be a regular (e.g. in a bar)

grȅm {a +ov (ext. pl) masc.; Nom Pl grèmovi} *sl* phonograph <Gre✍>

Grenóbl {a masc.} (lit. Grenoble) *sl-sex* ***Fac*** shapely <FreO*1>

greòta {ē fem.} Ser *col* pity <Slav>

grèpsti *See the following*

• **grèpsti pízdu** {VP} (lit. scratch one's cunt) *sl-fea* ***Obs*** lose time in useless activities, goof around

grèsli {part.} *dia* used to express uncertainty <Slav>

gréti {grém, grédū imperf. intr.} *dia* walk <Slav>

gȑglati {ām, ajū imperf.} *col* gurgle (creek, etc.) <Slav>

gȑgljānje {a neut.} *col* gurgling (of a river, stomach, throat, etc.) <Slav>

gȑgljati {ām, ajū imperf.} *col* gurgle (creek, etc.) <Slav>

gȑgljātor {a (acc. = gen.) masc.} (lit. gurgler) *sl-sex* ***Fac*** male homosexual, gay <Slav*1>

gȑgolj {a masc.} *col* gurgle (creek, etc.) <Slav>

grgòljav {a, o adj.} *col* gurgling (of a river, stomach, throat, etc.) <Slav>

grgòljēnje {a neut.} *col* gurgle (creek, etc.) <Slav>

grgòljiti {ljīm, ljē perf.} *col* gurgle (creek, etc.) <Slav>

grgòljiv {a, o adj.} *col* gurgling (of a river, stomach, throat, etc.) <Slav>

gȑgor {a masc.} *col* gurgle (creek, etc.) <Slav>

gȑgoran {rna, rno adj.} *col* gurgling (of a river, stomach, throat, etc.) <Slav>

grgòrēnje {a neut.} *col* gurgle (creek, etc.) <Slav>

grgòriti {gȑgorīm, rē imperf.} *col* gurgle (creek, etc.) <Slav>

gȑgot {a masc.} *col* gurgle (creek, etc.) <Slav>

grgòtānje {a neut.} *col* gurgle (creek, etc.) <Slav>

grgòtati {ām, ajū imperf. intr.} //gȑgoćēm, gȑgoćū imperf. intr./ *col* gurgle (creek, etc.) <Slav>

gȑgūt {a masc.} *col* gurgle (creek, etc.) <Slav>

grgùtānje {a neut.} *col* gurgle (creek, etc.) <Slav>

grgùtati {gȑgućēm, gućū imperf.} *col* gurgle (creek, etc.) <Slav>

grgùtav {a, o adj.} *col* gurgling (of a river, stomach, throat, etc.) <Slav>

grgùtavo {adv.} *col* gurgling (of a river, stomach, throat, etc.) <Slav>

grȉckalica {ē fem.} *col* crunchy snack <Slav>

grȉckati *See the following*

grȉckati pìhtije {VP} (lit. snack on some pork in jelly) *sl-fea* ***Fac*** have fear ☞ **grickati**

• **grȉckati pìhtije** {VP} (lit. snack on some pork in jelly) *sl-fea* ***Fac*** have fear

gȑf {a +ov (ext. pl) masc.; Nom Pl gȑfovi} **a.** *sl* trick, joke: *grif s loptom ball trick* <Ger*1> **b.** *sl* humor <Ger*2>

gȑmzlice {zlīcā fem. pl.} *sl* used for indefinite reference, anything

grisînī {īja masc.} *col* pretzel stick <BN>

grîsti {grízēm, grízū imperf. irreg.} (lit. bite) **a.** *col* attack, strike: *gristi protivnika attack one's enemy* <Slav*1> **b.** *col* be dangerous: *On grize, skloni mu se s puta. He bites, get out of his way.* <Slav*2>

- **grîsti stàklo** {VP} (lit. bite glass) *sl-fea* ***Fac*** be frightened, get scared
- **grîsti ȕdicu** {VP} (lit. bite a fish-hook) *sl* ***Fac*** be cheated, be swindled
- **grîsti ȕši** {VP} (lit. bite one's ears) *sl* ***Fac*** joke with, make a fool of

gȑva {ē fem.} *col* hair on the head <Slav*1>

grîz {a +ov (ext. pl) masc.; Nom Pl gȑzovi} (lit. bite) *sl* escape, flee <Slav*1>

grížnja *See the following*

- **grížnja sávesti** {NP} (lit. bite of conscience) SerE *col* guilty conscience
- **grížnja sávjesti** {NP} (lit. bite of conscience) *col* guilty conscience

grjehòta {ē fem.} *col* pity <Slav✍>

grjȅška {ē fem.; Dat grjȅški} [std. = greška] *col* mistake, error <Slav✍>

gȓk {a, o adj.} *col* bitter, tart <Slav>

Gȑkljan {a (acc. = gen.) masc.} (lit. throat) *sl* Greek (person) <SlavO✍>

gȑlīć {grlíća masc.} *sl-drugs* bottle neck used to smoke hashish <Slav*1>

gȑlo {a neut.} (lit. throat) **1** *sl* crowd, mob <Slav*1> **2** *sl-sex* attractive female <Slav*1> **3** *sl-music* singer <Slav*1>

gȓm {a +ov (ext. pl) masc.; Nom Pl gȓmovi} *dia* oak tree <Slav*1>

gȑmālj {a (acc. = gen.) masc.} *col* ***Der*** big-boned male <Slav>

gȑmčār {grmčára masc.} *dia* mill <Slav>

gȑmeti {mīm, mē perf.} SerE *col* thunder <Slav>

gȑmljava {ē fem.} *col* thunder <Slav>

gȑmljavina {ē fem.} *col* thunder <Slav>

gȓmno {adv.} (lit. thundering) *col* extremely loud, thundering: *svirati grmno play music extremely loud* <Slav>

gȑne *See the following*

- **Kvȁšenō ti gȑnejèbēm!** (lit. I fuck your sour dough!) {S} *dia* ***Off*** used as a moderate curse, Fuck you!

grȍb {gròba (acc. = gen.) +ov (ext. pl) masc.; Nom Pl gròbovi} (lit. grave) **1a.** *sl-fea* senior citizen <Slav*1> **b.** *sl-sex* elderly client of a prostitute **2** *sl* old house **4** *sl-fea* unattractive person

- **djȅčjī grȍb** {NP} (lit. child's grave) *sl* ***Fac*** large shoe
- **Grȍb ti jèbēm neòpevān!** {S} (lit. I fuck your unhallowed grave!) *col* ***Off*** used as a strong curse, Fuck you!
- **Grȍb ti òtvoren pòjebēm!** {S} (lit. I fuck your open grave!) *col* ***Off*** used as a strong curse, Fuck you!
- **ko grȍb** {PP} (lit. like a grave) *sl-fea* ***Der*** unattractive, ugly

grȍbār {a (acc. = gen.) masc.} /gròbār grobára (acc. = gen.) masc./ (lit. undertaker) **1** *sl-sports* player or fan of Partizan (a soccer team from Belgrade, Serbia) <Slav*1> **2** *sl* county clerk <Slav*1>

- **kò da ga je grȍbār pùstiō na òdsustvo** {PP} (lit. like an undertaker gave him a leave of absence) *sl-fea* ***Fac-Der*** extremely unattractive, ugly as sin

grȍbāreva pjȅsma {NP} (lit. undertaker's song) *sl* ***Fac*** funeral ☞ pjesma

grȍbārka {ē fem.; Dat grȍbārki} (lit. female undertaker) *sl-fea* unattractive female <Slav*1>

grôblje {a neut.} (lit. cemetery) **1** *sl-fea* senior citizen <Slav*1> **2** *sl-fea* unattractive person <Slav*1>

- **ko grôblje** {PP} (lit. like a graveyard) *sl-fea* ***Der*** unattractive, ugly

grȍbnica *See the following*

- **ko pòrodičnā grȍbnica** {PP} (lit. like a family tomb) *sl-fea* ***Der-Fac*** extremely unattractive, ugly as sin
- **pòrodičnā grȍbnica** {NP} (lit. family tomb) *sl-fea* extremely unattractive person

grȍf {a (acc. = gen.) +ov (ext. pl) masc.; Nom Pl gròfovi} (lit. count) *sl-fea* boaster, braggart, blowhard <Ger*1>

grȍfe {excl.} (lit. count) *sl* ***Fam*** used to address a male in direct informal communication, buddy <Ger*1>

grògan {a (acc. = gen.) masc.} *sl-fea* very important or influential person, big shot <Slav✍*1>

grȍgī {adj.} /grògī/ **a.** *sl-fea* groggy: *grogi bokser groggy boxer* <Eng*1> **b.i.** *sl-fea* drunk <Eng*2> **ii.** *sl-fea* beaten up <Eng*2>

grȍhot {a masc.} *col* burst of laughter <Slav>

grȍhotan {tna, tno adj.} *col* bursting (with laughter) <**Slav**>

grôm [1] {grȍma +ov (ext. pl) masc.; Nom Pl gròmovi} /grȍm/ **a.** *col* thunder <**Slav**> **b.i.** *col* effective move: *pustiti grom da i trznuti drota make an effective move and trick a cop* **ii.** *col* strong brandy

grôm [2] {adj.} /grȍm/ (lit. thunder) **a.** *col* strong, powerful (person, car, etc.) <**Slav***1> **b.** *col* excellent: *grom kola excellent car* <**Slav***2>
- **kao grȍm** {PP} /kao grȍm/ (lit. like thunder) *col* ***App*** excellent, awesome
- **ko grôm** {PP} /ko grȍm/ (lit. like thunder) *col* ***App*** excellent, awesome

gròmak {mka, mko adj.} (lit. thundering) *col* extremely loud, thundering <**Slav***1>

gròman {mna, mno adj.} *col* extremely loud, thundering <**Slav**>

gròmisati se {išēm, išū imperf. intr.} *sl* boast, brag <**Slav***1>

grȍmor {a masc.} *col* noise <**Slav**>

gròmovina {ē fem.} *sl* electric power <**Slav***1>

grȍš {gròša +ev (ext. pl) masc.; Nom Pl gròševi} (lit. Groschen *Austrian money*) *col* petty cash, chump change, peanuts <**Ger***1>

gròši {gróšā masc. pl.} (lit. Groschen *Austrian currency unit*) *col* money <**Ger***1>

gróza {ē fem.} *col* horror, terror <**Slav**>

grózda {ē fem.} *sl-drink* grape brandy <**Slav**>

gròzdovača {ē fem.} *sl-drink* grape brandy <**Slav**>

grôzje *See the following*
- **pȉčkino grôzje** {NP} (lit. cunt's berries) *dia* ***Obs*** nothing at all, fucking nothing

grȍzomōran {rna, rno adj.} *col* horrible, terrible <**Slav**>

grozomòrina {ē fem.} *sl-fea* dangerous female <**Slav***1>

grȍzomōrnica {ē fem.} *sl-fea* evil female, bitch <**Slav** ✣*1>

gȓrr {excl.} *col* the sound made by an angry dog, grr <**Slav**>

grȕ {excl.} *col* the sound made by an explosion, bang <**Slav**>

grûb {a, o adj.} Med *dia* unattractive, ugly <**Slav***1>

grȕbe {eta masc.} *sl* troublemaker, rowdy, ruffian <**Slav**✍>

grȕber {a (acc. = gen.) masc.} /grúber/ *sl* troublemaker, rowdy, ruffian <**Slav**✍>

grûbo rečèno {AdjP} (lit. roughly spoken) *col* used to introduce a sensitive topic, to put it crudely ☞ **reći**

grûbor {adj.} **a.** *sl* rude: *grubor frajer rude guy* <**Slav**✍> **b.** *sl* violent: *grubor faca violent guy* **c.** *sl* strong: *grubor vjetar strong wind*

grȕdānje {a neut.} (lit. snow-balling) *sl* fight (e.g. fist fight) <**Slav***1>

grûdi *See the following*
- **pobožne grûdi** {NP} (lit. religious breasts) *sl cor* ***Fac-Obs*** sagging female breast

grúhati [1] {grûhām, grúhajū imperf. intr.} *col* explode <**Slav**>

grúhati [2] {grûhām, grúhajū imperf.} **1a.** *col* shoot, fire <**Slav***1> **b.** *col* shell, bomb <**Slav***2> **2** *col* bang (loud and abrupt sound) <**Slav***2>

grȕntačiti {čīm, čē imperf.} *col* beat up <**Ger***1>

grȕpa {ē fem.} *col* band (music) <**Fre***1>

grȕpić {a masc.} *sl-sex* ***Fac-Obs*** group sex <**Fre** ✣*1>

grùpnjāk {grupnjáka masc.} *sl-sex* ***Obs*** group sex <**Fre** ✣*1>

grûv {a +ov (ext. pl) masc.; Nom Pl grúvovi} (lit. bang) *sl-sstu* mechanical learning <**Slav***1>

grûvanj {vnja neut.} **1** *col* gunshot <**Slav**> **2** *col* explosion <**Slav**>

grúvānje {a neut.} **a.** *col* shooting <**Slav**> **b.** *col* shelling, bombing <**Slav***1> **c.** *sl-stu* mechanical learning <**Slav***2>

grúvati {grûvām, grúvajū imperf.} **a.** *col* shoot loudly <**Slav**> **b.** *col* explode <**Slav***1> **c.** *col* shell, bomb <**Slav***2> **d.i.** *col* break wind loudly, fart loudly <**Slav***3> **ii.** *sl-sstu* learn mechanically <**Slav***3> **iii.** *sl* make noise <**Slav***3>

grùvīć {a masc.} *sl-sstu* difficult learning <**Slav**✍*1>

gû {excl.} *col* the sound made by a bird, coo <**Slav**>

gû-gû {excl.} *col* the sound made by a newborn, goo-goo <**Slav**>

gȕbār {a (acc. = gen.) masc.} **a.** *sl-fea* inhabitant of the countryside, hick, bumpkin **b.i.** *sl-fea* inquisitive person: *Taj gubar hoće sve da zna. That inquisitive person wants to know everything.* **ii.** *sl* official (in general): *vladin gubar government official*

gȕber {a (acc. = gen.) masc.} *sl-fea* inhabitant of the countryside, hick, bumpkin <**Hun**>

gȕbica {ē fem.} *col* mouth <**Slav***1>

gubìtāš {bitáša (acc. = gen.) masc.} *col* loser <**Slav**>

gùbiti se {bīm, bē imperf. intr.} (lit. lose oneself) *sl-fea* get confused <**Slav**[*1]>

gûc {a masc.} *col* sip <**Slav**>

gȕcati {ām, ajū perf.} *sl-drink* drink (alcohol) <**Slav**>

gȕckati {ām, ajū perf.} *sl-drink* drink (alcohol) <**Slav**>

gȕcnuti {nēm, nū perf.} *sl-drink* take a sip <**Slav**>
• **gȕcnuti ȁut** {VP} (lit. swallow an out) *sl-drugs* ***Fac*** miss one's vein while taking narcotic drugs

gȕča {ē fem.} *sl* dance <**Slav**[*1]>

gûd {a +ov (ext. pl) masc.; Nom Pl gúdovi} *col* the sound made by the gusle (a traditional stringed instrument) or similar string instrument <**Slav**>

gùdalo {a neut.} (lit. fiddle bow) *sl-sex* ***Fac-Obs*** penis, dick, prick <**Slav**[*1]>

gudèljati {ām, ajū imperf.} *sl-sex* ***Obs*** engage in sexual intercourse with (of a male) <**Slav**[*1]>

gudèrisati {išēm, išū imperf.; perm} **a.** *sl-sex* ***Obs*** engage in sexual intercourse with (of a male) <**Slav**[*1]> **b.** *sl* beat up <**Slav**[*2]>

gúditi {dīm, dē imperf.} *sl-sex* ***Fac-Obs*** engage in sexual intercourse with (of a male) <**Slav**[*1]>
• **gúdiō pȑdiō (nȉko te ne sluša)** {S} (lit. whether you play a string instrument or fart *nobody is listening to you*) *col* ***Obs-Fac*** used to indicate that any verbal action is pointless

gȕdra {e neut.; perm} /gùdra/ [std. = droga] *sl-drugs* narcotic drug, dope <**Fre**✍>

gȕdrica {e neut.; perm} [std. = droga] *sl-drugs* narcotic drug, dope <**Fre**✍>

gudrírati se {gùdrīrām, gudrírajū perf. intr.; perm} [std. = drogirati se] *sl-drugs* take narcotic drugs, do drugs <**Fre**✍>

gùdrisānje {a neut.; perm} *sl-drugs* intake of narcotic drugs, doing drugs <**Fre**❖✍>

gùdura {ē fem.} *col* impassible mountain <**Slav**>

gúđeti {dīm, dē imperf.} *dia* squeak <**Slav**✍>

gugúkati {gùgūčēm, ūčū imperf.} *col* coo (of birds) <**Slav**>

gȕgūt {a masc.} *col* cooing (of birds) <**Slav**>

gugùtati {tām, tajū imperf.} **a.** *col* coo (of birds) <**Slav**> **b.** *sl* blurp <**Slav**[*1]>

gugùtav {a, o adj.} *col* cooing (of birds) <**Slav**>

gugùtavo {adv.} *col* cooing (of birds) <**Slav**>

gùgutka {ē fem.; Dat gùgutki} *col* turtledove <**Slav**>

gugùtnjava {ē fem.} *col* weeping, crying <**Slav**[*1]>

gùjca {ē fem.} [std. = guzica] *sl-sex* ***Obs*** buttocks, butt <**Slav**✍>

gùjica {ē fem.} [std. = guzica] *sl-sex* ***Obs*** buttocks, butt <**Slav**✍>
• **u gùjicu na vášar** {PP} (lit. to the ass to a fair) *dia-col* ***Obs*** nowhere

gûk {a +ov (ext. pl) masc.; Nom Pl gȕkovi} **1** *col* cawing (of a crow) <**Slav**> **2a.** *col* cooing (of birds) <**Slav**> **b.** *col* pleasant voice <**Slav**[*1]>

gúkānje {a neut.} *col* cooing (of birds) <**Slav**>

gúkati {gûkām, gúkajū imperf. intr.} /gûčēm, čū imperf. intr./ *col* coo (of birds) <**Slav**>

gȕkav {a, o adj.} *col* cooing (of birds) <**Slav**>

gúknuti {gûknēm, nū perf.} **a.** *col* coo (of birds) <**Slav**> **b.** *sl* say, tell <**Slav**[*1]> **c.** *sl* admit, make a confession, come clean <**Slav**[*2]> **d.** *sl-thie* inform the police or other authorities, snitch, squeal <**Slav**[*3]>

gȕlāg {a (acc. = gen.) masc.} *sl-polit* Gulag (concentration camp for the opponents of the communist regime) <**RusO**>

gulámfer {a (acc. = gen.) masc.} *col* ***Der*** worthless or despicable person <**NE**[*1]> ☞ **gulanfer**

gulánfer[1] {a (acc. = gen.) masc.} **a.** *sl-fea* lazy or shiftless male, bum, good for nothing <**NE**[*1]> **b.i.** *sl-fea* poor male <**NE**[*2]> **ii.** *sl-sex* male homosexual, gay <**NE**[*2]> ☞ **gulamfer**

gȕlāš {a masc.} (lit. stew) *sl* unpleasant issue: *Baktanje s njom mi je gulaš. Dealing with her is unpleasant to me.* <**Hun**[*1]>

gúliti {gûlīm, lē imperf.} (lit. peel off) **1** *sl* work hard <**Slav**[*1]> **2** *sl* smoke <**Slav**[*1]> **3** *sl* overcharge, rip off <**Slav**[*1]> **5** *sl* devour, eat voraciously: *guliti slamu devour salami* <**Slav**[*1]> **6** *sl* walk **7a.** *sl* steal, swipe **b.** *sl-gamble* take another's money in gambling, rip off in gambling <**Slav**[*2]>
• **gúliti dlȁke** {VP} (lit. peel hairs) *sl-fea* get bored

gùljār {guljára (acc. = gen.) masc.} *sl-arch* snake <**Slav**[*1]>

guljàrica {ē fem.} **a.** *sl* leg (human) <**Slav**[*1]> **b.** *sl* shoe <**Slav**[*2]>

gùljārka {ē fem.} **a.** *sl* leg (human) <**Slav**[*1]> **b.** *sl* shoe <**Slav**[*2]>

guljáviti {gùljāvīm, vē imperf.} *sl* walk <**Slav**[*1]>

gùma {ē fem.} (lit. rubber) **1** *sl-sex* condom, rubber <**Gre**[*1]> **2** *sl* taxi <**Gre**[*1]>

gumárac {rca masc.} *sl* bus <**Gre**⁘*1>

gȕmati {ām, ajū imperf.} **1** *sl* devour, eat voraciously: *gumati piletinu devour chicken* <**Gre***1> **2** *sl-drink* drink (alcohol) <**Gre***1>

gùmātor {a (acc. = gen.) masc.} *sl* car, wheels <**Gre**⁘*1>

gȕmb {a masc.} Cro *col* button <**Hun**>

gùmbek {a (acc. = gen.) masc.} (lit. small button) Kajk *sl-sex* young prostitute <**Hun***1>

gȕmenī {ōg (acc. = gen.) masc.} (lit. the rubber one) *sl-crime* policeman, cop <**Gre***1>

gumènjāk {menjáka masc.} (lit. the rubber one) **1** *sl* bus station <**Gre**⁘*1> **2** *sl-sex* condom, rubber <**Gre**⁘*1> **3** *sl* rubber (inflatable) boat <**Gre**⁘*1>

gȕmi-štrúdla {ē fem.} (lit. rubber strudel) *sl-crime* billy club <**Gre-Ger***1>

gùmica {ē fem.} **/gȕmica/** *sl-sex* condom, rubber <**Gre***1>

gumigèleng {a masc.} *sl-auto* rubber joint (in transmission mechanism) <**Gre-Ger**>

gùndelj {a (acc. = gen.) masc.} *col* cockchafer, maybug <**Slav**>

gungùla {ē fem.} *col* crowd, mob <**NE**>

gȕnta {ē fem.} **1** *sl* rubber **2** *sl* cab, taxi

gùntbek {a (acc. = gen.) masc.} *sl-sex* ***Fac*** prostitute, hooker <**Ger**✍*1>

gûnj {a +ev (ext. pl) masc.; Nom Pl gúnjevi} *dia-col* fur jacket <**Gre**>

gurábija {ē fem.} (lit. a kind of oriental cookie) **a.** *sl* thing, object <**NE***1> **b.** *sl* trifle, thing of little importance or value <**NE***2>

guràčina {ē fem.} (lit. pushing) **1** *sl* game of chess <**Slav***1> **2** *sl* crowd, mob: *guračina u prodavnici crowd in the store* <**Slav***1>

gùrāć {guráća masc.} *sl* throat <**Slav**>

guràćica {ē fem.} (lit. pusher) **1** *sl* pipe (smoking) <**Slav***1> **2** *sl-arch* glass (in general) <**Slav***1>

gurálka {ē fem.} *sl* leg (human) <**Slav**>

gúralo *See the following*

• **međunòžnō gúralo** {NP} (lit. the thing which is pushed between one's legs) *sl* bicycle, bike

gûrām {excl.} *sl* used to express extreme disgust <**Slav***1>

gùrānka {ē fem.} *sl* leg (human) <**Slav***1>

gúrati {gûrām, gúrajū imperf.} (lit. push) **1** *col* live <**Slav***1> **2** *sl* run away, flee <**Slav***1>

• **gúrati dȑvca** {VP} (lit. push woods) *sl-sports* ***Fac*** play chess

guràvānjke {ī fem. pl.} *sl-arch* lumber <**Slav***1>

gurávinja {ē fem.} *sl-arch* burning wood <**Slav***1>

gùravka {ē fem.} *sl* leg (human) <**Slav***1>

gùrbet {a (acc. = gen.) masc.} **a.** *col* ***Off*** Gypsy (male) <**NE***1> **b.** *col* ***Off*** evil person <**NE***2>

gȕrbla {ē fem.} *sl-auto* crank <**Ger***1>

gûrka {ē fem.; Dat gûrki} **a.** *sl* pushing, showing <**Slav**⁘*1> **b.i.** *sl* fight (e.g. fist fight) <**Slav**⁘*2> **ii.** *sl* finding solution: *gurka za bubu u programu finding a solution to a bug in the program* <**Slav***2>

gȕrman {a masc.} *sl-media* grip (worker who pushes TV camera) <**Slav-Eng***1>

Gȕrnēm ti ga! {S} (lit. I stick it to you!) *col* ***Off*** used as a moderate curse, Fuck you! ☞ **gurnuti**

gùrnosi {adv.; perm} *sl* certainly, surely: *Gurnosi ću doći na dernek. I will come to the party for sure.* <**Slav**✍>

gȕrnuti {nēm, nū perf.} **/gúrnuti/** (lit. stick) *sl-sex* ***Obs*** engage in sexual intercourse with (of a male) <**Slav***1>

• **Gȕrnēm ti ga!** {S} (lit. I stick it to you!) *col* ***Off*** used as a moderate curse, Fuck you!

• **gúrnuti ga** {VP} (lit. push it) *sl-sex* ***Obs*** engage in sexual intercourse with (of a male)

gùrtna {ē fem.} **1** *col* belt <**Ger**> **2** *col* sash <**Ger**>

gȕs {excl.} *col* used to lure a goose <**Slav**>

gȕsa {excl.} *col* used to lure a goose <**Slav**>

gusáriti {gùsārīm, rē imperf.} *sl* take a risk, take a chance

gȕska {ē fem.; Dat gȕski} (lit. goose) **1** *sl-sex* ***Obs*** penis, dick, prick <**Slav***1> **2** *sl-fea* ***Der*** unintelligent female <**Slav***1>

gùslāč {gusláča (acc. = gen.) masc.} (lit. fiddler) *sl-sex* ***Fac-Obs*** male sexual partner (of a female) <**Slav***1>

gȕslār {a (acc. = gen.) masc.} (lit. fiddler) **1** *sl-crime* ***Der*** informer, stoolie, snitch <**Slav***1> **2** *sl-sex* male homosexual, gay <**Slav***1>

gȕslārka {ē fem.} (lit. fiddler) *sl* fifty-dinar bill <**Slav***1>

gùslati {ām, ajū imperf.} (lit. fiddle) **1a.** *sl-sex* ***Fac-Obs*** engage in sexual intercourse with (of a male) <**Slav***1> **b.** *sl-sex* ***Fac-Obs*** have prolonged sexual intercourse with <**Slav***2> **2** *sl* ***Der*** work slowly <**Slav***1>

gȕslēnje {a neut.} (lit. fiddling) *sl-sex* ***Fac-Obs*** sexual intercourse <**Slav***1>

gusliónica {ē fem.} (lit. fiddling place) *sl-sex* ***Fac-Obs*** place intended for sexual intercourse <Slav*1>

gȕsliti {līm, lē imperf.} (lit. fiddle) *sl-sex* ***Fac-Obs*** engage in sexual intercourse with (of a male) <Slav*1>

gûstā {ē fem. (adj. decl.)} (lit. the thick one) *sl-arch* woods, forest <Slav*1>

gùstijērna {ē fem.} *dia-col* reservoir <Lat>

gustírati {gùstīrām, gustírajū imperf.} **a.** *col* enjoy, like: *gustirati džez like jazz* <Lat✣*1> **b.** *col* clock, watch <Lat✣*2>

gùstīš *See the following*

• **gùstīš sa sódōm** {NP} (lit. the thick thing with soda) *sl-fea* ***Fac*** extremely dangerous situation

gûstō {ōg neut.} (lit. the thick one) *col* trouble, problem: *biti u gustom be in trouble* <Slav*1>

gȕša {ē fem.} *col* throat <Slav>

gùšāč {gušáča (acc. = gen.) masc.} (lit. strangler) *sl-fea* boring person, bore <Slav✣*1>

gùščetina {ē fem.} (lit. big goose) *sl-sex* ***Obs*** buttocks, butt <Slav✣>

gùšitelj {a (acc. = gen.) masc.} (lit. strangler) *sl-fea* boring person, bore <Slav*1>

gúšiti {gûšīm, gûšē imperf.} (lit. strangle) *sl-fea* annoy, bother, pester: *Komšija me gušio tri sata svojim pričama o fudbalu. My neighbor bothered me for two hours with his soccer stories.* <Slav*1>

gȕšt {a +ov (ext. pl) masc.; Nom Pl gùštevi} **a.** *col* taste, preferences <Lat✍> **b.** *col* pleasure: *Pušenje mi je gušt. Smoking is a pleasure for me.* <Lat✍*1>

gȕšter {a (acc. = gen.) masc.} (lit. lizard) **1** *sl-mil* rookie soldier, first-month soldier <Slav*1> **2a.** *sl-sex* prostitute, hooker <Slav*1> **b.** *sl* female <Slav*2> **c.** *sl* unattractive female, dog <Slav*3> **3** *sl* dollar, buck <Slav*1>

gût {a +ov (ext. pl) masc.; Nom Pl gútovi} **a.** *sl* money in a safe place <Ger*1> **b.** *sl* safe debt (sure to be repaid) <Ger*2>

gȕta {ē fem.} **1** *sl* multitude <Slav*1> **2** *sl* package (in general) <Slav*1>

gùtānje {a neut.} (lit. swallowing) *sl* wasting, using (e.g. of oil or gas by an engine) <Slav*1>

gùtati {ām, ajū imperf.} (lit. swallow) **1a.** *col* look attentively <Slav*1> **b.** *sl* be in love <Slav*2> **2** *sl* waste, use (e.g. oil or gas by an engine) <Slav*1> **3** *sl* believe, swallow <Slav*1>

• **gùtati kèfu** {VP} (lit. swallow a brush) *sl-fea* ***Fac*** be in love

• **gùtati zêca** {VP} (lit. swallow a rabbit) *sl-fea* ***Fac*** get frightened, freak

gȕtavo {adv.} *sl-fea* dangerous, dicey: *Bilo je gutavo kad su počeli da me ganjaju s pištoljima. It got dangerous when they started to chase me with guns.* <Slav*1>

gȕtnuti {nēm, nū perf.} *sl* make a mistake, screw up <Slav*1>

• **gȕtnuti ȁut** {VP} (lit. swallow an out) *sl-drugs* ***Fac*** miss one's vein while taking narcotic drugs

gúto {ē masc.} /ʹa masc./ *sl-fea* short person who keeps his or her head down <Slav✣*1>

guvèdo {a neut.} *dia* head of cattle <Slav✍>

gúvno {a neut.} *dia* threshing floor <Slav>

gûz {a +ov (ext. pl) masc.; Nom Pl gȕzovi} *sl-sex* ***Obs*** buttocks, butt <Slav>

• **nà guzove** {PP} (lit. over one's buttocks) *col* without deserving it

gûz-pàpīr {papíra masc.} /guzīc-pàpīr/ *sl-sex* ***Obs*** bathroom tissue, ass wipe <Slav✣>

gúza [1] {ē fem.} *sl-sex* ***Fam*** buttocks, butt <Slav>

gúza [2] {ē fem. & masc.} **1** *sl-fea* ***Der-Obs*** ingratiator (male), brownnoser, ass kisser: *Ona je guza, uvijek govori šta šef hoće da čuje. She's a brownnoser, she always tells things the boss wants to hear.* <Slav*1> **2** *sl-fea* intruder <Slav*1>

Guzánac {nca (acc. = gen.) masc.} (lit. McAss) *sl-sex* ***Fac-Obs*** a surname in Vojvodina, Yugoslavia <Slav>

Gùzanōv {a (acc. = gen.) masc.} *sl-sex* ***Fac-Obs*** a surname in Vojvodina <Slav>

gȕzānje {a neut.} *sl* ***Obs*** fast walking <Slav*1>

gȕzār {a (acc. = gen.) masc.} *dia* ***Obs*** metal or wooden basket used to catch fish <Slav*1>

gùzara {ē fem.} **a.** *sl-sex* ***Obs*** female with large buttocks <Slav✣> **b.** *dia* ***Obs*** basket used to catch sparrows <Slav✣*1>

gȕzas {sta, sto adj.} *sl-sex* ***Obs*** having big buttocks <Slav✣>

gȕzast {sta, sto adj.} *sl-sex* ***Obs*** having big buttocks <Slav✣>

gùzat {a, o adj.} **a.** *sl-sex* ***Obs*** having big buttocks <Slav✣> **b.** *sl-fea* ***Obs*** greedy, voracious (of food, money, etc.) <Slav✣*1>

gùzati {ām, ajū imperf.} *sl-fea* ***Obs*** walk fast <Slav✣*1>

gùzca {ē fem.} [std. = guzica] *sl-sex* ***Obs*** buttocks, butt <Slav✍>

gùzelja {ē fem.} *sl-sex* ***Obs*** buttocks, butt <Slav⁘>

guzèljati {ām, ajū imperf.} *sl-fea* ***Obs*** walk fast <Slav⁘[*1]>

gùzer {a (acc. = gen.) masc.} *dia* ***Obs*** wider end of an egg <Slav⁘[*1]>

guzerȁnt {a (acc. = gen.) masc.} *sl-sex* ***Der-Obs*** male homosexual, gay <Slav⁘-Ita✍[*1]>

gùzērka {ē fem.; Dat gùzērki} *sl* ***Obs*** front end of a wagon <Slav⁘[*1]>

guzèrnjāk {a masc.} *sl-sex* ***Obs*** buttocks, butt <Slav⁘>

guzètina {ē fem.} *sl-sex* ***Obs*** buttocks, butt <Slav⁘>

gùzic-pàpīr {papíra masc.} /guzȉc-pàpīr/ *sl-sex* ***Obs*** bathroom tissue, ass wipe <Slav⁘>

gùzica {ē f adj.} **a.** *sl-sex* ***Obs*** buttocks, butt <Slav⁘> **b.** *sl-fea* ***Obs*** worthless or despicable person, bum <Slav⁘[*1]> **c.** *sl-fea* ***Obs*** boaster, braggart, blowhard <Slav⁘[*2]>

• U gùzicu te jèbēm! {S} (lit. I fuck you in your ass!) *dia-col* ***Off*** used as a moderate curse, Fuck you!

gùzičār {a (acc. = gen.) masc.} **1** *sl-sex* ***Fac-Obs*** male homosexual, gay <Slav⁘[*1]> **2** *sl-sex* ***Der-Obs*** ingratiator (male), brownnoser, ass kisser <Slav⁘[*2]>

gùzičārka {ē fem.; Dat gùzičārki} **a.** *sl-sex* ***Fac-Obs*** attractive female <Slav⁘[*1]> **b.** *sl-sex* prostitute, hooker <Slav⁘[*2]>

gùzičas {sta, sto adj.} *sl-sex* ***Obs*** having big buttocks <Slav⁘✍>

gùzičast {sta, sto adj.} *sl-sex* ***Obs*** having big buttocks <Slav⁘✍>

guzičètina {ē fem.} *sl-sex* ***Obs*** buttocks, butt <Slav⁘>

gùzičica {ē fem.} /guzičíca/ *sl-sex* ***Obs*** buttocks, butt <Slav⁘>

gùzičina {ē fem.} /guzìčina/ *sl-sex* ***Obs*** buttocks, butt <Slav⁘>

gùzička {ē fem.; Dat gùzički} **a.** *sl-sex* ***Obs*** buttocks, butt <Slav⁘> **b.** *sl-sex* ***Obs*** female with large buttocks <Slav⁘[*1]> **c.** *sl-fea* ***Der-Obs*** greedy female (for food, money, etc.) <Slav⁘[*1]>

gùzičko {a (acc. = gen.) masc.} **a.** *sl-sex* ***Obs*** male with large buttocks <Slav⁘> **b.** *sl-sex* ***Fac-Obs*** male homosexual, gay <Slav⁘[*1]>

gùzičnjāk {a masc.} *sl-sex* ***Obs*** buttocks, butt <Slav⁘>

gȕzić {a (acc. = gen.) masc.} /gùzīć/ *sl-sex* ***Obs*** male homosexual, gay <Slav⁘[*1]>

gùzīle {a (acc. = gen.) masc.} *sl-sex* ***Obs*** male with large buttocks <Slav⁘>

Gȕzīn {a (acc. = gen.) masc.} (lit. McAss) *sl-sex* ***Fac-Obs*** a surname in Vojvodina, Yugoslavia <Slav>

Gùzina {ē masc.} (lit. McAss) *sl-sex* ***Fac-Obs*** surname in Bosna and Montenegro <Slav>

gúziti {gûzīm, zē imperf.} (lit. ass) *sl-sex* ***Obs*** engage in sexual intercourse with (of a male) <Slav⁘[*1]>

gúziti se {gûzīm, zē imperf. intr.} (lit. ass oneself) **1** *sl-fea* ***Obs*** be intrusive: *Guzio mi se u kući, pa nisam imao privatnosti. He was intrusive at my place, so I didn't have any privacy.* <Slav⁘[*1]> **2** *sl-fea* ***Obs*** work hard, bust one's ass <Slav⁘[*1]>

gùzna {ē fem.} (lit. the assy one) **a.** *sl-sex* ***Obs*** female with large buttocks <Slav⁘> **b.** *sl-sex* ***Der-Obs*** greedy female (for food, money, etc.) <Slav⁘[*1]>

gûznī {ā, ō adj.} *sl-sex* ***Obs*** buttocks, butt <Slav⁘>

gûznī sàlvēt {NP} (lit. ass wipe) *sl-sex* ***Fac-Obs*** bathroom tissue, ass wipe ☞ **salvet**

gúzo {a masc.; Voc gûzo} *sl-sex* ***Obs*** male with large buttocks <Slav⁘>

gȕzobād {a masc.} *dia* ***Obs*** thorny hay <Slav⁘[*1]>

gȕzobrīs {a masc.} (lit. ass wipe) *sl-sex* ***Obs-Fac*** bathroom tissue, ass wipe <Slav⁘[*1]>

guzodávac {vca (acc. = gen.) masc.} (lit. ass giver) *sl-sex* ***Fac-Obs*** male homosexual, gay <Slav⁘[*1]>

guzodŕpac {pca (acc. = gen.) masc.} (lit. ass catcher) *sl-fea* ***Fac-Obs*** feminized male <Slav⁘[*1]>

guzojébac {pca (acc. = gen.) masc.} (lit. butt fucker) **1** *sl-sex* ***Fac-Obs*** male homosexual, gay <Slav⁘[*1]> **2** *sl-fea* ***Der-Obs*** miser, tightwad, skinflint <Slav⁘[*1]>

guzojèbica {ē fem.} (lit. butt fucker) *sl-sex* ***Obs*** loose woman, slut <Slav⁘>

guzojèbīle {a masc.} (lit. one who engages in anal sexual intercourse) **1** *sl-sex* ***Fac-Obs*** male homosexual, gay <Slav⁘> **2** *sl-fea* ***Der-Obs*** miser, tightwad, skinflint <Slav⁘[*1]>

guzolízac {sca (acc. = gen.) masc.} (lit. buttocks licker) *sl-fea* ***Der-Obs*** ingratiator (male), brownnoser, ass kisser <Slav⁘[*1]>

gȕzoljūb {a (acc. = gen.) masc.} (lit. buttocks kisser) *sl-sex* ***Fac-Obs*** male homosexual, gay <Slav⁘[*1]>

guzoljúbac {pca (acc. = gen.) masc.} (lit. buttocks kisser) *sl-sex* ***Fac-Obs*** male homosexual, gay <Slav⁘[*1]>

Gȕzonić {a (acc. = gen.) masc.} /Gùzonić/ *sl-sex* ***Fac-Obs*** a surname in Serbia, Yugoslavia <Slav>

gúzonja {ē masc.} **a.** *sl-sex* ***Obs*** male with large buttocks <Slav❖> **b.** *sl-fea* ***Obs*** very important or influential person, big shot <Slav❖[*1]>

gúzonjica {ē fem. & masc.} (lit. little ass) *sl-fea* ***Fam-Obs*** worthless or despicable person, asshole <Slav❖[*1]>

gȕzonjić {a (acc. = gen.) masc.} /gùzonjić/ (lit. McAss) *sl-fea* ***Obs*** obese boy <Slav❖[*1]>

gȕzos {a masc.} *sl-sex* ***Obs*** buttocks, butt <Slav☞>

guzòser {a (acc. = gen.) masc.} (lit. ass shitter) *sl-fea* ***Obs*** worthless or despicable person, asshole <Slav❖>

guzòsera {ē fem.} (lit. ass shitter) *sl-fea* ***Obs-Der*** evil female, bitch <Slav❖[*1]>

guzotrèsina {ē masc.} (lit. ass shaker) *sl-fea* ***Der-Obs*** worthless or despicable person, asshole <Slav❖[*1]>

gȕzovi {ōvā masc. pl.} /gúzovi/ (lit. buttocks) *sl-crime* ***Obs*** stealing from a car <Slav[*1]>

gùzulja {ē fem.} (lit. asser) **a.** *sl-sex* ***Obs*** female with large buttocks <Slav❖> **b.** *sl-fea* ***Der-Obs*** greedy female (for food, money, etc.) <Slav❖[*1]>

gùzuljica {ē fem.} (lit. asser) **a.** *sl-sex* ***Obs*** female with large buttocks <Slav❖> **b.** *sl-fea* ***Der-Obs*** greedy female (for food, money, etc.) <Slav❖[*1]>

gùzuljičica {ē fem.} (lit. little asser) **a.** *sl-sex* ***Obs*** small buttocks <Slav❖> **b.** *sl-fea* ***Obs*** female with large buttocks **c.** ***Der-Obs*** greedy female (for food, money, etc.)

gúža {ē fem.} *sl-sex* ***Obs*** buttocks, butt <Slav☞>

gúžēnje {a neut.} **1** *sl-sex* ***Obs*** sexual intercourse <Slav❖[*1]> **2** *sl-fea* ***Obs*** hesitation: *Nismo iskoristili priliku zbog njegovog guženja. Due to his hesitation we didn't use the opportunity.* <Slav❖[*1]>

gȕžičnjāk {a masc.} *sl-sex* ***Obs*** buttocks, butt <Slav❖>

gûžnjak *See the following*

- **U gûžnjāk te jèbēm!** {S} (lit. I fuck you in your ass!) *dia* ***Off*** used as a moderate curse, Up yours!

gûžnjī {ā, ē adj.} *sl-sex* ***Obs*** buttocks, butt <Slav❖>

gûžva {ē fem.} **a.** *col* twisted piece of paper or fabric <Slav> **b.** *col* crowd, mob <Slav[*1]> **c.** *col* jam (e.g. traffic jam) <Slav[*2]>

- **gûžva pred gòlom** {NP} (lit. mess in front of the goal) *sl-sports* goal-scoring opportunity (e.g. in soccer)

gužvánac {nca masc.} **a.** *col* mess, disorder, disturbance <Slav❖> **b.** *col* crowd, mob <Slav❖[*1]>

gužvánjac {nca masc.} **a.** *col* mess, disorder, disturbance <Slav❖> **b.** *col* crowd, mob <Slav❖[*1]>

gȕžvānje {a neut.} (lit. wrinkling) *sl-fea* being in a crowd (e.g. on a rock concert) <Slav[*1]>

gȕžvati {ām, ajū imperf.} (lit. wrinkle) **a.** *sl* beat up <Slav[*1]> **b.** *sl-sex* engage in sexual intercourse with (of a male) <Slav[*2]>

gȕžvati se {ām, ajū imperf. intr.} (lit. wrinkle oneself) *sl-fea* be in a crowd <Slav[*1]>

gvantjêra {ē fem.} *dia* plate, dish <Ita>

gvàrdati {ām, ajū imperf.} *sl* look, watch, scope out <Ita>

gvȉnt {a +ov (ext. pl) masc.; Nom Pl gvìntovi} **1a.** *sl* trick, joke: *prevariti nekoga na gvint cheat somebody by using tricks* <Ger[*1]> **b.** *sl* joke <Ger[*2]> **c.** *sl* humor <Ger[*3]> **2** bottle cap

gvȉrcati {ām, ajū biasp.} *sl-drink* drink (alcohol) <Ger❖☞[*1]>

gvòzden {a, o--} /gvòzden/ (lit. iron) *sl* strong <Slav[*1]>

gvozdénac {nca masc.} (lit. the iron one) **1** *col* metal marble (the toy) <Slav❖> **2** *sl-drugs* metal syringe <Slav❖>

gvozdènjāk {denjáka masc.} *col* coin <Slav❖[*1]>

gvôžđa {ā neut. pl.} (lit. pieces of iron) *sl-crime* handcuffs, cuffs <Slav❖[*1]>

gvôžđe {a neut.} (lit. iron) **1** *sl-crime* handcuffs, cuffs <Slav[*1]> **2** *sl-drugs* metal ball used in smoking hashish <Slav[*1]>

gzz {a +ov (ext. pl) masc.; Nom Pl gzzòvi} *sl-sex* ***Obs*** buttocks, butt <Slav☞>

Hh

h {a +ov (ext. pl) masc.; Nom Pl hàovi} *sl* hour <Lat☞>

hȁ {excl.} **1** *col* used to make somebody go away <Slav> **2** *col* used to address a person in direct informal communication, hey, man <Slav> **3** *col* used to express hesitation, huh <Slav> **4** *col* the sound of laughing, ha <Slav>

hȁber {a masc.} /hàber/ BosM *col* message <NE[*1]>

hadezèovac {vca (acc. = gen.) masc.} *sl-polit* member of the HDZ (Hrvatska demokratska zajednica 'Croatian Democratic Union', a political party in Croatia) <Abb⁘>

hadezèovskī {ā, ō adj.} *sl-polit* pertaining to the HDZ (Hrvatska demokratska zajednica 'Croatian Democratic Alliance', a political party in Croatia) <Abb⁘>

hadezeóvština {ē fem.} *col* rule of the HDZ (Hrvatska demokratska zajednica 'Croatian Democratic Alliance', a political party in Croatia) <Abb⁘>

hȁdž {a +ev (ext. pl) masc.; Nom Pl hȁdževi} BosM *col* hadj (pilgrimage to the Muslim holy city of Mecca) <NE[*1]>

hádža {ē masc.} *sl-drugs* hashish, hash <NE[*1]>

hȁdžija {ē masc.} (lit. pilgrim to Mecca) **1** *col* very important or influential person, big shot <NE[*1]> **2** *sl-sex* elderly homosexual <NE[*1]> **3** *sl-sex* homosexual who takes the passive role, femme <NE[*1]>

hȁe {excl.} *col* used to command a cow to move on, go <Slav>

hȁferica {ē fem.} *sl-sports* sport shoe, sneaker <BN[*1]>

hàfif {a masc.} *sl-crime* criminal who is always broke <NE[*1]>

háfiz *See the following*

- **ko háfiz** {PP} (lit. like a person who knows the Qur'an by heart) Bos *col* completely, totally: *naučiti pjesmicu napamet ko hafiz learn a song by heart*

hȁhār {a (acc. = gen.) masc.} *sl* troublemaker, rowdy, ruffian <Hun>

hȁhoćūdan {dna, dno adj.} *sl* hated

hȁir {a masc.} BosM *col* happiness <NE[*1]>

hȁirala {excl.} *col* used to take leave of somebody informally, take care <NE[*1]>

haìrli {adv.} BosM *col* happily <NE>

hàisati {išēm, išū imperf.} *sl-sex* ***Obs*** engage in sexual intercourse with (of a male)

hâj [1] {excl.} /hȁj/ **1** *col* used to greet informally on arrival, hi <Eng> **2** *col* used in informal communication to make somebody do something, do it <NE> **3** *col* used in informal communication to draw attention, hey <NE>

hâj [2] {a +ev (ext. pl) masc.; Nom Pl hájevi} **a.** *col* high (mood, etc.) <Eng> **b.** *sl-drugs* high (on drugs) <Eng[*1]> **c.** *col* good mood <Eng[*2]>

hâj [3] {adj.} (lit. high) *sl-drink* drunk <Eng>

hâj-fâj {adj.} *col* ***App*** excellent, awesome <Eng[*1]>

hâj-fī {adj.} *col* ***App*** excellent, awesome <Eng[*1]>

hȁjati {ām, ajū biasp.} *sl* sleep, nap <Hun✍[*1]>

hâjbati {ām, ajū biasp.} *sl* drive a vehicle

hȁjcati {ām, ajū imperf.} /hâjcati/ *col* heat <Ger>

hâjčiti {čīm, čē imperf.} *sl* sleep, nap

hȁjd {excl.} /hȁjd/ *col* used in direct informal communication to make somebody do something, do it <NE✍> ☞ **aj, ajd, ajde, hajde**

hȁjda {excl.} *col* used in direct informal communication to make somebody do something, do it <NE✍>

hȁjdac {excl.} *sl* used to make somebody go away, beat it <NE✍>

hȁjde [1] {excl.} *col* used in direct informal communication to make somebody do something, do it <NE> ☞ **ajd, ajde**

- **Hȁjde jèbāč!** {S} (lit. Go ahead you fucker!) *col* ***Off*** used to stimulate to action and express a negative attitude toward, Come on, you fucker!
- **Hȁjde u kȕrac!** {S} (lit. Go to prick!) *col* ***Off*** used in angry dismissal, Fuck off!

hȁjde [2] {part.} *col* used as a question tag, really, indeed <NE[*1]> ☞ **ajde**

hajdùčija {ē fem.} *col* violent behavior <Slav>

hȁjfāć {a (acc. = gen.) masc.} *sl* radio amateur, ham <Eng[*1]>

hȁjfić {a (acc. = gen.) masc.} *sl-fea* person obsessed with musical appliances (such as stereo players, etc.), audio freak <Eng⁘[*1]>

hȁjfiš {a masc.} *col* garbage container <Ger[*1]>

hȁjhelicle {adj.} *sl-fea* obese, fat

hȁjkiti {kīm, kē imperf.} *sl* sleep, nap <Slav✍[*1]>

hȁjmo {excl.} *col* used to stimulate one or more persons to a common action, let's <Slav> ☞ **ajmo**

- **Hȁjmo se kárat!** {S} *sl-sex* ***Obs*** used to propose sexual intercourse

hȁjs {excl.} *col* used to command an ox to move on, go <Slav>

hȁjte {excl.} [std. = hajdete] **1** *col* used in direct informal communication with several persons or formal communication with one person to encourage them to act, do it: *Hajte sad uradite zadaću! Now do your homework!* <Slav> **2** *col* used in direct informal communication with several persons or formal communication with one person to encourage them to act, go ahead: *Hajte sa mnom! Come on with me!* <Slav> ☞ **ajte**

hàjvān {hajvána (acc. = gen.) masc.} **a.** BosM *col* cattle <NE*1> **b.** BosM *sl* troublemaker, rowdy, ruffian <NE*2>

hȁk {a +ov (ext. pl) masc.; Nom Pl hàkovi} *col* breathing <NE>

hȁker {a (acc. = gen.) masc.} /hàker/ *col* computer hacker <Eng>

hȁkī {īja masc.} /hàki/ *sl-drugs* hashish, hash <NE✍>

hàkl {a +ov (ext. pl) masc.; Nom Pl hàklovi} **1** *sl-sports* table soccer (game) <Ger> **2** *sl-sports* half-court basketball <Ger>

hȁknuti {hȑknēm, hȑknū perf.} *sl-crime* steal, swipe <Ger*1>

hȁkslī {īja masc.} *sl-drugs* hashish, hash <NE✍>

hâl {a masc.} *sl-sex* ***Obs*** vagina, cunt

hála [1] {ē fem.} **1** *sl-sex* bathroom: *smrdljiva hala stinking bathroom* <NE*1> **2** *sl* food: *Ima hale za tri dana. We have enough food for three days.* <NE*1>

hàla [2] {ē masc.} **a.** *sl-crime* policeman, cop <NE*1> **b.** *sl-crime* spy, spook <NE*2>

halàbučiti {čīm, čē imperf.} **a.** *col* make noise <Slav> **b.** *sl-sex* talk persistently and meaninglessly, blabber, chatter <Slav*1>

halàbuka {ē fem.} *col* noise <Slav>

haláknuti {hàlāknēm, nū perf.} **1** *sl-sex* ***Obs*** engage in sexual intercourse with (of a male) <NE*1> **2** *sl* sleep, nap <NE*1>

hàlāl [1] {excl.} **BosM** *col* be forgiven: *Halal ti one šljive što si mi ukro. May you be forgiven for those plums you have stolen from me.* <NE*1>

hàlāl [2] {halála masc.} BosM *col* forgiveness <NE*1>

haláliti {hàlālīm, lē biasp.} **a. BosM** *col* forgive, pardon: *halaliti dug forgive a debt* <NE> **b. BosM** *col* greet each other <NE*1> **c.** BosM *col* wish happiness <NE*2> **d.** BosM *col* bless <NE*4>

hàlāt {haláta masc.} [std. = alat] *sl* tools <NE✍>

hàlbaks {a masc.} (lit. half-axle) *sl* leg (human) <Ger*1>

hàlbaksa {ē fem.} *sl-crafts* half axle <Ger>

hàldisati {išēm, išū imperf.} *sl-sex* ***Obs*** engage in sexual intercourse with (of a male) <Gyp>

hâle {eta neut.} *sl-drugs* hashish, hash <NE✍>

halelúja {excl.} *col* hallelujah <Heb>

hàlisānje {a neut.} **1** *sl-drink* drinking (alcohol) <Gyp*1> **2** *sl-sex* ***Obs*** fellatio <Gyp*1>

hàlisati {išēm, išū imperf.} **1** *sl* eat, devour <Gyp*1> **2** *sl-sex* ***Obs*** engage in fellatio <Gyp*1>

hàliška {ē fem.; Dat hàliški} *sl* food <Gyp✍*1>

hàlka {ē fem.; Dat hàlki} *sl* food <NE*1>

hàlkati {ām, ajū imperf.} *sl* eat, devour <NE*1>

hȁlnuti {nēm, nū perf. intr.} *sl-sex* defecate <NE❖*1>

hȁlō {excl.} /halô, hàlo excl./ **a.** *col* used to open telephonic conversation or maintain the channel of communication, hello <Eng> **b.** *col* used to address a male in direct informal communication, hey <Eng*1> ☞ alo

hàltati {ām, ajū biasp.} *sl* stop <Ger>

hàlter {a masc.} *col* suspenders <Ger>

hàlūng {a masc.} *sl* food <Ger*1>

haljétak {tka masc.} *col* coat (outer garment) <Slav❖>

haljùkuša {ē fem.} *sl-fea* unintelligent female

háma {ē fem.} *sl* food <NE*1>

hàmāl {hamála (acc. = gen.) masc.} BosM *col* porter <NE*1>

hàmām {hamáma masc.} BosM *col* bath <NE*1>

hȁmati {ām, ajū imperf. intr.} *sl* eat, devour <Gyp*1>

hamburgèrāj {geràja masc.} *col* hamburger joint <Eng❖>

hamburgèrija {ē fem.} *col* hamburger joint <Eng❖>

hàmburgernica {ē fem.} *col* hamburger joint <Eng❖>

hȁmer {a masc.} *sl-crafts* hammer (the tool) <Ger>

Hàmlet {a (acc. = gen.) masc.} (lit. Hamlet) *sl* ***Der*** insane male, nut case <EngO*1>

hàmšišār {a (acc. = gen.) masc.} *sl-drugs* drug addict, junkie <NE✍>

hȁmzaga *See the following*

- **hȁmzaga hȍp** {NP} *sl-crime* steal, swipe; theft

hȁmziga *See the following*

- **hȁmziga hȍp** {NP} *sl-crime* steal, swipe; theft

hȁndriti {rīm, rē imperf.} *sl-sex* ***Obs*** engage in sexual intercourse with (of a male)

handrmólja {ē fem.} *col* trifle, thing of little importance or value <NE>

hȁndžār {a masc.} *col* knife <NE>

hȁniti {nīm, nē imperf.} *sl* eat

hȁnomāg {a masc.} *sl-sex* ***Obs*** penis, dick, prick <BN*1>

hȁnovān {vna, vno adj.} *sl* hungry

hanȕma {ē fem.} BosM *col* lady, woman <NE*1>

hȁnzaplast {a masc.} /hànzaplast/ *col* Band-Aid <BN>

hȁos [1] {excl.} (lit. chaos) *sl* used to express astonishment, unbelievable: *To je haos kako su ga isprebijali. That's unbelievable how they have beaten him up.* <Gre*1>

hȁos [2] {a masc.} (lit. chaos) **a.** *col* mess, disorder, disturbance <Gre*1> **b.** *sl* excellent object or plan, pearl, gem: *Njegova nova kola su haos. His new car is a pearl.* <Gre*2>

hȁos [3] {adv.} (lit. chaos) *sl* ***App*** excellent, awesome <Gre*1> *sl*

hȁos [4] {adj.} (lit. chaos) **a.** *sl* ***App*** excellent, awesome <Gre*1> **b.** *sl* ***App*** great <Gre*2>

hȁp {excl.} **1** *col* the sound made by a hiccup <NE*1> **2** *col* the sound made by swallowing, gulp <NE*1>

hápa {ē fem.} **1** *sl* food <Gyp*1> **2** *sl-crime* stealing, swiping <Gyp*1>

hápānje {a neut.} **1** *sl* catching, grabbing <Gyp*1> **2** *sl* eating <Gyp*1> **3** *sl-crime* theft <Gyp*1>

hápati {hâpām, hápajū imperf.} **1** *sl* catch, grab <Gyp*1> **2** *sl* eat, devour <Gyp*1> **3** *sl-crime* steal, swipe <Gyp*1>

hapávānje {a neut.} **1** *sl* catching, grabbing <Gyp*1> **2** *sl* eating <Gyp*1> **3** *sl* stealing <Gyp*1>

hapávati {hàpāvām, hapávajū biasp.} **1** *sl* catch, grab <Gyp*1> **2** *sl* eat, devour <Gyp*1> **3** *sl-crime* steal, swipe <Gyp*1>

hȁpavica {ē fem.} *sl* hand <NE*1>

hȁpiti {pīm, pē imperf.} **1** *sl* catch, grab <Gyp*1> **2** *sl* eat, devour <Gyp*1> **3** *sl-crime* steal, swipe <Gyp*1>

hȁps {a +ev (ext. pl) masc.; Nom Pl hàpsevi} *sl-crime* prison <Gre>

hȁpsa {ē fem.} *sl-crime* prison <Gre✍>

hapsȁna {ē fem.} *sl-crime* prison <Gre❖>

hȁptak {excl.} *sl* attention <Ger>

harabátija {ē fem.} *col* old and often malfunctioning car or mechanism, wreck <NE>

hàrāč {a masc.} **a.** *sl* tax <NE*1> **b.** *sl* stealing, swiping <NE*2>

hȁrati {ām, ajū imperf.} (lit. act violently) **a.** *sl* torture <NE*1> **b.** *sl* win <NE*2>

hàrem {a masc.} *sl-sex* ***Obs*** sexual intercourse <NE*1>

hàrisati {išēm, išū biasp.} **1** *sl-crime* steal, swipe <NE*1> **2** *sl* hurry up, rush <NE*1>

hȁriti {rīm, rē imperf.} *sl-sex* ***Obs*** engage in sexual intercourse with (of a male) <NE*1>

hȁrku {hàraku masc.; perm} *sl* cook <Slav✍>

hàrma {ē fem.} *sl-music* musical harmony <Gre✍>

harmòničiti {čīm, čē imperf.} (lit. play accordion) *sl-sex* ***Fac-Obs*** engage in sexual intercourse with (of a male) <Gre❖*1>

harmònika {ē fem.} (lit. accordion) *sl-fea* wrinkled face <Gre*1>

harmonìkāš {a (acc. = gen.) masc.} (lit. accordion player) **1a.** *sl-fea* elderly male with wrinkled forehead <Gre*1> **b.** *sl-fea* elderly male <Gre*2> **2** *sl-sex* penis <Gre*1>

hȁrnuti {nēm, nū perf.} *sl-crime* steal, swipe <NE*1>

hȁrtan {tna, tno adj.} *sl-fea* nice looking, cute <Ger*1>

hȁrtavo {adv.} *sl* confusing, not clear <Ger*1>

hȁs {a +ov (ext. pl) masc.; Nom Pl hàsovi} *sl* food <NE*1>

hȁsa {ē fem.} *sl* food <NE*1>

hȁsati {ām, ajū imperf.} **a.** *sl* eat, devour <Gyp*1> **b.** *sl* eat dinner <Gyp*2>

hȁsmiku {ua masc.} *sl-sex* ***Obs*** fellatio <Gyp>

hàsna {ē fem.} BosM *col* benefit, profit <NE>

hȁsniti {nīm, nē imperf. intr.} BosM *col* be useful: *Ona mi je žaga pravo hasnila. That saw was very useful.* <NE>

hàstal {a masc.} BosM *col* table <Hun✍>

hȁš [1] {a +ev (ext. pl) masc.; Nom Pl hàševi} *sl-drugs* hashish, hash <NE✍>

hâš [2] {a (acc. = gen.) +ev (ext. pl) masc.; Nom Pl hâševi} *sl-drugs* drug addict, junkie <NE❖*1>

hȁša [1] {excl.} *col* God save us, heaven help us <NE✍>

háša [2] {ē fem.} *sl-drugs* hashish, hash <NE✍>

hȁšiš {a masc.} *sl* cigarette, smoke <NE*1>

hȁšiš-dróga-mȉnās-kȁfa {ē fem.} **1** *sl-drugs* drug addict, junkie <NE-Fre-BN*1> **2** *sl-drugs* intake of narcotic drugs, doing drugs <NE-Fre-BN*1>

hȁšišār {a (acc. = gen.) masc.} *sl-drugs* drug addict, junkie <NE❖*1>

hȁškić {a masc.} *sl-drugs* drug addict, junkie <NE❖*1>

hȁšman {a (acc. = gen.) masc.} *sl-drugs* drug addict, junkie <NE✍>

hašòmān {šomána (acc. = gen.) masc.} /hašomân /a (acc. = gen.) masc./ **a.** *sl-drugs* drug addict, junkie <NE☞> **b.** male who dresses casually <NE☞*1>

hašòmānka {ē fem.} /hašòmanka /e fem./ **a.** *sl-drugs* drug addict, junkie <NE☞> **b.** *sl* female who dresses casually

hȁšu {ua masc.; perm} /hàšu/ *sl* chess <NE☞>

hàtīf {adj.} *sl* broke (financially) <NE*1>

hàtnati {ām, ajū biasp.} *sl* eat

hàuba {ē fem.} *sl-auto* hood (of a car) <Ger>

hàubaksa {ē fem.} *sl-sex* ***Fac-Obs*** buttocks, butt <Ger*1>

hàustor {a masc.} *col* entrance stairway <Ger>

hàustorče {eta neut.} *sl-fea* urban child <Ger✣*1>

hàuzmājstor {a (acc. = gen.) masc.} **a.** *col* janitor <Ger> **b.** *sl-drink* half liter of water served with wine <Ger*1>

hàva {ē fem.} **a.** BosM *col* air <NE> **b.** *sl* lack of success <NE*1>

Haváji {ā masc. pl.} (lit. Hawaii) *sl-crime* ***Iro*** name for Goli island prison (Croatia, where the former communist regime detained its political enemies) <EngO*1>

hàvājka {ē fem.} (lit. Hawaiian *female*) *sl-crime* ***Iro*** prison cell <Eng✣*1>

hàvārija {ē fem.} **1** *sl* unexpected message <Ita*1> **2a.** *sl-fea* stupid or mentally deficient person <Ita*1> **b.** *sl-fea* insane person, nut case <Ita*2>

havàrisati {šēm, šū biasp.} **a.** *sl* destroy, ruin <Ita✣*1> **b.** *sl* beat up <Ita✣*2>

hȁver {a (acc. = gen.) masc.} **1a.** *col* friend (male) <NE*1> **b.i.** *sl-crime* accomplice **ii.** *sl-crime* police investigator

hȁverica {ē fem.} SerE *col* friend (female) <NE✣*1>

havèrisati {išēm, išū imperf.} **a.** *col* make friends <NE✣*1> **b.** *sl-crime* act as an accomplice <NE✣*1>

hàvlija {ē fem.} BosM *col* kerchief <NE*1>

hȁznadār {a masc.} BosM *col* cashier <NE*1>

hazùrala {excl.} *col* get ready <NE*1>

hȅ {excl.} *col* used to express hesitation, huh <Slav>

hèbānje {a neut.} [std. = jebanje] *sl-sex* ***Obs*** sexual intercourse <Slav☞>

hèbati {bēm, bū biasp.} [std. = jebati] *sl-sex* ***Obs*** engage in sexual intercourse with (of a male) <Slav☞>

hȅc {a +ev (ext. pl) masc.; Nom Pl hècevi} *sl* joke <Ger>

hèćim {a (acc. = gen.) masc.} BosM *col* physician <NE*1>

héee {excl.} *col* used to express hesitation, huh <Slav>

hèfta {ē fem.} BosM *col* week <NE*1>

hèftānje {a neut.} (lit. basting) *sl-sex* ***Fac-Obs*** sexual intercourse <Ger*1>

hèftati {ām, ajū imperf.} (lit. baste) *sl-sex* ***Fac-Obs*** engage in sexual intercourse with (of a male) <Ger*1>

hèftati se {ām, ajū imperf. intr.} (lit. baste each other) *sl-sex* ***Fac-Obs*** engage in sexual intercourse with <Ger*1>

hêj {excl.} *col* used to draw attention in direct informal communication, hey <Slav>

héjbet [1] {a masc.} BosM *col* multitude <NE*1>

héjbet [2] {adv.} BosM *col* many, numerous: *Tamo je bilo hejbet raje. There was a whole bunch of people over there.* <NE*1>

hȅklānje {a neut.} (lit. crocheting) *sl-sex* ***Fac-Obs*** sexual intercourse <Ger*1>

hȅklati {ām, ajū imperf.} (lit. crochet) **a.** *col* crochet <Ger*1> **b.** *sl-sex* ***Fac*** engage in sexual intercourse <Ger*2>

hȅkler {a masc.} *sl-mil* automatic weapon <BN>

hèmiš {a masc.} *sl-sstu* chemistry (as a science course) <Gre☞>

hȅmke {eta neut.} *sl-sstu* chemistry teacher <Gre☞>

hȅmos {a (acc. = gen.) masc.} *sl-sstu* chemistry teacher <Gre☞>

hȅmosi {mōsā masc. pl.} *sl* hemorrhoids <Gre☞>

hèmpeš {a (acc. = gen.) masc.} *sl-fea* clumsy male, klutz

hȅndikep {a masc.} (lit. handicap) *sl-media* ***Iro*** happy ending (of a movie, etc.) <Eng*1>

hȅnkati {ām, ajū biasp.} **1** *sl* be in debt **2** *sl* sleep, nap

hȅp {a +ov (ext. pl) masc.; Nom Pl hèpovi} *sl-drugs* hashish consumer, hash head <Eng☞>

hȅpī {adj.} /hèpi/ *sl* happy <Eng>

heplírati {hèplīrām, rajū biasp.} *sl-crime* rob the same person several times

hȅplovati {lujēm, lujū imperf. intr.} *sl-crime* rob, fleece, rip off

hèrba {ē fem.} (lit. herbs) *sl-drugs* herbs (used as narcotic drugs) <Lat*1>

hèrberg {a masc.} (lit. hostel) *sl* railway station <Ger*1>

hȅrc-ròmān {romána masc.} (lit. heart novel) *sl* romance novel (usu. of low quality) <**Ger**[*1]>

hercegovánac {nca (acc. = gen.) masc.} (lit. 'Herzegoshitter': a contamination from 'Hercegovac' Herzegovinian and 'govno' excrement) *sl* Herzegovinian (inhabitant of the Southern part of Bosnia and Herzegovina) <**Slav**✍>

hȅrcfȅler {a masc.} (lit. heart condition) *sl* being in love <**Ger**[*1]>

hèrcig {adj.} *sl* lovely <**Ger**[*1]>

héro {a masc.} *sl-drugs* heroin, horse, smack <**Eng**✍>

hȅroš {a (acc. = gen.) masc.} *sl* hero <**Gre**[*1]>

hȅt {a +ov (ext. pl) masc.; Nom Pl hètovi} *sl* hat <**Eng**>

hètrik {a masc.} (lit. hat trick) [std. = het-trik] *sl-sports* hat trick (three goals scored by one player during one game of soccer) <**Eng**✍>

hèvina {ē fem.} **a.** *sl-sex* ***Obs*** vagina, cunt <**Gyp**> **b.** *sl-sex* ***Obs*** prostitute, hooker <**Gyp**[*1]> **c.** *sl* ***Obs*** female <**Gyp**[*2]>

- **strȍgā hèvina** {NP} **a.** *sl-fea* rich female **b.** *sl-fea* reasonable female

hȅznuti {nēm, nū perf.} *sl* hit, punch

hȉ {excl.} **1** *col* laughing sound <**Slav**> **2** *col* used to attract one's attention in informal communication, hey

hìbrīdan {dna, dno adj.} (lit. hybrid) *sl-fea* handsome, cute <**Lat**[*1]>

Híco {ē masc.} *sl* Hitler <**GerO**✍>

Hȉčkok *See the following*

- **Hȉčkok je ȉzabraō zà vās.** {S} (lit. Hitchcok has chosen for you.) *sl-sstu* ***Fac*** school test or quiz

Híća {ē masc.} *sl* Hitler <**GerO**✍>

Hićo {ē masc.} *sl* Hitler <**GerO**✍>

hidrocentrála {ē fem.} (lit. water power plant) *sl-drink* drink (alcohol) <**Gre**[*1]>

hȉhot {a masc.} **a.** *col* the sound of laughter, hah-hah <**Slav**> **b.** *col* giggle

hihòtānje {a neut.} *col* giggling <**Slav**>

hihòtati se {hìhoćēm, oćū imperf. intr.} *col* giggle <**Slav**>

hȉjo {excl.} *col* used to command a horse to move on, go <**Slav**>

hȉkī {īja masc.} *sl-fea* attack of hysteria, freak out <**Gre**✍>

Hȉl *See the following*

- **Kanârī Hȉl** {NP} (lit. Canary Hill) *sl* ***Fac*** Kanarevo Brdo (a neighborhood in Belgrade, Serbia)
- **Kukuríkū Hȉl** {NP} (lit. Cock-a-doodle-doo Hill) *sl* name for Petlovo brdo (a neighborhood in Belgrade Yugoslavia)

hȉljada *See the following*

- **Hȉljadu[PPRON] mâjki jèbēm!** {LSF} (lit. I fuck [PPRON] thousand mothers!) *col* ***Off*** used as a strong curse, Fuck you!

Hȉltōn {Hiltóna masc.} (lit. Hilton) **1** *sl-crime* ***Iro*** prison <**BN**[*1]> **2 Cro** *sl-polit* ***Iro*** Croatian Communist Party Headquarters in Zagreb, Croatia <**BN**[*1]>

hȉlja {ē fem.} *sl* thousand dinars; a thousand-dinar bill, a grand <**Gre**✍>

hiljadárka {ē fem.} *col* thousand dinars; a thousand-dinar bill, a grand <**Gre**✍>

hȉljka {ē fem.} *sl* thousand dinars; a thousand-dinar bill, a grand <**Gre**✍>

hìlzn {a masc.} *sl-auto* cartridge case <**Ger**>

Himaláji {a masc. pl.} (lit. the Himalayas) *sl-crime* police station <**SlavO**[*1]>

hȉnt {a masc.} *sl* hint, clue <**Eng**>

hínja {ē fem.} *sl-fea* miser, tightwad, skinflint

hȉpī {īja masc.} /hìpi/ **1** *col* hippie <**Eng**> **2** *sl* hippodrome

hipijána {ē fem.} *sl* hippies <**Eng**⁘>

hipijánović {a (acc. = gen.) masc.} *sl* hippie <**Eng**⁘>

hìpik {a (acc. = gen.) masc.} **a.** *sl* hippie <**Eng**⁘> **b.** *sl-drugs* drug addict, junkie <**Eng**⁘[*1]>

hipodrómac {a (acc. = gen.) masc.} (lit. the one from the hippodrome) *sl-fea* stupid or mentally deficient person <**Gre**⁘[*1]>

hȉps *See the following*

- **mâlī hȉps** {NP} *sl-drugs* small quantity of hashish

hìpten {adv.} *col* many, numerous <**NE**>

Hirohȉto {a masc.} **1** *sl-sstu* principal <**JapO**[*1]> **2** *sl* director, boss, manager <**JapO**[*1]>

hìstērija {ē fem.} (lit. hysteria) *sl-sstu* history <**Gre**[*1]>

histèrisati {išēm, išū imperf. intr.} *sl* go insane, freak out <**Gre**[*1]>

histerizírati {rìzīrām, rizírajū imperf. intr.} *sl* go insane, freak out <**Gre**[*1]>

hȉt {a +ov (ext. pl) masc.; Nom Pl hìtovi} *col* success, hit <**Eng**>

hȉtati kârte {VP} (lit. throw cards) *sl-gamble* play cards ☞ **hitati**

hȉtati se {ām, ajū imperf. intr.} (lit. throw oneself away) *sl* dance <**Slav***1>

- **hȉtati kârte** {VP} (lit. throw cards) *sl-gamble* play cards

hítiti 1 {tīm, tē imperf. intr.} BosM *col* hurry up, rush <NE*1>

hȉtiti 2 {tīm, tē perf.} **a.** *col* throw away, toss out <**Slav**> **b.** *sl* start working <**Slav***1> **c.** *sl* start flirting <**Slav***2>

- **hȉtiti pȉškeca** {VP} (lit. throw a piss) Cro *sl-sex* ***Fac-Obs*** urinate
- **hȉtiti rȉgleca** {VP} (lit. throw a vomit) Cro *sl-fea* vomit, throw up, puke

hȉtiti se {tīm, tē perf. intr.} **a.** *sl* start working <**Slav***1> **b.** *sl* start flirting <**Slav***2>

Hȉtler [PRON:ACC] je ìzvūkaō na lùtrijī. {LSF} (lit. *Adolf* Hitler has drawn [PRON:ACC] in a lottery!) *sl-fea* ***Fac*** used to indicate that someone is very unattractive, [PRON:NOM] is very ugly!: *Hitler ga je izvukao na lutriji! He is very ugly!* ☞ **Hitler**

- **kò da ga je Hȉtler ìzvūkō na lùtriji** {PP} (lit. like *Adolf* Hitler drew him in a lottery) *sl-fea* ***Fac-Der*** extremely unattractive, ugly as sin

hȉtnā {ē fem. (adj. decl.)} [std. = hitna pomoć] *col* emergency medical service <**Slav***1>

hȉtno *See the following*

- **pòd hitno** {PP} (lit. under urgent) *col* right away, now

hìtrī trȅn {NP} *sl* express train ☞ **tren**

hjȁ {excl.} *col* used to express hesitation, huh <**Slav**>

hládan *See the following*

- **mŕtav hládan** {AdjP} (lit. dead cold) *col* uninterested

hládan tȕš {NP} (lit. cold shower) *col* shock, cold shower ☞ **tuš**

hlàdetina {ē fem.} (lit. cold cut) *sl* ***Fac*** corpse, stiff <**Slav***1>

hláditi se {hlâdīm, dē imperf. intr.} (lit. cool off) *sl* play cards <**Slav***1>

hlâdnī òblog {NP} (lit. cold compress) *sl* unpleasant news ☞ **oblog**

hlâdno {adv.} *sl-sex* ***Der*** frigidly <**Slav***1>

hlâdno skȍntāno {AdjP} (lit. coldly calculated) *sl-fea* ***App*** clever, intelligent ☞ **skontati**

hladòvina {ē fem.} /hladovìna/ (lit. shade) **a.** *sl* place used to get some rest <**Slav***1> **b.** *sl* resting <**Slav***2> *sl* spending one's time in useless activities, fooling around, messing around <**Slav***3>

hlȅb {a +ov (ext. pl) masc.; Nom Pl hlèbovi} (lit. bread) **1 SerE** *sl-sex* ***Fac-Obs*** female breast, tit <**Slav***1> **2 SerE** *sl* ***App*** good and loved person <**Slav***1>

hlèbati {ām, ajū perf. intr.} (lit. bread) SerE *sl* relax, take it easy <**Slav**❖*1>

hlebínac {nca (acc. = gen.) masc.} *sl-fea* naive male <**SlavO***1>

Hlèbine {Hlȅbīnā fem. pl.} *sl-fea* naive person <**SlavO***1>

hljȅb {a +ov (ext. pl) masc.; Nom Pl hljèbovi} (lit. bread) **a. Ser** *col* work, labor <**Slav***1> **b. Ser** *col* job, gig <**Slav***2>

- **ko hljȅb** {PP} (lit. like bread) *col* ***App*** very good (of a person)

hm {excl.} *col* used to express hesitation, huh <**Slav**>

hmȅlj {hmèlja +ev (ext. pl) masc.; Nom Pl hmèljevi} (lit. hop) *sl-drink* beer <**Slav***1>

hmíliti {līm, lē imperf. intr.} BosM *col* move slowly (usu. of insects) <**Slav**✍>

hmíljeti {līm, lē imperf. intr.} BosM *col* move slowly (usu. of insects) <**Slav**✍>

hmm {excl.} *col* well <**Slav**>

hȍ {excl.} *col* hah <**Slav**>

hô-rȕk 1 {excl.} *col* used to stimulate somebody to a common action, heave-ho <**Slav**>

hô-rȕk 2 {adv.} *sl* carelessly <**Slav**>

hòbist {a (acc. = gen.) masc.} (lit. hobbyist) *sl-stu* student <**Eng***1>

hȍblānje {a neut.} (lit. planing) *sl-sex* ***Obs*** sexual intercourse <**Ger***1>

hȍblati {ām, ajū imperf.} (lit. plane) *sl-sex* ***Obs*** engage in sexual intercourse with (of a male) <**Ger***1>

hòblbank {a masc.} (lit. planing workbench) *sl-sex* ***Fac-Obs*** place intended for sexual intercourse <**Ger***1>

hȍbler {a masc.} (lit. one who planes) *sl-fea* ***Fac*** male with curly hair <**Ger***1>

hȍćan {ćna, ćno adj.} *col* willing <**Slav**>

Hòćemo li se kárat? {S} (lit. Are we going to fuck?) *sl-sex* ***Obs*** used to propose sexual intercourse ☞ **hteti, htjeti**

Hòćeš se sklízati? {S} (lit. Do you want to slide down?) *sl-sex* ***Fac-Obs*** used to propose sexual intercourse ☞ **hteti, htjeti**

hódalica {ē fem.} **1** *sl* leg (human) <Slav⁘> **2** *sl* cheap prostitute <Slav⁘[*1]>

hódāljka {ē fem.; Dat hódāljki} *sl* leg (human) <Slav⁘>

hódati {hôdām, hódajū imperf. intr.} **1** *sl* spend one's time in useless activities, fool around, mess around <Slav[*1]> **2** *col* date, go out with <Slav[*1]> **3** *sl-sex* work as a streetwalker <Slav[*1]>

hȍdi {excl.} *col* used to make somebody come, come over <Slav> ☞ **odi**

hòdulja {ē fem.} (lit. walker) *sl* leg (human) <Slav⁘[*1]>

hofírānje {a neut.} *sl* flirting <Ger[*1]>

hofírati {hòfīām, hofírajū biasp.} *sl* flirt <Ger[*1]>

hȍg *See the following*

- **mâlī hȍg** {NP} *sl* boss

hȍho {excl.} *col* used to express surprise, disbelief, etc., wow <Slav>

hȍhot {a masc.} *col* giggle <Slav>

hohòtānje {a neut.} *col* giggling <Slav>

hohòtati {hòhoćēm, oćū imperf. intr.} *col* giggle <Slav>

hohòtati se {hòhoćēm, oćū imperf. intr.} *col* giggle <Slav>

hohòtav {a, o adj.} *col* giggling <Slav>

hòhštapler {a (acc.= gen.) masc.} **a.** *sl-fea* impostor (male) <Ger> **b.** *sl-fea* status seeker, pretentious person, social climber (male), phony <Ger[*1]>

hohštaplèrāj {pleràja masc.} *sl-fea* the condition of a status seeker, pretentious person, social climber <Ger>

hòhštaplerka {ē fem.; Dat hòhštaplērki} **a.** *sl-fea* impostor (female) <Ger> **b.** *sl-fea* status seeker, pretentious person, social climber (male), phony <Ger>

hôj {excl.} *col* used to draw attention in direct informal communication, hey <Slav>

hȍjkānje {a neut.} *col* calling <Slav>

hȍjkati {ām, ajū imperf.} *col* call, shout <Slav>

hokèjāš {kejáša (acc. = gen.) masc.} (lit. hockey player) **a.** *sl-fea* ***Fac*** male who uses cane <Eng⁘[*1]> **b.** *sl-fea* ***Fac*** elderly male <Eng⁘[*2]>

Holàndija {ē fem.} (lit. Holland) *sl* ***Fac*** Banat (region in northeastern Serbia) <DutO[*1]>

hòlbaks {a masc.} *sl* muscular leg (of a woman) <Ger[*1]>

hòlcerica {ē fem.} *sl-sex* ***Obs*** vagina, cunt <Ger⁘[*1]>

Hòlivūd {a masc.} /Hòlivud/ (lit. Hollywood) *sl-sex* ***Fac*** bathroom <EngO[*1]>

hombòlēr {boléra masc.} *sl* female

hòmīć {homíća (acc. = gen.) masc.} *sl-sex* ***Der*** male homosexual, gay <Gre⁘[*1]>

hȍmos {a (acc. = gen.) masc.} *sl-sex* male homosexual, gay <Gre✍>

homosàpiens {a (acc. = gen.) masc.} (lit. Homo sapiens) *sl-sex* ***Fac*** male homosexual, gay <Lat[*1]>

hȍndić {a (acc. = gen.) masc.} *sl-auto* Honda (make of motorcycle) <BN✍>

hȍp {a +ov (ext. pl) masc.; Nom Pl hòpovi} *sl-drugs* opium <Slav[*1]>

hȍp-cȕp [1] {excl.} *col* used while dancing the kolo (a traditional folk dance) <Slav>

hȍp-cȕp [2] {neut.} *sl-sex* ***Fac-Obs*** sexual intercourse <Slav>

hȍpā {excl.} *col* used when jumping, hop <Slav>

- **hȍpā bâto** {ExcP} (lit. oh boy) *col* used to express astonishment, etc., oh boy

hȍpā-cȕpā [1] {excl.} *col* used while dancing kolo (a traditional folk dance) <Slav>

hȍpā-cȕpā [2] {neut.} *sl-sex* ***Fac-Obs*** sexual intercourse <Slav>

hȍpsā {excl.} *col* used when jumping, hop <Slav>

hȍpsalica {ē fem.} *sl* bus station <Slav⁘[*1]>

hòpsalīšte {a neut.} *sl* dance floor <Slav⁘[*1]>

hȍpsasā {ē masc.} **a.** *sl-fea* unattractive boy <Slav[*1]> **b.** *sl-fea* hated male, sob <Slav[*2]>

hȍpsati {ām, ajū imperf.} **a.** *col* hop <Slav⁘[*1]> **b.** *sl* dance <Slav⁘[*2]>

horizontála {ē fem.} **a.** *sl* sleeping <Gre[*1]> **b.** *sl* bed <Gre[*2]>

hòrmōnka {ē fem.} *sl-sports* steroid pill <Gre[*1]>

hȍrn {a +ov (ext. pl) masc.; Nom Pl hòrnovi} *sl-drugs* heroin, horse, smack <Eng>

hòrnīć {horníća masc.} *sl* radio

hȍrōz {a (acc. = gen.) masc.} Bos *dia-col* rooster <NE>

horòzić {a (acc. = gen.) masc.} Bos *dia-col* small rooster <NE⁘>

hôrs {a +ev (ext. pl) masc.; Nom Pl hórsevi} *sl-drugs* heroin, horse, smack <Eng>

Hôrs Sȉtī {NP} (lit. Horse City) Ser *sl* ***Fac*** name for Konjarnik (a neighborhood in Belgrade, Serbia) ☞ **Siti**

hȍštapler {a (acc. = gen.) masc.} **a.** *col* impostor (male) <Ger> **b.i.** *col* lazy or shiftless person, bum, good for nothing <Ger[*1]> **ii.** *col* status seeker, pretentious person, social climber, phony <Ger[*1]>

hȍt-dȍg {a masc.} *col* hot dog (the food) <Eng>

hotelȉška {ē fem.; Dat hotelȉški} /hotelȉška/ *sl* hotel <Fre✍>

hȍtlājn {a masc.} *col* hot line (telephone link) <Eng>

hráčak {čka masc.} *sl* spit <Slav>

hrȁčkati {ām, ajū imperf.} *sl* spit <Slav>

hrȁčnuti {nēm, nū perf.} *sl* spit <Slav>

hrákac {kca masc.} *sl* spit <Slav>

hrákati {hrâkām, hrákajū imperf.} //hrâčēm, čū imperf./ *sl* spit <Slav>

hráknuti {hrâknēm, nū perf.} *sl* spit <Slav>

hrána {ē fem.} (lit. food) *sl-drugs* narcotic drug, dope <Slav>

hranàrina {ē fem.} *sl* food <Slav[*1]>

hrániti {hrânīm, nē imperf.} **a.** *sl* persuade, convince <Slav> **b.** *sl* lie <Slav[*1]>
- **hrániti mȍstra** {VP} *sl* cheat a naive person
- **hrániti strâhom** {VP} (lit. feed with fear) *sl-fea* scare, frighten

Hȑbin {a (acc. = gen.) masc.} *sl* ***Fac*** a child from a Serbian-Croatian intermarriage <Slav❖>

hȑčiti {čīm, čē imperf.} *sl* eat, devour <Slav>

hȑda {ē fem.} *sl* food <Slav>

hrȅnōvke {ī fem. pl.} (lit. wieners) *sl* pantyhose <Slav[*1]>

hȑga {ē fem.; Dat hȑgi} **1** *sl* nose <Slav[*1]> **2** *sl* head <Slav[*1]> **3** *sl-fea* stupid or mentally deficient person <Slav[*1]>

hrȉp {a +ov (ext. pl) masc.; Nom Pl hrìpovi} *col* wheezing <Slav>

hrȉpa {ē fem.} *col* wheezing <Slav>

hrípānje {a neut.} *col* wheezing <Slav>

hrípati {hrîpām, hrípajū imperf. intr.} *col* wheeze <Slav>

hrȉpav {a, o adj.} *col* wheezy <Slav>

hȑk {a +ov (ext. pl) masc.; Nom Pl hŕkovi} *col* snoring <Slav>

hȑka {ē fem.; Dat hȑki} *col* snoring <Slav>

hŕkalo {a neut.} *col* snorer <Slav>

hrkánac {nca masc.} *col* sleeping <Slav❖>

hŕkānje {a neut.} *col* snoring <Slav>

hŕkati {hȑkām, hŕkajū imperf.} (lit. snore) *sl-sex* ***Obs*** engage in sexual intercourse with (of a male) <Slav>

hŕknuti {nēm, nū perf.} *sl-sex* ***Obs*** engage in sexual intercourse with (of a male) <Slav[*1]>

hrkobȕtnuti {nēm, nū perf.} *sl-sex* ***Obs*** engage in sexual intercourse with (of a male) <Slav✍>

hrònično pȍdān {AdjP} (lit. chronically subordinate) *sl-fea* ***Der*** easily falling in love ☞ **podan**

hrȍpot {a masc.} *col* snoring <Slav>

hropòtati {ròpoćēm, oćū imperf. intr.} *col* snore <Slav>

hȑpa {ē fem.} *col* pile, heap <Slav>
- **hȑpa gȍvānā** {NP} (lit. a pile, heap of shit) *sl* ***Der-Obs*** low-quality objects or ideas, pile of shit

hȑsuz {a (acc. = gen.) masc.} //a (acc. = gen.) masc./ BosM *col* ***Der*** worthless or despicable person <NE>

hrȕpiti {pīm, pē perf.} /hrúpiti/ *col* appear in large quantities <Slav>

hrȕstiti se {tīm, tē imperf. intr.} *sl* threaten

Hȑvāt *See the following*
- **pòtūrčenī Hȑvāt** {NP} (lit. a Croat converted into a Turk) *sl-fea* ***Off*** Bosnian Muslim

htȅti, htjȅti *See the following*
- **Hòćemo li se kárat?** {S} (lit. Are we going to fuck?) *sl-sex* ***Obs*** used to propose sexual intercourse
- **Hòćeš se sklízati?** {S} (lit. Do you want to slide down?) *sl-sex* ***Fac-Obs*** used to propose sexual intercourse
- **htȅti čúvati ôvce a némati štâp** {VP} (lit. want to keep sheep and not have a stick) *sl-fea* want to have fun without having any money
- **Nêćemo da kvârīmo.** {VP} (lit. We don't want to spoil it.) *sl* used to refer to a desired state of affairs, We don't want to spoil anything.
- **Ȍš prôđēš kroz jâ?** {S} (lit. Do you want to go through me?) *sl* used to refer to lack of consent, over my dead body
- **[PRON:NOM] hȍće da se jèbē a da [PRON:DAT] ne uđe.** used to indicate that a person would like to take an action without taking any related risks

hȕ {excl.} *col* used to express surprise, astonishment, etc. ugh <Slav>

hudòvica {ē fem.} [std. = udovica] BosM *col* widow <Slav✍>

hûj {excl.} *col* used to express surprise, astonishment, etc., ugh <Slav>

hȕja {ē fem.} **a.** *col* evil nature <NE*1> **b.** *col* outrage <NE*2>

hûk {a +ov (ext. pl) masc.; Nom Pl húkovi} *col* noise <Slav>

hȕka {ē fem.} *col* noise <Slav>

húkati {hûčēm, čū imperf. intr.} **1** *col* gasp <Slav> **2** *col* pant <Slav> **3** *col* pronounce 'huh' being in trouble <Slav>

húknuti {hûknēm, nū perf.} *col* pronounce 'huh' being in trouble <Slav>

hulahȍp {a +ov (ext. pl) masc.; Nom Pl hulahȍpi} *col* pantyhose <Eng*1>

hulahȍpke {i fem. pl.} *col* pantyhose <Eng⁘*1>

hȕlja {ē masc.} *col* ***Der*** worthless or despicable person <Slav>

hûm {a +ov (ext. pl) masc.; Nom Pl húmovi} *sl-sex* male easily cheated by a prostitute

hȕmīć {humíća (acc. = gen.) masc.} *sl-fea* joker, trickster, rascal

humorírati {mòrīrām, morírajū biasp. intr.} *sl* laugh <Lat⁘*1>

hùncut {a (acc. = gen.) masc.} *sl* troublemaker, rowdy, ruffian <Hun>

huncutàrija {ē fem.} *sl-fea* the condition of being a rowdy, troublemaker <Hun⁘>

hȕrā {excl.} *col* used to express joy, hurrah <Slav>

hȕrlīk {a masc.} [std. = urlik] *col* scream in pain, fear, or outrage <Slav✍>

hurlíkati {hùrlīčēm, čū imperf.} [std. = urlikati] *col* scream in pain, fear, or outrage <Slav✍>

hurlíknuti {hùrlīknēm, nū perf.} [std. = urliknuti] *col* scream in pain, fear, or outrage <Slav✍>

hvála {excl.} *col* used to express gratitude, thanks <Slav>

- **hvála Bȍgu** {NP} (lit. thank God) *col* used to express gratitude, thank God: *Hvala Bogu, sve je prošlo kako treba. Thank God, everything was as it should be.*
- **Hvála kûrcu!** {S} (lit. Thanks to the cock!) **1** *sl* ***Obs*** used to express the completion of a long awaited event, At last! Finally! **2** *sl* ***Obs*** used as a strong affirmative response, sure: *A: Jesi dobio karte? B: Hvala kurcu da jesam! A: Did you get the tickets? B: You bet!*
- **Hvála kûrcu na ȕdārcu!** {S} (lit. Thanks to the prick for this hit!) *sl* ***Fac-Obs*** used to express the completion of a long awaited event, At last! Finally!
- **Hvála pízdi!** {S} (lit. Thanks to the cunt!) *sl* ***Fac-Obs*** used to express the completion of a long awaited event
- **Hvála pízdi na pȍgotku!** {S} (lit. Thanks to the cunt for this hit!) *sl* ***Fac-Obs*** used to express the completion of a long awaited event, It's about fucking time!

hváliti {hvâlīm, lē imperf.} *col* miss, lack, be out of: *Hvali mi plivanje. I miss swimming.* ◊ *Hvali mi šećera u kući. I am out of sugar in my house.* <Slav*1>

hvȁtalo {a neut.} (lit. catcher) **a.** *sl* hand <Slav*1> **b.** arm <Slav*2>

hvȁtati *See the following*

- **hvȁtati ȁvu** {VP} (lit. catch air) *sl-fea* ***Fac*** spend one's time in useless activities, fool around, mess around
- **hvȁtati dȉm** {VP} (lit. catch smoke) *sl-fea* ***Fac*** spend one's time in useless activities, fool around, mess around
- **hvȁtati dȉm od lâđe i lokomotívē i prodávati ga** {VP} (lit. catch the steam from a ship and a locomotive and sell it) *sl-fea* ***Fac*** spend one's time in useless activities, fool around, mess around
- **hvȁtati krȉvine** {VP} (lit. catch turns) *sl-fea* escape, flee
- **hvȁtati krivìnu** {VP} (lit. hold a curve) *col* avoid work, shirk work
- **hvȁtati màglu** {VP} (lit. catch fog) *sl* run away, flee
- **hvȁtati na mȕšicu** {VP} (lit. catch on a fly) *sl* ***Fac*** flirt
- **hvȁtati na štósove** {VP} (lit. catch using tricks) *sl* trick, cheat, swindle
- **hvȁtati nȍkat** {VP} (lit. catch a nail) *sl* run away, flee
- **hvȁtati štúru** {VP} (lit. catch running) *sl* run away, flee
- **hvȁtati tȁlāse** {VP} (lit. catch waves) *sl* try to get in touch with
- **hvȁtati tûtanj** {VP} (lit. catch rumble) *col* run away, flee
- **hvȁtati zjȁla** {VP} *sl-fea* spend one's time in useless activities, fool around, mess around

hvȁtati se {ām, ajū imperf. intr.} (lit. catch each other) *sl-sex* ***Obs*** engage in sexual foreplay, pet, feel up <Slav*1>

Ii

i kvȉt {ConjP} *col* used to refer to the final state of affairs, period, that's it: *Ti si njega udario, on je tebe i kvit. You hit him, he hit you, and that's it.* ☞ **kvit**

I òca ti i mȁtēr jèbēm! {S} (lit. I fuck both your father and your mother!) *col* ***Off*** used as a strong curse ☞ otac

ȉ tō mi je nȇkakav štôs {S} (lit. and that is some trick) *col* ***Der*** used to belittle somebody's achievement, that's not worth shit ☞ štos

ȉ-hâ-hâ {adv.} **a.** *col* more than enough: *Hrane ima i-ha-ha za svakoga. There is more than enough food for everybody.* <**Slav**> **b.** too much, overwhelming <**Slav**[*1]>

ȉ-hā-hâj {adv.} **a.** *col* more than enough: *On ima para i-ha-haj. He's got more than enough money.* <**Slav**> **b.** too much, overwhelming <**Slav**[*1]>

i-i-ijȕ {excl.} *col* used to express excitement or joy, wow <**Slav**>

iâ {excl.} *col* the sound made by a donkey, hee-haw <**Slav**>

ibȅovac {vca (acc. = gen.) masc.} *sl-polit* supporter of Stalin in the Tito-Stalin conflict of 1948 <**Abb**⁘>

ibȅovskī {ā, ō adj.} *sl-polit* pertaining to supporters of Stalin in the Tito-Stalin conflict of 1948 <**Abb**⁘>

ȉber {excl.} *sl* one more <**Ger**[*1]>

iberàisovati se {išēm, išū biasp. intr.} *sl-crafts* wear out (make unusable through long or heavy use): *Iberaisovala se osovina. The axle is worn out.* <**Ger**[*1]>

ìberlauf {a masc.} *sl-crafts* overflow (usu. on an engine) <**Ger**>

ȉbić {a (acc. = gen.) masc.} *sl-polit* supporter of Stalin in the Tito-Stalin conflict of 1948 <**Abb**⁘[*1]>

ìbret {a masc.} *col* joke <**NE**[*1]>

Íća {ē fem.} *sl* ***Fam*** Italy <**SlavO**✍>

ìći {ìdēm, ìdu, ìď, ìš imperf. irreg.} **1** *col* be suitable, be fitting: *Ide li ova kravata uz ovo odijelo? Does this tie match this suit?* <**Slav**[*1]> **2** *col* date somebody <**Slav**[*1]> **3** *col* happen, occur: *Šta ide? What's happening?* <**Slav**[*1]>

- **ìći čìrike** {VP} *sl-sstu* skip classes, cut classes
- **ìći dvójkom** {VP} (lit. ride on the number two) *sl* ***Fac*** walk
- **ìći đònom** {VP} (lit. go with a sole) *sl* attack without any scruples, attack viciously (verbally)
- **ìći kao âlva** {VP} (lit. go like halva) *col* sell out quickly, sell like hotcakes
- **ìći kao hâlva** {VP} (lit. go like halva) *sl* sell out quickly, sell like hotcakes
- **ìći kao pòdmazāno**{VP} (lit. go like being lubricated) *col* go smoothly
- **ìći kod mòkrovića** {VP} (lit. go to the wet one) *sl-sex* ***Fac*** go to the bathroom
- **ìći na bùbrege** {VP} (lit. go to one's kidneys) *sl-fea* ***Fac*** get on one's nerves
- **ìći na čìtānje** {VP} (lit. go to the reading) *sl-fea* try to understand
- **ìći na deljáka** {VP} (lit. go to the splitting) SerE *sl-crime* share costs or loot
- **ìći na džȉgericu** {VP} (lit. go to one's liver) **a.** *sl-fea* ***Der*** be boring **b.** *sl-fea* ***Der*** get on one's nerves
- **ìći na đȍn** {VP} (lit. go to one's sole) *col* insinuate
- **ìći na gànglije** {VP} (lit. go to one's ganglia) *sl-fea* ***Der*** get on one's nerves
- **ìći na jája** {VP} (lit. go to one's balls) *sl-fea* ***Der-Obs*** be boring
- **ìći na jêdnjāk** {VP} (lit. go to one's gullet) *sl-fea* ***Der*** be boring
- **ìći na jȅtra** {VP} (lit. go to one's liver) *sl-fea* ***Der*** be boring
- **ìći na jȅtru** {VP} (lit. go to one's liver) *sl-fea* ***Der*** be boring
- **ìći na lêr** {VP} (lit. go into neutral gear) *sl* ***Fac*** engage in uncertain business
- **ìći na líniju** {VP} (lit. go to the line) *sl-crime* ***Fac*** go to steal
- **ìći na mínus dvâ dèci** {VP} (lit. go to the minus two decilitres) *sl-sex* ***Fac*** urinate, pee
- **ìći na Mȉrogōj** {VP} (lit. go to Mirogoj: central cemetery in Zagreb, Croatia) Cro *sl* ***Fac*** go to sleep
- **ìći na pȁlac** {VP} (lit. go to the thumb) *sl* ***Fac*** hitch-hike, thumb
- **ìći na prózivku** {VP} (lit. go to roll-call) *sl* go to a meeting
- **ìći na samoubòjstvo** {VP} (lit. go to suicide) *sl* ***Fac*** go to work
- **ìći na telèfōn** {VP} (lit. go to a telephone) *sl-sex* ***Fac*** go to the bathroom
- **ìći na tràmvaj** {VP} (lit. go to a streetcar) *sl* go to a meeting
- **ìći na vécu** {VP} *sl-sex* ***Fac*** go to the bathroom

• **ìći na žȉvce** {VP} (lit. go to one's nerves) *sl-fea* ***Der*** get on one's nerves

• **ìći po gànglijama** {VP} (lit. step on one's ganglia) *sl-fea* ***Der*** get on one's nerves

• **ìći po žȉvcima** {VP} (lit. step on one's nerves) *sl-fea* ***Der*** get on one's nerves

• **ìći se ubíjati** {VP} (lit. go to kill oneself) **a.** *sl-fea* ***Fac*** go to a party **b.** *sl-sex* ***Fac*** go to an orgy

• **ìći si páliti glâvu** {VP} (lit. go to burn one's head) Cro *sl-fea* ***Fac*** go to work

• **ìći tûći národ** {VP} (lit. go to beat people) *sl* ***Fac*** go to work

• **ìći ù krpe** {VP} (lit. go to the patches) *col* ***Fam*** go to sleep

• **ìći u žȉvot** {VP} (lit. go to life) *sl* go to a party

• **ìći uz dlȁku** {VP} (lit. go against one's hair) *col* ***Der*** oppose, be defiant

• **Ȉd u kȕrac!** {S} (lit. Go to the cock!) *col* ***Off*** used in angry dismissal, Fuck off!

• **Ìd u óčīn!** {S} (lit. Go to the father's *cock*!) *col-dia* ***Off*** used in angry dismissal, Fuck off!

• **Ìd u pízdu mȁterinu!** {S} (lit. Go to your mother's cunt!) *col* ***Off*** used in angry dismissal, Fuck off!

• **Ìdē ònā stvâr Hèlmuta Kôla Káro sam do bôla.** {S} (lit. They play that thing by Helmut Kohl, "I fucked until I had pain".) *sl* ***Fac-Obs*** used to refer to one's unfamiliarity with the music being played

• **Ȉdēš mi na jája!** {S} (lit. You're going on my balls!) *sl* ***Off*** used to express impatience toward one's interlocutor, You make me fucking nervous!

• **Ìdi bȅstrāga!** {S} (lit. Go to the place where there are no traces!) *col* used in angry dismissal, Go to hell!

• **ìdi brè** {VP} SerE *col* used to express disbelief

• **Ìdī dȍ đavola!** {S} (lit. Go to the devil!) *col* ***Off*** used in angry dismissal, Go to hell!

• **Ìdi do mòjēga!** {S} (lit. Go to my *prick*!) *col* ***Off*** used in angry dismissal, Fuck off!

• **ìdi mi dóđi mi!** {S} (lit. Go to me, come to me!) *col* used to refer to unidentified events, this and that

• **Ìdi mi ù kurac!** {S} (lit. Go to my prick!) *col* ***Off*** used in angry dismissal, Fuck off!

• **Ìdi nèsam te zvȁo s kȉćen kȕrac!** {S} (lit. Go away I did not call you with my decorated prick!) **SSer** *dia* ***Off*** used in angry dismissal, Fuck off!

• **Ìdi pȅcāj kàmile!** {S} (lit. Go and fish camels!) *sl* ***Fac*** used in angry dismissal, Beat it!

• **Ìdi pȉšāj pa se stȉšāj!** {S} (lit. Go take a piss and then calm down!) *sl* ***Fac-Obs*** used to calm down one's interlocutor, Cool off!

• **Ìdi pògledāj dȁ li sam iza ćȍška!** {S} (lit. Go and see if I am around the corner!) *sl* ***Fac*** used in angry dismissal, Beat it!

• **Ìdi tî u pízdu lêpū mȁterinu!** {S} (lit. Go to your nice mother's cunt!) **SerE** *col* ***Off*** used in angry dismissal, Fuck off!

• **Ìdi u bȍžjū mȁtēr!** {S} (lit. Go to God's mother!) *col* ***Off*** used in angry dismissal, Fuck off!

• **Ìdi u kȕrac!** {S} (lit. Go to cock!) *col* ***Off*** used in angry dismissal, Fuck off!

• **Ìdi u mâjčinu!** {S} (lit. Go to your mother's *cunt*!) *col* ***Off*** used in angry dismissal, Fuck off!

• **Ìdi u óčīn!** {S} (lit. Go to your father's *prick*!) *col-dia* ***Off*** used in angry dismissal, Fuck off!

• **Ìdi u péršun!** {S} (lit. Go to the parsley!) *sl* ***Fac*** used in facetious dismissal

• **Ìdi u pȉčku mȁterinu!** {S} (lit. Go to your mother's cunt!) *col* ***Off*** used in angry dismissal, Fuck you!

• **Ìdi u pízdu mȁterinu!** {S} (lit. Go to your mother's cunt!) *col* ***Off*** used in angry dismissal, Fuck you!

• **Ìdi u pízdu mȁternu!** {S} (lit. Go to your mother's cunt!) *col* ***Off*** used in angry dismissal, Fuck you!

• **Ìdi u pízdu mȁternjū!** {S} (lit. Go to your mother's cunt!) *col* ***Off*** used in angry dismissal, Fuck you!

• **Ìdi u pm!** {S} (lit. Go to your mc *mother's cunt*!) *col* ***Off*** used in angry dismissal, Fuck you!

• **Ìdi u trî pȉčke mâjčine!** {S} (lit. Go to *your* three mother's cunts!) *col* ***Off*** used in angry dismissal, Fuck you!

• **Ìdi u trî pízde mȁterine!** {S} (lit. Go to *your* three mother's cunts!) *col* ***Off*** used in angry dismissal, Fuck you!

• **Ìdi u vràžjū mȁtēr!** {S} (lit. Go to the devil's mother!) *col* ***Off*** used in angry dismissal, Fuck off!

• **Ìdi vȉdi ìmā li me nȁpolju!** {S} (lit. Go see if I am outside!) *sl* ***Fac*** used in angry dismissal, Beat it!

• **Ìdi zatvòri vráta izvàna!** {S} (lit. Go and close the door from outside!) *sl* ***Fac*** used in angry dismissal, Beat it!

• **Jèsi l ìšaō kȁd bez ȍka?** {S} (lit. Have you ever run without your eye?) *sl* ***Off*** used as a threat, I'm gonna beat the shit out of you!

• **Nek ìdē svȅ do kûrca!** {S} (lit. Let everything go to the prick!) *col* used to express lack of control over events, Fuck it!

ìćmet {a masc.} *col* multitude <**NE***[1]>

ìdāljka {ē fem.; Dat ìdāljki} *sl* leg (human) <**Slav**>

idéja {ē fem.} (lit. idea) *sl* leg (human) <**Gre***[1]>

• **fȉks idéja** {NP} *col* idee fixe, delusion

ìdeš {a (acc. = gen.) masc.} (lit. walker) *sl-sex* prostitute, streetwalker <**Slav**⁘*[1]>

Ìdēš mi na jája! {S} (lit. You're going on my balls!) *sl* ***Off*** used to express disgust toward one's interlocutor, You make me fucking nervous! ☞ **ići**

ìdi {excl.} *col* used to express disbelief, no kidding <**Slav**[*1]>

Ìdi bȅstrāga! {S} (lit. Go to the place where there are no traces!) *col* used in angry dismissal, Go to hell! ☞ **ići**

ìdi brè {VP} SerE *col* used to express disbelief, don't give me that shit ☞ **ići**

Ìdī dȍ đavola! {S} (lit. Go to the devil!) *col* ***Off*** used in angry dismissal, Go to hell! ☞ **ići**

Ìdi do mòjēga! {S} (lit. Go to my *prick*!) *col* ***Off*** used in angry dismissal, Fuck off! ☞ **ići**
• **ìdi mi dóđi mi!** {S} (lit. Go to me, come to me!) *col* used to refer to unidentified events, this and that ☞ **ići**

Ìdi mi ù kurac! {S} (lit. Go to my prick!) *col* ***Off*** used in angry dismissal, Fuck off! ☞ **ići**

Ìdi nèsam te zvȁo s kȉćen kȕrac! {S} (lit. Go away I did not call you with my decorated prick!) **SSer** *dia* ***Off*** used in angry dismissal, Fuck off! ☞ **ići**

Ìdi pȅcāj kàmile! {S} (lit. Go and fish camels!) *sl* ***Fac*** used in angry dismissal, Beat it! ☞ **ići**

Ìdi pìšāj pa se stìšāj! {S} (lit. Go take a piss and then calm down!) *sl* ***Fac-Obs*** used to calm down one's interlocutor, Cool off! ☞ **ići**

Ìdi pògledāj dȁ li sam iza ćòška! {S} (lit. Go and see if I am around the corner!) *sl* ***Fac*** used in angry dismissal, Beat it! ☞ **ići**

Ìdi tî u pízdu lêpū mȁterinu! {S} (lit. Go to your nice mother's cunt!) **SerE** *col* ***Off*** used in angry dismissal, Fuck off! ☞ **ići**

Ìdi u bȍžjū mȁtēr! {S} (lit. Go to God's mother!) *col* ***Off*** used in angry dismissal, Fuck off! ☞ **ići**

Ìdi u kȕrac! {S} (lit. Go to cock!) *col* ***Off*** used in angry dismissal, Fuck off! ☞ **ići**

Ìdi u mâjčinu! {S} (lit. Go to your mother's *cunt*!) *col* ***Off*** used in angry dismissal, Fuck off! ☞ **ići**

Ìdi u óčīn! {S} (lit. Go to your father's *prick*!) *col-dia* ***Off*** used in angry dismissal, Fuck off! ☞ **ići**

Ìdi u péršun! {S} (lit. Go to the parsley!) *sl* ***Fac*** used in facetious dismissal, Fuck off! ☞ **ići**

Ìdi u pȉčku mȁterinu! {S} (lit. Go to your mother's cunt!) *col* ***Off*** used in angry dismissal, Fuck you! ☞ **ići**

Ìdi u pízdu mȁterinu! {S} (lit. Go to your mother's cunt!) *col* ***Off*** used in angry dismissal, Fuck you! ☞ **ići**

Ìdi u pízdu mȁternu! {S} (lit. Go to your mother's cunt!) *col* ***Off*** used in angry dismissal, Fuck you! ☞ **ići**

Ìdi u pízdu mȁternjū! {S} (lit. Go to your mother's cunt!) *col* ***Off*** used in angry dismissal, Fuck you! ☞ **ići**

Ìdi u pm! {S} (lit. Go to your mc *mother's cunt*!) *col* ***Off*** used in angry dismissal, Fuck you! ☞ **ići**

Ìdi u trî pȉčke mâjčine! {S} (lit. Go to *your* three mother's cunts!) *col* ***Off*** used in angry dismissal, Fuck you! ☞ **ići**

Ìdi u trî pízde mȁterine! {S} (lit. Go to *your* three mother's cunts!) *col* ***Off*** used in angry dismissal, Fuck you! ☞ **ići**

Ìdi u vrȁžjū mȁtēr! {S} (lit. Go to the devil's mother!) *col* ***Off*** used in angry dismissal, Go to hell! ☞ **ići**

Ìdi vȉdi ìmā li me nȁpolju! {S} (lit. Go see if I am outside!) *sl* ***Fac*** used in angry dismissal, Beat it! ☞ **ići**

Ìdi zatvòri vráta izvàna! {S} (lit. Go and close the door from outside!) *sl* ***Fac*** used in angry dismissal, Beat it! ☞ **ići**

ìdidi {excl.} *sl* run (command) <**Slav**[*1]>

idìot {a (acc. = gen.) masc.} /**idiȍt** /a (acc. = gen.) masc./ **a.** *sl-fea* stupid or mentally deficient person <**Gre**> **b.** *sl-media* prompter (device in tv studios) <**Gre**[*1]>

idìotskī {ā, ō adj.} /**idiòtskī**/ (lit. idiotic) **a.** *sl-fea* unintelligent, idiotic: *idiotski plan idiotic plan* <**Gre**> **b.** *sl-fea* funny <**Gre**[*1]>

ìdiš {a masc.} *sl* ideal love, love of one's life <**Gre**⁘[*1]>

ȉdva {ē fem.} *sl* hardly any success

ȉđe {adv.} [std. = igd(j)e] *col-dia* anywhere: *Ima li iđe novina? Can I find the newspaper anywhere?* <**Slav**>

îđoš {perf.} *sl* walk <**Slav**>

ȉgđe {adv.} [std. = igd(j)e] *col-dia* anywhere: *Jesi li igđe vidio Muriza? Have you seen Muriz anywhere?* <**Slav**>

ȉglić {a masc.} *sl-sex* ***Fac*** male homosexual, gay <**Slav**⁘[*1]>

iglodȑkalo {a neut.} (lit. needle jackoff) *sl* turntable <**Slav**⁘[*1]>

ȉgrā [1] {excl.} *sl* used to express approval, okay <**Slav**>

ìgra [2] {ē fem.} (lit. game, play) **a.** *sl* plan: *igra za otvaranje firme plan to establish a company* <**Slav**[*1]> **b.** *sl* combination, tactics: *igra protiv predsjednika conspiration against the president* <**Slav**[*2]> **c.** *sl* conspiration <**Slav**[*2]>
• **drȕštvenē ìgre** {NP} (lit. social games) **1** *sl-gamble* ***Fac*** gambling **2** *sl-sex* ***Fac-Obs*** sexual intercourse

• ìgra s lȍptama {NP} (lit. play with the balls) *sl-sex* ***Fac-Obs*** rubbing female breast with the penis during sexual intercourse

igránac {nca masc.} (lit. dancing) *sl* dance <**Slav**❖*1>

ìgrānka {ē fem.} (lit. dancing) *sl* false incrimination, frame <**Slav***1>

igránjac {njca masc.} (lit. dancing) **a.** *sl* dance <**Slav**❖*1> **b.** party (social gathering) <**Slav**❖*2>

ȉgrānje *See the following*

• **ȉgrānje skriváča**{NP} (lit. hide-and-seek game) *sl-crime* ***Fac*** serving prison term on Goli island in Croatia (where the former communist regime detained its political enemies)

ȉgrati {ām, ajū imperf.} **1a.** *sl* be suitable, be fitting: *Igra mi taj stan. That condo is suitable for me.* <**Slav***1> **b.i.** *sl* be interesting: *Ova ulaznica igra sedam dana. This entrance ticket is valid for a week.* <**Slav***2> **ii.** *sl* be valid <**Slav***2> **iii.** be good, be cool: *Ona igra. She's cool.* 2 masturbate, beat off

• **ȉgrati čȁrdāš** {VP} (lit. dance the csardas *a Hungarian dance*) *sl-crime* ***Fac*** steal alcohol

• **ȉgrati džȅpnī bìljār** {VP} (lit. play pocket pool) **a.** *sl-sex* ***Fac-Obs*** play with one's testicles or penis through the pocket, play pocket pool **b.** *sl-sex* ***Fac-Obs*** masturbate, beat off

• **ȉgrati pìpirēvku** {VP} SerE *sl-fea* be obedient

• **ȉgrati ténis** {VP} (lit. play tennis) *sl* want to get acquainted with

• **Nè igrā!** {S} (lit. It doesn't play!) *col* used to refer to something impossible (usually in response to a request), No way!

• **nè igrā[PRON:DAT]** {LSF} (lit. It doesn't play to [PRON:ACC]) *col* used to refer to negative attitude: *Ne igra mi. I don't like it.*

ȉgrati se *See the following*

• **ȉgrati se glávōm** {VP} (lit. play with one's head) *col* risk, chance

ìgrica {ē fem.} *sl* computer game <**Slav**❖>

ȉh {excl.} *col* used to express strong emotions, such as excitement, impatience, grief, pain, etc. <**Slav**>

ȉh-ȉh-ȉh {excl.} *col* used to express strong emotions, such as excitement, impatience, grief, pain, etc. <**Slav**>

ȉhā {excl.} *col* used to express strong emotions, such as excitement, impatience, grief, pain, etc., ah <**Slav**>

ȉhāaa {excl.} *col* used to express strong emotions, such as excitement, impatience, grief, pain, etc., ah <**Slav**>

ȉhahâ {excl.} *col* the sound made by laughing, ha, ha <**Slav**>

ȉhāj {excl.} *col* used to express strong emotions, such as excitement, impatience, grief, pain, etc. <**Slav**>

ȉhnuti {nēm, nū perf. intr.} *col* pronounce 'ih' to express excitement, impatience, grief, pain, etc. <**Slav**>

ȉhū {excl.} *col* used to express strong emotions, such as excitement, impatience, grief, pain, etc. <**Slav**>

ȉhuhū {excl.} *col* used to express strong emotions, such as excitement, impatience, grief, pain, etc. <**Slav**>

ihuhúkati {hùhūčēm, čū imperf. intr.} *col* pronounce 'ih' <**Slav**>

iijȕ {excl.} *col* used to express excitement or joy, yippee, whoopee <**Slav**>

íja {ē masc.} *sl* ***Fam*** father, daddy <**Slav**>

ijȕ {excl.} *col* used to express excitement or joy, yippee, whoopee <**Slav**>

ȉka [1] {excl.} *col* used to make somebody go away <**Slav**>

ȉka [2] {ē fem.; Dat ȉki} *sl* silent disappearance, slink away <**Slav**>

ȉkamor {excl.} *sl* used to make somebody go away

ȉkati {ām, ajū imperf.} *sl* run away, flee <**Slav**>

ikebàna {ē fem.} /ikebána/ (lit. ikebana) *sl-fea* elderly female <**Jap***1>

ìkel {a (acc. = gen.) masc.} **a.** *sl-fea* stupid or mentally deficient person <**Gyp***1> **b.** *sl-fea* lazy or shiftless person, bum, good for nothing <**Gyp***2> **c.** *sl* male, guy <**Gyp***3>

ȉkele {excl.} *sl* used to draw someone's attention, look <**Gyp**☞>

ìkisati {išēm, išū imperf.} *sl* look, watch, scope out <**Gyp**>

ȉkiš [1] {excl.} *sl* used to check for the understanding on the part of one's interlocutor, Got it? <**Gyp**>

ìkiši [2] {excl.} *sl* used to draw someone's attention, look <**Gyp**>

ìkiši [3] {part.} *sl* question tag used to check if the import of the message has been captured, Got it? <**Gyp**>

íkiti {kīm, kē imperf.} **a.** *sl* look, watch, scope out <**Gyp***1> **b.** *sl* understand, realize <**Gyp***2>

ìklić-ždrákić {a masc.} *sl* look, glimpse <**Gyp-Slav.**☞*1>

ȉkra {ē fem.} (lit. caviar) *sl* child, kid <**Slav***1>

ȉkravica {ē fem.} (lit. the one full of caviar) *sl* pregnant female <Slav*1>

ȉks See the following

• **ȉks púta** {NP} (lit. x times) *col* many times

ȉkserice {rīcā neut. pl.} (lit. the x ones) *sl-fea* bandy legs <Lat❖>

ȉkši {excl.} *sl* used to point to something, look

il {c.} [std. = ili] *col* or <Slav✍>

ȉl je lȗd ȉl mu nȍge smȑdē {S} (lit. Either he is nuts or his feet stink) *col* used to express suspicion toward a third party, something is wrong with him ☞ **lud**

ȉl si lȗd ȉl ti nȍge smȑdē {S} (lit. Either you are nuts or your feet stink) *col* ***Fac*** used to express suspicion toward one's interlocutor, something is wrong with you ☞ **lud**

ilegálac {lca masc.} **1** *sl-stu* unregistered dormitory resident <Lat*1> **2** illegal pub

ilegàlisānje {a neut.} *sl-stu* illegal dormitory stay <Lat*1>

ilegàlisati {išēm, išū imperf.} *sl* stay or work illegally <Lat❖>

Ȉli stȉsni ili pȑdni! {S} (lit. close it or fart) *col* ***Obs*** used to stimulate a hesitant interlocutor to act, Shit or get off the pot! ☞ **stisnuti**

ȉljada {ē fem.} [std. = hiljada] *col* thousand <Gre✍>

iljadárka {ē fem.} [std. = hiljadarka] *col* thousand dinars; a thousand-dinar bill, a grand <Gre✍>

ìmati {ām, ajū imperf.} *sl* have a steady job <Slav*1>

• **Ìmā li làufa?** {S} (lit. Is there any place to run?) *sl* used to express disbelief, Really?

• **ìmā pa se prèlīvā** {S} (lit. [PRON:NOM] has and it spills over) *sl* ***Iro*** used to refer to a shortage: *A: Ima li on love? B: Ima pa se preliva. A: Does he have any money on him? B: Yeah, right! He ain't got anything.*

• **Ìmā[PRON:GEN].** {LSF} *col* used to refer to a large size of somebody or something: *Ima ga. He is big.*

• **Ìmāš ì pravo!** {S} *col* used to express approval, That's right!

• **Ìmāš li gùmē na cìpelama?** {S} (lit. Do you have any rubber on your shoes?) *col* ***Fac*** used in angry dismissal, Beat it!

• **ìmati adúte** {VP} (lit. have trumps) *sl-fea* have extraordinary qualities (usu. of a person)

• **ìmati cȗg** {VP} (lit. have a sip) *sl-drink* be a good drinker

• **ìmati čȕku** {VP} (lit. have a head) *sl-fea* know, have knowledge of

• **ìmati debèle ȍči** {VP} (lit. have a pair of fat eyes) *sl-sex* ***Fac-Obs*** engage in anal sexual intercourse with

• **ìmati (dobru) žváku** {VP} (lit. have *good* bubble gum) *sl* be outspoken

• **ìmati dugàčak fitīlj** {VP} (lit. have a long fuse) *sl-fea* ***Fac*** understand slowly

• **ìmati dȕnsta** {VP} (lit. have skill) **a.** *sl-fea* be smart: *Taj student ima dunsta. That student is smart.* **b.** *sl-fea* understand, realize: *imati dunsta za fudbal understand soccer*

• **ìmati dvê dlàke u trî rêda** {VP} (lit. have two hairs in three rows) *sl-fea* ***Iro*** be bald

• **ìmati Fìlipa** {VP} (lit. have Philip) *sl-sex* ***Fac*** suffer from syphilis, have the pox

• **ìmati fȋlm** {VP} (lit. have a movie) *sl-drugs* trip (on narcotic drugs)

• **ìmati fórē** {VP} *col* have an advantage over somebody

• **ìmati glâvu ko gòvnārskū kòfu** {VP} (lit. have a head as big as a bucket full of shit) *sl-fea* ***Der*** have an oversized head

• **ìmati gȍsta** {S} (lit. have a guest) *sl-crime* ***Iro*** be accompanied by an informer

• **ìmati jáke njȕpāvce** {S} (lit. have strong teeth) *sl-fea* be courageous, be brave

• **ìmati jèdno vèslo** {S} (lit. have just one oar) *sl-fea* ***Fac*** have just one arm

• **ìmati jèzik u ȍku** {VP} (lit. have a tongue in one's eye) *sl-fea* ***Fac*** be deaf and dumb

• **ìmati klìker (za [NOUN:ACC])** {VP} (lit. have a marble *for [NON:ACC])* *col* used to refer to someone's talent: *Ona ima kliker za matematiku! She is talented in math!*

• **ìmati kȍbru u džèpu** {VP} (lit. have a cobra in one's pocket) *sl-fea* ***Fac*** be tight with money, pinch pennies

• **ìmati kòvērtu** {VP} (lit. have an envelope) *sl* ***Fac*** have a steady job

• **ìmati krokodíla** {VP} (lit. have a crocodile) *sl* ***Fac*** have a pair of shoes

• **ìmati kȕrcšlus u mȍzgu** {VP} (lit. have a short circuit in one's brain) *sl-fea* ***Fac*** think unintelligently

• **ìmati kùršlus u mȍzgu** {VP} (lit. have a short circuit in one's brain) *sl-fea* ***Fac*** think unintelligently

• **ìmati màgacīn kéčēvā u rukávu** {VP} (lit. have a warehouse of aces up one's sleeve) *sl-gamble* ***Fac*** cheat at gambling

• **ìmati mȑkulju** {VP} (lit. have the black one) *sl-fea* ***Fac*** be blind

• **ìmati múda** {VP} (lit. have balls) *sl-fea* ***Obs*** be brave

• **ìmati Pèpicu od lúja** {VP} *sl-sex* ***Fac*** suffer from syphilis, have the pox

• **ìmati pētlju** {VP} (lit. have a knot) *sl-fea* ***App*** be courageous

• **ìmati pȉk** {VP} (lit. have a pick) *sl-fea* be malicious toward, pick at

• **ìmati pójma** {VP} (lit. have a concept) *sl-fea* know, have knowledge of

• **ìmati pòkvārene klíma-ȕređāje**{VP} (lit. have broken air-conditioning) *sl-fea* ***Fac*** have menopause

• **ìmati prèhlāđen kȃr** {VP} (lit. have a cold in one's prick) *sl-sex* ***Fac-Obs*** suffer from gonorrhea, have the clap

• **ìmati (dòbru) žváku** {VP} (lit. have a story) *sl* be outspoken

• **ìmati pȑvū rȗku** {VP} (lit. have the first hand) *sl-fea* know a major drug dealer

• **ìmati pȕtera na glávi** {VP} (lit. have butter on one's head) *sl-fea* have something on one's conscience

• **ìmati pȕtra na glávi** {VP} (lit. have butter on one's head) *sl-fea* have something on one's conscience

• **ìmati razbijène prózore** {VP} (lit. have broken windows) *sl-fea* ***Fac*** be blind

• **ìmati rázličite pȍglēde na svȇt**{VP} (lit. have different views of the world) *sl-fea* ***Fac*** be cross-eyed

• **ìmati rȕpu pod sȉsōm** {VP} (lit. have a hole below one's tit) *sl-fea* ***Fac-Obs*** suffer from tuberculosis, have TB

• **ìmati slȍmljeno kȍplje** {VP} (lit. have a broken spear) *sl-sex* ***Fac-Obs*** be impotent

• **ìmati smòlu** {VP} (lit. have some tar) **a.** Cro *col* have an accident **b.** Cro *col* have bad luck

• **ìmati stô gȍdīnā** {VP} (lit. have a hundred years) *sl-fea* ***Off*** be very old

• **ìmati tȑtu** {VP} (lit. have fear) *sl-fea* be afraid

• **ìmati trùle gȁmbe** {VP} (lit. have rotten legs) *sl-fea* ***Off*** limp

• **ìmati ùske pȍglēde na svȇt** {VP} (lit. have narrow views of the world) *sl-fea* ***Fac*** be cross-eyed

• **ìmati vèlikū špágu** {VP} (lit. have a big rope) *sl-fea* have good connections

• **ìmati vìjugu** {VP} (lit. have a convolution) *sl-fea* ***App*** be smart

• **ìmati visòko čèlo** {VP} (lit. have a high forehead) *sl-fea* ***Iro*** be bald

• **ìmati vȕnu** {VP} (lit. have wool) *sl-fea* be afraid

• **ìmati zȅnt** {VP} (lit. have seeing) **a.** *sl-fea* be seen: *imati zent u rulji be seen in the crowd* **b.** be afraid: *imati zent od krimosa be afraid of the criminals*

• **nêmā lȅba** {VP} (lit. no bread) SerE *col* used to refer to the futility of all efforts, it's no use

• **nêma problémā** {VP} *col* used to indicate that a problem can be solved, no problem, no big deal

• **némaš problémā** {VP} (lit. you don't have any problems) *col* used to refer to that a problem can be solved, no problem, no big deal: *Nemaš problema za čišćenje snega. Snow-clearing is no big deal.*

• **némati (blâgē) vȅzē** {VP} (lit. not have a *soft* connection) *col* be unaware of, be clueless

• **némati dȕnsta** {VP} (lit. be without skills) *sl* fail to understand

• **némati (ni) trî čȉste** {VP} (lit. be without the three clean) **1** *sl-fea* be insane, be nuts **2** *sl-fea* be a coward, be a chicken

• **némati (ni) trî čȕke** {VP} (lit. be without three hours) *sl-fea* be ignorant

• **némati nȍge** {VP} (lit. be without legs) *sl-drugs* be on narcotic drugs

• **némati šljàkaru** {VP} (lit. be without the one used for work *i.e. without one hand*) *sl-fea* be without one arm

ȉmbecil {a (acc. = gen.) masc.} *sl-fea* stupid or mentally deficient person, imbecile <Lat*1>

ȉmbić 1 {a (acc. = gen.) masc.} *sl-fea* stupid or mentally deficient person, imbecile <Lat✍>

ȉmbić 2 {adj.} *sl-fea* stupid or mentally deficient <Lat✍>

ȉme *See the following*

• **Ȉme ti jèbēm!** {S} (lit. I fuck your name!) *col* ***Off*** used as a moderate curse, Fuck you!

• **pȑvō ȉme** {NP} *col* first name, given name

iménce *See the following*

• **Iménce ti mȉlosnō jèbēm!** {S} (lit. I screw your dear little name!) *col-dia* ***Off*** used as a weak curse, Screw you!

ȉmidž {a masc.} /imidž/ *col* image, look <Eng>

imitírati {mìtīrām, mitírajū imperf.} *sl* lie <Lat*1>

ȉmpić 1 {a (acc. = gen.) masc.} *sl-sex* ***Der*** impotent male <Lat✍>

ȉmpić 2 {adj.} *sl-sex* ***Der*** impotent <Lat✍>

ȉmpoš 1 {a (acc. = gen.) masc.} *sl-sex* ***Der*** impotent male <Lat✍>

ȉmpoš 2 {adj.} *sl-sex* ***Der*** impotent <Lat✍>

ȉn 1 {adj.} *col* fashionable, in: *Nosio je neki in kaput. He wore an in coat.* <Eng>

ȉn 2 {adv.} *col* fashionably, in: *Ponašao se in. His behavior was in.* <Eng>

ìnād {a masc.} [std. = inat] BosM *col* defiance <NE✍>

ìndeks {a (acc. = gen.) masc.} (lit. university matriculation book) *sl-stu* university student <Lat*1>

Indíjac {jca (acc. = gen.) masc.} (lit. Indian) *sl-fea* ***Off*** Gypsy (male) <SlavO*1>

indíjac {jca masc.} (lit. Indian) *sl-drugs* hashish, hash <SlavO*1>

Indijánac {nca (acc. = gen.) masc.} (lit. American Indian) **1** *sl-fea* ***Off*** Gypsy (male) <SlavO*1> **2** *sl-fea* ***Der*** stupid or mentally deficient person <SlavO*1> **3a.** *sl-mil* soldier on patrol, scout <SlavO*1> **b.** *sl-mil* reconnaissance unit member <SlavO*2> **4** *sl* worm <SlavO*1>

Indijánci {jânācā masc. pl.} (lit. American Indians) *sl* large audience <SlavO*1>

indžìnjēr {džinjéra (acc. = gen.) masc.} [std. = inženjer, inžinjer] *col-dia* engineer <Ger⚘>

ȉnfić {a (acc. = gen.) masc.} (lit. clipping from Informbiro) *sl-polit* supporter of Stalin in the Tito-Stalin conflict of 1948 <Abb⚘>

infiltrírati se {filtrīrām, filtrírajū imperf. intr.} (lit. infiltrate) *sl* ***Fac*** enter (a room, building, etc.) <Lat*1>

informàtivka {ē fem.} *sl-sstu* notebook used for teacher's comments to the parent (usu. concerning child's behavior) <Lat❖*1>

informìsisati {išēm, išū biasp.} (lit. informisati 'inform' X sisati 'suck') *sl* ***Fac*** inform <Lat-Slav⚘>

Ingléskā {ē fem. (adj. decl.)} /Ȁnglēskā/ [std. = Engleska] *col-dia* England <SlavO⚘>

ingléskī {ā, ō adj.} /ȁnglēskī/ [std. = engleski] *col-dia* English <SlavO⚘>

inkasâtor {a (acc. = gen.) masc.} *sl-sports* stadium box office clerk <Ita>

inkubâtor {a masc.} (lit. incubator) *sl* maternity ward <Lat*1>

ȉnokosan {sna, sno adj.} (lit. independent, self-standing) *col-dia* lonely <Slav*1>

inspiréjšn {a masc.} *sl* inspiration <Eng>

ȉntačiti se {čīm, čē imperf. intr.} *sl-fea* be stubborn, be defiant

Ȉntālija {ē fem.} [std. = Italija] *col-dia* Italy <SlavO*1>

intelektuálac {lca (acc. = gen.) masc.} (lit. intellectual) *sl* five hundred dinars; a five hundred-dinar bill <Lat*1>
- **bùdūćī intelektuálac** {NP} (lit. future intellectual) *sl-sstu* ***Fac*** elite high-school student

intelektúkac {kca (acc. = gen.) masc.} (lit. intelektualac 'intellectual' X tukac 'turkey') *sl-fea* ***Fac-Der*** intellectual <Lat-Slav*1>

Ȉnter {a masc.} *sl* Intercontinental Hotel (Zagreb, Croatia) <BN⚘>

Interkȍntī {īja masc.} *sl* Intercontinental Hotel (Zagreb, Croatia) <BN⚘>

Interkȍntić {a masc.} *sl* Intercontinental Hotel (Zagreb, Croatia) <BN⚘>

intervjú *See the following*
- **intervjû Bibisìju** {NP} (lit. interview with the BBC) *sl-crime* ***Fac*** police interrogation

Ȉntić {a masc.} *sl* Intercontinental Hotel (Zagreb, Croatia) <BN⚘>

invàlīd {valída (acc. = gen.) masc.} (lit. cripple) *sl* parent <Lat*1>

invèntār {ventára masc.} (lit. inventory) *sl* frequent visitor, regular <Lat*1>

ȉo {excl.} *col* used to command an animal to move on, go <Slav>

ȉoklē {adv.} *col* from anywhere: *Ima li pomoći iokle? Is there any help from anywhere?* <Slav⚘> ☞ **ioklen**

ȉoklēn {adv.} *col* from anywhere: *Hoće li doći voz iokle? Is a train going to come from anywhere?* <Slav⚘> ☞ **iokle**

ȉole {part.} *col* barely, hardly, at all: *Da li me ti iole slušaš? Are you listening to me at all?* <Slav>

iotiàmisati {išēm, išū biasp.} *sl* love <Ita⚘>

ȉotklē {adv.} *col* from anywhere <Slav⚘>

ȉotklēn {adv.} *col* from anywhere <Slav⚘>

ìpsina {ē fem.} *sl* lie <Slav❖*1>

ȉrvās *See the following*
- **Gdȅ su ti ȉrvāsi?** {S} (lit. Where are your reindeer?) **SerE** *sl-fea* ***Fac*** used to express astonishment, Did you loose your mind? Are you nuts?

iscéditi {dīm, dē perf.} (lit. squeeze) **1** *sl* rob, fleece, rip off <Slav*1> **2** *sl-fea* bother, disturb <Slav*1>

iscijéditi {dīm, dē perf.} (lit. squeeze) *col* tire <Slav*1>
- **iscijéditi čȉr** {VP} (lit. squeeze an ulcer) *sl* tell secrets

iscúriti {rīm, rē perf.} **a.** *col* leak out, run out <Slav*1> **b.i.** *sl-crime* escape from prison <Slav*2> **ii.** *sl-fea* fail <Slav*2>

ìseći {iséčem, kū, ek, ek perf. irreg.} (lit. cut, slice) **1** **SerE** *sl* punish: *iseći dete zbog loših ocena punish a child for his/her bad grades* <Slav*1> **2** SerE *sl* beat up <Slav*1> **3** SerE *sl* frighten, scare <Slav*1>

iséći se {iséčem, kū, ek, ek a perf. irreg.} (lit. cut oneself all over) **a.** **SerE** *col* get frightened, get scared <Slav*1>

b. SerE *col* get nervous <Slav*2>

• **ìseći se ȍd strȃha** {VP} (lit. cut oneself out of fear) SerE *sl-fea* get frightened, get scared

isfašírati {fàšīrām, fašírajū perf.} **1** *sl* beat up <Fre*1> **2** *sl-music* sing out of tune <Fre*1>

isfazonírati {zònīrām, zonírajū perf.} **a.** *sl* make up, fabricate <Ger❖*1> **b.** cheat, swindle <Ger❖*2>

isfazonírati se {zònīrām, zonírajū perf. intr.} **1** *sl* put on make-up <Fre❖*1> **2** *sl* dress formally, dress up <Fre❖*1> **3** *sl* be in command <Fre❖*1>

isfenírati {fènīrām, fenírajū perf.} *sl-crafts* style one's hair with a blow-drier <Ger>

isfolírati {fòlīrām, folírajū perf.} *sl* cheat, swindle <Ita❖>

isfȕljati {ām, ajū perf. intr.} *sl* go out, leave <Slav>

ìsfur {a masc.} **1** *sl* evening out <Ger*1> **2** *sl* exit <Ger*1>

• **dèsnī ìsfur** {NP} (lit. right exit) *sl-polit* deportation from the Western-bloc countries

• **lêvī ìsfur** {NP} (lit. left exit) SerE *sl-polit* deportation from Eastern bloc countries

isfuranđèlī {īja masc.} *sl* outing <Ger☞>

isfúrati {ìsfūrām, isfúrajū perf. intr.} **a.** *sl* go out, leave <Ger❖> **b.** pass <Ger❖*1>

• **isfúrati iz fijòkē** {VP} (lit. escape from a drawer) *sl-crime* ***Fac*** escape from prison

isfurijanđèlī {īja masc.} *sl* outing <Ger☞>

isfuȑška {ē fem.; Dat isfuȑški} /isfuřška/ *sl* outing <Ger☞>

isisávānje {a neut.} (lit. sucking) **a.** *sl-gamble* taking money in gambling <Slav*1> **b.** *sl* earning (money) <Slav*2>

isisávati {sìsāvām, sisávajū imperf.} (lit. suck) **a.** *sl-gamble* take money in gambling, rip off in gambling <Slav*1> **b.** *sl* abuse financially, rip off <Slav*2>

iskápiti {ìskāpīm, pē perf.} *sl-drink* drink (alcohol) <Slav>

iskapljívati {kàpljujēm, ljujū imperf.} *sl-drink* drink (alcohol) <Slav>

iskašírati {kàšīrām, kašírajū perf.} *sl* beat up <Fre*1>

ìskati {ìšćēm, ìšćū imperf.} *dia-col* request <Slav>

ìskecati {ām, ajū perf.} **a.** *sl-sex* ***Obs*** engage in sexual intercourse with (of a male) <Slav> **b.** *sk* hit, punch <Slav*1> **c.** *sl* destroy, ruin <Slav*2>

ìskecati se {ām, ajū perf. intr.} **a.** *sl-sex* engage in sexual intercourse with <Slav> **b.** *sl* make a mistake, screw up <Slav*1>

iskèfati {ām, ajū perf.} (lit. brush off) *sl* reproach, scold <NE❖>

iskèmbati {ām, ajū perf.} *sl* take away, remove

iskembéciti {kèmbēcīm, cē perf.} *sl-sex* ***Obs*** engage in sexual intercourse with (of a male) <Slav*1>

iskembéčiti {kèmbēčīm, čē perf.} **a.** *sl* beat up <Slav*1> **b.** *sl* engage in sexual intercourse with (of a male) <Slav*2>

iskembóčiti se {kèmbōčīm, čē perf. intr.} *sl* stare at, be fixated on <Slav*1>

Ìskēnjām se jâ na [NP:ACC]! {LSF} (lit. I shit on that [NOUN:ACC]!) *sl* ***Off*** used to express disrespect or dissatisfaction, Fuck it!: *Iskenjam se ja na taj tvoj plan! I don't give a shit about that plan of yours!* ☞ **iskenjati se**

iskénjati {ìskēnjām, iskénjajū perf.} *sl-sex* ***Obs*** defecate, shit <Slav>

iskénjati se {ìskēnjām, iskénjajū perf. intr.} *sl-sex* ***Obs*** defecate, shit <Slav>

• **Ìskēnjām se jâ na** [NP:ACC]! {LSF} (lit. I shit on that [NOUN:ACC]!) *sl* ***Off*** used to express disrespect or dissatisfaction, Fuck it!: *Iskenjam se ja na taj tvoj plan! I don't give a shit about that plan of yours!*

iskiláviti se {kìlāvīm, vē perf. intr.} *sl* have a hard time, experience difficulties <Slav*1>

isklistírati {lìstīrām, listírajū perf.} **a.** *sl* defeat <Gre❖*1> **b.** *sl* reproach, scold <Gre❖*2>

iskȍčiti {ìskočīm, ìskočē perf.} (lit. pop out) **1** *col* blow (as of a fuse) <Slav*1> **2** *col* say something inappropriate <Slav*2>

• **Iskȍčile**[PRON:DAT] **ȍči.** {LSF} (lit. [PPRON] have popped out) *sl-fea* used to refer to astonishment of a third person: *Iskočile joj oči na golog muškarca. She stared at the naked man.*

• **Iskȍčile**[PRON:DAT] **ȍči na fédere.** {LSF} (lit. [PPRON] eyes have popped up on springs) *sl-fea* used to refer to astonishment of a third person: *Iskočile joj oči na federe od Marka. She stared at Marko.*

iskòpati *See the following*

• **iskòpati bȕnār** {VP} (lit. dig a well) *sl-crime* pick pockets

• **iskòpati ȍko** {VP} (lit. cut out an eye) *sl-fea* ***Fac*** be hesitant to lend any money

iskȍpčati se {ām, ajū perf. intr.} (lit. turn oneself off) *sl* exclude oneself <NE*1>

ìskopina {ē fem.} (lit. archeological find) *sl-sex* ***Fac*** elderly divorced female <Slav*1>

iskr̂cati se {ām, ajū perf. intr.} **1a.** *sl* meet a boyfriend or a girlfriend <Slav*1> **b.** *sl* start flirting <Slav*1> **2** *sl* pay (bills, etc.) <Slav*1>

iskrcávānje {a neut.} **1** *sl* making an acquaintance <Slav*1> **2** *sl* paying bills <Slav*1>

ìskrpati {ām, ajū perf.} *sl* beat up <Slav*1>

iskulírati {kùlīrām, kulírajū perf. intr.} **1** *sl* die, kick the bucket <Eng❖*1> **2** *sl* dump one's boyfriend or girlfriend <Eng❖*1> **3** *sl* calm somebody down <Eng❖*1> **4** *sl* calm down, cool off <Eng❖*1>

iskulírati se {kùlīrām, kulírajū perf. intr.} *sl* calm down, cool off <Eng❖>

iskùndačiti {čīm, čē perf.} **a.** *sl* beat up <NE❖*1> **b.** *sl-sex* engage in sexual intercourse with (of a male) <NE❖*2>

ìskurcati {ām, ajū perf.} (lit. iskrcati 'debark' X iskurcati 'deprick') *sl-mil* ***Obs*** debark (deploy military units on ship) <Slav☞>

ispàcati se {ām, ajū perf. intr.} *sl* take a bath

ȉspala {ē fem.} (lit. shooting) *sl* cheating, swindling <Slav>

Ìspale [PRON:DAT] **ȍči**. {LSF} (lit. [PPRON] eyes have fallen out) *sl-fea* used to refer to astonishment of the third person: *Ispale mu oči. He was very frightened.* ☞ ispasti

ispáliti {ìspālīm, lē perf.} **1a.** *sl* cheat, swindle <Slav*1> **b.** *sl* fail to keep a promise, go back on one's word <Slav*2> **2** *sl* hit, punch <Slav*1>

ìsparen {a, o adj.} (lit. evaporated) *sl* lost, without orientation <Slav*1>

ìspariti se *See the following*
- **ìspariti se u vídu lástinog rêpa** {VP} (lit. evaporate in the form of a swallow's tail) *sl-fea* ***Fac*** disappear, evaporate, vanish

ìspasti {anēm, anū perf. irreg.} *sl* fall down, kiss the floor <Slav*1>
- **Ìspale**[PRON:DAT] **ȍči**. {LSF} (lit. [PPRON] eyes have fallen out) *sl-fea* used to indicate astonishment of the third person, [PRON:NOM] was very frightened.: *Ispale mu oči. He was very frightened.*
- **ìspasti âcēnā strȁnka** {VP} (lit. turn out to be the party which is fucked) *sl-fea* ***Obs*** have a hard time, experience difficulties
- **ìspasti gȑbav** {VP} (lit. turn out to be hump-backed) **a.** *sl-fea* ***Fac*** be worse off: *ispasti grbav na trgovini paprikama be worse off on selling peppers* **b.** *sl-fea* ***Fac*** have a hard time, experience difficulties
- **ìspasti pèčūrka** {VP} (lit. turn out to be a mushroom) *sl* ***Fac*** pay for everything

ȉspaša {ē fem.} (lit. grazing) *sl-mil* dinner <Slav*1>

ìspeći {eknēm, eknū, ek, ek perf. irreg.} (lit. bake) *dia-col* make brandy <Slav*1>

ìspēglan {a, o- adj.} (lit. ironed) *sl* nice, cute (object or person) <Ger*1>

ìspēglati {ām, ajū perf.} (lit. iron) *sl* level <Ger*1>

ispenisável {perf.} *dia-col* study

ìspevati {ām, ajū perf.} (lit. sing out) SerE *sl-crime* inform the police or other authorities, sing <Slav*1>

ispéziti {ìspēzīm, zē perf.} *sl* get by begging

ispičkàrati {ām, ajū perf.} (lit. cunt out) *sl* ***Obs*** curse <Slav*1>

ispìjuša {ē fem.} (lit. sucker) *sl-sex* ***Fac*** female with an exaggerated interest in sex <Slav❖*1>

ispíranje *See the following*
- **ispírānje kûtnjākā** {NP} (lit. flushing one's molars) *sl* ***Fac*** kissing

ȉspišān {a, o adj.} *sl-sex* ***Obs*** urinated on <Slav>

ispíškiti se {kīm, kē perf. intr.} *col* urinate <Slav>
- **Ispíški se!** {S} (lit. Piss off!) *sl-fea* ***Fac-Obs*** used to make somebody go away, Piss off!

ìspiti {ìspijēm, jū perf.} *sl-drink* drink (alcohol) <Slav>

ispízditi {ìspīzdīm, dē perf. intr.} (lit. cunt out) **1** *sl-fea* ***Obs*** go insane, freak out <Slav*1> **2** *sl-fea* ***Obs*** give birth, have a baby: *ispizditi devojčicu give birth to a baby girl* <Slav*1>

ìspjevati {ām, ajū perf.} (lit. sing out) *sl-crime* inform the police or other authorities, sing <Slav*1>

ispláćiti {ìspčāćīm, ćē perf.} *sl* get, obtain <Slav*1>

ìsplaziti {zīm, zē perf. intr.} *sl* go out, leave <Slav*1>

ìsplaziti se {zīm, zē perf. intr.} (lit. stick out one's tongue) *sl* give money <Slav*1>

ìsplivati {ām, ajū perf. intr.} (lit. swim out) *col* overcome one's problems <Slav*1>

ìspljanuti {nēm, nū perf.} **a.** *sl* discover, find out: *ispljanuti intrigu discover an intrigue* <Slav*1> **b.** *sl* report, relate <Slav*2> **c.** *sl* say, tell <Slav*2>

ìspljugati {ām, ajū imperf.} (lit. smoke out) *sl-sex* ***Obs*** engage in fellatio <Slav❖*1>

ìspljunuti {nēm, nū perf.} (lit. spit out) **1** *sl* say, tell <Slav*1> **2** *sl* give money <Slav*1>

• ìspljunuti lóvu {VP} (lit. spit out the money) *col* pay (bills, etc.)

ispljùvati {ìspljujēm, ujū perf.} (lit. spit at) *col* denounce, criticize publicly, give a lot of flak: *Ispljuvali su ga zbog njegovog nepristojnog ponašanja u operi. He got a lot of flak for his rude behavior at the opera.* <**Slav***1>

ispod nóža {PP} (lit. from under a knife) *col* last-minute rescue ☞ **nož**

ispod pȕlta {PP} (lit. under the counter) *col* secretly, under the table, under the counter: *prodavati rakiju ispod pulta secretly sell brandy* ☞ **pult**

ispod tèzgē {PP} (lit. under the counter) *col* secretly, under the table, under the counter: *platiti ispod tezge pay secretly* ☞ **tezga**

ispod žȉta {PP} (lit. under the grains) *col* secretly, under the counter: *obaviti poso ispod žita do business secretly* ☞ **žito**

ispolívati {pòlīvām, polívajū perf.} *sl* beat up <**Slav***1>

isponàpiknuti {nēm, nū perf.} *sl-sex* ***Obs*** engage in sexual intercourse with (of a male) <**Slav**❖>

isponàpiknjuti {nēm, nū perf.} *sl* beat up <**Slav**❖>

isposécati {pòsēcām, posécajū perf.} **a. SerE** *sl* beat up <**Slav***1> **b. SerE** *sl-sex* engage in sexual intercourse with (of a male) <**Slav***2>

ispovȑteti {tīm, tē perf.} *sl* rotate, turn around <**Slav***1>

isprášiti {šīm, šē perf.} **a.** *sl* beat up <**Slav***1> **b.** *sl* defeat <**Slav***2>

ìspravljati *See the following*

• ìspravljati krȋvū Drínu {VP} (lit. try to correct the meandering Drina river) *col* do something in vain

ìsprcān {a, o adj.} /ìspr̄can /a, o adj./ **a.** *sl-sex* ***Obs*** engaged in sexual intercourse with <**Slav***1> **b.** *sl-sex* ***Obs*** sexually exhausted <**Slav***2>

ìsprcati {ām, ajū perf.} *sl-sex* ***Obs*** engage in sexual intercourse with (of a male) <**Slav***1>

ìsprcati se {ām, ajū perf. intr.} *sl-sex* ***Obs*** engage in sexual intercourse with to sateity <**Slav***1>

isprèdelati {ām, ajū perf.} Kajk *sl-sex* ***Obs*** engage in sexual intercourse with (of a male) <**Slav***1>

isprèpadati {ām, ajū perf.} (lit. frighten) *sl-sex* ***Fac-Obs*** begin with sexual foreplay <**Slav***1>

isprepalàpucati {ām, ajū perf.} **a.** *sl* beat up <**Slav**❖> **b.** *sl* engage in sexual intercourse with (of a male) <**Slav**❖*1>

ispreponàtaći {taknēm, taknū, tak, tak perf. irreg.} *sl-sex* ***Obs*** engage in sexual intercourse with (of a male) <**Slav**❖>

ispreponàtaći {àknēm, àknū, tak, tak perf. irreg.} **a.** *sl* beat up <**Slav**❖> **b.** *sl* engage in sexual intercourse with (of a male) <**Slav**❖*1>

isprèpucati {ām, ajū perf.} *sl* beat up <**Slav**❖>

ìspružiti se {žīm, žē imperf. intr.} **1** *sl* spend ample money: *Ispružio sam se na putu u Amsterdam. I spent lots of money on my trip to Amsterdam.* <**Slav***1> **2a.** *sl* be missing: *Marko se ispružio i niko ne može da ga nađe. Marko is missing and nobody can find him.* <**Slav***1> **b.** *sl* ***Fac*** die, kick the bucket <**Slav***2>

ìspucati {ām, ajū perf.} (lit. bang out) *sl-sex* ***Obs*** engage in sexual intercourse with (of a male) <**Slav***1>

ìspucati se {ām, ajū perf. intr.} (lit. shoot one's fill) **1** *sl* be left without any money: *ispucati se u inostranstvu be left abroad without any opportunities* <**Slav***1> **2** *sl* be left without opportunities <**Slav***1> **3** *sl-sex* have one's fill of sex <**Slav***1> **4** *col* spend (money, property, etc.) <**Slav***1>

ispúhati *See the following*

• ispúhati gùmu {VP} (lit. deflate a tire) *sl-fea* spend all the money, be broke

ìspūmpān {a, o adj.} (lit. flat) *sl-fea* helpless <**Ger***1>

ìspūmpati {ām, ajū biasp.} (lit. deflate) *sl* abuse financially, rip off <**Ger***1>

ìspušiti {šīm, še perf.} **a.** *sl-sex* ***Obs*** engage in fellatio <**Slav***1> **b.** *sl* ***Obs*** be cheated, be swindled <**Slav***2> **c.** *sl* lose a game <**Slav*****1>

ìspušten {a, o adj.} **a.** *sl-fea* disregarded <**Slav***1> **b.** *sl-fea* weary <**Slav***2> **c.** *sl-fea* insane, nuts <**Slav***3>

ìspužvati {ām, ajū perf.} *sl* beat up <**Slav***1>

ìspužvati se {ām, ajū perf. intr.} *sl-sex* ***Obs*** engage in sexual intercourse with <**Slav***1>

isšȁltati se {ām, ajū perf. intr.} **a.** *sl* be absent-minded <**Ger***1> **b.** *sl* exclude oneself <**Ger***1>

istabànati {ām, ajū biasp.} *sl* beat up <**NE**❖*1>

istábati {ìstābām, istábajū biasp.} /ìstabati/ *sl* beat up <**NE**>

istambùrati {ām, ajū biasp.} *sl* beat up <**NE**❖*1>

istapírati se {istàpīrām, istapírajū perf. intr.} *sl-gamble* lose money <**Fre**❖*1>

istèliti se {ìstelīm, ìstelē perf. intr.} *sl* have a hard time, experience difficulties <**Slav***1>

ìsterati *See the following*
• **ìsterati dûšu na flàutu** {VP} (lit. throw out one's soul on a flute) SerE *sl* ***Fac*** beat up

ìstesati {ešēm, ešū perf.} (lit. plane) *sl* beat up <Slav*1>

Ȉstī kȕrac! {AdjP} (lit. Same prick!) *col* ***Obs*** used to refer to lack of any change, Same old shit! ☞ **kurac**

Ȉstī kȕrac drȕgō pȁkovānje! {AdjP} (lit. Same prick in another package!) *col* ***Obs*** used to indicate lack of any change, Same old shit it just looks different! ☞ **kurac**

Ȉstō sránje! {NP} *col* ***Obs*** used to refer to lack of any change, Same old shit! ☞ **sranje**

Ȉstō sránje drȕgō pȁkovānje! {NP} (lit. Same shit in another package!) *col* ***Obs*** used to indicate lack of any change, Same old shit, just looks different! ☞ **sranje**

istoròkati {ām, ajū perf.} *sl* betray, turn to authorities <Slav*1>

istoròkati se {ām, ajū perf. intr.} *sl* talk one's fill <Slav*1>

ȉstovār {a masc.} *sl-sex* ***Obs*** defecating <Slav*1>
• **ȉstovār džȅpōvā** {NP} (lit. emptying of one's pockets) *sl-crime* pick pocketing
• **rùčnī ȉstovār** {NP} (lit. hand emptying) **1** *sl-sex* ***Obs*** masturbation, hand job **2** *sl-sex* ***Obs*** urination

istrȁžnjāk {ražnjáka (acc. = gen.) masc.} *sl-crime* magistrate, investigating judge <Slav❖*1>

istrȁžnjāk {istražnjáka masc.} *sl-crime* custody <Slav❖*1>

istr̀čati {ìstrčīm, čē perf. intr.} (lit. run out) **1** *sl* tell secrets, spill the beans <Slav*1> **2** *sl* overdo <Slav*1>

ìstrēsti se {istrésēm, istrésu perf. intr.} **1a.** *sl-sex* ***Obs*** ejaculate, cum <Slav*1> **b.** *sl-sex* ***Obs*** have one's fill of sex <Slav*2> **2** *sl* spend ample money <Slav*1>

istrkèljati {ām, ajū perf.} **1** *sl* make a mess while looking for something, rummage through: *istrkeljati stan rummage an apartment* <Slav*1> **2** *sl* tell, say <Slav*1> **3** *sl* write <Slav*1> get, obtain

istrkèljisati {išēm, išū perf.} **1** *sl* make a mess while looking for something, rummage through <Slav*1> **2** *sl* tell <Slav*1> **3** *sl* write <Slav*1>

istrónjati se {ìstrōnjām, istrónjajū perf. intr.} *sl-sex* ***Obs*** defecate, shit <Slav*1>

istròšiti se {ìstrošīm, ìstrošē perf. intr.} **a.** *sl* spend money <Slav*1> **b.i.** *sl-sex* have one's fill of sex <Slav*1> **ii.** *sl* lose <Slav*1>

ìstrzati {ìstrzām, ajū perf.} **1** *sl* frighten, scare <Slav*1> **2** *sl* start dating a female or male <Slav*1>

ìstrzati se {ām, ajū perf. intr.} *sl* be frightened, get scared <Slav*1>

istušírati {tùšīrām, tušírajū biasp.} *sl* beat up <Ger❖*1>

Ȉsus *See the following*
• **Ȉsusa ti tvôga!** {S} (lit. *I fuck* your Jesus!) *col* ***Off*** used as a weak curse, Damn you!

ȉš {excl.} *col* used to scare birds, shoo <Slav>

ȉša {excl.} *col* used to scare birds, shoo <Slav>

išȁltati se {ām, ajū perf. intr.} **a.** *sl* be absent-minded: *Išaltala se, pa je zaključala ključeve u kući. She was absent-minded and locked the keys in the house.* <Ger*1> **b.** *sl* exclude oneself, leave: *Išaltao se iz Saveta Univerziteta zbog razmimoilaženja s rektorom. He left the University council over differences with the president.* <Ger*1>

ìščačkati {ām, ajū perf.} *sl* find out (usu. secret information): *Iščačkao je da je predsjednik imao tri ljubavnice. He found out that the president had three mistresses.* <Slav*1>

ìščašen {a, o adj.} (lit. twisted) *sl-fea* ***Der*** insane, nuts <Slav*1>

ìščašiti *See the following*
• **ìščašiti beónjače** {VP} (lit. distort one's eyeballs) *sl-fea* ***Fac*** stare, glare at in surprise, gawk

iščepr̀kati {ām, ajū perf.} (lit. dig out) *col* find out (usu. secret information): *Iščeprkao je njegovo podmićivanje policije. He found out about his bribing the police.* <Slav*1>

išekètati {ām, ajū perf.} *sl* beat up <Slav❖ ✎>

ìšibān {a, o adj.} (lit. whipped) **1** *sl* rude <Slav*1> **2** *sl* beaten up, whipped <Slav*1>

ȉšijās *See the following*
• **ȉšijās trȅpavīca** {NP} (lit. sciatica of one's eyelashes) *sl-fea* ***Fac*** staring, glaring

ȉškati {ām, ajū imperf.} *col* chase birds away by pronouncing 'iš' <Slav>

ȉške {excl.} *col* used to scare a pig and other domestic animals, shoo <Slav>

iškòjiti se {jīm, jē perf. intr.} *sl* get, obtain: *Iškojio se za pedeset marona. He got fifty German marks.*

išórati {ìšōrām, išórajū perf.} *sl* beat up <Hun>

išórati se {ìšōrām, išórajū perf. intr.} *sl-sex* ***Obs*** urinate, piss <Hun>

ȉštati {ȉštēm, tū perf.} *col-dia* ask for: *Neko ište Mariju. Somebody is asking for Mary.* <Slav>

išuávljiti {šùāvljīm, ljē perf.} *sl* twist, sprain (arm, ankle, etc.)

išuljáviti {šùljāvīm, vē perf.} *sl* stab <Slav>

išupírati {šùpīrām, ajū perf.} *sl* throw out, kick out <Slav*1>

ìšutati {ām, ajū perf.} *sl* throw out, kick out <Eng*1>

išutírati {šùtīrām, šutírajū perf.} *sl* throw out, kick out <Eng*1>

ìtcri {īja masc.; perm} [std. = Ritz] *sl* name for Ritz bar (Zagreb, Croatia) <BN✍>

Ȉvica *See the following*

- **na Ȉvici** {PP} (lit. on the verge) *sl-fea* in love
- **na Ȉvici i mȁrici** {PP} (lit. on Hansel/verge and Gretel) *sl-fea* madly in love

Ȉvo *See the following*

- **Ȉjēpī Ívo** {NP} (lit. handsome Ivo) *sl-sex* ***Obs-Fac*** large penis

iz cûga {PP} *col* right away, right away ☞ **cug**

iz fàzōna {PP} (lit. for a trick) *col* for fun ☞ **fazon**

iz Fȉnskē {PP} (lit. from Finland *also: fin 'nice'*) *sl-fea* ***Fac*** kind, nice (of a person) ☞ **Finska**

Iz kôg si plȅmena? {S} (lit. From which tribe are you?) *sl-fea* ***Fac-Der*** used as a moderate offense, Where were you born? ☞ **pleme**

iz mȅsta {PP} (lit. from the spot) SerE *col* right away, now: *Zatvori prozor iz mesta, počeo je pljusak! Close the window right away it's starting to pour!* ☞ **mesto**

iz naftalína {PP} (lit. from mothballs) *col* very old, outdated: *pjesma iz naftalina very old song* ☞ **naftalin**

iz národnē pȅsmē {PP} (lit. from a folk song) SerE *sl-fea* ***Fac*** with permanently red face ☞ **pesma**

iz ȍvīh stôpā {PP} (lit. from these feet) *col* right away, now ☞ **stopa**

iz pìka {PP} *col* right away, now ☞ **pik**

iz štósa {PP} (lit. for trick) **a.** *col* just like that, just for the heck of it: *ukrasti auto iz štosa steal a car just for the heck of it* **b.** for fun ☞ **štos**

iz tôg špìla {PP} (lit. from that pack of cards) *sl-fea* of the same kind ☞ **špil**

iz tôka {PP} (lit. from the flow) *sl* right away, now ☞ **tok**

iz varikínē {PP} (lit. from the bleach) *sl-fea* ***Fac-Der*** boring ☞ **varikina**

iza brȁvē {PP} (lit. behind the lock) *col* in prison, behind the bars, locked up ☞ **brava**

iza úgla {PP} (lit. behind the corner) *col* secretly, under the counter ☞ **ugao**

iza zîda {PP} (lit. behind the wall) *sl-fea* secretly, under the counter ☞ **zid**

ìzāći *See the following*

- **ìzāći u sùsret** {VP} (lit. come out to a meeting) *col* permit, approve, go along with: *Izaći u susret prijatelju. Go along with one's friend's request.*

ìzakān {a, o adj.} *sl-fea* cheated <Slav*1>

ìzakati {ām, ajū perf.} **a.** *sl* destroy, ruin <Slav> **b.** *sl* beat up **c.** engage in sexual intercourse with (of a male)

izaláčiti se {čīm, čē perf. intr.} *sl-fea* vomit, throw up, puke

izàlaziti {zīm, zē imperf.} [std. = izlaziti] *sl* get out, leave <Slav✍>

izàpatiti {tīm, tē perf.} *sl* have a hard time, experience difficulties <Slav>

izàpatiti se {tīm, tē perf. intr.} *sl* have a hard time, experience difficulties <Slav>

Ȉzasrān {a, o adj.} (lit. shitted out) *sl-fea* worthless <Slav>

izbáciti *See the following*

- **izbáciti žmȉgavac** {VP} (lit. pull out the turn signal) *col* put on the blinker

ìzbačiti {čīm, čē perf.} [std. = izbaciti] **a.** *sl* throw away, toss out <Slav✍> **b.** *sl* fire, dismiss <Slav✍*1>

izbàštati {ām, ajū biasp.} *sl* beat up <Ita>

izbéčiti {ìzbēčīm, čē perf.} *col* open wide <Slav>

- **izbéčiti ȍči** {VP} (lit. stick out one's eyes) *col* stare, glare at in surprise, gawk

izbéčiti se {ìzbēčīm, čē perf. intr.} **1** *col* stare at, be fixated on <Slav> **2** *col* grimace, make faces (usu. in pain) <Slav>

izblamírati se {làmīrām, lamírajū perf. intr.} *sl-fea* make a fool of oneself <Fre>

izbljùvati se {ȉzbljujēm, ìzbljujū perf. intr.} *col* vomit copiously, puke one's guts out <Slav>

ìzboksati {ām, ajū perf.} (lit. box) **1** *sl* abuse financially, rip off <Eng⁘*1> **2** *sl* get something from somebody <Eng⁘*1>

izbombardírati {bàrdīrām, bardírajū perf.} (lit. bomb) **1** *sl* make, prepare, fix: *izbombardirati ručak fix dinner* <Fre⁘*1> **2** *sl* overburden with information <Fre⁘*1>

izbúbati {ìzbūbām, izbúbajū perf.} *sl* beat up <Slav*1>

izbubètati {ām, ajū perf.} *sl* beat up <Slav*1>

ìzbūljeno {adv.} *sl* clearly <Slav*1>

izbunàrisati {išēm, išū perf.} *sl-crime* pick pockets <NE⁘*1>

izbunáriti {bùnārīm, rē perf.} *sl-crime* take out of one's pocket <NE⁘*1>

izdàhnuti {ìzdahnēm, nū perf. intr.} (lit. breathe out) *sl* die, breathe one's last <Slav*1>

izdánje *See the following*

- **džèpnō izdánje** {NP} (lit. pocket edition) *sl-fea* ***Fac*** short female

ìzdeljati {ljēm, ljū perf.} **a.** *sl* beat up <Slav> **b.** *sl* engage in sexual intercourse with (of a male) <Slav*1>

izdevedesetdevètati {ām, ajū perf.} *sl* beat up <Slav✍>

izdevètati {ām, ajū perf.} *sl* beat up <Slav>

ìzdisati {išēm, išū imperf.} *sl* be in love <Slav*1>

izdòjiti se {jīm, jē perf. intr.} (lit. milk oneself) *sl-sex* ***Fac-Obs*** urinate one's fill <Slav*1>

ìzdrati se {dērēm, dērū perf. intr.} *sl* shout at <Slav*1>

ìzdrkān {a, o adj.} **a.** *sl-sex* ***Obs*** masturbated <Slav> **b.i.** *sl-fea* ***Der-Obs*** ill-tempered: *izdrkan komšija ill-tempered neighbor* <Slav*1> **ii.** *sl-fea* ***Der-Obs*** evil, mean, bad: *izdrkan šef mean boss* <Slav*1> **iii.** *sl-fea* ***Der-Obs*** used: *izdrkan auto used car* <Slav*1> **iv.** *sl-fea* ***Der-Obs*** ugly: *izdrkana zgrada ugly building* <Slav*1> **v.** *sl-fea* ***Der-Obs*** old: *izdrkan kamion old truck* <Slav*1> **vi.** *sl-fea* ***Der-Obs*** tired and weary: *biti izdrkan poslije teške semdice na poslu be tired and weary after a hard week at work* <Slav*1> **vii.** *sl-fea* ***Der-Obs*** undependable, unreliable: *izdrkan motor undependable motorcycle* <Slav*1>

- **ìzdrkān na lòpati** {VP} (lit. jacked off on a spade) **a.** *sl-fea* ***Der-Obs*** used: *kola izdrkana na lopati used car* **b.** *sl-fea* ***Der-Obs*** ugly **c.** *sl-fea* ***Der-Obs*** old **d.** *sl-fea* ***Der-Obs*** weary **e.** *sl-fea* ***Der-Obs*** undependable, unreliable

ìzdrkati {ām, ajū perf.} **a.** *sl-sex* ***Obs*** masturbate, beat off <Slav> **b.** *sl-sex* ***Obs*** ejaculate, cum <Slav*1>

ìzdrkati se {ām, ajū perf. intr.} (lit. masturbate) **1** *sl* shout at <Slav*1> **2** *sl* go insane, freak out <Slav*1>

izdrkávati se {dȑkāvām, drkávajū imperf. intr.} (lit. masturbate) *sl-sex* ***Der-Obs*** spend one's time in useless activities, fool around, mess around <Slav*1>

izdrkèljati {ām, ajū perf.} *sl* get, obtain <Slav*1>

izdrkèljisati {išēm, išū perf.} **a.** *sl-crime* steal, swipe <Slav*1> **b.** *sl* get, obtain <Slav*2>

- **izdrkèljisati pêrje** {VP} (lit. search through one's feathers) *sl-fea* ***Der-Obs*** dress formally, dress up

izdùrati {ām, ajū perf.} *sl* persist <NE*1>

izduvàčica {ē fem.} (lit. the one who takes her shoes off) *sl-sex* ***Fac*** old prostitute <Slav⁘*1>

izdúvati [1] {ìzdūvām, izdúvajū perf.} *sl* beat up <Slav*1>

izdúvati [2] {ìzdūvām, izdúvajū perf. intr.} **1a.** *sl* ***Fac*** die, kick the bucket <Slav*1> **b.** *sl* ***Fac*** be cheated, be swindled <Slav*2> **c.** *sl* lose a game <Slav*3> **2** *sl-drugs* smoke a joint <Slav*1>

izdúžiti se {ìzdūžīm, žē perf. intr.} **a.** *sl* pay (bills, etc.) <Slav*1> **b.** *sl* spend ample money <Slav*1>

izèbati {ìzebēm, bū perf.} **a.** *sl-sex* ***Obs*** engage in sexual intercourse with (of a male) <Slav✍> **b.** *sl* ***Obs*** beat up <Slav✍*1> **c.** *sl* ***Obs*** defeat <Slav✍*2>

Ȉzēm ga! {S} Vojv *dia* used to express dissatisfaction, Damn! ☞ **izeti**

ìzengovati {gujēm, gujū perf.} *sl* arrange, put in order

ìzēti *See the following*

- **Ȉzēm ga!** {S} Vojv *dia* used to express dissatisfaction, Damn!
- **Ȉzēš ga!** {S} Vojv *dia* used to express dissatisfaction, Damn!
- **Ȉzēš pòsō!** {S} Vojv *dia* used to express dissatisfaction, Damn!

izgafírati se {gàfīrām, gafírajū perf. intr.} *sl* make a fool of oneself <Fre*1>

ìzgengovati {gujēm, gujū perf.} (lit. take care of) SerE *sl* realize, become aware

izgiljáriti {gìljārīm, rē perf. intr.} **1** *sl* get out, leave <Gyp⁘> **2** *sl* walk for a long time

izgȉljati {ām, ajū perf. intr.} *sl* go out <Gyp⁘>

izgirigàrisati {išēm, išū perf.} *sl-crime* succeed in illegal business <Gyp⁘>

ìzgladiti {dīm, dē perf.} *sl* beat up <Slav*1>

ìzglancati {ām, ajū perf.} *col* polish, shine: *izglancati cipele polish shoes* <Ger⁘>

ȉzglēd *See the following*

- **repùblički ȉzglēd** {NP} (lit. republic look) *sl* stomach, belly, gut

izglúmiti {ìzglūmīm, mē perf.} **a.** *sl* cheat, swindle: *Izglumio je Mehu. He swindled Meho.* <Slav*1> **b.** *sl* lie: *Izglumio je da su ga ovamo poslali Amerikanci. He pretended that the Americans had sent him here.* <Slav*2>

izglupírati se {glùpirām, ajū perf. intr.} *sl* make a fool of oneself <Slav*1>

izgòreō {ela, elo adj.} (lit. burned) SerE *sl* robbed, ripped off <Slav*1>

izgòriti {ìzgorīm, rē perf.} (lit. burn) *sl* be destroyed, be ruined <Slav*1>

izgrafírati {gràfīrām, grafírajū perf. intr.} *sl* spend (money, property, etc.): *Izgrafirali smo sto maraka u onom restoranu. We spent one hundred German marks in that restaurant.*

izgrafírati se {gràfīrām, grafírajū perf. intr.} *sl-fea* make a fool of oneself <Fre⁘>

izgùbiti se {bīm, bē perf. intr.} (lit. loose oneself) *sl-fea* get confused <Slav*1>

izgustírati {gùstīrām, gustírajū perf.} *col* cease being interested in an object or issue, drop: *Djeca su izgustirala sve igračke kad im je bilo šesnaest godina. The children lost interest in all their toys when they were sixteen.* <Slav⁘>

izgustírati se {ām, ajū perf. intr.} *col* have one's fill of something <Ita⁘>

izgùtati {ām, ajū perf.} (lit. swallow) **a.** *sl* make a mistake, screw up: *izgutati u vožnji i napraviti sudar make a mistake in driving and have an accident* <Slav*1> **b.** *sl* lose money <Slav*2>

- **izgùtati trȉp** {VP} (lit. swallow a trip) *sl-drugs* take LSD

izigrávānje {a neut.} *sl* spending one's time in useless activities, fooling around, messing around <Slav⁘>

izigrávati {izìgrāvām, izigrávajū imperf.} **a.** *col* pretend <Slav⁘> **b.** *col* act as, impersonate: *izigravati Amerikanca impersonate an American* <Slav⁘*1>

- **izigrávati lȕster** {VP} (lit. play chandelier) *sl-fea* ***Fac*** be left on one's own, be left hanging
- **izigrávati prȅponu** {VP} (lit. play hurdle) *sl-fea* ***Fac*** be avoided
- **izigrávati sàksiju** {VP} (lit. play flower pot) *sl-fea* ***Fac*** be unimportant

izigrávati se {izìgrāvām, izigrávajū imperf. intr.} *sl* spend one's time in useless activities, fool around, mess around <Slav⁘>

izistȉnskī {adv.} *col* really, indeed <Slav⁘>

ìzjakati {ačēm, ačū perf.} **a.** *sl* betray, turn to authorities **b.** *sl* torture **c.** *sl* hug a female **d.** *sl* make angry, make mad

ȉzjebān {a, o adj.} **a.** *sl-sex* ***Obs*** engaged in sexual intercourse with <Slav*1> **b.** *sl-fea* ***Obs*** tired <Slav*2>

izjèbati {ìzjebēm, bū perf.} **a.** *sl-sex* ***Obs*** engage in sexual intercourse with (of a male) <Slav> **b.** *sl* ***Obs*** cheat, swindle: *izjebati profesora cheat one's professor* <Slav*1>

- **izjèbati ko sânskū kȍzu!** {VP} (lit. fuck like a Saanen she-goat) *sl-fea* ***Obs*** trick, cheat, swindle, fuck over
- **izjèbati ko vòla** {VP} (lit. fuck like an ox) *sl-fea* ***Obs*** trick, cheat, swindle, fuck over

izjúriti [1] {ìzjūrīm, rē perf.} *col* throw out, kick out: *Izjurili su ga iz tog restorana. He was kicked out of that restaurant.* <Slav*1>

izjúriti [2] {ìzjūrīm, rē perf. intr.} *col* leave hastily, split <Slav*1>

ȉzjutra {adv.} *dia-col* in the morning <Slav✍>

ìzlanuti se {nēm, nū perf. intr.} /izlànuti se/ (lit. bark out) *col* blurt out <Slav*1> ☞ **izlet(j)eti (se)**

izlápeti {pīm, pē imperf.} (lit. evaporate) SerE *col* turn senile <Slav*1>

izlapètis {a masc.} *sl-fea* going insane, freaking out <Slav✍>

- **izlapètis aproksimâlis** {NP} *sl-fea* ***Fac*** going senile

izlapìtis {a masc.} *sl-fea* going insane, freaking out <Slav✍>

izlazȉčati se {ām, ajū perf. intr.} *sl* vomit, throw up, puke <Slav*1>

izlémati {ìzlēmām, izlémajū perf.} *sl* beat up <Ger⁘*1>

izlèteti {ìzletīm, tē perf.} (lit. fly out) **1** **SerE** *sl* blurt out <Slav*1> **2** **SerE** *sl* get out, leave <Slav*1> **3** *sl* pay dearly <Slav*1> ☞ **izlanuti (se), izlajati (se)**

izlèteti se {ìzletīm, tē perf. intr.} SerE *sl* blurt out <Slav*1> ☞ **izlanuti (se), izlajati (se)**

izlètjeti {ìzletīm, tē perf. intr.} (lit. fly out) **1** *sl* blurt out <Slav*1> **2** *sl* get out, leave <Slav*1> **3** *sl* pay dearly <Slav*1> ☞ **izlanuti (se), izlajati (se)**

izlètjeti se {ìzletīm, tē perf. intr.} *sl* blurt out <Slav*1> ☞ **izlanuti (se), izlajati (se)**

ìzletnīk {a (acc. = gen.) masc.} (lit. picnicker) *sl-crime* just released prisoner <Slav*1>

ìzlīzānī kı̏t {NP} (lit. depleted dude) *sl* ***Fac*** waiter ☞ **kit**

Ìzlog {a (acc. = gen.) masc.} (lit. store window) *sl* name of a cafe on Ilica and Marinkovićeva streets in Zagreb, Croatia <Slav*1>

izljèći {egnēm, egnū, eg, eg perf. irreg.} *sl* get out, leave <Slav*1>

izmàltati {ām, ajū perf.} **a.** *sl-arch* beat up <Ger❖*1> **b.** *sl-arch* cheat, swindle <Ger❖*2>

izmàrisati {išēm, išū perf.} **a.** *sl* beat up <Gyp❖*1> **b.** *sl-crime* rob, rip off

izmasírati {màsīrām, masírajū perf.} **a.** *sl* beat up <Fre*1> **b.** *sl-fea* bother, annoy by talking <Fre*2>

izmávati {ìzmāvām, izmávajū perf.} *sl* beat up

ìzmazati {ažēm, ažū perf.} *sl* beat up <Slav*1>

ìzmećār {a (acc. = gen.) masc.} *sl-fea* ***Der*** servant <NE*1>

izméniti *See the following*

• **izméniti lȉčnī òpis** {VP} (lit. change someone's personal description) **SerE** *sl* beat up severely, rearrange someone's face

izmésiti {tīm, tē perf.} (lit. knead) SerE *sl-sex* ***Fac-Obs*** engage in sexual intercourse with (of a male) <Slav*1>

ìzmestiti {tīm, tē perf.} SerE *sl* beat up <Slav*1>

izmicàus {a masc.} *sl* silent disappearance, slinking away <Slav✎> ☞ **izmicauz**

izmicàuz {a masc.} *sl* silent disappearance, slinking away <Slav✎> ☞ **izmicaus**

izmisíriti *See the following*

• **izmisíriti bȕnār** {VP} (lit. dig out a well) *sl-crime* ***Fac*** cut somebody's pocket in order to steal her wallet

izmlátiti {tīm, tē perf.} **a.** *sl* beat up <Slav> **b.** *sl* cheat, swindle <Slav*1>

• **izmlátiti ko vòla u kùpusu** {VP} (lit. beat up like one beats an ox in the cabbage field) *col* beat up severely

• **izmlátiti na mȑtvō ìme** {VP} (lit. beat up to the dead name) *col* beat up severely

izmotàncija {ē fem.} *col* pretending, acting <Slav❖*1>

izmotávati se {mòtāvām, motávajū imperf. intr.} **a.** *col* act like a brat <Slav*1> **b.** *col* make jokes <Slav*2>

ìzmrdān {a, o adj.} (lit. moved) *sl-fea* tired <Slav*1>

ìzmrdati {ām, ajū perf.} (lit. move one's fill) **a.** *sl-sex* ***Fac-Obs*** engage in sexual intercourse with (of a male) <Slav*1> **b.** *sl* ***Obs*** make nervous, get on one's nerves <Slav*2>

ìzmućkati {ām, ajū perf.} (lit. stir) *sl* manage to do <Slav*1>

izmunđáriti {mùnđārīm, rē perf.} *sl* get, obtain

izmùntati {ām, ajū perf.} *sl* get, obtain <Ita*1>

ìzmūsti {izmúzēm, zū perf.} *sl* abuse financially, milk: *Izmuzao ju je za dve hiljade dinara. He squeezed two thousand dinars out of her.* <Slav*1>

ìzmuštrati {ām, ajū perf.} *sl* exercise discipline <Ger❖>

iznabádati {nàbādām, nabádajū perf. intr.} (lit. stab all over) *sl* beat up: *Juče ga je iznabadala Markova banda. Marko's gang beat him up yesterday.* <Slav*1>

ȉzoš {a (acc. = gen.) masc.} *sl-fea* person from the Eastern regions of the former Yugoslavia <Slav✎>

izráditi {ìzrādīm, dē perf.} *sl* cheat, swindle <Slav*1>

izràubovati {bujēm, bujū perf.} *sl* wear out (make unusable through long or heavy use) <Ger*1>

izrédati se {ìzrēdām, izrédajū perf. intr.} *sl-sex* ***Obs*** engage in group sex (of males who, one after another, engage in sexual intercourse with a single female), rape, gang bang <Slav*1>

ìzrenjkati {ām, ajū perf.} *sl* throw out, kick out

izrezbáriti {rèzbārīm, rē perf.} *sl* beat up <Slav*1>

izríbati {ìzrībām, izríbajū perf.} *sl* reproach, scold <Ger*1>

izrókati {ìzrōkām, izrókajū perf.} **a.** *sl* beat up <Slav❖*1> **b.** *sl-sex* engage in sexual intercourse with (of a male)

izrulètati {ām, ajū perf.} *sl* beat up <Fre*1>

izuličáriti {lìčārīm, rē perf.} (lit. street out) *sl* start dating a girl met on the street <Slav❖*1>

ìzuti se {ìzujēm, ujū perf. intr.} *sl* reach for one's wallet <Slav*1>

ìzvaditi *See the following*

• **Ìzvadi mi òvāj pânj iz ȍka!** {S} (lit. Take out this stump from my eye!) *sl* ***Fac*** used to express disbelief, Do you think I'm blind?

• **ìzvaditi nȍvū lȉčnū kártu** {VP} (lit. get a new ID) *sl* ***Fac*** beat up severely, rearrange someone's face

ìzvaditi se {dīm, dē perf. intr.} *sl* recover, get better <Slav*1>

izváliti {ìzvālīm, lē perf.} *col* say something unintelligent <Slav*1>

• **izváliti zûbe** {VP} (lit. push out one's teeth) *sl* beat up severely

izváliti se {ìzvālīm, lē perf. intr.} *sl* lay down (e.g. to sleep) <Slav*1>

izvaljívati {vàljujēm, ljujū imperf.} *col* keep pronouncing something preposterous <Slav*1>

izvanzemáljac {ljca (acc. = gen.) masc.} *col* extraterrestrial, alien <Slav>

ìzvatati {ām, ajū perf.} **a.** *sl* seduce <Slav*1> **b.** *sl* cheat, swindle <Slav*2>

izvatávati {vàtāvām, vatávajū imperf.} *sl* cheat, swindle <Slav*1>

ìzvesti {edēm, edū perf. irreg.} (lit. take out) *sl* ply with liquor in order to rob <Slav*1>

izvešpláviti {vèšplāvīm, vē perf.} (lit. blue the laundry) *sl* ***Fac*** beat up <Ger-Slav❖*1>

ìzvetriti {rīm, rē perf.} (lit. evaporate) SerE *sl* disappear, evaporate, vanish <Slav*1>

izvijátiti {vìjātīm, tē perf.} **a.** *sl* go out <Slav*1> **b.** *sl* leave a restaurant without having paid, run out on the tab <Slav*2>

ìzvimati {ām, ajū perf.} *col* clean thoroughly using chemical cleaners (usu. of house or apartment) <BN❖*1>

izvínte {excl.} [std. = izvinite] *col* used to express remorse or to make another give way, sorry, excuse me <Slav*1>

ìzvisiti {sīm, sē perf.} (lit. hang out) **a.** *sl* get nothing, come up empty <Slav*1> **b.i.** *sl* make a mistake, screw up <Slav*2> **ii.** *sl-gamble* lose money <Slav*2>

izvìždati se {ìzviždīm, dē perf. intr.} (lit. whistle out) *sl-sex* ***Obs*** urinate, piss <Slav*1>

izvláčiti *See the following*

• **izvláčiti iz naftalína** {VP} (lit. take out from naphthalene) *col* use something very old or passé (e.g. a dress, shirt)

izvòditi {ìzvodīm, dē imperf.} (lit. conduct) *col* pretend <Slav*1>

• **izvòditi bêsnē glíste** {VP} (lit. perform rabid worms) SerE *col* be a brat

• **izvòditi bijèsnē glíste**{VP} (lit. perform rabid worms) *col* be a brat

• **izvòditi gràđevīnskē rádove** {VP} (lit. perform construction works) *sl-sex* ***Fac-Obs*** masturbate, beat off

• **izvòditi krîvē Dríne** {VP} (lit. perform meandering Drina rivers) *col* be a brat

• **izvòditi krivìne** {VP} (lit. perform turns) *col* be a brat

• **Ne izvòdi bȉjēsnē glíste!** {S} (lit. Don't you perform rabid worms!) *col* used to express negative attitude (usu. toward a brat), Don't exaggerate!

izvòđāč {vođáča (acc. = gen.) masc.} *sl* boy who manages to do nothing more than to walk with his girlfriend <Slav*1>

izvòli {excl.} **1** *col* used when passing something in direct informal communication, here you go <Slav> **2** *col* used to express one's readiness to respond, what can I do for you <Slav> ☞ **izvolte, izvolite**

izvòlite {excl.} **1** *col* used when passing something in direct formal communication, here you go <Slav> **2** *col* used to express one's readiness to respond, what can I do for you <Slav> ☞ **izvoli, izvolte**

izvòlte {excl.} [std. = izvolite] **1** *col* used when passing something in direct formal communication, here you go <Slav> **2** *col* used to express one's readiness to respond, what can I do for you <Slav> ☞ **izvoli, izvolte**

izvózati {ìzvōzām, izvózajū imperf.} **a.** *sl* joke with, make a fool of <Slav*1> **b.** *sl* cheat, swindle <Slav*2> **c.** *sl* lie <Slav*3>

izvrndùpečiti se {čīm, čē perf. intr.} /izvrndupèčiti se/ *sl* lay down (e.g. to sleep) <Slav✍>

izvŕnuti *See the following*

• **izvŕnuti kŕzno** {VP} (lit. turn out one's fur) *sl-sex* ***Obs-Fac*** engage in sexual intercourse with

izvŕšiti *See the following*

• **izvŕšiti nȕždu** {VP} (lit. do what is necessary) *sl-sex* defecate, do one's business

ìzvūći *See the following*

• **ìzvūći iz naftalína** {VP} *col* use something very old or passé (e.g. a dress, shirt)

ȉža {ē fem.} *sl* home <Slav✍>

ȉžmikān {a, o adj.} (lit. squeezed) **a.** *sl-fea* exhausted <Slav*1> **b.** *sl-fea* abused (financially) <Slav*2>

ižmíkati {ìžmīčēm, ičū perf.} /ìžmikati /ām, ajū perf/ **a.** *sl* squeeze (sponge, etc.) <Slav*1> **b.** *sl* exhaust <Slav*2> **c.** *sl* abuse financially, rip off <Slav*3>

Jj

jà [1] {excl.} *col* used to express different emotions ranging from approval to outrage, oh <NE*1>

jâ [2] *See the following*

• **dà sam jâ s tȍbōm** {S} (lit. If I were with you) *col* used to introduce a piece of advice, if I were you: *Da sam ja s tobom, ne bih putovao po ovom vremenu. If I were you, I would not travel with the weather like this.*

• **Jâ bi da mî tô** [VERB:PRES 2pPL] {LSF} *col* used to stimulate to common action, Let us [VERB:PRES 2pPL] it

• **preko mȅne mŕtvōg** {PP} (lit. over my dead body) *col* used to refer to strong lack of approval, over my dead body

jȁ [3] {part.} *col* used as an independent affirmative response, of course, yeah <NE*1>

Jâ bi da mî tô [VERB:PRES 2pPL] {LSF} *col* used to stimulate to common action, Let us [VERB:PRES 2pPL] it ☞ **ja**

Jâ ga jèbēm a on pȑdī! {S} (lit. I screw him and he farts!) *sl* ***Off-Fac*** used as a moderate curse to a third party, Screw him! ☞ **jebati**

jâ ga kȑstīm, a ôn pȑdī {S} (lit. I am baptizing him but he is farting) *col* ***Obs-Fac*** used to indicate that a person does not pay attention to intensive persuasion

Jâ te jèbēm a ti pȑdīš! {S} (lit. I screw you and you fart!) *sl* ***Off-Fac*** used as a weak curse, Screw you! ☞ **jebati**

Jâ ti ga stȅra! {S} (lit. I will stick it to you!) *dia* ***Off*** used as a moderate curse, Fuck you! ☞ **sterati**

jȁblān {a (acc. = gen.) masc.} **1** *sl-fea* tall person <Slav*1> **2** *sl-sex* penis <Slav*1>

jȁbome {part.} *col* used as a strong affirmative response, of course, yeah, you bet <Slav>

jȁbukovača {ē fem.} *col* apple cider <Slav>

jȁc {excl.} *col* used to lure a goat <Slav>

jȁco {excl.} *col* used to lure a goat <Slav>

jȁd *See the following*

• **na jèdvītē jȁde** {PP} (lit. at very poor griefs) *col* with major difficulties

• **nȉ pō jȁda** {PP} (lit. not half the grief) **a.** *col* used to express that the outcome of a situation could have been even worse, not that bad: *To je ni po jada što su nas stavili u zatvor. That they put us in prison is not that bad.* **b.** *col* weak (lacking physical force or social importance): *ni po jada frajer weak guy*

jȁdan {excl.} *col* used to express compassion, poor thing <Slav*1>

• **jȁdna ti mâjka** {S} (lit. let your mother be sad) *col* used to indicate that one's interlocutor is doing something wrong, illegal, etc., What in the world are you doing! Oh God!: *Šta si uradio, jadna ti majka! Oh God, what have you done!*

jâdo [1] {excl.} *col* used to express compassion, poor thing <Slav*1>

jádo [2] {a masc.} /jádo /e masc./ *sl-fea* weak male, wimp <Slav*1>

jȁdovān {a (acc. = gen.) masc.} *col* poor male <Slav*1>

Jȁdrān *See the following*

• **plâvī Jȁdrān** {NP} (lit. blue Adriatic sea) *sl-crime* policeman, cop, man in blue

jaènce {a neut.} /jaènce /eta neut./ *sl-sex* ***Obs*** small testicle <Slav✍>

jaèšce {a neut.} /jaèšce /eta neut./ *sl-sex* ***Obs*** small testicle <Slav✍>

jàfina {ē fem.} **a.** *sl* forgery <NE❖*1> **b.** *sl* false incrimination, framing **c.** *sl* lie

jàgma {ē fem.} *col* looting <NE>

jagnjéšce {eta neut.} (lit. little lamb) *sl-fea* very young female, little girl <Slav*1>

jȁh {excl.} *col* used as a strong affirmative response, of course, yeah, you bet <NE*1>

jȁhati {jȁšēm, šū imperf.} (lit. ride) *sl-sex* ***Obs*** engage in sexual intercourse with (of a male) <Slav*1>

• **jȁhati skȁkavac** {VP} (lit. ride a jumping) *sl-fea* ***Fac*** be very happy

jàjān {jajána (acc. = gen.) masc.} (lit. the one with the eggs) *sl-fea* lively young male <Slav>

jàjara {ē fem.} (lit. the one with the eggs) **1** *sl-fea* extremely talkative person, chatterbox <Slav*1> **2a.** *sl-crime* petty thief <Slav*1> **b.** *sl-crime* crook, thief <Slav*2>

jájce {eta neut.} (lit. small egg) *sl-sex* ***Obs*** testicle, ball <Slav>

• **jájca od papagájca** {NP} (lit. little parrot's small balls) *col* nothing at all, fucking nothing

jáje {eta neut.} (lit. egg) **1** *sl-sex* ***Obs*** testicle, ball <Slav*1> **2** *sl-fea* bald male <Slav*1>

• **do jájā** {PP} (lit. to the balls) *sl* ***Obs*** excellent, awesome

• **Do jájā!** {PP} (lit. To the balls!) **1** *sl* used to express anger, Fuck it! **2** *sl* used to express satisfaction, Great!

• **jája od papagája** {NP} (lit. parrot's balls) *col* nothing at all, fucking nothing

• **jáje múćak tèbi za rúčak** {NP} (lit. rotten egg for your lunch) *sl-fea* used as a strong negative response, no way, never

jâk {jáka, jáko adj.} (lit. strong) **1** *col* handsome, cute: *jak frajer handsome male* <Slav*1> **2** *col* good, of high quality: *jaka kola good wheels* <Slav*1> **3** *col* important <Slav*1>

jâk štȉh {NP} *sl-fea* undependable person ☞ **štih**

jáka fȉrma {NP} (lit. strong firm) *col* ***Iro*** nothing special, no big deal: *Taj auto auto je jaka firma. That car is nothing special.* ☞ **firma**

jáka stvâr {AdjP} *col* ***Iro*** nothing special, no big deal ☞ **stvar**

jal {c.} [std. = ili] *dia* or <Slav✍>

jȁla {excl.} *col* used to command an action, do it <NE[*1]>

jȁlāh {excl.} *col* used to command an action, do it <NE[*1]>

jȁlija {ē fem.} **a.** *col* troublemakers, rowdies (collectively) <NE[*1]> **b.** *col* worthless or despicable persons <NE[*2]>

jȁlijāš {a (acc. = gen.) masc.} *sl-fea* troublemaker, rowdy, ruffian <NE>

jȁlla {excl.} BosM *col* God almighty <NE[*1]>

jȁma {ē fem.} (lit. chasm, hole) *sl-sex* ***Fac-Obs*** vagina, cunt <Slav[*1]>
- **sȅptičkā jȁma** {NP} (lit. sewage hole) *sl-sex* ***Obs*** vagina, cunt

jȁmāč {a (acc. = gen.) masc.} *sl-auto* Yamaha (make of motorcycle) <BN✍>

jȁmiti {mīm, mē perf.} *sl* take, get hold of, pick <Slav[*1]>

jȁmskī râdnik {NP} (lit. hole worker) *sl-sex* ***Fac-Obs*** male sexual partner (of a female) ☞ **radnik**

jȁnel {a masc.} *sl* jacket

jȁnpi {jȁnapi, jȁnopi adj.; perm} /jȁnpi/ [std. = pijan] *sl-drink* drunk, pickled <Slav✍>

jȁnpika {ē fem. & masc.; Dat jȁnpiki p} [std. = pijanac] *sl-drink* alcoholic, drunk <Slav✍>

jȁnuār {a (acc. = gen.) masc.} (lit. January) **1** *sl-fea* elderly male <Lat[*1]> **2** *sl-crime* policeman, cop <Lat[*1]>

jȁnje {eta neut.} (lit. lamb) *sl-sex* ***Fam*** virgin (female) <Slav[*1]>

jȁo {excl.} *col* used to express pain, grief, astonishment, etc., oh, woe <Slav>
- **jȁo pȁo** {S} (lit. ah it fell) *sl-sex* ***Fac*** impotent male

jȁoh {excl.} *col* used to express pain, grief, astonishment, etc., oh, woe <Slav>

jȁoj {excl.} *col* used to express pain, grief, astonishment, etc., oh, woe <Slav>

jȁok {a masc.} *col* scream in pain, fear, or outrage <Slav>

jaókati {jȁōčēm, čū imperf.} *col* scream in pain, fear, or outrage <Slav>

jaóknuti {jȁōknēm, nū perf.} *col* scream in pain, fear, or outrage <Slav>

Jȁorina {ē fem.} *dia* name for Jahorina (a mountain near Sarajevo, Bosnia) <Slav✍>

Japánac {nca (acc. = gen.) masc.} (lit. Japanese) *sl* child, kid <SlavO[*1]>

jȁpānka {ē fem.; Dat jȁpānki} (lit. Japanese) *sl-drink* alcoholic, drunk <SlavO[*1]>

Jȁpī {īja (acc. = gen.) masc.} **1a.** *sl* Japanese (person), Jap <SlavO✍[*1]> **b.** *sl* child, kid <SlavO✍[*1]> **2** *sl* yuppie <Eng>

jȁpija {ē fem.} **a.** *col* building material <NE> **b.** *sl* body <NE[*1]> **c.** *sl-fea* big-boned female <NE[*2]>

japučȉnskī {ōg (acc. = gen.) masc.} Cro *sl* father, dad <Slav✍>

jȁra {ē fem.} **1** *col* heat <Slav> **2** *sl* year <Ger✍>

jȁrac *See the following*
- **bȁbini jȁrčevi** {NP} (lit. old lady's goats) *col* hail

jȁrān {jarána (acc. = gen.) masc.} **a.** *col* friend (male) <NE[*1]> **b.** *sl-crime* detective <NE[*2]>

jȁrāne {excl.} *col* ***Fam*** used to address a male in direct informal communication, buddy <NE[*1]>

jarànica {ē fem.} Bos *col* female friend <NE⁘>

jarànika {ē masc.} Bos *dia-col* friend (male) <NE[*1]>

jarániti se {jȁrānīm, nē imperf. intr.} Bos *col* make friends <NE⁘>

jȁrānskī {ā, ō} Bos *col* friendly <NE⁘>

jaránstvo {a neut.} Bos *col* friendship <NE⁘>

jȁrba {ē fem.} *sl* grass (the plant) <Rum>

jȁrcati {ām, ajū imperf. intr.} *col* run around (e.g. school children on their break) <Slav[*1]>

jȁrdovina {ē fem.} *sl* bacon

járo {ē masc.} Bos *col* friend (male) <NE⁘>

jȁslara {ē fem.} *sl-fea* lazy or shiftless female, bum, good for nothing <Slav[*1]>

jȁslice {līcā fem. pl.} (lit. daycare) *sl-fea* prison, the pen <Slav[*1]>

jȁstrēb {a (acc. = gen.) masc.} *sl-polit* politician with extremist views, hawk <Slav[*1]>

jȁstučēnje {a neut.} *col* hitting with pillows <NE>

jȁstuk {a masc.} (lit. pillow) *sl-sex* ***Fac-Obs*** buttocks, butt <NE[*1]>
- **stârī jȁstuk** {NP} (lit. old pillow) *sl-fea* senior citizen

Jȁši mi na kȉtu! {S} (lit. Ride on my cock!) SerE *dia* ***Off*** used as a moderate curse, Up yours! ☞ **jašiti**

jàšika {ē fem.} (lit. riding) *sl-sex* ***Obs*** sexual intercourse <Slav*1>

jàšiti *See the following*

- **Jàši mi na kȉtu!** {S} (lit. Ride on my cock!) SerE *dia* ***Off*** used as a moderate curse, Up yours!
- **jàšiti na kȑpi** {VP} (lit. ride on a rag) *sl-sex* ***Fac*** have one's period
- **Kȍ te jàšī!** {S} (lit. Who is riding you?) *sl* ***Off*** used as a weak curse, Screw you!

jàšta {part.} *col* used as a strong affirmative response, of course, yeah, you bet <Slav>

jàšta râdī {ExcP} *col* used as a strong affirmative response, of course, yeah, you bet ☞ **raditi**

jaštàrica {ē fem.} *sl-arch* fire <Slav*1>

jàtismi se {jȅmsmi, jȕsmi imperf. intr.; perm} [std. = smijati se] *sl* laugh <Slav✍>

jàtnāč {a (acc. = gen.) masc.} *sl-auto* Yamaha (make of motorcycle) <BN✍>

jàto {a neut.} (lit. flock) **a.** *sl* company (group of people) <Slav*1> **b.** *sl* steady company, people one hangs with <Slav*2>

jàūk {a masc.} **a.** *col* scream in pain, fear, or outrage <Slav> **b.** *col* noise <Slav*1>

jaúkalac {kaoca (acc. = gen.) masc.} (lit. screamer) *col* person who often screams in pain <Slav✣>

jaúkalica {ē fem.} (lit. screamer) **1** *sl-fea* female who often screams in pain <Slav✣> **2** *sl-music* sad song <Slav✣>

jàukast {a, o adj.} **a.** *col* screaming in pain, fear, or outrage <Slav✣> **b.** *col* noisy <Slav✣*1>

jaúkati {jàūčem, čū imperf.} **a.** *col* scream in pain, fear, or outrage <Slav✣> **b.** *col* cry, shed tears, weep <Slav✣*1> **c.** *col* make noise <Slav✣*2>

jaùkav {a, o adj.} **a.** *col* screaming in pain, fear, or outrage <Slav✣> **b.** *col* noisy <Slav✣*1>

jaúkavac {vca (acc. = gen.) masc.} (lit. screamer) *col* person who often screams in pain <Slav✣>

jaùkljavina {ē fem.} *sl* screaming in pain, fear, or outrage <Slav✣>

jaùkljiv {a, o adj.} *col* screaming in pain, fear, or outrage <Slav✣>

jaùkljivo {adv.} *col* screaming in pain, fear, or outrage <Slav✣>

jaúknuti {jàūknēm, nū perf. intr.} **a.** *col* screams, shouts <Slav✣> **b.i.** *col* be robbed, be ripped off: *jauknuti za dvjesto marona be robbed of two hundred German marks* <Slav✣*1> **ii.aa.** *col* pay (bills, etc.) <Slav✣*1> **bb.** *col* overpay <Slav✣*2> **cc.** *sl-gamble* lose money <Slav✣*3>

jàuza {ē fem.} *sl* snack <Ger>

jàuzna {ē fem.} *sl* snack <Ger✍>

jáviti {jâvīm, vē perf.} *sl* hit, punch <Slav*1>

jâvka {ē fem.} (lit. the public one) **1** *sl* illegal meeting <Slav*1> **2** *sl* illegal connection

jàvnjāk {javnjáka masc.} (lit. the public one) *sl-sex* brothel, whorehouse <Slav*1>

Jàvōrka {ē fem.; Dat Jàvōrki} *sl* unknown female <Slav*1>

jàzavičārka {ē fem.} (lit. she-dachshund) *sl* loafer (shoe) <Slav*1>

jàzbec {a (acc. = gen.) masc.} *sl* servant <Slav*1>

jàzbina {ē fem.} **1** *sl* apartment <Slav*1> **2** *sl* home <Slav*1>

Jè l ti dànas bȍljē? {S} (lit. Are you feeling better today?) *sl* ***Fac*** used as an informal greeting, How are you doing! ☞ **bolje**

Jè l ti to svȅ ([NOUN:NOM]) il ìmā jȍš? {LSF} (lit. Is that all [NOUN:NOM] or is there more of it?) *sl* ***Der*** used to express negative attitude toward: *Je l to sve pričanje il ima još? What you're saying is worth shit!* ☞ **sve**

Jè s tî kod prȉvātnīka slúžio? {S} (lit. Did you serve in the private military forces?) *sl* ***Fac*** used to express negative attitude toward one's interlocutor's knowledge, Where did you go to school? ☞ **privatnik**

jȇb {a +ov (ext. pl) masc.; Nom Pl jébovi} **1** *sl-sex* ***Obs*** sexual intercourse <Slav✣> **2** *sl-sex* ***Obs*** sperm <Slav✣>

jéba {ē fem.} **1a.** *sl-sex* ***Obs*** sexual intercourse <Slav> **b.** *sl* ***Obs*** unpleasant situation, bummer: *Otpušten je - jeba. He was fired from his job. Bummer.* <Slav*1> **c.** *sl-fea* ***Obs*** trouble, problem <Slav*2> **d.** *sl-fea* boring event: *jeba na sastanku boring event in a meeting* <Slav*3> **2** *sl-sex* loose woman <Slav>

Jèbā ga tí! {S} (lit. You fuck it!) *dia* ***Obs*** used to express dissatisfaction, Fuck it! ☞ **jebati**

jèbac {pca (acc. = gen.) masc.} *sl-sex* ***Obs*** male sexual partner (of a female) <Slav>

jèbāč {jebáča (acc. = gen.) masc.} *sl-sex* ***Obs*** male sexual partner (of a female) <Slav>

jebàčica {ē fem.} *sl-sex* ***Obs*** female sexual partner (of a male) <Slav>

jebàčina {ē fem.} *sl-sex* ***Obs*** sexual intercourse <Slav>

jèbāčkī [1] {ā, ō adj.} (lit. fucking) *sl-sex* ***App-Obs*** excellent, awesome: *jebački uraditi test do excellent on a test* <**Slav**>

jèbāčkī [2] {adv.} (lit. fucking) *sl-fea* ***Obs*** skillfully <**Slav**>

Jèbaću [PRON:DAT] mȁtēr! {LSF} (lit. I will fuck [PPRON] mother!) *col* ***Off*** used as a threat of physical violence: *Jebaću mu mater! I will beat the shit out of him!* ☞ **jebati**

Jèbaću te nȍćas budȁlo! {S} (lit. I will fuck you tonight!) *col* ***Off*** used as a threat of physical violence, I'm gonna fuck you up! ☞ **jebati**

Jèbaću te u ústa! {S} (lit. I will fuck you in your mouth!) *col* ***Off*** used as a threat of physical violence, I'm gonna fuck you up! ☞ **jebati**

Jèbaću ti jâ mȁtēr ònū robìjāškū. {S} (lit. I will fuck that prisoner's mother of yours.) *col* ***Off*** used as a threat of physical violence, I'm gonna fuck you up! ☞ **jebati**

Jèbaću ti mâjku! {S} (lit. I will fuck your mother!) *col* ***Off*** used as a threat of physical violence, I'm gonna fuck you up! ☞ **jebati**

Jèbaću ti mâjku mâjčinu! {S} (lit. I will fuck your mother's mother!) *col* ***Off*** used as a threat of physical violence, I'm gonna fuck you up! ☞ **jebati**

Jèbaću ti mâjku u ústa! {S} (lit. I will fuck your mother in her mouth!) *col* ***Off*** used as a threat of physical violence, I'm gonna fuck you up! ☞ **jebati**

Jèbaću ti mȁmicu! {S} (lit. I will fuck your little mother!) *col* ***Off*** used as a threat of physical violence, I'm gonna fuck you up! ☞ **jebati**

Jèbaću ti nánu tvòju! {S} (lit. I will fuck your mother!) *col* ***Off*** used as a threat of physical violence, I'm gonna fuck you up! ☞ **jebati**

Jèbaću ti sèstru! {S} (lit. I will fuck your sister!) *col* ***Off*** used as a threat of physical violence, I'm gonna fuck you up! ☞ **jebati**

Jèbaću ti svȇ po spȉsku! {S} (lit. I will fuck all yours according to a list!) *col* ***Off*** used as a threat of physical violence, I'm gonna fuck you up! ☞ **jebati**

jebáda {ē fem.} **a.** *sl-sex* ***Obs*** sexual intercourse <**Slav**❖[*1]> **b.** *sl-fea* ***Obs*** unpleasant situation, bummer: *To da nismo dobili karte za koncert bila je prava jebada. Not getting concert tickets was a real bummer.* <**Slav**[*1]> **c.** *sl-fea* ***Obs*** trouble, problem <**Slav**[*2]> **d.** *sl-fea* ***Obs*** tedious job: *jebada oko rječnika tedious job on the dictionary* <**Slav**[*3]>

jèbāga {part.} *sl* intensifying particle <**Slav**[*1]>

Jebáji ga! {S} *col-dia* ***Obs*** used to express dissatisfaction, Fuck it! ☞ **jebavati**

Jebáji [NOUN:ACC]! {LSF} (lit. Fuck [NOUN:ACC]!) *col-dia* ***Obs*** used to express disrespect or dissatisfaction, Fuck it!: *Jebaji Halila, ko ga jebe! Fuck Halil, who gives a shit about him!* ☞ **jebavati**

Jèbal si ćȍk! {S} (lit. You fucked an egg!) SSer *dia* ***Obs*** used to express dissatisfaction, Fuck it! ☞ **jebati**

Jebal si čokavca! {S} (lit. You fucked an egg!) SSer *dia* ***Obs*** used to refer to a future difficult situation of one's interlocutor ☞ **jebati**

Jȅbāla [PRON:ACC] [NOUN:NOM]! {LSF} (lit. Let [NOUN:NOM] fuck [PRON:ACC]!) *col* ***Obs*** used to express disrespect or lack of interest in: *Jebala te zelena stolica, kup onu drugu! Fuck that green chair, buy the other one!* ☞ **jebati**

Jȅbàla te mâjka bȍžijā! {S} (lit. Let God's mother fuck you!) *col* ***Off*** used as a strong curse, Fuck you! ☞ **jebati**

Jȅbāle [PRON:ACC] [NOUN:NOM]! {LSF} (lit. Let [NOUN:NOM] fuck [PRON:ACC]!) *col* ***Obs*** used to express disrespect or lack of interest in: *Jebale te skupe cedeove! Fuck those expensive CDs!* ☞ **jebati**

Jȅbāli ih njȉhovi gròfovi! {S} (lit. Let their counts screw them!) *col-dia* ***Off*** used as a weak curse, Screw them! ☞ **jebati**

Jȅbāli [PRON:ACC] [NP:NOM]! {LSF} (lit. Let [NOUN: NOM] fuck [PRON:ACC]!) *col* ***Obs*** used to express disrespect or lack of interest in, Fuck that [NOUN:NOM]!: *Jebali ih glupi političari! Fuck their stupid politicians!* ☞ **jebati**

Jȅbālo [PRON:ACC] [NOUN:NOM] {LSF} (lit. Let [NOUN:NOM] fuck [PRON:ACC]!) *col-dia* ***Obs*** used to express disrespect or lack of interest in: *Jebalo ih dete! Fuck that kid!* ☞ **jebati**

jȅbān {a, o adj.} *sl-sex* ***Obs*** engaged in sexual intercourse with <**Slav**>

Jȅbānā ràbota! {NP} (lit. Fucked business!) *col* ***Obs*** used to express disrespect or lack of interest in ☞ **rabota**

jȅbānā strána {NP} (lit. the side which is fucked) *sl-fea* ***Obs*** cheated person, the one who is fucked ☞ **strana**

jȅbānā strȁnka {NP} (lit. the party which is fucked) *sl-fea* ***Obs*** cheated person, the one who is fucked ☞ **stranka**

jebánac {nca masc.} *sl-sex* ***Obs*** place intended for sexual intercourse <**Slav**>

jebàncija {ē fem.} **a.** *sl-sex* ***Obs*** sexual intercourse <Slav> **b.i.** *sl* ***Obs*** loss of time: *On misli da je odlazak u bioskop jebancija. He considers going to movies a loss of time.* <Slav*1> **ii.** *sl-fea* ***Obs*** mess, disorder, disturbance: *jebancija u kuhinji mess in the kitchen* <Slav*1> **iii.** *sl-fea* ***Obs*** job which does not bring enough money, low-paying job <Slav*1> **iv.** *sl-fea* ***Obs*** something boring <Slav*1>

jebànija {ē fem.} *sl-sex* ***Obs*** sexual intercourse <Slav>

jèbānje {a neut.} *sl-sex* ***Obs*** sexual intercourse <Slav>
- **jèbānje u bȍlestan mȍzak** {NP} (lit. fucking in a sick brain) *sl-fea* ***Obs*** trick, cheat, swindle, fuck over
- **jèbānje u zdrȁv mȍzak** {NP} (lit. fucking in a healthy brain) *sl-fea* ***Obs*** trick, cheat, swindle, fuck over

jebaónica {ē fem.} *sl-sex* ***Obs*** place intended for sexual intercourse <Slav>

jèbārnīk {a masc.} *sl-sex* ***Obs*** place intended for sexual intercourse <Slav>

jèbati {bēm, bū biasp.} **a.** *sl-sex* ***Obs*** engage in sexual intercourse with (of a male) <Slav> **b.i.** *sl-sports* ***Obs*** defeat: *jebati protivnika defeat one's adversary* <Slav*1> **ii.** *sl* ***Obs*** consider, respect: *jebati šefa respect one's boss* <Slav*1> **iii.** *sl* ***Obs*** cheat, swindle: *jebati naivca cheat a naive guy* <Slav*1> **iv.** *sl* ***Obs*** torture: *jebati drukera torture a stoolie* <Slav*1>
- **A jâ [PRON:DAT] (jèbēm) ([ADV]) (i) [NOUN: ACC] /rep/(i [NOUN:ACC])!** {LSF} (lit. And I fuck [ADV] *both* [NOUN] (and[NOUN]) to [PRON:ACC]) *col* ***Off*** used in response to another curse: *A ja tebi (jebem) bolje kevu! Fuck you too!*
- **da mi jèbēš mȁtēr** {S} (lit. you can fuck my mother) *col* ***Obs*** used to emphasize the truth of what has been said, I swear to God!
- **da mi jèbēš mȁtēr ako lȁžēm** {S} (lit. you can fuck my mother if I am lying to you) *col* ***Obs*** used to emphasize the truth of what has been said, I swear to God!
- **Da[PRON:DAT] jèbēm mâjku mȉlū.** {LSF} (lit. I fuck [PPRON] dear mother to [PRON:ACC]) *col* ***Off*** used as a threat of physical violence: *Da ti jebem majku milu! Fuck you!*
- **Dà ti jèbēm bȍga Ȉsusa!** {S} (lit. Let me fuck your God Jesus!) *col* ***Off*** used as a moderate curse, Fuck you!
- **Dà ti jèbēm mȁmicu mȓtvū!** {S} (lit. Let me fuck your little dead mother!) *col* ***Off*** used as a strong curse, Fuck you!
- **E jèbi ga!** {S} (lit. Well, fuck it!) *col* ***Obs*** used to express dissatisfaction and lack of control over events, Fuck it!
- **Jâ ga jèbēm a on pr̀dī!** {S} (lit. I screw him and he farts!) *sl* ***Off-Fac*** used as a moderate curse to a third party, Screw him!
- **Jâ te jèbēm a ti pr̀dīš!** {S} (lit. I screw you and you fart!) *sl* ***Off-Fac*** used as a weak curse, Screw you!
- **Jèbā ga tí!** {S} (lit. You fuck it!) *dia* ***Obs*** used to express dissatisfaction, Fuck it!
- **Jèbaću[PRON:DAT] mȁtēr!** {LSF} (lit. I will fuck [PPRON] mother!) *col* ***Off*** used as a threat of physical violence, I'm gonna fuck you up! : *Jebaću mu mater! I will beat the shit out of him!*
- **Jèbaću te nȍćas budàlo!** {S} (lit. I will fuck you tonight!) *col* ***Off*** used as a threat of physical violence, I'm gonna fuck you up!
- **Jèbaću te u ústa!** {S} (lit. I will fuck you in your mouth!) *col* ***Off*** used as a threat of physical violence, I'm gonna fuck you up!
- **Jèbaću ti jâ mȁtēr ȍnū robìjāškū.** {S} (lit. I will fuck that prisoner's mother of yours.) *col* ***Off*** used as a threat of physical violence, I'm gonna fuck you up!
- **Jèbaću ti mâjku!** {S} (lit. I will fuck your mother!) *col* ***Off*** used as a threat of physical violence, I'm gonna fuck you up!
- **Jèbaću ti mâjku mâjčinu!** {S} (lit. I will fuck your mother's mother!) *col* ***Off*** used as a threat of physical violence, I'm gonna fuck you up!
- **Jèbaću ti mâjku u ústa!** {S} (lit. I will fuck your mother in her mouth!) *col* ***Off*** used as a threat of physical violence, I'm gonna fuck you up!
- **Jèbaću ti mȁmicu!** {S} (lit. I will fuck your little mother!) *col* ***Off*** used as a threat of physical violence, I'm gonna fuck you up!
- **Jèbaću ti nánu tvòju!**{S} (lit. I will fuck your mother!) *col* ***Off*** used as a threat of physical violence, I'm gonna fuck you up!
- **Jèbaću ti sèstru!** {S} (lit. I will fuck your sister!) *col* ***Off*** used as a threat of physical violence, I'm gonna fuck you up!
- **Jèbaću ti svȅ po spȉsku!** {S} (lit. I will fuck all yours according to a list!) *col* ***Off*** used as a threat of physical violence, I'm gonna fuck you up!
- **Jèbal si ćȍk!** {S} (lit. You fucked an egg!) SSer *dia* ***Obs*** used to express dissatisfaction, Fuck it!
- **Jèbal si ćȍkavca!** {S} (lit. You fucked an egg!) **SSer** *dia* ***Obs*** used to refer to a future difficult situation of one's interlocutor
- **Jȅbāla[PRON:ACC] [NOUN:NOM]!** {LSF} (lit. Let [NOUN:NOM] fuck [PRON:ACC]!) *col* ***Obs*** used to express disrespect or lack of interest in: *Jebala te zelena stolica! Fuck that green chair!*
- **Jȅbȁla te mâjka bȍžijā!** {S} (lit. Let God's mother fuck you!) *col* ***Off*** used as a strong curse, Fuck you!
- **Jȅbāle[PRON:ACC] [NOUN:NOM]!** {LSF} (lit. Let [NOUN:NOM] fuck [PRON:ACC]!) *col* ***Obs*** used

to express disrespect or lack of interest in: *Jebale te skupe diskete! Fuck those expensive disks!*

• **Jèbāli ih njȉhovi grȍfovi!** {S} (lit. Let their counts screw them!) *col-dia* ***Off*** used as a weak curse, Screw them!

• **Jèbāli[PRON:ACC] [NP:NOM]!** {LSF} (lit. Let [NOUN:NOM] fuck [PRON:ACC]!) *col* ***Obs*** used to express disrespect or lack of interest in: *Jebali ih glupi političari! Fuck their stupid politicians!*

• **Jèbalo[PRON:ACC] [NOUN:NOM]** {LSF} (lit. Let [NOUN:NOM] fuck [PRON:ACC]!) *col-dia* ***Obs*** used to express disrespect or lack of interest in: *Jebalo ih dete! Fuck that kid!*

• **Jèbati ga!** {S} (lit. Fuck it!) *col* ***Obs*** used to express dissatisfaction, Fuck it!

• **jèbati jêža (u léđa)** {VP} (lit. fuck a hedgehog in its back) *col* ***Obs*** be in a very difficult situation

• **jèbati kévu** {VP} (lit. fuck one's mother) **a.** SerE *col* ***Obs*** defeat **b.** SerE *col* ***Obs*** cheat

• **jèbati mrtvàca** {VP} (lit. fuck a dead man) *sl-sex* ***Obs*** suffer from gonorrhea, have the clap

• **jèbati u zdrȁv mȍzak** {VP} (lit. fuck in a healthy brain) **a.** *sl-fea* ***Obs*** trick, cheat, swindle, fuck over **b.** *sl-fea* ***Obs*** make jokes with

• **jèbati znánje** {VP} (lit. fuck one's knowledge) *col* ***Obs*** defeat

• **jèbati[PRON:DAT] znánje** {LSF} (lit. fuck one's knowledge) *col* ***Obs*** defeat [PRON:ACC]: *Jebali su nam znanje na Olimpijadi. They defeated us in the Olympics.*

• **jèbē lûd zbûnjenōg** {VP} (lit. the crazy one is fucking the confused one) *col* ***Obs*** absolute mess, complete disorder

• **Jèbē mi se!** {S} (lit. I feel like fucking!) *col* ***Obs*** used to express indifference, I don't give a shit!

• **Jèbē mi se bȁš!** {S} (lit. I really fuck that!) *col* ***Obs*** used to express indifference, I really don't give a shit!

• **Jèbē mu se za sànkcije!** {S} (lit. He gives a fuck for the embargo!) *col* ***Obs*** used to express indifference of a third party male, He doesn't give a shit about anything.

• **Jèbē se [NP:DAT/PRON:DAT] za [NP:ACC/ PRON:ACC]** {LSF} *col* ***Obs*** used to express indifference: *Jebe se meni za Stojana! I don't give a shit about Stojan!*

• **Jèbē se [NOUN:DAT/PRON:DAT] za [NP:INS/ PRON:INS]!** {LSF} *col* ***Obs*** used to express indifference: *Jebe se meni za njim! I don't give a shit about him!*

• **Jèbēm ga!** {S} (lit. I fuck him!) *col* ***Off*** used as a moderate curse, Fuck you!

• **Jèbēm ga đe čȕō i đè nè čuō!** {S} (lit. I fuck him where he hears and where he does not hear.) *dia* ***Off*** used to express disrespect or lack of interest in, Fuck him!

• **Jèbēm ga kȍ te dȁde!** {S} (lit. I fuck the person who gave you!) *col* ***Off*** used as a moderate curse, Fuck you!

• **Jèbēm ga kȍ te ìmā!** {S} (lit. I fuck the person who has you!) *col* ***Off*** used as a moderate curse, Fuck you!

• **Jèbēm ga kȍ te nȁpravī!** {S} (lit. I fuck the person who made you!) *col* ***Off*** used as a moderate curse, Fuck you!

• **Jèbēm ga kȍ te ȍpasā!** {S} (lit. I fuck the person who put a belt on you!) *col* ***Off*** used as a moderate curse, Fuck you!

• **Jèbēm ga kȍ te rȍdī!** {S} (lit. I fuck the person who gave birth to you!) *col* ***Off*** used as a moderate curse, Fuck you!

• **Jèbēm ga kȍ te stvȍrī!** {S} (lit. I fuck the person who created you!) *col* ***Off*** used as a moderate curse, Fuck you!

• **Jèbēm ga kȍ te zȁdojī!** {S} (lit. I fuck the person you nursed from!) *col* ***Off*** used as a moderate curse, Fuck you!

• **Jèbēm ga kȍ te zdžȁde!** {S} *col* ***Off*** used as a moderate curse, Fuck you!

• **Jèbēm ga kȍ ti lȅba mêsī!** {S} (lit. I fuck the person who kneads your bread!) SerE *col* ***Off*** used as a moderate curse, Fuck you!

• **Jèbēm ga kȍ ti u grûdi dûvā!** {S} (lit. I fuck the person who blows in your breast!) Ser *sl* ***Off*** used as a moderate curse, Fuck you!

• **Jèbēm ga kȍj te jȕtrōs prȍbūdī!** {S} (lit. I fuck the person who woke you up this morning!) SSer *dia* ***Off*** used as a moderate curse, Fuck you!

• **Jèbēm ga kȍj ti dûvā u grûdi!** {S} (lit. I fuck the person who blows in your breast!) SSer *dia* ***Off*** used as a moderate curse, Fuck you!

• **Jèbēm ga kȍj ti pûvā u grûdi!** {S} (lit. I fuck the person who blows in your breast!) SSer *dia* ***Off*** used as a moderate curse, Fuck you!

• **Jèbēm ga kȍj ti se za kvȁku vȁtā!** {S} (lit. I fuck the person who grabs your doorknob!) SSer *dia* ***Off*** used as a moderate curse, Fuck you!

• **Jèbēm ga mŕtva u gròbu!** {S} (lit. I fuck him dead in the grave!) *sl* ***Off*** used as a strong curse, Fuck you!

• **Jèbēm ga od kȉlē!** {S} (lit. I fuck him from one kilogram!) *col* ***Off*** used as a moderate curse, Fuck you!

• **Jèbēm ga pa tàmān da mi je rȍđenī ćȁća!** {S} (lit. I fuck him even if he were my own father!) *col* ***Off*** used as a moderate curse, Fuck you!

• **Jèbēm ga što ti prȁg prèlazī!** {S} (lit. I fuck the person who passes your doorstep!) *col* ***Off*** used as a moderate curse, Fuck you!

• **Jèbēm ga u lûdū glâvu!** {S} (lit. I fuck him in his crazy head!) *col* ***Off*** used as a moderate curse, Fuck you!

• **Jèbēm li ga?** {VP} (lit. Do I fuck it?) 1 *col* used to refer to the futility of all efforts, it's no use 2 *col* used to refer to the lack of knowledge, I don't know. I haven't a clue.

• **Jèbēm li ga tàkva!** {S} (lit. I fuck him who is like that!) *col* ***Off*** used as a moderate curse, Fuck him!

• **Jèbēm li ti bȁbu!** {S} (lit. I screw your grandmother!) *col* ***Off*** used as a weak curse, Screw you!

• **Jèbēm li ti bȁbu uz tàrabu!** {S} (lit. I screw your grandmother near the fence!) *col* ***Off*** used as a weak curse, Screw you!

• **Jèbēm li ti bòkčići!** {S} (lit. I screw your little Gods!) SSer *dia* ***Off*** used as a weak curse, Screw you!

• **Jèbēm li ti bȍžjī čivìluk!** {S} (lit. I screw your God's hanger!) *sl* ***Off*** used as a weak curse, Screw you!

• **Jèbēm li ti bȍžjū letùrđiju!** {S} (lit. I fuck your God's church service!) *dia* ***Off*** used as a moderate curse, Fuck you!

• **Jèbēm li ti cȓkven dìrek!** {S} (lit. I screw your church pole!) *col* ***Off*** used as a weak curse, Screw you!

• **Jèbēm li ti cȓkvu Ravànicu!** {S} (lit. I fuck the church Ravanica to you!) *col* ***Off*** used as a moderate curse, Fuck you!

• **Jèbēm li ti čȅdo mȉlō!** {S} (lit. I fuck your dear child!) *col* ***Off*** used as a strong curse, Fuck you!

• **Jèbēm li ti ćérku i òca i mâjku!** {S} (lit. I fuck your daughter and father!) *col* ***Off*** used as a strong curse, Fuck you!

• **Jèbēm li ti dádu na lìvadu!** {S} (lit. I screw your sister on the meadow!) *dia* ***Off*** used as a weak curse, Screw you!

• **Jèbēm li ti đȅdu na grédu!** {S} (lit. I screw your grandfather on a bench!) *dia* ***Off*** used as a weak curse, Screw you!

• **Jèbēm li ti i nànku i tàtku!** {S} (lit. I fuck your mother and father!) SSer *dia* ***Off*** used as a moderate curse, Fuck you!

• **Jèbēm li ti i òca i mâjku a náročito mâjku!** {S} (lit. I fuck both your father and mother but I fuck your mother in particular!) *col* ***Off*** used as a strong curse, Fuck you!

• **Jèbēm li ti jȁsnū mȅsečinu!** {S} (lit. I screw your bright moonlight!) SerE *col* ***Off*** used as a weak curse, Screw you!

• **Jèbēm li ti kolàčići tvòji!** {S} (lit. I screw your cookies!) SSer *dia* ***Off*** used as a weak curse, Screw you!

• **Jèbēm li ti koriténce gde bôg pèrē nȍge!** {S} (lit. I screw your bowl where your God washes his legs!) *dia* ***Off*** used as a weak curse, Screw you!

• **Jèbēm li ti kùmicu!** {S} (lit. I screw your little maid of honor!) *col* ***Off*** used as a weak curse, Screw you!

• **Jèbēm li ti lêvū pàpučicu svêtē déve Màrijē!** {S} (lit. I screw your left slipper of the Virgin Mary!) SerE *dia* ***Off*** used as a weak curse, Screw you!

• **Jèbēm li ti mâjku!** {S} (lit. I fuck your mother!) *col* ***Off*** used as a strong curse, Fuck you!

• **Jèbēm li ti mâjku mȉlū!** {S} (lit. I fuck your dear mother!) *col* ***Off*** used as a strong curse, Fuck you!

• **Jèbēm li ti mâjku mȓtvū!** {S} (lit. I fuck your dead mother!) *col* ***Off*** used as a very strong curse, Fuck you!

• **Jèbēm li ti mȁmine dôjke!** {S} (lit. I fuck your mother's tits!) *col* ***Off*** used as a strong curse, Fuck you!

• **Jèbēm li ti mȉlō nànče!** {S} (lit. I fuck your dear mother!) SSer *dia* ***Off*** used as a moderate curse, Fuck you!

• **Jèbēm li ti mȉlō nȁne!** {S} (lit. I fuck your dear mother!) SSer *dia* ***Off*** used as a moderate curse, Fuck you!

• **Jèbēm li ti mȉlū sèstru!** {S} (lit. I fuck your dear sister!) *col* ***Off*** used as a strong curse, Fuck you!

• **Jèbēm li ti ȍblāk grȁdobitni!** {S} (lit. I screw your hail cloud!) *dia* ***Off*** used as a weak curse, Screw you!

• **Jèbēm li ti ȍca lópovskōg!** {S} (lit. I fuck your theiving father!) *col* ***Off*** used as a strong curse, Fuck you!

• **Jèbēm li ti Paraskévu!** {S} (lit. I fuck your Paraskeva: name of a Serbian saint!) *dia* ***Off*** used as a moderate curse, Fuck you!

• **Jèbēm li ti Pȍklade!** {S} (lit. I screw your carnival!) *dia* ***Off*** used as a weak curse, Screw you!

• **Jèbēm li ti pȍla bȍga!** {S} (lit. I screw one half of your God!) *col* ***Off-Fac*** used as a weak curse, Screw you!

• **Jèbēm li ti pòskurnicu!** {S} *col* ***Off*** used as a moderate curse, Fuck you!

• **Jèbēm li ti sêle golopìčestō!** {S} (lit. I fuck your naked-cunted sister!) SSer *dia* ***Off*** used as a moderate curse, Fuck you!

• **Jèbēm li ti sèstru grȅšnū!** {S} (lit. I fuck your sinful sister!) *col* ***Off*** used as a strong curse, Fuck you!

• **Jèbēm li ti sèstru mŕtvu!** {S} (lit. I fuck your dead sister!) *col* ***Off*** used as a very strong curse, Fuck you!

• **Jèbēm li ti sìtni kravàjčići!** {S} *col* ***Off*** used as a mild offense, Screw you!

• **Jèbēm li ti strȋnu na gȑbinu!** {S} (lit. I screw your aunt in her back!) *col* ***Off-Fac*** used as a weak curse, Screw you!

• **Jèbēm li ti strȋnu na lèdinu!** {S} (lit. I screw your aunt on the lawn!) *col* ***Off-Fac*** used as a weak curse, Screw you!

• **Jèbēm li ti sȗnce žȃrkō!** {S} (lit. I fuck your hot sun!) *col* ***Off*** used as a moderate curse, Fuck you!

• **Jèbēm li ti sȕpu!** {S} (lit. I screw your soup!) *col*

Off-Fac used as a weak curse, Screw you!

• **Jèbēm li ti svàstiku!** {S} (lit. I screw your wife's sister!) *col* ***Off*** used as a weak curse, Screw you!

• **Jèbēm li ti svêtū dévu Màriju!** {S} (lit. I fuck your holy Virgin Mary!) SerE *dia* ***Off*** used as a moderate curse, Fuck you!

• **Jèbēm li ti Svêtū nèdelju!** {S} (lit. I fuck your holy Sunday!) *col* ***Off*** used as a moderate curse, Fuck you!

• **Jèbēm li ti svêtū Paraskévu!** {S} (lit. I fuck your Paraskeva: name of a Serbian saint!) *col* ***Off*** used as a moderate curse, Fuck you!

• **Jèbēm li ti tètku!** {S} (lit. I screw your aunt!) *col* ***Off*** used as a weak curse, Screw you!

• **Jèbēm li ti tètku na rèšetku!** {S} (lit. I screw your aunt on the grid!) *col* ***Off-Fac*** used as a weak curse, Screw you!

• **Jèbēm li ti trȉsta i trî bȍga!** {S} (lit. I screw your three hundred and three gods!) *col* ***Off*** used as a weak curse, Screw you!

• **Jèbēm li ti zádušnice!** {S} (lit. I fuck your memorial service!) *dia* ***Off*** used as a moderate curse, Fuck you!

• **Jèbēm li ti žènicu!** {S} (lit. I fuck your little wife!) *col* ***Off*** used as a moderate curse, Fuck you!

• **Jèbēm li ti žènicu u rȉbicu!** {S} (lit. I screw your wife in her cunt!) *col* ***Off-Fac*** used as a weak curse, Screw you!

• **Jèbēm li ti žènīšte!** {S} (lit. I fuck your wife!) *col* ***Off*** used as a moderate curse, Fuck you!

• **Jèbēm li ti žènu dȑtu!** {S} (lit. I fuck your torn-apart wife!) *dia* ***Off*** used as a moderate curse, Fuck you!

• **Jèbēm li ti žènu gȍlū!** {S} (lit. I fuck your naked wife!) *col* ***Off*** used as a moderate curse, Fuck you!

• **Jèbēm li ti žènu gȑbavū!** {S} (lit. I fuck your hump-backed wife!) *col* ***Off*** used as a moderate curse, Fuck you!

• **Jèbēm li ti žènu grȅšnū!** {S} (lit. I fuck your sinful wife!) *col* ***Off*** used as a moderate curse, Fuck you!

• **Jèbēm li ti žènu pod lêvō kòleno!** {S} (lit. I screw your wife below her left knee!) SerE *col* ***Off*** used as a weak curse, Screw you!

• **Jèbēm li ti žènu u rásovu!** {S} *col* ***Off*** used as a moderate curse, Fuck you!

• **Jèbēm mu dijète u djètetu!** {S} (lit. I fuck his child in his child!) *col* ***Off*** used as a very strong curse, Fuck him!

• **Jèbēm mu fàmīliju!** {S} (lit. I fuck his family!) *col* ***Off*** used as a moderate curse, Fuck him!

• **Jèbēm mu lȅbac!** {S} (lit. I screw his bread!) *col* ***Off*** used as a weak curse, Screw him!

• **Jèbēm mu mȁtēr!** {S} (lit. I fuck his mother!) **a.** *col* ***Off*** used as a strong curse, Fuck him! **b.** ***Obs*** used to refer to the futility of all efforts, it's no use: *Ne znam šta da radim. Jebem mu mater! I don't know what to do. It's fucking hopeless!*

• **Jèbēm[PRON:DAT]** ònō što se jȍš nìje ròdilo! {S} (lit. I fuck all [PPRON] still unborn descendants!) *col* ***Off*** used as a strong curse: *Jebem mu ono što se još nije rodilo! Fuck him!*

• **Jèbēm mu svȅ do ùnučeta!** {S} (lit. I fuck his everything up to his grandson!) *col* ***Off*** used as a strong curse, Fuck him!

• **Jèbēm mu svȅ što mu sȑce vȍli!** {S} (lit. I fuck everything his heart likes!) *col* ***Off*** used as a moderate curse, Fuck him!

• **Jèbēm mu svéca!** {S} (lit. I fuck his saint!) *col* ***Off*** used as a moderate curse, Fuck him!

• **Jèbēm mu svȕ djȅcu!** {S} (lit. I fuck all his children!) *col* ***Off*** used as a very strong curse, Fuck him!

• **Jèbēm mu víno!** {S} (lit. I screw his wine!) *col* ***Off*** used as a moderate curse to a third party, Screw him!

• **Jèbēm[PRON:DAT]** ćêr! {LSF} (lit. I fuck [PPRON] daughter!) *col* ***Off*** used as a strong curse: *Jebem ti ćer! Fuck you!*

• **Jèbēm[PRON:DAT]** mȉša! {LSF} (lit. I screw your mouse!) *col* ***Obs*** used as a moderate curse: *Jebem im miša! Screw them!*

• **Jèbēm[PRON:DAT] [NUMBER]** mȁtērā! {LSF} (lit. I fuck [PPRON] [NUMBER] mothers!) *col* ***Off*** used as a strong curse: *Jebem joj trista matera! Fuck her!*

• **Jèbēm[PRON:DAT]** òca lópovskōg!. {LSF} (lit. I fuck [PPRON] theiving father!) *col* ***Off*** used as a strong curse: *Jebem ti oca lopovskog! Fuck you, thief!*

• **Jèbēm[PRON:DAT]** sèstru! {LSF} (lit. I fuck [PPRON] sister!) *col* ***Off*** used as a strong curse: *Jebem ti sestru! Fuck you!*

• **Jèbēm[PRON:DAT]** sȕnac! {LSF} (lit. I screw [PPRON] sun!) *col* ***Off*** used as a moderate curse: *Jebem ti sunac! Screw you!*

• **Jèbēm[PRON:DAT]** svȅ što ìmā i što će ìmati! {LSF} (lit. I fuck everything [PRON:NOM] has and [PRON:NOM] will have!) *col* ***Off*** used as a strong curse: *Jebem ti sve što imaš i što ćeš imati! Fuck you!*

• **Jèbēm te!** {S} (lit. I fuck you!) *col* ***Off*** used as a moderate curse, Fuck you!

• **Jèbēm te bȁlava!** {S} (lit. I fuck you beslobbered!) *col* ***Off*** used as a moderate curse, Fuck you!

• **Jèbēm te blêntava!** {S} (lit. I fuck you stupid!) *col* ***Off*** used as a moderate curse, Fuck you!

• **Jèbēm te blȅsavōga!** {S} (lit. I fuck you stupid!) *col* ***Off*** used as a moderate curse, Fuck you!

• **Jèbēm te bȍže!** {S} (lit. I fuck you God!) *col* ***Obs*** used to express dissatisfaction, Fuck it!

• **Jèbēm te budàlasta!** {S} (lit. I fuck you stupid!) *col* ***Off*** used as a moderate curse, Fuck you!

• **Jèbēm te ćȍpava!** {S} (lit. I fuck you limping!) *col* ***Off*** used as a moderate curse, Fuck you!

• **Jèbēm te ćȍrava!** {S} (lit. I fuck you half-blind!) *col* ***Off*** used as a moderate curse, Fuck you!

• **Jèbēm te ćȍravōga!** {S} (lit. I fuck you half-blind!) *col* ***Off*** used as a moderate curse, Fuck you!

• **Jèbēm te đè pìšāš!** {S} (lit. I fuck you where you piss!) *dia* ***Off*** used as a moderate curse, Fuck you!

• **Jèbēm te glúva!** {S} (lit. I fuck you deaf!) *col* ***Off*** used as a moderate curse, Fuck you!

• **Jèbēm te glúvōga!** {S} (lit. I fuck you deaf!) *col* ***Off*** used as a moderate curse, Fuck you!

• **Jèbēm te gȑbavōga!**{S} (lit. I fuck you hump-backed!) *col* ***Off*** used as a moderate curse, Fuck you!

• **Jèbēm te gȕbava!** {S} (lit. I fuck you leprous!) *col* ***Off*** used as a moderate curse, Fuck you!

• **Jèbēm te jȅbānōga!** {S} (lit. I fuck you fucked!) *col* ***Off*** used as a moderate curse, Fuck you!

• **Jèbēm te kad si bȉja mȁlecak!** {S} (lit. I fuck you when you were young!) SSer *dia* ***Off*** used as a moderate curse, Fuck you!

• **Jèbēm te kràkatōga!** {S} (lit. I fuck you short!) *col* ***Off*** used as a moderate curse, Fuck you!

• **Jèbēm te krmèljiva!**{S} (lit. I fuck you beslobbered!) *col* ***Off*** used as a moderate curse, Fuck you!

• **Jèbēm te làžljiva!** {S} (lit. I fuck you who lie!) *col* ***Off*** used as a moderate curse, Fuck you!

• **Jèbēm te lúda!** {S} (lit. I fuck you crazy!) *col* ***Off*** used as a moderate curse, Fuck you!

• **Jèbēm te lúdōga!** {S} (lit. I fuck you crazy!) *col* ***Off*** used as a moderate curse, Fuck you!

• **Jèbēm te màljena!** {S} (lit. I fuck you when you were small!) *dia* ***Off*** used as a moderate curse, Fuck you!

• **Jèbēm te mírnju!** {S} (lit. I fuck you peaceful!) *col* ***Off*** used as a moderate curse, Fuck you!

• **Jèbēm te mȑšava!** {S} (lit. I fuck you slim!) *col* ***Off*** used as a moderate curse, Fuck you!

• **Jébēm te mȑšavōga!** {S} (lit. I fuck you slim!) *col* ***Off*** used as a moderate curse, Fuck you!

• **Jèbēm te mŕtvōg!** {S} (lit. I fuck you dead!) *col* ***Off*** used as a strong curse, Fuck you!

• **Jèbēm te mŕtvōga!** {S} (lit. I fuck you dead!) *col* ***Off*** used as a strong curse, Fuck you!

• **Jèbēm te mȉtvosānōg!**{S} (lit. I fuck you half-dead!) *col* ***Off*** used as a strong curse, Fuck you!

• **Jèbēm te mȕšena!** {S} *dia* ***Off*** used as a moderate curse, Fuck you!

• **Jèbēm te mȕtava!** {S} (lit. I fuck you dumb!) *col* ***Off*** used as a moderate curse, Fuck you!

• **Jèbēm te ȍtpola a dȍpola nek te jèbē ćàća kòjī te tàko blȅsava nàpravio!** {S} (lit. I fuck one half of you and the second half of you should be fucked by your father who made you stupid like that!) *col* ***Off*** used as a moderate curse, Fuck you!

• **Jèbēm te pijàna!** {S} (lit. I fuck you drunk!) *col* ***Off*** used as a moderate curse, Fuck you!

• **Jèbēm te pòkvārenōga!** {S} (lit. I fuck you spoiled!) *col* ***Off*** used as a moderate curse, Fuck you!

• **Jèbēm te sàkata!** {S} (lit. I fuck you handicapped!) *col* ***Off*** used as a moderate curse, Fuck you!

• **Jèbēm te sàkatōga!** {S} (lit. I fuck you handicapped!) *col* ***Off*** used as a moderate curse, Fuck you!

• **Jèbēm te sijéda!** {S} (lit. I fuck you grey!) *col* ***Off*** used as a moderate curse, Fuck you!

• **Jèbēm te skȑčavōga!** {S} *dia* ***Off*** used as a moderate curse, Fuck you!

• **Jèbēm te slijépa!** {S} (lit. I fuck you blind!) *col* ***Off*** used as a moderate curse, Fuck you!

• **Jèbēm te slȉnjava!** {S} (lit. I fuck you beslobbered!) *dia* ***Off*** used as a moderate curse, Fuck you!

• **Jèbēm te smȁknūtōga!**{S} (lit. I fuck you decapitated!) *col* ***Off*** used as a moderate curse, Fuck you!

• **Jèbēm te smȍtāna!** {S} (lit. I fuck you clumsy) *col* ***Off*** used as a moderate curse, Fuck you!

• **Jèbēm te smȑdljiva!** {S} (lit. I fuck you stinky!) *col* ***Off*** used as a moderate curse, Fuck you!

• **Jèbēm te stàra!** {S} (lit. I fuck you old!) *col* ***Off*** used as a moderate curse, Fuck you!

• **Jèbēm te stàru!** {S} (lit. I fuck you old!) *col* ***Off*** used as a moderate curse, Fuck you!

• **Jèbēm te šȁšava!** {S} (lit. I fuck you crazy!) *col* ***Off*** used as a moderate curse, Fuck you!

• **Jèbēm te šȁšavōga!** {S} (lit. I fuck you crazy!) *col* ***Off*** used as a moderate curse, Fuck you!

• **Jèbēm te šȅpava!** {S} (lit. I fuck you limping!) *col* ***Off*** used as a moderate curse, Fuck you!

• **Jèbēm te tàkō presàmīćena!** {S} (lit. I fuck you so folded!) *col* ***Off*** used as a moderate curse, Fuck you!

• **Jèbēm te u dȕpe!** {S} (lit. I fuck you in the ass!) *col* ***Off*** used as a moderate curse, Fuck you!

• **Jèbēm te u dȕpe gȍlō!** {S} (lit. I fuck you in your naked ass!) *col* ***Off*** used as a moderate curse, Fuck you!

• **Jèbēm te u dȕpe lópovskō!** {S} (lit. I fuck you in your theiving ass!) *col* ***Off*** used as a moderate curse, Fuck you!

• **Jèbēm te u dȕpe rȕtavō!** {S} (lit. I fuck you in your hairy ass!) *col* ***Off*** used as a moderate curse, Fuck you!

• **Jèbēm te u dȕpe smȑdljivō!** {S} (lit. I fuck you in your stinking ass!) *col* ***Off*** used as a moderate curse, Fuck you!

• **Jèbēm te u dȕpe svìnjsko!** {S} (lit. I fuck you in your pig's ass) *col* ***Off*** used as a moderate curse, Fuck you!

• **Jèbēm te u dȕpe ȕsrānō!** {S} (lit. I fuck you in your shitty ass!) *col* ***Off*** used as a moderate curse, Fuck you!

• **Jèbēm te u dûšu dȕšmanskū!** {S} (lit. I fuck you in your enemy soul!) *col* ***Off*** used as a strong curse, Fuck you!

• **Jèbēm te u dûšu psѐćū!** {S} (lit. I fuck you in your dog's soul!) *col* ***Off*** used as a strong curse, Fuck you!

• **Jèbēm te u dûšu sȍtoninu!** {S} (lit. I fuck you in your devil's soul!) *col* ***Off*** used as a strong curse, Fuck you!

• **Jèbēm te u dûšu žȁlosnū!** {S} (lit. I fuck you in your sad soul!) *col* ***Off*** used as a strong curse, Fuck you!

• **Jèbēm te ȕ glāvu!** {S} (lit. I fuck you in your head!) *col* ***Off*** used as a moderate curse, Fuck you!

• **Jèbēm te u glâvu blѐsavū!** {S} (lit. I fuck your silly head!) *col* ***Off*** used as a moderate curse, Fuck you!

• **Jèbēm te u glâvu lûdū!** {S} (lit. I fuck you in your crazy head!) *col* ***Off*** used as a moderate curse, Fuck you!

• **Jèbēm te u glâvu šȁšavū!** {S} (lit. I fuck you in your crazy head!) *col* ***Off*** used as a moderate curse, Fuck you!

• **Jèbēm te u glâvu šûpljū!** {S} (lit. I fuck you in your empty head!) *col* ***Off*** used as a moderate curse, Fuck you!

• **Jèbēm te u glûvē ȕši!** {S} (lit. I fuck you in your deaf ears!) *col* ***Off*** used as a moderate curse, Fuck you!

• **Jèbēm te u gràmatičkō pódrūčje!** {S} (lit. I screw you in your grammar area!) *sl* ***Off-Fac*** used as a weak curse, Screw you!

• **Jèbēm te u gùjicu!** {S} (lit. I fuck you in your ass!) *dia* ***Off*** used as a moderate curse, Fuck you!

• **Jèbēm te u idéju!** {S} (lit. I screw you in the idea!) *sl* ***Off*** used as a weak curse, Screw you!

• **Jèbēm te u kȉšu!** {S} (lit. I screw you in the rain!) *dia* ***Off*** used as a weak curse, Screw you!

• **Jèbēm te u léđa!** {S} (lit. I fuck you in your back!) *col* ***Off*** used as a moderate curse, Fuck you!

• **Jèbēm te u mȁteri!** {S} (lit. I fuck you in your mother!) *col* ***Off*** used as a strong curse, Fuck you!

• **Jèbēm te u mȍzak!** {S} (lit. I fuck you in your brain!) *col* ***Off*** used as a moderate curse, Fuck you!

• **Jèbēm te ȕ nōs!** {S} (lit. I fuck you in your nose!) *col* ***Off*** used as a moderate curse, Fuck you!

• **Jèbēm te u njȍkalicu!** {S} (lit. I fuck you in your face!) *sl* ***Off*** used as a moderate curse, Fuck you!

• **Jèbēm te u njùškicu!** {S} (lit. I fuck you in your small snout!) *sl* ***Off*** used as a moderate curse, Fuck you!

• **Jèbēm te u njúšku!** {S} (lit. I fuck you in your snout!) *sl* ***Off*** used as a moderate curse, Fuck you!

• **Jèbēm te ȕ oči!** {S} (lit. I fuck your eyes!) *col* ***Off*** used as a moderate curse, Fuck you!

• **Jèbēm te ȕ oči dȑljavē!** {S} (lit. I fuck your dirty eyes!) *col* ***Off*** used as a moderate curse, Fuck you!

• **Jèbēm te ȕ oči zverȉnjavē!** {S} (lit. I fuck your beastly eyes!) *col* ***Off*** used as a moderate curse, Fuck you!

• **Jèbēm te ȕ oko!** {S} (lit. I fuck you in your eye!) *col* ***Off*** used as a moderate curse, Fuck you!

• **Jèbēm te u ȍko dȑljavō!** {S} (lit. I fuck you in your ugly eye!) *col* ***Off*** used as a moderate curse, Fuck you!

• **Jèbēm te ȕ oko pȍkvārenō!** {S} (lit. I fuck you in your rotten eye!) *col* ***Off*** used as a moderate curse, Fuck you!

• **Jèbēm te u pȉčku!** {S} (lit. I fuck you in your cunt!) *col* ***Off*** used as a moderate curse, Fuck you!

• **Jèbēm te u pȉčku lîčkū!** {S} (lit. I fuck you in your Lika cunt!; *Lika, a region in Croatia, used here to create a rhyme*) *sl* ***Off*** used as a moderate curse, Fuck you!

• **Jèbēm te u pízdu!** {S} (lit. I fuck you in your cunt!) *col* ***Off*** used as a moderate curse, Fuck you!

• **Jèbēm te u pŕkno!** {S} (lit. I fuck you in your ass!) *dia* ***Off*** used as a moderate curse, Fuck you!

• **Jèbēm te u pȑnjicu!** {S} (lit. I fuck you in your small ass!) *col* ***Off*** used as a moderate curse, Fuck you!

• **Jèbēm te u ȑku lópovskū!** {S} (lit. I fuck you in your theiving ass!) *dia* ***Off*** used as a moderate curse, Fuck you!

• **Jèbēm te u ȑnje!** {S} (lit. I fuck you in your ass!) *dia* ***Off*** used as a moderate curse, Fuck you!

• **Jèbēm tè u slȁbinu!** {S} (lit. I screw you in your thigh!) *col* ***Off*** used as a weak curse, Screw you!

• **Jèbēm te u slêpō crévo!** {S} (lit. I screw you in your appendix!) **SerE** *col* ***Off*** used as a weak curse, Screw you!

• **Jèbēm te u sȑce dȕšmanskō!** {S} (lit. I fuck you in your enemy heart!) *col* ***Off*** used as a strong curse, Fuck you!

• **Jèbēm te u sȑce nѐljudskō!** {S} (lit. I fuck you in your inhuman heart!) *col* ***Off*** used as a strong curse, Fuck you!

• **Jèbēm te u sȑce pácovskō!** {S} (lit. I fuck you in your rat's heart!) *col* ***Off*** used as a strong curse, Fuck you!

• **Jèbēm te u strȁžnjicu!** {S} (lit. I fuck you in your ass!) *col* ***Off*** used as a moderate curse, Fuck you!

• **Jèbēm te u šúpak!** {S} (lit. I fuck you in your ass!) *col* ***Off*** used as a moderate curse, Fuck you!

• **Jèbēm te u ústa!** {S} (lit. I fuck you in your mouth!) *col* ***Off*** used as a strong curse, Fuck you!

• **Jèbēm te u ústa grѐšnā!** {S} (lit. I fuck you in your sinful mouth!) *col* ***Off*** used as a strong curse, Fuck you!

• **Jèbēm te u ústa pògānā!** {S} (lit. I fuck you in your dirty mouth!) *col* ***Off*** used as a strong curse, Fuck you!

• **Jèbēm te u ústa smȑdelā!** {S} (lit. I fuck you in your stinking mouth!) *col* ***Off*** used as a strong curse, Fuck you!
• **Jèbēm te u ústa žvȁlavā!** {S} (lit. I fuck you in your big mouth!) *col* ***Off*** used as a strong curse, Fuck you!
• **Jèbēm te u ȕši!** {S} (lit. I fuck you in your ears!) *sl* ***Off*** used as a moderate curse, Fuck you!
• **Jèbēm te u zdrȁv mȍzak!** {S} (lit. I fuck you in your healthy brain!) *sl* ***Off*** used as a moderate curse, Fuck you!
• **Jèbēm te zȁborāvna!** {S} (lit. I fuck you forgetful!) *col* ***Off*** used as a moderate curse, Fuck you!
• **Jèbēm te zàgušēnōga!** {S} (lit. I fuck you smothered!) *dia* ***Off*** used as a moderate curse, Fuck you!
• **Jèbēm te zàmlāćenōga!** {S} (lit. I fuck you beaten up!) *col* ***Off*** used as a moderate curse, Fuck you!
• **Jèbēm te zgûrāna!** {S} (lit. I fuck you pressed!) *col* ***Off*** used as a moderate curse, Fuck you!
• **Jèbēm te zȉrava!** {S} (lit. I fuck you crooked-eyed!) *dia* ***Off*** used as a moderate curse, Fuck you!
• **Jèbēm te žívōga!** {S} (lit. I fuck you alive!) *col* ***Off*** used as a moderate curse, Fuck you!
• **Jèbēm ti!** {S} (lit. I fuck you!) *col* used to express dissatisfaction, Fuck it!
• **Jèbēm ti Ȁliju i svȅ tê muslȉmānskē kúrčeve!** {S} (lit. I fuck Alija and all Muslim cocks to you!) *col* ***Off*** used as a strong curse, Fuck you!
• **Jèbēm ti bêlī dân!** {S} (lit. I fuck your white day!) *col* ***Off*** used as a moderate curse, Fuck you!
• **Jèbēm ti bijèlū šèncu!** {S} (lit. I fuck your white wheat!) *dia* ***Off*** used as a moderate curse, Fuck you!
• **Jèbēm ti bȍga!** {S} (lit. I fuck your God!) *col* ***Off*** used as a moderate curse, Fuck you!
• **Jèbēm ti Bȍga bȍžjēg!** {S} (lit. I fuck your God's God!) *col* ***Off*** used as a moderate curse, Fuck you!
• **Jèbēm ti bȍga bȍžjēga!** {S} (lit. I fuck your God's God!) *col* ***Off*** used as a moderate curse, Fuck you!
• **Jèbēm ti Bȍga mȉlōga!** {S} (lit. I fuck your dear God!) *col* ***Off*** used as a moderate curse, Fuck you!
• **Jèbēm ti bȍga tvôga!** {S} (lit. I fuck your God!) *col* ***Off*** used as a moderate curse, Fuck you!
• **Jèbēm ti Bogoròdicu!** {S} (lit. I fuck your God's mother!) *col* ***Off*** used as a moderate curse, Fuck you!
• **Jèbēm ti Bòkčića!** {S} (lit. I screw your little God!) *dia* ***Off*** used as a weak curse, Screw you!
• **Jèbēm ti bȍžjē kàndilo!** {S} (lit. I screw your God's light in front of your icon!) *dia* ***Off*** used as a weak curse, Screw you!
• **Jèbēm ti bȍžjē mȉlovānje!** {S} (lit. I screw your God's petting!) *dia* ***Off*** used as a weak curse, Screw you!
• **Jèbēm ti bȍžjī čivìluk!** {S} (lit. I screw your God's hanger!) *dia* ***Off*** used as a weak curse, Screw you!
• **Jèbēm ti brâčnū drugàricu!** {S} (lit. I screw your spouse!) *col* ***Off*** used as a weak curse, Screw you!
• **Jèbēm ti bȓk!** {S} (lit. I screw your mustache!) *col* ***Off*** used as a weak curse, Screw you!
• **Jèbēm ti brȕču niz kòjū se zàdnjā kâp pȉšaćē cȉjēdī!** {S} (lit. I fuck the hair down which your last drop of urine goes!) *dia* ***Off*** used as a moderate curse, Fuck you!
• **Jèbēm ti càdūjku!** {S} *dia* ***Off*** used as a moderate curse, Fuck you!
• **Jèbēm ti cêlū fàmīliju!** {S} (lit. I fuck your whole family!) SerE *col* ***Off*** used as a strong curse, Fuck you!
• **Jèbēm ti cȓkvu!** {S} (lit. I fuck your church!) *col* ***Off*** used as a moderate curse, Fuck you!
• **Jèbēm ti cȓva u kòlevci!** {S} (lit. I fuck your worm in the crib!) *col* ***Off*** used as a very strong curse, Fuck you!
• **Jèbēm ti čának iz kògā kûsāš!** {S} (lit. I fuck the bowl from which you eat!) *dia* ***Off*** used as a moderate curse, Fuck you!
• **Jèbēm ti čȅdo!** {S} (lit. I fuck your child!) *col* ***Off*** used as a very strong curse, Fuck you!
• **Jèbēm ti čȅdo mȉlō!** {S} (lit. I fuck your dear child!) *col* ***Off*** used as a very strong curse, Fuck you!
• **Jèbēm ti čésnicu!** {S} (lit. I fuck your Christmas bread!) *dia* ***Off*** used as a moderate curse, Fuck you!
• **Jèbēm ti čivìluk gde bôg vȅšā gȁće!** {S} (lit. I screw the hanger where your God hangs his panties!) **SerE** *dia* ***Off*** used as a weak curse, Screw you!
• **Jèbēm ti čivìluk gde bôg zakàčuje kȁpu!** {S} (lit. I screw you the hanger where your God hangs his hat!) SerE *dia* ***Off*** used as a weak curse, Screw you!
• **Jèbēm ti čȍrbadžīku!** {S} (lit. I fuck your landlady!) SSer *dia* ***Off*** used as a moderate curse, Fuck you!
• **Jèbēm ti ćȁću!** {S} (lit. I fuck your father!) *dia* ***Off*** used as a moderate curse, Fuck you!
• **Jèbēm ti ćêr!** {S} (lit. I fuck your daughter!) *col* ***Off*** used as a very strong curse, Fuck you!
• **Jèbēm ti ćêr kȓvāvū!** {S} (lit. I fuck your bloody daughter!) *col* ***Off*** used as a very strong curse, Fuck you!
• **Jèbēm ti ćêr u ćèri!** {S} (lit. I fuck your daughter in your daughter!) *col* ***Off*** used as a very strong curse, Fuck you!
• **Jèbēm ti dàdicu!** {S} (lit. I fuck your sister!) SSer *dia* ***Off*** used as a moderate curse, Fuck you!
• **Jèbēm ti dádu!** {S} (lit. I fuck your sister!) SSer *dia* ***Off*** used as a strong curse, Fuck you!
• **Jèbēm ti dȅ je nȁjmilo!** {S} (lit. I fuck the dearest things to you!) **SSer** *dia* ***Off*** used as a strong curse, Fuck you!

• **Jèbēm ti déte kȑvavō!** {S} (lit. I fuck your bloody child!) SerE *col* ***Off*** used as a very strong curse, Fuck you!
• **Jèbēm ti déte nâjmìlijē!** {S} (lit. I fuck your dearest child!) SerE *col* ***Off*** used as a very strong curse, Fuck you!
• **Jèbēm ti déte ȕsrānō!** {S} (lit. I fuck your shitty child!) SerE *col* ***Off*** used as a very strong curse, Fuck you!
• **Jèbēm ti deténce!** {S} (lit. I fuck your small child!) SerE *col* ***Off*** used as a very strong curse, Fuck you!
• **Jèbēm ti Dèvicu Màriju!** {S} (lit. I fuck your Virgin Mary!) SerE *col* ***Off*** used as a moderate curse, Fuck you!
• **Jèbēm ti dijète!** {S} (lit. I fuck your child!) *col* ***Off*** used as a very strong curse, Fuck you!
• **Jèbēm ti dȑmavī!** {S} *dia* ***Off*** used as a moderate curse, Fuck you!
• **Jèbēm ti dûšu dúšinu!** {S} (lit. I fuck your soul's soul!) *col* ***Off*** used as a strong curse, Fuck you!
• **Jèbēm ti fàbriku na kòjū si ìzišō!** {S} (lit. I screw your factory from which you came out!) *sl* ***Off*** used as a weak curse, Screw you!
• **Jèbēm ti fàmīliju!** {S} (lit. I fuck your family!) *col* ***Off*** used as a strong curse, Fuck you!
• **Jèbēm ti fàmīliju cìganskū!** {S} (lit. I fuck your Gypsy family!) *col* ***Off*** used as a strong curse, Fuck you!
• **Jèbēm ti fàmīliju i kȍ je stvȍrī!** {S} (lit. I fuck your family and who created it!) *col* used as a strong curse, Fuck you!
• **Jèbēm ti fùrunu!** {S} (lit. I screw your stove!) *dia* ***Off*** used as a weak curse, Screw you!
• **Jèbēm ti gàzdaricu!** {S} (lit. I fuck your landlady!) *dia* ***Off*** used as a moderate curse, Fuck you!
• **Jèbēm ti gdȅ si se pȅkō!** {S} (lit. I fuck the place where you were baked!) SerE *sl* ***Off*** used as a moderate curse, Fuck you!
• **Jèbēm ti Góspu!** {S} (lit. I fuck you Holy Mary!) Med *dia* ***Off*** used as a moderate curse, Fuck you!
• **Jèbēm ti grȍb neòpevān!** {S} (lit. I fuck your grave!) *col* ***Off*** used as a very strong curse, Fuck you!
• **Jèbēm ti i kùmicu i starosvàticu!** {S} (lit. I fuck your little maid of honor and the best man!) *dia* ***Off*** used as a moderate curse, Fuck you!
• **Jèbēm ti i òca i mâjku!** {S} (lit. I fuck your father and mother!) *col* ***Off*** used as a very strong curse, Fuck you!
• **Jèbēm ti i òca i màtēr!** {S} (lit. I fuck both your father and mother!) *col* ***Off*** used as a very strong curse, Fuck you!
• **Jèbēm ti ìme i prézime!** {S} (lit. I fuck your name and surname!) *col* ***Off*** used as a moderate curse, Fuck you!
• **Jèbēm ti Ìsusa!** {S} (lit. I fuck your Jesus!) *col* ***Off*** used as a moderate curse, Fuck you!
• **Jèbēm ti jevànđēlje!** {S} (lit. I fuck your gospel!) *col* ***Off*** used as a moderate curse, Fuck you!
• **Jèbēm ti kalèndār!** {S} (lit. I screw your calendar!) *sl* ***Off*** used as a weak curse, Screw you!
• **Jèbēm ti kàšiku kòjōm kûsāš!** {S} (lit. I fuck the spoon you use to eat!) *col* ***Off*** used as a moderate curse, Fuck you!
• **Jèbēm ti kèstēn!** {S} (lit. I screw your chestnut!) *sl* ***Off*** used as a weak curse, Screw you!
• **Jèbēm ti kévinē kévē kévu!** {S} (lit. I fuck your mother's mother's mother!) SerE *col* ***Off*** used as a strong curse, Fuck you!
• **Jèbēm ti kévinu sìsu!** {S} (lit. I fuck your mother's tit!) SerE *col* ***Off*** used as a strong curse, Fuck you!
• **Jèbēm ti kévinu šùbaru!** {S} (lit. I fuck your mother's fur hat!) SerE *col* ***Off*** used as a strong curse, Fuck you!
• **Jèbēm ti kévu smȑdljivū!** {S} (lit. I fuck your stinking mother!) SerE *col* ***Off*** used as a strong curse, Fuck you!
• **Jèbēm ti klànjalo tvòje!** {S} *dia* ***Off*** used as a moderate curse, Fuck you!
• **Jèbēm ti klȉcu!** {S} (lit. I fuck your seed!) *dia* ***Off*** used as a moderate curse, Fuck you!
• **Jèbēm ti komšìče u panìče!** {S} (lit. I screw your little neighbor in her cunt!) *dia* ***Off*** used as a weak curse, Screw you!
• **Jèbēm ti kòmšinicu u gračànicu!** {S} (lit. I screw your neighbor in her cunt!) *dia* ***Off*** used as a weak curse, Screw you!
• **Jèbēm ti kȍsku mȑtvū!** {S} (lit. I fuck your death bone!) *dia* ***Off*** used as a strong curse, Fuck you!
• **Jèbēm ti kȑsnū slȁvu!** {S} (lit. I fuck your saint's day!) *col* ***Off*** used as a strong curse, Fuck you!
• **Jèbēm ti kȓst nad glávōm!** {S} (lit. I fuck the cross above your head!) *col* ***Off*** used as a strong curse, Fuck you!
• **Jèbēm ti krȕ!** {S} (lit. I fuck your bread!) *dia* ***Off*** used as a moderate curse, Fuck you!
• **Jèbēm ti krȕ kòjī jȅdēš!** {S} (lit. I fuck the bread you eat!) *dia* ***Off*** used as a moderate curse, Fuck you!
• **Jèbēm ti krȕ kòjī žděrēš!** {S} (lit. I fuck the bread you devour!) *dia* ***Off*** used as a moderate curse, Fuck you!
• **Jèbēm ti krȕšac!** {S} (lit. I fuck your bread!) *dia* ***Off*** used as a moderate curse, Fuck you!
• **Jèbēm ti krȕšnū mȑvu!** {S} (lit. I fuck your bread crumb!) *dia* ***Off*** used as a moderate curse, Fuck you!

• **Jèbēm ti kruzóvnicu!**{S} (lit. I fuck your corn storage!) *dia* ***Off*** used as a moderate curse, Fuck you!
• **Jèbēm ti kȓv!** {S} (lit. I fuck your blood!) *col* ***Off*** used as a moderate curse, Fuck you!
• **Jèbēm ti kȓv bȍžjī!** {S} (lit. I fuck your God's blood!) SSer *dia* ***Off*** used as a moderate curse, Fuck you!
• **Jèbēm ti kȓv bȍžjū!** {S} (lit. I fuck your God's blood!) *dia* ***Off*** used as a moderate curse, Fuck you!
• **Jèbēm ti kȓv Ȉsusovu!** {S} (lit. I fuck your Jesus's blood!) *dia* ***Off*** used as a moderate curse, Fuck you!
• **Jèbēm ti kȓv kȓvi!** {S} (lit. I fuck your blood's blood!) *col* ***Off*** used as a moderate curse, Fuck you!
• **Jèbēm ti kȓv tvòju!** {S} (lit. I fuck your blood!) *dia* ***Off*** used as a moderate curse, Fuck you!
• **Jèbēm ti kr̀vāća!** {S} (lit. I fuck your blood!) *dia* ***Off*** used as a moderate curse, Fuck you!
• **Jèbēm ti kŕzno kòjē ti je pr̀vī pût oko vrâta bílo!** {S} (lit. I screw the fur which was around your neck the first time!) *dia* ***Off*** used as a weak curse, Screw you!
• **Jèbēm ti kȕću bȍžju!** {S} (lit. I fuck your God's house!) *col* ***Off*** used as a moderate curse, Fuck you!
• **Jèbēm ti kȕću i kȕćīšte!** {S} (lit. I fuck your house and the place where it stands) *dia* ***Off*** used as a moderate curse, Fuck you!
• **Jèbēm ti kȕću lópovskū!**{S} (lit. I fuck your thieving house!) *col* ***Off*** used as a strong curse, Fuck you!
• **Jèbēm ti kȕću pòganū!** {S} (lit. I fuck your dirty house!) *col* ***Off*** used as a strong curse, Fuck you!
• **Jèbēm ti kukùruze!** {S} (lit. I screw your corn!) *dia* ***Off*** used as a weak curse, Screw you!
• **Jèbēm ti lȅbac!** {S} (lit. I fuck your bread!) SerE *dia* ***Off*** used as a moderate curse, Fuck you!
• **Jèbēm ti lèbārnīk!** {S} (lit. I fuck your bread storage!) SerE *dia* ***Off*** used as a moderate curse, Fuck you!
• **Jèbēm ti léglo đe si pr̀vī pût zàlegō!** {S} (lit. I fuck the nest where you first hatched!) *dia* ***Off*** used as a moderate curse, Fuck you!
• **Jèbēm ti lȉzaru!** {S} (lit. I fuck your licker!) *dia* ***Off*** used as a moderate curse, Fuck you!
• **Jèbēm ti lȕmu!** {S} *col* ***Off*** used as a moderate curse, Fuck you!
• **Jèbēm ti mâjku!** {S} (lit. I fuck your mother!) *col* ***Off*** used as a very strong curse, Fuck you!
• **Jèbēm ti mâjku àjdūčkū!** {S} (lit. I fuck your rebel mother!) *col* ***Off*** used as a very strong curse, Fuck you!
• **Jèbēm ti mâjku bȍžijū!** {S} (lit. I fuck your God's mother!) *col* ***Off*** used as a very strong curse, Fuck you!
• **Jèbēm ti mâjku bȑbljivū!**{S} (lit. I fuck your talkative mother!) *col* ***Off*** used as a very strong curse, Fuck you!
• **Jèbēm ti mâjku grȅšnū!** {S} (lit. I fuck your sinful mother!) *col* ***Off*** used as a very strong curse, Fuck you!
• **Jèbēm ti mâjku i kolijévku!** {S} (lit. I fuck your mother and crib!) *col* ***Off*** used as a very strong curse, Fuck you!
• **Jèbēm ti mâjku kȓvavū!** {S} (lit. I fuck your bloody mother!) *col* ***Off*** used as a very strong curse, Fuck you!
• **Jèbēm ti mâjku kûrvinskū!** {S} (lit. I fuck your whore-like mother!) *col* ***Off*** used as a very strong curse, Fuck you!
• **Jèbēm ti mâjku lópovskū!** {S} (lit. I fuck your criminal mother!) *col* ***Off*** used as a very strong curse, Fuck you!
• **Jèbēm ti mâjku lûdū!** {S} (lit. I fuck your crazy mother!) *col* ***Off*** used as a very strong curse, Fuck you!
• **Jèbēm ti mâjku mȉlosnū!** {S} (lit. I fuck your dear mother!) *col* ***Off*** used as a very strong curse, Fuck you!
• **Jèbēm ti mâjku mȉlū!** {S} (lit. I fuck your dear mother!) *col* ***Off*** used as a very strong curse, Fuck you!
• **Jèbēm ti mâjku mȓtvū!** {S} (lit. I fuck your dead mother!) *col* ***Off*** used as a very strong curse, Fuck you!
• **Jèbēm ti mâjku otìmāčkū!** {S} (lit. I fuck your robbing mother!) *col* ***Off*** used as a very strong curse, Fuck you!
• **Jèbēm ti mâjku pòganū!** {S} (lit. I fuck your dirty mother!) *col* ***Off*** used as a very strong curse, Fuck you!
• **Jèbēm ti mâjku pòkvārenū!** {S} (lit. I fuck your rotten mother!) *col* ***Off*** used as a very strong curse, Fuck you!
• **Jèbēm ti mâjku šȁšavū!** {S} (lit. I fuck your crazy mother!) *col* ***Off*** used as a very strong curse, Fuck you!
• **Jèbēm ti mâjku u čȉpku!** {S} (lit. I fuck your mother in her lace!) *dia* ***Off*** used as a very strong curse, Fuck you!
• **Jèbēm ti mâjku u čȉpku ispod pȕpka!** {S} (lit. I fuck your mother in her lace below her belly-button!) *dia* ***Off*** used as a very strong curse, Fuck you!
• **Jèbēm ti mâlō i vȅlikō!** {S} (lit. I fuck your small and big!) *col* ***Off*** used as a strong curse, Fuck you!
• **Jèbēm ti mȁmicu!** {S} (lit. I screw your mother!) *dia* ***Off*** used as a weak curse, Screw you!
• **Jèbēm ti mȁmicu tvòju!**{S} (lit. I screw your mother!) *dia* ***Off*** used as a weak curse, Screw you!
• **Jèbēm ti mȁmīn gùzīć!** {S} (lit. I fuck your mother's little ass!) *dia* ***Off*** used as a very strong curse, Fuck you!
• **Jèbēm ti mándžu nèsoljenū!** {S} (lit. I fuck your unsalted food!) *dia* ***Off*** used as a strong curse, Fuck you!
• **Jèbēm ti mȁtēr!** {S} (lit. I fuck your mother!) *col* ***Off*** used as a very strong curse, Fuck you!
• **Jèbēm ti mȁtēr bàlījskū!** {S} (lit. I fuck your Muslim mother!) *col* ***Off*** used as a very strong curse to a Bosnian Muslim, Fuck you!
• **Jèbēm ti mȁtēr bezòbraznū!** {S} (lit. I fuck your

indecent mother!) *col* ***Off*** used as a very strong curse, Fuck you!

• **Jèbēm ti mȁtēr blȅsavū!** {S} (lit. I fuck your crazy mother!) *col* ***Off*** used as a very strong curse, Fuck you!

• **Jèbēm ti mȁtēr čȅtničkū!** {S} (lit. I fuck your chetnik *Serbian soldier* mother!) *col* ***Off*** used as a very strong curse to a Serb, Fuck you!

• **Jèbēm ti mȁtēr mȁterinu!**{S} (lit. I fuck your mother's mother!) *col* ***Off*** used as a very strong curse, Fuck you!

• **Jèbēm ti mȁtēr muslìmānskū!** {S} (lit. I fuck your Muslim mother!) *col* ***Off*** used as a very strong curse, Fuck you!

• **Jèbēm ti mȁtēr nȅpismenū!** {S} (lit. I fuck your illiterate mother!) *col* ***Off*** used as a very strong curse, Fuck you!

• **Jèbēm ti mȁtēr òbrezānū!** {S} (lit. I fuck your circumcised mother!) *col* ***Off*** used as a very strong curse to a Bosnian Muslim, Fuck you!

• **Jèbēm ti mȁtēr štròkavū!** {S} (lit. I fuck your dirty mother!) *col* ***Off*** used as a very strong curse, Fuck you!

• **Jèbēm ti mȁtēr u čȉpku!** {S} (lit. I fuck your mother in her lace!) *dia* ***Off*** used as a very strong curse, Fuck you!

• **Jèbēm ti mȁtēr u** [NOUN:ACC]! {LSF} *col* ***Off*** used as a very strong curse, Fuck you!: *Jebem ti mater u usta! Fuck you!*

• **Jèbēm ti mȁtēr ȕstaškū!** {S} (lit. I fuck your Ustashi *Croatian soldier* mother!) *col* ***Off*** used as a very strong curse to a Croat, Fuck you!

• **Jèbēm ti mȁter vlȁškū!** {S} (lit. I fuck your Vlach *offensive name for a Serb* mother!) *col* ***Off*** used as a very strong curse to a Serb, Fuck you!

• **Jèbēm ti mȉlū màjčicu!** {S} (lit. I fuck your dear little mother!) *col* ***Off*** used as a very strong curse, Fuck you!

• **Jèbēm ti mȉlū mâjku!** {S} (lit. I fuck your dear mother!) *col* ***Off*** used as a very strong curse, Fuck you!

• **Jèbēm ti mȉlū mȁmicu!** {S} (lit. I fuck your dear mother!) *col* ***Off*** used as a very strong curse, Fuck you!

• **Jèbēm ti mȉša u duváru!** {S} (lit. I screw your mouse in the attic!) *dia* ***Off*** used as a weak curse, Screw you!

• **Jèbēm ti Mlâdū nèdelju!** {S} (lit. I fuck your young Sunday!) *dia* ***Off*** used as a moderate curse, Fuck you!

• **Jèbēm ti mȓtvā kókala!** {S} (lit. I fuck your dead bones.) *dia* ***Off*** used as a strong curse, Fuck you!

• **Jèbēm ti nebèsa bȍžjā!** {S} (lit. I fuck your God's skies!) *dia* ***Off*** used as a moderate curse, Fuck you!

• **Jèbēm ti nȅbo jȁsnō!** {S} (lit. I fuck your clear sky!) *col* ***Off*** used as a moderate curse, Fuck you!

• **Jèbēm ti nȅbo plâvō!** {S} (lit. I fuck your blue sky!) *col* ***Off*** used as a moderate curse, Fuck you!

• **Jèbēm ti nȅbo vȅdrō!** {S} (lit. I fuck your clear skies!) *col* ***Off*** used as a moderate curse, Fuck you!

• **Jèbēm ti nȅđelju!** {S} (lit. I fuck your Sunday!) *dia* ***Off*** used as a moderate curse, Fuck you!

• **Jèbēm ti nȍzdrve!** {S} (lit. I fuck your nostrils!) *col* ***Off*** used as a moderate curse, Fuck you!

• **Jèbēm ti njû što nije tû!** {S} (lit. I fuck her who is not here!) *col* ***Off*** used as a moderate curse, Fuck you!

• **Jèbēm ti òca màngupskōg!** {S} (lit. I fuck your jocular father!) *dia* used as a moderate curse

• **Jèbēm ti òca óčinōg!** {S} (lit. I fuck your father's father!) *dia* ***Off*** used as a strong curse, Fuck you!

• **Jèbēm ti palìlūj!** {S} *dia* ***Off*** used as a moderate curse, Fuck you!

• **Jèbēm ti pèćinu!** {S} (lit. I screw your cave!) *col* ***Off*** used as a weak curse, Screw you!

• **Jèbēm ti pȉčku mȁterinu!**{S} (lit. I fuck your mother's cunt!) *col* ***Off*** used as a strong curse, Fuck you!

• **Jèbēm ti plȁzajcu kòjōm si pȑvī pût plȁziō!** {S} (lit. I fuck the slide you slid the first time!) *dia* ***Off*** used as a moderate curse, Fuck you!

• **Jèbēm ti Pȍklade!** {S} (lit. I fuck your carnival!) *dia* ***Off*** used as a moderate curse, Fuck you!

• **Jèbēm ti pošténje!** {S} (lit. I fuck your straightness!) *col* ***Off*** used as a moderate curse, Fuck you!

• **Jèbēm ti rȁbotu tàkvu!** {S} (lit. I screw that work of yours!) *dia* ***Off*** used as a weak curse, Screw you!

• **Jèbēm ti rȉbīć!** {S} (lit. I fuck your cunt!) *dia* ***Off*** used as a moderate curse, Fuck you!

• **Jèbēm ti rȍda!** {S} *dia* ***Off*** used as a moderate curse, Fuck you!

• **Jèbēm ti sèstru!** {S} (lit. I fuck your sister!) *col* ***Off*** used as a strong curse, Fuck you!

• **Jèbēm ti sèstru kȓvavū!** {S} (lit. I fuck your bloody sister!) *col* ***Off*** used as a very strong curse, Fuck you!

• **Jèbēm ti sèstru nȅveselū!** {S} (lit. I fuck your sad sister!) *col* ***Off*** used as a strong curse, Fuck you!

• **Jèbēm ti sèstru pòganū!** {S} (lit. I fuck your dirty sister!) *col* ***Off*** used as a very strong curse, Fuck you!

• **Jèbēm ti sèstru pòkvārenū!** {S} (lit. I fuck your rotten sister!) *col* ***Off*** used as a very strong curse, Fuck you!

• **Jèbēm ti sîna mâlōga!** {S} (lit. I fuck your little son!) *col* ***Off*** used as a strong curse, Fuck you!

• **Jèbēm ti sȉrutku nȅslānū!**{S} (lit. I fuck your unsalted whey!) *dia* ***Off*** used as a moderate curse, Fuck you!

• **Jèbēm ti sìsić kòjī si póso!** {S} (lit. I fuck the tit which nursed you!) *dia* ***Off*** used as a moderate curse, Fuck you!

• **Jèbēm ti sȉsu kòjā te dòjila!** {S} (lit. I fuck the tit which hursed you!) *dia* ***Off*** used as a moderate curse, Fuck you!

• **Jèbēm ti sȉsu mȁterinu!** {S} (lit. I fuck your mother's tit!) *col* ***Off*** used as a moderate curse, Fuck you!
• **Jèbēm ti sjȁlo!** {S} (lit. I fuck your shiny spot!) *dia* ***Off*** used as a moderate curse, Fuck you!
• **Jèbēm ti sjȅme u sjȅmenu!** {S} (lit. I fuck your seed in the seed!) *dia* ***Off*** used as a strong curse, Fuck you!
• **Jèbēm ti slȁvca!** {S} (lit. I fuck your saint's day!) *dia* ***Off*** used as a moderate curse, Fuck you!
• **Jèbēm ti slȁvicu!** {S} (lit. I screw your little saint's day!) *dia* ***Off*** used as a weak curse, Screw you!
• **Jèbēm ti slȁvu!** {S} (lit. I fuck your saint's day!) *dia* ***Off*** used as a moderate curse, Fuck you!
• **Jèbēm ti slȁvu alàmunjsku!** {S} (lit. I fuck your irresponsible saint's day!) *dia* ***Off*** used as a moderate curse, Fuck you!
• **Jèbēm ti sôj živòtīnjskī!** {S} (lit. I fuck your animal kind!) *col* ***Off*** used as a strong curse, Fuck you!
• **Jèbēm ti sôrtu!** {S} (lit. I fuck your kind!) *col* ***Off*** used as a moderate curse, Fuck you!
• **Jèbēm ti sôrtu nȉkakvū!**{S} (lit. I fuck your unworthy kind!) *col* ***Off*** used as a strong curse, Fuck you!
• **Jèbēm ti stâru u šúpak!** {S} (lit. I fuck your old lady in her ass!) *sl* ***Off*** used as a strong curse, Fuck you!
• **Jèbēm ti stô bògōvā!** {S} (lit. I fuck your hundred gods!) *col* ***Off*** used as a moderate curse, Fuck you!
• **Jèbēm ti strînu!** {S} (lit. I screw your aunt!) *col* ***Off*** used as a weak curse, Screw you!
• **Jèbēm ti sȕnac!** {S} (lit. I screw your sun!) *dia* ***Off*** used as a weak curse, Screw you!
• **Jèbēm ti sûnce!** {S} (lit. I fuck your sun!) *col* ***Off*** used as a moderate curse, Fuck you!
• **Jèbēm ti sûnce jârkō!** {S} (lit. I fuck your bright sun!) *col* ***Off*** used as a moderate curse, Fuck you!
• **Jèbēm ti sûnce kalàjisānō!** {S} (lit. I screw your tin-covered sun!) *col* ***Off*** used as a weak curse, Screw you!
• **Jèbēm ti sûnce nȅbeskō!**{S} (lit. I fuck your heavenly sun!) *col* ***Off*** used as a moderate curse, Fuck you!
• **Jèbēm ti sûnce ònō što te grȅjē!** {S} (lit. I fuck the sun which heats you!) SerE *col* ***Off*** used as a moderate curse, Fuck you!
• **Jèbēm ti sûnce žȁrenō!** {S} (lit. I fuck your hot sun!) *col* ***Off*** used as a moderate curse, Fuck you!
• **Jèbēm ti sûnce žârkō!** {S} (lit. I fuck your hot sun!) *col* ***Off*** used as a moderate curse, Fuck you!
• **Jèbēm ti sûnce žârkō da ti jèbēm!** {S} (lit. I really fuck your sun!) *col* ***Off*** used as a moderate curse, Fuck you!
• **Jèbēm ti svȅ i svȁ!** {S} (lit. I fuck your everything!) *col* ***Off*** used as a moderate curse, Fuck you!
• **Jèbēm ti svȅ na gòmilu!**{S} (lit. I fuck your everything on a heap!) *col* ***Off*** used as a moderate curse, Fuck you!
• **Jèbēm ti svȅ na svétu!**{S} (lit. I fuck your everything in the world!) SerE *col* ***Off*** used as a strong curse, Fuck you!
• **Jèbēm ti svȅ po ȉme i prézime!** {S} (lit. I fuck your everything according to the name and surname!) *dia* ***Off*** used as a strong curse, Fuck you!
• **Jèbēm ti svȅ pò kuću!** {S} (lit. I fuck everything in your house!) *dia* ***Off*** used as a strong curse, Fuck you!
• **Jèbēm ti svȅ po spȉsak!** {S} (lit. I fuck everything yours according to a list!) *dia* ***Off*** used as a strong curse, Fuck you!
• **Jèbēm ti svȅ po spȉsku!** {S} (lit. I fuck everything yours according to a list!) *col* ***Off*** used as a strong curse, Fuck you!
• **Jèbēm ti svȅ svéce!** {S} (lit. I fuck all your saints!) *col* ***Off*** used as a strong curse, Fuck you!
• **Jèbēm ti svȅ Svêtē!** {S} (lit. I fuck all your saints!) *col* ***Off*** used as a strong curse, Fuck you!
• **Jèbēm ti svȅ šta ti u dȍm ùlazī!** {S} (lit. I fuck everything that enters your home!) *col* ***Off*** used as a moderate curse, Fuck you!
• **Jèbēm ti svȅ što ìmāš i što nêmāš!** {S} (lit. I fuck everything you have and you do not have!) *col* ***Off*** used as a strong curse, Fuck you!
• **Jèbēm ti svȅ što mu nȁ srcu lèžī!** {S} (lit. I fuck everything that is on your heart!) *col* ***Off*** used as a strong curse, Fuck you!
• **Jèbēm ti svȅ ù kući!** {S} (lit. I fuck everything in your home!) *col* ***Off*** used as a strong curse, Fuck you!
• **Jèbēm ti svȅ žívo i mŕtvo!** {S} (lit. I fuck all yours, alive and dead!) *col* ***Off*** used as a very strong curse, Fuck you!
• **Jèbēm ti svȅ žívo na svétu!** {S} (lit. I fuck all your alive in the world!) SerE *col* ***Off*** used as a strong curse, Fuck you!
• **Jèbēm ti svéca!** {S} (lit. I fuck your saint!) *col* ***Off*** used as a moderate curse, Fuck you!
• **Jèbēm ti svéću kȑštenū!** {S} (lit. I fuck your baptized candle!) SerE *dia* ***Off*** used as a moderate curse, Fuck you!
• **Jèbēm ti Svetȉliju!** {S} (lit. I fuck your St. Elias!) *dia* ***Off*** used as a moderate curse, Fuck you!
• **Jèbēm ti svêtōg Jována s bòse nȍge!** {S} (lit. I fuck your St. John with his bare feet!) *dia* ***Off*** used as a moderate curse, Fuck you!
• **Jèbēm ti svêtōg Nȉkolu s bêlū brádu!** {S} (lit. I fuck your St. Nicolas with his white beard!) *dia* ***Off*** used as a moderate curse, Fuck you!
• **Jèbēm ti svêtū Pêtku!** {S} (lit. I fuck your St. Petka!) *dia* ***Off*** used as a moderate curse, Fuck you!
• **Jèbēm ti svêtu Pêtku Paraskévu!** {S} (lit. I fuck your saint Petka Paraskeva!) *dia* ***Off*** used as a moderate

curse, Fuck you!

• **Jèbēm ti svȉralu kroz kòjū si pȑvī pût prosvírala!** {S} (lit. I fuck the flute you played the first time to you!) *dia Off* used as a moderate curse, Fuck you!

• **Jèbēm ti šèncu!** {S} (lit. I fuck your wheat!) *dia Off* used as a moderate curse, Fuck you!

• **Jèbēm ti što se nè setiš!** {S} (lit. I fuck the things you do not remember!) *col Off* used as a moderate curse, Fuck you!

• **Jèbēm ti što vȉđō i nè viđō!** {S} (lit. I fuck the things you saw and you did not see!) *dia Off* used as a moderate curse, Fuck you!

• **Jèbēm ti šûb!** {S} (lit. I fuck your fur coat!) *col Off* used as a moderate curse, Fuck you!

• **Jèbēm ti šȕbaru kévinu!** {S} (lit. I fuck your mother's fur cap!) *col Off* used as a moderate curse, Fuck you!

• **Jèbēm ti šúpak smȑdljivī!** {S} (lit. I fuck your stinking asshole!) *col Off* used as a moderate curse, Fuck you!

• **Jèbēm ti tâj žȉvot!** {S} (lit. I fuck that life!) *col Obs* used to express dissatisfaction, Fuck it!

• **Jèbēm ti tavnjàniək u kàndilo!** {S} (lit. I fuck your incense in its lamp!) *dia Off* used as a moderate curse, Fuck you!

• **Jèbēm ti tàvu!** {S} (lit. I screw your pan!) *col Off* used as a weak curse, Screw you!

• **Jèbēm ti tȅtku òšīšānū!** {S} (lit. I screw your aunt whose hair is cut off!) *sl Off* used as a weak curse, Screw you!

• **Jèbēm ti trȉsta bògōva!** {S} (lit. I fuck three hundred of your Gods!) *col Off* used as a moderate curse, Fuck you!

• **Jèbēm ti ȕjāk u kȕjnu!** {S} (lit. I screw your uncle in the kitchen!) *dia Off* used as a weak curse, Screw you!

• **Jèbēm ti ùjnicu u vȕnicu!** {S} (lit. I screw your little aunt in her little wool!) *sl Off* used as a weak curse, Screw you!

• **Jèbēm ti ùnuče ràno!** {S} (lit. I fuck your grandson early in the morning!) *col Off* used as a strong curse, Fuck you!

• **Jèbēm ti ústa!** {S} (lit. I fuck your mouth!) *col Off* used as a strong curse, Fuck you!

• **Jèbēm ti ústa pàrādnā!** {S} (lit. I fuck your parade mouth!) *col Off* used as a strong curse, Fuck you!

• **Jèbēm ti ȕtrobu kòja te nòsila!** {S} (lit. I fuck the womb which carried you!) *col Off* used as a strong curse, Fuck you!

• **Jèbēm ti ȕvo!** {S} (lit. I fuck your ear!) Ser *col Off* used as a moderate curse, Fuck you!

• **Jèbēm ti večérnicu tvòju!** {S} (lit. I fuck your evening church service!) *col Off* used as a moderate curse, Fuck you!

• **Jèbēm ti vénac na glávi!** {S} (lit. I fuck the wreath on your head!) SerE *dia Off* used as a moderate curse, Fuck you!

• **Jèbēm ti vèrige Ȉsusove!** {S} (lit. I fuck you Jesus's chains!) *dia Off* used as a moderate curse, Fuck you!

• **Jèbēm ti zákon bȍžī!** {S} (lit. I fuck your God's law!) *col Off* used as a moderate curse, Fuck you!

• **Jèbēm ti zákon dètinjī!** {S} (lit. I fuck your childish law!) SerE *dia Off* used as a moderate curse, Fuck you!

• **Jèbēm ti zákon domàćinskī!** {S} (lit. I fuck your landlord's law!) *dia Off* used as a moderate curse, Fuck you!

• **Jèbēm ti zákon tvôj dètinjī!** {S} (lit. I fuck your childish law!) *dia Off* used as a moderate curse, Fuck you!

• **Jèbēm ti zalogàjčić!** {S} (lit. I screw your small bite!) *dia Off* used as a weak curse, Screw you!

• **Jèbēm ti zvézdu!** {S} (lit. I screw your star!) SerE *dia Off* used as a weak curse, Screw you!

• **Jèbēm ti žènče u crévce!** {S} (lit. I screw your wife in her intestine!) SSer *dia Off* used as a weak curse, Screw you!

• **Jèbēm ti žènče u rȉpče!** {S} (lit. I screw your wife in her small fish!) *dia Off* used as a weak curse, Screw you!

• **Jèbēm ti žènu!** {S} (lit. I fuck your wife!) *col Off* used as a moderate curse, Fuck you!

• **Jèbēm ti žènu ćȅrastū!** {S} *dia Off* used as a moderate curse, Fuck you!

• **Jèbēm ti žènu da me pòznāvā!** {S} (lit. I fuck your wife so that she recognizes me!) *dia Off* used as a moderate curse, Fuck you!

• **Jèbēm ti žènu da pâmtī!** {S} (lit. I fuck your wife so that she remembers it!) *dia Off* used as a moderate curse, Fuck you!

• **Jèbēm ti žènu da se sȅćā!** {S} (lit. I fuck your wife so that she remembers it!) *dia Off* used as a moderate curse, Fuck you!

• **Jèbēm ti žènu kȑvavū!** {S} (lit. I fuck your bloody wife!) *dia Off* used as a strong curse, Fuck you!

• **Jèbēm ti žènu pòkvārenū!** {S} (lit. I fuck your rotten wife!) *dia Off* used as a strong curse, Fuck you!

• **Jèbēm ti žènu u gùzicu!** {S} (lit. I fuck your wife in her ass!) *dia Off* used as a moderate curse, Fuck you!

• **Jèbēm ti žènu u mêso kȉselō!** {S} (lit. I screw your wife in her sour meat!) *dia Off* used as a weak curse, Screw you!

• **Jèbēm ti žènu ùkapānū!** {S} *col Off* used as a moderate curse, Fuck you!

• **Jèbēm ti žȉvot!** {S} (lit. I fuck your life!) *col Obs* used to express dissatisfaction, Fuck it!

• **Jèbēm ti žȉvot ovàkav!** {S} (lit. I fuck life like this!) *col Off* used to express dissatisfaction, Fuck it!

• **Jèbēm ti žȉvot što ga žívīš!** {S} (lit. I fuck the life you've been living!) *col* ***Off*** used as a moderate curse, Fuck you!

• **Jèbēm ti životək tvôj!** {S} (lit. I fuck your small life!) *dia* ***Off*** used as a moderate curse, Fuck you!

• **Jèben pòsō!** {S} (lit. Fucking business!) *col* ***Obs*** used to express dissatisfaction, Fuck it!

• **Jèben svêt!** {S} (lit. Fucking people!) SerE *col* ***Off*** used to express disgust toward, Fuck them!

• **Jebèno vréme!** {S} (lit. Fucking time!) SerE *col* ***Obs*** used to express dissatisfaction, Fuck it!

• **Jèbēš dȑžavu!** {S} (lit. Fuck the state!) *col* ***Obs*** used to express dissatisfaction, Fuck it!

• **Jèbēš ga!** {S} (lit. Fuck it!) *col* ***Obs*** used to express dissatisfaction, Fuck it!

• **Jèbēš mi mȁtēr!** {S} (lit. You can fuck my mother!) *col* ***Obs*** used to emphasize one's point, It's fucking real!

• **Jèbēš mi svȅ!** {S} (lit. You can fuck all that is mine!) 1 *col* ***Obs*** used to express dissatisfaction, Fuck it! 2 ***Obs*** used to emphasize one's point, It's fucking real!

• **Jèbēš môme máčku mȁtēr!** {S} (lit. You can fuck my tomcat's mother!) *col* ***Fac-Obs*** used to express dissatisfaction, Fuck it!

• **Jèbēš pòso!** {S} (lit. Fuck the job!) *col* ***Obs*** used to express dissatisfaction, Fuck it!

• **Jèbēš[PRON:DAT] mȁtēr!** {LSF} (lit. You can fuck [PPRON] mother!) *col* used to express dissatisfaction, Fuck it!: *Jebeš mu mater! Fuck it!*

• **Jèbēš se ti u dȕpe!** {S} (lit. You fuck in your ass!) *col* ***Off*** used as a moderate curse, Fuck you!

• **Jèbēš svôj òbraz!** {S} (lit. Fuck your cheek!) *col* ***Off*** used as a moderate curse, Fuck you!

• **Jèbēš svòju rêč!** {S} (lit. Fuck your word!) *col* ***Obs*** used to express dissatisfaction, Fuck it!

• **Jèbi ga!** {S} (lit. Fuck it!) *col* ***Obs*** used to express dissatisfaction, Fuck it!

• **Jèbi ga grȍfe!** {S} (lit. Fuck it, you count!) **a.** *col* ***Obs*** used to express dissatisfaction, Fuck it! **b.** ***Obs*** used to express disbelief, Don't give me that shit!

• **Jèbi mȁtēr!** {S} (lit. Fuck your mother!) **1a.** *col* ***Obs*** used to express dissatisfaction, Fuck it! **b.** ***Obs*** used to express disbelief, Don't give me that shit! 2 ***Off*** used as a strong curse, Fuck you!

• **Jèbi me sȁd ako znâm!** {S} (lit. Fuck me if I knew it!) **a.** *col* ***Obs*** used to express disapproval, Fuck it! **b.** used to express unawareness, I got no fucking idea!

• **Jèbi se!** {S} (lit. Fuck you!) *col* ***Off*** used as a moderate curse, Fuck you!

• **Jèbi se tȋ u dȕpe!** {S} (lit. Fuck yourself in the ass!) *col* ***Off*** used as a moderate curse, Fuck you!

• **Jèbi se u kȕrac!** {S} (lit. Fuck yourself in your cock!) *col* ***Off*** used as a moderate curse, Fuck you!

• **Jèbi sèstru!** {S} (lit. Fuck your sister!) *col* ***Off*** used as a strong curse, Fuck you!

• **Jèbi si mȁtēr!** {S} (lit. Fuck your mother!) 1 *col* ***Off*** used as a strong curse, Fuck you! 2 ***Obs*** used to express disbelief, No shit?

• **Jèbi svôg ȍca!** {S} (lit. Fuck your father!) *col* ***Off*** used as a strong curse, Fuck you!

• **Jèbi ti svòju mȁtēr!** {S} (lit. Fuck your mother!) *col* ***Off*** used as a strong curse, Fuck you!

• **Jèbi ti svôm ȍcu ćérku!** {S} (lit. Fuck your father's daughter!) *col* ***Off-Fac*** used as a strong curse, Fuck you!

• **Jèbi ti tô!** {S} (lit. You fuck that!) *col* ***Obs*** used to express disbelief, Fuck it!

• **Jèbi ti tô što znâš!** {S} (lit. Fuck everything you know!) *col* ***Obs*** used to express disbelief, Fuck it!

• **Jèbite si džȁm!** {S} (lit. Fuck your soul!) *dia* ***Off*** used as a moderate curse, Fuck you!

• **Jèbō bi bùvu u skòku!** {S} (lit. He would fuck a jumping flea!) *col* ***Obs*** used to refer to exaggerated interest in sex of a third party male

• **Jèbō bi mùvu u létu!** {S} (lit. He would fuck a flying fly!) *col* ***Obs*** used to refer to exaggerated interest in sex of a third party male

• **Jèbō bi se za lóvu!** {S} (lit. He would fuck for money!) *col* ***Obs*** used to refer to miserly attitude of a third party male

• **Jèbō bi tȉcu u pícu!** {S} (lit. He would fuck a bird in its cunt!) *col* ***Obs*** used to refer to exaggerated interest in sex of a third party male

• **Jèbō bi zmìju u ȍko!** {S} (lit. He would fuck a snake in the eye!) *col* ***Obs*** used to refer to exaggerated interest in sex of a third party male

• **Jèbō ga!** {S} (lit. Fuck it!) *col* ***Obs*** used to express dissatisfaction, Fuck it!

• **Jèbō ga Bôg!** {S} (lit. God fuck him!) *col* ***Obs*** used to express dissatisfaction, Fuck!

• **Jèbō ga òtac!** {S} (lit. Let his father fuck him!) *col* ***Obs*** used to express dissatisfaction, Fuck!

• **jèbō ga tȋ** {S} (lit. you fuck it) *col* ***Obs*** used to emphasize one's point, you know: *Oni su došli, jebo ga ti. They came, you know.*

• **Jèbō ga tȋ!** {S} (lit. You fuck it!) *col* ***Obs*** used to express dissatisfaction, Fuck it!

• **Jèbō ih Bôg!** {S} (lit. Let God fuck them!) *col* ***Off*** used as a moderate curse, Fuck them!

• **Jèbō ih Bôg òtac!** {S} (lit. Let God fuck them!) *col* ***Off*** used as a moderate curse, Fuck them!

• **Jèbō ih nȍvī svètskī pòredak!** {S} (lit. Let the new world order screw them!) SerE *col* ***Fac-Obs*** used as a weak curse, Screw them!

• **Jèbō ih svêtī Jerònim!** {S} (lit. Let St. Hieronymus

fuck them!) *dia* ***Off*** used as a moderate curse, Fuck them!

• **Jèbō jâ tȅbe!** {S} (lit. Let me fuck you!) *col* ***Off*** used as a moderate curse, Fuck you!

• **Jèbō jâ tô!** {S} (lit. Let me fuck that!) *col* ***Obs*** used to express dissatisfaction, Fuck it!

• **Jèbō jêža u léđa!** {S} (lit. Let him fuck a hedgehog in its back!) *col* ***Obs*** used as a weak curse, Screw you!

• **Jèbō joj pȁs mȁtēr!** {S} (lit. Let a dog fuck her mother!) *col* ***Off*** used as a moderate curse, Fuck her!

• **Jèbō kòzu u bȓzōm vòzu!** {S} (lit. Let him screw a goat on a fast train!) *col* ***Fac-Obs*** used as a mild offense toward a third party male, Screw him!

• **Jèbō mȁmu!** {S} (lit. Let him fuck his mother!) *col* ***Obs*** used as a moderate curse, Fuck him!

• **jèbō mȁtēr** {S} (lit. let me fuck my mother) *col* ***Obs*** used to emphasize the truth of what has been said, I swear to God!

• **Jèbō mȁtēr sèljāčkū!**{S} (lit. Let him fuck his redneck mother!) *col* ***Off*** used as a moderate curse, Fuck him!

• **Jèbō me ònāj kò me sȁstavi s tȍbōm!** {S} (lit. Let me fuck the one who has connected me with you!) *col* ***Obs*** used as a moderate curse, Fuck you!

• **Jèbō mu pȁs mȁtēr!** {S} (lit. Let a dog fuck his mother!) *col* ***Off*** used as a very strong curse, Fuck him!

• **Jèbō pȁs mȁtēr njȉma!** {S} (lit. Let a dog fuck their mother!) *col* ***Off*** used as a very strong curse, Fuck them!

• **Jèbō[PRON:ACC] Bôg màhnitī!** {LSF} (lit. Let [PPRON:ACC] crazy God fuck [PRON:ACC]) *col* ***Off*** used as a moderate curse: *Jebo ih bog mahniti! Fuck them!*

• **Jèbō[PRON:ACC] [NP:NOM]!** {LSF} (lit. Let [NP:NOM] fuck [PRON:ACC]!) *col* ***Off*** used to express dissatisfaction or lack of interest in: *Jebo te ispit! Fuck that exam!*

• **Jèbō[PRON:DAT] [NOUN:NOM] mȁtēr u ústa!** {LSF} (lit. Let [NOUN:NOM] fuck [PPRON] mother in her mouth!) *col* ***Off*** used as a very strong curse: *Jebo ti policajac mater u usta! Fuck that policeman!*

• **Jèbō[PRON:DAT] pȁs mâjku!** {LSF} (lit. Let a dog fuck [PPRON] mother.) *col* ***Off*** used as a very strong curse: *Jebo ti pas majku! Fuck you!*

• **Jèbō si jêža!** {S} (lit. You fucked a hedgehog!) *col* ***Obs*** used to refer to a difficult situation of one's interlocutor, You really fucked up!

• **Jèbō si jêža u bòdljivō dȕpe!** {S} (lit. You fucked a hedgehog in his pricking ass!) *col* ***Obs*** used to refer to a difficult situation of one's interlocutor, You really fucked up!

• **Jèbō si jêža u léđa!** {S} (lit. You fucked a hedgehog in its back!) *col* ***Obs*** used to refer to a difficult situation of one's interlocutor, You really fucked up!

• **Jèbō si se u dȕpe!** {S} (lit. You fucked yourself in your ass!) *col* ***Obs*** used to refer to a difficult situation of one's interlocutor, You really fucked up!

• **Jèbō slȉku svòju!** {S} (lit. You screwed your picture!) *col* ***Obs*** used as a weak curse, Screw him!

• **Jèbō svȅsku!** {S} (lit. Screw a notebook!) *col* ***Obs-Fac*** used to express lack of interest in, Screw it!

• **Jèbō svòjē bàbē gȍlē sȉse!** {S} (lit. Fuck your grandmother's naked tits!) *col* ***Obs-Fac*** used as a moderate curse, Fuck you!

• **Jèbō svòjē mâjkē mȑtvačkē òpānke!** {S} (lit. Fuck your mother's dead peasant shoes!) *col* ***Off*** used as a very strong curse, Fuck you!

• **Jèbō svòju mâjku a mȉslio da je mòja!** {S} (lit. May you fuck your mother while thinking that it is my mother!) *col* ***Off-Fac*** used as a strong curse, Fuck you!

• **Jèbō te!**{S} (lit. Fuck you!) *col* ***Obs*** used to emphasize one's point

• **Jèbō te Àlija!**{S} (lit. Let Alija *Izetbegović, a prominent Bosnian-Muslim politician in the 1990s* fuck you!) *col* ***Off*** used as a moderate curse to a Bosnian Muslim, Fuck you!

• **Jèbō te blâgī Bôg!** {S} (lit. Let merciful God fuck you!) *col* ***Off*** used as a moderate curse, Fuck you!

• **Jèbō te bôg!** {S} (lit. Let God fuck you!) *col* ***Off*** used as a moderate curse, Fuck you!

• **Jèbō te bôg da te jȅbō!** {S} (lit. Let God fuck you, let God fuck you!) *col* ***Off*** used as a moderate curse, Fuck you!

• **Jèbō te bôg sȁkata!** {S} (lit. Let God fuck you handicapped!) *col* ***Off*** used as a moderate curse, Fuck you!

• **Jèbō te brȁt!** {S} (lit. Let your brother fuck you!) *col* ***Off*** used as a moderate curse, Fuck you!

• **Jèbō te ćȁća!** {S} (lit. Let your father fuck you!) *col* ***Off*** used as a moderate curse, Fuck you!

• **Jèbō te džȁndār!** {S} (lit. May a cop screw you!) *dia* ***Obs*** used as a weak curse, Screw you!

• **Jèbō te embȁrgo!** {S} (lit. May the embargo screw you!) *col* ***Obs*** used as a weak curse, Screw you!

• **Jèbō te faràōn!** {S} (lit. May a pharaon screw you!) *col* ***Fac-Obs*** used as a weak curse, Screw it!

• **Jèbō te Fránjo!**{S} (lit. Let Franjo *Tuđman, a prominent Croatian politician in the 1990s* fuck you!) *col* ***Off*** used as a moderate curse to a Croat, Fuck you!

• **Jèbō te grôm!** {S} (lit. Let lightning fuck you!) *col* ***Obs*** used to emphasize one's point, Fuck!

• **Jèbō te Hȉtler!** {S} (lit. I wish *Adolf* Hitler screws you!) *col* ***Obs*** used as a weak curse, Screw you

• **Jèbō te Ȉsus!** {S} (lit. Let Jesus fuck you!) *col* ***Obs*** used as a moderate curse, Fuck you!

• **Jèbō te jâ!** {S} (lit. Let me fuck you!) *col* ***Obs*** used as a moderate curse, Fuck it!

• **Jèbō te jâ u pȉčku!** {S} (lit. Let me fuck you in your cunt!) *col* ***Obs*** used as a moderate curse, Fuck you!

• **Jèbō te jâ u pȍla dvâ!** {S} (lit. Let me screw you at half past one!) *col* ***Fac-Obs*** used as a weak curse, Screw it!

• **Jèbō te kêr!** {S} (lit. Let a dog fuck you!) *col* ***Obs*** used as a moderate curse, Fuck you!

• **Jèbō te ko te glȅdā!** {S} (lit. Let those who look at you fuck you!) *col* ***Off*** used as a moderate curse, Fuck you!

• **Jèbō te ko te ìmā!** {S} (lit. Let those who have you fuck you!) *col* ***Off*** used as a moderate curse, Fuck you!

• **Jèbō te kò te nȁpravī!** {S} (lit. Let those who made you fuck you!) *col* ***Off*** used as a moderate curse, Fuck you!

• **Jèbō te ko te nìje!** {S} (lit. Let those who did not fuck you fuck you!) *col* ***Off*** used as a moderate curse, Fuck you!

• **Jèbō te kò te ȍlīzā!** {S} (lit. Let those who licked you fuck you!) *col* ***Off*** used as a moderate curse, Fuck you!

• **Jèbō te kò te ȍtelī!** {S} (lit. Let those who gave you birth fuck you!) *col* ***Off*** used as a moderate curse, Fuck you!

• **Jèbō te kò te ȍtesā!** {S} (lit. Let those who carved you fuck you!) *col* ***Off*** used as a moderate curse, Fuck you!

• **Jèbō te kò te rȍdī!** {S} (lit. Let those who gave birth to you fuck you!) *col* ***Off*** used as a moderate curse, Fuck you!

• **Jèbō te kò te ròdiō!** {S} (lit. Let one who gave birth to you fuck you!) *col* ***Off*** used as a moderate curse, Fuck you!

• **Jèbō te kò te stvòriō!** {S} (lit. Let those who created you fuck you!) *col* ***Off*** used as a moderate curse, Fuck you!

• **Jèbō te ko ti lȅba dâvā!** {S} (lit. Let those who give you bread fuck you!) **SerE** *dia* ***Off*** used as a moderate curse, Fuck you!

• **Jèbō te kȍnj!** {S} (lit. Let a horse fuck you!) *dia* ***Obs*** used to emphasize one's point, Fuck!

• **Jèbō te kùrčić!** {S} (lit. Let a small cock fuck you!) *dia* ***Obs*** used as a moderate curse, Fuck you!

• **Jèbō te lȅš!** {S} (lit. Let a corpse fuck you!) *dia* ***Obs*** used to emphasize one's point, Fuck!

• **Jèbō te marvènjāk!** {S} (lit. Let a cattle wagon fuck you!) *dia* ***Obs*** used as a moderate curse, Fuck you!

• **Jèbō te mȉš!** {S} (lit. May a mouse screw you!) *col* ***Obs*** used as a weak curse, Screw it!

• **Jèbō te mitropòlit!** {S} (lit. Let an archbishop fuck you!) *col* ***Fac-Obs*** used as a moderate curse, Fuck you!

• **Jèbō te môj kòmšija!** {S} (lit. Let my neighbor fuck you!) *col* ***Obs*** used as a moderate curse, Fuck you!

• **Jèbō te môme óči sîn!** {S} (lit. Let my father's son fuck you!) *dia* ***Fac-Off*** used as a moderate curse, Fuck you!

• **Jèbō te Musolînī!** {S} (lit. May Mussolini *prominent Italian politician in the 1930s and 1940s* screw you!) *col* ***Obs*** used as a weak curse, Screw it!

• **Jèbō te Nìkola Pȁšić!** {S} (lit. May Nikola Pašić *a prominent pre-WWII Serbian politician* screw you!) *col* ***Obs*** used as a weak curse, Screw it!

• **Jèbō te ôn!** {S} (lit. Let him fuck you!) *col* ***Obs*** used as a moderate curse, Fuck him!

• **Jèbō te ôn u dȕpe!** {S} (lit. Let him fuck you in your ass!) *col* ***Off*** used as a moderate curse, Fuck you!

• **Jèbō te ònāj kò te ȉzasrō!** {S} (lit. Let the one who shit you out fuck you!) *col* ***Off*** used as a moderate curse, Fuck you!

• **Jèbō te ònāj kò te jȕtrōs òbuvō!** {S} (lit. Let that one who put your shoes on this morning fuck you!) *col* ***Off*** used as a moderate curse, Fuck you!

• **Jèbō te ònāj kò te nȁpravī!** {S} (lit. Let that one who made you fuck you!) *col* ***Off*** used as a moderate curse, Fuck you!

• **Jèbō te ònāj kò te nàpraviō!** {S} (lit. Let the one who made you fuck you!) *col* ***Off*** used as a moderate curse, Fuck you!

• **Jèbō te ònāj kò ti dȁde vòlān!** {S} (lit. Let that one who gave you the steering wheel fuck you!) *col* ***Obs*** used to express negative opinion about one's interlocutor's driving abilities, You are a fucking bad driver!

• **Jèbō te ònāj kô ti mȅsto pȕpka nìje òdrezō glâvu!** {S} (lit. Let that one who did not cut off your head instead of your belly-button fuck you!) *col* ***Off*** used as a strong curse, Fuck you!

• **Jèbō te ȍsim Bôg!** {S} (lit. Let everybody except God fuck you!) *dia* ***Off*** used as a moderate curse, Fuck you!

• **Jèbō te òtac!** {S} (lit. Let your father fuck you!) *col* ***Off*** used as a strong curse, Fuck you!

• **Jèbō te pàndūr!** {S} (lit. Let your cop fuck you!) *col* ***Obs*** used to emphasize one's point, Fuck!

• **Jèbō te pâpa!** {S} (lit. Let the pope fuck you!) *col* ***Obs*** used to emphasize one's point, Fuck!

• **Jèbō te pàrip!** {S} (lit. Let your horse fuck you!) *col* ***Obs*** used to emphasize one's point, Fuck!

• **Jèbō te pȁs!** {S} (lit. Let a dog fuck you!) *col* ***Obs*** used to emphasize one's point, Fuck!

• **Jèbō te pátak!** {S} (lit. Let a duck fuck you!) *col* ***Obs*** used to emphasize one's point, Fuck!

• **Jèbō te rázrednī starȅšina!** {S} (lit. May your

classroom teacher screw you!) SerE *col* ***Obs-Fac*** used as a weak curse, Screw you!

• **Jèbō te rîmskī pâpa!** {S} (lit. Let the Roman pope fuck you!) *col* ***Obs*** used to emphasize one's point, Fuck!

• **Jèbō te sênj!** {S} (lit. May a millstone lever fuck you!) *dia* ***Obs*** used to emphasize one's point, Fuck!

• **Jèbō te slàvuj što dâvī ôvce!** {S} (lit. Let the nightingale who strangles sheep fuck you!) *dia* ***Obs*** used to emphasize one's point, Fuck!

• **Jèbō te Slóbo!** {S} (lit. Let Slobo *Milošević, a prominent Serbian politician in the 1990s* fuck you!) *col* ***Off*** used as a moderate curse to a Serb, Fuck you!

• **Jèbō te Šèšelj!** {S} (lit. Let Šešelj *a prominent Serbian politician in the 1990s* fuck you!) *col* ***Off*** used as a moderate curse to a Serb, Fuck you!

• **Jèbō te šȉnter!** {S} (lit. Let the dog-catcher fuck you!) *col* ***Obs*** used to emphasize one's point, Fuck!

• **Jèbō te tȁta!** {S} (lit. Let your father fuck you!) *col* ***Obs*** used to emphasize one's point, Fuck!

• **Jèbō te trȁktor!** {S} (lit. May a tractor screw you!) *col* ***Fac-Obs*** used as a weak curse, Screw it!

• **Jèbō te vlàdika!** {S} (lit. May a bishop screw you!) *col* ***Obs*** used as a weak curse, Screw it!

• **Jèbō te Vûk!** {S} (lit. Let Vuk *Drašković, a prominent Serbian politician in the 1990s* fuck you!) *col* ***Off*** used as a moderate curse to a Serb, Fuck you!

• **Jèbō te zêc što vúče kȍla!** {S} (lit. May a rabbit who pulls a cart screw you!) *dia* ***Obs*** used as a weak curse, Screw it!

• **Jèbō te žȅno!** {S} (lit. Let me fuck you, woman!) *col* ***Obs*** used as a moderate curse, Fuck you!

• **Jèbō ti dlȁke svòjē bákē!** {S} (lit. Fuck your grandmother's hairs!) *col* ***Obs*** used as a moderate curse, Fuck you!

• **Jèbō ti jâ mȁtēr!** {S} (lit. Let me fuck your mother!) *col* ***Off*** used as a very strong curse, Fuck you!

• **Jèbō ti kȍnj mȁtēr!** {S} (lit. Let a horse fuck your mother!) *col* ***Off*** used as a very strong curse, Fuck you!

• **Jèbō ti mâjku nȍsom u dȕpe!** {S} (lit. May you fuck your mother with your nose in her ass!) *col* ***Off*** used as a very strong curse, Fuck you!

• **Jèbō tî mȁtēr!** {S} (lit. May you fuck your mother!) *col* ***Off*** used as a very strong curse, Fuck you!

• **Jèbō ti ôn mȁtēr i tî njȅmu!** {S} (lit. Let him fuck your mother and you fuck his!) *col* ***Off*** used as a very strong curse, Fuck you!

• **Jèbō ti pȁs mȁtēr!** {S} (lit. Let a dog fuck your mother!) *col* ***Off*** used as a very strong curse, Fuck you!

• **Jèbō tî sȅbi mâjku!** {S} (lit. May you fuck your own mother!) *col* ***Off*** used as a very strong curse, Fuck you!

• **Jèbō tî svòju mȁtēr!** {S} (lit. May you fuck your mother!) *col* ***Off*** used as a very strong curse, Fuck you!

• **Jèbō ti svòju sèstru!** {S} (lit. May you fuck your sister!) *col* ***Off*** used as a very strong curse, Fuck you!

• **Jèbō ti svôme ȍcu i ȍtac tȅbi mâjku a jâ tȅbi i tvôm ȍcu mâjku!** {S} (lit. May you fuck your father's mother and your father fuck your mother and I fuck the mother of both of you!) *col* ***Off*** used as a very strong curse, Fuck you!

• **Jèbō tî tô!** {S} (lit. You fuck it!) *col* ***Obs*** used to emphasize one's point, Fuck!

• **Jèbū i razvàljujū!** {S} (lit. They fuck and destroy!) *col* ***Obs*** used to refer to the danger coming from a group of third persons

• **Kȍ[PRON:ACC] jèbē!** {LSF} (lit. Who fucks [PRON:ACC]!) *col* ***Off*** used to refer to indifference toward: *Ko ga jebe! Who gives a shit about him!*

• **Kȍ[PRON:DAT] jèbē mȁtēr!** {LSF} (lit. Who fucks [PPRON] mother!) *col* ***Off*** used to refer to indifference toward

• **Kȍ te jèbē!** {S} (lit. Who is fucking you?) *col* ***Off*** used to express disrespect, Fuck you!

• **Ma jèbi ga čȍveče!** {S} (lit. Fuck it, man!) *col* ***Obs*** used to express disrespect or dissatisfaction, Fuck it!

• **Ma jèbō te bôg!** {S} (lit. I hope God fucks you!) *col* ***Off*** used as a moderate curse, Fuck you!

• **Ne jèbē me tô!** {S} (lit. It doesn't fuck me!) *sl* ***Obs*** used to refer to one's indifference, I don't give a fuck!

• **Nè jèbēm nȉkogā!** {S} (lit. I don't fuck anybody!) *sl* ***Obs*** used to refer to one's indifference, I don't give a fuck!

• **Ne jèbēm[PRON:ACC] ni dvâ pȍstō!** {LSF} (lit. I don't fuck [PRON:ACC] not even two percent.!) *sl* ***Obs*** used to refer to one's indifference toward: *Ne jebem ga ni dva posto! I don't give a shit about him!*

• **Ne jèbēm[PRON:ACC] uȍpšte!** {LSF} (lit. I don't fuck [PRON:ACC] at all!) *sl* ***Obs*** used to refer to one's indifference toward: *Ne jebem te uopšte! I don't give a shit about you!*

• **Nè jèbēm[PRON:ACC] za sûhū šljȉvu!** {LSF} (lit. I don't fuck [PRON:ACC] for a prune!) *sl* ***Obs*** used to express indifference toward: *Ne jebem te ni za suhu šljivu. I don't give a fuck about you.*

• **Ne jèbēmo žȉvū sȉlu!** {S} (lit. We don't fuck live force!) *sl-mil* ***Obs*** used to refer to one's indifference, Fuck it!

• **Ne jèbi!** {S} (lit. Don't you fuck!) *sl* ***Obs*** used as a threat, Don't fuck with me!

• **Nè te jèbēm!** {S} (lit. I don't fuck you!) SSer *dia* ***Obs*** used to express indifference toward one's interlocutor, I don't give a fuck about you!

• **Nȅk si jèbē mȁtēr!** {S} (lit. Let him/her fuck his/her mother!) *col* ***Obs*** used as a strong curse, Fuck him/her!

• [NUMBER] [PRON:DAT] mâjki jèbēm! {LSF} (lit. I fuck [PPRON] [NUMBER] mothers!) *col* ***Off*** used as a strong curse, Fuck you!

• Pa da ga jèbēm màlo! {S} (lit. So that I fuck it a little!) *col* ***Obs*** used as a moderate curse, Fuck him!

• Ti jèbēm màtēr bezòbraznū! {S} (lit. I fuck your shameless mother!) *col-dia* ***Off*** used as a strong curse, Fuck you!

jèbati se {jèbēm, jebédu imperf. intr.} **a.** Vojv *sl-sex* ***Obs*** engage in sexual intercourse with <Slav> **b.** Vojv *sl* ***Der-Obs*** have problems with: *jebati se s pokvarenim kolima have problems with a broken-down car* <Slav[*1]>

jebávānje {a neut.} **a.** *sl-sex* ***Obs*** sexual intercourse <Slav> **b.i.** *sl* ***Obs*** destroying: *jebavanje plana destroying a plan* <Slav[*1]> **ii.** *sl* ***Obs*** cheating, swindling: *jebavanje staraca bamboozling one's parents* <Slav[*1]> **iii.** *sl-fea* ***Obs*** tedious job <Slav[*1]> **iv.** *sl* ***Obs*** torturing <Slav[*1]>

jebávati {jèbāvām, jebávajū imperf.} **a.** *sl-sex* ***Obs*** engage in sexual intercourse with (of a male) <Slav> **b.i.** *sl* ***Obs*** cheat, swindle <Slav[*1]> **ii.** *sl* ***Obs*** torture <Slav[*1]>

• Jebáji ga! {S} *col-dia* ***Obs*** used to express dissatisfaction, Fuck it!

• Jebáji [NOUN:ACC]! {LSF} (lit. Fuck [NOUN: ACC]!) *col-dia* ***Obs*** used to express disrespect or dissatisfaction, Fuck it!: *Jebaji Halila, ko ga jebe! Fuck Halil, who gives a shit about him!*

• jebávati ȁle {VP} (lit. fuck monsters) *sl* ***Obs*** spend one's time in useless activities, idle, do fucking nothing

• jebávati màtēr {VP} (lit. fuck someone's mother) **a.** *col* ***Obs*** tease, make fun of **b.** ***Obs*** make trouble for somebody: *Taj balavac mi je jebavo mater. That punk made me some troubles.*

• Málko me jèbāvāš! {S} (lit. You are fucking me over a little!) *col* ***Obs*** used to express disbelief, Don't give me that shit!

• Ne jèbāvā nȉkoga! {S} (lit. He doesn't fuck anybody!) *dia* ***Obs*** used to refer to indifference of a third party, He doesn't give a fuck!

• Nè te jèbāvām! {S} (lit. I don't fuck you!) SSer *dia* ***Obs*** used to express indifference toward one's interlocutor, I don't give a fuck about you!

jebécnuti {jèbēcnēm, nū perf.} *sl* curse <Slav>

jèbēćī {ā, ē adj.} *sl-sex* ***Obs*** engaging in sexual intercourse with <Slav>

jebèćina {ē fem.} *sl-sex* ***Obs*** sexual intercourse <Slav>

jebéknuti {jèbēknēm, nū perf.} *sl* curse <Slav>

jèben {a, o} **a.** *sl-sex* ***Obs*** engaged in sexual intercourse with <Slav> **b.i.** *sl-fea* ***Obs*** difficult: *jeben problem difficult problem* <Slav[*1]> **ii.** *sl-fea* ***Obs*** undependable, unreliable: *jeben partner undependable partner* <Slav[*1]>

jebengùzīle {ē masc.} (lit. fuck-ass) Mont *sl-sex* ***Fac-Obs*** male homosexual, gay <Slav[*1]>

jèbenī {ā, ō adj.} *sl-sex* ***Obs*** engaged in sexual intercourse with <Slav>

jebèno {adv.} (lit. fucked) *sl-fea* very difficult, screwed up: *Biće jebeno pobijediti njihovu ekipu. It'll be a bitch to beat their team.* <Slav>

jebenpízda {ē fem.} (lit. fuck-cunt) *sl-fea* evil female, bitch <Slav[*1]>

jèbeš {a (acc. = gen.) masc.} (lit. fucker) *sl-sex* ***Obs*** male sexual partner (of a female) <Slav>

jèbeša {ē masc.} (lit. fucker) *sl-sex* ***Obs*** male sexual partner (of a female) <Slav>

jèbeška {ē fem.; Dat jèbeški} (lit. fucker) *sl-sex* ***Obs*** loose woman, slut <Slav>

jèbeško {a masc.} /jebèško/ (lit. fucker) *sl-sex* ***Obs*** male sexual partner (of a female) <Slav>

Jebèvīć {bevíća masc.} (lit. Mount Fuck) *sl* ***Fac*** name for Mount Trebević (Bosnia) <Slav[illegible]>

jèbež {a masc.} *sl-sex* ***Obs*** sexual intercourse <Slav>

jebèžljiv {a, o adj.} **a.** *sl-sex* ***Obs*** easy to stimulate sexually <Slav> **b.** *sl-fea* ***Obs*** provocative <Slav[*1]>

jèbica {ē fem.} **a.** *sl-sex* ***Obs*** female sexual partner (of a male) <Slav> **b.** *sl-sex* ***Obs*** loose woman, slut <Slav[*1]>

jèbīč {jebíča (acc. = gen.) masc.} *sl-sex* ***Obs*** male sexual partner from Zagreb, Croatia <Slav>

jebìčina {ē fem.} *sl-sex* ***Obs*** sexual intercourse <Slav>

jèbiga {part.} (lit. fuck it) *col* intensifying particle <Slav>

jèbigūz {a (acc. = gen.) masc.} (lit. ass-fucker) **a.** *sl-sex* ***Obs*** male sexual partner (of a female) <Slav> **b.i.** *sl-sex* ***Fac-Obs*** male homosexual, gay <Slav[*1]> **ii.** *sl-fea* ***Der-Obs*** worthless or mean male, son of a bitch <Slav[*1]>

jèbiguza {ē fem.} (lit. ass-fucker) *sl-fea* evil female, bitch <Slav[*1]>

jebigùzica {ē fem.} (lit. ass-fucker) *sl-sex* ***Obs*** female sexual partner (of a male) <Slav>

jebigùzīle {a (acc. = gen.) masc.} (lit. ass-fucker) **a.** *sl-sex* ***Fac-Obs*** male homosexual, gay <Slav[*1]> **b.** *sl-fea* ***Der-Obs*** miser, tightwad, skinflint <Slav[*2]>

jebigûzović {a (acc. = gen.) masc.} (lit. ass-fucker) **1** *sl-fea* member of a disrespected family <Slav[*1]> 2 lover (male) <Slav[*1]>

jebìkānje {a neut.} **a.** *sl-sex* ***Obs*** sexual intercourse <Slav> **b.** *sl* ***Obs*** cursing <Slav[*1]>

jebìkati {ām, ajū imperf.} **a.** *sl-sex* ***Obs*** engage in sexual intercourse with (of a male) <Slav> **b.** *sl* ***Obs*** curse <Slav[*1]>

jebipízda {ē fem.} (lit. fuck-cunt) *sl-fea* evil female, bitch <Slav[*1]>

Jȅbisava {ē fem.} (lit. Fuckette) *sl* ***Fac-Obs*** Milosava (a woman's name) <Slav✍>

Jèbite si džȁm! {S} (lit. Fuck your soul!) *dia* ***Off*** used as a moderate curse, Fuck you! ☞ **jebati**

jébiti {bīm, bē imperf.} *sl-sex* ***Obs*** engage in sexual intercourse with (of a male) <Slav>

jèbivetar {tra (acc. = gen.) masc.} (lit. fuck-wind) **1** *sl-fea* ***Der-Obs*** worthless or despicable person <Slav[*1]> 2 *sl-fea* ***Der-Obs*** irresponsible person <Slav[*1]> 3 *sl-fea* ***Der-Obs*** loafer, idler <Slav[*1]>

jèbivjetar {tra masc.} (lit. fuck-wind) **1** *sl-fea* ***Der-Obs*** worthless or despicable person <Slav[*1]> 2 *sl-fea* ***Der-Obs*** irresponsible person <Slav[*1]> 3 *sl-fea* ***Der-Obs*** loafer, idler <Slav[*1]>

jȅbivljetar {tra masc.} (lit. fuck-wind) *dia* ***Der-Obs*** worthless or despicable person <Slav[*1]>

jȅbna {ē fem.} (lit. fucker) *sl-sex* ***Obs*** loose woman, slut <Slav[*1]>

jébo {a (acc. = gen.) masc.} (lit. fucker) *sl-fea* ***Der-OBs*** worthless or despicable person <Slav[*1]>

jèbōjka {ē fem.; Dat jèbōjki} (lit. fucker) *sl-sex* ***Obs*** loose woman, slut <Slav[*1]>

jébonja {ē masc.} (lit. fucker) *sl-fea* worthless or despicable person, bum <Slav[*1]>

jȅborēd {a masc.} (lit. fuckenda *jebati 'fuck' X raspored 'agenda'*) *sl* ***Fac-Obs*** agenda <Slav[*1]>

jȅbote {excl.} (lit. fuck you) *sl* used to express surprise, wow <Slav[*1]>

jèbovina {ē fem.} *sl-sex* ***Obs*** sperm <Slav>

jȅbozōv [1] {excl.} (lit. fuck-call) *sl* ladies choice (i.e. of their partner at a dance) <Slav[*1]>

jȅbozōv [2] {a masc.} (lit. fuck-call) **a.** *sl-sex* ***Obs*** proposition (for sexual intercourse) <Slav[*1]> **b.i.** *sl-mil* ***Fac-Obs*** telegram to a soldier <Slav[*2]> **ii.** *sl-drink* ***Obs*** name of a cafe in Zagreb, Croatia <Slav[*2]>

jȅbozōvan {vna, vno adj.} (lit. fuck-calling) **a.** *sl-sex* ***Obs*** attractive, hot <Slav[*1]> **b.** *sl-fea* ***Obs*** sexually provocative <Slav[*2]>

Jèbū i razvàljujū! {S} (lit. They fuck and destroy!) *col* ***Obs*** used to refer to the danger coming from a group of third persons ☞ **jebati**

jebùcānje {a neut.} *sl-sex* ***Obs*** sexual intercourse <Slav>

jebùcati {ām, ajū imperf.} *sl-sex* ***Obs*** engage in sexual intercourse with (of a male) <Slav>

jebùcati se {ām, ajū imperf. intr.} *sl-sex* ***Obs*** engage in sexual intercourse with <Slav>

jebùckati {ām, ajū imperf.} **a.** *sl-sex* ***Obs*** engage in sexual intercourse with (of a male) <Slav[*1]> **b.** *sl* ***Obs*** trick, cheat, swindle <Slav[*1]>

jȅbūd {a (acc. = gen.) masc.} *sl-sex* ***Fac-Obs*** would-be (desiring) male sexual partner <Slav>

jèbulja {ē fem.} **a.** *sl-sex* ***Obs*** loose woman, slut <Slav[*1]> **b.** *sl-sex* ***Obs*** loose woman who does not enjoy sexual intercourse <Slav[*2]>

jȅcāj {a masc.} *col* sob, weeping <Slav>

jȅcānje {a neut.} **a.** *col* crying, weeping <Slav> **b.** *sl* funeral <Slav[*1]>

jȅcati {ām, ajū imperf.} *col* cry, shed tears, weep <Slav>

jȅcavica {ē fem.} *sl* crying, weeping <Slav⁘>

jȅcavo {adv.} *col* crying, weeping <Slav>

jéčānje {a neut.} *col* moaning in pain <Slav>

jéčati {čīm, čē imperf.} *col* moan in pain <Slav>

jéčiti {čīm, čē imperf.} *col* moan in pain <Slav>

jèdan {jèna, jèno adj.} [std. = jedan, jedna, jedno] **a.** BosM *col* one (instead of standard jedan, jedna, jedno) <Slav> **b.** *col* a (instead of standard jedan, jedna, jedno) <Slav[*1]>

• **jèdan kroz jèdan** {NumP} (lit. one by one) *col* surely, certainly

jȅdan kròmpīr dvâ krompíra {NP} (lit. one potato two potatoes) *sl-sstu* ***Fac*** math course ☞ **krompir**

jȅdannēs {num.} [std. = jedanaest] BosM *col* eleven <Slav✍>

jedàred {adv.} *col-dia* once <Slav>

Jȅdē gôvna! {S} (lit. He eats shit!) *col* ***Obs*** used as a moderate curse, He is full of shit! ☞ **jesti**

Jȅdē gôvna kao Gȓk hȁjvār! {S} (lit. He eats shit like a Greek eats his relish!) *dia* ***Obs*** used as a moderate curse, He is really full of shit! ☞ **jesti**

Jèdē gôvna kao pìjan rȍtkvu! {S} (lit. He eats shit like a drunk eats radish!) *dia* ***Obs*** used as a moderate curse, He is really full of shit! ☞ **jesti**

Jȅdi gôvna! {S} (lit. Eat shit!) *col* ***Off*** used as a strong curse, Eat shit, man! ☞ **jesti**

Jèdi gôvna budàlo jèdna! {S} (lit. Eat shit you fool!) *col* ***Off*** used as a strong curse, Eat shit, you dumb-ass! ☞ **jesti**

Jèdi gôvna dèbela gôvna smr̀dljivā budàlo pȕ pȕ! {S} (lit. Eat shit, fat shit you stinking fool, phew!) *col* ***Off*** used as a strong curse, Eat shit, you dumb-ass! ☞ **jesti**

Jèdi gôvna i tvòja mâjka i òtac i svȉ! {S} (lit. Eat shit and your mother and your father and all!) *col* ***Off*** used as a strong curse, Your parents can eat shit, too! ☞ **jesti**

Jȅdi góvno! {S} (lit. Eat shit!) *col* ***Off*** used as a strong curse, Eat shit, man! ☞ **jesti**

Jȅdi kȕrac! {S} (lit. Eat cock!) *col* ***Off*** used as a strong curse, Blow me! ☞ **jesti**

jéditi se {dīm, dē imperf. intr.} *dia-col* be angry <**Slav**>

jèdnōč {adv.} *col* once <**Slav**✍>

jednòrupić {a (acc. = gen.) masc.} (lit. one-hole-dude) *sl-sex* ***Fac*** monogamous male <**Slav**[*1]>

jeftinòća {ē fem.} *col* low prices <**Slav**>

jègulja {ē fem.} (lit. eel) **1** *sl-sex* ***Obs*** penis, dick, prick <**Slav**[*1]> **2** *sl-drugs* narcotic drug, dope <**Slav**[*1]> **3** *sl-sex* prostitute, hooker <**Slav**[*1]>

jegùljāš {jeguljáša (acc. = gen.) masc.} (lit. eel seller) *sl-drugs* drug dealer, pusher <**Slav**⁘[*1]>

jêk {a +ov (ext. pl) masc.; Nom Pl jékovi} **a.** *col* the sound made by something moving abruptly, bang <**Slav**> **b.** *col* scream in pain, fear, or outrage <**Slav**[*1]>

jékati {jêkām, jékajū imperf.} *col* moan in pain <**Slav**>

jéknuti {jêknēm, nū perf.} *col* moan in pain <**Slav**>

jȅkser {a masc.} [std. = ekser] *dia* nail (fastening device) <**NE**✍>

jèktānje {a neut.} *col* moaning in pain <**Slav**>

jȅktati {jȅkćēm, kćū imperf.} *col* scream in pain, fear, or outrage <**Slav**>

jȅktavo {adv.} *col* screaming in pain, fear, or outrage <**Slav**>

jȅkteti {tīm, tē imperf.} SerE *col* scream in pain, fear, or outrage <**Slav**>

jel {part.} [std. = je li, jer] **1** *col* question tag: *Jel došo Suljo? Did Suljo arrive?* <**Slav**> **2** *col* because <**Slav**✍> **3** *col* if <**Slav**✍> **4** really, indeed

Jȅlac {jélca masc.} *sl* name for Jelačićev square (Zagreb, Croatia) <**SlavO**✍>

Jȅlčić {a masc.} *sl* name for Jelačićev square (Zagreb, Croatia) <**SlavO**✍>

jèlda {part.} *col* question tag: *On je tu, jelda? He is here, right?* <**Slav**>

jèldē {part.} /jèlde/ *col* question tag: *To je ona, jelde? That's her, right?* <**Slav**>

jèlēn *See the following*

- **bijèlī jèlēn** {NP} (lit. white deer) *sl-sex* ***Fac*** male homosexual

jȅlka {ē fem.} (lit. Christmas tree) *sl-sstu* failing grade <**Slav**[*1]>

jèlte {part.} *col* question tag <**Slav**>

jèmatva {ē fem.} Med *dia* harvest <**Slav**[*1]>

jèmēnje {a fem. pl.} *sl-sports* soccer shoes <**NEO**[*1]>

jènkrat {adv.} Kajk *dia* once <**Slav**>

jȅpkati {ām, ajū perf.} *sl-sex* ***Obs*** engage in sexual intercourse with (of a male) <**Slav**>

jèpstvo {a neut.} *sl-sex* ***Obs*** sexual intercourse <**Slav**[*1]>

jȅrbo {c.} *col-dia* because <**Slav**>

jerèbica {ē fem.} [std. = jarebica] *col-dia* partridge <**Slav**✍>

Jerèmija {ē masc.} (lit. Jeremiah) *sl-fea* elderly male <**HebO**[*1]>

jȅrfra {ē masc.; perm} /jèrfra jerafra (acc. = gen.) masc./ [std. = frajer] **a.** *sl* male, guy <**Ger**✍> **b.** *sl* boyfriend <**Ger**✍[*1]>

jèričiti {čīm, čē imperf. intr.} *sl* mock, ridicule

jèričiti se {čīm, čē imperf. intr.} *sl* mock, ridicule

jȅs {part.} *col* used as a strong affirmative response, of course, yeah, you bet <**Slav**>

jȅsenovānje {a neut.} *sl* ***Fac*** fall vacation <**Slav**⁘>

jȅsenovati {nujēm, nujū imperf.} *sl* ***Fac*** vacation in the fall <**Slav**[*1]>

Jȅsi dȍbar? {VP} (lit. Are you good?) *col* used as an informal greeting, How are you doing? ☞ **biti**

Jèsi l ìšaō kȁd bez ȍka? {S} (lit. Have you ever run without your eye?) *sl* ***Off*** used as a threat of physical violence ☞ **ići**

Jèsi l nȅkad tȑčaō za ȕšima? {S} (lit. Have you ever run after your ears?) *sl* ***Off*** used as a threat of physical violence ☞ **trčati**

Jèsi za žȉvot? {S} (lit. Are you for life?) *sl* ***Obs*** used to propose sexual intercourse ☞ **život**

jȅst {part.} /jȅste/ *col* used as a strong affirmative response, of course, yeah, you bet <**Slav**>

jȅsti *See the following*

• **Jèdē gôvna!** {S} (lit. He eats shit!) *col* ***Obs*** used as a moderate curse, He is full of shit!

• **Jèdē gôvna kao Gȑk hȁjvār!** {S} (lit. He eats shit like a Greek eats his relish.) *dia* ***Obs*** used as a moderate curse, He is really full of shit!

• **Jèdē gôvna kao pìjan rȍtkvu!** {S} (lit. He eats shit like a drunk eats radish.) *dia* ***Obs*** used as a moderate curse, He is really full of shit!

• **Jèdi gôvna!** {S} (lit. Eat shit!) *col* ***Off*** used as a strong curse, Eat shit, man!

• **Jèdi gôvna budàlo jèdna!** {S} (lit. Eat shit you fool!) *col* ***Off*** used as a strong curse, Eat shit you dumb-ass!

• **Jèdi gôvna dèbela gôvna smȑdljivā budàlo pȕ pȕ!** {S} (lit. Eat shit, fat shit you stinking fool, phew!) *col* ***Off*** used as a strong curse, Eat shit you dumb-ass!

• **Jèdi gôvna i tvòja mâjka i òtac i svȉ!** {S} (lit. Eat shit and your mother and your father and all!) *col* ***Off*** used as a strong curse, Your parents can eat shit, too!

• **Jèdi góvno!** {S} (lit. Eat shit!) *col* ***Off*** used as a strong curse, Eat shit, man!

• **Jèdi kȕrac!** {S} (lit. Eat cock!) *col* ***Off*** used as a strong curse, Blow me!

• **jȅsti džȉgericu** {VP} (lit. eat liver) *col* get on one's nerves

• **jȅsti frȁjeru iz kríla** {VP} (lit. eat from a dude's lap) *sl-sex* ***Fac-Obs*** engage in fellatio

• **jȅsti gôvna** {VP} (lit. eat shit) *col* ***Obs*** talk persistently and meaninglessly, have diarrhea of the mouth

• **jȅsti šèćer preko jàstuka** {VP} (lit. eat sugar over a pillow) *sl-sex* ***Fac-Obs*** engage in anal sexual intercourse

• **Ma jȅdi gôvna brȅ!** {S} (lit. But, eat shit, fella!) SerE *col* ***Off*** used as a strong curse, Eat shit, man!

• **Nè jedi gôvna!** {S} (lit. Don't you eat shit!) **a.** *col* ***Off*** used as a strong curse, Fuck you! **b.** *col* ***Off*** used to silence one's interlocutor, Shut up! **c.** *col* ***Off*** used to express disbelief, Don't give me that shit!

• **Nek jȅdē gôvna!** {S} (lit. Let him/her eat shit!) *col* ***Off*** used as a strong curse, He's full of shit!

• **Nek jȅdū tvôj òtac i mâjka gôvna!** {S} (lit. Let your father and mother eat shit!) *col* ***Off*** used as a strong curse, Your parents can eat shit, too!

jȅstīvo {a neut.} *col-dia* food <**Slav**>

Jéša {ē masc.} *sl-fea* ***Off*** Jew <**Gre**>

jȅtīm {jetíma (acc. = gen.) masc.} (lit. the baa one) *col* ***Der*** stupid or mentally deficient person

jevtinòća {ē fem.} *col* cheap prices <**Slav**>

jêz {a +ov (ext. pl) masc.; Nom Pl jézovi} **a.** *col* horror, terror <**Slav**[*1]> **b.** *sl* love <**Slav**[*2]>

jéza {ē fem.} **a.** *col* horror, terror <**Slav**[*1]> **b.** *sl* love <**Slav**[*2]>

Jèzdimīr {a (acc. = gen.) masc.} (lit. Jezdimir 'man's name' X jezditi 'to wander around') *sl-fea* ***Fac*** lonely male <**SlavO**[*1]>

jézditi {dīm, dē imperf.} *sl-auto* cruise (in a car, bus, etc.) <**Slav**[*1]>

jezèrača {ē fem.} Kajk *dia-col* thousand dinars; a thousand-dinar bill, a grand <**Hun**>

jȅzero {a neut.} Kajk *dia-col* thousand <**Hun**>

jèziš {adj.} *sl* horrible, terrible <**Slav**[*1]>

jèziv {a, o adj.} (lit. horrible) **1a.** *sl-fea* strange, weird: *jeziv frajer weird guy* <**Slav**[*1]> **b.** *sl-fea* genius, extraordinary: *jeziv učenik extraordinary student* <**Slav**[*2]> **c.** *sl-fea* excellent, awesome: *jeziva ćera awesome home* <**Slav**[*3]> **2** very bad

jklȍp {a masc.} *sl* used for indefinite reference, anything

jô [1] {pron.} [std. = ja] Med *dia* I <**Slav**>

jô [2] {excl.} *col* used to express grief, pain, astonishment, etc. etc., ah, ouch, woe <**Slav**>

jô-jā {excl.} *col* used to command an ox to stop <**Slav**>

jȍčkapinj {a masc.; perm} /jȍčkapinj jȍčkepinj fem./ [std. = pička] **a.** *sl-sex* ***Obs*** vagina, cunt <**Slav**> **b.** *sl* ***Obs*** female, cunt <**Slav**[*1]>

jȍčkicapinj {a masc.; perm} /jočkìcapinj /jȍčkicepinj fem./ [std. = pičkica] **a.** *sl-sex* ***Obs*** vagina, cunt <**Slav**> **b.** *sl* ***Obs*** young female, girl <**Slav**[*1]> ☞ **pičkica**

jȍčnjavatunj {a masc.; perm} /jȍčnjavatunj / jȍčnjavetunj fem./ [std. = tučnjava] *sl* fight (e.g. fist fight) <**Slav**>

jȍderpenj {a masc.; perm} /jȍderpenj /jȍderapenj (acc. = gen.) masc./ [std. = peder] **a.** *sl-sex* ***Obs*** male homosexual, gay <**Gre**> **b.** *sl-sex* ***Obs*** impotent male <**Gre**[*1]>

jȍdgranj {a masc.; perm} [std. = grad] *sl* city <**Slav**>

jȍgī {īja masc.} *col* mattress <**BN**[*1]>

jȍgī-dȕšek {a masc.} *col* mattress <**BN-NE**[*1]>

jȍgī-màdrac {NP} (lit. Yogi mattress) **a.** *col* mattress **b.** *col* bed ☞ **madrac**

jògurt-revolúcija {ē fem.} *sl-polit* rebellion against communist bureaucracy in Novi Sad, Serbia, 1988 <NE-Lat[*1]>

jogùrtati {ām, ajū biasp.} (lit. yogurt) *sl-sex* ***Obs*** engage in fellatio <NE[*1]>

jȍh {excl.} *col* used to express disbelief or pain, oh <Slav>

Jòhan {a (acc. = gen.) masc.} *sl-sex* ***Obs*** penis, dick, prick <GerO[*1]>

- **Jòhan Sebȁstijān** {NP} (lit. John Sebastian) *sl-sex* ***Fac-Obs*** penis, dick, prick

jȏj {excl.} *col* used to express disbelief or pain, oh <Slav>

jȍjkati {ām, ajū imperf.} *col* keep pronouncing 'joj' to express disbelief or pain <Slav>

jȍk {part.} *col* used as a strong negative response, no way, never <NE[*1]>

- **jȍk brȅ** {PartP} **a.** **SerE** *col* used as a negative particle, no **b.** used as a strong negative particle, no way

jȍkabanj {a masc.; perm} /jȍkabanj / jokebanj fem./ [std. = baka] *sl* grandmother, grandma <Slav✍>

jókānje {a neut.} *col* pronouncing 'jo' to express pain, disbelief, surprise, etc. <Slav>

jókati {jôkām, ajū imperf.} *col* keep pronouncing 'jo' to express pain, disbelief, surprise, etc. <Slav>

jȍkavac {part.} *col* negative response, no <NE❖>

jȍker {a (acc. = gen.) masc.} **1** *sl-fea* poor male <NE✍[*1]> **2** *sl-fea* handicapped person, cripple

jȍktordonj {a (acc. = gen.) masc.; perm} /jȍktordonj / joktoradonj (acc. = gen.) masc./ [std. = doktor] *sl* doctor, doc <Lat✍>

jȏle {eta masc.} (lit. Joseph) *sl-sex* ***Obs*** penis, dick, prick <SlavO[*1]>

jȍlpaz {a (acc. = gen.) masc.} **1** *sl-fea* spoiled child, brat <NE[*1]> **2** *sl-sex* penis <NE[*1]>

jòmpekpinj {a masc.; perm} /jòmpekpinj / jompekapinj masc./ [std. = pimpek] *sl-sex* ***Obs*** penis, dick, prick <Slav✍>

jȍndžaminj {a masc.; perm} /jòndžaminj / jondžeminj fem./ [std. = mindža] *sl-sex* ***Obs*** vagina, cunt <Ita✍>

jònobarkonj {a (acc. = gen.) masc.; perm} /jònobarkonj / jonobarakonj (acc. = gen.) masc./ [std. = konobar] *sl-drink* waiter <Ita✍>

jȍpē {adv.} [std. = opet] *dia-col* again <Slav✍>

jȍpēt {adv.} [std. = opet] *dia-col* again <Slav✍>

jȍrackunj {a masc.; perm} [std. = kurac] *sl-sex* ***Obs*** penis, dick, prick <Slav✍>

jȍrastanj {jòrestanj fem.; perm} [std. = stara] **1** *sl* mother <Slav✍> **2** *sl* girlfriend <Slav✍>

jȍrbanjetonj {jòrbanjatonj neut.; perm} [std. = torbanje] *sl-sex* ***Obs*** sexual intercourse <Slav✍>

jòrgan {a masc.} (lit. quilt) **a.** *sl* ten dinars; a ten-dinar bill <NE[*1]> **b.** *sl* thousand dinars; a thousand-dinar bill, a grand <NE[*2]>

jȍrgan-planìna {ē fem.} (lit. mountain quilt) *sl* thick quilt <NE-Slav[*1]>

jȍristanj {a (acc. = gen.) masc.; perm} [std. = stari] **1** *sl* father, dad <Slav✍> **2** *sl* friend (male) <Slav✍>

jòrnakanj {a masc.; perm} *sl* female

jòsatimunj {jòšemunj, jòšumunj imperf.; perm} [std. = musati] *sl* lie <Slav✍>

Jóso {a masc.} //ē masc./ (lit. Joseph) *sl-sex* ***Obs*** penis, dick, prick <SlavO[*1]>

jòstikranj {jodēmkranj, jodukranj imperf.; perm} [std. = krasti] *sl-crime* steal, swipe <Slav✍>

jòšatronj {a masc.; perm} [std. = šatro] *sl* slang <NE✍>

jȍšte {adv.} *col* still, without cessation: *On jošte radi. He is still working.* <Slav✍>

jòtaškrnj {a (acc. = gen.) masc.; perm} [std. = škrtac] *sl-fea* miser, tightwad, skinflint <Slav✍>

jòtrošanj {a masc.; perm} /jèšatronj fem./ [std. = šatro] *sl* slang <NE✍>

jȍzicagunj {a masc.; perm} //jòzicegunj fem./ [std. = guzica] *sl-sex* ***Obs*** buttocks, butt <Slav✍>

jòzičaritnunj {a masc.} *sl-music* musicians <Lat✍>

jȕ {excl.} *col* used to express surprise, fear, etc., oh <Slav>

jȕf {excl.} *col* used to express surprise, fear, etc., oh <Slav>

jȕfka {ē fem.; Dat jùfki} *col* phyllo (dough) <NE[*1]> ☞ **juvka**

Júga {ē fem.; Dat Júgi} **a.** *col* ***Fam*** Yugoslavia <Slav✍> **b.** *sl* name for Yugoslavia hotel (Belgrade, Serbia) <Slav✍[*1]>

Jȕgić {a (acc. = gen.) masc.} *col* ***Fam*** Yugoslav <Slav✍>

Jȕgić {a masc.} *col* ***Fam*** former Yugoexport company store (Zagreb, Croatia) <Slav✍>

Jugodȑp {a masc.} (lit. Yugoswipe) *sl-media* ***Fac*** name for Yugoslav Drama Theater (a theater in Belgrade, Serbia) <**Slav**✍>

jȕgonostàlgičār {a (acc. = gen.) masc.} *sl-polit* male who is emotionally attached to the former Yugoslavia, Yugo-nut <**Slav-Gre**>

jȕgonostàlgičārka {ē fem.; Dat jȕgonostàlgičārki} *sl-polit* female who is emotionally attached to the former Yugoslavia, Yugo nut <**Slav-Gre**>

jȕgonostàlgičārskī {ā, ō adj.} *sl-polit* pertaining to those who are emotionally attached to the former Yugoslavia <**Slav-Gre**>

Jȕgos {a (acc. = gen.) masc.} [std. = Jugosloven, Jugoslaven] *col* ***Fam*** Yugoslav <**Slav**✍>

jugoslòvēnskī {ōg masc.} Gast *sl* Serbo-Croatian (pertaining to the language) <**Slav**[*1]>

Jȕgošćāp {a masc.} (lit. Yugostick) *sl* ***Fac*** name for Yugoslav Drama Theater (a theater in Belgrade, Serbia) <**Slav**✍>

Jȕgović {a (acc. = gen.) masc.} [std. = Jugosloven, Jugoslaven] *col* ***Fam*** Yugoslav <**Slav**✍>

jȕgovićkī {ā, ō adj.} [std. = jugoslovenski, jugoslavenski] *col* ***Fam*** Yugoslav <**Slav**✍>

Jȕgovina {ē fem.} *col* ***Fam*** Yugoslavia <**Slav**✍>

jȕh {excl.} *col* used to express surprise, fear, etc. oh <**Slav**>

júha {ē fem.; Dat júhi} (lit. soup) **1** Cro *sl-drugs* narcotic drug, dope <**Slav**[*1]> **2** Cro *sl-auto* gasoline <**Slav**[*1]>

jȕha-hâj {excl.} *col* used to express great joy, whoopee, hurrah <**Slav**[*1]>

jȕj {excl.} *col* used to express surprise, fear, etc. oh <**Slav**>

jujúkānje {a neut.} /jùjukānje/ *col* pronouncing 'juj' to express surprise or fear <**Slav**>

jujùkati {ām, ajū imperf.} *col* keep pronouncing 'juj' to express surprise or fear <**Slav**>

jujúknuti {jùjūnēm, nū perf.} *col* pronounce 'juj' to express surprise or fear <**Slav**>

jujȕškānje {a neut.} *col* pronouncing 'juj' to express surprise or fear <**Slav**>

jujȕškati {ām, ajū imperf.} *col* ***Fam*** keep pronouncing 'juj' to express surprise or fear <**Slav**>

jùlār {julára masc.} **1** *sl-arch* golden or silver chain <**NE**[*1]> **2** *sl-arch* pocket watch <**NE**[*1]>

jûlovac {vca (acc. = gen.) masc.} *sl-polit* member of JUL (Jugoslovenska udružena levica 'United Yugoslav Left' a party in Serbia) <**Abb**⁘>

júnac {nca (acc. = gen.) masc.} (lit. calf) *sl* million <**Slav**[*1]>

junáctvo {a neut.} [std. = junaštvo] SSer *col* courageousness <**Slav**✍>

jùnfer {a masc.} /jȕnfer /a masc./ **a.** *sl-sex* ***Obs*** hymen <**Ger**[*1]> **b.** *sl-sex* ***Obs*** virgin <**Ger**[*2]> **c.** *sl-sex* ***Obs*** virginity <**Ger**[*3]>

jȕnferica {ē fem.} **1** *sl-sex* ***Obs*** virgin <**Ger**⁘[*1]> **2** *sl* ***Obs*** name of a cafe on Nikola Tesla in Zagreb, Croatia <**Ger**⁘[*1]>

jȕnferka {ē fem.; Dat jȕnferki} *sl-sex* ***Obs*** virgin <**Ger**⁘[*1]>

jùnferšaft {a masc.} *sl-sex* ***Obs*** virginity <**Ger**[*1]>

jȕnfić {a masc.} *sl-sex* ***Obs*** hymen <**Ger**✍>

jȕniōr {ē fem.} (lit. junior) *sl* teenager (male) <**Lat**[*1]>

jȕniōrka {ē fem.; Dat jȕniōrka} (lit. junior) *sl* teenager (female) <**Lat**[*1]>

jȕrcati {ām, ajū imperf.} *col* run <**Slav**>

jùrek {a (acc. = gen.) masc.} (lit. Georgie *i.e. St. George whose image appeared on the pre-WWII dinar bill*) *sl* thousand dinars; a thousand-dinar bill, a grand <**Slav**[*1]>

Jȕsos {a (acc. = gen.) masc.} (lit. JUS *i.e. Yugoslav Industrial Standard*) *sl-fea* person who wears clothing made in Yugoslavia <**Abb**⁘[*1]>

jutrènjāk {trenjáka masc.} *sl-sex* ***Obs*** early morning erection <**Slav**[*1]>

jûuuu {excl.} *col* used to express surprise, fear, etc., oh <**Slav**>

jùvka {ē fem.; Dat jùvki} *col* phyllo (dough) <**NE**[*1]> ☞ **jufka**

Kk

k.b.s.z [kəbəsəz] {part.} (Abbreviation of "kad bismo se zajebavali" 'if we were fooling around') **1** *sl* used to express uncertainty <**Abb**> **2** *sl* particle used to signal impossibility, no way <**Abb**>

ka {c.} [std. = kao] *col-dia* as <**Slav**✍>

kába {ē fem.} *col* the Kaaba (Muslim holy stone in Mecca) <NE>

kabadáhija {ē masc.} *sl-fea* troublemaker, rowdy, ruffian <NE>

kàban {a masc.} *sl* banknote

kabína {ē fem.} (lit. cabin) *sl-stu* ***Fac*** dormitory room <Fre[*1]>

kabláža {ē fem.} *sl-crafts* cables (esp. as a part of an engine) <Fre>

kabriòlet {adj.} (lit. convertible) *sl-fea* bald <Fre[*1]>

kabriòlet-cìpela {ē fem.} (lit. convertible shoe) *sl* ***Fac*** loafer (shoe) <Fre-Hun[*1]>

kabriòlet-mȁjica {ē fem.} (lit. convertible t-shirt) *sl-fea* ***Fac*** T-shirt with a very deep neck line <Fre❖[*1]>

kȁca {ē fem.} (lit. barrel) **a.** *col* wooden barrel <Slav> **b.i.** buttocks, **ii.x.** house, home **xx.** home

kàciga {ē fem.; Dat kàcigi} (lit. helmet) *sl-fea* short hair with bangs <Lat[*1]>

kȁč {adv.} *sl* how much: *Kač krompir? How much are potatoes?* <NE>

kačàmak {a masc.} *col* polenta <NE>

kačàmilka *See the following*

- **Kačàmilku ti jèbēm šȁjestū!** {S} SSer *dia* ***Off*** used as a moderate curse

kȁčara {ē fem.} *sl-drink* cottage used to distill brandy <Slav>

kȁčavac {vca (acc. = gen.) masc.} *sl-arch* potter <Slav>

kȁčiti {čīm, čē imperf.} (lit. hook, hang) *sl* understand, realize <Slav[*1]>

kȁčiti se {čīm, čē imperf. intr.} (lit. hook oneself) *sl* have a dispute <Slav>

kȁčka {ē fem.; Dat kȁčki} **1** *sl* manhunt <Slav[*1]> **2** *sl* bathtub <Slav[*1]> **3** *sl* name of a swimming pool on Daničićeva street in Zagreb, Croatia <Slav[*1]>

kȁčkati se {ām, ajū imperf. intr.} *sl* swim in shallow water <Slav[*1]>

kàd bi se zȅzali {AdvP} (lit. if we were joking) *col* used as a strong negative response, no way, never ☞ **zezati se**

kàd mèđedu gùzica zaráste {AdvP} (lit. when a bear's ass grows over) *dia* ***Obs*** never, not in a million years ☞ **međed**

kàd na vŕbi rȍdī grôžđe {AdvP} (lit. when grapes grow on a willow) *col* never, not in a million years ☞ **roditi**

kàd na vŕbi zasvŕbī {AdvP} (lit. when it starts to itch on a willow) *col* never ☞ **zasvrbeti**

kàd te lêpo mȍlīm {S} (lit. when I beg you nicely) SerE *col* used to emphasize one's request, pretty please ☞ **moliti**

kad te lêpo pîtām {S} (lit. when I ask you nicely) SerE *col* used to emphasize one's request, pretty please ☞ **pitati**

kàd te lijèpo mȍlīm {S} (lit. when I beg you nicely) *col* used to emphasize one's request, pretty please ☞ **moliti**

kad te lijèpo pîtām {S} (lit. when I ask you nicely) *col* used to emphasize one's request, pretty please ☞ **pitati**

Kàd te ràspīzdīm! {S} (lit. When I hit you in your cunt!) *col* ***Off*** used as a threat of physical violence ☞ **raspizditi**

káda {ē fem.} (lit. bathtub) Cro *sl* name of a swimming pool on Daničićeva street in Zagreb, Croatia <Slav[*1]>

kádar *See the following*

- **žútī kádar** {NP} (lit. yellow cadre *the yellow insignia of the lower-ranked military officers*) *sl-mil* NCOs, lower-ranked military officers

kàdija {ē masc.} *col* qadi (Muslim judge) <NE[*1]>

kadìkad {adv.} *col* a long time ago <Slav>

kȁdilāk {a (acc. = gen.) masc.} (lit. Cadillac) *sl-auto* ***Iro*** Wartburg (make of simple East German car) <BN[*1]>

- **bijèlī kȁdilāk** {NP} (lit. white Cadillac) *sl-drugs* phencyclidine

káditi {kâdīm, dē imperf.} **a.** *sl-fea* smoke (tobacco) <Slav[*1]> **b.** *sl* ingratiate, brownnose, kiss ass <Slav[*2]>

kadròvīk {a (acc. = gen.) masc.} *sl* ***Iro*** manager of the personnel department (e.g. in a company) <Rus>

kàduna {ē fem.} *col* prominent female <NE[*1]>

káđenje {a neut.} *sl-fea* ***Der*** ingratiate, brownnose, kiss ass <Slav[*1]>

kȁe {part.} *col* particle used to refer to the words of others: *Ona se kae popela na sam vrh. They say that she climbed all the way up.* <Slav✍>

kȁfa *See the following*

- **šlògīrānā kȁfa** {NP} (lit. apoplectic coffee) *sl-fea* coffee with cream

kȁfanskā stjuardȅsa {NP} (lit. bar's flight attendant) *sl* ***Fac*** female bathroom attendant ☞ **stjuardesa**

kafènisati {šēm, šū imperf. intr.} *col* ***Der*** engage in prolonged coffee drinking <NE>

kȁfez {a masc.} [std. = kavez] *col* cage <NE✍>

kȁfica {ē fem.} *col* ***Fam*** coffee <**NE***1>

kȁfīć {kafića masc.} *col* bar (drinking place) <**NE**❖>

kȁftor {a masc.} *sl-arch* stove

kȁhlica {ē fem.} *sl* hat <**Ger**❖>

kȁhva {ē fem.} **a.** BosM *col* coffee <**NE**> **b.** BosM *col* bar (drinking place) <**NE***1>

kahvȁna {ē fem.} BosM *col* bar (drinking place) <**NE**❖>

kahvènisati {išēm, išū biasp. intr.} BosM *col* engage in prolonged coffee drinking <**NE**❖>

kȁīć {kȁića masc.} Med *col-dia* boat <**Ita**>

kȁil {adj.} Bos *col* ready, set: *Kail sam poći. I'm ready to go.* <**NE**>

kȁiš {a masc.} /kȁiš/ **a.** *sl-crafts* belt driver <**NE***1> **b.** *sl* ten dinars; a ten-dinar bill <**NE***2>

kȁišnīk {a masc.} *sl-crafts* belt-driver cogwheel <**NE**❖>

kȁj {pron.} Kajk *dia* what (in any of its Serbo-Croatian meanings used in forms different from the standard) <**Slav**>

kája {ē fem.} *sl-drink* drink (alcohol)

kajâdo {excl.} *sl* used to silence one's interlocutor, shut up <**Gyp**>

kȁjāk *See the following*
- **kȁjāk rȉjāk** {NP} *sl-crime* bicycle cop

kȁjdo {excl.} *sl* used to silence one's interlocutor, shut up

kȁjgana *See the following*
- **Kȁjganu ti bȍžjū jèbēm!** {S} (lit. I screw your God's scrambled eggs!) *col* ***Off*** used as a weak curse, Screw you!
- **Kȁjganu ti jèbēm!** {S} (lit. I screw your scrambled eggs!) *col* ***Off*** used as a moderate curse, Screw you!
- **svêtōg Pȅtra kȁjgana** {NP} (lit. St. Peter's scrambled eggs) *sl-fea* expensive

kâjla {ē masc.} **1a.** *sl* trick, joke <**Ger***1> **b.** *sl-fea* good move: *Napravio je kajlu i zabio gol He made a good move and scored a goal.* <**Ger***2> **2a.** *sl* female <**Ger***1> **b.** *sl-fea* clumsy male, klutz <**Ger***2> **c.** *sl-fea* coward, chicken <**Ger***3>
- **stârā kâjla** {NP} (lit. old wedge) *sl-mil* old soldier

kȁjma {ē fem.} *sl* ten paras; a ten-para coin *sl* ten dinars; a ten-dinar bill

kȁjmak {a masc.} (lit. milk crust) **1** *sl-sex* ***Obs*** attractive female <**NE***1> **2** *sl* ***Obs*** profit, gain <**NE***1>

kȁjmān {kajmána (acc. = gen.) masc.} *sl-fea* unattractive person <**Ind***1>

kȁjna {ē fem.} *sl* ten paras; a ten-para coin

kȁjsijevača {ē fem.} *sl-drink* apricot brandy <**NE**❖>

kȁjsijovača {ē fem.} *sl-drink* apricot brandy <**NE**❖>

kȁk {adv.} *col-dia* how <**Slav**✍>

káka [1] {ē fem.; Dat káki} *sl-sex* ***Fam*** excrement <**Ger**>

káka [2] {adj.} *sl-fea* unattractive, ugly <**Ger***1>

kakadèmik {a (acc. = gen.) masc.} (lit. kaka 'stool' X akademik 'academician') *sl-fea* ***Fac-Obs*** academician <**Gre**✍>

kȁkān {a, o adj.} *sl-fea* unattractive, ugly <**Ger***1>

kȁkānje {a neut.} /kȁkānje/ *sl-sex* ***Fam*** defecating <**Ger**>

kȁkao {aa masc.} /kakȁo/ (lit. cocoa) *sl-fea* mulatto <**Spa***1>

kȁkati {ām, ajū imperf.} /kȁkati/ *sl-sex* ***Fam*** defecate <**Ger***1>

kȁkav {kaka, kako pron.} *col* which (in all its Serbo-Croatian meanings in the form different from the standard one) <**Slav**>

kȁkī [1] {part.} *col* used as a strong negative response, no way, never <**Slav**>

kȁkī [2] {a, o adj.} *col* which (in all its Serbo-Croatian meanings in the form different from the standard one) <**Slav**>

kȁkī [3] {adv.} *col* like what <**Slav**>

Kȁkī bákrači! {S} *col* used to express strong disbelief, No way! ☞ **bakrač**

kȁkī kȕrac {NP} (lit. what kind of cock) *col* ***Obs*** used as a strong negative response, no way, never ☞ **kurac**

Kȁkī kȕrac! {S} (lit. No cock!) *col* ***Obs*** used as a strong negation, No way! ☞ **kurac**

kákiti {kīm, kē imperf.} **a.** *sl-sex* ***Fam*** defecate <**Ger***1> **b.** ***Der*** talk persistently and meaninglessly, bullshit <**Ger***2>

kȁko *See the following*
- **kȁko bi se rèklo** {S} *col* used to express hesitation, You know
- **kȁko da kâžem** {S} *col* used to express hesitation, How shall I say
- **Kȁko je?** {S} *col* used as an informal greeting, What's up!

kȁko gȍd òkrēnēš {AdvP} (lit. any way you turn it) *col* at any rate ☞ **okrenuti**

kako mu se dȉgnē {AdvP} (lit. as it lifts to him) *col* ***Obs*** whenever he wants ☞ **dignuti se**

kako vàljā i trȅbujē {AdvP} (lit. as it is valid and as it is necessary) *dia* as it should be ☞ **valjati**

kakòkati {ām, ajū perf.} *col* cackle (hens, etc.) <**Slav**>

kàktus {a (acc. = gen.) masc.} (lit. cactus) *sl* father, dad <**Gre**^{*1}>

• **šlògīrānī kàktus** {NP} (lit. apoplectic cactus) *sl-fea* unattractive male

kakvbakráči {excl.} *col* used to express disapproval, No way! <**Slav-NE**^{*1}>

Kàkve su to fóre? {S} (lit. What kind of tricks are that?) *col* used to ask for additional information, What's up? ☞ **fora**

Kàkvi su to fólovi? {S} (lit. What kind of tricks are that?) *col* used to ask for additional information, What's up? ☞ **fol**

Kàkvi su to sistémi? {S} (lit. What kind of systems are that?) *col* used to ask for additional information, What's up? ☞ **sistem**

kâl {a +ov (ext. pl) masc.; Nom Pl kálovi} *sl* loss, detriment <**Slav**>

kaləc *See the following*

• **Kaləc ti jèbēm!** {S} SSer *dia* ***Off*** used as a moderate curse, Fuck you!

kȁla {ē fem.} *sl-fea* unattractive person <**Ita**^{*1}>

kalabàster {a masc.} *sl-sex* ***Obs*** large penis

kalàbura {ē fem.} *sl* nose

kàlac {lca (acc. = gen.) masc.} *sl-arch* horse (the animal)

kalafónac {nca (acc. = gen.) masc.} *sl-fea* ***Off*** Gypsy (male) <**Slav**✍>

kalahàster {a masc.} *sl-sex* ***Obs*** penis, dick, prick <**BN**^{*1}>

kàlaj *See the following*

• **Kàlaj ti jèbēm!** {S} (lit. I fuck your tin!) *dia* ***Off*** used as a moderate curse, Fuck you!

• **Kàlaj ti jèbēm na dnȍ kotəl gdè su se várile nȍge Ȉsusove!** {S} (lit. I fuck you the tin on the bottom of the pot where Jesus's legs were cooked!) SSer *dia* ***Off*** used as a moderate curse, Fuck you!

kalàmunja {ē fem.} *sl-fea* irresponsible person <**NE**^{*1}>

kalȁštura {ē fem.} **1** *sl-fea* ***Der*** senior citizen <**NE**^{*1}> **2** *sl-sex* ***Der*** prostitute, hooker **3a.** *sl-fea* ***Off*** Gypsy (female) **b.** *sl-fea* unattractively dressed female <**NE**^{*2}> **c.** *sl-fea* unattractive female <**NE**^{*2}>

kalàuz [1] {a (acc. = gen.) masc.} (lit. slim jim *the tool*) **a.** *sl* guide <**NE**^{*1}> **b.** *sl* friend (male) <**NE**^{*2}>

kalàuz [2] {a masc.} (lit. picklock) **1** *sl-sex* ***Obs*** penis, dick, prick <**NE**^{*1}> **2** *sl* connection, tie <**NE**^{*1}>

kàlcan {a (acc. = gen.) masc.} *sl-arch* priest (usu. Orthodox Christian)

kalcànica {ē fem.} *sl-arch* priest's wife (usu. Orthodox Christian)

kaldȑmisati *See the following*

• **kaldȑmisati njȕpāvce** {VP} (lit. pave one's eaters) *sl* ***Fac*** get fillings

kȁle {eta neut.} **1** *sl-arch* priest (usu. Orthodox Christian) **2** *sl-fea* very attractive female, hot number

kalèa [1] {ē masc.} *sl-fea* stupid or mentally deficient person

kalèa [2] {adj.} *sl-fea* ***Der*** insane, nuts

kaléja {ē masc.} *sl-fea* careless person

kȁlem {a (acc. = gen.) masc.} (lit. spool) *sl-fea* stupid or mentally deficient person <**NE**^{*1}>

kalemègdānskā prȉča {NP} (lit. Kalemegdan story *Kalemegdan is a fortress in Belgrade with many of parks where lovers meet*) *col* love ☞ **priča**

kalèndār {lendára masc.} (lit. calendar) *sl* year <**Lat**^{*1}>

kalendárac {rca (acc. = gen.) masc.} *sl-mil* peer <**Lat**❖^{*1}>

kalendàrisānje {a neut.} *sl* ample time <**Lat**❖^{*1}>

kȁlica {ē fem.} *sl-arch* mare

Kalifòrnija {ē fem.} *sl-drugs* narcotic drug, dope <**EngO**^{*1}>

kalírati {kàlīrām, kalírajū biasp. intr.} **a.** *sl* die, kick the bucket <**Ita**^{*1}> **b.i.** *sl* be very tired <**Ita**^{*2}> **ii.x.** *sl* lose money <**Ita**^{*2}> **x.x.** *sl-gamble* lose money <**Ita**^{*3}>

Kàliš {a masc.} *sl* name for Kalemegdan (a park in Belgrade, Serbia) <**NE**^{*1}>

kàlnuti {nēm, nū perf. intr.} **a.** *sl* die, kick the bucket <**Ita**^{*1}> **b.** *sl* lose money <**Ita**^{*2}>

kàlocnīk {a masc.} *sl-arch* bread

kàlosnīk {a masc.} *sl-arch* bread

kȁloš {a masc.} *sl* shoe <**Fre**^{*1}>

kalóša {ē fem.} *sl* shoe <**Fre**^{*1}>

kalpíranje {a neut.} *sl* hitting from behind, sucker punch

kàlpiš {a masc.} *sl-auto* car crash

kàluša {ē fem.} **1** *sl-fea* unattractive female <**Lat**✍^{*1}> **2** *sl-fea* very attractive female, hot number <**Lat**✍^{*1}>

kàluža {ē fem.} *col* puddle <**Slav**^{*1}>

kâlj {a +ev (ext. pl) masc.; Nom Pl káljevi} *sl-arch* oats

káljac {ljca (acc. = gen.) masc.} *sl-arch* horse (the animal)

kâljanā {ē fem. (adj. decl.)} *sl* coffee <**Slav**[*1]>

kàljav {a, o adj.} *col* dirty (not clean) <**Slav**>

kàljavac {vca (acc. = gen.) masc.} *sl-arch* potter <**Slav**[*1]>

kàljče {eta neut.} *sl-arch* colt (young horse)

kaljùgān {kaljugána masc.} *sl* shoe <**Slav**❖[*1]>

kàmač {a (acc. = gen.) masc.} *sl* boy, kid

kàmara {ē fem.} **1** *dia* room <**Ita**> **2a.** *col* pile, heap **b.** *col* multitude: *Imam kamaru stvari da uradim do kraja godine. I have a whole bunch of things to do before the end of the year.*

kamàrdžija {ē masc.} *sl-gamble* passionate gambler <**Ita**❖[*1]>

kàmate *See the following*
- **slòženē kàmate** {VP} (lit. compound interest rates) *sl* lending money to somebody

kambȅk {a masc.} /kàmbek /a masc./ *col* comeback, return <**Eng**>

kàmdžija {ē fem.} *col* whip <**NE**[*1]>

kȁmēn [1] {a masc.} (lit. stone) **1** *sl* coin <**Slav**[*1]> **2** prostitute, hooker <**Slav**[*1]> **3** name for Goli island prison, Croatia, where the former communist regime detained its political enemies <**Slav**[*1]>
- **kȁmēn na kȁmenu nìje òstaō** {S} (lit. not a single stone on another stone was left) *col* used to refer to extensive destruction
- **kȁmēn u bùbregu** {NP} (lit. kidney stone) *sl-sex* ***Fac*** old prostitute
- **ko kȁmēn za kùpus** {PP} (lit. like the sauerkraut stone, i.e. the stone traditionally put on the top of the heads of cabbage in a barrel with salty water *sauerkraut is not only shredded but also made from whole heads of cabbage*) *sl-fea* ***Fac*** big in size

kȁmen [2] {adj.} *sl-fea* strong <**Slav**[*1]>

kaménac {nca (acc. = gen.) masc.} (lit. sediment) *sl-sex* ***Fac*** prostitute, hooker <**Slav**[*1]>

kamènčić {a (acc. = gen.) masc.} (lit. pebble) *sl-sex* ***Fac*** prostitute, hooker <**Slav**[*1]>

kȁmenī {ōg (acc. = gen.) masc.} (lit. the one made of stone) *sl-fea* muscular male <**Slav**[*1]>

kamenòlom {a masc.} (lit. stone quarry) **a.** *sl* suspicious place <**Slav**[*1]> **b.** *sl* gathering place <**Slav**[*1]>

kamenjáriti {mènjārīm, rē imperf.} (lit. work with stone) *sl-sex* ***Fac*** work as a prostitute <**Slav**❖[*1]>

kamènjārka {ē fem.; Dat kamènjārki} (lit. stone viper) **a.** *sl-sex* ***Fac*** prostitute, hooker <**Slav**[*1]> **b.** *sl-fea* ***Fac*** unattractively dressed female <**Slav**[*2]>

kȁmer {a (acc. = gen.) masc.} *sl-fea* stranger (male) <**Eng**[*1]>

kamìjōn {mijóna masc.} [std. = kamion] *col-dia* truck <**Fre**☞>

kamikáza {ē fem.} (lit. kamikaze) *sl-sstu* school student <**Jap**[*1]>

kamikáze {masc.} (lit. kamikaze) *sl-sstu* school student <**Jap**[*1]>

kàmila {ē fem.} (lit. camel) **1** *sl-sex* ***Fac*** loose woman <**Gre**[*1]> **2** *sl-fea* hump-backed person <**Gre**[*1]>
- **pèčenā kàmila** {NP} (lit. baked camel) *sl-sex* ***Obs*** loose woman, slut

kàmilāvka {ē fem.} **a.** *sl* cap, hat <**Gre**[*1]> **b.** *sl-crime* police cap <**Gre**[*1]>

kamìlica {ē fem.} /kamilíca/ (lit. chamomile) *sl-drugs* low-quality hashish <**Lat**[*1]>

kàmīng *See the following*
- **kàmīng dâun** {NP} (lit. coming down) *sl-drugs* getting back to normal after the effect of narcotic drugs is over

kamìōn {a masc.} (lit. truck) *sl-fea* obese female <**Fre**[*1]>

kamiònčina {ē masc.} (lit. big truck) *sl-auto* truck <**Fre**❖>

kàmisovati {ām, ajū imperf.} *sl* search <**NE**[*1]>

kȁmiti {mīm, mē imperf.} **a.** *sl* search <**Gyp**> **b.** *sl* have, possess <**Gyp**[*1]>

kampanjóla {ē masc.} *sl-mil* military jeep with enclosed cabin <**Ita**[*1]>

kȁmsovati {sujēm, sujū imperf.} **1** *sl* eat, devour <**Gyp**[*1]> **2** *sl* have, possess <**Gyp**[*1]>

kána {ē fem.} *sl-sex* ***Obs*** buttocks, butt <**NE**[*1]>

kanáđanin {a (acc. = gen.) masc.} *col* Canadian dollar <**SlavO**[*1]>

kanáfa {ē fem.} *col* rope <**Ita**☞>

kànājka {ē fem.; Dat kànājki} **a.** *sl-arch* match (lighting device) <**Gyp**> **b.** *sl-arch* matchbox <**Gyp**[*1]> **c.** *sl-arch* fire <**Gyp**[*2]>

kànāl {kanála masc.} (lit. channel) **1** *sl-sex* ***Obs*** buttocks, butt <**Lat**[*1]> **2** *sl-sstu* ***Obs*** school bathroom <**Lat**[*1]>

kanalizácija {ē fem.} *sl-music* multitrack recording <**Lat**[*1]>

kànara {ē fem.} *sl* credit, loan <**NE**[*1]>

Kanârī Hīl {NP} (lit. Canary Hill) *sl* ***Fac*** Kanarevo Brdo (a neighborhood in Belgrade, Serbia) ☞ **hil**

kanarínac {nca (acc. = gen.) masc.} (lit. canary) **1 a.** *sl-music* singer <Slav*1> **b.** *sl-music* extremely talkative person, chatterbox <Slav*2> **c.** *sl-crime* informer, canary <Slav*3> **2** *sl* contoller (on public transportation) <Slav*1>

kancelàrija {ē fem.} (lit. office) *sl-sex* ***Obs*** bathroom <Lat*1>

kȁnda {part.} [std. = kao da] *col* used to express uncertainty <Slav✍>

kàndara {ē fem.} *sl* credit, loan <Hun*1>

kandeláber {a masc.} *sl-fea* tall male <Lat*1>

kandelábr {a masc.} *sl-fea* tall male <Lat*1>

kànder {a (acc. = gen.) masc.} *sl-sex* ***Obs*** person who breaks wind, farter <Gre✣*1>

kàndija {ē fem.} *sl-sex* ***Fac*** bathroom <Gre✣*1>

kȁndilāk {a (acc. = gen.) masc.} (lit. kandisati 'stink' X Cadillac) *sl-auto* Wartburg (make of simple East German car) <BN✍>

kàndīlce *See the following*

• **Kandìlce ti jèbēm!** {S} (lit. I fuck the hanging light in front of your icon!) *dia* ***Off*** used as a moderate curse, Fuck you!

kàndilīšte {a neut.} *sl-sex* ***Fac*** bathroom <Gre*1>

kàndilo {a neut.} (lit. hanging light before an icon) **1** *sl-sex* ***Fac-Obs*** buttocks, butt <Gre*1> **2** *sl-fea* ***Fac*** male who failed in having sex with a female <Gre*1>

kandìsara {ē fem.} *sl* station, stop (bus, train, streetcar, etc.) <Gre✣*1>

kàndisati {išēm, išū imperf.} *sl* smell, stink <Gyp✣*1>

kàndišē {excl.} *sl* used to express unpleasant smelling sensation, It stinks! <Gre✣*1>

kȁnditi {dīm, dē imperf.} *sl-fea* smell, stink <Gre✣*1>

kȁndra {ē fem.} *sl* loan, credit

kanìster {a masc.} *sl* closed portable container for liquids <Gre>

kániti {kânīm, nē imperf.} (lit. intend) **a.** *sl* search, seek <Slav*1> **b.** *sl* have, possess <Slav*2>

kȁnka {ē fem.; Dat kȁnki} **a.** *sl-sex* ***Obs*** buttocks, butt <Ger✍*1> **b.** *sl-sex* ***Obs*** anus, asshole <Ger✍*2>

kànkica {ē fem.} *sl-sex* ***Obs*** buttocks, butt

kȁnst *See the following*

• **na kȁnst** {PP} *sl-crime* using tricks, by cheating: *Zgrnuti lovu na kanst. Earn money by cheating.*

kánta {ē fem.} (lit. canister, bucket) **1** *sl-sex* ***Obs*** buttocks, can, butt <Ger*1> **2** *sl-sstu* grade C <Ger*1>

kantàrisānje {a neut.} *sl-sex* ***Obs*** sexual intercourse <Ger✣*1>

kàntaros {a masc.} *sl-sex* ***Obs*** buttocks, butt <Ger✍>

kàntati {ām, ajū imperf.} **a.** *sl* sing <Ita> **b.i.** *sl-sports* defeat <Ita*1> **ii.** *sl-sex* engage in sexual intercourse with (of a male) <Ita*1> **iii.** *sl* beat up <Ita*1>

• **kàntati gòlove** {VP} *sl-sports* score numerous goals (e.g. in soccer)

kȁnte {ea masc.} *sl* train <Ger*1>

kàntica {ē fem.} (lit. little canister) *sl-sex* ***Obs*** buttocks, can, butt <Ger✣*1>

kȁnuti {nēm, nū perf.} /kànuti/ **a.** *sl* pay (bills, etc.): *Kanuo sam cenera za novine. I have paid ten dinars for the newspaper.* <Slav*1> **b.** *sl* earn (money): *Kanula mi je milja. I have earned a grand.* <Slav*2>

• **kȁnuti lóvu** {VP} (lit. drop money) *sl* pay (bills, etc.)

kânj {a masc.} *sl-sex* ***Obs*** buttocks, butt <Gyp>

kánja {ē fem.} **a.** *sl-sex* ***Obs*** buttocks, butt <Gyp✣> **b.** *sl* head

kȁnjati {ām, ajū imperf.} **1** *sl-sex* ***Obs*** defecate, shit <Gyp✣> **2** *sl* sleep, nap <Gyp>

kȁnjavica {ē fem.} **a.** *sl* underpants, underwear <Gyp✣> **b.i.** *sl* panties, briefs <Gyp*1> **ii.** *sl* shirt <Gyp*1>

kánjiti {nīm, nē imperf.} *sl-sex* ***Obs*** engage in sexual intercourse with (of a male) <Gyp✣>

kȁo {part.} *col* used to express uncertainty <Slav>

kao bôg {PP} (lit. like a God) *col* ***App*** excellent, awesome: *stančuga kao bog awesome apartment* ☞ **bog**

kao bùbreg u lòju {AdvP} (lit. like a kidney in fat) *col* excellently (usu. in reference to one's lifestyle): *živjeti kao bubreg u loju live high on the hog* ☞ **bubreg**

kao dvâ plivadònčeka {AdvP} (lit. like two Tylenols) *sl-sex* ***Fac*** round female buttocks ☞ **plivadonček**

kao grôm {PP} /kao grȍm/ (lit. like thunder) *col* ***App*** excellent, awesome ☞ **grom**

ko grôm {PP} /ko grȍm/ (lit. like thunder) *col* ***App*** excellent, awesome ☞ **grom**

kao pèčūrka {PP} (lit. like a mushroom) *sl-fea* ***Der-Fac*** unintelligent, stupid, dumb ☞ **pečurka**

kao plèvē {PP} (lit. as much as a cockle) SerE *col* in large quantities, very many ☞ **pleva**

kao pljèvē {PP} (lit. as much as cockle) *col* in large quantities, very many ☞ **pljeva**

kao sȕza čȉst {PP} (lit. clean as a tear) *col* crystal-clear ☞ **suza**

kâp {excl.} *col* the sound made by dripping, drop <Slav>

kȁpa {ē fem.} (lit. cap) *sl-sex* ***Obs*** vagina, cunt <Ger*1>

kàpac {pca masc.} (lit. dripper) **1** *sl-sex* gonorrhea, the clap <Slav*1> **2** *col* small drop, droplet <Slav*1>

kapàklija {ē fem.} *sl-sex* ***Fac-Obs*** vagina with a large clitoris <NE*1>

kàpāljka *See the following*

• **na kàpāljku** {PP} (lit. at dripper) **1** *col* little by little **2** *col* in small quantities: *davati pare na kapaljku give money in small quantities*

kȁpānje {a neut.} *col* dripping (liquids) <Slav>

kȁpati {ām, ajū imperf. intr.} **a.** *col* drip: *Lavabo kapa. The sink leaks.* **b.** cry, shed tears, weep: *kapati za momkom cry over one's boyfriend* **c.** *sl-sex* suffer from gonorrhea, have the clap **e.** get money

kàpatka {ē fem.; Dat kàpatki} *col* small drop, droplet <Slav>

kȁpav {a, o adj.} *col* dripping (liquids) <Slav>

kȁpavica {ē fem.} *col* rainwater <Slav*1>

kapávko {a masc.} (lit. dripper) **1** *sl-sex* gonorrhea, the clap <Slav*1> **2a.** *sl-fea* ***Der*** crybaby <Slav*1> **b.** *sl-fea* coward, chicken <Slav*2>

kapedô {ôā masc.} (lit. KPD: Kazneno popravni dom, 'Detention Correction Center') **a.** *sl-crime* prison <Abb> **b.** *sl-crime* juvenile detention center, juvie <Abb*1>

kapedómac {mca (acc. = gen.) masc.} *sl-crime* juvenile inmate <Abb❖>

kapèla {ē fem.} (lit. chapel) *sl-fea* unattractive female <Ita*1>

kapèlica {ē fem.} (lit. small chapel) **1** *sl-drink* ***Fac*** bar (drinking place) <Ita*1> **2** Cro *sl-polit* former Croatian Communist Party Central Committee building <Ita*1>

kapètān {petána (acc. = gen.) masc.; Voc kȁpetāne} (lit. captain) *sl-fea* stupid or mentally deficient person <Lat*1>

kȁpica {ē fem.} (lit. small cap) *sl-sex* gonorrhea, the clap <Slav*1>

kapilárac {rca (acc. = gen.) masc.} *sl-drugs* heavy drug addict, big time junkie <Lat❖*1>

kapírati {kàpīrām, kapírajū imperf.} **a.** *sl* understand, realize: *kapirati problem understand the problem* <Lat> **b.** *sl* consider, think about <Lat*1>

kàpisati {išēm, išū imperf.} *sl* understand, realize: *kapisati plan understand the plan* <Lat>

kȁpiti {pīm, pē imperf.} *sl* understand, realize <Lat>

kapitulírati {tùlīrām, tulírajū imperf.} *sl-sex* ***Fac*** agree to have sexual intercourse with (of females) <Lat>

kȁplār {a (acc. = gen.) masc.} *sl-mil* corporal <Ita>

kȁplja {ē fem.} *col* drop (of liquid) <Slav>

kàpljati {kȃpljēm, ljū imperf.} (lit. drip, dribble) *col* come in small quantities but steadily (e.g. income) <Slav*1>

kȁpljavac {ljāvca (acc. = gen.) masc.} *sl* raincoat <Slav*1>

kapljèvit {a, o adj.} *col* dripping (liquids) <Slav>

kapljìcati {ām, ajū imperf.} *col* drip <Slav>

kàpljiv {a, o adj.} *col* dripping (liquids) <Slav>

kȁpnuti {nēm, nū perf. intr.} **1** *sl* die, kick the bucket <Slav*1> **2** *sl* earn (money) <Slav*1>

kâpo {oa masc.} **a.** *sl-crime* ring leader (of thieves) <Ita> **b.** *sl-mil* corporal <Ita*1>

kàpsati {ām, ajū biasp. intr.} /kàpsati /pšem, pšu perf. intr/ *sl* die, kick the bucket <Lat❖*1>

kapsóla {ē fem.} [std. = kapsula] *col* capsule (lunar, medicine, etc.) <Lat✍>

kȁpula {ē fem.} *dia-col* onions <Ita>

kapùtār {putára (acc. = gen.) masc.; Voc kȁputāru} *sl-fea* very important or influential person, big shot <Slav❖*1>

kaputírati {pùtīrām, putíajū biasp. intr.} *sl* ***Fac*** die, kick the bucket <Ger❖*1>

kaputȉška {ē fem.; Dat kaputȉški} /kaputȉška/ [std. = kaput] *sl* overcoat <Slav✍>

kâr [1] {a (acc. = gen.) +ev (ext. pl) masc.; Nom Pl kárevi} **a.** *sl-fea* ***Off*** Gypsy (male) <Gyp✍*1> **b.** *sl-fea* ***Der*** stupid or mentally deficient <Gyp✍*2>

kâr [2] {a +ev (ext. pl) masc.; Nom Pl kárevi} **1** *sl-sex* ***Obs*** penis, dick, prick <Gyp> **2** *sl-auto* car, wheels <Eng>

• **kâr od óvcē** {NP} (lit. sheep's prick) **a.** *sl* ***Obs*** nothing at all **b.** *sl-fea* ***Obs*** worthless object, junk **c.** *sl-fea* ***Obs*** useless object or device

• **Môj kâr!** {S} (lit. My prick!) *col* ***Obs*** used to express disappointment, Shit!

kâr-bùnār {kâr-bunára masc.} (lit. prick-well) *sl-sex* ***Fac-Obs*** vagina <Gyp-Slav*1>

kára {ē fem.} *sl-sex* ***Obs*** penis, dick, prick <Gyp>

karabúdžiti {ràbūdžīm, džē imperf.} **1** *sl-sex* ***Obs*** engage in sexual intercourse with (of a male) <Gyp> **2** *sl* build, construct, erect <Gyp>

kȁradža {ē fem.} *sl* train <NE[*1]>

karađòrđuša {ē fem.} *sl-fea* elderly female <SlavO[*1]>

Karagûzovac {zōvca masc.} (lit. Blackassville) *dia* place name in Serbia <Slav>

kàraka {ē fem.; Dat kàraki} *sl-sex* ***Obs*** prostitute, hooker <Gyp>

karakôndžula {ē fem.} **a.** *col* scarecrow <Gyp> **b.** *sl-fea* ***Der*** female with loud clothing and makeup <Gyp[*1]> **c.** *sl-fea* evil female, bitch <Gyp[*2]> **d.** unattractive person

karàkter {a masc.} (lit. character) *sl-sex* ***Fac-Obs*** penis, dick, prick <Gre[*1]>
• **tvȑd karàkter** {NP} (lit. hard character) *sl-sex* erect penis, hard on

karakušljívko {a (acc. = gen.) masc.} *sl-fea* mean or worthless person <NE-Slav[*1]>

Kârām ti séku! {S} (lit. I fuck your sister!) *sl* ***Off*** used as a strong curse, Fuck you! ☞ **karati**

karàmbōl {rambóla masc.} *sl-auto* car crash <Fre[*1]>

karamèla {ē fem.} (lit. toffee) **1a.** *sl-sex* ***Fac-Obs*** penis, dick, prick <Spa[*1]> **b.** *sl-sex* ***Fac-Obs*** small penis <Spa[*2]> **2** *sl* ***Fac*** Caravel (airplane model) <Slav[*1]>

karàmluk {a masc.} **a.** *sl* night <NE[*1]> **b.** *sl* darkness <NE[*2]>

karànfil {a (acc. = gen.) masc.} (lit. carnation *the flower*) **1** *sl-sex* male homosexual dandy <NE[*1]> **2** *sl-drink* alcoholic, drunk <NE[*1]>
• **šlògīrānī karánfil** {NP} (lit. apoplectic carnation *the flower*) *sl-fea* unattractive male

karánfilka {ē fem.; Dat karànfīlki} *sl-fea* foolish female <NE[*1]>

Karánović {a (acc. = gen.) masc.} *sl-sex* ***Fac-Obs*** seducer <Gyp>

karàntīn {rantína masc.} (lit. quarantine) *sl* train station <Lat[*1]>

kárānje {a neut.} *sl-sex* ***Obs*** sexual intercourse <Gyp>

karàta {ē fem.} *sl-crime* policeman, cop <Jap[*1]>

kárati {kârām, kárajū biasp.} **1** *sl-sex* ***Obs*** engage in sexual intercourse with (of a male) <Gyp> **2a.** *sl* ***Obs*** scold, punish <NE> **b.** *sl* ***Obs*** torture <NE[*1]>

• **Kârām ti séku!** {S} (lit. I fuck your sister!) *sl* ***Off*** used as a strong curse, Fuck you!

karaušlívko {a masc.} *sl-fea* homeless person, bum <NE-Slav[*1]>

karaušljívko {a masc.} **1** *sl-fea* ***Der*** crybaby <NE-Slav[*1]> **2** hairsplitter, nit picker <NE-Slav[*1]>

karavèla {ē fem.} (lit. caravelle) **1** *sl-sex* ***Obs*** buttocks, butt <Spa[*1]> **2** *sl-sports* ***Fac*** body builder <Spa[*1]>

karbìtuša {ē fem.} *sl-drink* low-quality brandy <Lat[*1]>

karburâtor {a masc.} **a.** *col* carburetor <Fre> **b.i.** *sl* nose <Fre[*1]> **ii.** *sl-crime* prison <Fre[*2]>

kàrdān {kardána masc.} **a.** *sl-auto* universal joint <BN> **b.** *sl-sex* penis <BN[*1]>

kàrdān-vȅla {ē fem.} *sl-auto* universal shaft <BN-Ger>

kàrdāš {kardáša (acc. = gen.) masc.} *sl* friend (male) <NE[*1]>

kardiològija {ē fem.} (lit. cardiology) *sl-fea* being in love <Gre[*1]>

kȁrē {part.} (lit. he says that) *col* particle used to express hesitation, as they say <Slav✍>

karfiōl {fiōla masc.} (lit. cauliflower) *sl-sex* ***Fac-Obs*** vagina, cunt <Ita[*1]>

kàrgōn {kargóna masc.} **a.** *sl* fear **b.** *sl* hesitation

kȁrī {īja masc.} *sl-sex* ***Obs*** penis, dick, prick <Gyp✍>

kàrica[1] {ē fem.} *sl-arch* pig (the animal) <Gyp>

kárica[2] {ē fem.} *sl-arch* small penis <Gyp>

kàridža {ē fem.} **a.** *sl-arch* pig (the animal) <Gyp> **b.** *sl-arch* sow (the animal) <Gyp[*1]>

karìdžalac {džaoca (acc. = gen.) masc.} *sl-arch* boar (the animal) <Gyp>

karidžànče {eta neut.} *sl-arch* pig (the animal) <Gyp>

karidžánče {eta neut.} *sl-arch* piglet <NE>

kàrika {ē fem.} *sl* finger ring <Hun[*1]>

karikaturírati {tùrīrām, turírajū biasp.} *sl* laugh <Ita[*1]>

kàrina {ē fem.} *sl-sex* ***Obs*** penis, dick, prick <Gyp>

karìnati {ām, ajū imperf.} *sl-sex* ***Obs*** engage in sexual intercourse with (of a male) <Gyp❖>

karìndža {ē fem.} **a.** *sl-arch* pig (the animal) <Gyp> **b.** *sl-arch* sow (the animal) <Gyp[*1]>

karìndžalac {lca (acc. = gen.) masc.} *sl-arch* boar (the animal) <Gyp>

karírati {kàrīrām, karírajū biasp.} *sl-sex* ***Fac-Obs*** engage in sexual intercourse with (of a male) <Gyp❖>

kàrisati {išēm, išū imperf.} *sl-sex* ***Obs*** engage in sexual intercourse with (of a male) <Gyp>

kàriška {ē fem.; Dat kàriški} *sl* admission ticket <Lat[*1]>

karkolòmija {ē fem.} *sl* dangerous situation <Slav[*1]>

karmìnisānje {a neut.} (lit. putting on lipstick) **a.** *sl* kissing <Ita[*1]> **b.** *sl* drinking (alcohol) <Ita[*2]>

karmìnisati {išēm, išū imperf.} *sl* kiss <Ita[*1]>

karmìnisati se {išēm, išū imperf. intr.} *sl-drink* get drunk <Ita❖[*1]>

kàrnī {īja masc.} *sl* meat <Ita✍>

kȁrnje {eta neut.} *sl* meat <Ita✍>

karȍca {ē fem.} (lit. coach) **a.** *sl-auto* car, wheels <Ita[*1]> **b.** *sl-auto* body (of a car) <Ita[*2]>

karolòmija {ē fem.} (lit. prick-breaking situation) *sl* dangerous event <Gyp-Slav❖[*1]>

kȁroljūb {a (acc. = gen.) masc.} (lit. prick-kisser) *sl-sex* ***Fac-Obs*** male homosexual, gay <Gyp-Slav❖[*1]>

kàrōn {karóna masc.} *sl-sex* ***Obs*** penis, dick, prick <Gyp✍>

karopljùgalo {a neut.} (lit. prick-smoker) *sl-sex* ***Fac-Obs*** male homosexual, gay <Gyp❖[*1]>

karosèrija {ē fem.} (lit. body *of a car*) *sl-sex* buttocks, butt <Fre[*1]>

kárta {ē fem.} **a.** *sl* ten dinars; a ten-dinar bill <Gre[*1]> **b.** thousand dinars; a thousand-dinar bill, a grand

- **kárta za ȉgrānje** {NP} (lit. playing card) *sl-gamble* dice altered to ensure winning, loaded dice
- **lȉčnā kárta** {NP} (lit. ID card) **1** *sl-drugs* narcotic drug, dope **2** *sl* steady girlfriend

kartiljèros {a masc.} *sl-gamble* playing card <Gre✍>

kàrtiška {ē fem.; Dat kàrtiški} *sl-gamble* playing card <Gre✍>

kartodrápec {a (acc. = gen.) masc.} (lit. ticket-tearer) *sl* train conductor, ticket taker (male) <Gre-Slav[*1]>

kartodràpka {ē fem.} (lit. ticket-tearer) *sl* train conductor, ticket taker (female) <Gre-Slav[*1]>

kartodŕpac {pca (acc. = gen.) masc.} (lit. ticket-tearer) *sl* supervisor (on public transportation) <Gre-Slav[*1]>

kartogrízac {sca (acc. = gen.) masc.} (lit. ticket-chewer) *sl* supervisor (on public transportation) <Gre-Slav[*1]>

kartònče {eta neut.} (lit. small cardboard) *sl-drugs* cardboard used as a filter for a joint <Fre❖[*1]>

kartonȉška {ē fem.; Dat kartonȉški} /kartonìška/ (lit. cardboard) [std. = karton] *sl-drugs* cardboard used as a filter in a joint <Fre✍[*1]>

kàrtōnka {ē fem.} (lit. the cardboard one) *sl-auto* Trabant (make of simple East German car) <Fre❖[*1]>

kàrulja {ē fem.} *sl-sex* ***Obs*** vagina, cunt <Gyp>

kâs {a +ev (ext. pl) masc.; Nom Pl kásevi} /kȁs/ *sl-music* tape recorder <Ita-Fre✍>

kasàba {ē fem.} *col* small town <NE[*1]>

kàsaper {a (acc. = gen.) masc.} **a.** *sl* butcher (literally) <NE> **b.** *sl* surgeon <NE[*1]>

kàsapin {a (acc. = gen.) masc.} (lit. butcher) **a.** *sl-fea* troublemaker, rowdy, ruffian <NE[*1]> **b.** *sl* surgeon <NE[*2]>

kàsapiti {pīm, pē imperf.} (lit. butcher) *sl* torture <NE[*1]>

kàsapljēnje {a neut.} (lit. butchering) *sl* torturing <NE[*1]>

kàsapnica {ē fem.} (lit. butcher's) *sl-stu* university exam <NE[*1]>

kasàrina {ē fem.} *sl-arch* building

kàsārna {ē fem.} (lit. barracks) **1** *sl* ***Dac*** store <Fre[*1]> **2** *sl* ***Dac*** home <Fre[*1]> **3** *sl* ***Fac*** cake <Fre[*1]>

kasètāš {kasetáša masc.} *col* tape recorder <Ita-Fre❖>

kaskàdēr {kadéra (acc. = gen.) masc.} (lit. stuntman) *sl* hired hand <Fre[*1]>

kaskadèros {a masc.} [std. = kaskader] *sl-media* stuntman <Fre✍>

kâsnō páljēnje {NP} (lit. slow ignition) *sl-fea* ***Fac*** slow understanding ☞ paljenje

kásti {kâžēm, kâžedū perf. irreg.} [std. = kazati] Vojv *dia-col* tell (in all its Serbo-Croatian meanings in the form different from the standard one) <Slav✍>

kastȉgati {ām, ajū imperf.} *col* punish <Ita>

kȁstra {ē fem.} *sl* church

kastrírati *See the following*

- **kastrírati tȅkst** {VP} (lit. castrate a text) *sl-media* ***Fac*** destroy a text by overediting

kȁšalj *See the following*

- **mȁčijī kȁšalj** {NP} (lit. cat's cough) **a.** *col* nothing at all **b.** *col* low quality object or performance
- **mȁčjī kȁšalj** {NP} (lit. cat's cough) **a.** *col* nothing at all **b.** *col* low-quality object or performance

kȁši {kěši fem.; perm} /kàši/ *sl* rain <Slav✍>

kȁšičica *See the following*

• na kȁšičicu {PP} (lit. on spoon) **1** *col* little by little **2** *col* in small quantities

kȁšika {ē fem.} (lit. spoon) *sl* match (lighting device) <NE[*1]>

kašȉkara {ē fem.} *sl-mil* hand grenade with spoon-shaped pin <NE❖[*1]>

kašírati {kàšīrām, kašírajū perf.} **a.** *sl* cover up, hide <Fre> **b.** *sl* throw away, toss out <Fre[*1]>

kašírati se {ām, ajū perf. intr.} *sl* cover up, hide <Fre>

kȁšta {ē fem.} *dia* home <Slav>

kaštȉgati {ām, ajū imperf.} *col* punish <Ita>

kȁt {adv.} [std. = kad] *dia* when <Slav✍>

kataglinègerovati {rujēm, rujū imperf.} *sl* buy

kataglîngerovati {rujēm, rujū imperf. intr.} *dia* buy

kàtanac {tānca masc.} (lit. lock) *sl-crime* prison, lock-up <Ita[*1]>

katapultírati {pùltīrām, pultírajū perf.} (lit. catapult) **a.** *sl* throw away, toss out <Gre❖[*1]> **b.** *sl* throw away, toss out <Gre❖[*1]> **c.** *sl* dismiss, fire (a person) <Gre[*2]>

kàtārka {ē fem.; Dat kàtārki} *sl* wallet <Gre[*1]>

katastròfičan {čna, čno--} *sl* catastrophic <Gre[*1]>

katastròfičār {a (acc. = gen.) masc.} *sl-fea* alarmist (male) <Gre❖[*1]>

katedrála {ē fem.} (lit. cathedral) *sl-fea* extremely tall and slender female, beanpole <Gre[*1]>

katedrâlis {a (acc. = gen.) masc.} *sl-fea* tall male <Gre✍[*1]>

kȁtfōr {a masc.} *sl* stove

kàtipla {čēmpla, čūpla imperf.; perm} [std. = plakati] *sl* cry, shed tears, weep <Slav✍>

kàtran {a masc.} (lit. tar) *sl-drugs* raw Macedonian opium <NE[*1]>

katrànica {ē fem.} (lit. tar thing) *sl* money <NE❖[*1]>

katrànjāk {ranjáka masc.} (lit. tar thing) *sl* coffee <NE❖[*1]>

kàtravoš {a masc.} *sl* beard <Gyp>

katȕnić {a (acc. = gen.) masc.} *sl-fea* person who habitually destroys everything <NE[*1]>

kàtvāroš {a masc.} *sl* beard

kȁu {excl.} *col* the sound made by a turkey <Slav>

kàubōj {a (acc. = gen.) masc.} (lit. cowboy) **a.** *sl-fea* stupid or mentally deficient person <Eng[*1]> **b.** troublemaker, rowdy, ruffian

• pròpalī kàubōj {NP} (lit. destroyed cowboy) *sl-fea* bowed-legged female

kaubójac {jca masc.} *sl-media* Western movie <Eng❖[*1]>

kȁučuk {a masc.} *sl* chewing gum <Eng[*1]>

kȁuguma {ē fem.} *sl* chewing gum <Ger>

kȁuk {a masc.} *col* cackling (of a turkey) <Slav>

kaùkānje {a neut.} *col* cackling (of a turkey) <Slav>

kaùkati {kàūčēm, kàūčū imperf.} **a.** *col* cackle (of a turkey) <Slav> **b.** *sl* cry, shed tears, weep <Slav[*1]>

kaùkavac {kāvca masc.} *col* sea gull <Slav>

kaùkčija {ē fem.} *col* person who cackles <Slav-NE[*1]>

kaúknuti {kàūnēm, nū perf.} **a.** *col* cackle (of a turkey) <Slav> **b.** *sl* cry, shed tears, weep <Slav[*1]>

kȁurī {īja (acc. = gen.) masc.} **a.** *sl* male, guy <NE[*1]> **b.** *sl* elderly male <NE[*2]>

kȁurin {a (acc. = gen.) masc.} *col* non-Muslim <NE>

kȁūrka {ē fem.; Dat kȁūrki} **a.** BosM *col* non-Muslim <NE❖[*1]> **b.** *sl* female <NE❖[*2]>

kàva {ē fem.} /káva/ (lit. coffee) **1** *sl-auto* Kawasaki (make of motorcycle) <BN✍> **2a.** *sl* female, **b.** *sl* anus

kavanȉška {ē fem.; Dat kavanȉški} /kavanȉška/ [std. = kavana] *sl-drink* ***Fam*** bar (drinking place) <NE✍>

kàvara {ē fem.} *sl* fear <NE>

kavènisati {šēm, šū imperf. intr.} *col* ***Der*** engage in prolonged coffee drinking <NE>

kàvez {a masc.} /kávez/ (lit. cage) **1** *sl-crime* custody <NE[*1]> **2** *sl* apartment <NE[*1]>

kȁvić {a masc.} *sl-auto* Kawasaki (make of motorcycle) <BN✍>

Kàvkāz {Kavkáza masc.} /Kȁvkaz /a masc./ (lit. Caucasus) *sl-drink* name for Kazališna kavana (a cafe near the Croatian National Theater, Zagreb, Croatia) <SlavO[*1]>

kȁvo {c.} [std. = kao] *dia* as <Slav✍>

kȁvurin {a masc.} SSer *sl-fea* evil male, s.o.b <NE[*1]>

kazačȍk {a masc.} (lit. Young Cossack) *sl-sex* ***Fac-Obs*** double consecutive sexual intercourse <Rus[*1]>

kàzan {a masc.} (lit. kettle) *col* boiler <NE[*1]>

kazàndžija {ē masc.} (lit. copper-smith) *sl-drink* person in charge of distilling brandy <NE❖[*1]>

kazànija {ē fem.} *sl-drink* fee for using boiler to distill brandy <NE[*1]>

kázati *See the following*

• **dok kȃžāš kȅks** {S} (lit. before you say "biscuit") *col* right away, before you can say "boo"

• **dok kȃžēš brȉtva** {S} (lit. before you say "razor") *col* right away, before you can say "boo"

• **dok nè kāžēš brȉtva** {S} (lit. before you don't say "razor") *col* right away, before you can say "boo"

• **dok nè kāžēš kȅks** {S} (lit. before you don't say "biscuit") *col* right away, before you can say "boo"

• **kázati slȍvo r** {VP} (lit. say a letter "r") *sl* tell somebody that he or she is too young

kàzīn {kazína masc.} **a.** *sl* mess, disorder, disturbance <Ita> **b.** *sl* scandal

kȁzniti {nīm, nē perf.} (lit. punish) *sl-sex* ***Fac-Obs*** engage in sexual intercourse with (of a male) <Slav*1>

KBZ [kəbz] {a +ov (ext. pl) masc.} (abbreviation from Kreditna Banka Zagreb 'Zagreb Credit Bank') *sl* loan (money) <Abb>

kéba {ē fem.} *sl* dagger (esp. one used as a weapon)

kèbanja {ē fem.} *sl* wagon (train car)

kebànjār {a (acc. = gen.) masc.} *sl-crime* person who steals from the train passengers

kébānje {a neut.} **a.** *sl* trouble, problem **b.** *sl* thing, object **c.** *sl* joke

kèbara {ē fem.} *sl* wallet

kébati {kêbām, kébajū imperf.} **a.** *sl* catch, grab **b.** *sl* chase

kebènjār {a (acc. = gen.) masc.} *sl-crime* person who steals from the train passengers

kèber {a masc.} *sl* child, kid

kèbera {ē fem.} *sl* wallet

kȅc [1] {excl.} **1** *col* used to drive away a goat <Slav> **2** *col* used at weddings to make the best man throw some money <Slav>

kêc [2] {kéca (acc. = gen.) +ev (ext. pl) masc.; Nom Pl kéčevi} **a.** *col* one <Hun> **b.i.** *sl-sstu* failing grade <Hun*1> **ii.** *sl-gamble* ace (cards) <Hun*1> **iii.** *sl-auto* Zastava 101 (make of car) <Hun*1> **iv.** *sl* streetcar line number one in Belgrade, Serbia <Hun* >

• **dvâ kéca** {NP} (lit. two aces) *sl* the number eleven trolley bus line in Belgrade, Serbia

kȅca [1] {excl.} **1** *col* used to drive away a goat <Slav> **2** *col* used at weddings to encourage the best man to throw some money <Slav>

kȅca [2] {ē masc.} *sl-fea* seducer

kȅcānje {a neut.} **1** *sl-sex* ***Obs*** sexual intercourse **2** pronouncing 'keca' at weddings to encourage the best man to throw some money

kècara {ē fem.} *sl-sex* ***Obs*** prostitute, hooker <Slav❖*1>

kȅcati {ām, ajū imperf.} **1a.** *sl-sex* ***Obs*** engage in sexual intercourse with (of a male) <Slav❖*1> **b.** *sl* ***Obs*** torture <Slav❖*2> **c.** *sl* ***Obs*** cheat, swindle <Slav❖*3> **2** *col-dia* keep pronouncing 'keca' to drive away a goat <Slav❖*1>

kȅcati se {ām, ajū imperf. intr.} *sl-sex* ***Obs*** engage in sexual intercourse with <Slav❖*1>

kècelja {ē fem.} (lit. apron) *sl* dress <Hun*1>

kèceriti se {rīm, rē imperf. intr.} *sl-fea* grin <Slav✍*1>

kȅckānje {a neut.} *col* pronouncing 'keca' <Slav>

kȅckati {ām, ajū imperf.} *sl* keep pronouncing 'keca' <Slav> ☞ **keca**

kȅckati se {ām, ajū imperf. intr.} **1** *sl* have an argument <Slav> **2** *sl-sex* engage in sexual intercourse with <Slav>

kèčara {ē fem.} *sl-sex* ***Fac*** prostitute, hooker <Eng❖*1>

kȅčēnje {a neut.} *sl* fight (e.g. fist fight) <Eng❖*1>

kečezkečkènisati {išēm, išū perf.} (lit. catch as catch can) *sl* beat up <Eng❖>

kèčiga {ē fem.; Dat kèčigi} (lit. sturgeon) **1** *sl-gamble* ace (cards) <Hun*1> **2** failing grade

kéčiti {kêčīm, čē imperf.} *sl* beat up <Eng❖*1>

kèčuga {ē fem.; Dat kèčugi} **1** *sl-gamble* ace (cards) <Hun❖> **2** *sl-sstu* failing grade <Hun❖*1>

kèćāš {kećáša masc.} *sl* tobacco

kećȁšica {ē fem.} *sl* beard

kèćija {ē fem.} *sl* eye (sight organ)

kećùralica {ē fem.} *sl* eye (sight organ)

kećùrati {rām, rajū imperf.} *sl-arch* look, watch, scope out

kèder {a masc.} *sl* ten dinars; a ten-dinar bill

kédža {ē masc.} *sl-drink* waiter <Ger✍>

kèfa {ē fem.} (lit. brush) **1a.** *sl-sex* ***Obs*** pubic hair <NE*1> **b.** *sl* ***Obs*** female <NE*2> **2** *sl* whim <NE*1> **3** *sl* love <NE*1>

kèfaćo {a masc.} *sl-fea* grimacer <Ita✍>

kèfalo {a neut.} /kȅfalo /a neut./ **a.** *sl* head <Gre*1> **b.** *sl* brain <Gre*2> **c.** *sl-fea* smart person, brain: *Pitaj ono kefalo, on će znati odgovor. Ask that brain, he'll know the answer.* <Gre*3>

kȅfati {ām, ajū imperf.} *sl* reproach, scold <**Hun**[*1]>

kégla {ē fem.} (lit. bowling pin) **1** *sl* rap, tap <**Ger**[*1]> **2** *sl* ten-para coin <**Ger**[*1]> **3a.** *sl* large round head <**Ger**[*1]> **b.** *sl-fea* person with large head <**Ger**[*2]>

kêglati se {ām, ajū imperf. intr.} (lit. bowl) *sl* find something highly humorous <**Ger**[*1]>

kȅhlati se {ām, ajū imperf. intr.} *sl* laugh

kȅhlav {a, o adj.} *sl-fea* humorous

kèjārnīk {a masc.} *sl-sex* ***Obs*** toilet <**Slav**✍[*1]>

kéka {ē fem.; Dat kéki} *sl* ten dinars; a ten-dinar bill

Kèkēnda {ē fem.} *dia* name for Kikinda (a town in Serbia) <**SlavO**✍>

kȅkēt {a masc.} *col* laughter <**Slav**>

kekètalica {ē fem.} *sl-fea* male who often laughs <**Slav**>

kekètalo {a neut.} *sl-fea* male who often laughs <**Slav**>

kekètati se {kèkećēm, ćū imperf. intr.} *sl* laugh <**Slav**>

kȅks {a +ev (ext. pl) masc.; Nom Pl kèksevi} (lit. biscuit) *sl-sex* ***Fac*** sexual intercourse <**Eng**[*1]>

kȅksānje {a neut.} (lit. wafering) *sl-sex* ***Obs*** sexual intercourse <**Eng**[*1]>

kȅksati {ām, ajū imperf.} (lit. biscuit) *sl-sex* ***Fac*** engage in sexual intercourse with (of a male) <**Eng**⁘[*1]>

kȅksić {a neut.} (lit. small biscuit) *sl-drugs* LSD, acid <**Eng**⁘[*1]>

kȅksovānje {a neut.} (lit. biscuiting) *sl-sex* ***Fac*** sexual intercourse <**Eng**⁘[*1]>

kȅlče {eta neut.} *sl-arch* dog (the animal) <**NE**✍>

kêle {eta neut.} *sl* mother <**Heb**✍>

keleràba {ē fem.} (lit. kohlrabi) **a.** *sl-fea* inhabitant of the countryside, hick, bumpkin <**Ger**[*1]> **b.** *sl-fea* stupid or mentally deficient person <**Ger**[*2]> **c.** *sl* naive male <**Ger**[*3]>

kȅleruj {a masc.} **1** *sl* dance **2** *sl* lively music

kelȉnče {eta neut.} *sl-arch* child, kid

kèlīnka {ē fem.} **a.** *sl-arch* daughter **b.** *sl* very young female, little girl

kéljati {kêljām, kéljajū imperf. intr.} *sl-fea* walk clumsily

keljávko {a masc.} *sl-fea* male with bandy legs

kémac {mca (acc. = gen.) masc.} *sl-fea* elderly male

kèmendeks {a masc.} *sl* ham and eggs <**Eng**✍>

kêmka {ē fem.} *sl-arch* dog (the animal)

kènče {eta neut.} *sl-arch* dog (the animal)

kènda {ē fem.} **a.** *sl-sex* ***Obs*** vagina, cunt **b.** *sl* ***Obs*** female, cunt

kéndža {ē masc.} *sl* Kent (cigarette brand) <**BN**✍>

kȅngūr {a (acc. = gen.) masc.} (lit. kangaroo) *sl* mailman <**Abo**[*1]>

kênka {ē fem.} *sl-arch* dog (the animal)

kȅntati {ām, ajū imperf.} *sl* throw away, toss out

kénja [1] {ē masc.} **1** *sl* Kent (cigarette brand) <**BN**✍> **2** *sl* waiter

kȅnja [2] {ē fem. & masc.} (lit. shitter) **a.** *sl-fea* ignorant person, dumb shit **b.** *sl-fea* clumsy person, klutz

kénjac {njca (acc. = gen.) masc.} **1** *dia* donkey <**Slav**[*1]> **2** *sl-fea* boring person, bore <**Slav**[*1]> **3** *sl-fea* clumsy male, klutz <**Slav**[*1]> **4** *sl-fea* extremely talkative person, chatterbox <**Slav**[*1]> **5a.** *sl-fea* teenager <**Slav**[*1]> **b.** *sl-fea* child, kid <**Slav**[*2]>

kènjāč {kenjáča (acc. = gen.) masc.} **a.** *sl-sex* ***Obs*** person who defecates <**Slav**⁘> **b.** *sl-fea* ***Der-Obs*** extremely talkative person, chatterbox <**Slav**⁘[*1]> **c.** *sl-fea* ***Der-Obs*** boring person, bore <**Slav**⁘[*2]>

kênjāj {excl.} *sl* used to silence one's interlocutor, shut up <**Slav**[*1]>

Kênjāj, kênjāj i brzȉne mênjāj! {S} (lit. Shit, shit and switch gears!) *sl* ***Obs*** used to make somebody go away ☞ **kenjati**

kènjara {ē fem.} **a.** *sl-sex* ***Obs*** buttocks, butt <**Slav**⁘> **b.** *sl-sex* anus <**Slav**⁘[*1]> **c.** *sl-fea* boring person, bore <**Slav**⁘[*1]>

kènjārnīk {a masc.} *sl-sex* ***Obs*** toilet <**Slav**⁘>

kénjati {kênjām, kénjajū imperf.} **a.** *sl-sex* ***Obs*** defecate, shit <**Slav**[*1]> **b.i.** *sl-fea* ***Obs*** talk persistently and meaninglessly, blabber, chatter <**Slav**[*2]> **ii.** *sl* ***Obs*** stay still <**Slav**[*2]> **iii.** *sl-thie* ***Obs*** spend term in prison <**Slav**[*2]> **iv.** *sl-fea* ***Obs*** spend one's time in useless activities, fool around, mess around <**Slav**[*2]> **c.** *sl* have, possess: *kenjati sto marona have one hundred German marks* <**Slav**[*1]> **d.** *sl* keep one's mouth shut <**Slav**[*1]>
• **Kênjāj, kênjāj i brzȉne mênjāj!** {S} (lit. Shit, shit and switch gears!) *sl* ***Obs*** used to make somebody go away
• **Kênjāj - mȁži glâvu!** {S} (lit. Shit and smear your head!) *sl* ***Obs*** used to silence one's interlocutor, Shut up!
• **kénjati gurábije** {VP} (lit. shit cakes) **a.** *sl-fea* ***Obs*** talk persistently and meaninglessly, bullshit **b.** *sl-fea* ***Obs*** lie

• **kénjati ko dȕmer** {VP} (lit. shit as a thinker) *sl-fea* ***Obs*** meditate

• **kénjati kvȁke** {VP} (lit. shit doorknobs) **a.** *sl-fea* ***Obs*** talk persistently and meaninglessly, blabber, chatter **b.** *sl-fea* ***Obs*** lie

• **kénjati šmȁjsere** {VP} (lit. shit machine-guns) **a.** *sl-fea* ***Obs*** talk persistently and meaninglessly, bullshit **b.** *sl-fea* ***Obs*** lie

• **kénjati žiléte** {VP} (lit. shit razor blades) **a.** *sl-fea* ***Obs*** talk persistently and meaninglessly, blabber, chatter **b.** *sl-fea* ***Obs*** lie

• **Nè kēnjāj!** {S} (lit. Don't shit!) **a.** *col* ***Off*** used to silence one's interlocutor, Shut up! **b.** *col* ***Off*** used to express disbelief **c.** *col* ***Off*** used to make somebody go away

kènjātor {a (acc. = gen.) masc.} (lit. shitter) **a.** *sl-fea* extremely talkative person, chatterbox <**Slav**❖> **b.i.** *sl-fea* boring person, bore <**Slav**❖[*2]> **ii.** *sl-fea* liar <**Slav**❖[*2]>

kenjáža {ē fem.} (lit. shitting) **a.** *sl-sex* ***Obs*** defecating <**Slav-Fre**[*1]> **b.** *sl-fea* ***Obs*** persistent and meaningless talk, blabber <**Slav-Fre**[*2]> **c.** *sl* ***Obs*** stupidity, lack of intelligence <**Slav-Fre**[*2]> **d.** *sl-fea* boredom <**Slav-Fre**[*3]> **e.** *sl-fea* boring event <**Slav-Fre**[*4]>

kènjka {ē fem.} *sl-arch* hen <**Gyp**>

kȅnjkati {ām, ajū biasp.} (lit. shit a little) **a.** *sl-sex* ***Obs*** defecate, shit <**Slav**> **b.** *sl-fea* ***Obs*** talk persistently and meaninglessly, blabber, chatter <**Slav**[*1]> **c.** *sl* ***Obs*** cry, shed tears, weep <**Slav**[*2]>

kȅnjkav {a, o adj.} **a.** *sl-fea* crying, fussy (as a baby) <**Slav**[*1]> **b.** *sl-fea* sickly <**Slav**[*2]>

képac {pca (acc. = gen.) masc.} *sl-fea* teenager <**NE**✍[*1]>

kȅpavac {vca masc.} *sl-crime* street policeman, beat cop <**NE**✍[*1]>

kȅpēc [1] {a (acc. = gen.) masc.} **a.** *sl-fea* short person <**NE**> **b.** *sl* child, kid <**NE**[*1]>

kèpec [2] {pca (acc. = gen.) masc.} *sl* boy, kid <**Slav**[*1]>

kêr [1] {a (acc. = gen.) +ov (ext. pl) masc.; Nom Pl kȇrovi} (lit. dog) **1** *sl-crime* policeman, cop <**Lat**[*1]> **2** *sl-fea* inhabitant of the countryside, hick, bumpkin <**Lat**[*1]> **3** *sl-fea* evil person <**Lat**[*1]> **4** *sl* male, guy <**Lat**[*1]>

kêr [2] {adj.} *sl-fea* unattractive, ugly <**Lat**[*1]>

kéra {ē fem.} *col-dia* dog (the animal) <**Lat**[*1]>

kȅravac {vca (acc. = gen.) masc.} *sl-crime* policeman, cop <**Lat**❖[*1]>

kerèbečiti se {čīm, čē imperf. intr.} *sl-fea* make faces, grimace <**Hun**❖[*1]>

kèrecvi {kèracvi masc. pl.; perm} [std. = cvikere] *sl* eyeglasses <**Ger**✍> ☞ **cvikere**

kereféka {ē fem.; Dat kereféki} *col* trick, joke <**Hun**>

kérēnje {a neut.} *sl* sleeping <**Lat**[*1]>

kèrija {ē fem.} **a.** *sl-drink* drink (alcohol) <**Gyp**> **b.** brandy

kerkína {ē fem.} *sl-drink* brandy <**Lat**[*1]>

kèrma {ē fem.; perm} [std. = marka] *sl* German mark <**Ger**✍>

kèrna {ē fem.} **a.** *sl-crime* hiding place (for things) **b.i.** *sl-drink* bar (drinking place) **ii.** *sl-auto* garage **iii.** *sl* barn **iv.** *sl* home

kȅrpo {kerapo masc.; perm} /kèrpo/ [std. = poker] *sl-gamble* poker <**Eng**✍>

kês {a +ov (ext. pl) masc.; Nom Pl késovi} *sl-fea* grin <**NE**[*1]>

kȅsa {ē fem.} (lit. bag) **1** *sl-sex* ***Obs*** sagging female breast <**NE**[*1]> **2** *sl-fea* affluent male, moneybags <**NE**[*1]>

kesáriti {kèsārīm, rē imperf.} *sl-crime* pick pockets <**NE**❖[*1]>

kèsāroš {a (acc. = gen.) masc.} *sl-crime* pickpocket <**NE**❖[*1]>

kèseriti se {rīm, rē imperf. intr.} *sl-fea* grin <**NE**[*1]>

kesírati {kèsīrām, kesírajū perf.} (lit. bag) *sl-crime* rob, rip off <**NE**[*1]>

kèskīr {keskíra masc.} *sl* tobacco

keslȉjānje {a neut.} *sl* laughter <**NE**❖[*1]>

kȅsnuti {nēm, nū perf.} *sl* sing <**NE**[*1]>

kesorézac {sca (acc. = gen.) masc.} (lit. bag-cutter) *sl-crime* criminal <**NE-Slav**[*1]>

kestènjāk {tenjáka (acc. = gen.) masc.} *sl-stu* professor, high-school teacher (male), prof <**Slav**❖[*1]>

kȅš {a +ev (ext. pl) masc.; Nom Pl kȅševi} **a.** *col* cash <**Eng**> **b.** *sl* ride on public transportation without paying fare <**Eng**[*1]>

• **u kèšu** {PP} (lit. in cash) *col* cash

kéša [1] {ē fem.} *sl* aunt

kéša [2] {ē masc.} **1** *sl-fea* senior citizen, **2** *sl-drink* waiter

kȅšadžija {ē masc.} *sl-fea* troublemaker, rowdy, ruffian

kȅšati se {ām, ajū imperf. intr.} **a.** *sl* look for trouble **b.** *sl* hang off the outside of a streetcar **c.** *sl* hang off anything

kèšātor {a (acc. = gen.) masc.} **1** *sl-fea* senior citizen, **2** *sl-sex* male who tries to get close to females on crowded public transportation

kȅšbōj {a (acc. = gen.) masc.} (lit. cash boy) *sl* garbage man <**Eng***1>

kêv {a +ov (ext. pl) masc.; Nom Pl kȅvovi} *sl* mother <**Heb***1>

kéva {ē fem.} **a.** *sl* mother <**Heb***1> **b.** *sl* school janitor (female) <**Heb***2>

• **Kéva da ti šȉznē!** {S} (lit. Let your mother freak out!) **SerE** *sl* ***Fac*** used to emphasize the truth of what has been said, I swear!

• **Kéva da ti šȉzne ako lȁžēm!** {S} (lit. Let your mother freak out if I lie!) *sl* used to emphasize the truth of what has been said, I swear!

• **Kévē mi!** {S} (lit. I swear by my mother!) **SerE** *sl* used to emphasize the truth of what has been said, I swear!

kévac {vca (acc. = gen.) masc.} **1** *sl* father, dad <**Heb**❖*1> **2** *sl* mother, mom <**Heb**❖*1> **3a.** *sl* grandfather, grandpa <**Heb**❖*1> **b.** *sl-fea* senior citizen <**Heb**❖*2> **4** *sl-sex* penis <**Heb**❖*1>

kevàna {ē fem.} *sl-crime* shelter (e.g. for homeless people) <**Heb**❖*1>

kèvati {ām, ajū imperf.} **a.** *sl* search <**Heb***1> **b.** *sl* have, possess: *kevati dobra kola have a good car* <**Heb***2>

kèvdža {ē fem.} *sl* mother, mom <**Heb**❖>

Kévē mi! {S} (lit. I swear by my mother!) **SerE** *sl* used to emphasize the truth of what has been said, I swear to my mother! ☞ **keva**

kevijánovićka {ē fem.; Dat kevijánovićki} *sl* mother, mom <**Heb**❖>

Kévinu ti zvézdu jèbēm! {S} (lit. I fuck your mother's star!) **SerE** *dia* ***Off*** used as a strong curse, Fuck you! ☞ **zvezda**

kȅvkati {ām, ajū imperf.} **a.** *sl-fea* talk persistently and meaninglessly, blabber, chatter **b.** *sl* talk

kȅvnuti {nēm, nū perf.} *sl* say, tell <**Slav**❖*1>

kêz {a +ov (ext. pl) masc.; Nom Pl kézovi} *sl* smile <**Slav**❖>

ki [1] {c.} *dia* as <**Slav**✍>

kî [2] {pron.} *dia* who (in all its Serbo-Croatian meanings in the form different from the standard) <**Slav** ✍>

kîb {a +ov (ext. pl) masc.; Nom Pl kíbovi} *sl* look, glimpse <**Ger**✍>

kȉbī {excl.} *sl* used to attract attention, look over there <**Ger**✍>

kìbīc {kibíca (acc. = gen.) masc.; Voc kȉbīče} *sl* bystander, observer <**Ger**>

kibìcēr {bicéra (acc. = gen.) masc.; Voc kȉbicēru} *sl* bystander, observer <**Ger**❖*1>

kìbicovanje {a neut.} *sl* observing, looking <**Ger**❖>

kìbicovati {cujēm, cujū imperf.} *sl* look, watch, scope out <**Ger**❖>

kìbicovati se {cujēm, cujū imperf. intr.} *sl* flirt <**Ger**❖*1>

kíbiti {bīm, be imperf.} **a.** *sl* look, watch, scope out <**Ger**✍> **b.** *sl* peep, look at others <**Ger**✍*1>

kíbla {ē fem.} **1** *sl-drink* bottle <**Ger***1> **2** prison bathroom <**Ger***1> **3** prison cell <**Ger***1> **4** *sl-sex* ***Obs*** penis, dick, prick <**Ger***1> **5** *sl* a poke, prod, or pinch on the buttocks, goose <**Ger***1>

kìblār {kiblára masc.} *sl-crime* prison <**Ger**❖*1>

kȉbnuti {nēm, nū perf.} *sl* look, watch, scope out <**Ger**❖>

kȉc {excl.} *sl-drugs* used to lure a pig <**Slav**>

kȉca {ē fem.} *sl-drink* brandy

kîcoš {a (acc. = gen.) masc.} *sl-fea* dandy, fop

kȋčma *See the following*

• **kȋčma trȁns**{NP} (lit. backbone transportation) *sl-drink* ***Fac*** alcohol rehabilitation clinic

kȋčmiti {mīm, mē imperf.} (lit. backbone) *sl* work, labor <**Slav**❖>

kìćati {ām, ajū imperf.} *sl* sell (exchange merchandise for money)

kȉd {a (acc. = gen.) +ov (ext. pl) masc.; Nom Pl kìdovi} *sl* male, guy <**Eng***1>

kída {ē fem.} *sl* escape, flee <**Gyp***1>

kȉdāj {excl.} *sl* used to make somebody go away, beat it <**NE***1>

kȉdānje {a neut.} (lit. chopping) *sl* running away, fleeing <**Slav***1>

kȉdati {ām, ajū imperf.} *sl* run away, flee <**Gyp***1>

kidavȅla [1] {excl.} *sl* used to make somebody go away, beat it <**Gyp**✍>

kidavȅla [2] {ē fem.} *sl* running away, fleeing <**Gyp**✍>

kidavȅlo {excl.} *sl* used to make somebody go away, beat it <**Gyp**✍>

kìdisati {išēm, išū imperf.} *sl* attack, strike: *kidisati na neprijatelja attack the enemy* <**Gre**>

kȉdnuti {nēm, nū perf. intr.} *sl* run away, flee <Gyp❖>

kidùrija {ē fem.} *sl* joke: *Taj njegov plan je obična kidurija. That plan of his is a real joke.* <Eng✍>

kȉf {a +ov (ext. pl) masc.; Nom Pl kìfovi} *sl-drugs* hashish, hash <Gre✍>

kȉfele {excl.} *col* used to make somebody go away <Hun>

kȉfeli {excl.} *sl* used to make somebody go away, beat it <Hun>

kífl {a masc.} [std. = kifla] *col* crescent roll <Ger✍>

kífla {ē fem.} (lit. crescent roll) *sl-sex* ***Obs*** penis, dick, prick <Ger[*1]>

kȉfli {excl.} *sl* used to make somebody go away, beat it <Hun✍>

kȉfliti {līm, lē imperf.} *sl* run <Hun>

kìhara {ē fem.} *sl* ***Fac*** nose <Slav❖>

kíhati {kîhām, kíhajū imperf. intr.} *col* sneeze <Slav>

kíhavica {ē fem.} *col* catarrh <Slav❖>

kijámet {a masc.} (lit. Judgement Day) Bos *col* bad weather (usu. snowstorm) <NE>

kìjara[1] {ē fem.} *sl-drink* brandy <NE✍>

kìjara[2] {kijēra fem.} *sl-drink* brandy <NE✍>

kijavìtis {a masc.} *sl* cold (illness) <Slav✍>

kȉkī {ija (acc. = gen.) masc.} **1** *sl-fea* unattractive person <GreO✍> **2** *sl-fea* very tall person, giant

kȉkica {ē fem.} (lit. small pig-tail) *sl-fea* naive young female <Slav❖[*1]>

kìkīć {kikíća (acc. = gen.) masc.; Voc kȉkīću} **a.** *sl-fea* young female, girl <Slav❖[*1]> **b.** *sl-fea* little boy, kid

kikìrēz {kiréza (acc. = gen.) masc.} *sl-fea* little boy, kid

kikirȉkī {ija masc.} (lit. peanut) **1** *sl-fea* pimple <Ind[*1]> **2** *sl* small business <Ind[*1]> **3** *s* trifle, thing of little importance or value <Ind[*1]>

kìklop {a (acc. = gen.) masc.} (lit. Cyclops) **a.** *sl-fea* very tall person, giant <Gre[*1]> **b.** *sl-fea* unattractive person <Gre[*1]> **c.** *sl-fea* stupid or mentally deficient person <Gre[*1]>

kȉknuti {nēm, nū perf. intr.} **a.** *sl* cry, shed tears, weep <Eng[*1]> **b.** *sl* go insane, freak out <Eng[*2]>

kìkoljiti se {ljīm, ljē imperf. intr.} *sl* laugh <Slav>

kikònder {a masc.} *sl-sstu* failing grade

kȉkot {a masc.} *sl* laughter <Slav>

kikòtānje {a neut.} *sl* laughter <Slav❖>

kikòtati {kìkoćēm, kìkoćū imperf.} *sl* laugh <Slav>

kikòtati se {kìkoćēm, kìkoćū imperf. intr.} *sl* laugh <Slav>

kikòtavac {vca (acc. = gen.) masc.} *sl-fea* laughing male <Slav❖>

kȉks {a +ev (ext. pl) masc.; Nom Pl kìksevi} *sl* mistake, error <Ger>

kȉks-idéja {ē fem.} (lit. kiks 'mistake' X fiks-ideja 'idee fixe') **a.** *sl-fea* fixation <Ger-Gre> **b.** *sl* stupid idea <Ger[*]Gre[*1]>

kȉksati {ām, ajū perf.} *sl* miss, fail: *kiksati u posljednjoj utakmici fail the last game* <Ger❖>

kiksírati {kìksīrām, kiksírajū perf.} *sl* miss, fail: *kiksirati posao fail to complete one's work* <Ger❖>

kȉksnuti {nēm, nū perf.} *sl* miss, fail <Ger❖>

kȉla {ē fem.} *sl-drink* liter <Gre[*1]>

kȉlav {a, o adj.} (lit. having a hernia) **a.** *sl-fea* clumsy, klutzy <Gre[*1]> **b.** *sl-fea* slow <Gre[*1]>

kȉlavac {lāvca (acc. = gen.) masc.} (lit. the one with a hernia) *sl-fea* clumsy male, klutz <Gre❖[*1]>

kiláviti {kìlāvīm, vē imperf.} (lit. have a hernia) *sl-fea* be slow <Gre❖[*1]>

kiláviti se {kìlāvīm, vē imperf. intr.} (lit. have a hernia) **a.** *sl-fea* strive, try hard, bust one's balls <Gre❖[*1]> **b.** *sl-fea* be slow <Gre❖[*2]>

kilávko {a masc.} (lit. the one with a hernia) *sl-fea* clumsy male, klutz <Gre❖[*1]>

kiláža {ē fem.} *sl* weight (usu. body) <Gre-Fre[*1]>

kìlāžnī {ā, ō adj.} *sl* weight (usu. body) <Gre-Fre[*1]>

kìlenc {a masc.} *sl-sex* ***Obs*** penis, dick, prick <Hun[*1]>

kȉler[1] {a (acc. = gen.) masc.} /kìler/ *sl-crime* killer <Eng>

kȉler[2] {a masc.} *sl-auto* radiator <Ger>

kȉliti {līm, lē imperf.} *sl* talk, have a conversation <Slav❖[*1]>

kȉlo {a neut.} **a.** *col* kilo <Gre> **b.i.** *sl* million <Gre[*1]> **ii.** *sl* liter <Gre[*1]>

kȉlometar-cȅler {a masc.} *sl-auto* odometer <Ger>

kílonja {ē masc.} *sl-fea* ***Der*** clumsy person, klutz <Gre❖[*1]>

kilòster {a (acc. = gen.) masc.} *sl-fea* ***Der*** clumsy person, klutz <Gre✍[*1]>

kȉlja {ē fem.} *sl* thousand dinars; a thousand-dinar bill, a grand <Gre✍>

kȉm {kìma +ov (ext. pl) masc.; Nom Pl kìmovi} *sl-arch* louse (the insect) <Ita*1>

kìnāf {kináfa (acc. = gen.) masc.; perm} [std. = fakin] **a.** *sl* boy, kid <Ita✍> **b.** *sl* male, guy <Ita✍*1>

kìndār {kindára masc.} *sl* dinar (Yugoslav currency unit) <Alb>

kȉnder {a (acc. = gen.) masc.} *sl* female <Ger>

Kìnēz [1] {Kinéza (acc. = gen.) masc.} (lit. Chinese *person*) *sl* Chinese restaurant, Zagreb, Croatia <SlavO*1>

kìnēz [2] {kinéza (acc. = gen.) masc.} (lit. Chinese *person*) *sl-fea* ***Fac*** relative living in one's apartment <SlavO*1>

kȉnfa {ē masc.; perm} /kìnfa /kìnafa masc./ [std. = fakin] **a.** *sl* boy, kid <Ita✍> **b.** *sl* male, guy <Ita✍*1>

kȉnfāć {a (acc. = gen.) masc.} [std. = fakin] **a.** *sl* boy, kid <Ita✍> **b.** *sl* male, guy <Ita✍*1>

Kȉng-kȍng {a (acc. = gen.) masc.} (lit. King Kong) *sl-fea* tall person <EngO*1>

kíno {a neut.} (lit. movie house) *col* funny event <Gre*1>

kȉnta {ē fem.} **a.** *sl* money (usu. a small quantity) <Alb*1> **b.** dinar (Yugoslav currency unit) <Alb*2>

kȉntāć {a masc.} **a.** *sl* money <Alb✣*1> **b.** *sl:* dinar (Yugoslav currency unit) <Alb✣*2>

kìntār {a (acc. = gen.) masc.} *sl-fea* affluent male, moneybags <Alb✣*1>

kȉntī {ija masc.} *sl* dinar (Yugoslav currency unit) <Alb✍*1>

kínuti {kînēm, nū perf. intr.} *col* sneeze <Slav✍>

kípiti {pīm, pē imperf. intr.} *sl-fea* go insane, freak out <Slav*1>

kȉpovati {ujēm, ujū imperf.} *sl-sex* ***Obs*** defecate, take a dump <Ger*1>

kíra {ē fem.} **a.** *sl* home <Gyp✍*1> **b.** *sl-drink* bar (drinking place) **c.** *sl-drink* restaurant

kȉrhner {a masc.} *sl-crafts* chisel (the tool) <Ger>

kirìjāš {rijáša (acc. = gen.) masc.} *sl-crime* roaming thief <NE*1>

kȉrner {a masc.} *sl-crafts* chisel (the tool) <Ger>

kìrurg {a masc.} (lit. surgeon) *sl-sex* ***Fac*** male homosexual, gay <Gre*1>

kȉs [1] {excl.} *col* used to lure a goat <Slav>

kȉs [2] {a +ev (ext. pl) masc.; Nom Pl kìsevi} *sl* kiss <Eng>

kȉsati {išēm, išū biasp.} //am, aju biasp. intr/ *sl* kiss <Eng✣>

kȉselā {ē fem. (adj. decl.)} (lit. the sour one) *col* mineral water <Slav✍>

kȉselā gláva {NP} (lit. sour head) *sl-drugs* notorious drug addict ☞ glava

kȉselī krȁstavac {NP} (lit. pickle) *sl* grandparent ☞ krastavac

kiselìna {ē fem.} (lit. acid) **a.** *sl-drugs* LSD, acid <Slav*1> **b.** *sl-drugs* drugs, dope <Slav*2>

kisèlīš {selíša masc.} (lit. the acid one) **1** *sl-drugs* LSD, acid <Slav*1> **2** *sl-drink* low-quality wine <Slav*1>

kȉseliti se {līm, lē imperf. intr.} (lit. sour oneself) *sl* stand in one place for a long time (usu. while waiting for someone) <Slav*1>

kisèljāk {seljáka (acc. = gen.) masc.} **1** *sl-fea* smart male, brain <Slav*1> **2** *sl-drink* bad wine <Slav*1>

kisimìzam {zma masc.} *sl* kissing <Eng✍>

kȉsko {a masc.} *sl* air <Slav*1>

kȉsnuti {nēm, nū imperf. intr.} **1** *sl* sit <Slav*1> **2** *sl* stand, be in an upright position: *Vojnici su kisnuli kod kapije tri sata. The soldiers stood at the gate for three hours.* <Slav*1>

kȉš {c.} *sl* look

kȉša *See the following*

- **Bȉće kȉšē!** {S} (lit. The rain is coming!) *sl-crime* used to refer to the approach of a dangerous situation
- **Bȉt će kȉšē!** {S} (lit. The rain is coming!) *sl-crime* used to refer to the approach of a dangerous situation
- **kȉše dòlazē** {S} (lit. the rains are coming) *sl-sex* ***Fac*** sagging female breast

kȉšiti {šīm, še imperf.} *sl* look, watch, scope out <Slav*1>

kíšnja {ē fem.} *sl* mosque <Slav>

kišóber {a masc.} [std. = kišobran] *sl* umbrella <Slav✍>

kȉšobrān {a masc.} (lit. umbrella) *sl* raincoat <Slav*1>

kȉštra {ē fem.} **a.** *col* box <Ger> **b.i.** *sl* head <Ger*1> **ii.** *sl* ship, vessel <Ger*1>

kȉt [1] {kìta (acc. = gen.) +ov (ext. pl) masc.; Nom Pl kìtovi} **a.** **Cro** *sl* boy, kid <Ger*1> **b.** **Cro** *sl* male, guy <Ger*1>

- **ìzlīzānī kȉt** {NP} (lit. depleted dude) *sl* ***Fac*** waiter
- **Kȉt ne jèbē nȉkoga.** {S} (lit. The guy doesn't fuck anybody.) **Cro** *sl-fea* ***Obs*** used to express lack of subordination of a third party male
- **kȉt od preko dèbelē bȁrē** {NP} (lit. the guy from the

other side of the great pond) **1** **Cro** *sl-fea* American (male) **2** Cro *sl-fea* Australian (male)

kȉt [2] {excl.} *col* used to drive away a cow <**Slav**>

kȉta {ē fem.} **1** *sl-sex* ***Fam*** penis <**Slav***1> **2a.** *sl* female <**Slav***1> **b.i.** *sl-sex* prostitute, hooker <**Slav***2> **ii.** *sl-fea* long hair <**Slav***2>
- **kȉta Mȁrjānova** {NP} (lit. Marjan's prick) *sl-fea* ***Obs*** worthless object, junk

kítac {kíca masc.} *sl-sex* ***Obs*** penis, dick, prick <**Slav**⁘*1>

kȉtāć {a masc.} *sl-sex* ***Obs*** penis, dick, prick <**Slav**⁘>

kitára {ē fem.} **a.** *sl-sex* ***Fac-Obs*** penis, dick, prick <**Gre***1> **b.** *sl-sex* ***Fac-Obs*** large penis <**Gre***2>

kitarésa {ē fem.} *sl-sex* ***Obs*** penis, dick, prick <**Slav**⁘*1>

kȉtica {ē fem.} *sl-sex* ***Fam*** penis <**Slav**⁘*1>

kȉtiti se *See the following*
- **kȉtiti se cvȅkima** {VP} **Cro** *sl-fea* be wrong, be mistaken: *Kitiš se cvekima ak misliš da bu došel. You are wrong if you think he'll come.*

kitolòmija {ē fem.} *sl* dangerous situation <**Slav**⁘*1>

kitolóvac {vca (acc. = gen.) masc.} *sl-sex* ***Fac-Obs*** male homosexual, gay <**Slav**⁘*1>

kȉtonja {ē masc.} **a.** *sl-sex* ***Obs*** male with a large penis <**Slav**⁘> **b.** *sl-sex* male sexual partner (of a female) <**Slav**⁘*1>

kȉtovati {tujēm, tujū imperf.} *sl* give flowers <**Slav**⁘*1>

kitùrina {ē fem.} *sl-sex* ***Obs*** large penis <**Slav**⁘>

kȉžiti {žīm, žē imperf.} *sl* look, watch, scope out

klȁckati {ām, ajū imperf.} **a.** *sl* walk <**Slav***1> **b.** *sl* be careless about: *Njemu se klacka hoće li proći ili pasti. He doesn't give a shit about passing or failing* <**Slav***2>
- **Kȍ[PRON:DAT] klȁckā kȍsti!** {LSF} (lit. Who is see-sawing [PPRON] bones!) *col* ***Off*** used to refer to indifference toward: *Ko mu klacka kosti! Who gives a shit about him!*
- **Kȍ ti klȁckā kȍsti!** {S} (lit. Who is see-sawing your bones?) *sl* ***Off*** used to express disrespect, Screw you!

klȁckavica {ē fem.} **a.** *col* seesaw <**Slav***1> **b.** *sl-drink* tremble from being drunk, have the shakes <**Slav***2>

klȁda {ē fem.} *sl-sex* ***Obs*** penis, dick, prick <**Slav***1>

klȁfrača {ē fem.} *sl-fea* extremely talkative person, chatterbox <**Ger***1>

klȁfrati {ām, ajū biasp.} **a.** *sl-fea* ***Der*** talk persistently and meaninglessly, blabber, chatter <**Ger***1> **b.** *sl* talk, have a conversation <**Ger***2>

klâj-klâj {adv.} *col* very slowly <**Slav**>

klàjber {a masc.} *sl* marble (the toy) <**Ger**✍>

klȁjduniti {nīm, nē perf. intr.} *sl* run away, flee <**Ger**⁘*1>

klȁjnuti {nēm, nū perf. intr.} *sl* run away, flee

klâk {a +ov (ext. pl) masc.; Nom Pl klákovi} *sl-crafts* lime (calcium oxide) <**Lat**>

klȁmati {ām, ajū imperf.} *sl* take: *klamati sendviče za put take some sandwiches for the trip* <**Ger***1> *sl* <**Ger***2>

klâmfa {ē fem.} (lit. cramp-iron) **a.** *sl-sex* ***Obs*** vagina, cunt <**Ger***1> **b.** *sl-sex* ***Obs*** prostitute, hooker <**Ger***2> **c.** *sl-sex* ***Obs*** loose woman, slut <**Ger***2>

klȁmfār {a (acc. = gen.) masc.} *sl* ***Fac*** dentist <**Ger**⁘*1>

klâmfati {ām, ajū imperf.} *sl-fea* talk persistently and meaninglessly, blabber, chatter <**Ger**⁘*1>

klâmpa {ē masc.} *sl* male

klânfa {ē fem.} **1** *sl-fea* female who cheats on her husband (i.e. sexually) <**Ger***1> **2** *sl-fea* senior citizen <**Ger***1>

klȁnjalo *See the following*
- **Klȁnjalo ti jèbēm!** {S} (lit. I fuck the place where you kneel and pray!) *dia* ***Off*** used as a moderate curse, Fuck you!

klȁp [1] {excl.} *col* the sound made by applause, clap <**Slav**>

klâp [2] {a +ov (ext. pl) masc.; Nom Pl klápovi} *sl-gamble* pat-a-cake <**Slav**>

klȁpa {ē fem.} **a.** *col* company (group of people) <**Slav**✍*1> **b.** *sl-crime* gang, group of one's close friends

klapàrānje {a neut.} *col* making noise <**Slav**>

klapàrati {ām, ajū imperf.} *col* make noise <**Slav**>

klȁpati {ām, ajū imperf.} **1a.** *sl-fea* talk persistently and meaninglessly, blabber, chatter: *klapati gluposti blabber about some nonsense* <**Slav***1> **b.** *sl* eat, devour: *klapati baklave eat baklawas* <**Slav***1> **2** *sl* agree: *klapati odlazak u kino agree to go to the movies* <**Ger**> **3** *sl* be convenient, be appropriate <**Ger**>

klapìnjati {njām, njajū imperf.} *col* make noise <**Slav**>

klȁpiti {pīm, pē perf.} *col* hit, punch <**Slav**>

klȁpna {ē fem.} *sl-crafts* lid <**Ger***1>

klára {ē fem.} *sl-music* clarinet <**Ita**✍>

klarìnēt [1] {rinéta (acc. = gen.) masc.; Voc klȁrinēte} *sl-fea* stupid or mentally deficient person <**Ita***1>

klarìnēt [2] {rinéta masc.} (lit. clarinet) *sl* ***Fac*** nose <**Ita***1>

klarinètista {ē masc.} (lit. clarinet player) *sl-fea* large-nosed male <**Ita**❖[*1]>

klàsa {ē fem.} (lit. class) *sl-mil* generation <**Lat**[*1]>
- **u drȕgū klàsu** {PP} (lit. in the second class) *sl-sex* ***Obs*** anally

klàse *See the following*
- **u cvàjte klàse** {PP} (lit. in the second class) *sl-sex* ***Obs*** anally

klàsīć {klasíća (acc. = gen.) masc.} *sl-mil* person from the same generation <**Lat**❖[*1]>

klàsika {ē fem.} *sl* nothing new <**Lat**[*1]>

klȁti {kȍljēm, kȍljū imperf.} (lit. slaughter) **1** *sl-sex* ***Obs*** engage in sexual intercourse with (of a male) <**Slav**[*1]> **2a.** *sl* torture <**Slav**[*1]> **b.** *sl-fea* annoy, bother, pester <**Slav**[*2]>

klȁti se {kȍljēm, kȍljū imperf. intr.} *col* fight (e.g. fist fight) <**Slav**[*1]>

klavijatúra {ē fem.} (lit. keyboard) **a.** *sl-sex* ***Fac-Obs*** feminine curves <**Lat**[*1]> **b.** *sl* ***Fac*** teeth <**Lat**>

klàvīr {klavíra masc.; Voc klȃvīru} (lit. piano) *sl-crime* ***Der*** informer, stoolie, snitch <**Fre**[*1]>

klavìrisati {išēm, išū imperf. intr.} (lit. play piano) *sl-crime* make excuses to the police for not carrying an ID <**Fre**❖[*1]>

klebècan {a (acc. = gen.) masc.} *sl-fea* stupid or mentally deficient person <**NE**❖>

kléber {a masc.} *sl* marble (the toy) <**Ger**[*1]>

klecaóna {ē fem.} (lit. trembling place) *sl* church <**Slav**[*1]>

klèhi {klêhā masc. pl.} *sl* teeth

klèkat {a masc.} *sl* screaming, shouting

klekètāš {ketáša (acc. = gen.) masc.; Voc klȇketāšu} *col* extraterrestrial, alien

klèkovača {ē fem.} *sl-drink* juniper brandy <**Slav**❖>

klȇkovačkī bùfalo {NP} *sl-fea* ***Fac*** high-quality shoe ☞ bufalo

klembècan {a (acc. = gen.) masc.} *sl-fea* stupid or mentally deficient person <**NE**❖>

klèmkača {ē fem.} *sl-arch* axe <**Ger**❖>

klèmna {ē fem.} *sl-crafts* clamp (the tool) <**Ger**>

klémpa [1] {ē fem.} *col* box (someone's ears) <**Slav**✐[*1]>

klémpa [2] {ē fem. & masc.} *sl-fea* ***Der*** lop-eared person <**Slav**✐[*1]>

klémpo {a masc.} *sl-fea* ***Der*** lop-eared person

klempùhec {a (acc. = gen.) masc.} *sl-fea* ***Der*** lop-eared person <**Slav**✐[*1]>

klȅnīšte {a neut.} *sl-arch* milk

klènkača {ē fem.} *sl-arch* axe

klȅnkānje {a neut.} *dia* planing (carpenter's)

klȅp {excl.} *col* the sound made by tapping, tap <**Slav**>

klȅpa [1] {excl.} *col* the sound made by tapping, tap <**Slav**>

klȅpa [2] {ē fem.} *col* ringing (bell, etc.) <**Slav**>

klépati {klȇpām, klépajū biasp.} *sl* learn <**Slav**❖[*1]>

klepèsati {klèpešēm, pešū imperf.} *col* tick-tock (clock, etc.) <**Slav**>

klȅpēt {klȅpeta masc.} *col* noise <**Slav**>

klepètac {eca masc.} *col* tongue (of a bell) <**Slav**>

klepètānje {a neut.} **a.** *sl-fea* prolonged and meaningless talk, blabber, chatter <**Slav**> **b.** *sl* making noise <**Slav**[*1]>

klepètati {klèpećēm, ećū imperf. intr.} **1** *col* make noise: *klepetati u tri sata noću make noise at three a.m.* <**Slav**[*1]> **2a.** *sl-fea* shake (an object, person, etc.): *klepetati od straha shake from fear* <**Slav**[*1]> **b.i.** *sl-fea* shiver (from cold): *klepetati od temperature na minus dvadeset stepeni shiver with the temperature at minus twenty degrees centigrade* <**Slav**[*2]> **ii.** *sl-fea* chatter <**Slav**[*2]>

klepètuša {ē fem.} **a.** *sl-fea* very young female, little girl <**Slav**❖[*1]> **b.** *sl-fea* unintelligent female <**Slav**❖[*2]>

klȅpiti {pīm, pē perf.} *sl* hit, punch <**Slav**❖>

klȅpkati {ām, ajū imperf.} *sl* hit, punch <**Slav**❖>

klȅpnuti {nēm, nū perf.} *sl* hit, punch <**Slav**❖>

klȅsār {a (acc. = gen.) masc.} (lit. sculptor) *sl-crime* long term prisoner <**Slav**[*1]>

klesárēnje {a neut.} (lit. making sculptures) *sl-crime* serving prison term at Goli island (Croatia, where the former communist regime detained its political enemies) <**Slav**[*1]>

klíber {a masc.} *sl* marble (the toy)

klíberiti se {rīm, rē imperf. intr.} /klìberiti se, klibériti se /rim, re imperf. intr./ *col* grin

klȉca *See the following*
- **Klȉcu ti čìvutskū!** {S} (lit. I fuck your Kike seed!) *dia* ***Off*** used as a strong curse to a Jewish person
- **Klȉcu ti jèbēm lȍšū!** {S} (lit. I fuck your bad seed!) *dia* ***Off*** used as a moderate curse, Fuck you!
- **Klȉcu ti jèbēm pòkvārenū!** {S} (lit. I fuck your rotten seed!) *dia* ***Off*** used as a strong curse, Fuck you!

klĩče *See the following*

• **Klĩče ti jèbēm!** {S} (lit. I fuck your small seed!) *dia Off* used as a moderate curse, Fuck you!

klíća [1] {ē masc.} *sl-sex Obs* clitoris <Gre✍>

Klíća [2] {ē masc.} (lit. Clitler, i.e. Klinton '*Bill* Clinton' X Hića '*Adolf* Hitler') *col Der* name for Bill Clinton used in Serbia (in particular during the military campaign against Yugoslavia in 1999) <Eng-GerO✍>

klĩk [1] {a (acc. = gen.) +ov (ext. pl) masc.; Nom Pl klìkovi} *sl* photographer <Slav*1>

klĩk [2] {a +ov (ext. pl) masc.; Nom Pl klíkovi} **a.** *col* strong voice <Slav*1> **b.** *col* high pitched sound <Slav*2> **c.** *col* bird's call <Slav*3> **d.** *col* call, shout

klĩk-klăk {masc.} *sl* money exchange (activity) <Slav>

klĩka {ē fem.; Dat klĩki} *col* cheering <Slav>

klíkati {klĩkām, klíkajū imperf.} **a.** *col* cheer for: *klikati za domaći tim cheer for the home team* <Slav⁘> **b.** *col* scream in pain, fear, or outrage <Slav⁘*1>

klĩkavac {vca (acc. = gen.) masc.} *col* falcon <Slav⁘*1>

klìker {a masc.} (lit. marbel) **1a.** *sl* idea, though <Ger*1> **b.** *sl* talent: *Ona ima kliker za klavir. She has talent for the piano.* <Ger*2> **c.** *sl* brain <Ger*2> **2** *sl-sex* small female breast <Ger*1>

likèrāš {keráša (acc. = gen.) masc.} **a.** *sl-fea* smart male, brain <Ger⁘*1> **b.** *sl-fea* inventive male <Ger⁘*2>

klĩknuti {nēm, nū perf.} **a.** *col* cheer for: *Nikad neću kliknuti za ove pedere. I'll never cheer for these dummies.* <Slav⁘> **b.** *col* scream in pain, fear, or outrage <Slav⁘*1>

klìktāš {kliktáša (acc. = gen.) masc.} *col* eagle <Slav⁘>

klĩmānje {a neut.} (lit. shaking) *sl-sex Obs* masturbation <Slav*1>

klĩmati {ām, ajū imperf.} (lit. shake) *sl-sex Obs* masturbate, beat off <Slav*1>

klimávko {a masc.} *sl-fea Der* coward, chicken <Slav⁘*1>

klìmīć {klimíća masc.} *sl* mother, mom

klĩmoglāv {a masc.} *sl* greeting <Slav*1>

klìmpac {a masc.} *sl-sex Obs* penis, dick, prick

klĩmpāč {a (acc. = gen.) masc.} *sl-sex Obs* penis, dick, prick

klĩn {a +ov (ext. pl) masc.; Nom Pl klìnovi} (lit. wedge) *sl-sex Obs* penis, dick, prick <Slav*1>

klĩnac {klĩnca (acc. = gen.) masc.} **a.** *col* child, kid <Slav*1> **b.** *sl-sex* penis <Slav*2>

• **kòjī klĩnac** {NP} (lit. which nail) *col* used to express disagreement: *Koji klinac ideš tamo? Why the hell are you going there?*

klĩnačkī {ā, ō adj.} *col* childish <Slav*1>

klincànica {ē fem.} *sl-arch* home

klincéza {ē fem.} *col* very young female, little girl <Slav✍*1>

klĩnconoša {ē fem.} /klincònoša/ (lit. infected person) *sl-sex Fac* pregnant female <Slav*1>

klinčàdija {ē fem.} **a.** *col* a group of small children <Slav⁘*1> **b.** *col* a group of teenagers

klinčànica {ē fem.} *sl-arch* house, home

klĩnče {eta neut.} *col* very young female, little girl <Slav⁘*1>

klìnček {a masc.} *sl-sex Obs* clitoris <Slav*1>

klìndōv {klindòva (acc. = gen.) masc.} **a.** *sl* son <Slav✍*1> **b.** *sl* child, kid <Slav✍*2> **c.** *sl* male, guy <Slav✍*3>

klìndōvka {ē fem.} **a.** *sl-fea* very young female, little girl <Slav✍*1> **b.i.** *sl* daughter **ii.** *sl-sex* prostitute, hooker

klíndža {ē fem.} *sl* marble (the toy) <Ger✍>

klĩng {a +ov (ext. pl) masc.; Nom Pl klìnovi} *col* doorbell <Slav*1>

klĩnka {ē fem.; Dat klĩnki} **a.** *col* very young female, little girl <Slav⁘*1> **b.** *sl* female <Slav⁘*2> **c.** *sl* lover (female) <Slav⁘*3> **d.** *sl-sex* prostitute, hooker <Slav⁘*4> **e.** *sl-drink* waitress <Slav⁘*5>

klìnkur {a (acc. = gen.) masc.} *sl-fea* average male <Slav*1>

klínja {ē masc.} **a.** *col* child, kid <Slav✍*1> **b.** *sl-sex* penis <Slav✍*2>

klínjo {a masc.} *col* child, kid <Slav✍*1>

klĩpa {ē fem.} (lit. log) *col Fac* nose <Slav>

klìpača {ē fem.} (lit. the knob one) *sl-drink* bottle of beer <Slav>

klìpan {a (acc. = gen.) masc.} **a.** *col* boy, kid <Slav*1> **b.i.** *sl-sex* penis <Slav*2> **ii.** *sl-fea* stubborn male, pigheaded guy <Slav*2>

klìpara {ē fem.} **1** *sl-drink* corncob brandy <Slav*1> **2** *sl-drink* beer

klĩs [1] {excl.} *col* used to make somebody go away, beat it <Slav>

klĩs [2] {a +ov (ext. pl) masc.; Nom Pl klísovi} *col* running away, fleeing <Slav>

klísnuti {klĩsnēm, nū perf. intr.} /klĩsnuti/ *col* run away, flee <Slav>

klȉstīr {klistíra (acc. = gen.) masc.} *sl-sex* ***Obs*** male homosexual, gay <**Gre**[*1]>

klistírati {lȉstīrām, listírajū biasp.} *sl-fea* bother, disturb <**Gre**[*1]>

klîš {excl.} *sl* used to make somebody go away <**Slav**>

klíša {ē fem.} **1** *sl* marble (the toy) <**Ger**✍> **2** *sl-sex* clitoris <**Lat**✍>

klȉšac {šca masc.} *sl* marble (the toy) <**Ger**✍>

klíšer {a masc.} *sl* marble (the toy) <**Ger**✍>

klíza {ē fem.} *col* slippery spot <**Slav**>

klízāljka {ē fem.} (lit. skate) *sl* ***Fac*** nose <**Slav**[*1]>

klô {excl.} *col* the sound made by gurgling, gurgle <**Slav**>

klobàrati {ām, ajū imperf.} *col* roar (engine, etc.) <**Slav**>

klȍbūk {a masc.} *col* hat <**Slav**>

klóca {ē fem.} *sl-sex* ***Fam*** bathroom <**Ger**✍>

klȍcati {ām, ajū imperf.} **a.** *col* click (produce a short, sharp, non-resonant sound) <**Slav**> **b.** *col* snip, clip <**Slav**[*1]> **c.** *col* chatter (of the teeth) <**Slav**[*2]>

klófer {a masc.} (lit. thrasher) *sl-crime* ***Der*** informer, stoolie, snitch <**Ger**>

klôk {excl.} *col* the sound made by gurgling, gurgle <**Slav**>

klòkan {a (acc. = gen.) masc.} (lit. kangaroo) **1** *sl-fea* homeless person, bum <**Fre**✍> **2** *sl-sex* fast lover, one who quickly finishes sexual intercourse **3** *sl-fea* stupid or mentally deficient person

klókati se {klôkām, klókajū imperf. intr.} *sl-fea* get nervous

klȍkī {īja (acc. = gen.) masc.} *sl-fea* homeless person, bum <**Fre**✍>

klȍkica {ē fem.} *sl-fea* homeless person, bum <**Fre**✍>

klokìnjati {ām, ajū imperf.} *col* gurgle (creek, etc.) <**Slav**>

klȍknuti {nēm, nū perf.} *col* sip (alcohol) <**Slav**>

klȍkoriti {rīm, rē imperf.} *col* make noise <**Slav**>

klȍkot {a masc.} *col* gurgle (creek, etc.) <**Slav**>

klokòtānje {a neut.} *col* gurgling (creek, etc.) <**Slav**>

klokòtati {klòkoćēm, ćū imperf. intr.} **a.** *col* gurgle (creek, etc.) <**Slav**> **b.** *sl* shoot, fire <**Slav**[*1]>

klokòtav {a, o adj.} *col* gurgling (creek, etc.) <**Slav**>

klómfer {a masc.} (lit. thrasher) *sl-sports* fan of OFK Beograd (a soccer team in Belgrade, Serbia) <**Ger**✍[*1]>

klȍntrāć {klȍntrāća (acc. = gen.) masc.} *sl* supervisor (on public transportation) <**Lat**✍[*1]>

klȍnuti {klȍnēm, nū perf.} *sl-drink* sip (alcohol) <**Slav**[*1]>

klónja {ē masc.} *sl-sex* ***Fam*** bathroom <**Ger**✍>

klònjara {ē fem.} (lit. the toilet one) *sl-sex* buttocks, butt <**Ger**✤[*1]>

klȍp [1] {excl.} *col* rap, tap <**Slav**>

klȍp [2] *See the following*

- **klȍp mâsti** {NP} (lit. a pack of fat) **a.** *sl* outrage **b.** *sl* fear

klópa {ē fem.} *sl-col* food <**Gyp**✤[*1]>

klopánac {nca masc.} **a.** *sl* food <**Gyp**✤[*1]> **b.** *sl* eating

klopánjac {njca masc.} **a.** *sl* food <**Gyp**✤[*1]> **b.** *sl* eating

klopàrati {ām, ajū imperf.} *col* make noise <**Slav**>

klȍpāroš {a (acc. = gen.) masc.} *sl-fea* voracious eater <**Gyp**✤[*1]>

klópati {klôpām, klópajū imperf.} *sl-col* eat, devour <**Gyp**✤[*1]>

klópati se {klôpām, klópajū imperf. intr.} *sl* ***Fac*** get nervous <**Gyp**✤[*1]>

klȍpavac {vca (acc. = gen.) masc.} *sl-fea* lazy or shiftless person, bum, good for nothing <**Gyp**✤[*1]>

klȍpiti {pīm, pē perf.} *sl* eat, devour <**Gyp**✤[*1]>

klȍpnuti {nēm, nū perf.} **a.** *sl* eat, devour <**Gyp**✤[*1]> **b.** *sl-crime* steal, swipe

klȍpot {a masc.} *col* the sound made by tapping, tap <**Slav**>

klopòtār {klopotára (acc. = gen.) masc.} *dia* bellwether <**Slav**✤[*1]>

klopòtati {klòpoćēm, oćū imperf. intr.} *col* make noise <**Slav**✤>

klȍšār {a (acc. = gen.) masc.} /klȍšār /ára (acc. = gen.) masc./ **a.** *sl-fea* homeless male, bum <**Fre**> **b.** *sl-fea* crude and ill-mannered male <**Fre**[*1]>

klošàrika {ē fem. & masc.} *sl-fea* homeless person, bum <**Fre**✍>

klošarȉška {ē masc.; Dat klošarȉški} /klošarȉška/ *sl-fea* homeless person, bum <**Fre**✍>

klošáriti {klȍšārīm, rē imperf.} *sl-fea* live like a homeless person <**Fre**✤>

klȍšārka {ē fem.} /klȍšārka /ē fem./ **a.** *sl-fea* homeless female, bum <**Fre**> **b.** *sl-fea* crude and ill-mannered female <**Fre**[*1]>

klȍt {a +ov (ext. pl) masc.; Nom Pl klòtovi} *col* front side (knitting) <Ger>

klȍvī {ija (acc. = gen.) masc.} *sl-crime* policeman, cop

klóvn {a (acc. = gen.) +ov (ext. pl) masc.} (lit. clown) *sl-crime* policeman, cop <Eng[*1]>

klòzetār {a (acc. = gen.) masc.} /klozètār/ *sl-mil* soldier who cleans toilets <Ger⁘[*1]>

klozètara {ē fem.} *sl music* acoustic guitar <Ger⁘[*1]>

klûb *See the following*

• **dìlkan klûb** {NP} (lit. mad man's club) *sl* ***Fac*** mental institution, madhouse

klȕfko {a neut.} [std. = klupko] *dia* ball (of wool) <Slav✍>

klúpa {ē fem.} *sl-crafts* desk

klȕpčati {ām, ajū imperf.} *sl-sex* ***Obs*** masturbate, beat off <Slav[*1]>

klȕpskē prostòrije {NP} (lit. club rooms) *sl-sstu* ***Fac*** school bathroom ☞ **prostorija**

klȕvko {a neut.} [std. = klupko] *dia* ball (of wool) <Slav✍>

kljáka {ē fem. & masc.; Dat kljáki} **a.** *sl-fea* senior citizen <Slav[*1]> **b.i.** *sl* mother, mom <Slav[*2]> **ii.** *sl-fea* handicapped person <Slav[*2]>

kljákac {kca (acc. = gen.) masc.} **a.** *sl* father, dad <Slav[*1]> **b.** *sl* grandfather, grandpa <Slav[*1]>

kljȁkav {a, o adj.} *sl-fea* handicapped <Slav[*1]>

kljȁker {a masc.} *sl-crime* thief, sticky fingers <Slav✍[*1]>

kljáko {ē masc.} *sl-fea* handicapped male <Slav>

kljȁks {a (acc. = gen.) +ev (ext. pl) masc.; Nom Pl kljàksevi} *sl-fea* unskilled person <Slav✍[*1]>

kljȁšmovac {mōvca (acc. = gen.) masc.} *sl-fea* stupid or mentally deficient person <Slav⁘[*1]>

kljâv {a +ov (ext. pl) masc.; Nom Pl kljávovi} *sl-music* piano <Fre✍>

kljáva {ē fem.} *sl-music* piano <Fre✍>

kljàver {a masc.} *sl-music* pianist <Fre✍>

kljéšta {a neut. pl.} *sl-crafts* pliers <Slav✍>

kljȋnčiti {čīm, čē imperf.} **a.** *sl* rise up **b.** *sl* sit

kljȉšiti {šīm, še imperf.} **a.** *sl* look, watch, scope out **b.** *sl* date, go out with

kljȍcati {ām, ajū imperf.} **a.** *col* click (produce a short, sharp, non-resonant sound) <Slav> **b.** *col* snip, clip <Slav[*1]> **c.** *col* chatter (of the teeth) <Slav[*2]>

kljȍknuti {nēm, nū perf. intr.} **a.** *sl* fall down, kiss the floor <Slav[*1]> **b.** *sl* get tired <Slav[*2]> **c.** *sl* die, kick the bucket <Slav[*3]>

kljȍva {ē fem.} /kljôva/ (lit. tusk) *sl* ***Fac*** tooth <Slav[*1]>

kljòvāč {kljováča (acc. = gen.) masc.; Voc kljȍvāču} (lit. the one with a pair of tusks) *sl* ***Fac*** dentist <Slav⁘[*1]>

kljòvār {kljovára (acc. = gen.) masc.; Voc kljȍvāru} (lit. the one with a pair of tusks) *sl-fea* bucktoothed person <Slav⁘[*1]>

kljòvātor {a (acc. = gen.) masc.} (lit. the one with a pair of tusks) *sl* ***Fac*** dentist <Slav⁘[*1]>

kljòvisanje {a neut.} *sl* laughing <Slav⁘[*1]>

kljȕcānje {a neut.} (lit. pecking) *sl-drugs* stumbling in effect of taking narcotic drugs <Slav[*1]>

kljȕcati {ām, ajū perf.} (lit. peck) *sl-drugs* stumble in effect of taking narcotic drugs <Slav[*1]>

kljȕcnuti {nēm, nū perf.} (lit. peck) *col* hit softly, tap <Slav[*1]>

kljûč {a +ev (ext. pl) masc.; Nom Pl kljúčevi} (lit. key) **1** *sl-sex* ***Fac-Obs*** penis, dick, prick <Slav[*1]> **2** *sl-drugs* drugs kept under lock and key <Slav[*1]>

• **fràncūskī kljûč** {NP} (lit. monkey wrench) *sl-sex* ***Fac*** penis

• **ko kljûč od lúdnicē** {PP} (lit. like the nuthouse key) *sl-fea* ***Fac*** big in size

• **sȑpskī kljûč** {NP} (lit. the Serbian wrench) *sl-sex* penis

kljȕčār {ključára (acc. = gen.) masc.} *sl-crime* burglar <Slav[*1]>

kljúčevi {čēvā masc. pl.} (lit. keys) *sl-crime* the police <Slav[*1]>

kljȕčkati {ām, ajū imperf. intr.} *sl-sex* ***Obs*** masturbate, beat off <Slav[*1]>

kljȕčnuti {nēm, nū perf. intr.} *sl-sex* ***Obs*** masturbate, beat off <Slav[*1]>

kljȕk {a +ov (ext. pl) masc.; Nom Pl kljúkovi} *sl-drugs* intake of narcotic drugs, doing drugs <Slav[*1]>

kljȕka {excl.} *col* the sound made by swallowing, gulp <Slav>

kljȕka {ē fem.; Dat kljȕki} *sl* ***Fac*** nose <Slav[*1]>

kljûn [1] {a (acc. = gen.) +ov (ext. pl) masc.; Nom Pl kljúnovi} (lit. beak) **1** *sl-crime* policeman, cop <Slav[*1]> **2** *sl-fea* offended person <Slav[*1]>

kljûn[2] {a +ov (ext. pl) masc.; Nom Pl kljúnovi} (lit. beak) **1a.** *sl* ***Fac*** nose, beak <Slav*1> **b.** *sl* mouth <Slav*2> **2** *sl* gun pistol <Slav*1>

kljùnār {a (acc. = gen.) masc.} *sl-fea* large-nosed male <Slav⁘*1>

kljúse {eta neut.} *col* old horse, nag <Slav>

kljùsina[1] {ē fem.} *col* old horse, nag <Slav>

Kljùsina[2] {ē masc.} (lit. nag) *sl* name of a coffee shop near Knez Mihailo Monument, Belgrade, Serbia <Slav*1>

kmávati {kmâvām, kmávajū imperf.} *sl* sleep, nap <Slav*1>

kméčati {čīm, čē imperf.} *col* cry, shed tears, weep <Slav>

kméza {ē fem.} *col* ***Der*** crybaby <Slav⁘>

kméziti {zīm, zē imperf.} *col* cry, shed tears, weep <Slav>

kmézo {ē masc.} *col* ***Der*** crybaby <Slav⁘>

kmȉca {ē fem.} *sl-fea* ***Off*** African American (female)

knȁp[1] {adv.} *col* exactly, as it should be <Ger>

knȁp[2] {adj.} *col* just right, as it should be <Ger>

knédla {ē fem.} (lit. dumpling) *sl-sports* ball <Ger*1>
- **njȕpati knédle** {VP} (lit. eat dumplings) *sl* ***Fac*** be cheated, be swindled

knedlírati {knèdlīrām, rajū biasp.} **a.** *sl* cheat, swindle <Ger⁘*1> **b.** *sl* lie <Ger⁘*1>

knèginja {ē fem.} (lit. duchess) *sl-sex* ***Fac*** male homosexual, queen <Slav*1>

Knêz {a +ov (ext. pl) masc.; Nom Pl Knȅzovi} *sl* name for Knez-Mihajlova street, Belgrade, Serbia <Slav*1>

Knèzmiš {a masc.} *sl* name for Knez-Mihajlova street, Belgrade, Serbia <Slav✍>

knȉndža {ē masc.} *sl-mil* Serbian rebel in Croatia in the1990s <SlavO-Jap*1>

knȍpr {knȁpr masc.; perm} /knòpr/ /prkno/ *sl-sex* ***Obs*** buttocks, butt <Slav✍>

knòriti {rīm, rē perf. intr.} **a.** *sl* die, kick the bucket <Slav✍*1> **b.** *sl* get tired

knȕt {knùta +ov (ext. pl) masc.; Nom Pl knùtovi} (lit. whip) *sl* apartment <Rus*1>

knjáva {ē fem.} **a.** *sl* sleeping <Slav> **b.i.** *sl* dream <Slav*1> **ii.** *sl* bed <Slav*2> **iii.** *sl* cap, hat
- **dèbelā knjáva** {NP} (lit. fat sleep) *sl* deep sleep

knjávati {knjâvām, knjávajū imperf.} *sl* sleep, nap <Slav>

knjávnica {ē fem.} *sl* name for Main Railroad Station restaurant, Zagreb, Croatia <Slav⁘*1>

knjévati {knjêvām, knjévajū imperf.} *sl* sleep, nap <Slav>

knjȉga *See the following*
- **cȓnā knjȉga** {NP} (lit. the black book) *sl-sstu* ***Fac*** grade book, black book
- **knjȉga ȕžāsa** {NP} (lit. the book of horror) *sl-mil* ***Fac*** daily log

knjȉškī móljac {NP} *col* book worm ☞ **moljac**

knjȉžār {a (acc. = gen.) masc.} /knjìžār/ (lit. book seller) *sl-polit* Communist, red, commie <Slav*1>

knjȉževīšte {eta neut.} *sl-sstu* school <Slav⁘*1>

knjȉžiti {žīm, žē imperf.} (lit. book) **1** *sl-sex* ***Obs*** masturbate, beat off <Slav*1> **2** *sl-sex* ***Obs*** engage in sexual intercourse with (of a male)

knjȉžiti se {žīm, žē imperf. intr.} *sl-fea* boast, brag <Slav*1>

knjòvānje {a neut.} *sl* sleeping <Slav>

knjòvati {ām, ajū imperf.} *sl* sleep, nap <Slav>

ko[1] {c.} [std. = kao] *col* as <Slav✍>
- **ko đȍjā** {PP} *dia* as if, kind of, sort of: *On ko đoja radi. He works, kind of.*

kȍ[2] *See the following*
- **kȍ o čèmu** [PRON/NOUN:NOM] o [PRON/NOUN:LOC] {S} (lit. who about what [PRON/NOUN:NOM] about [PRON/NOUN:LOC]) *col* *Ko o čemu, on o utakmici! He can't stop talking about that ball game!*

ko bêlā lála {PP} (lit. like a white tulip) SerE *col* obediently: *uraditi zadaću ko bela lala obediently do one's homework* ☞ **lala**

ko bìber po pìlavu {NP} (lit. like pepper over pilaf) BosM *col* favorably ☞ **biber**

ko blȁta {PP} (lit. as many as mud) *col* in large quantities, very many ☞ **blato**

ko bôg {PP} (lit. like a God) *col* ***App*** excellent, awesome: *supa ko bog awesome soup* ☞ **bog**

kò da ga je ćâle ìzdrkō na lòpati {PP} (lit. like his father jacked him off on a spade) **a.** *sl-fea* ***Der-Obs*** used: *auto ko da ga je ćale izdrko na lopati used car* **b.** *sl-fea* ***Der-Obs*** old **c.** *sl-fea* ***Der-Obs*** very unattractive, as if beaten with the ugly stick: *Taj frajer je ko da ga je ćale izdrko na lopati. That dude is very ugly.* **d.** *sl-fea* ***Der-Obs*** weary **e.** *sl-fea* ***Der-Obs*** undependable ☞ **ćale**

kò da ga je grȍbār pùstiō na ȍdsustvo {PP} (lit. like an undertaker gave him a leave of absence) *sl-fea* ***Fac-Der*** extremely unattractive, ugly as sin ☞ **grobar**

kò da ga je Hȉtler ìzvūkō na lùtriji {PP} (lit. like *Adolf* Hitler drew him in a lottery) *sl-fea* ***Fac-Der*** extremely unattractive, ugly as sin ☞ **Hitler**

kò da ga je izbácila kòbila u tŕku {PP} (lit. like the running mare has thrown him out) *sl-fea* ***Der-Fac*** extremely unattractive, ugly as sin ☞ **kobila**

kò da ga je izbácila pȍplava {PP} (lit. like the flood has flushed him out) **a.** *sl-fea* ***Der-Fac*** extremely unattractive, ugly as sin **b.** *sl-fea* ***Der-Fac*** sad, depressed: *Kad je saznao da nije dobio stipendiju, bio je ko da ga je izbacila poplava. He was depressed when he realized that he did not get the scholarship.* ☞ **poplava**

kò da glȅdām {PP} (lit. as if I have been watching it) *col* I can tell that ☞ **gledati**

kò da je iz Fînskē {PP} (lit. as if he is from Finland, also related to the adjective fin 'nice') *sl-fea* ***Fac*** very kind ☞ **Finska**

kò da je pòbegō grȍbāru s lòpatē {PP} (lit. as if he had escaped from the undertaker's spade) **SerE** *sl-fea* ***Der-Fac*** extremely unattractive, ugly as sin ☞ **pobeći**

kò da je rȍđen ispred fînskē ambásadē {PP} (lit. as if he was born in front of the Finnish embassy X fin 'nice') *sl-fea* ***Fac*** very kind ☞ **rođen**

ko dúša {PP} (lit. like soul) *col* very good (of a person) ☞ **duša**

ko đȍjā {PP} *dia* as if, kind of, sort of: *On ko đoja radi. He works, kind of.* ☞ **ko**

ko gòblēn {PP} (lit. like a Gobelin tapestry) *sl-fea* boring ☞ **goblen**

ko grȍb {PP} (lit. like a grave) *sl-fea* ***Der*** unattractive, ugly ☞ **grob**

ko grôblje {PP} (lit. like a graveyard) *sl-fea* ***Der*** unattractive, ugly ☞ **groblje**

ko háfiz {PP} (lit. like a person who knows the Qur'an by heart) **Bos** *col* completely, totally: *naučiti pjesmicu napamet ko hafiz learn a song by heart* ☞ **hafiz**

ko hljȅb {PP} (lit. like bread) *col* ***App*** very good (of a person) ☞ **hljeb**

ko iz dȕpeta {PP} (lit. as if it comes from the ass) *col* ***Der-Obs*** worthless, worth shit ☞ **dupe**

ko kàmēn za kùpus {PP} (lit. like the sauerkraut stone, i.e. the stone traditionally put on the top of the heads of cabbage in a barrel with salty water *sauerkraut is not only shredded but also made from whole heads of cabbage*) *sl-fea* ***Fac*** big in size ☞ **kamen**

ko kljûč od lúdnicē {PP} (lit. like the nuthouse key) *sl-fea* ***Fac*** big in size ☞ **ključ**

ko Králjević Mârko i pȉng-pȍng {PP} (lit. like crown prince Marko and ping-pong) *sl* ***Fac*** completely different ☞ **kraljević**

ko kȑme u Tȅherānu {PP} (lit. like a pig in Teheran) *sl-fea* ***Fac*** helplessly ☞ **krme**

ko krtȉčnjāk {PP} /ko kȑtičnjāk/ (lit. like a mole hole) *sl-fea* ***Der*** unattractive, ugly ☞ **krtičnjak**

ko lȉpa {PP} (lit. like a linden-tree) **1** *sl-fea* badly dressed, dressed without taste **2** *sl-fea* nicely dressed, tastefully dressed ☞ **lipa**

ko lópov {PP} (lit. like a thief) *sl-fea* extremely unattractive, ugly as sin ☞ **lopov**

ko nàkō {AdvP} *col* used to express usual state of affairs, so-so: *A. Kako je? B: Ko nako. A. How's life? B: Same-same.* ☞ **nako**

ko námērno pròbūđen kȍnj {PP} (lit. as if he is an intentionally awakened horse) *sl-fea* ***Fac*** insane, nuts ☞ **konj**

ko nè dāj Bȍže {PP} (lit. like God save us from that) *sl-fea* ***Der*** extremely unattractive, ugly as sin ☞ **Bog**

ko nèsrećan slȕčāj {PP} (lit. like an accident) *sl-fea* ***Der*** extremely unattractive, ugly as sin ☞ **slučaj**

ko ȍko {PP} (lit. like an eye) *sl-fea* filled, jam packed ☞ **oko**

ko paràgraf {PP} (lit. like a section mark) *sl-fea* ***Fac*** conceited, stuck-up ☞ **paragraf**

ko pȉčka u nȍvū kòšulju! {PP} (lit. like a cunt in a new shirt!) SSer *dia* ***Der-Obs*** evil, mean ☞ **pička**

ko pȉjanačkō góvno {PP} (lit. like a drunk's shit) *sl-fea* ***Der-Obs*** of unpleasant odor, stinking ☞ **govno**

ko pòdgrejān lȅš {PP} (lit. like a reheated corpse) SerE *sl-fea* ***Fac*** extremely unattractive, ugly as sin ☞ **leš**

ko pòpōv rùkāv {PP} (lit. like a priest's sleeve) *sl-sex* ***Fac-Obs*** large (of a vagina) ☞ **rukav**

ko pòrodičnā grȍbnica {PP} (lit. like a family tomb) *sl-fea* ***Der-Fac*** extremely unattractive, ugly as sin ☞ **grobnica**

ko prâse u plèhu {PP} (lit. like a piglet in a roasting pan) *sl-fea* ***Fac*** crumpet ☞ **prase**

ko prâvī {PP} (lit. like a real one) *col* ***App*** excellent, awesome ☞ **pravi**

ko próliv {PP} (lit. like diarrhea) *sl-fea* ***Der-Obs*** very boring ☞ **proliv**

Kȍ [PRON:ACC] jèbē! {LSF} (lit. Who fucks [PRON:ACC]!) *col* ***Off*** used to refer to indifference toward: *Ko ga jebe! Who gives a shit about him!* ☞ **jebati**

Kȍ [PRON:DAT] klȁckā kȍsti! {LSF} (lit. Who is see-sawing [PPRON] bones!) *col* ***Off*** used to refer to indifference toward: *Ko ti klacka kosti? Who gives a shit about you?* ☞ **klackati**

Kȍ [PRON:ACC] šîšā! {LSF} (lit. Who is giving [PRON: ACC] a haircut!) *col* ***Off*** used to refer to indifference toward: *Ko ga šiša? Who gives a shit about him?* ☞ **šišati**

Kȍ [PRON:DAT] jèbē mȁtēr! {LSF} (lit. Who fucks [PPRON] mother!) *col* ***Off*** used to refer to indifference toward ☞ **jebati**

ko s pȍslom {PP} (lit. like being on business) *col* used to refer to an usually illegal or inappropriate action performed without any hesitation, just like that: *ukrasti auto ko s poslom steal a car just like that* ☞ **posao**

ko salìven {PP} (lit. as if being molded) *col* perfect ☞ **saliven**

ko svȉ srȅtni {PP} (lit. like everybody is happy) *col* used to refer to an usually illegal or inappropriate action performed without any hesitation, just like that: *On, ko svi sretni, počeo da puši u kupeu za nepušače. He started to smoke in a non-smoker's compartment just like that.* ☞ **posao**

ko šêst bȁnki u sitnìni {PP} (lit. like sixty dinars in metal) *sl-fea* obese and unattractive ☞ **banka**

ko šifònjēr {PP} (lit. like a cupboard) *sl-fea* muscular ☞ **šifonjer**

Kȍ te drìblā! {S} (lit. Who is dribbling you?) *sl* ***Off*** used as a weak curse, Screw you! ☞ **driblati**

Kȍ te dȑndā! {S} (lit. Who is shaking you?) *sl* ***Off*** used as a weak curse, Screw you! ☞ **drndati**

Kȍ te jȁšī! {S} (lit. Who is riding you?) *sl* ***Off*** used as a weak curse, Screw you! ☞ **jašiti**

Kȍ te jèbē! {S} (lit. Who is fucking you?) *col* ***Off*** used to express disrespect, Fuck you! ☞ **jebati**

Ko te ȍnodī! {S} *dia* ***Off*** used to express disrespect, Fuck you! ☞ **onoditi**

kȍ te pîtā {S} (lit. who asks you) *col* used to indicate that one's interlocutor is not authorized to make decisions, Who asks you? ☞ **pitati**

Kȍ te sèdlā! {S} (lit. Who is putting a saddle on you?) *sl* ***Off*** used as a weak curse, Screw you! ☞ **sedlati**

Kȍ te sȉsā! {S} (lit. Who is sucking you?) *col* ***Off*** used to express disrespect, Fuck you! ☞ **sisati**

Kȍ te šévī! {S} (lit. Who is fucking you?) *sl* ***Off*** used to express disrespect, Fuck you! ☞ **ševiti**

Kȍ te šȅvkā! {S} (lit. Who is fucking you?) *sl* ***Off*** used to express disrespect, Fuck you! ☞ **ševkati**

Kȍ te šîšā! {S} (lit. Who is giving you a haircut?) *col* ***Off*** used to express disrespect, Screw you! ☞ **šišati**

Kȍ te šljívī! {S} (lit. Who is plumming you?) *col* ***Off*** used to express disrespect, Screw you! ☞ **šljiviti**

Kȍ te tȑtī! {S} (lit. Who is fucking you?) *sl* ***Off*** used to express disrespect, Fuck you! ☞ **trtiti**

Kȍ te vȑtī! {S} (lit. Who is turning you over?) *sl* ***Off*** used to express disrespect, Fuck you! ☞ **vrteti**

ko tésne gȁće {PP} (lit. like a tight pair of panties) SerE *sl-fea* very boring ☞ **gaće**

Kȍ ti klȁckā kȍsti! {S} (lit. Who is see-sawing your bones?) *sl* ***Off*** used to express disrespect, Screw you! ☞ **klackati**

Kȍ ti šmìrglā ȕši! {S} (lit. Who is polishing your ears?) *sl* ***Off*** used to express disrespect, Screw you! ☞ **šmirglati**

Kȍ ti štrìkā créva! {S} (lit. Who is knitting your intestines?) **SerE** *sl* ***Off*** used to express disrespect, Screw you! ☞ **štrikati**

ko trìper {PP} (lit. like gonorrhea) *sl-fea* boring ☞ **triper**

ko tròkrīlnī òrmān {PP} (lit. like a three-door cupboard) *sl-fea* muscular, pumped up ☞ **orman**

ko Zábāvnīk {PP} (lit. like Zabavnik *a multi-colored Yugoslav children's weekly*) *sl-fea* tattooed ☞ **zabavnik**

ko zdrâvlje {PP} (lit. like health) *sl-fea* excellent, awesome ☞ **zdravlje**

ko zmȁj {PP} (lit. like a dragon) **1** *col* excellent, awesome, **2** *sl-fea* very fast ☞ **zmaj**

ko zmìja u cévi {PP} (lit. like a snake in a gun barrel) SerE *sl-fea* in a helpless position, like fish in a barrel ☞ **zmija**

ko žûtī {PP} (lit. like the yellow one) *sl-fea* completely, totally ☞ **žuti**

kobajági {part.} *col* used to express uncertainty <**Slav-NE**[*1]>

kobàsica {ē fem.} (lit. sausage) **1** *sl-sex* ***Obs*** penis, dick, prick <**Slav**[*1]> **2** *sl-fea* ***Obs*** long routine talk <**Slav**[*1]>

3 *sl-media* article <Slav*1> 3 *sl* letter (correspondence) <Slav*1>

kòbila {ē fem.} (lit. mare) **a.** *sl-fea* big-boned female <Slav*1> **b.** *sl-fea* unattractive female, dog <Slav*2>
• **kò da ga je izbácila kòbila u tȑku** {PP} (lit. like the running mare has thrown him out) *sl-fea* ***Der-Fac*** extremely unattractive, ugly as sin
• **trȕlā kòbila** {NP} (lit. rotten mare) *col* leap frog (the game)

kȍbra {ē fem.} (lit. cobra) *sl-fea* female with eyeglasses, four-eyes <Lat*1>

kȍbradžija {ē masc.} (lit. cobra dude) *sl-fea* troublemaker, rowdy, ruffian <Lat❖*1>

kóca {ē fem.} **1** *sl-drugs* cocaine, coke <Spa✍> **2** *sl* Coca-Cola, coke <Spa✍> **3** *sl-gamble* gambler <Slav✍*1>

kȍcka {ē fem.; Dat kȍcki} (lit. cube) *sl-polit* the former Croatian Communist Party Central Committee building, Zagreb, Croatia <Slav*1>
• **stârā kȍcka** {NP} (lit. old square) *sl-mil* old soldier

kȍcoš {a masc.} *sl-gamble* gambler <Slav❖*1>

kóča {ē masc.} *sl* conductor (on a train, bus, or streetcar) <Fre✍>

kȍčija {ē masc.} (lit. chariot) *sl* cab, taxi <Hun*1>

kȍčijāš {a (acc. = gen.) masc.} /kočìjāš/ *sl* driver <Hun❖*1>

kȍčopēran {rna, rno adj.} *col* spry <Slav>

kȍćavac {ćāvca masc.} **a.** *sl-arch* egg **b.** *sl-sex* testicle, ball

kȍćka {ē fem.; Dat kȍćki} *sl-arch* hen <Slav✍>

kod práznōg stòla {PP} (lit. at an empty table) *Cro sl* name for the former Opera bar in Zagreb, Croatia ☞ **sto**

kódža {ē masc.} *sl-drugs* codeine <Eng✍>

kôdžos {a masc.} *sl-drugs* codeine <Eng✍>

kòfa {ē fem.} *sl* head <NE*1>

kòfer {a masc.} *sl* cab, taxi <Ger*1>

kofijánović {a masc.} *sl* coffee <Eng✍>

kòfrčiti se {čīm, čē imperf. intr.} *sl-fea* be conceited, be stuck-up

kȍhle {eta neut.} (lit. coal) *sl-drugs* drug money <Ger*1>

kȍj {pron.} *dia* who (in all its Serbo-Croatian meanings in the form different from the standard) <Slav✍>

Kȍj ćeš mi kȕrac! {S} (lit. Which prick do I need you!) *col* ***Off*** used in angry dismissal, Fuck off! ☞ **kurac**

Kȍj ćeš mi màtrāk! {S} *dia* ***Off*** used to make somebody go away, Beat it! ☞ **matrak**

Kȍj ćeš mi môj! {S} (lit. Which mine do I need you!) *dia* ***Off*** used in angry dismissal, Fuck off! ☞ **moj**

Kȍj ti je môj! {S} (lit. Which mine is it to you!) *dia* ***Off*** used in angry dismissal, Fuck off! ☞ **moj**

Kòjā cȓnā [NOUN:NOM]? {S} *col* used to ask for additional information, [NOUN:NOM] who: *Koja crna Marija? Marija who?* ☞ **kojii**

Kȍja si ti pȉčka od čovèka! {S} (lit. What kind of a cunt of man you are!) SerE *col* ***Off*** used to express disrespect, Fuck you! ☞ **pička**

Kȍjā ti je pízda màterina! {S} (lit. What kind of mother's cunt is it to you?) *col* ***Obs*** used to express negative attitude toward one's interlocutor ☞ **pizda**

Kȍjē su to fôre? {S} (lit. What kind of tricks are that?) *col* used to ask for additional information ☞ **fora**

kòjī *See the following*

Kòjī cȓnī[NOUN:NOM]? {S} *col* used to ask for additional information: *Koji crni Marko? Marko who?* ☞ **koji**

Kòjī će ([PRON:DAT]) **kȕrac?** {LSF} (lit. Which prick do/does [PRON] need it for?) *col* ***Obs*** used to refer to negative attitude toward an object: *Koji će ti kurac? What the hell do you need it for?* ☞ **kurac**

Kòjī ćeš kȕrac! {S} (lit. Which prick do you want?) *col* ***Off*** used in angry dismissal, Fuck off! ☞ **kurac**

kòjī klȉnac {NP} (lit. which nail) *col* used to express disagreement, why the hell: *Koji klinac ideš tamo? Why the hell are you going there?* ☞ **klinac**

kòjī kȕrac {NP} (lit. which prick) *col* ***Obs*** why: *Koji kurac ideš tamo? Why are you going there?* ☞ **kurac**

Kòjī kȕrac tî mène zajèbāvāš! {S} (lit. Which prick are you teasing me?) *col* ***Off*** used in angry dismissal, Fuck off! ☞ **kurac**

kòjī [PRON:DAT] **je kȕrac** {LSF} (lit. which cock is it to [PRON:ACC]) *col* ***Obs*** used to express negative attitude toward one's interlocutor: *koji im je kurac what's wrong with them* ☞ **kurac**

kòjī [PRON:DAT] **je đàvō** {LSF} (lit. what kind of devil is it with [PRON:ACC]) *col* used to express negative attitude toward one's interlocutor: *koji ti je đavo what's wrong with you* ☞ **đavo**

Kòjī ti je? {S} (lit. Which is it to you?) *col* used to express negative attitude toward one's interlocutor ☞ **koji**

Kòjī ti je àndrāk? {S} (lit. What kind of devil is it to you?) *dia* used to express negative attitude toward one's interlocutor ☞ **andrak**

Kòjī ti je kȍkot? {S} (lit. What kind of rooster is it to you?) *dia* used to express negative attitude toward one's interlocutor ☞ **kokot**

Kòjī ti je kȕrac? {S} (lit. Which cock is it with you?) *col* ***Obs*** used to express negative attitude toward one's interlocutor, What's wrong with you? ☞ **kurac**

kòjī *See the following*

- **Kòjā cȓnā[NOUN:NOM]?** {S} *col* used to ask for additional information: *Koja crna Marija? Marija who?*
- **Kòjī cȓnī[NOUN:NOM]?** {S} *col* used to ask for additional information: *Koji crni Marko? Marko who?*
- **Kòjī ti je?** {S} (lit. Which is it to you?) *col* used to express negative attitude toward one's interlocutor, What's wrong with you?

kojlektȉvnaja razvaljòtka {NP} (lit. collective destruction) *sl-sex* group sex ☞ **razvaljotka**

kȍjot {a (acc. = gen.) masc.} (lit. coyote) *sl-fea* beggar <**Spa**[*1]>

kóka {ē fem.; Dat kóki} (lit. hen) **1a.** *sl-sex* ***Obs*** vagina, cunt <**Slav**[*1]> **b.** *sl-sex* ***Obs*** prostitute, hooker <**Slav**[*2]> **c.** *sl* ***Obs*** female, cunt <**Slav**[*3]> **2** *sl-drugs* ***Obs*** cocaine, coke <**Slav**✍> **3** *sl-crime* ***Obs*** switch blade <**Slav**[*1]>

kokȁčina {ē fem.} **a.** *sl-sex* ***Obs*** sexual intercourse <**Slav**⁘[*1]> **b.** *sl* fight (e.g. fist fight)

kokaína {ē fem.} *sl-drugs* cocaine, coke <**Spa**✍>

kokalína {ē fem.} **1** *sl* bone: *makaroni s kokalinom meat pasta* <**Gre**> **2** *sl* meat <**Gre**>

kókānje {a neut.} **a.** *sl* beating up <**Slav**⁘[*1]> **b.** *sl* fight (e.g. fist fight) **c.** *sl* killing **d.** *sl* sexual intercourse

kòkara {ē fem.} **a.** *sl-sex* ***Obs*** prostitute, hooker <**Slav**⁘[*1]> **b.** *sl-fea* ***Obs*** female experienced in sex <**Slav**⁘[*2]> **c.** *sl-fea* ***Obs*** elderly female <**Slav**⁘[*3]>

kókati {kôkām, kókajū imperf.} **a.** *sl* beat up **b.i.** *sl* kill, murder **ii.** *sl-sex* engage in sexual intercourse with (of a male)

kókati se {kôkām, kókajū imperf. intr.} **a.** *sl* fight (e.g. fist fight) **b.** *sl* engage in sexual intercourse with (of a female)

kȍkavac {vca masc.} /kòkavac/ *sl* punch with one knuckle sticking out <**Slav**[*1]>

kokáža {ē fem.} *sl* fight (e.g. fist fight)

kȍkče {eta neut.} *sl-drugs* cocaine, coke <**Spa**✍>

kokèriti se {rīm, rē imperf. intr.} *sl* expose oneself, be conspicuous

kȍkī {īja masc.} /kòki/ *sl-drugs* cocaine, coke <**Spa**✍>

kȍkica {ē fem.} **1** *sl-drugs* cocaine, coke <**Spa**✍> **2** *sl-sex* prostitute, hooker <**Slav**⁘[*1]>

kókice {kīcā fem. pl.} *sl-drugs* cocaine, coke <**Slav**[*1]>

kȍknuti {nēm, nū perf.} *sl* kill, murder <**Slav**[*1]>

kokodákati {kòdāčēm, čū imperf.} (lit. cock-a-doodle-doo) *sl-fea* talk a lot, run one's month <**Slav**[*1]>

kȍkos {a masc.} (lit. coconut) *sl-drugs* cocaine, coke <**Spa**[*1]>

kȍkōš {i fem.} (lit. hen) **1** *sl-sex* ***Fac*** male homosexual, gay <**Slav**[*1]> **2** *sl-fea* ***Der*** foolish female <**Slav**[*1]>

kokȍšār {košára (acc. = gen.) masc.} (lit. poultry farmer) **1** *sl-crime* policeman, cop <**Slav**⁘[*1]> **2** *sl-fea* extremely talkative person, chatterbox **3** *sl-crime* petty thief

kokȍšārnīk {a masc.} (lit. hen-house) *sl-stu* girl's dormitory <**Slav**⁘[*1]>

kokošínjac {njca masc.} (lit. hen-house) **a.** *sl-fea* untidy apartment <**Slav**⁘[*1]> **b.** *sl* apartment <**Slav**⁘[*2]>

kokošínjac bâr {NP} (lit. hen-house bar) *sl-drink* Neboder bar, Zagreb, Croatia ☞ **bar**

kokȍšjā bȍlēst {NP} (lit. hen's disease) *sl-sex* anal sexual intercourse ☞ **bolest**

kokȍšjī abòrtus {NP} (lit. hen's abortion) *sl-drink* brandy and coke ☞ **abortus**

kòkōška {ē fem.; Dat kòkoški} /kòkoška, kȍkoška/ (lit. hen) **1a.** *sl* mucus, snot <**Slav**⁘[*1]> **b.** *sl* spit <**Slav**⁘[*2]> **2** *sl-fea* foolish female <**Slav**⁘[*1]>

kȍkot {a (acc. = gen.) masc.} (lit. rooster) **1** *sl-sex* ***Obs*** penis, dick, prick <**Slav**[*1]> **2** *sl-fea* moderately strong male <**Slav**[*1]>

- **Kòjī ti je kȍkot?** {S} (lit. What kind of rooster is it to you?) *dia* used to express negative attitude toward one's interlocutor, What's wrong with you?

kòkota {ē fem.} *sl-sex* prostitute, hooker <**Fre**[*1]>

kokòtān {kotána (acc. = gen.) masc.} **a.** *dia* rooster <**Slav**> **b.** *sl-sex* penis, cock

kokòtati {kòkoćēm, ćū imperf. intr.} *col* cackle (hens, etc.) <**Slav**>

kȍkotica {ē fem.} *sl-fea* kind of male hairstyle from WWII <**Slav**[*1]>

kokovèlisati {išēm, išū imperf.} *sl* lie

kȍks {a +ev (ext. pl) masc.; Nom Pl kòksevi} *sl-drugs* cocaine, coke <**Eng**[*1]>

kòktel {koktèla (acc. = gen.) masc.} (lit. cocktail) **1** *sl-sex* ***Obs*** sperm <**Eng**[*1]> **2** *sl-drugs* mixture of narcotic drugs <**Eng**[*2]>

kòkuz {a (acc. = gen.) masc.} **a.** *sl-fea* person out of money, person who is broke <**NE**> **b.** *sl-gamble* person who lost his/ her money in gambling <**NE**[*1]>

kȍla [1] {a neut. pl.} **1** *col* car, wheels <**Slav**[*1]> **2** *sl-gamble* playing card <**Slav**[*1]>

kóla [2] {a neut. pl.} Coca-Cola, coke <**Spa**✎>
- **kȍla za salátu** {NP} (lit. salad cart) *sl-crime* police van, paddy wagon

kòlac {kóca masc.} **1a.** *sl-sex* ***Fac-Obs*** penis, dick, prick <**Slav**[*1]> **b.** *sl-sex* ***Fac-Obs*** erect penis <**Slav**[*2]> **2** *sl-music* clarinet <**Slav**[*1]> **3** *sl-sstu* failing grade <**Slav**[*1]> **4** *sl-fea* slender leg <**Slav**[*1]>

kòlāč *See the following*
- **Kòlāč ti jèbēm!** {S} (lit. I fuck your cake!) *col* ***Fac*** used to emphasize one's point

kolàčārnica *See the following*
- **Kolàčārnicu ti jèbēm!** {S} (lit. I fuck your cake-bakery!) *dia* ***Fac*** used to emphasize one's point

kȍladžija {ē masc.} *sl* engineer <**Slav-NE**[*1]>

kòlājna {ē fem.} (lit. medal) *sl-fea* boaster, braggart, blowhard <**Ita**>

kólati {kôlām, kólajū imperf.} (lit. circulate) *sl-sex* ***Obs*** engage in sexual intercourse with (of a male) <**Slav**[*1]>

kòlbn {a masc.} *sl-auto* piston <**Ger**[*1]>

kòlbringa {ē fem.; Dat kòlbringi} *sl-auto* piston ring <**Ger**[*1]>

kòleba {ē fem.} *dia* shack <**Slav**✎>

kolèga {ē masc.; Dat kolégi} (lit. colleague) *sl-crime* ***Iro*** police investigator <**Lat**[*1]>

kòleno *See the following*
- **Brȉžitkino kòleno** {NP} (lit. Brigitte Bardot's knee) SerE *sl-fea* ***Fac*** bald head

kòlenović {a (acc. = gen.) masc.} SerE *col* ***App*** male from a respected family <**Slav**>

kòliba *See the following*
- **kòliba za komemoráciju** {NP} (lit. obituary shack) *sl* studio, efficiency apartment
- **Kòlibu ti jèbēm!** {S} (lit. I fuck your shack!) *dia* ***Obs*** used to emphasize one's point

kolíca {ā neut. pl.} *sl-auto* car, wheels <**Slav**⁘>

Kòliko cêpāš? {S} (lit. How much do you cut?) **SerE** *sl* used in bargaining (e.g. in a market, bazaar), How much? ☞ cepati

Kòlikō je dȍbar? {S} (lit. How good is he?) *sl* used to inquire about the financial state of a third party, How much money does he have? ☞ dobar

Kòlikō je téško? {S} (lit. How heavy is it?) *col* used to ask about quantity or price, How much? ☞ težak

Kòlikō je tèžak? {S} (lit. How heavy is he?) *col* used to inquire about the financial state of a third party, How much money does he have? ☞ težak

Kòlikō je zmíjā? {S} (lit. How many snakes?) *sl* used to inquire about the time, What time is it? ☞ zmija

kòliko sȕtra {AdvP} (lit. how much tomorrow) *col* first thing in the morning ☞ sutra

kòlīnje {a neut.} (lit. pig slaughtering) *sl-sex* ***Fac*** menstruation, period <**Slav**[*1]>

kòlko {adv.} [std. = koliko] *col* how much, how many: *Kolko imaš love? How much money do you have?* ◊ *Kolko ljudi ide na izlet? How many people are going on the field trip?* <**Slav**✎>
- **Kòlkō ònō bî?** {S} (lit. How much was it?) *col* used to ask about quantity or price, How much?

kȍlmovati {mujēm, mujū imperf.} *sl-fea* curl one's hair (as a style)

kȍlnuti {nēm, nū perf.} *sl* call (phone, etc.) <**Eng**>

kolodvorȉška {ē fem.; Dat kolodvorȉški} [std. = kolodvor] Cro *sl* main railroad station, Zagreb, Croatia <**Slav**✎>

kȍlpić {a masc.} *sl* news boy <**Fre**✎>

kolumbírati {lùmbīrām, lumbírajū perf.} (lit. Columbus) *sl* re-invent the wheel <**SpaO**[*1]>

kòljeno *See the following*
- **preko kòljena** {PP} (lit. over one's knee) *col* quickly and superficially

kòljka {ē fem.} *sl-arch* hen <**Slav**✎>

kòljenović {a (acc. = gen.) masc.} *col* ***App*** male from a respected family <**Slav**>

kòma {ē fem.} **a.** *sl* unconsciousness <**Gre**[*1]> **b.** *sl-drink* state of being drunk <**Gre**[*2]>

kòmād [1] {komáda (acc. = gen.) masc.; Voc kȍmáde} (lit. piece) **1a.** *sl* female, piece <**Gre**[*1]> **b.** *sl* attractive female <**Gre**[*2]> **2** *sl* male, guy <**Gre**[*1]>
- **dȍbar kòmād** {NP} (lit. a good piece) *sl-sex* ***App*** attractive, good-looking person

kòmād [2] {komáda masc.} (lit. piece) **1** *sl* ten dinars; a ten-dinar bill <**Gre**[*1]> **2** *sl-sstu* failing grade <**Gre**[*1]>

kòmanč-bêbi {fem.} (lit. Comanche) **1** *sl-fea* confrontational female <**Eng**[*1]> **2** *sl-fea* female with excessive makeup <**Eng**[*1]>

komàndo {a (acc. = gen.) masc.} (lit. commando) *sl-drugs* drug addict, junkie <**Eng**[*1]>

kòmāndos {a (acc. = gen.) masc.} (lit. commando) *sl-drugs* drug addict, junkie <**Eng**[*1]>

komárac {rca (acc. = gen.) masc.} (lit. mosquito) **1** *sl-mil* airman <**Slav**[*1]> **2** *sl* gardener <**Slav**[*1]>

komàrdžija {ē masc.} *sl-gamble* passionate gambler <**Slav**❖[*1]>

kòmāt [1] {komáta (acc. = gen.) masc.} (lit. piece) [std. = komad] **1** *sl* female <**Gre**✍[*1]> **2** *sl* boy, kid <**Gre**✍[*1]>

kòmāt [2] {komáta masc.} [std. = komad] *dia-col* piece, chunk <**Gre**✍>

kombìnīr-cánge {ī fem. pl.} *sl-crafts* pliers <**Ger**>

kombìnīr-cángle {ī fem. pl.} *sl-crafts* pliers <**Ger**>

kombìnīrke {ī fem. pl.} *sl-crafts* pliers <**Ger**>

kòmē mâjku {S} (lit. to whom are you cursing mother) *col* used to interrupt one's interlocutor by pretending to ask a question, what ☞ **majka**

komèndija {ē fem.} [std. = komedija] *dia-col* joke <**Gre**✍[*1]>

komendìjant {a (acc. = gen.) masc.} [std. = komedijant] *sl-fea* joker, trickster, rascal <**Gre**✍[*1]>

komfórnā {ē fem. (adj. decl.)} *sl-fea* attractive female <**Eng**[*1]>

komìnjati {ām, ajū imperf.} (lit. husk corn cobs) *sl-sex* ***Fac-Obs*** engage in sexual intercourse with (of a male) <**Slav**[*1]>

komírati se {kòmīrām, komírajū perf. intr.} *sl-drink* get very drunk, get smashed <**Gre**❖[*1]>

komìšāk {mišáka (acc. = gen.) masc.; Voc kȍmišāče} *sl-crime* policeman, cop <**Slav**[*1]>

kòmišnjāk {a (acc. = gen.) masc.; Voc kȍmišnjāče} *sl-crime* policeman, cop <**Slav**[*1]>

kòmita {ē masc.} (lit. Macedonian rebel) **a.** *sl-crime* accomplice <**Lat**[*1]> **b.** *sl-crime* person who sells various merchandise in night clubs <**Lat**[*2]>

kȍmka *See the following*

- **Kȍmku ti jèbēm!** {S} (lit. I screw your neighbor!) *dia* ***Off*** used as a weak curse, Screw you!

komoràna {ē fem.} **1** *sl-sex* ***Obs*** place intended for sexual intercourse <**Gre**[*1]> **2** *sl-gamble* gambling place <**Gre**[*1]> **3** *sl-gamble* hiding place <**Gre**[*1]>

kȍmōtan {tna, tno adj.} **a.** *col* relaxed, laid back <**Lat**> **b.** *sl-fea* affluent, loaded, fat <**Lat**[*1]>

kȍmōtno {adv.} *col* easily, without any difficulties <**Lat**[*1]>

kòmovača {ē fem.} *sl-drink* grape brandy <**Slav**❖>

kòmovica {ē fem.} *sl-drink* grape brandy <**Slav**❖>

kȍmp {a +ov (ext. pl) masc.} /*/a +ov (ext. pl) masc./* [std. = kompjuter, kompjutor] *sl* computer <**Eng**✍>

kȍmpa {ē fem.} **1a.** *sl* company (group of people) <**Fre**✍> **b.** *sl* friend (male) <**Fre**✍[*1]> **2** *sl* computer <**Lat**[*1]>

kompànija {ē fem.} **a.** *col* company (group of people) <**Fre**[*1]> **b.** *sl-crime* gang, group of one's close friends <**Fre**[*2]>

kȍmpić {a (acc. = gen.) masc.} /kòmpīć/ **1a.** *sl* partner <**Fre**✍> **b.** *sl* friend (male) <**Fre**✍[*1]> **2** *sl* computer <**Lat**✍>

kòmpiš {a (acc. = gen.) masc.} *sl-fea* lacking self-assurance: *biti kompiš na zabavi lack self-assurance at a party* <**Ita**✍[*1]>

kompletáža {ē fem.} *sl-crafts* completing <**Fre**>

komplètno {adv.} *col* completely, totally <**Lat**>

komšìče {eta neut.} SSer *dia-col* neighbor (female) <**NE**❖>

- **Komšìče ti jèbēm!** {S} (lit. I screw your neighbor!) SSer *dia* ***Off*** used as a weak curse, Screw you!

komšičénce *See the following*

- **Komšičénce ti malècko!** {S} (lit. *I screw* your little neighbor!) *dia* ***Off*** used as a weak curse, Screw you!

kòmšija {ē fem.} **Din** *col* neighbor (female) <**NE**[*1]>

kòmšika {ē fem.; Dat kòmšīki} *col* neighbor (female) <**NE**>

- **Komšìku ti jèbēm!** {S} (lit. I screw your neighbor!) *dia* ***Off*** used as a weak curse, Screw you!
- **Komšiłək ti cìganskī!** {S} (lit. *I screw* your Gypsy neighborhood!) *dia* ***Off*** used as a weak curse, Screw you!
- **Komšiłək ti jèbēm!** {S} (lit. I screw your neighborhood!) **SSer** *dia* ***Off*** used as a weak curse, Screw you!

komšiłək *See the following*

komšìluk {a masc.} **Din** *col* neighborhood <**NE**[*1]>

- **Komšìluk ti lópovskī!** {S} (lit. *I screw* your thieving neighborhood!) *col* ***Off*** used as a weak curse, Screw you!

kòmšinica {ē fem.} **Din** *col* neighbor (female) <**NE***1>

kòmšinjāk {a (acc. = gen.) masc.} *sl-crime* policeman, cop <**NE***1>

kómšo {ē masc.} **Din** *col* neighbor (male) <**NE***1>

kȍmunālnā vòda {NP} (lit. community water) *col* fresh water ☞ **voda**

kȍmunālnō {ōg neut.} *col* utilities (e.g. electricity) <**Lat***1>

komùnār {munára (acc. = gen.) masc.} *sl-polit* Communist, red, commie <**Fre**❖>

komùnjara {ē fem.} *sl-polit* Communist, red, commie <**Fre**❖>

komùnjārka {ē fem.; Dat komùnjārki} *sl-polit* Communist, red, commie <**Fre**❖>

komùnjārskī {ā, ō adj.} *sl-polit* Communist, red, commie <**Fre**❖>

kònak {a masc.} **Din** *col* overnight stay at another's apartment, sleepover <**NE***1>

koncèntrāt {centráta masc.} *sl* small quantity of something <**Lat***1>

kòncert {a masc.} (lit. concert) *sl-sex* ***Fac-Obs*** group sex <**Ita***1>

kônci {náca masc. pl.} (lit. threads) **a.** *sl* dress <**Slav***1> **b.** *sl* clothing, threads <**Slav***2>

kȍnda {ē fem.} *sl* fitness (physical or psychological) <**Lat**✍>

kóndo {a masc.} *col* conductor (on a train, bus, or streetcar) <**Fre**✍>

kȍndor {a (acc. = gen.) masc.} **1** *sl* conductor (on a train, bus, or streetcar) <**Fre**✍> **2** *sl-crime* policeman, cop

kȍnfić {a (acc. = gen.) masc.} *sl-crime* ***Der*** informer, stoolie, snitch <**Fre**✍*1>

konfjûz {adj.} *sl-fea* confused <**Eng**>

kòngrez {a masc.} [std. = kongres] *sl* congress (meeting) <**Lat**✍>

konkrȅtno {ōg neut.} *sl-drink* alcoholic beverage <**Lat***1>

konkrȅtno {adv.} *sl-drink* hard (of liquor) <**Lat***1>

konobarȉška {ē fem.; Dat konobarȉški} /konobarȉška/ [std. = konobar] *sl-drink* waiter <**Slav**✍>

kònop {a masc.} *col* rope <**Slav**>

kònstatovati {tujēm, tujū imperf.} **a.** *sl* have respect for: *ne konstatovati roditelje lack respect for one's parents* <**Lat***1> **b.** *sl* notice, observe <**Lat***2>

kòntara {ē fem.} *sl-drink* bar (drinking place)

kòntati {ām, ajū imperf.} **a.** *sl* compute <**Lat***1> **b.** *sl* understand, realize: *Ne kontam šta hoćeš da kažeš. I don't get what you want to say.* <**Lat***2> **c.** *sl* plan: *kontati put na more plan a trip to the seashore* <**Lat***3> **d.** *sl* think, ponder <**Lat***4>

kontèjnerka {ē fem.} /kontéjnerka/ (lit. the one from the garbage bin) **1** *sl* alley cat <**Eng**❖*1> **2** *sl-sex* prostitute, hooker <**Eng**❖*1>

kȍntić {a masc.} Cro *sl* Intercontinental Hotel (Zagreb, Croatia) <**BN**✍>

kȍnto *See the following*

- **a kȍnto** [NP:GEN] {c.conj} (lit. on account of [NP:GEN]) *col* regarding, with regard to [NP:ACC]: *Rekao mi je nešto a konto tebe. He told me something regarding you.*

kȍntra {ē fem.} *sl-sports* counterattack <**Lat**>

kȍntra ûma {PP} (lit. against the mind) *sl* headache: *pilula kontra uma headache remedy* ☞ **um**

kȍntrāš {kontráša (acc. = gen.) masc.} **1** *sl-fea* person opposed to everything, contrarian <**Lat**❖> **2** *sl* supervisor (on public transportation) <**Lat**❖> **3** *sl* male homosexual, gay <**Lat**>

kontràšica {ē fem.} *sl-sex* ***Fac-Obs*** female who enjoys anal sexual intercourse <**Lat**❖*1>

kȍntrić {a (acc. = gen.) masc.} *sl* supervisor (on public transportation) <**Fre**✍>

kontróla {ē fem.} *sl-gamble* counter move <**Fre***1>

kontròlōr {rolóra (acc. = gen.) masc.} *sl-drink* waiter <**Fre***1>

kòntuzovati se {zujēm, zujū perf. intr.} *sl-fea* be astonished, be amazed <**Lat***1>

kónusica {ē fem.} *sl* shoe <**BN***1>

kȍnvoj {a masc.} (lit. convoy) *sl-fea* package (in general) <**Fre***1>

kȍnj [1] {kònja (acc. = gen.) masc.} (lit. horse) **1a.** *sl-fea* stupid or mentally deficient person <**Slav***1> **b.** *sl-fea* clumsy person, klutz <**Slav***2> **2** *sl-fea* very young female, little girl <**Slav***1> **3** *sl* thousand dinars; a thousand-dinar bill, grand <**Slav***1> **4** *sl* ten thousand dinars; a ten thousand-dinar bill <**Slav***1> **5** *sl* hundred dinars; a hundred-dinar bill <**Slav***1> **6** *sl-drugs* heroin, horse, smack <**Slav***1> **7** *sl-sex* ***Obs*** anus, asshole <**Slav***1>

• **ko námērno prȍbūđen kȍnj** {PP} (lit. as if he is an intentionally awakened horse) *sl-fea* ***Fac*** insane, nuts

Kȍnj [2] {kȍnja (acc. = gen.) masc.} (lit. horse) **1** *sl* name of a coffee shop near Knez Mihailo Monument, Belgrade, Serbia <Slav*1> **2** *sl* name for Trg Republike in Belgrade <Slav*1>

kȍnjāk {a masc.} (lit. cognac) **1** *sl-auto* cab, taxi <Fre*1> **2** *sl-drugs* heroin, horse, smack <Fre*1>

kȍnjara {ē fem.} **a.** *sl-auto* garage <Slav*1> **b.** *sl-sex* buttocks, butt <Slav*2>

kȍnjica *See the following*

• **lȁkā kȍnjica** {NP} (lit. light cavalry) **1** *sl-sex* penis **2** *sl-sex* a group of prostitutes

kȍnjīć-gȑbonjić {konjíća-gȑbonjića (acc. = gen.) masc.} (lit. hump-backed horsie) *sl-sex* ***Fac-Obs*** penis, dick, prick <Slav*1>

kȍnjina {ē fem.} (lit. big horse) *sl-fea* worthless or despicable person, bum <Slav*1>

kȍnjosānje {a neut.} *sl* sleeping <Slav✤*1>

kȍnjosati {njošēm, šū imperf.} *sl* work hard (at manual labor) <Slav✤*1>

kȍnjosav {a (acc. = gen.) masc.} *sl-fea* ***Der*** clumsy person, klutz <Slav✤*1>

kȍnjoslav {a (acc. = gen.) masc.} *sl-fea* ***Der*** clumsy person, klutz <Slav✤*1>

kȍnjskā trúba {NP} (lit. horse trumpet) *sl-fea* boaster, braggart, blowhard ☞ **truba**

kȍnjskī {ā, ō adj.} (lit. horse) **a.** *sl-fea* big: *konjski obrok big meal* <Slav*1> **b.i.** *sl-fea* hard, difficult: *konjski zadatak difficult math problem* <Slav*2> **ii.** *sl-fea* strong, muscular <Slav*2>

kȍnju {excl.} (lit. you, horse) *col* ***Off*** used to offend one's interlocutor <Slav*1>

konjȕšār {njušára (acc. = gen.) masc.} (lit. stable boy *i.e. the stereotype that Croatians and Slovenes are servile to Austrian Germans like stable boys*) **1** Ser *sl-fea* ***Der*** Croat (person) <Slav*1> **2** Ser *sl-fea* ***Der*** Slovenian (person) <Slav*1>

kȍnzērva {ē fem.} (lit. canned goods) **1** *sl* package (in general) <Lat*1> **2** *sl-crime* prison, can <Lat*1> **3** *sl-auto* Trabant (make of simple East German car) <Lat*1> **4** *sl-auto* car, wheels <Lat*1> **5** *sl-auto* bus <Lat*1> **6** *sl-sex* ***Fac*** virgin <Lat*1> **7** *sl-sex* ***Der-Fac*** person with conservative views (usu. political) <Lat*1> **8** phonograph record <Lat*1> **9** *sl-music* conservatorium <Lat*1>

• **pûtnā kȍnzērva** {NP} (lit. travel can) *sl* streetcar

konzervírati {zȅrvīrām, zervīrajū imperf. intr.} *sl* converse, talk <Lat*1>

kȍnzum {a masc.} *col* consumption, spending <Lat>

kȍp [1] {a (acc. = gen.) +ov (ext. pl) masc.; Nom Pl kȍpovi} *sl* girlfriend <Slav*1>

kȍp [2] {a +ov (ext. pl) masc.; Nom Pl kȍpovi} **a.** *sl* work, labor <Slav*1> **b.** *sl* job, gig <Slav*2>

• **stâlnī kȍp** {NP} (lit. permanent digging place) *sl* steady girlfriend

kȍpāč {kopáča (acc. = gen.) masc.} (lit. digger) *sl-fea* worker <Slav*1>

kȍpānje {a neut.} (lit. digging) *sl* party (social gathering) <Slav*1>

kȍpati {ām, ajū imperf.} (lit. dig) **1** *sl* work <Slav*1> **2** *sl* search, look for: *kopati za cigarama look for the cigarettes* <Slav*1>

• **kȍpati bȕnār** {VP} (lit. dig a well) *sl-crime* pick pockets

kȍpātor {a (acc. = gen.) masc.} (lit. digger) *sl-sex* male looking for a loose woman, guy on the make <Slav✍*1>

kȍpatot {a (acc. = gen.) masc.} *sl-sex* male looking for a loose woman, guy on the make

kȍpčati {ām, ajū imperf.} (lit. button) *col-dia* understand, realize <NE*1>

kȍper {a (acc. = gen.) masc.} *sl-fea* inhabitant of the countryside, hick, bumpkin

kȍpitār {a (acc. = gen.) masc.} *sl-fea* inquisitive person <Slav*1>

kȍpito {a neut.} (lit. hoof) **1** *sl-crime* pistol, revolver <Slav*1> **2a.** *sl* foot <Slav*1> **b.** *sl* shoe <Slav*2>

kȍpljanīk {a (acc. = gen.) masc.} (lit. lancer) *sl-fea* ***Fac*** leaf collector <Slav*1>

kopljáriti {kȍpljārīm, rē imperf.} *sl* think, ponder <Slav✤*1>

kȍpljārnīk {a masc.} (lit. lancer) *sl-fea* leaf collector <Slav✤*1>

kȍplje {a neut.} (lit. lance) *sl-sex* ***Fac-Obs*** penis, dick, prick <Slav*1>

kȍpriva {ē fem.} (lit. stinging nettle) *sl-fea* attractive female <Slav*1>

kȍrālj *See the following*

• **cȓvenī korálji** {NP} (lit. red corals) *sl-sex* ***Fac*** menstruation, period

kȍravac {rāvca (acc. = gen.) masc.} *sl-fea* senior citizen <Gyp>

kȍravica {ē fem.} *sl-fea* senior citizen <Gyp>

kȍrca {ē fem.} *sl* mother, mom

kôrča {ē fem.} *sl-arch* mother, mom

kordàljēn {daljéna (acc. = gen.) masc.} *sl-arch* widower

kordaljènica {ē fem.} *sl-arch* widow

Koréja {ē fem.} (lit. Korea) Cro *sl* name of a bar at Bunićeva and Pucićeva streets, Zagreb, Croatia <SlavO*1>

korèla {ē fem.} *sl-fea* senior citizen

kȍrenov sôk {NP} (lit. root juice) *sl-drink* hard liquor ☞ sok

korída {ē fem.} (lit. corrida: bullfight) *sl-stu* university exam <Spa*1>

kòrito {a neut.} (lit. trough) *sl-sports* swimming pool <Slav*1>

korjánović {a masc.} *sl* coffee

kȍrka {ē fem.; Dat kȍrki} *sl-fea* senior citizen <Ger*1>

kórnjača {ē fem.} (lit. turtle) *sl-auto* Volkswagen (make of car) <Slav*1>

kòrosati {ošēm, ošū imperf.} *sl* cheat, swindle

kórpa {ē fem.} (lit. basket) **1** *sl* refusal <Ger*1> **2** *sl* unattractive female <Ger*1>

kòrpara {ē fem.} *sl* apartment <Ger⁘*1>

korpírati {kòrpīrām, korpírajū imperf.} (lit. basket) *sl* dump one's boyfriend or girlfriend <Ger⁘*1>

korpomânija {ē fem.} /korpomànija/ (lit. basketomania) *sl* fear of being dumped by one's girlfriend <Ger⁘*1>

korzijáner {a masc.} *sl* promenade <Ita✍>

kȍrzo {a neut.} *col* promenade <Ita>

kôs {sti fem.} [std. = kost] *sl* bone <Slav✍>

kòsa *See the following*

• **kòsa mu iz òčijū ráste** {S} (lit. his hair is growing from his eyes) *sl-fea* extremely unintelligent

kósati *See the following*

• **kósati pjȅnu** {VP} (lit. eat the foam) **1** *sl-sex* ***Obs*** engage in cunnilingus **2** *sl-fea* get nervous

kosijána {ē fem.} [std. = kosa] *sl* hair <Slav✍>

kosijáner [1] {a (acc. = gen.) masc.} *sl-fea* person with long hair, longhair <Slav✍>

kosijáner [2] {a masc.} [std. = kosa] *sl* hair <Slav✍>

kòsīnger {a masc.} [std. = kosa] *sl* hair <Slav✍>

kȍska {ē fem.} (lit. bone) **1a.** *sl* hand <Slav*1> **b.** *sl* arm <Slav*2> **2** *sl* bad playing card <Slav*1> **3** *sl-sstu* difficult problem (math, etc.) <Slav*1> **4** *sl-sports* bad pass (of a ball) <Slav*1> **5** *sl* cheating, swindling <Slav*1>

• **bez kȍske** {PP} (lit. without a bone) *sl-sports* swish (basketball shot that does not touch the rim)

• **do kȍskē** {PP} (lit. to the bone) *col* completely, totally, to the bone

• **Kȍsku ti jèbēm!** {S} (lit. I screw your bone!) *dia* ***Off*** used as a weak curse, Screw you!

• **stârā kȍska** {NP} (lit. old bone) *sl-mil* old soldier

kȍskati {ām, ajū imperf.} *sl* throw out, expel <Slav⁘*1>

kȍskica {ē fem.} (lit. small bone) *sl-fea* slender person <Slav⁘*1>

koslȉna {ē fem.} *sl* night club

kosmonàut {a (acc. = gen.) masc.} (lit. astronaut) *sl-fea* hairy male <Gre*1>

kosòokī {ōg (acc. = gen.) masc.} (lit. the slant-eyed one) **1** *sl-fea* ***Off*** Chinese (person), Slant <Slav*1> **2** *sl-fea* ***Off*** Japanese (person), Slant <Slav*1>

kôst {i fem.} (lit. bone) *sl-sex* ***Fac-Obs*** penis, bone <Slav*1>

• **kôst i kȍža** {NP} (lit. bone and skin) *sl-fea* extremely slender, skin and bone

• **mâsnā kôst** {NP} (lit. fat bone) *sl-sex* ***Fac-Obs*** male on the make

kostolómac {mca (acc. = gen.) masc.} (lit. bone-breaker) *sl-fea* troublemaker, rowdy, ruffian <Slav*1>

kȍstūr {a (acc. = gen.) masc.} (lit. skeleton) **1** *sl-fea* slender person, skeleton <Slav*1> **2** *sl* security guard <Slav*1>

kostúrac {rca (acc. = gen.) masc.} *sl-fea* weak person <Slav⁘*1>

kȍšara {ē fem.} (lit. basket) *sl* female <Slav*1>

košárac {rca masc.} [std. = košarka] *sl-sports* basketball game <Slav✍>

kȍšarica {ē fem.} [std. = košarka] *sl-sports* basketball game <Slav✍>

košarkȁšica {ē fem.} (lit. basketball player) *sl-sex* ***Fac*** pregnant female <Slav*1>

kȍškati {ām, ajū imperf. intr.} *sl-arch* throw out, expel <Slav*1>

kȍšnica {ē fem.} (lit. bee-hive) **1** *sl* ***Fac*** public transportation <Slav*1> **2** *sl* ***Fac*** crowd, mob <Slav*2>

kȍšos {a masc.} [std. = košulja] *sl* shirt <Slav✍>

koštùrača {ē fem.} (lit. skeleton) *sl-fea* slender female, walking skeleton

košuljijánović {a masc.} [std. = košula] *sl* shirt <**Slav**✐>

košuljȉška {ē fem.; Dat košuljȉški} **/**košuljìška**/** [std. = košulja] *sl* shirt <**Slav**✐>

kȍt {excl.} **1** *col* used to lure a bee <**Slav**> **2** *col* used to drive away a goose <**Slav**>

kòtāč {kotáča masc.} (lit. wheel) Cro *sl* bicycle, bike <**Slav***1>

kȍtār {a (acc. = gen.) masc.} *sl* tomcat <**Slav***1>

kòtara {ē fem.} *sl* cat <**Slav***1>

Kòtara {ē fem.} *sl-fea* ***Off*** German (person), Kraut <**Slav***1>

kotàrisati se {išēm, išū biasp. intr.} *sl* get rid of

kòtilo *See the following*
- **Kòtilo ti jèbēm!** {S} (lit. I screw your pot!) *dia* ***Off*** used as a weak curse, Screw you!

kȍtka {ē fem.; Dat kȍtki} *sl* cat <**Slav***1>

kȍtlār {a (acc. = gen.) masc.} *sl-drink* person in charge of distilling brandy <**Slav***1>

kòtlosān {a, o adj.} *sl* horrible, terrible: *kotlosan sudar horrible car crash* <**Slav***1>

kȍtomān {a (acc. = gen.) masc.} *sl* boss

kȍtomānka {ē fem.} *sl* lamp

kòtōn {kotóna masc.} **1** *col* condom, rubber <**Fre***1> **2** *sl-drugs* cotton used to filter opium <**Fre***1>

kȍtor {a (acc. = gen.) masc.} *sl* tomcat <**Slav***1>

kotùrača {ē fem.} (lit. roller) **a.** *sl-auto* old car, wreck <**Slav***1> **b.** *sl-auto* used car <**Slav***2>

kotùralo {a neut.} (lit. roller) *sl-drink* waiter <**Slav***1>

kotùrāš {turáša masc.} (lit. roller) *sl-auto* bus <**Slav***1>

kotùrati {ām, ajū imperf.} (lit. roll) **1** *sl-sex* get pregnant, get knocked up <**Slav***1> **2** *sl-sports* play soccer <**Slav***1>

kóva {ē fem.} **1** *sl-gamble* playing card **2** *sl* admission ticket **3** *sl* fare, ticket

kòvāč {kováča (acc. = gen.) masc.} (lit. blacksmith) *sl* ten dinars; a ten-dinar bill <**Slav***1>

kòvati {kȕjēm, kȕjū imperf.} (lit. forge, hammer) *sl-sex* ***Obs*** engage in sexual intercourse with (of a male) <**Slav***1>
- **kòvati u zvézde** {VP} (lit. forge into stars) SerE *sl-fea* praise

kòverat *See the following*
- **plâvī kòverat** {NP} (lit. blue envelope) *col* bribe

kovèrdžija {ē masc.} *sl* mailman <**Fre-NE***1>

kòvērta *See the following*
- **plâvā kòvērta** {NP} (lit. blue envelope) *col* bribe

kòviška {ē fem.; Dat kòviški} *sl-gamble* playing card

kovržànjci *See the following*
- **Kovržànjci ti jèbēm!** {S} (lit. I fuck your cakes!) SSer *dia* ***Off*** used as a weak curse, Screw you!

kòza {ē fem.} (lit. she-goat) **1** *sl-sex* ***Obs*** vagina, cunt <**Slav***1> **2** *sl-fea* ***Der*** unintelligent female <**Slav***1>

kȍzāk {zga masc.} (lit. Cossack) **1** *sl-fea* smart male, brain <**Rus***1> **2** *sl-fea* inhabitant of the countryside, hick, bumpkin <**Rus***1>

kozárac {rca masc.} *sl* slang <**Slav**⁘*1>

kozérva {ē fem.} [std. = konzerva] *col-dia* can <**Lat**✐>

kòziti se {zīm, zē imperf. intr.} (lit. play a goat) *sl-fea* hesitate, be skiddish

kòzle {eta neut.} *col-dia* young goat, kid <**Slav**>

kȍža {ē fem.} (lit. skin, leather) **1** *sl-sex* ***Obs*** vagina, cunt <**Slav***1> **2** *sl* ***Fac*** garment <**Slav***1>

Kȍžara {ē fem.} (lit. the leather one) *sl-fea* Russian (person) <**Slav***1>

kȍžīrān {a, o adj.} (lit. leathered) *sl-fea* nicely dressed, tastefully dressed <**Slav***1>

kožírati {kȍžīrām, kožírajū biasp.} (lit. leather) *sl-fea* dress formally, dress up <**Slav***1>

kožírati se {kȍžīrām, kožírajū biasp. intr.} (lit. leather oneself) **a.** *sl-fea* dress formally, dress up <**Slav***1> **b.** *sl* supply, furnish <**Slav***2>

kȍžiti se *See the following*

kȍžnuti se {nēm, nū perf. intr.} (lit. leather oneself) **a.** *sl-fea* ***Fac*** dress formally, dress up <**Slav**⁘*1> **b.** get something

kȍžnjāk [1] {kožnjáka masc.} (lit. the leather one) *col* leather jacket <**Slav**⁘>

kȍžnjāk [2] {kožnjáka (acc. = gen.) masc.} (lit. the leather one) *sl-crime* detective <**Slav**⁘*1>

kȍžolēpka {ē fem.; Dat kȍžolēpki} (lit. the one which stick to the skin) **1** **SerE** *sl-fea* thin dress <**Slav**⁘> **2** SerE *sl-fea* tight shirt <**Slav**⁘>

kožùrati se {ām, ajū imperf. intr.} (lit. get covered by skin) *sl* obtain, get <**Slav**>

kožúrica {ē fem.} (lit. small skin) *sl-sex* foreskin <Slav[*1]>

KP [kâ-pê] **dȍm** {NP} *sl-crime* juvenile detention center, juvie ☞ **dom**

kȓ {excl.} *col* the sound made by something cracking, crack <Slav>

krâ-krâ {excl.} *col* caw (of a crow) <Slav>

krába {ē masc.} (lit. crab) *sl* head <Fre[*1]>

krábar {bra, bro adj.} [std. = hrabar] *sl-fea* courageous <Slav✍>

kràfn {a masc.} (lit. doughnut) *sl-fea* black eye, shiner <Ger[*1]>

krágna {ē fem.} (lit. collar) *sl-crime* act of choking <Ger[*1]>

krȁjcati {ām, ajū biasp.} *sl* bypass, skirt <Slav>

krȁjcovati {cujēm, cujū imperf.} **1** *sl-sex* ***Obs*** engage in sexual intercourse with (of a male) <Slav[*1]> **2** *sl-crime* steal, swipe <Slav[*1]>

krâjka {ē fem.} *sl* one's own neighborhood <Slav>

krâjnīk {a (acc. = gen.) masc.} /kràjnīk /krajníka masc./ (lit. tonsil) *sl-fea* stupid or mentally deficient person <Slav[*1]>
- **do krâjnīkā**{PP} (lit. to the tonsils) *sl* ***Fac*** completely, totally

krâk {a +ov (ext. pl) masc.; Nom Pl krȁkovi} (lit. extremity) *sl* leg (human) <Slav>

krȁka[1] {excl.} *col* click (produce a short, sharp, non-resonant sound) <Slav>

kráka[2] {ē masc.; Dat kráki} (lit. the one with extremities) *sl-fea* tall person <Slav[*1]>

krȁka-krȁka {excl.} *col* click (short, sharp, non-resonant sound) <Slav>

krakàilo {a masc.} (lit. the one with extremities) *sl-fea* tall person <Slav⁘[*1]>

kràkat {a, o adj.} *sl-fea* with long legs and arms <Slav[*1]>

krakatílo {a masc.} (lit. the one with extremities) *sl-fea* ***Fac*** tall and slender male, beanpole <Slav⁘[*1]>

kráklja {ē fem. & masc.} (lit. the one with extremities) *sl-fea* ***Fac*** tall and slender person, beanpole <Slav✍[*1]>

kráknuti {krâknēm, nū perf.} *col* caw (of a crow) <Slav>

krȁkoš {a (acc. = gen.) masc.} (lit. the one with extremities) **1** *sl-fea* tall person <Slav✍[*1]> **2** *sl-fea* person with long legs and arms <Slav✍[*1]>

krâle {eta neut.} (lit. the one with extremities) *sl-fea* tall person <Slav✍[*1]>

krâlj {králja +ev (ext. pl) masc.; Nom Pl králjevi} (lit. king) *sl-fea* funny male <Slav[*1]>
- **krâlj Mȉlan** {NP} (lit. king Milan) **1a.** *sl-fea* boss **b.** *sl-fea* authority, expert **2** *sl-fea* attractive male
- **krâlj Mȉlan u tènku** {NP} (lit. king Milan in a tank) *sl-fea* very attractive male, hunk

kràljević *See the following*
- **ko Králjević Mârko i pȉng-pȍng** {PP} (lit. like crown prince Marko and ping-pong) *sl* ***Fac*** completely different
- **Králjević Mârko i pȉng-pȍng**{NP} (lit. crown prince Marko and ping-pong) *sl* ***Fac*** completely different

králjevskī {ā, ō adj.} (lit. regal, royal) *sl-fea* ***App*** excellent, awesome <Slav[*1]>

kràljica {ē fem.} (lit. queen) **1** *sl-sex* ***Fac*** male homosexual, queen <Slav[*1]> **2a.** *sl-sex* ***App*** funny female <Slav[*1]> **b.** *sl-sex* ***App*** excellent female, cool babe <Slav[*2]>

krâlju {excl.} (lit. my king) *sl* used to address a male in direct informal communication, my man <Slav[*1]>

krȁmp {kràmpa +ov (ext. pl) masc.; Nom Pl kràmpovi} (lit. pick) **1** *sl* bicycle, bike <Ger[*1]> **2** *sl-sex* unattractive female <Ger[*1]>

krampàljati {ām, ajū imperf. intr.} *sl* think, ponder <Ger⁘[*1]>

kràmpati {ām, ajū imperf.} (lit. pick) *sl* work hard (at manual labor) <Ger[*1]>

kràmper {a (acc. = gen.) masc.} (lit. picker) *sl* manual laborer <Ger[*1]>

kràmpus {a masc.} *sl-fea* unattractive female <Ger✍[*1]>

krángla {ē fem.} [std. = kragna] *dia* collar <Ger✍>

krâsnī *See the following*

kràstacka {ē fem.; Dat kràstacki} *sl* food

kràstačka {ē fem. (adj. decl.); Dat kràstački} *sl* food

krȁstavac {krȁstāvca (acc. = gen.) masc.} (lit. cucumber) *sl-fea* boy, kid <Slav[*1]>

krȁstavac {vca masc.} (lit. cucumber) **1** *sl-sex* ***Fac-Obs*** penis, dick, prick <Slav[*1]> **2** *sl* ***Fac-Obs*** nose <Slav[*1]> **3** *sl-sex* ***Fac-Obs*** small female breast <Slav[*1]>
- **kȉselī krȁstavac** {NP} (lit. pickle) *sl* grandparent

krȁstavica {ē fem.} [std. = krastavac] **a.** *col-dia* cucumber <Slav✍> **b.i.** *sl-sex* penis <Slav✍[*1]> **ii.** *sl-crime* picklock (tool), slim jim <Slav✍[*1]>

krȁstavice {a fem. pl.} *sl-crime* burglar's tools <Slav[*1]>

kr̀àsti {krádēm, krádū imperf. irreg.} *sl-arch* eat, devour <Slav*1>

kràtak {tka, tko adj.} (lit. short) **1a.** *sl-fea* without enough money, short <Slav*1> **b.** *sl-fea* indebted <Slav*2> **2** *sl-fea* stupid or mentally deficient <Slav*1>

kráter {a masc.} (lit. crater) *sl-fea* pimple <Gre*1>

krátež {a masc.} *sl-crime* sawed-off gun <Slav*1>

krátiti {krâtīm, tē imperf.} (lit. shorten) **a.** *sl* flirt <Slav*1> **b.** *sl* seduce <Slav*2>

kràtkī spôj {NP} (lit. short circuit) **1** *col* misunderstanding **2** *sl* memory blackout ☞ **spoj**

kratkotàlāsan {sna, sno adj.} (lit. short-wave) *sl-fea* unintelligent, stupid, dumb <Slav*1>

kratnpàtljati {ām, ajū imperf.} *sl* think, ponder

kr̀àva {ē fem.} (lit. cow) **1** *sl-fea* obese female, cow <Slav*1> **2** *sl-fea* unintelligent female <Slav*1> **3** *sl-music* saxophone, sax <Slav*1> **4** Cro *sl* name of a cafe on Frankopanska street, Zagreb, Croatia <Slav*1>

kr̀àva mùzara {NP} (lit. milking cow) **1** *sl-sex* ***Fac*** large-breasted female **2** *sl-fea* person from whom one takes money ☞ **krava**

- **kr̀àva mùzara** {NP} (lit. milk cow) **1** *sl-sex* ***Fac*** large-breasted female **2** *sl-fea* person from whom one takes money

kravàjče *See the following*

- **Kravàjče ti jèbēm!** {S} (lit. I fuck your bread!) *dia* ***Off*** used as a weak curse, Screw you!
- **Kravàjče ti u pèpel jèbēm!** {S} (lit. I fuck your bread in the ashes!) *dia* ***Off*** used as a moderate curse, Fuck you!

kràval {a masc.} *sl* unrest (e.g. social) <Ger>

kravàta {ē fem.} (lit. tie) **1** *sl-fea* elderly male <Slav*1> **2** *sl-fea* snob <Slav*1>

kr̃c {excl.} *col* the sound made by something cracking, crack <Slav>

kr̃calo {a masc.} **1** *sl-fea* ***Der*** coward, chicken <Slav*1> **2** *sl-fea* ***Der*** miser, tightwad, skinflint <Slav*1>

kr̃cānje {a neut.} *col* cracking (branch, etc.) <Slav>

kr̃cati {ām, ajū imperf.} *col* crack (branch, etc.) <Slav>

kr̃ckāj {a masc.} *col* cracking object <Slav>

kr̃ckānje {a neut.} **a.** *col* cracking (branch, etc.) <Slav> **b.** *col* spending <Slav*1>

kr̃ckati {ām, ajū imperf.} **a.** *col* crack (branch, etc.) <Slav> **b.** *col* spend (money, property, etc.) <Slav*1>

kr̃ckav {a, o adj.} *col* cracking (branch, etc.) <Slav>

kr̀culja {ē fem.} *sl* receipt

kŕčiti {čīm, čē imperf.} (lit. slash and burn) *sl-sex* ***Obs*** engage in sexual intercourse with (of a male) <Slav*1>

kr̃čule {eta neut.} *sl-arch* cap, hat

kŕdža [1] {ē fem.} **1** *sl* low-quality tobacco <NE*1> **2** low-quality marijuana

kr̀dža [2] {ē masc.} /kŕdža/ *sl-fea* short person <NE*1>

kr̀dža [3] {adj.} /kŕdža/ *sl-fea* worthless: *krdža roba worthless merchandise* <NE*1>

kŕdžo {ē masc.} *sl* low-quality tobacco <NE*1>

kreatívac {vca (acc. = gen.) masc.} *col* creative person <Lat❖>

krebèljānje {a neut.} *sl* laughter <Slav>

krèbil {krebìla (acc. = gen.) masc.} *sl-fea* stupid or mentally deficient person <Fre-Lat⇨>

kréca {ē fem. & masc.} *sl-fea* stupid or mentally deficient person <Fre⇨>

krecàna {ē fem.} *sl-fea* senile person <Fre*1>

krȅč [1] {krèča (acc. = gen.) +ev (ext. pl) masc.; Nom Pl krèčevi} (lit. lime, calcium oxide) *sl-fea* senile person <NE*1>

krȅč [2] {krèča +ev (ext. pl) masc.; Nom Pl krèčevi} (lit. lime, calcium oxide) *sl* fear <NE*1>

krečàna {ē fem.} (lit. lime pit) *sl-fea* senile person <NE*1>

krȅčār {a (acc. = gen.) masc.} (lit. lime pit worker) **a.** *sl-fea* senior citizen <NE*1> **b.** *sl-fea* senile person <NE*2>

krȅčiti se {čīm, čē imperf. intr.} (lit. put some lime on oneself) *sl* put on make-up <NE*1>

kréćati {krêćām, kréćajū imperf.} [std. = okretati] **a.** *dia-col* turn, revolve, move: *krećati jojo oka prsta turn a yo-yo around one's finger* <Slav⇨> **b.** *sl-sex* engage in sexual intercourse with (of a male) <Slav⇨*1>

kréći {excl.} *col* used to command somebody to move on, go ahead <Slav*1>

kréda {ē fem.} (lit. chalk) *col* loan, credit <Lat*1>

kréhati {krêhām, kréhajū imperf.} *sl* beat up

krêk {a +ov (ext. pl) masc.; Nom Pl krékovi} *col* crack (branch, etc.) <Slav>

kréka {ē fem.; Dat krékē} **1** *sl-arch* hen <Slav*1> **2** *sl* coal <SlavO>

krékac {kca (acc. = gen.) masc.} **a.** *sl-arch* rooster <Slav⁘[*1]> **b.** *sl-sex* penis, cock <Slav⁘[*2]>

krékavica {ē fem.} (lit. screamer) *sl-arch* hen <Slav⁘[*1]>

krèkče {eta neut.} *sl-arch* chicken (the animal) <Slav⁘[*1]>

krȅkete {excl.} *col* the sound made by an explosion, kaboom <Slav>

krélac {lca (acc. = gen.) masc.} *sl-fea* ***Der*** stupid or mentally deficient person <Fre☞>

krȇle {eta masc.} *sl-fea* ***Der*** stupid or mentally deficient person <Fre☞>

krelètān {letána (acc. = gen.) masc.} *sl-fea* ***Der*** stupid or mentally deficient person <Fre☞>

krȇlka {ē fem.; Dat krȇlki} **a.** *sl-fea* unintelligent female <Fre☞> **b.** *sl-fea* female <Fre☞[*1]>

krȇm {a +ov (ext. pl) masc.; Nom Pl krȇmovi} (lit. cream) **1** *sl-fea* stupid or mentally deficient person <Fre[*1]> **2** *sl-fea* high society, cream of society <Fre[*1]>

kréma {ē fem.} **a.** *col* high society, cream of society <Fre[*1]> **b.** *sl-crime* custody <Fre[*2]>

krematȏrijum {a masc.} (lit. crematorium) *sl-sstu* chemistry lab <Lat[*1]>

krèmbil {krembìla (acc. = gen.) masc.} (lit. kreten 'cretin' X debil 'imbecile') *sl-fea* stupid or mentally deficient person <Fre-Lat☞>

Kreménko {a masc.} /kreménko/ (lit. Fred Flintstone *cartoon character*) *sl-fea* stupid or mentally deficient person, Neanderthal <Slav☞[*1]>

krèmpita {ē masc.} *sl-fea* son of a very important or influential person <Fre-Gre[*1]>

krȅn {a +ov (ext. pl) masc.; Nom Pl krènovi} *sl-crime* naive patron in a restaurant susceptible to deception <Ger☞[*1]>

krȅna {ē fem.} **a.** *sl* match (lighting device) **b.** *sl* fire

kréniti {krȇnēm, nū perf. intr.} [std. = krenuti] *col-dia* begin, start <Slav☞>

krénuti {krȇnēm, nū perf. intr.} (lit. start) *col* succeed in business <Slav[*1]>
• **krénula prȋča** {S} (lit. the story has moved) *col* used to refer to the spread of false or private information, there was gossip

krèpati {ām, ajū perf. intr.} *sl* ***Der*** die, kick the bucket <Slav>
• **za krèpati** {PP} (lit. to die) *sl-fea* humorous, entertaining

krepatȏrijum {a masc.} (lit. die-torium) *sl* ***Fac*** crematorium <Lat☞>

krȅs [1] {excl.} *col* the sound made by an explosion, bang <Slav>

krȅs [2] {a +ov (ext. pl) masc.} *col* hit, punch <Slav>

krèsāč {kresáča (acc. = gen.) masc.} **a.** *sl-fea* troublemaker, rowdy, ruffian <Slav⁘[*1]> **b.** *sl-fea* lover (male) <Slav⁘[*2]>

krèsānje {a neut.} (lit. striking a spark) **a.** *sl* fight (e.g. fist fight) <Slav[*1]> **b.** *sl* sexual intercourse <Slav[*2]>

krȅsati {krȇšēm, krȇšū imperf.} (lit. strike a spark) *sl-fea* engage in sexual intercourse with (of a male), make sparks <Slav[*1]>

krȅsnūt {a, o adj.} *sl-fea* insane, nuts <Slav[*1]>

krȅsnuti {nēm, nū perf.} (lit. strike a spark) **1** *sl* hit, punch <Slav[*1]> **2** *sl* shoot, fire <Slav[*1]> **3a.** *sl* bang (loud and abrupt sound) <Slav[*1]> **b.** *sl* engage in sexual intercourse with (of a male) <Slav[*2]>

kréša {ē masc.} *sl-fea* stupid or mentally deficient person, cretin <Fre[*1]>

kréšta {ē fem. & masc.} *sl-fea* screaming person <Slav☞>

kréštavica {ē fem.} (lit. screamer) *sl-arch* hen <Slav[*1]>

krétati {krȇtām, krétajū imperf.} /krȇćēm, ćū imperf./ [std. = okretati] *sl* turn, revolve, move <Slav☞[*1]>

krètēn {kreténa (acc. = gen.) masc.} *sl-fea* stupid or mentally deficient person, cretin <Fre[*1]>
• **bȁlavī krètēn** {NP} (lit. the snotty cretin) *sl-sex* ***Fac-Obs*** penis, dick, prick

kretènčina {ē masc.} *sl-fea* stupid or mentally deficient person, cretin <Fre⁘[*1]>

kreténko {a masc.} (lit. Cretinstone: kreten 'cretin' X Kremenko 'Flintstone *cartoon character*') **a.** *sl-fea* stubborn male, pigheaded guy <Fre⁘[*1]> **b.** *sl-fea* stupid or mentally deficient person, cretin <Fre⁘[*2]>

krètēnskī {ā, ō adj.} *sl-fea* unintelligent, stupid, dumb <Fre⁘[*1]>

krȅtić {a masc.} *sl-fea* stupid or mentally deficient person, cretin <Fre☞[*1]>

kretonírati se {tònīrām, tonírajū biasp. intr.} *sl* make a fool of oneself <Fre⁘[*1]>

kréva {ē fem.} *sl* dancing

krevéljēnje {a neut.} *sl* making faces, grimacing <Slav>

krevètara {ē fem.} *sl-sex* ***Fac*** attractive female <Slav[*1]>

krevètārka {ē fem.; Dat krevètārki} *sl-sex* ***Fac*** attractive female <Slav⁘[*1]>

krȅvetibīlan {lna, lno adj.} *sl-sex* ***Fac*** sexy <Slav⁘[*1]>

krèvetovãnje {a neut.} *sl-sex* ***Obs*** sexual intercourse <Slav⁘[*1]>

krȅvkati {ām, ajū imperf.} *sl* laugh

kréza {adj.} [std. = krezub] *sl* toothless <Slav✍>

krȅzav {a, o adj.} *sl-fea* toothless <Sla>

krȅzavac {vca (acc. = gen.) masc.} *sl-fea* toothless male

krêzos {adj.} [std. = krezub] *sl-fea* toothless <Slav✍>

krèzub {a, o adj.} *sl-fea* toothless <Slav[*1]>

kŕhati {kȓhām, kŕhajū imperf.} *sl* break: *krhati stolice u bircu break chairs in a bar* <Slav[*1]>

kȓhor {a masc.} *col* the sound made by something cracking, crack <Slav>

kȓht {a, o adj.} *col* fragile, sensitive: *krhti tanjiri fragile saucers* <Slav✍>

krî {excl.} *col* the sound made by a bird, caw <Slav>

krî-krî {excl.} *col* the sound made by a bird, caw <Slav>

krȉcka {ē fem.; Dat krȉcki} **a.** *sl* screaming in pain, fear, or outrage <Slav> **b.** *sl* noise <Slav[*1]>

krikènjati {ām, ajū imperf.} *sl* have one's fill of something: *krikenjati gudricu have one's fill of dope* <Slav>

krikràčati {ām, ajū imperf.} *col* click (produce a short, sharp, non-resonant sound) <Slav>

krikrȉčati {čīm, čē imperf.} *col* caw (of a crow) <Slav>

krȉm {a +ov (ext. pl) masc.; Nom Pl krìmovi} *sl* mystery (movie, book) <Lat✍>

krȉmī {adj.} **a.** *col* crime <Lat✍> **b.** *col* mystery (movie, book) <Lat✍[*1]>

krìmīć {krimíća masc.} *col* mystery (movie, book) <Lat✍>

kriminálac {lca masc.} (lit. criminal) *col* mystery (movie, book) <Lat[*1]>

krìmiš {a masc.} *sl* mystery (movie, book) <Lat✍>

krȉmos {a (acc. = gen.) masc.} /krîmos/ *sl-crime* criminal <Lat✍>

krínjati {krînjām, krínjajū imperf. intr.} *sl* hide, cover up: *krinjati od drotova hide from the cops* <Slav✍>

krȉsnuti {nēm, nū perf.} **a.** *sl* scream in pain, fear, or outrage <Slav> **b.** *sl* shout at <Slav[*1]>

krìstāl {kristála (acc. = gen.) masc.} (lit. crystal) **a.** *sl-fea* foreign tourist who sells crystalware <Gre[*1]> **b.** *sl* tourist <Gre[*2]>

krìstāl-tùrist {a (acc. = gen.) masc.} *sl-fea* foreign tourist who sells crystalware <Gre-Fre[*1]>

krìstalno {adv.} (lit. crystal) *col* crystal (as in crystal clear) <Gre[*1]>

krîvā adrèsa {NP} (lit. wrong address) *col* failure ☞ adresa

Kríva je mâjka príroda i òtac karikatùrista! {S} (lit. It is the fault of his/her mother nature and the cartoonist father!) *sl-fea* extremely unattractive and unintelligent, ugly as sin and stupid ☞ **majka**

krìvača {ē fem.} *sl-crime* rifle <Slav[*1]>

krȉvaj *See the following*

- **Krȉvaj ti jèbēm!** {S} *col* ***Off*** used as a weak curse, Screw you!

krìvāk {kriváka masc.} (lit. the crooked one) *sl-sex* ***Obs*** penis, dick, prick <Slav[*1]>

krivìna {ē fem.} (lit. curve) **a.** *col* avoiding duties <Slav[*1]> **b.i.** *col* making a fool of oneself: *krivina na tulumu making a fool of oneself at the party* <Slav[*1]> **ii.** *col* one month of one's military service <Slav[*2]> **iii.** *col* nonsense <Slav[*2]>

krivináriti {vìnārīm, rē imperf. intr.} (lit. curve around) **a.** *sl-fea* avoid work, shirk work <Slav⁘[*1]> **b.** *sl-fea* make excuses <Slav⁘[*2]>

krivìnāš {vináša (acc. = gen.) masc.} (lit. one who curves around) **a.** *sl-fea* loafer, idler <Slav⁘[*1]> **b.** *sl-fea* liar <Slav⁘[*2]>

krivinášiti {vìnāšīm, šē imperf. intr.} (lit. curve around) *sl-fea* avoid work, shirk work <Slav⁘[*1]>

krivòguz {a, o adj.} (lit. crooked-assed) *sl-fea* having large buttocks <Slav⁘>

krivòguzā {ē fem. (adj. decl.)} (lit. crooked ass) *sl-fea* buttocks, butt <Slav⁘>

krivogùzati {ām, ajū imperf.} (lit. crooked-ass) *sl-fea* limp <Slav⁘[*1]>

krivogùzica {ē fem.} (lit. crooked ass) *sl-fea* buttocks, butt <Slav⁘>

krizírānje {a neut.} *sl* panicking <Gre⁘[*1]>

Krȉžanka {ē fem.} *sl-sstu* name of a high school on Križanićeva street, Zagreb, Croatia <SlavO[*1]>

krîžnī pût {NP} (lit. way of the Cross) Cro *sl* nursing home ☞ **put**

kȓk [1] {excl.} *col* the sound made by something cracking, crack <Slav>

kȓk [2] {a +ov (ext. pl) masc.; Nom Pl kŕkovi} **a.** *sl* hit, punch <Slav> **b.** *sl* eating <Slav[*1]>

kȑka {ē fem.; Dat kȑki} **a.** *sl* cracking (branch, etc.) <Slav> **b.** *sl* noise <Slav*1> **c.** crushing sound

kȑkac {excl.} *col* the sound made by something cracking, crack <Slav>

kȑkačē {adv.} *col* on one's back (usu. referring to carrying a child on one's back) <Slav>

kȑkačkē {adv.} *col* on one's back (usu. referring to carrying a child on one's back) <Slav>

kȑkan {a (acc. = gen.) masc.} *sl-fea* inhabitant of the countryside, hick, bumpkin <Slav*1>

krkáncija {ē fem.} **a.** *sl* abundant meal <Slav*1> **b.** *sl* eating <Slav*2>

kȑkanka {ē fem.} *sl-fea* female troublemaker, rowdy <Slav*1>

krkȁnluk {a masc.} *sl* eating <Slav*1>

krkánjac {njca masc.} **a.** *sl* eating <Slav*1> **b.** *sl* tasty food <Slav*2>

kŕkānje {a neut.} /kȑkānje/ *sl* eating <Slav*1>

kŕkati {kŕkām, kŕkajū imperf.} /kȑkati/ **a.** *sl* eat, devour <Slav*1> **b.** *sl* engage in sexual intercourse with (of a male) <Slav*2>

krkbùljisati {išēm, išū imperf.} *sl* kick in the buttocks <Slav✤*1>

kȑkete {ea masc.} /kȑkete/ **a.** *sl* hit, punch <Slav> **b.i.** *sl-fea* effective move: *napraviti krkete i izbjeći drotove make an effective move and avoid the police* <Slav*1> **ii.** *sl-auto* car crash <Slav*1>

krkljánac {nca masc.} **a.** *sl* mess, disorder, disturbance <Slav> **b.** *sl* attack, strike <Slav*1> **c.** *sl* fight (e.g. fist fight) <Slav*2> **d.** *sl* crowd, mob <Slav*3>

kȑkljānje {a neut.} *col* moaning in pain <Slav>

krkljáviti {kȑkljāvīm, vē perf.} *sl* shut somebody up <Slav*1>

kȑknuti {nēm, nū perf.} **a.** *sl* hit, punch <Slav*1> **b.** *sl* stick in, insert <Slav*2> **c.i.** *sl* eat, devour <Slav*3> **ii.** *sl-sex* engage in sexual intercourse with (of a male) <Slav*3> **ii.** *sl* die, kick the bucket <Slav*3>

krkubùljisati {išēm, išū biasp.} *sl* kick in the buttocks <Slav*1>

kȑkuša {ē fem.} *sl-fea* unattractive female <Slav*1>

kȓle {a (acc. = gen.) masc.} *sl-fea* ***Der*** stupid or mentally deficient person, cretin, idiot <Slav*1>

krlètān {letána (acc. = gen.) masc.} *sl-fea* ***Der*** stupid or mentally deficient person, cretin <Slav✍*1>

krletánović {a (acc. = gen.) masc.} *sl-fea* ***Der*** stupid or mentally deficient person, cretin <Slav✍*1>

kŕlja [1] {ē fem. & masc.} **a.** *sl-fea* boring person, bore <Slav*1> **b.** *sl-fea* intruder <Slav*2> **c.** *sl-fea* worthless or despicable person, bum <Slav*3>

kŕlja [2] {ē fem.} *sl-fea* poorly dressed male

kȑljāč {krljáča (acc. = gen.) masc.} *sl-sports* harsh soccer player <Slav✤*1>

kȑljānje {a neut.} **1a.** *sl-sex* ***Obs*** sexual intercourse <Slav*1> **b.** *sl* kissing <Slav*2> **2** *sl-sport* harsh play (in soccer) <Slav*1> **3** *sl-drugs* intake of narcotic drugs, doing drugs <Slav*1>

krljátak {tka masc.} *sl* tooth <Slav*1>

kȑljati {ām, ajū imperf.} **1** *sl* eat, devour <Slav*1> **2a.** *sl-sex* engage in sexual intercourse with (of a male) <Slav*1> **b.** *sl* kiss <Slav*2>

kȑljati ȍko {VP} (lit. stick one's eye) *sl-fea* peep, look at others ☞ **krljati**

kȑljati se {ām, ajū imperf. intr.} **1** *sl-drugs* take narcotic drugs, do drugs <Slav*1> **2** *sl* kiss <Slav*1>
- **kȑljati ȍko** {VP} (lit. stick one's eye) *sl-fea* peep, look at others
- **kȑljati ȕvo** {VP} (lit. stick one's ear) *sl* listen

krljáviti {kȑljāvīm, vē imperf.} *sl-sex* ***Obs*** French kiss <Slav*1>

kȑljnuti {nēm, nū perf.} *sl* hit, punch <Slav*1>
- **kȑljnuti jezìčinu** {VP} (lit. stick one's tongue) *sl* French kiss
- **kȑljnuti lȅngvidž** {VP} (lit. stick one's tongue) *sl* French kiss
- **kȑljnuti žvȁlu** {VP} *sl* French kiss

kȑmača {ē fem.} (lit. sow) **1** *sl-sports* ball which barely hits the side of a ping-pong table <Slav*1> **2a.** *sl-fea* ***Der*** obese female, porker <Slav*1> **b.i.** *sl-fea* ***Der*** hated female, witch <Slav*2> **ii.** *sl-sex* ***Fac*** female with attractive shape <Slav*2>

kŕmak {mka (acc. = gen.) masc.} (lit. hog) **1** *sl-fea* non-Muslim <Slav*1> **2** *sl-fea* dirty and untidy person, slob <Slav*1>

kȑmbučiti {čīm, čē imperf.} *sl-sex* ***Obs*** engage in sexual intercourse with (of a male) <Slav*1>

kȑme {eta neut.} (lit. hog) **1** *sl-fea* obese person, porker <Slav*1> **2a.** *sl-fea* non-Muslim <Slav*1> **b.** *sl-fea* ***Off*** Serb (person) <Slav*2> **3** *sl-fea* evil male, s.o.b <Slav*1>
- **ko kȑme u Tȅherānu** {PP} (lit. like a pig in Teheran) *sl-fea* ***Fac*** helplessly

krmèljati {ām, ajū imperf. intr.} *sl* sleep, nap <Slav*1>

kȑmisānje {a neut.} *sl* sleeping <Slav*1>

kȑnc {a +ev (ext. pl) masc.; Nom Pl kȑnčevi} *sl* belt, waist

kȑndelj {a (acc. = gen.) masc.} *sl-fea* unattractive person <Slav*1>

kŕntija {ē fem.} *col* old and often malfunctioning mechanism, wreck <NE>

kȑnuti {nēm, nū perf.} **a.** *sl* hit, punch <Slav> **b.i.** *sl* kiss <Slav*1> **ii.** *sl-sex* engage in sexual intercourse with (of a male) <Slav*1>

kŕnja {ē fem.} *sl-fea* toothless female <Slav>

kŕnjāš {krnjáša masc.} *sl* tooth <Slav❖*1>

krnjátak {tka masc.} *sl* tooth <Slav*1>

krnjàukānje {a neut.} *col* meow <Slav>

krnjàukati {učēm, učū imperf.} *col* meow <Slav>

kȑnjor {a masc.} *sl* meat

kȑnjotka {ē fem.; Dat kȑnjotki} *sl-sports* scratched marble (the toy) <Slav✍*1>

kȑnjozūb [1] {a (acc. = gen.) masc.} *sl-fea* toothless person <Slav*1>

kȑnjozūb [2] {a, o adj.} *sl-fea* without teeth, toothless <Slav*1>

kròātskī {ā, ō adj.} *col* Croatian (pertaining to a person or nation) <Lat>

kròfna {ē fem.} (lit. doughnut) *sl* female <Ger*1>

krokòdilka {ē fem.} (lit. the crocodile one) **1** *sl-crafts* clamp (the tool) <Gre❖*1> **2** *sl-fea* unattractive female, dog <Gre❖*1>

kròmpīr {krompíra masc.} **/kròmpir /a masc./** (lit. potato) **1** *sl* zero <Slav*1> **2** *sl* hole in one's sock <Slav*1> **3** *sl* blister <Slav*1>

- **jèdan kròmpīr dvâ krompíra** {NP} (lit. one potato two potato) *sl-sstu* ***Fac*** math course
- **vrȅlī kròmpīr** {NP} (lit. hot potato) *sl* uneasy affair, touchy matter, hot potato
- **vrûćī kròmpīr** {NP} (lit. hot potato) *sl-fea* uneasy affair, touchy matter, hot potato

krôv {krȍva +ov (ext. pl) masc.; Nom Pl kròvovi} (lit. roof) *sl* hat <Slav*1>

kroz sȉto i rèšeto {PP} *col* through thick and thin ☞ **sito**

kȑpa {ē fem.} (lit. kitchen cloth) **1a.** *sl* bill (of money) <Slav*1> **b.ii.** *sl* thousand dinars; a thousand-dinar bill, a grand **ii.** *sl* ten dinars; a ten-dinar bill **2a.** *sl* clothing, garment **b.i.** *sl* dress **ii.** *sl* shirt **3** *sl* fight (e.g. fist fight) **4** *sl-fea* ingratiator (male), brownnoser, ass kisser

kȑpānje {a neut.} (lit. mending) *sl* fight (e.g. fist fight) <Slav*1>

krpároš {a (acc. = gen.) masc.} (lit. the one with the rags) *sl-mil* lower-ranked officer <Slav❖*1>

kȑpati {ām, ajū imperf.} (lit. mend) *sl* beat up <Slav*1>

kȑpati se {ām, ajū imperf. intr.} (lit. mend each other) *sl* fight (e.g. fist fight) <Slav*1>

kȑpe {a fem. pl.} (lit. rags) **1a.** *sl* clothing <Slav*1> **b.i.** *sl* dress <Slav*2> **ii.** *sl* linen <Slav*2> **2** *sl* snow <Slav*1> **3** *sl* hundred dinars; a hundred-dinar bill <Slav*1>

krpènjača {ē fem.} *col* a soccer ball made of rags <Slav❖*1>

kȑpice {a fem. pl.} (lit. small rags) *sl* clothing <Slav*1>

kȑpiti {pīm, pē imperf.} (lit. mend) **a.** *sl* criticize <Slav*1> **b.** *sl* gossip, wag the tongue <Slav*2>

kȑpiti se {pīm, pē imperf. intr.} (lit. mend oneselves) *sl-fea* intrude, barge in <Slav*1>

kȑs *See the following*

- **Kȑs ti jèbēm!** {S} (lit. I fuck your cross!) *dia* ***Off*** used as a moderate curse, Fuck you!
- **Kȑs ti jèbēm bȍžjī!** {S} (lit. I fuck your God's cross!) *dia* ***Off*** used as a moderate curse, Fuck you!

kȑsak {ska masc.} *col* crack (branch, etc.) <Slav>

kȑskānje {a neut.} *col* cracking (branch, etc.) <Slav>

kȑskati {ām, ajū imperf.} *col* crack, produce the sound of cracking <Slav>

kȑst *See the following*

- **sêdmī kȑst** {NP} (lit. seventh cross) Cro *sl-drink* name of a bar on Trnjanska street in Zagreb, Croatia

krstək *See the following*

- **Krstək ti jèbēm!** {S} (lit. I fuck your little cross!) SSer *dia* ***Off*** used as a moderate curse, Fuck you!

kȑsta {kȑstā neut. pl.} *col* back (of a person) <Slav*1>

kȑstača *See the following*

- **Kȑstaču ti jèbēm!** {S} (lit. I fuck your cross!) *dia* ***Off*** used as a moderate curse, Fuck you!

kȑstačȍja {ē fem.} *sl* head

krstačȍjna {ē fem.} *sl* head

krstàrica {ē fem.} (lit. cruiser) *sl-fea* female with loud clothing and makeup <Slav*1>

kȑstāš {krstášā (acc. = gen.) masc.} *sl-fea* illiterate male <Slav*1>

kȑsten {a, o adj.} *col* baptized <**Slav*1**>
• **jâ ga kȑstīm, a ôn pȑdī** {S} (lit. I am baptizing him but he is farting) *col* ***Obs-Fac*** used to indicate that a person does not pay attention to intensive persuasion

kȑš {kȑša +ev (ext. pl) masc.; Nom Pl kȑševi} **a.** *sl-fea* old and often malfunctioning mechanism, wreck <**Slav*1**> **b.i.** *sl-sex* elderly prostitute <**Slav*2**> **ii.** *sl-fea* ruined and destroyed person or mechanism <**Slav*2**> **iii.** *sl-fea* mess, disorder, disturbance <**Slav*2**>

kȑšan {šna, šno adj.} *sl-fea* muscular, pumped up <**Slav*1**>
• **Ne kȑši kȕrac!** {S} (lit. Don't you break your prick!) *dia* ***Off*** used as a moderate curse, Fuck you!

krštènjāk {tenjáka masc.} *sl* birth certificate <**Slav⁘**>

kȑtica {ē fem.} *sl-fea* diligent male <**Slav*1**>

kȑtičnjāk *See the following*
• **ko krtȉčnjāk** {PP} /ko kȑtičnjāk/ (lit. like a mole hole) *sl-fea* ***Der*** unattractive, ugly

krtȉna {ē fem.} (lit. lean meat without any fat) *sl-sex* ***Obs*** buttocks, butt <**Slav*1**>

kȑtola {ē fem.} *dia-col* potato <**Slav**>

krȕ {krȕa +ov (ext. pl) masc.; Nom Pl krùovi} [std. = kruh] *dia-col* bread <**Slav✐**>

krûg {a +ov (ext. pl) masc.; Nom Pl krȕgovi} *col* a short ride <**Slav*1**>
• **dvójkīn krûg** {NP} (lit. the circle made by the streetcar number two) *Ser sl* downtown Belgrade

krȕh {a +ov (ext. pl) masc.; Nom Pl krùhovi} (lit. bread) *sl-drugs* narcotic drug, dope <**Slav*1**>

krȕlt {a +ov (ext. pl) masc.; Nom Pl krùltovi} *sl-drugs* narcotic drug, dope

krùmpīr [1] {krumpíra (acc. = gen.) masc.} (lit. potato) *Cro sl-crime* policeman, cop <**Slav*1**>

krùmpīr [2] {krumpíra masc.} (lit. potato) **1 Cro** *sl-music* long note <**Slav*1**> **2 Cro** *sl-drink* bar (drinking place) <**Slav*1**> **3** Cro *sl* name of a dance club at the former Žrtava fašizma Square in Zagreb, Croatia <**Slav*1**> **4** name of a cafe on Rački street in Zagreb, Croatia

krùmpīr-bâr {a +ov (ext. pl) masc.; Nom Pl krùmpīr-bȃrovi} **Cro** *sl* name of a dance club at the student dormitory complex in Zagreb, Croatia <**Slav-Eng*1**>

krumpìrāš {piráša (acc. = gen.) masc.; Voc krȕmpirāšu} (lit. potato-man) **1 Cro** *sl-fea* mainlander (so called by inhabitants of the coastal region) <**Slav⁘*1**> **2** Cro *sl-fea* obese male <**Slav⁘*1**> **3** Cro *sl-crime* policeman, cop <**Slav⁘*1**> **4** *sl-mil* soldier who is assigned to peeling potatoes <**Slav⁘*1**>

krùpnjāk {krupnjáka (acc. = gen.) masc.} *sl-fea* big-boned male <**Slav⁘**>

krȕška [1] {ē fem.; Dat krȕški} (lit. pear) *sl-sex* small firm female breast <**Slav*1**>

Krȕška [2] {ē fem.; Dat Krȕški} (lit. kruška 'pear' X Kruševac 'place name') *sl-crime* name of a prison in Kruševac, Serbia <**SlavO*1**>

krúška [3] {ē fem.; Dat krúški} (lit. pear) *sl-drink* pear brandy <**Slav⁘**>

krȕškovača {ē fem.} *sl-drink* pear brandy <**Slav⁘**>

krȕšnā pêć {NP} (lit. bread oven) *sl-sex* ***Fac*** large female buttocks ☞ **peć**

krútiti {krûtīm, tē imperf.} *sl* eat, devour <**Slav**>

krȕv {a +ov (ext. pl) masc.; Nom Pl krùvovi} [std. = kruh] *dia-col* bread <**Slav✐**>

krûžnā píla {NP} (lit. circular saw) *sl* opera singer ☞ **pila**

kȓv *See the following*
• **Kȓv ti jèbēm!** {S} (lit. I fuck your blood!) *col* ***Off*** used as a moderate curse, Fuck you!

krvàjca {ē fem.} *sl-arch* meat <**Slav**>

kȑvav {a, o adj.} (lit. bloody) **a.** *sl-fea* ***App*** good, cool: *krvav film good movie* <**Slav*1**> **b.** *sl-fea* funny <**Slav*2**> **c.** *sl-fea* nice <**Slav*3**>
• **kȑvav ko gèrla Ravȉjojla** {AdjP} (lit. as bloody as the girl Ravijojla, an epic character) *sl-fea* entertaining, funny

krvàvica {ē fem.} (lit. blood sausage) *sl-sex* ***Fac*** menstruation, period <**Slav*1**>

kȑvavo [1] {adv.} (lit. bloody) **a.** *sl-fea* hard, with difficulties: *krvavo raditi work hard* <**Slav*1**> **b.** *sl-fea* excellently, cool: *krvavo proći na turniru do excellently in a tournament* <**Slav*2**> **c.** *sl-fea* nicely <**Slav*3**>

kȑvavō [2] {ōg neut.} (lit. bloody) *sl* meat <**Slav*1**>

krvčək *See the following*
• **Krvčək ti jèbēm!** {S} (lit. I fuck your blood!) *SSer dia* ***Off*** used as a moderate curse, Fuck you!

kȑvčica *See the following*
• **Kȑvčicu ti jèbēm!** {S} (lit. I fuck your small blood!) *dia* ***Off*** used as a moderate curse, Fuck you!

kȑviš {adj.} *sl-fea* funny <**Slav✐*1**>

kȑvišan {šna, šno adj.} *sl-fea* ***App*** excellent, awesome <**Slav✐*1**>

kȑviti se {vīm, vē imperf. intr.} /kŕviti se/ **a.** *sl* argue, quarrel <Slav*1> **b.** *sl* fight (e.g. fist fight) <Slav*2>

kȑvljēnje {a neut.} **a.** *sl* prolonged and meaningless talk, blabber, chatter <Slav*1> **b.** *sl* argue, quarrel <Slav*2> **c.** *sl* fight (e.g. fist fight) <Slav*3>

krvoprolíće {a neut.} (lit. bloodshed) *sl-sex* ***Fac*** menstruation, period <Slav*1>

krznènjāk {nenjáka masc.} *sl* fur coat <Slav✤>

ks-ks {excl.} *sl* used to draw attention (usually of an attractive female) <Slav>

kš {excl.} *col* used to drive away a goat or a bird <Slav>

kúba {ē fem.} *sl-drugs* one cubic centimeter of liquid narcotic drug <Gre✍*1>

kùbān {kubána masc.} *sl* ten dinars; a ten-dinar bill <Gre✍*1>

kubikáža {ē fem.} *sl-auto* volume of an engine <Gre>

kùbura {ē fem.} *sl-crime* gun pistol <NE*1>

kúbus {a masc.} *sl* lie <Gre*1>

kȕc {excl.} *col* the sound made by knocking, knock <Slav>

kúca {ē masc.} SerE *col* ***Fam*** dog (the animal), doggie <Slav✍>

kȕcāj {a masc.} *col* knock (on a door, etc.) <Slav>

kûcanj {cnja masc.} *col* knock (on a door, etc.) <Slav>

kùcara {ē fem.} *sl* typewriter <Slav*1>

kȕcati {ām, ajū imperf. intr.} (lit. knock) *col* work, labor: *kucati do pet sati work until five o'clock* <Slav*1>

kȕcavac {vca (acc. = gen.) masc.} (lit. knocker) *sl* ***Fac*** telegraph operator <Slav✤*1>

kùcnjava {ē fem.} *col* knocking, rapping <Slav>

kûco {excl.} (lit. doggie) *col* ***Fam*** used to address a child in an intimate manner, peanut <Slav*1>

kùcōv {kucòva (acc. = gen.) masc.; Voc kùcove} *col-dia* dog <Slav✤>

kȕčadžija {ē fem.} *sl-fea* dog walker (male) <Slav✤>

kȕčadžījka {ē fem.} *sl-fea* dog walker (female) <Slav✤>

kȕčka {ē fem.; Dat kȕčki} (lit. bitch, female dog) **1** *sl* necktie <Slav*1> **2** *sl* prostitute, bitch <Slav*2>

kȕčkār {a (acc. = gen.) masc.} **a.** *sl* dog walker (male) <Slav✤*1> **b.** *sl-mil* army driver <Slav✤*1>

kȕća {ē masc.} **1 a.** *sl-crime* prison, the big house <Slav*1> **b.** *sl-crime* prison cell <Slav*2> **2** *sl-mil* barracks <Slav*1>

- **kȕća nȅobičnā** {NP} (lit. an extraordinary house) *sl-crime* prison
- **kȕćo stârā** {NP} (lit. old house) *col* used to address a male in direct informal communication
- **Kȕću ti jèbēm!** {S} (lit. I fuck your house!) *col* ***Off*** used as a moderate curse, Fuck you!
- **žûtā kȕća** {NP} (lit. yellow house) *sl-fea* mental institution, madhouse

kȕćica *See the following*

- **kȕćica u cvijèću** {NP} (lit. small house surrounded by flowers) *sl-polit* name of the former Croatian Communist Party Central Committee building in Zagreb, Croatia

kȕćnā bùva {NP} (lit. house flea) Ser *sl* housekeeper, maid ☞ **buva**

kȕćnī zmȁj {NP} (lit. house dragon) *sl* housekeeper, maid ☞ **zmaj**

kùćnjāk {a masc.} *sl* housekeeper, maid <Slav✤>

kȕćo stârā {NP} (lit. old house) *col* used to address a male in direct informal communication, pal ☞ **kuća**

Kȕću ti jèbēm! {S} (lit. I fuck your house) *col* ***Off*** used as a moderate curse, Fuck you! ☞ **kuća**

kud pȕklo da pȕklo {AdvP} (lit. wherever it bangs) [std. = pući] *col* used to indicate the willingness to act notwithstanding the consequences: *Idem na ljetovanje kud puklo da puklo. I'll use my summer vacation whatever happens.* ☞ **pući**

kùdē {adv.} [std. = kuda] *dia-col* where to, where do you want to go <Slav✍>

kudèljārka {ē fem.} SerE *sl-fea* female with dyed hair <Slav*1>

kȕdrav {a, o adj.} *sl-fea* curly (of hair) <Slav*1>

kùfer {a masc.} (lit. suitcase) **a.** *sl-crime* solitary prison cell <Ger*1> **b.** *sl-crime* prison <Ger*2> **c.** *sl-crime* unpleasant situation, bummer <Ger*2>

- **Kùfer mi je!** {S} (lit. It's a suitcase to me!) Cro *sl* used to refer to a dangerous situation

kȕga {ē fem.; Dat kȕgi} **1** *sl* apartment rent collector <Slav*1> **2** danger

kúgla {ē fem.} (lit. ball) *sl-sex* ***Obs*** large round female breast <Ger*1>

- **bìljārskā kúgla** {NP} (lit. billiard ball) *sl-fea* ***Fac*** bald male

kugláger {a masc.} *sl-crafts* ball bearing <Ger>

kuglàna {ē fem.} (lit. bowling alley) *sl* street <Ger*1>

kûglati {ām, ajū biasp.} *sl* abuse somebody's trust <Ger*1>

kûglati se {ām, ajū biasp. intr.} (lit. bowl) *sl* laugh <Ger[*1]>

• **kûglati se ȍd smijēha**{VP} (lit. bowl down in laughter) *sl* ***Fac*** find something highly humorous

kùglica *See the following*

• **slȁdostrasnē kùglice** {NP} (lit. lust balls) *sl-sex* testicles, balls

kùhača {ē fem.} (lit. cooking place) **Cro** *sl* the former workers' community center in Zagreb known for its dance parties <Slav[*1]>

kȕhānje {a neut.} (lit. cooking) **a.** *sl* flirting: *kuhanje s Mirom flirting with Mira* <Slav[*1]> **b.** *sl* persuasion <Slav[*2]> **c.** *sl* cheating, swindling <Slav[*3]>

kȕhār [1] {a (acc. = gen.) masc.} (lit. cook) **1** *sl-mil* officer <Slav[*1]> **2** *sl-crime* policeman, cop <Slav[*1]>

kȕhār [2] {a masc.} (lit. cookbook) *sl* flirting etiquette <Slav[*1]>

kȕhati {ām, ajū biasp.} (lit. cook) **a.** *sl* flirt: *kuhati sa susjetkom flirt with one's neighbor* <Slav[*1]> **b.** *sl* persuade, convince: *kuhati starce da daju lovu persuade one's parents to give some money* <Slav[*2]> **c.** *sl* cheat, swindle <Slav[*3]>

kùhčānje {a neut.} *sl-gamble* gambling (with cards) <Slav[*1]>

kȕhinja {ē fem.} (lit. cuisine) *col* intrigue <Slav[*1]>

kȕj {pron.} SSer *dia* who (in all its Serbo-Croatian meanings in the form different from the standard one) <Slav☞>

kȕja {ē fem.} /kúja/ (lit. bitch) **a.** *sl* female <Slav[*1]> **b.** *sl* unattractive female, dog <Slav[*2]> **c.** *sl* prostitute, hooker <Slav[*3]>

kûjda {ē fem.} *sl-arch* polenta

kûjdar {a masc.} *sl-arch* polenta

kûjka {ē fem.} *sl-arch* polenta

kujùndžija {ē masc.} *col* blacksmith <NE[*1]>

kujùndžīnica {ē fem.} *col* blacksmith's <NE[*1]>

kȕka {ē fem.; Dat kȕki} **1a.** *sl* year <Slav[*1]> **b.** *sl-crime* year in prison <Slav[*2]> **2** *sl-fea* look, glimpse <Slav[*1]> **3** *sl-fea* nose <Slav[*1]> **4** *sl-fea* arm <Slav[*1]>

kúkac {kca masc.} (lit. insect) *sl-fea* ***Der*** coward, chicken <Slav[*1]>

kȕkadžija {ē fem.} *sl-fea* dog walker (male) <Slav-NE[*1]>

kȕkadžika {ē fem.; Dat kȕkadžīki} *sl-fea* dog walker (female) <Slav-NE[*1]>

kȕkati {ām, ajū imperf. intr.} **a.** *sl* coo (of birds) <Slav[*1]> **b.** *sl* complain, whine <Slav[*2]> **c.** *sl* cry, shed tears, weep <Slav[*3]> **d.** *sl* sing <Slav[*4]>

• **kȕkala[PRON:DAT] mâjka** {LSF} (lit. let [PPRON] mother cry) *col* used to express compassion, poor thing: *Kukala mu majka, šta će sad? Poor thing, what is he going to do now?*

• **kȕkala ti mâjka** {S} (lit. let your mother weep) *col* used to indicate that one's interlocutor is doing something wrong, illegal, etc., What in the world are you doing! Oh God!: *Gdje ćeš, kukala ti majkà! Tamo je opasno! Oh God, where are you going! It is dangerous over there!*

kȕkavac {vca (acc. = gen.) masc.} **1** *sl-fea* pathetic person, poor thing <Slav[*1]> **2** *sl* ***Fac*** telegraph operator <Slav[*1]>

kukavȅla {ē fem.} *sl* objecting to everything, bitching <Slav☞>

kȕkavica {ē fem.} **a.** *col* cuckoo (the bird) <Slav[*1]> **b.i.** *sl* year <Slav[*2]> **ii.** *sl* ten dinars; a ten-dinar bill <Slav[*2]>

kukcològija {ē fem.} (lit. insectology) *sl-sstu* biology <Slav-Gre[*1]>

kȕkica {ē fem.} (lit. small hook) *sl-sstu* failing grade <Slav[*1]>

kuknjavȅla {ē fem.} *sl* objecting to everything, bitching <Slav☞>

kȕku {excl.} *col* used to express grief or sorrow <Slav>

• **kȕku lȅle** {ExcP} *col* used to express grief, woe

kukùmāvčiti {čīm, čē imperf. intr.} *sl-fea* complain, bitch <Slav>

kȕkurēk {a masc.} SerE *col* cock-a-doodle-doo <Slav>

kukurékati {ām, ajū imperf.} SerE *col* cock-a-doodle-doo <Slav>

kukurêku {excl.} *col* cock-a-doodle-doo <Slav>

kȕkurijēk {a masc.} *col* cock-a-doodle-doo <Slav>

kukurijêku {excl.} *col* cock-a-doodle-doo <Slav>

kȕkurīk {a masc.} *col* cock-a-doodle-doo <Slav>

kukuríkati {kùrīčēm, īčū imperf.} **a.** *col* cock-a-doodle-doo <Slav> **b.** *sl-fea* laugh <Slav[*1]>

kukuríknuti {kùrīknēm, nū perf.} (lit. cock-a-doodle-doo) *sl-sex* ***Fac-Obs*** engage in sexual intercourse with (of a male) <Slav>

kukurîku {excl.} *col* cock-a-doodle-doo <Slav>

Kukuríkū Hȉl {NP} (lit. Cock-a-doodle-doo Hill) *sl* name for Petlovo brdo (a neighborhood in Belgrade, Yugoslavia) ☞ **Hil**

Kukuríkū Sìtī {NP} (lit. Cock-a-doodle-doo City) *sl* name forPetlovo brdo (a neighborhood in Belgrade, Yugoslavia) ☞ **Siti**

kûl ¹ {adj.} *sl-fea* ***App*** excellent, awesome <Eng>

kûl ² {adv.} *sl-fea* ***App*** excellent, awesome <Eng>

kúla {ē fem.} (lit. the tower) *sl-crime* name of a prison in Stara Gradiška, Croatia <NE*1>
- **ćèle kúla** {NP} (lit. skull tower) *sl-drink* ***Fac*** name of a bar frequented by retirees in Zagreb, Croatia
- **Kúlu ti jèbēm!** {S} (lit. I screw your tower!) *dia* ***Off*** used as a weak curse, Screw you!

kulàna {ē fem.} *sl-crime* prison <Gyp*1>

kûle {eta masc.} **a.** *sl-fea* inhabitant of the countryside, hick, bumpkin **b.** troublemaker, rowdy, ruffian **c.** stupid or mentally deficient person, **d.** male

kuléga {ē masc.; Dat kulégi} (lit. colleague) [std. = kolega] *sl-crime* ***Iro*** police investigator <Lat✍*1>

kuléra {ē fem.} **a.** *sl* danger <Gre✍> **b.** *sl-crime* manhunt <Gre✍*1>

kulíranje {a neut.} **a.** *sl* calming down, cooling off <Eng*1> **b.** *sl* resting <Eng*2>

kulírati {kùlīrām, kulírajū perf.+ imperf.} **a.** *sl* calm down, cool off: *Kulirala je kad se pojavila policija. She cooled off when the heat arrived.* <Eng*1> **b.** *sl* get rest: *kulirati posle ručka get some rest after lunch* <Eng*2>

kùlōv {kulòva (acc. = gen.) masc.} **a.** *sl-fea* inhabitant of the countryside, hick, bumpkin **b.** *sl-fea* stupid or mentally deficient person **c.** *sl-fea* troublemaker, rowdy, ruffian **d.** *sl-sex* lover (male) **e.** *sl-fea* dandy, fop **f.** *sl* male

kulòvisānje {a neut.} *sl-fea* spending one's time in useless activities, fooling around, messing around

kulòvisati {išēm, išū imperf.} *sl-fea* spend one's time in useless activities, fool around, mess around

kùlōvka {ē fem.} **a.** *sl-sex* ***Der*** prostitute, hooker **b.** *sl* girlfriend

kulóvština {ē fem.} *sl-fea* spending one's time in useless activities, fooling around, messing around

kùlučār {a (acc. = gen.) masc.} *sl-fea* worker <NE*1>

kùlučiti {čīm, čē imperf.} *sl-crime* spend term in prison, do time <NE*1>

kúlja {ē fem.} *sl-sstu* failing grade

kûm {a (acc. = gen.) masc.} **1a.** *col* godfather (with whom both child and parents stay in a very close relationship all their lives) <Slav*1> **b.i.** *sl-crime* godfather <Slav*2> **ii.aa.** *sl* inhabitant of the countryside, hick, bumpkin <Slav*2> **bb.** *sl* male, guy <Slav*3> **2** *col* best man (with whom bride and groom stay in a very close relationship all their lives)

kúma {ē fem.} **1a.** *col* godmother (with whom both child and parents stay in a very close relationship all their lives) <Slav*1> **b.** *sl-fea* inhabitant of the countryside (female), hick, bumpkin <Slav*2> *col* bride of honor (with whom bride and groom stay in a very close relationship all their lives) <Slav*1>

kumàšin {a (acc. = gen.) masc.} *sl-fea* best man (with whom bride and groom stay in a very close relationship all their lives) <Slav❖>

kùmbura {ē fem.} *sl-crime* gun pistol <NE✍*1>

kùmek {a (acc. = gen.) masc.} **a.** **Kajk** *sl-fea* stupid or mentally deficient person <Slav*1> **b.** inhabitant of the countryside, hick, bumpkin

kumpànija {ē fem.} *sl* gang, group of one's close friends <Fre✍*1>

kúmstvo {a neut.} **1** *sl* being one's godfather <Slav*1> **2** *sl* being one's best man <Slav*1> ☞ **kum, kuma**

kùndak {a (acc. = gen.) masc.} *sl-crime* policeman, cop <NE*1>

kùndura {ē fem.} *sl* shoe <NE*1>

kȕnst {a +ov (ext. pl) masc.; Nom Pl kùnstovi} **1** *sl* profit, gain: *imati kunst od prodaje jaja make a profit from selling eggs* <Ger*1> **2** *sl* skillfulness: *Nije kunst prevariti naivca. It's no trick to cheat a naive guy.* <Ger*1>
- **na kȕnst** {PP} (lit. at arts) *sl-crime* using mischief

kȕnt {a +ov (ext. pl) masc.; Nom Pl kùntovi} **a.** *sl* room <Hun*1> **b.** *sl* apartment <Hun*2> **c.** *sl* hiding place <Hun*3> **d.** *sl* overnight stay at another's apartment, sleepover <Hun*4> **e.** *sl* sleeping <Hun*5>

kùntānje {a neut.} **a.** *sl* overnight stay at another's apartment, sleepover <Hun*1> **b.** *sl* sleeping <Hun*2>

kùntati {ām, ajū imperf.} **a.** *sl* stay overnight at another's apartment, sleepover <Hun*1> **b.** *sl* sleep, nap <Hun*2>

kuntírānje {a neut.} *sl* sleeping <Hun*1>

kuntírati {kùntīrām, kuntírajū imperf.} *sl* sleep, nap <Hun*1>

Kúnto *See the following*
- **Kúnto i Pánto** {NP} *col* used to refer to a group of different people (usu. a in derogatory context), just anybody: *Na toj zabavi se skupio i Kunto i Panto. Every Tom, Dick and Harry gathered at that party.*

kȕntovati {tujēm, tujū imperf.} *sl* sleep, nap <Hun*1>

kúnjati {kûnjām, kúnjajū imperf. intr.} *sl* sleep, nap <**Slav**[*1]>

kȕnjav {a, o adj.} **a.** *sl-fea* tired <**Slav**[*1]> **b.** *sl-fea* ill, sick <**Slav**[*2]>

kùnjavac {vca (acc. = gen.) masc.} *sl-fea* observer pretending to be sleeping <**Slav**[*1]>

kȕnjos {a (acc. = gen.) masc.} **a.** *sl-fea* sleepy person <**Slav**✍[*1]> **b.** *sl-fea* weak person <**Slav**✍[*2]> **c.** *sl-fea* patient <**Slav**✍[*3]>

kȕnjos {adj.} **a.** *sl-fea* sleepy <**Slav**✍[*1]> **b.** *sl-fea* sickly <**Slav**✍[*2]>

kùpalīšte {a neut.} (lit. bath, spa) *sl-crime* prison <**Slav**[*1]>

kúpati {kûpām, kúpajū imperf.} (lit. bathe) *sl* search <**Slav**[*1]>

• **kúpati zûbe** {VP} (lit. wash one's teeth) *sl-drink* drink (alcohol)

kȕpčānje {a neut.} *sl-gamble* a kind of a card game <**Slav**[*1]>

kùpēj {kupéja masc.} [std. = kupe] *sl* compartment on a train, etc. <**Fre**✍>

kȕpiti [1] {pīm, pē imperf.} (lit. pick) **a.** *sl* lift, rise <**Slav**[*1]> **b.** *sl* steal, swipe: *kupiti frajeru novčanik steal a wallet from a guy* <**Slav**[*2]> **c.** *sl* take <**Slav**[*3]>

• **kȕpiti fazóne** {VP} (lit. pick up tricks) *col* understand, realize

• **kȕpiti ga** {VP} (lit. pick it up) *sl-crime* pick pockets

• **kȕpiti óvcu** {VP} (lit. pick up a sheep) *sl-crime* pick pockets

• **kȕpiti pȑnje** {VP} (lit. pick up one's rugs) *sl* leave, go away

• **kȕpiti štôs** {VP} (lit. pick up a trick) **1** *sl* learn a trick **2** *sl* learn a joke **3** *sl* become skillful

• **kȕpiti štósove** {VP} (lit. pick up tricks) **1** *sl* learn a trick **2** *sl* learn a joke **3** *sl* become skillful

kúpiti [2] {kûpīm, pē perf.} *sl-col* believe, buy <**Slav**[*1]>

• **kúpiti bìlet** {VP} (lit. buy a ticket) *sl* get married, get hitched

• **kúpiti bìber** {VP} (lit. buy some pepper) *sl-sex* suffer from gonorrhea, have the clap

• **kúpiti čȉr** {VP} (lit. buy an ulcer) *sl-sex* suffer from syphilis, have the pox

kȕpiti se {pīm, pē imperf. intr.} (lit. pick oneself up) *col* leave, depart, walk <**Slav**[*1]>

• **Kȕpi se!** {S} (lit. Take yourself away!) *col* used to make somebody go away, Beat it!

kuplèrāj {lerája masc.} **a.** *sl-sex* brothel, whorehouse <**Ger**> **b.** *sl* chaos, mess: *imati kupleraj u kući have a mess in one's house* <**Ger**[*1]>

kȕplić {a masc.} *sl-sex* brothel, whorehouse <**Ger**✍>

kùplūng {a masc.} *sl-auto* clutch <**Ger**>

kûpljen {a, o adj.} (lit. bought) *sl-crime* informing the police, snitching: *kupljen jerfra snitching guy* <**Slav**[*1]>

kȕpus {a masc.} (lit. cabbage) **1** *sl-sstu* book <**Slav**[*1]> **2** *sl-sstu* notebook <**Slav**[*1]>

kupùsara [1] {ē fem.} (lit. the cabbage one) **1** *sl* head <**Slav**[*1]> **2** *sl-sstu* untidy notebook <**Slav**[*1]>

kupùsara [2] {ē fem.} (lit. the cabbage woman) **a.** *sl-fea* untidy female, slob <**Slav**[*1]> **b.** *sl-fea* unattractively dressed female <**Slav**[*2]>

kûr {a +ev (ext. pl) masc.; Nom Pl kúrevi} *sl-sex* ***Obs*** penis, dick, prick <**Slav**[*1]>

• **Kûr môj!** {S} (lit. My prick!) **a.** *col* ***Obs*** used as a strong negative response, no way, never **b.** *col* ***Obs*** used to express disbelief

• **Môj kûr!** {S} (lit. My prick!) *col* ***Obs*** used to express disappointment, Shit!

kûr-vȉnjāk {a masc.} (lit. prick brandy) *sl-drink* Courvoisier (a brand of cognac) <**Fre**✍>

kúra [1] {ē masc.} *sl-sex* ***Obs*** penis, dick, prick <**Slav**[*1]>

kúra [2] {ē fem.} **1** *sl-sex* ***Obs*** penis, dick, prick <**Slav**[*1]> **2** *sl-mil* military check-up (physical exam) <**Slav**[*1]>

kùrāba {ē fem.} /kurába /e fem./ *sl-sex* ***Fac-Obs*** prostitute, hooker <**Ger**✍>

kȕrac [1] {part.} *sl* used as a strong negative response, no way, never: *A: Hoćeš li mi pomoći! B: Hoću kurac! A: Are you going to help me! B: No way!* <**Slav**[*1]>

kȕrac [2] {excl.} (lit. prick) **a.** *sl* used to express disbelief or disagreement: *A: Bio sam na tom koncertu. B: Jesi kurac! A: A was at that concert. B: No shit!* <**Slav**[*1]> **b.** *sl* used as a strong negative response, no way, no deal: *A: Možeš li mi posuditi tri miljaka? B: Mogu kurac! A: Can you lend me three grand? B: No way!* <**Slav**[*2]>

kȕrac [3] {kûrca masc.} **a.** *sl-sex* ***Obs*** penis, dick, prick <**Slav**> **b.** *sl* ***Obs*** trifle, thing of little importance or value <**Slav**[*1]> **c.i.** *sl* ***Obs*** who knows what <**Slav**[*2]> **ii.** *sl* ***Obs*** trick, joke <**Slav**[*2]> **iii.** *sl* ***Obs*** nothing <**Slav**[*2]> **iv.** *sl* ***Obs*** something bad <**Slav**[*2]>

• **bȁbini kȕrčevi** {NP} (lit. old lady's pricks) *sl* ***Obs*** hail

• **Dò kūrca!** {PP} (lit. To the prick!) *sl* ***Obs*** used to express anger, Fuck it!

• E, jèsi kȕrac! {S} (lit. Yeah, you are my prick!) *col* ***Obs*** used as a strong negative response, no way, never

• Ȉstī kȕrac! {AdjP} (lit. Same prick!) *col* ***Obs*** used to refer to lack of any change

• Ȉstī kȕrac drȕgō pȁkovānje! {AdjP} (lit. Same prick in another package!) *col* ***Obs*** used to indicate lack of any change, Same old shit it just looks different!

• kàkī kȕrac {NP} (lit. what kind of cock) *col* ***Obs*** used as a strong negative response, no way, never

• Kàkī kȕrac! {S} (lit. No cock!) *col* ***Obs*** used as a strong negation, No way!

• Kȍj ćeš mi kȕrac! {S} (lit. Which prick do I need you!) *col* ***Off*** used in angry dismissal, Fuck off!

• Kòjī će ([PRON:DAT]) kȕrac? {LSF} (lit. Which prick do *you* need it for?) *col* ***Obs*** used to refer to a negative attitude toward an object: *Koji će ti kurac? What the hell do you need it for?*

• Kòjī ćeš kȕrac! {S} (lit. Which prick do you want?) *col* ***Off*** used in angry dismissal, Fuck off!

• kòjī kȕrac {NP} (lit. which prick) *col* ***Obs*** why: *Koji kurac ideš tamo? Why are you going there?*

• Kòjī kȕrac tî mȅne zajèbāvāš! {S} (lit. Which prick are you teasing me?) *col* ***Off*** used in angry dismissal

• kòjī[PRON:DAT] je kȕrac {LSF} (lit. which cock is it to [PRON:ACC]) *col* ***Obs*** used to express negative attitude toward one's interlocutor: *koji im je kurac what's wrong with them*

• Kòjī ti je kȕrac? {S} (lit. Which cock is it with you?) *col* ***Obs*** used to express negative attitude toward one's interlocutor, What's wrong with you?

• kȕrac na bàtini {NP} (lit. prick on a bat) **a.** *sl-fea* ***Obs*** nothing at all, fucking nothing **b.** *sl-fea* ***Obs*** worthless object, junk

• kȕrac od óvcē {NP} (lit. sheep's prick) **1** *sl-fea* ***Obs*** nothing at all **2** *sl-fea* unimportant person, nothing

• kȕrac tȉcē ródē {NP} (lit. stork's prick) **a.** *sl-fea* ***Obs*** nothing at all **b.** *sl-fea* ***Obs*** worthless object, junk

• kȕrac zȁ uši {NP} (lit. prick on one's ears) **a.** *sl-fea* ***Obs*** nothing at all **b.** *sl-fea* ***Obs*** worthless object, junk

• kûrcem u lèdinu {NP} (lit. with one's prick to a lawn) *sl* ***Obs*** die, kick the bucket

• nȁ kurac {PP} (lit. at a cock) *sl* ***Obs*** used to express disrespect or dissatisfaction, Fuck it!: *Na kurac sve te njegove planove. Fuck all his plans.*

• Ni kûrcu si ne kàzujē! {S} (lit. He doesn't tell it even to the prick!) SSer *dia* ***Obs*** used as a moderate curse, Fuck him!

• preko kûrca {PP} (lit. over one's prick) *col* unwillingly

• Prez kȕrac! {S} (lit. Through the prick!) *dia* ***Obs*** used as a strong negative response, no way, never

• têškī kȕrac {NP} (lit. heavy prick) **a.** *col* ***Der-Obs*** nothing at all **b.** *col* ***Der-Obs*** worthless object, junk

• U kȕrac! {S} (lit. In a prick!) *col* ***Obs*** used to express lack of control over events

• U kȕrac krâsnī! {S} (lit. In a nice prick!) *col-dia* ***Obs*** used to express lack of control over events

• U kȕrac lêpī! {S} (lit. In a beautiful prick!) SerE *dia-col* ***Obs*** used to express lack of control over events

• ȕ kūrcu {PP} (lit. in a prick) *col* far away, utterly remote

• za kòjī kȕrac {PP} (lit. for which prick) *col* ***Obs*** why

kȕrac-pȁlac {part.} (lit. prick-thumb) *sl* sexual intercourse <Slav*1>

• **kȕrac-pȁlac kriminálac** {NP} (lit. prick-thumb criminal) *sl-fea* ***Obs*** nothing at all

kuráda {ē fem.} *sl-crime* old unskillful criminal <Slav ✍>

kuràdāš {kuradáša masc.} *sl-sex* ***Obs*** male with a large penis <Slav*1>

kuradàšica {ē fem.} *sl-sex* ***Obs*** loose woman, slut <Slav⁘*1>

kuradàšlija {ē masc.} *sl-sex* ***Obs*** male with a large penis <Slav⁘*1>

kuràdija {ē fem.} *sl* male children, boys <Slav⁘*1>

kuràfte [1] {part.} *sl* used as a strong negative response, no way, never <Slav✍>

kuràfte [2] {ea masc.} *sl* error, mistake <Slav✍>

kuràica {ē masc.} **a.** *sl-sex* ***Obs*** male sexual partner (of a female) <Slav⁘*1> **b.** *sl-sex* ***Obs*** male with a large penis <Slav⁘*2>

Kuràica {ē masc.} (lit. the one with a prick) *sl* ***Fac*** nickname for a male <Slav ⁘*1>

Kuràičīn {a, o adj.} *sl* ***Fac-Obs*** pertaining to the nickname Kuraica <Slav⁘*1>

kuràile {a masc.} (lit. the one with a prick) *sl-sex* ***Obs*** male with a large penis <Slav⁘*1>

kuràjber {a (acc. = gen.) masc.} (lit. the one with a prick) **a.** *sl-sex* ***Obs*** male sexual partner (of a female) <Slav⁘*1> **b.** *sl-sex* ***Obs*** male with a large penis <Slav⁘*2> **c.** *sl-fea* ***Der-Obs*** mean or worthless person <Slav⁘*3> **d.** *sl-fea* irresponsible person <Slav⁘*4> **e.** *sl-fea* spoiled child, brat <Slav⁘*5>

• **Kuràjberu jèdan!** {S} (lit. You, guy with a big prick!) *col* ***Off*** used as a moderate curse, Fuck you!

kuràjlija {ē masc.} (lit. the one with a prick) *sl-sex* ***Obs*** male with a large penis <Slav⁘*1>

kùrājlo {a masc.} (lit. the one with a prick) *sl-sex* ***Obs*** male with a large penis **<Slav✣[*1]>**

kùrak {rka masc.} (lit. the one with a prick) *sl-sex* ***Obs*** penis, dick, prick **<Slav✣>**

kuràntīn {rantína masc.} (lit. prickrantine *kurac 'prick' X karantin 'quarantine'*) *sl-crime* hiding from a manhunt **<Slav-Lat>**

kùrat {a, o adj.} **a.** *sl-sex* ***Obs*** having a large penis **<Slav✣>** **b.** *sl-fea* ***Der-Obs*** unpleasant **<Slav✣[*1]>**

kuràtija {ē masc.} *sl* horse (the animal) **<Slav✣[*1]>**

kùratiti {tīm, tē imperf.} (lit. grow a bigger prick) *sl-fea* grow **<Slav✣[*1]>**

kùrātor {a (acc. = gen.) masc.} (lit. the one with a prick) *sl-sex* ***Obs*** male sexual partner (of a female) **<Slav✣>**

kȕrav {a, o adj.} (lit. prick's) *sl-fea* ***Obs*** dressed in loud and unattractive clothing **<Slav[*1]>**

kuráva {ē fem.} [std. = kurva] *sl-sex* prostitute, hooker **<Ger✍>**

kuravȅla {ē fem.} *sl-sex* ***Obs*** male sexual partner (of a female) **<Slav✍[*1]>**

kurávija {ē fem.} *sl-sex* ***Obs*** male sexual partner (of a female) **<Slav✍[*1]>**

kûrba {ē fem.} [std. = kurva] *sl-sex* prostitute, hooker **<Ger✍>**

• **Kûrba góspa!** {S} Med *col-dia* ***Obs*** used to express amazement, astonishment, etc., Fuck!

kurbàdūr {badúra masc.} *sl-sex* ***Fac*** male sexual partner (of a female) **<Slav✍[*1]>**

kùrbān {kurbána masc.} *col* Muslim animal sacrifice (esp. on Muslim holy days) **<NE>**

kùrbl {a +ov (ext. pl) masc.} *sl-auto* crank **<Ger>**

kùrbl-vȅla {ē fem.} *sl-auto* crank **<Ger>**

kùrbla {ē fem.} *sl-auto* crank **<Ger>**

kûrcem u lèdinu {NP} (lit. with one's prick to a lawn) *sl* ***Obs*** die, kick the bucket ☞ **kurac**

kurcoglávac {vca (acc. = gen.) masc.} *sl-fea* worthless or despicable person, dickhead **<Slav✣[*1]>**

kurcolízac {sca (acc. = gen.) masc.} (lit. prick-licker) *sl-sex* ***Fac-Obs*** male homosexual, gay **<Gyp✣[*1]>**

kurcòlōmka {ē fem.; Dat kurcòlōmki} (lit. prick-breaker) *sl-sex* ***Fac-Obs*** female who readily and indiscriminately engages in sexual intercourse, slut **<Slav✣[*1]>**

kȕrcoslāv {a (acc. = gen.) masc.} *sl-sex* ***Fac-Obs*** penis, dick, prick **<Slav✣[*1]>**

kȕrcšlus {a masc.} **a.** *sl-crafts* short circuit **<Ger>** **b.i.** *sl-fea* misunderstanding: *kurcšlus oko toga ko će platiti misunderstanding over who has to pay* **<Ger[*1]>** **ii.** *sl* five hundred dinars; a five hundred--inar bill **<Ger[*1]>** **iii.** *sl* memory blackout **<Ger[*1]>** **iv.** *sl-sex* penis **<Ger[*1]>**

kurčèkanja {ē fem.} *sl-sex* ***Obs*** penis, dick, prick **<Slav✣>**

kurčénce {eta neut.} *sl-sex* ***Obs*** small penis **<Slav✣>**

kȕrčēnje {a neut.} /kûrčēnje/ *sl-fea* boasting, bragging **<Slav[illegible][*1]>**

Kûrčēv [1] {Kûrčeva masc.} (lit. McPrick) *sl* ***Obs*** surname in Vojvodina, Serbia **<Slav✣>**

kûrčēv [2] {a, o adj.} *sl-sex* ***Obs*** pertaining to the penis **<Slav✣>**

Kûrčēv vòjnīk! {S} (lit. Prick's soldier!) *sl* ***Obs*** used as a moderate curse, Fuck him! ☞ **vojnik**

kûrčevē srȅćē {NP} (lit. of prick's happiness) *col* ***Obs*** not lucky at all ☞ **sreća**

kurčèvit {a, o adj.} **1** *sl-fea* ***Fac-Obs*** stubborn, pigheaded: *kurčevit pregovarač stubborn negotiator* **<Slav✣[*1]>** **2** *sl-fea* ***Fac-Obs-Der*** of very low-quality, lousy: *kurčevit bicikl shitty bike* **<Slav✣[*2]>**

kurčèvito {adv.} **a.** *sl-fea* ***Fac-Obs*** very difficult, screwed up: *Biće kurčevito da dobijemo te pare. It will be a bitch for us to get that money.* **<Slav✣[*1]>** **b.** *sl-fea* ***Fac-Obs-Der*** very bad **<Slav✣[*1]>**

Kȕrčī se! {S} (lit. He is showing his prick!) *sl-fea* ***Obs*** used to refer to conceited behavior of the third person ☞ **kurčiti se**

Kûrčīn blȁgoslōv! {S} (lit. Prick's blessing!) *dia* ***Obs*** used to express lack of interest in ☞ **blagoslov**

kùrčina {ē fem.} *sl-sex* ***Obs*** large penis **<Slav✣[*1]>**

kȕrčiti se {čīm, čē imperf. intr.} /kûrčiti se/ (lit. prick oneself) **a.** *sl-fea* ***Fac-Obs*** be conceited, be stuck-up: *Taj mali se kurči pa niko neće s njim da se igra. That boy is stuck-up so nobody wants to play with him.* **<Slav✣[*1]>** **b.** *sl-fea* ***Fac-Obs*** boast, brag **<Slav✣[*2]>** **c.** *sl-fea* show off **<Slav✣[*3]>**

• **Kȕrčī se!** {S} (lit. He is showing his prick!) *sl-fea* ***Obs*** used to refer to conceited behavior of the third person

kûrda {ē fem.} *sl-arch* polenta

kùrezina {ē fem.} *sl-sex* ***Obs*** large penis **<Slav✍>**

kȕriti {rīm, rē imperf.} *sl* smoke (tobacco) **<Slav>**

kȕrja {excl.} *sl* help, assist

Kȕrjāk[1] {a (acc. = gen.) masc.} (lit. wolf, i.e. the etymology of the name Vuk) *sl* name for Vuk Karadžić's monument in Belgrade, Serbia <Slav[*1]>

kȕrjāk[2] {a (acc. = gen.) masc.} (lit. wolf) *sl* guard, watchman <Slav[*1]>

kúro {ē masc.} *sl-sex* ***Obs*** penis, dick, prick <Slav ✣>

kȕro-mȕro {a masc.} *sl-fea* beloved person <Slav[*1]>

kȕrobaša {ē masc.} **a.** *sl-sex* ***Obs*** male with a large penis <Slav-NE[*1]> **b.** *sl-fea* ***Obs*** muscular male <Slav[*2]>

kȕrokrēt {a masc.} (lit. prick-flower) *sl* flirting <Slav ✣[*1]>

kurokr̀šina {ē fem.} (lit. prick-breaker) *sl-sex* ***Obs*** large penis <Slav✣[*1]>

kȕrolomka {ē fem.; Dat kȕrolōmki} (lit. prick-breaker) *sl-sex* ***Fac-Obs*** prostitute, hooker <Slav ✣[*1]>

kuromìcīn {micína masc.} (lit. kurac 'prick' X -micin 'a common ending of drug brand names') *sl-sex* ***Fac-Obs*** aphrodisiac <Slav-Lat[*1]>

kuromùdīle {a (acc. = gen.) masc.} (lit. prick-ball dude) *sl-sex* ***Obs*** male with a large penis <Slav✣[*1]>

kȕronosa {ē fem.} (lit. the prick-nosed one) *sl-fea* ***Fac-Obs*** female with a large nose <Slav✣[*1]>

kuronòsīle {a masc.} (lit. the prick-nosed one) *sl-fea* ***Fac-Obs*** male with a large nose <Slav✣[*1]>

kúronja {ē fem.} (lit. the one with a prick) **a.** *sl-sex* ***Obs*** male sexual partner (of a female) <Slav ✣> **b.** *sl-sex* ***Obs*** male with a large penis <Slav✣[*1]>

Kúronja {ē masc.} (lit. the one with a prick) *sl* ***Fac*** nickname for a male <Slav ✣>

kúronjica {ē masc.} (lit. the one with a prick) **a.** *sl-sex* ***Obs*** male sexual partner (of a female) <Slav ✣[*1]> **b.** *sl* ***Obs-Fam*** boy, kid <Slav✣[*2]>

kuropȅcati se {ām, ajū imperf. intr.} (lit. fish oneself on a prick) *sl-sex* ***Fac-Obs*** agree to have sexual intercourse with (of females) <Slav✣[*1]>

kuropùšāč {pušáča (acc. = gen.) masc.; Voc kuropȕšāču} (lit. prick-smoker) *sl-sex* ***Fac-Obs*** male homosexual, gay <Gyp✣[*1]>

Kȕrosava {ē fem.} (lit. Prickette) *sl* ***Fac-Obs*** Milosava (a woman's name) <Slav☞>

kȕroslada {ē fem.} (lit. sweet prick lover) **a.** *sl-sex* ***Obs*** prostitute, hooker <Slav✣[*1]> **b.** *sl-sex* ***Obs*** loose woman, prick lover , slut <Slav✣[*2]>

kurotrèsina {ē masc.} **a.** *sl-fea* ***Fac-Obs*** senior citizen <Slav✣[*1]> **b.** *sl-fea* ***Der-Obs*** mean or worthless person <Slav✣[*1]>

kȕrozeb[1] {a masc.} (lit. prick-freezing) *sl* ***Fac-Obs*** cold weather <Slav✣[*1]>

Kȕrozeb[2] {a masc.} (lit. prick-freezing) *sl* ***Obs*** a name of a peak in Montenegro <Slav✣>

kȕroždėr {a (acc. = gen.) masc.} (lit. prick-devourer) **a.** *sl-sex* ***Fac-Obs*** sexually aroused female, hot chick <Slav✣[*1]> **b.** ***Fac-Obs*** prostitute, hooker <Slav✣[*2]> **c.** ***Fac-Obs*** male homosexual, gay <Slav ✣[*3]>

kȕroždērka {ē fem.; Dat kȕroždērki} (lit. prick-devourer) **a.** *sl-sex* ***Fac-Obs*** sexually aroused female, hot chick <Slav✣[*1]> **b.** *sl-sex* ***Fac-Obs*** prostitute, hooker <Slav ✣[*2]>

kȕršlus {a masc.} /kùršlus/ **a.** *sl-crafts* short circuit <Ger> **b.** *sl* misunderstanding: *kuršlus oko mesta sastanka misunderstanding over the meeting place* <Ger[*1]> **c.** *sl* memory blackout <Ger[*2]>

kȕrta {ē masc.} *sl-fea* unattractive male <Slav ✣[*1]>

kurtàlisati {išēm, išū imperf.} *sl* get rid of <NE>

kurtàlisati se {išēm, išū biasp. intr.} *sl* get rid of <NE>

kùrtija {ē masc.} *sl* beloved child, apple of one's eye

kúrto[1] {a masc.} *sl* beloved child, apple of one's eye <Slav✣[*1]>

Kúrto[2] {a masc.} *sl* nickname for a male <Slav✣>

kurtoâzija {ē fem.} (lit. courtesy) *sl-sex* ***Fac*** homosexuality <Fre[*1]>

kùrtōn {kurtóna masc.} **a.** *sl-sex* ***Obs*** condom, rubber <Slav-Fre[*1]> **b.i.** *sl* ***Obs*** nothing at all: *dobiti kurton got fucking nothing* <Slav-Fre[*1]> **ii.** *sl* ***Obs*** cheating, swindling <Slav-Fre[*1]> **iii.** *sl-fea* unfavorable situation <Slav-Fre[*1]>

kùrtōnka {ē fem.} *sl* rubber raincoat <Slav-Fre[*1]>

kurùntīn {runtína masc.} *sl-crime* hiding from a manhunt

kùruz {a masc.} [std. = kukuruz] *dia-col* corn <Slav ☞>

kurúza[1] {ē fem.} (lit. corn bread) *sl-music* bad music <Slav☞>

kurúza[2] {adj.} (lit. corn bread) *sl-fea* crude <Slav☞[*1]>

kùruznā {ē fem. (adj. decl.)} (lit. the corn one) *sl-fea* redheaded female <Slav ☞[*1]>

kȗrva {ē fem.} **a.** *sl-sex* prostitute, hooker <Ger> **b.** *sl-sex* loose woman <Ger[*1]> **c.i.** *sl-fea* coward, chicken <Ger[*2]> **ii.aa.** *sl-fea* unfriendly person <Ger[*2]> **bb.** *sl-crime* informer, stoolie, snitch <Ger[*4]> **iii.** Ser *sl* bus line number thirteen in Belgrade, Serbia <Ger[*3]> **iv.** *sl* anus <Ger[*3]>

kȕrvāč {a masc.} *sl-drink* ***Fac*** Courvoisier (a brand of cognac) <**Fre**✍*1>

kurvànjluk {a masc.} *sl-sex* frequent changes of one's sexual partners <**Ger**❖*1>

kùrvār {kurvára (acc. = gen.) masc.; Voc kȕrvāru} (lit. whorer) **a.** *sl-sex* womanizer, male who frequently changes his sexual partners <**Ger**❖*1> **b.** *sl-sex* ***Obs*** anus, asshole <**Ger**❖*1>

kurvàrluk {a masc.} *sl-sex* frequent changes of one's sexual partners <**Ger**❖*1>

kùrvārskī {aj adj.} (lit. whorerish) *sl-sex* pertaining to a male who frequently changes his sexual partners <**Ger**❖*1>

kurvèštija {ē fem.} *sl-sex* ***Der*** prostitute, hooker <**Ger**✍>

kurvètina {ē fem.} **a.** *sl-sex* ***Der*** prostitute, hooker <**Ger**❖> **b.** *sl-sex* ***Der*** old prostitute <**Ger**❖*2> **c.** *sl-sex* ***Der*** loose woman <**Ger**❖*3> **d.** *sl-fea* necktie <**Ger**❖*3>

kùrvica {ē fem.} /krvíca/ *sl-sex* prostitute, hooker <**Ger**❖>

kȕrvič {a masc.} *sl-drink* ***Fac-Obs*** Courvoisier (a brand of cognac) <**Fre**✍*1>

kùrvinskī {adv.} (lit. whore-like) **a.** *sl-fea* ***Der*** cowardly <**Ger**❖> **b.** *sl-fea* ***Der*** unfriendly: *ponašati se kurvinski act unfriendly* <**Ger**❖*1> **c.** *sl-fea* ***Der*** crookedly <**Ger**❖*2>

kùrvinjāk {a masc.} (lit. whore-brandy) *sl-drink* ***Fac-Obs*** Courvoisier (a brand of cognac) <**Fre**✍*1>

kùrviš {a (acc. = gen.) masc.; Voc kȕrvāru} (lit. whorer) *sl-sex* womanizer, male who frequently changes his sexual partners <**Ger**❖*1>

kȕsnica {ē fem.} *sl-sex* ***Obs*** place intended for sexual intercourse <**Ger**❖*1>

kùstos {a (acc. = gen.) masc.} (lit. curator) *sl-drink* waiter <**Lat***1>

kùstura {ē fem.} *sl* knife <**Rum***1>

kȕš [1] {excl.} *col* used to silence one's interlocutor <**Fre**>

kȕš [2] {adv.} *col* where are you going to: *A: Kuš? B: Na plažu. A: Where are you going? B: To the beach.* <**Slav**✍>

kùšīn {kušína masc.} Med *dia* cushion <**Ita**>

kȕšovati {šujēm, šujū imperf.} **a.** *col* keep one's mouth shut <**Fre**❖> **b.** *col* throw out, expel <**Fre**❖*1>

kȕštra {ē fem.} *sl-fea* evil female, bitch <**Slav***1>

kȕštrav {a, o adj.} *sl-fea* dirty (not clean) <**Slav**>

kúštro {ē masc.} *sl-fea* kind male, nice guy <**Slav***1>

kût *See the following*

- **vînskī kût** {NP} (lit. wine corner) Cro *sl-fea* mental institution, madhouse

kutàrisati se {išēm, išū biasp. intr.} *sl* get rid of

kùtija {ē fem.} (lit. box) **1a.** *sl* haircut <**Slav***1> **b.** *sl* head <**Slav***2> **2** *sl* radio <**Slav***1> **3** *sl* hotel elevator <**Slav***1> **5** *sl-crime* prison <**Slav***1>

- **kùtija šȉbīcā** {NP} (lit. matchbox) **1** *sl* skyscraper **2** *sl* name for Trešnjevka dome in Zagreb, Croatia

kùtilo *See the following*

- **Kùtilo ti jèbēm!** {S} *dia* ***Off*** used as a weak curse, Screw you!

kȕtka {ē fem.; Dat kȕtki} *sl-sex* buttocks, butt <**Slav***1>

kùtlača {ē fem.} *col* big spoon, ladle <**Gre**>

kùtnek {a masc.} *sl-fea* stupid or mentally deficient person <**Slav**✍*1>

kùtōn {kutóna masc.} *sl-sex* condom, rubber <**Fre**>

kȕvān {a, o--} (lit. cooked, boiled) **a.** **Ser** *sl-fea* persuaded, convinced: *kuvan sumnjivac persuaded sceptic* <**Slav***1> **b.** *sl-fea* cheated: *kuvan idiot cheated idiot* <**Slav***2>

kȕvanā rȉba {NP} (lit. boiled fish) *sl-fea* conceited male, stuck-up dude ☞ **riba**

kȕvānje {a neut.} (lit. cooking, boiling) **a.** **Ser** *sl* persuasion <**Slav***1> **b.** *sl* ingratiating, brownnosing: *kuvanje šefu brownnosing one's boss* <**Slav***2>

kȕvār [1] {a (acc. = gen.) masc.} (lit. cook) Ser *sl-crime* policeman, cop <**Slav***1>

kȕvār [2] {a masc.} (lit. cookbook) Ser *sl* large book <**Slav***1>

kȕvarica *See the following*

- **Bȍžjū ti kȕvaricu!** {S} (lit. *I screw* your God's cook!) *col* ***Off-Fac*** used as a moderate curse or threat, Fuck you!
- **Kȕvaricu ti jèbēm!** {S} (lit. I screw your cook) *col* ***Off*** used as a weak curse, Screw you!

kȕvati {ām, ajū imperf.} (lit. cook, boil) **a.** **Ser** *sl* flirt: *kuvati dobru ribu flirt with a hot chick* <**Slav***1> **b.i.** *sl-fea* persuade, convince <**Slav***2> **ii.** *sl* ingratiate, brownnose, kiss ass: *Ona opet kuva šefu. She's brownnosing the boss again.* <**Slav***2> **iii.** *sl* request <**Slav***2>

kȕvī {excl.} *col* the sound made by a coocoo, coo <**Slav**>

kúza {ē fem. & masc.} *sl-arch* beggar

kȕzman {a masc.} *sl* vest

kȕžan {žna, žno adj.} **/kûžan/** (lit. infected with plague) *sl-fea* ill, sick <**Slav***1>

kȕždra {ē fem.} *sl-fea* curly hair <**Slav***1>

kûždrati {ām, ajū imperf. intr.} *sl* look, watch, scope out

kùžīna {ē fem.} Med *dia* kitchen <**Ita**>

kužírati {kùžīrām, kužírajū biasp.} *sl-fea* dress formally, dress up <**Ita**❖*1>

kužírati se {kùžīrām, kužírajū imperf. intr.} *sl* dress formally, dress up <**Ita**❖*1>

kužìrēr {žiréra (acc. = gen.) masc.} *sl-crime* skillful criminal <**Ita**❖*1>

kȕžiš {excl.} *col* used to check if the import of the message has been captured: *On ih je sve prevario, kužiš? He tricked them all, got it?* <**Ita**❖*1>

kȕžiti {žīm, žē imperf.} **/kúžiti/** **a.** *col* understand, realize: *kužiti ortakov plan understand one's partner's plan* <**Ita**❖*1> **b.** *col* lift, rise

• **ne kúžiti u dȉm** {VP} (lit. be unable to understand in smoke) *sl* fail to understand, be in a fog

kv [kâ-vê] {adj.} (lit. abbreviation of kvalifikovani/kvalificirani radnik 'skilled worker') *col* the title for a manual laborer who has some additional education <**Abb**>

kvȁčica {ē fem.} (lit. small hook) **a.** *sl-sex* prostitute, hooker <**Slav***1> **b.** **Cro** *sl-sex* streetwalker who works the Esplanade hotel and Svačićev square areas in Zagreb, Croatia <**Slav***1>

kvȁka {ē fem.} (lit. door knob) **1** *sl-fea* stupidity, lack of intelligence <**Slav***1> **2** *sl-fea* nose <**Slav***1> **3** *sl-fea* trap, catch <**Slav***1>

kvàkāč {kvakáča (acc. = gen.) masc.} *col* cawing bird <**Slav**>

kvákānje {a neut.} *col* cawing (of a crow) <**Slav**>

kvákati {kvâčēm, kvâčū imperf. intr.} *col* caw (of a crow) <**Slav**>

kvàktati {ām, ajū imperf. intr.} *col* caw (of a crow) <**Slav**>

kvâr {excl.} *col* cawing (of a crow) <**Slav**>

kváran {rna, rno adj.} **a.** *sl* rotten, decayed <**Slav***1> **b.i.** *sl* worthless <**Slav***2> **ii.** *sl-fea* evil, mean, bad <**Slav***2>

kvȁrat {rta masc.} Med *dia* quarter (one fourth of something) <**Ita**>

kvârijes {a masc.} (lit. kvar 'malfunction' X karijes 'caries') *col* caries (tooth decay) <**Fre**✍>

kváriti {kvârīm, rē imperf.} (lit. destroy) *sl* sing <**Slav***1>

kvàrnjāk {kvarnjáka masc.} **1** *sl* mean and deceiving action <**Slav**❖> **2** *sl* bad tooth <**Slav**❖>

kvásac *See the following*

• **Kvásac ti jèbēm!** {S} (lit. I screw your yeast!) *col* ***Off*** used as a weak curse, Screw you!

• **Kvásac ti u kvȁšaru jèbēm!** {S} (lit. I fuck your yeast in the yeast room!) *dia* ***Off*** used as a weak curse, Screw you!

Kvȁšenō ti gȑne jèbēm! {S} (lit. I fuck your sourdough!) *dia* ***Off*** used as a moderate curse, Fuck you! ☞ grne

Kvàtrić {a masc.} Cro *sl* name for Kvaternikov square in Zagreb, Croatia <**SlavO**✍>

kvéčānje {a neut.} *col* croaking (of a frog) <**Slav**>

kvéčati {čīm, čē imperf.} *col* croak (of a frog) <**Slav**>

kvȅčav {a, o adj.} *col* croaking (of a frog) <**Slav**>

kvêk {a +ov (ext. pl) masc.; Nom Pl kvèkovi} *col* lengthy sound <**Slav**>

kvȅka {ē fem.; Dat kvȅki} *col* the sound made by a rabbit <**Slav**>

kvȅker [1] {part.} *sl* used as a strong negative response, no way, never <**Slav**>

kvȅker [2] {a masc.} *sl* hit, punch <**Slav**>

kvekètati {kvèkećēm, ećū imperf.} *col* caw (of a crow) <**Slav**>

kvekètuša {ē fem.} *col* croaking frog <**Slav**>

kvéknuti {kvêknēm, nū perf.} **a.** *col* croak (of a frog) <**Slav**> **b.** *sl* be in a difficult situation <**Slav***1> **c.** *sl-crime* get arrested, get busted <**Slav***2> **d.** *sl* die, kick the bucket <**Slav***3>

kvíčati {čīm, čē imperf.} *col* squeak <**Slav**>

kvîk {a +ov (ext. pl) masc.; Nom Pl kvìkovi} *col* squeak <**Slav**>

kvȉka {ē fem.} *col* squeak <**Slav**>

kvíknuti {nēm, nū perf.} *col* squeak <**Slav**>

kvȉt [1] {excl.} *col* used to signal lack of willingness to negotiate, period: *Neću to da radim i kvit! I'm not going to do it. Period!* <**Fre**>

kvȉt [2] {adv.} *col* even, without any debts: *Vratio sam mu posuđeni novac, pa smo sad kvit. I gave him the borrowed money back, so we are even now.* <**Fre**>

• **i kvȉt** {ConjP} *col* used to refer to the final state of affairs, period, that's it: *Ti si njega udario, on je tebe i kvit. You hit him, he hit you, and that's it.*

kvȍc {excl.} *col* the sound made by a hen, cackle <Slav>

kvȍcānje {a neut.} *col* cackling <Slav>

kvȍcati {ām, ajū imperf. intr.} **a.** *col* cackle (hens, etc.) <Slav> **b.** *col* peck (with beak, etc.) <Slav*1>

kvȍcav {a, o adj.} *col* cackling <Slav>

kvòčetina {ē fem.} **a.** *col* egg-laying hen <Slav> **b.** *sl* female <Slav*1>

kvȍčka {ē fem.; Dat kvȍčki} (lit. hen) **1** *sl-fea* elderly female <Slav*1> **2** *sl-fea* unintelligent female <Slav*1>

kvȍčkica {ē fem.} **a.** *col* hen laying eggs, layer <Slav> **b.** *sl* female <Slav*1>

kvȑc [1] {excl.} *col* the sound made by something cracking, crack <Slav> **b.**

kvȑc [2] {a +ev (ext. pl) masc.; Nom Pl kvȑcevi} *col* misunderstanding: *Imali smo kvrc ali se sada dobro razumemo. We had a misunderstanding but now we understand each other well.* <Slav*1>

kvȑcānje {a neut.} *col* the sound made by tapping, tap <Slav>

kvȑcati {ām, ajū imperf. intr.} *col* tap <Slav>

kvȑcnut {a, o adj.} *sl-fea* slightly insane, nutty <Slav*1>

kvȑcnuti {nēm, nū perf.} *col* tap <Slav>

kvŕčānje {a neut.} *col* prolonged and meaningless talk, blabber, chatter <Slav>

kvŕčati {čīm, čē imperf. intr.} **a.** *col* squeak <Slav> **b.** *sl-fea* talk persistently and meaninglessly, blabber, chatter <Slav*1>

kvrȅka {ē fem.; Dat kvrȅki} *col* cackling <Slav>

kvrékati {ām, ajū imperf. intr.} *col* scream in pain, fear, or outrage <Slav>

kvréknuti {nēm, nū perf.} *col* squeak <Slav>

kvȑga {ē fem.; Dat kvȑgi} (lit. hump, bump) **1** *sl* year <Slav*1> **2** *sl-sstu* failing grade <Slav*1> **3** *sl-sex* penis <Slav*1> **4** *sl-mil* soldier <Slav*1> **5** *sl-fea* muscular male <Slav*1>

- **stârā kvȑga** {NP} (lit. old bump) *sl-mil* old soldier

kvȑk {excl.} *col* the sound made by something cracking, crack <Slav>

kvȑka {ē fem.} **1** *col* rabbit <Slav*1> **2** *col* squeaking <Slav*1>

kvȑkoriti {rīm, rē imperf.} *col* squeak <Slav>

kvŕljēnje {a neut.} *col* squeaking <Slav>

kvȑljiti {ljīm, ljē imperf.} *col* squeak <Slav>

Ll

l {part.} [std. = li] *col* question tag: *Je l došo? Did he come?* <Slav*1>

labȁznuti {nēm, nū perf.} *dia-col* hit, punch

lȁbīlan {lna, lno adj.} (lit. labile) *sl-sex* ***Fac*** impotent <Lat*1>

làbrec {a masc.} Kajk *sl-sstu* laboratory <Lat☞*1>

lȁbrnja {ē fem.} /làbrnja/ (lit. snout) **a.** *col* mouth <Slav> **b.i.** *col* lips <Slav*1> **ii.** *col* face (human) <Slav*1>

lȁbrnje {ī fem. pl.} /làbrnje/ *col* lips <Slav>

làbruža {ē fem.} *col* mouth <Slav>

lȁbūd [1] {adj.} (lit. swan) *sl-fea* careless <Slav*1>

lȁbūd [2] {a masc.} (lit. swan) **a.** *sl* dinar (Yugoslav currency unit) <Slav*1> **b.** *sl-gamble* gambling <Slav*2>

lȁbūd [3] {a (acc. = gen.) masc.} (lit. swan) **a.** *sl-sex* ***Fac*** male homosexual, gay <Slav*1> **b.** *sl-fea* ***Der*** stupid or mentally deficient person <Slav*2>

làbus {a masc.} **a.** *sl* foot <Hun> **b.** *sl* leg (human)

lȁcī [1] {ija masc.} **a.** *sl-fea* ***Off*** Gypsy (male) <Ger☞*1> **b.** *sl-music* musician <Ger☞*2>

lȁcī [2] {adj.} *sl* hungry <Slo☞>

lȁcman {a (acc. = gen.) masc.} *sl-fea* crook, thief <Ger*1>

lȁča {adv.} *sl* ***App*** excellent, awesome <Gyp>

làčan {a, o adj.} *sl* ***App*** excellent, awesome <Gyp❖>

làčano {adv.} *sl* ***App*** excellent, awesome <Gyp❖>

lȁčo [1] {a masc.} *sl* feeling, emotion <Gyp>

lȁčo [2] {adv.} *sl* ***App*** excellent, awesome <Gyp>

lȁća [1] {adv.} /láća/ *sl* easily <Slav*1>

lȁća [2] {ē fem.} /láća/ *sl* easy job, piece of cake, snap <Slav*1>

làćan {a, o adj.} *sl* ***App*** excellent, awesome <Gyp>

làćano [1] {adv.} **1** *sl* ***App*** excellent, awesome <Gyp> **2** *sl* easily <Gyp>

làćano [2] {a masc.} *sl-drugs* pleasant feeling induced by narcotic drugs, high <Gyp>

lȁćāran {rna, rno adj.} *sl-fea* ***App*** excellent, awesome <Gyp✍>

lȁće[1] {adj.} *sl* ***App*** excellent, awesome <Gyp✍>

lȁće[2] {adv.} *sl* ***App*** excellent, awesome <Gyp✍>

lȁćī {adj.} *sl* hungry <Slo✍[*1]>

lȁćo[1] {a masc.} *sl* feeling, emotion <Gyp>

lȁćo[2] {adv.} *sl* ***App*** excellent, awesome <Gyp>

lȃd {a +ov (ext. pl) masc.; Nom Pl ládovi} [std. = hlad] *col* shade (of a tree, etc.) <Slav✍>

láda {ē fem.} *sl* shoe

ládan {dna, dno adj.} [std. = hladan] **a.** *col* cold <Slav✍> **b.** *col* emotionally balanced <Slav✍[*1]>

lȁdica {ē fem.} (lit. drawer) *sl-crime* prison <Ger[*1]>

láditi se {dīm, dē imperf. intr.} (lit. cool off) [std. = hladiti se] *sl-gamble* play cards <Slav✍[*1]>

lȃdno {adv.} (lit. cold) [std. = hladno] *col* flatly: *Ladno je odbio njegovu ponudu. He flatly rejected his offer.* <Slav✍[*1]>

lȁdolēž *See the following*

- **šlȍgīrānī lȁdolēž** {NP} (lit. apoplectic ivy) *sl-fea* phlegmatic person

ladȍvina {ē fem.} /ladovína /e fem./ [std. = hladovina] **a.** *col* shady place <Slav> **b.** *col* resting, avoiding work <Slav[*1]>

lȃđa {ē fem.} (lit. ship) *sl* shoe <Slav[*1]>

lȁf[1] {a (acc. = gen.) +ov (ext. pl) masc.; Nom Pl lȁfovi} (lit. lion) [std. = lav] **a.** *col* ***App*** kind male, nice guy <Slav[*1]> **b.i.** *col* dandy, fop: *Laf se dotjerao. The dandy is dressed in his finest.* <Slav[*2]> **ii.** *col* very important or influential person, big shot <Slav[*2]> **iii.** *col* good friend <Slav[*2]>

- **lȁf iz Krȉstovē štȁlē** {NP} (lit. the lion from Christ's stable) **Cro** *sl-fea* unintelligent person who makes bad jokes

lȁf[2] {a +ov (ext. pl) masc.; Nom Pl lȁfovi} *sl* lie <NE>

lȁfanje {a neut.} **a.** *sl* cheating, swindling <NE❖[*1]> **b.** *sl* making jokes with somebody <NE❖[*2]>

lȁfati {ām, ajū imperf.} *sl* cheat, swindle <NE❖[*1]>

lȁfčina {ē fem.} **a.** *sl-fea* ***App*** kind male, nice guy <Slav[*1]> **b.** *sl-fea* ***App*** good friend <Slav[*2]>

lȁfica {ē fem.} *col* ***App*** kind female, nice lady <NE❖>

lȁfiti {fīm, fe perf.} *sl* lie <NE>

lȁfo[1] {masc.; perm} [std. = fol] *sl* joke, trick <Ita✍>

lȁfo[2] {ad adj.; perm} [std. = fol] *sl* as if, kind of, sort of: *On lafo radi. He pretends to be working.* <Ita✍> ☞ **šatro**

lȁgano {adv.} /lagáno/ *col* easily: *lagano položiti ispit pass an exam easily* <Slav>

láger {a masc.} *sl-crafts* bearing <Ger>

lagírati {lȁgīrām, lagírajū biasp.} *sl* lie <Slav✍>

lágiti {gīm, gē imperf.} *col* lie <Slav✍>

lȁhak {hka, hko adj.} [std. = lak] BosM *col* easy, light: *lahak problem easy problem* <Slav✍>

lȁhko {adv.} [std. = lako] BosM *col* easily, lightly: *lahko naći adresu easily find an address* <Slav✍>

lȁja {ē fem.} *dia* black sheep <Slav[*1]>

lȁjāč {lajáča (acc. = gen.) masc.} (lit. the one who barks) *sl* dog (the animal) <Slav❖[*1]>

lȁjati {jēm, jū imperf. intr.} (lit. bark) *sl* take part in a hunting trip <Slav[*1]>

lȁjavica {ē fem.} (lit. barking thing) **a.** *sl* mouth <Slav❖[*1]> **b.** *sl-fea* boaster <Slav❖[*1]>

lajávko {a masc.} (lit. the one who barks) *sl-fea* ***Der*** boaster, braggart, blowhard <Slav❖[*1]>

lȁjbek {a (acc. = gen.) masc.} **a.** *sl-fea* inhabitant of the countryside, hick, bumpkin <Ger> **b.** *sl-fea* naive person <Ger[*1]> **c.** *sl-crime* policeman, cop <Ger[*2]>

Lȃjka {ē fem.; Dat Lȃjki} (lit. Laika, the first dog in Space X lajati 'to bark') *sl-crime* ***Der*** informer, stoolie, snitch <RusO[*1]>

lájko {a masc.} (lit. the one who barks) *sl* dog (the animal) <Slav❖[*1]>

lȃjn {a +ov (ext. pl) masc.; Nom Pl lájnovi} (lit. line) *sl-drugs* line (of heroin or cocaine) <Eng[*1]>

lȁjne {eta neut.} *sl* nasal mucus, snot <Ger[*1]>

lȁk {a, o adj.} *sl-drink* light (of wine) <Slav[*1]>

lȁkā kȍnjica {NP} (lit. light cavalry) **1** *sl-sex* penis **2** *sl-sex* a group of prostitutes ☞ **konjica**

lȁkā žȅna {NP} (lit. easy woman) **a.** *sl-sex* prostitute, hooker **b.** *sl-sex* easy woman ☞ **žena**

lȁkavac {vca (acc. = gen.) masc.} *sl-fea* homeless person, bum <Slav❖[*1]>

lȁkāvče {eta neut.} *sl* dog (the animal) <Slav❖[*1]>

lȁkī[1] {ōg (acc. = gen.) masc.} *sl-fea* ***Der*** insane person, nut case <Slav[*1]>

Lȁkī [2]

• **Lȁkī Lučȃno** {NP} (lit. Lucky Luciano) *sl-fea* lazy or shiftless person, bum, good for nothing

lȁkī trȅn {NP} (lit. light train) *sl* passenger train ☞ **tren**

lȁkica {ē fem.} (lit. the easy one) **a.** *sl-sex* ***Fac*** prostitute, hooker <Slav❖[*1]> **b.** *sl-sex* ***Fac*** loose woman <Slav❖[*1]>

lȁko {adj.} *sl-fea* broke (financially) <Slav[*1]>

lakòća {e fem.} (lit. easiness) *sl-fea* stupid or mentally deficient person <Slav[*1]>

lȁkodājka {ē fem.; Dat lȁkodājki} (lit. easy giver) *sl-sex* ***Obs*** loose woman, easy woman, slut <Slav❖[*1]>

laktàncije {a masc.} /làktāncije /a masc./ (lit. the one with elbows) *sl-fea* person lacking any scruples <Slav✍>

laktovȉt {a (acc. = gen.) masc.} (lit. the one with elbows) *sl-fea* person lacking any scruples <Slav✍[*1]>

Lála {ē masc.} /lála /e masc./ (lit. tulip) **a.** *sl-fea* inhabitant of Vojvodina (a region in Yugoslavia) <NE[*1]> **b.** *sl-fea* player or fan of Vojvodina (a soccer team from Novi Sad, Serbia) <NE[*2]>

lála *See the following*

• **ko bêlā lála** {PP} (lit. like a white tulip) **SerE** *col* obediently: *uraditi zadaću ko bela lala obediently do one's homework*

lȁladi {a (acc. = gen.) masc.; perm} [std. = dilajla] *sl-fea* stupid or mentally deficient person <Ita✍>

lámpa {ē fem.} /lȃmpa /e fem./ (lit. lamp) **a.** *sl* head <Ger[*1]> **b.** *sl* face (human) <Ger[*2]> **c.** *sl* mouth <Ger[*3]>

lȁmpek {a masc.} *sl* boiler <Ger❖[*1]>

lánac {nca (acc. = gen.) masc.} (lit. chain) *sl* parent <Slav[*1]>

lȁnč {a +ev (ext. pl) masc.; Nom Pl lȁnčevi} *col* lunch <Eng>

lȁndara {ē fem.} /lȁndara/ *sl-fea* ***Der-Obs*** lazy or shiftless person, bum, good for nothing <Slav❖[*1]>

• **lȁndara pišȍre** {NP} **1** *sl* useless or worthless object **2** lazy or shiftless person, bum, good for nothing

landàralo {a neut.} *sl-fea* ***Der*** lazy or shiftless person, bum, good for nothing <Slav[*1]>

• **međubùtnō landàralo** {NP} (lit. the thing that swings between one's legs) *sl-sex* ***Fac-Obs*** penis, dick, prick

landàrānje {a neut.} /lȁndrānje/ *col* spending one's time in useless activities, fooling around, messing around <Slav❖[*1]>

landarapiškórac {rca (acc. = gen.) masc.} *sl-fea* extremely talkative person, chatterbox <Slav❖[*1]>

landarapišórac {rca (acc. = gen.) masc.} *sl-fea* extremely talkative person, chatterbox <Slav❖[*1]>

landàrati {ām, ajū imperf.} *sl-fea* walk aimlessly <Slav❖[*1]>

landarpišórac {rca (acc. = gen.) masc.} *sl-fea* extremely talkative person, chatterbox <Slav❖[*1]>

lȁndēnje {a neut.} *sl* carving <Ger[*1]>

landíranje {a neut.} *sl-fea* spending one's time in useless activities, fooling around, messing around <Ger[*1]>

landírati {ām, ajū biasp.} *sl-fea* spend one's time in useless activities, fool around, mess around <Ger[*1]>

lȁndra {ē fem.} *sl-fea* ***Der*** lazy or shiftless person, bum, good for nothing <Slav❖[*1]>

lȁndrānje {a neut.} /lȁndrānje/ *sl-fea* spending one's time in useless activities, fooling around, messing around <Slav❖[*1]>

lȁndrati {ām, ajū imperf.} /lȁndrati/ *sl-fea* spend one's time in useless activities, fool around, mess around <Slav❖[*1]>

lȁndrī {ija (acc. = gen.) masc.} **a.** *sl-fea* walker (person) <Slav❖[*]✍> **b.** *sl-fea* lazy or shiftless person, bum, good for nothing

lansírānje *See the following*

• **lansíranje r̄kōnjca**{NP} (lit. launching spit) *sl* spitting

lansírati {lȁnsīrām, lansírajū perf.} (lit. launch) *sl* hit, punch <Fre>

lȁnuti {lȁnēm, nū perf.} (lit. bark) *sl-fea* divulge a secret or forbidden matter, burst out <Slav[*1]>

Lȁp {a +ov (ext. pl) masc.; Nom Pl Lȁpovi} **Cro** *col* name for Lapidarij discotheque in Zagreb, Croatia <LatO✍>

lapàrānje {a neut.} *sl-fea* prolonged and meaningless talk, blabber, chatter <Slav[*1]>

lapàrati {ām, ajū imperf.} *sl-fea* talk persistently and meaninglessly, blabber, chatter <Slav[*1]>

lápati {lȃpām, lápajū imperf.} *sl-crime* steal, swipe <Slav[*1]>

lapèndus {a (acc. = gen.) masc.} *sl-fea* senior citizen <Slav✍>

Lȁpi me za balávka! {S} (lit. Catch my beslobbered one!) *sl* ***Obs*** used to refer to the state of not being jeopardized by one's interlocutor ☞ **lapiti**

lȁpina {ē fem.} **a.** *sl* mouth <Slav[*1]> **b.** *sl* face (human) <Slav[*2]>

làpis {a masc.} /lápis, lâpis/ *sl* pencil <Lat>

làpiti {pīm, pē perf.} *col* take <Slav>

- **Làpi me za balávka!** {S} (lit. Catch my beslobbered one!) *sl* ***Obs*** used to refer to the state of not being jeopardized by one's interlocutor

làpnuti {nēm, nū perf.} **a.** *sl-crime* steal, swipe <Slav> **b.** *sl* eat, devour <Slav[*1]>

lapónac {nca (acc. = gen.) masc.} (lit. Lapp X lapiti 'fade away') *sl-fea* elderly male <SlavO[*1]>

laprdānje {a neut.} **a.** *sl-fea* prolonged and meaningless talk, blabber, chatter <Slav> **b.** *sl-fea* constant and prolonged talk <Slav[*1]>

laprdati {ām, ajū imperf.} **a.** *sl-fea* talk persistently and meaninglessly, blabber, chatter <Slav> **b.** *sl-fea* talk persistently and meaninglessly, blabber, chatter <Slav[*1]>

làpte {eta neut.} *sl* milk <Rum>

làptec {a masc.} *sl-stu* laboratory <Lat✍>

lára {ē fem.} *sl* money

lârfa {ē fem.} **a.** *sl* mask <Lat> **b.** *sl-fea* female with loud makeup <Lat[*1]>

lârma {ē fem.} **a.** *col* noise <Ger> **b.** *sl* danger <Ger[*1]>

làrmāč {larmáča (acc. = gen.) masc.} *sl-fea* person who makes noise <Ger❖>

lârva {ē fem.} (lit. larva) *sl-fea* child, kid <Slav[*1]>

lâsi {lásā masc. pl.} Cro *col* hair <Slav>

làsno {adv.} [std. = lako] *dia* easily: *lasno stići u centar easily arrive downtown* <Slav✍>

làstavica {ē fem.} (lit. swallow) **1** *sl* female <Slav[*1]> **2** *sl-fea* homeless person, bum <Slav[*1]>

lástīn rêp {NP} *sl* running away, fleeing ☞ **rep**

làstiš {a (acc. = gen.) masc.} *sl-sex* ***Fac*** male homosexual, gay <BN>

làštarnica {ē fem.} *sl-arch* candle

làtīnka {ē fem.} (lit. Latin) **1** *sl-sstu* high school with emphasis on classical philology <Lat❖[*1]> **2** *sl-sstu* Latin teacher (female) <Lat❖[*1]>

làtiti se {tīm, tē imperf. intr.} **a.** *col* begin with an action: *latiti se pisanja referata begin writing a paper* <Slav> **b.** *col* take, get hold of, pick: *latiti se poklona accept a gift* <Slav[*1]>

làtrati {ām, ajū biasp.} *sl* talk, have a conversation <Slav[*1]>

làuf {a masc.} **a.** *sl* speeding (auto, etc.) <Ger[*1]> **b.** *sl* lie <Ger[*2]> **c.** *sl* falsely incriminate, frame <Ger[*3]>

làufati {ām, ajū imperf. intr.} **a.** *col* run <Ger> **b.** *col* walk <Ger[*1]>

làul {a masc.} *sl* garlic

làura {ē fem.} (lit. Laura) *sl-sex* prostitute, hooker <LatO[*1]>

lavabô {adj.} (lit. washbasin X labavo 'loose') *sl-fea* soft <Fre[*1]>

làvānje {a neut.} *sl* sleeping

làvati {ām, ajū imperf.} *sl* wash (in general) <Ita>

làver {a (acc. = gen.) masc.} /làver/ *sl* lover (male) <Eng>

lávež {a masc.} (lit. barking) *sl-fea* reproaching, scolding <Slav[*1]>

làviška {ē fem.; Dat làviški} *sl-crime* theft, swipe

làvōr {a masc.} (lit. wash-basin) *sl* pocket (on a coat, trousers, etc.) <Fre[*1]>

lavòrati {ām, ajū imperf. intr.} **1** Med *sl-fea* work, labor <Ita[*1]> **2** *sl-crime* steal, swipe <Ita[*1]>

làzār [1] {a masc.} **a.** *sl* key <SlavO[*1]> **b.** *sl-crime* picklock (tool), slim jim <SlavO[*2]>

làzār [2] {a (acc. = gen.) masc.} **a.** *sl-fea* victim <SlavO[*1]> **b.** *sl-fea* easily cheated male, easy mark <SlavO[*2]> **c.** *sl-fea* clumsy male, klutz <SlavO[*3]> **d.** *sl-sport* incompetent player (soccer, etc.) <SlavO[*4]>

làzārka {ē fem.; Dat làzārki} **a.** *sl-arch* week <SlavO[*1]> **b.** *sl-arch* year <SlavO[*2]>

lâž *See the following*

- **dnêvnē làži** {NP} (lit. daily lies) *sl* ***Fac*** daily newspaper

ležírānje {a neut.} *sl-sports* fixing games <Slav❖>

ležírati {lažīrām, ležírajū perf.} *sl-sports* fix a game <Slav❖>

lâžnī svjèdok {NP} (lit. false witness) *sl-drink* name of a bar at Amruševa street in the neighborhood of a court in Zagreb, Croatia ☞ **svjedok**

làžnjāk {lažnjáka masc.} **a.** *sl-fea* counterfeit money <Slav❖> **b.** *sl-fea* forfeited object <Slav❖[*1]>

lèb [1] {a (acc. = gen.) +ov (ext. pl) masc.; Nom Pl lèbovi} (lit. bread) [std. = hleb] **SerE** *sl-fea* ***App*** beloved person <Slav✍[*1]>

lèb [2] {a +ov (ext. pl) masc.; Nom Pl lèbovi} [std. = hleb] SerE *col-dia* bread <Slav✍>

- **Lèb ti jèbēm!** {S} (lit. I fuck your bread!) SerE *dia* ***Obs*** used to emphasize one's point
- **Lèba ti jèbēm!** {S} (lit. I fuck your bread!) SerE *dia* ***Obs*** used to emphasize one's point

lȅbac {pca masc.} [std. = hleb] SerE *dia* bread <Slav⁘>

• **Lȅbac ti jèbēm!** {S} (lit. I fuck your little bread!) SerE *dia* ***Off*** used as a moderate curse, Fuck you!

• **Lȅbac ti jèbēm i kȍj ga ȍmēsī!** {S} (lit. I fuck your bread and the one who baked it!) SerE *dia* ***Off*** used as a moderate curse, Fuck you!

• **Lȅbac ti jèbēm žènskī!** {S} (lit. I fuck your female bread!) SerE *dia* ***Off*** used as a moderate curse to a female, Fuck you!

• **Lȅbac ti kȑvav jèbēm što ga jȅdēš!** {S} (lit. I fuck your bloody little bread that you eat!) SerE *dia* ***Off*** used as a strong curse, Fuck you!

• **Lȅbac ti se ògadiō** {S} (lit. May you dislike the bread!) SerE *dia-col* ***Off*** used as a moderate curse, Fuck you!

lèbarnīk *See the following*

• **Lèbārnik ti jèb ēm!** {S} (lit. I fuck the place where you keep your bread!) SerE *dia* ***Obs*** used as a moderate curse, Fuck it!

lèbditi {dīm, dē imperf.} (lit. levitate) *sl* walk <Slav*1>

lȅcnuti se {nēm, nū perf. intr.} *sl-fea* get frightened, get scared <Slav>

léće {i fem. pl.} (lit. lenses) *sl-fea* eyeglasses, lenses <Slav*1>

lèći {lȅgnēm, lȅgnū, lȅg, lȅg perf. irreg.} (lit. lie down) **1** *sl-crime* get arrested, get busted: *Lego je za krađu kola. He got arrested for stealing cars.* <Slav*1> **2** *sl-sports* hit a ball: *Lopta mu je pravo legla. He hit that ball really hard.* <Slav*1>

• **ne lèzi vrâže** {VP} (lit. don't lay devil) *col* used to refer to an unfavorable event, shit happens

lȇd *See the following*

• **na lèdu** {PP} (lit. on ice) *col* suspended, on ice

lèdana {ē fem.} (lit. ice factory) *sl-fea* emotionally cold person <Slav*1>

• **ledàna Sísak** {NP} (lit. Sisak ice-factory) *sl-sex* ***Fac*** frigid female

lȅden {a, o adj.} (lit. cold) *sl-fea* dead <Slav*1>

ledènjāk {ledenjáka masc.} *sl-fea* scared male <Slav*1>

lȅdo {adv.; perm} /lèdo/ [std. = dole] *sl* down there, below, underneath: *Plaža je ledo. The beach is down there.* <Slav☞>

ledolómac {mca (acc. = gen.) masc.} (lit. ice breaker) *sl-fea* big-boned male <Slav*1>

léđa *See the following*

• **preko léđā** {PP} (lit. over one's back) *col* without deserving it

lègēnda {ē fem.} (lit. legend) **a.** *sl-fea* very famous person, legend <Lat*1> **b.** *sl-fea* nice individual, kind person <Lat*2>

• **žívā lègēnda** {NP} (lit. living legend) *col* very popular person, living legend

lègēndo {excl.} (lit. legend) *sl* ***Fam*** used to address a person in direct informal communication <Lat*1>

léglo {a neut.} (lit. litter) *sl* bed <Slav*1>

lȇgoš {a masc.} [std. = legitimacija] *sl* ID (separate document which every adult citizen of the former Yugoslavia had to carry on their person) <Lat☞>

lȅha {ē masc.; Dat lȇhi} *sl-crime* police investigator

lȇj {a (acc. = gen.) +ev (ext. pl) masc.; Nom Pl léjevi} *sl-drugs* place used to smoke narcotic drugs <Eng*1>

lȇjzī-bȇjzī {fem.} *sl-sex* lesbian <Gre⁘>

Lȅks {a masc.} (lit. the Lex) **Cro** *sl* Yugoslav (at present Croatian) Lexicographic Institute in Zagreb, Croatia <Gre☞>

Lȅksić {a masc.} (lit. the small Lex) **Cro** *sl* Yugoslav (at present Croatian) Lexicographic Institute in Zagreb, Croatia <Gre☞⁘>

lèksikon *See the following*

• **žívī lèksikōn** {NP} (lit. living lexicon) *col* omniscient person, walking dictionary

lèle {excl.} SerE *col* used to express grief, woe <Slav>

lelemȕde {neut.} SSer *sl-sex* ***Obs*** sexual intercourse <Slav>

lelùjati {ām, ajū imperf.} (lit. wave, surge) *sl-fea* cruise, walk through the town <Slav>

lémānje {a neut.} *sl* beating up <Ger*1>

lémati {lȇmām, lémajū imperf.} *sl* beat up <Ger*1>

lȅmba {ē fem.} *sl-arch* bread <Slav☞>

lèmisati {išēm, išū imperf.} *sl* beat up <Ger⁘*1>

lènguz {a (acc. = gen.) masc.} (lit. lazy ass) SerE *sl-fea* ***Obs-Der*** lazy or shiftless person, bum, good for nothing <Slav⁘*1>

lènguza {ē fem. & masc.} (lit. lazy ass) SerE *sl-fea* ***Obs-Der*** lazy or shiftless person, bum, good for nothing <Slav⁘*1>

lȅnkhēbl {a masc.} *sl-auto* connecting lever <Ger>

lȅnkrād {a masc.} *sl-auto* steering wheel <Ger>

lȇnta {ē fem.} *col* ribbon (in general) <Rus>

lentírati {lèntīrām, lentírajū biasp. intr.} *sl-crime* take photos for police files <Rus⁘*1>

lêntra {ē fem.} *sl-crime* photo in the police files, mug shot <Ita*1>

lèntrāš {lentráša (acc. = gen.) masc.} **a.** *sl-crime* police photographer <Ita❖*1> **b.** *sl-crime* spy, spook <Ita❖*2>

lênjā bȕba {NP} (lit. lazy bug) SerE *sl-fea* lazy or shiftless person, bum, good for nothing ☞ **buba**

Lȅo *See the following*

- **Lȅo Lèmešić** {NP} *sl-fea* troublemaker, rowdy, ruffian

lêp *See the following*

- **lêp ko frȕlica** {AdjP} (lit. as cute as a little flute) SerE *sl-fea* very pretty, cute as a button

lêpā gláva {NP} (lit. cute head) *sl-crime* name for the prison in Lepoglava, Croatia ☞ **glava**

lèpče {eta neut.} [std. = hlepče] SerE *dia* bread <Slav✍>

- **Lèpče ti jèbēm!** {S} (lit. I screw your little bread!) SerE *dia* ***Off*** used as a weak curse, Screw you!

lepèzān {pezána (acc. = gen.) masc.} (lit. fantail pigeon) *sl-fea* inhabitant of the countryside, hick, bumpkin <Slav*1>

lepezáner {a (acc. = gen.) masc.} (lit. fantail pigeon) *sl-fea* inhabitant of the countryside, hick, bumpkin <Slav*1>

lêpī [1] {ōg (acc. = gen.) masc.} (lit. the beautiful one) **a.** *sl-fea* dandy, fop <Slav*1> **b.** *sl-fea* good friend <Slav*2>

lêpī [2] {excl.} (lit. the handsome one) SerE *col* ***Fam*** used to address a male in direct informal communication <Slav*1>

Lȅpica {ē fem.} (lit. lep 'pretty' X Lepoglava 'place name') *sl-crime* name of a prison in Lepoglava, Croatia <SlavO>

lèpinja {ē fem.} (lit. flat bread) *sl-sex* ***Fac*** flat female breast, pancake <Slav*1>

- **Lèpinju ti jèbēm!** {S} (lit. I screw your round bread!) *col* ***Off*** used as a weak curse, Screw you!

lepìnjati {ām, ajū imperf.} (lit. bake small breads) *sl* beat up <Slav*1>

lépiti {lêpīm, pē imperf.} (lit. seal, glue) SerE *sl-sports* make defensive rebounds in basketball, clear the boards <Slav*1>

- **lépiti žváku** {VP} (lit. glue chewing gum) SerE *sl-fea* talk persistently and meaninglessly, blabber, chatter

lepòtica *See the following*

- **drȕmskā lepòtica** {NP} (lit. road beauty) SerE *sl-sports* ***Fac-Der*** bad soccer player

lȅpovānje {a neut.} *sl-crafts* reconstruction

lèpričār {a (acc. = gen.) masc.} (lit. leper) **a.** *sl-fea* person to be avoided <Gre❖*1> **b.** *sl-fea* boring person, bore <Gre❖*2>

lȅptīr {a (acc. = gen.) masc.} (lit. butterfly) **a.** *sl-sex* ***Fac*** male homosexual, gay <Slav*1> **b.** *sl-fea* ***Fac*** male model <Slav*2>

leptirȉška {ē fem.; Dat leptirȉški} (lit. small butterfly) **a.** *sl-sex* ***Fac*** male homosexual, gay <Slav✍*1> **b.** *sl-fea* ***Fac*** male model <Slav✍*2>

leptirȕška {ē fem.; Dat leptirȕški} (lit. small butterfly) **a.** *sl-sex* ***Fac*** male homosexual, gay <Slav✍*1> **b.** *sl-fea* ***Fac*** male model <Slav✍*2>

lêr [1] {a +ev (ext. pl) masc.; Nom Pl lérevi} (lit. neutral gear) **1** *sl* spending one's time in useless activities, fooling around, messing around <Ger*1> **2** *sl* uncertainty <Ger*1>

- **na lêr** {PP} (lit. in neutral gear) *sl* on credit

lêr [2] {adj.} (lit. neutral gear) *sl* broke (financially) <Ger*1>

lȅš [1] {a (acc. = gen.) +ev (ext. pl) masc.; Nom Pl lèševi} (lit. corpse) **a.** *sl-fea* senior citizen <Slav*1> **b.aa.** *sl-sstu* parent <Slav*2> **bb.** *sl-sstu* father <Slav*3> **c.aa.** *sl-sex* old prostitute <Slav*2> **bb.** *sl-sex* prostitute, hooker <Slav*3> **cc.** *sl* young female, girl <Slav*3>

lȅš [2] {a +ev (ext. pl) masc.; Nom Pl lèševi} (lit. corpse) *sl* fight (e.g. fist fight) <Slav*1>

- **ko pòdgrejān lȅš** {PP} (lit. like a reheated corpse) SerE *sl-fea* ***Fac*** extremely unattractive, like death warmed over

lèšac {šca (acc. = gen.) masc.} **1** *sl-arch* ox (the animal) **2** *sl-arch* goat (the animal)

- **lèšac ckȁmnī** {NP} *sl-arch* goat (the animal)

lèšče {eta neut.} *sl-arch* lamb (the animal)

lȅšēnje {a neut.} **1** *sl* fighting <Ger*1> **2** *sl-drink* drinking <Ger*1>

lȅšica {ē fem.} *sl-arch* sheep (the animal)

- **lȅšica ckȁmnā** {NP} *sl-arch* sheep (the animal)

lèšinār [1] {a (acc. = gen.) masc.} (lit. vulture) **1** *sl* supervisor (on public transportation) <Slav*1> **2** *sl-sstu* parent <Slav*1> **3** *sl-crime* thief who steals from drunks <Slav*1> **4** *sl-fea* person without any scruples <Slav*1>

lèšinār [2] {a (acc. = gen.) masc.} (lit. vulture) *sl* parent <Slav*1>

lešinárēnje {a neut.} *sl-crime* theft from a drunk <Slav*1>

lȅšiti {šīm, šē perf.} *sl* beat up <Ger*1>

lȅšiti se {šīm, šē imperf. intr.} *sl-drink* get drunk <Ger*1>

lȅško {a masc.} *sl-sex* procurer, pimp <Slav❖[*1]>

lȅšo {adv.} Med *col* boiled <Ita>

lȅt-lámpa {ē fem.} *sl-crafts* soldering iron <Ger>

lètāč {a masc.} (lit. flier) *sl-fea* ***Der*** insane person, nut case <Slav[*1]>

lȅtak {tka (acc. = gen.) masc.} (lit. leaflet) *sl-crime* policeman on a bicycle, bike cop <Slav[*1]>

lètēćā nòga {NP} (lit. flying leg) *sl-fea* lame person ☞ **noga**

lètēćā rȉba {NP} (lit. flying fish) *sl-sex* female who frequently changes boyfriends ☞ **riba**

lȅter {a (acc. = gen.) masc.} /lèter/ *sl* letter (correspondence) <Eng>

lèteti {tīm, tē imperf.} (lit. fly) SerE *sl-drugs* experience a strong drug effect

- **lèteti nȁpolje** {VP} (lit. fly out) *sl* be fired

lȅtkoln {a masc.} *sl-crafts* soldering iron <Ger[*1]>

lȅtkon {a masc.} *sl-crafts* soldering iron <Ger>

lȅtovānje {a neut.} (lit. summer vacation) **1** SerE *sl-crime* a short stay in prison <Slav[*1]> **2** *sl-crafts* soldering <Ger>

lȅtovati {tujēm, tujū biasp.} *sl-crafts* solder <Ger>

lètrika {ē fem.} [std. = elektrika] *col-dia* electricity <Gre✍>

letùrđija {ē fem.} [std. = liturgija] *dia* church service <Gre✍>

- **Letùrđiju ti jèbēm!**{S} (lit. I fuck your church service!) *dia* ***Off*** used as a moderate curse, Fuck you!

lȅtva {ē fem.} **a.** *col* plank <Slav> **b.i.** *sl-gamble* bad playing card <Slav[*1]> **ii.** *sl-fea* slender female <Slav[*2]> **iii.** *sl-drink* extremely drunk male <Slav[*2]>

leukèmičārka {ē fem.; Dat leukèmičārki} (lit. leukemia patient) *sl-fea* female in white socks <Gre[*1]>

lêvā rúka - dèsnī džȅp {NP} (lit. left hand - right pocket) **1** SerE *col* stealing **2** steal, swipe ☞ **ruka**

lèvača {ē fem.} **a.** SerE *col* hand <Slav[*1]> **b.** SerE *col* arm <Slav[*2]>

lèvāk [1] {leváka (acc. = gen.) masc.; Voc lȇvāče} **a.** *sl* stupid or mentally deficient person <Slav[*1]> **b.** *sl* clumsy person, klutz <Slav[*2]> **c.** *sl* naive person <Slav[*3]> **d.** *sl* strange person, weirdo <Slav[*4]> **e.** *sl* boring person, bore <Slav[*5]> **f.i.** *sl* unimportant person, nobody, nothing <Slav[*6]> **ii.** *sl* suspicious person <Slav[*6]>

lèvāk [2] {adj.} *sl* worthless <Slav[*1]>

lèvāt {leváta (acc. = gen.) masc.; Voc levátu} **a.** *sl-fea* stupid or mentally deficient person <Ita[*1]> **b.** *sl-fea* honest male, honest dude **c.i.** *sl-crime* inexperienced criminal **ii.** *sl* male

lèvati {ām, ajū imperf.} *sl* take along: *levati kofer take a suitcase along* <Ita[*1]>

lèvātka {ē fem.; Dat lèvātki} *sl* female <Ita❖[*1]>

lèvātor {a (acc. = gen.) masc.} *sl-fea* suspicious male <Ita❖[*1]>

lêvča {adv.} SerE *sl* left side <Slav✍>

lêvčiti {čīm, čē imperf.} *sl-sex* ***Obs*** engage in sexual intercourse with (of a male) <Slav✍>

lêvī [1] {ā, ō adj.} (lit. left) **1a.** **SerE** *sl-fea* ***Der*** insane, nuts <Slav[*1]> **b.** **SerE** *sl-fea* ***Der*** strange, weird: *levi plan weird plan* <Slav[*2]> **c.** SerE *sl-fea* ***Der*** unintelligent, stupid, dumb: *levi učenik stupid student* <Slav[*2]> **d.** SerE *sl-fea* ***Der*** worthless <Slav[*3]> **e.** SerE *sl-fea* ***Der*** unimportant <Slav[*4]> **2** SerE *sl-fea* counterfeit, false, fake <Slav[*1]>

lêvī [2] {ōg (acc. = gen.) masc.} (lit. left) **a.** **SerE** *sl-fea* stupid or mentally deficient person <Slav[*1]> **b.** **SerE** *sl-fea* insane person, nut case <Slav[*2]> **c.i.** SerE *sl-fea* strange person, weirdo <Slav[*3]> **ii.** SerE *sl-fea* naive male <Slav[*3]> **iii.** SerE *sl-fea* boring male, bore <Slav[*3]> **iv.** SerE *sl-fea* suspicious male **v.** SerE *sl-fea* unimportant person, nobody, nothing

lêvī ìsfur {NP} (lit. left exit) SerE *sl-polit* deportation from Eastern bloc countries ☞ **isfur**

lêvisice {a fem. pl.} /lévisice/ Cro *col* Levi's (blue jeans) <Eng❖>

lêviske {ī fem. pl.} /léviske/ *col* Levi's (blue jeans) <Eng❖>

léviti se {vīm, ve imperf. intr.} SerE *sl* laugh <Slav❖[*1]>

lȅvnuti {nēm, nū perf.} *sl* take

levòvēr {vovéra masc.} [std. = revolver] *dia-col* revolver <Eng✍>

lèzbača {ē fem.} *sl-sex* ***Der*** lesbian <Gre❖>

lȅzbos {a (acc. = gen.) masc.} *sl-sex* lesbian <Gre[*1]>

lȅzi-bȅzi {ïja masc.} *sl-sex* lesbian <Gre✍>

lezilébović {a (acc. = gen.) masc.} (lit. lie down bread) Ser *col* idler, loafer <Slav❖[*1]>

libánac {nca masc.} (lit. Lebanese) *sl-drugs* hashish, hash <SlavO[*1]>

libanónac {nca masc.} (lit. Lebanese) Cro *sl-drugs* hashish, hash <**SlavO**[*1]>

lîbar {bra masc.} *dia* book <**Ita**>

lȉbrati {ām, ajū imperf.} *sl* beat up

ličánjac {njca masc.} *sl* make-up, cosmetics <**Slav**✍>

lȉčnā {ē fem. (adj. decl.)} (lit. personal) *col* ID (separate document which every adult citizen of the former Yugoslavia had to carry on their person) <**Slav**[*1]>

lȉčnā kárta {NP} (lit. ID card) **1** *sl-drugs* narcotic drug, dope **2** *sl* steady girlfriend ☞ **karta**

lȉčnī ȍpis {NP} (lit. personal description) *sl* face (human) ☞ **opis**

ličnjàče {eta neut.} **SerE** *col* ID (separate document which every adult citizen of the former Yugoslavia had to carry on their person) <**Slav**❖[*1]>

lȉčnjāk {ličnjáka masc.} **a.** *col* ID (separate document which every adult citizen of the former Yugoslavia had to carry on their person) <**Slav**❖[*1]> **b.** *col* face (human) <**Slav**❖[*1]>

lȉd {a masc.} *sl-drugs* fifty joints of marijuana <**Eng**>

líder {a (acc. = gen.) masc.} (lit. leader) **a.** *sl* boss <**Eng**> **b.i.** *sl-music* band leader <**Eng**> **ii.** *sl-music* conductor (philharmonic, etc.) <**Eng**>

lîdo {a masc.} (lit. Lido, an island off the coast of Venice, Italy) **a.** *sl-sex* brothel, whorehouse <**ItaO**[*1]> **b.** *sl-sex* clandestine place where prostitutes gather <**ItaO**[*2]>

lȉft {a +ov (ext. pl) masc.; Nom Pl lȉftovi} *sl-drugs* advancement from a weaker to a stronger narcotic drug <**Eng**[*1]>

líga *See the following*

- **pȓvā líga** {NP} (lit. first division *eg in soccer*) **a.** *sl-fea* fun **b.** best quality

lȉht {adj.} *sl-fea* broke (financially) <**Ger**[*1]>

lȉhter {a (acc. = gen.) masc.} *sl-fea* person who is broke (financially) <**Ger**❖[*1]>

lihtèrisati se {išēm, išū imperf. intr.} *sl* become broke (financially) <**Ger**❖[*1]>

lijàne {a fem. pl.} *sl-crime* handcuffs, cuffs <**Fre**[*1]>

lijêpī {excl.} *col* ***Fam*** used to address a male in direct informal communication, hey <**Slav**>

lȉjēpī Ívo {NP} (lit. handsome Ivo) *sl-sex* ***Obs-Fac*** large penis ☞ **Ivo**

lijépiti {pīm, pē imperf.} (lit. seal, glue) *sl-sports* make defensive rebounds in basketball, clear the boards <**Slav**[*1]>

- **lijépiti màrku** {VP} (lit. stick on a stamp) *sl* beat up
- **lijépiti ȍdbaštānē prózore** {VP} *sl* turn a blind eye

lȉjēs {a +ov (ext. pl) masc.; Nom Pl ljȅsovi} (lit. coffin) **1** *sl* bed <**Slav**[*1]> **2** *sl* bass (voice) <**Slav**[*2]>

lȉjēvā rúka - dèsnī džȅp {NP} (lit. left hand - right pocket) *col* stealing *col* ☞ **ruka**

lȉjēvī {ōg (acc. = gen.) masc.} (lit. the left one) *sl-fea* stupid or mentally deficient person <**Slav**[*1]>

líka {ē fem.} *sl-sex* ***Obs*** urine, piss <**Slav**[*1]>

lȉkēr {likéra masc.} (lit. liqueur) *sl-sex* vaginal excretion <**Fre**[*1]>

lìkiš {a masc.} *sl-sstu* arts (school course) <**Slav**✍>

Lìkiš {a masc.} Ser *sl-stu* the fine arts academy in Belgrade, Serbia <**Slav**✍>

lȉkōvan {vna, vno adj.} *sl-fea* unintelligent, stupid, dumb <**Slav**[*1]>

likòvnjāk {kovnjáka (acc. = gen.) masc.} *col* artist (painter, sculptor, etc.) <**Slav**❖>

likvidírati {ām, ajū perf.} (lit. liquidate) *col* kill, murder <**Lat**[*1]>

lȉl {a +ov (ext. pl) masc.; Nom Pl lȉlovi} *sl* passport <**Gyp**>

lìlā {adj.} *col* purple <**Fre**>

lílati {ām, ajū imperf.} **a.** *col* swing (back and forth) <**Slav**✍[*1]> **b.** *sl-sex* engage in sexual intercourse with (of a male)

lȉliška {ē fem.; Dat lìliški} *sl* letter (correspondence) <**Gyp**>

lìluša {ē fem.} *sl* passport <**Gyp**>

lìluška {ē fem.; Dat lìluški} *sl* dog (the animal)

lȉm {a +ov (ext. pl) masc.; Nom Pl lȉmovi} (lit. sheet metal) *sl-crime* plate, saucer (in the prison cafeteria) <**Ita**>

lȉma {logma masc.; perm} /lìma/ [std. = mali] *sl* boy, kid <**Slav**✍>

lȉma {adj.; perm} /lìma/ [std. = mali] *sl* small <**Slav**✍>

lȉmāč {a (acc. = gen.) masc.; perm} /lìmāč/ [std. = mali] Cro *sl* boy, kid <**Slav**✍❖>

lȉmačica {ē fem.; perm} Cro *sl* female <**Slav**✍❖>

lìmanovo {a neut.} *sl-arch* cheese <**FreO**[*1]>

lȉmār {a (acc. = gen.) masc.} (lit. tin-smith) *sl-crime* ***Fac*** food server in prison <**Ita**❖[*1]>

lìmburg *See the following*

• **lìmburga mȅsēca**{NP} (lit. in the month of Limbourg) *col* never

• **u lìmburgu mȅsēcu kad se šíšajū màjmuni** {PP} (lit. in the month of Limbourg when they clip monkeys) SerE *col* never

• **u lìmburgu mjȅsēcu** {PP} (lit. in the month of Limbourg) *col* never

lìmēnka {ē fem.} (lit. can) *sl-sex* ***Fac*** virgin <Ita❖[*1]>

limènjāk {menjáka masc.} (lit. the sheet metal one) *sl-auto* car, wheels <Ita❖[*1]>

lȉmka {ē fem.} [std. = limuzina] **a.** *sl-auto* limousine, limo <FreO✍> **b.** *sl-auto* car, wheels <FreO✍[*1]>

lȉmūn {a masc.} (lit. lemon) *sl-sex* ***Obs*** small firm female breast <Ita[*1]>

limunáda {ē fem.} (lit. lemonade) **a.** *sl-fea* low-quality movie or novel, lemon <Ita❖[*1]> **b.i.** *sl-fea* boring person, bore <Ita❖[*2]> **ii.** *sl* love <Ita❖[*2]>

lȉmuz {a masc.} [std. = limuzina] *sl-auto* limousine, limo <FreO✍>

lȉmuza {ē fem.} [std. = limuzina] *sl-auto* limousine, limo <FreO✍>

limuzína {ē fem.} (lit. limousine) *sl* very frequent public bus <Fre[*1]>

lȉmza {ē fem.} [std. = limuzina] *sl-auto* limousine, limo <FreO✍[*1]>

lȉna {ē fem.} *sl* streetcar <Fre✍>

lìnafo [1] {part.; perm} [std. = folina] *sl* used to express uncertainty: *Ona linafo tamo radi. She sort of works there.* <Ita✍>

lȉnafo [2] {lȉnefo fem.; perm} [std. = folina] **a.** *sl* trick, joke <Ita✍> **b.** *sl* lie <Ita✍>

lìncura {ē fem.} *sl-drink* gentian root brandy <Slav>

lìndik {a masc.} *sl-sex* ***Obs*** clitoris <Gyp>

lȉndrānje {a neut.} **a.** *sl* haircut <Ita[*1]> **b.** *sl* beating

lȉndrati {ām, ajū imperf.} **a.** *sl* give a haircut <Ita[*1]> **b.** *sl* beat up

línija {ē fem.} (lit. line) **a.** *sl* promenade <Lat[*1]> **b.** *sl* border (between countries) <Lat[*1]>

linijáner {a masc.} *sl* promenade <Lat✍[*1]>

linìjāš {nijáša (acc. = gen.) masc.; Voc lȉnijāšu} *sl-crime* street policeman, beat cop <Lat❖✍[*1]>

linolèum {a masc.} *sl-fea* hairless masculine breast <Lat[*1]>

lȉnjāk {linjáka (acc. = gen.) masc.} Med *sl-fea* lazy or shiftless person, bum, good for nothing <Slav✍>

lìnjati {ām, ajū imperf.} /línjati/ *sl* beat up

lȉnjōv {linjòva (acc. = gen.) masc.} Med *sl-fea* lazy or shiftless person, bum, good for nothing <Slav✍>

lȋp {a, o adj.} [std. = lep, lijep] Med *dia* nice <Slav✍>

lȉpa [1] {ē fem.} (lit. linden tree) *sl-fea* ignorant person <Slav[*1]>

• **ko lȉpa** {PP} (lit. like a linden-tree) **1** *sl-fea* badly dressed, tastelessly dressed **2** *sl-fea* nicely dressed, tastefully dressed

lȉpa [2] {adj.} (lit. linden tree) **a.** *sl-fea* ignorant: *lipa nastavnik ignorant teacher* <Slav[*1]> **b.** *sl-fea* clumsy, klutzy <Slav[*2]>

lìpačēnje {a neut.} *sl-sex* ***Obs*** sexual intercourse

lȉpačiti {čīm, čē imperf.} *sl-sex* ***Obs*** engage in sexual intercourse with (of a male)

lípati [1] {lȋpām, lípajū imperf.} *dia* devour, eat voraciously

lìpati [2] {ām, ajū imperf.} *sl-drink* drink (alcohol) <Slav[*1]>

lipicáner {a (acc. = gen.) masc.} (lit. a stallion from Lipice) *sl-fea* dandy, fop <Slav-GerO[*1]>

lipicánerka {ē fem.; Dat lipicánērki} (lit. a mare from Lipice) *sl-sex* ***Fac*** prostitute, hooker <Slav-GerO[*1]>

lȉpsati {ām, ajū perf. intr.} //lȉpšēm, lȉpšū perf./ **a.** *col* die, croak <Slav[*1]> **b.** *col* get tired <Slav[*2]>

lìpsina {ē fem.} *sl* lie <Slav❖[*1]>

lȉptigūz {a (acc. = gen.) masc.} *sl-fea* ***Obs*** loafer, idler <Slav❖>

lȉra {ē fem.} **a.** *sl* lie <Gre[*1]> **b.** *sl* flirting <Gre[*2]>

• **na lȉru** {PP} (lit. on a lie) *sl* by lying

lȉrafōn {a (acc. = gen.) masc.} **a.** *sl-fea* liar <Gre[*1]> **b.** *sl-fea* crook, thief <Gre[*2]>

lȉrānje {a neut.} **a.** *sl* lying <Gre[*1]> **b.** *sl* deception <Gre[*1]>

lȉrati {ām, ajū imperf.} **a.** *sl* lie <Gre[*1]> **b.** *sl* cheat, swindle <Gre[*2]> **c.** *sl-auto* speed (auto, etc.) <Gre[*3]>

lȉrika {ē fem.} **1** *sl-sex* lesbian <Gre❖> **2a.** *sl* lie **b.** *sl* cheating, swindling **c.** *sl* flirting

lirìkati {ām, ajū imperf.} **a.** *sl* cheat, swindle <Gre[*1]> **b.** *sl* speed (auto, etc.) <Gre[*2]>

lìrisati {išēm, išū imperf.} *sl* cheat, swindle <Gre>

lȉrka {ē fem.} *sl-auto* speeding <Gre[*1]>

lȉrkati {ām, ajū imperf.} *sl* lie <Gre[*1]>

lĩsa {ē masc.} *sl-fea* joker, trickster, rascal <Slav☞*1>

lísac {sca (acc. = gen.) masc.} (lit. fox) **1** *sl-fea* sly male, fox <Slav*1> **2** *sl-fea* elderly male, old fox <Slav*1>

lìsica {ē fem.} (lit. fox) *sl-fea* sly male, fox <Slav*1>

lĩska {ē masc.} *sl-fea* troublemaker, rowdy, ruffian <Slav*1>

liskàluk {a masc.} *sl-fea* the condition of being a rowdy, troublemaker <Slav*1>

liskàna {ē fem.} *sl-fea* group of rowdies, gang of troublemakers <Slav*1>

lĩsnjāk {a masc.} **1 Cro** *sl* wallet <Slav✣> **2 Cro** *sl* name for Vatroslav Lisinski concert hall in Zagreb, Croatia <Slav✣>

lĩst *See the following*

- **lĩst kalendára** {NP} (lit. calendar page) *sl-fea* nursing home tenant

lìstati *See the following*

- **lìstati knjĩgu** {VP} (lit. browse through a book) *sl* think, ponder

lístiti *See the following*

- **lístiti knjĩgu** {VP} (lit. browse through a book) *sl* think, ponder

lĩstopādan {dna, dno adj.} (lit. leaf-falling) *sl-crime* easy to catch by the police <Slav*1>

lĩt {adj.} *sl-drugs* on narcotic drugs <Eng>

lĩtar {tra masc.} *sl* many, numerous <Gre*1>

lítavica {ē fem.} /lĩtavica/ *sl-sex* ***Obs*** excrement, shit <Slav✣*1>

lìtije *See the following*

- **Lìtije ti jèbēm!** {S} (lit. I fuck your procession!) *col* ***Off*** used as a moderate curse, Fuck you!

lìtipa {lĩmpa, lẽpa imperf.; perm} [std. = paliti] **1** *sl-crime* steal, swipe <Slav☞*1> **2a.** *sl* leave, depart, walk <Slav☞*1> **b.** *sl* run away, flee <Slav☞*2>

lítonja {ē masc.} *sl-fea* ***Der-Obs*** coward, chicken <Slav✣*1>

lĩtrati {ām, ajū biasp.} **a.** *sl* lie <Gre*1> **b.** *sl* cheat, swindle <Gre*2>

litráža {ē fem.} *sl-crafts* volume, capacity (of a containter, etc.) <Gre*1>

lìvada {ē fem.} (lit. meadow) *sl-sports* soccer field <Gre.*1>

lìvadić {a masc.} *sl-fea* naive male <Slav*1>

lĩvanjskī {a, o adj.} **a.** *sl* left <SlavO*1> **b.** *sl* clumsy, klutzy <SlavO*2>

lĩvanjskī br̀vnār {NP} (lit. lumberjack from Livno: a city in Bosnia) *sl* left pocket ☞ **brvnar**

lívati {lĩvām, lívajū imperf.} *sl* lie <Slav*1>

livòvēr {livovéra masc.} [std. = revolver] *dia-col* pistol, revolver <Eng☞>

lĩvpro {lìvapro masc.; perm} [std. = proliv] *sl* diarrhea, runs, trots <Slav☞>

lĩz {a +ev (ext. pl) masc.; Nom Pl lízovi} **a.** *col* lick <Slav> **b.** *sl-sex* cunnilingus <Slav*1>

líza {ē fem.} (lit. licking) *sl-sex* ***Obs*** cunnilingus <Slav☞*1>

lízalo {a neut.} *sl-sex* ***Fac*** male homosexual, gay <Slav✣*1>

lízānje *See the following*

- **lízānje dȕpeta** {NP} (lit. ass licking) *sl-fea* ***Der*** ingratiation, brownnosing, ass kissing

lízati {lĩžēm, žū imperf.} **1** *sl-sex* ***Obs*** engage in cunnilingus <Slav*1> **2** *sl* kiss <Slav*1>

- **lízati dȕpe** {VP} (lit. lick ass) *sl-fea* ***Der*** ingratiate, brownnose, kiss ass

lĩzgati {ām, ajū imperf.} *sl-drink* drink (alcohol) <Slav✣*1>

lìzigūz {a (acc. = gen.) masc.} /lìzguz/ (lit. ass licker) *sl-fea* ***Der-Obs*** ingratiator (male), brownnoser, ass kisser <Slav✣*1>

lìzika {ē fem.} *sl-sex* ***Obs*** cunnilingus <Slav✣>

lizimȉrov {a (acc. = gen.) masc.} (lit. licker) *sl-sex* ***Fac-Obs*** male homosexual, gay <Slav✣*1>

lĩzolēd {a masc.} (lit. lick ice) *sl* ***Fac*** ice cream <Slav✣*1>

lizȕckati {ām, ajū imperf.} *col* lick a little <Slav✣>

ližisàhan {a (acc. = gen.) masc.} *sl-fea* ***Der*** ingratiator (male), brownnoser, ass kisser <Slav-NE✣*1>

LJLj

Ljȕštimīr *See the following*

- **Ljȕštimīr Ljuštimírović** {NP} *sl-sex* ***Fac-Obs*** masturbator (male)

lòća {ē fem.} *sl-fea* untidy female, slob

lȍdžati {ām, ajū imperf. intr.} *dia* wander, roam

lòfaz {a masc.} [std. = lovac] *sl-sports* knight (in chess) <Slav☞>

lȍfra {ē fem.} /lôfra /e fem./ *sl-fea* female with loud clothing and makeup <Ger✍[*1]>

logarȉtmīrān {a, o adj.} *sl-fea* unattractive, ugly <Gre[*1]>

logórko {a masc.} *sl-fea* runaway, fugitive <Ger❖[*1]>

lȍgoš {a (acc. = gen.) masc.} *sl-mil* military fugitive, a.w.o.l. <Ger❖[*1]>

lȍjtra {ē fem.} (lit. ladder) Kajk *dia* tall and slender person, beanpole <Ger[*1]>

lokácija {ē fem.} (lit. location) **a.** *sl-drink* ***Fac*** drinking (alcohol) <Lat-Slav.[*1]> **b.** *sl-drink* ***Fac*** drinking place <Lat[*2]> **c.** *sl-drink* bar (drinking place) <Lat[*3]>

lȍkadžija {ē masc.} *sl-drink* ***Der*** alcoholic, drunk <Lat-Slav.[*1]>

lȍkānje {a neut.} /lókanje/ *sl-drink* ***Der*** drinking (alcohol) <Lat-Slav[*1]>

lȍkati {ām, ajū imperf.} /lókati lȍčēm, lȍčū imperf./ *sl-drink* ***Der*** drink (alcohol) <Lat-Slav[*1]>

lȍkatīv {a masc.} (lit. locative, the grammatical case) *sl-drink* ***Fac*** drinking (alcohol) <Lat-Slav[*1]>

lȍkātor {a (acc. = gen.) masc.} (lit. locator) *sl-drink* ***Fac*** alcoholic, drunk <Lat-Slav[*1]>

lȍkerica {ē fem.} *sl-sex* ***Obs*** large vagina <Lat-Slav.❖[*1]>

lȍknuti {nēm, nū perf.} *col* sip (alcohol) <Lat-Slav.❖[*1]>

lokomotíva {ē fem.} *sl* hit, punch <Lat[*1]>

lȍkos {a (acc. = gen.) masc.} **Cro** *sl-sports* player or fan of Lokomotiva (a basketball team from Zagreb, Croatia) <Lat✍[*1]>

lȍkot {a masc.} (lit. lock) **1** *sl-sex* ***Fac-Obs*** vagina, cunt <Ita[*1]> **2a.** *sl* ***Fac*** clock, watch <Ita[*1]> **b.** *sl* ***Fac*** pocket watch <Ita[*1]>

Lȍkvār [1] {a (acc. = gen.) masc.} (lit. the one from the pond) *sl-fea* ***Fac*** American <Slav[*1]>

lȍkvār [2] {a (acc. = gen.) masc.} (lit. the one from the pond) *sl-fea* stranger (male) <Slav[*1]>

lóla {ē masc.} **a.** *sl-fea* joyful person **b.i.** *sl-fea* rascal **ii.** *sl-drink* alcoholic, drunk

lȍma {adv.; perm} /lòma/ [std. = malo] *sl* a little, just a little bit: *Pomjeri se loma. Move a little.* <Slav✍>

lomàtati {ām, ajū imperf.} (lit. break) *sl-sex* ***Obs*** engage in sexual intercourse with (of a male) <Slav[*1]>

lomàtati se {ām, ajū imperf. intr.} *sl* be in an awkward position (physically) <Slav[*1]>

lȍmikūrka {ē fem.; Dat lȍmikūrki} (lit. prick-breaker) *sl-sex* ***Fac-Obs*** prostitute, hooker <Slav❖[*1]>

lȍmiti {mīm, mē imperf.} (lit. break) *sl* cheat, swindle <Slav[*1]>

- lȍmiti kȋčmu {VP} (lit. break one's spine) *sl-fea* be obedient

lȍmiti se {mīm, mē imperf. intr.} (lit. break) *col* be undecided <Slav[*1]>

lȍmokūrka {ē fem.; Dat lȍmokūrki} (lit. prick-breaker) *sl-sex* ***Fac-Obs*** prostitute, hooker <Slav❖[*1]>

lomòtati se {ām, ajū imperf. intr.} *sl* have a hard time, experience difficulties <Slav✍[*1]>

lònac {lónca masc.} (lit. pot) **1** *sl* ***Fac*** hat <Slav[*1]> **2** *sl* ***Fac*** cap, hat <Slav[*1]> **3** *sl* ***Fac*** head <Slav[*1]> **4** *sl* ***Fac*** prison <Slav[*1]>

- èkspres lònac {NP} (lit. express pot) *col* pressure cooker

lóne {a fem. pl.} [std. = pantalone] *sl* trousers, pants <Fre✍>

lònjara {ē fem.} *sl-crime* name of a prison in Stara Gradiška, Croatia

lȍp {excl.} *col* the sound made by tapping, tap <Slav>

lòpata {ē fem.} (lit. shovel) **1a.** *sl-sex* ***Fac*** prostitute, hooker <Slav[*1]> **b.** *sl-fea* ***Der*** unattractive female <Slav[*2]> **c.** *sl-sex* ***Der*** flat-breasted female <Slav[*3]> **2** *sl-sex* cunnilingus <Slav[*1]> **3a.** *sl-fea* stupid or mentally deficient person <Slav[*1]> **b.** *sl-fea* strange person, weirdo <Slav[*2]> **4** *sl* spoon <Slav[*1]>

lopàtānje {a neut.} (lit. shovelling) *sl-fea* prolonged and meaningless talk, blabber, chatter <Slav❖[*1]>

lȍpatār {adj.} (lit. the one with a shovel) **a.** *sl-fea* poor <Slav[*1]> **b.** *sl-fea* unattractive, ugly <Slav[*2]>

lopàtati {ām, ajū imperf.} (lit. shovel) *sl-fea* talk persistently and meaninglessly, blabber, chatter <Slav❖[*1]>

lȍpina {ē fem. & masc.} *sl-crime* thief, sticky fingers <Hun❖[*1]>

lópov *See the following*

- ko lópov {PP} (lit. like a thief) *sl-fea* extremely unattractive, ugly as sin

lopòvluk {a masc.} *sl-fea* the condition of being a thief <Hun-NE❖>

lȍptati se {ām, ajū imperf. intr.} (lit. play ball) *sl* argue, quarrel <Slav[*1]>

lȍptica {ē fem.} (lit. small ball) **a.** *sl* trick, joke <Slav❖[*1]> **b.** *sl* cheating, swindling <Slav❖[*2]>

lòpuža {ē masc.} *sl-crime* thief <**Hun**✤>

lóra {ē fem.} *sl-crime* theft, swipe

lȍst *See the following*
• **lȍst in spêjs**{AdjP} (lit. lost in space) *sl-fea* disoriented, lost in space

lȍš {a, e adj.} *sl-fea* unattractive, ugly <**Slav**[*1]>

lȍt {a +ov (ext. pl) masc.; Nom Pl lòtovi} *sl* gold <**Ger**[*1]>

lȍta {ē fem.} *sl-crime* accomplice <**Ger**✤[*1]>

Lȍtār {a (acc. = gen.) masc.} (lit. Lothar, a muscular comic-book character) *sl-fea* muscular male <**EngO**[*1]>

lótre {ī fem. pl.} *dia* ladder <**Ger**>

lôv {lȍva +ov (ext. pl) masc.; Nom Pl lòvovi} **1** *sl* money <**Gyp**☞> **2** *sl-crime* theft <**Slav**[*1]>
• **dèbelī lôv** {NP} (lit. fat hunting) *sl-crime* successful theft
• **tvȓd lôv** {NP} (lit. hard bucks) *sl* cold hard cash

lóva {ē fem.} *sl* money <**Gyp**>
• **sûvā lóva** {NP} Ser *col* cold hard cash
• **tvȓdā lóva** {NP} (lit. hard bucks) *sl* cold hard cash
• **žívā lóva** {NP} (lit. live bucks) *col* cold hard cash

lóvac {vca (acc. = gen.) masc.} /lòvac/ (lit. hunter) **1** *sl-fea* liar <**Slav**[*1]> **2** *sl-crime* detective <**Slav**[*1]>
• **lóvac na hȁrke** {NP} *sl-crime* pickpocket
• **lóvac u ȍbičnōj kȓpi** {NP} (lit. hunter in regular clothing) *sl-crime* undercover policeman

lȍvān {lována (acc. = gen.) masc.; Voc lȍvāne} (lit. the money one) *sl-fea* affluent male, moneybags <**Gyp**✤>

lȍvāš {lováša (acc. = gen.) masc.; Voc lȍvāšu} (lit. the money one) *sl-fea* affluent male, moneybags <**Gyp**✤>

lȍvātor {a (acc. = gen.) masc.} (lit. the money one) *sl-fea* affluent male, moneybags <**Gyp**✤>

lovčànīk {čaníka (acc. = gen.) masc.} (lit. lova 'money' X 'novčanik' wallet) *sl* wallet <**Gyp-Slav**[*1]>

lovijána {ē fem.} **1** *sl* money <**Gyp**☞> **2** *sl-fea* affluent male, moneybags <**Gyp**☞[*1]>

lovijànđer {a masc.} *sl* considerable amount of money <**Gyp**☞>

lovijánović {a masc.} *sl* money <**Gyp**☞>

lòvina {ē fem.} *sl* considerable amount of money <**Gyp**☞>

lòvīnđer {a masc.} *sl* money <**Gyp**☞>

lòviška {ē fem.; Dat lòviški} *sl* money <**Gyp**>

lȍvīšte *See the following*
• **vȅčnō lȍvīšte** {NP} (lit. eternal hunting ground) SerE *sl* ***Fac*** death

lȍvostāj {a masc.} (lit. non-hunting season X lova 'money' X staj 'congestion, level') **1** *sl* being broke (financially) <**Gyp-Slav**[*1]> **2** *sl* financial situation <**Gyp-Slav**[*1]>

lòvudža {ē fem.} *sl* sizable amount of money, big bucks <**Gyp**☞>

lòvuta {ē fem.} *sl* sizable amount of money, big bucks <**Gyp**☞>

lóza {ē fem.} *col* grape brandy <**Slav**>

lòzica *See the following*
• **Lòzicu ti jèbēm!** {S} (lit. I fuck your little family tree!) *col* ***Off*** used as a moderate curse

Lózić *See the following*
• **Vînko Lózić** {NP} (lit. Wineman Vinegrow) *sl-drink* alcoholic, drunk

lóziti {zīm, zē imperf.} (lit. vineyard) *sl-sex* ***Obs*** engage in sexual intercourse with (of a male) <**Slav**[*1]>

lòzovača {ē fem.} *col* grape brandy <**Slav**>

lóža *See the following*
• **šȍfērskā lóža** {NP} (lit. driver's balcony) *sl-media* first five rows in a theater

lòžāč {ložáča (acc. = gen.) masc.} (lit. stoker) **1** *sl-fea* liar <**Slav**[*1]> **2** *sl-fea* naive male <**Slav**[*1]>
• **lòžāč na bòingu** {NP} (lit. stoker on a Boeing) *sl-fea* big liar

ložàna {ē fem.} (lit. setting fire) *sl-fea* naive person <**Slav**✤[*1]>

lòžātor {a (acc. = gen.) masc.} (lit. stoker) **1** *sl-fea* liar <**Slav**✤[*1]> **2** *sl-fea* naive male <**Slav**✤[*2]>

lòžēnje {a neut.} (lit. burning, heating) **1** *sl* smoking (tobacco) <**Slav**[*1]> **2a.** *sl* lying <**Slav**[*1]> **b.** *sl* cheating, swindling <**Slav**[*2]>

lòžiti {žīm, žē imperf.} (lit. burn, heat) **1** *sl* smoke (tobacco) <**Slav**[*1]> **2a.** *sl* persuade, convince: *ložiti ribu da pođe na sastanak persuade a chick to go on a date* <**Slav**[*1]> **b.** *sl* lie <**Slav**[*2]> **c.** *sl* cheat, swindle <**Slav**[*3]> **3** *sl-auto* speed (auto, etc.) <**Slav**[*1]>
• **lòžiti šíljak** {VP} (lit. burn a sting) *sl* smoke

lòžiti se {žīm, žē imperf. intr.} (lit. heat oneself) **a.** *sl* be interested in something, be keen on <**Slav**[*1]> **b.** *sl* be in love <**Slav**[*2]>

lȍžnjava {ē fem.} (lit. heating) **a.** *sl* lying <**Slav**✤[*1]> **b.** *sl* cheating, swindling <**Slav**✤[*2]>

lubènica {ē fem.} (lit. watermelon) **1** *sl* head <**Slav**> **2** *sl-sex* buttocks, butt **3** **Cro** *sl* name of a cab stand at Britanski Square in Zagreb, Croatia

lùciprda {ē fem.} *sl-fea* joker, trickster, rascal <**Slav**☞>

lùcirda {ē fem.} **a.** *sl-fea* ***Der*** insane person, nut case <**Slav**☞> **b.** *sl-fea* stupid or mentally deficient person <**Slav**☞[*1]>

lȕcprda {ō fem.} **a.** *sl-fea* strange female, weird chick <**Slav**☞> **b.** *sl-fea* foolish female <**Slav**☞[*1]>

lȕče {eta neut.} *sl-fea* attractive person <**Slav**[*1]>

lûd [1] {lúda (acc. = gen.) +ov (ext. pl) masc.; Nom Pl lȕdovi} *sl-fea* ***App*** beloved person <**Slav**[*1]>

lûd [2] {a, o adj.} *sl-fea* adorable, lovable <**Slav**[*1]>

- **ìl je lûd ìl mu nȍge smȓdē** {S} (lit. Either he is nuts or his feet stink) *col* used to express suspicion toward a third party
- **ìl si lûd ìl ti nȍge smȓdē** {S} (lit. Either you are nuts or your feet stink) *col* ***Fac*** used to express suspicion toward one's interlocutor
- **lûd ko zvȍno** {AdjP} (lit. crazy as a bell) *sl-fea* completely insane, totally nuts
- **lûd stô grádī** {AdjP} (lit. a hundred degrees crazy) *col* completely insane, totally nuts
- **lûd stô nȁ sāt** {AdjP} (lit. crazy a hundred kilometers per hour) *col* completely insane, totally nuts

lȕda {ē fem.} *sl-fea* ***Der*** insane person, nut case <**Slav**>

- **dvòrskā lȕda** {NP} (lit. court fool) *sl-sex* ***Fac-Obs*** penis, dick, prick

ludáija {ē fem. & masc.} **a.** *sl-fea* ***Der*** insane person, nut case <**Slav**☞> **b.** *sl-fea* stupid or mentally deficient person <**Slav**☞[*1]>

ludája {ē fem. & masc.} **a.** *sl-fea* ***Der*** insane person, nut case <**Slav**☞> **b.** *sl-fea* stupid or mentally deficient person <**Slav**☞[*1]>

ludájia {ē fem. & masc.} *sl-fea* ***Der*** insane person, nut case <**Slav**☞>

lùdāk {ludáka (acc. = gen.) masc.; Voc lȕdāče} (lit. ludak 'insane person' X the letter L used to mark a car driven by a student driver) **1** *sl-sex* ***Obs*** penis, dick, prick <**Slav**[*1]> **2** *sl-fea* ***Der*** person learning to drive <**Slav**[*1]> **3** *sl-drugs* high-quality hashish, bad hash <**Slav**[*1]>

- **bȁlavī lùdāk** {NP} (lit. the snotty fool) *sl-sex* ***Fac-Obs*** penis, dick, prick

ludȁkos {a (acc. = gen.) masc.} (lit. the crazy one) *sl-fea* ***Der*** insane person, nut case <**Slav**☞>

lùdāndža {ē fem. & masc.} (lit. the crazy one) *sl-fea* ***Der*** insane person, nut case <**Slav**☞>

lùdara {ē fem.} (lit. the crazy one) **1** *sl-fea* psychiatric hospital, nuthouse <**Slav**[*1]> **2** *sl* head <**Slav**[*1]>

lúditi {dīm, dē imperf.} *col* become insane, freak out <**Slav**>

lúdnica {excl.} (lit. nuthouse) *col* ***App*** excellent, awesome <**Slav**[*1]>

lúdnica {adj.} *sl* ***App*** excellent, awesome <**Slav**[*1]>

- **Lúdnicē mi!** {S} (lit. I swear by my psychiatric hospital!) *sl* ***Fac*** used to emphasize the truth of what has been said, I swear!

lûdnjāk {a (acc. = gen.) masc.} **a.** *sl-fea* ***Der*** insane person, nut case <**Slav**☞> **b.** *sl-fea* stupid or mentally deficient person <**Slav**☞[*1]>

lûdō {ōg neut.} *sl-fea* psychiatric hospital, nuthouse <**Slav**[*1]>

lȕdoje {a masc.} (lit. the crazy one) *sl-sex* ***Fac-Obs*** penis, dick, prick <**Slav**[*1]>

lȕdos {a (acc. = gen.) masc.} *sl-fea* stupid or mentally deficient person <**Slav**☞>

lùdōv {ludòva (acc. = gen.) masc.} **a.** *sl-fea* ***Der*** insane person, nut case <**Slav**☞> **b.** *sl-fea* stupid or mentally deficient person <**Slav**☞[*1]>

lùdura {ē fem.} *sl* head <**Slav**❖>

lùduša {ē fem.} *sl-fea* foolish female <**Slav**❖>

lȕdvīg {adj.} *sl-fea* ***Der*** insane, nuts <**Slav**☞>

lùđāk {luđáka (acc. = gen.) masc.} (lit. ludak 'insane person' X the letter L used to mark a car driven by a student driver) *sl-auto* ***Fac*** person learning to drive <**Slav**[*1]>

lȕftānje {a neut.} **a.** *col* airing, ventilating <**Ger**[*1]> **b.** *sl-stu* skipping classes, cutting classes <**Ger**[*2]>

lȕftati {ām, ajū imperf.} **a.** *col* air, ventilate <**Ger**[*1]> **b.** *sl-stu* skip classes, cut classes <**Ger**[*2]>

lȕftbrèmzer {a (acc. = gen.) masc.} *sl-fea* ***Der*** lazy or shiftless person, bum, good for nothing <**Ger**[*1]>

lȕfter {a (acc. = gen.) masc.} **a.** *sl-fea* ***Der*** lazy or shiftless person, bum, good for nothing <**Ger**[*1]> **b.** *sl-fea* ***Der*** loafer, idler <**Ger**[*2]> **c.** *sl-fea* ***Der*** irresponsible person <**Ger**[*3]> **d.** *sl-thie* ***Der*** thief <**Ger**[*4]>

luftèrisānje {a neut.} *sl-fea* spending one's time in useless activities, fooling around, messing around <**Ger**❖[*1]>

lȕftērka {ē fem.; Dat lȕfterki} *sl-fea* ***Der*** worthless or despicable female <**Ger**❖[*1]>

lùftigūz {a (acc. = gen.) masc.} **a.** *sl-fea* ***Der*** lazy or shiftless person, bum, good for nothing <**Ger-Slav.**[*1]> **b.** *sl-fea* ***Der*** loafer, idler <**Ger**[*]**-Slav**[*2]> **c.** *sl-fea* ***Der*** irresponsible person <**Ger**[*]**-Slav**[*2]>

lùftika {ē fem. & masc.} *sl-fea* ***Der*** irresponsible person <**Ger**⁘[*1]>

luftírānje {a neut.} **a.** *col* airing, ventilating <**Ger**[*1]> **b.** *sl-fea* spending one's time in useless activities, fooling around, messing around <**Ger**[*2]>

luftírati {lùftīrām, luftírajū imperf.} *col* air, ventilate <**Ger**[*1]>

luftírati se {lùftīrām, luftírajū imperf. intr.} *sl-fea* spend one's time in useless activities, fool around, mess around <**Ger**⁘[*1]>

lûg {a +ov (ext. pl) masc.; Nom Pl lúgovi} *sl* male, guy <**Slav**[*1]>

lûj {a (acc. = gen.) +ev (ext. pl) masc.; Nom Pl lújevi} **1** *sl-crime* lamp reseller <**Lat**> **2** *sl-sex* syphilis, the pox

lùjika {ē fem.; Dat lùjiki} **1a.** *sl-fea* daydreamer <**Slav**✍[*1]> **b.** *sl-fea* strange female, weird chick <**Slav**✍[*2]> **c.** *sl-fea* foolish female <**Slav**✍[*2]> **d.** *sl-sex* loose woman <**Slav**✍[*4]> **e.** *sl-sex* sexually aroused female, hot chick <**Slav**✍[*5]> **2** *sl-fea* teenager (female) <**Slav**[*1]>

lújiti {jīm, jē imperf.} *sl-fea* act without inhibition <**Slav**✍>

lûjka {ē fem.} **1a.** *sl-fea* stupid or mentally deficient person <**Slav**✍[*1]> **b.** *sl* insanity, craziness <**Slav**✍[*2]> **c.** *sl* stupid idea <**Slav**✍[*3]> **2a.** *sl-fea* strange female, weird chick <**Slav**✍[*1]> **b.** *sl-fea* foolish female

lújo {ē masc.} *sl-sex* syphilis, the pox <**Lat**[*1]>

lùjza {ē fem.} *sl-gamble* pair of aces

lujzijàna {ē fem.} *sl-sex* skin and venereal diseases section of a hospital <**SlavO**[*1]>

lûk [1] {a +ov (ext. pl) masc.; Nom Pl lùkovi} *col* look, glimpse <**Eng**>

lȕk [2] *See the following*

• **ni lȕk jȅō, ni lȕk mȉrisaō** {S} (lit. neither eaten nor smelled any onions) *col* used to refer to lack of one's responsibility

lúka [1] {ē fem.} (lit. harbor) *sl-crime* hiding place (for people) <**Slav**[*1]>

lúka [2] {ē masc.} *sl* priest <**Gre.**[*1]>

lȕkac {kca masc.} (lit. onions) *sl* ten dinars; a ten-dinar bill <**Slav**[*1]>

lȕkānje {a neut.} *sl-fea* peeking <**Eng**⁘[*1]>

lȕkati {ām, ajū imperf.} *sl* peep, look at others <**Eng**⁘>

lȕkavac {vca (acc. = gen.) masc.} *sl* peeker <**Eng**⁘[*1]>

lȕkec {a masc.} Cro *sl* look, glimpse <**Eng**⁘[*1]>

lȕknja {ē fem.} *sl* hospital <**Ger**[*1]>

lùla {ē fem.} (lit. pipe) **1** *sl-sex* ***Fac-Obs*** penis, dick, prick <**NE.**[*1]> **2** *sl-sex* ***Fac-Obs*** fellatio <**NE.**[*1]> **3** *sl-sex* ***Fac*** condition of being a male homosexual <**NE**[*1]>

lùlek {a masc.} Cro *sl-sex* ***Obs*** penis, dick, prick <**NE.**✍[*1]>

lȕlos {a masc.} *sl-drugs* hashish pipe, hash pipe <**NE.**✍>

lumbètalo {a neut.} *dia* large bell <**Slav**✍>

lȕmpos {a masc.} *sl* party (social gathering) <**Ger**✍>

lȕmpos {a (acc. = gen.) masc.} *sl-drink* alcoholic, drunk <**Ger**✍>

lȕmpovati {pujēm, pujū imperf. intr.} *sl* party (engage in social gathering) <**Ger**⁘[*1]>

lùmpōvka {ē fem.} *sl-drink* drinking song <**Ger**⁘>

lȕngić {a masc.} *sl* roast (meat) <**Ger**✍>

lȕnta {ē fem.} *sl-crime* gun pistol <**Ger**[*1]>

lȕp {excl.} *col* the sound made by tapping, tap <**Slav**>

lȕpa {ē fem.} **a.** *sl* noise <**Fre**[*1]> **b.** *col* crashing <**Slav**>

lúpānje {a neut.} **a.** *col* making noise <**Slav**> **b.** *sl-fea* prolonged and meaningless talk, blabber, chatter <**Slav**[*1]>

lupàrānje {a neut.} *col* making noise <**Slav**⁘>

lupàrati {ām, ajū imperf. intr.} *col* make noise <**Slav**⁘>

lúpati {lûpām, lúpajū imperf.} (lit. make noise) **1a.** *sl* smash, break into pieces <**Slav**[*1]> **b.** *sl* beat up <**Slav**[*2]> **c.** *sl* defeat <**Slav**[*3]> **2** *sl* talk persistently and meaninglessly, blabber, chatter <**Slav**[*1]>

• **lúpati ko Màksim po dȉvīziji** {VP} (lit. bang like Max on the division) *col* talk persistently and meaninglessly, blabber, chatter

lupètānje {a neut.} (lit. making noise) *sl-fea* prolonged and meaningless talk, blabber, chatter <**Slav**⁘[*1]>

lupètati {ām, ajū imperf.} (lit. bang) *sl-fea* talk persistently and meaninglessly, blabber, chatter <**Slav**⁘[*1]>

lúpež {a (acc. = gen.) masc.} **a.** *col* ***Der*** thief (male), sticky fingers <**Slav**> **b.** *col* evil male <**Slav**[*1]>

lúpežica {ē fem.} **a.** *col* ***Der*** thief (female), sticky fingers <**Slav**> **b.** *col* evil female, bitch <**Slav**>

lȕpiti {pīm, pē perf.} *sl-fea* say something unintelligent <**Slav**[*1]>

• **lȕpiti iz pòtīljka** {VP} (lit. bang from the back of one's head) *sl* say something unintelligent, say something

off the wall
- **lȕpiti kvȅker** {VP} *sl* falsely incriminate, frame
- **lȕpiti po ȕšima** {VP} (lit. hit on the ears) *sl* borrow something without returning it
- **lȕpiti žvȁlu** {VP} *sl* kiss

lȕra {ē fem.} *sl* fight (e.g. fist fight) <Fre⁘[*1]>

lȕrati {ām, ajū imperf.} *sl* beat up <Fre⁘[*1]>

lȕriti {rīm, rē perf.} *sl* beat up <Fre⁘[*1]>

lȕster {adj.} (lit. ceiling lamp) *sl-fea* tricked, cheated <Fre[*1]>

lȕsteri {stērā masc. pl.} *sl* eyeglasses <Fre[*1]>

lúša {ē fem.} **a.** *sl-drugs* hashish pipe, hash pipe <Slav> **b.** *sl-sex* ***Obs*** penis, dick, prick <Slav[*1]>

lȕtka {ē fem.; Dat lȕtki} (lit. doll) **1** *sl-fea* attractive female, doll <Slav[*1]> 2 *sl-drugs* half gram of narcotic drugs <Slav[*1]>

lȕtrija {ē fem.} (lit. lottery) **1** *col* luck <Fre[*1]> 2 *col* risk, chance <Fre[*1]>

lúza {ē fem.} *sl* fight (e.g. fist fight)

lȕzati {ām, ajū imperf.} *sl* beat up

lȕzovati {zujēm, zujū imperf.} *sl* beat up <Ger⁘[*1]>

ljàdrožiti {žīm, žē imperf.} *sl-crime* steal, swipe <Ita⁘[*1]>

ljȁkse {ljàkasē masc.; perm} /ljàkse/ [std. = seljak] *sl-fea* inhabitant of the countryside, hick, bumpkin <Slav✍>

ljȁmta {ē fem.} *sl* razor

ljȁndēnje {a neut.} *sl-arch* planing

ljànkase {ljànkesē fem.; perm} [std. = seljanka] *sl-fea* inhabitant of the countryside, farmgirl <Slav✍>

ljȅpkomān {a (acc. = gen.) masc.} (lit. glue maniac) *sl-drugs* glue sniffer <Slav⁘[*1]>

jepljívko {a masc.} (lit. the sticky one) *sl-crime* pickpocket <Slav[*1]>

ljèpōjka {ē fem.} *col* beauty <Slav>

ljȅrga {ē fem.; Dat ljȅrgi} *sl-sex* ***Obs*** vagina, cunt <Slav[*1]>

ljèšnjanin {a masc.} *sl-auto* Zastava 101 (make of car) <Slav[*1]>

ljȅtovānje {a neut.} (lit. summer vacation) *sl-crime* short stay in prison <Slav[*1]>

ljȅvpro {ljèvapro masc.; perm} /ljèvpro/ [std. = proljev] *sl-sex* diarrhea, runs, trots <Slav✍>

ljȉga[1] {ē fem.; Dat ljȉgi} /ljíga/ (lit. the sleazy stuff) Der *sl-music* country or folk music <Slav[*1]>

ljȉga[2] {ē fem. & masc.; Dat ljȉgi} /ljíga/ (lit. the sleazy one) *sl-fea* worthless or despicable person <Slav[*1]>

ljȉgati {ām, ajū imperf.} *sl* run away in fear, scram <Slav[*1]>

ljȉgav {a, o adj.} (lit. slippery) *sl-fea* sly <Slav[*1]>
- **ljȉgav ko pízda** {AdjP} (lit. as slippery as a cunt) *sl-fea* ***Obs*** extremely despicable

ljȉgavac {vca masc.} *sl-fea* ***Der*** worthless or despicable male, scum <Slav[*1]>

ljȉljani {ljȉljānā masc. pl.} (lit. fleurs-de-lis *i.e. former Bosnian coat-of-arms*) *col* Bosnian passport <Slav[*1]>

ljȉzgavica {ē fem.} *col* slush, sleet <Slav[*1]>

ljȍc {excl.} *col* the sound made by tapping, tap <Slav>

ljȍckac {excl.} *col* the sound of tapping <Slav✍>

ljȍk {excl.} *col* used to drive away or lure a calf <Slav>

ljȍke {excl.} *col* used to drive away or lure a calf <Slav>

ljȍknuti {nēm, nū perf.} *sl-sex* ***Obs*** engage in sexual intercourse with (of a male) <Slav[*1]>

ljȍljnuti {nēm, nū perf.} **a.** *col* hit, punch <Slav> **b.i.** *sl-stu* fail an exam (flunk) <Slav[*1]> **ii.** *sl-sex* engage in sexual intercourse with (of a male) <Slav[*1]>

ljóskati {ljôskām, ljóskajū imperf.} *sl-drink* drink alcohol in large quantities <Slav[*1]>

ljȍsnuti {nēm, nū perf. intr.} **a.** *col* fall down, kiss the floor <Slav[*1]> **b.** *sl-sstu* fail an exam (flunk) <Slav[*1]>

ljúba {ē fem.} **1** *sl-sex* ***Obs*** buttocks, butt <Slav[*1]> 2 *col* love <Slav[*2]>

ljúbav *See the following*
- **ljúbav na pâsoš** {NP} (lit. love through a passport) *sl* pen-pal romance

ljȕbavnī mìšīć {NP} (lit. love muscle) *sl-sex* penis ☞ mišić

ljȕbica {ē fem.} Cro *col* love <Slav[*1]>

ljubičíca {ē fem.} (lit. violet *the flower*) *sl-crime* policeman, cop <Slav[*1]>
- **cȑnā ljubičíca** {NP} (lit. black violet *the flower*) *sl-sex* vagina

ljȕbić {a masc.} *col* love story (novel) <Slav⁘>

ljȕbilica {ē fem.} (lit. kisser) *sl* kissing <Slav⁘>

ljubišpíca {ē fem.} (lit. kiss-cunt) [std. = ljubičica] *sl* violet <Slav✍>

ljúbiti *See the following*
- **ljúbiti nirvànu** {VP} (lit. kiss nirvana) *sl* spend one's

time in useless activities, fool around, mess around

• **ljúbiti u dȕpe** {VP} (lit. kiss in ass) *sl* ingratiate, brownnose, kiss ass

Ljùbljanskā mlekârna {NP} (lit. Ljubljana *Slovenia capital city* dairy plant) *sl-sex* ***Fac*** large-breasted female ☞ **mlekarna**

ljubòvati {ljùbujēm, jū imperf.} *col* engage in a love affair <Slav>

ljȕckī {adv.} (lit. humanly) **a.** *col* properly, truly: *napisati zadaću ljucki do the homework properly* <Slav*1> **b.** *col* really, indeed <Slav*2>

ljȕdina {ē fem.} (lit. big man) *col* macho (person) <Slav*1>

ljȕdskī {adv.} (lit. humanly) **a.** *col* properly, truly: *ljudski očistiti frižider clean the fridge properly* <Slav*1> **b.** *col* fair <Slav*2>

ljûlj {a +ev (ext. pl) masc.; Nom Pl ljúljevi} **a.** *col* swing (at a playground) <Slav> **b.** *col* bang (loud and abrupt sound) <Slav*1>

ljúljati {ljûljām, ljúljajū imperf.} (lit. swing) **1** *sl-sex* ***Obs*** masturbate, beat off <Slav*1> **2** *sl-sex* ***Obs*** engage in sexual intercourse with (of a male) <Slav*1>

• **ljúljati màjmuna** {VP} (lit. swing the monkey) *sl-sex* ***Fac-Obs*** masturbate, spank the monkey

• **ljúljati vráta** {VP} (lit. swing doors) *sl-fea* spend one's time in useless activities, fool around, mess around

• **ljúljati vráta - pràviti prȍmaju** {VP} (lit. swing doors and make some draft) *sl-fea* spend one's time in useless activities, fool around, mess around

ljûljka {ē fem.} (lit. swinging) *sl-crime* police van, paddy wagon <Slav*1>

ljȕljkati {ām, ajū imperf.} (lit. swing a little bit) *sl-crime* imprison, put away <Slav*1>

ljȕljnuti {nēm, nū perf.} **1a.** *sl* stick in, insert <Slav*1> **b.i.** *sl-sex* masturbate, beat off <Slav*2> **ii.** *sl-sex* engage in sexual intercourse with (of a male) <Slav*2> **2** *sl-crime* be sent to prison <Slav*1> **3** *sl-gamble* win money in gambling <Slav*1> **4** *sl-drink* drink (alcohol) <Slav*1>

ljȕska {ē fem.} (lit. shell) **1** *sl* clothing <Slav*1> **2** *sl-fea* senior citizen <Slav*1>

Ljȕštimīr *See the following*

Ljȕštimīr Ljuštimírović {NP} *sl-sex* ***Fac-Obs*** masturbator (male) ☞ **Ljuštimir**

ljȕština {ē masc.} *sl-fea* stupid or mentally deficient person <Slav*1>

ljúštiti {ljûštīm, tē imperf.} (lit. peel) **1** *sl* beat up <Slav*1> **2** *sl-gamble* gamble <Slav*1> **3** *sl-sex* masturbate, beat off <Slav*1> **4** *sl* eat, devour <Slav*1> **5** *sl* drink (alcohol) <Slav*1> **6** *sl-fea* talk persistently and meaninglessly, blabber, chatter <Slav*1>

• **ljúštiti kârte** {VP} (lit. peel off playing cards) *sl-gamble* play cards

ljúštiti se {ljûštīm, tē imperf. intr.} (lit. peel off) *sl* take one's clothing off, strip <Slav*1>

ljȕštura {ē fem.} (lit. shell) *sl* bill (utilities, etc.) <Slav*1>

ljûtā {ē fem. (adj. decl.)} *sl-drink* strong brandy <Slav*1>

ljùtara {ē fem.} *sl-drink* brandy <Slav❖>

ljûtī {ā, ō adj.} *sl-fea* strong, muscular <Slav*1>

• **sȁmo mȁlo**{AdvP} *col* used to achieve a channel-related pause, hold on, hang on, one moment, please

Mm

mȁ [1] {conj.} Med *col* but: *Iša bi ma mi ne da ćaća. I would go there but my dad won't let me.* <Ita>

mâ [2] {fem.} [std. = mama] *dia* mother, mom <Slav>

mȁ [3] {part.} *col* intensifying particle: *Ko je tamo? Ma Mića? Who's there? Oh, it's Mića?* <Slav>

• **mȁ jȁ** {ExcP} *col* used as a strong affirmative response, sure

• **mȁ jok** {ExcP} *col* used as a strong negative response, no way, never

Ma jèbi ga čȍveče! {S} (lit. Fuck it, man!) *col* ***Obs*** used to express disrespect or dissatisfaction, Fuck it! ☞ **jebati**

Ma jèbō te bôg! {S} (lit. I hope God fucks you!) *col* ***Off*** used as a moderate curse, Fuck you! ☞ **jebati**

Ma jȅdi gôvna brȅ! {S} (lit. But, eat shit, fella!) SerE *col* ***Off*** used as a strong curse, Eat shit, man! ☞ **jesti**

mà môj {VP} (lit. well, yes) *col* affirmative used in response to 'ma nemoj', oh, yes ☞ **moj**

mà nèmōj {VP} (lit. oh, no) *col* used to express disbelief, no kidding ☞ **nemoj**

Ma pȕši ga u pȉčku mȁterinu! {S} (lit. Blow me to your mother's cunt!) *col* ***Off*** used as a strong curse, Fuck you! ☞ **pušiti**

Mà pȕši mi! {S} (lit. Blow me!) *col* ***Off*** used as a strong curse, Blow me! ☞ **puštiti**

mâ-mâ {excl.} *col* used to lure a cow <Slav>

máca {ē fem.} **a.** *col* ***Fam*** cat, kitty <Slav> **b.** *sl-sex* ***Obs*** vagina, pussy <Slav[*1]> **c.** *sl* female <Slav[*2]>

macafúknuti {fûknēm, nū perf.} *sl-sex* ***Obs*** engage in sexual intercourse with (of a male) <Slav-Eng⁘>

mȁckanje {a neut.} *sl-crime* murder <Slav[*1]>

mȁcnuti {nēm, nū perf.} *sl-crime* steal, swipe <Slav[*1]>

mâco {excl.} (lit. kitty) *col* ***Fam*** used to address children, peanut <Slav[*1]>

macóla {ē fem.} /macòla/ **a.** *col* sledge hammer <Ita> **b.** *sl* rap, tap

màcura {ē fem.} *sl-sports* checkmate <NE-Slav.O✍>

máčak {excl.} (lit. tomcat) *col* ***Fam*** used to express intimacy <Slav[*1]>

máčak {čka (acc. = gen.) masc.} (lit. tomcat) *sl-fea* feminized handsome male <Slav[*1]>

mȁče [1] {eta neut.} (lit. kitten) **a.** *sl* female <Slav[*1]> **b.** *sl-fea* handsome male, hunk <Slav[*2]>

mȁče [2] {excl.} (lit. kitten) *col* ***Fam*** used to address a female in an intimate manner, kitten <Slav[*1]>

mȁčijī kȁšalj {NP} (lit. cat's cough) **a.** *col* nothing at all **b.** *col* low quality object or performance ☞ **kašalj**

mačȉzam {zma masc.} *col* machismo <Spa[*1]>

mȁčjī kȁšalj {NP} (lit. cat's cough) **a.** *col* nothing at all **b.** *col* low-quality object or performance ☞ **kašalj**

mȁčka {ē fem.; Dat mȁčki} (lit. cat) *col* female <Slav[*1]>

mȁčkār {a (acc. = gen.) masc.} **1** *sl-crime* safe cracker <Slav[*1]> **2** *sl-fea* Italian (person), Dago <Slav[*1]>

mȁčko {excl.} (lit. cat) *col* ***Fam*** used to address a female in an intimate manner, kitten <Slav[*1]>

mȁčo {a masc.} *col* macho (person) <Slav>

mȁčo-mȅn {a (acc. = gen.) masc.} /mȁčo-mên/ *sl-fea* macho (person) <Spa-Eng[*1]>

mȁčōr {mačóra (acc. = gen.) masc.} (lit. tomcat) **1a.** *sl* male, tomcat <Slav[*1]> **b.** *sl-fea* dandy, fop <Slav[*2]> **c.** *sl-fea* boaster <Slav[*3]> **d.** *sl-fea* conceited male <Slav[*4]> **2** *sl-sex* penis <Slav[*1]>

mȁčos {a (acc. = gen.) masc.} *sl* female <Slav✍[*1]>

mȁčuga {ē fem.; Dat màčugi} (lit. bat) *sl-sex* ***Fac-Obs*** large penis <Slav[*1]>

màćuka {ē fem.; Dat màćuki} *sl-sports* check-mate <NE✍>

màdam pùšikār {NP} (lit. madam cocksucker) *sl-sex* ***Obs*** male homosexual, gay ☞ **pušikar**

màdo {excl.; perm} [std. = doma] Cro *sl* used to make somebody go away <Slav✍>

màdo {a neut.; perm} [std. = doma] Cro *sl* apartment <Slav✍>

màdrac *See the following*

• **jȍgī-màdrac** {NP} (lit. Yogi mattress) **a.** *col* mattress <BN-Ger> **b.** *col* bed

màdžar {a masc.} **a.** *sl* the sun <HunO[*1]> **b.** *sl* hot weather <HunO[*2]>

madžàron {a (acc. = gen.) masc.} *sl-fea* ***Der*** Hungarian (person) <HunO⁘>

màđār {mađára masc.} **a.** *sl* the sun <HunO[*1]> **b.** *sl* hot weather <HunO[*1]>

mȁf {a (acc. = gen.) +ov (ext. pl) masc.; Nom Pl màfovi} *sl-fea* joker, trickster, rascal

mâfija {ē fem.} /máfija/ **a.** *sl-crime* gang (criminal group) <Ita[*1]> **b.** *sl* company (group of people) <Ita[*2]>

mâfijāš {a (acc. = gen.) masc.} /mafìjāš/ *col* mobster <Ita⁘[*1]>

mâfijāškī {ā, ō adj.} /mafìjāškī/ *col* mafia <Ita⁘[*1]>

mâfijāštvo {a neut.} /mafijáštvo/ *col* mafia business <Ita⁘[*1]>

mâg {a +ov (ext. pl) masc.; Nom Pl mágovi} [std. = magnetofon] *sl-music* tape recorder <Gre✍>

màgacīn {a masc.} (lit. warehouse) *sl-sex* ***Fac*** buttocks, butt <NE[*1]>

màgare {eta neut.} (lit. donkey) *sl* three thousand dinars; a three thousand-dinar bill <Slav[*1]>

màgaza {ē fem.} /magàza, e fem./ (lit. warehouse) *sl* stomach, belly, gut <NE[*1]>

màgazīn {a masc.} (lit. warehouse) **a.** *sl-sex* ***Fac*** buttocks, butt <NE[*1]> **b.** *sl-sex* ***Fac*** anus <NE[*2]>

mâgija *See the following*

• **cȑnā mâgija** {NP} (lit. black magic) *sl-crime* ***Fac*** crime

màgiš {a masc.} *sl-music* tape recorder <Gre✍>

màgla [1] {excl.} (lit. fog) *col* used to make somebody go away <Slav[*1]>

màgla [2] {ē fem.} (lit. fog) *col* running away, fleeing <Slav[*1]>

màglenā svíla {NP} (lit. foggy silk) **a.** *sl-sex* expensive prostitute **b.** *sl-sex* prostitute, hooker ☞ **svila**

màgler {a (acc. = gen.) masc.} **1** *sl-fea* troublemaker, rowdy, ruffian <Slav❖[*1]> **2** *sl-fea* crook, thief <Slav❖[*2]>

màgnēt {adj.} (lit. magnet) *sl-fea* greedy (food, money, etc.) <Gre[*1]>

magnètisān {a, o adj.} (lit. magnetic) **a.** *sl-fea* enthusiastic <Gre[*1]> **b.** *sl-fea* fallen in love <Gre[*2]>

magnètisati {išēm, išū perf.} (lit. magnet) *sl* get a girlfriend ☞ **Gre***

màhalup {a (acc. = gen.) masc.} *sl-music* conductor (philharmonic, etc.)<Slav✍>

màhana {ē fem.} BosM *col* disadvantage <Slav✍>

màher [1] {a (acc. = gen.) masc.} **/màher/** **a.** *sl-fea* ***App*** skillful person <Ger[*1]> **b.** *sl-fea* crook, thief <Ger[*2]>

màher [2] {adj.} *sl-fea* skillful <Slav[*1]>

mahèrisānje {a neut.} **a.** *sl* attempts to solve a problem <Ger❖[*1]> **b.** *sl* cheating, swindling <Ger❖[*2]>

mahèrisati {išēm, išū biasp. intr.} **a.** *sl* attempt at solving a problem <Ger❖[*1]> **b.** *sl* cheat, swindle <Ger❖[*2]>

mahmùrluk {a masc.} [std. = mamurluk] BosM *sl-drink* hangover <NE✍>

màhovina {ē fem.} (lit. moss) *sl-fea* sparse hair <Slav[*1]>

màhrama {ē fem.} [std. = marama] BosM *col* scarf <NE>

mâj [1] {excl.} **1** *col* used when passing something to somebody <Slav✍> **2** *col* really, indeed <Slav✍>

màj [2] *See the following*

- **u mȅsēcu màju kad rúže cvètajū** {PP} (lit. in the month of May when roses bloom) SerE *sl* never
- **u mȅsēcu màju kad se màjmuni šíšajū** {PP} (lit. in the month of May when they clip monkeys) **SerE** *sl* never

mája [1] {ē fem.} **1** *col* ***Fam*** mother, mom <Slav❖> **2** *col* T-shirt <Slav❖>

màja [2] {ē fem.} *col* ***Fam*** T-shirt <Slav❖> *col*

màjara {ē fem.} *sl* ***Fam*** mother, mom <Slav✍>

màjčica /mâjčica/ *See the following*

- **Màjčicu ti jèbēm!** {S} (lit. I fuck your little mother!) *col* ***Off*** used as a strong curse, Fuck you!
- **Mȉlū li ti màjčicu!** {S} (lit. *I fuck* your dear mom!) *col* ***Off*** used as a moderate curse, Fuck you!

mâjčin *See the following*

- **Mâjčina vam!** {S} (lit. *I fuck* your mother's (cunt)!) *col* ***Off*** used as a strong curse, Fuck you!

mâjčīn sîne {NP} (lit. mother's son) *col* used as an intensifier in direct informal communication, yo ☞ **sin**

màjk {a +ov (ext. pl) masc.; Nom Pl màjkovi} *sl-music* mike, microphone <Eng>

mâjka {ē fem.} (lit. mother) *sl-fea* ***App*** good and loved person <Slav[*1]>

- **čìja mâjka cr̂nū vȕnu préde** {S} (lit. whose mother combs black wool) *col* used to refer to the situation in which it is uncertain who is going to be worse off
- **kòmē mâjku** {S} (lit. to whom are you cursing mother) *col* used to interrupt one's interlocutor by pretending to ask a question
- **Krı́va je mâjka príroda i òtac karikatùrista!** {S} (lit. it is the fault of his/her mother nature and the cartoonist father) *sl-fea* extremely unattractive and unintelligent
- **mâjka bežànija** {NP} (lit. mother skipping) SerE *sl-sstu* skipping class, cutting class
- **mâjka mu stàra** {S} (lit. his old mother to him) *col* used to emphasize a portion of discourse: *Majka mu stara zašto ne položiš taj zadnji ispit. Well then, why don't you pass that last exam of yours.*
- **Mâjka si!** {S} (lit. You are a mother!) *col* used to express appreciation
- **mâjka tramvája** {NP} (lit. the mother of all streetcars) Cro *sl* the streetcar line number one in Zagreb, Croatia
- **mâjkē mi** {NP} (lit. I swear by my mother) *col* used to emphasize the truth of what has been said, I swear!
- **mâjkē mi mȉlē** {NP} (lit. I swear by my dear mother) *col* used to emphasize the truth of what has been said, I swear!
- **mâjke[PRON:DAT]** {LSF} (lit. I swear to [PPRON] mother) *col* used to intensify one's point: *Pobedio sam, majke mi! I won, really!*
- **Màjke ti ga!** {S} (lit. *I fuck* your mother!) SSer *dia* ***Off*** ued as a strong curse, Fuck you!
- **Mâjke ti ga mȉlē nàmlātīm!** {S} (lit. I beat your dear mother!) SSer *dia* ***Off*** ued as a strong curse, Fuck you!
- **Màjke ti ga nabȉjem!** {S} (lit. I stick it to your mother!) SSer *dia* ***Off*** ued as a strong curse, Fuck you!
- **Màjke ti ga nabȕtam!** {S} (lit. I stick it to your mother!) SSer *dia* ***Off*** ued as a strong curse, Fuck you!
- **Màjke ti ga nakȍkam!** {S} (lit. I stick it to your mother!) SSer *dia* ***Off*** ued as a strong curse, Fuck you!
- **Màjke ti ga nàtēgnem!** {S} (lit. I stretch it to your mother!) SSer *dia* ***Off*** ued as a strong curse, Fuck you!
- **Màjke ti ga natrȅskam!** {S} (lit. I stick it to your mother!) SSer *dia* ***Off*** ued as a strong curse, Fuck you!
- **Màjke ti ga poplȁšim!** {S} (lit. I frighten it to your mother!) SSer *dia* ***Off*** ued as a strong curse, Fuck you!
- **Màjke ti ga pȕknem!** {S} (lit. I bang it to your mother!) SSer *dia* ***Off*** ued as a strong curse, Fuck you!
- **Màjke ti ga spalamȕdim!** {S} (lit. I put it to your

mother!) SSer *dia* ***Off*** ued as a strong curse, Fuck you!

• **Màjke ti ga spàlim!** {S} (lit. I burn it to your mother!) SSer *dia* ***Off*** ued as a strong curse, Fuck you!

• **Màjke ti ga stèram!** {S} (lit. I stick it to your mother!) SSer *dia* ***Off*** used as a strong curse, Fuck you!

• **Màjke ti ga zbibèrim!** {S} (lit. I pepper it to your mother!) SSer *dia* ***Off*** used as a strong curse, Fuck you!

• **Màjke ti ga zèznem!** {S} (lit. I trick it to your mother!) SSer *dia* ***Off*** used as a strong curse, Fuck you!

• **Màjke vam lȕde!** {S} (lit. *I fuck* your crazy mother!) SSer *dia* ***Off*** used as a strong curse, Fuck you!

• **Mâjku im jèbēm da im ne jèbēm!** {S} (lit. I fuck their mother, I really do!) *col* ***Off*** used as a strong curse, Fuck them!

• **Mâjku im jèbēm da im ne jèbēm plâćeničkū** {S} (lit. I fuck their mother, I really fuck their mercenary mother!) *col* ***Off*** used as a strong curse, Fuck them!

• **Mâjku im žȉcārskū!** {S} (lit. I fuck their begging mother!) *col* used as a strong curse, Fuck them!

• **Mâjku li ti òpālīm!** {S} (lit. I bang your mother!) *col* ***Off*** used as a strong curse, Fuck you!

• **mâjku mu** {NP} (lit. *I fuck* his mother!) *col* used to express disappointment, shit

• **Mâjku mu blèsavū!** {S} (lit. *I fuck* his crazy mother!) *col* used as a strong curse, Fuck him!

• **Mâjku ti blèsavu jèbēm!** {S} (lit. *I fuck* your crazy mother!) *col* ***Off*** used as a strong curse, Fuck you!

• **Mâjku ti bȍžjū!** {S} (lit. *I fuck* your God's mother!) *col* ***Off*** used as a strong curse, Fuck you!

• **Mâjku ti jèbēm!** {S} (lit. I fuck your mother!) *col* ***Off*** used as a strong curse, Fuck you!

• **Mâjku ti jèbēm kèlavū!** {S} (lit. I fuck your bald mother!) SSer *dia* ***Off*** used as a strong curse, Fuck you!

• **Mâjku ti jèbēm kȗrvinskū!** {S} (lit. I fuck your whore-like mother!) *col* ***Off*** used as a strong curse, Fuck you!

• **Mâjku ti jèbēm od kòjū si nàprajen!** {S} (lit. I fuck your mother that you are made from!) SSer *dia* ***Off*** used as a strong curse, Fuck you!

• **Mâjku ti jèbēm što te rȍdi!** {S} (lit. I fuck your mother who gave birth to you!) *col* ***Off*** used as a strong curse, Fuck you!

• **Mâjku ti lópovsku!** {S} (lit. *I fuck* your theiving mother!) *col* ***Off*** used as a strong curse, Fuck you!

• **Mâjku ti tvòju!** {S} (lit. *I fuck* your mother!) *col* ***Off*** used as a strong curse, Fuck you!

• **Mâjku ti ȕsrānū jèbēm!** {S} (lit. *I fuck* your shitty mother!) *col* ***Off*** used as a strong curse, Fuck you!

• **Mâjku ti vlàškū jèbēm!** {S} (lit. *I fuck* your Vlach mother!) *col* ***Off*** used as a strong curse to a Serb, Fuck you!

• **Mâjku vam jèbēm[ADJ:ACC]!** {S} (lit. I fuck your [ADJ] mother!) *col* ***Off*** used as a strong curse, Fuck you!

• **Stô ti mâjke jèbēm!** {S} (lit. I fuck your hundred mothers!) SSer *dia* ***Off*** used as a strong curse, Fuck you!

• **Trî ti mâjke jèbēm!**{S} (lit. I fuck your three mothers!) *col* ***Off*** used as a strong curse, Fuck you!

• **Trȉsta ti i trî mâjke jèbēm!** {S} (lit. I fuck your three hundred and three mothers) *col* ***Off*** used as a strong curse, Fuck you!

• **Trìsta ti mâjke mile!** {S} (lit. *I fuck* your three hundred dear mothers!) SSer *dia* ***Off*** used as a strong curse, Fuck you!

• **U bȍžjū mâjku!** {S} (lit. In God's mother!) *col* used to express lack of control over events, Fuck it!

màjkati {ām, ajū imperf. intr.} *sl* die, kick the bucket <Slav❖[*1]>

màjkica {ē fem.} (lit. little mother) **1** *sl-fea* moderately strong male <Slav[*1]> **2** *sl-sex* procuress, madam <Slav[*1]>

májkoviću {excl.} *col* used to address a male in an intimate manner, buddy, pal: *Nemoj ti, majkoviću, da mi se petljaš u poso! Man, don't interfere in my work!*

màjmun [1] {a (acc. = gen.) masc.} (lit. monkey) **1a.** *sl-fea* stupid or mentally deficient person <Slav[*1]> **b.** *sl-fea* child, little monkey <Slav[*2]> **2** *sl-sex* penis <Slav[*3]>

• **drògīrānī màjmun** {NP} (lit. stoned monkey) *sl-sports* ***Der*** incompetent goalie (soccer, etc.)

• **màjmun Đóka** {S} (lit. monkey George) *sl-sex* penis, dick

màjmun [2] {a masc.} (lit. monkey) **a.** *sl* ten dinars; a ten-dinar bill <Slav[*1]> **b.** *sl* foreign currency <Slav[*2]>

majmùnēz {majmunéza masc.} (lit. majmun 'monkey, ape' X majonez 'mayonnaise') *sl* ***Fac*** mayonnaise <Slav-Fre✍[*1]>

majmùnisati {išēm, išū biasp.} (lit. behave like a monkey) **1** *sl* spend one's time in useless activities, monkey around, mess around <Slav❖[*1]> **2** *sl* try to repair <Slav❖[*1]>

majmùnisati se {išēm, išū biasp.} (lit. behave like a monkey) *sl-fea* make a fool of oneself, make a monkey of oneself <Slav❖[*1]>

màjmunovo {a neut.} (lit. monkey's) *sl* partying day <Slav❖[*1]>

• **na màjmunovo** {PP} (lit. on Monkey's day) *sl* never

màjmunjāk {a masc.} (lit. the monkey place) Cro *sl* name of a cafeteria in Zagreb, Croatia <Slav❖[*1]>

màjōr {a masc.} (lit. major) *sl-sstu* failing grade <Lat[*1]>

mâjstor {a (acc. = gen.) masc.} (lit. master) **a.** *col* repairman <Ger[*1]> **b.** *col* kind male, nice guy <Ger[*2]>

mâjstore {excl.} (lit. my master) *col* ***Fam*** used to attract attention of a male in informal communication <Ger*1>

màjumun {a (acc. = gen.) masc.} (lit. monkey) [std. = majmun] **a.** *sl-fea* stupid or mentally deficient person <Slav✍*1> **b.** *sl-sports* incompetent goalie (soccer, etc.) <Slav✍*2>

màjzl {a +ov (ext. pl) masc.} *sl-crafts* chisel (the tool) <Ger>

mȁk *See the following*

• **za mȁk** {PP} (lit. for some poppy seed) *col* in a moment, soon

mȁkac {excl.} (lit. swipe) *col* used to make somebody go away, beat it! <Slav*1>

màkar *See the following*

• **màkar[PRON:DAT] to bílo zàdnjē** {LSF} (lit. even if this is the last thing [PRON:NOM] I do) *col* used to refer to the readiness to act notwithstanding the consequences: *Otići ću na skijanje, makar mi to bilo zadnje. I will go skiing, whatever happens.*

mȁkati {ām, ajū imperf.} *sl* eat, devour <Slav*1>

makedónac {nca masc.} (lit. Macedonian) *sl-drugs* unrefined Macedonian opium <SlavO*1>

màkina {ē fem.} /mȁkina/ (lit. machine) *sl-auto* car, wheels <Lat>

màkiš {a masc.} *sl* abroad, overseas

màkiša {ē fem.} *sl-sex* procurer, pimp

mȁklja {ē fem.} *sl* fight (e.g. fist fight)

màkljānje {a neut.} *sl* fight (e.g. fist fight)

màkljāroš {a (acc. = gen.) masc.} *sl-fea* troublemaker, rowdy, ruffian

màkljati {ām, ajū imperf.} *sl* beat up

màkljati se {ām, ajū imperf. intr.} *sl* fight (e.g. fist fight)

màkljātor {a (acc. = gen.) masc.} *sl-fea* troublemaker, rowdy, ruffian

makljáža {ē fem.} *sl* fight (e.g. fist fight)

màknī {īja (acc. = gen.) masc.} *sl-fea* unattractive person

màknuti {nēm, nū perf.} (lit. move) *sl-crime* steal, swipe <Slav*1>

mȁkō {oa masc.} *sl-fea* sly boy

mȁkoš {a masc.} *sl-sex* procurer, pimp

mȁks {adj.} (lit. max) *sl* the best <Lat*1>

mȁksī {adj.} /màksi/ (lit. maxi) *sl* the best <Lat*1>

Mȁksim *See the following*

• **Mȁksim Pízdić iz Rȕmē** {NP} (lit. Max McCunt from Ruma *a city in Serbia*) *sl-fea* ***Fac-Obs*** jokster

mȁksimālan {lna, lno adj.} **a.** *sl* ***App*** excellent, awesome <Lat*1> **b.** *sl* the best <Lat*2>

maksimȉlijān {adj.} /maksimilȉjān/ *sl* the best <Lat✍>

mȁksūz {part.} Bos *col* specially, intentionally: *Maksuz mi je sakrio torbu. He hid my bag intentionally.* <NE>

maksuzíja {ē fem.} BosM *col* special treat <NE❖>

mâl {a +ov (ext. pl) masc.; Nom. Pl. málovi} **a.** *dia-col* cattle <NE> **b.** *dia-col* property <NE*1>

mâlā [1] {excl.} (lit. the little one) *col* ***Fam*** used to address a female in direct informal communication <Slav*1>

mâlā [2] {ē fem. (adj. decl.)} (lit. the little one) **a.** *sl* female <Slav*1> **b.** *sl* male homosexual, gay <Slav*2>

Mâlā Floramî {NP} (lit. Little Florami, a ballet character) *sl-sex* male homosexual, gay ☞ **Florami**

mâlā góspa {NP} (lit. little Virgin Mary) **1** *sl-sex* ***Fac*** virgin **2** **Cro** *sl-fea* female from Zagorje, Croatia ☞ **gospa**

málac {lca (acc. = gen.) masc.} (lit. the small one) *col* boy, kid <Slav❖*1>

malája {ē masc.} *sl-fea* ***Der*** insane person, nut case <SlavO*1>

malalájac {jca (acc. = gen.) masc.} *sl* boy, kid <SlavO*1>

Mȁlbāč {a masc.} *sl* Marlboro (cigarette brand) <BN✍>

málčice {adv.} *col* just a little bit <Slav❖>

màlehan {hna, hno adj.} [std. = malen] *col* rather small <Slav✍>

mȁler [1] {a (acc. = gen.) masc.} *sl-fea* liar <Ger*1>

mȁler [2] {a masc.} /màlēr/ *col* misfortune, bad luck: *To što nismo dobili karte za kino je čisti maler. It's just bad luck that we did not get the movie tickets.* <Fre*1>

màlešan {šna, šno adj.} [std. = malen] *col* rather small <Slav✍>

mâlī {ōg (acc. = gen.) masc.} (lit. the little one) **a.** *col* boy, kid <Slav*1> **b.** *sl-sex* penis <Slav*2>

mâlī bóro {NP} (lit. little Boro) *sl* Marlboro (cigarette brand) ☞ **boro**

mâlī hȉps {NP} *sl-drugs* small quantity of hashish ☞ **hips**

mâlī hȍg {NP} *sl* boss ☞ **hog**

mâlī milȉōn {NP} (lit. little million) *col* multitude ☞ **milion**

mâli štàjg {NP} *sl* bus station ☞ **štajg**

malicána {ē fem.} **1a.** *sl-gamble* inexperienced gambler **b.** *sl-fea* naive male **c.** *sl-fea* rich naive male **2** *sl-crime* successful robbery

malìgānka {ē fem.} *sl-drink* barkeeper's daughter <**Fre**[*1]>

màlina {ē fem.} (lit. raspberry) *sl-fea* attractive female, tomato <**Slav**[*1]>

màliša {ē masc.} (lit. the small one) **a.** *col* boy, kid <**Slav⁘**[*1]> **b.** *col* short person <**Slav⁘**[*1]>

màlkalo {a neut.} *col* cat <**Slav**>

málkice {adv.} *col* just a little bit <**Slav**>

málko {adv.} *col* just a little bit <**Slav⁘**>

Málko me jèbāvāš! {S} (lit. You are fucking me over a little!) *col* ***Obs*** used to express disbelief, Are you fucking me! ☞ **jebavati**

màlo [1] {adj.} *sl* poor <**Slav**[*1]>

màlo [2] {a neut.} **1a.** *sl* pork <**Slav**[*1]> **b.i.** *sl* sausage <**Slav**[*2]> **ii.** *sl* smoked meat <**Slav**[*2]> **2** *sl-sex* penis <**Slav**[*1]> **3** *sl* money <**Slav**[*1]>

màlo [3] {adv.} (lit. little) *col* nothing special, no big deal: *A: Kako je? B: Evo, malo. A: What's up? B: Nothing special.* <**Slav**[*1]>

- **màlo ovàkō** {AdvP} *col* touchy or difficult: *Te stvari su malo ovako. Those are touchy matters.*

màlo mòrgen {AdvP} *col* never ☞ **morgen**

mâlō prâse {NP} (lit. little piglet) *sl-sex* ***Fac-Obs*** penis, dick, prick ☞ **prase**

màlo sȕtra {AdvP} *col* used as a strong negative response, no way, never ☞ **sutra**

màltati {ām, ajū imperf. intr.} *sl* cheat, swindle

maltrètmān {retmána masc.} *sl* torturing <**Fre**>

mâlj {a (acc. = gen.) +ev (ext. pl) masc.; Nom Pl máljevi} (lit. sledge hammer) *sl-fea* stupid or mentally deficient person <**Slav**[*1]>

maljáža {ē fem.} *sl* painting (as work of art) <**Slav**[*1]>

màma {ē fem.} (lit. mom) *sl* stomach, belly, gut <**Slav**[*1]>

- **Màmu li ti jèbēm!** {S} (lit. I screw your mother!) *col* ***Off*** used as a moderate curse, Screw you!
- **Màmu mu jèbēm!** {S} (lit. I fuck his mother!) *col* ***Off*** used as a strong curse, Fuck him!
- **Màmu ti jèbēm!** {S} (lit. I screw your mother!) *col* ***Off*** used as a moderate curse, Screw you!
- **Màmu ti jèbēm jâ!** {S} (lit. I screw your mother!) *col* ***Off*** used as a moderate curse, Screw you!
- **Màmu ti jèbēm jâ màlo!** {S} (lit. I screw your mother a little!) *col* ***Off*** used as a moderate curse, Screw you!
- **Màmu ti jèbēm ònū [ADJ:ACC]!** {S} (lit. I screw your [ADJ] mother!) *col* ***Off*** used as a moderate curse, Screw you!

màmče {eta neut.} *dia* ***Fam*** mother, mom <**Slav**☞>

- **Màmče ti jèbēm!** {S} (lit. I screw your little mother!) *dia* ***Off*** used as a weak curse, Screw you!
- **Mȉlō ti màmče jèbēm!** {S} (lit. I fuck your dear mom!) SerE *dia* ***Off*** used as a strong curse, Fuck you!

Màmē tvòjē trȕlē sȉse na tàvanu vȉsē! {S} (lit. Your mother's rotten tits are hanging in the attic!) *col* ***Off*** used as a strong curse, Fuck you! ☞ **sisa**

màmek {a (acc. = gen.) masc.; Voc màmek} (lit. little mom) **a.** Kajk *sl-sex* ***Fac*** prostitute, hooker <**Slav⁘**[*1]> **b.** Kajk *sl-sex* ***Fac*** female owner or manager of a brothel, madam <**Slav⁘**[*2]>

màmica {ē fem.} (lit. little mom) **a.** *sl-sex* ***Fac*** prostitute, hooker <**Slav**[*1]> **b.** *sl-sex* ***Fac*** female owner or manager of a brothel, madam <**Slav**[*2]>

- **Màmicu [PRON:DAT] jèbēm!** {LSF} (lit. I screw [PPRON] little mother!) *col* ***Off*** used as a weak curse toward a third party person: *Mamicu joj jebem! Screw her!*
- **Màmicu ti tvòju!** {S} (lit. I fuck your little mother!) *col* ***Off*** used as a strong curse, Fuck you!
- **Mȉlosnū ti màmicu jèbēm!** {S} (lit. I fuck your dear mom!) *col* ***Off*** used as a strong curse, Fuck you!

màmlaz {a (acc. = gen.) masc.} *sl-fea* stupid or mentally deficient person <**Hun**>

mamojébac {pca (acc. = gen.) masc.} (lit. motherfucker) *col* ***Der*** worthless or despicable person <**Heb**[*1]>

Màmu li ti jèbēm! {S} (lit. I screw your mother!) *col* ***Off*** used as a moderate curse, Screw you! ☞ **mama**

Màmu mu jèbēm! {S} (lit. I fuck his mother!) *col* ***Off*** used as a strong curse, Fuck him! ☞ **mama**

Màmu ti jèbēm! {S} (lit. I screw your mother!) *col* ***Off*** used as a moderate curse, Screw you! ☞ **mama**

Màmu ti jèbēm jâ! {S} (lit. I screw your mother!) *col* ***Off*** used as a moderate curse, Screw you! ☞ **mama**

Màmu ti jèbēm jâ màlo! {S} (lit. I screw your mother a little!) *col* ***Off*** used as a moderate curse, Screw you! ☞ **mama**

Màmu ti jèbēm ònū [ADJ:ACC]! {S} (lit. I screw your [ADJ] mother!) *col* ***Off*** used as a moderate curse, Screw you! ☞ **mama**

mȁmūran {rna, rno adj.} *sl-drink* having a hangover <NE>

mamùrluk {a masc.} **a.** *sl-drink* hangover <NE> **b.** *sl* ***Fac*** wedding <NE[*1]>

màmut {a (acc. = gen.) masc.} (lit. mammoth) *sl-fea* affluent elderly female <Rus[*1]>

• **màmut râjskī** {NP} (lit. heavenly mammoth) *sl-fea* mentally deficient person

mamùzati {ām, ajū imperf.} (lit. spur) *sl* abuse financially, rip off <NE[*1]>

mána {ē fem.} *col* malfunction <NE>

mánac {nca (acc. = gen.) masc.} *sl* boss <NE⁘[*1]>

mȁnastīrka {ē fem.; Dat mȁnastīrki} *sl-drink* type of brandy supposedly made in a monastery <Gre⁘[*1]>

mânča {ē masc.} **a.** *sl* gentleman <Gyp> **b.** *sl* boss <Gyp[*1]>

mȁnče {eta neut.} **a.** *sl* gentleman <Gyp> **b.** *sl* boss <Gyp[*1]>

màn̈četovica {ē fem.} **a.** *sl* lady, woman <Gyp⁘> **b.** *sl* boss's wife <Gyp⁘[*1]>

mánda {ē fem.} **a.** *sl-sex* ***Obs*** vagina, cunt <Gyp> **b.i.** *sl* ***Obs*** leg (human) <Gyp[*1]> **ii.** *sl-fea* ***Obs*** naive senior citizen <Gyp[*1]> **iii.** *sl-fea* senior citizen <Gyp[*1]>

màndār {mandára (acc. = gen.) masc.; Voc mȁndāru} *sl* boy, kid

màndara {ē fem.} *sl* leg (human)

màndāš {mandáša (acc. = gen.) masc.; Voc mȁndāšu} *sl-fea* poor male

mandóra {ē fem.} *sl-sex* prostitute, hooker <Gre[*1]>

màndōv {mandòva (acc. = gen.) masc.; Voc màndove} **a.** *sl-fea* ***Off*** Gypsy (male) **b.i.** *sl-fea* troublemaker, rowdy, ruffian **ii.** *sl-fea* unattractive male **iii.** *sl-fea* stupid or mentally deficient person,

màndōvka {ē fem.} *sl-sex* prostitute, hooker

màndrak {a masc.} *sl-crime* billy club <Gre[*1]>

màndril {a (acc. = gen.) masc.} *sl-fea* person with a face which resembles a monkey

mandŕknuti {màndr̄knēm, nū perf. intr.} *sl* ***Der*** die, kick the bucket <Gre⁘[*1]>

mandŕknuti {màndr̄knēm, nū perf.} *sl* ***Der*** steal, swipe <Gre⁘[*1]>

mándža {ē fem.} *sl* food <Ita☝[*1]>

màndžati {ām, ajū imperf.} *sl* eat, devour <Ita>

màndžovina {ē fem.} *sl* dinner <Ita⁘[*1]>

manđètna {ē fem.} [std. = manžetna] *sl* wedding ring <Fre☝>

mànevārskī mȅtak {NP} (lit. blank cartridge) *sl-sstu* school chalk ☞ **metak**

mȁnga {ē masc.; Dat mȁngi} *sl-fea* joker, trickster, rascal <Gyp☝>

mȁngāš {a (acc. = gen.) masc.} *sl-fea* troublemaker, rowdy, ruffian <Gyp☝>

màngisati {išēm, išū imperf.} *sl* beg, ask for money <Gyp[*1]>

màngōv {mangòva (acc. = gen.) masc.; Voc màngove} *sl-fea* troublemaker, rowdy, ruffian <Gyp☝>

màngup {a (acc. = gen.) masc.} *sl-fea* joker, trickster, rascal <Gyp>

mȁnī {īja masc.} /màni/ *sl* money <Eng>

• **mȁnī gòtovac** {NP} (lit. money in cash X proper name and surname) *sl* cash

Máni ga Mîto! {S} (lit. Leave it alone Mita!) SerE *col* used to express disbelief ☞ **manuti**

mȁnijāk {a (acc. = gen.) masc.} *col* maniac <Gre⁘>

mànit {a, o adj.} *col* ***Der*** insane, nuts <Heb⁘[*1]>

mànita {ē fem.} (lit. the crazy one) *sl-drugs* lactose mixed into heroin to deceive one's clients <Heb⁘[*1]>

manìtati {ām, ajū imperf. intr.} *sl-fea* go insane, freak out <Heb⁘[*1]>

manìtulja {ē fem.} *sl-fea* ***Der*** insane female, nut case <Heb⁘[*1]>

manìtuša {ē fem.} *sl-fea* ***Der*** insane female, nut case <Heb⁘[*1]>

mȁnkī {īja (acc. = gen.) masc.} *sl-fea* unattractive male <Eng[*1]>

mȁnos {a (acc. = gen.) masc.} *sl-fea* manual laborer <Lat☝[*1]>

mànot {a (acc. = gen.) masc.} *sl-arch* engineer

mánte {excl.} [std. = manite] **Vojv** *col* used to avoid discussion on a particular subject, leave that alone, don't ask me <Slav☝>

mánti {mânēm, mânū perf.} [std. = manuti] Vojv *sl* leave alone, cease boring <Slav☝>

mantìjāš {tijáša (acc. = gen.) masc.; Voc mântijāšu} *col* priest <Gre❖[*1]>

màntl {a +ov (ext. pl) masc.} (lit. trenchcoat) **1** *sl-sex* ***Fac*** condom, rubber <Ger[*1]> **2** *sl-sex* ***Fac*** foreskin <Ger[*2]>

manùčati se {ām, ajū imperf. intr.} *sl* get married, get hitched <**Gyp**>

mànuče {eta neut.} *sl-arch* child, kid <**Gyp**>

manuélac {lca (acc. = gen.) masc.} *sl-fea* manual laborer <**Lat**❖>

mànuk {a (acc. = gen.) masc.} *sl-arch* male, guy <**Gyp**>

mànuka {ē fem.} **1** *sl-arch* wife <**Gyp**> **2** *sl-arch* sister, sis <**Gyp**>

mànukot {a (acc. = gen.) masc.} **a.** *sl-arch* gentleman <**Gyp**> **b.** *sl-arch* boss <**Gyp**[*1]>

mánuti {mânēm, mânū perf.} *col* forget about <**Slav**[*1]>
• **mánuti se ćȍrava pòsla** {VP} (lit. give up the blind business) *col* give up, abandon
• **Máni ga Mîto!** {S} (lit. Leave it alone Mita!) SerE *col* used to express disbelief, Don't give me that shit!

mȁnja {ē fem.} *dia* mother, mom <**Slav**✍>

mànještra {ē fem.} (lit. soup) *dia* container <**Ita**[*1]>

mȁnjkati {ām, ajū biasp. intr.} (lit. miss) *sl* ***Fac*** die, kick the bucket <**Ita**[*1]>

manžèta {ē fem.} *sl* finger ring <**Fre**[*1]>

manžètna {ē fem.} *sl* finger ring <**Fre**[*1]>

mȁr [1] {excl.} *sl* used to make somebody go away, beat it <**Gyp**✍>

mâr [2] {a +ev (ext. pl) masc.; Nom Pl márevi} *sl* hit, punch <**Gyp**>

mára {ē fem.} **1a.** *sl* fight (e.g. fist fight) <**Gyp**> **b.** *sl* beating up <**Gyp**[*1]> **2** *sl-crime* police van, paddy wagon <**SlavO**[*1]> **3** *sl-drugs* marijuana, pot, grass <**SlavO**[*1]>

maràbunt {a (acc. = gen.) masc.} *sl-fea* foreign tourist without any money <**NE**[*1]>

maràhunt {a (acc. = gen.) masc.} *sl-fea* foreign tourist without any money <**NE**[*1]>

mȁrānje {a neut.} *sl* fight (e.g. fist fight) <**Gyp**>

maratónac {nca (acc. = gen.) masc.} (lit. marathon runner) *sl-fea* big liar <**Gre**[*1]>

maràtōnke {ī fem. pl.} *sl* bathing suit <**Gre**[*1]>

maravȅla {ē fem.} *sl* fight (e.g. fist fight) <**Gyp**>

màraz {a masc.} *sl* sickness <**NE**>

màrdelj {a masc.} **1** *sl-crime* prison <**Ita**✍[*1]> **2** *sl* city
• **Bêlī màrdelj** {NP} (lit. white prison) **1** *sl* countryside, the provinces **2** *sl* Belgrade, Serbia
• **gòtiv màrdelj** {NP} *sl-fea* country fair

màrdelja {ē fem.} *sl-crime* prison <**Ita**✍[*1]>

mardèljāš {deljáša (acc. = gen.) masc.; Voc mȁrdeljāšu} *sl-crime* prisoner <**Ita**❖✍[*1]>

mardèljati {ām, ajū imperf.} *sl-crime* stay in prison <**Ita**❖✍[*1]>

mardèljisati {išēm, išū imperf.} *sl-crime* stay in prison <**Ita**❖✍[*1]>

màrēnda {ē fem.} *col* morning or noon snack <**Ita**>

marèndati {ām, ajū imperf. intr.} *col* eat one's morning snack or lunch <**Ita**>

marendávati {èndāvām, endávajū imperf. intr.} *col* eat one's morning snack or lunch <**Ita**>

margàrīn {a masc.} (lit. margarine) *sl-fea* attractive female <**Fre**[*1]>

marginálac {lca (acc. = gen.) masc.} **a.** *sl-fea* unimportant person, nobody, nothing <**Lat**[*1]> **b.** *sl-fea* worthless or despicable person, bum <**Lat**[*2]>

Mȁrgot {a (acc. = gen.) masc.} *sl-sex* male homosexual, gay <**FreO**[*1]>

mȁrica {ē fem.} **1** *sl-crime* police van, paddy wagon <**SlavO**[*1]> **2** *sl-drugs* marijuana, pot, grass <**SlavO**[*1]>

Mȁričin sîn {NP} (lit. Mary's son) *sl-crime* policeman, cop ☞ **sin**

marifètluk {a masc.} **a.** *sl-fea* skill <**NE**> **b.** *sl-fea* evilness, maliciousness <**NE**[*1]>

Màrija {ē fem.} (lit. Mary) **1** *sl-sex* ***Fac*** virgin <**HebO**[*1]> **2** *sl-drugs* marijuana, Mary Jane <**HebO**[*1]>
• **dȑvenā Màrija** {NP} (lit. wooden Mary) *sl-fea* clumsy person, klutz

marijȁna {ē fem.} *sl-drugs* marijuana, Mary Jane <**SlavO**[*1]>

marinȅla {ē fem.} *sl-crime* theft, swiping <**Gyp**✍[*1]>

Màrīnko {a masc.} (lit. Marinko 'man's name') *sl-sex* ***Fac-Obs*** penis, dick, prick <**SlavO**[*1]>

mariȍla {ē fem.} **1** *sl* fight (e.g. fist fight) <**Gyp**✍> **2a.** *sl-crime* police van, paddy wagon <**SlavO**✍> **b.** *sl-crime* police <**SlavO**✍[*2]>

marisàna {ē fem.} *sl* fight (e.g. fist fight) <**Gyp**>

màrisānje {a neut.} **a.** *sl* fight (e.g. fist fight) <**Gyp**> **b.** *sl-crime* theft <**Gyp**[*1]>

màrisati {išēm, išū imperf.} **1** *sl* beat up <Gyp> **a.i.** *sl* steal, swipe <Gyp[*1]> **ii.** *sl-sex* engage in sexual intercourse with (of a male) <Gyp[*1]>

màrisati se {išēm, išū imperf. intr.} *sl* engage in fighting (e.g. with fists on the street) <Gyp>

màriš {a masc.} *sl-drugs* marijuana, Mary Jane <Spa✍>

màriška {ē fem.; Dat màriški} *sl-drugs* marijuana, Mary Jane <Spa✍>

máriti {rīm, rē imperf. intr.} *col* respect, obey <Slav>

màriti se {rīm, rē imperf. intr.} *sl* engage in fighting (e.g. with fists on the street) <Gyp>

màrka [1] {ē fem.; Dat màrki} **1a.** *sl-fea* ***Der*** clumsy person, klutz <Fre[*1]> **b.** *sl-fea* undependable person <Fre[*2]> **c.** *sl-fea* crybaby <Fre[*3]> **2** *sl-fea* nice male, cool guy <Fre[*1]> **3a.** *sl-fea* authority, expert <Fre[*1]> **b.** *sl-fea* very important or influential person, big shot <Fre[*2]>

- **tàksenā màrka** {NP} (lit. administrative fee stamp) *sl-fea* boring person, bore
- **vèlikā màrka** {NP} (lit. big brandname) *sl-fea* very important or influential person, big shot

màrka [2] {adj.} *sl-fea* undependable, unreliable <Fre[*1]>

markàcēr {a masc.} *sl-crime* theft from a drunk <Ger❖[*1]>

markàntna figúra {NP} (lit. remarkable figure) *sl-fea* person who earns his/her salary in German marks ☞ **figura**

màrkec {a masc.} *sl-crime* theft from a drunk <Ger❖[*1]>

markècēr {kecéra masc.} *sl-crime* theft from a drunk or sleeping person <Ger❖[*1]>

màrkecovānje {a neut.} *sl-crime* theft from a drunk <Ger❖[*1]>

màrkīrān {a, o adj.} **a.** *col* marked <Ger> **b.** *sl-sports* covered, guarded (soccer player, etc.) <Ger[*1]>

markírati {màrkīrām, markírajū imperf.} **1** *sl* act (in a theater play, etc.) <Fre[*1]> **2** *sl-sports* block a shot (in soccer, basketball, etc.) <Fre[*1]> **3** *sl-sstu* cut classes <Fre[*1]>

màrmārnik {a masc.} *sl-arch* church

màrnuti {nēm, nū perf.} **1** *sl-crime* steal, swipe <Gyp> **2** *sl* hit, punch <Gyp>

màrōd {adj.} *sl-fea* ill, sick <Fre>

marokánac {nca (acc. = gen.) masc.} *sl-drugs* hashish, hash <SlavO[*1]>

màrōn {maróna masc.} *sl* German mark <Ger✍>

maróni {ā masc. pl.} **1** *sl-crime* ammunition, ammo <Ger[*1]> **2** *sl-crime* police <Ger[*1]>

màrsovac {vca (acc. = gen.) masc.} (lit. Martian) *sl-crime* traffic policeman <Lat❖[*1]>

màrsōvka {ē fem.} (lit. Martian) *sl-fea* boring female, bore <Gre❖[*1]>

màrš [1] {excl.} **a.** *col* used to urge somebody on, go <Fre> **b.** *col* used to command dismissal, beat it <Fre[*1]>

- **Màrš odávde!** {S} (lit. Beat it!) *col* used to make somebody go away, Beat it!
- **Màrš píšonjo!** {S} (lit. Beat it you pisser!) *col* used in angry dismissal, Beat it!
- **Màrš pîzdo jèdna òbičnā!** {S} (lit. Beat it, you cunt!) *col* ***Off*** used in angry dismissal, Beat it!
- **Màrš u kȕrac!** {S} (lit. Go to a prick!) *col* ***Off*** used in angry dismissal, Fuck off!
- **Màrš u màterinu!** {S} (lit. Go to your mother's *cunt*!) *col* used as a strong curse, Fuck you!
- **Màrš u pȉčku màterinu!** {S} (lit. Go to your mother's cunt!) *col* ***Off*** used as a strong curse, Fuck you!
- **Màrš u pízdu màterinu!** {S} (lit. Go to your mother's cunt!) *col* ***Off*** used as a strong curse, Fuck you!

màrš [2] *See the following*

- **pòsmrtni màrš** {NP} (lit. funeral march) *sl* funeral

mârta {ē fem.} (lit. Martha) **a.** *sl-sex* prostitute, hooker <HebO[*1]> **b.** *sl-fea* suspicious female <HebO[*1]>

mârtićevac {vca (acc. = gen.) masc.} (lit. follower of Milan Martić, the minister of the interior in the Serbian region of Kraina in the 1990s) *col* Serbian fighter in Croatia in the1990s <SlavO❖>

màrtuna {ē fem.} **a.** *sl* lie, **b.** *sl* cheating, swindling

màrulja {ē fem.} *sl* German mark <Ger[*1]>

marvínče {eta neut.} *col-dia* head of cattle <Hun❖>

màsa {ē fem.} (lit. mass) **1** *sl-fea* obese male <Lat[*1]> **2** *sl* ten dinars; a ten-dinar bill <Lat[*1]>

másan {sna, sno adj.} (lit. fat) [std. = mastan] **a.** *sl-fea* obese, fat <Slav✍[*1]> **b.** *sl-fea* affluent, loaded, fat <Slav✍[*2]> **c.** *sl-fea* good, of high quality or skill, fat <Slav✍[*3]> **d.** *sl-fea* the best <Slav✍[*4]>

màsatiti {tīm, tē imperf.} *sl-arch* cut, slice

masáža {ē fem.} (lit. massage) *sl-fea* boredom <Fre[*1]>

màsēr {maséra (acc. = gen.) masc.} (lit. masseur) *sl-fea* boring person, bore <Fre[*1]>

maseràti {īja masc.} *sl-fea* boring person, bore <ItaO[*1]>

masírati {màsīrām, ajū imperf.} (lit. give massage) *sl* annoy, bother, pester <Fre[*1]>

màska {ē fem.} (lit. mask) *sl* face (human) <**Fre***1>

màskīrān {a, o adj.} (lit. masked) *sl-fea* with excessive make-up <**Fre***1>

maskírati se {màskīrām, maskírajū biasp. intr.} (lit. mask oneself) *sl-fea* put on make-up <**Fre***1>

maslàkān {lakána (acc. = gen.) masc.} *sl-sex* ***Obs*** penis, dick, prick

maslìkān {likána masc.} *sl-sex* ***Obs*** penis, dick, prick

maslìnjāk {màslinjāka masc.} (lit. olive field) *sl* five hundred dinars; a five-hundred dinar bill <**Slav***1>

mȁslo {a neut.} (lit. butter) **1** *sl-sex* ***Obs*** penis, dick, prick <**Slav***1> **2** *sl* female <**Slav***1> **3** *sl* money <**Slav***1>
• **[ADJ/PPRON] mȁslo** {LSF} (lit. [ADJ] butter) used to signal someone's fault: *Ta krađa je njegovo maslo. He had his fingers in that theft.*

mâsnā kôst {NP} (lit. fat bone) *sl-sex* ***Fac-Obs*** male on the make ☞ **kost**

mâsnē pàre {NP} (lit. fat money) *col* sizable amount of money, big bucks ☞ **pare**

mâsnī vȉc {NP} (lit. fat joke) *col* dirty joke ☞ **vic**

mâsno {adv.} (lit. fat) *sl-fea* big, many: *Masno su te zajebali. They fucked you over big.* <**Slav***1>

màsōvka {ē fem.} (lit. mass scene) *sl-sex* ***Fac-Obs*** group sex <**Lat**❖*1>

màspok {a masc.} (lit. mas*ovni* 'mass' pok(ret) 'movement') [std. = masovni pokret] *sl-polit* Croatian separatist movement in the 1970s <**Slav**❖>

màspokovac {vca (acc. = gen.) masc.} *sl-polit* member of the Croatian separatist movement in the 1970s <**Slav**❖>

màspokovskī {ā, ō adj.} *sl-polit* pertaining to the Croatian separatist movement in the 1970s <**Slav**❖>

maspokóvština {ē fem.} *sl-polit* Croatian separatist movement in the 1970s <**Slav**❖>

mâst {i fem.} (lit. fat, lard) **1** *sl* additional punishment <**Slav***1> **2** *sl* bribe <**Slav***1>

mástan {sna, sno adj.} (lit. fat, greasy) **a.** *sl-fea* obese, fat <**Slav***1> **b.** *sl-fea* affluent <**Slav***2> **c.** *sl-fea* good <**Slav***3>

màstilo {a neut.} (lit. ink) SerE *sl-fea* boring person, bore <**Slav***1>

mastȉljār {mastiljára (acc. = gen.) masc.} **1 SerE** *sl-sstu* high-school student <**Slav***1> **2 SerE** *sl* lower-ranked clerk (in an office) <**Slav***1>

mastȉljav {a, o adj.} (lit. ink-covered) *sl-crime* policeman, man in blue <**Slav***1>

mastȉljavī {ōg (acc. = gen.) masc.} (lit. the one covered with ink) *sl-crime* policeman, man in blue <**Slav***1>

mástiti {mâstīm, tē imperf.} (lit. fat) **1a.** *sl* lie <**Slav***1> **b.** *sl* cheat, swindle <**Slav***2> **2** *sl* smell, stink <**Slav***1>
• **mástiti bȓk** {VP} (lit. grease one's mustache) *col* eat, devour

mȁša {ē masc.} **1a.** *sl-fea* troublemaker, rowdy, ruffian <**NE***1> **b.** *sl-fea* boaster, braggart, blowhard <**NE***2> **c.** *sl-fea* conceited male <**NE***3> **2** *sl-drugs* marijuana, pot, grass <**NE***1>

mâšalā {excl.} **1** BosM *col* ***App*** used to express appreciation <**NE**> **2** BosM *col* finally <**NE**>

mâšalāh {excl.} BosM *col* ***App*** used to express appreciation <**NE**>

mašína {ē fem.} (lit. machine) **1** *col* car, wheels <**Lat***1> **2** *col* computer, machine <**Lat***1> **3** *col* gadget <**Lat***1>

mašínac {nca (acc. = gen.) masc.} **1** *col* mechanical engineering student <**Lat**❖*1> **2** *col* machine industry worker <**Lat**❖*1>

mašínica {ē fem.} (lit. small machine) *sl* matchbox <**Lat**❖*1>

mȁšīnka {ē fem.} (lit. machine gun) **1a.** *sl-sex* ***App*** seducer <**Lat**❖*1> **b.** *sl* ***App*** lover (female) <**Lat**❖*2> **c.** *sl-fea* ***App*** skillful person <**Lat**❖*3> **2** *sl-fea* dandy, fop <**Lat**❖*1>

mȁška {ē fem.; Dat mȁški} *sl-sex* ***Obs*** penis, dick, prick <**Fre**☞*1>

mȁšnjāk {a masc.} *sl* bowtie <**Ger**❖*1>

mȁštračēnje {a neut.} *sl-sex* ***Obs*** sexual intercourse <**NE***1>

mȁštračiti {čīm, čē imperf.} *sl-sex* ***Obs*** engage in sexual intercourse with (of a male) <**NE***1>

mȁštrafiti {fīm, fē biasp.} *sl* eat, devour <**NE***1>

mȁt[1] {excl.} *col* used to lure a queen-bee <**Slav**>

mȁt[2] *See the following*
• **mȁt iz nȅhāta**{NP} (lit. unintended checkmate) *sl-sports* incidental (not premeditated) checkmate

máta {ē fem.} *sl-sstu* mathematics <**Gre**☞>

matàruga {ē fem.; Dat matàrugi} *sl-sports* checkmate <**NE**☞>

Matàruškā Bȁnja {NP} (lit. Mataruška Banja, a spa in Serbia *the initial character sequence is the same as in mat 'checkmate'*) *sl-sports* checkmate ☞ **banja**

matemàtičār {a (acc. = gen.) masc.} (lit. mathematician) *sl-sstu* math teacher <Gre[*1]>

mȁtēr *See the following*

• **Mȁtēr mu blȅsavū!** {S} (lit. *I fuck* his crazy mother!) *col* used as a strong curse, Fuck him!

• **Mȁtēr ti jèbēm, da ti jèbēm!** {S} (lit. *I fuck* your mother, I really do!) *col* ***Off*** used as a strong curse, Fuck you!

• **Mȁtēr ti jèbēm džȕdžinskū!** {S} (lit. *I fuck* your redneck mother!) *col* ***Off*** used as a strong curse, Fuck you!

• **Mȁtēr ti tvòju!** {S} (lit. *I fuck* your mother!) *col* ***Off*** used as a strong curse, Fuck you!

• **Mȁtēr vam blȅsavū!**{S} (lit. *I fuck* your crazy mother!) *col* ***Off*** used as a strong curse, Fuck you!

• **Màterē mi!** {S} (lit. I swear by my mother!) *col* used to emphasize the truth of what has been said, I swear!

• **mȁterē ti** {NP} (lit. I swear by my mother) *col* really, indeed

• **U bȍžijū mȁtēr!** {S} (lit. In God's mother!) *col* used to express lack of control over events, Fuck it!

• **vrȁžijū mȁtēr** {NP} (lit. devil's mother) *col* nothing

mȁtera {ē fem.} *col-dia* mother <Slav>

mȁterinu {excl.} (lit. to the mother's) *col* used to express extreme dissatisfaction <Slav>

màthauzen {a (acc. = gen.) masc.} *sl-sports* checkmate <GerO[*1]>

màtilo {a neut.} *sl-drink* alcoholic beverage <Gyp>

matinéja {ē fem.} *sl* morning meeting of two spouse-cheaters, morning tryst <Fre[*1]>

màtiš {a masc.} *sl-sstu* mathematics <Gre✍>

màtiškinja {ē fem.} *sl-sstu* math teacher <Gre✍>

mȁtko {a masc.; perm} /mȁdko /madako masc./ (lit. piece) [std. = komad] *sl-fea* female with attractive shape <Slav✍[*1]>

Máto {ē masc.} (lit. Matthew) *sl-drink* waiter <SlavO[*1]>

màtor {a, o adj.} *sl-fea* old <Slav>

màtorā {ē fem. (adj. decl.)} (lit. the old one) *sl* mother, old lady <Slav>

matórac {rca (acc. = gen.) masc.} (lit. the old one) **a.** *sl-fea* senior citizen, old timer <Slav> **b.** *sl* parent, old folks **c.** *sl* father, old man

matòrān {matorána (acc. = gen.) masc.; Voc mȁtorāne} (lit. the old one) **a.** *sl-fea* senior citizen, old timer <Slav❖[*1]> **b.** *sl* parent, old folks <Slav❖[*2]> **c.** *sl* father, old man <Slav❖[*3]>

màtorī {ōg (acc. = gen.) masc.} (lit. the old one) *sl* father, old man <Slav>

màtōrka {ē fem.; Dat màtōrki} (lit. the old one) **a.** *sl-fea* elderly female, old timer <Slav> **b.** *sl* mother, old lady

mȁtrāk [1] {a (acc. = gen.) masc.} *sl-fea* evil male, s.o.b <Fre[*1]>

mȁtrāk [2] {a masc.} *sl-fea* unworthy object <Fre[*1]>

• **Kòj ćeš mi mȁtrāk!** {S} (lit. What kind of worthless object do I need you for!) *dia* ***Off*** used to make somebody go away, Beat it!

matrificírati {ām, ajū biasp. intr.} *sl-sports* checkmate <NE✍[*1]>

mȁtros {a (acc. = gen.) masc.} (lit. the old one) *sl-fea* senior citizen, old timer <Slav✍[*1]>

màtūf {matúfa (acc. = gen.) masc.; Voc mȁtūfe} **a.** *sl-fea* senior citizen <NE[*1]> **b.** *sl-fea* senile person <NE[*2]>

màtūh {matúha (acc. = gen.) masc.; Voc mȁtūhu} *sl-fea* senile person <NE[*1]>

maturálac {lca (acc. = gen.) masc.} *sl-fea* high school graduation trip <Lat❖>

màtūv {matúva (acc. = gen.) masc.; Voc mȁtūve} *sl-fea* senile person <NE[*1]>

mȁu {excl.} *col* the sound made by a cat, meow <Slav>

mȁu-mȁu {a masc.} *sl-gamble* a kind of simple card game <Slav>

mȁūk {a masc.} *col* meow <Slav>

maúkānje {a neut.} *col* meowing <Slav>

maúkati {màūčēm, màūčū imperf.} *col* meow <Slav>

maȕkav {a, o adj.} *col* meowing <Slav>

maȕkavā {ē fem.} *col* meow <Slav>

maȕkavac {vca masc.} *col* meowing <Slav>

màunka {ē fem.} *sl-arch* wife

mâz {excl.} *sl* used to encourage an action, go for it <Slav❖[*1]>

mȁzalo {a neut.} (lit. lubricant) **1** *sl* journalist <Slav[*1]> **2** *sl* painter (artist) <Slav[*1]>

mȁzānje {a neut.} (lit. lubricating) **a.** *sl* artistic painting <Slav[*1]> **b.i.** *sl* intake of narcotic drugs, doing drugs <Slav[*2]> **ii.** *sl* lying <Slav[*2]>

mȁzati {ažem, ažu imperf.} (lit. lubricate) **1** *sl* lie <Slav*1> **2** *sl-drugs* take narcotic drugs, do drugs <Slav*1> **3** *sl* engage in sexual intercourse with (of a male) <Slav*1> **4** *sl* bribe, lubricate <Slav*1> **5** *sl* devour, eat voraciously <Slav*1>

- **mȁzati ȍči** {VP} (lit. grease eyes) *col* lie

mȁzda *See the following*

- **mázda pȉterina** {NP} *sl* ***Off*** mother's vagina

màzga {ē fem.; Dat màzgi} (lit. mule) **a.** *sl-fea* unintelligent female <Slav*1> **b.** *sl-fea* stupid or mentally deficient person <Slav*2>

Màzgārnīk {a masc.} (lit. Muleville) *sl* name for Konjarnik (a neighborhood in Belgrade, Serbia) <Slav✍*1>

màzgōv {mazgòva masc.} (lit. mule) *sl-fea* stupid or mentally deficient person <Slav❖*1>

màzija [1] {ē fem.} *col-dia* iron (the metal) <NE>

mázija [2] {ē fem.; perm} [std. = zima] *sl* cold weather <Slav✍>

mazȉjati {ām, ajū imperf.} *sl-crime* steal, swipe <Slav❖*1>

mȁzīvo {a neut.} (lit. lubricant) *sl* bribe <Slav*1>

mȁznuti {nēm, nū perf.} **1** *sl-crime* steal, swipe <Slav❖*1> **2** *sl* catch **3** *sl-sex* engage in sexual intercourse with (of a male) **4** *sl* eat, devour **5** *sl* devour, eat voraciously **6** *sl-drink* drink (alcohol)

- **mȁznuti màjmuna** {VP} (lit. hit an ape) *sl-sex* ***Fac-Obs*** masturbate, spank the monkey
- **mȁznuti prófu** {VP} (lit. hit a professor) *sl-sex* engage in sexual intercourse with one's classmate

Máža {ē fem.} Ser *sl* name for Majestic hotel, Belgrade, Serbia <SlavO✍>

mážnja {ē fem.} *sl-crime* theft, swipe <Slav❖*1>

mažnjávānje {a neut.} *sl-crime* theft, swipe <Slav❖*1>

mažnjávati {màžnjāvām, mažnjávajū imperf.} *sl-crime* steal, swipe <Slav❖*1>

Mažuránac {nca (acc. = gen.) masc.} Cro *sl* name for Mažuranićev Square in Zagreb, Croatia <SlavO✍>

mê {excl.} *col* the sound made by a goat, baa <Slav>

mê-e-e {excl.} *col* the sound made by a goat, baa <Slav>

mȅblovati {lujēm, lujū imperf.} *sl* beat up <Ger*1>

méca [1] {ē fem.} (lit. teddy bear) **1** *sl-sex* ***Fam*** menstruation, period <Slav*1> **2** *sl-auto* ***Fam*** Mercedes (make of car) <Slav*1> **3** *sl-sex* ***Obs*** penis, dick, prick <Slav*1>

méca [2] {ē masc.} SerE *col* ***Fam*** teddy bear <Slav✍>

mȅčka {ē fem.; Dat mȅčki} (lit. she-bear) **1** *sl-crime* large safe <Slav*1> **2** *sl-fea* obese female <Slav*1> **3** *sl-auto* Mercedes (make of car) <Slav*1>

mȅčkār {a (acc. = gen.) masc.} (lit. bear trainer) *sl-crime* safe cracker <Slav*1>

Mȅdāk {a (acc. = gen.) masc.} Ser *sl* name for Medaković (a neighborhood in Belgrade, Serbia) <SlaO✍>

medecína {ē fem.} [std. = medicina] *col-dia* medicine <Lat✍>

mȅden {a, o adj.} (lit. honey) *sl-fea* disgusting <Slav*1>

medènjača {ē fem.} *col-dia* mead <Slav❖>

médo {ē masc.} *col* ***Fam*** teddy bear <Slav✍>

mèdved {a (acc. = gen.) masc.} (lit. bear) *sl-crime* person who steals from the train passengers <Slav*1>

mèdvedār {a (acc. = gen.) masc.} (lit. bear trainer) *sl-crime* person who steals from the train passengers <Slav*1>

mèdvjed {a (acc. = gen.) masc.} (lit. bear) **1a.** *sl* freight car <Slav*1> **b.** *sl* freight train <Slav*2> **2** *sl-sport* player or fan of Medveščak (a hockey team from Zagreb, Croatia) <Slav*1>

mȅdze {neut.} SSer *dia* snack <NE>

mèđed {a (acc. = gen.) masc.} (lit. bear) [std. = medvjed, medved] **a.** *dia* bear (the animal) <Slav> **b.** *col* big and clumsy person, oaf <Slav*1>

- **kàd mèđedu gùzica zaráste** {AdvP} (lit. when a bear's ass grows over) *dia* ***Obs*** never

međubùtnō landàralo {NP} (lit. the thing that swings between one's legs) *sl-sex* ***Fac-Obs*** penis, dick, prick ☞ **landaralo**

međunòga {ē fem.} (lit. between the legs) *sl-sex* ***Fac*** penis <Slav❖>

mȅđunōžje {a neut.} (lit. area between the legs) *sl-sex* ***Fac*** groin, crotch <Slav❖>

međunòžnō gúralo {NP} (lit. the thing which is pushed between one's legs) *sl* bicycle ☞ **guralo**

mȅg {a +ov (ext. pl) masc.; Nom Pl mègovi} *sl* tape recorder <Gre✍>

mèhak {hka, hko adj.} [std. = mek] BosM *col* soft (physically and psychologically) <Slav✍>

mehàničār {haničára (acc. = gen.) masc.; Voc mehàničāru} (lit. mechanic) *sl-sex* ***Fac*** frigid male <Gre*1>

mȅhko {adv.} [std. = meko] BosM *col* softly (physically and psychologically) <Slav✍>

mèit {a (acc. = gen.) masc.} BosM *col* dead <NE>

mèjātor {a (acc. = gen.) masc.} *sl-fea* extremely talkative person, chatterbox <**Slav**[*1]>

méjdān {mejdána masc.} *col* duel, fight <**NE**>

méjker *See the following*
- **pénis méjker** {NP} (lit. penis maker) *sl* ***Fac*** pacemaker

méjtef {a masc.} BosM *col* Muslim religious school <**NE**>

mȅka [1] {ē fem.; Dat mȅki} **a.** *col* bleating (of goat), baaing <**Slav**> **b.** *sl* money <**Slav**[*1]>

mȅkā [2] {ē fem. (adj. decl.)} (lit. the soft one) *sl-drink* soft brandy <**Slav**[*1]>

mekankìtis {a masc.} (lit. softitis) **a.** *sl-sex* ***Fac*** soft penis <**Slav**✎> **b.** *sl-sex* ***Fac*** impotence <**Slav**✎[*1]>

mékānje {a neut.} *col* bleating (of goat), baaing <**Slav**>

mékati {ām, ajū imperf.} **a.** *col* produce bleating sound of a goat or sheep, baa <**Slav**> **b.** *col* stare at, be fixated on <**Slav**[*1]>

mȅkāvka {ē fem.} *dia* bleating (of goat), baaing <**Slav**>

mekètānje {a neut.} *col* bleating (of sheep), baaing <**Slav**>

mekètati {mèkećēm, ećū imperf.} *col* produce bleating sound of a goat or sheep, baa <**Slav**>

mekètav {a, o adj.} *col* bleating (of goat), baaing <**Slav**>

mekìtis {a masc.} (lit. softitis) *sl-sex* penis of an impotent male <**Slav**✎>

mèkšati {ām, ajū biasp.} (lit. soften) *sl* cry, shed tears, weep <**Slav**[*1]>

mèktati {ām, ajū imperf.} *sl* stare at, be fixated on <**Slav**>

mekùrija {ē fem.} *col* softness <**Slav**✎>

mekúšac {šca masc.} (lit. mollusk) *sl-fea* irresolute male, spineless guy <**Slav**[*1]>

mȅldovati se {dujēm, dujū biasp. intr.} (lit. report) *sl* come, arrive <**Ger**[*1]>

mèljara {ē fem.} *sl* head <**Slav**[*1]>

mȅljavī {ōg (acc. = gen.) masc.} *sl-fea* obese male <**Slav**[*1]>

mèmljara {ē fem.} (lit. the place of dampness) *sl-crime* prison <**NE**[*1]>

mèmljiv {a, o adj.} *col* moist, damp <**NE**>

mènđuha {ē fem.; Dat mènđuhi} BosM *col* earring <**NE**>

mȅnga {ē fem.; Dat mȅngi} [std. = menstruacija] **1** *sl-sex* menstruation, period <**Lat**✎> **2** *sl* stone, rock

mȅngele {gēlā fem. pl.} *col* clamp (the tool) <**NE**>

menstruácija *See the following*
- **menstruácija mȍzga** {NP} (lit. brain menstruation) *sl-fea* being stunned

mèntōl {mentóla (acc. = gen.) masc.} (lit. menthol) *sl-fea* stupid or mentally deficient person <**Gre**[*1]>

mèntus {a (acc. = gen.) masc.} *sl-fea* stupid or mentally deficient person <**Lat**✎[*1]>

mènjāč {menjáča masc.} (lit. gear shift) **1** *sl-sex* ***Fac-Obs*** penis, dick, prick <**Slav**[*1]> **2** *sl* exchange (money, goods, etc.) <**Slav**[*1]>

ménjati *See the following*
- **ménjati žváku** {VP} (lit. change chewing gum) SerE *sl* chat, chew the cud

mènjāž {menjáža masc.} *sl* exchange (goods, money, etc.) <**Slav**✎>

menjáža {ē fem.} *sl* exchange (goods, money, etc.) <**Slav**✎>

mȅnza {ē fem.} (lit. cafeteria) **1** *sl* stomach, belly, gut <**Lat**[*1]> **2a.** *sl* mouth <**Lat**[*1]> **b.** *sl* face (human) <**Lat**[*2]> **3** *sl-sex* menstruation, period <**Lat**[*1]>

mènzis {a masc.} *sl-sex* menstruation, period <**Gre**>

mȅraba {excl.} BosM *col* used to greet on arrival, hello, hi <**NE**> ☞ **merhaba**

mèrāč {meráča masc.} *sl* day <**Slav**[*1]>

merája {ē fem.} BosM *col* open air: *sjediti na meraji sit in the open air* <**NE**[*1]>

mèrāk {meráka masc.} Bos *col* joy <**NE**>

mèrati {ām, ajū imperf.} *sl-crime* steal, swipe

mȅrati {rām, rajū biasp. intr.} *sl-crime* steal, swipe

mérdža {ē masc.} /mèrdža/ *sl-auto* Mercedes (make of car) <**BN**✎>

mȅrdžān {a masc.} *sl-auto* Mercedes (make of car) <**BN**✎>

mérdžo {ē masc.} /mérdžo /a masc./ *sl-auto* Mercedes (make of car) <**BN**✎>

mȅrhaba {excl.} BosM *col* hello, hi <**NE**> ☞ **meraba**

mȅrī [1] {īja (acc. = gen.) masc.} /mèri/ **1** *sl-sex* male homosexual, gay <**EngO**[*1]> **2** *sl-drugs* narcotic drug, dope <**EngO**[*1]>

Mȅrī [2] *See the following*
- **Mȅri Džȇjn** {NP} (lit. Mary Jane) *sl-drugs* marijuana, Mary Jane

mȅrica {ē fem.} SerE *sl* head <**Slav**[*1]>

mèridžovati se {džujēm, džujū biasp. intr.} *sl* get married, get hitched <Eng>

mȅrmērnica {ē fem.} (lit. the marble place) *sl-arch* church <NE*1>

mȅsār {a (acc. = gen.) masc.} (lit. butcher) *sl* ***Fac-App*** doctor, doc <Slav*1>

mèsara {ē fem.} (lit. butcher shop) **1a.** *sl-sex* ***Fac*** prostitute, hooker <Slav*1> **b.** *sl-sex* ***Fac*** place where prostitutes gather <Slav*2> **2** *sl* ***Fac*** hospital <Slav*1>

mesáriti {mèsārīm, rē imperf.} (lit. work as a butcher) **a.** *sl-fea* torture <Slav*1> **b.** *sl-sports* play aggressive soccer <Slav*2>

mèsatiti {tīm, tē imperf.} (lit. butcher) *sl-sports* play aggressive soccer <Slav>

mȅsečār {a (acc. = gen.) masc.} (lit. sleepwalker) SerE *sl-fea* hairy male <Slav*1>

mȅsečina {ē fem.} (lit. moonight) SerE *sl* poor illumination <Slav*1>

- **Mȅsečinu ti bȍžju!** {S} (lit. *I fuck* your God's moonlight!) SerE *col* ***Off*** used as a moderate curse, Fuck you!
- **Mȅsečinu ti jèbēm!** {S} (lit. I screw your moonlight!) SerE *col* ***Off*** used as a weak curse, Screw you!

mèsečiti {čīm, čē imperf.} SerE *sl* stand in the moonlight <Slav⁘>

mesírac {rca masc.} *sl-crime* knife <Ger☞>

mésiti {sīm, sē imperf.} (lit. knead) **1 SerE** *sl* beat up <Slav*1> **2a. SerE** *sl* persuade, convince <Slav*1> **b. SerE** *sl* annoy, bother, pester <Slav*2>

mésnica {ē fem.} (lit. butcher's) *sl* zipper, fly <Slav*1>

mêso {a neut.} (lit. meat) **1a.** *sl-sex* ***Fac*** female with attractive shape <Slav*1> **b.** *sl-sex* ***Fac*** prostitute, hooker <Slav*2> **c.** *sl* ***Fac*** female <Slav*3> **2** *sl-fea* muscular male <Slav*1>

mȅsto *See the following*

- **iz mȅsta** {PP} (lit. from the spot) **SerE** *col* right away, now: *Zatvori prozor iz mesta! Close the window right away!*
- **ȍnō mȅsto** {NP} (lit. that place) SerE *sl-sex* ***Obs*** bathroom

mȅšalica {ē fem.} (lit. mixer) SerE *sl-sex* ***Fac*** loose woman <Slav*1>

mȅšānje {a neut.} (lit. mixing) **1a. SerE** *sl-sex* ***Obs*** sexual intercourse <Slav*1> **b. SerE** *sl-sex* ***Obs*** shaking one's buttocks during sexual intercourse <Slav*2> **2** SerE *sl-sport* ***Fac*** wrestling <Slav*1>

mȅšati {mêšām, méšajū imperf.} (lit. mix) SerE *sl-sex* ***Obs*** shaking one's buttocks during sexual intercourse <Slav*1>

mȅšati se {mêšām, méšajū imperf. intr.} (lit. mix) SerE *sl-sex* ***Obs*** engage in sexual intercourse with <Slav*1>

mȅškoljiti se {ljīm, ljē imperf. intr.} /meškòljiti se/ *col* make faces in pain or fear <Slav☞*1>

Mȅštrović {a (acc. = gen.) masc.} *sl* fifty dinars (bill) <SlavO*1>

mȅt {a +ov (ext. pl) masc.; Nom Pl mètovi} *sl-drugs* methadone <BN☞>

méta {ē fem.} (lit. target) *sl* street <Lat*1>

mȅtak [1] {excl.} (lit. bullet) *sl* used to make somebody go away <Slav*1>

mȅtak [2] {tka masc.} (lit. bullet) **a.** *sl-sex* ***Fac*** penis <Slav*1> **b.** *sl-sex* ***Fac*** sexual intercourse <Slav*2>

- **mànevārskī mȅtak** {NP} (lit. blank cartridge) *sl-sstu* school chalk
- **pod mȅtak** {PP} (lit. under bullet) *sl-sex* ***Fac-Obs*** sexual intercourse

metálac {lca (acc. = gen.) masc.} *col* metal industry worker <Slav>

mȅtar {tra masc.} (lit. meter) **1** *sl* month <Gre*1> **2** *sl* many, numerous <Gre*1>

- **dvâ mȅtra ispod krȅča** {NP} (lit. two meters under the lime) *sl-fea* ***Fac*** very senile person
- **mȅtar dánā** {NP} (lit. a meter of days) *sl* one month
- **mȅtar i žìlēt** {AdjP} (lit. meter and razorblade tall) *sl-fea* short (in height)

metȉljav {a, o adj.} *col-dia* weak, irresolute: *metiljav tip wishy-washy guy* <Slav*1>

metiljávko {a masc.} **a.** *sl-fea* weak person <Slav*1> **b.** *sl-fea* slender person <Slav*2>

mȅtković {a masc.} (lit. Metković is a town in Croatia X metnuti - put X metak - bullet) *sl-sex* ***Fac*** sexual intercourse <SlavO*1>

mètla [1] {ē fem.} (lit. broom) **1** *sl* hair <Slav*1> **2a.** *sl-fea* slender female <Slav*1> **b.** *sl-fea* flat-breasted female <Slav*2> **3** *sl* beard <Slav*1>

mètla [2] {excl.} (lit. broom) *col* used to make somebody go away <Slav*1>

mètlārka {ē fem.} **a.** *sl* witch (the Serbo-Croatian equivalent of bogeyman) <Slav*1> **b.** *sl* unattractive person <Slav*2>

mȅtnuti {nēm, nū perf.} (lit. put) *sl-sex* ***Obs*** engage in sexual intercourse with (of a male) <Slav*1>

- **mȅtnuti na štrȉk** {VP} (lit. put on a rope) *sl-crime*

kill, murder
- **mȅtnuti pod mȅngu** {VP} *sl-crime* kill, murder

mètrō {ōa neut.} (lit. subway) **1** *sl-crime* police van, paddy wagon <**Fre**[*1]> **2** *sl-sex* toilet <**Fre**[*1]>

Mȅtro-Gȍldvin-Mȁjer {a (acc. = gen.) masc.} (lit. Metro-Goldwyn Mayer *movie studio*) *sl-fea* person who is in charge, head honcho <**BN**[*1]>

metuzálem {a (acc. = gen.) masc.} (lit. Methuselah) *sl-fea* senior citizen <**HebO**[*1]>

metùzko {a neut.} (lit. little Methuselah) *sl-fea* senior citizen <**HebO**✐[*1]>

mèza {ē fem.} *sl-drink* snack taken while drinking (alcohol) <**NE**>

mèzār {mezára masc.} BosM *col* grave <**NE**>

mèzārje {a neut.} BosM *col* cemetery <**NE**[*1]>

mèze {eta neut.} *sl-drink* snack taken while drinking (alcohol) <**NE**>

mèzimac {mca (acc. = gen.) masc.} *col* beloved child, apple of one's eye <**Slav**>

mèziti {zīm, zē perf.} *sl-drink* snack while drinking (alcohol) <**NE**>

mȉc {excl.} *col* used to lure a cat <**Slav**>
- **mȉc po mȉc** {NP} (lit. move by move) *col* little by little

mȉc-mȉc {adv.} *col* little by little: *Mic-mic i uveli su promjene u firmi. Little by little they introduced changes to the company.* <**Slav**>

míca[1] {ē fem.} **1a.** *sl* trap, catch <**Ger**[*1]> **b.** *sl* ambush <**Ger**[*2]> **2a.** *sl-sex* vagina <**Ger**[*1]> **b.** *sl* female <**Ger**[*2]>
- **míca trȁkalica** {NP} *sl-sex* loose woman
- **míca trȍfrtāljka** {NP} *sl-sex* loose woman

mȉca[2] {ē fem.} *sl* plan, project <**Slav**>

mícac {míca (acc. = gen.) masc.} /milicajac/ *sl-crime* policeman, cop <**Lat**✐>

micájac {jca (acc. = gen.) masc.} /milicajac/ *sl-crime* policeman, cop <**Lat**✐>

mȉcalo {a neut.} (lit. mover) *sl-sex* ***Fac*** penis <**Slav**[*1]>

Mìcika {ē fem.; Dat Mìciki} *sl-sex* ***Obs*** vagina, cunt <**HunO**[*1]>

mȋcoš {a (acc. = gen.) masc.} [std. = milicioner] *sl-crime* policeman, cop <**Lat**✐>

mìčigen {excl.} (lit. Michigan X micati, mičem 'to move') *sl* move over <**Eng-Slav**✐[*1]>

Míćo[1] {excl.} (lit. Mike) *sl* ***Fam*** used to address a person in direct informal communication <**SlavO**[*1]>

míćo[2] {ē masc.} *sl* chamber pot <**SlavO**[*1]>

mijȁū {excl.} *col* the sound made by a cat, meow <**Slav**>

mijȁūk {a masc.} *col* meow <**Slav**>

mijaùkānje {a neut.} *col* meowing <**Slav**>

mijaùkati {učem, uču imperf.} *col* meow <**Slav**>

mijénjati *See the following*
- **mijénjati fȃrbu** {VP} (lit. change colors) *col* blush, turn colors

mijéšati {mȉješām, mijéšajū imperf.} (lit. mix) *sl-sex* ***Obs*** shaking one's buttocks during sexual intercourse <**Slav**[*1]>
- **mijéšati slȋne** {VP} (lit. mix slobber) *sl* kiss

mìjōr {mijóra masc.} Med *dia* thousand dinars; a thousand-dinar bill, a grand <**Ita**>

mìjūr {mijúra masc.} Med *dia* thousand dinars; a thousand-dinar bill, a grand <**Ita**>

Mikȃdo {a (acc. = gen.) masc.} *sl-sstu* principal <**Jap**[*1]>

mìkan {a (acc. = gen.) masc.} *sl-fea* unintelligent male

mȉki {īja (acc. = gen.) masc.} (lit. Mike) *sl-sex* ***Obs*** penis, dick, prick <**EngO**[*1]>

Mȉkī-Šílja-Hòrācije {a masc.} (lit. Mickey-Goofy-Horace) *sl-sex* ***Fac-Obs*** masturbation <**EngO**[*1]>

mȉkica {ē masc.} **a.** *sl-fea* stupid or mentally deficient person <**EngO**[*1]> **b.** *sl* male, guy <**EngO**[*2]>

míkiti {kīm, kē imperf.} **a.** *sl-fea* ***Der*** ingratiate, brownnose, kiss ass **b.** *sl* persuade, convince

mȉkro[1] {a masc.} *sl* ear <**Gre**[*1]>

mȉkro[2] {adj.} *col* minute, very small <**Gre**[*1]>

mȉkrofōn *See the following*
- **mȉkrofōn je vȃš** {LSF} (lit. the mike is yours) *sl-sex* ***Fac-Obs*** fellatio

mȉkromèter {tra masc.} *sl-crafts* micrometer <**Gre**>

mȉks {a masc.} *sl-sports* mixed doubles (table tennis, etc.) <**Eng**>

mȉksati *See the following*
- **mȉksati jája** {VP} (lit. mix eggs) *sl-sex* ***Fac-Obs*** masturbate, beat off

mȉlāč {a (acc. = gen.) masc.} [std. = milicioner] *sl-crime* policeman, cop <**Lat**✐>

Mìlan {a (acc. = gen.) masc.} (lit. Milan, man's name X milicija 'police') *sl-crime* policeman, cop <**SlavO**[*1]>

Mȉldāć {a masc.} *sl* Milde Sorte (cigarette brand) <BN☞>

Mȉle {eta masc.} (lit. Mile, man's name X milicija 'police') *sl-crime* policeman, cop <SlavO[*1]>

Mȉlē li vam ga i pòkvarenē nánē nȁbijēm! {S} (lit. I fuck your dear and rotten mother!) SSer *dia* ***Off*** used as a strong curse, Fuck you! ☞ **nane**

mȉlek {a (acc. = gen.) masc.} *sl-crime* policeman, cop <Lat☞>

Mȉler {a (acc. = gen.) masc.} (lit. Miler, surname X milicija 'police') *sl-crime* policeman, cop <Lat☞>

Miléva {ē fem.} (lit. Mileva, woman's name) Ser *sl* female <SlavO[*1]>
- **sȉrotā Miléva** {NP} (lit. poor Mileva) *sl-fea* used to express compassion, poor thing

mȉlfāč {a (acc. = gen.) masc.} [std. = milicioner] *sl-crime* policeman, cop <Lat☞>

mȉlī {īja (acc. = gen.) masc.} (lit. dear X milicioner 'policeman') [std. = milicioner] *sl-crime* policeman, cop <Lat☞>

mȉlica {ē fem.} (lit. Milica, woman's name X milicija 'police') *sl-crime* police <Slo>

milìna {excl.} *col* used to express high satisfaction, awesome <Slav✣>
- **Milìna je pògledati!** {S} (lit. It is a beauty to look at!) *col* used to express appreciation, Something to look at!

milìōn *See the following*
- **mâlī milìōn** {NP} (lit. little million) *col* multitude

Mȉlisāv {a (acc. = gen.) masc.} (lit. Milisav, man's name X milicija 'police') *sl-crime* policeman, cop <SlavO[*1]>

mȉlk-šêjk {a +ov (ext. pl) masc.; Nom Pl mȉlk-šējkovi} *col* milk-shake <Eng>

mȉlkāč {a (acc. = gen.) masc.} [std. = milicioner] *sl-crime* policeman, cop <Lat☞>

mȉlkan {a (acc. = gen.) masc.} [std. = milicioner] *sl-fea* policeman, cop <Lat☞>

mȉlkavac {vca (acc. = gen.) masc.} *sl* boy, kid <Eng-Slav.✣[*1]>

mȉlkoš {a (acc. = gen.) masc.} [std. = milicioner] *sl-crime* policeman, cop <Lat☞>

Mȉlō li ti bòkče jèbēm! {S} (lit. I fuck your dear little God!) SerE *dia* ***Off*** used as a moderate curse or threat, Fuck you! ☞ **bokče**

Mȉlō ti deténce jèbēm! {S} (lit. I fuck your dear little child!) SerE *col* ***Off*** used as a very strong curse, Fuck you! ☞ **detence**

Mȉlō ti mȁmče jèbēm! {S} (lit. I fuck your dear mom!) SerE *dia* ***Off*** used as a strong curse, Fuck you! ☞ **mamče**

mȉlokūrka {ē fem.; Dat mȉlokūrki} (lit. dear-prick) *sl-sex* ***Fac*** prostitute, hooker <Slav✣>

mȉlomūd {a (acc. = gen.) masc.} *sl-sex* ***Fac*** male homosexual, gay <Slav✣[*1]>

Mȉlosnū ti mȁmicu jèbēm! {S} (lit. I fuck your dear mom!) *col* ***Off*** used as a strong curse, Fuck you! ☞ **mamica**

Mȉloš {a (acc. = gen.) masc.} /Milòša (acc. = gen.) masc./ (lit. the proper name Miloš has been resemantized because it partially coincides with milicija 'police') *sl-crime* policeman, cop <SlavO[*1]>

mȉlovati {lujēm, lujū imperf.} (lit. pet) *sl* tap <Slav[*1]>

milozvúčnica {ē fem.} (lit. the nice-sounding thing) *sl* streetcar <Slav✣[*1]>

Mȉlū li ti mȁjčicu! {S} (lit. *I fuck* your dear mom!) *col* ***Off*** used as a moderate curse, Fuck you! ☞ **majčica**

milùnēr {unéra (acc. = gen.) masc.} [std. = milioner, milijuner] *sl* millionaire <Ita✣☞>

mȉlja {ē fem.} /mȋlja/ **a.** *sl* thousand dinars; a thousand-dinar bill, a grand <Lat[*1]> **b.i.** *sl* ten dinars; a ten-dinar bill <Lat[*2]> **ii.** *sl* ten thousand dinars; a ten thousand-dinars bill <Lat[*2]>

mȉljāk {miljáka masc.} *sl* thousand dinars; a thousand-dinar bill, a grand <Lat[*1]>

mȋljka {ē fem.} **a.** *sl* thousand dinars; a thousand-dinar bill, a grand <Lat[*1]> **b.** *sl* ten dinars; a ten-dinar bill <Lat[*2]>

míljkovac {vca (acc. = gen.) masc.} *sl-crime* policeman, cop <Lat☞>

mȉmohōd {a masc.} (lit. walking by) **1** *sl-sex* ***Fac*** buttocks petting <Slav[*1]> **2** *sl* station, stop (bus, train, streetcar, etc.) <Slav[*1]>

mimóza {ē fem.} (lit. mimosa, the plant) *sl-sex* ***Fac*** male homosexual, gay <Lat[*1]>

mìmpek {a masc.} *sl-sex* ***Obs*** penis, dick, prick

mȋna {ē fem.} /mȋna /e fem./ (lit. mine) *sl* cheating, swindling <Ger[*1]>
- **nágaznā mȋna** {NP} (lit. land mine) *sl* excrement

mȉnāć {a masc.} *sl* miniskirt <Lat✣>

mȉndros {a masc.} *sl-fea* unattractive person <**Rom**[*1]>

míndža {ē fem.} **/**mìndža, mȉndža**/** **a.** *sl-sex* ***Obs*** vagina, cunt <**Gyp**> **b.** *sl* ***Obs*** female, cunt <**Gyp**[*1]>
• **míndža s kȉtōm na budàli** {NP} (lit. a cunt with a prick on a fool) *sl* female with a boyfriend in front of her

mìndžina {ē fem.} *sl-sex* ***Obs*** vagina, cunt <**Gyp**❖>

mȉndžocūr {a masc.} (lit. cunt-leak) *sl-sex* ***Obs*** menstruation, period <**Gyp-Slav**[*1]>

mindžȍsava {ē fem.} **a.** *sl-sex* ***Obs*** vagina, cunt <**Gyp**✍> **b.** *sl* ***Obs*** female, cunt <**Gyp**✍[*1]>

mȉndžoslava {ē fem.} **a.** *sl-sex* ***Obs*** vagina, cunt <**Gyp**✍> **b.** *sl* ***Obs*** female, cunt <**Gyp**✍[*1]>

mȉndžosprēj {a masc.} (lit. cunt-spray) *sl-sex* ***Fac-Obs*** vaginal deodorant <**Gyp-Eng**[*1]>

mìndžulja {ē fem.} **a.** *sl-sex* ***Obs*** vagina, cunt <**Gyp**✍> **b.** *sl* ***Obs*** female, cunt <**Gyp**✍[*1]>

mȉnfora {excl.} *sl* watch out, be careful

Minhàuzen {a (acc. = gen.) masc.} (lit. Munchhausen) **a.** *sl-fea* boaster, braggart, blowhard <**GerO**[*1]> **b.** *sl-fea* accomplished liar <**GerO**[*2]>

mȉnī-mȍzak {zga (acc. = gen.) masc.} (lit. mini-brain) *sl-fea* stupid or mentally deficient person, pea brain <**Lat-Slav**[*1]>

mȉnica {ē fem.} *col* miniskirt <**Lat**❖>

mìnīć {miníća masc.} **1** *sl-auto* Mini Morris (make of car) <**BN**❖> **2** *sl* miniskirt <**Lat**❖>

minìfora {excl.} *sl* watch out, be careful

mìnika {ē fem.} *sl* miniskirt <**Lat**✍>

minimálac {lca masc.} *col* minimum wage (lowest wage guaranteed by the state) <**Lat**❖>

minìmālke {i fem. pl.} *sl* panties, briefs <**Lat**❖>

minírati {mìnīrām, minírajū biasp.} (lit. mine, blow up) **1** *sl-fea* cheat, swindle <**Ger**[*1]> **2** *sl-fea* work against something or somebody <**Ger**[*1]>
• **minírati fȁcu** {VP} (lit. mine someone's face) *sl* punch in the face

ministrànt {a (acc. = gen.) masc.} *sl* ***Fac*** church beggar <**Lat**[*1]>

ministrírati {nìstrīrām, nisrírajū biasp.} *sl* ***Fac*** beg, ask for money <**Lat**[*1]>

mìniška {ē fem.; Dat mìniški} *sl* miniskirt <**Lat**✍>

minivâl {a masc.} *col* body wave (a type of permanent) <**Lat-Slav**>

Mȉnken {a masc.} [std. = Minhen] *Gast col* name for Munich (city, Germany) <**GerO**✍>

mȉnte {eta masc.} *sl-arch* mind, brain

mintȅlija {ē masc.} *sl-fea* smart person, brain

mínus {a masc.} (lit. minus) **a.** *col* deficit (e.g. in trade) <**Lat**[*1]> **b.** *col* drawback, undesirable feature <**Lat**[*2]>

minúta *See the following*
• **žȗtā minúta** {NP} (lit. yellow minute) *sl-fea* loss of self-control

minutáža {ē fem.} *col* length in minutes, running time <**Fre**>

minùtnjāk {excl.} *sl* used to achieve a pause in conversation, one moment, please <**Lat**❖[*1]>

mìnjāk {minjáka masc.} *sl* mini skirt <**Lat**✍>

miràjzla {ē fem.} *sl* trifle, thing of little importance or value

mirȉsati {mìrišēm, išū imperf.} (lit. smell) **1** *sl* lie: *Mirisali su ga da će dobiti povišicu. They lied to him that he would get a raise.* <**Slav**[*1]> **2** *sl* beat up <**Slav**[*1]> **3** *sl* like (usu. in the negative form): *Ne mirišem Marka. I don't like Marko.* <**Slav**[*1]>
• **mirȉsati trávu iz kȍrēna** {VP} (lit. smell grass from the roots) *sl* die, kick the bucket

mirȍvnjāk {rovnjáka (acc. = gen.) masc.} *col* peace activist <**Slav**❖>

mìrsāl {mirsála masc.} *sl-sex* female who strongly wiggles her buttocks while walking

mȉsa {ē fem.} (lit. sermon) *sl-sex* ***Fac*** the act of pronouncing obscenities during sexual intercourse <**Lat**[*1]>

mìsica {ē fem.} **a.** *sl-fea* Miss (beauty queen, etc.) <**Eng**❖> **b.** *sl-fea* attractive woman <**Eng**❖[*1]>

misìdžija {ē masc.} *sl-fea* troublemaker, rowdy, ruffian

mȉsīm {excl.} [std. = mislim] *col* used to express hesitation, I mean, you know <**Slav**✍[*1]> ☞ **mislim**

misírac {rca masc.} *sl-crime* knife <**Ger**❖>

misírati {misírām, misírajū biasp.} *sl* cut <**Ger**❖>

misíriti {mìsīrīm, rē imperf.} *sl-arch* cut, slice

mìsīrka {ē fem.} **1a.** *sl* knife <**Ger**❖> **b.** *sl* axe <**Ger**❖> **2** *sl* turkey (the animal) <**Heb**[*1]>

miskìnjav {a, o adj.} *dia-col* small

mȉslilo {a neut.} (lit. thinker) **a.** *sl* brain <**Slav**[*1]> **b.** *sl* head <**Slav**[*2]>

mȉslīm {excl.} (lit. I think) *col* used to express hesitation, I think, I mean, you know <Slav*1> ☞ **misim**

mȉsliti {līm, lē imperf.} (lit. think) *sl-sports* play chess <Slav*1>

mìstrija {ē fem.} *sl-crime* knife <Ita*1>

mȉš {a +ev (ext. pl) masc.; Nom Pl mìševi} (lit. mouse) **a.** *sl-fea* ***Der*** coward, chicken <Slav*1> **b.** *sl-fea* ***Der*** unimportant person, nobody, nothing <Slav*2>
- **mȉš bêlī** {NP} (lit. white mouse) SerE *sl-fea* scientist

míša {ē fem.} *sl* meat <Alb>

mìšīć {mišíća masc.} (lit. muscle) **1** *sl-sex* ***Fac*** penis, love muscle <Slav*1> **2** *sl* ***Fac*** female <Slav*1>
- **ljùbavnī mìšīć** {NP} (lit. love muscle) *sl-sex* penis

mȉška {ē fem.; Dat mȉški} *sl-arch* meat <Alb☙>

mìškira {ē fem.} *sl-arch* meat <Alb☙>

mȉško [1] {a masc.} (lit. teddy bear) **1** *sl-sex* ***Fac*** penis <SlavO*1> **2a.** *sl-fea* coward, chicken <SlavO*1> **b.** *sl-fea* stupid or mentally deficient person <SlavO*2>

Mȉško [2] {a masc.} (lit. Miško was the name of a bus driver in "Ko to tamo peva", a popular Yugoslav movie) *sl-auto* driver <SlavO>

mȉšolōvka {ē fem.} (lit. mouse trap) *sl-crime* prison <Slav*1>

mitèlija {ē masc.} *sl-fea* wiseguy, smartass

mitìngāš {mitingáša (acc. = gen.) masc.} *sl-polit* person who takes part in public rallies <Eng⁘>

mitingášiti {tìngāšīm, šē imperf.} *sl-polit* take part in public rallies <Eng⁘>

mitraljézac {sca (acc. = gen.) masc.} (lit. machine gunner) *sl-fea* person who speaks fast <Fre⁘>

mitròljēz {mitroljéza masc.} [std. = mitraljez] *sl-dia* machine gun <Fre☙>

mitroljézac {sca (acc. = gen.) masc.} [std. = mitraljez] *col-dia* machine gunner <Fre⁘☙>

mȉžēnje {a neut.} *sl* sleeping <Ita>

mȉžiti {žīm, žē imperf.} *sl* sleep, nap <Ita>

mjȅhūr {a masc.} (lit. bulb, bladder) *sl-sex* ***Fac-Obs*** vagina, cunt <Slav*1>

mjȅsečār {a (acc. = gen.) masc.} (lit. sleepwalker) *sl-crime* roof-top burglar <Slav*1>

mjȅsečina {ē fem.} (lit. moonlight) **1** *sl-fea* bald male <Slav*1> **2a.** *sl-sex* male sexual partner (of a female) <Slav*1> **b.** *sl-sex* very potent male <Slav*2>

mjȅsečnjāk {a (acc. = gen.) masc.} *sl-sex* menstruation, period <Slav*1>

mjèšina *See the following*
- **ùznojenā mjèšina** {NP} (lit. sweating bag) *sl-fea* obese person

mjèzimac {mca (acc. = gen.) masc.} *col* beloved child, apple of one's eye <Slav*1>

mjȕra {ē fem.} *sl-crime* custody

mjûz {a +ev (ext. pl) masc.; Nom Pl mjúzevi} *sl-music* music <Eng☙>

mjúza {ē fem.} *sl-music* music <Eng☙>

mkàlo {a neut.} *sl-arch* dinner <Slav>

mkánje {a neut.} *sl-arch* night <Slav>

mlàdīć {mladíća (acc. = gen.) masc.} (lit. young man) **a.** *sl* lover (male) <Slav*1> **b.** *sl* boyfriend <Slav*2>

mladòstāš {dostáša (acc. = gen.) masc.} *sl-sports* player or fan of Mladost (a water-polo team from Zagreb, Croatia) <Slav⁘>

mladostàšica {ē fem.} *sl-sports* player or fan of Mladost (a water-polo team from Zagreb, Croatia) <Slav⁘>

mladúnac {nca (acc. = gen.) masc.} *sl* male, guy <Slav*1>

mlȁđā séka {NP} (lit. younger sister) *sl-fea* male who only walks his girlfriend and nothing else ☞ **seka**

mlákonja {ē fem.} (lit. the tepid one) *sl-fea* irresolute male, spineless guy <Slav⁘>

mlàtati {ām, ajū imperf.} *sl* cheat, swindle <Slav*1>

mlatikárēnje {a neut.} *sl-fea* prolonged and meaningless talk, blabber, chatter <Slav*1>

mlatikáriti {tìkārīm, rē imperf.} *sl-fea* talk persistently and meaninglessly, blabber, chatter <Slav*1>

mlátiti {tīm, tē imperf.} (lit. thrash) **1** *col* beat up, thrash <Slav*1> **2** *col* earn amply <Slav*1>
- **mlátiti Dèsānku Šȁkić** {VP} (lit. hit the Right Hand) *sl-sex* ***Fac-Obs*** masturbate, beat off
- **mlátiti lóvu** {VP} (lit. thresh money) *col* earn amply
- **mlátiti màjmuna** {VP} (lit. hit one's monkey) *sl-sex* ***Fac-Obs*** masturbate, spank the monkey
- **mlátiti práznu slȁmu** {VP} (lit. thresh empty straw) *col* spend one's time in useless activities, fool around, mess around

mlátiti se {tīm, tē imperf. intr.} (lit. beat oneself up) **1** *sl* fight (e.g. fist fight) <Slav*1> **2** *sl-fea* behave foolishly <Slav*1>

mlàtnuti {nēm, nū perf.} **a.** *col* hit, punch <Slav> **b.aa.** *sl-sex* engage in sexual intercourse with (of a male) <Slav[*1]> **bb.** *sl-sex* masturbate, beat off <Slav[*2]> **c.** *sl* eat, devour <Slav[*1]>

mlâz {a +ev (ext. pl) masc.; Nom Pl mlázevi} (lit. jet) *sl* dating, going out with <Slav[*1]>

- **na dvâ mlâza** {PP} (lit. on two streams) *sl-sex* after the second date
- **na jèdan mlâz** {PP} (lit. at one stream) *sl-sex* after the first date
- **na mlâz** {PP} (lit. on stream) *sl* at once

mlâznjāk {a (acc. = gen.) masc.} [std. = mlažnjak] *col* jet (plane) <Slav✍>

mlêčnjāk {a masc.} (lit. milker) SerE *sl-sex* ***Obs*** female breast, tit <Slav✣[*1]>

mlèkara {ē fem.} (lit. dairy) **a.** SerE *sl-sex* ***Fac-Obs*** large female breast <Slav✣[*1]> **b.** SerE *sl-sex* large-breasted female <Slav✣[*1]>

mlekârna *See the following*

- **Ljùbljanskā mlekârna** {NP} (lit. Ljubljana *Slovenia capital city* dairy plant) *sl-sex* ***Fac*** large-breasted female

mlèkulja {ē fem.} (lit. milking cow) SerE *sl-sex* ***Fac-Obs*** large-breasted female <Slav[*1]>

mlȅti {mȅljēm, ljū imperf.} SerE *sl-fea* talk persistently and meaninglessly, blabber, chatter <Slav[*1]>

mlíko {a neut.} [std. = mleko, mlijeko] Med *sl* milk <Slav✍>

mlȉn {a +ov (ext. pl) masc.} (lit. mill) *sl* head <Slav[*1]>

mlȉnār {a (acc. = gen.) masc.} (lit. miller) *sl-fea* extremely talkative person, chatterbox <Slav[*1]>

mlȉtonja {ē masc.} *sl-fea* ***Der*** irresolute male, spineless guy <Slav>

mlȍgo {adv.} [std. = mnogo] *col-dia* many, numerous <Slav✍>

mlȍhav {a, o adj.} *col* soft <Slav>

mljà {excl.} **a.** *col* slurp <Slav> **b.** *col* squish <Slav[*1]>

mljȁc {excl.} **a.** *col* slurp <Slav> **b.** *col* squish <Slav>

mljȁcav {a, o adj.} *col* slurping <Slav>

mljȁckānje {a neut.} *col* slurping <Slav>

mljȁckati {ām, ajū imperf.} *col* slurp <Slav>

mljȁckav {a, o adj.} *col* slurping <Slav>

mljȁs {excl.} *col* slurp <Slav>

mljȁsānje {a neut.} *col* slurping <Slav>

mljȁsati {ām, ajū imperf.} *col* slurp <Slav>

mljȁskav {a, o adj.} *col* slurping <Slav>

mljȁti {mlîm, mlȉjū imperf.} Mont *dia* think, ponder <Slav>

mljâz {a (acc. = gen.) +ev (ext. pl) masc.; Nom Pl mljázevi} *sl-fea* street cleaner, street sweeper <Slav✍>

mljêčnjak {a masc.} (lit. milker) **1** *sl-sex* ***Fac*** female breast <Slav✣[*1]> **2** *col* dairy restaurant <Slav✣[*1]> **3** *sl-fea* inexperienced youngster <Slav✣[*1]>

mljèkara *See the following*

- **zágrebačkā mljèkara** {NP} (lit. Zagreb dairy) Cro *sl-sex* large female breast

mljekárstvo {a neut.} (lit. dairy) *sl-sex* ***Fac-Obs*** large female breast <Slav[*1]>

- **gràdskō mljekárstvo** {NP} (lit. city's dairy company) *sl-sex* ***Fac*** large female breasts

mljȅti {mlîm, mlê imperf.} (lit. mill, grind) *col* talk persistently and meaninglessly, blabber, chatter <Slav[*1]>

- **mljȅti glúposti** {VP} (lit. mill stupidities) *sl-fea* talk persistently and meaninglessly, blabber, chatter

mmm {excl.} /mmmm/ **1** *col* used to express satisfaction with food, mmm <Slav> **2** *col* used to express hesitation, mmm <Slav>

mnȍgo *See the following*

- **Mnȍgo mi se [VERB:PRESENT]** {S} (lit. [PRON] are/is [VERB:PRESENT] too much) *col* used to intensify one's claims, [PRON] are/is really [VERB:PRESENT]: *Mnogo mi se foliraš. You are really showing off.*

móca {ē fem.} *sl* female

móča {ē fem.} **1** *sl-drugs* hashish oil, hash oil <Slav[*1]> **2** *col* sauce <Slav[*1]>

mòčati {ām, ajū imperf.} (lit. wet) *sl-sex* ***Obs*** urinate <Slav[*1]>

mòčēnje {a neut.} (lit. wet) *sl-sex* ***Obs*** sexual intercourse <Slav[*1]>

Močigùzica {ē fem.} (lit. wet ass) *col* name of an island in Croatia <Slav>

mòčiti {čīm, čē imperf.} (lit. wet) *sl-sex* ***Obs*** engage in sexual intercourse with (of a male) <Slav[*1]>

mȍćan {ćna, ćno adj.} (lit. powerful) **a.** *col* skillful <Slav[*1]> **b.** *col* excellent, cool: *moćan sat cool watch* <Slav[*2]> **c.** *col* funny <Slav[*3]>

mòćati {ām, ajū imperf. intr.} *sl-sex* urinate <Slav[*1]>

mòći {perf. irreg.} *col* like (usu. in the negative form): *Ne mogu njegovu sestru nikako. I really don't like his sister.*

<Slav*1>

• **mòći pjȅvati bòrbenē** {VP} (lit. be able to sing combat songs) *col* be in a very difficult situation

• **mòći se slȉkati** {VP} (lit. be able to take one's photo) *sl-fea* be in a very difficult situation

• **Mȍgū da mi pljȕnū pod prózor!** {S} (lit. They can spit in front of my window!) *col* used to express the state of not being threatened, They can't do a thing to me!

• **Mȍgū da mi pȑdnū pod prózor!** {S} (lit. They can fart in front of my window!) *col* used to express the state of not being threatened, They can't do a thing to me!

• **mòre bȉt** {VP} (lit. it can be) *dia* supposedly

• **mȍre li òvā** {VP} (lit. can this go) *dia* used to stress one's point, how is this

• **mȍš mȉsiti** {VP} (lit. can you think) *col* ***Iro*** used to underestimate an object, plan, achievement, etc., big deal

• **mȍš mȉsliti** {VP} (lit. can you think) **a.** *col* ***Iro*** used to express surprise, astonishment, etc. **b.** used to underestimate an object, plan, achievement, etc., big deal

• **mȍšte mȉsiti** {VP} (lit. can you think) *col* ***Iro*** used to underestimate an object, plan, achievement, etc., big deal

• **mȍšte mȉsliti** {VP} (lit. can you think) **a.** *col* ***Iro*** used to express surprise, astonishment, etc. **b.** *col* used to underestimate an object, plan, achievement, etc., big deal

• **Mȍže da mi pljȕnē pod prózor!** {S} (lit. He/she can spit in front of my window!) *col* used to express the state of not being threatened, He/she can't do a thing to me!

• **Mȍže da mi pȑdnē pod prózor!** {S} (lit. He/she can fart in front of my window!) *col* used to express the state of not being threatened, You can't do a thing to me!

• **Mòže ì tāj kȕrac bȉti!** {S} (lit. That cock can be as well!) *col* ***Obs*** used to express a moderate probability

• **mȍže prȍć** {VP} (lit. it can pass) *col* used to express hesitant approval: *A: Kakav je bio film? B: Može proć. A: What was the movie like? B: Well, it was ok.*

• **Mȍžeš da mi pljȕnēš pod prózor!** {S} (lit. You can spit in front of my window!) *col* used to express the state of not being threatened, You can't do a thing to me!

• **Mȍžēš da mi pȑdnēš pod prózor!** {S} (lit. You can fart in front of my window!) *col* used to express the state of not being threatened, You can't do a thing to me!

• **Mȍžeš mi napúhati jája!** {S} (lit. You can inflate my testicles!) *col* used to express the state of not being threatened, You can't do a thing to me!

• **Mȍžeš múda od lȁbūda!** {S} (lit. You can swan's balls!) *col* used to express the state of not being threatened, You can't do a thing to me!

• **Mȍžeš tȋ da je pòpušīš!** {S} (lit. You can blow it!) *col* ***Off*** used to express the state of not being threatened, You can't do a thing to me!

• **mȍžete mȉsliti** {VP} (lit. can you think) *col* used to stress the fact considered unusual, Can you imagine that?

• **ne mògu ȍd smijēha**{VP} (lit. I cannot from laughing) **a.** *sl* used as a strong negative response, no way, never **b.** *sl* used to indicate the lack of money

• **Nêće mòći òvē nȍći!** {VP} (lit. It will be impossible this night!) *col* used as a strong negative response, no way, never

mȍćno {adv.} (lit. powerfully) *col* ***App*** excellent, awesome <Slav*1>

modèrnjāk {dernjáka (acc. = gen.) masc.} *sl-music* modern musical score <Slav❖>

môdnjāk {a (acc. = gen.) masc.} **1** *col* boutique <Fre❖> **2** *col* fashion journal <Fre❖>

mȍdrī cvȉjēt {NP} (lit. blue flower) *sl-sex* ***Fac-Obs*** buttocks, butt ☞ **cvijet**

mòdriti {rīm, rē imperf.} (lit. blue) *sl-sex* rape <Slav*1>

Mȍgu da mi dúvajū! {S} (lit. They can blow me!) *col* ***Obs*** used to express the state of not being threatened, You can't do a thing to me! ☞ **duvati**

môj {pron.} (lit. mine) *sl-sex* penis <Slav*1>

• **Dò mōga!** {PP} (lit. to mine) *sl* ***Obs*** used to express anger, Fuck it!

• **Do mòjēga!** {PP} (lit. to mine) *sl* ***Obs*** used to express anger, Fuck it!

• **Kȍj ćeš mi môj!** {S} (lit. Which mine do I need you!) *dia* ***Off*** used in angry dismissal, Fuck off!

• **Kȍj ti je môj!** {S} (lit. Which mine is it to you!) *dia* ***Off*** used in angry dismissal, Fuck off!

• **mà môj** {VP} (lit. well, yes) *col* affirmative used in response to 'ma nemoj', oh, yes

• **Môj ti o dèsno rȁme!** {S} (lit. My *prick* to your right sholder!) *col* ***Off-Fac*** used as a weak curse, Screw you!

• **Môj ti pod glàvicu!** {S} (lit. My *prick* to under your little head!) *col* ***Off*** used as a moderate curse, Fuck you!

• **Môj ti pod lêvō kòleno!** {S} (lit. My *prick* to your left knee!) SerE *col* ***Off*** used as a moderate curse, Fuck you!

• **Môj ti pod mȉšku!** {S} (lit. My *prick* in your armpit!) *col* ***Off*** used as a moderate curse, Fuck you!

• **Môj ti u dȕpe!** {S} (lit. My *prick* to your ass!) *col* ***Off*** used as a moderate curse, Fuck you!

• **Môj ti uz dȕpe!** {S} (lit. My *prick* up your ass!) *col* ***Off*** used as a moderate curse, Fuck you!

• **Môj ti za rȁdos!** {S} (lit. My *prick* for you to be happy!) *dia* ***Off*** used as a moderate curse, Fuck you!

• **Môj ti za vèčeru!** {S} (lit. My *prick* to your supper!) *col* ***Off*** used as a moderate curse, Fuck you!

• **Nà moj, cȅ!** {S} (lit. To my *prick*, yeah!) *dia* ***Off*** used as a moderate curse, Fuck you!

• **Nà moj, nȁ!** {S} (lit. To my *prick*, here!) *dia* ***Off*** used as a moderate curse, Fuck you!

• **Prez mòjēga!** {S} (lit. Through my *prick*!) *dia* ***Obs*** used as a strong negative response, no way, never

• **Za kȍj si môj!** {S} (lit. For which mine are you!) SerE *dia* ***Off*** used as a weak curse, Screw you!

• **za kòjī môj** {PP} (lit. for which mine) *sl* why

môj brâjko {NP} (lit. my bro) *col* used to address a male in direct informal communication, bro ☞ **brajko**

Môj kâr! {S} (lit. my prick) *col* ***Obs*** used to express disappointment, Fuck it! ☞ **kar**

Môj kûr! {S} (lit. my prick) *col* ***Obs*** used to express disappointment , Fuck it! ☞ **kur**

môj náklon {NP} (lit. My bow!) *col* used to greet ☞ **naklon**

mòja {pron.} (lit. mine) *sl-sex* vagina <**Slav*1**>

mȍjne {excl.; perm} /mòjne/ [std. = nemoj] *sl* used to prevent action <**Slav✍**>

Mȍjne tȉsra! {S} (lit. Don't shit!) *sl* ***Obs*** used to express disbelief, Don't give me that shit! ☞ **tisra**

mòjnegadèntro {excl.; perm} *sl* used to prevent the action of putting something in a wrong place, Don't put it where it does not belong! <**Slav✍**>

mòjnegastèrmo {excl.} *sl* used to prevent the action of putting something in a wrong place, Don't put it where it does not belong! <**Slav✍**>

mójo {a masc.} *sl-drugs* smuggled narcotic drugs

mȍkar {mòkra, kro adj.} (lit. wet) *sl-drink* ***Fac*** drunk, pickled <**Slav*1**>

• **mȍkar do pápka** {AdjP} (lit. wet to his hoofs) **a.** *sl-fea* sweating **b.** *sl-sex* sexually aroused, hot, wet

mokasína {ē fem.} (lit. moccasin) **a.** *sl-sex* ***Fac*** hymen <**Ind*1**> **b.** *sl-sex* ***Fac*** virginity <**Ind*2**>

mȍkī [1] {īja (acc. = gen.) masc.} /mòki/ *sl-fea* stupid or mentally deficient person <**Eng✍**>

mȍkī [2] {īja masc.} /mòki/ *sl-drugs* morphine <**Gre✍**>

mȍkica {ē fem.} /mòkica/ *sl-drugs* morphine <**Gre✍**>

mókiti {kīm, kē imperf. intr.} *sl-sex* urinate <**Slav✍**>

mȍkrā {ē fem. (adj. decl.)} /mòkra/ (lit. the wet one) *sl-sex* passionate female <**Slav*1**>

mȍkrī brȁt {NP} (lit. wet brother) *sl-drink* alcoholic, drunk ☞ **brat**

mòkriti {rīm, rē imperf.} (lit. wet) **1** *sl-sex* urinate <**Slav*1**> **2** *sl* cry, shed tears, weep <**Slav*1**>

mòkriti se {rīm, rē imperf. intr.} (lit. wet oneself) *sl* wash oneself <**Slav*1**>

mȍlću fȋno {VP} (lit. I will ask you nicely) *col* used to support one's request, please ☞ **moliti**

mȍlću lêpo {VP} (lit. I will ask you nicely) SerE *col* used to emphasize one's request, please ☞ **moliti**

molèkula {ē fem.} (lit. molecule) *sl-sstu* chemistry teacher <**Gre*1**>

mȍler {a (acc. = gen.) masc.} *col* wall painter <**Ger**>

mȍlīm {excl.} *col* used to respond to thanking, you are welcome <**Slav**>

mòliti *See the following*

• **kàd te lêpo mȍlīm** {S} (lit. when I beg you nicely) SerE *col* used to emphasize one's request, pretty please

• **kàd te lijèpo mȍlīm** {S} (lit. when I beg you nicely) *col* used to emphasize one's request, pretty please

• **mòlću fȋno** {VP} (lit. I will ask you nicely) *col* used to support one's request, please

• **mòlću lêpo** {VP} (lit. I will ask you nicely) SerE *col* used to emphasize one's request, please

• **mòlīću fȋno** {VP} (lit. I will ask you nicely) *col* used to emphasize one's request, please

• **mòlīću lêpo** {VP} (lit. I will ask you nicely) SerE *col* used to emphasize one's request, please

• **mȍlīm lêpo** {VP} (lit. I am asking you nicely) SerE *col* used to express approval, so be it

• **mȍlīm lijèpo** {VP} (lit. I am asking you nicely) *col* used to express approval, so be it

• **mȍlīm te** {VP} (lit. I am asking you) *col* used to stress the fact considered unusual, Can you imagine that?: *Ona, molim te, obojila kosu u zeleno. She dyed her hair green, can you imagine that!*

• **mȍlīm vas** {VP} (lit. I am asking you) *col* used to stress the fact considered unusual, Can you imagine that?

mòlitva *See the following*

• **Mòlitvu ti jèbēm!** {S} (lit. I fuck your prayer!) *dia* ***Off*** used as a moderate curse, Fuck you!

mȍlovān {a, o adj.} (lit. painted) *sl-fea* with make-up on, painted <**Ger*1**>

mȍlovati {lujēm, lujū imperf.} (lit. paint) **a.** *sl-fea* lie <**Ger*1**> **b.** *sl-fea* cheat, swindle <**Ger*2**>

móljac {ljca (acc. = gen.) masc.} (lit. moth) **1** *sl-fea* bald male <**Slav*1**> **2** *sl-sstu* high-school senior <**Slav*1**> **3** *sl-fea* boring person, bore <**Slav*1**>

• **knjȉškī móljac** {NP} *col* book worm (figuratively)

mòmak {mka (acc. = gen.) masc.} (lit. young man) **a.** *col* lover (male) <**Slav*1**> **b.** *col* boyfriend <**Slav*2**>

mômče {eta neut.} *col-dia* boy, kid <Slav>

mòmčina {ē masc.} (lit. big boy) *sl-fea* big-boned male, big boy <Slav>

mòmenat {excl.} (lit. moment) *col* used to ask for a pause, one moment <Lat[*1]> ☞ **moment, sekundu, trenutak**

mòment {excl.} (lit. moment) *col* used to ask for a pause, one moment <Lat[*1]> ☞ **momenat, sekundu, trenutak**

momòruz {a masc.} *dia* corn

momòruza {ē fem.} *dia-col* corn

mȍnd {a masc.} **a.** *sl* coat (outer garment) <Ger[*1]> **b.** *sl-sex* condom, rubber <Ger[*2]>

mòndiš {adj.} *sl-fea* modern <Ger>

monòkl {a masc.} (lit. monocle) *sl-fea* eye bruise, shiner <Gre-Lat[*1]>

mònsūnskī perìod {NP} (lit. monsoon period) *sl* crying time ☞ **period**

montárac {rca masc.} **a.** *sl* coat (outer garment) <BN❖[*1]> **b.** *sl-sex* condom, rubber <BN❖[*2]>

montáža {ē fem.} **a.** *sl-crafts* assembly <Fre> **b.** *sl* intrigue <Fre[*1]>

Montenegríner {a (acc. = gen.) masc.} *sl-fea* ***Der*** Montenegrin (person) <ItaO✍>

Monteníger {a (acc. = gen.) masc.} *sl-fea* ***Off*** Montenegrin (person) <ItaO✍>

mòntēr {montéra (acc. = gen.) masc.} (lit. assembler) *sl-fea* gynecologist <Fre[*1]>

mòntēr grâbā {NP} (lit. cunt assembler) *sl-sex* ***Fac-Obs*** gynecologist's dispensary ☞ **graba**

montírānje {a neut.} **a.** *sl-crafts* assembling <Fre[*1]> **b.i.** *sl-fea* intriguing <Fre[*2]> **ii.** *sl-sex* sexual intercourse <Fre[*2]>

montírati {mòntīrām, montajū biasp.} **a.** *sl-crafts* assemble, mount <Fre[*1]> **b.i.** *sl-fea* insinuate <Fre[*2]> **ii.** *sl-sex* engage in sexual intercourse with (of a male) <Fre[*2]>

montírati se {mòntīrām, ajū biasp.} (lit. assemble oneself) *sl-fea* dress formally, dress up <Fre[*1]>

monumȅnt {a masc.} (lit. monument) *sl* promenade <Lat[*1]>

mopasân {adv.} *col* by the way <Fre✍>
- **nȍćnā mòra** {NP} *col* nightmare

mòrāl {morála masc.} (lit. moral) *sl-drink* brandy <Lat[*1]>

mȍre {excl.} *col* used to address a person in direct informal communication, hey <NE>
- **Mòre kòmē mâjku brȅ!** {S} (lit. To whom *are you fucking* mother!) **SerE** *col* ***Off*** used as a threat in response to a strong curse, Fuck you!
- **Mòre mâjku ti màngupskū!** {S} (lit. *I fuck* your joker's mother!) *col* ***Off*** used as a strong curse, Fuck you!

mȍrfo {a neut.} [std. = morfin] *sl-drugs* morphine <Gre✍>

mòre bȉt {VP} (lit. it can be) *dia* supposedly ☞ **moći**

mȍre li òvā {VP} (lit. can this go) *dia* used to stress one's point, how is this ☞ **moći**

mòrgen *See the following*
- **màlo mòrgen** {AdvP} *col* never

mȍri {excl.} *dia* used to address a person in direct informal communication, hey <Gre>

mòrica {ē fem.} **1** *sl-arch* flea (the insect) **2** *sl-arch* louse (the insect)

mòriti se {rīm, rē imperf. intr.} (lit. get tired) **a.** *sl* long, desire <Slav[*1]> **b.** *sl* daydream <Slav[*2]>

mòriza {ē fem.} **1** *sl* flea (the insect) **2** *sl* louse (the insect)

mòrnār {mornára (acc. = gen.) masc.} (lit. sailor) BosM *col* pork <Slav[*1]>

mòrōn {moróna (acc. = gen.) masc.} *sl-fea* stupid or mentally deficient person <Gre[*1]>

mòrskā gáža {NP} (lit. seashore gig) *sl-music* summer job for an orchestra ☞ **gaža**

mòrskī {ā, ō adj.} (lit. seashore) **a.** *sl-fea* unintelligent, stupid, dumb <Slav[*1]> **b.** *sl-fea* strange, weird <Slav[*2]>

mòrskī trȅn {NP} (lit. seashore train) *sl* steam ship ☞ **tren**

mòrtus [1] {adj.} **1** *sl-fea* broke (financially) <Lat[*1]> **2** *sl-fea* tired <Lat[*1]> **3** *sl-drink* drunk <Lat[*1]>

mòrtus [2] {adv.} *sl* completely, totally, dead: *mortus pjan dead drunk* <Lat[*1]>

mòrtus pìjan {AdjP} (lit. dead drunk) *col* very drunk, dead drunk ☞ **pijan**

mòrtus pjȁn {AdjP} (lit. dead drunk) *col* very drunk, dead drunk ☞ **pijan**

mòrzeovac {vca (acc. = gen.) masc.} **1** *sl-fea* ***Der*** informer, stoolie, snitch <EngO[*1]> **2** *sl-fea* person who speaks with unintelligible pronunciation <EngO[*1]>

Mosòrija {ē fem.} Cro *sl* name for Mosor restaurant at Jelačićev Square in Zagreb, Croatia <SlavO[*1]>

môst {mȍsta +ov (ext. pl) masc.; Nom Pl mȍstovi} (lit. bridge) *sl-sports* sign 1 (home team wins) and 2 (visitors win) on a sport betting coupon (i.e. one bets that a game of soccer will not end with a tied score) <Slav[*1]>

mòstati {ām, ajū imperf.} *sl* keep one's mouth shut

mòstiti {tīm, tē imperf.} *sl* keep one's mouth shut

mȍš mȉsiti {VP} (lit. can you think) *col* ***Iro*** used to underestimate an object, plan, achievement, etc., big deal ☞ **moći**

mȍš mȉsliti {VP} (lit. can you think) **a.** *col* ***Iro*** used to express surprise, astonishment, etc. **b.** *col* used to underestimate an object, plan, achievement, etc. ☞ **moći**

móša {ē fem.} **1** *sl* sister, sis **2** *sl* game based on hitting each other in the stomach

mȍšt {a +ov (ext. pl) masc.; Nom Pl mȍštovi} (lit. must, unfermented or fermenting juice) *sl-sex* ***Fac-Obs*** large vagina <Ger[*1]>

mȍšte mȉsiti {VP} (lit. can you think) *col* ***Iro*** used to underestimate an object, plan, achievement, etc. ☞ **moći**

mȍšte mȉsliti {VP} (lit. can you think) **a.** *col* ***Iro*** used to express surprise, astonishment, etc. **b.** *col* used to underestimate an object, plan, achievement, etc. ☞ **moći**

mòtārnīk {a masc.} *sl-sex* ***Fac-Obs*** bathroom

mòtati {ām, ajū imperf.} (lit. roll) **1** *col* eat, devour <Slav[*1]> **2a.** *col* flirt <Slav[*1]> **b.** *col* cheat, swindle <Slav[*2]> **c.** *col* joke with, make a fool of <Slav[*3]> **3** *col* roll a cigarette or joint <Slav[*1]>
- **mòtati oko (mâlōg) pȑsta** {VP} (lit. wind around the pinkie) *col* manipulate a person: *Njegova žena mota ga oko malog prsta. His wife manipulates him.*

motavȉška {adj.; Dat motavȉški} /motavìška/ *sl-fea* intelligent, smart, bright <Gyp>

mòtika {ē fem.} *sl-fea* unattractive female <Slav[*1]>

mótiti {tīm, tē imperf.} *sl* run away, flee

mȍtka {ē fem.; Dat mȍtki} (lit. stick) **1a.** *sl-fea* slender person <Slav[*1]> **b.** *sl-fea* tall and slender female, beanpole <Slav[*2]> **c.** *sl* fashion model <Slav[*2]> **2** *sl-sstu* math <Slav[*1]>

motocángle {i fem. pl.} (lit. biker's pliers) *sl-crafts* ***Fac*** name for a nonexistent kind of pliers used to joke with people without knowledge of tools <Ger✍>

motorȉška {ē fem.; Dat motorȉški} /motorìška/ *sl-auto* motorcycle <Lat✍>

mótovi {tōvā masc. pl.} *sl-sex* ***Obs*** excrement

mȍzak {zga masc.} (lit. brain) **1** *sl* head <Slav[*1]> **2** *col* smart person, brain <Slav[*1]>
- **u bȍlestan mȍzak** {PP} *col* against common sense
- **u mâlī mȍzak**{PP} *col* intensely (usu. being disturbed, bothered, etc.)
- **u mȍzak** {PP} (lit. in the brain) *sl-fea* skillfully
- **U mȍzak te jèbēm!** {S} (lit. I fuck you in your brain!) *col-dia* ***Off*** used as a moderate curse, Fuck you!
- **u zdrȁv mȍzak** {PP} (lit. in the healthy brain) *col* against common sense

mòzgāroš {a (acc. = gen.) masc.} *sl-fea* smart male, brain <Slav✣>

mòzgati {ām, ajū imperf. intr.} (lit. use one's brain) *col* think, ponder (usu. in an attempt to find a solution to a problem) <Slav✣[*1]>

mȍzges *See the following*
- **dès mȍzges** {NP} *sl-fea* smart person, brain

mòžda {part.} *col* maybe <Slav>

Mȍže da mi pljȕnē pod prózor! {S} (lit. He/she can spit in front of my window!) *col* used to express the state of not being threatened ☞ **moći**

Mȍže da mi pȑdnē pod prózor! {S} (lit. He/she can fart in front of my window!) *col* used to express the state of not being threatened ☞ **moći**

Mȍže ì tāj kȕrac bȉti! {S} (lit. That cock can be as well!) *col* ***Obs*** used to express a moderate probability ☞ **moći**

mȍže prôć {VP} (lit. it can pass) *col* used to express hesitant approval, well, ok: *A: Kakav je bio film? B: Može proć. A: What was the movie like? B: Well, it was ok.*

Mȍžeš da mi pljȕnēš pod prózor! {S} (lit. You can spit in front of my window!) *col* used to express the state of not being threatened ☞ **moći**

Mȍžèš da mi pȑdnēš pod prózor! {S} (lit. You can fart in front of my window!) *col* used to express the state of not being threatened ☞ **moći**

Mȍžeš mi napúhati jája! {S} (lit. You can blow my balls!) *col* used to express the state of not being threatened ☞ **moći**

Mȍžeš múda od lȁbūda! {S} (lit. You can swan's balls!) *col* used to express the state of not being threatened ☞ **moći**

Mȍžeš tî da je pòpušīš! {S} (lit. You can blow it!) *col* ***Off*** used to express the state of not being threatened ☞ **moći**

mȍžete mȉsliti {VP} (lit. can you think) *col* used to stress the fact considered unusual, Can you imagine that? ☞ moći

mráčan {čna, čno adj.} /mrâčan/ (lit. dark) 1 *sl-fea* blind <Slav*1> 2 *sl-fea* excellent, awesome <Slav*1>

mrâčnjāk {a (acc. = gen.) masc.} /mràčnjāk/ (lit. dark one) 1 *sl* night train <Slav⁘*1> 2 *sl-fea* evil person <Slav⁘*1> 3 *sl* female <Slav⁘*1>

mrâk [1] {a (acc. = gen.) +ov (ext. pl) masc.; Nom Pl mrȁkovi} (lit. darkness) *sl-fea* stupid or mentally deficient person <Slav*1>

mrâk [2] {a +ov (ext. pl) masc.; Nom Pl mrȁkovi} (lit. darkness) 1 *sl-sex* ***Fac*** virginity <Slav*1> 2 *sl-fea* ***Der*** stupidity, lack of intelligence <Slav*1> 3 *sl-fea* ***App*** something excellent, something cool <Slav*1>

mrâk [3] {adj.} (lit. darkness) *sl-fea* ***App*** excellent, awesome: *Kupila je neku mrak suknju. She bought an awesome skirt.* <Slav*1>

mrâk [4] {adv.} (lit. darkness) *sl-fea* ***App*** excellent, awesome: *U diskoteci je bilo mrak. We had an awesome time in the discotheque.* <Slav*1>

mrȁka {ē fem.; Dat mrȁki} (lit. the dark place) *sl-crime* prison cell <Slav⁘*1>

mràkača {ē fem.} (lit. big darkness) *sl* darkness <Slav⁘>

mràkanja {ē fem.} (lit. darkness) *sl-crime* prison <Slav⁘*1>

mrákonja {ē masc.} (lit. dark one) *sl-fea* ***Off*** African American (male) <Slav*1>

mràkuša [1] {ē fem.} *sl-fea* darkness <Slav✍>

mràkuša [2] {adj.} (lit. darkness) *sl-fea* ***App*** excellent, awesome <Slav✍>

mravìjati {ām, ajū biasp.} *sl* walk <Slav>

mràvinjāk {a masc.} (lit. ant hill) *sl* dance floor <Slav*1>

mravírati {mràvīrām, mravírajū biasp.} 1 *sl* walk <Slav*1> 2 *sl* work, labor <Slav*1>

mȑc {a (acc. = gen.) masc.} [std. = mrtvac] *dia-col* dead person <Slav✍>

mȑcan {a (acc. = gen.) masc.} (lit. corpse) *sl-fea* senior citizen <Slav✍*1>

mȑcī {īja (acc. = gen.) masc.} *sl-fea* senior citizen <Slav✍>

mȑcina {ē fem.} (lit. corpse) 1 *sl-fea* senior citizen <Slav⁘*1> 2 *sl-fea* weak male, wimp <Slav⁘*1>

mȑcko {a (acc. = gen.) masc.} (lit. small corpse) *sl-fea* senior citizen <Slav*1>

mrcodáviti {còdāvīm, vē imperf.} *sl-sex* ***Fac-Obs*** engage in sexual intercourse with (of a male) <Slav✍>

mȑcoš {a (acc. = gen.) masc.} *sl-fea* senior citizen <Slav*1>

mȑčēnje {a neut.} *sl-sex* ***Obs*** sexual intercourse <Slav*1>

mȑčiti {čīm, čē imperf.} *sl-sex* ***Obs*** engage in sexual intercourse with (of a male) <Slav*1>

mȑdāljka {ē fem.} /mȑdāljka/ (lit. mover) **a.** *sl-sex* ***Fac*** loose woman <Slav*1> **b.** *sl-sex* ***Fac*** lover (female) <Slav*2>

mȑdānje {a neut.} **a.** *sl* fidgeting: *Njeno neprestano mrdanje me nervira. Her constant fidgeting gets on my nerves.* <Slav*1> **b.** *sl-crime* stealing, swiping <Slav*2> **c.** *sl-sex* sexual intercourse <Slav*3>

mȑdati {ām, ajū imperf.} **a.** *sl* fidget: *Ne mrdaj ispred televizora. Don't fidget in front of the tv.* <Slav> **b.** *sl-sex* engage in sexual intercourse with (of a male) <Slav*1>

mȑdnuti {nēm, nū perf.} **a.** *sl* move, change the position of <Slav*1> **b.** *sl* hit, punch: *mrdnuti frajera u njušku hit a guy in the face* <Slav*2> **c.** *sl-crime* steal, swipe: *mrdnuti novčanik steal a wallet* <Slav*3> **d.** *sl-sex* engage in sexual intercourse with (of a male) <Slav*4>

mȑđati {ām, ajū imperf.} *sl* mumble <Slav⁘>

mrȅlo {a neut.} *sl-arch* umbrella <Ita✍>

mrèljāš {mreljáša (acc. = gen.) masc.} *sl-crime* prisoner <Ita✍*1>

mrȅškati se {ām, ajū imperf. intr.} (lit. wrinkle) *sl* move in an effort to assume a position

mȑga {ē masc.; Dat mȑgi} *sl-fea* muscular male <Slav*1>

mȑgūd {a (acc. = gen.) masc.} *sl-fea* gloomy person <Slav*1>

mȑha {ē masc.; Dat mȑhi} *sl-fea* muscular male

mrìdžati {ām, ajū imperf.} *sl* mumble <Slav⁘>

mȑka {ē fem.} *sl* night <Slav⁘>

mȑkālj {a (acc. = gen.) masc.} *dia* black ram <Slav>

mŕkānje {a neut.} *sl-arch* night <Slav*1>

mŕkati {mȑkām, mŕkajū imperf.} *sl-sex* engage in sexual intercourse with (of sheep) <Slav>

mȑklā {ē fem. (adj. decl.)} *sl-fea* night <Slav*1>

mŕknuti [1] {mȑknēm, nū perf.} /mȑknuti/ *sl-crime* steal, swipe <Slav*1>

mȑknuti [2] {nēm, nū perf.} (lit. darken) *sl* hit, punch <Slav*1>

mȑkonja {ē masc.} *sl-arch* eating dinner <Slav>

mȑkonju {adv.} *sl* at night <**Slav**✍>

mr̀kōv {mrkòva (acc. = gen.) masc.} *col* dark-colored horse <**Slav**⁘[*1]>

mȑkšan {a masc.} *sl-arch* night <**Slav**✍>

mr̀kšant {a masc.} *sl* night <**Slav**✍>

mr̀kulja {ē fem.} (lit. the dark one) *sl-crime* name of a prison in Stara Gradiška, Croatia <**Slav**[*1]>

mȑkva {ē fem.} (lit. carrot) **1** *sl* ***Fac*** nose <**Slav**[*1]> **2** *sl-fea* redheaded person, carrot top <**Slav**[*1]>

mȑlja {ē fem.} (lit. stain) *sl-fea* ten dinars; a ten-dinar bill <**Slav**[*1]>

mȑljav {a, o adj.} (lit. with stains) *sl-fea* weak, lacking physical strength <**Slav**[*1]>

mrljáviti {mȑljāvīm, vē imperf.} **1** *sl-fea* work <**Slav**[*1]> **2** *sl-fea* eat poorly <**Slav**[*1]>

mr̀ljimuda {ē masc.} *sl-fea* ***Der-Fac*** worthless or despicable person <**Slav**⁘[*1]>

mȑma *See the following*

• **mȑma dròbātor u rȕpi** {NP} *sl* night bar janitor

mȑmāč {a (acc. = gen.) masc.} *sl-fea* priest <**Slav**⁘[*1]>

mŕmak {mka (acc. = gen.) masc.} *sl-crime* clothing thief <**Slav**[*1]>

mr̀mljānje {a neut.} *col* mumbling <**Slav**>

mr̀mljati {ām, ajū imperf.} *sl-fea* mumble <**Slav**>

mr̀mljavac {vca (acc. = gen.) masc.} *sl-fea* mumbling male, mumbles <**Slav**⁘[*1]>

mŕmljo {ē masc.} *sl-fea* mumbling male, mumbles <**Slav**⁘[*1]>

mrmòkati {očēm, očū imperf.} *col* mumble <**Slav**>

mr̀moljiti {ljīm, ljē imperf.} *col* mumble <**Slav**>

mȑmor {a masc.} *col* gurgle (creek, etc.) <**Slav**>

mrmòrav {a, o adj.} *col* gurgling (creek, etc.) <**Slav**>

mr̀morēnje {a neut.} *col* gurgling (creek, etc.) <**Slav**>

mr̀moriti {rīm, rē imperf.} *col* gurgle (creek, etc.) <**Slav**>

mr̀mositi {sīm, sē imperf.} *col* gurgle (creek, etc.) <**Slav**>

mȑmot {a (acc. = gen.) masc.} **a.** *col* gopher <**Slav**> **b.i.** *sl* male, guy <**Slav**[*1]> **ii.** *sl-fea* stupid or mentally deficient person <**Slav**[*1]>

mrmòtati {mr̀moćēm, oćū imperf. intr.} *col* gurgle (creek, etc.) <**Slav**>

mr̀motka {ē fem.; Dat mr̀motki} *sl* female <**Slav**[*1]>

mȑndžānje {a neut.} *sl-fea* prolonged and meaningless talk, blabber, chatter <**Slav**>

mȑndžati {ām, ajū imperf.} *sl-fea* talk persistently and meaninglessly, blabber, chatter <**Slav**>

mŕsiti {mr̂sīm, sē imperf.} *sl* spoil, interfere, mess up: *Šef mi je pomrsio planove za odmor. My boss has spoiled my vacation plans.* <**Slav**[*1]>

• **mŕsiti múda** {VP} (lit. mix one's balls) *sl-fea* spend one's time in useless activities, fool around, mess around

• **Ne mŕsi múda!** {S} (lit. Don't you mix your balls!) *dia* ***Obs*** used to express disbelief

mȑsomūd {a (acc. = gen.) masc.} (lit. ball-winder) *sl-fea* lazy or shiftless person, bum, good for nothing <**Slav**⁘[*1]>

mrsomúdonja {ē fem. & masc.} (lit. ball-winder) *sl-fea* lazy or shiftless person, bum, good for nothing <**Slav**⁘[*1]>

mȑš {excl.} *col* used to make somebody go away, Beat it! <**Slav**>

• **Mȑš u pízdu mȁterinu!** {S} (lit. Go to your mother's cunt!) *sl-fea* ***Off*** used as a strong curse, Fuck you!

mŕšiti *See the following*

• **Ne mŕši múda!** {S} (lit. Don't you mix your balls!) *dia* ***Obs*** used to express disbelief

mršȕljav {a, o adj.} *sl-fea* ***Fam*** slender, skinny <**Slav**⁘>

mŕtav [1] {tva (acc. = gen.) masc.} (lit. dead) *sl-fea* joker, trickster, rascal <**Slav**[*1]>

mŕtav [2] {tva, tvo adj.} **/mr̀tav/** (lit. dead) **1a.** *sl-fea* ***App*** good, neat, cool: *mrtav motor cool bike* <**Slav**[*1]> **b.** *sl-fea* ***App*** skillfull <**Slav**[*2]> **c.** *sl-fea* funny <**Slav**[*3]> **2** *sl-fea* empty (room, hall, etc.) <**Slav**[*1]>

• **mŕtav za šprȅhu** {AdjP} (lit. dead for talking) *sl-fea* deaf person

mŕtav pìjan {AdjP} *col* very drunk, dead drunk ☞ **pijan**

mŕtav ȕmōran {AdjP} *sl-fea* very tired, dead tired ☞ **umoran**

mŕtav-hládan {AdjP} (lit. dead cold) *col* uninterested ☞ **hladan**

mȑtkovati {kujēm, kujū imperf.} *sl-sex* ***Obs*** engage in sexual intercourse with (of a male) <**Slav**[*1]>

mr̀tljan {a (acc. = gen.) masc.} *sl-fea* policeman, cop <**Slav**[*1]>

mr̂tvā príroda {NP} (lit. still life) *sl-mil* lunch packet ☞ **priroda**

mr̂tvā vójska {NP} (lit. dead army) *sl* funeral ☞ **vojska**

mr̀tvac {a (acc. = gen.) masc.} **/mr̀tvāc/** (lit. dead) **1** *sl-fea* parent <**Slav**[*1]> **2** *sl-fea* broke male <**Slav**[*1]> **3** *sl* cigarette butt <Slav*1>

• vȅselī mȑtvac {NP} (lit. merry dead, the bar is adjacent to the central cemetery) Cro *sl-drink* name of a bar on Mirogojska street in Zagreb, Croatia

mȑtvačkī {ā, ō adj.} *sl-fea* ***App*** excellent, awesome <Slav*1>

mȑtvāčnica {ē fem.} (lit. morgue) **1a.** *sl-fea* boredom <Slav*1> **b.** *sl-fea* bed time <Slav*2> **2** *sl-sstu* teachers' room <Slav*1>

• **glȁvnā mȑtvāčnica** {NP} (lit. main morgue) *sl-fea* ***Fac*** name for Petrinjska street prison, Zagreb, Croatia

mȑtvāk {mrtváka (acc. = gen.) masc.} (lit. the dead) **a.** *sl-fea* phlegmatic male <Slav*1> **b.** *sl-fea* unattractive male <Slav*2>

mrtvàkuša {ē fem.} (lit. dead) *sl-fea* ***Fac*** physically and intellectually slow female <Slav*1>

mȓtvō púhalo {NP} (lit. dead blower) **a.** *sl-fea* lazy or shiftless person, dead beat **b.** *sl-fea* unskilled person ☞ **puhalo**

mȓtvō púvalo {NP} (lit. dead blower) *sl-fea* boaster, braggart, blowhard ☞ **puvalo**

mrùljān {mruljána (acc. = gen.) masc.} *sl-fea* blind male

mȑviti {vīm, vē imperf.} *sl-fea* talk persistently and meaninglessly, blabber, chatter <Slav*1>

mȓz {a +ev (ext. pl) masc.; Nom Pl mŕzevi} *sl* hatred <Slav✍>

mŕzeti *See the following*

• **mŕzi[PRON:ACC]** {LSF} (lit. It hates [PRON: ACC]) *col* used to indicate unwillingness to act: *Mrzi me da idem u kupovinu. I don't feel like going shopping.*

mȑzlā píva {NP} (lit. frozen beer) Cro *sl* a bar at Magazin road and Katina street in Zagreb, Croatia ☞ **piva**

mȑzlā pízda {NP} (lit. frozen cunt) *sl-fea* ***Obs*** conceited person ☞ **pizda**

mrzojébac {pca (acc. = gen.) masc.} *sl-sex* ***Fac-Obs*** male sexual partner (of a female) <Slav❖*1>

mû {excl.} *col* the sound made by a cow, moo <Slav>

mȕa {ē fem.} [std. = muva, muha] *dia-col* fly (the insect) <Slav✍>

mȕcānje {a neut.} (lit. stuttering) *sl-fea* persistent and meaningless talk, blabber <Slav*1>

mȕcati {ām, ajū imperf. intr.} *sl-fea* talk persistently and meaninglessly, blabber, chatter <Slav*1>

• **mȕcati na jèdnu nȍgu** {VP} (lit. stutter on one leg) *sl-fea* limp

mùcek {múcka (acc. = gen.) masc.} (lit. cat) Kajk *sl-sex* ***Fac*** male homosexual, gay <Slav*1>

mucuváljak {ljka masc.} *sl-arch* egg <Slav>

mucuvánjak {njka masc.} *sl-arch* egg

mucvánjak {njka masc.} *sl-arch* egg <Slav>

mȕča {ē fem.} *sl-drugs* hashish oil, hash oil <Slav*1>

mùčati {čīm, čē imperf.} /múčati/ *dia-col* keep quiet <Slav>

mȕčenica {ē fem.} (lit. martyr) *sl-drink* strong plum brandy <Slav*1>

mȕčenīk {a (acc. = gen.) masc.} (lit. martyr) *sl-sstu* ***Fac*** high-school student <Slav*1>

mùčibabić {a (acc. = gen.) masc.} (lit. the one who tortures grandmas) **1** *sl-sex* ***Fac*** male sexual partner of elderly females <Slav❖*1> **2** *sl* ***Fac*** dentist <Slav❖*1>

mučiónica {ē fem.} (lit. torture chamber) **a.** *sl-sstu* school <Slav*1> **b.** *sl-sstu* classroom <Slav*2>

mùčitelj {a (acc. = gen.) masc.} (lit. torturer) **1** *sl-sstu* teacher <Slav*1> **2** *sl-mil* corporal <Slav*1>

mȕčkavac {kāvca masc.} *sl-arch* egg <Slav*1>

múćak [1] {excl.} *col* used as a strong negative response, no way, never <Slav*1>

múćak [2] {ćka (acc. = gen.) masc.} **a.** *sl-fea* crook, thief: *Taj mućak će svakoga prevariti. That crook will cheat anybody.* <Slav*1> **b.i.** *sl-fea* evil person <Slav*2> **ii.** *sl-fea* undependable person <Slav*2> **iii.** *sl-fea* abnormal person, weirdo <Slav*2>

mùćibabić {a (acc. = gen.) masc.} **1** *sl-sex* ***Fac*** male sexual partner of elderly females <Slav*1> **2** *sl* ***Fac*** dentist <Slav*1>

mȕćka {ē fem.; Dat mȕćki} (lit. stirring) **a.** *sl* cheating, swindling <Slav*1> **b.** *sl* immoral activity <Slav*2> **b.** *sl-crime* illegal business (in general) <Slav*3>

mȕćkalica {ē fem.} (lit. stirring) *sl-fea* immoral activity <Slav*1>

mȕćkalo {a neut.} (lit. stirrer) *sl-arch* egg <Slav*1>

mȕćkānje {a neut.} (lit. stirring) *sl-fea* cheating, swindling <Slav*1>

mȕćkāroš {a (acc. = gen.) masc.} (lit. stirrer) **a.** *sl-crime* crook, thief <Slav*1> **b.** *sl-fea* skillful person <Slav*2>

mȕćkati {ām, ajū biasp.} (lit. stir) *sl-fea* cheat, swindle <Slav*1>

mȕćkavac {vca masc.} *sl-arch* egg <Slav*1>

mùćūrla {ē fem.} *sl-arch* head <Slav✍[*1]>

múda {ē fem.} *sl-fea* evil female, bitch <Slav[*1]>

- **múda Màrijānova** {NP} (lit. Marijan's balls) *col* nothing
- **múda od làbūda!** {NP} (lit. swan's balls) *col* nothing at all
- **múda tȉcē ródē** {NP} (lit. stork's balls) *sl* ***Obs-Fac*** nothing at all
- **múda u slȁdoledu** {NP} (lit. balls in ice-cream) *col* nothing at all
- **trȕlā múda pòkōjnōg làbūda** {S} (lit. rotten balls of a deceased swan) *sl* ***Obs*** nothing at all

mudája {ē fem.} *dia* twin fruit <Slav⁘[*1]>

mudàlija {ē masc.} *sl-sex* ***Fac-Obs*** male with large testicles <Slav⁘>

mudalína {ē fem.; perm} *sl* lemonade <Slav✍>

mȕdālj {a masc.} *sl-sex* ***Obs*** male with large testicles <Slav⁘>

mȕdāljēv {a, o adj.} *sl-fea* pertaining to a male with large testicles <Slav⁘>

mùdān {mudána (acc. = gen.) masc.} *sl-sex* ***Obs*** male with large testicles <Slav[*1]>

mudánce {eta neut.} *sl-sex* ***Obs*** small testicle <Slav⁘>

mùdānte {i fem.} Med *col-dia* underpants, underwear <Ita>

mudàntīne {ā fem. pl.} Med *col-dia* male bathing suit <Ita>

mùdānje {a neut.} *sl-fea* spending one's time in useless activities, fooling around, messing around <Slav⁘[*1]>

mùdara {ē fem.} *sl-fea* white plum <Slav⁘[*1]>

mudárko {a masc.} *sl-fea* male with large testicles <Slav>

mùdāš {mudáša (acc. = gen.) masc.} *sl-sex* ***Obs*** animal with large testicles <Slav⁘>

mudášce {eta neut.} *sl-sex* ***Obs*** small testicle <Slav>

mùdat {a, o adj.} *sl-sex* ***Obs*** having large testicles <Slav[*1]>

mùdati {ām, ajū imperf.} **1** *sl-fea* spend one's time in useless activities, fool around, mess around <Slav[*1]> **2** *sl-fea* annoy, bother, pester <Slav[*1]>

mùdatiti {tīm, tē imperf.} *sl-sex* ***Obs*** have bigger testicles <Slav⁘>

mudénce {eta neut.} *sl-sex* ***Obs*** small testicle <Slav⁘>

mudèško {a masc.} *sl-fea* boring small person <Slav⁘>

mùdežina {ē fem.} *sl-sex* ***Obs*** testicular skin <Slav[*1]>

mùdīle {a masc.} *sl-sex* ***Obs*** animal with large testicles <Slav⁘>

mûdnī {ā, ō adj.} *sl-sex* ***Obs*** testicular <Slav>

múdnica {ē fem.} *sl-sex* ***Obs*** testicular skin <Slav[*1]>

múdo {a neut.} *sl-sex* ***Obs*** testicle <Slav[*1]>

mudòbolja {ē fem.} *sl-sex* ***Obs*** pain in the testicles <Slav⁘>

mȕdoglād {a (acc. = gen.) masc.} (lit. the one who pets testicles) *sl-sex* ***Fac-Obs*** male homosexual, gay <Slav⁘[*1]>

mȕdogrīz {a (acc. = gen.) masc.} (lit. ball-biter) *sl-crime* ***Der-Obs*** investigating judge, ball-busting judge <Slav⁘[*1]>

mȕdomīr {a (acc. = gen.) masc.} *sl-sex* ***Fac-Obs*** male homosexual, gay <Slav⁘[*1]>

múdonja {ē masc.} **a.** *sl-sex* ***Obs*** male with large testicles <Slav> **b.i.** *sl-fea* ***Obs*** courageous male, guy with balls <Slav[*1]> **ii.aa.** *sl-fea* ***Obs*** very important or influential person, big shot <Slav[*1]> **bb.** *sl-polit* ***Obs*** dictator <Slav[*2]> **cc.** *sl-mil* ***Obs*** officer <Slav[*3]> **iii.aa.** *sl-fea* ***Obs*** boaster, braggart, blowhard <Slav[*1]> **bb.** ***Obs*** conceited male <Slav[*2]> **iv.** ***Obs*** high-paying hotel guest <Slav[*1]> **c.** ***Obs*** male, **d.** *sl* ***Obs*** boy, kid <Slav[*2]>

múdonjica {ē masc.} *sl-sex* ***Obs*** male with large testicles <Slav[*1]>

múdonjić {a (acc. = gen.) masc.} *sl-fea* ***App-Obs*** courageous male, guy with balls <Slav[*1]>

múdonjīn {a, o adj.} *sl-fea* pertaining to a male with large testicles <Slav⁘>

mùdōrka {ē fem.} *dia* twin fruit <Slav⁘[*1]>

mùdovača {ē fem.} *dia* twin fruit <Slav⁘[*1]>

mûdović {a (acc. = gen.) masc.} (lit. the one with the balls) *sl-fea* ***App-Obs*** courageous male, guy with balls <Slav⁘[*1]>

mudòvolja {ē fem.} (lit. ball-willing) *dia* wild grapes <Slav⁘[*1]>

mùdrica {ē fem. & masc.} *sl-fea* smart person, brain <Slav⁘>

mȕdrogriz {a (acc. = gen.) masc.} (lit. ball-biter) *sl-crime* police investigator <Slav⁘[*1]>

mudròlija {ē fem.} (lit. wisdom) *col* ***Der*** pretentious discourse or idea without any value <Slav⁘[*1]>

mudròser {a (acc. = gen.) masc.} (lit. wise shitter) *sl-fea* ***Der*** person who exaggerates in theorizing, smart ass <Slav⁘[*1]>

mudžahèdīn {mudžahedína (acc. = gen.) masc.} *sl-fea* ***Off*** Bosnian Muslim <NE*1>

mùđūrla {ē fem.} *sl-arch* head <Slav✍*1>

mȕf {mùfa +ov (ext. pl) masc.; Nom Pl mùfovi} (lit. fur) **a.** *sl-sex* ***Fac-Obs*** pubic hair <Ger*1> **b.** *sl-sex* ***Fac-Obs*** vagina, muff <Ger*2> **c.** *sl* ***Fac-Obs*** female, cunt <Ger*3>

mȕfčina {ē fem.} (lit. big fur) *sl-sex* ***Fac-Obs*** large vagina <Ger✣>

mùflōn {muflóna (acc. = gen.) masc.} **1** *sl-fea* ***Der*** cunning male <Slav*1> **2** *sl* parent <Slav*1>

mùfljūz [1] {mufljúza (acc. = gen.) masc.; Voc mȕfljūzu} **a.** *sl-fea* person who is broke (financially) <NE*1> **b.** *sl-fea* evil person <NE*2> **c.i.** *sl-fea* troublemaker, rowdy, ruffian <NE*2> **ii.aa.** *sl-fea* crook, thief <NE*2> **bb.** *sl-fea* worthless person, bum <NE*3> **cc.** *sl-fea* stupid or mentally deficient person <NE*3>

mùfljūz [2] {mufljúza masc.} *sl-gamble* gambling loss <NE*1>

mùfōnka {ē fem.} *sl-fea* ***Der*** cunning female <Slav*1>

mȕftadžija {ē masc.} *sl-fea* person who abuses others (usu. financially), parasite, leech <NE✣>

mùftār {muftára masc.} *sl* jacket <NE*1>

muftáre {a fem. pl.} *sl* trousers, pants <NE✣>

mùftāš {muftáša (acc. = gen.) masc.} *sl-fea* person who abuses others (usu. financially), parasite, leech <NE✣>

mùftē {adv.} **a.** Din *col* free, gratis <NE> **b.** *col* inexpensive, cheap <NE*1>
- **na mùfte** {PP} **1** *col* free, gratis **2** *col* illegally

mȕfter {a masc.} *sl* fur jacket <NE✣>

mùha [1] {ē fem.; Dat mùhi} (lit. fly) *sl-fea* boring person, bore <Slav*1>

mùha [2] {adj.} (lit. fly) *sl-fea* boring <Slav*1>

muhádžer {a (acc. = gen.) masc.} BosM *col* refugee <NE>

muhádžir {a (acc. = gen.) masc.} BosM *col* refugee <NE>

muháđer {a (acc. = gen.) masc.} BosM *col* refugee <NE>

mȕholōvka {ē fem.} (lit. fly trap) *sl-sex* ***Fac-Obs*** vagina, cunt <Slav*1>

mȕhūr {a masc.} BosM *col* seal, stamp <NE>

mujáket *See the following*
- **ni mujáket** {PP} Bos *col* nothing

mȕka {ē fem.} (lit. pain, torture) **1** *sl-sex* ***Obs*** vagina, cunt <Slav*1> **2** *sl-drink* ***Fac*** brandy <Slav*1>
- **nȉ pō mȕkē** {PP} (lit. not half of pain) *col* used to indicate that a problem can be solved, no problem, no big deal

mukájet {adj.} BosM *col* laborious, tedious <NE>
- **ni mukájet** {PP} Bos *col* without a single word

múkati {mûčēm, mûčū imperf.} *col* moo <Slav>

mùktatos {adv.} Din *sl-fea* free, gratis <NE✍>

mȕkte {adv.} **a.** Din *col* free, gratis <NE> **b** *col* inexpensive, cheap <NE*1>

mùktiti {tīm, tē imperf.} *sl* work, labor <NE✣*1>

mȕla {ē fem.} **a.** *sl-sex* ***Fac*** male sexual partner (of a female) <NE*1> **b.** *sl-sex* ***Fac*** sexually potent male <NE*2>

múlac {lca (acc. = gen.) masc.} **a.** *sl-fea* young male, boy, kid <Ita✍*1> **b.** *sl-fea* joker, trickster, rascal **c.** *sl-fea* stupid or mentally deficient person

mulàrija {ē fem.} Med *col* youth <Ita*1>

mûlj {a +ev (ext. pl) masc.; Nom Pl múljevi} (lit. mud) **1** *sl-fea* name for river Sava <Slav*1> **2** *sl-drink* alcoholic beverage <Slav*1> **3** *sl-drink* low-class bar, dive <Slav*1>

múlja {ē masc.} *sl-fea* crook, thief <Slav✍*1>

muljáriti {mùljārīm, rē imperf.} *sl-fea* lie <Slav✣*1>

múljati {ām, ajū imperf.} **1** *sl-fea* devour, eat voraciously <Slav*1> **2** *sl-sex* shake one's buttocks <Slav*1> **3a.** *sl-fea* lie <Slav*1> **b.** *sl-fea* cheat, swindle <Slav*2> **c.** *sl-fea* be involved in dirty business

mùljātor {a (acc. = gen.) masc.} **a.** *sl-fea* liar <Slav✣*1> **b.** *sl-fea* cheater, swindler <Slav✣*2>

mȕljnuti {nēm, nū perf.} *sl-crime* steal, swipe <Slav*1>
- **Mȕljnēm ti ga!** {S} (lit. I stick it to you!) *col* ***Off*** used as a moderate curse, Fuck you!

mȕljos {a (acc. = gen.) masc.} *sl-fea* crook, thief <Slav✍>

mȕljte {adv.} *col* much, very <Ita✍*1>

mȕljtesta {ē fem.} **a.** *sl-fea* official (in general) **b.** *sl-fea* government representative

mùmak {mka (acc. = gen.) masc.} [std. = momak] *dia* boy, kid <Slav>

mȕmati {ām, ajū imperf.} *sl-fea* mumble <Slav>

mumificíranje {a neut.} (lit. mummifying) *sl-drink* drinking (alcohol) <NE✣*1>

mumificírati se {ficīrām, ficírajū biasp.} (lit. mummify) *sl-drink* get drunk, get pickled <NE*1>

mûmija {ē fem.} (lit. mummy) **a.** *sl-fea* senior citizen <NE*1> **b.** *sl* parent <NE*2>

mùmlati {ām, ajū imperf.} *col* mumble <Slav>

mùmljati {ām, ajū imperf.} *col* mumble <Slav>

munára {ē fem.} *sl-sex* ***Fac*** male homosexual who takes the passive role, femme <NE>

mȕnd {a +ov (ext. pl) masc.; Nom Pl mùndovi} *sl* coat (outer garment) <Fre✍>

múnđa {ē fem.} *sl-fea* cheating, swindling

munđàrati {ām, ajū imperf.} **a.** *sl-fea* cheat, swindle **b.** *sl-fea* smuggle

munđárēnje {a neut.} *sl-fea* cheating, swindling

munđáriti {rīm, rē imperf.} *sl-fea* cheat, swindle

mùnđāroš {a (acc. = gen.) masc.} **a.** *sl-fea* cheater, swindler **b.i.** *sl-crime* smuggler **ii.aa.** *sl-fea* crook, thief **bb.** *sl-fea* skillful person

mùnđati {ām, ajū imperf.} *sl-fea* cheat, swindle

mȕnđica {ē fem.} /mûnđica/ *sl* earring <NE✣*1>

mȕnēm {excl.} *dia* used to express extreme dissatisfaction <Slav*1>

Mȕnēm ti ga! {S} (lit. I bang it to you!) *col* ***Off*** used as a moderate curse, Fuck you! ☞ **munuti**

mȕngos {a (acc. = gen.) masc.} (lit. mongoose) **a.** *sl-fea* fast runner, speedster <Spa*1> **b.** *sl-fea* stupid or mentally deficient person <Spa*2>

mȕngosica {ē fem.} (lit. she-mongoose) *col* child's orthopedic shoe <Ind✣*1>

mùnīcija {ē fem.} (lit. ammunition) *sl-mil* dry food rations <Lat*1>

mȕnt {a (acc. = gen.) +ov (ext. pl) masc.; Nom Pl mùntovi} *sl* coat (outer garment) <Fre✍>

mȕnta {ē fem.} *sl* coat (outer garment) <Fre✍>

mùntām {num.} *sl* seven <Ita*1>

mùntānje {a neut.} *sl* cheating, swindling <Ita*1>

muntárac {rca masc.} **a.** *sl* coat (outer garment) <Fre*1> **b.** *sl* jacket <Fre*2>

muntáre {a fem. pl.} *sl* trousers, pants <Fre*1>

muntàrica {ē fem.} *sl* coat (outer garment) <Fre*1>

mùntārke {i fem. pl.} *sl* trousers, pants <Fre*1>

muntátac {rca masc.} *sl* coat (outer garment) <Fre*1>

mùntati {ām, ajū imperf.} *sl* cheat, swindle <Ita>

mùntērke {i fem. pl.} *sl* trousers, pants <Fre*1>

mùntīrke {i fem. pl.} *sl* trousers, pants <Fre*1>

mȕnuti {nēm, nū perf.} /múnuti/ *sl* hit, punch
- **Mȕnēm ti ga!** {S} (lit. I bang it to you!) *col* ***Off*** used as a moderate curse

múnja [1] {ē fem.} (lit. lightning) **1** *sl-fea* ***App*** skillful person <Slav*1> **2** *sl* big earring <Slav*1> **3a.** *sl* streetcar <Slav*1> **b.** *sl* trolley bus <Slav*2> **4** *sl-fea* unusual event: *Pričao mi je kako se zaglavio u liftu i neke slične munje. He told me that he got stuck in an elevator and some similar unusual events.* <Slav*1>

múnja [2] {adj.} *sl-fea* skillful <Slav*1>

munjtárac {rca masc.} *sl* coat (outer garment) <Fre*1>

mȕpovac {vca (acc. = gen.) masc.} (lit. from MUP, Ministarstvo unutarnjih poslova 'Ministry of Interior') **1** *col* Croatian policeman in the early 1990s <Abb✣> **2** *col* Serbian policeman in the late 1990s

mûr {a +ev (ext. pl) masc.; Nom Pl múrevi} **Din** *dia* seal, stamp <NE✍>

mȕra {ē fem.} *sl-crime* custody <Ita*1>

múrija [1] {ē fem.} **a.** *sl-crime* police <Ita*1> **b.** *sl-crime* prison <Ita*2> **c.** *sl-crime* custody <Ita*3> **d.** *sl-crime* police van, paddy wagon <Ita*4>

múrija [2] {ē masc.} *sl-crime* policeman, cop <Ita*1>
- **bijèlā múrja** {NP} (lit. white cops) *sl-crime* bribed police officers, cops on the take

múrijāš {a (acc. = gen.) masc.} /murìjāš/ *sl-crime* policeman, cop <Ita*1>

mùrīrān {a, o adj.} *sl-crime* imprisoned <Ita*1>

murirànt {a (acc. = gen.) masc.} *sl-crime* prisoner <Ita*1>

murírati {mùrīrām, murírajū biasp.} **1** *sl-crime* arrest: *Murirali su ga u krađi kola. He got arrested while stealing cars.* <Ita*1> **2** *sl-crime* be in prison <Ita*1>

mùrisati {mùrišēm, išū biasp.} *sl-crime* arrest: *Murisali su ga i strpali u zatvor. They have arrested him and put him in jail.* <Ita*1>

mȕrīvo {a neut.} *sl-arch* cheese

múrja {ē fem.} **a.** *sl-crime* the police <Ita*1> **b.** *sl-crime* custody <Ita*2> **c.** *sl-crime* police van, paddy wagon

múrja {ē masc.} *sl-crime* policeman, cop <Ita*1>
- **cȑnā múrja** {NP} (lit. black police) *sl-mil* military police

mùrjāk {a (acc. = gen.) masc.} *sl-crime* policeman, cop <Ita*1>

mùrjān {a (acc. = gen.) masc.} *sl-crime* policeman, cop <**Ita**[*1]>

mȕrjāš {a (acc. = gen.) masc.} *sl-crime* policeman, cop <**Ita**[*1]>

mûrka [1] {ē masc.; Dat mûrki} *sl-crime* policeman, cop <**Ita**[*1]>

mûrka [2] {ē fem.; Dat mûrki} **a.** *sl-crime* police <**Ita**[*1]> **b.** *sl-crime* custody <**Ita**[*2]> **c.** *sl-crime* police van, paddy wagon <**Ita**[*3]>

mùrkac {a (acc. = gen.) masc.} *sl-crime* policeman, cop <**Ita**[*1]>

mȕrkāč {a (acc. = gen.) masc.} *sl-crime* policeman, cop <**Ita**[*1]>

mùrkan {a (acc. = gen.) masc.} *sl-crime* policeman, cop <**Ita**[*1]>

mȕrnuti {nēm, nū perf.} *sl-crime* arrest <**Ita**[*1]>

mùruz {a masc.} *dia* corn <**Slav**☝>

mûrva {ē fem.} **1a.** *dia* mulberry tree **b.** *dia* mulberry fruit 2 *sl-sex* prostitute, hooker <**Lat**☝>

mȕs rȕnda {NP} *sl-sex* ***Fac-Obs*** group sex ☞ **runda**

mȕsati {ām, ajū biasp.} *sl-crime* lie

mȕsav {a, o adj.} *sl-fea* dirty (not clean) <**Slav**>

mùstang {adj.} *sl-fea* wild (temperament, personality, etc.) <**Eng**[*1]>

mȕster {a masc.} *sl-sex* naive victim of a prostitute

mûsti {múzēm, múzū perf. irreg.} **/músti/** (lit. milk) *sl-fea* abuse financially, milk <**Slav**[*1]>

mȕstovati {tujēm, tujū imperf.} **/mùstovati/** *sl* keep one's mouth shut

mȕstra {ē fem.} **/mùstra/** 1 *sl-fea* conceited person <**Ger**[*1]> 2 *sl-sex* male on the make <**Ger**[*1]>

mùšica *See the following*

• **vînskā mùšica** {NP} (lit. wine fly) *sl-drink* alcoholic, drunk

mùškāć {muškáća (acc. = gen.) masc.} **a.** *sl-fea* male, guy <**Slav**❖> **b.** *sl-fea* boy, kid <**Slav**❖[*1]>

mùškī ginekòlog {NP} (lit. male gynecologist) *sl-sex* ***Fac*** male homosexual, gay ☞ **ginekolog**

mùškīć {muškíća (acc. = gen.) masc.; Voc mȕškīću} *sl-sex* male, guy <**Slav**❖[*1]>

mȕšmula {ē fem.} 1 *sl-sex* ***Fac*** male homosexual, gay <**Gre**[*1]> 2 *sl* ***Fac*** female <**Gre**[*1]>

mȕštavica {ē fem.} *sl* shirt

mȕštavice {a fem. pl.} *sl* panties, briefs

mùštikla {ē fem.} (lit. cigarette holder) *sl-crime* ***Fac*** penis <**Ger**>

mȕštrānje {a neut.} *sl* prolongation <**Ger**[*1]>

mȕštrati {ām, ajū imperf.} *sl* exercise discipline <**Ger**[*1]>

muštùluk {a masc.} **a. Din** *col* reward for a person who brings good news of any kind <**NE**> **b. Din** *col* good news <**NE**[*1]>

mútan {tna, tno adj.} (lit. opaque) **a.** *sl-fea* ***Der*** cunning, sly, slick <**Slav**[*1]> **b.** *sl-fea* ***Iro*** skillful <**Slav**[*2]> **c.** *sl-fea* ***Der*** drunk <**Slav**[*3]> **d.** *sl-fea* ***Der*** depressed, blue <**Slav**[*4]> **e.** *sl-fea* ***Der*** suspicious <**Slav**[*5]> **f.** *sl-fea* hungry <**Slav**[*5]>

mȕtav {a, o adj.} **a.** *sl-fea* mute <**Slav**> **b.i.** *sl-fea* clumsy, klutzy <**Slav**[*1]> **ii.** *sl-fea* hungry <**Slav**[*2]>

mutàvdžījskī {ōg masc.} (lit. mute man's speech) *sl* slang <**Slav-NE**[*1]>

mutavȅla {ē fem.} *sl-drink* hangover <**Slav-Gyp**>

mȕtavskī {ōg masc.} (lit. mute man's speech) *sl* slang <**Slav**❖[*1]>

mȕter {a masc.} *sl-drugs* marijuana, pot, grass <**Ger**[*1]>

mȕterica {ē fem.} *sl* mother, mom <**Ger**❖>

mùtikaša {ē fem.} (lit. stew stirrer) *sl-fea* intriguer <**Slav**❖[*1]>

mùtikašu {ua masc.} (lit. stew stirrer) *sl* cook <**Slav**☝[*1]>

mùtikesa {ē fem.} (lit. bag stirrer) **a.** *sl-fea* intriguer <**Slav**❖[*1]> **b.** *sl-fea* cheater, swindler <**Slav**❖[*2]> **c.** *sl-crime* thief <**Slav** ❖[*3]>

mutírati {mùtīrām, mutírajū imperf.} (lit. mutate) *sl* beat up <**Ger**[*1]>

mútiti {mûtīm, tē imperf.} **a.** *col* cheat, swindle <**Slav**[*1]> **b.i.aa.** *col* persuade, convince: *mutiti starce da se uzmu kola persuade one's parents to use the car* <**Slav**[*2]> **bb.** *sl* sell (exchange merchandise for money): *mutiti deterdžent sell detergent* <**Slav**[*3]> **cc.** *sl* resell <**Slav**[*4]> **ii.** *col* flirt <**Slav**[*2]>

mùtivoda {ē fem.} **a.** *sl-fea* intriguer <**Slav**❖[*1]> **b.** *sl-fea* cheater, swindler <**Slav**❖[*2]>

mȕtka {ē fem.; Dat mȕtki} *sl* mother, mom <**Ger**☝>

mutljárēnje {a neut.} *sl* cheating, swindling <**Slav**❖[*1]>

mùtljavina {ē fem.} (lit. stirring) **a.** *sl-fea* ***Der*** immoral activity <**Slav**[*1]> **b.** *sl-fea* suspicious person <**Slav**[*2]> **c.** *sl-fea* cheat, swindle <**Slav**[*3]>

mutljávko {a masc.} (lit. stirrer) *sl-fea* abnormal male, weirdo <Slav✣*1>

mutljívko {a masc.} (lit. stirrer) **a.** *sl-fea* crook, thief <Slav✣*1> **b.** *sl-fea* undependable male <Slav✣*2>

mutnjáković {a (acc. = gen.) masc.} (lit. stirrer) **a.** *sl-fea* crook, thief <Slav✣*1> **b.** *sl-fea* suspicious person <Slav✣*2>

múto {a masc.} (lit. mute person) *sl-fea* stupid or mentally deficient person <Slav✣>

mȕūr {a +ev (ext. pl) masc.; Nom Pl mȕurevi} Din *col* seal, stamp <NE✍>

mùva {ē fem.} Ser *sl* food <Slav*1>

mùva {adj.} Ser *sl-fea* bald <Slav*1>

muvàna {ē fem.} Ser *sl* mess, disorder, disturbance <Slav✣*1>

mȕvānje {a neut.} **1** *sl* ***Der*** ingratiate, brownnose, kiss ass <Slav*1> **2** *sl* eating <Slav*1> **3** *sl* flirting <Slav*1>

muváriti {mùvārīm, rē imperf. intr.} *sl* flirt without going too far: *On je muvario svaku ribu u tom kafiću. He only flirted with the chicks in that cafe.* <Slav✍*1>

mȕvati {ām, ajū imperf.} **1** *sl* ***Der*** ingratiate, brownnose, kiss ass: *muvati profesorima brownnose one's professors* <Slav*1> **2** *sl* eat, devour: *muvati piletinu eat chicken* <Slav*1> **3a.** *sl* lie <Slav*1> **b.** *sl* cheat, swindle <Slav*2> **c.** *sl* flirt <Slav*3> **d.** *sl* sell (exchange merchandise for money) <Slav*4>

mȕvati se {ām, ajū imperf. intr.} **a.** *col* mess around, fool around: *Neki besposličari muvaju se ispred kuće. Some loafers are fooling around in front of the house.* <Slav✣> **b.** *sl* walk <Slav✣*1> **c.** *sl* flirt <Slav✣*2>

mùvātor {a (acc. = gen.) masc.} **a.** *sl-fea* suspicious male <Slav✣*1> **b.i.** *sl-fea* skillful male <Slav✣*2> **ii.aa.** *sl-fea* liar <Slav✣*2> **bb.** *sl-fea* cheater, swindler <Slav✣*3>

múving {a masc.} (lit. moving) **1** *sl* walk <Eng*1> **2** *sl* pushing, showing <Eng*1>

muvosèrina {ē fem.} Ser *dia* fly dirt, fly shit <Slav>

múza {ē fem.} *sl-sstu* music class <Gre✍>

mùzara {ē fem.} (lit. milking cow) **1** *sl-fea* person from whom one frequently borrows, cash cow <Slav✣*1> **2** *sl-sex* large-breasted female <Slav✣*1>

mùzēj *See the following*

• **mùzēj òhlāđenīh** {NP} (lit. museum of the frozen ones) *sl* ***Fac*** morgue

• **mùzēj vòštānīh fìgūrā** {NP} (lit. wax *figure* museum) Cro *sl* ***Fac*** former Opera restaurant in Zagreb, Croatia

mȕzgav {a, o adj.} *col-dia* dirty (not clean) <Slav>

muzicírati {zìcīrām, zicírajū imperf.} (lit. play music) *sl-fea* talk persistently and meaninglessly, blabber, chatter <Gre*1>

mùzičār {a (acc. = gen.) masc.} (lit. musician) **1** *sl-crime* policeman, cop <Gre*1> **2** *sl-fea* stupid or mentally deficient person <Gre*1>

mùzika {ē fem.} (lit. music) **a.** *sl-sex* gonorrhea, the clap <Gre*1> **b.** *sl-crime* police <Gre*2>

mȕžika {ē fem.} [std. = muzika] Med *dia* music <Gre✍>

Nn

nȁ {excl.} *col* used when passing something to somebody, here <Slav>

na bàrjāk {PP} (lit. to a flag) *col* on credit: *kupiti kola na barjak buy a car on credit* ☞ **barjak**

na bàtērije i na strúju {PP} (lit. plug and battery powered) *sl-sex* ***Fac*** bisexual, AC/DC ☞ **baterija**

na blȉnd {PP} (lit. on blind) *col* haphazardly ☞ **blind**

na bȓk {PP} (lit. on a mustache) *sl* on credit: *kupiti kuću na brk buy a house on credit* ☞ **brk**

na bȑzac {PP} (lit. on a quickie) *col* quickly ☞ **brzac**

na brzàca {PP} (lit. on a quickie) *col* quickly ☞ **brzac**

na brzáka {PP} (lit. on a quickie) *col* quickly ☞ **brzak**

na cŕno {PP} (lit. on black) *col* illegally ☞ **crn**

na cȑtu {PP} (lit. on line) *sl* on credit ☞ **crta**

na divljáka {PP} (lit. on wild) **a.** *col* illegally **b.** *col* secretly, under the counter **c.** *col* without a ticket (enter a performance, ball game, etc.) **d.** by cheating ☞ **divljak**

na dȉvljē {PP} (lit. on wild) **a.** *col* secretly, under the counter **b.** without a ticket (enter a performance, ball game, etc.) **c.** illegally ☞ **divlje**

na dȕgē stàze {PP} (lit. on long paths) *col* for a long time ☞ **staza**

na dȕgū prúgu {PP} (lit. on long rails) *col* long-term: *investicija na dugu prugu long-term investment* ☞ **pruga**

na dvâ mlâza {PP} (lit. on two streams) *sl-sex* after the second date ☞ **mlaz**

na finjáka {PP} (lit. on niceness) *sl* nicely ☞ **finjak**

na fôl {PP} (lit. on trick) *col* using mischief ☞ **fol**

na fúri {PP} (lit. on the line) *sl-sex* on the street (of prostitutes) ☞ **fura**

nà guzove {PP} (lit. over one's buttocks) *col* without deserving it ☞ **guz**

na ȉvici {PP} (lit. on the verge) *sl-fea* in love ☞ **ivica**

na ȉvici i mȁrici {PP} (lit. on Hansel/verge and Gretel) *sl-fea* madly in love ☞ **ivica**

na jèdan mlâz {PP} (lit. at one stream) *sl-sex* after the first date ☞ **mlaz**

na jèdvītē jȁde {PP} (lit. at very poor griefs) *col* with major difficulties ☞ **jad**

na kȁnst {PP} *sl-crime* using tricks, by cheating: *zgrnuti lovu na kanst get money by cheating* ☞ **kanst**

na kàpāljku {PP} (lit. at dripper) **1** *col* little by little **2** *col* in small quantities: *davati pare na kapaljku give money in small quantities* ☞ **kapaljka**

na kȁšičicu {PP} (lit. on spoon) **1** *col* little by little **2** *col* in small quantities ☞ **kašičica**

Na kȍjū fóru? {PP} (lit. on which trick?) *sl* used to ask for additional information, How? ☞ **fora**

na krȁju baládē {PP} (lit. at the end of the ballad) *col* in the end ☞ **balada**

na kȕnst {PP} (lit. at arts) *sl-crime* using mischief ☞ **kunst**

nà kurac {PP} (lit. at a cock) *sl* ***Obs*** used to express disrespect or dissatisfaction, Fuck it!: *Na kurac sve te njegove planove. Fuck all his plans.* ☞ **kurac**

na lèdu {PP} (lit. on ice) *col* suspended, on ice ☞ **led**

na lêr {PP} (lit. in neutral gear) *sl* on credit ☞ **ler**

na lȉru {PP} (lit. on a lie) *sl* by lying ☞ **lira**

na màjmunovo {PP} (lit. on Monkey's day) *sl* never ☞ **majmunovo**

na mlâz {PP} (lit. on stream) *sl* at once ☞ **mlaz**

Nà moj, cȅ! {S} (lit. To my *prick*, yeah!) *dia* ***Off*** used as a moderate curse, Fuck you! ☞ **moj**

Nà moj, nȁ! {S} (lit. To my *prick*, here!) *dia* ***Off*** used as a moderate curse, Fuck you! ☞ **moj**

na mȕfte {PP} **1** *col* free, gratis **2** *col* illegally ☞ **mufte**

na ȍblāk {PP} (lit. at a cloud) *sl* occasionally ☞ **oblak**

na ȍdmet {PP} (lit. at castoff) *col* useless ☞ **odmet**

na Pâlmu de Majôrku {PP} (lit. to Palma de Mallorca) Cro *sl* to Čateške toplice (a spa in Croatia) ☞ **Palma**

na pȍla trî {PP} (lit. at half past two) *sl-fea* sick, ill ☞ **tri**

na prózivku {PP} (lit. to the roll-call) **1** *sl* at designated time **2** *sl* for a walk: *Uzeo je cucka na prozivku. He took the dog for a walk.* ☞ **prozivka**

na prúgi {PP} (lit. at a strip) *sl* on the spot, at a designated place or a place of an event: *Bio je na prugi kad su ubili predsjednika. He was there when they killed the president.* ☞ **pruga**

na rûke {PP} (lit. to one's arms) *col* in cash: *Plaćen je na ruke. He was paid in cash.* ☞ **ruka**

na sabáhu {PP} (lit. at morning) Bos *col* in the morning ☞ **sabah**

na sȍbu {PP} (lit. to the room) **1** *sl-sex* ***Fac*** to sexual intercourse **2** *sl* on credit ☞ **soba**

nà sreću {PP} (lit. to luck) *sl-crime* without being observed ☞ **sreća**

na svêtī Nȉkad {PP} (lit. on holy neverday) *col* never ☞ **nikad**

na svêtō nigdárjevo {PP} (lit. on holy neverday) *col* never ☞ **nigdarjevo**

na svêtō nȉkad {PP} (lit. on holy never) *col* never ☞ **nikad**

na štráfti {PP} (lit. at the line) *sl* on the spot, at a designated place or a place of an event ☞ **štrafta**

na tàvan {PP} (lit. to the attic) *sl-crime* to a convenient place for stealing ☞ **tavan**

na televîzoru {PP} (lit. on a tv set) [std. = na televiziji] *col* on tv ☞ **televizor**

na tràsu {PP} (lit. to a tour) *sl* on credit ☞ **trasa**

na trî ćȍška {NumP} (lit. at three corners) *col* disordered, messy ☞ **ćošak**

na zâpadu nȉšta nȍvo {PP} (lit. nothing new in the West) *sl-sstu* failing grade ☞ **zapad**

nába {ē fem.} *sl-auto* hub (on a wheel) <**Ger**>

nabacȉnđel {a masc.} /nabacìnđel/ *sl* flirting <**Slav**✍[*1]>

nabacȉška {ē masc.; Dat nabacȉški} /nabacìška/ *sl* seducer <**Slav**✍[*1]>

nabáciti {cīm, cē perf.} (lit. throw at) **1a.** *col* get, obtain: *nabaciti novi televizor get a new tv* <**Slav**[*1]> **b.** *col* buy: *nabaciti litar mlijeka buy a liter of milk* <**Slav**[*2]> **c.** *col* dress <**Slav**[*2]> **2** *sl* flirt <**Slav**[*2]>

• **nabáciti ânđeoskī kêz** {VP} (lit. put on an angelic grin) *sl-fea* laugh

• **nabáciti fârbu** {VP} (lit. put on color) **1** *col* blush, turn colors **2** *col* get a sun tan

• **nabáciti gârdos** {VP} (lit. put on wardrobe) *sl-fea* dress formally, dress up

• **nabáciti kônce** {VP} (lit. put on threads) *sl-fea* dress formally, dress up

• **nabáciti mȍnopōl** {VP} (lit. put on monopoly) *sl-fea* be the most important

• **nabáciti pêrje** {VP} (lit. put on feathers) *sl-fea* dress formally, dress up

• **nabáciti tàmnjāk** {VP} (lit. put on the dark one) *sl-fea* dress in black

nabáciti se {nàbācīm, ce perf. intr.} (lit. throw oneself at) *col* flirt, throw oneself at: *Nabacio se Miri čim ju je sreo. He threw himself at Mira as soon as he met her.* <Slav*1>

nabacìvāč {civáča (acc. = gen.) masc.} (lit. thrower at) *sl-sex* male sexual partner (of a female) <Slav⁘*1>

nabacívānje {a neut.} (lit. throwing at) **a.** *col* pushing, showing <Slav*1> **b.** *col* flirting <Slav*1>

nabacívati se {cujēm, cujū imperf. intr.} (lit. throw oneself at) **a.** *col* flirt, throw oneself at: *Nabacuje se svakoj djevojci koju sretne. He throws himself at each and every girl he meets.* <Slav*1> **b.** *col* be boring <Slav*2>

nabacóka [1] {ē masc.; Dat nabacóki} (lit. thrower at) *sl* seducer <Slav✍*1>

nabacóka [2] {ē fem.; Dat nabacóki} **1** *sl* pushing, shoving <Slav✍*1> **2** *sl-sports* kick in front of the adversaries' goal <Slav✍*1> *sl* flirting <Slav✍*1>

nabádāljka {ē fem.} /**nabàdāljka**/ (lit. one that sticks on) **1** *sl* ***Fac*** leg (human) <Slav⁘*1> **2** *sl-sex* ***Fac*** prostitute, hooker <Slav⁘*1>

nabádānje {a neut.} (lit. sticking on) *sl-sex* ***Obs*** sexual intercourse, poking <Slav*1>

nabádati {nàbādām, nabádajū imperf.} (lit. keep sticking on) *sl-sex* ***Obs*** engage in sexual intercourse with (of a male), poke <Slav*1>

nàbaniti {nīm, nē perf.} **a.** *sl* make, construct, build **b.** falsely incriminate, frame

• **nabániti žáru** {VP} *sl-arch* set fire

nabanjívati {bànjujēm, jū imperf.} *sl* make, construct, build

nàbāren {ā, ō adj.} (lit. cooked) *sl-drink* ***Fac*** drunk, pickled <Slav*1>

nabáriti se {nàbārīm, rē perf. intr.} (lit. cook oneself) *sl-drink* get drunk, get toasted <Slav*1>

nabàrtati {ām, ajū perf.} **a.** *sl* find, locate **b.** *sl* get, obtain

nabìflati {ām, ajū perf.} *sl* learn <Ger⁘>

nàbiflati se {ām, ajū aiv+v} *sl-fea* put on make-up <Ger⁘*1>

nabigùzica {ē fem.} (lit. push ass) **a.** *sl-fea* ***Der-Obs*** lazy or shiftless person, bum, good for nothing <Slav⁘*1> **b.** *sl-fea* ***Der-Obs*** loafer, idler <Slav⁘*1>

Nabigùzice {zīcā fem. pl.} (lit. push asses) *sl-fea* ***Obs*** a place of extreme wretchedness or squalor, hellhole <Slav⁘*1>

nabìjāč {bijáča (acc. = gen.) masc.} (lit. stuffer) *sl-sex* ***Fac*** male sexual partner (of a female) <Slav⁘*1>

nabíjati {nàbījām, nabíjajū imperf.} (lit. keep sticking, keep stuffing) **1** *sl-sex* ***Obs*** engage in sexual intercourse with (of a male) <Slav*1> **2** *sl-sports* ***Der*** play bad soccer <Slav*1>

• **nabíjati rȍgove** {VP} (lit. stick horns) *col* cheat on one's lover or spouse

Nȁbijēm ga! {S} (lit. I stick it!) *col* ***Off*** used as a moderate curse, Fuck you! ☞ **nabiti**

Nȁbijēm te! {S} (lit. I stick you!) *col* ***Off*** used as a strong curse, Fuck you! ☞ **nabiti**

Nȁbijēm te na bàtinu! {S} (lit. I stick you on my bat!) *col* ***Off*** used as a strong curse, Fuck you! ☞ **nabiti**

Nȁbijēm te nà kurac! {S} (lit. I stick you on my prick!) *col* ***Off*** used as a strong curse, Fuck you! ☞ **nabiti**

Nȁbijēm ti ga! {S} (lit. I stick it to you!) *col* ***Off*** used as a strong curse, Fuck you! ☞ **nabiti**

nabìjen {a, o adj.} (lit. stuffed) *sl-fea* muscular, pumped up <Slav*1>

nàbildovan {a, o adj.} (lit. built) *sl-fea* muscular, pumped up <Eng⁘*1>

nàbildovānōst {i fem.} (lit. being built) *sl-fea* muscularity <Eng⁘*1>

nàbildovati se {dujēm, dujū perf.} (lit. build oneself) *sl-fea* become muscular <Eng⁘*1>

nàbiti {ijēm, ijū perf.} (lit. stick) **1** *sl* beat up <Slav*1> **2a.** *sl-sex* engage in sexual intercourse with (of a male) <Slav*1> **b.i.** *sl* overcharge, rip off <Slav*1> **ii.** *sl-sports* score numerous goals (e.g. in soccer) <Slav*1>

• **Nȁbijēm ga!** {S} (lit. I stick it!) *col* ***Off*** used as a moderate curse, Fuck you!

• **Nȁbijēm te!** {S} (lit. I stick you!) *col* ***Off*** used as a strong curse, Fuck you!

• **Nȁbijēm te na bàtinu!** {S} (lit. I stick you on my bat!) *col* ***Off*** used as a strong curse, Fuck you!

• **Nàbijēm te nà kurac!** {S} (lit. I stick you on my prick!) *col* ***Off*** used as a strong curse, Fuck you!

• **Nàbijēm ti ga!** {S} (lit. I stick it to you!) *col* ***Off*** used as a strong curse, Fuck you!

• **nàbiti cijénu** {VP} (lit. stick a price) **a.** *col* overcharge, rip off **b.** *col* overestimate

• **nàbiti fôl** {VP} (lit. stick a trick) *sl* trick, cheat, swindle

• **nàbiti gùzicu** {VP} (lit. stick one's ass) *sl* ***Obs*** profit without doing anything

• **nàbiti nà kurac** {VP} (lit. stick onto one's prick) **a.** *sl-sex* ***Obs*** engage in sexual intercourse with **b.** *sl* ***Obs*** underestimate **c.** *sl* offend

• **nàbiti rezùltāt** {VP} (lit. stick result) *sl-sports* beat in sports by a high margin, trounce, smear

• **nàbiti rȍgove** {VP} (lit. put horns to) *col* cheat on one's lover or spouse

• **nàbiti špȉcu** {VP} (lit. stick seed) **a.** *sl* throw away, toss out **b.** *sl* dump one's boyfriend or girlfriend

nàbosti {bodēm, bodū perf. irreg.} (lit. stick on) **1** *sl-sex* ***Obs*** engage in sexual intercourse with (of a male), poke <Slav[*1]> **2** *sl* come to the best solution <Slav[*1]>

nabúbati {ām, ajū perf.} **1** *sl-sstu* learn by rote <Slav[*1]> **2** *sl* beat up <Slav[*1]>

nàbūdžen {a, o adj.} **1** *sl-fea* strong <NE⁘[*1]> **2** *sl-auto* upgraded <NE⁘[*1]> ☞ **budžiti**

nabudžénko {a masc.} *sl-fea* ***Iro*** muscular male <NE⁘[*1]>

nabúšiti {nàbūšīm, šē perf.} (lit. perforate) **a.** *sl-sports* score numerous goals (e.g. in soccer) <Slav[*1]> **b.** *sl-sports* defeat <Slav[*1]>

nàbuškati {ām, ajū perf.} (lit. perforate) **a.** *sl-sports* score numerous goals (e.g. in soccer) <Slav⁘[*1]> **b.** *sl-sports* defeat <Slav⁘[*1]>

nacementírati se {mèntīrām, mentírajū perf. intr.} (lit. cover oneself with concrete) *sl* stand in one place for a long time (usu. while waiting for someone), have cement shoes <Lat⁘[*1]>

nacépiti se {nàcēpīm, pē perf. intr.} (lit. be fully immunized) SerE *sl-drink* get drunk <Slav[*1]>

nacériti se {nàcērīm, rē perf. intr.} *sl* grin <Slav⁘[*1]>

nàcīcān {a, o adj.} *sl-drink* drunk

nacícati se {nàcīcām, nacícajū perf. intr.} *sl-drink* get drunk

nacinkróciti se {cìnkrōcīm, cē perf. intr.} *sl-fea* dress formally, dress up

nacìrisān {a, o adj.} *sl-drink* drunk <Slav⁘[*1]>

nacìrisati se {šēm, šū perf. intr.} (lit. be fully immunized) *sl-drink* get drunk <Slav⁘[*1]>

nacíriti se {nàcīrīm, rē perf. intr.} (lit. be fully immunized) *sl-drink* get drunk <Slav⁘[*1]>

nàcirkān {a, o adj.} *sl-drink* drunk <Slav⁘[*1]>

nàcirkati se {ām, ajū perf. intr.} *sl-drink* get drunk <Slav⁘[*1]>

nacrtān {a, o adj.} (lit. drawn) *sl-fea* with excessive make-up <Slav[*1]>

nàcrtati se {ām, ajū perf. intr.} (lit. draw oneself) *col* show up <Slav[*1]>

nàcuclān {a, o adj.} (lit. had one's fill of a pacifier) *sl-drink* drunk <Slav⁘[*1]>

nàcuclati se {ām, ajū perf. intr.} (lit. have one's fill of a pacifier) *sl-drink* get drunk <Slav⁘[*1]>

nàcugān {a, o adj.} *sl-drink* drunk <Ger⁘[*1]>

nàcugati {ām, ajū imperf.} *sl-drink* make drunk <Ger⁘>

• **nàcugati fràjkana** {VP} (lit. make a guy drunk) *sl* make somebody agitated

• **nàcugati Sávē** {VP} (lit. make someone drink the Sava river) *sl-crime* kill, murder

nàcugati se {ām, ajū perf. intr.} *sl-drink* get drunk <Ger⁘[*1]>

Nàcvr̄cām ti ga! {S} (lit. I fry it to you!) *dia* ***Off*** used as a strong curse, Fuck you! ☞ **nacvrcati**

nàcvr̄cān {a, o adj.} *sl-drink* drunk <Slav⁘[*1]>

nacvŕcati *See the following*

nacvŕcati se {nàcvr̄cām, nacvŕcajū perf. intr.} *sl-drink* get drunk <Slav⁘[*1]>

• **Nàcvr̄cām ti ga!** {S} (lit. I fry it to you!) *dia* ***Off*** used as a strong curse, Fuck you!

nàcvrckān {a, o adj.} *sl-drink* drunk <Slav⁘[*1]>

nàcvrckati se {ām, ajū perf. intr.} *sl-drink* get drunk <Slav⁘[*1]>

nàčičkati {ām, ajū perf.} *col* overload, overburden <Slav⁘[*1]>

nàčičkati se {ām, ajū perf. intr.} *sl* annoy, bother, pester <Slav⁘[*1]>

nȁčisto {adv.} (lit. cleanly) *col* completely, totally <Slav[*1]>

nàčr̄čkati {ām, ajū perf.} Cro *col* scribble, write illegibly <Slav>

Nàčukām ti ga! {S} (lit. I knock it to you!) *dia* ***Off*** used as a strong curse, Fuck you! ☞ **načukati**

nàčukati *See the following*
- **Nàčukām ti ga!** {S} (lit. I knock it to you!) *dia* ***Off*** used as a strong curse, Fuck you!

naćeflèisati se {išēm, išū perf. intr.} *dia-col* get drunk <NE❖*1>

naćevlèisān {a, o adj.} *dia-col* drunk, pickled <NE❖*1>

náći *See the following*
- **náći jêža** {VP} (lit. find a hedgehog) *sl* be mistaken
- **náći za shȍdno** {VP} (lit. find appropriate) **a.** *col* decide **b.** *col* approve, confirm, sanction
- **náći žȉcu** {VP} (lit. find a wire) *col* hit the spot, be very appropriate

náći se {nâđem, nâđu, náđ, nàš perf. irreg.} (lit. find oneself) *sl-drugs* find one's vein while inserting a drug needle <Slav*1>

nȁćve {ī fem. pl.} (lit. dough-tray) *sl-sex* ***Fac*** large female breast <Slav*1>

náda {ē fem.} (lit. hope) *col* talent, talented person <Slav*1>

nàdariti {rīm, rē perf.} (lit. gift) *sl* ***Iro*** throw away, toss out <Slav*1>

nadèrati {nàderēm, rū perf. intr.} Vojv *col* be in a difficult situation <Slav*1>

nadéviti se {nàdēvīm, vē perf. intr.} *sl-drink* get drunk <NE❖*1>

nàdizati se {ižēm, ižū imperf. intr.} (lit. raise) *sl-fea* ***Fac*** raise one's cultural level <Slav*1>

nȁdničarka {ē fem.; Dat nȁdničārki} /nàdničarka/ (lit. daily-wage worker) *sl-sex* ***Fac*** prostitute, hooker <Slav*1>

nadovezívānje {a neut.} (lit. connecting) *sl* prolonged and meaningless talk, blabber, chatter <Slav*1>

nadovezívati {ām, ajū imperf.} (lit. connect) *sl* talk persistently and meaninglessly, blabber, chatter <Slav*1>

nàdrgljati se {ām, ajū perf. intr.} *sl-drink* get drunk <Slav*1>

nàdrilovati se {lujēm, lujū perf. intr.} *sl-drink* get drunk <Eng❖*1>

nàdrinkati se {ām, ajū perf. intr.} *sl-drink* get drunk <Eng❖*1>

nàdrkān {a, o adj.} (lit. erect) **a.** *sl* angry, mad <Slav❖*1> **b.** *sl-fea* nervous <Slav❖*2>

nàdrkati {ām, ajū perf.} (lit. erect) **a.** *sl-sex* ***Obs*** stimulate to achieve erection <Slav❖> **b.** *sl* provoke, incite <Slav❖*1>

nàdrkati se {ām, ajū perf.} (lit. erect oneself) **a.** *sl-fea* get nervous <Slav❖> **b.** *sl-fea* get angry <Slav❖*1>

nadŕljati {nàdr̄ljām, nadŕljajū perf. intr.} (lit. harrow) *col* be in a difficult situation <Slav*1>
- **nadŕljati ko žûtī** {VP} (lit. have problems like the yellow one) *sl-fea* be in a very difficult situation

nàdrmān {a, o adj.} (lit. shook) *sl-drink* drunk <Slav*1>

nàdrmati se {ām, ajū perf. intr.} (lit. shake oneself) *sl-drink* get drunk <Slav*1>

nàdr̄ndān {a, o adj.} (lit. shook) **a.** *sl-fea* nervous <Slav❖*1> **b.** *sl-fea* insane, nuts <Slav❖*1>

nàdr̄ndati se {ām, ajū perf.} **a.** *sl-fea* get nervous <Slav❖*1> **b.** *sl-fea* get mad <Slav❖*1>

nàdrukān {a, o adj.} *sl-sex* pregnant, knock up <Ger❖*1>

nàdrukati {ām, ajū perf.} *sl-auto* pump the gas pedal <Ger❖*1>

nàduti {dmem, dmu perf.} (lit. swell) *sl* defeat <Slav*1>

nàduvān {a, o adj.} (lit. inflated) **1** *sl-fea* conceited, stuck-up <Slav*1> **2** *sl-drugs* under the strong influence of narcotic drugs, stoned <Slav*1>

nadúvati {nàdūvām, nadúvajū perf.} (lit. inflate) **1a.** *sl-drugs* smoke narcotic drugs <Slav*1> **b.** *sl-drugs* make somebody smoke narcotic drugs <Slav*2> **2** *sl* beat up <Slav*1>

nadúvati se {ām, ajū perf. intr.} (lit. inflate oneself) **1** *sl-drugs* have one's fill of hashish <Slav*1> **2** *sl-drugs* have one's fill of glue-sniffing <Slav*1>

nàdžag-bȁba {ē fem.} *sl-fea* ill-tempered female <NE-Slav.*1>

nàdžakbaba {ē fem.} *sl-fea* ill-tempered female <NE-Slav.*1>

nadžàlisati {išēm, išū perf.} *sl* find, locate

nadžibrániti se {nīm, nē perf. intr.} *sl-drink* get drunk <NE❖*1>

nadžȍdžeriti se {rīm, rē perf. intr.} *sl* assume an awkward position (e.g. sitting in a chair) <NE❖*1>

nadžókati se {ām, ajū perf. intr.} *sl-drink* get drunk <NE❖*1>

nađáriti {nàđārīm, rē perf.} *sl* throw away, toss out

nàđubriti *See the following*
- **nàđubriti créva** {VP} (lit. fertilize one's intestines) SerE *sl* eat one's fill, be stuffed

nȁe [1] {part.} [std. = ne] *sl* negative response, no <Slav✍>

nȁe [2] {excl.} [std. = ne] *sl* it is worthless <Slav✍>

nàfājtān {a, o adj.} *sl-drink* drunk <Ger⁘*1>

nàfājtati {ām, ajū perf.} *col* sprinkle the laundry before pressing <Ger⁘*1>

nàfājtati se {ām, ajū perf. intr.} *sl-drink* get drunk <Ger⁘*1>

nafàka {ē fem.; Dat nafàki} BosM *col* loan, credit <NE*1>

nafalàtati {ām, ajū perf.} Vojv *col-dia* cut into pieces <Hun>

nàfatati {ām, ajū perf.} *col* catch one's fill (of anything) <Slav☞>

nafàtirān {a, o adj.} (lit. covered with cotton) *sl-fea* affluent, in the clover <Slav⁘*1>

nafatírati se {ām, ajū perf. intr.} (lit. put some cotton around oneself) *sl* secure oneself, be safe <Slav⁘*1>

nàfilān {a, o adj.} (lit. stuffed) *sl-sex* ***Fac*** pregnant, knocked up <Ger*1>

nàfilati {ām, ajū perf.} **a.** *col* stuff <Ger⁘*1> **b.** *sl-sex* make pregnant, knock up <Ger⁘*2>

nàfistati se {ām, ajū perf. intr.} *sl-drink* get very drunk, get smashed

nàfrulān {a, o adj.} *sl-drink* drunk <Slav⁘*1>

nafrùlati se {ām, ajū perf. intr.} *sl-drink* get drunk <Slav⁘*1>

nȁfta {ē fem.} (lit. oil) **a.** *sl-auto* diesel fuel <Gre*1> **b.** *sl-drink* ***Fac*** alcoholic beverage <Gre*2>

naftàlīn {a masc.} (lit. mothballs) *sl-fea* old or outdated item <Gre*1>
• **iz naftalína** {PP} (lit. from mothballs) *col* very old, outdated: *pjesma iz naftalina very old song*

naftàlīnka {ē fem.} (lit. the one from mothballs) *sl-drink* ***Fac*** brandy <Gre⁘*1>

nȁftarica {ē fem.} *col* oil stove <Gre⁘*1>

nàftāš {naftáša (acc. = gen.) masc.} (lit. oiler) **1** *sl-auto* car with diesel engine, diesel <Gre⁘*1> **2** *sl-sex* male looking for a loose woman, guy on the make <Gre⁘*1>

nafúrati {nàfūrām, nafúrajū perf. intr.} *sl* arrive, come <Ger⁘*1>

nàfuren {a, o adj.} *sl-fea* angry, mad

nàfutrān {a, o adj.} *sl-fea* affluent <Ger⁘*1>

nàfutrati {ām, ajū perf.} (lit. stuff) **a.** *sl* lie <Ger⁘*1> **b.** cheat, swindle <Ger⁘*2>

nàfutrati se {ām, ajū perf. intr.} *sl-fea* become affluent <Ger⁘*1>

nàgariti {rīm, rē perf.} /nagáriti/ (lit. soot) **1** *sl-auto* speed (auto, etc.) <Slav*1> **2** *col* heat (a room, etc.) <Slav*1> **3** *sl-sex* engage in sexual intercourse with (of a male) <Slav*1>

nàgaziti {zīm, zē perf.} (lit. step onto) **1** *sl* be trapped, be without a way out <Slav*1> **2a.** *sl* find, locate <Slav*1> **b.** *sl* discover, find out <Slav*2> **3** *sl-auto* speed (auto, etc.) <Slav*1> **3** *sl-sex* engage in sexual intercourse with (of a male) <Slav*1> **4** *sl* heat (a room, etc.) <Slav*1>

nágaznā mîna {NP} (lit. land mine) *sl* excrement, piece of shit [illegible] mina

nàglāncati {ām, ajū perf.} *col* polish, shine <Ger⁘*1>

naglàvān {glavána masc.} *sl* ***Fac*** hat <Slav☞*1>

nagrabúsiti {gràbūsīm, sē perf.} *col* be in a difficult situation <Slav*1>

nagràisati {išēm, išū perf.} /nagràjisati /išem, išu perf./ *col* be in a difficult situation <NE*1>

nagrànisati se {išēm, išū perf. intr.} *sl-drink* get drunk <Slav⁘*1>

nagŕnuti {nàgr̄nēm, nū perf. intr.} *col* arrive in large quantities <Slav*1>

nȁgro {adv.} *sl* easily

nagrúvati {nàgrūvām, nagrúvajū perf.} (lit. bang) *sl-sstu* learn well <Slav*1>

nàgumati se {ām, ajū perf. intr.} *sl* eat one's fill, be stuffed

nagúrati {nàgūrām, nagúrajū perf. intr.} *sl* give, pass <Slav*1>

nàguz [1] {a (acc. = gen.) masc.} (lit. at the buttocks) *sl-sex* ***Fac-Obs*** male homosexual, gay <Slav⁘*1>

nàguz [2] {adv.} (lit. at the buttocks) *col* ***Obs*** backwards <Slav⁘*1>

nàguzac {sca (acc. = gen.) masc.} (lit. at the buttocks) *sl-sex* ***Fac-Obs*** male homosexual who takes the passive role, femme <Slav⁘*1>

nàguzac {sca masc.} (lit. at the buttocks) *sl* ***Fac-Obs*** short jacket <Slav⁘*1>

naguzàčkē {adv.} (lit. asswards) *col* ***Obs*** backwards <Slav⁘*1>

nàguzār {a (acc. = gen.) masc.} /nagùzār/ (lit. at the buttocks) *sl-sex* ***Fac-Obs*** male homosexual who takes the passive role, femme <Slav⁘*1>

nagùzara {ē masc.} (lit. at the buttocks) *sl-sex* ***Fac-Obs*** male homosexual who takes the passive role, femme <Slav⁘*1>

naguzèljez {a masc.} (lit. at the buttocks) *dia* ***Obs*** crab <Slav❖*1>

nagúziti {nàgūzīm, zē perf.} **a.** *col* ***Obs*** show or stick out one's buttocks <Slav❖*1> **b.** *sl-sex* ***Obs*** engage in sexual intercourse with (of a male) <Slav❖*2> **c.** *sl* ***Obs*** have a hard time, experience difficulties <Slav❖*3>

nagúziti se {nàgūzīm, zē perf.} **a.** *col* ***Obs*** show or stick out one's buttocks <Slav❖*1> **b.** *col* ***Obs*** be in a position which disturbs somebody else <Slav❖*2>

naguzívalo {a masc.} *sl-fea* ***Obs*** person who sticks out his/her buttocks while walking <Slav❖*1>

náguznīk {a masc.} *dia* ***Obs*** rump cover for a horse <Slav❖*1>

náguznjāk {a masc.} *dia* ***Obs*** buttocks (of poultry) <Slav❖*1>

nagváždalo {a neut.} *sl-fea* ***Der*** extremely talkative person, chatterbox

nagváždānje {a neut.} *sl-fea* ***Der*** prolonged and meaningless talk, blabber, chatter

nagváždati {ām, ajū imperf. intr.} *sl-fea* talk persistently and meaninglessly, blabber, chatter

nàhājcati {ām, ajū perf.} *col* heat up (room, house, etc.) <Ger❖>

nahàlisati se {išēm, išū perf. intr.} *sl* have one's fill of food <NE❖*1>

nàhamati se {ām, ajū perf. intr.} *sl* have one's fill of food

nàhanovān {a, o adj.} *sl-fea* full (of food), stuffed

nàhanovati se {nūjēm, nūjū perf. intr.} *sl* eat one's fill, be stuffed

nahàsati se {ām, ajū perf. intr.} /nahàsati se/ *sl* have one's fill of food, be stuffed <NE❖*1>

nàhēren {a, o adj.} *col* slanting <Slav❖*1>

nȁhēro {adv.} *col* slanting <Slav❖*1>

nahoróziti se {zīm, zē perf. intr.} *sl-fea* be stubborn, be defiant <NE❖*1>

nahòrōžen {a, o adj.} *sl-fea* stubborn, pigheaded <NE❖*1>

nàhrupiti {pīm, pē perf.} /nahrúpiti/ *col* appear in large quantities <Slav❖*1>

naíva {ē fem.} *col* naiveness <Fre❖*1>

nȁīvan *See the following*

- **nȁīvan ko kèlner** {AdjP} (lit. as naive as a waiter) *sl-fea* not naive at all, savvy
- **nȁīvan ko sȍbarica** {AdjP} (lit. as naive as a hotel maid) *sl-fea* not naive at all, savvy

naìvčina {ē fem. & masc.} *sl-fea* naive person <Fre❖*1>

nâj 1 {excl.} *sl* used when offering something to somebody <Slav>

nâj 2 {excl.} *sl* used to prevent action <Slav>

nâj-hâj {adj.} *sl-fea* ***App*** excellent, awesome <Slav-Eng*1>

nâj-nâj {adj.} *sl* excellent, awesome <Slav>

nája {ē fem. & masc.} *sl-fea* senior citizen <Slav*1>

nàjarcān {a, o adj.} *sl-fea* excited

najàrcati {ām, ajū perf. intr.} *sl-fea* speed (auto, etc.)

nȁje {part.} *sl* negative response, no <Slav☞>

najèbati {bēm, bū perf. intr.} **a.** *col* ***Obs*** be in a difficult situation <Slav*1> **b.** *sl* be beaten up <Slav*1>

- **Nȁjebā ga!** {S} (lit. He fucked it up!) *dia* ***Obs*** used to refer to a difficult situation of a third party, He's fucked!
- **Najèbaćeš kô žûtī!** {S} (lit. You will be fucked up like the yellow one!) *col* ***Obs*** used to refer to a difficult situation of one's interlocutor in the future, You really fucked up!
- **najèbati kô žûtī** {VP} (lit. be fucked up like the yellow one) *sl* ***Obs*** be beaten up
- **Nȁjebō je!** {S} (lit. He is fucked up!) *col* ***Obs*** used to refer to a difficult situation of a third party, He's fucked!
- **Nȁjebō je ko jêž!** {S} (lit. He is fucked up like a hedgehog!) *col* ***Obs*** used to refer to a difficult situation of a third party male, He's fucked!

najèbati se {bēm, bū perf. intr.} *sl-sex* ***Obs*** have one's fill of sex <Slav>

- **Nàjebēm ti se aláha i jèbenōg tvôg hȍdžē!** {S} (lit. I fuck my fill of your God and your fucking imam!) *col* ***Off*** used as a strong curse to a Bosnian Muslim, Fuck you!
- **Nàjebēm ti se mȁterinē pȉčkē!** {S} (lit. I fuck my fill of your mother's cunt!) *col* ***Off*** used as a strong curse, Fuck you!

Nàjedi se gȍvānā pȕno pa díši! {S} (lit. Eat your fill of shit and then breathe!) *col* ***Off*** used as a strong curse, Eat shit! ☞ **najesti se**

najèsti se {nàjedēm, edū perf. irreg.} *col* eat too much, gorge, pig out <Slav*1>

- **Nàjedi se gȍvānā pȕno pa díši!** {S} (lit. Eat your fill of shit and then breathe!) *col* ***Off*** used as a strong curse, Eat shit!
- **nàjesti se gérmē** {VP} (lit. eat one's fill of yeast) *sl-fea* get pregnant, get knocked up
- **nàjesti se hlȅba** {VP} (lit. eat one's fill of bread) SerE

col profit, gain

• **nàjesti se kàktusa** {VP} (lit. eat one's fill of cactus) *sl-drugs* take some mescaline

najéžiti {nàjēžīm, žē perf. intr.} *sl* ***Fac*** be in a difficult situation <Slav❖*1>

nâjlaf {a (acc. = gen.) masc.} **a.** *sl* boss <Slav-NE*1> **b.** *sl-fea* very important or influential person, big shot <Slav-NE*1>

nájlak {adv.} BosM *col* slowly <NE*1>

nàjlōn {adj.} (lit. nylon) **1a.** *sl-fea* weak, irresolute: *najlon frajer wishy-washy guy* <BN*1> **b.i.** *sl-fea* cowardly: *najlon šef cowardly boss* <BN*2> **ii.** *sl-fea* unhealthy: *najlon hrana unhealthy food* <BN*2>

nàjlōn pláža {NP} (lit. nylon beach) *col* nudist beach ☞ **plaža**

nàjlōn vȉskī {NP} (lit. nylon whiskey) *sl-drink* tea served instead of whiskey when a person buys a drink for the people at another table ☞ **viski**

nȁjo {part.} *sl* negative response, no <Slav✍>

nâjprvō {adv.} *col* first <Slav✍>

nâjvećī {ā, ē adj.} *sl-fea* ugliest <Slav*1>

nàkačiti {čīm, čē perf.} (lit. hook on) *sl* put on, dress <Slav*1>

nàkačiti se {čīm, čē perf. intr.} (lit. hook oneself to) *sl* get acquainted with (job, task, etc.) <Slav*1>

nakàntati {ām, ajū biasp.} **a.** *sl* beat up <Ger❖*1> **b.** *sl-sports* defeat <Ger❖*1>

nakarakȕrčiti se {čīm, čē perf. intr.} /nakarakûrčiti se/ *col* ***Obs*** stand in such a way to disturb others <Slav-NE*1>

nakarmìnisati se {išēm, išū perf. intr.} (lit. put some lipstick on) *sl-drink* get drunk <Ita❖*1>

nákav {pron.} [std. = nekakav] *col* some <Slav✍>

nàkava {ē fem.} [std. = kavana] *sl-drink* bar (drinking place) <NE✍>

nâkaza {ē fem.} /nàkaza/ (lit. monster) *sl-fea* unattractive person <Slav*1>

nakésiti se {nàkēsīm, sē perf.} *sl* smile <Slav❖*1>

• **nakésiti se do pápka** {VP} (lit. smile up to one's hooves) *sl* find something highly humorous

nakinđúriti se {kìnđūrīm, rē perf. intr.} *sl-fea* dress formally, dress up

nakìtaćiti {ćīm, ćē perf.} (lit. prick on) *sl-sex* ***Obs*** engage in sexual intercourse with (of a male) <Slav❖*1>

nàkititi {tīm, tē perf.} (lit. prick on) **a.** *sl-sex* ***Fac-Obs*** engage in sexual intercourse with (of a male) <Slav❖*1> **b.** *sl* fall asleep, doze off <Slav❖*1>

nàkititi se {tīm, tē perf. intr.} (lit. put decorations on) **a.** *sl* get formally dressed, dress up <Slav*1> **b.** get drunk <Slav*2>

nȁkjučē {adv.} *col* two days before today <Slav>

naklápānje {a neut.} *sl-fea* persistent and meaningless talk, blabber, chatter <Slav❖*1>

naklápati {ām, ajū imperf.} **1** *sl-fea* talk persistently and meaninglessly, blabber, chatter <Slav❖*1> **2** engage in sexual intercourse with (of a male) <Slav❖*1>

náklon *See the following*

• **môj náklon** {NP} (lit. My bow!) *col* used as a greeting, Hello!

naklópati se {nàklōpām, naklópajū perf. intr.} *col* eat one's fill, be stuffed <Gyp❖*1>

nàkljucati se {ām, ajū perf. intr.} *sl-drink* get drunk <Slav*1>

nàkljukati {ām, ajū perf.} *sl-sex* ***Obs*** engage in sexual intercourse with (of a male) <Slav*1>

nàkljukati se {ām, ajū perf. intr.} *col* have one's fill of food, be stuffed <Slav>

nàkō {adv.} [std. = onako] *col-dia* just like that, just for the heck of it: *On je nako ukro frajeru novčanik. He stole the guy's wallet just like that.* <Slav✍>

• **ko nàkō** {AdvP} *col* used to express usual state of affairs, same-same: *A. Kako je? B: Ko nako. A. How's life? B: Same-same.*

nakókati se {nàkōkām, nakókajū perf. intr.} *sl-drink* get drunk <Slav*1>

nakòkeriti se {rīm, rē perf. intr.} *sl* assume an awkward position (e.g. sitting in a chair) <Slav❖*1>

nàkresān {a, o adj.} *sl-drink* drunk <Slav*1>

nàkresati se {rešēm, rešū biasp. intr.} *sl-drink* get drunk <Slav*1>

nàkrīvljen {a, o adj.} (lit. elevated) **a.** *sl-fea* ***Der*** insane, nuts <Slav*1> **b.** ***Der*** strange, weird <Slav*2> **c.** ***Der*** slow to learn <Slav*3>

nakrivopízditi se {vòpīzdīm, dē perf. intr.} *sl-fea* ***Obs*** be in a bad mood <Slav❖*1>

nakŕkati se {nàkr̄kām, nakŕkajū perf. intr.} *col* eat, devour <Slav❖*1>

nȁksutra {adv.} *col* two days after tomorrow <Slav>

nàktiti {tīm, tē imperf.} *sl* sleep, nap <Ger❖*1>

nàkūrčen {a, o adj.} **a.** *sl-fea* nervous: *nakurčena žena nervous female* <Slav❖*1> **b.** *sl-fea* in a bad mood: *biti nakurčen na žurci be in a bad mood at the party* <Slav❖*2>

nakurìkati {ām, ajū perf.} *col* repair, fix <Slav❖*1>

nàkūrnjāk {a masc.} (lit. on-the-prick) *sl-sex* ***Fac-Obs*** condom, rubber <Slav>

nàlafrati se {ām, ajū perf. intr.} *sl-fea* put on loud make-up

nalèteti {nàletīm, tē perf.} (lit. fly at) **SerE** *col* come across, bump into: *naleteti na školskog druga bump into one's old school mate* <Slav*1>

• **nalèteti na mînu** {VP} (lit. hit a mine) SerE *sl-sstu* get a failing grade, flunk

nalètilić {a (acc. = gen.) masc.} **1** *sl-fea* naive male <Slav❖*1> **2** *sl-fea* troublemaker, rowdy, ruffian <Slav❖*1>

nalètiti {nàletīm, tē imperf.} *sl* be cheated, be swindled <Slav❖*1>

nalévānje {a neut.} (lit. pouring) SerE *sl-drink* drinking (alcohol) <Slav*1>

nálik {adj.} *col* similar <Slav>

nalílati se {nàlīlām, nalílajū perf. intr.} *sl-drink* get drunk <Slav*1>

nàlirkati se {ām, ajū perf. intr.} *sl-drink* get drunk

nàliti *See the following*

• **nàliti tàracu** {VP} (lit. sprinkle the porch) *sl-drink* get drunk

nàliti se {nàlijēm, jū perf. intr.} (lit. soak oneself) *sl-drink* get drunk <Slav*1>

nalìven {a, o adj.} (lit. soaked) *sl-drink* drunk <Slav*1>

nalízati se {nàlīžem, ižū perf. intr.} (lit. lick one's full) *sl-drink* get drunk <Slav*1>

nȁlo {a masc.} *sl-crime* third-rate criminal (albeit being one for a long time)

nàlofrati se {ām, ajū perf. intr.} *sl-fea* put on loud make-up

nàlokān {a, o adj.} *sl-drink* drunk <Slav*1>

nàlokati se {očem, oču perf. intr.} /nalókati se/ *sl-drink* get drunk <Slav*1>

nalòkmačiti se {čīm, čē perf. intr.} *sl-drink* get drunk <Slav☞*1>

nalòžiti {žīm, žē perf.} (lit. burn) *sl* cheat, swindle <Slav*1>

nalòžiti se {žīm, že perf. intr.} (lit. burn oneself) **a.** *sl-fea* fall in love <Slav*1> **b.** be aroused (emotionally) **c.** believe, trust

nalsùvati *See the following*

• **Nàlsuva ga!** {S} SSer *dia* ***Off*** used as a moderate curse, Fuck you!

nàlugovati {gujēm, gujū perf.} *sl-arch* bargain

nalukávati se {lùkāvām, lukávajū imperf. intr.} *sl* peep, look at others <Eng❖*1>

nȁluzaj {adv.} *sl* quickly

nàluzati {ām, ajū perf.} *sl* get ready

nàljeći {nàljegnēm, gnū, eg, eg perf. irreg.} *dia* attack, strike <Slav*1>

nàljōskān {a, o adj.} *sl-drink* drunk <Slav*1>

naljóskati se {ām, ajū perf. intr.} *sl-drink* get drunk <Slav*1>

naljúljati se {nàljūljām, naljúljajū perf. intr.} (lit. swing one's full) *sl-drink* get drunk <Slav*1>

namàčkariti se {rīm, vē perf. intr.} (lit. cat oneself on) *sl-fea* put on excessive make-up <Slav❖*1>

namàknuti {nàmaknēm, nū perf.} **1** *sl-sex* ***Obs*** engage in sexual intercourse with (of a male) <Slav*1> **2** *col* arrange for: *namaknuti povišicu arrange for a raise* <Slav*1>

• **namàknuti kȉntu** {VP} (lit. push some money) *sl* earn amply

• **namàknuti lóvu** {VP} (lit. push some money) *sl* earn amply

namàndžati se {ām, ajū perf. intr.} *sl* eat one's fill, be stuffed <Ita❖>

nȁmastīr {a masc.} [std. = manastir] *dia* monastery <Gre☞>

nàmazān {a, o adj.} (lit. lubricated) **a.** *sl-fea* experienced: *namazan fudbaler experienced soccer player* <Slav*1> **b.** *sl-fea* skillful: *namazan kriminalac skillful criminal* <Slav*2> **c.** *sl-fea* sly <Slav*3>

• **nàmazan svîm bòjama** {AdjP} (lit. painted with all colors) *col* very sly

• **nàmazān svîm fârbama** {AdjP} (lit. painted with all colors) *col* very sly

• **nàmazān svîm mástima** {AdjP} (lit. painted with all colors) *col* very sly

nàmazati *See the following*

• **nàmazati frȁjeru prózor** {VP} (lit. lubricate a window for a guy) *sl* trick, cheat, swindle

nàmazati se {ažēm, ažū perf. intr.} (lit. lubricate oneself) *sl* eat one's fill, be stuffed <Slav*1>

nàmestiti {tīm, tē perf.} (lit. fix) **1 SerE** *sl* beat up <**Slav***1> **2 SerE** *col* fix, arrange something for somebody (usu. illegal) <**Slav***1>
- **nàmestiti ìgru** {VP} (lit. set a play) SerE *col* falsely incriminate, frame

nȁmeštāj {a masc.} (lit. furniture) **1 SerE** *sl-sex* ***Fac*** female body <**Slav***1> **2 SerE** *sl-drink* ***Fac*** wine with soda <**Slav***1>

naméštāljka {ē fem.} /naméštaljka/ **1 SerE** *sl-sports* fixed game <**Slav***1> **2 SerE** *sl* false incrimination, frame <**Slav***1>

naméštānje {a neut.} SerE *col* gossiping <**Slav***1>

naméštati {ām, ajū imperf.} **1 SerE** *sl* falsely incriminate, frame <**Slav***1> **2 SerE** *sl* prearrange so as to ensure a desired fraudulent outcome, fix <**Slav***1>
- **naméštati ìgru** {VP} (lit. set a play) SerE *col* falsely incriminate, frame

namìcāljka {ē fem.} *sl-sex* ***Fac*** prostitute, hooker <**Slav***1>

namìrisān {a, o adj.} /nȁmirisān/ (lit. perfumed) *sl-fea* affluent, loaded, fat <**Slav***1>

namirìsati {mìrišēm, mìrišū perf.} (lit. sniff) *sl* feel, sense <**Slav***1>

nàmjestiti {tīm, tē perf.} (lit. fix) **1** *col* falsely incriminate, frame <**Slav***1> **2** *col* prearrange so as to ensure a desired fraudulent outcome, fix <**Slav***1>
- **nàmjestiti ìgrānku** {VP} (lit. set a dancing party) *col* falsely incriminate, frame
- **nàmjestiti ìgru** {VP} (lit. set a play) *col* falsely incriminate, frame
- **nàmjestiti mȉnu** {VP} (lit. set a mine) *sl* falsely incriminate, frame
- **nàmjestiti pȕšku** {VP} (lit. set a rifle) *sl* trick, cheat, swindle

nȁmještāj {a masc.} (lit. furniture) *sl-sex* ***Fac*** female body <**Slav***1>

namjéštāljka {ē fem.} **1 SerE** *col* false incrimination, frame <**Slav***1> **2 SerE** *col* prearranged competition or contest <**Slav***1>

namlátiti {nàmlātīm, tē perf.} (lit. thrash) **1** *col* beat up <**Slav***1> **2** *col* earn (money) <**Slav***1>

namontírati {mòntīrām, montírajū perf.} (lit. assemble) **1** *sl* falsely incriminate <**Fre**⁘*1> **2** *sl* prearrange so as to ensure a desired fraudulent outcome, fix, frame <**Fre**⁘*1>
- **namontírati nogáre** {VP} (lit. assemble legs) *sl* run away, flee

namontírati se {mòntīrām, montírajū perf. intr.} (lit. assemble oneself) *sl-fea* dress formally, dress up <**Fre**⁘*1>

nána {ē fem.} **1** *dia* grandmother, grandma <**NE**> **2** *dia* mother, mom <**NE**>
- **Mȉlē li vam ga i pòkvarenē nánē nȁbijēm!** {S} (lit. I fuck your dear and rotten mother!) **SSer** *dia* ***Off*** used as a strong curse, Fuck you!
- **Nȁne li ti ga!** {S} (lit. *I fuck* to your mother!) SSer *dia* ***Off*** used as a strong curse, Fuck you!
- **Nȁne mu ga!** {S} (lit. *I fuck* his mother!) SSer *dia* ***Off*** used as a strong curse, Fuck him!
- **Nȁne ti ga mile!** {S} (lit. *I fuck* your dear mother!) SSer *dia* ***Off*** used as a strong curse, Fuck you!
- **Nȁne ti ga nabȉjēm!** {S} (lit. I stick it to your mother!) SSer *dia* ***Off*** used as a strong curse, Fuck you!
- **Nȁne ti kȑvavō!** {S} (lit. *I fuck* your bloody mother!) SSer *dia* ***Off*** used as a very strong curse, Fuck you!
- **Nȁne ti tvòje!** {S} (lit. *I fuck* your mother!) SSer *dia* ***Off*** used as a strong curse, Fuck you!
- **Nȁne vi ga!** {S} (lit. *I fuck* your mother!) SSer *dia* ***Off*** used as a strong curse, Fuck you!
- **Nánu mu pogȁnu!** {S} (lit. *I fuck* his dirty mother!) *dia* ***Off*** used as a strong curse, Fuck him!

nánati {nânām, nánajū imperf.} *col* rock a child <**Slav**>

nȁnče {eta neut.} *sl-fea* elderly female <**NE**⁘*1>

nánica *See the following*
- **Nȁnicu li ti!** {S} (lit. *I fuck* your little mother!) SSer *dia* ***Off*** used as a strong curse, Fuck you!
- **Nȁnicu ti mȉlu!** {S} (lit. *I fuck* your dear mother!) SSer *dia* ***Off*** used as a strong curse, Fuck you!

nȁnovača {ē fem.} *sl-drink* mint brandy <**NE**⁘*1>

Nánu mu pogȁnu! {S} (lit. *I fuck* his dirty mother!) *dia* ***Off*** used as a strong curse, Fuck him! ☞ **nana**

nȁnjupati se {ām, ajū perf. intr.} /nanjúpati se/ *col* eat one's fill, be stuffed <**Ita**⁘*1>

naočárac {rca (acc. = gen.) masc.} *sl-fea* male with eyeglasses, four-eyes <**Slav**⁘*1>

nȁočari {čārā masc. pl.} (lit. eyeglasses) *sl-fea* ***Fac*** black eye, shiner <**Slav***1>
- **Belmȍndo nȁočāri** {NP} (lit. Belmondo, French actor popular in the 1970s, eyeglasses) *sl* ***Fac*** black eye, shiner

nȁočārka {ē fem.; Dat nȁočārki} (lit. cobra) *sl-fea* female with eyeglasses, four-eyes <**Slav**⁘*1>

nâpad {a masc.} (lit. attack) *sl* dating, going out with <**Slav***1>

napakȉnđel {a neut.} *sl-gamble* cheating in cards <**Ger**✎>

nàpakovati {kujēm, kujū perf.} (lit. pack) *sl* insinuate <Ger❖*1>

napáliti {nàpālīm, lē perf.} *sl* lie <Slav*1>

napáliti se {npālīm, lē perf. intr.} (lit. burn oneself) **a.** *sl-fea* fall in love <Slav*1> **b.** *sl-fea* be aroused (emotionally) <Slav*1> **c.** *sl* believe, trust <Slav*2> ☞ **naložiti se**

nàpāljen {a, o adj.} (lit. burning) **a.** *sl-fea* in love <Slav*1> **b.** *sl-fea* aroused, hot <Slav*2> **c.** *sl-sex* aroused, hot <Slav*3>

napánjati se {nàpānjām, napánjajū perf. intr.} *sl* eat one's fill, be stuffed <Ita❖*1>

napásati *See the following*

- **napásati ȍči** {VP} (lit. graze one's eyes) **1** *sl-fea* observe a female for a long time **2** *sl-fea* watch sexually explicit material

nàpasti {adnēm, adnū perf. irreg.} (lit. attack) *sl* go somewhere <Slav*1>

napèndečiti {čīm, čē perf.} *sl-sex* ***Obs*** engage in sexual intercourse with (of a male) <Slav*1>

nȁpet *See the following*

- **nȁpēt ko pȕška** {AdjP} (lit. as tense as a rifle) *sl-fea* very tense

nȁpētō {ōg neut.} (lit. tense) *sl* fun <Slav*1>

nàpevati {ām, ajū perf.} (lit. sing a lot) **a.** **SerE** *sl* promise <Slav*1> **b.** **SerE** talk persistently and meaninglessly, blabber, chatter <Slav*2>

nàpičiti {čīm, čē perf.} (lit. cunt on) **a.** *sl-sex* ***Obs*** engage in sexual intercourse with (of a male) <Slav*1> **b.** *sl* ***Obs*** kick in the buttocks <Slav*2>

nàpičnjāk {a masc.} *sl-sex* ***Obs*** pubic hair (female) <Slav❖*1>

napíjati {nàpījām, napíjajū imperf.} *col* make drunk <Slav*1>

napikávati {pìkāvām, pikávajū imperf.} *sl-sex* ***Obs*** engage in sexual intercourse with (of a male) <Slav*1>

nàpiknuti {nēm, nū perf.} *sl-sex* ***Obs*** engage in sexual intercourse with (of a male) <Slav*1>

nàpiti {nàpijēm, ijū perf.} *col* make drunk <Slav*1>

nàpljugān {a, o adj.} **1** *sl-drink* drunk **2** *sl-drugs* stoned (on hashish or marijuana)

nàpljugati se {ām, ajū perf. intr.} **1** *sl-drink* get drunk **2** *sl-drugs* smoke one's fill of hashish or marijuana

napljùvati {ljujēm, ljujū perf.} (lit. spit on) *col* criticize publicly <Slav*1>

nápoj {a (acc. = gen.) masc.} *sl-fea* stupid or mentally deficient person <Slav*1>

nápoj {a masc.} **1a.** *sl* soup <Slav*1> **b.** meal <Slav*2> **c.** low-quality food, slop <Slav*3> **2** wine

nàpojen {a, o adj.} (lit. filled with water) *sl-sex* ***Fac*** pregnant, knocked up <Slav*1>

nápon *See the following*

- **vìsokī nápon** {NP} (lit. high voltage) *sl-sex* ***Fac*** lust, sexual urge

nápōran {rna, rno adj.} (lit. tiring) *col* boring: *naporan film boring movie* <Slav*1>

nàpraviti *See the following*

- **nàpraviti cȑtu** {VP} (lit. make a line) *sl* run away, flee, make tracks
- **nàpraviti frȅsku** {VP} (lit. make a fresco) *sl* beat up
- **nàpraviti sránje** {VP} (lit. make shit) *col* cause problems
- **nàpraviti stȑvinu** {VP} (lit. make a corpse) *sl* beat up
- **nàpraviti zbȕnjēvku** {VP} (lit. make confusion) *sl* confuse, mix up
- **nàpraviti zîd** {VP} (lit. make a wall) *sl-crime* cover for a pickpocket while he is stealing

nàprčen {a, o adj.} *sl-fea* arrogant <Slav*1>

nàprčiti se {čīm, čē perf. intr.} *sl-fea* be conceited, be stuck-up <Slav*1>

nàprednā {ē fem. (adj. decl.)} (lit. the forward one) *sl-sex* ***Fac*** large-breasted female <Slav*1>

napríčati *See the following*

- **Štȁ mi nȁprīča!** {S} (lit. What did you tell to me!) *col* used to express disbelief, Unbelievable!

napr̀ndečiti {čīm, čē perf.} *sl-sex* ***Obs*** engage in sexual intercourse with (of a male) <Slav✍*1>

náprsnjāk {a masc.} (lit. thimble) *sl-sex* ***Fac*** small female breast <Slav*1>

nàpucati {ām, ajū perf.} (lit. shoot at) **1a.** *sl* beat up <Slav*1> **b.** *sl* hit, punch <Slav*2> **c.** *sl* hit another car, have a fender bender <Slav*3> **2** *sl* direct against somebody (usu. a dog) <Slav*1>

nàpucati se {ām, ajū perf. intr.} (lit. bang oneself) *col* eat one's fill, be stuffed <Slav*1>

napuhávati {pùhāvām, puhávajū imperf.} (lit. inflate) *sl-fea* aggrandize <Slav*1>

- **napuhávati jája** {VP} (lit. blow one's balls) *sl-sex* ***Obs*** engage in fellatio

napuhávati se {pùhāvām, puhávajū imperf. intr.} (lit. inflate oneself) *sl-fea* boast, brag, puff oneself up <Slav*1>

nàpūjdati {ām, ajū perf.} *col* make someone act against a third party, stir up: *Marko je napujdao Jovana na Mariju. Marko stirred Jovan up against Marija.* <Hun*1>

nàpumpān {a, o adj.} (lit. inflated) **1** *sl-sex* ***Fac*** pregnant, knocked up <Ger❖*1> **2** *sl-fea* ***Fac*** muscular, pumped up <Ger❖*1> **3** *sl-fea* ***Fac*** full of ideas <Ger❖*1>

nàpūmpati {ām, ajū perf.} (lit. inflate) **1 a.** *sl* lie <Ger❖*1> **b.** *sl* persuade, convince <Ger❖*2> **2** *sl-sex* make pregnant, knock up <Ger❖*1>

nàpunjen {a, o adj.} (lit. stuffed) *sl-sex* ***Fac*** pregnant, knocked up <Ger❖*1>

napúpeo {ela, elo adj.} SerE *sl-fea* pregnant, knocked up <Slav*1>

napúpeti {nàpūpīm, pē perf. intr.} (lit. bud) SerE *sl-fea* get pregnant, get knocked up <Slav*1>

nàpušen {a, o adj.} (lit. smoked) *sl-drugs* pertaining to the person who feels the effects of marijuana or hashish <Slav*1>

Nàputam ti ga! {S} (lit. I stick it to you!) *dia* ***Off*** used as a strong curse, Fuck you! ☞ **naputati**

nàputati *See the following*
- **Nàputam ti ga!** {S} (lit. I stick it to you!) *dia* ***Off*** used as a strong curse, Fuck you!

napuvávati {pùvāvām, puvávajū imperf.} *col* inflate, blow up <Slav*1>

nàrāndža {ē fem.} (lit. orange) *sl-fea* very young female, little girl <NE*1>

naràuhati se {ām, ajū perf. intr.} *sl-drugs* smoke one's fill of hashish or marijuana <Ger❖*1>

naràvnati *See the following*
- **naràvnati lìčnjāk** {VP} (lit. flatten one's ID) *sl* beat up severely, rearrange someone's face

náravskī {adv.} (lit. naturally) *col* used as a strong affirmative response, of course, yeah, you bet <Slav*1>

nàrdžija {ē masc.} *sl-crime* pickpocket <NE✍*1>

nȁre {excl.} *sl-arch* used to express absence

narédati {nàrēdām, narédajū perf.} *sl* tell, say <Slav*1>

naréditi {nàrēdīm, dē perf.} *sl-fea* persuade, convince <Slav*1>

naredívati *See the following*
- **Narèduj nȅgatīvno!** {S} (lit. Talk negatively!) *sl* used to stimulate one's interlocutor to lie

nárednīk {a (acc. = gen.) masc.} *sl-mil* sergeant <Slav*1>

nàrenjkati {ām, ajū perf.} *sl* force, coerce

narezíliti {rèzīlīm, lē perf.} *col* reproach, scold <NE*1>

nȁrgo {adv.} *sl* easy, simple (of a problem, etc.)

nȁrgu {adv.} *sl* easy, simple (of a problem, etc.)

nàrisati {išēm, išū biasp.} (lit. draw) Cro *sl* daydream <Slav*1>

nàrisati se {išēm, išū perf. intr.} (lit. draw oneself) Cro *sl* arrive, come <Slav*1>
- **Nàriši se!** {S} (lit. Draw yourself!) Cro *sl* used to refer to something impossible (usu. in response to a request), No way!

nȁrkić {a (acc. = gen.) masc.} /nàrkīć/ *sl-drugs* junkie <Gre✍>

nȁrko {-*} *sl-drugs* narcotic drug, dope: *narko-mafija drug mafia* <Gre✍>

narkohòličār {a (acc. = gen.) masc.} (lit. narcoholic) **1** *sl-fea* ***Der*** insane person <Gre❖*1> **2** *sl-drink* ***Der*** alcoholic, drunk <Gre❖*1> **3** *sl-drugs* ***Der*** drug addict, junkie <Gre❖*1>

nȁrkos {a (acc. = gen.) masc.} /nârkos/ *sl-drugs* drug addict, junkie <Gre✍>

narkòtičār {a (acc. = gen.) masc.} (lit. drug addict) *sl-drugs* alcoholic, drunk <Gre❖>

narkóza {ē fem.} (lit. narcosis) **a.** *sl-drink* alcoholic beverage <Gre❖> **b.** *sl-drink* wine <Gre❖>

nárockī {ā, ō adj.} [std. = narodski] *col-dia* folk, country <Slav✍>

narȍdnjāčkī {ā, ō adj.} (lit. people's) *sl-music* folk, country <Slav*1>

narȍdnjāk {rodnjáka (acc. = gen.) masc.} *sl-music* country or folk music performer <Slav*1>

narȍdnjāk {rodnjáka masc.} *sl-music* country or folk song <Slav*1>

národskī {ā, ō adj.} (lit. people's) *col* folk, country <Slav>

narókati se {nàrōkām, narókajū perf. intr.} **1** *sl-drink* get drunk <Eng❖*1> **2** *sl-drugs* take narcotic drugs, do drugs <Eng❖*1>

nàrōljān {a masc.} *sl-drink* drunk, pickled <Ger❖*1>

naróljati se {nàrōljām, naróljajū perf. intr.} *sl-drink* get drunk <Ger❖*1>

nárukvica {ē fem.} (lit. bracelet) *sl* ***Fac*** cash payment <Slav*1>

nárukvice {kvīcā fem. pl.} (lit. bracelets) *sl-crime* ***Fac*** handcuffs, bracelet <Slav*1>

nasáditi {nàsādīm, dē perf.} (lit. stick on) **a.** *sl-sex* ***Obs*** engage in sexual intercourse with (of a male), poke <Slav*1> **b.** *sl* cheat, swindle <Slav*2>

nasáditi se {dīm, dē perf. intr.} (lit. stick oneself on) **1** *col* be mistaken <Slav*1> **2** *col* stand in one place for a long time (usu. disturbing others): *Njena prijateljica se nasadila na telefon, pa sam morao čekati. Her friend was hanging on the phone, so I had to wait.* <Slav*1>

nàsaftān {a, o adj.} (lit. juicy) **1** *sl-drink* drunk, juiced <Ger✤*1> **2** *sl-sex* sexually aroused, wet <Ger✤*1>

nasandŕćiti se {sàndr̄ćīm, ćē perf. intr.} *col* stand in one place for a long time (usu. disturbing others) <Slav*1>

nàsānkati {ām, ajū perf.} *col* cheat, swindle <Slav*1>

nàsānkati se {ām, ajū imperf. intr.} (lit. have one's fill of sledding) *sl* be mistaken <Slav*1>

nasàntraćiti {ćīm, ćē perf.} *sl-sex* ***Obs*** engage in sexual intercourse with (of a male) <Slav*1>

nàsānjkati {ām, ajū perf.} (lit. ride on a sled) *col* cheat, swindle, take for a ride <Slav*1>

nàsānjkati se {ām, ajū perf.} (lit. have one's fill of riding on a sled) *col* be mistaken <Slav*1>

nàseći se {naséčem, naséeku, nasék, nasék perf. irreg.} (lit. cut one's fill) SerE *sl-drink* get drunk <Slav*1>

nasekìrati {ām, ajū perf.} *col* make nervous, get on one's nerves <NE>

nasekìrati se {ām, ajū perf. intr.} **a.** *sl* get nervous, worry <NE> **b.** *sl-drink* get drunk <NE*1>

nàsesti {ednēm, ednū perf. irreg.} (lit. sit on) SerE *col* be mistaken <Slav*1>

nàsipati se {ām, ajū perf. intr.} (lit. pour one's fill) *sl-drink* get drunk <Slav*1>

nàsisān {a, o adj.} (lit. sucked) *sl-drink* drunk <Slav*1>

nàsisati se {išēm, išū perf. intr.} (lit. suck one's fill) *sl-drink* get drunk <Slav*1>

nàsjeći se {nasjéčem, nasjéku, nàsjēk, nàsjēk perf. irreg.} (lit. cut one's fill) *sl-drink* get drunk <Slav*1>

nàsjesti {ednēm, ednū perf. irreg.} (lit. sit on) *col* be mistaken <Slav*1>

nàslikati se {ām, ajū perf. intr.} (lit. paint oneself) *col* come, arrive <Slav*1>

náslon {a masc.} (lit. back *of chair, bench, etc.*) *sl* nudist beach <Slav*1>

náslovnā strána {NP} (lit. front page) *sl-sex* ***Fac-Obs*** sexual intercourse in which the female partner lies on her back ☞ **strana**

nàsmicati {ām, ajū perf.} *sl* cheat, swindle <Slav*1>

nȁsmijān {jna, jno adj.} (lit. smiley) *col* happy <Slav*1>

nàsrati {serēm, serū perf.} **a.** *sl-sex* ***Obs*** defecate one's fill <Slav*1> **b.** *sl* ***Obs*** lie <Slav*2>

nàsrati se {serēm, seru perf. intr.} (lit. shit one's fill) **1 a.** *sl* arrive uninvited <Slav*1> **b.** *sl* show up <Slav*2> **2** *sl-fea* talk persistently and meaninglessly <Slav*1>

nȁsta {ē masc.} *sl* janitor <Slav✍>

nàstaviti {vīm, vē perf.} (lit. continue) *col* put on water to boil: *Nastavi kafu. Put water on to boil for the coffee.* <Slav*1>

nastrádati {nàstrādām, nastrádajū perf. intr.} *col* die, kick the bucket <Slav*1>

nástrešnica {ē fem.} [std. = nadstrešnica] *col* porch <Slav✍>

nasúkati se {nàsučem, učū imperf. intr.} **1** *sl-fea* be in a difficult situation <Slav*1> **2** *sl-fea* be mistaken <Slav*2>

nàsvīrān {a, o adj.} *sl-drink* drunk <Slav*1>

nasvírati se {nàsvīrām, nasvírajū perf. intr.} (lit. play one's fill of music) *sl-drink* get drunk <Slav*1>

nàsvitkati se {nàsvitkām, ajū perf. intr.} *sl-drink* get drunk <Slav*1>

našárati {nàšārām, našárajū perf.} *col* write <Slav*1>

našèšeriti se {rīm, rē perf. intr.} *sl* annoy, bother, pester: *Našešerili su mi se neki rođaci. Some relatives of mine have been bothering me.* <Slav✤✍*1>

našešíriti se {našèšīrīm, rē perf. intr.} *sl* be very boring <Slav✤*1>

nȁšīkān {a, o adj.} *sl-drink* drunk <Slav✤*1>

našíkati {nàšīkām, našíkajū perf.} *sl-sex* ***Obs*** engage in sexual intercourse with (of a male) <Slav✤*1>

našíkati se {nàšīkām, našíkajū perf. intr.} *sl-drink* get drunk <Slav✤*1>

nàšljēmān {a, o adj.} *sl-drink* drunk <Slav✤*1>

našljémati se {nàšljēmām, našljémajū perf. intr.} *sl-drink* get drunk <Slav✤*1>

našljískati *See the following*

- **Nàšljiskām ti ga!** {S} (lit. I stick it to you!) *dia* ***Off*** used as a strong curse, Fuck you!

našljíviti {nàšljīvīm, vē perf.} (lit. plum on) *sl* cause a black eye <**Slav**[*1]> ☞ šljiva

nàšljōkān {a, o adj.} *sl-drink* drunk <**Slav**❖[*1]>

našljókati se {nàšljōkām, našljókajū perf. intr.} *sl-drink* get drunk <**Slav**❖[*1]>

nàšmīnkati {ām, ajū perf.} (lit. put on make-up) *sl* beat up severely <**Ger**[*1]>

nàšmīnkati se {ām, ajū perf. intr.} (lit. put on make-up) *sl-drink* get drunk <**Ger**[*1]>

nàšōdrati se {ām, ajū perf. intr.} *sl* have one's fill of food, be stuffed

nàšpanān {a, o adj.} **a.** *sl-crafts* tight <**Ger**[*1]> **b.** *sl-fea* tense <**Ger**[*2]>

nàšpanovān {a, o adj.} **a.** *sl-crafts* tight <**Ger**[*1]> **b.** *sl-fea* tense <**Ger**[*2]>

nàšpanovati {nūjēm, nūjū perf.} *sl-crafts* tighten <**Ger**[*1]>

našprícati se {nàšprīcām, našprícajū perf. intr.} *sl-drink* get drunk <**Ger**[*1]>

naštéliti {nàštēlīm, lē perf.} *col* fix, arrange something for somebody (usu. illegal) <**Ger**[*1]>

nàštelovati {lujēm, lujū perf.} *sl-crafts* adjust, tune <**Ger**[*1]>

nàštimati {ām, ajū perf.} **a.** *col* adjust, tune <**Ger**[*1]> **b.** *sl* persuade, convince <**Ger**[*2]>

naštimávati {štìmāvām, štimávajū imperf.} **a.** *col* tune, adjust, fix <**Ger**[*1]> **b.** persuade, convince <**Ger**[*2]> **c.** flirt <**Ger**[*3]>

nàšvasān {a, o adj.} *sl-drink* drunk <**Ger**[*1]>

nàšvasati se {ām, ajū imperf. intr.} *sl-drink* get drunk <**Ger**[*1]>

našvŕljati {nàšvrljām, našvŕljajū perf.} *col* scribble, write illegibly <**Slav**>

nàtaći {takēnm, taknū, tak, tak perf. irreg.} (lit. stick on) *sl-sex* ***Obs*** engage in sexual intercourse with (of a male) <**Slav**[*1]>

natàkariti {rīm, rē perf.} (lit. stick) **1** *sl-sex* ***Obs*** engage in sexual intercourse with (of a male) <**Slav**❖[*1]> **2** *sl* dress, put on (clothing, etc.) <**Slav**❖[*1]>

natàknuti {nàtaknēm, nū perf.} (lit. stick) *sl-sex* ***Obs*** engage in sexual intercourse with (of a male) <**Slav**[*1]>
- **natàknuti na kàlup** {VP} (lit. stick on a form) *sl-sex* ***Fac-Obs*** engage in sexual intercourse with
- **natàknuti na rážanj** {VP} (lit. stick on a roasting-spit) *sl-sex* ***Fac-Obs*** engage in sexual intercourse with
- **natàknuti na rôg** {VP} (lit. stick on a horn) *sl-sex* ***Fac-Obs*** engage in sexual intercourse with

nàtankān {a, o adj.} *sl-drink* drunk <**Ger**[*1]>

nàtankati {ām, ajū perf.} *sl auto* fill up with gas <**Ger**[*1]>

nàtankati se {ām, ajū perf. intr.} *sl-drink* get drunk <**Ger**[*1]>

natànkīrān {a, o adj.} *sl-drink* drunk <**Ger**[*1]>

nàtankovati {kujēm, kujū perf.} *sl auto* fill up with gas <**Ger**[*1]>

natégnuti {nàtēgnēm, nū perf.} (lit. stretch) *sl-sex* ***Obs*** engage in sexual intercourse with (of a male) <**Slav**[*1]>
- **natégnuti múda do kòljena** {VP} (lit. pull one's balls down to one's knee) *sl-fea* ***Obs*** work hard, bust one's balls

natenáne {adv.} *col* without any rush, in an elaborate manner, step-by-step (usu. in reference to telling a story) <**NE**>

natèzāč {tezáča (acc. = gen.) masc.} (lit. stretcher) *sl-music* rock guitarist <**Slav**[*1]>

natézati {nàtēžem, ēžu imperf.} (lit. keep stretching) *sl-drink* drink (alcohol) <**Slav**[*1]>

natìkača {ē fem.} *sl-sex* ***Fac*** prostitute, hooker <**Slav**[*1]>

nȁtkāsna {ē fem.} *col* nightstand <**Ger**>

nȁtkos {a (acc. = gen.) masc.} *sl-drugs* drug addict, junkie <**Gre**☞>

natnàzati se {ām, ajū perf. intr.} *sl* eat one's fill, be stuffed

natocìljati {ām, ajū perf.} *col* cheat, swindle

natocìljati se {ām, ajū perf. intr.} *sl* come, arrive <**Slav**[*1]>

natòčiti {nàtočīm, čē perf.} **a.** *sl* falsely incriminate, frame <**Slav**[*1]> **b.** *sl* cheat, swindle <**Slav**[*2]>

natòčiti se {čīm, čē perf. intr.} *sl-drink* get drunk <**Slav**[*1]>

natòvaren {a, o adj.} (lit. loaded) *sl-fea* affluent, loaded, fat <**Slav**[*1]>

natòvariti {rīm, rē perf.} (lit. load) *sl* falsely incriminate, frame <**Slav**[*1]>

natòviti se {nàtovīm, vē perf. intr.} *sl-fea* gain weight <**Slav**[*1]>

nàtpevati {ām, ajū perf.} (lit. outsing) **a.** SerE *sl* be louder than somebody else <**Slav**[*1]> **b.** SerE *sl* defeat <**Slav**[*1]>

nàtpičnjāk {a masc.} (lit. above the cunt) *sl-sex* ***Obs*** pubic area (female) <**Slav**❖>

natpíjati {nàtpījām, natpíjajū imperf.} *col* drink more alcohol than somebody else, outdrink <Slav>

nàtpiti {nàtpijēm, ijū perf.} *col* drink more alcohol than somebody else, outdrink <Slav>

natȑčati {nàtrčīm, čē perf.} (lit. run into) *col* come, arrive <Slav*1>

natŕćiti se {nàtrćīm, ćē perf. intr.} *sl-fea* stick out one's buttocks <Slav*1>

nàtrēskān {a, o adj.} **a.** *sl-drink* drunk <Slav*1> **b.** *sl-fea* in love <Slav*2>

natréskati se {ām, ajū perf. intr.} /nàtreskati se/ **a.** *sl-drink* get drunk <Slav*1> **b.** *sl-fea* fall in love <Slav*2>

nàtrēsti {trésēm, trésū perf. irreg.} *sl-drink* drink (alcohol) <Slav*1>

nàtrēsti se {natrésēm, sū perf. intr.} *sl-drink* get drunk <Slav*1>

nàtrgati se {ām, ajū perf. intr.} *sl-drink* get drunk <Slav*1>

natrkèljisati {išēm, išū perf.} **a.** *sl* stick in, insert <Slav*1> **b.** *sl-sex* engage in sexual intercourse with (of a male) <Slav*2>

natȑpati *See the following*

- **natȑpati bunáre** {VP} (lit. put in wells) *sl-fea* get rich

nàtrtiti {tīm, tē perf.} /natŕtiti/ *sl-sex* ***Obs*** engage in sexual intercourse with (of a male) <Slav*1>

natŕtiti se {nàtȓtīm, tē perf. intr.} *sl-fea* stick out one's buttocks <Slav*1>

nàtucati *See the following*

- **nàtucati klînca** {VP} (lit. hit a kid) *sl-sex* make pregnant, knock up

nàtūći {natúčem, natúku, nàtūk, nàtūk perf. irreg.} **1** *sl-mil* step on a mine <Slav*1> **2** *sl* have a hard time, experience difficulties: *natući u ratu have a hard time during the war* <Slav*1> **3** *sl* beat up <Slav*1>

- **nàtūći klînca** {VP} (lit. hit a kid) *sl-sex* make pregnant, knock up

naȕčiti {nàučīm, čē perf. intr.} (lit. learn) *col* get used to: *Naučila sam na buku od tramvaja. I got used to the streetcar noise.* <Slav*1>

- **dòtle bi i óvca naȕčila da ȉgrā míce s brȁbōnjcima** {S} (lit. by that time even a sheep would learn to play checkers with its shit) *sl* ***Fac*** used to refer to impatience

naujglàvica {ē fem.} *sl-fea* conceited male <Slav⁘*1>

náuman {mna, mno adj.} **a.** *col* having the intention to: *biti nauman kupiti nova kola have the intention to buy a new car* <Slav*1> **b.** *col* willing: *biti nauman otići na more be willing to go to the seashore* <Slav*1>

naȕmpasti {adnēm, adnū perf. irreg.} /nàumpasti/ *col* have an idea <Slav⁘>

naváliti {nàvālīm, lē imperf.} (lit. try hard) *sl-sex* ***Obs*** attempt to engage in sexual intercourse with (of a male) <Slav*1>

- **naváliti ko mȕtav na telèfōn** {VP} (lit. insist on using like a mute a telephone) *sl-fea* be very intrusive

naváliti se *See the following*

- **Naváli se na mòjēga!** {S} (lit. Lean on my *prick*!) *dia* ***Off*** used as a strong curse, Fuck you!

nȁvēk {adv.} SerE *col* forever <Slav*1>

navíjati *See the following*

- **Ne nàvījāj!** {S} (lit. Don't roll it!) *sl* used to express disbelief, No shit?

navínuti *See the following*

- **navínuti pílu** {VP} (lit. roll a saw) *sl-auto* speed on a motorcycle

nàviti *See the following*

- **nàviti féder** {VP} (lit. wind a spring) *col* make nervous, get on one's nerves: *Navila mi feder zbog male plate. He/she is teasing me over a low salary.*

navláčiti {nàvlāčīm, čē imperf.} **1a.** *col* cheat, swindle <Slav*1> **b.** *col* tease <Slav*2> **2a.** *sl-sex* engage in sexual intercourse with (of a male) <Slav*1> **b.** *sl-sex* engage in sexual foreplay, pet, feel up <Slav*2>

nâvlaka {ē fem.} **1** *sl* T-shirt <Slav*1> **2a.** *sl* something one gets addicted to <Slav*1> **b.** *sl* trap, catch <Slav*2>

navlàkuša {ē fem.} *col* cheating, swindling <Slav⁘*1>

nȁvlāš {adv.} *dia* intentionally, on purpose <Slav*1>

navózati se {nàvōzām, navózajū perf. intr.} (lit. have one's fill of driving) *sl-drink* get drunk <Slav*1>

nàvr {adv.} [std. = navrh] *dia-col* on the top, over, above something <Slav>

navŕnuti {nàvȓnēm, nū perf. intr.} *col* stop by, drop in on <Slav*1>

navȕčen {vučèna, no adj.} *sl-drugs* addicted to narcotic drugs <Slav*1>

nàvūći {navúčem, navúkū, nàvūk, nàvūk perf. irreg.} (lit. pull over) **1** *sl* ***Obs*** engage in sexual intercourse with (of a male) <Slav*1> **2** cheat, swindle **3** *col* catch, get something unwillingly: *Navukla je prehladu. She has caught cold.* <Slav*1>

- **nàvūći klînca** {VP} (lit. drag a kid) *sl-sex* get pregnant, get knocked up

• **nàvūći na dupljáka** {VP} (lit. drag on duplicity) *sl-crime* run away through a two-exit building

• **nàvūći na plúća** {VP} (lit. draw on one's lungs) *sl* hug

• **nàvūći na šifónjer** {VP} (lit. draw onto a cupboard) *sl* hug

• **nàvūći zâvesu** {VP} (lit. pull curtains) *sl* shut up

nàvūći se {navúčem, navúkū, nàvūk, nàvūk imperf. intr.} (lit. pull oneself over) **1** *sl* fall in love <Slav*1> **2** *sl-drugs* be on narcotic drugs <Slav*1>

Navukodonòsōr {nosóra (acc. = gen.) masc.} (lit. Nebuchadnezzar X navuko do nosa, pulled-to-the-nose) *sl-fea* elderly divorced female <Slav⁘*1>

nàzadnā {ē fem. (adj. decl.)} (lit. the backward one) *sl-sex* ***Fac*** female with large buttocks <Slav*1>

nàzdraviti {vīm, vē perf. intr.} *col* offer a toast (speech) <Slav*1>

nàzdravljati {âm, ajū imperf. intr.} *col* offer a toast (speech) <Slav*1>

nàzobati se {ām, ajū perf. intr.} *sl* eat one's fill, be stuffed <Slav*1>

nȁzōr {adv.} *sl-fea* without being able to stand it, over one's needs or capabilities: *Pije nazor, pa će ga ujutro boljeti glava. He's been drinking more than he can handle and will have a headache in the morning.* <NE>

naždèrati se {nàžderēm, derū perf. intr.} *col* eat one's fill, be stuffed <Slav*1>

nȁždrati se {nàžderēm, derū perf. intr.} *col* eat one's fill, be stuffed <Slav*1>

nȁže {nȅže fem.; perm} /nàže/ [std. = žena] *sl* female <Slav☝>

nažljókati se {nàžljōkām, nažljókajū perf. intr.} *sl-drink* get drunk <Slav⁘*1>

nažvákati se {nàžvāčem, āčū perf. intr.} (lit. chew one's fill) *sl-drink* get drunk <Slav*1>

nȁžvaliti se {līm, lē perf. intr.} *sl-drink* get drunk <Slav*1>

nažvŕljati {nàžvr̄ljām, nažvŕljajū perf.} *col* scribble, write illegibly <Slav>

nè biti ni rôd ni pomòzibôg {VP} (lit. be neither a relative nor God to you) *col* be totally unrelated: *Možda ličimo, ali on mi nije ni rod ni pomozibog. We may look alike but are totally unrelated.* ☞ **biti**

nè biti nȍrmālan {VP} (lit. be abnormal) *sl-fea* be insane, be off ☞ **biti**

nè biti pri čȉstōj svésti {VP} (lit. lack clear consciousness) SerE *col* be insane, be nuts ☞ **biti**

nè biti sâm {VP} (lit. be with somebody) *sl-fea* be insane, be nuts ☞ **biti**

nè biti sâm {VP} (lit. not be alone) *sl-fea* be insane, be nuts ☞ **biti**

nè biti zdrȁv {VP} (lit. be unhealthy) *col* be insane, be nuts ☞ **biti**

nè dírājte mi ravnȉcu {VP} (lit. don't touch my flatlands) *sl-sex* ***Fac*** small female breast ☞ **dirati**

nè gȉnē [PRON:DAT] ([NOUN:NOM]) {LSF} (lit. [NOUN: NOM] doesn't die to [PRON:ACC]) *col* used to refer to inevitability of an event: *Ne gine ti zatvor. You cannot avoid going to jail.* ☞ **ginuti**

Nè igrā! {S} (lit. It doesn't play!) *col* used to refer to something impossible (usu. in response to a request), No way! ☞ **igrati**

nè igrā [PRON:DAT] {LSF} (lit. It doesn't play to [PRON: ACC]) *col* used to refer to a negative attitude: *Ne igra mi. I don't like it.* ☞ **igrati**

Ne izvòdi bȉjēsnē glíste! {S} (lit. Don't perform rabid worms!) *col* used to express a negative attitude (usu. toward a brat) ☞ **izvoditi**

Ne jèbāvā nȉkoga! {S} (lit. He doesn't fuck anybody!) *dia* ***Obs*** used to indicate indifference of a third party, Fuck him! ☞ **jebavati**

Ne jèbē me tô! {S} (lit. It doesn't fuck me!) *sl* ***Obs*** used to refer to one's indifference, I don't give a fuck! ☞ **jebati**

Nè jèbēm nȉkogā! {S} (lit. I don't fuck anybody.) *sl* ***Obs*** used to refer to one's indifference, I don't give a fuck! ☞ **jebati**

Ne jèbēm [PRON:ACC] ni dvâ pȍstō! {LSF} (lit. I don't fuck [PRON:ACC] not even two percent.!) *sl* ***Obs*** used to refer to one's indifference toward: *Ne jebem ga ni dva posto! I don't give a fuck about him!* ☞ **jebati**

Ne jèbēm [PRON:ACC] uȍpšte! {LSF} (lit. I don't fuck [PRON:ACC] at all!) *sl* ***Obs*** used to refer to one's indifference toward: *Ne jebem te uopšte! I don't give a fuck about you!* ☞ **jebati**

Nè jèbēm [PRON:ACC] za sûhū šljȉvu! {LSF} (lit. I don't fuck [PRON:ACC] for a prune!) *sl* ***Obs*** used to express indifference toward one's interlocutor: *Ne jebem te ni za suhu šljivu. I don't give a fuck about you.* ☞ **jebati**

Ne jèbēmo žîvū sȉlu! {S} (lit. We don't fuck live force!) *sl-mil* ***Obs*** used to refer to one's indifference, We don't give a fuck! ☞ **jebati**

Ne jèbi! {S} (lit. Don't fuck!) *sl* ***Obs*** used as a threat of physical violence, Don't fuck with me! ☞ **jebati**

Nè jedi gôvna! {S} (lit. Don't eat shit!) **a.** *col* ***Off*** used as a strong curse, Eat shit! **b.** *col* ***Off*** used to silence one's interlocutor, Shut up! **c.** *col* ***Off*** used to express disbelief, No shit! ☞ **jesti**

Nè kēnjāj! {S} (lit. Don't shit!) **a.** *col* ***Off*** used to silence one's interlocutor, Shut up! **b.** *col* used to express disbelief, No shit! **c.** *col* used to make somebody go away ☞ **kenjati**

Ne kȑši kȕrac! {S} (lit. Don't break your prick!) *dia* ***Off*** used as a moderate curse, Screw you! ☞ **kršiti**

ne kúžiti u dȉm {VP} (lit. be unable to understand in smoke) *sl* fail to understand, be in a fog ☞ **kužiti**

ne lèzi vrâže {VP} (lit. devil don't lay) *col* used to refer to unfavorable event, shit happens ☞ **leći**

Ne me zajèbāvāj! {S} (lit. Don't fuck me over!) SSer *dia* ***Obs*** used to express disbelief, No fucking way! ☞ **zajebavati**

ne mògu ȍd smijēha {VP} (lit. I cannot from laughing) **a.** *sl* used as a strong negative response, no way, never **b.** *sl* used to indicate the lack of money ☞ **moći**

Ne mŕsi múda! {S} (lit. Don't mix your balls!) *dia* ***Obs*** used to express disbelief, No shit! ☞ **mrsiti**

Ne mŕši múda! {S} (lit. Don't mix your balls!) *dia* ***Obs*** used to express disbelief, No shit! ☞ **mršiti**

Ne nàvījāj! {S} (lit. Don't roll it!) *sl* used to express disbelief ☞ **navijati**

Ne palamúdi! {S} (lit. Don't drop your balls!) **1** *col* ***Obs*** used as a weak curse, Screw you! **2a.** *col* used to silence one's interlocutor, Shut up! **b.** *col* used to express disbelief ☞ **palamuditi**

nè pāli {V} (lit. it doesn't fire) **a.** *col* used as a strong negative response, no way, never ☞ **paliti**

Nè pizdri se! {S} (lit. Don't act like a cunt!) *dia* ***Off*** used in angry dismissal, Fuck off! ☞ **pizdriti se**

nè pravi prȍmaju {VP} (lit. don't make a draft) *sl* shut up, cease talking ☞ **praviti**

nè rādī bibliotéka {S} (lit. the library is closed) *sl* ***Fac*** used to confuse one's interlocutor ☞ **raditi**

ne razumijévati {V} (lit. be unable to understand) *col* fail to understand ☞ **razumijevati**

Ne rȉse! {S} (lit. Don't bullshit!) *sl* ***Off*** used to express disbelief, Don't bullshit me! ☞ **tisra**

Ne sèri! {S} (lit. Don't bullshit!) **1** *col* ***Off*** used as a strong curse, Fuck you! **2** *col* used to silence one's interlocutor, Bullshit! **3** *col* used to refer to strong disbelief, Don't bullshit me! ☞ **srati**

Nè svīrāj! {S} (lit. Don't play!) *col* ***Off*** used as a moderate curse, Fuck you! ☞ **svirati**

Nè svīrāj kȗrcu! {S} (lit. Don't play to a prick!) *col* ***Off*** used as a moderate curse, Fuck you! ☞ **svirati**

Nè te jèbāvām! {S} (lit. I don't fuck you!) **SSer** *dia* ***Obs*** used to express indifference toward one's interlocutor , I don't give a fuck about you! ☞ **jebavati**

Nè te jèbēm! {S} (lit. I don't fuck you!) SSer *dia* ***Obs*** used to express indifference toward one's interlocutor , I don't give a fuck about you! ☞ **jebati**

Ne túli kȕrac! {S} (lit. Don't hide your cock!) *dia* ***Off*** used as a moderate curse, Fuck you! ☞ **tuliti**

nè videti (ni) bélu mȁčku {VP} (lit. be unable to see even a white cat) **a.** **SerE** *col* be very drunk, be blind drunk **b.** SerE *col* be unable to see anything ☞ **videti**

ne vrijédī nȉ pō pízdē hládnē vòdē {S} (lit. that is not worth even a half cunt of cold water) *col* used to refer to worthless items or ideas, it ain't worth shit ☞ **vrijediti**

Ne zajèbāvāj! {S} (lit. Don't fuck over!) **1** *col* ***Obs*** used as a moderate curse, Fuck you! **2** *col* used to silence one's interlocutor, Shut up! **3** *col* used to express disbelief, No fucking way! ☞ **zajebavati**

Ne zajèbāvāj me! {S} (lit. Don't fuck me over!) **a.** *col* used as a moderate curse **b.** *col* used to silence one's interlocutor, Shut up! **c.** *col* used to express disbelief, No fucking way! ☞ **zajebavati**

ne zarezívati ni za súvu šljȋvu {VP} (lit. be unwilling to cut even for a prune) **Ser** *col* not care about, not give a fig about ☞ **zarezivati**

Nè znā se ni kȍ pȉjē ni kȍ plâćā. {S} (lit. One doesn't know who drinks and who pays.) *col* total disorder, complete mess ☞ **piti**

nȅā problémā {VP} (lit. no problems) *sl* used to refer to approval, consent, etc., no problem, no big deal: *A: Hvala za kredit! B: Nea problema. A: Thanks for the loan! B: No big deal.* ☞ **biti**

nȅakav {pron.} [std. = nekakav] Cro *col* some <**Slav**✍>

neandertálac {lca (acc. = gen.) masc.} (lit. Neanderthal) **a.** *sl-fea* stupid or mentally deficient person <**Ger**[*1]> **b.** very unintelligent person **c.** worthless person, bum

nȅbo *See the following*

- **Nebèsa ti bȍžjā tvòja!** {S} (lit. *I fuck* your God's heaven!) *col* ***Off*** used as a moderate curse, Fuck you!
- **Nebèsa ti jèbēm!** {S} (lit. I fuck your heaven!) *col* ***Off*** used as a moderate curse, Fuck you!
- **Nȅbo ti jèbēm!** {S} (lit. I fuck your sky!) *col* ***Off*** used as a moderate curse, Fuck you!

nȅboslōv {a masc.} (lit. sky-talker) *sl-fea* homeless person, bum <Slav[*1]>

nȅbulōzan {zna, zno adj.} **a.** *sl-fea* absurd, idiotic: *nebulozan prijedlog absurd proposal* <Lat[*1]> **b.** *sl-fea* unintelligent, stupid, dumb <Lat[*2]>

nȅčesōv {a, o adj.} [std. = nečiji] *dia* somebody's <Slav✍>

nȅčī {pron.} [std. = nečiji] *dia* somebody's <Slav✍>

nȅčitav {a, o adj.} **a.** *sl-fea* slightly insane, nutty <Slav[*1]> **b.** *sl-fea* insane, nuts <Slav[*2]>

Nêće mòći òvē nȍći! {VP} (lit. It will be impossible this night!) *col* used as a strong negative response, no way, never ☞ **moći**

nêće prôći {VP} (lit. It will not pass) *col* used as a strong negative response, no way, never ☞ **proći**

Nêćemo da kvârīmo. {VP} (lit. We don't want to spoil it.) *sl* used to indicate a desired state of affairs ☞ **hteti**

néda {ē fem.} *sl-sex* ***Fac*** female who does not readily engage in sexual intercourse <Slav[*1]>

nèdelja *See the following*

- **Bȍžjū ti nèdelju!** {S} (lit. *I fuck* your God's Sunday!) **SerE** *col* ***Off*** used as a moderate curse or threat, Fuck you!

nedòđija {ē fem.} *sl-fea* place of extreme wretchedness or squalor, hellhole <Slav[*1]>

nȅdojebān {a, o adj.} *sl-sex* ***Obs*** person who did not finish sexual intercourse <Slav[*1]>

nedokùrčiv {a, o adj.} (lit. nedokučiv 'unreachable' X kurčiv 'prick's') *sl-fea* unreachable, out of range (e.g. a very important or influential person) <Slav[*1]>

nedòmujica {ē fem.} *sl* doubt <Slav✍>

nȅdotupāvan {vna, vno adj.} *sl-fea* unintelligent, stupid, dumb <Slav⁘[*1]>

nȅđe {adv.} [std. = negdje] *col-dia* somewhere <Slav✍>

nȅfēr {adj.} *col* unfair <Eng⁘[*1]>

nȅg {c.} [std. = nego] *col* than <Slav✍>

negatívac {vca (acc. = gen.) masc.} (lit. the negative one) **1** *sl-crime* police investigator <Lat⁘[*1]> **2** strict judge **3** sly male, fox

nȅgatīvan {vna, vno adj.} (lit. negative) **1** *sl* false <Slav[*1]> **2a.** *sl* poor: *negativna porodica poor family* <Slav[*1]> **b.** *sl* hopeless: *negativan plan hopeless plan* <Slav[*1]> **c.** *sl* gloomy: *negativan stan gloomy apartment* <Slav[*3]>

negatíviti {negàtīvīm, vī imperf.} *sl* hate, despise <Slav⁘[*1]>

nȅgđe {adv.} [std. = negdje] *col-dia* somewhere <Slav✍>

neglìžàntan {tna, tno adj.} *sl-fea* relaxed, laid back <Fre[*1]>

nȅgo {part.} *col* well <Slav>

negotívac {vca (acc. = gen.) masc.} *sl-fea* unattractive person <Ger⁘[*1]>

nȅgotīvan {vna, vno adj.} **a.** *sl-fea* unattractive, ugly **b.** *sl-fea* bad

nȅgovānā sàksija {NP} (lit. cherished flower pot) *sl-fea* attractive elderly female ☞ **saksija**

néjde {excl.} /nêjde/ [std. = ne ide] Kajk *col-dia* used to express impossibility <Slav✍>

néjmati {nêjmām, néjmajū imperf.} [std. = nemati] BosM *col* lack, be without <Slav✍>

nȅk {part.} [std. = neka] *col* used to express willingness or approval of an event, let: *Nek djeca idu napolje. Let the children go out.* <Slav✍>

- **Nȅk je srȅćno!** {S} (lit. Let it be lucky!) Ser *col* used to express good wishes, Good luck!
- **Nȅk je sà srećōm!** {S} (lit. Let it be with luck!) *col* used to express good wishes, Good luck!
- **Nȅk je srȅćno i berìćetno!** {S} (lit. Let it be lucky and profitable!) **Ser** *col* used to express good wishes, Good luck!
- **Nȅk je srȅtno!** {S} (lit. Let it be lucky!) *col* used to express good wishes, Good luck!
- **Nȅk je srȅtno i berìćetno!** {S} (lit. Let it be lucky and profitable!) *col* used to express good wishes, Good luck!
- **Nȅk vam je sà srećōm!** {S} (lit. Let it be with happiness to you!) *col* used to express favorable attitude toward, Good luck!

Nek ìdē svȅ do kûrca! {S} (lit. Let everything go to the prick!) *col* used to express lack of control over events, Fuck it! ☞ **ići**

Nek jȅdē gôvna! {S} (lit. Let him/her eat shit!) *col* ***Off*** used as a strong curse, Fuck him! ☞ **jesti**

Nek jȅdū tvôj òtac i mâjka gôvna! {S} (lit. Let your father and mother eat shit!) *col* ***Off*** used as a strong curse, Fuck you! ☞ **jesti**

Nȅk si jèbē mȁtēr! {S} (lit. Let him/her fuck his/her mother!) *col* ***Obs*** used as a strong curse, Fuck him/her! ☞ **jebati**

nȅkak {adv.} [std. = nekako] Cro *col-dia* somehow <Slav✍>

nekaširati {kàšīrām, kaširajū perf.} *sl* be refused, be denied, be turned down

nȅkat {a masc.} *sl* night

nèkcija {ē fem.} [std. = injekcija] *dia-col* shot, injection (medical) <Lat✍>

nȅkoj {pron.} [std. = neko] *dia* somebody <Slav✍>

néma {excl.} *col* used as a strong negative response, no way, never <Slav[*1]>

nêmā grȅškē {VP} (lit. no mistake) *col* used to indicate that a problem can be solved, no problem, no big deal: *Nema greške za parkiranje. Parking is no big deal.* ☞ **biti**

nêmā hljȅba {VP} (lit. no bread) *col* used to indicate the futility of an effort, it's no use ☞ **biti**

nêmā lȅba {VP} (lit. no bread) SerE *col* used to indicate the futility of all efforts, it's no use ☞ **imati**

nêma problémā {VP} *col* used to refer to that a problem can be solved, no problem, no big deal ☞ **imati**

nêmā šȁnsē {VP} (lit. no chance) *col* used as a strong negative response, no way, never ☞ **biti**

nêmā šansónē {VP} (lit. no chanson) *sl* used as a strong negative response, no way, never ☞ **biti**

nêmā tèōrijē {VP} (lit. no theory) *col* used as a strong negative response, no way, never ☞ **biti**

nêmā tȉjē pârā {VP} (lit. no money like that) *dia* used to indicate that something is priceless, money cannot buy it ☞ **biti**

nêmā vȅzē {VP} (lit. no connection) *col* used to indicate irrelevance of something, doesn't matter ☞ **biti**

nêmā zímē {VP} (lit. no winter) *col* used to indicate that a problem can be solved ☞ **biti**

Nêmā žíva ròba. {S} (lit. Not a live slave is here.) *sl* used to indicate that a place is empty, Nobody there. ☞ **biti**

némaš problémā {VP} (lit. you don't have any problems) *col* used to indicate that a problem can be solved, no problem, no big deal: *Nemaš problema za čišćenje snega. Snow-clearing is no big deal.* ☞ **imati**

némati {nêām, némajū imperf.} [std. = nemati, nemam] *col* lack, be without <Slav✍>

némati (blâgē) vȅzē {VP} (lit. not have a *soft* connection) *col* be unaware of, be clueless ☞ **imati**

némati dȕnsta {VP} (lit. be without skills) *sl* fail to understand ☞ **imati**

némati (ni) trî čȉste {VP} (lit. be without the three clean) **1** *sl-fea* be insane, be nuts **2** *sl-fea* be a coward, be a chicken ☞ **imati**

némati (ni) trî čȕke {VP} (lit. be without three hours) *sl-fea* be ignorant ☞ **imati**

némati nȍge {VP} (lit. be without legs) *sl-drugs* be on narcotic drugs ☞ **imati**

némati šljàkaru {VP} (lit. be without the one used for work *i.e. without one hand*) *sl-fea* be without one arm ☞ **imati**

Nèmčuga {ē fem.; Dat Nèmčugi} SerE *col* ***Off*** German (person), Kraut <Slav✣>

nèmō {excl.} [std. = nemoj] *col* used to prevent action <Slav✍>

nèmōj {excl.} *col* used to prevent action <Slav>

- **mà nèmōj** {VP} (lit. oh, no) *col* used to express disbelief, no kidding

Nèmōj mi srȁt! {S} (lit. Don't bullshit me!) *col* used to refer to strong disbelief, Don't bullshit me! ☞ **srati**

Nèmōj srȁt! {S} (lit. Don't bullshit!) *col* used to refer to strong disbelief, Don't bullshit me! ☞ **srati**

Nèmoj zajebávati! {S} (lit. Don't fuck over!) *col* ***Obs*** used to express disbelief, No fucking way! ☞ **zajebavati**

Nèmōj zajebávati! {S} (lit. Don't fuck me over!) **a.** *col* used as a moderate curse, Fuck you! **b.** *col* used to express disbelief, No fucking way! ☞ **zajebavati**

Nèmōj zajebávati? {S} (lit. Don't fuck me over?) *col* used to express disbelief, No fucking way! ☞ **zajebavati**

néna {ē fem.} *col* grandmother, grandma <NE[*1]>

- **Nénu ti jèbēm kràkatū!** {S} (lit. I fuck your sister with long legs!) *dia* ***Off*** used as a strong curse, Fuck you!
- **Nénu ti oplàjvāzīm!** {S} (lit. I fuck your sister!) *dia* ***Off*** used as a strong curse, Fuck you!

nenadjèbiv {a, o adj.} (lit. unfuckable) *sl-fea* invincible, untouchable <Slav[*1]>

nenadjèljiv {a, o adj.} **a.** *sl-fea* skillful <Slav*1> **b.** *sl-fea* mighty <Slav*2> **c.** *sl-fea* honest person, one who cannot be framed <Slav*3>

neosùđīvān {a, o adj.} (lit. unconvicted) *sl-sex* ***Fac*** virgin <Slav*1>

neòvejān {a, o adj.} SerE *sl-fea* sly <Slav*1>

Nèpāl {Nepála masc.} (lit. Nepal) **a.** *sl-sex* ***Obs*** penis, dick, prick <SlavO*1> **b.** *sl-sex* ***Obs*** erect penis, hard on <SlavO*2>

nepálac {lca masc.} *sl-drugs* hashish, hash <SlavO*1>

nèpče *See the following*

- **Nèpče ti tvòje!** {S} (lit. *I fuck* your little sky!) *dia* ***Off*** used as a moderate curse, Fuck you!

nȅpīc-fràjer {a (acc. = gen.) masc.} *sl-sex* ***Obs*** sexually inexperienced male <Slav-Ger*1>

nȅpoćūdan {dna, dno adj.} **a.** *sl-fea* unattractive, ugly <Slav*1> **b.** *sl-fea* negative, undesired <Slav*2> **c.** *sl-fea* hostile <Slav*3>

nèpoznāt {a, o adj.} (lit. unknown) *sl-fea* strange, weird <Slav*1>

nȅpoznātā {ē fem. (adj. decl.)} (lit. unknown quantity, i.e. X in mathematics) *sl-fea* female with bandy legs <Slav*1>

neprejèbiv {a, o adj.} (lit. unoverfuckable) **1** *sl-fea* invincible, untouchable <Slav❖*1> **2** unavoidable <Slav❖*1>

nȅren {a, o adj.} *sl* bad

nerénac {nca (acc. = gen.) masc.} *sl-fea* elderly male

nȅrga {ē fem.; Dat nȅrgi} *sl* female

nèrvčik {a (acc. = gen.) masc.} *sl-fea* nervous person, nail biter <Lat❖*1>

nesalòmljivī {īh masc. pl.} (lit. invincibles) *sl-sstu* school council <Slav*1>

nȅskafa {ē fem.} (lit. Nescafe *coffee brand*) *col* instant coffee <BN❖>

nȅslān {a, o adj.} (lit. unsalty) *sl-fea* unskilled <Slav*1>

nèsrećan slȕčāj {NP} (lit. accident) **1** *sl-fea* unattractive person **2** *sl-fea* poor person ☞ **slučaj**

nèsrećo {excl.} *col* used to express compassion, poor thing <Slav*1>

nèstati {nēm, nū perf. intr.} (lit. disappear) *sl* die, kick the bucket <Slav*1>

nȅsvrstān {a, o adj.} **/nèsvrstān/** (lit. non-aligned) *sl-fea* ***Fac*** introvert <Slav*1>

nȅšta {pron.} [std. = nešto] *col* something <Slav✍>

neukapìrljiv {a, o adj.} **a.** *sl-fea* opaque, unclear, difficult to grasp <Ita❖*1> **b.** *sl-fea* excellent, cool <Ita❖*2>

neukapìrljivo {adv.} **a.** *sl-fea* unclear, opaquely <Ita❖*1> **b.** *sl-fea* excellent, cool <Ita❖*2>

nȅūm {a masc.} (lit. not-mind X Neum, a city on the Adriatic coast) *sl* stupidity, lack of intelligence <Slav*1>

nȅurōzan {zna, zno adj.} *col* nervous <Lat❖>

nevàljas {sta, sto adj.} [std. = nevaljast] *col* bad <Slav✍>

nèvesta *See the following*

- **Nèvestu ti jèbēm!** {S} (lit. I fuck your bride!) SerE *dia* ***Off*** used as a moderate curse, Fuck you!
- **Nèvestu ti nȅvenčānu jèbēm!** {S} (lit. I fuck your unmarried bride!) SerE *dia* ***Off*** used as a moderate curse, Fuck you!

nèvestica *See the following*

- **Nèvesticu ti tvòju!** {S} (lit. *I fuck* your little bride!) SSer *dia* ***Off*** used as a moderate curse, Fuck you!

nèviđeno {adv.} (lit. unseen) *sl-fea* excellent, superb <Slav*1>

nezgodácija {ē fem.} *col* difficult or unpleasant situation <Slav✍>

nezgodácija {adj.} *sl-fea* unpleasant <Slav✍>

nèznalica {ē fem.} *col* unintelligent male <Slav*1>

Ni kȗrcu si ne kàzujē! {S} (lit. He doesn't tell it even to the prick!) SSer *dia* ***Obs*** used as a moderate curse, Fuck him! ☞ **kurac**

ni lȕk jȅō, ni lȕk mȉrisaō {S} (lit. neither eaten nor smelled any onions) *col* used to refer to lack of one's responsibility ☞ **luk**

ni mujáket {PP} Bos *col* nothing ☞ **mujaket**

ni mukájet {PP} Bos *col* without a single word ☞ **mukajet**

nȉ pō jȁda {PP} (lit. not half the grief) **a.** *col* used to express that the outcome of a situation could have been even worse, not half bad, not bad: *To je ni po jada što su nas stavili u zatvor na godinu dana. That they put us in prison for a year is not that bad.* **b.** *col* weak (lacking physical force or social importance): *ni po jada frajer weak guy* ☞ **jad**

nȉ pō mȕkē {PP} (lit. not half of pain) *col* used to indicate that a problem can be solved, not half bad, not bad ☞ **muka**

ni pȑdac {PP} (lit. not even a fart) *sl* shut up, cease talking ☞ **prdac**

ni za žívu glâvu {PP} (lit. not even for a live head) *col* used as a strong negative response, no way, never ☞ glava

nì zbog čeg {PP} (lit. for nothing) *col* for no reason whatsoever, for nothing ☞ šta

Niagàra {ē fem.} (lit. Niagara) *sl-sex* ***Fac*** soft female breast <EngO[*1]>

nȉcaj {excl.} *sl* used to prevent action

nȉcam {part.} [std. = nisam] *sl* negative response, no <Slav✍>

nȉcati {ām, ajū imperf.} (lit. grow) *sl* ***Iro*** lack, be without <Slav[*1]>

nȉckam {adv.} *sl* not a bit

nȉcom {part.} [std. = nisam] *sl* negative response, no <Slav✍>

ničégović {a (acc. = gen.) masc.} *sl-fea* worthless or despicable person <Slav❖>

nídl {a +ov (ext. pl) masc.} *sl-drugs* syringe, needle <Eng>

nȉđe {adv.} [std. = nigdje] *col-dia* nowhere <Slav✍>

nigdárjevo *See the following*

- **na svêtō nigdárjevo** {PP} (lit. on holy neverday) *col* never

nȉgdi {adv.} [std. = nikad] *dia* never <Slav✍>

nìje mi nȕmera {VP} (lit. not my number) *sl* used to express dissatisfaction, not my number, not my style, not for me ☞ biti

nìje nȁpēto {VP} (lit. it is not tense) *sl* boredom ☞ biti

nìje nȍrmālno {VP} (lit. it is not normal) *col* used to refer to something unusual or insane: *Kakva dobra kolica, nije normalno! What a cool car, I can't believe it!* ☞ biti

nìje ròdilo {VP} (lit. no yields) *sl* used to refer to one's shortage of something ☞ biti

Nìje šèćer ȕ vodu! {S} (lit. Sugar did not get into the water!) *col-dia* used to indicate that ample time is available ☞ biti

nìje ti ćâle staklorézac {S} (lit. your old man is not a glass cutter) SerE *sl* used to express that somebody is blocking one's view, You make a better door than a window! ☞ biti

nìje ti stâri stȁklār {S} (lit. your old man is not a glass cutter) *sl* used to express that somebody is blocking one's view, You make a better door than a window! ☞ biti

nìje zà prīču {PP} (lit. not for talking) *col* used to refer to confidential matters, (this is) confidential, hush-hush ☞ priča

nȉkad *See the following*

- **na svêtī Nȉkad** {PP} (lit. on holy neverday) *col* never
- **na svêtō nȉkad** {PP} (lit. on holy never) *col* never
- **nȉkad bȍljē** {AdvP} (lit. never better) *col* used in response to "How are you doing?", Never better!
- **nȉkad gȍrē** {S} (lit. never worse) *col* used in response to "How are you doing?", Horrible!

nȉkāko {excl.} (lit. like nothing) *col* response to the question "How are you doing?", Horrible! <Slav[*1]>

nìkanōr {part.} *col* negative response, no <Slav✍>

nikdárjevo {a neut.} Cro *sl* day which never comes <Slav✍>

nȉkesto {ōg neut.} *sl-arch* lamb (the animal)

nȉko *See the following*

- **nȉkom nȉšta** {ProP} (lit. nothing to anyone) *col* used to express lack of negative consequences, nothing has happened, everything's fine

nikòtaka {ē fem.; Dat nikòtaki} (lit. nobody touched her) *sl-sex* ***Fac*** virgin <Slav❖[*1]>

nikòtīn {kotína masc.} (lit. nicotin) *sl* cigarette, smoke <FreO[*1]>

nȉks {part.} *col* negative response, no <Ger>

nȉkson {a (acc. = gen.) masc.} (lit. Nixon) *sl* ten-centimeter long cigarette with filter <EngO[*1]>

nimfèta {ē fem.} (lit. nymphet) *sl-sex* ***Fac*** promiscuous young female, nymphet <Fre[*1]>

nȉmfić {a (acc. = gen.) masc.} (lit. nymphomaniac) *sl-sex* ***Fac*** loose woman <Gre✍>

nȉnak {a masc.} *sl* pantyhose

nȉndža {ē masc.} *col* ninja <Jap>

nȉoklē {adv.} [std. = niotkud] *col-dia* from nowhere <Slav✍>

nísam frȁjer {VP} (lit. I am not a dude) *sl* used to indicate one's knowledge of the dangers in a situation ☞ biti

Nísam vèslo sȉsaō! {S} (lit. I didn't suck an oar!) *sl* used to indicate one's knowledge of a situation ☞ biti

Nísam vèslo sȉsō! {S} (lit. I didn't suck an oar!) *sl* used to indicate one's knowledge of a situation ☞ biti

Nísi ni zà kurac! {S} (lit. You are not even for a prick!) *sl* ***Off*** used as a moderate curse, Screw you! ☞ **biti**

nȉspe {nìsape masc.; perm} /nìspe/ [std. = penis] *sl-sex* ***Obs*** penis, dick, prick <**Lat**✍>

nȉš {pron.} [std. = ništa] Cro *dia-col* nothing <**Slav**✍>

Nîš-Pȉrot {masc.} (lit. Nis - Pirot *two towns in Southern Serbia*) *sl-sex* ***Fac-Obs*** masturbation <**SlavO**>

ništa *See the following*

- **nȉšta me nè pītāj** {S} (lit. never worse) *col* used in response to "How are you doing?", Horrible!

ništačȍvek {a (acc. = gen.) masc.} /ništačòvek/ SerE *sl-fea* worthless or despicable person <**Slav**❖[*1]>

ništačȍvjek {a (acc. = gen.) masc.} /ništačòvjek/ *sl-fea* worthless or despicable person <**Slav**❖[*1]>

ništarȍba [1] {ē fem.} *sl-fea* worthless, low-quality merchandise, junk <**Slav**❖[*1]>

ništarȍba [2] {ē fem. & masc.} *dia* idler, loafer <**Slav**❖>

nȉštāroš {a (acc. = gen.) masc.} *sl-fea* worthless or despicable person <**Slav**❖[*1]>

nȉt {c.} [std. = niti] *col* neither <**Slav**>

nìtna {ē fem.} *sl-crafts* rivet <**Ger**>

nìtnāš {nitnáša (acc. = gen.) masc.} (lit. riveter) *sl-sex* ***Fac*** male sexual partner (of a female) <**Ger**❖[*1]>

nȉtnovati {nūjēm, nūjū imperf.} **a.** *sl-crafts* rivet <**Ger**> **b.** *sl-sex* engage in sexual intercourse with (of a male) <**Ger**[*2]> **c.** masturbate, beat off <**Ger**[*2]>

nȉtovānje {a neut.} *sl-crafts* riveting <**Ger**[*1]>

nȉtovati {tujēm, tujū imperf.} (lit. rivet) *sl-sex* ***Fac-Obs*** engage in sexual intercourse with (of a male) <**Ger**[*1]>

nivèlisānje {a neut.} (lit. levelling) *sl* punishment <**Fre**[*1]>

nivèlisati {išēm, išū biasp.} (lit. level) *sl* punish <**Fre**[*1]>

nȍ {part.} *col* intensifying particle, well <**Slav**>

- **nȍ nȍ** {ExcP} (lit. no no) **1** *col* used to silence one's interlocutor, Shut up! **2** used to prevent an action, don't do it

nȍaj {part.} *sl* used to express absence, there isn't

nȍč {fem.} [std. = noć] SSer *dia* night <**Slav**✍>

nòčica *See the following*

- **Nòčicu ti lȅtnjū jèbēm!** {S} (lit. I screw your little summer night!) **SSer** *dia* ***Off*** used as a weak curse, Screw you!

nòćnā mòra {NP} *col* nightmare ☞ **mora**

nòćnī brȁvār {NP} (lit. nighttime locksmith) *sl-crime* ***Fac*** burglar ☞ **bravar**

nòga [1] {excl.} (lit. foot, leg) *sl* used to make somebody go away, beat it <**Slav**[*1]>

nòga [2] {ē fem.} (lit. foot, leg) **1a.** *sl-fea* stupid or mentally deficient person <**Slav**[*1]> **b.** *sl-drink* alcoholic, drunk <**Slav**[*2]> **2** *sl* throwing away, tossing out <**Slav**[*1]>

- **ćȍpavā nòga** {NP} (lit. lame leg) *sl-drink* name of a night club in Zagreb, Croatia called Corson
- **gòveđā nòga** {NP} (lit. beef leg) *sl-sex* ***Fac*** penis
- **lètēćā nòga** {NP} (lit. flying leg) *sl-fea* lame person
- **nȍge ȕ vīs** {NP} (lit. legs high) *sl-sex* ***Fac-Obs*** prostitute, hooker
- **svrȁčijē nȍge** {NP} (lit. magpie's legs) *col* slender legs
- **trȅćā nòga** {NP} (lit. the third leg) *sl-sex* ***Fac-Obs*** penis, the third leg

nȍgač {a masc.} (lit. the foot-thing) **1** *sl* bicycle, bike <**Slav**❖[*1]> **2** *sl-sports* soccer <**Slav**❖[*1]>

nȍgāć {a masc.} (lit. the foot-thing) **1** *sl* bicycle, bike <**Slav**❖[*1]> **2** *sl* soccer <**Slav**❖[*1]>

nogára {ē fem.} *sl* leg (of a female) <**Slav**❖[*1]>

nogárica {ē fem.} *sl* pretty leg (of a female) <**Slav**❖[*1]>

nogàvica {ē fem.} /nògavica /e fem./ *sl* pretty leg (of a female) <**Slav**❖[*1]>

nogàvice {a fem. pl.} /nògavice /a fem. pl./ *sl* trousers, pants <**Slav**❖[*1]>

nògica *See the following*

- **stȁklenā nògica** {NP} (lit. glass little leg) *sl-auto* bus station

nògīrān {a, o adj.} (lit. footed) **a.** *col* thrown away, tossed out <**Slav**❖[*1]> **b.** *col* dismissed, fired <**Slav**❖[*2]> **c.** *col* dumped by a boyfriend or a girlfriend <**Slav**❖[*3]>

nogírati {nògīrām, nogírajū biasp.} (lit. foot) **a.** *col* throw away, toss out <**Slav**❖[*1]> **b.** *col* dismiss, fire (a person) <**Slav**❖[*2]> **c.** *col* dump one's boyfriend or girlfriend <**Slav**❖[*3]>

nȍgomēt {a masc.} (lit. soccer X foot-work) *sl* throwing away, tossing out <**Slav**❖[*1]>

nȍgoš [1] {a (acc. = gen.) masc.} (lit. the foot-thing) *sl-sports* soccer player <**Slav**❖[*1]>

nȍgoš [2] {a masc.} (lit. the foot-thing) *sl-sports* soccer <**Slav**❖[*1]>

nȍgovati {gujēm, gujū perf.} (lit. foot) *sl* throw away, toss out <**Slav**❖[*1]> *sl* fire <**Slav**❖[*2]>

nȍkat [1] {excl.} (lit. finger nail) **1** *sl* used to make somebody go away, beat it <**Slav**❖[*1]> **2** *sl* used to express disbelief, impossible <**Slav**❖[*1]>

nȍkat [2] {kta masc.} (lit. finger nail) **a.** *sl* danger <**Slav**❖[*1]> **b.** *sl* running away, fleeing <**Slav**❖[*2]>

nokautírati {kaùtīrām, kautírajū imperf.} *sl-sports* knock out (boxing) <**Eng**>

nȍki [1] {īja masc.} *sl* nose <**Slav**✍>

nȍki [2] {nȁki neut.; perm} [std. = kino] *sl* movie house, theater <**Gre**✍>

nòknvela {ē fem.} *sl-auto* camshaft <**Ger**>

nòkotče {eta neut.} *sl* young female, girl

nòkotka {ē fem.; Dat nòkotki} *sl* female

nòktati {ām, ajū biasp.} *sl* run <**Slav**[*1]>

nòktīrān {a, o adj.} (lit. finger-nailed) **1** *sl-fea* ***Fac*** dumped by a boyfriend or a girlfriend <**Slav**[*1]> **2** *sl-fea* ***Fac*** dismissed, fired <**Slav**[*1]>

noktírati {nòktīrām, noktírajū biasp.} **a.** *sl* throw away, toss out <**Slav**[*1]> **b.** *sl* escape from prison <**Slav**[*2]>

nȍktogrīz {a (acc. = gen.) masc.} (lit. nail biter) *sl-fea* nervous person, nail biter <**Slav**[*1]>

nôle {eta neut.} *sl* nose <**Slav**✍>

nȍn stȍp {NP} (lit. nonstop) **a.** *col* day and night **b.** *col* always ☞ **stop**

nȍn-stȍp {a +ov (ext. pl) masc.; Nom Pl nȍn-stòpovi} *sl* hitch-hiking <**Eng**>

nôna {ē fem.} *dia-col* grandmother, grandma <**Ita**>

nôndā {adv.} [std. = onda] *dia* then <**Slav**✍>

nȍnica {ē fem.} *col* chamber pot

nôno {a masc.} *dia-col* grandfather, grandpa <**Ita**>

nonšalàncija {ē fem.} *col* nonchalance, carefreeness <**Fre**>

nȍnšantālan {lna, lno adj.} [std. = nonšalantan] *sl-fea* nonchalant <**Fre**✍>

nórac {rca (acc. = gen.) masc.} Cro *dia* ***Der*** insane person, nut case <**Ger**>

nȍrc {a (acc. = gen.) +ev (ext. pl) masc.; Nom Pl nòrčevi} Cro *dia* strange person, weirdo <**Ger**>

nòrēnje {a neut.} Cro *sl-fea* being insane, being nuts <**Ger**>

nòrmālka {ē fem.; Dat nòrmalki} *col* normal state of affairs <**Lat**>

normàlnjāk {malnjáka (acc. = gen.) masc.} *sl-fea* average male <**Lat**❖[*1]>

nôs *See the following*

- **Ȕ nōs te jèbēm!** {S} (lit. I fuck you in your nose!) *col-dia* ***Off*** used as a moderate curse, Fuck you!

nósati {nôsām, nósajū imperf.} *col* carry, have along <**Slav**>

Nòsi se u pízdu mȁterinu! {S} (lit. Carry yourself to your mother's cunt!) *col* ***Off*** used in angry dismissal, Fuck off! ☞ **nositi se**

Nòsi se u trȋ lêpē mȁterine! {S} (lit. Carry yourself to three nice mother's *cunts*.) **SerE** *col* used in angry dismissal, Fuck off! ☞ **nositi se**

nòsī tèle u mùdāntama {VP} (lit. he carries a calf in his pants) Med *sl-sex* ***Fac-Obs*** very potent male ☞ **nositi**

nòsīnger {a masc.} *sl* ***Fac*** nose <**Slav**✍>

nòsiti *See the following*

- **Nòsi se u pízdu mȁterinu!** {S} (lit. Carry yourself to your mother's cunt!) *col* ***Off*** used in angry dismissal, Fuck off!
- **Nòsi se u trȋ lêpē mȁterine!** {S} (lit. Carry yourself to three nice mother's *cunts*.) **SerE** *col* used in angry dismissal, Fuck off!
- **nòsī tèle u mùdāntama** {VP} (lit. he carries a calf in his pants) Med *sl-sex* ***Fac-Obs*** very potent male
- **nòsiti cíglu** {VP} (lit. carry a brick) *sl-sex* ***Fac*** have one's period
- **nòsiti fènjer** {VP} (lit. carry a lantern) *col* be the last one (competition, line, etc.)
- **nòsiti kònja** {VP} (lit. carry a horse) *sl-fea* be insane, be nuts
- **nòsiti krȋž** {VP} (lit. carry a cross) *sl-fea* be lame
- **nòsiti lúju** {VP} (lit. carry syphilis) *sl-sex* ***Fac*** suffer from syphilis, have the pox
- **nòsiti mrtvàce srȁt** {VP} (lit. carry the dead to take a shit) *sl-fea* do something useless
- **nòsiti mȓtvīma vȍdu** {VP} (lit. carry water to the dead) *sl-fea* sleep deeply
- **nòsiti pèrike na drȉkere** {VP} (lit. carry wigs on pressure) *sl-fea* be very untidy
- **nòsiti pèriku na drȉkere** {VP} (lit. carry a wig on pressure) *sl-fea* be of very low quality
- **nòsiti tèle u mùntarama** {VP} (lit. carry a calf in one's pants) *sl-sex* ***Fac-Obs*** have a large penis

nósonja {ē masc.} **a.** *sl-fea* large-nosed person <**Slav**❖> **b.i.** *sl-crime* police investigator <**Slav**❖[*1]> **ii.aa.** *sl-fea* very important or influential person, big shot <**Slav**❖[*1]> **bb.** *sl-fea* boss <**Slav**❖[*2]>

nȍsūrda {ē fem.} *sl-fea* large nose <Slav❖>

nóša {ē fem.} *col* chamber pot <Ger✍[*1]>

nóta *See the following*

• **U nótu te krȋvū jȅbēm!** {S} (lit. I fuck you in a crooked note!) *dia-col* ***Off*** used as a moderate curse, Fuck you!

• **vȅdrā nóta** {NP} (lit. a clear note) *sl-sex* ***Fac*** breaking wind, farting

[NOUN:NOM] nà sūnce! {S} (lit. [NOUN:NOM] in the sunlight!) *col* used to ask for something: *Pare na sunce pa ću ti dati! Show me your money and I will give it to you!* ☞ **sunce**

[NOUN:NOM] nà sūnce! {S} (lit. [NOUN:NOM] in the sunlight!) *col* used to ask for something: *Pare na sunce pa ću ti dati! Show me your money and I will give it to you!* ☞ **sunce**

Nȍvāć {Nováća masc.} Ser *sl* name for New Belgrade (Serbia) <SlavO✍>

novàjlija {ē masc.} *col* rookie <Slav-NE>

Nȍvāk [1] {Nováka masc.} Ser *sl* name for New Belgrade (Serbia) <SlavO✍>

nȍvāk [2] {nováka masc.} /Nȍvāk/ (lit. the new one) *sl* New Year's Eve: *Gde ćeš za novaka? Where are you going to celebrate the New Year?* <Slav[*1]>

nȍvī {ōg (acc. = gen.) masc.} (lit. the new one) *sl-crime* recently-hired police investigator <Slav[*1]>

Nȍvī Ȍdmā {NP} (lit. New Now *'odma' and 'sad' are synonymous*) *sl* ***Fac*** Novi Sad (a city in Yugoslavia) ☞ **Odma**

novogȍvor {a masc.} (lit. new speech) *col* newspeak, incomprehensible political jargon <Slav>

novokompȍnīrān {a, o adj.} **a.** *sl-music* country (as of music) <Slav-Lat> **b.** *sl-fea* new and of low quality <Slav-Lat[*1]>

novokòmponovān {a, o adj.} **a.** *sl-music* country (as of music) <Slav-Lat> **b.** *sl-fea* ***Der*** new and of low quality <Slav-Lat[*1]>

nôž *See the following*

• **ispod nóža** {PP} (lit. from under a knife) *col* last-minute rescue

• **Nôž ti jȅbēm!** {S} (lit. I fuck your knife!) *col* ***Off*** used as a moderate curse, Fuck you!

• **pod nôž** {PP} (lit. under the knife) **a.** *col* to have surgery, go under the knife: *Neću da idem pod nož samo da bi ne bih imala bore. I don't want to go under the knife just to get rid of my wrinkles.* **b.** *col* urgently: *Taj rukopis mi je potreban pod nož - časopis izlazi sutra. I need that manuscript urgently - the journal goes to press tomorrow.*

nožȍvīnje {a neut.} *dia* knife <Slav❖>

nȕ {excl.} *col* used to draw someone's attention, look <Slav>

nȕderica {ē fem.} *sl* nudist beach <Lat❖>

nȕdić {a (acc. = gen.) masc.} /nùdīć/ *sl* nudist <Lat❖>

nȕdiška {ē fem.; Dat nûdiški} *sl* nudist beach <Lat❖>

núdla {ē fem.} (lit. noodle) *sl-sex* ***Fac*** female nudist <Ger[*1]>

núđe {adv.} [std. = ondje] *dia* there <Slav✍>

nùkliš {adj.} *col* nuclear <Lat✍>

nùkliš senzácija {NP} (lit. nuclear revelation) *sl-fea* big revelation, bombshell ☞ **senzacija**

nȕla {ē fem.} **a.** *sl-fea* worthless or despicable person, a zero <Lat[*1]> **b.i.** *sl-fea* university student <Lat[*2]> **ii.** *sl-fea* stupid or mentally deficient person <Lat[*2]>

• **dùplā nȕla** {NP} (lit. double zero) *sl-sex* ***Fac-Obs*** buttocks, butt

• **nȕla trȋ** {NumP} (lit. zero three) **1** *sl-auto* Fiat 126P (a car brand) **2** *sl-fea* short

nȕlerica {ē fem.} (lit. the zero one) **1** *sl-sex* ***Fac-Obs*** buttocks, butt <Lat❖[*1]> **2** *sl-fea* ***Fac*** bald head <Lat❖[*1]>

nȕltī sât {NP} (lit. class zero) Cro *sl-sex* ***Fac-Obs*** sexual intercourse between two high-school students ☞ **sat**

nȕltī sèrvīs {NP} (lit. zero service) *sl-auto* first check-up after a new vehicle has been purchased ☞ **servis**

[NUMBER] [PRON:DAT] mâjki jȅbēm! {LSF} (lit. I fuck [PPRON] [NUMBER] mothers!) *col* ***Off*** used as a strong curse: *Sto ti majki jebem! Fuck you!* ☞ **jebati**

nȕmera {ē fem.} /nùmera/ (lit. number) **1** *sl* female <Lat[*1]> **b.** *sl-sex* suitable sexual partner <Lat[*2]> **c.** *sl-sex* sexual intercourse

numizmàtičār {a (acc. = gen.) masc.} (lit. numismatist) *sl-fea* person with numerous pimples, pimple face <Gre[*1]>

núnati {nûnām, núnajū imperf.} *col* rock a child <Slav>

nȕpoš {a masc.} *sl* outrage

nȕrkati {ām, ajū imperf.} *sl* build, construct, erect

nȕšiti se {šīm, še imperf. intr.} *sl* kiss <Slav✍[*1]>

nȕt {excl.} *col* used to draw someone's attention, look <Slav>

nȕti {excl.} *col* used to draw someone's attention, look <Slav>

nȕto {excl.} *col* used to draw someone's attention, look <Slav>

• **nȕtō dȅ** {ExcP} *dia* used to draw someone's attention, look

NJnj

njȁjke {excl.; perm} /njàke/ [std. = kenjaj] *sl* used to silence one's interlocutor, shut up <Slav✍[*1]>

njákati {njâčem, âču imperf.} /njákati /am, aju imperf. intr/ (lit. bray) **1** *sl-fea* talk persistently and meaninglessly, blabber, chatter <Slav[*1]> **2a.** *sl-fea* beat up <Slav[*1]> **b.** *sl-fea* torture <Slav[*2]> **3** *sl-fea* laugh <Slav[*1]>

njȁma {ē fem.} *sl-sex* ***Obs*** sexual intercourse <Slav[*1]>

njȁmnuti {nēm, nū perf.} *sl* snatch, grab <Slav[*1]>

njȁsvi {njēsvi fem.; perm} /njàsvi/ (lit. pig) [std. = svinja] *sl* politician <Slav✍[*1]>

njȅgra {ē fem.} *sl-sex* ***Obs*** vagina, cunt

njȅrga {ē fem.; Dat njȅrgi} *sl-sex* ***Obs*** vagina, cunt

njȅsra {ē fem.; perm} /njèsra/ [std. = sranje] **a.** *sl-fea* excrement <Slav✍> **b.** *sl-fea* prolonged and meaningless talk, diarrhea of the mouth <Slav✍[*1]> **c.** *sl-fea* difficult situation, deep shit <Slav✍[*1]>

njȇšto {pron.} [std. = nešto] *dia* something <Slav✍>

njȅzga {ē fem.; Dat njȅzgi} *sl-sex* ***Obs*** vagina, cunt

njȉhova pòsla {NP} *col* used to express disrespect, their dirty business, that's typical of them ☞ posla

njîn {pron.} [std. = njihov] *dia* their <Slav✍>

njȉva {ē fem.} *sl-fea* easily cheated person, easy mark <Slav[*1]>

njȍān {pron.} [std. = njen] *dia* her <Slav✍>

njȍfra [1] {ē fem.; perm} /njòfra/ [std. = Franjo] Cro *sl* boy, kid <SlavO[*1]>

njȍfra [2] {excl.; perm} /njòfra/ [std. = Franjo] **Cro** *sl* used to draw attention in direct informal communication, hey <SlavO✍[*1]>

njójzīn {pron.} [std. = njen, njezin] *dia* her <Slav✍>

njókac {kca (acc. = gen.) masc.} **a.** *col* donkey <Slav❖[*1]> **b.** stupid or mentally deficient person

njȍkalica {ē fem.} **a.** *sl* face (human) <Slav❖[*1]> **b.** *sl* nose

njȍknuti {nēm, nū perf.} *col* fall flat: *Poskliznuo se i njoknuo na lice kad je bježo od drotova. He slipped and fell flat on his face while running from the cops.* <Slav❖[*1]>

njónja {ē masc.} **1** *sl-fea* troublemaker, rowdy, ruffian <Slav❖[*1]> **2** *sl* nose <Slav❖>

njôrča {ē masc.} *sl-fea* sleepy person, sleepy head <Slav❖[*1]>

njȍriti {rīm, rē imperf. intr.} *dia-col* sleep long <Slav❖[*1]>

njȍrnuti {nēm, nū perf.} *sl-sex* ***Obs*** engage in sexual intercourse with (of a male) <Slav❖[*1]>

njȕferica {ē fem.} *sl-sex* virgin <Ger✍[*1]>

njȕknuti {nēm, nū perf.} *sl-sex* ***Obs*** engage in sexual intercourse with (of a male)

njȕnjoriti {rīm, rē imperf.} /njunjòriti/ *sl-fea* talk persistently and meaninglessly, blabber, chatter <Slav❖[*1]>

njúpa {ē fem.} *sl* food <Ita❖✍[*1]>

njȕpalica {ē fem.} /njúpalica/ *sl* mouth <Ita❖✍[*1]>

njupàluk {a masc.} *sl* food <Ita❖✍[*1]>

njȕpānje {a neut.} **a.** *sl* eating <Ita❖✍[*1]> **b.** *sl* being nervous

njȕpati {ām, ajū imperf.} *sl* eat, devour <Ita❖✍[*1]>

• **njȕpati cúcke** {VP} (lit. eat dogs) Cro *sl-fea* suffer from tuberculosis, have TB

• **njȕpati pȅpel** {VP} (lit. eat ashes) Cro *sl-fea* suffer from tuberculosis, have TB

• **njȕpati sìrovī krȕmpir** {VP} (lit. eat raw potatoes) Cro *sl-fea* grimace, make faces (usu. in pain)

njȕpati se {ām, ajū imperf. intr.} *sl* get angry <Ita❖✍[*1]>

njȕpavac {vca masc.} **1** *sl* tooth <Ita❖✍[*1]> **2** *sl* bread

njȕpavica {ē fem.} **a.** *sl* mouth <Ita❖✍[*1]> **b.** *sl* jaw

njupáža {ē fem.} **a.** *sl* eating <Ita❖✍[*1]> **b.i.** *sl* being nervous **ii.** *sl* drug

njȕpiti {pīm, pē perf.} *sl* eat, devour <Ita❖✍[*1]>

njȕpnuti {pnēm, pnū perf.} *col* snatch, grab <Ita❖✍[*1]>

njȕpoš {excl.} *sl* the sound made by eating <Ita❖✍[*1]>

njûs {a masc.} *sl-media* news (in general) <Eng>

njušènjāk {šenjáka masc.} (lit. the one who sniffs) *sl* ***Fac*** nose <Slav❖[*1]>

njȕšiti {šīm, šē imperf.} (lit. sniff) **a.** *sl* feel, sense <Slav[*1]> **b.** *sl* understand, realize <Slav[*2]>

njȕšiti se {šīm, šē imperf. intr.} (lit. sniff one another) *sl* kiss <Slav❖[*1]>

njúška {ē fem.} /njȕška/ (lit. snout) **1i.a.** *sl* face, snout <Slav*1> **b.** *sl* nose <Slav*2> **ii.a.** *sl-crime* skillful criminal <Slav*1> **b.** *sl-fea* worthless person, bum <Slav*2>
- **slânā njúška** {NP} (lit. salty snout) *sl-fea* unattractive face

njȕškalo {a neut.} (lit. sniffer) **a.** *sl-crime* policeman, cop <Slav❖*1> **b.** *sl-crime* detective <Slav❖*2> **c.** *sl-crime* informer, stoolie, snitch <Slav❖*3> **d.** *sl-fea* intrusive person <Slav❖*4>

njùškara {ē fem.} *sl* head <Slav❖*1>

njȕškati {ām, ajū imperf.} (lit. sniff) *sl* search, sniff out <Slav❖*1>

njȕškati se {ām, ajū imperf. intr.} (lit. sniff one another) *sl* kiss <Slav❖*1>

Oo

ô {excl.} *col* used to express wish or surprise, oh, hey <Slav>

ô-jê {excl.} *col* the sound made by yawning <Slav>

ô-ôj {excl.} *col* used to draw attention in direct informal communication, hey <Slav>

ô-rȕk {excl.} *col* used to stimulate somebody to a common effort, heave <Slav>

ȍbala {ē fem.} (lit. coast) *sl-fea* stupid or mentally deficient person <Slav*1>

òbaliti [1] {līm, lē perf.} (lit. beslobber) *sl* engage in fellatio <Slav*1>

obáliti [2] {òbālīm, lē perf.} *dia* throw down <Slav>
- **Òbali ga!** {S} (lit. Beslobber it!) *sl-sex* ***Off*** used as a moderate curse, Blow me!

obáriti {rīm, rē perf.} (lit. cook) **a.** *sl* persuade, convince <Slav*1> **b.** *sl* seduce **c.** *sl* get a girlfriend

ȍbaška {adv.} Bos *col* separately, individually, each on his/her own <NE*1>

obavȅzno {adv.} /ȍbavezno/ (lit. obligatorily) **1** *col* always: *On obavezno popije ljutu prije ručka. He always drinks a shot of schnapps before dinner.* <Slav*1> **2** *col* of course: *Hoćeš li doći? Obavezno! Will you come? Of course!* <Slav*1>

òbed *See the following*
- **Ȍbēd ti jèbēm!** {S} (lit. I screw your meal!) SerE *dia* ***Off*** used as a weak curse, Screw you!

óber {a (acc. = gen.) masc.} **1** *sl-drink* waiter <Ger> **2** *sl* railroad supervisor <Ger>

óberlihti {līhtā masc. pl.} *sl* eyeglasses <Ger*1>

Obèsiću te za múda na òrah! {S} (lit. I will hang you by your balls on a walnut tree!) *col* ***Obs*** used as a threat of physical violence, I'm gonna beat the shit out of you! ☞ **obesiti**

òbesiti *See the following*
- **Obèsiću te za múda na òrah!** {S} (lit. I will hang you by your balls on a walnut tree!) *col* ***Obs*** used as a threat of physical violence

obèspariti {rīm, rē perf.} *sl* go broke (financially) <NE❖>

obešènjāk {šenjáka masc.} SerE *sl* ***Fac*** clothes tree <Slav*1>

ȍbge *See the following*
- **Ȍbge ti jèbēm!** {S} (lit. I fuck your cakes!) *dia* ***Off*** used as a moderate curse, Fuck you!

òbīći {īđēm, īđū perf.} (lit. go around) *sl* leave alone, cease boring <Slav*1>

òbiknuti {nēm, nū perf. intr.} *col-dia* get used to <Slav☞>

obìlaziti *See the following*
- **obìlaziti pógone** {VP} (lit. supervise departments of a plant) *sl-drink* go to bars looking for companions

objáviti *See the following*
- **objáviti kònkurs** {VP} (lit. advertise a job) *sl-fea* start incriminating falsely, start framing

objektivírati {tìvīrām, tivírajū imperf.} (lit. materialize) *sl-sex* ***Fac*** engage in sexual intercourse with (of a male) <Lat*1>

òbjesiti se {sīm, sē imperf. intr.} (lit. hang oneself) *sl* ***Fac*** get married, get hitched <Slav*1>

òbješen {a, o adj.} (lit. hung) **1** *sl* married, hitched <Slav*1> **2** *sl* popular <Slav*1>

ȍblāčan {čna, čno adj.} (lit. cloudy) *sl-fea* dangerous, dicey <Slav*1>

ȍblāčno {adv.} (lit. cloudy) *sl-fea* dangerous but inviting (situation, event, etc.) <Slav*1>

òblajati {jēm, jū perf.} *sl* falsely incriminate, frame <Slav*1>

òblajmiti {mīm, mē perf.} *sl* hit, punch

ȍblāk {a (acc. = gen.) masc.} (lit. cloud) *sl-fea* ***Der*** insane person, nut case <Slav*1>
• **na ȍblāk** {PP} (lit. at a cloud) *sl* occasionally

òblānda *See the following*
• **u dùplōj òblāndi** {PP} (lit. in double cover) *sl-fea* dressed formally, dressed up

òblanjati {ām, ajū perf.} (lit. plane) *sl-sex* ***Fac-Obs*** engage in sexual intercourse with (of a male) <Slav*1>

oblȅka {ē fem.; Dat oblȅki} Cro *col* clothing <Slav>

oblíjati se {òblíjām, oblíjajū imperf. intr.} *sl-drink* get drunk <Slav❖*1>

òblog *See the following*
• **hlâdnī òblog** {NP} (lit. cold compress) *sl* unpleasant news

òbložen {a, o adj.} *sl-fea* affluent <Slav*1>

ȍbnōć {adv.} *col* in the night <Slav>

obojàdisati {išēm, išū perf.} *col* paint (wall, ceiling, etc.) <NE❖>

obòriti {òborīm, rē perf.} (lit. throw down) **1** *sl-drink* drink (alcohol), throw down <Slav*1> **2** *sl* eat, throw down <Slav*1> **3** *sl-sex* engage in sexual intercourse with (of a male) <Slav*1>

ȍbračun *See the following*
• **ȍbračun kod O.K.**[ô-kê] **Korála** {NP} (lit. shootout at the OK Corral) *sl-sstu* make-up exam

obráditi {òbrādīm, dē perf.} **a.** *col* cheat, swindle <Slav*1> **b.** *col* get, obtain <Slav*2>

obrađívānje {a neut.} **a.** *col* indoctrination <Slav*1> **b.** *col* persuasion <Slav*2> **c.** *col* cheating, swindling <Slav*3>

obrađívati {ràđujēm, đujū imperf.} **a.** *col* indoctrinate <Slav*1> **b.** *col* persuade, convince <Slav*2> **c.i.** *col* seduce <Slav*3> **ii.** *col* cheat, swindle <Slav*3>

òbrati *See the following*
• **òbrati bòstan** {VP} (lit. pick up the melons) *col* have a hard time, experience difficulties

òbraz {a masc.} (lit. cheek) *col* honor <Slav*1>

obràzli [1] {adj.} BosM *col* honorable <Slav❖*1>

obràzli [2] {adv.} BosM *col* honorably <Slav❖*1>

òbrazovati se {zujēm, zujū biasp. intr.} *sl* ***Fac*** dance cheek-to-cheek <Slav*1>

òbrazōvka {ē fem.} *sl-sstu* school <Slav*1>

òbresti se {obrétem, étu perf. irreg.} *col* find oneself (in a situation, country, etc.) <Slav>

òbrezānī {ōg (acc. = gen.) masc.} (lit. the circumcised one) *col* ***Off*** Bosnian Muslim <Slav*1>

obrȉjati {jēm, jū perf.} (lit. shave) *sl* rob, fleece, rip off <Slav*1>

òbrisati se {išēm, išū perf. intr.} *sl* lose <Slav*1>

obŕnuti {òbr̄nēm, nū perf.} (lit. turn over) **a.** *sl-sex* ***Obs*** engage in sexual intercourse with (of a male) <Slav*1> **b.** cheat, swindle

obŕnuti se {òbr̄nēm, nū perf. intr.} (lit. turn over) *sl* make a mistake, screw up <Slav*1>

òbrok *See the following*
• **tȍplī òbrok** {NP} (lit. hot meal) **1** *sl-sex* ***Obs*** fellatio **2** *col* salary supplement intended to cover lunch, lunch money

obŕstiti {òbr̄stīm, tē perf.} (lit. graze off) *sl-crime* rob, rip off <Slav*1>

òbrukati {ām, ajū perf.} *col* ashame, bring disgrace to <Slav❖*1>

òbūći se {obúčem, obúku, òbūk, òbūk perf. irreg.} (lit. dress) *sl-fea* get an education <Slav*1>
• **òbūći se ù šumi** {VP} (lit. get dressed in the woods) *sl-fea* limp

ȍbzīrom {c.} [std. = s obzirom na] *col* with respect to <Slav✍>

Òca mi! {S} (lit. I swear by my father!) *col* used to emphasize the truth of what has been said, I swear! ☞ otac

Òca ti dètīnjēg! {S} (lit. *I fuck* your childish father!) *col* ***Off*** used as a moderate curse, Fuck you! ☞ otac

Òca ti jèbēm! {S} (lit. I fuck your father!) *col* ***Off*** used as a strong curse, Fuck you! ☞ otac

Òca ti jèbēm, mȑtvōg! {S} (lit. I fuck your dead father!) *col* ***Off*** used as a very strong curse, Fuck you! ☞ otac

Òca ti kȑvavōg jèbēm! {S} (lit. I fuck your bloody father!) *col* ***Off*** used as a very strong curse, Fuck you! ☞ otac

Òca ti tvôg! {S} (lit. *I fuck* your father!) *col* ***Off*** used as a strong curse, Fuck you! ☞ otac

Òca ti tvôga! {S} (lit. *I fuck* your father!) *col* ***Off*** used as a strong curse, Fuck you! ☞ otac

òcariniti {nīm, nē perf.} /ocàriniti/ **a.** *sl* look, watch, scope out <Slav*1> **b.** *sl* steal, swipe <Slav*2>

oceániti {cèānīm, nē imperf.} *sl-fea* cry, shed tears, weep <Gre❖*1>

ocinkáriti {cìnkārīm, rē perf.} *sl-crime* inform the police or other authorities, snitch, squeal <**Ger❖**[*1]>

ocìpljati {ām, ajū perf.} *sl* leave, depart, walk <**Hun❖**[*1]>

ocugánac {nca (acc. = gen.) masc.} *sl-drink* alcoholic, drunk <**Ger❖**[*1]>

òcvancovati {cujēm, cujū perf.} *sl* grade (in school) <**Ger❖**[*1]>

ȍcvrki {ȍcvr̄kā masc. pl.} *sl* cracklings <**Slav**[*1]>

ȍčāj {excl.} *col* horror, terror <**Slav**>

ȍčājan {jna, jno adj.} *col* bad <**Slav**[*1]>

očàlāš {očaláša (acc. = gen.) masc.; Voc ȍčalāšu} *sl-fea* male with eyeglasses, four-eyes <**Ita❖**>

očále {ā fem. pl.} **a.** Med *col* eyeglasses <**Ita**> **b.** *sl-sex* bra <**Ita**[*1]>

očalíner {a (acc. = gen.) masc.} *sl-fea* male with eyeglasses, four-eyes <**Ita❖**[*1]>

òčas {adv.} *col* quickly <**Slav**>

očèpiti {òčepīm, pē perf.} *col* hit, punch <**Slav**[*1]>

očèpulja {ē fem.} *sl-fea* female gossiper <**Slav❖**[*1]>

očerùpati se {pām, pajū perf. intr.} *sl* take one's dress off, strip <**Slav**[*1]>

očèšati se {ām, ajū perf. intr.} (lit. scratch oneself) *col* get for free <**Slav**[*1]>

očèšljati {ām, ajū perf.} (lit. comb) **a.** *sl* hit, punch <**Slav**[*1]> **b.** take away, remove <**Slav**[*2]> **c.** rob, fleece, rip off <**Slav**[*3]>

ȍči {òčijū masc. pl.} (lit. eyes) *sl-sex* ***Fac-Obs*** nipples (of a female) <**Slav**[*1]>

ȍči ko šêst bànkī {NP} (lit. eyes like six dinars) *sl-fea* big, wide eyes ☞ **oko**

Ȍči su mu òtišle u čvȍr. {S} (lit. His eyes went into a knot.) *sl-fea* used to refer to the astonishment of a third person male, He was stunned. ☞ **oko**

Ȍči ti ìspale! {S} (lit. May your eyes fall out!) *col* ***Off*** used as a strong offense, Damn you! ☞ **oko**

Òčijū mi! {S} (lit. I swear by my eyes!) *col* used to emphasize the truth of what has been said, I swear! ☞ **oko**

óčīn {excl.} (lit. father's *cock*) *dia* used as a strong negative response, no way, never <**Slav**[*1]>

òčinjī {ā, ē adj.} *dia-col* eye's <**Slav**>

òčistiti {tīm, tē perf.} (lit. clean) *sl-crime* steal, swipe <**Slav**[*1]>

• **òčistiti drôb** {VP} (lit. clean entrails) *sl* get all the money (e.g. in gambling)

òčukati {ām, ajū perf.} *sl-crime* break into <**Slav**[*1]>

očùpati *See the following*

• **očùpati r̀ibu** {VP} (lit. clean fish) *sl-sex* ***Fac-Obs*** abuse a female (usu. sexually)

òćerati {ām, ajū imperf.} [std. = otjerati] *dia* throw away, toss out <**Slav**✐>

ȍćno {òćino fem.; perm} [std. = noć] *sl* night <**Slav**✐>

oćoráviti {ćòrāvīm, vē perf.} (lit. lose sight) **1** *sl-drugs* be down (after the effects of narcotic drugs) <**NE**[*1]> **2** *sl* fall in love <**NE**[*1]>

od glávē do pétē {PP} (lit. from head to heel) *col* from head to toe, completely ☞ **glava**

od rúkē {PP} (lit. from hand) **a.** *col* right away, now **b.** *col* conveniently, handy ☞ **ruka**

od šûba {PP} (lit. at once) *sl* right away, at once ☞ **šub**

od zûba do zûba dvâ dâna jàhānjā {PP} (lit. from one tooth to another two days of riding) *sl-fea* gaps between the teeth ☞ **zub**

od zûba do zûba trî dâna jàhānja {PP} (lit. from one tooth to another three days of riding) *sl-fea* gaps between the teeth ☞ **zub**

odàlamiti {mīm, mē perf.} /odalámiti/ **a.** *sl* hit, punch <**Lat-Ita**[*1]> **b.** *sl-sex* engage in sexual intercourse with (of a male)

odàpēti {òdapnēm, pnū perf. intr.} (lit. bang) **1** *sl-sex* ***Obs*** engage in sexual intercourse with (of a male), bang <**Slav**[*1]> **2** *sl* ***Der*** die, kick the bucket <**Slav**[*1]> **3** *sl-drugs* overdose (on drugs) <**Slav**[*1]>

odàpinjānje {a neut.} (lit. banging) **a.** *sl* dying <**Slav**[*1]> **b.** *sl-drugs* down (after the effects of narcotic drugs) <**Slav**[*2]>

odàpinjati {ām, ajū imperf. intr.} (lit. bang) *sl* ***Der*** die, kick the bucket <**Slav**[*1]>

odbàrtati {ām, ajū perf. intr.} **1** *sl-arch* take away, remove **2** *sl-arch* drive away, drive off

odbàštati {ām, ajū perf.} **1** *sl-crime* break into **2** *sl* walk **3** *sl* beat up

odbaštávati *See the following*

• **odbaštávati dàsku** {VP} (lit. bang a plank) *sl* open the door

odbáštiti {tīm, tē perf.} **a.** *sl* open (door, window, etc.) <**NE❖**[*1]> **b.** *sl-crime* break into <**NE❖**[*2]>

òdbīj {excl.} *col* used to make somebody go away, beat it <Slav*1>

odbrìjati {ām, ajū perf.} *col* beat up <Slav*1>

odbrojávati {bròjāvām, brojávajū imperf.} (lit. count down) *sl-fea* be in a nursing home <Slav*1>

óde {adv.} [std. = ovd(j)e] *dia-col* here <Slav✍>

Òde litùrgija u pȉčku! {S} (lit. Church service went to a cunt!) *dia* ***Obs*** used to express lack of control over events, Fuck it! ☞ **otići**

ódedama {adv.} [std. = ovd(j)e] *dia* here <Slav✍>

òdeljati {ām, ajū perf.} SerE *sl* beat up <Slav*1>

ódenā {adv.} [std. = ovd(j)e] *dia-col* here <Slav✍>

odèrati {òderēm, rū perf.} (lit. rip off) **1** *sl-gamble* beat, win money from somebody <Slav*1> **2** *sl* overcharge, rip off <Slav*2>
- **odèrati kȍžu** {VP} (lit. peel off skin) *col* rob, fleece, rip off

odgalopírati {lòpīrām, lopírajū perf.} *sl* run away, flee <Fre*1>

odgàmbati {ām, ajū perf.} *sl* depart, leave <Ita⁘>

odgambávānje {a neut.} *sl* departure <Ita⁘>

òdgibāj {excl.} *sl* used to make somebody go away, beat it <Slav*1>

odgíbati {òdgībām, odgíbajū perf.} *sl* walk away, leave <Slav*1>

odgìljati {ām, ajū perf.} /odgíljati/ *sl* walk away, leave <Gyp⁘*1>

òdgledati *See the following*
- **òdgledati nȉzbrdo** {VP} (lit. look downhill) *sl* look at one's open zipper

odglúmiti {òdglūmīm, òdglúmē perf.} (lit. act out) *col* pretend <Slav*1>
- **odglúmiti màglu** {VP} (lit. act fog) *sl* run away, flee

òdgnjusān {a, o adj.} *sl-fea* unattractive, ugly

ȍdi [1] {excl.} *col* used to make somebody join you, come over <Slav✍> ☞ **hodi**

ódi [2] {adv.} [std. = ovd(j)e] *dia* here <Slav✍>

òdigrati {ām, ajū perf.} (lit. play out) **1** *sl* lose one's sympathy <Slav*1> **2** *sl* lose value <Slav*1>
- **òdigrati bilìjār s jájima** {VP} (lit. play billiards with one's balls) *sl* hit somebody in the testicles
- **òdigrati strìptīz** {VP} (lit. play striptease) *sl* admit, make a confession, come clean

odigrávati {odìgrāvām, odigrávajū imperf.} **a.** *sl-fea* be suitable, be fitting: *Odigrava li ova torba? Is this bag suitable?* <Slav*1> **b.** *sl-fea* be valid <Slav*2> **c.** *sl-fea* be interesting <Slav*3> **d.** *sl-fea* be excellent <Slav*4>

ódikā {adv.} [std. = ovd(j)e] *dia* here <Slav✍>

ȍdīm {imperf.} [std. = hodam] SSer *dia* go (in all its Serbo-Croatian meanings in the form different from the standard one) <Slav✍>

òdjahati {ašēm, ašū perf. intr.} (lit. ride away) *sl* leave, depart, walk <Slav*1>

odjèbati {òdjebēm, bū perf.} **1a.** *sl* dump one's boyfriend or girlfriend <Slav*1> **b.** *sl* send away, dismiss <Slav*2> **c.** *sl* cease boring <Slav*3> **2** *sl-sex* engage in sexual intercourse with (of a male) <Slav*1>
- **odjèbati karijéru** {VP} (lit. fuck off one's career) *sl* dump one's boyfriend or girlfriend

odjèbi {excl.} *col* used to make somebody go away, beat it <Slav*1>

odjèdriti {òdjedrīm, rē perf.} (lit. sail away) **1** *sl* leave, beat it <Slav*1> **2** *sl* be destroyed, be ruined <Slav*1>

òdlahnuti {nēm, nū perf. intr.} BosM *col* ease up, take it easy <Slav✍>

òdlajati {jēm, jū perf.} (lit. bark out) *sl-crime* inform the police or other authorities, snitch, squeal <Slav*1>

òdlāndrati {ām, ajū perf.} *sl* leave, walk, depart, walk <Slav⁘*1>

odlépiti {òdlēpīm, pē perf. intr.} (lit. unstitch) **a.** SerE *sl* go insane, become unglued, freak out: *On je odlepio pa priča gluposti. He went nuts and he is blabbling nonsense.* <Slav*1> **b.** SerE *sl* fall in love: *odlepiti na komšinicu fall in love with one's neighbor* <Slav*1> **c.** SerE *sl* be interested in something, be keen on: *odlepiti na tenis be interested in tennis* <Slav*1>

odlepršati {ām, ajū perf.} **a.** *col* fly away <Slav*1> **b.** *col* go away, leave <Slav*2> **c.** *sl* die, kick the bucket <Slav*3>

odlèteti {òdletīm, tē perf.} (lit. fly away) **a.** SerE *sl* leave, depart, walk <Slav*1> **b.** SerE *sl* get angry <Slav*2>

ȍdmā {adv.} [std. = odmah] *col* right away, now <Slav✍>
- **Nȍvī Ȍdmā** {NP} (lit. New Now *'odma' and 'sad' are synonymous*) *sl* ***Fac*** Novi Sad (a city in Yugoslavia)

odmàgliti {òdmaglīm, lē perf.} /ȍdmagliti/ (lit. fog off) *col* run away, flee <Slav⁘*1>

odmàralīšte {a neut.} (lit. vacation resort) *sl* hospital <Slav*1>

odmardèljati {ām, ajū perf.} *sl-crime* spend one's term in prison <Ita❖[*1]>

òdmet *See the following*

- **na òdmet** {PP} (lit. at castoff) *col* useless

odmòri {excl.} [std. = odmori se] *col* used to calm down one's interlocutor, cool off <Slav✍>

Odmòri se na mòjēga! {S} (lit. Rest on my *prick*!) SSer *dia* ***Off*** used as a moderate curse, Fuck you! ☞ **odmoriti se**

odmorìška {ē fem.; Dat odmorìški} /odmorìška/ *sl* vacation resort <Slav✍>

odmòriti {òdmorīm, rē perf.} [std. = odmoriti se] *col* take a rest, take a break, relax <Slav✍>

- **Odmòri se na mòjēga!** {S} (lit. Rest on my *prick*!) SSer *dia* ***Off*** used as a moderate curse, Fuck you!
- **odmòriti ga** {VP} (lit. rest it) *sl-sex* ***Fac-Obs*** cease one's engagement in sexual intercourse

òdnesti {esēm, esū perf. irreg.} (lit. take away) [std. = odn(ij)eti] Cro *sl-crime* steal, swipe <Slav✍>

Òdnosīm ti se s kévōm! {S} (lit. I relate with your mother!) *sl* ***Off*** used as a strong curse, Fuck you! ☞ **odnositi se**

odnòsiti se {sīm, sē imperf. intr.} (lit. relate to) *sl-sex* ***Obs*** engage in sexual intercourse with <Slav[*1]>

- **Òdnosīm ti se s kévōm!** {S} (lit. I relate with your mother!) *sl* ***Off*** used as a strong curse, Fuck you!

òdojak *See the following*

- **rěš pěčenī òdojak** {NP} (lit. well done piglet) *sl-fea* bald male

ȍdovlē {adv.} /odóvlē/ [std. = odavde] *dia* from here <Slav✍>

ȍdovlēk {adv.} *dia* from here <Slav✍>

ȍdovlēn {adv.} /odóvlē/ [std. = odavde] *dia* from here <Slav✍>

odráditi {òdrādīm, dē perf.} (lit. finish work) **1** *sl-sex* ***Fac-Obs*** cease one's engagement in sexual intercourse <Slav[*1]> **2** *sl* seduce <Slav[*1]>

òdralkati {ām, ajū perf.} *sl* dump one's boyfriend or girlfriend

odrápiti {òdrāpīm, pē perf.} **a.** *sl* hit, punch **b.i.** *sl-sex* engage in sexual intercourse with (of a male) **ii.** *sl* overcharge, rip off

òdrati {derēm, derū perf.} **1a.** *col* steal, swipe <Slav[*1]> **b.** *sl-gamble* take someone's money in gambling <Slav[*2]> **2** beat up severely, trash

odráziti se {zīm, zē perf. intr.} *sl* speak out <Slav[*1]>

odrèagovati {gujēm, gujū perf.} *col* react <Lat❖>

odréditi {òdrēdīm, dē perf.} *sl* do, accomplish <Slav[*1]>

òdrizati {ižēm, izū perf.} [std. = odrezati] Med *dia* cut off, chop off <Slav✍>

òdrukati {ām, ajū perf. intr.} (lit. print out) *sl-crime* ***Fac*** inform the police or other authorities, snitch, squeal <Ger[*1]>

òdruknuti {nēm, nū perf.} *sl-crime* inform the police or other authorities, snitch, squeal <Ger❖[*1]>

òdskočnā dàska {NP} (lit. springboard) *col* springboard (for one's career) ☞ **daska**

odsmr̀di {excl.} (lit. stink out) *sl* used to make somebody go away, get out <Slav[*1]>

odsmr̀diti {dīm, dē perf.} *sl* get rid of <Slav[*1]>

odstondírati {stòndīrām, stondírajū perf.} *sl-drugs* lie down while being stoned <Eng❖>

odstúpiti {òdstūpīm, pē perf.} *sl* cease boring <Slav[*1]>

odsúkati {òdsúkām, odsúkajū perf.} *sl-sports* play a game <Slav[*1]>

odsúkati se {òdsúkām, odsúkajū perf. intr.} *sl* separate from somebody (e.g. from one's spouse) <Slav[*1]>

òdsustvo *See the following*

- **sèksuālnō òdsustvo** {NP} (lit. sexual leave of absence) *sl-mil* ***Fac*** exceptional leave of absence in the military

odsvírati *See the following*

- **odsvírati hîmne** {VP} (lit. play the national anthems) *sl* greet each other
- **odsvírati sèt** {VP} (lit. play a set) **a.** *sl* play several songs **b.** *sl* be destroyed, be ruined

òdšacati {ām, ajū perf.} *sl* take a careful look, check out <Ger❖[*1]>

òdšājbati {ām, ajū perf.} **1** *sl* run away, flee <Ger❖[*1]> **2** *sl* engage in sexual intercourse with (of a male) <Ger❖[*1]>

odšaráfiti {šàrāfīm, fē perf.} *col* unscrew <Ger❖>

odšeráfiti {šèrāfīm, fē perf.} *col* unscrew <Ger❖>

odšéviti {òdšēvīm, vē perf.} *sl-sex* ***Obs*** engage in sexual intercourse with (of a male) <Slav[*1]>

òdšibati {ām, ajū perf.} *sl-sex* ***Obs*** engage in sexual intercourse with (of a male) <Slav[*1]>

òdšlepati {ām, ajū perf. intr.} *sl* date, go out with <Ger❖>

òdšrafiti {fīm, fē perf.} **a.** *col* unscrew <Ger❖> **b.** *col* hit, punch <Ger❖[*1]>

odùjmiti {mīm, mē perf.} *sl-drink* drink a little (alcohol) <Slav*1>

odúljiti {òdūljīm, ljē perf.} *sl-gamble* win in gambling or marbles game <Slav*1>

odušèviti se *See the following*

• **odušèviti se ko kȕče u lȉftu** {VP} (lit. be thrilled like a dog in an elevator) *sl-fea* be very enthusiastic

odùzēti *See the following*

• **odùzeti jȕnfer** {VP} (lit. take someone's hymen) *sl-sex* ***Obs*** deflower

odùzēti se {òdzmēm, zmū perf. intr.} *sl-drink* get very drunk, get dead drunk <Slav*1>

ȍdvaditi {dīm, dē perf.} (lit. take out) **1** *sl* ease up, take it easy <Slav*1> **2** *sl* cease lying <Slav*1>

• **ȍdvaditi bȍtu** {VP} *sl* slap, smack

odvàjāč {vajáča (acc. = gen.) masc.} *sl-sex* male sexual partner (of a female) <Slav*1>

odvájati {òdvājām, odvájajū imperf.} **1** *sl* flirt <Slav*1> **2** *sl* work, labor <Slav*1> **3** *sl* pay (bills, etc.) <Slav*1>

• **odvájati rášu** {VP} *sl-sex* ***Obs*** watch other's sexual intercourse

• **odvájati žváku** {VP} (lit. separate chewing gum) *sl-fea* talk, have a conversation

odváliti {òdvālīm, lē perf.} *col* say something unintelligent <Slav*1>

• **odváliti krèvet** {VP} (lit. hit a bed) *sl-sex* ***Obs*** engage in sexual intercourse with

• **odváliti pešáka** {VP} (lit. hit walking) SerE *sl* walk

• **odváliti žváku** {VP} (lit. hit chewing gum) *sl-fea* talk, have a conversation

odvèslati {ām, ajū perf. intr.} *sl* leave, depart, walk <Slav*1>

ȍdvisiti {sīm, sē perf.} **a.** *sl* be ruined, be destroyed <Slav*1> **b.** *sl* lose money <Slav*1>

odvȍjiti {ȍdvojīm, jē perf.} (lit. separate) **1a.** *sl* take, get hold of, pick: *odvojiti knjige take some books* <Slav*1> **b.** *sl* flirt <Slav*2> **c.** *sl* get a girlfriend <Slav*3> **2** *sl* stop <Slav*1>

• **odvȍjiti čmâr** {VP} (lit. separate an asshole) *sl* follow, go behind somebody

• **odvȍjiti dèvōjku** {VP} (lit. separate a girl) *sl* commence a love affair

• **odvȍjiti đánu** {VP} (lit. separate a look) *sl* look, watch, scope out

• **odvȍjiti ìkilić-ždràkić** {VP} (lit. separate staring) *sl* look, watch, scope out

• **odvȍjiti ȍko** {VP} (lit. separate an eye) *sl* take a look, scope out

• **odvȍjiti rȉbu** {VP} (lit. separate a fish) *sl* commence a love affair

• **odvȍjiti sòvān** {VP} (lit. separate an owl) *sl* sleep, nap

• **odvȍjiti sòvāž** {VP} (lit. separate sleeping) *sl* sleep, nap

• **odvȍjiti sovijáner** {VP} (lit. separate sleeping) *sl* sleep, nap

• **odvȍjiti sôvku** {VP} (lit. separate sleeping) *sl* sleep, nap

• **odvȍjiti sóvu** {VP} (lit. separate an owl) *sl* sleep, nap

• **odvȍjiti tàbane** {VP} (lit. separate one's feet) *sl* walk

• **odvȍjiti ȕvo** {VP} (lit. separate one's ear) *sl* listen

• **odvȍjiti žváku** {VP} (lit. separate chewing gum) *sl* talk persistently and meaninglessly, blabber, chatter

odzújati {ȍdzūjīm, jē perf.} (lit. buzz away) **a.** *sl* leave, depart, walk <Slav*1> **b.** *sl* end one's term in prison <Slav*2>

odzvȉždati {òdzviždīm, dē perf.} /odzvíždati/ (lit. whistle away) **a.** *sl* discover, find out: *odzviždati nepravilnosti discover irregularities* <Slav*1> **b.i.** *sl-crime* inform the police or other authorities, blow the whistle <Slav*2> **ii.** *sl* prevent, block: *odzviždati velike probleme prevent big troubles* <Slav*2>

odzvòniti {òdzvonīm, nē perf.} (lit. ring away) **a.** *sl* be destroyed, be ruined <Slav*1> **b.** *sl* die, kick the bucket <Slav*2>

ȍdža {ē masc.} [std. = hodža] *dia* imam <NE✍>

ȍdžak {odžáka masc.} /ȍdžāk/ (lit. chimney) *sl-fea* chain smoker, chimney <NE*1>

odžàkānje {a neut.} *sl-drink* drinking (alcohol) <NE❖*1>

odžàkati {ām, ajū perf.} *sl* throw away, toss out <NE❖*1>

odžàkati se {ām, ajū perf. intr.} **1** *sl-drink* get drunk <NE❖*1> **2** *sl-drugs* smoke (tobacco) <NE❖*1>

odžódžiti {òdžōdžīm, džē perf.} **a.** *sl* spend one's time in useless activities, fool around, mess around <NE❖*1> **b.** *sl* take a rest, take a break, relax **c.** *sl-sex* cease one's engagement in sexual intercourse

ođànisati {išēm, išū perf.} **a.** *sl* look, watch, scope out <Gyp❖> **b.** *sl* feel, sense <Gyp❖*1>

óđe {adv.} [std. = ovd(j)e] *dia* here <Slav✍>

óđekarce {adv.} [std. = ovd(j)e] *dia* here <Slav✍>

óđekare {adv.} [std. = ovd(j)e] *dia* here <Slav✍>

óđena {adv.} [std. = ovd(j)e] *dia* here <Slav✍>

ófa {ē masc.} *sl-mil* officer <Lat✍>

òfajditi se {dīm, dē perf. intr.} *sl* profit, gain <**NE❖**[*1]>

òfaliti {līm, lē perf.} *sl* get worse <**Ger❖**[*1]>

ofanzívac {vca (acc. = gen.) masc.} *sl-sports* offensive player <**Lat**[*1]>

òfārbati {ām, ajū perf.} (lit. paint) *sl* cheat, swindle <**Ger❖**[*1]>

Òfēlija {ē fem.} (lit. Ophelia) *sl-sex* ***Fac*** prostitute, hooker <**EngÓ**[1]>

òfentāl {a masc.} Gast *col* residence permit (for ex-Yugoslav guest workers in Germany) <**Ger✍**>

oficīr {oficíra (acc. = gen.) masc.} (lit. officer) *sl-fea* inhabitant of the countryside, hick, bumpkin <**Fre**[*1]>

oficīrka {ē fem.; Dat oficīrki} (lit. the officer's one) *sl-mil* low-cut boots <**Lat❖**[*1]>

òfićak {ćka masc.} *col* splinter <**NE❖**[*1]>

òfinger {a masc.} **a.** *sl* clothes hanger <**Ger✍**> **b.** *sl* shoulder <**Ger✍**>

ofírati {òfīrām, ofírajū perf.} **1a.** *sl* discover, find out: *ofirati jeftin dućan discover a cheap store* <**Eng❖**[*1]> **b.** *sl* inform the police or other authorities, snitch, squeal <**Eng❖**[*2]> **2** *sl* leave somebody: *ofirati devojku leave one's girlfriend* <**Eng❖**[*1]>

ofírati se {ām, ajū perf. intr.} *sl* leave somebody: *ofirati se od poznanika leave one's acquaintance* <**Eng❖**[*1]>

òfita {ē masc.} *sl-gamble* lucky gambler

ȍfos {a (acc. = gen.) masc.} *sl-mil* officer <**Lat✍**>

òfraštiti {štīm, šte perf.} *sl-sex* ***Obs*** engage in sexual intercourse with (of a male)

ofráziti se {zīm, zē perf. intr.} *sl* express oneself <**Gre❖**[*1]>

òfrčen {a, o adj.} *sl-fea* old

òfrčija {ē fem.} *sl-fea* senior citizen

ofrkéstiti se {fr̀kēstīm, tē perf.} *sl* regain consciousness, come to

ȍfrljē {adv.} *col* approximately <**Slav**[*1]>

ȍfsājd {a masc.} *sl* trouble, problem <**Eng**[*1]>

- **u ȍfsājdu** {PP} (lit. off side) **a.** *sl-fea* outside **b.** *sl-fea* ill, sick

òfūcān {a, o adj.} **a.** *sl-fea* used <**Slav**[*1]> **b.** *sl-fea* in old clothing **c.** *sl-fea* looking bad

òfuljiti {ljīm, ljē perf.} /ofúljiti/ **1** *sl-gamble* win money from, come out ahead **2** *sl* hit, punch

ȍgāvan {vna, vno adj.} *col* gross, nasty: *ogavna hrana repulsive food* <**Slav**>

ogávština {ē fem.} *col* gross thing or situation <**Slav**>

ȍgbo {excl.; perm} [std. = bog] **1 Cro** *sl* used to greet informally on arrival, hi <**Slav✍**> **2 Cro** *sl* used to take leave of somebody informally, bye <**Slav✍**>

ògizditi {dīm, dē perf.} *sl* hit, punch

oglàbātor {a (acc. = gen.) masc.} *sl-fea* beggar

oglòžiti *See the following*

- **oglòžiti do kȍžē** {VP} (lit. peel off up to one's skin) *sl-gamble* take all one's money in gambling

ȍgnjište *See the following*

- **Ȍgnjīšte ti jèbēm!** {S} (lit. I fuck your fireplace!) *dia* ***Off*** used as a moderate curse, Fuck you!

ȍgradica *See the following*

- **ȍgradica za cvêće** {NP} (lit. flower fence) *sl-fea* mentally deficient person

ogràničen {a, o adj.} (lit. limited) *sl-fea* unintelligent, stupid, dumb <**Slav**[*1]>

- **ogràničen ko bàlkōn** {AdjP} (lit. as restricted as a balcony) *sl-fea* unintelligent, stupid, dumb
- **ogràničen ko ȍbala** {AdjP} (lit. as restricted as a shore) *sl-fea* unintelligent, stupid, dumb
- **ogràničen ko tàcna** {AdjP} (lit. as restricted as a tray) *sl-fea* unintelligent, stupid, dumb
- **ogràničen ko teràsa** {AdjP} (lit. as restricted as a porch) *sl-fea* unintelligent, stupid, dumb

ogrèbati se {ògrebēm, bū perf. intr.} (lit. scratch oneself) *col* get for free <**Slav**[*1]>

- **ogrèbati se za dúgu** {VP} (lit. scratch for a card) *sl-gamble* get a suitable playing card

ògrepsti se {ògrebēm, ebū perf. irreg.} (lit. scratch oneself) *col* get for free <**Slav**[*1]>

ògriz {a masc.} *sl* female <**Slav**[*1]>

ògrjev {a masc.} *col* fuel <**Slav**[*1]>

ȍgroz {a masc.} *col* female <**Slav**[*1]>

ogùglati {ām, ajū perf. intr.} *sl-fea* get used to (usu. something unpleasant) <**Gyp**>

ogúliti {ògūlīm, lē perf.} (lit. peel off) *col* rob, rip off <**Slav**[*1]>

- **ogúliti na kúbi** {VP} (lit. peel off on Cuba) *sl-gamble* take money from somebody in gambling

ògūljen {a, o adj.} (lit. peeled off) *sl-fea* bald <**Slav**[*1]>

ȍh {excl.} *col* used to express surprise, pain, etc. oh <**Slav**>

ȍhā {excl.} **1** *col* used to command a horse to stop, stop <**Slav**> **2** used to express approval, great

ȍhēj {excl.} *col* used to command a horse to move on, go <Slav>

ohláditi {ȍhlādīm, dē perf.} (lit. cool off) **1a.** *col* cease talking, put a cork in <Slav[*1]> **b.** *col* cease boring <Slav[*2]> **2a.** *col* beat up <Slav[*1]> **b.** *sl-crime* kill, murder <Slav[*2]>

• **ohláditi kàpislu** {VP} (lit. cool off a shell) *sl* shut up, cease talking

• **ohláditi u kàpislu** {VP} (lit. cool off into a shell) *sl* calm down, cool off

ohláditi se {ȍhlādīm, dē perf. intr.} (lit. cool off) **1** *sl-fea* relax, cool off <Slav[*1]> **2** *sl* die, kick the bucket <Slav[*1]>

ȍhō {excl.} *col* used to express surprise, wow <Slav>

ȍho-hô {adv.} *col* ample, plenty of: *Hrane ima oho-ho, bujrum. There is a whole bunch of food left, help yourself.* <Slav>

ȍhoho {excl.} *col* used to express surprise, wow <Slav>

ȍhōj {excl.} *col* used to express surprise, wow <Slav>

ôj {excl.} *col* used to draw attention in direct informal communication, hey <Slav>

ȍjā {excl.} *col* used to express joy, great <Slav>

òjaditi {dīm, dē perf.} (lit. make sad) **a.** *sl* beat up <Slav[*1]> **b.** *sl* rob, rip off <Slav[*2]> **c.** *sl* defeat <Slav[*3]>

ȍjc {excl.} *dia-col* used to drive away an ox <Slav>

òjebina {ē fem.} *sl* ***Fac-Obs*** half eaten crescent (roll) <Slav[*1]>

ojèzičiti se {čīm, čē perf. intr.} (lit. tongue oneself) *sl-fea* start talking extensively <Slav❖[*1]>

ojìkare {kārā fem. pl.} *sl* eyeglasses <Slav❖[*1]>

ȍka {ē fem.} [std. = oko] *sl-fea* ***Fam*** eye (sight organ) <Slav✍>

ókac {kca (acc. = gen.) masc.} *sl-fea* person in eyeglasses, four-eyes <Slav❖[*1]>

òkačiti se {čīm, čē perf. intr.} (lit. hang oneself) *col* ***Fac*** hang up one's coat <Slav[*1]>

òkatī {ōg (acc. = gen.) masc.} (lit. the big-eyed one) *sl-fea* boss <Slav[*1]>

okàuz {a masc.} *sl* eye (sight organ) <Slav✍>

ókca {ē fem.} *sl-drugs* hashish, hash

ókce *See the following*

• **U ókce te jèbēm!** {S} (lit. I fuck you in your small eye!) *dia* ***Off*** used as a moderate curse, Fuck you!

• **U ókce te jèbēm, kȗrvinskō!** {S} (lit. I fuck you in your hooker little eye!) *dia* ***Off*** used as a moderate curse, Fuck you!

òkefati {ām, ajū perf.} *col* brush (e.g. to clean garment) <Hun❖>

okêj {excl.} *col* okay, fine, great <Eng>

okèseriti {rīm, rē perf.} *sl-sex* ***Obs*** engage in sexual intercourse with (of a male)

okešávānje {a neut.} *sl-sex* ***Obs*** sexual foreplay, petting, feeling up

ȍkica {ē fem.} *sl-drugs* opium <Gre✍>

okiláviti se {vīm, ve perf. intr.} (lit. develop a hernia) *sl-fea* work hard, bust one's balls <Gre❖[*1]>

okináva {ē fem.} **1** *sl-crime* bloody street fight <Slav✍> **2** *sl-stu* failed exam <Slav✍>

òkinuti {nēm, nū perf.} **1** *sl-sex* ***Obs*** engage in sexual intercourse with (of a male) <Slav[*1]> **2** *sl* ***Der*** die, kick the bucket <Slav[*1]> **3** *sl-stu* fail an exam (flunk) <Slav[*1]> **4** *sl-sex* break wind, fart

òkisati {išēm, išū imperf.} *sl* look, watch, scope out <Slav❖>

òkita {ē masc.} *sl-gamble* lucky gambler

Oklahȍma {ē fem.} (lit. Oklahoma) Cro *sl* name of a bar on Trnjanska street in Zagreb, Croatia <EngO[*1]>

òklamati {ām, ajū perf.} *sl* take, get hold of, pick

ȍklē {adv.} [std. = odakle] *dia-col* from where <Slav✍>

ȍklēn {adv.} [std. = odakle] *dia-col* from where <Slav✍>

òklocati se {ām, ajū perf. intr.} *sl-fea* lose weight <Slav❖[*1]>

òklok {a masc.} (lit. o'clock) **a.** *sl* hour <Eng[*1]> **b.** *sl* clock, watch <Eng[*2]>

òkljīnčiti {čīm, čē perf.} *sl* leave, depart, walk

ȍko [1] {a neut.} (lit. eye) *sl-crime* ***Der*** informer, stoolie, snitch <Slav[*1]>

ȍko [2] {excl.} (lit. eye) *col* ***Fam*** used to address a person in an intimate manner, dear <Slav[*1]>

• **gȍtivnō ȍko** {NP} (lit. nice eye) *sl* clock, watch

• **ko ȍko** {PP} (lit. like an eye) *sl-fea* filled, jam packed

• **ȍči ko šêst bȁnkī** {NP} (lit. eyes like six dinars) *sl-fea* big and wide eyes

• **Ȍči su mu òtišle u čvȍr.** {S} (lit. His eyes went into a knot.) *sl-fea* used to refer to the astonishment of a third person male, He was stunned.

• **Ȍči ti ìspale!** {S} (lit. May your eyes fall out!) *col* ***Off*** used as a strong curse

• **Òčijū mi!** {S} (lit. I swear by my eyes!) *col* used to emphasize the truth of what has been said, I swear!

• **pícino ȍko** {NP} (lit. cunt's eye) *col* ***Obs*** very clean, clean as a whistle

• **pod ȍkom** {PP} (lit. under eye) *col* under surveillance, being watched

• **sȍcijalnē ȍči** {NP} (lit. social eyes) *sl-fea* eyeglasses

• **spȅcijalnē ȍči** {NP} (lit. special eyes) *sl-fea* eyeglasses

okolokȕćnīpìšātor {a masc.} (lit. round-the-house pisser) *sl* ***Fac*** gutter <Slav❖[*1]>

okolotȑbušnī pantalodŕžac {NP} (lit. round-belly trousers-holder) *sl* ***Fac*** waist, belt ☞ **pandalodržac**

okolotȑbušnī pantalodȑžāč {NP} (lit. round-belly trousers-holder) *sl* ***Fac*** waist, belt ☞ **pantalodržač**

okòpniti {òkopnīm, nē perf. intr.} (lit. melt) *sl* ***Fac*** die, kick the bucket <Slav[*1]>

ȍkoslāv {a masc.} *sl* eye (sight organ) <Slav✍>

okoslavírati {slàvīrām, slavírajū imperf.} *sl* look, watch, scope out <Slav❖✍>

ȍkovān {a, o adj.} (lit. in chains) *sl-fea* ***Fac*** married, hitched <Slav[*1]>

okovánje {a neut.} (lit. being in chains) *sl-crime* spending term in prison <Slav[*1]>

okȍvati se {òkujēm, jū perf. intr.} *sl* ***Fac*** marry, tie the knot <Slav[*1]>

òkovi {ōvā masc. pl.} *sl* ***Fac*** marriage <Slav[*1]>

òkoziti se {zīm, zē perf. intr.} (lit. give birth to goat) *sl-fea* have a hard time, experience difficulties <Slav[*1]>

okréćati {òkrēćēm, ćū imperf.} (lit. turn around) [std. = okretati] **a.** *col-dia* turn, revolve, move <Slav✍> **b.** *col-dia* engage in sexual intercourse with (of a male) <Slav✍[*1]>

okrénuti {òkrēnēm, nū perf.} (lit. turn around) **1** *sl-sex* ***Obs*** engage in sexual intercourse with (of a male) <Slav[*1]> **2a.** *sl-crime* cheat, swindle **b.** *sl-crime* steal

• **kàko gȍd òkrēnēš** {AdvP} (lit. any way you turn it) *col* at any rate

• **okrénuti ćȕrak nàopāko** {VP} (lit. turn one's hat the other way around) *col* turn over a new leaf

• **okrénuti lîst** {VP} (lit. turn a page) *col* turn over a new leaf

okrénuti se {òkrēnēm, nū perf. intr.} (lit. turn around) *sl* make a mistake, screw up <Slav[*1]>

okrètljiv {a, o adj.} (lit. movable) *col* undependable, unreliable <Slav[*1]>

okrȍčiti {òkročīm, čē perf.} *dia* ***Obs*** engage in sexual intercourse with (of a male) <Slav[*1]>

òkrpiti se {òkrpīm, pē perf.} (lit. mend oneself) **1** *sl* earn amply <Slav[*1]> **2** *sl* get ample new things <Slav[*1]>

òkrūgaō *See the following*

• **okrúglo pa na ćóše** {AdjP} (lit. round with corners) *col* undetermined: *Njegovi politički stavovi su sve nešto okruglo pa na ćoše. His political attitudes are undetermined.*

okrùgljača {ē fem.} *sl* lightbulb <Slav❖[*1]>

òkrūžen {a, o adj.} *sl-fea* unattractive, ugly <Slav[*1]>

ȍkserice {a fem. pl.} *sl-fea* bow legs <Slav❖[*1]>

oksidácija {ē fem.} (lit. oxidation) *sl-gamble* playing cards <Gre[*1]>

ȍksigenskā sȉjalica {NP} (lit. oxygen light bulb) *sl-sex* ***Fac-Obs*** very attractive female, hot number ☞ **sijalica**

ȍktopōd {a (acc. = gen.) masc.} (lit. octopus) *sl* female <Gre[*1]>

ȍkuka {ē fem.} (lit. turn) **1** *sl* avoiding <Slav[*1]> **2** *sl-mil* one month of one's military service <Slav[*1]>

okulári {lārā masc. pl.} *col* eyeglasses <Ita[*1]>

okúpati {òkūpljām, ajū perf. intr.} *sl-crime* find, locate <Slav[*1]>

okupâtor {a (acc. = gen.) masc.} (lit. occupier, i.e. Benito Mussolini, who occupied a part of the former Yugoslavia during WWII) *sl-drink* Mussolini (a kind of wine and juice cocktail) <Lat[*1]>

okùpīran {a, o adj.} (lit. occupied) **1** *sl-fea* ***Fac*** married <Lat[*1]> **2** *sl-fea* busy <Lat[*1]>

òkusiti *See the following*

• **òkusiti mȕstera** {VP} (lit. taste a dude) *sl* profit, gain

ȍkvīr {a masc.} (lit. frame) **1** *sl* door <Slav[*1]> **2** window <Slav[*1]>

ȍla-ôl {excl.} *col* used to express surprise, excitement, joy, etc., oh my <Slav>

òlabaviti {vīm, vē perf.} /olàbaviti, olabáviti/ **a.** *col* ease up, take it easy: *Juče je bila nervozna ali je danas olabavila. She was nervous yesterday but she eased it up today.* <Slav[*1]> **b.** *col* stop <Slav[*1]> **c.** *col* shut up <Slav[*3]>

oládi {excl.} [std. = ohladi] *col* used to calm down one's interlocutor, cool off <Slav✍[*1]>

Oládi ga da ti ga nȁbijēm! {S} (lit. Cool it off so that I can stick it to you!) **a.** *col* ***Off*** used as a moderate curse, Fuck you! **b.** *col* used to silence one's interlocutor, Shut up! ☞ **oladiti**

oláditi {òlādīm, dē perf.} [std. = ohladiti] **1a.** *sl* beat up <Slav✍[*1]> **b.** *sl-sports* knock out (boxing) <Slav✍[*2]> **c.** *sl* shut up <Slav✍[*3]> **d.** *sl-crime* kill, murder <Slav✍[*4]> **e.** *sl-crime* steal from, rip off <Slav✍[*5]> **f.** *sl* be sent to prison <Slav✍[*6]> **2a.** *sl* ease up, take it easy <Slav✍[*1]> **b.** *sl* calm down, cool off <Slav✍[*2]> **3** *sl* dump one's girlfriend or boyfriend

• **Oládi ga da ti ga nȁbijēm!** {S} (lit. Cool it off so that I can stick it to you!) **a.** *col* ***Off*** used as a moderate curse, Fuck you! **b.** *col* used to silence one's interlocutor, Shut up!

• **oláditi pápke** {VP} (lit. cool off one's hooves) *sl* die, kick the bucket

olàkšati {ām, ajū perf.} (lit. make lighter) *sl-crime* steal from, rip off <Slav[*1]>

olàktati {tām, tajū perf.} (lit. elbow) *sl-crime* steal from, rip off <Slav⁘[*1]>

òlalije *See the following*

• **Òlālije ti jèbēm!** {S} *dia* ***Off*** used as a moderate curse, Fuck you!

òlanjati {ām, ajū imperf.} *sl* wash one's face

òlanjati se {ām, ajū imperf. intr.} *sl* wash one's face

òlešiti {šīm, šē perf.} /olèšiti/ **1** *sl-sex* ***Obs*** engage in sexual intercourse with (of a male) <Slav[*1]> **2** *sl* beat up <Slav[*1]>

òlešiti se {šīm, šē perf.} /olèšiti se/ **1** *sl-drink* drink too much (alcohol) <Slav[*1]> **2** *sl-drugs* overdose <Slav[*1]>

ȍlfo {òlafo masc.; perm} /òlfo/ [std. = fol] *sl* trick, joke <Ita✍>

ȍli [1] {c.} [std. = ili] *dia* or <Slav✍>

ȍli [2] {excl.} [std. = hoćeš li] *dia* used to check if one's interlocutor wants something <Slav✍>

oligáviti {ìgāvīm, vē perf.} *sl* wash one's face

òlikō {adv.} [std. = ovoliko] *dia* this many <Slav✍>

òlīndrati {ām, ajū perf.} **1** *sl* beat up **2** *col* give a very short haircut

òlio {ija masc.} (lit. Ollie) *sl-fea* ***Der*** clumsy person, klutz <EngO[*1]>

òlipati {ām, ajū perf. intr.} *sl* hit, punch

olȉstati {ām, ajū perf.} *sl-fea* dress formally, dress up <Slav[*1]>

ȍloš {a masc.} *col* worthless or despicable person <Slav[*1]>

ȍlošār {a (acc. = gen.) masc.} *sl-fea* ***Der*** worthless or despicable person <Slav⁘[*1]>

olováriti se {olòvārīm, rē perf. intr.} *sl-fea* become affluent <Gyp⁘[*1]>

òltar *See the following*

• **Òltār ti jèbēm!** {S} (lit. I fuck your altar!) *dia* ***Off*** used as a moderate curse, Fuck you!

òluk {a masc.} (lit. gutter) **1a.** *sl-crime* concealed exit <NE[*1]> **b.** *sl-crime* exit <NE[*2]> **2** *sl* source of income <NE[*1]>

òlupina {ē fem.} (lit. wreck) *sl-fea* senior citizen <Slav[*1]>

oljóskati se {òljōskām, oljóskajū perf. intr.} *sl-drink* get drunk <Slav⁘[*1]>

òljūštiti {tīm, tē perf.} (lit. peel off) *sl-sex* ***Obs*** engage in sexual intercourse with (of a male) <Slav[*1]>

ȍmā {adv.} [std. = odmah] *dia-col* right away, now <Slav✍>

omáciti se {òmācīm, cē perf. intr.} (lit. have kittens) *sl* vomit, throw up, puke <Slav[*1]>

omàknuti *See the following*

• **Òmaknēm ti ga!** {S} (lit. I miss it to you!) *dia* ***Off*** used as a moderate curse, Fuck you!

omȁnučiti se {čīm, čē perf. intr.} *sl* get married, get hitched

òmānūt {a, o adj.} *sl-fea* ***Der*** insane, nuts <Slav[*1]>

ománuti {òmānēm, nū perf.} (lit. miss) **1** *sl-sex* ***Fac-Obs*** engage in sexual intercourse with (of a male) <Slav[*1]> **2** *sl* make a mistake, screw up <Slav[*1]>

• **ománuti petáka** {VP} (lit. miss a grade A) *sl-sstu* get the highest grade

ȍmanjī {ā, ē adj.} *col* smallish <Slav>

omástiti *See the following*

• **omástiti ȁsfalt** {VP} (lit. lubricate asphalt) *sl-auto* fall from a motorcycle, kiss the pavement

omástiti se {òmāstīm, tē perf. intr.} (lit. eat fat) *sl* earn amply <Slav[*1]>

• **omástiti bȓk** {VP} (lit. lubricate one's mustache) **a.** *sl* eat one's fill, be stuffed **b.** *sl* earn amply

omatúfeti {màtūfīm, fē perf.} SerE *sl-fea* turn senile <NE⁘>

ȍmča {ē fem.} (lit. noose) *sl* ***Fac*** marriage <Slav[*1]>

òmīš {omíša (acc. = gen.) masc.} *sl-fea* talented male

ȍmmā {adv.} [std. = odmah] BosM *dia* instantly <Slav✍>

ȍmrka {ē fem.} *sl-sex* ***Obs*** sexual intercourse (of sheep) <Slav✍>

òmudina {ē fem.} *sl-sex* ***Obs*** area around testicles <Slav⁘>

ôn *See the following*
- **Ôn je sî.** {S} (lit. He is OK.) *sl-fea* used to express one's appreciation toward a third party male, He's OK.

ona stvâr {NP} (lit. that thing) *sl-sex* sexual intercourse ☞ **stvar**

onàdati {ām, ajū perf.} *sl-sex* ***Obs*** engage in sexual intercourse with (of a male)

ònāj *See the following*
- **Ònāj ko te jȅbō!** {S} (lit. The one who fucked you!) *col* ***Off*** used as a moderate curse in response to a question, Fuck you!: *A: Ko je pitao za tvoje mišljenje? B: Onaj ko te jebo! A: Who asked for your opinion? B: Fuck you!*

onàkō {part.} *col* particle used to express undetermined state, so-so <Slav>

ònām {adv.} [std. = onamo] *col-dia* there <Slav✍>

onanȉ-onanȁ {ē fem.} (lit. ob-la-di, from Beatles' song transformed to coincide with the noun onanija 'onanism') *sl-sex* ***Fac-Obs*** masturbation <Gre✍>

ȍndāj {adv.} [std. = onda] *dia* then <Slav✍>

ȍndāk {adv.} [std. = onda] *dia* then <Slav✍>

ȍndār {adv.} [std. = onda] *dia* then <Slav✍>

ònī {pron.} [std. = onaj] *dia-col* that <Slav✍>

òno [1] {pron.} *col* depreciatory pronoun usually used in reference to young persons: *Ono će mi reći šta da radim! That thing is not going to tell me what to do!* <Slav[*1]>

ònō [2] {pron.} (lit. that) **1** *col* bribe <Slav[*1]> **2** *sl-sex* sexual intercourse <Slav[*1]> **3** *col* used to make a vague reference to anything: *Mi smo tamo ono. We did, ya know.* <Slav[*1]>
- **ònō Mîle** {NP} (lit. that Mile) *sl* used to express lack of idea what to do next, what now

ònō mȅsto {NP} (lit. that place) SerE *sl-sex* ***Obs*** bathroom ☞ **mesto**

onòditi *See the following*
- **Kȍ te ȍnodī!** {S} (lit. Who did it to you!) *dia* ***Off*** used to express disrespect, Fuck you!

onúdijēn {adv.} [std. = ond(j)e] *dia* there <Slav✍>

ôooj {excl.} *col* used to draw attention in direct informal communication, hey <Slav>

ȍp [1] {excl.} *col* used when jumping, hop <Slav>

ȍp [2] {a +ov (ext. pl) masc.; Nom Pl òpovi} *sl-drugs* opium <Slav>

ȍpā {excl.} /òpā/ *col* used to express surprise, astonishment, etc., oh <Slav>
- **ȍpā bâto** {ExcP} (lit. oh boy) *col* used to express astonishment, wow
- **ȍpā Mȉkī** {ExcP} (lit. oh boy) *col* used to express astonishment, wow

ȍpadnica {ē fem.} **a.** *sl* hand <Slav[*1]> **b.** *sl* arm <Slav[*2]>

opàjdār {opajdára (acc. = gen.) masc.} *sl-sex* ***Fac*** male homosexual, gay <Slav❖[*1]>

opàjdara {ē fem.} **a.** *sl-sex* ***Der*** prostitute, hooker <Slav❖[*1]> **b.** *sl-fea* ***Der*** extremely talkative female, chatterbox <Slav❖[*2]>

opàjdariti {rīm, rē perf.} *sl* hit, punch <Slav❖[*1]> *sl* engage in sexual intercourse with (of a male)

ȍpalā {excl.} /òpalā/ *col* used to express surprise, wow <Slav>

ȍpalāc {excl.} /òpalāc/ *col* used to express surprise, wow <Slav>

opálija {ē fem.} *sl-sex* ***Fac*** prostitute, hooker <Slav✍>

Òpālīm te! {S} (lit. I bang you!) *col* ***Off*** used as a moderate curse, Fuck you! ☞ **opaliti**

Òpālīm te gòlīm! {S} (lit. I bang you with my naked *prick*!) *col* ***Off*** used as a moderate curse in response to a question, Fuck you!: *A: Molim? B: Opalim te golim! A: Pardon me? B: Fuck you!* ☞ **opaliti**

opalìndati {ām, ajū perf.} *sl-sex* ***Obs*** engage in sexual intercourse with (of a male) <Slav✍[*1]>

opáliti {òpālīm, lē perf.} (lit. bang) **a.** *sl* hit, punch <Slav[*1]> **b.i.** *sl* engage in sexual intercourse with (of a male) <Slav[*2]> **ii.** *sl* break wind, fart <Slav[*2]> **iii.** *sl* tell, say <Slav[*2]>
- **Òpālīm te!** {S} (lit. I bang you!) *col* ***Off*** used as a moderate curse, Fuck you!
- **Òpālīm te gòlīm!** {S} (lit. I bang you with my naked *prick*!) *col* ***Off*** used as a moderate curse in response to a question, Fuck you!: *A: Molim? B: Opalim te golim! A: Pardon me? B: Fuck you!*
- **opáliti kȕnt** {VP} (lit. bang a sleep) *sl* sleep, nap
- **opáliti lîz** {VP} (lit. bang a lick) *sl-sex* ***Obs*** engage in cunnilingus
- **opáliti màjmuna** {VP} (lit. bang a monkey) *sl-sex* ***Fac-Obs*** masturbate, spank the monkey
- **opáliti mȅtak** {VP} (lit. bang a bullet) *sl-sex* ***Fac-Obs*** engage in sexual intercourse with, bang
- **opáliti múvīng** {VP} (lit. bang a move) *sl* walk
- **opáliti pešáka** {VP} (lit. bang a walker) SerE *sl* walk
- **opáliti po plômbi** {VP} (lit. bang one's filling) *sl-sex* ***Obs*** deflower

• opáliti u tȉkvu na dúgi {VP} (lit. bang a pumpkin on a card) *sl-gamble* win the bank

opaljívānje {a neut.} (lit. banging) *sl-sex* ***Obs*** sexual intercourse, banging <Slav*1>

opaljȍt {a masc.} 1 *sl-sex* ***Fac-Obs*** sexual intercourse <Slav✍ *1> 2 *sl-stu* failed exam <Slav✍ *1>

opàmbrčiti {čīm, čē perf.} 1 *sl* hit, punch <Slav*1> 2 *sl-sex* engage in sexual intercourse with (of a male) <Slav*1>

opàmprčiti {čīm, čē perf.} 1 *sl* hit, punch <Slav*1> 2 *sl-sex* engage in sexual intercourse with (of a male) <Slav*1>

opanàčkē {adv.} (lit. naopačke 'upside down' X opanak 'peasant shoe') [std. = naopačke] *col* upside down <Slav✍>

òpanak {òpānka masc.} (lit. peasant shoe) *sl-fea* inhabitant of the countryside, hick, bumpkin

opàndrčiti {čīm, čē perf.} 1 *sl* hit, punch <Slav*1> 2 *sl-sex* engage in sexual intercourse with (of a male) <Slav*1>

opanjkávati {opànjkāvām, opanjkávajū imperf.} *col* gossip, wag the tongue <Slav⁘ *1>

opàprčiti {čīm, čē perf.} *sl-sex* ***Obs*** engage in sexual intercourse with (of a male) <Slav*1>

opàrmačiti {čīm, čē perf.} *sl-sex* ***Obs*** engage in sexual intercourse with (of a male)

opasúljiti se {opàsūljīm, ljē perf. intr.} (lit. be-bean oneself) *sl* come to terms, become reasonable <Slav*1>

opàtica {ē fem.} (lit. nun) *sl-sex* ***Fac*** virgin <Aram*1>

Opàtija {ē fem.} *sl-crime* ***Iro*** solitary prison cell <SlavO*1>

opàučiti {čīm, čē perf.} a. *col* hit, punch <Slav*1> b. *col* engage in sexual intercourse <Slav*2>

òpcigovati {gujēm, gujū biasp. intr.} *col* subtract <Ger*1>

ȍpē {adv.} [std. = opet] *col-dia* again <Slav✍>

òpeći se {òpečēm, òpekū, òpek, òpek perf. irreg.} (lit. burn oneself) *sl-fea* be in a difficult situation <Slav*1>

opèlješiti {šīm, še perf.} /opeljéšiti/ *col* rob, rip off <Slav⁘ *1>

ȍpera *See the following*

• sàpunskā ȍpera {NP} (lit. soap opera) *col* soap opera

operácija {ē fem.} (lit. operation) *sl-fea* ***Der*** clumsy person, klutz <Lat*1>

• ȕniverzalnā operácija {NP} (lit. universal operation) *sl-fea* very clumsy person, complete klutz

ȍperacionī stô {NP} (lit. surgical table) *sl-gamble* gambling table ☞ sto

opèrāš {operáša (acc. = gen.) masc.; Voc ȍperāšu} Cro *sl* a visitor at the Opera bar in Zagreb, Croatia <Lat⁘ *1>

operdášiti {opèrdāšīm, šē perf.} *sl-sex* ***Obs*** engage in sexual intercourse with (of a male)

opèrisān {a, o adj.} (lit. operated) *sl-fea* clumsy, klutzy <Lat*1>

operȕšati {ām, ajū perf.} *sl* rob, rip off <Slav*1>

ȍpēt {a, o adj.} a. *sl-fea* affluent <Slav*1> b. *sl-fea* excellent, cool <Slav*2>

òpičen {a, o adj.} (lit. hit at the cunt) a. *sl-fea* ***Der*** insane, nuts <Slav*1> b. *sl-fea* ***App*** extravagant <Slav*1>

òpičiti {čīm, čē perf.} (lit. hit the cunt) a. *sl-sex* ***Obs*** hit, punch <Slav⁘> b. *sl-sex* ***Obs*** engage in sexual intercourse with (of a male) <Slav⁘ *1>

opijúkati {opìjūčem, ūčū perf.} *sl-sex* ***Obs*** engage in sexual intercourse with (of a male) <Slav*1>

òpis *See the following*

• lȉčnī òpis {NP} (lit. personal description) *sl* face (human)

opísati se {òpīšēm, īšū perf. intr.} *sl* eat one's fill, be stuffed <Slav*1>

òpizdina {ē fem.} *sl-sex* ***Obs*** area around vagina <Slav⁘ *1>

opízditi {òpīzdīm, dē perf.} (lit. cunt) a. *sl-sex* ***Obs*** hit, punch <Slav⁘ *1> b. *sl* ***Obs*** engage in sexual intercourse with (of a male) <Slav⁘ *2>

ȍpklada {ē fem.} *col* bet <Slav>

opkopávati {kòpāvām, kopávajū imperf.} (lit. dig around) *sl* lie <Slav*1>

oplajváziti {làjvāzīm, zē perf.} (lit. pencil) *sl-sex* ***Obs*** engage in sexual intercourse with (of a male) <Ger⁘ *1>

• Oplàjvāzīm te! {S} (lit. I pencil you!) *col* ***Off*** used as a moderate curse, Fuck you!

• oplájvaziti Šáćira {VP} (lit. to pencil Šaćir, a Muslim given name) *sl-sex* ***Fac-Obs*** masturbate, beat off

opláviti {vīm, ve perf.} (lit. blue) 1 *sl* beat up <Slav*1> 2 *sl* annoy, bother, pester <Slav*1>

òplesti {òpletēm, etū perf. irreg.} (lit. knit around) a. *sl-sex* ***Fac*** hit, punch <Slav*1> b. *sl-sex* ***Fac-Obs*** engage in sexual intercourse with (of a male) <Slav*2>

òplet {a masc.} *sl* paneling <Slav*1>

oplèten {a, o adj.} (lit. knitted) *sl-crime* robbed, ripped off <Slav*1>

opléviti {òplēvim, òplēvē imperf.} (lit. weed) *sl-crime* pick somebody's pockets <Slav*1>

oplìndrati {ãm, ajũ perf.} *sl-crime* rob, rip off

òpljunuti {nẽm, nũ perf.} (lit. spit on) *sl-fea* criticize publicly <Slav*1>

òpnãš {opnáša (acc. = gen.) masc.; Voc ȍpnãšu} *sl-fea* stupid or mentally deficient person <Slav*1>

Òpni se! {S} *dia* ***Off*** used as a moderate curse, Fuck you! ☞ **opnuti se**

òpnuti se *See the following*

• **Òpni se!** {S} *dia* ***Off*** used as a moderate curse, Fuck you!

oporúčiti {pòrũčīm, čẽ perf.} *sl* kill, murder <Slav*1>

òpraljati {ãm, ajũ imperf.} [std. = opravljati] *sl-crafts* repair, fix <Slav✍>

oprcóknuti {pȑcōknēm, nũ perf.} *sl-sex* ***Obs*** engage in sexual intercourse with (of a male) <Slav❖>

oprédmetiti {tīm, tẽ perf.} *sl-sex* ***Obs*** engage in sexual intercourse with (of a male) <Slav*1>

ȍprēm {excl.} *col* used to express extreme disgust

• **Ȍprēm bâto!** {S} (lit. I push it, brother!) *col* used to stimulate to an action

• **Ȍprēm dòbro!** {S} (lit. I push it well!) *col* used to express disrespect or lack of interest in

• **Ȍprēm sêko!** {S} (lit. I push it, sister!) *col* used to express disrespect or lack of interest in

òprēti se *See the following*

• **Òpri se!** {S} (lit. Push yourself!) *col* used as a moderate curse, Fuck it!

oprèznjãk {opreznjáka (acc. = gen.) masc.} *sl-fea* cautious male <Slav❖>

oprìndačiti {čīm, čẽ perf.} *sl-sex* ***Obs*** engage in sexual intercourse with (of a male) <Slav*1>

opȑndačiti {čīm, čẽ perf.} *sl-sex* ***Obs*** engage in sexual intercourse with (of a male) <Slav*1>

òpružen {a, o adj.} (lit. stretched) **a.** *sl-fea* unattractive, ugly: *opružena riba ugly chick* <Slav*1> **b.** *sl-fea* unimportant <Slav*2>

òpruženo {adv.} (lit. stretched) *sl* distantly <Slav*1>

òpružiti se {žīm, žẽ perf.} (lit. stretch oneself) *sl* pay (bills, etc.) <Slav*1>

opservatôrij *See the following*

• **sȅksuālnī opservatôrīj** {NP} (lit. sexual observatory) **Cro** *sl-sex* ***Fac*** name of a bar at Ilica and Marinkovićeva streets in Zagreb, Croatia

opsèsija {ẽ fem.} (lit. obsession) *sl* ***Fac*** cigarette, smoke <Lat*1>

ȍpšīran {rna, rno adj.} (lit. extensive) *sl-fea* boring <Slav*1>

Òpšticemo vam s mâjkōm. {S} (lit. We will communicate with your mother.) *sl* ***Off*** used as a strong curse, Fuck you! ☞ **opštiti**

Òpštīm ti se s mâjkōm! {S} (lit. I communicate with your mother!) *sl* ***Off*** used as a strong curse, Fuck you! ☞ **opštiti**

ȍpština *See the following*

• **za célu ȍpštinu** {PP} (lit. for the whole county) **SerE** *col* too much, overwhelming

òpštiti {tīm, tẽ perf.} (lit. communicate) *sl-sex* ***Obs*** engage in sexual intercourse with <Slav*1>

• **Òpšticemo vam s mâjkōm.** {S} (lit. We will communicate with your mother.) *sl* ***Off*** used as a strong curse, Fuck you!

• **Òpštīm ti se s mâjkōm!** {S} (lit. I communicate with your mother!) *sl* ***Off*** used as a strong curse, Fuck you!

optalidónac {nca (acc. = gen.) masc.} (lit. Optalidon, common prescription drug) *sl-drugs* first time drug user <BN❖*1>

opticírati {tìcīrãm, ticírajũ imperf.} *sl* look, watch, scope out <Gre❖*1>

òptić {a masc.} *sl-drugs* Optalidon pill <BN❖>

òptika {ẽ fem.} *sl* eyeglasses <Gre*1>

òptike {ȍptīka masc. pl.} *sl* eyeglasses <Gre*1>

opúhati {òpūhãm, opúhajũ perf.} (lit. blow away) *sl-crime* steal, swipe <Slav*1>

òpuliti {līm, lẽ perf.} *sl* lift, rise

òpurkati {ãm, ajũ imperf.} *sl-crime* steal, swipe

òrahovača {ẽ fem.} *sl-drink* plum brandy made with walnuts <Slav❖*1>

orandžína {ẽ fem.} *sl-fea* obese female <Fre✍>

órаõ {rla (acc. = gen.) masc.} (lit. eagle) **1** *sl* friend (male) <Slav*1> **2** *sl* group leader <Slav*1>

• **Órao krûžī.** {S} (lit. The eagle is circling around.) *sl-crime* used to indicate imminent danger from the police

òraovača {ẽ fem.} [std. = orahovača] *sl-drink* plum brandy made with walnuts <Slav❖✍>

òrasi {òrãhã masc. pl.} (lit. nuts) **1** *sl-sex* ***Fac*** testicles, nuts <Slav*1> **2** *sl* money <Slav*1>

òrati {òrēm, rũ imperf.} (lit. plough) *sl-sex* ***Fac-Obs*** engage in sexual intercourse with (of a male) <Slav*1>

òrãtor {a (acc. = gen.) masc.} (lit. orator) *sl-crime* ***Der*** informer, stoolie, snitch <Lat*1>

ȍrdēn {a masc.} (lit. decoration) *sl-fea* bruise <Lat[*1]>

òrdija {ē fem.} *sl-drink* wine <NE[*1]>

òrdijān {ordijána masc.} *sl-arch* wine

òrdīn {ordína masc.} *sl-drink* wine <NE[*1]>

ȍrdūj {a masc.} *sl-drink* wine <NE[*1]>

orezíliti se {orèzīlīm, lē perf. intr.} *sl-fea* make a fool of oneself <NE❖[*1]>

òrgān {orgána (acc. = gen.) masc.} (lit. organ) *sl-crime* policeman, cop <Gre[*1]>

- **drûg òrgān** {NP} (lit. comrade organ) *sl-crime* ***Fac-Der*** policeman, cop

organìzam {zma masc.} (lit. organism) [std. = orgazam] *sl-sex* ***Fac-Obs*** orgasm <Gre✍>

orgànizovati se {zujēm, zujū perf. intr.} (lit. get organized) *sl-sex* have an orgasm <Gre[*1]>

òrgija {ē fem.} *col* orgy <Gre>

òrijāš [1] {orijáša (acc. = gen.) masc.; Voc ȍrijāšu} *sl-fea* giant <Hun>

orìjāš [2] {orijáša masc.} **a.** *dia* village <Hun[*1]> **b.** *sl* building block <Hun[*2]>

ȍrjan {a masc.} *sl-drink* wine <NE[*1]>

ȍrk {a +ov (ext. pl) masc.; Nom Pl òrkovi} [std. = orkestar] *sl-music* orchestra <Gre✍>

ôrka {ē fem.; Dat ôrki} (lit. killer whale) *sl-sex* ***Fac*** male homosexual, gay

òrkestar {tra masc.} (lit. orchestra) *sl-crime* police manhunt <Gre[*1]>

orlùšina {ē fem.} (lit. large eagle) **a.** *sl* friend (male) <Slav❖[*1]> **b.** *sl* group leader <Slav❖[*2]>

òrmān [1] {ormána (acc. = gen.) masc.} (lit. cupboard) *sl-fea* muscular male <NE[*1]>

òrmān [2] {ormána masc.} **1** *sl* cupboard <NE[*1]> **2** *sl* novel <Fre✍>

- **ko trȍkrīlnī òrmān**{PP} (lit. like a three-door cupboard) *sl-fea* muscular
- **trȍkrīlnī òrmān** {NP} (lit. three-door cupboard) *sl-fea* muscular male
- **trȍkrīlnī òrmār** {NP} (lit. three-door cupboard) *sl-fea* muscular male

ormànljika {ē fem.} *sl-arch* tree <NE❖[*1]>

ormànjlika {ē fem.} *sl-arch* woods, forest <NE❖[*1]>

òrmār {ormára (acc. = gen.) masc.} *sl-fea* muscular male <Fre[*1]>

ȍrōz {a (acc. = gen.) masc.} Bos *dia-col* rooster <NE>

ȍrpa {òrapa (acc. = gen.) masc.; perm} [std. = paor] **a.** *sl-fea* inhabitant of the countryside, hick, bumpkin <Slav✍> **b.** *sl-fea* father, daddy <Slav✍[*1]>

òrtāk {ortáka (acc. = gen.) masc.} **a.** *col* friend (male) <NE> **b.** *col* partner <NE[*1]> **c.** *col* accomplice <NE[*2]>

ortàkinja {ē fem.} *sl* friend (female) <NE❖>

osèdlati *See the following*

- **osèdlati krȁvu** {VP} (lit. saddle a cow) *sl-fea* marry an older woman
- **osèdlati krȁvu s tèletom** {VP} (lit. saddle a cow with a calf) *sl-fea* marry a woman with a child

ȍsēk {a masc.} SerE *dia* fence, wall <Slav>

ȍsiēk {a masc.} *dia* fence, wall <Slav>

osigùrāč {osiguráča (acc. = gen.) masc.} (lit. fuse) *sl* relative <Slav[*1]>

ȍsijēk {a masc.} *dia* fence, wall <Slav>

òsīk {osíka masc.} *dia* fence, wall <Slav>

ȍsīljka {e fem.} *sl-arch* louse (the insect)

ȍskār {a (acc. = gen.) masc.} **1** *sl* parent <EngO[*1]> **2** *sl* failing grade <Eng>

oslàjpičiti {čīm, čē perf.} *sl* hit, punch <Slav❖[*1]>

ȍslić {a (acc. = gen.) masc.} (lit. hake) *sl-auto* Austin (make of car)

òsmāk {osmáka masc.} *sl* eight <Slav✍>

osmérac {rca (acc. = gen.) masc.} (lit. the team of eight men manning a racing boat) *sl-sstu* ***Fac*** eight-year high-school student (instead of the usual four) <Slav[*1]>

osmogòdišnjāk {a (acc. = gen.) masc.} (lit. eight years old) *sl-fea* ***Iro*** manager who has only an elementary school diploma <Slav[*1]>

òsnova *See the following*

- **po svîm òsnovama** {PP} (lit. on all bases) *col* on all counts

osokòliti se {osòkolīm, lē perf. intr.} (lit. falcon oneself) **a.** *sl-fea* become courageous <Slav❖[*1]> **b.** *sl-drink* ***Fac*** get drunk <Slav❖[*2]>

osovljávati se {osòvljāvām, osovljávajū imperf. intr.} *sl* fall asleep, doze off <Slav[*1]>

ostáci {ȍstatākā masc. pl.} (lit. leftovers) *sl-drugs* leftovers from a previous fix <Slav[*1]>

òstati *See the following*

- **ȍstati bez nȍvācā** {VP} (lit. stay without any money) *sl* be cheated, be swindled

• òstati kràtak {VP} (lit. stay short) *col* lose money

• òstati kràtkīh rukávā{VP} (lit. stay with short sleeves) **a.** *col* be unsuccessful **b.** *col* lose money

• òstati pȕn {VP} (lit. stay full) *sl-sex* get pregnant, get knocked up

• òstati u čàbru {VP} (lit. stay in a wash basin) *sl* be worse off

òstaviti *See the following*

• òstaviti pȕno pjȅsāmā {VP} (lit. leave a handful of songs) *sl* start a discussion and leave

ȍstos {a masc.} *sl-drugs* leftovers of a drug in a syringe <Slav✍[*1]>

ostràguša {ē fem.} (lit. the behind one) **1** *sl-sex* ***Fac-Obs*** female who engages in anal sex <Slav[*1]> **2** *sl-sex* ***Obs*** anus, asshole <Slav[*1]> **3** *sl-sex* ***Fac-Obs*** male homosexual who takes the passive role, femme <Slav[*1]>

òstria {ē fem.} *sl-fea* stupid or mentally deficient person <Ita[*1]>

òstrići {ostrížem, ostrígu, òstrīg, òstrīg perf. irreg.} *dia* give a haircut <Slav✍>

ȍstriga {ē fem.; Dat ȍstrigi} (lit. oyster) *sl-fea* stupid or mentally deficient person <Ita[*1]>

òstrūgānī {a, o adj.} (lit. the scratched one) *sl-fea* bald <Slav[*1]>

ostrúgati {òstrūgām, ostrúgajū perf.} (lit. scratch) *sl* shave <Slav[*1]>

ostrúgati se {òstrūgām, ostrúgajū perf. intr.} (lit. scratch oneself) *sl* shave <Slav[*1]>

ȍstrvo {a neut.} (lit. island) *sl* swelling <Slav[*1]>

osùnećen {a, o adj.} *col* circumcised <NE❖>

osùnetiti {tīm, tē perf.} *col* circumcise <NE❖>

òsūšen {a, o adj.} (lit. dried) *sl-fea* broke (financially) <Slav[*1]>

osúšiti {òsūšīm, še perf.} (lit. dry) *sl* hit, punch <Slav[*1]>

òsūti se {ȍspēm, spu perf. intr.} *sl-fea* get nervous <Slav[*1]>

òsvetnīk *See the following*

• cŕnī òsvetnīk {NP} (lit. the black avenger) *sl-sstu* ***Fac*** grade book, black book

ȍš {excl.} [std. = hoćeš li] **1** *col* used to check if one's interlocutor wants something <Slav✍> **2** *col* used to drive away a dog, shoo <Slav>

Ȍš prôđēš kroz jâ? {S} (lit. Do you want to go through me?) *sl* used to refer to lack of consent, Over my dead body! ☞ **hteti**

ȍša {excl.} *col* used to drive away a dog, shoo <Slav>

òšacati {ām, ajū perf.} *sl* take a careful look, check out <Ger❖[*1]>

ȍšacovati {cujem, cujū perf.} **a.** *col* estimate, guess <Ger> **b.** *col* look, watch, scope out <Ger[*1]>

ošàjbudžiti {džīm, džē perf.} **a.** *sl* hit, punch <Slav❖✍[*1]> **b.** *sl* engage in sexual intercourse with (of a male) <Slav❖✍[*2]>

ošàjdariti {rīm, rē perf.} **a.** *sl* hit, punch <Slav❖✍[*1]> **b.** *sl* engage in sexual intercourse with (of a male) <Slav❖✍[*2]>

ošàmaren *See the following*

• ošàmaren po mȍzgu {AdjP} (lit. slapped on his brain) *sl-fea* insane, nuts

ošàmariti *See the following*

• ošàmariti ga {VP} (lit. give it a slap) *sl-sex* ***Fac-Obs*** masturbate, beat off

• ošàmariti pàtos {VP} (lit. slap floor) SerE *sl* fall down, hit the ground

ošàrnariti {ȍšarnarīm, rē perf.} (lit. slap) *sl-crime* look for an opportunity to pick pockets

ošášoljiti {ljīm, ljē perf.} *col* hit, punch

ošàuknuti {nēm, nū perf.} *sl* hit, punch

ȍšinūt {a, o adj.} *sl-fea* ***Der*** insane, nuts <Slav[*1]>

ȍšinuti {nēm, nū perf.} /ošínuti/ **a.** *col* hit, punch <Slav> **b.** *col* engage in sexual intercourse with (of a male), bang <Slav[*1]>

ošíšati *See the following*

• ošíšati vȁka {VP} (lit. give a haircut) **a.** *sl* earn amply **b.** *sl* rob, rip off

ȍškljabati {ām, ajū perf.} *sl-crime* rob, rip off

ȍškrtati {ām, ajū perf.} *sl* open (door, window, etc.)

ošlàjpičiti {čīm, čē perf.} *sl* hit, punch <Slav❖[*1]>

ošljáriti {ȍšljārīm, rē imperf.} *col* do something superficially

ošošóljiti {ošȍšōljīm, ljē perf.} *sl-fea* dazzle using effective words, snow <Slav❖[*1]>

ȍšrat {a masc.; perm} [std. = šatro] *sl* slang <NE✍>

ȍštar {tra, tro adj.; perm} (lit. sharp) [std. = šatra] **1** *col* strict <Slav[*1]> **2** *col* smart, sharp <Slav[*1]>

oštàrija {ē fem.} *sl-drink* bar (drinking place) <Ita>

oštŕljnuti {ȍštrljnēm, nū perf.} *sl* hit by car

ȍštrō {ōg neut.} (lit. the sharp stuff) *sl-drink* hard liquor <Slav[*1]>

òšuriti {rīm, rē perf.} *sl-fea* rob, rip off <Slav[*1]>

òšuriti se {rīm, rē perf.} **a.** *col* burn oneself <Slav> **b.** *col* make a mistake, screw up <Slav[*1]>

ošvorcírati {vòrcīrām, vorcírajū perf.} *sl* hit, punch <Ger❖[*1]>

ošvorcírati se {vòrcīrām, vorcírajū perf. intr.} *sl-fea* lose all one's money, go broke <Ger❖>

òšeć {ečem, eku, ek, ek perf. irreg.} [std. = odsjeći] *dia* cut off, chop off <Slav☞>

ośètljiv {a, o adj.} *dia* sensitive, touchy <Slav[*1]>

òtac *See the following*

- **I òca ti i mȁtēr jèbēm!** {S} (lit. I fuck both your father and your mother!) *col* ***Off*** used as a strong curse, Fuck you!
- **Òca mi!** {S} (lit. I swear by my father!) *col* used to emphasize the truth of what has been said, I swear!
- **Òca ti dètīnjēg!** {S} (lit. *I fuck* your kiddish father!) *col* ***Off*** used as a moderate curse, Fuck you!
- **Òca ti jèbēm!** {S} (lit. I fuck your father!) *col* ***Off*** used as a strong curse, Fuck you!
- **Òca ti jèbēm, mȑtvōg!** {S} (lit. I fuck your dead father!) *col* ***Off*** used as a very strong curse, Fuck you!
- **Òca ti kȑvavōg jèbēm!** {S} (lit. I fuck your bloody father!) *col* ***Off*** used as a very strong curse, Fuck you!
- **Òca ti tvôg!** {S} (lit. *I fuck* your father!) *col* ***Off*** used as a strong curse, Fuck you!
- **Òca ti tvôga!** {S} (lit. *I fuck* your father!) *col* ***Off*** used as a strong curse, Fuck you!
- **Sâm te òtac jèbō!** {S} (lit. Let your father himself fuck you!) *col* ***Off*** used as a strong curse, Fuck you!

ȍtafrljē {adv.} *dia-col* approximately <Slav☞[*1]>

ȍtālē {adv.} [std. = odatle] *col-dia* from there <Slav☞>

otàljati {ām, ajū perf.} *sl-fea* do something unwillingly and superficially <Slav❖>

otambùrati {ām, ajū perf. intr.} *sl* beat up <NE❖[*1]>

otánjiti {òtānjīm, njē perf.} (lit. become narrower) *col* get worse <Slav[*1]>

otàslačiti {čīm, čē perf.} *sl-sex* ***Obs*** engage in sexual intercourse with (of a male)

otasterírati {tèrīrām, terírajū perf.} *sl-crime* inform the police or other authorities, snitch, squeal <Ger❖[*1]>

otastèrisati {išēm, išū perf.} *sl-crime* inform the police or other authorities, snitch, squeal <Ger❖[*1]>

otcinkáriti {cìnkārīm, rē perf.} *sl-crime* inform the police or other authorities, snitch, squeal <Ger❖[*1]>

òtcinkati {ām, ajū perf.} *sl-crime* inform the police or other authorities, snitch, squeal <Ger❖[*1]>

otcìpljati {ām, ajū perf.} *sl* leave, depart, walk <Hun❖[*1]>

òtčukati {ām, ajū perf.} *sl-crime* inform the police or other authorities, snitch, squeal <Slav[*1]>

otégnuti *See the following*

- **otégnuti jája do kòljena** {VP} (lit. pull one's balls down to one's knees) *sl* work hard, bust one's balls
- **otégnuti pápke** {VP} (lit. stretch one's hooves) *sl* die, kick the bucket

òtekaō {kla, klo adj.} (lit. swollen) *sl-sex* ***Fac-App*** attractive, hot <Slav[*1]>

òteklaō {kla, klo adj.} (lit. swell) *sl-fea* attractive, hot <Slav[*1]>

òterati *See the following*

- **Òteraj me mȍlīm te u pȉčku mȁterinu!** {S} (lit. Send me to my mother's cunt, please!) **SerE** *sl* ***Obs*** used to express disbelief, No fucking way!
- **òterati u grȍb** {VP} (lit. send to the grave) **SerE** *col* ruin, destroy: *Njegove loše ocene će me oterati u grob. His bad grades will be the ruin of me. (parent of a chid)*
- **òterati u slépce** {VP} (lit. send to the blind people) SerE *sl* rob, rip off

òterati se {ām, ajū perf. intr.} SerE *sl* sleep, nap <Slav[*1]>

òtesati {ešēm, ešū perf.} *sl* beat up <Slav[*1]>

òtēti se {òtmēm, òtmū perf. intr.} (lit. release oneself) **1** *sl-drink* get drunk <Slav[*1]> **2** *sl* die, kick the bucket <Slav[*1]> **3** *sl* be surprised <Slav[*1]>

otézati se {òtēžem, ēžū imperf. intr.} (lit. stretch, extend *used in reference to a period of time*) *sl* stretch (warm-up before physical activity) <Slav[*1]>

otfikariti {rīm, rē perf.} /otfikáriti/ *col* cut off, chop off <NE❖[*1]>

òtfućkati {ām, ajū perf.} *sl* prevent somebody from talking, shut somebody up <Slav❖[*1]>

òtfur {a masc.} *sl* departure <Ger❖>

otfúrati {òtfūrām, otfūrajū perf. intr.} **a.** *col* leave, depart, walk <Ger❖[*1]> **b.** *col* take along <Ger❖[*2]>

- **otfúrati na dùrkan** {VP} *sl-crime* take somebody to a house with two exits and run away from them

otfurȉška {ē fem.; Dat otfurȉški} *sl* departure <Ger☞>

òtīći {òdēm, òdū, òtiđ, òtiš perf. irreg.} *col* malfunction <Slav[*1]>

- **Òde litùrgija u pȉčku!** {S} (lit. Church service went to a cunt!) *dia* ***Obs*** used to express lack of control over events, Fuck it!

- **òtīći u àut** {VP} (lit. go out of bounds) *sl* be knocked out
- **òtīći u kȕrac** {VP} (lit. go to a prick) *sl* ***Obs*** be in a very difficult situation
- **òtīći u kȕrac krâsnī** {VP} (lit. go to a nice prick) *col* ***Obs*** be in a very difficult situation
- **òtīći u legendu** {VP} (lit. go to legend) *sl* die, kick the bucket
- **òtīći u Mȍkricu** {VP} (lit. go to the Wetplace) Cro *sl* go to the bathroom
- **òtīći u pàkaō** {VP} (lit. go to hell) *sl* die, kick the bucket
- **òtīći u pȉčku mȁterinu** {VP} (lit. go to mother's cunt) *sl* ***Obs*** be in a very difficult situation
- **òtīći u râj** {VP} (lit. go to heaven) *sl* die, kick the bucket
- **òtīći u tandàriju** {VP} (lit. go to the bangland) *sl* be destroyed, be ruined
- **òtīći u Tùngūziju** {VP} (lit. go to Tunguska, a Russian province X guz 'buttocks') *sl* go far away, go to the end of the world

òtimānje {a neut.} (lit. grabbing) *sl-drink* drinking (alcohol) <Slav*1>

òtimati se {ām, ajū imperf.} (lit. resist) *sl-drink* get drunk <Slav*1>

òtintati *See the following*

- **òtintati pápke** {VP} (lit. color one's hooves) *sl-crime* get fingerprinted

òtipkati {ām, ajū perf.} *sl-crime* inform the police or other authorities, snitch, squeal <Ger✣*1>

òtišō {šla, šlo adj.} *sl-fea* malfunctioning, crashed, gone <Slav*1>

òtjecati {ečēm, ečū imperf.} (lit. swell) *sl-sex* ***Obs*** masturbate, beat off <Slav*1>

òtkačen {a, o adj.} (lit. unhooked) **a.** *col* unconventional, bohemian <Slav*1> **b.** strange, weird **c.** slightly insane, nutty

otkačénko {a masc.} (lit. the unhooked one) *sl-fea* strange male, weirdo <Slav✣*1>

òtkačenōst {i fem.} (lit. being unhooked) *sl-fea* lack of conventionality, bohemian life style <Slav*1>

òtkači {excl.} (lit. unhook) *col* used to make somebody go away, beat it, back off <Slav*1>

òtkači se {excl.} (lit. unhook) *col* used to make somebody go away, beat it, back off <Slav*1>

otkačȉška {ē fem. & masc.; Dat otkačȉški} **1a.** *sl-fea* strange person, weirdo <Slav✍*1> **b.** *sl-fea* insane person, nut case <Slav✍*2> **2** *sl* insanity, craziness <Slav✍*1>

òtkačiti {čīm, čē perf.} (lit. unhook) **a.** *sl-fea* become insane, become unhinged <Slav*1> **b.** *sl-fea* fall in love <Slav*2>

- **òtkačiti zȅzalicu** {VP} (lit. unhook a joke) *sl* have a great time

òtkačiti se {čīm, čē perf. intr.} (lit. unhook oneself) **1** *sl-fea* become insane, become unhinged <Slav*1> **2** *sl* get rid of <Slav*1>

- **òtkači se** {V} (lit. unhook) *col* used to make somebody go away, get off my back

otkàntati {ām, ajū biasp.} **1** *sl-sex* ***Obs*** engage in sexual intercourse with (of a male) <Ita✣*1> **2** *sl* dump one's boyfriend or girlfriend

ótkid {a masc.} **1** *sl-fea* very sad event <Slav*1> **2** *sl-fea* very pleasant event: *Imali smo otkid preko vikenda. We had a very pleasant time over the weekend.* <Slav*1>

otkídati[1] {òtkīdām, otkídajū imperf.} *sl* call, shout <Slav*1>

otkídati[2] {òtkīdām, otkídajū imperf. intr.} *sl-fea* become insane, freak out <Slav*1>

òtkinuti {nēm, nū perf.} **a.** *sl-fea* go insane, freak out <Slav*1> **b.** *sl-fea* fall in love <Slav*2> **c.** *sl* be excited <Slav*3> **d.** *sl* laugh <Slav*4>

- **òtkinuti flȅku** {Vp} (lit. take off a stain) *sl* run away, flee

òtkinuti se {nēm, nū perf. intr.} **1** *sl-fea* become insane, freak out <Slav*1> **2** *sl* get rid of <Slav*1>

òtkljinčiti {čīm, čē perf.} *sl* leave, depart, walk <Eng✣*1>

otknjávati {òtknjāvām, otknjávajū perf.} *sl* sleep, nap <Slav✣>

òtkriti *See the following*

- **òtkriti Amèriku** {VP} (lit. discover America) *col* ***Iro*** used to indicate that what was said is nothing new, reinvent the wheel
- **òtkriti tòplu vȍdu** {VP} (lit. discover hot water) *col* ***Iro*** used to refer to that what was said is nothing new, reinvent the wheel

otkùčāč {kucáča (acc. = gen.) masc.} *sl-crime* ***Der*** informer, stoolie, snitch <Slav✣*1>

otkùcalo {a neut.} *sl-crime* ***Der*** informer, stoolie, snitch <Slav✣*1>

otkùčār {otkucāra (acc. = gen.) masc.} *sl-crime* ***Der*** informer, stoolie, snitch <Slav✣*1>

òtkucati {ām, ajū perf.} 1 *sl-crime* inform the police or other authorities, snitch, squeal <Slav❖*1> 2 *sl* die, kick the bucket <Slav❖*1>

otkucávati {kùcāvām, kucávajū imperf.} *sl-crime* inform the police or other authorities, snitch, squeal <Slav❖*1>

otkùlučiti {čīm, čē perf.} (lit. finish one's hard labor) *sl-crime* serve one's time in prison <NE❖*1>

ȍtolē {adv.} [std. = odatle] *dia-col* from there <Slav☞>

ȍtomān {a masc.} *col* couch <NE>

otórbiti {bīm, bē perf.} *sl* give birth, have a baby <Slav❖*1>

òtova {ē fem.} *dia* second grass (on a pasture, etc.) <Slav>

ȍtovac {ȍtōvca (acc. = gen.) masc.} *sl-sstu* technology teacher (male) <Abb❖>

ȍtōvka {ē fem.} *sl-sstu* technology teacher (female) <Abb❖>

otperjášiti {pèrjāšīm, šē perf.} **a.** *col* disappear, evaporate, vanish: *otperjašiti poslije tuluma disappear after the party* <Slav*1> **b.** *col* get lost <Slav*2> **c.** *col* run away, flee <Slav*3>

otpèrjati {ām, ajū perf.} **a.** *col* disappear, evaporate, vanish: *otperjati sa sastanka get lost from a meeting* <Slav*1> **b.** *col* get lost <Slav*2> **c.** *col* run away, flee <Slav*3>

òtpevati {ām, ajū perf.} (lit. sing out) 1 **SerE** *sl-fea* be worse off: *otpevati na razmjeni be worse off in an exchange* <Slav*1> 2 SerE *sl-crime* inform the police or other authorities, snitch, squeal <Slav*1>

• **òtpevati balādu** {VP} (lit. sing a ballad) **a.** **SerE** *sl-crime* inform the police or other authorities, snitch, squeal **b.** SerE *sl* end up in a very difficult situation

otpíjati {òtpījām, ajū imperf.} *sl-drink* drink a little (alcohol) <Slav*1>

òtpisān {a, o adj.} (lit. written off) *sl-fea* retired <Slav*1>

òtpīsānī {ōg (acc. = gen.) masc.} *sl-fea* retiree <Slav*1>

otpísati {òtpīšēm, išū perf.} *sl* cease counting on <Slav*1>

òtpiti {òtpijēm, ijū perf.} *sl-drink* drink a little (alcohol) <Slav*1>

otpízditi {òtpīzdīm, dē perf.} *sl-fea* brutally send away <Slav❖*1>

òtpjevati {ām, ajū perf.} (lit. sing out) *sl-crime* inform the police or other authorities, snitch, squeal <Slav*1>

òtplaziti {zīm, zē perf.} (lit. creep away) *sl* leave, slink away <Slav*1>

òtplaziti {zīm, zē perf.} (lit. crawl away) *sl* leave, slink away <Slav*1>

Òtplivāj! {excl.} (lit. Swim away!) *sl* used to make somebody go away, Beat it! <Slav*1>

òtplivati {ām, ajū perf.} (lit. swim away) **a.** *sl* disappear, evaporate, vanish <Slav*1> **b.** *sl* go away, leave <Slav*1>

otplòviti {òtplovīm, vē perf.} (lit. sail or float away) *sl* leave, depart, walk <Slav*1>

otporâtor {a (acc. = gen.) masc.} *sl-crime* burglar <Slav☞*1>

ȍtpozadnīk {a (acc. = gen.) masc.} (lit. the behind one) *sl-sex* ***Obs*** male homosexual, gay <Slav*1>

otpŕhnuti {òtpr̄hnēm, nū perf. intr.} (lit. fly away) **a.** *sl* disappear, evaporate, vanish <Slav*1> **b.** *sl* go away, leave <Slav*1>

otpúhniti {òtpūhnēm, nū perf.} *sl* leave, depart, walk <Slav*1>

otpúši {excl.} *sl* used to make somebody go away <Slav*1>

òtrcān {a, o adj.} *col* used up <Slav*1>

ȍtrēmčiti {čīm, čē perf.} SerE *sl* get married, get hitched <Slav❖*1>

ȍtrēmčiti se {čīm, čē perf. intr.} SerE *sl* get married, get hitched <Slav❖*1>

ȍtrēsti {trésēm, trésū perf. irreg.} (lit. shake off) *sl-sex* ***Obs*** ejaculate, cum <Slav*1>

otròmbōljen {a, o adj.} *sl-fea* soft <Slav*1>

otrombóljiti {tròmbōljīm, ljē perf.} *sl-fea* become sluggish <Slav*1>

òtrov {a (acc. = gen.) masc.} (lit. poison) 1 *sl-fea* ***App*** skillful person <Slav*1> 2 *sl-sex* seducer <Slav*1>

ȍtrōvan {vna, vno adj.} (lit. poisonous) *sl-fea* malicious <Slav*1>

otròvati {òrujēm, òtrujū perf.} (lit. poison) *sl* excite, arouse <Slav*1>

• **otròvati kònja** {VP} (lit. poison a horse) *sl* sleep, nap

• **otròvati sòvān** {VP} (lit. poison a sleep) *sl* sleep, nap

• **otròvati sòvāž** {VP} (lit. poison a sleep) *sl* sleep, nap

• **otròvati sovijáner** {VP} (lit. poison a sleep) *sl* sleep, nap

• **otròvati sôvku** {VP} (lit. poison a sleep) *sl* sleep, nap

• **otròvati sóvu** {VP} (lit. poison an owl) **a.** *sl* sleep, nap **b.** be completely rested

otróvnjača {ē fem.} (lit. the poisonous one) *sl-sex* ***Fac-App*** attractive female <Slav❖[*1]>

otúciti {cīm, cē perf.} *sl-crime* steal, swipe

otúđiti {đīm, đē perf.} (lit. alienate) *col* steal, swipe <Slav[*1]>

òtur {excl.} *sl* sit down <Slav>

otvòriti {òtvorīm, rē perf.} (lit. open) **a.** *sl-sex* ***Obs*** engage in sexual intercourse with (of a male) <Slav[*1]> **b.** *sl-sex* ***Obs*** deflower <Slav[*1]>

out [ȁut][1] {adj.} *sl* out, eliminated <Eng>

out [ȁut][2] {adv.} *sl* out, eliminated <Eng>

òvāj {excl.} **1** *col* used to express hesitation or uncertainty, uh <Slav> **2** *col* operator used to mark a point the speaker wishes to clarify, well, now, let's see, look <Slav>

òvāj râd {NP} (lit. this work) *sl* used to support gestures (usu. hand movements), like this ☞ **rad**

òvajditi se {dīm, dē perf. intr.} *col* make a profit <NE❖>

ovàko {excl.} *col* used to mark the beginning of the point or purpose of conversation, listen up, here is the deal <Slav[*1]>

ovàkva je stvâr {S} *col* used to introduce a point, Listen up, here's the deal ☞ **stvar**

òvan {óvna (acc. = gen.) masc.} /óvan /vna (acc. = gen.) masc./ (lit. ram) **1** *sl* male sexual partner (of a female) <Slav[*1]> **2** *sl-fea* stubborn male, pigheaded guy <Slav[*1]> **3** *sl-fea* naive male <Slav[*1]>

• **dȍbrovōljnī óvan** {NP} (lit. voluntary ram) *sl-fea* ***Fac*** person susceptible to deception, easy mark

ovàrisati {išēm, išū imperf.} **a.** *col* guess <NE[*1]> **b.** *col* learn <NE[*2]>

óvca {ē fem.} (lit. sheep) **1a.** *sl-fea* stupid or mentally deficient person <Slav[*1]> **b.** *sl-fea* naive person <Slav[*2]> **c.** *sl-fea* victim <Slav[*3]> **2** *sl* female <Slav[*1]> **3** *sl-fea* person with curly hair <Slav[*1]>

• **ôvcu na rážanj** {NP} (lit. sheep to roasting spit) *sl-sex* ***Obs*** sexual intercourse

òvčār {ovčára (acc. = gen.) masc.} (lit. shepherd) **a.** *sl-fea* inhabitant of the countryside, hick, bumpkin <Slav[*1]> **b.i.** *sl-fea* stupid or mentally deficient person <Slav[*2]> **ii.** *sl-fea* unattractive male <Slav[*2]>

óvdek {adv.} [std. = ovd(j)e] *dia* here <Slav✍>

óvdi {adv.} [std. = ovd(j)e] *dia* here <Slav✍>

óvdinā {adv.} [std. = ovd(j)e] *dia* here <Slav✍>

óvđe {adv.} [std. = ovd(j)e] *dia* here <Slav✍>

óvđen {adv.} [std. = ovd(j)e] *dia* here <Slav✍>

ȍvećī {ā, ē adj.} *col* rather big <Slav>

òveriti *See the following*

• **òveriti sèmestar** {VP} (lit. have a semester approved) SerE *sl* have a girlfriend

• **òveriti šȉšārku** {VP} (lit. certify a fir cone) SerE *sl* engage in sexual intercourse with

òveriti se {rīm, rē perf. intr.} (lit. certify oneself) SerE *sl-drugs* take a shot of narcotic drugs, shoot up <Slav[*1]>

òvō {pron.} (lit. this) *col* used to refer to the current social and political situation (particularly to the events in the 1990s in the former Yugoslavia) <Slav[*1]>

• **òvō nêmā nȉgde** {S} (lit. this does not exist anywhere) SerE *col* used to express astonishment, this is unbelievable

• **òvō nêmā nȉgdje** {S} (lit. this does not exist anywhere) *col* used to express astonishment, this is unbelievable

òvō-ònō {excl.} *col* used to express hesitation, things like that <Slav>

òvod {adv.} /ovôd adv./ [std. = ovd(j)e] *dia* here <Slav✍>

ovóđen {adv.} [std. = ovd(j)e] *dia* here <Slav✍>

ovolìčkī {adj.} *col* that small <Slav❖>

ovolìpackī {ā, ō adj.} *col* that small <Slav❖>

ovòlkačkī {ā, ō adj.} *col* that big <Slav❖>

ovòlkī {ā, ō adj.} [std. = ovoliki] *col* that big <Slav✍>

òvsen {a, o adj.} *sl-arch* rare, uncommon <Slav[*1]>

ovúdekā {adv.} [std. = ovuda] *dia* this way <Slav✍>

òzdō {adv.} [std. = odozdo] *col-dia* from below <Slav✍>

òzgō {adv.} [std. = odozgo] *col-dia* from above <Slav✍>

ȍznojān {a, o adj.} [std. = oznojen] *col* sweating <Slav✍>

oznòjiti *See the following*

• **oznòjiti plúća** {VP} (lit. sweat one's lungs) *sl-drugs* smoke strong drugs

oznòjiti se *See the following*

• **Oznòjilo mi se góvno u dȕpetu.** {S} (lit. The shit in my ass was sweating.) *sl* ***Fac-Obs*** used to refer to very high air temperature, It's hot as shit.

oždrljékati se {òždrijēkām, oždrijékajū perf. intr.} *sl-drink* get drunk <Slav>

ȍžeći {ežēm, egū, eg, eg perf. irreg.} (lit. burn) **1** *sl-sports* play aggressively <Slav[*1]> **2** *sl-sex* engage in sexual intercourse with (of a male) <Slav[*1]>

ožèniti se {nīm, nē perf. intr.} (lit. get married) *sl-gamble* win money <Slav*1>

ožèžen {a, o adj.} *col* burned <Slav>

ožèži {excl.} (lit. burn) **1** *col* used to ask musicians to play a song <Slav*1> **2** *sl-mil* fire <Slav*1>

ȍžno {ȍžano masc.; perm} [std. = nož] *sl* knife <Slav✍>

ožúčiti {ȍžūčīm, čē perf.} *sl* make sad, sadden <Slav❖*1>

ȍžujak {jka masc.} (lit. March) Cro *sl-drink* beer <Slav*1>

ožujáner {a masc.} Cro *sl-drink* beer <Slav❖*1>

Pp

p.p.p. [pê-pê-pê] {excl.} (lit. *p*rimi p(uno) p(ozdrava) - receive many regards) *sl* best regards <Abb>

pȁ [1] {part.} **1** *col* particle used to express hesitation, well <Slav> **2** *col* particle used at beginning of the sentence that moves the conversation along, so, well, and <Slav>

pâ [2] {excl.} **1** *col* the sound made by a gun, bang <Slav> **2** *col* ***Fam*** used as informal farewell, bye <Slav>

Pa da ga jèbēm mȁlo! {S} (lit. So that I fuck it a little!) *col* ***Obs*** used as a moderate curse, Fuck him! ☞ **jebati**

pa džȁ ili bȕ {ExcP} (lit. either dža or bu) *col* used to indicate willingness to act notwithstanding the consequences ☞ **dža**

pȁ-pâ {excl.} *col* ***Fam*** used to take leave of somebody informally, bye-bye <Slav>

pa-pȁk {excl.} *col* the sound made by a gun, bang <Slav>

pȁc {a +ev (ext. pl) masc.; Nom Pl pȁčevi} *sl* bath <Ger*1>

pȁcānje {a neut.} *sl* cooking <Ger*1>

pàcati se {ām, ajū imperf. intr.} *sl* take a bath <Ger*1>

pȁcer {a (acc. = gen.) masc.} /pàcer/ **a.** *col* clumsy male, klutz <Ger> **b.** *sl-sports* incompetent player (soccer, etc.) <Ger*1>

pacijȅnt {a (acc. = gen.) masc.} (lit. patient) **1** *sl-fea* ***Der*** unimportant person, nobody, nothing <Lat*1> **2** *sl-fea* ***Der*** unattractive male <Lat*1> **3** *sl* ***Der*** victim <Lat*1> **4** *sl-fea* ***Der*** stupid or mentally deficient person <Lat*1>

pȁciti {cīm, cē perf.} **1** *sl* walk **2** *sl-crime* steal, swipe

pácov {a (acc. = gen.) masc.} (lit. rat) **1** *sl-fea* muscle <Slav*1> **2** *sl-sex* tampon <Slav*1> **3** *sl-fea* unattractive person <Slav*1>

• **čȅtnī pácov** {NP} (lit. company rat) *sl-mil* worker in military storehouse

pȁčeška {ē fem.; Dat pȁčeški} *sl-arch* beard

pȁčiti {čīm, čē imperf.} *sl* lie <Ita*1>

pȁdati *See the following*

• **pȁdati na fólove** {VP} (lit. fall on tricks) *sl-fea* be susceptible to deception

pȁdavica {ē fem.} (lit. epilepsy) *sl-fea* nervousness <Slav*1>

pȁdavičār {a (acc. = gen.) masc.} (lit. epileptic) *sl-fea* male who wears old jeans <Slav*1>

pȁdavičārka {ē fem.; Dat pȁdavičārki} (lit. epileptic) **1** *sl-fea* female who wears old jeans <Slav*1> **2** *sl-sex* sexually aroused female, hot chick <Slav*1>

pȁdavine {vīnā fem. pl.} (lit. precipitations) *sl-sex* ***Fac*** excrement <Slav*1>

pádež {a masc.} (lit. grammatical case) **a.** *sl* ***Fac*** fall (physical) <Slav*1> **b.** *sl* ***Fac*** failure <Slav*2>

• **drȕgi pádež** {NP} (lit. the second case) *col* another issue, separate matter

pȁdī {īja masc.} *sl-drugs* Caucasian hashish

Pàdinburg {a masc.} **a.** Ser *sl-crime* ***Fac*** name for Padinska Skela (a town near Belgrade, Serbia) <Slav✍> **b.** *sl-crime* ***Fac*** the name of a prison in Padinska Skela <Slav✍*1>

Padìnjāk {dinjáka masc.} **a.** Ser *sl-crime* name for Padinska Skela (a town near Belgrade, Serbia) <Slav✍> **b.** Ser *sl-crime* name of a prison in Padinska Skela <Slav✍*1>

padobránac {nca (acc. = gen.) masc.} (lit. parachuter) **1** *col* ***Fac*** person who breaks into a line <Slav*1> **2** *col* ***Fac*** intruder <Slav*1>

Pâdova {ē fem.} (lit. Padua, a city in Italy) *sl-sstu* ***Fac*** failed exam <ItaO-Slav*1>

padovànskī {ā, ō adj.} (lit. McFalldown) *sl-sex* ***Fac*** impotent <Slav✍*1>

pȁdže {masc.; perm} /pàdže/ [std. = džep] *sl* pocket (on a coat, trousers, etc.) <NE✍>

pȁf {excl.} *col* the sound made by an explosion, bang <Slav>

pahȕljača {ē fem.} (lit. the snow-flaked one) *sl-sex* ***Obs*** vagina, cunt <Slav*1>

pahùljica {ē fem.} (lit. snow flake) *sl-sex* ***Fac*** male homosexual, gay <**Slav**[*1]>

pâj {excl.} [std. = pazi] *col* used to draw attention in direct informal communication, attention <**Slav**✍>

- **Pȁj ȍvō!** {S} (lit. watch this) *col-dia* used to attract attention, Listen up!
- **Pȁj sȁd!** {S} (lit. watch this) *col-dia* used to attract attention, Listen up!
- **Pȁj sȁd ȍvō!** {S} (lit. watch this now) *col-dia* used to attract attention, Listen up!

pája {ē masc.} (lit. Donald Duck) *sl-crime* policeman, cop <**NE**[*1]>

pàjac {pajàca (acc. = gen.) masc.} (lit. bozo) *sl-crime* policeman, cop <**Ita-NE**[*1]>

pàjdāš {pajdáša (acc. = gen.) masc.} **a.** *col* friend (male) <**Hun**> **b.** *sl-sstu* roommate (male) <**Hun**[*1]>

pájdo {a (acc. = gen.) masc.} **1** *sl* friend (male) <**Hun**✍> **2a.** *sl-drugs* narcotic drug, dope <**Hun**✍[*1]> **b.** *sl-drugs* heroin, horse, smack <**Hun**✍[*2]>

pàjkan {a (acc. = gen.) masc.} *sl-crime* policeman, cop <**NE**[*1]>

pajkanalizácija {ē fem.} (lit. copsewage, i.e. pajkan 'cop' X kanalizacija 'sewage') *sl-crime* ***Fac*** the police <**NE**✍>

pájkēnje {a neut.} *col* ***Fam*** sleeping <**Slav**>

pájkiti {kīm, kē imperf.} *col* ***Fam*** sleep, nap <**Slav**>

pȁjp {a +ov (ext. pl) masc.; Nom Pl pàjpovi} **a.** *sl-drugs* hashish pipe, hash pipe <**Eng**> **b.** *sl* pipe (smoking) <**Eng**>

pȁjs {excl.} *col* used to lure a pig <**Slav**>

pàjser {a masc.} **a.** *sl-crafts* iron lever <**Ger**[*1]> **b.** *sl-sex* penis

pajsèrisati se {išēm, išū imperf. intr.} *sl-fea* be conceited, be stuck-up <**Ger**⁘[*1]>

pȁjt {a (acc. = gen.) +ov (ext. pl) masc.; Nom Pl pàjtovi} **a.** *sl* friend (male) <**Hun**✍> **b.** *sl-sstu* roommate (male) <**Hun**✍[*1]>

pàjtāš {pajtáša (acc. = gen.) masc.} **a.** *col* friend (male) <**Hun**> **b.** *sl-sstu* roommate (male) <**Hun**[*1]>

pȁjtos {a (acc. = gen.) masc.} **a.** *sl* friend (male) <**Hun**✍> **b.** *sl-sstu* roommate (male) <**Hun**✍[*1]>

pȁk {a +ov (ext. pl) masc.; Nom Pl pàkovi} (lit. pack) *sl-gamble* deck of cards <**Eng**>

pȁker {a (acc. = gen.) masc.} /pàker/ (lit. packer) **1a.** *sl-fea* cheater, swindler <**Ger**[*1]> **b.** *sl-gamble* professional gambler, pro gambler <**Ger**[*2]> **2** *sl-sports* midfielder (soccer) <**Ger**[*1]>

pàkēt {éta masc.} (lit. packet) *sl-gamble* deck of cards <**Fre**[*1]>

pȁkī {īja (acc. = gen.) masc.} /pàki/ *sl-crime* policeman, cop <**NE**✍>

pakírati {pàkīrām, ajū biasp.} (lit. pack) **a.** *sl-fea* falsely incriminate, frame: *pakirati susjeda frame one's neighbor* <**Ger**[*1]> **b.** *sl-fea* cheat, swindle: *pakirati na ispitu cheat on an exam* <**Ger**[*2]> **c.** *sl-fea* gossip, wag the tongue <**Ger**[*3]>

pakistánac {nca masc.} (lit. Pakistani) *sl-drugs* hashish, hash <**SlavO**[*1]>

pȁklen {a, o adj.} (lit. hellish) *sl-fea* excellent, superb, awesome: *Maja je paklena riba. Maja is an awesome chick.* <**Slav**[*1]>

páкljo {ē masc.} *sl-fea* one-armed man

pàkn {a +ov (ext. pl) masc.; Nom Pl pàknovi} *sl-auto* brake pad <**Ger**>

pàkna {ē fem.} *sl-auto* brake pad <**Ger**>

pȁkosan {sna, sno adj.} [std. = pakostan] *sl-fea* malicious <**Slav**✍>

pȁkovānje {a neut.} (lit. packing) *sl-gamble* deceiving in cards <**Ger**[*1]>

pȁkovati {kujēm, kujū imperf.} (lit. pack) **a.** *sl-fea* falsely incriminate, frame <**Ger**[*1]> **b.** *sl-fea* cheat, swindle <**Ger**[*2]>

paksìjān {paksijána (acc. = gen.) masc.} **a.** *sl-fea* malicious person **b.** *sl-fea* enemy **c.** *sl-fea* aggressor

pȁkšu {pàkašu masc.; perm} /pàkšu/ *sl-sex* ***Obs*** anus, asshole <**Slav**✍> ☞ **šupak**

Pȁla [PRON:DAT] sjèkira ȕ mēd. {LSF} (lit. [PPRON] axe has fallen into honey.) *col-dia* used to refer to a favorable situation of the third party: *Pala joj je sjekira u med. She is favored by luck.* ☞ **pasti**

pȁlac {pâlca masc.} (lit. thumb, the phrase "sisati palac", literally 'to suck a thumb' means 'to be naive') **a.** *sl-fea* naive male <**Slav**[*1]> **b.** *sl-fea* coward, chicken <**Slav**[*2]>

pàlača {ē fem.} (lit. palace) *sl-crime* prison where one sleeps on planks <**Ita**[*1]>

palačínka [1] {ē fem.} (lit. pancake) **1** *sl* bowtie <**Hun**[*1]> **2** *sl-drugs* intake of narcotic drugs, doing drugs <**Hun**[*1]> **3** *sl-sex* flat female breast, pancake <**Hun**[*1]>

palačínka [2] {adj.} (lit. pancake) *sl-fea* bald <**Hun**[*1]>

palačínke {ī fem. pl.} /palačínke /naka masc. pl./ (lit. pancakes) *sl-sex* ***Fac*** group sex <Hun*1>

palàmār {lamára masc.} (lit. rope) *sl-sex* ***Obs*** penis, dick, prick <NE*1>

palamùdija {ē fem. & masc.} *sl-fea* boring person, bore <Slav❖*1>

palamúditi {làmūdīm, dē imperf.} (lit. drop one's balls) **1** *sl-sex* ***Obs*** engage in sexual intercourse with (of a male) <Slav*1> **2a.** *sl-fea* ***Der-Obs*** talk persistently and meaninglessly, blabber, chatter <Slav*1> **b.** *sl-fea* ***Der-Obs*** lie <Slav*2> **c.** *sl-fea* ***Der-Obs*** annoy, bother, pester <Slav*3> **d.** *sl-fea* ***Der-Obs*** annoy, bother, pester <Slav*4>

• **Ne palamúdi!** {S} (lit. Don't drop your balls!) **1** *col* ***Obs*** used as a weak curse, Screw you! **2a.** *col* used to silence one's interlocutor, Shut up! **b.** *col* used to express disbelief, Don't give me that shit!

palamùdžija {ē masc.} (lit. mister Drop-the-balls) **a.** *sl-fea* ***Der*** worthless or despicable male, scum <Slav❖*1> **b.** *sl-fea* ***Der*** boring male, bore <Slav❖*2>

palàmūr {lamúra masc.} (lit. rope) *sl-sex* ***Obs*** penis, dick, prick <NE✍*1>

pàlāndra {ē fem.} *sl-sex* prostitute, hooker <FreO*1>

pâle {eta masc.} **a.** *sl* friend (male) <Hun✍> **b.** *sl-sstu* roommate (male) <Hun✍*1>

Pàle su mi rolète! {S} (lit. My blinds have fallen!) *sl-fea* used to refer to loss of consciousness in the past, I blacked out! ☞ **pasti**

pálenje {a neut.} *sl-auto* ignition <Slav✍>

pâlī {excl.} *sl* ***App*** excellent, awesome <Slav*1>

páli {excl.} (lit. fire) **1** *sl* used to make somebody go away, beat it <Slav> **2** *sl* used to command to run away, run <Slav*1>

pàlida {ē fem.} (lit. burner) **a.** *sl-sex* sexually aroused person, hot person <Slav✍> **b.** *sl-sex* seductive female, hot babe <Slav✍*1>

pàlija {ē fem.} *dia-col* bat, stick, rod

Palìlulos {a (acc. = gen.) masc.} [std. = Palilulac] **Ser** *sl* inhabitant of Palilula (a neighborhood in Belgrade, Serbia) <SlavO✍>

palȉndati {ām, ajū biasp.} *sl-crime* steal, swipe

pàlīnka {ē fem.} (lit. burner) *sl-drink* brandy <Hun>

páliti {pâlīm, lē imperf.} (lit. burn) **1** *sl* function, work well: *plan pali the plan works well* <Slav*1> **2** *sl* be valid: *karta pali the ticket is valid* <Slav*2> **3** *sl* make noise <Slav*1> **4a.** persuade, convince <Slav*1> **b.aa.** steal, swipe <Slav*2> **bb.** pick pockets <Slav*3> **c.aa.** cheat, swindle <Slav*2> **bb.** lie <Slav*3>

• **nè pāli** {V} (lit. it doesn't fire) **a.** *col* used as a strong negative response, no way, never

• **páliti gȓlo** {VP} (lit. burn one's throat) *sl-drink* drink too much

• **páliti kȁsno** {VP} (lit. start the engine late) *sl-fea* be slow to understand

• **páliti muštèriju** {VP} (lit. burn one's customer) *sl-crime* pick pockets

páliti se {pâlīm, lē imperf. intr.} (lit. burn oneself) **1a.** *sl-fea* get upset <Slav*1> **b.** *sl-sex* get sexually aroused, get hot <Slav*2> **2** *sl-fea* be excited <Slav*1> **3** *sl-fea* be easily cheated <Slav*1>

Pàlma *See the following*

• **na Pâlmu de Majôrku** {PP} (lit. to Palma de Mallorca) Cro *sl* to Čateške toplice (a spa in Croatia)

pȁlo s kȉšōm {VP} (lit. fallen with rain) *sl* something new ☞ **pasti**

palùrān {palurána masc.} *sl-arch* cabbage

pàljār {paljára masc.} *sl* groschen (the coin)

pȁlje {a neut.} *sl-arch* bread

páljēnje {a neut.} (lit. burning) *sl* making interested <Slav*1>

• **kâsnō páljēnje** {NP} (lit. slow ignition) *sl-fea* ***Fac*** slow understanding

pàljevina {excl.} *sl* run <Slav*1>

pàljevina {ē fem.} (lit. burning) **1** *sl-sex* sexually aroused person, hot person <Slav*1> **2a.** *sl* theft, swiping <Slav*1> **b.** *sl* lying <Slav*2> **c.** *sl* lie <Slav*3> **3** *sl-fea* easily cheated person, easy mark <Slav*1>

pàljīnka {ē fem.} (lit. burner) *sl-drink* brandy <Hun>

pàljkara {ē fem.} *sl* leg (human)

pàljkuš {a masc.} *sl-arch* beans <Lat✍*1>

pàljōr {paljóra masc.} *sl-drink* brandy

pàljōrka {ē fem.} *sl-drink* brandy

pȁmēt *See the following*

• **dà ti pȁmēt stȁnē** {S} (lit. so that your mind stops working) *col* used to refer to the unusual feature of an object or event, that's mind boggling: *Kakva dobra kola, da ti pamet stane. What a car, that's unbelievable.*

• **pȁmēt ȕ glāvu** {NP} (lit. mind to the head) *col* be careful

• **zèčijā pȁmēt** {NP} (lit. hare's mind) *sl* escape, flee

pamètnica {ē fem. & masc.} *sl-fea* ***App*** smart person, brain <**Slav**❖>

pametnjáković {a (acc. = gen.) masc.} **a.** *sl-fea* smart male, brain <**Slav**[*1]> **b.** *sl-fea* person who bothers others with his comments <**Slav**[*2]>

pàmfla {ē fem.} *sl-sex* sexually aroused female, hot chick

pàmflek {a masc.} *sl-fea* stomach, belly, gut

pàmprčiti {čīm, čā imperf.} *sl-sex* ***Obs*** engage in sexual intercourse with (of a male) <**Slav**❖[*1]>

pàmpuk {a masc.} *sl* hit, punch <**Slav**[*1]>

pàmpur[1] {part.} *sl* negative particle, no <**Fre**[*1]>

pàmpur[2] {excl.} *sl* used to express disbelief, no way <**Fre**[*1]>

pàmūr {pamúra masc.} *sl* restaurant

panáija *See the following*

• **Panàiju ti svêtū pòjebēm!** {S} (lit. *I fuck* your holy boiled wheat!) *dia* ***Off*** used as a moderate curse, Fuck you!

panàjlija {ē fem.} *sl-crime* golden religious objects stolen from a church <**Gre**[*1]>

pȁnčosi {ōsā masc. pl.} /pânčosi/ *sl* trousers, pants <**Fre**✍>

pàndisanje {a neut.} *sl-fea* making a fool of oneself

pàndisati {išēm, išū imperf.} *sl* make a fool of oneself

pandȑknuti {pàndr̄knēm, nū perf.} *sl-fea* be ruined, be destroyed <**Slav**❖[*1]>

pàndūr {pandúra (acc. = gen.) masc.} **1** *sl-crime* policeman, cop <**Hun**[*1]> **2** *sl-stu* failing grade <**Hun**[*2]>

• **pàndūr fefèrōn** {NP} (lit. hot pepper cop) *sl-crime* dangerous policeman (i.e. one who is successful in catching criminals)

pandurácija {ē fem.} **a.** *sl-crime* the police <**Hun**✍[*1]> **b.** *sl-crime* police station <**Hun**✍[*2]>

pandùrčina {ē masc.} **a.** *sl-crime* policeman, cop <**Hun**❖[*1]> **b.** *sl-crime* good and highly professional policeman <**Hun**❖[*2]>

pandùrija {ē fem.} **a.** *sl-crime* the police <**Hun**✍[*1]> **b.** *sl-crime* police station <**Hun**✍[*2]>

pàndžija {ē fem.} *sl-arch* polenta <**NE**>

pȁnica *See the following*

• **Pànicu ti jèbēm!** {S} (lit. I fuck your little boiled wheat!) *dia* ***Off*** used as a moderate curse, Fuck you!

pàničār {a (acc. = gen.) masc.} *col* alarmist (male) <**Gre**❖[*1]>

paničara {ē fem.} (lit. panicker) *sl-fea* alarmist (male) <**Gre**[*1]>

pàničārka {ē fem.; Dat pàničārki} (lit. panicker) *sl-fea* alarmist (female) <**Gre**[*1]>

pànija {ē fem.} *sl* water <**Gyp**>

pȁnk {a +ov (ext. pl) masc.; Nom Pl pànkovi} (lit. punk) *sl-music* punk rock <**Eng**>

pȁnker {a (acc. = gen.) masc.} /pànker/ (lit. punker) *sl-music* punker (male) <**Eng**>

pȁnkērka {ē fem.; Dat pȁnkērki} /pànkērka/ (lit. punker) *sl-music* punker (female) <**Eng**>

panknȁ**rkomānka** {ē fem.} (lit. punk-junkie) *sl-drugs* drug addict, junkie <**Eng-Gre**[*1]>

pàntale {pȁntālā fem. pl.} *col* trousers, pants <**Fre**✍> ☞ **pantole**

pantalodȑžac {šca masc.} *sl* ***Fac*** waist, belt <**Slav**❖>

• **okolotȑbušnī pantalodȑžāc** {NP} (lit. round-belly trousers-holder) *sl* ***Fac*** waist, belt

pantalodȑžāč {držáča masc.} *sl* ***Fac*** waist, belt <**Slav**❖>

• **okolotȑbušnī pantalodȑžāč** {NP} (lit. round-belly trousers-holder) *sl* ***Fac*** waist, belt

pàntara {ē fem.} *sl-sstu* school

pànterōv znôj {NP} (lit. panther's sweat) *sl-drink* hard liquor ☞ **znoj**

pàntiške {i fem. pl.} *sl* trousers, pants <**Fre**✍>

pantljìčara {ē fem.} (lit. tapeworm) *col* ticket for multiple rides <**Ger**[*1]>

pàntljika {ē fem.} *col* band, waist <**Ger**>

pàntole {pȁntōlā fem. pl.} *col* trousers, pants <**Fre**✍> ☞ **pantole**

pȁntosi {osa masc. pl.} /pântosi/ *sl* trousers, pants <**Fre**✍>

pȁnuti {nēm, nū perf. intr.} [std. = pasti] *dia-col* fall (physically) <**Slav**✍>

pȃnj[1] {a (acc. = gen.) +ev (ext. pl) masc.; Nom Pl pánjevi} (lit. tree-stump) **a.** *sl-fea* stupid or mentally deficient person <**Slav**[*1]> **b.** *sl-fea* senior citizen <**Slav**[*2]>

pȃnj[2] {a +ev (ext. pl) masc.; Nom Pl pánjevi} (lit. tree-stump) **1** *sl-drugs* cigarette with hashish and tobacco mixed <**Slav**[*1]> **2** *sl* suitcase <**Slav**[*1]> **3** *sl-crime* safe <**Slav**[*1]> **4** *sl* package (in general) <**Slav**[*1]> **5** *sl* unshredded piece of tobacco found in cigarette <**Slav**[*1]>

• **u pánjevima** {PP} (lit. in tree-stumps) *col* never

pánja {ē fem.} **a.** *sl* bread <**Ita**> **b.** *sl* food <**Ita**[*1]>

pánja {adj.} (lit. bread) *sl-fea* ***App*** good, neat, cool <Ita*1>

pȁnjānje {a neut.} **a.** *sl-fea* anger <Ita✣*1> **b.** *sl-fea* nervousness <Ita✣*2>

pȁnjār {a (acc. = gen.) masc.} *sl-crime* thief who steals from suitcases <Slav✣*1>

pànjati {ām, ajū biasp.} *sl* eat, devour <Ita✣*1>

pȁnjega {ē fem.; Dat pȁnjegi} *dia* hole, opening

pànjislas {a masc.} *sl* bread <Ita✎>

panjóka {ē fem.; Dat panjóki} *sl* one kilogram of bread <Ita✎>

pànjota {ē fem.} *sl* bread <Ita✎>

Pȁō *See the following*

- **Pȉm Pȅk Pȁō** {NP} (lit. The-Cock-Has-Fallen) *sl-sex* impotent

Pȁō mi je rȍlo! {S} (lit. My blinds have fallen down!) *sl-fea* used to refer to loss of consciousness in the past, I blacked out! ☞ **pasti**

pȁō s katedrálē {AdjP} (lit. fallen from a cathedral) *sl-fea* insane, nuts ☞ **pasti**

papâ 1 {excl.} *col* ***Fam*** used to take leave of somebody informally, bye <Slav>

pápa 2 {ē fem.} **1** *col* ***Fam*** food <Slav> **2** *col* ***Fam*** slipper <Slav>

pâpa 3 *See the following*

- **pâpa pȉšu** {NP} *sl-sex* fellatio

papàgāj {pagája (acc. = gen.) masc.} (lit. parrot) **1** *sl-crime* pickpocket <Ger*1> **2** *sl-mil* liaison soldier <Ger*1> **3** *sl-crime* informer, stoolie, snitch <Ger*1> **4** *sl-fea* male in loud clothing <Ger*1>

papàgāj-cánge {ī fem. pl.} (lit. parrot tongs) *sl-crafts* tongs <Ger>

papàgāj-cángle {ī fem. pl.} (lit. parrot tongs) *sl-crafts* tongs <Ger✎>

papàgājke {ī fem. pl.} (lit. parrot tongs) *sl-crafts* tongs <Ger✣>

pápak 1 {pka (acc. = gen.) masc.} *sl-fea* inhabitant of the countryside, hick, bumpkin <Slav*1> *sl-fea* father, daddy <Slav*1>

pápak 2 {pka masc.} (lit. hoof) **a.** *sl* finger <Slav*1> **b.** *sl* foot <Slav*1> **c.i.** *sl* leg (human) <Slav*3> **ii.** *sl* shoe <Slav*3>

- **rȅstānī pápak** {NP} (lit. fried hoof) *sl-fea* old shoe

pàpan {a (acc. = gen.) masc.} **a.** *sl-fea* inhabitant of the countryside, hick, bumpkin <Slav✎*1> **b.** *sl-fea* stupid or mentally deficient person

pàpanka {ē fem.; Dat pàpanki} *sl-fea* inhabitant of the countryside, hick, bumpkin <Slav✎*1>

paparàco {a (acc. = gen.) masc.} *col* photographer of celebrities, paparazzo <Ita>

pȁpati {ām, ajū biasp.} **a.** *col* ***Fam*** eat, devour <Slav> **b.** *sl-sex* ***Obs*** engage in fellatio <Slav*1>

papazjànija {ē fem.} **1** *col* mess, disorder, disturbance <NE> **2** *sl* mother <NE*1>

pâpe {eta neut.} /pápe/ Med *dia-col* ***Fam*** father, papa <Ita>

pȁpī {īja (acc. = gen.) masc.} *sl-sex* ***Fac*** male homosexual, gay <Slav*1>

pȁpica {ē masc.} **1** *sl* ***Fam*** father, papa <Ita✣> **2a.** *col* ***Fam*** meal <Slav*1> **b.** *sl* food <Slav*2>

pàpika {ē masc.} *sl-crime* policeman, cop

pàpīr 1 {papíra (acc. = gen.) masc.} (lit. paper) *sl-fea* harmless person <Gre*1>

pàpīr 2 {papíra masc.} (lit. paper) **a.** *col* documents <Gre*1> **b.** *sl* money <Gre*2> **c.** *sl* law <Gre*3> **d.** *sl* newspaper <Gre*4>

papiȉška {ē fem.; Dat papiȉški} /papiȉška/ (lit. small paper) *sl* money <Gre✎*1>

pȁpiti {pīm, pē imperf.} **a.** *col* ***Fam*** eat, devour <Slav> **b.** *sl-sex* ***Obs*** engage in fellatio <Slav*1>

papkijóber {a masc.} (lit. over-the-hoof) *sl* ***Fac*** shoe <Slav-Ger✎*1>

pàplī {īja masc.} *sl* work, labor

pȁpliti {līm, lē imperf.} *sl* work, labor *sl*

pȁprica *See the following*

- **Pȁpricu ti jèbēm!** {S} (lit. I fuck your millstone lever!) *dia* ***Off*** used as a moderate curse, Fuck you!

pàprika {ē fem.} (lit. pepper) *sl-sex* ***Fac-Obs*** penis, dick, prick <Slav*1>

pȁprikāš {a masc.} /papȑkāš/ (lit. vegetable stew) *sl* suitcase <Slav*1>

pàpučār {a (acc. = gen.) masc.} *col* husband dominated by his wife, henpecked husband <NE*1>

pàpučica {ē fem.} (lit. small slipper) *sl-fea* husband dominated by his wife, henpecked husband <NE✣*1>

pâr *See the following*

- **brâčni pâr** {NP} (lit. spouses) *sl-sex* ***Fac*** testicles

pàra [1] {ē fem.} **a.** *col* twenty-five-para coin <**NE***1> **b.** *col* money <**NE***2>

pȁra [2] *See the following*

• **pod pȁrōm** {PP} (lit. under steam) *sl-drink* slightly drunk, tipsy

paráda {ē fem.} **1** *sl-crime* court session <**Fre***1> **2** *sl-sports* effective action by a soccer goalie <**Fre***1>

paradȁjz {a masc.} (lit. tomato) **1** *sl-fea* foreign tourist without any money <**Ger***1> **2** *sl* nose <**Ger***2>

paradȁjzović {a (acc. = gen.) masc.} (lit. McTomato) *sl-fea* shy male <**Ger**⁘*1>

parafȁmfula {ē fem.} *sl* female <**Fre**⁘*1>

paràgraf {a (acc. = gen.) masc.} /pàragraf/ (lit. paragraph) *sl-fea* conceited person <**Gre***1>

• **ko paràgraf** {PP} (lit. like a section mark) *sl-fea* ***Fac*** conceited, stuck-up

paràjlija {ē masc.} *sl-fea* affluent person, moneybags <**Slav-NE**>

paraláža {ē fem.} *col* big lie <**Gre-Slav**>

parampàrčād {i fem.} *col* shards (usu. of broken glass), smithereens <**NE**>

pȁrano {a masc.} [std. = paranoja] *sl-drugs* fear of being followed <**Gre**☞>

paranòičār {a (acc. = gen.) masc.} *col* alarmist (male) <**Gre**⁘*1>

paranòisati {išēm, išū imperf.} **a.** *sl-fea* panic, freak out <**Gre***1> **b.** *sl-fea* get scared, get frightened <**Gre***2>

paranȍja {ē fem.} /paranòja/ **a.** *sl* fear <**Gre***1> **b.** *sl-drugs* strong fear <**Gre***2>

paràstos {a masc.} *col* requiem (in Orthodox church) <**Gre**>

pàrati {rīm, rē imperf.} *col-dia* look like, seem <**Ita**>

parazȉt {a (acc. = gen.) masc.} /paràzit/ (lit. parasite) *col* person who abuses others (usu. financially), parasite, leech <**Gre***1>

parcȅla {ē fem.} (lit. lot) *sl* grave <**Fre***1>

pàrcov {parcòva (acc. = gen.) masc.} *col-dia* rat (the animal) <**Slav***1>

párče {eta neut.} **a.** *col* piece, chunk <**NE**> **b.** *sl* female <**NE***1>

• **dòbro párče** {NP} (lit. good piece) *sl-sex* ***App*** attractive, good-looking person

pàrdovina {ē fem.} *sl* dress

pàrdovine {vīnā fem. pl.} *sl* clothing

pàre *See the following*

• **mâsnē pàre** {NP} (lit. fat money) *col* sizable amount of money, big bucks

pàriti [1] {rīm, rē imperf. intr.} Med *col-dia* look like, seem: *Pari mi da će kiša. It looks like we'll get some rain.* <**Ita**>

pȁriti [2] *See the following*

• **pȁriti ȍči** {VP} (lit. steam one's eyes) **1** *sl-fea* observe a female for a long time **1** *sl-fea* watch sexually explicit material

parízer {a masc.} *col* bologna <**Ger***1>

parkírati se {pàrkīrām, parkírajū biasp. intr.} (lit. park) **1a.** *sl* stop by <**Fre***1> **b.** *sl-drink* drink a little (alcohol) <**Fre***2> **2** *sl* lie <**Fre***1>

• **parkírati se u kòfer** {VP} (lit. park in a suitcase) *sl* ***Iro*** die, kick the bucket

• **parkírati se u sànduk** {VP} (lit. park in a coffin) *sl* ***Iro*** die, kick the bucket

pàrlati {ām, ajū imperf.} *sl* talk, have a conversation <**Ita**>

pȁrljāk {a masc.} (lit. tree-stump) *sl-sex* ***Obs*** penis, dick, prick <**Slav**☞*1>

pàrmak {a (acc. = gen.) masc.} (lit. finger) *sl-sstu* failing grade <**NE***1>

partája {ē fem.} *sl-gamble* a game of cards <**Ger***1>

pàrtēr {adj.} (lit. ground floor) *sl-fea* depressed <**Fre***1>

pártī {īja masc.} *col* party (social gathering) <**Eng**>

partizánovac {nōvca (acc. = gen.) masc.} *sl-sports* fan of Partizan (soccer team in Belgrade, Serbia) <**Fre***1>

pȁrtoš {a (acc. = gen.) masc.} *sl-polit* Communist, red, commie <**Fre**☞*1>

pȁru {pěru masc.; perm} /pàru/ (lit. hole) [std. = rupa] **a.** *sl-sex* ***Obs*** vagina, cunt <**Slav**☞*1> **b.** *sl* ***Obs*** female, cunt <**Slav**☞*2>

pȁs {psa (acc. = gen.) masc.} (lit. dog) *sl-fea* unattractive person <**Slav***1>

pâs {a +ov (ext. pl) masc.; Nom Pl pásovi} *sl-sports* pass (in soccer) <**Eng**>

pȁsati [1] {ām, ajū biasp. intr.} *col* be suitable, be fitting: *Pasa mi taj hotel tačno je u centru. That hotel is right downtown, very convenient.* <**Ita**>

pàsati [2] {ām, adū perf.} Med *dia-col* pass (of time) <**Ita**>

pasírati {pàsīrām, pasírajū imperf.} **1** *sl-sports* pass the ball <**Fre**> **2** *sl-gamble* pass (in gambling) <**Fre**> **3** *sl-fea* annoy, bother, pester <**Fre**> **4** *sl-fea* happen, occur <**Fre**>

pasírati se {pàsīrām, pasírajū perf. intr.} *sl* happen, occur <Fre>

pasívac {vca (acc. = gen.) masc.} (lit. the passive one) *sl-sex* ***Fac*** male homosexual who takes the passive role, femme <Lat❖*1>

pàsjakovača {ē fem.} *sl-drink* low-quality brandy <Slav❖>

pâsoš *See the following*

• **pâsoš za pàkaō** {NP} (lit. passport to hell) *sl-sstu* school record book

pȁsovati {sujēm, sujū biasp.} **1a.** *sl* pass by <Ger> **b.** *sl-sports* pass the ball <Ger*1> 2 *col* be adequate, be ok <Ger*1>

pàstēr {a (acc. = gen.) masc.} *sl-crime* ***Der*** informer, stoolie, snitch <FreO*1>

pȁsti [1] {adnēm, adnū perf. irreg.} (lit. fall down) **1** *sl* pay (bills, etc.) <Slav*1> **2a.** *sl-crime* get arrested, get busted <Slav*1> **b.** *sl-crime* get arrested for dealing drugs, get busted for dealing <Slav*2>

• **da pȁdnēš na dȕpe** {S} (lit. you can fall on your ass) *col* ***Obs*** excellent, awesome

• **da pȁdnēš na ȍko** {S} (lit. you can fall on your eye) *col* excellent, awesome

• **da pȁdnēš na trȅpavice** {S} (lit. you can fall on your eyelashes) *sl* ***Fac*** excellent, awesome

• **da pȁdnēš na trèpiš** {S} (lit. you can fall onto your eyelashes) *sl* ***Fac*** excellent, awesome

• **Pȁla[PRON:DAT] sjèkira ȕ mēd.** {LSF} (lit. [PPRON] axe has fallen into honey.) *col-dia* used to refer to a favorable situation of the third party: *Pala joj je sjekira u med. She is favored by luck.*

• **Pȁle su mi rolète!** {S} (lit. My blinds have fallen!) *sl-fea* used to refer to a loss of consciousness in the past, I blacked out!

• **pȁlo s kȉšōm** {VP} (lit. fallen with rain) *sl* something new

• **Pȁō mi je rȍlo!** {S} (lit. My blinds have fallen down!) *sl-fea* used to refer to a loss of consciousness in the past, I blacked out!

• **pȁō s katedrálē** {AdjP} (lit. fallen from a cathedral) *sl-fea* insane, nuts

• **pȁsti mȑtav** {VP} (lit. drop dead) *sl* die, kick the bucket

• **pȁsti na dȕpe** {VP} (lit. fall on one's ass) *sl* be surprised, be knocked on one's ass

• **pȁsti na grȉf** {VP} (lit. fall on a trick) *sl* be cheated, be swindled

• **pȁsti na ljépak** {VP} (lit. fall on glue) *sl* be cheated, be swindled

• **pȁsti nȁ oko** {VP} *col* be very surprised

• **pȁsti na štôs** {VP} (lit. fall on trick) **a.** *sl* believe, trust **b.** *sl* be persuaded **c.** *sl* be cheated, be swindled

• **pȁsti na trȅpavice** {VP} (lit. fall on one's eyelashes) *sl-fea* be very excited, freak out

• **pȁsti na trèpiš** {VP} (lit. fall on one's eyelashes) *sl-fea* be very excited, freak out

• **pȁsti na ȕho** {S} (lit. fall on one's ear) *sl* be shocked

• **pȁsti s bȉka** {VP} (lit. fall from a bull) *sl-fea* be dumped by one's girlfriend

• **pȁsti s Mȁrsa** {VP} (lit. fall from Mars) *sl-fea* be uninformed

• **pȁsti u dúbak** {VP} (lit. fall into a cradle) *sl-gamble* lose money

• **pȁsti u frâs** {VP} *col* get frightened, get scared

• **pȁsti za màrdelj** {VP} (lit. fall for prison) *sl-crime* get arrested, get busted

• **pȁsti za slobòdu** {VP} (lit. fall for freedom) *sl-crime* get arrested, get busted

pâsti [2] {pásēm, sū imperf. irreg.} /pásti/ (lit. graze) **1** *sl-sex* wait for a customer (of a prostitute) <Slav*1> **2** *sl-fea* stare at, be fixated on <Slav*1> **3** *sl* eat, devour <Slav*1>

pàstīr {pastíra (acc. = gen.) masc.} (lit. shepherd) **1** *sl-fea* ***Fac*** retiree <Slav*1> **2** *sl-sex* ***Fac*** procurer, pimp <Slav*1>

pàstūh {a (acc. = gen.) masc.} (lit. stud) *sl-sex* adequate male sexual partner <Slav*1>

pasùljara {ē fem.} (lit. the beany one) **1** *sl-fea* ***Der*** rude female <Lat❖*1> **2a.** *sl-fea* sexually experienced female <Lat❖*1> **b.i.** *sl-fea* senior citizen <Lat❖*2> **ii.aa.** *sl-sex* inexpensive prostitute <Lat❖*2> **bb.** *sl-sex* prostitute, hooker <Lat❖*3>

pasùljčina {ē fem.} *col* beans <Lat❖>

pȁša {ē fem.} (lit. grazing) *sl-mil* eating <Slav*1>

pašàluk {a masc.} (lit. pasha's land) *sl-sex* ***Fac*** bar where many females often gather <NE*1>

pȁšica {ē fem.} (lit. small pasture) *sl* food <Slav*1>

pȁšmage {a neut.} *dia* peasant shoes <NE>

pȁt {excl.} *col* used to lure a duck <Slav>

pȁta-kârte {ī fem. pl.} *sl-gamble* even number of cards taken by two or more players during one game <Ita*1>

pátak {tka (acc. = gen.) masc.} (lit. duck) **1** *sl-fea* short male <Slav*1> **2** *sl-fea* short-legged male <Slav*1> **3** *sl-sex* penis <Slav*1>

pàtakac {kca (acc. = gen.) masc.} (lit. little duck) **1** *sl-fea* short male <Slav☞*1> **2** *sl-fea* short-legged male <Slav☞*2>

pàtakos {a (acc. = gen.) masc.} (lit. little duck) **1** *sl-fea* short male <**Slav** ✍[*1]> **2** *sl-fea* short-legged male <**Slav** ✍[*2]>

patamȕzovānje {a neut.} **a.** *sl* persuasion: *patamuzovanje mušterija persuasion of one's clients* <**Slav** ❖[*1]> **b.** *sl* lying

patamȕzovati {zujēm, zujū imperf.} *sl* lie <**Slav** ❖[*1]>

patàčōn {tačóna (acc. = gen.) masc.} *sl-fea* short male <**Slav** ✍[*1]>

páter {a (acc. = gen.) masc.} (lit. father *priest*) *sl-sex* ***Fac*** male homosexual, gay <**Lat**[*1]>

patètičan {čna, čno adj.} (lit. pathetic) *sl-fea* ***App*** good, cool <**Gre**[*1]>

pátež {a (acc. = gen.) masc.} *sl* sufferer <**Slav** ✍>

pȁticvr̄k {a (acc. = gen.) masc.} *sl-fea* short male <**Slav**[*1]>

pȁtiti {tīm, tē imperf.} (lit. suffer) *sl-drink* get drunk <**Slav**[*1]>

- **pȁtiti kao od TBC-a** [tê-bê-cèa] {VP} (lit. suffer like from TB) *sl-fea* be without a girlfriend
- **pȁtiti kao pàtika** {VP} (lit. suffer like a tennis shoe) *sl-fea* suffer considerably
- **pȁtiti kao patȉšpānj** {VP} (lit. suffer like a sweet bread) *sl-fea* suffer considerably

pȁtka {ē fem.; Dat pȁtki} (lit. duck) **1** *sl-sex* ***Obs*** penis, dick, prick <**Slav**[*1]> **2** *col* rumor <**Slav**[*1]>

pàtkac {a (acc. = gen.) masc.} (lit. duck) *sl-fea* short male <**Slav** ✍[*1]>

patȍfne {ī fem. pl.} *sl* slippers <**Ger**[*1]>

pȁtoka {ē fem.; Dat pȁtoki} *sl-drink* low-quality plum brandy <**Slav**>

patològija {ē fem.} (lit. pathology) *sl-fea* slightly insane, nutty <**Gre**[*1]>

pàtos {a masc.} (lit. floor) SerE *sl* defeat <**Gre**[*1]>

patosírati {tòsīrām, tosírajū biasp.} (lit. send to the floor) SerE *sl* knock down, floor <**Gre** ❖[*1]>

patosírati se {tòsīrām, tosírajū biasp. intr.} (lit. hit the floor) **1** **SerE** *sl-fea* be surprised, be floored <**Gre** ❖[*1]> **2** SerE *sl-drink* ***Fac*** get drunk <**Gre** ❖[*1]>

pàtosman {a (acc. = gen.) masc.} (lit. floor-man) **1** **SerE** *sl-fea* ***Fac*** short male <**Gre-Eng**[*1]> **2** **SerE** *sl-fea* ***Fac*** short-legged male <**Gre-Eng**[*2]>

pàtosmen {a (acc. = gen.) masc.} (lit. floor-man) SerE *sl-fea* ***Fac*** short male <**Gre-Eng**[*1]>

patrànjača {ē fem.} *sl-sex* ***Fac-Obs*** penis, dick, prick

patŕljak {ljka masc.} (lit. stump) *sl-sex* ***Fac-Obs*** small penis <**Slav**[*1]>

patȑnjača {ē fem.} (lit. stump) *sl-sex* ***Fac-Obs*** penis, dick, prick <**Slav**[*1]>

patróla {ē fem.} (lit. patrol) *sl-sex* ***Fac-Obs*** quick sexual intercourse, quickie <**Fre**[*1]>

patúljak {ljka (acc. = gen.) masc.} (lit. dwarf) *sl-fea* short male <**Slav**[*1]>

pȁučina {ē fem.} (lit. spiderweb) *sl-fea* limp hair <**Slav**[*1]>

Pȁučina {ē fem.} (lit. spiderweb) *sl* Internet, Web <**Slav**[*1]>

pȁūk {a (acc. = gen.) masc.} (lit. spider) **1** *col* tow truck <**Slav**[*1]> **2** *sl-crime* policeman, cop <**Slav**[*1]>

pȁūn {a (acc. = gen.) masc.} (lit. peacock) *sl-fea* dandy, fop <**Slav**[*1]>

paùnisati se {išēm, išū imperf. intr.} (lit. peacock) *sl-fea* boast, brag <**Slav** ❖[*1]>

pàuza {excl.} (lit. break) *sl* used to prevent one's interlocutor from speaking, shut up <**Lat**[*1]>

pȁverica {ē fem.} *sl* fire <**Ita** ❖[*1]>

pȁvernjāk {a masc.} *sl-arch* pan, pot <**Ita** ❖[*1]>

pȁvijān {a (acc. = gen.) masc.} (lit. baboon) *sl-fea* stupid or mentally deficient person <**Ger**[*1]>

pàzārka {ē fem.; Dat pàzārki} (lit. merchant) *sl-sex* ***Fac*** prostitute, hooker <**NE** ❖[*1]>

pàzarnī {ā, ō adj.} *col* vending <**NE**[*1]>

pȁzi {excl.} **1** *col* used to draw attention in direct informal communication, listen up <**Slav**[*1]> **2** *col* used to intensify one's own utterance, you know <**Slav**[*1]>

pcòvati {cūjēm, cūjū imperf.} [std. = psovati] SSer *dia* ***Obs*** curse <**Slav** ✍>

pčèlica {ē fem.} (lit. small bee) *col* smart male, brain <**Slav**[*1]>

pčȅnica {ē fem.} [std. = pšenica] *dia* wheat <**Slav** ✍>

pȅ {num.} [std. = pet] *col-dia* five <**Slav** ✍>

péca {ē fem.} *sl-sex* ***Fac*** male homosexual, gay <**Slav** ✍[*1]>

pècāljka {ē fem.; Dat pècāljki} (lit. fishing rod) **1a.** *sl* ***Fac*** hand <**Slav**[*1]> **b.** *sl* arm <**Slav**[*2]> **2** *sl* leg (of a female) <**Slav**[*1]>

pècānje {a neut.} (lit. fishing) **a.** *sl* catching: *pecanje lopova catching thieves* <**Slav**[*1]> **b.** *sl-crime* theft <**Slav**[*2]>

pècāroš {a (acc. = gen.) masc.} (lit. fisherman) **a.** *sl* male who attempts to catch or grasp something <**Slav**[*1]> **b.** *sl-crime* thief <**Slav**[*1]>

pȅcati {ām, ajū imperf.} (lit. fish) **a.** *sl* search, fish for <**Slav*1**> **b.** *sl* catch <**Slav*2**> **c.** *sl-crime* steal, swipe <**Slav*3**>

• **pȅcati bârku** {VP} (lit. fish for a boat) *sl-crime* pick pockets

pȅcati se {ām, ajū imperf. intr.} (lit. get caught on a hook) *sl* believe (usu. in something which is either unrealistic or with hidden disadvantages), be hooked <**Slav*1**>

• **pȅcati se na žúljeve** {VP} (lit. be fished on blisters) *sl* work, labor

pȅcka {ē fem.; Dat pȅcki} *sl-fea* slender leg

péčak {čka masc.} *sl* fifty dinars (bill) <**Slav✎**>

pèčat {a masc.} (lit. seal) *sl* finger ring <**Slav*1**>

pèčen {a, o adj.} (lit. baked) **1** *sl-fea* ***Der*** cunning, sly, slick: *pečen povlo cunning thief* <**Slav*1**> **2** *sl-fea* lost: *pečen u nepoznatom gradu lost in an unknown city* <**Slav*1**> **3** *sl-fea* beaten up <**Slav*1**> **4** *sl-fea* experienced <**Slav*1**> **5** *sl-fea* indoctrinated <**Slav*1**> **6** *sl-fea* ruined <**Slav*1**>

• **rȅš pèčen** {AdjP} (lit. well done *baking*) *sl-drink* drunk, toasted

pèčenā kàmila {NP} (lit. baked camel) *sl-sex* ***Obs*** loose woman, slut ☞ **kamila**

pèčūrka {ē fem.; Dat pèčūrki} (lit. mushroom) **1** *sl-sex* ***Fac*** male homosexual, gay <**Slav*1**> **2** *sl* ***Fac*** imam <**Slav*1**> **3a.** *sl-fea* ***Fac*** naive male <**Slav*1**> **b.** *sl-fea* stupid or mentally deficient person <**Slav*2**> **c.** *sl-fea* foolish female <**Slav*3**> **3** *sl-sex* head of a penis <**Slav*1**>

• **kao pèčūrka** {PP} (lit. like a mushroom) *sl-fea* ***Der-Fac*** unintelligent, stupid, dumb

pêć *See the following*

• **krȕšnā pêć** {NP} (lit. bread oven) *sl-sex* ***Fac*** large female buttocks

pèći {pèčēm, pèkū, ek, ek imperf. irreg.} (lit. bake) *sl-drink* distill alcoholic beverages <**Slav*1**>

pèćina {ē fem.} (lit. cave) **1a.** *sl* home <**Slav*1**> **b.** *sl* apartment <**Slav*2**> **c.** *sl* room <**Slav*3**> **d.** *sl-sex* room used by a prostitute, trick room <**Slav*4**> **2** *sl-sex* vagina <**Slav*1**>

pȅda {ē masc.} *sl-sex* male homosexual, gay <**Gre✎**>

pèdāl [1] {pedála (acc. = gen.) masc.; Voc pȅdale} (lit. pedal) *sl-sex* ***Fac*** male homosexual, gay <**Gre✎**>

pèdāl [2] {pedála masc.} *sl* pedal <**Fre**>

pedála {ē fem.} **a.** *sl* pedal <**Fre**> **b.** *sl-sex* male homosexual, gay <**Gre✎**>

• **pedála gâsa** {NP} (lit. gas pedal) *sl-auto* gas pedal

pedalína {ē fem.} *col* paddle boat <**Fre❖**>

pedálo {a neut.} (lit. pedal) *sl-sex* ***Fac*** male homosexual, gay <**Gre✎**>

péder {a (acc. = gen.) masc.} **a.** *sl-sex* ***Der*** male homosexual, gay <**Gre✎**> **b.i.** *sl-fea* ***Der*** long-haired musician <**Gre✎*1**> **ii.** *sl-fea* ***Der*** inhabitant of Zagreb, Croatia <**Gre✎*1**> **iii.** *sl-fea* ***Der*** unfriendly person <**Gre✎*1**> **iv.** *sl-fea* ***Der*** coward, chicken <**Gre✎*1**>

péder štȁjg {NP} (lit. faggot promenade) **Cro** *sl-sex* ***Der*** name of a place in Zagreb, Croatia where homosexuals are known to gather ☞ **štajg**

péder-bâr {a +ov (ext. pl) masc.; Nom Pl péder-bárovi} (lit. faggot bar) **a.** *sl-sex* ***Fac*** public bathroom <**Gre-Eng*1**> **b.** Cro *sl-sex* ***Fac*** name of a public toilet at Zrinjevac in Zagreb, Croatia, where male homosexuals gather <**Gre-Eng*2**>

pedèrāj [1] {deràja (acc. = gen.) masc.} *sl-sex* ***Fac*** male homosexual, gay <**Gre✎**>

pedèrāj [2] {deràja masc.} **a.** *sl-sex* ***Fac*** homosexuality <**Gre✎**> **b.** *sl-sex* ***Fac*** difficult or unpleasant situation <**Gre✎*1**>

pedèrāš {deráša (acc. = gen.) masc.; Voc pȅderāšu} *sl-sex* ***Fac*** male homosexual, gay <**Gre✎**>

pederàško {a masc.} *sl-sex* ***Fac*** male homosexual, gay <**Gre✎**>

péderbâl {a masc.} (lit. faggot ball) *sl-sex* ***Fac*** party without females <**Gre✎-Fre*1**>

pedèrčina {ē masc.} (lit. big faggot) **a.** *sl-sex* ***Der*** male homosexual, gay <**Gre❖*1**> **b.** *sl-fea* ***Der*** unfriendly person <**Gre❖*2**>

péderica {ē fem.} (lit. faggot stuff) *sl-fea* small-sized attaché case <**Gre❖*1**>

péderice {ā fem. pl.} (lit. faggot wear) *sl-fea* tight trousers <**Gre❖*1**>

pederȉko {a (acc. = gen.) masc.} *sl-sex* ***Fac*** male homosexual, gay <**Gre✎**>

pedèrīn {derína (acc. = gen.) masc.} *sl-sex* ***Fac*** male homosexual, gay <**Gre✎**>

pederȉška {ē fem.; Dat pederȉški} /pederìška/ *sl-sex* ***Fac*** male homosexual, gay <**Gre✎**>

péderskī {ā, ō adj.} **a.** *sl-sex* male homosexual, gay <**Gre**> **b.** *sl* ***Der*** unfriendly <**Gre*1**>

pedèruša {ē fem.} (lit. faggot stuff) **a.** *sl-fea* evil male <Gre❖[*1]> **b.** *sl* small-sized attaché case <Gre❖[*1]>

pedesètača {ē fem.} *col* fifty dinars (bill) <Slav❖[*1]>

pȅdī {īja (acc. = gen.) masc.} *sl-sex* ***Fac*** male homosexual, gay <Gre☞>

pedigrȅ *See the following*

• **bez pedigrȅa** {PP} (lit. without a pedigree) **a.** *sl-crime* ***Fac*** of suspicious origin **b.** *sl-crime* ***Fac*** stolen

pedìkēr {dikíra (acc. = gen.) masc.} (lit. pedicure) *sl-sex* ***Fac*** male homosexual, gay <Gre☞>

pedìkīr {dikíra (acc. = gen.) masc.} (lit. pedicure) *sl-sex* ***Fac*** male homosexual, gay <Gre☞>

pȅdos {a (acc. = gen.) masc.} *sl-sex* ***Fac*** male homosexual, gay <Gre☞>

pêdrānje {a neut.} (lit. faggoting) **1** *sl-sex* anal sexual intercourse <Gre☞[*1]> **2** *sl-sex* anus <Gre☞[*1]>

pêdro {a neut.} (lit. Pedro) *sl-sex* ***Fac*** male homosexual, gay <Gre☞>

pedrolazàrija {ē fem.} *sl-sex* ***Fac*** male homosexual, gay <Gre☞>

pedrològija {ē fem.} (lit. Pedrology) *sl-sex* ***Fac*** homosexuality <Gre☞>

pȅdu {pètadu neut.; perm} [std. = dupe] *sl-sex* ***Obs*** buttocks, butt <Slav☞>

pȅđa {ē masc.} *sl-sex* ***Fac*** male homosexual, gay <Gre☞>

pefàzōn {fazóna (acc. = gen.) masc.} *sl-crime* ***Der*** policeman, cop

pefèzōn {fezóna (acc. = gen.) masc.} *sl-crime* policeman, cop

pȅgavac {gāvca (acc. = gen.) masc.} (lit. the one with spots) *sl-fea* evil male <Slav[*1]>

pégla {ē fem.} (lit. iron) **1** *sl* fist <Ger[*1]> **2** *sl-fea* boring person, bore <Ger[*1]> **3** *sl-drink* vomit, throw up, puke <Ger[*1]> **4** *sl-auto* Fiat 125P (make of car) <Ger[*1]> **5** *sl* orthopedic shoe <Ger[*1]> **6** *sl-sex* loose woman <Ger[*1]>

pèglāč {pegláča (acc. = gen.) masc.} (lit. the one who irons) *sl-fea* troublemaker, rowdy, ruffian <Ger❖[*1]>

pêglānje {a neut.} /péglānje/ (lit. ironing) **1** *sl* ***Fac*** beating up <Ger[*1]> **2** *sl-sex* ***Fac-Obs*** masturbating <Ger[*1]> **3** *sl-sex* ***Fac-Obs*** sexual intercourse <Ger[*1]>

pèglara {ē fem.} (lit. ironing thing) *sl* street <Ger☞[*1]>

pêglati {ām, ajū imperf.} /pèglati/ (lit. iron) **1** *sl-sex* ***Fac*** beat up <Ger[*1]> **2a.** *sl-sex* ***Fac-Obs*** masturbate, beat off <Ger[*1]> **b.** *sl* ***Fac-Obs*** engage in sexual intercourse with (of a male) <Ger[*2]> **3** *sl* reproach, scold <Ger[*1]> **4** *sl* lie <Ger[*1]>

• **péglati Lázu** {VP} (lit. iron one's Dick) *sl-sex* ***Obs*** masturbate, beat off

• **péglati po mózgu** {VP} (lit. iron over one's brain) *sl-fea* bore, disturb

• **péglati sa stránē** {VP} (lit. iron aside) *sl* cheat on one's lover or spouse

péglica {ē fem.} (lit. small iron) **1** *sl-auto* Fiat 126P (a model of a simple Polish car) <Ger[*1]> **2** *sl-auto* Renault 4 (make of car) <Ger[*1]> **3** Cro *sl* former train from Zagreb to Samobor, Croatia <Ger[*1]>

pêgula [1] {ē masc.} **a.** Med *dia* person who has bad luck, ill-starred person <Ita[*1]> **b.** Med *dia* clumsy male, klutz <Ita[*1]>

pêgula [2] {ē fem.} Med *dia* bad luck <Ita[*1]>

pȅh {a +ov (ext. pl) masc.; Nom Pl pèhovi} (lit. bad luck) *col* accident <Ger>

pèhist {a (acc. = gen.) masc.} *sl-fea* person having bad luck <Ger❖>

pèkara {ē fem.} (lit. bakery) *sl-sex* ***Fac-Obs*** buttocks, butt <Slav[*1]>

pȅke {excl.} *sl* okay, fine, great <NE☞>

pȅkī {excl.} *sl* okay, fine, great <NE☞>

pèkiš {a masc.} *sl* pen (writing instrument) <Ska☞[*1]>

pèkljārka {ē fem.} *sl* wallet <Ger☞[*1]>

pèkmez [1] {a (acc. = gen.) masc.} (lit. jam) *sl-fea* ***Der*** crybaby <NE[*1]>

pèkmez [2] {a masc.} (lit. jam) *sl* mess, disorder, disturbance <NE[*1]>

pekméza {ē fem. & masc.} (lit. jam child) *sl-fea* ***Der*** crybaby <NE[*1]>

pelánovićka {ē fem.; Dat pelánovićki} *sl-sex* prostitute

pȅlcati {ām, ajū imperf.} (lit. immunize) *sl-sex* ***Fac-Obs*** engage in sexual intercourse with (of a male) <Ger[*1]>

pȅlcer {a (acc. = gen.) masc.} (lit. graft) *sl-fea* slender female <Ger[*1]>

pȅlcovānje {a neut.} (lit. immunization) *sl-sex* ***Fac-Obs*** sexual intercourse <Ger[*1]>

pȅlcovati {cujēm, cujū imperf. intr.} *col* immunize <Ger>

pȅle {eta masc.} /pêle/ (lit. Pele) *sl-sex* ***Fac*** male homosexual, gay <Gre☞>

pelètān {letána (acc. = gen.) masc.} *sl-sex* ***Fac*** male homosexual, gay <Gre☞>

pelìkān {likána (acc. = gen.) masc.} (lit. pelican) **1** *sl-sex* ***Fac*** male homosexual, gay <**Gre**✍> **2** *sl-fea* large-nosed male <**Gre**[*1]>

pèlīn {a masc.} (lit. wormwood) *sl-drink* Jaegermeister beer <**Slav**[*1]>

pèljača {ē fem.} *sl-arch* mare <**Slav**❖[*1]>

pèlješiti {šīm, še imperf.} *sl-crime* steal from, rip off <**Slav**[*1]>

Pémac {mca (acc. = gen.) masc.} *col-dia* Czech <**Ger**✍>

pȅna {ē fem.} Gast *sl-fea* ***Der*** lazy or shiftless person, bum, good for nothing <**Ger**✍>

penàldžija {ē fem.} *sl-sports* soccer player who specialized in penalty kicks <**Lat-NE**[*1]>

penàvisati {išēm, išū biasp.} *sl* show, display

pénce {eta neut.} [std. = dupence] **a.** *sl-sex* ***Fam*** small buttocks <**Slav**✍> **b.** *sl-sex* ***Fac-Fam*** short attractive female <**Slav**✍[*1]>

pencìlīnskī {ā, ō adj.} (lit. penicillin) *sl-fea* horrible, terrible <**Lat**[*1]>

pèndrāč {a masc.} *sl-crime* policeman, cop <**Ger**❖[*1]>

pèndrečiti {čīm, čē imperf.} **a.** *sl-crime* beat with a billy club <**Ger**❖> **b.** *sl-sex* engage in sexual intercourse with (of a male) <**Ger**❖[*1]>

pèndrek {a masc.} **a.** *sl-crime* billy club <**Ger**> **b.** *sl-sex* penis <**Ger**[*1]>

pêndžer {a masc.} *col-dia* window <**NE**>

pèndžera {ē fem.} *col-dia* window <**NE**>

pèndžeri {džērā masc. pl.} (lit. windows) *sl* ***Fac*** eyeglasses <**NE**[*1]>

pènezi {pȇnēzā masc. pl.} Kajk *dia-col* money <**Ger**[*1]>

pȅngi {ā masc. pl.} *dia-col* money <**Hun**[*1]>

penicìlīn {cilína masc.} (lit. penicillin) *sl-fea* ***App*** successful person <**Lat**[*1]>

pènicilīnskī {ā, ō adj.} (lit. penicillin) *sl-fea* excellent, awesome <**Lat**[*1]>

pénis *See the following*

pénis méjker {NP} (lit. penis maker) *sl* ***Fac*** pacemaker ☞ **mejker**

penìsati {pènišēm, išū imperf.} *sl* talk, have a conversation <**Gyp**>

penìsēr {niséra (acc. = gen.) masc.} (lit. penis player) *sl-sex* ***Fac*** male sexual partner (of a female) <**Lat**❖[*1]>

penkála [1] {ē masc.} (lit. pen *writing device*) *sl-crime* ***Der*** informer, stoolie, snitch <**SlavO**[*1]>

penkála [2] {ē masc.} *sl-crime* pen (writing device) <**SlavO**[*1]>

penkálo {a masc.} **a.** *col* pen (writing device) <**SlavO**[*1]> **b.** *sl-sex* penis <**SlavO**[*2]>

pènkiš {a masc.} *sl* pen (writing device) <**SlavO**✍[*1]>

pèntek {a (acc. = gen.) masc.} *sl-crime* jailer

penziònīrān {a, o adj.} (lit. retired) *sl-crime* serving a long term in prison <**Lat**[*1]>

pȅnzos {a (acc. = gen.) masc.} *sl-fea* retiree <**Lat**✍>

pènjati se *See the following*

- **pènjati se nà kurac** {VP} (lit. climb on somebody's prick) *sl* ***Obs*** bother, disturb, be on someone's ass

pènjer {a masc.} *sl-arch* cheese

pênžeri {žērā masc. pl.} (lit. windows) *sl* eyeglasses <**NE**[*1]>

pènjez {a masc.} *dia-col* money <**Ger**✍[*1]>

pènjisati {išēm, išū imperf. intr.} *sl* talk, have a conversation

pȅpel {a (acc. = gen.) masc.} (lit. ashes) *sl-gamble* poker player who went broke <**Slav**[*1]>

pepèljara {ē fem.} (lit. ashtray) *sl-fea* unattractive female <**Slav**[*1]>

pȅpeljata {ē fem.} **1** *sl* head <**Slav**[*1]> **2** *sl-auto* Fiat 125P (make of car) <**Slav**[*1]>

pepèljuga {ē fem.; Dat pepèljugi} /Pepèljuga/ (lit. Cinderella) **a.** *sl-sex* ***Fac*** male homosexual, gay <**Gre**✍> **b.** *sl-fea* naive person <**Slav**[*1]> **c.** *sl-fea* naive customer <**Slav**[*2]>

pȅpī [1] {īja (acc. = gen.) masc.} /pèpi/ *sl-sex* ***Fac*** male homosexual, gay <**Gre**✍>

pȅpī [2] {īja masc.} /pèpi/ *sl-drugs* preludine (a kind of narcotic drug) <**BN**✍>

pèpika {ē fem.} *sl-sex* ***Fac*** male homosexual, gay <**Gre**✍>

pepîno {a masc.} **a.** *sl-sex* ***Fac*** male homosexual, gay <**Gre**✍> **b.** *sl-fea* ***Fac*** feminized male <**Gre**✍[*1]>

pȅpos {a (acc. = gen.) masc.} *sl-sex* male homosexual, gay <**Gre**✍>

pèpsika {ē fem.} **a.** *sl* Pepsi <**BN**✍> **b.** *sl-fea* stranger (male) <**BN**✍[*1]>

perája {ē fem.} (lit. fin) *sl* arm <**Slav**[*1]>

pérce {eta neut.} (lit. feather) *sl-fea* slender person <**Slav**[*1]>

pȅrfa {adj.} *sl* perfect: *perfa plan perfect plan* <**Lat**✍>

pȅrger {a (acc. = gen.) masc.} *sl-crime* pickpocket

pȅrī {īja masc.} *sl-drugs* preludine (a kind of narcotic drug)

pȅrica {ē masc.} (lit. Pete) *sl-sex* ***Fac*** male homosexual, gay <Gre☞>

pèrika {ē fem.} (lit. wig) *sl-fea* thick hair <Fre[*1]>

pèrikle {ea masc.} *sl* wig <Fre☞>

pèrilka {ē fem.} **1** *sl* babysitter <Slav⁘[*1]> **2** *sl* kitchen help

pèriljek {a masc.} **a.** *sl-fea* unattractive thing <Slav[*1]> **b.** *sl-fea* crude and ill-mannered female, Neanderthal <Slav[*2]>

perȉod {a masc.} (lit. period) *sl-sex* menstruation, period <Eng>

- **mònsūnskī perȉod** {NP} (lit. monsoon period) *sl* crying time
- **perȉod monsúna** {NP} (lit. monsoon period) *sl-fea* crying time

perióda {ē fem.} (lit. period) *sl-sex* menstruation, period <Gre[*1]>

pèriskopi {kōpā masc. pl.} /pȅriskopi/ (lit. periscopes) *sl* eyeglasses <Gre[*1]>

pèrislav {a (acc. = gen.) masc.} **a.** *sl-fea* ***Der*** clumsy person, klutz <Slav⁘[*1]> **b.** *sl-fea* ***Der*** beggar <Slav⁘[*2]>

perjáriti {pèrjārīm, rē imperf.} (lit. trade with feathers) **1a.** *sl* trade <Slav[*1]> **b.** *sl* carry small trade <Slav[*2]> **2** *sl-crime* steal something of little value <Slav[*1]>

pèrjati {ām, ajū imperf.} (lit. spread feathers) *col* leave, depart, walk <Slav[*1]>

pȇrje {a neut.} (lit. feathers) **1a.** *sl* garment, suit <Slav[*1]> **b.** *sl* dress <Slav[*2]> **c.** *sl* nice clothing <Slav[*3]> **2** *sl* facial hairs <Slav[*1]>

- **Pȇrje će da leti.** {S} (lit. The feathers will fly.) *col* used to refer to a dangerous situation in the future

pèrkan {a (acc. = gen.) masc.} **a.** *sl* boy, kid **b.** *sl-fea* stupid or mentally deficient person, **c.i.** *sl-crime* policeman, cop **ii.** *sl-sex* male homosexual, gay **iii.** *sl-sex* male cheated by a prostitute

pèrmant {a masc.} *sl-auto* antifreeze <BN[*1]>

pèro [1] {a neut.} (lit. feather) *sl* pocket knife <Slav[*1]>

- **trȋ pèra na šešíru** {NP} (lit. three feathers on a hat) *sl-sex* gonorrhea, the clap

Péro [2] {ē masc.} (lit. Peter) **a.** *sl* male, guy <SlavO[*1]> **b.** *sl-fea* clumsy male, klutz <SlavO[*2]>

perpendikùlisati {išēm, išū imperf.} (lit. perpendiculate) *sl* circulate around <Lat[*1]>

Pérsa {ē fem.} (lit. Persa, woman's name) **a.** *sl* female <SlavO[*1]> **b.** *sl* male homosexual, gay <SlavO[*2]>

pèrsu {adv.; perm} [std. = super] *col* ***App*** excellent, awesome <Lat>

péršin {a masc.} (lit. parsley) *sl* flowers <Slav[*1]>

pèrtla {ē fem.} *col* shoelace <Ger>

pȅrtlovati se {lujēm, lujū imperf. intr.} (lit. tie one's shoe-laces) *sl-fea* walk slowly, amble <Ger⁘[*1]>

perȕšati {ām, ajū imperf.} *sl* steal, swipe <Slav[*1]>

pèrvert {a (acc. = gen.) masc.} **a.** *sl-fea* pervert, weirdo <Lat⁘> **b.** *sl-sex* male homosexual, gay <Lat⁘[*1]>

pervèrznjāk {vrznjáka (acc. = gen.) masc.} *sl-fea* pervert, weirdo <Lat>

pȅs {psa (acc. = gen.) masc.} [std. = pas] **a.** **Kajk** *dia* dog (the animal) <Slav☞> **b.i.** **Kajk** *sl-sex* male homosexual, gay <Slav☞[*1]> **ii.** Kajk *sl-crime* informer, stoolie, snitch <Slav☞[*2]>

pèsek {ska (acc. = gen.) masc.} [std. = pas] Kajk *col* dog (the animal) <Sla>

pȅsma *See the following*

- **iz národnē pȅsmē** {PP} (lit. from a folk song) SerE *sl-fea* ***Fac*** with permanently red face

pešáčiti {pèšāčīm, čē imperf.} (lit. go on foot) SerE *sl-sex* ***Obs*** engage in sexual intercourse with (of a male) <Slav[*1]>

pèšadīnka {ē fem.} SerE *sl-mil* high-top boot <Slav⁘[*1]>

pèšāk {pešáka (acc. = gen.) masc.; Voc pȅšāče} (lit. pedestrian) SerE *sl-sex* ***Fac*** male homosexual, gay <Gre☞>

pešáka {adv.} *sl* on foot <Slav☞>

pèškeš {a masc.} **a.** *col* gift, present <NE> **b.** *col* tip, gratuity <NE>

pèškīr {peškíra (acc. = gen.) masc.} (lit. towel) *sl-sex* ***Fac*** male homosexual, gay <Gre☞>

pȅško {a masc.} **a.** *sl-sex* ***Fac*** male homosexual, gay <Gre☞> **b.** *sl-fea* ***Fac*** weak and irresolute male, wimp <Gre☞[*1]>

péšo {a masc.} /péšo /e masc/ *sl-sex* ***Fac*** male homosexual, gay <Gre☞[*1]>

pešòvān {šována (acc. = gen.) masc.} *sl-sex* ***Fac*** male homosexual, gay <Gre☞>

pešovànder {a (acc. = gen.) masc.} *sl-sex* ***Fac*** male homosexual, gay <Gre☞>

pêt sȕrkī za krȗnu {NP} (lit. five grand for a crown) *sl* five-thousand dinar reward ☞ **surka**

péta *See the following*

• **vȉšekatnā péta** {NP} (lit. multi-storey heel) Cro *sl-fea* high heel (of a shoe)

petája {ē fem.} *sl* hand <**Slav**⁘*1>

pètāk {petáka masc.} **1** *sl* five <**Slav**⁘> **2** *sl-sstu* A (the highest grade) <**Slav**⁘> **3** *sl* fifty dinar bill <**Slav**⁘> **4** *sl* five thousand dinars; a five-thousand dinar bill <**Slav**⁘*1>

Pȅtar {tra (acc. = gen.) masc.} (lit. Peter) **1a.** *sl* victim <**SlavO***1> **b.** *sl-sex* victim of a prostitute <**SlavO***2> **2** *sl-crime* policeman, cop <**SlavO***1>

pètēljka {ē fem.} (lit. stalk) *sl-sex* ***Obs*** penis, dick, prick <**Slav***1>

pètica {ē fem.} (lit. five) **1** *sl-auto* Fiat 125 (make of car) <**Slav***1> **2** *sl-fea* attractive female <**Slav***1> **3** *sl-drugs* high-quality marijuana <**Slav***1> **4** *sl-drugs* five grams of any narcotic <**Slav***1>

pètīng {a masc.} *sl-sex* sexual foreplay, petting, feeling up <**Eng**>

pètlīć *See the following*

• **šlògīrānī pètlīć** {NP} (lit. apoplectic small rooster) SerE *sl-fea* unattractive male, dog

pétlovac {tlōvca masc.} SerE *sl* the bus line to Petlovo Brdo in Belgrade, Serbia <**SlavO**⁘>

Pétlovača {ē fem.} *sl* name for Petlovo brdo (a neighborhood in Belgrade Yugoslavia) <**Slav**✍>

pȅtlja {ē fem.} (lit. knot) *sl-fea* bravery <**Slav***1>

petljàncija {ē fem.} *col* entanglement, complex issue <**Slav**⁘*1>

pètljār {petljára (acc. = gen.) masc.} *sl-crime* pick-pocket <**Slav***1>

pètljara {ē fem.} **1** *sl* spy, spook <**Slav***1> **2** *sl* leg (human) <**Slav***1>

petljáriti {pètljārīm, rē imperf.} (lit. tie) **1** *sl-crime* pick pockets <**Slav***1> **2a.** *sl-fea* work slowly <**Slav***1> **b.i.** *sl-fea* work clumsily <**Slav***1> **ii.** *sl-fea* be bored at work <**Slav***2> **3** *sl-fea* intrigue <**Slav***1>

pètljārka {ē fem.} (lit. the one who ties) **1** *sl* wallet <**Slav***1> **2** *sl-crime* petty thief <**Slav***2> **3** *sl-crime* informer, stoolie, snitch <**Slav***1>

• **Pètljārka mi sjâ jèktiku.** {S} (lit. My knot-thing is shining.) *sl-fea* used to refer to the state of being broke

pètljārnik {a (acc. = gen.) masc.} (lit. the one who ties) *sl-crime* ***Der*** informer, stoolie, snitch <**Slav***1>

pètljārnik {a masc.} (lit. the one who ties) *sl* wallet <**Slav***1>

pètljāroš {a (acc. = gen.) masc.} (lit. complicator) **a.** *sl-fea* person who habitually makes everything more complicated <**Slav***1> **b.** *sl-crime* pickpocket <**Slav***2>

pètljavina {ē fem.} (lit. tying) **a.** *sl* complication <**Slav***1> **b.** *sl* lying <**Slav***2>

pètljati {ām, ajū imperf. intr.} **a.** *col* lie <**Slav**> **b.** *col* cheat, swindle <**Slav**> **c.** *col* be bureaucratic <**Slav**>

pètljati se {ām, ajū imperf. intr.} *col* intrude, barge in <**Slav***1>

pètnaēs {num.} [std. = petnaest] *col-dia* fifteen <**Slav**✍>

pètnēs {num.} [std. = petnaest] *col-dia* fifteen <**Slav**✍>

petòglavac {vca masc.} (lit. the five-headed one) *sl* five-dinar coin <**Slav***1>

petokolònāš {lonáša masc.} (lit. member of the fifth column) *sl* ***Fac*** fifty dinars (bill) <**Slav**⁘*1>

Petrijáner {a (acc. = gen.) masc.} *sl-crime* name of a prison on Petrinjska street in Zagreb, Croatia <**SlavO***1>

pévac {vca (acc. = gen.) masc.} (lit. rooster) **1** SerE *sl* stutterer <**Slav***1> **2** *sl-sex* penis, cock <**Slav***1>

pèvāč [1] {peváča (acc. = gen.) masc.} (lit. singer) **1 SerE** *sl* ***Fac*** beans <**Slav***1> **2 SerE** *sl* person who makes noise <**Slav***1> **3** SerE *sl-crime* informer, stoolie, snitch <**Slav***2> **4** SerE *sl-sports* incompetent player (soccer, etc.) <**Slav***1> ***Fac***

pèvāč [2] {peváča masc.} (lit. singer) SerE *sl-crime* machine gun <**Slav***1>

pevàčica {ē fem.} (lit. singer) SerE *sl-fea* female with skinny legs <**Slav***1>

pȅvalica {ē fem.} (lit. singer) SerE *sl* mouth <**Slav***1>

pèvāljka {ē fem.} (lit. singer) SerE *sl-music* ***Der*** country or folk music performer (female) <**Slav***1>

pȅvānje {a neut.} (lit. singing) SerE *sl-crime* ***Fac*** informing police or other authorities, singing <**Slav***1>

pȅvati {ām, ajū imperf.} (lit. sing) **1 SerE** *sl-crime* inform the police or other authorities, sing <**Slav***1> **2 SerE** *sl* talk, have a conversation <**Slav***1>

• **pȅvati ko slàvūj** {VP} (lit. sing like a nightingale) SerE *sl-fea* have skinny legs

• **pȅvati lêpo** {VP} (lit. sing nicely) SerE *sl-fea* have skinny legs

• **pȅvati Opàtiju** {VP} (lit. sing at the Opatija pop-music festival) SerE *sl-fea* cry on departure

• **pȅvati Rigolȅto** {VP} (lit. sing Rigoletto) SerE *sl* vomit, throw up, Ralph

pèvče {eta neut.} (lit. little rooster) SerE *sl-sex* ***Obs*** penis, cock <**Slav***1>

pȅvnuti {nēm, nū perf.} (lit. sing) **1a.** **SerE** *sl* tell, say <**Slav***1> **b.** **SerE** *sl-crime* inform the police or other authorities, sing <**Slav***2> 2 SerE *sl* die, kick the bucket <**Slav***1>

• **pȅvnuti Rigolȅto** {VP} (lit. sing Rigoletto) SerE *sl* vomit, throw up, Ralph

pevúšiti {pèvūšīm, šē imperf.} SerE *col* sing <**Slav**>

péza {ē fem.} *sl-auto* Fiat 125 PZ (make of car) <**BN**✍>

pezéjac {jca (acc. = gen.) masc.} *sl-auto* Fiat 125 PZ (make of car) <**BN**✍>

pèzēljka {ē fem.} *sl-auto* Fiat 125 PZ (make of car) <**BN**✍>

péziti {pêzīm, zē imperf.} *sl-fea* ***Der*** ingratiate, brownnose, kiss ass

pȅzos {a masc.} (lit. peso) *sl* ***Fac*** dinar (Yugoslav currency unit) <**Spa***1>

pèžō {pežòa masc.} (lit. Peugeot *a make of car*) *sl-sex* ***Fac*** male homosexual, gay <**Gre**✍>

pff {excl.} *col* puff (produce the sound) <**Slav**>

pȉ {excl.} **1** *col* the sound made by spitting, phew <**Slav**> 2 *col* used to lure chicken <**Slav**>

pȉ-pī {excl.} *col* used to lure chicken <**Slav**>

pîc {a +ev (ext. pl) masc.; Nom Pl pícevi} *sl-sex* ***Obs*** vagina, cunt <**Slav**✍>

píca {ē fem.} **a.** *sl-sex* ***Obs*** vagina, cunt <**Slav**> **b.** *sl* ***Obs*** female, cunt <**Slav***1>

• **píca na kvàdrāt** {NP} (lit. the cunt to the second power) *sl-sex* ***App-Obs*** attractive female

• **túrbo píca** {NP} (lit. turbo cunt) *sl-sex* ***App-Obs*** attractive female

pìcāć {pìcāća masc.; Voc pȉcāću} *sl-sex* ***Obs*** vagina, cunt <**Slav**>

picàizla {ē fem.} *sl-sex* pubic louse, crabs <**Slav**>

picàjzl {a masc.} *sl-sex* pubic louse, crabs <**Slav**>

picàjzla {ē fem.} **a.** *sl-sex* pubic louse, crabs <**Slav**> **b.** *sl-fea* ***Der*** hairsplitter, nit picker <**Slav***1> **c.** *sl-fea* ***Der*** extremely orderly person, neatness <**Slav***2>

pȉcalo {a neut.} *sl-sex* ***Obs*** vagina, cunt <**Slav**✍>

pìcān {picána (acc. = gen.) masc.} (lit. cunter) *sl-fea* dandy, fop <**Slav**❖*1>

picániti se {pìcānīm, nē imperf. intr.} (lit. cunt up) **a.** *sl-fea* dress formally, dress up <**Slav**❖*1> **b.** *sl-fea* be conceited, be stuck-up <**Slav**❖*2>

pìcara {ē fem.} **a.** *sl-sex* ***Obs*** vagina, cunt <**Slav**❖> **b.** *sl* ***Obs*** female, cunt <**Slav**❖*1>

pȉcati {ām, ajū imperf.} *sl-sstu* skip classes, cut classes <**Slav**✍*1>

pìcek [1] {adj.} *sl-fea* short <**Slav**✍*1>

pìcek [2] {a (acc. = gen.) masc.} (lit. cunter) **a.** *sl-fea* feminized male <**Slav**❖*1> **b.** *sl-fea* inhabitant of Zagreb, Croatia <**Slav**❖*2>

pȉcī {adj.} *sl-fea* dressed formally, dressed up <**Ita**✍*1>

pìcig {adj.} *sl-fea* dressed formally, dressed up <**Ita**✍*1>

pîcijus *See the following*

• **po pîcijusu** {PP} (lit. according to the cunt's standard) *sl* ***Fac*** according to the Yugoslav Industrial Standard

picikȁto {adj.} /picikâto/ **1** *sl-fea* dressed formally, dressed up <**Ita***1> 2 *sl-fea* excellent, cool <**Ita***1>

pícīn {a, o adj.} *sl-sex* ***Obs*** vagina, cuntl <**Slav**>

pícīn dȉm {NP} (lit. cunt's smoke) *sl* ***Obs*** unimportant issue or object: *Taj ispit, to je bio picin dim! That exam, that was fucking nothing!* ☞ **dim**

pícina vòda {NP} (lit. cunt's water) *sl* ***Obs*** unimportant issue or object ☞ **voda**

pìcīng {adj.} *sl-fea* nicely dressed, tastefully dressed <**Ita***1>

pícino ȍko {NP} (lit. cunt's eye) *col* ***Obs*** very clean, clean as a whistle ☞ **oko**

pìciplac {a masc.} (lit. cunt-place) *sl-sex* ***Fac-Obs*** late-night bar frequented by prostitutes <**Slav-Ger***1>

pìckāroš {a (acc. = gen.) masc.} (lit. cunter) *sl-sex* ***Obs*** male sexual partner (of a female) <**Slav**❖*1>

pȉcko {a masc.} (lit. cunter) *sl-fea* dandy, fop <**Slav***1>

pȉckoš {a (acc. = gen.) masc.} (lit. cunter) *sl-sex* ***Obs*** male sexual partner (of a female) <**Slav***1>

pȉcnuti se {nēm, nū perf. intr.} *sl-fea* dress formally, dress up <**Slav**>

pȉcodēr {a masc.} (lit. cunt-thorn) *sl-fea* very distant part of a village <**Slav**❖*1>

picòglav {a, o adj.} (lit. cunt-headed) *sl-fea* small-headed <**Slav**❖*1>

picòglava {ē fem.} (lit. the cunt-headed one) *sl-fea* small-headed female <Slav❖[*1]>

picoglàvīle {a (acc. = gen.) masc.} (lit. the cunt-headed one) *sl-fea* small-headed male <Slav❖[*1]>

pìcōjka {ē fem.} (lit. cuntess) **a.** *sl-sex* ***Obs*** loose woman, slut <Slav❖[*1]> **b.** *sl* ***Obs*** female, cunt <Slav❖[*2]>

picóka {ē fem.; Dat picóki} *sl-sex* ***Obs*** female, cunt <Slav✍[*1]>

picòlīn {picolína masc.} *sl-sex* ***Obs*** vagina, cunt <Slav✍>

picolóvac {vca (acc. = gen.) masc.} (lit. cunt-fisher) **a.** *sl-sex* ***Fac-Obs*** male sexual partner (of a female) <Slav❖[*1]> **b.** *sl-sex* ***Fac-Obs*** lover (male) <Slav❖[*2]>

picóljak {ljka masc.} *sl-sex* ***Obs*** vagina, cunt <Slav✍>

picomehànìčār {haničára (acc. = gen.) masc.} (lit. cunt mechanic) *sl-sex* ***Fac-Obs*** gynecologist <Slav-Lat❖[*1]>

picopévac {vca (acc. = gen.) masc.} (lit. cunt singer) **a.** SerE *sl-fea* ***Obs*** short male <Slav❖[*1]> **b.** *sl-fea* ***Obs*** weak and irresolute person, wimp <Slav❖[*2]> **c.** *sl-fea* ***Obs*** worthless or despicable male, bum <Slav❖[*3]>

picòpēvka {ē fem.; Dat picòpēvki} (lit. cunt singer) SerE *sl-sex* ***Fac-Obs*** prostitute, hooker <Slav❖[*1]>

pîcoš {a (acc. = gen.) masc.} *sl-sex* ***Obs*** female, cunt <Slav❖[*1]>

picòvān {cována (acc. = gen.) masc.} (lit. cunter) *sl-fea* ***Obs*** dandy, fop <Slav❖[*1]>

picúknuti {pìcūknēm, nū perf.} (lit. cunt up) *sl-fea* ***Fac-Obs*** make a mistake, screw up <Slav[*1]>

picùlīn {culína masc.} *sl-sex* ***Obs*** vagina, cunt <Slav✍>

piculīnčić {a masc.} **a.** *sl-sex* ***Obs*** vagina, cunt <Slav✍[*1]> **b.** *sl-sex* ***Obs*** attractive female <Slav[*2]>

picùlīnka {ē fem.; Dat picùlīnki} **a.** *sl-sex* ***Obs*** vagina, cunt <Slav✍> **b.** *sl-sex* ***Obs*** loose woman, slut <Slav✍[*1]>

picúljak {lja masc.} *sl-sex* ***Obs*** vagina, cunt <Slav✍>

picùljān {culjána masc.} *sl-sex* ***Obs*** vagina, cunt <Slav✍>

picùljica {ē fem.} *sl-sex* ***Obs*** vagina, cunt <Slav✍>

picúrak {rka masc.} **a.** *sl-sex* ***Obs*** vagina, cunt <Slav✍> **b.** *sl-fea* ***Obs*** young female, girl <Slav✍[*1]>

Picùrić {a (acc. = gen.) masc.} (lit. McCunt) *sl* ***Fac-Obs*** a male nickname <Slav❖>

picùrina {ē fem.} *sl-sex* ***Obs*** large vagina <Slav✍>

pìcuša {ē fem.} **a.** *sl-sex* ***Obs*** small vagina <Slav❖> **b.** *sl-sex* ***Obs*** vagina, cunt <Slav❖[*1]> **c.** *sl* ***Obs-Der*** female, cunt <Slav❖[*2]>

píčak {čka masc.} **a.** *sl-sex* ***Obs*** vagina, cunt <Slav❖> **b.** *sl* ***Obs*** female, cunt <Slav❖[*1]>

pȉčānje {a neut.} (lit. cunting) **1** *sl* ***Obs*** fight (e.g. fist fight) <Slav❖[*1]> **2** *sl-music* ***Obs*** volume (of sound) <Slav❖[*1]> **3** *sl* intensity <Slav❖[*1]>

pičárēnje {a neut.} (lit. cunting) *sl-sex* ***Obs*** looking for females, scoping for babes <Slav❖[*1]>

pičáriti {pìčārīm, rē imperf.} (lit. cunt) *sl-sex* ***Obs*** look for females <Slav❖[*1]>

pìčat {a, o adj.} (lit. cunty) *sl-sex* ***Obs*** having a large vagina <Slav❖[*1]>

pȉčēnje {a neut.} (lit. cunting) **1** *sl-sex* ***Obs*** masturbation <Slav❖[*1]> **2** *sl-sex* ***Obs*** sexual intercourse <Slav❖[*1]> **3** *sl* ***Obs*** intensity <Slav❖[*1]> **4** *sl-auto* ***Obs*** fast driving <Slav❖[*1]> **5** *sl* ***Obs*** fight (e.g. fist fight) <Slav❖[*1]> **6a.** *sl-music* ***Obs*** volume (of sound) <Slav❖[*1]> **b.** *sl-music* ***Obs*** loud music <Slav❖[*2]> **6** *sl-fea* ***Obs*** fast walking <Slav❖[*1]>

pìčetina {ē fem.} /pičètina/ **a.** *sl-sex* ***Obs*** large vagina <Slav❖> **b.** *sl-sex* ***Obs*** vagina, cunt <Slav❖[*1]> **c.** *sl* ***Fac-Obs*** females, cunts <Slav❖[*2]>

pìčetnjāk {a masc.} (lit. cunt shoe) *dia* ***Fac-Obs*** low-quality peasant shoe <Slav❖[*1]>

pìčevina {ē fem.} *sl-sex* ***Obs*** vagina, cunt <Slav❖>

Pìčevina {ē fem.} (lit. Cuntville) *dia* ***Obs*** a place name in Herzegovina <Slav❖[*1]>

Pȉči brâle! {S} (lit. Speed it brother!) *col-dia* used to sanction action, Go ahead! ☞ **pičiti**

pȉčica {ē fem.} *sl-sex* ***Obs*** small vagina <Slav❖>

pȉčīć {pičíća (acc. = gen.) masc.} **a.** *sl-sex* ***Obs*** vagina, cunt <Slav❖> **b.** *sl* ***Obs*** female, cunt <Slav❖[*1]> **c.** *sl-sex* ***Obs*** attractive female <Slav❖[*2]> **d.** *sl-sex* ***Obs*** short attractive female <Slav❖[*3]> **e.** *sl-fea* ***Obs*** very young female, little girl <Slav❖[*4]>

- **pȉčīć ko kolàčić** {NP} (lit. small cunt like a cookie) *sl-sex* ***Obs*** short attractive female

pȉčija {ē fem.} (lit. cunter) *sl* ***Der-Obs*** female, cunt <Slav❖[*1]>

pȉčiti {čīm, čē imperf.} (lit. cunt) **1** *sl-sex* ***Obs*** engage in sexual intercourse with (of a male) <Slav❖[*1]> **2** *sl* ***Obs*** speed (auto, etc.) <Slav❖[*1]> **3** *sl* ***Obs*** live one's life <Slav❖[*1]> **4a.** *sl-music* ***Obs*** play a musical instrument excellently <Slav❖[*1]> **b.** *sl-music* ***Obs*** play rock and roll (in a band) <Slav❖[*2]> **5** *sl-fea* ***Obs*** work quickly <Slav❖[*1]> **6** *sl-fea* ***Obs*** walk quickly <Slav❖[*1]> **7** *sl* travel <Slav❖[*1]>

• **Pȉči brâle!** {S} (lit. Speed it brother!) *col-dia* used to sanction action, Go ahead!

• **pȉčiti niz Jȁhorinu** {VP} (lit. speed down Jahorina mountain) *sl* hurry up, rush

pȉčka {ē fem.; Dat pȉčki} **1.i.aa.** *sl-sex* ***Obs*** vagina, cunt <Slav> **bb.** *sl* ***Obs*** female, cunt <Slav*1> **cc.** *sl-fea* ***Der-Obs*** worthless or mean female, bitch <Slav*2> **ii.** *sl* ***Obs*** mouth <Slav*1> **iii.** *sl-crime* ***Der-Obs*** informer, stoolie, snitch <Slav*2> worthless or despicable male, bum <Slav*3>

• **ko pȉčka u nȍvū kòšulju!** {PP} (lit. like a cunt in a new shirt) SSer *dia* ***Der-Obs*** evil, mean

• **Kȍja si ti pȉčka od čovèka!** {S} (lit. What kind of a cunt of man you are!) SerE *col* ***Off*** used to express disrespect or dissatisfaction, Fuck it!

• **Pȉčka im mâjčina!** {S} (lit. Their mother's cunt to them!) *col* ***Off*** used as a strong curse, Fuck them!

• **Pȉčka im mȁterina!** {S} (lit. Their mother's cunt to them!) *col* ***Off*** used as a strong curse, Fuck them!

• **Pȉčka mu mȁterina!** {S} (lit. His mother's cunt to him!) **a.** *col* ***Off*** used as a strong curse, Fuck him! **b.** *col* used to emphasize one's point, Fuck!

• **Pȉčka mu strȋnina!** {S} (lit. His aunt's cunt to him!) **a.** *col* ***Off*** used as a moderate curse, Fuck him! **b.** used to emphasize one's point, Fuck!

• **Pȉčka ti mȁterina!** {S} (lit. Your mother's cunt to you!) *col* ***Off*** used as a strong curse, Fuck you!

• **Pȉčka ti mȁterina sèljāčkā!** {S} (lit. Your peasant's mother's cunt to you!) *col* ***Off*** used as a strong curse, Fuck you!

• **Pȉčka ti se ògadila!** {S} (lit. Let the cunt become disgusting to you!) *col* ***Off*** used as a moderate curse, Fuck you!

• **Pȉčka ti strínina pȉčko!** {S} (lit. Your aunt's cunt to you, you cunt!) *col* ***Off*** used as a strong curse, Fuck you!

• **pȉčko jèdna** {NP} (lit. you cunt) *col* ***Off*** used as a strong curse, Fuck you!

• **Pȉčko jèdna!** {S} (lit. You cunt!) *col* ***Off*** used as a strong curse, Fuck you!

• **Pȉčko jèdna klȍpavā!** {S} (lit. You lop-cunted cunt!) *col* ***Off*** used as a strong curse, Fuck you!

• **Pȉčko jèdna smȑdljivā!** {S} (lit. You stinking cunt!) *col* ***Off*** used as a strong curse, Fuck you!

• **Pȉčko klȍmpavā!** {S} (lit. You lop-cunted cunt!) *col* ***Off*** used as a strong curse, Fuck you!

• **Pȉčko smȑdljivā!** {S} (lit. You stinking cunt!) *col* ***Off*** used as a strong curse, Fuck you!

• **Pȉčku ću ti polúpati!** {S} (lit. I will smash your cunt!) *col* ***Off*** used to threaten physical violence, I'm gonna beat the shit out of you!

• **Pȉčku ȍko prȍdāvā!** {S} (lit. The eye is selling a cunt!) *dia* ***Obs*** used to express disrespect or dissatisfaction, Fuck it!

• **U pȉčku lêpū mȁterinu!** {S} (lit. To nice mother's cunt!) SerE *col-dia* ***Off*** used to express lack of control over events, What the fuck!

• **U pȉčku mȁterinu!** {S} (lit. To mother's cunt!) *col* ***Obs*** used to express lack of control over events, What the fuck!

pȉčkalīšte {a neut.} (lit. cunt place) *sl-sports* ***Obs*** boxing ring <Slav✣*1>

pȉčkār {a (acc. = gen.) masc.} /pìčkār/ (lit. cunter) *sl-sex* ***Obs*** male sexual partner (of a female) <Slav✣*1>

pȉčkara {ē fem.} (lit. cunter) *sl-sex* ***Obs*** loose woman, slut <Slav✣*1>

pičkàrānje {a neut.} (lit. cunting) **1** *sl-sex* ***Obs*** sexual intercourse <Slav✣*1> **2** *sl-fea* ***Obs*** cursing <Slav✣*1>

pičkàrati {ām, ajū imperf.} (lit. cunt) **1** *sl-sex* ***Obs*** engage in sexual intercourse with (of a male) <Slav✣*1> **2** *sl-fea* ***Obs*** curse <Slav✣*1>

pičkàrati se {ām, ajū imperf. intr.} (lit. cunt each other) *sl* ***Obs*** fight, argue <Slav✣*1>

pičkárēnje {a neut.} (lit. cunting) *sl-sex* ***Obs*** sexual intercourse <Slav✣*1>

pičkàrija {ē fem.} (lit. cunt-thing) *sl-fea* ***Obs*** trifle, thing of little importance or value <Slav✣*1>

pȉčkāroš {a (acc. = gen.) masc.} (lit. cunter) **a.** *sl-sex* ***Obs*** male looking for a loose woman, guy on the make <Slav✣*1> **b.** *sl-sex* ***Obs*** male sexual partner (of a female) <Slav✣*2> **c.** *sl-fea* ***Obs*** womanizer <Slav✣*3> **d.** *sl-fea* ***Obs*** worthless or despicable male <Slav✣*4>

pičkaròšēnje {a neut.} (lit. cunting) *sl-sex* ***Obs*** sexual intercourse <Slav✣*1>

pičkaròšiti {šīm, šē imperf.} (lit. cunt) *sl-sex* ***Obs*** engage in sexual intercourse with (of a male) <Slav✣*1>

pȉčkati se {ām, ajū imperf. intr.} **1** *sl-gamble* ***Obs*** play marbles <Slav✣*1> **2** *sl-gamble* ***Obs*** drop out of a game <Slav✣*1>

pičkáža {ē fem.} (lit. cunting) *sl* ***Obs*** fight (e.g. fist fight) <Slav✣*1>

pičkètina {ē fem.} **1** *sl-sex* ***Obs*** large vagina <Slav✣> **2** *sl-sex* ***App-Obs*** attractive female <Slav✣>

pȉčkica {ē fem.} **a.** *sl-sex* ***Obs*** small vagina <Slav✣> **b.** *sl-sex* ***Obs*** vagina, cunt <Slav✣*1> **c.** *sl-fea* ***Der-Obs*** coward, chicken <Slav✣*2> **d.** ***Der-Obs*** stupid or mentally deficient person <Slav✣*3>

pìčkīle {a masc.} *sl-sex* ***Obs*** male sexual partner (of a female) <Slav❖*1>

pi̍čkīn dȉm {NP} (lit. cunt's smoke) *col* ***Obs*** unimportant issue or object: *Akra je pičkin dim za Bagdad. Accra is fucking nothing in comparison with Baghdad.* ☞ **dim**

pi̍čkīn dȕšmanin {NP} (lit. cunt's enemy) *sl-sex* ***Fac-Obs*** very potent male ☞ **dušmanin**

pi̍čkina vòda {NP} (lit. cunt's water) *col* ***Obs*** nothing at all ☞ **voda**

pi̍čkino grôzje {NP} (lit. cunt's berries) *dia* ***Obs*** nothing at all ☞ **grozje**

pi̍čkino vesélje {NP} (lit. cunt's joy) *dia* ***Obs*** nothing at all ☞ **veselje**

pičkòba {ē fem.} (lit. cunter) *sl* ***Obs*** female, cunt <Slav❖*1>

pi̍čkobaša {ē fem. & masc.} (lit. cunt ruler) **1** *sl-sex* ***Obs*** male sexual partner (of a female) <Slav❖*1> **2** *sl-fea* ***Obs*** strong female <Slav❖*1>

pi̍čkodēr {a masc.} (lit. cunt tearer) *sl-sex* ***Fac-Obs*** penis, dick, prick <Slav❖*1>

pičkojèbina {ē fem.} (lit. cunt fucking) **a.** *sl-sex* ***Obs*** sexual intercourse <Slav❖*1> **b.** *sl-fea* ***Obs*** remote and unpleasant place <Slav❖*2>

pi̍čkolīz {a (acc. = gen.) masc.} *sl-sex* ***Obs*** cunnilingus <Slav❖>

pičkolízac {sca (acc. = gen.) masc.} **a.** *sl-sex* ***Obs*** male who engages in cunnilingus <Slav❖> **b.** *sl-fea* ***Obs*** ingratiator, brownnoser <Slav❖*1>

píčkonja {ē masc.} (lit. cunter) **a.** *sl-sex* ***Obs*** male sexual partner (of a female) <Slav❖*1> **b.** *sl-fea* ***Obs*** worthless or despicable male <Slav❖*4>

pi̍čkoprēž {a (acc. = gen.) masc.} (lit. cunt puller) *sl-sex* ***Obs*** male sexual partner (of a female) <Slav❖*1>

pičkoprèžina {ē fem.} (lit. cunt puller) *sl-sex* ***Obs*** male sexual partner (of a female) <Slav❖*1>

Píčkovac {vca masc.} (lit. Cunt's Spring) *dia* ***Obs*** name of a water source in Serbia <Slav❖*1>

Pi̍čkovden {a masc.} (lit. Cunt Day) *sl* ***Fac*** the day which never comes <Slav❖*1>

pi̍čkulja {ē fem.} (lit. cunter) **a.** *sl-sex* ***Obs*** loose woman, slut <Slav❖*1> **b.** *sl* ***Obs*** female, cunt <Slav❖*1>

pičkùljina {ē fem.} (lit. big cunt) **a.** *sl-sex* ***Obs*** loose woman, slut <Slav❖*1> **b.** *sl* ***Obs*** female, cunt <Slav❖*2>

pičkùrina {ē fem.} *sl-sex* ***Obs*** large vagina <Slav❖>

pìčkuša {ē fem.} **a.** *sl-sex* ***Obs*** loose woman, slut <Slav❖*1> **b.** *sl* ***Obs*** female <Slav❖*2>

pičórak {rka (acc. = gen.) masc.} (lit. cunter) *sl-fea* ***Der-Obs*** short female <Slav❖*1>

pi̍čos {a masc.} (lit. cunter) *sl* ***Obs*** female, cunt <Slav❖*1>

pi̍čuga {ē fem.; Dat pìčugi} *sl-drink* ***Obs*** beer <Slav❖*1>

pičúljak {ljka (acc. = gen.) masc.} **a.** *sl-sex* ***Obs*** vagina, cunt <Slav❖> **b.** *sl-sex* ***Obs*** attractive female <Slav❖*1>

pičúrak {rka masc.} **a.** *sl-sex* ***Obs*** small vagina <Slav❖> **b.** *sl-fea* ***Obs*** young female, girl <Slav❖*1>

pi̍čvajs {a masc.} **a.** *sl-sex* ***Obs*** vagina, cunt <Slav❖> **b.** *sl-sex* ***Obs*** sexual intercourse <Slav❖*1> **c.i.** *sl-auto* ***Obs*** speeding (auto, etc.) <Slav❖*2> **ii.** ***Obs*** loud music <Slav❖*2>

pi̍čvajz {a masc.} **1** *sl* ***Obs*** fight (e.g. fist fight) <Slav❖*1> **2** *sl-fea* ***Obs*** mess, disorder, disturbance <Slav❖*1>

píće *See the following*

- **píće za mladíće** {NP} (lit. a drink to the boys) *sl-drink* another round (of alcoholic drinks)
- **píće za spermíće** {NP} (lit. a drink to little sperms) *sl* ***Fac*** Coca-Cola, coke

pićénce {a neut.} /pićénce /eta neut./ *sl-drink* drink (usu. alcohol) <Slav❖>

pićóka {ē fem.; Dat pićóki} **a.** *sl-sex* ***Obs*** vagina, cunt <Slav✍> **b.** *sl* ***Obs*** female, cunt <Slav✍*1>

pićókara {ē fem.} **a.** *sl-sex* ***Obs*** vagina, cunt <Slav✍> **b.** *sl* ***Obs*** female, cunt <Slav✍*1>

pȉf {excl.} *col* the sound made by slapping, slap <Slav>

pȉf-pȁf {excl.} *col* the sound made by slapping, slap <Slav>

pìfla {ē fem.} *col* whistle <Slav>

pȉg {a +ov (ext. pl) masc.; Nom Pl pìgovi} (lit. pig) *sl-drugs* drug addict who takes all kinds of narcotic drugs <Eng*1>

pi̍gati {ām, ajū biasp.} (lit. pig) *sl-fea* make nervous, get on one's nerves <Eng❖*1>

pi̍gati se {ām, ajū biasp. intr.} (lit. pig oneself) *sl-fea* get angry <Eng❖*1>

pìgist {a (acc. = gen.) masc.} (lit. pigist) *sl-sex* ***Obs*** male homosexual, gay <Eng❖*1>

pìgista {ē masc.} (lit. pigist) *sl-sex* ***Obs*** male homosexual, gay <Eng❖*1>

pi̍glu {adj.; perm} [std. = glupi] *sl* unintelligent, stupid, dumb <Slav✍>

pȉh {excl.} 1 *col* the sound made by spitting, phew <Slav> 2 *col* used to lure chicken <Slav> 3 *col* used to express disappointment <Slav>

pȉha {excl.} 1 *col* the sound made by spitting, phew <Slav> 2 *col* used to lure chicken <Slav>

pìjac {a masc.} [std. = pijaca] *col* market <Ita✍>

pìjaca *See the following*

- **bùvljā pìjaca** {NP} (lit. flea market) *sl-sstu* ***Fac*** high-school students on break

pìjača {ē fem.} **a.** *sl-drink* alcoholic beverages <Slav> **b.** *sl-drink* drinking (alcohol) <Slav[*1]>

pìjan *See the following*

- **mòrtus pìjan** {AdjP} (lit. dead drunk) *col* very drunk, dead drunk
- **mòrtus pjȁn** {AdjP} (lit. dead drunk) *col* very drunk, dead drunk
- **mȑtav pìjan** {AdjP} *col* very drunk, dead drunk
- **pìjan ko avìōn** {AdjP} (lit. as drunk as an airplane) *sl-drink* very drunk, drunk as a skunk
- **pìjan ko cȓnā zèmlja** {AdjP} (lit. as drunk as the black earth) *sl-drink* very drunk, drunk as a skunk
- **pìjan ko čȅp** {AdjP} (lit. as drunk as a cork) *sl-drink* very drunk, drunk as a skunk
- **pìjan ko ćúskija** {AdjP} (lit. as drunk as a crowbar) *sl-drink* very drunk, drunk as a skunk
- **pìjan ko déva** {AdjP} (lit. as drunk as a camel) Cro *sl-drink* very drunk, drunk as a skunk
- **pìjan ko dȕpe** {AdjP} (lit. as drunk as an ass) *sl-drink* very drunk, drunk as a skunk
- **pìjan ko gùzica** {AdjP} (lit. as drunk as an ass) *sl-drink* ***Obs*** very drunk, drunk as a skunk
- **pìjan ko lȅtva** {AdjP} (lit. as drunk as a plank) *sl-drink* very drunk, drunk as a skunk
- **pìjan ko mâjka** {AdjP} (lit. as drunk as a mother) *sl-drink* very drunk, drunk as a skunk
- **pìjan ko Rȕs** {AdjP} (lit. as drunk as a Russian) *sl-drink* very drunk, drunk as a skunk
- **pìjan ko svínja** {AdjP} (lit. as drunk as a pig) *sl-drink* very drunk, drunk as a skunk
- **pìjan ko tréska** {AdjP} (lit. as drunk as a splinter) *sl-drink* very drunk, drunk as a skunk
- **pìjan ko zèmlja** {AdjP} (lit. as drunk as earth) *sl-drink* very drunk, drunk as a skunk

pìjanā {ē fem. (adj. decl.)} (lit. drunk) *sl-sex* ***Fac*** frigid female <Slav[*1]>

pijánac {nca (acc. = gen.) masc.} *sl-drink* alcoholic, drunk <Slav❖>

pìjānčiti {čīm, čē imperf.} *sl-drink* drink (alcohol) in large quantities <Slav[*1]>

pijàndura {ē masc.} *sl-drink* alcoholic, drunk <Slav❖>

pìjanī Čȅh {AdjP} (lit. drunk Czech) *sl* streetcar line ☞ **Čeh**

pìjanī tȕljān {AdjP} (lit. drunk seal) Cro *sl-fea* inhabitant of the countryside, hick, bumpkin ☞ **tuljan**

pìjanis {a (acc. = gen.) masc.} *sl-drink* alcoholic, drunk <Slav✍>

pijànist {a (acc. = gen.) masc.} (lit. piano player) *sl-drink* alcoholic, drunk <Slav✍[*1]>

pìjānka {ē fem.} **a.** *sl-drink* drinking party <Slav[*1]> **b.** *sl* party (social gathering) <Slav[*2]>

pìjat {a masc.} Med *col-dia* plate, dish <Ita[*1]>

pȉjavica {ē fem.} (lit. leech) **a.** *sl-fea* boring person, bore <Slav[*1]> **b.** *sl-sex* procurer, pimp <Slav[*2]>

pijavȉška {ē fem.; Dat pijavȉški} (lit. small leech) *sl-drink* alcoholic, drunk <Slav-Gyp✍>

Pȉjēm pîvo, jèbe mi se žîvo! {S} (lit. I've been drinking my beer, and I don't give a shit about anything!) *col* ***Obs*** used to express indifference, I don't give a shit! ☞ **piti**

pȉjkati {ām, ajū imperf.} 1 *sl* steal a glance, peep <Slav> 2 *col* chirp (of a chick) <Slav>

pìjoža {adj.} *sl-fea* shy

pȉjū {excl.} *col* the sound made by a chick, chirp <Slav>

pijujúkati {jùjūčēm, jūčū imperf.} 1 *col* peep (sound) <Slav> 2 *col* chirp (of a chick) <Slav[*1]>

pȉjūk {a masc.} **a.** *col* the sound made by a small bird, tweet <Slav> **b.** *col* peep (sound) <Slav[*1]>

pijúkānje {a neut.} **a.** *col* chirp (of a chick) <Slav[*1]> **b.** *col* peeping, looking at others <Slav[*2]>

pijúkati {pìjūčēm, pìjūčū imperf.} **a.** *col* chirp (of a chick) <Slav> **b.** *col* peep, look at others <Slav[*1]>

pijùkav {a, o adj.} *col* peeping, looking at others <Slav[*1]>

pijúkavac {jùkāvca (acc. = gen.) masc.} /pijùkavac/ *col* a kind of peeping bird (Eudromias morinellus or Charadrius pluvialis) <Slav❖[*1]>

pȉk [1] {excl.} 1 *col* used to stop an action, that's enough <Slav> 2 *col* that doesn't count <Slav[*1]>

pȉk [2] {pìka +ov (ext. pl) masc.; Nom Pl pìkovi} 1 *col* disaffection toward <Slav> 2 *col* pick on somebody <Slav>

- **iz pìka** {PP} *col* right away, now
- **u pìku** {PP} 1 *sl* used as a strong affirmative response, sure 2 *sl* right away, now

píka {ē fem.; Dat píki} *sl-sex* ***Fam-Obs*** vagina, cunt <Slav✍>

pȉkati {ām, ajū imperf.} **a.** *sl* kick, strike <Slav> **b.** *sl-sports* play soccer <Slav*1>
• **pȉkati lȍptu** {VP} (lit. kick the ball) *sl-sports* play soccer

pȉkati se {ām, ajū imperf. intr.} *sl-drugs* stick in a syringe needle <Slav⁘>

pȉkavac {kāvca masc.} *col* cigarette butt <Slav*1>

pȉkavac {kāvca (acc. = gen.) masc.} (lit. cigarette butt) **1** *sl-fea* little boy, kid <Slav*1> **2** *sl-sex* small penis

pȉkčer {a masc.} (lit. picture) *sl* photo <Eng>

pȉkica {ē fem.} *sl-auto* streetcar trailer

pȉklja {ē fem.} *sl-auto* Fiat 850 sport (make of car)

pìknik {a masc.} *col* picnic <Eng>

pȉknuti {nēm, nū perf.} **a.** *sl* kick, strike <Ger⁘*1> **b.i.** *sl-sex* engage in sexual intercourse with (of a male) **ii.** *sl* die, kick the bucket

pikolína {ē fem.} *sl* female <Slav✍*1>

pȉkolo {adj.} *sl-fea* small, little <Ita>

pȉks {a +ev (ext. pl) masc.; Nom Pl pìksevi} *sl-drugs* small dose of narcotic drugs <Eng✍*1>

pȉksa {ē fem.} *sl* head <Ger*1>

piksàjzla {ē fem.} /piksájzla/ *sl* ashtray <Ger✍*1>

pìksla [1] {excl.} (lit. ashtray) *sl* used to make somebody go away <Ger*1>

pìksla [2] {ē fem.} **a.** *sl* ashtray <Ger> **b.i.** *sl-gamble* apartment used for gambling <Ger*1> **ii.** *sl-fea* short obese female <Ger*1>

pikslàjza [1] {ē fem.} *sl* ashtray <Ger*1>

pikslájza [2] {ē fem.} *sl* ashtray <Ger✍>

pìksle {ī fem. pl.} *sl-fea* thick eyeglasses <Ger*1>

pikslijána {ē fem.} *sl* ashtray <Ger✍>

pikslijàšica {ē fem.} *sl* ashtray <Ger✍>

pȉksna {ē fem.} *sl-crafts* cartridge case <Ger✍>

pìkzibner {adj.} *sl-fea* worthless

píla {ē fem.} (lit. saw) **1** *sl* female <Slav*1> **2** *sl-sex* sexual intercourse <Slav*1> **3** *sl-auto* motorcycle <Slav*1> **4** *sl-music* violin <Slav*1> **5** *sl-fea* boring person, bore <Slav*1>
• **krȗžnā píla** {NP} (lit. circular saw) *sl* opera singer

pilàna {ē fem.} (lit. saw-mill) **1** *sl* boredom <Slav*1> **2** *sl* teasing <Slav*1>

pȉlār {pilára (acc. = gen.) masc.} (lit. sawer) *sl-sex* ***Fac*** boring sexual partner <Slav*1>

pìlārnica {ē fem.} (lit. saw-mill) *sl-sex* ***Fac*** place intended for sexual intercourse <Slav*1>

pilàvče {eta neut.} *sl* dinar (Yugoslav currency unit)

pìlāvka {ē fem.} *sl* gold coin

pȉle {excl.} (lit. my chick) *col* ***Fam*** used to address a person in an intimate manner, honey <Slav*1>

pilèćina {ē fem.} [std. = piletina] *dia-col* chicken meat <Slav✍>

pílēnje {a neut.} (lit. sawing) **1** *sl-sex* ***Fac-Obs*** sexual intercourse <Slav*1> **2** *sl-fea* boredom <Slav*1>

pìletina {e fem.} (lit. chicken meat) **1** *sl* group of females <Slav*1> **2** *sl* female, chick <Slav*1>

pȉlić {a masc.} (lit. chicken) *sl-music* synthesizer <Slav*1>

pilìćār {pilićára (acc. = gen.) masc.} (lit. chicken farm owner) **1** *sl-crime* petty thief <Slav*1> **2** *sl-auto* local bus or train (which makes frequent stops) <Slav*1>

pilićárēnje {a neut.} *sl-fea* petty trade <Slav⁘*1>

pilićáriti {lìćārīm, rē imperf. intr.} *col* do petty trade <Slav⁘*1>

pilìćārka {ē fem.; Dat pilìćārki} (lit. poultry woman) *sl-fea* lazy or shiftless female, bum, good for nothing <Slav*1>

pilìćārnīk {a masc.} (lit. chicken farm) *sl-auto* train from Belgrade, Serbia to Split, Croatia <Slav*1>

píliti {līm, lē imperf.} (lit. saw) **1** *sl-sex* ***Fac-Obs*** engage in sexual intercourse with (of a male), screw <Slav*1> **2** *sl-fea* annoy, bother, pester <Slav*1>
• **píliti zȕbove** {VP} (lit. saw one's teeth) *sl-sex* French kiss

pȉlka {ē fem.} (lit. small saw) *sl* female

pȉlke {i fem. pl.} *sl* money

pȉlo {excl.} *col* used to lure chicken <Slav>

pìlōt *See the following*
• **próbnī pìlōt** {NP} (lit. test pilot) *sl-crime* car thief

pilotírati {lòtīrām, lotírajū biasp.} (lit. pilot) **a.** *sl-fea* flirt <Fre*1> **b.** *sl-fea* cheat on one's lover or spouse <Fre*2>

pìlove {lōvā masc. pl.} *sl* money

pìlovina {ē fem.} (lit. saw-dust) *sl-fea* senile male <Slav*1>

pȉlula {ē fem.} /pìlula/ (lit. pill) *sl* female <Lat*1>

píljak {ljka masc.} **a.** *col-dia* gravel, pebbles <Slav> **b.** *sl* coin <Slav[*1]>

piljáve {ī fem. pl.} *sl-arch* money

píljiti {ljīm, ljē imperf. intr.} *sl-fea* stare at, be fixated on <Slav[*1]>

pȉljkati {ām, ajū biasp.} (lit. throw pebbles) *sl-gamble* gamble <Slav[*1]>

Pȉm Pȅk Pȃõ{NP} (lit. the-Cock-Has-Fallen) *sl-sex* impotent ☞ Pao

pȉmpāč {a masc.} *sl-sex* ***Obs*** penis, dick, prick <Ger✍[*1]>

pìmpek [1] {a (acc. = gen.) masc.} **1** *sl* male, guy <Ger✍[*1]> 2 *sl-fea* boring male, boring dude <Ger✍[*1]>

pìmpek [2] {a masc.} *sl-sex* ***Obs*** penis, dick, prick <Ger✍>

pimpèkdžija {ē fem.} *sl-fea* strange person, weirdo <Ger-NE[*1]>

pȉmpić {a masc.} *sl-sex* ***Obs*** penis, dick, prick <Ger✍[*1]>

pȉmplānje {a neut.} **1** *sl-fea* prolonged and meaningless talk, blabber, chatter <Ger[*1]> 2 *sl-sports* boring game (soccer, etc.) <Ger[*1]> 3 *sl-fea* slow work <Ger[*1]>

pȉmplati {ām, ajū imperf.} **1** *sl-fea* talk persistently and meaninglessly, blabber, chatter <Ger[*1]> 2 *sl-sports* play monotonously (soccer, etc.) <Ger[*1]> 3 *sl-fea* work slowly <Ger[*1]>

pȉmpler {a (acc. = gen.) masc.} **1** *sl-fea* overly talkative person, chatterbox <Ger[*1]> 2 *sl-sports* incompetent player (soccer, etc.) <Ger[*1]> 3 *sl-fea* slow worker <Ger[*1]>

pȉmplovānje {a neut.} 1 *sl-fea* prolonged and meaningless talk, blabber, chatter <Ger[*1]> 2 *sl-fea* monotonous game (soccer, etc.) <Ger[*1]>

pȉmplovati {lujēm, lujū imperf.} **1** *sl-fea* talk persistently and meaninglessly, blabber, chatter <Ger[*1]> 2 *sl-sports* play monotonously (soccer, etc.) <Ger[*1]>

pȉmzlati {ām, ajū biasp.} *sl-sex* ***Obs*** rub one's partner's vagina with one's penis <Ger[*1]>

pȉnam {a masc.} *sl* ashtray

pȉngāč {a masc.} *sl-sports* ping-pong <Eng✍>

pȉngāć {a masc.} *sl-sports* ping-pong <Eng✍>

pȉngić {a masc.} *sl-sports* ping-pong <Eng✍>

pìngiš {a masc.} *sl-sports* ping-pong <Eng✍>

pìngvīn {pingvína (acc. = gen.) masc.; Voc pȉngvīne} (lit. penguin) 1 *sl* ***Fac*** nun, penguin <Lat[*1]> 2 *sl-fea* ***Der*** stupid or mentally deficient person <Lat[*1]> 3 *sl* ***Fac*** waiter <Lat[*1]>

- **pingvíni pȁdajū ȕ nesvēst** {S} (lit. the penguins are fainting) SerE *col* very cold

pȉnka {ē fem.; Dat pȉnki} *sl-gamble* money which goes to the host

pìnkāroš {a (acc. = gen.) masc.} *sl-gamble* person who rents out his/her apartment for gambling

pìnkl {a masc.} *sl* bundle <Ger[*1]>

pȉnklić {a masc.} *sl* slope of a hill <Ger✣[*1]>

Pinȍkio {a masc.} /Pinòkio/ (lit. Pinocchio) *sl-sex* ***Fac-Obs*** boy's penis <ItaO[*1]>

pȉnta {ē fem.} (lit. pint) *sl* head <Eng[*1]>

pìnjāta {ē fem.} *dia* pan, pot <Ita>

pìnjave {ī fem. pl.} *sl* money

piònīr {pioníra (acc. = gen.) masc.} (lit. pioneer) *sl-fea* young boy <Fre[*1]>

Pionírac {rca masc.} Ser *sl* the Pionir dome in Belgrade, Serbia <Fre✍>

piònīrka {a (acc. = gen.) masc.} (lit. pioneer) *sl-fea* young female, girl <Fre[*1]>

pípa {ē fem.} **a.** *col* faucet <Lat> **b.i.** *sl-sex* cunnilingus <Lat[*1]> **ii.** *sl-sex* fellatio <Lat[*1]> **iii.** *sl-drink* drinking <Lat[*1]>

pípak {pka masc.} (lit. tentacle) **a.** *sl* finger <Slav[*1]> **b.** *sl* glove <Slav[*2]>

pȉpānje {a neut.} (lit. touching) *sl-sex* sexual foreplay, petting, feeling up <Slav[*1]>

pìpek {a masc.} *sl-sex* ***Obs*** boy's penis <Ger✣[*1]>

pȉpī {īja masc.} **1** *sl* Fanta juice <Slav[*1]> 2 *sl-sex* urinating <Slav[*1]>

pȉpica {ē fem.} *sl-sex* ***Obs*** vagina, cunt <Slav[*1]>

pipiȑpī {īja masc.} *sl-sex* ***Obs*** penis, dick, prick <Slav[*1]>

pȉpničārka {ē fem.; Dat pȉpničārki} *sl-sex* ***Obs*** female who rubs the penis <Slav✣[*1]>

pȉpos {a masc.} *sl* shoe <Slav✍>

pȉps *See the following*

- **mâli pȉps** {NP} (lit. small pips) *sl-drugs* small piece of hashish

pìrinač {nča masc.} (lit. rice) SerE *sl* pearl (jewelry) <NE[*1]>

píriti {pîrīm, rē imperf.} *col* blow (e.g. to cool off hot soup) <Slav[*1]>

- **píriti vȁtru** {VP} (lit. blow fire) *sl* cause unrest

pirlìtati {ām, ajū imperf. intr.} *col* behave or talk indecently <Slav[*1]>

pirot'ānac {nca (acc. = gen.) masc.} Ser *sl-fea* inhabitant of Southern Serbia <Slav✍>

pȉrs {a +ev (ext. pl) masc.; Nom Pl pìrsevi} *sl* body piercing <Eng>

pȉs [1] {excl.} *col* used to drive away a cat <Slav>

pȉs [2] {a (acc. = gen.) +ev (ext. pl) masc.; Nom Pl písevi} **a.** *sl-fea* miser, tightwad, skinflint **b.** *sl-crime* informant, stoolie **c.** *sl-fea* worthless or despicable person

pîs [3] {a +ev (ext. pl) masc.; Nom Pl písevi} *sl-drugs* small quantity of narcotic drugs <Eng[*1]>

pȉs [4] {adj.} *sl-fea* unattractive, ugly

pîsak {ska masc.} (lit. mouthpiece) *sl-sex* ***Fac-Obs*** penis, dick, prick <Slav[*1]>

písalica {ē fem.} (lit. writing thing) *sl* pencil <Slav❖[*1]>

pisánac {nca masc.} (lit. writing thing) *sl* letter (correspondence) <Slav❖[*1]>

pisànija {ē fem.} *col* scribbling <Slav❖[*1]>

písati *See the following*

- **píši kȕći pròpalo** {VP} (lit. write home that it has failed) *col* used to express impossibility or unfavorable outcome
- **píši pròpalo** {VP} (lit. write that it has failed) *col* used to express impossibility or unfavorable outcome

piskàralo {a neut.} (lit. scribbler) **1** *sl-media* journalist <Slav❖[*1]> **2** *sl* writer <Slav❖[*1]> **3** *sl-crime* informant, stoolie <Slav❖[*1]>

písmo {a neut.} (lit. letter) *col* tails (of a coin) <Slav[*1]>

- **písmo-gláva** {NP} (lit. heads or tails) *sl-sex* ***Fac-Obs*** 69 (sexual position)
- **svêtō písmo** {NP} (lit. Holy Bible) *sl* law

písmo-gláva {excl.} (lit. letter-head) *col* heads or tails (of a coin) <Slav[*1]>

pȉsnuti {nēm, nū perf.} **1** *col* talk, have a conversation <Slav[*1]> **2** *col* call (phone, etc.) <Slav[*1]>

pȉsta {ē fem.} (lit. runway) *sl-mil* building corridor <Fre>

pȉš [1] {excl.} *col* the sound made by urination <Slav>

pîš [2] {a +ev (ext. pl) masc.; Nom Pl pîševi} (lit. piss) *col* ridiculous thing, absurd event <Slav[*1]>

- **žîvī pîš** {NP} (lit. living piss) *sl-fea* ***Obs*** highly humorous event or person

pȉš-pȉš {a masc.} *sl-sex* ***Fam*** urinating, peeing <Slav[*1]>

píša {ē fem.} **a.** *sl-sex* ***Fam*** urine, pee <Slav❖> **b.i.** *sl-sex* ***Fam*** vagina <Slav❖[*1]> **ii.** *sl* ***Fam*** female <Slav[*2]> **c.** *sl-sex* boy's penis <Slav[*1]>

pìšaća {ē fem.} *sl-sex* ***Obs*** urine, piss <Slav>

pìšaćka {ē fem.; Dat pìšaćki} *sl-sex* ***Obs*** urine, piss <Slav>

píšak {ška masc.} *sl-sex* ***Obs*** urine, piss <Slav❖>

pìšaka {ē fem.} *sl-sex* ***Obs*** urine, piss <Slav>

pìšalo {a neut.} (lit. pisser) *sl-sex* ***Obs*** penis, pisser <Slav❖[*1]>

Pȉšām ti se u ústa! {S} (lit. I piss in your mouth!) *col* ***Off*** used as a strong curse, Piss on you! ☞ **pišati se**

pišánac {nca (acc. = gen.) masc.} (lit. pisser) *sl-sex* ***Obs*** urinator, pisser <Slav❖>

pȉšānī {ā, ō adj.} (lit. pissed on) *sl-fea* ***Obs*** worthless <Slav❖[*1]>

pišánjak {njka masc.} *sl-sex* ***Obs*** urine, piss <Slav❖>

pìšānje {a neut.} **a.** *sl-sex* ***Obs*** urinating, pissing <Slav> **b.** *sl* ***Obs*** humor <Slav[*1]> **c.** *sl-fea* ***Obs*** ridiculous thing, absurd event <Slav[*2]>

pišaónica {ē fem.} (lit. pissing place) **a.** *sl-sex* ***Obs*** bathroom <Slav❖[*1]> **b.** *sl-fea* ***Obs*** mess, disorder, disturbance <Slav❖[*2]>

pišapȕšī {ija masc.} (lit. pissing is smoking) *sl-sex* ***Obs*** school bathroom <Slav✍>

pìšara {ē fem.} (lit. pisser) *sl-drink* ***Obs*** low-quality brandy <Slav❖[*1]>

pìšati {ām, ajū imperf.} *sl-sex* ***Obs*** urinate, piss <Slav>

- **pìšati bùbrege** {VP} (lit. piss one's kidneys) *sl-fea* work hard
- **pìšati krv** {VP} (lit. piss blood) *sl-fea* work hard
- **pìšati kroz sȉto** {VP} (lit. piss through a sieve) *sl-sex* ***Obs*** suffer from syphilis, have the pox

pìšati se {ām, ajū imperf. intr.} *sl-sex* ***Obs*** urinate, piss <Slav[*1]>

- **Pȉšām ti se u ústa!** {S} (lit. I piss in your mouth!) *col* ***Off*** used as a strong curse, Piss on you!

pȉšēnje {a neut.} *sl-sex* ***Obs*** urinating, pissing <Slav✍>

píši kȕći pròpalo {VP} (lit. write home that it has failed) *col* used to express impossibility or unfavorable outcome ☞ **pisati**

píši pròpalo {VP} (lit. write that it has failed) *col* used to express impossibility or unfavorable outcome ☞ **pisati**

pȉšica {ē fem.} (lit. little pisser) *sl-sex* ***Obs*** vagina, cunt <Slav❖[*1]>

pȉšicav {a, o adj.} (lit. pissed on) *sl-fea* ***Obs*** worthless <**Slav**>

pȉšičan {čna, čno adj.} (lit. pissing) *sl-fea* ***Obs*** very funny <**Slav**[*1]>

pìšičav {a, o adj.} (lit. pissed on) *sl-fea* ***Obs*** worthless <**Slav**>

pìšigaća {ē masc.} (lit. pant pisser) *sl-sex* ***Der-Obs*** urinator , pisser <**Slav**❖[*1]>

pišijáda {ē fem.} (lit. pissing) **a.** *sl-fea* ***Obs*** fun <**Slav**✍[*1]> **b.** *sl-fea* ***Obs*** ridiculous thing, absurd event <**Slav** ✍[*2]>

pȉšiti {šīm, šē imperf.} *sl-sex* ***Obs*** urinate, piss <**Slav**✍>

pȉškā pantalȉška {VP} (lit. Your pants are pissing.) *sl* used to warn one's interlocutor that his zipper is open ☞ **piškati**

pìškan {a, o adj.} *sl* hit in marbles <**Slav**✍>

piškàrati {ām, ajū imperf.} *sl-sex* ***Obs*** urinate, piss <**Slav**❖>

pȉškati {ām, ajū imperf.} *sl-sex* ***Obs*** urinate, piss <**Slav**❖>
- **pȉškā pantalȉška** {VP} (lit. Your pants are pissing.) *sl* used to warn one's interlocutor that his zipper is open

pȉškati se {ām, ajū imperf.} (lit. piss) *sl-gamble* ***Obs*** leave a game <**Slav**❖>

pȉškavac *See the following*
- **slàdak pȉškavac** {NP} (lit. sweet pisser) *sl-sex* sexual intercourse

pȉškica {ē fem.} (lit. little pisser) *sl-sex* ***Obs*** vagina, cunt <**Slav**❖[*1]>

píškiti {kīm, kē biasp.} *sl-sex* ***Fam*** urinate, pee <**Slav**❖>

piškopéja {ē fem.} (lit. Pissville) *sl-fea* ***Obs*** a place of extreme wretchedness or squalor, hellhole <**Slav** ❖>

pìškūr {pìškura (acc. = gen.) masc.} (lit. piss-cock) *sl-fea* ***Der-Obs*** coward, chicken <**Slav**❖[*1]>

pȉšljiv {a, o adj.} (lit. pissed on) *sl-fea* ***Obs*** worthless <**Slav**>

pȉšna {ē fem.} **a.** *sl-sex* ***Obs*** urinator, pisser <**Slav**❖[*1]> **b.** *sl-fea* ***Der-Obs*** evil female, bitch <**Slav**❖[*1]>

pȉšnūt {a, o adj.} (lit. pissed on) *sl-fea* ***Der-Obs*** insane, nuts <**Slav**❖[*1]>

pȉšnuti {nēm, nū perf.} *sl-sex* ***Obs*** urinate, piss <**Slav** ❖>

píšo [1] {a (acc. = gen.) masc.; Voc pîšo} (lit. pisser) *sl-fea* ***Obs*** beloved child, apple of one's eye <**Slav**❖[*1]>

Pȉšo [2] {a (acc. = gen.) masc.; Voc Pȉšo} (lit. Piss) *dia* ***Fac-Obs*** Radisav (man's name) <**Slav**❖[*1]> ☞ **Pišov**

pišóka {ē fem.; Dat pišóki} **a.** *sl-sex* ***Obs*** urine, piss <**Slav**❖> **b.** *sl-drink* wine with soda <**Slav**❖[*1]>

píšonja {ē fem.} *sl-sex* ***Obs*** urinator , pisser <**Slav**❖[*1]>

pišôre {excl.} *sl* nonsense <**Slav**✍[*1]>

Píšōv {a, o adj.} (lit. Piss') *dia* ***Fac-Obs*** Radisav's (referring to the proper name) <**Slav**❖[*1]> ☞ **Pišo**

Pȉšta {ē masc.} (lit. Pista: a common Hungarian name 'Steve') *sl-fea* ***Der*** Hungarian (person) <**HunO**[*1]>

pȉštōlj {pištólja (acc. = gen.) masc.} (lit. gun) *sl-fea* person who is broke (financially) <**Ita**[*1]>

pȉšulja {ē fem.} (lit. pisser) **a.** *sl-sex* ***Obs*** vagina, cunt <**Slav**❖[*1]> **b.** *sl* ***Obs*** female, cunt <**Slav**❖[*2]> **c.** *sl* ***Der-Obs*** girl <**Slav**❖[*3]>

pìšura {ē fem.} (lit. pisser) **a.** *sl-sex* ***Obs*** vagina, cunt <**Slav**❖[*1]> **b.** *sl* ***Obs*** female, cunt <**Slav**❖[*2]>

pišúrak {rka masc.} *sl-sex* ***Obs*** urine, piss <**Slav**✍>

pišùrija {ē fem.} (lit. pissing) *sl-fea* ***Obs*** ridiculous thing, absurd event <**Slav** ❖[*1]>

Pitàgora {ē fem.} (lit. Pythagoras) *sl-drink* waiter <**GreO**[*1]>

pȉtār {a (acc. = gen.) masc.} (lit. pie-eater) *sl-sports* fan of Sarajevo (a soccer team in Sarajevo, Bosnia) <**Slav**✍[*1]>

pítati *See the following*
- **kad te lêpo pîtām** {S} (lit. when I ask you nicely) SerE *col* used to emphasize one's request, pretty please
- **kad te lijèpo pîtām** {S} (lit. when I ask you nicely) *col* used to emphasize one's request, pretty please
- **kȍ te pîtā** {S} (lit. who asks you) *col* used to indicate that one's interlocutor is not authorized to make decisions
- **Pîtāj si čȕk!** {S} (lit. Ask your prick!) *dia* used to express lack of information
- **Pîtāj si Đóku!** {S} (lit. Ask your Dick!) SSer *dia* used to express lack of information
- **Pîtāj si ga!** {S} (lit. Ask it!) SSer *dia* used to express lack of information
- **Pîtāj si kȕrac!** {S} (lit. Ask your prick!) SSer *dia* ***Obs*** used to express lack of information
- **Pítām si kâr!** {S} (lit. I am asking my prick!) *dia* used to express lack of information
- **Pîtām si kûr!** {S} (lit. I am asking my prick!) *dia* used to express lack of information
- **Pîtām si mòjēga!** {S} (lit. I am asking my *prick*!) *dia* used to express lack of information

pitekàntrop {a (acc. = gen.) masc.} (lit. caveman) *sl-fea* ***Fac*** senior citizen <**Gre**[*1]>

pȉti *See the following*
- **Nè znā se ni kȍ pȉjē ni kȍ plâćā.** {S} (lit. One

doesn't know who drinks and who pays.) *col* total disorder, complete mess

- **Pȉjēm pȋvo, jèbe mi se žȋvo!** {S} (lit. I've been drinking my beer, and I don't give a shit about anything!) *col* ***Obs*** used to express indifference, I don't give a shit!
- **pȉti ko dúga** {VP} (lit. drink like a rainbow) *sl-drink* overindulge in alcoholic beverages
- **pȉti ko Rȕs** {VP} (lit. drink like a Russian) *sl-drink* overindulge in alcoholic beverages
- **pȉti ko smûk** {VP} (lit. drink like an Aesculapius' snake) *sl-drink* overindulge in alcoholic beverages
- **pȉti šprȉcer iz kȍžnē čàšē** {VP} (lit. drink wine with water from a leather glass) *sl-sex* ***Fac-Obs*** engage in fellatio

pìtom {a (acc. = gen.) masc.} (lit. the domesticated one) *sl-fea* quiet male **<Slav[*1]>**

pitòmo {adv.} (lit. domesticated) *sl* really, indeed: *On te pitomo gotivi. He really likes you.* **<Slav[*1]>**

pìtōn {pitóna (acc. = gen.) masc.} (lit. python) **1** *sl-sex* ***Fac-Obs*** penis, dick, prick **<Gre[*1]>** **2a.** *sl-fea* ***Fac*** overly talkative person, chatterbox **<Gre[*1]>** **b.** *sl-fea* ***Fac*** boring person, bore **<Gre[*2]>**

pitònčić {a (acc. = gen.) masc.} (lit. small python) *sl-sex* ***Fac-Obs*** penis, dick, prick **<Gre❖[*1]>**

pitùrati {ām, ajū imperf.} Med *col-dia* dye **<Ita[*1]>**

pȉu-pȉu {excl.} *col* the repeated sound made by a chick, chirp-chirp **<Slav>**

píva {ē fem.} [std. = pivo] *col* beer **<Slav✍>**

- **mȓzlā píva** {NP} (lit. frozen beer) Cro *sl* a bar at Magazin road and Katina street in Zagreb, Croatia

pívac {vca (acc. = gen.) masc.} [std. = pjevac, pevac] Med *dia* rooster **<Slav✍>**

pìvara {ē fem.} *sl-drink* beer **<Slav[*1]>**

pȉvati {ām, ajū imperf.} [std. = pjevati, pevati] Med *dia* sing **<Slav✍>**

pívce {eta neut.} *sl-drink* beer **<Slav❖>**

pìvceps {a masc.} (lit. beerceps *pivo 'beer' X biceps 'biceps'*) *sl-fea* ***Fac*** beer belly **<Slav-Lat✍>**

pìvčuga {ē fem.; Dat pìvčugi} *sl-drink* beer **<Slav❖>**

pȉvdža {ē masc.} [std. = pivo] *sl-drink* beer **<Slav✍>**

pìvdžān {a masc.} *sl-drink* beer **<Slav✍>**

pìvīć {pivíća masc.} [std. = pivo] *sl-drink* beer **<Slav✍>**

pìvkan {a masc.} *sl-drink* beer **<Slav✍>**

pivòpija {ē masc.} *sl-drink* beer drinker **<Slav❖>**

pízda {ē fem.} **a.** *sl-sex* ***Obs*** vagina, cunt **<Slav>** **b.i.** *sl* ***Obs*** female, cunt **<Slav[*1]>** **ii.** *sl-fea* ***Der-Obs*** miser, tightwad, skinflint **<Slav[*2]>** **iii.** *sl-fea* hairsplitter, nit picker **<Slav[*3]>** **iv.aa.** *sl-fea* unfriendly person **<Slav[*4]>** **bb.** *sl-crime* informer, stoolie, snitch

- **E u pízdu màterinu!** {S} (lit. Well, into *your* mother's cunt!) *col* ***Obs*** used to express dissatisfaction and lack of control over events, Fuck it!
- **Kȍjā ti je pízda màterina!** {S} (lit. What kind of mother's cunt is it to you?) *col* ***Obs*** used to express negative attitude toward one's interlocutor, Fuck you!
- **mȓzlā pízda** {NP} (lit. frozen cunt) *sl-fea* ***Obs*** conceited person
- **Pízda im màterina!** {S} (lit. Their mother's cunt to them!) *col* ***Off*** used as a strong curse, Fuck them!
- **Pízda li ti màterina!** {S} (lit. Your mother's cunt to you!) *col* ***Off*** used as a strong curse, Fuck you!
- **pízda nêmā zûbe** {S} (lit. a cunt does not have teeth) *col* ***Obs-Fac*** used to indicate that a female is inferior to a male
- **Pízda ti màterina!** {S} (lit. Your mother's cunt to you!) *col* ***Off*** used as a strong curse, Fuck you!
- **Pízda ti màterina ònā lópovskā!** {S} (lit. Your theiving mother's cunt to you!) *col* ***Off*** used as a strong curse, Fuck you!
- **Pízda ti strȋnina!** {S} (lit. Your aunt's cunt to you!) *col* ***Off*** used as a moderate curse, Fuck you!
- **Pízdo jèdna!** {S} (lit. You cunt!) *col* ***Off*** used as a strong curse
- **U pízdu màterinu!** {S} (lit. To mother's cunt!) *col* ***Obs*** used to express lack of control over events, Fuck it!
- **u pízdu màterinu** {S} (lit. to mother's cunt) *col* ***Obs*** far away, utterly remote
- **U trî pízde màterine!** {S} (lit. To the three mother's cunts!) *sl* ***Obs*** used to emphasize one's point, Fuck!
- **u trî pízde màterine** {S} (lit. to the three mother's cunts!) *sl* ***Obs*** far away, utterly remote

Pȉzdac {a masc.} (lit. Cuntville) *dia* ***Obs*** a pasture in Lika **<Slav>**

pìzdača {ē fem.} (lit. cunter) *sl* female **<Slav❖[*1]>**

pìzdār {pizdára (acc. = gen.) masc.} (lit. cunter) *sl-fea* ***Der-Obs*** worthless or despicable person **<Slav❖[*1]>**

pìzdara {ē fem.} (lit. cunter) **a.** *sl-sex* ***Obs*** female with a large vagina **<Slav❖>** **b.** *sl* ***Obs*** female, cunt **<Slav❖[*1]>**

pizdàrija {ē fem.} (lit. cunt-stuff) **1** *sl-fea* unpleasant situation, bummer **<Slav[*1]>** **2** *sl-fea* easy thing to do **<Slav[*1]>** **3** *sl-fea* mess, disorder, disturbance **<Slav[*1]>**

pìzdatā {ē fem. (adj. decl.)} (lit. cunty) *sl-sex* ***Obs*** female with a large vagina **<Slav[*1]>**

pìzdek[1] {a (acc. = gen.) masc.} (lit. cunter) *sl-fea* inhabitant of Zagreb, Croatia <Slav❖*1>

pìzdek[2] {a (acc. = gen.) masc.} (lit. cunt-guy) **a.** *sl-fea* egotistic male <Slav*1> **b.** miser, tightwad, skinflint <Slav❖*2> **c.** *sl-fea* undependable friend <Slav❖*3>

pizdèkān {pizdekána (acc. = gen.) masc.} (lit. cunter) **a.** *sl-fea* egotist <Slav❖*1> **b.** *sl-fea* miser, tightwad, skinflint <Slav❖*2> **c.** *sl-fea* undependable friend <Slav❖*2>

pízdeti {dīm, dē imperf. intr.} (lit. cunt) **a.** **SerE** *sl-fea* be nervous <Slav❖*1> **b.** **SerE** *sl-fea* go insane, freak out <Slav❖*2>

pizdètina {ē fem.} (lit. big cunt) **a.** *sl-fea* ***Der-Obs*** worthless or despicable female, bitch <Slav❖*1> **b.** *sl-fea* ***Der-Obs*** worthless or mean male, son of a bitch <Slav❖*2>

pízdica {ē fem.} *sl-sex* ***Obs*** small vagina <Slav❖>

pízdin dȉm {NP} (lit. cunt's smoke) **a.** *col* ***Obs*** unimportant issue or thing, fucking nothing: *Sva ta politika, to je pizdin dim! All that politics, it's just fucking nothing!* **b.** *col* ***Obs*** worthless object, junk ☞ **dim**

pízdina pȍbuna {NP} (lit. cunt's rebellion) *sl-sex* ***Fac-Obs*** menstruation, period ☞ **pobuna**

pȉzdīšte {a neut.} (lit. cunt place) **1** *dia* ***Obs*** place where a robbery has taken place <Slav❖*1> **2** *dia* ***Obs*** abandoned terrain <Slav❖*1>

pízditi {dīm, dē imperf. intr.} (lit. cunt) **a.** *sl-fea* be nervous <Slav❖*1> **b.i.** *sl* cry, shed tears, weep <Slav❖*2> **ii.** *sl* complain, bitch <Slav❖*2>

pîzdo {excl.} *col* ***Off*** used to express extreme dissatisfaction <Slav❖*1>

pizdojèbina {ē fem.} (lit. cunt fucking) **a.** *sl-sex* ***Obs*** sexual intercourse <Slav❖*1> **b.** *sl-fea* ***Obs*** a place of extreme wretchedness or squalor, hellhole <Slav❖*2>

pizdȍjēpka {ē fem.; Dat pizdȍjēpki} (lit. cunt-fucker) **1** *sl-sex* ***Obs*** lesbian <Slav❖*1> **2a.** *sl-sex* ***Obs*** prostitute, hooker <Slav❖*1> **b.** *sl-sex* ***Obs*** loose woman, slut <Slav❖*1>

pizdolízac {sca (acc. = gen.) masc.} (lit. cunt-licker) **a.** *sl-sex* ***Obs*** male who engages in cunnilingus <Slav❖> **b.** *sl-fea* ***Der-Obs*** worthless or despicable person, bum <Slav❖*1> **c.** *sl-fea* ***Der-Obs*** ingratiator (male), brownnoser, ass kisser <Slav❖*2>

pȉzdriti se *See the following*

• **Nè pizdri se!** {S} (lit. Don't you act like a cunt!) *dia* ***Off*** used in angry dismissal, Fuck off!

pìzdulja {ē fem.} (lit. cunter) **1** *sl-fea* boring female, bore <Slav❖*1> **2** *sl-fea* unfriendly person <Slav❖*1>

pìzdūn {pizdúna (acc. = gen.) masc.} /pizdûn /a (acc. = gen.) masc./ (lit. cunter) **a.** *sl-fea* egotist <Slav❖*1> **b.i.** *sl-fea* miser, tightwad, skinflint <Slav❖*2> **ii.** *sl-fea* cunning male <Slav❖*2>

pizdúnče {eta neut.} (lit. cunt-baby) *sl-fea* ***Obs*** baby, newborn <Slav❖*1>

pizdùrčina {ē fem.} *sl-sex* ***Obs*** large vagina <Slav❖>

pizdùrina {ē fem.} **a.** *sl-sex* ***Obs*** large vagina <Slav❖> **b.i.** *sl-fea* ***Der-Obs*** worthless or mean female, bitch <Slav❖*1> **ii.aa.** *sl-fea* ***Der-Obs*** egotist <Slav❖*1> **bb.** worthless or mean male, son of a bitch <Slav❖*2>

pìzduša {ē fem.} (lit. cunter) *sl* female, cunt <Slav❖*1>

• **Pìzdušo jèdna!** {S} (lit. You cunt-lady!) *col* ***Off*** used as a strong curse, Fuck you!

pȉzma {ē fem.} *dia* maliciousness <Gre>

piždrùljina {ē fem.} *sl-sex* ***Obs*** large vagina <Slav✍>

pjȁc {pjàca +ev (ext. pl) masc.; Nom Pl pjàcevi} Med *dia-col* market <Ita>

pjȁca {ē fem.} Med *col* market <Ita>

pjȁn {a, o adj.} [std. = pijan] *sl-drink* drunk <Slav✍>

pjánac {nca (acc. = gen.) masc.} [std. = pijanac] *sl-drink* alcoholic, drunk <Slav✍>

pjáno {ē masc.} [std. = pijanac] *sl-drink* alcoholic, drunk <Slav✍>

pjȁnskā prîča {NP} (lit. drunk's story) *sl-drink* drunk talk ☞ **priča**

pjȁt {pjàta masc.} Med *dia-col* plate, dish <Ita>

pjȅniti se {nīm, nē imperf. intr.} (lit. foam) *sl-fea* get nervous <Slav*1>

pjȅsma {ē fem.} (lit. song) *sl-stu* political economics (an obligatory subject at universities in the former Yugoslavia) <Slav*1>

• **grȍbāreva pjȅsma** {NP} (lit. undertaker's song) *sl* ***Fac*** funeral

pjȅsmarica {ē fem.} (lit. songbook) *sl-fea* senior citizen <Slav*1>

pjȅsnīk {a (acc. = gen.) masc.} (lit. poet) *sl-crime* ***Der*** informer, stoolie, snitch <Slav*1>

pjȅšadīnka {ē fem.} *sl-mil* high-top boot <Slav❖*1>

pjȅšāk {pješáka (acc. = gen.) masc.} (lit. pedestrian) *sl-sex* ***Fac*** male homosexual, gay <Slav*1>

pjévac {a (acc. = gen.) masc.} (lit. rooster) *sl-fea* stupid or mentally deficient person <Slav*1>

pjèvāč {pjeváča (acc. = gen.) masc.} (lit. singer) *sl-crime* informer, stoolie, snitch <Slav*1>

pjevàčica {ē fem.} (lit. singer) *sl-fea* female with slender legs <Slav*1>

pjȅvalica {ē fem.} (lit. singer) *sl* mouth <Slav*1>

pjȅvalo *See the following*
- **vȅlikō pjȅvalo** {NP} (lit. big singer) *sl-fea* boaster, braggart, blowhard

pjȅvati {ām, ajū imperf.} (lit. sing) **a.** *sl-crime* inform the police or other authorities, sing <Slav*1> **b.** *sl* admit, make a confession, come clean <Slav*1>
- **pjȅvati o bômbama** {VP} (lit. sing about the bombs) *sl-fea* reveal secret information

pjȅvica {ē fem.} (lit. singer) *sl* female <Slav*1>

pjevúšiti {pjèvūšīm, šē imperf.} (lit. sing) *sl-fea* talk persistently and meaninglessly, blabber, chatter <Slav*1>

pjȕgara {ē fem.} *sl* cigarette, smoke <Slav❖*1>

pjȕgati {ām, ajū imperf.} *sl* smoke (tobacco) <Slav❖*1>

pjȕva {ē fem.} *sl* cigarette, smoke <Slav*1>

PKB [pê-kâ-bê] {a masc.} (lit. Belgrade Dairy) Ser *sl-sex* ***Fac*** large-breasted female <BN*1>

pkȉca {ē fem.} *sl-drugs* hashish, hash

Plàčigūz {a masc.} (lit. Cryassville) *dia* ***Obs*** a place name in Bosnia <Slav>

plàčipička {ē fem.; Dat plàčipički} (lit. cry-cunt) **a.** *sl-fea* ***Der*** crybaby <Slav❖*1> **b.** *sl-fea* coward, chicken <Slav❖*1>

plȁčko {a masc.} (lit. crier) **a.** *sl-fea* ***Der*** crybaby <Slav❖> **b.** *sl-fea* coward, chicken <Slav❖*1>

plȁčkoljiti {ljīm, ljē imperf.} (lit. cry) *sl* cry, shed tears, weep <Slav❖>

plâćenī pȍštār {NP} (lit. paid mailman) *sl-crime* informer, stoolie, snitch ☞ **poštar**

plàfōn {plafóna masc.} (lit. ceiling) *sl-gamble* the highest bid in cards <Fre*1>

plȁhta {ē fem.} (lit. sheet) **1** *sl* hundred dinars; a hundred-dinar bill <Slav*1> **2** *sl* million dinars; a million-dinar bill <Slav*1> **3** *sl* face (human) <Slav*1> **4** *sl* ghost <Slav*1> **5** *sl* ***Fac*** Vjesnik daily, Zagreb, Croatia <Slav*1> **6** *sl* long newspaper article <Slav*1>

plȁhtica *See the following*
- **plȁhtica bȍžjā** {NP} (lit. small God's sheet) *sl* five hundred dinars; a five-hundred dinar bill

plȁjvāz 1 {a (acc. = gen.) masc.} (lit. pencil) *sl* male, guy <Ger>

plȁjvāz 2 {a masc.} **a.** *sl* pencil <Ger> **b.** *sl-sex* ***Fac*** penis <Ger*1>

plàkāt {plakáta (acc. = gen.) masc.} (lit. poster) **a.** *sl-fea* boring male, bore <Dut*1> **b.** *sl-fea* intruder <Dut*2>

plákati 1 {plâkām, plákajū imperf.} //plâčēm, plâčū imperf./ *col* barely wash <Slav>

plȁkati 2 {ačēm, ačū imperf. intr.} (lit. cry) *sl* ***Der*** complain, whine <Slav*1>
- **plȁkati za gȍvnārom** {VP} (lit. cry over a shithead) *sl-sex* ***Obs*** engage in anal sexual intercourse

pláknuti {plâknēm, nū perf.} *col* barely wash <Slav>

pláknuti se {plâknēm, nū perf. intr.} **a.** *col* barely wash oneself <Slav> **b.** *sl* run away, flee <Slav*1>

plàkosati {ošēm, ošū imperf.} *sl-fea* get frightened, get scared <Slav❖*1>

plàmćeti {tīm, tē imperf.} [std. = plamtjeti] *dia* burn <Slav✍>

plân *See the following*
- **zèlenī plân** {NP} (lit. green plan) *sl* five thousand dinars; a five-thousand dinar bill

plȁndovānje {a neut.} *dia-col* resting, having a break <Slav>

plȁndovati {dujēm, dujū imperf.} *dia-col* get some rest <Slav>

plànina {ē fem.} (lit. mountain) *sl-crime* name of a prison in Lepoglava, Croatia <Slav*1>

planinàriti {nìnārīm, rē imperf.} (lit. hike) *sl-sex* ***Fac-Obs*** engage in sexual foreplay, pet, feel up <Slav*1>
- **planinàriti nȅrve** {VP} (lit. climb on one's nerves) *sl-fea* make nervous, get on one's nerves
- **planinàriti po nȅrvima** {VP} (lit. climb on one's nerves) *sl-fea* make nervous, get on one's nerves

plànīnka {ē fem.} (lit. hiker) *sl-fea* female who often refuses advances from males <Slav*1>

plȁnkerica {ē fem.} *sl* streetcar line <Ger❖*1>

plantávko {a masc.} *sl-fea* clumsy male, klutz

plànuti {plȁnēm, nū perf.} /plȁnuti/ (lit. burn) *col* burst in outrage, blow up, lose one's cool <Slav*1>

plàskosati se {ošēm, ošū imperf. intr.} *sl-arch* get frightened, freak

plàstičār {a (acc. = gen.) masc.} (lit. plastic worker) *sl-fea* young male, boy, kid <Gre❖*1>

plastikánac {nca (acc. = gen.) masc.} (lit. plastic stuff) *sl-auto* Trabant (make of simple East German car) <**Gre**⁘[*1]>

plàta {ē fem.} **a.** *sl-crafts* board, plank <**Ger**> **b.** *sl* cigarette paper <**Ger**[*1]>

platfùsist {a masc.} (lit. flat-footed person) *sl-fea* trifle, thing of little importance or value <**Ger**[*1]>

platfusist {a (acc. = gen.) masc.} (lit. flat footed person) *sl-fea* ***Der*** lazy or shiftless person, bum, good for nothing <**Ger**[*1]>

pláti pa se kláti {S} (lit. pay and then swing) *col* you have to pay for it before you use it ☞ **platiti**

plàtine {a fem. pl.} (lit. platinum) *sl-auto* breaker points (on an automobile distributor) <**Spa**[*1]>

plátiti *See the following*

• **pláti pa se kláti** {S} (lit. pay and then swing) *col* you have to pay for it before you use it

plâvā kòvērta {NP} (lit. blue envelope) *col* bribe ☞ **koverta**

plávac {vca (acc. = gen.) masc.} (lit. the blue one) *sl-crime* policeman, man in blue <**Slav**⁘[*1]>

plàvāč {plaváča (acc. = gen.) masc.} (lit. the blue one) *sl-crime* policeman, man in blue <**Slav**⁘[*1]>

plâvī {ōg (acc. = gen.) masc.} (lit. the blue one *both the police uniform and the jerseys of the teams below are blue*) **1** *sl-crime* policeman, man in blue <**Slav**[*1]> **2** *sl-sports* player for Yugoslav national team <**Slav**[*1]> **3** *sl-sports* player for Dinamo (in the 1990s Croatia, a soccer team from Zagreb, Croatia) <**Slav**[*1]> **4** *sl-sports* player for Budućnost (a soccer team from Podgorica, Yugoslavia) <**Slav**[*1]> **5** *sl-sports* player for Željezničar (a soccer team from Sarajevo, Bosnia) <**Slav**[*1]>

plâvī ânđeō {NP} (lit. blue angel) *sl-crime* policeman, man in blue ☞ **anđeo**

plâvi g {NP} (lit. blue g) *sl-crime* policeman, man in blue ☞ **g**

plâvī Jàdrān {NP} (lit. blue Adriatic sea) *sl-crime* policeman, man in blue ☞ **Jadran**

plâvī kòverat {NP} (lit. blue envelope) *col* bribe ☞ **koverat**

pláviti *See the following*

• **pláviti vrât** {VP} (lit. blue one's neck) *sl-fea* bore, disturb

plàvnjika {ē fem.} *sl* fifty dinars (bill) <**Slav**⁘[*1]>

plàvuša {ē fem.} *col* blond female <**Slav**⁘[*1]>

plazánac {nca (acc. = gen.) masc.} (lit. crawling) *sl* walk <**Slav**⁘[*1]>

plȁziti [1] {zīm, zē imperf. intr.} (lit. crawl) *sl* walk <**Slav**[*1]>

plȁziti [2] {zīm, zē imperf.} (lit. stick one's tongue out) *sl* offend: *plaziti profesora* *offend one's professor* <**Slav**[*1]>

• **plȁziti jèzik pred pȍštōm i lépiti màrke** {Vp} (lit. stick out one's tongue in front of a post office and seal the stamps) ŠerE *sl-fea* spend one's time in useless activities, fool around, mess around

pláža *See the following*

• **nàjlōn pláža** {NP} (lit. nylon beach) *col* nudist beach

plȁžēnje {a neut.} (lit. crawling) **a.** *sl* walk <**Slav**[*1]> **b.** *sl* dating a female <**Slav**[*2]>

plebéjac {jca (acc. = gen.) masc.} (lit. plebeian) *sl-polit* labor union activist <**Lat**[*1]>

plȅh {plèha +ov (ext. pl) masc.; Nom Pl plèhovi} **a.** *col* sheet metal <**Ger**> **b.** *sl-auto* car, wheels <**Ger**[*1]>

plȅh-šâjba {ē fem.} *sl-crafts* tin washer <**Ger**>

plȅh-šàjbna {ē fem.} *sl-crafts* tin washer <**Ger**>

plehàna {ē fem.} (lit. tinning) *sl* hitting, punching <**Ger**⁘[*1]>

pléhānje {a neut.} (lit. tinning) *sl* hitting, punching <**Ger**⁘[*1]>

pléhati {ām, ajū imperf.} (lit. tin) *sl* hit, punch <**Ger**⁘[*1]>

plȅhnjāk {a (acc. = gen.) masc.} **1** *sl-auto* car, wheels <**Ger**⁘[*1]> **2** *sl* raincoat <**Ger**⁘[*1]>

plêjka {ē fem.} *sl-music* long-playing phonograph record, LP <**Eng**✍[*1]>

plȅme *See the following*

• **Iz kôg si plȅmena?** {S} (lit. From which tribe are you?) *sl-fea* ***Fac-Der*** used as a moderate curse, You hick!

plesnìvec {vca masc.} (lit. mouldy person) *sl-fea* introvert person <**Slav**✍[*1]> *sl-fea* sly person, fox <**Slav**✍[*2]>

plêsnjāk {a masc.} (lit. dancer) *col* dance floor <**Slav**⁘>

plèšare {a fem. pl.} (lit. sheet-metal scissors) *sl-crafts* tin-snips <**Ger**>

plèškare {a fem. pl.} (lit. sheet-metal scissors) *sl-crafts* tin-snips <**Ger**>

pletènice {a fem. pl.} (lit. tresses) *sl-fea* crooked teeth <**Slav**[*1]>

plȅva *See the following*

• **kao plȅvē** {PP} (lit. as much as a cockle) SerE *col* in large quantities, very many

plezȉrčina {ē fem.} *sl-fea* high pleasure <Fre⁘>

plȉcak {excl.} *col* the sound made by splashing, splash <Slav>

plíća {ē fem.} (lit. shallow area) *sl-fea* stupid or mentally deficient person <Slav⁘*1>

plȉćāk {plićáka (acc. = gen.) masc.; Voc plȉćāku} (lit. shallow area) *sl-fea* stupid or mentally deficient person <Slav*1>

plȉnara {ē fem.} (lit. gas works) **1a.** *sl-sex* ***Fac-Obs*** buttocks, butt <Slav*1> **b.** *sl-sex* ***Fac-Obs*** anus, asshole <Slav*2> **2** *sl-fea* ***Fac*** senior citizens (collectively) <Slav*2>

• **Tȅrēzijinā plȉnara** {NP} (lit. Theresia's gas works) *sl-crime* name of a prison in Stara Gradiška, Croatia

plȋnčiti {čīm, čē imperf.} *sl* cry, shed tears, weep

plȋndrati {ām, ajū imperf.} **a.** *sl* steal from, rip off <Ger> **b.** *sl* cheat, swindle <Ger*1>

plȉtak {tka, tko adj.} (lit. shallow) *sl-fea* unintelligent, stupid, dumb <Slav*1>

plȉvāč {pliváča (acc. = gen.) masc.; Voc plȋvāču} (lit. swimmer) *sl-fea* easily cheated person, easy mark <Slav*1>

plivàdōn {vadóna (acc. = gen.) masc.; Voc plȋvadōne} (lit. Plivadon is a brand name of painkiller) *sl* friend (male) <BN*1>

plivadònček *See the following*

• **kao dvâ plivadònčeka** {AdvP} (lit. like two Tylenols) *sl-sex* ***Fac*** round female buttocks

plȋvati *See the following*

• **plȋvati u lóvi** {VP} (lit. swim in bucks) **1** *sl-fea* possess a significant amount of money, be swimming in dough **2a.** *sl-fea* be endangered **b.** *sl-fea* lose (money, goods, etc.) **c.** *sl-fea* be cheated, be swindled **3** be successful

pljàčipička {ē fem.; Dat pljàčipički} (lit. cry-cunt) **a.** *sl-fea* ***Der*** crybaby <Slav⁘*1> **b.** *sl-fea* coward, chicken <Slav⁘*1>

pljȕnuti lóvu {VP} (lit. spit the money) *col* pay, cough up the dough ☞ **pljunuti**

plȍča {ē fem.} (lit. plate) *sl* fifty-dinar coin <Slav*1>

plômba {ē fem.} (lit. leaden seal) *sl-sex* ***Fac*** virgin <Fre*1>

plônđa {ē fem.} *sl* female

plóska {ē fem.} *sl-drink* flat bottle (usu. filled with alcohol) <Slav⁘>

plôt {a +ov (ext. pl) masc.; Nom Pl plòtovi} (lit. fence) **1** *sl* comb <Slav*1> **2** *sl* teeth <Slav*1>

• **trȕlī plôt** {NP} (lit. rotten fence) *sl-fea* decayed teeth

plóvak {vka masc.} (lit. float) *sl* shoe <Slav*1>

plòviti {vīm, ve imperf. intr.} (lit. float) *sl* walk <Slav*1>

plúća {a neut. pl.} (lit. lungs) *sl-sex* ***Fac*** large female breast <Slav*1>

plȕmbati {ām, ajū imperf.} *sl-drink* drink (alcohol)

pluvánac {nca masc.} *sl* tobacco <Slav⁘*1>

pljȁca {ē fem.} [std. = pijaca] *dia-col* market <Ita✍>

pljȁče {eta neut.} *sl-arch* bride

pljȁfnuti {nēm, nū perf.} **1** *col* clap <Slav> **2** *col* splash <Slav*1>

pljȁka {ē fem.; Dat pljȁki} *sl* female

pljakȕrina {ē fem.} *sl* female

pljȁs {excl.} **1** *col* the sound made by clapping, clap <Slav> **2** *col* the sound made by splashing, splash <Slav*1>

pljȁska {ē fem.} *col* splash <Slav>

pljȁskānje {a neut.} *col* splash <Slav>

pljȁskati {ām, ajū imperf.} **a.** *col* splash <Slav> **b.** *sl* fall (physically) <Slav*1>

pljȁt {a masc.} Med *dia-col* saucer <Ita>

pljȅs {excl.} *col* the sound made by clapping, clap <Slav>

pljȅs-pljȅs {excl.} *col* the sound made by clapping, clap <Slav>

pljêsak {ska masc.} **1** *col* applause <Slav⁘> **2** *col* splash <Slav⁘> **3** *sl* ***Fac*** hamburger <Slav✍*1>

pljèskac {excl.} *col* the sound made by clapping, clap <Slav>

pljèskara {ē fem.} *sl* face (human) <Slav*1> *sl* head <Slav*2>

pljȅskavica {ē fem.} (lit. hamburger) *sl* hit, punch <Slav*1>

pljèsniv rȍb {VP} (lit. mouldy slave) *sl-crime* old prisoner ☞ **rob**

Pljȅška {ē fem.; Dat Pljȅški} Cro *sl-drink* Plješevica bar in Zagreb, Croatia <SlavO✍>

pljȅva *See the following*

• **kao pljȅvē** {PP} (lit. as much as cockle) *col* in large quantities, very many

pljôjka {ē fem.} *sl-sex* ***Fac-Obs*** flat female breast <Slav☞*1>

pljòviti {vīm, vē imperf.} *sl-fea* ***Der*** ingratiate, brownnose, kiss ass

pljùbārka {ē fem.; Dat pljùbārki} *sl-drink* suburban bar <Slav❖*1>

pljȕc {excl.} *col* the sound made by spitting, phew <Slav>

pljúca {ē fem.} (lit. spitter) **1** *sl-auto* Fiat 750 (make of car) <Slav❖*1> **2** *sl* mouth <Slav❖*1> **3** *sl-crime* pistol, revolver <Slav❖*1>

pljȕcak {cka masc.} (lit. spitter) *sl-crime* pistol, revolver <Slav❖*1>

pljȕckalica {ē fem.} (lit. spitter) *sl-crime* machine gun <Slav❖*1>

pljȕckānje {a neut.} (lit. spitting) *sl* smoking (tobacco) <Slav*1>

pljȕckati {ām, ajū imperf.} (lit. spit) *sl* smoke (tobacco) <Slav❖*1>

pljȕckavica {ē fem.} (lit. spitter) *sl-fea* average person <Slav❖*1>

pljȕcko {a masc.} (lit. spitter) *sl-fea* boaster, braggart, blowhard <Slav❖*1>

pljȕf {excl.} *col* the sound made by splashing, splash <Slav>

pljȕf-pljȕf {excl.} *col* the sound made by splashing, splash <Slav>

pljúga {ē fem.; Dat pljúgi} /pljūga/ **a.** *sl* cigarette, smoke <Slav❖*1> **b.** *sl-drugs* joint

pljùgāljka {ē fem.} (lit. smoker) *sl-sex* ***Fac*** prostitute, hooker <Slav❖*1>

pljugánac {nca masc.} (lit. smoking) **1** *sl* tobacco <Slav❖*1> **2** *sl-sex* fellatio

pljȕgānje {a neut.} **a.** *sl* smoking (tobacco) <Slav❖*☞> **b.i.** *sl-drink* drinking (alcohol) **ii.** *sl* milking

pljùgara {ē fem.} **1** *sl* cigarette, smoke <Slav❖*1> **2a.** *sl-drink* suburban bar **b.** *sl-drink* bar (drinking place) **3** *sl* tobacco

pljugàrdžija {ē masc.} (lit. smoker) *sl-drink* barkeeper <Slav-NE*1>

pljȕgarica {ē fem.} (lit. smoker) *sl-drink* bar (drinking place) <Slav❖*1>

pljùgārka {ē fem.} (lit. smoker) **1** *sl-sex* ***Fac*** prostitute, hooker <Slav❖*1> **2** *sl-drink* bar (drinking place) <Slav❖*1>

pljùgārnica {ē fem.} *sl-arch* bar (drinking place) <Slav❖*1>

pljȕgati {ām, ajū imperf.} **a.** *sl* smoke (tobacco) <Slav❖*1> **b.i.** *sl-drugs* smoke drugs **ii.** *sl-sex* engage in fellatio

pljȕgavac {vca masc.} *sl* tobacco <Slav❖*1>

pljȕgerica {ē fem.} *sl-sex* ***Fac*** female who frequently engages in fellatio <Slav❖*1>

pljúgica {ē fem.} *sl* cigarette, smoke <Slav❖*1>

pljȕniti {nēm, nū perf.} (lit. spit) **1** *sl* hit, punch <Slav*1> **2** *sl* pay dearly <Slav*1> **3** *sl* live close to something: *Meni je pljuniti do posla. I live very close to my work.* <Slav*1>

pljȕnūt {a, o adj.} (lit. spit) *col* identical, exactly the same <Slav*1>

pljȕnuti {nēm, nū perf.} (lit. spit) **1** *sl* hit, punch <Slav*1> **2** *sl* pay dearly <Slav*1> **3** *sl* live close to something: *Meni je pljunuti do posla. I live very close to my work.* <Slav*1>

• **pljȕnuti lóvu** {VP} (lit. spit the money) *col* pay, cough up the dough

pljȕs {excl.} *col* the sound made by splashing, splash <Slav>

pljȕsk {excl.} *col* the sound made by splashing, splash <Slav>

pljùskac {excl.} *col* the sound made by splashing, splash <Slav>

pljȕskānje {a neut.} *col* splashing <Slav>

pljùskara {ē fem.} **1** *sl* face (human) <Slav❖*1> **2** *sl* head <Slav❖*1>

pljȕskati {ām, ajū imperf.} **1** *col* pour <Slav> **2** *col* gurgle (creek, etc.) <Slav> **3** *sl* flow <Slav>

pljȕsnuti {nēm, nū perf.} (lit. splash) **a.** *col* splash <Slav> **b.** *sl* die, kick the bucket <Slav*1>

pljùšāč {pljušáča (acc. = gen.) masc.; Voc pljȕšāču} *sl-music* brass player (brass instrument musician) <Slav☞*1>

pljȕva {ē fem.} (lit. spitter) *sl* cigarette, smoke <Slav*1>

pljuvánac {a masc.} (lit. spitter) *sl-arch* tobacco <Slav❖*1>

pljùvati {pljȕjēm, pljȕjū imperf.} *col* spit <Slav>

• **pljùvati mêso** {VP} (lit. spit meat) *sl-fea* suffer from tuberculosis, have TB

• **pljùvati slȋnu** {VP} (lit. spit mucus) *sl* laugh

pljȗvka {ē fem.} (lit. spitter) *sl* cigarette, smoke <Slav*1>

pȍ [1] {excl.} *col* used when jumping, hop <Slav>

pò* [2] {adv.} *col* rather *: *On je polijen. He is rather lazy.* <**Slav**>

po pîcijusu {PP} (lit. according to the cunt's standard) *sl* ***Fac*** according to the Yugoslav Industrial Standard ☞ **picijus**

po ps-u [pê-ȅsu] {PP} (lit. by the military code of conduct) *sl-mil* as the rule says ☞ **ps**

po svîm ȍsnovama {PP} (lit. on all bases) *col* on all counts ☞ **osnova**

po žnóri {PP} (lit. on a rope) **a.** Cro *sl* easily **b.** Cro *sl* as planned ☞ **žnora**

pȍa {excl.} *col* used when jumping, hop <**Slav**>

pòarati {ām, ajū perf. intr.} [std. = poharati] *col-dia* steal, swipe <**NE**✍*1>

pòbāčen {a, o adj.} (lit. aborted) **1** *sl-fea* short <**Slav***1> **2** *sl-fea* undeveloped: *pobačeno dijete underdeveloped child* <**Slav***1>

pòbanjati {ām, ajū perf.} (lit. bathroom) *sl-sex* ***Obs*** urinate, piss <**Ita**⁘*1>

pòbanjiti {njīm, njē perf.} (lit. bathroom) *sl-sex* ***Obs*** urinate, piss <**Ita**⁘*1>

pòbeći *See the following*

- **kò da je pòbegō grȍbāru s lòpatē** {PP} (lit. as if he had escaped from the undertaker's spade) **SerE** *sl-fea* ***Der-Fac*** extremely unattractive, ugly as sin

pobègulja {ē fem.} SerE *col-dia* female who leaves her husband <**Slav***1>

pobéleti {pòbēlīm, lē perf. intr.} (lit. turn white) SerE *sl-fea* get scared, turn white <**Slav***1>

pobenáviti {bènāvīm, vē perf. intr.} *sl-fea* go insane, freak out <**NE**⁘>

pobjègulja {ē fem.} *col-dia* female who leaves her husband <**Slav***1>

pȍbogu [1] {part.} *col* intensifying particle, dear God <**Slav**⁘>

pȍbogu [2] {excl.} *col* for heaven's sake <**Slav**⁘>

- **pȍbogu brȁte** {NP} (lit. my brother in God) *col* used to address a male in an intimate manner, buddy, pal

pȍbožnē grûdi {NP} (lit. religious breasts) *sl-sex* ***Fac-Obs*** sagging female breast ☞ **grudi**

pobŕkati {pòbr̄kām, pobŕkajū perf.} /pòbrkati/ *col* mix up, confuse <**Slav***1>

pobrljáviti {br̀ljāvīm, vē perf.} **1** *sl-drink* get very drunk <**Slav***1> 2 go insane, freak out <**Slav***1>

póbro {ē masc.} *col* blood-brother <**Slav**>

pobudàlilā rȉba {NP} (lit. crazy fish) *sl* stolen money ☞ **riba**

pobudàliti {līm, lē perf. intr.} **1** *sl-fea* go insane, freak out <**NE**⁘*1> **2** *sl-fea* disappear, evaporate, vanish <**NE**⁘*1>

pȍbuna *See the following*

- **pízdina pȍbuna** {NP} (lit. cunt's rebellion) *sl-sex* ***Fac-Obs*** menstruation, period
- **pȍbuna vȅšānīh** {NP} (lit. rebellion of the hung ones) SerE *sl-sstu* skipping class, cutting class

pocépati {pòcēpām, pocépajū perf.} (lit. tear apart) **1a.** **SerE** *sl-sex* ***Fac-Obs*** engage in sexual intercourse with (of a male) <**Slav***1> **b.** *sl-sex* ***Fac-Obs*** engage in intense sexual intercourse with (of a male) <**Slav***2> **2** *sl* beat up severely <**Slav***1> **3** *sl-sports* defeat <**Slav***1>

pocijépati {pòcijēpām, pocijépajū biasp.} **1** *sl-sex* ***Fac-Obs*** engage in intensive sexual intercourse with (of a male) <**Slav***1> **2** *sl* beat up severely <**Slav***1>

pockùljati {ām, ajū perf.} *sl-sex* ***Obs*** defecate, shit

pòcokiti *See the following*

- **Pòcokīš mi pŕžu!** {S} (lit. Suck my prick!) *col* ***Off*** used as a strong curse, Blow me!

pocrkívati {cr̀kīvām, crkívajū imperf. intr.} *sl-arch* look, watch, scope out

pòcugati {ām, ajū biasp.} *sl-drink* drink up (alcohol) <**Ger**⁘*1>

pȍčasnica {ē fem.} *col* song in somebody's honor <**Slav**⁘>

pȍčeti *See the following*

pȍčkati {ām, ajū biasp.} *sl* pay (bills, etc.)

počkùljati {ām, ajū perf.} *sl-sex* ***Obs*** defecate, shit

pȍčohati se {ām, ajū perf. intr.} **1** *sl* scratch oneself: *počohati se po leđima scratch one's back* **2** *sl* fight (e.g. fist fight): *počohati se s komšijom fight with one's neighbor*

pòćerati {ām, ajū perf.} [std. = potjerati] *dia* begin to drive <**Slav**✍*1>

- **pòćerati ôvce** {VP} (lit. drive away the sheep) *sl-sstu* take students out of class (e.g. to have their break outside)

póći {pôđem, pôđu, póđ, pòš perf. irreg.} (lit. start going) *dia-col* begin, start: *Marko ih je pošo tuć al smo ga zadržali. Marko started to beat them up, but we stopped him.* <**Slav***1>

pod ćȕprijōm {PP} (lit. under a bridge) *sl-sex* ***Obs*** homosexual intercourse ☞ **ćuprija**

pod drógōm {PP} (lit. under drugs) *sl-drink* drunk ☞ **droga**

pod gâsom {PP} (lit. under gas) *sl-drink* drunk, gassed ☞ **gas**

pod gȍrīvom {PP} (lit. under fuel) *sl-drink* drunk, tanked ☞ **gorivo**

pòd hitno {PP} (lit. under urgent) *col* right away, now ☞ **hitno**

pod mȅtak {PP} (lit. under bullet) *sl-sex* ***Fac-Obs*** sexual intercourse ☞ **metak**

pod nôž {PP} (lit. under the knife) **a.** *col* to have surgery, go under the knife: *Neću da idem pod nož samo da bi ne bih imala bore. I don't want to go under the knife just to get rid of my wrinkles.* **b.** *col* urgently: *Taj rukopis mi je potreban pod nož - časopis izlazi sutra. I need that manuscript urgently - the journal goes to press tomorrow.* ☞ **nož**

pod ȍkom {PP} (lit. under eye) *col* under surveillance, being watched ☞ **oko**

pod pȁrōm {PP} (lit. under steam) *sl-drink* slightly drunk, tipsy ☞ **para**

pȍdān {a, o adj.} (lit. dominated) *sl-fea* fallen in love <**Slav***1>

- **hrȍnično pȍdān** {AdjP} (lit. chronically subordinate) *sl-fea* ***Der*** easily falling in love

Pòdbigūz {a masc.} (lit. Bangassville) *dia* ***Obs*** a place name in Bosnia <**Slav**⁘>

podbòčiti se *See the following*

- **Podbòči se s mòjēga!** {S} (lit. Lean it on my *prick*!) *dia* ***Off-Fac*** used as a weak curse, Screw you!

podèbljati {ām, ajū perf.} (lit. thicken) *sl* turn the volume up, pop up the volume <**Slav***1>

podéliti *See the following*

- **podéliti dlànove** {VP} (lit. share palms) SerE *sl* fight (e.g. fist fight)
- **podéliti znȁčke** {VP} (lit. share pins) SerE *sl* fight (e.g. fist fight)

podèrati {pòderēm, rū perf.} (lit. tear apart) *sl-sex* ***Obs*** engage in intensive sexual intercourse with (of a male) <**Slav***1>

- **podèrati ko lùdāk Polìtiku** {VP} (lit. tear apart like a madman does with the Politika daily) **Ser** *sl* destroy, ruin
- **podèrati ko Oslobođénje** {VP} (lit. tear apart like the Oslobođenje daily) *sl* destroy, ruin
- **podèrati ko Vȅselū svèsku** {VP} (lit. tear apart like the Vesela sveska children's weekly) *sl* destroy, ruin
- **podèrati žbûn** {VP} (lit. tear apart the bush) *sl-sex* ***Obs*** engage in anal sexual intercourse

pòdgladiti {dīm, dē perf.} (lit. pet under) *sl* hit, punch <**Slav***1>

podgúrnuti {pòdgūrnēm, nū perf.} *col* push, shove <**Slav**>

podgùzāš {guzáša (acc. = gen.) masc.; Voc pȍdguzāšu} *sl-fea* ***Der-Obs*** ingratiator (male), brownnoser, ass kisser <**Slav**⁘*1>

pòdgūznī {a, o adj.} *sl-sex* ***Obs*** buttocks, butt <**Slav**⁘>

pòdići {ignēm, ignū, ig, ig perf. irreg.} (lit. pick up) *sl-crime* steal, swipe <**Slav***1>

podijéliti *See the following*

- **podijéliti dlànove** {VP} (lit. share palms) *sl* fight (e.g. fist fight)

podìlaziti {zīm, zē imperf. intr.} *sl-fea* ***Der*** ingratiate, brownnose, kiss ass <**Slav***1>

podilèjisati {išēm, išū perf. intr.} **a.** *sl-fea* get angry <**Ita**⁘*1> **b.** *sl-fea* go insane, freak out <**Ita**⁘*2>

podilkániti {dìlkānīm, nē perf. intr.} *sl-fea* go insane, freak out <**Ita**✐⁘*1>

pòdjājčiti {čīm, čē imperf.} (lit. underball) *sl-fea* ***Der*** ingratiate, brownnose, kiss ass <**Slav**⁘*1>

podjèbati {pòdjebēm, bū perf.} (lit. underfuck) *sl-sex* ***Obs*** cheat, swindle <**Slav***1>

podjebávānje {a neut.} (lit. underfucking) **a.** *sl-fea* cheating, swindling <**Slav***1> **b.** *sl-fea* annoying, bothering <**Slav***2> **c.** *sl-fea* teasing <**Slav***3>

podjebávati {jèbāvām, jebávajū imperf.} (lit. underfuck) **a.** *sl* cheat, swindle <**Slav***1> **b.** *sl* annoy, bother, pester <**Slav***2> **c.** *sl* tease <**Slav***3>

pòdmazati {ažēm, ažū perf.} (lit. lubricate, grease) *col* bribe, lubricate <**Slav***1>

pòdmazati se {ažēm, ažū perf. intr.} (lit. lubricate oneself) *sl-drink* drink a little (alcohol), get lubricated <**Slav***1>

pódmōrnica {ē fem.} /pòdmōrnica/ (lit. submarine) *sl* disco, discotheque <**Slav***1>

pódmorničārka {ē fem.; Dat pódmorničārki} /pòdmorničārk/ (lit. submarine soldier) *sl* female <**Slav**⁘*1>

pȍdnapīt {a, o adj.} *sl-drink* slightly drunk, tipsy <**Slav**⁘>

pódnē {eva neut.} (lit. noon) SerE *sl* the bus line number twelve in Belgrade, Serbia <**Slav***1>

podrápati {pòdrāpām, podrápajū imperf.} (lit. tear apart) *sl-sex* ***Obs*** engage in sexual intercourse with (of a male) <**Slav***1>

podrèpāš {repáša (acc. = gen.) masc.; Voc pòdrepāšu} **1** *sl-sex* ***Fac*** male homosexual, gay <Slav❖[*1]> **2** *sl-fea* ***Der*** ingratiator (male), brownnoser, ass kisser <Slav❖[*2]>

podrigívati {rìgujēm, gujū imperf.} *col* burp, belch <Slav>

podrìguša {ē fem.} (lit. burper) *sl-fea* low-quality salami <Slav✍[*1]>

pòdrklo *See the following*

• **Pòdrklo ti jèbēm!** {S} *dia* ***Off*** used as a moderate curse, Fuck you!

pòdrum {a masc.} (lit. basement) *sl-drink* bar (drinking place) <Slav[*1]>

podrùmār {rumára (acc. = gen.) masc.} (lit. the one from the basement) *sl-fea* male who does not have his own apartment <Slav❖[*1]>

podrùmlija {ē masc.} (lit. the one from the basement) *sl-fea* homeless person, bum <Slav❖[*1]>

Podùdlāj mi ga! {S} (lit. Suck it to me!) *sl-sex* ***Off*** used as a strong curse, Blow me! ☞ **podudlati**

podùdlati {ām, ajū perf.} (lit. suck) *sl-sex* ***Obs*** engage in fellatio <Slav[*1]>

• **Podùdlāj mi ga!** {S} (lit. Suck it to me!) *sl-sex* ***Off*** used as a strong curse, Blow me!

podúvati {ām, ajū perf.} (lit. blow) *sl-drugs* smoke hashish <Slav[*1]>

podváliti {pòdvālīm, lē perf.} (lit. trick) *sl* give money <Slav[*1]>

pódvodnī rìbolōv {NP} (lit. underwater fishing) *sl-sex* ***Fac-Obs*** sexual intercourse in water ☞ **ribolov**

pòdvūći se {podvúčem, podvúkū, pòdvūk, pòdvūk perf. irreg.} (lit. squeeze underneath) **1** *sl-fea* ***Der*** ingratiate, brownnose, kiss ass: *podvući se šefu brownnose one's boss* <Slav[*1]> **2** *sl* cheat, swindle <Slav[*1]>

pódzēmlje {a neut.} (lit. underground) **1** *sl* pedestrian tunnel <Slav[*1]> **2** *sl* alternative political or cultural stream, underground <Slav[*1]>

podžápati se {pòdžāpām, podžápajū imperf. intr.} *col* start fighting <NE[*1]>

podževèljati se {ām, ajū perf. intr.} *sl* fight (e.g. fist fight) <NE❖[*1]>

podževèljisati se {išēm, išū perf. intr.} *col-dia* fight (e.g. fist fight) <NE[*1]>

pođòniti {pòđonīm, nē perf.} (lit. sole) *sl-sstu* prepare crib-sheets for an exam <NE❖[*1]>

• **pođòniti vȁške** {VP} (lit. put soles on one's fleas) *sl* get some money

• **pođòniti zȍbnice** {VP} (lit. put soles on one's feed-bag) *sl* have one's teeth fixed

pòēzija {ē fem.} *col* ***App*** something excellent, something cool <Gre[*1]>

• **čìstā pòēzija** {NP} (lit. pure poetry) *col* ***App*** excellent, pure poetry

Pòfājčiš mi kȍkota péderu! {S} (lit. Smoke my cock, you faggot!) *sl-sex* ***Off*** used as a strong curse, Suck my dick! ☞ **pofajčiti**

pòfājčiti {čīm, čē perf.} **a.** *sl-sex* ***Obs*** engage in fellatio <Ger❖[*1]> **b.** *sl-sex* ***Obs*** engage in sexual intercourse with (of a male) <Ger❖[*2]>

• **Pòfājčiš mi kȍkota péderu!** {S} (lit. Smoke my cock, you faggot!) *sl-sex* ***Off*** used as a strong curse, Suck my dick!

Poflaùtāj mi ga! {S} (lit. Play the flute on my cock!) *sl-sex* ***Off*** used as a strong curse, Suck my dick! ☞ **poflautati**

poflaùtati {ām, ajū perf.} (lit. play flute) *sl-sex* ***Obs*** engage in fellatio <Ita❖[*1]>

• **Poflaùtāj mi ga!** {S} (lit. Play the flute on my cock!) *sl-sex* ***Off*** used as a strong curse, Suck my dick!

pofríkiti {pòfrīkīm, kē perf.} *sl-fea* be very frightened, freak out <Eng❖>

pofrtùtma {ē fem.} *col-dia* mess, disorder, disturbance <Slav✍[*1]>

pofúkati {pòfūkām, pofúkajū perf.} *sl-sex* ***Obs*** engage in sexual intercourse with (of a male) <Eng❖[*1]>

pofurtùtma {ē fem.} *col-dia* noise <Slav✍[*1]>

pògača *See the following*

• **Pògaču ti jèbēm!** {S} (lit. I screw your bread!) *dia* ***Off*** used as a weak curse, Screw you!

• **Pògaču ti présnu jèbēm!** {S} (lit. I screw your raw bread!) SerE *dia* ***Off*** used as a weak curse, Screw you!

pògačica {ē fem.} (lit. flat bread) *sl-sex* ***Fac*** small female breast <Slav[*1]>

pògačice {čīcā fem. pl.} (lit. flat breads) *sl-fea* thick eyeglasses <Slav[*1]>

pògan [1] {a, o adj.} *col-dia* evil, mean, bad: *pogan frajer mean guy* <Slav[*1]>

pȍgān [2] {i fem.} *col-dia* dirt <Slav[*1]>

pogánac *See the following*

• **Pogánca ti u dȗvku jèbēm!** {S} (lit. I fuck your dirty kid in its cradle!) *dia* ***Off*** used as a very strong curse, Fuck you!

pogòditi *See the following*

• **pogòditi u žȉcu** {VP} (lit. hit the string) *col* find a vulnerable spot

• **pogòditi žȉcu** {VP} (lit. hit the string) *col* find a vulnerable spot

pogòvnati {gòvnām, ajū perf.} *sl-sex* ***Obs*** defecate, shit, <Slav❖>

pògrješka {ē fem.; Dat pògrješki} [std. = pogreška] *col-dia* error, mistake <Slav☞>

pȍhara {ē fem.} *col-dia* robbery <NE❖[*1]>

pòharati {ām, ajū perf.} *col-dia* rob, fleece, rip off <NE❖[*1]>

pòhasati {ām, ajū perf.} *sl* eat, devour <NE❖[*1]>

pohásiti se {sīm, sē imperf. intr.} *col-dia* try to do something beyond one's capabilities <NE❖[*1]>

pohíti {excl.} BosM *col* used to urge somebody to move <Slav>

pohítiti {pòhītīm, tē perf. intr.} BosM *col* hurry up, rush <Slav>

pòhoblati {ām, ajū perf.} /pohòblati /ām, ajū perf./ (lit. plane) *sl-sex* ***Obs*** engage in sexual intercourse with (of a male) <Ger❖[*1]>

pȍhovānā šȁmlica {NP} (lit. breaded chair) *sl* female ☞ šamlica

pòhvatati se {ām, ajū perf. intr.} (lit. catch each other) *sl-sex* ***Obs*** engage in sexual foreplay, pet, feel up <Slav[*1]>

poìzdignuti {nēm, nū perf.} (lit. lift up considerably) *sl* start singing <Slav[*1]>

pòjam *See the following*

• **geògrafskī pójam** {NP} (lit. geographical concept) **a.** *sl-fea* ***Fac*** boring person, bore **b.** *sl-fea* ***Fac*** unimportant person, nobody, nothing

• **pójma nêmām** {VP} (lit. I have no concept) *col* used to refer to lack of knowledge, I don't know, I haven't a clue

pòjān {pojána masc.} *sl-arch* paper (e.g. sheets of paper)

pojèbati {pòjebēm, bū perf.} *sl-sex* ***Obs*** engage in sexual intercourse with (of a male) <Slav❖>

pojèbati se {pòjebēm, bū perf.} *sl-sex* ***Obs*** engage in sexual intercourse with <Slav❖>

Pòjel jájca od zȁmlatu! {S} (lit. He has eaten scrambled eggs!) SSer *dia* ***Obs*** used as a moderate curse, Fuck you! ☞ pojesti

pòjesti *See the following*

• **Pòjeo je múda óvnova!** {S} (lit. He has eaten a ram's balls!) *col* ***Obs*** used as a moderate cure, Fuck you!

• **pòjeo vûk màgare** {VP} (lit. a wolf has eaten a donkey) *col* nothing has happened

• **pòjesti Francúza** {VP} (lit. eat a Frenchman) *sl-sex* ***Obs*** suffer from syphilis, have the pox

• **pòjesti jêža** {VP} (lit. eat a hedgehog) *sl* be badly mistaken

• **pòjesti žȉlēt** {VP} (lit. eat a razor blade) *sl-fea* be surprised

pòjesti se {edēm, edu perf. intr.} (lit. eat one self) *col* get nervous <Slav[*1]>

pòjiti {jīm, jē imperf.} (lit. water) **a.** *sl-fea* talk persistently and meaninglessly, blabber, chatter <Slav[*1]> **b.** *sl* cheat by convincing into <Slav[*2]>

pójma nêmām {VP} (lit. I have no concept) *col* used to refer to lack of knowledge, I don't know, I haven't a clue ☞ pojam

pòjmāš {pojmáša (acc. = gen.) masc.; Voc pȍjmāšu} *sl-fea* stupid or mentally deficient person <Slav❖>

pokákiti se {pòkākīm, kē perf. intr.} *sl-sex* ***Fam*** defecate, shit <Ger❖>

pȍkāl {pokála masc.} (lit. cup) *sl-sex* ***Fac*** buttocks, butt <Fre[*1]>

pokarabúsati {ràbūsām, rabúsajū } *col* destroy, ruin <NE❖[*1]>

pokazívati *See the following*

• **pokazívati bùbrege** {VP} (lit. show one's kidneys) *sl* laugh

pokénjati {pòkēnjām, pokénjajū perf.} (lit. shit) *sl-fea* offend <Slav❖>

pokénjati se {pòkēnjām, pokénjajū perf. intr.} *sl-sex* ***Obs*** defecate, shit <Slav❖>

pokeríca {ē fem.} *sl-gamble* poker <Eng❖>

pokerȉška {ē fem.; Dat pokerȉški} /pokerȉška/ *sl-gamble* poker <Eng☞>

pòkisao {a, o adj.} (lit. soaked) *sl-fea* sad: *On je pokisao jer mu je umro pas. He is sad 'cause his dog died.* <Slav[*1]>

poklápa {ē fem.} **a.** *sl-gamble* a kind of card game where players try to flip over their playing cards <Slav❖> **b.** *sl-sex* sexual intercourse <Slav❖[*1]>

pòklop {a masc.} (lit. cover) *sl-fea* cheat, swindle <Slav[*1]>

pòklopac {pca masc.} (lit. lid) *sl* cap, hat <Slav[*1]>

poklópati {pòklōpām, poklópajū perf.} *sl* eat, devour: *poklopati dva puna tanjira devour two plate-fulls* <Gyp❖[*1]>

poklópati se {pòklōpām, poklópajū perf. intr.} (lit. eat oneself) *sl-fea* get nervous <**Gyp**✣*1>

pòklopljen {a, o adj.} (lit. covered) *sl-fea* deaf <**Slav***1>

pòkop {a masc.} (lit. burial) *sl* effective joke <**Slav***1>

pȍkopān frȁjer {NP} (lit. buried guy) *sl-fea* ruined male (e.g. financially) ☞ **frajer**

pokòpati {ām, ajū perf.} (lit. bury) **1** *sl* reply, answer <**Slav***1> **2** *sl* destroy, ruin <**Slav***1> **3** defeat: *Zvezda je pokopala Partizana pet nula. Red Star has buried Patizan five zip.*

pokòrnjāk {kornjáka (acc. = gen.) masc.} (lit. the obedient one) *sl-fea* ***Der*** ingratiator (male), brownnoser, ass kisser <**Slav**✣*1>

pòkošenī {ā, ō adj.} (lit. mowed) *sl-fea* bald <**Slav***1>

pòkotče {eta neut.} *sl-fea* very young female, little girl

pokúnjiti {pòkūnjīm, njē perf.} *sl* ashame, bring disgrace to <**Slav***1>

pokúnjiti se {pòkūnjīm, njē perf. intr.} *sl* be very sad <**Slav***1>

pòkupiti {pīm, pē perf.} (lit. pick up) **1** *sl* get, obtain: *pokupiti dve karte za utakmicu get two ball game tickets* <**Slav***1> **2** *sl* hit, punch: *pokupiti frajera u stomak hit a guy in the gut* <**Slav***1>

• **pòkupiti čȁure** {VP} (lit. pick up bullet shells) *sl* shut up, cease talking

• **pòkupiti kȁjmak** {VP} (lit. skim) *col* get the best part of something, skim off the cream

• **pòkupiti pȑnje** {VP} (lit. get one's rags) *col* leave, depart, walk

• **pòkupiti šlâg** {VP} (lit. pick up cream) *col* get the best part of something, skim off the cream

• **pòkupiti vȑhnje** {VP} (lit. pick up sour cream) *col* get the best part of something, skim off the cream

pòkupiti se {pīm, pē perf.} (lit. pick oneself up) *sl* leave abruptly and silently <**Slav***1>

pòkvāren {a, o adj.} (lit. rotten) *col* bad, mean, immoral: *pokvarena gazdarica mean landlady* <**Slav***1>

pȍla-cijélo {a neut.} *sl-gamble* a kind of game with collector's cards where one has to guess if two cards will fall at the same side <**Slav***1>

pȍla rȉba - pȍla rȉba {NP} (lit. half fish-half fish) *sl* ***Fac*** mermaid ☞ **riba**

pȍlāganā smȑt {NP} (lit. slow death) *sl-fea* boring person, bore ☞ **smrt**

pȍlāk {adv.} [std. = polako] *col-dia* easy, in no hurry <**Slav**✍>

polakírati se {làkīrām, lakírajū biasp. intr.} (lit. put on some lacquer) *sl* ***Fac*** die, kick the bucket <**Fre**✣*1>

• **polégnuti pílu** {VP} (lit. lay down the saw) *sl-auto* fall from a motorcycle on a curve

polèteti {tīm, tē perf.} (lit. start flying) SerE *sl* pay (bills, etc.) <**Slav***1>

polètjeti {tīm, tē perf.} (lit. start flying) *sl* pay (bills, etc.) <**Slav***1>

polevátiti {lèvātīm, tē imperf.} *sl-crime* steal from, rip off

pòlica {ē fem.} (lit. shelf) *sl* female

pòlīć {polića masc.} (lit. halfer) *sl* half-dinar coin <**Slav**✣*1>

polírānje {a neut.} (lit. polishing) *sl-sex* ***Fac-Obs*** sexual intercourse <**Lat***1>

polìtičkī {ōg (acc. = gen.) masc.} (lit. the political one) *sl-polit* political prisoner <**Gre***1>

polìtika [1] {excl.} (lit. politics) *sl* watch out, be careful <**Gre***1>

polìtika [2] {ē fem.} (lit. politics) *col-dia* ***Der*** cunning, sly, slick <**Gre***1>

polìtka {ē fem.} (lit. politics) [std. = politika] *col-dia* ***Der*** cunning, sly, slick <**Gre**✍*1>

polivȁčina {ē fem.} (lit. pouring) *sl* fight (e.g. fist fight) <**Slav***1>

polívānje {a neut.} (lit. watering) *sl* fighting <**Slav***1>

polívati *See the following*

• **polívati bȃštu** {VP} (lit. water one's garden) *sl-fea* live a quiet family life

polívati se {pòlīvām, polívajū imperf. intr.} (lit. pour water on oneself) *sl* fight (e.g. fist fight) <**Slav***1>

polížati *See the following*

• **polízati tȁnjīr** {VP} (lit. lick one's plate) *col* eat one's meal entirely, eat everything: *Djeco, poližite tanjir! Eat everything kids!*

pòlizgati {ām, ajū perf.} *sl-arch* drink up (alcohol)

pôlka {ē fem.; Dat pôlki} (lit. half) *sl* half-dinar coin <**Slav**✣*1>

polòmiti {pòlomīm, mē perf.} (lit. break) **a.** *sl* beat up severely, trash <**Slav***1> **b.** *sl-sex* engage in sexual intercourse with (of a male) <**Slav***2>

polòmiti se {pòlomīm, mē perf. intr.} (lit. break oneself) **1** *sl-fea* boast, brag <**Slav***1> **2** *sl-fea* strive, try hard <**Slav***1>

pòloram {a masc.} *sl-arch* cabbage

polóvnjača {ē fem.} (lit. halfer) **a.** *sl-fea* female over 25 years old <**Slav**❖[*1]> **b.** *sl-fea* sexually experienced female <**Slav**❖[*2]> **c.** *sl-fea* divorced female <**Slav**❖[*3]>

polòvnjāk {lovnjáka (acc. = gen.) masc.} (lit. halfer) *sl-auto* used car <**Slav**❖[*1]>

polòžiti {žīm, žē perf.} (lit. put down) **1** *sl-fea* say something unintelligent <**Slav**[*1]> **2** *sl-sex* engage in sexual intercourse with (of a male) <**Slav**[*1]>

• **polòžiti za bìzōna** {VP} (lit. pass the bison exam) *sl-fea* get old

• **polòžiti žìvot** {VP} (lit. lay down one's life) *sl* die, kick the bucket

pòltrōn {poltróna (acc. = gen.) masc.; Voc pȍltrōne} *sl-fea* ***Der*** ingratiator (male), brownnoser, ass kisser <**Fre**[*1]>

pòluknuti {nēm, nū perf.} *sl* peep, look at others <**Eng**❖>

polúpati *See the following*

• **polúpati lónčiće** {VP} (lit. break all little pots) *col* make a mistake, screw up

pȍlusvijēt {a +ov (ext. pl) masc.; Nom Pl pȍlusvjȇtovi} (lit. half-world) *sl-fea* ***Der*** worthless or despicable persons, scum <**Slav**❖>

polùtān {lutána (acc. = gen.) masc.} (lit. halfer) *sl-fea* worker-peasant <**Slav**❖>

pȍlutka {ē fem.; Dat pȍlutki} /pòlutka/ (lit. half) *sl-drugs* half gram of narcotic drugs <**Slav**[*1]>

pòljāk {poljáka (acc. = gen.) masc.; Voc pȍljāče} (lit. Pole) *sl-fea* person who stares <**Slav**[*1]>

pȍljār {a masc.} *sl* groschen (the coin) <**Slav**[*1]>

poljúbiti *See the following*

• **Poljúbi me u dȕpe!** {S} (lit. Kiss my ass!) *col* ***Off*** used as a moderate curse, Kiss my ass!

• **Poljúbi pa òstavi!** {S} (lit. Kiss and then leave it!) *col* used in response to complaints about something, usu. when a child complains about food, Take it or leave it!

• **poljúbiti dlànovac** {VP} (lit. kiss a palm hit) *sl* ***Fac*** get a slap

• **poljúbiti pàrkēt** {VP} (lit. kiss the floor) *sl* fall down, kiss the floor

• **poljúbiti pàtos** {VP} (lit. kiss the floor) *sl* fall down, kiss the floor

• **poljúbiti pȍd** {VP} (lit. kiss the floor) *sl* fall down, kiss the floor

• **poljúbiti pòpa** {VP} (lit. kiss a priest) *sl* ***Iro*** fall down, kiss the floor

• **poljúbiti brȁvu** {VP} (lit. kiss a lock) *col* find nobody at home

• **poljúbiti (zàtvorena) vráta** {VP} (lit. kiss a *closed* door) *col* find nobody at home

poljuprȉvreda {ē fem.} [std. = poljoprivreda] *col-dia* agriculture <**Slav**✍>

pòmaći se *See the following*

pomáda {ē fem.} *col* cosmetic cream <**Fre**>

pòmagā-vi-bôg {excl.} (lit. God helps you) Ser *dia* used to greet a religious person <**Slav**❖>

pòmāgābog {excl.} (lit. God helps) Ser *dia* used to greet a religious person <**Slav**❖>

pomágati *See the following*

• **pomágati nerazvìjenē** {VP} (lit. help the undeveloped ones) *sl-sex* ***Fac-Obs*** engage in sexual intercourse with an unattractive female

pomahnítati {màhnītām, mahnítajū perf. intr.} *sl-fea* go insane, freak out <**Heb**❖[*1]>

Pomàknula mu se dàska u glávi. {S} (lit. A plank in his head has moved.) *sl-fea* used to refer to insanity of a third party ☞ **pomaknuti se**

pòmaknūt {a, o adj.} (lit. moved) *sl-fea* ***Der*** insane, nuts <**Slav**[*1]>

pomàknuti se *See the following*

• **Pomàknula mu se dàska u glávi.** {S} (lit. A plank in his head has moved.) *sl-fea* used to refer to insanity of a third party

pomàrisati se {išēm, išū imperf. intr.} *sl* fight (e.g. fist fight): *pomarisati se s tri frajera fight against three guys* <**Gyp**❖[*1]>

pòmed {a (acc. = gen.) masc.} *sl-fea* very important or influential person, big shot

pòmeriti se *See the following*

• **Pòmeri se s mȅsta!** {S} (lit. Move from that place!) **SerE** *col* used in response to unwanted news or prediction

pòmesti {etēm, etū perf. irreg.} (lit. sweep out) *sl-crime* steal, swipe <**Slav**[*1]>

pomìjār {mijára (acc. = gen.) masc.} (lit. the one who has to deal with slops) *sl-mil* soldier on kp. <**Slav**❖[*1]>

pomìjara {ē fem.} (lit. slops place) **1** *sl* mouth <**Slav**❖[*1]> **2** *sl-fea* person who eats anything, garbage gut <**Slav**❖[*1]>

pòmije {pȍmījā fem. pl.} (lit. slops) *sl-polit* politician <**Slav**[*1]>

pòmilovati {lujēm, lujū perf. intr.} (lit. pet) *sl* hit, punch <**Slav**[*1]>

pomòčati {ām, ajū perf.} (lit. water) *sl-sex* ***Obs*** urinate, piss <Slav❖*1>

pòmoći *See the following*

• **Pòmoći će mu ko mȑtvōm ȍbloge.** {S} (lit. That will help him like compresses will a dead person.) *col* ***Iro*** used to refer to the futility of all efforts, It's no use

pòmrdati {ām, ajū perf.} (lit. move) *sl-sex* ***Obs*** engage in sexual intercourse with (of a male) <Slav*1>

ponájlak {adv.} BosM *col* slowly <NE*1>

pȍnī èkspres {NP} (lit. pony express) Cro *sl* streetcar line number two in Zagreb, Croatia ☞ **ekspres**

pònistra {ē fem.} Med *col-dia* balcony <Ita>

pónor {a masc.} (lit. abyss) *sl-sex* ***Fac*** bathroom <Slav*1>

pònjava {ē fem.} (lit. shawl) *sl* cigarette paper <Slav*1>

ponjàvče {eta neut.} *col-dia* shawl <Slav❖>

pȍp {pòpa (acc. = gen.) +ov (ext. pl) masc.; Nom Pl pòpovi} (lit. priest) **1** *sl-crime* policeman, cop <Slav*1> **2** *sl-sstu* professor, high-school teacher (male), prof <Slav*1> **3** *sl-sex* male homosexual, gay <Slav*1> **4** *sl* groschen (the coin) <Slav*1>

pòpadati {ām, ajū perf.} (lit. fall) *col* laugh intensively, fall down laughing <Slav*1>

popalìndati {ām, ajū biasp.} *sl-crime* steal, swipe

popáliti {pòpālīm, lē perf.} (lit. burn out) **a.** *sl* persuade, convince <Slav*1> **b.** *sl-crime* steal, swipe <Slav*2>

popáliti se {pòpālīm, lē perf. intr.} (lit. burn) *sl-fea* get interested <Slav*1>

popàrisati {išēm, išū perf.} *sl-crime* steal, swipe <Slav❖*1>

pòpēti se *See the following*

• **pòpēti se nà kurac** {VP} (lit. climb on the prick) *col* ***Obs*** be very boring

• **pòpēti se na telèfōn** {VP} (lit. climb on the telephone) *col* hang on the telephone for a long period of time

popičkàrati se {ām, ajū perf.} *sl* ***Obs*** have an argument <Slav❖*1>

popingvíniti {pìngvīnīm, nē perf. intr.} (lit. penguin out) *sl-fea* go insane, freak out <Lat❖*1>

pòpiš {a masc.} *sl-sex* ***Obs*** urinating, pissing <Slav✍*1>

Popìšām ti se jâ nà tō! {S} (lit. I piss on it to you!) *col* ***Off*** used to express disrespect or dissatisfaction, Fuck it! ☞ **popišati se**

pȍpišān {a, o adj.} **a.** *sl-sex* ***Obs*** covered with urine <Slav> **b.** *sl-fea* ***Obs*** ashamed: *Bio je popišan kad su svi saznali za njegov skandal. He was ashamed when everybody learned about his scandal.* <Slav*1> **c.** *sl-fea* ***Obs*** sad, depressed <Slav*2>

popìšati {ām, ajū perf.} *sl-sex* ***Obs*** urinate, piss <Slav>

popìšati se {ām, ajū perf. intr.} *sl-sex* ***Obs*** urinate, piss <Slav>

• **Popìšām ti se jâ nà tō!** {S} (lit. I piss on it to you!) *col* ***Off*** used to express disrespect or dissatisfaction, Fuck it!

popíškiti se {pòpīškīm, kē perf. intr.} *sl-sex* urinate <Slav❖>

popišmániti se {pìšmānīm, nē perf. intr.} *col* ***Der*** change one's mind <NE*1>

popìšulja {ē fem.} (lit. pisser) **a.** *sl-fea* very young female, little girl <Slav❖*1> **b.** *sl* female <Slav❖*2>

pòpiti [1] {pȍpijēm, ijēdu perf.} *sl-drink* drink (alcohol) <Slav✍>

pòpiti [2] {pȍpijēm, ijū perf.} *sl-fea* be beaten up <Slav*1>

• **pòpiti àsa** {VP} (lit. drink an ace) *sl* get a failing grade, flunk

• **pòpiti bàtine** {VP} (lit. drink beating) *sl* be beaten up

• **pòpiti blȃm** {VP} (lit. drink shame) *sl-fea* boast, brag

• **pòpiti hàsana** {VP} (lit. drink an ace) *sl* get a failing grade, flunk

• **pòpiti kanalizáciju** {VP} (lit. drink sewage) *sl-drink* get drunk

• **pòpiti kéca** {VP} (lit. drink an ace) *sl* get a failing grade, flunk

• **pòpiti klàsiku** {VP} (lit. drink classical) *sl* be knocked out

• **pòpiti máru** {VP} (lit. drink beating) *sl* be beaten up

• **pòpiti nȍgu** {VP} (lit. drink a foot) *sl* get fired

• **pòpiti nȍkat** {VP} (lit. drink a nail) *sl* miss, fail

• **pòpiti pàrkēt** {VP} (lit. drink floor) *sl* fall down, kiss the floor

• **pòpiti pàtos** {VP} (lit. drink floor) **a.** *sl* fall down, kiss the floor **b.** *sl* be defeated

• **pòpiti pedálu** {VP} (lit. drink a pedal) *sl* get fired

• **pòpiti péglu** {VP} (lit. drink an iron) *sl* be knocked out

• **pòpiti pèndrek** {VP} (lit. drink a billyclub) *sl* ***Fac*** be beaten up

• **pòpiti pȍd** {VP} (lit. drink floor) **a.** *sl* fall (physically) **b.** *sl* be defeated

• **pòpiti pričánjac** {VP} (lit. drink talking) *sl-fea* chat

• **pòpiti sòvān** {VP} (lit. drink sleeping) *sl* sleep, nap

• **pòpiti sòvān** {VP} (lit. drink sleeping) *sl* sleep, nap

• **pòpiti sòvāž** {VP} (lit. drink sleeping) *sl* sleep, nap

• **pòpiti sovijáner** {VP} (lit. drink sleeping) *sl* sleep, nap

• **pòpiti sôvku** {VP} (lit. drink sleeping) *sl* sleep, nap

• **pòpiti sóvu** {VP} (lit. drink sleeping) *sl* sleep, nap

• **pòpiti šopéna** {VP} (lit. drink Chopin) *sl-sex* ***Fac-Obs*** engage in fellatio

popizdeti {pópizdim, dē perf. intr.} (lit. cunt out) **a.** SerE *sl-fea* go insane, freak out <Slav❖[*1]> **b.** SerE *sl-fea* get angry <Slav❖[*2]>

popízditi {pòpīzdīm, dē perf. intr.} (lit. cunt out) *sl-fea* go insane, freak out <Slav❖[*1]>

popizdìtis {a masc.} *sl-fea* nervousness <Slav✐[*1]>

popláhnuti {pòplāhnēm, nū perf.} *sl* hit, punch <Slav>

pòplašiti {šīm, še perf.} (lit. frighten) **1** *sl-sex* ***Fac-Obs*** engage in sexual intercourse with (of a male) <Slav[*1]> **2** *sl-fea* ***Fac*** steal, swipe <Slav[*1]>

pȍplava {ē fem.} (lit. flood) *sl-fea* too short trousers, flood pants <Slav[*1]>

• **kò da ga je izbácila pȍplava** {PP} (lit. like the flood has flushed him out) **a.** *sl-fea* ***Der-Fac*** extremely unattractive, ugly as sin **b.** *sl-fea* ***Der-Fac*** sad, depressed: *Kad je saznao da nije dobio stipendiju, bio je ko da ga je izbacila poplava. He was depressed when he realized that he did not get the scholarship.*

popláviti *See the following*

• **Poplávíće mi vrât!** {S} (lit. My neck is going to be blue!) *sl-fea* used to express the feeling of being bored with somebody, You are boring!

pòplīnđati {ām, ajū perf. intr.} *sl-crime* steal, swipe

pòpljugati {ām, ajū perf.} **a.** *sl* smoke (tobacco) <Slav❖[*1]> **b.** *sl-sex* engage in fellatio **c.** *sl-fea* be cheated, be swindled

• **pòpljugati fóru** {VP} (lit. smoke a trick) *sl* be cheated, be swindled

pòpōv štȁkor {NP} (lit. priest's rat) *sl-sex* ***Fac-Obs*** penis of an elderly male ☞ **štakor**

pòpraviti {vīm, vē imperf.} (lit. repair) *sl* beat up <Slav[*1]>

pòpraviti se {vīm, ve perf. intr.} *col* gain weight <Slav[*1]>

poprditi *See the following*

• **Pòprdīš mi ga!** {S} (lit. You fart it to me!) *sl-sex* ***Off*** used as a strong curse

poprdùckati {ām, ajū imperf.} (lit. fart a little) *sl-fea* talk persistently and meaninglessly, blabber, chatter <Slav❖[*1]>

poprȉčekati {ām, ajū perf.} *col* wait <Slav❖>

pòpunjen {a, o adj.} (lit. fitted) *sl-fea* obese, fat <Slav[*1]>

• **elegàntno pòpunjen** {AdjP} (lit. elegantly stuffed) *col* ***Iro*** obese, fat

pòpuši {excl.} *sl-sex* ***Off-Obs*** used to express one's extreme disgust and to offend one's interlocutor, Blow me! <Slav[*1]>

Pòpuši kȕrac! {S} (lit. Smoke a prick!) *sl-sex* ***Off*** used as a strong curse, Blow mw! ☞ **popušiti**

pòpušiti {šīm, šē perf.} (lit. smoke) **a.** *sl-sex* ***Obs*** engage in fellatio <Slav[*1]> **b.** *sl-fea* be cheated, be swindled <Slav[*2]>

• **Pòpuši kȕrac!** {S} (lit. Smoke a prick!) *sl-sex* ***Off*** used as a strong curse, Blow me!

• **Pòpuši mi!** {S} (lit. Smoke it to me!) *sl-sex* ***Off*** used as a strong curse, Blow me!

• **Pòpuši mi káru!** {S} (lit. Smoke my prick!) *sl-sex* ***Off*** used as a strong curse, Blow me!

• **Pòpuši mi kȍdžāka!** {S} (lit. Smoke my Kojak!) *sl-sex* ***Off*** used as a strong curse, Blow me!

• **Pòpuši mi kȕrac!** {S} (lit. Smoke my prick!) *sl-sex* ***Off*** used as a strong curse, Blow me!

• **Pòpuši mi kȕrac smȑdljivī!** {S} (lit. Smoke my stinky prick!) *sl-sex* ***Off*** used as a strong curse, Blow me!

• **Pòpuši mi pàtiku kad stȁnēm u góvno!** {S} (lit. Smoke my tennis shoe when I step on a piece of shit!) *sl* ***Off*** used as a strong curse, Fuck you!

• **Pòpuši mi púždru!** {S} (lit. Smoke my prick!) *sl-sex* ***Off*** used as a strong curse, Blow me!

• **Pòpuši môj sunny boy!** {S} (lit. Smoke my sunny boy!) *sl-sex* ***Off*** used as a strong curse, Blow me!

• **Pòpuši péderu!** {S} (lit. Smoke it, you faggot!) *sl-sex* ***Off*** used as a strong curse, Blow me!

• **pòpušiti fóru** {VP} (lit. smoke a trick) **1** *sl* be cheated, be swindled **2** *sl* be mistaken

• **pòpušiti kȕrac** {VP} (lit. smoke a prick) *sl-sex* ***Obs*** engage in fellatio

• **pòpušiti máru** {VP} (lit. smoke beating) *sl* be beaten up

pòrajfati {ām, ajū perf.} *sl-drink* drink (alcohol) <Ger❖[*1]>

poràptati {ām, ajū perf.} *sl-sex* ***Obs*** defecate, shit

pòrašpati {ām, ajū perf.} (lit. file) *sl-sex* ***Fac-Obs*** engage in sexual intercourse with (of a male) <Ger❖[*1]>

poràuhati {ām, ajū perf.} (lit. smoke) *sl-drugs* smoke hashish <Ger❖[*1]>

pȍrdāk {a (acc. = gen.) masc.} *sl-arch* dog (the animal)

pòrdok {a (acc. = gen.) masc.} *sl-arch* dog (the animal)

poredívati {rèdujēm, rèdujū imperf.} *sl* speak slang <Ger❖[*1]>

• **poredívati gȅpavačkī** {VP} (lit. speak criminalese) *sl* speak slang

• poredívati šătrovačkī {VP} (lit. speak slang) *sl* speak slang

poređívati {rèđujēm, rèđujū imperf. intr.} *sl* speak slang <Ger❖[*1]>

pòreznīk {a (acc. = gen.) masc.} (lit. taxman) *sl-drink* waiter <Slav[*1]>

pȍrijān {a (acc. = gen.) masc.} *sl-crime* policeman, cop <Gyp>

pòriti *See the following*

• pòriti frȁjera {VP} (lit. tear a guy apart) *sl-crime* pick pockets

pòrnīć {porníća masc.} *sl-sex* pornographic magazine or movie, porn mag or flick <Gre❖>

pôrno* {a adj.} /pòrno*/ *sl-sex* pornographic, porno <Gre>

pòrod *See the following*

• Pòrod ti jèbēm! {S} (lit. I fuck your kids!) *sl* ***Off*** used as a very strong curse, Fuck you!

pòrodičnā grȍbnica {NP} (lit. family tomb) *sl-fea* extremely unattractive person ☞ grobnica

pȍrpa {ē fem.} *sl-fea* unattractive female

portábl [1] {a masc.} (lit. portable) *sl* small quantity of something <Fre[*1]>

portábl [2] {adj.} (lit. portable) *sl* small <Fre[*1]>

pòrtviš {a masc.} *sl-fea* short male <Ger[*1]>

pôs {sta +ov (ext. pl) masc.; Nom Pl pòstovi} [std. = post] *col-dia* fasting <Slav✍>

• Pôs ti jèbēm! {S} (lit. I fuck your fasting!) *dia* ***Off*** used as a moderate curse, Fuck you!

• Pôs ti tvôj! {S} (lit. I fuck your fasting!) *dia* ***Off*** used as a moderate curse, Fuck you!

pòsā {sla masc.} [std. = posao] *dia-col* job, gig <Slav✍>

pȍsada {ē fem.} (lit. crew) *sl* company (group of people) <Slav[*1]>

pòsaō *See the following*

• ko s pòslom {PP} (lit. like being on business) *col* used to refer to an often illegal or inappropriate action performed without any hesitation: *ukrasti auto ko s poslom steal a car just like that*

posàugati {ām, ajū perf.} (lit. suck) **1** *sl-drink* drink (alcohol) <Ger[*1]> **2** *sl-sex* ***Obs*** engage in fellatio <Ger[*1]>

pòseći se *See the following*

• pòseći se na dlȁku {VP} (lit. cut oneself on a hair) **a.** *sl-fea* make a fool of oneself **b.** *sl-sex* fail in sex

poselámiti {sèlāmīm, mē perf. intr.} *col* send regards <NE[*1]>

pòser {a masc.} *sl-sex* ***Obs*** defecating <Slav❖>

Pòserēm ti se jâ nà tō! {S} (lit. I shit on that to you!) *col* ***Off*** used to express disrespect or dissatisfaction, Fuck it! ☞ posrati se

pòserkija {ē fem.} *dia* saber, sword <Slav❖[*1]>

pòserkinja {ē fem.} *dia* saber, sword <Slav❖[*1]>

posèrulja {ē fem.} (lit. shitter) *sl-fea* ***Der*** unclean female <Slav❖[*1]>

pòsijati {jēm, jū perf.} (lit. plant) **a.** *col* lose <Slav[*1]> **b.** *col* give away <Slav[*2]>

• pòsijati pàpriku {VP} (lit. seed peppers) *sl* get rid of

pòsla *See the following*

• [ADJ/PPRON] pòsla {NP} (lit. [ADJ] business) *col* ***Off*** used to denote a negative feature specific to a given group: *ciganska posla Gypsy dirty business, That's typical of Gypsies*

• njȉhova pòsla {NP} *col* used to express disrespect or dissatisfaction, their dirty business, that's typical of them

pòslati *See the following*

• Pòslaćemo ih u pízdu mȁterinu! {S} (lit. We will send them to their mother's cunt!) *sl* ***Obs*** used as a threat of physical violence to a group of third persons

• pòslati bômbu {VP} (lit. send a bomb) *sl* hit, punch

• pòslati čèkić {VP} (lit. send a hammer) *sl-crime* kill, murder

• pòslati gèbis {VP} (lit. send one's jaw) *sl* lose one's teeth

• pòslati mȍzak na ȉspašu {VP} (lit. send one's brain to graze) *col* take a rest, take a break, relax

• pòslati mȍzak na òtavu {VP} (lit. send one's brain to graze) *col* take a rest, take a break, relax

• pòslati mȍzak na pȁšu {VP} (lit. send one's brain to graze) *col* take a rest, take a break, relax

• pòslati po bùrek {VP} (lit. send to get some meat pies) *sl* trick, cheat, swindle

• pòslati po ćevápe{VP} (lit. send to get some meatballs) *sl* trick, cheat, swindle

• pòslati u mȅsto rođénja {VP} (lit. send to the birthplace) SerE *sl* curse, cuss

• pòslati u miròvinu {VP} (lit. retire) *sl-crime* kill, murder

Pȍslijē Tȉta - kȉta! {S} (lit. After Tito it's prick!) *sl-polit* ***Obs*** used to complain about the situation in the former Yugoslavia in the 1980s and 1990s ☞ Tito

poslòvnjāk {lovnjáka (acc. = gen.) masc.} *col* businessman <Slav❖>

pȍsluga {ē fem.; Dat pȍslugi} [std. = samoposluga] *col* grocery store <**Slav**✍>

pòsljednjī vlâk za Katàngu {NP} (lit. the last train to Katanga) **Cro** *sl-fea* dying person ☞ **vlak**

pòsmrtni mȁrš {NP} (lit. funeral march) *sl* funeral ☞ **marš**

pòsō {sla masc.} [std. = posao] *col* work, labor <**Slav**✍>

pòsraćkati {ām, ajū perf.} *sl-sex* ***Obs*** defecate, shit <**Slav**>

pȍsrān {a, o adj.} (lit. full of shit) **a.** *sl-fea* ***Obs*** defecated on <**Slav**[*1]> **b.** *sl-fea* ***Obs*** ashamed <**Slav**[*2]> **c.** *sl-fea* ***Obs*** depressed <**Slav**[*3]>

Pȍsrān-glàvica {ē fem.} (lit. Mt. Shithead) *dia* ***Obs*** a place name in Montenegro <**Slav**❖>

posrànče {eta neut.} (lit. shit-baby) *sl-fea* ***Obs*** small child <**Slav**❖[*1]>

pòsranica {ē fem.} (lit. shitter) *sl-fea* ***Der-Obs*** worthless or despicable female, shithead <**Slav**❖[*1]>

pòsranīk {posraníka (acc. = gen.) masc.; Voc pȍsranīče} /posrànīk/ (lit. shitter) **1** *sl-fea* ***Der-Obs*** worthless or despicable male, shithead <**Slav**❖[*1]> **2** member of Yugoslav parliament <**Slav**✍[*1]>

posránje {a neut.} *sl-sex* ***Obs*** defecating <**Slav**❖>

pòsrati {serēm, serū perf.} (lit. shit) **a.** *sl-sex* ***Obs*** defecate, shit <**Slav**> **b.** *sl* ***Obs*** destroy, ruin <**Slav**[*1]>

- **za pòsrati** {PP} (lit. to shit) *sl-fea* ***Obs*** worthless, worth shit

pòsrati se {serēm, seru perf. intr.} *sl-sex* ***Obs*** defecate, shit <**Slav**>

- **Pòserēm ti se jâ nà tō!** {S} (lit. I shit on that to you!) *col* ***Off*** used to express disrespect or dissatisfaction, Fuck it!

posrijédi *See the following*

- **posrijédi je** {PP} *col* used to stress one's point, the point is

pósro {a masc.} /le masc./ *sl-fea* ***Der-Obs*** worthless or despicable person <**Slav**❖[*1]>

posrògaća {ē fem. & masc.} (lit. underpants-shitter) **a.** *sl-fea* ***Der-Obs*** worthless or despicable person, shithead <**Slav**❖[*1]> **b.** *sl-fea* ***Der-Obs*** coward, chicken <**Slav**❖[*2]>

pȍsrogūz {a masc.} (lit. ass-shitter) *sl-fea* ***Der-Obs*** worthless or despicable male, shithead <**Slav**❖[*1]>

posròguza {ē fem. & masc.} (lit. ass-shitter) *sl-fea* ***Der-Obs*** worthless or despicable person, shithead <**Slav**❖[*1]>

pósronja {ē fem. & masc.} (lit. ass-shitter) *sl-fea* ***Der-Obs*** worthless or despicable person, shithead <**Slav**❖[*1]>

pȍsrorēp {a (acc. = gen.) masc.} (lit. tail-shitter) **a.** *sl-fea* ***Der-Obs*** weak ox <**Slav**❖[*1]> **b.** *sl-fea* weak and irresolute person, wimp <**Slav**❖[*2]>

posròrepa {ē fem.} (lit. tail-shitter) **a.** *sl-fea* ***Der-Obs*** weak cow <**Slav**❖[*1]> **b.** *sl-fea* ***Der-Obs*** weak female <**Slav**❖[*2]>

pôsrović {a (acc. = gen.) masc.} (lit. shitter) *sl-fea* ***Der-Obs*** worthless or despicable person, shithead <**Slav**❖[*1]>

pòsrulja {ē fem.} (lit. shitter) *sl-fea* ***Der-Obs*** worthless or despicable female, shithead <**Slav**❖[*1]>

pȍstava *See the following*

- **pȑvā pȍstava** {NP} (lit. first lineup) *sl* steady company, people one hangs with

pòstaviti *See the following*

- **pòstaviti mînu** {VP} (lit. plant a mine) *sl* trick, cheat, swindle

pòsteja {ē fem.} [std. = postelja] *dia-col* bed <**Slav**✍>

postèljārka {ē fem.} (lit. bed-person) **Cro** *sl-fea* female who rents rooms for one night at the train station in Zagreb, Croatia <**Slav**❖[*1]>

posteljìna {ē fem.} *sl* ***Fac*** lining (of a jacket) <**Slav**[*1]>

pòstiti {tīm, tē imperf. intr.} (lit. fast) *sl-sex* ***Fac*** refrain from engaging in sexual intercourse with <**Slav**[*1]>

posúditi *See the following*

- **posúditi frȁjeru óvna** {VP} (lit. lend a ram to a guy) *sl* pass a client to somebody else
- **posúditi žváku** {VP} (lit. borrow bubble-gum) *sl* kiss

pȍšājbati se {ām, ajū perf. intr.} *sl* fight (e.g. fist fight) <**Ger**❖[*1]>

pošandŕcati {ām, ajū perf. intr.} /pošandȑcati/ *sl-fea* go insane, freak out <**Slav**❖[*1]>

pošašáviti {šàšāvīm, vē perf. intr.} *sl-fea* go insane, freak out <**NE**❖[*1]>

pošéviti {pòšēvīm, vē perf.} *sl-sex* ***Obs*** engage in sexual intercourse with (of a male) <**Slav**❖[*1]>

pošéviti se {pòšēvīm, vē perf. intr.} *sl-sex* ***Obs*** engage in sexual intercourse with <**Slav**❖[*1]>

pošízeti {pòšīzīm, zē perf. intr.} SerE *sl-fea* go insane, freak out <**Gre**❖[*1]>

pošíziti {pòšīzīm, zē perf. intr.} *sl-fea* go insane, freak out <**Gre**❖[*1]>

pòškicnuti {nēm, nū perf.} *sl* look, watch, scope out

pòšlī {adv.} *sl-fea* the late: *njegov pošli otac his late father* <Slav*1>

pošljàjzditi {pòšljazdīm, dē perf. intr.} *sl-fea* go insane, freak out

pòšljednjī {ā, ē adj.} [std. = posljednji] *dia* last, being at the end: *Bio sam pošljednji u redu za mlijeko. I was the last in the milk line.* <Slav✍>

pòšōdrati {ām, ajū imperf.} *sl-sex* ***Obs*** engage in sexual intercourse with (of a male) <Ger❖*1>

pošórati se {pòšōrām, pošórajū perf. intr.} **1** *sl-sex* ***Obs*** urinate, piss <Ger❖*1> **2** *sl* fight (e.g. fist fight)

pȍštār {a (acc. = gen.) masc.} (lit. mailman) **1** *sl-crime* policeman from a foreign country <Fre*1> **2** *sl-crime* informant, stoolie <Fre*1>

- **plâćenī pȍštār** {NP} (lit. paid mailman) *sl-crime* informer, stoolie, snitch
- **Pȍštār njȕšī.** {S} (lit. The mailman is sniffing.) *sl-crime* used to indicate that an informer is nearby

pȍštarica {ē fem.} (lit. mailwoman) *sl-sex* ***Obs*** female who readily and indiscriminately engages in sexual intercourse, slut <Fre*1>

poštarìlos {a (acc. = gen.) masc.} *sl* mailman <Fre✍>

poštarìška {ē masc.; Dat poštarìški} /poštarìška/ *sl* mailman <Fre✍>

poštèno {adv.} (lit. honestly) *col* much, very: *pošteno se najesti eat a good meal* <Slav*1>

pošténje *See the following*

- **Pošténje ti jèbēm!** {S} (lit. I fuck your honesty!) *col* ***Off*** used as a moderate curse, Fuck you!
- **Pošténje ti tàkvō jèbēm!** {S} (lit. I fuck that kind of honesty that you have!) *col* ***Off*** used as a moderate curse, Fuck you!

poštósati {pòštōsām, poštósajū perf.} (lit. bang) *sl-sex* ***Obs*** engage in sexual intercourse with (of a male) <Ger❖*1>

poštovànskī {excl.} [std. = poštovanje] **1** *sl* ***Fac*** used to greet informally on arrival, hi <Slav✍> **2** *sl* ***Fac*** used to take leave of somebody informally, bye-bye <Slav✍>

poštovánje {excl.} *col* used to greet mostly in direct formal communication, hello <Slav>

pośèđeti {pòśedīm, edē perf.} [std. = posjedjeti] *dia* sit for a while <Slav✍>

pȍt {a +ov (ext. pl) masc.; Nom Pl pòtovi} **1** *sl-drugs* hashish, hash <Eng> **2** *sl-drugs* marijuana, pot, grass <Eng>

potàflati {ām, ajū perf.} *sl-sex* ***Obs*** engage in sexual intercourse with (of a male) <Ger❖*1>

pòtēgānō {ōg neut.} *sl-arch* meat <Slav❖*1>

potégnuti {pòtēgnēm, nū perf.} (lit. pull) *sl-drink* drink (alcohol) <Slav*1>

- **potégnuti ga zà uho** {VP} (lit. pull his ear) *sl-sex* ***Fac-Obs*** masturbate, beat off

pòterati *See the following*

- **pòterati na súvo** {VP} (lit. drive to dry land) SerE *sl-fea* introduce strict discipline

potfȑknuti {pòtfȑknēm, nū perf.} *col* roll up (e.g. sleeves) <Ger❖>

potfukávanje {a neut.} (lit. underfucking) *sl-fea* cheating, swindling <Eng❖*1>

potfukávati {fùkāvām, fukávajū imperf.} (lit. underfuck) *sl-fea* cheat, swindle <Eng❖*1>

potkopávati *See the following*

- **potkopávati pénziju** {VP} (lit. dig retirement money) *sl* work

pȍtkova {ē fem.} /pòtkova/ (lit. horse-shoe) **1** *sl-sex* ***Obs*** vagina, cunt <Slav*1> **2** *sl* fifty dinars; a fifty-dinar coin <Slav*1>

pòtkovān {a, o adj.} (lit. iron-shod) **a.** *sl-fea* affluent <Slav*1> **b.** *sl-fea* very important, very influential <Slav*2> **c.** *sl-fea* competent, knowledgeable, good: *biti potkovan iz matematike be good in math* <Slav*3>

potkòvati {pòtkujēm, kujū perf.} (lit. shoe a horse) *sl-fea* shoe a horse <Slav*1>

pòtkožen {a, o adj.} (lit. having the fat under the skin) *sl-fea* affluent <Slav❖*1>

pòtkožiti se {žīm, žē perf. intr.} (lit. get some fat under the skin) *sl-fea* become affluent <Slav❖*1>

potkùbati {pòtkubām, ajū perf.} *sl* bribe, lubricate

pòtkuriti {rīm, rē perf.} *sl* cheat, swindle <Slav*1>

potkusùrati se {ām, ajū perf. intr.} *col* settle mutual financial issues <NE❖*1>

potkusurívati se {sùrīvām, sùrujū imperf. intr.} *col* settle mutual financial issues <NE❖*1>

pȍtljē {adv.} [std. = poslije] *dia* later <Slav✍>

pòtok {a masc.} (lit. creek) *sl-crime* prison <Slav*1>

- **Bûbanj pòtok** {NP} (lit. Drum creek) *sl-crime* ***Fac*** prison

potòrbati {ām, ajū perf.} (lit. bag) *sl-sex* ***Obs*** engage in sexual intercourse with (of a male) <Slav❖*1>

potpáliti {pòtpālīm, lē perf.} (lit. set fire) *sl* make interested: *potpaliti ženu za kupovinu novih kola make one's wife interested in buying a new car* <**Slav*1**>

potpáliti se {pòtpālīm, lē perf. intr.} (lit. catch fire) *sl* get interested: *potpaliti se za odlazak na more get turned on to go to the seashore* <**Slav*1**>

potpaljìvāč {ljiváča (acc. = gen.) masc.} (lit. fire setter) *sl-sex* ***Fac*** male sexual partner (of a female) <**Slav*1**>

pòtpičnjāk [1] {a (acc. = gen.) masc.} (lit. Mr. Undercunt) *sl-fea* bearded male <**Slav❖*1**>

pòtpičnjāk [2] {a masc.} (lit. undercunt) *sl-sex* ***Obs*** area below vagina <**Slav❖*1**>

pȍtplata {ē fem.} (lit. sole) *col* inner pocket (of a jacket) <**Slav*1**>

potrbȕškē {adv.} *col* prone, lying on one's stomach <**Slav❖**>

pòtrefiti {fīm, fē perf.} *col-dia* hit, punch <**Ger❖**>

pòtrefiti se {fīm, fē perf. intr.} *col* happen (used usu. when two or several things coincide): *Tako se potrefilo da su nam se isti dan rodila djeca. It happened that our kids were born on the same day.* <**Ger❖**>

potrízdeti {pòtrīzdīm, dē perf. intr.} (lit. popizdeti 'get angry' has been modified to include the number three, which signals a higher intensity of being angry) SerE *sl-fea* get very angry <**Slav✍*1**>

potŕkati {pòtr̄kām, potŕkajū perf.} *sl-sex* ***Obs*** engage in sexual intercourse with (of a male) <**Slav*1**>

potrošábl {adj.} *sl-fea* used <**Slav-Fre❖**>

potrȍšiti {šīm, šē perf.} (lit. wear out) *sl-sex* ***Obs*** engage in sexual intercourse with (of a male) <**Slav*1**>

potrȍšiti se {šīm, šē perf. intr.} (lit. wear oneself out) *sl-drink* get drunk <**Slav*1**>

pòtrtkati {ām, ajū perf.} *sl-sex* ***Obs*** engage in sexual intercourse with <**Slav✍*1**>

pòtruhnuti {nēm, nū perf. intr.} [std. = potrunuti] *col* rotten, decayed <**Slav✍**>

pòtucati {ām, ajū perf.} (lit. crush) *sl-sex* ***Obs*** engage in sexual intercourse with (of a male) <**Slav*1**>

pòtucati se [1] {ām, ajū perf. intr.} (lit. crush each other) *sl-sex* ***Obs*** engage in sexual intercourse with <**Slav*1**>

potúcati se [2] {pòtūčām, potúcajū imperf. intr.} *col* wander, roam <**Slav*1**>

potùmplati {ām, ajū perf.} *sl-sex* ***Obs*** engage in sexual intercourse with (of a male) <**Ger❖*1**>

pòtūrčenī Hȑvāt {NP} (lit. a Croat converted into a Turk) *sl-fea* ***Off*** Bosnian Muslim ☞ **Hrvat**

pòtūrčenī Sȑbin {NP} (lit. a Serb converted into a Turk) *sl-fea* ***Off*** Bosnian Muslim ☞ **Srbin**

poturčènjāk {poturčenjáka (acc. = gen.) masc.; Voc pȍturčenjāče} (lit. converted Turk) *sl-fea* Bosnian Muslim <**Slav*1**>

pòturica {ē masc.} (lit. converted Turk) **1** *sl-fea* Bosnian Muslim <**Slav*1**> **2** *sl-fea* defector, traitor <**Slav*1**>

poubíjati se *See the following*

- **poubíjati se od [NOUN:GEN]** {LSF} (lit. kill each other because of [NOUN:NOM]) *sl-fea* be very [ADJ]: *Poubijali su se od rada. They were very diligent in their work.*

pȍva {ē fem.} *sl* wallet

povaćáriti {vàćārīm, vàćārē perf.} (lit. catch around) *sl-crime* steal, swipe <**Slav*1**>

pováliti {pòvālīm, lē perf.} (lit. lay down) *sl-sex* ***Obs*** engage in sexual intercourse with (of a male) <**Slav*1**>

pòvatati {pòvatām, ajū perf.} [std. = pohvatati] **a.** *col* catch <**Slav✍**> **b.** *sl-sex* sexually stimulate, turn on <**Slav✍*1**>

pòvatati se {pòvatām, ajū perf. intr.} [std. = pohvatati se] *sl-sex* ***Obs*** engage in sexual foreplay, pet, feel up <**Slav✍*1**>

povìzati {pòvižem, ižū imperf.} *sl-sex* ***Obs*** become aroused, get wet

pȍvlaka {ē fem.} [std. = pavlaka] *col-dia* sour cream <**Slav✍**>

pȍvlo {pòvalo masc.; perm} /pòvlo/ [std. = lopov] thief <**Hun✍**>

povrátiti *See the following*

- **povrátiti sȇrvu** {VP} (lit. return a serve) *sl* vomit, throw up, puke

povrátii se *See the following*

- **povrátiti se u pȑvō líce** {VP} (lit. get back in the first person) *sl-fea* regain consciousness, come to

povúci-potégni {adv.} (lit. grab it, don't give it) *col* used to refer to a situation which involves intensive bargaining, going back and forth: *Bilo je povuci-potegni, ali smo se na kraju dogovorili. We went back and forth for a while, and eventually reached an agreement.* ☞ **drž-nedaj**

pòvūći {povúčēm, povūkū, povúk, povúk perf. irreg.} (lit. pull) **1** *sl-drink* get drunk <**Slav*1**> **2** *sl-crime* take from one's pocket <**Slav*1**>

- **Povúci me zà kurac preko kúrca!** {S} (lit. Pull my

prick over my prick!) *col* ***Off*** used as a strong curse, Fuck you!

• **pòvūći bârku** {VP} (lit. pull a boat) **1** *sl-crime* steal someone's wallet **2** *sl* flush a toilet **3** *sl* shut up, cease talking

• **pòvūći Bȍga za jája** {VP} (lit. pull God's balls) *col* make an extraordinary achievement

• **pòvūći Bȍga za múda** {VP} (lit. pull God's balls) *col* make an extraordinary achievement

• **pòvūći kâr za ȕho** {VP} (lit. pull one's prick's ear) *sl-sex* ***Fac-Obs*** masturbate, beat off

• **pòvūći nȍgu u štôs** {VP} (lit. pull one's leg in a trick) **a.** *sl-fea* feel excellent **b.** *sl* continue to party

• **pòvūći[PRON:ACC]** za jèzik {LSF} (lit. pull [PPRON] tongue) *col* make [PRON:ACC] talk: *Povukao me za jezik, pa sam mu rekla sve šta mislim o njemu. He made me talk, so I told him what I really thought about him.*

• **pòvūći vȍdu** {VP} (lit. pull water) *sl* shut up, cease talking

pòvuriti {rīm, rē perf.} (lit. burn) *dia-col* eat

pòzadina {ē fem.} (lit. background) **a.** *sl-sex* ***Fac*** buttocks, back side, butt <Slav*1> **b.** *sl-sex* ***Fac*** attractive buttocks <Slav*2>

pozadínac {nca (acc. = gen.) masc.} (lit. rear-echelon soldier) *sl-sex* ***Fac*** male homosexual, gay <Slav✣*1>

pȍzdrav *See the following*

• **pȍzdrāv papírom** {NP} (lit. greeting in paper) *sl* tip, gratuity

pòzēr {pozéra (acc. = gen.) masc.} *sl-fea* dandy, fop <Fre*1>

póziv *See the following*

• **vôjnī póziv** {NP} (lit. call to military service) *sl-fea* unattractive female

pȍzniš {a masc.} [std. = poznavanje prirode] *sl-sstu* environment course (in elementary school) <Slav☞>

pozorìšnjāk {pozorišnjāka (acc. = gen.) masc.; Voc pȍzorišnjāče} *sl-media* theater worker <Slav✣*1>

pòždirati {rēm, ru imperf.} (lit. devour) *col* eat too much, gorge, pig out <Slav*1>

pòždrēti {rēm, ru perf.} (lit. devour) SerE *col* eat too much, gorge, pig out <Slav*1>

prȁčkānje {a neut.} (lit. shooting with a sling) *sl* fight (e.g. fist fight) <Slav✣*1>

prȁćka {ē fem.; Dat prȁćki} **a.** *col* sling <Slav> **b.i.** *sl-crime* gun pistol <Slav*1> **ii.** *sl* nose <Slav*1> **iii.** *sl* female <Slav*1> **iv.** *sl-fea* fast person, speedster <Slav*1>

pràđed {a (acc. = gen.) masc.} [std. = pradjed] *dia-col* great-grandfather <Slav☞>

prâh {a +ov (ext. pl) masc.; Nom Pl práhovi} (lit. powder) *sl-drugs* narcotic drug, dope <Slav*1>

• **ânđeoskī prâh** {NP} (lit. angel dust) *sl-drugs* phencyclidine

prája {ē fem.} [std. = praćka] *sl* sling <Slav☞>

pràkljača {ē fem.} *sl-fea* unattractive female

prȁkljos {a (acc. = gen.) masc.} *sl-fea* unattractive female

pràmac {mca masc.} (lit. bow *front end of a vessel*) *sl-sstu* school bathroom <Slav*1>

pràngija {ē fem.} (lit. small cannon) **1** *sl-fea* senior citizen <FreO> **2** *sl-sex* cheap prostitute **3** *sl-crime* gun pistol

pránje *See the following*

• **pránje glávē** {NP} (lit. head washing) **1** *sl* reproach, scold **2** *sl-sex* fellatio

• **pránje glávē i vrâta**{NP} (lit. head and neck washing) *sl-sex* ***Fac-Obs*** cunnilingus

• **pránje mȍzga** {NP} (lit. brain washing) **1** *sl* strong reprimand **2** *sl* questioning, interrogation

prâsak {ska masc.} (lit. bang) *sl-sex* ***Obs*** sexual intercourse <Slav*1>

prâse {eta neut.} (lit. piglet) **1** *sl-fea* obese person, porker <Slav*1> **2** *sl-sex* large penis <Slav*1>

• **ko prâse u plèhu** {PP} (lit. like a piglet in a roasting pan) *sl-fea* ***Fac*** narrow, tight

• **mâlō prâse** {NP} (lit. little piglet) *sl-sex* ***Fac-Obs*** penis, dick, prick

práskānje {a neut.} (lit. banging) *sl-sex* ***Obs*** sexual intercourse <Slav*1>

práskati {ām, ajū imperf.} (lit. bang) *sl-sex* ***Obs*** engage in sexual intercourse with (of a male), bang <Slav*1>

prȁsnūt {a, o adj.} (lit. banged) *sl-fea* ***Der*** insane, bonkers <Slav*1>

prȁsnuti {nēm, nū perf.} (lit. bang) *sl-sex* ***Obs*** engage in sexual intercourse with (of a male), bang <Slav*1>

prášak {ška masc.} (lit. powder) *sl-drugs* narcotic drug, dope <Slav*1>

prȁšinār {a (acc. = gen.) masc.} /prašȉnār /šinára (acc. = gen.) masc/ (lit. dust-dude) *sl-mil* infantry soldier, ground pounder <Slav✣*1>

prašȉnjār {šinjára (acc. = gen.) masc.} (lit. dust-dude) *sl-mil* infantry soldier, ground pounder <Slav*1>

prâšiti {prâšīm, šē imperf.} (lit. dust) **1** *sl-sex* ***Obs*** engage in sexual intercourse with (of a male) <**Slav**[*1]> **2** *sl-music* play a musical instrument <**Slav**[*1]>

prȁti *See the following*

• **prȁti flȁše nògama** {VP} (lit. wash bottles with one's legs) *sl-fea* have skinny legs

• **prȁti glâvu** {VP} (lit. wash one's head) **1** *sl* reproach, scold **2** *sl-sex* engage in fellatio

• **prȁti rajnglu** {VP} (lit. wash a stove ring) *sl-sex* ***Fac-Obs*** engage in cunnilingus

pràvac [1] {excl.} /**právac**/ *col* used to urge somebody to move straight ahead <**Slav**[*1]>

pràvac [2] {adv.} *col* directly, straight <**Slav**[*1]>

prâvī *See the following*

• **ko prâvī** {PP} (lit. like a real one) *col* ***App*** excellent, awesome

prȁviti *See the following*

• **nè pravi prȍmaju** {VP} (lit. don't make a draft) *sl* shut up, cease talking

• **prȁviti bèlāj** {VP} (lit. make a mess) BosM *col* create problems, cause trouble

• **prȁviti dȅcu** {VP} (lit. make kids) **1** **SerE** *sl* joke with, make a fool of **2a.** *sl-sex* torture **b.** *sl-fea* engage in sexual intercourse with

• **prȁviti pȉpī** {VP} (lit. make pee) *sl-sex* ***Fam*** urinate, pee

• **prȁviti situáciju** {VP} (lit. make the situation) *sl-fea* boast, brag

• **prȁviti štènčiće** {VP} (lit. make puppies) *sl-sex* ***Obs*** engage in sexual intercourse with

• **prȁviti ventiláciju** {VP} (lit. make ventilation) *sl-fea* talk persistently and meaninglessly, flap one's jaws

• **prȁvljen na dȕpe pa prètākān** {AdjP} (lit. made on the ass and then poured into another container) **a.** *sl-fea* absolutely insane, totally nuts **b.** *sl-fea* worthless (object, person, etc.)

prȁviti se {vīm, vē imperf. intr.} (lit. make oneself) **a.** *col* pretend: *Ona se samo pravi da je tamo šef. She just pretends to be a boss over there.* <**Slav**[*1]> **b.** *col* boast, brag <**Slav**[*2]>

• **prȁviti se Ȅnglēz** {VP} (lit. pretend to be an Englishman) **a.** *col* act calm, act cool **b.** *col* turn a blind eye **c.** *col* pretend to be uninformed **d.** *col* pretend not to understand

• **prȁviti se Tóša** {VP} (lit. pretend to be Joe) **a.** **SerE** *col* pretend to be uninformed **b.** *col* pretend to be unintelligent

prâvō {adv.} **1** *col* really, indeed <**Slav**[*1]> **2** *col* very much: *Pravo mu se sviđaš. He likes you very much.* <**Slav**[*1]>

prȁvopīs {a masc.} (lit. orthography) *sl-sex* ***Fac-Obs*** manual insertion of the penis into one's vagina <**Slav**[*1]>

prâznā {ē fem. (adj. decl.)} (lit. the empty one) *sl-sex* ***Der*** frigid female <**Slav**[*1]>

prâznīk {a (acc. = gen.) masc.} (lit. empty person) *sl-sex* ***Fac*** impotent male <**Slav**[*1]>

prâzno {adv.} *sl-fea* difficult, bad <**Slav**[*1]>

praznòguz [1] {a (acc. = gen.) masc.} (lit. the empty buttocks) *sl-fea* poor male <**Slav**[*1]>

praznòguz [2] {a, o adj.} (lit. empty-butted) *sl-fea* poor <**Slav**[*1]>

pȑc [1] {a +ev (ext. pl) masc.; Nom Pl pŕcevi} *sl* ***Fea*** breaking wind, farting <**Slav**[*1]>

PȐC [2] {a masc.} /**pȑc**/ (abbreviation *p*rivate r(ecreational) c(enter) X prcati 'to fuck') *sl* ***Fac*** private lot (usu. with a cottage on it) <**Abb**[*1]>

pŕca {ē masc.} *sl-fea* ***Der*** short person <**Slav**[*1]>

pȑcānje {a neut.} *sl-sex* ***Obs*** sexual intercourse <**Slav**>

pȑcapȑcati {ām, ajū imperf.} *sl-sex* ***Obs*** engage in sexual intercourse with (of a male) <**Slav**>

pȑcati {ām, ajū imperf.} *sl-sex* ***Obs*** engage in sexual intercourse with (of a male) <**Slav**>

• **pȑcati mȕšice** {VP} (lit. fuck flies) *sl* ***Obs*** spend one's time in useless activities, fool around, mess around

pȑckati {ām, ajū imperf.} *sl-sex* ***Obs*** engage in sexual intercourse with (of a male) <**Slav**>

pȑcknedl {a (acc. = gen.) masc.} (lit. fart-dumpling) *sl-fea* short person <**Slav-Ger**[*1]>

Pȑcković {a (acc. = gen.) masc.} (lit. McFart) *sl* a surname <**Slav**❖[*1]>

pȑcnuti {nēm, nū perf.} **1** *sl-sex* ***Obs*** engage in sexual intercourse with (of a male) <**Slav**❖> **2** *sl-sex* ***Obs*** break wind, fart <**Slav**❖>

pŕco {a masc.} /**pŕco** /e masc./ *sl-fea* short male <**Slav**[*1]>

prcòjgenz {a masc.} *sl-sex* brothel, whorehouse <**Slav**☞>

pȑcokoz {a masc.} (lit. goat-fuck) *sl-sex* ***Obs*** sexual intercourse (of goats) <**Slav**❖>

pȑcvoljak {ljka (acc. = gen.) masc.} **1** *sl-fea* little boy, kid <**Slav**❖[*1]> **2** *sl-fea* young female, girl <**Slav**❖[*1]> **3** *sl* chip, chunk <**Slav**❖[*1]> **4** *sl-sex* small penis <**Slav**❖[*1]>

pȑča {ē fem.} *sl* female <**Slav**☞>

přčast {a, o adj.} *sl-fea* small (of the nose) <**Slav**[*1]>

přčiti {čīm, čē imperf.} (lit. strut) *sl-sex* ***Obs*** engage in sexual intercourse with (of a male) <**Slav**[*1]>

přčiti se {čīm, čē imperf. intr.} (lit. strut) *sl-fea* be conceited, be stuck-up <**Slav**[*1]>

přčkati {ām, ajū imperf. intr.} *col* work on something <**Slav**>

přća {ē fem.} *sl-fea* pug-nosed person <**Slav**❖>

přćāknūt {a, o adj.} *sl-fea* slightly insane, wacky <**Slav**❖[*1]>

přćiti {ćīm, ćē imperf.} (lit. strut) *sl-sex* ***Obs*** engage in sexual intercourse with (of a male) <**Slav**[*1]>

přćnuti {nēm, nū perf. intr.} *sl-sex* ***Obs*** engage in sexual intercourse with (of a male) <**Slav**>

přćos {a masc.} *sl-fea* short-nosed person <**Slav**☞>

přda {ē fem.} (lit. farter) *sl-sex* ***Obs*** buttocks, butt <**Slav**❖[*1]>

přdac[1] {rca (acc. = gen.) masc.} (lit. fart) **1** *sl-fea* ***Der-Obs*** stupid or mentally deficient person <**Slav**❖[*1]> **2** *sl-fea* ***Der-Obs*** extremely talkative person, chatterbox <**Slav**❖[*1]>

přdac[2] {rca masc.} *sl-sex* ***Obs*** breaking wind, farting <**Slav**❖>

• **ni přdac** {PP} (lit. not even a fart) *sl* shut up, cease talking

přdāč {prdáča (acc. = gen.) masc.} **a.** *sl-sex* ***Obs*** person who breaks wind <**Slav**❖> **b.** *sl-fea* ***Der-Obs*** extremely talkative person, chatterbox <**Slav**❖[*1]> **c.i.aa.** *sl-fea* snob <**Slav**❖[*2]> **bb.** young snob <**Slav**❖[*3]> **ii.** moron

prdàčina {ē fem.} (lit. farting) *sl* ***Fac-Obs*** fun <**Slav**❖[*1]>

přdalica {ē fem.} (lit. farter) **1** *sl-sex* ***Obs*** buttocks, butt <**Slav**❖[*1]> **2** *sl-auto* ***Fac*** motorcycle <**Slav**❖[*1]> **3** *sl-auto* ***Fac*** engine <**Slav**❖[*1]>

přdalo {a neut.} (lit. farter) **1** *sl-sex* ***Obs*** buttocks, butt <**Slav**❖[*1]> **2** *sl-auto* ***Fac*** car, wheels <**Slav**❖[*1]> **3** *sl-auto* ***Fac*** motorcycle <**Slav**❖[*1]>

• **U přdalo te jèbēm!** {S} (lit. I fuck you in your farting thing!) *dia-col* ***Off*** used as a moderate curse, Fuck you!

přdāljka {ē fem.} (lit. farter) *sl-sex* ***Obs*** buttocks, butt <**Slav**❖>

prdáljko {a masc.} (lit. farter) *sl-auto* ***Fac-Obs*** motorcycle <**Slav**❖[*1]>

přdara {ē fem.} (lit. farter) **1** *sl-sex* ***Obs*** buttocks, butt <**Slav**❖[*1]> **2** *sl-fea* ***Der-Obs*** boring female, bore <**Slav**❖[*1]> **3a.** *sl-fea* ***Der-Obs*** foolish female <**Slav**❖[*1]> **b.** *sl-fea* rude female <**Slav**❖[*2]> **c.** *sl* female <**Slav**❖[*3]>

prdàrluk {a masc.} (lit. farting) *sl-fea* ***Fac-Obs*** nonsense, bullshit <**Slav**❖[*1]>

přdavac {vca masc.} (lit. farter) *sl* ***Fac-Obs*** cheese <**Slav**❖[*1]>

prdécnuti {přdēcnēm, nū perf. intr.} *sl-sex* ***Obs*** break wind, fart <**Slav**❖[*1]>

prdekàna {ē fem.} (lit. farting place) *sl-crime* ***Fac-Obs*** prison <**Slav**❖[*1]>

prdéknuti {přdēknēm, nū perf. intr.} **a.** *sl-sex* ***Obs*** break wind, fart <**Slav**❖> **b.** *sl* ***Fac*** die, kick the bucket <**Slav**❖[*1]>

přdeti {dīm, dē imperf. intr.} **a.** **SerE** *sl-sex* ***Obs*** break wind, fart <**Slav**> **b.** **SerE** *sl-fea* ***Fac-Obs*** talk persistently and meaninglessly, blabber, chatter <**Slav**[*1]> **c.i.** *sl* ***Fac-Obs*** lie <**Slav**[*2]> **ii.** *sl-fea* ***Fac-Obs*** be boring <**Slav**[*2]>

přdež {a masc.} /pŕdež/ *sl-sex* ***Obs*** breaking wind, farting <**Slav**❖>

přdežmen {a (acc. = gen.) masc.} (lit. fart-man) **a.** *sl-fea* ***Der-Obs*** talkative loafer <**Slav**❖[*1]> **b.** *sl-fea* ***Der-Obs*** irresponsible male <**Slav**❖[*2]>

prdìkara {ē fem. & masc.} (lit. farter) *sl-fea* ***Der-Obs*** spendthrift <**Slav**❖[*1]>

přdimiš {adj.} *col* ***Obs-Fac*** grey <**Slav**❖[*1]>

přditi {dīm, dē imperf. intr.} **a.** *sl-sex* ***Obs*** break wind, fart <**Slav**> **b.** *sl-fea* ***Fac-Obs*** talk persistently and meaninglessly, blabber, chatter <**Slav**❖[*1]> **c.** *sl* ***Fac-Obs*** lie <**Slav**❖[*2]>

• **sīlōm přdī, ȑđōm smr̀dī** {S} (lit. farts with force, smells of rust) *col* ***Obs*** used to indicate that one is pretending to be affluent or influential while being weak and unimportant

přdizvēk {a (acc. = gen.) masc.} *sl-sex* ***Obs-Fac*** person who breaks wind frequently or loudly <**Slav**❖[*1]> ☞ **prdozvek**

pŕdlja {ē masc.} *sl* ***Fac*** beans <**Slav**❖[*1]>

přdnuti {nēm, nū perf. intr.} *sl-sex* ***Obs*** break wind, fart <**Slav**❖>

• **Přdni mi na čȕk!** {S} (lit. Fart on my prick!) *dia* ***Off*** used as a moderate curse, Fuck you!

• **Přdni mi na stójka!** {S} (lit. Fart on my dick!) *dia* ***Off*** used as a moderate curse, Fuck you!

• **přdnuti na pamet** {VP} (lit. fart on one's mind) *col* ***Obs*** decide, feel like doing

• **přdnuti na ròsu** {VP} (lit. fart on dew) *sl* die, kick the bucket

• pȑdnuti na svijéću {VP} (lit. fart on a candle) *sl* die, kick the bucket

• pȑdnuti u čàbar {VP} (lit. fart in a bowl) *sl* die, kick the bucket

• pȑdnuti u fènjer {VP} (lit. fart in a lantern) *sl* die, kick the bucket

• pȑdnuti u varíćak {VP} (lit. fart in a bowl) *col* ***Obs*** be unable to do anything

pȑdnjati {ām, ajū imperf.} *sl-fea* ***Der-Obs*** talk persistently and meaninglessly, blabber, chatter <Slav❖*1>

pȑdonja {ē masc.} (lit. farter) *sl-fea* ***Der-Obs*** senior citizen, old fart <Slav❖*1>

pȑdozvēk {a (acc. = gen.) masc.} *sl-sex* ***Obs-Fac*** person who breaks wind frequently or loudly <Slav❖*1> ☞ **prdizvek**

prdùckānje {a neut.} **a.** *sl-sex* ***Obs*** breaking wind, farting <Slav❖> **b.** *sl-fea* ***Fac-Obs*** persistent and meaningless talk, blabber <Slav❖*1>

prdùckati {ām, ajū imperf. intr.} **a.** *sl-sex* ***Obs*** break wind, fart <Slav❖> **b.** *sl-fea* ***Fac-Obs*** talk persistently and meaninglessly, blabber, chatter <Slav❖*1>

prèbiti {prȅbijēm, ijū imperf.} (lit. crush) **a.** *sl* beat up <Slav*1> **b.** *sl-sex* deflower <Slav*2>

• prèbiti kô vòla u kùpusu {VP} (lit. break like an ox in cabbage) *col* beat up severely

• prèbiti na mȑtvō ȉme {VP} (lit. break on a dead name) *col* beat up severely

prebròditi {prèbrodīm, dē perf.} (lit. sail through) *col* overcome, surmount, get past <Slav*1>

precìrisati {išēm, išū perf.} *sl-drink* drink too much (alcohol) <Slav❖*1>

prècirkati se {ām, ajū perf. intr.} *sl-drink* get very drunk, get smashed <Slav❖*1>

precópati se {prècōpām, precópajū perf. intr.} *sl-fea* fall madly in love <Slav❖*1>

prècvikati {ām, ajū perf.} *col* cut (with scissors, etc.) <Ger❖*1>

prècvikovati {kujēm, kujū perf. intr.} *sl* cut (with scissors, etc.) <Ger>

prècvovkati {ām, ajū perf.} *col* cut (with scissors, etc.) <Ger❖*1>

préći {prêđēm, prêđū, préđ, prèš perf. irreg.} (lit. overrun) *sl* cheat, swindle <Ger*1>

• préći ko bicìkl slòna {VP} (lit. trick like a bike would trick an elephant) *sl* be unable to cheat or outwit somebody

• préći ko mȑtvac dàsku {VP} (lit. trick like a dead person tricks a plank) *sl* be unable to cheat or outwit somebody

• préći ko pégla rèšō {VP} (lit. trick like an iron tricks a stove) *sl* be unable to cheat or outwit somebody

préći se {prêđēm, prêđū, préđ, prèš perf. irreg.} (lit. overrun) *col* make a mistake, screw up <Ger*1>

precòrlti {precòrlīm, ie imperf.} **a.** *sl* oversleep (fail to wake up at a certain time) <NE❖*1> **b.** *sl-sex* engage in sexual intercourse with (of a male) <NE❖*2>

pred vràtima {PP} (lit. in front of the door) *col* just around the corner: *Zima je pred vratima. Winter is just around the corner.* ☞ **vrata**

prȅdak {tka (acc. = gen.) masc.} (lit. ancestor) *sl* parent, old folks <Slav*1>

predevèrati {ām, ajū perf.} **a.** *col* live through <NE❖> **b.** *col* endure, survive <NE❖*1>

prȅdnjāk {a masc.} /prèdnjāk/ **1** *sl* inner pocket (of a jacket) <Slav❖*1> **2** *sl* lining (of a jacket) <Slav❖*1>

prèdriblati {ām, ajū perf.} **a.** *sl-sports* dribble (e.g. in basketball) <Eng> **b.** *sl* cheat, swindle <Eng*1>

prȅdvojničkā {ē fem. (adj. decl.)} (lit. the pre-military one) *sl-sstu* student's military training <Slav❖>

prȅđe {adv.} [std. = prije] *dia* before <Slav✍>

prêđen {a, o adj.} (lit. walked over) *sl-fea* cheated <Slav*1>

prȇf {prèfa +ov (ext. pl) masc.; Nom Pl prèfovi} [std. = preferans] *sl-gamble* preference (a kind of card game) <Fre✍>

prèfakuta {ē fem.} *sl-fea* ***Der*** cunning female

prèfarbān {a, o adj.} (lit. dyed) **1** *sl-fea* experienced: *prefarban kriminalac experienced criminal* <Ger❖*1> **2** *sl-fea* fallen in love <Ger❖*1> **3** *sl-fea* cheat, swindle <Ger❖*2>

• prefárbān svîm bòjama {AdjP} (lit. painted with all colors) *col* very sly

prèfārbati {ām, ajū perf.} (lit. dye) *sl-fea* cheat, swindle <Ger❖*1>

prefàzōn {fazóna (acc. = gen.) masc.} *sl-crime* policeman, cop

prefòlīrān {a, o adj.} *sl-fea* cheated <Ita❖*1>

prefolírati {fòlīrām, folírajū perf.} *sl-fea* cheat, swindle <Ita❖*1>

prefòrsīrān {a, o adj.} *sl-fea* overused: *preforsiran motor overused engine* <Fre❖*1>

preforsírati {fòrsīrām, forsírajū imperf.} *sl-fea* overuse, wear out: *preforsirati auto overuse a car* <**Fre**❖*✍>

prèfrigān {a, o adj.} *sl-fea* ***Der*** cunning, sly, slick <**Ita**❖*1>

prefrigánac {nca (acc. = gen.) masc.} *sl-fea* ***Der*** cunning male <**Ita**❖*1>

prefúrati {prèfūrām, prefúrajū perf.} (lit. run through) *sl-drugs* overdose <**Ger**❖*1>

pregòreti {prègorīm, rē perf. intr.} (lit. burn out) SerE *sl* ***Fac*** die, kick the bucket <**Slav***1>

pregòrjeti {prègorīm, rē perf. intr.} (lit. burn out) *sl* die, kick the bucket <**Slav***1>

pregráditi se {prègrādīm, dē perf. intr.} (lit. separate) *sl* make a mistake, screw up <**Slav***1>

prejèbati {prèjebēm, bū perf.} *sl-fea* cheat, swindle, fuck over <**Slav**❖*1>

prejebávānje {a neut.} *sl-fea* cheating, swindling, fucking over <**Slav**❖*1>

prèjehati {ām, ajū perf.} (lit. override) **1** *sl* cheat, swindle <**Slav***1> 2 *sl-auto* overtake (pass another car on the road) <**Slav***1>

prèkini {excl.} (lit. break it) *col* used to silence one's interlocutor, cut it out <**Slav***1>

preklàpača {ē fem.} **a.** *sl-mil* blanket on the rim of one's bed (which is the required procedure for soldiers) <**Slav**❖> **b.** *sl-sex* female with large vaginal lips <**Slav**❖*1> **c.** *sl* female <**Slav**❖*2>

prêko {a neut.} (lit. across) **a.** *sl* Italy <**Slav***1> **b.** *sl* abroad, overseas <**Slav***2>

preko kòljena {PP} (lit. over one's knee) *col* quickly and superficially ☞ **koljeno**

preko kûrca {PP} (lit. over one's prick) *col* unwillingly ☞ **kurac**

preko léđā {PP} (lit. over one's back) *col* without deserving it ☞ **leđa**

preko mène mȑtvōg {PP} (lit. over my dead body) *col* used to refer to strong lack of approval, over my dead body ☞ **ja**

prȅkomānda {ē fem.} *sl-mil* redeployment <**Slav**❖>

prekòntati {ām, ajū perf.} *sl-fea* make a wrong estimate <**Lat**❖*1>

prekòntati se {ām, ajū perf. intr.} *sl-fea* make a wrong estimate <**Lat**❖*1>

prèkrīžen {a, o adj.} (lit. crossed out) *sl-mil* dismissed from the military, booted out of the military <**Slav***1>

préla {ē fem.} *sl-drugs* preludine (a kind of narcotic drug) <**BN**✍>

prelástiti {prèlāstīm, tē perf.} *sl-sex* ***Obs*** engage in sexual intercourse with (of a male)

prélaz {a masc.} (lit. crossing) **a.** *sl* cheating, swindling <**Slav***1> **b.** *sl* mistake, error <**Slav***2>

prèlaziti {zīm, zē imperf.} (lit. cross) *sl* cheat, swindle <**Slav***1>

prelistávati *See the following*

• **prelistávati lèksikōn sȅksuālnīh ȉzrāzā** {VP} (lit. leaf through a lexicon of sexual expressions) *sl-sex* ***Fac*** talk about girls

préliti se {līm, lē perf.} *col* spill over (from a glass, etc.) <**Slav**>

prélo {a neut.} *col-dia* rural party (social gathering) <**Slav**>

prelòmiti {mīm, mē perf.} (lit. break) *sl* beat up severely, trash <**Slav***1>

prèmazān {a, o adj.} (lit. lubricated) *sl-fea* ***Der*** cunning, sly, slick <**Slav***1>

• **prèmazān svîm mástima** {AdjP} (lit. lubed with all creams) *col* sly, slick

premijéra {ē fem.} (lit. premiere) *sl-fea* very important or influential person, big shot <**Fre***1>

premijéra {adj.} (lit. premiere) *sl-fea* superb, awesome <**Fre***1>

prèmijērka {ē fem.; Dat prèmijērki} *sl-fea* naive female <**Fre**❖*1>

premiròtina {ē fem.} *sl-fea* ***Der*** coward, chicken <**Slav**❖*1>

premiròtka {ē fem.; Dat premirōtki} /premiròtka/ *sl-fea* ***Der*** coward, chicken <**Slav**❖*1>

premùntati {ām, ajū perf.} **a.** *sl* cheat, swindle <**Ita**❖*1> **b.** *sl* abuse financially, rip off

prépad {a masc.} (lit. ambush) *sl-sstu* surprise quiz, pop quiz <**Slav***1>

preparírānje {a neut.} (lit. taxidermy) *sl* persuasion <**Lat***1>

preparírati {prepàrīrām, preparírajū biasp.} (lit. stuff) **1** *sl* beat up <**Lat***1> 2 *sl* persuade, convince <**Lat***1> **3** *sl* resign, quit <**Lat***1>

prepečènica {ē fem.} (lit. double distilled) *sl-drink* strong brandy <**Slav**❖>

prepèčēnka {ē fem.} (lit. double distilled) *sl-drink* plum brandy <**Slav**❖>

prèpičiti {čīm, čē perf.} (lit. cunt over) **1** *sl* cheat, swindle <Slav❖*1> **2** *sl-auto* overtake (pass another car on the road) <Slav❖*1>

prepíjati {prèpījām, prepíjajū imperf.} *sl-drink* drink too much (alcohol) <Slav❖>

prepìšati {ām, ajū perf.} (lit. piss over) **1** *sl* cheat, swindle <Slav❖*1> **2** *sl-auto* overtake (pass another car on the road) <Slav❖*1>

prepišávati {pìšāvām, pišávajū imperf.} (lit. piss over) **1** *sl* cheat, swindle <Slav❖*1> **2** *sl-auto* overtake (pass another car on the road) <Slav❖*1>

prepucávānje {a neut.} (lit. shooting at each other) **1** *col* arguing <Slav❖*1> **2** *col* fight (e.g. fist fight) <Slav❖*1>

prepucávati se {pùcāvām, pucávajū imperf. intr.} (lit. shoot at each other) *col* argue, quarrel <Slav❖*1>

prèpušiti [1] {šīm, šē perf.} (lit. smoke too many cigarettes) *sl-sex* ***Obs*** engage in sexual intercourse with (of a male) <Slav❖*1>

prèpušiti [2] {šīm, šē perf. intr.} *sl* smoke too many cigarettes <Slav❖>

prerádíti {prèrādīm, dē perf.} (lit. work over) *sl-fea* cheat, swindle <Slav❖*1>

prerádíti se {prèrādīm, dē perf. intr.} (lit. work over) *sl-fea* make a mistake, screw up <Slav❖*1>

prèrāđen {a, o adj.} (lit. worked over) *sl-fea* cheated <Slav❖*1>

prèrpati {ām, ajū perf.} *sl* cut somebody's throat <Slav*1>

presáditi *See the following*

• **presáditi bùbreg** {VP} (lit. transplant a kidney) *sl* beat up

presaldúmiti {sàldūmīm, mē perf.} *sl* change somebody's attitude <NE❖*1>

presaldúmiti se {sàldūmīm, mē perf. intr.} *sl* change one's attitude <NE❖*1>

presamítiti {sàmītīm, tē perf.} *col* fold, bend <Slav❖*1>

presàugati {ām, ajū perf.} *sl-auto* overchoke <Ger❖>

prèseći {preséčēm, presékū, prèsēk, prèsēk perf. irreg.} (lit. cut) **1 SerE** *sl* put a ring on one's finger <Slav*1> **2** SerE *sl* drink hard liquor after beer or wine, drink boilermakers <Slav*1>

• **prèseći èkser** {VP} (lit. cut a nail) SerE *sl* get frightened, freak

prèseći se {preséčēm, presékū, prèsēk, prèsēk perf. irreg.} (lit. cut oneself) SerE *sl* get frightened, get scared <Slav*1>

presèliti se *See the following*

• **presèliti se na ahíret** {VP} (lit. move to heaven) BosM *col* die, pass on

• **presèliti se na ònāj svêt** {VP} (lit. move to the other world) SerE *col* die, pass on

• **presèliti se na ònāj svìjēt** {VP} (lit. move to the other world) *col* die, pass on

preserávānje {a neut.} **a.** *sl-fea* ***Der-Obs*** prolonged and meaningless talk, blabber, chatter <Slav❖*1> **b.** *sl-fea* ***Obs*** being funny <Slav❖*2>

preserávati se {sèrāvām, serávajū imperf. intr.} **1** *sl-fea* ***Obs*** be funny <Slav❖*1> **2** *sl-fea* ***Der-Obs*** be conceited, be stuck-up <Slav❖*1>

prèsipānje *See the following*

• **prèsipānje iz šúpljēg u prázno** {NP} (lit. pouring from the hollow to the empty) **1** *sl-fea* ***Fac*** talk persistently and meaninglessly, blabber, chatter **2** *sl-sports* basketball

prèsipati *See the following*

• **prèsipati iz šúpljēg u prázno** {VP} (lit. pour from the hollow to the empty) **1** *sl-fea* talk persistently and meaninglessly, blabber, chatter **2** *sl-sports* ***Fac*** play basketball

prèsjeći {presjéčem, sjéku, sjȅk, sjȅk perf. irreg.} (lit. cut) *sl-drink* drink hard liquor after beer or wine, drink boilermakers <Slav*1>

prèskok {a masc.} (lit. jump) Cro *sl* connecting streetcar ticket in Zagreb, Croatia <Slav*1>

prèslišati [1] {ām, ajū perf.} (lit. examine) **a.** *col* reproach, scold <Slav*1> **b.** *sl-sports* defeat <Slav*2>

prèslišati [2] {šām, šajū perf.} *sl-sports* defeat <Slav*1>

preslišávati {lìšāvām, ajū imperf.} (lit. examine) **a.** *col* reproach, scold <Slav*1> **b.** *sl-sports* defeat <Slav*2>

preslušávānje {a neut.} (lit. interrogation) *sl-stu* exam <Slav*1>

presóviti {prèsōvīm, vē perf.} *sl* sleep at another's place, sleep over <Slav❖*1>

prèsvisnuti {nēm, nū perf. intr.} **a.** *sl* die, kick the bucket <Slav*1> **b.** *sl-fea* get very tired <Slav*2>

prȅsvlaka {ē fem.; Dat prȅsvlaki} (lit. change) *sl-crime* the act of robbing garment <Slav*1>

prèsvući {presvúčem, presvúkū, prèsvūk, prèsvūk perf. irreg.} (lit. change) *sl-crime* rob, fleece, rip off <Slav*1>

prȅša {ē fem.} Med *col-dia* urgent situation <Ita*1>

prèšājbati {ām, ajū perf.} *sl-auto* overtake (pass another car on the road) <Ger❖*1>

prešàltati se {ām, ajū perf. intr.} (lit. switch one's gears) *sl* switch, change: *prešaltati se na novu telefonsku kompaniju switch to a new phone company* <Ger❖*1>

prèšaltovati se {tujēm, tujū perf. intr.} (lit. switch one's gears) *sl* switch, change: *prešaltovati se na slabije cigare switch to milder cigarettes* <Ger❖*1>

prȅšati {ām, ajū imperf.} **a.** *col-dia* urge, press: *Urednik me preša da predam članak. The editor is urging me to submit my article.* <Ita❖*1> **b.** *sl-fea* annoy, bother, pester <Ita❖*2>

prèšibati {ām, ajū perf.} **1** *sl* beat up <Slav❖*1> **2** *sl-auto* overtake (pass another car on the road) <Slav❖*1>

prešíšati {prèšīšām, prešíšajū perf.} **1** *sl-auto* overtake (pass another car on the road) <Slav❖*1> **2** *sl* miss by passing or driving by: *Prešišali smo izlaz 39. We missed exit 39.* <Slav❖*1>

prȅšno {adv.} Med *col-dia* urgent <Ita>

prèšpilovati {lujēm, lujū imperf.} *sl* make sure, be certain <Ger❖*1>

pretákānje {a ncut.} (lit. pour from one container to another) *sl-fea* prolonged and meaningless talk, blabber, chatter <Slav*1>

pretákati {prètāčēm, prètāčū imperf.} //ačem, aču imperf./ (lit. pour from one container to another) *sl-fea* talk persistently and meaninglessly, blabber, chatter <Slav*1>
- **pretákati slȋnu** {VP} (lit. pour one's spit from one place to another) *sl* kiss

prètitrovan {a, o adj.} *sl-drink* drunk <Slav❖*1>

prètitrovati se {rujēm, rujū perf. intr.} *sl-drink* get drunk <Slav❖*1>

prȅtpālēnje {a neut.} *sl-auto* pre-ignition <Slav❖>

prètrgnuti se {nēm, nū perf. intr.} **a.** *col* do one's best <Slav*1> **b.** *col* ***Iro*** invest minimal effort in doing something <Slav*2>

prȅtrka {ē fem.} (lit. running through) Cro *sl* connecting streetcar ticket in Zagreb, Croatia <Slav❖*1>

pretrkèljisati {išēm, išū perf.} *sl* make a mess while looking for something, rummage through <Slav❖*1>

pretumbácija {ē fem.} *col* rearrangement <NE❖*1>

pretùmbati {ām, ajū perf.} *col* flip over <NE❖*1>

pretùmbati se {ām, ajū perf. intr.} *col* flip over <NE❖*1>

prevèslati {ām, ajū perf.} (lit. row over) *sl* cheat, swindle <Slav*1>

prèviti {prȅvijēm, ijū perf.} (lit. change one's bandages) *sl* beat up <Slav*1>

prevŕnuti {prèvr̄nēm, nū perf.} (lit. turn over) *sl-sex* ***Obs*** engage in sexual intercourse with (of a male) <Slav*1>

Prez kȕrac! {S} (lit. Through the prick!) *dia* ***Obs*** used as a strong negative response, No way, Never ☞ **kurac**

Prez mòjēga! {S} (lit. Through my *prick!*) *dia* ***Obs*** used as a strong negative response, No way, Never ☞ **moj**

pŕhati {pr̂hām, pŕhajū imperf.} *col* rot, decay <Slav*1>

pȑhkati {ām, ajū imperf.} *col* rot, decay <Slav❖*1>

prhȑnuti {pȑhrnēm, nū perf. intr.} *col* rot, decay <Slav❖*1>

pricvŕljiti {prȉcvr̄ljīm, ljē perf.} *sl-sex* ***Obs*** engage in sexual intercourse with (of a male) <Slav❖*1>

prȋča *See the following*
- **čȋča-mȋča gòtova prȋča** {S} (lit. the story is over) used to indicate the end of something (originally of a fairy tale) that's it, that's all she wrote
- **kalemègdānskā prȋča** {NP} (lit. Kalemegdan story *Kalemegdan is a fortress in Belgrade with plenty of parks where lovers meet*) *col* love
- **nȉje zà prīču** {PP} (lit. not for talking about) *col* used to refer to confidential matters, (this is) confidential, touchy, hush-hush
- **pjȁnskā prȋča** {NP} (lit. drunk's story) *sl-drink* drunk talk
- **prȋče za mȃlū dȅcu** {NP} (lit. stories for little kids) SerE *col* lies, made-up events
- **prȋče za mȃlū djȅcu** {NP} (lit. stories for little kids) *col* lies, made-up events
- **šúpljā prȋča** {NP} (lit. a hollow story) **a.** *col* lie **b.** *col* unintelligent talk
- **trȕlā prȋča** {NP} (lit. rotten story) *col* lie
- **zà prīču** {PP} (lit. for talking about) *col* very strange

pričánac {nca masc.} *col* long conversation <Slav❖>

pričánjac {njca masc.} *sl-fea* prolonged and meaningless talk, blabber, chatter <Slav❖>

príčati *See the following*
- **Dȁ mi je nȅko pričō nè bi vȅrovō!** {S} (lit. If somebody told me this, I would not believe it!) SerE *col* used to express disbelief, astonishment, etc., Unbelievable! <da>
- **Dȁ mi je nȅko pričō nè bi vjȅrovō!** {S} (lit. If somebody told me this, I would not believe it!) *col* used to express disbelief, astonishment, etc., Unbelievable! <da>
- **príčati bȃjke** {VP} (lit. tell fairy tales) *col* tell lies
- **príčati lȇvē dríne** {VP} (lit. tell the left Drina rivers)

SerE *col* lie

• **príčati prîču** {VP} (lit. tell a story) *col* lie

prîče za mâlū dȅcu {NP} (lit. stories for little kids) SerE *col* lies, made-up events ☞ **priča**

prîče za mâlū djȅcu {NP} (lit. stories for little kids) *col* lies, made-up events ☞ **priča**

prȉčes *See the following*

• **Prȉčēs ti jèhēm tvôj!** {S} (lit. I fuck your communion!) *dia* ***Off*** used as a moderate curse, Fuck you!

pričéstiti se {prìčēstīm, tē perf. intr.} (lit. take communion) *sl-drink* drink a little (alcohol) <Slav*1>

pričvŕljiti {prìčvrljīm, ljē imperf.} (lit. sizzle by) *sl-sex* ***Obs*** engage in sexual intercourse with (of a male) <Slav✍*1>

pricóriti {prìćōrīm, rē perf.} *sl-crime* arrest for a short time <NE❖*1>

prìdačiti {čīm, čē perf.} *sl-sex* ***Obs*** engage in sexual intercourse with (of a male) <Slav❖*1>

pridȑžati *See the following*

• **pridȑžati pàzār** {VP} (lit. keep the day's receipts) *sl-crime* rob, rip off

pridržávati *See the following*

• **pridržávati ćóše** {VP} (lit. keep a corner) **Din** *sl-fea* spend one's time in useless activities, fool around, mess around

prìdurmiti se {mīm, mē perf. intr.} *sl* feel sleepy <Ita❖*1>

prìfatiti {tīm, tē perf.} [std. = prihvatiti] *col-dia* take <Slav✍>

prìfatiti se {tīm, tē perf. intr.} [std. = prihvatiti se] *col-dia* stick with, stay with: *prifatiti se svoje priče stick with one's story* <Slav✍>

prìfur {a masc.} *sl* approaching <Ger❖*1>

prifúrati {prìfūrām, prifúrajū perf.} *sl* approach, draw near <Ger❖*1>

prìglavak {lāvka masc.} *dia-col* wool sock <Slav❖>

prigȕšāč {gušáča neut.} [std. = prigušivač] *sl-crime* silencer (on a gun) <Slav✍>

príja [1] {ē fem.} *col-dia* mother of one's son's or daughter's spouse <Slav❖>

príja [2] {adv.} [std. = prije] *col-dia* before <Slav✍>

prȉjatelj {a (acc. = gen.) masc.} *col-dia* father of one's son's or daughter's spouse <Slav*1>

prȉjātno {excl.} **1** *col* used as a polite farewell or acknowledgment, Fine, You're welcome, Sure <Slav> **2** *col* bon appetite <Slav>

prijáviti {vīm, vē perf.} *col* tell <Slav*1>

• **prijáviti čeličànu** {VP} (lit. report one's iron mill) *sl-fea* show one's strong muscles

• **prijáviti gâbora** {VP} (lit. report an ugly creature) *sl* introduce a girl to one's companions

• **prijáviti mȁčku** {VP} (lit. report a cat) *sl* introduce a girl to one's companions

• **prijáviti u klȁpu** {VP} (lit. report into the company) *sl* introduce to one's companions

• **prijavljívati nòvac** {VP} (lit. report money) *sl-crime* inform the police or other authorities, snitch, squeal

prijèbati se {bēm, bū perf. intr.} *sl-sex* ***Obs*** feel the urge to engage in sexual intercourse <Slav❖>

prijèkcija {ē fem.} *sl* appendix (the organ)

prijòniti {nīm, nē perf.} [std. = prionuti] *col-dia* stick to something: *Školjka je prijonila za stijenu. A shell has stuck to a rock.* <Slav✍>

prȉka [1] {ē masc.; Dat prȉki} *col-dia* friend (male) <Slav❖>

prȉka [2] {excl.} *col-dia* used to address a male in direct informal communication, buddy <Slav❖>

prìkan {a (acc. = gen.) masc.} **a.** *col-dia* male, guy <Slav❖*1> **b.** *sl-sex* penis <Slav❖*2> **c.** *sl-crime* policeman, cop <Slav❖*3>

prȉkaza {ē fem.} *sl* ghost <Slav❖>

prikéljiti se {prìkēljīm, ljē perf. intr.} *sl* be with somebody <Slav❖*1>

prikénjati {ām, ajū perf. intr.} (lit. shit up) **1** *sl* add (numbers): *prikenjati još dvadeset dinara add an additional twenty dinars* <Slav❖*1> **2** *sl* sit: *prikenjati na klupi sit on a bench* <Slav❖*1> **3** *sl* shut up <Slav❖*1> **4** *sl* approach, draw near <Slav❖*1>

prikénjati se {ām, ajū perf. intr.} *sl-sex* ***Obs*** feel an urge to defecate, have to go: *Prikenjalo mu se času. He had to go during the class.* <Slav❖>

prȉkī {īja (acc. = gen.) masc.} **a.** *sl* male, guy <Slav✍*1> **b.** *sl-sex* penis <Slav✍*2> **c.** *sl-crime* policeman, cop <Slav✍*3>

prìkolica {ē fem.} (lit. trailer) **1a.** *sl* female <Slav*1> **b.i.** *sl* girlfriend <Slav*2> **ii.** *sl* wife <Slav*2> **2** *sl-crime* additional punishment <Slav*1> **3** *sl* child, kid <Slav*1> **4** *sl-thie* policeman with a dog

prìkrpati se {ām, ajū perf. intr.} *sl-fea* horn in, butt in <Slav❖*1>

prìkrpiti se {pīm, pē perf. intr.} *sl-fea* get close to somebody <**Slav**⁘[*1]>

prìkucati *See the following*
• **prìkucati među rȍgove** {VP} (lit. hammer between the horns) *sl* hit in the face

prìkucati se {ām, ajū perf. intr.} (lit. nail down) *sl-drugs* take a dose of narcotic drugs <**Slav**[*1]>

prikúčiti {prìkūčīm, čē perf.} *col-dia* drag something close to oneself <**Slav**⁘>

prìlepak {pka masc.} (lit. sticker) SerE *sl-fea* person one cannot get rid of <**Slav**[*1]>

prìlipak {pka masc.} (lit. sticker) [std. = priljepak] **1** **Med** *sl-sex* ***Fac*** small female breast <**Slav**✍[*1]> **2a.** Med *sl-fea* intruder <**Slav**✍[*1]> **b.** Med *sl-fea* boring person, bore <**Slav**✍[*2]>

pȑm {a (acc. = gen.) +ov (ext. pl) masc.; Nom Pl prìmovi} *sl-fea* crude and ill-mannered person, Neanderthal <**Lat**✍>

príma fȍrpās {NP} (lit. superb trick) *sl-fea* an unimportant person, nobody ☞ **forpas**

prìmāćā {ē fem. (adj. decl.)} (lit. the one for receptions) *col* living room, reception room <**Slav**⁘>

prìmalja {ē fem.} (lit. obstetric nurse) *sl-sex* ***Fac*** prostitute, hooker <**Slav**[*1]>

primârijus {a (acc. = gen.) masc.} /prìmārijus/ (lit. head doctor) **a.** *sl-fea* crude and ill-mannered person, Neanderthal <**Lat**[*1]> **b.** *sl-fea* person susceptible to deception <**Lat**[*1]>

prímati se {prîmām, prímajū imperf. intr.} **1** *sl-fea* like <**Slav**[*1]> **2** *sl-fea* be cheated, be swindled <**Slav**[*1]>

pȑmić {a (acc. = gen.) masc.} *sl-fea* crude and ill-mannered person, Neanderthal <**Lat**✍>

prímiti {prîmīm, mē perf.} (lit. receive) **1** *sl-sex* ***Obs*** engage in sexual intercourse with (of a female) <**Slav**[*1]> **2** *sl* believe, trust <**Slav**[*1]>

prímiti se {prîmīm, mē perf. intr.} **1** *sl-fea* like, appreciate <**Slav**[*1]> **2** *sl-fea* be cheated, be swindled <**Slav**[*1]>

pȑmos {a (acc. = gen.) masc.} *sl-fea* crude and ill-mannered person, Neanderthal <**Lat**✍>

pȑmoš {a (acc. = gen.) masc.} *sl-fea* crude and ill-mannered person, Neanderthal <**Lat**✍>

princéza {ē fem.} (lit. princess) *sl-sex* ***Fac*** male homosexual who takes the passive role, femme <**Lat**[*1]>

prȉpīt {a, o adj.} *sl-drink* drunk <**Slav**✍>

Prìpizdina {ē fem.} *sl-fea* ***Der*** a place of extreme wretchedness or squalor, hellhole

prìprāvnīk {a (acc. = gen.) masc.} (lit. intern) *sl-mil* lower-ranked officer <**Slav**[*1]>

prìpuz {a (acc. = gen.) masc.} (lit. the one who crept by) **1** *sl-fea* ***Der*** newcomer <**Slav**[*1]> **2** *sl-fea* male who lives with his in-laws <**Slav**[*1]>

prȉpuza {ē fem.} (lit. crawler) *sl-fea* male who lives with his in-laws <**Slav**[*1]>

príroda *See the following*
• **mȓtvā príroda** {NP} (lit. still life) *sl-mil* lunch bag

prislòniti *See the following*
• **prislòniti kȁšiku** {VP} (lit. move one's spoon closer) *sl* die, kick the bucket

prisluškìvāč {kiváča masc.} (lit. listener) *sl-crime* ***Der*** informer, stoolie, snitch <**Slav**[*1]>

prȉšapnuti {nēm, nū perf.} (lit. whisper) *sl* tell, say <**Slav**[*1]>

prišaráfiti {šàrāfīm, fē perf.} (lit. screw) **1** *sl* tame <**Ger**⁘[*1]> **2** *sl* falsely incriminate, frame <**Ger**⁘[*1]>

prȉšipetlja {ē fem.} *sl-fea* intruder <**Slav**⁘[*1]>

prȉšiti {prȉšijēm, ijū perf.} (lit. sew on) **a.** *sl* add <**Slav**[*1]> **b.** *sl* blame, accuse <**Slav**[*2]>

prȉšiti se {prȉšijēm, ijū perf. intr.} (lit. sew oneself on) *sl* get close to somebody (physically or emotionally) <**Slav**[*1]>

prȉšlopiti se {pīm, pē perf. intr.} *sl* have one's photo taken <**Slav**⁘[*1]>

prȉštekati {ām, ajū perf.} **a.** *sl* plug in (e.g. an electronic device) <**Ger**⁘[*1]> **b.** *sl* necktie <**Ger**⁘[*2]>

prȉštīć {prištíća masc.} (lit. small pimple) *sl-sex* ***Fac*** small female breast <**Slav**[*1]>

pritéći {tégnēm, tégnū, tég, tég perf. irreg.} *col* tighten <**Slav**>

prìterati {ām, ajū perf.} (lit. drive) **SerE** *sl-sex* ***Obs*** feel an urge to urinate or defecate, have to go: *Priteralo me na sastanku. I had to go during the meeting.* <**Slav**[*1]>

prìvatiti {tīm, tē perf.} [std. = prihvatiti] *col* catch, grab <**Slav**✍>

privàtluk {a masc.} *col* private business <**Lat-NE**[*1]>

prȉvātnīk *See the following*
• **Jè s tî kod prȉvātnīka slúžio?** {S} (lit. Did you serve in the private military forces?) *sl* ***Fac*** used to express negative attitude toward one's interlocutor's knowledge, Where did you learn it?

privàtnjāk {vatnjáka (acc. = gen.) masc.} (lit. private person) *sl-fea* introvert <Lat❖*1>

prìvesti {edēm, edū perf.} (lit. put under arrest) **1** *sl-sex* ***Fac-Obs*** engage in sexual intercourse with (of a male) <Slav*1> **2** *sl* ***Fac*** bring home (usu. a girlfriend or a boyfriend to meet one's parents) <Slav*1>

prìvjesak {ska (acc. = gen.) masc.} (lit. hanger) **a.** *sl-fea* intruder <Slav*1> **b.** *sl-fea* boring person, bore <Slav*2>

prizemljénje {a neut.} (lit. landing) **1** *sl-drugs* down (after the effects of narcotic drugs) <Slav*1> **2** *sl-fea* realizing the actual state of affairs <Slav*1>

prizèmljiti se {prìzemljīm, prìzemljē perf. intr.} (lit. landing) **1** *sl-drugs* come down (after the effect of narcotic drugs is over) <Slav*1> **2** *sl-fea* realize the actual state of affairs <Slav*1>

prȉzme {i fem. pl.} (lit. prisms) *sl* eyeglasses <Gre*1>

pȑknci {nākā masc. pl.} *sl-fea* worthless clothing <Slav*1>

pŕkno {a neut.} *sl-sex* ***Obs*** anus, asshole <Slav>

• **U pŕkno te jèbēm!** {S} (lit. I fuck you in your ass!) *dia* ***Off*** used as a moderate curse, Fuck you!

pȑknos {a masc.} *sl-sex* ***Obs*** anus, asshole <Slav✍>

pŕle {eta neut.} *sl-fea* ***Der*** coward, chicken <Slav✍*1>

pŕlja {ē fem.} **1** *sl* dress <Slav*1> **2** *sl-drink* brandy <Slav*1>

pȑljav vȅš {NP} (lit. dirty laundry) *col* dirty laundry ☞ veš

pȑna {ē fem.} *sl-fea* weak male, wimp <Slav*1>

pȑndačiti {čīm, čē imperf.} *sl-sex* ***Obs*** engage in sexual intercourse with (of a male) <Slav*1>

pȑnuti {nēm, nū perf. intr.} **a.** *sl-sex* ***Obs*** break wind, fart <Slav> **b.** *sl* ***Fac-Obs*** run away, flee <Slav*1>

pŕnjci {pȓnjākā masc. pl.} *sl-fea* inexpensive clothing <Slav*1>

pȑnje {ā fem. pl.} /pȓnje/ (lit. rags) *sl-fea* clothing <Slav*1>

pròaktān *See the following*

• **pròaktān kao vrédan** {AdjP} (lit. seen as valuable) *sl-fea* known for giving big tips

proàktati {ām, ajū perf.} **1** *sl* discover, find out <Lat❖*1> **2** *sl* understand, realize <Lat❖*1>

probekrìjati {ām, ajū perf.} *sl-drink* have a great time (usu. while drinking alcohol) <NE❖*1>

próbnī pìlōt {NP} (lit. test pilot) *sl-crime* car thief ☞ pilot

pròborovati {rujēm, rujū perf.} **a.** *sl-crafts* drill through <Ger❖> **b.** *sl-sex* engage in sexual intercourse with (of a male), drill <Ger❖*1>

pròbušenā {ē fem. (adj. decl.)} (lit. the one with a hole) *sl-sex* ***Fac-Obs*** former virgin <Slav*1>

pròbūšenī dȍlār {NP} (lit. drilled dollar) *sl-sex* ***Obs*** former virgin ☞ dolar

probúšiti {pròbūšīm, šē perf.} (lit. make a hole) *sl-sex* deflower <Slav*1>

procijéditi {pròcijēdīm, dē perf.} /procijèditi/ (lit. strain) *sl-crime* pass through the customs without any difficulties <Slav*1>

procvètati {ām, ajū perf.} (lit. bloom) SerE *sl-fea* be successful <Slav*1>

procvjètati {ām, ajū perf.} (lit. bloom) *col* be happy <Slav*1>

pròčačkati {ām, ajū perf.} *sl* discover a secret <Slav*1>

• **pròčačkati fárove** {VP} (lit. stick the headlights) *sl* have one's vision checked

pročèšljati {ām, ajū perf.} (lit. comb) **1** *col* search, comb <Slav*1> **2** *sl* walk <Slav*1>

pročìtati {ām, ajū imperf.} (lit. read) *col* know someone's intentions, read someone <Slav*1>

• **pročìtati ko Oslobođénje** {VP} (lit. read like the Oslobođenje daily) *sl* know someone's intentions, read someone

• **pročìtati ko Vȅselū Svȅsku** {VP} (lit. read like the Vesela sveska, children's weekly) *sl* know someone's intentions, read someone

pròćērdati {ām, ajū perf.} *col* spend (money, property, etc.) <Gre❖*1>

próći *See the following*

• **nȇće prȏći** {VP} (lit. it will not pass) *col* used as a strong negative response, no way, never

• **próći od pízdē** {VP} (lit. go through out of a cunt) *sl* ***Obs*** turn a blind eye (usu. in order to avoid work)

prȍdak {a (acc. = gen.) masc.} *sl-arch* dog (the animal)

pròdati *See the following*

• **pròdati čȉpku** {VP} (lit. sell lace) *sl-sex* ***Obs*** engage in sexual intercourse for the first time

• **pròdati gevéru** {VP} (lit. sell arms) *sl-crime* pick pockets

• **pròdati zȕhe** {VP} (lit. sell nothing) *sl-gamble* cheat

• **skûpo pròdati svòju kȍžu** {VP} (lit. sell one's skin expensively) *col* fight to the end

prodavàčica *See the following*

• **prodavàčica cȓnīh ljubičícā** {NP} (lit. seller of black violets) *sl-sex* ***Obs*** prostitute, hooker

prodávati *See the following*

• **prodávati bùreke** {VP} (lit. sell meat pies) *sl-fea* chatter

• **prodávati bùve** {VP} (lit. sell fleas) **a.** *sl* use new phrases **b.** *sl* lie

• **prodávati cvíku** {VP} (lit. sell fear) *sl-sex* ***Obs*** suffer from gonorrhea, have the clap

• **prodávati dȋvča žváke**{VP} (lit. sell wild bubblegum) *sl* lie

• **prodávati fazóne** {VP} (lit. sell tricks) **a.** *sl* trick, cheat, swindle **b.** *sl* lie **c.** *sl* use new phrases

• **prodávati fólove** {VP} (lit. sell tricks) **a.** *sl* trick, cheat, swindle **b.** *sl* lie

• **prodávati fóre** {VP} (lit. sell tricks) **a.** *sl* trick, cheat, swindle **b.** *sl* lie, **c.** *sl* use new phrases

• **prodávati kȍžu** {VP} (lit. sell one's skin) *sl* look for a job

• **prodávati krȍmpīr u mùštiklu**{VP} (lit. sell a potato in a cigarette holder) *sl* lie

• **prodávati màglu** {VP} (lit. sell fog) *col* spend one's time in useless activities, fool around, mess around

• **prodávati mòder**{VP} *sl* lie

• **prodávati múda za bùbrege** {VP} (lit. sell balls as kidneys) *col* trick, cheat, swindle

• **prodávati pálčeve**{VP} (lit. sell thumbs) *sl* hitch-hike, thumb

• **prodávati štósove** {VP} (lit. sell tricks) **a.** *sl* lie **b.** *sl* cheat, swindle **c.** *sl* use new phrases

• **prodávati zjȁke** {VP} (lit. sell nothing) *col* spend one's time in useless activities, fool around, mess around

• **prodávati zjȁla** {VP} (lit. sell nothing) *col* spend one's time in useless activities, fool around, mess around

prodávati se {pròdajēm, ajū imperf. intr.} (lit. sell oneself) *sl-fea* boast, brag <Slav*1>

prodilèjisati {išēm, išū perf. intr.} *sl-fea* go insane, freak out <Lat⁘*1>

producírati se {dùcīrām, ducírajū biasp. intr.} (lit. produce oneself) **a.** *col* show up in public <Lat*1> **b.** *sl-fea* be conceited, be stuck-up <Lat*2>

prodúljiti {pròdūljīm, ljē perf.} (lit. extend) *sl-sex* defecate <Slav*1>

pròdumati {ām, ajū perf.} *sl* think over, mull over <Rus⁘*1>

prođániti {pròđānīm, nē perf.} *sl* discover, find out <Gyp⁘>

prófa {ē fem. & masc.} *sl-stu* professor, high-school teacher, prof <Lat✍>

prȍfāč {a (acc. = gen.) masc.} *sl-stu* professor, high-school teacher (male), prof <Lat✍>

prȍfačica {ē fem.} *sl-stu* professor, high-school teacher (female), prof <Lat✍>

pròfān {profána (acc. = gen.) masc.} *sl-stu* professor, high- teacher (male), prof <Lat✍>

profànder {a (acc. = gen.) masc.} *sl-stu* professor, high-school teacher (male), prof <Lat✍>

profàndērka {ē fem.; Dat profànderki} *sl-stu* professor, high-school teacher (female), prof <Lat✍>

profaràōn {raóna (acc. = gen.) masc.} (lit. profesor 'professor' X faraon 'pharaoh') *sl-stu* ***Fac*** professor, high-school teacher (male), prof <Lat✍>

profaràōnka {ē fem.; Dat profaràōnki} (lit. profesor 'professor' X faraon 'pharaoh') *sl-stu* professor, high-school teacher (female), prof <Lat✍>

profesiònālka {ē fem.} (lit. female professional) *sl-sex* prostitute, hooker <Lat*1>

prȍfī [1] {īja (acc. = gen.) masc.} /pròfi/ **a.** *col* professional athlete, pro <Lat✍> **b.** *col* a professional of any kind, pro <Lat✍*1>

prȍfī [2] {adj.} *col* professional, pro <Lat✍>

prȍfica {ē fem.} *sl-stu* professor, high-school teacher, prof <Lat✍>

prȍfić {a (acc. = gen.) masc.} **1** *sl-stu* professor, high-school teacher (male), prof <Lat✍> **2** *sl* professional athlete, pro <Lat✍>

prȍfisor {a (acc. = gen.) masc.} [std. = profesor] *col-dia* professor, high-school teacher (male), prof <Lat✍>

pròfućkati {ām, ajū perf.} (lit. whistle out) *sl* lose <Slav⁘*1>

profùkljača {ē fem.} *sl-sex* ***Der*** prostitute, hooker <Eng⁘*1>

profùknjača {ē fem.} *sl-sex* ***Der*** prostitute, hooker <Eng⁘*1>

pròfulati {ām, ajū perf.} **a.** *sl* miss, fail <Ita⁘*1> **b.** *sl* make a mistake, screw up

pròfur {a masc.} *sl* passing by <Ger*1>

profúrati {pròfūrām, profúrajū perf. intr.} **a.** *sl* pass by <Ger*1> **b.** *sl* have fun downtown <Ger*2>

• **profúrati mínu** {VP} (lit. pass by a mine) *sl-crime* pass through the customs without any difficulties

profurávati {fùrāvām, furávajū imperf.} *sl* pass by <Ger*1>

profúzati se {pròfūzām, profúzajū imperf. intr.} *sl* lay back

prògljārnica {ē fem.} *sl-arch* railroad

progùtati {gùtām, ajū perf.} (lit. swallow) **a.** *sl* understand, realize <Slav*1> **b.** *sl* believe, swallow <Slav*2>

- **progùtati bȕmbāra** {VP} (lit. swallow a bumble bee) *sl-sex* ***Fac*** get pregnant, get knocked up
- **progùtati lȍptu** {VP} (lit. swallow a ball) *sl-fea* have a sizable belly

proizvòditi {ìzvodīm, dē imperf.} (lit. produce) **a.** *sl* ***Fac*** work, labor <Slav*1> **b.** *sl* be employed <Slav*2> **c.** *sl* have a steady job <Slav*3>

projèbati se {pròjebēm, bū perf. intr.} *sl-sex* ***Obs*** start having sex frequently <Slav✤>

projèkcija {ē fem.} (lit. projection) *sl* addendum <Lat*1>

prokišnjávati {kìšnjāvām, ajū imperf.} (lit. leak) *sl* bleed <Slav*1>

pròkljucati {ām, ajū perf.} (lit. peck through) *sl-sex* ***Fac-Obs*** break the hymen <Slav*1>

prokljùvati {pròkljujēm, ujū perf.} (lit. peck through) *sl* discover, find out <Slav*1>

prokljúviti {pròkljūvīm, vē perf.} (lit. peck through) **a.** *sl* discover, find out <Slav*1> **b.** *sl* get information <Slav*2>

pròknjižen *See the following*

- **pròknjižen za náuku** {AdjP} (lit. registered for science) *sl-sstu* school student

pròknjiženo {adv.} (lit. booked) *sl* understandable <Slav*1>

pròknjižiti {žīm, žē perf.} (lit. book) **1** *sl* seduce <Slav*1> **2** *sl* go through <Slav*1>

pròkuhāno {adv.} (lit. boiled) *sl* clear <Slav*1>

Pròkurcal následstvo! {S} (lit. He fucked up his inheritance!) SSer *dia* ***Obs*** used as a moderate curse, Fuck him! ☞ prokurcati

prokùrcati *See the following*

- **Pròkurcal následstvo!** {S} (lit. He fucked up his inheritance!) SSer *dia* ***Obs*** used as a moderate curse, Fuck him!

pròkūrčiti se {čīm, čē perf. intr.} (lit. prick up) **a.** *sl-fea* ***Obs*** begin to act wild <Slav✤*1> **b.** *sl-fea* ***Obs*** show off <Slav✤*2>

pròkuvati {ām, ajū perf. intr.} (lit. boil) *sl-fea* get angry <Slav*1>

prokúžiti {pròkūžīm, žē perf.} **a.** *sl* discover, find out <Ita✤*1> **b.** *sl* understand, realize

prólaz {a masc.} (lit. passage) *sl* station, stop (bus, train, streetcar, etc.) <Slav*1>

prólaznā vèčera {NP} (lit. transient supper) *sl-stu* one-time cafeteria supper ☞ večera

prólaznī bôn {NP} (lit. transient coupon) *sl-stu* temporary food coupon (for use in a cafeteria) ☞ bon

prólaznī rúčak {NP} (lit. transient lunch) *sl-stu* one-time cafeteria dinner ☞ ručak

próliv *See the following*

- **ko próliv** {PP} (lit. like diarrhea) *sl-fea* ***Der-Obs*** very boring

prolívati {pròlīvām, prolívajū imperf.} (lit. spill) *sl-fea* talk persistently and meaninglessly, blabber, chatter <Slav*1>

prolúpati {pròlūpām, prolúpajū perf. intr.} (lit. start rumbling) **1** *sl-fea* go insane, freak out: *Prolupao je poslije smrti žene. He went nuts after his wife died.* <Slav*1> **2** *sl-crafts* start malfunctioning: *Kola su mi prolupala. My car started to malfunction.* <Slav*1>

prolúpō {ala, alo adj.} *sl-crafts* malfunctioning <Slav*1>

prolúziti {pròlūzīm, zē perf.} *sl* sell (exchange merchandise for money)

proljećárac {rca (acc. = gen.) masc.} (lit. the spring-time one *separatist movement culminated in the spring*) *sl-polit* member of the Croatian separatist movement in the 1970s <Slav✤*1>

proljepòtati se {ām, ajū perf. intr.} *col* improve, get better (of the weather) <Slav*1>

prȍmaha {ē fem.; Dat prȍmahi} [std. = promaja] *col* draft (i.e. stream of air) <Slav⇗>

proméniti *See the following*

- **proméniti lȉčnī òpis** {VP} (lit. change someone's personal description) **SerE** *sl* beat up severely, rearrange someone's face
- **proméniti bòje klûba** {VP} (lit. change the colors of one's club) **SerE** *sl-sports* transfer to another club (soccer, basketball, etc.)
- **proméniti tišlèrāj** {VP} (lit. change someone's carpentry) SerE *sl* hit, punch

promijéniti *See the following*

- **promijéniti bàtērije** {VP} (lit. replace the batteries) *sl* take a rest, take a break, relax
- **promijéniti fasádu** {VP} (lit. change the front) *sl-fea* beat up severely, rearrange someone's face
- **promijéniti lȉčnī òpis** {VP} (lit. change someone's personal description) *sl-fea* beat up severely, rearrange someone's face
- **promijéniti plȍču** {VP} (lit. change the record) *col* talk about something else, swich to another topic of

conversation

• Promjéni plȍču! {S} (lit. Change the record!) *col* used to make one's interlocutor change the subject of conversation, Change the subject!

pròmuvati se {ām, ajū perf. intr.} *col* breeze around, tool around (e.g. walk around at a party) <Slav*1>

[PRON:NOM] hȍće da se jèbē a da [PRON:DAT] ne uđe. (lit. [PRON:NOM] wants to fuck but not to have it [PRON:REFLEXIVE) used to indicate that a person would like to take an action without willingness to take any related risks ☞ **hteti, htjeti**

propađȍt [1] {a (acc. = gen.) masc.} *sl-fea* ***Der*** worthless or despicable person <Slav✐*1>

propađȍt [2] {adj.} *sl-fea* destroyed <Slav✐*1>

pròpalca {ē masc.} [std. = propalica] *col* ***Der*** worthless or despicable person <Slav✐*1>

pròpalī kàubōj {NP} (lit. destroyed cowboy) *sl-fea* bow-legged female ☞ **kauboj**

pròpalica {ē fem. & masc.} *col* ***Der*** worthless or despicable person <Slav*1>

propalìtēt {litéta (acc. = gen.) masc.} **a.** *col* ***Der*** worthless or despicable person <Slav✐*1> **b.** *sl-sex* ***Der-Fac*** prostitute, hooker <Slav✐*2>

pròpasti *See the following*

• **pròpasti u zȅmlju** {VP} (lit. drop into the earth) *sl* die, be six feet under

propȅler {a masc.} /propèlēr/ **a.** *col* propeller <Lat> **b.** *sl-fea* lazy or shiftless person, bum, good for nothing <Lat*1>

propènjisati {išēm, išū perf. intr.} *sl* talk, have a conversation

pròpeti se *See the following*

• **pròpēti se na propèlānku** {VP} *sl-fea* be destroyed, be ruined

• **pròpēti se na propȅleru** {VP} *sl-fea* be destroyed, be ruined

pròpevati {ām, ajū perf. intr.} (lit. start singing) SerE *sl-crime* inform the police or other authorities, sing <Slav*1>

propíjati {pròpījām, propíjajū imperf.} *sl-drink* spend money on alcohol <Slav❖>

pròpiti {ijēm, ijū perf.} *sl-drink* spend money on alcohol <Slav❖>

pròpjevati {ām, ajū perf.} (lit. start singing) **a.** *sl-crime* inform the police or other authorities, sing <Slav*1> **b.** *sl* start talking <Slav*2>

prȍpūh {a masc.} **a.** *col* draft (i.e. stream of air) <Slav> **b.** *sl* motel <Slav*1>

propùpati {ām, ajū perf.} (lit. grow buds) *sl-fea* be happy <Slav*1>

pròpupčiti {čīm, čē perf.} *sl-sex* abort, miscarry <Slav❖*1>

pròpustnica {ē fem.} (lit. entrance ticket) *sl* face (human) <Slav*1>

proserávānje {a neut.} (lit. shitting out) *sl-fea* ***Obs*** prolonged and meaningless talk, diarrhea of the mouth <Slav*1>

proserávati {sèrāvām, serávajū imperf.} (lit. shit out) *sl-fea* ***Obs*** joke <Slav*1>

proserávati se {sèrāvām, serávajū imperf. intr.} (lit. shit oneself out) *sl-fea* ***Obs*** talk persistently and meaninglessly, have diarrhea of the mouth <Slav*1>

pròsipānje *See the following*

• **pròsipānje mȍzga** {NP} (lit. spilling the brains) *sl-sex* ***Fac-Obs*** masturbate, beat off

pròsipati {ām, ajū imperf.} (lit. spill) *sl* preach, give lectures to <Slav*1>

• **pròsipati mu mȍzak** {VP} (lit. spill his brain) *sl-sex* ***Fac-Obs*** masturbate, beat off

pròsnifati {ām, ajū perf.} (lit. sniff through) **1** *sl* be sure <Eng❖*1> **2** *sl* find out, sniff out <Eng❖*1>

pròstiti *See the following*

• **da pròstē** [NP:NOM] (lit. may [NP:NOM] forgive me) used to introduce an obscene element of discourse

• **da pròstī** [NP:NOM] (lit. may [NP:NOM] forgive me) used to introduce an obscene element of discourse, pardon my French

• **da pròstīš** {S} (lit. forgive me) *col* used to introduce an obscene element of , pardon my French

prostitȕtkinja {ē fem.} *sl-sex* prostitute, hooker <Lat✐>

prostòrija *See the following*

• **klȕpskē prostòrije** {NP} (lit. club rooms) *sl-sstu* ***Fac*** school bathroom

pròsūti {prȍspēm, spū perf.} (lit. spill) **a.** *sl-fea* say something unintelligent <Slav*1> **b.** *sl* say, spill <Slav*2>

• **pròsūti bùvu** {VP} (lit. spill a flea) **1** Ser *sl* lie **2** *sl* introduce a new joke

• **pròsūti fàzōn** {VP} (lit. spill a trick) **1** *sl* lie **2** *sl* introduce a new joke

• **pròsūti fóru** {VP} (lit. spill a trick) **1** *sl* lie **2** *sl* introduce a new joke

• **pròsūti ìznutricu** {VP} (lit. spill the innards) *sl-crime* stab

• **pròsūti lóvu** {VP} (lit. spill money) *sl* spend money
• **pròsūti sìrće** {VP} (lit. spill vinegar) *sl* make a mistake, screw up

pròšacati {ām, ajū perf.} *sl* estimate, guess <**Ger**❖*1>

pròšājbati {ām, ajū perf.} **a.** *sl-auto* speed (auto, etc.) <**Ger**❖*1> **b.i.** *sl-auto* go for a quick ride <**Ger**❖*2> **ii.** *sl-auto* ride <**Ger**❖*2>

prošétati [1] {pròšētām, prošétajū perf. intr.} (lit. walk) *sl* leave, depart, walk <**Slav***1>

prošétati [2] {pròšētām, prošétajū perf.} (lit. walk) *sl* cheat, swindle: *prošetati naivku cheat a naive female* <**Slav***1>
• **Pròšētāj mu kȍžu!** {S} (lit. Walk its skin!) *sl-sex* ***Off*** used as a moderate curse, Fuck you!
• **prošétati blokèjčiće** {VP} (lit. walk the blocks) *sl* leave, depart, walk
• **prošétati pitóna** {VP} (lit. walk a python) *sl* leave, depart, walk
• **prošétati sȕrlu** {VP} (lit. walk one's trunk) *sl* go out

prošétati se {pròšētām, prošétajū perf. intr.} (lit. take a walk) *sl* leave alone, cease boring <**Slav***1>
• **Pròšētāj se!** {S} (lit. Take a walk!) *sl* used to make somebody go away, Take a hike!

pròšibati {ām, ajū perf.} *sl-auto* speed (auto, etc.) <**Slav***1>

prošíšati {pròšīšām, prošíšajū perf. intr.} (lit. cut hair through) *col* miss by passing or driving by <**Slav***1>

prȍšlica {ē fem.} **1** *sl* rain <**Slav***1> **2** *sl* water <**Slav***1> **3** *sl* winter <**Slav***1> **4** *sl-drink* brandy <**Slav***1>

prošnjófati {pròšnjōfām, prošnjōfajū perf.} **a.** *sl* find out, sniff out <**Ger**❖*1> **b.** *sl* understand, realize

prošnjúrati {pròšnjūrām, prošnjúrajū biasp. intr.} **1a.** *sl* walk <**Ger**❖*1> **b.** *sl-crime* investigate, look into: *prošnjurati ubistvo investigate a homicide* <**Ger**❖*2> **c.** *sl* patrol <**Ger**❖*3> **2** *sl-crime* smuggle: *prošnjurati augu preko grane smuggle booze across the border* <**Ger**❖*1>

prošvérati {pròšvērām, prošvérajū perf.} *col* smuggle <**Ger***1>

pròšvercati {ām, ajū perf.} *col* smuggle <**Ger***1>

pròšvercovati {cujēm, cujū perf.} *col* smuggle <**Ger***1>

prošvírati {pròšvīrām, prošvírajū perf. intr.} *sl-fea* go insane, freak out

pròšvrcati se {ām, ajū perf. intr.} *sl* take a walk

prošvŕljati {pròšvr̄ljām, prošvŕljajū perf. intr.} *col* wander, roam: *prošvrljati kroz prodavnice go on a shopping spree* <**Gre**❖*1> *col* <**Gre**❖*1>

pròtek {a masc.} *sl* flow <**Slav***1>

protȉnjača {ē fem.} *sl-arch* sewing needle

protȉnjavac {vca (acc. = gen.) masc.} *sl-arch* tailor

protinjàvskī {ā, ō adj.} *sl-arch* tailor's

prȍtivu {gen.} [std. = protiv] *col* against, counter: *biti protivu iznesenog rešenja be against the proposed solution* <**Slav**☞>

protretírati {trètīrām, tretírajū perf.} *sl* get a favorable opinion about somebody <**Fre**❖*1>

prȍtuha {ē fem.; Dat prȍtuhi} *sl* ***Der*** worthless or despicable person <**Slav***1>

protúrati *See the following*
• **protúrati lȅptīra** {VP} (lit. push the butterfly through) *sl* lie
• **protúrati lȅptīre**{VP} (lit. push the butterflies through) *sl* lie
• **protúrati pȕške** {VP} (lit. push the guns through) *sl* lie

protȕtnjati *See the following*
• **protȕtnjati cȓtu** {VP} (lit. run past the line) *sl-crime* pass through customs without any difficulties

prȍtuva {ē fem.} Ser *sl* ***Der*** worthless or despicable person <**Slav***1>

prȍvala {ē fem.} (lit. break in) **1** *sl* betrayal <**Slav***1> **2** *sl* stupidity, lack of intelligence <**Slav***1> **3** *sl* joke <**Slav***1>
• **prȍvala ȍblākā** {NP} (lit. cloud burst, torrential downpour) *sl-sex* ***Fac-Obs*** ejaculation

provalȉška {ē fem.; Dat provalȉški} /provalìška/ (lit. break in) *sl-crime* informing the police or other authorities, snitching, squealing <**Slav**☞*1>

prováliti {pròvālīm, lē perf.} (lit. break) **1** *sl* discover, find out: *provaliti jeftinu prodavnicu discover an inexpensive store* <**Slav***1> **2** *sl-crime* inform the police or other authorities, snitch, squeal <**Slav***1> **3** *sl* unmask: *provaliti mućku unmask an intrigue* <**Slav***1> **4** *sl* understand, realize: *provaliti fazon understand a trick* <**Slav***1> **5** *sl-fea* say something unintelligent <**Slav***1> **6** *sl-fea* tell a joke <**Slav***1>
• **prováliti bùvu** {VP} (lit. burst a flea) *sl-fea* say something unintelligent
• **prováliti fóru** {VP} (lit. break a trick) *sl* solve a problem, have a breakthrough
• **prováliti na drȕk** {VP} (lit. burst on pressure) *sl* denounce, criticize publicly

prováliti se {pròvālīm, lē perf. intr.} (lit. break out) *sl* say something unintelligent <**Slav***1>

provaljívati {vàljīvām, valjívajū imperf.} //vàljujēm, vàljujū imperf./ (lit. break in) **1** *sl* discover, find out <Slav*1> **2** *sl-crime* inform the police or other authorities, snitch, squeal <Slav*1> **3** *sl* unmask <Slav*1> **4** *sl* understand, realize <Slav*1> **5** *sl-fea* say something unintelligent <Slav*1>

provaljívati se {vàljīvām, valjívajū imperf. intr.} /vàljujēm, vàljujū imperf. intr./ (lit. break out) *sl-fea* say something unintelligent <Slav*1>

proverávati se {vèrāvām, verávajū imperf. intr.} (lit. check each other) SerE *sl-sex* ***Fac-Obs*** engage in sexual intercourse with (of a male) <Slav*1>

provózati {pròvōzām, provózajū perf.} (lit. drive around) **a.** *sl-sex* ***Fac-Obs*** engage in sexual intercourse with (of a male) <Slav*1> **b.** *sl-fea* ***Fac*** cheat, swindle <Slav*2>
• **provózati na rìngišpīlu** {VP} (lit. give a ride on a merry-go-around) **a.** *sl-sex* ***Fac-Obs*** engage in sexual intercourse with **b.** *sl* cheat, swindle

provózati se {pròvōzām, provózajū perf. intr.} (lit. take a ride) *sl* be cheated, be taken for a ride <Slav*1>

prozènisati {išēm, išū perf.} **1** *sl* make sure, be certain: *Prozeniši da ona dođe na vreme. Make sure that she arrives on time.* <San❖*1> **2** *sl* look, watch, scope out <San❖*1>

prozévati *See the following*
• **prozévati čmâr** {VP} (lit. yawn one's asshole) SerE *sl-fea* get frightened, freak

prozìntati {ām, ajū perf.} *sl* discover, find out

prȍzīrnā {ē fem. (adj. decl.)} (lit. the transparent one) *sl-drink* vodka <Slav*1>

prozívati {pròzīvām, prozívajū imperf.} (lit. call someone's name) *col* criticize publicly <Slav*1>

prózivka {ē fem.} (lit. roll-call) **1** *sl* meeting of a group of people who meet each other frequently <Slav*1> **2** *sl* public critique <Slav*1>
• **na prózivku** {PP} (lit. to the roll-call) **1** *sl* at the designated time **2** *sl* for a walk: *Uzeo je cucka na prozivku. He took the dog for a walk.*

prózor {a masc.} (lit. window) **1** *sl* eye (sight organ) <Slav*1> **2** *sl* open lips <Slav*1>

prózori {zōrā masc. pl.} (lit. windows) *sl-fea* eyeglasses <Slav*1>

prozorȉška {ē fem.; Dat prozorȉški} /prozorȉška/ *sl* window <Slav☞>

prozújati {pròzūjīm, jē perf. intr.} **a.** *col* buzz by: *prozujati na motoru buzz by on a bike* <Slav❖> **b.aa.** *sl* walk: *prozujati po glavnoj ulici walk down the main street* <Slav❖*1> **bb.** *sl* breeze through town or a bar <Slav❖*2>

prozùmbati {ām, ajū perf.} *col* drill through <NE❖*1>

pròzvati {zovēm, zovū perf.} **a.** *col* criticize publicly <Slav*1> **b.i.** *col* offend in public <Slav*2> **ii.** *sl* falsely incriminate, frame <Slav*2>

prožderávati se {dèrāvām, derávajū imperf. intr.} (lit. eat through) *col* eat too much, gorge, pig out <Slav❖>

prȍždraka {ē fem.} *sl* window <Slav*1>

pȑpa[1] {excl.} *col* used to accuse someone of being frightened, you're scared <Slav*1>

pȑpa[2] {ē fem.} *sl* fear <Slav*1>

pȑpisati {išēm, išū imperf.} *sl-fea* get scared, get frightened <Slav❖*1>

pŕpiti {pīm, pē perf. intr.} /pȑpiti /pim, pe perf. intr./ *sl-fea* have fear <Slav❖*1>

pŕskati {pȓskām, pŕskajū imperf.} (lit. sprinkle) *sl* cry, shed tears, weep <Slav*1>

pȑsnevāl {a masc.} *sl* finger ring

pȓst {a masc.} (lit. finger) *sl-sex* ***Fac-Obs*** penis, dick, prick <Slav*1>
• **trȇćī pȓst** {NP} (lit. the third finger) *sl-sex* ***Fac-Obs*** penis, dick, prick

pȑstac {prstàca masc.} **a.** *sl* poke, prod, or pinch on the buttocks, goose <Slav❖*1> **b.** *sl* ***Der*** any kind of childish game <Slav❖*2>

pȑstača {ē fem.} (lit. the one with a finger) *sl-sex* ***Obs*** masturbator (female) <Slav❖*1>

pȑstāć {a masc.} **a.** *sl-sex* ***Obs*** sexual foreplay, petting, feeling up <Slav*1> **b.** *sl-sstu* ***Obs*** a poke, prod, or pinch on the buttocks, goose <Slav*2>

prsténac {nca masc.} (lit. fingering) **1** *sl-sex* ***Obs*** sexual foreplay, petting, feeling up <Slav❖*1> **2** *sl-sstu* ***Obs*** a poke, prod, or pinch on the buttocks, goose <Slav❖*1>

pȑtlja {ē fem.} **1** *sl* shirt <Slav> **2** *sl* dress <Slav*1>

pȑtljānje {a neut.} *sl-fea* persistent and meaningless talk, blabber <Slav*1>

pȑtljati {ām, ajū imperf.} *sl-fea* talk persistently and meaninglessly, blabber, chatter <Slav>

prȕćnuti {nēm, nū perf.} (lit. splash) *sl-sex* ***Obs*** engage in sexual intercourse with (of a male) <Slav*1>

prȕćnuti se {nēm, nū perf. intr.} **a.** *col* lay down (e.g. to sleep) <Slav*1> **b.** *sl* die, kick the bucket <Slav*2>

prúga *See the following*
- **na dȕgū prúgu** {PP} (lit. on long rails) *col* long-term: *investicija na dugu prugu long-term investment*
- **na prúgi** {PP} (lit. at a strip) *sl* on the spot, at a designated place or a place of an event: *Bio je na prugi kad su ubili predsjednika. He was on the spot when they killed the president.*

prût {prúta +ov (ext. pl) masc.; Nom Pl prútovi} *col-dia* stick, bat <Slav>

prȕžiti *See the following*
- **prȕžiti pȍtu u prózor** {VP} *sl* punch in the eye

pr̀vā {ē fem. (adj. decl.)} (lit. the first one) *sl* new girlfriend <Slav[*1]>

pr̀vā líga {NP} (lit. first division *e.g., in soccer*) **a.** *sl-fea* fun **b.** best quality, first rate, major league ☞ **liga**

pr̀vā pȍstava {NP} (lit. first lineup) *sl* steady company, people one hangs with ☞ **postava**

pr̀vāk {adj.} (lit. champion) *sl-fea* handsome, cute <Slav[*1]>

pr̀vāk {prváka masc.} (lit. champion) **1** *sl-fea* effective move <Slav[*1]> **2** *sl-fea* good idea <Slav[*1]> **3** *sl-fea* good joke <Slav[*1]>

prvénac {nca masc.} (lit. firstborn child) *sl-drink **Fac*** first brandy (of a drinking session) <Slav[*1]>

pr̀vō ȉme {NP} *col* first name, given name ☞ **ime**

prvobórac {rca (acc. = gen.) masc.} (lit. veteran from the first year of WW II in the former Yugoslavia) *sl **Fac*** young lover <Slav[*1]>

pŕznica {ē fem. & masc.} *sl-fea* untidy person, slob <Slav[*1]>

pŕzniti {pȓznīm, nē imperf. intr.} *sl-fea* make mess, litter <Slav[*1]>

pržióna *See the following*
- **pržióna kȁvē** {NP} (lit. coffee roaster) *sl* seashore beach

pȓžūn {a masc.} *sl-crime* prison <Ita⇗>

ps [pê-ȇs] *See the following*
- **po ps-u** [pê-ȇsu] {PP} (lit. by the military code of conduct) *sl-mil* as the rule says, by the book

psȅto {a neut.} (lit. dog) **1** *sl-fea* unattractive person, dog <Slav[*1]> **2** *sl-fea* unfriendly person <Slav[*1]>

psìhički {adv.} *col* psychologically <Gre⇗>

psȉk {a +ov (ext. pl) masc.; Nom Pl psìkovi} **a.** *col* the sound of abrupt movement, wham <Slav> **b.** *col* the sound of a car-horn, beeping (alarm, etc.) <Slav>

psȉka {ē fem.; Dat psȉki} **a.** *col* the sound of abrupt movement, wham <Slav> **b.** *col* the sound of a car-horn, beeping (alarm, etc.)<Slav>

psȉkāč {psikáča (acc. = gen.) masc.} *col* beeper <Slav❖>

psȉkānje {a neut.} *col* beeping (alarm, etc.) <Slav>

psȉkati {ām, ajū imperf.} *col* beep (produce a sharp-picthed sound) <Slav❖>

psȉkav {a, o adj.} *col* beeping (alarm, etc.) <Slav❖>

psȉknuti {nēm, nū perf.} *col* beep (alarm, etc.) <Slav❖>

psȉna {ē fem.} (lit. big dog) **1a.** *sl-fea* senior citizen <Slav[*1]> **b.** *sl-fea* unattractive person, dog <Slav[*2]> **c.** *sl-crime* police investigator, bloodhound <Slav[*3]> **2** *sl* problem, trouble <Slav[*1]> **3** *sl* lie <Slav[*1]>

psôvka *See the following*
- **psôvka od čovȅka** {NP} (lit. a curse of a man) SerE *sl-fea* worthless or despicable person

psst {excl.} *col* used to silence one's interlocutor, hush <Slav>

pst {excl.} *col* used to silence one's interlocutor, hush <Slav>

Ptàraši {raši (acc. = gen.) masc.; perm} /Ptàrši/ *sl-fea **Off*** Albanian (person) <Alb⇗>

Ptàrši {Ptàraši (acc. = gen.) masc.; perm} /Ptàrši/ *sl-fea **Off*** Albanian (person) <Alb⇗>

ptȉca {ē fem.} (lit. bird) *sl* female <Slav[*1]>
- **ptȉca rúgalica** {NP} (lit. mocking bird) *sl-fea* mockingbird
- **ptȉce znȁjū** {S} (lit. birds know) *col* used to refer to lack of knowledge, who knows

ptȉčica {ē fem.} **1a.** *sl-sex **Fac-Obs*** vagina, cunt <Slav[*1]> **b.** *sl* female <Slav[*2]> **2** *sl-crime* criminal <Slav[*1]>

pȕ {excl.} *col* the sound made by spitting, phew <Slav>

pȕb {pùba (acc. = gen.) +ov (ext. pl) masc.; Nom Pl pùbovi} **1a.** *sl-crime* policeman, cop <Ger[*1]> **b.** *sl-crime* police investigator <Ger[*2]> **2** *sl* the bus line number twelve in Belgrade, Serbia <Ger[*1]>

pubertȅtlija {ē fem.} *col* teenager <Lat❖>

pubijáner {a (acc. = gen.) masc.} **1a.** *sl-crime* policeman, cop <Ger❖[*1]> **b.** *sl-crime* police investigator <Ger❖[*2]> **2** *sl-fea* teenager <Lat❖[*1]> **3** Ser *sl* the bus line number twelve in Belgrade, Serbia <Ger❖[*1]>

pùbiš {a (acc. = gen.) masc.} **1a.** *sl-crime* policeman, cop <Ger⇗[*1]> **b.** *sl-crime* police investigator <Ger⇗[*2]> **2** *sl-fea* teenager <Lat⇗[*1]> **3** *sl* the bus line number twelve in Belgrade, Serbia <Ger⇗[*1]>

pȕbiti {bīm, bē perf.} [std. = poljubiti] *sl* kiss <Slav✍>

pubòvija {ē fem.} *sl-crime* police station <Ger❖^{*1}>

púca [1] {ē fem.} (lit. shooter) **1** *sl-crime* pistol, revolver <Slav❖^{*1}> **2a.** *sl-sex* inexpensive prostitute <Slav❖^{*1}> **b.** *sl-sex* amateur prostitute <Slav❖^{*2}>

pȕca [2] {eta neut.} Med *col-dia* button

Pȕcā mi pȑsluk. {S} (lit. My vest is cracking.) *col* used to express indifference, I don't give a damn! ☞ **pucati**

Pȕcajū mi kòpite! {S} (lit. My hooves are cracking!) *dia* used to express indifference, I don't give a damn! ☞ pucati

pȕcalica {ē fem.} (lit. shooter) **1** *sl-sex* ***Fac*** prostitute, hooker <Slav❖^{*1}> **2** *sl-crime* pistol, revolver <Slav❖^{*1}>

pùcāljka {ē fem.; Dat pùcāljki} *sl-crime* pistol, revolver <Slav❖^{*1}>

pȕcati {ām, ajū imperf.} (lit. shoot) **1** *sl-sex* ***Obs*** engage in sexual intercourse with (of a male) <Slav^{*1}> **2** *sl* cheat, swindle <Slav^{*1}> **3** *sl* throw away, toss out <Slav^{*1}>

- **Pȕcā mi pȑsluk.** {S} (lit. My vest is cracking.) *col* used to express indifference, I don't give a damn!
- **Pȕcajū mi kòpite!** {S} (lit. My hooves are cracking!) *dia* used to express indifference, I don't give a damn!
- **pȕcati na** [NP:ACC] {VP} (lit. shoot at) *col* have somebody or something in mind

pȕce {eta neut.} *col-dia* button

pȕcnuti {nēm, nū perf.} (lit. shoot) *sl* cheat, swindle <Slav^{*1}>

pȕcvāl {a masc.} *col* tow <Ger✍>

pȕcvol {a masc.} *col* tow <Ger✍>

pȕcvola {ē fem.} *col* tow <Ger✍>

pȕčavac {vca (acc. = gen.) masc.} *sl-arch* blind male

pùčavnica {ē fem.} *sl* mosque

pȕć {excl.} **1** *col* the sound made by splashing, splash <Slav> **2** *col* used to lure a turkey <Slav> **3** *col* the sound made by a turkey, gobble <Slav>

pȕć-purȕć {excl.} *col* the sound made by a turkey, gobble <Slav>

pȕći {pȕknēm, pȕknū, pȕk, pȕk a perf. irreg.} (lit. burst, crack) **1a.** *sl-fea* be in a difficult situation <Slav^{*1}> **b.** *sl-fea* be defeated <Slav^{*2}> **c.** *sl-fea* lose a game: *Pukli smo protiv Mađara. Our team lost to the Hungarians.* <Slav^{*3}> **d.** *sl* die, kick the bucket <Slav^{*4}> **2** *sl-fea* go insane, freak out <Slav^{*1}> **3** *sl-sex* lose one's virginity <Slav^{*1}> **4** *sl* spend (money, property, etc.): *Puko sam sto maraka. I spent one hundred German marks.* <Slav^{*1}>

- **kud pȕklo da pȕklo** {AdvP} (lit. wherever it bangs) [std. = pući] *col* used to refer to the willingness to act notwithstanding the consequences, whatever happens: *Idem na ljetovanje kud puklo da puklo. I'll my take my summer vacation whatever happens.*
- **pȕći među rȍgove** {VP} (lit. bang between horns) *sl* hit, punch
- **pȕći rêpom o lèdinu** {VP} (lit. hit with one's tail on a lawn) *dia* fall on one's back
- **Pȕkla mi zèzāljka.** {S} (lit. My funny thing is broken.) *sl-fea* used to express one's state of not being in the mood, I am not in the mood.
- **pȕkla stȍtka** {VP} (lit. his 100 has broken) *sl-mil* less than one hundred days of one's military service left

pùćkac {excl.} **1** *col* the sound made by puffing, puff <Slav> **2** *col* the sound made by a turkey, gobble <Slav>

pȕćkati {ām, ajū imperf.} **1** *col* puff (produce the sound) <Slav^{*1}> **2** *col* gobble (of a turkey) <Slav^{*1}>

pȕćpulik {a masc.} *col* gobble <Slav^{*1}>

pùćpura {ē fem.} *col* gobble <Slav^{*1}>

pućpuríkānje {a neut.} *col* gobbling <Slav^{*1}>

pućpuríkati {ām, ajū imperf. intr.} //ríčēm, čū imperf. intr./ *col* gobble <Slav^{*1}>

pȕćpuruć {a masc.} *col* gobble <Slav❖>

pȕćpuruka {ē fem.} *col* gobble <Slav❖>

púder {a masc.} (lit. powder) *sl-drugs* powdered opium <Fre^{*1}>

pùdīng {a masc.} (lit. pudding) *sl-sex* ***Fac*** female breast <Eng^{*1}>

pȕf [1] {excl.} **1** *sl* no <Slav^{*1}> **2** *col* the sound of tapping, tap <Slav^{*1}>

pȕf [2] {a +ov (ext. pl) masc.; Nom Pl pùfovi} *sl-drugs* opium <Eng^{*1}>

pufèrāš {feráša (acc. = gen.) masc.} **1** *sl* male who hangs from a streetcar <Ger❖^{*1}> **2** *sl* streetcar conductor <Ger❖^{*1}>

pȕfnuti {nēm, nū perf. intr.} *sl-sex* ***Obs*** break wind, fart <Slav❖^{*1}>

pȕh {a +ov (ext. pl) masc.; Nom Pl pȕhovi} (lit. dormouse) **1** *sl* night train <Slav^{*1}> **2** *col* puff (the sound) <Slav^{*1}>

púhalo *See the following*

- **mȑtvō púhalo** {NP} (lit. dead blower) **a.** *sl-fea* lazy or shiftless person, bum, good for nothing **b.** *sl-fea* unskilled person

púhānje {a neut.} *col* blowing, exhaling <Slav>

púhati {pûšēm, šū imperf. intr.} *col* blow, exhale <Slav>
- **púhati na hládno** {VP} (lit. blow on something cold) *col* be cautious
- **púhati na vrúće** {VP} (lit. blow on something hot) *col* ***Iro*** be cautious

pȕhica {ē fem.} *sl* nose <Slav⁘[*1]>

púhnuti {pûhnēm, nū perf.} (lit. blow) *sl-crime* steal, swipe <Slav[*1]>

pȕj *See the following*
- **pȕj pȉke ne vážī**{VP} (lit. phew, it's not valid anymore) *col* used by children to signal that one cannot change what has been done
- **pȕj pȉke prȁćke, néma vȉšē vrȁćkē** {VP} (lit. phew, sling, no more return) *col* used by children to signal that one cannot change what has been done

pûjdānje {a neut.} *sl-fea* stimulation to an action <Hun⁘[*1]>

pûjdati {ām, ajū imperf. intr.} *col* stimulate to action, rouse <Hun[*1]>

pȕk {excl.} *col* a minor explosion, bam <Slav>

pȕkī [1] {excl.} *sl* used to express the absence of readiness to reach an agreement, no deal: *A: Hoćeš li mi to prodati? B: Puki! A: Are you going to sell this to me? B: No deal!* <Slav>

pȕkī [2] {īja (acc. = gen.) masc.} **1** *sl-crime* policeman, cop <Slav✍[*1]> **2** *sl-mil* colonel <Slav✍> **3** *sl* the bus line number twelve in Belgrade, Serbia <Slav✍[*1]>

pȕkica {ē masc.} **1** *sl-crime* policeman, cop <Slav✍[*1]> **2** *sl* the bus line number twelve in Belgrade, Serbia <Slav✍[*1]>

Pȕkla mi zèzāljka. {S} (lit. My funny thing is broken.) *sl-fea* used to express one's state of not being in the mod, I am not in the mood. ☞ **pući**

pȕkla stȍtka {VP} (lit. his 100 has broken) *sl-mil* less than one hundred days of one's military service left ☞ **pući**

pȕklja {ē masc.} *sl-stu* student <Slav[*1]>

pȕknūt {a, o adj.} (lit. cracked) *sl-fea* ***Der*** insane, cracked <Slav[*1]>

pȕknuti [1] {nēm, nū perf. intr.} (lit. crack) *sl-fea* get angry <Slav[*1]>

pȕknuti [2] {nēm, nū perf.} (lit. crack) **a.** *col* hit, punch <Slav[*1]> **b.i.** *col* kick, strike <Slav[*2]> **ii.** *sl-sex* engage in sexual intercourse with (of a male) <Slav[*2]>
- **Pȕknulo[PRON:DAT] ȕ glāvu!** {LSF} (lit. It has banged in [PPRON] head!) *sl* used to indicate that the message has been understood: *Puknulo im u glavu! They have gotten it!*
- **pȕknuō fȉlm** {VP} (lit. broken film) *col* used to refer to strong discontent
- **Pȕknuo[PRON:DAT] fȉlm.** {LSF} (lit. [PPRON] film has broken.) *col* used to refer to strong discontent: *Puknuo mi je film od toga. I was sick and tired of that.*
- **pȕknuti ka cúrčak** {VP} (lit. crack like a little girl) *sl-fea* go insane, crack up
- **pȕknuti po šȁvu** {VP} (lit. crack at the seams) *sl-fea* go insane, crack up
- **Pȕkō féder.** {S} (lit. The spring has broken) *sl-fea* used to refer to strong discontent, That tears it!
- **Pȕkō fȉlm.** {S} (lit. The film has broken.) *col* used to refer to strong discontent, That tears it!
- **Pȕkō mu klȉker.** {S} (lit. His marble has broken) *sl-fea* used to indicate that a third party has understood the message, He's got it.

púla {ē fem.} *sl* wallet

pûle {eta masc.} **1** *sl-crime* policeman, cop <Slav✍[*1]> **2** *sl-mil* colonel <Slav✍[*1]> **3** *sl* wallet <Slav✍[*1]>

pùlēn {puléna (acc. = gen.) masc.} **1** *sl* friend (male) <Fre[*1]> **2** *sl-sports* player <Fre[*1]>

pulfèrāš {feráša (acc. = gen.) masc.} *sl* male who hangs from a streetcar <Ger⁘[*1]> *sl* streetcar conductor <Ger⁘[*1]>

pȕlke {eta neut.} *sl-crime* the police

pȕlovānje {a neut.} *sl-sports* keeping horses in race (of a jockey) <Eng[*1]>

pȕlovati {lujēm, lujū imperf.} *sl-sports* keep horses in race (of a jockey) <Eng[*1]>

pȕlt *See the following*
- **ispod pȕlta** {PP} (lit. under the counter) *col* secretly, under the counter: *prodavati rakiju ispod pulta sell brandy under the counter*

pùljosati {ošēm, ošū imperf.} *sl-crime* steal, swipe

pûmpa {ē fem.} (lit. pump) **1** *sl-drugs* hypodermic needle <Ger[*1]> **2** *sl-crime* billy club <Ger[*1]>

pumpánjac {njca masc.} (lit. pumping) *sl* heart <Ger⁘[*1]>

pȕmpānje {a neut.} (lit. pumping) **1** *sl* persuasion <Ger⁘[*1]> **2** *sl-sex* sexual intercourse <Ger⁘[*1]>

pûmpati {ām, ajū perf.} (lit. pump) **1** *sl-sex* ***Fac-Obs*** engage in sexual intercourse with (of a male), pump <Ger[*1]> **2** *sl-fea* abuse financially, rip off <Ger[*1]> **3** *sl* persuade, convince <Ger[*1]>
- **pȕmpati žȉlu** {VP} (lit. pump the vein) *sl-drugs* prepare to take a shot of drugs

pùmpica {ē fem.} (lit. small pump) *sl-sex* ***Fac-Obs*** penis, dick, prick <Ger❖[*1]>

pũn *See the following*

• **dùpke pũn** {AdjP} *col* completely filled with, jam packed

• **pũn fazónā ko mȁčka búvā** {AdjP} (lit. full of tricks like a cat is full of fleas) *sl-fea* highly humorous

• **pũn kȁšpe** {AdjP} (lit. full of bacon) *sl-polit* politician

• **pũn ko brôd** {AdjP} (lit. full like a ship) *sl-fea* rich person

• **pũn ko ȍko** {AdjP} (lit. full like an eye) *sl-fea* filled, jam packed

• **Pũn mi je kùfer!** {S} (lit. My suitcase is full!) *col* used to express strong discontent, I've had it! I've had enough!

• **Pũn mi je kũrac!** {S} (lit. My prick is full!) *col* ***Obs*** used to express strong discontent, I've had it! I've had enough!

• **Pũn mi je kũrac, s njȅga!** {S} (lit. My prick is full of him!) SSer *dia* ***Obs*** used as a moderate curse, Fuck him!

• **Pũn mi te šévac!** {S} (lit. My fucker is full of you!) *sl* ***Off*** used to express strong discontent, Fuck you!

• **Pũn[PRON:DAT] je kũrac**. {LSF} (lit. [PRON:DAT] prick is full of that.) *col* ***Obs*** used to express strong discontent: *Pun mu je kurac He is sick and tired of all this.*

• **pũn pũtra**{AdjP} (lit. full of butter) **a.** *sl-fea* suspicious **b.** *sl-crime* wanted by the police

• **pũn vòdē** {AdjP} (lit. full of water) *sl-drink* drunk

• **pùna šȁka dlâkā** {AdjP} (lit. full fist of hairs) *sl-sex* attractive female

pũnā {ē fem. (adj. decl.)} (lit. the full one) *sl-sex* pregnant female <Slav[*1]>

pũniti {nīm, nē imperf.} (lit. stuff) **1** *sl* lie <Slav[*1]> **2** *sl* ***Obs*** engage in sexual intercourse with (of a male) <Slav[*1]>

• **pũniti crijéva** {VP} (lit. stuff one's intestines) *sl* eat, devour

• **pũniti krvàvice** {VP} (lit. stuff blood sausages) *sl-fea* suffer from tuberculosis, have TB

• **pũniti sàrmu** {VP} (lit. stuff cabbage rolls) *sl-sex* engage in sexual intercourse with a not fully erect penis

pũno *See the following*

• **pùno ko blȁta** {AdvP} (lit. as much as mud) *col* in large quantities, very many

punoglávac {vca (acc. = gen.) masc.} (lit. tadpole) *sl-sex* ***Fac-Obs*** penis, dick, prick <Slav[*1]>

punturìtis {a masc.} *sl* fear <Slav✍[*1]>

pũnjenica {ē fem.} *col* ***Fac*** mother-in-law <Slav❖[*1]>

pũp {excl.} **1** *col* the sound made by tapping, tap <Slav[*1]> **2** *col* the sound made by a small explosion, pop <Slav[*1]>

pũpa {ē fem.} *sl* ***Fam*** stomach, belly, tummy <Slav✍[*1]>

pũpak {pka (acc. = gen.) masc.} (lit. navel) *sl-sex* ***Fac*** male homosexual, gay <Slav[*1]>

• **U pũpak te jèbēm!** {S} (lit. I screw you in your navel!) *dia-col* ***Off*** used as a weak curse, Screw you!

• **vézati pũpak** {VP} (lit. tie one's navel) *sl-fea* marry, tie the knot

pùpati {ām, ajū imperf.} (lit. bud) *col* enjoy, like <Slav[*1]>

pũpavac {vca (acc. = gen.) masc.} *sl-fea* obese person <Slav❖[*1]>

pùpčić {a masc.} (lit. small navel) *sl-sex* ***Obs*** vagina, cunt <Slav[*1]>

pũpnuti {nēm, nū perf. intr.} (lit. bud) *sl-sex* ***Obs*** break wind, fart <Slav[*1]>

pũr {excl.} *col* the sound made by a turkey, gobble <Slav>

puràniti se {pùrānīm, nē imperf. intr.} (lit. turkey) *sl-fea* be conceited, be stuck-up <Slav❖[*1]>

pũrca {ē masc.} *sl-crime* thief <Slav>

pũrča {ē masc.} *sl-fea* loafer, idler

pũrče {eta neut.} *sl* child, kid

pũre {eta neut.} (lit. young turkey) *sl* child, kid <Slav[*1]>

Pũrgar {a (acc. = gen.) masc.} *sl-fea* name of inhabitant of Zagreb, Croatia <Ger❖[*1]>

Pũrger[1] {a (acc. = gen.) masc.} **a.** *sl-fea* name of inhabitant of Zagreb, Croatia <Ger❖[*1]> **b.** *sl-fea* Croat (person) <Lat❖[*2]>

pũrger[2] {a (acc. = gen.) masc.} (lit. the pure one) *sl-fea* city boy <Ger❖[*1]>

pùrkāč {a (acc. = gen.) masc.} **a.** *sl-fea* loafer, idler <Slav❖[*1]> **b.** *sl-fea* lazy or shiftless person, bum, good for nothing <Slav❖[*2]> **c.** *sl-crime* thief <Slav❖[*3]>

pũrkati {ām, ajū imperf. intr.} *sl-crime* steal, swipe <Slav[*1]>

pũrnuti {nēm, nū perf.} *sl-crime* steal, swipe <Slav✍>

pùrnjati {ām, ajū imperf.} **1** *sl-fea* get angry <Slav❖[*1]> **2** *sl-fea* speed (auto, etc.) <Slav❖[*1]> **3** *sl-fea* smoke tobacco frequently <Slav❖[*1]>

pùrzek {a (acc. = gen.) masc.} *sl-arch* dog (the animal)

pũsa {ē fem.} *col* ***Fam*** kiss <Ger>

• **Pũsu bráci!** {S} (lit. A kiss to brother!) *sl-sex* ***Fac-Obs*** used as a moderate curse

pustàlja {ē masc.} SSer *col-dia* troublemaker, rowdy, ruffian <Slav⁘*1>

pústinja {ē fem.} (lit. desert) *sl-sex* ***Obs*** vagina, cunt <Slav*1>

pùstiti *See the following*

• **pùstiti bùvu** {VP} (lit. release a flea) **a.** *sl* spread the news **b.** *sl* lie

• **pùstiti fàzōn** {VP} (lit. release a joke) *sl* lie

• **pùstiti fóru** {VP} (lit. release a trick) *sl* lie

• **pùstiti gȍlūba** {VP} (lit. release a pigeon) *sl-sex* break wind, pass gas, fart

• **pùstiti gȍlūba u čȍporu másnīh kòstī** {VP} (lit. release a pigeon in a pack of fat bones) *sl-sex* break wind in the presence of important or influential persons

• **pùstiti gȍlūbu** {VP} (lit. let to the pigeon) **1** SerE *sl-sex* ***Obs*** masturbate, beat off **2** SerE *sl-sex* ***Obs*** urinate, piss

• **pùstiti ȉkru** {VP} (lit. release caviar) *sl-sex* engage in sexual intercourse with

• **pùstiti jȅbozōv** {VP} (lit. release a fuck call) *sl-sex* ***Obs*** look for attention

• **pùstiti kanaríncu vȍdu** {VP} (lit. release some water to a canary) *sl-sex* ***Obs*** urinate, piss

• **pùstiti múlcu kȓv** {VP} (lit. let the kid bleed) **1** *sl-sex* ***Obs*** masturbate, beat off **2** *sl-sex* ***Obs*** urinate, piss

• **pùstiti pévca** {VP} (lit. release a rooster) SerE *sl-sex* ***Obs*** urinate, piss

• **pùstiti pévcu kȓv** {VP} (lit. let the rooster bleed) **1** SerE *sl-sex* ***Obs*** masturbate, beat off **2** SerE *sl-sex* ***Obs*** urinate, piss

• **pùstiti pijétlu kȓv** {VP} (lit. let the rooster bleed) **1** *sl-sex* ***Obs*** masturbate, beat off **2** *sl-sex* ***Obs*** urinate, piss

• **pùstiti pijévcu žȉlu** {VP} (lit. release rooster's vein) **1** *sl-sex* ***Obs*** masturbate, beat off **2** *sl-sex* ***Obs*** urinate, piss

• **pùstiti rȍgove** {VP} (lit. grow horns) *sl* get up (from bed, etc.)

• **pùstiti rȍgove** {VP} (lit. grow horns) *sl* get up (from bed, etc.)

• **pùstiti se u prómet** {VP} (lit. come to traffic) *sl-sex* ***Obs*** start having sex frequently

• **pùstiti sȕzu za Hȉtlera** {VP} (lit. shed a tear for Hitler *Adolf Hitler*) *sl-sex* ***Fac-Obs*** urinate, piss

• **pùstiti šéjtana** {VP} (lit. release the devil) *sl-sex* ***Fac-Obs*** break wind, pass gas, fart

• **pùstiti vȍdu** {VP} (lit. release water) *sl* ***Obs*** shut up, cease talking

• **pùstiti vȍdu na slobòdu** {VP} (lit. free water) *sl-sex* ***Fac-Obs*** urinate

Pȕsu bráci! {S} (lit. a kiss to brother) *sl-sex* ***Fac-Obs*** used as a moderate curse, Blow me! ☞ **pusa**

pùšāč {pušáča (acc. = gen.) masc.} (lit. smoker) **a.** *sl-fea* boring person, bore <Slav*1> **b.** *sl-fea* extremely talkative male, chatterbox <Slav*2> **c.** *sl-fea* evil male <Slav*3> **c.** *sl-fea* liar <Slav*4> **e.** *sl-fea* insinuator <Slav*5> **f.** *sl-fea* chatterbox <Slav*6> *sl-fea* stupid or mentally deficient person <Slav*6>

pušàčica {ē fem.} (lit. smoker) *sl-sex* ***Obs*** female who frequently engages in fellatio <Slav*1>

púšćati {ām, ajū impert.} [std. = puštati] *dia* let, allow, permit <Slav✍>

pȕšēnje {a neut.} (lit. smoking) *sl-sex* ***Obs*** fellatio <Slav*1>

pȕši {excl.} *sl-sex* used to express extreme disgust and to offend one's interlocutor <Slav*1>

Pȕši ga! {S} (lit. Smoke it!) *sl-sex* ***Off*** used as a moderate curse, Blow me! ☞ **pušti**

Pȕši kȕrac! {S} (lit. Smoke prick!) *sl-sex* ***Off*** used as a strong curse, Blow me! ☞ **pušti**

Pȕši mȁlo pȓst! {S} (lit. Smoke my finger a little bit!) *sl* ***Off*** used to express the state of not being threatened, You can't do a fucking thing to me! ☞ **pušiti**

Pȕši mi kȕrac! {S} (lit. Smoke my prick!) *sl-sex* ***Off*** used as a moderate curse, Blow me! ☞ **pušiti**

Pȕši mi mȁlo pȓst! {S} (lit. Smoke my finger a little bit!) *sl* ***Off*** used to express the state of not being threatened, You can't to a fucking thing to me! ☞ **pušiti**

Pȕši rȁcku mȁlo! {S} (lit. Smoke my prick a little bit!) *sl-sex* ***Off*** used as a strong curse, Blow me! ☞ **pušiti**

Pȕši sâm sȅbi òbrezānī kȕrac! {S} (lit. Smoke your circumcised prick!) *sl-sex* ***Off*** used as a strong curse, Blow me! ☞ **pušiti**

pȕšik {a (acc. = gen.) masc.} (lit. smoker) **a.** *sl-fea* boring person, bore <Slav✍*1> **b.i.** *sl-fea* extremely talkative person, chatterbox <Slav✍*2> **ii.** *sl-fea* evil male <Slav✍*2> **iii.** *sl-fea* liar <Slav✍*2> **iv.** *sl-fea* insinuator <Slav✍*2> **v.** *sl-fea* chatterbox <Slav✍*2> **vi.** *sl-fea* stupid or mentally deficient person <Slav✍*3>

pȕšika {ē fem.; Dat pȕšiki} (lit. smoker) *sl-sex* ***Fac*** prostitute, hooker <Slav⁘*1>

pȕšikar *See the following*

• **màdam pȕšikār** {NP} (lit. madam cocksucker) *sl-sex* ***Obs*** male homosexual, gay

pȕšikurac {rca (acc. = gen.) masc.} (lit. prick smoker) *sl-fea* ***Der-Obs*** worthless or despicable person <Slav⁘*1>

pȕšikūrka {ē fem.; Dat pȕšikūrki} (lit. prick smoker) *sl-sex* ***Fac-Obs*** prostitute, hooker <Slav⁘*1>

pušióna {ē fem.} (lit. smoking room) **1** *sl-fea* difficult or unpleasant situation <Slav⁘*1> **2** *sl-fea* boredom <Slav⁘*1> **3** *sl-sstu* school bathroom <Slav⁘*1>

pȕšiti {šīm, šē imperf.} (lit. smoke) **a.** *sl-sex* ***Obs*** engage in fellatio <Slav*1> **b.i.** *sl-fea* be cheated, be swindled <Slav*2> **ii.** *sl-drugs* take (narcotic) drugs <Slav*2>

• **Ma pȕši ga u pȉčku mȁterinu!** {S} (lit. Blow me to your mother's cunt!) *col* ***Off*** used as a strong curse, Blow me!

• **Pȕši ga!** {S} (lit. Smoke it!) *sl-sex* ***Off*** used as a moderate curse, Blow me!

• **Pȕši kȕrac!** {S} (lit. Smoke prick!) *sl-sex* ***Off*** used as a strong curse, Blow me!

• **Pȕši mȁlo pȑst!** {S} (lit. Smoke my finger a little bit!) *sl* ***Off*** used to express the state of not being threatened, You can't do a fucking thing to me!

• **Pȕši mi kȕrac!** {S} (lit. Smoke my prick!) *sl-sex* ***Off*** used as a moderate curse, Blow me!

• **Pȕši mi mȁlo pȑst!** {S} (lit. Smoke my finger a little bit!) *sl* ***Off*** used to express the state of not being threatened, You can't do a fucking thing to me!

• **Pȕši rȁcku mȁlo!** {S} (lit. Smoke my prick a little bit!) *sl-sex* ***Off*** used as a strong curse, Blow me!

• **Pȕši sâm sȅbi ȍbrezānī kȕrac!** {S} (lit. Smoke your circumcised prick!) *sl-sex* ***Off*** used as a strong curse, Blow me!

• **Pȕšīm zȅtu!** {S} (lit. I am smoking my son-in-law's bone!) *sl* ***Off*** used in angry dismissal, Blow me!

• **Pȕšite mi svȅ ȍbrezānē bȁlije!** {S} (lit. Y'all circumcised Muslims, smoke it to me!) *col* ***Off*** used as a strong curse to a Bosnian Muslim, Blow me!

• **pȕšiti fazóne** {VP} (lit. smoke tricks) *sl-fea* believe, trust

• **pȕšiti kao Tȕrčin** {VP} (lit. smoke like a Turk) *sl-fea* smoke heavily, smoke like a chimney

• **pȕšiti kâr** {VP} (lit. smoke prick) *sl-sex* ***Obs*** engage in fellatio

• **pȕšiti lùlu míra** {VP} (lit. smoke a peace pipe) *sl-sex* ***Fac-Obs*** engage in fellatio

• **pȕšiti trúbu** {VP} (lit. smoke a trumpet) *sl-sex* ***Fac-Obs*** engage in fellatio

pȕška [1] {excl.} (lit. gun, rifle) **1** *sl* used to express appreciation, great, excellent <Slav*1> **2** *sl* used to express satisfaction, great, excellent <Slav*1>

pȕška [2] {ē fem.; Dat pȕški} (lit. gun, rifle) **1** *sl-sex* ***Fac-Obs*** penis, rod <Slav*1> **2a.** *sl-sex* ***App*** attractive female <Slav*1> **b.** *sl-sex* sexually aroused female, hot chick <Slav*2> **3** *sl-fea* danger <Slav*1> **4** *sl-fea* mistake, error: *Napravili smo pušku kad smo mu dali da vozi. We made a mistake when we let him drive.* <Slav*1> **5** *sl-fea* nose <Slav*1>

• **Bíla je pȕška.** {S} (lit. There was a gun.) *sl-crime* used to refer to a dangerous situation in the past: *Bila nam je puška kad su nas zaganjali drotovi. We were in danger when the heat was chasing us.*

pȕška [3] {adj.} (lit. gun, rifle) **1** *sl* ***App*** excellent <Slav*1> **2** *sl* tense <Slav*1>

pȕškār {a masc.} (lit. gunman) *sl-sex* ***Fac*** male homosexual, gay <Slav⁘*1>

puškáriti {pùškārīm, rē imperf.} (lit. shoot) *sl* cheat, swindle <Slav⁘*1>

puškáriti {pùškārīm, rē imperf. intr.} (lit. shoot) **a.** *sl-sstu* take crib-sheets to one's exam <Slav⁘*1> **b.** *sl-sstu* prepare crib-sheets for an exam <Slav⁘*2>

pȕškāš {a (acc. = gen.) masc.} (lit. gunman) *sl-fea* large-nosed male <Slav⁘*1>

puškètina {ē fem.} (lit. big gun, big rifle) *sl-crime* machine gun <Slav⁘*1>

pȕškica {ē fem.} *sl-sstu* crib sheet, cheat sheet <Slav⁘*1>

pùškīn {excl.} *sl* used to refer to an unwillingness to make a transaction, no deal: *A: Hoćeš li mi prodati auto? B: Puškin! A: Are you going to sell me your car? B: No deal!* <Slav✍*1>

púšnica {excl.} *sl* ***App*** excellent, awesome <Slav*1>

pȕšnuti {nēm, nū perf.} *sl* push, shove <Eng>

púštati *See the following*

• **púštati balóne** {VP} (lit. release balloons) *sl* lie

• **púštati bùve** {VP} (lit. release fleas) Ser *sl* lie

• **púštati gȍlubove** {VP} (lit. release pigeons) *sl-sex* ***Fac*** break wind, pass gas, fart

• **púštati nȍžice** {VP} (lit. grow little legs) *sl* run away, flee

• **púštati pȁru** {VP} (lit. release steam) *sl-sex* ***Fac*** break wind silently, fart silently

• **púštati plȋn** {VP} (lit. release gas) *sl-sex* ***Fac*** break wind, pass gas, fart

pȕštiti {pȕštīm, tē perf.} [std. = pustiti] *dia* leave alone <Slav✍>

• **Mà pȕši mi!** {S} (lit. Blow me!) *col* ***Off*** used as a strong curse, Blow me!

pût *See the following*

• **ȁsfaltnī pût** {NP} (lit. pavement road) *sl-sex* ***Fac*** overly stiff hymen

• **krȋžnī pût** {NP} (lit. way of the Cross) Cro *sl* nursing home

• **pût na mȅsēc** {NP} (lit. trip to the moon) SerE *sl-drugs* taking narcotic drugs

• **pût u vìsokō drúštvo** {NP} (lit. road to high society) *sl-sstu* elite high school

pȕter {a (acc. = gen.) masc.} /pùter/ (lit. butter) **a.** *sl-fea* young female, girl <**Ger**[*1]> **b.** *sl-fea* attractive young female <**Ger**[*2]> **c.** *sl-fea* attractive female <**Ger**[*3]>

pȕterica {ē fem.} /pùter/ (lit. butter girl) **a.** *sl-fea* young female, girl <**Ger**[*1]> **b.** *sl-fea* attractive young female <**Ger**[*2]> **c.** *sl-fea* attractive female <**Ger**[*3]>

pȕtka {ē fem.; p, Dat pȕtki} /pȕtka /pùtaka masc./ [std. = kaput] *sl* coat (outer garment) <**Slav**✍>

pûtnā kònzērva {NP} (lit. travel can) *sl* streetcar ☞ **konzerva**

pûtnīk {a (acc. = gen.) masc.} (lit. traveller) **1** *sl-crime* thief who steals on trains, train thief <**Slav**[*1]> **2** *sl-sex* ***Fac*** gonorrhea, the clap <**Slav**[*1]>

pûu {excl.} *col* the sound made by spitting, phew <**Slav**>

pȕvadžija {ē masc.} **a.** *sl-fea* boaster, braggart, blowhard <**Slav**✣[*1]> **b.** *sl-fea* conceited male <**Slav**✣[*2]>

puvàkati {ām, ajū imperf.} *sl-fea* boast, brag <**Slav**✣[*1]>

puvàkati se {ām, ajū imperf. intr.} Ser *sl-fea* boast, brag <**Slav**✣[*1]>

púvalo *See the following*

• **mȑtvō púvalo** {NP} (lit. dead blower) *sl-fea* boaster, braggart, blowhard

puvànder {a (acc. = gen.) masc.} **a.** *sl-fea* boaster, braggart, blowhard <**Slav**✣[*1]> **b.** *sl-fea* conceited male <**Slav**✣[*2]>

púvati se {pûvām, púvajū imperf. intr.} *sl-fea* boast, brag <**Slav**✣[*1]>

pùvātor {a (acc. = gen.) masc.} **a.** *sl-fea* boaster, braggart, blowhard <**Slav**✣[*1]> **b.** *sl-fea* conceited male <**Slav**✣[*2]>

pûz {a +ev (ext. pl) masc.; Nom Pl púzevi} *sl-sex* ***Obs*** vagina, cunt <**Slav**[*1]>

pȕzati {ām, ajū imperf.} (lit. crawl) *sl-fea* ***Der*** ingratiate, brownnose, kiss ass <**Slav**[*1]>

pȕzavac {vca (acc. = gen.) masc.} (lit. crawler) *sl-fea* ***Der*** ingratiator (male), brownnoser, ass kisser <**Slav**✣[*1]>

púzdro {a masc.} *sl-fea* stupid or mentally deficient person

pùzla {ē fem.} *sl* puzzle (game) <**Eng**✍>

pûž {a +ev (ext. pl) masc.; Nom Pl púževi} (lit. snail) **1** *sl-sex* ***Obs*** vagina, cunt <**Slav**[*1]> **2** *sl-fea* ***Der*** slow person, slowpoke <**Slav**[*1]>

pùžek {a (acc. = gen.) masc.} (lit. small snail) *sl-sex* ***Fac-Obs*** small penis <**Slav**[*1]>

Rr

rabìnara {ē fem.} *sl-sex* prostitute

râboš-mȁjstor {a (acc. = gen.) masc.} *sl-crafts* belt repairman <**Hun-Lat**✣[*1]>

rȁbota {ē fem.} /ràbota/ **a.** *col* suspicious activities: *Policija istražuje njegove rabote. The police have been investigating his suspicious activities.* <**Slav**[*1]> **b.** *col* hard work <**Slav**[*2]> **c.** *sl* work, labor <**Slav**[*3]>

• **Jèbānā ràbota!** {NP} (lit. Fucked business!) *col* ***Obs*** used to express disrespect or lack of interest in, Fuck it!

ràbotnīk {a (acc. = gen.) masc.} *col* worker <**Slav**>

Rȁc {a +ev (ext. pl) masc.; Nom Pl Racevi} *sl-fea* ***Off*** Slav <**Hun**>

rȁca {ē fem.} (lit. duck) *sl-fea* short female <**Slav**[*1]>

rȁcka {ē fem.; Dat rȁcki p} *sl-sex* ***Obs*** penis, dick, prick <**Slav**✍> ☞ **kurac**

rȁcko {a masc.; perm} *sl-sex* ***Obs*** penis, dick, prick <**Slav**✍> ☞ **kurac**

rȁcku {masc.; perm} /ràcku/ *sl-sex* ***Obs*** penis, dick, prick <**Slav**✍> ☞ **kurac**

rȁči *See the following*

• **Rȁči ti vèniālnū jèbēm!** {S} SerE *dia* ***Off*** used as a moderate curse, Fuck you!

râd *See the following*

• **òvāj râd** {NP} (lit. this work) *sl* used to support gestures (usu. hand movements)

• **râd na sȉc** {NP} (lit. work at sitting) *sl-fea* work at home

• **rùčnī râd** {NP} (lit. handwork) *sl-sex* ***Fac-Obs*** masturbation, hand job

radàjner {a masc.} *col* Radenska mineral water <**BN**✍>

rȁdapcīger {a masc.} *sl-auto* wheel remover (the tool) <**Ger**>

rȁdār {a masc.} (lit. radar) *sl* ear <**Eng**[*1]>

radàrista {ē masc.} (lit. radar operator) *sl-fea* lop-eared person <**Eng**[*1]>

rȁdētan {tna, nto adj.} *col-dia* laborious, tedious <**Slav**>

radìjālka {ē fem.; Dat radìjālki} (lit. radial tire) *sl-sex* ***Fac*** loose woman <**Lat**✣[*1]>

radijâtōrke {i fem. pl.} (lit. the radiator ones) *sl* velvet trousers <Lat❖*1>

radìkāl {dikála (acc. = gen.) masc.} *sl-polit* member of the Radical Party (a political party in Serbia) <Lat*1>

râdio {a neut.} (lit. radio) *sl* head <Lat*1>

• **râdio Miléva** {NP} (lit. radio Mileva, proper name) *col* rumors

radiónica *See the following*

• **glavarskā radiónica** {NP} (lit. headman's workshop) *sl-fea* ***Fac*** psychiatric hospital, nuthouse

ráditi 1 {râdīm, dē imperf.} (lit. work) **1a.** *sl* cheat, swindle <Slav*1> **b.** *sl* make jokes <Slav*2> **c.** *sl* lie <Slav*3> **2a.** *sl-crime* steal, swipe: *Ne radim više automobile, sada radim samo stanove. I do not swipe cars anymore, now I only do apartments.* <Slav*4> **b.** *sl-crime* pick pockets **3** *sl-sex* engage in sexual intercourse with (of a male) **4** *sl-drugs* influence (of drugs): *Radi ga LSD. He's on LSD.*

• **jàšta râdi** {ExcP} *col* used as a strong affirmative response, of course, yeah, you bet

• **nè rādī bibliotéka** {S} (lit. the library is closed) *sl* ***Fac*** used to confuse one's interlocutor

• **ráditi kô vòla u kùpusu** {VP} (lit. work like an ox in cabbage) *col* trick, cheat, swindle

• **ráditi Mīkī-Šílja-Hòrācije** {VP} (lit. do Mickey-Goofy-Horace) *sl-sex* ***Fac-Obs*** masturbate, beat off

• **ráditi pòsaō** {VP} (lit. work the job) **a.** *sl-fea* fit, be suitable **b.** *sl-drugs* be strong enough (of drugs)

• **ráditi rádnju** {VP} (lit. do the job) **1** *sl-gamble* gamble **2** *sl-sex* ***Obs*** engage in sexual intercourse with **3** *col* fit, be suitable **4** *sl-drugs* be strong enough (of drugs)

• **ráditi u fùšu** {VP} (lit. moonlight *work*) *sl-fea* cheat on one's lover or spouse

• **ráditi u mòzak** {VP} (lit. work in brains) *sl* joke with, make a fool of

• **ráditi u pìvari** {VP} (lit. work in a brewery) *sl-fea* have skinny legs

• **ráditi za èksere** {VP} (lit. work for nails) *sl* work without being rewarded adequately, work for peanuts: *Ona radi za eksere. She works for peanuts.*

• **ráditi za kikirìkī** {VP} (lit. work for peanuts) *sl* work without being rewarded adequately, work for peanuts

• **ráditi za masláčak** {VP} (lit. work for dandelion) *sl* work without being rewarded adequately, work for peanuts

ráditi 2 {râdīm, râdidū imperf.} Vojv *col-dia* work, labor <Slav☞>

ráditi se {râdīm, dē imperf.} **1** *sl-drink* get drunk <Slav*1> **2** *sl-drugs* take narcotic drugs, do drugs <Slav*1>

Ràdivoje {a masc.} (lit. Radivoje, man's name X radio) *sl* radio <Lat☞>

ràdkapna {ē fem.} **a.** *sl-auto* hubcap <Ger☞> **b.** *sl-fea* extremely stupid or mentally deficient person <Ger*1>

râdnīk {a (acc. = gen.) masc.} (lit. worker) *sl-crime* pickpocket <Slav*1>

• **jàmskī râdnik** {NP} (lit. hole worker) *sl-sex* ***Fac-Obs*** male sexual partner (of a female)

ràdnuti {nēm, nū perf.} (lit. work a little) *sl* cheat, swindle <Slav*1>

rádnja {ē fem.} **1a.** *col* store <Slav> **b.** *sl-sex* sexual intercourse <Slav*1> **c.** *sl* cheating, swindling <Slav*2> **2** *col* zipper, fly <Slav*1>

• **Rádnja râdī.** {S} (lit. shop is open) **1** *sl-sex* ***Obs*** sexual intercourse **2** *sl-gamble* gambling

Râdnjāk {a (acc. = gen.) masc.} (lit. the worker's one) Cro *sl* name of a dance club at Workers' center in Zagreb, Croatia <BN☞>

ràdodājka {ē fem.; Dat ràdodājki} /radòdājka, radodâjka, radodàjka/ (lit. glad giver) **a.** *sl-sex* ***Fac*** prostitute, hooker <Slav❖*1> **b.** *sl-sex* ***Fac*** loose woman <Slav❖*2>

radoholìzam {zma masc.} *col* workaholism <Slav-Eng*1>

Ràdōjka {ē fem.; Dat Ràdōjki} (lit. Radojka woman's name X rado 'gladly') *sl-sex* ***Fac*** loose woman <SlavO*1>

ràdōst *See the following*

• **dèčijā ràdōst** {NP} (lit. children's joy) SerE *sl-mil* bread spread with marmalade on it

• **djèčijā ràdōst** {NP} (lit. children's joy) *sl-mil* bread spread with marmalade

radóševićka {ē fem.; Dat radóševićki} (lit. the glad one) *sl-sex* ***Fac*** loose woman <Slav☞*1>

radùckati {ām, ajū imperf.} (lit. work a little) *col* work slowly <Slav❖>

ràfa {ē fem.} *sl-fea* unattractive female

ràfūng {a masc.} *sl-sex* ***Obs*** vagina, cunt

ràga {ē fem.; Dat ràgi} (lit. old horse) **1** *sl-fea* unattractive female <Slav*1> **2** *sl-fea* old car, wreck <Slav*1>

ráhat {adj.} Bos *col* comfortable (of a person), doing great: *Izašao je iz bonice, pa je rahat. He is out of the hospital and he is doing great.* <NE>

ràhat-lòkum {a masc.} BosM *col* Turkish delight (type of candy) <NE>

ráhmet {a masc.} BosM *col* death <NE>

• **Ráhmeta mi dédinōg!** {S} (lit. *I swear* by my

grandfather's death!) BosM *col* used to emphasize the truth of what has been said, I swear!

rahmètli {adj.} BosM *col* the late (dead) <NE>

rahmètli-pȍster {a masc.} BosM *sl* obituary <NE-Eng[*1]>

ràin {a (acc. = gen.) masc.} *sl-crime* policeman, cop <Gyp>

ràinac {nca (acc. = gen.) masc.} *sl-crime* policeman, cop <Gyp>

rȃj {a +ev (ext. pl) masc.; Nom Pl ràjevi} (lit. paradise) *sl* freedom <Slav[*1]>

rája {ē fem.} **a.** *col* people <NE[*1]> **b.** *col* company (group of people) <NE[*2]> **c.** *col* gang, group of one's close friends <NE[*3]> **d.** masses, rabble <NE[*4]>

ràjber {a (acc. = gen.) masc.} **a.** *sl-fea* ***Der*** unfriendly person <Ger[*1]> **b.** *sl-fea* ***Der*** worthless or despicable person, bum <Ger[*2]>

rȁjc {a +ev (ext. pl) masc.; Nom Pl ràjcevi} **a.** *sl-sex* ***Obs*** lust, sexual urge <Ger[*1]> **b.** *sl-sex* ***Obs*** sexual stimulation <Ger[*2]>

rȁjcati {ām, ajū imperf.} /rȁjcati/ *sl-sex* ***Obs*** stimulate sexually, turn on <Ger[*1]>

rȁjcati se {ām, ajū imperf. intr.} /rȁjcati se/ **a.** *sl-sex* ***Obs*** get sexually aroused, get hot <Ger[*1]> **b.** *sl* ***Obs*** get excited, get turned on <Ger[*2]>

ràjcūng {a masc.} *sl-sex* ***Obs*** lust, sexual urge <Ger[*1]>

ràjfa {ē fem.} *sl-drink* drink (alcohol) <Ger[*1]>

rȁjfānje {a neut.} *sl-drink* drinking (alcohol) <Ger[*1]>

ràjfati {ām, ajū imperf.} **1** *sl* cheat, swindle <Ger[*1]> **2** *sl-auto* speed (auto, etc.) <Ger[*1]> **3** *sl-drink* drink (alcohol) <Ger[*1]>

ràjīnke {ī fem. pl.} *sl* money <Gyp>

rájko {a masc.} *sl-arch* the sun <Slav[*1]>

rájngla {ē fem.} (lit. stove ring) **a.** *sl-sex* ***Fac-Obs*** vagina, cunt <Ger[*1]> **b.** *sl-sex* ***Fac*** prostitute, hooker <Ger[*2]>

Rȃjskā se svijéća upálila! {S} (lit. Heavenly candle is lighted!) *sl* used to indicate that a favorable state of affairs has been reached, I made it! I succeeded! ☞ svijeća

rȃjskō {ōg masc.} *sl-arch* the sun <Slav[*1]>

rȁjsnēdl {a masc.} *col* pin (fastening device) <Ger>

rȁjsnēgla {ē fem.} *col* pin (fastening device) <Ger>

ràjūng {a masc.} *sl-sex* ***Obs*** vagina, cunt

rȁka {ē fem.; Dat rȃki} (lit. grave) *sl-sex* ***Fac-Obs*** vagina, cunt <Slav[*1]>

rakèta {ē fem.} (lit. rocket) *sl-sex* ***App*** highly attractive female, bombshell <Ger[*1]>

rakȉjati {ām, ajū imperf.} *sl-drink* drink plum brandy <NE⁘>

ràkijīca {ē fem.} *sl-drink* shot of schnapps <NE⁘>

rakírati {ràkīrām, rakíraju biasp.} *sl-fea* walk slowly, amble <Slav⁘[*1]>

ràkonjac {njca masc.} *sl-sex* ***Obs*** penis, dick, prick <Slav[*1]>

rakréčiti se {ràkrēčīm, čē perf. intr.} [std. = raskrečiti se] *col* spread one's legs <Slav✍>

ràkūn {rakúna (acc. = gen.) masc.; Voc rȃkune} (lit. raccoon) *sl-fea* male with a black eye <Eng[*1]>

rȁlica {ē fem.} (lit. ploughshare) *sl* leg (human) <Slav[*1]>

rȁlje {a fem. pl.} (lit. jaws) **1** *sl* mouth <Slav[*1]> **2** *sl-sex* vagina <Slav[*1]>

rámpa {ē fem.} /rȃmpa/ (lit. ramp, barrier) **a.** *sl-sex* ***Fac-Obs*** erect penis <Fre[*1]> **b.i.** *sl* state border <Fre[*2]> **ii.** *sl* ***Fac*** nose <Fre[*2]>

rȁna {ē fem.} (lit. wound) *sl-sex* ***Obs*** vagina, cunt <Slav[*1]>

rȁnč {a +ev (ext. pl) masc.; Nom Pl rànčevi} (lit. ranch) **1** *col* property (usu. with a house) in the vicinity visited during weekends <Spa[*1]> **2** *sl* street <Spa[*1]>

ràndes {a masc.} *col* dating, going out with <Fre✍>

rániti {ranīm, ranē imperf.} [std. = hraniti] *col-dia* feed, give food to <Slav✍>

ránkovićevac {vca (acc. = gen.) masc.} (lit. the Rankovič's one) *sl-polit* follower of Aleksandar Ranković (a hard-line communist politician in the former Yugoslavia) <SlavO⁘>

ranorànilac {ioca (acc. = gen.) masc.} (lit. early riser) *sl-drink* person who leaves a bar early in the morning <Slav⁘>

ràsan {sna, sno adj.} (lit. purebred) *sl-sex* ***App*** attractive, hot: *rasna riba hot chick* <Spa[*1]>

ràsate {rasetē fem.; perm} [std. = terasa] *sl* terrace <Fre✍>

rascópati {ām, ajū perf.} *col* smash, crush <Slav[*1]>

rashihȉšati se {ām, ajū perf. intr.} *sl* laugh <Slav✍>

rashihòtati se {ām, ajū perf. intr.} *sl* laugh <Slav✍>

ráshodovati {dujēm, dujū biasp.} *col* write off (e.g. office equipment) <Slav>

rashohòtati se {ām, ajū perf. intr.} *sl* laugh <Slav✣>

rȁska {ē fem.} *sl-sstu* homeroom teacher <Slav✍>

raskàntati {ām, ajū perf.} /ràskantati/ *sl* defeat <Ger✣[*1]>

raskàntati se {ām, ajū perf. intr.} /ràskantati se/ **1** *sl* separate <Ger✣[*1]> **2** *sl* argue, quarrel <Ger✣[*1]>

ràskinuti {nēm, nū perf. intr.} (lit. break) *sl-crime* break out of prison <Slav[*1]>

ràsklamfan {a, o adj.} *sl-fea* in a bad mood <Ger✣[*1]>

raskokodákati se {kòdāčēm, kòdāčū perf. intr.} **a.** *col* cackle (hens, etc.) <Slav> **b.** *sl-fea* talk persistently and meaninglessly, blabber, chatter

raskòpati {ām, ajū perf.} (lit. dig out) *sl* get angry <Slav[*1]>

ràskrēčen {a, o adj.} *col* astride <Slav[*1]>

raskȑstiti {tīm, tē perf.} **a.** *col* settle an issue: *Raskrstili su dugove. They settled their debts.* <Slav✣[*1]> **b.** *col* get rid of: *raskrstiti sa starim kolima get rid of an old car* <Slav✣[*2]>

ràskućiti {ćīm, ćē perf.} (lit. de-house) *col* lose one's property <Slav[*1]>

raskukurékati se {ām, ajū perf. intr.} **a.** SerE *col* cock-a-doodle-doo <Slav> **b.** SerE *sl-fea* talk persistently and meaninglessly, blabber, chatter <Slav[*1]>

rȁskupusān {a, o adj.} *sl-fea* untidy, messy <Slav✣[*1]>

raskurážiti se {kùrāžīm, žē perf. intr.} (lit. get discouraged) *sl* take one's dress off, strip <Fre✣[*1]>

raskurcávati {kùrcāvām, ajū imperf.} (lit. prick away) *sl* destroy, ruin <Slav✣[*1]>

raskusùrati se {ām, ajū perf. intr.} *col* settle mutual financial issues <NE✣[*1]>

raskusurívati se {sùrīvām, sùrujū imperf. intr.} *col* settle mutual financial issues <NE✣[*1]>

raskȕžnjati {ām, ajū perf.} *sl* understand, realize

raskužnjávati {kùžnjāvām, kužnjávajū imperf.} **a.** *sl* feel, sense: *raskužnjavati vrelinu feel the heat* **b.** *sl* understand, realize **c.** *sl* know, have knowledge of **d.** discover, find out

ràskvocati se {ām, ajū perf. intr.} /raskvócati se/ **a.** *col* cackle (hens, etc.) <Slav> **b.** *sl-fea* talk persistently and meaninglessly, blabber, chatter <Slav[*1]>

rȁsnā {ē fem. (adj. decl.)} *sl-sex* ***App-Obs*** attractive female <NE✣[*1]>

ràspadati se {ām, ajū imperf. intr.} (lit. fall apart) *sl-fea* be sick <Slav[*1]>

raspáliti {ràspālīm, lē perf.} (lit. burn) **1a.** *col* hit, punch <Slav[*1]> **b.** *col* fire, shoot <Slav[*1]> **2** *col* make happy <Slav[*1]> **3** *col* commence an action: *Raspaliti cuganje. Start digging.* <Slav[*1]>

raspáliti se {ràspālīm, lē perf. intr.} (lit. burn) *sl-fea* get angry, burn <Slav[*1]>

raspaljȍtka {ē fem.; Dat raspaljȍtki} /raspaljòtka/ **a.** *sl* party (social gathering) <Slav✍[*1]> **b.** *sl-sex* orgy <Slav✍[*2]>

raspaméti {excl.} *sl* fire (command) <Slav[*1]>

raspamétiti se {pàmētīm, tē perf. intr.} (lit. lose one's mind) **1** *sl* ***App*** have a good time <Slav[*1]> **2** *sl-fea* be enthusiastic about, be crazy about <Slav[*1]>

raspandȑkača {ē fem.} *sl-sex* ***Fac*** prostitute, hooker <Slav✣[*1]>

raspandŕknuti {pàndrknēm, nū perf.} *sl* hit hard

raspèkmeziti {zīm, zē perf.} /raspekméziti /zim, ze perf./ (lit. jam) *col* spoil (of children) <Slav✣[*1]>

raspèkmeziti se {zīm, zē perf. intr.} /raspekméziti se /zim, ze perf. intr./ (lit. jam) *sl-fea* become soft, be irresolute <Slav✣[*1]>

ràspičiti {čīm, čē perf.} (lit. cunt out) **a.** *sl-sex* ***Obs*** break the hymen <Slav✣[*1]> **b.** *sl* ***Obs*** hit, punch <Slav✣[*2]> **c.** *sl* ***Obs*** destroy, ruin <Slav✣[*3]>

ràspičkati {ām, ajū perf.} **1** *sl* spend (money, property, etc.) <Slav✣[*1]> **2** *sl* beat up <Slav✣[*1]>

ràspičkati se {ām, ajū perf.} (lit. decunt oneself) *sl* ***Obs*** have an argument <Slav✣[*1]>

ràspigan {a, o adj.} *sl-fea* angry, mad

ràspigati {ām, ajū perf.} *sl* make angry, make mad

raspiláviti se {pìlāvīm, vē imperf. intr.} **a.** *col* ***App*** feel good <NE✣[*1]> **b.** *col* be nice and tender (of food) <NE✣[*2]>

raspištóljiti se {ljīm, ljē perf. intr.} *sl-fea* slip into something comfortable (usu. scanty) <Cze✣[*1]>

raspitívati se {tujēm, tujū imperf. intr.} (lit. ask around) *sl-sex* ***Fac-Obs*** play with one's sexual partner's breast, feel up <Slav[*1]>

raspízditi {ràspīzdīm, dē perf.} (lit. cunt out) **a.** *sl* hit, punch <Slav✣[*1]> **b.** *sl* get upset <Slav✣[*2]>

- **Kàd te ràspīzdīm!** {S} (lit. When I hit you in your cunt!) *col* ***Off*** used as a threat of physical violence

raspízditi se {ràspīzdīm, dē perf. intr.} (lit. cunt out) *sl* cry, shed tears, weep <**Slav**❖*1>

ràspljuskati {ām, ajū perf.} *col* splash <**Slav**❖>

raspolòžiti se {žīm, že perf. intr.} *col* cheer up <**Slav**❖>

ràsprcati se {ām, ajū perf. intr.} *sl-sex* ***Obs*** start having sex frequently <**Slav**❖>

raspȑdeti sc {ràsprdīm, dē perf. intr.} **a. SerE** *sl-sex* ***Obs*** break wind frequently <**Slav**❖> **b. SerE** *sl-fea* ***Fac-Obs*** lie a lot <**Slav**❖*1>

ràsprodān {a, o adj.} (lit. sold) *sl-fea* busy <**Slav**❖*1>

ràsprodāt {a, o adj.} (lit. sold) *sl-fea* busy <**Slav**❖*1>

rasprskávānje {a neut.} *col* blowing up (explosives, etc.) <**Slav**❖*1>

ràsprsnuti {nēm, nū perf.} *col* blow up (explosives, etc.) <**Slav***1>

ràspucati {ām, ajū perf.} (lit. burst) *col* make nervous, get on one's nerves <**Slav***1>

ràspucati se {ām, ajū perf. intr.} (lit. burst oneself) *col* get nervous <**Slav***1>

ràstā {rēsta fem.; perm} /e fem./ [std. = stara] **1** *sl* mother <**Slav**✍> **2.** *sl-fea* elderly female <**Slav**✍> **b.** *sl* girlfriend <**Slav**✍*1>

rastáliti {ràstālīm, lē perf.} *sl* divide, split <**NE**❖*1>

rastaljívati {tàljujēm, ljujū imperf.} (lit. melt) *sl* share, split <**Slav***1>

rastézāljka {ē fem.} (lit. stretcher) *sl-music* accordion, squeeze box <**Slav***1>

rȃsti *See the following*

rastírati {ràstīrām, rastírajū perf.} *sl-crime* get back from prison

rastrúbiti {ràstrūbīm, bē perf.} (lit. trumpet around) *col* talk all around <**Slav***1>

rastùrača {ē fem.} (lit. destroyer) *sl-sex* prostitute, hooker <**Slav***1>

rasturàčina {ē fem.} (lit. destruction) **1a.** *sl-music* loud music <**Slav**❖*1> **b.** *sl-music* rock music <**Slav**❖*2> **2** *sl* fun <**Slav**❖*1> **3** *sl-sex* sexual intercourse <**Slav**❖*1>

ràsturiti {rīm, rē perf.} (lit. destroy) **a.** *sl* defeat <**Slav***1> **b.** *sl* beat up severely, destroy <**Slav***2> **c.** *sl-sex* engage in sexual intercourse with (of a male) <**Slav***3>

ràsturiti brȃk {VP} (lit. destroy a marriage) *sl* be a home wrecker ☞ **rasturiti**

ràsturiti se {rīm, rē perf.} (lit. destroy oneself) *sl-drink* get very drunk, get dead drunk <**Slav***1>

• **ràsturiti brȃk** {VP} (lit. destroy a marriage) *sl* be a home wrecker

rásturnica *See the following*

• **Rástūrnicu ti jèbēm!** {S} (lit. I fuck your destroyer!) *dia* ***Off*** used as a moderate curse, Fuck you!

ráša {ē fem.} *sl-sex* ***Obs*** buttocks, butt <**Slav***1>

rašamònac {nca (acc. = gen.) masc.} *sl-sex* ***Fac*** male homosexual, gay <**Jap**✍*1>

raščepòtina {ē fem.} *sl-sex* ***Fac*** loose woman <**Slav***1>

raščepȑkati {ām, ajū perf. intr.} *col* hurt a wound <**Slav***1>

raščèpulja {ē fem.} *sl-sex* ***Fac-Obs*** prostitute, hooker <**Slav**❖*1>

ràščistiti {tīm, tē perf.} (lit. clear up) *sl* clear up an issue: *Hajmo raščistiti plaćanje poreza. Let's clear up the issue paying the tax.* <**Slav***1>

ràšćerati {ām, ajū perf.} [std. = rastjerati] *col-dia* expel, throw out <**Slav**✍>

ràškōv {raškòva (acc. = gen.) masc.} **a.** *sl* horse (the animal) **b.** *sl-fea* male inhabitant of the countryside, hick, bumpkin **c.** *sl-fea* naive male

ràškovica {ē fem.} *sl-arch* mare

rȁšlje {ī fem. pl.} (lit. fork) *sl-arch* priest <**Gyp**>

rašȍmōn {šomóna (acc. = gen.) masc.} *sl-sex* ***Fac*** voyeur <**Jap***1>

rašomónac {nca (acc. = gen.) masc.} **1** *sl-sex* ***Fac*** male homosexual, gay <**Jap***1> **2** *sl-sex* ***Fac*** voyeur <**Jap***1>

rašomonijáda {ē fem.} (lit. from the film 'Rashomon', Akira Kujrosawa) *col* event which can be interpreted in a number of ways <**Jap**✍*1>

rašomònisānje {a neut.} *sl-sex* ***Fac*** voyeurism <**Jap**✍*1>

rašomònisati {išēm, išū imperf.} *sl-sex* ***Fac*** peep, look at others <**Jap**✍*1>

rȁšpānje {a neut.} (lit. filing) *sl-sex* ***Fac-Obs*** sexual intercourse <**Ger***1>

rȁšpati {ām, ajū imperf.} (lit. file) *sl-sex* ***Fac-Obs*** engage in sexual intercourse with (of a male) <**Ger***1>

ràšeći {rašéčēm, rašéku, ràšēk, ràšēk perf. irreg.} [std. = rasjeći] *sl* cut, slice <**Slav**✍>

ràtkapa {ē fem.} *sl-auto* hubcap <**Ger**>

ràtkapna {ē fem.} *sl-auto* hubcap <**Ger**>

ratosìljati se {ām, ajū imperf. intr.} *col* get rid of: *ratosiljati se ispita get rid of one's exams* <**Gre**✣[*1]>

rȁtovānje {a neut.} (lit. waging war) *sl-gamble* gambling <**Slav**[*1]>

rȁtovati {tujēm, tujū imperf. intr.} (lit. wage war) *sl-gamble* gamble <**Slav**[*1]>

ràubovati {bujēm, bujū imperf.} **a.** *col* wear out (make unusable through long or heavy use) <**Ger**> **b.** *sl* abuse financially, rip off <**Ger**[*1]>

ràuhati {ām, ajū imperf.} **a.** *sl* smoke (tobacco) <**Ger**[*1]> **b.** *sl-drugs* smoke hashish <**Ger**[*2]>

ráva {ē fem.} [std. = kurva] *sl-sex* prostitute, hooker <**Ger**✍>

ràvaku {ràveku fem.; perm} [std. = kurva] *sl-sex* prostitute, hooker <**Lat**✍>

rȁvčo {ràvačo, ràvočo adj.; perm} [std. = ćorav] *sl-fea* blind <**NE**✍>

rȁvćo {ràvačo, ràvočo adj.; perm} /ràvćo/ [std. = ćorav] *sl-fea* blind <**NE**✍>

ràvnati se {ràvnām, ràvnajū imperf. intr.} (lit. make straight) *col* compare with: *Nemoj ti mene ravnati s Marinom. Do not compare me to Marina.* <**Slav**[*1]>

ràvulja {ē fem.} [std. = kurva] *sl-sex* prostitute, hooker <**Ger**✍>

rȁzbacān {a, o adj.} (lit. thrown around) *sl-fea* muscular, pumped up <**Slav**[*1]>

• **rȁzbacān ko trî bȁnke u dvâ džèpa** {AdjP} (lit. muscular like three dinars in two pockets) *sl-fea* pretending to be strong

rȁzbacānā {ē fem. (adj. decl.)} (lit. the thrown one) *sl-fea* obese female, porker <**Slav**[*1]>

razbacánko {a masc.} (lit. the thrown one) *sl-fea* muscular male <**Slav**✣[*1]>

razbaškáriti se {bàškārīm, rē perf. intr.} *col* lay back and get some rest <**NE**✣>

razbȁštati {ām, ajū perf.} **a.** *sl* destroy, ruin <**Slav**✣[*1]> **b.** *sl* break through (a window, door, etc.) <**Slav**✣[*2]>

razbȁštavac {tāvca (acc. = gen.) masc.} *sl-fea* troublemaker, rowdy, ruffian <**Slav**✣[*1]>

ràzbiti {rȁzbijēm, ijū perf.} (lit. crush) *sl* beat up, crush, trash <**Slav**[*1]>

• **ràzbiti ko gâjbu** {VP} (lit. smash like a crate) *sl* beat up, crush, trash

ràzbiti se {rȁzbijēm, ijū perf. intr.} (lit. break oneself) *sl-drink* get very drunk, get smashed <**Slav**[*1]>

rázbōjnik {a masc.} (lit. robber) *sl-mil* private first class <**Slav**✣[*1]>

ràzboškati {ām, ajū perf.} *sl-arch* destroy, ruin

razbúcati {ām, ajū perf.} **a.** *col* tear apart, destroy <**Slav**> **b.** *col* destroy, ruin <**Slav**[*1]> **c.** *sl* beat up <**Slav**[*2]> **d.** *sl-sex* engage in intensive sexual intercourse with (of a male) <**Slav**[*3]>

ràzgaćiti se {ćīm, ćē perf. intr.} *sl-fea* slip into something comfortable (usu. scanty) <**Slav**✣[*1]>

razgihávānje {a neut.} *sl-crime* serving prison term at Goli island (Croatia, where the former communist regime detained its political enemies)

razgotíviti {gòtīvīm, vē perf.} *sl* beat up severely

razgovòruša {ē fem.} (lit. the talkative one) *col* second coffee served to one's guests <**Slav**✣[*1]>

razgrànati se {ām, ajū perf. intr.} (lit. branch) *sl* pull strings, use connections <**Slav**[*1]>

razgúliti {ràzgūlīm, lē perf.} *sl* run away, flee <**Slav**✣[*1]> ☞ **stušiti**

razgúziti {ràzgūzīm, zē perf.} *sl-sex* ***Obs*** shake one's buttocks <**Slav**✣[*1]>

razguzívati {gùzívām, ajū imperf.} *sl-sex* ***Obs*** shake one's buttocks <**Slav**✣[*1]>

ràzići se {zīđem, zīđu perf. intr.} (lit. disperse) *sl* leave (of a group of people, usu. leaving a gathering of some kind) <**Slav**[*1]>

razjebànica {ē fem.} *sl-sex* ***Obs*** loose woman, slut <**Slav**✣[*1]>

razjèbati {bēm, bū perf.} /ràzjebati/ **a.** *sl-sex* ***Obs*** engage in sexual intercourse with (of a male) <**Slav**[*1]> **b.** *sl* ***Obs*** destroy, ruin, fuck up <**Slav**[*2]>

razjebòtina {ē fem.} *sl-fea* ruined and destroyed person or mechanism <**Slav**✣[*1]>

ràzjehati {ām, ajū perf.} (lit. ride over) **a.** *sl* destroy, ruin <**Slav**[*1]> **b.** *sl* smash, crush <**Slav**[*2]> **c.** *sl-sex* exhaust sexually <**Slav**[*3]>

rázlika *See the following*

• **Rázlika je u definîcijī.** {S} (lit. There is a difference in the definition.) *sl* used to refer to lack of difference, There is no difference at all.

ràzliti {ijēm, ijū perf.} (lit. spill) *sl* ashame, bring disgrace to <**Slav**[*1]>

razmazánko {a masc.} *sl-fea* weak person, wimp <**Slav**✣[*1]>

razmenjívati *See the following*
- **razmenjívati pljùvāčku** {VP} (lit. exchange saliva) SerE *sl* French kiss

razmòntīrān {a, o adj.} (lit. disassembled) *sl-fea* tired <Fre*1>

raznìtati {ām, ajū perf.} *sl* make angry, make mad <Ger✤*1>

raznògīrān {a, o adj.} *sl-fea* thrown away, tossed out <Slav✤*1>

ràznjupān {pna, pno adj.} *sl-fea* angry, mad <Ita✤*1>

ràznjupati {ām, ajū perf.} 1 *sl-fea* get angry <Ita✤*1> 2 *sl-fea* make angry, make mad

ràzrāđen *See the following*
- **ràzrāđen ko sòlūnskā còkula** {AdjP} (lit. as worked out as a boot from the Salonika front *in WWI*) *sl-sex* ***Obs*** sexually experienced

razređívati {rèđujēm, rèđujū imperf.} *sl* talk, have a conversation <Slav*1>

razùmeti se *See the following*
- **razùmeti se kô Mára u krȋvi kȕrac** {VP} (lit. understand like Mary about a crooked prick) **SerE** *sl-sex* ***Obs*** used to refer to one's lack of ability, not know dick
- **razùmeti se kô Màrica u krȋvi kȕrac** {VP} (lit. understand like little Mary about a crooked prick) **SerE** *sl-sex* ***Obs*** used to refer to one's lack of ability, not know dick
- **razùmjeti se kô Mára u krȋvi kȕrac** {VP} (lit. understand like Mary about a crooked prick) *sl-sex* ***Obs*** used to refer to one's lack of ability, not know dick
- **razùmjeti se kô Màrica u krȋvi kȕrac** {VP} (lit. understand like little Mary about a crooked prick) *sl-sex* ***Obs*** used to refer to one's lack of ability, not know dick

razumijévati *See the following*
- **ne razumijévati** {V} (lit. be unable to understand) *col* fail to understand

razùmjeti se *See the following*

razùmjeti se kô Mára u krȋvi kȕrac {VP} (lit. understand like Mary about a crooked prick) *sl-sex* ***Obs*** used to indicate one's lack of ability, not know dick ☞ **razumeti se**

razùmjeti se kô Màrica u krȋvi kȕrac {VP} (lit. understand like little Mary about a crooked prick) *sl-sex* ***Obs*** used to indicate one's lack of ability, not know dick ☞ **razumeti se**

razváliti {ràzvālīm, lē perf.} (lit. destroy) 1 *sl-sex* ***Obs*** engage in sexual intercourse with (of a male) <Slav*1> 2 *sl-sports* defeat, destroy <Slav*1> 3 *sl* hit, punch <Slav*1>

razváliti se {ràzvālīm, līm, lē perf.} *sl-drink* get very drunk, get smashed <Slav*1>

razvalìtis {a masc.} /razvalítis/ *sl* appetite <Slav✍*1>

razvaljívati {vàljūjēm, ljūjū imperf.} (lit. destroy) 1 *sl-fea* be skillful <Slav*1> 2 *sl-sex* ***Obs*** engage in sexual intercourse with (of a male)

razvaljȍtka /razvaljòtka/ *See the following*
- **kojlektȉvnaja razvaljȍtka** {NP} (lit. collective destruction) *sl-sex* group sex

razvijátiti {vìjātīm, tē perf. intr.} **a.** *col* run away, flee <Slav✤*1> **b.** *col* go away, leave <Slav✤*2>

razvìjōjla {ē fem.} (lit. the developed one) *sl-sex* ***App*** female with large breasts and big buttocks <Slav✍*1>

razvijȍtka {ē fem.; Dat razvijȍtki} /razvijòtka/ (lit. the developed one) 1 *sl-sex* ***App*** female with large breasts and big buttocks <Slav✍*1> 2 *sl-fea* ***App*** body builder <Slav✍*1> 3 *sl-music* ***Fac*** accordion, squeeze box <Slav✍*1>

rázvodnica {ē fem.} 1 *sl-fea* divorced female <Slav✤> 2 *sl-fea* female homewrecker <Slav✤>

rázvodnīk {a (acc. = gen.) masc.} (lit. private first class) 1 *sl-fea* seducer <Slav*1> 2 *sl-fea* boy who manages to do nothing more than to walk with his girlfriend <Slav*1>

razvòdniti {ràzvodnīm, nē perf.} (lit. dilute) *sl-fea* dilute a story, make a story less spectacular <Slav*1>

razvodnjávati {vòdnjāvām, vodnjávajū imperf.} (lit. dilute) *sl-fea* be boring <Slav*1>

razvòđāč {vođáča (acc. = gen.) masc.} *sl-fea* boy who manages to do nothing more than to walk with his girlfriend <Slav*1>

ráža {ē fem.} (lit. ray) *sl-fea* unattractive female <Slav*1>

rdžȁ {fem.} [std. = rđa] SSer *dia* rust <Slav✍>

ȑđa {ē fem.} *sl-fea* evil person <Slav*1>

ȑđav {a, o adj.} *col* evil, mean, bad <Slav*1>

rebàrica {ē fem.} (lit. the Rebar's one) *sl-drink* name for Vila Rebar restaurant in Zagreb, Croatia <SlavO✤>

rebètati {ām, ajū imperf. intr.} //rèbećēm, ćū imperf. intr./ *sl* laugh

rȅbnuti {nēm, nū perf.} **a.** *sl* hit, punch: *rebnuti u glavu hit in the head* <Slav*1> **b.** *sl* surprise unpleasantly: *Rebnulo me njegovo ponašanje. His behavior has been an unpleasant surprise.* <Slav*2> **c.** *sl* overcharge, rip off: *Rebnuo nas konobar. The waiter has ripped us off.* <Slav*3>

Rèci stârōj da pòdgrijē pàpriku. {S} (lit. Tell your old lady to heat up the peppers.) *sl-sex* ***Off-Fac*** used as a strong curse, Fuck you! ☞ **reći**

rècimo {part.} (lit. let us say) **a.** *sl* particle used to introduce thought meant to be taken hypothetically or quasi-hypothetically: *Recimo da on dođe, šta ćemo onda? Suppose he comes, what are we going to do then?* <**Slav**[*1]> **b.** *sl* particle used to indicate approximation: *Bilo ih je recimo pedeset. There were fifty of them, more or less.* <**Slav**[*2]>

rȅcka {ē fem.; Dat rȅcki} (lit. small cut) **1** *sl* knife <**Slav**[*1]> **2** *sl-mil* one month of one's military service <**Slav**[*1]>

rȅcnuti {nēm, nū perf.} (lit. cut a little) *sl* say, tell <**Slav**✍>

rêč *See the following*

- **čàsnā rêč** {NP} (lit. word of honor) **SerE** *col* used to emphasize the truth of what has been said, I swear!

rèćemo {part.} (lit. let's say) [std. = recimo] **a.** *sl* particle used to introduce thought meant to be taken hypothetically or quasi-hypothetically: *Rećemo da će doći svi pozvani. Suppose all invited would come.* <**Slav**✍[*1]> **b.** *sl* particle used to indicate approximation: *Do tamo je rećemo pet kilometara. It is more or less five kilometers to that place.* <**Slav**✍[*2]>

rèći {rȅknēm, rȅknū, rȅk, rȅk perf. irreg.} *col* say, tell <**Slav**>

- **dok si rȅkaō brȉtva** {S} (lit. before you said "razor") *col* right away, before you can say "boo"
- **dok si rȅkō brȉtva** {S} (lit. before you said "razor") *col* right away, before you can say "boo"
- **dok si rȅkō kȅks** {S} (lit. before you said "biscuit") *col* right away, before you can say "boo"
- **grûbo rečèno** {AdjP} (lit. roughly spoken) *col* used to introduce a sensitive topic, to put it crudely
- **Rèci stârōj da pòdgrijē pàpriku.** {S} (lit. Tell your old lady to heat up the peppers.) *sl-sex* ***Off-Fac*** used as a strong curse, Fuck you!

rédalica {ē fem.} *sl-sex* ***Fac-Obs*** group sex <**Slav**[*1]>

redáljak {ljka masc.} *sl-sex* ***Fac-Obs*** group sex <**Slav**❖[*1]>

rédāljka {ē fem.} /rèdāljka/ **1** *sl-sex* ***Obs*** group sex <**Slav**❖[*1]> **2** *sl-sex* ***Obs*** loose woman, slut <**Slav**❖[*1]> **3** *sl* ***Fac*** group beating <**Slav**❖[*1]>

rédati {rêdām, rédajū imperf.} (lit. put one after another) **a.** *sl* beg, ask for money <**Slav**[*1]> **b.** *sl* talk, have a conversation <**Slav**[*1]>

- **rédati gȍtīvno** {VP} (lit. speak well) *sl* beg, ask for money

redávati {rèdāvām, redávajū imperf. intr.} *sl* talk, have a conversation <**Ger**❖>

rèdiška {ē fem.; Dat rèdiški} *sl-sex* ***Fac-Obs*** group sex <**Slav**✍[*1]>

rèdnjara {ē fem.} **a.** *sl-crime* ***Der*** informer, stoolie, snitch **b.** *sl-crime* prison informer, stoolie

rèdnjāroš {a (acc. = gen.) masc.} *sl-crime* ***Der*** informer, stoolie, snitch

rèfija {ē fem.} *sl-mil* military (armed forces in general)

règāl {regála (acc. = gen.) masc.; Voc rȅgāle} (lit. cabinet) *sl-fea* ***Fac-App*** obese person <**Lat**[*1]>

rȅget {a masc.} *col* croaking (of a frog) <**Slav**>

regètati {ām, ajū imperf. intr.} /règećēm, règećū imperf. intr/ *col* croak (of a frog) <**Slav**❖>

regláža {ē fem.} *sl-auto* regulation <**Fre**>

règlāžnī {ā, ō adj.} *sl-auto* regulating <**Fre**>

rȅgler {a masc.} /règler/ *sl-auto* regulator <**Fre**>

reglírānje {a neut.} *sl-auto* regulation <**Fre**>

rȅgnuti {nēm, nū perf.} *col* growl (of an animal) <**Slav**>

rȅgo {adv.} /règo/ [std. = gore] *sl* upstairs <**Slav**✍>

réja {ē fem.} *sl-mil* military reserve

rèkēt {rȅketa masc.} *sl-crime* racket (criminal) <**Eng**>

reketírati {kètīrām, ketírajū biasp. intr.} *sl-crime* carry on a racket (criminal) <**Eng**>

rekláma *See the following*

- **rekláma za DDT** {NP} (lit. DDT commercial) *sl-fea* very unattractive person
- **rekláma za gôrkū sô** {NP} (lit. Epsom salts *laxative* commercial) *sl-fea* extremely unattractive person

rȅko {part.} (lit. I said) *col* used to emphasize one's own point, I swear to God! <**Slav**[*1]>

rèksača {ē fem.} *sl-fea* unattractive female

rȅlo {a masc.} *sl-fea* senior citizen

rȅm {a +ov (ext. pl) masc.; Nom Pl rèmovi} *sl* chip, chunk <**NE**>

réma {ē masc.} SerE *sl-mil* rookie soldier, first month soldier

rémac {mca (acc. = gen.) masc.} *sl-mil* rookie soldier, first month soldier

remàdija {ē fem.} *sl-mil* military (armed forces in general)

remíza {ē fem.} (lit. depot) **1** *sl-crime* prison <**Fre**[*1]> **2** *sl-sports* tied score <**Fre**[*1]>

rémo {a masc.} /**rémo** /e masc./ *sl-mil* rookie soldier, first month soldier

rȅn [1] {a +ov (ext. pl) masc.; Nom Pl rènovi} [std. = hren] *dia* horse radish <Slav✍>

rȅn [2] {adj.} (lit. horse radish) [std. = hren] *sl-fea* ***App*** good, neat, cool <Slav✍*1>

rèndisati {išēm, išū imperf.} (lit. grate) *sl-sex* ***Fac-Obs*** engage in sexual intercourse with (of a male) <NE⁘*1>

rentgènāl {gnála masc.} *sl-fea* slender person <GerO*1>

rȅnjkati {ām, ajū imperf.} *sl* throw away, toss out

rêp {a +ov (ext. pl) masc.; Nom Pl rȇpovi} (lit. tail) *sl-sex* ***Fac-Obs*** buttocks, butt <Slav*1>
- **lástīn rêp** {NP} *sl* running away, fleeing
- **rêpom u lèdinu** {NP} (lit. with one's tail on the field) *sl* fall down, kiss the floor
- **U rêp te jèbēm!** {S} (lit. I fuck you in your tail!) *dia-col* ***Off*** used as a moderate curse, Fuck you!
- **u vídu lástinōg rêpa** {PP} (lit. in the form of a swallow's tail) *col* quickly

rȅpa {ē fem.} /rèpa/ (lit. beets) *sl* money, cabbage <Slav*1>

rȅpavica {ē fem.} **a.** *sl-arch* hand <Slav⁘*1> **b.** *sl-arch* arm <Slav⁘*2>

rèpetē {adv.} /rèpete/ (lit. seconds *of a meal*) *sl* again: *Sad repete radimo isti posao. Now we have to do the same job again.* <Fre*1>

rèpevica {ē fem.} **a.** *sl* hand **b.** *sl* arm

rȅpka {ē fem.; Dat rȇpki} [std. = reprezentacija] *sl-sports* national team (soccer, basketball, etc.) <Lat✍>

réponja {ē masc.} (lit. the one who has a tail) *sl-mil* rookie soldier, first month soldier <Slav⁘*1>

Rèptīl {Reptìla (acc. = gen.) masc.} (lit. reptile) *sl-fea* inhabitant of Split, Croatia <Lat*1>

repùblički ȉzglēd {NP} (lit. republic look) *sl* stomach, belly, gut ☞ **izgled**

repùblika *See the following*
- **banána repùblika** {NP} (lit. banana republic) *sl-media* ***Der*** country dominated by a foreign power

rérna {ē fem.} (lit. oven) *sl-sex* ***Fac-Obs*** vagina, cunt <Ger*1>

rèsavac {vca (acc. = gen.) masc.} (lit. member of Resava medieval transcription school) *sl-sstu* transcriber <SlavO*1>

résaviti {vīm, vē imperf.} (lit. work as a transcriber at Resava school) **a.** *sl-sstu* transcribe <SlavO⁘*1> **b.** *sl-sstu* cheat on an exam <SlavO⁘*2>

reskírati {rèskīrām, reskírajū imperf.} *col* risk, chance <Fre*1>

rèspekt {a masc.} *col* respect, obey <Lat>

rȅspo {rèzapo masc.; perm} /rèspo/ [std. = porez] *sl* tax <Slav✍>

rȅst {a +ov (ext. pl) masc.; Nom Pl rèstovi} **1** *sl-crime* prison <Ger*1> **2** *sl* remains, leftovers <Ger*1>

rȅstānī pápak {NP} (lit. fried hoof) *sl-fea* old shoe ☞ **papak**

rȅstić {a masc.} [std. = restoran] *sl-drink* restaurant <Lat✍>

rèstiti {tīm, tē imperf.} *sl* falsely incriminate, frame

rȅš {adj.} *col* well done: *reš odrezak well done steak* <Ger*1>

rȅš pèčen {AdjP} (lit. well done *baking*) *sl-drink* drunk, toasted ☞ **pečen**

rȅš pèčenī òdojak {NP} (lit. well done piglet) *sl-fea* bald male ☞ **odojak**

rèšō {adj.} (lit. small stove) *sl-fea* shy <Fre*1>

rȅšpekt {a masc.} [std. = respekt] *col-dia* respect, obey <Lat✍>

rȅšt {a +ov (ext. pl) masc.; Nom Pl rèštovi} *sl-crime* prison <Lat✍>

retrovîzori {zōrā masc. pl.} (lit. rear view mirrors) *sl-fea* eyeglasses <Lat*1>

reumáriti {reùmārīm, rē imperf.} (lit. rheum) *sl* work, labor <Gre⁘*1>

réva {ē masc.} [std. = revizor] *sl* supervisor (on public transportation) <Lat✍>

révac {vca masc.} [std. = revolver] *sl-crime* revolver <Eng✍>

rèvār {revára masc.} [std. = revolver] *sl-crime* revolver <Eng✍>

rèvati {ām, ajū imperf.} **a.** *col* bray (of a donkey) <Slav> **b.i.** *sl* cry, shed tears, weep <Slav*1> **ii.** *sl* attack verbally, denonuce <Slav*1>

revolúcija *See the following*
- **cȓvenā revolúcija** {NP} (lit. red revolution) *sl-sex* ***Fac*** menstruation, period

revòlvēr {volvéra masc.} (lit. revolver) *sl* key <Lat*1>

rezánac {nca (acc. = gen.) masc.} **/rèzanac** /nca (acc. = gen.) masc/ (lit. pasta) **1** *sl-crime* policeman, cop <Slav*1> **2** *sl-drink* waiter <Slav*1>

rezánci {zânāca masc. pl.} **/rèzanci** /aca masc. pl/ (lit. pasta) **1** *sl* mucus, snot <Slav*1> **2** *sl-fea* small teeth <Slav*1> **3** *sl-fea* sparse hair <Slav*1>

rȅzānje {a neut.} (lit. cutting) *sl-sex* ***Obs*** sexual intercourse <Slav*1>

rȅzati {ežem, ežu imperf.} (lit. cut) *sl-sex* ***Obs*** engage in sexual intercourse with (of a male) <Slav*1>

rȅzervār {a masc.} [std. = rezervoar] *sl-auto* gas tank <Fre☞>

rezervòār {voára masc.} (lit. gas tank) *sl* ***Fac*** stomach, belly, tank <Fre*1>

rezíliti {rèzīlīm, lē imperf.} **1** *col* joke with, make a fool of <NE✣*1> **2** *col* worry about: *reziliti oko gubljenja posla worry about losing one's job* <NE✣*1> **3** *col* reproach, scold: *reziliti neposlušno dijete reprimand a naughty child* <NE✣*1>

rèzna {ē fem.} *sl-drink* wine <Gyp>

rezùltāt {zultáta masc.} (lit. result) *sl-crime* prison <Lat*1>

réžānje {a neut.} **a.** *col* growling (of an animal) <Slav> **b.** *sl-crafts* growling (a symptom of a malfunction) <Slav*1>

réžati {žīm, žē imperf.} *col* growl (of an animal) <Slav>

rgètati {ām, ajū imperf. intr.} *col* clang (produce a sharp metal sound) <Slav>

rȉba {ē fem.} (lit. fish) **1a.** *sl-sex* ***Obs*** vagina, cunt <Slav*1> **b.** *sl* female, fox <Slav*2> **2** *sl* money, clams <Slav*1> **3** silence <Slav*1>

- **kȕvanā rȉba** {NP} (lit. boiled fish) *sl-fea* conceited male
- **lètēćā rȉba** {NP} (lit. flying fish) *sl-sex* female who frequently changes boyfriends
- **pobudàlilā rȉba** {NP} (lit. crazy fish) *sl* stolen money
- **pȍla rȉba - pȍla rȉba** {NP} (lit. half fish half fish) *sl* ***Fac*** mermaid
- **sìtna rȉba** {NP} (lit. small fish) **a.** *sl-fea* unimportant person, small fry **b.** *sl-fea* worthless or despicable person, bum
- **sìtna rȉba pljȕckavica** {NP} (lit. small spitting fish) *sl-fea* unimportant person, small fish
- **tùđā rȉba** {NP} (lit. other's fish) *sl-crime* stolen money
- **zapendžètīrāna rȉba** {NP} (lit. windowed fish) *sl-sex* virgin

ribánjac {njca masc.} (lit. rubbing) *sl* cleaning <Slav*1>

rîbānje {a neut.} (lit. rubbing) **1** *sl* fight (e.g. fist fight) <Slav*1> **2** *col* reproaching, scolding <Slav*1>

rȉbār {a (acc. = gen.) masc.} (lit. fisherman) *sl-crime* pickpocket <Slav*1>

rîbati {rîbām, rîbajū imperf.} (lit. rub) **1** *sl* beat up: *ribati protivnika beat up one's adversary* <Slav*1> **2** *col* reproach, scold: *ribati lijenog službenika reprimand a lazy employee* <Slav*1>

- **rȉbati kljȍve** {VP} (lit. brush one's tusks) *sl* brush one's teeth

rîbati se {rîbām, rîbajū imperf. intr.} (lit. rub each other) *sl* argue <Ger*1>

rȉbica {a masc.} (lit. small fish) **a.** *sl-sex* ***Obs*** vagina, cunt <Slav*1> **b.** *sl-fea* young female, girl <Slav*2>

rìbīč {ribíča (acc. = gen.) masc.} (lit. fisherman) *sl-sex* ***Fac*** male homosexual, gay <Slav*1>

ribìčija[1] {ē masc.} *sl* fishing <Slav*1>

Ribìčija[2] {ē masc.} Cro *sl* name for Ribnjak dance floor in Zagreb, Croatia <Slav*1>

ribìčōn {bičóna masc.} (lit. small fish) *sl* female <Slav*1>

rìbīć {ribíća masc.} (lit. small fish) *sl-sex* ***Obs*** vagina, cunt <Slav✣*1>

rȉbīzla {ē fem.} (lit. currant) **a.** *sl* brain <Slav*1> **b.** *sl-fea* wise male <Slav*1> **c.aa.** *sl-fea* very young female, little girl <Slav*1> **bb.** female <Slav*2>

rȉbo {a masc.} *sl-sex* ***App*** attractive female <Slav*1>

rȉbolōv {a masc.} (lit. fishing) *sl* ***Fac*** looking for females, fishing for chicks <Slav*1>

- **pódvodnī rȉbolōv** {NP} (lit. underwater fishing) *sl-sex* ***Fac-Obs*** sexual intercourse in water

rìbōn {ribóna masc.} (lit. fish) **a.** *sl-sex* ***Fac-App*** attractive female <Slav*1> **b.** *sl* female <Slav*2>

rȉbovānje {a neut.} (lit. fishing) *sl-sex* ***Fac-Obs*** sexual intercourse <Slav*1>

rȉbovati {bujēm, bujū imperf.} (lit. fish) *sl-sex* ***Fac-Obs*** engage in sexual intercourse with (of a male) <Slav*1>

rìcinus {a (acc. = gen.) masc.} (lit. castor oil) **a.** *sl-fea* ***App*** skillful person <Lat*1> **b.** *sl-fea* ***App*** diligent person <Lat*1>

rîč {i fem.} [std. = riječ, reč] Med *dia* word <Slav☞>

rȉči {excl.} *sl* used to make somebody go away

rȉčiti {čīm, čē perf. intr.} *sl* run away, flee

rȉčka {ē fem.; Dat rȉčki} *sl* female <Slav☞*1>

rȉdati {ām, ajū imperf. intr.} (lit. wipe) *sl* laugh <Slav*1>

rídža {ē fem.} **1** *sl-auto* reverse (gear) <**EngO*1**> **2** *sl* supervisor (on public transportation) <**EngO*1**>

ridžòvān {džována (acc. = gen.) masc.} *sl* supervisor (on public transportation) <**EngO*1**>

Rȉdžvēj {a (acc. = gen.) masc.} *sl* supervisor (on public transportation) <**EngO*1**>

rȉđa {ē masc.} /**ríđa**/ *sl* supervisor (on public transportation) <**EngO*1**>

rìđan {a (acc. = gen.) masc.} /**rìđān**/ (lit. brown-haired horse) *sl* supervisor (on public transportation) <**Slav*1**>

riđòkosī {ōg (acc. = gen.) masc.} (lit. the redheaded one) *sl* supervisor (on public transportation) <**Slav*1**>

riđòvān {đována (acc. = gen.) masc.} (lit. the redheaded one) *sl* supervisor (on public transportation) <**EngO*1**>

rìfle {ī fem. pl.} /**rífle**/ (lit. Rifle: popular brand name of jeans) *col* jeans <**Eng*1**>

rȉflja {ē fem.} *sl* female <**Ger*1**>

rìfljānje {a neut.} (lit. cutting land) *sl-sex* ***Fac-Obs*** sexual intercourse <**Ger*1**>

rìfljati {ām, ajū imperf.} (lit. cut land) *sl-sex* ***Fac-Obs*** engage in sexual intercourse with (of a male) <**Ger*1**>

rȉgati {ām, ajū imperf.} **1** *sl* have, possess <**Slav*1**> **2a.** *col* vomit, throw up, puke <**Slav*1**> **b.** *sl* lose money <**Slav*2**>

rìglec {a masc.} Kajk *sl* vomiting, throwing up, puking <**Slav✍**>

rȉgnuti {nēm, nū perf.} **a.** *sl* vomit, throw up, puke <**Slav*1**> **b.** *sl* be forced to pay <**Slav*1**> **c.** *sl-gamble* lose money <**Slav*2**>

rigolètati {ām, ajū imperf.} (lit. Rigoletto) *col* vomit, throw up, Ralph <**ItaO*1**>

rigolèto {a masc.} (lit. Rigoletto) *col* vomiting, throwing up, Ralphing <**ItaO*1**>

rȉja {ē fem.} **a.** *sl-crime* policeman, cop <**Ita✍**> **b.** *sl-crime* jailer <**Ita✍*1**>

rȉjāk {a (acc. = gen.) masc.} **a.** *sl-crime* policeman, cop <**Ita✍**> **b.** *sl-crime* jailer <**Ita✍*1**>

rìjamu {jēmu masc.; perm} *sl-crime* policeman, cop <**Ita✍*1**>

rijàna {ē fem.} *sl-sex* gonorrhea, the clap

rijédak {tka, tko adj.} (lit. rare) *sl-fea* slim <**Slav*1**>

rijéšiti se {rijêšīm, šē perf. intr.} *col* get rid of, dump <**Slav*1**>

rȋkati {ām, ajū imperf. intr.} /**rȋkati** /ríčēm, íčū imperf. intr./ **a.** *col* roar (of an animal) <**Slav*1**> **b.** *sl* die, kick the bucket <**Slav*2**>

rȉkavac {vca (acc. = gen.) masc.} (lit. roarer) *sl-arch* ox (the animal) <**Slav⁘*1**>

rikávati {rìkāvām, rikávajū imperf. intr.} **1** *sl* die, kick the bucket <**Slav⁘*1**> **2** *sl* break <**Slav⁘*2**> **3** *sl-gamble* lose money <**Slav⁘*3**>

rikavȅla {ē fem.} **a.** *sl* death <**Slav✍*1**> **b.** *sl-crime* being arrested <**Slav✍*2**> **c.** *sl* disaster: *Ako ne platimo na vrijeme neće biti rikavela. It won't be a disaster if we do not pay on time.* <**Slav✍*3**>

rȉkavica {ē fem.} (lit. roarer) *sl-arch* cow <**Slav✍*1**>

rȉkī {ija (acc. = gen.) masc.} *sl* supervisor (on public transportation) <**EngO*1**>

rȋknuō {ula, ulo adj.} *sl-fea* malfunctioning, crashed, gone <**Slav⁘*1**>

rȋknuti {nēm, nū perf. intr.} **1** *sl* die, kick the bucket: *riknuti u osamdesetoj godini die at eighty* <**Slav⁘*1**> **2** *sl-crafts* break: *riknuti ogradu break a fence* <**Slav⁘*1**> **3** *sl* pay (bills, etc.): *riknuti dvaes soma pay twenty dinars* <**Slav⁘*1**> **4** *sl-crime* get arrested, get busted: *riknuti za krađu get arrested for a theft* <**Slav⁘*1**> **5** *sl* resign, quit: *riknuti šefovsko mesto resign from being a boss* <**Slav*1**> **6** *sl* push, shove: *riknuti čoveka u tramvaju push a guy on a streetcar* <**Slav*1**> **7** *sl-drugs* overdose <**Slav*1**> **8** *sl-stu* fail an exam (flunk): *riknuti iz matiša fail a math exam* <**Slav*1**> **9** *sl-gamble* lose money: *riknuti na pokeru lose money playing poker* **10** *sl-fea* get very tired: *Toliko sam radio da sam riknuo. I worked so much that I got very tired.* <**Slav*1**>

riknjávati {rìknjāvām, riknjávajū imperf.} *sl* spend money <**Slav⁘*1**>

rìkverc [1] {a (acc. = gen.) masc.} (lit. reverse *gear*) *sl-fea* handicapped child <**Ger*1**>

rìkverc [2] {a masc.} *sl-auto* reverse (gear) <**Ger**>

rilètne {a fem. pl.} *sl-fea* fun: *Bile su riletne u gradu. It was fun in the city.*

rȉlo {a neut.} *sl* ***Fac*** nose <**Slav*1**>

rȋljati {ām, ajū imperf. intr.} *sl-fea* work hard

rȉmtitu vȕlo u pȁdže {VP} (lit. I stick some money into your pocket) *sl* bribe ☞ **rititu**

Rȉmtu ti tȕki! {S} (lit. I stick my prick in you!) *sl* ***Off*** used as a moderate curse, Fuck you! ☞ **rititu**

rinfúza {ē fem.} *sl-drink* wine <**Ita*1**>

rȉng-šlȉsl {a +ov (ext. pl) masc.; Nom Pl rȉng-šlȉslovi} *sl-crafts* ring wrench (the tool) <Ger*1>

rȉnga {ē fem.; Dat rȉngi} *sl-crafts* ring (part of a mechanism) <Ger*1>

rìngāš {ringáša (acc. = gen.) masc.} **a.** *sl-crime* ring seller <Ger*1> **b.** *sl-crime* person who resells stolen watches, watch fence <Ger*2>

ríngla {ē fem.} (lit. stove ring) *sl* wedding ring <Ger*1>

rínglica {ē fem.} *sl-fea* small African American <Ger*1>

rinìtis {a masc.} (lit. rhinitis) *sl-sex* ***Fac-Obs*** sexual intercourse <Lat*1>

rȉnta {ē fem.} *sl* work, labor

rȉntati {ām, ajū biasp. intr.} *sl-fea* work hard

ripicàjzla {ē fem.} *sl-fea* dangerous female <Ger✥*1>

rȉpida {ē fem.} (lit. creature) **a.** *sl-fea* tall person <Gre*1> **b.** *sl-fea* long-legged female <Gre*2>

rȉpiti {pīm, pē perf.} *col* jump <Slav>

rìsōvče {eta neut.} *dia* beef <Slav*1>

rȉsta {ē masc.; perm} //rȍgsta masc./ (lit. old man) [std. = stari] **a.** *sl* father, old man <Slav✐> **b.** *sl* friend (male) <Slav✐*1>

rȉstić {a (acc. = gen.) masc.; perm} (lit. old man) *sl* father <Slav✐>

rȉstićka {ē fem.; Dat rȉstićki p} (lit. old lady) *sl* mother, old lady <Slav✐>

rìsūljka {ē fem.} *sl-arch* cow <Slav*1>

rȉša {ē masc.} (lit. the old one) [std. = stariša] *sl-fea* senior citizen, old timer <Slav✐>

rȉšasta {rišesta masc.; perm} //e masc./ (lit. the old one) [std. = stariša] *sl-fea* senior citizen, old timer <Slav✐>

rȉševac {vca (acc. = gen.) masc.} (lit. old man) [std. = stariša] *sl-fea* elderly male <Slav✐>

rȉta {ē fem.} (lit. rag) *sl* money <Slav*1>

rȉti {ijēm, ijū imperf.} (lit. dig) *sl-sex* ***Fac-Obs*** rape <Slav*1>

rȉtica {ē fem.} *sl-sex* ***Obs*** buttocks, butt <Slav✥>

rȉtimor se {rīmmo, rēmo perf. intr.; perm} [std. = umoriti se] *sl-fea* get tired <Slav✐>

rȉtitu {rīmtu, rētu perf.; perm} [std. = turiti] *sl* stick in, insert <Slav✐>

- **rȉmtitu vȕlo u pȁdže** {VP} (lit. I stick some money into your pocket) *sl* bribe

- **Rȉmtu ti tȕki!** {S} (lit. I stick my prick in you!) *sl* ***Off*** used as a moderate curse, Fuck you!

rȉtobrīs {a masc.} (lit. ass wipe) *sl-sex* ***Fac-Obs*** bathroom tissue, ass wipe <Slav✥*1>

ritoznòjičār {a (acc. = gen.) masc.} (lit. ass-sweater) **a.** *sl-sex* ***Fac-Obs*** male homosexual, gay <Slav✥*1> **b.** *sl-sex* ***Fac-Obs*** male homosexual who takes the passive role, femme <Slav✥*2>

rízla {ē fem.} (lit. Rizla: a popular brand name of cigarette paper) *sl* cigarette paper <BN*1>

ríža {ē fem.} (lit. rice) *sl* snow <Slav*1>

rjȁmu {rjēmu fem.; perm} /rjàmu/ [std. = murija] *sl-crime* the police <Ita✐>

ješávati se {rjèšāvām, rješávajū imperf. intr.} (lit. get rid of) *sl-crime* resell, fence <Slav*1>

ȑka {ē fem.; Dat ȑki} (lit. rag) **a.** *col-dia* old clothing <Slav*1> **b.** *col-dia* noise <Slav*2>

ȑkāč {a (acc. = gen.) masc.} [std. = hrkač] *col-dia* snorer <Slav✐*1>

ŕkati {ȑkām, ŕkajū imperf.} [std. = hrkati] **a.** *col-dia* snore <Slav✐> **b.** *sl* beat up <Slav✐*1>

ȑkavac {vca masc.} [std. = hrkavac] *sl* spit <Slav✐*1>

ȑke-kȍke {neut.} *sl-sex* sexual intercourse <Slav*1>

ȑknūt {a, o adj.} *sl-fea* ***Der*** insane, nuts <Slav✐*1>

ȑknuti {nēm, nū perf.} **1** *sl-sex* ***Obs*** engage in sexual intercourse with (of a male) <Slav✐*1> **2** *col* throw away, toss out <Slav✐*2>

ȑkonjac {kōnjca masc.} *col-dia* mucus, snot <Slav✥*1>

ȑmbalija {ē masc.} *col-dia* hard worker <Slav✥>

ȑmbati {ām, ajū imperf.} **a.** *col-dia* work hard (at manual labor) <Slav> **b.** *sl-sex* engage in sexual intercourse with (of a male) <Slav*1>

ȑmpalija {ē masc.} /ȑmpalija/ *sl-fea* troublemaker, rowdy, ruffian <Slav✥>

mâli pȉps {NP} (lit. small pips) *sl-drugs* small piece of hashish ☞ **pips**

ȑnja *See the following*

- **U ȑnju te jèbēm!** {S} (lit. I fuck you in your ass!) *dia* ***Off*** used as a moderate curse, Fuck you! Up yours!

rȍb *See the following*

- **plјèsniv rȍb** {VP} (lit. mouldy slave) *sl-crime* old prisoner

rȍba {ē fem.} (lit. merchandise) **1a.** *col-dia* clothing <Ita> **b.** *col-dia* laundry <Ita[*1]> **2** *sl* female <Ita>

ròbara {ē fem.} *sl* department store <Ita❖[*1]>

Robespjêr {a (acc. = gen.) masc.} (lit. Robespierre) *sl-fea* dandy, fop <FreO[*1]>

ròbija {ē fem.} (lit. long prison term) **1** *sl-fea* troublemaker, rowdy, ruffian <Slav[*1]> **2** *sl-sstu* poke, prod, or pinch on the buttocks, goose <Slav[*1]> **3** *sl* ***Fac*** marriage <Slav[*1]> **4** *sl-sstu* ***Fac*** school <Slav[*1]>

robȉjāš {bijáša (acc. = gen.) masc.} (lit. long-term prisoner) **1** *sl-fea* ***Fac*** married man <Slav[*1]> **2** *sl-fea* ***Fac*** school student <Slav[*1]>

robijàšica {ē fem.} (lit. long-term prisoner) **1** *sl-fea* married woman <Slav[*1]> **2** *sl-fea* high-school student <Slav[*1]>

robȉjāšnica {ē fem.} (lit. strict prison) **1** *sl-fea* factory <Slav[*1]> **2** *sl-sstu* school <Slav[*1]>

ròbnjāk {robnjáka masc.} *sl* department store <Ita❖[*1]>

rȍbot {a (acc. = gen.) masc.} (lit. robot) **1** *sl-auto* car, wheels <Cze[*1]> **2** *sl-auto* motorcycle <Cze[*1]>

rôd *See the following*

- **Rôd ti jèbēm!** {S} (lit. I fuck your family!) *col* ***Off*** used as a strong curse, Fuck you!
- **Rôd ti lópovskī!** {S} (lit. *I fuck* your theiving family!) *col* ***Off*** used as a strong curse, Fuck you!
- **Rôd ti pòkvāren!** {S} (lit. *I fuck* your rotten family!) *dia* ***Off*** used as a strong curse, Fuck you!

Róda [1] {ē fem.} (lit. stork) Cro *sl-drink* name of a bar on Petrova street in Zagreb, Croatia <Slav[*1]>

róda [2] {ē fem.} (lit. stork) **a.** *sl-fea* long-legged female <Slav[*1]> **b.** *sl* female <Slav[*1]> **c.** *sl-fea* insane female <Slav[*2]>

Ròdēzija {ē fem.} (lit. Rhodesia) *sl-fea* tall and slender female, beanpole <SlavO[*1]>

ròdilo {excl.} **1** *sl* used to signal that everything is well <Slav[*1]> **2** *sl* used to signal possession <Slav[*1]>

ròditēljka {ē fem.} (lit. she-parent) *col* mother <Slav❖[*1]>

ròditi *See the following*

- **kàd na vŕbi rȍdī grôžđe** {AdvP} (lit. when grapes grow on a willow) *col* never

rȍdnā {ē fem.} /rȍdna /rodana masc./ [std. = narodna] *sl-music* country or folk music <Slav✍>

rȍdoljūb {a (acc. = gen.) masc.} (lit. patriot) *sl-fea* manual laborer <Slav[*1]>

rȍđāk {a (acc. = gen.) masc.} (lit. relative) *col* friend (male) <Slav[*1]>

rȍđen *See the following*

- **kò da je rȍđen ispred fȉnskē ambásadē** {PP} (lit. as if he were born in front of the Finnish embassy X fin 'nice') *sl-fea* ***Fac*** very kind

rȍđenā gènga {NP} (lit. own money) *sl* money earned at one's work ☞ **genga**

ròđenī [1] {excl.} (lit. the born one, the dear one) *col* ***Fam*** used to address one or more persons in direct informal communication, buddy <Slav[*1]>

ròđenī [2] {ōg (acc. = gen.) masc.} (lit. the born one, the dear one) *sl-sports* player or fan of Velež (a soccer team from Mostar, Bosnia) <Slav[*1]>

róđo [1] {ē masc.} **a.** *col* relative <Slav❖> **b.** *col* friend (male) <Slav❖[*1]>

rôđo [2] {excl.} *col* used to address one or more persons in direct informal communication, buddy <Slav❖>

ròfit {a, o adj.} [std. = rovit] *col-dia* barely boiled <Slav✍>

rôg {a +ov (ext. pl) masc.; Nom Pl rȍgovi} (lit. horn) **1** *sl-sex* ***Fac-Obs*** penis, dick, prick <Slav[*1]> **2** *sl* knife <Slav[*1]>

rogírānje {a neut.} *sl* cheating, swindling <Slav❖[*1]>

rogírati {rògīrām, rogírajū biasp.} *sl* cheat, swindle <Slav❖[*1]>

rógonja {ē masc.} (lit. the one with horns) *sl-fea* cheated husband <Slav[*1]>

rȍgovi {gōvā masc. pl.} (lit. horns) *sl* forehead <Slav[*1]>

ròjīnke {ī fem. pl.} *sl-arch* money

rókānje {a neut.} **1** *sl* fight (e.g. fist fight) <Slav[*1]> **2** *sl-mil* shelling, bombing <Slav[*1]> **3** *sl-sex* sexual intercourse <Slav[*1]> **5** *sl-drink* drinking <Slav[*1]>

rókati {rôkām, rókajū imperf.} **1** *sl-mil* shell, bomb <Slav[*1]> **2** *sl-sex* engage in sexual intercourse with (of a male) <Slav[*1]> **3** *sl-drugs* take narcotic drugs, do drugs <Slav[*1]>

rókati se {rôkām, rókajū imperf. intr.} **1** *sl-drugs* take narcotic drugs intravenously, mainline, shoot up <Slav[*1]> **2** *sl-sex* engage in sexual intercourse with <Slav[*1]>

rȍker {a (acc. = gen.) masc.} /ròker/ **a.** *sl-music* rock musician, rocker <Eng> **b.** *sl-fea* ***Fac*** pig (the animal) <Slav-Eng>

rȍkerskī {ā, ō adj.} /ròkerskī/ *sl-music* rock and rol <Eng>

rȍkić {a masc.} *sl-music* rock music <Eng❖>

rȍklja {ē fem.} *sl-sex* ***Obs*** vagina, cunt <Slav❖[*1]>

rȍkmōn {a masc.} **a.** *sl-music* monotonous sound **b.** *col* dripping (liquids)

Rȍknēm ti ga! {S} (lit. I bang it to you!) *col-dia* ***Off*** used as a moderate curse, Fuck you! ☞ **roknuti**

rȍknuti {nēm, nū perf.} **1** *sl* engage in fellatio <Slav[*1]> 2a. *sl* hit, punch <Slav[*1]> **b.** *sl-sex* engage in sexual intercourse with (of a male) <Slav[*2]> **2a.** *sl* fail <Slav[*1]> b. *sl-stu* fail an exam (flunk) **3** *sl-drugs* take narcotic drugs intravenously, mainline, shoot up <Slav[*1]>
• **Rȍknēm ti ga!** {S} (lit. I bang it to you!) *col-dia* ***Off*** used as a moderate curse, Fuck you!

rȍkot {a masc.} *col* grunt (of an animal) <Slav>

rȍksa {ē fem.} *sl-fea* elderly female <Slav❖[*1]>

rȍksovānje {a neut.} *sl-sex* ***Obs*** sexual intercourse <Slav❖[*1]>

rȍksovati {sujēm, sujū imperf.} **1** *sl-sex* ***Obs*** engage in sexual intercourse with (of a male) <Slav❖[*1]> **2** *sl-music* dance to rock and roll

ròktānje {a neut.} /rȍktānje/ *col* grunting (of an animal) <Slav>

ròktati {rȍkćēm, kćū imperf.} /rȍktati/ *col* grunt (of an animal) <Slav>

rȍktav {a, o adj.} *col* grunty (of an animal) <Slav>

rȍktavo {adv.} *col* grunty (of an animal) <Slav[*1]>

rôl-krágna {ē fem.} *col* turtleneck (on a shirt) <Ger>

rolèta {ē masc.} (lit. blind) **1** *sl* mouth <Ger[*1]> **2** *sl* eyelid <Ger[*1]>

rolètne {ī fem. pl.} (lit. blinds) *sl-polit* backward attitudes <Ger[*1]>

ròlingstōn {a (acc. = gen.) masc.} (lit. rolling stone) *sl-fea* ***Fac*** Herzegovinian (inhabitant of the Southern part of Bosnia and Herzegovina) <Eng[*1]>

rôlka {ē fem.} **a.** *col* turtleneck (on a shirt) <Ger❖> **b.** *sl-sex* foreskin <Ger❖[*1]>

rȍlovati {lujēm, lujū imperf.} *sl-music* dance to rock and roll <Eng❖>

ròlōvka {ē fem.} *col* turtleneck shirt <Ger❖>

rȍm {a, o adj.} [std. = hrom] *dia-col* lame (limping) <Slav✍>

romàntičār {a (acc. = gen.) masc.} (lit. romantic) *sl-sports* player or fan of OFK Beograd (a soccer team from Belgrade, Serbia) <Fre[*1]>

rȍmbāč {a (acc. = gen.) masc.} *sl* child's scooter <Fre-Lat✍>

Ròmče {eta neut.} *sl-fea* Gypsy child <Slav❖>

rȍmī {ija (acc. = gen.) masc.} /ròmi/ *sl-drugs* rominal (narcotic drug) <BN✍>

ròmīć {romíća (acc. = gen.) masc.} *sl-fea* ***Off*** Gypsy (male) <Slav✍>

ròmiška {ē masc.; Dat ròmiški} *sl-fea* ***Off*** Gypsy (male) <Slav✍>

romònisati {išēm, išū imperf.} *col* drip <Slav❖[*1]>

romònit {a, o adj.} *col* dripping (liquids) <Slav❖[*1]>

ròmonjēnje {a neut.} *col* dripping (liquids) <Slav[*1]>

rȍmor {a masc.} *col* dripping (liquids) <Slav>

rȍmōran {rna, rno adj.} *col* dripping (liquids) <Slav>

ròmorenje {a neut.} *col* dripping (liquids) <Slav>

ròmoriti {rīm, rē imperf.} **a.** *col* drip <Slav> **b.** *col* gurgle (creek, etc.) <Slav[*1]>

rȍn-tȍn-tȍn {a (acc. = gen.) masc.} *sl-fea* very unintelligent person <FreO[*1]>

rónac {nca (acc. = gen.) masc.} (lit. diver) *sl-drink* alcoholic, drunk <Slav[*1]>

ròncati {ām, ajū imperf.} /rôncati/ *col* cry, shed tears, weep <Slav✍[*1]>

rondàrānje {a neut.} *col* roaring (a symptom of malfunction of an auto, etc.) <Slav>

rondàrati {ām, ajū imperf.} *col* roar (engine, etc.) <Slav>

ròndati {ām, ajū imperf.} /rôndati/ *col* grumble, mumble <Slav[*1]>

rȍndža {ē fem.} **a.** *sl-sex* ***Obs*** vagina, cunt **b.** *sl* ***Obs*** female, cunt **c.** *sl-fea* ***Der*** female with loud clothing and makeup

rȍnđa {ē fem.} **a.** *sl-sex* ***Obs*** vagina, cunt **b.** *sl* ***Obs*** female, cunt **c.** *sl-fea* ***Der*** female with loud clothing and makeup

ròniti *See the following*
• **ròniti u dubòko** {VP} (lit. dive in the deep) *sl-sex* ***Obs*** engage in cunnilingus

rȍnjke {i fem. pl.} *sl* money

ropopírati {pòpīrām, popírajū perf. intr.} *sl* answer, respond

rȍpot {a masc.} *col* noise <Slav>

ropòtati {ròpoćēm, oćū imperf. intr.} //ròpoćēm, ćū imperf. intr/ *col* make noise <Slav>

rȍra {ē fem.} (lit. tube) **1** *sl-sex* ***Obs*** buttocks, butt <Ger[*1]> **2a.** *sl-crime* concealed exit <Ger[*1]> **b.** *sl* exit <Ger[*2]>

rôrcánge {ī fem. pl.} *sl-crafts* tubular pliers <Ger>

rôrcángle {ī fem. pl.} *sl-crafts* tubular pliers <Ger>

ròsiti {sīm, sē imperf. intr.} (lit. dew) *sl-sex* ***Fac-Obs*** break wind, fart <Slav*1>

rosòmān {somána masc.} *sl* stone, rock

ròspija {ē fem.} *col* evil female, bitch <NE*1>

róša {ē fem.} (lit. hole used in the game of marbles) *sl-sex* ***Fac-Obs*** loose woman, slut

ròšat {a masc.; perm} /rȁšat masc./ [std. = šatro] *sl* slang <Gyp✍>

rošȍmōn {šomóna masc.} *sl-sex* voyeur <JapO✍*1>

rošomónac {nca (acc. = gen.) masc.} **1** *sl-sex* voyeur <JapO✍*1> **2** *sl-sex* male homosexual, gay <JapO✍*1>

rošomònisānje {a neut.} *sl-sex* voyeurism <JapO✍*1>

rošomònisati {išēm, išū imperf.} *sl-sex* peep, look at others <JapO✍*1>

ròštīlj {roštílja masc.} (lit. barbecue) **1** *sl-fea* malfunctioning lighter <Ger*1> **2** *sl-auto* additional trunk on the top of an automobile <Ger*1> **3** *sl* factory <Ger*1>

roštiljáda {ē fem.} *col* barbecuing competition (cook off) <Ger⁘>

roštȉljati {ām, ajū biasp.} **a.** *col* barbecue, grill <Ger⁘> **b.i.** *sl-sports* play table soccer <Ger⁘*1> **ii.** *sl-sex* engage in sexual intercourse with (of a male) <Ger⁘*1>

roštiljijáda {ē fem.} *col* barbecuing competition (cook off) <Ger⁘>

rotáviti {ròtāvīm, vē imperf.} *sl-arch* be able to

róvac[1] {vca (acc. = gen.) masc.} (lit. mole-cricket) **1** *sl* supervisor (on public transportation) <Slav*1> **2** *sl-fea* naive male <Slav*1>

rôvac[2] {vca masc.} (lit. mole-cricket) *sl* funeral <Slav*1>

ròvāš {rováša (acc. = gen.) masc.; Voc rȍvāšu} (lit. mole-cricket) *sl-fea* male who counts the females he has had sex with <Slav*1>

rovȅlo {a neut.} *sl-crime* pistol, revolver <Gyp*1>

roviskáriti {vìskārīm, rē perf.} *sl* falsely incriminate, frame

ròvit {a, o adj.} **a.** *col* barely boiled <Slav> **b.** *sl-sports* injured, hurt <Slav*1>

Rôvka {ē fem.} *sl* name for Rovinj (a town in Croatia) <Slav>

róza {ē fem.} **a.** *sl-fea* sclerosis <Ger*1> **b.** *sl-fea* sclerotic person <Ger*2>

ròzbīf {a masc.} (lit. roast beef) *sl-sex* ***Fac-Obs*** vagina, cunt <Eng*1>

r̀pa {ē fem.} [std. = hrpa] *col-dia* pile, heap <Slav✍>

r̀pačkē {i fem. pl.} *sl-arch* scissors

r̄palo {a neut.} *sl* knife

r̄pānje {a neut.} *sl-crime* slaughtering (of people)

r̄pati {ām, ajū imperf.} *sl-crime* slaughter (people)

r̄pnuti {nēm, nū perf.} *sl-arch* cut, slice <Slav*1>

rpolívati {pòlīvām, polívajū imperf.} *sl-fea* talk persistently and meaninglessly, blabber, chatter

r̀suz {a (acc. = gen.) masc.} //a (acc. = gen.) masc./ BosM *col* ***Der*** worthless or despicable person <NE>

r̄š {excl.} *sl* used to make somebody go away <Slav>

r̀štati {tīm, tē imperf.} *col* crunch (under foot) <Slav>

r̀šum {a masc.} *col* mess, disorder, disturbance <NE>

r̀tanja *See the following*

- **R̀tanju ti jèbēm!** {S} (lit. I fuck your ass!) *dia* ***Off*** used as a moderate curse, Fuck you!

rȕblja {ē fem.} (lit. Ruble) *sl* dinar (Yugoslav currency unit) <Rus*1>

rȕbvīz {a masc.} **a.** *sl-drink* alcoholic beverages **b.** *sl-drink* wine

rȕcka {ē fem.; p Dat rȕcki} *sl-sex* ***Obs*** penis, dick, prick <Slav✍> ☞ **kurac**

rúčak *See the following*

- **prólaznī rúčak**{NP} (lit. transient lunch) *sl-stu* one-time cafeteria dinner

rȕčati {rûčām, rúčajū imperf.} *sl* make noise <Slav*1>

rȕčiti {čīm, čē perf.} *sl* make noise <Slav*1>

rȕčka {ē fem.; Dat rȕčki} (lit. handle) *sl-sex* ***Fac-Obs*** penis, dick, prick

rȕčnā {ē fem. (adj. decl.)} /rȕčnā/ *sl-auto* emergency brake <Slav>

rȕčni bàcāč {NP} (lit. hand thrower) **1** *sl-mil* mortar **2** *sl-mil* bazooka ☞ **bacač**

rȕčnī ȉstovār {NP} (lit. hand emptying) **1** *sl-sex* ***Obs*** masturbation, hand job **2** *sl-sex* ***Obs*** urination ☞ **istovar**

rȕčnī râd {NP} (lit. handwork) *sl-sex* ***Fac-Obs*** masturbation, hand job ☞ **rad**

rȕčnīk {ručníka (acc. = gen.) masc.} (lit. towel) *sl-sex* ***Fac*** male homosexual, gay <Slav*1>

rudáriti {rùdārīm, rē imperf.} (lit. work as a miner) *sl-fea* work hard (at manual labor) <**Slav**[*1]>

rȕdlav {a, o adj.} *col* curly (of hair) <**Slav**>

rúdo {a neut.} (lit. shaft) *sl-sex* ***Fac-Obs*** erect penis <**Slav**[*1]>

rȕdokōp {a masc.} (lit. mine) *sl* factory <**Slav**[*1]>

Rúja {ē masc.} *col* Russian (person) <**Slav**✍>

Rȕjān {a (acc. = gen.) masc.} /Rùjan/ *col* Russian (person) <**Slav**✍>

Rújo {a masc.} /Rújo /e masc./ *col* Russian (person) <**Slav**✍>

rúka *See the following*

• **lêvā rúka - dèsnī džȅp** {NP} (lit. left hand - right pocket) **1** SerE *col* stealing **2** steal

• **lìjēvā rúka - dèsnī džȅp** {NP} (lit. left hand - right pocket) *col* stealing *col*

• **na rûke** {PP} (lit. into one's hands) *col* in cash: *Plaćen je na ruke. He was paid in cash.*

• **od rúkē** {PP} (lit. from hand) **a.** *col* right away, now **b.** *col* conveniently, handy

rùkāv *See the following*

• **ko pòpōv rùkāv** {PP} (lit. like a priest's sleeve) *sl-sex* ***Fac-Obs*** large (of a vagina)

rȕknuti {nēm, nū perf.} **1** *sl-crime* steal, swipe <**Slav**[*1]> **2** *sl* hit, punch <**Slav**[*1]>

rȕkomēt {a masc.} (lit. handball *a European ball game similar to soccer, but played in arenas and the ball is thrown by hand, not kicked*) *sl-sex* ***Fac-Obs*** sexual foreplay, petting, feeling up <**Slav**[*1]>

rukomètāš {metáša (acc. = gen.) masc.; Voc rȕkometāšu} (lit. handball player *a European ball game similar to soccer, but played in arenas and the ball is thrown by hand, not kicked*) *sl-sex* ***Fac-Obs*** male who only pets his girlfriend, one who only gets to second base <**Slav**[*1]>

rȕkoš {a masc.} *sl-sports* handball (a European ball game similar to soccer, but played in arenas and the ball is thrown by hand, not kicked) <**Slav**✍>

rukotvòrina {ē fem.} (lit. handwork) *sl-fea* bruise <**Slav**[*1]>

rukotvòrine {rīnā fem. pl.} (lit. handworks) **1** *sl-sex* ***Fac-Obs*** masturbation, hand job <**Slav**[*1]> **2** *sl-sex* ***Fac-Obs*** sexual foreplay, petting, feeling up <**Slav**[*1]>

rukovòdilac {ioca (acc. = gen.) masc.} (lit. C.E.O.) *sl-fea* ***Fac*** boy who manages to do nothing more than to hold his girlfriend's hand <**Slav**[*1]>

rȕksāk {a masc.} (lit. back pack) **1** *sl-sex* ***Fac-Obs*** buttocks, butt <**Ger**[*1]> **2** *sl* child, kid <**Ger**[*1]>

rùktānje {a neut.} *col* barking (of a dog) <**Slav**>

rùktati {ām, ajū imperf.} *col* bark (of a dog) <**Slav**>

rùlet *See the following*

• **rȕskī rùlet** {NP} (lit. Russian roulette) *sl-fea* risky situation

• **sȑpskī rùlēt** {NP} (lit. Serbian roulette) *sl* a game where one speeds through a red light at a busy intersection

Rȕlovac {vca masc.} *sl* Russian (person) <**Slav**✍>

rȕlja {ē fem.} (lit. crowd) **1** *col* company (group of people) <**Slav**[*1]> **2** *col* people <**Slav**[*1]>

rùmija {ē fem.} *sl-arch* flour

rȕnda {ē fem.} /rúnda/ *sl-drink* round (drinks in a bar) <**Ger**>

• **mȕs rȕnda** {NP} *sl-sex* ***Fac-Obs*** group sex

rȕndosava {ē fem.} (lit. the curly one) *sl* vagina <**Slav**⁘[*1]>

rùndulja {ē fem.} *sl-sex* ***Obs*** vagina, cunt

rùnkōv {a (acc. = gen.) masc.} *sl-arch* horse (the animal) <**Slav**⁘[*1]>

rȕnja {ē fem.} **a.** *sl* hairs (on one's body) <**Slav**> **b.** *sl-fea* curly hair <**Slav**[*1]> **c.** *sl-sex* vagina <**Slav**[*2]>

rȕnjav {a, o adj.} *sl-fea* hairy <**Slav**>

rúnjo {ē masc.} *sl-fea* male with long hair, long hair <**Slav**>

Rȕpa [1] {ē fem.} (lit. hole) Ser *sl* the name for Arts Academy Club in Belgrade, Serbia <**Slav**[*1]>

rȕpa [2] {ē fem.} (lit. hole) **1a.** *sl-sex* ***Obs*** vagina, hole <**Slav**[*1]> **b.** *sl* ***Obs*** female, cunt <**Slav**[*2]> **2** *sl-sex* brothel, whorehouse <**Slav**[*1]> **3a.** *sl* bad apartment, dump: *Ne mogu više da živim u ovoj rupi. I cannot live in this dump any more.* <**Slav**[*1]> **b.** *sl* apartment <**Slav**[*2]> **4a.** *sl-drink* joint, low-class bar <**Slav**[*1]> **b.** bar (drinking place) <**Slav**[*2]> **5a.** *sl-thie* prison <**Slav**[*1]> **b.** *sl-thie* custody **6** *sl* a distant and unpleasant place, hellhole <**Slav**[*1]>

• **stârā rȕpa** {NP} (lit. old hole) Cro *sl-drink* name of a bar at the Central Station in Zagreb, Croatia

rȕpica {ē fem.} (lit. small hole) *sl-sex* ***Obs*** vagina, cunt <**Slav**[*1]>

rùpīnger {a masc.} (lit. the one with a hole) **a.** *sl* hole, opening <**Slav**✍> **b.i.** *sl* female <**Slav**✍[*1]> **ii.** *sl* apartment <**Slav**✍[*1]> **iii.** *sl-sex* brothel, whorehouse <**Slav**✍[*1]> **iv.** *sl-drink* bar (drinking place) <**Slav**✍[*1]> **v.** *sl-crime* prison <**Slav**✍[*1]>

rȕra {ē fem.} (lit. tube) *sl-crime* policeman, cop <**Ger**[*1]>

rùsija {ē fem.} (lit. Russia) **1** *sl-sex* ***Fac*** female with very large breasts and very big buttocks <**Slav**[*1]> **2** *sl-sex* ***Fac*** large buttocks <**Slav**[*1]>

rȕska {ē fem.} *sl* word

rȕskī rùlet {NP} (lit. Russian roulette) *sl-fea* risky situation ☞ **rulet**

rȕsvāj {a masc.} **/rùsvaj/ a.** *col* mess, disorder, disturbance <**NE**> **b.** *col* fight (e.g. fist fight) <**NE**[*1]>

rȕša {ē fem.} *sl-drink* wine <**Ita**[*1]>

rùštati {tīm, tē imperf.} *col* crunch (under foot) <**Slav**>

rȕvo {a neut.} [std. = ruho] *dia-col* clothing <**Slav**✍>

rúža *See the following*

• **rúža vjètrōvā** {NP} (lit. rose of winds) *sl-sex* ***Obs*** hymen

rúžan *See the following*

• **rúžan ko lópov** {AdjP} (lit. as ugly as a thief) *sl-fea* extremely unattractive, ugly as sin

• **rúžan ko màjmun** {AdjP} (lit. as ugly as a monkey) *sl-fea* extremely unattractive, ugly as sin

• **rúžan ko trȅćī svjètskī rȁt** {AdjP} (lit. as ugly as the Third World War) *sl-fea* extremely unattractive, ugly as sin

ružióna {ē fem.} *sl* fun <**Slav**[*1]>

rúžiti {žīm, že imperf. intr.} (lit. reprimand) **1a.** *sl* party (social gathering): ***ružiti do tri u noći*** *party until three a.m.* <**Slav**[*1]> **b.** *sl* have fun: ***ružiti na utakmici*** *have fun at a ball game* <**Slav**[*2]> **2** *sl* lie: *Ona stalno ruži. She constantly lies.* <**Slav**[*1]>

rvàku {rvȅku fem.; perm} [std. = kurva] *sl-sex* prostitute, hooker <**Lat**✍>

r̄zāč {rzáča (acc. = gen.) masc.; Voc r̄zāču} (lit. neigher) *sl-arch* horse (the animal) <**Slav**[*1]>

r̄zānje {a neut.} *col* neighing <**Slav**>

r̄zati {r̄žēm, r̄žū imperf. intr.} **a.** *col* neigh <**Slav**> **b.** *sl* laugh <**Slav**[*1]>

r̄žāč {ržáča (acc. = gen.) masc.} *sl-arch* horse (the animal) <**Slav**⁘>

Ss

s.s. [ȅs ȅs] {masc.} (lit. *super* s(permos)) *sl-sex* ***Fac*** sexually potent male <**Lat**✍>

sǝs {acc.} [std. = sa] *dia* with <**Slav**✍>

sa sȉrom na njúški {PP} (lit. with some cheese on the snout) *sl-sex* ***Obs*** with sperm on one's face ☞ **sir**

sàbāh {sabáha masc.} *col-dia* morning <**NE**>

• **na sabáhu** {PP} (lit. at morning) Bos *col* in the morning

sàbājle {adv.} *col* at dawn, early in the morning <**NE**>

sȁblāst {i fem.} *sl-sstu* parent <**Slav**[*1]>

sȁblja {ē fem.} (lit. saber) **1** *sl-sex* ***Fac-Obs*** penis, dick, prick <**Slav**[*1]> **2** *sl* ***Fac*** knife <**Slav**[*1]>

sačèkuša {ē fem.} *sl-crime* killing from an ambush <**Slav**⁘[*1]>

sačulátac {láca (acc. = gen.) masc.} *sl* unimportant issue

sȁd *See the following*

• **Sȁd ću da te fȑcām!** {S} (lit. I will bang you now!) *dia-col* ***Off*** used as a moderate curse, Fuck you!

• **Sȁd ću da te kȃrām!** {S} (lit. I will fuck you now!) *col-dia* ***Off*** used as a moderate curse, Fuck you!

• **Sȁd si nȁjebō!** {S} (lit. You are fucked up now!) *col* ***Off*** used to refer to an imminent difficult situation of one's interlocutor, You're fucked!

• **sàd tî ùzmi** {AdvP} (lit. now you take it) *col* used to sum up one's point, That's how it is!

sadàka {ē fem.; Dat sadàki} BosM *col* mercy <**NE**>

sàdē {adv.} [std. = sada] *col-dia* now <**Slav**✍>

sàdēk {adv.} [std. = sada] *col-dia* now <**Slav**✍>

sàdēkarcē {adv.} [std. = sada] *col-dia* now <**Slav**✍>

sàdēkare {adv.} [std. = sada] *col-dia* now <**Slav**✍>

sàdēna {adv.} [std. = sada] *col-dia* now <**Slav**✍>

sádnica {ē fem.} (lit. seedling) *sl-fea* stupid or mentally deficient person <**Slav**[*1]>

sȁfatati {ām, ajū imperf.} (lit. juice) **a.** *col* catch, grab <**Slav**✍[*1]> **b.** *sl* annoy, bother, pester <**Slav**✍[*2]> **c.** *sl* date <**Slav**✍[*3]>

sȁft {a +ov (ext. pl) masc.; Nom Pl sȁftovi} (lit. juice) **1** *sl-drink* drink (alcohol), juice <Ger[*1]> **2** *sl-sex* ***Obs*** vaginal excretion <Ger[*1]>

sȁftāć {a masc.} (lit. juicer) **1** *sl-fea* sentimental movie <Slav✣[*1]> **2** *sl-fea* sentimental novel <Slav✣[*1]>

saftàli {adj.} BosM *col* juicy <Ger-NE>

sȁftānje {a neut.} (lit. juicing) *sl-drink* drinking (alcohol), juicing <Ger✣[*1]>

sȁftati {ām, ajū biasp.} (lit. juice) **1** *sl-drink* drink (alcohol), juice <Slav✣[*1]> **2** *sl-sex* engage in cunnilingus <Slav✣[*1]> **3** *col* cry, shed tears, weep <Slav✣[*1]>

sàfūn {safúna masc.} [std. = sapun] *col-dia* soap

safùnica {ē fem.} [std. = sapunica] *col-dia* soap foam

safùnjati {ām, ajū imperf.} [std. = sapunati] *col-dia* wash with soap

sàglja {ē fem.} *sl-arch* bag <Fre✍>

sagòreti {sàgorīm, rē perf. intr.} (lit. burn up) SerE *sl* die, kick the bucket <Slav[*1]>

sagòriti {sàgorīm, rē perf. intr.} (lit. burn up) *sl* ***Fac*** die, kick the bucket <Slav[*1]>

sagòrjeti {sàgorīm, rē perf. intr.} (lit. burn up) *sl* ***Fac*** die, kick the bucket <Slav[*1]>

sàgradan {a masc.} *sl-drink* imitation plum brandy <NE[*1]>

sagȑdān {rdána masc.} *sl-drink* imitation plum brandy <NE[*1]>

sàgulja {ē fem.} *sl* bag <Ger✍>

sȁhat {a masc.} [std. = sat] **a.** BosM *col* hour <NE✍> **b.** BosM *col* clock tower <NE✍[*1]>

sahrániti {sàhrānīm, nē perf.} (lit. bury) **1** *col* destroy, ruin <Slav[*1]> **2** *sl* cheat, swindle <Slav[*1]>

sàjber {adj.} (lit. cyber) **a.** *sl* cyber <Eng> **b.** *sl-fea* excellent, awesome

sàjdžija {ē masc.} *col* watchmaker <NE>

sȁjla[1] {ē fem.} *col* cord <Ger>

sȁjla[2] {ē masc.} (lit. cord) *sl-fea* troublemaker, rowdy, ruffian <Ger>

sàjlovati se {sȁjlujēm, lujū biasp. intr.} (lit. rope oneself) *sl-fea* get confused <Ger✣[*1]>

sàjmonica {ē fem.} (lit. Simon's shoe *after Simon and Garfunkel*) *col* antelope leather shoe <EngO[*1]>

sakalȕda {ē fem.} *sl-fea* stupid or mentally deficient person <NE✣[*1]>

sàkat {a masc.} **1** *sl* coat (outer garment) <NE[*1]> **2** *sl* jacket <NE[*1]>

sakatája {ē fem.} *sl-fea* handicapped person <NE✍>

sakàtija {ē fem.} *sl-fea* handicapped person <NE✍>

sakàto {a masc.} *sl-fea* beggar <NE[*1]>

sàksija {ē fem.} (lit. flower pot) **1** *sl-sex* ***Fac*** attractive elderly female <NE[*1]> **2** *sl-fea* average man <NE[*1]>
- **nȅgovānā sàksija** {NP} (lit. cherished flower pot) *sl-fea* attractive elderly female

sȁksofōn {a (acc. = gen.) masc.} (lit. saxophone) *sl-fea* stupid or mentally deficient person <EngO-Gre[*1]>

sàlaziti {zīm, zē imperf.} [std. = silaziti] *col-dia* descend <Slav✍>

salȉven *See the following*
- **ko salȉven** {PP} (lit. as if being molded) *col* perfect

sàlvet *See the following*
- **gûznī sàlvēt** {NP} (lit. ass napkin) *sl-sex* ***Fac-Obs*** bathroom tissue, ass wipe

sâm *See the following*
- **sámo pò sebi** {AjdP} (lit. alone by itself) **a.** *col* obviously **b.** *col* self-evidently

Sâm te òtac jȅbō! {S} (lit. Let your father himself fuck you!) *col* ***Off*** used as a strong curse, Fuck you! ☞ **otac**

sambijánović {a masc.} *sl-music* samba <Port✍>

sàmiš {a masc.} *sl* grocery store <Slav✍>

sàmiška {ē fem.; Dat sàmiški} *sl* grocery store <Slav✍>

sȁmizdat {a masc.} *col* self-publishing <Rus>

sȁmo {part.} *col* just: *A: Šta ću sad? B: Samo ti radi. A: What shoud I do now? B: Just keep working.* <Slav>

sȁmo mȁlo {AdvP} (lit. just a little) *col* used to achieve a channel-related pause, one moment, please ☞ **mȁlo**

Sȁmo mu cȉpele vírē. {S} (lit. Only his shoes are sticking out.) *sl-fea* used to refer to ingratiation of a third party male ☞ **cipele**

sámo pò sebi {AjdP} (lit. alone by itself) **a.** *col* obviously **b.** *col* self-evidently ☞ **samo**

sȁmo sekùndu {NP} *col* used to achieve a channel-related pause, one moment, please ☞ **sekundu**

sȁmo tȁkō {AdvP} (lit. only like that) *sl-fea* fun ☞ **tako**

sȁmo trenútak {NP} *col* used to achieve a channel-related pause, hold on, hang on, one moment, please ☞ **trenutak**

Samobòrček {a (acc. = gen.) masc.} **Kajk** *col* name of a narrow-gauge train which used to run from Zagreb to Samobor, Croatia <**SlaO**>

sȁmogon {a masc.} (lit. self-made brandy) *sl* fear <**Rus**[*1]>

sȁmojēd {a (acc. = gen.) masc.} *sl* dog (the animal) <**Slav**[*1]>

samopȍsluga {ē fem.; Dat samopȍslugi} (lit. grocery store) *sl-crime* easily accessible wallet (e.g. to a pickpocket) <**Slav**[*1]>

sȁmotok {a masc.} *sl-drink* name of a dry white wine from Herzegovina <**Slav**>

sȁmpās {a masc.} *col* being without any restrictions <**Slav**>

sàmūn {samúna masc.} [std. = somun] BosM *col* home-made bread <**NE**✍>

sandolína {ē fem.} (lit. boat) *sl-fea* long shoe <**Ita**[*1]>

sandolírānje {a neut.} *sl* walk <**Ita**✤[*1]>

sandolírati {dòlīrām, dolírajū imperf.} *sl* walk <**Ita**✤[*1]>

sandùčara {ē fem.} (lit. trunk-like thing) **1** *sl-fea* unattractive communist-style architecture building <**NE**✤[*1]> **2** *sl-sex* loose woman <**NE**✤[*1]>

sȁnšājn {a masc.} (lit. sunshine) *sl-drugs* narcotic drug, dope <**Eng**[*1]>

sánjati *See the following*
- **sánjati u kolóru** {VP} (lit. dream in color) *sl-sex* ***Obs*** dream of sexual intercourse

saobràćājka {ē fem.} **a.** *sl-auto* car crash <**Slav**✤> **b.** *sl* dating, going out with <**Slav**✤[*1]>

sàpēt {a, o adj.} *col* tied <**Slav**[*1]>

sȁpu {sepu fem.; perm} /sàpu/ [std. = pusa] *sl* kiss <**Slav**✍>

sapùnār {punára (acc. = gen.) masc.} (lit. soap maker) *sl-sex* ***Fac*** male homosexual, gay <**Slav**✤[*1]>

sapùnati {ām, ajū imperf.} (lit. soap) **1** *sl-sex* ***Fac-Obs*** engage in sexual intercourse with (of a male) <**Slav**[*1]> **2** *sl* reproach, scold <**Slav**[*1]>

sapùnica {ē fem.} (lit. soap foam) *sl-fea* soap opera <**Slav**[*1]>

sàpunskā ȍpera {NP} (lit. soap opera) *col* soap opera ☞ **opera**

sapùnjārka {ē fem.; Dat sapùnjārki} (lit. soap maker) *sl-sex* ***Fac*** lesbian <**Slav**✤[*1]>

Saràjlija {ē masc.} (lit. inhabitant of Sarajevo) *sl-sports* fan of Sarajevo (a soccer team in Sarajevo, Bosnia) <**SlavO**[*1]>

Sàrājvo {a neut.} [std. = Sarajevo] *col* name for Sarajevo (a city in Bosnia) <**Slav**✍>

sȁrana {ē fem.} [std. = sahrana] *col* funeral <**Slav**✍>

saràniti {sàrānīm, nē perf.} [std. = sahraniti] **a.** *col* bury <**Slav**✍> **b.** *col* destroy, bury <**Slav**✍[*1]>

saranjívati {rànjīvām, ajū imperf.} //rànjujēm, rànjujū imperf./ [std. = sahranjivati] *col* bury <**Slav**✍>

Sàrdīnija {ē fem.} (lit. Sardinia X sardina 'sardine') *sl-fea* ***Fac*** crowded bus, bus packed like sardines <**ItaO**[*1]>

sardìnisati se {išēm, išū biasp. intr.} (lit. sardine oneself) *sl* ***Fac*** board a bus <**ItaO**[*1]>

sȁrme {i fem. pl.} (lit. cabbage rolls) *sl-fea* big eyes <**NE**[*1]>

sàseći {saséčem, sasékū, sàsek, sàsek perf. irreg.} (lit. cut) SerE *sl* steal somebody's girlfriend <**Slav**[*1]>

sàsranak {nka masc.} [std. = sastanak] *sl* ***Fac*** meeting <**Slav**✍>

sàstančārskī {ā, ō adj.} *col* ***Der*** pertaining to frequent and lengthy meetings <**Slav**✤>

sàstānčiti {čīm, čē imperf.} *col* ***Der*** spend too much time in meetings <**Slav**✤>

sàstaviti {vīm, vē perf.} (lit. connect) **a.** *col* hit, punch <**Slav**[*1]> **b.** *sl-drink* get drunk, get smashed <**Slav**[*2]>
- **sàstaviti sa zèmljōm** {VP} (lit. connect with the Earth) *col* beat up, level, flatten

sasúnuti {sàsūnēm, nū perf.} *sl-sex* ***Obs*** engage in sexual intercourse with (of a male)

sàsūti {sàspēm, spu perf.} (lit. pour in) *sl-sex* ***Obs*** engage in sexual intercourse with (of a male) <**Slav**[*1]>

sȁš čȕt {VP} (lit. you will hear it now) *col* used to express the incoming information in one's discourse, just wait ☞ **čuti**

sašàptati {ām, ajū perf.} //sàšapćēm, sàšapćū imperf./ *col* whisper <**Slav**✤>

sašaptávānje {a neut.} *col* the sound made by whispering <**Slav**✤>

sašaptávati {šàptāvām, šatptávajū imperf.} *col* whisper <**Slav**✤>

sašaptávati se {ām, ajū imperf. intr.} *col* whisper <**Slav**✤>

• **Dòbro sȁšīto!** {S} (lit. Well sewed!) *sl* used to express satisfaction, appreciation, etc., Everything's fine!

sȁšīto {adv.} *sl* done <Slav*1>

sašȉven {adj.} (lit. sewn) *sl-fea* deaf-and-dumb <Slav*1>

sašúćeti {sàšūtīm, ūtē perf.} [std. = zašutjeti] *dia-col* be silent <Slav✍>

sât *See the following*
• **nȕltī sât** {NP} (lit. hour zero) Cro *sl-sex* ***Fac-Obs*** sexual intercourse between two high-school teenagers

sȁtara {ē fem.} (lit. butcher's axe) *sl* female <NE*1>

sataràniti {tàrānīm, nē perf.} 1 *sl* destroy, ruin <Slav*1> 2 *sl* beat up severely, trash <Slav*1>

satelȉt {a (acc. = gen.) masc.} /satèlit/ (lit. satelite) *sl-fea* ***Der*** ingratiator (male), brownnoser, ass kisser <Lat*1>

sàterati {ām, ajū perf.} (lit. drive in) *sl-sex* ***Obs*** engage in sexual intercourse with (of a male) <Slav*1>
• **sàterati u ćȍšak** {VP} (lit. drive to the corner) SerE *col* corner somebody

sàtimu {sȁmmu, sàjumu imperf.; perm} [std. = musati] *sl* lie

sàtjerati {ām, ajū perf.} (lit. drive in) *sl-sex* ***Obs*** engage in sexual intercourse with (of a male) <Slav*1>
• **sàtjerati u ćȍšak** {VP} (lit. drive to the corner) SerE *col* corner somebody

sàtljik {a masc.} *sl-drink* drinking glass (of alcohol) <Ger>

sàtrati {sàtarēm, rū perf.} (lit. rub out) *col-dia* kill in a driving accident: *Traktor je satrao pješaka. A tractor has killed a pedestrian.* <Slav*1>

sȁug {a masc.} *sl-auto* choke <Ger>

sàugati {ām, ajū biasp.} 1 *sl* vacuum <Ger❖> 2 *sl-drink* drink (alcohol) <Ger❖*1> 3 *sl-sex* engage in fellatio <Ger*1>

sàuna [1] {ē fem.} (lit. sauna) *sl-fea* extremely hot room, sauna <Fin*1>

sàuna [2] {adj.} (lit. sauna) *sl-fea* obese, fat <Fin*1>

sàvatati {ām, ajū imperf.} [std. = sahvatati] **a.** *col* catch, get hold of (person, etc.) <Slav✍> **b.** *col* annoy, bother, pester <Slav✍*1> **c.** *col* date, go out with <Slav✍*2>

sàviti *See the following*
• **sàviti kȉčmu u čvȍr** {VP} (lit. bend someone's backbone into a knot) *sl* beat up, beat into a pretzel

sȁvra {ē fem.} *sl* rifle

savrakèlac {lca masc.} *sl* rifle

savȕljaga {ē fem.; Dat savȕljagi} [std. = sovuljaga] *col* owl <Slav✍>

sažȁrēn {sažaréna masc.} *sl-arch* lime (calcium oxide) <Slav*1>

scȅna {ē fem.} *col* event <Gre*1>

scipeláviti {vīm, vē perf.} *sl* beat up <Hun❖*1>

sȅc {a +ov (ext. pl) masc.} (lit. snip) **1** SerE *sl-fea* boasting, bragging <Slav*1> **2** *sl-gamble* betting <Slav*1>

sècāroš {a (acc. = gen.) masc.} (lit. snipper) SerE *sl-gamble* bettor <Slav*1>

sȅcati {ām, ajū imperf.} (lit. snip) **1** SerE *sl* carry, bear <Slav*1> **2** SerE *sl* drag, move <Slav*1>

sȅcovānje {a neut.} (lit. snipping) SerE *sl-gamble* betting <Slav*1>

sȅcovati {cujēm, cujū imperf.} (lit. snip) SerE *sl-gamble* bet <Slav*1>

sečèno {adj.} SerE *col* agreed <Slav*1>

sȅća {adj.} *sl-fea* handsome, cute

sȅći {séčem, séku, sȅk, sȅk imperf. irreg.} (lit. cut) SerE *sl* annoy, bother, pester <Slav*1>
• **sȅći krivìnu** {VP} (lit. cut a curve) SerE *sl* run away, flee

sȅćija {ē fem.} **a.** *col* sofa <NE> **b.** last row of seats (on a bus, streetcar, etc.) <NE*1>

sèćira {fem.} [std. = sekira] SSer *dia* axe <Slav✍>

sèdam *See the following*
• **sèdam cèntimetārā dúšē** {NP} (lit. seven centimeters of soul) *sl-sex* ***Obs*** impotence
• **sèdam smȑtnīh grijéhā** {NP} (lit. seven deadly sins) Cro *sl-drink* a bar in Zagreb, Croatia

sedàmnājs {num.} [std. = sedamnaest] *col* seventeen <Slav✍>

sedàmnājsti {num.} [std. = sedamnaesti] *col* seventeenth <Slav✍>

sedàmnēs {num.} [std. = sedamnaest] *col* seventeen <Slav✍>

sèdlati {ām, ajū biasp.} (lit. saddle) *sl* work hard (at manual labor) <Slav*1>
• **Kȍ te sèdlā!** {S} (lit. Who is putting a saddle on you?) *sl* ***Off*** used as a weak curse, Screw you!

sêdmī kȓst {NP} (lit. seventh cross) Cro *sl-drink* name of a bar on Trnjanska street in Zagreb, Croatia ☞ **krst**

sèdmica {ē fem.} (lit. seven) **a.** *sl-sex* prostitute, hooker <Slav*1> **b.** *sl-sex* loose woman <Slav*2>

sèfta {ē fem.} *sl* rap received from one's peers after getting a haircut <NE[*1]>

sehára {ē fem.} BosM *col* box or chest used to store valuables <NE>

séja {ē fem.} *col* ***Fam*** sister, sis <Slav✐>

séka {ē fem.; Dat séki} **a.** *col* ***Fam*** sister, sis <Slav✐> **b.** *sl* female <Slav✐[*1]> **c.** *sl-sex* prostitute, hooker <Slav✐[*2]>
- **čàsnā séka** {NP} (lit. nun) *sl-sex* ***Fac*** prostitute, hooker
- **mlȁđā séka** {NP} (lit. younger sister) *sl-fea* male who does nothing more than walk his girlfriend
- **sèka Pérsa** {NP} (lit. sis Persa) *col* sissy, effeminate

sekìrati se {ām, ajū imperf. intr.} *col* be upset <NE>

sȅks-šéma {ē fem.} (lit. sex scheme) *sl-sex* agreement to have sexual intercourse with (of females) <Eng-Gre[*1]>

sȅks-šȍp {a +ov (ext. pl) masc.; Nom Pl sȅks-šòpovi} *col* sex shop <Eng>

sèksača {ē fem.} (lit. sexer) *sl-sex* ***Obs*** loose woman, slut <Eng⁘[*1]>

sȅksānje {a neut.} (lit. sexing) **a.** *sl-sex* ***Obs*** sexual intercourse <Eng⁘> **b.** *sl-sex* ***Obs*** masturbation <Eng⁘[*1]>

sèksara {ē fem.} (lit. sexer) *sl* leg (human) <Eng⁘[*1]>

sȅksati {ām, ajū imperf.} (lit. sex) **a.** *sl-sex* ***Obs*** engage in sexual intercourse with (of a male) <Eng⁘[*1]> **b.** *sl-sex* ***Obs*** masturbate, beat off <Eng⁘[*2]>

sȅksī {adj.} /sèksi/ *col* sexy <Eng>

sȅksī-mašína {ē fem.} (lit. sex machine) **a.** *sl-sex* ***Fac*** loose woman <Eng[*1]> **b.** *sl-fea* ***Fac*** evil female, bitch <Eng[*2]>

sèksilīšte {a neut.} (lit. sex-place) *sl-sex* ***Fac-Obs*** group sex <Eng⁘[*1]>

seksírati {sèksīrām, rajū biasp.} (lit. sex) *sl-sex* ***Obs*** engage in sexual intercourse with (of a male) <Eng⁘[*1]>

seksndràjsig {a masc.} (lit. thirty-six) **a.** *sl-sex* ***Fac-Obs*** sexual intercourse <Ger✐[*1]> **b.** *sl-sex* ***Fac-Obs*** masturbation <Ger✐[*2]>

seksndràjsik {a masc.} (lit. thirty six) *sl-sex* ***Fac-Obs*** engage in fellatio <Ger✐[*1]>

sȅksuālnī opservatôrīj {NP} (lit. sexual observatory) **Cro** *sl-sex* ***Fac*** a bar at Ilica and Marinkovićeva streets in Zagreb, Croatia ☞ **opservatorij**

sȅksuālnō òdsustvo {NP} (lit. sexual leave of absence) *sl-mil* ***Fac*** exceptional leave of absence in the military ☞ **odsustvo**

sekùndu {excl.} *col* used to ask for a pause, hang on, hold on, one moment <Lat[*1]> ☞ **moment, momenat, trenutak**
- **sȁmo sekùndu** {NP} *col* used to achieve a channel-related pause, hold on, hang on, one moment, please

sèlām[1] {excl.} BosM *col* salaam (Islamic greeting) <NE[*1]>

sèlām[2] {seláma masc.} BosM *col* salaam (Islamic greeting) <NE>

selámet {a masc.} BosM *col* profit, gain <NE>

sêle *See the following*
- **Sêle li ti tvòje!** {S} (lit. *I fuck* your sister!) *dia* ***Off*** used as a strong curse, Fuck you!
- **Sêle li ti tvòje mǝlècko!** {S} (lit. *I screw* your little sister!) **SSer** *dia* ***Off*** used as a weak curse, Screw you!

sèlo *See the following*
- **špânskā sèla** {NP} (lit. Spanish villages) *col* unknown concepts or ideas, Greek (as in: it's Greek to me)

sȅlotējp {a masc.} *col* Scotch tape, adhesive tape <BN>

sȅlpo {slapo masc.; perm} /sèlpo/ **a.** Kajk *sl* work, labor <Slav✐> **b.** Kajk *sl* job, gig <Slav✐>

seljàčina {a (acc. = gen.) masc.} (lit. big peasant) **a.** *sl-fea* inhabitant of the countryside, hick, bumpkin <Slav[*1]> **b.** *sl-fea* male with bad manners, total crude <Slav[*2]>

sèljāk {seljáka (acc. = gen.) masc.; Voc sȅljāče} (lit. peasant) **a.** *sl-fea* inhabitant of the countryside, hick, bumpkin <Slav[*1]> **b.** *sl-fea* male with bad manners <Slav[*2]>
- **sèljāk bez grȕnta** {NP} (lit. peasant without land) *sl-fea* mentally deficient person

seljóber {a (acc. = gen.) masc.} **a.** *sl-fea* inhabitant of the countryside, hick, bumpkin <Slav✐[*1]> **b.** *sl-fea* stupid or mentally deficient person <Slav✐[*2]>

sȅmafōr {a (acc. = gen.) masc.} (lit. traffic lights) **1a.** *sl-fea* person who frequently blushes <Gre[*1]> **b.** *sl-fea* boaster, blowhard <Gre[*2]> **2** *sl-fea* bald male <Slav[*1]>

semafòrisati {išēm, išū imperf.} (lit. shine like traffic lights) *sl-fea* blush, turn colors <Gre⁘[*1]>

semafóriti {màfōrīm, rē imperf.} (lit. shine like traffic lights) *sl-fea* blush, turn colors <Gre⁘[*1]>

Sȅmenārskā akadèmija - Ȍdsēk za leblèbije {NP} (lit. Chick-pea Department of the Seed academy) **SerE** *sl-fea* ***Fac*** substandard vocational school ☞ **akademija**

semènkara {ē fem.} (lit. the seed one, i.e. the one worn by the low-class people who sell seeds) *sl-fea* cheap and unattractive tennis shoe <Slav⁘[*1]>

sȅmerīng {a masc.} *sl-auto* collector ring on a piston <Ger>

sèmka *See the following*

• **Sȅmku ti jèbēm!** {S} (lit. I fuck your sister!) *dia* ***Off*** used as a strong curse, Fuck you!

sȅndvīč {a masc.} (lit. sandwich) *sl-auto* streetcar bumper <Eng*1>

• **u sȅndvīču** {PP} (lit. in sandwich) *sl-sex* ***Obs*** being between two partners during sexual intercourse

Senegálac [1] {lca (acc. = gen.) masc.} (lit. Senegalese) **a.** *sl-fea* inhabitant of the countryside, hick, bumpkin <SlavO*> **b.** *sl-fea* soldier from the countryside <SlavO* *1>

senílac {lca (acc. = gen.) masc.} **a.** *sl-fea* senile person <Lat> **b.i.** *sl-fea* senior citizen <Lat*1> **ii.** *sl-fea* stupid or mentally deficient person <Lat*1> **iii.** *sl-fea* father <Lat*1>

sènīlka {ē fem.} (lit. senile woman) *sl-fea* elderly female <Slav*1>

sênka {ē fem.} (lit. shadow) SerE *sl* spy, spook <Slav*1>

sêno {a neut.} (lit. hay) SerE *sl* money <Slav*1>

sèntiš {adj.} *col* sentimental <Lat*1>

sèntiš {a masc.} **1** *col* sentimental song <Lat*1> **2** *col* sentimental dance <Lat*1>

sèntiška {ē fem.; Dat sèntiški} *sl-music* sentimental music <Lat*1>

senzácija *See the following*

• **nùkliš senzácija** {NP} (lit. nuclear revelation) *sl-fea* big revelation, bombshell

sèptičkā jȁma {NP} (lit. sewage hole) *sl-sex* ***Obs*** vagina, cunt ☞ **jama**

sȅptić {a masc.} *sl-music* septet <Lat✍>

séra {ē fem.} (lit. shitter) *sl-sex* ***Obs*** female bathroom attendant <Slav❖>

sérac {rca (acc. = gen.) masc.} (lit. shitter) *sl-fea* ***Der-Obs*** extremely talkative person, chatterbox <Slav❖*1>

sèrāč {seráča (acc. = gen.) masc.} (lit. shitter) **1** *sl-fea* ***Obs-Der*** extremely talkative person, chatterbox <Slav❖*1> **2** *sl-fea* ***Obs-Der*** boring person, bore <Slav❖*2>

sèrātor {a (acc. = gen.) masc.} (lit. shitter) **1** *sl-fea* ***Fac*** extremely talkative person, chatterbox <Slav❖*1> **2** *sl-polit* ***Fac*** senator <Slav❖*1>

sèrbez [1] {adj.} BosM *col* careless <NE>

sèrbez [2] {adv.} **a.** BosM *col* slowly: *uraditi posao serbez work slowly* <NE> **b.** BosM *col* indifferently: *Gleda serbez na onoga ko ga je optužio. He looks indifferently at his accuser.* <NE*1>

Serejòtija {ē fem.} (the abbreviation SRJ, Federal Republic of Yugoslavia X srati, to shit) *sl-polit* ***Fac-Obs*** the Federal Republic of Yugoslavia <Abb✍>

serejòtskī {ā, ō adj.} *sl-polit* ***Fac-Obs*** pertaining to the Federal Republic of Yugoslavia <Abb✍>

Sȅrēm ti se na! {S} (lit. I shit on that!) *col* ***Off*** used to express indifference, I don't give a shit! ☞ **srati se**

Sȅrem ti se u [NOUN:ACC]! {LSF} (lit. I shit in [NP:ACC]) *col* used to express disrespect or dissatisfaction, Fuck it!: *Serem ti se u taj plan. Fuck that plan of yours.* ☞ **srati se**

serèmak {a (acc. = gen.) masc.} *sl-fea* poor male <Slav*1>

sèriglāva {ē fem. & masc.} (lit. shithead) **a.** *sl-fea* ***Der-Obs*** extremely talkative person, chatterbox <Slav❖*1> **b.** *sl-fea* ***Der-Obs*** boring person, bore <Slav❖*2>

sȅrkati {ām, ajū imperf.} (lit. shit a little) **1** *sl-sex* ***Obs*** defecate, shit <Slav❖*1> **2** *sl-fea* ***Der-Obs*** talk persistently and meaninglessly, have diarrhea of the mouth <Slav❖*2>

séronja {ē masc.} (lit. shitter) **a.** *sl-fea* ***Der-Obs*** worthless or despicable person <Slav❖*1> **b.** *sl-fea* ***Der-Obs*** extremely talkative person, chatterbox <Slav❖*2> **c.** *sl-fea* ***Der-Obs*** coward, chicken <Slav❖*3> **d.** *sl-fea* ***Der-Obs*** boring person, bore <Slav❖*3>

Sȅrtić {a masc.} Cro *sl* name of a dance club at Vrapče near Zagreb, Croatia <Slav*1>

serȕckati {ām, ajū biasp.} **a.** *sl-sex* ***Obs*** defecate in small quantities <Slav> **b.** *sl-fea* ***Der-Obs*** talk persistently and meaninglessly, blabber, chatter <Slav*1>

servílac {lca (acc. = gen.) masc.} *sl-fea* ***Der*** ingratiator (male), brownnoser, ass kisser <Lat❖*1>

sȅrvīs {servísa masc.} **a.** *col* service (in general) <Fre> **b.** *col* check-up <Fre*1>

• **nȕltī sèrvīs** {NP} (lit. zero service) *sl-auto* first check-up after a new vehicle has been purchased

servisírati {vìsīrām, visírajū biasp.} *col* service <Fre>

sȅrvīz {servíza masc.} (lit. service) [std. = servis] *col* china <Fre✍>

sèsil {a masc.} *sl-drugs* mark on a shot glass <Fre*1>

sȅsti *See the following*

• **Sȅdnēš mi na kȉtu!** {S} (lit. Sit on my prick!) SSer *col* ***Off*** used as a moderate curse, Fuck you!

• **Sèdni mi na mòjēga!** {S} (lit. Sit on my *prick!*) SSer *dia* ***Off*** used as a moderate curse, Fuck you!

sèstra {ē fem.} (lit. sister) **1** *sl* I (when a female refers to herself) <Slav*1> **2** *sl* female <Slav*1> **3** *sl-sex* lesbian <Slav*1> **4** *sl* female friend <Slav*1>

• **čàsnā sèstra** {NP} (lit. nun) *sl-sex* ***Fac*** prostitute, hooker

• **Sèstrē mi!** {S} (lit. *I swear* by my sister!) *col* used to emphasize the truth of what has been said, I swear!

• **Sèstrē mi mȉlē!** {S} (lit. *I swear* by my dear sister!) *dia* used to emphasize the truth of what has been said, I swear!

• **Sèstre ti ga!** {S} (lit. *I bang* it to your sister!) SSer *dia* ***Off*** used as a strong curse, Fuck you!

• **Sèstre ti ga mȕnēm!** {S} (lit. I bang it to your sister!) SSer *dia* ***Off*** used as a strong curse, Fuck you!

• **Sèstre ti ga skaràbūdžīm!** {S} (lit. I bang it to your sister!) SSer *dia* ***Off*** used as a strong curse, Fuck you!

• **Sèstre ti ga spotȁknēm!** {S} (lit. I stick it to your sister!) SSer *dia* ***Off*** used as a strong curse, Fuck you!

• **Sèstre ti ga šȉbnēm!** {S} (lit. I stick it to your sister!) SSer *dia* ***Off*** used as a strong curse, Fuck you!

• **Sèstre ti ga ùbācīm!** {S} (lit. I insert it to your sister!) SSer *dia* ***Off*** used as a strong curse, Fuck you!

• **Sèstre ti ga ùtopīm!** {S} (lit. I drown it to your sister!) SSer *dia* ***Off-Fac*** used as a strong curse, Fuck you!

• **Sèstre ti ga zabòbrčīm!** {S} (lit. I bang it to your sister!) SSer *dia* ***Off*** used as a strong curse, Fuck you!

• **Sèstru li ti!** {S} (lit. *I fuck* your sister!) *col* ***Off*** used as a strong curse, Fuck you!

• **Sèstru li ti tvòju!** {S} (lit. *I fuck* your sister!) *col* ***Off*** used as a strong curse, Fuck you!

• **Sèstru li ti tvòju jèbēm!** {S} (lit. I fuck your sister!) *col* ***Off*** used as a strong curse, Fuck you!

• **Sèstru li ti zbárīm!** {S} (lit. I boil your sister!) *col* ***Off*** used as a strong curse, Fuck you!

• **Sèstru ti jèbēm mȉlū!** {S} (lit. I fuck your dear sister!) *col* ***Off*** used as a strong curse, Fuck you!

• **Sèstru ti tvòju!** {S} (lit. *I fuck* your sister!) *col* ***Off*** used as a strong curse, Fuck you!

• **Sèstru ti u pičək!** {S} (lit. *I fuck* your sister in her cunt!) SSer *dia* ***Off*** used as a strong curse, Fuck you!

• **Sèstru ti u pȉčicu!** {S} (lit. I fuck your sister in her small cunt!) *col-dia* ***Off*** used as a strong curse, Fuck you!

• **Sèstru ti u pìšalo!** {S} (lit. *I fuck* your sister in her pissing thing!) *col* ***Off*** used as a strong curse, Fuck you!

• **Sèstru ti u pìzdicu!** {S} (lit. *I screw* your sister in her cunt!) *col* ***Off*** used as a weak curse, Screw you!

sèstrica *See the following*

• **Dà ti sèstricu na tràvicu!** {S} (lit. Let me *screw* your little sister on the grass!) SSer *dia* ***Off-Fac*** used as a weak curse, Screw you!

• **Dà ti sèstricu u vodènicu!** {S} (lit. Let me *screw* your little sister in a watermill!) SSer *dia* ***Off-Fac*** used as a weak curse, Screw you!

• **Sèstricu ti u gùzicu!** {S} (lit. *I screw* your sister in her ass!) *col-dia* ***Off*** used as a weak curse, Screw you!

• **Sèstricu ti u rȉbicu!** {S} (lit. *I screw* your sister in her little fish!) *col-dia* ***Off*** used as a weak curse, Screw you!

sȅstro {excl.} (lit. my sister) *sl* ***Fam*** used to address a female in direct informal communication, sister <Slav*1>

Sèstru li ti! {S} (lit. *I fuck* your sister!) *col* ***Off*** used as a strong curse, Fuck you! ☞ **sestra**

Sèstru li ti tvòju! {S} (lit. *I fuck* your sister!) *col* ***Off*** used as a strong curse, Fuck you! ☞ **sestra**

Sèstru li ti tvòju jèbēm! {S} (lit. I fuck your sister!) *col* ***Off*** used as a strong curse, Fuck you! ☞ **sestra**

Sèstru li ti zbárīm! {S} (lit. I boil your sister!) *col* ***Off*** used as a strong curse, Fuck you! ☞ **sestra**

Sèstru ti jèbēm mȉlū! {S} (lit. I fuck your dear sister!) *col* ***Off*** used as a strong curse, Fuck you! ☞ **sestra**

Sèstru ti tvòju! {S} (lit. *I fuck* your sister!) *col* ***Off*** used as a strong curse, Fuck you! ☞ **sestra**

Sèstru ti u pičək! {S} (lit. *I fuck* your sister in her cunt!) SSer *dia* ***Off*** used as a strong curse, Fuck you! ☞ **sestra**

Sèstru ti u pȉčicu! {S} (lit. I fuck your sister in her small cunt!) *col-dia* ***Off*** used as a strong curse, Fuck you! ☞ **sestra**

Sèstru ti u pìšalo! {S} (lit. *I fuck* your sister in her pissing thing!) *col* ***Off*** used as a strong curse, Fuck you! ☞ **sestra**

Sèstru ti u pìzdicu! {S} (lit. *I screw* your sister in her cunt!) *col* ***Off*** used as a weak curse, Screw you! ☞ **sestra**

sȇvāj {excl.} (lit. lighten *meteorol.*) SerE *col* used to make somebody go away, beat it <Slav*1>

sȅvāp {sevápa masc.} **a.** BosM *col* mercy <NE> **b.** BosM *col* good deed <NE*1>

sevàpli {adj.} BosM *col* merciful <NE*1>

sévati {ām, ajū imperf.} (lit. lighten *meteorol.*) **1** SerE *sl-fea* be pretty <Slav*1> **2** SerE *sl* run away, flee <Slav*1>

• **sévati ȍčima** {VP} (lit. lighten with one's eyes) SerE *col* look at with hatred, glare at

sèvdāh {sevdáha masc.} **a.** BosM *col* yearning for love <NE> **b.** BosM *col* a kind of nostalgic folk music <NE[*1]>

sevdàlija {ē masc.} **a.** BosM *col* love-struck male, love-sick guy <NE[*1]> **b.** BosM *col* singer of love songs <NE[*2]>

sevdàlisati {išēm, išū biasp. intr.} BosM *col* yearn for love <NE[*1]>

sèvdisati {išēm, išū biasp. intr.} BosM *col* yearn for love <NE>

sevèljče {eta neut.} *sl* cigarette, smoke

sȅverina {ē fem.} *sl-drink* herbal brandy

sévnuti {sêvnēm, nū perf. intr.} (lit. lighten *meteorol.*) SerE *sl* ***Fac*** die, kick the bucket <Slav[*1]>

sezóna {ē fem.} (lit. season) *sl-sex* ***Fac*** time of separation between a male and a female <Fre[*1]>

sezónac {nca (acc. = gen.) masc.} *col* seasonal worker <Fre✤>

sfìnga {ē fem.; Dat sfìngi} (lit. Sphinx) *sl-fea* widow <Gre[*1]>

sfìtīljen {a, o adj.} **a.** *sl-fea* affluent <NE[*1]> **b.** *sl-fea* well off <NE[*1]>

sfȕćkati {ām, ajū perf.} (lit. whistle) *sl* spend (money, property, etc.) <Slav✤[*1]>

sî {part.} **a.** *sl* used as a strong affirmative response, of course, yeah, you bet <Ita> **b.** *sl* used as an independent affirmative response, ok, ok <Ita>

• **sî Mîle** {ExcP} (lit. yes Mile) *sl* affirmative response, yes

• **sî Mîle-bȕba-jêž** {ExcP} (lit. yes Mile, bug, hedgehog) *sl* affirmative response, yes

• **sî Miléva** {ExcP} (lit. yes Mileva) *sl* affirmative response, yes

sȉc {a +ev (ext. pl) masc.; Nom Pl sìcevi} *col* seat <Ger>

sȉcer {a masc.} **1** *sl-sports* fixed game <Ger[*1]> **2a.** *sl* false incrimination, frame <Ger[*1]> **b.** *sl* trap, catch <Ger[*2]>

sȉć {a +ev (ext. pl) masc.; Nom Pl sìćevi} *sl-drugs* narcotic drug, dope

síća {ē fem.} **a.** *sl* petty cash, chump change, peanuts <Slav✤[*1]> **b.i.** *sl* something of little importance <Slav✤[*2]> **ii.** *sl-mil* few number of days until the end of one's military term <Slav✤[*3]> **iii.** *sl-crime* small number of days until the end of one's prison term <Slav✤[*3]>

sìćanovo {a neut.} *sl* village

sići *See the following*

• **sići s kȗrca** {VP} (lit. descend from one's prick) *sl* leave alone, cease boring, fuck off

sída {ē fem.} *col* AIDS <Fre>

sìdāš {sidáša (acc. = gen.) masc.; Voc sȉdāšu} *col* AIDS patient <Fre✤>

sìdrāš {sidráša (acc. = gen.) masc.; Voc sȉdrāšu} **a.** *sl-sports* water-polo player who stays at adversaries' goal <Slav✤[*1]> **b.** *sl-fea* male who stays in one place (e.g. in a bar) <Slav✤[*1]>

sìdžim {a masc.} BosM *col* rope <NE>

síđa {ē fem.} *sl-sex* ***Obs*** female breast, tit <Slav[*1]>

sȉf {a +ov (ext. pl) masc.; Nom Pl sìfovi} [std. = sifilis] *sl-sex* syphilis, the pox <Gre✎>

sífa {ē fem.} [std. = sifilis] *sl-sex* syphilis, the pox <Gre✎>

sȉfić {a masc.} [std. = sifilis] *sl-sex* syphilis, the pox <Gre✎>

sifìlitika {ē fem.} [std. = sifilis] **a.** *sl-sex* syphilis, the pox <Gre✎> **b.** *sl-fea* difficult or unpleasant situation <Gre✎[*1]>

sȉfke {eta masc.} *sl-sex* ***Fac*** syphilis, the pox <Gre✎>

sìflis bâr {NP} (lit. syphilis bar) Cro *sl-drink* name for Tingl-Tangl bar in Zagreb, Croatia ☞ **bar**

sìfōn {sifóna masc.} (lit. syphon) *sl-sex* ***Obs*** female breast, tit <Gre[*1]>

sifònjērka {ē fem.} *sl-sex* ***Fac*** prostitute, hooker <Gre✤[*1]>

signalizácija {ē fem.} (lit. signalling) *sl* correspondence <Lat[*1]>

sìgrati se {sȉgrām, sȉgrajū imperf. intr.} /sȉgrati se/ [std. = igrati se] *dia-col* play a game <Slav✎>

sigurácija {ē fem.} *col* safety, security <Slav✎>

sìhrōn {sihróna masc.} [std. = sinhron] *sl-crafts* synchronizing mechanism <Gre✎>

sȉjalica {ē fem.} (lit. light bulb) *sl-fea* moon <Slav[*1]>

• **ȍksigenskā sȉjalica** {NP} (lit. oxygen light bulb) *sl-sex* ***Fac-Obs*** very attractive female, hot number

sìjati {ām, ajū imperf.} (lit. shine) *sl* have, possess <Slav[*1]>

• **sìjati dvâ lêvā ȍka** {VP} (lit. shine two left eyes) SerE *sl-fea* be cross-eyed

• **sȉjati pȅpel** {Vp} (lit. sow ashes) *sl-fea* suffer from a disease

• sȉjati sífu {VP} (lit. sow syphilis) *sl-sex* ***Obs*** transmit syphilis

• sȉjati trȉšu {VP} (lit. sow gonorrhea) *sl-sex* ***Obs*** transmit gonorrhea

sijévati *See the following*

• sijévati òčima {VP} (lit. lighten *meteorol.* with one's eyes) *col* look at with hatred, glare at

sijévnuti {nēm, nū perf. intr.} /sijèvnuti/ (lit. lighten *meteorol.*) *sl* remember <Slav[*1]>

sìjuks {a (acc. = gen.) masc.} (lit. Sioux) *sl-fea* female with too much makeup <Eng[*1]>

sȉk {excl.} *col* the sound made by a goose, honk <Slav>

síka {ē fem.; Dat síki} *sl-sex* ***Fam*** female breast <Slav❖>

sȉkānje {a neut.} /síkanje/ *col* honking (of a goose) <Slav>

sìkati {sȉktīm, tē imperf. intr.} /síkati/ **1** *col* hiss (snake, gas, etc.) <Slav> **2** *col* honk (of a goose) <Slav> **3** *col* blow, exhale <Slav>

sìkira {ē fem.} [std. = sjekira] *dia-col* axe <Slav✍>

sikirácija {ē fem.} *col* being upset, worried <NE>

sȉknuti {nēm, nū perf. intr.} **1** *col* hiss (snake, gas, etc.) <Slav> **2** *col* honk (of a goose) <Slav> **3** *col* blow, exhale <Slav>

sikòtati {sìkoćēm, oćū imperf. intr.} **1** *col* hiss (snake, gas, etc.) <Slav> **2** *col* honk (of a goose) <Slav> **3** *col* blow, exhale <Slav>

sȉktānje {a neut.} **1** *col* hissing (snake, gas, etc.) <Slav> **2** *col* blowing, exhaling <Slav>

sìktati {sȉkćēm, kćū imperf. intr.} **1** *col* hiss (snake, gas, etc.) <Slav> **2** *col* honk (of a goose) <Slav> **3** *col* blow, exhale <Slav>

sȉktav {a, o adj.} **1** *col* hissing (snake, gas, etc.) <Slav> **2** *col* honking (of a goose) <Slav> **3** *col* blowing, exhaling <Slav>

sȉktavica {ē fem.} *col* hissing snake <Slav❖[*1]>

sȉktavo {adv.} **1** *col* hissing (snake, gas, etc.) <Slav> **2** *col* blowing, exhaling <Slav>

siktèćiv {a, o adj.} *col* hissing (snake, gas, etc.) <Slav>

sȉkter {excl.} **Din** *col* used to make somebody go away, beat it <NE>

siktèrisati {išēm, išū imperf.} **a. Din** *col* drive away, expel <NE❖> **b. Din** *sl* resign, quit <NE❖[*1]>

siktèruša {ē fem.} BosM *col* ***Fac*** last coffee served to one's guests <NE❖[*1]>

sìlazak *See the following*

• sìlazak ânđela {NP} (lit. descent of the angels) *sl-sex* ***Obs*** looking at a woman's vagina

silèsija {ē fem.} *col* multitude <Slav NE[*1]>

silìkōn {silikóna masc.} (lit. silicone) *sl-sex* ***Fac*** female breast <Lat[*1]>

silìkōnka {ē fem.} (lit. the silicone one) *sl-sex* ***Fac*** female breast <Lat[*1]>

silìkōnskā tréba {NP} (lit. silicone chick) *sl-sex* attractive female ☞ **treba**

sȋlka {ē fem.} *sl-sex* ***Obs*** rape <Slav✍>

sȉlōm pȑdī, ȑđōm smȑdī {S} (lit. farts with force, smells of rust) *col* ***Obs*** used to indicate that one is pretending to be affluent or influential, while being weak and unimportant

sȉlos {a (acc. = gen.) masc.} *sl-fea* troublemaker, rowdy, ruffian <Slav✍>

sìlovānje *See the following*

• sȉlovānje iz nȅhāta {NP} (lit. unintended rape) *sl* joking with, fooling with

sȉm {adv.} [std. = ovamo] Cro *col* here <Slav✍>

sȉmāj {excl.} Cro *sl* come, arrive <Slav❖[*1]>

simèntālka {ē fem.; Dat simèntālki} (lit. Simental cow) *sl-sex* ***Fac*** large-breasted female <GerO[*1]>

sȉmiti {mīm, mē biasp. intr.} Cro *sl* come, arrive <Slav✍>

sȉmo {adv.} Cro *col-dia* here, in this direction <Slav>

sȉmovati {mujēm, mujū biasp. intr.} *sl* come, arrive <Slav✍>

sȉmpa {adj.} [std. = simpatičan] *sl* likable <Gre✍>

sȋn {a (acc. = gen.) +ov (ext. pl) masc.; Nom Pl sȋnovi} (lit. son) *sl-fea* female from a white-collar family <Slav[*1]>

• mâjčīn sîne {NP} (lit. mother's son) *col* used as an intensifier in direct informal communication, hey

• Màričīn sîn {NP} (lit. Mary's son) *sl-crime* policeman, cop

sìnče *See the following*

• Sȉnče ti kalàjisānō! {S} (lit. *I fuck* your tin covered little son!) *dia-col* ***Off*** used as a very strong curse, Fuck you!

sìnčić {a (acc. = gen.) masc.} /sìnčīč sinčíća (acc. = gen.) masc/ (lit. sonny) *sl-fea* very young female, little girl <Slav[*1]>

sȉndos {a (acc. = gen.) masc.} **a.** *sl* union activist <Gre✍> **b.** *sl-fea* snob <Gre✍*1>

sȉndža {ē fem.} **a.** *sl* lie <NE*1> **b.** *sl* joke <NE*2>

sȉndžīr {sindžíra masc.} /sȉndžīr/ Din *col* chain <NE>

sínđa {ē fem.} **a.** *sl* trick, joke: *Ima sinđa kako da se ne plati kazna. There is a trick to avoid paying the fine* <Gre✍> **b.i.** *sl* lie <Gre✍*1> **ii.** *sl* effective move: *napraviti sinđu i dobiti hrpu love make an effective move and earn big bucks* <Gre✍*1> **iii.** *sl* joke

sȉnđos {a (acc. = gen.) masc.} **1** *sl* union activist <Gre*1> **2** *sl-fea* snob <Gre*1> **3** *sl-fea* average male <Gre*1>

sȉne {excl.} /sîne/ (lit. my son) *sl* ***Fam*** used to address a person younger than oneself in direct informal communication, sonny <Slav*1>

sinemàskop {a masc.} (lit. cinemascope) *sl-sex* ***Obs*** wide buttocks <Gre*1>

sȉnfa {ē fem.} *sl-sex* female breast <Slav✍>

sȉngati {ām, ajū imperf.} *sl* sing <Eng>

sȉnger {a masc.} /sìnger/ **a.** *sl-music* singer <Eng> **b.** *sl-sex* very attractive female, hot number <Eng*1>

sȉngl {a +ov (ext. pl) masc.; Nom Pl sìnglovi} *sl-music* "single" phonograph record <Eng>

sȉnglica {ē fem.} *sl-music* "single" phonograph record <Eng❖>

sȉnglka {ē fem.; Dat sìnglki} *sl-music* "single" phonograph record <Eng❖>

sȋnko {excl.} (lit. my son) *sl* ***Fam*** used to address a person younger than oneself in direct informal communication, sonny <Slav*1>

sinòvac {vca (acc. = gen.) masc.} (lit. nephew) *sl-fea* female from a blue-collar family <Slav*1>

sinòvica {ē fem.} (lit. niece) *sl-fea* female from a blue-collar family <Slav*1>

sínuti {sînēm, sînū perf.} (lit. shine) **1a.** *sl* pay (bills, etc.) <Slav*1> **b.** *sl* get, obtain <Slav*2> **c.** *sl* have, possess <Slav*3> **2** *col* remember <Slav*1>
- **sínuti lóvu** {VP} (lit. shine money) *sl* pay (bills, etc.)

sȉnjati {ām, ajū imperf.} *sl* see

sȉpak {pka, pko adj.} (lit. loose) *sl-fea* undependable, unreliable <Slav*1>

sipljívko {a (acc. = gen.) masc.} (lit. loose dude) *sl-fea* sickly person <Slav*1>

sípnja {ē fem.} (lit. pouring) *col* asthma <Slav*1>

sȉpot {a masc.} *col* asthma <Slav✍*1>

sȉr {a (acc. = gen.) +ev (ext. pl) masc.; Nom Pl sìrevi} (lit. cheese) *sl-fea* person with pale skin <Slav*1>
- **sa sȉrom na njúški** {PP} (lit. with some cheese on the snout) *sl-sex* ***Obs*** with sperm on one's face
- **sȉra i vôjnē mùzikē** {NP} (lit. cheese and military music) *col* nothing at all, Not much!: *Šta ima? Sira i vojne muzike! What's up? Not much!*

sȉrak {a (acc. = gen.) masc.} *col-dia* orphan <Slav>

sirâno {a neut.} (lit. Cyrano) *sl-drugs* syringe, needle <FreO*1>

sirânž {a masc.} *sl-drugs* syringe, needle <Fre*1>

sirànžēr {ranžéra masc.} *sl-drink* wine with soda <Fre❖*1>

sirènjāvka *See the following*
- **Sirènjāvku ti jèbēm!** {S} *dia* ***Off*** used as a moderate curse, Fuck you!

sȉrīšte *See the following*
- **Sȉrište ti jèbēm!** {S} (lit. I fuck your rennet) *dia* ***Off*** used as a moderate curse, Fuck you!

sírnica {ē fem.} (lit. cheese-pie) *sl-sex* ***Obs*** buttocks, butt <Slav*1>

siròmā {áa masc.} [std. = siromah] *col* poor male <Slav✍>

siròmāk {romáka (acc. = gen.) masc.} [std. = siromah] *col* poor male <Slav✍>

sȉrotā Miléva {NP} (lit. poor Mileva) *sl-fea* used to express compassion, poor thing ☞ **Mileva**

sirotánović {a (acc. = gen.) masc.} *sl-fea* poor male <Slav✍>

siròtko {a masc.} *sl-fea* poor male <Slav✍>

siròvina {ē fem.} /sirovìna/ (lit. raw material) **1** *sl-fea* ***Der*** stupid or mentally deficient person <Slav*1> **2** *sl-fea* ***Der*** rude person <Slav*1> **3a.** *sl-fea* ***Der*** troublemaker, rowdy, ruffian <Slav*1> **b.** *sl-fea* ***Der*** body builder <Slav*2>
- **siròvinā ljûtā** {NP} (lit. hot raw material) *sl-fea* mentally deficient person

siròvnjāk {sirovnjáka (acc. = gen.) masc.} **a.** *sl-fea* inhabitant of the countryside, hick, bumpkin <Slav❖*1> **b.** *sl-fea* troublemaker, rowdy, ruffian <Slav❖*2>

sȉsa[1] {ē fem.} **a.** *sl-sex* female breast <Slav> **b.** *sl-fea* ***Der*** coward, chicken <Slav*1>
- **Mȁmē tvòjē trȕlē sȉse na tàvanu vȉsē!** {S} (lit. Your mother's rotten tits are hanging in the attic!) *col* ***Off*** used as a strong curse, Fuck you!
- **Sȉsu ti jèbēm kȑvavū!** {S} (lit. I fuck your bloody tit!) *col* ***Off*** used as a strong curse, Fuck you!
- **trȅćā sȉsa** {NP} (lit. the third tit) *sl-sex* ***Fac-Obs***

penis, dick, prick
• U sȉsu te jèbēm! {S} (lit. I fuck you in your tit!) *col* ***Off*** used as a moderate curse, Fuck you!

sísa [2] {ē fem.} *sl-sex* ***Obs*** large-breasted female <Slav❖*1>

sìsača {ē fem.} *sl-sex* ***Obs*** large-breasted female <Slav❖*1>

Sȉsāj ga! {S} (lit. Suck it!) *col* ***Off*** used as a strong curse, Suck it! ☞ sisati

Sȉsāj kȕrac! {S} (lit. Suck my prick!) *col* ***Off*** used as a strong curse , Suck my prick! ☞ sisati

sìsana {ē fem.} *sl-sex* ***Obs*** large-breasted female <Slav❖>

sȉsānče {eta neut.} (lit. sucker) *sl-fea* naive male, sucker <Slav*1>

sȉsānje {a neut.} (lit. sucking) **1** *sl-drink* drinking (alcohol) <Slav*1> 2 *sl-sstu* exam <Slav*1>

sȉsār {a (acc. = gen.) masc.} (lit. mammal) *sl-drink* alcoholic, drunk <Slav*1>

sìsara {ē fem.} *sl-sex* ***Obs*** large-breasted female <Slav❖*1>

sȉsat {a, o adj.} *sl-sex* ***Obs*** having large breasts, busty <Slav*1>

sȉsati {ām, ajū biasp.} (lit. suck) *sl-drink* ***Fac*** drink (alcohol) <Slav*1>
• **Kȍ te sȉsā!** {S} (lit. Who is sucking you?) *col* ***Off*** used to express disrespect, Fuck you!
• **Sȉsāj ga!** {S} (lit. Suck it!) *col* ***Off*** used as a strong curse, Suck it!
• **Sȉsāj kȕrac!** {S} (lit. Suck my prick!) *col* ***Off*** used as a strong curse, Suck my prick!
• **sȉsati ćȍšak od Ȁvalē** {VP} (lit. suck a corner of the Avala mountain) *sl-fea* ***Fac*** be very naive, be a sucker
• **sȉsati ćȍšak od helikòptera** {VP} (lit. suck a corner of a helicopter) *sl-fea* ***Fac*** be very naive, be a sucker
• **sȉsati ćȍšak od hȉpodrōma** {VP} (lit. suck a corner of a hippodrome) *sl-fea* ***Fac*** be very naive, be a sucker
• **sȉsati ćȍšak od stòla** {VP} (lit. suck a corner of a table) *sl-fea* ***Fac*** be very naive, be a sucker
• **sȉsati ćȍšak od tròliša** {VP} (lit. suck a corner of a trolleybus) *sl-fea* ***Fac*** be very naive, be a sucker
• **sȉsati vèslo** {VP} (lit. suck an oar) *sl-fea* be naive, be a sucker: *Nisam ja sisao velso. I'm not a sucker.*

sȉsavac {sāvca (acc. = gen.) masc.} (lit. mammal X the one who sucks) **1** *sl* ***Fac*** vacuum cleaner <Slav*1> 2 *sl* ***Der*** boy, kid <Slav*1>

sȉseška {ē fem.; Dat sìseški} *sl-sex* ***Obs*** large-breasted female <Slav❖*1>

sisètina {ē fem.} *sl-sex* ***Obs*** large female breast <Slav❖*1>

sȉsī {īja masc.} *sl-sex* ***Fac*** male homosexual who takes the passive role, femme <Slav✍*1>

sìsica {ē fem.} *sl-sex* small female breast <Slav❖>

sìsīć {sisíća masc.} *sl-sex* ***Obs*** small female breast <Slav❖*1>

sȉsikūr {a masc.} (lit. cock-sucker) *sl-sex* ***Fac-Obs*** male homosexual, gay <Slav❖*1>

sìsna {ē fem.} *sl-sex* ***Obs*** large-breasted female <Slav✍*1>

sȉsobrān {a masc.} (lit. tit protector) *sl-sex* ***Obs*** bra <Slav❖*1>

sȉsodrmka {ē fem.} (lit. tit-shaker) *sl-sex* ***Obs*** prostitute, hooker <Slav❖*1>

sisodŕžac {šca masc.} (lit. tit holder) *sl-sex* ***Obs*** bra <Slav❖*1>

sisodȑžāč {džáča masc.} (lit. tit holder) *sl-sex* ***Obs*** bra <Slav❖*1>

Sȉsoe {a masc.} (lit. McTit) *sl* ***Fac-Obs*** masculine first name <Slav✍*1>

Sȉsoević {a (acc. = gen.) masc.} (lit. McTit) *sl* ***Fac-Obs*** surname <Slav✍*1>

sȉsoje [1] {a masc.} *sl-fea* naive male, sucker <Slav❖*1>

Sȉsoje [2] {a masc.} *sl-sex* ***Fac*** large-breasted male <Slav❖*1>

sìsōn {sisóna masc.} *sl-sex* ***Obs*** female breast, tit <Slav✍>

sȉsonja {ē fem. & masc.} *sl-fea* ***Obs*** animal with large breasts <Slav❖*1>

sisoprihvàtāč {vatáča masc.} (lit. tit catcher) *sl-sex* ***Obs*** bra <Slav❖*1>

sìstēm *See the following*
• **Kàkvi su to sistémi?** {S} (lit. What kind of systems are those?) *col* used to ask for additional information, What's all that? What's with that?
• **stȅreo sìstēm** {NP} (lit. stereo system) *sl-drugs* shooting narcotic drugs in both arms

sistèmāš {a (acc. = gen.) masc.} (lit. system player) *sl-gamble* gambler or lottery player who uses systems in playing <Gre❖*1>

sistémi {ā masc. pl.} (lit. systems) *sl* cheating, swindling <Gre*1>

Sȉsu ti jèbēm kȑvavū! {S} (lit. I fuck your bloody tit!) *col* ***Off*** used as a strong curse, Fuck you! ☞ sisa

sisúljak {ljka masc.} *sl-sex* ***Obs*** female breast, tit <Slav❖>

sìsūrda {ē fem.} *sl-sex* ***Obs*** female breast, tit <Slav❖>

sisùrina {ē fem.} *sl-sex* ***Obs*** large female breast <Slav❖>

sȉt {a, o adj.} (lit. full) *sl-fea* affluent <Slav*1>

sȉtī {ija masc.} *col* city <Eng>
- **Hôrs Sȉtī** {NP} (lit. Horse City) Ser *sl* ***Fac*** name for Konjarnik (a neighborhood in Belgrade, Serbia)
- **Kukurȉkū Sȉtī** {NP} (lit. Cock-a-doodle-doo City) *sl* name for Petlovo brdo (a neighborhood in Belgrade Yugoslavia)

sȉtnā {ē fem. (adj. decl.)} *sl-mil* military (armed forces in general) <Slav*1>

sìtna rȉba {NP} (lit. small fish) **a.** *sl-fea* unimportant person, small fry **b.** *sl-fea* worthless or despicable person, bum

sìtna rȉba pljȕckavica {NP} (lit. small spitting fish) *sl-fea* unimportant person, small fish ☞ **riba**

sȉto {a neut.} **1** *sl* fairground <Slav*1> **2** *sl-crime* policeman, cop <Slav*1>
- **kroz sȉto i rèšeto** {PP} *col* through thick and thin

sívac {vca (acc. = gen.) masc.} (lit. grey man) **1** *sl-fea* average person <Slav⁘*1> **2** *sl-polit* union activist <Slav⁘*1> **3** *sl-fea* snob <Slav⁘*1> **4** *sl-sex* syphilis, the pox <Slav⁘*1>

sîvī {ōg (acc. = gen.) masc.} (lit. the grey one) **1** *sl-fea* average person <Slav⁘*1> **2** *sl-polit* union activist <Slav⁘*1> **3** *sl-fea* snob <Slav⁘*1>

sîvka {ē fem.} (lit. grey thing) *sl* church <Slav⁘*1>

sȉvor {a (acc. = gen.) masc.} **1** *sl* gentleman <Ita✍*1> **2** *sl* boss

sȉvorī {ija (acc. = gen.) masc.} *sl-crime* policeman, cop <Ita✍*1>

Sȉzif {a (acc. = gen.) masc.} (lit. Sisyphus) *sl-sex* ***Fac*** impotent male <GreO*1>

sjȁhati {jāšēm, jāšū perf.} (lit. dismount) **a.** *col* get off somebody's back <Slav*1> **b.** *col* cease boring <Slav*2>
- **sjȁši Kȕrta da ùzjašē Mȕrta** {S} (lit. get off Kurta, let Murta ride) *col* used to refer to lack of any change (usu. when referring to political life), tweedle dum and tweedle dee

sjâj *See the following*
- **u pȕnōm sjáju** {PP} (lit. in the full shine) *col* in full glory
- **vìsokī sjâj** {NP} (lit. high shine) *sl-sex* ***Fac*** cunnilingus

sjȁknuti {nēm, nū perf.} *sl* remember

sjaràniti se {jàrānīm, nē perf. intr.} Bos *col* make friends <NE⁘>

sjȁriti {rīm, rē perf.} *sl-sex* ***Obs*** engage in sexual intercourse with (of a male) <Slav*1>

sjȁši {excl.} (lit. dismount) *col* used to make somebody go away, beat it <Slav*1>

sjȁši Kȕrta da ùzjašē Mȕrta {S} (lit. get off Kurta, let Murta ride) *col* used to refer to lack of any change (usu. when referring to political life), tweedle dum and tweedle dee ☞ **sjahati**

sjȁšiti {šīm, šē perf.} (lit. dismount) *col* avoid <Slav*1>

sjáviti {sjâvīm, vē perf.} **a.** *dia* bring one's cattle down from the mountain <Slav> **b.** *col* pop up, appear <Slav*1>

sjȅbān {a, o adj.} (lit. fucked up) **a.** *sl-fea* defeated <Slav*1> **b.** *sl-fea* sad, depressed <Slav*2>
- **sjȅbān ȕ glāvu** {AdjP} (lit. fucked up in his head) *sl-fea* insane, fucked in the head

sjèbati {bēm, bū perf.} (lit. fuck up) **a.** *col* destroy, ruin: *sjebati kola destroy a car* <Slav*1> **b.** *sl-fea* defeat: *sjebati protivnika defeat one's adversary* <Slav*2> **c.** *sl-fea* make sad, sadden <Slav*3>
- **sjèbati znánje** {VP} (lit. fuck up knowledge) *sl* laugh at, tease
- **Sjȅbō si stvâr!** {S} (lit. You fucked up the thing!) *col* ***Obs*** used to express a strong reprimand, Fuck you!

sjèbati se {bēm, bū perf. intr.} (lit. fuck oneself up) **1a.** *sl-fea* be ruined, be destroyed: *sjebati se u poslu s ribama be ruined in the fish business* <Slav⁘*1> **b.i.** *sl-fea* fall in love: *sjebati se s Marijom fall in love with Marija* <Slav⁘*2> **ii.** *sl-fea* be in a difficult situation <Slav⁘*2> **2** *sl* be mistaken: *Sjebo se kad je mislio da će lako položiti ispit. He was mistaken when he thought that he would pass that exam easily.* <Slav⁘*1> **3** *sl* fall down, kiss the floor: *Sjebao se niz stepenice. He fell down the stairs.* <Slav*1>

sjecikèsāroš {a masc.} *sl-crime* pickpocket <Slav⁘*1>

sjèdac {adj.} (lit. sitter) *sl-sex* ***Fac*** impotent <Slav*1>

sjȅdalo {a neut.} (lit. seat) *sl-sex* buttocks, seat, butt <Slav*1>

sjȅdati *See the following*
- **sjȅdati na mȕku** {VP} (lit. sit on one's trouble) *col* make someone's situation even worse

sjèdēljka {ē fem.} (lit. sitting) *sl-sstu* exam <Slav*1>

sjȅsti {jȅdnēm, jȅdnū perf. irreg.} (lit. sit) *sl-sports* hit a ball <Slav*1>
- **Sjȅlo je.** {S} (lit. It sat.) *sl-fea* used to express satisfaction, It is cool!

sjévnuti {sjêvnēm, nū perf. intr.} (lit. lighten *meteorol.*) **1** *sl* die, kick the bucket <Slav*1> **2** *sl* remember <Slav*1>

Sjûrīm ti ga! {S} (lit. I speed it to you!) *col* ***Off*** used as a moderate curse, Fuck you! ☞ sjuriti

sjúriti {sjûrīm, rē perf.} (lit. run into) **a.** *col* stick in, insert <Slav*1> **b.** *sl-sex* engage in sexual intercourse with (of a male) <Slav*2>
- **Sjûrīm ti ga!** {S} (lit. I speed it to you!) *col* ***Off*** used as a moderate curse, Fuck you!

Skȁdar {dra masc.} (lit. Skadar *a city in Albania*) Ser *sl* Skadarlija (a street in Belgrade) <SlavO✍>

Skádža {ē fem.} Ser *sl* Skadarlija (a street in Belgrade) <SlavO✍>

skákati *See the following*
- **skákati na lévo** {VP} (lit. jump to the left) SerE *sl-fea* limp

skȁkavac [1] {kāvca (acc. = gen.) masc.} (lit. grasshopper) **1** *sl-fea* obedient person <Slav*1> **2** *sl-crime* burglar who enters apartments through windows <Slav*1>

skȁkavac [2] {kāvca masc.} (lit. grasshopper) *sl-crime* switchblade <Slav*1>

skȁkavica {ē fem.} (lit. hopper) *sl* female <Slav*1>

skalabrȉjati {jēm, jū imperf.} *sl-sex* ***Obs*** engage in sexual intercourse with (of a male)

skalamèrija {ē fem.} **1** *col* mechanism <Ita✣*1> **2** *col* innovative construction **3** *col* unattractive building

skâle {a fem. pl.} Med *dia* stairway <Ita*1>

skȁlp {a +ov (ext. pl) masc.; Nom Pl skȁlpovi} (lit. scalp) **a.** *sl* skin <Lat*1> **b.i.** *sl-sex* hymen <Lat*2> **ii.** *sl* hairstyle <Lat*2>

skalpírati {kàlpīrām, kalpírajū biasp.} (lit. scalp) *sl-sex* ***Obs*** deflower <Lat*1>

skȁmnī {ā, ō adj.} *sl-fea* worthless

Skandinâvija {ē fem.} (lit. Scandinavia) *sl* ***Fac*** applause <Lat✍*1>

Skȁndināvka {ē fem.; Dat Skȁndināvka} /Skandȉnāvka/ (lit. Scandinavian) *sl-sex* ***Fac*** loose woman <LatO*1>

skandírānje {a neut.} *col* ovations <Lat*1>

skȁngale {ā masc. pl.} *sl* trifles, things of little importance or value

skȁpati {ām, ajū perf. intr.} **a.** *sl* die, kick the bucket <Slav*1> **b.** *sl* work hard (at manual labor) <Slav*2>

skapávati {skàpāvām, skapávajū imperf. intr.} **a.** *sl* die, kick the bucket <Slav*1> **b.** *sl* starve <Slav*2>

skapírati {kàpīrām, kapírajū perf.} **a.** *sl* understand, realize <Lat> **b.** *sl* consider, think about <Lat*1>

skarabúdžiti {karàbūdžīm, dže perf.} **1** *col* build quickly and shabbily <NE*1> **2** *sl-sex* have quick sexual intercourse, have a quickie <NE*1>
- **Skaràbūdžīm ti ga!** {S} (lit. I bang it to you!) *dia* ***Off*** used as a moderate curse, Fuck you!

skarlíknuti {skàrlīknēm, nū perf. intr.} *sl* die, kick the bucket

skȁtula {ē fem.} Med *col-dia* box <Ita> ☞ škatulja

SKC [skəc] {masc.} *col* name for Student Cultural Center in Belgrade, Serbia <Abb>

skȅla {ē fem.} (lit. ferry) *sl-drink* bar (drinking place) <NE*1>

skȅlet {a (acc. = gen.) masc.} (lit. skeleton) *sl-sstu* parent <Gre*1>

skèmbati {ām, ajū perf.} /skȅmbati/ **1** *sl* put, place: *skembati štoljaš u ormar put a gun in a cupboard* **2** *sl* lose, be unable to find: *skembati ključeve lose one's keys*

skèntati {ām, ajū perf.} *sl-crime* steal, swipe

skénjati {skênjām, skénjajū perf.} (lit. shit at) **1a.** *sl-fea* destroy, ruin: *skenjati kompjuter destroy a computer* <Slav✣*1> **b.** *sl-fea* defeat <Slav✣*2> **c.** *sl-crime* kill, murder <Slav✣*3> **2** *sl* spend (money, property, etc.): *skenjati hiljadu dolara spend a thousand bucks* <Slav✣*1>

skénjati se {kênjām, kénjajū perf. intr.} (lit. shit oneself) *sl* ***Obs*** fall down, kiss the floor: *Skenjao se s motora. He has fallen from his motorbike.* <Slav*1>

skȅrak {a masc.} *sl-crafts* hammer (the tool)

skíčānje {a neut.} *col* squeaking <Slav>

skíčati {čīm, čē imperf.} *col* squeak <Slav>

skidȁčica {ē fem.} *sl-sex* stripper (female) <Slav*1>

skídati *See the following*
- **skídati blȁto** {VP} (lit. remove mud) *sl* wash oneself
- **skídati pȁučinu** {VP} (lit. remove spiderwebs) *sl-sex* ***Obs*** engage in sexual intercourse with
- **skídati pȉnku** {VP} (lit. remove the chip) *sl* earn money by renting a room for sex
- **skídati pȍglēd** {VP} (lit. take off the view) **a.** *sl-sex* wait for a customer (of a prostitute) **b.** *sl* walk

skȋk {a +ov (ext. pl) masc.; Nom Pl skȋkovi} *col* hiss (snake, gas, etc.) <Slav>

skȉka {ē fem.} **1** *col* hissing (snake, gas, etc.) <Slav> **2** *col* screaming in pain, fear, or outrage <Slav*1> **3** *col* noise <Slav*2>

skíknuti {nēm, nū perf. intr.} **1** *col* hiss (snake, gas, etc.) <**Slav**> **2** *col* be stolen <**Slav**[*1]> **3a.** *col* die, kick the bucket <**Slav**[*1]> **b.** *sl-gamble* lose all one's money <**Slav**[*2]>

skȉksati {ām, ajū perf.} *sl* fail: *skiksati na ispitu fail at an exam* <**Ger⁘**[*1]>

skȉksnuti {nēm, nū perf. intr.} *sl* be in a difficult situation <**Ger⁘**[*1]>

skilìkānje {a neut.} *col* hissing (snake, gas, etc.) <**Slav**>

skilìkati {ām, ajū imperf. intr.} *col* hiss (snake, gas, etc.) <**Slav**>

skȉnuti {nēm, nū perf.} (lit. take off) **1** *sl-crime* kill, murder <**Slav**[*1]> **2** *sl-sports* win: *skinuti zlatnu medalju win a gold medal* <**Slav**[*1]> **3** *sl* take from: *Skinuo je sat Marku. He took a watch from Marko.* <**Slav**[*1]> **4** *sl* impersonate, imitate: *Super je skinula Stinga. She imitated Sting perfectly.* <**Slav**[*1]>

- **skȉnuti đánu** {VP} (lit. remove hymen) *sl-sex* ***Obs*** deflower
- **skȉnuti jȕnfer** {VP} (lit. remove hymen) *sl-sex* ***Fac*** deflower
- **skȉnuti mrâk (s ȍčijū)** {VP} (lit. remove darkness *from someone's eyes*) *sl-sex* ***Obs-Fac*** deflower
- **skȉnuti pȁučinu s krajníkā** {VP} (lit. remove the spiderweb from someone's tonsils) *sl* ***Fac*** French kiss
- **skȉnuti pȑstēn** {VP} (lit. remove the ring) *sl-sex* deflower
- **skȉnuti s kȗrca** {VP} (lit. remove from one's prick) *sl* ***Obs*** finish something, get rid of: *Skinuo sam s kurca taj posao. I've finished that job.*
- **skȉnuti trólu** {VP} (lit. remove a trolley) *sl* divorce

skȉnuti se {nēm, nū perf. intr.} (lit. undress) **1** *col* leave alone, cease boring <**Slav**[*1]> **2** *col* cease taking narcotic drugs or alcohol <**Slav**[*1]>

- **Skȉn se s kȗrca!** {S} (lit. Get off my prick!) *col* ***Off*** used in angry dismissal, Fuck off!
- **Skȉni mi se!** {S} (lit. Get off!) *col* ***Off*** used in angry dismissal, Fuck off!
- **Skȉni mi se s kȗrca!** {S} (lit. Get off my prick!) *col* ***Off*** used in angry dismissal, Fuck off!
- **skȉnuti se s ìglē** {VP} (lit. get off the needle) *sl-drugs* be clean (of drugs)
- **skȉnuti se s vrâta** {VP} (lit. get off someone's neck) *sl* leave alone, cease boring

skȉsnuti {nēm, nū perf. intr.} *sl* be in a difficult situation

skìtara {ē fem.} *sl-fea* homeless female, bum <**Slav⁘**>

skívati {skîvām, skívajū imperf.} (lit. smith) **a.** *sl* be cautious <**Slav**[*1]> **b.** *sl* look, watch, scope out <**Slav**[*2]>

sklȅčkān {a, o adj.} *sl-fea* careless

sklépān {a, o adj.} *sl-fea* improvised <**Slav**[*1]>

sklépati {ām, ajū perf.} /sklȅpati/ *col* create an improvised construction, slap something together <**Slav**[*1]>

sklìpsati {ām, ajū perf. intr.} *sl* die, kick the bucket <**Slav**[*1]>

sklȉsati {līšēm, līšū biasp.} *sl* run away, flee <**Slav**[*1]>

sklȉzav {a, o adj.} (lit. slippery) *sl-fea* ***Der*** insane, nuts <**Slav**[*1]>

sklòniti *See the following*

- **sklòniti njúšku** {VP} (lit. hide one's snout) *sl* abstain from interfering in the affairs of others, keep one's nose out of other people's business

sklòpiti *See the following*

- **sklòpiti se ko pȅrorēz** {VP} (lit. fold down like a pocket knife) *sl* calm down
- **sklòpiti stàklēnke** {VP} (lit. close glasses) *sl* close one's eyes

skȍbālj {a masc.} *sl-sex* ***Obs*** penis, dick, prick <**Slav**[*1]>

skȍckān {a, o adj.} **1** *sl-fea* well-dressed <**Slav⁘**[*1]> **2** *sl-drink* drunk <**Slav⁘**[*1]>

skȍckati se {ām, ajū perf. intr.} **1** *sl-fea* dress formally, dress up <**Slav⁘**[*1]> **2** *sl-drink* get drunk **3** *sl* be as wished or planned: *Sve se skockalo, pa je dobio tu stipendiju. Everything went as planned and he won that grant.*

skočánjiti se {skòčānjīm, njē perf. intr.} *col* freeze <**Slav**[*1]>

skòčiti {kȍčīm, čē perf.} (lit. jump) *col* make a short trip, hop to: *skòčiti do mora hop to the seashop* <**Slav**[*1]>

skókati *See the following*

- **Skôkām ti ga!** {S} (lit. I bang it to you!) *dia-col* ***Off*** used as a moderate curse, Fuck you!

skȍknuti {nēm, nū perf. intr.} **1** *col* go to get or buy something <**Slav**[*1]> **2** *col* make a short trip <**Slav**[*1]>

skȍmpati se {ām, ajū perf. intr.} *sl* be very close to each other (of friends) <**Ita⁘**[*1]>

skȍnčati {čām, čajū perf.} *col* die, kick the bucket <**Slav**[*1]>

skȍntati {ām, ajū perf.} **a.** *sl* understand, realize <**Lat⁘**[*1]> **b.** *sl* agree

- **hlâdno skȍntāno** {AdjP} (lit. coldly calculated) *sl-fea* ***App*** clever, intelligent

skopàče {eta neut.} *sl-fea* very young female, little girl

skȍpak {a (acc. = gen.) masc.} *sl-fea* very young female, little girl

skòpati *See the following*

• **skòpati fàcu** {VP} (lit. dig out the face) *sl* grimace, make faces (usu. in pain)

skòpčati {ām, ajū biasp.} *sl* understand, realize <Slav*1>

skopízditi se {kòpīzdīm, dē perf. intr.} *sl* ***Obs*** freeze <Slav✣*1>

skoromòbil {a masc.} (lit. quickmobile) *sl-auto* ***Fac*** tractor <Slav☞*1>

skȍt {a (acc. = gen.) +ov (ext. pl) masc.; Nom Pl skòtovi} (lit. beast) **a.** *col* unattractive person <Slav*1> **b.** *col* worthless or despicable person, bum <Slav*2> **c.** *col* evil person <Slav*3>

skȍtan {tna, tno adj.} *sl-sex* ***Obs*** pregnant, knock up <Slav*1>

skȍžen {a, o adj.} (lit. with skin) **a.** *sl-fea* affluent <Slav✣*1> **b.** *sl-fea* very important, very influential <Slav✣*2>

skȑcati {ām, ajū perf. intr.} *sl* waste, spend <Slav✣*1>

skrénuti {skrênēm, nū perf. intr.} (lit. turn) *col* go insane, freak out <Slav*1>

• **skrénuti ûmom** {VP} (lit. turn with one's mind) *col* get frightened, get scared

skrȅsati {ām, ajū perf.} (lit. strike fire) *col* say bluntly <Slav*1>

• **skrȅsati u bȓk** {VP} (lit. strike a spark to somebody's mustache) *col* say bluntly

skŕhati {skȓhām, skŕhajū perf.} *sl-fea* destroy, ruin <Slav*1>

skŕkati {skȓkām, skŕkajū perf.} **1** *sl-fea* destroy, ruin: *skrkati bicikl destroy a bike* <Slav*1> **b.** *sl-fea* spend (money, property, etc.): *skrkati petsto dolara spend five hundred bucks* <Slav*2> **c.** *sl-fea* eat, devour <Slav*3>

skrôz {adv.} *col* completely, totally <Slav✣*1>

skrozírati {kròzīrām, krozírajū perf.} *sl* see through (lit. and fig.) *sl* be in a difficult situation

skȑšiti {kȓšīm, šē perf.} **a.** *sl-fea* destroy, ruin <Slav*1> **b.** *sl-fea* beat up <Slav*2>

skȑšiti se {kȓšīm, šē perf. intr.} (lit. break oneself) **1a.** *sl* get injured <Slav*1> **b.** *sl-drink* get drunk <Slav*2> **2** *sl* fall down, kiss the floor <Slav*1>

skȑta {ē fem.} *sl* door

skùbačiti {čīm, čē imperf.} *sl-sex* ***Obs*** engage in sexual intercourse with (of a male)

skùbati {ām, ajū biasp.} *sl* cheat, swindle

skùbina {ē fem.} *sl-sex* ***Der*** loose woman

skȕhān {a, o adj.} (lit. boiled) **1** *sl-fea* persuaded, convinced <Slav*1> **2** *sl-fea* cheated <Slav*2>

skȕhāno *See the following*

• **tȍplo skȕhāno** {NP} (lit. cooked hot) *sl-crime* stolen, hot

skȕhati {ām, ajū perf.} (lit. boil) **a.** *sl* persuade, convince: *Skuhao je šefa da ga pusti na konferenciju. He persuaded his boss to let him go to a conference.* <Slav*1> **b.** *sl-fea* cheat, swindle: *skuhati naivca cheat a sucker* <Slav*2> **c.** *sl* outwit, outsmart <Slav*3> *sl-sex* engage in sexual intercourse with (of a male) <Slav*1>

skulírati se {kùlīrām, kulírajū perf. intr.} **1** *sl* calm down, cool off <Eng✣*1> **2** *sl* continue a love affair after breaking it for a while <Eng✣*1>

skȕp [1] {skùpa +ov (ext. pl) masc.; Nom Pl skùpovi} (lit. gathering) *col* fair <Slav*1>

skûp [2] {a, o adj.} (lit. expensive) *sl-fea* affluent <Slav*1>

skùpa {adv.} *col* together <Slav>

skúpljati *See the following*

• **skúpljati pràšinu** {VP} (lit. gather dust) *col* sit around (of different objects): *Tvoje igračke samo skupljaju prašinu, uopšte ih ne koristiš. Your toys are just gathering dust, you have not been using them at all.*

skûpo {adv.} (lit. expensive) *sl-fea* obese, fat <Slav*1>

skûpo pròdati svòju kȍžu {VP} (lit. sell one's skin dearly) *col* fight to the end ☞ **prodati**

skȕpština {ē fem.} (lit. Parliament) **1** *sl* five thousand dinars; a five-thousand dinar bill <Slav*1> **2** *sl* fifty dinars (bill) <Slav*1>

skùrcati {ām, ajū perf.} (lit. prick up) *sl-sex* ***Obs*** engage in sexual intercourse with (of a male) <Slav✣*1>

skȕša {ē fem.} (lit. mackerel) **1** *sl-fea* slender female <Slav*1> **2** *sl-fea* Dalmatian (inhabitant of Dalmatia, Croatia) <Slav*1>

skutùrati {ām, ajū perf.} *sl-crime* steal, swipe

skȕvān {a, o adj.} (lit. cooked) **a.** *sl-fea* defeated <Slav*1> **b.** *sl-fea* cheated, swindled <Slav*2>

skȕvati {ām, ajū perf.} (lit. boil) **a.** *sl* persuade, convince <Slav*1> **b.** *sl* defeat <Slav*2>

skȕžīrān {a, o adj.} *sl-fea* dressed formally, dressed up <Ita✣*1>

skužírati se {kùžīrām, kužírajū perf. intr.} *sl-fea* dress formally, dress up <Ita✣*1>

skúžiti {kûžīm, žē imperf.} **a.** *sl* understand, realize <Ita✣*1> **b.** *sl* see

skȕžnuti {nēm, nū perf.} *sl* understand, realize <Ita❖[*]✍>

skvŕčiti {vȓčīm, čē perf.} *col* wrap <Slav>

skvȑčiti {čīm, čē perf.} *col* contract (muscle, etc.) <Slav>

skvȑčiti se {čīm, čē perf. intr.} *col* become contracted (of a muscle, etc.) <Slav>

slȁb {a, o adj.} *col* weak <Slav[*1]>

slàba stòlica {NP} (lit. weak chair) *sl-fea* ***Iro*** obese male ☞ **stolica**

slabòtinja {ē fem.} (lit. weakness) *dia* illness <Slav❖>

slàdak pȉškavac {NP} (lit. sweet pisser) *sl-sex* sexual intercourse ☞ **piškavac**

slàdīć {ladíća masc.} *sl* ***Fac*** ice cream <Slav✍>

sláditi se {dīm, dē imperf. intr.} **1** *col* enjoy, like <Slav❖[*1]> **2** *col* rejoice, triumph <Slav❖[*1]>

sladogúzac {sca (acc. = gen.) masc.} (lit. sweet-ass dude) *sl-sex* ***Fac-Obs*** male homosexual, gay <Slav❖[*1]>

sladolèdār {ledára (acc. = gen.) masc.} (lit. ice-cream man) *sl-sex* male looking for a loose woman, guy on the make <Slav❖[*1]>

slȁdostrasnē kùglice {NP} (lit. lust balls) *sl-sex* testicles, balls ☞ **kuglica**

sladúnac {a (acc. = gen.) masc.} (lit. sweetie) *sl-fea* very young female, little girl <Slav❖[*1]>

slágati *See the following*

- **slágati štrȉke** {VP} (lit. assemble knitting) *sl-sex* defecate
- **slágati vȁtru** {VP} (lit. assemble fire) *sl-fea* get angry, get hot

slàgātor *See the following*

- **slàgātor čȁpli** {NP} (lit. record assembler) *sl-music* DJ

slȁma {ē fem.} (lit. straw) *sl* money <Slav[*1]>

slȁmarica {ē fem.} (lit. straw-bed) *sl* head <Slav[*1]>

slámati {slâmām, slámajū biasp.} (lit. break) *sl* think, ponder <Slav[*1]>

slânā njúška {NP} (lit. salty snout) *sl-fea* unattractive face ☞ **njuška**

slànīk {slaníka masc.} (lit. salt shaker) *sl* clock, watch <Slav[*1]>

slánjača {ē fem.} (lit. the salty thing) *sl-arch* sea <Slav❖[*1]>

slásta {ē fem.} *sl* pastry shop <Slav✍>

slàstičār {a (acc. = gen.) masc.} (lit. pastry chef) *sl-sex* ***Fac*** male who engages in cunnilingus <Slav[*1]>

slât *See the following*

- **Slât ti jèbēm!** {S} *dia* ***Off*** used as a moderate curse, Fuck you!

slȁti *See the following*

- **slȁti pódmōrnice** {VP} (lit. send submarines) *sl* follow, go behind somebody
- **slȁti sȉsāvce da se pròtēgnū** {VP} (lit. send mammals to stretch themselves) *sl* send away, dismiss

slàtkara {ē fem.} *sl* pastry shop <Slav✍>

slàtkīć {slatkíća (acc. = gen.) masc.} (lit. sweetie) *sl-fea* attractive male <Slav[*1]>

slatkokȕrast {a, o adj.} (lit. sweet-pricked) *sl-sex* ***Fac-Obs*** inclined toward sexual intercourse <Slav❖[*1]>

slȁvica *See the following*

- **Slȁvicu ti jèbēm!** {S} (lit. I fuck your small saint's day!) *dia* ***Off*** used as a moderate curse, Fuck you!
- **Slȁvicu ti jèbēm što je slȁvīš!** {S} (lit. I fuck the small saint's day you celebrate!) *dia* ***Off*** used as a moderate curse, Fuck you!

Slávko {a neut.} *sl-fea* stupid or mentally deficient person <SlavO[*1]>

slȁvkobe {adj.} *sl-fea* foolish <Slav✍>

Slȁvōnka {ē fem.; Dat Slȁvōnki} (lit. woman from Slavonia *a region in Croatia*) *sl* thousand dinars; a thousand-dinar bill, a grand <SlavO[*1]>

slȁvūj {slavúja (acc. = gen.) masc.} (lit. nightingale) *sl-fea* slender female <Slav[*1]>

slépac {pca (acc. = gen.) masc.} (lit. blind) **1** **SerE** *sl-fea* person who is broke (financially) <Slav[*1]> **2** *sl-fea* senior citizen <Slav[*1]> **3** *sl-fea* ignorant <Slav[*1]>

slèpčina {ē fem. & masc.} (lit. the big blind) SerE *sl-fea* ignorant <Slav[*1]>

slevắčiti {lèvāčīm, čē perf.} SerE *col* do something superficially <Slav❖[*2]>

slídža {ē fem.} *sl-sports* collector card <Slav✍>

slȉkān {a, o adj.} (lit. pictured) *col* similar <Slav[*1]>

slȉkānje {a neut.} (lit. picturing) *col* showing in public <Slav[*1]>

slȉkār {a (acc. = gen.) masc.} (lit. painter) *sl-fea* naive male <Slav[*1]>

slȉkati se {ām, ajū imperf. intr.} (lit. have one's pictures taken) *col* show in public <Slav[*1]>

slȉke-bijélo {a neut.} *sl-gamble* a kind of game with collector cards where one has to guess if two cards will fall on the side where the picture is <Slav[*1]>

slȋnak {a masc.} *sl* cigarette butt <Slav❖*1>

slìnara {ē fem.} (lit. the place full of spit) *sl* ***Fac*** pastry shop <Slav❖*1>

slinàrkapa {ē fem.} (lit. saliva-cap) *sl-sex* ***Fac-Obs*** vagina, cunt <Slav❖*1>

slȋnavac {vca (acc. = gen.) masc.} *sl* boy, kid <Slav*1>

slȋnāvka {ē fem.} *sl* crying <Slav*1>

slȉnčār {a masc.} *sl* home <Slav❖*1>

slȋniti [1] {nīm, nē imperf. intr.} (lit. slobber) **a.** *sl* cry, shed tears, weep <Slav*1> **b.** *sl* talk persistently and meaninglessly, blabber, chatter <Slav*2>

slȋniti [2] {nīm, nē imperf.} (lit. slobber) *sl* kiss <Slav*1>

slíno {ē masc.} *sl-fea* dirty boy <Slav❖*1>

slípiti {pīm, pē imperf.} *sl* sleep, nap <Eng❖>

slístiti {slȋstīm, tē perf.} **a.** *col* destroy, ruin, kill: *slistiti dušmanina ruin the enemy* <Slav*1> **b.i.** *col* eat, devour: *slistiti cijelu tortu devour a whole cake* <Slav*2> **ii.** *col* spend (money, property, etc.): *slistiti dva miliona spend two million* <Slav*2>

Slòbist {a (acc. = gen.) masc.} (lit. follower of Slobodan Milošević) *sl-fea* ***Off*** Serb (person) <SlavO❖*1>

Slóbo {ē masc.} (lit. Slobodan Milošević) *sl-fea* ***Off*** Serb (person) <SlavO*1>

slobòda *See the following*

• **Slobòdē mi!** {S} (lit. I swear by my freedom!) *sl-crime* used to emphasize the truth of what has been said, I swear!

Slobòdan {a (acc. = gen.) masc.} /Slobòdān /bodána (acc. = gen.) masc./ (lit. Liberty) *sl-crime* ***Fac*** lawyer, attorney <SlavO*1>

slobòdānka [1] {ē fem.; Dat slobòdānki} (lit. freedom thing) *sl-crime* ***Iro*** police van, paddy wagon <Slav*1>

Slobòdānka [2] {ē fem.; Dat slobòdānki} (lit. Slobodan's *i.e. Slobodan Milošević* thing) *sl-crime* ***Fac-Der*** Politika daily newspaper <Slav*1>

slobodáriti {bòdārīm, rē imperf.} (lit. be free) *sl* wander, roam <Slav*1>

slȍbodnā fȁca {NP} (lit. free face) *sl-fea* insane person, nut case ☞ **faca**

slobòdnjāk {bodnjáka masc.} (lit. the free one) *sl-sports* free kick <Slav❖*1>

slobòdnjāk {bodnjáka (acc. = gen.) masc.; Voc slȍbodnjāče} (lit. free man) *sl-fea* self-employed person <Slav❖*1>

Sloboslâvija {ē fem.} (lit. Slobo *Slobodan Milošević* X Yugoslavia) *sl-polit* ***Iro-Fac*** Federal Republic of Yugoslavia <SlavO❖*1>

slòmiti *See the following*

• **slòmiti kȋčmu** {VP} (lit. break someone's backbone) *sl* beat up

• **slòmiti pȉčku** {VP} (lit. break the cunt) *sl* ***Obs*** beat up

slȍn {a (acc. = gen.) +ov (ext. pl) masc.; Nom Pl slònovi} (lit. elephant) **1** *sl-fea* stupid or mentally deficient person <Slav*1> **2** *sl-fea* obese person <Slav*1> **3** *sl-fea* clumsy person, klutz <Slav*1>

slòtija {ē fem.} *sl-fea* unattractive female

slȍvo {a neut.} (lit. word) *sl* journalist <Slav*1>

slȍženē kàmate {VP} (lit. compound interest rates) *sl* lending money to somebody ☞ **kamate**

slòžiti *See the following*

• **slòžiti prȋču** {VP} (lit. assemble a story) *sl* lie

• **slòžiti štósom** {VP} (lit. assemble with a trick) *sl* hit, punch

slòžiti se {žīm, že perf. intr.} (lit. compose oneself) **a.** *sl* fall down <Slav*1> **b.** *sl-drink* get very drunk <Slav*2>

slȕčaj *See the following*

• **ko nèsrećan slȕčāj** {PP} (lit. like an accident) *sl-fea* ***Der*** extremely unattractive

• **nèsrećan slȕčāj** {NP} (lit. accident) **1** *sl-fea* unattractive person **2** *sl-fea* poor person

slúga {ē fem. & masc.; Dat slúgi} (lit. servant) *sl-drink* waiter <Slav*1>

slùhista {ē masc.} (lit. the one with hearing) *col* male with talent for music <Slav❖*1>

slȕnjavica {ē fem.} (lit. the beslobbered one) *sl-sex* ***Fac-Obs*** vagina, cunt <Slav❖*1>

slȗpān {a, o adj.} (lit. crashed) *sl-fea* distorted <Slav*1>

slȕrpati {ām, ajū imperf.} (lit. slurp) *sl* kiss <Eng*1>

slȕšalica {ē fem.} (lit. headphone) *sl* ear <Slav*1>

slȕta {ē fem.} **a.** *sl-fea* untidy female, slob **b.** *sl-fea* unattractively dressed female

slȕzavica {ē fem.} (lit. the beslobbered one) *sl-sex* ***Fac-Obs*** vagina, cunt <Slav❖*1>

slúznica {ē fem.} (lit. the beslobbered one) *sl-sex* ***Fac-Obs*** vagina, cunt <Slav❖*1>

slȕžba {ē fem.} (lit. service) *col* job, gig <Slav*1>

sljàjpik {a masc.} *sl* wallet

smandȑljati {ām, ajū perf.} *col* do something superficially <Slav*1>

smánjiti *See the following*

• **smánjiti dȍživljāj** {VP} (lit. reduce the feeling) *sl-fea* calm down

smárati {smârām, smárajū imperf. intr.} (lit. make tired) **1** *sl* die, kick the bucket <Slav*1> **2** *sl-fea* annoy, bother, pester <Slav*1>

smárati se {smârām, smárajū imperf. intr.} *sl-arch* die, pass on <Slav*1>

smàriti {rīm, rē perf.} *sl-crime* steal, swipe

smȁzati {ažēm, ažū perf.} **a.** *col* eat, devour <Slav*1> **b.** *sl* beat up severely <Slav*2> **c.** *sl-sports* defeat <Slav*3>

smèćar {a (acc. = gen.) masc.} (lit. garbage man) *sl-mil* soldier on kp. <Slav✣*1>

smèjalica {ē fem.} (lit. laughter) **1** *sl* jocular word <Slav✣*1> **2** *sl* joke <Slav✣*1>

smȅstiti *See the following*

• **smȅstiti na elèktričnū stòlicu** {VP} (lit. put in the electric chair) SerE *sl* ***Fac*** force to get a haircut

smȅtnuti *See the following*

• **smȅtnuti s úma** {VP} (lit. remove from one's mind) *col* forget

smétnje *See the following*

• **tȅhničkē smétnje** {NP} (lit. technical interference) *sl-sex* ***Fac*** menstruation, period

smȉcati {ām, ajū imperf.} *sl* cheat, swindle <Slav*1>

smìntača {ē fem.} *sl-fea* unattractive female

smíriti *See the following*

• **smíriti ìgru** {VP} (lit. make the game less passionate) **a.** *sl-sports* slow the tempo of a game (e.g. in soccer) **b.** *sl-fea* calm down, cool off

smȉrk {a +ov (ext. pl) masc.; Nom Pl smìrkovi} *sl-crafts* sandpaper <Ger* >

smìslāš {misláša (acc. = gen.) masc.} (lit. the one with senses) **a.** *sl-fea* smart male, brain <Slav✣*1> **b.** *sl-fea* talented male <Slav✣*2>

smìslāškī {adv.} *sl-fea* skillfully <Slav✣*1>

smíšnica {ē fem.} (lit. funny thing) Med *sl-sex* ***App*** attractive female <Slav✣☞*1>

smjȅško {a masc.} (lit. laughter) *sl-fea* witty male, clever guy <Slav*1>

smǝkle {eta neut.} *sl-fea* stupid or mentally deficient person

smǝklje {eta neut.} *sl-fea* stupid or mentally deficient person

smlȁta {ē fem.} *sl-fea* ***Der*** clumsy person, klutz <Slav✣*1>

smlȁviti {vīm, vē perf.} *col* beat up severely <Slav>

smȍk {smòka +ov (ext. pl) masc.; Nom Pl smòkovi} *col-dia* greasy food <Slav>

smȍkī {īja masc.} /smòki/ (lit. Smokey) *sl-sex* ***Fac-Obs*** small penis <Eng*1>

smȍkić {a masc.} *sl-sex* ***Fac-Obs*** small penis <Eng☞*1>

smòkīng {a masc.} *sl* cigarette, smoke <Eng*1>

smòkovača {ē fem.} *sl-drink* fig brandy <Slav✣*1>

smȍkva {ē fem.} (lit. fig) *sl-sex* ***Obs*** vagina, cunt <Slav*1>

smȍkvica {ē fem.} (lit. small fig) *sl-sex* ***Fac*** male homosexual, gay <Slav*1>

smòla {ē fem.} (lit. resin) **a.** *col* accident <Slav*1> **b.** *col* bad luck <Slav*2>

smólja {ē masc.} **a.** *sl-fea* ***Der*** clumsy person, klutz <Slav☞*1> **b.** *sl-fea* ***Der*** untidy male, slob <Slav☞*2>

smȍljav {a, o adj.} *sl-fea* quiet <Slav✣*1>

smoljávko {a masc.} **a.** *sl-fea* ***Der*** clumsy person, klutz <Slav✣*1> **b.** *sl-fea* ***Der*** untidy male, slob <Slav✣*2>

smortírati {mòrtīrām, mortírajū perf. intr.} *sl-arch* get dark, approach evening <Ita✣*1>

smȍtān {a, o adj.} (lit. wrapped, rolled) **a.** *col* clumsy, klutzy <Slav*1> **b.i.** *sl-fea* unattractive, ugly <Slav*2> **ii.** *sl-fea* cheated, swindled <Slav*2> **iii.** *sl-crime* stolen, hot <Slav*2>

• **smȍtān ko sȁjla** {AdjP} (lit. as wrapped as a cord) *sl-fea* clumsy, klutzy

• **smȍtān ko šȕferica** {AdjP} *sl-fea* clumsy, klutzy

• **smȍtān ko záštitnā màska** {AdjP} (lit. as wrapped as a protective mask) *sl-fea* ***Fac*** clumsy, klutzy

smotanája {ē masc.} *sl-fea* ***Der*** clumsy person, klutz <Slav☞*1>

smotánko {a (acc. = gen.) masc.} *col* ***Der*** clumsy person, klutz <Slav✣*1>

smòtati {ām, ajū perf.} (lit. wrap, roll) **1** *sl-crime* steal, swipe <Slav*1> **2** *sl* cheat, swindle <Slav*1> **3** *sl-sex* engage in sexual intercourse with (of a male) <Slav*1>

smȍždīti {mȍždīm, dē perf.} (lit. take with the brains) *col* beat up severely <Slav✣>

smrâd {a +ov (ext. pl) masc.; Nom Pl smrȁdovi} (lit. stench) *col* ***Der*** worthless or despicable person <Slav*1>

smràdara {ē fem.} (lit. the stinky female) *sl-fea* messy woman, untidy female <Slav⁘*1>

smrádo {ē masc.} (lit. the stinky male) *sl-fea* ***Der*** worthless or despicable person <Slav⁘*1>

smȑčkati {ām, ajū imperf.} *col* sniff, smell <Slav⁘>

smr̀deti {dīm, dē imperf.} (lit. stink) *sl-fea* be boring <Slav*1>

smȑdež {a masc.} /smr̀dež/ *col* smell, stench <Slav⁘>

smr̀dibuba {ē fem.} (lit. stinking bug) *sl-sex* ***Fac*** prostitute, hooker <Slav*1>

smrdljévak {vka masc.} (lit. a stinking herb) *sl* ***Fac*** commercial (such as the one on TV) <Slav*1>

smrdljìčko {a (acc. = gen.) masc.} (lit. the stinking one) *sl-fea* moderately strong male <Slav☞*1>

smr̀dljiv {a, o adj.} (lit. stinking) **a.** *sl-fea* unattractive, ugly <Slav*1> **b.** *sl-fea* hostile <Slav*2>

smr̀dljivac {ljīvca (acc. = gen.) masc.} (lit. stinker) **a.** *sl-fea* unattractive male <Slav*1> **b.** *sl* cigarette, smoke <Slav*1>

smr̀dulja {ē fem.} (lit. the stenchy one) **1** *sl-sex* ***Obs*** vagina, cunt <Slav*1> **2** *sl-crime* ***Der*** prison cell <Slav*1>

smȑklje {eta neut.} *sl-arch* fool

smȑmuviti {vīm, vē perf.} *sl-sex* ***Obs*** engage in sexual intercourse with (of a male) <Slav☞*1>

smȑt *See the following*

• **pȍlāganā smȑt** {NP} (lit. slow death) *sl-fea* boring person, bore

smȑtnīk {a masc.} (lit. mortal) *sl-crime* capital punishment <Slav*1>

smȑtnjāk {smrtnjáka masc.} *sl-crime* capital punishment <Slav⁘*1>

smȓviti *See the following*

• **smȓviti ko béba zvȅčku** {VP} (lit. crush like a baby crush a rattle) **a.** *sl* destroy, ruin **b.** *sl* beat up

smȑznuti se *See the following*

• **dà se smȑznēš** {VP} (lit. it makes you freeze) *col* very frightening, very scary: *Film je bio da se smrzneš. The movie was very frightening.*

smúcati se {smûcām, smúcajū imperf. intr.} *col* wander, roam <Slav>

smûćen {a, o adj.} (lit. shaken) **a.** *sl-crime* ***Der*** insane, nuts <Slav*1> **b.** *sl-crime* ***Der*** slightly insane, nutty <Slav*2>

smûk {a (acc. = gen.) +ov (ext. pl) masc.; Nom Pl smúkovi} (lit. Aesculapius' snake) **1** *sl-drink* alcoholic, drunk <Slav*1> **2** *sl-fea* skillful person <Slav*1>

smȕkle {eta neut.} *sl-fea* stupid or mentally deficient person

smȕklje {eta neut.} *sl-fea* stupid or mentally deficient person

smùmlati {ām, ajū perf.} *col* mumble <Slav⁘>

smùmljati {ām, ajū perf.} *col* mumble <Slav⁘>

smûšen {a, o adj.} *col* clumsy, klutzy <Slav*1>

smùšujēnje {a neut.} *sl-crime* theft, swipe <Slav☞*1>

smùtljivac {vca masc.} **a.** *sl-sex* ***Fac*** bathroom <Slav*1> **b.** Cro *sl-sex* ***Fac*** name of a public toilet at Jelačić square in Zagreb, Croatia <Slav*2>

smȕvati {ām, ajū perf.} **a.** *col* persuade, convince <Slav*1> **b.** *col* cheat, swindle <Slav*2>

smȕvati se {ām, ajū perf. intr.} *sl* start dating a female or male <Slav*1>

snâ {aē fem.} [std. = snaja, snaha] *dia-col* sister-in-law <Slav☞>

snàgātor {a (acc. = gen.) masc.} (lit. the one with power) *col* troublemaker, rowdy, ruffian <Slav⁘*1>

snâjka {ē fem.; Dat snâjki} *col-dia* sister-in-law <Slav⁘>

snàjper {a (acc. = gen.) masc.} (lit. sniper) **a.** *col* sniper (person) <Eng*1> **b.** *sl-fea* person wearing eyeglasses, four-eyes <Eng*1>

snàjperi {pērā masc. pl.} (lit. snipers) *sl* eyeglasses <Eng*1>

snajpèrist {a (acc. = gen.) masc.} (lit. sniper) *sl-fea* male with eyeglasses, four-eyes <Eng⁘*1>

snàjpērka {ē fem.} (lit. sniper) *sl-fea* female with eyeglasses, four-eyes <Eng⁘*1>

snàjprka {ē fem.; Dat snàjprki} (lit. sniper) *sl-fea* female with eyeglasses, four-eyes <Eng⁘*1>

snàlaziti se {zīm, zē imperf. intr.} (lit. surmount difficulties) *sl-sex* ***Fac*** work as a prostitute <Slav*1>

snáša {ē fem.} *sl-fea* inhabitant of the countryside (female) <Slav*1>

snegòvila {ē fem.} (lit. snow fairy) SerE *dia-col* beauty <Slav⁘*1>

snȅka {ē fem.; Dat snȅki} *sl* evening

snȅkiti se {kīm, kē perf. intr.} *sl* get dark, approach evening

snȅska {ē fem.; Dat snȅski} *sl* mother <Slav✍*1>

snȅsko {a (acc. = gen.) masc.} *sl* father, dad <Slav✍*1>

snȉfā {excl.} *sl* used to express the unpleasant smelling sensation <Eng*1>

snȉfati {ām, ajū biasp.} (lit. sniff) *sl-drugs* sniff glue <Eng*1>

snȉfer {a (acc. = gen.) masc.} *sl-drugs* drug addict who sniffs narcotic drugs or glue <Eng*1>

snímati {nîmām, nímajū imperf. intr.} (lit. take pictures) **1** *sl* look, watch, scope out <Slav*1> **2** *col-dia* take off, strip <Slav*1>

snímiti {nîmīm, nîmē perf.} **1** *sl* see, observe <Slav*1> **2** *col-dia* take off, strip <Slav*1>

sȍba *See the following*

- **na sȍbu** {PP} (lit. to the room) **1** *sl-sex* ***Fac*** to sexual intercourse **2** *sl* on credit
- **sȍba zâvjerē** {NP} (lit. conspiracy room) *sl-sstu-sl-sex* school bathroom
- **šȍk sȍba** {NP} (lit. intensive care unit) *sl-sex* room intended for sexual intercourse

socijála {ē fem.} (lit. benefits) **1** *col* story intended to evoke compassion <Lat*1> **2** *col* social aid <Lat*1>

sȍcijalnē ȍči {NP} (lit. social eyes) *sl-fea* eyeglasses ☞ oko

sȍća {ē fem.} *sl* female <Slav*1>

sòfija {ē fem.} (lit. Sophia) *sl* sleeping <Ger*1>

sòfkara {ē fem.} *sl* eye (sight organ) <Gyp*1>

sȍfkati {ām, ajū imperf.} *sl* sleep, nap <Gyp>

sȍfke {eta neut.} *sl-fea* ***Der*** child from the countryside <SlavO*1>

sȍfra {ē fem.} BosM *col* table <NE>

sòfūn {sofúna masc.} *sl* bacon

sôjka {ē fem.; Dat sôjki} *sl* female <Slav*1>

sôk *See the following*

- **kȍrenov sôk** {NP} (lit. root juice) *sl-drink* hard liquor

sokàčara {ē fem.} (lit. the one from alleys) *sl-sex* ***Fac*** prostitute, streetwalker <NE❖*1>

sòkiš {a masc.} *sl* skyscraper <Fre✍>

sȍkō {ola (acc. = gen.) masc.} (lit. falcon) *sl* female <Slav*1>

sokòćalo {a neut.} *sl-arch* radio <Slav❖*1>

sokòćilo {a neut.} *sl-arch* car, wheels <Slav❖*1>

sokòlac {kóca (acc. = gen.) masc.} **1a.** *sl-fea* ***App*** skillful person <Slav*1> **b.** *sl-fea* joke teller <Slav*2> **2** *sl* female <Slav*1>

sokolàna {ē fem.} **1** *sl* low-class fun (carnivals, etc.) <Slav*1> **2** *sl* ecstasy <Slav*1>

sokoláner {a (acc. = gen.) masc.} (lit. falconer) *sl* female <Slav✍*1>

sôl {a +ov (ext. pl) masc.; Nom Pl sòlovi} *sl-crime* prison cell <Slav*1>

- **Sôl ti jèbēm!** {S} (lit. I screw your salt!) *dia* ***Off*** used as a weak curse, Screw you!

sòlara {ē fem.} *sl-crime* prison cell <Slav*1>

sòlčica *See the following*

- **Sòlčicu ti jèbēm!** {S} (lit. I fuck your small salt!) *dia* ***Off*** used as a moderate curse, Fuck you!

sôldi {ā fem. pl.} Med *dia* money <Ita>

sȍler {a (acc. = gen.) masc.} (lit. soloist) **a.** *sl-fea* lonely male <Ita❖*1> **b.** *sl-fea* stranger (male) <Ita❖*2>

sȍlerica {ē fem.} (lit. soloist) **a.** *sl-fea* stranger (female) <Ita❖*1> **b.** *sl-fea* lonely female <Ita❖*2>

sȍlīdan {dna, dno adj.} *sl-fea* reliable <Lat*1>

sȍlidno {adv.} *sl-fea* rather well: *uraditi posao solidno do a job rather well* <Lat*1>

solírānje {a neut.} (lit. playing solo) *sl* being lonely <Ita*1>

solírati {sòlīrām, solírajū imperf.} (lit. play solo) **a.** *sl* be alone <Ita*1> **b.i.** *sl-drink* drink alone <Ita*2> **ii.** *sl-sex* urinate, piss <Ita*2>

sȍlist {a (acc. = gen.) masc.} (lit. soloist) *sl-fea* lonely male <Ita*1>

sòlista *See the following*

- **sòlista na fȕćkāljki** {NP} (lit. whistle soloist) *sl-crime* policeman, cop

sȍlistica {ē fem.} /solȉstica/ (lit. soloist) *sl-fea* lonely female <Ita*1>

solȉtērka {ē fem.} (lit. skyscraper woman) *sl-fea* tall and slender female, beanpole <Fre❖*1>

sòliti *See the following*

- **sòliti pȁmēt** {VP} (lit. salt one's mind) *col* preach, patronize

sôlo {adj.} (lit. solo) *col* alone, unaccompanied, solo <Ita*1>

sôlotrȉnker {a (acc. = gen.) masc.} *sl-drink* alcoholic who drinks alone <Ger>

sȍm [1] {sòma (acc. = gen.) +ov (ext. pl) masc.; Nom Pl sòmovi} (lit. catfish) *sl-fea* stupid or mentally deficient person <Slav[*1]>

sȍm [2] {sòma +ov (ext. pl) masc.; Nom Pl sòmovi} (lit. catfish) **a.** *sl* thousand dinars; a thousand-dinar bill, a grand <Slav[*1]> **b.i.** *sl* one dinar; a one-dinar coin <Slav[*2]> **ii.** *sl* ten paras; a ten-para coin <Slav[*2]> **iii.** *sl* ten dinars; a ten-dinar coin <Slav[*2]> **iv.** *sl* thousand <Slav[*2]>

somotnjáci {njákā masc. pl.} *col* tight velvet trousers <Ger⁘[*1]>

somòtnjare {a fem. pl.} *col* velvet trousers <Ger⁘[*1]>

sòmovac {vca (acc. = gen.) masc.} *sl-fea* very affluent male <Slav⁘[*1]>

sȍmovati {ujēm, ujū imperf.} (lit. catfish) *sl* pay (bills, etc.): *sȍmovati račun u restoranu pay the check in the restaurant* <Slav⁘[*1]>

sòmūn {somúna masc.} **a.** BosM *col* flat Near Eastern bread <NE> **b.** *sl-sex* buttocks, butt <NE[*1]>

somùnjara {ē fem.} *sl* ***Fac*** bakery <NE⁘[*1]>

sȍngati {ām, ajū biasp.} *sl-music* sing <Eng⁘>

sȍnger {a (acc. = gen.) masc.} *sl-music* singer <Eng⁘[*1]>

sòptānje {a neut.} *col* panting <Slav>

sòptati {tīm, tē imperf.} *col* pant <Slav>

sȍptav {a, o adj.} *col* panting <Slav>

sòptiti {tīm, tē imperf.} *col* pant <Slav>

sôrta *See the following*

- **Sôrtu ti pòganū jèbēm!** {S} (lit. I fuck your dirty kind!) *col* ***Off*** used as a strong curse, Fuck you!

sôs {a +ov (ext. pl) masc.; Nom Pl sósovi} (lit. sauce) **a.** *col* unpleasant situation, bummer <Fre[*1]> **b.** *col* very difficult situation <Fre[*2]>

sȍška {ē fem.; Dat sȍški} /sòška/ *sl* passport <Rus[*1]>

sȍšpa {ē fem.; perm} /sòšpa /sòšapa fem./ *sl* passport <Lat✍>

sóva {ē fem.} (lit. owl) **1a.** *sl* sleeping <Gyp> **b.** *sl* prostitute, hooker <Gyp[*1]> **c.** *sl-sex* female <Gyp[*2]> **2** *sl-fea* inhabitant of the countryside, hick, bumpkin <Slav[*1]> **3** *sl-fea* senior citizen <Slav[*1]> **4** *sl-fea* person wearing eyeglasses, four-eyes <Slav[*1]>

sòvān {sována masc.} *sl* sleeping <Gyp⁘[*1]>

sòvārnik {a masc.} (lit. owl-place) *sl* bedroom <Gyp[*1]>

sòvati {sȕjēm, sȕjū imperf.} [std. = psovati] *col-dia* curse <Slav✍>

sòvāž {sováža masc.} *sl* sleeping <Slav✍[*1]>

sôvčiti {čīm, čē imperf.} (lit. owl) *sl* sleep, nap <Gyp⁘[*1]>

sòvēljka {ē fem. & masc.} *sl-arch* dangerous female

sòvēr {sovéra (acc. = gen.) masc.} *sl-crime* night train thief <Gyp⁘[*1]>

sovijáner {a masc.} *sl* sleeping <Gyp✍[*1]>

Sovȉljara {ē fem.} Cro *sl-drink* name of a bar at the Central Station in Zagreb, Croatia <Gyp✍[*1]>

sòvīnger *See the following*

- **sòvīnger na òfīnger** {NP} (lit. sleeping on a hanger) *sl* sleeping on the upper bunk

sòvisati {išēm, išū imperf.} *sl* sleep, nap <Gyp⁘[*1]>

sòviška {ē fem.; Dat sòviški} *sl* sleeping <Gyp✍[*1]>

sóviti {vīm, vē imperf.} (lit. owl) *sl* sleep, nap <Gyp⁘[*1]>

sôvka {ē fem.} *sl* sleeping <Gyp⁘[*1]>

sȍvkānje {a neut.} *sl* sleeping <Gyp⁘[*1]>

sȍvkati {ām, ajū imperf.} (lit. owl) *sl* sleep, nap <Gyp⁘[*1]>

sȍvra *See the following*

- **Sȍvru ti jèbēm!** {S} (lit. I fuck your table!) *dia* ***Off*** used as a moderate curse, Fuck you!

sovùljaga {ē fem.; Dat sovùljagi} *sl-fea* unattractive female <Slav[*1]>

spàcati {ām, ajū perf.} *sl* destroy, ruin

spáča {ē masc.} *sl-auto* small Citroen (make of car) <BN✍>

spàček {a (acc. = gen.) masc.} *sl-auto* small Citroen (make of car) <BN✍>

spȁdalo {a neut.} *col* ***Der*** **a.** lazy or shiftless person, bum, good for nothing <Slav⁘[*1]> **b.** funny person, clown <Slav⁘[*2]>

spagìtār {gitára masc.} *sl-auto* Citroen (make of car)

spȁguār {a (acc. = gen.) masc.} (lit. spaček *a small Citroen car* X Jaguar (a luxurious car)) *sl-auto* small Citroen (make of car) <BN✍[*1]>

spájati {spâjām, spájajū imperf.} (lit. connect) *sl* understand, get it <Slav[*1]>

- **spájati kônce** {VP} (lit. connect the threads) *sl* understand, get it

spȁjk {a +ov (ext. pl) masc.; Nom Pl spàjkovi} *sl-auto* small Citroen (make of car) <BN✍>

spȁjker {a masc.} *sl-fea* boaster, braggart, blowhard <Eng[*1]>

spâk {a +ov (ext. pl) masc.; Nom Pl spákovi} *sl-auto* small Citroen (make of car) <BN✍>

spakírati {pàkīrām, pakírajū perf.} (lit. pack) **a.** *sl* falsely incriminate, frame <Ger❖*1> **b.** *sl* blame, accuse <Ger❖*2> **c.** *sl-crime* imprison, put away <Ger❖*3>

spȁkovati {kujēm, kujū perf.} (lit. pack) **1** *sl* falsely incriminate, frame <Ger❖*1> **2** *sl* beat up <Ger❖*1>

spâle {eta neut.} *sl-auto* small Citroen (make of car) <BN✍>

spáliti {spâlīm, lē perf.} (lit. burn) *sl* spend money, burn money <Slav*1>

spànđati se {ām, ajū imperf. intr.} /spànđati se/ **a.** *sl* date, go out with <Ger❖*1> **b.** *sl* spend time together with

spȁnjga {ē fem.; Dat spȁnjgi} *sl-crime* handcuffs, cuffs <Ger❖*1>

spȁnjka {ē fem.} *sl-crime* handcuffs, cuffs <Ger❖*1>

spȁpštiti {šīm, še perf.} *dia* support, cheer for

spȁrkati {ām, ajū imperf.} (lit. spark) *sl-sex* ***Obs*** engage in sexual intercourse with (of a male) <Eng❖*1>

spȁrkati se {ām, ajū perf. intr.} (lit. park oneself) *sl-auto* park <Eng❖*1>

sparȕtati {ām, ajū perf.} *sl-crime* steal, swipe <Slav✍*1>

spȁsoje {a (acc. = gen.) masc.} *sl-auto* ***Fac*** small Citroen (make of car) <SlavO*1>

Spâsovdan {dāna masc.} (lit. Salvation) *sl* ***Fac*** payday <SlavO*1>

spàvāćā {ē fem. (adj. decl.)} (lit. the sleeping one) *col* bedroom <Slav*1>

spavánac {nca masc.} **a.** *sl* sleeping <Slav✍> **b.** *sl* hit, punch <Slav✍*1>

spavánjac {njca masc.} *sl* sleeping <Slav✍>

spàvātor {a (acc. = gen.) masc.} *sl* sleepy person <Slav✍*1>

spȅcijalnē ȍči {NP} (lit. special eyes) *sl-fea* eyeglasses ☞ oko

spȅcijālno {adv.} *col* in particular <Lat>

spèkīrān {a, o adj.} *sl-crime* caught, busted <Ger❖*1>

spelávati {spèlāvām, spelávajū imperf.} Cro *sl* make happy <Slav*1>

spèngati {ām, ajū perf.} *sl-crime* arrest <Ita*1>

spèrmara {ē fem.} (lit. the one who is full of sperm) **a.** *sl-sex* ***Fac-Obs*** prostitute, hooker <Gre❖*1> **b.** *sl-sex* ***Fac-Obs*** sexually aroused female, hot chick <Gre❖*2>

spèrmātorka {ē fem.; Dat spèrmātorki} (lit. the one who is full of sperm) **a.** *sl-sex* ***Fac-Obs*** prostitute, hooker <Slav❖*1> **b.** *sl-sex* ***Fac-Obs*** loose woman, slut <Slav❖*2> **c.** *sl-sex* ***Fac-Obs*** sexually aroused female, hot chick <Slav*3>

spèrmić {a masc.} /spèrmīć/ (lit. spermer) **1a.** *sl-sex* ***Fac-Obs*** masturbator (male) <Slav❖*1> **b.** *sl* ***Fac-Obs*** boy, kid <Slav❖*2> **2** *sl-drink* ***Fac-Obs*** name of a bar at Ilica and Marinkovićeva streets in Zagreb, Croatia <Slav*1>

spèrmuša {ē fem.} (lit. spermer) **a.** *sl-sex* ***Fac-Obs*** prostitute, hooker <Slav❖*1> **b.** *sl-sex* ***Fac-Obs*** sexually aroused female, hot chick <Slav*2>

sperȕtati {ām, ajū perf. intr.} *sl-arch* steal, swipe <Slav*1>

spètljati se {ām, ajū imperf. intr.} *col* start dating a female or male <Slav*1>

spȅvati {ām, ajū perf.} (lit. compose) SerE *sl* talk, have a conversation <Slav*1>

spȉčiti {čīm, čē perf.} (lit. cunt) *sl* break <Slav❖*1>

spȉčiti se {čīm, čē perf. intr.} (lit. cunt to) *sl* ***Obs*** agree <Slav*1>

spȉčkati {ām, ajū perf.} (lit. cunt out) **a.** *sl* spend (money, property, etc.) <Slav❖*1> **b.** *sl* destroy, ruin <Slav❖*2> **c.** *sl* lose <Slav❖*3>
• **Spȉčkaću te!** {S} (lit. I will cunt you!) *col* ***Off*** used as a threat, Fuck you!

spîd {a +ov (ext. pl) masc.; Nom Pl spídovi} (lit. speed) **1a.** *sl-drugs* speed (auto, etc.) <Eng*1> **b.i.** *sl-drugs* intake of LSD <Eng*2> **ii.** *sl-drugs* narcotic drug, dope <Eng*2> **2** *sl-auto* speed (auto, etc.) <Eng>

spídērka {ē fem.; Dat spídērki} (lit. speeder) *sl-fea* troublemaker, rowdy, ruffian <Eng❖*1>

spidírati {ām, ajū biasp.} *sl-auto* speed (auto, etc.) <Eng❖*1>

spȉka {ē fem.; Dat spȉki} **a.** *sl* speech <Eng> **b.i.** *sl* one's style of expression <Eng*1> **ii.** *sl* the content of what has been said <Eng*1>

spìkati {ām, ajū imperf.} *sl* speak <Eng❖>

spìkl {a +ov (ext. pl) masc.} **a.** *sl* talk, have a conversation <Eng✍*1> **b.** *sl* language <Eng✍*2>

spirȉtuša {ē fem.} *sl-drink* strong brandy <Lat❖*1>

spôj {a +ev (ext. pl) masc.; Nom Pl spòjevi} (lit. connection) *sl* dating, going out with <Slav*1>
• **kràtkī spôj** {NP} (lit. short circuit) **1** *col* misunderstanding **2** *sl* memory blackout

spòjiti {jīm, jē perf.} (lit. connect) *sl* meet a boyfriend or girlfriend <Slav*1>

spôjka {ē fem.} (lit. clutch) **1** *sl* dating, going out with <Slav*1> **2** *sl-sex* sexual intercourse <Slav*2>

spȍmenīk {a masc.} (lit. monument) *sl-fea* ***Fac*** belly, stomach, tummy <Slav*1>

• **spȍmenīk pȁlōm herόju** {NP} (lit. a monument to a fallen hero) **1** *sl-fea* male with a large belly **2** *sl-sex* impotent male

sponzòruša {ē fem.} *sl-fea* ***Fac*** female who dates affluent males <Lat❖*1>

spȍr *See the following*

• **zàmr̄šen spȍr** {NP} (lit. complicated argument) *sl* pyrrhic victory

spòrāć {sporáća (acc. = gen.) masc.} *sl-fea* slow person, slowpoke <Slav❖*1>

spòrāć {sporáća masc.} *sl* slow dance <Slav❖*1>

spȍrtsnjāk {a masc.} *sl-auto* sports car <Eng❖*1>

spotàpiknuti {nēm, nū perf.} *sl-sex* ***Obs*** engage in sexual intercourse with (of a male) <Slav☞*1>

sprášiti {sprâšīm, šē perf.} (lit. dust) **a.** *sl* stick in, insert <Slav*1> **b.** *sl-sex* engage in sexual intercourse with (of a male) <Slav*2>

spȑcati {ām, ajū perf.} **a.** *sl-sex* ***Obs*** engage in sexual intercourse with (of a male) <Slav*1> **b.i.** *sl* ***Obs*** be cheated, be swindled <Slav*2> **ii.** *sl* spend (money, property, etc.) <Slav*2>

spȑčiti {čīm, čē perf.} *sl-sex* ***Obs*** engage in sexual intercourse with (of a male) <Slav*1>

spȑćiti {ćīm, ćē perf.} *sl-sex* ***Obs*** engage in sexual intercourse with (of a male) <Slav*1>

sprdàčina {ē fem.} *sl* joking with, fooling with <Slav*1>

spȑdati se {ām, ajū imperf. intr.} *sl* joke <Slav*1>

spr̀diti {dīm, dē perf.} (lit. fart) *sl-sex* ***Obs*** engage in sexual intercourse with (of a male) <Slav*1>

sprόvod {a masc.} (lit. funeral) *sl* ***Iro*** wedding <Slav*1>

Spȑporīm ti ga! {S} (lit. I bang it to you!) *dia* ***Off*** used as a moderate curse, Fuck you! ☞ sprporiti

spȑporiti *See the following*

• **Spȑporīm ti ga!** {S} (lit. I bang it to you!) *dia* ***Off*** used as a moderate curse, Fuck you!

spȑžiti {žīm, žē perf.} (lit. burn) *sl-sex* ***Obs*** engage in sexual intercourse with (of a male) <Slav*1>

spȕcati {ām, ajū perf.} **a.** *sl* hit, punch <Slav*1> **b.** *sl-sex* engage in sexual intercourse with (of a male) <Slav*2>

spȕst {a +ov (ext. pl) masc.; Nom Pl spùstovi} (lit. downhill) *sl* false incrimination, frame <Slav*1>

spùstiti {spȕstīm, tē perf.} /spústiti/ (lit. put down) **a.** *sl-sex* ***Obs*** engage in sexual intercourse with (of a male) <Slav*1> **b.** *sl* cheat, swindle <Slav*2> **c.** *sl* take revenge <Slav*3> **d.** *sl* outwit, outsmart <Slav*4>

• **spùstiti dùrbīn** {VP} (lit. put one's binoculars down) *sl-fea* suffer from depression

• **spùstiti rolètnu** {VP} (lit. put one's blinds down) *sl* be beaten up

spȕšiti {šīm, šē perf.} (lit. put down) *sl* be beaten up <Slav☞*1>

spúštalica {ē fem.} **a.** *sl* a joke about somebody <Slav*1> **b.** *sl* effective reply <Slav*2>

spúštanje *See the following*

• **spúštānje u pòdrum** {NP} (lit. descent to the basement) **1** *sl-sex* fellatio **2** *sl-sex* cunnilingus

spûž {a (acc. = gen.) +ev (ext. pl) masc.; Nom Pl spȕževi} [std. = puž] *dia-col* snail (the animal) <Slav☞>

spȕžva {ē fem.} (lit. sponge) *sl-fea* person with a good memory <Slav*1>

• **spȕžva za prȁt prόzore** {NP} (lit. window-washing sponge) *sl-sex* penis of an elderly male

srâč {sráča (acc. = gen.) +ev (ext. pl) masc.; Nom Pl sráčevi} (lit. shitter) **a.** *sl-fea* ***Der-Obs*** extremely talkative person, chatterbox <Slav❖*1> **b.** *sl-fea* ***Der-Obs*** boring person, bore <Slav❖*2>

srâć {sráća +ev (ext. pl) masc.; Nom Pl sráćevi} *sl-sex* ***Obs*** defecator <Slav❖*1>

sràćara {ē fem.} (lit. shitter) *sl-sex* ***Obs*** buttocks, butt <Slav❖*1>

srȁćka {ē fem.; Dat srȁćki} **a.** *sl-sex* ***Obs*** diarrhea, runs, trots <Slav> **b.** *sl-sex* ***Obs*** worthless trifle <Slav*1>

srȁćkalica {ē fem.} **a.** *sl-sex* ***Obs*** diarrhea, runs, trots <Slav> **b.i.** *sl-sex* ***Fac-Obs*** prolonged and meaningless talk, blabber, chatter <Slav*1> **ii.** *sl-fea* worthless trifle <Slav*1>

srȁćkati {ām, ajū biasp.} **a.** *sl-sex* ***Obs*** defecate in small quantities <Slav> **b.** *sl* ***Fac-Obs*** talk persistently and meaninglessly, blabber, chatter <Slav*1>

sráćnica {ē fem.} (lit. shitter) **1** *sl-sex* ***Obs*** buttocks, butt <Slav❖*1> **2** *sl-sex* ***Obs*** bathroom <Slav❖*1>

srȁlja {ē fem.} (lit. shitter) *sl-sex* ***Obs*** female bathroom attendant <Slav❖*1>

srâm *See the following*

• **Srâm te bílo!** {S} (lit. Shame on you!) *col* used as a reprimand, Shame on you!

sramòtnjāk {motnjáka masc.} (lit. the one who is ashamed) *sl-sex* ***Fac-Obs*** penis, dick, prick <Slav[*1]>

sránje [1] {excl.} *col* used to express negative attitude, shit, bullshit, nonsense <Slav>

sránje [2] {a neut.} **a.** *col* excrement <Slav> **b.** *col* unpleasant situation, bummer <Slav[*1]> **c.** *col* prolonged and meaningless talk, blabber, chatter <Slav[*2]> **d.i.** *col* lie <Slav[*4]> **ii.** *col* boring thing or event <Slav[*4]> **iii.** *col* stupidity, lack of intelligence <Slav[*4]>

• **Bȉće sránja!** {S} (lit. Shit will happen!) *sl-crime* used to refer to the approach of a dangerous situation, It is getting dangerous!

• **flášīrāno sránje** {NP} (lit. bottled shit) *sl* ***Fac-Obs*** diarrhea, runs, trots

• **Ȉstō sránje!** {NP} (lit. Same shit!) *col* ***Obs*** used to refer to lack of any change, Same old shit!

• **Ȉstō sránje drȕgō pȁkovānje!** {NP} (lit. Same shit in another package!) *col* ***Obs*** used to refer to lack of any change, Same old shit, just looks different!

• **sránje kroz apotèkarskī lêvak** {NP} (lit. taking a shit through a pharmaceutical funnel) **SerE** *col* very difficult situation, deep shit

• **sránje kroz gûstō grânje** {NP} (lit. taking a shit through thick bushes) *col* very difficult situation, deep shit

• **têškō sránje** {NP} (lit. heavy shit) *sl-fea* very difficult situation, deep shit

srâsti {srástēm, stū perf. irreg.} *sl* smell, stink <Slav[*1]>

srȁti {sȅrēm, sȅrū imperf.} **a.** *col* defecate, shit <Slav> **b.** *col* talk persistently and meaninglessly, bullshit <Slav[*1]> **c.i.** *col* be boring: *Toliko je srao da sam skoro zaspao. He was so boring that I almost fell asleep.* <Slav[*2]> **ii.** preach, give lectures to <Slav[*2]> **iii.aa.** persuade, convince <Slav[*2]> **bb.** lie <Slav[*3]>

• **Sȅrēm ti se na!** {S} (lit. I shit on that!) *col* ***Off*** used to express indifference, I don't give a shit!

• **Sȅrem ti se u [NOUN:ACC]!** {LSF} (lit. I shit in [NP:ACC]) *col* used to express disrespect or dissatisfaction, Fuck it!: *Serem ti se u taj plan. Shit on that plan of yours.*

• **Ne sȅri!** {S} (lit. Don't you bullshit!) **1** *col* ***Off*** used as a strong curse, Fuck you! **2** *col* used to silence one's interlocutor, Shut up! **3** *col* used to refer to strong disbelief, Don't bullshit me!

• **Nèmōj mi srȁt!** {S} (lit. Don't bullshit me!) *col* used to refer to strong disbelief, Don't bullshit me!

• **Nèmōj srȁt!** {S} (lit. Don't bullshit!) *col* used to refer to strong disbelief, Don't bullshit me!

• **srȁti flánce** {VP} (lit. shit the latest fashion) **1** *sl-fea* ***Obs*** overdo **2** cry, shed tears, weep

• **srȁti gȁlebove** {VP} (lit. shit gulls) *sl-fea* ***Obs*** talk persistently and meaninglessly, bullshit

• **srȁti krȇč** {VP} (lit. shit lime) *sl-fea* ***Obs*** talk persistently and meaninglessly, bullshit

• **srȁti kvȁke** {VP} (lit. shit door-knobs) **1** *sl-fea* ***Obs*** talk persistently and meaninglessly, bullshit **2** *sl* lie

• **srȁti òkove** {VP} (lit. shit chains) **1** *sl-fea* ***Obs*** talk persistently and meaninglessly, bullshit **2** lie

• **srȁti se u [NOUN:ACC]** {LSF} (lit. shit in [NOUN: ACC]) *sl-fea* be indifferent toward, be uninterested in: *Serem se ja u te propise. I don't give a shit about those rules.*

• **srȁti tànkē drȇke** {VP} (lit. shit thin hairs) *sl-fea* eat insufficiently

Sȓbēnda {ē masc.} **a.** *sl-fea* ***App*** real Serb, one who behaves in compliance with ethnic customs <SlavO⁘> **b.** *sl-fea* Serb (person) <SlavO⁘[*1]>

Sȓbin {a (acc. = gen.) masc.} (lit. Serb) *sl-sstu* Serbian language teacher (male) <SlavO[*1]>

• **pòtūrčenī Sȓbin** {NP} (lit. a Serb converted into a Turk) *sl-fea* ***Off*** Bosnian Muslim

srbočȅtnīk {a (acc. = gen.) masc.} *sl-fea* ***Off*** Serb (person) <Slav⁘[*1]>

srbomŕzac {sca (acc. = gen.) masc.} *col* Serb hater, Serb basher <Slav⁘>

Srboslâvija {ē fem.} (lit. Serbs X Yugoslavia) *sl-polit* ***Fac*** former Yugoslavia <Slav✍[*1]>

sȑboždēr {a (acc. = gen.) masc.} (lit. Serb eater) *col* Serb hater, Serb basher <Slav⁘[*1]>

sȑboždēran {rna, rno adj.} (lit. Serb-eating) *col* hating Serbs <Slav⁘[*1]>

sȑboždērskī {ā, ō adj.} (lit. Serb-eating) *col* hating Serbs <Slav⁘[*1]>

sȓce [1] *See the following*

• **sȓce[ADJ:VOC]** {NP} (lit. [ADJ:VOC] heart) *col* ***Fam*** used to address one's interlocutor in an intimate manner, dear heart: *sȓce dȅdino honey, darling*

• **sȓce mòje** {NP} (lit. my heart) *col* used to address one's interlocutor in an intimate manner, dear heart

• **Sȓce[PRON:DAT] je nà mjestu** {S} (lit. [POS: PRON] is at its place) *col* used to refer to satisfaction: *Da li ti je sad srce na mjestu? Are you satisfied now?*

• **U sȓce te jèbēm!** {S} (lit. I fuck you in your heart!) *col* ***Off*** used as a moderate curse, Fuck you!

sȑce [2] {excl.} (lit. my heart) *col* ***Fam*** used to address a person in an intimate manner, dear heart <Slav[*1]>

sȑča {ē fem.} /sȓča/ *col* broken glass <NE>

sȑčka {ē fem.} *sl* heart attack <Slav[*1]>

sȑdžba {ē fem.} /sŕdžba/ *col* anger <Slav>

srèbro *See the following*

• **stârō srèbro** {NP} (lit. old silver) *sl-sex* sexually experienced female

srȅćno {adv.} [std. = srećno] *col* happily <Slav✍>

srȅća *See the following*

• **kûrčevē srȅćē** {NP} (lit. of prick's happiness) *col* ***Obs*** not lucky at all

• **nà sreću** {PP} (lit. to luck) *sl-crime* without being observed

• **Nȅk vam je sà srećōm!** {S} (lit. Let it be with happiness to you!) *col* used to express favorable attitude toward, Good luck!

• **srȅćo mòja** {NP} (lit. my luck) *col* used to address one's interlocutor in an intimate manner, dear heart

• **Srȅću ti jèbēm!** {S} (lit. I fuck your luck!) *col-dia* ***Off*** used as a moderate curse, Fuck you!

srȅćan *See the following*

• **srȅćan ko kȕče** {AdjP} (lit. as happy as a dog) Ser *sl-fea* very happy

Srȅćko {a (acc. = gen.) masc.} (lit. Lucky) *sl-sex* ***Fac-Obs*** young male's penis <SlavO[*1]>

srȅćo {excl.} (lit. my happiness) *col* ***Fam*** used to address a person in an intimate manner, honey <Slav[*1]>

srȅćo mòja {NP} (lit. my luck) *col* used to address one's interlocutor in an intimate manner, honey ☞ **sreća**

Srȅću ti jèbēm! {S} (lit. I fuck your luck!) *col-dia* ***Off*** used as a moderate curse, Fuck you! ☞ **sreća**

sréditi {srêdīm, dē perf.} (lit. settle) **a.** *col* arrange for <Slav[*1]> **b.** *col* beat up severely, trash <Slav[*2]> **c.** *col* destroy, ruin <Slav[*3]>

sréditi se {srêdīm, dē perf. intr.} (lit. settle) *sl-drugs* take narcotic drugs intravenously, mainline, shoot up <Slav[*1]>

srȅdnja žȁlōst {NP} (lit. average sadness) *col* poor, of rather low quality ☞ **žalost**

srèdstvo *See the following*

• **srèdstvo kȍntra ûma** {NP} (lit. means against mind) *sl* ***Fac*** headache pill

srêm {sréma (acc. = gen.) +ov (ext. pl) masc.; Nom Pl srémovi} *sl-sports* coach

srȅtan *See the following*

• **ko svȉ srȅtni** {PP} (lit. like everybody is happy) *col* used to refer to an usually illegal or inappropriate action performed without any hesitation: *On, ko svi sretni, počeo da puši u kupeu za nepušače. He started to smoke in a non-smoking compartment just like that.*

srȉtan {tna, tno adj.} [std. = sretan] Med *dia* happy <Slav✍>

sȓk [1] {excl.} *col* slurp <Slav>

sȓk [2] {a +ov (ext. pl) masc.; Nom Pl sŕkovi} *col* slurp <Slav>

sȑkāj {a masc.} *col* slurp <Slav>

sŕkānje {a neut.} *col* slurping <Slav>

sŕkati {sȓkām, sŕkajū imperf.} //sȓčēm, sȓčū imperf./ **a.** *col* slurp <Slav> **b.** *sl* sniff <Slav[*1]>

sŕknuti {sȓknēm, nū perf.} **a.** *col* slurp <Slav> **b.** *sl* sniff, snort <Slav[*1]>

sȑkūt {a masc.} *col* slurp <Slav>

srkùtānje {a neut.} **a.** *col* slurping <Slav> **b.** *sl* sniffing <Slav[*1]>

srkùtati {sȑkućēm, ućū imperf.} **a.** *col* slurp <Slav❖> **b.** *sl* sniff, snort <Slav❖[*1]>

sŕpa {ē fem.} *sl-sstu* Serbian language (school course) <Slav✍>

Sȓpkinja {ē fem.} (lit. Serbian) *sl-sstu* Serbian-language teacher (female) <SlavO[*1]>

sȓpskī kljûč {NP} (lit. the Serbian wrench) *sl-sex* penis ☞ **ključ**

sȓpskī rùlēt {NP} (lit. Serbian roulette) *sl* a game where one speeds through a red light at a busy intersection ☞ **rulet**

sȓpskī stôund {NP} (lit. Serbian stoned) *sl* ***Col*** afternoon siesta ☞ **stound**

srȕšiti {šīm, šē perf.} (lit. destroy) **a.** *sl* arrange for <Slav[*1]> **b.** *sl* trick, cheat, swindle <Slav[*2]> **c.** *sl-music* conduct (philharmonic, etc.) <Slav[*2]>

sȓž *See the following*

• **do sȓži** {PP} (lit. to the bone marrow) *col* completely, totally, to the bone: *pokvaren do srži completely ill-natured*

stùmbati se {ām, ajū perf. intr.} *col* roll down a slope <NE❖>

stàcīn {stacína masc.} Med *dia* station, stop (bus, train, streetcar, etc.) <Ita>

stȁf {a +ov (ext. pl) masc.; Nom Pl stȁfovi} (lit. stuff) *sl-drugs* hashish, hash <Eng*1>

stȁja {ē fem.} (lit. barn) *sl-crime* prison cell <Slav*1>

stàjati *See the following*

- **stàjati ko pȉletu còkule** {VP} (lit. fit like hard shoes on a chicken) *sl-fea* be unsuitable
- **stàjati ko pȉletu sȉse** {VP} (lit. fit like tits on a chicken) *sl-fea* ***Fac-Obs*** be unsuitable

stȁjkati {ām, ajū imperf.} **1** *sl* work, labor <Slav❖*1> **2** *sl* stay, linger <Slav❖*1>

stàkla {kālā neut. pl.} *sl* eyeglasses <Slav*1>

stȁklenā nògica {NP} (lit. glass little leg) *sl-auto* bus station ☞ **nogica**

Staklénac {nca masc.} (lit. the glass one) **Ser** *sl* name of a shopping mall at Republika Square in Belgrade, Serbia <Slav❖*1>

staklénac [1] {nca (acc. = gen.) masc.} (lit. the glass one) **a.** *sl-fea* intellectual <Slav❖*1> **b.** *sl-fea* incompetent boxer <Slav❖*1> **c.** *sl-sex* prostitute, hooker <Slav❖*1>

staklénac [2] {nca masc.} **a.** *sl-sports* glass marble (the toy) <Slav❖*1> **b.** *sl* glass eye <Slav❖*2>

stàklēnka {ē fem.} (lit. jar) *sl* eye (sight organ) <Slav❖*1>

staklènjāk {lenjáka (acc. = gen.) masc.} (lit. the glass one) *sl-fea* blind male <Slav❖*1>

stȁklić {a masc.} (lit. small glass) *sl-drugs* bottle neck used to smoke hashish <Slav❖*1>

staklíći {ā masc. pl.} (lit. small glasses) *sl* eyeglasses <Slav❖*1>

stȁklo {a neut.} (lit. glass) *sl* coin <Slav*1>

stȁlenac {nca (acc. = gen.) masc.} *sl* unimportant issue or object

stâlnī kȍp {NP} (lit. permanent digging place) *sl* steady girlfriend ☞ **kop**

stân {excl.} [std. = stani] *col* used to ask for a pause, wait <Slav✍>

stȁn de {VP} *col-dia* used to achieve a channel-related pause, hold on, hang on, one moment, please ☞ **stati**

stȁnār {stanára (acc. = gen.) masc.} (lit. tenant) *sl* ***Fac*** louse (the insect) <Slav*1>

stànara {ē fem.} *sl* home <Slav*1>

stȁnčuga {ē fem.; Dat stȁnčugi} *sl-fea* big apartment <Slav❖>

stȁndard {adv.} (lit. standard) *col* always <Eng*1>

stȁni {excl.} *col* used to ask for a pause, wait <Slav>

stȁni-pȁni {adv.} *sl* very urgent, do or die <Slav❖*1>

stànica {ē fem.} (lit. station) *sl* apartment <Slav*1>

stȁniška {ē fem.; Dat stȁniški} (lit. apartment) *sl* train station <Slav✍*1>

stánje *See the following*

- **zakìntīrānō stánje** {NP} (lit. the state of no-buck) *sl-fea* lack of money

stánjiti *See the following*

- **stánjiti lòpatu** {VP} (lit. thin one's shovel) *sl* talk less

stȁr *See the following*

- **stȁr ko bìblija** {AdjP} (lit. as old as the Bible) *sl-fea* very old, as old as the hills

stârā {ē fem. (adj. decl.)} (lit. the old woman) **1** *col* mother, old lady <Slav*1> **2** *col* friend (female) <Slav*1> **3** *sl-sex* old prostitute <Slav*1>

- **stârē mi** {NP} (lit. *I swear* by my old lady) *col* used to emphasize the truth of what has been said, I swear!

stárā džȍmba {NP} (lit. old bump) *sl-mil* old soldier ☞ **džomba**

stârā kâjla {NP} (lit. old wedge) *sl-mil* old soldier ☞ **kajla**

stârā kȍcka {NP} (lit. old square) *sl-mil* old soldier ☞ **kocka**

stârā kȍska {NP} (lit. old bone) *sl-mil* old soldier ☞ **koska**

stârā kvȑga {NP} (lit. old bump) *sl-mil* old soldier ☞ **kvrga**

stârā rȕpa {NP} (lit. old hole) Cro *sl-drink* name of a bar at the Central Station in Zagreb, Croatia ☞ **rupa**

stȁrac {stârca (acc. = gen.) masc.} (lit. geezer) **1** *sl* parent, old folks <Slav*1> **2** *sl* ten dinars; a ten-dinar bill <Slav*1>

starčàdija {ē fem.} *col* senior citizens (collectively) <Slav❖>

stârī {ōg (acc. = gen.) masc.} **1** *sl* father, dad, old man <Slav*1> **2** *sl* friend (male) <Slav*1> **3** *sl-crime* prison administrator <Slav*1>

stârī bórac {NP} (lit. old fighter) *sl-mil* the conscript who has only a short time left until his discharge ☞ **borac**

stârī jàstuk {NP} (lit. old pillow) *sl-fea* senior citizen ☞ **jastuk**

stârī šàjser {NP} (lit. old shitter) *sl-fea* senile male ☞ **šajser**

starijána {ē fem.} (lit. the old one X Stara Gradiška 'the placename: Old Gradiška') *sl-crime* name of a prison in Stara Gradiška, Croatia <SlavO✍*1>

stàriša {ē masc.} *sl-fea* senior citizen <Slav⁘>

stàrka [1] {ē fem.; Dat stârki} /stârka /e fem./ **a.** *sl-fea* senior citizen <Slav⁘> **b.** *sl-sex* elderly prostitute <Slav⁘*1> **c.** *sl-sex* prostitute who supports her lover financially <Slav⁘*2>

stàrka [2] {ē fem.; Dat stàrki} *sl* tennis shoe, sneaker <BN>

stârō srèbro {NP} (lit. old silver) *sl-sex* sexually experienced female ☞ **srebro**

stȁrtati {ām, ajū perf.} *sl-sex* begin to flirt <Eng⁘*1>

stȁrtovānje {a neut.} *sl* initial flirting <Eng⁘*1>

stȁrtovati {tujēm, tujū perf. intr.} *sl* start flirting <Eng*1>

starùdija {ē fem.} (lit. wrecks) **a.** *sl-fea* old things, old junk <Slav✍> **b.** *sl-fea* senior citizens (collectively) <Slav✍*1>

stàrulja {ē fem.} (lit. the old one) *sl-crime* name of a prison in Stara Gradiška, Croatia <SlavO✍*1>

stàti *See the following*

- **stȁn de** {VP} *col-dia* used to achieve a channel-related pause, hold on, hang on, one moment, please

stàtist {a (acc. = gen.) masc.} (lit. extra) *sl-fea* unimportant person, nobody, nothing <Gre*1>

stàtista {ē masc.} (lit. extra) **1** *sl-sports* ***Der*** bad soccer player <Gre*1> **b.** *sl-fea* ***Fac*** average person <Gre*1>

statíva {ē fem.} (lit. post) *sl-fea* strong leg <Lat*1>

stàviti {vīm, vē perf.} (lit. stick) *sl-sex* ***Obs*** engage in sexual intercourse with (of a male) <Slav*1>

stàza *See the following*

- **na dȕgē stàze** {PP} (lit. on long paths) *col* for a long time

stáža {ē masc.} *sl-mil* intern sergeant <Fre✍*1>

stàžista {ē masc.} *sl-mil* intern sergeant <Fre⁘*>

stážo {a masc.} /stážo /e masc./ *sl-mil* intern sergeant <Slav✍*1>

stègnat {a (acc. = gen.) masc.} **1** *sl-crime* policeman, cop **2** *sl-mil* soldier

stènjara {ē fem.} (lit. moaning place) *sl-crime* name of a prison in Stara Gradiška, Croatia <Slav⁘*1>

stènjati *See the following*

- **stènjati u plȁhti** {VP} (lit. moan in a sheet) *sl-fea* suffer from tuberculosis, have TB

stȅpati {ām, ajū perf.} Cro *col-dia* hit, punch <Slav*1>

stepávānje {a neut.} *sl* labor of love <Slav*1>

stèpsti {pēm, pū perf.} Cro *dia-col* hit, punch <Slav✍>

- **stèpsti pápcima** {VP} (lit. bang with one's hoofs) *sl* die, kick the bucket
- **stèpsti za lóvu** {VP} (lit. bang for money) *sl-crime* take money from

stȅrati {ām, ajū perf.} (lit. drive in) SerE *sl-sex* ***Obs*** engage in sexual intercourse with (of a male) <Slav*1>

- **Jâ ti ga stȅra!** {S} (lit. I will stick it to you!) *dia* ***Off*** used as a moderate curse, Fuck you!
- **Stȅrām ti ga!** {S} (lit. I stick it to you!) SerE *dia-col* ***Off*** used as a moderate curse, Fuck you!

stȅreo gljȁva {NP} (lit. stereo shoe) *sl-fea* high-quality shoe ☞ **gljava**

stȅreo gljȁvica {NP} (lit. stereo little shoe) *sl-fea* high-quality shoe ☞ **gljavica**

stȅreo sìstēm {NP} (lit. stereo system) *sl-drugs* shooting narcotic drugs in both arms ☞ **sistem**

stériti {rīm, rē imperf.} *sl* stare at, be fixated on <Eng>

stêvka {ē fem.; Dat stêvki} *sl* female flight attendant <SlavO*1>

stèznat {a (acc. = gen.) masc.} **a.** *sl-fea* miser, tightwad, skinflint **b.** *sl-fea* coward, chicken

stȉcānje {a neut.} (lit. accruing) *sl-sex* seducing <Slav*1>

stȉcati {stȉčēm, stȉčū imperf.} (lit. accrue) *sl* seduce <Slav*1>

stȉći *See the following*

- **Stȉgo ti ȕgalj!** {S} (lit. Coal has reached you!) *sl-fea* used to express the feeling of being bored with somebody, You are boring!

stídan {dna, dno adj.} [std. = stidljiv] *col* shy <Slav✍>

stídnā dlȁčica {NP} (lit. shame hair) *sl-sex* pubic hair ☞ **dlačica**

stȉf {a +ov (ext. pl) masc.; Nom Pl stȉfovi} *sl-fea* obese male <Eng*1>

stȉja {excl.} *col* the sound made by the goose <Slav>

stijéna {ē fem.} /stijèna/ (lit. rock) *sl-fea* muscular male <Slav*1>

stȉjo {excl.} *col* the sound made by the goose <Slav>

stȉmapro {stȉmepro fem.} *sl-crime* stealing, swiping

stína {ē fem.} [std. = stijena, stena] Med *dia* stone, rock <Slav✍>

stȉpsa {ē fem.} /stȉpsa/ **a.** *sl-fea* miser, tightwad, skinflint <Gre[*1]> **b.** *sl-fea* egotist <Gre[*2]>

stȉpu {excl.; perm} /stȉpu/ [std. = pusti] **a.** *sl* leave it alone, it does not matter <Slav✍> **b.** *sl* let it be <Slav✍[*1]>

stȉpuj {excl.; perm} [std. = pusti] *sl* leave it alone <Slav✍>

stȋsak {ska masc.} (lit. grip) **a.** *sl* arrogance <Slav[*1]> **b.** *sl* bravery <Slav[*1]>

stȉska {ē fem.} (lit. squeezing) *sl-fea* crowd, mob <Slav[*1]>

stískati se {stȋskām, stískajū imperf. intr.} /stȉskati se/ *sl-fea* slow dance <Slav[*1]>

stȉskavac {vca masc.} (lit. catcher) **1** *sl-fea* close dance <Slav⁘[*1]> **b.** *sl* fear <Slav⁘[*1]>

stȉsnuti {nēm, nū perf.} /stísnuti/ (lit. grip) *sl* dare, have courage to do something <Slav[*1]>

- **Ȉli stȉsni ili pȑdni!** {S} (lit. Close it or fart!) *col* ***Obs*** used to stimulate a hesitant interlocutor to act, Shit or get off the pot!
- **stȉsnuti pȅtlju** {VP} (lit. press the knot) *col* dare
- **stȉsnuti zûbe** {VP} (lit. clench one's teeth) *col* endure, survive

stȉsnuti se {nēm, nū perf. intr.} /stísnuti se/ (lit. squeeze) **1** *sl-fea* be sad <Slav[*1]> **2** *sl-fea* be tight with money, pinch pennies <Slav[*1]> **3** *sl-fea* get frightened, get scared <Slav[*1]>

stȉtpu {stȋmpu, stȅpu perf.; perm} [std. = pustiti] *sl* let, allow, permit <Slav✍>

stjènica {ē fem.} (lit. bedbug) *sl-fea* boring male, bore <Slav[*1]>

stjȅrati {ām, ajū perf.} (lit. drive in) **a.** *sl* stick in, insert <Slav[*1]> **b.** *sl-sex* engage in sexual intercourse with (of a male) <Slav[*2]>

- **stjȅrati ga** {VP} (lit. stick it) *sl-sex* engage in sexual intercourse with

stjȅti {òću, òćē imperf.} [std. = htjeti] *col-dia* want, wish (in all its meanings in the form different from the standard) <Slav✍>

stjuardȅsa {ē fem.} /skiardèsa/ (lit. flight attendant) *sl-sex* ***Fac*** prostitute who often changes her place of residence <Eng[*1]>

- **kàfanskā stjuardȅsa** {NP} (lit. bar's flight attendant) *sl* ***Fac*** female bathroom attendant

stjúca {ē fem.} [std. = stjuardesa] *sl* female flight attendant <Eng✍>

stô [1] *See the following*

- **kod práznōg stòla** {PP} (lit. at an empty table) Cro *sl* name for the former Opera bar in Zagreb, Croatia
- **ȍperacionī stô** {NP} (lit. surgical table) *sl-gamble* gambling table

stô [2] *See the following*

- **stô dèbelīh mȁjmūna** {NumP} (lit. hundred fat monkeys) *sl* hundred thousand dinars (amount and its bill)
- **stô pȍstō** {NumP} (lit. hundred percent) *col* for sure
- **Stô púta ti jèbēm mȁtēr!** {S} (lit. I fuck your mother a hundred times!) *col* ***Off*** used as a strong curse, Fuck you!

stô grâmā džigérnjačē {NumP} (lit. hundred grams of liver) *sl* hit in the plexus ☞ **džigernjača**

Stô ti mâjke jèbēm! {S} (lit. I fuck your hundred mothers!) SSer *dia* ***Off*** used as a strong curse, Fuck you! ☞ **majka**

stòbanak {nka masc.} *sl* ten dinars; a ten-dinar bill <Slav⁘>

stòēćī {ā, ē adj.} (lit. standing) [std. = stojeći] *dia* for special occasions: *stoeće odijelo suit for a special occasion* <Slav✍[*1]>

stója {ē fem.} *col* hundred dinars; a hundred-dinar bill or coin <Slav✍[*1]>

stojàdin {a (acc. = gen.) masc.} *col* Zastava 101 (make of car) <Slav✍[*1]>

stojàdīnka {ē fem.; Dat stojàdīnki} *sl-auto* Zastava 101 (make of car) <Slav✍[*1]>

Stòjan {a masc.} (lit. Stojan, man's name X stojati 'stand') *sl-sex* ***Fac-Obs*** penis, dick, prick <SlavO[*1]>

stòjānka {ē fem.} *sl* ten dinars; a ten-dinar coin <SlavO[*1]>

stôjčiti {čīm, čē perf.} *sl-sex* ***Obs*** engage in sexual intercourse with (of a male) <Slav[*1]>

Stójko {a masc.} (lit. Stojko, man's name X stojati 'stand') *sl-sex* penis, dick <SlavO[*1]>

stȍka {ē fem.; Dat stȍki} (lit. cattle) *col* ***Der*** worthless or despicable person or group of persons, scum <Slav[*1]>

stòkuća {ē fem.} (lit. hundred-house) *sl-fea* female who frequently visits other people's houses (usu. to gossip), busybody <Slav⁘[*1]>

stòlāš {stoláša (acc. = gen.) masc.; Voc stȍlāšu} (lit. deskman) *sl-polit* politician <Slav⁘[*1]>

stòlica *See the following*

- **slàba stòlica** {NP} (lit. weak chair) *sl-fea* obese male

stòlijēvī {ā, ō adj.} **a.** *sl-fea* clumsy, klutzy <Slav⁘*1> **b.** *sl-fea* unintelligent, stupid, dumb <Slav⁘*2>

stòlovi {lōvā masc. pl.} (lit. tables, desks) *sl-gamble* two aces with two tens (in poker) <Slav*1>

stòljetnjāk {a (acc. = gen.) masc.} (lit. the hundred-year-old one) *sl-fea* boaster, braggart, blowhard <Slav⁘*1>

stomàklija {ē fem.} (lit. the belly one) **1** *sl-drink* herbal brandy <Slav✍*1> **2** *sl-sex* pregnant female <Slav✍*1>

stôn 1 {a +ov (ext. pl) masc.; Nom Pl stónovi} *sl-drugs* used as a strong narcotic effect, speed, rush <Eng*1>

stôn 2 {adj.} *sl-drugs* under the strong influence of narcotic drugs, stoned <Eng>

• **stôn ko búlja** {AdjP} (lit. as stoned as an ass) *sl-drugs* completely stoned

stônd 1 {a +ov (ext. pl) masc.; Nom Pl stóndovi} *sl-drugs* used as a strong narcotic effect, speed, rush <Eng*1>

stônd 2 {adj.} *sl-drugs* stoned <Eng*1>

stòndiran {a, o adj.} *sl-drugs* under the strong influence of narcotic drugs, stoned <Eng>

stònoga {ē fem.} (lit. centipede) *sl-crime* police patrol <Slav*1>

stȍp {a masc.} (lit. stop) *sl-sex* ***Fac*** menstruation, period <Eng*1>

• **nȍn stȍp** {NP} (lit. nonstop) **a.** *col* day and night **b.** *col* always

stȍpa {ē fem.} *sl-mil* one month of one's military service <Slav*1>

• **iz òvīh stôpā** {PP} (lit. from these feet) *col* right away, now

stòpička {ē fem.; Dat stòpički} (lit. hundred-cunt) *sl-sex* ***Fac-Obs*** prostitute, hooker <Slav⁘*1>

stopírānje {a neut.} *col* hitch-hiking <Eng>

stopírati {stòpīrām, stopírajū imperf.} **1** *sl-auto* hitch-hike <Eng⁘*1> **2** *sl* stop <Eng⁘>

stȍrī {īja masc.} *sl* story <Eng>

stȍtka {ē fem.; Dat stȍtki} /stòtka/ *sl* hundred dinars; a hundred-dinar bill <Slav⁘*1>

stôun {a +ov (ext. pl) masc.; Nom Pl stóunovi} *sl-drugs* narcotic drug, dope <Eng*1>

stôund 1 {a masc.} *sl-drugs* strong influence of narcotic drugs <Eng>

• **sȑpskī stôund** {NP} (lit. Serbian stoned) *sl* ***Col*** afternoon siesta

stôund 2 {adj.} *sl-drugs* under the strong influence of narcotic drugs, stoned <Eng*1>

strâ {aa masc.} [std. = strah] *col-dia* fear <Slav✍>

strâdati {strâdam, strâdaju imperf. intr.} *sl* die, kick the bucket <Slav*1>

strȁhobālān {lna, lno adj.} (lit. horrible) *sl-fea* ***App*** excellent, bad, mean <Slav*1>

strahohálnōst {i fem.} (lit. being horrible) *sl-fea* greatness <Slav*1>

strahòvit {a, o adj.} (lit. horrible) *sl-fea* ***App*** excellent, bad, mean <Slav*1>

strána *See the following*

• **jèbānā strána** {NP} (lit. the side which is fucked) *sl-fea* ***Obs*** cheated person, the one who is worse off

• **náslovnā strána** {NP} (lit. front page) *sl-sex* ***Fac-Obs*** sexual intercourse in which the female partner lies on her back

strȁnka *See the following*

• **âčenā strȁnka** {NP} (lit. the side which is fucked) **SSer** *dia* ***Obs*** person who is worse off: *Ispao je ačena stranka u poslu s Čečencima. He was worse off on that deal with the Chechens.*

• **jèbānā strȁnka** {NP} (lit. the party which is fucked) *sl-fea* ***Obs*** cheated person, the one who is worse off

strȁobālan {lna, lno adj.} (lit. horrible) **a.** *sl-fea* ***App*** excellent, bad, mean <Slav✍*1> **b.** *sl-fea* strange, weird <Slav✍*2> **c.** *sl-fea* very funny <Slav✍*3>

straobálnōst {nosti fem.} (lit. being horrible) *sl-fea* greatness <Slav✍*1>

strášan {šna, šno adj.} (lit. horrible) **a.** *sl-fea* exciting <Slav*1> **b.i.** *sl-fea* cunning, sly, slick <Slav*2> **ii.aa.** *sl-fea* strange, weird <Slav*2> **bb.** *sl-fea* very funny <Slav*3>

strášno {adv.} (lit. horribly) *sl-fea* ***App*** excellent, bad, mean <Slav*1>

stráva 1 {ē fem.} /strȁva/ **a.** *col* horror, terror <Slav✍> **b.** *sl-fea* insanity, craziness <Slav✍*1>

stráva 2 {excl.} (lit. horror) *col* ***App*** excellent, awesome <Slav*1>

stráva 3 {adj.} (lit. horror) *col* ***App*** excellent, awesome <Slav*1>

strȁvičan {čna, čno adj.} (lit. horrible) **a.** *sl-fea* exciting <Slav*1> **b.** *sl-fea* cunning, sly, slick <Slav*2> **c.** *sl-fea* strange, weird <Slav*3> **d.** *sl-fea* very funny <Slav*4>

strȁvično {adv.} (lit. horribly) *sl-fea* very <Slav*1>

strȅfiti {fīm, fe perf.} 1 *col* hit, punch <Ger*1> 2 *col* shock <Ger*1>

strȅfiti se {fīm, fe perf. intr.} *col* happen, occur <Ger*1>

strêjndž {adv.} *sl* strange <Eng>

strêjt[1] {adj.} *sl* normal, straight <Eng>

strêjt[2] {adv.} *sl* normal, straight <Eng>

strèjtāš {strejtáša (acc. = gen.) masc.; Voc strȅjtāšu} *sl-fea* normal person, one having generally acceptable attitudes and behavior <Eng>

strêlka {ē fem.; Dat strêlki} *sl* entrance ticket to the first five rows in the movie house <Slav⁘*1>

strȅlovān {vna, vno adj.} (lit. shot) *sl-fea* in love <Slav*1>

strȅlovānā {ē fem. (adj. decl.)} (lit. the shot one) *sl-sex* ***Fac*** former virgin <Slav*1>

strȅlovānje {a neut.} (lit. shooting) *sl-sex* ***Fac-Obs*** sexual intercourse <Slav*1>

streljàna {ē fem.} (lit. shooting range) *sl-sex* ***Fac-Obs*** room intended for sexual intercourse <Slav*1>

strȅndžer {a (acc. = gen.) masc.} /stréndžer/ *sl* stranger (male) <Eng>

strȅndžerica {ē fem.} /stréndžerica/ *sl* stranger (female) <Eng⁘>

strèndžerka {ē fem.; Dat strèndžerki} /stréndžerka/ *sl* stranger (female) <Eng⁘>

streptomìcīn[1] {micína (acc. = gen.) masc.} (lit. Streptomycin) *sl-fea* ***App*** skillful person <BN*1>

streptomìcīn[2] {adj.} (lit. Streptomycin) **a.** *sl-fea* ***Fac-App*** excellent, awesome <BN*1> **b.** *sl-fea* dominant <BN*2>

streptomìnđīn {minđína (acc. = gen.) masc.} (lit. Streptomicine, a drug brand name X minđa, cunt) *sl-fea* ***App*** skillful person <BN*1>

strêsti se {résēm, résū perf. irreg.} /strésti se/ (lit. shake) **a.** *sl* die, kick the bucket <Slav*1> **b.** *sl* get frightened, get scared <Slav*2>

stȓgānī {ā, ō adj.} (lit. teared off) *sl-fea* lame (limping) <Slav*1>

stȓgati *See the following*

• **stȓgati ȍko** {VP} (lit. tear apart an eye) *sl-fea* stare, glare at in surprise, gawk

strîc {stríca (acc. = gen.) +ov (ext. pl) masc.; Nom Pl stríčevi} (lit. uncle) **a.** *col* male, guy <Slav*1> **b.** *sl* retiree <Slav*2>

strìček {a (acc. = gen.) masc.} (lit. little uncle) Cro *sl-sex* ***Fac-Obs*** small penis <Slav*1>

strȉgati {ām, ajū imperf.} /strígati/ (lit. shear, clip *sheep, etc.*) 1**a.** *sl* look, watch, scope out <Slav*1> **b.** *sl* get interested <Slav*2> 2 *sl* give a haircut <Slav*1>

strîna {ē fem.} (lit. aunt) 1 *sl-sex* prostitute, hooker <Slav*1> 2 *sl-sex* buttocks, butt <Slav*1> 3 *sl-fea* weak person <Slav*1>

• **Strîne ti ga!** {S} (lit. *I screw* your aunt!) *dia* ***Off*** used as a weak curse, Screw you!

• **Strínu ti jèbēm!** {S} (lit. I screw your aunt!) *col* ***Off*** used as a weak curse, Screw you!

• **Strínu ti tvȍju!** {S} (lit. I screw your aunt!) *col* ***Off*** used as a weak curse, Screw you!

strînka {ē fem.} *dia* ***Fam*** aunt (paternal) <Slav⁘>

• **Strînke ti ga!** {S} (lit. *I screw* your little aunt!) *dia* ***Off*** used as a weak curse, Screw you!

Strínu ti jèbēm! {S} (lit. I screw your aunt!) *col* ***Off*** used as a weak curse, Screw you! ☞ **strina**

Strínu ti tvȍju! {S} (lit. I screw your aunt!) *col* ***Off*** used as a weak curse, Screw you! ☞ **strina**

strìperka {ē fem.} *sl* female stripper <Eng⁘>

strȉpovati {pujēm, pujū biasp.} (lit. strip) *sl* let go, release: *stripovati lopova let a thief go* <Eng⁘*1>

strjèlica {ē fem.} [std. = strelica] BosM *col* arrow <Slav✍>

stȓk[1] {a +ov (ext. pl) masc.; Nom Pl stŕkovi} *sl* dating, going out with <Slav*1>

stȓk[2] {a +ov (ext. pl) masc.; Nom Pl stŕkovi} *sl* meeting <Slav✍*1>

stȓka {ē fem.} *sl-fea* mess, disorder, disturbance <Slav⁘*1>

stŕkati {ām, ajū perf.} *sl* beat up <Slav*1>

strméknuti {stȓmēknēm, nū perf.} *sl-sex* ***Obs*** engage in sexual intercourse with (of a male) <Slav*1>

strméknuti se {stȓmēknēm, nū perf. intr.} *col* fall (physically) <Slav>

strmopízditi se {mòpīzdīm, dē perf. intr.} *sl* fall (physically) <Slav⁘*1>

stȑndžosati {ošēm, ošū imperf.} *sl-sex* ***Obs*** engage in sexual intercourse with (of a male)

stȑndžōv {strndžòva (acc. = gen.) masc.} *sl-fea* inhabitant of the countryside, hick, bumpkin

stȑnđōv {strnđòva (acc. = gen.) masc.} *sl-fea* inhabitant of the countryside, hick, bumpkin

stȑnkōv {strnkòva (acc. = gen.) masc.} *sl-fea* inhabitant of the countryside, hick, bumpkin

strnovrátiti {nòvrātīm, tē perf.} *sl-sex* ***Obs*** engage in sexual intercourse with (of a male) <**Slav*1**>

stròberī {īja masc.} (lit. strawberry) *sl-drugs* strawberry (narcotic drug) <**Eng*1**>

strȍg {a, o adj.} (lit. strict) **a.** *sl-fea* ***App*** excellent, awesome <**Slav*1**> **b.i.** *sl-fea* affluent <**Slav*2**> **ii.** *sl-fea* reasonable <**Slav*2**> **iii.** *sl-fea* real <**Slav*2**>

strȍg fôl {NP} (lit. strict joke) **a.** *sl-fea* successful trick **b.** perfect lie ☞ **fol**

strȍgā hèvina {NP} **a.** *sl-fea* rich female **b.** *sl-fea* reasonable female ☞ **hevina**

strȍgo {adv.} (lit. strictly) *sl-fea* very <**Slav*1**>

strogòća {ē fem.} *col* rigor <**Slav⁘**>

strôj {strȍja +ev (ext. pl) masc.; Nom Pl strȍjevi} (lit. machine) **1** *sl-sex* ***Obs*** buttocks, butt <**Slav*1**> **2** *sl-auto* car, wheels <**Slav*1**>

strôuberī {īja masc.} (lit. strawberry) *sl-drugs* LSD, acid <**Eng*1**>

strpùsati {ām, ajū perf.} (lit. stick in) *sl-sex* ***Obs*** engage in sexual intercourse with (of a male) <**Slav✍*1**>

strúgānje {a neut.} (lit. scraping) **1** *col* snoring <**Slav*1**> **2** *sl-sex* sexual intercourse <**Slav*1**> **3** *sl* lying <**Slav*1**>

strúgati {strûžēm, žū imperf.} (lit. scrape) **1** *col* snore <**Slav*1**> **2** *sl-sex* engage in sexual intercourse with (of a male) <**Slav*1**> **3** *sl* shave <**Slav*1**> **4** run away, flee <**Slav*1**>

- **strúgati atmosféru** {VP} (lit. scrape the atmosphere) *sl* worry about
- **strúgati kȍžu** {VP} (lit. scrape skin) *sl-fea* have a hard time, experience difficulties
- **strúgati pízdu** {VP} (lit. scratch one's cunt) *sl-fea* ***Obs*** lose time in useless activities, goof around
- **strúgati vȍlju** {VP} (lit. scrape will) *sl* try hard, give one's best

strȕgisati {išēm, išū imperf.} (lit. scrap) *sl* run away, flee <**Slav✍*1**>

strúgnuti {strûgnēm, nū perf. intr.} (lit. scrap) *sl* run away, flee <**Slav*1**>

strȕhnuti {nēm, nū perf. intr.} [std. = strunuti] BosM *col* rotten, decayed <**Slav✍*1**>

strúja {ē fem.} (lit. electricity) **1** *sl-crime* manhunt <**Slav*1**> **2** *sl-crime* the police <**Slav*1**> **3** *sl* streetcar conductor <**Slav*1**>

strȕjīć {rujíća (acc. = gen.) masc.} *sl* electrician <**Slav⁘*1**>

strújnica {ē fem.} *sl-sex* attractive female breast <**Slav⁘*1**>

strȕna {ē fem.} (lit. cord) **1a.** *sl* street <**Slav*1**> **b.** *sl* road <**Slav*2**> **2** *sl* hair <**Slav*1**>

strùnjača {ē fem.} (lit. mat) *sl* female <**Slav*1**>

strúsiti {strȕsīm, sē perf.} *sl-drink* drink up (alcohol) <**Slav*1**>

str̀vina {ē fem.} (lit. corpse) **1** *sl-fea* ***Der*** worthless or despicable person <**Slav*1**> **2a.** *sl-fea* ***Der*** troublemaker, rowdy, ruffian <**Slav*2**> **b.** *sl-fea* muscular male <**Slav*3**> **c.** *sl-fea* inhabitant of the countryside, hick, bumpkin <**Slav*4**>

strvináriti {vȉnārīm, rē imperf.} *sl* learn <**Slav⁘*1**>

stû {excl.} *col* used to command an ox to pull back <**Slav**>

stȕa {ē fem.} [std. = stuha] **a.** *sl* ghost <**Slav✍**> **b.** *sl-fea* ***Der*** evil female, bitch <**Slav✍*1**>

stȕba {ē fem.} Cro *col* stair <**Slav**>

Stubáki {ā masc. pl.} Cro *sl* name for Stubičke toplice (a spa in Croatia) <**SlavO✍**>

Stubičnjâk {a masc.} Cro *sl* name for Stubičke toplice (a spa in Croatia) <**SlavO✍**>

Stubinjâk {a masc.} Cro *sl* name for Stubičke toplice (a spa in Croatia) <**SlavO✍**>

stùdent *See the following*

- **stùdent fȉzikē** {NP} (lit. student of physics) *sl-fea* manual laborer

studentàrija {ē fem.} *col* university students (taken collectively) <**Lat⁘**>

studèntnjāk {dentnjáka masc.} **1** *sl-stu* dormitory, dorm <**Lat⁘*1**> **2** *sl-stu* campus <**Lat⁘*1**>

Studènjāk {denjáka masc.} (lit. the students' one) *sl-stu* name of a campus dormitory complex in Belgrade, Serbia <**Slav⁘**>

stȕdoš {a (acc. = gen.) masc.} [std. = student] **a.** *sl-stu* student <**Lat✍**> **b. Cro** *sl* name of a dance club at the Studentski centar Zagreb, Croatia <**Lat✍*1**>

stȕha {ē fem.; Dat stȕhi} *sl-fea* ***Der*** evil female, bitch <**Slav*1**>

Stuháki {ā masc. pl.} Cro *sl* name for Stubičke toplice (a spa in Croatia) <**SlavO✍*1**>

stȕka {ē fem.} *col* bang (loud and abrupt sound) <**Slav**>

stȕkānje {a neut.} *col* bang (loud and abrupt sound) <**Slav**>

stȕkati {ām, ajū imperf.} *col* pronounce the exclamation "stu" to make an ox pull back <**Slav*1**>

stûp {a +ov (ext. pl) masc.; Nom Pl stúpovi} (lit. pole) *sl-fea* strong leg (of a female) <Slav*1>

stȕpa {ē fem.} *sl-drink* booth (in a bar, restaurant) <Slav*1>

stȕpār {stupára (acc. = gen.) masc.} **a.** *sl-fea* loafer, idler <Slav❖*1> **b.** *sl-fea* worthless or mean male, bum <Slav❖*2> **c.** *sl-fea* cheating, swindling <Slav❖*3>

stȕpovi {pōvā masc. pl.} (lit. poles) *sl* border (between countries) <Slav*1>

sturnovrátiti {nòvrātīm, tē perf.} *sl-sex* ***Obs*** engage in sexual intercourse with (of a male)

stúšiti {stûšīm, šē perf.} *sl* run away, flee <Slav❖*1> ☞ **stušiti**

stȕštiti se {tīm, tē perf. intr.} *col* arrive quickly and with high intensity (of storm, offense in sports, etc.) <Slav*1>

stvâr *See the following*

- **jáka stvâr** {AdjP} (lit. strong thing) *col* ***Iro*** nothing special, no big deal
- **ònā stvâr** {NP} (lit. that thing) *sl-sex* sexual intercourse
- **ovàkva je stvâr** {S} (lit. the thing is like this) *col* used to introduce a point, Listen up, Here's the deal.
- **Stvâr hôdā.** {S} (lit. The thing walks.) *col* used to refer to a favorable state of affairs, Everything is going well.
- **stvâr je u tome da** {S} *col* used to stress one's point, the point is

stvâri {stvárī fem. pl.} (lit. things) *sl-sex* ***Fac*** menstruation, period <Slav*1>

stvârno {part.} /stvárno/ *col* really, indeed <Slav>

stvȍr {a +ov (ext. pl) masc.; Nom Pl stvòrovi} (lit. creature) **a.** *col* person <Slav*1> **b.** *sl-fea* unattractive person <Slav*2>

su [1] {ins.} [std. = sa] *dia* with <Slav✍>

su* [2] {adj.} *col* slightly: *Bili su supijani. They were slightly drunk.* <Slav>

sublimírati {lìmīrām, limírajū biasp.} (lit. sublimate) *sl* disappear, evaporate, vanish <Lat*1>

sȕdār {a masc.} (lit. car crash) *sl* dating, going out with <Slav*1>

sudarȉška {ē fem.; Dat sudarȉški} (lit. car crash) *sl* dating, going out with <Slav✍*1>

sudòpera {ē masc.} (lit. kitchen sink) *sl-sstu* monitor (pupil who for one day keeps the blackboard clean) <Slav*1>

sȕfler {a (acc. = gen.) masc.} (lit. prompter) *sl-crime* ***Der*** informer, stoolie, snitch <Fre*1>

sûh {a, o adj.} (lit. dry) *sl-fea* broke (financially) <Slav*1>

sȕjmez {a (acc. = gen.) masc.} *sl-drink* alcoholic, drunk <NE*1>

sujùmez {a (acc. = gen.) masc.} *sl-drink* alcoholic, drunk <NE*1>

sukȁrno {a masc.} (lit. Sukarno, Indonesian president X sukati 'lie') **1** *sl* cheating, swindling <IndoO*1> **2** *sl* falsely incriminating, framing <IndoO*1>

súkati {sûčēm, sûčū imperf.} (lit. twist) **1** *sl-drink* drink (alcohol) <Slav*1> **2** *sl* lie, twist the truth <Slav*1>

Sûknēm ti ga! {S} (lit. I stick it to you!) *col-dia* ***Off*** used as a weak curse, Screw you! ☞ **suknuti**

súknuti {sûknēm, nū perf.} (lit. twist) **1** *sl-drink* drink (alcohol) <Slav*1> **2a.** *sl* lie, twist the truth <Slav*1> **b.** *sl* cheat, swindle <Slav*2> **c.** *sl* falsely incriminate, frame <Slav*3> **3** *sl-sex* engage in sexual intercourse with (of a male)

- **Sûknēm ti ga!** {S} (lit. I stick it to you!) *col-dia* ***Off*** used as a weak curse, Screw you!

sȕknja {ē fem.} (lit. skirt) *sl* female <Slav*1>

sȕknjica {ē fem.} (lit. small skirt) *sl-fea* very young female, little girl <Slav*1>

sulìnār {linára masc.} *sl-drink* tobacco pipe <NE*1>

sulùndār {lundára masc.} (lit. funnel) *sl-mil* bazooka <NE*1>

sȕljpa {sùljapa masc.; perm} [std. = pasulj] *col* beans <Lat✍>

sȕljpāš {a masc.; perm} [std. = pasulj] *sl* beans <Lat✍>

sùmāhnūt {a, o adj.} [std. = sumanut] *sl-fea* ***Der*** insane, nuts <Slav✍>

sùmānūt {a, o adj.} *col* ***Der*** insane, nuts <Slav>

sȕnac *See the following*

- **Sȕnac ti tvôj!** {S} (lit. *I screw* your little sun!) *dia* ***Off*** used as a weak curse, Screw you!

sùnanac *See the following*

- **Sùnanac ti jèbēm!** {S} (lit. I screw your little sun!) *dia* ***Off*** used as a weak curse, Screw you!

sûnce *See the following*

- **[NOUN:NOM] nà sūnce!** {S} (lit. [NOUN:NOM] in the sunlight!) *col* used to ask for something: *Pare na sunce! Show me your money!*
- **Sûnce li ti nȅbesnō!** {S} (lit. *I screw* your heavenly sun!) *col-dia* ***Off*** used as a weak curse, Screw you!

• **Sûnce li ti tvòje!** {S} (lit. *I screw* your sun!) *col-dia* ***Off*** used as a weak curse, Screw you!
• **Sûnce ti gàravō!** {S} (lit. *I screw* your soothy sun!) *col-dia* ***Off*** used as a weak curse, Screw you!
• **Sûnce ti jârkō!** {S} (lit. *I screw* your bright sun!) *col-dia* ***Off*** used as a weak curse, Screw you!
• **Sûnce ti jèbēm!** {S} (lit. I screw your sun!) *col* ***Off*** used as a weak curse, Screw you!
• **Sûnce ti jèbēm kȓvavō!** {S} (lit. I screw your bloody sun!) *col* ***Off*** used as a weak curse, Screw you!
• **Sûnce ti jèbēm žàrenō!** {S} (lit. I screw your hot sun!) *col-dia* ***Off*** used as a weak curse, Screw you!
• **Sûnce ti jèbēm žârkō!** {S} (lit. I screw your hot sun!) *col-dia* ***Off*** used as a weak curse, Screw you!
• **Sûnce ti kȓvavō!** {S} (lit. *I screw* your bloody sun!) *col-dia* ***Off*** used as a weak curse, Screw you!
• **Sûnce ti nȅbeskō!** {S} (lit. *I screw* your heavenly sun!) *col-dia* ***Off*** used as a weak curse, Screw you!
• **Sûnce ti tvòje!** {S} (lit. *I screw* your sun!) *col-dia* ***Off*** used as a weak curse, Screw you!
• **Sûnce ti ùsijānō jèbēm!**{S} (lit. I screw your glowing sun!) *col-dia* ***Off*** used as a weak curse, Screw you!
• **Sûnce ti žàranō!** {S} (lit. *I screw* your hot sun!) *col-dia* ***Off*** used as a weak curse, Screw you!
• **Sûnce ti žàrenō!** {S} (lit. *I screw* your hot sun!) *col-dia* ***Off*** used as a weak curse, Screw you!
• **Sûnce ti žârkō!** {S} (lit. *I fuck* your hot sun!) *col-dia* ***Off*** used as a moderate curse, Fuck you!
• **Sûnce ti žȅženō!** {S} (lit. *I screw* your glowing sun!) *col-dia* ***Off*** used as a weak curse, Screw you!
• **Sûnce vam jârkō!** {S} (lit. *I screw* your bright sun!) *col-dia* ***Off*** used as a weak curse, Screw you!

sùnčalīšte {a neut.} (lit. sunbathing beach) *sl-crime* name for Goli island prison (Croatia, where the former communist regime detained its political enemies) <**Slav***1>

sȕnčānje {a neut.} (lit. sunbathing beach) *sl-crime* serving prison term at Goli island (Croatia, where the former communist regime detained its political enemies) <**Slav***1>

sûnčati *See the following*
• **sûnčati zȗbe** {VP} (lit. sunbathe one's teeth) *sl* laugh

sùndžer {a masc.} (lit. sponge) [std. = sunđer] *sl-drink* alcoholic, drunk <**NE**✍*1>

sùnđer {adj.} (lit. sponge) *sl-fea* soft <**NE***1>

sùnđer {a (acc. = gen.) masc.} (lit. sponge) **1** *sl-sstu* diligent student <**NE***1> **2** *sl-drink* alcoholic, drunk <**NE***1>

sùnet {a masc.} BosM *col* circumcision <**NE**>

sùnetiti {tīm, tē imperf.} BosM *col* circumcise <**NE**>

sȕnovrātan {tna, tno adj.} *sl-fea* intrusive <**Slav***1>

sȕnuti {nēm, nū perf.} **1.** *sl* stick in, insert <**Slav***1> **b.i.** *sl-sex* engage in sexual intercourse with (of a male) <**Slav***2> **ii.** *sl* visit, pop in, stop by <**Slav***2>

sȕp *See the following*
• **sȕp bjelòglavī**{NP} (lit. white-headed vulture) *sl-crime* detective

sȕpa *See the following*
• **sȕpa za tetùrānje** {NP} (lit. stumbling soup) *sl-crime* drink (alcohol)

sùpentof {a masc.} *col* soup bowl <**Ger**>

sȕper {adv.} *col* ***App*** excellent, awesome <**Lat**>

superȉška {adv.; Dat superȉški} *col* ***App*** excellent, awesome <**Lat**>

sȕpić {a (acc. = gen.) masc.} **a.** *sl-crime* policeman, cop <**Abb**⁘*1> **b.** *sl-sports* junior player <**Slav***1>

sȕpijan {a, o adj.} *sl-drink* slightly drunk, tipsy <**Slav**⁘>

sȕpovac {pōvca (acc. = gen.) masc.} **a.** *sl-crime* policeman, cop <**Abb**⁘*1> **b.** *sl-crime* detective <**Abb**⁘*2> **c.** *sl-crime* spy, spook <**Abb**⁘*3>

supstànca {ē fem.} (lit. substance) *sl* personality <**Lat***1>

surčínac {a (acc. = gen.) masc.; Voc sȕrčīnče} (lit. the one from the Surcin airport, Belgrade, Serbia) *sl-crime* policeman, cop <**SlavO***1>

sùrduk {a masc.} *col* abyss <**NE**>

Sùrdūknēm ti ga! {S} (lit. I stick it to you!) *dia* ***Off*** used as a moderate curse, Fuck you! ☞ **surduknuti**

surduknúće {a neut.} *sl-sex* ***Obs*** sexual intercourse <**NE**⁘*1>

surdúknuti {sùrdūknēm, nū perf.} **a.** *col* stick in, insert <**NE**⁘*1> **b.** *sl-sex* engage in sexual intercourse with (of a male) <**NE**⁘*2>
• **Sùrdūknēm ti ga!** {S} (lit. I stick it to you!) *dia* ***Off*** used as a moderate curse, Fuck you!

surdùljuša {ē fem.} *sl-fea* foolish female <**NE**⁘*1>

surdúmiti {sùrdūmīm, mē perf.} *sl-sex* ***Obs*** engage in sexual intercourse with (of a male) <**NE**⁘*1>

sȕrka *See the following*
• **pêt sȕrkī za krȕnu** {NP} (lit. five grand for a crown) *sl* five thousand dinar reward

sȕrla {ē fem.} /sûrla/ (lit. elephant trunk) **1** *sl* face (human) <**Slav***1> **2a.** *sl* nose <**Slav***1> **b.** large nose <**Slav***2>

sùrlāš {surláša (acc. = gen.) masc.} (lit. the one with the elephant trunk) *sl-fea* male with a large nose <**Slav**⁘*1>

sùrlek {a (acc. = gen.) masc.} (lit. the one with a nose) *sl-fea* male with a large nose <Slav⁘*1>

Sȕrtūknēm ti ga! {S} (lit. I stick it to you!) *dia* ***Off*** used as a moderate curse, Fuck you! ☞ **surtuknuti**

surtúknuti *See the following*
- **Sȕrtūknēm ti ga!** {S} (lit. I stick it to you!) *dia* ***Off*** used as a moderate curse, Fuck you!

sȕrutka {ē fem.; Dat sȕrutki} *col-dia* whey, water left after making cheese <Slav>

sùrvati se {ām, ajū perf. intr.} /sȕrvati se/ *col* fall down, kiss the floor <Slav*1>

sùsrati {ām, ajū perf.} (lit. shit at) *sl* ***Fac-App*** meet unwillingly <Slav⁘*1>

sûša {ē fem.} /sȕša/ (lit. drought) **1** *sl-fea* being broke (financially) <Slav*1> **2** *sl* bad day <Slav*1> **3** *sl-sex* sexless period <Slav*1>

sušióna {ē fem.} (lit. drying place) **1** *sl-fea* nursing home <Slav*1> **2** *sl-crime* prison <Slav*1>

sûšnā gȍdina {NP} (lit. dry year) *sl-fea* a year when one cannot go to the seashore for a vacation ☞ **godina**

súšnica {ē fem.} (lit. drying place) *sl-drink* ***Fac*** bar (drinking place) <Slav*1>

sùtlija {ē fem.} (lit. rice with milk) *sl-sex* ***Fac-Obs*** sperm <NE*1>

sùtlijāš {a masc.} (lit. rice with milk) *sl-sex* sperm <NE*1>

sȕtra {adv.} (lit. tomorrow) *sl* ***Fac*** never <Slav*1>
- **kòliko sȕtra** {AdvP} (lit. how much tomorrow) *col* first thing in the morning
- **mȁlo sȕtra** {AdvP} *col* used as a strong negative response, no way, never

sûvā lóva {NP} Ser *col* cash ☞ **lova**

suvárak [1] {rka (acc. = gen.) masc.} (lit. dry burning log) *sl-fea* slender male <Slav⁘*1>

suvárak [2] {rka masc.} (lit. dry burning log) *sl* cash <Slav⁘*1>

suvogùsas {sta, sto adj.} (lit. dry-assed) *sl-fea* ***Obs*** slender, skinny <Slav☞⁘*1>

suvòguza {ē fem.} (lit. dry-assed woman) *sl-fea* slender female <Slav⁘*1>

suvogȕzas {sta, sto adj.} (lit. dry-assed) *sl-fea* ***Obs*** slender, skinny <Slav☞⁘*1>

suvònjav {a, o adj.} (lit. skinny) *sl-fea* unnecessary <Slav*1>

suvòta {ē fem.} *col* dry place <Slav>

suvremènjāk {menjáka (acc. = gen.) masc.} Cro *col* modern person <Slav⁘*1>

sȕza {ē fem.} (lit. tear) *sl-sex* ***Fac*** gonorrhea, the clap <Slav*1>
- **kao sȕza čȉst**{PP} (lit. clean as a tear) *col* crystal-clear

sȕziti {zīm, zē imperf.} **a.** *sl* cry, shed tears, weep <Slav*1> **b.** *sl-sex* suffer from gonorrhea, have the clap <Slav*2>

svȁk {pron.} [std. = svako] *col* everyone <Slav☞>

svȁkā čâst {NP} (lit. every honor *to you*) *col* used to express appreciation, good for you ☞ **čast**

svȁkā [PRON:DAT] čâst {LSF} (lit. every honor to [PRON:ACC]) *col* used to express appreciation, good for [PRON:ACC]: *Položio si! Svaka ti čast! You passed the test! Good for you!* ☞ **čast**

Svȁkā ti se dála! {S} (lit. Let every girl give it to you!) *sl* ***App*** used to express appreciation, Thanks a lot! ☞ **svaki**

svȁka vȁška ȍbaška {NP} (lit. each louse on its own) *col* separately, individually, each on his/her own ☞ **vȁška**

svȁkī *See the following*
- **Svȁkā ti se dála!** {S} (lit. Let every girl give it to you!) *sl* ***App*** used to express appreciation, Thanks a lot!

sváriti {svârīm, rē perf.} (lit. digest) *col* become accustomed to, get used to <Slav*1>

svàstiče *See the following*
- **Svàstiče ti jȅbnēm!** {S} (lit. I fuck a little your little wife's sister!) SSer *dia* ***Off*** used as a weak curse, Screw you!

svàstika *See the following*
- **Svàstike ti ga!** {S} (lit. *I screw* your wife's sister!) SSer *dia* ***Off*** used as a weak curse, Screw you!
- **Svàstike ti ga mȕljnēm!** {S} (lit. I squish it to your wife's sister!) SSer *dia* ***Off*** used as a weak curse, Screw you!
- **U svàstiku ti ga zàbodēm!** {S} (lit. I stick it in your wife's sister!) *dia-col* ***Off*** used as a moderate curse, Fuck you!

svȁšta {excl.} (lit. everything) *col* used to express disbelief, unbelievable <Slav*1>

svȅ *See the following*
- **Jè l ti to svȅ** ([NOUN:NOM]) **il ìmā jȍš?** {LSF} (lit. Is that all [NOUN:NOM] or is there more of it?) *sl* ***Der*** used to express negative attitude toward: *Je l to sve tvoj rad il ima još? Your work is worth shit!*
- **svȅ gô** [NOUN:NOM] {PronP} *col* ***Der*** used to refer to the high presence of a group of people, They are

all [NOUN:NOM]: *Sve go Hrvat. They're all Croats.*

• **svȅ i svȁšta** {ProP} (lit. all and everything) *col* just anything

• **Svȅ mōj do mòjēga!** {S} (lit. All mine next to mine!) *col* ***Fac-Obs*** used to express disrespect, Fuck it!

• **Svȅ skùrcaō!** {S} (lit. I hope you prick out everything!) *dia-col* ***Off*** used as a weak curse, Screw you!

• **Svȅ, svȅ, ali...** {ProP} (lit. All, all, but...) *col* used to express disagreement, Yes, but

• **Svȅ ti jèbēm!** {S} (lit. I fuck everything to you!) *col* ***Off*** used as a strong curse, Fuck you!

• **Svȅ ti na gòmilu jèbēm!** {S} (lit. I fuck everything to you on a pile!) *col-dia* ***Off*** used as a strong curse, Fuck you!

• **Svȅ ti na kȕp pòjebēm!** {S} (lit. I fuck everything to you on a pile!) *dia-col* ***Off*** used as a strong curse, Fuck you!

• **Svȅ ti na svetək pòjebēm!** {S} (lit. I fuck everything in this little world to you!) SSer *dia* ***Off*** used as a strong curse, Fuck you!

• **Svȅ ti na svétu jèbēm!** {S} (lit. I fuck everything in the world to you!) SerE *col* ***Off*** used as a strong curse, Fuck you!

• **Svȅ ti na vrȁ jèbēm!** {S} (lit. I fuck everything on the top to you!) SSer *dia* ***Off*** used as a strong curse, Fuck you!

• **Svȅ ti odjedàmput pòjebēm!**{S} (lit. I fuck everything at once to you!) *col-dia* ***Off*** used as a moderate curse, Fuck you!

• **Svȅ ti po kalèndār jèbēm!** {S} (lit. I fuck everything yours in accordance with the calendar!) SSer *dia* ***Off*** used as a moderate curse, Fuck you!

• **Svȅ ti pò kuću pòjebēm!** {S} (lit. I fuck everything in your house!) SSer *dia* ***Off*** used as a strong curse, Fuck you!

• **Svȅ ti pòjebēm!** {S} (lit. I fuck everything to you!) *col* ***Off*** used as a strong curse, Fuck you!

• **Svȅ ti smȑdljivō jèbēm!** {S} (lit. I fuck everything stinky to you!) *col-dia* ***Off*** used as a strong curse, Fuck you!

• **Svȅ ti žívo jèbēm!** {S} (lit. I fuck everything alive to you!) *col* ***Off*** used as a strong curse, Fuck you!

Svéca mu njègovōg! {S} (lit. *I screw* his saint!) *col-dia* ***Off*** used as a weak curse, Screw you! ☞ **svetac**

Svéca ti jèbēm dȅčijēg! {S} (lit. I screw your childish saint!) SerE *col-dia* ***Off*** used as a weak curse, Screw you! ☞ **svetac**

Svéca ti tvôga! {S} (lit. *I screw* your saint!) *col-dia* ***Off*** used as a weak curse, Screw you! ☞ **svetac**

svéća {ē fem.} (lit. candle) **1** *sl-fea* person who is disturbing a love pair <Slav*1> **2** *sl-sports* high ball falling down <Slav*1>

• **Svéću ti jèbēm!** {S} (lit. I screw your candle!) SerE *dia-col* ***Off*** used as a weak curse, Screw you!

svêtā Ȁna {NP} (lit. St. Ann) *sl-sex* female who engages in fellatio, Betty Blow Job ☞ **Ana**

svétac *See the following*

• **Svéca mu njègovōg!** {S} (lit. *I screw* his saint!) *col-dia* ***Off*** used as a weak curse, Screw you!

• **Svéca ti jèbēm dȅčijēg!** {S} (lit. I screw your childish saint!) SerE *col-dia* ***Off*** used as a weak curse, Screw you!

• **Svéca ti tvôga!** {S} (lit. *I screw* your saint!) *col-dia* ***Off*** used as a weak curse, Screw you!

svètina {ē fem.} SerE *col* crowd, mob <Slav*1>

svȅtlo *See the following*

• **zèlenō svȅtlo** {NP} (lit. green light) SerE *col* acceptance

svêtō písmo {NP} (lit. Holy Bible) *sl* law ☞ **pismo**

svêtōg Pȅtra kȁjgana {NP} (lit. St. Peter's scrambled eggs) *sl-fea* expensive ☞ **kajgana**

svèznadār {a masc.} (lit. the one who knows everything) *sl-fea* braggart, know-it-all <Slav*1>

svèznalica {ē fem.} (lit. the one who knows everything) *sl-sex* ***Fac-Obs*** female who uses different objects to masturbate <Slav*1>

svȉ *See the following*

• **Svȉ ti mȑtvī pòjebēm!** {S} (lit. I fuck all your dead!) SSer *dia* ***Off*** used as a very strong curse, Fuck you!

svíja {ē fem.} *sl-sports* edgeball (in ping-pong) <Slav✣*1>

svijéća *See the following*

• **Râjskā se svijéća upálila!** {S} (lit. Heavenly candle is lighted!) *sl* used to indicate that a favorable state of affairs has been reached, I made it! I succeeded!

svijȅćica {ē fem.} [std. = svjećica] *sl-auto* spark plug <Slav✍>

svȉkati {ām, ajū imperf. intr.} *sl-arch* look, watch, scope out

svȉktati {ām, ajū imperf.} *sl-drink* drink (alcohol)

svíla *See the following*

• **mȁglenā svíla** {NP} (lit. foggy silk) **a.** *sl-sex* expensive prostitute **b.** *sl-sex* prostitute, hooker

svìlati {ām, ajū imperf.} *sl-sex* ***Obs*** engage in sexual intercourse with (of a male)

svìlen {svilèna, svilèno adj.} (lit. silky) *sl-fea* scared <Slav*1>

svìlenī {ōg (acc. = gen.) masc.} (lit. the silky one) *sl-fea* ***Der*** crybaby <Slav❖*1>

svilènjāk {lenjáka (acc. = gen.) masc.} (lit. the silky one) **a.** *sl-fea* ***Der*** crybaby <Slav❖*1> **b.** *sl-sex* ***Der*** male homosexual, gay <Slav❖*2>

svȉnga {ē fem.; Dat svȉngi} (lit. Sphynx) [std. = sfinga] *sl-fea* widow <Gre⇪>

svínja {ē fem.} (lit. pig) **1** *sl-fea* ***Der*** worthless or despicable person <Slav*1> **2** *sl-fea* ***Der*** obese person, porker <Slav*1>

svìnjāk {svinjáka (acc. = gen.) masc.} (lit. the pig stuff) **a.** *sl* wallet <Slav❖*1> **b.** *sl* old stolen wallet <Slav❖*2>

svinjàrija {ē fem.} (lit. piggery) **1** *sl* ***Fac*** pork <Slav*1> **2** *sl* unpleasant situation, bummer <Slav*1>

svìrājka {ē fem.} *dia-col* flute <Slav❖>

svìrala {ē fem.} *col-dia* flute <Slav❖>

svírānje {a neut.} (lit. playing an instrument) *sl-fea* prolonged and meaningless talk, blabber, chatter <Slav*1>

- **svírānje hîmnē** {NP} (lit. playing the national anthem) *sl-sstu* rising of school children when the teacher enters
- **svírānje kûrcu** {NP} (lit. playing to the prick) *col* lying

svírati {svîrām, svírajū imperf.} (lit. play an instrument) **1** *sl-sex* ***Obs*** engage in sexual intercourse with (of a male) <Slav*1> **2** *sl-sex* suffer from gonorrhea, have the clap <Slav*1> **3a.** *sl-fea* ***Der*** talk persistently and meaninglessly, blabber, chatter <Slav*1> **b.** *sl-fea* ***Der*** preach, give lectures to <Slav*2>

- **Nè svīrāj!** {S} (lit. Don't you play!) *col* ***Off*** used as a moderate curse, Fuck you!
- **Nè svīrāj kûrcu!** {S} (lit. Don't you play to a prick!) *col* ***Off*** used as a moderate curse, Fuck you!
- **svírati frùlu** {VP} (lit. play the flute) *sl-sex* ***Obs*** engage in fellatio
- **svírati gràmofōn** {VP} (lit. play on a turntable) *sl-sex* ***Obs*** engage in sexual intercourse with an underaged teen
- **svírati klàvīr** {VP} (lit. play a piano) **1** *sl-crime* inform the police or other authorities, sing **2** *sl-crime* leave one's fingerprints **3** *sl-crime* be handcuffed
- **svírati kûrcu** {VP} (lit. play to the prick) *sl-fea* ***Obs*** talk persistently and meaninglessly, blabber, chatter
- **svírati na bàtāk** {VP} (lit. play on a chicken leg) *sl* eat, devour
- **svírati na žȉli** {VP} (lit. play on a vein) *sl-sex* ***Obs*** engage in fellatio
- **svírati zùbnī òrkestar** {VP} (lit. play the dental orchestra) *sl-fea* chatter (of the teeth, when feeling cold)

svìrigūz {a (acc. = gen.) masc.} (lit. ass-player) *sl-fea* ***Obs*** poor male <Slav❖*1>

svirigùzati {ām, ajū imperf.} (lit. play one's ass) *sl-fea* ***Obs*** walk around barely dressed <Slav❖*1>

svìripīzda {ē fem.} (lit. cunt-player) *sl-sex* ***Fac-Obs*** loose woman, slut <Slav❖*1>

svîrka {ē fem.} (lit. playing) **a.** *sl-music* musical concert <Slav❖*1> **b.** *sl* work (at one's work) <Slav❖*2>

svȉrnuti {nēm, nū perf.} (lit. play a little) *sl-sex* ***Obs*** engage in sexual intercourse with (of a male) <Slav❖*1>

svȉsnuti {nēm, nū perf. intr.} *sl* die, kick the bucket <Slav*1>

svȉtlati {ām, ajū perf.} *sl-sex* ***Obs*** engage in sexual intercourse with (of a male) <Slav*1>

Svȉtnem ti ga! {S} (lit. I band it to you!) *dia* ***Off*** used as a weak curse, Screw you! ☞ **svitnuti**

svȉtnuti *See the following*

- **Svȉtnem ti ga!** {S} (lit. I bang it to you!) *dia* ***Off*** used as a weak curse, Screw you!

svjèdok *See the following*

- **lȁžnī svjèdok** {NP} (lit. false witness) *sl-drink* name of a bar at Amruševa street in the neighborhood of a court in Zagreb, Croatia

svjètina {ē fem.} *col* crowd, mob <Slav*1>

svjȅtlo *See the following*

- **cȓvenō svjȅtlo** {NP} (lit. red light) *sl-sex* ***Fac*** menstruation, period
- **zèlenō svjȅtlo** {NP} (lit. green light) *col* acceptance

svôj {pron.} (lit. one's own) *sl-sex* penis <Slav*1>

svòja {pron.} (lit. one's own) *sl-sex* vagina <Slav*1>

svračáriti {svràčārīm, rē imperf.} (lit. crow) *sl* think, ponder <Slav❖*1>

svrȁčijē nȍge {NP} (lit. magpie's legs) *col* slender legs ☞ **noga**

svrȁka {ē fem.; Dat svrȁki} (lit. magpie) **1a.** *sl-fea* talkative elderly female <Slav*1> **b.** *sl-fea* noisy senior citizen <Slav*2> **2** *sl-fea* female with slender legs <Slav*1>

svȑbeti {bīm, bē perf. intr.} (lit. itch) **SerE** *sl-fea* bother, disturb: *Svrbi me to što nemam dozvolu za rad. Not having a work permit bothers me.* <Slav*1>

svȑbiti {bīm, bē perf. intr.} (lit. itch) *sl-fea* bother, disturb: *Svrbi ga žena. His wife disturbs him.* <Slav*1>

svr̂daō {dla masc.} (lit. drill *the tool*) *sl-sex* ***Fac-Obs*** penis, dick, prick <Slav*1>

svr̂dla {ē fem.} *sl-sex* ***Obs*** vagina, cunt <Slav*1>

svr̂dlati {ām, ajū imperf.} (lit. drill) *sl-sex* ***Obs*** engage in sexual intercourse with (of a male) <Slav*1>

svr̂dlo {a neut.} (lit. drill, bore) *sl-sex* ***Fac-Obs*** male homosexual who takes the active role <Slav*1>

svŕnuti {svr̂nēm, nū perf. intr.} *col* stop by, drop in on <Slav*1>

svršávati {svr̀šāvām, svršávajū imperf. intr.} (lit. cum) **a.** *sl-sex* ***Obs*** ejaculate, cum <Slav*1> **b.** *sl-fea* ***Obs*** be very happy <Slav*2>

svŕšiti {svr̂šīm, šē perf. intr.} **a.** *sl-sex* ***Obs*** ejaculate, cum <Slav*1> **b.i.** *sl* ***Fac-Obs*** cease boring <Slav*2> **i.** *sl* have one's fill of something <Slav*2>

svȕđ {adv.} [std. = svugdje] *dia-col* everywhere <Slav☞>

š.l.b. {adj.} (abbreviation from šašav, lud, blesav *crazy, nuts, koo-koo*) *sl-fea* ***Der*** insane, koo-koo <Abb*1>

š-š-š {excl.} *col* used to silence one's interlocutor, hush <Slav>

šȁ[1] {pron.} [std. = šta] *col* what (in any of its Serbo-Croatian meanings used in forms different from the standard) <Slav☞>

šȁ[2] {excl.} *col* the sound made by a bird, tweet <Slav>

Šàban {a (acc. = gen.) masc.} *sl-fea* inhabitant of the countryside, hick, bumpkin <NEO>

šàbečēnje {a neut.} *sl-sex* ***Obs*** sexual intercourse <NE❖*1>

šàber {a masc.} *sl-crafts* scraper

šȁcan {a (acc. = gen.) masc.} *sl-sstu* professor, high-school teacher (male), prof <Ger❖*1>

šȁcati {ām, ajū biasp.} **a.** *sl* estimate, guess <Ger❖> **b.** *sl* look, watch, scope out <Ger❖*1> *sl*

šȁcnuti {nēm, nū perf.} *col* look, watch, scope out <Ger❖*1>

šȁcovānje {a neut.} *col* watching <Ger❖*1>

šȁcovati {cujēm, cujū imperf.} **a.** *sl* estimate, guess: *Šacujem da je do tamo pet kilometara. I guess that it's five kilometers to that place.* <Ger❖> **b.** *sl* look, watch, scope out: *šacovati na znak look at a sign* <Ger❖*1> **c.** *sl* choose, select: *šacovati haljinu choose a dress* <Ger❖*2>

šáder {a masc.} *sl* money <Ger☞*1>

šȃfla {ē fem.} *sl* head <Ger☞*1>

šȁhista {ē fem.} (lit. chess player) *sl-sports* person who thinks for a long time before moving <NE*1>

šahóvnica {ē fem.} (lit. checker board) *col* Croatian flag or coat of arms <Slav❖*1>

šȁht {a +ov (ext. pl) masc.; Nom Pl šàhtovi} (lit. manhole) *sl-sex* ***Fac-Obs*** large vagina <Ger*1>

šàin {a masc.} *sl-crime* theft from a counter

šája {ē fem.} [std. = šah] *sl-sports* chess <NE☞>

šȃjba {ē fem.} **1** *sl-crafts* washer (on a bolt) <Ger> **2** *sl-auto* windshield <Ger>

šȃjbati {ām, ajū imperf.} **1** *sl-sex* ***Fac-Obs*** engage in sexual intercourse with (of a male) <Ger*1> **2a.** *sl-auto* speed (auto, etc.) <Ger*1> **b.** *sl-auto* overtake (pass another car on the road) <Ger*2> **3** *sl* play a game <Ger*1>

šȃjbe {i fem. pl.} *sl-fea* eyeglasses <Ger*1>

šàjbna {ē fem.} *sl-crafts* washer (on a bolt) <Ger☞>

šàjkača {ē fem.} (lit. Central Serbia peasant's cap) **a.** *sl-sex* ***Fac-Obs*** large vagina <Slav*1> **b.** *sl-sex* ***Fac-Obs*** vagina, cunt <Slav*2>

šȁjkan {a (acc. = gen.) masc.} *sl-fea* stupid or mentally deficient person

šàjser {a (acc. = gen.) masc.} (lit. shitter) **1** *sl-fea* senior citizen <Ger❖*1> **2** *sl-fea* coward, chicken <Ger❖*1>
- **stȃrī šàjser** {NP} (lit. old shitter) *sl-fea* senile male

šȁka *See the following*
- **šȁka jȁda** {NP} (lit. a fistful of misery) *sl-fea* weak male, wimp

šȁkār {a masc.} (lit. fister) *sl-sex* ***Fac*** masturbator (male) <Slav❖*1>

šakètānje {a neut.} *sl* fight (e.g. fist fight) <Gyp>

Šȁkić *See the following*
- **Dèsānka Šȁkić** {NP} (lit. Desanka, a proper name, and Šakić is derived from šaka *fist*. Combined, this is related to the right fist (desna šaka)) *sl-sex* ***Fac-Obs*** masturbation, Madam Rosy Palm and her five daughters

šakírati {šàkīrām, šakírajū perf.} (lit. fist) *sl-sex* ***Fac-Obs*** masturbate, beat off <Slav❖*1>

šȁkopīs {a masc.} (lit. fist-writing) *sl-fea* handwriting <Slav❖*1>

šakùrčić {a masc.} *sl-sports* chess <NE-Slav.☞>

šála *See the following*
- **šálu nȁ strānu** {NP} (lit. kidding aside) *col* used to switch to a more serious narrative, no kidding now

šalabàhter [1] {a masc.} *sl-sstu* crib sheet, cheat sheet <NE✍*1>

šalabàhter [2] {a (acc. = gen.) masc.} **a.** *sl-fea* ***Der*** clumsy person, klutz <NE*1> **b.** *sl-fea* loafer, idler <NE*2> **c.i.** *sl-fea* troublemaker, rowdy, ruffian <NE*3> **ii.** *sl-fea* dandy, fop <NE*4> **e.** *sl-fea* worthless or despicable male, bum <NE*5> **f.** *sl-fea* irresponsible person <NE*6> **g.** *sl* male, guy <NE*7>

šalabȁjzānje {a neut.} **1** *sl-fea* making a fool of oneself <NE*1> **2** *sl-fea* talk persistently and meaninglessly, blabber, chatter <NE*1>

šalabâjzati {ām, ajū imperf.} *sl-fea* talk persistently and meaninglessly, blabber, chatter <NE*1>

šalabàjzer {a (acc. = gen.) masc.} **a.** *sl-fea* ***Der*** clumsy person, klutz <NE*1> **b.** *sl-fea* loafer, idler <NE*2> **c.i.** *sl-fea* troublemaker, rowdy, ruffian <NE*3> **ii.** *sl-fea* dandy, fop <NE*4> **e.** *sl-fea* worthless or despicable male, bum <NE*5> **f.** *sl-fea* irresponsible person <NE*6>

šalabàjzerka {ē fem.} *sl-fea* ***Der*** worthless or despicable female, bitch <NE>

šalabázati {làbāzām, labázajū imperf. intr.} *sl-fea* spend one's time in useless activities, fool around, mess around

šâlē {adv.} *col-dia* easily <Slav✍*1>

šȁlfa {ē fem.} Cro *sl* name of a dance floor at Šalata hall in Zagreb, Croatia <SlavO✍>

šȁlīn {šalína (acc. = gen.) masc.} **a.** *sl-fea* stupid or mentally deficient person <Slav✍*1> **b.** *sl-fea* insane person, nut case <Slav✍*2>

šȁltati {ām, ajū imperf.} *sl-auto* shift gears <Ger❖>

šȁlter [1] {a (acc. = gen.) masc.} (lit. light switch) *sl-fea* social climber (male) <Ger*1>

šȁlter [2] {a masc.} *col* counter, window (e.g. in a bank) <Ger>

šȁlterskī {ā, ō adj.} *col* counter <Ger>

šȁlthēbl {a masc.} *sl-auto* gear stick <Ger>

šȁmar {a masc.} (lit. slap) *sl-sstu* failing grade <Slav*1>

šamàrānje *See the following*

- **šamàrānje krâjnīkā** {NP} (lit. slapping one's tonsils) *sl* French kissing

šamàrati {ām, ajū imperf.} (lit. slap) *sl-sex* ***Fac-Obs*** engage in cunnilingus <Slav*1>

- **šamàrati džèpove** {VP} (lit. slap one's pockets) *sl-crime* steal, swipe
- **šamàrati knjȉgu** {VP} (lit. slap a book) *sl-sstu* learn laboriously
- **šamàrati kràjnīke** {VP} (lit. slap one's tonsils) **a.** *sl* ***Fac*** French kiss, swab one's tonsils **b.** *sl-sex* ***Fac-Obs*** engage in cunnilingus
- **šamàrati màjmuna** {VP} (lit. slap the monkey) *sl-sex* ***Obs*** masturbate, spank the monkey

šamàrati se {ām, ajū imperf. intr.} (lit. slap oneself) *sl-sex* ***Fac-Obs*** masturbate, beat off <Slav*1>

šamàrčina {ē fem.} *col* slap, smack <Slav❖>

šȁmlica {ē fem.} *col* footstool <Ger>

- **pȍhovānā šȁmlica** {NP} (lit. breaded footstool) *sl* female

šȁmličast {a, o adj.} *sl-fea* sly <Ger❖*1>

šampanjírati *See the following*

- **šampanjírati kȃr** {VP} (lit. champagne a prick) *sl-sex* ***Fac-Obs*** engage in fellatio

šȁmrl {a masc.} **a.** *sl* small chair <Ger> **b.** *sl* ***Fac*** high sole shoe <Ger*1>

šȁmrla {ē fem.} **a.** *sl* small chair <Ger> **b.** *sl* ***Fac*** high sole shoe <Ger*1>

šȁmšula {ē fem.} **a.** *sl-fea* stupid or mentally deficient person **b.i.** *sl-fea* foolish female **ii.** *sl-fea* absent-minded person

šána {ē fem.} **1a.** *sl-crime* theft, swipe **b.** *sl-crime* stolen goods, hot stuff **2** *sl-sports* chess

- **Šâno, dûšo!** {S} (lit. Nut, my darling!) *sl-fea* ***Off*** used as a weak curse, You're nuts!

šȁnčēr {šančéra (acc. = gen.) masc.} (lit. the trench-man) *sl-fea* digger, manual worker on a digging assignment

šandrmácija {ē fem.} **a.** *sl-fea* joking with, fooling with <Slav✍*1> **b.** *sl* cheating, swindling

šandrmírānje {a neut.} **a.** *sl-fea* joking with, fooling with <Slav✍*1> **b.** *sl* cheating, swindling

šandrmírati {dȑmīrām, drmírajū imperf.} *sl* cheat, swindle <Slav✍*1>

šáner {a (acc. = gen.) masc.} **a.** *sl-crime* thief (male), sticky fingers **b.** *sl-fea* inhabitant of the countryside, hick, bumpkin

šánērka {a (acc. = gen.) masc.; Dat šánerki} **a.** *sl-crime* thief (female), sticky fingers **b.** *sl-fea* inhabitant of the countryside (female), hick, bumpkin

šánerskī {ā, ō adj.} **a.** *sl-crime* thief's **b.** *sl-fea* crude

Šȁngaj *See the following*

- **u Šȁngāj** {PP} (lit. to Shanghai) *sl* used to make somebody go away, Beat it!

šȁngājka {ē fem.; Dat šàngājki} *sl* tennis shoe, sneaker <BN>

Šànika {ē fem.} *sl-fea* ***Der*** insane person, nut case

šanírati {šànīrām, šanírajū imperf.} *sl-crime* steal, swipe

šȁnk {a +ov (ext. pl) masc.; Nom Pl šànkovi} *sl-drink* bar (drinking place) <Ger>

šȁnker {a (acc. = gen.) masc.} /šànker/ *sl-drink* bartender <Ger>

šȁnkerica {ē fem.} /šànkerica/ *sl-drink* barmaid <Ger>

Šȁno {a masc.} *sl-fea* stupid or mentally deficient person

Šâno, dûšo! {S} (lit. Nut, my darling!) *sl-fea* ***Off*** used as a weak curse, You're nuts! ☞ šana

šansóna {ē fem.} *sl* chance <Fre*1>

šansonȅta {ē fem.} *sl* slim chance <Fre*1>

šȁnt {a +ov (ext. pl) masc.; Nom Pl šàntovi} *sl* social connection

šȁntav {a, o adj.} **a.** *sl-fea* slightly insane, nutty <Slav*1> **b.i.** *sl-fea* insane, nuts <Slav*2> **ii.** *sl-fea* clumsy, klutzy <Slav*2>

šantrê {èa masc.} *sl-drink* wine <BN*1>

šȁnž {šánža +ev (ext. pl) masc.; Nom Pl šànževi} *sl* hidden money <Fre*1>

šanžírati {šànžīrām, šanžírajū biasp.} *sl* hide, cover up <Fre❖*1>

šȁp {a +ov (ext. pl) masc.; Nom Pl šàpovi} **1** *sl-crime* accomplice's share of stolen goods, take **2** *sl-crime* bribe

šápa {ē fem.} (lit. paw) **a.** *sl* hand <Slav*1> **b.** *sl* arm <Slav*2> **c.** *sl-crime* accomplice's share of stolen goods, take <Slav*2>

šapírati {šàpīrām, šapírajū imperf.} **1a.** *sl* take <Slav*1> **b.** *sl* grab, snatch: *šapirati besplatno pivo grab a free beer* <Slav*2> **c.** *sl-crime* steal, swipe <Slav*3> **2** *sl* bribe, lubricate: *šapirati drota bribe a cop*

šȁpist {a (acc. = gen.) masc.} *sl-crime* unskilled pickpocket <Slav❖*1>

šȁpka {ē fem.; Dat šàpki} (lit. cap) *sl-sex* ***Fac-Obs*** large vagina <NE*1>

šàptāč {šaptáča (acc. = gen.) masc.; Voc šȁptāču} (lit. prompter) *sl-crime* ***Der-Fac*** informer, stoolie, snitch <Slav*1>

šȁptigūz {a (acc. = gen.) masc.} (lit. whispering ass) *sl-crime* ***Der-Obs*** informer, stoolie, snitch <Slav❖*1>

šára {ē fem.} (lit. scribble) **1** *sl* certificate, diploma <Slav*1> **2** *sl* passport <Slav*1> **3** *sl* ID (separate document which every adult citizen of the former Yugoslavia had to carry on their person) <Slav*1> **4** *sl* certificate, diploma <Slav*1> **5** *sl-auto* driver's license <Slav*1> **6** *sl-mil* soldier's ID <Slav*1> **7** *sl* draft notice <Slav*1> **8** *sl* newspaper <Slav*1> **9** *sl* signature **10** Cro *sl* name of a dance club at the Šarengrad Street in Zagreb, Croatia <Slav*1>

šára-mára {ē fem.} *sl-sstu* cut classes <Slav✍*1>

šárac {rca masc.} **1** *sl* pencil <Slav❖*1> **2** *sl-sex* pornographic magazine <Slav❖*1>

šàrāč {šaráča (acc. = gen.) masc.; Voc šȁrāču} (lit. scribbler) *sl* exhibitionist, flasher <Slav❖*1>

šàrāf {šaráfa masc.} *col* screw (fastening device) <Ger>

šàrāf {adv.} *sl-fea* ***App*** excellent <Ger*1>

šarafcíger {a masc.} *col* screwdriver <Ger>

šaràfštok {a masc.} *sl-crafts* clamp (the tool) <Ger>

šàran {a (acc. = gen.) masc.} (lit. carp) **1** *sl-fea* affluent male, moneybags <Slav*1> **2** stupid or mentally deficient male <Slav*1>

šárati {ām, ajū biasp.} (lit. scribble) **a.** *sl* write <Slav*1> **b.** *sl* lie <Slav*1> **c.** *sl* cheat, swindle <Slav*2> **d.i.** *sl* cheat on one's lover or spouse <Slav❖*3> **ii.** *sl* be in illegal business <Slav*3>

šȁre {eta neut.} **1** *sl* certificate, diploma <Slav✍*1> **2** *sl* passport <Slav✍*1> **3** *sl* ID (separate document which every adult citizen of the former Yugoslavia had to carry on their person) <Slav✍*1> **4** *sl* certificate, diploma <Slav✍*1> **5** *sl-auto* driver's license <Slav✍*1> **6** *sl-mil* soldier's ID <Slav✍*1> **7** *sl-mil* draft notice <Slav✍*1> **8** newspaper

šàren {a, o adj.} (lit. multicolored) *sl-fea* suspicious <Slav*1>

šȁrenī {ōg (acc. = gen.) masc.} (lit. the multicolored one) *sl-fea* boaster, braggart, blowhard <Slav*1>

šarènica {ē fem.} **1** *sl* certificate, diploma <Slav❖*1> **2** *sl* certificate, diploma <Slav❖*1> **3** *sl* passport <Slav❖*1> **4** *sl* ID (separate document which every adult citizen of the former Yugoslavia had to carry on their person) <Slav❖*1> **5** *sl* driver's license <Slav❖*1> **6** *sl-mil* soldier's ID <Slav❖*1> **7** *sl-mil* draft notice <Slav❖*1> **8** *sl* newspaper <Slav❖*1> **9** signature <Slav❖*1>

šarènīš {reníša masc.} **a.** *sl* colorful things <Slav✍> **b.** *sl-fea* miscellany <Slav✍*1>

šarírati {šàrīrām, šarírajū imperf.} **1** *sl* write a letter of reference <Slav❖*1> **2** *sl* check one's ID <Slav❖*1>

šàrklo {šàraklo masc.; perm} (lit. hobo) [std. = klošar] **a.** *sl-fea* homeless person, bum <Fre✍[*1]> **b.** *sl-fea* stupid or mentally deficient person

šarplanínac {a (acc. = gen.) masc.} (lit. Šarplaninac is a sheep dog breed) **1a.** *sl-fea* inhabitant of the countryside, hick, bumpkin <SlavO[*1]> **b.** *sl-fea* stupid or mentally deficient person <SlavO[*2]> **2** *sl-fea* male wearing fur <SlavO[*1]>

šàrulja {ē fem.} *sl-gamble* playing card <Slav❖[*1]>

šȁša {ē fem.} *sl* noise <NE❖[*1]>

šȁša {ē masc.} *sl-fea* inhabitant of the countryside, hick, bumpkin <NE❖[*1]>

šȁšav {a, o adj.} /šȁšāv/ **a.** *sl-fea* insane, nuts <NE❖[*1]> **b.** *sl-fea* strange, weird <NE❖[*2]>

šȁškast {a, o adj.} **a.** *sl-fea* slightly insane, nutty <NE❖[*1]> **b.** *sl-fea* strange, weird <NE❖[*2]>

šȁtipi {šȁmpi, šàjupi imperf.; perm} *sl-sex* ***Obs*** urinate, piss <Slav✍> ☞ **pišati**

šàtltati {ām, ajū imperf.} *sl-auto* shift gears <Ger>

šȁtornja {ē fem.} *sl-crime* prison <NE✍[*1]>

šȁtra {ē fem.} *sl* slang <NE[*1]>

šàtrānđa {ē fem.} *sl-crime* prison <NE✍[*1]>

šȁtrati {ām, ajū biasp.} *sl* lie <NE❖[*1]>

šatràundža {ē fem.} *sl-crime* prison <NE✍[*1]>

šȁtrav {a (acc. = gen.) masc.} *sl* criminal <NE❖[*1]>

šȁtri {šȅtri masc.; perm} *sl-sex* ***Obs*** gonorrhea, the clap <Ger✍> ☞ **triša**

šatrírati {šàtrīrām, šatrírajū imperf.} **a.** *sl* speak slang <NE❖[*1]> **b.** *sl* lie <NE❖[*2]> **c.** *sl* cheat, swindle <NE❖[*3]>

šȁtro [1] {part.} *sl* used to express uncertainty: *On šatro tamo radi. He sort of works there.* <NE[*1]>

šȁtro [2] {a masc.} *sl* slang <NE❖[*1]>

šȁtro [3] {adj.} *sl-fea* false <NE❖[*1]>

šȁtro [4] {ad adj.} [std. = fol] *sl* as if, kind of, sort of: *On šatro radi. He pretends to be working.* <Ita✍> ☞ **lafo**

šȁtro-amàtēr {šȁtro-amatéra (acc. = gen.) masc.} *sl-sports* professional player who pretends to be an amateur, ringer <Lat❖[*1]>

šatrològija {ē fem.} *sl* lying <NE❖[*1]>

šàtrōn {šatróna masc.} *sl-crime* prison <NE✍[*1]>

šatronáda {ē fem.} *sl-crime* prison <NE✍[*1]>

šàtrōnđa {ē fem.} *sl-crime* prison <NE✍[*1]>

šàtronja {ē fem.} /šȁtronja/ *sl-crime* prison <NE[*1]>

šȁtrovac {trōvca (acc. = gen.) masc.} **a.** *sl-crime* criminal <NE❖[*1]> **b.** *sl-crime* thief, sticky fingers <NE❖[*2]> **c.** *sl-crime* crook, thief <NE❖[*3]> **d.i.** *sl-gamble* gambler <NE❖[*4]> **ii.** *sl-fea* homeless person, bum

šȁtrovačkī {ōg masc.} **a.** *col* slang <Slav❖[*1]> **b.** *col* syllabic permutations in speech (e.g. bari instead of riba 'fish, female...') <Slav❖[*2]>

šȁtrovica {ē fem.} *sl-sex* prostitute, hooker <Slav❖[*1]>

šatrovírānje {a neut.} **a.** *sl* speaking in slang <Slav❖[*1]> **b.** *sl* cheating, swindling <Slav❖[*2]>

šatrovírati {ròvīrām, rovírajū imperf.} **a.** *sl* speak slang <Slav❖[*1]> **b.** *sl* cheat, swindle <Slav❖[*2]> **c.** *sl* pretend <Slav❖[*3]> **d.** *sl* lie <Slav❖[*3]>

šàtrūndža {ē fem.} *sl-crime* prison <NE[*1]>

šavàtsere {šavàmserē, šàvajuserē imperf. intr.; perm} [std. = rješavati se] *sl-crime* resell, fence <Slav✍>

ščâmčiti {čīm, čē perf.} *sl-sex* ***Obs*** engage in sexual intercourse with (of a male) <Slav[*1]>

ščâp {ščápa +ov (ext. pl) masc.; Nom Pl ščápovi} *sl-crime* theft, swipe <Slav[*1]>

ščȁriti {rīm, rē biasp.} *sl* sell (exchange merchandise for money)

ščegetàuček {a masc.} Kajk *sl-sex* ***Obs*** clitoris

ščȅnđati {ām, ajū perf.} *sl* sell (exchange merchandise for money)

ščèpati {ām, ajū perf.} *col* grab, snatch <Slav>

ščvȑgati {ām, ajū biasp.} *sl* beat up <Slav[*1]>

ščvȑljnuti {nēm, nū perf.} *sl-sex* ***Obs*** engage in sexual intercourse with (of a male) <Slav[*1]>

ščvȑljugnuti {nēm, nū perf.} *sl-sex* ***Obs*** engage in sexual intercourse with (of a male) <Slav[*1]>

šćâp {šćápa +ov (ext. pl) masc.; Nom Pl šćápovi} [std. = štap] *dia* cane, walking stick <Slav✍>

šćȁpiti {pīm, pē perf.} **a.** *col* grab, snatch <Slav[*1]> **b.** *sl-crime* steal, swipe <Slav[*2]>

šćène {eta neut.} [std. = štene] *dia* puppy <Slav✍>

šćêr {i fem.} [std. = kćer] *dia-col* daughter <Slav✍>

šćȉpito {adv.} *sl-fea* tight

šèbečiti {čīm, čē imperf.} *sl-sex* ***Obs*** engage in sexual intercourse with (of a male) <NE❖[*1]>

šèbočiti {čīm, čē imperf.} *sl-sex* ***Obs*** engage in sexual intercourse with (of a male) <NE❖*1>

šećérko {a neut.} *sl-fea* diabetic <Slav❖*1>

šećerléma {ē fem.} *col* sweet pastry or candies <NE❖*1>

šećèruša {ē fem.} *sl-drink* schnapps made from sugar <Slav❖*1>

šȅf {a +ov (ext. pl) masc.; Nom Pl šèfovi} (lit. chief) *sl-drink* waiter <Fre*1>

šȅfe {excl.} (lit. chief) *col* used to address a male in direct formal communication, boss, chief <Fre*1>

šȅfka {ē fem.; Dat šȅfki} *sl-sex* ***Obs*** sexual intercourse

šefkàna {ē fem.} *sl-sex* ***Obs*** brothel, whorehouse

šèfkārna {ē fem.} *sl-sex* ***Obs*** brothel, whorehouse

šèfkārnīk {a masc.} *sl-sex* ***Obs*** brothel, whorehouse

šȅfovati {jēm, jū imperf. intr.} *col* act as a boss <Fre❖*1>

šȅfovica {ē fem.} *col* boss's wife <Fre❖*1>

šéga {ē fem.; Dat šégi} 1 *sl-fea* fun <NE> 2 *sl-crafts* saw (the tool) <Ita>

šegáčēnje {a neut.} *col* joking with, fooling with <NE❖>

šegáčiti se {šègāčīm, čē imperf. intr.} /šègačiti se/ *sl-fea* joke <NE❖>

šègānje {a neut.} *sl* joking with, fooling with <NE❖>

šegebèdečiti {čīm, čē imperf.} 1 *sl-sex* ***Obs*** engage in sexual intercourse with (of a male) <Ita-Slav.*1> 2 *sl* cheat, swindle *sl-fea* joke

Šȅher {a masc.} BosM *col* ***App*** name for Sarajevo (a city in Bosnia) <NE*1>

šèhīd {šehída (acc. = gen.) masc.} BosM *col* hero <NE>

šéjtan {a (acc. = gen.) masc.} BosM *col* devil <NE>

šejtanizácija {ē fem.} (lit. devil's business) *sl-sex* ***Fac*** breaking wind, farting <NE❖*1>

šekètānje {a neut.} *sl* fight (e.g. fist fight) <Slav☞*1>

Šȅkspīr {a (acc. = gen.) masc.} (lit. Shakespeare) 1 *sl-sex* ***Fac*** male homosexual, gay <EngO*1> 2 *sl-fea* expert <EngO*1>

Šȅkspīr-tîp {a (acc. = gen.) +ov (ext. pl) masc.; Nom Pl Šȅkspīr-típovi} (lit. Shakespeare-type) *sl-fea* masochist, male who likes to suffer (esp. in love) <EngO*1>

šȅlna {ē fem.} 1 *sl- craf* ring (part of a mechanism) <Ger> 2 *sl-crafts* clamp (the tool) <Ger>

šȅm {a +ov (ext. pl) masc.; Nom Pl šȅmovi} *sl-fea* fun <NE*1>

šéma {ē fem.} (lit. scheme) 1 *sl-fea* fun <Gre*1> 2 *sl* arrangement <Gre*1> 3 *sl* love affair <Gre*1> 4 *sl* job, gig: *Imam neku šemu za soma maraka. I have a gig for a thousand German marks.* <Gre*1>

šȅmati {ām, ajū imperf.} *sl-fea* enjoy, like <Gre❖*1>

šemsòati {šȅmsujēm, sujū imperf.} *sl-fea* enjoy, like <NE❖*1>

šènica {ē fem.} [std. = pšenica] *dia* wheat <Slav☞>

šéniti {nīm, nē imperf.} (lit. beg *of a dog*) *sl-fea* request <NE*1>

šènlučiti {čīm, čē imperf. intr.} *col* drink too loud and celebrate too loud <NE*1>

šénluk {a masc.} Din *col* excessive celebration with drinking <NE>

šénuti {nēm, nū perf.} *sl-fea* go insane, freak out <NE❖*1>

šépa {ē fem.} *sl* female <Slav*1>

šèpārčiti {čīm, čē imperf.} *sl-sex* engage in sexual intercourse with (of a male)

šepèračiti {čīm, čē perf.} *sl-sex* ***Obs*** engage in sexual intercourse with (of a male)

šépo {a masc.} /šépo /e masc./ *sl-fea* lame male <Slav❖*1>

šèrāf {šeráfa masc.} *col* screw (fastening device) <Ger>

šèrbet {a masc.} *sl-drugs* weak drug <NE*1>

šèrīf {šerífa (acc. = gen.) masc.} (lit. sheriff) 1 *sl-fea* director, boss, manager <Eng*1> 2 *sl-fea* principal <Eng*1>

šérpa {ē fem.} (lit. pan) 1 *sl-sports* incompetent goalie (soccer, etc.) <Ger*1> 2 *sl* hat <Ger*1>

šês {num.} [std. = šest] *col* six <Slav☞>

šȅsan {sna, sno adj.} Med *dia* handsome, cute <Ita> ☞ šestan

šȅsnā {ē fem.} Med *sl-sex* attractive female <Ita*1>

šèsnēs {num.} [std. = šesnaest] *col* sixteen <Slav☞>

šést glávā {NP} (lit. six heads) *sl-gamble* gambling success ☞ glava

šèstalo {a neut.} *sl-crime* pistol, revolver

šȅstan {sna, sno adj.} Med *dia* handsome, cute <Ita> ☞ šesan

šèšīr {šešíra (acc. = gen.) masc.} (lit. hat) *sl-sex* ***Fac*** male homosexual, gay <Slav*1>

šešîrdžija {ē masc.} (lit. one with a hat) *col* person who habitually dresses formally <NE❖*1>

šèšken {a (acc. = gen.) masc.} *sl-fea* stupid or mentally deficient person

šètāč {šetáča (acc. = gen.) masc.} (lit. walker) **1** *sl-fea* walker (boy who can only get his girlfriend to walk with him) <Slav[*1]> **2** *sl-crime* policeman, cop <Slav[*1]> **3** *sl-polit* protester <Slav[*1]>

šètāj {excl.} (lit. take a walk) *sl* used to make somebody go away, beat it, take a walk, hit the road <Slav[*1]>

šétalica {ē fem.} (lit. walker) *sl-sex* ***Fac*** prostitute, streetwalker <Slav⁘[*1]>

šétanje *See the following*

• **šétanje gâlījā po Dȕnāvu** {NP} (lit. walking galleys down the Danube river) *sl* conversation, talk

šétati {šêtām, šétajū imperf.} (lit. walk) *sl* cheat, swindle <Slav[*1]>

• **šétati cìpele** {VP} (lit. walk one's shoes) *sl* walk

• **šétati gàće** {VP} (lit. walk one's pants) *sl-fea* boast, brag

• **šétati gâlije po Dȕnāvu** {VP} (lit. walk galleys down the Danube river) *sl* talk, have a conversation

• **šétati kȍžicu** {VP} (lit. walk one's penis skin) *sl-sex* masturbate, beat off

• **šétati kȍžu** {VP} (lit. walk one's skin) *sl-fea* dress formally, dress up

• **šétati nȍge** {VP} (lit. walk one's legs) *sl* walk

• **šétati pantalóne** {VP} (lit. walk one's trousers) *sl* walk

• **šétati pêrje** {VP} (lit. walk one's feathers) *sl-fa* show off

• **šétati pitóna** {VP} (lit. walk one's python) *sl* leave, depart, walk

šéva {ē fem.} **1** *sl-sex* ***Obs*** sexual intercourse <Slav[*1]> **2a.** *sl-sports* dribbling <Slav[*1]> **b.** *sl-fea* joking with, fooling with <Slav[*2]> **c.** *sl-fea* cheating, swindling <Slav[*2]>

šévac {vca (acc. = gen.) masc.} **1** *sl-sex* ***Obs*** penis, dick, prick <Slav⁘[*1]> **2** *sl-sex* ***Obs*** male sexual partner (of a female) <Slav⁘[*2]> **3** *sl-auto* Chevrolet (make of car) <BN⌀>

šèvāk {ševáka masc.} *sl-sex* ***Obs*** penis, dick, prick <Slav⁘[*1]>

šévānje {a neut.} **1** *sl-sex* ***Obs*** sexual intercourse <Slav⁘[*1]> **2a.** *sl-sports* dribbling <Slav⁘[*1]> **b.** *sl* cheating, swindling <Slav⁘[*1]> **c.** *sl* joking with, fooling with <Slav⁘[*2]>

šèvārnīk {a masc.} *sl-sex* ***Obs*** brothel, whorehouse <Slav⁘[*1]>

šévati {šêvām, šévajū imperf.} **1** *sl-sex* ***Obs*** engage in sexual intercourse with (of a male) <Slav⁘[*1]> **2a.** *sl-sports* dribble (e.g. in basketball) <Slav⁘[*1]> **b.** *sl* cheat, swindle <Slav⁘[*1]>

šévati se {šêvām, šévajū imperf. intr.} *sl-sex* ***Obs*** engage in sexual intercourse with <Slav⁘[*1]>

šèvātor {a (acc. = gen.) masc.} *sl-sex* ***Obs*** male sexual partner (of a female) <Slav⁘[*1]>

šèvčina {ē fem.} *sl-sex* ***Obs*** penis, dick, prick <Slav⁘[*1]>

šéviti {vīm, vē imperf.} *sl-sex* ***Obs*** engage in sexual intercourse with (of a male) <Slav⁘[*1]>

• **Kȍ te šévī!** {S} (lit. Who is fucking you?) *sl* ***Off*** used to express disrespect, Fuck you!

šéviti se {vīm, vē imperf. intr.} *sl-sex* ***Obs*** engage in sexual intercourse with <Slav⁘[*1]>

šèvkalica {ē fem.} *sl-sex* ***Obs*** vagina, cunt <Slav⁘[*1]>

šèvkānje {a neut.} *sl-sex* ***Obs*** sexual intercourse <Slav⁘[*1]>

šèvkārnīk {a masc.} *sl-sex* ***Obs*** brothel, whorehouse <Slav⁘[*1]>

šèvkati {ām, ajū imperf.} *sl-sex* ***Obs*** engage in sexual intercourse with (of a male) <Slav⁘[*1]>

• **Kȍ te šèvkā!** {S} (lit. Who is fucking you?) *sl* ***Off*** used to express disrespect, Fuck you!

šèvkati se {ām, ajū imperf. intr.} *sl-sex* ***Obs*** engage in sexual intercourse with <Slav⁘[*1]>

šezdesetȍsmāš {tosmáša (acc. = gen.) masc.; Voc šezdesetȍsmāšu} *sl-polit* student protester from the 1968 protests in the former Yugoslavia <Slav⁘[*1]>

šezdesetȍsmāškī {ā, ō adj.} *sl-polit* pertaining to the 1968 student protests in the former Yugoslavia <Slav⁘[*1]>

šȉba {ē fem.} (lit. stick) *sl* fight (e.g. fist fight) <Slav[*1]>

šibácija {ē fem.} (lit. whipping) **1** *sl* fight (e.g. fist fight) <Slav⁘[*1]> **2** *sl-sex* masturbation, beating off <Slav⁘[*1]> **3** *sl* beating up <Slav⁘[*1]>

šibàčina {ē fem.} (lit. whipping) *sl* fight (e.g. fist fight) <Slav⁘[*1]>

šȉbadžija {ē masc.} **1a.** *sl-fea* stupid or mentally deficient person <Slav-NE[*1]> **b.** *sl-fea* strange person, weirdo <Slav-NE[*2]> **c.** *sl-sex* masturbator (male) <Slav-NE[*3]> **d.** *sl-fea* unfriendly person <Slav-NE[*4]> **e.** *sl-fea* boring person, bore <Slav-NE[*5]> **f.** *sl-fea* egotist <Slav*NE[*6]> **2** *sl-fea* troublemaker, rowdy, ruffian <Slav*NE[*1]>

šȉbadžīka {ē fem.; Dat šȉbadžīki} **1a.** *sl-fea* boring female, bore <Slav-NE[*1]> **b.** *sl-fea* foolish female <Slav-NE[*2]> **2** *sl-sex* masturbator (male) <Slav-NE[*3]> **3** *sl-fea* unfriendly person <Slav-NE[*3]> **4** *sl-fea* stupid or mentally deficient person <Slav-NE[*3]>

šibadžīnka {ē fem.; Dat šibadžīnki} *sl-fea* egotist <Slav-NE*1>

šibađija {ē masc.} (lit. whipper) *sl-fea* hairsplitter, nit picker <Slav❖*1>

šibāj {excl.} (lit. whip it) **1** *col* used to make somebody go away, beat it <Slav❖*1> **2** *col* hurry up, rush <Slav❖*2>

šibānje {a neut.} (lit. whipping) **1** *sl* fight (e.g. fist fight) <Slav❖*1> **2** *sl-sex* masturbation, beating off <Slav❖*1> **3** *sl* beating up <Slav❖*1>

šibati {ām, ajū imperf.} (lit. whip) **1** *sl-sex* ***Obs*** engage in sexual intercourse with (of a male) <Slav❖*1> **2** *sl-sex* ***Obs*** masturbate, beat off <Slav❖*1> **3** *sl* beat up <Slav❖*1> **4** *sl-auto* speed (auto, etc.) <Slav❖*1>

šibati se {ām, ajū imperf.} (lit. whip) **1** *sl-sex* ***Obs*** engage in sexual intercourse with <Slav❖*1> **2** *sl-sex* ***Obs*** masturbate, beat off <Slav❖*1> **3**

šibáža {ē fem.} *sl* fighting <Slav❖*1>

šibe {excl.} *col* used to make somebody go away, beat it <Slav❖*1>

šiber [1] {a (acc. = gen.) masc.} **a.** *sl-fea* ***Der*** lazy or shiftless person, bum, good for nothing <Ger*1> **b.** *sl-fea* ***Der*** stupid or mentally deficient person <Ger*2> **c.** *sl-fea* ***Der*** strange person, weirdo <Ger*3> **d.** *sl-fea* hairsplitter, nit picker <Ger*4> **e.** *sl-fea* egotist <Ger*5> **f.** *sl-fea* masturbator (male) <Ger*6> **g.** *sl-fea* unfriendly person <Ger*7> **h.** *sl-fea* boring person, bore

šiber [2] {a masc.} **a.** *sl-crafts* adjustable measure <Ger*1> **b.** *sl-sstu* a poke, prod, or pinch on the buttocks, goose <Ger*2>

šibica {ē fem.} (lit. match) *sl-fea* redheaded person <Slav*1>

šibicār {a (acc. = gen.) masc.} /šibìcār /šibicára (acc. = gen.) masc./ *sl-gamble* street gambler <Slav❖*1>

šibicáriti {bìcārīm, rē imperf.} *sl-gamble* gamble on the street using matchboxes <Slav❖*1>

šibigūz {a (acc. = gen.) masc.} (lit. whip-ass) *sl-fea* ***Der-Obs*** lazy or shiftless person, bum, good for nothing <Slav❖*1>

šibigûzović {a (acc. = gen.) masc.} (lit. McWhipass) *sl-fea* a child of a worthless or mean person <Slav❖*1>

Šibnēm ti ga! {S} (lit. I whip it to you!) *col-dia* ***Off*** used as a weak curse, Screw you! ☞ **šibnuti**

šibnuti {nēm, nū perf.} (lit. whip) **a.** *sl* hit, punch <Slav❖*1> **b.i.** *sl-sex* engage in sexual intercourse with (of a male) <Slav*2> **ii.** *sl* throw away, toss out <Slav❖*1>

• **Šibnēm ti ga!** {S} (lit. I whip it to you!) *col-dia* ***Off*** used as a weak curse, Screw you!

šibos {a (acc. = gen.) masc.} *sl-fea* troublemaker, rowdy, ruffian <Slav❖*1>

šic {excl.} *col* used to drive away a cat, scat <Slav>

šica {excl.} *col* used to drive away a cat, scat <Slav>

šicati {šicām, šicajū imperf.} **1** *col* drive away a cat <Slav❖*1> **2** *col* aim, direct <Ger❖*1>

šićār {šićára masc.} BosM *col* profit, gain <NE>

šićàrdžija {ē masc.} BosM *col* profiter <NE❖>

šifònjēr {šifonjéra (acc. = gen.) masc.} (lit. cupboard) **1** *sl-fea* muscular male, pumped up guy <Gre❖*1> **2** *sl-fea* obese female <Gre❖*1>

• **ko šifònjēr** {PP} (lit. like a cupboard) *sl-fea* muscular

šifonjéri {ā masc. pl.} (lit. cupboards) *sl* lungs, gills <Gre❖*1>

šija *See the following*

• **U šiju te jèbēm!** {S} (lit. I screw you in your neck!) *dia* ***Off*** used as a weak curse, Screw you!

šik {excl.} *col* used to make somebody go away, scram <Slav>

šikàna {ē fem.} *sl-sex* ***Obs*** place intended for sexual intercourse <Slav❖*1>

šíkati {šīkām, šíkajū imperf.} (lit. burst) **1a.** *sl* beat up <Slav❖*1> **b.** *sl-sex* engage in sexual intercourse with (of a male) <Slav❖*2> **2** *sl* carry, bear <Slav*1>

šike {excl.} *col* used to drive away a pig <Slav>

šikić {a (acc. = gen.) masc.} *sl-sex* ***Obs*** male sexual partner (of a female) <Slav❖*1>

šíknuti {šīknēm, nū perf.} **1a.** *sl* hit, punch <Slav*1> **b.** *sl-sex* engage in sexual intercourse with (of a male) <Slav*2> **2** *sl* throw away, toss out <Slav*1>

šikoi {excl.} *sl* look

šíljak {ljka masc.} *sl* cigarette, smoke <Slav*1>

šiljbočiti {čīm, čē imperf.} *sl-sex* ***Obs*** engage in sexual intercourse with (of a male)

šiljeg {a (acc. = gen.) masc.} *dia* young sheep <Slav>

šilježe {eta neut.} *dia* young sheep <Slav>

šiljgūz {a (acc. = gen.) masc.} (lit. sharp ass) *sl-sex* ***Obs*** person with pointed buttocks <Slav❖>

šiljgùza {ē fem. & masc.} (lit. sharp ass) *sl-sex* ***Obs*** person with pointed buttocks <Slav❖>

šíljiti {šîljīm, ljē imperf.} (lit. sharpen) **1** *sl-sex* ***Obs*** engage in sexual intercourse with (of a male) <Slav*1> **2** *sl* lie <Slav*1> **3** *sl* annoy, bother, pester <Slav*1>

šȉljka {ē fem.} *sl-arch* pepper

Šíljko {a masc.} *sl-fea* ***Off*** German (person), Kraut

šíljo {ē masc.} *sl* boy, kid <EngO*1>

šȉljobočiti {čīm, čē imperf.} *sl-sex* ***Obs*** engage in sexual intercourse with (of a male)

šȉljogūz {a (acc. = gen.) masc.} (lit. sharp ass) *sl-sex* ***Obs*** person with pointed buttocks <Slav*1>

šȉljòguz {a, o adj.} (lit. sharp-assed) *sl-sex* ***Obs*** with pointed buttocks <Slav⁘>

šȉljòguza {ē fem.} (lit. sharp ass) *sl-sex* ***Obs*** person with pointed buttocks <Slav⁘>

šȉljokūr [1] {a (acc. = gen.) masc.} (lit. sharp prick) *sl-sex* ***Obs*** male with a sharp-tipped penis <Slav⁘>

šȉljòkur [2] {a, o adj.} (lit. sharp prick) *sl-sex* ***Obs*** having a pointed penis <Slav⁘>

šiljòkurac {kūrca (acc. = gen.) masc.} (lit. sharp prick) **a.** *sl-fea* ***Der-Obs*** worthless or despicable person <Slav⁘*1> **b.** *sl-fea* ***Der-Obs*** young dandy <Slav⁘*2> **c.** *sl-fea* ***Der-Obs*** irresponsible person <Slav⁘*3> **d.** *sl-fea* ***Der-Obs*** boy, kid <Slav⁘*4>

šiljokùrān {kurána (acc. = gen.) masc.} **a.** *sl-fea* ***Der-Obs*** worthless or despicable person <Slav⁘*1> **b.** *sl-fea* ***Der-Obs*** young dandy <Slav⁘*2> **c.** *sl-fea* ***Der-Obs*** irresponsible person <Slav⁘*3> **d.** *sl-fea* ***Der-Obs*** boy, kid <Slav⁘*4>

šȉljokùrānskī {ā, ō adj.} *sl-fea* ***Der-Obs*** pertaining to a worthless or mean person <Slav⁘*1>

šȉljokùrīle {a masc.} *sl-sex* ***Obs*** male with a sharp-tipped penis <Slav⁘>

šȉma {excl.} *sl* used to silence one's interlocutor, shut up

šȉmāj {excl.} *sl* used to make somebody go away, beat it

šȉmati {ām, ajū imperf.} *sl* run away, flee

šȉmbovati {bujēm, bujū imperf.} *sl* run away, flee

šimírati {šȉmīrām, šimírajū imperf.} *sl* run away, flee

šȉmiti {mīm, mē imperf.} *sl* run away, flee

šȉmkovati {kujēm, kujū imperf.} *sl* run away, flee

šȉmler {a (acc. = gen.) masc.} **a.** *sl-fea* clumsy male, klutz **b.** *sl-fea* strange male, weirdo

šȉmovati {mujēm, mujū imperf.} *sl* run away, flee

šȉnati {excl.; perm} [std. = tišina] *sl* used to silence one's interlocutor, shut up <Slav✍>

šindivíla {ē fem.} *sl-fea* loose woman

šȉntār {a (acc. = gen.) masc.} (lit. dog-catcher) **1** *sl* doctor, doc <Ger✍*1> **2** *sl-fea* evil person <Ger✍*1>

šȉnter {a (acc. = gen.) masc.} /šínter/ (lit. dog-catcher) **1** *sl* supervisor (on public transportation) <Ger*1> **2** *sl-fea* unattractive female, dog <Ger*1>

šȉnuti {nēm, nū perf.} *sl* throw away, toss out <Slav*1> • **šȉnuti po brázdi** {VP} (lit. hit the furrow) *sl-sex* ***Obs*** engage in sexual intercourse with

šínja {ē fem.} [std. = šina] *sl* rail (railroad) <Slav✍>

šȉo mi ga Đúra {VP} (lit. Jack has tailored it for me) SerE *sl* used to refer to indifference toward ☞ **šiti**

šȉpak {excl.} (lit. rose hip) *col* used to express disbelief or negative attitude <Slav*1>

šípak {pka masc.} (lit. rose hip) *col* nothing <Slav*1>

šȉpàrica {ē fem.} *col* very young female, little girl <Slav⁘*1>

šȉpčiti {čīm, čē imperf. intr.} *col* walk for a long time <Slav*1>

šȉpkica {ē fem.} *col* stick, bat <Slav⁘>

Šȉpu ga! {S} (lit. Smoke it!) *sl* used as a strong curse, Suck my dick! ☞ **šitipu**

Šȉpu ràcku! {S} (lit. Smoke my prick!) *sl* used as a strong curse, Suck my prick! ☞ **šitipu**

šȉritcānge {i fem. pl.} *sl-crafts* pincers <Ger>

šȉritcāngle {i fem. pl.} *sl-crafts* pincers <Ger✍>

šȉrok {a masc.} (lit. wide) *col* city <Slav*1>

šȉsnjati {ām, ajū imperf.} *sl* spring (of a water source, etc.) <Slav*1>

šȉš {excl.} **1** *col* used to drive away poultry, shoo <Slav> **2** *col* smash, crush <Slav*1>

šȉša {ē fem.} **a.** *sl-drink* bottle <NE> **b.** *sl-drink* brandy <NE*1>

šíšānje {a neut.} (lit. haircut) **1** *sl-sex* ***Fac-Obs*** sexual intercourse <Slav*1> **2** *sl-auto* overtaking (passing another car on the road) <Slav*1>

šȉšārka {ē fem.; Dat šȉšārki} (lit. gall-nut) *sl* female <Slav*1>

šíšati {šȋšām, šíšajū imperf.} (lit. give a haircut) **1** *sl-sex* ***Obs*** engage in sexual intercourse with (of a male) <Slav*1> **2a.** *sl* appreciate, enjoy, like <Slav*1> **b.** *sl* respect, obey <Slav*2> **c.** *sl* take care of <Slav*3> **3a.** *sl-auto* speed (auto, etc.) <Slav*1> **b.** *sl-auto* overtake (pass another car on the road) <Slav*2> **4** *sl* overcharge, rip off <Slav*1>

• **Kȍ[PRON:ACC] šȉšā!** {LSF} (lit. Who is giving [PRON:ACC] a haircut!) *col* ***Off*** used to refer to indifference toward: *Ko ga šiša? Who gives a damn about him?*

• **Kȍ te šȉšā!** {S} (lit. Who is giving you a haircut?) *col* ***Off*** used to express disrespect, Screw you!

šíšati se *See the following*

• **šíšati se peškírom** {VP} (lit. use a towel to shave) *sl-fea* be bald

šišȁtor {a (acc. = gen.) masc.} (lit. the one who cuts hair) **1** *sl* ***Fac*** barber <Slav⁘*1> **2** *sl* ***Fac*** hairdresser <Slav⁘*1>

šȉše {eta neut.} **a.** *sl-drink* bottle <NE> **b.** *sl-drink* shot glass <NE*1>

šȉšibeka {ē fem.; Dat šȉšibeki} **a.** *sl-sex* ***Obs*** loose woman, slut **b.** *sl-fea* ***Der*** unattractive female

šíšiti {šȉšīm, šē imperf.} *sl* drip <Slav>

šȉšnuti {nēm, nū perf.} **a.** *sl* hit, punch <Slav*1> **b.** *sl-sex* have quick sexual intercourse, have a quickie <Slav*2> **c.** *sl-sex* engage in sexual intercourse with (of a male) <Slav*3> **d.** *sl* stick in, insert <Slav*4>

šȉšnuti se {nēm, nū perf. intr.} *sl* get a haircut <Slav⁘*1>

šȉšnjava {ē fem.} **a.** *sl* speed (auto, etc.) <Slav*1> **b.** *sl* running away, fleeing <Slav*2>

šȉštānje {a neut.} *col* hissing (snake, gas, etc.) <Slav*1>

šȉštati {tīm, tē imperf. intr.} **a.** *col* hiss (snake, gas, etc.) <Slav> **b.** *sl* whisper <Slav*1> **c.** *col* squeak <Slav*2>

šȉštav {a, o adj.} *col* hissing (snake, gas, etc.) <Slav*1>

šȉštavo {adv.} *col* hissing (snake, gas, etc.) <Slav>

šȉt [1] {excl.} *col* used to express extreme dissatisfaction <Eng>

šȉt [2] {a +ov (ext. pl) masc.; Nom Pl šȉtovi} **a.** *sl-sex* ***Obs*** excrement, shit <Eng> **b.i.aa.** *sl-drugs* low-quality hashish <Eng*1> **bb.** *sl-drugs* drugs, dope <Eng*2> **ii.** *sl* trifle, thing of little importance or value <Eng*2>

šȉt [3] {adv.} *col* difficult <Eng>

šȉtara {ē fem.} *sl-sex* ***Obs*** buttocks, butt <Eng⁘*1>

šȉti {ijēm, ijū imperf.} (lit. sew) **1a.** *sl-auto* overtake (pass another car on the road) <Slav*1> **b.** *sl* outwit, outsmart <Slav*2> **c.** *sl* be better than somebody else <Slav*3> **d.** *sl* defeat <Slav*4> **2** *sl-sex* engage in sexual intercourse with (of a male) <Slav*1>

• **šȉo mi ga Đúra** {VP} (lit. Jack has tailored it for me) SerE *sl* used to refer to indifference toward

• **šȉti dȕmine** {VP} (lit. sew lies) *sl* lie

šȉtipu {šȉmpu, šēpu imperf.; perm} (lit. smoke) [std. = pušiti] *sl-sex* ***Obs*** engage in fellatio <Slav✍*1>

• **Šȉpu ga!** {S} (lit. Smoke it!) *sl* used as a strong curse, Suck my dick!

• **Šȉpu rȁčku!** {S} (lit. Smoke my prick!) *sl* used as a strong curse, Suck my prick!

šívati {šȉvām, šívajū imperf.} (lit. sew) **1a.** *sl-auto* overtake (pass another car on the road) <Slav*1> **b.** *sl* outwit, outsmart <Slav*2> **c.** *sl* be better than somebody else <Slav*3> **d.** *sl* defeat <Slav*3> **2** *sl-sex* engage in sexual intercourse with (of a male)

• **šívati gȕmb** {VP} (lit. sew a button) Cro *sl-sex* rub clitoris

šȉz [1] {a (acc. = gen.) +ev (ext. pl) masc.; Nom Pl šízevi} *sl-fea* schizophrenic <Gre✍*1>

šȉz [2] {adj.} *sl-fea* strange, weird <Gre✍*1>

šȉza [1] {ē fem.} **a.** *sl-fea* ***Der*** insanity, craziness <Gre✍*1> **b.** *sl-fea* ***Der*** hysteria <Gre✍*2> **c.** *sl* dance <Gre✍*3>

šíza [2] {adj.} **a.** *sl-fea* eccentric, extravagant, weird <Gre✍*1> **b.** *sl-fea* insane, nuts <Gre✍*2>

šizbláza {ē fem.} **a.** *sl-fea* stupid or mentally deficient person <Gre✍*1> **b.** *sl-fea* foolish female <Gre✍*2>

šízēnje {a neut.} *sl-fea* eccentric behavior, weirdness <Gre✍*1>

šizijáda {ē fem.} **a.** *sl-fea* ***Der*** insanity, craziness <Gre✍*1> **b.** *sl* noise <Gre✍*1>

šȉzik [1] {a (acc. = gen.) masc.} *sl-fea* ***Der*** insane person, nut case <Gre✍*1>

šȉzik [2] {adj.} *sl-fea* slightly insane, nutty <Gre✍*>

šȉzika {ē fem.} **a.** *sl-fea* ***Der*** insane female, nut case <Gre✍*1> **b.** *sl-sex* loose woman <Gre✍*2>

Šȉzilȋšte {a neut.} Ser *sl* name of a coffee shop near Knez Mihailo Monument, Belgrade, Serbia <Gre⁘*1>

šíziti {zīm, zē imperf.} **1a.** *sl-fea* go insane, freak out <Gre⁘*1> **b.** *sl-fea* be very happy <Gre⁘*2> **c.** *sl* dance <Gre⁘*3> **2a.** *sl-fea* get nervous <Gre⁘*1> **b.** *sl-fea* get upset <Gre⁘*2>

šȉznica {ē fem.} *sl-fea* psychiatric hospital, nuthouse <Slav⁘*1>

šȉznuti {nēm, nū perf. intr.} *sl-fea* go insane, freak out <Slav⁘>

šizobláza {ē fem.} *sl-fea* stupid or mentally deficient person <Slav✍[*1]>

šizofrèničār {a (acc. = gen.) masc.} (lit. schizophrenic) *sl-fea* strange person, weirdo <Gre[*1]>

šizofrèničārka {ē fem.; Dat šizofrèničārki} (lit. schizophrenic) *sl-fea* strange female, weird chick <Slav⁘[*1]>

šjȏr {a masc.} Med *dia* used to address a male in direct informal communication, mister, sir <Ita>

šjȏra {ē fem.} Med *dia* used to address a female in direct formal communication, madam <Ita>

škȃf {a +ov (ext. pl) masc.; Nom Pl škȁfovi} *sl-sex* ***Fac-Obs*** large vagina <Lat[*1]>

škȁliti {līm, lē imperf.} *sl* harm, damage

škàmut {a masc.} *col* barking of a young dog <Slav⁘[*1]>

škamùtānje {a neut.} *col* barking of a young dog <Slav⁘[*1]>

škamùtati {ām, ajū imperf.} **a.** *col* yelp (of a young dog) <Slav⁘[*1]> **b.** *col* bark (of a dog)

škàndāl {kandála masc.} Med *dia* scandal <Ita>

škȁr {a +ov (ext. pl) masc.; Nom Pl škàrovi} [std. = škart] *col* malfunctioning devices <Ita✍>

škàrnicl {a masc.} **1** *sl* hat <Ita-Ger[*1]> **2** *sl-crime* prison

škàrpīna {ē fem.} (lit. red snapper) *sl-fea* unattractive female <Ita[*1]>

škȁrt {a +ov (ext. pl) masc.; Nom Pl škàrtovi} **a.** *col* low-quality merchandise, junk <Ita[*1]> **b.** worthless people <Ita[*2]>

škartírati {škàrtīrām, škartírajū perf.} (lit. trash) **a.** *sl* resign, quit <Ita⁘[*1]> **b.** *sl* throw away, toss out <Ita⁘[*2]> **c.** *sl* dump one's boyfriend or girlfriend <Ita⁘[*3]>

škàtalja {ē fem.} **1** *sl* streetcar <Ita⁘> **2** *sl* ship, vessel

škȁtula {ē fem.} *col-dia* box <Ita> ☞ **škatulja**

škȁtulja {ē fem.} Med *col-dia* box <Ita> ☞ **skatula**
- **škȁtulja šȉbīcā** {NP} (lit. matchbox) Cro *sl-sports* name of a sports dome in Zagreb, Croatia

škȅmbav {a, o adj.} *sl-sex* pregnant, knocked up <NE[*1]>

škȅmbavā tréba {NP} (lit. plump chick) *sl-sex* pregnant female ☞ **treba**

škèmbe {eta neut.} **a.** *sl* stomach, belly, gut <NE[*1]> **b.** *sl-fea* obese person <NE[*2]>

škémbo {a masc.} /ē masc./ *sl-fea* obese male <NE✍[*1]>

škémbonja {ē masc.} *sl-fea* obese person <NE✍[*1]>

škèmbreg {a masc.} *sl-sex* ***Obs*** vagina, cunt <NE✍[*1]>

škȉcati {ām, ajū imperf.} *sl* look, watch, scope out <Slav[*1]>

škȉcēr {a (acc. = gen.) masc.} (lit. sketcher) *sl-crime* detective <Ger⁘[*1]>

škȉcnuti {nēm, nū perf.} *sl* glance <Slav⁘[*1]>

škȉljān {a (acc. = gen.) masc.} *sl-fea* boy who likes to be hugged <Slav⁘[*1]>

škiljávko {a masc.} *sl-stu* student <Slav⁘[*1]>

šklȁp {a +ov (ext. pl) masc.; Nom Pl šklápovi} *col* click (short, sharp, non-resonant sound) <Slav[*1]>

šklòpōcija[1] {ē fem.} **a.** *col* old and often malfunctioning mechanism, wreck <Slav✍[*1]> **b.** *sl-auto* old car, wreck <Slav✍[*2]>

šklopòtati {šklòpoćēm, oćū imperf. intr.} //lòpoćēm, lòpočū imperf. intr./ *col* make noise <Slav>

šklj [šəklj] {adj.} *col* of lowest quality, cheap: *Bili smo u nekom šklj hotelu, a ti se hvališ. We were in a cheap hotel, and you are boasting about it.* <Slav[*1]> ☞ **žnj**

škljȍc {excl.} *col* click (short, sharp, non-resonant sound) <Slav>

škljȍcāj {a masc.} *col* click (short, sharp, non-resonant sound) <Slav>

škljȍcati {ām, ajū imperf.} *col* click (produce a short, sharp, non-resonant sound) <Slav⁘>

Škȍdilāk {a (acc. = gen.) masc.} (lit. Škoda *a simple Eastern European car* X Cadillac) *sl-auto* Škoda (make of car) <BN✍>

škȍjne {excl.} *sl* watch out, be careful

škȏla *See the following*
- **bèčkā škȏla** {NP} (lit. Vienna school) **a.** *col* elegance **b.** *col* very elegant person
- **bèčkā škȏla ìsturenō odelénje Nȋš** {NP} (lit. Vienna school branch office in Niš *a city in Southern Serbia*) SerE *col* ***Fac*** provincial snob: *Mića je bečka škola istureno odelenje Niš. Miça is a provincial snob.*

školárac {rca masc.} *sl-sstu* school <Slav⁘[*1]>

škȍlarina {ē fem.} /škòlārina, školarína/ (lit. tuition) *sl-drugs* understanding that bogus narcotic drugs have been purchased <Slav⁘[*1]>

škȍlkić {a masc.} *sl-sstu* school student <Slav⁘[*1]>

škȏlnjāk {a (acc. = gen.) masc.} *sl-sstu* educational TV program <Slav⁘[*1]>

škȏljka {ē fem.} (lit. shell) *sl-sex* ***Fac-Obs*** vagina, cunt <Slav[*1]>

škȍrnja {ē fem.} *sl* shoe

Škȍt {a (acc. = gen.) masc.} (lit. Scot) **1** *sl-fea* ***Der*** male in tight trousers <EngO[*1]> 2 *sl-fea* miser, tightwad, skinflint

Škòtkinja {ē fem.} *sl-fea* miser, tightwad, skinflint (female) <EngO[*1]>

škrábalo {a neut.} (lit. scribbler) **1** *sl-fea* journalist <Slav❖[*1]> **2** *sl* pencil <Slav❖[*1]> **3** *sl-fea* bad writer <Slav❖[*1]>

škrábati {ām, ajū biasp.} *sl* write <Ger[*1]>

škrȁbljica {ē fem.} *sl-sex* ***Obs*** vagina, cunt <Slav❖[*1]>

škȑcnuti {nēm, nū perf.} *col* click (produce a short, sharp, non-resonant sound) <Slav❖>

škrebètati {rèbećēm, rebećū imperf.} **a.** *col* squeak <Slav❖> **b.** *col* chatter (of the teeth, in outrage) <Slav❖[*1]>

škrehètāljka {ē fem.} *sl-auto* old car, wreck <Slav❖[*1]>

škȑge {škȑgā fem. pl.} (lit. gills) **a.** *sl* lungs, gills <Slav[*1]> **b.** *sl-sex* female breast <Slav[*2]>

škȑgūt {a masc.} *col* chattering (of the teeth) <Slav❖>

škrîp {a +ov (ext. pl) masc.; Nom Pl škrípovi} *col* squeak <Slav>

škrȉpa {ē fem.} *col* squeak <Slav❖>

škrȉpav {a, o adj.} *col* squeaking <Slav❖>

škrȉplja {ē fem.} (lit. clamp) **a.** *sl-fea* ***Der*** worthless or despicable person <Slav❖[*1]> **b.** *sl-sex* prostitute, hooker <Slav❖[*2]> **c.** *sl-fea* ***Der*** unfriendly person <Slav❖[*3]> **3a.** *sl* lover (female) <Slav❖[*1]> **b.** *sl* female <Slav❖[*2]> **c.** *sl-fea* naive female <Slav❖[*3]> **d.** *sl-fea* ***Der*** foolish female <Slav❖[*4]>

škrȉpūt {a masc.} *col* soft squeak <Slav❖[*1]>

škrȍbot {a masc.} *col* gnashing (of one's teeth in outrage) <Slav❖>

škrobòtānje {a neut.} *col* gnashing (of one's teeth in outrage) <Slav❖>

škrobòtati {ròbоćēm, ròbоćū imperf. intr.} *col* gnash (one's teeth in outrage) <Slav❖>

škrofulóza {ē fem.} *sl-fea* spoiled child, brat <Lat[*1]>

škȓtalo {a neut.} *sl* pencil <Slav❖[*1]>

škȕda {ē fem.} **1a.** *sl* money <Lat[*1]> **b.** *sl* metal two-dinar coin <Lat[*2]> **2** *sl* fight (e.g. fist fight) <Lat[*1]>

škudírānje {a neut.} **a.** *sl* beating up <Lat❖[*1]> **b.** *sl* fight (e.g. fist fight) <Lat❖[*2]>

škudírati {kùdīrām, kudírajū biasp.} *sl* beat up <Lat❖[*1]>

škȕlja {ē fem.} *sl-sex* ***Obs*** vagina, cunt

škȕljica {ē fem.} *sl-sex* ***Obs*** vagina, cunt

škȕta {ē fem.} **a.** *sl* inner pocket (of a jacket) **b.** *sl* inner pocket (of a jacket)

Škȕtor {a (acc. = gen.) masc.} *sl-fea* Herzegovinian (inhabitant of the Southern part of Bosnia and Herzegovina) <Lat[*1]>

škvâdra {ē fem.} *col-dia* company (group of people) <Ita[*1]>

šlâfgust {a masc.} *sl-sex* paid sex <Ger[*1]>

šlága {ē fem.; Dat šlági} **1** *col* slap, smack <Ger[*1]> **2** *sl-gamble* game of guessing numbers on currency bills <Ger[*1]>

šláger [1] {a (acc. = gen.) masc.} (lit. hit song) **1** *sl-fea* stupid or mentally deficient person <Ger[*1]> **2** *sl-sex* very attractive female, hot number <Ger[*1]>

šláger [2] {adj.} (lit. hit) *sl-fea* ***App*** excellent, awesome <Ger[*1]>

šlagírati {šlàgīrām, šlagírajū biasp.} *sl* slap, smack <Ger❖[*1]>

šlagírati se {šlàgīrām, šlagírajū biasp. intr.} *sl-fea* go insane, freak out <Ger❖[*1]>

šlȁjfānje {a neut.} **a.** *sl-crafts* polishing <Ger[*1]> **b.** *sl-sex* ***Obs*** sexual intercourse <Ger[*2]>

šlȁjfati {ām, ajū imperf.} **a.** *sl-crafts* polish <Ger[*1]> **b.** *sl-sex* engage in sexual intercourse with (of a male) <Ger[*2]>

šlȁjferica {ē fem.} **a.** *sl-crafts* ***Fac*** polishing machine <Ger❖> **b.** *sl-sex* lesbian <Ger❖[*1]>

šlȁjfovati {fujēm, fujū imperf.} **a.** *sl-crafts* polish <Ger[*1]> **b.** *sl-fea* stutter <Ger[*2]>

šlâjka {ē fem.} *sl* spit with mucus <Ger♁>

šlȁjm [1] {adv.} *sl-fea* bad <Ger[*1]>

šlȁjm [2] {a +ov (ext. pl) masc.; Nom Pl šlȁjmovi} *col* mucus, snot <Ger[*1]>

šlȁjmara {ē fem.} *sl* spit with mucus <Ger>

šlȁjmisati {išēm, išū biasp.} *sl* spit <Ger❖[*1]>

šlȁjpek {a masc.} *col* wallet <Ger>

šlȁjpik {a masc.} **1** *col* wallet <Ger> **2** *sl-fea* female from a blue-collar family <Ger[*1]>

šlȁmpast {a, o adj.} *col* clumsy, klutzy <Ger>

šlȁmpav {a, o adj.} *col* clumsy, klutzy <Ger>

šlàtānje {a neut.} *sl-sex* ***Obs*** sexual foreplay, petting, feeling up

šlàtati {ām, ajū biasp.} **a.** *sl-sex* ***Obs*** engage in sexual foreplay, pet, feel up **b.** *sl-sex* ***Obs*** stimulate sexually, turn on

šlàuf {a masc.} **a.** *col* hose <**Ger**> **b.** *sl-sex* penis <**Ger***1>

šlèpānje {a neut.} **1** *sl-gamble* keeping one card (in poker) <**Ger**❖*1> **2** *sl* intrusion <**Ger**❖*1>

šlèpati {ām, ajū biasp.} **a.** *sl-gamble* keep a card (in poker) <**Ger***1> **b.** *sl* take one's girlfriend along <**Ger***1>

šlèpati se {ām, ajū biasp. intr.} **1** *sl* compete <**Ger**❖*1> **2a.** *sl* go along, accompany <**Ger**❖*1> **b.** *sl-fea* intrude, barge in <**Ger**❖*2>

šlèper [1] {a (acc. = gen.) masc.} (lit. trailer-truck) **a.** *sl-fea* intruder <**Ger***1> **b.** *sl-fea* boring person, bore <**Ger***2>

šlèper [2] {a masc.} *sl-auto* trailer truck <**Ger**>

šlèpovānje {a neut.} **1** *sl-gamble* keeping a card (in poker) <**Ger**❖*1> **2** *sl* intrusion <**Ger**❖*1>

šlèpovati {pujēm, pujū imperf.} **1a.** *sl* take one's girlfriend home to meet one's parents <**Ger**❖*1> **b.** *sl* take one's girlfriend along <**Ger**❖*2> **c.** *sl* take somebody along (e.g. to a party) <**Ger***3> **2** *sl-gamble* keep a card (in poker)

šlìc {šlìca +ev (ext. pl) masc.} *col* zipper, fly <**Ger**>

šlîf {a +ov (ext. pl) masc.; Nom Pl šlìfovi} *col* style, kind <**Ger***1>

šlîfovān {a, o adj.} *col* stylish <**Ger**❖*1>

šlìhtara {ē fem.} *sl-fea* ingratiator (male), brownnoser, ass kisser <**Ger**>

šlîhtati se {ām, ajū imperf.} *sl-fea* ***Der*** ingratiate, brownnose, kiss ass <**Ger***1>

šlîs {excl.} *col* the sound made by slapping, slap <**Slav**>

šlìsl {a masc.} *sl-crafts* key <**Ger**>

šlofìnjāk {finjáka masc.} *sl* bed <**Ger**❖*1>

šlòg [1] {excl.} *col* used to express the state of being shocked <**Ger**>

šlòg [2] {a (acc. = gen.) +ov (ext. pl) masc.; Nom Pl šlògovi} **a.** *sl-fea* retarded person, retard <**Ger***1> **b.** *sl-fea* insane person, nut case <**Ger***2> **c.** *sl-fea* unattractive person <**Ger***3>

šlòg [3] {a +ov (ext. pl) masc.; Nom Pl šlògovi} *col* stroke, apoplexy <**Ger**>

šlògati {ām, ajū biasp.} *sl-gamble* play cards <**Ger**❖*1>

šlògī-drògī [1] {īja (acc. = gen.) masc.} *sl-fea* stupid or mentally deficient person <**Ger-Fre***1>

šlògī-drògī [2] {adj.} *sl-fea* ***Der*** insane, nuts <**Ger-Fre***1>

šlògīrān {a, o adj.} (lit. having a stroke) **1** *sl-fea* clumsy, klutzy <**Ger**❖*1> **2** *sl-fea* excellent, cool <**Ger**❖*1>

šlògīrānā kàfa {NP} (lit. apoplectic coffee) *sl-fea* coffee with whipped cream ☞ **kafa**

šlògīrānī kàktus {NP} (lit. apoplectic cactus) *sl-fea* unattractive male ☞ **kaktus**

šlògīrānī karánfil {NP} (lit. apoplectic carnation *the flower*) *sl-fea* unattractive male ☞ **karanfil**

šlògīrānī làdolēž {NP} (lit. apoplectic ivy) *sl-fea* phlegmatic person ☞ **ladolež**

šlògīrānī pètlīć {NP} (lit. apoplectic small rooster) SerE *sl-fea* unattractive male ☞ **petlić**

šlogìruša {ē fem.} *sl-fea* strong coffee <**Ger**❖*1>

šlòpnuti {nēm, nū perf.} *col* the sound made by tapping, tap <**Slav**❖>

šlùs [1] {excl.} *col* used to stop an action, that's enough <**Ger**>

šlùs [2] {a +ev (ext. pl) masc.; Nom Pl šlùsevi} *col* end, cessation <**Ger**>

šljâfgust {a masc.} *sl-sex* paid sex <**Ger**✍>

šljága {ē fem.; Dat šljági} /šljàga/ **1a.** *col* slap, smack <**Ger**> **b.** *col* hit, punch <**Ger***1> **2** *sl* cream <**Ger**✍>

šljagárac {rca masc.} *sl* hit, punch <**Ger**✍*1>

šljagírati {ljàgīrām, šljagírajū biasp.} *sl* hit, punch <**Ger**❖*1>

šljàjpik {a masc.} (lit. wallet) *sl-fea* female from a blue-collar family <**Ger***1>

šljàk {a +ov (ext. pl) masc.; Nom Pl šljàkovi} *sl* cigarette, smoke <**Slav**✍*1>

šljàka {ē fem.} **a.** *sl* work, labor <**Ger***1> **b.** *sl* dangerous job

- **šljàka na mútno** {NP} (lit. work in murky waters) *sl-fea* suspicious job

šljakánac {nca masc.} *sl* work, labor <**Ger**❖*1>

šljakaóna {ē fem.} *sl-fea* factory <**Ger**❖*1>

šljàkār {a (acc. = gen.) masc.} *sl-fea* worker <**Ger**❖*1>

šljakárac {rca masc.} **a.** *sl* work, labor <**Ger**❖*1> **b.** *sl* job, gig

šljakáriti {ljàkārīm, rē perf.} *sl* work, labor <**Ger**❖*1>

šljàkārnica {ē fem.} *sl-fea* factory <**Ger**❖*1>

šljàkāroš {a (acc. = gen.) masc.} **a.** *sl* worker <**Ger**❖*1> **b.i.** *sl-crime* thief **ii.** *sl-crime* pickpocket

šljȁkati {ām, ajū imperf.} **a.** *sl* work, labor <Ger⁘*1> **b.i.** *sl* learn, study **ii.** *sl-crime* steal

• **šljȁkati Amerikánca** {VP} (lit. work an American) *sl-crime* pretend to be an American

• **šljȁkati na cȉstērni** {VP} (lit. work on a tanker) *sl-drink* hang out at the bar

• **šljȁkati prvénstvo** {VP} (lit. work the World Cup) *sl-sports* watch World Cup soccer

• **šljȁkati skȁkāvce** {VP} (lit. work grasshoppers) *sl-crime* rob via balcony

šljȁkātor {a (acc. = gen.) masc.} **a.** *sl-crime* worker <Ger⁘*1> **b.i.** *sl* pickpocket **ii.** *sl-crime* thief, sticky fingers

šljȁkavac {vca (acc. = gen.) masc.} *sl-fea* manual laborer <Ger⁘*1>

šljȁker {a (acc. = gen.) masc.} **a.** *sl* worker <Ger⁘*1> **b.i.** *sl-crime* thief **ii.** *sl-crime* pickpocket

šljȁknuti {nēm, nū perf.} *sl-crime* steal, swipe <Ger⁘*1>

šljȁm {a +ov (ext. pl) masc.; Nom Pl šljàmovi} /šljâm/ *col* ***Der*** worthless or despicable persons, scum <Ger*1>

šljȁpat {a masc.} *col* splash <Slav⁘>

šljàpati {ām, ajū imperf.} *col* splash <Slav⁘>

šljȁpavica {ē fem.} **a.** *sl* hand <Slav⁘*1> **b.** *sl* arm <Slav⁘*2>

šljȁpica {ē fem.} *sl* shoe <Ger⁘*1>

šljȁpiti {pīm, pē imperf.} *col* splash <Slav⁘>

šljàporiti {rīm, rē imperf.} *col* splash <Slav⁘>

šljapùtati {ām, ajū imperf.} *sl-fea* talk persistently and meaninglessly, blabber, chatter <Slav⁘*1>

šljȁs {excl.} *col* the sound made by slapping, slap <Slav>

šljàštiti {tīm, tē imperf.} /šljáštiti/ *sl-fea* be loud (colors) <Slav⁘*1>

šljàštiti se {tīm, tē imperf. intr.} /šljáštiti se/ *sl* speed (auto, etc.) <Slav⁘*1>

šljâz {adj.} *sl-fea* unattractive, ugly as sin <Slav*1>

šljȅći {egnēm, egnū, eg, eg perf. irreg.} [std. = sići] *dia* descend <Slav☞>

šljȅmānje {a neut.} *sl-drink* drinking (alcohol) <Ger⁘*1>

šljȅmati {ām, ajū biasp.} *sl-drink* get drunk <Ger⁘*1>

šljȅpkati {ām, ajū imperf.} *col* splash <Slav⁘>

šljéviti {šljêvīm, vē imperf.} *sl-sex* ***Obs*** urinate, piss <Slav⁘*1>

šljȉs {excl.} *col* the sound made by slapping, slap <Slav>

šljȉskānje {a neut.} *sl-drink* drinking (alcohol) <Slav⁘*1>

šljȉsnuti *See the following*

• **Šljȉsnēm ti ga!** {S} (lit. I squish it to you!) *col-dia* ***Off*** used as a weak curse, Screw you!

šljȉva [1] {ē fem.} (lit. plum) **1** *col* bruise <Slav*1> **2** *sl-crime* policeman, cop <Slav*1> **3** *sl-sex* vagina <Slav*1> **4** *sl-sex* unsuitable sexual partner <Slav*1>

• **za sûvū šljȉvu** {PP} (lit. for a prune) **Ser** *col* at all: *Ne zarezuje ju za suvu šljivu. He does not give a fig about her.*

šljíva [2] {ē fem.} **1** *sl-drink* plum brandy <Slav⁘> **2** *sl-sex* ***Obs*** vagina, cunt <Slav⁘*1>

šljȉvāč {a (acc. = gen.) masc.} (lit. plummer) *sl-crime* policeman, man in blue <Slav⁘*1>

šljȉvār {a (acc. = gen.) masc.} (lit. plummer) *sl-crime* policeman, man in blue <Slav⁘*1>

šljíviti {vīm, vē imperf.} (lit. plum) *col* respect, obey: *On ne šljivi svoje roditelje. He does not respect his parents.* <Slav⁘*1>

• **Kȍ te šljívī!** {S} (lit. Who is plumming you?) *col* ***Off*** used to express disrespect, Screw you!

šljȉvosati {ošēm, ošū imperf.} (lit. plum) *sl* respect, obey <Slav⁘*1>

šljȍfinjāk {šljofinjáka masc.} *sl* bed <Ger☞*1>

šljóka {ē fem.; Dat šljóki} **a.** *sl-drink* alcoholic beverage <Slav⁘*1> **b.** *sl-drink* brandy

šljókānje {a neut.} *sl-drink* drinking (alcohol) <Slav⁘*1>

šljȍkara {ē fem.} *sl-drink* alcoholic, drunk <Slav⁘*1>

šljokárac {rca masc.} *sl-drink* drinking (alcohol) <Slav⁘*1>

šljókati {šljôkām, šljókajū imperf.} *sl-drink* get drunk <Slav⁘*1>

šljȍknuti {nēm, nū perf.} **1** *sl-drink* drink (alcohol) <Slav⁘*1> **2** *sl* die, kick the bucket <Slav⁘*1> **3** *sl-crime* steal, swipe <Slav⁘*1>

šljȕcati {ām, ajū imperf.} *sl* kick, strike <Slav⁘*1>

šljúnak {nka (acc. = gen.) masc.} (lit. pebbles) **1a.** *sl-sex* ***Fac*** prostitute, hooker <Slav*1> **b.** *sl-sex* ***Fac*** loose woman <Slav*2> **2** *sl* ***Fac*** rice <Slav*1>

šljûnčiti {čīm, čē imperf.} *sl* cry, shed tears, weep <Slav⁘*1>

šljȕnta {ē fem.} *sl-fea* stupid or mentally deficient person

šljȕnuti {nēm, nū perf.} *sl-stu* fail an exam (flunk) <Slav⁘*1>

• šljȕnuti lóvu {VP} (lit. swing money) *sl* spend money

šljȕpati {ām, ajū biasp.} *sl-sex* ***Obs*** engage in cunnilingus <Slav✤*1>

šmȁjhlati {ām, ajū biasp.} *sl-sex* ***Obs*** engage in sexual foreplay, pet, feel up <Ger✤*1>

šmȁjser {a masc.} (lit. machine gun) *sl-sex* ***Obs*** penis, dick, prick <Ger✤*1>

šmȅk {šmèka +ov (ext. pl) masc.; Nom Pl šmèkovi} **a.** *col* taste, preferences <Ger> **b.** *sl* look, glimpse <Ger*1>

šmȅkār {a (acc. = gen.) masc.} *sl-crime* skillful criminal who has not been caught <Ger✤*1>

šmekáriti {mèkārīm, mèkārē imperf.} *sl* look at with interest, check out <Ger✍*1>

šmȅkati {ām, ajū imperf.} *sl* look at with interest, check out <Ger*1>

šmȅker {a (acc. = gen.) masc.} /šmèker/ **a.** *sl-fea* ***Der*** cunning male <Ger*1> **b.** *sl-sex* seducer <Ger*2> **c.** *sl-sex* male sexual partner (of a female) <Ger*3> **d.** *sl-sex* voyeur <Ger*4> **e.i.** *sl-fea* dandy, fop <Ger*5> **ii.** *sl* observer <Ger*5>

šmȅkeriti {rīm, rē biasp.} **a.** *sl* look, watch, scope out <Ger✤*1> **b.** *sl* like, appreciate <Ger✤*2>

šmȅkos {a (acc. = gen.) masc.} **a.** *sl-sex* seducer <Ger✍*1> **b.** *sl-fea* lover (male) <Ger✍*2> **c.** *sl-sex* male sexual partner (of a female) <Ger✍*3> **e.** *sl-fea* dandy, fop <Ger✍*4> **f.i.** observer **ii.** skillful person

šmȅkovānje {a neut.} *sl* looking, watching, scoping out <Ger✤*1>

šmȅkovati {kujēm, kujū biasp.} *sl* look, watch, scope out <Ger✤*1>

šmêle {eta masc.} *sl-fea* attractive male <Ger✍*1>

šmînka {ē fem.; Dat šmínki} (lit. make-up) **1** *col* high society <Ger*1> **2** *sl* cheating, swindling <Ger*1> **3** *sl-fea* boasting, bragging <Ger*1>

šmȉnkačica {ē fem.} (lit. the one who puts on make-up) *sl-fea* female who dresses fashionably <Ger✤*1>

šmȉnkānje {a neut.} (lit. putting on make-up) **1** *sl-drink* drinking (alcohol) <Ger✤*1> **2** *sl-fea* boasting, bragging <Ger✤*1> **3** *sl* cheating, swindling <Ger✤*2>

šmînkati se {ām, ajū biasp. intr.} (lit. put on make-up) **1a.** *sl-fea* dress formally, dress up <Ger✤*1> **b.** *sl-fea* show off <Ger✤*2> **c.** *sl-fea* be conceited, be stuck-up <Ger✤*3> **2** *sl-drink* get drunk <Ger✤*1>

šmȉnker {a (acc. = gen.) masc.} /šmìnker/ (lit. male who puts on make-up) **a.** *sl-fea* dandy, fop <Ger✤*1> **b.** *sl-fea* stupid or mentally deficient person <Ger✤*2> **c.** *sl-fea* crook, thief <Ger✤*3> **d.** *sl-fea* liar <Ger✤*4> **e.** *sl-fea* boaster, braggart, blowhard <Ger✤*5> **f.** *sl-fea* conceited male <Ger✤*6> **g.** *sl-fea* inhabitant of the countryside, hick, bumpkin <Ger✤*7>

šminkèrāj {keràja masc.} (lit. make-up) **a.** *sl-fea* dressing formally, dressing up <Ger✤*1> **b.** *sl-fea* being conceited, being stuck up <Ger✤*2>

šminkerȉkī {īja masc.} *sl-fea* attractive male <Ger✍*1>

šmȉnkerka {ē fem.} (lit. female who puts some make-up on) **a.** *sl-fea* female who dresses fashionably <Ger✤*1> **b.** *sl-fea* conceited female <Ger✤*2>

šmȉrati {ām, ajū imperf.} (lit. lubricate) *sl* lie <Ger*1>

šmȉrglānje {a neut.} **a.** *sl-crafts* polishing <Ger✤> **b.** reproaching, scolding <Ger✤*1>

šmȉrglati {ām, ajū imperf.} **a.** *sl* polish <Ger✤> **b.i.** *sl* take care <Ger✤*1> **ii.** *sl* reproach, scold <Ger✤*1>
• **Kȍ ti šmȉrglā ȕši!** {S} (lit. Who is polishing your ears?) *sl* ***Off*** used to express disrespect, Screw you!

šmízla {ē fem.} **a.** *sl-fea* spoiled female <Ger> **b.** *sl-sex* loose woman <Ger*1>

šmȍkljan {a (acc. = gen.) masc.} **a.** *sl-fea* stupid or mentally deficient person <Ger✤*1> **b.** *sl-fea* clumsy person, klutz

šmȍkljos {a (acc. = gen.) masc.} **a.** *sl-fea* stupid or mentally deficient person <Ger✤*1> **b.** *sl-fea* clumsy person, klutz **c.** *sl-fea* weak person, wimp

šmólja [1] {ē fem.} *sl-fea* untidy female, slob <Ger✤*1>

šmólja [2] {ē masc.} **a.** *sl-fea* clumsy male, klutz <Ger✤*1> **b.** *sl-fea* unattractive male

šmŕca {ē fem.} *sl-fea* very young female, little girl <Slav✤*1>

šmȑcāj {a masc.} **a.** *sl* cry, shed tears, weep <Slav> **b.** *sl* short deep breath <Slav*1>

šmȑcati {ām, ajū imperf.} **a.** *col* cry, shed tears, weep <Slav> **b.** *col* cry, shed tears, weep <Slav*1>

šmȑcna {ē fem.} *sl-fea* child, kid <Slav✤*1>

šmȑćkati {ām, ajū imperf.} *col* splash <Slav✤*1>

šmŕkati {šmȑčēm, šmȑčū imperf.} *col* sniff, snort <Slav✤>

šmȑkavac {kávca (acc. = gen.) masc.} **a.** *sl-fea* weak person, wimp <Slav✤*1> **b.** *sl-fea* child, kid <Slav✤*2>

šmȑkavica {ē fem.} *sl-fea* child, kid <Slav✤*1>

šmŕljiti {ljīm, ljē imperf.} *sl* cry, shed tears, weep <Slav✤*1>

šmȕgnuti {nēm, nū perf. intr.} *sl-fea* run away, flee

šmȕk {šmùka +ov (ext. pl) masc.; Nom Pl šmȕkovi} *sl* jewelry <Ger>

šnȁjd {a +ov (ext. pl) masc.; Nom Pl šnàjdovi} *sl-sex* ***Obs*** lust, sexual urge <Ger[*1]>

šnȁjder {a (acc. = gen.) masc.} /šnàjder/ **a.** *col* tailor <Ger❖> **b.** *sl* kid (goat) <Ger❖[*1]>

šnâl {a masc.} *sl-crafts* clamp (the tool) <Ger>

šnȁpati {ām, ajū biasp.} *sl* squeeze (sponge, etc.) <Ger❖[*1]>

šnȁperica {ē fem.} (lit. snapper) *sl-sex* ***Fac-Obs*** vagina, cunt <Ger❖[*1]>

šnê {šnēa masc.} *col* icing on a cake <Ger>

šnȅka {ē fem.; Dat šnȅki} *sl-auto* snail (part of steering mechanism) <Ger>

šnȋr {a +ev (ext. pl) masc.; Nom Pl šnírevi} **1** *sl* cheating, swindling <Ger[*1]> **2** *sl-sports* dribbling <Ger[*1]>

šnírānje {a neut.} *sl-sports* dribbling <Ger[*1]>

šnírati {šnȋrām, šnírajū imperf.} **a.** *sl* tie (shoelaces, etc.) <Ger> **b.i.** *sl-sports* dribble (e.g. in basketball) <Ger[*1]> **ii.** *sl* walk fast <Ger[*1]>

šnȉtati {ām, ajū imperf.} *sl-sex* ***Fac-Obs*** engage in sexual intercourse with (of a male) <Ger❖[*1]>

šnjȁjd {a +ov (ext. pl) masc.; Nom Pl šnjàjdovi} *sl-sex* ***Obs*** desire for sex, horniness <Ger[*1]>

šnjȍf {a masc.} *sl* smell, sniff <Ger✍>

šnjófalica {ē fem.} *sl* ***Fac*** nose <Ger❖[*1]>

šnjȍfati {ām, ajū biasp.} *sl* smell <Ger❖[*1]> *sl* investigate, look into

šnjóka {ē fem.; Dat šnjóki} *sl-drink* brandy

šnjûr {a +ev (ext. pl) masc.; Nom Pl šnjúrevi} *sl-gamble* one chip in <Ger✍[*1]>

šnjúrati {šnjûrām, šnjúrajū} investigate, nose around <Ger❖[*1]>

šnjúrati se {šnjûrām, šnjúrajū imperf. intr.} *sl* walk <Ger❖[*1]>

šnjùvara {ē fem.} *sl* walker (person) <Ger❖[*1]>

šȍ {pron.} [std. = zašto] *col* why <Slav✍>

šóder [1] {a (acc. = gen.) masc.} (lit. pebbles) **1** *sl* male, guy <Ger[*1]> **2** *sl-sex* prostitute, hooker <Ger[*1]>

šóder [2] {a masc.} **a.** *col* gravel, pebbles <Ger[*1]> **b.i.** *sl-sex* vagina <Ger[*2]> **ii.aa.** *sl-sex* money <Ger[*2]> **bb.** *sl* abundance <Ger[*3]> **iii.** *sl-drugs* drug <Ger[*2]>

šóder [3] {adv.} (lit. pebbles) *sl* ample, plenty of: *Tamo je šoder povrća. There are plenty of vegetables over there.* <Ger[*1]>

šóder-grȁba {ē fem.} *sl-sex* ***Fac-Obs*** vagina, cunt <Ger[*1]>

šóditi {šôdīm, dē perf.} *sl* engage, participate, take part in

šȍfēr {šoféra (acc. = gen.) masc.} **a.** *sl-auto* driver <Fre> **b.** *sl-crime* pickpocket <Fre[*1]>

šoferírati {šoferīrām, šoferírajū imperf.} **a.** *sl-auto* drive (a vehicle) <Fre❖> **b.** *sl-mil* clean a long corridor <Fre❖[*1]>

šȍfērka {ē fem.; Dat šȍfērki} *sl-auto* driver (female) <Fre>

šȍfērskā lóža {NP} (lit. driver's balcony) *sl-media* first five rows in a theater ☞ loža

šȍferšājba {ē fem.} **a.** *col* windshield <Ger> **b.** **Cro** *sl* name of a bar on Petrinjska street in Zagreb, Croatia <Ger[*1]>

šȍferšājbe {ī fem. pl.} *sl* eyeglasses <Ger[*1]>

šoferšàjbna {ē fem.} *col* windshield <Ger>

šoferšàjbne {ī fem. pl.} *sl* eyeglasses <Ger[*1]>

šȍjka {ē fem.; Dat šȍjki} (lit. jay) *sl-fea* ***Der*** ingratiator (male), brownnoser, ass kisser <Slav[*1]>

šȍjkan {a (acc. = gen.) masc.} **a.** *sl-fea* stupid or mentally deficient person <Slav❖[*1]> **b.** *sl-fea* clumsy male, klutz <Slav❖[*2]>

Šȍk [1] {a (acc. = gen.) +ov (ext. pl) masc.; Nom Pl Šȍkovi} *sl-fea* Albanian (person) <Alb[*1]>

šȍk [2] {a +ov (ext. pl) masc.; Nom Pl šȍkovi} *sl-fea* person visibly different from others, oddball <Alb[*1]>

šȍk sȍba {NP} (lit. intensive care unit) *sl-sex* room intended for sexual intercourse ☞ soba

šȍkac {kca (acc. = gen.) masc.} *sl-fea* ***Off*** Croat (person) <SlavO[*1]>

šȍkačkī {ā, ō adj.} *sl-fea* ***Off*** Croatian (pertaining to a person or nation) <SlavO[*1]>

šȍkīng-blû {ua masc.} *sl* shock, astonishment <Eng[*1]>

šôlde {i fem. pl.} Med *dia-col* money <Ita>

šólja [1] {ē fem.} (lit. cup) **a.** *sl-sex* ***Fac-Obs*** vagina, cunt <Ger[*1]> **b.** *sl-fea* boring female, bore <Ger[*2]> **c.** *sl-fea* unattractive female <Ger[*3]> **d.** *sl-fea* foolish female <Ger[*4]> **e.** *sl* female <Ger[*5]>

šólja [2] {ē masc.} (lit. cup) *sl-fea* stupid or mentally deficient person <Ger[*1]>

šȍntav {a, o adj.} *sl-fea* clumsy, klutzy <Slav*1>

šónja {ē masc.} *sl-fea* ***Der*** clumsy person, klutz <Slav❖>

šónjca {ē masc.} *sl-fea* very unintelligent male, complete moron <Slav❖>

šȍnjča {ē fem. & masc.} **a.** *sl-fea* stupid or mentally deficient person <Slav✍*1> **b.** *sl-fea* clumsy person, klutz

šȍpati {ām, ajū imperf.} **a.** *col* force-feed poultry by inserting food into their beak <Ger> **b.i.** *sl* beat up <Ger*1> **ii.aa.** *sl* lie <Ger*1> **bb.** *sl* cheat, swindle <Ger*2> **iii.** *sl-fea* overdo <Ger*1>

šȍpka {ē fem.; Dat šȍpki} *sl* box above one's ear <Slav*1>

šóra {ē fem.} *sl* fight (e.g. fist fight) <Hun*1>

šórānje {a neut.} **a.** *sl* beating up <Hun❖*1> **b.** *sl-sex* urinating

šórati {šôrām, šórajū biasp.} **1** *sl-sex* ***Obs*** urinate, piss <Hun❖*1> **2** *sl* beat up <Hun❖*1> **3** *sl-sports* play soccer <Hun❖*1>

šórati se {šôrām, šórajū imperf. intr.} *sl* fight (e.g. fist fight) <Hun❖*1>

šȍrc {a +ev (ext. pl) masc.; Nom Pl šȍrcevi} *col* shorts <Eng>

šȍre {eta neut.} *sl-drink* wine

šȍrka {ē fem.} **1** *sl* fight (e.g. fist fight) <Hun*1> **2** *sl-sex* ***Obs*** urine, piss

šȍrnuti {nēm, nū perf.} **1** *sl-sex* ***Obs*** urinate, piss <Hun❖*1> **2** *sl* beat up <Hun❖*1> **3** *sl-sports* play soccer <Hun❖*1>

šȍška {ē fem.; Dat šȍški} *sl* passport <Rus*1>

šȍškār {a (acc. = gen.) masc.} *sl-crime* forger <Rus❖*1>

šȍšōn {šošóna (acc. = gen.) masc.; Voc šȍšōne} (lit. Shoshone) **a.** *sl-fea* inhabitant of the countryside, hick, bumpkin <EngO*1> **b.** *sl-fea* stupid or mentally deficient person <EngO*2>

šȍtka {ē fem.; Dat šȍtki} **a.** *col* wider end of an egg <Slav> **b.** *sl-sex* buttocks, butt <Slav*1>

šȍtrī {īja masc.; perm} *sl-sex* gonorrhea, the clap <Ger✍> ☞ trišo

šȍu [1] {ua masc.} **1** *sl* scandal <Eng*1> **2** *sl* spectacular scene <Eng*1>

šȍu [2] {excl.} *sl* used to signal something being highly humorous <Eng>

šȍvēn {šovéna (acc. = gen.) masc.} *sl-fea* chauvinist <FreO*1>

špâg {a +ov (ext. pl) masc.; Nom Pl špágovi} /špȁg/ **1** *col-dia* rope <Ita> **2** **Med** *col-dia* pocket (on a coat, trousers, etc.) <Ita>

špága {ē fem.; Dat špági} *col-dia* rope <Ita>

špagáta {ē fem.} *col-dia* rope <Ita>

špágerica {ē fem.} *sl* shoe made of ropes <Ita❖*1>

Špagètār {getára (acc. = gen.) masc.; Voc Špȁgetāru} (lit. spaghetti-eater) *sl-fea* Italian (person), Dago <Ita❖*1>

špàjhla {ē fem.} *sl* leg (human) <Ger*1>

špȁjz {a masc.} (lit. storage room) *sl* ***Fac*** stomach, belly, gut <Ger*1>

špȁnati {ām, ajū biasp.} (lit. span) **a.** *sl* play a game <Ger*1> **b.** *sl-sports* play soccer <Ger*2>

špánga {ē fem.; Dat špángi} *sl-crime* leather belt with spikes used to transport dangerous criminals <Ger*1>

špânskā sèla {NP} (lit. Spanish villages) *col* unknown concepts or ideas, Greek (as in: it's Greek to me) ☞ selo

špárati {špârām, špárajū imperf. intr.} *col* save money, sock money away: *Deset godina smo šparali za kuću. We saved money for ten years to buy a house.* <Ger>

špȁret {a masc.} *col* kitchen stove <Ger>

špȁrhet {a masc.} (lit. stove) *sl-music* ***Fac*** studio tape recorder <Ger*1>

špârkàsa {ē fem.} (lit. piggy bank) *sl-fea* bedroom <Ger*1>

špârtati {ām, ajū imperf.} **a.** *col* cruise, walk through the town <Ger*1> **b.** *col* walk <Ger*2> **c.** *sl-sex* engage in sexual intercourse with (of a male) <Ger*3>

špâs {a +ov (ext. pl) masc.; Nom Pl špásovi} *sl-fea* joy <Ger>

špèditi {dīm, dē imperf.} *sl-sex* cheat on one's lover or spouse

špȅhati {ām, ajū biasp.} **a.** *sl* follow, tail <Ger*1> **b.** *sl* look, watch, scope out <Ger*2>

špȅk [1] {a (acc. = gen.) +ov (ext. pl) masc.; Nom Pl špèkovi} (lit. bacon) *sl-sex* ***Fac*** female with large breasts and big buttocks <Ger*1>

špȅk [2] {a +ov (ext. pl) masc.; Nom Pl špèkovi} (lit. bacon) *sl* stomach, belly, gut <Ger*1>

špèkcija {ē fem.} [std. = inspekcija] *sl-crime* lookout (during theft) <Lat✍*1>

špȅkjēger {a (acc. = gen.) masc.} (lit. bacon hunter) *sl-fea* beggar <Ger*1>

špȅkula {ē fem.} *sl* eye (sight organ) <Lat*1>

špèlūnka {ē fem.} *sl-drink* low-class bar, dive <**Lat**[*1]>

špȅra {ē fem.} **1** *sl-crime* picklock (tool) <**Ger**[*1]> **2** *sl-crime* prison <**Ger**[*1]>

špìc {a +ov (ext. pl) masc., Nom Pl špìcovi} (lit. tip) **1** *sl-sports* offense <**Ger**[*1]> **2** *sl-sex* penis <**Ger**[*1]> **3** *sl-auto* traffic jam <**Ger**[*1]>

špȉc-ìgrāč {a (acc. = gen.) masc.} *sl-sports* top player <**Ger-Slav**[*1]>

špȉca {ē fem.} (lit. seed) **1** *sl-fea* very young female, little girl <**Ger**[*1]> **2a.** *sl-sex* loose woman <**Ger**[*1]> **b.** *sl* female <**Ger**[*2]> **c.** *sl-fea* cowardly female, chicken <**Ger**[*3]> **3** *sl* coin <**Ger**[*1]> **4aa.** *sl* square <**Ger**[*1]> **bb.** Cro *sl* name for Jelačićev square in Zagreb, Croatia <**Ger**[*1]> **5** *sl-drugs* rush, high <**Ger**[*1]> **6** *col* peak (traffic, etc.) <**Ger**[*1]>

špìcara {ē fem.} (lit. the pointed one) *sl* shoe <**Ger**❖[*1]>

špȉccānge {i fem. pl.} *sl-crafts* pincers <**Ger**>

špȉccāngle {i fem. pl.} *sl-crafts* pincers <**Ger**>

špȉcerice {ā masc. pl.} **1** *sl* pointy-toed shoes <**Ger**❖[*1]> **2** *sl* trousers, pants <**Ger**❖[*1]>

špìcl {a (acc. = gen.) +ov (ext. pl) masc.; Nom Pl špìclovi} **a.** *sl-crime* police investigator <**Ger**[*1]> **b.** *sl-crime* undercover agent <**Ger**[*2]> **c.** *sl-crime* informer, stoolie, snitch

špȉclati {ām, ajū biasp. intr.} **a.** *sl* follow, tail <**Ger**[*1]> **b.** *sl-crime* inform the police or other authorities, snitch, squeal <**Ger**[*2]>

špìclov {a (acc. = gen.) masc.} **a.** *sl-fea* ***Der*** cunning male <**Ger**[*1]> **b.** *sl-fea* skillful male <**Ger**[*2]>

špicóka {ē fem.; Dat špicóki} *sl-fea* pointy-toed shoe <**Ger**❖[*1]>

špìčōk {a masc.} **1** *sl-fea* pointy-toed shoe <**Ger**✍[*1]> **2** trousers, pants <**Ger**✍[*1]>

špìgeta {ē fem.} Med *dia-col* shoelace <**Ita**>

špígl {a +ov (ext. pl) masc.; Nom Pl špíglovi} **a.** *col* mirror <**Ger**> **b.** *sl* hotel <**Ger**[*1]>

špígli {ā masc. pl.} *sl* eyeglasses <**Ger**[*1]>

špíglo {a neut.} *col-dia* mirror <**Ger**✍>

špìjūn {špijúna masc.} (lit. spy) *sl-crafts* gap measuring plates <**Ita**[*1]>

špȉkati {ām, ajū imperf.} *sl* speak <**Eng**✍>

špȉl *See the following*

- **iz tȏg špȉla** {PP} (lit. from that pack of cards) *sl-fea* of the same kind

špȉlati {ām, ajū biasp.} **1** *sl-gamble* play cards <**Ger**[*1]> **2** *sl-fea* pretend: *špilati Engleza pretend to be an Englishman* <**Ger**[*2]> **3** *sl-fea* be conceited, be stuck-up: *Mali špila, pa niko neće da se igra s njim. The kid is stuck-up and nobody wants to play with him.* <**Ger**[*3]>

špíler {a (acc. = gen.) masc.} (lit. player) *sl-gamble* gambler <**Ger**[*1]>

špilhózer {a (acc. = gen.) masc.} *sl-fea* child, kid <**Ger**[*1]>

špilhózner {a (acc. = gen.) masc.} *sl-fea* child, kid <**Ger**[*1]>

špilhóznerka {ē fem.} *sl-fea* ***Fac*** female child, girl <**Ger**❖[*1]>

špíliti {līm, lē imperf.} *sl-gamble* play cards <**Ger**❖[*1]>

špȉlja {ē fem.} (lit. cave) **1** *sl* home <**Slav**[*1]> **2** hotel <**Slav**[*1]>

špìōn {špióna masc.} *sl-crafts* gap measuring plates <**Ita**[*1]>

špìrāl féder {NP} (lit. spiral spring) *sl-crafts* spiral spring ☞ **feder**

špirijáda {ē fem.} *sl-crime* police <**Ita**❖[*1]>

špȉrit {a masc.} *sl-drink* denatured alcohol <**Lat**[*1]>

špȍret {a masc.} *col* kitchen stove <**Ger**>

špȏrkā {ē fem. (adj. decl.)} (lit. the dirty one) *sl-fea* low-quality cigarette <**Ita**[*1]>

špȏrkī {a, o adj.} Med *dia-col* dirty (not clean) <**Ita**>

špȏrko {adv.} Med *dia-col* dirty (not clean) <**Ita**>

špòrkulja {ē fem.} (lit. the dirty female) Med *sl-fea* untidy female, slob <**Ita**❖[*1]>

šprâhfeler {a masc.} *sl-fea* speech disorder <**Ger**>

šprȅha {ē fem.; Dat šprȅhi} *sl* speech <**Ger**>

šprȅhati {ām, ajū biasp.} *sl* speak <**Ger**❖>

šprȅng-šâjba {ē fem.} *sl-crafts* spring washer <**Ger**>

šprȅng-šâjbna {ē fem.} *sl-crafts* spring washer <**Ger**>

šprȉca {ē fem.} (lit. syringe) *sl* escape, flee <**Ger**>

- **bez šprȉcē** {PP} (lit. without a syringe) *sl-sex* ***Fac*** without any venereal diseases (usu. of a prostitute)

šprícānje {a neut.} (lit. spraying) **1** *sl-sex* ***Obs*** ejaculation <**Ger**❖[*1]> **2** *sl-drugs* intravenous intake of narcotic drugs, mainlining, shooting up <**Ger**❖[*1]>

šprícati {šprȋcām, šprícajū imperf.} (lit. spray) **1** *sl-sex* ***Obs*** ejaculate, cum <**Ger**❖[*1]> **2** *sl-music* play a musical instrument <**Ger**❖[*1]>

šprícati se {šprȋcām, šprícajū imperf. intr.} *sl-drugs* take narcotic drugs intravenously, mainline, shoot up <**Ger**❖[*1]>

šprȉcer {a masc.} /šprìcer/ *col* wine with water <**Ger**>

špricèrāš {ceráša (acc. = gen.) masc.} *sl-drink* person who drinks wine with water <**Ger**❖>

šprȉh {adj.} *sl-fea* fast <**Ger***1>

šprȉntati {ām, ajū biasp.} (lit. sprint) *sl* run <**Eng**❖>

šprȉnterica {ē fem.} (lit. sprinter) *sl-sex* ***Fac-Obs*** diarrhea, runs, trots <**Eng**❖>

špúra [1] {excl.} *sl* run <**Ger***1>

špúra [2] {ē fem.} **a.** *sl-auto* track (of a wheel) <**Ger**> **b.** *sl* running away, fleeing <**Ger***1>

špúrati {špûrām, špúrajū biasp.} *sl* run <**Ger***1>

špûrijus {a masc.} *col* foreboding <**Ger**>

špȕrnuti {nēm, nū perf. intr.} *sl* run <**Ger**❖*1>

šrȁf {a +ov (ext. pl) masc.; Nom Pl šràfovi} *sl-crafts* screw (fastening device) <**Ger**>

šràfcīger [1] {a (acc. = gen.) masc.} (lit. screwdriver) *sl-fea* student from a blue-collar family <**Ger***1>

šràfcīger [2] {a masc.} **a.** *sl-crafts* screwdriver <**Ger**> **b.** *sl-sex* penis <**Ger***1>

šràfcigerskī {ā, ō adj.} *sl-crafts* assembly <**Ger**❖*1>

šrafcijáner {a (acc. = gen.) masc.} *sl-fea* student from a blue-collar family <**Ger**✍*1>

šràfštok {a masc.} *sl-crafts* clamp (the tool) <**Ger**>

šréber {a (acc. = gen.) masc.} **a.** *sl-sstu* overly diligent student <**Ger***1> **b.** *sl-fea* ingratiator (male), brownnoser, ass kisser <**Ger***2>

šrȍt {a (acc. = gen.) +ov (ext. pl) masc.; Nom Pl šròtovi} *sl-fea* unattractive female <**Ger***1>

štȁ *See the following*

- **nȉ zbog čeg** {PP} (lit. for nothing) *col* for no reason whatsoever, for nothing
- **štȁ bî** {VP} (lit. what was there) *col* used to ask for additional information, What happened?
- **Šta ìmā?** {S} (lit. What is there?) *col* used as a greeting, What's up?
- **šta ìmā** {VP} (lit. what is there) *col* used as an informal greeting, What's up!
- **Štȁ je bílo, bílo je!** {S} (lit. What has happened, has happened!) *col* used to indicate that what has happened cannot be reversed, It's all over now!
- **Štȁ je klȍšāri?** {S} (lit. What's up bums?) *col* used as a greeting, What's up?
- **šta kôštā da kôštā** {S} (lit. whatever it costs) *col* used to refer to readiness to purchase something notwithstanding its price, whatever it costs, price is no object
- **štȁ li** {ProP} (lit. what not) *col* used to refer to lack of knowledge, who knows what
- **Štȁ me bòlī kȕrac!** {S} (lit. What it hurts my prick!) *col* ***Obs*** used to express indifference, I don't give a damn!
- **Štȁ me bòlī ȕvo?** {S} (lit. What my ear hurts me?) Ser *col* used to express indifference, I don't give a damn!
- **Štȁ se dȉrā?** {S} (lit. What is being done?) *col* used as a greeting, What's up?
- **Štȁ se râdi?** {S} (lit. What is being done?) *col* used as a greeting, What's up?
- **Štȁ tî znâš ko môj kȕrac!** {S} (lit. What do you know, like my prick!) *col* ***Obs*** used to express disrespect or dissatisfaction, Fuck it!
- **Štȁ zévāš?** {S} (lit. What are you yawning?) SerE *col* used to ask for additional information, What?
- **Zȁ šta si?** {S} (lit. For what are you?) *col* used to offer something, usu. drinks or food, What would you like?

Štȁ mi nȁprīča! {S} (lit. What did you tell to me!) *col* used to express disbelief, Unbelievable! ☞ **napríčati**

štâbovac {bōvca (acc. = gen.) masc.} *sl-mil* headquarters officer <**Ger**❖*1>

štȁjg {a +ov (ext. pl) masc.; Nom Pl štàjgovi} *sl-sex* gathering place for prostitutes <**Ger***1>

- **mâli štȁjg** {NP} *sl* bus station
- **péder štȁjg** {NP} (lit. faggot promenade) **Cro** *sl-sex* ***Der*** name of a place in Zagreb, Croatia where homosexuals are known to gather

štȁjga {ē fem.; Dat štȁjgi} /štâjga/ **a.** *sl* promenade <**Ger**> **b.i.** *sl-crime* pickpocket's working area <**Ger***1> **ii.aa.** *sl-sex* surroundings of the train station where prostitutes gather <**Ger***1> **bb.i.** *sl* station, stop (bus, train, streetcar, etc.) <**Ger***2> **ii.** *sl* stop (bus, etc.) <**Ger***2>

štȁjgati {ām, ajū biasp.} *sl-fea* get angry <**Ger**❖*1>

štàjger {a masc.} Cro *sl* the streetcar line number two in Zagreb, Croatia <**Ger**❖*1>

štȁjgerica {ē fem.} *sl-sex* prostitute, hooker <**Ger**❖*1>

štàjgerka {ē fem.; Dat štàjgerki} *sl-sex* low-class prostitute <**Ger**❖*1>

štȁka {ē fem.; Dat štȁki} (lit. crutch) **a.** *sl-drugs* narcotic drug, dope <**Ger***1> **b.** *sl* leg (human)

štàkara {ē fem.} (lit. the one with crutches) *sl-fea* long-legged female <**Ger**❖*1>

štȁkor {a (acc. = gen.) masc.} (lit. rat) **1** *sl-fea* ***Der*** cunning male <**Slav***1> **2** *sl-fea* unattractive person <**Slav***1> **3** *sl-auto* Vespa (model of motorcycle)

<Slav*1>
• **pòpōv štàkor** {NP} (lit. priest's rat) *sl-sex* ***Fac-Obs*** penis of an elderly male

štàla {ē fem.} (lit. stable) **1** *sl-auto* garage <**Ger***1> **2** *sl* dance floor <**Ger***1>

štàmbīlj {štambílja masc.} **a.** *col* seal, stamp <**Ger***1> **b.** *sl-stu* credit for a course at the university <**Ger**>

štambìljati {ām, ajū imperf.} (lit. stamp) *sl-sex* ***Fac-Obs*** engage in sexual intercourse with (of a male) <**Ger**✣*1>

štàmpajzer {a (acc. = gen.) masc.} *sl-fea* stupid or mentally deficient person <**Ger**✍*1>

štȁncati {ām, ajū imperf.} *sl* assemble, mount <**Ger***1>

štȁncovati {cujēm, cujū imperf.} *sl* assemble, mount <**Ger***1>

štánga {ē fem.; Dat štángi} (lit. pole) **a.** *col* rod <**Ger**> **b.** *sl-fea* slender female

štȁngās {a masc.} *sl-auto* hand gas <**Ger**>

štángla {ē fem.} *col* rod <**Ger**>

štâp {a +ov (ext. pl) masc.; Nom Pl štápovi} (lit. stick) **1** *sl-sex* ***Fac-Obs*** penis, dick, prick <**Slav***1> **2** *sl* cigarette, smoke <**Slav***1>
• **dvâ štápa u dvê tȉkve** {NP} (lit. two sticks in two pumpkins) *sl-fea* ***Fac*** having skinny legs

štȁpovati {pujēm, pujū imperf.} *sl* beat with a billy club <**Slav**✣*1>

štȁrt {a +ov (ext. pl) masc.; Nom Pl štàrtovi} *sl* flirting <**Ger***1>

štȁrtānje {a neut.} *sl* flirting <**Ger**✣*1>

štȁrtati {ām, ajū biasp.} **1** *sl* run fast <**Ger**✣*1> **2** *sl* flirt <**Ger**✣*1>
• **štȁrtati na gòlo** {VP} (lit. start at the naked) *sl* wander, roam

štȁrter {a (acc. = gen.) masc.} *sl* flirting male <**Ger**✣*1>

štȁš [1] {excl.} [std. = šta ćeš] *col* what do you want <**Slav**✍>

štȁš [2] {excl.} [std. = šta ćeš] *col* used to express indifference, that's how it is <**Slav**✍>

štédnja *See the following*
• **vêzānā štédnja** {NP} (lit. bound savings) *sl-sex* ***Fac*** incest

štȅk {a +ov (ext. pl) masc.; Nom Pl štèkovi} **a.** *sl-crime* hiding place <**Ger***1> **b.** *sl* savings <**Ger***1>

štȅk-šlȉsl {a +ov (ext. pl) masc.; Nom Pl štȅk-šlȉslovi} *sl-crafts* stick-on key <**Ger**>

štéka {ē fem.; Dat štéki} **1.** *col* door knob <**Ger**> **b.i.** *sl* fight (e.g. fist fight) <**Ger***1> **ii.** *sl* cigarette carton <**Ger***1> **2** *sl* savings <**Ger***1>

štȅkati {ām, ajū imperf.} (lit. plug in) **a.** *col* plug in (e.g. an electronic device) <**Ger**> **b.** *sl* understand, get clued in, be plugged in <**Ger***1>

štȅker {a (acc. = gen.) masc.} **1** *sl-fea* miser, tightwad, skinflint <**Ger***1> **2** *sl-crime* accomplice <**Ger***1> **3** *sl-fea* troublemaker, rowdy, ruffian <**Ger***1> **4** *sl-crime* informer, stoolie, snitch <**Ger***1>

štȅkovati {kujēm, kujū imperf.} **a.** *sl* hide, cover up <**Ger**✣*1> **b.** *sl* save money, sock money away <**Ger**✣*2>

štèktati {tèkćēm, tèkćū imperf. intr.} *col* hiss (snake, gas, etc.) <**Slav**>

štéla {ē fem.} *col* connection, tie <**Ger***1>

štéliti {štêlīm, lē imperf.} *col* fix, arrange something for somebody (usu. illegal): *šteliti posao za druga arrange a job for a friend* <**Ger***1>

štȅlovānje {a neut.} *sl-crafts* tuning, adjusting, fixing <**Ger**>

štȅlovati {lujēm, lujū imperf.} *sl-crafts* tune, adjust, fix <**Ger**> *sl-crafts* improve, get better <**Ger***1>
• **štȅlovati pòēziju** {VP} (lit. adjust poetry) *sl* lie

štèlūng {a masc.} *sl-crafts* tuning, adjusting, fixing <**Ger**>

štȅma {ē fem.} *sl* fight (e.g. fist fight) <**Ger**✣*1>

štȅmati {ām, ajū imperf.} (lit. hollow out, deepen) *sl-sex* ***Fac-Obs*** engage in sexual intercourse with (of a male) <**Ger***1>

štȅmer {a (acc. = gen.) masc.} *sl-fea* troublemaker, rowdy, ruffian <**Ger**✣*1>

štènara {ē fem.} (lit. doghouse) **a.** *sl-crime* prison <**Slav***1> **b.** *sl-crime* prison cell <**Slav***2>

štȅp {a +ov (ext. pl) masc.; Nom Pl štèpovi} **1** *sl-crime* proficient theft <**Ger***1> **2** *sl-sex* sexual intercourse <**Ger***1>

štȅpati {ām, ajū imperf.} (lit. stitch) **1** *sl-sex* ***Fac-Obs*** engage in sexual intercourse with (of a male) <**Ger***1> **2** *sl* date <**Ger***1>

štètnanje {a neut.} *sl* fighting <**Slav**✍*1>

štètnati {ām, ajū biasp.} **a.** *sl* beat up <**Slav**✍*1> **b.** *sl-sex* engage in sexual intercourse with (of a male) <**Slav**✍*2>

štȉcovānje {a neut.} *sl-crime* black-market money exchange <**Ger**✣*1>

štìcūng {a masc.} *sl-crime* black-market money exchange <**Ger***1>

štȉft {a (acc. = gen.) +ov (ext. pl) masc.; Nom Pl štȉftovi} *sl-crime* desperate criminal <**Ger***1>

štìglec {a (acc. = gen.) masc.} *sl-crime* ***Der*** informer, stoolie, snitch <**Ger***1>

štiglèta {ē fem.} *sl* shoe <**Ger**❖*1>

štȉh [1] {a (acc. = gen.) +ov (ext. pl) masc.; Nom Pl štȉhovi} *sl-fea* undependable person <**Ger***1>

štȉh [2] {a +ov (ext. pl) masc.; Nom Pl štȉhovi} **a.** *sl* stabbing <**Ger**> **b.** *sl-sex* sexual intercourse <**Ger***1>
- **jâk štȉh** {NP} *sl-fea* undependable person

štȉhati {ām, ajū biasp.} *sl-crime* kill, murder <**Ger**❖*1>

štìkla {ē fem.} **a.** *sl* high heel (of a shoe) <**Ger**> **b.** *sl-fea* slender female <**Ger***1>

štȉma {excl.} *col* used to indicate acknowledgment of message, That's right! <**Ger**>

štȉmānje {a neut.} (lit. tuning) **a.** *sl* flirting <**Ger***1> **b.** *sl* persuasion <**Ger***2>

štȉmati [1] {ām, ajū biasp.} (lit. tune) **a.** *sl* persuade, convince <**Ger***1> **b.** *sl* flirt <**Ger***2> **c.** *sl* be fitting, be in tune with <**Ger***3>

štȉmati [2] {ām, ajū biasp. intr.} (lit. tune) *col* be convenient, be appropriate <**Ger**>

štìmūng {a masc.} *col* atmosphere <**Ger**>

štítiti {štȋtīm, tē imperf.} *sl* give, pass <**Slav***1>

štô {pron.} [std. = zašto] *col* why <**Slav**✍>
- **štȍ bi se rèklo** {S} (lit. what one would say) *col* used to express hesitation, you know, as they say
- **štȍ bi tȋ rȅkō** {S} (lit. which you would tell) *col* used to express hesitation and to establish closer contact with one's interlocutor, you know, as they say
- **Štȍ si pízda!** {S} (lit. Why are you a cunt!) *col* ***Off*** used as a reprimand, Shame on you!
- **Štȍ si[NOUN:NOM]!** {S} (lit. Why are you such a [NOUN:NOM]!) *col* ***Off*** used to express dissatisfaction, Why are you such a jerk?: *Što si peder! Why are you such a jerk!*
- **Štȍ ti je [NOUN:NOM]!** {LSF} (lit. What is [NOUN:NOM]!) *col* used to stress one's point, That's [NOUN:NOM]!: *Što ti je rat. Sve je uništeno i nikom nije dobro. That's the war. Everything has been destroyed and nobody is well off.*

štȍf {a masc.} *sl* topic of conversation <**Ger***1>

štòfika {ē fem.; Dat štòfiki} *sl-sex* ***Obs*** penis, dick, prick <**Ger**✍*1>

štògođ {pron.} [std. = štogod] *dia-col* some <**Slav**✍>

štògoj {pron.} [std. = štogod] *dia-col* some <**Slav**✍>

štòkfiš {adj.} *sl-fea* stiff <**Ger**❖*1>

štȍkrl {a masc.} **a.** *sl* small chair <**Ger**> **b.** *sl* ***Fac*** high sole shoe <**Ger***1>

štȍkrla {ē fem.} **a.** *sl* small chair <**Ger**> **b.** *sl* ***Fac*** high sole shoe <**Ger***1>

štȍljāš {a masc.} (lit. actor) [std. = pištolj] *sl-crime* pistol, revolver <**Cze**✍*1>

štȍljpi {štòljapi masc.; perm} (lit. actor) [std. = pištolj] *sl-crime* pistol, revolver <**Cze**✍*1>

štȍnō {c.} *col* as: *On je, štono kažu, štreber. He is, as they say, a geek.* <**Slav**>
- **Štȍno kâžē** {S} *col-dia* used to express hesitation, You know, As they say
- **Štȍno kâžū** {S} *col-dia* used to express hesitation, You know, As they say

štȍperica {ē fem.} (lit. stopwatch) *sl-sex* ***Fac*** prostitute who charges by the hour <**Ger***1>

štòpl {a +ov (ext. pl) masc.} *sl-crafts* stopper <**Ger**>

štȍplīn {štoplína masc.} Cro *sl* name of a cab stand on Anke Butorac street in Zagreb, Croatia <**Ger**✍*1>

štôs [1] {štósa (acc. = gen.) +ov (ext. pl) masc.; Nom Pl štósovi} (lit. trick) *sl-sex* ***App*** attractive female <**Ger***1>

štôs [2] {štósa +ov (ext. pl) masc.; Nom Pl štósovi} **a.** *sl* trick, joke <**Ger**> **b.** *sl* thing, object <**Ger***1> **c.** *sl* intrigue <**Ger***2> **d.** *sl* good idea <**Ger***3> **e.** *sl* joke <**Ger***4> **f.i.** *sl* interesting event <**Ger***5> **ii.** *sl-fea* skillfulness <**Ger***5> **iii.** *sl* example <**Ger***5>
- **ì tō mi je nȅkakav štôs** {S} (lit. and that is some trick) *col* ***Der*** used to belittle somebody's achievement, that's not worth shit
- **iz štósa** {PP} (lit. for trick) **a.** *col* just like that, just for the heck of it: *ukrasti auto iz štosa steal a car just for the heck of it* **b.** for fun
- **štósa rȁdi** {PP} (lit. for a joke) *col* just like that, just for the heck of it

štósati {štôsām, štósajū imperf.} (lit. hit) *sl-sex* ***Fac-Obs*** engage in sexual intercourse with (of a male) <**Ger**❖*1>

štôsdèmfa {ē fem.} (lit. shock absorber) *sl-sex* ***Fac-Obs*** female breast, tit <**Ger***1>

štôsdèmfer {a masc.} **a.** *sl-auto* shock absorber <**Ger**> **b.** *sl-sex* female breast <**Ger***1>

štósēr {štoséra (acc. = gen.) masc.} **a.** *sl-fea* joke teller <**Ger**❖*1> **b.** *sl-fea* skillful person <**Ger**❖*2> **c.** *sl-sex* male sexual partner (of a female) <**Ger**❖*3>

štôsno {adv.} *sl-fea* effectively <Ger⁘*1>

štȍsnuti {nēm, nū perf.} *sl-sex* ***Obs*** engage in sexual intercourse with (of a male) <Ger⁘*1>

štosòvit {a, o adj.} *sl-fea* funny <Ger⁘*1>

štráfta {excl.} (lit. line) *col* used to make somebody go away, beat it <Ger*1>

štráfta {ē fem.} **1a.** *col* promenade <Ger*1> **b.** *col* meeting place <Ger*1> **2** *sl* border (between countries) <Ger*1>
- **na štráfti** {PP} (lit. at the line) *sl* on the spot, at a designated place of an event

štrȁftāč {štraftáča (acc. = gen.) masc.} *sl-fea* person who walks regularly <Ger*1>

štrȁjfati {ām, ajū imperf.} *sl* touch <Ger*1>

štránga {ē fem.; Dat štrángi} *sl* rope <Ger>

štrâp {a +ov (ext. pl) masc.; Nom Pl štrâpovi} *sl* walking <Ger✍>

štràpac {rapàca masc.} *sl-fea* long walk <Ger✍*1>

štrapacírānje {a neut.} *sl-fea* walking for a long time <Ger*1>

štrapànzl {a masc.} *sl* longer walk <Ger✍*1>

štrapanzlišingèlīrka {ē fem.} *sl* promenade <Ger✍*1>

štràpati {ām, ajū imperf. intr.} *sl-fea* walk for a long time <Ger✍*1>

štȑcāljka {ē fem.; Dat štȑcāljki} (lit. syringe) **1** *sl-crime* machine gun <Ger⁘*1> **2** *sl-crime* rifle <Ger⁘*1>

štrébati {štrêbām, štrébajū imperf.} **a.** *sl-sstu* learn mechanically <Ger*1> **b.** *sl-fea* be overly serious, be stuffy <Ger*2>

štréber {a (acc. = gen.) masc.} **a.** *sl-sstu* overly diligent student <Ger> **b.** *sl-fea* ingratiator (male), brownnoser, ass kisser <Ger*1>

štrȅcnuti se {nēm, nū perf.} *col* get frightened, get scared <Slav⁘*1>

štrȉcī {īja (acc. = gen.) masc.} *sl-sex* pimp <Ger✍*1>

štrȉgati se {ām, ajū imperf. intr.} *sl* get a haircut <Slav✍>

štrȉherica {ē fem.} (lit. knitter) *sl-sex* ***Fac*** prostitute, hooker <Ger*1>

štrȉk {a +ov (ext. pl) masc.; Nom Pl štrȉkovi} (lit. rope) **1** *sl* ***Fac*** necktie <Ger*1> **2** *sl-sex* ***Fac*** penis <Ger*1>

štrȉkānje {a neut.} (lit. knitting) *sl-music* long rock'n'roll solo <Ger*1>

štrȉkati {ām, ajū imperf.} (lit. knit) **1** *sl-sex* ***Fac-Obs*** engage in sexual intercourse with (of a male) <Ger*1> **2a.** *sl-fea* ***Fac*** walk fast <Ger*1> **b.i.** *sl-fea* run away, flee <Ger*2> **ii.** *sl-fea* work quickly <Ger*2>
- **Kȍ ti štrȉkā créva!** {S} (lit. Who is knitting your intestines?) **SerE** *sl* ***Off*** used to express disrespect, Screw you!

štrȉkerica {ē fem.} (lit. knitter) *sl-sex* ***Fac*** prostitute, hooker <Ger*1>

štȑk {a +ov (ext. pl) masc.; Nom Pl štȑkovi} *sl* starch <Ger*1>

štȑklja {ē fem.} *sl-fea* tall person <Slav⁘*1>

štȑkljan {a (acc. = gen.) masc.} *sl-fea* tall male <Slav⁘*1>

štȑkljast {a, o adj.} *col* tall and slender (of a person) <Slav>

Štrȍc {a +ev (ext. pl) masc.; Nom Pl štrȍcevi} **Cro** *sl* name for Strossmayerovo Promenade in Zagreb, Croatia <SlavO✍*1>

štrȍka {ē fem.; Dat štrȍki} (lit. dirt) **a.** *sl-fea* dirt <Slav⁘*1> **b.** *sl-fea* ***Der*** dirty and untidy female, slob

štrȍkav {a, o adj.} **a.** *col* dirty (not clean) <Slav⁘*1> **b.** *sl-fea* unattractive, ugly

štrȍkōvan {vna, vno adj.} *sl-fea* dirty (not clean) <Slav⁘*1>

štrȕca {ē fem.} **a.** *col* loaf <Ger> **b.** *sl* child, kid <Ger*1>

štrúdla {ē fem.} (lit. strudel) *sl* female <Ger*1>

štrȕka {ē fem.} **a.** *sl* advice <Ita*1> **b.** *sl* instruction <Ita*2>

štrȕker {a (acc. = gen.) masc.} *sl* instructor <Ita⁘*1>

štrȕmf-mašína {ē fem.} *sl* anything <GerO*1>

štrumfèta {ē fem.} (lit. Smurfette) *sl-sex* ***Fac*** loose woman <GerO*1>

štrȕmfnuti {nēm, nū perf.} (lit. smurf) *sl* cheat, swindle <GerO*1>

štrȕmfovati {fujēm, fujū imperf.} (lit. smurf) **1** *sl* work, labor <GerO*1> **2** *sl* live <GerO*1>

štȕca {ē fem.} *sl-music* record or turntable which skips portions of a song <Slav⁘*1>

štȕcānje {a neut.} (lit. hiccups) *sl-drugs* being under a strong influence of narcotic drugs, being dead stoned <Slav*1>

štȕcati {ām, ajū imperf.} (lit. have hiccups) **1a.** *sl-crime* help in pickpocketing <Slav*1> **b.** *sl-crime* cover for one's accomplice <Slav*2> **2** be under a strong influence of narcotic drugs, be dead stoned <Slav[*1]>

- **štȕcati kljȍve** {VP} (lit. have hiccups with one's tusks) *sl* kiss
- **štȕcati zȗbe** {VP} (lit. have hiccups with one's teeth) *sl* kiss

štȕce {a (acc. = gen.) masc.} *sl-crime* accomplice

štȕcer {a (acc. = gen.) masc.} *sl-crime* pickpocket's helper <Ger[*1]>

štucírati {štùcīrām, štucírajū imperf.} *sl* push, shove <Ger[*1]>

štùcna {ē fem.} *sl-sports* soccer upper sock <Ger>

štȕcovati {cujēm, cujū imperf.} *sl-crime* help in pickpocketing <Ger[*1]>

študírati {štùdīrām, študírajū imperf.} [std. = studirati] *sl* plan <Lat✍[*1]>

štȕka {ē fem.} (lit. pike *fish*) **1a.** *sl-sex* ***Fac-Obs*** vagina, cunt <Slav[*1]> **b.** *sl-sex* ***Fac*** prostitute, hooker <Slav[*2]> **2** *sl* big money <Slav[*1]>

štȕkati {ām, ajū imperf.} *sl* run away, flee <Slav❖[*1]>

štȕlati {ām, ajū perf.} *sl* leave, depart, walk <Ger❖[*1]>

štúra [1] {excl.} *sl* used to make somebody go away, beat it <Ger[*1]>

štúra [2] {ē fem.} **a.** *sl* escape, flee <Ger[*1]> **b.** *sl* running away, fleeing <Ger[*2]>

štȕrnuti {nēm, nū perf.} **1** *sl* resign, quit <Ger❖[*1]> **2** *sl* push, shove <Ger❖[*1]>

šȕ-šȕ {excl.} *col* the sound made by whispering, shh-shh <Slav>

šȕb *See the following*

- **od šȗba** {PP} (lit. at once) *sl* right away, now

šȕbara {ē fem.} (lit. fur hat) **1** *sl-sex* ***Fac-Obs*** vagina, cunt <Slav[*1]> **2** *sl-fea* moderately strong male <Slav[*1]>

šúber {a masc.} *sl-crafts* nose <Ger✍[*1]>

šȕbler {a masc.} *sl-crafts* adjustable measure <Ger>

šȕć-mȕć *See the following*

- **šȕć-mȕć pa prolij** {ExcP} *col* used to express dissatisfaction, nothing special

šȕćmurast {a, o adj.} *sl-fea* complicated

šȕfnūdl {a masc.} *sl-sex* ***Fac-Obs*** penis, dick, prick <Ger[*1]>

šȕfnūdla {ē fem.} **1** *sl-fea* nudist <Ger[*1]> **2** *sl-fea* crybaby <Ger[*1]>

šȕft {a (acc. = gen.) +ov (ext. pl) masc.; Nom Pl šȕftovi} *sl-fea* ***Der*** worthless or despicable person <Ger[*1]>

šȕga {ē fem.; Dat šūgi} *sl-fea* unattractive thing <NE[*1]>

šugàmān {gamána masc.} Med *dia* towel <Ita>

šȕgav {a, o adj.} *sl-fea* bad <NE>

šȕha {a masc.; Dat šȕhi} BosM *col* foreboding <NE>

šúhnuti {šȗhnēm, nū perf.} *sl-drink* drink (alcohol) <NE❖[*1]>

šȕhva {a masc.} BosM *col* foreboding <NE>

šuhvèli {adj.} BosM *col* foreboding <NE[*1]>

šȗjka {ē fem.} *sl* shoe

šȕkadžija {ē masc.} *sl-drink* alcoholic, drunk <NE❖[*1]>

šȕkar {adv.} *sl* much, very: *imati šukar love have much money* <Gyp>

šúkati {šȗkām, šúkajū imperf.} **1** *sl-drink* drink (alcohol) <NE❖[*1]> **2** *sl* lie <NE❖[*1]>

šúknuti {šȗknēm, nū perf.} *sl-drink* drink (alcohol) <NE❖[*1]>

šúle *See the following*

- **víner šúle** {NP} (lit. Vienna school) *sl-fea* very elegant person
- **víner šúle ìsturenō odelénje Nîš** {NP} (lit. Vienna school, Niš *a city in Serbia* branch) SerE *sl-fea* provincial snob

šuléja {ē masc.} *sl-drink* alcoholic, drunk <NE✍[*1]>

šúlja {ē fem.} **1** *sl-drink* brandy **2** *sl* shirt <Slav✍>

- **šúlja na botàniku** {NP} (lit. botanical pattern shirt) *sl-fea* flowered shirt, Hawaiian shirt

šȗljka {ē fem.} [std. = košulja] *sl-fea* shirt <Slav✍>

Šȕma [1] {ē fem.} (lit. Woods) Ser *sl* name of Šumatovac (a restaurant in Belgrade, Serbia) <SlavO✍>

šȕma [2] {ē fem.} (lit. woods) **1a.** *sl-sex* ***Fac-Obs*** pubic hair <Slav[*1]> **b.** *sl-sex* ***Fac-Obs*** vagina, cunt <Slav[*2]> **2** *sl* ***Fac*** hair <Slav[*1]> **3** *sl* village <Slav[*1]> **4a.** *sl-mil* guerilla <Slav[*1]> **b.** *sl-mil* guerilla warfare <Slav[*2]> **5** *sl-thie* police formation (group of policeman) <Slav[*1]>

šȕma [3] {adv.} (lit. woods) *col* many, numerous <Slav[*1]>

šumagȅle {excl.} *sl* used to make somebody go away, beat it <Gyp[*1]>

šȕmāk {šumáka masc.} *sl-fea* male out of control, wild man <Slav❖[*1]>

šȕman {mna, mno adj.} (lit. noisy) **1** *sl-fea* young <Slav[*1]> **2** *sl-fea* good <Slav[*1]>

šumangȅle {excl.} *sl* used to make somebody go away, beat it <Gyp[*1]>

šȕmār {a (acc. = gen.) masc.} (lit. forester) **a.** *sl-fea* inhabitant of the countryside, hick, bumpkin <**Slav***1> **b.** *sl-fea* troublemaker, rowdy, ruffian <**Slav***2>

Šȕmica {ē fem.} (lit. small forest) **1** *sl-sex* ***Fac-Obs*** pubic hair, bush <**Slav***1> **2** *sl-sex* vagina <**Slav***1>

šumíder {a (acc. = gen.) masc.} *sl-fea* average person

šumíder {a masc.} *sl* lie

šȕmiti {mīm, mē imperf.} **a.** *col* blow (wind, etc.) <**Slav***1> **b.** *col* roar (engine, etc.) <**Slav***2>

šûmka {ē fem.; Dat šûmki} [std. = šunka] *dia-col* ham <**Slav**✎>

šúmnā bičànica {NP} *sl-arch* saber, sword ☞ **bičanica**

šûmnjāk {a (acc. = gen.) masc.} **1a.** *sl* gentleman <**Slav***1> **b.** *sl* boss <**Slav***2> **c.** *sl-fea* affluent male, moneybags <**Slav***3> **2** inhabitant of the countryside, hick, bumpkin

• **šúmnjak za gáru** {NP} *sl-arch* sugar

šȕmor {a masc.} *col* noise <**Slav**⁘>

šumovláčiti {mòvlāčīm, čē imperf.} *sl* sneak, attempt not to be observed <**Slav**⁘>

šȕmovlāk {a masc.} *sl* sneaking, attempting not to be observed <**Slav**⁘>

šȕngrād {a masc.} *sl-crafts* flywheel <**Ger**>

šûnka {ē fem.; Dat šúnki} (lit. ham) **a.** *sl* cheek <**Slav***1> **b.** *sl* face (human) <**Slav***2>

šúnto {ē masc.} *sl-crime* jailer <**Gyp**>

šȕp {excl.} *col* the sound made by tapping, tap <**Slav**>

šȕp-kárta {ē fem.} *col* hit, punch <**Ger***1>

šȕpa {ē fem.} (lit. basement) **1** *sl-sex* ***Fac-Obs*** buttocks, butt <**Ger***1> **2** *sl* ***Der-Fac*** apartment <**Ger***1>

šúpak {pka (acc. = gen.) masc.} **a.** *sl-sex* ***Obs*** anus, asshole <**Slav**> **b.** *sl-fea* ***Der-Obs*** stupid or mentally deficient person <**Slav***1> **c.** *sl-fea* ***Der-Obs*** inhabitant of the countryside, hick, bumpkin <**Slav***2>

• **Šúpak je!** {S} (lit. It's an asshole!) *sl-fea* ***Obs*** used to refer to a dangerous situation

• **Šúpak jèdan!** {S} (lit. You, one asshole!) *col* ***Off*** used as a strong curse, Asshole!

• **Šúpak mi je!** {S} (lit. It's an asshole to me!) *sl-fea* ***Obs*** used to refer to one's fear

• **U šúpak te jèbēm!** {S} (lit. I fuck you in your asshole!) *col* ***Off*** used as a moderate curse, Fuck you!

šúpalj {plja, plje adj.} **a.** *sl* hollow <**Slav***1> **b.i.aa.** *sl-sports* incompetent (of a player) <**Slav***2> **bb.** *sl-fea* insane, nuts <**Slav***2> **ii.** broke (financially) **iii.** poor

šȕpānje {a neut.} *sl* touching <**Ger**⁘*1>

šȕpati {ām, ajū imperf.} *sl* touch <**Ger**⁘*1>

šȕpčēnje {a neut.} *sl-sex* ***Obs*** sexual intercourse <**Slav**⁘*1>

šȕpčić {a masc.} *sl-sex* ***Obs*** small anus <**Slav**⁘>

šȕpčina {ē fem.} **a.** *sl-sex* ***Obs*** big anus <**Slav**⁘> **b.** *sl-fea* ***Der-Obs*** evil person <**Slav**⁘*1> **c.** *sl-fea* ***Der-Obs*** stupid or mentally deficient person <**Slav**⁘*2>

šȕpčiti {čīm, čē imperf.} (lit. asshole) *sl-sex* ***Obs*** engage in sexual intercourse with (of a male) <**Slav**⁘*1>

šȕpćina {ē masc.} (lit. big ass) *sl-sex* ***Obs*** anus, asshole <**Slav**✎>

šupeljàčina {ē masc.} *sl-fea* obese child <**Slav**⁘*1>

šupéljak {ljka (acc. = gen.) masc.} *sl-fea* obese child <**Slav**⁘*1>

šupèljānje {a neut.} *sl-fea* slow walk <**Slav**⁘*1>

šupèljati {ām, ajū imperf.} *sl-fea* walk slowly, amble <**Slav**⁘*1>

šupèndara {ē fem.} *sl-sex* ***Obs*** prostitute, hooker <**Slav**✎*1>

šȕpēndra {ē fem.} *sl-sex* ***Obs*** prostitute, hooker <**Slav**✎*1>

šȕper {a (acc. = gen.) masc.} *sl-sports* incompetent player (soccer, etc.) <**Slav**✎*1>

šȕpguza {ē fem.} *sl-sex* ***Obs*** female with large buttocks <**Slav**⁘*1>

šȕpika {ē fem.} *sl-sex* ***Obs*** prostitute, hooker <**Slav**⁘*1>

šupírānje {a neut.} *sl* throwing away, tossing out <**Ger**⁘*1>

šupírati {šȕpīrām, šupírajū biasp.} *sl* throw away, toss out <**Ger**⁘*1>

šȕpiti {pīm, pē perf.} *sl* arrive unexpectedly, appear out of nowhere, pop in <**Ger**⁘*1>

šȕpka {ē fem.; Dat šȕpki} *sl-sex* ***Obs*** female with large buttocks <**Ger**⁘*1>

šȕpkara {ē fem.} *sl-sex* ***Obs*** female with large buttocks <**Ger**⁘*1>

šȕpkīle {a masc.} *sl-sex* ***Obs*** male with large buttocks <**Slav**✎*1>

šúpkonja {ē masc.} *sl-sex* ***Obs*** male with large buttocks <**Slav**⁘*1>

šúpljā prȉča {NP} (lit. a hollow story) **a.** *col* lie **b.** *col* unintelligent talk ☞ **priča**

šȕpljāk *See the following*

• **U šȕpljāk te jèbēm!** {S} (lit. I fuck you in your hollow place!) *col-dia* ***Off*** used as a moderate curse, Fuck you!

šûpljē [1] {ēg neut.} (lit. the hollow one) **1** *sl-crime* pistol, revolver <**Slav**[*1]> **2** *sl-crime* rifle <**Slav**[*1]>

šúplje [2] {adv.} *sl-fea* difficult, bad <**Slav**[*1]>

šûpljī {pljēg (acc. = gen.) masc.} (lit. the hollow one) *sl-sports* incompetent goalie (soccer, etc.) <**Slav**[*1]>

šupljìkāt {ljikáta masc.} **a.** *sl* lie <**Slav**✍[*1]> **b.** *sl-fea* prolonged and meaningless talk, blabber, chatter <**Slav**✍[*2]>

šȕpljikàvo {adv.} *sl-fea* with too many disadvantages <**Slav**[*1]>

šúpljiti {ljīm, ljē imperf.} *col* drill (using tools) <**Slav**❖>

šȕpnuti {nēm, nū perf.} *sl* throw away, toss out <**Ger**❖[*1]>

Šúponja {ē masc.} (lit. the asshole one) *dia* ***Obs*** ox (the animal) <**Slav**❖[*1]>

šúponja {ē masc.} (lit. the asshole one) *sl-fea* short obese male <**Slav**❖[*1]>

šȕrka {ē fem.; Dat šȕrki} *sl-sex* ***Obs*** penis, dick, prick

šȕs {a +ev (ext. pl) masc.; Nom Pl šȕsevi} **a.** *sl* shot (firearms) <**Ger**> **b.i.** *sl-sex* sexual intercourse <**Ger**[*1]> **ii.** *sl* whim <**Ger**[*1]>

šȕster {a (acc. = gen.) masc.} *col* shoe repairman <**Ger**>

šȕša {ē fem.} **1** *sl-sex* ***App*** attractive female <**Slav**[*1]> **2** *sl-fea* ***Der*** unworthy person <**Slav**[*1]>

šúšak {ška masc.} *col* noise <**Slav**❖>

šȕšanj {šnja masc.} **a.** *col* noise <**Slav**❖> **b.i.** *sl* currency note <**Slav**❖[*1]> **ii.** *sl* fallen leaves <**Slav**❖[*1]>

šȕška {ē fem.; Dat šȕški} **1** *sl* bill (of money) <**Slav**❖[*1]> **2** *sl* hundred dinars; a hundred-dinar bill <**Slav**❖[*1]> **3** *sl* ten dinars; a ten-dinar bill <**Slav**❖[*1]> **4** *sl-fea* naive person **5** *sl-fea* stupid or mentally deficient person

šȕškalica {ē fem.} *sl* currency note <**Slav**❖[*1]>

šuškàrati {ām, ajū imperf.} *col* make noise <**Slav**❖>

šȕškati {ām, ajū imperf.} **a.** *col* make moderate noise <**Slav**❖> **b.** whisper: *Ne šuškaj nego govori glasno! Don't whisper, speak up!* **c.** spread rumors: *Šuška se da će ga otpustiti. There are rumors that he will be fired.*

šȕškavac {kāvca masc.} **1** *sl-drink* beer <**Slav**❖[*1]> **2** *col* thin rain coat <**Slav**❖[*1]>

šȕške {ī fem. pl.} *sl* money <**Slav**❖[*1]>

šȕškor {a masc.} *col* moderate noise <**Slav**✍>

šȕškoriti {rīm, rē imperf.} *col* make moderate noise <**Slav**❖>

šȕšljiga {ē fem.; Dat šȕšljigi} *sl-drink* brandy

šȕšmula {ē fem.} *sl-fea* ***Der*** harsh female, bitch

šúšnja {ē fem.} *col* noise <**Slav**❖>

šȕšnjava {ē fem.} *col* noise <**Slav**❖>

šȕšt {a +ev (ext. pl) masc.; Nom Pl šȕštevi} *col* noise <**Slav**❖>

šȕštanj {a masc.} *col* noise <**Slav**❖>

šȕštānje {a neut.} *col* noise <**Slav**[*1]>

šȕštati {tīm, tē imperf.} /šúštati/ *col* make noise <**Slav**❖>

šȕštavac {tāvca masc.} *sl* passport <**Slav**❖[*1]>

šȕštavica {ē fem.} **1** *sl* currency note <**Slav**❖[*1]> **2** *sl-gamble* playing card <**Slav**❖[*1]>

šušulìjēr {lijéra (acc. = gen.) masc.} *sl-drink* barkeeper

šušȕmiga {ē fem. & masc.; Dat šušȕmigi} **1** *sl-fea* ***App*** skilled person **2** *sl-fea* ***Der*** foolish female **3** *sl-fea* ***Der*** stupid or mentally deficient person

šút [1] {excl.} [std. = šuti] *col* used to silence one's interlocutor, shut up <**Slav**✍>

šȕt [2] {šȕta +ov (ext. pl) masc.; Nom Pl šȕtovi} *sl-sex* ***App*** attractive female <**Eng**[*1]>

šȕtara {ē fem.} *sl-crime* prison cell <**Eng**❖[*1]>

šutírati {šȕtīrām, šutírajū imperf.} *col* kick, strike <**Eng**>

šȕtīrati se {šȕtīrām, šutírajū imperf. intr.} *sl* fight (e.g. fist fight) <**Eng**[*1]>

šȕtka {ē fem.; Dat šȕtki} (lit. kicking) **1** *sl* fight (e.g. fist fight) <**Eng**❖[*1]> **2** *sl* a game of dancing to punk rock and kicking each other <**Eng**❖[*1]>

šȕtnuti {nēm, nū perf.} *sl* resign, quit <**Eng**[*1]>

šuvàrica {ē fem.} (lit. from the name of Dr. Stipe Šuvar who introduced school reform) *sl-sstu* used in reference to high schools after the school reform in the 1970s in the former Yugoslavia <**SlavO**[*1]>

šȕza {ē fem.} *sl* shoe <**Eng**✍[*1]>

Švába {ē masc.} *col* ***Off*** German (male), Kraut <**Slav**>
• **Švába tra-la-lâ** {NP} (lit. Kraut toot-toot-toot) SerE *sl* extremely talkative person, chatterbox

Švàbica {ē fem.} *col* ***Off*** German (female), Kraut <**Slav**>

Švâbija {ē fem.} *sl* Germany <**Slav**✍>

Švábo {ē masc.} *col* ***Off*** German (male), Kraut <**Slav**>
• **Švábo tra-la-lâ** {NP} (lit. Kraut toot-toot-toot) *sl* extremely talkative person, chatterbox

Švȁbos {a (acc. = gen.) masc.} *sl-fea* ***Off*** German (male), Kraut <**Slav**✍>

Švàbōv {Švabòva (acc. = gen.) masc.} *sl-fea* ***Off*** German (male), Kraut <**Slav**✍>

šváca [1] {ē masc.} **a.** *sl* ***Fam*** lover (male) <**Fre**✍*1> **b.** *sl* ***Fam*** boyfriend <**Fre**✍*2>

šváca [2] {ē masc. & fem.} *sl-sex* lover <**Fre**✍>

švȁj {excl.} *sl-crime* used to warn and command hiding of some object (usu. from the police), hide it <**Slav**✍*1>

švajcárac {rca (acc. = gen.) masc.} *sl* Swiss franc <**GerO***1>

švȁjznuti {nēm, nū perf.} *sl* hit, punch <**Ger***1>

švȁler {a (acc. = gen.) masc.} /švàlēr /švaléra (acc. = gen.) masc./ **a.** *col* seducer <**Fre***1> **b.** *col* lover (male) <**Fre***2> **c.** *col* boyfriend <**Fre***3>
- **dȅkoratīvan švȁler** {NP} (lit. decorative lover) *sl-fea* male who just walks with females only to be seen with them

švalerácija {ē fem.} **a.** *col* flirting <**Fre***1> **b.** *sl-sex* sexual intercourse <**Fre***2>

švalèrānje {a neut.} **a.** *col* flirting <**Fre***1> **b.** *sl-sex* sexual intercourse <**Fre***2>

švalèrati se {ām, ajū imperf. intr.} *col-dia* cheat on one's lover or spouse <**Fre***1>

švalèrisānje {a neut.} **a.** *col* flirting <**Fre***1> **b.** *sl-sex* sexual intercourse <**Fre***2>

švàlērka {ē fem.; Dat švàlērki} **a.** *col* lover (female) <**Fre***1> **b.** *col* girlfriend <**Fre***2>

Švàpčanin {a (acc. = gen.) masc.} *sl-fea* ***Off*** German (male), Kraut <**Slav**✍>

švàpskī {ā, ō adj.} *sl-fea* ***Off*** German (pertaining to a person or nation), Kraut <**GerO***1>

švȁsānje {a neut.} (lit. welding) **1** *sl-sex* ***Fac-Obs*** sexual intercourse <**Ger***1> **2** *sl-drink* drinking <**Ger***1>

švȁsati {ām, ajū imperf.} (lit. weld) **1** *sl-sex* ***Fac-Obs*** engage in sexual intercourse with (of a male) <**Ger***1> **2** *sl-drink* ***Fac*** drink (alcohol) <**Ger***1>

švȁser {a (acc. = gen.) masc.} (lit. welder) *sl-sex* ***Fac-Obs*** male sexual partner (of a female) <**Ger***1>

Švéca [1] {ē fem.} *sl* Sweden <**Ger**✍>

švéca [2] {ē fem.} *sl* sister, sis <**Ger**✍>

švȇj {excl.} *sl-crime* used to warn and command hiding of some object (usu. from the police), hide it <**Slav***1>

švéjati {švȇjām, švéjajū imperf. intr.} *sl* hide, cover up

Švȇjk {a (acc. = gen.) +ov (ext. pl) masc.; Nom Pl Švéjkovi} (lit. The good soldier Švejk is a character from a novel by Czech writer Jaroslav Hašek) *sl-mil* soldier <**CzeO***1>

švȅnkī {īja (acc. = gen.) masc.} /švènki/ **a.** *sl-fea* stupid or mentally deficient person <**Ger**✍*1> **b.** *sl-fea* insane male, nut case <**Ger**✍*2>

švȅnkovati {kujēm, kujū imperf.} *sl-media* pan (with a movie or television camera) <**Ger**>

švéra {ē fem.} *sl* cheating on one's lover or spouse <**Ger***1>

švérānje {a neut.} *sl* cheating on one's lover or spouse <**Ger***1>

švȅrc {a +ev (ext. pl) masc.; Nom Pl švèrcevi} *col* smuggling <**Ger***1>

švȅrcānje {a neut.} *col* smuggling <**Ger***1>

švȅrcati {ām, ajū imperf.} *col* smuggle <**Ger***1>

švȅrcer {a (acc. = gen.) masc.} /švèrcer/ *col* smuggler <**Ger***1>

švȅrcovānje {a neut.} *col* smuggling <**Ger***1>

švȅrcovati {cujēm, cujū imperf.} *col* smuggle <**Ger***1>

švȇsta [1] {ē fem.} *sl* sister, sis <**Ger**✍>

Švȇsta [2] {ē fem.} *sl* Sweden <**Ger**✍>

švȇsterica {ē fem.} *sl* sister <**Ger**⁘>

švȇstērka {ē fem.; Dat švȇstērki} *sl* sister <**Ger**⁘>

švȉcati {ām, ajū biasp.} *sl-fea* work hard (at manual labor) <**Ger***1>

švȉcgerla {ē fem.} *sl-fea* ***Der*** dirty and untidy female, slob <**Ger**⁘>

švȉmati se {ām, ajū imperf. intr.} *sl* swim <**Ger**⁘>

švìndl {a +ov (ext. pl) masc.; Nom Pl švìndlovi} *sl* cheating, swindling <**Ger**>

švȉndler {a (acc. = gen.) masc.} *sl-fea* cheater, swindler <**Ger**>

švindlèrāj {švindleràja masc.} *sl* cheating, swindling <**Ger**>

švȉndlovānje {a neut.} *sl* cheating, swindling <**Ger**>

švȉndlovati {lujēm, lujū biasp.} *sl* cheat, swindle <**Ger**⁘>

švȍrc {adj.} *col* broke (financially) <**Ger**>

švȍrcer {a (acc. = gen.) masc.} *sl-fea* person who is broke (financially) <**Ger**>

švorcírati se {švòrcīrām, švorcírajū imperf. intr.} *sl-fea* be broke, be out of money <**Ger**⁘>

švrȁkopīs {a masc.} (lit. crow writing) *col* illegible handwriting, chicken scratching <Slav❖[*1]>

švŕca {ē fem.} *sl-fea* very young female, little girl <Slav✍>

švŕća {ē masc.} **1** *sl* wallet <Slav✍> **2** *sl* child, kid <Slav✍>

švŕćo {a masc.} //e m, / *sl* child, kid <Slav✍>

švȓle {eta masc.} **a.** *sl-fea* ***Fam*** little boy, kid **b.** *sl-fea* ***Fam*** small child, kiddo

švŕljati {švȓljām, švŕljajū imperf. intr.} **1** *col* wander, roam: *švrljati uokolo u potrazi za dobrim restoranom wander around looking for a good restaurant* <Gre❖[*1]> **2** *col* scribble, write illegibly: *švrljati u svesci scribble in a notebook* <Gre❖[*1]>

Śś

śȁ {pron.} [std. = šta] **Bos** *col-dia* what (in any of its Serbo-Croatian meanings used in forms different from the standard) <Slav✍>

śȁe {excl.} [std. = šta je] Bos *col-dia* what is going on, what's up <Slav✍>

śȁnuti {nēm, nū perf.} [std. = šapnuti] Bos *col* whisper <Slav✍>

śȇći {śéčem, śéku, śȇk, śȇk perf. irreg.} [std. = sjeći] *dia* cut, disrupt <Slav✍>

śȅdok {śedòka (acc. = gen.) masc.; Voc śȅdoče} [std. = svjedok] *dia* witness <Slav✍>

śȅđeti {śèdīm, śèdē imperf. intr.} [std. = sjedjeti] Mont *dia* sit <Slav✍>

śèkira {ē fem.} [std. = sjekira] *dia* axe <Slav✍>

śȇs {śȇdnēm, śȇdnū, śȇd, śȇ perf. irreg.} [std. = sjesti] *dia* sit <Slav✍>

śȇsti {śȇdēm, śȇdu perf. irreg.} [std. = sjesti] *dia* sit <Slav✍>

śȅtan {tna, tno adj.} [std. = sjetan] *dia* sad, depressed <Slav✍>

śȇver {a masc.} [std. = sjever] *dia* North <Slav✍>

śȉđeti {śèdīm, śèdē imperf.} [std. = sjedjeti] Mont *dia* sit <Slav✍>

śó {pron.} [std. = zašto] Bos *col* why <Slav✍>

Tt

tȁ [1] {excl.} **1** *col* well <Slav> **2** *col* but <Slav> **3** *col* oh <Slav>

tâ [2] {tâa masc.} Med *dia* father, daddy <Slav✍>

tába {ē fem.} **a.** *sl* fight (e.g. fist fight) <NE✍[*1]> **b.** *sl-sex* sexual intercourse <NE✍[*2]>

tàbāč {tabáča (acc. = gen.) masc.} *sl* troublemaker, rowdy, ruffian <Slav❖[*1]>

tabàčina {ē fem.} *sl* beating up <Slav❖[*1]>

tȁbadžija {ē masc.} *sl-fea* troublemaker, rowdy, ruffian <NE❖[*1]>

tàban [1] {excl.} (lit. foot-sole) *sl* used to make somebody go away, beat it <NE[*1]>

tàban [2] {a masc.} (lit. foot-sole) **1** *sl* running away, beating feet <NE[*1]> **2** *sl* shoe <NE[*1]> **3** *sl* intellectual <NE[*1]>

- **dȕs tàbani** {NP} *col* flat feet

tabànānje {a neut.} (lit. walk on foot) **a.** *col* walking <NE❖[*1]> **b.** *sl-fea* persistent and meaningless talk, blabber <NE❖[*2]>

tabànāš {banáša (acc. = gen.) masc.} (lit. foot-walker) **1** *sl-crime* street policeman, beat cop <NE❖[*1]> **2** *sl-sex* male looking for a loose woman, guy on the make <NE❖[*1]>

- **têškī tabànāš od bȁrē** {NP} (lit. heavy walker from the pond) *sl-fea* rich foreigner

tabànati {ām, ajū imperf. intr.} (lit. walk on foot) **a.** *col* walk <NE❖[*1]> **b.** *sl* run <NE❖[*2]> **c.** *sl-fea* talk persistently and meaninglessly, blabber, chatter <NE❖[*3]>

tabànisati {išēm, išū imperf. intr.} (lit. walk on foot) **a.** *sl* walk <NE❖[*1]> **b.** *sl* run away, flee <NE❖[*2]>

tȁbanovića fijáker {NP} (lit. foot cart) *col* walking ☞ fijaker

tabánjac {njca masc.} *sl* beating up <NE❖[*1]>

tȁbānje {a neut.} **a.** *sl* beating up <NE❖[*1]> **b.** *sl-sex* sexual intercourse <Slav❖[*2]>

tȁbati {ām, ajū imperf.} **a.** *sl* beat up <NE❖[*1]> **b.** *sl-sex* engage in sexual intercourse with (of a male) <Slav❖[*2]>

tȁbati se {ām, ajū imperf. intr.} *sl* fight (e.g. fist fight) <NE✣[*1]>

tàbātor {a (acc. = gen.) masc.} **a.** *sl-fea* troublemaker, rowdy, ruffian <NE✣[*1]> **b.i.** *sl-crime* policeman, cop <Slav✣[*2]> **ii.** *sl-sex* lover (male) <Slav✣[*2]>

tabáža {ē fem.} *sl* fight (e.g. fist fight) <NE✣[*1]>

tábla {ē fem.} (lit. blackboard) *sl-fea* stupid or mentally deficient person <Lat[*1]>

tabletòmān {a (acc. = gen.) masc.} /tabletòmān/ (lit. pill maniac) **a.** *sl-drugs* person who takes too many pills, pill popper <Fre✣[*1]> **b.** *sl-drugs* drug addict, junkie <Fre✣[*2]>

tabletomànija {ē fem.} (lit. pill mania) *sl-drugs* habit of taking too many pills <Fre✣[*1]>

tȁblić {tablíća (acc. = gen.) masc.} *sl-drugs* drug addict who takes pills, pill popper <Lat✣[*1]>

tȁblīć {tablíća masc.} *sl-gamble* a kind of simple card game <Lat✣>

tablijána {ē fem.} *sl-gamble* a kind of simple card game <Lat✣[*1]>

tabòisānje {a neut.} *sl-sex* ***Obs*** sexual intercourse <NE✍[*1]>

tabòisati {išēm, išū imperf.} *sl-sex* ***Obs*** engage in sexual intercourse with (of a male) <NE✍[*1]>

tàbut {a masc.} BosM *col* coffin <NE>

tȁca {ē fem.} (lit. tray) *sl-drink* ***Fac*** bar (drinking place) <Ger[*1]>

tàcna {ē fem.} (lit. tray) *sl* female <Ger[*1]>

tȁčka *See the following*
- **bêlā tȁčka** {NP} (lit. the white spot) SerE *sl-sports* penalty kick (in soccer)

tȁčko {a masc.} *sl* bicycle, bike <Slav✍[*1]>

tâć {a +ev (ext. pl) masc.; Nom Pl táćevi} *sl* rap, tap

tàdēr {adv.} [std. = tada] *dia* then <Slav✍>

tȁdro {a (acc. = gen.) masc.; perm} /tàdro/ *sl-crime* policeman, cop <Ger✍[*1]>

tȁflati {ām, ajū imperf.} *sl-sex* ***Obs*** engage in sexual intercourse with (of a male) <Ger✣[*1]>

tahȉtī {īja masc.} *sl-auto* cab, taxi <PoliO[*1]>

tȁhta {ē fem.} BosM *col* plank <NE>

Tâj fìlm nêćeš glȅdati! {S} (lit. You will not see that movie!) *col* used to express the improbability of an event, No way! ☞ **film**

tája {ē masc.} **a.** *col* ***Fam*** father, daddy <Slav✍> **b.** *sl-crime* ***Fac*** elderly victim of a pickpocket <Slav✍[*1]>

tȁjger {a masc.} *sl-drugs* Tigar glue (sniffed by drug addicts) <Eng[*1]>

tájko {a masc.} *col* ***Fam*** father, daddy <Slav✍>

tájo {ē masc.} *col* ***Fam*** father, daddy <Slav✍>

tȁk [1] {excl.} *col* the sound made by tapping, tap <Slav>

tȁk [2] {adv.} [std. = tako] **1** *col* so much <Slav✍> **2** *col* that way <Slav✍>

taka {excl.} **1** *col* the sound made by knocking, knock <Slav> **2** *col* the sound made by tapping, tap <Slav>

tàkī {ā, ō adj.} [std. = takav] *col* such <Slav✍>

Tȁknēm ti ga! {S} (lit. I touch it to you!) *dia* ***Off-Fac*** used as a weak curse, Screw you! ☞ **taknuti**

tȁknuti *See the following*
- **Tȁknēm ti ga!** {S} (lit. I touch it to you!) *dia* ***Off-Fac*** used as a weak curse, Screw you!

tȁknūto-mȁknūto {excl.} **a.** *sl-sports* used in a game of chess to inform one's adversary that he/she has to move the piece he/she has picked up, rather than returning it to its initial position and taking a new one <Slav[*1]> **b.** *col* used to express the opinion that one has to continue the job he/she started <Slav[*2]>

tȁkō {part.} *col* thus, so <Slav>
- **sȁmo tȁkō** {AdvP} (lit. only like that) *sl-fea* fun

tȁksenā màrka {NP} (lit. administrative fee stamp) *sl-fea* boring person, bore ☞ **marka**

tȁksī {īja masc.} /tȁksi, tàksi/ (lit. cab) *sl-fea* ***Fac*** boy who manages to do nothing more than to walk with his girlfriend <Gre[*1]>

tȁksī-gèrla {ē fem.} /tȁksi-gèrla, tàksi-gèrla/ (lit. cab girl) *sl-sex* ***Fac*** prostitute, streetwalker <Gre-Eng[*1]>

taksìkati {ām, ajū imperf.} (lit. give a cab ride) *sl* take somebody along (e.g. to a party) <Gre✣[*1]>

taksírati {tàksīrām, taksírajū imperf.} (lit. give a cab ride) *sl* take one's girlfriend to her home after a date <Gre✣[*1]>

tàksista {ē masc.} (lit. cab driver) *sl-fea* ***Fac*** boy who manages to do nothing more than to walk with his girlfriend <Gre[*1]>

taktȉlisati se {išēm, išū imperf.} *sl* touch <Lat✣[*1]>

takùlīn {kulína masc.} *sl* wallet <Ita>

tâl {a +ov (ext. pl) masc.; Nom Pl tálovi} **a.** *col* share, split <Ger> **b.i.** *sl-crime* one's part of a loot, one's take <Ger[*1]> **ii.** *sl* deal, agreement (in general) <Ger[*1]>

talàsānje {a neut.} (lit. creating waves) *sl-fea* prolonged and meaningless talk, blabber, chatter <Slav[*1]>

talàsati {ām, ajū imperf.} (lit. create waves) **a.** *sl-fea* talk persistently and meaninglessly, blabber, chatter <Slav*1> **b.** *sl-fea* annoy, bother, pester <Slav*2> **c.** *sl-fea* panic, freak out <Slav*3>

tâle {eta neut.} [std. = tašta] *sl* mother-in-law <Slav✍>

tàličan {čna, čno adj.} **a.** *col* lucky <NE❖> **b.** *sl-fea* ***Iro*** unlucky <NE❖*1>

tâlija {ē fem. & masc.} **a.** *sl-fea* lucky person <NE> **b.** *sl-fea* ***Iro*** unlucky indiviudual <NE*1>

tâlija {ē fem.} **1a.** *sl* luck <NE> **b.** *sl-gamble* one's last money in gambling <NE*1> **2** *sl* lie <NE*1>

Talijanı̏ška {ē fem.; Dat Talijanı̏ški} /Talijanı̀ška/ [std. = Italijan] *sl-fea* Italian (person), Dago <SlavO✍>

táliti {tâlīm, lē imperf.} *col* share, split <NE❖*1>

táliti se {tâlīm, lē imperf. intr.} *col* conspire, plot <NE❖*1>

tàljiga {ē fem.; Dat tàljigi} *sl* shoe <Slav*1>

taljìgati {ām, ajū imperf.} *sl* run away, flee <Slav❖*1>

taljìzgati {ām, ajū imperf.} *sl-fea* talk persistently and meaninglessly, blabber, chatter <Slav✍*1>

tàmān {adv.} /tamàn adv/ *col* exactly, precisely <NE>

- **tàmān pòsla** {AdvP} (lit. exactly business) *col* used to refer to an unwanted object or event, that's the last thing I need right now

tamániti {tàmānīm, nē imperf.} (lit. eradicate) **1a.** *col* ***Fac*** eat, devour <NE*1> **b.** *col* ***Fac*** eat too much, gorge, pig out <NE*2> **2** *sl* ***Fac*** kill, rub out <NE*1>

tàmbati {ām, ajū biasp.} *sl* beat up <NE✍*1>

tàmbura {ē fem.} (lit. tamburica - mandolin-like folk instrument) **1a.** *sl-sex* ***Obs*** vagina, cunt <NE*1> **b.** *sl-sex* female <NE*2> **2** *sl-crime* prison <NE*1> **3** *sl* hospital <NE*1> **4** *sl* fight (e.g. fist fight) <NE*1> **5** *sl* mouth <NE*1>

- **dȑžāvnā tàmbura** {NP} (lit. government tamburica - mandolin-like folk instrument) *sl-crime* ***Fac*** prison

tambùrānje {a neut.} (lit. playing the tamburica - mandolin-like folk instrument) *sl-fea* prolonged and meaningless talk, blabber, chatter <NE❖*1>

tambùrāš {buráša masc.} (lit. tamburica *mandolin-like folk instrument* player) *sl-crime* policeman, cop <NE❖*1>

tambùrati {ām, ajū imperf.} **a.** *col* play the tamburica (traditional string instrument) <NE❖> **b.i.** *sl* beat up <NE❖*1> **ii.** *sl* talk persistently and meaninglessly, blabber, chatter <NE❖*1>

tȁmburica {ē fem.} (lit. tamburica - mandolin-like folk instrument) *sl* female <NE❖*1>

tàmīć {tamíća masc.} **a.** *sl-auto* small TAM (make of truck) <BN> **b.** *sl-drink* ***Fac*** quantity of beer one has consumed <BN*1>

tȁmo-vâmo {excl.} (lit. here and there) *col* used to express hesitation <Slav✍*1>

tȁnāhan {hna, hno adj.} [std. = tanan] BosM *col* thin <Slav✍>

tànak {nka masc.} *sl-arch* thread <Slav*1>

tànak {nka, nko adj.} (lit. thin) **a.** *col* bad: *tanak film bad movie* <Slav*1> **b.** *col* weak: *tanak radnik weak worker* <Slav*2> **c.** *col* broke (financially): *tanak gazda broke owner* <Slav*3>

tȁnc {a +ev (ext. pl) masc.; Nom Pl tàncevi} *sl* dancing <Ger>

tàncāljka {ē fem.; Dat tàncāljki} *sl* dancing <Ger❖*1>

tȁncovati {cujēm, cujū imperf.} *sl* dance <Ger❖>

tȁndara-brȍć {excl.} *sl* nonsense <NE❖*1>

tȁndara-mȁndara-brȍć {excl.} *sl* nonsense <NE✍*1>

tandàrija {ē masc.} *col* nothing <NE✍*1>

tandáriti {tàndārīm, rē imperf.} *sl-sex* ***Obs*** engage in sexual intercourse with (of a male) <NE❖*1>

tàndēm *See the following*

- **Tàndēm jȁšē králjevı́ću Mȃrko.** {S} (lit. Crown prince Marko is riding on a tandem bike.) *sl-fea* used to express unfavorable opinion on something

tȁndr̄ {excl.} *col* rumble (e.g. a cart on a rocky road) <Slav>

tandŕčak {čka masc.} (lit. a bit of rumbling) **a.** *sl* dance <Slav❖*1> **b.** *sl-gamble* game <Slav❖*2>

tandȑček {čka masc.} (lit. a bit of rumbling) **a.** *sl* dance <Slav❖*1> **b.** *sl-gamble* game <Slav❖*2>

tȁndrčiti {čīm, čē imperf.} (lit. rumble) *sl-sex* ***Obs*** engage in sexual intercourse with (of a male) <Slav❖*1>

tȁndr̄k {a masc.} *col* rumbling <Slav>

tandȑkāje {a neut.} *col* noise <Slav>

tandȑkalo {a neut.} **1** *sl* alarm clock <Slav❖*1> **2** *sl* bell <Slav❖*1> **3** *sl-fea* stupid or mentally deficient person <Slav❖*1>

tandȑkānje {a neut.} **a.** *col* rumbling <Slav❖*1> **b.** *col* noise <Slav❖*2> **c.** *sl-fea* prolonged and meaningless talk, blabber, chatter <Slav❖*3> **d.** *sl-fea* spending one's time in useless activities, fooling around, messing around

tandȑkati {ām, ajū imperf.} **a.** *col* rumble (e.g. a cart on a rocky road) <Slav❖*1> **b.** *sl-fea* talk persistently and meaninglessly, blabber, chatter <Slav❖*2> **c.** *sl-fea* preach, give lectures to <Slav❖*3>

tandr̄knuti {tàndr̄nēm, nū perf.} (lit. rumble) **a.** *col* make a mistake, screw up <Slav❖*1> **b.** *col* be in a difficult situation <Slav❖*2> **c.** *sl-gamble* lose money <Slav❖*3> **d.** *sl-sports, sl-gamble* lose a game <Slav❖*4>

tàndžara {ē fem.} *sl-crime* rifle <NE>

tȁne *See the following*

- **Táne ti gósino!** {S} (lit. *I screw* your Lord's bullet!) *dia* ***Off*** used as a weak curse, Screw you!

tȁnec {nca masc.} Kajk *dia* dance <Ger☞>

tȁnga {ē fem.; Dat tȁngi} *sl-fea* attractive female <Poli*1>

tangírati {tàngīrām, tangírajū imperf.} *sl-fea* make somebody nervous <Lat*1>

tȁnk {a +ov (ext. pl) masc.; Nom Pl tànkovi} *sl-auto* gas tank <Ger>

tȁnkānje {a neut.} *sl-auto* filling up with gas <Ger❖>

tankárēnje {a neut.} *sl-auto* filling up with gas <Ger❖>

tankáriti {tànkārīm, rē imperf. intr.} *sl-auto* fill up with gas <Ger❖>

tȁnkāroš {a (acc. = gen.) masc.} *sl* gas station worker <Ger❖*1>

tȁnkati {ām, ajū imperf. intr.} *sl-auto* fill up with gas <Ger❖>

tànker {a masc.} *sl* army-style coat <BN>

tȁnkerice {ā fem. pl.} *sl* jeans <BN*1>

tȁnko {adv.} (lit. thin) **a.** *col* poorly <Slav*1> **b.** *col* weakly <Slav*2>

tankoserìtis {a masc.} (lit. thin shit) *sl-sex* ***Fac*** diarrhea, runs, trots <Slav❖*1>

tȁnkovati {kujēm, kujū imperf.} *sl-auto* fill up with gas <Ger❖>

tantàrānčiti {čīm, čē imperf.} *sl-sex* ***Obs*** engage in sexual intercourse with (of a male) <Slav❖*1>

tȁnte *See the following*

- **tȁnte za tȁnte** {NP} Din *col* pay back, take revenge

tânj {a +ev (ext. pl) masc.; Nom Pl tànjevi} *sl* bribe

tȁnjarnica {ē fem.} *sl* shopkeeper (female) <Slav*1>

tánjež {i fem.} (lit. thinness) *sl-fea* something of rather low quality <Slav*1>

tánjiti {tânjīm, njē imperf.} (lit. make thinner) *sl* sell (exchange merchandise for money) <Slav*1>

tànjūr {tanjúra masc.} (lit. saucer) *sl* city square <Slav*1>

tȁp [1] {excl.} *col* the sound made by tapping, tap <Slav>

tȁp [2] {tàpa +ov (ext. pl) masc.; Nom Pl tàpovi} **1** *sl-drugs* narcotic drug, dope <Slav*1> **2** *sl-fea* silent walking <Slav*1>

tȁp-tȁp {excl.} *col* the sound made by tapping, tap <Slav>

tȁpa-tȁpa {excl.} *col* the sound made by tapping, tap <Slav>

tȁpāt {a masc.} *col* applause <Slav*1>

tàpati {ām, ajū imperf.} **1** *col* tap <Slav❖*1> **2** *sl* walk silently <Slav❖*1>

- **tàpati po pr̄dalu** {VP} (lit. tap somebody's farting thing) *sl-sex* ***Obs*** pet somebody's buttocks

tapètār {tapetára (acc. = gen.) masc.} (lit. wallpaper layer) *sl-sex* ***Fac*** male homosexual, gay <Gre❖*1>

tȁpī {īja (acc. = gen.) masc.} *sl-gamble* losing gambler

tápija {ē fem.} /tàpija/ BosM *col* bad luck <NE*1>

tapírati se {tàpīrām, tapírajū imperf. intr.} (lit. have a permanent) *sl-gamble* lose money <Fre*1>

tapisèrija {ē fem.} (lit. tapestry) *sl-fea* hairy masculine chest <Fre*1>

tȁpka [1] {ē fem.; Dat tȁpki} **a.** *sl* rap, tap <Slav❖*1> **b.** game with collector's cards where one tries to flip over a card

tȁpka [2] {ē masc.; Dat tȁpki} *sl-gamble* losing gambler <Slav❖*1>

tapkárēnje {a neut.} *sl-crime* scalping tickets <Slav❖*1>

tapkáriti {tàpkārīm, rē imperf.} *sl-crime* scalp tickets <Slav❖*1>

tȁpkāroš {a (acc. = gen.) masc.} *sl-crime* ticket scalper <Slav❖*1>

tȁpkati {ām, ajū imperf.} **a.** *sl-fea* walk silently <Slav❖*1> **b.** *sl-crime* scalp tickets <Slav❖*2>

tȁpke {eta neut.} *sl-gamble* playing cards <Slav❖*1>

tȁpos {a (acc. = gen.) masc.} *sl-crime* ticket scalper <Slav☞*1>

tàpšati {tȁpšēm, šū imperf.} *col* tap <Slav*1>

tára {ē fem.} *sl-drink* brandy

tàraba {ē fem.} **a.** *col* fence, walls <NE> **b.i.** *sl-fea* clumsy person, klutz <NE*1> **ii.** *sl-crime* policeman, cop <NE*1> **iii.** *sl-fea* flat-breasted male <NE*1> **iv.**

tàrabār {a (acc. = gen.) masc.} *sl-fea* male without his own apartment <NE❖*1>

tàrador {a (acc. = gen.) masc.; perm} *sl-crime* policeman, cop <Ger✍[*1]>

tàradro {ē fem.; perm} *sl-crime* policeman, cop <Ger✍[*1]>

Taràna {ē fem.} **a.** *sl-fea* male who wears shoulder straps <NE[*1]> **b.** *sl-fea* male without his own apartment <NE[*2]>

tarapàna {ē fem.} **a.** *col* mess, disorder, disturbance <NE> **b.** *col* fight (e.g. fist fight) <NE[*1]>

târča {ē fem.} **a.** *sl-drink* grape brandy **b.** *sl-drink* brandy

tàrdija {ē fem.} *sl-drink* brandy

tȁrdža {ē fem.} 1 *sl-drink* plum brandy 2 *sl-drink* grape brandy

tàrigūz [1] {a masc.} (lit. rub-ass) *sl-sex* ***Fac-Obs*** bathroom tissue, ass wipe <Slav✣[*1]>

tàrigūz [2] {a (acc. = gen.) masc.} (lit. rub-ass) *sl-fea* ***Der-Obs*** ingratiator (male), brownnoser, ass kisser <Slav✣[*1]>

tarlàhati {ām, ajū imperf.} *sl-sex* ***Obs*** engage in sexual intercourse with (of a male)

tarnbùrati {ām, ajū biasp.} (lit. play the tamburica - mandolin-like folk instrument) *sl* beat up <NE✍[*1]>

tàrnjār {tarnjára (acc. = gen.) masc.; Voc tȁrnjāru} *sl* merchant (male)

tàrnjarica {ē fem.} *sl* boss's wife

tàrzanica {ē fem.} *sl-fea* Tarzan-style hairstyle <EngO✣[*1]>

tàslačēnje {a neut.} *sl-sex* ***Fac-Obs*** sexual intercourse <NE[*1]>

tàslačiti {čīm, čē imperf.} *sl-sex* ***Obs*** engage in sexual intercourse with (of a male) <NE[*1]>

tȁster {a (acc. = gen.) masc.} (lit. key) *sl-crime* ***Der*** informer, stoolie, snitch <Lat[*1]>
- **tȁster stàcīn** {NP} (lit. button station) *sl* radio

tastèrāš {teráša (acc. = gen.) masc.; Voc tȁsterāšu} (lit. user of keys) *sl-crime* ***Der*** informer, stoolie, snitch <Lat✣[*1]>

tȁš [1] {a +ev (ext. pl) masc.; Nom Pl tàševi} [std. = tašta] *sl* mother-in-law <Slav✍>

Tȁš [2] {a +ev (ext. pl) masc.; Nom Pl Tàševi} Ser *col* name for Tašmajdan, the park in Belgrade, Serbia <NEO✍>

tàšak {a masc.} **a.** *dia* egg <NE> **b.** *dia* testicle <NE[*1]> **c.** *sl-sex* penis <NE[*2]>

tàšanče {eta neut.} *dia* lamb (the animal) <NE✣[*1]>

Tašmájdan {a masc.} (lit. Tašmajdan is a neighborhood in Belgrade, Serbia) **a.** Ser *sl-fea* skinhead <NEO[*1]> **b.** Ser *sl-fea* bald head <NEO[*2]>

tȁšnēr {tašnéra (acc. = gen.) masc.} (lit. purse maker) *sl-crime* purse thief, purse snatcher <Ger[*1]>

tȁštnjāk {a masc.} [std. = tašta] *sl* mother-in-law <Slav✍>

tȁta *See the following*
- **tȁta máta** {NP} **a.** *col* expert **b.** *sl* boss

tȁtica *See the following*
- **Tȁticu li ti jèbēm!** {S} (lit. I screw your little dad!) *col-dia* ***Off*** used as a weak curse, Screw you!
- **Tȁticu ti mȓtvōga jèbēm!** {S} (lit. I fuck your dead dad!) *col-dia* ***Off*** used as a very strong curse, Fuck you!

tȁtko *See the following*
- **Tȁtka li ti tvôga!** {S} (lit. *I fuck* your little dad!) SSer *dia* ***Off*** used as a moderate curse, Fuck you!

tàvan {a masc.} (lit. attic) *sl* skyscraper <NE[*1]>
- **na tàvan** {PP} (lit. to the attic) *sl-crime* to a convenient place for stealing

tàvati {ām, ajū imperf.} *sl* cook <Gyp>

tàviti {vīm, vē imperf.} *sl* cook <Gyp>

tàvla {ē fem.} BosM *col* backgammon <NE>

tàvnjan *See the following*
- **Tàvnjan ti jèbēm!** {S} (lit. I screw your incense!) *dia* ***Off*** used as a weak curse, Screw you!

tàzbina {ē fem.} *col* in-laws <Slav✣>

táze {adv.} Din *col* fresh <NE>

tážiti {tâžīm, žē imperf.} *sl* be (in any of its Serbo-Croatian meanings used in forms different from the standard): *tažiti na poslu be at work.* ◊ *tažiti kao policajac be a policeman* <Slav[*1]>

TBC [tê-bê-cê] {a masc.} (lit. TB) *sl-fea* macho (person) <Abb[*1]>

te ... te {c.} *col* both ... and <Slav>

téča {ē masc.} (lit. uncle) SerE *sl* I (when a male refers to himself) <Slav[*1]>

tèdbeš {adj.} *sl* identical, exactly the same

tèfić {a masc.} *sl* telephone, phone <Gre✍>

tèfter {a masc.} BosM *col* notebook <NE>

tèfteriti {rīm, rē imperf.} BosM *col* write <NE✣>

tȅget {a (acc. = gen.) masc.} (lit. dark blue) *sl-crime* policeman, man in blue <GerO[*1]>

tégla {ē fem.} (lit. jar) **1a.** *sl-fea* stupid or mentally deficient person <Lat*1> **b.** *sl-fea* phlegmatic person <Lat*2> **2** *sl* female <Lat*1>

tȅh {excl.} *col* used to express resignation, ah <Slav>

Tȅherān {a masc.} (lit. Tehran) *sl* ***Der-Fac*** name for Sarajevo (a city in Bosnia) <NEO*1>

tèhničār {a (acc. = gen.) masc.} (lit. technician) **1** *sl-sex* ***Fac*** male homosexual, gay <Gre*1> **2** *sl-sex* ***Fac-Obs*** small penis <Gre*1>

tȅhničkē smétnje {NP} (lit. technical disturbances) *sl-sex* ***Fac*** menstruation, period ☞ **smetnje**

tèhnika *See the following*

- **bêlā tèhnika** {NP} (lit. white technology) SerE *col* kitchen appliances
- **bìjēlā tèhnika** {NP} (lit. white technology) *col* kitchen appliances

têjp {a +ov (ext. pl) masc.; Nom Pl téjpovi} *sl* tape (in general) <Eng*1>

tèkma {ē fem.} *sl-sports* ball game (in general) <Slo>

Tȅksās {a (acc. = gen.) masc.} /Tèksas/ (lit. Texas) **Cro** *sl-sports* name for Trešnjevka (a neighborhood in Zagreb, Croatia) <EngO*1>

tȅkst {a +ov (ext. pl) masc.; Nom Pl tèkstovi} (lit. text) **a.** *sl* word <Lat*1> **b.** *sl* the content of what is being said <Lat*2>

tèkstīl {tekstíla masc.} (lit. textile) *sl* clothing <Lat*1>

tektónac {nca (acc. = gen.) masc.} (lit. the tectonic one) *sl-fea* distressed person <Gre✣*1>

télac {lca (acc. = gen.) masc.} (lit. calf) *sl-fea* stupid or mentally deficient person <Slav*1>

tȅle {eta neut.} (lit. calf) *sl-fea* muscular male, pumped up dude <Slav*1>

telèfōn [1] {telefóna masc.} (lit. phone) **1** *sl* punch in the head <Gre*1> **2** *sl-sex* bathroom <Gre*1>

telèfōn [2] {telefóna (acc. = gen.) masc.} (lit. telephone) *sl-crime* ***Der*** informer, stoolie, snitch <Gre*1>

telefònati {ām, ajū biasp.} [std. = telefonirati] *sl* telephone, phone <Gre✍>

telefònīk {foníka masc.} *sl* telephone book, phonebook <Gre✣>

telefònist {a (acc. = gen.) masc.} (lit. operator) *sl-crime* informer, stoolie, snitch <Gre*1>

telefonȉška {ē fem.; Dat telefòniški} /telefonȉška/ [std. = telefon] *sl* telephone, phone <Gre✍>

telefùnken {a masc.} *sl* telephone, phone <Gre-BN*1>

tȅlefūr {a masc.} *sl-gamble* signaling (in cards as a form of cheating) <Gre-Ger*1>

telefúrati {lèfūrām, lefúrajū biasp.} *sl-gamble* signal (in cards as a form of cheating) <Gre-Ger*1>

telègraf {a (acc. = gen.) masc.} (lit. telegraph) *sl-crime* ***Der*** informer, stoolie, snitch <Gre*1>

telepàtija {ē fem.} (lit. telepathy) *sl* church <Gre*1>

teleprìnter {a (acc. = gen.) masc.} /teleprìnter/ (lit. teleprinter) *sl-crime* ***Der*** informer, stoolie, snitch <Gre*1>

tȅlerād {a masc.} *sl-crafts* cogwheel <Ger>

tȅleskopi {ā masc. pl.} (lit. telescopes) *sl* eyeglasses <Gre*1>

Televîzor {a masc.} (lit. tv set) **Cro** *sl-drink* name of a bar on Ilica and Marinkovićeva streets in Zagreb, Croatia <Gre*1>

- **na televîzoru** {PP} (lit. on a tv set) [std. = na televiziji] *col* on tv

tèlezūr {a masc.} *sl* television (set and medium) <Lat-Slav✍*1>

tȅliš {a masc.} [std. = televizija] *sl* ***Fam*** television (set and medium) <Gre-Lat✍>

tèliti se {līm, lē imperf. intr.} (lit. give birth to a calf) **a.** *col* have a hard time, experience difficulties <Slav*1> **b.** *sl* complain, have a cow <Slav*2> **c.** *sl* cry, shed tears, weep <Slav*3>

tȅlka {ē fem.; Dat telki} [std. = televizija] *sl* ***Fam*** television (set and medium) <Gre-Lat✍>

tȅlkāč {a masc.} [std. = televizija] *sl* ***Fam*** television (set and medium), <Gre-Lat✍>

tȅlkica {ē fem.} [std. = televizija] *sl* ***Fam*** television (set and medium) <Gre-Lat✍>

tȅlkić {a masc.} [std. = televizija] *sl* ***Fam*** television (set and medium) <Gre-Lat✍>

têlo {a neut.} (lit. body) **1** **SerE** *sl-sex* ***Fac-Obs*** penis, dick, prick <Slav*1> **2** **SerE** *sl-sex* ***Fac*** attractive female <Slav*1> **3** SerE *sl* ***Fac*** knife <Slav*1>

temèrut {a (acc. = gen.) masc.} *sl-fea* clumsy male, klutz

tempèrīrān {a, o adj.} (lit. with constant temperature) *sl-drink* drunk <Lat*1>

téna {ē fem.} *sl-sports* tennis shoe, sneaker <Eng✍*1>

tènder {a masc.} *sl-sex* ***Fac*** female breast <Eng*1>

tènisica {ē fem.} *col* tennis shoe, sneaker <Eng✣*1>

téniska {ē fem.; Dat. téniski} *col* tennis shoe, sneaker <Eng✣[*1]>

tȅnk {a +ov (ext. pl) masc.; Nom Pl tènkovi} (lit. tank *military vehicle*) *sl-fea* obese person <Eng[*1]>
• **tȅnk júrī vȅlikū mȁčku** {S} (lit. a tank is chasing a big cat) *sl* ***Fac*** used to express gratitude, thanks

tȅnkre {ea (acc. = gen.) masc.; perm} /tènkre /tenakre (acc. = gen.) masc./ [std. = kreten] *sl-fea* stupid or mentally deficient person <Fre✍>

têntati {ām, ajū imperf.} *col* urge somebody to an action (usu. something immoral or dangerous) <Lat[*1]>

Tȅodor {a (acc. = gen.) masc.} (lit. Theodore) *sl-crime* policeman, cop <SlavO[*1]>

tepeljèzgati {ām, ajū imperf.} *sl-fea* talk persistently and meaninglessly, blabber, chatter <Slav✍[*1]>

tèpih {a masc.} (lit. carpet) *sl-drink* ***Fac*** bar (drinking place) <Ger[*1]>

tepljèzgati {ām, ajū imperf.} *sl-fea* talk persistently and meaninglessly, blabber, chatter <Slav✍[*1]>

tèpsija {ē fem.} **a.** *col* pan, pot <NE> **b.** *sl* head <NE[*1]>

terapèut {a (acc. = gen.) masc.} (lit. therapist) *sl-fea* boring person, bore <Gre[*1]>

terénac {nca masc.} *sl-auto* sport utility vehicle <Fre✣[*1]>

teretàna {ē fem.} *sl-sports* gym <Slav✣[*1]>

terètnjāk {retnjáka (acc. = gen.) masc.} (lit. heavy truck) *sl-fea* complicated person <Slav✣[*1]>

terèvēnčiti {čīm, čē imperf. intr.} *sl-drink* party (engage in social gathering) <NE[*1]>

terèvēnka {ē fem.} *sl-drink* party (social gathering) <NE[*1]>

Tèrēzijinā plìnara {NP} (lit. Theresia's gas works) *sl-crime* name of a prison in Stara Gradiška, Croatia ☞ **plinara**

tȅrs [1] {a +ov (ext. pl) masc.; Nom Pl tèrsovi} **1** *sl-gamble* loaded dice <NE[*1]> **2** *sl-gamble* marked card <NE[*1]>

tȅrs [2] {adj.} *sl* fake, phoney <NE>

tȅsati {tȇšēm, tȇšū imperf.} **a.** *sl* beat up <Slav[*1]> **b.i.** *sl-sex* engage in sexual intercourse with (of a male) <Slav[*2]> **ii.** *sl-drink* drink (alcohol) <Slav[*2]> **iii.** *sl* drill, exercise: *tesati vojnike drill soldiers* <Slav[*2]>

Tȅsla {ē masc.} (lit. Tesla *a Serbian-American inventor*) *sl* five hundred dinars; a five-hundred dinar bill <SlavO[*1]>

Tȅslić {a masc.} (lit. Teslić is a town in Bosnia, but the name of the bill is derived from Tesla, a Serbian-American inventor) *sl* five hundred dinars; a five-hundred dinar bill <SlavO✣[*1]>

tȅstati {ām, ajū imperf.} (lit. test) *sl* beat up <Eng✣[*1]>

testèrāš {testeráša (acc. = gen.) masc.} (lit. saw worker) *sl-crime* ***Der*** informer, stoolie, snitch <NE>

testèrisati {išēm, išū imperf.} (lit. saw) **1** *col* snore, saw logs <NE✣[*1]> **2** *sl-sex* engage in sexual intercourse with (of a male) <NE✣[*1]>

testírānje {a neut.} (lit. testing) *sl-sex* ***Fac-Obs*** sexual intercourse <Eng✣[*1]>

testírati {tèstīrām, testírajū biasp.} (lit. test X testis 'testicle') **1** *sl* kick or punch in the testicles, low blow <Eng✣[*1]> **2** *sl-sex* engage in sexual intercourse with (of a male <Eng✣[*1]>

têškī [1] {ā, ō adj.} (lit. heavy) *col* real, big, major: *On je teški folirant. He is a real con man.* <Slav[*1]>

têškī [2] {ōg (acc. = gen.) masc.} (lit. the heavy one) **a.** *sl-fea* troublemaker, rowdy, ruffian <Slav[*1]> **b.** *sl-crime* criminal <Slav[*2]>

têškī kȕrac {NP} (lit. heavy prick) **a.** *col* ***Der-Obs*** nothing at all **b.** *col* ***Der-Obs*** worthless, unimportant object or issue ☞ **kurac**

têškī tabànāš od bȁrē {NP} (lit. heavy walker from the pond) *sl-fea* rich foreigner ☞ **tabanaš**

têškī trȅn {NP} (lit. heavy train) *sl* freight train ☞ **tren**

têškō sránje {NP} (lit. heavy shit) *sl-fea* very difficult situation, deep shit ☞ **sranje**

têškō úlje {NP} (lit. heavy oil) *sl-drink* 40 proof brandy ☞ **ulje**

têško {excl.} (lit. hardly) *col* used to signal impossibility, hardly <Slav[*1]>
• **Têško bȍgami!** {AdvP} (lit. Difficult, I swear to God!) *sl* used to refer to impossibility or improbability of an event, No way!
• **Têško sîne!** {AdvP} (lit. Difficult, my son!) *sl* used to express disagreement, No way, Jose!

tȅta {excl. } *col* used to address adult women older than oneself, ma'am <Slav[*1]>
• **tȅta fantéza** {NP} (lit. lady Fantese) *sl* Fanta (a brand of juice)
• **tȅta sȉsa bȁkse** {NP} *sl-sex* ***Obs*** elderly female who pays males for their sexual services

tètanus {a (acc. = gen.) masc.} (lit. tetanus) *sl-fea* ***App*** skillful person <Gre[*1]>

tȇti {òću, òćē imperf.} [std. = hteti] **SerE** *col* want, wish (in all its meanings in the form different from the standard) <Slav✍>

tȅtka {ē fem.; Dat tȅtki} (lit. aunt) **1a.** *sl-sex* ***Fac*** male homosexual, gay <Slav*1> **b.** *sl-sex* ***Fac*** male homosexual who takes the passive role, femme <Slav*2> **2** *sl-sex* ***Obs*** buttocks, butt <Slav*1> **3** *sl-fea* ***Der*** female who looks older than she actually is <Slav*1>
- **čȉja tȅtka cȓnū vȕnu préde** {S} (lit. whose aunt combs black wool) *col* used to refer to a situation in which it is uncertain who is going to be worse off: *Tući ću se s njim pa da vidimo čija majka crnu vunu prede. I will fight him and we will see who gets the short end.*
- **Tȅtke ti ga!** {S} (lit. *I screw* your aunt!) SSer *dia* ***Off*** used as a weak curse, Screw you!
- **Tȅtku li ti jèbēm!** {S} (lit. You screw your aunt!) *col-dia* ***Off*** used as a weak curse, Screw you!
- **Tȅtku ti tvòju!** {S} (lit. *I screw* your aunt!) *col-dia* ***Off*** used as a weak curse, Screw you!

tȅtkica {ē fem.} (lit. little aunt) **a.** *col* school janitor (female) <Slav*1> **b.** *sl-sex* ***Der*** male homosexual, gay <Slav*1>

tetovírati se *See the following*
- **tetovírati se od rȁdosti** {VP} (lit. tattoo oneself from being so happy) *sl-fea* be very happy

tȅtrapak {a (acc. = gen.) masc.} /tètrapak/ (lit. Tetra pack) **1** *sl-auto* Trabant (make of simple East German car) <BN*1> **2** *sl-auto* Fiat 126P (a model of a simple Polish car) <BN*1>

tȅtrēb {a (acc. = gen.) masc.} (lit. grouse) **1** **SerE** *sl-crime* ***Der*** policeman, cop <Slav*1> **2** **SerE** *sl-sex* ***Fac*** prostitute, hooker <Slav*1>

tȅtrijēb {a (acc. = gen.) masc.} (lit. grouse) *sl-fea* stupid or mentally deficient person <Slav*1>

tȅtrijēb {a (acc. = gen.) masc.} (lit. grouse) **1** *sl-crime* policeman, pig <Slav*1> **2** *sl-sex* prostitute, hooker <Slav*1> **3** *sl-fea* love-struck male, love-sick guy <Slav*1>

tetùrati {ām, ajū imperf.} (lit. stumble) *sl* look for something in different places <Slav*1>

tetùrati se {ām, ajū imperf.} (lit. stumble) **a.** *sl* walk clumsily, stumble along <Slav*1> **b.** *sl* get drunk <Slav*2>

téva {ē fem.} [std. = television] **a.** *sl* television (set and medium) <Gre-Lat✍> **b.** *sl* watching television <Gre-Lat✍*1>

tevábija {ē fem.} BosM *col* relatives <NE>

têvê {adj.} [std. = televizija] *col* television (set and medium) <Gre-Lat✍>

tèviš {a masc.} [std. = televizija] *sl* ***Fam*** television (set and medium) <Gre-Lat✍>

tèzga {ē fem.; Dat tèzgi} **a.** *col* desk, counter, workbench, stand <NE*1> **b.** *col* moonlighting (work) <NE*2>
- **ispod tèzgē** {PP} (lit. under the counter) *col* secretly, under the counter: *platiti ispod tezge pay secretly*

tèzgār {tezgára (acc. = gen.) masc.} *col* person who has an additional job, moonlighter <NE❖*1>

tezgàrati {ām, ajū imperf.} *col* have an additional job, moonlight <NE❖*1>

tezgárēnje {a neut.} *col* person who has an additional job, moonlighting <NE❖*1>

tezgáriti {tèzgārīm, rē imperf.} *col* have an additional job, moonlight <NE❖*1>

tèzgāroš {a (acc. = gen.) masc.} *col* person who has an additional job, moonlighter <NE❖*1>

téžak {ška, ško adj.} (lit. heavy) **1a.** *sl-fea* introvert <Slav*1> **b.** *sl-fea* unintelligent, light-weight <Slav*2> **c.** *sl-fea* boring <Slav*3> **d.** *sl-fea* miserly, stingy <Slav*4> **2** *sl-fea* used in reference to the amount of money one has or what something is worth: *On je težak dva miliona dolara. He's got two million bucks* <Slav*1>
- **[ADJ] kòlikō je téžak** {AdjP} (lit. as [ADJ] as heavy) *col* used to denote a high intensity (usu. of a negative personality trait): *On je pokvaren koliko je težak. He is very sly.*
- **Kòlikō je téško?** {S} (lit. How heavy is it?) *col* used to ask about quantity or price, How much?
- **Kòlikō je téžak?** {S} (lit. How heavy is he?) *col* used to inquire about the financial state of a third party, How much money does he have?
- **téžak kao ćùskija** {AdjP} (lit. as heavy as a crowbar) *sl-fea* very heavy
- **tȅžī slȕčāj** {NP} (lit. a heavier case) *col* used to indicate that an unfavorable situation cannot be changed, too bad

tfȕ {excl.} *col* the sound made by spitting, phew <Slav>

th {excl.} *col* the sound of spitting pronounced to indicate underestimation of something or someone, phew <Slav>

thȅ {excl.} *col* well <Slav>

thȉ {excl.} *col* the sound of spitting pronounced to indicate underestimation of something or someone, phew <Slav>

thjȁ {excl.} *col* well <Slav>

Ti jèbēm mȁtēr bezòbraznū! {S} (lit. I fuck your shameless mother!) *col-dia* ***Off*** used as a strong curse, Fuck you! ☞ jebati

tî *See the following*
- **Tî si môj kȕrac!** {S} (lit. You are my prick!) *col* ***Off*** used as a weak curse, Screw you!

• **Tî si pízda od čovjèka!** {S} (lit. You are a cunt of a man!) *col* ***Off*** used as a strong curse, Fuck you!

tíba {ē fem.} *col* ***Fam*** stomach, belly, tummy <**Slav**✍>

tíbica {ē fem.} *col* ***Fam*** stomach, belly, tummy <**Slav**✍>

tibùljāk {tibuljāka masc.} *col* ***Fam*** stomach, belly, tummy <**Slav**✍>

tȉca [1] {excl.} [std. = ptica] *col* used when taking photos, cheese <**Slav**✍[*1]>

tȉca [2] {ē fem.} (lit. bird) [std. = ptica] *sl-crime* quiet criminal <**Slav**✍[*1]>

tȉć {a +ev (ext. pl) masc.; Nom Pl tȉćevi} (lit. young bird) *sl* airplane <**Slav**[*1]>

tȉćokrōv {a +ov (ext. pl) masc.; Nom Pl tićokròvovi} (lit. bird roof) *sl* airport <**Slav**⁘[*1]>

tȉću {excl.; perm} /tȉću/ [std. = ćuti] **1** *col* used to silence one's interlocutor in a specific speech act or in general, shut up, be silent about this <**Slav**✍>

tìfusār {a (acc. = gen.) masc.} (lit. typhus patient) **1** *sl-fea* poor male <**Gre**[*1]> **2** *sl-sports* passionate fan, fanatic <**Gre**[*1]>

tìgerice {ā fem. pl.} (lit. tigers) *sl-music* organ (musical instrument) <**Ger**⁘[*1]>

Tìhomīr {a (acc. = gen.) masc.} (lit. Theo) *sl-sex* ***Fac*** silent discharge of intestinal gas, s.b.d. (silent fart) <**SlavO**[*1]>

tȉjēsto {a neut.} (lit. dough) *sl-sex* ***Fac*** soft female breast <**Slav**[*1]>

tȉk-tȁk {a +ov (ext. pl) masc.; Nom Pl tȉk-tȁkovi} *col* ticking (clock, etc.) <**Slav**>

tíka {ē fem.} [std. = patika] *sl* tennis shoe, sneaker <**NE**✍>

tȉka-tȁk {excl.} *col* tick-tock (clock, etc.) <**Slav**>

tȉkānje {a neut.} *col* ticking (clock, etc.) <**Slav**>

tikatàkānje {a neut.} *col* ticking (clock, etc.) <**Slav**>

tikatàkati {ām, ajū imperf.} *col* tick-tock (clock, etc.) <**Slav**>

tȉkati {ām, ajū imperf.} *col* knock (on a door, etc.) <**Slav**>

tȉki-tȁk {excl.} *col* tick-tock (clock, etc.) <**Slav**>

tikitȁkovānje {a neut.} *col* ticking (clock, etc.) <**Slav**>

tikitȁkovati {kujēm, kujū imperf.} *col* tick-tock (clock, etc.) <**Slav**>

tikȉtati {ām, ajū imperf.} *col* tick-tock (clock, etc.) <**Slav**>

tiktàkānje {a neut.} *col* ticking (clock, etc.) <**Slav**>

tiktàkati {ām, ajū imperf.} *col* tick-tock (clock, etc.) <**Slav**>

tiktȉkati {ām, ajū imperf.} *col* tick-tock (clock, etc.) <**Slav**>

tȉkva [1] {ē fem.} (lit. pumpkin) **1a.** *sl-fea* skinhead <**Slav**[*1]> **b.** *sl-fea* stupid or mentally deficient person <**Slav**[*2]> **c.** *sl-fea* stupid or mentally deficient person, melon-head <**Slav**[*3]> **2** *sl* head <**Slav**[*1]>

tȉkva [2] {adj.} (lit. pumpkin) *sl-fea* bald <**Slav**[*1]>

tìkvan {a (acc. = gen.) masc.} **a.** *sl-fea* stupid or mentally deficient person, melon-head <**Slav**⁘[*1]> **b.** *sl-fea* person with large head <**Slav**⁘[*2]>

tikvánko {a masc.} (lit. pumpkin-man) *sl-fea* stupid or mentally deficient person, melon-head <**Slav**⁘[*1]>

tìkvanja {ē fem.} *sl* head <**Slav**⁘[*1]>

tìkvara {ē fem.} *sl* head <**Slav**⁘[*1]>

tȉkvić {a (acc. = gen.) masc.} (lit. pumpkin-man) *sl-fea* stupid or mentally deficient person <**Slav**⁘[*1]>

tȉkvos {a (acc. = gen.) masc.} (lit. pumpkin-man) *sl-fea* stupid or mentally deficient person <**Slav**⁘[*1]>

tȉl *See the following*

• **U tȉl te vȁšljiv jèbēm!** {S} (lit. I fuck you in your ass which is full of lice!) *dia* ***Off*** used as a moderate curse, Fuck you!

tȉlī {part.} *col* very <**Slav**[*1]>

tîljka {ē fem.} *sl-arch* hen

tȉm-tȉm {excl.} *col* the sound made by a bell, ding ding <**Slav**>

tìmberlēnka {ē fem.} *sl* sharp-tipped shoe <**BN**[*1]>

tȋn {a (acc. = gen.) +ov (ext. pl) masc.; Nom Pl tínovi} *sl-fea* teenager (male) <**Eng**>

tìna {ē fem.} *sl-fea* teenager (female) <**Eng**⁘>

tìnaba {ē fem.; perm} (lit. bat) [std. = batina] *sl-sex* ***Obs*** penis, dick, prick <**Slav**✍[*1]>

Tîne *See the following*

• **Tîne i Ràdōjka** {NP} (lit. Tine and Radojka: first names of two persons from a popular accordion duo) *sl-auto* articulated bus

tînka {ē fem.; Dat tînki} *sl-fea* teenager (female) <**Eng**⁘>

tȉnksti {kšēm, kšū imperf.} *sl* ring (a bell, etc.) <**Slav**>

tînta {ē fem.} (lit. ink) *sl-crime* taking fingerprints <**Lat**[*1]>

tìntara {ē fem.} *sl* head <**Lat**⁘[*1]>

tȉntolōvka {ē fem.} *sl* head <Lat❖*1>

tìnjati {ām, ajū imperf.} (lit. glow) *sl* give, pass <Slav*1>

tinjávati {tìnjāvām, tinjávajū imperf.} (lit. glow) **a.** *sl* give, pass <Slav*1> **b.** *sl* pay (bills, etc.) <Slav*2>

tȋp [1] {a (acc. = gen.) +ov (ext. pl) masc.; Nom Pl típovi} **a.** *col* male, guy <Gre*1> **b.** *sl-fea* undependable male <Gre*2> **c.** *sl-fea* suspicious male <Gre*3> **d.** *sl-fea* strange male, weirdo <Gre*4> **e.i.** *sl-fea* stranger (male) <Gre*5> **ii.** *sl-fea* worthless or despicable person, bum <Gre*4>

- **čètvrtast tȋp** {NP} (lit. square guy) *sl-fea* unintelligent and rigid clerk
- **dȉnārskī tȋp** {NP} (lit. dinar type) *sl-fea* ***Fac*** person with big income (in any business), money bags

tȉp [2] {a +ov (ext. pl) masc.; Nom Pl típovi} *col* favorite <Gre*1>

tȉp-tȍp {adj.} *col* ***App*** excellent, tip-top <Eng>

tȉpa-tȁpa {excl.} *col* the sound made by a metal object, clang <Slav>

tìpčina {ē fem.} **1** *sl-fea* ***Der*** worthless or despicable male, scum <Gre❖*1> 2 *sl-fea* ***App*** excellent male, cool guy <Gre❖*1>

tȉpka {ē fem.; Dat tȉpki} (lit. key) *sl-crime* ***Der*** informer, stoolie, snitch <Ger*1>

tȉpkāč {tipkáča (acc. = gen.) masc.} (lit. typist) *sl-crime* ***Der*** informer, stoolie, snitch <Ger❖*1>

tȉpkati {ām, ajū imperf.} (lit. type) *sl-crime* inform the police or other authorities, snitch, squeal <Ger*1>

tȉpovati {pujēm, pujū biasp.} *sl-gamble* bet <Gre❖*1>

típus {a (acc. = gen.) masc.} /tȋpus/ **a.** *sl* male, guy <Gre*1> **b.** *sl-fea* strange male, weirdo <Gre*2> **c.i.** *sl-fea* stranger (male) <Gre*3> **ii.** worthless or despicable person, bum <Gre*3>

tipusáner {a (acc. = gen.) masc.} *sl-fea* very suspicious person <Ger✍*1>

tȋr [1] {excl.} *col* used to calm down a she-goat <Slav>

tȉr [2] {a +ev (ext. pl) masc.; Nom Pl tìrevi} *sl-auto* heavy truck <Abb*1>

tìrita {ē fem.} **a.** *sl-arch* book <NE❖*1> **b.** *sl-arch* letter (correspondence) <NE❖*1> **c.** *sl-arch* paper (e.g. sheets of paper) <NE❖*1>

tiritnjâk {a masc.} *sl* fur jacket <NE❖*1>

tȉrke {eta masc.} *sl* Tirol salami (a low quality salami in the former Yugoslavia) <GerO✍*1>

tȉrovac {vca (acc. = gen.) masc.} *sl-auto* heavy-truck driver <Abb❖*1>

tȉrta {ē fem.} **a.** *sl* paper (e.g. sheets of paper) <NE❖*1> **b.** *sl* book

tȉsnuti {nēm, nū imperf.} (lit. push) *sl-sex* ***Obs*** engage in sexual intercourse with (of a male) <Slav*1>

tȉsra {rȅmse, rȉse imperf.; perm} /tȉsra/ [std. = srati] **a.** *sl-sex* ***Obs*** defecate, shit <Slav✍> **b.** *sl-sex* ***Der-Obs*** talk persistently and meaninglessly, have diarrhea of the mouth <Slav✍*1>

- **Mȍjne tȉsra!** {S} (lit. Don't shit!) *sl* ***Obs*** used to express disbelief, Don't give me that shit!
- **Ne rȉse!** {S} (lit. Don't you bullshit!) *sl* ***Off*** used to express disbelief, Don't give me that bullshit!

tȉšler {a (acc. = gen.) masc.} *sl-crafts* carpenter <Ger>

tišlèrāj {lerája masc.} *col* furniture <Ger>

tišnòća {excl.} *col* used to silence one's interlocutor, shut up <Slav✍>

tȉta {excl.} *col* used to prevent children from doing something <Slav>

Tȉto *See the following*

- **Pȍslijē Tȉta - kȉta!** {S} (lit. After Tito it's prick!) *sl-polit* ***Obs*** used to complain about the situation in the former Yugoslavia in the 1980s and 1990s

titòist {a (acc. = gen.) masc.} *sl-polit* Titoist (follower of Josip Broz Tito, communist dictator in the former Yugoslavia) <SlavO❖*1>

titòista {ē masc.} *sl-polit* Titoist (follower of Josip Broz Tito, communist dictator in the former Yugoslavia) <SlavO❖*1>

titoìstičkī {ā, ō adj.} *sl-polit* pertaining to the followers of Josip Broz Tito (communist dictator in the former Yugoslavia) <SlavO❖*1>

titoìzam {zma masc.} *sl-polit* Titoism (ideology of Josip Broz Tito, communist dictator in the former Yugoslavia) <SlavO❖*1>

Tȉtrā mi! {S} (lit. It vibrates to me!) *sl* used to refer to satisfaction, It rings true for me! ☞ **titrati**

tȉtrati {ām, ajū imperf.} (lit. oscillate) **1** *sl-fea* ***Der*** ingratiate, brownnose, kiss ass <Slav*1> 2 *sl-fea* ***Der*** be convenient, be appropriate <Slav*1>

- **Tȉtrā mi!** {S} (lit. It vibrates to me!) *sl* used to refer to satisfaction, It rings true for me!
- **tȉtrati jája** {VP} (lit. vibrate someone's balls) *sl-fea* ***Obs*** ingratiate, brownnose, kiss ass

• **tĩtrati múda** {VP} (lit. vibrate someone's balls) *sl-fea* ***Obs*** ingratiate, brownnose, kiss ass

tĩtrovānje {a neut.} *sl-drink* drinking (alcohol) <**Slav**❖[*1]>

tívica {ē fem.} [std. = televizija] *sl* television (set and medium) <**Gre-Lat**✍>

tjȁ {excl.} *col* well <**Slav**>

tjȅrati *See the following*

• **tjȅrati mȁjmuna da pòvraćā** {VP} (lit. make monkey throw up) *sl-sex* masturbate, spank the monkey

• **tjȅrati ptȉcu** {VP} (lit. drive the bird) *sl-sex* masturbate, beat off

• **tjȅrati šégu** {VP} (lit. drive a joke) [std. = tjerati] *col* joke with, make a fool of

tkȁlu {tkelu fem.; perm} /tkȁlu/ (lit. doll) [std. = lutka] *sl-sex* ***App*** attractive female, doll <**Slav**✍[*1]>

tkȁti {tkâm, tkȁjū imperf.} (lit. weave) *sl-sstu* learn <**Slav**[*1]>

tkȍ *See the following*

• **Tkȍ te jèbē!** {S} (lit. Who fucks you!) Cro *col* ***Off*** used as a moderate curse, Fuck you!

• **Tkȍ te šljívi!** {S} (lit. Who plums you!) Cro *sl* ***Der*** used to express depreciation, Who gives a shit about you!

• **Tkȍ te šmìrglā!** {S} (lit. Who sandpapers you!) Cro *sl* ***Der*** used to express depreciation, Who gives a shit about you!

tlȁčiti {čīm, čē perf.} (lit. pressure) *sl-fea* annoy, bother, pester <**Slav**[*1]>

tlȁka {ē fem.; Dat tlȃki} (lit. pressure) *sl* boredom <**Slav**[*1]>

tlčȁnj {a masc.} *sl-sex* ***Obs*** penis, dick, prick <**Slav**✍>

tô *See the following*

• **tô bi se jȅbālo a u pȉčku nè bi díralo** {S} (lit. it would like to fuck without its cunt being touched) *col* ***Obs-Der*** used to indicate that a person would like to take an action without willingness to take any related risks

• **Tô je drȕgī pádež.** {S} (lit. That is another case.) *col* used to refer to the difference between two situations, that's something completely different

• **Tô je kȕrac od óvcē!** {S} (lit. That is a sheep's prick!) *col* ***Obs*** used to express disrespect, Fuck it!

• **tȍ je ònō prâvō** {S} (lit. That's the right thing) *sl-sex* sexual intercourse

• **Tȍ je svȅ pȉčkīn dȉm!** {S} (lit. All that is cunt's smoke!) *col* ***Obs*** used to express disrespect, Fuck it!

• **Tô je svȅ za môj kȕrac!** {S} (lit. All that is for my prick!) *col* ***Obs*** used to express disrespect, Fuck it!

• **tô je tâ ȁka** {S} (lit. that's the thing) *dia* used to sum up one's point, That's how it is!

• **tô je tô** {S} (lit. that is that) *col* used to sum up one's point, That's how it is!

• **Tô je vȅć nȅšto.** {S} (lit. That is something.) *col* used to express admiration of a repeated offer or achievement, That's already something.

• **Tô ni kȗrca ne vrédī!** {S} (lit. That is not even worth a prick!) **SerE** *col* ***Der-Obs*** used to express disrespect, Fuck it!

tòbdžija {ē masc.} (lit. artillery man) *sl-sex* ***Fac*** male homosexual, gay <**NE**[*1]>

toblerône {rónā fem. pl.} (lit. Toblerone *a brand of chocolate*) *sl* teeth <**BN**>

tȍbogān {a masc.} (lit. slide) *sl* ***Fac*** nose <**Eng**[*1]>

tȍbož {part.} *col* used to express uncertainty: *On tobož studira. He kind of goes to school.* <**Slav**✍>

tȍbože {part.} *col* used to express uncertainty: *Ona ga tobože voli. She kind of loves him.* <**Slav**>

tòcilo {a neut.} *sl-fea* stupid or mentally deficient person <**Slav**[*1]>

tòčak [1] {čka (acc. = gen.) +ov (ext. pl) masc.} (lit. wheel) *sl-fea* stupid or mentally deficient person <**Slav**[*1]>

tòčak [2] {čka +ov (ext. pl) masc.} **a.** *col-dia* water source <**Slav**> **b.** *sl-drink* alcoholic beverages <**Slav**[*1]>

• **zȁdnjī tòčak** {NP} (lit. rear wheel) *sl-sex* buttocks, rear end, butt

tòčiti {čīm, čē imperf.} **a.** *col* pour <**Slav**> **b.** *sl-sex* urinate, take a leak <**Slav**[*1]> **c.** *sl* harm <**Slav**[*2]>

tȍčka {ē fem.; Dat tȍčki} (lit. dot) *sl* thousand dinars; a thousand-dinar bill, a grand <**Rus**[*1]>

tȍčkovi {tȍčkōvā masc. pl.} (lit. wheels) *sl-auto* car, wheels <**Slav**[*1]>

Tȍd-ÂÔ {masc.} (lit. wide movie screen) *sl-fea* wide hips <**BN**[*1]>

tȍh {excl.} *col* the sound made by an explosion, bang <**Slav**>

tòjaga {ē fem.; Dat tòjagi} [std. = toljaga] *dia* bat, stick, rod <**Slav**✍>

tôk *See the following*

• **iz tôka** {PP} (lit. from the flow) *sl* right away, now

tóle {a fem. pl.} [std. = pantalone] *sl* trousers, pants <**Fre**✍>

tolȉšnī {a, o adj.} *col* that small <**Slav**❖>

tòlkī {ā, ō adj.} [std. = toliki] *col* that big <**Slav**✍>

tòljaga {ē fem.; Dat tòljagi} **a.** *col* bat, stick, rod <Slav> **b.** *sl-sex* penis <Slav*1>

toljàgati {ām, ajū imperf.} (lit. hit with a bat) **a.** *sl* beat up <Slav❖> **b.** *sl* think, ponder <Slav❖*1> **c.** *sl* worry about <Slav❖*2>

Tȍmāš *See the following*

- **zèlenī Tȍmāš** {NP} (lit. green Tom) *sl-crime* police van (in pre-WWII Yugoslavia)

tȍmbola {ē fem.} (lit. bingo) *col* unclear situation <Ita>

Tomislávac {vca masc.} **1** Cro *sl* name for King Tomislav square in Zagreb <SlavO❖*1> **2** Cro *sl* name for Sljeme mountain shelter in Croatia <SlavO❖*1>

tòmpus {a masc.} (lit. cigar) *sl-sex* ***Fac-Obs*** penis, dick, prick <Fre*1>

tȍna *See the following*

- **tȍnu stàkla** {NP} (lit. one ton of glass) *sl-auto* car, wheels

Tònček {a masc.} (lit. little Tony) *sl-sex* ***Fac*** condom, rubber, Jimmy <SlavO❖*1>

Tônka {ē fem.; Dat Tônki} (lit. Tony) *sl-sex* ***Fac*** male homosexual, gay <SlavO*1>

tònuti {nēm, nū imperf. intr.} (lit. drown) *col* go broke (financially) <Slav*1>

tȍnjār {a (acc. = gen.) masc.} *sl* merchant (male) <Ita❖*1>

tȍp [1] {a (acc. = gen.) +ov (ext. pl) masc.; Nom Pl tòpovi} (lit. cannon) **a.** *sl-fea* deaf person <NE*1> **b.** *sl-fea* person with hearing difficulties <NE*2> **c.** *sl-fea* stupid or mentally deficient person <NE*1>

tȍp [2] {a +ov (ext. pl) masc.; Nom Pl tòpovi} (lit. cannon) **1** *sl-sstu* failing grade <NE*1> **2** *sl-sex* ***Obs*** penis, dick, prick <NE*1> **3** *sl* key <NE*1>

tȍp-lȉsta {ē fem.} (lit. hit parade) *sl* ***Fac*** obituary <Eng*1>

tȍpče {eta neut.} (lit. small cannon) *sl-sex* ***Fac*** a poke, prod, or pinch on the buttocks, goose <NE*1>

tòpina {ē fem.} (lit. big cannon) *sl-fea* deaf person <NE❖*1>

tòpiti *See the following*

toplàna {ē fem.} (lit. heating plant) *sl-sex* ***Fac*** male homosexual, gay <Slav*1>

tȍplī {ōg (acc. = gen.) masc.} (lit. the warm one) *sl-sex* ***Fac*** male homosexual, gay <Slav❖*1>

tȍplī brȁt {NP} (lit. warm brother) *sl-sex* ***Der*** male homosexual, gay ☞ **brat**

tȍplī òbrok {NP} (lit. hot meal) **1** *sl-sex* ***Obs*** fellatio **2** *col* a salary supplement intended to cover lunch ☞ **obrok**

tȍplice {a fem. pl.} (lit. spa) *sl-crime* ***Iro*** prison <Slav*1>

tȍplo skȕhāno {NP} (lit. cooked hot) *sl-crime* stolen, hot ☞ **skuhano**

tòpljāk {topljáka (acc. = gen.) masc.} (lit. the warm one) *sl-sex* ***Fac*** male homosexual, gay <Slav❖*1>

tȍpoglēdno {adv.} *col* in that respect <Slav❖>

tȍpot {a masc.} **a.** *col* thud <Slav> **b.** *col* noise <Slav*1>

topòtānje {a neut.} *col* thud <Slav>

topòtati {tòpoćēm, oćū imperf. intr.} *col* thud <Slav>

topòtljiv {a, o adj.} *col* thudding <Slav❖>

topóvnjača {ē fem.} (lit. gun-boat) *sl-sex* ***Fac-App*** highly attractive female, bombshell <Slav*1>

tȍpovskā cȉjēv {NP} (lit. cannon barrel) *sl-sex* ***Fac-Obs*** anus, asshole ☞ **cijev**

tȍptāj {a masc.} *col* thud <Slav>

tòptati {tȍpćēm, tȍpćū imperf.} *col* thud <Slav>

tȍpuz {a masc.} (lit. mace *medieval weapon*) *sl-sex* ***Fac-Obs*** penis, dick, prick <NE*1>

topùzārnīk {a masc.} (lit. mace place) *sl-crime* prison <NE❖*1>

tȏr {a +ov (ext. pl) masc.; Nom Pl tȍrovi} /tȍr/ (lit. animal pen) *sl* street <Slav*1>

tóranj [1] {rnja (acc. = gen.) masc.} (lit. tower) *sl-fea* tall person <Slav*1>

tóranj [2] {rnja masc.} (lit. tower) *sl-sex* ***Fac*** large female breast <Slav*1>

tórba {ē fem.} (lit. bag) *sl-sex* ***Fac-Obs*** vagina, cunt <Slav*1>

tȍrbālj {a masc.} *sl-sex* ***Obs*** sexual intercourse <Slav❖*1>

tòrbānje {a neut.} *sl-sex* ***Obs*** sexual intercourse <Slav❖*1>

- **tòrbānje u búlju** {NP} (lit. bagging in the ass) *sl-sex* ***Obs*** anal sexual intercourse

tòrbār {a (acc. = gen.) masc.} (lit. marsupial) **1** *sl* courier <Slav*1> **2** *sl-crime* thief who steals using a bag to store the stolen goods <Slav*1>

torbáriti {tòrbārīm, rē imperf.} (lit. bag) *sl* sell (exchange merchandise for money) <Slav❖*1>

tòrbati {ām, ajū imperf.} (lit. bag) *sl-sex* ***Obs*** engage in sexual intercourse with (of a male) <Slav❖*1>

tòrbljāk {torbljáka masc.} *sl* bag <Slav✍>

torbùljak {torbuljáka masc.} /torbúljak/ *sl* bag <Slav✍>

torbùljār {torbuljára (acc. = gen.) masc.} *sl-sex* ***Fac*** male homosexual, gay <Slav❖[*1]>

torcída {ē fem.} *sl-sports* the fans of Hajduk (a soccer team in Split, Croatia) <Spa[*1]>

toreâdor {a (acc. = gen.) masc.} (lit. toreador) *sl-sstu* ***Fac*** high-school teacher <Spa[*1]>

tòrlati {ām, ajū imperf.} *sl-fea* talk persistently and meaninglessly, blabber, chatter <NE[*1]>

tôro {excl.} *col* the sound made by meaningless and prolonged talk, blah-blah <Slav>

tȍro-tȍro {excl.} *col* the sound made by meaningless and prolonged talk, blah-blah <Slav>

toròkalo {a neut.} *sl-fea* extremely talkative person, chatterbox <Slav❖[*1]>

toròkānje {a neut.} *sl-fea* prolonged and meaningless talk, blabber, chatter <Slav❖[*1]>

toròkati {ām, ajū imperf.} //tòročēm, tòročū impperf. intr/ *col* talk persistently and meaninglessly, blabber, chatter <Slav[*1]>

toròkuša {ē fem.} *sl-fea* extremely talkative female, chatterbox <Slav❖[*1]>

torpedírati {pèdīrām, pedírajū biasp.} (lit. torpedo) *sl* get rid of <Lat[*1]>

tortȉljos {a masc.} (lit. torta 'cake' X tortilja 'tortilla') [std. = torta] *sl* cake <Lat✍[*1]>

tòrtiška {ē fem.; Dat tòrtiški} [std. = torta] *sl* cake <Lat✍[*1]>

tȍrtos {a masc.} [std. = torta] *sl* cake <Lat✍[*1]>

tȍšāk {a (acc. = gen.) masc.} (lit. John Toshak, a soccer player who was considered stupid) *sl-fea* stupid or mentally deficient person

tȍtālno {adv.} /tòtālno/ *col* completely, totally <Lat>

tòtrk {a masc.} *sl* pecking (with the beak, etc.) <Slav>

totȑkānje {a neut.} *sl* pecking (with the beak, etc.) <Slav>

totȑkati {ām, ajū imperf.} *sl* peck (with beak, etc.) <Slav>

totȑkav {a, o adj.} *sl* woodpecker-like <Slav>

tòvar {a (acc. = gen.) masc.} (lit. donkey) *sl-fea* inhabitant of Split, Croatia <Slav[*1]>

- **tòvar kòji gòrī** {NP} (lit. burning load) *sl-crime* stolen goods, hot stuff

tòvarić {a (acc. = gen.) masc.} (lit. small donkey) *sl-crime* policeman, pig <Slav[*1]>

tovàriš {a (acc. = gen.) masc.} *sl* ***Fac*** porter <Rus[*1]>

trà-la-la {excl.} *col* the sound made by meaningless and prolonged talk, blah-blah <Slav>

trȁ-ta {excl.} *col* the sound of repeated soft noise, wah-wah <Slav>

trabâkula {ē fem.} Med *col* twin-masted sailboat <Ita>

trabùnjati {ām, ajū imperf.} *sl-fea* talk persistently and meaninglessly, blabber, chatter <Slav>

trȁč {a +ev (ext. pl) masc.; Nom Pl tràčevi} *col* gossip, wag the tongue <Ger>

trâčak *See the following*

- **tráčak rȁja** {NP} (lit. a ray of heaven) *sl-sex* ***Fac*** gonorrhea, the clap

tràčara {ē fem.} *sl-fea* gossiper <Ger❖>

trȁčati {ām, ajū imperf. intr.} *col* gossip, wag the tongue <Ger>

trȁčerskī {ā, ō adj.} /tráčerskī/ *col* gossipy <Ger>

trádža {ē fem.} **1** *sl-drink* grape brandy **2** *sl* pocket radio

tràfika {ē fem.} *col* newsstand <Ita>

tràfka {ē fem.; Dat trâfki} **a.** *sl* cigarette, smoke <Slav[*1]> **b.** *sl-drugs* hashish, hash <Slav[*2]>

trȁg {a (acc. = gen.) +ov (ext. pl) masc.; Nom Pl trȁgovi} (lit. trace) *sl* male, guy <Slav[*1]>

tràjana {ē fem.} *sl-sex* gonorrhea, the clap

tràjca {ē fem.} *sl* bag <Ger✍[*1]>

trâjna {ē fem.} *col* permanent (hair style), perm <Slav[*1]>

tràjvan {a masc.} [std. = tramvaj] *col-dia* streetcar <Eng✍>

trȁk [1] {excl.} *col* the sound made by a metal object, clang <Slav>

trâk [2] {a +ov (ext. pl) masc.; Nom Pl tràkovi} *col* trace, vestige <Slav>

trȁkalica {ē fem.} (lit. tapeworm) **1** *sl-sex* ***Obs*** vagina, cunt <Slav[*1]> **2** *sl* eye (sight organ) <Slav[*1]> **3** *sl-sex* bathroom tissue, ass wipe <Slav[*1]> **4** *sl* ambush <Slav[*1]>

trȁkānje {a neut.} *sl* looking, watching, scoping

trakáriti {tràkārīm, rē imperf.} **a.** *sl* investigate, look into <Slav❖[*1]> **b.** *sl* patrol <Slav❖[*2]>

trȁkati {ām, ajū imperf.} **1a.** *sl* look, watch, scope out <Slav[*1]> **b.** *sl* investigate, look into <Slav[*2]> **c.** *sl* patrol <Slav[*3]> **2** *sl* dance <Slav[*1]>

trakàtrāljka {ē fem.} *sl* clock, watch <Slav[*1]>

trȁkavica {ē fem.} **1** *sl-gamble* game <Slav[*1]> 2 *sl-music* tape <Slav[*1]>

tràkeljara {ē fem.} *sl* store <Slav[*1]>

trakèljati {ām, ajū imperf.} **1** *sl* sell (exchange merchandise for money) <Slav[*1]> 2 *sl* dance

tràkljac {a masc.} *sl* dinar (Yugoslav currency unit) <Slav[*1]>

trȁkoš {excl.} **a.** *sl* look out <Slav> **b.** *sl* used to draw someone's attention, look <Slav[*1]>

trȁktor {a (acc. = gen.) masc.} (lit. tractor) *sl-fea* stupid or mentally deficient person <Lat[*1]>

traktòrist {a (acc. = gen.) masc.} (lit. tractor driver) *sl-auto* unskilled driver <Lat[*1]>

trȁktorka {ē fem.} (lit. the tractor one) *sl-fea* obese female <Lat❖[*1]>

tralákānje {a neut.} *sl-fea* prolonged and meaningless talk, blabber, chatter <Slav>

tralákati {tràlāčēm, tràlāčū imperf.} *sl-fea* talk persistently and meaninglessly, blabber, chatter <Slav>

trȁlala [1] {excl.} *col* the sound made by meaningless and prolonged talk, blah-blah <Slav>

trȁlala [2] {ē fem.} **a.** *sl-fea* unattractive boy <Slav> **b.** *sl-fea* unloved boy <Slav[*1]>

trȁlalāj {a (acc. = gen.) masc.} *sl-fea* careless person <Slav[*1]>

tralalákānje {a neut.} *sl-fea* prolonged and meaningless talk, blabber, chatter <Slav>

tralalákati {làlāčēm, làlāčū imperf.} *sl-fea* talk persistently and meaninglessly, blabber, chatter <Slav>

tralalíkānje {a neut.} *sl-fea* prolonged and meaningless talk, blabber, chatter <Slav[*1]>

tralalíkati {làlīčēm, làlīčū imperf.} *sl-fea* talk persistently and meaninglessly, blabber, chatter <Slav[*1]>

tralatùnjati {ām, ajū imperf. intr.} *sl* think, ponder <Slav[*1]>

trambàlāj {balája masc.} [std. = tramvaj] *sl* streetcar <Eng✍>

trambèlāj {belája masc.} [std. = tramvaj] *sl* streetcar <Eng✍>

tràmbulja {ē fem.} *sl* bush, shrub

tràmpa {ē fem.} *col* exchange (money, goods, etc.) <NE>

trȁmpiti {pīm, pē biasp.} /trâmpiti/ *col* exchange (money, goods, etc.) <NE❖>

trȁmpiti se {pīm, pē perf. biasp.} *col* exchange (money, goods, etc.) <NE❖[*1]>

tràmvaj {a (acc. = gen.) masc.} /tràmvāj/ (lit. streetcar) *sl-crime* policeman, cop <Eng[*1]>

tràndati {ām, ajū imperf.} *col* the sound made by tapping, tap <Slav[*1]>

trándža {ē masc.} 1 *sl* pocket radio <Lat-Eng✍> 2 *sl* streetcar <Eng✍>

trȁndžić {a masc.} *sl-sex* ***Obs*** sexual intercourse <Lat-Eng✍[*1]>

trandžírānje {a neut.} (lit. carving) *sl-sex* ***Fac-Obs*** sexual intercourse <Lat-Eng✍[*1]>

trándžiti {trândžīm, džē imperf.} (lit. carve) **1** *sl-sex* ***Fac-Obs*** engage in sexual intercourse with (of a male) <Lat-Eng✍[*1]> 2 *sl* dance <Lat-Eng✍[*1]>

tránđa {ē masc.} [std. = tranzistor] *sl* pocket radio <Lat-Eng✍[*1]>

transfirzírati {rzīrām, zírajū biasp.} *sl-sex* ***Fac-Obs*** engage in cunnilingus <Lat✍[*1]>

transformâtor {a (acc. = gen.) masc.} (lit. transformer) *sl-drugs* drug courier <Lat[*1]>

trànsfūzija {ē fem.} (lit. blood transfusion) *sl-sex* ***Fac-Obs*** sexual intercourse <Lat[*1]>

trȁnja {ē fem.} *sl* money <Slav[*1]>

tránjac {njca masc.} *sl-crime* prison

trȁnjār {a (acc. = gen.) masc.} **1** *sl-fea* senior citizen <Slav❖[*1]> 2 *sl* merchant (male) <Slav❖[*1]> 3 *sl* boss <Slav❖[*1]> 4 *sl-fea* unattractive male <Slav❖[*1]>

tránjci {trânjākā masc. pl.} *sl* money <Slav❖[*1]>

trȁnjerica {ē fem.} **1** *sl-fea* elderly female <Slav❖[*1]> 2 *sl* mistress, extramarital lover (female) <Slav❖[*1]> 3 *sl* boss's wife <Slav❖[*1]>

tranjèrija {ē fem.} *sl* shopkeeper (male) <Slav❖[*1]>

trȁnzić {a masc.} [std. = tranzistor] *sl* pocket radio <Lat-Eng✍[*1]>

trànzistor [1] {a (acc. = gen.) masc.} (lit. transistor) **1** *sl-fea* short male <Lat-Eng[*1]> 2 *sl-fea* male slow to understanding <Lat-Eng[*1]>

trànzistor [2] {a masc.} (lit. transistor) **a.** *sl* pocket radio <Lat-Eng[*1]> **b.i.** *sl* small quantity of something <Lat-Eng[*2]> **ii.** *sl-crime* magazine (for bullets on a machine gun) <Lat-Eng[*2]>

trȁp [1] {excl.} *col* the sound made by a clumsy and noisy style of walking <Slav>

trȁp ² {a (acc. = gen.) +ov (ext. pl) masc.; Nom Pl trȁpovi} *sl-crime* prison <Slav*1>
- **zȁdnjī trȁp** {NP} (lit. rear suspension) *sl-sex* buttocks, rear end, butt

trȁp-trȁp {excl.} *col* clumsy and noisy style of walking <Slav>

trapađója {ē masc.} *sl-fea* ***Der*** clumsy person, klutz <Slav✍*1>

trapađóza {ē fem.} *sl-fea* ***Der*** clumsy person, klutz <Slav✍*1>

trapađózla {ē fem.} *sl-fea* unskilled female <Slav✍*1>

trapàrati {ām, ajū imperf.} *col* walk clumsily and noisily <Slav✤*1>

trȁpavičār {a (acc. = gen.) masc.} *sl-fea* clumsy male, klutz <Slav✤*1>

trȁpavičārka {ē fem.; Dat trȁpavičārki} (lit. the clumsy one) *sl-fea* unskilled female dancer <Slav✤*1>

trȁper {a (acc. = gen.) masc.} (lit. trapper) *sl-fea* stupid or mentally deficient person <Eng*1>

trȁperice {rīcā fem. pl.} (lit. trapper's wear) *col* jeans <Eng✤*1>

tràpet {a (acc. = gen.) masc.} *sl-fea* male

trȁpke {i fem.} *sl* jeans <Eng✍*1>

trȁpša {ē fem. & masc.} *sl-fea* ***Der*** clumsy person, klutz <Slav✍*1>

traràkati {ām, ajū imperf.} *sl-music* play (e.g. a trumpet) <Slav>

trȁrara {excl.} *col* the sound made by trumpet, toot <Slav>

trȁs {excl.} **1** *col* the sound made by an explosion, bang <Slav> **2** *col* the sound made by slamming, wham <Slav*1>

tràsa *See the following*
- **na tràsu** {PP} (lit. to a tour) *sl* on credit

tráskalo {a neut.} *sl-fea* extremely talkative person, chatterbox <Slav✤*1>

trȁskānje {a neut.} *col* bang (loud and abrupt sound) <Slav✤*1>

trȁskati {ām, ajū imperf.} *col* bang (loud and abrupt sound) <Slav✤>

trȁsu {adv.; perm} /tràsu/ [std. = sutra] *sl* tomorrow <Slav✍>

trȁšta {ē fem.} *sl* bag <Gyp>

traumírati {traùmīrām, traumírajū biasp.} *sl* hit, punch <Gre*1>

tráva {ē fem.} (lit. grass) **1** *sl-drugs* hashish, hash <Slav*1> **2** *sl-drugs* marijuana, pot, grass <Slav*1> **3a.** *sl-drugs* tobacco <Slav*1> **b.** *sl* low-quality cigarette <Slav*1> **4a.** *sl-drink* herbal brandy <Slav*1> **b.** *sl-drink* weak brandy <Slav*2>
- **tráva stískavac** {NP} (lit. squezing grass) *sl-fea* fear
- **trávā tèkućā** {NP} (lit. liquid grass) *sl-drink* herbal brandy

tràvanja {ē fem.} *sl-arch* plum (the fruit) <Slav✤*1>

tràvār {travára (acc. = gen.) masc.} /trȁvār/ (lit. herbal healer) *sl-drugs* drug addict, junkie <Slav*1>

trȁvarica {ē fem.} /travàrica/ **a.** *sl-drink* herbal brandy <Slav✤*1> **b.** *sl* reproach, scold <Slav✤*2>

trȁvčār {a (acc. = gen.) masc.} **1** *sl-arch* boss <Slav✤*1> **2** *sl-arch* merchant (male) <Slav✤*1> **3** *sl-arch* monkey, ape <Slav✤*1>

travčàrica {ē fem.} **1** *sl* mistress, extramarital female lover <Slav✤*1> **2** *sl* merchant (male) <Slav✤*1> **3** *sl* boss's wife <Slav✤*1>

travèrzna {ē fem.} *sl-auto* traverse <Lat>

travìnjār {a (acc. = gen.) masc.} **a.** *sl* merchant (male) <Slav*1> **b.** *sl* boss <Slav*2>

travinjàrica {ē fem.} **1** *sl* merchant (female) <Slav*1> **2** *sl* mistress, extramarital female lover <Slav*1> **3** *sl* boss's wife <Slav*1>

trȁvka {ē fem.} /trâvka/ (lit. grass) **1** *sl-drugs* marijuana, pot, grass <Slav*1> **2** *sl* tobacco <Slav*1> **3** *sl-drugs* drugs, dope <Slav*1> **4** *sl-drink* weak brandy <Slav*1>

tràvosānje {a neut.} (lit. grassing oneself) *sl-drugs* smoking marijuana, smoking a joint <Slav✤*1>

tràvosati se {ošēm, ošū biasp. intr.} (lit. grass oneself) *sl-drugs* take narcotic drugs, do drugs <Slav✤*1>

trážiti *See the following*
- **trážiti sȉsu** {VP} (lit. look for a tit) *sl-drink* ***Fac-Obs*** order a drink

tȑba {ē fem.} *col* ***Fam*** stomach, belly, gut <Slav✤>

tȑbonja {ē masc.} **a.** *sl-fea* obese male <Slav✤*1> **b.** *sl-fea* very important or influential person, big shot <Slav✤*2>

tȑbu {ua masc.} [std. = trbuh] *col* stomach, belly, gut <Slav✍>

tȑbuv {a masc.} [std. = trbuh] *dia-col* stomach, belly, gut <Slav✍>

tȑc-vȑc {excl.} *col* used to express hesitation <Slav*1>

tȑčak {čka (acc. = gen.) masc.} *sl* journalist <Slav✤*1>

tȑčati *See the following*

• **Jèsi l nȅkad tȑčaō za ȕšima** {S} (lit. Have you ever run after your ears?) *sl* ***Off*** used as a threat of physical violence

tȑčic {a (acc. = gen.) masc.} (lit. runner) *sl* courier <Slav❖[*1]>

tȑčipīš {a (acc. = gen.) masc.} (lit. run-piss) *sl-fea* crook, thief <Slav❖[*1]>

tȑčkalica {ē fem.} (lit. runner) *sl-sex* ***Fac*** diarrhea, runs, trots <Slav❖[*1]>

tȑčkalo {a neut.} (lit. runner) **1** *sl-drink* waiter <Slav❖[*1]> **2** porter

trčkàralo {a neut.} (lit. runner) *sl-crime* jailer <Slav❖[*1]>

Tȑčko *See the following*

• **Tȑčko Tȑčković** {NP} (lit. Runnie Runner) *sl* ***Fac*** mailman

Tŕća {ē fem.} *sl* Trieste (Italy, a popular shopping destination for ex-Yugoslavs) <ItaO✍> ☞ **Trst**

tȑdek {a (acc. = gen.) masc.} *sl-fea* miser, tightwad, skinflint <Slav✍[*1]>

tréba {ē fem.} **a.** *sl* female <Alb[*1]> **b.** *sl-sex* prostitute, hooker <Alb[*2]>

• **silìkōnskā tréba** {NP} (lit. silicone chick) *sl-sex* attractive female

• **škȅmbavā tréba**{NP} (lit. plump chick) *sl-sex* pregnant female

• **tréba opàjdara** {NP} (lit. banging chick) *sl-sex* female who readily and indiscriminately engages in sexual intercourse, slut

• **tréba s gȑbōm** {NP} (lit. chick with a hump) *sl-sex* pregnant female

• **tréba u patróli** {NP} (lit. chick on patrol) **a.** *sl-sex* prostitute, streetwalker

trȅbati *See the following*

• **trȅbā mi[NOUN:NOM]** {LSF} (lit. I need [NOUN: NOM]) **1** *col* used to ask for a person: *Treba mi Sabaheta. Can I speak with Sabaheta.* **2** *col* used to ask for something: *Treba mi malo brašna. Can I have some flour?*

• **trȅbaō bi [NOUN:ACC]** {LSF} (lit. I would need [NOUN:ACC]) **1** *col* used to ask for a person: *Trebao bi Ivana. Could I speak with Ivan?* **2** *col* used to ask for something: *Trebao bih jedno pivo. Can I have a bear.*

• **trȅbaō bih[NOUN:ACC]** {LSF} (lit. I would need [NOUN:ACC]) **1** *col* used to ask for a person: *Trebala bih Petra. Could I speak with Peter* **2** *col* used to ask for something

trȅćā nòga {NP} (lit. the third leg) *sl-sex* ***Fac-Obs*** penis, the third leg ☞ **noga**

trȅćā sȉsa {NP} (lit. the third tit) *sl-sex* ***Fac-Obs*** penis, dick, prick ☞ **sisa**

trećepózivac {zīvca (acc. = gen.) masc.} (lit. member of the contingent which is third to be drafted) *sl-sex* ***Fac*** male homosexual, gay <Slav[*1]>

trȅćī pȑst {NP} (lit. the third finger) *sl-sex* ***Fac-Obs*** penis, dick, prick ☞ **prst**

trȅf {a +ov (ext. pl) masc.; Nom Pl trȅfovi} *sl* luck <Fre[*1]>

trȅfijans {a masc.} [std. = tref] *sl-gamble* spade (card suit) <Fre✍>

trȅfiti {fīm, fe perf.} *col* hit, punch <Ger[*1]>

• **Trȅfiō[PRON:ACC] frâs!** {S} (lit. The stroke has hit me!) *col* used to refer to astonishment in the past: *Trefio me fras od toga šta je rekao! I was shocked by what he said!*

trȅhnuti {nēm, nū perf.} [std. = tresnuti] *col* fall down, kiss the floor: *tresnuti s kruške fall down from a pear tree* <Slav✍>

trêm {a (acc. = gen.) +ov (ext. pl) masc.; Nom Pl trȇmovi} *sl* male, guy <Alb[*1]>

trèmče {eta neut.} SerE *sl* child, kid <Alb❖[*1]>

Trèmens *See the following*

• **drûg Trèmens** {NP} (lit. comrade tremens) *sl-drink* ***Fac*** alcoholic, drunk

trȅmka {ē fem.} *sl* female <Alb❖[*1]>

trȅn {a +ov (ext. pl) masc.; Nom Pl trènovi} **a.** *sl* train <Eng> **b.** *sl* streetcar <Eng[*1]>

• **hìtrī trȅn** {NP} *sl* express train

• **lȁkī trȅn** {NP} (lit. light train) *sl* passenger train

• **mòrskī trȅn** {NP} (lit. seashore train) *sl* steam ship

• **têškī trȅn** {NP} (lit. heavy train) *sl* freight train

trenútak {excl.} *col* used to ask for a pause, one moment <Slav[*1]> ☞ **moment, momenat, sekundu**

• **sȁmo trenútak** {NP} *col* used to achieve a channel-related pause, hold on, hang on, one moment, please

trénje {a neut.} (lit. friction) *sl-sex* ***Fac-Obs*** sexual intercourse <Slav[*1]>

trȅpavičārka {ē fem.; Dat trȅpavičārki} **a.** *sl-fea* female with obviously false eyelashes <Slav❖[*1]> **b.** *sl-sex* loose woman <Slav❖[*2]>

trȅpiš {a masc.} *sl* eyelash <Slav✍>

trȅs [1] {excl.} *col* the sound made by an explosion, bang <Slav>

trȅs [2] {a +ov (ext. pl) masc.; Nom Pl trèsovi} *col* bang (loud and abrupt sound) <Slav>

trȇsak {ska masc.} **a.** *col* loud sound <Slav> **b.** *col* crashing <Slav[*1]> **c.** *col* blast <Slav[*2]>

trȅska {ē fem.} (lit. shaking) **a.** *col* loud sound <Slav> **b.i.aa.** *col* crashing <Slav[*1]> **bb.** *col* blast <Slav[*2]> **ii.** *sl* streetcar <Slav[*1]> **iii.aa.** *sl* train <Slav[*1]> **bb.x.** station, stop (bus, train, streetcar, etc.) **xx.aa.** railway **bb.** theft on public transportation **iv.** dance

Tréska {ē fem.; Dat Tréski} *col* name for Treskavica (a mountain near Sarajevo, Bosnia) <SlavO✍>

trèskac {excl.} *col* the sound made by slapping, slap <Slav>

trȅskāć {a masc.} /trèskāć/ (lit. shaker) *sl-drugs* dose of narcotic drug <Slav⁘[*1]>

trȅskāj {a masc.} (lit. shake, bang) **a.** *col* loud sound <Slav> **b.** *col* crashing <Slav[*1]> **c.** *col* blast <Slav[*2]>

tréskānje {a neut.} (lit. shaking) *sl-drugs* intravenous intake of narcotic drugs, mainlining, shooting up <Slav[*1]>

tréskati {trȇskām, tréskajū imperf.} *col* bang (loud and abrupt sound) <Slav>

trȅskavac {vca (acc. = gen.) masc.} (lit. shaker) **1a.** *sl* dancer <Slav⁘[*1]> **b.** *sl-sports* player <Slav⁘[*2]> **2** *sl-fea* epileptic <Slav⁘[*1]>

trȅskavac {vca masc.} (lit. shaker) **1** *sl* dance <Slav⁘[*1]> **2** *sl* train <Slav⁘[*2]>

trȅskāvci {kavācā masc. pl.} (lit. shakers) *sl* chains <Slav⁘[*1]>

trȅskavica {ē fem.} **1** *sl* cart (e.g. oxcart) <Slav⁘[*1]> **2** *sl* dancer <Slav⁘[*1]> **3** *sl* dance <Slav[*1]>

trȅskavice {vīcā fem. pl.} (lit. shakers) *sl* ox chart <Slav⁘[*1]>

trȅsko {a masc.} (lit. shaker) *sl-sex* ***Fac*** male looking for a loose woman, guy on the make <Slav⁘[*1]>

trȅskot {a masc.} *col* bang (loud and abrupt sound) <Slav>

treskòtānje {a masc.} *col* bang (loud and abrupt sound) <Slav>

treskòtati {ām, ajū imperf.} /trèskoćēm, trèskoćū imperf./ *col* bang (loud and abrupt sound) <Slav>

trȅsnuti {nēm, nū perf.} (lit. bang) **a.** *sl* hit, punch <Slav[*1]> **b.i.** *sl-sex* engage in sexual intercourse with (of a male), bang <Slav[*2]> **ii.** *sl-sex* say something unintelligent <Slav[*2]>

trȅsnuti se {nēm, nū perf. intr.} **a.** *col* hit oneself (e.g. to become sober) <Slav> **b.i.** *sl-sex* engage in sexual intercourse with, bang <Slav[*1]> **ii.** *sl-drugs* take narcotic drugs intravenously, mainline, shoot up <Slav[*1]> **iii.** *sl-fea* say energetically <Slav[*1]> **iv.** *sl-fea* say something unintelligent <Slav[*1]>

trȅsomān {a (acc. = gen.) masc.} (lit. banger) *sl-music* rock musician, head banger <Slav-Eng⁘[*1]>

trȇsti {trésēm, trésū imperf. irreg.} /trésti/ (lit. shake) *sl-gamble* play cards <Slav[*1]>

- **trésti se ko vȑšalica** {VP} (lit. shake like a threshing machine) *sl-fea* be frightened, get scared
- **trésti búljōm** {VP} (lit. shake one's ass) *sl* think, ponder
- **trésti mȇso** {VP} (lit. shake one's meat) *sl-sex* masturbate, beat off
- **trésti znánje** {VP} (lit. shake knowledge) *sl-sstu* do well on an exam

trȇsti se {trésēm, trésū x imperf. intr.} /trésti/ (lit. shake) **1** *sl* cry, shed tears, weep <Slav[*1]> **2** *sl* dance <Slav[*1]> **3** *sl* get scared, get frightened <Slav[*1]>

Trȇšće {a neut. pl.} [std. = Trst] *sl* Trieste (Italy, a popular shopping destination for ex-Yugoslavs) <ItaO✍>

trȅšnjevača {ē fem.} *sl-drink* cherry brandy <Slav⁘>

tréštati {tīm, tē imperf.} *col* play (music) loud <Slav[*1]>

tretírati {trètīrām, tretírajū imperf.} **a.** *sl* respect, obey <Fre[*1]> **b.** *sl* like, appreciate <Fre[*2]> **c.** *sl* think well of somebody <Fre[*3]>

trezvènjāk {venjáka (acc. = gen.) masc.} *col* teetotaler <Slav⁘>

Tȓgāč {a masc.} (lit. the square) Cro *sl* name for Jelačićev square (Zagreb, Croatia) <Slav✍[*1]>

Tȓgīć {a masc.} (lit. the square) Cro *sl* name for Jelačićev square (Zagreb, Croatia) <Slav✍[*1]>

tȑgnuti {nēm, nū perf.} **a.** *sl-drink* drink (alcohol) quickly, chug <Slav[*1]> **b.** *sl-drink* drink, sip (usu. alcohol) <Slav[*2]>

trî *See the following*

- **na pȍla trî** {PP} (lit. at half past two) *sl-fea* sick, ill

trî pèra na šešíru {NP} (lit. three feathers on a hat) *sl-sex* gonorrhea, the clap ☞ **pero**

Trî ti bȍga jèbēm! {S} (lit. I fuck your three gods!) SSer *dia* ***Off*** used as a moderate curse, Fuck you! ☞ **Bog**

Trî ti mȃjke jèbēm! {S} (lit. I fuck your three mothers!) *col* ***Off*** used as a strong curse, Fuck you! ☞ **majka**

trìbūng {a masc.} *sl-auto* transmission <Ger[*1]>

trȉca {ē fem.} **1** *sl-sports* three pointer (basketball) <Slav[*1]> **2** *sl-gamble* a kind of game played with three cards in hand <Slav[*1]> **3** *sl-sstu* grade C <Slav[*1]>

trȉes {num.} [std. = trideset] *col* thirty <Slav✍>

trȉfilis {a masc.} (lit. triper 'gonorrhea' X stifles 'syphilis') [std. = sifilis] *sl-sex* ***Fac*** syphilis, the pox <Gre✍>

trifȓtāljke {ī fem. pl.} /trȉfrtāljke/ (lit. three quarters) *col* small panties <Slav-Ger[*1]>

trijána {ē fem.} *sl-sex* gonorrhea, the clap <Ger✍>

trijáne {ā fem. pl.} *sl-gamble* a kind of game played with three cards in hand <Slav✍[*1]>

trijáner {a masc.} **1** *sl-gamble* a kind of game played with three cards in hand <Slav✍[*1]> **2** *sl-sex* gonorrhea, the clap <Ger[*1]>

trikolóri {ā masc. pl.} *sl-sports* members of the French national team <Fre>

triléma {ē fem.} (lit. The prefix 'di' *two* has been replaced with 'tri' (three)) *sl* ***Fac*** highly intricate dilemma, touchy case <Gre✍>

trȉlīng {a masc.} (lit. triple) **1** Ser *sl* the streetcar line number three in Belgrade, Serbia <Ger[*1]> **2** *sl-sex* gonorrhea, the clap <Ger✍>

trȉngeld {a masc.} *sl-drink* gratuity, tip <Ger>

trȉp {a +ov (ext. pl) masc.; Nom Pl trȉpovi} (lit. trip) **1** *sl-drugs* LSD, acid <Eng[*1]> **2** *sl-drugs* a small quantity of narcotic drug <Eng[*1]> **3** *sl-drugs* absolute tranquility <Eng[*1]> **4a.** *sl-drugs* pleasant feeling induced by narcotic drugs, high <Eng[*1]> **b.** *sl* imagination <Eng[*1]>
- **bȅd trȉp** {NP} (lit. bad trip) *sl-drugs* unpleasant effect of narcotic drugs, bad trip

trȉper {a masc.} **a.** *sl-sex* gonorrhea, the clap <Ger> **b.** *sl-fea* something very boring <Ger[*1]>
- **ko trȉper** {PP} (lit. like gonorrhea) *sl-fea* boring

trȉper-kombinácija {ē fem.} *sl* unintelligent plan, dumb idea <Ger-Lat[*1]>

tripèrisati {pèrišēm, šū imperf. intr.} *sl-fea* bother, disturb <Ger✤[*1]>

triperȉška {ē fem.; Dat triperȉški} /triperȉška/ Cro *sl* the former Opera bar in Zagreb, Croatia <Ger✍[*1]>

trȉpica {ē fem.} (lit. tripe) *sl-sex* ***Fac*** prostitute, hooker <Slav✤[*1]>

trȉpovati {pujēm, pujū imperf. intr.} **a.** *sl-drugs* be under the influence of narcotic drugs, be stoned <Eng✤[*1]> **b.** *sl-drugs* take narcotic drugs, do drugs <Eng✤[*2]> **c.** *sl* imagine <Eng✤[*3]>

Trȉsta li ti bȍga jèbēm! {S} (lit. I fuck your three hundred gods!) SSer *dia* ***Off*** used as a moderate curse, Fuck you! ☞ Bog

Trȉsta ti i trȋ mâjke jèbēm! {S} (lit. I fuck your three hundred and three mothers!) *col* ***Off*** used as a strong curse, Fuck you! ☞ majka

Trȉsta ti mâjke mȉlē! {S} (lit. *I fuck* your three hundred dear mothers!) SSer *dia* ***Off*** used as a strong curse, Fuck you! ☞ majka

trȉstāć {tristáća (acc. = gen.) masc.} *sl-auto* Fiat 1300 (make of car) <Slav✤[*1]>

tristènjāk {tenjáka (acc. = gen.) masc.} *sl-auto* Fiat 1300 (make of car) <Slav✤[*1]>

trȉstnjāk {a (acc. = gen.) masc.} *sl-auto* Fiat 1300 (make of car) <Slav✤[*1]>

tríša {ē fem.} [std. = triper] *sl-sex* gonorrhea, the clap <Ger✍>

tríšo {ē masc.} [std. = triper] *sl-sex* gonorrhea, the clap <Ger✍>

tȓka {ē fem.} (lit. race *the competition*) **1** *sl* cheating performed in a short time <Slav[*1]> **2** *sl-crime* quick unloading of stolen goods <Slav[*1]>

tȓkāč {a (acc. = gen.) masc.} (lit. runner) **1** *sl-fea* gloomy person <Slav[*1]> **2** *sl-fea* coward, chicken <Slav[*1]>

tȓkalica {ē fem.} *sl-sex* ***Fac*** diarrhea, runs, trots <Slav[*1]>

trkèljati {ām, ajū imperf.} *sl* make a mess while looking for something, rummage through <Slav[*1]>

trkèljisānje {a neut.} **1** *sl-fea* prolonged and meaningless talk, blabber, chatter <Slav[*1]> **2** *sl-fea* rummaging through apartment or things <Slav[*1]>

trkèljisati {išēm, išū imperf.} **a.** *sl* make a mess while looking for something, rummage through <Slav[*1]> **b.** *sl* search <Slav[*2]> **c.** *sl-crime* steal, swipe <Slav[*3]>

tȓknūt {a, o adj.} *sl-fea* ***Der*** insane, nuts <Slav[*1]>

tȓknuti {nēm, nū perf.} (lit. run) *sl-sstu* fail to pass a grade in school, flunk <Slav[*1]>

tȓkopīš {a (acc. = gen.) masc.} (lit. run-pisser) *sl-fea* crook, thief <Slav✤[*1]>

tȓlica {ē fem.} *sl* saber, sword <Slav✤[*1]>

tȓljati *See the following*
- **tȓljati pízdu** {VP} (lit. rub one's cunt) *sl-fea* ***Obs*** lose time in useless activities, goof around
- **tȓljati jèzičinu** {VP} (lit. rub one's big tongue) *sl* French kiss
- **tȓljati jèzik** {VP} (lit. rub one's tongue) *sl* French

kiss
• tŕljati žlézdu {VP} (lit. rub a gland) SerE *sl-sex* ***Obs*** engage in sexual intercourse with

tȑnbiti {bīm, bē imperf.} **a.** *sl-fea* talk persistently and meaninglessly, blabber, chatter <Slav✍[*1]> **b.** *sl-fea* gossip, wag the tongue <Slav❖[*2]> **c.** *sl-fea* be boring <Slav❖[*3]>

trndáriti {tȑndārīm, rē imperf.} *sl* search <Slav[*1]>

tȑndosati {ošem, ošu imperf.} *sl-sex* ***Obs*** engage in sexual intercourse with (of a male) <Slav✍[*1]>

tȑndžati {ām, ajū imperf.} *sl-sex* ***Obs*** engage in sexual intercourse with (of a male) <Slav✍[*1]>

tȑnigūz {a (acc. = gen.) masc.} (lit. numb-ass) *sl-fea* ***Fac-Obs*** person who sits for a long time <Slav❖[*1]>

tȑnjavac {vca masc.} *sl* fear <Slav❖[*1]>

tròati {trȕjēm, rūjū imperf.} [std. = trovati] *sl* lie <Slav✍[*1]>

trȍba {adj.} *sl-fea* broke (financially) <Ita✍[*1]>

tròbanak {nka masc.} (lit. three bucks) Ser *sl* the streetcar line number three in Belgrade, Serbia <Slav-Lat[*1]>

trȍfāznī {ā, ō adj.} (lit. the one with three phases) Cro *sl-fea* ***Fac*** Orthodox Christian <Slav-Gre[*1]>

trȍfrtāljke {ī fem. pl.} /trofȑtāljke/ (lit. three quarters) *col* short trousers, flood pants <Slav-Ger[*1]>

troglòdit {a (acc. = gen.) masc.} *sl-fea* stupid or mentally deficient person <Gre[*1]>

tròguz {a (acc. = gen.) masc.} (lit. three-asses) *sl-fea* ***Obs*** male with large buttocks <Slav[*1]>

tròjān [1] {trojána (acc. = gen.) masc.; Voc trȍjāne} (lit. Trojan) *sl-fea* stupid or mentally deficient person <Slav[*1]>

tròjān [2] {trojána masc.} (lit. Trojan) *sl-gamble* a kind of game played with three cards in hand <Slav[*1]>

trojánac {nca (acc. = gen.) masc.} (lit. Trojan) *sl-fea* stupid or mentally deficient person <GreO[*1]>

trokìrāš {kiráša (acc. = gen.) masc.; Voc trȍkirāšu} *sl-fea* stutterer

trokírati {tròkīrām, trokírajū imperf.} **1a.** *sl* work improperly (of an engine, mechanism, etc.) **b.** *sl* miss, fail **c.** *sl-fea* stutter **2** die, kick the bucket

trokrílac {lca (acc. = gen.) masc.} (lit. three-door cupboard) *sl-fea* muscular male, pumped up dude <Slav[*1]>

tròkrīlnī òrmān {NP} (lit. three-door cupboard) *sl-fea* muscular male, pumped-up dude ☞ **orman**

tròkrīlnī òrmār {NP} (lit. three-door cupboard) *sl-fea* muscular male, pumped-up dude ☞ **orman**

trȍkūt {a masc.} (lit. triangle) **1** *sl-sex* ***Obs*** vagina, cunt <Slav[*1]> **2** *sl* small panties <Slav[*1]> **3** Cro *sl* name of a cab station at Masarykova and Preradovićeva streets in Zagreb, Croatia <Slav[*1]>

trokùtice {ā fem. pl.} (lit. the triangular ones) *sl* small panties <Slav❖[*1]>

trokùtić {a masc.} (lit. small triangle) *sl-sex* ***Obs*** vagina, cunt <Slav[*1]>

tróla {ē fem.} (lit. traction) **1** *sl* trolley bus <Eng[*1]> **2** *sl* streetcar <Eng[*1]> **3** *sl-sex* penis <Eng[*1]>

tròliš {a masc.} *sl* trolley bus <Eng✍>

trȍm {a, o adj.} (lit. slow) *sl-fea* jobless <Slav[*1]>

tròmbl {a +ov (ext. pl) masc.} *sl* drums <Ger✍>

tròml {a +ov (ext. pl) masc.} *sl* drums <Ger>

trónjati {trônjām, trónjajū imperf.} *sl-sex* ***Obs*** defecate, shit <Slav❖[*1]>

trónja {ē fem. & masc.} **a.** *sl* fear <Slav❖[*1]> **b.** *sl-fea* weak person, wimp **c.** *sl-fea* coward, chicken

trónjac {njca masc.} *sl-crime* prison <Slav❖[*1]>

trònjār {tronjára (acc. = gen.) masc.} **1** *sl* merchant (male) <Slav❖[*1]> **2** *sl* gentleman <Slav❖[*1]> **3** *sl* boss <Slav❖[*1]> **4** *sl* monkey, ape <Slav❖[*1]>

trȍnjarica {ē fem.} **1** *sl* mistress, extramarital female lover <Slav❖[*1]> **2** *sl* lady, woman <Slav❖[*1]> **3** *sl* boss's wife <Slav❖[*1]> **4** *sl* female shop keeper <Slav❖[*1]>

trónjati {trônjām, trónjajū imperf.} *sl-sex* ***Obs*** defecate, shit <Slav❖[*1]>

trȍnjavac {njāvca (acc. = gen.) masc.} **a.** *sl-fea* weak person <Slav❖[*1]> **b.** *sl-fea* coward, chicken

trônjča {ē masc.} *sl-fea* ***Der*** coward, chicken <Slav❖[*1]>

trópa [1] {ē masc.} /tròpa/ *sl-stu* person who failed an exam <Ita[*1]>

trópa [2] {adj.} /tròpa/ **a.** *sl-fea* lost <Ita> **b.** *sl-fea* broke (financially) <Ita[*1]> **c.** *sl-fea* destroyed <Ita[*2]> **d.** *sl-fea* failed <Ita[*3]> **e.** *sl-fea* dead <Ita[*4]>

tròpačka {ē fem.; Dat tròpački} **1** *sl-arch* sewing machine **2** *sl-arch* shoe

trȍpasto {adv.} *sl-fea* expensive <Ita❖[*1]>

tropírati {tròpīrām, tropírajū biasp.} **1** *sl* be beaten up <Ita❖[*1]> **2** *sl-sstu* fail an exam (flunk) <Ita❖[*1]>

trȍpnuti {nēm, nū perf. intr.} **1** *sl* be beaten up <Ita❖[*1]> **2** *sl-sstu* fail an exam (flunk) <Ita❖[*1]>

trȍpo {adv.} *sl-fea* expensive <Ita❖[*1]>

tròsisa {ē fem.} (lit. three tits) *sl-fea* ***Der-Obs*** greedy female (for food, money, etc.) <Slav❖*1>

tròsobnjāk {trosobnjáka (acc. = gen.) masc.} *sl* two-bedroom apartment <Slav❖*1>

trȍša {ē fem.} /trȍša /treša fem./ *sl* slang <NE✍*1>

trȍšan {šna, šno adj.} (lit. shabby) **a.** *sl-fea* tired <Slav*1> **b.** *sl-fea* unwilling <Slav*2>

trošávati {tròšāvām, trošávaju imperf.} *sl-fea* pay (bills, etc.) <Slav❖*1>

tròšiti {šīm, šē imperf.} (lit. spend) *sl* sell (exchange merchandise for money) <Slav*1> *sl* give, pass <Slav*2>

tròšiti se {šīm, šē imperf. intr.} (lit. spend oneself) *sl* enjoy, like <Slav*1>

tròtiš {a masc.} *sl* scooter (children's toy) <Fre✍*1>

tròtl {a (acc. = gen.) +ov (ext. pl) masc.} *sl-drink* waiter <Ger*1>

trȍtoārka {ē fem.; Dat trȍtoārki} /trotòārka/ (lit. curb chick) *sl-sex* ***Fac*** prostitute, streetwalker <Fre❖*1>

trȍtoslāv {a (acc. = gen.) masc.} *sl-fea* lame person <Slav❖*1>

tròvāč {trováča (acc. = gen.) masc.} (lit. poisoner) **a.** *sl-fea* seducer <Slav*1> **b.** *sl-fea* liar <Slav*2>

tròvānje {a neut.} (lit. poisoning) **1** *sl* lying <Slav*1> **2** *sl* flirting <Slav*1> **3** *sl* ingratiate, brownnose, kiss ass <Slav*1>

tròvati {trȕjēm, trȕjū imperf.} (lit. poison) **a.** *sl* lie <Slav*1> **b.i.aa.** *sl* persuade, convince <Slav*2> **bb.** *sl* flirt <Slav*3> **ii.** *sl* gossip, wag the tongue <Slav*2>

- **tròvati sòvān** {VP} (lit. poison sleeping) *sl* sleep, nap
- **tròvati sòvāž** {VP} (lit. poison sleeping) *sl* sleep, nap
- **tròvati sóve** {VP} (lit. poison owls) *sl* sleep, nap
- **tròvati sovijáner** {VP} (lit. poison sleep) *sl* sleep, nap
- **tròvati sôvku** {VP} (lit. poison sleep) *sl* sleep, nap
- **tròvati sóvu** {VP} (lit. poison an owl) *sl* sleep, nap

tȑpati {ām, ajū biasp.} (lit. put in) **1** *sl* eat, devour <Slav*1> **2** *sl* ***Obs*** engage in sexual intercourse with (of a male) <Slav*1>

Tr̀pimīr {a (acc. = gen.) masc.} (lit. Trpimir 'man's name' X trpiti 'suffer') *sl-fea* person who suffers <SlavO*1>

Tȓš {a +ev (ext. pl) masc.; Nom Pl Tȓševi} *sl* Trieste (Italy, a popular shopping destination for ex-Yugoslavs) <ItaO✍>

tȓt *See the following*

- **tȓt Mìlōjka** {ExcP} (lit. bang Milojka, a proper name) Ser *col* used as a strong negative response, no way, never

tȓt-mȓt [1] {excl.} *col* used to express hesitation, this and that: *Nemoj mi tȓt-mȓt nego počni da radiš. Do not hesitate, just start to work.* <Slav>

tȓt-mȓt [2] {a +ov (ext. pl) masc.; Nom Pl tȓt-mr̀tovi} **1** *col* confusion <Slav*1> **2** *col* jitters <Slav*1> **3** *col* fear: *Bilo je tȓt-mȓt kad su počeli da pucaju na nas. We had fear when they started to shoot at us.* <Slav*1> **4** *sl* hesitation <Slav*1>

tr̀ta {ē fem.} **1** *sl-sex* ***Obs*** buttocks, butt <Slav*1> **2** *sl* fear <Slav*1>

tȓta-vȓta {ē fem.} *col* nothing <Slav*1>

trtàrati se {ām, ajū imperf. intr.} *sl* fear <Slav❖*1>

tr̀tāroš {a (acc. = gen.) masc.} *sl-fea* ***Der*** coward, chicken <Slav❖*1>

tr̀tāš {trtáša (acc. = gen.) masc.; Voc tr̀tāšu} **1** *sl-fea* ***Der*** ingratiator (male), brownnoser, ass kisser <Slav❖*1> **2** *sl-sex* ***Der*** male with large buttocks <Slav❖*1> **3** *sl-fea* ***Der*** coward, chicken <Slav❖*1>

trtášiti {tr̀tāšīm, še biasp.} *sl-fea* fear <Slav❖*1>

tȓtav {a, o adj.} *sl-fea* obese, fat <Slav*1>

tȓte-mȓte {excl.} *col* used to express hesitation, this and that: *Nema trte-mrte nego radite kako vam je naređeno. Do not hesitate, just do what you were ordered to do.* <Slav>

tr̀tica {ē fem.} (lit. posterior) *sl-sex* ***Obs*** buttocks, butt <Slav>

tȓtiti {tīm, tē imperf.} *sl-sex* ***Obs*** engage in sexual intercourse with (of a male) <Slav❖*1>

- **Kȍ te tȓtī!** {S} (lit. Who is fucking you?) *sl* ***Off*** used to express disrespect, Fuck you!

tȓtiti se {tīm, tē imperf. intr.} **1** *sl-fea* boast, brag <Slav❖*1> **2** *sl-sex* engage in sexual intercourse with <Slav❖*1>

tȓtka {ē fem.; Dat tȓtki} *sl-sex* ***Obs*** buttocks, butt <Slav❖*1>

tȓtljāk {trtljáka (acc. = gen.) masc.} *sl-fea* inhabitant of the countryside, hick, bumpkin

tȓtnjāk {trtnjáka (acc. = gen.) masc.} *sl-arch* peasant <Slav*1>

trtomúditi se {tòmūdīm, dē imperf. intr.} *sl-fea* intrude, barge in <Slav❖*1>

tȓtonja {ē masc.} /tŕtonja/ (lit. shitter) **1** *sl-fea* boaster, braggart, blowhard <Slav❖*1> **2** *sl-fea* conceited male

<Slav❖[*2]> 3 *sl-fea* obese male <Slav❖[*3]> 4 *sl-fea* very important or influential person, big shot <Slav❖[*1]>

tȑtos {a (acc. = gen.) masc.} 1 *sl-fea* ***Der*** ingratiator (male), brownnoser, ass kisser <Slav✍[*1]> 2 *sl-sex* ***Der*** male with large buttocks <Slav✍[*1]>

tȑtositi {sīm, sē imperf.} *sl-fea* talk persistently and meaninglessly, blabber, chatter <Slav✍[*1]>

tȑtoš {a (acc. = gen.) masc.} *sl-fea* ***Der*** ingratiator (male), brownnoser, ass kisser <Slav✍[*1]>

tȑtošiti {šīm, šē imperf.} *sl-fea* talk persistently and meaninglessly, blabber, chatter <Slav❖[*1]>

trúba [1] {ē fem.} (lit. trumpet) 1 *sl-sex* ***Obs*** excrement, shit <Slav[*1]> **2a.** *sl-fea* ***Der*** average person <Slav[*1]> **b.** *sl-fea* ***Der*** stupid or mentally deficient person <Slav[*2]> **c.i.** *sl-fea* ***Der*** clumsy person, klutz <Slav[*3]> **ii.** *sl-sex* ***Der*** impotent male <Slav[*3]> **iii.** *sl-fea* cheated male **iv.** *sl-fea* person who is broke (financially) **3** *sl-sex* failed sex **4** *sl-fea* stupidity, lack of intelligence

- **bijèsnā trúba** {NP} (lit. rabid trumpet) *sl* female
- **kȍnjskā trúba** {NP} (lit. horse trumpet) *sl-fea* boaster, braggart, blowhard

trúba [2] {adj.} (lit. trumpet) *sl-fea* worthless <Slav[*1]>

- **trúba frȁjer** {NP} (lit. trumpet guy) **a.** *sl-sex* ***Der*** impotent male **b.** *sl-fea* ***Der*** unimportant person, nobody, nothing **c.** *sl-fea* ***Der*** clumsy male, klutz **d.** *sl-fea* financially broke male **e.** *sl-fea* loser

trúba fóra {NP} (lit. trumpet trick) *sl* cheating, swindling ☞ fora

trúbac {pca (acc. = gen.) masc.} (lit. trumpeter) *sl-drink* alcoholic, drunk <Slav❖[*1]>

trùbāč {trubáča (acc. = gen.) masc.} (lit. trumpeter) **1a.** *sl-fea* average person <Slav[*1]> **b.** *sl-fea* cheated male <Slav[*2]> **c.i.** *sl-fea* person who is broke (financially) <Slav[*3]> **ii.** *sl-sex* impotent male <Slav[*1]> **2** *sl-drink* drunk <Slav[*1]> **3** *sl-sex* male homosexual, gay <Slav[*1]>

trubàdūr {badúra (acc. = gen.) masc.} (lit. troubadour) **a.** *sl-fea* average person <Fre[*1]> **b.** *sl-fea* stupid or mentally deficient person <Fre[*2]> **c.** *sl-fea* clumsy male, klutz <Fre[*3]> **d.** *sl-sex* impotent male <Fre[*4]> **e.** *sl-fea* cheated male <Fre[*4]>

trùbāk {trubáka masc.} *sl* hearing (human perceptive ability) <Slav❖[*1]>

trubalȇska {ē fem.; Dat trubalȇski} *sl-fea* interesting event <Slav✍[*1]>

trubèntati {ām, ajū biasp.} (lit. play trumpet) *sl-fea* talk persistently and meaninglessly, blabber, chatter <Slav✍[*1]>

trȕber {a (acc. = gen.) masc.} (lit. trumpeter) *sl-crime* ***Der*** informer, stoolie, snitch <Slav❖[*1]>

trúbica {ē fem.} (lit. small trumpet) *sl* female <Slav[*1]>

trúbiti {trúbīm, bē imperf.} (lit. play trumpet) *sl-fea* be boring <Slav[*1]>

trȕc {a +ev (ext. pl) masc.; Nom Pl trùcevi} *sl-fea* stubbornness <Ger>

trucírati {trùcīrām, trucúrajū biasp.} *sl-fea* be stubborn, be defiant <Ger❖>

trȕckavac {kāvca (acc. = gen.) masc.} *sl-crime* petty thief <Slav❖[*1]>

trȕcke {ī fem. pl.} *col* a wild see-saw ride <Slav❖[*1]>

trȕćānje {a neut.} *sl-fea* prolonged and meaningless talk, blabber, chatter <Slav❖[*1]>

trȕćati {ām, ajū imperf.} *sl-fea* talk persistently and meaninglessly, blabber, chatter <Slav❖[*1]>

trȕhaō {trùhla, trùhlo adj.} [std. = truo] BosM *col* rotten, decayed <Slav✍>

trȕhlo {adv.} [std. = trulo] BosM *col* rotten, decayed <Slav✍>

trȕhnuti {nēm, nū imperf. intr.} [std. = trunuti] BosM *col* rotten, decayed <Slav✍>

trȕker {a (acc. = gen.) masc.} *sl-crime* policeman, cop <Ger[*1]>

trȕlā fóra {NP} (lit. rotten trick) *sl* cheating, swindling ☞ fora

trȕlā kòbila {NP} (lit. rotten mare) *col* leap frog (the game) ☞ **kobila**

trȕlā múda pòkōjnōg làbūda {S} (lit. Rotten balls of a deceased swan.) *sl* ***Obs*** nothing at all ☞ **muda**

trȕlā príča {NP} (lit. rotten story) *col* lie ☞ **priča**

trulârios {a (acc. = gen.) masc.} *sl-fea* obese male <Slav✍[*1]>

trȕlī plôt {NP} (lit. rotten fence) *sl-fea* decayed teeth ☞ plot

trȕlī Zâpad {NP} (lit. rotten West) **a.** *col* ***Fac*** the decadent West **b.** *col* ***Fac*** Western European countries (in general) ☞ Zapad

trȕliti {līm, lē imperf.} (lit. rotten) *sl-fea* smell, stink <Slav[*1]>

trȕlo {adv.} (lit. rotten) **1** *sl-fea* falsely: *trulo optužiti accuse falsely* <Slav[*1]> **2** *sl-fea* unfair: *ponašati se trulo prema nekome act unfairly toward somebody* <Slav[*1]> **3** *sl-fea* stupidly: *trulo izgubiti lovu lose one's money stupidly* <Slav[*1]>

trȕmbekulōzan {zna, zno adj.} [std. = tuberkulozan] *sl-fea* tubercular <Lat✍>

trȕndžast {a, o adj.} *sl* orange (color)

trȕnjav {a, o adj.} *sl-fea* sly <Slav[*1]>

trȕō {trùla, trùlo adj.} (lit. rotten) *sl-fea* false <Slav[*1]>

trȗp {excl.} *col* the sound made by tapping, tap <Slav>

trȕpa {excl.} *col* the sound made by tapping, tap <Slav>

trùpac {pca (acc. = gen.) masc.} (lit. log) *sl-fea* stupid or mentally deficient person <Slav⁘[*1]>

trȕpānje {a neut.} *col* making noise while walking <Slav[*1]>

trupàrānje {a neut.} *col* making noise while walking <Slav[*1]>

trupàrati {ām, ajū imperf.} *col* make noise while walking <Slav[*1]>

trȕpati {ām, ajū imperf.} *col* make noise while walking <Slav[*1]>

trùpina {ē fem.} (lit. big log) *sl-sex* ***Fac*** attractive body <Slav[*1]>

truplijáner {a masc.} *sl* body <Slav✍[*1]>

tȑzānje {a neut.} **1** *sl* flirting <Slav[*1]> **2** *sl* observing, looking <Slav[*1]> **3** *sl-fea* ingratiation, brownnosing, ass kissing <Slav[*1]> **4** *sl-fea* seducing <Slav[*1]> **5** *sl-crafts* irregular, frequently interrupted (work of an engine) <Slav[*1]>

tȑzati {ām, ajū imperf.} (lit. twitch) **1a.** *sl* like <Slav[*1]> **b.** *sl* flirt <Slav[*2]> **c.** *sl* love <Slav[*3]> **2** *sl* draw <Slav[*1]> **3** *sl* look, watch, scope out <Slav[*1]> **4** *col* run unevenly (engine, etc.) <Slav[*1]>
- **tȑzati na žȕč** {VP} (lit. shake at one's gall-bladder) *sl-fea* make nervous, get on one's nerves

tȑzati se {ām, ajū imperf. intr.} (lit. twitch) *sl-fea* be frightened, get scared <Slav[*1]>

tȑzātor {a (acc. = gen.) masc.} (lit. twitcher) *sl-fea* seducer <Slav⁘[*1]>

tȑzav {a, o adj.} (lit. twitchy) *sl-fea* nervous <Slav[*1]>

tȑzavica {ē fem.} (lit. twitcher) *sl-music* electric guitar <Slav[*1]>

tȑznuti {nēm, nū perf.} (lit. twitch) **1** *sl* fall in love: *Ivan se trznuo na Mariju na prvi pogled. John fell in love with Mary at first sight.* <Slav[*1]> **2** *sl-drink* drink, sip (usu. alcohol): *trznuti ljutu have a shot of schnapps* <Slav[*1]> **3** *sl* cheat, swindle: *trznuti gazdu radnje cheat a shopkeeper* <Slav[*1]>

tȑžnica {ē fem.} (lit. market place) *sl-sex* ***Fac*** prostitute, hooker <Slav[*1]>

tȗ {excl.} *col* the sound made by a trumpet, toot <Slav>

túba {ē fem.} (lit. tuba) *sl-fea* tuberculosis patient <Lat[*1]>

tùbāš {trubáša (acc. = gen.) masc.; Voc trȕbāšu} (lit. tuba player) *sl-sex* ***Fac*** male homosexual, gay <Lat[*1]>

tubèrān {tuberána (acc. = gen.) masc.; Voc tȕberāne} *sl-fea* tuberculosis patient <Lat⁘[*1]>

tuberóza {ē fem.} *sl-fea* tuberculosis patient <Lat⁘[*1]>

tubijáner {a (acc. = gen.) masc.} *sl-fea* tuberculosis patient <Lat⁘[*1]>

tùbiš {a (acc. = gen.) masc.} *sl-fea* tuberculosis patient <Lat⁘[*1]>

tȕc {excl.} *col* the sound made by a smallish explosion, bam <Slav>

tȕc-mȕc [1] {excl.} **1** *col* stuttering sound <Slav> **2** *col* this and that <Slav>

tȕc-mȕc [2] {adv.} *col* having difficulties in expressing oneself <Slav>

túcak {cka (acc. = gen.) masc.} (lit. crusher) *sl-sex* ***Fac*** male sexual partner (of a female) <Slav⁘[*1]>

tùcāljka {ē fem.; Dat tùcāljki} (lit. crusher) **1** *sl-sex* ***Fac-Obs*** prostitute, hooker <Slav⁘[*1]> **2** *sl-sex* ***Obs*** sexual intercourse <Slav⁘[*1]>

tȕcānje {a neut.} (lit. crushing) *sl-sex* ***Obs*** sexual intercourse <Slav⁘[*1]>

tùcār {tucára (acc. = gen.) masc.; Voc tȕcāru} *sl-fea* beggar <Slav⁘[*1]>

tȕcati {ām, ajū imperf.} (lit. crush) **1** *sl-sex* ***Obs*** engage in sexual intercourse with (of a male) <Slav[*1]> **2** *sl* lose time <Slav[*1]>
- **tȕcati žȉcu** {VP} (lit. bang wire) *sl* beg, ask for money

tȕcati se {ām, ajū imperf. intr.} (lit. crush each other) *sl-sex* ***Obs*** engage in sexual intercourse with (of a male) <Slav[*1]>

tȕcer {a (acc. = gen.) masc.} *sl-fea* beggar <Slav⁘[*1]>

tȕcić {a (acc. = gen.) masc.} (lit. crusher) **a.** *sl-sex* ***Obs*** male sexual partner (of a female) <Slav⁘[*1]> **b.** *sl* lover (male) <Slav⁘[*2]>

tùckac {excl.} *col* the sound made by a smallish explosion, bam <Slav>

tuckàrati {ām, ajū imperf.} *col* beep (alarm, etc.) <Slav⁘[*1]>

Tȕcman {a masc.} (lit. Bang-man) **1** Cro *sl* name forTucić dance school in Zagreb, Croatia <SlavO✍[*1]> 2 Cro *sl* name of a dance club on Maršal Tito square in Zagreb, Croatia <SlavO✍[*1]>

tûcović {a (acc. = gen.) masc.} (lit. crusher) **a.** *sl-sex* ***Obs*** male sexual partner (of a female) <Slav✤[*1]> **b.** *sl* lover (male) <Slav✤[*2]>

tȕče {eta neut.} *sl-sex* male sexual partner (of a female) <Slav✍[*1]>

tûći {túčēm, túkū, tûk, tûk perf. irreg.} **a.** *col* beat up <Slav[*1]> **b.** *sl-sports* defeat <Slav[*2]>

- **tûći kȑpe** {VP} (lit. beat rugs) *sl-crime* pick pockets
- **tûći lȕtkicu** {VP} (lit. beat the little doll) *sl-sex* ***Obs*** masturbate, beat off
- **tûći màjmuna** {VP} (lit. beat the monkey) *sl-sex* ***Obs*** masturbate, spank the monkey
- **túći žȉcu** {VP} (lit. beat the wire) *sl* beg, ask for money

túde {adv.} [std. = tu] *dia-col* here <Slav✍>

túdi {adv.} [std. = tu] *dia-col* here <Slav✍>

túdik {adv.} [std. = tu] *dia-col* here <Slav>

tȕdom {excl.} *sl* used to signal that import of the message has been captured <Hun>

tudòmisati {išēm, išū biasp.} **a.** *sl* understand, realize <Hun✤> **b.** *sl* know, have knowledge of <Hun✤[*1]>

tùdum {a masc.} *sl-drink* low-quality wine

tùdum {a (acc. = gen.) masc.} *sl-fea* stupid or mentally deficient person

tùdup {a (acc. = gen.) masc.} **a.** *sl-fea* unattractive boy **b.** *sl-fea* unloved boy

tùđā rȉba {NP} (lit. other's fish) *sl-crime* stolen money ☞ riba

Tȕđmanovac {nōvca (acc. = gen.) masc.} (lit. follower of Franjo Tudjman *Croatian president in the 1990s*) *sl-fea* ***Der*** Croat (person) <SlavO✤[*1]>

tȕf {excl.} *col* the sound made by a smallish explosion, bam <Slav>

tȕhnuti {nēm, nū perf.} *sl* cheat, swindle <◊✍>

tȕj [1] {excl.} *col* the sound made by a turkey, gobble <Slav>

tûj [2] {adv.} [std. = tu] *dia-col* here <Slav✍>

tùjkā {adv.} [std. = tu] *dia-col* here <Slav✍>

tȕk {excl.} *col* the sound made by a smallish explosion, bang <Slav>

tȕka {ē fem.} *col* noise <Slav[*1]>

tȕknuti {nēm, nū perf. intr.} *col* smell, stink <Slav[*1]>

tûl {a +ov (ext. pl) masc.; Nom Pl túlovi} *sl-drink* bar (drinking place) <NE✍[*1]>

túlac [1] {lca (acc. = gen.) masc.} *sl-fea* clumsy male, klutz <Slav[*1]>

túlac [2] {lca masc.} *sl* party (social gathering) <NE✍[*1]>

tùlek {a (acc. = gen.) masc.} *sl-crime* policeman, cop <NE[*1]>

tulìpān {lipána (acc. = gen.) masc.; Voc tȕlipāne} (lit. tulip) **a.** *sl-fea* stupid or mentally deficient person <NE[*1]> **b.** *sl-fea* ruined person <NE[*2]>

túliti {līm, lē imperf.} *sl* sing <Slav[*1]>

- **Ne túli kȕrac!** {S} (lit. Don't you hide your cock!) *dia* ***Off*** used as a moderate curse, Fuck you!

tùlum {a masc.} **a.** *sl* party (social gathering) <NE[*1]> **b.** *sl* fun <NE[*2]>

tulumáriti {lùmārīm, rē imperf.} /tulumàriti/ *sl* party (engage in social gathering) <NE✤[*1]>

tulumátiti {lùmātīm, lùmātē imperf.} /tulumàtiti/ *sl* party (engage in social gathering) <NE✤[*1]>

tulumȉška {ē fem.; Dat tulumȉški} /tulumìška/ *sl* party (social gathering) <NE✍[*1]>

tȕlja {ē fem.} *sl* country, nation <NE[*1]>

tȕljān {a (acc. = gen.) masc.} (lit. seal) **1** Cro *sl-fea* Italian (person), Dago <Slav[*1]> **2a.** *sl-fea* stupid or mentally deficient person <Slav[*1]> **b.** *sl-sex* male who is easily cheated by prostitutes <Slav[*2]>

- **pìjanī tȕljān** {AdjP} (lit. drunk seal) Cro *sl-fea* inhabitant of the countryside, hick, bumpkin

tùljara {ē fem.} *sl-drink* late-night bar

tùljezga {ē masc.; Dat tùljezgi} *sl-fea* ***Der*** coward, chicken

tumaròlog {a (acc. = gen.) masc.} (lit. wanderologist) *sl-fea* ***Fac*** homeless person, bum <Slav-Gre✤[*1]>

tumarològija {ē fem.} (lit. wanderology) *sl-fea* ***Fac*** being a homeless person <Slav-Gre✤[*1]>

tùmbati se {ām, ajū imperf. intr.} **a.** *col* roll down a slope <NE✤> **b.** *col* ride (on a bus, etc.) uncomfortably <NE✤[*1]>

tȕmbe {adv.} *sl-fea* upside-down <NE>

tȕmplānje {a neut.} *sl-sex* ***Obs*** sexual intercourse <Ger[*1]>

tȕmplati {ām, ajū imperf.} *sl-sex* ***Obs*** engage in sexual intercourse with (of a male) <Ger[*1]>

tûn {adv.} [std. = tu] *col* there <Slav✍>

tũna [1] {ē fem.} (lit. tuna fish) **a.** *sl* money, clams <Slav[*1]> **b.** *sl* wallet <Slav[*2]>

tûnā [2] {adv.} [std. = tu] *dia-col* here <Slav✍>

tùnēl {tunéla masc.} (lit. tunnel) *sl-sex* ***Obs*** vagina, love tunnel <Eng[*1]>

tùnezga {ē fem.; Dat tùnezgi} **a.** *sl-fea* weak person, wimp **b.** *sl-fea* crybaby **c.** *sl-fea* coward, chicken

Tùngũzija {ē fem.} (lit. Tungusia *a province in Russia* X guz 'ass') *sl-fea* a place of extreme wretchedness or squalor, hellhole <SlavO[*1]>

tũnjav {a, o adj.} *sl-fea* unskilled

tùnjezga {ē masc.; Dat tùnjezgi} *sl-crime* reluctant criminal

tũp [1] {excl.} *col* the sound made by a smallish explosion, bang <Slav>

tûp [2] {a, o adj.} **a.** *col* unintelligent, stupid, dumb <Slav[*1]> **b.** *sl* insane, nuts <Slav[*2]>

tũpa-lũpa {excl.} *col* the sound made by objects colliding, crash <Slav>

tũpadžija {ē masc.} (lit. the dull one) **a.** *sl-fea* stupid or mentally deficient person <Slav-NE[*1]> **b.** *sl-fea* extremely talkative person, chatterbox <Slav-NE[*2]> **c.** *sl-fea* boring person, bore <Slav-NE[*3]>

tupamȁros {a (acc. = gen.) masc.} (lit. tup 'dull' X Tupamaros 'a terrorist movement') **a.** *sl-fea* extremely talkative person, chatterbox <Slav✍[*1]> **b.** *sl-fea* boring person, bore <Slav✍[*2]>

tupàrati {ām, ajū imperf.} *sl-fea* move while making noise (as of a train) <Slav[*1]>

tũpavac {pāvca (acc. = gen.) masc.} *col* ***Der*** stupid or mentally deficient person <Slav❖[*1]>

tũpe-lũpe {excl.} *col* the sound made by tapping, tap <Slav>

tùpičnica *See the following*

• **bùbnā tùpičnica** {NP} (lit. the place of grinding and preaching) *sl-sstu* ***Fac*** school

tùpiglāv {a (acc. = gen.) masc.} (lit. dullhead) *sl-stu* student <Slav❖[*1]>

tùpilo {a neut.} *sl-fea* boredom <Slav❖[*1]>

tùpisānje {a neut.} *sl-fea* prolonged and meaningless talk, blabber, chatter <Slav❖[*1]>

tùpisati {išēm, išū imperf.} (lit. dull) **a.** *sl-fea* do something stupid <Slav❖[*1]> **b.** *sl-fea* talk persistently and meaninglessly, blabber, chatter <Slav❖[*2]> **c.** *sl-fea* be boring <Slav❖[*3]> **d.i.** *sl-fea* act unintelligently <Slav❖[*4]> **ii.** *sl-fea* preach, give lectures to <Slav❖[*4]>

túpiti {tûpīm, pē imperf.} (lit. dull) **a.** *sl-fea* talk persistently and meaninglessly, blabber, chatter <Slav[*1]> **b.** *sl-fea* annoy, bother, pester <Slav[*2]> **c.i.** *sl-fea* act unintelligently <Slav[*3]> **ii.aa.** preach, give lectures to **bb.** talk

• **túpiti mòtku** {VP} (lit. dull a stick) *sl-fea* bother, disturb

• **túpiti o Rùsijī** {VP} (lit. dull about Russia) *sl-fea* talk about something one is not competent in

• **túpiti zûbe** {VP} (lit. dull one's teeth) *sl-fea* bore, disturb

tũpkānje {a neut.} *col* tapping <Slav❖>

tũpkati {ām, ajū imperf.} *col* the tap <Slav❖>

túpljenje {a neut.} (lit. blunting) *col* prolonged and meaningless talk, blabber, chatter <Slav❖>

tupòljev {adj.} /tupòljev/ (lit. Tupolev 'make of Russian airplane' X tup 'dull, stupid') *sl-fea* unintelligent, stupid, dumb <BN[*1]>

túponja {ē masc.} (lit. dull person) *sl-fea* stupid or mentally deficient person <Slav❖[*1]>

tũposlāv {a (acc. = gen.) masc.} *sl-fea* stupid or mentally deficient person <Slav❖[*1]>

tùpsōn {tupsóna (acc. = gen.) masc.} *sl-fea* ***Der*** stupid or mentally deficient person <Slav✍[*1]>

Tũrak {rka (acc. = gen.) masc.} (lit. Turk) *sl-fea* ***Off*** Bosnian Muslim (male) <SlavO[*1]>

tũrbo {adj.} /tùrbo/ *sl-fea* ***App*** excellent, awesome <Lat[*1]>

túrbo píca {NP} (lit. turbo cunt) *sl-sex* ***App-Obs*** attractive female ☞ **pica**

tũrbo-kóka {ē fem.; Dat tũrbo-kóki} /tùrbo-kóka/ (lit. turbo chick) *sl-sex* ***Fac-Obs*** attractive female <Eng-Slav[*1]>

Tùrčin [1] {a (acc. = gen.) -in (rd. pl.) masc.; Nom Pl Tûrci} (lit. Turk) *sl-fea* ***Off*** Bosnian Muslim (male) <SlavO[*1]>

• **cȓnī Tùrčin** {NP} (lit. black Turk) *sl* ***Fac*** night train

tùrčin [2] {a masc.} (lit. Turk) *sl-drugs* hashish, hash <SlavO[*1]>

Tũri ga jèzik u dũpe bȉće ti slȁđē! {S} (lit. Stick your tongue in your ass, it'll be sweeter!) SSer *dia* ***Obs*** used as a strong curse, Fuck you! ☞ **turiti**

Tũrio kũrac u! {S} (lit. He put his prick into!) *dia* ***Obs*** used as a strong curse, Fuck you! ☞ **turiti**

turírati {tùrīrām, turírajū biasp. intr.} *sl-auto* shift an engine into high gear <Fre[*1]>

tùrist {a (acc. = gen.) masc.} (lit. tourist) **1** *sl-sex* ***Fac*** male sexual partner (of a female) <Fre*1> **2** *sl-crime* ***Fac*** prisoner with a short sentence <Fre*1>

tȕriti {rīm, rē perf.} **a.** *sl* stick in, insert <Slav> **b.** *sl-sex* engage in sexual intercourse with (of a male) <Slav*1>

• **Tȕri ga jèzik u dȕpe bȉće ti slȁđē!** {S} (lit. Stick your tongue in your ass, it'll be sweeter!) SSer *dia* ***Obs*** used as a strong curse, Fuck you!

• **Tȕrio kȕrac u!** {S} (lit. He put his prick into!) *dia* ***Obs*** used as a strong curse, Fuck you!

turìzam {zma masc.} (lit. tourism) *sl-sex* ***Obs*** buttocks, butt <Fre*1>

Tȕrković {a (acc. = gen.) masc.} (lit. McTurk) *sl-fea* ***Off*** Bosnian Muslim (male) <SlavO⁘*1>

tùrnjāk {turnjáka (acc. = gen.) masc.} *sl* boy, kid

turpijáner {a masc.} *sl-fea* boring event <NE✍*1>

turpìjati {ām, ajū imperf.} (lit. file) **1** *sl-sex* ***Obs*** engage in sexual intercourse with (of a male) <Slav⁘*1> **2.** *sl-fea* talk persistently and meaninglessly, blabber, chatter <Slav*1> **b.** *sl-fea* preach, give lectures to <Slav*2> **c:.** *sl-fea* annoy, bother, pester <Slav⁘*3>

• **turpìjati dávež** {VP} (lit. file choking) *sl-fea* be bothered, be disturbed

tȕrskī akumulâtor {NP} (lit. Turkish battery) *sl-fea* person who thinks slowly, dim bulb ☞ **akumulator**

tȕršija {ē fem.} *col* marinated vegetables, preserves <NE>

• **Tùršiju ti òplulū jèbēm!** {S} (lit. I fuck your spitting food for winter!) *dia* ***Off*** used as a moderate curse, Fuck you!

tȕspās {a masc.} **1** *sl* arrival <Slav⁘*1> **2** *sl* layover, stopover <Slav⁘*1>

tuspásiti se {tùspāsīm, sē perf. intr.} **1** *sl* arrive, come <Slav⁘*1> **2** *sl* stop for a short time <Slav⁘*1>

tȕš *See the following*

• **hládan tȕš** {NP} (lit. cold shower) *col* shock, cold shower

tušírati {tùšīrām, tušírajū biasp.} (lit. shower) *sl* beat up <Slav*1>

Tȕškić {a masc.} Cro *sl* name for Tuškanac park in Zagreb, Croatia <SlavO✍>

tȕt *See the following*

• **tȕt òvāmo, tȕt ònāmo** {AdvP} (lit. toot here, toot there) *dia* here and there, all over

túta {ē fem.} **1a.** *col* chamber pot <Slav*1> **b.i.** *sl* broom <Slav*2> **ii.** *col* clumsy person, klutz <Slav*2>

tȕtāć {a masc.} *sl-auto* car, wheels

tȗtanj [1] {excl.} (lit. rumbling) *col* used to make somebody go away, beat it <Slav*1>

tȗtanj [2] {tnja masc.} **a.** *col* rumble (e.g. a cart on a rocky road) <Slav*1> **b.** *col* running away, fleeing <Slav*2>

tùtanja {ē fem.} *sl* head

tùtati {ām, ajū biasp.} *sl* sleep, nap

tutavȅla [1] {excl.} *col* used to make somebody go away, beat it <Slav-Gyp*1>

tutavȅla [2] {ē fem.} *col* running away, fleeing <Slav-Gyp*1>

tȕti-frȕti {īja masc.} *col* stupidity, lack of intelligence <Ita*1>

tȕtka {ē fem.; Dat tȕtki} [std. = prostitutka] *sl-sex* prostitute, hooker <Lat✍>

tȕtkati {ām, ajū imperf.} **a.** *col* beep (alarm, etc.) <Slav⁘> **b.** *col* honk, blow a horn <Slav⁘*1>

tȕtle *See the following*

• **tȕtle mȁlo** {AdvP} (lit. bang a little) *dia* never

tȕtnuti {nēm, nū perf.} **a.** *col* stick in, insert <Slav*1> **b.** *sl* bang (loud and abrupt sound) <Slav*2> **c.** *sl-sex* engage in sexual intercourse with (of a male) <Slav*3>

tûtos {a (acc. = gen.) masc.} *sl* tutor <Lat✍*1>

tùtuk {a masc.} **a.** *col* beep (alarm, etc.) <Slav> **b.** *col* honk (of a horn) <Slav*1>

tùtumrāk {a (acc. = gen.) masc.} **a.** *sl-fea* stupid or mentally deficient person <Slav⁘*1> **b.** *sl-fea* ignorant person <Slav⁘*1>

tùtun [1] {a (acc. = gen.) masc.} (lit. tobacco) **a.** *sl-crime* cigarette seller in prison <NE*1> **b.** *sl-fea* informer, stoolie, snitch <NE*1>

tùtun [2] {a masc.} *dia* tobacco <NE*1>

tutùnjati {tùtnjīm, njē imperf.} *col* mumble <Slav*1>

tuturȕtū {tua (acc. = gen.) masc.} **1** *sl-fea* person who is broke (financially) <Slav*1> **2** *sl-fea* average person <Slav*1>

tuturȕtū frȁjer {NP} (lit. toot guy) **a.** *sl-fea* clumsy person, klutz **b.** *sl-fea* loser ☞ **frajer**

tȕžibaba {ē fem.} *sl-fea* child who always informs parents or teachers about his/her peers, tattletale <Slav⁘*1>

tȕžideda {ē fem.} *sl-fea* child who always informs parents or teachers about his/her peers, tattletale <Slav⁘*1>

tȕz {a +ov (ext. pl) masc.; Nom Pl tȕzovi} BosM *col* salt <NE>

tvèntī sȅnčerī fȍks {NP} (lit. Twentieth Century Fox) *sl-fea* cross-eyed person ☞ **foks**

tvȉgī {fem.} (lit. Twiggy, a popular model from the 1970s) *sl-fea* slender female <Eng*1>

tvȉgica {ē fem.} (lit. Twiggy, a popular model from the 1970s) *sl-fea* slender female <Eng*1>

tvȉst {a +ov (ext. pl) masc.; Nom Pl tvȉstovi} (lit. twist) *sl-drugs* marijuana cigarette, joint <Eng*1>

tvȉster {a (acc. = gen.) masc.} (lit. twister) *sl-drugs* person who smokes marijuana, pot head <Eng*1>

tvȍrza {tvoraza masc.; perm} [std. = zatvor] *sl-crime* prison <Slav[illegible]>

tvȓd [1] {excl.} (lit. hard) *dia* used to express extreme disgust <Slav*1>

tvȓd [2] {a, o adj.} (lit. hard) **1** *sl-fea* abundant <Slav*1> **2** *sl-drink* drunk <Slav*1> **3** *sl-fea* miserly, stingy <Slav*1>

tvȓd karàkter {NP} (lit. hard character) *sl-sex* erect penis ☞ **karakter**

tvȓd lôv {NP} (lit. hard bucks) *sl* cold hard cash ☞ **lov**

tvȓdā lóva {NP} (lit. hard bucks) *sl* cold hard cash ☞ **lova**

tvrdnjáković {a (acc. = gen.) masc.} *sl-fea* miser, tightwad, skinflint <Slav❖*1>

tvrdòuk {a, o adj.} *sl-fea* hard to learn <Slav❖>

tvȓtko {a (acc. = gen.) masc.} (lit. Tvrtko, man's name X tvrd 'hard') **1** *sl-sex* ***Fac-Obs*** erect penis <Slav❖*1> **2** *sl-fea* miser, tightwad, skinflint <Slav❖*1> **3** *sl-drink* alcoholic, drunk <Slav❖*1>

Uu

ȕ {excl.} **1** *col* used to express various emotions, such as satisfaction, surprise, delight, dislike, or pain, oh <Slav> **2** *col* walk <Slav>
- **Ȕ jè!** {S} *sl* used to express astonishment, Wow!
- **Ȕ jèbote!** {S} (lit. Wow, you be fucked!) *sl* ***Obs*** used to express astonishment, Wow!

u ȁutu {PP} (lit. in out) **a.** *sl-fea* expelled: *On je u autu iz Amerike za špijuniranje. He was expelled from the United States for spying.* **b.** *sl-fea* suspended ☞ **aut**

u bóbu {PP} (lit. in berry) *col* exactly, precisely ☞ **boba**

u bȍlestan mȍzak {PP} *col* against common sense ☞ **mozak**

U bȍžijū mȁtēr! {S} (lit. In God's mother!) *col* used to express lack of control over events, Fuck it! ☞ **mater**

U bȍžjū mâjku! {S} (lit. In God's mother!) *col* used to express lack of control over events, Fuck it! ☞ **majka**

u bȗbnju {PP} (lit. in a drum) *sl-crime* in custody waiting to be convicted ☞ **bubanj**

U crévce te jèbēm! {S} (lit. I screw you in your small intestine!) **SerE** *dia* ***Off*** used as a weak curse, Screw you! ☞ **crevce**

U crévo te jèbēm! {S} (lit. I screw you in your intestine!) SerE *dia* ***Off*** used as a weak curse, Screw you! ☞ **crevo**

u cúgu {PP} *col* at once ☞ **cug**

u cvàjte klȁse {PP} (lit. in the second class) *sl-sex* ***Obs*** anally ☞ **klase**

u čȁbru {PP} (lit. in bowl) *col* in a difficult situation ☞ **čabar**

U čèmu je gréda? {S} (lit. In what is the beam?) *col-dia* used to ask for additional information, What's happening? ☞ **greda**

u dlȁku {PP} (lit. in hair) *col* exactly, precisely ☞ **dlaka**

u drȕgū klȁsu {PP} (lit. in the second class) *sl-sex* ***Obs*** anally ☞ **klasa**

u dùmini {PP} **a.** *sl* as if **b.** *sl* never ☞ **dumina**

ù dupe na vášar {PP} (lit. to the ass to a fair) *col* nowhere ☞ **dupe**

Ù dupe te jèbēm! {S} (lit. I fuck you in your ass!) *col* ***Off*** used as a moderate curse, Fuck you! ☞ **dupe**

Ù dupe te pȑtenō jèbēm! {S} (lit. I fuck you in your linen ass!) *dia* ***Off*** used as a moderate curse, Fuck you! ☞ **dupe**

Ù dupe te šȕgavō jèbēm! {S} (lit. I fuck you in your mangy ass!) *dia-col* ***Off*** used as a moderate curse, Fuck you! ☞ **dupe**

U dupénce te jèbēm! {S} (lit. I fuck you in your small ass!) *dia-col* ***Off*** used as a moderate curse, Fuck you! ☞ **dupence**

u dȕplōj òblāndi {PP} (lit. in double cover) *sl-fea* dressed formally, dressed up ☞ **oblanda**

u dȕre {PP} (lit. in order) *sl* affirmative response, ok, no problem ☞ **dure**

U džȉgerice ti ga kȍknēm! {S} (lit. I bang it in your liver!) SSer *dia* ***Off*** used as a weak curse, Screw you! ☞ **džigerica**

u fȁsu {PP} *sl* used as a strong affirmative response, sure ☞ **fas**

u filterima {PP} (lit. in the filters) *sl* never ☞ **filter**

u fôl {PP} (lit. in the trick) *sl* as if ☞ **fol**

U glȁvicu te jèbēm! {S} (lit. I screw you in your small head!) *dia-col* ***Off*** used as a weak curse, Screw you! ☞ **glavica**

U glâvu te jèbēm! {S} (lit. I fuck you in your head!) *dia-col* ***Off*** used as a moderate curse, Fuck you! ☞ **glava**

u gùjicu na vášar {PP} (lit. to the ass to a fair) *dia-col* ***Obs*** nowhere ☞ **gujica**

U gùzicu te jèbēm! {S} (lit. I fuck you in your ass!) *dia-col* ***Off*** used as a moderate curse, Fuck you! ☞ **guzica**

U gûžnjāk te jèbēm! {S} (lit. I fuck you in your ass!) *dia* ***Off*** used as a moderate curse, Fuck you! ☞ **gužnjak**

u kèšu {PP} (lit. in cash) *col* cash ☞ **keš**

U kȕrac! {S} (lit. In a prick!) *col* ***Obs*** used to express lack of control over events, Fuck it! ☞ **kurac**

U kȕrac krâsnī! {S} (lit. In a nice prick!) *col-dia* ***Obs*** used to express lack of control over events, Fuck it! ☞ **kurac**

U kȕrac lêpī! {S} (lit. In a beautiful prick!) SerE *dia-col* ***Obs*** used to express lack of control over events, Fuck it! ☞ **kurac**

ù kūrcu {PP} (lit. in a prick) *col* far away, utterly remote ☞ **kurac**

u lìmburgu mȅsēcu kad se šíšajū màjmuni {PP} (lit. in the month of Limbourg when they clip monkeys) SerE *col* never ☞ **limburg**

u lìmburgu mjȅsēcu {PP} (lit. in the month of Limbourg) *col* never ☞ **limburg**

u mâlī mȍzak {PP} *col* intensely (usu. being disturbed, bothered, etc.) ☞ **mozak**

u mȅsēcu màju kad rúže cvètajū {PP} (lit. in the month of May when roses bloom) SerE *sl* never ☞ **maj**

u mèsēcu màju kad se màjmuni šíšajū {PP} (lit. in the month of May when they clip monkeys) SerE *sl* never ☞ **maj**

u mȍzak {PP} (lit. in the brain) *sl-fea* skillfully ☞ **mozak**

U mȍzak te jèbēm! {S} (lit. I fuck you in your brain!) *col-dia* ***Off*** used as a moderate curse, Fuck you! ☞ **mozak**

Ȕ nōs te jèbēm! {S} (lit. I fuck you in your nose!) *col-dia* ***Off*** used as a moderate curse, Fuck you! ☞ **nos**

U nótu te krîvū jèbēm! {S} (lit. I fuck you in a crooked note!) *dia-col* ***Off*** used as a moderate curse, Fuck you! ☞ **nota**

u ȍfsājdu {PP} (lit. off side) **a.** *sl-fea* outside **b.** *sl-fea* ill, sick ☞ **ofsajd**

U ókce te jèbēm! {S} (lit. I fuck you in your small eye!) *dia* ***Off*** used as a moderate curse, Fuck you! ☞ **okce**

U ókce te jèbēm, kûrvinskō! {S} (lit. I fuck you in your hooker little eye!) *dia* ***Off*** used as a moderate curse, Fuck you! ☞ **okce**

u pánjevima {PP} (lit. in tree-trumps) *col* never ☞ **panj**

U pȉčku lêpū mȁterinu! {S} (lit. To nice mother's cunt!) SerE *col-dia* ***Off*** used to express lack of control over events, Fuck it! ☞ **pička**

U pȉčku mȁterinu! {S} (lit. To mother's cunt!) *col* ***Obs*** used to express lack of control over events, Fuck it! ☞ **pička**

u pìku {PP} **1** *sl* used as a strong affirmative response, sure **2** *sl* right away, now ☞ **pik**

U pívskū flȁšu! {S} (lit. To beer bottle!) *col-dia* used to express lack of control over events, Fuck it! ☞ **flaša**

U pízdu mȁterinu! {S} (lit. To mother's cunt!) *col* ***Obs*** used to express lack of control over events, Fuck it! ☞ **pizda**

u pízdu mȁterinu {S} (lit. to mother's cunt) *col* ***Obs*** far away, utterly remote ☞ **pizda**

U pȑdalo te jèbēm! {S} (lit. I fuck you in your farting thing!) *dia-col* ***Off*** used as a moderate curse, Fuck you! ☞ **prdalo**

U pŕkno te jèbēm! {S} (lit. I fuck you in your ass!) *dia* ***Off*** used as a moderate curse, Fuck you! ☞ **prkno**

u pȕnōm sjáju {PP} (lit. in the full shine) *col* in full glory ☞ **sjaj**

U pȕpak te jèbēm! {S} (lit. I screw you in your navel!) *dia-col* ***Off*** used as a weak curse, Screw you! ☞ **pupak**

U rêp te jèbēm! {S} (lit. I fuck you in your tail!) *dia-col* ***Off*** used as a moderate curse, Fuck you! ☞ **rep**

U ȑnju te jèbēm! {S} (lit. I fuck you in your ass!) *dia* ***Off*** used as a moderate curse, Fuck you! Up yours! ☞ **rnja**

u sȅndvīču {PP} (lit. in sandwich) *sl-sex* ***Obs*** being between two partners during sexual intercourse ☞ **sendvič**

U sȉsu te jèbēm! {S} (lit. I fuck you in your tit!) *col* ***Off*** used as a moderate curse, Fuck you! ☞ **sisa**

U sȑce te jèbēm! {S} (lit. I fuck you in your heart!) *col* ***Off*** used as a moderate curse, Fuck you! ☞ **srce**

U svàstiku ti ga zàbodēm! {S} (lit. I stick it in your wife's sister!) *dia-col* ***Off*** used as a moderate curse, Fuck you! ☞ **svastika**

u Šȁngāj {PP} (lit. to Shanghai) *sl* used to make somebody go away ☞ **Šangaj**

U šȉju te jèbēm! {S} (lit. I screw you in your neck!) *dia* ***Off*** used as a weak curse, Screw you! ☞ **šija**

U šúpak te jèbēm! {S} (lit. I fuck you in your asshole!) *col* ***Off*** used as a moderate curse, Fuck you! ☞ **šupak**

U šùpljāk te jèbēm! {S} (lit. I fuck you in your hollow place!) *col-dia* ***Off*** used as a moderate curse, Fuck you! ☞ **šupljak**

U tȉl te vàšljiv jèbēm! {S} (lit. I fuck you in your ass which is full of lice!) *dia* ***Off*** used as a moderate curse, Fuck you! ☞ **til**

ù tōm gȑmu lèži zêc {S} (lit. the rabbit lies in that bush) *col* used to sum up one's point, That's how it is! ☞ **zec**

ù tomē je fàzōn {S} (lit. that's where the trick is) *col* used to sum up one's point, That's how it is! ☞ **fazon**

ù tomē je fôl {S} (lit. that's where the trick is) *col* used to sum up one's point, That's how it is! ☞ **fol**

ù tomē je fóra {S} (lit. that's where the trick is) *col* used to sum up one's point, That's how it is! ☞ **fora**

U trȋ pízde mȁterine! {S} (lit. To the three mother's cunts!) *sl* ***Obs*** used to emphasize one's point ☞ **pizda**

u trȋ pízde mȁterine {S} (lit. to the three mother's cunts) *sl* ***Obs*** far away, utterly remote ☞ **pizda**

U ústa te blâženā! {S} (lit. *I fuck* you in your beatified mouth!) *col-dia* ***Off*** used as a strong curse, Fuck you! ☞ **usta**

U ústa te jèbēm! {S} (lit. I fuck you in your mouth!) *col* ***Off*** used as a strong curse, Fuck you! ☞ **usta**

U ústa te kȑvavā! {S} (lit. *I fuck* you in your bloody mouth!) *col-dia* ***Off*** used as a strong curse, Fuck you! ☞ **usta**

U ústa te mȓtvā! {S} (lit. *I fuck* you in your dead mouth!) *col-dia* ***Off*** used as a strong curse, Fuck you! ☞ **usta**

U ústa te pògana jèbēm! {S} (lit. I fuck you in your dirty mouth!) *col-dia* ***Off*** used as a strong curse, Fuck you! ☞ **usta**

U ústa te pòkvārenā jèbēm! {S} (lit. I fuck you in your rotten mouth!) *col-dia* ***Off*** used as a strong curse, Fuck you! ☞ **usta**

U ustânča te jèbēm! {S} (lit. I fuck you in your small mouth!) *dia-col* ***Off*** used as a strong curse, Fuck you! ☞ **ustanca**

U ȕvo te glûvō jèbēm! {S} (lit. I fuck you in your deaf ear!) Ser *dia-col* ***Off*** used as a moderate curse, Fuck you! ☞ **uvo**

u vídu lástinōg rêpa {PP} (lit. in the form of a swallow's tail) *col* quickly ☞ **rep**

U vȕnu te jèbēm! {S} (lit. I fuck you in your wool!) *dia* ***Off*** used as a moderate curse, Fuck you! ☞ **vuna**

u zdrȁv mȍzak {PP} (lit. in the healthy brain) *col* against common sense ☞ **mozak**

Ù zdrāvlje! {S} (lit. In health!) *col* used as a toast, Cheers! To your health! ☞ **zdravlje**

U zûb te zlátan jèbēm! {S} (lit. I screw you in your gold tooth!) *dia-col* ***Off*** used as a weak curse, Screw you! ☞ **zub**

u žȉvot {PP} (lit. in life) *col* out (to have some fun): *Otišli su u život poslije devet sati. They went out after nine o'clock.* ☞ **život**

u žútu {PP} (lit. in yellow) *col-dia* never ☞ **žuto**

ȕā {excl.} *col* used to express public disagreement, boo <Slav>

ȕār {a masc.} [std. = uvar] *dia-col* profit, gain <Slav>

ùara {excl.} *col* used to express joy, hurrah <Slav>

ubacȉška {ē fem.; Dat ubacȉški} /ubacȉška/ **a.** *sl-fea* intruder <Slav*1> **b.** *sl-fea* ingratiator (male), brownnoser, ass kisser <Slav*2>

ubáciti {ùbācīm, cē perf.} **a.** *sl* insert, stick in <Slav*1> **b.** *sl-sex* ***Obs*** engage in sexual intercourse with (of a male) <Slav*2>

- **ubáciti u mašínu** {VP} (lit. put in the machine) *sl* joke with, make a fool of
- **ubáciti u rȉkverc** {VP} (lit. put into reverse gear) *sl* withdraw

ubáciti se {ùbācīm, cē perf. intr.} (lit. insert oneself) **a.** *sl* begin to flirt <Slav*1> **b.** *sl* introduce oneself <Slav*2>

• **ubáciti se u trȉp** {VP} (lit. insert oneself into the trip) *sl-drugs* feel the effect of narcotic drugs

ubacívati se {bàcujēm, cujū imperf. intr.} (lit. keep inserting oneself) *sl* begin to flirt <Slav*1>

ubacóka {ē fem.; Dat ubacóki} **a.** *sl-fea* ***App*** skillful person <Slav✣*1> **b.** *sl-fea* person who wants to push into a group of people without being invited <Slav✣*2>

ubȁčiti {čīm, čē perf.} /ubȁčiti/ [std. = ubaciti] **a.** *sl* insert, stick in <Slav☞> **b.** *sl-sex* ***Obs*** engage in sexual intercourse with (of a male) <Slav☞*1>

ubádati {ùbādām, ubádajū imperf.} (lit. stab) **1a.** *sl* catch <Slav*1> **b.** *sl-crime* arrest <Slav*2> **2** *sl-sex* engage in sexual intercourse with (of a male) <Slav*1> **3** *sl* guess <Slav*1>

ubaláviti se {bàlāvīm, vē perf. intr.} (lit. beslobber oneself) *sl-sex* ***Obs*** ejaculate prematurely <Slav*1>

ùbaniti {nīm, nē perf.} *sl-crime* kill, murder

ubȁštati se {bȁštām, bȁštajū perf. intr.} *sl-crime* kill, murder <Ita*1>

ubȁštrati {ām, ajū perf.} **1** *sl-crime* kill, murder <Ita*1> **2** *sl* get, obtain <Ita*1> **3** *sl* eat, devour <Ita*1> **4** *sl-drink* drink (alcohol) <Ita*1>

ubȁštrati se {ām, ajū perf. intr.} *sl-fea* force oneself on somebody <Ita*1>

ubetonírati se {tònīrām, tonírajū perf. intr.} (lit. cement oneself) *sl-drink* get very drunk, get plastered <Lat✣*1>

ùbi [PRON:ACC] [NOUN:NOM] {LSF} (lit. [NOUN: NOM] killed [PRON:ACC]) *col* used to refer to suffering from something: *Ubi me ovo hodanje! This walking is killing me!* ☞ **ubiti**

ubíjanje *See the following*

• **ubíjānje oka** {NP} (lit. killing one's eye) *sl* sleep, nap

ubíjati {ùbījām, ubíjajū imperf.} (lit. kill) *sl-sex* ***Obs*** engage in sexual intercourse with (of a male) <Slav*1>

• **ubíjati ȍko** {VP} (lit. kill one's eye) *sl* sleep, nap

• **ubíjati u vrednòću** {VP} (lit. kill in diligence) SerE *sl-fea* bore, disturb

• **ubíjati vréme** {VP} (lit. kill time) SerE *col* wait for a certain period of time to pass

• **ubíjati vrijéme** {VP} (lit. kill time) *col* wait for a certain period of time to pass

ubístven {a, o adj.} (lit. killing) **a.** *sl-fea* ***App*** excellent, awesome <Slav*1> **b.** *sl-fea* very funny <Slav*2>

ȕbitāčan {adj.} (lit. deadly) *sl-fea* excellent, awesome <Slav*1>

ùbiti {ȕbijēm, ijū perf.} (lit. kill) **a.** *sl* beat up <Slav*1> **b.i.** *sl* devour, eat voraciously <Slav*2> **ii.** *sl-sex* engage in sexual intercourse with (of a male) <Slav*2> **iii.aa.** *sl* make big money <Slav*2> **bb.** *sl* get money <Slav*3> **iv.** *sl* drink (alcohol) <Slav*2>

• **ùbi[PRON:ACC] [NOUN:NOM]** {LSF} (lit. [NOUN:NOM] killed [PRON:ACC]) *col* used to refer to suffering from something: *Ubi me ovo hodanje! This walking is killing me!*

• **ùbiti ȁsa** {VP} (lit. kill an ace) *sl-sstu* get a failing grade, flunk

• **ùbiti bȍga** {VP} (lit. kill a God) *col* beat up

• **ùbiti bȍga u [PRON:LOC]** {LSF} (lit. kill a God in [NOUN:ACC]) *col* beat up severely: *Ubili su boga u njemu. They beat the shit ouf of him.*

• **ùbiti bùgera** {VP} **1** *sl-sstu* get a failing grade, flunk **2** *sl* find a girlfriend

• **ùbiti dešnjáka** {VP} (lit. kill the righthanded one) *sl-auto* turn right

• **ùbiti drȕgū** {VP} (lit. kill the second one) *sl-drink* continue to drink

• **ùbiti ìspit** {VP} (lit. kill an exam) *sl-stu* pass an exam

• **ùbiti lȅptīra** {VP} (lit. kill a butterfly) *sl-sex* ***Obs*** find and leave a girl

• **ùbiti levāka** {VP} (lit. kill the lefthanded one) SerE *sl-auto* turn left

• **ùbiti Némca** {VP} (lit. kill a German) SerE *sl-sstu* get a failing grade, flunk

• **ùbiti nȍkat** {VP} (lit. kill a nail) *sl* run away, flee

• **ùbiti ròlōv** {VP} (lit. kill rolling) *sl-sstu* skip classes, cut classes

• **ùbiti sòvān** {VP} (lit. kill a sleep) *sl* sleep, nap

• **ùbiti sòvāž** {VP} (lit. kill a sleep) *sl* sleep, nap

• **ùbiti sovijáner** {VP} (lit. kill a sleep) *sl* sleep, nap

• **ùbiti sôvku** {VP} (lit. kill a sleep) *sl* sleep, nap

• **ùbiti sóvu** {VP} (lit. kill a sleep) *sl* sleep, nap

• **ùbiti tûtanj** {VP} (lit. kill rumbling) *sl* run away, flee

• **ùbiti u pójam** {VP} (lit. kill in one's concept) [std. = ùbiti] *col* defeat

ùbiti se {ȕbijēm, ijū perf. intr.} (lit. kill oneself) **1** *sl* fight (e.g. fist fight) <Slav*1> **2** *sl-drink* get very drunk, get dead drunk <Slav*1>

• **ùbiti se ko pȕška** {VP} (lit. kill oneself like a rifle) *sl-drink* get very drunk, get dead drunk

• **ùbiti se [VERB:ACTIVE PARTICIPLE]** {VP} **a.** *col* [VERB] really hard: *Ubi se radeći. He works really hard.* **b.** *col* ***Iro*** [NOT] [VERB] at all.: *Ubio se učeći. He did not learn at all.*

ȕbleha {ē fem.; Dat ȕblehi} *sl* cheating, swindling

ùbod {a masc.} (lit. stab) *sl-sex* ***Obs*** sexual intercourse <Slav*1>

ùbosti {odēm, odū perf. irreg.} (lit. prick, stab) **1** *sl* hit, punch <Slav*1> **2** *sl-sex* engage in sexual intercourse with (of a male), poke <Slav*1> **3** *sl-drugs* take narcotic drugs intravenously, mainline, shoot up <Slav*1> **4** *sl* guess correctly <Slav*1> **5a.** *sl* find, locate <Slav*1> **b.** *sl* get, obtain <Slav*2>
- **ùbosti aviònče** {VP} (lit. poke a small plane) *sl-sstu* get a failing grade, flunk
- **ùbosti dešnjáka** {VP} (lit. poke the righthanded one) *sl-auto* turn right
- **ùbosti leváka** {VP} (lit. poke the lefthanded one) SerE *sl-auto* turn left

ùbrati {berēm, berū perf.} (lit. pick) **1** *sl-crime* kill, murder <Slav*1> **2a.** *sl* see <Slav*1> **b.** *sl* understand, realize <Slav*2>

ùbrisati se {išēm, išū perf. intr.} *sl* be unable to count on: *Možeš se ubrisati s njegovom pomoću. You cannot count on his help.* <Slav*1>

ubúciti se {ùbūcīm, cē perf. intr.} (lit. get chubby) *sl-fea* gain weight <Slav⁘*1>

ubùfati {ām, ajū perf.} *sl-crime* kill, murder

ubùftati {ām, ajū perf.} *sl-crime* kill, murder

ubunàrisati {išēm, išū perf.} *sl* put into one's pocket, pocket <NE⁘*1>

ȕc {excl.} *dia* used to make a dog retrieve <Slav>

ùcakati {ām, ajū perf. intr.} *col* catch, grab <Slav*1>
- **ùcakati u fijóku** {VP} (lit. stick in the drawer) *sl-crime* apprehend, put under arrest

ucànjati {ām, ajū perf.} *sl* catch, grab <Slav*1>

ucécati {ùcēcām, ucécajū perf.} *sl-crime* kill, murder <Slav*1>

ucíriti se {ùcīrīm, rē perf. intr.} *sl-drink* get drunk

ùcirkati se {ām, ajū perf. intr.} *sl-drink* get drunk <Ger⁘*1>

ucmékati {ùcmēkām, ucmékajū perf.} *sl-crime* kill, murder <Slav*1>

ucȑvati se {ām, ajū perf. intr.} (lit. putrefy) *sl-sex* have syphilis, have the pox <Slav*1>

ùcupati {ām, ajū perf.} *sl-crime* kill, murder

ùcvikati {ām, ajū perf.} *sl-fea* get frightened, get scared <Ger⁘*1>

ùćaknūt {a, o adj.} *sl-crime* under police surveillance

ućániti {ùćānīm, nē perf.} *sl* understand, get it

ućapírati {ćàpīrām, ćapírajū perf.} *sl* catch, grab <Slav⁘*1>

ućáriti {ùćārīm, ùćārē perf.} Bos *col* have profit, gain <NE>

ućátiti {ùćātīm, tē perf.} *sl* write in (fill in) <NE⁘*1>

Ùćerām ti! {S} (lit. I stick it to you!) *dia* ***Off*** used as a moderate curse, Fuck you! ☞ **ućerati**

ùćerati {ām, ajū perf.} [std. = utjerati] *dia-col* drive in <Slav☞>
- **Ùćerām ti!** {S} (lit. I stick it to you!) *dia* ***Off*** used as a moderate curse, Fuck you!

ućériti {ùćērīm, rē perf.} *sl* understand, get it

úći *See the following*
- **úći u bȉznis** {VP} (lit. get introduced into the business) *col* get acquainted with (job, task, etc.)
- **úći u klȋnč** {VP} (lit. enter a clinch) *sl* fight (e.g. fist fight)

ućòrisati {išēm, išū perf.} *sl-crime* steal, swipe <NE⁘*1>

ućorkírati {ćòrkīrām, ćorkīrajū perf.} *sl-crime* arrest <NE⁘*1>

ùdarati *See the following*
- **ùdarati glȁnc** {VP} (lit. hit the shine) **1** *sl-sex* ***Fac-Obs*** engage in cunnilingus **2** *sl-sex* ***Fac-Obs*** masturbate, beat off **3** *sl* dress formally, dress up
- **ùdarati màjmuna** {VP} (lit. bang the monkey) *sl-sex* ***Obs*** masturbate, spank the monkey
- **ùdarati pèlcūg** {VP} (lit. bang a shot) *sl-sex* ***Obs*** engage in sexual intercourse with
- **ùdarati po ùšima** {VP} (lit. bang in the ears) *sl-sex* ***Obs*** masturbate, beat off
- **ùdarati sóvu** {VP} (lit. hit the owl) *sl* sleep, nap
- **ùdarati u talàmbase** {VP} (lit. beat the drums) *col* excessively spread the news

ùdaren {a, o adj.} (lit. hit) *sl-fea* ***Der*** insane, nuts <Slav*1>
- **ùdaren mòkrōm čàrapōm** {AdjP} (lit. hit with a wet sock) *sl-fea* insane, touched in the head
- **ùdaren mòkrōm kȑpōm** {AdjP} (lit. hit with a wet rag) *sl-fea* insane, touched in the head
- **ùdaren u glâvu** {AdjP} (lit. hit in head) *sl-fea* insane, touched in the head

ùdariti {rīm, rē perf.} (lit. hit) *sl-sex* ***Fac-Obs*** masturbate, beat off <Slav*1>
- **ùdariti brîs** {VP} (lit. hit erasing) *sl* run away, flee
- **ùdariti cijénu** {VP} (lit. hit a price) *col* overprice
- **ùdariti čȁvlinu** {VP} (lit. hit a big nail) *sl* dump one's boyfriend or girlfriend
- **ùdariti čȅšalj** {VP} (lit. hit the comb) **a.** *sl* obtain, get **b.i.** *sl* hit, punch **i.** *sl* beg, ask for money
- **ùdariti čvóku** {VP} (lit. hit the rap, tap) *sl-sex* ***Obs***

engage in sexual intercourse with

• **ùdariti đȍn** {VP} (lit. hit the sole) **a.** *sl* attack, strike **b.** *sl* falsely incriminate, frame

• **ùdariti farbijáner** {VP} (lit. hit a colored thing) *sl-fea* fear

• **ùdariti frȋz** {VP} (lit. hit a hairstyle) *sl* get a haircut

• **ùdariti glȁnc** {VP} (lit. hit the shine) *sl-sex* ***Obs*** engage in cunnilingus

• **ùdariti glazúru** {VP} (lit. hit the coating) *sl-sex* ***Obs*** engage in cunnilingus

• **ùdariti kéglu** {VP} (lit. hit a bowling pin) **1** *sl* the sound made by tapping, tap **2** *sl* ridicule, mock

• **ùdariti kȗrcem u lèdinu** {VP} (lit. hit one's cock on the lawn) *sl* ***Obs*** die, kick the bucket

• **ùdariti lȋru** {VP} (lit. hit lie) **a.** *sl* trick, cheat, swindle **b.** *sl* lie **c.** *sl* flirt

• **ùdariti màjmunovo** {VP} (lit. hit the monkey stuff) *sl-sex* ***Obs*** masturbate, spank the monkey

• **ùdariti mȃr** {VP} (lit. hit the beating) *sl-crime* steal, swipe

• **ùdariti mȅtak** {VP} (lit. hit a bullet) *sl-sex* ***Obs*** engage in sexual intercourse with

• **ùdariti Mòrzea** {VP} (lit. hit the Morse) *sl-sex* ***Obs*** masturbate using one finger, beat off

• **ùdariti na dȕplō gȍlo** {VP} (lit. hit at double nothing) *sl-sex* ***Obs*** meet a male homosexual

• **ùdariti nabacìnđel** {VP} (lit. hit the intruding) *sl* flirt

• **ùdariti nabacóku** {VP} (lit. hit the intruding) *sl* flirt

• **ùdariti nìtnu** {VP} (lit. hit a rivet) **a.** *sl* falsely incriminate, frame **b.** *sl-sex* ***Obs*** engage in sexual intercourse with

• **ùdariti palačínku** {VP} (lit. hit a pancake) *sl-drugs* take narcotic drugs, do drugs

• **ùdariti pèčat na prògpustnicu** {VP} (lit. hit a seal on an entrance ticket) *sl* slap, smack

• **ùdariti pȉčkōm o plàfōn** {VP} (lit. hit one's cunt on the ceiling) *sl* ***Obs*** die, kick the bucket

• **ùdariti pȉčkōm po plafónu** {VP} (lit. hit one's cunt on the ceiling) *sl-fea* ***Obs*** be nervous about something that cannot be reversed

• **ùdariti po bȁjsu** {VP} (lit. hit on the bass) *sl-sex* ***Obs*** engage in sexual intercourse with

• **ùdariti po cìferblatu** {VP} *sl-sex* ***Obs*** engage in sexual intercourse with

• **ùdariti po cilìndru** {VP} (lit. hit on the cylinder) *sl-sex* ***Obs*** engage in sexual intercourse with

• **ùdariti po glávi maslikána** {VP} (lit. hit the monkey on the head) *sl-sex* ***Obs*** masturbate, spank the monkey

• **ùdariti po kȁpslu** {VP} (lit. hit on the capsule) *sl-sex* ***Obs*** engage in sexual intercourse with

• **ùdariti po míndži** {VP} (lit. hit on the cunt) *sl-sex* ***Obs*** engage in sexual intercourse with

• **ùdariti po pȉčki** {VP} (lit. hit on the cunt) *sl-sex* ***Obs*** engage in sexual intercourse with

• **ùdariti po tàmburi** {VP} (lit. hit on the tambourine) *sl-sex* ***Obs*** engage in sexual intercourse with

• **ùdariti po ȕšima** {VP} (lit. hit on the ears) *sl-sex* ***Obs*** trick, cheat, swindle

• **ùdariti politúru** {VP} (lit. hit some polish) *sl-crime* engage in cunnilingus

• **ùdariti prȅsvlaku** {VP} (lit. hit the cover) *sl-sex* ***Obs*** steal clothing

• **ùdariti rȋg** {VP} (lit. hit a puke) *sl* vomit, throw up, puke

• **ùdariti rigolȅto** {VP} (lit. hit Rigoletto) *sl* vomit, throw up, puke

• **ùdariti rínglu** {VP} (lit. hit the stove ring) *sl-sex* ***Obs*** engage in sexual intercourse with

• **ùdariti spavánac** {VP} (lit. hit sleeping) *sl* sleep, nap

• **ùdariti spavánjac** {VP} (lit. hit sleeping) *sl* sleep, nap

• **ùdariti tušijànder** {VP} (lit. hit taking a shower) *sl* take a shower

• **ùdariti tušijáner** {VP} (lit. hit taking a shower) *sl* take a shower

• **ùdariti zvȓčku** {VP} (lit. hit rap) **a.** *col* the sound made by tapping, tap **b.** *col* ridicule, mock

• **ùdariti žȉcu** {VP} (lit. hit the wire) *col* beg, ask for money

ùdarničkā znȁčka {VP} (lit. champion worker's pin) *sl* bruise ☞ **značka**

ùdārnik {a (acc. = gen.) masc.} (lit. champion worker) *sl-fea* troublemaker, rowdy, ruffian <Slav*1>

ùdati {ām, ajū perf.} *sl* sell worthless merchandise, sell junk <Slav*1>

ȕdāv {a (acc. = gen.) masc.} (lit. python) **a.** *sl-fea* extremely talkative person, chatterbox <Slav*1> **b.** *sl-fea* boring person, bore <Slav*2> **c.** *sl-fea* stupid or mentally deficient person <Slav*3>

udávati {ùdāvām, udávajū biasp.} //ùdjēm, ùdājū imperf./ (lit. marry) *sl* sell (exchange merchandise for money) <Slav*1>

udáviti {ùdāvīm, vē perf.} (lit. strangle) *sl-fea* annoy, bother, pester <Slav*1>

ùdbāš {udbáša (acc. = gen.) masc.; Voc ȕdbāšu} *sl-polit* member of UDBA (communist secret police in the former Yugoslavia) <Abb⁘>

ùdbāškī {ā, ō adj.} *sl-polit* pertaining to communist secret police in the former Yugoslavia <Abb⁘>

ùdbić {a (acc. = gen.) masc.} **a.** *sl-polit* ***Fac*** undercover agent <Abb✍[*1]> **b.** *sl-crime* ***Fac*** detective <Abb✍[*2]>

ùdbovac {vca (acc. = gen.) masc.} *sl-polit* member of communist secret police in the former Yugoslavia <Abb❖[*1]>

ùdesiti {sīm, sē imperf.} (lit. decorate) *sl* beat up, tattoo <Slav[*1]>

udičáriti {ùdičārīm, rī imperf.} (lit. fish with a hook) *sl-crime* pick pockets <Slav❖[*1]>

ȕdlū {adj.; perm} [std. = lud] *sl-fea* ***Der*** insane, nuts <Slav✍>

udòmiti {ùdomīm, mē perf.} (lit. find a home for) *sl* sell worthless merchandise, sell junk <Slav[*1]>
- **udòmiti skakáča** {VP} (lit. find home for one's jumper) *sl-sex* ***Obs*** engage in sexual intercourse with

Udòvica {ē fem.} (lit. the Widow) Ser *sl* Beograđanka (a highrise in Belgrade, Serbia) <Slav[*1]>

ùdriskati {ām, ajū perf.} *sl* destroy, ruin

ùdriti {drīm, drē perf.} [std. = udariti] *col-dia* hit, punch <Slav✍>

udròbiti {ùdrobīm, bē perf.} (lit. soak pieces of bread in soup or stew) *sl-sex* ***Fac-Obs*** engage in sexual intercourse with (of a male) <Slav[*1]>

udvòjiti *See the following*
- **udvòjiti gȋljke** {VP} (lit. double one's legs) *sl* beat up

uđànisati {išēm, išū perf.} **a.** *sl* look, watch, scope out <Gyp❖> **b.** *sl* feel, sense <Gyp❖[*1]> **c.** *sl* understand, realize **d.** *sl* remember

uđániti {nīm, nē perf.} **a.** *sl* look, watch, scope out <Gyp❖> **b.** *sl* understand, realize <Gyp❖[*1]> **c.** *sl* remember <Gyp❖[*1]>

uđériti {rīm, rē perf.} **a.** *sl* look, watch, scope out **b.** *sl* understand, realize **c.** *sl* remember

ȕf {excl.} **1** *col* used to express hesitation, huh <Slav> **2** *col* used to express disbelief, oh, really <Slav>

ùfačkati {ām, ajū perf.} *sl* beg, ask for money <Slav>

ùfaćkati {ām, ajū perf.} *sl* catch, grab <Slav>

ufàlčovan {a, o adj.} *sl-fea* banded <Ger❖[*1]>

ùfanjati {ām, ajū perf.} *sl* catch, grab <Slav✍[*1]>

ùfatiti {tīm, tē perf.} [std. = uhvatiti] *sl* catch <Slav✍>

ùfatiti se *See the following*
- **ùfatiti se nȍgē** {VP} (lit. catch one's foot) *col* run away, flee, beat feet

ùfērčiti {čīm, čē perf.} *col* understand, realize <Ger❖[*1]>

ùfiksati se {ām, ajū perf. intr.} *sl-drugs* take narcotic drugs intravenously, mainline, shoot up <Eng❖[*1]>

ufitíljiti se {fitīljīm, fitīljē perf. intr.} *sl-fea* be conceited, be stuck-up <NE❖[*1]>

ufrekéstiti {rèkēstīm, tē perf.} *sl* freeze <Ger❖[*1]>

ufrekéstiti se {rèkēstīm, tē perf. intr.} *sl* freeze <Ger❖[*1]>

ùfrikovati {kujem, kujū perf.} *sl-fea* get frightened, get scared <Eng❖[*1]>

ufúljati se {ùfūljām, ufúljajū imperf. intr.} *sl-sex* ***Obs*** break wind, fart <Slav[*1]>

ùfur {a masc.} *sl* entrance <Ger❖[*1]>

ufúrati {ùfūrām, ufúrajū perf.} *sl* get in, enter <Ger❖[*1]>

ufúrati se {ùfūrām, ufúrajū perf. intr.} **a.** *sl-fea* force oneself on somebody <Ger❖[*1]> **b.** *sl-fea* intrude, barge in <Ger❖[*2]>

ufurávati se {ùfūrāvām, ufurávajū imperf. intr.} **1** *sl-fea* ***Der*** ingratiate, brownnose, kiss ass <Ger❖[*1]> **2a.** *sl-fea* ***Der*** force oneself on somebody <Ger❖[*1]> **b.** *sl-fea* ***Der*** intrude, barge in <Ger❖[*2]>

ufurijánović {a masc.} *sl* entrance <Ger✍>

ufurȉška {ē fem.; Dat ufurȉški} /ufurȉška/ *sl* entering <Ger✍[*1]>

ugáđati *See the following*
- **ugáđati kao čȉru na gùzici** {VP} (lit. please like the ulcer on your butt) *sl-fea* ***Obs*** please in every way

ugajbírati se {gàjbīrām, gajbírajū perf. intr.} (lit. be put in a cage) *sl* ***Fac*** get married, get hitched <Ita❖[*1]>

ùgajbiti {bīm, bē perf.} *sl-crime* imprison, put away <Ita❖[*1]>

úgaō {gla masc.} (lit. corner) *sl* one dinar; a one-dinar coin <Slav[*1]>
- **iza úgla** {PP} (lit. behind the corner) *col* secretly, under the counter

ugásiti {ùgāsīm, sē perf. intr.} (lit. turn off) **a.** *sl* die, kick the bucket <Slav[*1]> **b.** *sl* have a bad time <Slav[*2]>

ùgaziti {zīm, zē perf.} (lit. step in) *sl* beat up <Slav[*1]>

ugȉljati {ām, ajū perf.} /ugȉljati/ *sl* enter <Gyp>

ùginuti {nēm, nū perf. intr.} *sl* ***Der*** die, kick the bucket <Slav[*1]>

Ùglješa {ē masc.} /Ùglješa/ **1** *sl-fea* ***Off*** Gypsy (male) <Slav[*1]> **2** *sl-fea* ***Off*** African American (male) <Slav[*1]> **3** *sl-fea* ***Der*** nervous person, nail biter <Slav[*1]>

ùgnati {ām, ajū perf.} (lit. drive in) *sl-sex* ***Obs*** engage in sexual intercourse with (of a male) <Slav*1>

ugráditi {ùgrādīm, dē perf.} (lit. build in) *sl-sex* ***Obs*** engage in sexual intercourse with (of a male) <Slav*1>
• **ugráditi ga** {VP} (lit. install it) *sl-sex* ***Obs*** engage in sexual intercourse with

ugráditi se {dīm, dē perf. intr.} (lit. build oneself in) *sl* pay money for something (usu. for a common effort) <Slav*1>

ùgrīsti {ugrízēm, izū perf. irreg.} (lit. bite) *sl* eat, devour <Slav*1>

ùgrūhān {a, o adj.} BosM *col* having contusions (usu. from falling down), black and blue <Slav*1>

ugrúhati se {ām, ajū perf.} BosM *col* get contusions (usu. from falling down) <Slav*1>

ùgrūvān {a, o adj.} *col* with contusions (usu. from falling down), black and blue <Slav*1>

ugrúvati se {ām, ajū perf.} *col* get contusions (usu. from falling down) <Slav*1>

ugùrsuz {a (acc. = gen.) masc.} *sl-fea* troublemaker, rowdy, ruffian <NE>

ugursùzluk {a masc.} *sl-fea* rowdyism <NE>

ugúziti se {ùgūzīm, zē perf. intr.} *sl-fea* ***Der-Obs*** ingratiate, brownnose, kiss ass <Slav❖*1>

ùhā {excl.} **1** *col* used to express astonishment, wow <Slav> **2** *col* used to express relief, huh <Slav>

ùhīj {excl.} **a.** *col* the sound used when laughing at somebody <Slav> **b.** *col* the sound used to express pain or discomfort <Slav*1>

ùhkati {ām, ajū imperf.} *col* pant <Slav❖*1>

uhljebljénje {a neut.} (lit. inbreadment) *col* job, gig <Slav❖*1>

ùholaža {ē fem.} (lit. earwig) *sl-crime* ***Der*** informer, stoolie, snitch <Slav*1>

ùhoslav {a masc.} *sl* ear <Slav✍*1>

uhoslavírati {làvīrām, lavírajū imperf.} *sl* hear <Slav✍*1>

uhosláviti {uhòslāvīm, vē imperf.} *sl* hear <Slav✍*1>

ùhū {excl.} **a.** *col* the sound used when laughing at somebody <Slav> **b.** *col* the sound used to express pain or discomfort <Slav*1>

uhúkānje {a neut.} *col* hooting, jeering <Slav*1>

uhúkati {ùhūčēm, čū imperf. intr.} *col* hoot, jeer <Slav❖>

ùhvaćen {a, o adj.} (lit. caught) *sl-fea* frightened <Slav*1>

Ùhvati me za kâr! {S} (lit. Catch my prick!) *sl* ***Off*** used as a moderate curse, Fuck off! ☞ **uhvatiti**

ùhvatiti *See the following*
• **Ùhvati me za kâr!** {S} (lit. Catch my prick!) *sl* ***Off*** used as a moderate curse, Fuck off!
• **Ùhvati me za kȕrac!** {S} (lit. Catch my prick!) *col* ***Off*** used as a moderate curse, Fuck off!
• **Ùhvatila[PRON:ACC] [NOUN:NOM]** {LSF} *col* used to refer to suffering from something: *Uhvatila ga promaja pa drhti. Cold has caught him and made him shiver.*
• **Ùhvatila[PRON:ACC] zèčijā pȁmēt.** {LSF} (lit. Hare's mind has caught [PRON:ACC].) *sl-fea* used to refer to one's fleeing (usu. in fear): *Uhvatila me zečija pamet od mafioza. I ran away from the mob.*
• **Ùhvatiō[PRON:ACC] [NOUN:NOM]** {LSF} *col* used to refer to suffering from something: *Uhvatila ga nostalgija. Homesickness has suddenly got him.*
• **ùhvatiti brîs** {VP} (lit. catch some erasing) *sl* run away, flee
• **ùhvatiti drâmskī zálet** {VP} (lit. catch a dramatic run) *sl* run away, flee
• **ùhvatiti džádu** {VP} (lit. catch the road) Din *sl* run away, flee
• **ùhvatiti màglu** {VP} (lit. catch the fog) *sl* run away, flee
• **ùhvatiti máju** {VP} (lit. catch a mother) *sl-sex* ***Obs*** have an extramarital child
• **ùhvatiti prȍmaju** {VP} (lit. catch a draft) *sl-sex* ***Obs*** lose one's virginity
• **ùhvatiti rȅn** {VP} (lit. catch some horseradish) *sl* leave, depart, walk
• **ùhvatiti šȉšnjavu** {VP} (lit. catch some hissing) *sl* run away, flee
• **ùhvatiti štúru** {VP} (lit. catch some running) *sl* run away, flee
• **ùhvatiti tûtanj** {VP} (lit. catch some rumbling) *sl* run away, flee

ȕj {excl.} *col* used to drive away a crow <Slav>

ȕjā [1] {excl.} **1** *col* used to command cessation of an action, stop, enough <Slav> **2** *col* used to signal readiness (in hide-and-seek game), we are ready

ȕja [2] {ē fem.} **a.** *sl-fea* evil nature **b.** *sl-fea* outrage

úja [3] {ē masc.} (lit. uncle) SerE *sl-fea* ***Off*** Croat (person) <Slav❖*1>

újac {jca masc.} *dia-col* uncle (mother's brother) <Slav✍>

ùjārčiti {čīm, čē perf.} *sl* sell (exchange merchandise for money) <Slav❖*1>

újčevina {ē fem.} *col* mother's relatives <Slav❖*1>

ujdùrma {ē fem.} *col* intrigue: *Namestili su mu ujdurmu da ne postane direktor. They were intriguing against him to prevent him from becoming the boss.*

ujèbati {bēm, bē perf.} *sl* cheat, swindle <Slav*1>

ùjesti {edēm, edū perf. irreg.} (lit. bite) **1** *sl* eat, devour <Slav*1> 2 *sl* beat up <Slav*2>

újka {ē masc.; Dat újki} (lit. uncle) **1** *sl-fea* stupid or mentally deficient person <Slav*1> 2 *sl-fea* ***Off*** Croat (person) <Slav❖*1>

ùjkisati {išēm, išū biasp.} *sl* look, watch, scope out <Slav❖*1>

újko {a masc.} /ȕjko /e masc./ (lit. uncle) *sl-fea* ***Off*** Croat (person) <Slav❖*1>

ȗjna *See the following*

- **Ȗjne ti ga!** {S} (lit. *I screw* your aunt!) SSer *dia* ***Off*** used as a weak curse, Screw you!
- **Ȗjnu li ti jèbēm!** {S} (lit. I screw your aunt!) *col-dia* ***Off*** used as a weak curse, Screw you!
- **Ȗjnu li ti jèbēm u čàrapu!** {S} (lit. I screw your aunt in her stocking!) SSer *dia* ***Off*** used as a weak curse, Screw you!
- **Ȗjnu ti dètīnju!** {S} (lit. *I screw* your childish aunt!) SerE *dia-col* ***Off*** used as a weak curse, Screw you!
- **Ȗjnu ti tvòju!** {S} (lit. *I screw* your aunt!) *col-dia* ***Off*** used as a weak curse, Screw you!

újo {ē masc.} (lit. uncle) *sl-fea* ***Off*** Croat (person) <Slav❖*1>

ȕjū {excl.} **1** *col* help, assist <Slav> 2 *col* hurrah <Slav>

ȕjutru *See the following*

ukákiti {ùkākīm, kē perf.} *sl-sex* ***Fam*** defecate, take a dump <Ger❖*1>

ukákiti se {ùkākīm, kē perf. intr.} **a.** *sl-sex* ***Fam*** defecate in one's pants <Ger❖*1> **b.** *sl-fea* ***Fac*** be afraid <Ger❖*2>

ukàlupiti {pīm, pē perf.} (lit. mold) *sl-sex* ***Obs*** engage in sexual intercourse with (of a male) <NE❖*1>

ukàntati {ām, ajū perf.} **a.** *sl-sports* defeat <Ger❖*1> **b.** *sl-crime* kill, murder <Ger❖*2>

ukàntati se {ām, ajū perf. intr.} *sl* commit suicide <Ger❖*1>

ukapírati {kàpīrām, kapírajū perf.} *sl* understand, realize <Ita❖*1>

ukàrgoljen {a, o adj.} *sl-fea* frightened

ukargóniti {kàrgōnīm, nē perf. intr.} *sl-fea* get scared, get frightened

ukargóniti se {kàrgōnīm, nē perf. intr.} *sl-fea* get scared, get frightened

ukébati {ùkēbām, ukébajū perf.} **a.** *sl* catch **b.i.** *sl-crime* arrest **ii.** *sl-crime* kill, murder

ùkēnjān {a, o adj.} (lit. shitty) *sl-fea* ***Obs*** frightened <Slav*1>

ukénjati {ùkēnjām, ukénjajū perf.} **a.** *sl-sex* ***Obs*** defecate, shit **b.i.** *sl* ***Fac-Obs*** die, croak <Slav*2> **ii.** *sl-fea* ***Fac-Obs*** destroy, ruin <Slav*2>

ukénjati se {ùkēnjām, ukénjajū perf. intr.} **a.** *sl* defecate, shit <Slav*1> **b.** *sl-fea* get scared, get frightened <Slav*1>

ȕkfu {ùkafu masc.; perm} [std. = fuk] *sl-sex* ***Obs*** sexual intercourse <Eng⇄>

ùknjižen {a, o adj.} (lit. booked) *sl-fea* lived through <Slav*1>

ùknjižiti {žīm, žē perf.} (lit. book) **1** *sl-sex* ***Fac-Obs*** engage in sexual intercourse with (of a male) <Slav*1> 2 *sl* get married, get hitched <Slav*1>

ukočánjiti se {kòčānjīm, njē perf. intr.} *sl-fea* be very cold <Slav*1>

ukóčiti {ùkōčīm, čē perf. intr.} (lit. stiffen) *sl* die, kick the bucket <Slav*1>

ukóčiti se {ùkōčīm, čē perf. intr.} (lit. stiffen) *sl-drink* get drunk <Slav*1>

ukókati {ùkōkām, ukókajū perf.} **1** *sl-crime* kill, murder <Slav❖*1> 2 *sl-drink* drink up (alcohol) <Slav❖*1>

ukokávānje {a neut.} *sl-crime* killing <Slav❖*1>

ukòpati {ām, ajū perf.} **a.** *sl-fea* worsen somebody's situation <Slav*1> **b.** *sl-fea* ruin somebody (emotionally or financially) <Slav*2>

- **ukòpati nȍge** {VP} (lit. dig one's legs) *sl* die, kick the bucket

ukòpati se {ām, ajū perf. intr.} *sl-fea* stand in one place for a long time (usu. while waiting for someone) <Slav*1>

ukòpčati {ām, ajū perf.} (lit. turn on) *sl* understand, get it <Slav*1>

ukoràviti se *See the following*

- **Ukoràvija se ko kȕrac u prèsolac!** {S} (lit. He has turned stiff like a prick!) SSer *dia* ***Obs*** used to express disrespect, Fuck him!

ukȑcati se {ām, ajū perf. intr.} (lit. get on board) **a.** *sl* begin to flirt <Slav*1> **b.** *sl* start to meet with a group of people regularly <Slav*1>

ukrcávānje {a neut.} (lit. getting on board) *sl* flirting <Slav*1>

ukrcávati se {kȑcāvām, krcávajū imperf. intr.} (lit. get on board) *sl* flirt <Slav*1>

ukròtiti {ùkrotīm, tē perf.} (lit. tame) *sl* get a girlfriend <Slav*1>

ùkucati se {ām, ajū perf. intr.} (lit. nail oneself down) *sl-drugs* take narcotic drugs intravenously, mainline, shoot up <Slav*1>

ukucávānje {a neut.} (lit. nailing) *sl-sports* slamming (basketball, etc.) <Slav*1>

ukukurúziti se {kùrūzīm, zē perf. intr.} (lit. corn) *sl-sex* ***Obs*** have an erection <Slav❖*1>

ukùrcati {ām, ajū perf.} (lit. ukrcati, board X kurac, prick) [std. = ukrcati] *sl* ***Fac*** board (a ship, plane, etc.) <Slav✎>

ùkūrčiti se {čīm, čē perf. intr.} **a.** *sl-fea* be conceited, be stuck-up <Slav❖*1> **b.** *sl-crime* handle police investigators with dignity <Slav❖*2>

ùlār {ulára masc.} (lit. halter) **1a.** *sl* watch chain <NE*1> **b.** *sl* pocket watch <NE*2> **2** *sl* necktie <NE*1>

ulàufati se {ām, ajū perf. intr.} *sl* get in, enter <Ger❖*1>

ulèćeti {ùletīm, ùletē perf.} [std. = uletjeti] **1** *col* fly in <Slav✎> **2** *col* fly out <Slav✎*1>

ulèditi se {ùledīm, dē perf. intr.} (lit. freeze) *sl* ***Fac*** die, kick the bucket <Slav*1>

ùlēknut {a, o adj.} *sl-fea* deepened <Slav*1>

ulèma {ē fem.} BosM *col* Muslim clergy <NE>

ùlešiti se {šīm, šē perf. intr.} (lit. corpse) **1** *sl* lie down <Slav❖*1> **2** *sl-drink* get drunk, get pickled <Slav❖*1>

uletávānje {a neut.} (lit. flying in) *sl-fea* forcing oneself on somebody <Slav*1>

ulèteti {ùletīm, tē perf. intr.} (lit. fly in) SerE *sl* contribute, chip in <Slav*1>

- **ulèteti u dèčjī dodátak** {VP} (lit. run into children allowance) **1 SerE** *sl-fea* get married, get hitched **2 SerE** *sl-fea* give birth, have a baby
- **ulèteti u fàzōn** {VP} (lit. run into a trick) SerE *sl* become skilled or adept

ùletviti se {vīm, ve perf. intr.} (lit. plank) *sl-drink* get drunk <Slav❖*1>

ùlēvčiti se {čīm, čē perf. intr.} (lit. turn left) SerE *sl-drink* get drunk <Slav❖*1>

uličáriti {lìčārīm, rē imperf.} (lit. be a streetwalker) **1** *sl-sex* ***Fac*** approach females on the street in order to make acquaintance <Slav❖*1> **2** *sl-sex* ***Fac*** work as a streetwalker <Slav❖*1>

ȕličārka {ē fem.; Dat ȕličārki} (lit. streetwalker) *sl-sex* ***Fac*** prostitute, hooker <Slav*1>

ȕliti se {ȕlijēm, ijū perf. intr.} (lit. pour oneself in) *sl-drink* get drunk <Slav*1>

úlog {a masc.} /úlog/ (lit. deposit) *sl* money <Slav*1>

ùlokviti {vīm, vē perf.} (lit. pond) *sl-sex* ***Fac-Obs*** urinate <Slav❖*1>

ùlokviti se {vīm, vē perf. intr.} (lit. pond oneself) *sl-sex* ***Fac-Obs*** urinate <Slav❖*1>

ulòviti *See the following*

- **ulòviti zêca** {VP} (lit. catch a rabbit) *sl-sex* ***Obs*** get pregnant, the rabbit died

ulóviti se {ùlōvīm, vē perf. intr.} (lit. cash oneself) *sl* make a considerable amount of money <Gyp❖>

ùluzati {ām, ajū perf.} (lit. English lose with the s-cr prefix u) *sl-crime* kill, murder <Eng❖*1>

ûlje {a masc.} (lit. oil) *sl* money <Slav*1>

- **têškō úlje** {NP} (lit. heavy oil) *sl-drink* 40 proof brandy

uljèpšati {ām, ajū perf.} (lit. beautify) *sl* beat up <Slav*1>

ûm *See the following*

- **kȍntra ûma** {PP} (lit. against the mind) *sl* headache: *pilula kontra uma headache pill*

ùmagliti {līm, lē perf.} (lit. fog in) *sl* drive away, drive off <Slav❖*1>

ùmagliti se {līm, lē perf. intr.} (lit. fog oneself in) *sl* leave, depart, walk <Slav❖*1>

ùmak {a masc.} (lit. dip) *sl-sex* ***Obs*** sexual intercourse <Slav*1>

umákānje {a neut.} (lit. dipping) **1** *sl* kissing <Slav*1> **2** *sl-sex* quick sexual intercourse, quickie <Slav*1>

ùmetan {tna, tno adj.} (lit. insertive) *sl-fea* skillful <Slav*1>

ùmetnīk {a (acc. = gen.) masc.} (lit. artist X umetnuti 'insert') **1** *sl-fea* intruder <Slav*1> **2a.** *sl-sex* male sexual partner (of a female) <Slav*1> **b.** *sl* lover (male) <Slav*2>

ùmirānje {a neut.} (lit. dying) *sl* laughing <Slav*1>

ùmirati {rēm, rū imperf.} (lit. die) *sl* laugh <Slav*1>

umíriti {ùmīrīm, ùmīrē perf.} (lit. tranquilize) *sl* beat up <Slav*1>

ȕmīt {a, o adj.} (lit. with one's face washed) [std. = umiven] *sl* washed <Slav✎>

ùmjetnō gnȍjīvo {NP} (lit. artificial fertilizer) Cro *sl-drugs* drug addict, junkie ☞ gnojivo

umlátiti {tīm, tē perf.} (lit. thrash) *sl* beat up, crush, trash <Slav❖*1>

ȕmobōlan {lna, lno adj.} (lit. mind-sick) *sl-fea* the most beautiful <Slav*1>

umòčiti {ùmočīm, čē perf.} (lit. dip in) *sl-sex* ***Fac-Obs*** engage in sexual intercourse with (of a male) <Slav*1>

umòčiti se {čīm, čē perf. intr.} (lit. dip oneself) **1** *sl-fea* be in a difficult situation <Slav*1> **2a.** *sl-sex* engage in sexual intercourse with (of a male) <Slav*1> **b.** *sl-sex* engage in quick sexual intercourse with (of a male), have a quickie <Slav*2> **3** *sl* destroy, ruin <Slav*1>

ùmor {a masc.} /úmor/ *col* fatigue <Slav>

ȕmōran *See the following*
- **mȑtav ȕmōran** {AdjP} *sl-fea* very tired, dead tired

ùmr̄kati se {ām, ajū perf. intr.} *sl-drink* get drunk <Slav*1>

umtaràsa {ē fem.} *sl* female

umúliti se {ùmūlīm, lē perf. intr.} *sl-fea* be in a bad mood <Slav*1>

umúsiti se {ùmūsīm, sē perf. intr.} *sl-fea* be in a bad mood <Slav*1>

ùmuvati se {ām, ajū perf. intr.} *sl-fea* force oneself in <Slav✣*1>

ȗn {pron.} [std. = on] *dia* he <Slav✍>

ùnāj {pron.} [std. = onaj] *dia* that <Slav✍>

ùncut {a (acc. = gen.) masc.} *sl-fea* crook, thief <Ger*1>

ȕnča {ē fem.} **a.** *sl* apartment **b.** *sl* home

úndā {adv.} [std. = onda] *dia* then <Slav✍>

ȕndža {ē fem.} **a.** *sl* apartment **b.** *sl* house, home

ȕndža-vàla {ē fem.} *sl-crime* breaking into an apartment

ùndžān {undžána masc.} *sl* store

ùndžāroš {a (acc. = gen.) masc.} **a.** *sl-crime* burglar **b.** *sl-crime* thief who works a railroad station

ȕnđa {ē fem.} *sl* house, home

ùnđāroš {a (acc. = gen.) masc.} **a.** *sl-crime* burglar **b.** *sl-crime* thief who works a railroad station

ueréditi {nèrēdīm, dē perf.} (lit. make a mess) *sl-sex* defecate <Slav*1>

unerédíti se {nèrēdīm, dē perf. intr.} (lit. make a mess of oneself) **1** *sl-sex* defecate <Slav*1> **2** *sl-sex* get drunk, get messed up <Slav*1>

unervóziti se {nèrvōzīm, zē perf. intr.} *sl-fea* get nervous <Lat✣*1>

unezgóditi {nèzgōdīm, dē perf.} *col* cause inconvenience to somebody <Sla>

unezvériti se {nèzvērīm, rē perf. intr.} /unèzveriti se/ *sl-fea* go insane, freak out <Slav*1>

ùnīći {ùnīđem, īđu, uníđ, ùniš perf. irreg.} [std. = ući] *col-dia* enter <Slav✍>

uništávati {nìštāvām, ništávajū imperf.} (lit. destroy) *sl* eat, devour <Slav*1>

uništávati ždȇr {VP} (lit. destroy devouring) *sl* eat, devour ☞ žder

ùništiti *See the following*
- **ùništiti u drȕgī kànāl** {VP} (lit. destroy in the second channel) *sl-sex* ***Obs*** anal sexual intercourse

ȕniverzalnā operácija {NP} (lit. universal operation) *sl-fea* very clumsy person, complete klutz ☞ operacija

únka {ē fem.; Dat únki} *sl* dog (the animal) <NE*1>

ȕnkta {ē masc.} *sl* dog (the animal) <NE*1>

unóšiti se {šīm, še perf. intr.} (lit. potty oneself) *sl-fea* have fear <Slav✣*1>

unprofórac {rca (acc. = gen.) masc.} *col* a member of the UN protection forces in Bosnia in 1990s <Abb*1>

unprofúrac {rca (acc. = gen.) masc.} *col-dia* a member of the UN protection forces in Bosnia in 1990s <Abb✍*1>

ȕnta {ē fem.} *sl* dog (the animal) <NE*1>

ùnuče {eta neut.} (lit. grandchild) *sl-drink* small drinking bottle <Slav*1>

unučȉnja {ē fem.} SSer *dia* grand-daughter <Slav✍>

ùnūtra {adv.} (lit. inside) *sl-crime* in prison, behind the bars <Slav*1>

unútri {adv.} [std. = unutra] *dia* inside <Slav✍>

unútrima {adv.} [std. = unutra] *dia* inside <Slav✍>

ȕnjkati {ām, ajū perf. intr.} *col* mispronounce (usu. with additional nasal articulation) <Slav*1>

uokvíriti *See the following*
- **uokvíriti kùtiju** {VP} (lit. frame one's box) *sl-fea* get a haircut

uòlafiti se {fīm, fē perf. intr.} **1** *sl-drink* drink too much (alcohol) **2** *sl-drugs* overdose (on drugs)

uortáčiti se {čīm, čē perf. intr.} *col* become partners <NE✣*1>

úpad {a masc.} *sl* going out (to a restaurant, movies, etc.) <Slav*1>

upáliti {ùpālīm, lē perf.} (lit. burn) **a.** *sl* succeed, make it <Slav*1> **b.i.** *sl-sex* engage in sexual intercourse with (of a male) <Slav*2> **ii.** *sl-crime* steal, swipe <Slav*2>

upáliti se *See the following*

- **Upálila[PRON:DAT]** se lámpa. {S} (lit. His lamp has lit.) *sl* used to indicate that somebody has understood something, The light went on!
- **Upálila[PRON:DAT]** se làmpica. {S} (lit. His little lamp has lit.) *sl* used to indicate that somebody has understood something, The light went on!
- **Upálila[PRON:DAT]** se sȉjalica. {S} (lit. His little lamp has lit.) *sl* used to indicate that somebody has understood something, The light went on!

ùpanuti {nēm, nū perf. intr.} [std. = pasti] *col-dia* fall down, kiss the floor <Slav☞>

ùpasti {adnēm, adnū a perf. irreg.} *col* enter <Slav*1>

- **ùpasti u mrȉžu** {VP} (lit. drop into a net) Med *sl-fea* fall in love

ùpecati {ām, ajū perf.} (lit. fish) **1** *sl-crime* steal, swipe <Slav*1> **2** *sl* catch, grab <Slav*1> **3** *sl-crime* imprison, put away <Slav*1>

ùpecati se {ām, ajū perf. intr.} (lit. catch oneself) *sl-fea* fall in love <Slav*1>

ùpeći {eknēm, eknū, ek, ek perf. irreg.} *col* be extremely hot (of the outdoor temperature) <Slav*1>

upériti {ùpērim, rē perf.} /upèriti/ *col* point <Slav>

upicániti se {nīm, nē perf. intr.} *sl-fea* dress formally, dress up <Slav❖*1>

upìcānjen {a, o adj.} *sl-fea* dressed formally, dressed up <Slav❖*1>

upíciti {ùpīcīm, cē perf.} (lit. cunt in) *sl-fea* mature (of women) <Slav❖*1>

ùpičkiti {kīm, kē perf.} (lit. cunt up) *sl* destroy, ruin <Slav❖*1>

upìjača {ē fem.} (lit. absorber) *sl-drugs* opium product <Slav*1>

ùpīsān {a, o adj.} (lit. registered) *sl-fea* lived through <Slav*1>

ùpiš {a masc.} *sl-fea* ridiculous thing, absurd event <Slav❖*1>

upišàljče {eta neut.} (lit. pisser) *sl-fea* child, kid <Slav❖*1>

ȕpišān {a, o adj.} *sl-sex* ***Obs*** urinated on <Slav>

upišànče {eta neut.} (lit. urinator) *sl-fea* child, kid <Slav❖*1>

upišaníče {eta neut.} (lit. pisser) *sl-fea* child, kid <Slav❖*1>

upišànīk {šaníka (acc. = gen.) masc.} *sl-sex* ***Obs*** urinator , pisser <Slav❖*1>

upišánko {a (acc. = gen.) masc.} **a.** *sl-sex* ***Obs*** urinator, pisser <Slav❖*1> **b.** *sl-fea* ***Der-Obs*** coward, chicken <Slav❖*2>

upìšati {ām, ajū perf.} *sl-fea* urinate <Slav>

upišávānje {a neut.} (lit. urinating) **a.** *sl-fea* ridiculous thing, absurd event <Slav*1> **b.** *sl-fea* making laugh <Slav*2>

upišávati se {pìšāvām, pišávajū imperf. intr.} (lit. urinate) *sl-fea* find something highly humorous <Slav*1>

upìšulja {ē fem.} **a.** *sl-sex* ***Obs*** urinator, pisser <Slav❖*1> **b.** *sl-fea* ***Der-Obs*** female child, girl <Slav❖*2>

ùplakati se {ačēm, ačū perf. intr.} //ām, ajū perf. intr./ (lit. cry) **a.** *sl* make a mistake, screw up <Slav*1> **b.** *sl* lose <Slav*2>

upljùvati se {ùpljūjēm, ùpljūjū perf. intr.} (lit. spit oneself) *sl-fea* talk persistently and meaninglessly, blabber, chatter <Slav*1>

upokòjiti {upòkojīm, jē perf.} (lit. tranquilize) *sl* kill, neutralize <Slav*1>

upokòjiti se {upòkojīm, jē perf. intr.} (lit. tranquilize) *sl* ***Fac*** die, kick the bucket <Slav*1>

ȕprav {adv.} [std. = upravo] *col* exactly, precisely <Slav☞>

upražnjávati *See the following*

- **upražnjávati krȁvu** {VP} (lit. use a cow) *sl-fea* have very tidy hair

upȑditi {ùprdīm, dē perf. intr.} (lit. fart in) **a.** *sl-sex* ***Obs*** break wind frequently <Slav*1> **b.** *sl-crime* ***Der-Obs*** kill, murder <Slav*2>

uprimpícu {adv.} (lit. in cuntiple; u principu, in principle X pica, cunt) [std. = u principu] *sl* ***Fac*** in principle <Lat☞>

upropástiti {pròpāstīm, tē perf.} (lit. destroy) *sl* intimidate, frighten <Slav*1>

upŕskati {ùpr̄skām, upŕskajū perf.} (lit. bespatter) **a.** *sl* miss, fail <Slav*1> **b.** *sl-fea* destroy, ruin <Slav*2>

ùpucati {ām, ajū perf.} (lit. shoot) **1** *sl-fea* intrude, barge in <Slav*1> **2** *sl-crime* kill, murder <Slav*1>

upucávati se {pùcāvām, pucávajū imperf. intr.} **1** *sl* decide <Slav*1> **2** *sl-crime* shoot at each other <Slav*1>

upúvati se {ùpūvām, púvajū imperf. intr.} *sl-sex* break wind, fart <Slav*1>

ȗra {ē fem.} /ȗra/ Med *col* hour <Ger>

uráditi {ùrādīm, ùrādē perf.} (lit. do) *col* rob, fleece, rip off: *Uradili su stan za deset minuta. They cleaned the apartment in ten minutes.* <Slav*1>

urámiti {ùrāmīm, mē perf.} (lit. frame) *sl* ***Fac*** get married, get hitched <Slav*1>

urànista {ē masc.} *sl-sex* ***Der*** male homosexual, gay <Gre>

urésiti se {ùrēsīm, sē perf. intr.} (lit. dress up, decorate oneself) *sl-drink* get very drunk, get smashed <Slav*1>

ȗrica {ē fem.} /ȕrica/ *col* clock, watch <Ger*1>

urìnisati {išēm, išū biasp.} *sl-sex* ***Fac*** urinate, pee <Lat⁘*1> *sl*

ùrlati {ām, ajū imperf.} *col* scream in pain, fear, or outrage <Ita>

urlíkalo {a neut.} *sl-music* singer <Ita⁘*1>

ùrnisati {išēm, išū biasp.} **a.** *col* destroy, ruin <Lat*1> **b.** *col* beat up <Lat*2>

ùrok {a masc.} *sl-fea* black magic <Slav*1>

urókati {ùrōkām, urókajū perf.} *sl-crime* kill, murder <Slav⁘*1>

urókati se {ùrōkām, urókajū perf. intr.} **1** *sl-drink* get drunk <Slav⁘*1> 2 *sl-drugs* take narcotic drugs, do drugs

uróljati se {ùrōljām, uróljajū perf. intr.} *sl-drink* get drunk <Slav*1>

ȕrvina {ē fem.} *dia* valley <Slav>

ùrviz {a masc.} *sl-drink* wine

ȕsa {excl.} *col* used to drive away a pig <Slav>

usáditi se {dīm, dē perf. intr.} (lit. plant oneself in) *sl* be in one particular position <Slav*1>

ùsaftati se {ām, ajū perf. intr.} (lit. be in the sauce) *sl-fea* sweat <Ger⁘*1>

usafùnjati se {ām, ajū perf. intr.} (lit. soap oneself) *sl-fea* smell, stink <Slav⇗*1>

usàhnuti {nēm, nū perf. intr.} (lit. wither) *sl* die, kick the bucket <Slav*1>

userávānje {a neut.} (lit. shitting) *sl-fea* fear <Slav*1>

usidjèlica {ē fem.} *sl-fea* elderly unmarried female <Slav*1>

ùsidriti *See the following*

- **ùsidriti čàktar** {VP} (lit. anchor one's prick) *sl-sex* ***Obs*** engage in sexual intercourse with

ùsidriti se {rīm, rē perf. intr.} (lit. throw anchor) **1** *sl* stand in one place for a long time (usu. while waiting for someone), drop anchor <Slav*1> 2 *sl* date the same female for a long time <Slav*1>

ùsijanā gláva {NP} (lit. a glowing head) *sl-fea* quick-tempered or impetuous person, hothead ☞ **glava**

usijávānje {a neut.} (lit. glowing) *sl-fea* anger <Slav*1>

ùsis {a masc.} *sl-auto* suction <Slav>

uskòkuša {ē fem.} (lit. the jump-in one) *sl* loafer (shoe) <Slav⁘*1>

uskopístiti se {kòpīstīm, tē perf. intr.} *sl-fea* be stubborn, be defiant <Slav*1>

uskopízditi se {kòpīzdīm, dē perf. intr.} *sl-fea* be stubborn, be defiant <Slav*1>

ùskurac {adv.} (lit. up the prick) *sl* in spite of everything <Slav*1>

ùskūrčiti se {čīm, čē perf. intr.} *sl-fea* be stubborn, be defiant <Slav*1>

ȕsmenī {ōg (acc. = gen.) masc.} (lit. oral *exam*) *sl-sex* ***Fac-Obs*** fellatio <Slav*1>

usmerávati *See the following*

- **usmerávati na sȅver i zâpad** {VP} (lit. direct to the north and the west) **SerE** *sl-crime* take photos in prison

usmerènjāk {renjáka (acc. = gen.) masc.} **SerE** *sl-sstu* high-school student after the school reform in the 1970s in the former Yugoslavia <Slav⁘*1>

usmjerènjāk {renjáka (acc. = gen.) masc.} *sl-sstu* high-school student after the school reform in the 1970s in the former Yugoslavia <Slav⁘*1>

ȕsna *See the following*

- **vrȅlā ȕsna** {NP} (lit. hot lip) *sl* female

ùsnāći {ā masc. pl.} *dia* mustache <Slav⁘*1>

usósiti {ùsōsīm, sē perf.} (lit. sauce) *sl* give somebody a hard time <Fre⁘*1>

usósiti se {ùsōsīm, sē perf. intr.} (lit. be in th sauce) *sl* get into problems <Fre⁘*1>

uspávati {ùspāvām, uspávajū perf.} (lit. put to sleep) *sl* beat up <Slav*1>

úsra {ē fem.} *sl-fea* ***Der*** dirty and untidy female, slob <Slav⁘*1>

ȕsrān {a, o adj.} **a.** *sl-sex* ***Obs*** defecated on, shitty <Slav> **b.** *sl-fea* ***Der-Obs*** worthless <Slav*1> **c.** *sl-fea* ***Der-Obs*** insane, nuts <Slav*2>

usrànica {ē fem.} (lit. shitter) *sl-fea* ***Der*** dirty and untidy female, slob <Slav⁘*1>

ùsranīk {usraníka (acc. = gen.) masc.} (lit. shitter) *sl-fea* ***Der*** dirty and untidy male, slob <Slav⁘*1>

usránko {a (acc. = gen.) masc.} (lit. shitter) **a.** *sl-fea* ***Der*** dirty and untidy male, slob <Slav❖*1> **b.** *sl-fea* ***Der*** coward, chicken <Slav❖*2>

ȕsrati {serēm, serū perf.} **a.** *sl-sex* ***Obs*** defecate, shit <Slav> **b.i.** *sl-fea* ***Der-Obs*** destroy, ruin <Slav*1> **ii.** *sl* ***Obs*** beat up <Slav*1>

- **ȕsrati mȍtku** {VP} (lit. shit a stick) *sl-fea* destroy, ruin

ȕsrati se {serēm, serū perf. intr.} **a.** *sl-sex* ***Obs*** defecate in one's pants <Slav> **b.** *sl-fea* ***Obs*** get frightened, get scared <Slav*1>

ȕsrećiti {ćīm, ćē perf.} (lit. make happy) **1** *sl-sex* ***Fac-Obs*** engage in sexual intercourse with <Slav*1> **2** *sl-fea* ***Iro*** cause problems <Slav*1>

úsro {a masc.} /le masc./ **1** *sl-fea* ***Der-Obs*** coward, chicken <Slav❖*1> **2** *sl-fea* dirty and untidy male, slob <Slav❖*1>

ústa *See the following*

- **U ústa te blȃženā!** {S} (lit. *I fuck* you in your beatified mouth!) *col-dia* ***Off*** used as a strong curse, Fuck you!
- **U ústa te jèbēm!** {S} (lit. I fuck you in your mouth!) *col* ***Off*** used as a strong curse, Fuck you!
- **U ústa te kȑvavā!** {S} (lit. *I fuck* you in your bloody mouth!) *col-dia* ***Off*** used as a strong curse, Fuck you!
- **U ústa te mȓtvā!** {S} (lit. *I fuck* you in your dead mouth!) *col-dia* ***Off*** used as a strong curse, Fuck you!
- **U ústa te pòganā jèbēm!** {S} (lit. I fuck you in your dirty mouth!) *col-dia* ***Off*** used as a strong curse, Fuck you!
- **U ústa te pòkvārenā jèbēm!** {S} (lit. I fuck you in your rotten mouth!) *col-dia* ***Off*** used as a strong curse, Fuck you!

ustánca *See the following*

- **U ustánca te jèbēm!** {S} (lit. I fuck you in your small mouth!) *dia-col* ***Off*** used as a strong curse, Fuck you!

ȕstaša {ē masc.} (lit. Ustasha *a member of Croatian nazi troops during WWII*) *sl-fea* ***Off*** Croat (person) <Slav*1>

ustašòīd {ustašoída (acc. = gen.) masc.} *sl-fea* follower of Ustasha (Croatian nazi) ideology <Slav❖>

ȕstašoīdan {dna, dno adj.} *sl-fea* Ustasha-like (Croatian nazi) <Slav❖>

ustašoídnōst {i fem.} *sl-fea* being Ustasha-like (Croatian Nazi during World War II) <Slav❖>

ustondírati se {tòndīrām, tondírajū perf. intr.} *sl-drugs* get intoxicated on narcotic drugs, get high <Eng❖*1>

ustréliti {ȕstrēlīm, lē perf.} (lit. shoot with bow and arrow) *sl* find incidentally <Slav*1>

ȕstrēljen {a, o adj.} (lit. shot with an arrow) *sl-fea* in love <Slav*1>

ustrtáriti se {tȑtārīm, rē perf. intr.} *sl-fea* get frightened, get scared <Slav❖*1>

ȕš {excl.} *col* used to drive away various animals <Slav>

ȕša {excl.} *col* used to drive away various animals <Slav>

ušȁče {eta neut.} *dia* young donkey <Slav❖*1>

ušȁltati se {ām, ajū perf. intr.} *sl* stay with somebody, stick with somebody <Ger❖*1>

ušapírati {šȁpīrām, šapírajū perf.} *sl-crime* steal, swipe <Fre❖*1>

ušapíriti {šȁpīrīm, rē perf.} *sl-crime* steal, swipe <Fre❖*1>

ušárati {ȕšārām, ušárajū perf.} *sl* write down, jot down <Slav❖*1>

ušárati se {ȕšārām, ušárajū perf. intr.} *sl* put one's name on a list <Slav❖*1>

ȕšarnūt {a, o adj.} *sl-crime* under police surveillance <Slav❖*1>

ušȁtafiti {fīm, fē perf.} *sl-crime* resell, fence

ušćȁknuti {ȕšćaknēm, nū perf.} Bos *col* hurt, feel pains (in one's back)

ȕše {excl.} *col* quick <Slav>

ušémiti se {ȕšēmīm, ȕšēmē perf. intr.} (lit. get into a scheme) *sl* start dating a female or male: *Ušemio se s Marijom čim ju je sreo. He started to date Marija as soon as he met her.* <Lat❖*1>

ušíkati se {ȕšīkām, ušíkajū perf. intr.} *sl-drink* get drunk <Slav❖*1>

ušíljiti se {ȕšīljīm, ljē perf. intr.} (lit. become pointed) *sl-fea* lose weight <Slav*1>

ušimicvòkliti se {līm, lē perf. intr.} *sl-fea* dress formally, dress up <Slav✍*1>

ȕšinuti {nēm, nū perf.} *col* twist, sprain (arm, ankle, etc.) <Slav*1>

ȕšiti {ȕšijēm, ijū perf.} (lit. mend) **1** *sl-sports* defeat <Slav*1> **2** *sl-auto* overtake (pass another car on the road) <Slav*1> **3** *sl* answer, respond <Slav*1>

ušlogírati se {šlògīrām, šlogírajū perf. intr.} *sl-fea* faint <Ger❖*1>

ȕšljakati {ām, ajū perf.} *sl-crime* steal, swipe <Slav*1>

ùšljakati se {ām, ajū perf. intr.} *sl* join, take part in <Slav*1>

ušljéviti se {ùšljēvīm, vē perf. intr.} *sl-sex* ***Obs*** urinate in one's pants <Slav❖*1>

ùšljiskati se {ām, ajū perf. intr.} *sl-drink* get drunk <Slav❖*1>

ušljíviti {ùšljīvīm, vē perf.} (lit. plum) *sl* hit, punch <Slav❖*1>

ušljókati se {ùšljōkām, ušljókajū perf. intr.} *sl-drink* get drunk <Slav❖*1>

ùšmekati {ām, ajū perf. intr.} *sl* notice, observe: *Ušmekao je slobdan sto. He noticed a free table.* <Ger❖*1>

ušnīrati *See the following*

- **ušnírati pȉčku** {VP} (lit. tie one's cunt) *sl* ***Obs*** shut up, cease talking

ȕšnuti {nēm, nū perf.} (lit. ear) *sl* whisper <Slav❖*1>

ušórati {ùšōrām, ušórajū perf.} *sl* beat up severely <Slav❖*1>

ušórati se {ùšōrām, ušórajū perf. intr.} **a.** *sl-sex* ***Obs*** urinate in one's pants <Slav❖*1> **b.** *sl-fea* ***Obs*** get frightened, get scared <Slav❖*2>

ušpárati {ùšpárām, ušpárajū perf.} *col* save money, sock money away: *ušparati hiljadu maraka save a thousand German marks* <Ger>

ùštafiti {tīm, tē perf.} *sl* take out a mortgage (house, etc.)

ùštekati {ām, ajū perf.} **a.** *col* plug in (e.g. an electronic device) <Ger❖> **b.i.** *col* turn on (radio, tv, etc.) <Ger❖*1> **ii.** *sl-sex* engage in sexual intercourse with (of a male) <Ger❖*1> **iii.** *sl* understand, get clued in, be plugged in <Ger❖*1>

ȕštimati {ām, ajū perf.} **a.** *col* tune, adjust, fix <Ger❖> **b.** *col* coordinate <Ger❖*1>

uštimávati {tìmāvām, timávajū imperf.} *col* tune, adjust, fix <Ger❖>

ùštīrkān {a, o adj.} (lit. starched) *sl-fea* dressed formally, dressed up <Ger❖*1>

uštirkánko {a masc.} (lit. the starched one) *sl-fea* formally dressed male <Ger❖*1>

ùštītkān {a, o adj.} (lit. starched) **a.** *sl-fea* stiff <Ger✍*1> **b.** *sl-fea* conceited, stuck-up <Ger✍*2>

ùštogljen {a, o adj.} **a.** *sl-fea* formal **b.** *sl-fea* dressed up

ùštopati {ām, ajū perf.} **a.** *sl-sports* stop, block (soccer ball, etc.) <Ger❖> **b.** *col* mend (garment) <Ger❖*1>

ùštopovati {pujēm, pujū perf.} **a.** *sl-sports* stop, block (soccer ball, etc.) <Ger❖> **b.** *col* mend (garment) <Ger❖*1>

ȕštva {ē fem.} *sl-fea* ***Der*** worthless or despicable person <Slav*1>

ùšutati se {tām, tajū perf. intr.} (lit. get silent) *sl-drink* get drunk <Slav*1>

ȕt {a (acc. = gen.) +ov (ext. pl) masc.; Nom Pl ùtovi} *sl-arch* king

utàbaniti {nīm, nē perf.} *sl* tame <NE❖*1>

utábati {ùtābām, utábajū perf.} **/ùtabati/** **a.** *sl* beat up severely <NE❖*1> **b.** *sl-crime* kill, murder <NE❖*2>

utàmbati {ām, ajū perf.} *sl-crime* kill, murder <NE✍*1>

utánjiti {ùtānjīm, njē perf.} (lit. get thinner) **1** *sl-fea* be broke, be out of money <Slav*1> **2** *sl* sell (exchange merchandise for money) <Slav*1> **3** *sl* spend (money, property, etc.) <Slav*1>

utápati {ùtāpām, utápajū imperf. intr.} (lit. drown) *sl-crime* resell, fence <Slav*1>

- **utápati vréme** {VP} (lit. drown one's time) **SerE** *sl-fea* spend one's time in useless activities, fool around, mess around
- **utápati vrijéme** {VP} (lit. drown one's time) *sl-fea* spend one's time in useless activities, fool around, mess around

utápljati {ùtāpljām, utápljajū biasp.} *sl* sell (exchange merchandise for money) <Slav*1>

- **utápljati vrijème** {VP} (lit. drown one's time) *sl-fea* spend one's time in useless activities, fool around, mess around

ȕteče prâse {VP} (lit. the pig will run away) *sl-fea* used to indicate that the room will cool off (usu. when one opens a door or a window in the winter) ☞ **uteći**

ùteći {eknēm, eknū, ek, ek perf. irreg.} *col-dia* run away, flee <Slav*1>

- **ȕteče prâse** {VP} (lit. the pig will run away) *sl-fea* used to indicate that the room will cool off (usu. when one opens a door or a window in the winter)

ùtēntati {ām, ajū perf. intr.} **1** *sl* die, kick the bucket <Lat❖*1> **2** *sl* arrange for <Lat❖*1>

utépati {ùtépām, ajū perf.} *sl-crime* kill, murder <Slav❖*1>

ùterati *See the following*

- **Ùterām ti ga!** {S} (lit. I stick it to you!) SerE *col-dia* ***Off*** used as a moderate curse, Fuck you!
- **Ùterām ti mâjci!** {S} (lit. I stick it to your mother!) SerE *dia-col* ***Off*** used as a strong curse, Fuck you!

ùtiti se {tīm, tē perf. intr.} *sl-drink* get drunk <Slav*1>

ȕtnuti {nēm, nū perf.} *sl-sex* ***Obs*** engage in sexual intercourse with (of a male) <Slav*1>

ùtok {a masc.} *sl-crime* gun, pistol

ȕtoka {ē fem.; Dat ȕtoki} *sl-crime* gun, pistol

utòpiti {ùtopīm, pē perf.} (lit. drown) **1** *sl* sell (exchange merchandise for money) <Slav*1> **2** *sl* destroy, ruin <Slav*1>

• **utòpiti na kȍntu** {VP} (lit. drown on one's account) *sl* sell on credit

útōrnīk {a masc.} [std. = utorak] *col* Tuesday <Slav✍>

ùtrampiti {pīm, pē perf.} *col* sell using persuasion <NE❖*1>

• **ùtrampiti jêža** {VP} (lit. give a hedgehog) *sl* trick, cheat, swindle

• **utràmpiti šȁmar gȁćama** {VP} (lit. give a slap to one's underpants) *sl-sex* ***Obs*** masturbate, beat off

ùtrapiti {pīm, pē perf.} **a.** *col* give something unwanted <Slav❖*1> **b.** *col* sell (exchange merchandise for money) <Slav❖*2> **c.** *sl* cash (a check, etc.) <Slav❖*3>

utȑčati {ùtrčīm, čē perf.} (lit. run in) **1** *sl* contribute, chip in <Slav*1> **2** *sl-fea* be trapped, be without a way out <Slav*1> **3** *sl* understand, get it <Slav*1>

utrčávati {tȑčāvām, trčávajū imperf.} (lit. run in) **1** *sl* blame, accuse <Slav*1> **2** *sl-fea* flirt <Slav*1> **3** *sl* boast, brag <Slav*1>

• **utrčávati kao tvȍr kad mu dûnēš pod rêp** {VP} (lit. run in like a skunk when you under below his tail) *sl-fea* boast, brag

ùtripovati {pujēm, pujū perf. intr.} *sl* have false expectations, just think: *Utripovala je da će otići u Ameriku. She only thinks she is going to the States.* <Eng❖*1>

utróljati se {ùtrōljām, utróljajū perf. intr.} *sl-fea* get frightened, get scared <Slav✍*1>

utrónjati se {ùtrōnjām, utrónjajū perf. intr.} *sl-fea* get frightened, get scared <Slav✍*1>

utȑpati se {ām, ajū perf. intr.} **1** *col* join or force one's way into a group of people <Slav*1> **2** *sl* start dating a female <Slav*1>

utucávati {tùcāvām, tucávajū imperf.} (lit. crush) *sl-fea* talk persistently and meaninglessly, blabber, chatter <Slav❖*1>

utúviti {ùtūvīm, vē perf.} **a.** *sl* remember <Slav*1> **b.** *sl* learn <Slav*2>

• **utúviti ȕ glāvu** {VP} (lit. push into *some*one's head) **1** *col* teach **2** *col* learn

ȕū {excl.} **1** *col* used in searching in hide-and-seek <Slav> **2** *col* the sound used to express the feeling of being cold <Slav>

uvaćáriti {vàćārīm, rē perf. intr.} (lit. catch around) *sl-fea* get some kind of profit: *Uvaćario je na promeni vlasti. He profited from the change of regime.* <Slav✍*1>

uvalàkāč {lakáča (acc. = gen.) masc.} *sl-fea* ***Der*** ingratiator (male), brownnoser, ass kisser <Slav❖*1>

uvalakáčević {a (acc. = gen.) masc.} *sl-fea* ***Der*** ingratiator (male), brownnoser, ass kisser <Slav❖*1>

uváliti {ùvālīm, lē perf.} (lit. insert) **1** *sl-sex* ***Obs*** engage in sexual intercourse with (of a male) <Slav*1> **2a.** *sl* sell worthless merchandise, sell junk <Slav*1> **b.** *sl* persuade, convince <Slav*2> **c.** *sl* cheat, swindle <Slav*3> **d.** *sl* falsely incriminate, frame <Slav*4>

• **uváliti dȉvča žváku** {VP} (lit. give wild bubblegum) *sl* lie

• **uváliti jèzik** {VP} (lit. insert one's tongue) *sl* French kiss

• **uváliti jèzičinu** {VP} (lit. insert one's big tongue) *sl* French kiss

• **uváliti ludáka** {VP} (lit. insert one's fool) *sl-sex* ***Obs*** engage in sexual intercourse with

• **uváliti lȕdoja** {VP} (lit. insert one's fool) *sl-sex* ***Obs*** engage in sexual intercourse with

• **uváliti máru** {VP} (lit. insert some beating) *sl* beat up

• **uváliti pàkēt** {VP} (lit. insert a package) *sl-gamble* trick, cheat, swindle

• **uváliti vrûć kròmpir** {VP} (lit. give a hot potato) *col* pass a problem to somebody else, pass a hot potato

• **uváliti žváku** {VP} (lit. insert bubblegum) *sl* lie

uváliti se {ùvālīm, lē imperf. intr.} **1** *col* get into problems <Slav*1> **2** *sl-fea* intrude, barge in <Slav*1>

uváljati {ùvāljām, uváljajū perf.} (lit. roll) *sl* sell worthless merchandise, sell junk <Slav*1>

uvaljivanje {a neut.} *col* insertion <Slav*1>

uvaljívati {ām, ajū imperf.} //vàljujēm, vàljujū imperf./ (lit. insert) *sl* sell worthless merchandise, sell junk <Slav*1>

• **uvaljívati dȉvča žváku** {VP} (lit. keep inserting wild bubblegum) *sl* lie

• **uvaljívati pȁške** {VP} **a.** *sl* trick, cheat, swindle **b.** *sl* joke with, make a fool of

• **uvaljívati pȕške** {VP} (lit. keep inserting rifles) **a.** *sl* lie **b.** *sl* cheat, swindle

• **uvaljívati žváku** {VP} (lit. keep inserting bubblegum) *sl* lie

ȕvār {a masc.} *col-dia* profit, gain <Slav>

ùvatiti {tīm, tē perf.} [std. = uhvatiti] **a.** *col-dia* catch <Slav✍> **b.** *col-dia* get, obtain <Slav✍[*1]>

ùvesti *See the following*

• **ùvesti strúju** {VP} (lit. connect to the powerline) *sl-sex* ***Obs*** manually stimulate the vagina

uvláčiti se {ùvlāčīm, čē imperf. intr.} *sl-fea* ***Der*** ingratiate, brownnose, kiss ass <Slav[*1]>

uvlàkāč {lakáča (acc. = gen.) masc.} *sl-fea* ***Der*** ingratiator (male), brownnoser, ass kisser <Slav⁘[*1]>

uvlakáčević {a (acc. = gen.) masc.} *sl-fea* ***Der*** ingratiator (male), brownnoser, ass kisser <Slav⁘[*1]>

uvlakàčica {ē fem.} *sl-fea* ***Der*** ingratiator (female), brownnoser, ass kisser <Slav⁘[*1]>

uvlákčević {a (acc. = gen.) masc.} *sl-fea* ***Der*** ingratiator (male), brownnoser, ass kisser <Slav⁘[*1]>

ȕvle {eta neut.} *sl-fea* ***Der*** ingratiator (male), brownnoser, ass kisser <Slav✍[*1]>

ȕvo *See the following*

• **U ȕvo te glûvō jèbēm!** {S} (lit. I fuck you in your deaf ear!) Ser *dia-col* ***Off*** used as a moderate curse, Fuck you!

uvòštiti {ùvoštīm, tē perf. intr.} **1** *sl* die, kick the bucket <Slav[*1]> **2** *sl* beat up severely <Slav[*1]>

uvòštiti se {ùvoštīm, tē perf. intr.} *sl-drink* get drunk <Slav[*1]>

ùvrnūt {a, o adj.} (lit. twisted) *sl-fea* ***Der*** insane, nuts <Slav[*1]>

ùvūći se {uvúčēm, uvúkū, ùvūk, ùvūk perf. irreg.} (lit. get in) *sl-fea* ingratiate, brownnose, kiss ass <Slav[*1]>

• **ùvūći se ù dupe** {VP} (lit. squeeze to someone's ass) *sl-fea* ingratiate, brownnose, kiss ass

• **ùvūći se u gùzicu** {VP} (lit. squeeze to someone's ass) *sl-fea* ***Der-Obs*** ingratiate, brownnose, kiss ass

• **ùvūći se u šúpak** {VP} (lit. squeeze to someone's asshole) *sl-fea* ***Der-Obs*** ingratiate, brownnose, kiss ass

ùzak {ska, sko adj.} (lit. narrow) *sl-fea* miserly, stingy <Slav[*1]>

uzbihuzúriti {hùzūrīm, rē perf.} BosM *col* annoy, bother, pester <NE[*1]>

úzda {ē fem.} (lit. rein) *sl-fea* ***Fac*** married woman <Slav[*1]>

uzelèniti {zèlenīm, nē perf.} (lit. paint in green) *sl-fea* be in a difficult situation, paint oneself into a corner <Slav[*1]>

• **uzelèniti rádnju** {VP} (lit. green a store) *sl-fea* destroy, ruin

uzèmljiti {ùzemljīm, ljē perf.} (lit. ground) *sl* confront somebody with reality <Slav[*1]>

ùzentati se {ām, ajū perf. intr.} *sl-fea* get frightened, freak

uzèntovati se {ùzentujēm, jū perf. intr.} *sl-fea* get frightened, freak

ùzēti {ȕzmēm, ȕzmū perf.} *col* start doing <Slav[*1]>

• **ùzēti flȁster** {VP} (lit. take a Band Aid) *sl* shut up, cease talking

• **ùzēti jȕnfer** {VP} (lit. take someone's hymen) *sl-sex* ***Obs*** deflower

• **ùzēti kàjmak** {VP} (lit. skim off the cream) *col* get the best part of something, skim off the cream

• **ùzēti mèru** {VP} (lit. take someone's measure) **a.** SerE *col* beat up **b.i.** *col* cheat, swindle **ii.** *sl-sports* defeat **iii.** write out a traffic ticket

• **ùzēti mjèru** {VP} (lit. take one's measure) *col* beat up

• **ùzēti na mȉndros** {VP} *sl* be malicious toward, pick at

• **ùzeti zdrȁvo za gòtovo** {VP} (lit. take healthy for finished) *col* take as a sure fact

uzjèbati se {bēm, bū perf. intr.} *sl-fea* get worse <Slav[*1]>

ùznojenā mjèšina {NP} (lit. sweating bag) *sl-fea* obese person ☞ **mješina**

uzortírati se {zòrtīrām, zortírajū perf. intr.} *sl-fea* frighten, scare <NE⁘[*1]>

uzvìjōjla {ē fem.} **a.** *sl-sex* ***App*** attractive female <Slav[*1]> **b.** *sl-sex* loose woman <Slav[*2]>

uzvìjuša {ē fem.} **a.** *sl-sex* ***App*** attractive female <Slav[*1]> **b.** *sl-sex* loose woman <Slav[*2]>

ȕžās {excl.} *col* horror, terror <Slav>

ùžditi {dīm, dē perf.} /ȕždīti /ijem, iju perf./ **a.** *sl* burn <Slav[*1]> **b.i.** *sl* hit, punch <Slav[*2]> **ii.** *sl-fea* run fast <Slav[*2]>

uždrákiti {ùždrākīm, kē perf.} *col* look, watch, scope out <Slav✍[*1]>

úže {eta neut.} /ȕžē/ (lit. rope) *col* necktie <Slav[*1]>

užežènica {ē fem.} *sl-fea* prostitute, hooker <Slav[*1]>

ùžganica {ē fem.} *sl-fea* prostitute, hooker <Slav[*1]>

ȕžicati {ām, ajū perf.} *col* beg, ask for money <Slav⁘[*1]>

ùžickati {ām, ajū perf.} *col* beg, ask for money <Slav❖[*1]>

ùžljakati {ām, ajū perf.} *sl-crime* steal someone's wallet

ùžljakiti {kīm, kē perf.} *sl-crime* steal a wallet

užútiti {ùžūtīm, tē perf.} (lit. yellow) *sl-sex* ***Obs*** defecate, shit <Slav[*1]>

Vv

v.d. {adj.} *col* temporary <Abb[*1]>

v.d. [vê-dê] **àuto** {NP} (lit. deputy car) *sl-auto* ***Fac*** Trabant (make of simple East German car) ☞ **auto**

vábiti {vâbīm, bē imperf.} *col-dia* call, shout <Slav[*1]>

vȁća {ē fem.} *sl-sex* ***Obs*** sexual foreplay, petting, feeling up <Slav✍[*1]>

vȁćānje {a neut.} *dia* catching, grasping <Slav✍[*1]>

vaćárēnje {a neut.} **1** *sl* cheating, swindling <Slav✍[*1]> **2** *sl-sex* sexual foreplay, petting, feeling up <Slav✍[*1]>

vaćáriti {vàćārīm, rē imperf.} **1** *sl* cheat, swindle <Slav✍[*1]> **2** *sl* flirt <Slav✍[*1]>

vȁćati {ām, ajū imperf.} SSer *dia* catch <Slav✍>

vaćàtina {ē fem.} **1** *sl* cheating, swindling <Slav✍[*1]> **2** *sl-sex* sexual foreplay, petting, feeling up <Slav✍[*1]>

vàdičep {a (acc. = gen.) masc.} (lit. corkscrew) *sl-sex* ***Fac-Obs*** male who deflowers virgins <Slav[*1]>

vàdičepovati {pujēm, pujū imperf. intr.} *sl-sex* ***Fac-Obs*** deflower <Slav❖[*1]>

vȁditi {dīm, dē imperf.} (lit. take out) *col* save <Slav[*1]>
- **vȁditi flȅke** {VP} (lit. take out stains) **1** *sl-drink* cure one's hangover **2** *sl* recover, get better
- **vȁditi iz gȍvānā** {VP} (lit. take out from shit) *sl* save, rescue
- **vȁditi kȓv na slâmku** {VP} (lit. take blood using a straw) **a.** *sl-fea* bore, disturb **b.** *sl* give a hard time
- **vȁditi mâst** {VP} (lit. take out some fat) **a.** *sl-fea* bore, disturb **b.i.** *sl-fea* give a hard time **ii.** *sl-fea* provoke, incite
- **vȁditi mâst na slàmčicu** {VP} (lit. take out some fat using a small straw) *sl* provoke, incite
- **vȁditi skȉju iz ȍka** {VP} (lit. take out a ski from your eye) *sl* lie

vȁditi se {dīm, dē imperf. intr.} **1** *sl* avoid <Slav[*1]> **2** *col* make excuses <Slav[*1]>

vȁđēnje {a neut.} (lit. taking out) *col* excuse <Slav[*1]>

vágen {a masc.} (lit. car) *sl-auto* Volkswagen (make of car) <Ger[*1]>

vagína {ē fem.} (lit. vagina) **1** *sl* female <Lat[*1]> **2** *sl-auto* Volkswagen (make of car), bug, beetle <Lat[*1]>
- **vagína pȅktoris** {NP} (lit. vagina pectoris) *sl* ***Fac*** angina pectoris

vȁgla {ē fem.; perm} /vágla /vegla fem./ [std. = glava] *sl* head <Slav✍>

vàgōn {vagóna masc.} (lit. wagon) *sl-auto* car, wheels <Eng[*1]>

vâj {excl.} *col* ugh <Slav>

vàjda {ē fem.} *col* profit, gain <NE>

vàjdica {ē fem.} *col* small profit, peanuts <NE❖>

vȁjēk {adv.} [std. = uvijek] *dia-col* always <Slav✍>

vȁjk {adv.} [std. = uvijek] *dia-col* always <Slav✍>

vàjme {excl.} *col* ugh <Slav>

vàjmeh {excl.} *col* ugh <Slav>

vȁjska {ē fem.} *sl* female <Alb>

vȁjza {ē fem.} **a.** *sl* daughter <Alb> **b.** *sl* female <Alb[*1]>

vajzȉnče {eta neut.} *sl* very young female, little girl <Alb[*1]>

vàjzīnka {ē fem.; Dat vàjzínki} *sl* very young female, little girl

vȁjzor {a (acc. = gen.) masc.} **a.** *sl* daughter <Alb> **b.** *sl* female <Alb[*1]>

vajzùrina {ē fem.} *sl-fea* big-boned female

vȁka {ē fem.; Dat vȁki p} /vȁka /veka fem./ [std. = kava] *sl* coffee <NE✍>

vȁkat {kta masc.} **a.** BosM *col* time (in general) <NE> **b.** BosM *col* period, era <NE[*1]> **c.** BosM *col* age <NE[*2]>

vàkī {pron.} [std. = ovakav] *col-dia* like this, this kind of: *Odavno nije bilo vakog vina. We haven't had a wine like this for quite some time.* <Slav✍>

vàkō {adv.} [std. = ovako] *col* this way <Slav✍>

vàlā[1] {part.} *col* really, indeed <NE[*1]>

vála[2] {excl.} [std. = hvala] *dia-col* used to express gratitude, thanks <Slav✍>

vàla[3] {ē fem.} 1 Med *col* lagoon, bay <Lat> 2 *sl-crime* burglary <Lat*1>

vàlēr {valéra (acc. = gen.) masc.} *sl-crime* burglar <Lat⁘*1>

vàlidža {ē fem.} Med *dia-col* suitcase <Fre>

valírati {vàlīrām, valírajū biasp.} *sl-crime* steal, swipe <Lat⁘*1>

vàlista {ē masc.} *sl-crime* burglar <Lat⁘*1>

vȁlo {velo fem.; perm} /vȁlo/ [std. = lova] *sl* money

vàlter {a masc.} **a.** *sl* cheating, swindling <GerO*1> **b.** *sl* deception <GerO*2>

• **Vàlter brânī Sàrajēvo** {NP} (lit. Valter defends Sarajevo: title of a popular Yugoslav movie) *sl-sex* large-breasted female

Vȁlja ì tō! {S} (lit. That is valid as well!) *col* used to express approval, That's right! ☞ **valjati**

vȁlja se {VP} (lit. it's valid) *col* used to signal agreement, that's right ☞ **valjati**

váljanje *See the following*

• **váljānje divljákā** {NP} (lit. rolling the wild stuff) 1 *sl-gamble* matchbox gambling 2 *sl* selling low-quality merchandise 3 *sl* laughing **4a.** *sl-drugs* drug dealing **b.** *sl* illegal business (in general)

• **váljānje topíćā** {NP} (lit. rolling small cannons) *sl-gamble* matchbox gambling

váljati[1] {vâljām, váljajū imperf.} (lit. roll) **a.** *sl* cheat <Slav*1> **b.i.** *sl-gamble* play with marked cards <Slav*2> **ii.** *sl-drugs* sell drugs <Slav*2> **iii.** *sl* sell (exchange merchandise for money) <Slav*2> **iv.** *sl* lie <Slav*2>

• **váljati dîvča žváku** {VP} (lit. roll wild bubblegum) *sl* lie

• **váljati divljáka** {VP} (lit. roll the wild dude) *sl* lie

• **váljati divljáke** {VP} (lit. roll the wild stuff) 1 *sl-crime* sell worthless merchandise, sell junk 2 *sl-gamble* play with loaded dice

• **váljati topíće** {VP} (lit. roll small cannons) *sl-gamble* gamble with matchboxes

vȁljati[2] {ām, ajū imperf.} (lit. roll) *sl* be good, be cool <Slav*1>

• **kako vȁljā i trȅbujē** {AdvP} (lit. as it is valid and as it is necessary) *dia* as it should be

• **Vȁlja ì tō!** {S} (lit. That is valid as well!) *col* used to express approval, That's right!

• **vȁljā se** {VP} (lit. it's valid) *col* used to express agreement, One should do it that way!

váljati se {vâljām, váljajū imperf. intr.} (lit. roll down) *sl* laugh <Slav*1>

vàljātor {a (acc. = gen.) masc.} **a.** *sl-crime* reseller <Slav⁘*1> **b.** *sl-fea* suspicious looking male <Slav⁘*2> **c.** *sl-fea* worthless or despicable person, bum <Slav*3>

vàljda {part.} *col* probably <Slav*1>

vàljuga {ē fem.; Dat vàljugi} 1 *sl-fea* skillfulness <Slav✍*1> 2 *sl* thing, object <Slav✍*1> 3 *sl-fea* interesting event <Slav✍*1> 4 *sl* joke <Slav✍*1>

vàmīlija {ē fem.} *dia-col* family <Lat✍>

vâmo {adv.} [std. = ovamo] *col-dia* here <Slav✍>

vàmpijēr {a (acc. = gen.) masc.} [std. = vampir] *dia* vampire <Slav✍>

vàmpīr {vampíra (acc. = gen.) masc.} (lit. vampire) *col* evil female, witch, bitch <Slav>

vȁmpor {a masc.} Med *dia* ship, vessel <Ita✍>

vȁna {ē fem.} *sl* bathtub <Ger>

vàncaga {ē fem. & masc.} /vàncaga/ *sl-fea* homeless person, bum <Ger*1>

vȁndrovati {rujēm, rujū imperf.} *sl* run away, flee <Ger⁘>

vȁni {adv.} **a.** *col* outside <Slav> **b.** *col* abroad, overseas <Slav*1>

vȁnta {ē fem.} **a.** *sl* forehead <Ita*1> **b.** *sl* head

vanzemáljac {ljca (acc. = gen.) masc.} *col* extraterrestrial, alien <Slav⁘>

vanzèmāljka {ē fem.} *col* extraterrestrial, alien <Slav⁘>

vâpor {a masc.} Med *dia* ship, vessel <Ita>

varàkati {ām, ajū imperf.} *col* cheat, swindle <Slav⁘>

varàkati se {ām, ajū imperf. intr.} *col* live very poorly, live from one day to another <Slav*1>

varáknuti {vàrāknēm, nū perf.} *col* cheat, swindle <Slav⁘>

vȁrati {ām, ajū imperf.} *col* cheat, swindle <Slav>

vârba {ē fem.} [std. = farba] *dia-col* paint (wall, ceiling, etc.) <Ger✍>

varbordȋnī {ija masc.} (lit. Wartburg *a very simple Eastern European car* X Lamborghini) *sl-auto* Wartburg (make of simple East German car) <BN✍>

varburgînī {ija masc.} (lit. Wartburg *a very simple Eastern European car* X Lamborghini) *sl-auto* Wartburg (make of simple East German car) <BN✍>

vȁrcaga {ē fem.} /vàrcaga/ **a.** *sl-fea* troublemaker, rowdy, ruffian **b.** *sl-fea* lazy or shiftless person, bum, good for nothing

vârda {excl.} *col* used to express a dangerous situation, watch out <Ita✍*1>

vâren {a, o adj.} **a.** *col* boiled <Slav> **b.** *col* persuaded, convinced <Slav[*1]>

varènika {ē fem.} *dia* milk <Slav>

várēnje {a neut.} *sl-crafts* welding <Slav[*1]>

varijȁnta {ē fem.} 1 *col* plan <Lat[*1]> 2 *col* possibility <Lat[*1]>
• **varijȁnta nògē** {NP} (lit. leg combination) *sl-polit* emigration from one's country

varikína *See the following*
• **iz varikínē** {PP} (lit. from the bleach) *sl-fea* ***Fac-Der*** boring

varírati {vàrīrām, varírajū imperf.} *sl* be suitable, be fitting <Lat[*1]>

váriti {vârīm, rē imperf.} *sl-crafts* weld <Slav[*1]> *sl* like <Slav[*1]> *sl* be suitable, be fitting <Slav[*2]>

váriti se {vârīm, rē imperf. intr.} *sl* be suitable, be fitting <Lat[*1]>

varȉvce *See the following*
¥ **Varȉvce ti i grnénce pòjebēm!** {S} (lit. I screw your meal and the dish!) SSer *dia* ***Off*** used as a weak curse, Screw you!
• **Varȉvce ti jèbēm!** {S} (lit. I screw your meal!) SSer *dia* ***Off*** used as a weak curse, Screw you!

vȁrīvo {a neut.} *col* boiled food <Slav>
• **Vȁrīvo ti nedòvārenō jèbēm!** {S} (lit. I screw your uncooked meal!) *dia* ***Off*** used as a weak curse, Screw you!

vároš {i fem.} *col* city <Hun>

vàrteksica {ē fem.} *sl-sex* prostitute who stands by the Varteks store at Jelačićev Square in Zagreb, Croatia <BN❖[*1]>

vàrzelj {a (acc. = gen.) masc.} 1 *sl-fea* inhabitant of the countryside, hick, bumpkin 2 *sl* priest

vàrzilo {a neut.} *sl-crime* burglar's tools

vȁs {pron.} [std. = sav] *col-dia* whole, entire <Slav◊✍>

vȁscijēlī {ā, ō adj.} [std. = sav] *col-dia* whole, entire <Slav✍>

vaseljéna {ē fem.} *col* universe, cosmos <Slav>

vȁservāga {ē fem.; Dat vȁservāgi} (lit. leveling ruler) *sl* being beaten up by two people <Ger[*1]>

vȁsvijēk {adv.} *col-dia* always <Slav>

vášar {a masc.} (lit. fair) *col* mess, disorder, disturbance <Hun[*1]>

vȁška {ē fem.; Dat vȁški} (lit. louse) **1** *sl-fea* ***App*** good idea <Slav[*1]> **2a.** *sl-fea* hairsplitter, nit picker <Slav[*1]> **b.** *sl-fea* boring person, bore <Slav[*2]> **3** *sl* joke <Slav[*1]>
• **svȁka vȁška ȍbaška** {NP} (lit. each louse on its own) *col* separately, individually, each on his/her own

vȁške {i fem. pl.} (lit. lice) *sl* money <Slav[*1]>

vatȁčina {ē fem.} *sl-sex* ***Obs*** sexual foreplay, petting, feeling up <Slav✍[*1]>

vatȁćina {ē fem.} *sl-sex* ***Obs*** sexual foreplay, petting, feeling up <Slav✍[*1]>

vȁtānje {a neut.} [std. = hvatanje] *col* sexual foreplay, petting, feeling up <Slav✍>

vatárac {rca masc.} **a.** *sl-sex* ***Obs*** sexual foreplay, petting, feeling up <Slav✍[*1]> **b.** *sl* flirting <Slav✍[*2]>

vatáriti {vàtārīm, rē biasp.} **a.** *sl* catch, grab <Slav✍[*1]> **b.i.aa.** *sl* cheat, swindle <Slav✍[*2]> **bb.** *sl-crime* steal, swipe <Slav✍[*3]> **ii.** *sl-sex* engage in sexual foreplay, pet, feel up <Slav✍[*2]>

vatatȁčina {ē fem.} *sl-sex* ***Obs*** sexual foreplay, petting, feeling up <Slav✍[*1]>

vȁtati {ām, ajū imperf.} **a.** *sl* catch, grab <Slav✍[*1]> **b.i.** *sl* cheat, swindle <Slav✍[*2]> **ii.** *sl-sex* engage in sexual foreplay, pet, feel up <Slav✍[*2]>
• **vȁtati na štósove** {VP} (lit. catch on tricks) *col* trick, cheat, swindle
• **vȁtati zjȁla** {VP} (lit. catch nothing) *sl-fea* spend one's time in useless activities, fool around, mess around
• **vȁtati zjȁla pa im čùpati krílca** {VP} (lit. catch nothing and then pluck their wings) *sl-fea* ***Fac*** spend one's time in useless activities, fool around, mess around
• **vȁtati zjȁle** {VP} (lit. catch nothing) *sl-fea* spend one's time in useless activities, fool around, mess around

vȁtati se {ām, ajū imperf. intr.} (lit. catch each other) *sl-sex* ***Obs*** engage in sexual foreplay, pet, feel up <Slav[*1]>

vatáža {ē fem.} *sl-sex* ***Obs*** sexual foreplay, petting, feeling up <Slav✍[*1]>

vàterpōlo {a neut.} (lit. water polo) *sl-sex* ***Fac-Obs*** sexual intercourse in which the female sweats considerably <Eng[*1]>

vàtīrān {a, o adj.} (lit. full of cotton) *sl-fea* affluent <NE[*1]>

vàtiže {vȁmže, vàjuže imperf.} *sl* enjoy, like <Slav✍>

vȁtle {vàtale masc.; perm} [std. = levat] *sl-fea* ***Der*** stupid or mentally deficient person <Lat✍>

vȁtpje {vȁmpje, vàjupje imperf.; perm} /vàtpje/ [std. = pjevati] *sl* sing <Slav✍>

vȁtra {ē fem.} (lit. fire) **1** *sl* high temperature, fever <Slav*1> **2** *sl-sex* sexually aroused person, hot person <Slav*1> **3** *sl-fea* danger <Slav*1> **4** *sl* mess, disorder, disturbance <Slav*1> **5** *sl* noise <Slav*1> **6** *sl* short deadline <Slav*1> **7** *sl-crime* manhunt <Slav*1>

vȁtrenā bȁro {NP} (lit. sizzling hot merchandise) *sl-crime* merchandise which can cause problems to its possessor, hot stuff ☞ **baro**

vȁtrenā vȍda {NP} (lit. fire water) *sl-drink* ***Fac*** drink (alcohol, esp. hard liquor) ☞ **voda**

vȁtrenī {ōg masc.} (lit. the fiery one) *sl-sports* player for Croatian national team <Slav*1>

vatrènjāk {trenjáka masc.} *sl-auto* bus station <Slav✣*1>

vȁtrić {a masc.} Cro *sl* name for Vatroslav Lisinski concert hall in Zagreb, Croatia <SlavO✣*1>

vatrírati {vàtrīrām, vatrírajū biasp. intr.} **1** *sl-fea* go insane, freak out <Slav*1> **2** *sl* make noise <Slav*1> **3** *sl* create a mess <Slav*1> **4** *sl-fea* reproach, scold <Slav✣*1> **5** *sl-fea* get nervous <Slav✣*1>

vatrogásac {sca (acc. = gen.) masc.} (lit. firefighter) *sl-sex* ***Fac*** male who engages in sexual intercourse with elderly females <Slav*1>

vȁtrovati se {rujēm, rujū imperf. intr.} (lit. fire at each other) *sl* argue, quarrel <Slav*1>

vȁu {excl.} *col* the sound made by the dog, arf <Slav>

vȁvijēk {adv.} [std. = uvijek] *dia-col* always <Slav✍>

vȁzda {adv.} *col-dia* always <Slav✍>

vȁzdān {adv.} *col-dia* always <Slav✍>

vȁzde {adv.} *dia-col* always <Slav✍>

vazèlīn {vazelína (acc. = gen.) masc.} (lit. vaseline) *sl-fea* ***Der-Fac*** ingratiator (male), brownnoser, ass kisser <Fre*1>

vazelínac {nca (acc. = gen.) masc.} (lit. vaseliner) **1** *sl-fea* ***Der-Fac*** ingratiator (male), brownnoser, ass kisser <Fre✣*1> **2** *sl-sex* ***Der-Fac*** male homosexual, gay <Fre✣*1>

vazelínko {a masc.} (lit. vaseliner) *sl-fea* ***Der-Fac*** ingratiator (male), brownnoser, ass kisser <Fre✣*1>

vážī {excl.} *col* used to signal readiness to accept what has been proposed, it's a deal <Slav>

vážna fȁca ko trȍjānskī kȍnj {NP} (lit. face as important as the Trojan horse) *sl-fea* conceited male ☞ **faca**

vê-cê {ea masc.} (lit. toilet) *sl-stu* ***Der-Fac*** university cafeteria <Eng*1>

véca {ē fem.} /Véca/ *sl-sex* ***Fam*** bathroom <Eng✍>

vȅcati {ām, ajū imperf.} (lit. toilet) *sl-sex* ***Fac*** urinate, pee <Eng✍*1>

vècējka {ē fem.} *sl-sex* ***Fac*** female bathroom attendant <Eng✍*1>

vecêovac {vca (acc. = gen.) masc.} (lit. toilet man) *sl-sex* ***Fac*** male homosexual, gay <Eng✍*1>

véčānje {a neut.} *col* bleating (of goat), baaing <Slav>

véčati {čīm, čē imperf. intr.} *col* bleat (of goat), baa <Slav>

vèčera *See the following*

- **prólaznā vèčera** {NP} (lit. transient supper) *sl-stu* one-time cafeteria supper

vèčerica *See the following*

- **Vèčericu ti pòjebēm!** {S} (lit. I screw your little supper!) *dia* ***Off*** used as a weak curse, Screw you!

Večernjâk {a (acc. = gen.) masc.} Cro *col* Večernji list (a daily paper from Zagreb, Croatia) <SlavO✍>

vȅčnō lȍvīšte {NP} (lit. eternal hunting ground) SerE *sl* ***Fac*** death, happy hunting ground ☞ **lovište**

vȅć {acc.} *col* than <Slav>

vèdež {a masc.} *sl* food bowl

vȅdrā nóta {NP} (lit. a clear note) *sl-sex* breaking wind, farting ☞ **nota**

vȅdžba {ē fem.} [std. = vežba] SSer *dia* practice, exercise <Slav✍>

vȅdžbati {ām, ajū imperf.} [std. = vežbati] SSer *dia* practice, exercise <Slav✍>

vegetácija {ē fem.} (lit. vegetation) *sl* ***Fac*** hair <Lat*1>

vèhnuti {nēm, nū imperf. intr.} [std. = venuti] BosM *col* faint <Slav✍>

vȅka {ē fem.; Dat vȅki} *col* bleating (of goat), baaing <Slav>

vȅkav {a, o adj.} *col* bleating (of goat) <Slav>

vȅkēt {a masc.} *col* bleating (of goat), baaing <Slav>

vekètānje {a neut.} *col* bleating (of goat), baaing <Slav>

vekètati {vèkećēm, vèkećū imperf. intr.} *col* bleat (of goat), baa <Slav>

vȅla {ē fem.} *sl-auto* shaft <Ger>

vȅlečasnī {ā, ō adj.} (lit. reverend) **1** *sl-fea* ***Der*** cowardly <Slav*1> **2** *sl-fea* bald <Slav*1>

vèlī {excl.} *col-dia* used to refer to the words of others, as they say <Slav*1>

vȅlikā góspa {NP} (lit. Assumption, Great Lady') **1** *sl-sex* virgin **2** Cro *sl-fea* female from Split, Croatia ☞ **gospa**

vȅlikā màrka {NP} (lit. big brandname) *sl-fea* very important or influential person, big shot ☞ **marka**

vȅlikō pjȅvalo {NP} (lit. big singer) *sl-fea* boaster, braggart, blowhard ☞ **pjevalo**

vȅljī {ā, ē adj.} [std. = veliki] *dia* big <Slav✍>

vȅlju {excl.} [std. = velim] Mont *dia-col* used to open a portion of text with one's own thoughts, I say <Slav✍>

vendèta {ē fem.} *col* revenge, payback <Ita>

vȅndovati {dujēm, dujū biasp.} *sl-gamble* cease gambling and pretending to play without money <Ger❖*1>

Vènēcija {ē fem.} (lit. Venice) *sl-sex* ***Fac*** bathroom <ItaO*1>

Vènera {ē fem.} (lit. Venus) *sl-sex* ***Iro*** female with venereal disease <GreO*1>

ventilâtor {a (acc. = gen.) masc.} (lit. fan) *sl-fea* homeless person, bum <Lat*1>

vènuti *See the following*

• **vènuti ko zȕmbul** {VP} (lit. wilt like a hyacinth) *sl-fea* suffer in love

vȅpar {pra (acc. = gen.) masc.} *col* boar (the animal) <Slav>

vȅra *See the following*

• **Vȅru li ti tvòju jèbēm!** {S} (lit. I screw your faith!) SerE *dia-col* ***Off*** used as a weak curse, Screw you!

• **Vȅru li vam dètīnjū!** {S} (lit. *I screw* your childish faith!) SerE *dia-col* ***Off*** used as a weak curse, Screw you!

• **Vȅru ti cȉganskū jèbēm!** {S} (lit. I screw your Gypsy faith!) SerE *dia-col* ***Off*** used as a weak curse, Screw you!

• **Vȅru ti jèbēm!** {S} (lit. I screw your faith!) SerE *dia-col* ***Off*** used as a weak curse, Screw you!

• **Vȅru ti pòkvārenū jèbēm!** {S} (lit. I screw your rotten faith!) SerE *dia-col* ***Off*** used as a weak curse, Screw you!

• **Vȅru ti prevȑtlivū jèbēm!** {S} (lit. I screw your changeable faith!) SerE *dia-col* ***Off*** used as a weak curse, Screw you!

vèrem {a masc.} *sl* tuberculosis <NE>

verèsija {ē fem.} *col* credit (usu. given informally by a bartender or shopkeeper) <NE>

vèrglānje {a neut.} *sl-fea* prolonged and meaningless talk, blabber, chatter <Ita❖*1>

vèrglati {ām, ajū imperf.} *sl-fea* talk persistently and meaninglessly, blabber, chatter <Ita❖*1>

vèrige {vȅrīgā fem. pl.} *col-dia* chain kept above the fireplace to hang a kettle <Slav>

vèritās {a masc.} *sl-drink* wine <Lat*1>

vȅrk {a +ov (ext. pl) masc.; Nom Pl vèrkovi} **a.** *sl* hour <Ger*1> **b.i.** *sl* clock, watch <Ger*2> **ii.** *sl* clock, watch <Ger*2>

vèrna {ē fem.} *sl-sex* ***Obs*** vagina, cunt

veronáuka {ē fem.} (lit. catechism) **a.** *sl* ***Fac*** Marxism <Slav*1> **b.** *sl* ***Fac*** sociology <Slav*2>

Vésa {ē fem.} *sl-sex* ***Fam*** bathroom <Eng✍>

vȅselī mȑtvac {NP} (lit. merry dead, the bar is adjacent to the main cemetery) Cro *sl-drink* name of a bar on Mirogojska street in Zagreb, Croatia ☞ **mrtvac**

vesèlica {ē fem.} *sl-fea* happy female <Slav*1>

vesèlin [1] {a (acc. = gen.) masc.} *sl-fea* boy who manages to do nothing more than to walk with his girlfriend <Slav❖*1>

Vesèlin [2] {a (acc. = gen.) masc.} (lit. Veselin, man's name X WC [ve-ce] 'bathroom') *sl-sex* ***Fac*** bathroom <SlavO*1>

vèsēlko {a masc.} *sl-sex* ***Fac-Obs*** penis, dick, prick <SlavO*1>

vèsēlnīk {a (acc. = gen.) masc.} *sl-fea* boy who manages to do nothing more than to walk with his girlfriend <Slav❖*1>

vesélje *See the following*

• **pȉčkino vesélje** {NP} (lit. cunt's joy) *dia* ***Obs*** nothing at all

vèslo {a neut.} (lit. oar) *sl* fork <Slav*1>

vésti {vézēm, vézū perf. irreg.} (lit. knit) **1** *sl-stu* do well on an exam <Slav*1> **2** *sl-fea* talk persistently and meaninglessly, blabber, chatter <Slav*1> **3** *sl-sports* play soccer well <Slav*1>

vȅš {a +ev (ext. pl) masc.; Nom Pl vèševi} *col* laundry <Ger>

• **pȑljav vȅš** {NP} (lit. dirty laundry) *col* dirty laundry

vȅš-mašína {ē fem.} (lit. washer) *sl-auto* Fiat 125 (make of car) <Ger>

vešpláviti {vèšplāvīm, vē imperf.} *sl* beat up <Ger-Slav.*1>

vetèrān {veterána (acc. = gen.) masc.} (lit. veteran) *sl-stu* ***Fac*** eternal student, professional student <Lat*1>

veterìnārnica {ē fem.} (lit. animal hospital) *sl-stu* student dispensary <Lat*1>

vȅtkre {ea masc.; perm} /vètkre /vetakre masc./ [std. = krevet] *sl* bed <Slav✍>

vetrènjača {ē fem.} (lit. windmill) SerE *sl* radar <**Slav**[*1]>

vȅverica {ē fem.} (lit. squirrel) *sl-fea* naive person <**Slav**[*1]>

vȅza {ē fem.} (lit. link) **1** *col* connection, tie <**Slav**[*1]> **2** *col* love affair <**Slav**[*1]>

- **bez vȅzē** {PP} (lit. without a connection) **a.** *col* evil, mean: *frajer bez veze mean guy* **b.i.** *col* stupid: *bez veze knjiga stupid book* **ii.** *col* nothing special, no big deal: *A: Kakav je bio film? B: Bilo je bez veze. A: How was the movie? B: It was nothing special.*

vêzānā štédnja {NP} (lit. connected savings) *sl-sex* incest, sexual intercourse between relatives ☞ **štednja**

vèzara {ē fem.} **a.** *sl-fea* stupid or mentally deficient person <**Slav**❖[*1]> **b.** *sl-fea* ignorant person <**Slav**❖[*1]>

vézati *See the following*

vézati pȕpak {VP} (lit. tie one's navel) *sl-fea* marry, tie the knot ☞ **pupak**

vèzist {a (acc. = gen.) masc.} **1** *sl-sports* midfielder (soccer) <**Slav**❖[*1]> **2a.** *sl-fea* stupid or mentally deficient person <**Slav**❖[*1]> **b.** *sl-fea* ignorant person <**Slav**❖[*2]>

vèzista {ē masc.} **a.** *sl-sports* midfielder (soccer) <**Slav**❖[*1]> **b.** *sl-fea* ignorant person <**Slav**❖[*2]>

vȉbrić {a masc.} *sl-music* vibraphone, vibes <**Lat**✍[*1]>

vȉbros {a (acc. = gen.) masc.} (lit. the vibrant one) **a.** *sl-fea* ***App*** skillful male <**Lat**✍[*1]> **b.** *sl-fea* crook, thief <**Lat**✍[*2]>

vȉc *See the following*

- **čȍkolādnī vȉc** {NP} (lit. chocolate joke) *sl-polit* ***Fac*** dangerous political joke
- **mâsnī vȉc** {NP} (lit. fat joke) *col* dirty joke (usu. sexual)

vicematurȁnt {a (acc. = gen.) masc.} *sl-sstu* high-school junior <**Lat**[*1]>

vȉcī {excl.} *col* used to lure a pig <**Slav**>

vȉckāroš {a (acc. = gen.) masc.} *sl-fea* joker, trickster, rascal <**Ger**❖[*1]>

vȉckast {a, o adj.} *sl-fea* humorous (of a person) <**Ger**❖>

vîd {excl.} [std. = vidi] *col* used to draw someone's attention, look <**Slav**✍>

vȉdār {a (acc. = gen.) masc.} *col-dia* healer, one who practices non-conventional medicine <**Slav**❖>

vȉdati {ām, ajū imperf.} *col-dia* heal <**Slav**❖>

vȉdē {excl.} [std. = vidi] *col-dia* used to draw someone's attention, look <**Slav**✍>

vȉdelo *See the following*

- **Vȉdelo ti jèbēm!** {S} (lit. I screw your daylight!) SerE *dia* ***Off*** used as a weak curse, Screw you!

vȉdeo {a masc.} **1** *col* TV clip <**Lat**[*1]> **2** *col* VCR <**Lat**[*1]>

vȉdeti *See the following*

- **Bôg te vȉdiō!** {S} (lit. Let God see you!) *col* used to express astonishment, Unbelievable!
- **Da vidimo čija majka crnu vȕnu prede!** {S} (lit. Let us see whose mother combs black wool!) *col* used as a threat, Let 's see who's gonna pay for this!
- **nè videti (ni) bélu mȁčku** {VP} (lit. be unable to see even a white cat) **a.** **SerE** *col* be very drunk, be blind drunk **b.** SerE *col* be unable to see anything
- **vȉdeti dȕplo** {VP} (lit. see double) SerE *sl-drink* be drunk
- **vȉdeti svȅ zvézde** {VP} (lit. see all the stars) SerE *sl-fea* be hit, see stars
- **vȉdeti zvézde** {VP} (lit. see the stars) SerE *sl-fea* be hit, see stars

vidíkovac {vca masc.} /vȉdikovac/ **1** *sl* panorama <**Slav**[*1]> **2** *sl-drink* name of a bar at Ilica and Marinkovićeva streets in Zagreb, Croatia <**Slav**[*1]>

- **dȍnje vidíkovac** {NP} (lit. one promenade deck) *sl* one example: *Daj mi donje vidikovac da je lagao pa ću ti vjerovati. Give me one example of him lying and I will believe you.*

vîdno {adv.} (lit. visible) **a.** *sl* free, gratis <**Slav**[*1]> **b.** *sl-crime* no police <**Slav**[*2]>

vȉdoje {a masc.} *sl-fea* person wearing eyeglasses, four-eyes <**Slav**❖[*1]>

vȉdra [1] {ē fem.} (lit. otter) **1** *sl-fea* ***App*** skillful male: *Taj dečak je prava vidra u sportu. That boy is really skillful in sports.* <**Slav**[*1]> **2** *sl-sex* prostitute, hooker <**Slav**[*2]>

vȉdra [2] {adj.} (lit. otter) *sl-fea* skillful: *vidra igrač skillful player* <**Slav**[*1]>

viđen {a, o adj.} **a.** *sl-fea* sure <**Slav**[*1]> **b.** *sl-fea* predestined <**Slav**[*2]>

vȉđi {excl.} [std. = vidi] Mont *dia* used to draw someone's attention, look <**Slav**✍>

vȉđu {excl.} [std. = vidi] Mont *dia* used to draw someone's attention, look <**Slav**✍>

vijȁgra {ē fem.} (lit. Viagra) *sl-sex* ***Fac*** loose woman <**BN**[*1]>

vȉjalica {ē fem.} (lit. snowstorm) *sl-crime* warrant <**Slav**❖[*1]>

vijátović {a masc.} *sl* disappearing <**Slav**✍[*1]>

vijètnāmka {ē masc.} *sl* army-style coat <BN>

vìjuga {ē fem.; Dat vìjugi} (lit. convolution) **a.** *sl-fea* talent <Slav[*1]> **b.** *sl-fea* smartness <Slav[*2]> **c.** *sl* idea, thought <Slav[*3]>

vìjuge {i fem. pl.} (lit. convolutions) *sl* brain <Slav[*1]>

víkati se {vîkām, víkajū imperf. intr.} //vîčēm, čū imperf. intr/ *sl* have a name, be called <Slav⁘[*1]>

vìkendica {ē fem.} /vìkēndica/ (lit. cottage house) *sl* ***Fac*** grave <Eng⁘[*1]>

víkniti {vîknēm, nū perf.} (lit. scream) **1** *sl-sex* ***Fac-Obs*** engage in sexual intercourse with (of a male) <Slav[*1]> 2 *sl-drink* buy a drink for someone <Slav[*1]>

víknuti {vîknēm, nū perf.} (lit. scream) **1** *sl-sex* ***Obs*** engage in sexual intercourse with (of a male) <Slav[*1]> 2 *sl* pay (bills, etc.) <Slav[*1]> 3 *sl-drink* buy a drink for someone <Slav[*1]> 4 *sl* ring (a bell, etc.) <Slav[*1]>

• **víknuti píće** {VP} (lit. call a drink) *col* buy a drink for someone

víla[1] *See the following*

• **vȉla Ćȕpić** {NP} (lit. Ćupić villa) *sl-fea* psychiatric hospital, nuthouse

• **vȉla šȁška** {NP} (lit. nut villa) *sl-fea* ***Fac*** psychiatric hospital, nuthouse

víla[2] *See the following*

• **Víle su**[PRON:ACC] pronósale! {LSF} (lit. Fairies have carried [PRON:ACC]!) *col* used to indicate that someone had luck in a dangerous situation, [PRON:NOM] had lots of luck!: *Vile su nas pronosale na toj utakmici. We had lots of luck at that ball game.*

vilèneti {nīm, nē imperf. intr.} (lit. act like a fairy) SerE *sl-fea* act insanely, freak out <Slav[*1]>

vilèniti {nīm, nē imperf. intr.} (lit. act like a fairy) *sl-fea* act insanely, freak out <Slav[*1]>

vilènjāk {vilenjáka (acc. = gen.) masc.} *col-dia* fairy's son <Slav[*1]>

vȉlice {a fem. pl.} (lit. jaws) *sl* face (human) <Slav[*1]>

vìmara {ē fem.} (lit. the one with an udder) *sl-sex* ***Fac-Obs*** large-breasted female <Slav⁘[*1]>

vȉmati {ām, ajū imperf.} *col* clean thoroughly using chemical cleaners (usu. of house or apartment) <BN⁘[*1]>

vȉme {ena neut.} (lit. udder) *sl-sex* ***Fac-Obs*** female breast, tit <Slav[*1]>

vìnālka {ē fem.} Cro *sl* name of a bar on Preradovićeva street in Zagreb, Croatia

vȉnāz {a masc.} *col* raw material used to produce tiles <BN[*1]>

vìnčina {ē fem.} *sl-drink* wine <Slav⁘>

vìnčuga {ē fem.; Dat vìnčugi} *sl-drink* wine <Slav⁘>

vìnd-jàkna {ē fem.} *col* windbreaker (jacket) <Ger>

vìndjaka {ē fem.; Dat vìndjaki} *col* windbreaker (jacket) <Ger>

víner šúle {NP} (lit. Vienna school) *sl-fea* very elegant person ☞ **šule**

víner šúle ìsturenō odeljénje Nîš{NP} (lit. Vienna school, Niš *a city in Serbia* branch) SerE *sl-fea* provincial snob ☞ **šule**

vìnkleroš {a (acc. = gen.) masc.} **a.** *sl-fea* stupid or mentally deficient person <Ger⁘[*1]> **b.i.** *sl-fea* naive male <Ger⁘[*2]> **ii.** *sl-fea* male with long hair, long hair <Ger[*2]>

Vînko Lózić {NP} (lit. Wineman Vinegrow) *sl-drink* alcoholic, drunk ☞ **Lozić**

vìnogrād {a masc.} (lit. vineyard) *sl-sstu* failing grades in school <Slav[*1]>

vinòpija {ē fem.} *sl-drink* wine drinker <Slav⁘>

vînskā mùšica {NP} (lit. wine fly) *sl-drink* alcoholic, drunk ☞ **mušica**

vînskī brȁt {NP} (lit. wine brother) *sl-drink* alcoholic, drunk ☞ **brat**

vînskī kût {NP} (lit. wine corner) Cro *sl-fea* psychiatric hospital, nuthouse ☞ **kut**

vȉnjāk {a masc.} *col* brandy <Slav⁘>

vȉnjav {a, o adj.} *sl-fea* unattractive, ugly

violína {ē fem.} (lit. violin) *sl* slender person <Ita[*1]>

vȉp {a +ov (ext. pl) masc.; Nom Pl vìpovi} (abbreviated from veze i protekcija *connections and protection*) *sl* connection, tie <Abb[*1]>

vȉpovac {vca (acc. = gen.) masc.} *sl-fea* male with connections <Abb⁘[*1]>

vìrdžīnija {ē fem.} (lit. Virginia) *sl-sex* ***Fac*** virgin (female) <EngO[*1]>

virdžinijána {ē fem.} *sl-sex* ***Fac*** virgin (female) <EngO☞[*1]>

virdžinìjānka {ē fem.} *sl-sex* ***Fac*** virgin (female) <EngO☞[*1]>

víriti {rīm, rē perf.} *col* peep, look at others <Slav>

vȉršl {a masc.} (lit. frankfurter) **1** *sl-sex* ***Fac-Obs*** narrow penis <**Ger***1> **2** *sl-sex* ***Fac-Obs*** penis, dick, prick <**Ger***1>

vȉršla {ē fem.} (lit. frankfurter) *sl-sex* ***Fac-Obs*** penis, dick, prick <**Ger***1>

virtȕoz {a (acc. = gen.) masc.} (lit. virtuoso) *sl-sex* ***Fac*** extremely potent male <**Ita***1>

vȉsāš {visáša (acc. = gen.) masc.; Voc visašu} *sl-sports* high jumper <**Slav**⁘*1>

vȉsēćī vȑt {NP} (lit. hanging garden) *sl-sex* sagging female breast ☞ **vrt**

vȉsibaba {ē masc.} (lit. snowdrop *the flower*) **1** *sl-sex* ***Fac*** impotent male <**Slav***1> **2** *sl-sex* ***Fac*** sagging female breast <**Slav***1>

vȉsibabić {a (acc. = gen.) masc.} (lit. snowdrop *the flower* dude) *sl-sex* ***Fac*** impotent male <**Slav***1>

visijáner {a masc.} *sl-fea* failure <**Slav**✍*1>

vȉsimīr {a masc.} (lit. hanger) **1** *sl-sex* ***Fac*** impotent male <**Slav**⁘*1> **2** *sl-sex* ***Fac-Obs*** penis, dick, prick <**Slav**⁘*1>

• **Vȉsimīr Međunógić** {NP} (lit. Hangfellow Betweenthelegs) *sl-sex* penis

vȉsiti {sīm, sē imperf. intr.} (lit. hang) **1** *col* spend ample time at one place, be a regular <**Slav***1> **2** *sl-fea* be indebted <**Slav***1> **3** *sl-fea* lose money or chances <**Slav***1> **4** *sl-fea* be left on one's own, be left hanging <**Slav***1>

• **vȉsiti ko lȕster** {VP} (lit. hang like a chandelier) **a.** *sl-fea* be left on one's own, be left hanging **b.** *sl-fea* be left without any money

vȉskāč {a (acc. = gen.) masc.} *sl-drink* whiskey <**Eng**✍>

vȉskī *See the following*

• **nȁjlōn vȉskī** {NP} (lit. nylon whiskey) *sl-drink* tea served instead of whiskey when a person buys a drink for the people at another table

vȉsok *See the following*

• **vȉsok mȅtar i mȉlimetar** {AdjP} (lit. a meter and a millimeter tall) *sl-fea* short (in height)

• **vȉsok mȅtar i žȉlēt**{AdjP} (lit. a meter and a razorblade tall) *sl-fea* short (in height)

vȉsokī nápon {NP} (lit. high voltage) *sl-sex* lust, sexual urge ☞ **napon**

vȉsokī sjȃj {NP} (lit. high shine) *sl-sex* cunnilingus ☞ **sjaj**

visȍko {adv.} (lit. high) *sl-fea* expensive <**Slav***1>

visúljak {ljka masc.} (lit. hanger) **1** *sl* mistake, error <**Slav***1> **2** *sl* failure <**Slav***1> **3** *sl-sex* impotent male <**Slav***1> **4** *sl-fea* poor male <**Slav***1>

vȉsūng [1] {a (acc. = gen.) masc.} (lit. hanging) *sl-gamble* losing gambler <**Slav**✍*1>

vȉsūng [2] {a masc.} (lit. hanging) *sl* mistake, error <**Slav**✍*1>

vȉsūng [3] {adj.} (lit. hanging) *sl* tricked, cheated <**Slav**✍*1>

vȋš {excl.} [std. = vidiš] *col* used to draw someone's attention, look <**Slav**✍>

vȉšekatnā péta {NP} (lit. multistorey heel) Cro *sl-fea* high heel (of a shoe) ☞ **peta**

višȉna {ē fem.} [std. = visina] **a.** *col-dia* multitude <**Slav**✍*1> **b.** *col-dia* majority <**Slav**✍*2>

vȉšnjevača {ē fem.} *sl-drink* sour cherry brandy <**Slav**⁘*1>

vȉt {excl.} *col* used to lure pigeons <**Slav**>

vȉta {excl.} *col* used to lure pigeons <**Slav**>

vitȁmīn {tamínā (acc. = gen.) masc.} (lit. vitamin) *sl-fea* ***App*** skillful male <**Lat***1>

vitamínac {nca (acc. = gen.) masc.} (lit. vitamin-man) *sl-fea* healthy boy <**Slav**⁘*1>

vitamȉnčić {a (acc. = gen.) masc.} (lit. small vitamin) *sl-sex* ***Fac-App*** sexy teenage girl <**Slav**⁘*1>

vitamȉndžija {ē masc.} (lit. vitamin-man) **1** *sl-fea* very tall person, giant <**Slav**⁘*1> **2** *sl-fea* healthy boy <**Slav**⁘*1>

víza {ē fem.} **1** *sl* rain <**Hun**> **2** *sl* winter <**Hun**> **3** *sl* water <**Hun**>

vȉzati se {ām, ajū imperf. intr.} *sl-sex* ***Obs*** urinate, piss <**Slav**>

vjedógonja {ē masc.} *dia* evil ghost <**Slav**>

vjȅš {šta, što adj.} [std. = vješt] *dia* skillful <**Slav**✍>

vjȅšala {a neut. pl.} (lit. gallows) *sl-sex* ***Fac*** medical check-up for prostitutes <**Slav***1>

vjȅštalica {ē fem.} [std. = vješalica] *sl* hanger (for clothes) <**Slav**✍>

vjetrȅnjāk {renjáka masc.} **1** *sl-auto* bus station <**Slav**⁘*1> **2** *sl-fea* homeless person, bum <**Slav**⁘*1>

vlȁh {a (acc. = gen.) masc.} (lit. Vlach) *sl-fea* ***Off*** Serb (person) <**Slav***1>

vlȃhović {a masc.} *sl-drink* Vlahov (a brand of hard liquor sold in the former Yugoslavia) <**BN**✍>

vlȁj {a (acc. = gen.) masc.} *sl-fea* inhabitant of Croatian mainland <**Slav**✍*1>

vlâk *See the following*

• **pòsljednjī vlâk za Katàngu** {NP} (lit. the last train to Katanga) Cro *sl-fea* dying person

vlk {masc.} [std. = vuk] SSer *dia* wolf (the animal) <**Slav**✍>

vljȅš {vljèšta, vljèšto adj.} [std. = vješt] *sl-fea* skillful <**Slav**✍>

vljéštac {šca (acc. = gen.) masc.} [std. = vještac] *dia* witch (the Serbo-Croatian equivalent of bogeyman) <**Slav**✍>

vljȅštica {ē fem.} [std. = vještica] *dia* witch (the Serbo-Croatian equivalent of bogeyman) <**Slav**✍>

vnȕč {a +ev (ext. pl) masc.; Nom Pl vnùčevi} *sl-fea* smell, stench

vnȕčiti {čīm, čē imperf.} *sl-fea* smell, stink

vȍč {excl.} *col* used to lure or drive away a cow <**Slav**>

vȍčke {excl.} *col* used to lure or drive away a cow <**Slav**>

vȍćka *See the following*

• **vȍćka pȍslijē kȉšē** {NP} (lit. fruit after rain) *sl-fea* ***Fac*** impotence

vòda {ē fem.} (lit. water) **1** *sl-fea* boredom <**Slav**[*1]> **2a.** *sl-fea* stupid or mentally deficient male <**Slav**[*1]> **b.** *sl-fea* weak male, wimp <**Slav**[*2]>

• **kȍmunālnā vòda** {NP} (lit. community water) *col* fresh water

• **pícina vòda** {NP} (lit. cunt's water) *sl* ***Obs*** unimportant issue or object

• **pȉčkina vòda** {NP} (lit. cunt's water) *col* ***Obs*** nothing at all

• **vȁtrenā vòda** {NP} (lit. fire water) *sl-drink* ***Fac*** drink (alcohol, esp. hard liquor)

vòdenja {ē fem.} (lit. the watery one) *sl-sex* ***Obs*** penis, dick, prick <**Slav**❖[*1]>

vodènjāk[1] {denjáka (acc. = gen.) masc.} (lit. the watery one) *sl* sailor <**Slav**❖[*1]>

vodènjāk[2] {denjáka masc.} (lit. the watery one) **1** *sl* rain <**Slav**❖[*1]> **2** *sl-sex* erect penis <**Slav**❖[*1]>

vòdīč {vodíča (acc. = gen.) masc.} (lit. guide) **1** *sl-drugs* drug addict who introduces newcomers to the habit <**Slav**[*1]> **2** *sl-sex* procurer, pimp <**Slav**[*1]>

• **vòdīč pásā** {NP} (lit. dog-walker) *sl-mil* army driver

vòditi *See the following*

• **vòditi na bîka** {VP} (lit. take to a bull) *sl-sex* ***Fac*** engage in sexual intercourse with

vȍdorāvan {vna, vno adj.} (lit. horizontal) *sl-fea* indifferent <**Slav**[*1]>

vóđe {adv.} [std. = ovdje] *dia-col* here <**Slav**✍>

vóđekā {adv.} [std. = ovdje] *dia-col* here <**Slav**✍>

vóđekarcē {adv.} [std. = ovdje] *dia-col* here <**Slav**✍>

vóđekārē {adv.} [std. = ovdje] *dia-col* here <**Slav**✍>

vóđenāke {adv.} *dia* here <**Slav**✍>

vȍj {adv.} [std. = ovdje] *dia-col* here <**Slav**✍>

vȍjāk {a (acc. = gen.) masc.} /vòjāk/ *col* soldier <**Slav**✍>

vȍjkā {adv.} [std. = ovdje] *dia-col* here <**Slav**✍>

vójko {a masc.} *sl-mil* soldier <**Slav**✍>

vôjnī póziv {NP} (lit. call to military service) *sl-fea* unattractive female ☞ **poziv**

vȍjnīk *See the following*

• **Kûrčēv vȍjnīk!** {S} (lit. Prick's soldier!) *sl* ***Obs*** used as a moderate curse, Fuck him!

vojnìkinja {ē fem.} (lit. she-soldier) *sl-fea* ***Der*** insane female, nut case <**Slav**[*1]>

vójska *See the following*

• **mȓtvā vójska** {NP} (lit. dead army) *sl* funeral

vòkmen {a masc.} *col* walkman <**BN**[*1]>

vôl *See the following*

• **vôl bez rȍga** {NP} (lit. ox without one horn) *sl-fea* one-armed man

vòleti {vòlēm, vòlū imperf.} **SerE** *col* prefer, give advantage to: *Voli popiti nego išta. He likes to drink more than anything else.* <**Slav**✍>

vòleti se *See the following*

• **vòleti se ko kònji** {VP} (lit. love each other like horses) *sl-fea* be madly in love

volìdžānje {a neut.} *sl-fea* prolonged and meaningless talk, blabber, chatter

volìdžati {ām, ajū imperf.} *sl-fea* talk persistently and meaninglessly, blabber, chatter

vòlina {ē fem. & masc.} **a.** *col* big ox <**Slav**❖> **b.** *sl-fea* stupid or mentally deficient person <**Slav**❖[*1]>

vòliti *See the following*

• **vòliti cvàjtere** {S} (lit. like the second one) *sl-sex* enjoy anal sexual intercourse

• **vòliti tȍplō mêso** {VP} (lit. love hot meat) *sl-sex* ***Fac*** enjoy anal sexual intercourse

Vȍlkswāgen {a masc.} (lit. Volkswagen, a make of car) *sl-sex* ***Fac*** loose woman <**Ger**[*1]>

vòljati {ām, ajū imperf.} *sl* promise <**Slav**❖[*1]> *sl* make noise <**Slav**❖[*2]>

vòljkārnīk {a masc.} *sl-sex* ***Obs*** bathroom <**Slav**❖[*1]>

vònjara {ē fem.} **1a.** *sl-sex* ***Obs*** buttocks, butt <**Slav**❖[*1]> **b.** *sl-sex* ***Obs*** anus, asshole <**Slav**❖[*2]> 2 *sl* border (between countries) <**Slav**❖[*1]>

vònjifer {a (acc. = gen.) masc.} *sl-fea* boring person, bore <**Slav**✍[*1]>

vonjifèrisati {išēm, išū biasp.} *sl-fea* smell, stink <**Slav**✍[*1]>

vồpi {vapi neut.; perm} /vòpi/ [std. = pivo] *sl-drink* beer <**Slav**✍>

vorkaholìzam {zma masc.} *col* workaholism <**Eng**>

vồsak {ska (acc. = gen.) masc.} (lit. wax) **a.** *sl-fea* pale-complexioned person <**Slav**[*1]> **b.** *sl-fea* sick person <**Slav**[*2]>

vồštac {excl.} *col* used to drive away a cat, scat <**Slav**✍[*1]>

vồštiti {tīm, tē imperf.} (lit. wax) *col* beat up, wax <**Slav**[*1]>

vồtnjāk {a masc.} [std. = voćnjak] *dia* orchard <**Slav**✍>

vôz {a +ov (ext. pl) masc.; Nom Pl vòzovi} (lit. train) **1** *sl* carton of cigarettes <**Slav**[*1]> 2 *sl* cheating, swindling <**Slav**[*1]>

vóžānje {a neut.} (lit. driving) **1a.** *sl-sports* dribbling <**Slav**[*1]> **b.** *sl* cheating, swindling <**Slav**[*2]> 2 *sl-drink* drinking (alcohol) <**Slav**[*1]>

vózati {vôzām, vózajū imperf.} (lit. give a ride) **1a.** *sl* cheat, swindle <**Slav**[*1]> **b.** *sl* lie <**Slav**[*2]> 2 *sl-sports* dribble (e.g. in basketball) <**Slav**[*1]>

vózati se {vôzām, vózajū imperf. intr.} (lit. take a ride) **1** *sl-drink* get drunk <**Slav**[*1]> 2 *sl-drugs* be under the influence of narcotic drugs, be stoned <**Slav**[*1]>

vồzdra {excl.; perm} /vòzdra/ [std. = zdravo] **1** *sl* used to greet informally on arrival, hi <**Slav**✍> 2 *sl* used to take leave of somebody informally, bye <**Slav**✍>

Vòzi Mĩško! {S} (lit. Drive Mike! *a line from a popular Yugoslav movie*) *col* used to stimulate one's interlocutor to commence a common trip, Let's go James! ☞ **voziti**

vòziti {vồzīm, zē imperf.} (lit. drive) **1** *sl-sex* ***Fac-Obs*** engage in sexual intercourse with (of a male) <**Slav**[*1]> 2 *sl* beat up <**Slav**[*1]> 3 *sl-gamble* play cards <**Slav**[*1]> 4 *sl-fea* cheat, swindle <**Slav**[*1]>

- **Vòzi Mĩško!** {S} (lit. Drive Mike! *a line from a popular Yugoslav movie*) *col* used to stimulate one's interlocutor to commence a common trip, Let's go James!

vòziti se {vồzīm, zē imperf. intr.} [std. = ride] *sl-drugs* be on narcotic drugs <**Slav**[*1]>

vồžd {a (acc. = gen.) +ov (ext. pl) masc.; Nom Pl vòždovi} **a.** *sl-polit* leader <**Slav**> **b.** *sl* Serbian nationalist leader <**Slav**[*1]>

vồžnja {ē fem.} (lit. ride) **1a.** *sl* sexual intercourse <**Slav**[*1]> **b.** *sl-sex* cheating, swindling <**Slav**[*2]> 2 *sl-drugs* narcotic drug effect, trip <**Slav**[*1]>

vrâg *See the following*

- **Vrâg mu mầtēr!** {S} (lit. Devil with his mother!) Cro *col* ***Off*** used as a weak curse, Screw him!
- **Vrâg te jềbō!** {S} (lit. May the devil screw you!) *col* ***Off*** used as a weak curse, Screw you!
- **Vrâg te ồdneō!** {S} (lit. May the devil carry you away!) *col* ***Off*** used as a weak curse, Screw you!

vragòta {ē fem.} *sl* sister <**Slav**❖[*1]>

vràgotnīk {a (acc. = gen.) masc.} *sl* brother <**Slav**❖[*1]>

vrân {a, o adj.} *col* black <**Slav**>

vràncūskī {ā, ō adj.} [std. = francuski] *dia-col* French <**Slav**O✍>

vráta *See the following*

- **cȑkvenā vráta** {NP} (lit. church door) *sl-sex* ***Fac-Obs*** shaved vagina
- **gềnerālnā vráta** {NP} (lit. general door) *sl* danger, dangerous situation
- **pred vràtima** {PP} (lit. in front of the door) *col* on the doorstep, just around the corner: *Zima je pred vratima. Winter is just around the corner.*

vratarizírati {rìzīrām, rizírajū imperf.} *sl* open and close the door frequently <**Slav**❖[*1]>

vrầžijū mầtēr {NP} (lit. devil's mother) *col* nothing ☞ **mater**

vȑc {excl.} *col* hop <**Slav**>

vȑčāj {a masc.} *col* squeak <**Slav**>

vȑcati *See the following*

- **vȑcati mêd** {VP} (lit. separate, extract honey) *sl-sex* defecate, take a dump

vȑč {vȑča +ev (ext. pl) masc.; Nom Pl vȑčevi} (lit. pitcher) *sl-sex* ***Obs*** vagina, cunt <**Slav**[*1]>

vȑčati {čīm, čē imperf.} **1** *col* growl (of animal, engine, etc.) <**Slav**> 2 *col* hiss (snake, gas, etc.) <**Slav**>

vréčati {čīm, čē imperf. intr.} *col* bleat (of goat), baa <**Slav**>

vrềća {ē fem.} (lit. bag) **1** *sl-sex* ***Fac-Obs*** sagging female breast <**Slav**[*1]> 2 *sl-fea* ***Der*** elderly female, old bag <**Slav**[*1]> 3 *sl-sex* ***Der*** pregnant female <**Slav**[*1]> 4 *sl* dress <**Slav**[*1]>

• vrȅća búvā {NP} (lit. flea bag) Ser *sl-fea* dog, flea bag

vrȅka {ē fem.} *col* bleating (of goat), baaing <Slav>

vrȅkānje {a neut.} *col* bleating (of goat), baaing <Slav>

vrékati {vrêčēm, čū imperf. intr.} *col* bleat (of goat), baa <Slav>

vrȅlā ȕsna {NP} (lit. hot lip) *sl* female ☞ **usna**

vrȅlī krȍmpīr {NP} (lit. hot potato) *sl* uneasy, touchy matter, hot potato ☞ **krompir**

vrȅmeplōv {a masc.} (lit. time-machine) **1** *sl* clock, watch <Slav*1> **2** *sl* hour <Slav*1>

vréštati {tīm, tē imperf. intr.} *col* bleat (of goat), baa <Slav>

vȑgodnīk {a (acc. = gen.) masc.} *sl* brother <Slav*1>

vȑgotnica {ē fem.} *sl* sister <Slav*1>

vȑgotnīk {a (acc. = gen.) masc.} *sl* brother <Slav*1>

vrȉća {ē fem.} [std. = vreća] *dia* bag, wrap <Slav✍>

vrijéditi *See the following*

• **ne vrijédī nȉ pō pízdē hládnē vȍdē** {S} (lit. that is not worth even a half cunt of cold water) *col* used to refer to worthless items or ideas

vrijéme *See the following*

• **za vrijéme cȁra** {PP} (lit. in the czar's times) *col* in the pre-WWII Yugoslavia

vrîsak {ska masc.} (lit. scream) **1** *col* very modern thing <Slav*1> **2** *col* ridiculous thing, absurd event <Slav*1> **3** *col* shot (firearms) <Slav*1> **4** *col* effective move <Slav*1> **5** *col* loud clothing <Slav*1>

vrísnuti {vrîsnēm, nū perf.} (lit. scream) **1a.** *sl* overpay <Slav*1> **b.** *sl* be overcharged, be ripped off <Slav*2> **c.** *sl* pay (bills, etc.) <Slav*3> **d.** *sl-gamble* lose money <Slav*4> **2** *sl-crime* get arrested, get busted <Slav*1> **3** *sl* die, kick the bucket <Slav*1> **4** *sl-drink* buy a drink for someone <Slav*1> **5** *sl* disappear, evaporate, vanish <Slav*1>

vrȉšćati {ćīm, ćē imperf.} [std. = vrištati] *dia* scream in pain, fear, or outrage <Slav✍>

vrištánjac {njca masc.} (lit. screaming) *sl-fea* loud sweater <Slav❖*1>

vrȉštati {tīm, tē imperf. intr.} (lit. scream) *sl-fea* laugh intensely: *Vrištala sam kad mi je ispričao vic. I was rolling on the floor when he told me that joke* <Slav*1>

• **vrȉštati ko mȅtla** {VP} (lit. scream like a broom) **1** *sl-fea* wear something loud **2** *sl-fea* be intrusive

• **vrȉštati ko siréna** {VP} (lit. scream like a siren) **1** *sl-fea* wear something loud **2** *sl-fea* be intrusive

• **vrȉštati od srȅće** {VP} (lit. scream from happiness) *col* be very happy

vrȉštēćī {ā, ē adj.} (lit. screaming) *sl-fea* ***App*** excellent, awesome <Slav*1>

vrȉtić {a masc.} [std. = vrtić] *col* kindergarten <Slav✍>

vrȉtnjāk {a masc.} (lit. in-the-butt) **a.** *sl* kick in the buttocks <Slav❖*1> **b.** *sl* dismissing, firing <Slav❖*2>

vȑljav {a, o adj.} **a.** *sl-fea* cross-eyed <Slav*1> **b.** *sl-fea* superficial <Slav*2>

vȑljika {ē fem.} *sl-crime* rifle <Slav*1>

vŕnuti {vȓnēm, nū perf. intr.} *col* return, come back <Slav*1>

vŕnuti se {vȓnēm, nū perf. intr.} *col* return, come back <Slav*1>

vŕpōljiti se {ljīm, ljē imperf. intr.} *col* be unable to sit still <Slav>

vȑštati {ām, ajū imperf.} **a.** *col* squish <Slav✍> **b.** *col* squeak <Slav✍*1>

vȑt *See the following*

• **vìsēćī vȑt** {NP} (lit. hanging garden) *sl-sex* ***Fac*** sagging female breast

vȑtačkē {ī fem. pl.} *sl* cart (e.g. oxcart) <Slav❖*1>

vȑtēška {ē fem.} (lit. merry-go-round) *sl-music* turntable <Slav*1>

vȑteti {tīm, tē imperf.} (lit. spin) **a.** **SerE** *sl* beat up <Slav*1> **b.** **SerE** *sl-sex* engage in sexual intercourse with (of a male) <Slav*2> **c.** SerE *sl* cheat, swindle

• **Kȍ te vȑtī!** {S} (lit. Who is turning you over?) *sl* ***Off*** used to express disrespect, Fuck you!

vȑtigūz {a (acc. = gen.) masc.} (lit. ass shaker) **1** *sl-fea* lively child <Slav❖*1> **2a.** *sl-fea* worthless or despicable person, bum <Slav❖*1> **b.** *sl-fea* idler, loafer <Slav❖*1>

vȑtiguza {ē fem.} (lit. ass shaker) **1** *sl-fea* ***Der-Obs*** worthless or despicable person, bum <Slav❖*1> **2** *sl-sex* ***Der-Obs*** sexually aroused female, hot chick <Slav❖*1>

vȑtipraška {ē fem.; Dat vȑtipraški} *sl-fea* irresponsible person <Slav❖*1>

vȑtirupa {ē fem.} *sl-fea* ***App*** skillful person <Slav❖*1>

vrtoglávititi {tȍglāvīm, vē imperf.} (lit. feel dizzy) *sl-sex* ***Fac-Obs*** engage in cunnilingus <Slav❖*1>

vrtúljak {ljka masc.} (lit. merry-go-round) *sl* event <Slav*1>

vrûćī kròmpīr {NP} (lit. hot potato) *sl-fea* uneasy affair, touchy matter, hot potato ☞ **krompir**

vrućȉnčina {ē fem.} *col* heat <Slav❖>

vrȗsak {ska masc.} [std. = vrisak] *col* squeak <Slav✍>

vrȕskati {ām, ajū imperf.} [std. = vriskati] *col* squeak <Slav✍>

vrȕskav {a, o adj.} [std. = vriskav] *col* squeaking <Slav✍>

vrútak {tka masc.} (lit. source) *sl-sex* ***Obs*** vagina, cunt <Slav[*1]>

vȑz {gen.} SSer *dia* above <Slav✍>

vȑzgānje {a neut.} **a.** *sl* joking with, fooling with <Slav❖[*1]> **b.** *sl* cheating, swindling <Slav❖[*2]>

vȑzgati {ām, ajū imperf.} *sl* cheat, swindle <Slav❖[*1]>

vȑzgati se {ām, ajū imperf. intr.} *sl-fea* spend one's time in useless activities, fool around, mess around <Slav❖[*1]>

vȑždati {dīm, dē imperf.} *col* whiffle <Slav>

vȑždeti {dīm, dē imperf.} SerE *col* whiffle <Slav>

všȕšnuti {nēm, nū perf.} *sl-sstu* skip classes, cut classes <Slav✍[*1]>

vucàrati se {ām, ajū imperf. intr.} *sl-fea* spend one's time in useless activities, fool around, mess around <Slav❖[*1]>

vucibàtina {ē fem. & masc.} **1** *sl-fea* ***Der*** lazy or shiftless person, bum, good for nothing <Slav❖[*1]> **2** *sl-crime* policeman, cop <Slav❖[*1]>

Vùcīnj {Vucínja masc.} [std. = Ulcinj] *sl* name for Ulcinj (a city on the Montenegrin coast) <SlavO✍>

vȕčād {i fem.} **a.** *col* wolf cubs <Slav> **b.** *col* stubborn children <Slav[*1]>

vùčica {ē fem.} (lit. she-wolf) *sl-fea* unattractive female, dog <Slav[*1]>

vúde {adv.} [std. = ovdje] *dia-col* here <Slav[*1]>

vúdenā {adv.} [std. = ovdje] *dia-col* here <Slav✍>

vúdenākā {adv.} [std. = ovdje] *dia-col* here <Slav✍>

vùdžagla {ē fem.; perm} //vegla fem./ [std. = glavudža] *sl* head <Slav✍[*1]>

vȕga {ē fem.; Dat vȕgi} (lit. golden oriole) *sl-fea* stinking person, person with B.O. <Slav[*1]>

vȕgla {ē fem.; perm} /vùgla /vegla fem./ [std. = glava] *sl* head <Slav✍>

vùglec {a masc.} **1** Kajk *sl* coal <Slav✍> **2** Kajk *sl* angle, corner <Slav✍>

vȕglerica {ē fem.} (lit. the one from the corner) Kajk *sl-sex* prostitute, streetwalker <Slav✍[*1]>

vȕgliti {līm, lē imperf.} **1** *col* drag, move <Slav[*1]> **2** *sl* beat up <Slav[*1]>

vùgorek {a masc.} *sl* nose <Slav✍[*1]>

vȕho {a neut.} (lit. ear) [std. = uho] **a.** Kajk *dia* ear <Slav✍> **b.** Kajk *sl* neighbor <Slav✍[*1]>

vȗk {a (acc. = gen.) +ov (ext. pl) masc.; Nom Pl vȕkovi} (lit. wolf) **1** *sl-fea* ***Der*** unattractive male, dog <Slav[*1]> **2a.** *sl-fea* ***Der*** unattractive female, dog <Slav[*1]> **b.** *sl* female <Slav[*2]> *sl-fea* experienced male, one who knows life <Slav[*2]>

- **vȗk s pȉčkom** {NP} (lit. wolf with a cunt) *col* ***Obs-Der*** strong and resolute female

vukòdlak {a (acc. = gen.) masc.} *col* werewolf <Slav>

vukòdlak {a masc.} (lit. werewolf) *sl* night train <Slav[*1]>

vukojèbina {ē fem.} (lit. wolf fuck) *sl-fea* a place of extreme wretchedness or squalor, hellhole <Slav❖[*1]>

vȗkovac {kōvca (acc. = gen.) masc.} (lit. A student) Ser *sl-fea* ***Fac*** person who looks for a (usu. simple) job around Vuk Karadžić's monument in Belgrade, Serbia <Slav❖[*1]>

vȕksa {ē fem.} *sl-sex* ***Der*** prostitute, hooker <Ger✍[*1]>

vȕla {ē fem.} *sl* money

vùlkān {vulkána masc.} (lit. volcano) *sl* ulcer <Slav[*1]>

vȕna [1] {excl.} (lit. wool) *col* used to signal another's being frightened <Slav[*1]>

vȕna [2] {ē fem.} (lit. wool) *col* fear <Slav[*1]>

- **U vȕnu te jèbēm!** {S} (lit. I fuck you in your wool!) *dia* ***Off*** used as a moderate curse, Fuck you!
- **vȕna Kȋćo** {NP} (lit. wool, Sweepy) Ser *col* used to refer to the fear of one's interlocutor, You are scared!

vȕnč {a +ev (ext. pl) masc.; Nom Pl vùnčevi} *sl-fea* smell, stench

vȕnčiti {čīm, čē biasp.} *sl-fea* smell, stink

vùnek {a (acc. = gen.) masc.} (lit. the woolen one) *sl-fea* ***Der*** coward, chicken <Slav❖[*1]>

vunìca {ē fem.} /vuníca/ (lit. wool) *sl* ***Fac*** hair <Slav[*1]>

vunovlačárēnje {a neut.} *sl-fea* prolonged and meaningless talk, blabber, chatter <Slav[*1]>

vunovlačáriti {làčārīm, rē imperf.} **a.** *sl-fea* talk persistently and meaninglessly, blabber, chatter <Slav[*1]> **b.** *sl-fea* be boring <Slav[*2]>

vȕpa {ē fem.} [std. = pivo] *sl-drink* beer <Slav✍>

VÙPĪ {īja neut.} *sl-auto* Fiat 128 (make of car)

vùra {ē fem.} [std. = ura] Kajk *dia* hour <Ger✍>

vùrica {ē fem.} [std. = urica] Kajk *dia* hour <Ger✍>

vùriti {rīm, rē imperf.} *col-dia* eat, devour

vùskati {ām, ajū imperf.} **a.** *sl* sew **b.** *sl* work, labor

vutèčina {ē fem.} *sl* neighborhood with a specific jargon (e.g. Gornji Grad in Zagreb, Croatia)

vùtra {ē fem.; perm} /vùtra /vetra fem./ [std. = trava] *sl-drugs* marijuana, pot, grass <Slav✍>

vùzbāl {a masc.} [std. = fudbal] *dia-col* soccer <Ger✍>

vùzel {zla masc.} (lit. knot) Kajk *dia* necktie <Slav✍>

vùzgala {a neut. pl.} *dia* sled <Slav❖>

Vùznēm ti ga! {S} (lit. I stick it to you!) *dia* ***Off*** used as a moderate curse, Fuck you! ☞ **vuznuti**

vùznuti *See the following*
- **Vùznēm ti ga!** {S} (lit. I stick it to you!) *dia* ***Off*** used as a moderate curse, Fuck you!

Yû-hàšiš {a masc.} (lit. Yugo hashish) *sl* Morava (cigarette brand) <Eng-NE[*1]>

Zz

za célu čètu {PP} (lit. for the whole company) SerE *col* too much, overwhelming ☞ **četa**

za célu òpštinu {PP} (lit. for the whole county) SerE *col* too much, overwhelming ☞ **opština**

za cijélu čètu {PP} (lit. for the whole company) *col* too much, overwhelming ☞ **četa**

za čìjē bàbē zdrâvlje {NP} *col* why ☞ **zdravlje**

za dlàku {AdjP} (lit. for a hair) *col* closely ☞ **dlaka**

za dòbar dân {PP} (lit. for a good day) *col* used to indicate that something has been performed without any hesitation, just like that ☞ **dan**

za džə {PP} *sl* free, gratis ☞ **dž**

za èksere {PP} (lit. for the nails) *sl-fea* without being properly paid ☞ **ekser**

zà glāvu {PP} (lit. for head) *col* urgently ☞ **glava**

za kìnēskū àrmiju {PP} (lit. for Chinese army) *col* too much, overwhelming ☞ **armija**

Za kòj si môj! {S} (lit. For which mine are you!) SerE *dia* ***Off*** used as a weak curse, Screw you! ☞ **moj**

za kòjī kùrac {PP} (lit. for which prick) *col* ***Obs*** why ☞ **kurac**

za kòjī môj {PP} (lit. for which mine) *sl* why ☞ **moj**

za krèpati {PP} (lit. to die) *sl-fea* humorous, entertaining ☞ **krepati**

za kûrčevo zdrâvlje {PP} (lit. for prick's health) *col* for no reason whatsoever, for nothing ☞ **zdravlje**

za màk {PP} (lit. for some poppy seed) *col* in a moment, soon ☞ **mak**

za pòsrati {PP} (lit. to shit) *sl-fea* ***Obs*** worthless, worth shit ☞ **posrati**

zà prīču {PP} (lit. for talking) *col* very strange ☞ **priča**

za sûvū šljìvu {PP} (lit. for a prune) Ser *col* at all: *Ne zarezuje ga za suvu šljivu. He does not give a fig about him at all.* ☞ **šljiva**

Zà šta si? {S} (lit. For what are you?) *col* used to offer something, usu. drinks or food, What would you like? ☞ **šta**

za vrijéme càra {PP} (lit. in the czar's times) *col* in the pre-WWII Yugoslavia ☞ **vrijeme**

Zába {ē masc.} *col* Politikin zabavnik (youth magazine from Belgrade, Serbia) <SlavO✍>

zabadàva {adv.} /zabàdava, zabadáva/ *col* free, gratis <NE❖>

zabalabùćkati {ām, ajū perf.} *sl-fea* do something superficially <Slav✍[*1]>

zabàštati {ām, ajū perf.} **a.** *sl* hit, punch <Ita❖[*1]> **b.** *sl-crime* imprison, put away <Ita❖[*2]>
- **zabàštati bàljaz** {VP} *sl* shut up, cease talking

zabàštati se {ām, ajū perf. intr.} **1** *sl* run into, hit <Ita❖[*1]> **2** *sl* hit, punch <Ita❖[*1]>

zabatáliti {bàtālīm, lē perf.} *col* abandon <NE❖[*1]>

zàbavljati se *See the following*
- **zàbavljati se hònorārno**{VP} (lit. have fun part-time) *sl-sex* change one's partners every now and then

Zábavnīk *See the following*
- **ko Zábāvnīk** {PP} (lit. like Zabavnik *a multi-colored Yugoslav children's weekly*) *sl-fea* tattooed

zabàvnjāk [1] {bavnjáka (acc. = gen.) masc.} *sl-music* pop musician <Slav❖[*1]>

zabàvnjāk [2] {bavnjáka masc.} *sl-music* pop music song <Slav❖*1>

zàbela {ē fem.} (lit. Zabela is a very well known prison in Požarevac, Yugoslavia) *sl-crime* prison <SlavO*1>

zabetònīrān {a, o adj.} (lit. cemented) *sl-fea* unintelligent, dense <Fre❖*1>

zabetonírati se {tònīrām, tonírajū perf. intr.} (lit. cement oneself) *sl-drink* get drunk, get plastered <Lat❖*1>

zabezéknuti se {bèzēknēm, nū perf. intr.} *sl-fea* be very surprised <Slav❖>

zabìberiti {rīm, rē perf.} (lit. pepper) **1a.** *sl* cheat, swindle <NE❖*1> **b.** *sl* falsely incriminate, frame <NE❖*2> **2** *sl-sex* engage in sexual intercourse with (of a male) <NE❖*1>

zabídžiti {zàbīdžīm, džē perf.} *sl-fea* be stubborn, be defiant

Zàbijēm ti ga! {S} (lit. I stick it to you!) *col-dia* ***Off*** used as a moderate curse, Fuck you! ☞ **zabiti**

Zàbijēm ti ga mâjci! {S} (lit. I stick it to your mother!) *col-dia* ***Off*** used as a strong curse, Fuck you! ☞ **zabiti**

zabìlježiti {žīm, žē perf.} (lit. register) *sl* achieve <Slav*1>

zabírati {zàbīrām, zabírajū perf. intr.} *sl-drink* drink beer in large quantities <Ita❖*1>

zàbiti {zàbijēm, bijū perf.} (lit. stick) **1** *sl-sex* ***Obs*** engage in sexual intercourse with (of a male) <Slav*1> **2** *sl-crime* kill, murder <Slav*1>

- **Zàbijēm ti ga!** {S} (lit. I stick it to you!) *col-dia* ***Off*** used as a moderate curse, Fuck you!
- **Zàbijēm ti ga mâjci!** {S} (lit. I stick it to your mother!) *col-dia* ***Off*** used as a strong curse, Fuck you!
- **zàbiti cvíku** {VP} (lit. stick fear) *sl* trick, cheat, swindle
- **zàbiti cvíku** {VP} (lit. stick fear) *sl* trick, cheat, swindle
- **zàbiti kâjlu** {VP} (lit. stick a wedge) **1a.** *sl* trick, cheat, swindle **b.** *sl* falsely incriminate, frame **2** *sl* spit
- **zàbiti[NUMBER] komádā.** {LSF} (lit. stick [NUMBER] goals) *sl-sports* used to refer to the number of goals scored, shoot [NUMBER] goals.: *Zabili su im sedam komada. They shot seven goals against the other team.*

zablokírati {blòkīrām, blokírajū perf.} *sl* cease working (mechanism, etc.) <Fre❖*1>

zablokírati se {blòkīrām, blokírajū perf. intr.} (lit. block oneself) **1** *col* be unable to remember <Fre❖*1> **2** *col* malfunction <Fre❖*1>

zablombírati {blòmbīrām, blombírajū perf.} (lit. seal) *sl* beat up <Fre❖*1>

zabòraviti *See the following*

- **zabòraviti dísati** {VP} (lit. forget to breathe) *sl* die, kick the bucket

zàbosti *See the following*

- **zàbosti kòlac** {VP} (lit. drive in a stake) *sl-sstu* give a failing grade, flunk somebody

zabrìjati {zàbrijēm, jū perf.} (lit. shave) **a.** *sl-fea* enjoy, like <Slav*1> **b.** *sl-fea* stay up all night drinking and partying <Slav*2>

zabrìjati se {zàbrijēm, jū perf.} (lit. shave) **a.** *sl-fea* enjoy, like <Slav*1> **b.** *sl-fea* stay up all night drinking and partying <Slav*2>

zabúbati {zàbūbām, zabúbajū perf.} *sl* run into, hit <Slav*1>

zabúljiti se {zàbūljīm, ljē perf. intr.} *sl* stare at, be fixated on <Slav❖*1>

zabunkèrisati se {išēm, išū perf.} (lit. stay in a bunker) *sl* stay at home <Eng❖*1>

zabùrdisati {išēm, išū perf.} **a.** *sl* stick in, insert <Fre❖*1> **b.** *sl-sex* engage in sexual intercourse with (of a male)

zabušânt {a (acc. = gen.) masc.} *col* loafer, idler <Slav❖*1>

zabušávati {bùšāvām, bušávajū imperf.} *col* avoid work, shirk work <Slav❖*1>

zabúšiti {zàbūšīm, šē perf.} *sl* run into <Slav❖*1> *sl* hit, punch <Slav❖*2>

zabúšiti se {zàbūšīm, še perf. intr.} **1** *sl* run into, hit <Slav❖*1> **2** *sl* hit, punch <Slav❖*1>

zacemèntīrān {a, o adj.} (lit. cemented) **1** *sl-fea* rather unintelligent, pretty dense <Lat❖*1> **2** *sl-fea* difficult to remove <Lat❖*1>

zacéniti se {zàcēnīm, nē perf. intr.} *col* laugh <Slav*1>

zacépiti {zàcēpīm, pē perf.} SerE *sl-crime* steal from (usu. in a restaurant), rip off <Slav❖>

zàcōpān {a, o adj.} *sl-fea* in love <Slav❖*1>

zacópati se {zàcōpām, zacópajū perf. intr.} *sl-fea* fall in love <Slav❖*1>

zacrvèneti *See the following*

- **zacrvèneti mu ȕši** {VP} (lit. make its ears red) SerE *sl-sex* ***Obs*** masturbate, beat off

zacvŕcati {zacvŕcām, zacvŕcajū perf.} *sl-sex* ***Obs*** engage in sexual intercourse with (of a male) <Slav❖*1>

začèpiti {zàčepīm, pē perf.} (lit. cork) *sl* cease talking, put a cork in it <Slav*1>

• **začèpiti usta** {VP} (lit. cork someone's mouth) *col* outwit, outsmart

• **začèpiti žvȁle** {VP} (lit. cork one's bit) *sl* cease talking, put a cork in it

zàćorēn {a, o adj.} *sl-fea* fallen in love <NE❖*1>

zaćóriti {zàćōrīm, rē perf.} *sl* sleep, nap <NE❖*1>

zaćóriti se {rīm, rē perf. intr.} *sl-fea* fall in love <NE❖*1>

záda {ē fem.} [std. = zadaća] *sl-sstu* ***Fam*** homework, assignment <Slav✍>

zadáviti *See the following*

• **zadáviti lȕtku**{VP} (lit. strangle the doll) *sl-sex* ejaculate by masturbating

zàdesti {zàdenēm, denū perf. irreg.} (lit. find) *sl-sex* ***Obs*** engage in sexual intercourse with (of a male) <Slav*1>

zàdjenuti {nēm, nū perf.} *sl* stick in, insert <Slav*1>

zàdnjāk {zadnjáka masc.} **1** *sl* rear pocket <Slav❖*1> **2** *sl-auto* bus station <Slav❖*1>

zàdnjī {ā, ō adj.} (lit. the last) *sl-fea* worst <Slav*1>

zàdnjī tòčak {NP} (lit. rear wheel) *sl-sex* buttocks, rear end, butt ☞ **točak**

zàdnjī trȁp {NP} (lit. rear suspension) *sl-sex* buttocks, rear end, butt ☞ **trap**

zadrìbālda {ē fem.} *sl-fea* stubborn person, pigheaded person

zàđenuti {nēm, nū perf.} [std. = zadjenuti] *dia* stick in, insert <Slav✍>

záđevica {ē fem.} [std. = zadjevica] *dia* argument, quarrel <Slav✍>

zađónjiti {nīm, nē perf.} **1** *sl* sleep, nap <NE❖*1> **2** *sl* tease

zaèbati {ām, ajū perf.} *sl* cheat, swindle <Slav✍*1>

zaebávānje {a neut.} *sl* joking with, fooling with <Slav✍*1>

zaebávati {jèbāvām, jebávajū imperf.} *sl* make jokes with <Slav✍*1>

zafijúkati {fijūčem, fijūčū perf.} (lit. wham) *sl-sex* ***Obs*** engage in sexual intercourse with (of a male) <Slav*1>

zàfikati {ām, ajū perf.} *sl-sex* ***Obs*** engage in sexual intercourse with (of a male) <Ger❖>

zafrkàncija {ē fem.} *col* cheating, swindling <Ger>

zafrkȁnt {a (acc. = gen.) masc.} *sl-fea* joker, trickster, rascal <Slav❖*1>

zafrkȁntskī {ā, ō adj.} /zafrkàntskī/ *sl* joking with, fooling with <Slav❖*1>

zafrkávānje {a neut.} **a.** *sl* joking with, fooling with <Slav❖*1> **b.** *sl* cheating, swindling <Slav❖*2> **c.** *sl* making a fool of <Slav❖*3>

zafrkávati {fr̀kāvām, frkávajū imperf.} **a.** *col* joke with, make a fool of <Slav❖*1> **b.** *col* cheat, swindle <Slav❖*2> **c.** *col* tease <Slav❖*3>

zafrkávati se {fr̀kāvām, frkávajū imperf. intr.} *col* joke <Slav❖*1>

zàfrknuti {nēm, nū perf.} *col* cheat, swindle <Slav❖*1>

zafrljácnuti {fr̀ljācnēm, nū perf.} *col* throw away, toss out <Slav❖*1>

zàfrljiti {ljīm, ljē imperf.} *sl* sell (exchange merchandise for money) <Slav❖*1>

zafr̀ndati {ām, ajū perf.} *sl-sex* ***Obs*** engage in sexual intercourse with (of a male) <Slav❖*1>

Zȁgī {īja (acc. = gen.) masc.} /Zàgi/ *sl-fea* ***Der*** inhabitant of Zagreb, Croatia <SlavO✍>

zàginuti {nēm, nū perf. intr.} **a.** *sl* die, kick the bucket <Slav*1> **b.** *sl* stay up all night drinking and partying <Slav*2>

zaglábati {zàglābām, zaglábajū imperf.} *sl* snatch, grab <Slav*1>

zaglavìnjati {ām, ajū perf.} **1** *sl* be in a hurry <Slav❖*1> **2** *sl* be in a difficult situation <Slav❖*1>

zagláviti {zàglāvīm, vē perf.} **1** *sl-sex* ***Obs*** engage in sexual intercourse with (of a male) <Slav*1> **2a.** *sl-crime* be in a difficult situation <Slav*1> **b.i.** *sl-fea* get arrested, get busted <Slav*2> **ii.** *sl-sex* get pregnant, get knocked up <Slav*2> **3** *sl* stay long (usu. partying) <Slav*1>

• **zagláviti kȍla za salátu** {VP} (lit. stick the salad cart) *sl-crime* get arrested, get busted

• **zagláviti ròbiju** {VP} (lit. stick a long prison term) *sl-crime* go to prison

zagláviti se {zàglāvīm, vē perf. intr.} (lit. get sticked) *sl* stop by <Slav*1>

zaglíbiti {zàglībīm, bē perf.} **a.** *sl-sex* ***Obs*** engage in sexual intercourse with (of a male) <Slav*1> **b.** *sl-fea* have fun <Slav*2> **c.** *sl* stay up all night drinking and partying <Slav*3>

zaglíbiti se {zàglībīm, bē perf. intr.} *sl-fea* have a hard time, experience difficulties <Slav*1>

zagòreti {zàgorīm, rē perf.} (lit. burn) *sl-sex* ***Obs*** abstain from sexual intercourse for a long time <Slav*1>

zagòriti {zàgorīm, rē perf.} (lit. burn) *sl-sex* ***Obs*** abstain from sexual intercourse for a long time <Slav✍*1>

zagòrjeti {zàgorīm, rē perf.} (lit. burn) *sl-sex* ***Obs*** abstain from sexual intercourse for a long time <Slav[*1]>

Zágōrka {ē fem.; Dat Zágórki} (lit. female inhabitant of Hrvatsko zagorje in Croatia) *sl-crime* name of a prison in Lepoglava, Croatia <SlavO[*1]>

zagòvnati {ām, ajū perf.} *sl-sex* ***Obs*** defecate, shit <Slav❖[*1]>

zágrebačkā mljèkara {NP} (lit. Zagreb dairy) Cro *sl-sex* large female breast ☞ mljekara

zagrèbāš {zagrebáša (acc. = gen.) masc.} (lit. the Zagreb one) *sl-sports* player or fan of Zagreb (a soccer team in Zagreb, Croatia) <SlavO❖[*1]>

zagrebávati {zagrèbāvām, zagrebávajū imperf.} (lit. scratch *but derived from zajebavati 'fuck over'*) **a.** *sl* tease <Slav[*1]> **b.** *sl* make jokes with <Slav[*2]>

zàgrejati *See the following*

• **zàgrejati stòlicu** {VP} (lit. heat a chair) [std. = zagrejati] SerE *col* learn thoroughly and seriously

Zagrejèbić {a (acc. = gen.) masc.} (lit. Zagreb fucker) **a.** *sl-fea* ***Fac*** male inhabitant of Zagreb, Croatia <Slav✍> **b.** *sl-sex* ***Fac*** inadequate male sexual partner <Slav✍[*1]>

zàgrijati *See the following*

• **zàgrijati stòlicu** {VP} (lit. heat a chair) [std. = zagrejati] *col* learn thoroughly and seriously

zàgrīsti {grízēm, grízū perf. irreg.} (lit. bite) **1a.** *col* get interested <Slav[*1]> **b.** *col* fall in love <Slav[*2]> **c.** *sl* flirt <Slav[*3]> **2** *sl-fea* be caught, be captured <Slav[*1]> **3** *sl-fea* hurry up, rush <Slav[*1]>

zȁgu {zēgu fem.; perm} /zàgu/ [std. = guza] *sl-sex* ***Obs*** buttocks, butt <Slav✍>

zagùljāč {guljáča masc.} *sl-fea* conceited male <Slav❖[*1]>

zàgūljen {a, o adj.} **a.** *sl-fea* complicated <Slav[*1]> **b.** *sl-fea* difficult <Slav[*2]> **c.** *sl-fea* ill-tempered <Slav[*3]> **d.** *sl-fea* undependable, unreliable <Slav[*4]>

zaguljénko {a (acc. = gen.) masc.} **a.** *sl-fea* gloomy person <Slav❖[*1]> **b.** *sl-fea* stubborn person, pigheaded person <Slav❖[*2]> **c.** *sl-fea* undependable person <Slav❖[*3]>

zagústiti {zàgūstīm, tē perf. intr.} *sl-fea* be in a difficult situation: *Zagustilo im je kad nisu dobili pare koje su očekivali. They were in a very difficult situation when they did not get the money they expected.* <Slav[*1]>

zagušòtina {ē fem.} *sl-fea* conceited male <Slav❖[*1]>

zàgutaviti se {vīm, vē perf. intr.} *sl* become dangerous (of a situation) <Slav❖[*1]>

zàguzak {ska masc.} *sl-fea* short person <Slav❖[*1]>

zàguzast {a, o adj.} *sl-fea* very unpleasant <Slav❖[*1]>

zagúziti {zàgūzīm, zē perf.} *sl-sex* ***Obs*** engage in sexual intercourse with (of a male) <Slav❖[*1]>

zàhaklān {a, o adj.} *sl-fea* married, hitched

zàhenkati {ām, ajū biasp.} *sl* fall asleep, doze off

záhodār {a (acc. = gen.) masc.} (lit. restroom guy) *sl-sex* ***Fac*** male homosexual, gay <Slav❖[*1]>

zahȑđati {ām, ajū perf. intr.} [std. = zarđati] BosM *col* rust <Slav✍>

zàigrati *See the following*

• **Zàigraće mȅčka i pred** [ADJ/PPRON] **vràtima.** {S} (lit. A bear will dance in front of their door as well.) *col* used to indicate that revenge for indecent actions will come: *Zaigraće mečka i pred njihovim vratima za tu uvredu. They will pay for that insult one day.*

zaìskati {zàišćēm, išćū perf.} *col-dia* request <Slav>

zàjahati {ašēm, ašū perf.} (lit. ride on) *sl-fea* annoy, bother, pester <Slav[*1]>

zàjān {zajána (acc. = gen.) masc.} *sl-fea* joker, trickster, rascal

zájeb {a masc.} *sl-fea* ***Obs*** cheating, swindling <Slav❖[*1]>

Zȁjebāli ste se! {S} (lit. You have fucked over yourselves!) *col* used as a reprimand, Shame on you! ☞ **zajebati se**

zȁjebān {a, o adj.} **a.** *sl-fea* ***Obs*** bad <Slav❖[*1]> **b.i.** *sl-fea* unintelligent, stupid, dumb <Slav❖[*2]> **ii.** *sl-fea* unattractive, ugly <Slav❖[*2]> **iii.** *sl-fea* excellent, awesome <Slav❖[*2]> **iv.** *sl-fea* dangerous, dicey <Slav❖[*2]>

zajebàncija {ē fem.} **1a.** *sl-fea* ***Obs*** spending one's time in useless activities, fooling around, messing around <Slav❖[*1]> **b.** *sl-fea* ***Obs*** fun <Slav[*2]> **2** *sl-fea* ***Obs*** problem, trouble <Slav[*1]> **3** *sl* effort <Slav[*1]>

zȁjebāno {adv.} *sl-fea* ***Obs*** highly dangerous or unpleasant: *Ako ne platimo kiriju biće zajebano. If we do not pay our rent, it will be bad.* <Slav❖[*1]>

zajebȁnt {a (acc. = gen.) masc.} *sl-fea* ***Obs*** joker, trickster, rascal <Slav❖[*1]>

zajèbati {bēm, bū perf.} /zàjebati/ **1** *sl* ***Obs*** cheat, swindle <Slav❖[*1]> **2** *sl-fea* ***Obs*** destroy, ruin <Slav❖[*1]>

• **Zajèbi ga!** {S} (lit. Fuck him over!) *col* used to express disrespect, Fuck him!

• **Zajèbi me!** {S} (lit. Fuck me over!) *col* used to express disbelief, Fuck me!

• **Zȁjebō bȁbicu!** {S} (lit. He fucked his little

grandmother over!) *col-dia* used to express disrespect, Fuck it!

zajèbati se {bēm, bū perf. intr.} /zàjebati se/ *sl-fea* ***Obs*** be mistaken <Slav❖[*1]>

• **Zȁjebāli ste se!** {S} (lit. You have fucked over yourselves!) *col* used as a reprimand, Shame on you!

zajebávānje {a neut.} *sl* ***Obs*** cheating, swindling <Slav❖[*1]>

zajèbāvāš {excl.} *sl* ***Obs*** used to express disbelief or distrust <Slav❖[*1]>

zajebávati {jèbāvām, jebávajū imperf.} **a.** *sl-fea* ***Obs*** make nervous, get on one's nerves <Slav❖[*1]> **b.** *sl* ***Obs*** tease <Slav❖[*2]> **c.** *sl* ***Obs*** cheat, swindle <Slav❖[*3]>

• **Ne me zajèbāvāj!** {S} (lit. Don't you fuck me over!) SSer *dia* ***Obs*** used to express disbelief, Fuck me!

• **Ne zajèbāvāj!** {S} (lit. Don't you fuck over!) **1** *col* ***Obs*** used as a moderate curse, Fuck you! **2** *col* used to silence one's interlocutor, Shut up! **3** *col* used to express disbelief, Fuck me!

• **Ne zajèbāvāj me!** {S} (lit. Don't you fuck me over!) **a.** *col* used as a moderate curse, Fuck you! **b.** *col* used to silence one's interlocutor, Shut up! **c.** *col* used to express disbelief, Fuck me!

• **Nèmoj zajebávati!** {S} (lit. Don't you fuck over!) *col* ***Obs*** used to express disbelief, Fuck me!

• **Nèmōj zajebávati!** {S} (lit. Don't you fuck me over!) **a.** *col* used as a moderate curse, Fuck you! **b.** *col* used to express disbelief, Fuck me!

• **Nèmōj zajebávati?** {S} (lit. Don't you fuck me over?) *col* used to express disbelief, Fuck me!

• **Zajèbāvāš me!** {S} (lit. You are fucking me over!) *col* used to express disbelief, Fuck me!

• **Zajèbāvāš nas!** {S} (lit. You are fucking us over!) *col* used to express disbelief, Fuck me!

zajebávati se {jèbāvām, jebávajū imperf. intr.} *sl-fea* ***Obs*** spend one's time in useless activities, fool around, mess around <Slav❖[*1]>

zajèbāvšī {ā, ē adj.} *sl-sex* ***Obs*** engaged in sexual intercourse with <Slav❖[*1]>

zajèbi {excl.} *sl* ***Obs*** used to express dissatisfaction <Slav❖[*1]>

Zajèbi ga! {S} (lit. Fuck him over!) *col* used to express disrespect, Fuck him! ☞ zajebati

Zajèbi me! {S} (lit. Fuck me over!) *col* used to express disbelief, Fuck me! ☞ zajebati

Zȁjebō bȁbicu! {S} (lit. He fucked his little grandmother over!) *col-dia* used to express disrespect, Fuck it! ☞ zajebati

zajebúniti se {jèbūnīm, nē perf. intr.} (lit. zajebati se 'fuck one self over' X zabuniti se 'be mistaken') [std. = zabuniti se] *sl* ***Obs*** make a mistake, screw up <Slav✐>

zȁjec [1] {a masc.} [std. = zec] *dia* rabbit <Slav✐>

zȁjec [2] {adj.} [std. = zec] *sl* the last one <Slav✐[*1]>

zàjehati {ām, ajū biasp.} (lit. ride on) *sl* cheat, swindle <Slav[*1]>

zàkačiti {čīm, čē perf.} (lit. hook) **1** *sl-sex* get pregnant, get knocked up <Slav[*1]> **2** *sl* be inflicted with a disease <Slav[*1]>

zàkājlati {ām, ajū perf.} **a.** *sl-sex* ***Obs*** engage in sexual intercourse with (of a male) <Ger❖[*1]> **b.** *sl* cheat, swindle <Ger❖[*2]>

zakalafírati {làfīrām, lafírajū perf.} **a.** *sl* stick in, insert <Ita❖[*1]> **b.** *sl-sex* engage in sexual intercourse with (of a male)

zakalàmbačiti {čīm, čē perf.} *sl-sex* ***Obs*** engage in sexual intercourse with (of a male)

zakalambàsati {ām, ajū perf.} *sl-sex* ***Obs*** engage in sexual intercourse with (of a male)

zakalàmfisati {išēm, išū perf.} **a.** *sl* stick in, insert **b.** *sl-sex* engage in sexual intercourse with (of a male)

zakaldȑmisān {a, o adj.} *sl* unintelligent, stupid, dumb <NE❖[*1]>

zakàntati {ām, ajū perf.} **1a.** *sl* stick in, insert <Ger❖[*1]> **b.** *sl-sex* engage in sexual intercourse with (of a male) <Slav❖[*2]> **2** *sl* kill, murder <Slav❖[*1]>

zakarabúdžiti {ràbūdžīm, džē perf.} **a.** *sl* stick in, insert <Gyp❖[*1]> **b.** *sl-sex* engage in sexual intercourse with (of a male)

zakekéčiti {kèkēčīm, čē perf.} **a.** *sl* ***Obs*** stick in, insert **b.** *sl-sex* engage in sexual intercourse with (of a male)

zakérati {zàkērām, zakérajū imperf. intr.} (lit. be-dog) *sl-fea* complain, bitch

zakèrečiti {čīm, čē perf.} **a.** *sl* stick in, insert **b.** *sl-sex* engage in sexual intercourse with (of a male)

zakéviti {zàkēvīm, zàkēvē perf. intr.} (lit. become mother) *sl-sex* get pregnant, get knocked up <Heb❖[*1]>

zàkinderiti {rīm, rē perf.} *sl-sex* ***Obs*** engage in sexual intercourse with (of a male) <Ger❖[*1]>

zakìntīrānō stánje {NP} (lit. the state of no-buck) *sl-fea* lack of money ☞ stanje

zàkinuti {nēm, nū perf.} *col* deny, refuse <Slav[*1]>

zàkitati {ām, ajū perf.} **1** *sl-sex* ***Obs*** engage in sexual intercourse with (of a male) <Slav❖*1> **2** *sl-sex* ***Obs*** get close to a female in a crowd <Slav❖*1>

zakitávati {kìtāvām, kitávajū imperf.} *sl-sex* ***Obs*** get close to a female in a crowd <Slav❖*1>

zȁklān {a, o adj.} (lit. with his throat cut) *sl-gamble* who lost money in gambling <Slav*1>

zàklati {zàkoljēm, koljū perf.} (lit. cut throat) **1** *sl-drink* drink (alcohol) <Slav☞*1> **2** *sl* overcharge, rip off <Slav*1> **3** *sl-gamble* take money <Slav*1> **4** *sl-sex* engage in sexual intercourse with <Slav*1>

zaklincóriti {klìncōrīm, rē perf.} *sl-sex* ***Obs*** engage in sexual intercourse with (of a male) <Slav☞*1>

zaklinčóriti {klìnčōrīm, rē perf.} **a.** *sl* stick in, insert <Slav☞*1> **b.** *sl-sex* engage in sexual intercourse with (of a male) <Slav☞*2>

zaklìnderiti {rīm, rē perf.} **a.** *sl* stick in, insert <Slav☞*1> **b.** *sl-sex* engage in sexual intercourse with (of a male) <Slav☞*2>

zaknjávati {zàknjāvām, zaknjávajū biasp.} *sl* fall asleep, doze off <Slav❖*1>

zákon *See the following*
- **Zákon ti jèbēm**! {S} (lit. I screw your law!) *dia-col* ***Off*** used as a weak curse, Screw you!

zakòpati {ām, ajū perf.} **1** *sl* do, create <Slav*1> **2a.** *sl* worsen somebody's situation <Slav*1> **b.** *sl* ruin somebody (emotionally or financially) <Slav*2>
- **zakòpati klínca** {VP} (lit. dig a kid) *sl-sex* ***Obs*** make pregnant, knock up

zakòpati se {ām, ajū perf. intr.} (lit. dig oneself) *sl-fea* stay at home <Slav*1>

zȁkopčān {a, o adj.} (lit. buckled up) **a.** *sl-fea* distant <Slav*1> **b.** *sl-fea* unfriendly <Slav*2>

zakòpčati se {ām, ajū perf. intr.} (lit. buckle up) *sl* stay at home <Slav☞*1>
- **zakòpčati se na léđa** {VP} (lit. buckle up on one's back) *sl-fea* be careless

zakòvati {zàkujēm, kujū perf.} *sl* kill, murder <Slav*1>

zakovìtlati {ām, ajū perf.} *col* swing something before throwing it <Slav>

zakovŕnuti {kòvr̄nēm, nū perf. intr.} **1** *sl* ***Fac-Der*** die, kick the bucket <Slav❖*1> **2** *sl* cheat, swindle <Slav❖*1>

zȁkr̄čen {a, o adj.} (lit. blocked) *sl-sex* sexually inactive <Slav*1>

zȁkrečen {a, o adj.} *sl-sex* sexually inactive <NE❖*1>

zȁkrpān {a, o adj.} (lit. mended) *sl-fea* poor <Slav*1>
- **zȁkrpān frȁjer** {NP} (lit. mended dude) *sl-fea* tuberculosis patient

zȁkrpāno {adv.} (lit. mended) **a.** *sl* done (e.g. a deal) <Slav*1> **b.** *sl-fea* finished, completed <Slav*1>

zȁkucati {ām, ajū perf.} (lit. nail down) **1** *sl-sports* slam <Slav*1> **2** *sl-music* record rock music <Slav*1>

zȁkucati se {ām, ajū perf. intr.} (lit. nail down oneself) *sl-drugs* take narcotic drugs intravenously, mainline, shoot up <Slav*1>

zakùndačiti {čīm, čē perf.} **a.** *sl* stick in, insert <NE❖*1> **b.** *sl-sex* engage in sexual intercourse with (of a male) <NE❖*2>

zȁkuriti {rīm, rē perf.} **1a.** *sl* begin to smoke a cigarette <Slav*1> **b.** *sl* light a cigarette <Slav*2> **2** *sl* run away, flee <Slav*1>

zȁkvrčān {a, o adj.} *sl-fea* old <Slav❖*1>

zàleći {egnēm, egnū, eg, eg perf. irreg.} *sl* lie down <Slav❖>

zalèmiti {zàlemīm, mē perf.} (lit. solder) *sl* hit, punch <Ger*1>

zalépiti {zàlēpīm, pē perf.} (lit. glue) SerE *sl* outwit, outsmart <Slav*1>
- **zalépiti šȁmar** {VP} (lit. stick a slap) SerE *sl* slap, smack

zȁletovān {a, o adj.} *sl-crafts* welded <Ger❖>

zȁletovati {tujēm, tujū perf.} *sl-crafts* weld <Ger❖>

zalijépiti *See the following*
- **zalijépiti ȍko** {VP} (lit. glue one's eye) *sl* sleep, shut eye
- **zalijépiti šȁmar** {VP} (lit. stick a slap) *sl* slap, smack

zalijépiti se {zàlijēpīm, pē perf. intr.} (lit. stick onto) *sl* bother, disturb <Slav*1>

zalijévati *See the following*
- **zalijévati vȑt** {NP} (lit. pour one's garden) Cro *sl-fea* live a quiet family life

zalílati {zàlīlām, zalílajū perf.} (lit. swing) *sl-sex* ***Obs*** engage in sexual intercourse with (of a male) <Slav❖*1>

zàlimfati {ām, ajū perf.} (lit. lymph) **a.** *sl-sex* ***Obs*** engage in sexual intercourse with (of a male) <Lat❖*1> **b.** *sl* cheat, swindle <Lat❖*2>

zalípiti se {zàlīpīm, pē perf. intr.} (lit. glue oneself, stick to) Med *sl-fea* fall in love, be stuck on <Slav☞>

zȁliti {zȁlijēm, lijū perf. intr.} (lit. swing) *sl-drink* have a drink (alcohol) <Slav*1>

zàliti se {zàlijēm, lijū perf. intr.} (lit. swing) *sl-drink* get drunk <Slav[*1]>

zalívānje {a neut.} (lit. pouring water) *sl-drink* drinking (alcohol) <Slav[*1]>

zálog {a masc.} *sl-gamble* any object used in a children's game where the person in possession of that object has to do something <Slav⁘>

zalòmiti {zàlomīm, mē perf.} **a.** *sl-sex* ***Obs*** engage in sexual intercourse with (of a male) <Slav[*1]> **b.** *sl-fea* have fun <Slav[*2]>

zalòmiti se {zàlomīm, mē perf. intr.} *col* happen (used usu. when two or several things coincide) <Slav[*1]>

zálotan {a, o adj.} *sl-fea* married, hitched

zalòžiti {zàložīm, žē perf.} *sl* hit, punch <Slav⁘[*1]>

zalòžiti se {zàložīm, žē perf. intr.} *col* snack <Slav⁘[*1]>

zalúditi {zàlūdīm, dē perf.} (lit. make nuts) *sl-fea* enjoy, like <Slav⁘[*1]>

zaluđìvāč {đivāča (acc. = gen.) masc.} (lit. the one who makes other people nuts) *sl-sstu* A-student, student who makes As <Slav⁘[*1]>

zaluđívānje {a neut.} *sl-stu* intensive learning, cramming <Slav⁘[*1]>

zaluđívati {lùđujēm, đujū imperf.} (lit. make nuts) *sl-fea* frighten, scare <Slav⁘[*1]>

zaluđívati se {lùđujēm, đujū imperf. intr.} (lit. get nuts) *sl-fea* work hard (at manual labor) <Slav⁘[*1]>

zàluftati {ām, ajū perf.} (lit. ventilate) *sl-sstu* cut classes <Ger⁘[*1]>

zamàglisati {išēm, išū perf.} (lit. fog) *sl-arch* do something superficially <Slav⁘[*1]>

zámahac {hca masc.} [std. = zamajac] BosM *col* cogwheel <Slav✍>

zamajávati {màjāvām, majávajū imperf.} *col* lose time <Slav⁘[*1]>

zamajávati se {màjāvām, majávajū imperf. intr.} *col* lose time <Slav⁘[*1]>

zamàndaliti {līm, lē perf.} /zamandáliti/ **a.** *sl* close one's gate <NE⁘> **b.** *sl* insert, stick in <NE⁘[*1]> **c.** *sl-sex* engage in sexual intercourse with (of a male) <NE⁘[*2]>

zamàntati *See the following*
- **zamàntati mȍzgon** {VP} (lit. swing one's brain) Med *sl-fea* fall in love

zàmazati *See the following*
- **zàmazati ȍči** {VP} (lit. besmear eyes) *col* trick, cheat, swindle

zamazìjati {ām, ajū perf.} *sl-crime* steal, swipe <Fre⁘[*1]>

zamenjívati *See the following*
- **zamenjívati pljùvāčku** {VP} (lit. exchange saliva) SerE *sl* kiss

zameráčiti {mèrāčīm, čē perf.} Din *col* crave <NE⁘[*1]>

zâmjenīk {a (acc. = gen.) masc.} (lit. deputy) **a.** *sl-sex* ***Fac-Obs*** anus, asshole <Slav[*1]> **b.** *sl-sex* ***Fac-Obs*** buttocks, butt <Slav[*2]>

zȁmlata {ē fem.} **a.** *sl-fea* idler, loafer <Slav⁘[*1]> **b.** *sl-fea* stupid or mentally deficient person <Slav⁘[*1]>

zàmr̄šen *See the following*

zàmr̄šen spȍr {NP} (lit. complicated argument) *sl* pyrrhic victory ☞ **spor**

zanemáriti {nèmārīm, rē perf.} (lit. disregard) *sl* leave alone, cease boring <Slav[*1]>

Zanèsi mi mȁlo! {S} (lit. Swing it to me a little bit!) *dia* ***Off*** used as a weak curse, Screw you! ☞ **zanijeti**

zanéti *See the following*
- **Zanèsi mi mȁlo!** {S} (lit. Swing it to me a little bit!) *dia* ***Off*** used as a weak curse, Screw you!

zanimácija {ē fem.} *col* exercise, workout <Slav⁘[*1]>

zànitati {ām, ajū perf.} (lit. rivet) *sl* cheat, swindle <Ger⁘[*1]>

zànitati se {ām, ajū perf. intr.} (lit. rivet oneself) *sl* be cheated, be swindled <Ger⁘[*1]>

zanȍsiti *See the following*
- **zanȍsiti ko múda na kȍsidbi** {VP} (lit. swing like one's balls in mowing) *dia* ***Obs*** deviate from a trajectory significantly

zanjíbati *See the following*
- **zanjíbati fr̀ăk** {VP} *sl* leave a restaurant without having paid, run out on the tab

zaòbīći {obīđēm, obīđū, obīđ, òbiš perf. irreg.} /zaobíći/ (lit. circumvent) *col* avoid <Slav[*1]>

zaopráve {adv.} *col-dia* really, indeed <Slav>

zaorgìjati {ām, ajū perf. intr.} (lit. orgy) *sl-sex* ***Obs*** engage in sexual intercourse with <Gre⁘[*1]>

zàpaciti {cīm, cē imperf.} *sl* run away, flee

zâpad[1] *See the following*
- **Dìvljī zâpad** {NP} (lit. the Wild West) **a.** *col* rough environment, chaotic community **b.** *col* mess, disorder,

disturbance

• **na zâpadu nȉšta nȍvo** {PP} (lit. nothing new in the West) *sl-sstu* failing grade

Zâpad ² *See the following*

• **trȕlī Zâpad** {NP} (lit. rotten West) **a.** *col* ***Fac*** the decadent West **b.** *col* ***Fac*** Western European countries (in general)

Zâpadnjāk {a masc.} (lit. the Western one) **Cro** *sl-fea* name for Western Railroad Station in Zagreb, Croatia <Slav❖*1>

zapáli {excl.} (lit. burn it) *sl* used to offer a cigarette to one's interlocutor <Slav*1>

zapalìndati {ām, ajū perf.} *sl* run away, flee <Slav✍*1>

zapáliti {zàpālīm, lē perf.} (lit. burn) **1** *sl* smoke (tobacco) <Slav*1> **2** *sl* run away, flee <Slav*1> **3** *sl-crime* steal, swipe <Slav*1>

• **zapáliti dàdeka** {VP} (lit. fire one's little daddy) *sl* pretend

zapaljénje {a neut.} (lit. ignition) **a.** *sl* match (lighting device) <Slav*1> **b.** *sl* matchbox <Slav*2>

zàpapriti {rīm, rē perf.} (lit. pepper) *sl-fea* spit <Slav❖*1>

zapèčen {a, o adj.} *sl-fea* burnt <Slav❖>

zàpekō {la, lo adj.} *sl-fea* burnt <Slav❖>

zapendžètīrāna rȉba {NP} (lit. windowed fish) *sl-sex* virgin ☞ **riba**

zàpeniti {nīm, nē perf.} (lit. foam) SerE *sl-fea* get angry, foam at the mouth <Slav*1>

zapesíniti {pèsīnīm, nē perf.} *sl-sex* make pregnant, knock up <Slav❖*1>

zapésniti {zàpēsnīm, nē perf.} *sl-sex* make pregnant, knock up <Slav✍*1>

zapésnuti {zàpēsnēm, nū perf.} *sl-sex* make pregnant, knock up <Slav✍*1>

zàpēti {zȁpnēm, pnū perf. intr.} (lit. get stuck) *col* have problems <Slav*1>

zapìšati {ām, ajū perf.} *sl-sex* ***Obs*** urinate on (physically) <Slav❖>

zapìzdati {ām, ajū perf.} *sl-fea* ***Obs*** get stronger <Slav❖*1>

zapízditi ¹ {zàpīzdīm, dē perf. intr.} (lit. cunt on) *sl* ***Obs*** start going <Slav❖*1>

zapízditi ² {zàpīzdīm, dē perf.} (lit. cunt up) *sl* ***Obs*** destroy, ruin <Slav❖*1>

zàpjeniti {nīm, nē perf.} (lit. foam) *sl-fea* become angry, foam at the mouth <Slav*1>

zaprášiti {zàprāšīm, šē perf. intr.} (lit. dust) *col* run away, flee <Slav*1>

zaprášiti {zàprāšīm, še perf.} (lit. dust) *sl-sex* ***Obs*** engage in sexual intercourse with (of a male) <Slav*1>

zaprdékati {pȑdēkām, prdékajū perf. intr.} **1** *sl-sex* ***Obs*** break wind, fart <Slav❖> **2** *sl-sex* ***Fac-Obs*** engage in sexual intercourse with (of a male) <Slav❖*1>

zapȑditi {zàprdīm, dē perf.} **1 a.** *sl* insert, stick in <Slav❖*1> **b.** *sl-sex* engage in sexual intercourse with (of a male) <Slav❖*2> **c.** *sl-sex* make pregnant, knock up <Slav❖*3> **2** *sl-sex* break wind, fart <Slav❖*1>

zapŕzniti {zàprznīm, nē perf.} *col* make untidy, make messy <Slav>

zàpržiti *See the following*

• **zàpržiti čórbu** {VP} (lit. make the soup thicker) *col* set an intrigue to: *zapržiti čorbu šefu intrigue against the boss*

zapurnjáviti {pùrnjāvīm, vē perf.} *sl-fea* blush, turn colors <Slav❖*1>

zàpušen {a, o adj.} (lit. corked) *sl-sex* sexually inactive <Slav*1>

zàpušiti {šīm, šē perf.} (lit. cork) **1** *sl-sex* ***Obs*** engage in sexual intercourse with (of a male) <Slav*1> **2** *sl* cease talking, put a cork in <Slav*1>

• **zàpušiti kanalizáciju** {VP} (lit. stick sewage) *sl* shut up, cease talking

• **zàpušiti pljúcu** {VP} (lit. stick spitting thing) *sl* shut up, cease talking

zâr {a +ov (ext. pl) masc.; Nom Pl zárovi} *sl-gamble* dice <NE>

zarakìjati se {ām, ajū imperf. intr.} *sl-drink* get drunk <NE❖*1>

zarèndati {ām, ajū perf.} *sl* scratch <NE❖*1>

zàrenjkati {ām, ajū perf.} *sl* patch, mend

zarèvati {ām, ajū imperf. intr.} *sl-arch* fall asleep, doze off <Fre❖>

zarezívati {rèzujēm, zujū imperf.} *col* respect, obey: *Ona ne zarezuje nastavnike. She does not respect her teachers.* <Slav❖*1>

• **ne zarezívati ni za súvu šljȉvu**{VP} (lit. be unwilling to cut even for a prune) **Ser** *col* not care about, not give a fig about

zaríbati {ām, ajū perf.} **1** *sl-sex* ***Obs*** engage in sexual intercourse with (of a male) <Slav*1> **2** *sl* cease working (mechanism, etc.) <Slav*1> **3** *sl* die, kick the bucket

<Slav*1> 4 *sl* get very ill <Slav*1> 5 *sl* cheat, swindle <Slav*1>

zaríbati se {zàrībām, zaríbajū perf. intr.} **1** *sl* be cheated, be swindled <Slav*1> **2** *sl* cease working (mechanism, etc.) <Slav*1>

zaribávānje {a neut.} *sl-crafts* malfunctioning <Slav*1>

zaríbō {ala, alo adj.} *sl-crafts* malfunctioning <Slav*1>

zàrigljanā {ē fem. (adj. decl.)} *sl-fea* married woman

zaròniti {zàronīm, nē perf. intr.} (lit. dive) *sl* die, kick the bucket <Slav*1>

zàrov {a masc.} *sl-gamble* dice <NE❖>

zàrūčen {a, o adj.} (lit. engaged) *sl-crime* ***Fac*** in handcuffs, cuffed <Slav*1>

zarúžiti {zàrūžīm, žē perf.} *sl-fea* enjoy, like <Slav❖*1>

zasáditi *See the following*

• **zasáditi rúžu** {VP} (lit. plant a rose) *sl-sex* ***Obs*** engage in sexual intercourse for the first time

zàsaftān {a, o adj.} (lit. saucy) *sl-sex* ***Obs*** aroused, hot <Ger❖*1>

zâseda {ē fem.} (lit. ambush) SerE *sl-sstu* quiz <Slav*1>

zàsedlān {a, o adj.} (lit. saddled) *sl-fea* married <Slav❖*1>

zaslípiti {zàslīpīm, pē perf.} *sl* fall asleep, doze off <Eng❖>

zasmr̀deti {zàsmrdīm, dē perf.} (lit. start stinking) SerE *sl-sex* ***Fac-Obs*** defecate, shit <Slav*1>

zasmr̀djeti {dīm, dē perf.} (lit. start stinking) *sl-sex* ***Fac-Obs*** defecate, shit <Slav*1>

zàsofkati {ām, ajū perf.} *sl* fall asleep, doze off

zàsrati {serēm, serū perf.} **a.** *sl-sex* ***Obs*** defecate, shit <Slav❖> **b.** *sl-fea* ***Der-Obs*** talk persistently and meaninglessly, have diarrhea of the mouth <Slav❖*1> **c.** *sl-fea* ***Der-Obs*** destroy, ruin <Slav❖*2>

zâstava *See the following*

• **cr̀venā zâstava** {NP} (lit. red flag) **1** *sl-sex* ***Fac*** menstruation, period **2** *sl-sex* ***Fac*** bloody sheet after sexual intercourse with a female having her period

zâstave {i fem. pl.} (lit. flags) *sl-fea* ***Fac*** baggy trousers <Slav*1>

zástori {tōrā masc. pl.} (lit. blinds) *sl* eyeglasses <Slav*1>

zasúkati {zàučēm, učū perf.} (lit. tuck up) *sl-drink* get very drunk, get smashed <Slav*1>

zasvŕbeti *See the following*

• **kàd na vŕbi zasvŕbī** {AdvP} (lit. when it starts to itch on a willow) *col* never

zašamúditi {šàmūdīm, dē perf.} *sl* cast a spell on

zašárati {zàšārām, zašárajū perf.} (lit. scribble) *sl-sex* cheat on one's lover or spouse <Slav*1>

zašíšati {zàšīšām, zašíšajū perf.} (lit. give a haircut) *sl-sex* ***Obs*** engage in sexual intercourse with (of a male) <Slav❖*1>

zȁškatati {ām, ajū perf.} *sl* close (e.g. a counter or a store)

zȁšktati {ām, ajū perf.} *sl-arch* close (e.g. a counter or a store)

zašnírati {zàšnīrām, ajū perf.} (lit. lace up) **1** *col* tie one's shoelaces <Ger❖> **2** *sl-crime* cheat one's accomplice <Ger❖*1> **3** *sl* cease talking, shut up <Ger❖*1>

zȁšōdrati {ām, ajū perf.} *sl* overprice <Ger❖*1>

zašórati {zàšōrām, zašórajū perf. intr.} *sl* beat up <Hun❖*1>

zȁšrafiti {fīm, fē perf.} SerE *col* screw (nut, etc.) <Ger>

zȁštekaō {ala, alo adj.} *sl-fea* malfunctioning <Ger*1>

zȁštekovati {kujēm, kujū imperf.} *sl* hide, cover up <Ger*1>

zȁštemati {ām, ajū perf.} *sl* beat up <Ger*1>

zȁštihtati {ām, ajū perf.} **a.** *sl-crime* cut somebody's throat <Ger*1> **b.** *sl-crime* kill, murder <Ger*2>

zašùštati {zàšuštīm, zàšuštē perf. intr.} (lit. start rustling, start making noise) *sl* spend money: *Zašuštao je 200 marona u Ricu. He spent 200 German marks at the Ritz.* <Slav*1>

zȁšvajsovati {sujēm, sujū perf.} *sl-crafts* weld <Ger❖>

zatábati {zàtābām, zatábajū perf.} *sl* beat up <NE❖*1>

zatàknuti *See the following*

• **zatàknuti u mûlj** {VP} (lit. stick in the mud) *sl-crime* kill, murder

zatàmbati {ām, ajū perf.} *sl* kill, murder

zatàrabiti {bīm, bē perf.} *col-dia* close (e.g. a counter or a store) <NE*1>

zàteći {eknēm, eknū, ek, ek perf. irreg.} *sl* find, locate <Slav*1>

zatèfteriti {rīm, rē perf.} (lit. write down) **1** *sl-sex* ***Obs*** engage in sexual intercourse with (of a male) <NE❖*1> **2** *sl* falsely incriminate, frame <NE❖*1>

zȁtelebān {a, o adj.} *sl-fea* in love

zatelèbati se {ām, ajū perf. intr.} *sl-fea* fall in love

zatetrébiti {tètrēbīm, bē perf.} **1** SerE *sl-fea* fall in love <Slav❖[*1]> **2** *sl-fea* run away, flee <Slav❖[*1]>

zatetrébiti se {tètrēbīm, bē perf. intr.} SerE *sl-fea* fall in love <Slav❖[*1]>

zàtrēskan {a, o adj.} *sl-fea* fallen in love <Slav❖[*1]>

zatréskati se {zàtrēskām, zatréskajū perf. intr.} /zàtreskati se/ *sl-fea* fall in love <Slav❖[*1]>

zatrìdečiti {čīm, čē perf.} *sl-sex* ***Obs*** engage in sexual intercourse with (of a male) <Slav✍[*1]>

zatȉndečiti {čīm, čē perf.} *sl-sex* ***Obs*** engage in sexual intercourse with (of a male) <Slav✍[*1]>

zàtrpān {a, o adj.} (lit. buried under) *sl-fea* deaf <Slav[*1]>
- **zàtrpān u pàpīr** {AdjP} (lit. dug in paper) *sl-fea* rich, loaded

zàtūći {túčēm, túkū, zàtūk, zàtūk perf. irreg.} (lit. beat up) *sl-sex* ***Obs*** engage in sexual intercourse with (of a male), bang <Slav[*1]>

zatulumáriti {lùmārīm, rē perf.} *sl-fea* enjoy, like <NE❖[*1]>

zátvor {a masc.} (lit. prison) *sl-sstu* ***Iro*** school <Slav[*1]>

zaùrlati {ām, ajū perf.} (lit. scream) *sl* cheat, swindle <Ita❖[*1]>

zàuška {ē fem.; Dat zàuški} *col* slap, smack <Slav[*1]>

zaváliti {zàvālīm, lē perf.} *sl-sex* ***Obs*** engage in sexual intercourse with (of a male) <Slav[*1]>
- **zaváliti kȍsku** {VP} (lit. stick in a bone) *sl* create problems, cause trouble

zaváliti se {zàvālīm, lē perf. intr.} *col* lie on one's back <Slav❖[*1]>

zaváriti {zàvārīm, rē perf.} (lit. weld) *sl* laugh <Slav❖[*1]>

zàvatiti {tīm, tē perf.} [std. = zahvatiti] *col-dia* afflict <Slav✍>

zàvēzān {a, o adj.} (lit. tied) *sl-fea* married, hitched <Slav[*1]>

zavézati {zàvēžēm, ežū perf.} (lit. tie) **1** *sl* cut, slice <Slav[*1]> **2** *sl* shut up <Slav[*1]> **3** *sl-drink* get very drunk, tie one on <Slav[*1]>

zavéži {excl.} *col* used to silence one's interlocutor, shut up <Slav[*1]>

zàvīličiti {čīm, čē perf.} **a.** *sl* insert, stick in <Slav❖[*1]> **b.** *sl-sex* engage in sexual intercourse with (of a male) <Slav❖[*2]>

zavìngeriti {rīm, rē perf.} **a.** *sl* insert, stick in <Eng❖[*1]> **b.** *sl-sex* engage in sexual intercourse with (of a male) <Eng❖[*2]>

zavitlȁnt {a (acc. = gen.) masc.} *sl-fea* joker, trickster, rascal <Slav❖[*1]>

zavitlávānje {a neut.} *col* joking with, fooling with <Slav❖[*1]>

zavitlávati {vìtlāvām, vitlávajū imperf.} **a.** *col* joke <Slav❖[*1]> **b.** *col* cheat, swindle <Slav❖[*2]>

zavitlávati se {vìtlāvām, vitlávajū imperf. intr.} *col* joke <Slav❖[*1]>

zavláčiti *See the following*
- **zavláčiti pod vrgánje** {VP} (lit. squeeze under mushrooms) *sl-drink* be very drunk

zàvrckānō {ōg masc.} *sl-arch* letter (correspondence)

zavȑljačiti {čīm, čē perf.} /zavrljáčiti/ *col-dia* throw away, toss out <Slav❖[*1]>

zavŕnuti {zàvȓnēm, nū perf.} (lit. twist) **1** *sl-fea* cheat, swindle <Slav❖[*1]> **2** *sl-auto* turn the steering wheel <Slav❖[*1]> **3** *sl-sports* change the trajectory of a soccer ball <Slav❖[*1]>

zȁvȑtanj {tnja (acc. = gen.) masc.} (lit. screw) *sl-fea* stupid or mentally deficient person <Slav[*1]>

zàvrtati {rćēm, rćū imperf.} (lit. screw) *sl-fea* lie <Slav[*1]>

zavȑteti *See the following*
- **zavȑteti dȕpetom** {VP} (lit. swing one's butt) SerE *sl-fea* gain weight
- **Zàvrtīm ti ga!** {S} (lit. I swing it to you!) *col-dia* ***Off*** used as a weak curse, Screw you!

zavrzlàma {ē fem.} /zavrzláma/ **1** *col* mess, disorder, disturbance <Slav✍[*1]> **2** *col* intrigue <Slav✍[*1]> **2** *col* complicated situation <Slav✍[*1]>

zàvūći {zavúčem, zavúku, zàvūk, zàvūk perf. irreg.} **a.** *sl-sex* ***Obs*** engage in sexual intercourse with (of a male) <Slav[*1]> **b.** *sl-fea* cheat, swindle <Slav[*2]>

zàzati {ām, ajū imperf.} *sl-fea* joke

zazebéknuti se {zèbēknēm, nū perf. intr.} *sl-fea* be stunned <Slav✍>

zȁždìti {dijēm, dijū perf.} *sl* start running (moving quickly) <Slav>

zažmíriti {zàžmīrīm, rē perf. intr.} (lit. close one's eyes) *sl* ***Fac*** die, kick the bucket <Slav[*1]>

zbȁbiti se {bīm, bē perf. intr.} (lit. become a grandmother) *sl-fea* get visibly older <Slav>

zbânčiti {čīm, čē perf.} **a.** *sl* beat up <Ita❖[*1]> **b.** *sl* defeat

zbànđati {ām, ajū perf.} *sl* throw away, toss out <Ita❖[*1]>

zbáriti {zbârīm, rē perf.} (lit. boil) **a.** *sl* get a girlfriend <Slav❖[*1]> **b.** *sl* persuade, convince <Slav❖[*2]>

zbȁviti se {vīm, vē perf.} *sl* start dating a female or male <Slav[*1]>

zbèlilo {a neut.} SerE *sl* miracle <Slav❖[*1]>

zbȉb {a +ov (ext. pl) masc.; Nom Pl zbíbovi} *sl-fea* naive male, sucker

Zbìberīm ti ga! {S} (lit. I pepper it to you!) *col-dia* ***Off*** used as a weak curse, Screw you! ☞ **zbiberiti**

zbìberiti {rīm, rē perf.} (lit. pepper) **a.** *sl* insert, stick in <NE❖[*1]> **b.i.aa.** *sl-sex* engage in sexual intercourse with (of a male) <NE❖[*2]> **bb.** *sl-fea* cheat, swindle <NE❖[*3]> **ii.** *sl* score (in sports) <NE❖[*2]>
- **Zbìberīm ti ga!** {S} (lit. I pepper it to you!) *col-dia* ***Off*** used as a weak curse, Screw you!

zbȉčiti {čīm, čē perf.} **a.** *sl* stick in, insert <Slav❖[*1]> **b.** *sl-sex* engage in sexual intercourse with (of a male) <Slav❖[*2]> **c.** *sl* cheat, swindle <Slav❖[*3]>
- **zbȉčiti ga** {VP} (lit. whip it) *sl* trick, cheat, swindle

zbȉčlati {ām, ajū perf.} *sl* cheat, swindle

zbìglati {ām, ajū perf.} **a.** *sl* stick in, insert <Ger❖[*1]> **b.** *sl-sex* engage in sexual intercourse with (of a male) <Ger❖[*2]>

zbȉjēm {excl.} *sl* used to express extreme disgust <Slav[*1]>

Zbȉjēm ti ga! {S} (lit. I stick it to you) *col-dia* ***Off*** used as a moderate curse, Fuck you! ☞ **zbiti**

zbȉksati {ām, ajū perf.} **1** *sl* reproach, scold <Ger❖[*1]> **2** *sl-fea* dress formally, dress up <Ger❖[*1]>

zbírati {zbîrām, zbírajū imperf.} *sl* learn, study: *zbirati matiš learn math* <Slav[*1]>

zbȉti *See the following*
- **Zbȉjēm ti ga!** {S} (lit. I stick it to you) *col-dia* ***Off*** used as a moderate curse, Fuck you!

zblȁnūt {a, o adj.} *sl-fea* confused <Slav✍[*1]>

zblànuti se {zblȁnēm, nū perf. intr.} *sl-fea* be confused <Slav✍[*1]>

zbog sìtnē dècē {PP} (lit. because of the small kids) SerE *sl* without any particular reason ☞ **dete**

zbȍksati {ām, ajū perf.} **1** *sl* obtain, get <Eng❖[*1]> **2** *sl* beg, ask for money <Eng❖[*1]>

zbȍmbati {ām, ajū perf.} **1** *sl* beat up <Fre❖[*1]> **2** *sl* lie <Fre❖[*1]>

zbȍr *See the following*
- **zbȍr biráčā** {NP} (lit. voters' meeting) *sl-crime* court council
- **zbȍr gȍlubōvā** {NP} (lit. pigeons' meeting) *sl-sex* gathering of prostitutes
- **zbȍr pjeváčā** {NP} (lit. singers' meeting) *sl-crime* interrogation in custody
- **zbȍr tȁmbūrā** {NP} (lit. tamburicas' *mandolin-like folk instrument* meeting) *sl-crime* group of policemen
- **zbȍr tamburášā** {NP} (lit. tamburica *mandolin-like folk instrument* players' meeting) *sl-crime* group of prisoners

zbòriti {rīm, rē imperf.} *col-dia* talk, have a conversation <Slav[*1]>

zbórnica {ē fem.} (lit. gathering place) *sl* street <Slav[*1]>

zbòsti {zbòdēm, zbòdū perf. irreg.} *sl-crime* steal, swipe <Slav❖[*1]>

zbȍškati {ām, ajū perf.} *sl-arch* make

zbòtati {ām, ajū biasp.} *sl-crime* kill, murder

zbrájalica {ē fem.} (lit. game of addition) *sl-sex* ***Fac-Obs*** group sex <Slav❖[*1]>

zbȓčkata *See the following*
- **zbȓčkata na jàjcite** {NP} (lit. shaking of eggs) *sl* ***Fac*** scrambled eggs

zbȓda *See the following*
- **zbȓda zdȍla** {AdvP} (lit. from the hill and valley) **1** *col* haphazardly **2** **Ser** *sl* from Banovo Brdo (a nieghborhood in Belgrade, Serbia)

zbrȉsati {išēm, išū perf.} (lit. erase) **a.** *sl* run away, flee <Slav[*1]> **b.** *sl-sstu* cut class, skip class <Slav[*2]>
- **zbrȉsati cȓtu** {VP} (lit. erase a line) *sl-polit* escape abroad
- **zbrȉsati ko déte slȋnu** {VP} (lit. erase like a kid does with saliva) **1** SerE *sl* run away, flee **2** *sl* beat up
- **zbrȉsati s čȁsa** {VP} (lit. wipe out from a class) *sl-sstu* cut classes

zbȓljān {a, o adj.} *sl-fea* clumsy, klutzy <Slav[*1]>

zbrljéknuti {bȑljēknēm, nū perf.} **a.** *sl* make a mistake, screw up <Slav❖[*1]> **b.** *sl-fea* do something superficially <Slav❖[*2]>

zbrokváriti {ròkvārīm, rē perf.} *sl* dump one's boyfriend or girlfriend

zbúbati {zbûbām, zbúbajū perf.} *sl* eat, devour <Slav❖[*1]>

zbunjȍla {ē fem.} (lit. confuser) *sl-fea* stupid or mentally deficient person <**Slav**✍[*1]>

zbȕtām {excl.} *sl* used to express extreme disgust <**Slav**[*1]>

Zbȕtām ti ga! {S} (lit. I stick it to you!) *dia* ***Off*** used as a moderate curse, Fuck you! ☞ zbutati

zbȕtati *See the following*

• **Zbȕtām ti ga!** {S} (lit. I stick it to you!) *dia* ***Off*** used as a moderate curse, Fuck you!

zbȕtnuti {nēm, nū perf.} **a.** *sl* insert, stick in <**Slav**⁘[*1]> **b.** *sl-sex* engage in sexual intercourse with (of a male) <**Slav**⁘[*2]> **c.** *sl-fea* cheat, swindle <**Slav**⁘[*3]> **d.** *sl* falsely incriminate, frame <**Slav**⁘[*4]>

zdȁpi {zdȅpi fem.; perm} /zdàpi/ [std. = pizda] *sl-sex* ***Obs*** vagina, cunt <**Slav**✍>

zdȅbljān {a, o adj.} (lit. swell) *sl-fea* affluent, loaded, fat <**Slav**⁘[*1]>

zdȅksati {ām, ajū perf.} *sl* beat up

zdȉgnuti {nēm, nū perf.} (lit. lift up) *sl-crime* steal, lift <**Slav**⁘[*1]>

zdȉmati {ām, ajū perf.} **a.** *sl* catch quickly <**Slav**⁘[*1]> **b.** *sl-crime* steal, swipe <**Slav**⁘[*2]>

zdȉmiti [1] {mīm, mē perf.} (lit. smoke) **1** *sl-crime* steal, swipe <**Slav**⁘[*1]> **2** *sl* hit, punch <**Slav**⁘[*1]>

zdȉmiti [2] {mīm, mē perf. intr.} *col* run away, flee <**Slav**⁘[*1]>

zdȉper {a (acc. = gen.) masc.} *sl-crime* thief, sticky fingers <**Slav**✍[*1]>

zdȉpiti {pīm, pē perf.} *sl-crime* steal, swipe <**Slav**[*1]>

zdȉpnuti {nēm, nū perf.} *sl-crime* steal, swipe <**Slav**[*1]>

zdȉti {dīm, dē imperf.} *sl* think, ponder

zdȍksati {ām, ajū perf. intr.} *sl* die, kick the bucket <**Gre**⁘[*1]>

zdrȁo {excl.} [std. = zdravo] **1** *col* used to greet informally on arrival, hi <**Slav**✍> **2** *col* used to take leave of somebody informally, bye <**Slav**✍>

• **Zdrȁo, žúrīm!** {S} (lit. Hi, I'm in a hurry!) *col* used to make somebody go away, Hi, good-bye!

zdrȁufnuti {nēm, nū perf.} *sl-sex* ***Obs*** engage in sexual intercourse with (of a male) <**Ger**⁘[*1]>

zdrávko {excl.} **1** *sl* used to greet informally on arrival, hi <**Slav**✍> **2** *sl* used to take leave of somebody informally, bye <**Slav**✍>

zdrâvlje *See the following*

• **ko zdrâvlje** {PP} (lit. like health) *sl-fea* excellent, awesome

• **Ȕ zdrāvlje!** {S} (lit. In health!) *col* used as a toast, To your health! Cheers!

• **za čìjē bȁbē zdrâvlje** {NP} *col* why

• **za kûrčevo zdrâvlje** {PP} (lit. for prick's health) *col* ***Obs*** for no reason whatsoever, for nothing

• **Zdrâvlja mi!** {S} /Zdrȁvlja mi!/ (lit. I swear by my health!) *col* used to emphasize the truth of what has been said, I swear!

zdrȁvo {adv.} **a.** *col* really, indeed: *On je zdravo lud. He is really nuts.* <**Slav**[*1]> **b.** *col* very: *Njena baka je zdravo bolesna. Her grandmother is very sick.* <**Slav**[*1]>

zdrȁvo {excl.} **1** *col* used to greet informally on arrival, hi <**Slav**> **2** *col* used to take leave of somebody informally, bye <**Slav**>

• **zdrȁvo đáci** {AdvP} (lit. Hi, pupils) *col* used to sum up one's point, That's how it is!

• **Zdrȁvo, žúrīm!** {S} (lit. Hi, I'm in a hurry!) *col* used to make somebody go away, Hi, good-bye!

zdȑkān {a, o adj.} **a.** *sl-sex* ***Obs*** masturbating <**Slav**✍> **b.** *sl-fea* ***Obs*** tired <**Slav**✍[*1]> **c.** *sl-fea* ***Fac-Obs*** clumsy, klutzy <**Slav**✍[*2]>

zdrkánac {nca (acc. = gen.) masc.} (lit. the jacked-off one) **Cro** *sl-fea* lazy or shiftless person, bum, good for nothing <**Slav**⁘[*1]>

zdȑmati {ām, ajū perf.} *sl* hit, punch <**Slav**[*1]>

• **zdȑmati u brúndu** {VP} (lit. shake in the head) *sl* punch in the head

zdròbiti {bīm, bē perf.} *sl* spend (money, property, etc.) <**Slav**[*1]>

zdȕa {ē fem.} *dia* outrage <**Slav**✍>

zdúbiti {zdûbīm, bē perf.} (lit. carve) *sl-sex* ***Fac-Obs*** engage in sexual intercourse with (of a male) <**Slav**⁘[*1]>

zdúšiti {zdûšīm, šē perf.} *sl* run away, flee <**Slav**⁘[*1]> ☞ stušiti

zdȕva {ē fem.} *dia* outrage <**Slav**✍[*1]>

zdȕvāč {a (acc. = gen.) masc.} *dia* ghost <**Slav**✍[*1]>

zȅbrast {a, o adj.} (lit. zebra-like) *sl-fea* suspicious <**Ita**[*1]>

zȅbrica {ē fem.} (lit. small zebra) *sl* female <**Ita**[*1]>

zȅbromīr {a (acc. = gen.) masc.} *sl-fea* worker who paints pedestrian crossings <**Ita**⁘[*1]>

zêc {a (acc. = gen.) +ev (ext. pl) masc.; Nom Pl zȅčevi} (lit. hare) **1** *sl-sex* ***Fac*** person who ejaculates prematurely <**Slav**[*1]> **2** *sl-fea* ***Fac*** coward, chicken <**Slav**[*1]>

• **ù tōm gŕmu lȅži zêc** {S} (lit. the rabbit lies in that bush) *col* used to sum up one's point, That's how it is!

zèčijā pȁmēt {NP} (lit. hare's mind) *sl* escape, flee ☞ pamet

zȅgnuti {nēm, nū perf.} *sl* tell, say

zȅka {ē fem.; Dat zȅki} *sl-sex* ***Obs*** sexual intercourse <Slav❖*1>

zȅkati {ām, ajū imperf.} **a.** *sl* insert, stick in <Slav❖*1> **b.** *sl-sex* engage in sexual intercourse with (of a male) <Slav❖*2>

zȅkavac {vca (acc. = gen.) masc.} *sl-fea* ***Der*** coward, chicken <Slav❖*1>

zȅkiti {kīm, kē imperf.} *sl* look, watch, scope out <Slav❖*1>

zékiti se {kīm, kē imperf. intr.} **a.** *sl-fea* make jokes with <Slav*1> **b.** *sl-fea* have fun <Slav*2> **c.** *sl-sex* engage in sexual intercourse with <Slav*3> **d.** *sl* cheat, swindle <Slav*4>

zelèmbāć [1] {lembáća (acc. = gen.) masc.} (lit. green lizard) **a.** *sl-fea* inexperienced male, greenhorn <Slav❖*1> **b.** *sl-fea* youngster, kid <Slav❖*2>

zelèmbāć [2] {lembáća masc.} (lit. the green one) **1** *sl* US dollar, greenback <Slav❖*1> **2** *sl* five hundred dinars; a five hundred-dinar bill <Slav❖*1> **3** *sl* hundred dinars; a hundred-dinar bill <Slav*1>

zèlen {a, o adj.} **1** *sl-fea* young <Slav*1> **2** *sl-polit* environmentalist <Slav*1>

zèlenā {ē fem. (adj. decl.)} (lit. the green one) **1** *sl-sex* ***Fac*** virgin (female) <Slav*1> **2** *sl-drink* herbal brandy <Slav*1> **3** *sl* watermelon <Slav*1>

zèlenā bèretka {NP} (lit. green beret) *sl-mil* Bosnian Muslim soldier ☞ **beretka**

zelènāš [1] {lenáša (acc. = gen.) masc.} *sl-fea* park guard <Slav❖*1>

zelènāš [2] {lenáša masc.} (lit. the green one) *sl* money <Slav*1>

zelenȁšica {ē fem.} (lit. green woman) *sl-sex* ***Fac*** virgin (female) <Slav❖*1>

zelènbāč {lenbáča masc.} (lit. green lizard) [std. = zelembać] *sl* US dollar, greenback <Slav❖✍*1>

zelènbāć {lenbáća masc.} (lit. green lizard) *sl* five hundred dinars; a five-hundred dinar bill <Slav❖*1>

zèlenī {ōg masc.} (lit. the green one) *sl* US dollar, greenback <Slav*1>

zèlenī plân {NP} (lit. green plan) *sl* five thousand dinars; a five-thousand dinar bill ☞ **plan**

zèlenī Tȍmāš {NP} (lit. green Tom) *sl-crime* police van (in pre-WWII Yugoslavia) ☞ **Tomaš**

zelènika {ē fem.} (lit. the green one) *sl-arch* woods, forest <Slav❖*1>

zelènilo {a neut.} (lit. green) *sl* sickness <Slav*1>

zèlenō svȅtlo {NP} (lit. green light) SerE *col* acceptance ☞ **svetlo**

zèlenō svjȅtlo {NP} (lit. green light) *col* acceptance ☞ **svjetlo**

Zelènjāk {a masc.} Ser *sl* name for Zeleni Venac (a neighborhood in Belgrade) <SlavO✍>

zelenjáva {adj.} (lit. greens) *sl-sex* ***Fac*** inexperienced, green <Slav*1>

zȅlja {ē fem.} *sl-sex* ***Obs*** vagina, cunt <Slav❖*1>

zêlje {a neut.} (lit. cabbage) **1** *sl* money <Slav*1> **2** *sl* documents <Slav*1> **3** **Cro** *sl* name of an army swimming pool in Zagreb, Croatia <Slav*1>

zȅljkati {ām, ajū imperf.} *sl-sex* ***Obs*** urinate, piss <Slav❖*1>

zéma {ē masc.} SerE *col* ***Fam*** fellow countryman <Slav✍*1>

zèmān {zemána masc.} BosM *col-dia* time (in general) <NE*1>

zèmbīlj {zembílja masc.} BosM *col-dia* basket <NE>

zèmlja {ē fem.} (lit. earth) *sl-sex* ***Fac-Obs*** vagina, cunt <Slav*1>

• **Zȅmljo, otvòri se!** {S} (lit. Open up, earth!) *col* used to express shame

zèmljāk {zemljáka (acc. = gen.) masc.} (lit. compatriot) **1** *sl-crime* corpse, stiff <Slav*1> **2** *sl-crime* policeman, cop <Slav*1>

zèmljosānje {a neut.} *sl-drink* drinking (alcohol) <Slav❖*1>

zèmljosati {ošēm, ošū imperf.} (lit. earth) *sl-drink* get drunk <Slav❖*1>

zèmljosati se {ošēm, ošū imperf. intr.} (lit. earth oneself) *sl-drink* get very drunk, get smashed <Slav❖*1>

zȅmljotrēs {a masc.} (lit. earthquake) *sl-drink* rum and coke <Slav*1>

zémo {ē masc.} /zémo /a masc./ *col* ***Fam*** fellow countryman <Slav✍*1>

zȅn {a +ov (ext. pl) masc.; Nom Pl zènovi} *sl-drugs* LSD, acid

zȅnga {ē fem.; Dat zȅngi} *sl-polit* member of Croatian national guard <Abb✍>

zȅngnuti {nēm, nū perf.} *sl* tell, say <Ger✍*1>

zȅngovati {gujēm, gujū imperf.} *sl* arrange for

zènisati {išēm, išū biasp.} *sl* look, watch, scope out <Sans⁘*1>

zȅnt {a +ov (ext. pl) masc.; Nom Pl zèntovi} **1** *sl-fea* danger **a.i.** *sl-fea* mess, disorder, disturbance **ii.** *sl* fear

zèntara {ē fem.} **1** Cro *sl-drink* name of a bar at the Central Station in Zagreb, Croatia **2** *sl-fea* coward, chicken

zèntati {ām, ajū biasp.} **1** *sl* look, watch, scope out **2** *sl* dance

zentírati {zèntīrām, zentírajū perf.} *sl* discover, find out

zȅntovati {tujēm, tujū imperf.} **1** *sl* feel, sense **2** *sl* discover, find out

zȅntovati se {tujēm, tujū imperf.} *sl* have fear *sl*

zȅnuti {nēm, nū perf.} *sl* hit, punch

zȅpa {ē fem.} *sl* mouth

zêpsti {zébēm, zébū imperf.} *sl-crime* pick pockets <Slav*1>

zèra {ē fem.} Din *col* small quantity of something <NE>

zèricu {adv.} Bos *col* a little, just a little bit: *Skreni zericu ulijevo! Turn just a little bit to the left!* <NE⁘>

zèriti {rīm, rē imperf.} **a.** *sl* grab, snatch <NE*1> **b.** *sl* catch <NE*2> **c.** *sl-crime* steal, swipe <NE*3>

zèru {adv.} Bos *col* a little, just a little bit: *pomjeriti se zeru move just a little bit* <NE>

zȅsta drȉnk {NP} *sl-drink* drink (alcohol) ☞ **drink**

ZȄT {a ov masc.; Nom Pl ZÈTovi} (lit. Zagreb electric trams) Cro *sl-sex* ***Fac-Obs*** group sex <Abb*1>

Zȅtovac {tōvca (acc. = gen.) masc.} (lit. worker of the Zagreb electric trams) *sl-crime* streetcar pickpocket <Abb⁘*1>

zèus {a (acc. = gen.) masc.} (lit. Zeus) *sl-crime* stupid or mentally deficient person <Gre*1>

zévalica {ē fem.} (lit. yawner) SerE *sl-sex* ***Fac-Obs*** vagina, cunt <Slav*1>

zévati {ām, ajū imperf.} (lit. yawn) **1** SerE *sl-fea* stare at, be fixated on <Slav*1> **2** *sl-fea* be bored <Slav*1>

- **zévati čmâr** {VP} (lit. yawn one's asshole) SerE *sl-fea* ***Obs*** get frightened, freak
- **zévati ko pròmūkla mȁčka** {VP} (lit. yawn like a hoarse cat) SerE *sl-fea* talk persistently and meaninglessly, blabber, chatter

zȅvzečiti se {čīm, čē perf. intr.} *sl-fea* spend one's time in useless activities, fool around, mess around <NE⁘*1>

zèvzek {a (acc. = gen.) masc.} **a.** *sl-fea* stupid or mentally deficient person <NE*1> **b.** *sl-fea* insane person, nut case <NE*2> **c.** *sl-fea* worthless or despicable person, bum <NE*3>

zêz {a +ov (ext. pl) masc.; Nom Pl zȅzovi} *sl-fea* trick, joke <Slav⁘*1>

zèzāč {zezáča (acc. = gen.) masc.} *sl-fea* joker, trickster, rascal <Slav⁘*1>

zezȁčina {ē fem.} *sl-fea* extensive joking <Slav⁘>

zȅzāje {a neut.} *sl-fea* joking with, fooling with <Slav⁘*1>

zȅzalica {ē fem.} **1** *sl-fea* fun <Slav⁘*1> **2** *sl* arm <Slav⁘*1> **3** *sl* toy <Slav⁘*1>

zezàncija {ē fem.} **a.** *sl-fea* fun <Slav⁘*1> **b.** *sl-fea* joking with, fooling with <Slav⁘*2> **c.** *sl* cheating, swindling <Slav⁘*3>

zȅzānje {a neut.} **1a.** *sl-fea* joking with, fooling with <Slav⁘*1> **b.** *sl-fea* teasing <Slav⁘*2> **c.** *sl-fea* cheating, swindling <Slav⁘*3> **2** *sl-drugs* intravenous intake of narcotic drugs, main-lining, shooting up <Slav⁘*1>

zȅzati {ām, ajū imperf.} **a.** *sl-fea* joke with, make a fool of <Slav⁘*1> **b.** *sl-fea* tease <Slav⁘*2> **c.** *sl* cheat, swindle <Slav⁘*3> **d.** *sl* torture <Slav⁘*4> **e.** *sl-sex* engage in sexual intercourse with (of a male) <Slav⁘*5>

- **kàd bi se zȅzali** {AdvP} (lit. if we were joking) *col* used as a strong negative response, no way, never
- **zȅzati u mâlī mȍzak** {VP} (lit. joke in the little brain) **a.** *sl-fea* joke with, make a fool of **b.** *sl-fea* cheat, swindle
- **zȅzati u mȍzak** {VP} (lit. joke in the brain) **a.** *sl* joke with, make a fool of **b.** *sl* cheat, swindle

zȅzati se {ām, ajū imperf. intr.} **a.** *sl-fea* make jokes with <Slav*1> **b.** *sl-fea* have fun <Slav*2> **c.** *sl-sex* engage in sexual intercourse with <Slav*3> **d.** *sl* cheat, swindle <Slav*4>

zèzātor {a (acc. = gen.) masc.} *sl-fea* joker, trickster, rascal <Slav⁘*1>

zȅznuti {nēm, nū perf.} **a.** *sl-fea* joke with, make a fool of <Slav⁘*1> **b.** *sl* cheat, swindle <Slav⁘*2>

- **zȅznūti u mȍzak** {VP} (lit. joke in the brain) *sl-fea* trick, cheat, swindle

zȅznuti se {nēm, nū perf. intr.} *sl* make a mistake, screw up <Slav⁘*1>

zezȕckati {ām, ajū imperf.} *sl* cheat, swindle <Slav⁘*1>

zezȕckati se {ām, ajū imperf. intr.} *sl* cheat, swindle <Slav⁘*1>

zgȁsnuti {nēm, nū perf. intr.} **1** *sl* die, kick the bucket <**Slav**[*1]> **2** *sl-sports* lose a game <**Slav**[*1]> **3** *sl-fea* be destroyed, be ruined <**Slav**[*1]>

zgȁziti *See the following*

• **zgȁziti ko mȁčka ciklámu** {VP} (lit. squish like a cat does with cyclamen) *sl* beat up

zgȅngovati {gujēm, gujū perf.} *sl* realize, become aware of

zgepàrluk {a masc.} **1** *sl-crime* loot, pillage <**Slav❖**[*1]> **2** *sl-crime* theft

zgȅpiti {pīm, pē perf.} *sl-crime* steal, swipe <**Slav❖**[*1]>

zgíbati {zgîbām, zgíbajū perf.} *sl-sstu* cut classes <**Slav❖**[*1]>

zgȉljati {ām, ajū perf.} /zgíljati/ *sl* run away, flee <**Gyp❖**[*1]>

zglàjzati {ām, ajū perf.} **1a.** *sl* make a mistake, screw up <**Ger❖**[*1]> **b.** *sl* miss, fail <**Ger❖**[*2]> **2** *sl-polit* get removed from political life <**Ger❖**[*1]> **3** *sl-fea* overdo partying <**Ger❖**[*1]>

zglȁjznuti {nēm, nū perf. intr.} **1a.** *sl* make a mistake, screw up <**Ger❖**[*1]> **b.** *sl* miss, fail <**Ger❖**[*2]> **2** *sl-polit* get removed from political life <**Ger**[*1]>

zgȍdno {excl.} *col* ***App*** used to express appreciation <**Slav**[*1]>

zgòmbati {ām, ajū perf.} *sl* beat up

zgòreti {rīm, rē perf.} (lit. burn) *sl-fea* be destroyed, be ruined <**Slav**[*1]>

zgotíviti {zgòtīvīm, vē perf.} **a.** *sl* make, create **b.** *sl* take **c.** *sl* persuade, convince **d.** *sl* arrange for **e.** *sl* fall in love

zgotòviti {zgòtovīm, vē perf.} (lit. prepare) **a.** *sl* take <**Slav**[*1]> **b.** *sl* persuade, convince <**Slav**[*2]> **c.** *sl* arrange for <**Slav**[*3]>

zgȍvnati {ām, ajū perf.} (lit. shit) **a.** *sl* destroy, ruin <**Slav❖**[*1]> **b.** *sl* beat up severely <**Slav❖**[*1]>

zgrȁbiti {bīm, bē perf.} *col* snatch, grab <**Slav**[*1]>

zgrȁmziti {zīm, zē perf.} *sl* rape

zgrànuti se {rānēm, nū perf. intr.} *col* be surprised <**Slav❖**[*1]>

zgȑbiti {bīm, bē perf.} (lit. hump) *sl-sex* ***Obs*** engage in sexual intercourse with (of a male) <**Slav**[*1]>

zgȑtati *See the following*

• **zgȑtati pàre lòpatōm** {VP} (lit. collect money with a shovel) *sl-fea* posess a significant amount of money, rake in the dough

zgrȕdati {ām, ajū perf.} (lit. snowball) *sl* beat up <**Slav❖**[*1]>

zgùbidān {a (acc. = gen.) masc.} (lit. the one who loses days) Kajk *col* loafer, idler <**Slav✍**[*1]>

zgúditi {dīm, dē perf.} (lit. fiddle) *sl-sex* ***Obs*** engage in sexual intercourse with (of a male) <**Slav❖**[*1]>

zgustírati se {gùstīrām, gustírajū perf. intr.} *sl* have enough of, be sick and tired of <**Ita❖**[*1]>

zgûza {adv.} (lit. asswards) *sl* ***Obs*** from behind <**Slav❖**>

zgúziti {zgûzīm, zē perf.} (lit. ass) **a.** *sl* ***Obs*** hit from behind <**Slav❖**[*1]> **b.** *sl-sex* engage in sexual intercourse with (of a male) <**Slav❖**[*2]>

zgȕžvati {ām, ajū perf.} (lit. wrinkle) *sl* beat up <**Slav**[*1]>

• **zgȕžvati cȉferblat** {VP} *sl* destroy somebody's face by hitting it, rearrange somebody's face

zíbene {a masc.} *sl* seven <**Ger✍**>

zȉc {a +ev (ext. pl) masc.; Nom Pl zȉcevi} (lit. seat) *sl-sex* ***Fac*** buttocks, seat, butt <**Ger**[*1]>

zȉcagu {zȉcegu fem.; perm} [std. = guzica] *sl-sex* buttocks, butt <**Slav✍**>

zȉcer {a masc.} **1** *sl-sports* position from which it is easy to score a basket <**Ger**[*1]> **2** *sl* any situation with a certain outcome, sure thing <**Ger**[*2]> **2** *sl-crime* ambush <**Ger**[*1]>

zȉcnuti {nēm, nū perf. intr.} *sl* sit <**Ger❖**>

zîd {a +ov (ext. pl) masc.; Nom Pl zȉdovi} (lit. wall) **1** *sl* cover, disguise <**Slav**[*1]> **2** *sl* neighbor <**Slav**[*1]>

• **iza zîda** {PP} (lit. behind the wall) *sl-fea* secretly, under the counter

zȉdār {zidára (acc. = gen.) masc.; Voc zȉdāru} (lit. bricklayer) *sl-crime* pickpocket's accomplice <**Slav**[*1]>

zídati {zîdām, zídajū imperf.} (lit. build) **1** *sl-sex* ***Fac-Obs*** engage in sexual intercourse with (of a male) <**Slav**[*1]> **2a.** *sl-crime* help in pickpocketing <**Slav**[*1]> **b.** *sl-crime* look for one's accomplice <**Slav**[*2]>

zȉft {a +ov (ext. pl) masc.; Nom Pl zȉftovi} *col* sediment <**Ger**[*1]>

zigoráknuti {gòrāknēm, nū perf.} *sl* beat up severely

zȉgovānje {a neut.} *sl-sex* ***Obs*** sexual intercourse <**Gre❖**[*1]>

zȉgovati {gujēm, gujū imperf.} *sl-sex* ***Obs*** engage in sexual intercourse with (of a male) <**Gre❖**[*1]>

zȉher {a masc.} *col* any situation with a certain outcome, sure thing <**Ger**[*1]>

zȉher {adv.} *col* certainly, surely: *On je ziher kod kuće. He is surely home.* <**Ger**[*1]>

zihèrāš {a (acc. = gen.) masc.} **a.** *sl-fea* cautious male <Ger> **b.** *sl-crime* burglar <Ger[*1]>

zihèrāškī {ā, ō adj.} *sl* safe <Ger❖>

zȉherica {ē fem.} **a.** *col* safety pin <Ger> **b.** *sl-fea* any situation with a certain outcome, sure thing <Ger[*1]>

zȉherūng {a masc.} *sl-crafts* fuse <Ger>

zìjān[1] {zijána masc.} BosM *col* being lost <NE[*1]>

zìjān[2] {adj.} BosM *col* lost <NE[*1]>

zijánćer {a (acc. = gen.) masc.} *sl-fea* troublemaker, rowdy, ruffian <NE❖[*1]>

zijániti {zìjānīm, nē perf.} BosM *col* lose, be unable to find <NE❖[*1]>

zijániti se {zìjānīm, nē perf. intr.} BosM *col* become lost <NE❖[*1]>

zìjati {ām, ajū imperf.} /zíjati/ **1** *col* stare at, be fixated on <Slav[*1]> **2** *sl* shout at <Slav[*1]>

zijévānje {a neut.} /zijèvānje/ (lit. yawning) *sl* laughter <Slav[*1]>

zijévati /zijèvati/ *See the following*
- **zijévati u dȉm** {VP} (lit. yawn into smoke) *sl-fea* suffer from tuberculosis, have TB

zijévnuti {zijêvnēm, nū perf. intr.} /zijèvnuti/ (lit. yawn) *sl* die, kick the bucket <Slav[*1]>

zȉk {excl.} *col* the sound made by slamming, wham <Slav>

zíka {ē fem.; Dat zíki} [std. = muzika] *sl-music* music <Lat✍>

zíkiti {kīm, kē imperf.} *sl-fea* peep, look at others <Slav✍[*1]>

zîljka {ē fem.} *sl* eye (sight organ)

zimárac {rca masc.} *sl* winter coat <Slav✍[*1]>

zìmnjāk {zimnjáka masc.} *sl* winter coat <Slav❖[*1]>

zimòvnīk {a masc.} Cro *sl-drink* name of a restaurant at the Central station in Zagreb, Croatia <Slav❖[*1]>

zȉnbu {ua masc.} *sl-auto* gasoline

zìndān {zindána masc.} (lit. dark place) *sl-crime* strict prison <NE[*1]>

zìnden {a masc.} (lit. dark place) *sl-crime* strict prison <NE[*1]>

Zȉni da ti kâžēm! {S} (lit. Open your mouth so that I can tell you!) **1** *col* used to make somebody go away, Get lost! **2** *col* used to express unwillingness to release information, I'm not gonna tell you that! ☞ **zinuti**

zìntati {ām, ajū imperf.} *sl* look, observe

zȉnuti {nēm, nū perf. intr.} (lit. open one's eyes wide) **a.** *col* stare at, be fixated on <Slav[*1]> **b.** *col* be surprised <Slav[*2]> **c.** *col* wonder, be puzzled <Slav[*3]>
- **Zȉni da ti kâžēm!** {S} (lit. Open your mouth so that I can tell you!) **1** *col* used to make somebody go away, Get lost! **2** *col* used to express unwillingness to release information, I'm not gonna tell you that!
- **zȉnuti kao sȍm** {VP} (lit. open up one's mouth like a catfish) *sl-fea* be very surprised
- **zȉnuti ko pȇš** {VP} *col* open one's mouth wide

zìnzōv {zinzòva (acc. = gen.) masc.} *sl-fea* stupid or mentally deficient person

zȉpa {excl.; perm} /zìpa/ [std. = pazi] **1** *sl* used to draw someone's attention, look <Slav✍[*1]> **2** *sl* watch out, be careful <Slav✍[*1]>

zipàrati {ām, ajū imperf.} **a.** *sl* reproach, scold **b.** *sl-fea* talk persistently and meaninglessly, blabber, chatter

zipáriti {zìpārīm, rē imperf.} **a.** *sl* reproach, scold **b.** *sl-fea* talk persistently and meaninglessly, blabber, chatter

zȉrkati {ām, ajū imperf.} *col* look, watch, scope out <Slav[*1]>

zȉtovānje {a neut.} *sl-sex* ***Obs*** sexual intercourse

zȉtovati {tujēm, tujū imperf.} *sl-sex* ***Obs*** engage in sexual intercourse with (of a male)

zjàkara {ē fem.} *sl* head <Slav❖[*1]>

zjȁker {a masc.} **a.** *sl-fea* loafer, idler <Slav❖[*1]> **b.** *sl-fea* homeless person, bum <Slav❖[*2]>

zjápiti *See the following*
- **zjápiti prázan** {VP} (lit. yawn empty) *col* be empty

zjȁšiti {šīm, še perf.} (lit. ride) *sl-sex* ***Fac-Obs*** engage in sexual intercourse with (of a male) <Slav❖[*1]>

zjévalo {a neut.} (lit. yawner) *sl-music* singer <Slav❖[*1]>

zjȍdlati {ām, ajū perf.} (lit. yodel) *sl-sex* ***Fac-Obs*** engage in sexual intercourse with (of a male) <Ger❖[*1]>

zjòsatibrinj {a masc.; perm} [std. = zbrisati] *sl* escape, flee <Slav✍[*1]>

zlâtnjāk {a masc.} (lit. the gold one) *sl-fea* gold tooth <Slav❖[*1]>

zlȍptati {ām, ajū perf.} (lit. ball) *sl* beat up <Slav❖[*1]>

zlòtvor {a masc.} (lit. evil-doer) *sl-sex* ***Fac-Obs*** penis, dick, prick <Slav[*1]>

zmȁj[1] {zmàja (acc. = gen.) +ev (ext. pl) masc.; Nom Pl zmàjevi} (lit. dragon) **1** *sl* housekeeper, maid <Slav[*1]> **2** *sl-fea* elderly female who sits in her apartment all the time <Slav*1> 3 *sl-fea* one's mother who spends all her time at home <Slav*1>

zmȁj 2 {adj.} (lit. dragon) **a.** *sl-fea* ***App*** excellent, awesome <Slav*1> **b.** *sl-fea* ***App*** handsome and strong <Slav*2>

• **ko zmȁj** {PP} (lit. like a dragon) **1** *col* excellent, awesome 2 *sl-fea* very fast

• **kȕćnī zmȁj** {NP} (lit. house dragon) *sl* housekeeper, maid

zmȁjček {a (acc. = gen.) masc.} (lit. small dragon) *sl-sports* player or fan of Olimpija (a soccer and basketball team from Ljubljana, Slovenia) <Slav❖*1>

zmajèvit {a, o adj.} (lit. dragon-like) *sl-fea* ***App*** excellent, awesome <Slav*1>

zmájko {a masc.} (lit. small dragon) **1** *sl* housekeeper, maid <Slav❖*1> 2 *sl* housewife, lady of the house <Slav❖*1>

zmátati {zmâtām, zmátajū imperf.} *sl* sell (exchange merchandise for money) <Slav❖*1>

zmesáriti {mèsārīm, rē perf.} (lit. butcher) *sl* beat up, butcher <Slav❖*1>

zmìja {ē fem.} /zmíja/ (lit. snake) **1** *sl-fea* ***Der*** evil person, snake <Slav*1> 2 *sl-fea* ***App*** talented male <Slav*1> 3 *sl-fea* slender female <Slav*1> 4 *sl-fea* elderly female <Slav*1> 5 *sl-fea* prostitute, hooker <Slav*1> 6 *sl-fea* motorcycle <Slav*1>

• **ko zmìja u cévi** {PP} (lit. like a snake in a gun barrel) SerE *sl-fea* in a helpless position, like fish in a barrel

• **Kòlikō je zmíjā?** {S} (lit. How many snakes?) *sl* used to inquire about the time

zmijoglávac {vca masc.} (lit. snake-head) *sl-sex* ***Fac-Obs*** penis, dick, prick <Slav❖*1>

zmijoglávac {vca (acc. = gen.) masc.} (lit. snake-head) *sl* male, guy <Slav❖*1>

zmjȅsiti {sīm, sē perf.} (lit. knead) *sl* beat up <Slav❖*1>

zmȍtān {a, o adj.} (lit. wrapped) *sl-fea* distressed <Slav✍*1>

zmòtati {ām, ajū perf.} (lit. wrap) *sl* cheat, swindle <Slav✍*1>

znâči {excl.} *col* used to sum up one's point, that means, so, you see <Slav*1>

znȁčka {ē fem.; Dat znȁčki} (lit. pin) *sl-fea* pimple <Slav*1>

• **ùdarničkā znȁčka** {VP} (lit. champion worker's pin) *sl* bruise

znâš 1 {excl.} *col* used to draw attention, you know <Slav>

znâš 2 {excl.} **1** *col* used to express hesitation, you know <Slav*1> 2 *col* used to check if the channel of communication is open, got it <Slav*1>

znȁti *See the following*

• **kȍ će ga znȁti** {S} *col* used to express lack of knowledge, who knows: *Ko će ga znati kad će se popraviti vrijeme. Who knows when the weather will improve.*

• **znȁti s[NOUN:INS]** {LSF} (lit. know with [NOUN: ACC]) *col* be good with [NOUN:ACC]: *On zna s parama. He is good with money.*

znogírati {nògīrām, nogírajū perf.} (lit. kick out) **1** *sl* dump one's boyfriend or girlfriend <Slav❖*1> 2 *sl* throw away, toss out <Slav❖*1>

znôj *See the following*

• **cȑnačkī znôj** {NP} (lit. African American sweat) *sl* ***Fac*** weak black coffee

• **pànterōv znôj** {NP} (lit. panther's sweat) *sl-drink* hard liquor

znòjalica {ē fem.} (lit. sweater) *sl* sock, stocking <Slav❖*1>

znòjara {ē fem.} (lit. sweater) *sl* shirt <Slav❖*1>

znȍjavica {ē fem.} (lit. sweater) *sl* sock, stocking <Slav❖*1>

znòjīć {znojíća masc.} (lit. small sweat) *sl-sex* ***Fac-Obs*** sexual intercourse <Slav❖*1>

znôjka {ē fem.} (lit. the sweaty one) *sl* sock, stocking <Slav❖*1>

znȍjogūz {a masc.} (lit. sweat-ass) Cro *sl-drink* ***Fac-Obs*** Ritoznojčan (a brand of wine) <Slav❖*1>

znjánje {a neut.} *sl* walk <Slav✍*1>

zôb {i fem.} (lit. oats) **1** *sl-mil* ammunition, ammo <Slav*1> 2 *sl* money <Slav*1>

zòbati {zȍbām, zòbajū biasp.} (lit. peck) *sl* eat, devour <Slav*1>

zobljáriti {zòbljārīm, rē imperf.} *sl-crime* steal, swipe

zȍbnice {nīcā masc. pl.} (lit. oat bags) *sl* ***Fac*** teeth <Slav*1>

zȍlka {ē fem.} *sl* eye (sight organ)

zôo {a masc.} (lit. zoo) *sl* dance floor <Gre*1>

zôr {a +ev (ext. pl) masc.; Nom Pl zórevi} **1** *col-dia* effort <NE> 2 *col-dia* pride <NE*1>

zȍrli {adv.} *col-dia* very: *On je zorli tvrdoglav. He is very pigheaded.* <NE❖*1>

zórnjača *See the following*
• **Zórnjaču ti jèbēm!** {S} (lit. I screw your early morning star!) *dia* ***Off*** used as a weak curse, Screw you!

zòrnjāk {zornjáka masc.} **1** *sl-sex* ***Obs*** early morning sexual intercourse <**Slav**✣[*1]> 2 *sl-sex* ***Obs*** early morning erection <**Slav**✣[*1]>

zòrōm {adv.} *col* in the morning <**Slav**✣>

zȍrt [1] {excl.} *col* used to signal that another person is frightened <**NE**>

zȍrt [2] {a +ov (ext. pl) masc.; Nom Pl zòrtovi} *col* fear <**NE**>

zȍtskā bukùrlija {NP} *sl-arch* mosque ☞ **bukurlija**

zôvnūt {a, o adj.} (lit. called) *sl-fea* slightly insane, nutty <**Slav**[*1]>

zráčiti {zrâčīm, čē imperf. intr.} (lit. emit, radiate) *sl* look at with interest, check out <**Slav**[*1]>

zrȁkalica {ē fem.} *sl* eye (sight organ) <**Slav**✣[*1]>

zrȁkati {ām, ajū imperf.} *sl* chase <**Slav**[*1]>

zrȁkavica {ē fem.} *sl* eye (sight organ) <**Slav**✣[*1]>

zráknuti {zrâknēm, nū perf.} *sl* look, watch, scope out <**Slav**[*1]>

zrȁkoš {excl.} *sl* warning signal <**Slav**✐[*1]>

zrȁšiti {šīm, še perf.} *sl-sex* ***Obs*** engage in sexual intercourse with (of a male)

zrȅzati {zrȅžēm, zrȅžū perf.} (lit. cut) *sl-sex* ***Fac-Obs*** engage in sexual intercourse with (of a male) <**Slav**✣[*1]>

zrȅzati se {zrȅžēm, zrȅžū perf. intr.} *sl* make a mistake, screw up <**Slav**✣[*1]>

zrȉhtān {a, o adj.} Kajk *sl-fea* tuned up (of any mechanism) <**Ger**✣[*1]>

zrìhtati {ām, ajū perf.} *col-dia* settle an issue <**Ger**>

zríka {ē fem. & masc.} *sl-fea* cross-eyed person <**Slav**[*1]>

zrȉkati {ām, ajū imperf.} **1** *sl* estimate, guess <**Ger**✣[*1]> **2a.** *sl* stare at, be fixated on <**Ger**✣[*1]> **b.** *sl* peep, look at others <**Ger**✣[*2]> **c.** *sl* take a look, scope out <**Ger**✣[*3]>

zrȉkav {a, o adj.} *sl-fea* cross-eyed <**Slav**[*1]>

zrȉkī {īja (acc. = gen.) masc.} /zrìki/ *sl-fea* miser, tightwad, skinflint

zríkiti {kīm, kē imperf.} *col* squint <**Slav**[*1]>

zrȉktati {ām, ajū perf.} **1** Kajk *sl* repair, fix <**Ger**✣[*1]> 2 Kajk *sl* arrange for <**Ger**✣[*2]>

zrìlīng [1] {a (acc. = gen.) masc.} *sl-fea* stupid or mentally deficient person <**Ger**✣[*1]>

zrìlīng [2] {adj.} *sl-fea* ***Der*** insane, nuts <**Ger**✣[*1]>

zrȉngati {ām, ajū perf.} *sl* ring (a bell, etc.) <**Ger**✣[*1]>

zrȋnskī {ōg (acc. = gen.) masc.} (lit. Zrinski was a Croatian noble) *sl-crime* detective <**SlavO**[*1]>

Zrínjevac {vca masc.} (lit. Zrinjevac is a name for Zrinski Square in Zagreb, Croatia) **Cro** *sl-drink* Zrinski (a brand of Croatian brandy) <**SlavO**[*1]>

zrȉpovati {pujēm, pujū perf.} *sl-drugs* take LSD, drop acid <**Eng**✣[*1]>

zrȉsati {išēm, išū biasp.} (lit. erase) Cro *sl* cheat, swindle <**Slav**✣[*1]>

zȑkī {īja (acc. = gen.) masc.} *sl-fea* miser, tightwad, skinflint

zŕnce *See the following*
• **bêlā kȑvnā zŕnca** {NP} (lit. white blood cells) SerE *sl-sex* ***Fac-Obs*** sperm

zȑnija {ē fem.} *dia* salt <**Slav**✣[*1]>

zûb [1] {a (acc. = gen.) masc.} (lit. tooth) *sl-crime* policeman, cop <**Slav**[*1]>

zûb [2] {a masc.} (lit. tooth) *sl* knife <**Slav**[*1]>
• **od zûba do zûba dvâ dâna jȁhānjā** {PP} (lit. from one tooth to another two days of riding) *sl-fea* gaps between the teeth
• **od zûba do zûba trî dâna jȁhānja** {PP} (lit. from one tooth to another three days of riding) *sl-fea* gaps between the teeth
• **U zûb te zlátan jèbēm!** {S} (lit. I screw you in your gold tooth!) *dia-col* ***Off*** used as a weak curse, Screw you!
• **zúbi na rázdeljak** {NP} (lit. parting teeth) SSer *sl-fea* gaps between the teeth
• **zúbi u fôrcìmeru** {NP} (lit. teeth in the lobby) *sl-fea* uneven teeth

zubárēnje {a neut.} *sl* laughter <**Slav**✣[*1]>

zubàtac {bàca (acc. = gen.) masc.} (lit. dentex fish) *sl-fea* male with crooked teeth <**Slav**[*1]>

zùbisānje {a neut.} *sl* laughing <**Slav**✣[*1]>

zúbiti {bīm, bē imperf.} (lit. tooth) *sl* eat, devour <**Slav**✣[*1]>

zubočùpāč {čupáča (acc. = gen.) masc.} (lit. tooth-puller) *sl* dentist <**Slav**✣[*1]>

zubolómac {mca masc.} (lit. tooth-smasher) *sl-crime* brass knuckles <**Slav**✣[*1]>

zȕc [1] {excl.} *col* the sound made by a fly, buzz <**Slav**>

zȕc [2] {a +ev (ext. pl) masc.; Nom Pl zùcevi} *col* whisper <**Slav**>

zúca {ē fem.} *sl-gamble* a kind of game where one has to guess who hit him/her <Slav[*1]>

zȕcati {ām, ajū imperf.} *col* whisper <Slav✣[*1]>

zȕckati {ām, ajū imperf.} *col* whisper <Slav✣[*1]>

zȕcniti {nēm, nū perf.} *sl* look, watch, scope out <Slav✣[*1]>

zȕcnuti {nēm, nū perf.} **1a.** *col* tell, say <Slav[*1]> **b.** *sl* admit, make a confession, come clean <Slav[*2]> 2 *sl* remember somebody <Slav[*1]> 3 *sl* look, watch, scope out <Slav[*1]>

zúčati {čīm, čē imperf.} *col* buzz loudly <Slav✣>

zûj {a +ev (ext. pl) masc.; Nom Pl zújevi} *col* buzz (bee, buzzer, etc.) <Slav>

zúja {ē fem.} **a.** *col* buzz (bee, buzzer, etc.) <Slav> **b.** *sl* pocket radio <Slav[*1]>

zùjāč {zujáča (acc. = gen.) masc.} *col* buzzing insect <Slav✣[*1]>

zùjača {ē fem.} *col* buzzing fly <Slav✣[*1]>

zujàčina {ē fem.} *sl-fea* boredom <Slav✣[*1]>

zújak {jka masc.} *col* dung beetle <Slav✣[*1]>

zújala {ē fem.} *col* buzzing fly <Slav✣[*1]>

zújalica {ē fem.} **a.** *col* buzzer (e.g. on a door) <Slav✣> **b.** *col* buzzing fly <Slav✣[*1]>

zújan {jna, jno adj.} *col* buzzing (bee, buzzer, etc.) <Slav✣>

zújānje {a neut.} *col* buzzing (bee, buzzer, etc.) <Slav✣>

zújati {jīm, jē imperf.} **a.** *col* buzz (bee, buzzer, etc.) <Slav✣> **b.i.aa.** *sl* walk <Slav✣[*1]> **bb.** *sl* breeze through town or bar <Slav✣[*2]> **ii.** *sl* sleep, nap <Slav✣[*2]>

zȕjav {a, o adj.} *col* buzzing (bee, buzzer, etc.) <Slav✣>

zújavac {vca masc.} *sl* phone <Slav✣[*1]>

zújēnje {a neut.} *col* buzzing (bee, buzzer, etc.) <Slav✣[*1]>

zujìkati {ām, ajū imperf.} *col* buzz (bee, buzzer, etc.) <Slav✣>

zújiti {jīm, jē imperf.} *col* buzz (bee, buzzer, etc.) <Slav✣>

zûjka {ē fem.} *sl* rain <Slav✣[*1]>

zȕjkānje {a neut.} *col* buzzing (bee, buzzer, etc.) <Slav✣>

zȕjkati {ām, ajū imperf.} *col* buzz (bee, buzzer, etc.) <Slav✣>

zûjno {adv.} *col* buzzing (bee, buzzer, etc.) <Slav✣>

zȕjnuti {nēm, nū perf. intr.} *col* start buzzing (bee, buzzer, etc.) <Slav✣>

zȕk {a +ov (ext. pl) masc.; Nom Pl zȕkovi} **a.** *col* buzz (bee, buzzer, etc.) <Slav> **b.** *col* noise <Slav✣[*1]>

zȕka {ē fem.} **a.** *col* buzz (bee, buzzer, etc.) <Slav✣> **b.** *col* noise <Slav✣[*1]>

zùkača {ē fem.} *col* buzzing fly <Slav✣[*1]>

zȕkānje {a neut.} **a.** *col* buzzing (bee, buzzer, etc.) <Slav✣> **b.** *col* noise <Slav✣[*1]>

zùkara {ē fem.} *col* buzzing fly <Slav✣[*1]>

zȕkasto {adv.} *col* buzzing (bee, buzzer, etc.) <Slav✣>

zúkati {zûčēm, čū imperf.} *col* buzz (bee, buzzer, etc.) <Slav✣>

zúknuti {zûknēm, nū perf.} *col* buzz (bee, buzzer, etc.) <Slav✣>

zúktati {tīm, tē imperf.} *col* buzz (bee, buzzer, etc.) <Slav✣>

zùkvan {a (acc. = gen.) masc.} *sl-fea* stupid or mentally deficient person <Slav✣[*1]>

zȕler {a (acc. = gen.) masc.} *sl* aviator

zȕlfa {ē fem.} *sl* female <NE[*1]>

zulukàfer {a (acc. = gen.) masc.} *sl* male, guy <NE⇝[*1]>

zùlum {a masc.} BosM *col* terror, tyranny <NE[*1]>

zulùmćār {lumćára (acc. = gen.) masc.} BosM *col* troublemaker, rowdy, ruffian <NE✣>

zûljka {ē fem.} *sl-arch* rain

zȕm {a +ov (ext. pl) masc.; Nom Pl zùmovi} *col* zoom (loud noise) <Eng>

zumírati {rām, rajū imperf. intr.} (lit. zoom) *sl* stare at, be fixated on <Eng[*1]>

zundàrača {ē fem.} *col* buzzing fly <Slav✣[*1]>

zundàrati {ām, ajū imperf.} *col* buzz loudly <Slav✣>

zùndulja {ē fem.} *col* buzzing fly <Slav✣[*1]>

zȕnuti {nēm, nū perf.} /zúnuti/ **a.** *col* buzz (bee, buzzer, etc.) <Slav✣> **b.** *col* hit, punch <Slav✣>

zȕnzāk {a (acc. = gen.) masc.} *col* dung beetle <Slav✣[*1]>

zùnzara {ē fem.} (lit. buzzing fly) *sl-fea* ***Der*** lazy or shiftless person, bum, good for nothing <Slav[*1]>

zunzàrānje {a neut.} *col* buzzing (bee, buzzer, etc.) <Slav✣>

zunzàrati {ām, ajū imperf. intr.} **a.** *col* buzz (bee, buzzer, etc.) <Slav✣> **b.** *sl-fea* talk persistently and meaninglessly, blabber, chatter <Slav✣[*1]>

zunzáriti {rīm, rē imperf. intr.} **a.** *col* buzz (bee, buzzer, etc.) <Slav✣> **b.** *sl-fea* talk persistently and meaninglessly, blabber, chatter <Slav✣[*1]>

zupčànik {čanīka (acc. = gen.) masc.} (lit. gearwheel) *sl-stu* mechanical engineering student <Slav[*1]>

zùra {ē fem.} *sl-arch* water

zȕrak {a masc.} *sl-crime* ***Der*** informer, stoolie, snitch <Slav✣[*1]>

zùrilo {a neut.} *sl* mirror <Slav✣[*1]>

zúriti {rīm, rē imperf.} *col* stare at, be fixated on <Slav✣[*1]>

zȗrka {ē fem.} [std. = frizura] *sl* haircut <Ger☞>

zȕrkati {ām, ajū imperf.} *sl* look, watch, scope out <Slav✣[*1]>

zùrna {ē fem.} *sl-drink* alcoholic, drunk <NE[*1]>

zȕza {ē fem.} *sl* housekeeper, maid <Slv>

zuzàrati {ām, ajū imperf.} (lit. buzz) *sl-fea* preach, give lectures to <Slav✣[*1]>

zuzáriti {zùzārīm, rē imperf.} (lit. buzz) *sl-fea* reproach, scold <Slav✣[*1]>

zȕznuti {nēm, nū perf.} (lit. buzz) **a.** *sl* tell, say <Slav✣[*1]> **b.** *sl* look, watch, scope out <Slav✣[*1]>

zȕzos {a masc.} *sl* housekeeper, maid <Slv☞>

zuzùckati {ām, ajū imperf.} *col* buzz (bee, buzzer, etc.) <Slav✣>

zùzuk {a masc.} *col* buzz (bee, buzzer, etc.) <Slav✣>

zuzùkānje {a neut.} *col* buzzing (bee, buzzer, etc.) <Slav✣>

zuzùkati {zùzūčēm, ūčū imperf.} *col* buzz (bee, buzzer, etc.) <Slav✣>

zuzùkav {a, o adj.} *col* buzzing (bee, buzzer, etc.) <Slav✣>

zvâr {excl.} *col* the sound made by roaring, roar <Slav>

zvȅckac {a masc.} *col* clang (sharp metal sound) <Slav✣>

zvȅckāj {a masc.} *col* clang (sharp metal sound) <Slav✣>

zvȅckānje {a neut.} *col* clang (sharp metal sound) <Slav✣>

zvȅckast {a, o adj.} *col* clanging (producing a sharp metal sound) <Slav✣>

zvȅckati {ām, ajū imperf. intr.} *col* clang (alarm, etc.) <Slav✣>

zvȅckav {a, o adj.} *col* clanging (producing a sharp metal sound) <Slav✣>

zvȅcnuti {nēm, nū perf. intr.} *col* clang (produce a sharp metal sound) <Slav✣>

zvȅčāj {a masc.} *col* clanging (producing a sharp metal sound) <Slav>

zvéčak {čka masc.} *dia* tongue (of a bell) <Slav✣[*1]>

zvȇčan {čna, čno adj.} *col* noisy <Slav✣>

zvéčānje {a neut.} *col* noise <Slav✣>

zvéčati {čīm, čē perf. intr.} *col* clang (produce a sharp metal sound) <Slav✣>

Zvȅčić {a masc.} Cro *sl-drink* name of a bar on Masarykova street in Zagreb, Croatia <BN☞>

Zvȅčka [1] {ē fem.; Dat Zvȅčki} Cro *sl-drink* name of a bar on Masarykova street in Zagreb, Croatia <Slav[*1]>

zvȅčka [2] {ē fem.; Dat zvȅčki} **a.** *col* rattle (the toy) <Slav✣> **b.** *sl-drink* cognac <Slav✣[*1]>

zvêk {a +ov (ext. pl) masc.; Nom Pl zvékovi} *col* clang (sharp metal sound) <Slav✣>

zvȅka {ē fem.; Dat zvȅki} *col* clang (sharp metal sound) <Slav✣>

zvèkan {a (acc. = gen.) masc.} **1** *sl-fea* stupid or mentally deficient person <Slav✣[*1]> **2** *sl-drink* Zvečevo (a brand of brandy) <BN☞>

zvȅkec {excl.} *col* the sound made by a metal object, clang <Slav>

zvȅkēt {a masc.} *col* clang (sharp metal sound) <Slav>

zvekètalo {a neut.} *col-dia* bell <Slav✣[*1]>

zvȅkētan {a, o adj.} *col* clanging (producing a sharp metal sound) <Slav✣>

zvekètānje {a neut.} *col* clanging (producing a sharp metal sound) <Slav✣>

zvekètati {zvèkećēm, ećū imperf. intr.} *col* clang (produce a sharp metal sound) <Slav✣>

zvekètav {a, o adj.} *col* clanging (producing a sharp metal sound) <Slav✣>

zvekètljiv {a, o adj.} *col* clanging (producing a sharp metal sound) <Slav✣>

zvekétnuti {zvèkētnēm, nū perf. intr.} *col* clang (produce a sharp metal sound) <Slav✣>

zvȅknuti {nēm, nū perf. intr.} **a.** *col* clang (produce a sharp metal sound) <Slav✣> **b.** *sl* hit, punch <Slav✣[*1]>

zvèktānje {a neut.} *col* clanging (producing a sharp metal sound) <Slav✣[*1]>

zvèktati {zvȅkćēm, ćū imperf. intr.} *col* clang (produce a sharp metal sound) <Slav✣>

zvȅktav {a, o adj.} *col* clanging (producing a sharp metal sound) <Slav❖ >

zvekùtati {zvèkućēm, ućū imperf. intr.} *col* clang (produce a sharp metal sound) <Slav❖>

zvêrka {ē fem.; Dat zvêrki} (lit. beast) SerE *col* very important or influential person, big shot: *Moj direktor je zverka. My boss is a bigshot.* <Slav*1>

zvézda *See the following*

• **Kévinu ti zvézdu jèbēm!**{S} (lit. I fuck your mother's star) SerE *dia* ***Off*** used as a strong curse, Fuck you!

• **Zvézdu li ti!** {S} (lit. *I screw* your star!) SerE *dia* ***Off*** used as a weak curse, Screw you!

• **Zvézdu li ti jèbēm!** {S} (lit. I screw your star!) SerE *dia* ***Off*** used as a weak curse, Screw you!

• **Zvézdu ti jârkū!** {S} (lit. *I screw* your bright star!) SerE *dia* ***Off*** used as a weak curse, Screw you!

• **Zvézdu ti jèbēm što te nȍću vȍdī!** {S} (lit. I screw your star which leads you at night!) SerE *dia* ***Off*** used as a weak curse, Screw you!

• **Zvézdu ti sjâjnū!** {S} (lit. *I screw* your shining star!) SerE *dia* ***Off*** used as a weak curse, Screw you!

zvezdánjac {njca masc.} SerE *sl* night <Slav❖*1>

zvèzdarnīk *See the following*

• **Zvèzdārnik ti tvôj jèbēm!** {S} (lit. I screw your constellation!) SerE *dia* ***Off*** used as a weak curse, Screw you!

zvèzdāš {zvezdáša (acc. = gen.) masc.; Voc zvȅzdāšu} *sl-sports* fan of Crvena Zvezda (a soccer team in Belgrade, Serbia) <Slav❖*1>

Zvézdu li ti! {S} (lit. *I screw* your star!) SerE *dia* ***Off*** used as a weak curse, Screw you! ☞ **zvezda**

Zvézdu li ti jèbēm! {S} (lit. I screw your star!) SerE *dia* ***Off*** used as a weak curse, Screw you! ☞ **zvezda**

Zvézdu ti jârkū! {S} (lit. *I screw* your bright star!) SerE *dia* ***Off*** used as a weak curse, Screw you! ☞ **zvezda**

Zvézdu ti jèbēm što te nȍću vȍdī! {S} (lit. I screw your star which leads you at night!) SerE *dia* ***Off*** used as a weak curse, Screw you! ☞ **zvezda**

Zvézdu ti sjâjnū! {S} (lit. *I screw* your shining star!) SerE *dia* ***Off*** used as a weak curse, Screw you! ☞ **zvezda**

zvíjati {zvȉjām, zvíjajū biasp.} (lit. wrap) *sl* disappear, evaporate, vanish <Slav*1>

zvȉjēr {i fem.} (lit. beast) *sl-fea* muscular male, pumped up guy <Slav*1>

zvȉjū {a (acc. = gen.) masc.} *sl-fea* irresponsible person <Slav*1>

zvȉjūk {a (acc. = gen.) masc.} **a.** *sl-fea* loafer, idler <Slav❖*1> **b.** *sl-fea* lazy or shiftless person, bum, good for nothing <Slav❖*2>

zvȉjūk {a masc.} *col* whistle (the sound) <Slav❖*1>

zvijùkānje {a neut.} *col* whistle (the sound) <Slav❖*1>

zvijùkati {zvȉjūčēm, zvȉjūčū imperf.} *col* whistle (produce the sound) <Slav❖*1>

zvínuti {zvînēm, nū perf.} *col* slap, smack <Slav*1>

zvȋr {a +ov (ext. pl) masc.; Nom Pl zvȉrovi} (lit. beast) [std. = zvijer] *sl-auto* motorcycle <Slav*1>

zvȉruša {ē fem.} (lit. she-beast) [std. = zvjeruša] *sl-auto* motorcycle <Slav*1>

zvȉsiti {sīm, sē perf. intr.} (lit. hang) **a.** *sl-fea* have a bad time <Slav❖*1> **b.** *sl-fea* lose money <Slav❖*2>

zvȉška {ē fem.; Dat zvȉški} *col* whistle (the instrument) <Slav❖>

zvȉz {a +ev (ext. pl) masc.; Nom Pl zvízovi} *col* wham (e.g. of a door slammed shut) <Slav>

zvȉzak {ska masc.} *col* whistle (the sound) <Slav❖>

zvȋzd {a +ov (ext. pl) masc.; Nom Pl zvízdovi} *col* whistle (the sound) <Slav❖>

zvȉzga {ē fem.; Dat zvȉzgi} **1** *col* hissing (snake, gas, etc.) <Slav❖> **2** *col* whistle (the sound) <Slav❖>

zvȉzgac {vca masc.} *col* wham (e.g. of a door slammed shut) <Slav❖>

zvȉzgāj {a masc.} *col* whistle (the sound) <Slav❖>

zvȉzgav {a, o adj.} *col* whistling <Slav❖>

zvȉzgljiv {a, o adj.} *col* whistling (pertaining to the sound) <Slav❖>

zvȉznuti {nēm, nū perf.} **a.** *sl* hit, punch <Slav❖*1> **b.i.** *sl-sex* engage in sexual intercourse with (of a male) <Slav❖*2> **ii.** *sl* die, kick the bucket <Slav❖*1>

• **Zvȉznēm ti ga!** {S} (lit. I slam it to you!) *col-dia* ***Off*** used as a weak curse, Screw you!

• **zvȉznuti ga** {VP} (lit. slam it) *sl-sex* engage in sexual intercourse with

zvȋžd {a +ov (ext. pl) masc.; Nom Pl zvíždovi} *col* whistle (the sound) <Slav❖>

zvȉždāj {a masc.} *col* whistle (the sound) <Slav❖>

zvȉždāk [1] {zviždáka (acc. = gen.) masc.} *col* whistling bird <Slav❖*1>

zvìždāk [2] {zviždáka masc.} *col* whistle (the instrument) <Slav⁘>

zvìždalica {ē fem.} *col* whistle (the instrument) <Slav⁘>

zvìždalo {a neut.} *col* whistle (the instrument) <Slav⁘>

zvìždāljka {ē fem.} *col* whistle (the instrument) <Slav⁘>

zvìždānje {a neut.} *col* whistle (the sound) <Slav⁘>

zvìždati {dīm, dē imperf.} **a.** *col* whistle (produce the sound) <Slav⁘> **b.** *sl-sex* urinate <Slav⁘[*1]>

zvȉždav {a, o adj.} *col* whistling (pertaining the sound) <Slav⁘>

zvȉždavac {vca (acc. = gen.) masc.} *col* whistling bird <Slav⁘[*1]>

zvȉždūk {a masc.} *col* whistle (the sound) <Slav⁘>

zviždùkānje {a neut.} *col* whistle (the sound) <Slav⁘>

zviždùkati {zvìždučēm, učū imperf.} *col* whistle (produce the sound) <Slav⁘>

zviždúknuti {zvìždūknēm, nū perf.} *col* whistle (produce the sound) <Slav⁘>

zvìžđēnje {a neut.} *col* whistle (the sound) <Slav⁘>

zvìžđeti {ždīm, ždē imperf.} *col* whistle (produce the sound) <Slav⁘>

zvȉžnuti {nēm, nū perf.} *col* whistle (produce the sound) <Slav⁘>

zvjèrati {ām, ajū imperf.} *col* stare at, be fixated on <Slav[*1]>

zvȍcānje {a neut.} (lit. clanging) *col* objecting <Slav⁘[*1]>

zvȍcati {ām, ajū imperf.} **a.** *col* objecting <Slav⁘> **b.** *col* reproach, scold <Slav⁘[*1]> **c.** *col* nag <Slav⁘[*2]> **d.** *col* preach (as a priest) <Slav⁘[*3]>

zvȍcnuti {nēm, nū perf. intr.} *col* clang (produce a sharp metal sound) <Slav⁘[*1]>

zvokòtati {zvòkoćem, oćū imperf. intr.} *col* clang (produce a sharp metal sound) <Slav⁘>

zvokòtnuti {zvòkotnēm, nū perf. intr.} *col* clang (produce a sharp metal sound) <Slav⁘>

zvȍn {a +ov (ext. pl) masc.; Nom Pl zvònovi} **a.** *col* clang (sharp metal sound) <Slav⁘> **b.** *col* bell <Slav⁘[*1]>

zvònac {nca (acc. = gen.) masc.} *sl-crime* ***Der*** informer, stoolie, snitch <Slav⁘[*1]>

zvȍnak {nka, nko adj.} *col* sound <Slav⁘>

zvȍnār {a (acc. = gen.) masc.} /zvònār /zvonára masc./ (lit. bellman) **a.** *sl-fea* extremely talkative person, chatterbox <Slav⁘[*1]> **b.** *sl-crime* informer, stoolie, snitch <Slav⁘[*2]>

zvónca {naca neut. pl.} (lit. bells) *sl-fea* bell-bottom pants <Slav⁘[*1]>

zvòncare {cārā fem. pl.} *sl-fea* bell-bottom pants <Slav⁘[*1]>

zvȍnčav {a, o adj.} *col* clanging (producing a sharp metal sound) <Slav⁘>

Zvònimīr {a (acc. = gen.) masc.} (lit. Zvonimir, man's name X zvoniti 'to ring') *sl-sex* ***Fac*** loud discharge of intestinal gas, loud fart <SlavO[*1]>

zvòniti {nīm, nē imperf.} (lit. clang) *sl-crime* inform the police or other authorities, snitch, squeal <Slav⁘[*1]>

zvȍnkati {ām, ajū imperf.} *col* ring (a bell, etc.) <Slav⁘>

Zvónko *See the following*

- **Zvónko Spásić** {NP} (lit. Bell the Savior) *sl-sstu* school bell at the end of a class

zvȍno {a neut.} (lit. bell) *col* ear <Slav⁘[*1]>

zvonjàkati {ām, ajū imperf. intr.} *col* clang (produce a sharp metal sound) <Slav⁘>

zvònjava {e neut.} **a.** *col* clanging (producing a sharp metal sound) <Slav⁘> **b.** *col* ringing (bell, etc.) <Slav⁘>

zvònjavina {ē fem.} **a.** *col* clang (sharp metal sound) <Slav⁘> **b.** *col* ringing (bell, etc.) <Slav⁘>

zvònjēnje {a neut.} *col* clanging (producing a sharp metal sound) <Slav⁘>

zvòziti {zvȍzīm, zē imperf.} *sl* cheat, swindle <Slav⁘[*1]>

zvȑc {excl.} **1** *col* the sound made by ringing, ring <Slav⁘[*1]> **2** *col* the sound made by tapping, tap <Slav⁘> **3** *sl-fea* used to express disregard, lack of appreciation, etc. <Slav⁘>

zvȑcānje {a neut.} *col* tapping <Slav⁘[*1]>

zvȑcati {ām, ajū imperf.} *col* tap <Slav⁘[*1]>

zvȑcnuti {nēm, nū perf. intr.} **a.** *col* buzz (bee, buzzer, etc.) <Slav⁘> **b.** *col* rap, tap <Slav⁘[*1]>

zvŕčak {čka masc.} *col* top (the toy) <Slav⁘[*1]>

zvȑčāljka {ē fem.; Dat zvȑčāljki} *col* top (the toy) <Slav⁘[*1]>

zvŕčati {čīm, čē imperf. intr.} **a.** *col* hiss (snake, gas, etc.) <Slav⁘> **b.** *col* buzz (bee, buzzer, etc.) <Slav⁘[*1]> **c.** *col* ring (a bell, etc.) <Slav⁘[*2]> **d.** *col* reproach, scold <Slav⁘[*3]>

zvȑčav {a, o adj.} *col* hissing (snake, gas, etc.) <Slav⁘>

zvȑčavo {adv.} *col* hissing (snake, gas, etc.) <Slav⁘>

zvřčina {ē fem.} *col* buzzer (e.g. on a door) <Slav⁘[*1]>

zvřčka {ē fem.; Dat zvřčki} **1** *col* rap, tap <Slav⁘[*1]> **2** *col* top (the toy) <Slav⁘[*1]>

zvřda {ē fem.} *sl-sex* ***Obs*** vagina, cunt <Slav⁘[*1]>

zvřdānje {a neut.} **a.** *col* buzzing (alarm, etc.) <Slav⁘> **b.** *col* roaring (engine, etc.) <Slav⁘[*1]>

zvȓj {a +ev (ext. pl) masc.; Nom Pl zvŕjevi} *col* roaring (engine, etc.) <Slav>

zvŕjānje {a neut.} **a.** *col* roaring (engine, etc.) <Slav⁘> **b.** *sl-fea* spending one's time in useless activities, fooling around, messing around <Slav⁘[*1]>

zvŕjati {jīm, jē imperf.} **a.** *col* wander, roam <Slav⁘[*1]> **b.** *sl-fea* spend one's time in useless activities, fool around, mess around <Slav⁘[*2]> **2** *sl* roar (engine, etc.) <Slav⁘[*1]>

zvřjav {a, o adj.} *col* roaring (engine, etc.) <Slav⁘[*1]>

zvřk {a +ov (ext. pl) masc.} **a.** *col* roaring (engine, etc.) <Slav⁘> **b.** *col* top <Slav⁘[*1]>

zvřka {ē fem.} *col* roaring (engine, etc.) <Slav⁘>

zvŕkalo {a neut.} (lit. roarer) *sl* phone <Slav⁘[*1]>

zvŕkānje {a neut.} *col* roaring (engine, etc.) <Slav⁘>

zvrkétnuti {zvrkètnēm, nū perf. intr.} *col* roar (engine, etc.) <Slav⁘>

zvȑknuti {nēm, nū perf.} **a.** *col* roar (engine, etc.) <Slav⁘> **b.** *col* clang (produce a sharp metal sound) <Slav⁘[*1]>

zvȑktati {tīm, tē imperf. intr.} *col* roar (engine, etc.) <Slav⁘>

zvȑkteti {tīm, tē imperf.} SerE *col* roar (engine, etc.) <Slav⁘>

zvȑkulja {ē fem.} *col* buzzing fly <Slav⁘[*1]>

zvȑlati {ām, ajū imperf.} *col* buzz (bee, buzzer, etc.) <Slav⁘>

zvŕlja {ē fem.} *col* button on a thread used to produce sparks <Slav⁘[*1]>

zvŕljati {ljīm, ljē imperf.} *col* buzz (bee, buzzer, etc.) <Slav⁘>

zvȓncati {ām, ajū imperf.} **a.** *col* buzz (bee, buzzer, etc.) <Slav⁘> **b.** *col* roar (engine, etc.) <Slav⁘[*1]>

zvȓnčati {ām, ajū imperf.} **a.** *col* buzz (bee, buzzer, etc.) <Slav⁘> **b.** *col* roar (engine, etc.) <Slav⁘[*1]>

zvȓnda {ē fem.} *sl-sex* ***Obs*** vagina, cunt <Slav⁘[*1]>

zvȑndalo {a neut.} *sl* dentist <Slav⁘[*1]>

zvȑndara {ē fem.} *col* buzzing fly <Slav⁘[*1]>

zvȓndati {ām, ajū imperf.} **a.** *col* buzz (bee, buzzer, etc.) <Slav⁘> **b.i.** *col* roar (engine, etc.) <Slav⁘[*1]> **ii.** *col* preach, give lectures to <Slav⁘[*1]> **iii.** *col* reproach, scold <Slav⁘[*1]>

zvȓndati {ām, ajū imperf.} *col* ring (a bell, etc.) <Slav⁘>

zvȓndati {ām, ajū imperf. intr.} *col* talk persistently and meaninglessly, blabber, chatter <Slav[*1]>

zvȑndōv {zvrndòva (acc. = gen.) masc.} **a.** *sl-fea* stupid or mentally deficient person **b.** *sl-fea* lazy or shiftless person, bum, good for nothing

zvȓr {excl.} *col* the sound made by ringing, ring <Slav>

zvûčnīk {a masc.} (lit. loudspeaker) *sl* ***Fac*** ear <Slav[*1]>

Žž

ž [žə] {a +ov (ext. pl) masc.} *sl* clock, watch <Slav✍>

žȁba {ē fem.} (lit. frog) **1a.** *sl-sex* ***Fac-Obs*** buttocks, butt <Slav[*1]> **b.** *sl-sex* prostitute, hooker <Slav[*2]> **2** *sl-auto* big Citroen (make of car) <Slav[*1]>

Žábac {pca (acc. = gen.) masc.} (lit. frog) *sl-fea* Italian (person), Dago <Slav[*1]>

žȁbačiti {čīm, čē imperf.} *sl-fea* be conceited, be stuck-up <Slav⁘[*1]>

žȁbačiti se {čīm, čē imperf. intr.} *sl-fea* boast, brag <Slav⁘[*1]>

žȁbār {a (acc. = gen.) masc.} (lit. frog-eater) **1** *sl-fea* continental male <Slav[*1]> **2** *sl-fea* Italian (person), Dago <Slav[*1]> **3** *sl-fea* rookie <Slav[*1]>

žáca {ē masc.} *sl-crime* policeman, cop <Fre✍>

žȁcli {žȅcli fem.; perm} [std. = žlica] Cro *sl* spoon <Slav✍>

žȁcman {a (acc. = gen.) masc.} *sl-crime* policeman, cop <Slav✍>

žága {ē fem.; Dat. žági} *dia-col* saw (the tool) <Ita✍>

žâgor {a masc.} *col* noise <Slav⁘>

žȁgōran {rna, rno adj.} *col* noisy <Slav⁘>

žagòrav {a, o adj.} *col* noisy <Slav⁘>

žȁgorēnje {a neut.} *col* making noise <Slav⁘>

žȁgoriti {rīm, rē imperf.} *col* make noise <Slav⁘>

žagòrljiv {a, o adj.} *col* noisy <Slav⁘>

žȁhica {ē fem.} *sl* wallet

žȁlōst *See the following*

• **srȅdnja žȁlōst** {NP} (lit. average sadness) *col* poor, of rather low quality

žȁlostan *See the following*

• **žȁlosna ti mâjka** {S} (lit. let your mother be sad) *col* used to indicate that one's interlocutor is doing something wrong, illegal, etc., What in the world are you doing! Oh God!: *Žalosna ti majka, uhapsiće te zbog toga! What in the world are you doing! You gonna get arrested for that!*

žȁmorēnje {a neut.} *sl-fea* prolonged and meaningless talk, blabber, chatter <Slav⁘>

žȁmoriti {rīm, rē imperf.} **a.** *sl-fea* make noise <Slav⁘> **b.** talk persistently and meaninglessly, blabber, chatter <Slav⁘[*1]>

Žȁn *See the following*

• **Žȁn Pôl Zȁjebūn** {NP} (lit. Jean Paul Fuckover) *sl-sstu* tricky mathematical problem

žȁndār {a (acc. = gen.) masc.} **a.** *sl-crime* policeman, cop <Fre[*1]> **b.** *sl-gamble* knight (card which counts twelve in some games) <Fre[*2]> **c.** Ser *sl* bus line number twelve in Belgrade, Serbia <Fre[*3]>

žandàrisati {išēm, išū biasp. intr.} **a.** *sl-fea* ***Fac*** supervise <Fre⁘[*1]> **b.** *sl-fea* ***Fac*** torture <Fre⁘[*2]>

žȁndarm {a (acc. = gen.) masc.} *sl-crime* policeman, cop <Fre>

žandàrmisati {išēm, išū biasp.} *sl* torture <Fre⁘[*1]>

žȁpla {ē fem.; perm} [std. = plaža] *sl* beach <Fre☞>

žára {ē fem.} *sl* fire, flames <Slav⁘[*1]>

žárac {rca masc.} *sl-crime* gunpowder <Slav⁘[*1]>

žȁrdīn {žardína masc.} Med *dia* garden <Fre>

žarènīk {reníka masc.} *dia* gold coin <Slav⁘[*1]>

žárēnje {a neut.} **a.** *sl* gold coin <Slav[*1]> **b.** *sl* outrage <Slav[*2]>

žáriti *See the following*

• **žáriti i páliti** {VP} *col* be very successful

žȃrnīk {a masc.} *sl* gold coin <Slav⁘[*1]>

žȁrulja {ē fem.} *sl* idea, thought <Slav[*1]>

žbȋr {a +ov (ext. pl) masc.; Nom Pl žbírovi} **1** *sl-crime* policeman, cop <Ita[*1]> **2** *sl-crime* informer, stoolie, snitch <Ita[*1]>

žbùnjara {ē fem.} *sl-fea* attractive female <Slav⁘[*1]>

ždȇr {a +ov (ext. pl) masc.; Nom Pl ždérovi} *sl* food <Slav☞[*1]>

• **uništávati ždȇr** {VP} (lit. destroy devouring) *sl* eat, wolf

ždéra {ē fem.} *sl* food <Slav☞[*1]>

ždèrāč *See the following*

• **ždèrāč spȅrmē** {NP} (lit. sperm devourer) *sl-sex* male homosexual, gay

ždèrača {ē fem.} *sl* food <Slav⁘[*1]>

ždèrānje {a neut.} (lit. eating) *sl* anger <Slav[*1]>

ždèrāti *See the following*

• **ždèrati mȁslo** {VP} (lit. devour fat) *sl-sex* engage in fellatio

• **ždèrati rȍzbīf** {VP} (lit. devour roast beef) *sl-sex* engage in cunnilingus

ždèrati se {rēm, rū imperf. intr.} (lit. eat oneself) *sl-fea* get nervous <Slav[*1]>

ždȅravac {rāvca masc.} **1** *sl* hunger <Slav⁘[*1]> **2** *sl* stomach, belly, gut <Slav⁘[*1]>

ždrȃk {a +ov (ext. pl) masc.; Nom Pl ždrákovi} *sl* look, glimpse <Slav☞[*1]>

ždrȁka {ē fem.; Dat ždrȁki} *sl* food <Slav☞[*1]>

ždráka {ē fem. & masc.; Dat ždráki} *sl-fea* person with eyeglasses, four-eyes <Slav☞[*1]>

ždrȁkānje {a neut.} *sl* looking, watching, scoping <Slav>

ždrȁkati {ām, ajū imperf.} *sl* look, watch, scope out <Slav⁘[*1]>

ždrȁkavac {vca masc.} *sl* window <Slav⁘[*1]>

ždrȁkavica {ē fem.} *sl* eye (sight organ) <Slav⁘[*1]>

ždrȃkno {adv.} **a.** *sl-fea* visibly <Slav⁘[*1]> **b.** *sl-fea* obviously <Slav⁘[*2]>

ždrȁknuti {nēm, nū perf.} *sl* look, watch, scope out <Slav⁘[*1]>

ždràufnuti {nēm, nū perf.} *sl-sex* ***Obs*** engage in sexual intercourse with (of a male) <Slav[*1]>

ždrébac {pca (acc. = gen.) masc.} (lit. stud) **1** *sl-drink* cognac <Slav[*1]> **2** *sl-fea* seducer <Slav[*1]>

ždrébe {eta neut.} (lit. calf) SerE *sl* fifteen hundred dinars <Slav[*1]>

ždrȉkati {ām, ajū imperf.} *sl* look, watch, scope out <Slav⁘[*1]>

ždrókati {ždrôkām, ždrókajū imperf.} *sl-drink* drink (alcohol) quickly, chug <Slav⁘[*1]>

ždrȍplja {ē fem.} a. *sl-sex* ***Der*** prostitute, hooker <Ita*1> b. *sl-sex* ***Der*** loose woman <Ita*2>

ždvrljúgnuti {dvȑljūgnēm, nū perf.} *sl-sex* ***Obs*** engage in sexual intercourse with (of a male)

žȅdovati {dujēm, dujū imperf.} *sl-fea* be thirsty <Slav✣>

žégati se {žêgām, žégaju imperf. intr.} *sl-sex* engage in sexual intercourse with (of a female) <Ita*1>

želàtīn {želatína masc.} (lit. gelatin) *sl-drugs* thick drug substance <Fre*1>

žȅlē {èa masc.} (lit. gel) *sl-drugs* thick drug substance <Fre*1>

žȅlja {ē fem.} (lit. wish) *sl-sex* ***Fac-Obs*** vagina, cunt <Slav*1>

željèzara {ē fem.} (lit. steel-mill) *sl* coin <Slav*1>

Žéljo {ē masc.} /Žéljo /a masc./ *sl-sports* name for Željezničar (a soccer team in Sarajevo, Bosnia) <Slav☞>

žéljovac {ljōvca (acc. = gen.) masc.} *sl-sports* fan of Željezničar (a soccer team in Sarajevo, Bosnia) <Slav☞*1>

žȅmička {ē fem.; Dat žȅmički} (lit. bun) *sl-sex* ***Fac-Obs*** the contour of the vagina, camel toe <Slav*1>

žȅmlja {ē fem.} (lit. bun) *sl-sex* ***Fac-Obs*** vagina, cunt <Slav*1>

žȅmskā {ē fem. (adj. decl.)} [std. = ženska] *col-dia* female <Slav☞*1>

žȅna {ē fem.} (lit. woman) *sl-sex* ***Fac*** prostitute, hooker <Slav*1>

• làkā žȅna {NP} (lit. easy woman) a. *sl-sex* prostitute, hooker b. *sl-sex* loose woman

• Žȅne ti ga žvȁjznēm! {S} (lit. I slap it to your wife!) SSer *dia* ***Off*** used as a moderate curse, Fuck you!

• Žȅnu li ti ìzgorīm! {S} (lit. I burn your wife!) *dia* ***Off*** used as a moderate curse, Fuck you!

• Žȅnu ti i u vȗnu jèbēm! {S} (lit. I fuck your wife in her wool!) *dia* ***Off*** used as a moderate curse, Fuck you!

• Žȅnu ti jèbēm! {S} (lit. I fuck your wife!) *col* ***Off*** used as a moderate curse, Fuck you!

• Žȅnu ti kȉselū! {S} (lit. *I fuck* your sour wife!) *dia* ***Off*** used as a moderate curse, Fuck you!

• Žȅnu ti kȉselū jèbēm! {S} (lit. I fuck your sour wife!) *dia* ***Off*** used as a moderate curse, Fuck you!

• Žȅnu ti mȁznēm! {S} (lit. I steal your wife!) *col-dia* ***Off*** used as a moderate curse, Fuck you!

• Žȅnu ti nàgūzīm! {S} (lit. I buttfuck your wife!) *col-dia* ***Off*** used as a moderate curse, Fuck you!

• Žȅnu ti ošàjdarīm! {S} (lit. I slap your wife!) *dia* ***Off*** used as a moderate curse, Fuck you!

• Žȅnu ti tvȍju! {S} (lit. *I fuck* your wife!) *col-dia* ***Off*** used as a moderate curse, Fuck you!

• Žȅnu ti u cvetək pȍjebēm! {S} (lit. I fuck your wife in her flower!) SSer *dia* ***Off*** used as a moderate curse, Fuck you!

• Žȅnu ti u pȉčku smȑdelū! {S} (lit. *I fuck* your wife in her stinking cunt!) SerE *dia* ***Off*** used as a moderate curse, Fuck you!

• Žȅnu ti u rȗno jèbēm! {S} (lit. I fuck your wife in her fur!) *dia* ***Off*** used as a moderate curse, Fuck you!

• Žȅnu ti u rȕpicu jèbēm! {S} (lit. I fuck your wife in her hole!) *dia* ***Off*** used as a moderate curse, Fuck you!

• Žȅnu ti u rȕpu jèb ēm! {S} (lit. I fuck your wife in her hole!) *dia* ***Off*** used as a moderate curse, Fuck you!

• Žȅnu ti u šùbaru! {S} (lit. *I fuck* your wife in her fur hat!) *dia* ***Off*** used as a moderate curse, Fuck you!

• Žȅnu ti zgûzīm! {S} (lit. I buttfuck your wife!) *col* ***Off*** used as a moderate curse, Fuck you!

žȅnče {eta neut.} *dia* wife <Slav✣*1>

• Žȅnče ti jèbēm! {S} (lit. I screw your little wife!) SSer *dia* ***Off*** used as a weak curse, Screw you!

• Žȅnče ti tvȍje! {S} (lit. *I screw* your little wife!) SSer *dia* ***Off*** used as a weak curse, Screw you!

• Žȅnče ti u tȑticu jèb ēm! {S} (lit. I screw your wife in her ass!) SSer *dia* ***Off*** used as a weak curse, Screw you!

ženètina {ē fem.} (lit. big woman) *col* female <Slav*1>

žȅnica *See the following*

• Žȅnicu ti jèbēm! {S} (lit. I fuck your little wife!) *col* ***Off*** used as a moderate curse, Fuck you!

žȅnskā {ē fem. (adj. decl.)} *col* female <Slav*1>

žȅnskāć {a (acc. = gen.) masc.} *sl* female <Slav☞*1>

žȅnskāć {ženskáća masc.} *col* female <Slav*1>

žȅnskica {ē fem.} /žȅnskica /e fem./ *col* female <Slav✣*1>

Žȅnu li ti ìzgorīm! {S} (lit. I burn your wife!) *dia* ***Off*** used as a moderate curse, Fuck you! ☞ žena

Žȅnu ti i u vȗnu jèbēm! {S} (lit. I fuck your wife in her wool!) *dia* ***Off*** used as a moderate curse, Fuck you! ☞ žena

Žȅnu ti jèbēm! {S} (lit. I fuck your wife!) *col* ***Off*** used as a moderate curse, Fuck you! ☞ žena

Žȅnu ti kȉselū! {S} (lit. *I fuck* your sour wife!) *dia* ***Off*** used as a moderate curse, Fuck you! ☞ žena

Žȅnu ti kȉselū jèbēm! {S} (lit. I fuck your sour wife!) *dia* ***Off*** used as a moderate curse, Fuck you! ☞ žena

Žȅnu ti mȁznēm! {S} (lit. I steal your wife!) *col-dia* ***Off*** used as a moderate curse, Fuck you! ☞ žena

Žènu ti nàgūzīm! {S} (lit. I buttfuck your wife!) *col-dia Off* used as a moderate curse, Fuck you! ☞ **žena**

Žènu ti ošȁjdarīm! {S} (lit. I slap your wife!) *dia Off* used as a moderate curse, Fuck you! ☞ **žena**

Žènu ti tvòju! {S} (lit. *I fuck* your wife!) *col-dia Off* used as a moderate curse, Fuck you! ☞ **žena**

Žènu ti u cvetək pòjebēm! {S} (lit. I fuck your wife in her flower!) SSer *dia Off* used as a moderate curse, Fuck you! ☞ **žena**

Žènu ti u pȉčku smȉdelū! {S} (lit. *I fuck* your wife in her stinking cunt!) SerE *dia Off* used as a moderate curse, Fuck you! ☞ **žena**

Žènu ti u rȕno jèbēm! {S} (lit. I fuck your wife in her fur!) *dia Off* used as a moderate curse, Fuck you! ☞ **žena**

Žènu ti u rȕpicu jèbēm! {S} (lit. I fuck your wife in her hole!) *dia Off* used as a moderate curse, Fuck you! ☞ **žena**

Žènu ti u rȕpu jèb ēm! {S} (lit. I fuck your wife in her hole!) *dia Off* used as a moderate curse, Fuck you! ☞ **žena**

Žènu ti u šȕbaru! {S} (lit. *I fuck* your wife in her fur hat!) *dia Off* used as a moderate curse, Fuck you! ☞ **žena**

Žènu ti zgûzīm! {S} (lit. I buttfuck your wife!) *col Off* used as a moderate curse, Fuck you! ☞ **žena**

žȅpa {ē fem.} *sl* simple shoe made of canvas with a rubber sole <BN[*1]>

žȅsta {ē fem.} *sl-drink* hard liquor <Slav⁘[*1]>

žestȉna {ē fem.} *sl-drink* hard liquor <Slav⁘[*1]>

žȅstok {a, o adj.} **1** *col* hot, spicy <Slav[*1]> **2** *sl-drink* hard (of liquor) <Slav[*1]>

žȅšćī {ā, ē adj.} *col* ***App*** excellent, awesome <Slav[*1]>

žȅtōn {žetóna masc.} (lit. token) *sl-drugs* narcotic drug, dope <Fre[*1]>

žfȁknuti {nēm, nū perf.} *sl* look, watch, scope out <Slav⁘[*1]>

žgȁba {ē fem.} *sl-fea* unattractive female

žgàdija {ē fem.} **a.** *col* small animals <Slav[*1]> **b.** *col* small children <Slav[*1]>

žgánci *See the following*

- **Žgánci su mi pròšli krȍz noge.** {S} (lit. Cornmeal mush has gone through my legs.) Cro *sl-fea* used to refer to one's fear in the past, I was scared shitless!

žgèbe {eta neut.} **a.** *dia* child, kid <Slav[*1]> **b.** *dia* baby, newborn <Slav[*2]>

žgèpče {eta neut.} **a.** *dia* child, kid <Slav[*1]> **b.** *dia* baby, newborn <Slav[*2]>

žglȁviti {vīm, vē imperf.} **a.** *sl-fea* preach, give lectures to <Slav✍[*1]> **b.** *sl-fea* talk persistently and meaninglessly, blabber, chatter <Slav✍[*2]>

žgȍbavica {ē fem.} *sl-fea* unattractive female <Slav⁘[*1]>

žgólja {ē fem. & masc.} SerE *sl-fea* ***Der*** slender person <Slav✍>

žgȍljav {a, o adj.} *sl-fea* slender, skinny

žgȍljavica {ē fem.} *sl-fea* ***Der*** slender female <Slav⁘[*1]>

žgoljávko {a masc.} *sl-fea* slender male

žȉbati {ām, ajū imperf.} *sl* walk

žȉc {a +ev (ext. pl) masc.; Nom Pl žìcevi} *sl-crime* policeman, cop <Fre✍[*1]>

žȉca {ē fem.} (lit. wire) **1** *sl-fea* curly hair <Slav[*1]> **2** *sl* streetcar <Slav[*1]> **3** trolley bus <Slav[*1]> **4** *sl-fea* talent <Slav[*1]> **5** *sl* begging <Slav[*1]> **6** *sl-crime* capital punishment <Slav[*1]> **7** *sl* request <Slav[*1]> **8** *sl-fea* ingratiation, brownnosing, ass kissing

- **žȉca gê** {NP} (lit. G string) **1** *sl* request **2** *sl-fea* ingratiation, brownnosing, ass kissing

žȉcānje {a neut.} **1** *col* begging <Slav⁘[*1]> **2** *sl-fea* ingratiation, brownnosing, ass kissing <Slav⁘[*2]>

žȉcār {a (acc. = gen.) masc.} **a.** *sl-fea* loafer, idler <Slav⁘[*1]> **b.i.** *sl-fea* social parasite <Slav⁘[*2]> **ii.** *sl-fea* homeless male, bum <Slav⁘[*2]>

žȉcārēnje {a neut.} **1** *sl-fea* begging <Slav⁘[*1]> **2** *sl-fea* ingratiation, brownnosing, ass kissing <Slav[*2]>

žicáriti {žȉcārīm, rē imperf.} **1** *col* beg, ask for money <Slav[*1]> **2** *sl-fea* ingratiate, brownnose, kiss ass <Slav[*2]>

žȉcāroš {a masc.} **a.** *sl-fea* loafer, idler <Slav⁘[*1]> **b.** *sl-fea* social parasite <Slav⁘[*2]> **c.** *sl-fea* homeless male, bum <Slav⁘[*3]>

žicáš {žicáša (acc. = gen.) masc.} *sl-fea* beggar

žȉcati {ām, ajū imperf.} **1** *col* beg, ask for money <Slav[*1]> **2** *sl-fea* ingratiate, brownnose, kiss ass <Slav[*2]>

žȉcer {a (acc. = gen.) masc.} **a.** *sl-fea* loafer, idler <Slav⁘[*1]> **b.** *sl-fea* social parasite <Slav⁘[*2]> **c.** *sl-fea* homeless male, bum <Slav⁘[*3]>

žȉckānje {a neut.} *sl-fea* begging <Slav⁘[*1]>

žȉckati {ām, ajū imperf.} *sl-fea* beg, ask for money <Slav⁘[*1]>

žȉcu {masc.} *sl-fea* begging <Slav✍*1>

žȉdnuti se {nēm, nū perf. intr.} *sl-crime* escape from the police <Slav✍*1>

Žȉdov {a (acc. = gen.) masc.} **a.** Ser *sl-fea* ***Off*** Jew <Slav*1> **b.** *sl-fea* ***Off*** miser, tightwad, skinflint <Slav*2>

Žȉga {ē fem.; Dat Žȉgi} *sl-fea* ***Off*** Jew <Slav✍>

žȉgica {ē fem.} (lit. match *lighting device*) *sl-fea* ***Off*** Jew <Slav*1>

žȉgolo {a masc.} *sl-fea* ***Off*** Jew <Slav✍*1>

žȉkati {ām, ajū imperf.} [std. = kužiti] *sl* understand, realize <Ita✍*1>

žȉknuti {nēm, nū perf.} **a.** *sl* look, watch, scope out <Ita✍*1> **b.** *sl* understand, grasp

žȉku {excl.; perm} [std. = kuži] *sl* used to draw someone's attention, look <Ita✍*1>

žȉla {ē fem.} (lit. vein) **1** *sl-sex* ***Fac-Obs*** penis, dick, prick <Slav*1> **2** *sl-stu* professor, high-school teacher (male), prof <Slav*1>

žiláviti {žȉlāvīm, vē imperf.} **a.** *sl-fea* annoy, bother, pester <Slav❖*1> **b.** *sl* work (usu. slowly and ineffectively) <Slav❖*2> **c.** *sl-fea* talk persistently and meaninglessly, blabber, chatter <Slav❖*2> **d.** preach, give lectures to

žiláviti se {žȉlāvīm, vē imperf. intr.} *sl-fea* be in a difficult situation <Slav❖*1>

žȉlāvka {ē fem.} (lit. Žilavka is a sort of wine from Herzegovina) *sl-fea* boring person, bore <Slav❖*1>

žilávljēnje {a neut.} *sl-fea* prolonged and meaningless talk, blabber, chatter <Slav❖*1>

žȉlēt [1] {žiléta (acc. = gen.) masc.} (lit. razor blade) **a.** *sl-fea* slender person <FreO*1> **b.** *sl-fea* short person <FreO*1>

žȉlēt [2] {žiléta masc.} *sl* month <FreO*1>

žilètić {a (acc. = gen.) masc.} *sl-fea* child, kid <FreO*1>

žȉlka {ē fem.} *sl* job, gig

žȉmku {excl.; perm} /žȉmku/ [std. = kužim] *sl* used to signal that import of message is captured, I got it <Ita✍*1>

žȉnadru {žȉnedru fem.; perm} [std. = družina] *sl-crime* gang, group of one's close friends <Slav✍>

žȉntara {ē fem.} *sl* goldsmith's

žȉpčiti {čīm, čē perf. intr.} *sl-fea* walk for a long time

žȉr {a +ov (ext. pl) masc.; Nom Pl žȉrovi} (lit. acorn) *sl-sex* ***Fac-Obs*** buttocks, butt <Slav*1>

žiràfa {ē fem.} (lit. giraffe) **1** *sl-sports* basketball player <NE*1> **2** **Cro** *sl* name for Zagrepčanka skyscraper in Zagreb, Croatia <NE*1>

žȉrak {a masc.} *sl* bank checking account <Fre✍*1>

žirantòbil {a (acc. = gen.) masc.} *sl-crime* accomplice <Fre✍*1>

žȉrati {ām, ajū imperf.} *sl* walk

žȉrić {a masc.} *sl* bank checking account <Fre✍*1>

žȉto *See the following*

• **ispod žȉta** {PP} (lit. under the grains) *col* secretly, under the counter: *obaviti poso ispod žita do business secretly*

žȉv [1] {excl.} *col* the sound made by a sparrow, tweet <Slav>

žȋv [2] *See the following*

• **žȋv bȉō** {VP} (lit. be alive) *col* used to stimulate a male to act, please: *Hajde, živ bio, kupi novine! Would you please buy the newspaper!*

žȋv bȉō! {VP} (lit. be alive) *col* used as a complementary phrase, Long live!

• **žȋv se pòjesti** {VP} (lit. eat oneself alive) *col* get nervous

• **žíva bíla** {VP} (lit. be alive) *col* used to stimulate a male to act, please: *Živa bila, dodaj mi naočale! Pass me my glasses, please!*

• **žívi bíli** {VP} (lit. be alive) *col* used to stimulate a group of people to act, please: *Djeco, živi bili, pospremite sobu! Kids, would you do your room, please!*

• **žívi bíli pa vȉdeli** {S} (lit. let us be alive and we will see) **SerE** *col* used to refer to a situation with unpredictable outcomes, let's wait and see what is going to happen

• **žívi bíli pa vȉdjeli** {S} (lit. let us be alive and we will see) *col* used to refer to a situation with unpredictable outcomes, let's wait and see what is going to happen

žívā enciklopêdija {NP} (lit. living encyclopedia) *col* omniscient person, walking encyclopedia ☞ **enciklopedija**

žívā lègēnda {NP} (lit. living legend) *col* very popular person, living legend ☞ **legenda**

žívā lóva {NP} (lit. live bucks) *col* cash ☞ lova

žȉvac [1] {vca (acc. = gen.) masc.} /žívac/ **a.** *col* nervous person, nail biter <Slav*1> **b.** *sl-crime* recidivist <Slav*2>

žȉvac [2] {adj.} *col* nervous <Slav*1>

živcírānje {a neut.} *col* being nervous <Slav❖*1>

živcírati {žȉvcīrām, živcírajū imperf.} *col* make nervous, get on one's nerves <Slav*1>

živcírati se {žìvcīrām, živcírajū imperf. intr.} *col* get nervous <Slav❖>

živčènjāk {čenjáka (acc. = gen.) masc.} *sl-fea* nervous male <Slav❖[*1]>

žíveli {excl.} **1** SerE *col* used to take leave of a group of persons informally, bye <Slav[*1]> **2** SerE *col* used to greet a group of persons, hi <Slav[*1]> **3** SerE *col* used as a toast to a group of people, cheers <Slav[*1]>

živèrkati {ām, ajū, imperf.} *col* produce the sound of a small bird, tweet <Slav❖>

žívī lèksikōn {NP} (lit. living lexicon) *col* omniscient person, walking dictionary ☞ **leksikon**

žîvī pîš {NP} (lit. living piss) *sl-fea* ***Obs*** highly humorous event or person ☞ **piš**

žívila {excl.} **1** *col* used to take leave of a female informally, bye <Slav[*1]> **2** *col* used to greet a female informally, hi <Slav[*1]> **3** *col* used as a toast to a female, cheers <Slav[*1]>

žívili {excl.} /žìvilī/ **1** *col* used to take leave of a group of people informally, bye <Slav[*1]> **2** *col* used to greet a group of people informally, hi <Slav[*1]> **3** *col* used as a toast to a group of people, cheers <Slav[*1]>

žìvīnka {ē fem.} *col-dia* animal <Slav❖[*1]>

žíviō {excl.} /žìviō/ **1** *col* used to take leave of a male informally, bye <Slav[*1]> **2** *col* used to greet a male informally, hi <Slav[*1]> **3** *col* used as a toast to a male, cheers <Slav[*1]>

žíviti *See the following*

- **žíviti od kónca** {VP} (lit. live from thread) *sl-fea* suffer from tuberculosis, have TB

žívjeli {excl.} **1** *col* used to take leave of a group of persons informally, bye <Slav[*1]> **2** *col* used to greet a group of persons informally, hi <Slav[*1]> **3** *col* used as a toast to a group of people, cheers <Slav[*1]>

žìvodēr {a (acc. = gen.) masc.} (lit. dog-catcher) *sl-mil* officer <Slav[*1]>

žìvot *See the following*

- **Jèsi za žìvot?** {S} (lit. Are you for life?) *sl* ***Obs*** used to propose sexual intercourse
- **u žìvot** {PP} (lit. in life) *col* out (to have some fun): *Otišli su u život u kafanu. They went out afterwards to the bar.*
- **živòta ti** {NP} (lit. swear by your life) *col* used to emphasize one's request, please: *Daj mi hleb, života ti! Pass me the bread, please!*

životinjáriti {tìnjārīm, rē imperf.} *sl* ***Fac*** vegetate, veg out <Slav❖[*1]>

živžìkati {ām, ajū imperf.} *col* produce he sound of a sparrow, tweet <Slav❖>

žlàbrati {ām, ajū biasp.} **a.** *sl* talk, have a conversation <Slav❖[*1]> **b.** *sl-fea* talk persistently and meaninglessly, blabber, chatter <Slav❖[*2]>

žlàjfa {ē fem.} *sl* female <Ger❖[*1]>

žlàjfe {i fem. pl.} *sl-auto* brakes <Ger❖[*1]>

žlàrnbrati {ām, ajū biasp.} *sl* talk

žlèpati {ām, ajū biasp.} *sl-drink* drink (alcohol) <Ger[*1]>

žlèva {ē fem.} *sl-drink* drink (alcohol)

žlèviti {vīm, vē imperf.} *sl-drink* drink (alcohol)

žlézda *See the following*

- **bȍlesnā žlézda** {NP} (lit. sick gland) SerE *sl-sex* ***Fac*** large female breast

žlȕndra {ē fem.} **1** *sl-sex* ***Obs*** vagina, cunt <Slav[*1]> **2** *sl-sex* ***Obs*** penis, dick, prick <Slav[*1]> **3** *sl-sex* ***Obs*** the penis of an elderly male <Slav[*1]> **4** *sl-fea* slender female <Slav[*1]>

žljȅva {ē fem.} *sl-drink* drink (alcohol)

žljȅviti {vīm, ve imperf.} *sl-drink* drink (alcohol)

žljóka {ē fem.; Dat žljóki} *sl-drink* weak brandy

žmìgavac {vca masc.} (lit. turn signal) *sl* eye (sight organ) <Slav[*1]>

žmìk {a +ov (ext. pl) masc.} *sl-crime* stupid or mentally deficient person

žmírē {adv.} *col* with closed eyes <Slav✍[*1]>

žmíra {ē fem.} *col* hide-and-seek <Slav✍[*1]>

žmŕćkati {ām, ajū imperf.} *col* splash <Slav❖[*1]>

žmȕke {excl.} *col* the sound made by slamming, wham <Slav>

žmȕljiti {ljīm, ljē imperf.} **1** *sl* cry, shed tears, weep <Slav❖[*1]> **2** *sl* kiss <Slav❖[*2]>

žmûr {a +ev (ext. pl) masc.; Nom Pl žmúrevi} **a.** *sl* sleeping <Slav✍[*1]> **b.i.** *sl* dream <Slav✍[*2]> **ii.** *sl* rest <Slav✍[*2]>

žmúrka {ē fem.} *col* hide-and-seek <Slav✍[*1]>

žmúrkē {adv.} SerE *col* with closed eyes <Slav✍[*1]>

žnàbl {a +ov (ext. pl) masc.} *sl* mouth <Ger[*1]>

- **žnábl na pókus** {NP} (lit. experimental mouth) *sl* French kiss

žnìranac {rānca masc.} Cro *col-dia* shoelace <Ger❖[*1]>

žnírãnje {a neut.} **1 Cro** *sl-sports* well-played soccer <**Ger**✤*1> **2a. Cro** *sl* cheating, swindling <**Ger**✤*1> **b.** Cro *sl-crime* theft <**Ger**✤*2>

žnȉrati {ãm, ajū imperf.} Cro *col-dia* tie one's shoelaces <**Ger**✤>

žnírati {žnîrãm, žnírajū biasp. intr.} **1** *sl-sports* play good soccer <**Ger**✤*1> **2a.** *sl* cheat, swindle <**Ger**✤*1> **b.** *sl-crime* steal, swipe <**Ger**✤*2>

žnóra [1] {ē fem.} **a.** Cro *col* necktie <**Ger***1> **b.i.** Cro *sl-sports* game <**Ger***1> **ii.** Cro *sl* connection, tie <**Ger***1>

žnòra [2] {ē fem.} Kajk *dia-col* rope <**Ger**>
- **po žnóri** {PP} (lit. on a rope) **a.** Kajk *sl* easily **b.** Cro *sl* as planned

žnȍranac {rãnca masc.} Cro *col-dia* shoelace <**Ger**✤*1>

žnj [žənj] {adj.} *sl-fea* of lowest quality, cheap: *To su neka žnj kola. That'a bottom-of-the line car.* <**Slav***1> ☞ **šklj**

žnjȁpati {ãm, ajū imperf.} *sl* eat, devour <**Slav**✍*1>

žnjȁrati {ãm, ajū imperf.} *sl-sex* ***Obs*** engage in sexual foreplay, pet, feel up <**Slav**✍*1>

žnjȁriti {rīm, rē imperf.} *sl-sex* ***Obs*** engage in sexual foreplay, pet, feel up <**Slav**✍*1>

žnjȉkati {ãm, ajū imperf. intr.} *sl-arch* look, watch, scope out

žnjȉriti {rīm, rē imperf.} *sl* laugh <**Slav**✍*1>

žóga {ē fem.; Dat žógi} *sl-sports* ball <**Slo**>

žȍhãr {a (acc. = gen.) masc.} (lit. roach) **1** *sl-music* note <**Slav***1> **2** *sl-fea* moderately strong male <**Slav***1> **3** *sl-fea* worthless person, bum <**Slav***1>

žrâk {a +ov (ext. pl) masc.} *sl* look, glimpse <**Slav**✍*1>

žrȁkãnje {a neut.} *sl* looking <**Slav**✍*1>

žrȁkati {ãm, ajū imperf.} *sl* look, watch, scope out <**Slav**✍*1>

žráknuti {žrâknēm, nū perf.} *sl* look, watch, scope out

žènskãroš {a (acc. = gen.) masc.} **a.** *sl-sex* male sexual partner (of a female) <**Ger**✤*1> **b.** *sl-sex* ***Obs*** male with exaggerated interest in sex <**Ger**✤*1>

žtèmisati {išēm, išū biasp.} *sl* love <**Fre**✤>

žȗbor {a masc.} **a.** *col* gurgling (creek, etc.) <**Slav**✤> **b.** *col* noise <**Slav**✤*1>

žȗbōran {rna, rno adj.} *col* gurgling (creek, etc.) <**Slav**✤>

žubòrav {a, o adj.} *col* gurgling (creek, etc.) <**Slav**✤>

žubòrēnje {a neut.} *col* gurgling (creek, etc.) <**Slav**✤>

žȗborīšte {a neut.} *col* water source <**Slav**✤*1>

žubòriti {rīm, rē imperf. intr.} **a.** *col* gurgle (creek, etc.) <**Slav**✤> **b.** *col* make noise <**Slav**✤*1> **c.** *sl-sex* urinate, piss <**Slav**✤*1>

žȗc {a (acc. = gen.) +ov (ext. pl) masc.; Nom Pl žùcovi} *sl* dog (the animal)

žȗč {a (acc. = gen.) +ev (ext. pl) masc.; Nom Pl žùčevi} *sl* dog (the animal)

žȗja {ē fem.} **1** *sl-drink* beer <**Slav***1> **2a.** *dia* sheep with yellow spots <**Slav***1> **b.** *sl-fea* blond female <**Slav***1>

žȗjãn {a (acc. = gen.) masc.} *sl-fea* blond male <**Slav**✤*1>

žújka {ē fem.} *sl* ten paras; a ten-para coin <**Slav**✤*1>

žûlj {a +ev (ext. pl) masc.; Nom Pl žúljevi} (lit. blister) **1** *sl-sex* ***Fac-Obs*** vagina, cunt <**Slav***1> **2** *sl* ***Fac*** fat belly <**Slav***1> **3** *sl* shoe <**Slav***1> **4** *sl* potato <**Slav***1>

žùljati {ãm, ajū imperf.} **1a.** *sl-sex* ***Fac-Obs*** engage in sexual intercourse with (of a male) <**Slav**✤*1> **b.** *sl-sex* ***Fac-Obs*** engage in prolonged sexual intercourse with (of a male) <**Slav**✤*2> **2** *sl* wander, roam <**Slav***1>

žúljiti *See the following*
- **žúljiti dân** {VP} (lit. blister the day) *sl-fea* be bothered, be disturbed

žùntara {ē fem.} *sl* goldsmith's <**Slav**✤*1>

žúpa {ē fem.} (lit. parish) *sl-sex* ***Iro*** brothel, whorehouse <**Slav***1>

žûr {a +ev (ext. pl) masc.; Nom Pl žúrevi} Ser *col* party (social gathering) <**Fre**>

žurája {ē fem.} *sl* party (social gathering) <**Fre**✍>

žuréza {ē fem.} *sl* party (social gathering) <**Fre**✍>

žûrka {ē fem.} Ser *col* party (social gathering) <**Fre**✤>

žȕrkata *See the following*
- **žȕrkata na akrȅpite** {NP} (lit. scorpion party) *sl-sstu* ***Fac*** school board meeting

žûtā {ē fem. (adj. decl.)} (lit. the yellow one) *sl* outrage <**Slav***1>

žûtā kȕća {NP} (lit. yellow house) *sl-fea* psychiatric hospital, nuthouse ☞ **kuća**

žûtā minúta {NP} (lit. yellow minute) *sl-fea* loss of self-control ☞ **minuta**

žȕtača {ē fem.} (lit. the yellow one) *sl-sex* ***Obs*** buttocks, butt <**Slav**✤*1>

žùtan {a masc.} *sl* gold coin <**Slav**✤*1>

žùtara {ē fem.} (lit. the yellow one) **1** *sl-sex* ***Obs*** buttocks, butt <Slav❖*1> **2** *sl* goldsmith's <Slav❖*1> **3** *sl* psychiatric hospital, nuthouse <Slav❖*1>

žȕtavica {ē fem.} *sl* mouth <Slav❖*1>

žûtī {ōg (acc. = gen.) masc.} (lit. the yellow one) **1** *sl-sports* player or fan of Jugoplastika (now POP 84 a basketball team from Split, Croatia) <Slav*1> **2** *sl-crime* policeman, cop <Slav*1> **3** *sl-fea* blond male <Slav*1>
• **ko žûtī** {PP} (lit. like the yellow one) *sl-fea* completely, totally

žûtī kádar {NP} (lit. yellow cadre *the yellow insignia of the lower-ranked military officers*) *sl-mil* NCOs, lower ranked military officers ☞ **kadar**

žùtica {ē fem.} (lit. jaundice) *sl* gold <Slav*1>

žȕtka {ē fem.; dat žȕtki} (lit. the yellow one) *sl-sex* ***Obs*** buttocks, butt <Slav❖*1>

žûtō {a neut.} /žúto/ (lit. the yellow stuff) **1** *sl* gold <Slav*1> **2** *sl* excrement <Slav*1> **3** *sl* heroin, horse, smack <Slav*1>
• **u žútu** {PP} (lit. in yellow) *col-dia* never

žutokljúnac {nca (acc. = gen.) masc.} (lit. yellow beak) *sl-fea* ***Der*** young male, boy, kid <Slav❖*1>

žvȁcnuti {nēm, nū perf.} *sl* eat, devour <Slav❖*1>

žvàćkalica {ē fem.} *sl* mouth <Slav❖*1>

žvȁjznuti {nēm, nū perf.} **a.** *sl* hit, punch <Slav❖*1> **b.** *sl-sex* engage in sexual intercourse with (of a male) <Slav❖*1>
• **Žvȁjznēm ti ga!** {S} (lit. I swing it to you!) *col* ***Off*** used as a moderate curse, Fuck you!

žváka {ē fem.; Dat žváki} **a.** *col* chewing gum <Slav❖> **b.i.** *sl-fea* babbling <Slav❖*1> **ii.** *sl* pasta <Slav❖*1> **iii.** *sl-fea* boring song <Slav❖*1> **iv.** *sl-fea* boring story <Slav❖*1> **v.** *sl* joke <Slav❖*1> **vi.** *sl* social skills <Slav❖*1>
• **dívča žváka** {NP} (lit. wild chewing gum) *sl* lie

žvákalica {ē fem.} (lit. chewer) **1** *sl-fea* very young female, little girl <Slav❖*1> **2** *sl-sex* male homosexual, gay <Slav❖*1>

žvákati {žvâćem, ćū imperf.} (lit. chew) **a.** *sl* eat, devour <Slav*1> **b.** read <Slav*2>
• **žvákati gaćerónce** {VP} (lit. chew one's pants) *sl-fea* be frightened, get scared

žvakerîno {a masc.} *sl* chewing gum <Slav❖>

žvakèrōn {a masc.} *sl* chewing gum <Slav❖>

žvȁknuti {nēm, nū perf.} *sl* eat, devour <Slav❖*1>

žvȁkonjiti {njīm, njē imperf.} *sl* eat, devour <Slav❖*1>

žvȁkos {a masc.} *sl* chewing gum <Slav✍>

žvȁla {ē fem.} (lit. bit) *sl* kiss <Slav*1>

žvaláriti {žvàlārīm, rē imperf.} *sl-fea* talk persistently and meaninglessly, blabber, chatter <Slav❖*1>

žvȁlati {ām, ajū imperf.} *sl-fea* talk persistently and meaninglessly, blabber, chatter <Slav*1>

žvaláviti {žvàlāvīm, vē imperf.} *sl-fea* talk persistently and meaninglessly, blabber, chatter <Slav❖*1>

žvaláviti se {žvālāvīm, vē imperf. intr.} *sl* kiss <Slav❖*1>

žvalávko {a masc.} *sl-fea* male with a large mouth <Slav❖*1>

žvalávko {a masc.} **1** *sl-fea* child, kid <Slav❖*1> **2** *sl-fea* boring person, bore <Slav❖*1>

žvalávljēnje {a neut.} *sl* kissing <Slav*1>

žvȁle {a fem. pl.} *sl* mouth <Slav*1>

žvȁliti {līm, lē imperf.} **1** *sl-fea* talk persistently and meaninglessly, blabber, chatter <Slav❖*1> **2** *sl* kiss <Slav❖*1>

žválo {ē masc.} //a (acc. = gen.) masc./ (lit. moose lips) *sl-fea* male with a large mouth <Slav❖>

žvȁljac {ljca masc.} *sl* kiss <Slav❖*1>

žvȁljati {ām, ajū biasp.} *sl* eat, devour <Slav❖*1>

žvȁlje {a fem. pl.} (lit. bit) *sl* mouth <Slav*1>

žváljo {ē masc.} *sl-fea* male with a large mouth <Slav❖*1>

žvȁnj-žvȁnj [1] {masc.} **a.** *sl-fea* ***Fac*** sermon <Slav*1> **b.** *sl-fea* ***Fac-Der*** reproach, scold <Slav*1>

žvȁnj-žvȁnj [2] {perf.} *sl-fea* preach, give lectures to <Slav*1>

žvȁnje {eta neut.} **a.** *sl* pig (the animal) <Slav❖*1> **b.** *sl* piglet <✍>

žvànjet {a masc.} *sl* baking <Slav❖*1>

žvánjež {a masc.} *sl* baking <Slav❖*1>

žvȁnjkānje {a neut.} *sl-fea* ***Fac*** sermon <Slav*1>

žvȁnjkati {ām, ajū imperf.} **a.** *sl-fea* preach, give lectures to <Slav*1> **b.** *sl-fea* reproach, scold <Slav*1>

žvàtān {tna, tno adj.} **a.** *sl-fea* stupid or mentally deficient person <✍> **b.** *sl-fea* inhabitant of the countryside, hick, bumpkin <✍>

žvékānje {a neut.} *sl* fight (e.g. fist fight) <Slav❖*1>

žvékati {ām, ajū imperf.} *sl* beat up <Slav❖*1>

žvȅknuti {nēm, nū perf.} *sl* hit, punch <Slav✍*1>

žvŕljati {ljím, ljé imperf.} *sl* scribble, write illegibly <**Slav**❖[*1]>

Źź

źènica {ē fem.} [std. = zjenica] *dia* pupil (of the eye) <**Slav**⇯>

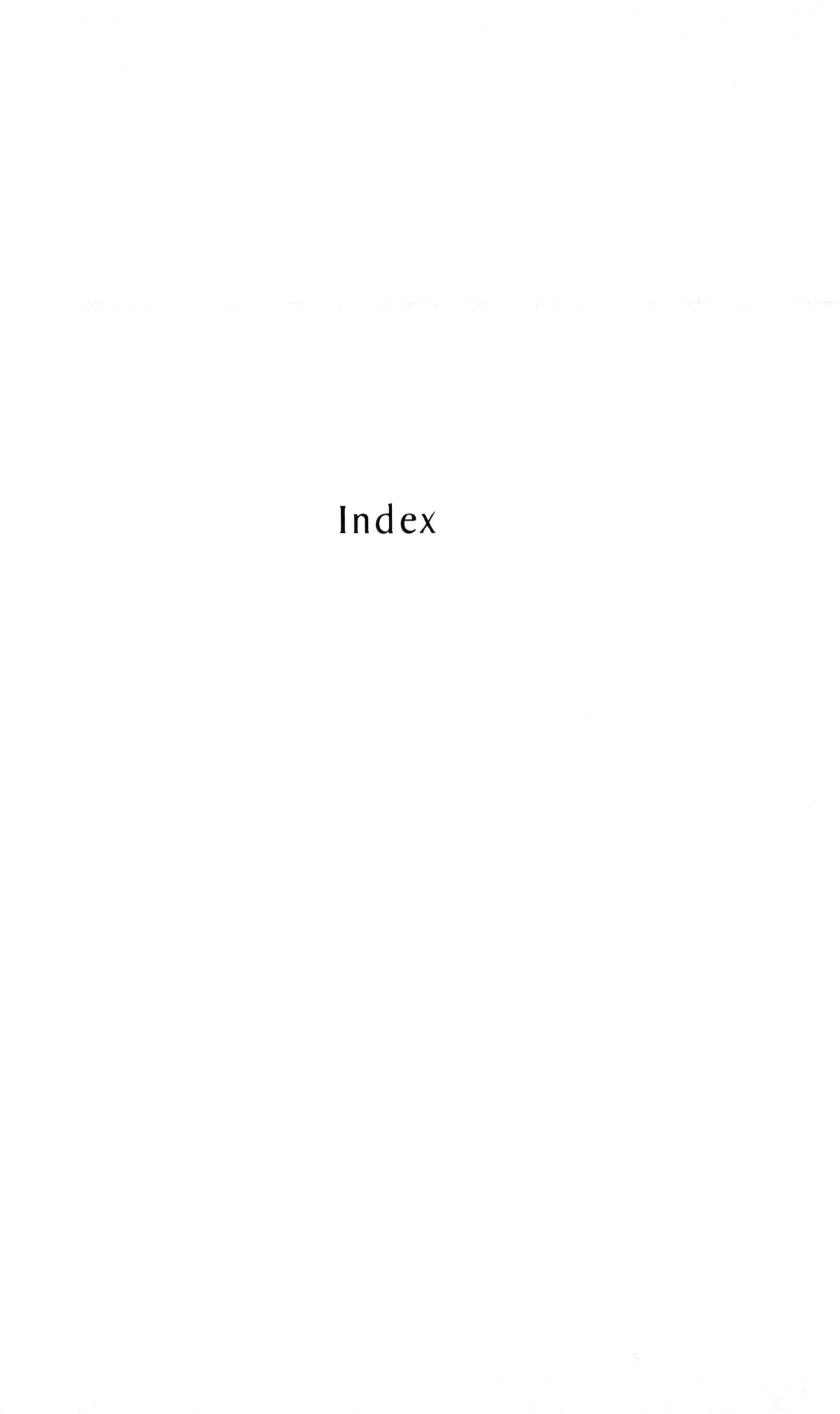

Index

a (instead of standard jedan, jedna, jedno): jèdan

A (the highest grade): pètāk

A-student, student who makes As: bȕbī-bubī, zaluđìvāč

aba (a kind of thick woolen fabric used for clothing, usu. homemade): àba

abandon: zabatáliti

abandoned terrain: pȉzdīšte

abnormal male, weirdo: mutljávko

abnormal person, weirdo: múćak [2]

abort, miscarry: pròpupčiti

abortion (of a fetus): ȁbić, abortȉška, čȉšćēnje

about, concerning: akȍnto

above: vȑz

above, upstairs: goríkā

abrasion: ȁbānje

abroad, overseas: gȍre, màkiš, prêko, vàni

absent-minded person: šȁmšula

absolute tranquility: trȉp

absolutely free: džȁb-džàbē

absolutely, totally, completely: apsalūtno

absorb shocks: federírati

abstain from sexual intercourse for a long time: pòstiti, zagòreti, zagòriti, zagòrjeti

absurd, idiotic: nȅbulōzan

abundance: šóder [2]

abundant: tvȓd [2]

abundant meal: krkáncija

abuse (usu. financially): grèbati se, ìspūmpati, isisávati, ìzboksati, ìzmūsti, ižmíkati, mamùzati, mûsti, premùntati, pûmpati, ràubovati

abuse somebody's trust: kûglati

abused (financially): ìžmikān

abuser (of others): grèbātor, grèbātorka

abyss: sùrduk

academician: kakadèmik

academy: dèmija [1]

accident: pȅh, smòla

accomplice: ȁver, hȁver, kòmita, lȍta, òrtāk, štȅker, štȕce, žirantòbil

accomplice's share of stolen goods, take: šȁp, šápa

accomplished liar: maratónac, Minhàuzen

accordion player: armonìkāš, crèvār

accordion, squeeze box: armònika, crijévo, rastézāljka, razvijȍtka

ace (cards): kêc [2], kèčiga, kèčuga

achieve: zabìlježiti

acoustic guitar: klozètara

act (in a theater play, etc.): markírati

act poorly (e.g. in a movie, theater play): glumàtati

act as a boss: šȅfovati

act as a Serbian guerilla fighter in the Ottoman Empire: àjdukovati

act as a troublemaker: džigèrisati

act as an accomplice: havèrisati

act as, impersonate: izigrávati

act insanely, freak out: vilèneti, vilèniti

act like a brat: izmotávati se

act like a coward: džigèrisati se

act of choking: krágna

act of playing cards: dȕganje

act of pronouncing obscenities during sexual intercourse: mȉsa

act of reselling tickets illegally, scalping tickets: dugárēnje

act of robbing garment: prȅsvlaka

act of running away: brisavȅla, brȉtva [3]

act of running away from: brȉs [2], brȉsānje

act unintelligently: tùpisati, túpiti

act without inhibition: lújiti

add (numbers): prikénjati

add: dògljati [1], prìšiti

addendum: projèkcija

addict in need of narcotic drugs, junkie needing a fix: gȁper

addicted to narcotic drugs: navùčen

additional punishment: mâst, prìkolica

additional trunk on the top of an automobile: ròštīlj

address (mail, etc.): andrèsa, andresírati

adequate female sexual partner: cvìkerica

adequate male sexual partner: filcmâjstor, pàstūh

adjust, tune: nàštelovati, nàštimati

adjustable measure: šíber [2], šȕbler

admission ticket: kàriška, kóva

admit, make a confession, come clean: gúknuti, pjȅvati, zȕcnuti

adorable, lovable: lûd [2]

advancement from a weaker to a stronger narcotic drug: lȉft

adventure: àviška, dogodóvština

advice: štrȕka

afflict: zàvatiti

affluent: gȍtīvan, mástan, nàfutrān, òbložen, ȍpēt, pȍtkovān, pòtkožen, sfìtīljen, sȉt, skȍžen, skûp [2], strȍg, vàtīrān

affluent elderly female: màmut

affluent male, moneybags: bùržūj, kȅsa, kìntār, lòvān, lòvāš, lòvātor, lovijána, šàran, šûmnjāk

affluent person, moneybags: paràjlija

affluent senior citizen: đȕva

affluent, in the clover: nafàtirān

affluent, loaded, fat: kȍmōtan, másan, namìrisān, natòvaren, zdȅbljān

Afghani hash: afganistánac, àvgān, avganistánac

African American (female): cȑnka

African American (male): banána, cȑnčina, cȑnčuga, Cȓnja, čàmuga, čokoláda, čȍkolādnī, dȉmnjačār, džàmuga, kmȉca, mrákonja, Ȕglješa

afterlife: ahíret

again: jȍpē, jȍpēt, ȍpē, rȅpetē

against, counter: prȍtivu

age: vàkat

agenda: jèborēd
aggrandize: napuhávati
aggressive person, bully: agresívac
aggressive play (e.g. in soccer): cjépānje
aggressive soccer player: cèpāroš, cjèpāroš
aggressor: paksìjān
agree: klȁpati, skòntati, spȉčiti se
agree to have sexual intercourse with (of females): dȁti, kapitulírati, kuropȅcati se
agreed: sečèno
agreement to have group sexual intercourse with: džȉnfis
agreement to have sexual intercourse with (of females): sȅks-šéma
agriculture: poljuprȉvreda
AIDS: sída
AIDS patient: sìdāš
aim, direct: šícati
air: ârija, àva, hàva, kȉsko
air, ventilate: lȕftati, luftírati
airing, ventilating: lȕftānje, luftírānje
airman: komárac
airplane: avìjōn, tȉć
airport: tȉćokrōv
alarm clock: tandȑkalo
alarmist (female): pàničārka
alarmist (male): drȁmer, fȑkāroš, fȑkātor, katastròfičār, pàničār, panȉčara, paranòičār
Albanian (person): Arbànas, Arnàut, Ptàraši, Ptȁrši, Šȍk [1]
Albanian (pertaining to a person): arbànaškī, arnàutskī
Albanian cognac: Ènverić
alcoholic beverage: ȁlk, bljȕva, bûz, cȉra, cȉrka, cúga, cugàluk, cugánjac, cȕgeher, drȉnk, dróga, glô-glô, konkrȅtno, màtilo, mûlj, nȁfta, narkóza, šljóka
alcoholic beverages: pìjača, rȕbvīz, tòčak [2]
alcoholic who drinks alone: sôlotrȉnker
alcoholic, drunk: ȁlhos, ȁlkić, alkokòličār, ȁlkos, bèćār, bèkrija, blȅfer, bonbòndžija, bonbònđija, cepànica, cìrer, cìrkāroš, cȉrke, cjepànica, cȕcler, cùgāroš, cȕger [1], cugèrāš, cȕgos, cȕgoš, delírko, drȉnker, drȍger, džȉberskī, fènjer, jànpika, jàpānka, karànfil, lȍkadžija, lòkātor, lóla, lȕmpos, narkohòličār, narkòtičār, nòga [2], ocugánac, pijánac, pijàndura, pìjanis, pijànist, pijavȉška, pjánac, pjáno, rónac, sȉsār, smûk, sùjmez, sujùmez, sùndžer, sùnđer, šljòkara, šȕkadžija, šuléja, trúbac, tvȑtko, zùrna
alley cat: kontèjnerka
alone, unaccompanied, solo: sôlo
alternative artist (in general): alternatívac
alternative political or cultural stream, underground: pódzēmlje
alternative politician (outside mainstream politics): alternatívac
always: obavȅzno, stàndard, vȁjēk, vȁjk, vȁsvijēk, vàvijēk, vȁzda, vȁzdān, vȁzde
amateur prostitute: púca [1]
amber: ćéhlìbār
ambush: míca [1], trȁkalica, zȉcer
America: Amèrka
American (person): Ȁmer, Amerȉgos, Lȍkvār [1]
ammunition, ammo: džebàna, grȁh, grášak, maróni, zôb
amphetamine, benny: ȁmf, ȁmfī, ȁmfić
ample time: kalendàrisānje
ample, plenty of: šóder [3], ȍho-hô
ampoule of methedrine: ȁmp
Amsterdam (Holland): Dȁm
anal sexual intercourse: ȁjsovānje, pêdrānje
anecdote: bȉks [2]
anger: gȉftānje, pȁnjānje, sȑdžba, usijávānje, ždèrānje
angle, corner: vùglec
angry, mad: nàdrkān, nàfuren, ràspigan, ràznjupān
animal: žȉvīnka
animal with large breasts: sísonja
animal with large testicles: mùdāš, mùdīle
annoy, bother, pester: ȁkati, bihuzúriti, céditi, dȁnfati, dáviti, džangȉzati, džárati, fitȉljiti, gúšiti, klȁti, masírati, mésiti, mùdati, nàčičkati se, nasȅšeriti se, opláviti, palamúditi, palamúditi, pasírati, pȉliti, podjebávati, prȅšati, sàfatati, sàvatati, sȅći, smárati, šȉljiti, talàsati, tlȁčiti, túpiti, turpìjati, udáviti, uzbihuzúriti, zàjahati, žiláviti
annoying, bothering: ȁkānje, podjebávānje
answer, respond: ropopírati, ùšiti
antelope leather shoe: sàjmonica
antifreeze: pèrmant
antique store: antȉkvārnjāk
anus: ȁlka, ȁlkica, analȉtičār [2], analȉtičārka, centrála, cvàjter, dùbara, dȕckī, đȕbre, kȁnka, kàva, kènjara, kȍnj [1], kûrva, kùrvār, mȁgazīn, ostràguša, pȁkšu, pêdrānje, plȉnara, pŕkno, pȑknos, šúpak, šȕpćina, vònjara, zâmjenīk
any in a series of numbers, nth: ȅntī
any institution affiliated with the regime in Serbia in the 1990s: bastȉlja
any kind of childish game: pȉstac
any object used in a children's game where the person in possession of that object has to do something: zálog
any situation with a certain outcome, sure thing: zȉcer, zȉher, zȉherica
anything: štrȕmf-mašína
anywhere: ȉđe, ȉgđe
apart, separately, individually: bàška [2]
apartment: ambasáda, ȁnsta, bȁčva, bŕlog, čȃrda, gȃjba, gajbijána, gajbijȁšica, gnézdo, jȁzbina, kàvez, knȕt, kokošínjac, kòrpara, kȕnt, màdo, pèćina, rȕpa [2], rùpīnger, stànica, šȕpa, ȕnča, ȕndža
apartment rent collector: kȕga
apartment used for gambling: pìksla [2]
aphrodisiac: kuromìcīn
appear in large quantities: hrȕpiti, nàhrupiti
appear, arrive at a meeting point: cȑtati se
appearance: fȁzōn
appendix (the organ): prijèkcija
appetite: apetìtis, razvalìtis
applause: pljȇsak, Skandinȃvija, tȁpāt

apple cider: jȁbukovača

appreciate, enjoy, like: brȅnovati, céniti, fȅrmati, gotíviti, šíšati

approach females on the street in order to make acquaintance: uličáriti

approach, draw near: prifúrati, prikénjati

approaching: prȉfur

approve, confirm, sanction: áminovati

approximately: ȍfrljē, ȍtafrljē

apricot brandy: kàjsijevača, kàjsijovača

archbishop: drenòvān

archenemy: dîn-dȕšman, dîn-dȕšmanin

area around testicles: òmudina

area around vagina: òpizdina

area below vagina: pòtpičnjāk [2]

argue, quarrel: kȑviti se, kȑvljēnje, lȍptati se, prepucávati se, raskàntati se, vȁtrovati se

arguing: prepucávānje

argument, quarrel: záđevica

arm: bȁnalica, gȅpavac, gȅpavica, gràbulja, hvȁtalo, kȍska, kȕka, lèvača, òpadnica, pècāljka, peràja, rȅpavica, rèpevica, šápa, šljȁpavica, zȅzalica

army driver: kȕčkār

army green, olive drab: esembê

army-style coat: tànker, vijètnāmka

aroused, hot: nàpāljen, nàpāljen, zàsaftān

arrange for: namàknuti, srédíti, srȕšiti, ùtēntati, zȅngovati, zgotòviti, zgotíviti, zrȉktati

arrange, put in order: ìzengovati

arrangement: šéma

arrest: ćorkírānje, ćorkírati, murírati, mùrisati, mȕrnuti, spèngati, ubádati, ućorkírati, ukébati

arrest for a short time: prićóriti

arrested: đȉgnūt, dȑpljen

arrival: dofurijánović, dogambávānje, tȕspās

arrive in large quantities: nagŕnuti

arrive quickly: dòkuriti, dòsprintati, dòšprintati, dòštartati

arrive quickly and with high intensity (of storm, offense in sports, etc.): stȕštiti se

arrive unexpectedly, appear out of nowhere, pop in: bàhnuti, bànuti, bȁpnuti, bȕbiti, bȕbnuti, šȕpiti

arrive uninvited: nàsrati se

arrive with difficulty: dogégati se

arrive, come: arȉvati, aterírati, dofúrati, dofúrati se, dògambati, dogíbati, dogȉljati, dògljati [2], dògnjati, dogurívati, dòhajbati, dolepȑšati, dopèrjati, dòplaziti, dòpuzati, dorȉvati se, dòšājbati, dòslepati, nafúrati, nàrisati se, tuspásiti se

arrogance: stȋsak

arrogant: nàprčen

arrow: strjèlica

article: kobàsica

artist (painter, sculptor, etc.): likòvnjāk

artistic painting: mȁzānje

arts (school course): lìkiš

Arts Academy club in Belgrade, Serbia: Dèmija [2], Rȕpa [1]

as: ka, kȁvo, ki [1], ko [1], štònō

as a matter of fact: dodúšē

as if, kind of, sort of: lȁfo [2], šȁtro [4]

as long as: dògod

ashame, bring disgrace to: brȕkati, òbrukati, pokúnjiti, ràzliti

ashamed: pȍpišān, pȍsrān

ashtray: čikobérnica, piksàjzla, pìksla [2], pikslàjza [1], pikslájza [2], pikslijána, pikslijàšica, pȉnam

ask for: ìštati

asphalt: àsvalt

assemble, mount: montírati, štȁncati, štȁncovati

assembling: montírānje

assembly: montáža, šràfcigerskī

assistance, help: apanírānje

assume an awkward position (e.g. sitting in a chair): nadžòdžeriti se, nakòkeriti se

asthma: sȋpot, sípnja

astride: ràskrēčen

at night: mȑkonju

atmosphere: štȉmūng

attack: grȋsti, nàljeći, špȉc

attack of hysteria, freak out: hȉkī

attack verbally, denonuce: rèvati

attack, strike: dȑkati se, kìdisati

attempt at solving a problem: mahèrisati

attempt to engage in sexual intercourse with (of a male): naváliti

attempts to solve a problem: mahèrisānje

attention: hȁptak

attractive body: trùpina

attractive buttocks: pòzadina

attractive elderly female: bábac, babùrina, babùskara, babùskera, sàksija

attractive female: apsìkulja, avìōn, avìōnka, bȁtāk, bulahȅtka, bùter, búzda, cáva, čkìcapi, gȑlo, gùzičārka, kàjmak, kòmād [1], komfórnā, kòpriva, krevètara, krevètārka, margàrīn, otróvnjača, pètica, piculȉnčić, pȉčīć, pičkètina, pičúljak, pȕška [2], pȕter, pȕterica, rȁsnā, rȉbo, rȉbōn, smíšnica, šȅsnā, štôs [1], šȕša, šȕt [2], tȁnga, têlo, tȕrbo-kóka, uzvȉjōjla, uzvȉjuša, žbùnjara

attractive female breast: strújnica

attractive female, bombshell: bômba [2]

attractive female, doll: Bàrbika, lȕtka, tkȁlu

attractive female, tomato: màlina

attractive individual: lȕče

attractive leg (of a female): getríbe

attractive legs (of a female): bùtevi

attractive male: slàtkīć, šmêle, šminkerȉkī

attractive woman: mìsica

attractive young female: pȕter, pȕterica

attractive, hot: jȅbozōvan, òtekaō, òteklaō, ràsan

auditorium: dvorhàna

aunt (mother's sister or mother's brother's wife): dàidžīnica

aunt (paternal): strȋnka

aunt (wife of father's brother): àmidžīnica

aunt: kéša [1]

Austin (a car make): ȍslić

authority, expert: màrka [1]

auto with high performance engine, souped up car: àbart

automatic weapon: hȅkler

average male: cikètān, cmólja, klȉnkur, normàlnjāk, sàksija, sȉnđos

average person: bezvèznjāk, crévce [2], pljȕckavica, sȋvī, stàtista, sívac, šumíder, trúba [1], trùbāč, trubàdūr, tuturȕtū

aviator: zȕler

avoid: sjȁšiti, vȁditi se, zaòbīći

avoid duties: čùpati se

avoid work, shirk work: eskivírati, krivinàriti, krivinášiti, zabušávati

avoiding: eskiváža, eskuváža, krivìna, ȍkuka

avoiding duties: čùpānje

avoiding the law: folijánac

away from here: ćȁ

axe: bàltija, klèmkača, klènkača, mìsīrka, sèćira, sìkira, śȅkira

axle: ȁksa, àkšēnka

babbling: žváka

baby brother: bráco [1]

baby, newborn: bebèrōn, bebijáner, bebìrōn, bèpče, ȅmbriōn, pizdúnče, žgèbe, žgèpče

babysitter: pèrilka

back (of a person): àrka, gȑbača, kȑsta

backbone: čmȁki

backgammon: tàvla

background, the ground or scenery behind something: bȅkgrâund

backward attitudes: rolètne

backwards: nàguz [2], naguzàčkē

bacon: jàrdovina, sòfūn

bad apartment, dump: rȕpa [2]

bad day: sûša

bad hair day: àntifrīz

bad joke: dȑkopīš

bad luck: pêgula [2], smòla, tápija

bad mood, down: dâun

bad movie: filmčina

bad music: kurúza [1]

bad pass (of a ball): kȍska

bad playing card: dàska, kȍska, lȅtva

bad tooth: kvàrnjāk

bad weather (usu. snowstorm): kijámet

bad wine: kisèlīš, kisèljāk

bad writer: škrábalo

bad, malfunctioning: fȍrpās [2]

bag: bàngalo, čûrka, sȁglja, sàgulja, tòrbljāk, torbùljak, tràjca, trȁšta

bag, wrap: vrȉća

baggy trousers: zâstave

baker: ekmèčija

bakery: somùnjara

baking: žvànjet, žvánjež

balcony: pònistra

bald: bosòglav, bȕljav, ćȕslav, dekòltirān, glàtkī, kabriòlet, mùva, ògūljen, òstrūgānī, palačínka [2], pòkošenī, tȉkva [2], vȅlečasnī

bald head: dlȁka, glóbus, nȕlerica, Tašmájdan

bald male: ablènder, čùtura, ćélo, ćùslāv, dekoltê, jáje, mjȅsečina, móljac, sȅmafōr

ball (esp. soccer ball): bàlūn

ball (of wool): klȕfko, klȕvko

ball: ćȅsa, knédla, žóga

ball bearing: kugláger

ball game (in general): tèkma

ball game similar to soccer but in which one is not supposed to score a goal but rather to avoid scoring it: dùrdur

ball which barely hits the side of a ping-pong table: kȑmača

banal talk: bljùvotina

banana: bahána

band (music): grȕpa

band (usu. rock music): bȅnd

band leader: líder

band, waist: pàntljika

Band-Aid: hȁnzaplast

banded: ufàlčovan

bandy legs: ȉkserice

bang (loud and abrupt sound): cknȕti, grúhati [2], krȅsnuti, ljȗlj, stȕka, stȕkānje, trȁskānje, trȁskati, trȅs [2], tréskati, trȅskot, treskòtānje, treskòtati, tȕtnuti

bank checking account: žȉrak, žȉrić

banker: bȁnkār

banknote: kàban

baptize (into a church): ànjesti

baptized: kȑsten

bar (drinking place): bìfēj, bȉfić, bȕrza, cârda, cèpārnica, cìsterna, cȑkva, čārda, dȁščara, kàfīć, kàhva, kahvàna, kapèlica, kavanȉška, kèrna, kòntara, kíra, krùmpīr [2], lokácija, nàkava, pljùgara, pljùgārka, pljȕgarica, pljùgārnica, pòdrum, rȕpa [2], rùpīnger, skȅla, súšnica, šȁnk, tàca, tèpih, tȗl

bar where many females often gather: pašàluk

bar with large windows: akvârīj, akvârijum

bar, tavern (usu. a low-class one), dive: bȉrc, bìrcuz, bȉrt, bìrtija, oštàrija

barbecue, grill: gràdele, roštȉljati

barbecuing competition (cook off): roštiljáda, roštiljijáda

barber: bríca [2], bríco, cȍbri, grebènār, šìšātor

barely boiled: ròfit, ròvit

barely wash: plákati [1], pláknuti

barely wash oneself: pláknuti se

barely, hardly, at all: ȉole
bargain: nàlugovati
bark (of a dog): rùktati, škamùtati
barkeep, bar-owner (female): birtàšica
barkeep, bar-owner (male): bȉrtāš, pljugàrdžija, šušulȉjēr
barkeeper's daughter: malȉgānka
barking (of a dog): rùktānje
barking of a young dog: škàmut, škamùtānje
barmaid: birtàšica, šȁnkerica
barn: kerna
barracks: kȕća
bartender: bȉrtāš, šȁnker
basement: ȁndergrâund
basket: zèmbīlj
basket used to catch sparrows: gùzara
basketball game: košárac, kòšarica
basketball player: žiràfa
bass (musical instrument or tone): ȁsba, bȁjs, lȉjēs
bat, stick, rod: baštánac, batínac, bàtunjac, ćùtek, degènek, pàlija, tòjaga, tòljaga
bath: banjáža, hàmām, pȁc
bathe: bàdati, bàdati se, bȑčkati se
bathing suit: maràtōnke
bathroom: ckȕljān, čkùljān, čùkljān, ćnȇf, dàščara, hála [1], Hòlivūd, kancelàrija, kàndija, kàndilīšte, klóca, klónja, mòtārnīk, pišaónica, pónor, smùtljivac, sráćnica, telèfōn [1], véca, Vènēcija, Vésa, Vesèlin [2], vòljkārnīk
bathroom tissue, ass wipe: bȕljobrīs, gûz-pàpīr, gùzic-pàpīr, gȕzobrīs, ȑtobrīs, tàrigūz [1], trȁkalica
bathroom, crapper: gȍvnāć [2], gòvnara
bathtub: kȁčka, vȁna
bay (horse): àlat [1]
bazaar, indoor market place: bezìstān, bezìsten
bazooka: erbéjac, sulùndār
be (in any of its Serbo-Croatian meanings used in forms different from the standard): bȉti [1], bȉti [2], tážiti
be: bȉdnuti
be able to: rotáviti
be absentminded: isšȁltati se, išȁltati se
be adequate, be ok: pȁsovati
be afraid: ukákiti se
be alone: čȁmuti, solírati
be angry: dȑkati se, jéditi se
be aroused (emotionally): nalòžiti se, napáliti se
be as wished or planned: skȍckati se
be astonished, be amazed: kòntuzovati se
be baptized (into a church): ànjesti se
be beaten up: dòbiti, fȁsovati, najèbati, pòpiti [2], spȕšiti, trȍpnuti, tropírati
be better than somebody else: šȉti, šívati
be bored: davežírati se, dáviti se, zévati
be bored at work: petljáriti
be boring: bàzditi, ćumùrati, dogúliti, dòklīnčiti, dòkūrčiti, dopíliti, dopízdeti, dopízditi, dopížđeti, nabacívati se, pȑdeti, razvodnjávati, smȑdeti, srȁti, tȑnbiti, trúbiti, tùpisati, vunovlačáriti
be broke, be out of money: izlihtèrisati (se), izlihtírati (se), švorcírati se, utánjiti
be broken, malfunction, die: cȓći
be bureaucratic: pètljati
be careless about: klȁckati
be caught, be captured: zàgrīsti
be cautious: skívati
be cheated, be swindled: ìspušiti, izdúvati [1], nalètiti, pòpljugati, pòpušiti, prímati se, prímiti se, pȕšiti, spȑcati, zànitati se, zarībati se
be cheated, be taken for a ride: provózati se
be conceited, be stuck-up: barònisati, búdžiti se, dȑknuti se, drkúniti se, dŕviti se, džibèrisati se, folírati se, glúmiti, kòfrčiti se, kȕrčiti se, nàprčiti se, pajsèrisati se, picániti se, pȑčiti se, preserávati se, producírati se, puràniti se, šmînkati se, špìlati, ufītīljiti se, ùkūrčiti se, žàbačiti
be confused: zblȁnuti se
be convenient, be appropriate: klȁpati, štȉmati [2], tȉtrati
be dangerous: grȉsti
be defeated: pȕći
be destroyed, be ruined: ablatírati, izgòriti, odjèdriti, òdvisiti, odzvòniti, pandŕknuti, sjèbati se, zgȁsnuti, zgòreti
be down (after the effects of narcotic drugs): oćoráviti
be easily cheated: páliti se
be employed: proizvòditi
be enthusiastic about, be crazy about: raspamétiti se
be excellent: odigrávati
be excited: cvȁsti, òtkinuti, páliti se
be extremely hot (of the outdoor temperature): ùpeći
be fitting, be in tune with: štȉmati [1]
be fond of, like: gotòviti
be forced to pay: rȉgnuti
be forgiven: hàlāl [1]
be friends: duèliti
be frightened, get scared: ìstrzati se, tȑzati se
be frigid sexually: eskimírati
be funny: preserávati se
be good, be cool: ȉgrati, vàljati [2]
be happy: cvȁsti, procvjètati, propùpati
be in a bad mood: nakrivopízditi se, umúliti se, umúsiti se
be in a crowd: gȕžvati se
be in a difficult situation: bàldisati, kvéknuti, nadèrati, nadŕljati, nagrabúsiti, nagràisati, najèbati, najéžiti, nasúkati se, òpeći se, pȕći, sjèbati se, skȉksnuti, skȉsnuti, skrozírati, tandŕknuti, umòčiti se, zaglavìnjati, zagláviti, zagústiti, žiláviti se
be in a difficult situation, paint oneself into a corner: uzelèniti
be in a good mood: raspiláviti se
be in a hurry: glavìnjati, zaglavìnjati
be in a nursing home: odbrojávati
be in a position which disturbs somebody else: nagúziti se
be in a state of shock: frasírati se

be in an awkward position (physically): lomàtati se
be in command: isfazonírati se
be in debt: hȇnkati
be in illegal business: šárati
be in love: ȁšikovati, gùtati, ìzdisati, lòžiti se
be in one particular position: usáditi se
be in prison: bàjbočiti, murírati
be indebted: vȉsiti
be inflicted with a disease: zàkačiti
be interested in: bàcati se, fúrati se, lòžiti se
be interested, be turned on: odlépiti
be interesting: ȉgrati, odigrávati
be intrusive: gúziti se
be involved in dirty business: múljati
be late: dòcniti
be left on one's own, be left hanging: vȉsiti
be left without any money: ìspucati se
be left without opportunities: ìspucati se
be loud (colors): šljȁštiti
be louder than somebody else: nàtpevati
be miserly, be a tightwad, be a skinflint: cicijášiti
be missing: ìspružiti se
be mistaken: nasáditi se, nàsānkati se, nàsānjkati se, nàsesti, nàsjesti, nasúkati se, sjèbati se, zajèbati se
be nervous: pízdeti, pízditi
be offended: fȕriti se
be on narcotic drugs: nàvūći se, vòziti se
be overcharged, be ripped off: vrísnuti
be overly serious, be stuffy: štrébati
be pretty: sévati
be proud of, beam with pride: blȉstati
be refused, be denied, be turned down: nekašírati
be robbed, be ripped off: jaúknuti
be sad: stȉsnuti se
be sent to prison: ljȕljnuti, oláditi
be sick: ràspadati se
be silent: sašúćeti
be skillful: razvaljívati
be slow: kiláviti, kiláviti se
be stolen: skȉknuti
be stubborn, be defiant: ìntačiti se, nahoróziti se, trucírati, uskopístiti se, uskopízditi se, ùskūrčiti se, zabídžiti
be stunned: zazebéknuti se
be successful: procvètati
be suitable, be fitting: ȉći, ȉgrati, odigrávati, pȁsati [1], váriti, váriti se, varírati
be suitable, fit: ćúćati
be sure: pròsnifati
be surprised: òtēti se, zgrànuti se, zȉnuti
be surprised, be floored: patosírati se
be thirsty: žȅdovati
be tight with money, pinch pennies: stȉsnuti se
be tired (from work, sports, etc.): cȓći
be trapped, be without a way out: nàgaziti, utȓčati
be unable to count on: ùbrisati se
be unable to find something or find one's way due to limited visibility: ćorétati
be unable to remember: zablokírati se
be unable to sit still: vŕpōljiti se
be undecided: lòmiti se
be under a strong influence of narcotic drugs, be dead stoned: štȕcati
be under the influence of narcotic drugs, be stoned: trȉpovati, vózati se
be upset: sekìrati se
be useful: hȁsniti
be valid: ȉgrati, odigrávati, páliti
be very boring: našešíriti se
be very close to each other (of friends): skòmpati se
be very cold: ukočánjiti se
be very frightened, freak out: pofríkiti
be very happy: svršávati, šíziti
be very hot, feel intense heat: čvȁriti se
be very sad: pokúnjiti se
be very surprised: zabezéknuti se
be very tired: kalírati
be with somebody: prikéljiti se
be worn out, be exhausted: bàldisati
be worse off: òtpevati
beach: fùruna, žȁpla
beans (served without meat): gȍlō
beans: ćúčavac, dinàmit, fȑčule, pàljkuš, pasùljčina, pèvāč [1], pŕdlja, sȕljpa, sȕljpāš
bear (the animal): mèđed
beard: čȅtka, kàtravoš, kàtvāroš, kećȁšica, mètla [1], pàčeška
bearded male: bráda [2], čèkinjo, fȑčalija, pòtpičnjāk [1]
bearing: láger
beast (the animal): bèstija, bȅštija, dzvȅr
beat: gájtaniti
beat energetically (as of heart), beat like crazy: đȉpiti
beat music (the style): bȉtić
beat up: ȁknuti, akušírati, bȁšaliti, bȁštati, bekendírati, bȅnešiti, betonírati, bȕftati, cjépati, čȉbučiti, čȍhati, degènečiti, dȅljati, devètati, flȉkati, flȉknuti, fȕtiti, gȁziti, glȁditi, gnjéčiti, grèbati, grùntačiti, gudèrisati, gȕžvati, havàrisati, ìseći, isfašírati, iskašírati, iskembéčiti, ìskrpati, iskùndačiti, ispolívati, isponàpiknjuti, isposécati, ispráštiti, isprepalàpucati, ispreponàtaći, isprèpucati, ìspužvati, istabànati, istábati, istambùrati, ìstesati, istušírati, išekètati, išórati, ìzakati, izbȁštati, izbúbati, izbubètati, ìzdeljati, izdevedesetdevètati, izdevètati, izdúvati [2], izèbati, ìzgladiti, izlémati, izmàltati, izmàrisati, izmasírati, izmávati, ìzmazati, ìzmestiti, izmlátiti, iznabádati, izrezbáriti, izrókati, izrulètati, izvešpláviti, kàntati, kečezkečkènisati, kéčiti, kókati, kréhati, kȑpati, lémati, lèmisati, lepìnjati, lȅšiti, lȉbrati, lȉndrati, lìnjati, lúpati, lȕrati, lȕriti, lȕzati, lȕzovati, ljúštiti, màkljati, màrisati, mȅblovati, mésiti, mirìsati, mutírati, nàbiti, nabúbati, nadúvati, nakàntati, nàmestiti, namlátiti, nàpucati, nàtūći, njákati, odbȁštati, odbrìjati, òdeljati, ohláditi, òjaditi,

oláditi, òlešiti, òlīndrati, opláviti, otambùrati, òtesati, pêglati, pòpraviti, prèbiti, preparírati, prèšibati, prèviti, ràspičkati, razbúcati, ríbati, ŕkati, scipeláviti, skȑšiti, spȁkovati, stŕkati, ščvȑgati, šȉbati, šíkati, škudírati, šȍpati, šórati, šȍrnuti, štètnati, tȃbati, tàmbati, tambùrati, tambùrati, tȅsati, tȅstati, toljàgati, tȗći, tušírati, ùbiti, ùgaziti, ùjesti, uljèpšati, umíriti, ùrnisati, uspávati, ùsrati, vešpláviti, vòziti, vȑteti, vȗgliti, zablombírati, zašórati, zàštemati, zatábati, zbȃnčiti, zbòmbati, zdȅksati, zgòmbati, zgrȗdati, zgùžvati, zlȍptati, zmjȅsiti, žvékati

beat up severely: faširati, nàšmīnkati, pocépati, pocijépati, razgotíviti, smȁzati, smlȁviti, smòžditi, uvòštiti, zgòvnati, zigoráknuti

beat up severely, destroy: ràsturiti

beat up severely, trash: òdrati, polòmiti, prelòmiti, sataràniti, sréditi, ušórati, utábati

beat up, butcher: zmesáriti

beat up, crush, trash: ràzbiti, umlátiti

beat up, tattoo: ùdesiti

beat up, thrash: mlátiti

beat up, wax: vòštiti

beat with a billy club: pèndrečiti, štȃpovati

beat, defeat: bȉti [3]

beat, win money from somebody: odèrati

beaten up: derìvāt, grȍgī, pèčen

beaten up, whipped: ìšibān

beating up: akuširānje, degènek, kókānje, mára

beating up: bàštānje, devètānje, lémānje, lȉndrānje, pêglānje, šibácija, šȉbānje, škudírānje, šórānje, tabàčina, tabánjac, tȃbānje

beating up by two people: vȁservāga

beautiful: dȅkoratīvan

beauty: ljèpōjka, snegòvila

because: jel, jȅrbo

become sluggish: otrombóljiti

become accustomed to, get used to: sváriti

become affluent: nàfutrati se, olováriti se, pòtkožiti se

become angry, foam at the mouth: zàpjeniti

become aroused, get wet: povìzati

become broke (financially): lihtèrisati se

become contracted (of a muscle, etc.): skvȑčiti se

become courageous: osokòliti se

become dangerous (of a situation): zàgutaviti se

become insane, become unhinged: òtkačiti, òtkačiti se

become insane, flip out, go nuts: flȉpnuti

become insane, freak out: lúditi, otkídati [2], òtkinuti se

become lost: dȇti se, zijániti se

become muscular: nàbildovati se

become partners: uortáčiti se

become soft, be irresolute: raspèkmeziti se

bed: dàske, horizontála, knjáva, léglo, lȉjēs, pòsteja, šlofìnjāk, šljòfinjāk, vȅtkre

bed time: mȑtvāčnica

bedroom: sòvārnik, spàvāćā, špȃrkàsa

beef: rȉsōvče

beep (alarm, etc.): cìčati, cìčiti, cilìnkati, cilíkati, cvŕčati, psȉkati, psȉknuti, tuckàrati, tȗtkati

beeper: psȉkāč

beeping (alarm, etc.): cȉlīk, cilìnkānje, cilíkānje, cvȑljūk, psȉkānje, psȉkav, tùtuk

beer: bȉra, bȉrić, hmȅlj, klìpara, òžujak, ožujáner, pìčuga, pìvara, pìvčuga, pȉvdža, pìvdžān, pìvīć, pìvkan, píva, pívce, šȗškavac, vȍpi, vȗpa, žȗja

beer belly: pìvceps

beer drinker: pivòpija

before: prȅđe, príja [2]

beg, ask for money: čèšati se, fȅktati, màngisati, ministrírati, rédati, ùfačkati, ùžickati, zbȍksati, žicáriti, žȉcati, ùžicati, žȉckati

beggar: drȍpljār, kȍjot, kúza, oglàbātor, pèrislav, sakàto, špèkjēger, tùcār, tȗcer, žicáš

beggar who pretends to limp: gȅgavac

begging: žȉca, žȉcānje, žȉcārēnje, žȉckānje, žȉcu

begin dating a female or male: ìstrzati, smȗvati se, spètljati se, ušémiti se, zbȃviti se

begin to act wild: pròkūrčiti se

begin to drive: pòćerati

begin to flirt: stȃrtati, ubáciti se, ubacívati se, ukȑcati se

begin to smoke a cigarette: zàkuriti

begin to take effect (of narcotic drugs): dȉzati

begin with an action: lȃtiti se, raspáliti

begin with sexual foreplay: isprèpadati

begin, start: kréniti, póći

behave: cȁnjati se

behave foolishly: mlátiti se

behave or talk indecently: pirlìtati

being broke, being out of money: dekintácija

being a homeless person: tumarològija

being absent: ȃutsajd

being arrested: rikavȅla

being broke (financially): glȃd, lȍvostāj, sûša

being conceited, being stuck up: šminkèrāj

being funny: preserávānje

being in a crowd (e.g. on a rock concert): gùžvānje

being in love: hȅrcfȅler, kardiològija

being insane, being nuts: nòrēnje

being lonely: solírānje

being lost: zìjān [1]

being nervous: njȗpānje, njupáža, živcírānje

being one's best man: kúmstvo

being one's godfather: kúmstvo

being under a strong influence of narcotic drugs, being dead stoned: štȗcānje

being upset: sikirácija

being Ustasha-like (Croatian Nazi during World War II): ustašoídnōst

being without any restrictions: sȃmpās

believe (usu. in something which is either unrealistic or with hidden disadvantages), be hooked: pȅcati se believe, buy: kúpiti [2]

believe, swallow: gùtati, progùtati

believe, trust: nalòžiti se, napáliti se, prímiti

bell: dȉn-dȍn, dzvȍno, tandȑkalo, zvekètalo, zvȍn

bell-bottom pants: zvónca, zvòncare

bellwether: klopòtār

beloved child, apple of one's eye: kùrtija, kúrto [1], mèzimac, mjèzimac, pȉšo [1]

belt driver: kàiš

belt repairman: râboš-mâjstor

belt, waist: gùrtna, kȑnc

belt-driver cogwheel: kàišnīk

bench: bȁnak

benefit, profit: hàsna

Benzedrine, benny: béndža

beret: francùzica

berry (in general): bóba

best: mȁks, mȁksī, mȁksimālan, maksimȉlijān, másan

best man (with whom bride and broom stay in a very close relationship all their lives): kûm

best man (with whom bride and groom stay in a very close relationship for all their life): kumàšin

best regards: p.p.p. [pê-pê-pê]

bet: ȍpklada, sȅcovati, tȉpovati

betray, turn in to authorities: dȁnfati

betray, turn to authorities: istoròkati, ȉzjakati

betrayal: prȍvala

betting: sȅc, sȅcovānje

bettor: sècāroš

bicycle, bike: bacȉklo, becȉklo, déva, dvotòčkāš, kòtāč, krȁmp, nȍgač, nȍgāć, tȁčko

big apartment: stànčuga

big Citroen (make of car): àjkula, žȁba

big earring: múnja [1]

big eyes: sàrme

big lie: paraláža

big money: štȕka

big nose: nòsūrda, sȕrla

big ox: vòlina

big spoon, ladle: kùtlača

big, awesome: ȁša

big, many: mâsno

big-boned and clumsy person, oaf: mèđed

big-boned female: bedèvija, jàpija, kòbila, vajzùrina

big-boned female, whale: àjkula

big-boned male:

big-boned male: degènek, gorògan, krùpnjāk

big-boned male: gȑmālj

big-boned male: ledolómac

big-boned male, big boy: mòmčina

big-boned mare: bedèvija

big-boned person: grdòsija

big-eyed person: buljóka

big-nosed male: klarinètista, kljùnār, pelȉkān, pȕškāš

big-nosed person: nósonja

bike, bicycle: bȁjc, bȁjk, bȁjs, bîc, bicȉklo, bȉciš, bȉciška, bicíkla

bill (utilities, etc.): ljȕštura

bill (of money): kȑpa, šȕška

billy club: gȕmi-štrúdla, màndrak, pèndrek, pûmpa

biology: kukcològija

bird's call: klîk [2]

birth certificate: krštènjāk

bisexual, AC/DC: àmfȋbija, dùplī [2], dùplōnka, dvòcjēvka

bitch (female dog): ćȅmica, ćȅvka

bite (a bone, etc.): glàbati

bitter coffee: gòrkīć

bitter, tart: gȓk

black: vrân

black eye, shiner: kràfn, nȁočari

black magic: ùrok

black ram: mȑkālj

black sheep: lȁja

black-market money exchange: štȕcovānje, štȉcūng

blacksmith: kujùndžija

blacksmith's: kujùndžīnica

blame, accuse: prȉšiti, spakírati, utrčávati

blank cartridge: ćórak [1]

blanket on the rim of one's bed (which is the required procedure for soldiers): preklàpača

blast: trêsak, trȅska, trȅskāj

bleat (of goat), baa: bekètati, véčati, vekètati, vréčati, vrékati, vréštati

bleat (of sheep), baa: békati, béknuti, bléjati [1]

bleating (of goat): vȅkav

bleating (of goat), baaing: bekètānje, mȅka [1], mékānje, mȅkāvka, mekètav, véčānje, vȅka, vȅkēt, vekètānje, vrȅka, vrȅkānje

bleating (of sheep): bléjānje, blêk, blȅka

bleating (of sheep), baaing: bȅka, békānje, mekètānje

bleed: prokišnjávati

bless: haláliti

blind: mráčan, rȁvčo, rȁvćo

blind male: mrȕljān, pȕčavac, staklènjāk

blink: fercèrati

blister: kròmpīr

block a shot (in soccer, basketball, etc.): markírati

block, prevent: blokírati

blocked shot (in basketball): banána

blocked, prevented: blòkīrān

blocking, preventing: blokírānje

blond female: plàvuša, žȕja

blond male: ȅmentāler, žȕjān, žûtī

blood-brother: póbro

bloody street fight: okináva

blow (as of a fuse): iskòčiti

blow (e.g. to cool off hot soup): píriti

blow (wind, etc.): dúhati, fijùkati, fijúknuti, šȕmiti

blow up (explosives, etc.): ràsprsnuti

blow, exhale: púhati, sìkati, sȉknuti, sikòtati, sìktati

blowing (wind, etc.): dúhānje, fȉjūk, fijùkānje, fijùkav

blowing up (explosives, etc.): rasprskávānje

blowing, exhaling: púhānje, sìktānje, sȉktav, sȉktavo

blue jeans: fàrmerice, fàrmērke, fȃrmosi

bluff, pretend: blȅf, blȅfati, blefírati

bluffer: blȅfer

bluffing: blefírānje

blurp: gugùtati

blurt out: ìzlanuti se, izlèteti, izlèteti se, izlètjeti, izlètjeti se

blush, turn colors: semafòrisati, semafóriti, zapurnjáviti

BMW (a car make), Bimmer: bȅmbāč, bèńcta, béndža, béndžo, benđóla

boar (the animal): dosánac, dòsinac, karìdžalac, vȅpar

boar: karìndžalac

board (a ship, plane, etc.): ukùrcati

board: plȃta

board a bus: sardȉnisati se

boast, brag: barònisati, búdžiti, drȁmiti, dupètati se, džekírati, džekírati se, fáliti se, frȉjati se, glúmiti, gròmisati se, knjȉžiti se, kȕrčiti se, paùnisati se, polòmiti se, prȁviti se, prodávati se, puvàkati, puvàkati se, púvati se, tȑtiti se, utrčávati, žàbačiti se

boast, brag, puff oneself up: napuhávati se

boaster, braggart, blowhard: bàlōn [1], dȑkūn, dȕvadžija, duvànder, grȁmofōn, grȍf, gùzica, kòlājna, lȁjavica, lajávko, màčōr, mȁša, Minhàuzen, múdonja, pljȕcko, pȕvadžija, puvànder, pùvātor, sȅmafōr, spȁjker, stòljetnjāk, šàrenī, šmȉnker, tȑtonja

boasting, bragging: frajèrisānje, frȉjka, kȕrčēnje, sȅc, šmȋnka, šmȉnkānje

boat: kàīć

body (of a car): karȍca

body: jàpija, truplijáner

body builder (female): bìlderka

body builder (male): bȉks [1], bìlder, bȍdī-bìlder, karavèla, razvijȍtka, siròvina

body builder:

body building: bȍdī-bìldīng

body man, mechanic: blȁtobrān [1]

body piercing: pȉrs

bohemian, one who lives unconventionally: alternatívac

boiled: lȅšo, vȃren

boiled food: vȁrīvo

boiler: kàzan, làmpek

bologna: parízer

bolt (mechanical part): čȉvija

bomb: bȏnba

bon appetite: prȉjātno

bone: kokalína, kȏs

book: ćìtāb, ćìtāp, kùpus, lȋbar, tìrita, tȉrta

boot: bùnār, čȉzmāk, čizmijána, čizmindȅros

booth (in a bar, restaurant): stȕpa

border (between countries): bȁra [2], cȑta [2], grána, línija, stȕpovi, štráfta, vònjara

boredom: čȁmos, čàmura, gnjávež, kenjáža, masáža, mȑtvāčnica, pilàna, pílēnje, pušióna, tlȁka, tùpilo, vòda, zujàčina

boring: mùha [2], nápōran, ȍpšīran, téžak

boring event: jéba, kenjáža, turpijáner

boring female, bore: mȁrsōvka, pìzdulja, pȑdara, šȉbadžīka, šólja [1]

boring game (soccer, etc.): pȉmplānje

boring issue: dávež [2]

boring male, bore: cikètān, lȇvī [2], palamùdžija, plàkāt, stjènica

boring male, boring dude: pìmpek [1]

boring or unpleasant matter, hassle: gnjaváža

boring person, bore: cȇđ, ćùmur [1], dávež [1], dávid, dàvitelj, dȑkelja, filòksera, fizioterapèut, gnjàvātor, gnjávež, gȕšāč, gȕšitelj, kénjac, kènjāč, kènjara, kènjātor, kŕlja [1], lèpričār, lèvāk [1], limunáda, màsēr, maserȁti, màstilo, móljac, mùha [1], palamùdija, pégla, pȉjavica, pìtōn, píla, prìlipak, prìvjesak, pùšāč, pùšik, sèrāč, sèriglāva, séronja, srȃč, šíber [1], šȉbadžija, šlȅper [1], terapèut, tȕpadžija, tupamȁros, ȕdāv, vȁška, vònjifer, žȉlāvka, žvalávko

boring sexual partner: automàtičār, pìlār

boring small person: mudèško

boring song: žváka

boring story: žváka

boring thing or event: sránje [2]

boring, uninteresting: akùstičan

borrowed money not intended to be returned: čȉp

Bosnia and Herzegovina: Bȇ-Hȃ [1], Bȇhȃ [1], Džamahȋrija [1]

Bosnian (person): Bosančȅros

Bosnian (pertaining to a person): bȇ-hȃ [2], bȇhȃ [2]

Bosnian Muslim (female): balȉnkuša, bȕštra, bùštura, Fáta

Bosnian Muslim (male): bàlija, džȉhādovac, mudžahèdīn, òbrezānī, poturčènjāk, pòturica, Tȕrak, Tùrčin [1], Tȕrković

Bosnian Muslim (pertaining to a person): bàlījskī, bàlīnskī, bàlīskī

Bosnian passport: ljìljani

Bosnians: Bȍsnatrans

boss: àga, Ȁtamān, bȃn [2], Bȍnd, bȍs [1], čȋf, đȁvō, ȅfše, gȁzda, gȁzdarica, génja, glȁfōr, gòlēmča, gòlēmša, kȍtomān, líder, mánac, mȃnča, mȃnče, mànukot, nȃjlaf, nósonja, ȍkatī, sȉvor, šȕmnjāk, trȁnjār, trȁvčār, travìnjār, trònjār

boss's wife: mànčetovica, šȅfovica, tàrnjarica, trȁnjerica, travčàrica, travinjàrica, trȍnjarica

both ... and: te ... te

bother with, waste time over: bàkćati se, bàktati se

bother, annoy by talking: izmasírati

bother, disturb: cȉmati, fašírati, gnjáviti, iscéditi, klistírati, svȑbeti, svȑbiti, tripèrisati, zalijépiti se

bottle: bocijáner, bùtelja, kíbla, šíša, šíše

bottle cap: gvȉnt

bottle neck used to smoke hashish: gȑlīć, stȁklić

bottle of beer: klìpača

boutique: môdnjāk

bow legs: ȍkserice

bowl (food container): čának, ćása

bowtie: mȁšnjāk, palačínka [1]

box (someone's ears): klémpa [1]

box: čèkmeče, kȉštra, skȁtula, škȁtula, škȁtulja

box above one's ear: šȍpka

box office: bȍks-ȍfis

box or chest used to store valuables: sehára

boxing ring: pìčkalīšte

boy who likes to be hugged: škȉljān

boy who manages to do nothing more than to hold his girlfriend's hand: rukovòdilac

boy who manages to do nothing more than to walk with his girlfriend: fasàdēr, izvòđāč, rázvodnīk, razvòđāč, tàksī, tàksista, vesèlin [1], vèsēlnīk

boy's penis: cigarèta, Pinȍkio, pìpek, píša

boy, kid: àrap, bôjs, cúrac, cùrān, Džȅk, đélac, đȍkica, fȅrgajn, fȕkić, kàmač, kèpec [2], kìnāf, kȉnfa, kȉnfāć, kȉt [1], klìpan, kòmāt [1], krȁstavac, kúronjica, lȉma, lȉmāč, málac, malalájac, mȃlī, màliša, màndār, mȉlkavac, mômče, mùškāć, múdonja, mùmak, njȍfra [1], pèrkan, sȉsavac, slȉnavac, spȅrmić, šíljo, šiljòkurac, šiljokùrān, tùrnjāk

boyfriend: abàžur, dasòvān, dȅčko [2], đuvègija, đuvèglija, frȁjer, jȅrfra, mlàdīć, mòmak, šváca [1], švȁler

boys: čkȉde

bra: blȕhī, brûshàlter, cìcncȅker, cìcntréger, očále, sȉsobrān, sisodŕžac, sisodȑžāč, sisoprihvàtāč

braggart, know-it-all: svèznadār

brain: bùbreg, kèfalo, klȉker, mȉslilo, rȉbīzla, vìjuge

brake: brȅmza, brȅmz-pedála

brake pad: pàkn, pàkna

brakes: žlȁjfe

brand name of prescription drug used by drug addicts to produce a narcotic effect: àrtān

brandy: bêlā, bèlača, bômba [2], cûjka, dàskovača, dróga, gotȉvica, kèrija, kerkína, kȉca, kȉjara [1], kȉjara [2], ljùtara, mòrāl, mȕka, naftàlīnka, pàlīnka, pàljīnka, pàljōr, pàljōrka, pŕlja, prȍšlica, šljóka, šnjóka, šíša, šúlja, šùšljiga, tára, târča, tàrdija, vȉnjāk

brandy drinker: džȉber, džȉbronja

brandy made from wood splinters: dàskovača

brass knuckles: bòkser, bokserȉška, zubolómac

brass player (brass instrument musician): pljùšāč

bravery: pȅtlja, stîsak

bray (of a donkey): rèvati

bread: bòkār, bȍkor, bùkar, cȉglja, kàlocnīk, kàlosnīk, krȕ, krȕv, lȅb [2], lȅbac, lȅmba, lèpče, njȕpavac, pȁlje, pánja, pànjislas, pànjota

break: rikávati, ríknuti

break into an apartment: òčukati, odbàštati, odbáštiti

break out of prison: ràskinuti

break the hymen: pròkljucati, ràspičiti

break through (a window, door, etc.): razbàštati

break wind frequently, fart alot: raspȑdeti se, upȑditi

break wind loudly, fart loudly: grúvati

break wind silently, fart silently: fȕljiti se

break wind while defecating: drȍćkati, drȍćnuti

break wind, fart: dȁmfati, òkinuti, opáliti, pȑcnuti, prdécnuti, prdéknuti, pȑdeti, pȑditi, pȑdnuti, prdùckati, pȑnuti, pȕfnuti, pȕpnuti, ròsiti, ufúljati se, upúvati se, zaprdékati, zapȑditi

break, disintegrate: kŕhati

break, disrupt: spȉčiti

breaker points (on an automobile distributor): plȁtine

breakfast: frȕštuk

breaking into an apartment: ȕndža-vȁla

breaking wind: gnjúrac, gȍlūb, pȑc [1], pȑdac [2], pȑdež, prdùckānje, šejtanizácija

breathe: díhati

breathing: díhānje, hȁk

breeze around, tool around (e.g., walk around at a party): pròmuvati se

breeze through town or a bar: prozújati, zújati

bribe: mâst, mȁzīvo, ònō [2], šȁp, tânj

bribe, lubricate: mȁzati, pòdmazati, potkùbati, šapírati

brick: ćôrka

bricklayer: bȍškāč, bȍškāć

bride: pljȁče

bride of honor (with whom bride and groom stay in a very close relationship all their lives): kúma

bridge player: brìdžer

brief: brȉfovati

briefcase: àktn-tȁška, àktn-tàšna, ȁktōvka

brigade (military): bregáda

brilliantine (hairdressing cream): diláber [2]

bring: docìpljati, dòvući

bring along: dobàrtati, dȍčkati, dočkòjati

bring home (usu. a girlfriend or a boyfriend to meet one's parents): prìvesti

bring one's cattle down from the mountain: sjáviti

broke (financially): dekìntīrān, hàtīf, lȁko, lêr [2], lȉht, mòrtus [1], òsūšen, sûh, šúpalj, švȍrc, tànak, trȍba, trópa [2]

broke (financially), cleaned out: čȉst

broke male: mȑtvac

broken glass: sȑča

broken, malfunctioning, dead: cȑkaō, cȑkō

broom: bráda [1], túta

brothel client: bádža

brothel, whorehouse: àbaša, cèpārnica, jàvnjāk, kuplèrāj, kȕplić, lîdo, prcòjgenz, rȕpa [2], rùpīnger, šefkàna, šèfkārna, šèfkārnīk, šèvārnīk, šèvkārnīk, žúpa

brother: bȁki [1], bâle [1], bàtan, bȁte, báto [2], bȕmbār, bȕrāz [1], burázer, vràgotnīk, vȑgodnīk, vȑgotnīk

brother-in-law: đȅver

brotherhood: bràstvo

bruise: ȍrdēn, rukotvòrina, šljȉva [1]

brunette: cȑnka, gȁra

brush (e.g. to clean garment): òkefati

brutally send away: otpízditi
bucktoothed person: kljòvār
bug (insect): bȕbos
build quickly and shabbily: skarabúdžiti
build, construct, erect: bȁniti, karabúdžiti, nȕrkati
building: kasàrina
building block: orȉjāš[2]
building corridor: pȉsta
building material: jàpija
bullet: fìšek
bullet or knife wound: bága
bump (usu. in road): džòmba, džȍmbe
bumping into and picking somebody's pockets: àduak
bundle: pȉnkl
bundle of money: bȕt, dȅme, dȅtne
burglar: dumbèrāš, filèksīr, kljȕčār, otporâtor, ùndžāroš, ùnđāroš, vàlēr, vàlista, zihèrāš
burglar who enters apartments through windows: skȁkavac[1]
burglar's kit: krȁstavice, vàrzilo
burglary: vȁla[3]
burn: plàmćeti, ȕžditi
burn oneself: òšuriti se
burned: ožèžen
burning wood: gurávinja
burnt: zapèčen, zàpekō
burp, belch: podrigívati
burr, burdock: cȉkālj
burst in outrage, blow up, lose one's cool: plànuti
burst of laughter: grȍhot
bursting (with laughter): grȍhotan
bury: sarániti, saranjívati
bus (usu. in public transportation): antibiòtik
bus: bȁs, bȕs, bùsanja, ćíro, gumárac, kònzērva, kotùrāš
bus line number thirteen in Belgrade, Serbia: dáma, kûrva
bus line number twelve in Belgrade, Serbia: žȁndār
bus line number twelve in Belgrade, Serbia: pódnē, pȕb, pùbiš, pubijáner, pȕkī[2], pȕkica
bus line number twenty in Belgrade, Serbia: dvòbanka
bus line to Petlovo Brdo in Belgrade, Serbia: pétlovac
bus station: gumènjāk, hȍpsalica, vatrènjāk, vjetrènjāk, zàdnjāk
bush, shrub: àndrak[2], džbûn, tràmbulja
business (any kind of): bȉznis
businessman: poslòvnjāk
busy: okùpīran, rȁsprodān, rȁsprodāt
but: mȁ[1], tȁ[1]
butcher (literally): džèlāt, kàsaper
buttocks (of poultry): náguznjāk
buttocks petting: mȉmohōd
buttocks, back side, butt: pòzadina
buttocks, butt: ȁlka, ȁlkica, àubakse, brȁva[2], bûlj, búlja[1], buljáfer, buljáker, buljàkser, buljànder, buljànfer, buljàsker, bùljāf, bùljina, bùljkāf, bùljōn, bȕljos, buljòsava, bȕljoš, bȕta, centrála, crèvara, čmára, dȉndara[1], dȉndulja, dròbara, dùbara, dȕckī, dùgme, dùkat, dùlavka, dȕpe, dùpinger, dúša, đȕlāvka, èkrān, fȑka, gèpek, gladiòla, gùjca, gùjca, gùjica, gòvnara, gȕščetina, gûz, gúza[1], guzèrnjāk, guzètina, guzičètina, gùzičica, gùzičina, gùzička, gùzičnjāk, gûznī, gȕzos, gúža, gûžnjī, gùzca, gùzelja, gùzica, gzz, gùžičnjāk, hàubaksa, jàstuk, jòzicagunj, kȁca, kána, kànāl, kàndilo, kȁnka, kànkica, kàntaros, kânj, kánja, karavèla, karosèrija, kènjara, klònjara, knȍpr, kònjara, krivòguzā, krivogùzica, krtìna, kȕtka, lubènica, ljúba, mȁgacīn, mȁgazīn, nȕlerica, pȅdu, pòkara, plìnara, pòdgūznī, pȍkāl, pȑda, pȑdalica, pȑdalo, pȑdāljka, pȑdara, ráša, rêp, rȉtica, rȍra, rȕksāk, sírnica, sòmūn, sràćara, sráćnica, strîna, strôj, šȉtara, šȍtka, šȕpa, tȅtka, tȑta, tȑtica, tȑtka, turȉzam, vònjara, zȁgu, zâmjenīk, zȉcagu, žȁba, žîr, žùtača, žùtara, žȕtka
buttocks, can, butt: kánta, kàntica
buttocks, seat, butt: sjȅdalo, zȉc
buttocks, tail, butt: àuspūh
button: gȕmb, pȕca[2], pȕce
button on a thread used to produce sparks: zvŕlja
buy: kataglinègerovati, kataglîngerovati, nabáciti
buy a drink for someone: víkniti, víknuti, vrísnuti
buzz (alarm, etc.): zvŕčati, zvȑlati, zvŕljati, zvȑncati, zvȑnčati, zvȑndati
buzz (bee, buzzer, etc.): zújati, zujȉkati, zújiti, zȕjkati, zȕk, zȕka, zúkati, zúknuti, zúktati, zȕnuti, zunzàrati, zunzáriti, zuzùckati, zùzuk, zuzùkati
buzz (usu. of flies): bzȉkati
buzz: zûj, zúja, zvȑcnuti
buzz by: prozújati
buzz loudly: zúčati, zundàrati
buzzer (e.g., on a door): zújalica, zvȑčina
buzzing (bee, buzzer, etc.): zújan, zújānje, zȕjav, zújēnje, zȕjkānje, zûjno, zȕkānje, zȕkasto, zunzàrānje, zuzùkānje, zuzùkav, zvȑdānje
buzzing fly: zùjača, zùkača, zùkara, zùndulja, zújala, zújalica, zundàrača, zvȑkulja, zvȑndara
buzzing insect: zùjāč
by the way: mopasân
bypass, skirt: krȁjcati
bystander, observer: kìbīc, kibȉcēr
cab, taxi: glòba, gȕnta, kȍčija, kòfer, kȍnjāk, tahȉtī
cabbage: palùrān, pòloram
cable, wire: gájtan
cables (esp. as a part of an engine): kabláža
cackle (hens, etc.): kakòkati, kaúknuti, kokòtati, kvȍcati, raskokodákati se, ràskvocati se
cackle (of a turkey): kȁuk, kaùkānje, kaùkati
cackling (hens, etc.): kvȍcānje, kvȍcav, kvrȅka
cafe: fìćka
cage: kȁfez
cake: kàsārna, tortȉljos, tòrtiška, tȍrtos
call (phone, etc.): kȍlnuti, pȉsnuti
call, shout: hȍjkati, klȋk[2], otkídati[1], vábiti
calling: hȍjkānje
calm down, cool off: iskulírati, iskulírati se, kulírati, oláditi,

skulírati se
calm somebody down: iskulírati
calming down, cooling off: kulíranje
campus: studèntnjāk
camshaft: nòknvela
can: kozérva
can opener: deflorâtor
Canadian dollar: kanáđanin
candle: cûrka, ćȕka, džûrka, đûrka, lȁštarnica
candy: bȍnkāč
cane, walking stick: šćâp
cap, hat: gláva, kàmilāvka, knjáva, kȑčule, lònac, pòklopac
capital punishment: smȑtnīk, smȑtnjāk, žȉca
capsule (lunar, medicine, etc.): kapsóla
car battery: bàtērija
car crash: kàlpiš, karàmbōl, kȑkete, saobràćājka
car mechanic, grease monkey: avtomehàničār
car theft: àkcija
car with diesel engine, diesel: dizèlāš, nȁftāš
car, auto: àvto, àutīć, àuto
car, wheels: apàrāt, četvorotòčkāš, gùmātor, kâr [2], karȍca, kȍla, kolíca, kònzērva, limènjāk, lȉmka, màkina, mašína, plȇh, plȇhnjāk, pȑdalo, rȍbot, sokòćilo, strôj, tòčkovi, tȕtāć, vàgōn
car-mechanic: avtomehàničārskī
Caravel (airplane model): karamèla
carburetor: fergázer, karburâtor
card gambling: bilȉjara
card playing: dugànija
cardboard used as a filter for a joint: kartònče
cardboard used as a filter in a joint: kartonȉška
careless: ȁljkav, ávetast, lȁbūd [1], sèrbez [1], sklȅčkān
careless person: àjmana, kaléja, trȁlalāj
careless, irresponsible, and sloppy female: ȁljkavica, aljkàvuša
careless, irresponsible, and sloppy male: ȁljkavac
carelessly: hô-rȕk [2]
caries (tooth decay): kvârijes
carpenter: tȉšler
carry on a racket (criminal): reketírati
carry small trade: perjáriti
carry, bear: cȕglati, sȅcati, šíkati
carry, have along: bàrtati, nósati
cart (e.g. oxcart): čkòjači, trȅskavica, vȑtačkē
carton of cigarettes: bȍks, vôz
cartoon (film): cȑtāć, cȑtānī, crtánko, crtènjāk, cȑtić
cartridge case: hȉlzn, pìksna
carving: lȁndēnje
cash: kȅš, suvárak [2], ùtrapiti
cash payment: nárukvica
cashier: hȁznadār
cast a spell on: cȍprati, zašamúditi
castigate: gŕditi
cat: kòtara, kȍtka, màlkalo
cat, kitty: máca
catarrh: kȉhavica
catastrophic: katastròfičan
catch: fȁćkati, mȁznuti, pȅcati, pòvatati, ubádati, ùfatiti, ukébati, ùvatiti, vȁćati, zèriti
catch one's fill (of anything): nàfatati
catch quickly: zdȉmati
catch, get hold of (person, etc.): sàvatati
catch, get something unwillingly: nàvūći
catch, grab: ćopávati, fȁnjati, hápati, hapávati, hȁpiti, fȁtati, kébati, prȉvatiti, sàfatati, ùcakati, ucànjati, ućapírati, ùfaćkati, ùfanjati, ùpecati, vatáriti, vȁtati
catching: pȅcānje
catching, grasping: ćopávānje, hápānje, hapávānje, vȁćānje
cattle: hàjvān, mâl
Caucasian hashish: pȁdī
caught, busted: spèkīrān
cause a black eye: našljíviti
cause inconvenience to somebody: unezgóditi
cause problems: ùsrećiti
cautious gambling: bètōn [2]
cautious male: oprèznjāk, zihèrāš
caw (of a crow): grâk, grȁka, gràkāt, grákati, gráknuti, gràktati, krâ-krâ, kráknuti, krikrȉčati, kvákati, kvàktati, kvekètati
cawing (of a crow): gràktānje, grȁktav, gûk, kvákānje, kvâr
cawing bird: kvàkāč
ceaase talking, shut up: zašnírati
cease an action: aterírati
cease being interested in an object or issue, drop: izgustírati
cease bothering, stop disturbing: apsolvírati, cirkùlisati, odjèbati, odstúpiti, ohláditi, sjȁhati, svŕšiti
cease counting on: otpísati
cease gambling after having earned certain amount of money: dȉgnuti se
cease gambling and pretend to play without money: vȅndovati
cease lying: òdvaditi
cease one's engagement in sexual intercourse: odráditi, odžóđžiti
cease taking narcotic drugs or alcohol: skȉnuti se
cease talking, put a cork in: ohláditi, začèpiti, zàpušiti
cease working (mechanism, etc.): zablokírati, zarȉbati, zarȉbati se
cease, stop: fèrmati, hàltati, odvòjiti, òlabaviti, stopírati
celebration: aldùmāš
cement: cìmenat, cìment, cȉmēnta
cemetery: bòrovice, mèzārje
Centedrine: cèment [2], cȇnt [2]
central prison: Cȇzār
certainly, surely: gùrnosi, zȉher
certificate, diploma: céga [2], čitába, ćába, šára, šára, šȁre, šȁre, šarènica, šarènica

chain: sìndžīr

chain kept above the fireplace to hang a kettle: vèrige

chain smoker, chimney: òdžak

chains: trȇskāvci

chair: dȕpetrōn

chamber pot: míćo [2], nȍnica, nóša, túta

chance: šansóna

change one's attitude: presaldúmiti se

change one's mind: popišmániti se

change somebody's attitude: presaldúmiti

change the trajectory of a soccer ball: zavŕnuti

changeable mind: fanfuljȃgis

chaos, mess: kuplèrāj

charcoal barbecue (cooking device): bárbekju, bárbikju

chase: kébati, zrȁkati

chase birds away by pronouncing 'iš': ȉškati

chat: ćakùlati, ćȃskati

chatter (of the teeth): cvokòtati, cvòktati, klȍcati, kljȍcati

chatter (of the teeth, in outrage): škrebètati

chatter: klepètati

chatterbox: pùšāč, pùšik

chattering (of the teeth): cvokòtav, cvòktānje, škȑgūt

chattering (of the teeth, when feeling cold): cȅpēt

chauvinist: šòvēn

cheap and unattractive tennis shoe: semènkara

cheap brandy: balègara

cheap prices: jevtinòća

cheap prostitute: hódalica, pràngija

cheat by convincing into: pòjiti

cheat in marbles: đȉdati

cheat on an exam: résaviti

cheat on one's lover or spouse: pilotírati, šárati, špèditi, švalèrati se, zašárati

cheat one's accomplice: zašnírati

cheat, swindle: bacàkati, blȉcati, blȉcnuti, cinculírati, cȕcnuti, đȉći, dȑiblovati, drìbljati, facírati, fȃrbati, fȅršati, folírati, frùlati [1], fȕtrati, isfazonírati, isfolírati, ispáliti, izglúmiti, izjèbati, izmàltati, izmlátiti, izráditi, ȉzvatati, izvatávati, izvózati, jèbati, jebávati, kȅcati, knedlírati, kòrosati, kȕhati, lȁfati, lȉrati, lirìkati, lìrisati, lȉtrati, lòmiti, lòžiti, mahèrisati, màltati, mástiti, minírati, mlàtati,, mȍlovati, mòtati, mùtljavina, mȕćkati, múljati mùnđati, munđàrati, munđáriti, mùntati, mútiti, mȕvati, mùvātor, nȁfutrati, nalòžiti, nasáditi, nàsānkati, nàsmicati, natocìljati, natòčiti, navláčiti, nàvūći, obráditi, obrađívati, obŕnuti, òfārbati, okrénuti, pȃkovati, pakírati, páliti, pètljati, plȉndrati, podjèbati, podjebávati, pòdvūći se, pòklop, potfukávati, pòtkuriti, préći, prèdriblati, prèfarbān, prȅfārbati, prefolírati, prèjehati, prèlaziti, premùntati, prèpičiti, prepìšati, prepišávati, preráditi, prevèslati, prošétati [1], provózati, pȕcati, pȕcnuti, puškáriti, ráditi [1], rȁdnuti, ràjfati, rogírati, sahrániti, skùbati, skȕhati, smȉcati, smòtati, smȕvati, spùstiti, stȕpār, súknuti, šandrmírati, šárati, šatrovírati, šatrírati, šegebèdečiti, šétati, ševati, šȍpati, štrȕmfnuti, švȉndlovati, tȑznuti, tȕhnuti, ujèbati, uváliti, vaćáriti, váljati, varàkati, varáknuti, vȃrati, vatáriti, vȃtati, vózati, vòziti, vȑteti, vȑzgati, zabìberiti, zaèbati, zafrkávati, zàfrknuti, zajèbati, zajebávati, zàjehati, zàkājlati, zakovŕnuti, zàlimfati, zànitati, zarȉbati, zaùrlati, zavitlávati, zavŕnuti, zàvūći, zbìberiti, zbȉčiti, zbȉčlati, zbȕtnuti, zékiti se, zȅzati, zȅzati se, zezùckati, zezùckati se, zȅznuti, zmòtati, zrȉsati, zvòziti, žnírati

cheat, swindle, fuck over: prejèbati

cheat, swindle, take for a ride: nàsānjkati

cheated: ȉzakān, kȕvān, prȇđen, prefòlīrān, prèrāđen, skȕhān, skȕvān, smȍtān

cheated husband: rógonja

cheated male: trúba [1], trùbač, trubàdūr

cheated male, sucker: čàbar [2]

cheater, swindler: ȁpāš, dȑibljer, folirȃnt, mùljātor, mùnđāroš, mùtikesa, mùtivoda, pȃker, švȉndler

cheating (usu. by a waiter), ripping off: blȉcānje

cheating in cards: pȃkovānje

cheating in playing cards: napakȉnđel

cheating on one's lover or spouse: švéra, švérānje

cheating performed in a short time: tȑka

cheating, swindling: cȕcānje, čarlàma, fȃrbānje, fȏl [2], fòlina, folirȁncija, folírānje, forlírānje, fȕtrānje, ȉspalajebávānje, kȍska, kȕhānje, kùrtōn, lȃfanje, lìrika, lȍptica, lȍžēnje, lȍžnjava, mahèrisānje, màrtuna, mȋna, mȕćka, mȕćkānje, múnđa, munđārēnje, mùntānje, mutljárēnje, navlàkuša, obrađívānje, podjebávānje, potfukávanje, prélaz, rádnja, rogírānje, sistémi, sukȁrno, šandrmácija, šandrmírānje, šatrovírānje, šéva, ševānje, šmȉnka, šmȉnkānje, šnȋr, švìndl, švindlèrāj, švȉndlovānje, ȕbleha, vaćárēnje, vaćàtina, vàlter, vȏz, vózānje, vóžnja, vȑzgānje, zafrkȁncija, zafrkávānje, zájeb, zajebávānje, zezȁncija, zȅzānje, žnírānje

cheating, swindling: lȉrānje, vàlter

cheating, swindling, fucking over: prejebávānje

check one's ID: šarírati

check, make sure: čekírati

check-mate: màcura, màćuka, matàruga, màthauzen, matrificírati

check-up: sèrvīs

cheek: šȗnka

cheer for: klȉknuti, klíkati

cheer for, root for: drȕkati

cheer up: raspolòžiti se

cheering: klȉka

cheese: brȉza, bȓnza, lìmanovo, mȕrīvo, pènjer, pȑdavac

chemistry (as a science course): hèmiš

chemistry lab: krematȏrijum

chemistry teacher: hȅmke, hȅmos, molèkula

cherry brandy: trȅšnjevača

chess: hȃšu, šája, šakùrčić, šána

Chevrolet (make of car): ševac

chewing gum: kȃučuk, kȃuguma, žváka, žvakerȉno, žvakèrōn, žvȃkos

chicken (the animal): krèkče

chicken meat: čiketina, pilèćina

child from a Serbian-Croatian intermarriage: Hȑbin

child from high-rise building: blòkēj

child from the countryside: sȍfke

child of a worthless or mean individual: šibigûzović

child who always informs parents or teachers about his/her peers, tattle tale: tùžibaba, tùžideda

child's scooter: rȍmbāč

child, kid: balávko, bòkče, dȅrīšte, dèrle, díte, đâle, đálac, đàvlac, đȁvle, đelàrče, đéte, đȅtić, gòvnār, ȉkra, Japánac, Jȁpī, kèber, kelìnče, kénjac, kȅpēc [1], klȋnac, klìndōv, klínja, klínjo, lârva, mànuče, prìkolica, pȕrče, pȕre, rȕksāk, šmŕcna, šmȑkavac, šmȑkavica, špilhózer, špilhózner, štrȕca, švŕća, švŕćo, trèmče, upišàljče, upišànče, upišaníče, žgèbe, žgèpče, žilètić, žvalávko

child, little monkey: màjmun [1]

childish: klȋnačkī

children orthopedic shoe: mȕngosica

china: sèrvīz

Chinese (person), Slant: kosòokī

Chinese restaurant, Zagreb, Croatia: Kìnēz [1]

chip (in poker): čȉp

chip, chunk: pȑcvoljak, rȅm

chirp (of a bird, cricket etc.): cvŕčati, cvrgúknuti, cvŕkati, cvȑknūt

chirp (of a chick): pijúkānje, pȉjkati, pijujúkati, pijúkati

chirping (of a bird, cricket, etc.): cvȑka, cvŕkānje, cvȑljūk

chirping sound: cvȑč

chisel (the tool): kȉrhner, kȉrner, màjzl

Chivas Regal (a brand of whiskey): čívac

choke: čȍk [1], sȃug

choose, select: bȉćkati, šȁcovati

church: bìsērka, bukùrija, bukùrlija, kȁstra, klecaóna, màrmārnik, mèrmēmica, sîvka, telepàtija

church beggar: ministrȃnt

church service: letùrđija

cigarette butt: čȉk [2], ćòrtan [2], dȁd, dȕd, mȑtvac, pȉkavac, slȋnak

cigarette carton: štéka

cigarette holder: cigàršpic

cigarette paper: plȁta, pònjava, rízla

cigarette seller in prison: tùtun [1]

cigarette smoke: cûg, dȉmac

cigarette with hashish and tobacco mixed: pânj [2]

cigarette, smoke: bàgōv, cigára, cigarȉlos, cȉgos, dìmara, dȉmnjāk, dùvān, fȕma, gàraci, gȁrka, hàšiš, nikòtīn, opsèsija, pjùgara, pjȕva, pljùgara, pljúga, pljúgica, pljȕva, pljûvka, sevèljče, smòkīng, smȑdljivac, šȉljak, šljȁk, štâp, trȁfka

cineaste, film maker: fìlmadžija, filmȃš

circle: đȉr

circulate around: perpendikùlisati

circumcise: osùnetiti, sùnetiti

circumcised: osùnećen

circumcision: sùnet

cistern: bìstērna, bìstijērna

Citroen (a car make): spagìtār

city: ćàršija, džùngla, jòdgranj, màrdelj, sȋtī, šȉrok, vároš

city boy: pȕrger [2]

city square: tànjūr

civil engineering student: građevínac

civilian clothing one buys right before one leaves the military, civies: civilizácija, cìvīlka

clamp (the tool): banána, klèmna, krokòdilka, mȅngele, šaràfštok, šèlna, šnȃl, šrȁfštok

clandestine brothel: bùnker

clandestine gambling place: àrdija

clandestine place intended for sexual intercourse: àrdija

clandestine place where prostitutes gather: lîdo

clang (produce a sharp metal sound): čukàrati, rgètati, zvȅckati, zvȅcnuti, zvéčati, zvekètati, zvekétnuti, zvȅknuti, zvèktati, zvekùtati, zvȍcnuti, zvokòtati, zvokòtnuti, zvonjàkati, zvȑknuti

clang (sharp metal sound): zvȅckac, zvȅckāj, zvȅckānje, zvêk, zvȅka, zvȅkēt, zvȍn, zvònjavina

clanging (producing a sharp metal sound): zvȅckast, zvȅckav, zvȅčāj, zvȅkētan, zvekètānje, zvekètav, zvekètljiv, zvèktānje, zvȅktav, zvȍnčav, zvònjava, zvònjēnje

clap: pljȁfnuti

clarinet: frùla, klára, kòlac

classroom: mučiónica

clean a long corridor: šoferírati

clean thoroughly using chemical cleaners (usu. of house or apartment): ìzvimati, vȉmati

clean, purified drug: čȉstāk

cleaning: ribánjac

clear: pròkuhāno

clear up an issue: ràščistiti

clearly: ìzbūljeno

click (produce a short, sharp, non-resonant sound): cmȍknuti, klȍcati, kljȍcati, krȁka [1], krikràčati, škljȍcati, škȑcnuti

click (short, sharp, non-resonant sound): krȁka-krȁka, šklȁp, škljȍc, škljȍcāj

click (sound made with the lips): cvȑktati

clitoris: Dràžen, Grȅgor, klíća [1], klìnček, klíša, lìndik, ščegetàuček

clock tower: sȁhat

clock, watch: gràstano, gustírati, lȍkot, òklok, slànīk, trakàtrāljka, ûrica, vȅrk, vȅrk, vrȅmeplōv, ž [žə]

close (e.g. a counter or a store): zàškatati, zàšktati, zatàrabiti

close dance: stȉskavac

close friend, good buddy: àhbāb

close one's gate: zamàndaliti

closed: brȁva [1]

closed portable container for liquids: kanȉster

closing time, last call: fàjronat [2], fàjront [1], fàjront [2]

clothes hanger: ȍfinger

clothes tree: obešènjāk

clothing: duljȉne, kȑpe, kȑpice, ljȕska, oblȅka, pàrdovine, pȑnje, ròba, rȕvo, tèkstīl

clothing thief: mŕmak

clothing, garment: àba, ambálaža, gàrdiš, gàrdos, kȑpa

clothing, threads: kônci

clown around: áčiti se

clumsy and noisy style of walking: trȁp-trȁp

clumsy female, klutz: bezveznjákovićka

clumsy male, klutz: bezvèznjāk, bezveznjáković, bìzgōv, cipovànder, cmólja, fȍrpās[3], frȉk[1], gȁfer, hèmpeš, kâjla, kénjac, kȉlavac, kilávko, lȁzār[2], pȁcer, pêgula[1], Péro[2], plantávko, šȉmler, šmólja[2], šòjkan, temèrut, trȁpavičār, trubàdūr, túlac[1]

clumsy person, klutz: bìlmez, čìnpek, Džȉm, kȅnja[2], kilòster, kílonja, kȍnj[1], kònjosav, kònjoslav, lèvāk[1], màrka[1], òlio, operácija, pèrislav, slȍn, smlȁta, smólja, smoljávko, smotanája, smotánko, šalabàhter[2], šalabàjzer, šmòkljan, šmȍkljos, šónja, šȍnjča, tàraba, trapađója, trapađóza, trȁpša, trúba[1], túta

clumsy, klutzy: búšan, dȓven, kȉlav, lȉpa[2], lìvanjskī, mȕtav, opèrisān, smȍtān, smûšen, stòlijēvī, šȁntav, šlȁmpast, šlȁmpav, šlògīrān, šȍntav, zbȓljān, zdȑkān

clutch: kùplūng

coach: srêm

coal: ćùmur[2], glȅnār, kréka, vùglec

coat (outer garment): drónjak, haljétak, mȍnd, montárac, mȕnd, mȕnt, mȕnta, muntárac, muntàrica, muntátac, munjtárac, pȕtka, sàkat

Coca-Cola, coke: kóca, kóla

cocaine: čȁrlī

cocaine, coke: dȕst, kóca, kóka, kokaína, kòkče, kȍkī, kȍkica, kókice, kȍkos, kȍks

cock-a-doodle-doo: kȕkurēk, kukurékati, kukurêku, kȕkurijēk, kukurijêku, kȕkurīk, kukurȋku, kukurȋkati, raskukurékati se

cockchafer, maybug: gùndelj

codeine: kódža, kôdžos

coffee: bàculja, cȓnā, čàđa, čòrbavina, čòrbovina, čòrbovinja, fíca, gȁra, gȁravica, kàfica, kàhva, kâljanā, katrànjāk, kofijánović, korjánović, vȁka

coffee with milk: askèrōl, eskàrōl

coffin: tàbut

cognac: zvȅčka[2], ždrébac

cogwheel: bèndiks, cênrād, tȅlerād, zámahac

coin: gvozdènjāk, kȁmēn[1], píljak, stàklo, špȉca, željèzara

cold (illness): kijavìtis

cold: cvȍkotno, frȉgīdno, ládan

cold temperature:

cold weather: gôlje, kȕrozeb[1], mázija[2]

collar: krángla

collect (e.g. stamps): džídžati

collectively: čȍporatīvno

collector card: slídža

collector ring on a piston: sȅmerīng

colonel: pȕkī[2], pûle

colorful things: šarènīš

colt (young horse): cukàrče, kàljče

comb: češljùgār, grȁblje, grȁhlje, plôt

comb wool: dȑndati

combination, tactics: ìgra[2]

come across, bump into: nalèteti

come down (after the effect of narcotic drugs is over): prizèmljiti se

come in small quantities but steadily (e.g., income): kàpljati

come to terms, become reasonable: opasúljiti se

come to the best solution: nàbosti

come, arrive: mȅldovati se, nàslikati se, natocìljati se, natȑčati, sȉmāj, sȉmiti, sȉmovati

comeback, return: kambȅk

comfortable (of a person), doing great: ráhat

command a donkey to move on: ćȕškati

commercial (such as the one on TV): smrdljévak

commit suicide: ukàntati se

Communist, red, commie: cȑven[1], cȑvenī[2], crvènjāk, knjȉžār, komùnār, komùnjara, komùnjārka, komùnjārskī, pȁrtoš

community: džèmāt, đèmāt

company (group of people): bràtija, ekípa, jȁto, klȁpa, kȍmpa, kompànija, mâfija, pȍsada, rája, rȕlja, škvâdra

compare with: rȁvnati se

compartment on a train, etc.: kùpēj

compete: šlȅpati se

competent, knowledgeable, good: pȍtkovān

complain, bitch: cvȉliti, kukùmāvčiti, pízditi, zakérati

complain, have a cow: tèliti se

complain, whine: kȕkati, plȁkati[2]

complete overhaul: genèrālka

completely, totally: dibidȕs, dibidȕz, dimidȕs, dȕzdibidȕs, gȁjnc, komplȅtno, nȁčisto, skrôz, tȍtālno

completely, totally, dead: mòrtus[2]

completing: kompletáža

complicated: šùćmurast, zàgūljen

complicated person: terètnjāk

complicated situation: zavrzlàma

complication: pètljavina

compute: kòntati

computer: kȍmp, kȍmpa, kȍmpić

computer game: ìgrica

computer hacker: hâker

computer, machine: mašína

comrade (communist party official): drȕks

concealed exit: òluk, rȍra

conceited female: drkùnica, drkùnjača, šmȉnkerka

conceited male: duvànder, gȉgantostrȁka, mȁčōr, mȁša, múdonja, naujglàvica, pȕvadžija, puvànder, pùvātor, šmȉnker, tȓtonja, zagùljāč, zagušòtina

conceited person: mȕstra, paràgraf

conceited, stuck-up: nàduvān, ùštītkān

concept, idea: čȕkalj

condition of a status seeker, pretentious person, social climber: hohštaplèrāj

condition of being a male homosexual: lùla

condition of being a rowdy, troublemaker: huncutàrija,

liskàluk

condition of being a thief: lopòvluk

condition of being broke: bèdāk[2]

condition of being despicable or worthless individual: fakináža

condom, rubber: gùma, gùmica, gumènjāk, kòtōn, kùrtōn, kùtōn, màntl, mȍnd, montárac, nàkūrnjāk

condom, rubber, Jimmy: Tònček

conduct (philharmonic, etc.): srȕšiti

conductor (on a train, bus, or streetcar): abasàmis, dùgār, kóča, kóndo, kȍndor

conductor (philharmonic, etc.): líder, màhalup

cone (usu. made of paper and used by street merchants to package seeds or roasted chestnuts): fìšek

cone: ćórac

cone-shaped container used to drink hard liquor: čȍkānj

confederate in shell game: folirȁnt

confront somebody with reality: uzèmljiti

confrontational female: kòmanč-bêbi

confuse, mix up: bŕkati

confused: konfjûz, zblȁnūt

confusing, not clear: hȁrtavo

confusion: tȑt-mȑt[2]

congress (meeting): kòngrez

connecting lever: lènkhēbl

connecting rod: blȁjštānga

connecting streetcar ticket in Zagreb, Croatia: prèskok, prȇtrka

connection, tie: kalàuz[2], štéla, vȅza, vȉp, žnóra[1]

conservatorium: kònzērva

consider, respect: jèbati

consider, think about: kapírati, skapírati

considerable amount of money: lovijànđer, lòvina

conspiration: ìgra[2]

conspire, plot: domunđávati se, táliti se

constant and prolonged talk: lapȑdānje

constantly: fȕrt

construction worker: dùnđer, građevínac

construction worker's: dùnđerskī

consumption, spending: kònzum

container: mànještra

contemplate, think: ȁktati, aladùmati

content of what has been said: spȉka

content of what is being said: tȅkst

continental male: žȁbār

continue a love affair after breaking it for a while: skulírati se

contoller (on public transportation): kanarínac

contour of the vagina, camel toe: žȇmička

contract (muscle, etc.): skvȑčiti

contract for a band: gáža

contribute, chip in: ulèteti, utȑčati

convenient place for stealing: eldorâdo

conversation, talk: èglen

converse, talk: konzervírati

conviction (for a crime): bèrba

coo (of birds): gugúkati, gugùtati, gúkati, gúknuti, kȕkati

cooing (of birds): gȕgūt, gugùtav, gugùtavo, gûk, gúkānje, gȕkav

cook: hȁrku, mùtikašu, tàvati, tàviti

cook in a Turkish-style restaurant: àščija

cooking: pȁcānje

coordinate: ùštimati

cord: sȁjla[1]

corn: kùruz, momòruz, momòruza, mùruz

cornbread: bukètāš, đȍmka, đȍnka

corncob brandy: klìpara

corner (in a house): bùdžāk

corner (of a building, room, etc.): ćòšak

corporal: kȁplār, kâpo, mùčitelj

corpse, stiff: hlàdetina, zèmljāk

correspondence: signalizácija

corridor, hall: àutostráda

cosmetic cream: pomáda

cosmopolitan: belosvètskī

cost: dôći

cottage used to distill brandy: kàčara

cotton: fȁta

cotton used to filter opium: kòtōn

couch: ȍtomān

counter: šȁlterskī

counter attack: kȍntra

counter move: kontróla

counter, window (e.g., in a bank): šȁlter[2]

counterfeit money: làžnjāk

counterfeit ticket: dìvjāk, fàlšara, fàlšārka

counterfeit, false, fake: lêvī[1]

country (as of music): novokompònīrān

country established by a foreign force: bantùstān

country or folk music: ćirìlica

country or folk music performer: naròdnjāk

country or folk muslic performer (female): pèvāljka

country or folk song: naròdnjāk

country, nation: tȕlja

county (as of music): novokòmponovān

county clerk: grȍbār

courageous: krábar

courageous male, guy with balls: múdonja, múdonjić, mûdović

courageous person: àjdūk

courageousness: junáctvo

courier: dvònožac, tȍrbār, tȑčic

course, class: dosađínstvo

court of law: cèpārnīk, cjèpārnik

court session: cépānje, paráda

courthouse: blagovaóna

Courvoisier (a brand of cognac): kȕrvāč, kùrvič kûr-vı̏njāk, kùrvinjāk,

cousin (mother's brother's or mother's sister's son): dàidžić

cousin (paternal): àmidžić

cover for one's accomplice: dȅkovati, štȕcati

cover up, hide: dȅkovati, kašírati, kašírati se

cover with a blanket and beat up: ćȅbovati

cover, disguise: zîd

cover, lid: dèkl, dèkla, dèklica, dȅkmantl, dèkna

covered with mucus, snotty: bȁlav

covered with urine: pȍpišān

covered, guarded (soccer player, etc.): màrkīrān

covering with a blanket and beating up: ćȅbovānje

cow: bȁčka, bȍčka, rȉkavica, rìsūljka

cow bell: cìngara

coward, chicken: améba, cȉcko, cvìkāroš, cvȉkato, cvìkātor, cvȉkos, cvȉkoš, ćépa, dèrpe, febètār, gȉrica, góvno[2], Gȑčkā, kâjla, kapávko, klimávko, kȑcalo, kúkac, kûrva, lítonja, mȉš, mȉško[1], pȁlac, péder, pȉčkica, pìškūr, plàčipička, plȁčko, pljàčipička, posrògaća, premiròtina, premirȍtka, pȓle, séronja, sȉsa[1], stèznat, šȁjser, tȑkāč, trónja, trȍnjavac, trônjča, tȑtāroš, tȑtāš, tùljezga, tùnezga, upišánko, usránko, úsro, vùnek, zêc, zȅkavac, zèntara

cowardly: kùrvinskī, nàjlōn, vȅlečasnī

cowardly female, chicken: špȉca

crab: naguzèljez

crack (branch, etc.): čvȍgnuti, čvóka, čvȍknuti, čvȓgnuti, čvȓknuti, kȑcati, kȑckati, kȑskati, krêk, kȑsak

cracking (branch, etc.): cvȓknūt, kȑcānje, kȑckānje, kȑckav, kȑka, kȑskānje

cracking object: kȑckāj

cracklings: ȍcvrki

crank: gùrbla, kùrbl, kùrbla, kùrbl-vȅla

crashing: lȕpa, trêsak, trȅska, trȅskāj

crave: zameráčiti

crawl to (usu. of an infant): dobaùljati

crawl, creep: baùljati

cream: šljága

create a mess: vatrírati

create an improvised construction: sklépati

creative person: kreatívac

credit (usu. given informally by a bartender or shopkeeper): verèsija

credit for a course at the university: štàmbīlj

credit, loan: bàrjāk, kànara, kàndara

creep (of a lizard, child, etc.): bahùljati

crematorium: krepatôrijum

crescent roll: kífl

crib sheet, cheat sheet: đȍn, pȕškica, šalabàhter[1]

cricket (the insect): cvŕkavac

crime: krȉmī

criminal: dȅlkos, dušogúbac, kesorézac, krȉmos, ptȉčica, šȁtrav, šȁtrovac, têškī[2]

criminal who is always broke: hàfif

criminal who is good at pretending to be innocent: glúmac

criticize publicly: kȓpiti, napljùvati, òpljunuti, prozívati, prȍzvati

croak (of a frog): kvéčati, kvéknuti, regètati

croaking (of a frog): kvéčānje, kvȅčav, rȅget

croaking frog: kvekètuša

Croat-Muslim Federation (in Bosnia): Federácija[2]

Croatian (person): konjùšār, Pȕrger[1], šòkac, Tȕđmanovac, úja[3], újko, újo, ȕstaša, újka

Croatian (pertaining person): kròātskī, šòkačkī

Croatian Communist Party Headquarters in Zagreb, Croatia: Hìltōn

Croatian flag or coat of arms: šahóvnica

Croatian policeman in the early 1990s: mȕpovac

Croatian separatist movement in the 1970s: màspok, maspokóvština

crochet: hȅklati

crook, thief: folijȃnt, jàjara, làcman, lȉrafōn, màgler, mȃher[1], mùćkāroš, mùfljūz[1], mùnđāroš, múćak[2], múlja, mȕljos, mutljívko, mutnjáković, šȁtrovac, šmȉnker, tȑčipīš, tȑkopīš, ùncut, vȉbros

crooked teeth: pletènice

crookedly: kùrvinskī

crops: birìćet

cross-eyed: dȕdnūt, vȓljav, zrȉkav

cross-eyed person: búljko, zrȉka

crossbreed dog, mongrel, mutt: avlijáner, dȍdž, džúkac, džùkela

crowd, mob: bulùmēnta, bȕljūk, gòmila, gȓlo, gungùla, guràčina, gûžva, gužvánac, gužvánjac, kȍšnica, krkljánac, stȉska, svètina, svjètina

crowded bus, bus packed like sardines: Sàrdīnija

croze: fȁlc

crude: kurúza[2], šánerskī

crude and ill-mannered female, Neanderthal: čaršijánerka, klȍšārka, pèriljek

crude and ill-mannered male, Neanderthal: čaršijáner, klȍšār

crude and ill-mannered people: čàršija

crude and ill-mannered person, Neanderthal: prȉm, primârijus, prȉmić, prȉmos, prȉmoš

cruise (in a car, bus, etc.): jézditi

cruise, walk through the town: lelùjati, špârtati

crunch (under foot): ȑštati, rùštati

crunchy snack: grȉckalica

crush, break, squish: cknȕti

crushing sound: kȑka

cry in grief: gènditi, gȅnđiti

cry, shed tears, weep: baláviti, bȁliti, cêndrati, cjéditi, cmȉzdriti, cmóljiti, cvȉliti, cvíliti, djȅditi, fafȕnjati, jaúkati, jȅcati, kȃpati, kàtipla, kaùkati, kaúknuti, kȅnjkati, kȉknuti, kméčati, kméziti, kȕkati, mèkšati, mòkriti, oceániti, plàčkoljiti, plȉnčiti, pŕskati, pízditi, raspízditi se, rèvati, ròncati, sȁftati, slȉniti[1], sȕziti, šljûnčiti, šmȓcāj, šmȓcati, šmŕcati, šmŕljiti, tèliti se, trêsti se, žmȕljiti

crybaby: kapávko, karaušljívko, kméza, kmézo, màrka[1],

pèkmez[1], pekméza, plàčipička, plȃčko, pljàčipička, svìlenī, svilènjāk, šȕfnūdla, tùnezga

crying: balávljēnje, bȁljēnje, cvȑka, slȉnāvka

crying, fussy (as with a baby): kȅnjkav

crying, weeping: jȅcānje, jȅcavica, jȅcavo

crystal (as in crystal clear): krìstalno

cuckoo (the bird): kȕkavica

cucumber: krȁstavica

cunnilingus: dùdljānje, lîz, lìzika, lòpata, líza, pȉčkolīz, pípa

cunning female: mùfōnka, prèfakuta

cunning male: mùflōn, pìzdūn, prefrigánac, šmȅker, špìclov, štȁkor

cunning, sly, slick: mútan, pèčen, polìtika[2], polìtka, prèfrigān, prèmazān, strášan, stràvičan

cupboard: òrmān[2]

curl one's hair (as a style): kȍlmovati

curly (of hair): kȕdrav, rȕdlav

curly hair: kȕždra, rȕnja, žȉca

currency note: šȕšanj, šȕškalica, šȕštavica

curse: ispičkàrati, jebécnuti, jebéknuti, jebìkati, pcòvati, pičkàrati, sòvati

curse, profanity: glágol

cursing: jebìkānje, pičkàrānje

cushion: kùšīn

custody: istràžnjāk, kàvez, kréma, mjȕra, mȕra, múrija[1], múrja, mûrka[2], rȕpa[2]

custom, habit: ádet

customs officer: còlāš

cut (with scissors, etc.): prècvikati, prècvikovati, prècvovkati

cut: misírati

cut class, skip class: zbrȉsati

cut classes: markírati, šára-mára, zàluftati, zgíbati

cut into pieces: nafalàtati

cut into pieces, slices (e.g. bread, sausage, etc.): falàtati

cut off, chop off: abortírati, òdrizati, òseć, otfikariti

cut somebody's throat: prèrpati, zàštihtati

cut with knife, slice (e.g., a tomato, potato): bȁšnuti

cut, disrupt: sȅći

cut, slice: màsatiti, misíriti, ràseći, ȑpnuti, zavézati

cutlery: ȅscājg

cutting classes, skipping classes: avijàtika

cutting pliers: cvȉkcánge, cvȉkcángle

cyber: sàjber

cylinder casing: ànzac

Czech: Pémac

dad: glávonja

dagger (esp. one used as a weapon): čàkija, đȕla, kéba

dagger (esp. one used as a weapon): àndžār

daily wage: dȍlga

dairy restaurant: mljêčnjak

Dalmatian (inhabitant of Dalmatia, Croatia): blȉtvāš, dalmatàjner, Dȃlmoš, gȉrica, skȕša

dance: ćȁga, ćȁgati, dȑmati se, đȕska, đȕskati, đȕskavac, gàlop, gȕča, hȉtati se, hȍpsati, igránac, igránjac, kȅleruj, šíza[1], šíziti, tȁncovati, tandŕčak, tandȑček, tȁnec, trȁkati, trakèljati, trándžiti, trȅska, trȅskavac, trȅskavica, trêsti se, zèntati

dance cheek-to-cheek: òbrazovati se

dance floor: đȕskavac, hòpsalīšte, mràvinjāk, plêsnjāk, štȁla, zôo

dance to rock and roll: rȍksovati, rȍlovati

dancer: ćȁger, ćȁgerica, trȅskavac, trȅskavica

dancing: bugárac, čȁga, ćàgānac, ćȁgānje, drmáža, dŕmež, kréva, tȃnc, tàncāljka

dandy, fop: dȅndī, Džȅk, englézer, fàzān, fićfirić, fȉžbajn, gàmen, gotȉvnjāk, gotívac, kîcoš, kùlōv, lȃf[1], lêpī[1], lipicáner, màčōr, màšīnka, pȁūn, pìcān, pȉcko, picòvān, pòzēr, Robespjêr, šalabàhter[2], šalabàjzer, šmȅker, šmȅkos, šmȉnker

danger: kȕga, kuléra, lârma, nȍkat[2], pȕška[2], vȁtra, zȅnt

dangerous but inviting (situation, event, etc.): ȍblāčno

dangerous event: karolòmija

dangerous female: grozomòrina, ripicàjzla, sòvēljka

dangerous job: šljȁka

dangerous male, one who acts violently: gàdnjāk

dangerous place, powder keg: barutàna

dangerous situation: karkolòmija, kitolòmija

dangerous, dicey: gȕtavo, ȍblāčan, zȁjebān

dare, have courage to do something: stȉsnuti

dark-colored horse: mȑkōv

darkness: karàmluk, mràkača, mràkuša[1]

date the same female for a long time: ùsidriti se

date, go out with: gȁziti, fúrati, hódati, ìći, kljȉšiti, òdšlepati, sȁfatati, sàvatati, spàn̄dati se, štȅpati

date, going out with: čvȅnk, dȁrsu, fúrānje, furijandžȅlī, , furijan̄đȅlī, furijánović, mlâz, nâpad, plȁžēnje, ràndes, saobràćājka, spôj, spôjka, stȓk[1], sȕdār, sudarȉška

daughter: ćéra[2], đéte, kèlīnka, klȉndōvka, šćêr, vȁjza, vȁjzor

day: ȁnda, dȅn, đȕn, glȁvnīk, mèrāč

day which never comes: nikdárjevo, Pȉčkovden

daydream: mòriti se, nàrisati

daydreamer: lùjika

dazzle using effective words, snow: ošošóljiti

dead: bîvšī, lȅden, mèit, trópa[2]

dead end: ćȍrsokāk

dead person: mȓc

deaf: pòklopljen, zȁtrpān

deaf person: dȅfos, glùvāć, glùvara, tȍp[1], tòpina

deaf senior citizen: glùvara

deaf-and-dumb: sašȉven

deaf-and-dumb person: blȅkēt

deal (playing cards): dèlisati, dèlkati, dȅlnuti

deal narcotic drugs, be a pusher: dȉlati, dȉlovati

deal with, arrange, take care of (usu. with authorities of some kind): gánjati

deal with, bother with: devèrati

deal, agreement (in general): tâl

deal, business: dȋl

dealer (e.g., car dealer): dȋler

dealing drugs: àkcija

death: Bȃre, ráhmet, rikavȇla

debark (deploy military units on ship): ìskurcati

decagram (10 grams): dȅka[2]

decay, rot: àmbisati se

decent behavior: fȉnjāk

deceptive face: fàsadeks

decide: upucávati se

deck of cards: pȁk, pàkēt

decorate (a person, house, etc.): džídžati

decorate: fȉlovati

decoration: dekurácija

deepened: ùlēknut

defeat: čèšljati, dèrati, isklistírati, isprášiti, izèbati, jèbati, kàntati, lúpati, nabúšiti, nàbuškati, nàduti, nakàntati, nàtpevati, òjaditi, pàtos, pocépati, pokòpati, prèslišati[1], prèslišati[2], preslišávati, raskàntati, ràsturiti, razváliti, sjèbati, skénjati, skȕvati, smȁzati, šȉti, šívati, tȗći, ukàntati, ùšiti, zbȃnčiti

defeated: sjȅbān, skȕvān

defecate: đȕbriti, gȁziti, hȁlnuti, kȁkati, kákiti, kȅnjkati, prodúljiti, unerédititi, unerédititi se,

defecate in small quantities: serùckati, srȁćkati

defecate one's fill: nàsrati

defecate quickly: drȍćnuti

defecate, shit: čkȕljati, čkȕljiti, drȉskati, drȉstati, gòvniti, iskénjati, iskénjati se, istrónjati se, kȁnjati, kénjati, pockùljati, počkùljati, pokákiti se, pokénjati se, poràptati, pòsraćkati, pòsrati, pòsrati se, sȅrkati, srȁti, tȉsra, trónjati, trónjati, ukénjati, ukénjati se, ùsrati, užútiti, zagòvnati, zasmȑdeti, zasmȑdjeti, zàsrati

defecate in one's pants: ukákiti se, ùsrati se

defecate, shit, take a dump: pogòvnati

defecate, take a dump: kȉpovati, ukákiti

defecated on: pȍsrān

defecated on, shitty: gȍvnav, gȍvnen, ȕsrān

defecating: ȉstovār, kàkānje, kenjáža, pòser, posránje

defecator: srȃć

defect: dèfekt

defect identification within the process of repairing: defektáža

defect in the code or routine of a computer program, bug: bȕba

defector, traitor: pòturica

defenseman (soccer): defanzívac

defensive soccer: bùnker

defiance: ȉnād

deficit (e.g. in trade): mínus

deflower: otvòriti, prèbiti, probúšiti, skalpírati, vàdičepovati

delinquency: delikvèncija

denatured alcohol: đȉkan, špȉrit

denim: dènim

denounce, criticize publicly, give a lot of flak: ispljùvati

dentist: klȁmfār, kljòvāč, kljòvātor, mùčibabić, mùćibabić, zubočùpāč, zvȉndalo

deny, refuse: zàkinuti

depart, leave: odgàmbati

department store: ròbara, ròbnjāk

departure: odgambávānje, òtfur, otfurȉška

dependable: fȃmōzan

depreciatory pronoun usually used in reference to young persons: òno[1]

depressed: pȁrter, pȍsrān

depressed, blue: mútan

descend: sàlaziti, šljȅći

desire of sex, horniness: šnjȁjd

desk: klúpa, tèzga

desperate criminal: štȉft

destroy, bury: saràniti

destroy, ruin: ȁkati, bŕljati[1], fùrdačiti, havàrisati, ìskecati, ìzakati, pokarabúsati, pokòpati, pòsrati, raskurcávati, ràspičiti, razbȁštati, ràzboškati, razbúcati, razjèbati, ràzjehati, sahrániti, satarániti, sjèbati, skénjati, skŕhati, skŕkati, skȑšiti, slístiti, spàcati, spȉčkati, srédititi, ùdriskati, ukénjati, umòčiti se, ùpičkiti, upŕskati, ùrnisati, ùsrati, utòpiti, zajèbati, zapízditi[2], zàsrati, zgòvnati

destroyed: propađȍt[2], trópa[2]

destroying: jebávānje

detail: drangùlija

detective: àgiš, àgiša, alijánović, dèkster, đȍrđić, gènter, jàrān, kòžnjāk[2], lóvac, njȕškalo, sȕpovac, škìcēr, ȕdbić, zrȋnskī

devil: àndrak[1], ckȁmnjāk, đȁvol, gàgul, šéjtan

devour, eat voraciously: gúliti, gȕmati, lípati[1], mȁzati, mȁznuti, múljati, ùbiti

dexedrine: dȅks

dezoxine: dȅkica, dȅtī, dȅzī

diabetic: šećérko

diarrhea, runs, trots: lȉvpro, ljȅvpro, srȁćka, srȁćkalica, šprȉnterica, tankoserȉtis, tȑčkalica, tȑkalica

dice: bíbice, ćȁrke, zȃr, zàrov

dictator: dȑmātor, glávonja, múdonja

die, breathe one's last: izdàhnuti

die, croak: lìpsati, ukénjati

die, kick the bucket: arlaúknuti, cȁpnuti[2], cíknuti, crkávati, cȑknuti, fijúknuti, iskulírati, ìspružiti se, izdúvati[1], kȁlnuti, kalírati, kȁpnuti, kàpsati, kaputírati, kljȍknuti, knòriti, krèpati, kȑknuti, kvéknuti, mȁjkati, mandŕknuti, mȁnjkati, nastrádati, nèstati, odàpēti, odàpinjati, odlepȑšati, odzvòniti, ohláditi se, òkinuti, okòpniti, òtēti se, òtkucati, pȅvnuti, pȉknuti, pljȕsnuti, polakírati se, prdéknuti, pregòreti, pregòrjeti, prèsvisnuti, prȕćnuti se, pȕći, rikávati, ríkati, ríknuti, sagòreti, sagòriti, sagòrjeti, sévnuti, sjévnuti, skàpati, skapávati, skarlíknuti, skíknuti, sklȉpsati, skònčati, smárati, strádati, strȇsti se, svȉsnuti, šljȍknuti, trokírati, ugásiti, ùginuti, ukóčiti, ulèditi se, upokòjiti se, usàhnuti, ùtēntati, uvòštiti, vrísnuti, zàginuti, zakovŕnuti, zarȉbati, zaròniti, zažmíriti, zdȍksati, zgȁsnuti, zijévnuti, zvȉznuti

die, pass on: smárati se

diesel engine (usu. of a train): dízēlka

diesel fuel: dízel, nȁfta

different drȕkčī, drȕkšī

differently: drȕkčē, drȕkšē

difficult: fȅrku, jèben, šȉt[3], zàgūljen

difficult learning: grùvīć

difficult or unpleasant situation: nezgodácija, pedèrāj[2], pušióna, sifilȉtika

difficult problem (math, etc.): kȍska

difficult situation, deep shit govnàrija, njȅsra

difficult to remove: zacemèntīrān

difficult, bad: prâzno, šúplje[2]

difficult, hairy: čȕpavo

difficult, requiring hard work: cȑnačkī

digger, manual worker on a digging assignment: šànčēr

diligent male: kȑtica

diligent person: cȓv, rìcinus

diligent student: sùnđer

dilute a story, make a story less spectacular: razvòdniti

dim headlights: àblendovati

dinar (Yugoslav currency unit): bélac[2], đȉndžī, díndža, gláva, kìndār, kînta, kȉntāć, kȉntī, lȁbūd[2], pȅzos, pilàvče, rȕblja, tràkljac

dinner: ȉspaša, màndžovina, mkàlo

diple (double flute, a traditional musical instrument) player: dìplāš

direct against somebody (usu. a dog): nàpucati

directly, straight: dìrekt, drȅto, drȉto, pràvac[2]

director, boss, manager: đȉksī, đȉlfa, dìšān, đȉšomor, díša, Hirohȉto, šèrīf

dirt: pȍgān[2], štrȍka

dirty (not clean): kȁljav, kȕštrav, mȕsav, mȕzgav, špôrkī, špôrko, štròkav, štròkōvan

dirty and untidy female, slob: gàdulja, gàdura, štrȍka, švȉcgerla, úsra, usrànica

dirty and untidy male, slob: cȉganin, kŕmak, ùsranīk, usránko, úsro

dirty boy: slíno

dirty object: drȅk[1]

disadvantage: màhana

disaffection toward: pȉk[2]

disappear, evaporate, vanish: abmarkírati, ȉspariti (se), ȉzvetriti, otperjášiti, otpèrjati, òtplivati, otpŕhnuti, pobudàliti, sublimírati, vrísnuti, zvíjati

disappearing: vijátović

disaster: rikavȅla

disco, discotheque: dìskāč, dìskāć, dìskara, diskijáner, pódmōrnica

discourse operator used to mark an end of one's own words: dòsta

discover a secret: pròčačkati

discover, find out: ȉspljanuti, nàgaziti, odzvȉždati, ofírati, proàktati, prođániti, prokljúviti, proklјùvati, prokúžiti, prováliti, provaljívati, prozȉntati, raskužnjávati, zȅntovati, zentírati

disgusting: mȅden

disliked action or situation: gadàrija

dismiss, fire (a person): katapultírati, nogírati

dismiss, fire (a person): ȉzbačiti, nȍgovati

dismissed from the military, booted out of the military: prèkrīžen

dismissed, fired: nògīrān, nòktīrān

dismissing, firing: vrȉtnjāk

disregarded: ȉspušten

distant: zȁkopčān

distant and unpleasant place, hellhole: rȕpa[2]

distantly: òpruženo

distill alcoholic beverages: pèći

distorted: slûpān

distressed: zmȍtān

distressed person: tektónac

distributor head: fertàjler, frtàjler

divide, split: rastáliti

divorced female: polóvnjača, rázvodnica

divulge a secret or forbidden matter, burst out: lànuti

do manual labor: fizikàlisati

do one's best: prètrgnuti se

do petty trade: pilićáriti

do something quickly and superficially: sleváčiti

do something stupid: tùpisati

do something superficially: ošljáriti, sleváčiti, smandȑljati, zabalabùćkati, zamàglisati, zbrljéknuti

do something unwillingly and superficially: otàljati

do something very slowly: dáviti, gnjáviti

do well on an exam: vésti

do, accomplish: odréditi

do, create: dȅlati, zakòpati

doctor, doc: bélac[1], dóca, dȍk, dȍktoš, dȍktūr, dòtūr, jòktordonj, mȅsār, šȉntār

doctored wine, wine diluted with water: delánac, fȉlić

document (in general): cȅdulja, čitába, ćȁge

documents: pàpīr[2], zêlje

dog (the animal): ćȉkljavac, čkȉljavac, ćèlče, ćêm, džȕkljavac, đêm, đèvče, đúkac, kȅlče, kêmka, kènče, kênka, kéra, kùcōv, làjāč, lájko, lȁkāvče, lȉluška, pȅs, pèsek, pȍrdāk, pòrdok, prȍdak, pùrzek, sȁmojēd, únka, ȕnkta, ȕnta, žȕc, žȕč

dog (the animal), doggie: cúko, ćúko, kúca

dog of any breed: džúkac

dog walker (female): kȕčadžījka, kȕkadžika

dog walker (male): kȕčadžija, kȕčkār, kȕkadžija

dog, flea bag: buvoskùpljāč

doing nothing, fooling around: dembȅlisānje

dollar, buck: bȁks, bȁksi, gȕšter

dominant: streptomȉcīn[2]

done (deal): zàkrpāno

done: sȁšīto

donkey: kénjac, njókac

door: ȍkvīr, skȑta

door hinge: baglàma
door knob: štéka
door window: bùljilo
doorbell: klīng
dormitory room: kabína
dormitory, dorm: studèntnjāk
dose of narcotic drug: trȅskāć
double (of double size or quantity): dùplī [1]
double (shot of alcohol): dùpljāk [2]
double coffee: dùpljāk [2]
double consecutive sexual intercourse: kazačȍk
double-barrelled gun: dvòcēvka, dvòcjēvka
doubt: nedòmujica
down (after the effects of narcotic drugs): dâun, odàpinjānje, prizemljénje
down there, below, underneath: lȅdo
downtown: céja, čàršija
draft (i.e., stream of air): prȍmaha, prȍpūh
draft notice: šára, šȃre, šarènica
drag something close to oneself: prikúčiti
drag, move: sȅcati, vȕgliti
dragon: aždàha
draw: tȑzati
drawback, undesirable feature: mínus
drawer: čèkmeče
dream: knjáva, žmȗr
dress (female garment): àljina, àljna
dress: duljȉna, kècelja, kônci, kȑpa, kȑpe, nabáciti, pàrdovina, pêrje, pŕlja, pȑtlja, vrȅća
dress formally, dress up: isfazonírati se, kȍžnuti se, kožírati, kožírati se, kužírati, kužírati se, montírati se, nacinkróciti se, nakinđúriti se, namontírati se, olȉstati, picániti se, pȉcnuti se, skȍckati se, skužírati se, šmȋnkati se, upicániti se, ušimicvòkliti se, zbȉksati
dress rehearsal: genèrālka
dress, put on (clothing, etc.): natàkariti
dressed formally, dressed up: bandàžīrān, pȉcī, pìcig, picikȃto, skùžīrān, upìcānjen, ùštīrkān
dressed in loud and unattractive clothing: kȕrav
dressed in used and dirty clothing: drȍnjav
dressed up: ùštogljen
dressing formally, dressing up: fazonírānje, šminkèrāj
dribble (e.g. in basketball): drȉbljati, prȅdriblati, šévati, šnírati, vózati
dribbler (e.g. in basketball): drȉbljer
dribbling: šéva, šévānje, šnȋr, šnírānje, vózānje
drill (tool): bórer
drill (using tools): bȍrovati, šúpljiti
drill through: prȍborovati, prozȕmbati
drill, exercise: tȅsati
drink (alcohol): bàlsamovati, báriti, bléjati [2], bonbònisati, cícati, cȕclati, cedȉliti, cépati, cépiti, cêvčiti, cȉmati, cȉmnuti, cȉrisati, cȉrkati, cȉrnuti, cȕgati, cȕgnuti, cȕnuti, cvȑcnuti, čȕgati, ćȅpī, ćȉrisati, drȉnkati, drȉnkovati, dȑmati, drogírati se, drváriti, džókati, fistati, glô, gȕcati, gȕckati, gȕmati, gvȉrcati, hidrocentrála, iskápiti, iskapljívati, ìspiti, kája, kèrija, lȉpati [2], lȉzgati, lȍkati, ljȕljnuti, ljúštiti, mȁznuti, natézati, nàtrēsti, plȕmbati, pòpiti [1], pòrajfati, posàugati, potégnuti, rȁjfa, rȁjfati, sàugati, sȉsati, súkati, súknuti, svȉktati, šljȍknuti, šúhnuti, šúkati, šúknuti, švȁsati, tȅsati, ubȁštrati, ubìti, zàklati, zlèpati, zlȅva, zlȅviti, žljȅva, žljȅviti
drink (alcohol) in large quantities: pȉjānčiti
drink (alcohol) quickly, chug: tȑgnuti, ždrókati
drink (alcohol), juice: sȁft, sȁftati
drink (alcohol), throw down: obòriti
drink (usu. alcohol): pićénce
drink a little (of alcohol): odùjmiti, òtpiti, otpíjati, parkírati se, pričȅstiti se
drink a little (of alcohol), get lubricated: pòdmazati se
drink alcohol in large quantities: ljóskati
drink alcohol in the evening: akšȁmlučiti
drink alone: solírati
drink beer: bȉpovati
drink beer in large quantities: zabírati
drink boilermakers: betonírati
drink hard liquor after beer or wine, drink boilermakers: prèseći, prèsjeći
drink made of one half wine and one half water: fȉftić
drink more alcohol than somebody else, outdrink: nàtpiti, natpíjati
drink plum brandy: rakȉjati
drink too loud and celebrate too loud: šènlučiti
drink too much (of alcohol): òlešiti se, precȉrisati, prepíjati, uòlafiti se
drink up (alcohol): pòcugati, pòlizgati, strúsiti, tȑgnuti, tȑznuti, ukókati
drinking (alcohol): lȍkatīv, mumificíranje
drinking (alcohol): aldùmāš, ȁlko, alkohòlisānje, bàlsamovānje, bonbònisānje, cépānje, cícānje, cêvčēnje, cȉrisānje, cȉrka, cȕclānje, cugánjac, cȕgānje, ćȉrisānje, drȉnk, drmáža, drogírānje, džókānje, hàlisānje, karmȉnisānje, lokácija, lȍkānje, nalévānje, odžàkānje, òtimānje, pȉjača, pljȕgānje, rȁjfānje, sȉsānje, šljȅmānje, šljȉskānje, šljókānje, šljokárac, šmȉnkānje, tȉtrovānje, vózānje, zalívānje, zèmljosānje
drinking (alcohol) in the evening: akšàmluk
drinking (alcohol), juicing: sȁftānje
drinking: dȑmānje, lȅšēnje, pípa, rókānje, švȁsānje
drinking bout: ȁlko-trȉp
drinking glass (of alcohol): sàtljik
drinking party: pȉjānka
drinking place: lokácija
drinking song: lùmpōvka
drip: cȁpkati, cȁpnuti [2], kȁpati, kȁpati, kaplȉcati, romònisati, rȍmoriti, šȉšiti
dripping (liquids): kȁpānje, kȁpav, kapljèvit, kàpljiv, rȍkmōn, romònit, rȍmonjēnje, rȍmor, rȍmōran, rȍmorenje
drive (a vehicle): drȁjvati, drajvírati, gòniti, hȃjbati, šoferírati
drive (e.g. animals to pasture): gòniti
drive away cats: šícati

drive away, drive off: odbàrtati, ùmagliti

drive away, expel: siktèrisati

drive in: ùćerati

drive to: dòćerati

driver (female): šòfērka

driver: kȍčijāš, Mȉško [2], šòfēr

driver's licence: šára, šȃre, šarènica

drop (of liquid): kȁplja

drop out of a game: pȉčkati se

drug: njupáža, šóder [2]

drug addict who introduces newcomers to the habit: vòdīč

drug addict who sniffs narcotic drugs or glue: snȉfer

drug addict who takes all kinds of narcotic drugs: pȉg

drug addict who takes pills, pill popper: tȁblić

drug addict, junkie: dizàjner, drògāroš, dròger, drogèrāš, drȍgī, drogirȁnt, drȍgomān, drȍgomānka, drȍgos, drȍgoš, džȁnkī, đȁnkī, đankóza, fiksac, fiksāć, fȉkser, hàmšišār, hȃš [2], hàšišār, hàšiš-dróga-mȉnās-kàfa, hȃškić, hȁšman, hašòmān, hašòmānka, hìpik, komàndo, kòmāndos, narkohòličār, nȁrkos, nȁtkos, panknȁrkomānka, tabletòmān, tràvār

drug courier: transformâtor

drug dealer, pusher: bȁgman, dȉler, jegùljāš

drug money: kȍhle

drug paraphernalia: artiljèrija, bȉz, fȉt

drug session: diližȃnsa, džȅga

drug-induced hallucination: film

drugs kept under lock and key: ključ̂

drugs, dope: kiselìna, šȉt [2], tràvka

drugstore, pharmacy: apatéka, ȁpos, aspìrīn

drummer: drȁmer, drȁrner

drums: drȁmati, drȁmeri, tròmbl, tròml

drunk: ćìrisān, drȉnkī, drògīrān, grȍgī, hȃj [3], mòrtus [1], mútan, nàcīcān, nacìrisān, nàcirkān, nàcuclān, nàcugān, nàcvr̄cān, nàcvrckān, nàdrmān, nàfȁjtān, nàfrulān, nàkresān, nalìven, nàlokān, nàljōskān, nàpljugān, nàsisān, nàsvīrān, nàšīkān, nàšljēmān, nàšljōkān, nàšvasān, nàtankān, natànkīrān, nàtrēskān, pjȁn, prètitrovan, prȉpīt, skȍckān, tempèrīrān, trùbāč, tvȑd [2]

drunk, hammered, smashed: cêpān

drunk, juiced: nàsaftān

drunk, pickled: bàlsamovān, balzàmīrān, jȁnpi, mȍkar, nàbāren, naćevlèisān, nàrōljān

drunk, plastered: betònīrān

dry food rations: mùnīcija

dry place: suvòta

Dubrovnik (a city in Croatia): Dúba, Dubijána

duel, fight: méjdān

dull, uninterested: bélo [1]

dump one's boyfriend or girlfriend: dèponovati, iskulírati, korpírati, nogírati, odjèbati, òdralkati, oláditi, otkàntati, škartírati, zbrokváriti, znogírati

dumped by a boyfriend or a girlfriend: nògīrān, nòktīrān

dung beetle: zújak, zȕnzāk

dunum (surface measure of approx. 100 square yards): dùlum

duplicitous person: dùpljāk [1]

duty free shop: djȕtić

Dušanovac (a neighborhood in Belgrade): Dùškec, Dȕško

dye: pitùrati

dyed in the wood communist: bètōn [1]

dying: odàpinjānje

dying person: fitīlj [2], fitiljȉška

dynamo: dináma

e-mail somebody: emajlírati

eagle: klȉktāš

ear: anténa, blȁtobrān [2], mȉkro [1], rȁdār, slȕšalica, ȕhoslav, vȕho, zvȍno, zvȗčnīk

ear-ring: bȑnjica

early morning erection: jutrènjāk, zòrnjāk

early morning sexual intercourse: zòrnjāk

earn (money): cvètati, kȁnuti, kȁpnuti, namlátiti

earn amply: mlátiti, òkrpiti se, omástiti se

earring: mènđuha, mȕnđica

earth, soil: bòtača, cȓnka

ease up, take it easy: òdlahnuti, òdvaditi, òlabaviti, oláditi

easily: glȁt, glȁtko, lȁća [1], làćano [1], lȁgano, lȁsno, nȁgro, šȃlē

easily accessible wallet (e.g., to a pickpocket): samopȍsluga

easily cheated male: lȁzār [2], njȉva

easily cheated person, easy mark: pàljevina, plìvāč

easily, lightly: lȁhko

easily, without any difficulties: kȍmōtno

easy job, piece of cake, snap: lȁća [2]

easy thing to do: pizdàrija

easy to catch by the police: lȉstopādan

easy to stimulate sexually: jebèžljiv

easy, in no hurry: pȍlāk

easy, light: lȁhak

easy, simple (of a problem, etc.): nȁrgo, nȁrgu

eat dinner: hȁsati

eat greedily, wolf, stuff one's face: domìnati

eat in great quantities, pig out: búbati

eat one's fill, be stuffed: nàgumati se, nàhanovati se, naklópati se, namàndžati se, nàmazati se, nànjupati se, napánjati se, nàpucati se, natnàzati se, nàzobati se, nažděrati se, nàždrati se, opísati se

eat one's morning snack or lunch: marèndati, marendávati

eat poorly: mrljáviti

eat too much, be stuffed: dáviti se

eat too much, gorge, pig out: najèsti se, prožderávati se, pȍždirati, pȍždrēti, tamániti

eat, devour: ȁniti, àpisati, ȁpiti, ȁpnuti, àždíti, drȁpiti, fȕriti, hàlisati, hàlkati, hȁmati, hȁniti, hápati, hapávati, hȁpiti, hȁsati, hàtnati, hȑčiti, kȁmsovati, klȁpati, klópati, klȍpiti, klȍpnuti, krȁsti, kȑkati, kȑknuti, kȑljati, krútiti, lȁpnuti, ljúštiti, mȁkati, màndžati, mȁštrafiti, mȁznuti, mlȁtnuti, mòtati, mȕvati, nakȑkati se, njȕpati, njȕpiti, pànjati, pȁpati, pȁpiti, pâsti [2], pȍhasati, poklópati, pòvuriti, skȑkati, slístiti, smȁzati, tamániti, tȑpati, ubȁštrati, ùgrīsti, ùjesti, uništávati, vȕriti, zbúbati, zòbati, zúbiti, žděrati, žnjȁpati, žvȁcnuti, žvákati, žvȁknuti, žvȁkonjiti, žvȁljati

eat, throw down: obòriti

eating: hápānje, hapávānje, klopánac, klopánjac, kȑk [2], krkáncija, krkànluk, krkánjac, kŕkānje, mȕvānje, njȕpānje, njupáža, pȁša

eating dinner: mȑkonja

eccentric (not perfectly round) soccer ball: frljóka

eccentric behavior, weirdness: šízēnje

eccentric point (e.g. on a shaft): ekscènder

eccentric, extravagant, weird: šíza [2]

ecstasy (narcotic drug): ȅks [2], èkser, ekstáza, ȅkstazī

ecstasy: sokolàna

edgeball (in ping-pong): svíja

educational TV program: škôlnjāk

effective action by a soccer goalie: paráda

effective joke: pòkop

effective move: díndža, grôm [1], kȑkete, pȑvāk, sínđa, vrîsak

effective reply: bȑzalica, spúštalica

effectively: štôsno

efficiency, studio (apartment): gàjbica, gȁrsić

effort: zajebàncija, zôr

egg: àrniška, cvànjek, čàmīć, čmčić, ćȍkavac, kȍćavac, mucuváljak, mucuvánjak, mucvánjak, mȕčkavac, mȕćkalo, mȕćkavac, tàšak

egg-laying hen: kvòčetina

egotist: dȕpe-gláva, pizdèkān, pìzdūn, pizdùrina, stȋpsa, šíber [1], šȉbadžija, šȉbadžīnka

egotistic male: pìzdek [2]

eight: òsmāk

eight-year high-school student (instead of the usual four): osmérac

ejaculate: ìstrēsti se, ìzdrkati, òtrēsti, svršávati, svŕšiti, šprícati

ejaculate prematurely: ubaláviti se

ejaculation: šprícānje

elbowing, maneuvering: bàštrānje

elderly client of a prostitute: grȍb

elderly divorced female: ìskopina, Navukodonòsōr

elderly female: babùrina, babùskara, babùskera, bàkuta, dàsulja, frȃjla, ikebàna, karađòrđuša, kvȍčka, nànče, rȁstā, rȍksa, sènīlka, trȁnjerica, zmìja

elderly female: bȁba [2], kòkara, màtōrka

elderly female who sits in her apartment all the time: zmȁj [1]

elderly female, old bag: vrȅća

elderly homosexual: hàdžija

elderly male: arhìvār, čȉča, čiláger, čílac, číle, geògraf, gȉcle, građevínac, harmonìkāš, hokèjāš, jȁnuār, Jerèmija, kȃurī, kémac, kravàta, lapónac, nerénac, rȉševac

elderly male with wrinkled forehead: harmonìkāš

elderly male, old fox: lísac

elderly prostitute: drapačóza, kȑš, stȁrka [1]

elderly unmarried female: usidjèlica

elderly victim of a pickpocket: tája

electric guitar: tȑzavica

electric power: gròmovina

electrician: strùjīć

electricity: lètrika

elegant: èleg

elegant male: đȅnt, fȉšbajn

elegantly: gàlant

elevator: dizúljak

eleven: jèdannēs

eliminator: elimināṫor

emancipated: emancìpicovan

emergency brake: rȕčnā

emergency medical service: hȉtnā

emigrant: emȉgos

emotional person: emotívac

emotionally balanced: ládan

emotionally cold person: lèdana

empty (room, hall, etc.): akùstičan, mŕtav [2]

end one sexual intercourse: dojèbati

end one's term in prison: odzújati

end, cessation: šlȕs [2]

endure, survive: predevèrati

enemy: dȕšmanin, paksìjān

energetic boy: dȑmpuc

engage in a fight (fists, etc.): flastèrisati se, fȕtiti se

engage in a love affair: ljubòvati

engage in anal sexual intercourse with (of a male): ȃjsovati

engage in casual sexual intercourse with (of females): dávati

engage in cunnilingus: dȕdlati, fȁjfati, lízati, sȃftati, šamàrati, šljȕpati, transfirzírati, vrtogláviti

engage in fellatio: cùclati, dȕdlati, fȁfati, fȃjčiti, fȃjfati, flaùtati, fȕmati, glòckati, glȍcnuti, glȍđati, hàlisati, ìspljugati, ìspušiti, jogùrtati, òbaliti [1], pȃpati, pȃpiti, pljȕgati, podùdlati, pòfȃjčiti, poflaùtati, pòpljugati, pòpušiti, posàugati, pȕšiti, rȍknuti, sàugati, seksndràjsik, šȉtipu

engage in fighting (e.g., with fists on the street): màrisati se, mȁriti se

engage in group sex (of males who, one after another, engage in sexual intercourse with a single female), rape, gang bang: izrédati se

engage in intensive sexual intercourse with (of a male): dèrati, pocijépati, pocépati, podèrati, razbúcati

engage in prolonged coffee drinking: kafènisati, kahvènisati, kavènisati

engage in prolonged sexual intercourse with (of a male): žùljati

engage in quick sexual intercourse with (of a male), have a quickie: umòčiti se

engage in quick sexual intercourse with, have a quickie: bȑzati

engage in sexual foreplay, pet, feel up: dŕpati, fȁćkati, fȁtati, fȁtati se, fȉlcovati, hvȁtati se, navláčiti, planináriti, pòhvatati se, pòvatati se, šlàtati, šmȁjhlati, vatáriti, vȁtati, vȁtati se, žnjȁrati, žnjȁriti

engage in sexual intercourse out of boredom (of a male):

čaklanìati

engage in sexual intercourse with (of a female): kókati se, prímiti, žégati se

engage in sexual intercourse with (of a male): ȁkati, ȁknuti, ȃrčiti, bȁjsati, bȁsniti, bȁti, bàtije, bȁtje, blȁnjati, bȕtnuti, cȅpnuti, cevrljúgnuti, cȕcati, cȕckati, cvàjcvrkovati, čèrečiti, čèšljati, čìbučiti, čȉjati, čȕkati, čȕknuti, ćóriti [1], dȅrnuti, drápati, dȑknuti, dunìjati, džárati, džidžibúdžiti, džȉndžati, džukèljisati, đalafȕsnuti, đunìjati, fȃjčiti, fȁkati, fȁnjati, fazonírati, fȉštiti, fljȕzgati, fȑljnuti, fȑnditi, ftȁknuti, ftȅrati, fȕkati, fȕndati, fȕntiti, fȕtati, gácati, gájtaniti, gȁziti, glȃncati, glòdati, gnjéčiti, grèbati, gùslati, gudèljati, gudèrisati, gúditi, gȕrnuti, gȕsliti, gúziti, gȕžvati, hàisati, haláknuti, hàldisati, hȁndriti, hȁriti, harmòničiti, hèbati, hȅftati, hȍblati, hŕkati, hŕknuti, hrkobȕtnuti, ìskecati, iskembéciti, iskembéćiti, iskùndačiti, isponàpiknuti, isposécati, ìsprcati, isprèdelati, isprepalàpucati, ispreponàtaći, ispreponàtaći, ìspucati, ȉzakati, ȉzdeljati, izèbati, izjèbati, izmésiti, ȉzmrdati, izrókati, jȁhati, jèbati, jebávati, jebìkati, jébiti, jebùcati, jebùckati, jȅpkati, kàntati, kánjiti, karabúdžiti, kárati, karȉnati, kàrisati, karírati, kȁzniti, kȅcati, kȅksati, klȁti, knjȉžiti, kókati, kólati, komȉnjati, kòvati, krȁjcovati, kŕčiti, kréćati, krȅsnuti, kŕkati, kȑknuti, kȑljati, kȑmbučiti, kȑnuti, kukuríknuti, lȇvčiti, lȉpačiti, lȉlati, lomàtati, lóziti, ljȍknuti, ljȍljnuti, ljúljati, ljȕljnuti, macafúknuti, màrisati, mȁštračiti, mȁzati, mȁznuti, mȅtnuti, mlȁtnuti, mòčiti, montírati, mrcodáviti, mŕčiti, mȑdati, mȑdnuti, mȑtkovati, nàbiti, nabíjati, nàgariti, nàgaziti, nagúziti, nakȉtaćiti, nàkititi, naklápati, nàkljukati, namàknuti, napèndečiti, nàpičiti, napikávati, nàpiknuti, naprȉndečiti, nasàntraćiti, naśíkati, nàtaći, natàkariti, natàknuti, natégnuti, natrkèljisati, nàtrtiti, navláčiti, nàvȕći, nȉtnovati, nȉtovati, njȍrnuti, njȕknuti, objektivírati, òblanjati, obòriti, obŕnuti, odàlamiti, odjèbati, odrápiti, òdšȁjbati, odšéviti, òdšibati, òfraštiti, okèseriti, òkinuti, okréćati, okrénuti, okròčiti, òlešiti, òljȗštiti, ománuti, onàdati, opàjdariti, opalȉnđati, opáliti, opàmbrčiti, opàmprčiti, opàndrčiti, opàprčiti, opàrmačiti, opàučiti, operdášiti, òpičiti, opijúkati, oplajváziti, òplesti, oprcóknuti, oprédmetiti, oprȉndačiti, oprȉndačiti, opízditi, òrati, ošȁjbudžiti, ošàjdariti, otàslačiti, otkàntati, otvòriti, òžeći, palamúditi, pàmprčiti, pȇglati, pȅlcati, pèndrečiti, pešáćiti, pȉčiti, pičkàrati, pičkaròšiti, pȉknuti, pocépati, podrápati, pòfȃjčiti, pofúkati, pòhoblati, pojèbati, polòmiti, polòžiti, pòmrdati, pòplašiti, pòrašpati, pošéviti, pòšȍdrati, poštósati, potȁflati, potòrbati, potŕkati, potròšiti, pòtucati, potùmplati, popáliti, prášiti, pȑcapȑcati, pȑcati, pȑckati, pȑcnuti, pȑčiti, pŕćiti, pŕćnuti, precóriti, prelástiti, prèpušiti [1], prevŕnuti, pricvŕljiti, pričvŕljiti, prȉdačiti, prȉvesti, prȉndačiti, proverávati se, provózati, prȕćnuti, pȕknuti[2], pȕniti, ráditi [1], ràsturiti, rȁšpati, razjèbati, razváliti, razvaljívati, rèndisati, rȅzati, rȉbovati, rȉfljati, ȑknuti, ȑmbati, rókati, rȍknuti, rȍksovati, roštȉljati, sapùnati, sasúnuti, sàsȗti, sàterati, sàtjerati, sȅksati, seksírati, sjȁriti, sjúriti, skalabrȉjati, skùbačiti, skùrcati, skȕhati, smòtati, smȑmuviti, spȁrkati, spotàpiknuti, sprášiti, spŕcati, spȑčiti, spŕćiti, spȑditi, spȑžiti, spȕcati, spùstiti, stȁviti, stȅrati, stjȅrati, stȏjčiti, strméknuti, stȑndžosati, strnovrátiti, strpùsati, strúgati, sturnovrátiti, súknuti, sȕnuti, surdúknuti, surdúmiti, svȉlati, svȉrnuti, svȉtlati, svírati, svȑdlati, šȃjbati, šćȃmčiti, šćvȑljnuti, šćvȑljugnuti, šèbečiti, šèbočiti, šegebèdečiti, šèpȃrčiti, šepèračiti, šévati, šéviti, šȅvkati, šȉbati, šȉbnuti, šȉljbočiti, šȉljobočiti, šȉšnuti, šȉti, šíkati, šíknuti, šlȁjfati, šíljiti, šnȉtati, špȁrtati, šíšati, štambȉljati, štȅmati, štȅpati, štètnati, štósati, štȍsnuti, štȑkati, šȕpčiti, švàsati, šívati, tȁbati, tabòisati, tȁflati, tandáriti, tàndrčiti, tantàrȃnčiti, tarlàhati, tàslačiti, tȅsati, testèrisati, testírati, tȉsnuti, tòrbati, trándžiti, tȑndosati, tȑndžati, tȑpati, tȑtiti, tȕcati, tȕcati se, tȕmplati, tȕriti, turpȉjati, tȕtnuti, ubáciti, ubàčiti, ubádati, ubíjati, ùbiti, udròbiti, ùgnati, ugráditi, ukàlupiti, ùknjižiti, umòčiti, umòčiti se, upáliti, ùštekati, ȕtnuti, uváliti, víkniti, víknuti, vòziti, vȑteti, zabȉberiti, zàbiti, zabùrdisati, zacvŕcati, zàdesti, zafijúkati, zàfikati, zafȑndati, zagláviti, zaglíbiti, zagúziti, zàkȃjlati, zakalafírati, zakalàmbačiti, zakalambàsati, zakalàmfisati, zakàntati, zakarabúdžiti, zakekéčiti, zakèrečiti, zàkinderiti, zàkitati, zaklincóriti, zaklinčóriti, zaklȉnderiti, zakùndačiti, zàlimfati, zalȉlati, zalòmiti, zamàndaliti, zaprášiti, zaprdékati, zapȑditi, zàpušiti, zaríbati, zašíšati, zatèfteriti, zatȑidečiti, zatȑndečiti, zaváliti, zàvȋličiti, zavȉngeriti, zàvȕći, zbȉberiti, zbȉčiti, zbȉglati, zbȕtnuti, zídati, zdràufnuti, zdúbiti, zȅkati, zȅzati, zgȑbiti, zgúditi, zgúziti, zȉgovati, zȉtovati, zjȁšiti, zjòdlati, zrȁšiti, zrȅzati, zvȉznuti, ždràufnuti, ždvrljúgnuti, žùljati, žvȁjznuti

engage in sexual intercourse with (of a male), bang: ȁjsnuti [2], bȉcnuti, gáđati, odàpȇti, òšinuti, práskati, prȁsnuti, pȕcati, trȅsnuti, zàtȕći

engage in sexual intercourse with (of a male), drill: bȍrovati, burgȉjati, pròborovati

engage in sexual intercourse with (of a male), make sparks: krȇsati

engage in sexual intercourse with (of a male), poke: bȍsti, nabádati, nàbosti, nasáditi, ùbosti

engage in sexual intercourse with (of a male), pump: pȗmpati

engage in sexual intercourse with (of a male), screw: pȉliti

engage in sexual intercourse with (of sheep): mŕkati

engage in sexual intercourse with: ȁkati se, cépati se, čȉjati se, dèrati se, fȉrcati se, flȅkati se, fȑljati se, fȑndati, hèftati se, hȅklati, ìskecati se, ìspužvati se, jèbati se, jebùcati se, kȅcati se, kȅckati se, méšati se, odnòsiti se, ȍpštiti, pojèbati se, pošéviti se, pòtrtkati, pòtucati se [1], rókati se, ševati se, šéviti se, šȅvkati se, šȉbati se, tȑtiti se, ùsrećiti, zàklati, zaorgȉjati, zékiti se, zȅzati se

engage in sexual intercourse with to sateity: ìsprcati se

engage in sexual intercourse with, bang: trȅsnuti se

engage, participate, take part in: šóditi

engaged in sexual intercourse with: ìsprcȃn, ȉzjebȃn, jȅbȃn, jèben, jèbenȋ, zajèbȃvšȋ

engaging in sexual intercourse with: bȍckȃnje, jèbȇćȋ

engine: pȑdalica

engineer: četiriȍčko, indžȉnjȇr, kȍladžija, mànot

England: Ingléskȃ

English (pertaining to a person): ingléskȋ

English teacher (female): Ènglȇskinja

English teacher (male): Ènglȇz

enjoy, like: ćȇjfiti, drváriti, pùpati, sláditi se, šȅmati, šemsòati, tròšiti se, vàtiže, zabrȉjati, zabrȉjati se, zalúditi, zarúžiti, zatulumáriti, gustírati

enjoying: fúralica

entaglement, complex issue: petljàncija

enter (a room, building, etc.): infiltrírati se

enter: ugȉljati, ùnȋći, ùpasti

entering: ufurȉška

enthusiastic: magnètisȃn

entrance: ùfur, ufurijánović

entrance stairway: hàustor

entrance ticket or fare: biljètić

entrance ticket to the first five rows in the cinema: strêlka

environment course (in elementary school): pȍzniš

environmentalist: zèlen

epileptic: trȅskavac

equal: barabȁr [1]

equally: barabȁr [2]

erect (of one's penis): dȉgnuti se

erect penis: digitâlis, kòlac, Nèpāl, rámpa, rúdo, tvȑtko, vodènjāk [2]

error, mistake: fàlīnka, kuràfte [2], pògrješka

escalator: dòlāp

escape from prison: iscúriti, noktírati

escape from the police: žȉdnuti se

escape, flee: đáda [2], furijanȅlī, furijánović, gìljer, grȉz, kída, šprȉca, štúra [2], zjòsatibrinj

escape, getaway: dȉm [2]

escape, show one's heels: cìpela [2]

estimate, guess: céniti, fàrisati, òšacovati, pròšacati, šàcati, šȁcovati, zrȉkati

eternal student, professional student: vetèrān

even number of cards taken by two or more players during one game: pàta-kârte

even, without any debts: kvȉt [2]

evening: snȅka

evening drinker, person who prefers to drink alcohol in the evening: akšàmlučār

evening out: ìsfur

event: àkcija, scȅna, vrtúljak

event which can be interpreted in a number of ways: rašomonijáda

everyone: svȁk

everywhere: svȕđ

evil: ȑđav

evil female, bitch: avétinja, ćémka, golopíca, golopízda, gòvnulja, gòvnuša, grȍzomōrnica, guzòsera, jebenpízda, jèbiguza, jebipízda, karakôndžula, kȕštra, lúpežica, múda, pȉšna, ròspija, sȅksī-mašína, stȕa, stȕha, vàmpīr

evil ghost: vjedógonja

evil male: lúpež, pedèruša, pȅgavac, pùšāč, pùšik

evil male, s.o.b: kȁvurin, kȑme, mȁtrāk [1]

evil nature: hȕja, ȕja [2]

evil person: àbdika, gùrbet, kêr [1], mrâčnjāk, múćak [2], mùfljūz [1], ȑđa, šȉntār, šùpčina

evil person, beast: bèštija

evil person, snake: zmìja

evil, mean, bad: izdrkán, kváran, nȅgotīvan, nȅren, nevàljas, ȍčājan, pògan [1], pòkvāren, šlȁjm [1], šȕgav, tànak, zȁjebān

evilness, maliciousness: marifètluk

ex, former: ȅks [1], ȅx

exactly, as it should be: knȁp [1]

exactly, precisely: bȁš, tàmān, ȕprav

exaggerate: búdžiti

exam: preslušávānje, sȉsānje, sjèdēljka

example: bȉks [2], štôs [2]

excellent: fȁmōzan, grôm [2], pȕška [3], šàrāf

excellent female, cool babe: kràljica

excellent male, cool guy: tìpčina

excellent movie: fȉlmčina, fȉlmčuga

excellent object or plan, pearl, gem: hȁos [2]

excellent, awesome: bésan, bijésan, bôgbògōva, bògovskī, bômba [1], bȍžje, čakulit, dūzdibidȕn, fantàstičan, gȁla [2], gȍtīvan, gȍtīvno, gȍtvan, hâj-fâj, hâj-fī, hȁos [3], hȁos [4], jèbāčkī [1], jèziv, králjevskī, kȑvišan, kûl [1], kûl [2], lȁča, làčan, làčano, lȁčo [2], làćan, làćano [1], làćāran, lȁće [1], lȁće [2], lȁćo [2], lúdnica, lúdnica, mȁksimālan, mȍćno, mráčan, mrâk [3], mrâk [4], mràkuša [2], mȑtvačkī, nâj-hâj, nâj-nâj, pâlī, pènicilīnskī, pȅrsu, púšnica, sàjber, stráva [2], stráva [3], streptomìcīn [2], strȍg, sȕper, superȉška, šláger [2], tȕrbo, ȕbitāčan, ubístven, vrȉštēćī, zȁjebān, zmȁj [2], zmajèvit, žȅšćī

excellent, bad, mean: strȁhobālān, strahòvit, strȁobālan, strášno

excellent, big time: gȁla [1]

excellent, cool: mȍćan, neukapìrljiv, neukapìrljivo, ȍpēt, picikàto, šlògīrān

excellent, sharp, awesome: brȉtva [2], brȉtva [4]

excellent, superb: nèviđeno

excellent, superb, awesome: apsolȕtan, pȁklen

excellent, tip-top: tȉp-tȍp

excellently, cool: kȑvavo [1]

excessive celebration with drinking: šénluk

exchange, swap (money, goods, etc.): čȅnčati

exchange, swap: čȅnč, đôr, đóra, đórānje, đórati, đórati se, mènjāč, mènjāž, menjáža, tràmpa, trȁmpiti, trȁmpiti se

excite, arouse: otròvati

excited: nàjarcān

exciting: strášan, stràvičan

exclude oneself: iskòpčati se, isšȁltati se

exclude oneself, leave: išȁltati se

excrement: drȅk [1], govnàrija, góvno [2], káka [1], lítavica, mótovi, njȅsra, pȁdavine, sránje [2], šȉt [2], trúba [1], žȕtō

excuse: vȁđēnje

exercise discipline: ìzmuštrati, mȕštrati

exercise, workout: zanimácija

exhaust: ižmíkati

exhaust pipe, tail pipe: àuspuf, àuspūh

exhaust sexually: ràzjehati

exhausted: ȉžmikān

exhibitionist, flasher: šàrāč

exit: ìsfur, òluk, rȍra

expel, throw out: ràšćerati

expensive: trȍpasto, trȍpo, visòko

expensive, steep: debèlo

experience a strong drug effect: lèteti

experienced: nàmazān, pèčen, prèfarbān

experienced male, one who knows life: vûk

expert: Šèkspīr

explode: grúhati [1], grúvati

explosion: grȗvanj

expose oneself, be conspicuous: kokèriti se

express oneself: ofráziti se

express, quick: èkspres [1], èkspresan

express, quickly: èkspres [2]

extensive joking: zezàčina

extra, additionally: ȅkstra [1]

extraordinary high-quality item: čȕdo

extraordinary male: džáfer

extraordinary matter: egzòtika

extraterrestrial, alien: izvanzemáljac, klekètāš, vanzemáljac, vanzèmāljka

extravagant: òpičen

extremely drunk male: lètva

extremely hot room, sauna: sàuna [1]

extremely loud, thundering: gȓmno, gròmak, gròman

extremely orderly person, neatness: picàjzla

extremely potent male: virtùoz

extremely slender individual, walking skeleton: bijȁfra [2]

extremely strong male, bull, ox: bivòlčina

extremely stupid or mentally deficient person: ràdkapna

extremely talkative female, chatterbox: alàpača, džȁftara, opàjdara, toròkuša

extremely talkative male, chatterbox: dȑmadžija, dȑndāš, dȑndos, dȑndoš, dròćkāš, pȑdac [1], pȑdāč, pùšāč

extremely talkative person, chatterbox: àbronoša, bùbnjār, blebètalo, dávež [1], dávid, dupepévac, jàjara, kanarínac, kénjac, kènjāč, kènjātor, klàfrača, kokòšār, landarapiškórac, landarapišórac, landarpišórac, mèjātor, mlȋnār, nagvážđalo, pùšik, sérac, sèrāč, sèrātor, sèriglāva, séronja, srâč, toròkalo, tráskalo, tȕpadžija, tupamȃros, ȕdāv, zvȍnār

extremely tall female: katedrála

extremist: èkstrēm

eye (sight organ): fildžān, ȁktalica, cîljka, ckȉvalo, cvȉkalo, dzîljka, fâr, fènjer, glèdāljka, kèćija, kećùralica, ȍka, okàuz, ȍkoslāv, prózor, sòfkara, stàklēnka, špȅkula, trȁkalica, zîljka, zȍlka, zrȁkalica, zrȁkavica, ždrȁkavica, žmȉgavac

eye bruise, shiner: monòkl

eye's: òčinjī

eyeglasses: cvìkeri, ćórci, ćòrīle, ćȍroskopi, dalekòzor, dijòptrije, diòptrije, dùrbīn, durbíni, dvȍglēd, dzîljke, džȍzeri, džȍzluci, đòrzluci, đȍzle, đȍzluci, đȍzluk, đȕzle, ekráni, kèrecvi, lȕsteri, óberlihti, očále, ojȉkare, okulári, òptika, òptike, pèndžeri, pênžeri, pèriskopi, prȉzme, prózori, retrovîzori, snàjperi, stàkla, staklíći, šȃjbe, šòferšājbe, šoferšàjbne, špígli, tȅleskopi, zástori

eyeglasses, lenses: léće

eyelash: trèpiš

eyelid: rolèta

eyes: fárovi

face (human): cȁfa, cìferblat, cȕfa, fȁca, fȁjercāg, fȁjercajg, fasáda, fȁsūng, frnjóka, frnjókalica, frnjókica, lȃbrnja, lámpa, làpina, lȉčnjāk, màska, mȅnza, njȍkalica, plȃhta, pljèskara, pljùskara, pròpustnica, sȕrla, šûnka, vȉlice

face, snout: njúška

facial hairs: pêrje

factory: robìjāšnica, rȍštīlj, rȕdokōp, šljakaóna, šljàkārnica

fail: iscúriti, rȍknuti, skȉksati

fail an exam (flunk): cȍcnuti, drȍcnuti, drȍknuti, ljȍljnuti, ljȍsnuti, òkinuti, ríknuti, rȍknuti, šljȕnuti, trȍpnuti, tropírati

fail to engage in sexual intercourse, be refused: čàbrisati

fail to keep a promise, go back on one's word: ispáliti

fail to pass a grade in school, flunk: tȑknuti

failed: trópa [2]

failed exam: okináva, opaljȍt, Pâdova

failed sex: čàbar [1], ćórak [1], trúba [1]

failing grade: àdam, àdūt, ȁs, ȃver, aviònče, bandéra, búger, càjper, cvíka, cvȍk [2], cvȍker, fȍto-šȍk, jêlka, kêc [2], kèčiga, kèčuga, kikònder, kòlac, kòmād [2], kȕkica, kúlja, kvȑga, màjōr, ȍskār, pàndūr, pàrmak, šàmar, tȍp [2]

failing grades in school: vìnogrād

failure: pádež, visijáner, visúljak

faint: ušlogírati se, vèhnuti

fair: dèrnek, ljùdskī, skȕp [1]

fairground: sȉto

fairy's son: vilènjāk

faith, religion: dîn

fake, phoney: tȅrs [2]

faked merchandise: dùpljāk [2]

falcon: klȉkavac

fall (physical): pádež

fall (physically): pȁnuti, pljȁskati, strméknuti se, strmopízditi se

fall asleep, doze off: nàkititi, osovljávati se, zàhenkati, zaknjávati, zarèvati, zaslípiti, zàsofkati

fall down, kiss the floor: ìspasti, kljȍknuti, ljȍsnuti, sjèbati se, skénjati se, skȑšiti se, slòžiti se, sùrvati se, trȅhnuti, ùpanuti

fall flat: njȍknuti

fall in love: nalòžiti se, napáliti se, natréskati se, nàvūći se, oćoráviti, odlépiti, ȍtkačiti, ȍtkinuti, sjèbati se, ùpecati se, zacópati se, zaćóriti se, zȁgrīsti, zatelèbati se, zatetrébiti, zatetrébiti se, zatréskati se

fall in love with: tȑznuti, zgotíviti

fall in love, be stuck on: zalípiti se

fall madly in love: precópati se

fall vacation: jȅsenovānje

fallen in love: magnètisān, pȍdān, prèfarbān, zàćorēn, zȁtrēskan

fallen leaves: šûšanj

false: fȃlš [1], nȅgatīvan, šȁtro [3], trȕō

false incrimination, frame: cinculírānje, ȉgrānka, naméštāljka, namjéštāljka, sȉcer, spȕst

false incrimination, framing: jȁfina

false information, rumor: bùva

false name: dìvljāk [2]

false news: bàlōn [2], bômba [2]

false, counterfeit, faked: dìvljī

falsely: trȕlo

falsely incriminate, frame: fèrcandrgovati, lȁuf, nàbaniti, naméštati, nàmjestiti, namontírati, natòčiti, natòvariti, òblajati, pȁkovati, pakírati, prišaráfiti, pròzvati, rèstiti, roviskáriti, spȁkovati, spakírati, súknuti, uváliti, zabìberiti, zatèfteriti, zbȕtnuti

falsely incriminating, framing: sukȁrno

family: fȁmeja, fȁmīlija, vàmīlija

famous: fȁmōzan

fan of Crvena Zvezda (a soccer team in Belgrade, Serbia): cȉganin, dèlija, zvèzdāš

fan of Željezničar (a soccer team in Sarajevo, Bosnia): žéljovac

fan of OFK Beograd (a soccer team in Belgrade, Serbia): klómfer

fan of Partizan (soccer team in Belgrade, Serbia): partizánovac

fan of Sarajevo (a soccer team in Sarajevo, Bosnia): pȉtār, Saràjlija

fan or player for Čelik (a soccer team in Zenica, Bosnia): čèlikovac

fan or player for Dinamo (in the 1990s called Croatia, a soccer team from Zagreb, Croatia): dȉnamovac

fancy: fènsī

fans of Hajduk (a soccer team in Split, Croatia): torcída

Fanta juice: pȉpī

fare, ticket: kóva

fascist: fȁšer

fashion journal: môdnjāk

fashion model: mòtka

fashionable, in: ȉn [1]

fashionably, in: ȉn [2]

fast: gòtīvan, šprȉh

fast driving: pȉčēnje

fast lover, one who quickly finishes sexual intercourse: klòkan

fast melody: fȁstica

fast person, speedster: prȁćka

fast run: gàlop

fast runner, antelope, gazelle: antilòpa

fast runner, speedster: bȑzac [1], mȕngos

fast train, express train: bȑzac [2], bȑzāk

fast walking: gȕzānje, pȉčēnje

fasting: pôs

fat belly: žûlj

father: ćȁća, ćȁćos, ćálac, ćâle, lȇš [1], rȉstić, senílac

father of one's son's or daughter's spouse: prȉjatelj

father's, pop's, dad's: ćâletōv

father, dad: japučȉnskī, jòristanj, kàktus, kévac, kljákac, snȅsko, stârī

father, daddy: ȁpa [2], bába [1], bábo, bášta [2], ída, ȍrpa, pápak [1], tâ [2], tája, tájko, tájo

father, old man: matórac, matòrān, màtorī, rȉsta

father, papa: pâpe, pȁpica

fatigue: ùmor

faucet: pípa

faulty: gȑbav

favorite: tîp [2]

fax: fȁks

fear: cvíka, cvȍk [2], cvòker, frȉk [2], fȑka, fȕfka, gȑč, kàrgōn, kàvara, krȅč [2], paranȍja, pȑpa [2], punturȉtis, sȁmogon, stȉskavac, strâ, tȑnjavac, trónja, tȑta, trtàrati se, trtášiti, tȑt-mȑt [2], userávānje, vȕna [2], zȅnt, zȍrt [2]

fear of being dumped by one's girlfriend: korpomânija

fear of being followed: pàrano

Federal Republic of Yugoslavia: Serejòtija

Federal Republic of Yugoslavia: Sloboslâvija

fee for using boiler to distill brandy: kazànija

feed, give food to: rániti

feel a thief stealing one's wallet: drȁjfovati

feel an urge to defecate, have to go: prikénjati se

feel an urge to urinate or defecate, have to go: prìterati

feel good: raspiláviti se

feel hot (temperature): bȁnjati se

feel hot (temperature), bake: báriti se

feel sleepy: prìdurmiti se

feel the urge to engage in sexual intercourse: prijèbati se

feel, sense: namirȉsati, njȕšiti, ođànisati, raskužnjávati, uđànisati, zȅntovati

feeling, emotion: lȁčo [1], lȁćo [1]

feet: fȉt

fellatio: cùclānje, dùdlānje, fȁf, fȁfānje, hàlisānje, hȁsmiku, lùla, pljugánac, pípa, pȕšēnje, ȕsmenī

fellow countryman: zéma, zémo

female: àjkuna, bànkara, bȁtre, báza, bùkēt, bȕba, búlja [1], bȕra, bȕtra, cáca, câjka, cáva, cȉca, cùcika, cucùrojka, cȕpa, cȕra, câvka, čćȅ, čȅče, čȉstīlka, čkȁma, ćónta, čùvadārka, ćȍška, dásīnica, dásīnka, dȉmulja, drndàljka, dȉndulja, drȍcica, drúsla, đȁnferica, féla, félja, fljȁška, frȁjerica, frȁjērka, frâjla, fȑlja, fulágerka, fȕndra, fùnkīn, gâbor, gèrla, glavȍbolja, glòdalica, glônđa, gréba, gȕšter, hèvina, hombòlēr, jòrnakanj, kâjla, kȁūrka, kàva, kèfa, kènda, kȉnder, kȉta, klȉnka, kòmāt [1], kòšara, krêlka, kròfna, kȕja, kvòčetina, kvȍčkica, lȁstavica, lèvātka, lȉmačica, máca, mȁče [1], mȁčka, mȁčos, mâlā [2], màslo, míca [1], mêso, Miléva, mȉšić, móca, mrȁčnjāk, mȉrnotka, mȕšmula, nȁže, nȅrga, nòkotka, nȕmera, ȍgriz, ȍgroz, ȍktopōd, óvca, parafȁmfula, párče, píčak, Pérsa, pȉčić, pȉčija, pȉčka, pičkòba, pȉčkulja, pičkȕljina, pȉčkuša, pȉčos, pikolína, pȉlka, pȉlula, pȉšulja, pȉšura, pȉzdača, pjèvica, píla, plônđa, pljȁka, pljakùrina, pódmorničārka, pòlica, popȉšulja, prȁćka, pȑča, pȑdara, preklàpača, prȉkolica, píša, ptȉca, ptȉčica, pízda, ribȉčōn, rȉbīzla, rìbōn, rȉčka, rȉflja, rȍba, róda [2], rùpīnger, sȁtara, séka, sèstra, skȁkavica, sȍća, sôjka, sȍkō, sokòlac, sokoláner, sóva, strùnjača, sȕknja, šépa, šȉšārka, škrȉplja, šólja [1], špȉca, štrúdla, tàcna, tàmbura, tàmburica, tégla, tréba, trȅmka, trúbica, umtaràsa, vagína, vȁjska, vȁjza, vȁjzor, vûk, zȅbrica, zȕlfa, žȅmskā, ženètina, žȅnskā, žȅnskāć, žȅnskāć, žȅnskica, žlȁjfa

female bathroom attendant: séra, srȁlja, vècējka

female body: nȁmeštāj, nȁmještāj

female breast: amortȉzēr, bàcāč, bàlkōn, bàlōn [2], cȅca, cȉca, cȉkica, čȉpsa, deltòid, dȕda[1], hlȇb, mlȇčnjāk, mljȇčnjak, pùdīng, sífa, sȉfōn, silȉkōn, silȉkōnka, sȉnfa, sȉsa[1], sȉsōn, sisúljak, sȉsūrda, síka, škȓge, štȏsdèmfa, štȏsdèmfer, tènder, vȉme

female child, girl: đevòjčica, špilhóznerka, upȉšulja

female drug addict, female junkie: dizàjnērka

female experienced in sex: kòkara

female flight attendant: stȇvka, stjúca

female friend: jarànica, sèstra

female from a blue-collar family: brȍš, sinòvac, sinòvica, šlàjpik, šljàjpik

female from a respected family: čȅgovićka

female from a white-collar family: sȋn

female gossiper: očèpulja

female homewrecker: rázvodnica

female in white socks: leukèmičārka

female nudist: núdla

female orthopedic shoe: borosána

female over 25 years old: polóvnjača

female owner or manager of a brothel, madam: màmek, màmica

female pubic hairs, bush: džbûn

female sexual partner: cȍca, dásīnica, dásīnka, dàskalica, jebàčica, jèbica, jebigùzica

female sexual partner of a married male (of a male): cvàjterica

female shop keeper: trȍnjarica

female stripper: strȉperka

female troublemaker, rowdy: kȓkanka

female who abuses males: cèhulja

female who approaches males (usu. offering sexual favors to them): dočèkuša

female who cheats on her husband (i.e. sexually): klȃnfa

female who dates affluent males: sponzòruša

female who does not readily engage in sexual intercourse: néda

female who dresses casually: hašòmānka

female who dresses fashionably: šmȉnkačica, šmȉnkerka

female who engages in anal sex: ostràguša

female who enjoys anal sexual intercourse: analȉtičārka, kontràšica

female who financially abuses males: glȍdārka

female who frequently engages in fellatio: bajadéra, dudlàšica, fafàčica, pljȕgerica, pušàčica

female who frequently visits other people's houses (usu. to gossip), busybody: stòkuća

female who has had an abortion or miscarriage: àbortovānā

female who is emotionally attached to the former Yugoslavia, Yugo-nut: jȕgonostàlgičārka

female who leaves her husband: pobègulja, pobjègulja

female who looks older than she actually is: tȅtka

female who often refuses advances from males: plànīnka

female who often screams in pain: jaúkalica

female who peeps, peeper: gìcīnka

female who readily and indiscriminately engages in sexual intercourse, slut: kurcòlōmka, pȍštarica

female who rents rooms for one night at the train station in Zagreb, Croatia: postèljārka

female who rubs the penis: pȉpničārka

female who simultaneously engages in sexual intercourse with two males: dvòcjēvka

female who stands at the entrance to greet visitors (usu. to one's own home): dočèkuša

female who strongly wiggles her buttocks while walking: mìrsāl

female who uses different objects to masturbate: svèznalica

female who wears old jeans: pādavičārka

female with a large nose: kȕronosa

female with a large vagina: pìzdara, pìzdatā

female with an exaggerated interest in sex: ispȉjuša

female with attractive shape: kȓmača, mȁtko, mȇso

female with bandy legs: nȅpoznātā

female with dyed hair: kudèljārka

female with excessive makeup: kòmanč-bȇbi

female with eyeglasses, four eyes: cvikeràšica, cvȉkerica, kȍbra, nȁočārka, snàjpērka, snàjprka

female with large breasts and big buttocks: razvȉjōjla, razvijȍtka, špȅk[1]

female with large breasts and buttocks: buhalȅtka

female with large buttocks: debèljāk, dupètara, dùpetina, gùzara, gùzička, gùzna, gùzulja, gùzuljica, gùzuljičica, nàzadnā, šùpkara, šȕpguza, šȕpka

female with large buttocks: dùpeška

female with large vaginal lips: preklàpača

female with loud clothing and makeup: karakȏndžula, krstàrica, lȍfra, rȍndža, rȍnđa

female with loud makeup: lȃrfa

female with nail polish: àutolakȉrērka

female with obviously false eyelashes: trȅpavičārka

female with skinny legs: pevàčica

female with slender legs: pjevàčica, svrȁka

female with too much makeup, babe with loud makeup: sȉjuks

female with venereal disease: Vènera

female with very large breasts and very big buttocks: rùsija

female, chick: bȃri, pìletina

female, cunt: cána, cȃpi, cȕpī, čkȃpi, džùmina, jòčkapinj, kóka, míndža, mindžòsava, mȉndžoslava, mìndžulja, mȕf, pȃru, píca, pìcara, pìcōjka, picóka, pȋcoš, pìcuša, pićóka, pićókara, pìzdara, pìzduša, rȍndža, rȍnđa, rȕpa[2]

female, fox: rȉba

female, piece: kòmād[1]

females: pìčetina

females dated by a single male: ergȅla

feminine curves: klavijatúra

feminized handsome male: máčak

feminized male: fȅmka, guzodŕpac, pepȋno, pìcek[2]

fence, wall: tàraba, ȍsēk, ȍsiēk, ȍsijēk, ȍsīk

fever: čȁmalica

few number of days until the end of one's military term:

síća
Fiat (a car make): frižìdēr
Fiat 124 (a car model): četvórka
Fiat 125 (a car model): pètica, vȅš-mašína
Fiat 128 (a car model): VȖPĪ
Fiat 125 PZ (a car model): péza, pezéjac
Fiat 125P (a car model): pégla, pȅpeljata
Fiat 125PZ (a car model): pèzēljka
Fiat 126P (a model of a simple Polish car): péglica, tȅtrapak
Fiat 1300 (a car model): trìstāć, tristènjāk, trìstnjāk
Fiat 750 (a car model): fíća, figúra, filip, filop, fíkus, pljúca
Fiat 850 sport (a car model): pȉklja
fidget: mȑdati
fidgeting: mȑdānje
fifteen: pètnaēs, pètnēs
fifteen hundred dinars: ždrébe
fifty dinar bill: gȕslārka, pètāk
fifty dinar coin: plȍča
fifty dinars (bill): Mȅštrović, péčak, pedesètača, petokolònāš, plàvnjika, skȕpština
fifty dinars; a fifty-dinar coin: pȍtkova
fifty joints of marijuana: lȉd
fifty-fifty, halfs: fifti-fifti
fig: fȉga
fig brandy: smòkovača
fight (e.g. fist fight): aplàuz, bàšanica, bàšta[1], baštánac, baštànija, bàštati se, cépati se, cepáža, cjépānje, cjepáža, čȍha, čȍhānje, dàngānje, dȁr-mȃr, dekívānje, dilkániti, dȗr-mȃr, džápati se, fȁjt, fáma, fȉrka, gédžānje, grȕdānje, gȗrka, jòčnjavatunj, kȅčēnje, klȁti se, kokàčina, kókānje, kókati se, kokáža, krèsānje, krkljánac, kȓpa, kȓpānje, kȓpati se, kȑviti se, kȑvljēnje, lȅš[2], lȕra, lúza, mȁklja, màkljānje, màkljati se, makljáža, mára, mȁrānje, maravȅla, mariȍla, marisàna, màrisānje, mlátiti se, pȉčānje, pȉčēnje, pičkáža, pȉčvajz, pȍčohati se, podževèljati se, podževèljisati se, polivàčina, polívati se, pomàrisati se, pȍšājbati se, pošórati se, prȁčkānje, prepucávānje, rȉbānje, rȉbati se, rókānje, rȕsvāj, šakètānje, šekètānje, šȉba, šibácija, šibàčina, šȉbānje, škȕda, škudírānje, šóra, šórati se, šȍrka, štéka, štȅma, šùtīrati se, šȕtka, tába, tàbati se, tabáža, tàmbura, tarapàna, ùbiti se, žvékānje
fight, argue: pičkàrati se
fighter: fàjter
fighting: bàštānje, lȅšēnje, polívānje, šibáža, štètnanje
fill up with gas: nàtankati, nàtankovati, tankáriti, tȁnkati, tȁnkovati
fill, stuff: fȕndati
filling (e.g. in a tooth): blȏmba
filling up with gas: tȁnkānje, tankárēnje
filter (in general): filter[1]
finally: mȃšalā
financial abuse: gréba
financial situation: lȍvostāj
find incidentally: ustréliti
find one's vein while inserting a drug needle: náći se
find oneself (in a situation, country, etc.): ȍbresti se
find out (usu. secret information): ìščačkati, iščepȑkati
find out, sniff out: pròsnifati, prošnjófati
find something highly humorous: kȇglati se, upišávati se
find, locate: nabàrtati, nadžàlisati, nàgaziti, okúpati, ùbosti, zàteći
finding solution: gȗrka
finding, discovery: bȉks[2]
fine arts academy in Belgrade, Serbia: Lìkiš
fine, nicely (e.g. dressed): fȉno
finger: bólao[2], drȕpavac, dȓpavac, gȅpavac, pápak[2], pípak
finger on the distributor head (auto body): finger
finger ring: àlka, kàrika, manžèta, manžètna, pèčat, pȑsnevāl
finished, completed: zàkrpāno
fire (command): ožèži, raspaméti
fire: cȑvēn[2], jaštàrica, kànājka, krȅna, pȁverica, žára
fire, shoot: raspáliti
first: nȃjprvō
first brandy (of a drinking session): prvénac
first coffee served to one's guests: dočèkuša
first sexual intercourse in one's life, one's first time: čàjānka
first time drug user: optalidónac
fish: bòluk, bùluk
fishing: ribȉčija[1]
fist: pégla
fitness (physical or psychological): kȍnda
five: pȇ, pètāk
five grams of any narcotic: pètica
five hundred dinars; a five hundred-dinar bill: intelektuálac, kȕrcšlus, zelèmbāć[2]
five hundred dinars; a five-hundred dinar bill: maslȉnjāk, pètāk, skȕpština, Tȅsla,
five-dinar coin: petògłavac
fixation: kȉks-idéja
fixed game: naméštāljka, sȉcer
fixing games: lažírānje
flag: bàjrāk, bàrjāk
flash (effect of narcotic drugs): flȅš
flashback: flȅš-bȅk
flat (e.g. tire): búšan
flat bottle (usu. filled with alcohol): plóska
flat female breast, pancake: lèpinja, palačínka[1], pljȏjka
flat Near Eastern bread: sòmūn
flat pliers: flȁhcānge, flȁhcāngle
flat-breasted female: dàcka, dàska, dàščara, lòpata, mètla[1]
flat-breasted male: tàraba
flatly: lȃdno
flea (the insect): bȕvos, mòrica, mòriza
flea market: bùvljāk
flight, running away: bežànija
flip over (a box, etc.): pretùmbati
flip over: pretùmbati se
flirt: àšikovati, bàcati se, flȅrt, flȅrtovati, hofírati, kìbicovati se, krátiti, kȕhati, kȕvati, mòtati, mútiti, mȕvati, mȕvati se,

nabáciti, naštimávati, odvájati, odvòjiti, pilotírati, štȁrtati, štȉmati [1], tròvati, tȑzati, ukrcávati se, utrčávati, vaćáriti, zàgrīsti

flirt without going too far: muváriti

flirt, throw oneself at: nabáciti se, nabacívati se

flirting: ašìkluk, flȅrtovānje, hofírānje, kȕhānje, kȕrokrēt, lȉra, lȉrika, mȕvānje, nabacȉnđel, nabacóka [1], nabacívānje, štȁrt, štȁrtānje, štȉmānje, švalerácija, švalèrānje, švalèrisānje, tròvānje, tȑzānje, ukrcávānje, vatárac

flirting etiquette: kȕhār [2]

flirting male: štȁrter

flour: rùmija

flour brandy: brȁšnjevača

flow: pljȕskati, pròtek

flower: cvît

flower garden: albȁšča

flowers: drâč, péršin

flute: ćȕrlika, svìrājka, svìrala

fly (the insect): mȕa

fly away: odlepȑšati

fly dirt, fly shit: muvosèrina

fly in: ulèćeti

fly out: ulèćeti

flyer, leaflet: flájer

flywheel: šȕngrād

fold, bend: presamítiti

folk (pertaining to the style of music): fȍlk [2]

folk or country music: dȑnka, dȑnka-dȑnka, drȕka-drȕka, fȍlk [1], ljȉga [1], rȍdnā

folk, country: nárockī, naròdnjāčkī, národskī

follow, tail: špȇhati, špȉclati

follower of Aleksandar Ranković (a hard-line communist politician in the former Yugoslavia): ránkovićevac

follower of Ustashi (Croatian nazi) ideology: ustašòīd

food: ánež, ánjež, ápa [1], hála [1], hàliška, hàlka, hàlūng, háma, hápa, hȁs, hȁsa, hranàrina, hȑda, jȅstīvo, klópa, klopánac, klopánjac, kràstacka, kràstačka, mándža, mùva, njúpa, njupàluk, pánja, pápa [2], pȁpica, pȁšica, ždêr, ždéra, ždèrača, ždrȁka

food bowl: vèdež

food ration: fàsūnga

food server in prison: lȉmār

fool: smȑklje

foolish: cvȑknūt, čvȃknūt, slàvkobe

foolish child: dèkrēt

foolish female: čȉvurica, dilbèruša, karánfilka, kȍkōš, kòkōška, lùduša, lȕcprda, lùjika, lûjka, pèčūrka, pȑdara, surdùljuša, šȁmšula, šȉbadžīka, šizbláza, škȑplja, šólja [1], šušùmiga

foolish female, turkey: ćȕrka

foot: gȉlja [1], kòpito, làbus, pápak [2]

footstool: šȁmlica

for heaven's sake: pȍbogu [2]

for special occasions: stòēćī

force oneself in: ùmuvati se

force oneself on somebody: ubàštrati se, ufúrati se, ufurávati se

force, coerce: nàrenjkati

force, power, strength: dzôr

force-feed poultry by inserting food into their beak: šȍpati

forcing oneself on somebody: uletávānje

foreboding: špûrijus, šȕha, šȕhva, šuhvèli

forehead: rȍgovi, vȁnta

foreign currency: màjmun [2]

foreign tourist who sells crystal ware: krìstāl, krìstāl-tùrist

foreign tourist without any money: maràbunt, maràhunt, paradȁjz

foreskin: kožúrica, màntl, rôlka

forever: nȁvēk

forfeited object: lȁžnjāk

forger: šȍškār

forgery: jàfina

forget about: mánuti

forgive, pardon: aláliti, haláliti

forgiveness: àlāl [1], hàlāl [2]

fork: vèslo

formal: ùštogljen

formally dressed male: uštirkánko

former Croatian Communist Party Central Committee building: kapèlica

former Croatian Communist Party Central Committee building, Zagreb, Croatia: kȍcka

former Opera bar in Zagreb, Croatia: triperȉška

former student dormitory on Tvrtko street in Zagreb, Croatia: Bijȁfra [1]

former train from Zagreb to Samobor, Croatia: péglica

former virgin: pròbušenā, strȅlovānā

former workers' community center in Zagreb known for its dance parties: kùhača

former Yugo export company store (Zagreb, Croatia): Jȕgić

former Yugoslavia: Srboslâvija

fortune-teller: bȃjalica

forty: četères, čȅtrēs

forty year old female: fircigerica

forty year old male: firciger

four: čètir, čȅtri, čvȑka

fragile, sensitive: kȑht

franc (French currency unit): fáronja, fránja

fraudulent, counterfeit: fôl [3]

free items or services: džabàlučina

free kick: slobòdnjāk

free time: dòkonōst

free, gratis: badàva, badàvad, bȁmbadàva, bȁnbadàva, dž, džə, džȁba, džabáka, džabalèskū, džabàli, džȁbē, đȁbē, frȁj, mȕftē, mùktatos, mùktē, vȋdno, zabadàva

freedom: rȃj

freeze: skočánjiti se, skopízditi se, ufrekéstiti, ufrekéstiti se

freight car: mèdvjed

freight train: mèdvjed

French: francùzljiv, vràncūskī
French kiss: krljáviti
Frenchman: fràncek
frequent changes of one's sexual partners: kurvànjluk, kurvàrluk
frequent visitor, regular: invèntār
fresh: frèšak, táze
fridge, refrigerator: frȉgos
friend (esp. from the military), buddy: bórac
friend (female): frendica, haverica, ortakinja, stara
friend (male): àrap, ȁver, bája[1], bȁja[2], bâle[1], bàtan, bȕrāz[1], burázer, cȁr, drùgār[1], drùškan, frȅnd, frȅndāć, frȅndić, frȅntāč, hȁver, jàrān, jarànika, járo, jòristanj, kalàuz[1], kàrdāš, kȍmpa, kȍmpić, óraō, orlùšina, òrtāk, pàjdāš, pájdo, pȁjt, pàjtāš, pȁjtos, pâle, plivàdōn, prȉka[1], pùlēn, rȉsta, rȍđāk, róđo[1], stârī
friendly: jàrānskī
friendly barkeeper: čȁrdāš
friendship: jaránstvo
frighten, scare: ìseći, ìstrzati, uzortírati se, zaluđívati
frightened: ùhvaćen, ukàrgoljen, ùkēnjān
frigid female: frižìdērka, pìjanā, prâznā
frigid male: mehàničār
frigidly: hlâdno
from above: òzgō
from anywhere: ȉoklē, ȉoklēn, ȉotklē, ȉotklēn
from behind: zgûza
from below: òzdō
from here: ȍdovlē, ȍdovlēk, ȍdovlēn
from nowhere: nȉoklē
from there: ȍtālē, ȍtolē
from time to time: đèkad
from where: ȁokle, ȍklē, ȍklēn
front end of a wagon: gùzērka
front side (knitting): klȍt
fruit: àlkica, ánalica
fruit juice: bebìrōn, berbijáner
fruitful, bountiful: berìćetan, birìćetan
fruitfully: berìćetno
fry: čvȁriti, frȉgati
fuel: ògrjev
fugitive, runaway: avijàtičār, gìljer
full (of food), stuffed: nàhanovān
full of ideas: nàpumpān
full, packed: fȕl
fun: dumbarȅska, fȁn, gíbalica, nȁpētō, pišijáda, prdàčina, rasturàčina, rilètne, ružióna, šéga, šȅm, šéma, tùlum, zajebàncija, zȅzalica, zezàncija
function, operate: funkcionànisati
function, work well: páliti
funeral: dženáza, đenáza, glúma, jȅcānje, rôvac[2], sȁrana
funny: idìotskī, kȑvav, kȑviš, mȍćan, mŕtav[2], štosòvit
funny event: kíno
funny female: kràljica
funny male: krâlj
fur: bùndara
fur coat: kr̀znènjāk
fur jacket: gûnj, mȕfter, tiritnjâk
furious, livid: bésan
furniture: tišlèrāj
furrier: ćùrčija
fuse: zȉherūng
futile discussion: dȓkalica
gadget (any device considered to be unnecessary or of low quality): blèsimetar, blèsometar
gadget: drangùlija, mašína
gain weight: búciti se, bȕcnuti se, natòviti se, pòpraviti se, ubúciti se
gallant: aȉgdžija
gamble: dȕgati se, ljúštiti, pȉljkati, rȁtovati
gamble on the street using matchboxes: šibicáriti
gambler: kóca, kȍcoš, šȁtrovac, špíler
gambler or lottery player who uses systems in playing: sistèmāš
gambling (with cards): kùhčānje
gambling: cȃrka, lȁbūd[2], rȁtovānje
gambling loss: bȕla, mùfljūz[2]
gambling place: komoràna
game: tandŕčak, tandȑček, trȁkavica
game based on hitting each other into stomach: móša
game of cards: partája
game of chess: guràčina
game of dancing to punk rock and kicking each other: šȕtka
game of guessing numbers on currency bills: šlága
game of speed chess: cȕgerica
game with collector's cards where one tries to flip over a card: tȁpka[1]
gang (criminal group): bânda, mâfija
gang leader: gȁzda, glàvnī[2]
gang, group of one's close friends: drùžina, ekípa, klȁpa, kompànija, kumpànija, rája, žȉnadru
gap measuring plates: cèntipleh, čȅšalj[2], špìjūn, špȉōn
garage: ȁmbār, kèrna, kònjara, štȁla
garbage: džȕba
garbage can: đubrijéra
garbage container: hàjfiš
garbage man: bȑljos, džȕbār, džȕber, dȕbos, đȕbos, kȅšbōj
garden (vegetable, flower, etc.): bȁšča, bȁšća
garden: gȃj, žȁrdīn
gardener: Bȕgar, komárac
garlic: lȁul
garment: kȍža
garment, suit: pȇrje
gas station worker: tànkāroš
gas tank: rȅzervār, tȁnk
gasket: dȉhtūng
gasoline: čórba, júha, zȉnbu

gasp: húkati

gathering place (for a group of people): báza

gathering place: kamenòlom

gathering place for drug addicts: ȁerodrom

gathering place for prostitutes: štȃjg

gear stick: šȁlthēbl

gearbox: getrîba

general: đenèrāl, gȅne [2], géša, gláva

generation: klàsa

genius: čȉnjenica, čȉnjenica, genijálac, genitálac, géša

genius, extraordinary: jèziv

gentian root brandy: lìncura

Gentile, Goy: gôj, gója

gentleman: bádža, balavnȉška, čkávac, efȅndija, génja, gòlēmča, gòlēmša, mânča, mȁnče, mànukot, sȉvor, šûmnjāk, trònjār

geography (as a science course): gègiš

geometry teacher (female): cȑtānka

geometry teacher (male): crtánko

German (female), Kraut: Švàbica

German (male), Kraut: Germánac, Kòtara, Nèmčuga, Šîljko, Švába, Švábo, Švȃbos, Švàbōv, Švàpčanin

German (pertaining to a person), Kraut: švȁpskī

German mark: dȍjčmàrka, kèrma, màrōn, màrulja

Germany: Alemànja, Dòjčland, filatèlija, Švâbija

get a failing grade, flunk: cȍcnuti

get a girlfriend: magnètisati, obáriti, odvòjiti, ukròtiti, zbáriti

get a haircut: šȉšnuti se, štȑgati se

get a promotion: àvanzovati

get acquainted with (job, task, etc.): nàkačiti se

get agitated: čápati se

get ample new things: òkrpiti se

get an education: òbūći se

get angry: fȕljiti se, fȕriti se, gȉftati se, nàdrkati se, njȕpati se, odlèteti, pȉgati se, podilèjisati, popízdeti, pròkuvati, pȕknuti [1], pùrnjati, raskòpati, ràznjupati, štȃjgati

get angry, burn: raspáliti se

get angry, foam at the mouth: zàpeniti

get arrested for dealing drugs, get busted for dealing: pȃsti [1]

get arrested, get busted: kvéknuti, lèći, pȃsti [1], rîknuti, vrísnuti, zagláviti

get back from prison: rastírati

get by begging: ispéziti

get close to a female in a crowd: zàkitati, zakitávati

get close to somebody (physically or emotionally): prìšiti se

get close to somebody: prìkrpiti se

get confused: gùbiti se, izgùbiti se, sàjlovati se

get contusions (usu. from falling down): ugrúhati se, ugrúvati se

get dark, approach evening: smortírati, snȅkiti se

get dressed: drȅsovati (se)

get drunk: karmìnisati se, lȅšiti se, nacícati se, nacépiti se, nacìrisati se, nàcirkati se, nacíriti se, nàcuclati se, nàcugati se, nacvŕcati se, nàcvrckati se, naćeflèisati se, nadéviti se, nàdrgljati se, nàdrilovati se, nàdrinkati se, nàdrmati se, nadžibràniti se, nadžókati se, nàfȃjtati se, nafrùlati se, nagrànisati se, nakarmìnisati se, nàkititi se, nàkljucati se, nakókati se, nàkresati se, nàlirkati se, nàliti se, nalîlati se, nàlokati se, nalòkmačiti se, nalízati se, naljóskati se, naljúljati se, nàpljugati se, narókati se, naróljati se, nàseći se, nasekìrati se, nàsipati se, nàsisati se, nàsjeći se, nàsvitkati se, nasvírati se, našíkati se, našljémati se, našljókati se, nàšmīnkati se, našprícati se, nàšvasati se, nàtankati se, natòčiti se, natréskati se, nàtrēsti se, nàtrgati se, navózati se, nažljókati se, nažvákati se, nàžvaliti se, oblíjati se, odžàkati se, oljóskati se, osokòliti se, òtēti se, òtimati se, oždrljékati se, pȃtiti, patosírati se, potrȍšiti se, pòvūći, prètitrovati se, ráditi se, skȍckati se, skȑšiti se, šljȅmati, šljókati, šmînkati se, tetùrati se, ucíriti se, ùcirkati se, ukóčiti se, ùletviti se, ùlēvčiti se, ùliti se, ùmȓkati se, urókati se, uróljati se, ušíkati se, ùšljiskati se, ušljókati se, ùšutati se, ùtiti se, uvòštiti se, vózati se, zàliti se, zarakìjati se, zèmljosati

get drunk, get messed up: unerédìti se

get drunk, get pickled: bàlsamovati se, mumificírati se, ùlešiti se

get drunk, get plastered: zabetonírati se

get drunk, get smashed: sàstaviti

get drunk, get toasted: báriti se, nabáriti se

get excited, get turned on: rȃjcati se

get favorable opinion about somebody: protretírati

get for free: očȅšati se, ogrèbati se, ògrepsti se

get formally dressed, dress up: nàkititi se

get frightened, get scared: cvȉkati, lȅcnuti se, iséći se, plàskosati, plàkosatise, prèseći se, strêsti se, štrȅcnuti se, ùsrati se, stȉsnuti se, ùfrikovati, ustrtáriti se, ušórati se, utróljati se, utrónjati se, uzèntovati se, ùzentati se, ùcvikati

get in, enter: ufúrati, ulàufati se

get information: prokljúviti

get injured: skȑšiti se

get interested: popáliti se, potpáliti se, strȉgati, zàgrȉsti

get into problems: usósiti se, uváliti se

get intoxicated on narcotic drugs, get high: ustondírati se

get lost: otperjášiti, otpèrjati

get mad: nàdȓndati se

get married, get hitched: burmànisati se, diplomírati, manùčati se, mèridžovati se, òbjesiti se, omànučiti se, òtrēmčiti, òtrēmčiti se, ugajbírati se, ùknjižiti, urámiti

get money: kȃpati, ùbiti

get nervous: iséći se, klókati se, klópati se, nàdrkati se, nàdȓndati se, òsūti se, pjȅniti se, pòjesti se, poklópati se, ràspucati se, šíziti, unervóziti se, vatrírati, ždèrati se, živcírati se

get nervous, wory: nasekìrati se

get nothing, come up empty: ìzvisiti

get off somebody's back: sjȃhati

get out, leave: izàlaziti, izgiljáriti, izlèteti, izlètjeti, izljèći

get pregnant, get knocked up: kotùrati, napúpeti, zagláviti, zàkačiti, zakéviti

get ready: hazùrala, nàluzati

get removed from political life: zglàjzati, zglȃjznuti

get rest: kulírati

get rich quickly: dȓmnuti

get rid of: amputírati, kotàrisati se, kurtàlisati, kurtàlisati se, kutàrisati se, odsmȑditi, òtkačiti se, òtkinuti se, raskȑstiti, ratosìljati se, torpedírati

get rid of, do away with: alásiti se

get rid of, dump: rijéšiti se

get scared, get frightened: gȑčiti se, paranòisati, pȑpisati, trêsti se, ukargóniti, ukargóniti se, ukénjati se

get scared, turn white: pobéleti

get sexually aroused, get hot: páliti se, rȁjcati se

get some kind of profit: uvaćáriti

get some rest: plȁndovati

get something: kȍžnuti se

get something from somebody: ìzboksati

get stronger: zapìzdati

get tired: kljȍknuti, knòriti, lìpsati, rȉtimor se

get tired, exhausted (from work, sports, etc.): cȓknuti

get upset: páliti se, raspízditi, šíziti

get used to (usu. something unpleasant): ogùglati

get used to: naùčiti, òbiknuti

get very angry: potrízdeti

get very drunk, get dead drunk: odùzēti se, ràsturiti se, ùbiti se

get very drunk, get plastered: betonírati, betonírati se, pobrljáviti, ubetonírati se

get very drunk, get smashed: komírati se, nȁfistati se, prècirkati se, ràzbiti se, razváliti se, slòžiti se, urésiti se, zasúkati, zèmljosati se

get very drunk, tie one on: zavézati

get very ill: zarȉbati

get very tired: prèsvisnuti, ríknuti

get visibly older: zbȁbiti se

get worse: òfaliti, otánjiti, uzjèbati se

get, obtain: kožùrati se, zbȍksati

get, obtain: ispláćiti istrkèljati, iškòjiti se, izdrkèljati, izdrkèljisati, izmùntati, izmunđáriti, nabáciti, nabàrtati, obráditi, pòkupiti, sínuti, ubȁštrati, ùbosti, ùvatiti

ghost: plȃhta, prȉkaza, stȗa, zdȗvāč

giant: òrijāš [1]

gift, present: pèškeš

giggle: hȉhot, hihòtati se, hȍhot, hohòtati, hohòtati se

giggling: hihòtānje, hohòtānje, hohòtav

girl: pìšulja

girl's: cȕrskī

girl's dormitory: kokòšārnīk

girlfriend: dèfōjka, dèvōjka, djèvōjka, jòrastanj, kùlōvka, kȍp [1], prìkolica, švàlērka, rȁstā

give a haircut: lȉndrati, òstrići, strȉgati

give a very short haircut: òlīndrati

give away: pòsijati

give birth, have a baby: ispízditi, otórbiti

give cigarettes: duvániti

give flowers: kȉtovati

give money: ìsplaziti se, ìspljunuti, podváliti

give somebody a hard time: usósiti

give something unwanted: ùtrapiti

give, pass: dèlisati, nagúrati, štítiti, tȉnjati, tinjávati, tròšiti

glance: škȉcnuti

glass (in general): càklo, guràćica

glass container for liquids, demijohn: demìdžana, demìjuna

glass eye: staklénac [2]

glass marble (the toy): staklénac [2]

gloomy: nȅgatīvan

gloomy person: dàrker, mȑgūd, tȑkāč, zaguljénko

glove: futróla, pípak

glue sniffer: ljȅpkomān

gnash (one's teeth in outrage): škrobòtati

gnashing (of one's teeth in outrage): škrȍbot, škrobòtānje

go (in all its Serbo-Croatian meanings in the form different from the standard one): ȍdīm

go along, accompany: šlȅpati se

go astray (usu. of a ball): fȅlšati

go away, leave: ìspariti (se), odlepȑšati, òtplivati, otpȑhnuti, razvijátiti

go broke (financially): obèspariti, tònuti

go for a quick ride: pròšājbati

go insane, freak out: brljáviti, budàliti, dilkániti, géknuti, histèrisati, histerizírati, ispízditi, ìzdrkati se, kȉknuti, kípiti, manìtati, odlépiti, òtkinuti, pobenáviti, pobrljáviti, pobudàliti, podilèjisati, podilkániti, pomahnítati, popingvíniti, popízdeti, popízditi, pošandŕcati, pošašáviti, pošljàjzditi, pošízeti, pošíziti, prodilèjisati, prolúpati, prošvírati, pȕći, pízdeti, skrénuti, šénuti, šȉznuti, šlagírati se, šíziti, unezvériti se, vatrírati

go out: izgìljati, izvijátiti

go out, leave: isfùljati, isfúrati, ìsplaziti

go somewhere: nàpasti

go through: pròknjižiti

go to get or buy something: skȍknuti

go, be directed to: glàvati

goal (in soccer, water polo, etc.): brȃnka, gȃjba, gȏ

goat (the animal): ckȁmnī [2], lèšac

gobble (of a turkey): pȕćkati

gobble: pùćpura, pȕćpulik, pućpuríkati, pȕćpuruć, pȕćpuruka

gobbling: pućpuríkānje

God: érić [1]

God almighty: jȁlla

God save us, heaven help us: hȁša [1]

godfather (with whom both child and parents stay in a very close relationship all their lives): kûm

godfather: kûm

godmother (with whom both child and parents stay in a very close relationship all their lives): kúma

going insane, freaking out: aproksimȃlis, ȁut [1], frȉkaut, izlapètis, izlapìtis

going out (to a restaurant, movies, etc.): úpad

gold: lȍt, žȕtica, žûtō

gold coin: gàlban, gàlzīn, pìlāvka, žarènīk, žárēnje, žȃrnīk,

žùtan
gold tooth: zlâtnjāk
golden or silver chain: jùlār
golden religious objects stolen from a church: panàjlija
goldsmith's: žìntara , žùntara, žùtara
gonorrhea, the clap: čîr, fràncūz, gnójac, kàpac, kapávko, kȁpica, mùzika, pûtnīk, rijàna, sȕza, šȁtri, šȍtrī, tràjana, trijána, trijáner, trìlīng, trȉper, tríša, tríšo
good: mástan, šȕman
good and highly professional policeman: pandùrčina
good and loved male: cȁr, dobrotánović, gotívac
good and loved person: hlȅb, kȕro-mȕro, lȅb [1], lûd [1] mâjka
good behavior, moral behavior: àhlak
good deed: sèvāp
good feeling induced by narcotic drug effect, high: džȁmpȁp
good friend: lȁf [1], làfčina, lêpī [1]
good idea: bȉser [1], pȉvāk, štôs [2], vȁška
good joke: gȁf, pȉvāk
good looking male, hunk: flȉt
good luck, lucky strike, run of luck: alavȉja, birìćet
good mood: hâj [2]
good move: kâjla
good news: dragȉčka, muštùluk
good playing card: dújo
good, cool: kȑvav, patètičan
good, neat: àpsik, bȁrdo
good, neat, cool: mŕtav [2], pánja, rȅn [2]
good, of high quality: jâk
good, of high quality or skill, fat: másan
gopher: mȑmot
gossip, wag the tongue: kȑpiti, opanjkávati, pakírati, trȁč, trȁčati, tȑnbiti, tròvati
gossiper: tràčara
gossiping: naméštānje
gossipy: trȁčerskī
government representative: mùljtesta
grab, snatch: ćȁpiti, ćȍpiti, fȑknuti, šapírati, šćèpati, šćȁpiti, zèriti
grade (in school): ȍcvancovati
grade C: kánta, trȉca
grade D: búger
graduating university student: ȁpsić
grand-daughter: unučȉnja
grandfather, grandpa: bákac, dédo, déka [1], dekúta, dekutáner, đȅd, đȅt, kévac, kljákac, nôno
grandmother, grandma: bȁku, bàkuta, bakùtān, bakutáner, jòkabanj, nána, néna, nôna
grape brandy: grózda, grȍzdovača, kòmovača, kòmovica, lóza, lòzovača, târča, tàrdža, trádža
grass (the plant): grâs, jàrba
gratuity, tip: trìngeld
grave: mèzār, parcȅla, vìkendica
gravel, pebbles: píljak, šóder [2]

greasy food: smȍk
great: hȁos [4]
great-grandfather: pràđed
greatness: strahobálnōst, straobálnōst
greedy (food, money, etc.): ȁlav, màgnēt
greedy female (for food, money, etc.): ȁlavica, gùzička, gùzna, gùzulja, gùzuljica, gùzuljičica, tròsisa
greedy male (for food, money, etc.): ȁlavac, dupèško
greedy, voracious (of food, money, etc.): gùzat
Greek (person): Gȅrkos, Gȑkljan
green peas: brȅmze
greet each other: haláliti
greeting: klȉmoglāv
grey: pȉdimiš
grief: dȅrt
grimace, make faces (to entertain others): áčiti se
grimace, make faces (usu. in pain): izbéčiti se
grimace, make faces to entertain or mock: béčiti se, bekéljiti se, benáviti se
grimacer: kèfaćo
grin: cêr, cerèkati se, kèceriti se, kês, kèseriti se, klíberiti se, nacériti se
grinding machine: frézer
grip (worker who pushes TV camera): gȕrman
grocery store: bàkālnica, grànap, pȍsluga, sàmiš, sàmiška
groggy: grȍgī
groin, crotch: mȅđunōžje
groschen (the coin): pàljār, pȍljār, pȍp
gross thing or situation: ogávština
gross, nasty: ȍgāvan
group beating: rédāljka
group leader: órаō, orlùšina
group of females: pìletina
group of masturbators: čaplajàna, čàplājna
group of rowdies, gang of troublemakers: liskàna
group of small children: klinčàdija
group of teenagers: klinčàdija
group sex: grȕpić, grùpnjāk, kòncert, màsōvka, palačínke, rédalica, redáljak, rédāljka, rèdiška, sèksilīšte, zbrájalica, ZȄT
grow: kùratiti
growl (of animal, engine, etc.): vȑčati
growl (of an animal): rȅgnuti, réžati
growling (a symptom of a malfunction): réžānje
growling (of an animal): réžānje
grumble, mumble: ròndati
grunt (of an animal): rȍkot, ròktati
grunting (of an animal): ròktānje
grunty (of an animal): rȍktav, rȍktavo
guard, watchman: čúkac, kȕrjāk [2]
guerilla warfare: šȕma [2]
guess: ovàrisati, ubádati
guess correctly: ùbosti

guest worker: cŕnac, delègāt, gastarbàjter, gastarbàjterka, gȁster, gȁstić, gȁstos

guest worker's: gastarbàjterskī

guide: kalàuz [1]

guilty: gȑbav

guitar: đȉtra

Gulag (concentration camp for the oponents of the communist regime): gȕlāg

gun, pistol: gȁn, garàbīn, kljûn [2], kùbura, kùmbura, lȕnta, prȁčka, prȁngija

gun, pistol: ùtok, ȕtoka

gunpowder: žárac

gunshot: grûvanj

gurgle (creek, etc.): bȑbot, brbòtānje, brbòtati, brbùkati, brbùtati, gòlgolj, golgòljiti, gòlgot, golgòtati, gȑglati, gȑgljati, gȑgolj, grgòljēnje, grgòljiti, gȑgor, grgòrēnje, gȑgot, grgòtānje, grgòtati, gȑgūt, grgùtānje, grgùtati, grgòriti, klokȉnjati, klȍkot, klokòtati, mȑmor, mȑmoriti, mȑmositi, mrmòtati, pljȕskati, ròmoriti, žubòriti

gurgling (creek, etc.): brbùkānje, brbòtav, glògotānje, gȑgljānje, grgòljav, grgòljiv, gȑgoran, grgùtav, grgùtavo, klokòtānje, klokòtav, mrmòrav, mȑmorēnje, žȕbor, žȕbōran, žubòrav, žubòrēnje

gurgling:

gutter: okolokȕćnīpìšātor

gym: bilderàna, teretàna

gynecologist: mòntēr, picomehàničār

Gypsy (female): kalàštura

Gypsy (male): Afrikánac, cíga, cígo, cigòjner, cîgoš, Firàun, Fȉrga, Fȉrgoš, Gȁnci, Gàncimetar, garàvān, gùrbet, Indijánac, Indíjac, kalafónac, kâr [1], lȁcī [1], màndōv, ròmīć, ròmiška, Ȕglješa

Gypsy child: Ròmče

habit of taking too many pills: tabletomànija

habitual casual dresser: džempèrāš

hadj (pilgrimage to the Muslim holy city of Mecca): hȁdž

hah: hȍ

hair: čȕpa, kosijána, kosijáner [2], kòsīnger, lâsi, mètla [1], strȕna, šȕma [2], vegetácija, vunȉca

hair on the head: flóra, grȉva

haircut: frîz, kùtija, lȉndrānje, zûrka

hairdresser: šȉšātor

hairdresser's: frizèrāj

hairless masculine breast: linolèum

hairs (on one's body): rȕnja

hairsplitter, nit picker: cèpidlaka, karaušljívko, picàjzla, pízda, šíber [1], šȉbađija, vȁška

hairsplitting, nitpicking: cèpidlačkī

hairstyle: skȁlp

hairy: rȕnjav

hairy male: čèkinjos, kosmonàut, mȅsečār

hairy male, hairy ape: bȕsēn

hairy masculine chest: tapisèrija

hairy musician: dugolásec

hairy person, ape: čȕpa

half axle: àlbaksa, hàlbaksa

half eaten crescent (roll): òjebina

half gram of narcotic drugs: lȕtka, pȍlutka

half liter of water served with wine: hàuzmājstor

half-court basketball: hàkl

half-dead: cîknūt

half-dinar coin: pòlīć, pôlka

halleluia: halelúja

halves, splitting costs: dèljāk

ham: šûmka

ham and eggs: kemèndeks

hamburger: pljêsak

hamburger joint: hamburgèrāj, hamburgèrija, hàmburgernica

hammer (the tool): čȕkalica, ćȍkle, hȁmer, skȅrak

hand: bȁnalica, dŕpalica, fȁtalo, gȅpavac, gȅpavica, gràbulja, hȁpavica, hvȁtalo, kȍska, lèvača, òpadnica, pècāljka, petája, rȅpavica, rèpevica, šápa, šljȁpavica

hand ball (in soccer): ȅnac

hand gas: štȁngās

hand grenade with spoon-shaped pin: kašȉkara

handball (an European ball game similar to soccer, but played in arenas and the ball is thrown by hand, not kicked): rȕkoš

handcuffs, bracelet: nárukvice

handcuffs, cuffs: amerȉkanke, bukágije, cvànciger, gvôžđa, gvôžđe, lijàne, spȁnjga, spȁnjka

handicapped: kljȁkav

handicapped child: rȉkverc [1]

handicapped male, cripple: kljáko

handicapped person, cripple: jȍker, kljáka, sakatája, sakàtija

handle police investigators with dignity: ùkūrčiti se

handsome and strong: zmȁj [2]

handsome male, hunk: avijàtičār, dèlija, gotȉvnjāk, gotívac, mȁče [1]

handsome, cute: càkan, hìbrīdan, jâk, pȉvāk, sȅća, šȅsan, šȅstan

handwriting: šȁkopīs

hang off anything: kȅšati se

hang off the outside of a streetcar: kȅšati se

hang up one's coat: òkačiti se

hanger (for clothes): àufīnger, vjèštalica

hangover: flȅka, mahmùrluk, mamùrluk, mutavȅla

haphazardly, by pure luck: blȉnd

happen (used usu. when two or several things coincide): pòtrefiti se, zalòmiti se

happen, occur: ìći, pasírati, pasírati se, strȅfiti se

happily: haìrli, srȅčno

happiness: hȁir

happy: hȅpī, nȁsmijān, srȉtan

happy ending (of a movie, etc.): hȅndikep

happy female: vesèlica

hard (of liquor): konkrȅtno, žèstok

hard liquor: destȉlāt, ȍštrō, žȅsta, žestȉna

hard times: bèdāk [2]

hard to learn: tvrdòuk

hard work: ràbota

hard worker: ȓmbalija

hard, with difficulties: kȍnjskī, kȓvavo [1]

hard-currency bank account: devìznjāk

hard-soled shoe: bàkāndža, còkula, gòjzerica

hard-working person: cŕnac

hardened criminal: bája [1], bȃja [2], dȅčko [2]

hardly any success: ȉdva

harm: tòčiti

harm, damage: škàliti

harsh female, bitch: šȕšmula

harsh play (in soccer): kr̀ljānje

harsh soccer player: kr̀ljāč

harvest jèmatva

hashish consumer, hash head: hȇp

hashish oil, hash oil: móča, mȕča

hashish or marijuana: dúvānje, dûvka

hashish pipe, hash pipe: čȉlām, lȕlos, lúša, pȁjp

hashish, hash: gàndža, gnâs, gȍvo, hádža, hȁkī, hȁkslī, hâle, hȁš [1], háša [2], indíjac, kȉf, libánac, libanónac, marokánac, nepálac, ókca, pakistánac, pkȉca, pȍt, stȁf, tràfka, tráva, tùrčin [2]

hat: glàntāš, gláva, hȅt, kȁhlica, klòbūk, krôv, lònac, naglàvān, šérpa, škàrnicl

hat trick (three goals scored by one player during one game of soccer): hètrik

hate, despise: negatíviti

hated: hȁhoćūdan

hated elderly female: babùrina, babùskara, babùskera

hated female, witch: kȓmača

hated male, sob: hȍpsasā

hating Serbs: sr̄boždēran, sr̄boždērskī

hatred: mȑz

have a bad time: ugásiti, zvȉsiti

have a dispute: kȁčiti se

have a drink (of alcohol): zàliti

have a good time: raspamétiti se

have a great time (usu. while drinking alcohol): probekrìjati

have a hard time, experience difficulties: gȑčiti se, istèliti se, izàpatiti, izàpatiti se, iskiláviti se, iznàpatiti (se), lomòtati se, nagúziti, nàtūći, ȍkoziti se, tèliti se, zaglíbiti se

have a hard time, struggle:

have a name, be called: víkati se

have a quick snack: čalabŕcnuti

have a slight ache: bolùckati

have a steady job: ìmati, proizvòditi

have an additional job, moonlight: tezgàrati, tezgáriti

have an argument: kȅckati se, popičkàrati se, ràspičkati se

have an erection: ukukurúziti se

have an idea: naùmpasti

have an orgasm: orgànizovati se

have bigger testicles: mùdatiti

have enough of, be sick and tired of: dodìjati, dopízdeti, dopízditi, dopížđeti, dozlogŕditi, zgustírati se

have false expectations, just think: ùtripovati

have fear: pŕpiti, unóšiti se, zȅntovati se

have fun: rúžiti, zaglíbiti, zalòmiti, zékiti se, zȅzati se

have fun downtown: profúrati

have one's check paid by others: grèbati se

have one's fill of food: nahàlisati se, nàhamati se

have one's fill of food, be stuffed: nahàsati se, nàkljukati se, nàšōdrati se

have one's fill of glue-sniffing: nadúvati se

have one's fill of hashish: nadúvati se

have one's fill of sex: ìspucati se, ìstrēsti se, istròšiti se, najèbati se

have one's fill of something: izgustírati se, krikènjati, svŕšiti

have one's period: dòbiti

have one's photo taken: prȉslopiti se

have problems: zàpēti

have problems with: jèbati se

have profit, gain: ućáriti

have prolonged sexual intercourse with: gùslati

have quick sexual intercourse, have a quickie: skarabúdžiti, šȉšnuti

have respect for: bèndati, kònstatovati

have sexual foreplay, pet, feel up: drápati se

have sexual intercourse with: bȁpnuti

have syphilis, have the pox: ucr̀vati se

have, posses: cȁnjati, gájiti, gotíviti, kȁmiti, kȁmsovati, kániti, kénjati, kèvati, rȉgati, sìjati, sínuti

having a hangover: mȁmūran

having a large penis: kùrat

having a large vagina: pìčat

having a pointed penis: šiljòkur [2]

having contusions (usu. from falling down), black and blue: ùgrūhān, ȕgrūvān

having difficulties in expressing oneself: tȕc-mȕc [2]

having difficulties in seeing: ćȍrav

having excessive make-up: màskīrān, nàcrtān

having large breasts, busty: sìsat

having large buttocks: gȕzas, gȕzast, gùzat, gùzičas, gùzičast, krivòguz

having large testicles: mùdat

having long legs and arms: kràkat

having make-up on, painted: mȍlovān

having pointed buttocks: šiljòguz

having the intention to: náuman

having too many disadvantages: šùpljikàvo

having untidy clothing: dȓljav

having white buttocks: bjelòguz [2]

hay: àvtuga

he: ûn

head: atmosféra, brúnda, bȕća, budàla, bùklija, búlja [1], bùljāk, čèlēnka, čèlo, ćónta, ćòntara, ćùtura, ćȁbu, ćȉverica, ćónta, ćȕpa, fȕlja, fànfara, fàntara, glàvir, glàvudža, glàvūrda, glàvuša, hȑga, kánja, kèfalo, kȉštra, kòfa, krába, kȑstačòja, krstačȍjna, kupùsara[1], kùtija, lámpa, lùdara, lùdura, lònac, lubènica, mùćūrla, mùđūrla, mèljara, mȅrica, mȉslilo, mlȉn, mȍzak, njùškara, pȅpeljata, pȉksa, pȉnta, pljèskara, pljùskara, râdio, slȁmarica, šȃfla, tèpsija, tȉkva[1], tìkvanja, tìkvara, tìntara, tȉntolōvka, tùtanja, vȁgla, vȁnta, vùdžagla, vȕgla, zjàkara

head of a penis: pèčūrka

head of cattle: guvèdo, marvínče

head, pumpkin: bùndeva

headquarters officer: štȃbovac

heads (of a coin): gláva

heads or tails (of a coin): písmo-gláva

heal: vȉdati

healer, one who practices non-conventional medicine: alternatívac, vȉdār

healthy boy: vitamìndžija, vitamínac

hear: uhosláviti, uhoslavírati

hearing (human perceptive ability): trùbāk

heart: čȕka, čukárac, čȕkica, pumpánjac

heart attack: sȑčka

heat (a room, etc.): nàgariti, nàgaziti

heat: hȁjcati, jȁra, vrućìnčina

heat up (room, house, etc.): nàhājcati

heaven (religion): džènet

heavy drug addict, big time junkie: kapilárac

heavy truck: tȉr[2]

heavy-truck driver: tȉrovac

hell (religion): džehènnem

hello, hi: mȅrhaba

help in pickpocketing: štȕcati, štȕcovati, zídati

help, assist: kȕrja, ȕjū

helpless: ìspūmpān

hemorrhoids: hȅmosi

hen: kènjka, kȍćka, kòljka, kréka, krékavica, kréštavica, tȉljka

hen laying eggs, layer: kvȍčkica

her: njȍān, njójzīn

herbal brandy: sȅverina, stomàklija, tráva, trȁvarica, zèlenā

herbs (used as narcotic drugs): hèrba

here: ȅo, èvē, óde, ódedama, ódenā, ódi[2], ódikā, óđe, óđekarce, óđekare, óđena, óvdek, óvdi, óvdinā, óvđe, óvđen, òvod, ovóđen, sȉm, tùjkā, túde, túdi, túdik, tȗj[2], tȗnā[2], vâmo, vóđe, vóđekā, vóđekarcē, vóđekārē, vóđenāke, vòj, vòjkā, vúde, vúdenā, vúdenākā

here and there, all over: ȁvȓlj-bȁvȓlj, đèđe

here and there, every now and then: đȅne-đȅne

here, in this direction: sȉmo

heritage, inheritance: amánet

hero: àđār, hȅroš, šèhīd

heroin, horse, smack: bêlō[2], dôp, dôup, èsid, héro, hȍrn, hôrs, kȍnj[1], kònjāk, pájdo, žûtō

Herzegovinian (inhabitant of the Southern part of Bosnia and Herzegovina): Éra, Èrcegovac, Éro, hercegovánac, ròlingstōn, škȕtor

hesitate, be shy: fȅmisati se, fȅmkati se

hesitate, be skiddish: kòziti se

hesitate, stall: balabȕćkati, glístiti se, gnjáviti

hesitating: cinculíranje

hesitation: cȉc-mȉc, gúžēnje, kàrgōn, tȓt-mȓt[2]

hidden money: šânž

hide (usu. from the police): dȅkovati se

hide from a manhunt, be on the lamb: barúniti

hide from publicity, lay low: bunkèrisati, bunkèrisati se, bunkerírati se

hide, cover up: dȅknuti, dȅmfati, krínjati, šanžírati, štȅkovati, švéjati, zàštekovati

hide-and-seek: žmíra, žmúrka

hideout: bŕlog, bùljkāf

hiding: dȅkovānje

hiding from a manhunt: kuràntīn, kurùntīn

hiding place (for people): lúka[1]

hiding place (for things): búđa, kèrna

hiding place: bùkljāf, komoràna, kȕnt, štȅk

hiding place for stolen goods, stash: garáža

high (mood, etc.): hâj[2]

high (on drugs): hâj[2]

high ball falling down: svéća

high heel (of a shoe): štȉkla

high jumper: vìsāš

high performance (of cars), souped up: àbartovān

high pitched sound: klȋk[2]

high pleasure: plezìrčina

high school: đȉmnā, garnìzōn, gìmna

high school graduation trip: maturálac

high school junior: vicematurȁnt

high school senior: móljac

high school student: mastȉljār, mȕčenīk, robijàšica

high school student after the school reform in the 1970s in the former Yugoslavia: usmerènjāk, usmjerènjāk

high school teacher: toreâdor

high school with emphasis on classical philology: làtīnka

high society: šmînka

high society, cream of society: krêm, kréma

high sole shoe: šȁmrl, šȁmrla, štȍkrl, štȍkrla

high temperature, fever: vȁtra

high-paying hotel guest: múdonja

high-quality hashish, bad hash: lùdāk

high-quality marijuana: pètica

high-top boot: pèšadīnka, pjèšadīnka

highest bid in cards: plàfōn

highly attractive female, bombshell: rakèta, topóvnjača

highly attractive female, knockout: fȑstuša

highly attractive male, hunk: fȑstāk

highly dangerous or unpleasant: zȁjebāno

highly humorous: genijálština

highly humorous person, laugh, scream: genijálac

highly intricate dilemma, touchy case: triléma

hill: ćùvīk

hint, clue: hȉnt

hip: flȁnka

hippie: hȉpī, hipijánović, hìpik

hippies: hipijána

hippodrome: hȉpī

hired hand: kaskàdēr

hiss (snake, gas, etc.): fȑskānje, fȑskati, sìkati, sȉknuti, sikòtati, sìktati, skȋk, skilìkati, skíknuti, štèktati, vȑčati, zvŕčati, šȉštati

hissing (snake, gas, etc.): sìktānje, sȉktav, sȉktavo, siktèćiv, skȉka, skilìkānje, šȉštānje, šȉštav, šȉštavo, zvȉzga, zvȑčav, zvȑčavo

hissing snake: sȉktavica

history: hìstērija

hit a ball: lèći, sjȅsti

hit another car, have a fender bender: nàpucati

hit by car: oštŕljnuti

hit from behind: zgúziti

hit hard: raspandŕknuti

hit in marbles: pìškan

hit oneself (e.g., to become sober): trȅsnuti se

hit softly, tap: kljȕcnuti

hit with a bottle (e.g. in a street fight): flȁšovati

hit, punch: ȁjsnuti [2], aplàuz, bekendírati, bȉcnuti, bŕknuti, celívati, ciglírati, čȕkati, ćȕšnuti, ćȕtnuti, dòkačiti, drȁjfnuti, dȑknuti, dúnuti, dȕrnuti, flȉknuti, fȕtiti, géknuti, hȅznuti, ìskecati, ispáliti, jáviti, klȁpiti, klȅpiti, klȅpkati, klȅpnuti, krȇs [2], krȅsnuti, kȑk [2], kȑkete, kȑknuti, kȑljnuti, kȑnuti, kvȅker [2], labàznuti, lansírati, lokomotíva, ljȍljnuti, mâr [2], mȁrnuti, mlȁtnuti, mȑdnuti, mȑknuti [2], mȕnuti, nàpucati, òblajmiti, očèpiti, očèšljati, odàlamiti, odrápiti, òdšrafiti, òfuljiti, ògizditi, òlipati, opàjdariti, opáliti, opàmbrčiti, opàmprčiti, opàndrčiti, opàučiti, òpičiti, òplesti, opízditi, oslàjpičiti, osúšiti, ošàjbudžiti, ošàjdariti, ošášoljiti, ošàuknuti, òšinuti, ošlàjpičiti, ošvorcírati, pàmpuk, pléhati, pljȅskavica, pljȕniti, pljȕnuti, pòdgladiti, pòkupiti, pòmilovati, popláhnuti, pòtrefiti, pȕknuti [2], raspáliti, ràspičiti, raspízditi, razváliti, rȅbnuti, rȍknuti, rȕknuti, sàstaviti, spavánac, spȕcati, stȅpati, stèpsti, strȅfiti, šȉbnuti, šȉšnuti, šíknuti, šljága, šljagárac, šljagírati, šȕp-kárta, švȁjznuti, traumírati, trȅfiti, trȅsnuti, ùbosti, ùdriti, ušljíviti, ùžditi, zabàštati, zabàštati se, zabúšiti, zabúšiti se, zalèmiti, zalòžiti, zđȉmiti [1], zdȑmati, zȅnuti, zȕnuti, zvȅknuti, zvȉznuti, žvȁjznuti, žvȅknuti

hitch-hike: stopírati

hitch-hiking: nȍn-stȍp, stopírānje

Hitler: Híco, Híća, Híćo

hitting from behind, sucker punch: kalpírānje

hitting with pillows: jàstučēnje

hitting, punching: plehàna, pléhānje

hole in one's sock: kròmpīr

hole, opening: àlka, pȁnjega, rùpīnger

hollow: šúpalj

holy: ćȅlav

home: bȕre, cârda, ćȉku, ȉža, jȁzbina, kȁca, kàsārna, kȁšta, kèrna, klincànica, kíra, pèćina, slȉnčār, stànara, špȉlja, ȕnča

home-made: dòmāćī

home-made bread: sàmūn

homeless female, bum: klȍšārka, skìtara

homeless male, bum: klȍšār, žȉcār, žȉcāroš, žȉcer

homeless person, bum: àdrapovac, bùnjalo, džȍndra, đȉlkoš, frènter, golopìzdalo, karaušlívko, klòkan, klȍkī, klòkica, klošàrika, klošarȉška, lȁkavac, lȁstavica, nȅboslōv, podrùmlija, šȁrklo, šȁtrovac, tumaròlog, vȁncaga, ventilâtor, vjetrènjāk, zjȁker

homeroom teacher: rȁska

homework, assignment: záda

homosexual who takes the passive role, femme: hàdžija

homosexuality: kurtoâzija, pedèrāj [2], pedrològija

Honda (make of motorcycle): hȍndić

honest male, honest dude: lèvāt

honest person, one who cannot be framed: nenadjèljiv

honk (of a goose): sìkati, sȉknuti, sikòtati, sìktati

honk (of a horn): tùtuk

honk, blow a horn: tȕtkati

honking (of a goose): sȉkānje, sȉktav

honor: òbraz

honorable: čȁzben, obràzli [1]

honorably: obràzli [2]

hood (of a car): hàuba

hoot, jeer: uhúkati

hooting, jeering: uhúkānje

hop: hȍpsati, vȑc

hopeless: nȅgatīvan

horn in, butt in: prìkrpati se

horrible, terrible: grȍzomōran, jèziš, kòtlosān, pencìlīnskī

horror, terror: gróza, jêz, jéza, ȍčāj, stráva [1], ȕžās

horse (the animal): ȁhat, ȁt, cȕkar [2], džȕka, đȉ-đȉ [1], đógo, kàlac, káljac, kuràtija, ràškōv, rùnkōv, ȓzāč, ȓžāč

horse radish: rȅn [1]

horse whip: điјòtāljka, đȉjotka

hose: šlȁuf

hospital: lȕknja, mèsara, odmàralīšte, tàmbura

hostile: nȅpoćūdan, smȑdljiv

hot dog (the food): hȍt-dȍg

hot line (telephone link): hȍtlājn

hot weather: màdžar, màđār

hot, spicy: žèstok

hotel: bína, hotelȉška, špígl, špȉlja

hotel elevator: kùtija

hotel room: ćèlija

hour: ȁuer, čȕka, h, òklok, sȁhat, ȗra, vȅrk, vrȅmeplōv, vȕra, vȕrica

house with two entrances: dùrkan

house, home: céra [1], kȁča, klinčànica, ȕndža, ȕnđa

housekeeper, maid: kùćnjāk, zmȃj [1], zmájko, zȕza, zȕzos

housekeeping: dosađínstvo

housewife, lady of the house: zmájko

housing: gehȁjz

how: kȃk

how much, how many: kȁč, kòlko
hub (on a wheel): nába
hubcap: ràdkapna, ràtkapa, ràtkapna
hug a female: ìzjakati
hugging, embracing: dávljēnje
hum, hiss: brújati
humor: grȉf, gvȉnt, pìšānje
humorous (of a person): vȉckast
humorous: kȅhlav
hump-backed person: kàmila
humpbacked individual: glȁvoseča
hundred currency units; a hundred-unit bill: bȁnka
hundred dinar bill: kȓpe
hundred dinars; a hundred-dinar bill: crvènkapica, gláva, kȍnj [1], plȁhta, stȍtka, šȕška, zelèmbāć [2]
hundred dinars; a hundred-dinar bill or coin: stója
hundred German marks: gláva
Hungarian (person): Đȁrma, madžàron, Pȉšta
hunger: žděravac
hungry: bokalȉška, hȁnovān, lȁcī [2], lȁćī, mútan, mȕtav
hurrah: ȕjū
hurry up, rush: gȁriti, hàrisati, hítiti [1], pohítiti, šȉbāj, zàgrīsti, zalàufati (se)
hurt a wound: raščepȑkati
hurt, feel pains (in one's back): ušćàknuti
hurt, feel pains: bòliti
hurtful statement, caustic remark: bljùvotina
husband: čȍek, čȍjek, čȍvek, gòrnjāk [1]
husband dominated by his wife, henpecked husband: pàpučār, pàpučica
hymen: džána, džànfer, džȁnifer, đána, jùnfer, jȕnfić, mokasína, skȁlp
hypodermic needle: pûmpa
hysteria: šíza [1]
I (when a female refers to herself): sèstra
I (when a male refers to himself): bája [1], bȁja [2], brȁt, číka, číko, téča
I: jô [1]
ice cream: ȉzolēd, slàdīć
icing on a cake: šnê
ID (separate document which every adult citizen of the former Yugoslavia had to carry on their person): bumȁška, ćagèta, lêgoš, ȉčnā, ličnjàče, ȉčnjāk, šára, šȁre, šarènica
idea, thought: dȉhtūng, klȉker, vȉjuga, žȁrulja
ideal love, love of one's life: ìdiš
identical, exactly the same: pljȕnūt, tèdbeš
idler, loafer: lezilébović, ništarȍba [2], vȉtigūz, zȁmlata
ždrȍplja
if: ak, el, jel
IFOR (Implementation Forces for Dayton Peace Agreement in Bosnia in the 1990s): ȁjfōr
ignition: pálenje
ignition coil: bobína, bombína
ignorant: ȉpa [2], slépac, slèpčina
ignorant person: ȉpa [1], tùtumrāk, vèzara, vèzist, vèzista
ignorant person, dumb shit: kȅnja [2]
ignorant person, dunce: dȕnster
ill, sick: bólnica [2], cȉknūt, kȕnjav, kȕžan, màrōd
ill-behaved youngster, brat: dzìndzōv
ill-tempered: ìzdrkān, zàgūljen
ill-tempered female: nàdžag-bȁba, nàdžakbaba
illegal business (in general): mȕćka
illegal cab driver: dìvljāk [1]
illegal connection: jȃvka
illegal distillery, still: bùnker
illegal dormitory stay: ilegàlisānje
illegal meeting: jâvka
illegal pub: ilegálac
illegible handwriting, chicken scratching: švrȁkopīs
illiterate male: kȓstāš
illness: bȍlēs, slabòtinja
image, look: ȉmidž
imagination: trȉp
imagine: trȉpovati
imam: ȍdža, pèčūrka
imitation plum brandy: sàgradan, sagȓdān
immoral activity: mȕćka, mȕćkalica, mùtljavina
immoral group of individuals: gȁmād
immunize: pȅlcovati
impassible mountain: gùdura
impersonate somebody else, be a con artist: folírati se
impersonate, imitate: skȉnuti
important: jȃk
impostor (female): hòhštaplerka
impostor (male): hȍštapler
impostor (male), con man: hòhštapler
impotence: mekankìtis
impotent: ćórak [2], ȉmpić [2], ȉmpoš [2], lȃbīlan, padovànskī, sjèdac
impotent male: bèzjājnīk, ȉmpić [1], ȉmpoš [1], jòderpenj, prâznīk, Sìzif, trúba [1], trùbāč, trubàdūr, vìsibaba, vìsibabić, vìsimīr, visúljak
imprison, put away: ljȕljkati, ùpecati, spakírati, ùgajbiti, zabȁštati
imprisoned: mùrīrān
imprisonment: brȁva [2]
improve, get better (of the weather): proljepòtati se
improve, get better: štȅlovati
improvement: boljítak
improvised: sklépān
impudent or insolent female: brezòbraznica
impudent or insolent male: brezòbraznīk
impudent, insolent: brezòbrazan
in a bad mood: nàkūrčen, ràsklamfan
in a difficult situation: bógīn
in a stuttering manner: bȅkavo
in handcuffs, cuffed: zàrūčen

in love: nàpāljen, nàtrēskān, strèlovān, ùstrēljen, zàcōpān, zàtelebān

in old clothing: òfūcān

in one's home country: dȍle

in particular: spȅcijālno

in principle: uprimpícu

in prison, behind the bars: ùnūtra

in spite of everything: ùskurac

in that respect: tòpoglēdno

in the evening: dȍvečē

in the morning: ȉzjutra, sàbājle, zòrōm

in the night: ȍbnōć

in vain, for nothing: badàva, badàvad, džàba, džàbāk, džàbē, đàbē

in-laws: tàzbina

inadequate male sexual partner: Zagrejȅbić

inclined toward sexual intercourse: slatkokūrast

incompetent female laborer: fúšerka

incompetent (of a player): šúpalj

incompetent boxer: staklénac [1]

incompetent goalie (soccer, etc.): bûšnī, màjumun, šérpa, šûpljī

incompetent laborer: fúšer

incompetent player (soccer, etc.): lâzār [2], pȁcer, pèvāč [1], pȉmpler, stàtista, šȕper

incompetently or superficially performed job: fušèrāj

incomplete: fàličan

inconvenience, boring or unpleasant matter: gnjávež

incurable alcoholic, hopeless drunk: delȉričār

indebted: kràtak

indecent action: đȍn

indeed, really: bȉla, bȉlāh, bȉlāhī, bìlaj, bȍgam, bȍgami

Independent State of Croatia (Croatian Nazi state during WWII): endeâzija

indicator (on a machine, gadget, etc.): cáger

indifferent: vȍdorāvan

indifferently: sèrbez [2]

indoctrinate: obrađívati

indoctrinated: pèčen

indoctrination: obrađívānje

inexpensive clothing: pŕnjci

inexpensive jewelry: đinđuha, đinđuva

inexpensive prostitute: pasùljara, púca [1]

inexpensive, cheap: bagatèla [2], èvtin, mùftē, mùktē

inexpensively, cheaply: bagatèla [3]

inexperienced criminal: lèvāt

inexperienced gambler: malicána

inexperienced male, greenhorn: zelèmbāć [1]

inexperienced youngster: mljȇčnjak

inexperienced, green: zelenjáva

infamous, notorious: fȁmōzan

infantry soldier, ground pounder: pràšinār, prašȉnjār

inflate, blow up: napuvávati

influence (of drugs): ráditi [1]

inform: informìsisati

inform the police or other authorities, blow the whistle: odzvìždati

inform the police or other authorities, sing: ìspevati, ìspjevati, pȅvati, pȅvnuti, pjȅvati, pròpevati, pròpjevati

inform the police or other authorities, snitch, squeal: cinkáriti, cȉnkati [2], cȉnkovati, drȕkati, drȕknuti, drȕkovati, gajgerírati, gúknuti, ȉzlajati (se), ocinkáriti, ofírati, òdlajati, òdrukati, òdruknuti, otastèrisati, otasterírati, otcinkáriti, òtcinkati, òtčukati, òtipkati, òtkucati, otkucávati, òtpevati, òtpjevati, prováliti, provaljívati, špȉclati, tȉpkati, zvòniti

information passed to the police or other authorities: cȉnk [2]

informer, canary: kanarínac

informer, stoolie, snitch: àvaz [2], ȁver, bugàčica, cȉnk [3], cìnkāroš, cȉnker, čȍmbe, daktilògraf, dostàvljāč, drùkātor, drȕker, gàjger, glȁsnī, gôst, gȕslār, klàvīr, klófer, kȍnfić, kûrva, Lâjka, mòrzeovac, njȕškalo, ȍko [1], òrātor, otkùčāč, otkùcalo, otkùcār, papàgāj, pàstēr, penkála [1], pȅs, pètljārka, pètljārnik, pèvāč [1], pȉčka, pȉs [2], piskàralo, pjȅsnīk, pjèvāč, prisluškìvāč, pízda, pȍštār, rèdnjara, rèdnjāroš, sȕfler, šàptāč, šàptigūz, špìcl, štȅker, štȕglec, tȁster, tastèrāš, telèfōn [2], telefònist, telègraf, teleprȉnter, testèrāš, tȉpka, tìpkāč, trȕber, tùtun [1], ȕholaža, zȕrak, zvònac, zvȍnār, žbîr

informing police or other authorities, singing: pȅvānje

informing the police or other authorities, snitching, squealing: drȕk, provalȉška

informing the police, snitching: kûpljen

ingratiate, brownnose, kiss ass: cilemilezírānje, cilemilezírati, cilemizírānje, čépiti se, čmàrisati, čmúrati se, glȁditi, káditi, káđenje, kȕvānje, kȕvati, míkiti, mȕvānje, mȕvati, péziti, pljòviti, podȉlaziti, pòdjājčiti, pòdvūći se, pȕzati, šlȉhtati se, tȉtrati, tròvānje, ufurávati se, ugúziti se, uvláčiti se, ùvūći se, žicáriti, žȉcati

ingratiation, brownnosing, ass kissing: tȑzānje, žȉca, žȉcānje, žȉcārēnje

ingratiator (female), brownnoser: uvlakàčica

ingratiator (male), brownnoser, ass kisser: bicìklista, buljouvlàčilac, buljouvlàkāč, čȅp [1], čèpulja, čmárko, čmáronja, dupelízac, dȕper, gmâz, gmȉza, gmȉzavac, gnjȉda, gúza [2], guzolízac, gùzičār, kȑpa, lȉzigūz, ližisàhan, pizdolízac, podgùzāš, podrèpāš, pokòrnjāk, pòltrōn, pȕzavac, satelȉt, servílac, šlȉhtara, šȏjka, šréber, štréber, tàrigūz [2], tȑtāš, tȑtos, tȑtoš, ubacȉška, uvalàkāč, uvalakáčević, uvlàkāč, uvlakáčević, uvlákčević, ȕvle, vazèlīn, vazelínac, vazelínko

ingratiator, brownnoser: pičkolízac

inhabitant of Croatian islands: bòdul

inhabitant of Croatian mainland: vlȁj

inhabitant of Kruševac, Serbia: čaràpān

inhabitant of Palilula (a neighborhood in Belgrade, Serbia): Palȉlulos

inhabitant of Southern Serbia: pirot'ȁnac

inhabitant of Split, Croatia: Rèptīl, tòvar

inhabitant of the countryside (female), hick, bumpkin: čùšpajzica, dèsīnka, kúma, snáša, šánērka

inhabitant of the countryside, farmgirl: ljànkase

inhabitant of the countryside, hick, bumpkin: bàlvan [1],

beločaràpāš, bernardínac, bjeločàrapić, bȑđanin, cálac, cáva, čaràpān, čaràpār, čéda, čkȁlja, čòban, čòbanin, dàsina, desòvān, dȋvča[1], Divčibárac, dizèlāš, džȋber, džòvān, džȕdža, džudžòvān, džudžovànder, džúkac, džùkela, džùkser, đùkser, geàčina, gȅāk, geàkinja, gédža, gédžo, gedžòvān, géđa, gȅgula, geguláner, gilènder, glènder, glênđer, gòrštāk, gràfičār, gràfikos, grȁfos, gȕbār, gȕber, kelerába, kêr[1], kȍper, kȍzāk, kȑkan, kûle, kùlōv, kûm, kùmek, làjbek, lepèzān, lepezáner, ljȁkse, oficȋr, òpanak, ȍrpa, òvčār, pápak[1], pàpan, pàpanka, seljàčina, sèljāk, seljóber, Senegálac[1], siròvnjāk, sóva, stȑndžōv, stȑnđōv, stȑnkov, strvina, Šaban, šaner, šarplaninac, šȕša, šmȋnker, šòšōn, šȕmār, šûmnjāk, šúpak, tȑtljāk, vàrzelj, žvàtān

inhabitant of Užice (a city in Serbia): Éra, Éro

inhabitant of Vojvodina (a region in Serbia): Lála

inhabitant of Zagreb, Croatia: péder, pìcek[2], pìzdek[1], Zȁgī

initial flirting: ànlaserovānje, ànlasovānje, stȁrtovānje

injection nozzle: àjnšprel-dízna, ànšpric-dízna

injured, hurt: ròvit

inner pocket (of a jacket): pȍtplata, prȅdnjāk, škȕta, škȕta

innovative construction: skalamèrija

inquisitive person: gȕbār, kòpitār

insane female: róda[2]

insane female, nut case: bolèsnica, fòjnikina, manìtulja, manìtuša, šȉzika, vojnìkinja

insane male, nut case: Hàmlet, švȅnkī

insane person, nut case: bàtina, bȅzjak, blȅsa, blèsan, bolèsnīk, dègēn, diláber[1], dìldika, dìlkan, dȋvča[1], flȉper, hàvārija, lȁkī[1], lètāč, lêvī[2], lùcirda, lȕda, ludáija, ludája, lùdāndža, ludájia, ludȁkos, lûdnjāk, lùdōv, malája, narkohòličār, nórac, ȍblāk, otkačȉška, šàlīn, Šànika, šȉzik[1], šlȍg[2], zèvzek

insane, bonkers: bȕbnūt, prȁsnūt

insane, cracked: pȕknūt

insane, koo-koo: š.l.b.

insane, nuts: ȁšav, bȁngav, bȅdast, bȅnas, bȅnast, bȅnav, betònīrān, bèzvezan, bijésan, blêntav, blȅsav, bȍlestan, čȕknūt, čvâknūt, dȉlke[2], dȑknūt, dȑmnūt, dûnūt, ìspušten, ìščašen, kalèa[2], krȅsnūt, lêvī[1], lȕdvīg, mànit, nàdrndān, nàkrīvljen, nȅčitav, ȍmānūt, òpičen, ȍšinūt, pȉšnūt, pòmaknūt, ȑknūt, sklȉzav, smûćen, sùmāhnūt, sùmānūt, šàntav, šȁšav, šlȍgī-drȍgī[2], šúpalj, šíza[2], tȑknūt, tûp[2], ùdaren, ȕdlū, ȕsrān, ùvrnūt, zrìlīng[2]

insane, touched in the head: čvôknūt

insanity, craziness: dilèjisānje, flȉp, flȉper, lûjka, otkačȉška, stráva[1], šizijáda, šíza[1]

insects: gȁmād

insensitive male, cold dude: dȑvo

insert, stick in: ubáciti, ubàčiti, zamàndaliti, zapȑditi, zàvīličiti, zavìngeriti, zbìberiti, zbȕtnuti, zȅkati

insertion: uvaljivanje

inside: unútri, unútrima

insincere excuse: fȅmisānje

insincerely: dȕplo, fȁlš[2], fôl[4]

insinuate: montírati, nàpakovati

insinuator: Bòrdžija, pùšāč, pùšik

insist: forsírati

inspiration: inspiréjšn

instance of impudence, insolence: brezobràzluk

instant coffee: nȅskafa

instantly: ȍmmā

instruction: štrȕka

instructor: štrȕker

intake of LSD: spîd

intake of narcotic drugs, doing drugs: fiksòtis, gùdrisānje, hàšiš-dróga-mȉnās-kàfa, kljȕk, kȑljānje, mȁzānje, palačínka[1]

intellectual: intelektúkac, staklénac[1], tàban[2]

intelligent, smart, bright: bȉstar, motavȉška

intensifying particle: al, àlāj[2], àlāl[2], dêr, jèbāga, jèbiga, mȁ[3]

intensifying particle, ah: a[2]

intensifying particle, dear God: pȍbogu[1]

intensifying particle, really, indeed: bòme

intensifying particle, well: nȍ

intensifying particle, wow: àlā[3]

intensity: pȉčānje, pȉčēnje

intensive learning, cramming: zaluđívānje

intentionally, on purpose: ašćáre, nàvlāš

interest in something: ȁber

interesting event: štôs[2], trubalȅska, vàljuga

intern sergeant: stáža, stàžista, stážo

Internet, Web: Pȁučina

interrupted game: čòsik

intimate friend: gotívac

intimidate, frighten: upropástiti

intrauterine device, IUD: andarmólja, fȕk-féder

intravenous drug use, main lining: bȍckānje

intravenous intake of narcotic drugs, main-lining, shooting up: dizàjn, fiks, fiksānje, šprícānje, tréskānje, zȅzānje

intrigue: kȕhinja, montáža, petljáriti, štôs[2], ujdùrma, zavrzlàma

intriguer: mùtikaša, mùtikesa, mùtivoda

intriguing: montíranje

introduce oneself: ubáciti se

introvert: nȅsvrstān, privàtnjāk, téžak

introvert person: plesnìvec

intrude, barge in: kȑpiti se, pètljati se, šlȅpati se, trtomúditi se, ufúrati se, ufurávati se, ùpucati, uváliti se

intruder: čivìluk, filòksera, flȁster, gúza[2], kȑlja[1], padobránac, plàkāt, prìlipak, prìšipetlja, prìvjesak, šlȅper[1], ubacȉška, ùmetnīk

intrusion: šlȅpānje, šlȅpovānje

intrusive: sȕnovrātan

intrusive person: njȕškalo

invented word, word which does not exist: frfòkljica

inventive male, inventive dude: klikèrāš

invest minimal effort in doing something: prètrgnuti se

investigate, look into: čàčkati, prošnjúrati, šnjȍfati, trakáriti, trȁkati

investigating judge, ball-busting judge: mȕdogrīz

investigating judge, magistrate: bábo

invincible, untouchable: nenadjèbiv, neprejèbiv

iron (the metal): màzija [1]

iron lever: pàjser

irregular, frequently interrupted (work of an engine): tȓzānje

irresolute male, spineless guy: mekúšac, mlákonja, mlȉtonja

irresponsible male: pȓdežmen

irresponsible person: alàmunja, dàndara, dȑndara [2], džȁmbās, jèbivetar, jèbivjetar, kalàmunja, kuràjber, lȕfter, lùftigūz, lùftika, šalabàhter [2], šalabàjzer, šiljokùrān, šiljòkurac, vȑtipraška, zvȉjū

Islamic country: džamahȋrija [2]

it is worthless: nȃe [2]

it's gone: fȕč, fȕć

Italian (person): mȁčkār, žȁbār, Borsalȋno, Špagètār, Talijanȉška, tȕljān, Žábac

Italian (person), Dago: Dȉgić, Dígo, Dìgol

Italy: Íća, Dìgićija, Ȉntālija, prȇko

items of no value or importance: drangùlije

jacket: džȍka, jànel, mùftār, muntárac, sàkat

Jaegermeister beer: pèlīn

jailer: fírer, pèntek, ȑja, ȑjāk, šúnto, trčkàralo

jam (e.g. traffic jam): gȗžva

janitor: hàuzmājstor, nȁsta

Japanese (person), Jap: Jàpī

Japanese (person), Slant: kosòokī

jaw: njȕpavica

jazz music: džȅzerica

jazz musician: bàndīt

jeans: džȋnserice, ȑfle, tȁnkerice, trȃperice, trȁpke

jeans jacket: gòrnjāk [2]

jet (plane): mlȃznjāk

Jew: čȉfut, čȉfutin, čȉvut, ćífo, ćȉfut, Jéša, Žȉdov, Žȉga, žȉgica, žȉgolo

jewelry: šmȕk

jitters: tȑt-mȑt [2]

job which does not bring enough money, low-paying job: jebàncija

job, gig: àrbajt, sȅlpo

job, gig: gáža, hljȅb, kȍp [2], pòsā, slùžba, šéma, šljakárac, uhljebljénje, žȉlka

jobless: trȍm

jocular word: smèjalica

join a group of people: utȑpati se

join, take part in: ùšljakati se

joint (a part of a mechanism): gèleng

joint: pljúga

joint, low-class bar: rȕpa [2]

joke (usu. a practical one): čȉvija

joke: bunàrisati, bùrgija, bùva, cáka, fàzōn, fȉnta, gevéra, gȑč, gvȉnt, hȅc, ìbret, kébānje, kidùrija, komèndija, proserávati, prȍvala, sȉndža, smèjalica, sínđa, spȑdati se, šegáčiti se, šegebèdečiti, štȏs [2], vàljuga, vȁška, zafrkávati se, zavitlávati, zavitlávati se, zàzati, žváka

joke about somebody: spúštalica

joke around: bacàkati

joke teller: càkāroš, fazònēr, sokòlac, štósēr

joke with, make a fool of: izvózati, mòtati, rezíliti, zafrkávati, zȅzati, zȅznuti

joke, trick: lȃfo [1]

joker, clown: cirkuzȃnt

joker, trickster, rascal: àlčak, drípac, hȕmīć, komendȉjant, lȉsa, lùciprda, mȃf, mànga, màngup, mŕtav [1], múlac, vìckāroš, zafrkȁnt, zàjān, zajebȁnt, zavitlȁnt, zèzāč, zèzātor

joking with, fooling with: cȕcānje, čarlàma, sprdàčina, šandrmácija, šandrmírānje, šegáčēnje, šȅgānje, šéva, šévānje, vȓzgānje, zaebávānje, zafrkȁntskī, zafrkávānje, zavitlávānje, zȅzāje, zezàncija, zȅzānje

journalist: mȁzalo, piskàralo, slȍvo, škrábalo, tŕčak

joy: mèrāk, špȃs

joyful person: lóla

judgement: fȅtva

jug: bȍjalija

juice: đȕs

juicy: saftàli

jump: đȉpati se, đȉpiti, đípati, ȑpiti

jump abruptly, leap: đȉsiti

junior player: sȕpić

juniper brandy: klèkovača

junkie: nȁrkić

just: sȁmo

just a little bit: málčice, málkice, málko

just like that, just for the heck of it: nàkō

just released prisoner: ìzletnīk

just right, as it should be: knȃp [2]

juvenile detention center, juvie: bàlvan [2], kapedȏ

juvenile inmate: kapedómac

Kaaba (Muslim holy stone in Mecca): ćába

Kaaba (Muslim holy stone in Mecca): kába

Kawasaki (make of motorcycle): kàva, kȁvić

keep: gájiti

keep a card (in poker): šlȅpati, šlȅpovati

keep hitting: ćúškati

keep horses in race (of a jockey): pȕlovati

keep one's mouth shut: čkòliti, kénjati, kȕšovati, mòstati, mòstiti, mȕstovati

keep pronouncing 'ae' to express satisfaction, surprise, delight, dislike, pain, etc.: aékati

keep pronouncing 'ajs' to urge an ox to move on: ȁjskati

keep pronouncing 'eh' to express different emotions ranging from satisfaction to grief: ȅhkati

keep pronouncing 'ej' to draw attention: ȅjkati

keep pronouncing 'jo' to express pain, disbelief, surprise, etc.: jókati

keep pronouncing 'joj' to express disbelief or pain: jȍjkati

keep pronouncing 'juj' to express surprise or fear: jujùkati, jujȕškati

keep pronouncing 'keca': kȅckati

keep pronouncing 'keca' to drive away a goat: kȅcati

keep pronouncing something preposterous: izvaljívati

keep quiet: mùčati

keeping a card (in poker): šlȅpovānje

keeping horses in race (of a jockey): pȕlovānje

keeping one card (in poker): šlȅpānje

Kent (cigarette brand): kéndža, kénja [1]

kerchief: hàvlija

key: čȕklju, lȁzār [1], revòlvēr, šlìsl, tȍp [2]

key ring: fȕk-féder

kick in front of the adversaries' goal: nabacóka [1]

kick in the buttocks: krkbùljisati, krkubùljisati, nàpičiti, vrȉtnjāk

kick or punch in the testicles, low blow: testírati

kick, strike: cȁknuti [1], džilítnuti, pȉkati, pȉknuti, pȕknuti [2], šljȕcati, šutírati

kid (goat): šnȁjder

kill in a driving accident: sàtrati

kill, murder: dȅknuti, kókati, kȍknuti, likvidírati, ohláditi, oláditi, oporúčiti, skénjati, skȉnuti, štȕhati, ùbaniti, ùbrati, ùcupati, ùluzati, ubàštati (se), ubàštati se, ubàštrati, ubùfati, ubùftati, ucécati, ucmékati, ukàntati, ukébati, ukókati, upȑditi, ùpucati, urókati, utábati, utàmbati, utépati, zàbiti, zakàntati, zakòvati, zàštihtati, zatàmbati, zbòtati

kill, neutralize: upokòjiti

kill, rub out: tamániti

killer: kȉler [1]

killing: flȉnt, kókānje, ukokávānje

killing from an ambush: sačèkuša

kilo: kȉlo

kind female, nice lady: làfica

kind male, nice guy: bája [1], bȁja [2], kúšťro, lȁf [1], làfčina, mȃjstor

kind of a card game: kȕpčānje

kind of bird (Tringa alpina): čiríkavac

kind of Bosnian Muslim heroic song: fahríja

kind of card game where players try to flip over their playing cards: poklápa

kind of coin-throwing game where one tries to place coins as close to a wall or a line as possible, pitching pennies, lagging: blíža

kind of game played with three cards in hand: trȉca, trijáne, trijáner, tròjān [2]

kind of game where one has to guess who hit him/her: zúca

kind of game with collector cards where one has to guess if two cards will fall on the side where the picture is: slȉke-bijélo

kind of game with collector's cards where one has to guess if two cards will fall at the same side: pȍla-cijélo

kind of jump-rope played by girls with an elastic band: èma-èsesa

kind of male hairstyle from WWII: kȍkotica

kind of mush made of cheese, fat and corn flour: cȉcvara

kind of nostalgic folk music: sèvdāh

kind of peeping bird (Eudromias morinellus or Charadrius pluvialis): pijúkavac

kind of round pepper: bàbura

kind of simple card game: mȁu-mȁu, tàblīć, tablijána

kind of songbird: belnèguza, belengùzac, belòguza, bjelènguza, bjelòguzā

kind of token in a children's game where the person with the token has to do something (usu. sensitive or unpleasant): fóta

kindergarten: vrȉtić

king: ȕt

king-size bed: fȕkodrōm

kiss: cmȁknuti, cmókati, cmȍknuti, cmokòtati, cmòktati, cmóljiti, cȍkiti, cȍknuti, cvȍkati, karmìnisati, kȉs [2], kȉsati, kȑljati, kȑljati se, kȑnuti, lízati, nȕšiti se, njȕšiti se, njȕškati se, pȕbiti, pȕsa, sȃpu, slȉniti [2], slȕrpati, žmȕljiti, žvȁla, žvaláviti se, žvȁliti, žvàljac

kiss loudly and conspicuously: cmákati, cmákati se

kissing: buvárēnje, cmókānje, cmokòtānje, cvȍkōt, karmìnisānje, kisimìzam, kȑljānje, ljùbilica, umákānje, žvalávljēnje

kitchen: kùžīna

kitchen help: pèrilka

kitchen stove: špȁret, špȍret

knife: bȁke, bíčak, bóca, bȍcka, đȕla, hȁndžār, kùstura, mesírac, mìsīrka, misírac, mìstrija, nožòvīnje, ȍžno, rȅcka, rȏg, ȑpalo, sȁblja, têlo, zûb [1]

knife, dagger: dȅžbo

knight (card which counts twelve in some games): žȁndār

knight (in chess): lòfaz

knock (on a door, etc.): čukàrati, kȕcāj, kûcanj, tȉkati

knock (on the door, etc.): čȕkati

knock down, floor: asfaltírati, patosírati

knock out (boxing): nokautírati, oláditi

knocking, rapping: kùcnjava

know someone's intentions, read someone: pročìtati

know, have knowledge of: dìvati, đànisati, raskužnjávati, tudòmisati

Škoda (make of car): Škȍdilāk

labor of love: stepávānje

labor union activist: plebéjac

laboratory: làbrec, làptec

laborious, tedious: mukájet, rȁdētan

lack of conventionality, bohemianism: òtkačenōst

lack of intelligence, stupidity: amàkluk

lack of success: hàva

lack of time: càjtnot

lack, be without: néjmati, némati, nȉcati

lacking self-assurance: kòmpiš

lactose mixed into heroin to deceive one's clients: mànita

ladder: lótre

ladies choice (i.e. of their partner at a dance): jȅbozōv [1]

lady, woman: efendínīca, èrćava, góspa, gȍspoja [2], hanùma, mànčetovica, trȍnjarica

lagoon, bay: vȃla [3]

lamb (the animal): bèkan, lèšče, nȉkesto, tàšanče

lame: ȁksav, bȁngav, bangéja [2], bȁngja, ćȍpav, rȍm, stȑgānī
lame excuse: fȅmkānje
lame male: aksávko, baštòvān, cóto, ćȍpavī, šépo
lame person: bangéja [1], bángo, baštovàndžika, trȍtoslāv
lame, gimpy: dȕdnūt, gȅgav
lament: fȅstivāl
lamp: fȅncia, fȅnđa, fèrāl, kȍtomānka
lamp reseller: lȗj
landlady: gȁzdarica
landlord: gȁzda
language: spìkl
large: džȁmbo, kȍnjskī, vȅljī
large anus: šȕpčina
large audience: Indijánci
large bell: lumbètalo
large book: kȕvār [2]
large buttocks: bùljara, buljèskara, dùpeška, dùpetina, rùsija
large female breast: mlèkara, mljekárstvo, nāćve, plúća, sisètina, sisùrina, tóranj [2]
large penis: cvànciger, kitára, kùrčina, kùrezina, kurokȑšina, mȁčuga, prȃse
large penis: kalabàster, kitùrina
large round female breast: kúgla
large round head: kégla
large safe: mȅčka
large shoe: čámac
large silver coin: grȁndić
large stomach: brèntača
large vagina: lȍkerica, mȍšt, mùfčina, picùrina, pìčetina, pičkètina, pičkùrina, pizdùrčina, pizdùrina, piždrùljina, šȁht, šȁjkača, šȁpka, škȁf
large-breasted female: dòjčura, dòjkara, mlèkara, mlèkulja, mùzara, nàprednā, PKB [pê-kâ-bê], simèntālka, sìsača, sìsana, sìsara, sìseška, sìsna, sísa [2], vìmara
large-breasted male: Sȉsoje [2]
last coffee served to one's guests: siktèruša
last one: zȁjec [2]
last place finisher (in any competition): fenjèrāš, fenjèrdžija
last row of seats (on a bus, streetcar, etc.): sèćija
last, being at the end: pȍšljednjī
late (dead): rahmètli
late: dòckan
late: pȍšlī
late-night bar: ȁrba, bàriška, bùnker, tùljara
late-night bar frequented by prostitutes: pìciplac
later: dòcnijē, pȍtljē
lathe: drébank
Latin teacher (female): làtīnka
laugh: cirùkati, čkȁljiti se, humorírati, jàtismi se, karikaturírati, kȅhlati se, kekètati se, kìkoljiti se, kikòtati, kikòtati se, krȅvkati, kȗglati se, kukuríkati, léviti se, njákati, òtkinuti, rashihìšati se, rashihòtati se, rashohòtati se, rebètati, rȉdati, ȑzati, ùmirati, váljati se, zacéniti se, zaváriti, žnjȉriti

laugh aloud: cerèkati se
laugh intensely: vrìštati
laugh intensively, fall down laughing: pòpadati
laughing: kljòvisanje, ùmirānje, zùbisānje
laughing male: kikòtavac
laughing sound: hȉ
laughter: dúrēnje, glúma, gòrēnje, kȅkēt, keslìjānje, kȉkot, kikòtānje, krebèljānje, zijévānje, zubárēnje
laundry: rȍba, vȅš
law: bìblija, pàpīr [2]
lawyer, attorney: fiškāl, Slobòdan
lay back: profúzati se
lay back and get some rest: razbaškáriti se
lay down (e.g. to sleep): izváliti se, izvrndùpečiti se, prȕćnuti se
layover, stopover: tȕspās
laziness, a fit of laziness: fjȁka
lazy or shiftless female, bum, good for nothing: jàslara, pilìćārka
lazy or shiftless person, bum, good for nothing: ȁmza, badavàdžija, bázalo, bèćār, bèkrija, dèmbel, džùlōv, Firàun, fȕndra, gàmen, gȃnča, gȅāk, gràfikos, gulánfer [1], hòštapler, ìkel, lȁndara, landàralo, lȁndra, lȁndrī, lènguz, lènguza, lȉnjāk, lȉnjōv, lȕftbrèmzer, lȕfter, lùftigūz, mȑsomūd, mrsomúdonja, nabigùzica, pȅna, platfùsist, propèler, pȕrkāč, spȁdalo, šíber [1], šȉbigūz, vȁrcaga, vucibàtina, zdrkánac, zùnzara, zvȉjūk, zvȉndōv
lazy person, lazybones: klȍpavac
leader: gȁzda, vȍžd
leaf collector: kȍpljanīk, kòpljārnīk
leak (in a tire): dèfekt
leak out, run out: iscúriti
leap frog (the game): bìber-štrȕc
learn: gàmbati, klépati, nabȉflati, ovàrisati, strvináriti, šljȁkati, tkȁti, utúviti, zbírati
learn by rote: nabúbati
learn mechanically: bìflati, grúvati, štrébati
learn well: nagrúvati
leather bag: cánta, čȁnta
leather belt with spikes used to transport dangerous criminals: špánga
leather jacket: kȍžnjāk [1]
leave (of a group of people, usu. leaving a gathering of some kind): ràzići se
leave a game: pȉškati se
leave a restaurant without having paid, run out on the tab: izvijátiti
leave abruptly and silently: pòkupiti se
leave alone, stop boring: cirkùlisati, mánti, òbīći, prošétati se, skȉnuti se, zanemáriti
leave hastily, split: dúnuti, izjúriti [2]
leave it alone: stȉpuj
leave it alone, it does not matter: stȉpu
leave somebody: ofírati, ofírati se
leave without finishing, lose interest in, drop: batáliti

leave, beat it: odjèdriti

leave, depart, walk: lìtipa, kȕpiti se, ocìpljati, òdjahati, odlèteti, odvèslati, odzújati, òkljīnčiti, òdlāndrati otcìpljati, otfúrati, òtkljinčiti, otplòviti, otpúhniti, pèrjati, prošétati[2], pùštiti, štȕlati, ùmagliti se

leave, slink away: òtplaziti, òtplaziti

left: lìvanjskī

left side: lêvča

leftovers from a previous fix: ostáci

leftovers of a drug in a syringe: [illegible]

leg (human): ȁksavica, bàndara, bȕt, cȉplja, cìrkla, čkȍjalica, čkôjka, čkôrka, dùrača, gȁmba, gȁno, gȁnu, gȁrka, gȁzalica, gȁzalo, gìljarica, gìljārka, giljàrōn, glavàljica, gljȁka[2], gljârka, gljȁvica, gùljārka, gùrānka, gùravka, guljàrica, gurálka, hàlbaks, hódalica, hódāljka, hòdulja, ìdāljka, idéja, krâk, làbus, mánda, màndara, nabádāljka, pàljkara, pápak[2], pètljara, ràlica, sèksara, špàjhla, štȁka

leg (of a female): bàtāk, câpka, gȁmbavica, gȁmbica, nogára, pècāljka

lemonade: mudalína

length in minutes, running time: minutáža

lengthy sound: kvêk

lesbian: dȁjk, glȁncerica, lêjzī-bêjzī, lèzbača, lȅzbos, lȅzi-bȅzi, lìrika, pizdòjēpka, sapùnjārka, sèstra, šlȁjferica

let go, release: strȉpovati

let it be: stȉpu

let, allow, permit: púšćati, stìtpu

letter (correspondence): kobàsica, lȅter, lìliška, pisánac, tìrita, zàvrckānō

level: ìspēglati

levelling: egalìzīrka

Levi's (blue jeans): lêvisice, lêviske

liaison soldier: papàgāj

liar: bàrōn, bȉšop, bòmbāš, bùvātor, dȉmničār, fȍler, folijánović, gȁnča, kènjātor, krivìnāš, lȉrafōn, lóvac, lòžāč, lòžātor, mȁler[1], mùljātor, mùvātor, pùšāč, pùšik, šmȉnker, tròvāč

library: bìbliš

lick: lîz

lick a little: lizùckati

lid: klàpna

lie: ȁšati, bȁjati, bâjka, baladírati, bálo[2], baròniṡati, baronírati, barùnisati, bȉks[2], bljùvotina, bômba[2], bombášiti, bùva, cìtrīrati, ćumùrati, dȑblovati, dròbiti, dumbàrati, dùmina, dumírati, fȁrba, fârbati, fȉlovati, flȁntati, folìnjati, fòrtati, fȕtrati, gȁniti, gàtila, glúmiti, hrániti, imitírati, ìpsina, izglúmiti, izvózati, jàfina, jòsatimunj, knedlírati, kokovèlisati, kúbus, lȁf[2], lȁfiti, lágiti, lagírati, lȁuf, lìnafo[2], lìpsina, lȉra, lȉrati, lìrika, lȉrkati, lȉtrati, lòžiti, lívati, màrtuna, mástiti, mȁzati, mirìsati, mȍlovati, muljáriti, múljati, mȕsati, mȕvati, nàfutrati, napáliti, nàpūmpati, nàsrati, opkopávati, pȁčiti, páliti, pàljevina, parkírati se, patamȕzovati, pêglati, pètljati, pȑdeti, pȑditi, psȉna, pȕniti, ráditi[1], rúžiti, sàtimu, sȉndža, sínđa, sránje[2], srȁti, šárati, šȁtrati, šatrovírati, šatrírati, šȉljiti, šmȉrati, šȍpati, šúkati, šumíder, šupljìkāt, tâlija, tròati, tròvati, válјati[1], vózati, zàvrtati, zbòmbati

lie a lot: raspȑdeti se

lie down: ùlešiti se, zàleći

lie down while being stoned: odstondírati

lie on one's back: zaváliti se

lie to: palamúditi

lie, twist the truth: súkati, súknuti

lies, made-up events: baròn ije

lifeguard: gorȉla

lifestyle: fûrka

lift, rise: kȕpiti[1], kȕžiti, òpuliti

light (of wine): lȁk

light a cigarette: zàkuriti

lightbulb: okrùgljača

lighter: fȁjercāg, fȁjercajg, fȍjerbah

likable: sȉmpa

likable person: Bôg

like (usu. in the negative form): mirìsati, mòći

like: gotíviti, prímati se, tȑzati, váriti

like this: vàkī

like what: kàkī[3]

like, appreciate: džániti, prímiti se, šmèkeriti, tretírati

lime (calcium oxide): bèlāč, čamùrnjāš, klâk, sažàrēn

limousine, limo: lȉmka, lìmuz, lìmuza, lȉmza

limp: gégati se, gèljati, krivogùzati

limp hair: pàučina

limp penis: crévo

line (of heroin or cocaine): cȑta[2], lâjn

line (thin continuous mark): ćíza

linen: kȓpe

linen bag: càglja

lining (of a jacket): posteljìna, prȅdnjāk

lips: làbrnja, làbrnje

lisp, mispronounce dental consonants due to physiological reasons: fȑskati

lisping, mispronouncing of dental consonants due to physiological reasons: fȑskānje

liter: kȉla, kȉlo

litter (used on construction sites): cìvare

little boy, kid: kìkīć, kikìrēz, pȉkavac, pȑcvoljak, švȑle

little boy, sprout: bàmbus[2]

little by little: mȉc-mȉc

little, just a little bit: lȍma, zèricu, zèru

live: gúrati, štrȕmfovati

live at another's expense, leech off somebody: čèšati se

live close to something: pljȕniti, pljȕnuti

live from day to day: bȉvkati

live like a homeless person: klošáriti

live one's life: pȉčiti

live through: predevèrati

live very poorly, live from one day to another: varàkati se

live, exist: fúrati se

lived through: ùknjižen, ùpīsān

lively child: vȑtigūz

lively music: kèleruj

lively young male: jàjān

liver (the organ): džìgera

living at another's expense, leeching off somebody: čèšānje, čèšljānje, grèbānje

living room, reception room: prìmāćā

loaded dice: tȅrs[1]

loaf: štrȕca

loafer (shoe): jàzavičārka, kabriòlet-cìpela, uskòkuša

loafer, idler: bànzāč, bànzōv, dànguba, džabalèbār, gânča, glȍdār, glúvac, jèbivetar, jèbivjetar, krivìnāš, lìptigūz, lȕfter, lùftigūz, nabigùzica, pȕrča, pȕrkāč, stȕpār, šalabàhter[2], šalabàjzer, zabušânt, zgùbidān, zjȁker, zvȉjūk, žȉcār, žȉcāroš, žȉcer

loan (money): KBZ [kəbz]

loan, credit: bȑk, kȁndra, kréda, nafȁka

local bus or train (which makes frequent stops): pilìćār

lock (of hair): fȑč

logs: drvljànīk

lolita: frȁjerica

lonely: ȉnokosan

lonely female: sȍlerica, sòlistica

lonely male: Jèzdimīr, sòlist

lonely person: sȍler

long conversation: pričánac

long hair: džùngla, kȉta

long jumper: dàljāš

long newspaper article: plȁhta

long note: krùmpīr[2]

long rock'n'roll solo: štȉkānje

long routine talk: kobàsica

long shoe: sandolína

long term prisoner: klȅsār

long time ago: kadìkad

long walk: štràpac

long, desire: mòriti se

long-haired musician: péder

long-legged female: rìpida, róda[2], štàkara

long-playing phonograph record, LP: plêjka

long-term female sexual partner: abonȇntica, abonȇntkinja

longer walk: štrapànzl

look at with interest, check out: šmekáriti, šmȅkati, zráčiti

look attentively: gùtati

look back at somebody: àblendovati

look for an opportunity to pick pockets: ošàrnariti

look for clients (of prostitutes): faćkáriti, fȁćkati

look for females: pičáriti

look for one's accomplice: zídati

look for something in different places: tetùrati

look for trouble: kȅšati se

look like, seem: pàrati, pàriti[1]

look out: trȁkoš

look, glimpse: đȁnel, ìklić-ždrákić[2], kîb, kȕka, lȕk[1], lȕkec, ždrâk

look, image: šmȅk

look, watch, scope out: àšikovati, đànisati, glédìti, gvàrdati, kíbiti, kȉšiti, kljȉšiti, skívati, snímati, strȉgati, šmȅkovati, špȅhati, tȑzati, zȅkiti, zìntati, zȉrkati, ȁktati, čkȉljnuti, dzìljati, dždráknuti, đániti, đȁnkati, đènisati, đȅriti, đȕšiti, ènē, ìkisati, kećùrati, kȉbnuti, íkiti, kȉžiti, kûždrati, òcariniti, ođànisati, òkisati, okoslavírati, opticírati, òšacovati, pocrkívati, pòškicnuti, prozènisati, svȉkati, šàcati, šȁcnuti, šȁcovati, škȉcati, šmèkeriti, trȁkati, uđànisati, uđániti, uđériti, ùjkisati, uždrákiti, zènisati, zèntati, zráknuti, zȕcniti, zȕcnuti, zȕrkati, zȕznuti, ždrȁkati, ždrȁknuti, ždrȉkati, žfȁknuti, žȉknuti, žnjȉkati, žrȁkati, žráknuti

looking bad: òfȕcān

looking for females, fishing for chicks: rȉbolōv

looking for females, scoping for babes: pičárēnje

looking, watching, scoping: đànisānje, fȁrkānje, šmȅkovānje, trȁkānje, ždrȁkānje, žrȁkānje

lookout (accomplice): bòrbāš

lookout (during theft): špèkcija

loose woman: abonȇntkinja, àrgō, bicìklistkinja, bùšotina, cáva, čépa, ćêlka, ćòškara, dáda[2], Dȁnkinja, darèžljīvka, dȑmāljka, dróca, drȍlja, dȕšodājnā, flȉćkica, frȉzērka, fȕfa, fȕfica, fȕga, fulágerka, grànit, guzojèbica, jéba, jèbeška, jèbica, jèbna, jèbōjka, jèbulja, kàmila, klâmfa, kuradàšica, kûrva, kurvètina, lȁkica, lùjika, méšalica, mȑdāljka, nȉmfić, pȁdavičārka, pàmfla, pégla, pìcōjka, picùlīnka, pìčkara, pičkùljina, pìčkulja, pìčkuša, pizdòjēpka, pȕška[2], radìjālka, rȁdodājka, Ràdōjka, radóševićka, raščepòtina, razjebànica, rédāljka, róša, sandȕčara, sèdmica, sèksača, sȅksī-mašína, Skȁndināvka, skùbina, spèrmara, spèrmātorka, , spèrmuša, svìripīzda, šindivíla, šȉšibeka, šȉzika, šljúnak, šmízla, špȉca, štrumfèta, trȅpavičārka, uzvìjōjla, uzvìjuša, vijȁgra, Vȍlkswāgen, vȑtiguza,

loose woman who does not enjoy sexual intercourse: jèbulja

loose woman, easy woman: lȁkodājka

loose woman, prick lover: kȕroslada

loot, pillage: ȁrati, zgepàrluk

looting: jàgma

lop-eared person: klémpa[2], klémpo, klempùhec, radàrista

lose (usu. in a game): pȕći

lose: ìspušiti, izdúvati[1], istrȍšiti se, òbrisati se, pròfućkati, pòsijati, spȉčkati, tandŕknuti, ùplakati se, zgȁsnuti

lose all one's money: skíknuti

lose all one's money, go broke: ošvorcírati se

lose money: crkávati, istapírati se, izgùtati, ìzvisiti, jaúknuti, kȁlnuti, kalírati, kalírati, òdvisiti, rȉgati, rȉgnuti, rikávati, ríknuti, tandŕknuti, tapírati se, vrísnuti, zvȉsiti

lose money or chances: vȉsiti

lose one's property: ràskućiti

lose one's sympathy: òdigrati

lose one's virginity: pȕći

lose time: tȕcati, zamajávati, zamajávati se

lose value: òdigrati

lose weight: òklocati se, ušȉljiti se

lose, be unable to find: skèmbati, zijániti

loser: gubìtāš

losing gambler: tȃpī, tȃpka[2], vìsūng[1]

loss of consciousness: bèhūt

loss of time: jebàncija

loss, detriment: bȕda[1], dokurcàna, džȉga, kȃl

lost: pèčen, trópa[2], zìjān[2]

lost, without orientation: ìsparen

loud and angry person: džèvātor

loud clothing: vrȋsak

loud discharge of intestinal gas, loud fart: Zvònimīr

loud kiss: cmȍk[2], cmòkac

loud laugh: cȅrēk

loud laughing: cerèkānje

loud music: pȉčēnje, pȉčvajs, rasturàčina

loud rock music: cjepáža

loud sound: trȇsak, trȅska, trȅskāj

loud sweater: vrištánjac

louse (the insect): cȉka, cȉtra, cȋvka, ckȁmnā, kȉm, mòrica, mòriza, ȍsīljka, stànār

love (in general): bȁvlju

love: ȁšik, gájiti, iotiàmisati, jȇz, jéza, kèfa, limunáda, ljúba, ljȕbica, tȑzati, žtèmisati

love affair: šéma, vȅza

love story (novel): ljȕbić

love whisper: gȓč

love-struck male, love-sick guy: sevdàlija, tȅtrijēb

lovely: hèrcig

lover (female): ȁmfora, àmōrka

lover (female): klȋnka, mȑdāljka, švàlērka

lover (male): dìbler, gȍlūb, jebigȗzović, krèsāč, kùlōv, lȁver, màšīnka, mlàdīć, picolóvac, škȑplja, šmȅkos, šváca[1], šváca[2], švȁler, tàbātor, tȕcić, tȗcović

low income: cȑkavica

low prices: jeftinòća

low-class bar, dive: bȃjta, ćùmez, mȗlj, špèlūnka

low-class fun (carnivals, etc.): sokolàna

low-class prostitute: ȁšōv, štàjgerka

low-class tavern or inn (esp. in Ottoman times): ȃn[1]

low-cut boots: ofìcīrka

low-proof plum brandy: cȗjka

low-quality (usu. in reference to merchandise), junk: bófl[2]

low-quality brandy: džȉbra, gòvnara, karbìtuša, pàsjakovača, pȁtoka, pìšara

low-quality cigarette: špȏrkā, tráva

low-quality food, slop: bȕćkurīš, nápoj

low-quality hard liquor, rot gut: bendžèluk

low-quality hashish: bȉle, bȋlje, bȋljka, kamìlica, šȉt[2]

low-quality marijuana: kŕdža[1]

low-quality merchandise, junk: bófl[1], dìvljāk[2], džȉbra, škȁrt

low-quality movie: bóza[1]

low-quality movie or novel, lemon: limunáda

low-quality peasant shoe: pìčetnjāk

low-quality salami: podrìguša

low-quality tobacco: kŕdža[1], kŕdžo

low-quality wine: tùdum

low-quality, cheap: bèzvezan, blȉjēd

lower-ranked clerk (in an office): mastìljār

lower-ranked officer: krpároš, prìprāvnīk

lowest passing grade: blìzanac, dvánja, dvónja, dvójka[1]

LSD, acid: dróge, dȕh, èsid, kȅksić, kiselìna, kisèlīš, strȏuberī, trȉp, zȅn

luck: lùtrija, tȃlija, trȅf

lucky: tàličan

lucky gambler: òfito, òkita

lucky person: tȃlija

lumber: guràvānjke

lunch: lȁnč

lungs, gills: šifonjéri, škȓge

lure chickens: ćȕkati

luring chickens: ćȕkānje

lust, sexual urge: ȅros, rȁjc, ràjcūng, šnȁjd

lying: dumbàrānje, folírānje, lȉrānje, lòžēnje, lòžnjava, mȁzānje, pàljevina, patamȕzovānje, pètljavina, strúgānje, šatrològija, tròvānje

mace (medieval weapon): buzdòhān[2]

machine gun: čȁčkalica, mitròljēz, pèvāč[2], pljȕckalica, puškètina, štȑcāljka

machine gunner: mitroljézac

machine industry worker: mašínac

machismo: mačȉzam

macho (person): ljùdina, mȁčo, mȁčo-mȅn, TBC [tê-bê-cê]

mafia: mȃfījāškī

mafia business: mȃfijāštvo

magazine (for bullets on a machine gun): trȁnzistor[2]

magistrate, investigating judge: istràžnjāk

mailman: kȅngūr, kovèrdžija, poštarȉlos, poštarȉška

main idea: bȉks[2]

main railroad station, Zagreb, Croatia: kolodvorȉška

main thing, most important thing: bȉks[2]

mainlander (so called by inhabitants of the coastal region): krumpìrāš

Mažuranićev Square in Zagreb, Croatia: Mažuránac

majority: višȉna

make: zbȍškati

make a considerable amount of money: ulóviti se

make a fool of oneself: blamírati se, gafírati se, glupírati se, izblamírati se, izgafírati se, izglupírati se, izgrafírati se, kretonírati se, majmùnisati se, orezíliti se, pàndisati

make a mess while looking for something, rummage through: istrkèljati, istrkèljisati, pretrkèljisati, trkèljati, trkèljisati

make a mistake, mess up: make a mistake, screw up: bŕljati[2], brljáviti, cȕcnuti se, čàbrisati, čabrírati, èkscesnuti, fȁliti[2], fȑljati se, gȕtnuti, ìskecati se, izgùtati, ìzvisiti, obŕnuti se, okrénuti se, ománuti, ȍšuriti se, picúknuti, préći se, pregráditi se, preráditi se, pròfulati, tandŕknuti, ùplakati se, zajebúniti se, zbrljéknuti, zȅznuti se, zglàjzati, zglȁjznuti, zrȅzati se

make a profit: òvajditi se

make a short trip: skòčiti, skȍknuti

make a wrong estimate: prekòntati, prekòntati se

make angry, make mad: ìzjakati, ràspigati, raznìtati, ràznjupati

make big money: ùbiti

make brandy: ìspeći

make defensive rebounds in basketball, clear the boards: lépiti, lijépiti

make drunk: nàcugati, nàpiti, napíjati

make excuses: kriviváriti, vȁditi se

make excuses to the police for not carrying an ID: klavìrisati

make faces in pain or fear: mèškoljiti se

make faces, grimace: kerèbečiti se

make friends: havèrisati, jaràniti se, sjaràniti se

make happy: raspáliti, spelávati

make interested: potpáliti

make jokes: izmotávati se, ráditi [1]

make jokes with: facírati, zaebávati, zagrebávati, zékiti se, zȅzati se

make mess, litter: pŕzniti

make moderate noise: šȕškati, šȕškoriti

make nervous, get on one's nerves: ìzmrdati, nasekìrati, pȉgati, ràspucati, zajebávati, živcírati

make noise: dȑndati, džȁkati, fȑkisati, glomòtati, glòmtati, gràktati, grúvati, halàbučiti, jaúkati, klapàrati, klapìnjati, klepètati, klȍkoriti, klopàrati, klopòtati, lupàrati, páliti, ropòtati, rùčati, rȕčiti, šklopòtati, šȕštati, šuškàrati, vatrírati, vòljati, žȁgoriti, žȁmoriti, žubòriti

make noise while walking: trupàrati, trȕpati

make pregnant, knock up: nàfilati, nàpūmpati, zapesíniti, zapésniti, zapésnuti, zapȑditi

make preparations for an action of some kind: àšikovati

make sad, sadden: ožúčiti, sjèbati

make somebody nervous: tangírati

make somebody smoke narcotic drugs: nadúvati

make someone act against a third party, stir up: nàpūjdati

make sure, be certain: prèšpilovati, prozènisati

make untidy, make messy: zapŕzniti

make up, fabricate: isfazonírati

make, construct, build: nàbaniti, nabanjívati

make, create: zgotíviti

make, prepare, fix: izbombardírati

make-up, cosmetics: ličánjac

making a fool of: cinculírānje, zafrkávānje

making a fool of oneself: glupírānje, krivìna, pàndisanje, šalabàjzānje

making an acquaintance: iskrcávānje

making faces, grimacing: krevéljēnje

making interested: páljēnje

making jokes with somebody: lȃfanje

making laugh: upišávānje

making noise: gràktānje, klapàrānje, klepètānje, lúpānje, lupàrānje, žȁgorēnje

making noise while walking: trȕpānje, trupàrānje

male bathing suit: mudàntīne

male cheated by a prostitute: pèrkan

male children, boys: kuràdija

male easily cheated by a prostitute: hȗm

male from a respected family: čȅgović, kòlenović, kòljenović

male habitually on the lookout for females: automàtičār

male homosexual dandy: karànfīl

male homosexual intercourse: alkárēnje, ćùprija

male homosexual who takes the active role: aktȉvist, aktȉvista, aktívac, svȑdlo

male homosexual who takes the passive role, femme: bȕzer, buzerànt, munára, nàguzac, nàguzār, nagùzara, ostràguša, pasívac, princéza, ritoznòjičār, sȉsī, tȅtka

male homosexual, gay: barùnica, bȁštrac, bȁštrāč, beločaràpāš, bìljčica, bulájko, bùljāš, bȕzić, buzorànt, buzurànt, bùzićār, čèlista, čèstitār: dȅpre, dèrape, dèrpe, dȅrpe, dȅrpić, dlȁkār, dràjfer, dùdek, dȕdloje, dupedávac, dupètāš, dùplōnka, dupojébac, gulánfer [1], gȕslār, gùzičko, fȁfer, féder, fȅsko, fȅško, fȉfī, fȉšbajn, fȉzbajn, Floramȋ, gánjalo, gȇj, glàvīć, golánfer, gȍspođica, gȑgljātor, guzerȁnt, gȕzić, guzodávac, guzojébac, guzojèbīle, gȕzoljūb, guzoljúbac, gùzičār, hòmīć, hȍmos, homosàpiens, ȉglić, jebengùzīle, jèbigūz, jebigùzīle, jòderpenj, kȁroljūb, karopljùgalo, kìrurg, kitolóvac, klȉstīr, kȍkōš, kòntrāš, kurcolízac, kuropùšāč, kȕrožder, lȁbūd [3], làstiš, lȅptīr, leptirȉška, leptirȕška, lizimȉrov, lízalo, mȃlā [2], Mȁrgot, mȅrī [1], mȉlomūd, mimóza, mùcek, mȕdoglād, mȕdomīr, mȕšmula, nàguz [1], opàjdār, ȏrka, ȍtpozadnīk, pahùljica, pȃpī, páter, péca, pèčūrka, pȅđa, pèdāl [1], pedála, pedálo, péder, pedèraj [1], pedèrāš, pederàško, pedèrčina, pederȉko, pedèrīn, pederȉška, péderskī, pȅdī, pedȉkēr, pedȉkīr, pȅdos, pȇdro, pedrolazàrija, pȅđa, pȅle, pelètān, pelȉkān, pepèljuga, pȅpī [1], pèpika, pepȋno, pȅpos, pȅrica, pèrkan, Pérsa, pèrvert, pȅs, pèšāk, pèškīr, pȅško, péšo, pešȍvān, pešovànder, pèžō, pìgist, pìgista, pjèšāk, podrèpāš, pȍp, pozadínac, pȕpak, pȕškār, rašamónac, rašomónac, rìbīć, ritoznòjičār, rošomónac, rùčnīk, sapùnār, sìsikūr, sladogúzac, smȍkvica, svilènjāk, Šȅkspīr, šèšīr, tapètār, tèhničār, tȅtka, tȅtkica, tòbdžija, Tȏnka, toplàna, tȍplī, tòpljāk, torbùljār, trùbāč, trećepózivac, tùbāš, uranista, vazelínac, vecȇovac, záhodār, žvákalica

male homosexual, queen: knèginja, kràljica

male in loud clothing: papàgāj

male in tight trousers: Škȍt

male inhabitant of the countryside, hick, bumpkin: ràškōv

male inhabitant of Zagreb, Croatia: Zagrejȅbić

male looking for a loose woman, guy on the make: bȁri, gòvedo, kòpātor, kòpatot, nàftāš, pìčkāroš, sladolèdār, tabànāš, trȅsko

male lover: Bòžidār, mòmak, ùmetnīk

male model: lȅptīr, leptirȉška, leptirȕška

male nickname: Picùrić

male on the make: mȕstra

male out of control, wild man: šùmāk

male protector (usu. in relation to a female): abàžur

male sexual partner (of a female): bùldožder, dàsina, Frézer, fùkāč, gùslāč, jèbac, jèbāč, jèbeš, jèbeša, jèbeško, jèbigūz, kȉtonja, kuràica, kuràjber, kùrātor, kuravȅla, kurávija, kurbàdūr, kúronja, kúronjica, mjȅsečina, mrzojébac, mũla, nabacìvāč, nabȉjāč, nȉtnāš, òvan, píčkonja, penìsēr, pìckāroš, pȉckoš, picolóvac, pȉčkār, pìčkāroš, pìčkīle, pȉčkobaša, pȉčkoprēž, pičkoprèžina, potpaljìvāč, šévac, šèvātor, šȉkić, šmȅker, šmȅkos, štósēr, švȁser, túcak, tȕcić, tȗcović, tȕče, tùrist, ùmetnīk, žènskāroš

male sexual partner: odvàjāč

male sexual partner from Zagreb, Croatia: jèbīč

male sexual partner of elderly females: mùčibabić, mùćibabić

male slow to understanding: trànzistor[1]

male student who cuts classes: avijàtiko

male waiting for his date to arrive: džònjāroš

male wearing fur: šarplanínac

male who attempts to catch or grasp something: pècāroš

male who behaves unconventionally, weirdo: degenèrik[2]

male who breaks wind while defecating: dròćkāš

male who counts the females he has had sex with: ròvāš

male who deflowers virgins: vàdičep

male who does not have his own apartment: podrùmār

male who dresses casually: hašòmān

male who engages in anal sexual intercourse: analìtičār[1]

male who engages in cunnilingus: pičkolízac, pizdolízac, slàstičār

male who engages in sexual intercourse with elderly females: ȁgbaba, antìkvār, babojébac, bagèrist, vatrogásac

male who failed in having sex with a female: kàndilo

male who hangs from a streetcar: pufèrāš, pulfèrāš

male who is easily cheated by prostitutes: tȕljān

male who is emotionally attached to the former Yugoslavia, Yugo-nut: jȕgonostàlgičār

male who lives with his in-laws: domàzet, prìpuz, prȉpuza

male who often laughs: kekètalica, kekètalo

male who only pets his girlfriend, one who only gets to second base: rukomètāš

male who stays in one place (e.g., in a bar): sìdrāš

male who uses cane: hokèjāš

male who uses tries to get close to females on crowded public transportation: kèšātor

male who wears old jeans: pȁdavičār

male who wears shoulder straps: Taràna

male with a black eye: ràkūn

male with a large nose: kuronòsīle, sùrlāš, sùrlek

male with a large penis: kȉtonja, kuràdāš, kuradȁšlija, kuràica, kuràile, kuràjber, kuràjlija, kùrājlo, kȕrobaša, kuromùdīle, kúronja

male with a sharp-tipped penis: šȉljokūr[1], šiljokùrīle

male with bad manners: seljàčina, sèljāk

male with bandy legs: keljávko

male with connections: vȉpovac

male with crooked teeth: zubàtac

male with curly hair: hȍbler

male with dark complexion: gàragan

male with exaggerated interest in sex: žènskāroš

male with eyeglasses, four eyes: cvikèrāš, ćòrkan, ćóro, naočárac, očàlāš, očalíner, snajpèrist

male with large buttocks: dúpac, dupèško, dupetárović, gúzo, gúzonja, gùzičko, gùzīle, šùpkīle, šúpkonja, trògüz, tȑtāš, tȑtos

male with large testicles: mùdān, mudàlija, mȕdālj, mudárko, múdonja, múdonjica

male with long arms: čȉta, čȉtos, čìtuljos

male with long hair, long hair: bìtlis, bìtls, čȕpavac[1], čȕpko, čúpo, rúnjo, vìnkleroš

male with talent for music: slùhista

male with white buttocks: bjèlogūz[1]

male witha a large mouth: žvalávko, žválo, žváljo

male without a beard, clean shaver: ćóso

male without his own apartment: tàrabār, Taràna

male, guy: bádža, bȍškāč, bȍškāć, brȁt, cúrac, čȉkovac, čkávac, čkàvela, čȍek, čȍjāk, čȍjek, čȏk[2], čòvik, čùvadār, ćálac, ćélac, dása, dasòvān, đȁvlāš, fȁca, fàcan, fèrgajn, fráca, frȁjer, fràjkan, frȅnk, gȍlūb, ìkel, jȅrfra, kȁurī, kȇr[1], kȉd, kȉt[1], kìnāf, kȉnfa, kȉnfāć, klȁmpa, klȉndōv, kòmād[1], kȗle, kùlōv, kȗm, lèvāt, lȗg, mànuk, mȉkica, mladúnac, mȑmot, mùškāć, mùškīć, múdonja, Péro[2], pìmpek[1], plȁjvāz[1], prìkan, prȉkī, strȋc, šalabàhter[2], šóder[1], tȋp[1], típus, trȃg, trȇm, tràpet, zmijoglávac, zulukàfer

male, tomcat: màčōr

malfunction: mána, òtīći, zablokírati se

malfunctioning: zaribávānje

malfunctioning devices: škȁr

malfunctioning lighter: rȍštīlj

malfunctioning, crashed, gone: òtišō, ríknō, zarībō, zȁštekaō

malicious: ȍtrōvan, pȁkosan, prolúpō,

malicious person: paksìjān

maliciousness: pȉzma

manage to do: ìzmućkati

manager of the personnel department (e.g. in a company): kadròvīk

manager who has only an elementary school diploma: osmogòdišnjāk

manhunt: baràčit, kȁčka, kuléra, strúja, vȁtra

maniac: mȁnijāk

manipulate (an instrument, vehicle): baràtati

manner: fazóna

manual insertion of the penis into one's vagina: prȁvopīs

manual laborer: ȁrgat, fȉzičār, fizikálac, fizikáner, fȉzikos, fȉzikus, fȉzos, kràmper, mȁnos, manuélac, rȍdoljūb, šljȁkavac

many, numerous: héjbet[2], hìpten, lȉtar, mȅtar, mlȍgo, šȕma[3]

marble (the toy): fŕnja, klàjber, klȉber, kléber, klȉšac, klíndža, klȉša, klíšer

mare: cukàrica, kȁlica, pèljača, rȁškovica

marijuana cigarette, joint: džȍint, džȍjnt, tvȉst

marijuana, Mary Jane: Màrija, marijȁna, màriš, màriška

marijuana, pot, grass: bàtine, domàćica, grȃs, mára, mȁrica, mȁša, mȕter, pȍt, tráva, trȁvka, vȕtra

marinated vegetables: tùršija

mark on a shot glass: cȑta [2], sèsil

mark on a shot glass showing one deciliter: cècil

marked: màrkīrān

marked card: tȅrs [1]

marker (writing device): flóka, flòkiš, flȍks, flòmīć

market: pìjac, pjȁc, pjȁca, pljȁca

Marlboro (cigarette brand): Mȁlbāč

marriage: gìljotina, òkovi, ȍmča, ròbija

married: okùpīran, zàsedlān

married man: robìjāš

married woman: robijàšica, úzda, zàrigljanā

married, hitched: òbješen, ȍkovān, zàhaklān, zálotan, zàvēzān

marry, tie the knot: okòvati se

Marxism: veronáuka

masculine first name: Sȉsoe

mashed potatoes: cèment [2]

mask: lârfa

masochist, male who likes to suffer (esp. in love): Šȅkspīr-tîp

masturbate: apcìgati, biljáriti, čaplàjisati, dȑkati, dȑkati se, drkèljisati, dȑmati, dŕviti, ȉgrati, ìzdrkati, klȉmati, klȕpčati, kljȕčkati, kljȕčnuti, knjȉžiti, ljúljati, ljȕljnuti, ljúštiti, nȉtnovati, òtjecati, pêglati, sȅksati, šakírati, šamàrati se

masturbate, beat off: mlȁtnuti, šȉbati, šȉbati se, ùdariti

masturbated: ìzdrkān

masturbating: čaplàjisānje, dȑmānje, pêglānje, zdȑkān

masturbation: dȑkānje, klȉmānje, Mȉkī-Šȉlja-Hòrācije, Nȉš-Pȉrot, onanȉ-onanȁ, pȉčēnje, sȅksānje, seksndràjsig

masturbation, beating off: šibácija, šȉbānje

masturbation, hand job: rukotvòrine

masturbator (female): dȑkadžījka, pȉstača

masturbator (male): čaplàjist, dȑkadžija, dȑkezina, dȑkoš, dȑkšezina, dȑmadžija, dȑmātor, gladijâtor, spȅrmić, šȁkār, šíber [1], šȉbadžija, šȉbadžīka

match (lighting device): ćȉber, ćȉbra, ćȉbre, dȑvo, kànājka, kàšika, krȅna, zapaljénje

matchbox: ćȉbra, kànājka, mašínica, zapaljénje

maternity ward: inkubâtor

math: mȍtka

math teacher: dìgitrōn, matemàtičār, màtiškinja

mathematics: máta, màtiš

mattress: jȍgī, jȍgī-dùšek

mature (of women): upíciti

maybe: mòžda

mayonnaise: majmùnēz

mead: medènjača

meal: nápoj, pȁpica

mean and deceiving action: kvàrnjāk

mean individual: fùnjara [1]

mean or worthless individual: karakušljívko, kuràjber, kurotrèsina

meaningless: dȕbiōzan, glȕpav

meaningless talk, blabber: balávljēnje

measure for opium: fȁn

meat: kàrnī, kȁrnje, kokalína, kȑnjor, krvàjca, kȑvavō [2], mȉška, mȉškira, mȉša, pòtēgānō

mechanical engineering student: mašínac, zupčànik

mechanical learning: grȗv, grúvānje

mechanical studying: búbanje

mechanism: skalamèrija

medal, decoration: dekorácija

medical check-up for prostitutes: vjȅšala

medicine: medecína

meet a boyfriend or a girlfriend: iskȑcati se, spòjiti

meet unwillingly: sùsrati

meeting: sàsranak, stȓk [2]

meeting of a group of people who meet each other frequently: prózivka

meeting place: štráfta

member of a disrespected family: jebigȗzović

member of any subcultural group which worships evil: dàrker

member of communist secret police in the former Yugoslavia: ȕdbovac

member of Croatian national guard: zȅnga

member of JUL (Jugoslovenska udružena levica 'United Yugoslav Left' a party in Serbia): jûlovac

member of the Croatian separatist movement in the 1970s: màspokovac, proljećárac

member of the HDZ (Hrvatska demokratska zajednica 'Croatian Democratic Union', a political party in Croatia): hadezȅovac

member of the Radical Party (a political party in Serbia): radȉkāl

member of the SDP (Socijaldemokratska partija 'Social Democratic Party', a party in Croatia): esdepȅovac

member of the SDS (Srpska demokratska stranka 'Serbian Democratic Party', a Serbian party in Bosnia): esdeȅsovac

member of the SPS (Socijaldemokratska partija Srbije 'Social Democratic Party of Serbia', a party in Serbia): espeȅsovac

member of the UN protection forces in Bosnia in 1990s: unprofórac, unprofúrac

member of the Yugoslav Communist Party: crvèndāć

member of UDBA, communist secret police in the former Yugoslavia: ùdbāš

member of Yugoslav parliament: pòsranīk

members of the French national team: trikolóri

memory blackout: kȕrcšlus, kȕršlus

mend (garment): ȕštopati, ȕštopovati

menstruating female: grànīčārka

menstruation, period: cȉkla, cûrka, kòlīnje, krvàvica, krvoprolíće, méca [1], mȅnga, mȅnza, mènzis, mȉndžocūr, mjȅsečnjāk, perìod, perióda, stȍp, stvâri

mention, hit on: dòkačiti

meow: krnjàukānje, krnjàukati, mȁūk, maúkati, maùkavā, mijaùkati, mijȁūk

meowing: maùkav, maùkavac, maúkānje, mijaùkānje

Mercedes (a car make): budžóbus, mérdža, mȅrdžān,

mérdžo
Mercedes (make of car): méca [1], mȅčka
mercenary: ajlùgdžija, àjlučār
merchandise: bȁro [2]
merchant (female): travinjàrica
merchant (male): tàrnjār, tȍnjār, trȁnjār, trȁvčār, travčàrica, travìnjār, trònjār
merciful: sevàpli
mercy: sadàka, sèvāp
mess around, fool around: mùvati se
mess, disorder, disturbance: alàvānta, bèlāj, čȕnak, dȁr-mâr, džéva, džȕmbus, fáma, fertùtma, fȑka, frtùtma, gužvánac, gužvánjac, hȁos [2], jebàncija, kàzīn, krkljánac, kȑš, muvàna, papazjànija, pèkmez [2], pȉčvajz, pišaónica, pizdàrija, pofrtùtma, ȑšum, rȕsvāj, stȑka, tarapàna, vášar, vȁtra, zavrzlàma, zȅnt
message: ȁber, àbər, hȁber
messy woman, untidy female: smràdara
messy, disorderly: ȁljav
metal ball used in smoking hashish: gvôžđe
metal industry worker: metálac
metal marble (the toy): gvozdénac
metal or wooden basket used to catch fish: gȕzār
metal syringe: gvozdénac
metal two-dinar coin: škȕda
methadone: mȅt
micrometer: mȉkromèter
midfielder (soccer): pȁker, vèzist, vèzista
mighty: nenadjèljiv
mike, microphone: mȁjk
Milde Sorte (cigarette brand): Mȉldāć
military (armed forces in general): armáda [1], armáta, àskara, askèrija, rèfija, remàdija, sìtnā
military check-up (physical exam): kúra [1]
military commander (esp. in Ottoman times): àlājbeg
military commander's (esp. in Ottoman times): àlājbegov
military fugitive, a.w.o.l.: lògoš
military ID: bȕkvica
military jeep with enclosed cabin: kampanjóla
military rank: čvárak
military reserve: réja
milk: klȅnīšte, lȁpte, mlíko, varènika
milk sugar used as a substitute for heroin: bonìta
milk-shake: mȉlk-šȇjk
milking: pljȕgānje
mill: gȑmčār
million: júnac, kȉlo
million dinars or units of any other currency; a million-dinar bill: cígla
million dinars; a million-dinar bill: plȁhta
millionaire: galòpēr, milùnēr
Milosava (a woman's name): Jèbisava, Kȕrosava
mind: fitȋlj [1]
mind, brain: mȉnte

mineral water: kȉselā
Mini Morris (a car make): mìnīć
mini skirt: dòmindžos, dòmindžos-sȕknja, dòminđos, dòminđos-sȕknja, fasáda-mìnjāk, mȉnāć, mȉnica, mìnīć, mìnika, mìniška, mìnjāk
miniature (small bottle of alcoholic beverage): bòmbica
minimal dose of a drug: ćȅlavac
minimal wage: minimálac
minor car crash, fender bender: čukánjac
minor explosion, bam: pȕk
minor leagues, bush leagues: fildžān-líga
mint brandy: nànovača
minute (unit of time): cvȑkla, dekíka
minute, very small: mȉkro [2]
miracle: zbèlilo
mirror: glȉpši, špígl, špíglo, zùrilo
miscellany: šarènīš
miser (female), tightwad: Škȍtkinja
miser, tightwad, skinflint: bùnket, cìcija, cicìjāš, cȉcoš, cìculja, cȉncarin, cȉncer, cȉncoš, dramòser, guzojébac, guzojèbīle, hínja, jebigùzīle, jòtaškrnj, kȑcalo, pȉs [2], pìzdek [2], pizdèkān, pìzdūn, pízda, stèznat, stȉpsa, Škȍt, štȅker, tȑdek, tvrdnjáković, tvȑtko, zȑkī, zȑkī, Žȉdov
miserly, stingy: téžak, tvȓd [2], ùzak
misfortune, bad luck: mȁler [2]
mispronounce (usu. with additional nasal articulation): ȕnjkati
Miss (beauty queen, etc.): mìsica
miss by passing or driving by: prešíšati, prošíšati
miss, fail: čabrírati, kȉksati, kȉksnuti, kiksírati, pròfulati, trokírati, upŕskati, zglȁjzati, zglȁjznuti
miss, fail to hit: fȕlati
miss, lack, be out of: hváliti
miss, long for, be without: fȁliti [1]
missing one's vein: ȁut [1]
missy: gȍspojica
mistake, error (usu. in social relations): gȁf
mistake, error: fȅler, grjȅška, kȉks, prélaz, pȕška [2], visúljak, vìsūng [2]
mistery (movie, book): krìmiš
mistress, extramarital female lover: trȁnjerica, travčàrica, travinjàrica, trȍnjarica
misunderstanding: kȕrcšlus, kȕršlus, kvȑc [2]
misuse: fȑljati se
mix up, confuse: pobŕkati
mixed doubles (table tennis, etc.): mȉks
mixture of narcotic drugs: kòktel
mixture of soda water and mineral water: amerikáner
moan in pain: jéčati, jéčiti, jékati, jéknuti
moaning in pain: jéčānje, jèktānje, kȑkljānje
mobster: mâfijāš
moccasin: crnògōrka
mock, ridicule: jèričiti, jèričiti se
moderate noise: šȕškor

moderate politician, dove: gòlūb

moderately strong male: čòporac, čȕčko, kȍkot, màjkica, smrdljȉčko, šùbara, žȍhār

modern: mòndiš

modern and popular place, hip place: dèndiš

modern musical score: modèrnjāk

modern person: suvremènjāk

moist, damp: mèmljiv

moment: cȗg

monastery: nȁmastīr

money (usu. a small quantity): kȋnta

money: cȉfra, džȅga, dženga, đȅnge, đȇngi, fȅndža, fôle, frȁnkopān, gáža, gȅnga, gôld, gròši, katrànica, kȉntāć, lára, lôv, lóva, lovijána, lovijánović, lòvīnđer, lòviška, mȃlo [2], mȁnī, mȁslo, mȅka [1], òrasi, pàpīr [2], papirȉška, pàra [1], pènezi, pȅngi, pènjez, pȉlke, pȉlove, piljáve, pìnjave, ràjīnke, rȉta, ròjīnke, rȍnjke, sêno, slȁma, sôldi, šáder, škȕda, šóder [2], šôlde, šȕške, trȁnja, tránjci, úlog, ȗlje, vȃlo, vȁške, vȕla, zelènāš [2], zȇlje, zôb

money belt: bùbreg

money exchange (activity): klȉk-klȃk

money in a safe place: gȗt

money which goes to the host: pȉnka

money, cabbage: rȅpa

money, clams: rȉba, tȕna [1]

monitor (pupil who for one day keeps the blackboard clean): sudòpera

monkey wrench: amerikáner, frȁncūz

monkey, ape: banànāš, banàndžija, trȁvčār, trònjār

monogamous male: jednòrupić

monotonous game (soccer, etc.): pȉmplovānje

monotonous sound: rȍkmōn

Montenegrin (person): đȅtić, Montenegríner, Monteníger

month: mȅtar, žȉlēt [2]

monthly wage earner: àjlučār, ajlùgdžija

moo: múkati

moon: sȉjalica

moonlighting (work): tèzga

Morava (cigarette brand): Yȗ-hàšiš

more than enough: ȉ-hâ-hâ, ȉ-hā-hâj

morning: sàbāh

morning meeting of two spouse cheaters, morning tryst: matinéja

morning or noon snack: màrēnda

moron: pȑdāč

morphine: èmsel, gȁnk, mȍkī [2], mȍkica, mȍrfo

mosque: bȕkva, kíšnja, pùčavnica

most beautiful: ȕmobōlan

motel: prȍpūh

motel where spouse cheaters meet, no-tell motel: Abortàna, Brakolómac

mother: dȃjka, dàre, jòrastanj, kêle, kêv, kéva, mȁtera, papazjànija, rȁstā, ròditēljka, snȅska

mother of one's son's or daughter's spouse: príja [1]

mother's relatives: újčevina

mother, mom: dáda [1], dádica, kévac, kèvdža, kevijánovićka, klȉmīć, kljáka, kȍrca, kôrča, mâ [2], mája [1], màjara, màmče, mȁnja, mȕterica, mȕtka, nána

mother, old lady: màtorā, màtōrka, rȉstićka, stârā

mother-in-law: pȕnjenica, tâle, tȃš [1], tȃštnjāk

motorcycle: motorȉška, píla, pȑdalica, pȑdalo, prdáljko, rȍbot, zmìja, zvȋr, zvìruša

mouth: bàljaz, bàljoz, cùpina, dròbilica, frnjókalica, golùbārnīk, gòvnara, gȕbica, kljûn [2], lȁbrnja, làbruža, lȁjavica, lámpa, làpina, mȅnza, njȕpalica, njȕpavica, pȅvalica, pȉčka, pjȅvalica, pljúca, pomìjara, rȁlje, rolèta, tàmbura, zȅpa, žnàbl, žȕtavica, žvàćkalica, žvȃle, žvȃlje

mouth, muzzle, face: bȑnjica, fàmfulja, fànfrlja

move in an effort to assume a position: mrȅškati se

move over: mìčigen

move slowly (usu. of insects): hmíliti, hmíljeti

move while making noise (as of a train): tupàrati

move, change the position of: ćúlati, mȑdnuti

movie house, theater: bìjus, bȋk [1], bȉonja, bioskopìjān, bioskopijáner, bioskopijánović, bȉs [2], bìskis, bìskiš, bíša, bùvar, nȍki [2]

much, very: debèlo, dòbro [2], mȕljte, poštèno, šȕkar

mucus, snot: kòkōška, rezánci, ȓkonjac, šlȃjm [2]

mud: glȋb

muddy terrain: blȁga, bȑčkavica

mulatto: kàkao

mulberry fruit: mûrva

mulberry tree: mûrva

multicolored: baljùško

multitrack recording: kanalizácija

multitude: bȕljūk, gȕta, héjbet [1], ìćmet, kàmara, silèsija, višȉna

mumble: mȑđati, mrìdžati, mȑmljati, mrmòkati, mȑmoljiti, mȕmati, mùmlati, mùmljati, smùmlati, smùmljati, tutùnjati

mumbling: mȑmljānje

mumbling male, mumbles: mȑmljavac, mŕmljo

murder: mȁckānje

muscle: čvȍr, pácov

muscular: čvȍrnovat

muscular female: buhalȅtka, džòmba, džȍmbe

muscular leg (of a woman): hòlbaks

muscular male: báto [2], bȉk [2], bìlder, čeličàna, flȉt, gorȉla, kȁmenī, kȕrobaša, kvȑga, Lȍtār, mêso, mȑga, mȑha, nabudžénko, òrmān [1], òrmār, razbacánko, stijéna, stȑvina

muscular male, pumped up dude: tèle, trokrílac

muscular male, pumped up guy: šifònjēr, zvȉjēr

muscular, pumped up: kȑšan, nabìjen, nàbildovan, nàpumpān, rȁzbacān

muscularity: čeličàna, nàbildovānōst

music: mjȗz, mjúza, mùžika, zíka

music class: múza

music festival: fȅstica, fèstira

music from one's own country: domàćica

music shool: glazbènjāk

musical concert: svȋrka

musical harmony: hàrma

musician: bàndīt, bàpist, fíro, lȁcī [1]

musicians: jòzičaritnunj

Muslim animal sacrifice (esp. on Muslim holy days): kùrbān

Muslim clergy: ulèma

Muslim female: bȕla

Muslim religious book (in general): ćìtāb, ćìtāp

Muslim religious community: džèmāt, đèmāt

Muslim religious school: mḗjtef

Mussolini (a kind of wine and juice cocktail): okupâtor

mustache: ùsnāći

mute: mȕtav

my generation: gȅne [1], génjo

mystery (movie, book): krȉm, krȉmī, krìmīć, kriminálac

nag: zvȍcati

nail (fastening device): čavȑkān, èsker, jèkser

naive customer: pepèljuga

naive female: prèmijērka, škȑplja

naive inhabitant of the countryside: bugojánac

naive male: abàžur, àbīb, bicìklista, cáva, diléja, diletànt, flòrijān, Generȁlić, gràfičār, grȁfos, hlebínac, keleràba, lêvī [2], lìvadić, lòžāč, lòžātor, malicána, nalètilić, òvan, pȁlac, pèčūrka, ràškōv, róvac [1], sȉsānče, sȉsoje [1], slȉkār, vìnkleroš, zbȉb

naive patron in a restaurant susceptible to deception: krȅn

naive person: bášta [2], Hlèbine, làjbek, lèvāk [1], ložàna, naìvčina, óvca, pepèljuga, šȕška, vȅverica

naive senior citizen: mánda

naive victim of a prostitute: mȕster

naive young female: kȉkica

naiveness: naíva

naked (of a female): golopìčast

naked (of a male): gȍlokūr, golòmud

naked: gològuz, gològuzas, gològuzast, golòtrbas, gȍljāhan

naked male: gologùzīle

nakedness: golòtinja

name for a nonexistent kind of pliers used to joke with people without knowledge of tools: motocángle

name for Banat (region in northeastern Serbia): Holàndija

name for Baščaršija (a late medieval neighborhood in Sarajevo, Bosnia): Čàršija

name for Bill Clinton used in Serbia (in particular during the military campaign against Yugoslavia in 1999): Klíća [2]

name for the cab stand at Britanski Square in Zagreb, Croatia: lubènica

name for the cab stand on Anke Butorac street in Zagreb, Croatia: štòplīn

name for the high school on Križanićeva street, Zagreb, Croatia: Krȉžanka

name for the prison at Goli island (Croatia, where the former communist regime detained its political enemies): Gòljāk, kȁmēn [1], Haváji, sùnčalīšte

name for the prison in Stara Gradiška, Croatia: dugàna, kúla, lònjara, mȑkulja

name of a bar at Ilica and Marinkovićeva streets in Zagreb, Croatia: akvârīj

name of a bar at Nikola Tesla street in Zagreb, Croatia: đȁnf

name of a bar frequented by retirees in Zagreb, Croatia: ćȅle-kúla

name of a bar on Ilica street in Zagreb, Croatia: Televîzor

name of a bar on Masarykova street in Zagreb, Croatia: Zvȅčić, Zvȅčka [1]

name of a bar on Petrinjska street in Zagreb, Croatia: šòferšājba

name of a bar on Petrova street in Zagreb, Croatia: Ròda [1]

name of a bar on Preradovićeva street in Zagreb, Croatia: vìnālka

name of a bar on Trnjanska street in Zagreb, Croatia: Oklahòma

name of a bar with large windows at the Albania building in Belgrade, Serbia: akvârijum

name of a cafe in Zagreb, Croatia: jȅbozōv [2]

name of a cafe on Frankopanska street, Zagreb, Croatia: krȁva

name of a cafe on Ilica street in Zagreb, Croatia: Ìzlog

name of a cafe on Nikola Tesla street in Zagreb, Croatia: jȕnferica

name of a cafe on Rački street in Zagreb, Croatia: krùmpīr [2]

name of a cafeteria in Zagreb, Croatia: màjmunjāk

name of a dance club at Jakšić dance school in Zagreb, Croatia: Džȅksōn

name of a dance club at the former Žrtava fašizma Square in Zagreb, Croatia: krùmpīr [2]

name of a dance club at the student dormitory complex in Zagreb, Croatia: krùmpīr-bâr

name of a dance club at the Studentski centar Zagreb, Croatia: stȕdoš

name of a dance club at Vrapče near Zagreb, Croatia: Sȅrtić

name of a dance club at Workers' center in Zagreb, Croatia: Râdnjāk

name of a dance club in Fijanova street in Zagreb, Croatia: Fijáker

name of a dance club on Bogović's street in Zagreb, Croatia: Bȉgāč

name of a dance club on Brešč street in Zagreb, Croatia: Brȅšč

name of a dance club on Maršal Tito square in Zagreb, Croatia: Tȕcman

name of a dance club on Trnjanska cesta, Zagreb, Croatia: baràka

name of a dance cub at the Šarengrad Street in Zagreb, Croatia: šára

name of a dry white wine from Herzegovina: sȁmotok

name of a field in Lika, Croatia: Dèrigūz

name of a peak in Montenegro: Kȕrozeb [2]

name of a place where prostitutes gather in Zagreb, Croatia near the train station: Àvēnija

name of a restaurant at the Main Railroad Station in Zagreb, Croatia: knjávnica

name of a restaurant at the main train station in Zagreb, Croatia: dȉmnica name of a restaurant on Margaretska street, Zagreb, Croatia: Dũda[2]

name of a water source in Serbia: Píčkovac

name of an island in Croatia: Močigùzica

name of Belgrade (Serbia): Bȃngkok, Bȃnkok, Bègiš

name of Beograđanka (a highrise in Belgrade, Serbia): Udòvica

name of Bijelo dugme (a very popular rock band in the former Yugoslavia during the 1970s and 1980s): Dugmíći

name of Britanski trg (a square in Zagreb, Croatia): Británac

name of Gradski podrum, a restaurant in Zagreb, Croatia: Gêpê

name of Željezničar (a soccer team in Sarajevo, Bosnia): Žéljo

name of inhabitant of Zagreb, Croatia: Pȕrgar, Pȕrger[1]

name of Intercontinental Hotel (Zagreb, Croatia): Ȉnter, Interkȍntī, Interkȍntić, Ȉntić, kȍntić

name of Jahorina (a mountain near Sarajevo, Bosnia): Jàorina

name of Jarun lakes (Zagreb, Croatia): Bágeri

name of Jelačićev square (Zagreb, Croatia): Jèlac, Jêlčić, špȉca, Tȓgāč, Tȓgīć

name of Kalemegdan (a park in Belgrade, Serbia): Kàliš

name of Kazališna kavana (i.e. a cafe near the Croatian National Theater, Zagreb, Croatia): Kàvkāz

name of Kikinda (a town in Serbia): Kèkēnda

name of King Tomislav square in Zagreb, Croatia: Tomislávac

name of Knez-Mihajlova street in Belgrade, Serbia: Knêz, Knèzmiš

name of Konjarnik (a neighborhood in Belgrade, Serbia): Màzgārnīk

name of Kvaternikov square in Zagreb, Croatia: Kvȃtrić

name of Lapidarij discotheque in Zagreb, Croatia: Lȃp

name of Majestic hotel, Belgrade, Serbia: Máža

name of Medaković (a neighborhood in Belgrade, Serbia): Mȅdāk

name of Mosor restaurant at Jelačićev Square in Zagreb, Croatia: Mosòrija

name of Mount Trebević (Bosnia): Jebèvīć

name of Munich (city, Germany): Mȉnken

name of New Belgrade (Serbia): Nòvāć, Nòvāk[1]

name of Padinska Skela (a town near Belgrade, Serbia): Pàdinburg, Padȉnjāk

name of Patria Movie Theater (formerly called Triglav, Zagreb, Croatia): bàhara

name of Petlovo brdo (a neighborhood in Belgrade Serbia): Pétlovača

name of Pionir dome in Belgrade, Serbia: Pionírac

name of Ritz bar (Zagreb, Croatia): ìtcri

name of Rovinj (a town in Croatia): Rôvka

name of Sarajevo (a city in Bosnia): Sàrājvo, Šȅher, Tȅherān

name of Strossmayerovo Promenade in Zagreb, Croatia: Štrȍc

name of Stubičke toplice (a spa in Croatia): Stubinjâk, Stuháki

name of Stubičke toplice (a spa in Croatia): Stubáki, Stubičnjâk

name of Student Cultural Center in Belgrade, Serbia: SKC [skəc]

name of Tašmajdan, the park in Belgrade, Serbia: Tȃš[2]

name of the army swimming pool in Zagreb, Croatia: zêlje

name of the bar at Bunićeva and Pucićeva streets, Zagreb, Croatia: Koréja

name of the bar at Ilica and Marinkovićeva street in Zagreb, Croatia: spȅrmić, vidíkovac

name of the bar at the Central Station in Zagreb, Croatia: Sovȉljara, zèntara

name of the cab station at Masarykova and Preradovićeva streets in Zagreb, Croatia: trȍkūt

name of the campus dormitory complex in Belgrade, Serbia: Studènjāk

name of the Cepelin discotheque (in Belgrade, Serbia): Cȅp

name of the coffee shop near Knez Mihailo Monument, Belgrade, Serbia: Kljùsina[2], Kȍnj[2], Šȉzilīšte

name of the dance club at Šalata hall in Zagreb, Croatia: šȃlfa

name of the department store in the Beograđanka high-rise in Belgrade, Serbia: akvârijum

name of the Fine Arts Academy Club (Belgrade, Serbia): Â[3]

name of the hotel Esplanade in Zagreb, Croatia: Ȅspa, Ȅspić

name of the juvenile detention center in Glina, Croatia: Glinènjāk, Glȉnica

name of the juvenile detention center in Lepoglava, Croatia: glùbara

name of the narrow-gauge train which used to run from Zagreb to Samobor, Croatia: Samobòrček

name of the prison at Padinska Skela, Serbia: Pàdinburg, Padȉnjāk

name of the prison in Lepoglava, Croatia: Lȅpica, Zágōrka

name of the prison in Kruševac, Serbia: Krȕška

name of the prison in Lepoglava, Croatia: plànina

name of the prison in Stara Gradiška, Croatia: cȓvara

name of the prison in Stara Gradiška, Croatia: Gradijáner

name of the prison in Stara Gradiška, Croatia: starijána, stàrulja, stènjara

name of the prison on Petrinjska street in Zagreb, Croatia: Petrijáner

name of the public toilet at Jelačićev square in Zagreb, Croatia: smùtljivac

name of the public toilet at Zrinjevac in Zagreb, Croatia, where male homosexuals gather: péder-bâr

name of the Ribnjak dance club in Zagreb, Croatia: Ribȉčija[2]

name of the river Sava: mûlj

name of the shopping mall at Republika Square in Belgrade, Serbia: Staklénac

name of the Sljeme mountain shelter in Croatia: Tomislávac

name of the streetcar line number nine in Zagreb, Croatia: Désa name of the swimming pool on Daničićeva street in Zagreb, Croatia: Dànica , kȁčka, káda

name of the Western train station in Zagreb, Croatia: Zâpadnjāk

name of the Zagrepčanka skyscraper in Zagreb, Croatia: žiràfa

name of theVuk Karadžić's monument in Belgrade, Serbia: Kȕrjāk[1]

name of Treskavica (a mountain near Sarajevo, Bosnia): Tréska

name of Trešnjevka (a neighborhood in Zagreb, Croatia): Tèksās

name of Trešnjevka soccer field in Zagreb, Croatia: grȁha

name of Trg Republike in Belgrade, Serbia: Kȍnj[2]

name of Tucić dance school in Zagreb, Croatia: Tȕcman

name of Tuškanac park in Zagreb, Croatia: Tȕškić

name of Ulcinj (a city on the Montenegrin coast): Vùcīnj

name of Vatroslav Lisinski concert hall in Zagreb, Croatia: lȉsnjāk

name of Vatroslav Lisinski concert hall in Zagreb, Croatia: vȁtrić

name of Vila Rebar restaurant in Zagreb, Croatia: rebàrica

name of Yugoslav Drama Theater (a theater in Belgrade, Serbia): Jugodȑp, Jȕgošćāp

name of Yugoslavia hotel (Belgrade, Serbia): Júga

name of Zagreb, Croatia: Grȅbza

name of Zeleni Venac (a neighborhood in Belgrade): Zelènjāk

name of Šumatovac (a restaurant in Belgrade, Serbia): Šȕma[1]

nap: drêmka, haláknuti

narcotic drug effect, trip: vóžnja

narcotic drug in the form of a dense substance: cr̀njāk

narcotic drug, dope: aspiríni, bònbōn, dȅršo, dôp, dôup, džȁnk, fiks, gȁdro, gȕdra, gȕdrica, hrána, jègulja, júha, Kalifòrnija, krȕh, krȕlt, mȅrī[1], nȁrko, pájdo, prâh, prášak, sȁnšājn, sȉć, spîd, stôun, štȁka, tȁp[2], žètōn

narcotic drugs hidden in one's anus: fìnger

narrow penis: vìršl

narrow-gauge train: ćíra, ćíro

nasal mucus, snot: bȁla, lȁjne

national border: brȉtva[3]

national team (soccer, basketball, etc.): rȅpka

near, close by: blízo

necktie: bȕnt, čvȍr, kȕčka, kurvètina, prȉštekati, štrȉk, ùlār, úže, vùzel, žnóra[1]

needle: Džȍnī, gȁn

negative particle, no: ȁš, pàmpur[1]

negative response, no: jȍkavac, nȁe[1], nȁje, nȁjo, nȉcam, nȉcom, nìkanōr, nȉks

negative, undesired: nȅpoćūdan

neigh: ȓzati

neighbor (female): komšȉče, kòmšija, kòmšika, kòmšinica

neighbor (male): kómšo

neighbor: vȕho, zîd

neighborhood: komšȉluk

neighborhood with a specific jargon (e.g. Gornji Grad in Zagreb, Croatia): vutèčina

neighing: ȓzānje

neither: nȉt

nephew (one's brother's son): bratùčed

nervous: nàdrkān, nàdr̄ndān, nàkūrčen, nȅurōzan, tȑzav, žȉvac[2]

nervous male: živčènjāk

nervous person, nail biter: nèrvčik, nȍktogrīz, Ȕglješa, žȉvac[1]

nervousness: pȁdavica, pȁnjānje, popizdȉtis

never: nȉgdi, sȕtra

new and of low quality: novokompònīrān, novokòmponovān

new girlfriend: pr̀vā

new newspaper: frȉškić

New Year's Eve: nòvāk[2]

newcomer: dȍđoš, dóšlo, dotepénac, pr̀ipuz

news (in general): ȁber, àbər, cvéba, njûs

news boy: kȍlpić

newspaper: pàpīr[2], šára, šȁre, šarènica

newspeak, incomprehensible political jargon: novogȍvor

newsstand: trȁfika

nice and kind female: Fȉnkinja

nice and kind male: Fínac

nice clothing: pêrje

nice individual, kind person: lègēnda

nice male, cool guy: dȅda, màrka[1]

nice woman, friendly female: cȁrica

nice, cool: bâjan

nice, cute (object or person): fȉn, hȁrtan, ìspēglan, kȑvav, lîp

nice, kind: fȉnskī

nicely: kȑvavo[1]

nicely dressed, tastefully dressed: kȍžīrān, pìcīng

nicely furnished room: golùbārnīk

nicely shaped glass marble (the toy): Amerikánac

niceness, kindness: finòća

nickname for a male: Kuràica, Kúronja, Kúrto[2]

night: karàmluk, mkánje, mȑka, mŕkānje, mȑklā, mȑkšan, mr̀kšant, nȅkat, nȍć, ȍćno, zvezdánjac

night club: koslȉna

night train: mrȃčnjāk, pȕh, vukòdlak

night train thief: sòvēr

night-shift policeman: bèskućnīk

nightstand: nȁtkāsna

ninja: nȉndža

nipples (of a female): ȍči

no: pȕf[1]

no police: vîdno

no problem, no big deal: fȍrpās[1]

noble or aristocratic female: ȅrcavā

noise: cȉkot, cìktānje, cȉrlīk, deràčina, drȅka, džȁka, džéva, glȍmot, grája, grȍmor, halàbuka, hûk, hȕka, jàūk, klȅpēt, krȉcka, kȑka, lârma, lȕpa, pofurtùtma, ȑka, rȍpot, skȉka, šȁša, šizijáda, šȕmor, šúšak, šûšanj, šúšnja, šȕšnjava, šȕštānje, šûšt, šûštanj, tandȑkāje, tandȑkānje, tȍpot, tȕka, vȁtra, zȕk, zȕka, zȕkānje, zvéčānje, žȃgor, žȕbor

noisy: àukast, jaùkav, jzvêčan, žȃgōran, žagòrav, žagòrljiv

noisy senior citizen: svrȁka

non-Muslim: ćáfir, ćȁur, ćȁurin, dòmuz, đȁur, đȁurin, kȁurin, kȁūrka, kŕmak, kȑme

nonchalance, carefreeness: nonšalàncija

nonchalant: nȍnšantālan

nonsense: bašibòzuk, dȑn-zvȑc, dȑn-zvȑc, krivìna, pišôre, prdàrluk, tȃndara-brȍć, tȃndara-mȃndara-brȍć

normal: čȉst

normal individual, one having generally acceptable attitudes and behavior: strèjtāš

normal state of affairs: nòrmālka

normal, straight: strêjt [1], strêjt [2]

North: sȅver

nose: bàbura, cùfla, flàuta, frùla, frnjóka, hȑga, kalàbura, karburâtor, kìhara, klarìnēt [2], klȉpa, klízāljka, kljȕka, krȁstavac, kȕka, kvȁka, mȑkva, nȍki [1], nôle, nòsīnger, njȍkalica, njónja, njušènjāk, njúška, paradȃjz, prȁćka, pȕhica, pȕška [2], rámpa, rȉlo, sȕrla, šnjófalica, šúber, tȍbogān, vùgorek

nose, beak: kljûn [2]

not a bit: nȉckam

not real, fake: gȉstro [1]

not to mention: bàška [1]

note: žȍhār

notebook: kùpus, tèfter

notebook used for teacher's comments to the parent (usu. concerning child's behavior): informàtivka

nothing: kȕrac [3], nȉš, šípak, tandàrija, tȑta-vȑta

nothing at all: kùrtōn

nothing new: klàsika

nothing special, no big deal: mȁlo [3]

notice a pickpocket at work: centírati

notice, observe: čekírati, kònstatovati, ùšmekati

novel: ȍrmān [2]

now: sàdē, sàdēk, sàdēkarcē, sàdēkare, sàdēna

nowhere: nȉđe

nozzle: dízna

nuclear: nùkliš

nudist: gòlāć, nȕdić, šȕfnūdla

nudist beach: gȍlā, golijána, náslon, nȕderica, nùdiška

number two streetcar line in Zagreb, Croatia: dúja

nun, penguin: pìngvīn

nursing home: sušióna

oak tree: gȓm

oats: kȃlj

obedient person: skȁkavac [1]

obese boy: dȉmpuc, gȕzonjić

obese child: šupeljàčina, šupéljak

obese female: avìōn, avìōnka, bùncek, drúsnjača, đuvègija, kamìōn, kȉmača, mȅčka, orandžína, rȁzbacānā, šifònjēr, trȁktorka

obese female, cow: krȁva

obese male: bȁčva, bȕbastī, búca, bȕcko, crevokȅnjastī, déba, débo, debeljúca, dùnlop, đúle, fȅtī, gíca, gíco, gȍvnojēd, krumpìrāš, màsa, mȅljavī, règāl, stȉf, svínja, škémbe, škémbo, tènk, tȑbonja, tȑtonja, trulârios

obese male homosexual: gêjša

obese, fat: bajbèlide, bȕav, bȕcmas, dèžmekas, dèžmekast, hàjhelicle, másan, mástan, pòpunjen, sàuna [2], skûpo, tȑtav

obituary: rahmètli-pȍster, tȍp-lȉsta

object used as a hideout: fasáda

object, criticize: drȍncati

objecting: zvȍcānje, zvȍcati

objecting to everything, bitching: kukavȅla, kuknjavȅla

objecting, criticism, bitching: drȍncānje

observe (somebody or something): ȁktati

observe, look: kìbicovati

observer: šmȅker, šmȅkos

observer pretending to be sleeping: kùnjavac

observing, looking: džànisānje, kìbicovanje, tȑzānje

obviously: ždrȃkno

occasion ripe for stealing: adrèsa, Amèrika

occasional joke: bȉzalica

occupy, reserve: bèzecovati

ocean: bȁra [2]

odometer (or any other counter on a mechanism): cȅler

odometer: kȉlometar-cȅler

of course: obavȅzno

of lowest quality, cheap: šklj [šəklj], žnj [žənj]

of very low-quality, lousy: kurčèvit

offend: plȁziti [2], pokénjati

offend in public: prȍzvati

offended person: kljûn [1]

offense, epithet: epìtēt

offensive player: ofanzívac

offer a toast (speech): nàzdraviti, nàzdravljati

officer: kȕhār [1], múdonja, ófa, ȍfos, žȉvodēr

official (in general): gȕbār, mùljtesta

oh: tȁ [1]

oil can: èlkānta

oil pump: èlpūmpa

oil stove: nȁftarica

okay, fine, great: dȉvre, okêj, pȅke, pȅkī

old (of a person): dâvnjī

old: dâmnjī, fȑčen, gȑbav, ìzdrkān, màtor, ȍfrčen, zȁkvrčān

old and malfunctioning mechanism, wreck: arábatija, harabátija, kŕntija, kȑš, šklȍpōcija [1]

old car, wreck: fòrdāljka, kotùrača, rȁga, šklȍpōcija [1], škrehètāljka

old clothing: ȓka

old horse, nag: kljúse, kljùsina [1]

old house: grȍb

old or outdated item: naftàlīn

old prostitute: ditòpljača, đȕka, flândra, flînta, flôndra, flûndra, flȕndra, izduvàčica, kurvètina, lȇš [1], stârā
old shoe: gòndola
old soldier: džòmba, džȍmbe
old stolen wallet: svìnjāk
old things: starȕdija
old trousers: bùcina
old unskillful criminal: kuráda
old-fashioned, passé: ȁut [2]
on foot: cipeltransom, pešaka
on narcotic drugs: lȉt
on one's back (usu. referring to carrying a child on one's back): kȑkačē, kȑkačkē
on the top, over, above something: nàvr
once: èdnōm, jedàred, jèdnōč, jènkrat
one (instead of standard jedan, jedna, jedno): jèdan
one: dȍnje, kêc [2]
one chip in: šnjûr
one cubic centimeter of liquid narcotic drug: kúba
one dinar; a one-dinar coin: bêlka, glàvica, glàvka, sȍm [2], úgaō
one fourth, quarter: fȑtālj
one hundred dinars; a hundred-dinar bill: céner, crvèndāć, cȕger [2]
one kilogram of bread: panjóka
one kilogram of marijuana, brick: brȉk
one month of one's military service: krivìna, ȍkuka, rȅcka, stȍpa
one more: ȉber
one or another: đèko
one's last money in gambling: tâlija
one's mother who spends all her time at home: zmȁj [1]
one's older brother: bája [1], bȁja [2]
one's own neighborhood: krâjka
one's part of a loot, one's take: tâl
one's style of expression: spȉka
one's wife and children: čȅljād
one-armed man: čandávko, pákljo
one-bedroom apartment: dvosòbnjāk
one-deciliter bottle of alcoholic beverage: bóbica
one-eyed: ćȍrav
one-room attic apartment: golùbinjāk
onions: čȃpa, kȃpula
onset of drug effect: ȁp [2]
opanak (a kind of peasant shoe): čámac, čàrup
opaque, unclear, difficult to grasp: neukapìrljiv
open (door, window, etc.): odbáštiti, ȍškrtati
open air: merája
open and close the door frequently: vratarizírati
open lips: prózor
open wide: izbéčiti
operator used to mark a point the speaker wishes to clarify, well, now, let's see, look: òvāj
opium: hȍp, ȍkica, ȍp [2], pȕf [2]
opium pipe: gȍng
opium product: upìjača
opposing, having objections to: antiprȍtīvan
opposite side (knitting): fȑkēt
Optalidon pill: ȍptić
or: el, il, jal, ȍli [1]
orange (color): trȕndžast
orchard: vȍtnjāk
orchestra: ȍrk
organ (musical instrument): tìgerice
orgasm: organìzam
orgy: òrgija, raspaljȍtka
ornamental coin (usu. worn as a part of a folk costume): albȁšča
orphan: sȉrak
Orthodox Christian: trȍfāznī
orthopedic shoe: pégla
out of money, broke: ćȅlav
out, eliminated: ȁut [2], out [ȁut] [1], out [ȁut] [2]
outing: isfuranđȅlī, isfurijanđȅlī, isfurȉška
outpatient department (of a hospital): abulȁnta
outrage: hȕja, nȕpoš, ȕja [2], zdȕa, zdȕva, žárēnje, žûtā
outside: vàni
outwit, outsmart: dòakati, dòhakati, skȕhati, spùstiti, šȉti, šívati, zalépiti
ovations: skandírānje
overburden with information: izbombardírati
overcharge, rip off: cȅpnuti, cjépati, dèrati, gúliti, nàbiti, odèrati, odrápiti, rȅbnuti, šíšati, zàklati
overchoke: presàugati
overcoat: kaputȉška
overcome one's problems: ìsplivati
overcome, surmount, get past: prebròditi
overdo: istȑčati, šȍpati
overdo partying: zglàjzati
overdose (on drugs): odàpēti, uòlafiti se
overdose: òlešiti se, prefúrati, ríknuti
overflow (usu. on an engine): ìberlauf
overload, overburden: nàčičkati
overly diligent student: šréber, štréber
overly talkative person, chatterbox: pȉmpler, pìtōn
overnight stay at another's apartment, sleepover: kònak, kȕnt, kùntānje
overpay: jaúknuti, vrísnuti
overprice: zàšōdrati
oversleep (fail to wake up at a certain time): prećóriti
overtake (pass another car on the road): prèjehati, prèpičiti, prepìšati, prepišávati, prèšājbati, prèšibati, prešíšati, šȃjbati, šíšati, šȉti, šíšati, šívati
overtaking (passing another car on a street or road): šíšānje
overuse, wear out: preforsírati
overused: prefòrsīrān

owl: savùljaga

owner of a Turkish-style restaurant: àščija

ox (the animal): bòčkan, lèšac, r̄kavac, Šúponja

ox chart: trȅskavice

package (in general): gȕta, kȍnvoj, kònzērva, pânj [2]

paddle boat: pedalína

paid sex: šlâfgust, šljâfgust

pain in the testicles: mudòbolja

paint (wall, ceiling, etc.): bojàdisati, fârba, fârbati, obojàdisati, vârba

painter (artist): mȁzalo

painting (as work of art): maljáža

painting: fârbānje

pair of aces: lùjza

pale-complexioned person: vȍsak

pan (with a movie or television camera): švȅnkovati

pan, pot: pȁvernjāk, pìnjāta, tèpsija

paneling: òplet

panic, freak out: drȁmiti, fȑka, fȑkisati, paranòisati, talàsati

panicking: krizírānje

panorama: vidíkovac

pant: húkati, sòptati, sòptiti, ȕhkati

panties, briefs: kȁnjavica, minìmālke, mȕštavice

panting: sòptānje, sȍptav

pantyhose: hrȅnōvke, hulahȍp, hulahȍpke, nȉnak

paper (e.g. sheets of paper): ȁrtija, pòjān, tȉrita, tȉrta

parent: fòsīl, gȍvnār, invàlīd, lánac, lȅš [1], lèšinār [1], lèšinār [2], mȑtvac, mùflōn, mûmija, ȍskār, sȁblāst, skèlet

parent, old folks: matórac, matòrān, prȅdak, stȁrac

parents, old folks: cȑkavci

park: spȁrkati se

park guard: zelènāš [1]

particle used at beginning of the sentence that moves the conversation along, so, well, and: pȁ [1]

particle used in strong negation, no way: dȋ [1]

particle used to establish a communication channel (usu. in telephonic conversation), yeah, yes, hello, hi: dȁ

particle used to express active listening, uhuh, ok, gotcha: dòbro [1]

particle used to express affirmation or approbation in response to adjacent statement or sequence, good, fine, well: dòbro [1]

particle used to express disbelief: gdȅ

particle used to express hesitation, as they say: kȁrē

particle used to express hesitation, well: pȁ [1]

particle used to express uncertainty, I think, if I am not mistaken: bívā

particle used to express undetermined state, so-so: onàkō

particle used to indicate approximation: rècimo, rèćemo

particle used to introduce thought meant to be taken hypothetically or quasi-hypothetically: rècimo, rèćemo

particle used to maintain communication channel (usu. in telephonic conversation), yeah, huh-huh, ok: dȁ

particle used to refer to the words of others: kȁe

particle used to signal a contradiction between two parts of a discourse or to amend previous information, well: dodúšē

particle used to signal impossibility, no way: k.b.s.z [kəbəsəz]

particle used to signal one's intention: dȁ

particle used to sum up a point and: dàklem

particle used to sum up previous facts: èlem

partner: kȍmpić, ȍrtāk

partridge: jerèbica

party (engage in social gathering): bânčiti, bekr̀jati, lȕmpovati, tulumáriti, tulumátiti

party (social gathering): aldùmāš, cúga, cȕgeher, ćȁga, ćȁgati, dèrnek, durgárac, fȅšta, GLP [gê-ȅl-pê], igránjac, kòpānje, lȕmpos, pártī, pìjānka, raspaljȍtka, rúžiti, terèvēnčiti, terèvēnka, túlac [2], tùlum, tulumȉška, žûr, žurája, žuréza, žûrka

party without females: péderbâl

partying day: màjmunovo

pass (in gambling): pasírati

pass (in soccer): pâs

pass (of time): pàsati [2], pȁsovati

pass: isfúrati

pass by: profúrati, profurávati

pass the ball: pȁsovati, pasírati

pass through the customs without any difficulties: procijéditi

passing by: pròfur

passionate fan, fanatic: tìfusār

passionate female: mȍkrā

passionate female dancer (one who makes exaggerated moves while dancing): dokolèničārka

passionate female, hot female: fefèrōnka

passionate gambler: kamàrdžija, komàrdžija

passionate male sexual partner: Fáruk

passport: lȉl, lìluša, sȍška, sȍšpa, šára, šȁre, šarènica, šȍška, šȕštavac

pasta: žváka

pastry shop: slásta, slàtkara, slȉnara

pasture in Lika: Pìzdac

pat-a-cake: klâp [2]

patch (used to repair hoses): bàndāž

patch, mend: zàrenjkati

pathetic individual, poor thing: kȕkavac

patient: kȕnjos

patrol: prošnjúrati, trakáriti, trȁkati

pay (bills, etc.): cȁlnuti, càltati, cólati, cȍlovati, iskȑcati se, izdúžiti se, jaúknuti, kȁnuti, odvájati, òpružiti se, pȁsti [1], pòčkati, polèteti, polètjeti, rȋknuti, sínuti, sȍmovati, tinjávati, trošávati, vȋknuti, vrísnuti

pay dearly: izlèteti, izlètjeti, pljȕniti, pljȕnuti

pay money for something (usu. for a common effort): ugráditi se

payday: Spâsovdan

paying bills: iskrcávānje

peace activist: miròvnjāk

peach brandy: brȅskovača

peak (traffic, etc.): špȉca

pear brandy: krúška, krȕškovača

pearl (jewelry): pȉrinač

peasant: tȑtnjāk

peasant shoe: gljárnica

peasant shoes: pȁšmage

peck (with beak, etc.): kvȍcati, totȑkati

pecking (with the beak, etc.): tòtrk, totȑkānje

pedal: pèdāl[2], pedála

pedestrian tunnel: pódzēmlje

peeker: lȕkavac

peeking: lȕkānje

peep (sound): pijujúkati, pȉjūk

peep, look at others: gíciti, kíbiti, lȕkati, nalukávati se, pijúkati, pòluknuti, rašomònisati, rošomònisati, víriti, zíkiti, zrȉkati

peeping, looking at others: pijúkānje, pijùkav

peer: kalendárac

pen (for writing): fȉlac

pen (writing device): penkála[2], penkálo, pènkiš

pen (writing instrument): pèkiš

pencil: làpis, plȁjvāz[2], písalica, šárac, škrábalo, škȑtalo

penis: àdūt, bàmbus[1], banána, cùcla, crévo, čèšnjāk[2], čȉk[2], delègāt, džìngiskān, Džȍnī, fȁjfa, fȕkalo, glávonja, glísta, harmonìkāš, jȁblān, jòlpaz, kàrdān, kȁrī, kévac, kȉtica, klȉnac, klȉpan, klínja, krȁstavica, kítac, kȕrcšlus, kvȑga, màčōr, màjmun[1], mȃlī, mȁlo[2], međunòga, mȅtak[2], mȉcalo, mìmpek, mȉško[1], mȏj, mȕštikla, pàjser, pátak, pèndrek, penkálo, plȁjvāz[2], prìkan, prȉkī, pȕška[2], svȏj, šlȁuf, špȉc, šràfcīger[2],, štȑk, tàšak, tòljaga, tróla

penis of an elderly male: žlȕndra

penis of an impotent male: mekìtis

penis, bone: kȏst

penis, cock: kokòtān, krékac, pévac, pèvče

penis, dick, prick: àrkan, arkàna, bagađóra, bajònēt, balávko, bàltazār, bàlvan[2], bàrjāk, bàrtol, bȁtāk, bàtina, báto[2], bímbo, blȁjzna, bȍljēt, bórer, budàlāš, búdža, buđóla, buzdòvān[2], cigára, čȕkalo, čȕpko, ćàvāp, ćèvāp, ćúna, deflorȃtor, Dȉgić, digitȁlis, dȉkan, dòkan, dȕda[1], dugòvratī, džìndōv, džȍna, đóka, đòkan, đȍkica, đóko, đȏle, fȁlce, fàlkōn, gȁta, gìngibas, gùdalo, gȕska, hȁnomāg, jègulja, Jòhan, jȏle, jòmpekpinj, jòrackunj, Jóso, kalahàster, kalàuz[2], kȃr[2], kára, karàkter, karamèla, kàrina, kàrōn, kíbla, kífla, kìlenc, kȉta, kȉtāč, kitára, kitarésa, klȁda, klìmpac, klȉmpāč, klȉn,kljȗč, kobàsica, kȍkot, kòlac, kònjīć-gȑbonjić, kȍplje, krȁstavac, krìvāk, kȗr, kúra[1], kúra[2], kȕrac[3], kùrak, kȕrcoslāv, kurčèkanja, kúro, lùdāk, lȕdoje, lùla, lùlek, lúša, Màrīnko, maslàkān, maslìkān, màslo, màška, méca[1], mènjāč, mȉki, SNèpāl, nȉspe, palàmār, palàmūr, pàprika, pȁrljāk, pȁtka, patrànjača, patȑnjača, pètēljka, pȉčkodēr, pȉmpāč, pìmpek[2], pȉmpić, pipirȉpī, pȋsak, pìtōn, pitònčić, pȑst, pùmpica, punoglávac, ràcka, ràcko, ràcku, ràkonjac, rȏg, rȕcka, rȕčka, sȁblja, skȍbālj, sramòtnjāk, Stójko, svȑdaō, šévac, šèvāk, šèvčina, šmàjser, štȃp, štòfika, šȕfnūdl, šȕrka, tȇlo, tìnaba, tlčànj,tòmpus, tȍp[2], tòjan, tòpuz, vèsēlko, vìršl, vìršla, vìsimīr, vòdenja, zlòtvor, zmijoglávac, žȉla, žlȕndra

penis, drill: bùrgija

penis, love muscle: mìšīć

penis, pisser: pìšalo

penis, tool: àlāt[2]

people: bȁgra, rája, rȕlja

pepper: gòripetlja, šȉljka

Pepsi: pèpsika

perfect: pȅrfa

performing artist: cirkuzant

period in which one holds one's breath: dùšak

period without sexual intercourse: bèzjebica

period, era: vȁkat

permanent (hair style), perm: trȃjna

persist: izdùrati

persistent and meaningless talk, blabber: eglènisati, kenjáža, mȕcānje, naklápānje, prdùckānje, pìtljānje, tabànānje

person: stvȍr

person from the Eastern regions of the former Yugoslavia: ȉzoš

person from the same generation: klàsīć

person from whom it is easy to steal, easy mark: bášta[2]

person from whom one frequently borrows, cash cow: mùzara

person having bad luck: pèhist

person in charge of distilling brandy: kazàndžija, kȍtlār

person in charge of distributing hard liquor at parties: dòlibaša

person in eyeglasses, four eyes: ókac

person in love: fiksácija

person in question (female): dòtičnā

person in question (male): dòtičnī

person lacking any scruples: laktàncije, laktovȉt

person learning to drive: lùdāk, lùđāk

person obsessed with musical appliances (such as stereo players, etc.), audio freak: hȁjfić

person one cannot get rid of: prìlepak

person opposed to everything, contrarian: kòntrāš

person out of money, person who is broke: kòkuz

person susceptible to deception: primȃrijus

person to be avoided: lèpričār

person visibly different from others, oddball: šȍk[2]

person wearing eyeglasses, four eyes: astrònom, snàjper, sóva, vȉdoje

person who abuses others (usu. financially), parasite, leech: čèšalj[1], čèšātor, fȁćkalica, glòbār, grèbāroš, grèbātor, grèbātorka, mȕftadžija, mùftāš, parazȉt

person who avoids his/her duties, shirker: eskivȃtor

person who behaves unconventionally, weirdo: čȕnkos

person who borrows frequently: grèbāroš

person who bothers others with his comments: pametnjáković

person who breaks into a line: padobránac

person who breaks wind: kànder, pȑdāč
person who breaks wind frequently or loudly: pȑdizvēk, pȑdozvēk
person who cackles: kaùkčija
person who defecates: kènjāč
person who destroys escalators out of sheer boredom: fȁraga
person who did not finish sexual intercourse: nȅdojebān
person who dresses in black: dàrker
person who drinks wine with water: špricèrāš
person who eats anything, garbage gut: pomìjara
person who ejaculates prematurely: zêc
person who engages in sexual intercourse: bórac
person who exaggerates in theorizing, smart ass: mudròser
person who failed an exam: trópa [1]
person who frequently and gladly engages in fights: fàjtara
person who frequently blushes: sȅmafōr
person who habitually destroys everything: katùnić
person who habitually dresses formally: šešȉrdžija
person who habitually makes everything more complicated: pètljāroš
person who has an additional job, moonlighter: tèzgār, tèzgāroš
person who has an additional job, moonlighting: tezgárēnje
person who has bad luck, ill-starred person: pêgula [1]
person who illegally exchanges money: gèngāš
person who is both a factory worker and a farmer: duplikânt, duplikȁnt, duplìkāt
person who is broke (financially): fȍler, lȉhter, mùfljūz [1], pìštōlj, slépac, švȍrcer, trúba [1], trùbāč, tuturȕtū
person who is disturbing a love pair: svéća
person who is in charge, head honcho: Mȅtro-Gȍldvin-Mȁjer
person who is likely to be beaten: fìtīlj [2], fitiljȉška
person who leaves bar early in the morning: ranorànilac
person who likes to pet females: fàćkāroš
person who lives at another's expense, leech: čèšāroš
person who lives off of others' successes: dunàjeger
person who looks for a (usu. simple) job around Vuk Karadžić's monument in Belgrade, Serbia: vûkovac
person who lost his/her money in gambling: kòkuz
person who makes noise: bùdžātor, džèvātor, fȑkātor, làrmāč, pèvāč [1]
person who often screams in pain: jaúkalac, jaúkavac
person who pays the check in a restaurant, host: cȅhmâjstor
person who picks up leaves and garbage in parks: faćaljȉst, fataljȉst
person who rents out his/her apartment for gambling: pìnkāroš
person who resells stolen watches: fìrlī
person who resells stolen watches, watch fence: rìngāš
person who saves or who is in possession of German marks: filatèlist, filatèlista
person who sells fake gold rings: fìrlī
person who sells various merchandise in night clubs: kòmita
person who sits for a long time: tȑnigūz
person who smokes hashish: dùvāč
person who smokes marijuana, pot head: tvȉster
person who speaks fast: mitraljézac
person who speaks with unintelligible pronunciation: mòrzeovac
person who spends his/her time in useless activities, slacker: džabalèbović
person who spends time in useless activities: džabalèbāroš
person who stares: pòljāk
person who steals from the train passengers: kebànjār, kebènjār, mèdved, mèdvedār
person who steals without discriminating either victims or objects stolen: blȉnder
person who sticks out his/her buttocks while walking: naguzívalo
person who studies mechanically: búbalica, búbalo, bùbant
person who suffers: Tȑpimīr
person who takes part in public rallies: mitìngāš
person who takes too many pills, pill popper: tabletòmān
person who thinks for a long time before moving: šàhista
person who walks regularly: štràftāč
person who wants to push into a group of people without being invited: emigrȁnt, ubacóka
person who wears clothing made in Yugoslavia: Jȕsos
person who wears eyeglasses, four eyes: đòzluk
person with a face which resembles a monkey: màndril
person with a good memory: spȕžva
person with a large head: čòntāš, glàvnī [2]
person with a pale skin: sȉr
person with conservative views (usu. political): kònzērva
person with curly hair: óvca
person with dark complexion: džȍker
person with eyeglasses, four eyes: ždráka
person with flat feet: dustabànlija
person with hearing difficulties: tȍp [1]
person with large buttocks: dùpēnda
person with large head: kégla, tìkvan
person with long hair, longhair: kosijáner [1]
person with long legs and arms: kràkoš
person with numerous pimples, pimple face: numizmàtičār
person with pointed buttocks: šȉljgūz, šiljgùza, šȉljogūz, šiljògūza
person with seeing difficulties: čȍkī
person with snot on his/her face: bálo [1], bálonja
person with university degree: fakultètlija
person with white buttocks: bȅlogūz [1]
person without any scruples: lèšinār [1]
personality: supstȃnca
persuade, convince: báriti, gotíviti, hrániti, kȕhati, kȕvati, lòžiti, mésiti, míkiti, mútiti, nàpūmpati, narédíti, nȁštimati, naštimávati, obáriti, obrađívati, páliti, popáliti, preparírati, pûmpati, skȕhati, skȕvati, smȕvati, sràti, štȉmati [1], tròvati,

uváliti, zbáriti, zgotòviti, zgotíviti

persuaded, convinced: kȕvān, skȕhān, vâren

persuasion: kȕhānje, kȕvānje, obrađívānje, patamȕzovānje, preparírānje, pȕmpānje, štȉmānje

pertaining to a bar, tavern (usu. low-class): bìrtījskī

pertaining to a despicable or worthless individual: baràbīn, baràbōv

pertaining to a male who frequently changes his sexual partners: kùrvārskī

pertaining to a male with large testicles: mȕdāljōv, múdonjīn

pertaining to a person with white buttocks: bȅloguz [2]

pertaining to a physically or psychologically underdeveloped person: abòrtus

pertaining to a soup kitchen: àščījskī

pertaining to a Turkish-style restaurant àščījskī

pertaining to a worthless or mean individual: šiljokùrānskī

pertaining to Bosnian Muslims: džȉhādskī

pertaining to communist secret police in the former Yugoslavia: ùdbāškī

pertaining to frequent and lengthy meetings: sàstančārskī

pertaining to one who prefer to drink alcohol in the evening: akšàmlučārskī

pertaining to silent persons: ćutòloškī

pertaining to supporters of Stalin in Tito-Stalin conflict in the1948: ibȅovskī

pertaining to testament, will: amánetnī

pertaining to the afterlife: ahíretskī

pertaining to the bleating of sheep: blȅjav

pertaining to the Croatian separatist movement in the 1970s: màspokovskī

pertaining to the Federal Republic of Yugoslavia: serejòtskī

pertaining to the followers of Josip Broz Tito (communist dictator in the former Yugoslavia): titoìstičkī

pertaining to the HDZ (Hrvatska demokratska zajednica 'Croatian Democratic Alliance', a political party in Croatia): hadezȅovskī

pertaining to the Independent State of Croatia (Croatian nazi state during WWII): endèhāški

pertaining to the nickname Kuraica: Kuràičīn

pertaining to the penis: kûrčēv [2]

pertaining to the person who feels the effects of marijuana or hashish: nàpušen

pertaining to the soccer team "Sarajevo" from Sarajevo, Bosnia: bòrdō

pertaining to the1968 student protests in the former Yugoslavia: šezdesetòsmāškī

pertaining to those who are emotionally attached to the former Yugoslavia,: jȕgonostàlgičārskī

pervert, weirdo: pèrvert, pervèrznjāk

pessimism: bèdāk [2]

petty cash, chump change, peanuts: cȑkavica, cvàncik, cvónjak, grȍš, síća

petty thief: àpan, jàjara, kokȍšār, pètljārka, pilìćār, trȕckavac

petty trade: pilićárēnje

phlegmatic female: Èskīmka

phlegmatic male: Èskīm, Eskímac, mȑtvāk

phlegmatic person: flègma, tégla

phone: gôvna, zújavac, zvŕkalo

phonograph: grȅm

phonograph record: čȁplo, kònzērva

photo: fȍtka, fȍtos, pȉkčer

photo in the police files, mug shot: lêntra

photographer: klȉk [1]

photographer of celebrities, paparazzo: paparàco

photographic camera: fȍtić

photographic slide: dȉjāč

phyllo (dough): jùfka, jùvka

physically and intellectually slow female: mrtvàkuša

physician: hèćim

physics (as a school course): fȉzis, fíza

physics teacher: fizičār, fizikos, fíza

pianist: kljàver

piano: kljâv, kljáva

pick on somebody: pȉk [2]

pick pockets: brȉjati, bunáriti, džepáriti, izbunàrisati, kesáriti, páliti, petljáriti, ráditi [1], udičáriti, zêpsti

pick somebody's pockets: opléviti

pick-pocket: pètljār

picking pockets: bunárēnje

picklock (tool): špȅra

picklock (tool), slim jim: krȁstavica, lȁzār [1]

pickpocket who has been caught: cȅnt [1]

pickpocket: bàrkist, bòmbāš, bunàrdžija, bùnāroš, dùmbāroš, dumbòrāš, dumèrāš, džèpāroš, džȅpos, gèngāš, gȅposlāv, gotívac, kèsāroš, ljepljívko, nàrdžija, papàgāj, pȅrger, pètljāroš, râdnīk, rȉbār, sjecikèsāroš, šljàkāroš, šljàkātor, šljàker, šòfēr

pickpocket's accomplice: zìdār

pickpocket's helper: štȕcer

pickpocket's working area: štȃjga

picnic: pìknik

piece of paper, scrap of paper: cȅdulja

piece, chunk: fȁlat, fȅta, kòmāt [2], párče

pig (the animal): dasánče, dósa, dòsānče, dòsānka, kàrica [1], kàridža, karidžȁnče, karȉndža, rȍker, žvȁnje

piglet: dósa, dòsānče, dòsānka, karidžánče, žvȁnje

pile, heap: hȉpa, kàmara, ȉpa

pimp: štrȉcī

pimple: bubùljōn, crvotòčina, kikirȉkī, kráter, znȁčka

pin (fastening device): rȁjsnēdl, rȁjsnēgla

pincers: šȉritcānge, šȉritcāngle, špȉccānge, špȉccāngle

pine brandy: bòrovica

ping (produce a sharp metal sound): cȁknuti [2], fȑskati, fȑsnuti

ping (sharp metal sound): cȁkat

ping-pong: pȉngāč, pȉngāć, pȉngić, pìngiš

pinging (producing a sharp metallic sound): fȑskānje

pipe (smoking): gaćàrica, guràćica, pȁjp

pirated CD (produced in Bulgaria): bȕgarin

pistol, revolver: àktēr, čȕkalo, gȁra, kòpito, livòvēr, pùcāljka, pljúca, pljȕcak, púca [1], pȕcalica, rovȅlo, šèstalo, štȍljāš, štȍljpi, šûpljē [1]

piston: kòlbn

piston ring: kòlbringa

pitcher (container for liquids): bȁjalija

pity: greòta, grjehòta

place intended for gambling, gambling den: bùljkāf

place intended for sexual intercourse: bùljkāf, fukaóna, gusliónica, hòblbank, jebánac, jebaónica, jèbārnīk, komoràna, kȕsnica, pìlārnica, šikàna

place name in Bosnia: Plàčigūz, Pòdbigūz

place name in Herzegovina: Pìčevina

place name in Montenegro: Pȍsrān-glàvica

place name in Serbia: Karagûzovac

place name in Srem, Serbia: Gològuzā

place of extreme wretchedness or squalor, hellhole: bestrágija, Nabigùzice, nedòđija, piškopéja, pizdojèbina, Prìpizdina, Tùngūzija, vukojèbina

place swarming with females: akvârijum

place used to get some rest: hladòvina

place used to smoke narcotic drugs: lêj

place where a robbery has taken place: pȉzdīšte

place where movies prohibited by censorship are stored: bùnker

place where one can eat and sleep for free: dibàldus

place where prostitutes gather: mèsara

plan: ìgra [2], kòntati, študírati, varijȁnta

plan, project: mȉca [2]

planing (carpenter's): klȅnkānje

planing: ljȁndēnje

plank: lȅtva, tȃhta

plate, dish: gvantjêra, pìjat, pjȁt

plate, saucer (in the prison cafeteria): lȋm

play (music) loud: tréštati

play a game: odsúkati, sìgrati se, špȁnati, žnóra [1]

play a game: šâjbati

play a musical instrument: bapírati, prášiti, šprícati

play a musical instrument: traràkati

play a musical instrument excellently: pȉčiti

play aggressive soccer: mesáriti, mèsatiti

play aggressively: ȍžeći

play bad soccer: nabíjati

play cards: biljáriti, dijalogizírati, dugáriti, hláditi se, láditi se, šlȍgati, špìlati, špíliti, trêsti, vòziti

play chess: mȉsliti

play good soccer: žnírati

play guitar: đȉtrati

play marbles: pȉčkati se

play monotonously (soccer, etc.): pȉmplati, pȉmplovati

play music (usu. in reference to the disliked type): čandȑkati

play rock and roll (in a band): pȉčiti

play soccer: kotùrati, pȉkati, šórati, šȍrnuti, špȁnati

play soccer well: vésti

play speed chess: cȕgati, cugèrisati

play table soccer: roštȉljati

play the diple (double flute, a traditional musical instrument): dȉpliti

play the tamburica (traditional string instrument): tambùrati

play with marked cards: váljati [1]

play with one's sexual partner's breast, feel up: raspitívati se

player: pùlēn, trȅskavac

player for Budućnost (a soccer team from Podgorica, Montenegro): plâvī

player for Croatian national team: vàtrenī

player for Crvena Zvezda (a soccer team from Belgrade, Serbia): cȑveno-bêlī, cȑveno-bijéli

player for Dinamo (in the 1990s Croatia, a soccer team from Zagreb, Croatia): plâvī

player for Željezničar (a soccer team from Sarajevo, Bosnia): plâvī

player for Yugoslav national team: plâvī

player or fan of Cibona (a basketball team from Zagreb, Croatia): cȉbos

player or fan of Hajduk (a soccer team from Split, Croatia): bîlī

player or fan of Jugoplastika (now POP 84 a basketball team from Split, Croatia): žûtī

player or fan of Lokomotiva (a basketball team from Zagreb, Croatia): lȍkos

player or fan of Medveščak (a hockey team from Zagreb, Croatia): mèdvjed

player or fan of Mladost (a water-polo team from Zagreb, Croatia): mladòstāš, mladostàšica

player or fan of OFK Beograd (a soccer team from Belgrade, Serbia): romàntičār

player or fan of Olimpija (a soccer and basketball team from Ljubljana, Slovenia): zmàjček

player or fan of Partizan (a soccer team from Belgrade, Serbia): grȍbār

player or fan of Velež (a soccer team from Mostar, Bosnia): rȍđenī [2]

player or fan of Vojvodina (a soccer team from Novi Sad, Serbia): Lála

player or fan of Zagreb (a soccer team in Zagreb, Croatia): zagrèbāš

players for Cibona (a basketball team from Zagreb, Croatia): Cȉbosi

players for Partizan (a soccer team from Belgrade, Serbia): cŕno-bêlī, cŕno-bijélī

players on an Italian national team (e.g. soccer, basketball): Azúri

playing card: dúga, kartiljèros, kàrtiška, kȍla, kóva, kòviška, šàrulja, šȕštavica

playing cards: ćagèta, oksidácija, tȃpke

playing music (usu. in reference to the disliked type): čandȑkānje

pleasant feeling induced by narcotic drugs, high: bȍk, bôl, làćano [2], trȉp pleasant voice: gûk

pleasure: gȕšt

plenty of money, stack of cash: ergȅla

pliers: cánge, cángle, kliješta, kombìnīr-cánge, kombìnīr-cángle, kombìnīrke

Plješevica bar in Zagreb, Croatia: Pljȅška

plug in (e.g. an electronic device): prìštekati, ùštekati, štȅkati

plum (the fruit): tràvanja

plum brandy: prepećenka, taruža

plum brandy: šljíva [2]

plum brandy made with wallnuts: òrahovača, òraovača

ply with liquor in order to rob: ìzvesti

pocket (on a coat, trousers, etc.): àmbār, bùnār, džèpiner, làvōr, pȁdže, špâg

pocket knife: pèro [1]

pocket picking: džȅp, džepárēnje, džȅpka

pocket radio: trádža, trándža, tránđa, trȁnzić, trànzistor [2], zúja

pocket watch: džèpnjāk, jùlār, lòkot, ùlār

pocketbook: džèpnjāk

pockmarked face: fŕnjo

point: upériti

pointy-toed shoe: špicóka, špìčōk

pointy-toed shoes: špȉcerice

poison, venom: àbdika

poke, prod, or pinch on the buttocks, goose: càjper, pȑstac, ròbija

poke, prod, or pinch on the buttocks, goose: kíbla, pȑstāć, prsténac, šíber [2], tòpče

poker: kȅrpo, pokeríca, pokerȉška

poker player who went broke: pȅpel

polenta: kačàmak, kûjda, kûjdar, kûjka, kûrda, pàndžija

police: bòrba, mariȍla, maróni, mȉlica, múrija [1], mûrka [2], mùzika, špirijáda

police: cȉja, kljúčevi, múrja, pajkanalizácija, pandurácija, pandùrija, pȕlke, rjȁmu, strúja

police cap: kàmilāvka

police dog: đùklija

police formation (group of policeman): šȕma [2]

police interrogation: čèšljānje

police investigator: ȁla [1], ȁver, glȍdār, hȁver, koléga, kuléga, lȅha, mȕdrogriz, negatívac, nósonja, psȉna, pȕb, pubijáner, pùbiš, špìcl

police manhunt: òrkestar

police patrol: stònoga

police photographer: lèntrāš

police station: Himaláji, pandurácija, pandùrija, pubòvija

police van, paddy wagon: ljȗljka, mára, mȁrica, mariȍla, mètrō, múrija [1], múrja, mûrka [2], slobòdānka [1]

policeman from a foreign country: pȍštār

policeman on a bicycle, bike cop: lȅtak

policeman with a dog: prìkolica

policeman, cop: àgiša, ȁla [1], âle, anđèlčić, ânđeō, ȁver, aždàja, bȁbāj, balavnȉška, barȉtān, bȍbī, bórder, brôjnīk, bȕmbār, cája, cájac, câjka, càjkan, cȁjkoš, cájo, ćȍškāš, dȅver [1], drékalica, drȍt, drȍtār, drȍter, dròver, dùrpan, džȁndār, fȉć, fȉćātor, gȁvrān, glȍdār, gȕmenī, hȁla [2], jȁnuār, karàta, kêr [1], kȅravac, klȍvī, klóvn, kljûn [1], kokòšār, komìšāk, kòmišnjāk, kòmšinjāk, kȍndor, krùmpīr [1], krumpiraš, kȕlin [1], kùndak, kȕvār [1], làjbek, ljubičíca, mícac, micájac, mîcoš, mȉlāč, Mȉlan, Mîle, mìlek, Mȉler, mȉlfāč, mȉlī, Mȉlisāv, mȉlkāč, mìlkan, mȉlkoš, Mȉloš, míljkovac, mȉtljan, múrija [2], múrijāš, múrja, mùrjāk, mùrjān, mùrjāš, , mûrka [1], mùrkac, mȕrkāč, mùrkan mùzičār, njȕškalo, òrgān, pája, pàjac, pàjkan, pȁkī, pàndūr, pandùrčina, pàpika, pȁūk, pefàzōn, pefèzōn, pèndrāč, pèrkan, Pȅtar, pȍp, porijan, prefàzōn, prìkan, prȉkī, pȕb, pubijáner, pùbiš, pȕkī [2], pȕkica, pûle, ràin, ràinac, rezánac, rȉja, rȉjāk, rìjamu, rȕra, sȉto, sȉvorī, stègnat, sȕpić, sȕpovac, surčínac, šètāč, šljȉva [1], tàbātor, tȁdro, tambùrāš, tàraba, tàrador, tàradro, Tȅodor, tȅtrēb, tràmvaj, trȕker, tùlek, vucibàtina, zèmljāk, zûb [1], žáca, žȁcman, žȁndār, žȁndarm, žbîr, žȉc, žûtī

policeman, man in blue: mastȉljav, mastȉljavī, plávac, plàvāč, plâvī, šljȉvāč, šljȉvār, tȅget

policeman, pig: tȅtrijēb, tòvarić

polish: šlȁjfati, šlȁjfovati, šmìrglati

polish, shine: glâncati, ìzglancati, nàglāncati

polishing: frȅzovānje, šlȁjfānje, šmìrglānje

polishing machine: belégija, šlȁjferica

political agitation: agitȉška

political economics (an obligatory subject at universities in the former Yugoslavia): pjȅsma

political emigrant to Argentina: Argentíner

political prisoner: polìtičkī

politician: glávonja, njȁsvi, pòmije, stòlāš

politician with extremist views, hawk: jȁstrēb

Politika daily newspaper: Slobòdānka [2]

Politikin zabavnik (youth magazine from Belgrade, Serbia): Zába

poor (of a male): gòlokūr, golòmud

poor: gològuz, gȑdan, lòpatār, mȁlo [1], nȅgatīvan, praznòguz [2], šúpalj, zàkrpān

poor female: gològuza, golopìzdalo, golopìzduša

poor illumination: mȅsečina

poor male: gològuz, gòlokūr, golokùrīle, gulánfer [1], jȁdovān, jȍker, màndāš, praznòguz [1], serèmak, siròmā, siròmāk, sirotánović, siròtko, svìrigūz, tȉfusār, visúljak

poor person: drònjčina, fukàra [1], govnòćera

poorly: tànko

poorly dressed male: kŕlja [2]

poorly dressed person: gologùzica

pop music song: zabàvnjāk [2]

pop musician: zabàvnjāk [1]

pop up, appear: sjáviti

popular: òbješen

popular and beloved female, goddess: bòginja

porch: nástrešnica

pork: mȁlo [2], mòrnār, svinjàrija

pork rind: bònbōn

pornographic magazine: šárac

pornographic magazine or movie, porn mag or flick: pòrnīć

pornographic, porno: pôrno*

porter: àmāl, hàmāl, tovàriš, tr̃čkalo

position from which it is easy to score a basket: zȉcer

position, duty one performs: fúkcija

possibility: varijȁnta

potato: kȑtola, žûlj

potter: kàčavac, kȁljavac

pour: pljȕskati, tòčiti

powdered opium: púder

practice body building: bìldati, bȉldovati

practice law: àdverbovati

practice, exercise: vȇdžba, vȇdžbati

pre-ignition: prȅtpālēnje

pre-WW II Yugoslavia: đȉlda

preach, give lectures to: cvȍcati, dȑviti, džvȁnjkati, pròsipati, srȁti, svírati, tandȑkati, tùpisati, túpiti, turpìjati, zuzàrati, zvȍcati, zvȑndati, žglȁviti, žiláviti, žvȁnjkati, žvȁnj-žvȁnj[2]

prearrange so as to ensure a desired fraudulent outcome, fix: lažírati, nàmestiti, naméštati, nàmjestiti, naštéliti, štéliti

prearrange so as to ensure a desired fraudulent outcome, fix: namontírati

prearranged competition or contest: namjéštāljka

predestined: viđen

prefer, give advantage to: vòleti

preference (a kind of card game): prȅf

pregnant female: brȅnta, ȉkravica, klȉnconoša, košarkàšica, pȕnā, stomàklija, vrȅća

pregnant, knocked up: nàdrukān, nàfilān, nàpojen, nàpumpān, nàpunjen, napúpeo, skȍtan, škȅmbav

preludine (a kind of narcotic drug): pȅpī[2], pȅrī, préla

prepare crib-sheets for an exam: đòniti, pođòniti, puškáriti

pressure bearing: drȕklāger

pretend: drȁmiti se, glúmiti, izigrávati, izvòditi, odglúmiti, prȁviti se, šatrovírati, špȉlati

pretending: fèmisānje, folirància

pretending, acting: izmotàncija

pretending, as if: bajági

pretentious discourse or idea without any value: mudròlija

pretty leg (of a female): nogárica, nogàvica

pretzel stick: grisînī

prevent somebody from talking, shut somebody up: òtfućkati

prevent, block: odzvȉždati

price tag: etikêcija

pride: zôr

priest (usu. Orthodox Christian): kàlcan, kȁle

priest: čȁtr̄lj, čatȑljān, dȅrpe, gàlāh, lúka[2], mantȉjāš, mȑmač, rȁšlje, vàrzelj

priest's wife (usu. Orthodox Christian): kalcànica

principal: dȉksī, dìreks, dȉrš, dȉrša, dȉšomor, dȉša, Hirohȉto, Mikâdo, šèrīf

prison: ȁps, ȁpsa, apsàna, bàhara, bàjbok, bajbokàna, bàjbuk, bàksara, bàlvani, bȁnja[2], bàrunja, bètōn[2], bȉjaro, bùksara, bólnica[1], bùrdelj, bûbanj, bùhara, bȕksa, bùvara, ckȁmnī[1], čkȁmni, ćôrka, ćȕtka, ćúza, ćuzbekàna, đȕtka, đuzbekàna, ègede, fijóka, frižȉdēr, fȕk[2], gâjba, Glàvnjača, glùbara, hȁps, hȁpsa, hapsàna, Hȉltōn, kapedô, karburâtor, kȉblār, kùfer, kulàna, kùpalīšte, kùtija, lȁdica, lònac, màrdelj, màrdelja, mèmljara, mȉšolōvka, mràkanja, múrija[1], pòtok, prdekàna, pȑžūn, remíza, rȅst, rȅšt, rezùltāt, rȕpa[2], rùpīnger, sušióna, šȁtornja, šàtrānđa, šatràundža, šàtrōn, šatronáda, šàtrōnđa, šàtronja, šàtrūndža, škàrnicl, špȅra, štènara, tàmbura, tȍplice, topùzārnīk, tránjac, trȁp[2], trónjac, tvȍrza, zȁbela

prison administrator: bábo, bŕko, genèrāl, stârī

prison bars: gitáre

prison bathroom: kíbla

prison cell: ćȅla, ćȅlica, ćêlka, hàvājka, kíbla, kȕća, mrȁka, smȑdulja, sôl, sòlara, stȁja, štènara, šùtara

prison informer, stoolie: rèdnjara

prison solitary: đȉlnica

prison term: furijáda

prison where one sleeps on planks: pàlača

prison, can: kònzērva

prison, lock-up: kàtanac

prison, the big house: ambasáda, kȕća

prison, the pen: jȁslice

prisoner: ćȍrker, mardèljāš, mrèljāš, murirȁnt

prisoner at the prison in Turopolje, Croatia: falsifìkāt

prisoner with a short sentence: tùrist

private business: privàtluk

private first class: rázbōjnik

private lot (usu. with a cottage on it): PȐC[2]

probably: vàljda

problem child, brat: àrambaša

problem, trouble: dubióza, gréda, psȉna, zajebàncija

procurer, pimp: cùplīnger, cùprīnger, dìlkāš, lȅško, màkiša, mȁkoš, pàstīr, pȉjavica, vòdič

procuress, madam: màjkica

produce bleating sound of a goat or sheep, baa: mékati, mekètati

professional athlete, pro: prȍfī[1], prȍfić

professional gambler, pro gambler: pȁker

professional of any kind, pro: prȍfī[1]

professional player who pretends to be an amateur, ringer: šȁtro-amàtēr

professional, pro: prȍfī[2]

professor, high school teacher (female), prof: prȍfačica, profàndērka, profaràōnka

professor, high school teacher (male), prof: cvȉker, kestènjāk, pȍp, prȍfāč, pròfān, profànder, profaràōn, prȍfić, prȍfisor, šàcan, žȉla

professor, high school teacher, prof: prófa, prȍfica

proficient theft: štȅp

profit: àir, àsna, berìćet, fȁjda, kàjmak, kȕnst, ȍfajditi se, selámet, sȉćār, ȕār, ȕvār, vàjda

profitable: berìćetan, birìćetan

profitably: berìćetno

profiter: šićàrdžija

prolongation: mȕštrānje

prolonged and meaningless talk, blabber, chatter: avètānje, balègānje, baljèzgānje, barlìjānje, bavr̀ljanje, benávljenje, benètānje, bèntānje, blâ-blâ[1], blȁvorēnje, blebètānje,bubètānje, bȕgarēnje, bulážēnje, bulážnjēnje, bunàcānje, bunárēnje, bùncānje, buvárēnje, cvȍkānje, cvokòtānje, čȁntrānje, ćapr̀dānje, dȑkānje, dȓndānje, dumbàrānje, džvȁnjkānje, đȕbrēnje, frajèrisānje, fȓfljānje, fŕljānje, klepètānje, kȑvljēnje, kvŕčānje, lapàrānje, lapìdānje, lopàtānje, lúpānje, lupètānje, mlatikárēnje, mȑndžānje, nadovezívānje, nagváždānje, pȉmplānje, pȉmplovānje, preserávānje, pretákānje, pričánjac, srȁćkalica, sránje[2], svírānje, šupljìkāt, talàsānje, tambùrānje, tandr̀kānje, toròkānje, tralákānje, tralalákānje, tralalíkānje, trkèljisānje, trȕćānje, tùpisānje, túpljenje, vèrglānje, volìdžānje, vunovlačárēnje, žȁmorēnje, žilávljēnje

prolonged and meaningless talk, diarrhea of the mouth: dupodèrānje, gòvnānje, njȇsra, proserávānje

promenade: cȓta[2], fúra, korzijáner, kȍrzo, linijáner, línija, monumȇnt, štȁjga, štráfta, štrapanzlišingèlīrka

prominent female: kàduna

promiscuous young female, nymphet: nimfèta

promise: nàpevati, vòljati

prompter (device in tv studios): idìot

prone, lying on one's stomach: potrbȕškē

pronounce 'ae' to express satisfaction, surprise, delight, dislike, pain, etc.: aéknuti

pronounce 'ajs' to urge an ox to move on: ȁjsnuti[1]

pronounce 'ccc' to express disbelief: cȍknuti, còktati

pronounce 'huh' being in trouble: húkati, húknuti

pronounce 'ih': ihuhúkati

pronounce 'ih' to express excitement, impatience, grief, pain, etc.: ȉhnuti

pronounce 'juj' to express surprise or fear: jujúknuti

pronounce the exclamation 'stu' to make an ox pull back: stȕkati

pronouncing 'aha' when grasping the import of conversation: ahàluk

pronouncing 'ajs' to urge an ox to move on: ȁjskānje

pronouncing 'ej' to draw attention: ȅjkānje

pronouncing 'jo' to express pain, disbelief, surprise, etc.: jókānje

pronouncing 'juj' to express surprise or fear: jujúkānje, jujȕškānje

pronouncing 'keca': kȅckānje

pronouncing 'keca' at weddings to encourage the best man to throw some money: kȅcānje

propeller: propȅler

properly, truly: ljùckī, ljùdskī

property (usu. with a house) in the vicinity visited during weekends: rȃnč

property: mâl

proposition (for sexual intercourse): jȅbozōv[2]

prostitute who charges by the hour: štȍperica

prostitute who engages in sexual intercourse with foreigners: dèvīznā

prostitute who often changes her place of residence: stjuardȇsa

prostitute who stands by the Varteks store at Jelačićev Square in Zagreb, Croatia: vàrteksica

prostitute who supports her lover financially: stȁrka[1]

prostitute, bitch: kȕčka

prostitute, hooker: ȁla[1], àpljara, bicìklistkinja, džògara, džùboks, bitùmen, blûdnica, càfuta, cépāljka, cèpulja, cjèpāljka, čâvka, čèšāljka, čèšātorka, čèšljārka, čùkara, dèvōjka, djèvōjka, dróca, dròcika, drȍcka, dròculja, drȍksa, drȍlja, dròmbulja, dròmfulja, drònfulja, drónja, drȍplja, dròpljača, džȕklja, fȃćkalica, fànfulja, fàtāljka, fljakafljóca, fljȁška, fiaška, fȋfa, fȋfica, flȉcka, flȉćka, flȉćkica, flȋnta, flôjsa, fùnjara[1], fȏlks-vagína, folksvagína, frakafljȍca, frakàfulja, frakfljóca, fràkfulja, fȓntulja, fúca, fȕfa, fȕfica, fùfika, fȕga, fȕka, fukàra[1], fùkara[2], fȕkī, fȕkica, fȕkos, fukòura, fȕksa, fȕnfa, fûr, gâbor, gèrla, glȍdārka, grànit, grèbāljka, gȕšter, gùntbek, gȕzičārka, hèvina, jègulja, kalȁštura, kȁmēn[1], kaménac, kamènčić, kamènjārka, kàraka, kècara, kèčara, kȋta, klâmfa, klȉndōvka, klȋnka, kóka, kòkara, kȍkica, kòkota, kontèjnerka, kùrāba, kùrvica, kȕja, kùlōvka, kuráva, kûrba, kȕrolomka, kȕroslada, kȕroždeр, kȕroždērka, kûrva, kurvèštija, kurvètina, kvȁčica, làkica, làura, lȇš[1], lipicánerka, lòmikūrka, lȍmokūrka, lòpata, màmek, mȁmica, mandóra, màndōvka, mârta, mèsara, mêso, mȉlokūrka, mûrva, nabádāljka, nȁdničarka, namìcāljka, natìkača, Ȍfēlija, opàjdara, opálija, pàlāndra, pasùljara, pàzārka, pelánovićka, picòpēvka, pizdòjēpka, pljùgāljka, pljùgārka, pr̀imalja, profesiònālka, profùkljača, profùknjača, propalìtēt, prostitȕtkinja, pȕcalica, pùšika, pùšikūrka, rabìnara, rȁdodājka, rájngla, raspandr̀kača, rastùrača, raščèpulja, ráva, ràvaku, ràvulja, rvàku, sèdmica, séka, sifònjērka, sȉsodr̄mka, smr̀dibuba, sóva, spèrmara, spèrmātorka, spèrmuša, staklénac[1], stòpička, strȋna, šȁtrovica,škr̀iplja, šljúnak, šóder[1], štȁjgerica, štr̀iherica, štr̀ikerica, štȕka, šupèndara, šùpēndra, šùpika, tùcāljka, tȅtrēb, tȅtrijēb, tréba, tr̀ipica, tŕžnica, tȕtka, ȕličārka, užežènica, ùžganica, vȉdra[1], vȕksa, zmìja, žȁba, ždr̀oplja, žȅna

prostitute, streetwalker: ìdeš, šétalica, àsfalterica, asfȁltērka, asfȁltuša, ćȍškara, sokàčara, tȁksī-gèrla, trȍtoārka, vȕglerica

protecting: dȅkovānje

protester: šètāč

provocative: jebèžljiv

provocatively dressed female: golopíca, golopȉčka, golopízda

provoke, incite: čȁčkati, frustrírati, nàdrkati

psychiatric hospital, nut house: ćȁlapr-kȕća, dilkàna, dilkànica, dìlkārnica, lùdara, lûdō, šȉznica, žùtara

psychologically: psìićkī

pubic area (female), muff: cȕbok, nàtpičnjāk

pubic hair (female): nàpičnjāk

pubic hair: čȁj, kèfa, mȕf, šȕma[2]

pubic hair, bush: šȕmica

pubic hair, fur: bûnda

pubic louse, crabs: picàizla, picàjzl, picàjzla

public bathroom: péder-bâr

public critique: prózivka

public transportation: kȍšnica

puddle: kàluža
puff (produce the sound): pff, pŭćkati
puff (the sound): pŭh
pug-nosed individual: pŕća
pull strings, use connections: razgrànati se
pull, tug: cȉmati
pump the gas pedal: nàdrukati
punch (the tool): dȕršlāg
punch in the head: bándža, dlànovac, telèfōn [1]
punch with one knuckle sticking out: kȍkavac
punch, hit
punish: ìseći, kastȉgati, kaštȉgati, nivèlisati
punishment: nivèlisānje
punk rock: pȁnk
punker (female): pȁnkērka
punker (male): pȁnker
pupil (of the eye): źènica
puppy: ćèmče, šćène
purple: lȉlā
purse thief, purse snatcher: tàšnēr
push, shove: fȕrnuti [2], podgúrnuti, pȕšnuti, ríknuti, štucírati, štȕrnuti
pushing, showing: bàštrānje, gûrka, múving, nabacóka [1], nabacívānje
put a ring on one's finger: prèseći
put excessive make-up: namàčkariti se
put into one's pocket, pocket: ubunàrisati
put on loud make-up: nàlafrati se, nàlofrati se
put on make-up: isfazonírati se, krȅčiti se, maskírati se, nàbiflati se
put on water to boil: nàstaviti
put on, dress: nàkačiti
put one's name on a list: ušárati se
put under arrest: ȁpsiti
put up resistance: batȑgati se
put, place: skèmbati
putty: gȉt
puttying: gȉtovānje
puzzle (game): pùzla
qadi (Moslem judge): kàdija
quadriplegic: bȉljka
quantity of beer one has consumed: tàmīć
quarreling: džangrìzav
quarrelsome female: bórac
quarter (one fourth of something): kvȁrat
quarter of a cc (measure for narcotic drugs): fȑtālj
question tag: ȁjdē [1], jel, jèlda, jèldē, jèlte
question tag used to check if the import of the message has been captured, Got it?: ìkiši [3]
quick: ȕše
quick sexual intercourse, quickie: bȑzāk, patróla, umákānje
quick unloading of stolen goods: tȑka
quickly: bȑzovōzno, nȁluzaj, òčas
quiet: smȍljav
quiet criminal: tȉca [2]
quiet male: pìtom
quiz: zâseda
rabbit: kvȑka, zȁjec [1]
races (usu. auto or motorcycle): dȉrke
racket (criminal): rèkēt
radar: vetrènjača
Radenska mineral water: radȁjner
radiator: kȉler [2]
radio: bȑbljivac [2], dȉora, hòrnīć, kùtija, Ràdivoje, sokòćalo
radio amateur, ham: hȁjfāć
Radisav (a man's name): Píšo [2]
Radisav's (referring to the proper name Radisav): Píšōv
rail (railroad): šínja
railroad: prògljārnica
railroad supervisor: óber
railway: trȅska
railway station: hèrberg
rain: kȁši, prȍšlica, vodènjāk [2], víza, zûjka, zûljka
raincoat: kȁpljavac, kȉšobrān, plȅhnjāk
rainwater: kȁpavica
raise one's cultural level: nàdizati se
raise, bring up: gòjiti
rake (the tool): grèbulje
rap received from one's peers after getting a haircut: sèfta
rap, tap: čvȍgnuti, čvóka, čvȍknuti, čvȑga, čvȑgnuti, čvȑknuti, kégla, klȍp [1], kvȑcati, kvȑcnuti, macóla, mȉlovati, šlȍpnuti, tràndati, tâć, tàpati, tȁpka [1], tàpšati, tȕpkati, zvȑcati, zvȑcnuti, zvȑčka
rape: mòdriti, rȉti, sȋlka, zgrȁmziti
rapist: fàntōm
rare, uncommon: òvsen
rascal: lóla
rat (the animal): pàrcov
rather *: pò* [2]
rather big: ȍvećī
rather small: màlehan, màlešan
rather unintelligent, pretty dense: zacemèntīrān
rather well: sȍlidno
rattle (the toy): zvȅčka [2]
raw Macedonian opium: kàtran
raw material used to produce tiles: vȉnāz
Ray Ban sunglasses: bânke
razor: bičànica, frîzmāher, ljȁmta
re-invent the wheel: kolumbírati
reach for one's wallet: ìzuti se
reach, bring an object closer to oneself: dòkūčiti
react: odrèagovati
read: žvákati
ready, set: kàil
real: gȉstro [1], strȍg, têškī [1]
real Serb, one who behaves in compliance with ethnic

customs: Sr̀bēnda

realize the actual state of affairs: prizèmljiti se

realize, become aware: ìzgengovati

realize, become aware of: zgȅngovati

realizing the actual state of affairs: prizemljénje

really, indeed: bāš, fȁkat [1], fùrtum, izistìnskī, jel, ljùckī, mâj [1], pitòmo, prâvō, stvârno, vàlā [1], zaopráve, zdrȁvo

rear pocket: zàdnjāk

rearrangement: pretumbácija

reasonable: sùbg

rebel leader: àrambaša

rebellion against communist bureaucracy in Novi Sad, Yugoslavia, 1988: jògurt-revolúcija

receipt: kr̀culja

recently-hired police investigator: nȍvī

recidivist: ćélo, devètān, žȉvac [1]

reconnaissance unit member: Indijánac

reconstruction: lȅpovānje

record or turntable which skips portions of a song: štȕca

record rock music: zàkucati

recover, get better: glístiti, ìzvaditi se

red wine: cr̀njāk

redeployment: prȅkomānda

redhead (female): kùruznā

redhead: šȉbica

redhead, carrot top: mȑkva

referring to the one who has earned some money: dȍbar [1]

refugee: dòbeg, dòbjeg, muhádžer, muhádžir, muháđer

refusal: kórpa

regain consciousness, come to: ofrkéstiti se

regimental colors: àlāj-bàrjāk

regulating: règlāžnī

regulation: regláža, reglírānje

regulator: rȅgler

rejoice, triumph: sláditi se

related to the Croat-Muslim Federation (in Bosnia): fȅderālnī

relative (person): osigùrāč, róđo [1]

relative living in one's apartment: kìnēz [2]

relatives: fâjta, tevábija

relax, cool off: ohláditi se

relax, take it easy: hlèbati

relaxed, laid back: kȍmōtan, negližântan

release mucus: bȁliti

release mucus involuntarily: baláviti

releasing mucus: balávljēnje, bȁljēnje

reliable: sȍlīdan

reluctant criminal: tùnjezga

remains, leftovers: rȅst

remember: sijévnuti, sjȁknuti, sjévnuti, sínuti, uđànisati, uđániti, uđériti, utúviti

remember somebody: zȕcnuti

remote and unpleasant place: pičkojèbina

Renault 4 (a car model): četvórka, gòjzerica, péglica

repair, fix: nakuȑkati, òpraljati, zȑiktati

repairman: mâjstor

repeated sound made by a chick, chirp-chirp: pȉu-pȉu

repeated sound made by a small bell, ding-ding: bȉm-bȁm, cȁn-cȁn, cȉn-cȁn, cȉnk-cȉnk

repeated sound made by metal objects, clang-clang: cȁka-cȁka, cȁk-cȁk

repeated sound made by splashing, splash-splash: bȑč-brč

reply, answer: pokòpati

report, relate: ìspljanuti, ìzlajati (se)

reproach, scold: bȕkvica, cvȍcati, čântrati, džȁkati, džvȁnjkati, iskèfati, isklistírati, izríbati, kȅfati, narezíliti, pêglati, prèslišati [1], preslišávati, ríbānje, ríbati, rezíliti, sapùnati, šmìrglānje, šmìrglati, trȁvarica, vatrírati, zbȉksati, zipàrati, zipáriti, zuzáriti, zvȍcati, zvŕčati, zvȓndati, žvȁnjkati, žvȁnj-žvȁnj [1]

reproaching, scolding: lávež

Republic of Serbska (so called by the Bosnian Muslims): Entȉtēt

reputation (usu. good): fȉrma [1]

request: glȁditi, ìskati, kȕvati, šéniti, zaìskati, žȉca

requiem (in Orthodox church): paràstos

resell: mútiti

resell tickets illegally, scalp tickets: dugáriti

resell, fence: dȉlovati, đabàskati, frkolévati, rješávati se, šavàtsere, ušàtafiti, utápati

reseller of stolen merchandise: bànkīr, vàljātor

reserve, book: begènisati

reservoir: gùstijēma

residence permit (for ex-Yugoslav guest workers in Germany): òfentāl

resign, quit: preparírati, ríknuti, siktèrisati, škartírati, štȕrnuti, šȕtnuti

respect, obey: brȅnovati, fèrmati, máriti, rèspekt, rèšpekt, šljìvosati, šljíviti, šíšati, tretírati, zarezívati

response to the question "How are you doing?", Horrible!: nȉkāko

rest: žmûr

restaurant: kíra, pàmūr, rȅstić

restaurant at the Central station in Zagreb, Croatia: zimòvnīk

resting: hladòvina, kulíranje

resting, avoiding work: ladòvina

resting, having a break: plàndovānje

retarded person, retard: šlȍg [2]

retired: òtpisān

retiree: òtpīsānī, pàstīr, pȅnzos, strîc

return, come back: vŕnuti, vŕnuti se

return, get back: curíknuti se

revelation, bombshell: bômba [2]

revenge, payback: vendèta

reverse (gear): rídža, rȉkverc [2]

revolver: levòvēr, révac, rèvār

reward for a person who brings good news of any kind:

muštùluk
ribbon (in general): lênta
rice: šljúnak
rich male: glàvnī [2], gotívac
rich naive male: malicána
rich person: Amèrika
ride (on a bus, etc.) uncomfortably: tùmbati se
ride: pròšājbati
ride on public transportation without paying fare: kȅš
ridiculous thing, absurd event: cepùrija, pȋš [2], pìšānje, pišijáda, pišùrija, ùpiš, upišávānje, vrȋsak
riding (horseback): đī-đī [2]
rifle: bàštūnka, cêvka, čȁčkalica, krìvača, sȁvra, savrakèlac, štȉcāljka, šûpljē [1], tàndžara, vȉljika
right (as contrasted to left): dùvanjskī
right away, now: fȕrtom, ȍdmā, ȍmā
rigor: strogòća
Rijeka soccer team fan club from Rijeka, Croatia: Armáda [2]
ring (a bell, etc.): cangàrati, cȁnjkati, cincàkati, cincìkati, cȉnkati [1], tȉnksti, víknuti, zrȉngati, zvònkati, zvŕčati, zvȓndati
ring (part of a mechanism): rȉnga, šèlna
ring (small bell): cingàrati
ring leader (of thieves): kâpo
ring seller: rìngāš
ring wrench (the tool): rȉng-šlìsl
ringing (bell, etc.): cangàrānje, klȅpa [2], zvònjava, zvònjavina
rip off: fȉknuti
rip, tear apart: búcati
rise up: kljȋnčiti
risk, chance: lùtrija, reskírati
Ritoznojćan (a brand of wine): znȍjogūz
rivet: bìksna, nìtna, nȉtnovati
riveting: nȉtovānje
rning money: isisávānje
roach (insect): bȕbos
road: džáda [2], đáda [2], gljârnīk, strȕna
roaming thief: kirìjāš
roar (engine, etc.): klobàrati, rondàrati, šȕmiti, zvŕjati, zvrkétnuti, zvȑknuti, zvȑktati, zvȑkteti, zvȓncati, zvȓnčati, zvȓndati
roar (of an animal): ríkati
roaring (engine, etc.): dȓnda, dȓndav, rondàrānje, zvȑdānje, zvȓj, zvŕjānje, zvȑjav, zvȑk, zvȑka, zvŕkānje
roast (meat): lȕngić
rob the same individual several times: heplírati
rob, fleece, rip off: brìjati, hȅplovati, iscéditi, obrìjati, očèšljati, pòharati, prèsvući, uráditi
rob, rip off: izmàrisati, kesírati, obŕstiti, ogúliti, òjaditi, opèlješiti, operùšati, oplìndrati, ȍškljabati, ȍšuriti
robbed, ripped off: izgòreō, oplèten
robber, thief: aràčlija
robbery: bèrba, pȍhara
robin: cȉkavica
rock a child: nánati, núnati
rock guitarist: natèzāč
rock music: cepáža, rasturàčina, rȍkić
rock musician, head banger: trȅsomān
rock musician, rocker: rȍker
rock or pop musician: elèktričār
rock'n'roll: rȍkerskī
rod: štánga, štángla
roll a cigarette or joint: mòtati
roll down a slope: stùmbati se, tùmbati se
roll up (e.g. sleeves): potfȑknuti
romance novel (usu. of low quality): hȅrc-ròmān
rominal (narcotic drug): rȍmī
roof-top buglar: mjȅsečār
rookie: brȕjān, novàjlija, žȁbār
rookie soldier, first month soldier: fàzān, gȕšter, réma, rémac, rémo, réponja
room: gâjba, gajbijána, gajbijàšica, kàmara, kȕnt, pèćina
room intended for sexual intercourse: fȕkodrōm, streljàna
room used by a prostitute, trick room: pèćina
roommate (female): cȉmērka, frȅndica
roommate (male): cȉmer, frȅnd, frȅndāć, frȅntāč, pàjdāš, pȁjt, pàjtāš, pȁjtos, pâle
rooster: hȍrōz, kokòtān, krékac, ȍrōz, pívac
rope: cŕnec, kanáfa, kònop, sìdžim, špâg, špága, špagáta, štránga, žnòra [2]
rot, decay: pŕhati, pȑhkati, prhȉnuti
rotate, turn around: ispovȉteti
rotten, decayed: kváran, pòtruhnuti, strȕhnuti, trȕhaō, trȕhlo, trȕhnuti
round (drinks in a bar): rȕnda
rowdyism: ugursùzluk
rub one's partner's vagina with one's penis: pȉmzlati
rubber (inflatable) boat: gumènjāk
rubber: gȕnta
rubber joint (in transmission mechanism): gumigèleng
rubber raincoat: kùrtōnka
rude: dȋvča [2], grûbor, ìšibān
rude female: pasùljara, pȉdara
rude male: džèbrak
rude person: siròvina
ruin somebody (emotionally or financially): dòtūći, ukòpati, zakòpati
ruined (emotionally or financially): pèčen
ruined and destroyed person or mechanism: kȑš, razjebòtina
ruined person: tulìpān
rule of the HDZ (Hrvatska demokratska zajednica 'Croatian Democratic Alliance', a political party in Croatia): hadezeóvština
rum and coke: zȅmljotrēs
rumble (e.g. a cart on a rocky road): tȃndr̄, tandȑkati, tûtanj [2]
rumbling: tȃndȑk, tandȑkānje

rummaging through apartment or things: trkèljisānje

rumor: pȁtka

rump cover for a horse: náguznīk

run (command): ìdidi

run: džàdati, gàmbati, jùrcati, kȉfliti, làufati, nòktati, pàljevina, šprȉntati, špúra[1], špúrati, špȕrnuti, tabànati, zafúrati (se)

run around (e.g. school children on their break): jàrcati

run away in fear, scram: ljȉgati

run away, flee: brȉsati, brísnuti, cȉpliti, cȉpljati, čkòjiti, dìmisati, dȉmiti, dimírati, džàdisati, džȁdnuti, đàlisati, đȁlnuti, fȕati, fȕrnuti[1], gljȁnuti, gljȁti, gnjȁti, gúrati, ȉkati, kȉdati, kȉdnuti, klȁjduniti, klȁjnuti, klísnuti, lìtipa, mótiti, odgalopírati, odmàgliti, òdšājbati, otperjášiti, otpèrjati, pláknuti se, pȑnuti, razgúliti, razvijátiti, rȉčiti, sévati, sklȉsati, strúgati, strùgisati, strúgnuti, stúšiti, šȉmati, šȉmbovati, šȉmiti, šȉmkovati, šȉmovati, šimírati, šmȕgnuti, štrȉkati, štȕkati, tabànisati, taljìgati, ùteći, vȁndrovati, zàkuriti, zàpaciti, zapalìndati, zapáliti, zaprášiti, zatetrébiti, zbrȉsati, zdȉmiti[2], zdúšiti, zgìljati

run fast: galopírati, štȁrtati, ùžditi

run into: zabúšiti

run into, hit: zabàštati se, zabúbati, zabúšiti se

run unevenly (engine, etc.): tȑzati

runaway, fugitive: logórko

running away, beating feet tàban[2]

running away, fleeing: bježànija, čìstac[2], furijandžēlī, furijanđēlī, gàmbātor, kȉdānje, kidavȅla[2], klȉs[2], màgla[2], nȍkat[2], šȉšnjava, špúra[2], štúra[2], tȗtanj[2], tutavȅla[2]

rural party (social gathering): prélo

rush, high: špȉca

rush, hurry: fȓka

Russian (person): Bàćuška[2], Kòžara, Rúja, Rȕjān, Rújo, Rȕlovac

rust: rdžȁ, zahȑđati

saber, sword: pòserkija, pòserkinja, tȑlica

sad: dèrtli, pòkisao, šȅtan

sad song: jaúkalica

sad, depressed: pȍpišān, sjȅbān

safe: bunàrče, pȃnj[2], zihèrāškī

safe cracker: mȁčkār, mȅčkār

safe debt (sure to be repaid): gȗt

safety pin: zȉherica

safety, security: sigurácija

sagging female breast: kȅsa, vrȅća, vìsibaba

sailor: fȍka, vodènjāk[1]

salaam (Islamic greeting): sèlām[1], sèlām[2]

salt: tȕz, zȓnija

samba: sambijánović

sandal (shoe), Jesus boot: àpostōlka

sandpaper: smȉrk

sanitary napkin: bugàčica

sash: gùrtna

satisfaction: godrìna

sauce: móča

saucer: pljȁt

sauerkraut: atòmnjāk

sausage: čȗrka, mȁlo[2]

Sava (river, former Yugoslavia): Bȁra[1]

save: vȁditi

save money, sock money away: čarapírati, špárati, štȅkovati, ušpárati

savings: štȅk, štéka

saw (the tool): žága

saw (tool): džága

saw: bȏgnsȅk, šéga

sawed-off gun: krátež

saxophone, sax: fȁjfa, krȁva

say bluntly: skrȅsati

say energetically: trȅsnuti se

say something unintelligent: odváliti

say something inappropriate: iskòčiti

say something unintelligent: izváliti, lȕpiti, polòžiti, pròsūti, prováliti, prováliti se, provaljívati, provaljívati se, trȅsnuti, trȅsnuti se

say something unintelligent, blurt out: bȕbnuti

say, spill: pròsūti

say, tell: gúknuti, ìspljanuti, ìspljunuti, kȅvnuti, rȅcnuti, rèći

scalp tickets: tapkáriti, tȃpkati

scalping tickets: tapkárēnje

scandal: kàzīn, škàndāl, šȏu[1]

scarab, dung beetle: gȍvnovālj

scarecrow: karakȏndžula

scared: svìlen

scared male: ledènjāk

scarf: màhrama

scary: frikòvit

schizophrenic: šȋz[1]

schnapps made from sugar: šećèruša

school: bastȉlja, knjȉževīšte, mučiónica, òbrazōvka, pàntara, ròbija, robìjāšnica, školárac, zátvor

school bathroom: čikobérnica, kànāl, pišapȕšī, pràmac, pušióna

school council: nesalòmljivī

school janitor (female): čȅtkica, kéva, tȅtkica

school student: đȁker, đȁkomo, gòlāć, kamikáza, kamikáze, robìjāš, škȍlkić

scissors: crapàjce, cȓpājce, ȓpačkē

sclerosis: róza

sclerotic person: róza

scold, punish: kárati

scooter (children's toy): tròtiš

score (in sports): zbìberiti

score numerous goals (e.g. in soccer): nàbiti, nabúšiti, nàbuškati

Scotch tape, adhesive tape: sèlotējp

scraper: šȁber

scratch: zarèndati

scratch oneself: čȍmati se, pȍčohati se

scratch-off lottery: gréba

scratched marble (the toy): kȑnjotka

scream (in pain, fear, or outrage): arlaúkati, arlaúknuti, cìčati, cìčiti, cijùkati, cȋk[2], cìkljevina, cȋktāj, cilìnkati, cilíkati, cíkati, cíknuti, dèrnjati se, dréčati, drékniti, dréknuti, hȕrlīk, hurlíkati, hurlíknuti, jȁok, jaókati, jaóknuti, jàūk, jaúkati, jaúknuti, jêk, jèktati, jèkteti, klȋknuti, klíkati, kvrékati, vrìšćati, krȉsnuti, ùrlati

screaming (in pain, fear, or outrage): cijùkānje, cȋka, cȋkav, cìktānje, cȉlīk, cilìnkānje, cilíkānje, jaùkav, jaùkljavina, jaùkljiv, jàukast, jaùkljivo, jȅktavo, klèkat, krȉcka, skȋka

screaming person: kréšta

screw (fastening device): šàrāf, šèrāf, šrȃf

screw (nut, etc.): zàšrafiti

screwdriver: šarafcíger, šràfcīger[2]

scribble, write illegibly: nàčrčkati, našvŕljati, nažvŕljati, švŕljati, žvŕljati

scribbling: pisànija

sea: bȁra[2], slánjača

sea gull: kaùkavac

seal, stamp: mȕhūr, mȗr, mȕūr, štàmbīlj

search: kàmisovati, kȁmiti, kèvati, kúpati, trkèljisati, trndáriti

search, comb: pročèšljati

search, fish for: pȅcati

search, look for: cȕnjati[1], čàčkati, dìkljati, grabùljati, grèbati, kòpati

search, seek: kániti

search, sniff out: njȕškati

seasonal worker: sezónac

seat: sȉc

second: gȉdru

second coffee served to one's guests: razgovòruša

second grass (on a pasture, etc.): òtova

second Yugoslavia (1945-1990): Avnoslȃvija

secure oneself, be safe: nafatírati se

security guard: kȍstūr

sediment: zȋft

seduce: báriti, gotíviti, ìzvatati, krátiti, obáriti, obrađívati, odráditi, pròknjižiti, stȉcati

seducer: Karánović, kȅca[2], màšīnka, nabacȉška, nabacóka[2], òtrov, rázvodnīk, šmȅker, šmȅkos, švȁler, tròvāč, tȓzātor, ždrébac

seducing: stȉcānje, tȓzānje

see: sìnjati, skúžiti, ùbrati

see through (lit. and fig.): skrozírati

see, look, spot: đȉviti

see, observe: snímiti

seesaw: klȁckavica

self-employed person: slobòdnjāk

self-publishing: sȁmizdat

self-service store: dȑpārnica

selfish person: fȕksa

sell (exchange merchandise for money): dàtipro, dȃtpro, džanjávati, džnjávati, ferkìćati, frkávati, frkìćati, kìćati, mútiti, mȕvati, prolúziti, šćȁriti, šćȅnđati, tánjiti, torbáriti, trakèljati, ùjārčiti, tròšiti, udávati, utánjiti, utápljati, utòpiti, ùtrapiti, váljati[1], zàfrljiti, zmátati

sell drugs: váljati[1]

sell using persuasion: ùtrampiti

sell worthless merchandise, sell junk: ùdati, udòmiti, uváliti, uváljati, uvaljívati

senator: sèrātor

send away, dismiss: dvojkírati, odjèbati

send regards: poselámiti

senile male: pȉlovina

senile person: galapȃgos, krecàna, krȅč[1], krečàna, krȅčār, màtūf, màtūh, màtūv, seníac

senior citizen: ȁmfora, bábac, bȁbos, bàbula, bàbule, bákac, bàkūt, bakùtān, bakutáner, bàmbus[2], barutàna, bìblija, bȍgoljūb, čèšnjāk[1], dèkūt, , dekùtāndràplja, dȓklje, dȓtle, đutùrum, fòsīl, gȉcka, gȓba, grȍb, grȏblje, kalàštura, kéša[2], kèšātor, kévac, klȃnfa, kljáka, kȍravac, kȍravica, korèla, kȍrka, krȅčār, kurotrèsina, lapèndus, lȅš[1], ljȕska, mánda, màtūf, metuzálem, metùzko, mȑcan, mȑcī, mȑcina, mȑcko, mȑcoš, mȗmija, nája, òfrčija, òlupina, pȃnj[1], pasùljara, pitekàntrop, pjȅsmarica, pràngija, psȉna, rȅlo, senílac, slépac, sóva, stàriša, stȁrka[1], šàjser, trȁnjār

senior citizen, old fart: pȑdonja

senior citizen, old goat: bìzōn

senior citizen, old timer: matórac, matòrān, mȁtros, rȉša, rȉšasta

senior citizens (collectively): plìnara, starčàdija, starùdija

sensitive, touchy: ośètljiv

sentimental: sèntiš

sentimental dance: sèntiš

sentimental movie: sȁftāć

sentimental music: sèntiška

sentimental novel: sȁftāć

sentimental song: sèntiš

separate: raskàntati se

separate from somebody (e.g. from one's spouse): odsúkati se

separately, individually, each on their own: bȁmbàška, ȍbaška

septet: sȅptić

Serb (female): četnìkuša

Serb hater, Serb basher: srbomŕzac, sȑboždēr

Serbian (male): čédo, čȅtnīk, čéto, ćédo, ćȅtnīk, ćéto, kȑme, Slòbist, Slóbo, Sȑbēnda, srbočȅtnīk, vlȃh

Serbian fighter (male): ćédo, ćȅtnīk, čȅtnīk, čéto

Serbian fighter in Croatia in the1990s: knȉndža, mȃrtićevac

Serbian from Serbia proper: gédža, gédžo, gedžòvān

Serbian guerilla fighter during the Ottoman Empire: àjdūk

Serbian language (school course): sŕpa

Serbian language teacher (female): Sȑpkinja

Serbian language teacher (male): Sȑbin

Serbian nationalist leader: vȍžd

Serbian policeman in the late 1990s: mȕpovac

Serbian rebellion in Kraina (a province of Croatia) in the

early 1990s: bàlvan-revolúcija

Serbo-Croatian (pertaining to the language): jugoslòvēnskī

sergeant: nárednīk

series of weak adversaries (e.g. in a tournament): eldorâdo

sermon: žvȁnjkānje, žvȁnj-žvȁnj [1]

servant: ìzmećār, jàzbec

serve one's time in prison: otkùlučiti

service (in general): sèrvīs

service: servisírati

serving a long term in prison: penziònīrān

serving prison term at Goli island (Croatia, where the former communist regime detained its political enemies): klesárēnje, razgihávānje, sȕnčānje

setting fire to someone's fingers: gitára

setting fire to someone's toes, giving someone a hotfoot: bicìkl

settle an issue: raskȑstiti, zrìhtati

settle mutual financial issues: potkusùrati se, potkusurívati se, raskusùrati se, raskusurívati se

seven: mùntām, zíbene

seven-inch long penis: dèkān

seventeen: sedàmnājs, sedàmnēs

seventeenth: sedàmnājsti

sew: vȕskati

sewing machine: tròpačka

sewing needle: bòdača, bòdāljka, bódlja, protìnjača

sex shop: sȅks-šȍp

sexless period: sûša

sexual foreplay, petting, feeling up: ćaplàisānje, dŕpānje, drpáža, ȅros, fȉlcovānje, okešávānje, pètīng, pȉpānje, pȓstāć, prsténac, rȕkomēt, rukotvòrine, šlàtānje, vȁća, vaćárēnje, vaćàtina, vatàčina, vatàćina, vȁtānje, vatárac, vatatàčina, vatáža

sexual intercourse (of goats): pȑcokoz

sexual intercourse (of sheep): ȍmrka

sexual intercourse: ȁkānje, bànjeje, bùkarenje, bòdēnje, cépānje, čèrečēnje, čȕkānje, fìrcānje, fȕk [2], fukánac, fȕkānje, gácānje, gàjtarēnje, gatárēnje, glágol, glôd, gȕslēnje, gúžēnje, hàrem, hèbānje, hèftānje, hȅklānje, hȍblānje, hȍpā-cȕpā [2], hȍp-cȕp [2], jàšika, jêb, jéba, jebàčina, jebáda, jebàncija, jebànija, jèbānje, jebávānje, jebèćina, jȅbež, jebìčina, jebìkānje, jebùcānje, jèpstvo, jòrbanjetonj, kantàrisānje, kárānje, kȅcānje, kȅks, kȅksānje, kȅksovānje, kokàčina, kókānje, krèsānje, krȅvetovānje, kȑljānje, kȕrac-pȁlac, lelemȕde, lìpačēnje, màštračēnje, méšānje, mȅtak [2], mȅtković, mòčēnje, montírānje, mŕčēnje, mȑdānje, nȕmera, njȁma, ònō [2], opaljȍt, opaljívānje, pêglānje, pȅlcovānje, pȉčēnje, pičkàrānje, pičkárēnje, pičkaròšēnje, pičkojèbina, pȉčvajs, píla, pizdojèbina, pílēnje, poklápa, polírānje, prâsak, práskānje, pŕcānje, pȕmpānje, rádnja, rasturàčina, rȁšpānje, rȅzānje, rȉbovānje, rìfljānje, rinìtis, ȓke-kȍke, rókānje, rȍksovānje, sȅksānje, seksndràjsig, spôjka, strȅlovānje, strúgānje, surduknúće, šàbečēnje, šȅfka, šéva, šévānje, šȅvkānje, šlàjfānje, šíšānje, štȅp, štȉh [2], šùpčēnje, šȕs, švalerácija, švalèrānje, švalèrisānje, švȁsānje, tába, tȃbānje, tabòisānje, tàslačēnje, testírānje, tȍrbālj, tòrbānje, trȁndžić, trandžírānje, trànsfȕzija, trénje, tùcāljka, tȕcānje, tȕmplānje, ùbod, ȕkfu, ùmak, vóžnja, zȅka, zȉgovānje, zȉtovānje, znòjīć

sexual intercourse in which the female sweats considerably: vàterpōlo

sexual intercourse with simultaneous mutual oral stimulation, 69: dȕpe-gláva

sexual intercourse, banging: gáđānje

sexual intercourse, poking: nabádānje

sexual stimulation: rȁjc

sexually aroused female, hot chick: àjkula, kȕrožder, kȕroždērka, lùjika, pàlida,

sexually aroused person, hot person: pàlida, pàljevina, vȁtra

sexually aroused, hot: nàsaftān

sexually exhausted: ìsprcān

sexually experienced female: pasùljara, polóvnjača

sexually frigid female: Ȅskīmka, frìgita, frȉgos

sexually inactive: zàkȓčen, zàkrečen, zàpušen

sexually inexperienced male: nȅpīc-frȁjer

sexually potent male: alàtljikār, mȕla, s.s. [ȅs ȅs]

sexually provocative: jȅbozōvan

sexually stimulate, turn on: pòvatati

sexy: krȅvetibīlan, sȅksī

sexy teenage girl: vitamìnčić

shack: kòleba

shade (of a tree, etc.): deknlàntl, lâd

shady place: ladòvina

shaft (e.g. of an engine): bòlcn, bòlcna

shaft: vȅla

shag carpet: čȕpavac [2]

shake (an object, person, etc.): drmùsati, klepètati

shake (usu. in outrage), boil: cèpteti

shake one's buttocks: múljati, razgúziti, razguzívati

shaking one's buttocks during sexual intercourse: méšānje, méšati, mijéšati

shame, disgrace, scandal: blȁm, brȕka

shapely: Grenóbl

shards (usu. of broken glass), smithereens: parampàrčād

share, split: dîl, rastaljívati, tâl, tálitì

sharing: dèljāk

sharp knife: ćȕla

sharp sound (e.g. of a steam whistle): cȉkūt

shave: ostrúgati, ostrúgati se, strúgati

shawl: ponjàvče

she-wolf: ćȅmica

sheep: békavica, blejȉkuša, blèkača, lȅšica

sheep with yellow spots: žȕja

sheet metal: plȅh

shell, bomb: đúle, grúhati [2], grúvati, rókati

shelling, bombing: grúvānje, rókānje

shelter (e.g. for homeless people): kevàna

shelter for drug addicts: ȁndergrâund

shepherd: čòban, čòbanin

shift an engine into high gear: turírati

shift gears: šàltati, šàtltati

shine (on any polished object): glȁnc

shine (reflect light): càkliti se

ship, vessel: kȉštra, škàtalja, vȁmpor, vâpor

shirt: kȁnjavica, kȍšos, košuljijánović, košuljȉška, kȑpa, mȕštavica, pȑtlja, šúlja, šûljka, znòjara

shiver (from cold): klepètati

shiver from cold or fright: dȑktati

shock: strȅfiti

shock absorber: štôsdèmfer

shock absorption system: federácija[1]

shock, astonishment: šòkīng-blû

shoe: bùfalo, cipelȉška, cipijánović, cȉpos, còkula, čûn, gȉlja[1], gìljalica, gìljār, gìljara, gìljarica, gìljārka, giljàrōn, gîljka, gȉlja[2], gljâjka, gljȁka[2], gljȁra, gljárak, gljârka, gljárnica, gòndola, gràpiška, guljàrica, gùljārka, kȁloš, kalóša, kaljùgān, kónusica, kòpito, kùndura, láda, lâđa, pápak[2], papkijóber, pȉpos, plóvak, škȍrnja, šljȁpica, špìcara, štiglèta, šûjka, šȕza, tàban[2], tàljiga, tìmberlēnka, tròpačka, žûlj

shoe a horse: potkòvati

shoe made of ropes: špágerica

shoe repairman: šȕster

shoelace: pèrtla, špìgeta, žnȉranac, žnòranac

shoot at each other: upucávati se

shoot loudly: grúvati

shoot, fire: grúhati[2], klokòtati, krȅsnuti

shooting: grúvānje

shopkeeper (female): tȃnjarnica

shopkeeper (male): tranjèrija

shopping (i.e., the goods one has bought): bakàluk

shopping: bazárēnje

shopping bag: céger, cȅker

short (in height, of a person): abòrtīrān

short: pìcek[1], pòbāčen

short attractive female: pénce, pìčīć

short circuit: kȕrcšlus, kȕršlus

short coat with elongated wooden buttons: đubretárac

short deadline: vȁtra

short deep breath: šmȑcāj

short female: déva, dokolènica, pičórak, rȁca

short hair: čȅtka, čȅtkica

short hair with bangs: kàciga

short hashish pipe: ćìlim

short jacket: nàguzac

short male: pátak, pàtakac, pàtakos, patàšōn, pȁticvȑk, pàtkac, pàtosman, pàtosmen, patúljak, picopévac, pòrtviš, pŕco, trȁnzistor[1]

short obese female: pìksla[2]

short obese male: šúponja

short person: bádža, cȑcoljak, cȑcvoljak, crévce[1], kȅpēc[1], kȑdža[2], màliša, pŕca, pȑcknedl, zàguzak, žȉlēt[1]

short person who keeps his or her head down: gúto

short ride: krûg

short sound made by metal objects, ping: fȑc

short stay in prison: ljȅtovānje

short stay in prison: lȅtovānje

short trousers, flood pants: trȍfrtāljke

short-legged male: pátak, pàtakac, pàtakos, pàtosman

short-nosed individual: pȑćos

short-sighted male: búlja[2]

shorts: šȍrc

shot (firearms): šȕs, vrîsak

shot and beer, boilermaker: bètōn[2]

shot glass: fićok, šȉše

shot of schnapps: ràkijīca

shot, injection (medical): nèkcija

shoulder: òfinger

shout at: krȉsnuti, zìjati, ìzdrati se, ìzdrkati se

show in public: slȉkati se

show off: kȕrčiti se, pròkūrčiti se, šmînkati se

show or stick out one's buttocks: nagúziti, nagúziti se

show up: nàcrtati se, nàsrati se

show up in public: producírati se

show, display: penàvisati

showing in public: slȉkānje

shut somebody up: krkljáviti

shut up: òlabaviti, oláditi, prikénjati, zavézati

shy: pìjoža, rèšō, stídan

shy male: paradȁjzović

sick joke: cȑnjāk, crnjànskī

sick person: vȍsak

sick, ill: bîvšī, bùbini

sickish person: sipljívko

sickly: bolèšljiv, kȅnjkav, kȕnjos

sickness: boléština, màraz, zelènilo

side by side, jointly: barabȁr[2]

side dish: čùšpajz

side or edge of something: bânda

side, flank: flȁnka

sign 1 (home team wins) and 2 (visitors win) on a sport betting coupon, i.e. one bets that a game of soccer will not end with a tied score: môst

signal (in cards as a form of cheating): telefúrati

signaling (in cards as a form of cheating): tȅlefūr

signature: šára, šarènica

silence: rȉba

silencer (on a gun): prigùšāč

silent disappearance, slink away: ȉka[2]

silent disappearance, slinking away: izmicàus, izmicàuz

silent discharge of intestinal gas, s.b.d. (silent fart): Tȉhomīr

silent person: ćutòlog

silent walking: tȁp[2]

similar: nálik, slȉkān

simple but effective solution: blàjbinger

simple shoe made of canvas and with rubber sole: žȅpa

simple soup with flour only: àjnpren-čórba

simple, easy: bȕkvār

simply, just: čȉsto

sing: kàntati, kȅsnuti, kȕkati, kváriti, pevúšiti, pȉvati, singati, sȍngati, túliti, vȁtpjo

sing Christmas carols: čaprazdivániti

sing monotonously and in one voice, drone: cindàrati

sing out of tune: falšírati, isfašírati

singer: gȑlo, kanarínac, sȉnger, sȍnger, urlíkalo, zjévalo

singer of love songs: sevdàlija

singing one day a week on a contract (usu. during the summer season): čvȑga

"single" phonograph record: sìngl, sìnglica, sìnglka

sip (alcohol): ćȅvnuti, klȍknuti, klònuti, lȍknuti

sip: gûc

sipping (of alcohol): cêvčēnje

sister: dâjka, švȅsterica, švȅstērka, vragòta, vȉgotnica

sister, sis: dáda [1], mànuka, móša, séja, séka, švéca [2], švȅsta [1]

sister-in-law: snâ, snâjka

sit: kȉsnuti, kljȉnčiti, prikénjati, śèđeti, śês, śȅsti, śȉđeti, zȉcnuti

sit down: òtur

sit for a while: pośèđeti

six: šês

sixteen: šèsnēs

sizable amount of money, big bucks: lòvudža, lòvuta

sizzle (of bacon on a frying pan): cvŕčati

sizzling sound: cvȑč

Skadarlija (a street in Belgrade): Skȁdar, Skádža

skill: marifètluk

skilled person: šušùmiga

skillful: mȍćan, múnja [2], mútan, nàmazān, nenadjèljiv, ùmetan, vȉdra [2], vjȅš, vljȅš

skillful and adept male: akrȍbat, akrȍbata, balètān

skillful criminal: đȍlī, framàzōn, kužìrēr, njúška

skillful criminal who has not been caught: šmȅkār

skillful male: ćalȉškān, ćalȉškīn, glàvnī [2], mùvātor, špìclov, vȉbros, vȉdra [1], vitàmīn

skillful person: fȁhman, fazȍnēr, fifik, filadèlfija [1], mȁher [1], màšīnka, mùćkāroš, mùnđāroš, múnja [1], òtrov, rȉcinus, smûk, sokòlac, streptomìcīn [1], streptomìnđīn, šmȅkos, štósēr, tètanus, ubacóka, vȑtirupa

skillful, adept: mȁher [2], mŕtav [2]

skillfully: jèbāčkī [2], smìslāškī

skillfulness: bȉks [2], fitīlj [1], kȕnst, štôs [2], vàljuga

skin: skȁlp

skin and venereal diseases section of a hospital: lujzijàna

skinhead (a person with shaved head): glóbus

skinhead: skìnhed, Tašmájdan, tȉkva [1]

skip classes, cut classes: lȕftati, pȉcati, všȕšnuti

skipping classes, cutting classes: lȕftānje

skirt: dògaćnica

sky: érić [2]

skyscraper: sòkiš, tàvan

slam (a door, etc.): fȕknuti

slam: zàkucati

slamming (basketball, etc.): ukucávānje

slang: ȁštro, dlȁkārskī, gȅgavačkī, gȅgavskī, jòšatronj, jòtrošanj, kozárac, mutàvdžījskī, mȕtavskī, òšrat, ròšat, šàtra, šȁtro [2], šȁtrovačkī, trȍša

slang word: frcòkla

slanting: nàhēren, nȁhēro

slap, smack: aplàuz, ćȕška, dàndara, dȁnga, dȁngla, dlȁn, dlànovac, fȕska, šamàrčina, šlága, šlagírati, šljága, zàuška, zvínuti

slaughter (people): ȓpati

slaughtering (of people): ȓpānje

Slav: Rȁc

sled: vȕzgala

sledge hammer: macóla

sleep at another's place, sleep over: presóviti

sleep long: njȍriti

sleep, nap: bújati, búji-báji, bújiti, bújkiti, čmávati, ćóriti [1], drȉncati, dȓncati, dȕrmiti, džófa, džȍfra, džónjati, đónjati, fljéjiti, hȁjati, hâjčiti, hȁjkiti, hȅnkati, kȁnjati, kmávati, knjáva, knjávati, knjévati, knjòvati, kònjosānje, krmèljati, kùntānje, kùntati, kȕntovati, kuntírānje, kuntírati, kúnjati, làvānje, mȉžiti, nàktiti, òterati se, otknjávati, pájkiti, slípiti, sȍfija, sȍfkati, sóva, sòvān, sòvāž, sôvčiti, sovijáner, sòvisati, sóviti, sôvka, sȍvkānje, sȍvkati, spavánac, spavánjac, tùtati, zaćóriti, zađónjiti, zújati, žmûr

sleeping: ćoránac, ćórānje, ćórēnje, džónjānje, horizontála, hrkánac, kérēnje, knjòvānje, kȑmisānje, kȕnt, mȉžēnje, pájkēnje

sleeping, snooze: sòviška

sleepy: kȕnjos

sleepy person: kȕnjos, spàvātor

sleepy person, sleepy head: čmávalo, njôrča

slender boy: čókljo

slender female: ȁfīnger, àkrep, àufīnger, àufīngerka, cȅlorouk, cȅlrouk, dȑvārnica, džȉglja, lȅtva, mètla [1], pȅlcer, skȕša, slàvūj, suvòguza, štánga, štȉkla, tvȉgī, tvȉgica, zmìja, žgȍljavica, žlȕndra

slender female, walking skeleton: koštùrača

slender leg: kòlac, pȅcka

slender male: bakàlār, dupepévac, suvárak [1], žgoljávko

slender person: fȍsna, glȉpši, glísta, kȍskica, metiljávko, mȍtka, pérce, rentgènāl, violína, žgólja, žȉlēt [1]

slender person, skeleton: kȍstūr

slender, skinny: mršùljav, suvogùsas, suvogùzas, žgȍljav

slightly: su* [2]

slightly curly hair (a type of permanent): minivâl

slightly drunk, tipsy: ćeflèisān, pȍdnapīt, sȕpijan

slightly insane, nutty: ćáknūt, fàličan, kvȑcnut, nȅčitav, òtkačen, patològija, smûćen, šȁntav, šȁškast, šȉzik [2], zôvnūt

slightly insane, touched in the head: cvȑcnūt

slightly insane, wacky: pȑćāknūt

slim: rijédak

slim chance: šansonȅta

sling: prȁćka, prája

slip into something comfortable (usu. scanty): raspištóljiti se, ràzgaćiti se

slip of tongue: bìser [1]

slipper: pápa [2]

slippers: patòfne

slippery spot: klíza

slope of a hill: bȁir, pȉnklić

Slovenia: dežȅla

Slovenian (person): konjùšār

Slovenian (pertaining to a person): dežèlāškī

slow: kȉlav

slow dance: spòrāć, stískati se

slow in understanding: dugotàlāsan

slow person, slowpoke: pûž, spòrāć

slow to learn: nàkrīvljen

slow walk: šupèljānje

slow work: pȉmplānje

slow worker: pȉmpler

slowly: nájlak, ponájlak, sèrbez [2]

slurp: bljȁncati, mljȁ, mljȁc, mljȁckati, mljȁs, mljȁsati, sȑk [1], sȑk [2], sȑkāj, sŕkati, sŕknuti, sȑkūt, srkùtati

slurping: mljȁcav, mljȁckānje, mljȁckav, mljȁsānje, mljȁskav, sŕkānje, srkùtānje

slush, sleet: bljúzga, bljȕzgavica, ljȉzgavica

sly: ljȉgav, nàmazān, neòvejān, šàmličast, trȕnjav

sly boy: mȁkō

sly male, fox: lìsica, lísac, negatívac

sly person, fox: plesnìvec

small (of the nose): pȑčast

small: lȉma, miskìnjav, portábl [2]

small African American: rínglica

small animals: žgàdija

small anus: šùpčić

small bit, small amount: bìber [1]

small business: kikirȉkī

small buttocks: dupénce, dúza, gùzuljičica, pénce

small chair: šȁmrl, šȁmrla, štȍkrl, štȍkrla

small child: posrànče

small child, kiddo: švȑle

small children: žgàdija

small Citroen (make of car): spàček, spâk, spâle, spȁsoje, spáča, spȁguār, spȁjk

small decorative element (e.g. on garment): džídža, džídža-bídža

small dog, puppy: cùcek

small dose of narcotic drugs: pȉks

small drinking bottle: ùnuče

small drop, droplet: kàpac, kàpatka

small female breast: klȉker, krȁstavac, náprsnjāk, pògačica, prìlipak, prȉštīć, sȉsica, sìsīć

small female child, little girl: cȕrica

small finger: ćevàpčić

small firm female breast: krȕška, lȉmūn

small garden (vegetable, flower, etc.): bȁščica

small glass jug: bokàlić

small Near Eastern-style coffee cup: fildžān

small number of days until the end of one's prison term: síća

small panties: trifȑtāljke, trȍkūt, trokùtice

small penis: čèvāp, ćàvāp, ćèvāp, ćevàpčić, karamèla, kárica [2], kurčénce, patfljak, pȉkavac, pȑcvoljak, pùžek, smȍkī, smȍkić, strȉček, tèhničār

small piece of excrement: govánce

small piece of paper: cedùljče

small profit, peanuts: fȁjdica, vàjdica

small quantity of narcotic drug: trȉp

small quantity of narcotic drugs: pîs [3]

small quantity of something: bóba, drȁm, koncèntrāt, portábl [1], trànzistor [2], zèra

small room: gàjbica

small rooster: horòzić

small TAM (make of truck): tàmīć

small teeth: rezánci

small testicle: jaènce, jaèšce, mudánce, mudášce, mudénce

small tie knot: brȁbonjac, brȁbonjak

small town: kasàba

small vagina: čȕbica, pìcuša, pȉčica, pȉčkica, pičúrak, pízdica

small yellow coins of any currency (pennies): Bȕgari

small, little: pȉkolo

small-headed: picòglav

small-headed female: picòglava

small-headed male: picoglàvīle

small-sized attaché case: péderica, pedèruša

smallish: ȍmanjī

smart: filter [2]

smart individual, sharp cookie: brȉtva [3]

smart male (esp. in math): digitrónac

smart male: fàjter

smart male, brain: kisèljāk, klikèrāš, kȍzāk, mòzgāroš, pametnjáković, pčèlica, smìslāš

smart person: bȉstrica

smart person, brain: glávonja, kèfalo, mintȅlija, mȍzak, mùdrica, pamètnica

smart, sharp: brȉtva [4], ȍštar

smartness: vȉjuga

smash, break into pieces: lúpati

smash, crush: rascópati, ràzjehati, šȉš

smell: šnjȍfati

smell, sniff: šnjȍf

smell, stench: smȑdež, vnȕč, vȕnč

smell, stink: bàzdeti, bàzditi, čȕti se, dȁmfati, kàndisati, kȁnditi, místiti, srâsti, trȕliti, tȕknuti, usafȕnjati se, vnȕčiti, vonjifèrisati, vȕnčiti

smile: kêz, nakésiti se

smoke (tobacco): čȉkati, čûr, čȕrati, čvȁriti, dȉmiti, drȍgati, duvániti, dúvati, džȁmiti, đȁmiti, fȁjfati, fȕmati, káditi,

kȕriti, lòžiti, odžàkati se, pjȕgati, pljȕckati, pljȕgati, pòpljugati, ràuhati, zapáliti
smoke (tobacco): baràlisati
smoke: gúliti
smoke a joint: izdúvati [1]
smoke drugs: dúvati, pljȕgati
smoke hashish: podúvati, poràuhati, ràuhati
smoke narcotic drugs: nadúvati
smoke one's fill of hashish or marijuana: nàpljugati se, naràuhati se
smoke tobacco frequently: pùrnjati
smoke too many cigarettes: prèpušiti [2]
smoked meat: mȁlo [2]
smoking (hashish or marijuana): dúvānje, dûvka
smoking (tobacco): lòžēnje, pljȕckānje, pljȕgānje
smoking marijuana, smoking a joint: tràvosānje
smuggle: munđàrati, prošnjúrati, prošvérati, prȍšvercati, prȍšvercovati, švȅrcati, švȅrcovati
smuggled narcotic drugs: mójo
smuggled tobacco: dìvina
smuggler: mùnđāroš, švȅrcer
smuggling: švȅrc, švȅrcānje, švȅrcovānje
snack: jàuza, jàuzna, mȅdze, zalòžiti se
snack taken while drinking (alcohol): mèza, mèze
snack while drinking (alcohol): mèziti
snail (part of steering mechanism): šnȅka
snail (the animal): spûž
snake: gùljār
snatch, grab: njȁmnuti, njȕpnuti, zaglábati, zgrȁbiti
sneak, attempt not to be observed: àlijeriti, šumovláčiti
sneaking, attempting not being observed: šȕmovlāk
sneeze: kíhati, kínuti
sniff glue: snȉfati
sniff snort: sŕkati, sŕknuti, srkùtati
sniff, smell: smȑčkati, šmŕkati
sniffing: srkùtānje
sniffing glue: dúvānje
snip, clip: klȍcati, kljȍcati
sniper (person): snàjper
snob: artičòka, dôđoš, džȉbronja, džòvān, džȕdža, džudžòvān, džùkser, frìkulja, kravàta, pȑdāč, sîndos, sȉnđos, sîvī, sívac
snore: hropòtati, ŕkati, strúgati
snore, saw logs: testèrisati
snorer: hŕkalo, ȑkāč
snoring: hȑk, hȑka, hŕkānje, hrȍpot, strúgānje
snow: kȓpe, ríža
so much: tȃk [2]
soap: sàfūn
soap foam: safùnica
soap opera: sapùnica
sob, weeping: jȅcāj
soccer: bȁlfica, fúca, fȕtić, fȕzbāl, nȍgač, nȍgāć, nȍgoš [2], vȕzbāl
soccer ball: bubamára
soccer ball made of rags: krpènjača
soccer field: lìvada
soccer player: nȍgoš [1]
soccer player who specialized in penalty kicks: penàldžija
soccer shoes: jèmēnje
soccer upper sock: štùcna
social aid: socijála
social climber (male): šȁlter [1]
social connection: šȃnt
social gathering (usu. in the evening): drugárac
social parasite: žȉcār, žȉcāroš, žȉcer
social skills: žváka
sociology: veronáuka
sock, stocking: cára, znòjalica, znȍjavica, znôjka
sofa: sèćija
soft (physically and psychologically): mèhak
soft: lavabô, mlȍhav, otròmbōljen, sùnđer
soft brandy: mȅkā [2]
soft female breast: Niagàra, tȉjēsto
soft penis: mekankìtis
soft squeak: škȑpūt
softly (physically and psychologically): mȅhko
softly: cîle-mîle
softness: mekùrija
solder: lȅtovati
soldering: lȅtovānje
soldering iron: lȅtkoln, lȅtkon, lȅt-lámpa
soldier: àsker, esembȅovac, kvȑga, stègnat, Švêjk, vȍjāk, vójko
soldier from the countryside: Senegálac [1]
soldier on kp.: pomìjār, smȅćar
soldier on patrol, scout: Indijánac
soldier who cleans toilets: klòzetār
soldier who is assigned to peeling potatoes: krumpìrāš
soldier who serves only one year: gòdišnjāk [2]
soldier's ID: šára, šȃre, šarènica
solitary prison cell: ćȅlica, kùfer, Opàtija
solution, answer to the problem: cáka
solve a problem: devèrati
some: nákav, nȅakav, štògođ, štògoj
somebody: nȅkoj
somebody's: nȅčesōv, nȅčī
somehow: nȅkak
something: nȅšta, njȅšto
something available for free, freebie: frȁjština
something bad: kȕrac [3]
something boring: jebàncija
something excellent: bȁnja [2]
something excellent, something cool: mrâk [2], pòēzija
something important: gédžānje

something of little importance: síća
something of rather low quality: tánjež
something one gets addicted to: nâvlaka
something or someone excellent: gȍldāć
something unattractive: grdòba
something very boring: trȉper
something very good: Amèrika
somewhere: nȅđe, nȅgđe
son: fàćok, klȉndōv
son of a very important or influential person: krèmpita
song in somebody's honor: pòčasnica
sort of: gȉstro[2]
sort, kind of: fâjta, fazóna, féla
soul: džân
sound: zvȍnak
sound made by a bell: cȉnkaj
sound made by a bell, ding: dȁn[1]
sound made by a bird, caw: krî, krî-krî
sound made by a bird, chirr: cvȓ, cvȓk
sound made by a bird, coo: gû
sound made by a bird, tweet: šȁ[2]
sound made by a cat, meow: mȁu, mijȁū
sound made by a chick, chirp: pȉjū
sound made by a clock, tick-tock: cȁk-cȁk
sound made by a clumsy and noisy style of walking: trȁp[1]
sound made by a coocoo, coo: kȕvī
sound made by a cow, moo: mû
sound made by a dog, arf: ȁv
sound made by a donkey, hee-haw: iâ
sound made by a fly, buzz: zȕc[1]
sound made by a goat, baa: mê, mê-e-e
sound made by a goose, honk: gâ, sȉk
sound made by a gun, bang: dȕ, pâ[2], pa-pȁk
sound made by a hen, cackle: kvȍc
sound made by a hiccup: hȁp
sound made by a hit or strike, bang, bop: bȕp
sound made by a metal object, clang: tȉpa-tȁpa, trȁk[1], zvȅkec
sound made by a mild collision, bap: bȁp
sound made by a newborn, goo-goo: a[1], gâ-gâ, gû-gû
sound made by a rabbit: kvȅka
sound made by a sheep, baa: bâ, bêk
sound made by a small bell, ding: cȁn, cȉn, cȉnk[1]
sound made by a small bird, tweet: cȉ, cijùkānje, cȉju, cȉjūk, cȉk[2], cȉk[1], cȉka, cȉkav, cìkljevina, cȉn, cȉn-cȁn, črȉk, đȉk, pȉjūk
sound made by a small explosion, bang: cȅc
sound made by a small explosion, pop: pȕp
sound made by a smallish explosion, bam: tȕc, tùckac, tȕf
sound made by a smallish explosion, bang: čȁvlik, tȕk, tȕp[1]
sound made by a sparrow, tweet: džȉv-džȉv, đȉv-đȉv, žȉv[1]
sound made by a trumpet, toot: tû
sound made by a turkey, gobble: dùrdur, pȕć, pùćkac, pȕć-purȕć, pȕr, tȕj[1]
sound made by an abrupt movement, wham: fȕk[1]
sound made by an angry dog, grr: gȓ, gȓrr
sound made by an explosion, bang: bȁm, bȕb, čvȓk, dȁn[1], dȕm, grȕ, krȇs[1], pȁf, tȍh, trȁs, trȇs[1]
sound made by an explosion, boom: bȓb, bȕ, bȕm[1]
sound made by an explosion, kaboom: krȅkete
sound made by applause, clap: klȁp[1]
sound made by chatter: cvȍk[1]
sound made by clapping, clap: pljȁs, pljȅs, pljèskac, pljȅs-pljȅs
sound made by cutting with scissors, snip: fȉk
sound made by dripping, drop: kâp
sound made by eating: njȕpoš
sound made by gurgling, gurgle: klô, klôk
sound made by knocking, knock: čȕk, kȕc, tȁka
sound made by laughing, ha, ha: ȉhahâ
sound made by machine gun, rat-a-tat-tat: đȁra
sound made by meaningless and prolonged talk, blah-blah: blâ-blâ[2], tôro, tȍro-tȍro, trà-la-la, trȁlala[1]
sound made by metal objects, clang: cȁk
sound made by objects colliding, crash: tȕpa-lȕpa
sound made by pricking: bȍc
sound made by puffing, puff: pùćkac
sound made by rapid movement, whoosh: fȓk
sound made by ringing, ring: zvȓc, zvȓrr
sound made by roaring, roar: zvâr
sound made by slamming, wham: trȁs, zȉk, žmȕke
sound made by slapping, slap: fȉs, fȉskac, pȉf, pȉf-pȁf, šlȉs, šljȁs, šljȉs, trèskac
sound made by slapping, smack: ćùškac
sound made by sneezing, achoo: cȉh, cȉhā
sound made by something cracking, crack: kȓ, kȓc, kȓhor, kȓk[1], kȑkac, kvȓc[1], kvȓk
sound made by something moving abruptly, bang: jêk
sound made by spalshing, splash: fljȁs
sound made by spanking, spank: čȁvlik, fljȉs
sound made by spitting, phew: pȉ, pȉh, pȉha, pljȕc, pȕ, pûu, tfȕ
sound made by splashing, splash: bȕć, fljȕs, plȉcak, pljȁs, pljȕf, pljȕf-pljȕf, pljȕs, pljȕsk, pljùskac, pȕć
sound made by swallowing, gulp: ȁp[1], hȁp, kljȕka
sound made by taking away, snatch: cȁp
sound made by taking objects, whoosh: ćȁp
sound made by tapping, tap: klȅp, klȅpa[1], klȍpot, lȍp, lȕp, ljȍc, pȕp, šȕp, tȁk[1], tȁka, tȁp[1], tȁpa-tȁpa, tȁp-tȁp, trûp, trȕpa, tȕpe-lȕpe, zvȓc
sound made by the dog, arf: vȁu
sound made by the goose: stȉja, stȉjo
sound made by the gusle (a traditional stringed instrument) or similar string instrument: gûd
sound made by the turkey: kȁu
sound made by trumpet, toot: trȁrara
sound made by urination: pȉš[1]

sound made by whispering: sašaptávānje, šȕ-šȕ
sound made by yawning: ô-jê
sound of a bell, ding-dong: bȕm-bȁm
sound of a car-horn, beeping: psȉk, psȉka
sound of a clock, tick-tack: cȍkot
sound of a loud kiss: cmȍk[1]
sound of abrupt movement, wham: psȉk, psȉka
sound of laughing, ha: hȁ
sound of laughter, hah-hah: hihot
sound of made by a bell, ding ding: tȉm-tȉm
sound of repeated soft noise, wah-wah: trȁ-ta
sound of spitting pronounced to indicate underestimation of something or someone, phew: th, thȉ
sound of tapping: ljȍckac
sound of tapping, tap: pȕf[1]
sound used by laughing at somebody: ȕhīj, ȕhū
sound used to express pain or discomfort: ȕhīj, ȕhū
sound used to express the feeling of being cold: ȕū
soup: čórba, nápoj
soup bowl: sùpentof
soup kitchen: àščīnica
sour cherry brandy: vȉšnjevača
sour cream: pȍvlaka
source of income: òluk
Soviet Union: Bàćuška[1]
sow (the animal): kàridža, karȉndža
spade (card suit): trèfijans
spank: fljȉsnuti
spark plug: svijèćica
sparrow: džȉvdža
sparse hair: màhovina, rezánci
speak: spìkati, špȉkati, šprȅhati
speak out: odráziti se
speak out, bark: ìzlajati (se)
speak slang: poredívati, poređívati, šatrovírati, šatrírati
speak with difficulties, stutter due to physiological reasons: fȑfljati
speaking in slang: šatrovírānje
speaking with difficulties, stuttering due to physiological reasons: fȑfljānje
special treat: maksuzíja
specially, intentionally: màksūz
spectacular scene: šôu[1]
speech: spȉka, šprȅha
speech disorder: šprâhfeler
speed (auto, etc.): drápati se, fànđosati, fúrati, lȉrati, lirȉkati, lòžiti, nàgariti, nàgaziti, najàrcati, pȉčiti, pròšājbati, pròšibati, pùrnjati, ràjfati, spȋd, spȋd, spidírati, šâjbati, šȉbati, šȉšnjava, šljȁštiti se, šíšati
speed chess player: cugèrāš
speed chess tournament: cȕger[2]
speed, step on the gas: gȁziti
speeding (auto, etc.): fúrānje, lȉrka, lâuf, pȉčvajs

spend (money, property, etc.): ìspucati se, izgrafírati, kȑckati, pròćērdati, pȕći, ràspičkati, sfȕćkati, skénjati, skŕkati, slístiti, spȉčkati, spȑcati, utánjiti, zdròbiti
spend ample money: ìspružiti se, ìstrēsti se, izdúžiti se
spend ample time at one place, be a regular: vȉsiti
spend money: istròšiti se, riknjávati, zašȕštati
spend money on alcohol: pròpiti, propíjati
spend money, burn money: spáliti
spend one's term in prison: odmardèljati
spend one's time in useless activities, fool around, mess around: ȁkati se, badavàdžisati, blejati[1], činčulírati, cúnjati[2], džabalebárēnje, džabalebáriti, džabalèbisati, džabàlučiti, frajèrisati, gluhárȉti, gluváriti, hódati, izdrkávati se, izigrávati se, kénjati, kulòvisati, landírati, lȁndrati, luftírati se, majmùnisati, mùdati, odžódžiti, šalabázati, vȑzgati se, vucàrati se, zajebávati se, zèvzečiti se, zvŕjati
spend term in prison: kénjati
spend term in prison, do time: kùlučiti
spend time together with: spànđati se
spend too much time in meetings: sàstānčiti
spend, squander: ârčiti
spending: kȑckānje
spending one's time in useless activities, fooling around, messing around: džabalèbisānje, frajèrisānje, gluvárenje, glûvka, hladòvina, izigrávānje, kulòvisānje, kulóvština, landàrānje, landíranje, lȁndrānje, lêr[1], luftèrisānje, luftírānje, mùdānje, tandȑkānje, zajebàncija, zvŕjānje
spending term in prison: okovánje
spendthrift: prdìkara
sperm: jêb, jèbovina, kòktel, sùtlija, sȕtlijāš
spill over (from a glass, etc.): préliti se
spit: hráčak, hrȁčkati, hrȁčnuti, hrákac, hrákati, hráknuti, kòkōška, pljùvati, ȑkavac, šlàjmisati, zàpapriti
spit with mucus, spit with snot: šlâjka, šlàjmara
splash: bȑč, bȑčak, bȑčkati, fljȁsnuti, fljȕsnuti, pljȁfnuti, pljȁska, pljȁskānje, pljȁskati, pljêsak, pljȕsnuti, ràspljuskati, šljȁpat, šljàpati, šljȁpiti, šljàporiti, šljȅpkati, šmȑćkati, žmȑćkati
splashing: bȑčkānje, pljȕskānje
splinter: òfićak
spoil (of children): raspèkmeziti
spoil, interfere, mess up: mŕsiti
spoiled child, brat: dèrle, drònjguz, đȁvō, jòlpaz, kuràjber, škrofulóza
spoiled female: šmízla
spoon: lòpata, žȁcli
sport shoe, sneaker: hȁferica
sport utility vehicle: terénac
sports car: spȍrtsnjāk
spread new slang words: buváriti
spread one's legs: rakrèčiti se
spread rumors: bòmbati, šȕškati
spring (mechanical part): féder
spring (of a water source, etc.): šȉsnjati
spring ring: féder-rȉnga

spring washer: féder-šȃjba, féder-šàjbna, šprȅng-šȃjba, šprȅng-šàjbna

sprinkle the laundry before pressing: nàfājtati

spry: kȍčopēran

spy, spook: ȁla [1], àlka, ȁver, aždàja, cȉja, flȁster, hȁla [2], lèntrāš, pètljara, sênka, sȕpovac

square: špȉca

squeak: cȉktāj, fȑškati, fȑštati, gúđeti, kvíčati, kvȋk, kvȉka, kvíknuti, kvŕčati, kvréknuti, kvȑkoriti, kvȑljiti, skíčati, šȉštati, škrebètati, škrȋp, škrȉpa, vȑcāj, vȑštati, vrûsak, vrȕskati

squeaking: cikȉljav, kvȑka, kvŕljēnje, skíčānje, škrȉpav, vrȕskav

squeeze (sponge, etc.): ižmíkati, šnȁpati

squint: ćóriti [1], zríkiti

squish: mljȁ, mljȁc, vȑštati

stab: išuljáviti

stabbing: štȉh [2]

stadium box office clerk: inkasȃtor

stain: flȅka

stain oneself: flȅkati se

stair: bȁsamak, stȕba

stairway: skȃle

stale (usu. food, esp. bread): bàjat

stand for a long time: džédžati, džónjati

stand in one place for a long time (usu. disturbing others): napenáliti (se), nasáditi se, nasandŕćiti se

stand in one place for a long time (usu. while waiting for someone): ȁjnštancovati, dȕdovati, džéđiti, kȉseliti se, ukòpati se

stand in one place for a long time (usu. while waiting for someone), drop anchor: ùsidriti se

stand in one place for a long time (usu. while waiting for someone), have cement shoes: nacementírati se

stand in such a way to disturb others: nakarakȕrčiti se

stand in the moonlight: mèsečiti

stand on one's head: dúbiti

stand still: cementírati

stand, be in an upright position: kȉsnuti

standing in one place for a long period of time (usu. while waiting for someone): dȕdovānje, džédžānje, džónjānje

star (celestial body): dzvȅzda

starch: štȉrk

stare at, be fixated at: béčiti se, béljiti, béljiti se, bléjati [1], bléjiti, blȅnuti, buljáriti, búljiti, ćóriti [1], fiksírati, filcírati, iskembéčiti se, ispéčiti (se), izbéčiti se, mékati, mèktati, pâsti [2], píljiti, stériti, zabúljiti se, zévati, zȉjati, zȉnuti, zrȉkati, zumírati, zúriti, zvjèrati

staring: bléjānje

start buzzing (bee, buzzer, etc.): zȕjnuti

start dating a female: utȑpati se

start dating a girl met on the street: izuličáriti

start doing: ùzēti

start fighting: podžápati se

start flirting: aterírati, hȉtiti [2], hȉtiti se, iskȑcati se, stȁrtovati

start going: zapízditi [1]

start having sex frequently: projèbati se, ràsprcati se

start malfunctioning: prolúpati

start running (moving quickly): zȁžditi

start singing: poȉzdignuti

start talking: pròpjevati

start talking extensively: ojèzičiti se

start to meet with a group of people regularly: ukȑcati se

start working: hȉtiti [2], hȉtiti se

starter: ȁnlaser

starve: skapávati

state border: rámpa

state of being drunk: kòma

state of shock: frȃs

station, stop (bus, train, streetcar, etc.): dvȍtko, kandȉsara, mȉmohōd, prólaz, stàcīn, štȁjga, trȅska

status of a guest worker: gastarbȁjterstvo

status seeker, pretentious person, social climber (male), phony: hòhštapler, hòhštaplerka

status seeker, pretentious person, social climber, phony: hòštapler

stay at home: zabunkèrisati se, zakòpati se, zakòpčati se

stay in prison: mardèljati, mardèljisati

stay long (usu. partying): zagláviti

stay or work illegally: ilegȁlisati

stay overnight at another's apartment, sleepover: kùntati

stay still: kénjati

stay up all night drinking and partying: zabrȉjati, zabrȉjati se, zȁginuti, zaglíbiti

stay with somebody, stick with somebody: ušȁltati se

stay, linger: stȁjkati

steady company, people one hangs with: jȁto

steal a glance, peep: pȉjkati

steal a wallet: ȕžljakiti

steal from (usu. in a restaurant), rip off: zacépiti

steal from, rip off: gotíviti, oláditi, olàkšati, olàktati, pèlješiti, plȉndrati, polevátiti

steal somebody's girlfriend: sàseći

steal someone's wallet: ȕžljakati

steal something of little value: perjáriti

steal, lift: zdȉgnuti

steal, swipe: ȁknuti, àpisati, ȁpiti, ȁpnuti, ȁpsnuti, bunàrisati, cȁpnuti [1], cȕrkati, čȉstiti, čòpeti, čȍreti, čȕknuti, čváknuti, ćȁpiti, ćapírati, ćopávati, ćòpisati, ćȍpiti, ćòrisati, ćȍriti [2], ćȍrnuti, dȅkrati, dȉći, dȉgnuti, dȉpiti, drápati, dȑmnuti, drpáriti, dŕpati, dȑpisati, dȑpiti, dȑpnuti, fȅtiti, gȅpiti, gràbljati, gúliti, hȁknuti, hápati, hapávati, hȁpiti, hàrisati, hȁrnuti, izdrkèljisati, jòstikranj, klȍpnuti, krȁjcovati, kȕpiti [1], lápati, lȁpnuti, lavòrati, lȉtipa, ljàdrožiti, mȁcnuti, màknuti, mandŕknuti, màrisati, mȁrnuti, mazȉjati, mȁznuti, mažnjávati, mèrati, mȅrati, mȑdnuti, mŕknuti [1], mȕljnuti, òcariniti, òčistiti, òdnesti, òdrati, okrénuti, opúhati, òpurkati, otúciti, otúđiti, páliti, pȅcati, pȁciti, palȉndati, perȕšati, pȕljosati, pòarati, pòdići, pòmesti, popalȉndati, popáliti, popàrisati, pòplašiti, pòplȉnđati, povaćáriti, púhnuti, pȕrkati, pȕrnuti, ráditi [1], rȕknuti, skèntati, skutùrati, smȁriti, smòtati, sparȕtati, sperȕtati, šanírati, šapírati, šćȁpiti, šljȁkati, trkèljisati, šljȁknuti, šljȍknuti, ućòrisati, upáliti, ušapírati, ušapíriti, valírati, vatáriti, zamazìjati, zapáliti, zbòsti, zdȋmati, zdȋmiti [1], zdȋpiti, zdȋpnuti, zèriti, zgȅpiti, zobljáriti, žnírati

stealing from a car: gȕzovi

stealing, swiping: hápa, hapávānje, hàrāč, [illegible], stìmapro

steering wheel: đèvrek, lȅnkrād

step back, make way: abmarkírati se

step on a mine: nàtūći

step over: gìljati

stepchild: fàćok

stereo set: círa

steroid pill: hòrmōnka

stick in a syringe needle: pȉkati se

stick in, insert: fȕrnuti [2], kȓknuti, ljȕljnuti, natrkèljisati, ȑititu, sjúriti, sprášiti, stjȅrati, sȕnuti, surdúknuti, šȉšnuti, tȕriti, tȕtnuti, zabùrdisati, zàdjenuti, zàđenuti, zakalafírati, zakalàmfisati, zakàntati, zakarabúdžiti, zakekéčiti, zakèrečiti, zaklinčóriti, zaklȉnderiti, zakùndačiti, zbȉčiti, zbìglati

stick out one's buttocks: natŕćiti se, natŕtiti se

stick to something: fȁtati se, prijòniti

stick with, stay with: prìfatiti se

stick, bat: búdža, prȗt, šȉpkica

stick-on key: štȅk-šlìsl

stiff: dȓven, štòkfiš, ùštītkān

still, without cessation: jȍšte

stimulate sexually, turn on: rȁjcati, šlàtati

stimulate to achieve erection: nàdrkati

stimulate to action, rouse: pûjdati

stimulation to action: pûjdānje

stink intensely, stink to high Heaven: cȕhnuti

stinking person, person with B.O.: vūga

stir: bŕkati

stolen: smȍtān

stolen goods, hot stuff: šána

stolen money: ćôr

stolen, hot: dîvča [2], dìvljī, dȓpljen

stomach, belly, gut: akumulâtor, ždȅravac, bùrāg, bùrat, búša, dòmovina, flȃm, màgaza, mȃma, mȅnza, pàmflek, spȍmenīk, škèmbe, špȁjz, špȅk [2], tŕba, tȑbu, tȑbuv

stomach, belly, tank: rezervòār

stomach, belly, tummy: pȕpa, tíba, tíbica, tibùljāk

stone, rock: čamùrnjāš, mȅnga, rosòmān, stína

stoned (on hashish or marijuana): nàpljugān

stoned: stônd [2]

stop (bus, etc.): štȁjga

stop by, drop in on: navŕnuti, parkírati se, svŕnuti, zagláviti se

stop for a short time: tuspásiti se

stop, block (soccer ball, etc.): ùštopati, ùštopovati

stopper: štòpl

store: bànež, bùtīga, dùćān, kàsārna, rádnja, tràkeljara, ùndžān

story: stȍrī

story intended to evoke compassion: socijála

stove: fùruna, kȁftor, kȁtfōr

straight jacket: džèmper

straight, clean: čȉst

strange: strȇjndž

strange female, weird chick: lȕcprda, lùjika, lûjka, šizofrèničārka

strange male, weirdo: otkačénko, šȉmler, tîp [1], típus

strange person, weirdo: bolèsnīk, lèvāk [1], lêvī [2], lòpata, nȍrc, otkačȉška, pimpèkdžija, šíber [1], šȉbadžija, šizofrèničār

strange, weird: jèziv

strange, weird: lêvī [1], mòrskī, nàkrīvljen, nèpoznāt, òtkačen, strȁobālan, strášan, stràvičan, šȁšav, šȁškast, šîz [2]

stranger (female): sȍlerica

stranger (male): àrap, dȍšljār, kȁmer, lȍkvār [2], pèpsika, sȍler, strȅndžer, strȅndžerica, strȅndžerka, tîp [1], típus

strawberry (narcotic drug): stròberī

street: gìljarica, kuglàna, méta, pèglara, rȁnč, strȕna, tôr, zbórnica

street child: dȕfter

street cleaner, street sweeper: cȅstolīz, dòmlāznjāk, mljâz

street fight: alàvānta

street gambler: šȉbicār

street policeman, beat cop: kȅpavac, linìjāš, tabànāš

streetcar: lȉna, milozvúčnica, múnja [1], škàtalja, tràjvan, trambàlāj, trambèlāj, tránđža, trȅn, trȅska, tróla, žȉca

streetcar bumper: sèndvīč

streetcar conductor: pufèrāš, pulfèrāš, strúja

streetcar line: plȁnkerica

streetcar line number nine in Zagreb, Croatia: dèfektnā

streetcar line number one in Belgrade, Serbia: kêc [2]

streetcar line number one in Zagreb, Croatia: ȁs

streetcar line number three in Belgrade, Serbia: trìlīng, tròbanak

streetcar line number two in Belgrade, Serbia: búger

streetcar line number two in Zagreb, Croatia: cvíčak

streetcar line number two in Zagreb, Croatia: štȁjger

streetcar pickpocket: Zȅtovac

streetcar trailer: pȉkica

streetwalker who works the Esplanade hotel and Svačićev square areas in Zagreb, Croatia: kvȁčica

stretch (of a person in a gym): otézati se

strict: ȍštar

strict judge: negatívac

strict prison: bȁnja [2], zìndān, zìnden

strict teacher: ȁla [1], aždàja

string beans: burànija

stripper (female): skidàčica

strive, try hard: bacàkati se, gȉnuti, polòmiti se

strive, try hard, bust one's balls: kiláviti se

stroboscope: bȉckalica

stroke, apoplexy: šlȍg [3]

stroller (for children): dúbak

strong: grûbor, gvȍzden, kȁmen [2], nàbūdžen

strong brandy: grôm [1], ljûtā, prepečènica, spirìtuša

strong coffee: šlogìruša

strong fear: paranȍja

strong female: pīčkobaša

strong heroin: bòmbe

strong influence of narcotic drugs: stôund [1]

strong leg (of a female): stûp

strong leg: statíva

strong legs: bàlvani

strong plum brandy: batȑgača, mȕčenica

strong voice: klȋk [2]

strong, muscular: dȍbar [2], kȍnjskī, ljûtī

strong, powerful (person, car, etc.): grôm [2]

stubborn children: vȕčād

stubborn male, pigheaded guy: bídža, gȉgantostrȁka, klȉpan, kreténko, òvan

stubborn person, pigheaded person: àrdžija, àrlija, bandòglavac, bȍrčula, zadrìbālda, zaguljénko

stubborn, pigheaded: bandòglav, kurčèvit, nahòrōžen

stubbornness: trȕc

student: hòbist, pȕklja, stȕdoš, škiljávko, tùpiglāv

student dispensary: veterìnārnica

student driver: ȅlovac

student from a blue-collar family: fȉžbajn, grafijáner, grȁfos, šràfcīger [1], šrafcijáner

student protester from the 1968 protests in the former Yugoslavia: šezdesetòsmāš

student who learns mechanically: bìflant

student's military training: prȅdvojničkā

studio (painter's etc.): golùbārnīk

studio tape recorder: špȁrhet

study: ispenisável

study mechanically: búbati

stuff: nàfilati

stumble in effect of taking narcotic drugs: kljȕcati

stumbling in effect of taking narcotic drugs: kljȕcānje

stuntman: kaskadèros

stupid idea: bìser [1], glùpača, glùpuša, kȉks-idéja, lûjka

stupid or mentally deficient: dùduk, glȕpav, ȉmbić [2], kâr [1], kràtak

stupid or mentally deficient male: ávetnīk, bléso, glùpāk, glùpan, vòda

stupid or mentally deficient person: abderíćanin, avétinja, balàban, bàlvan [1], baštòvān, baštovàndžika, bàtina, bèdāk [1], bȅna, bernardínac, bèstija, bètōn [1], bȅzjak, bezvèzist, bȉk [2], bìlmez, bȋljka, bìser [2], bisérko, bìzgōv, bléćak, blȅka, blénta, blénto, blȅsa, blèsan, blȅska, bílja, bòban, bolèsnīk, bòlīd, Bȍško, bȕda [2], budàla, budàlčina, bȕkva, bùkvan, busogrȕdadžija, búzda, buzdòhān [1], buzdòvān [1], cèment [1], cepànica, cipovànder, cjepànica, čȁjnīk, čáva, čìnpek, čȕkadžija, ćála, ćálo, ćàlōv, ćȕpa, ćùskija, ćùtuk, dàlabu, dèbīl, debìlčina, dȅbos [2], dȅdāk, dȅfus, dègēn, degenèrik [2], dèkrēt, diàbola, dibdiléja, dijabóla, dilàber [1], dilàjla, dȉlber, dȉldik, dȉldika, dilèa, diléja, diletânt, dȉlkan, dȉlke [1], dȉlkoš, dìmbōn, Dimìtrije, divànija, dȍn, dòrat, dȑkotina, dȑndōv, drndòvčina, dùdek, dȕdos, dûdoš, dùduk, dupévac, dúšo [1], dzìndzōv, Džȅf, Džȉm, džìndžōv, džùlōv, fȅbruār, frȁjērka, gédža, gédžo, gedžòvān, gilènder, glupànder, glupàntrop, glùpērda, glùpsan, glùpson, hàvārija, hipodrómac, hȑga, idìot, ìkel, Indijánac, jètīm, kalèa [1], kȁlem, kapètān, kàubōj, keleràba, kìklop, klarìnēt [1], klebècan, klembècan, klòkan, kljȁšmovac, kùmek, kȍnj [1], krâjnīk, krèbil, kréca, krélac, krȇle, krelètān, krêm, krèmbil, kùlōv, kûle, kùtnek, lȁbūd [3], lakòća, làladi, lùdōv, lèvāk [1], lèvāt, lêvī [2], lȉjēvī, lòpata, lùcirda, ludáija, ludája, lûdnjāk, lȕdos, lûjka, ljùština, màjmun [1], màjumun, mâlj, màmlaz, màndōv, màzga, màzgōv, mèntōl, mèntus, mùfljūz [1], mȉkica, mȉško [1], mòkī [1], mòrōn, mrâk [1], mȑmot, múlac, mȕngos, múto, mùzičār, nápoj, neandertálac, nòga [2], nȕla, njókac, ȍbala, òpnāš, òstria, ȍstriga, óvca, òvčār, pacijȅnt, pânj [1], pàpan, pȁvijān, pèčūrka, pèrkan, pȉčkica, pìngvīn, pjévac, plíća, plȉćāk, pòjmāš, pȑdac [1], pùšāč, pùšik, púzdro, sádnica, sakalȕda, sȁksofōn, seljóber, senílac, siròvina, Slávko, slȍn, smǝkle, smǝklje, smȕkle, smȕklje, sȍm [1], šàjkan, šȁlīn, šȁmšula, Šȁno, šȁrklo, šarplanínac, šȉber [1], šȅšken, šȉbadžija, šȉbadžīka, šizbláza, šizobláza, šláger [1], šlȍgī-drȍgī [1], šljȕnta, šmìnker, šmȍkljan, šmȍkljos, šòjkan, šólja [2], šȍnjča, šòšōn, štàmpajzer, šúpak, šùpčina, šȕška, šušùmiga, švȅnkī, tábla, tandȑkalo, tégla, télac, tȅnkre, tètrijēb, tȉkva [1], tȉkva [1], tìkvan, tikvánko, tȉkvić, tȉkvos, tòcilo, tòčak [1], tȍp [1], tȍšāk, tràktor, trȁper, troglòdit, tròjān [1], trojánac, trúba [1], trubàdūr, trùpac, tùdum, tulìpān, tȕljān, tȕpadžija, tȕpavac, túponja, tȕposlāv, tùpsōn, tùtumrāk, ȕdāv, újka, vȁtle, vèzara, vèzist, vìnkleroš, vòlina, zȁmlata, zȁvr̄tanj, zbunjòla, zèus, zèvzek, zìnzōv, zrìlīng [1], zvèkan, zvȑndōv, žmȉk, zùkvan, žvàtān

stupid or mentally deficient person, cretin: kréša, krètēn, kretènčina, kreténko, krȅtić, krlètān, krletánović

stupid or mentally deficient person, cretin, idiot: kȓle

stupid or mentally deficient person, imbecile: ȉmbecil, ȉmbić [1]

stupid or mentally deficient person, Neanderthal: Kreménko

stupid or mentally deficient person, one who is "bananas": banànāš, banàndžija

stupid or mentally deficient person, pea brain: mȉnī-mȍzak

stupidity, lack of intelligence: amàluk, bakráči [2], bedastòća, bljúzga, bljȕzgavica, brȍć, budàlastōst, budaláština, kenjáža, kvȁka, mrâk [2], nȅūm, prȍvala, sránje [2], trúba [1], tȕti-frȕti

stupidly: trȕlo

stutter: šlȁjfovati, trokírati

stutter word, uh: ê [2]

stutterer: békavac, pévac, trokìrāš

stuttering: bȅkav

stuttering sound: tȕc-mȕc [1]

style hair with a blow drier: fenírati

style of behavior: fàzōn

style one's hair with a blow-drier: isfenírati

style, kind: fàzōn, šȉif

stylish: šlȉfovān

subtract: òpcigovati

suburban bar: pljùbārka, pljùgara

succeed in business: krénuti

succeed in illegal business: izgirigàrisati

succeed, make it: upáliti
succeed, separate, part from: alavèrtisati se
succesfull robbery: malicána
success, hit: hȉt
successful criminal: dèsnī
successful gambler: dèsnī
successful gambling: dȕse
successful person: penicìlīn
such: taki
suction: ùsis
suffer from gonorrhea, have the clap: kȁpati, sȕziti, svírati
sufferer: pátež
suffering: dokurcàna
sugar: blâg, cȕkar [1], cȕker
suitable sexual partner: nȕmera
suitcase (construed as an object of stealing): brôd
suitcase: bârka, pânj [2], pȁprikāš, vàlidža
suitor: aȉgdžija
Sun: érić [2]
sun: màdžar, màđār, rájko, râjskō
sunbathe: guštèrisati (se)
sunburned person: bubašvàbista
sunglasses: cvȉške
sunset, evening: àkšam
superb, awesome: dȕzdibidȕs, ȅkstra [2], fȁjn [1], fȁjn [2], fȅnomenālan, fȅnomenālno, filadèlfija [3], premijéra
superb, big time: filadèlfija [2]
superficial: bȁngav, vȑljav
superficial female: fúšerka
superficial person: fúšer
supervise: žandàrisati
supervisor (on public transportation): cepodȉpāč, kartodŕpac, kartogrízac, klòntrāć, kòntrāš, kȍntrić, lèšinār [1], rídža, réva, ridžòvān, Rȉdžvēj, rȉđa, rìđan, riđòkosī, riđòvān, rȉkī, róvac [1], šȉnter
supply in a clandestine manner, give on the sly: dòturiti
supply, furnish: kožírati se
support, cheer for: spȁpštiti
supporter of Stalin in the Tito-Stalin conflict of 1948: ibȅovac, ȉbić, ȉnfić
sure: viđen
surfer: dàskāš
surgeon: kàsaper, kàsapin
surgery: aperácija
surname: Pȑcković, Sȉsoević
surname in Bosna and Montenegro: Gùzina
surname in Serbia: Gȕzonić
surname in Vojvodina: Guzánac, Gȕzīn, Gùzanōv
surname in Vojvodina, Serbia: Kûrčēv [1]
surprise quiz, pop quiz: prépad
surprise unpleasantly: rȅbnuti
surroundings of the train station where prostitutes gather: štȁjga
suspenders: hàlter
suspicious: mútan, šàren, zȅbrast
suspicious activities: rȁbota
suspicious female: mârta
suspicious looking male: vàljātor
suspicious male: lèvātor, lêvī [2], mùvātor, tîp [1]
suspicious person: lèvāk [1], mùtljavina, mutnjáković
suspicious place: kamenòlom
sweater: džemperȉška
sweating: ȍznojān
sweating: ùsaftati se
sweatshirt: ambálaža
Sweden: Švéca [1], Švȅsta [2]
sweet pastry or candies: šećerléma
swelling: ȍstrvo
swift mountain river or spring: bȉstrica
swim: bȁnjati se, švȉmati se
swim in shallow water: kȁčkati se
swimming: banjáža
swimming pool: kòrito
swing (at the playground=: ljûlj
swing (back and forth): lílati
swing something before throwing it: zakovìtlati
Swiss franc: švajcárac
switch blade: kóka
switch, change: prešàltati se, prèšaltovati se
switchblade: skȁkavac [2]
syllabic permutations in speech (eg. bari instead of riba 'fish, female...'): šȁtrovačkī
synchronizing mechanism: sìhrōn
synthesizer: pȉlić
syphilis with symptoms appearing on one's face: fŕljo
syphilis, the pox: cifilìnder, fŕnjo, lûj, lújo, sífa, sȉf, sȉfić, sifilìtika, sȉfke, sívac, trìfilis
syringe, needle: bóca, nídl, sirâno, sirânž
T-shirt: mája [1], mȁja [2], nâvlaka
T-shirt with a very deep neck line: kabriòlet-mȁjica
table: hàstal, sȍfra
table soccer (game): hàkl
table, desk: àstāl
tailor: protìnjavac, šnȁjder
tailor's: protinjàvskī
tails (of a coin): písmo
take (narcotic) drugs: pȕšiti
take (usu. narcotic drugs), do: dȉpovati
take: àpisati, ȁpiti, ȁpnuti, bŕknuti, dȑpnuti, fȑknuti, gràpsiti, jȁmiti, klȁmati, kȕpiti [1], lȁpiti, lȁtiti se, lȅvnuti,odvòjiti, ȍklamati, prȉfatiti, šapírati, zgotòviti, zgotíviti
take a bath: ispàcati se, pàcati se
take a careful look, check out: ȍdšacati, ȍšacati
take a dose of narcotic drugs: prȉkucati se
take a look, scope out: zrȉkati
take a rest, take a break, relax: dȕškati, odmòriti, odžódžiti

take a risk, take a chance: gusáriti

take a shot of narcotic drugs, shoot up: òveriti se

take a sip: gȕcnuti

take a walk: prošnjúrati (se), pròšvrcati se

take along: lèvati, otfúrati

take another's money in gambling, rip off in gambling: gúliti

take away, remove: iskèmbati, očèšljati, odbàrtati

take care: šmìrglati

take care of: šíšati

take cigarettes from the others, bum smokes: grèbati se

take crib-sheets to one's exam: puškáriti

take from: skȉnuti

take from one's pocket: pòvūći

take LSD, drop acid: zȑpovati

take money: zàklati

take money in gambling, rip off in gambling: isisávati

take money without giving narcotic drugs in return: eskivírati

take narcotic drugs intravenously, mainline, shoot up: bȍckati se, fiksati, fiksati se, ùfiksati se, ùkucati se, rókati se, rȍknuti, srédíti se, špŕícati se, trȅsnuti se, ùbosti, zàkucati se

take narcotic drugs, do drugs: čváknuti, fiksovati, gáđati se, gudrírati se, kȑljati se, mȁzati, narókati se, ráditi se, rókati, tràvosati se, trȉpovati, urókati se

take narcotics drugs for recreational purposes: folírati

take off, strip: snímati, snímiti

take one's clothing off, strip: ljúštiti se

take one's dress off, strip: čerùpati se, očerùpati se, raskurážiti se

take one's girlfriend along: šlȅpati, šlȅpovati

take one's girlfriend home to meet one's parents: šlȅpovati

take one's girlfriend to her home after a date: taksírati

take out a mortgage (house, etc.): ùštafiti

take out of one's pocket: izbunáriti

take out, remove, get rid of: abortírati

take part in a hunting trip: lȁjati

take part in public rallies: mitingášiti

take photos for police files: lentírati

take revenge: spùstiti

take somebody along (e.g. to a party): fìrovati, šlȅpovati, taksìkati

take someone's money in gambling: òdrati

taking away, snatching: cȁpkānje

taking fingerprints: tȉnta

taking money in gambling: isisávānje

talc: fédervajs

talent: klȉker, vìjuga, žȉca

talent, talented person: náda

talented male: òmīš, smìslāš, zmìja

talk a lot, run one's month: kokodákati

talk all around: rastrúbiti

talk loud: galopírati

talk one's fill: istoròkati se

talk persistently and meaninglessly: nàsrati se

talk persistently and meaninglessly, blabber, chatter: àrlati, avètati, baláviti, balègati, baljèzgati, barlìjati, bavȑljati, benáviti, benètati, bêntati, blȁvoriti, blebètati, bljezgáriti, bljùvati, bȑbljati, bùrljati, brljáviti, búbati, bubètati, bulázniti, bunàcati, bunàrati, bùncati, buváriti, càcoriti, calapȑdati, cigùljati, cmìljati, cvȍkati, cvȍkōt, ćântrati, čapljèzgati, čapljȉzgati, čegȑtati, ćalapȑdati, ćapȑdati, dȑskati, dȑkati, drkèljisati, dȑndati, dròbiti, drȍćkati, dúljiti, dumbàrati, dupètati se, dupodèrati, džavȑljati, đȕbriti, frajèrisati, fȑfljati, fȑljati, fȕfljati, fúnjati, halàbučiti, kénjati, kȅnjkati, kȅvkati, klȁfrati, klâmfati, klȁpati, kvŕčati, lapàrati, lapȑdati, lapȑdati, lopàtati, lúpati, lupètati, ljúštiti, mlatikáriti, mlȅti, mljȅti, mȑndžati, mȑviti, mȕcati, muzicírati, nadovezívati, nagvážđati, naklápati, nàpevati, njákati, njȕnjoriti, palamúditi, pȉmplati, pȉmplovati, pjevúšiti, pòjiti, poprdùckati, pȑdeti, pȑditi, pȑdnjati, prdùckati, pretákati, prolívati, pȑtljati, raskokodákati se, raskukurékati se, ràskvocati se, rpolívati, serùckati, slȉniti [1], sràćkati, svírati, šalabȁjzānje, šalabâjzati, šljapùtati, tabànati, talàsati, taljȉzgati, tambùrati, tandȑkati, tepeljèzgati, tepljèzgati, tòrlati, toròkati, trabùnjati, tralákati, tralalákati, tralalíkati, tȑnbiti, tȑtositi, tȑtošiti, trubèntati, trȕćati, tùpisati, túpiti, turpìjati, upljùvati se, utucávati, vèrglati, vésti, volìdžati, vunovlačáriti, zipàrati, zipáriti, zunzàrati, zunzáriti, zvȑndati, žȁmoriti, žglȁviti, žiláviti, žlȁbrati, žvaláriti, žvȁlati, žvaláviti, žvȁliti

talk persistently and meaninglessly, bullshit: gòvnati, kákiti, srȁti

talk persistently and meaninglessly, have diarrhea of the mouth: proserávati se, sèrkati, tȉsra, zàsrati

talk persistently on trivial topics: čavȑljati

talk, have a conversation: àrlati, barlìjati, benáviti, divániti, dìvati, đȁkati, eglènisati, folȉnjati, kȅvkati, kȉliti, klȁfrati, lȁtrati, pàrlati, pȉsnuti, penìsati, pènjisati, pȅvati, propènjisati, razređívati, rédati, redávati, spȅvati, spìkl, túpiti, zbòriti, žlȁbrati, žlȁmbrati

talkative elderly female: svrȁka

talkative loafer: pȑdežmen

talkative male, chatterbox: bȑbljivac [1]

talkative person, chatterbox: čàrapa

talking, chatting: eglènisānje

tall and female, beanpole: mȍtka, Ròdēzija, solìtērka

tall and slender (of a person): džȉgljast, štȑkljast

tall and slender male, beanpole: krakatílo

tall and slender person, beanpole: kráklja, lòjtra

tall male: ćòrtan [1], kandeláber, kandelábr, katedrâlis, štȑkljan

tall person: anténa, bandéra, čȁplja, čivìluk, jàblān, Kȉng-kȍng, kráka [2], krakàilo, krȁkoš, krâle, rȉpida, štȑklja, tóranj [1]

tall young male: cìpōv

tame: prišaráfiti, utàbaniti

tampon: pácov

tape (in general): têjp

tape: trȁkavica

tape measure: còlštok

tape recorder: kâs, kasètāš, mâg, màgiš, mȅg

tapping: kvȑcānje, tȕpkānje, zvȑcānje

tarpaulin: ceráda, ciráda

Tarzan-style hairstyle: tàrzanica

taste, preferences: gȕšt, šmȅk

tasteless food: bȑčkotina

tasteless, gross: bljȕtav

tasty bite, morsel: čȁlabȑc

tasty food: krkánjac

tax: àrāč, hàrāč, rȅspo

taxi: gùma

tea with rum: ćàjćirom

teacher: bȁba[2], mùčitelj

teachers' room: mȑtvāčnica

tear apart, destroy: razbúcati

tease: bȍckati, navláčiti, podjebávati, zađónjiti, zafrkávati, zagrebávati, zajebávati, zȅzati

teasing: bȍckānje, pilàna, podjebávānje, zȅzānje

technology teacher (female): ȍtōvka

technology teacher (male): ȍtovac

teddy bear: méca[2], médo

tedious job: jebáda, jebávānje

teenager (female): jȕniōrka, lùjika, tȋna, tînka

teenager (male): fȕkić, jȕniōr, tîn

teenager: gljȉvica, kénjac, képac, pubertètlija, pubijáner, pùbiš

teeth: dȍmine, gȅba, gȅha, glòdāljka, klavijatúra, klȅhi, plôt, toblerône, zȍbnice

teetotaler: trezvènjāk

telegram to a soldier: jȅbozōv[2]

telegraph operator: kȕcavac, kȕkavac

telephone book, phonebook: telefònīk

telephone, phone: bȑzac[2], fòntele, tȅfić, telefùnken, telefònati, telefonȉška

television (set and medium): tèlezūr, tèliš, tȅlka, tȅlkāč, tȅlkica, tȅlkić, téva, têvê, tèviš, tívica

tell (in all its Serbo-Croatian meanings in the form different from the standard one): kásti

tell: istrkèljisati, prijáviti

tell a joke: prováliti

tell fortunes: gonétati

tell secrets, spill the beans: istȑčati

tell, say (usu. in the negative): béknuti

tell, say: istrkèljati, narédati, opáliti, pȅvnuti, prȉšapnuti, zȅgnuti, zȅngnuti, zȕcnuti, zȕznuti

temporary: v.d.

ten: céner, dȅst

ten currency units; a ten-unit bill: bȁnka, céner

ten days of military service: bȁnka

ten dinars; a ten-dinar bill: bànčura, bôn, bumȁška, čȑvenā, desètāk, đòrđija, đȕrđa, gȉrica, jòrgan, kàiš, kàjma, kárta, kèder, kéka, kòmād[2], kòvāč, kȓpa, kùbān, kȕkavica, lȕkac, màjmun[2], màsa, mȉlja, mîljka, mȑlja, stȁrac, stòbanak, šȕška

ten dinars; a ten-dinar coin: bȁnak, gláva, sȍm[2], stòjānka

ten paras; a ten-para coin: bȁnak, gláva, kàjma, kàjna, sȍm[2], žújka

ten thousand dinars; a ten thousand-dinar bill: cígla, desètāk, kȍnj[1], mȉlja

ten years: bȁnka

ten-centimeter long cigarette with filter: nȉkson

ten-para coin: kégla

tennis shoe, sneaker: stàrka[2], šàngājka, téna, tènisica, téniska, tíka

tense: nàšpanān, nàšpanovān, pȕška[3]

term in prison: bìjaro

terrace: ràsate

terror: zùlum

testament, will: ȁber, amánet

testicle: múdo, tàšak

testicle, ball: jájce, jáje, kȍćavac

testicles, nuts: òrasi

testicular: mûdnī

testicular skin: mùdežina, múdnica

than: nȅg, vȅć

that: ònī, ùnāj

that big: ovòlkačkī, ovòlkī, tòlkī

that doesn't count: pȉk[1]

that small: ovolìckī, ovolìpackī, tolìšnī

that way: tȁk[2]

theater worker: pozorȉšnjāk

theft: ćopávānje, dizàjn, drpáža, hápānje, lôv, màrisānje, pȅcānje, zgepàrluk, žnírānje

theft from a counter: šàin

theft from a drunk: lešinárēnje, markàcēr, màrkec, màrkecovānje

theft from a drunk or sleeping person: markècēr

theft on public transportation: trȅska

theft, swipe: dŕpež[1], dȑpisānje, gȅpa, làviška, lóra, mážnja, mažnjávānje, smȕšujēnje, šána, šćâp

theft, swiping: dȓp, dŕpānje, drpárēnje, marinȅla, pàljevina

their: njîn

then: nôndā, ȍndāj, ȍndāk, ȍndār, tàdēr, úndā

there: ànamo, núđe,ònām, onúdijēn, tûn

thick drug substance: želàtīn, žèlē

thick eyeglasses: pìksle, pògačice

thick hair: pèrika

thick quilt: jòrgan-planìna

thick sweatshirt: dȕks, dȕkserica, dȕks-màjica

thief (female), sticky fingers: lúpežica, šánērka

thief (male), sticky fingers: lúpež, šáner

thief: čàruga, gânča, lòpuža, lȕfter, mùtikesa, pècāroš, pȍvlo, pȕrca, pȕrkāč, šljàkāroš, šljȁker

thief who steals from drunks: lèšinār[1]

thief who steals from suitcases: pȁnjār

thief who steals in trains: pûtnīk

thief who steals using a bag to store the stolen goods: tȍrbār

thief who works a railroad station: ùndžāroš, ùnđāroš

thief's: šánerskī

thief, sticky fingers: ćȍpić, dȉvljāk [1], dizàjner, dȑpāroš, dŕpež [2], đàpan, gȅpār, gȅpavac, kljȁker, lòpina, šȁtrovac, šljàkātor, zdȉper

thigh: bȕtka

thin: tànāhan

thin dress: kȍžolēpka

thin rain coat: šȕškavac

thing of little importance or value, trifle: andȑmōlj, andrmólja

thing, object: ȁrstva, gréda, gurábija, kébānje, štôs [2], vàljuga

think over, mull over: pròdumati

think well of somebody: tretírati

think, ponder (usu. in an attempt to find a solution of a problem): mòzgati

think, ponder: čvȁkriti, čvȁljiti, dȕmati, kòntati, kopljáriti, krampàljati, kratnpàtljati, mljȁti, slámati, svračáriti, toljàgati, tralatùnjati, zdȉti

thinker: dȕmer

thinking, pondering: dȕmānje

third-rate criminal (albeit being one for a long time): nȁlo

thirty: trȉes

this and that: tȕc-mȕc [1]

this many: òlikō

this way: ovúdekā, vàkō

thorny field: dèrig ūz

thorny hay: gȕzobād

thorny plant: drȁča

thousand: ȉljada, jȅzero, sȍm [2]

thousand currency units; a thousand-unit bill, a grand: bȁnka

thousand dinars; a thousand-dinar bill, grand: bôn, bumȁška, Đôrđe, đȕrač, đȕrać, đûrđa, golùbica, hȉlja, hiljadárka, hȉljka, iljadárka, jezèrača, jòrgan, jùrek, kárta, kȉlja, kȍnj [1], kȑpa, mìjōr, mìjūr, mȉlja, mìljāk, mîljka, Slàvōnka, sȍm [2], tȍčka

thread: tànak

threaten: hrȕstiti se

three pointer (basketball): trȉca

three thousand dinars; a three thousand-dinar bill: màgare

threshing floor: gúvno

throat: gègeš, gùrāć, gȕša

throw away, toss out: ȁknuti, bȁčiti, cȉbati, cipelírati, cȉtba, cȕnjati [1], ćúlati, fȉknuti, frljácnuti, frljáknuti, fȑljnuti, frljóknuti, hȉtiti [2], ȉzbačiti, kašírati, katapultírati, katapultírati, kȅntati, nàdariti, nađáriti, nȍgovati, nogírati, noktírati, ȍćerati, odžȁkati, pȕcati, rȅnjkati, ȑknuti, šȉbnuti, šȉnuti, škartírati, šíknuti, šȕpnuti, šupírati, zafrljácnuti, zavȑljačiti, zbànđati, znogírati

throw down: obáliti [2]

throw out, expel: kȍskati, kȍškati, kȕšovati

throw out, kick out: išupírati, ȉšutati, išutírati, izjúriti [1], ȉzrenjkati

throwing away, tossing out: fŕljānje, nòga [2], nȍgomēt, šupírānje

thrown away, tossed out: cipèlirān, nògīrān, raznògīrān

thud: tȍpot, topòtānje, topòtati, tȍptāj, tòptati

thudding: topòtljiv

thunder: gȑmeti, gȑmljava, gȑmljavina, grôm [1]

thus, so: tàkō

tick-tock (clock, etc.): klepèsati, tȉka-tȁk, tikatàkati, tȉki-tȁk, tikitȁkovati, tikȉtati, tiktàkati, tiktȉkati

ticket for multiple rides: pantljȉčara

ticket scalper: tàpkāroš, tȁpos

ticket, fare: dúga

ticking (clock, etc.): tȉkānje, tikatàkānje, tikitȁkovānje, tȉk-tȁk, tiktàkānje

tidy and orderly male, neatnik: cȉkić

tie (shoelaces, etc.): šnírati

tie one's shoelaces: zašnírati, žnȉrati

tied: sàpēt

tied score: remíza

Tigar glue (sniffed by drug addicts): tàjger

tight: nàšpanān, nàšpanovān, šćȉpito

tight shirt: kȍžolēpka

tight trousers: anàtomke, frùla-pantalóne, frùle, frùlice, péderice

tight vagina: barȉlček

tight velvet trousers: somotnjáci

tighten: nàšpanovati, pritéći

time of prosperity, boom: bȕm [2]

time of separation between a male and a female: sezóna

time, period: cȁjt, vȁkat, zèmān

tin washer: plȅh-šȃjba, plȅh-šȁjbna

tin-snips: plèšare, plèškare

tiny, minute (of a person, object, etc.): bìber [2]

tip, gratuity: pèškeš

tire: iscijéditi

tired: ȉzjebān, ȉzmrdān, kȕnjav, mòrtus [1], razmòntīrān, trȍšan, zdȑkān

tired and weary: ȉzdrkān

Tirol salami (a low quality salami in the former Yugoslavia): tìrke

title for a manual laborer who has some additional education: kv [kâ-vê]

Titoism (ideology of Josip Broz Tito, communist dictator in the former Yugoslavia): titoȉzam

Titoist (follower of Josip Broz Tito, communist dictator in the former Yugoslavia): titòist, titòista

tobacco: čȁdālnik, čȕrāvnik, ćȕrōv, ćùrovnīk, đȕrōv, đȕrōvnīk, kèćāš, kèskīr, pluvánac, pljugánac, pljùgara, pljȕgavac, pljuvánac, tráva, trȁvka, tùtun [2]

tobacco pipe: sulȉnār

today: dèneska

together: skùpa

together, collectively: đȕturē

toilet: cv [cê-vê], ćúčavac, ćènef, ćenífa, ćènīf, ćinífa, kèjārnīk, kènjārnīk, mètrō

tomato: cȑvenī [1]

tomcat: grèbāč, grȅbān, kȍtār, kȍtor

tomorrow: trȁsu

tongs: papàgāj-cánge, papàgāj-cángle, papàgājke

tongue (of a bell): klepètac, zvéčak

tongue twister: bȑzalica

too much, overwhelming: cȕfīl, ȉ-hâ-hâ, ȉ-hā-hâj

too short trousers, flood pants: pȍplava

tools: hàlāt

tooth: čȅp[2], čèpina, dàndiška, dȍmino, gȅbis, glȍdavac, kljȍva, krljátak, kŕnjaš, krnjátak, njȕpavac

toothless: kréza , krȅzav, krêzos, krèzub

toothless female: kŕnja

toothless male: krȅzavac

toothless person: kȓnjozūb[1]

top (the toy): zvŕčak, zvȑčāljka, zvȑčka

top: zvȑk

top player: špȉc-ìgrāč

topic of conversation: štȍf

torture: fòrtati, hȁrati, ìzjakati, jèbati, jebávati, kárati, kàsapiti, kȅcati, klȁti, mesáriti, njákati, zȅzati, žandàrisati, žandàrmisati

torture gradually: cȕcati, cȕckati

torturing: jebávānje, kàsapljēnje, maltrètmān

totally, completely, fully: gȁnc

touch: džárati, džȁrkati, štrȁjfati, šȕpati, taktìlisati se

touch or play with, fiddle with, fool with: bambȑljati

touch, put one's hands onto, mess with: bȁrkati

touching: šȕpānje

tourist: fùrešt, krìstāl

tow: pȕcvāl, pȕcvol, pȕcvola

tow truck: dizàjner, pȁūk

towel: šugàmān

toy: zȅzalica

Trabant (a make of simple East German car): kàrtōnka, kònzērva, tȅtrapak

Trabant (a make of simple East German car): plastikánac

trace, vestige: trâk[2]

track (of a wheel): špúra[2]

tractor: skoromòbil

trade: perjáriti

traffic jam: špȉc

traffic policeman: mȁrsovac

trailer truck: šlȅper[2]

train: ȁkvla, búlac, kȁnte, kȁradža, trȅn, trȅska, trȅskavac

train conductor, ticket taker (female): kartodràpka

train conductor, ticket taker (male): kartodrápec

train from Belgrade, Serbia to Split, Croatia: pilìćārnīk

train station: bánōf, karàntīn, stàniška

transcribe: résaviti

transcriber: rèsavac

transmission: trìbūng

transport of new prisoners: cȕvaks

trap, catch: fȁćkalica, kvȁka, míca[1], nâvlaka, sȉcer

travel: pȉčiti

traverse: travèrzna

treat well: gotíviti

tree: baštúnjac, bȁtalica, ormànljika

tremble from being drunk, have the shakes: klȁckavica

trick, cheat, swindle: baciti, bajati, balabúćati, fàzōn, fȉnta, fôl[2], jebùckati srȕšiti

trick, joke: bȉks[2], càfuta, cáka, fòlina, fòluška, fóra[2], gevéra, grȉf, gvȉnt, kâjla, kȕrac[3], kereféka, lìnafo[2], lȍptica, ȍlfo, sínđa, štôs[2], zêz

tricked, cheated: lȕster, vìsūng[3]

Trieste (Italy, a popular shopping destination for ex-Yugoslavs): Tŕća, Trȇšće, Tȓš

trifle, thing of little importance or value: andarmólja, dȑkalica, džídža, džídža-bídža, đȉnđuha, đȉnđuva, gurábija, handrmólja, kikirȉkī, kȕrac[3], miràjzla, pičkàrija, platfùsist, šȉt[2]

trifles, things of little importance or value: čàpārci, skȁngale

tripe: čkembíći

trolley bus: múnja[1], tróla, tròliš, žȉca

troubemaler, rowdy: dizèlāš

trouble, problem: àndrak[2], bèlāj, bȕla, dȅver[2], durgùzica, gûstō, jéba, jebáda, kébānje, ȍfsājd

troublemaker, rowdy, ruffian: àjdūk, bȁbāč, bàlvan[1], bȁšter, bìzgōv, bombàrdēr, bȍrčula, bubuléja, bùdžātor, cȅstār, čàruga, čȕkāč, dàndara, Dìlinger, Divčibárac, dizàjner, dȑndara[2], drípac, dušogúbac, džȁmbās, gàner, gelìpter, grȕbe, grȕber, hȁhār, hàjvān, hùncut, jȁlijāš, kabadáhija, kàsapin, kàubōj, kȅšadžija, kȍbradžija, kostolómac, krèsāč, kûle, kùlōv, lȉska, màgler, màkljāroš, màkljātor, màndōv, mȁngāš, màngōv, mȁša, misìdžija, mùfljūz[1], nalètilić, njónja, pèglāč, pustàija, razbȁštavac, ȓmpalija, ròbija, sȁjla[2], sȉlos, siròvina, siròvnjāk, snàgātor, spídērka, stȑvina, šalabàhter[2], šalabàjzer, šȉbadžija, šȉbos, štȅker, štȅmer, šȕmār, tàbāč, tȁbadžija, tàbātor, têškī[2], ùdārnik, ugùrsuz, vȁrcaga, zijánćer, zulùmćār

troublemakers, rowdies (collectively): jàlija

trousers, pants: bȅčke, blȅferi, cȉjēvi, čàkšire, čȅhla, čùčehla, dògaćnica, gaćeróne, lóne, muftáre, muntáre, mùntārke, mùntērke, mùntīrke, nogàvice, pȁnčosi, pàntale, pàntiške, pàntole, pȁntosi, špȉcerice, špȉčōk, tóle

truck: kamìjōn, kamiònčina

trunk (of a car): gèpek

truth: fȁkat[2]

try to do something beyond one's capabilities: pohásiti se

try to repair: majmùnisati

try, strive for: glȅdati

tubercular: trȕmbekulōzan

tuberculosis: vèrem

tuberculosis patient: túba, tubèrān, tuberóza, tubijáner, tùbiš

tubular pliers: rôrcánge, rôrcángle

Tuesday: útōrnīk

tune an engine for high performance (usu. of an automobile), soup up a car: àbartovati

tune or rebuild an engine for maximum performance, soup up a car: frizírati

tune, adjust, fix: cícati, naštimávati, štȅlovati, ùštimati, uštimávati

tuned up (of any mechanism): zrȉhtān

tuning, adjusting, fixing: cícānje, štȅlovānje, štèlūng
turkey (the animal): mìsīrka
Turkish delight (type of candy): rȁhat-lòkum
Turkish-style restaurant: àščīnica
turn (e.g., wide turns of a truck): ȁjnšlājg
turn (eg. when riding a bicycle): đȉr
turn on (radio, tv, etc.): ùštekati
turn senile: izlápeti, omatúfeti
turn the steering wheel: zavŕnuti
turn the volume up, pop up the volume: podèbljati
turn, revolve, move: kréćati, krétati, okréćati
turntable: grádža, grȁmfić, grándža, iglodȑkalo, vȉtēška
turtledove: gùgutka
turtleneck (on a shirt): rôlka, rôl-krágna
turtleneck shirt: dolčevȉta, ròlōvka
tutor: tûtos
TV clip: vȉdeo
tweet: cijùkati, čȉvkati, živèrkati, živžȉkati
tweeting bird: đȉkavac
tweety (sound made by a small bird): cijùkav, cikìljav
twelve: dvánajs, dvánēs, dvánest
twenty: dvàes, dvàjes
twenty-five-para coin: pàra [1]
24-hour convenience store: drádža, dràgiša, dràgstor, dráža
twin fruit: mùdōrka, mùdovača, mudája
twin-masted sailboat: trabâkula
twist, sprain (arm, ankle, etc.): išuávljiti, ùšinuti
twisted piece of paper or fabric: gûžva
two aces with two kings (in poker): bètōn [2]
two aces with two tens (in poker): stòlovi
two days after tomorrow: nȁksutra
two days before today: nȁkjučē
two dinars; a two-dinar coin: čvȑka, dvòglāvka
two-bedroom apartment: tròsobnjāk
two-liter bottle (usu. of wine): dvòguza
type (on a keyboard, etc.): čȕkati
type of brandy supposedly made in a monastery: mȁnastīrka
type of wide-shouldered jacket: bonavèna
typewriter: kùcara
ugh: vâj, vàjme, vàjmeh
ugliest: nâjvećī
ugly: ìzdrkān
ulcer: vùlkān
umbrella: àmrēl, amréla, kišóber, mrȅlo
unable to serve in the military for any reason: dȕs
unattractive boy: hȍpsasā, trȁlala [2], tùdup
unattractive building: skalamèrija
unattractive clothing: àmbulja
unattractive communist-style architecture building: sandȕčara
unattractive elderly female, hag: babùrina, babùskara, babùskera, fùndača
unattractive female, dog: aligâtorica, aligâtōrka, àšōv, aždàha, aždàja, čùšpajzica, dròkljača, glȍdārka, gonoréja, grȍbārka, gȕšter, kalàštura, kàluša, kapȅla, kòbila, kórpa, krȁmp, kràmpus, kȑkuša, krokòdilka, kȕja, lòpata, mòtika, pepȅljara, pȍrpa, pràkljača, prȁkljos, rȁfa, rȁga, ráža, rèksača, slòtija, smìntača, sovùljaga, šȉnter, šȉšibeka, škàrpīna, šólja [1], šrȍt, vùčica, vûk, žgȁba, žgȍbavica
unattractive male: mȑtvāk
unattractive male, ape: čȉta, čȉtos, čȉtuljos
unattractive male, dog: aligâtor, bȁrbar, čâjnīk, drȁkulić, Dràkulović, drâle, gìbōn, kȕrta, màndōv, mȁnkī, òvčār, pacijȅnt, smȑdljivac, šmólja [2], trȁnjār, vûk
unattractive male, Frankenstein: Frànkenštajn
unattractive person: àkrap, àkrep, avétinja, drȁkula, dràkūt, džȍndra, džȕbos, džȕklja, gâbor, grdòba, gȑđa, grȍb, grôblje, kàjmān, kȁla, karakôndžula, kȉkī, kìklop, kȑndelj, màknī, mètlārka, mȉndros, nâkaza, negotívac, pácov, pȁs, psȅto, psȉna, skȍt, stvȍr, šlȍg [2], štȁkor
unattractive thing: pèriljek, šȕga
unattractive, ugly: bljȕtav, bljuvoȉzazōvan, ckȁmnī, degenèrik [1], demòlīrān, demòntīrān, gȓd, gȓdan, grûb, káka [2], kȁkān, kêr [2], logarȉtmīrān, lòpatār, lȍš, nȅgotīvan, nȅpoćūdan, òdgnjusān, òkrūžen, òpružen, pȉs [4], smȍtān, smȑdljiv, štrȍkav, vȉnjav, zȁjebān
unattractive, ugly as sin: šljâz
unattractively dressed female: dȓkotina, kalàštura, kamènjārka, kupùsara [2], slȕta
unavoidable: neprejèbiv
uncertainty: lêr [1]
uncle (father's brother): àmidža, čȉča, číka, číko
uncle (mother's brother or mother's sister's husband): dàidža, dàjdža
uncle (mother's brother): újac
uncle (term of address to male of one's father's generation): číka, číko
unclean female: posèrulja
unclear situation: tȍmbola
unclear, opaquely: neukapìrljivo
unconsciousness: kòma
unconventional, bohemian: òtkačen
unconventional, weird: degenèrik [1]
undependable friend: pìzdek [2], pizdèkān
undependable male: čàrapa, màrka [1], múćak [2], mutljívko, štȉh [1], tîp [1], zaguljénko
undependable, unreliable: ìzdrkān, jèben, màrka [2], okrètljiv, sìpak, zàgūljen
under police surveillance: ùćaknūt, ȕšarnūt
under the strong influence of narcotic drugs, stoned: nàduvān, stôn [2], stòndiran, stôund [2]
undercover agent: àlkica, glȍdār, špìcl, ȕdbić
undercover policeman, plainclothes cop: cìvīl, civìlnjāk
underground (organization): ȁndergrâund
underground movie or music: ȁndergrâund
underpants, underwear: ćȅga, gaćerónci, gaćeróne, kȁnjavica, mùdānte
understand someone's intentions, read someone: čȉtati
understand, get clued in, be plugged in: štȅkati, ùštekati

understand, realize: džànisati, džániti, ȉkiti, kȁčiti, kàpisati, kȁpiti, kapírati, kòntati, kòpčati, kȕžiti, njȕšiti, proàktati, progùtati, prokúžiti, prošnjófati, prováliti, provaljívati, raskužnjávati, raskùžnjati, skapírati, skòntati, skòpčati, skúžiti, skȕžnuti, spájati, ućániti, tudòmisati, ùbrati, ućériti,uđànisati, uđániti, uđériti, ùfērčiti, ukapírati, ukòpčati, utȑčati, žȉkati, žȉknuti

understandable: pròknjiženo

understanding that bogus narcotic drugs have been purchased: škȍlarina

understanding, realizing: dȕnst

undeveloped: pòbāčen

unemployed person: glúvac

unexpected message: hàvārija

unfair: nȅfēr, trȕlo

unfavorable situation: bȅd, bèdiška, kùrtōn

unfriendly: kùrvinskī, péderskī, zȁkopčān

unfriendly person: čȍmbe, kȗrva, péder, pedèrčina, pìzdulja, psȅto, pízda, ràjber, šíber[1], šȉbadžija, šȉbadžīka, škȑplja

unharmful person: pàpīr[1]

unhealthy: nàjlōn

unimportant: bèzvezan, lêvī[1], òpružen

unimportant issue: sačulátac

unimportant issue or object: stàlenac

unimportant person, nobody, nothing: burànija, lèvāk[1], lêvī[2], marginálac, mȉš, pacijȅnt, stàtist

unintelligent female: gȕska, haljùkuša, klepètuša, kòza, krȁva, krêlka, kvȍčka, màzga

unintelligent male: mìkan, nèznalica

unintelligent plan, dumb idea: trȉper-kombinácija

unintelligent, dense: zabetònīrān

unintelligent, idiotic: idìotskī

unintelligent, light weight: téžak

unintelligent, stupid, dumb: bèzvezan, blàziš, dádo, ȅrlav, kratkotȁlāsan, krètēnskī, lêvī[1], lȉkōvan, mòrskī, nȅbulōzan, nȅdotupāvan, ogràničen, pȉglu, plìtak, stòlijēvī, tȗp[2], tupȍljev, zȁjebān, zakaldȑmisān

union activist: sȉndos, sȉnđos, sîvī, sívac

universal joint: kàrdān

universal shaft: kàrdān-vȅla

universe, cosmos: vaseljéna

university: fȁk[1], fàkiš, fȁks

university cafeteria: vê-cê

university exam: kàsapnica, korída

university student: ìndeks, nȕla

university students (taken collectively): studentàrija

unknown: ȁpoznāt, bèzvezan

unknown female: Jàvōrka

unloved boy: trȁlala[2], tùdup

unlucky: tàličan

unlucky indiviudual: tâlija

unmanly husband (in all aspects of life): bèskūrčević

unmask: prováliti, provaljívati

unnecessary: suvònjav

unpleasant: ȁprijātan, kùrat, nezgodácija

unpleasant fact: dupodèrina

unpleasant feeling: bȅd, bèdiška

unpleasant female, bitch: fùnjara[1]

unpleasant issue: gȕlāš

unpleasant odor, stench: bâz, bâzd

unpleasant situation, bummer: čàbar[1], jéba, jebáda, kùfer, pizdàrija, sôs, sránje[2], svinjàrija

unreachable, out of range (e.g. a very important or influential person): nedokùrčiv

unrefined Macedonian opium: makedónac

unregistered dormitory resident: ilegálac

unrest (e.g. social): kràval

unscrew: odšaráfiti, odšeráfiti, òdšrafiti

unshredded piece of tobacco found in cigarette: pânj[2]

unskilled: nȅslān, tȕnjav

unskilled driver: traktòrist

unskilled female: trapađózla

unskilled female dancer: trȁpavičārka

unskilled person: kljȁks

unskilled pickpocket: šàpist

unsolvable problem: fòrdāljka

unsuitable sexual partner: šljȉva[1]

untidy apartment: kokošínjac

untidy female, slob: bŕlja, kupùsara[2], lȍća, slȕta, šmólja[1], špòrkulja

untidy male, slob: cmólja, smólja, smoljávko

untidy notebook: kupùsara[1]

untidy person, slob: pŕznica

untidy place (e.g., apartment or room): ćùmez

untidy, messy: ȁljav, rȁskupusān

untie: dréšiti, drijéšiti

unusual event: múnja[1]

unwilling: trȍšan

unworthy object: mȁtrāk[2]

unworthy person: šȕša

up-side-down: tȕmbe

upgrade: búdžiti

upgraded: nàbūdžen

upside down: opanȁčkē

upstairs: rȅgo

urban child: hàustorče

urge somebody to an action (usu. something immoral or dangerous): têntati

urge, press: prȅšati

urgent: prȅšno

urgent situation: prȅša

urging, pressing: agitȉška

urinate: ispȉškiti se, pošórati se, pȉškiti, ùlokviti, ùlokviti se, upìšati, vȅcati, zvìždati, žubòriti

urinate in one's pants: ušljéviti se, ušórati se

urinate on (physically): zapìšati

urinate one's fill: izdòjiti se

urinate, pee: pȉškiti, urìnisati, vȅcati

urinate, piss: išórati se, izvȉždati se, mòčati, mòćati, mókiti, mòkriti, pìšati, pìšati se, pȉšiti, piškàrati, pȉškati, pȉšnuti, pòbanjati, pòbanjiti, pomòčati, popìšati, popìšati se, popíškiti se, solírati, šàtipi, šljéviti, šórati, šȍrnuti, vȉzati se, zȅljkati,

urinate, take a leak: tòčiti

urinated on: ȉspišān, ȕpišān

urinating: pȉpī, pìšānje, pȉšēnje, pȉš-pȉš, pòpiš, šórānje

urinator: pišánac, pìšigaća, pìšna, píšonja, upišànīk, upišánko, upìšulja

urine: pìšaka, píša, píšak, šôrka

urine, piss: bȁnja [2], líka, pìšaća, pìšaćka, pišánjak, pišóka, pišúrak,

US dollar, buck: dolarȉška, dolôres, drȍljār

US dollar, greenback: zelèmbāć [2], zelènbāč, zèlenī

used in direct informal communication to make somebody do something, do it: hȁjda

used in direct informal communication with another person to encourage him/her to act: àjd

used in direct informal communication with another person to encourage him/her to move: àjd

used in informal communication to draw attention, hey: hâj [1]

used in informal communication to make somebody do something, do it: hâj [1]

used (not new): dòtrajān

used: ìzdrkān, òfūcān, potrošábl

used after a joke or trick is played on April Fools' day, April fool!: aprìlīlī

used after making one's interlocutor scared: cvȉk-cvȉk

used and dirty clothing: drónjak

used as a polite farewell or acknowledgment, Fine, You're welcome, Sure: prȉjātno

used as a question tag, really, indeed: hàjde [2]

used as a stron narcotic effect, speed, rush: stôn [1], stônd [1]

used as a stron negative response, no way, no deal: kȕrac [2]

used as a strong affirmative response, of course, yeah, you bet or similar expression: bèli, bezbèli, bòme, dabgòme, dabòme, dàkako, glȉtā, jȁbome, jȁh, jàšta, jȅs, jȅst, náravskī, sî

used as a strong negative response, no way, never or similar expression: fȑcāngle, frcòkla, jȍk, kàkī [1], kȕrac [1], kuràfte [1], kvȅker [1], múćak [1], néma, óčīn

used as a toast to a group of people, cheers: žíveli, žívili, žívjeli

used as a toast to a single female, cheers: žívila

used as a toast to a single male, cheers: žíviō

used as an independent affirmative response, of course, yeah: jâ [3], sî

used as informal farewell, bye: pâ [2]

used at weddings to encourage the best man to throw some money: kȅca [1]

used at weddings to make the best man throw some money: kȅc [1]

used car: kotùrača, polòvnjāk

used clothing store: drȍnjavac

used for indefinite reference, anything: grȉmzlice, jklȍp

used in a game of chess to inform one's adversary that he/she has to move the piece he/she has picked up, rather than returning it to its initial position and taking a new one: tȁknūto-mȁknūto

used in direct informal communication: ćûj [1]

used in direct informal communication to make somebody do something, do it: hàjd, hàjde [1]

used in direct informal communication with another person to encourage him/her to act: àjde [2]

used in direct informal communication with another person to encourage him/her to move on: àjde [2]

used in direct informal communication with one person to urge him/her to do something, do it, why don't you, go ahead: àj

used in direct informal communication with one person to urge him/her to move, come on: àj

used in direct informal communication with one person, hey: bȅ

used in direct informal communication with several persons or formal communication with one person to encourage them to act or move: àjte, àjte

used in direct informal communication with several persons or formal communication with one person to encourage them to act, do it: hàjte

used in direct informal communication with several persons or formal communication with one person to encourage them to act, go ahead: hàjte

used in folk songs without any semantic content: alabânda

used in general reference: fȑcāngla

used in informal direct communication to make somebody transfer an object: dȃvāj

used in reference to high schools after the school reform in the 1970s in the former Yugoslavia: šuvàrica

used in reference to the amount of money one has or what something is worth: téžak

used in searching in hide-and-seek: ȕū

used to accuse someone of being frightened, you're scared: pȑpa [1]

used to achieve a pause in conversation, one moment, please: minùtnjāk

used to address a child in an intimate manner, peanut: kûco

used to address a female in direct formal communication, madam: šjôra

used to address a single female in an intimate manner, kitten: mȁče [2], mȁčko

used to address a single female in direct informal communication: mâlā [1]

used to address a single female in direct informal communication, dear: bêjbī

used to address a single female in direct informal communication, hey, yo: bóna

used to address a single female in direct informal communication, sister: sȅstro

used to address a single individual in an intimate manner, dear: ȍko [2]

used to address a single individual in an intimate manner, dear heart: sȑce [2]

used to address a single individual in an intimate manner,

honey: pȉle, srȅćo

used to address a single individual in an intimate manner, my dear: dûšo[2]

used to address a single male in an intimate manner, buddy, pal, or similar expression: májkoviću

used to address a single male in direct informal communication: lêpī[2]

used to address a single male in direct informal communication, bro: bâto[1]

used to address a single male in direct informal communication, brother: bȁki[2], bâle[2], bràcika, brâco[2]

used to address a single male in direct informal communication, buddy: bȁja[3], jàrāne

used to address a single male in direct informal communication, hey: bȍlan, lijêpī

used to address a single male in direct informal communication, hey: ȁlō, bân[1], brȁte, hȁlō

used to address a single male in direct informal communication, man: čȍče, čȍveče, ćȍeće

used to address a single male in direct informal communication, mister, sir: efèndi, gȍsn, gȍsn, šjôr

used to address a single male in direct informal communication, my man: cȁre, krâlju

used to address a single male in direct informal communication, pal, buddy: drùgār[2]

used to address a single male in direct informal communication, yo, my brother, my friend: buráz[2], burázeru

used to address a single male, in direct communication, boss, chief: šȅfe

used to address a single person in direct informal communication, hey, man: hȁ

used to address a single person younger than oneself in direct informal communication, sonny: sȉne, sînko

used to address a single young male in direct informal communication, boy, son: dȅčko[1]

used to address adult women older than oneself, ma'am: tȅta

used to address children, peanut: mâco

used to address one male in direct informal communication: drágoviću

used to address one male in direct informal communication, buddy: grȍfe, prȉka[2]

used to address one or more individuals in direct informal communication: bâ

used to address one or more individuals in direct informal communication with various additional meanings ranging from disapproval to familiarity, etc., hey you, man; the hell, damn it; for heaven's sake, wow: brȅ

used to address one or more individuals in direct informal communication, buddy: ròđenī[1], rôđo[2]

used to address one person in direct informal communication: lègēndo, Míćo[1]

used to address one person in direct informal communication, hey: mȍre, mȍri

used to address or refer to an older male (esp. by children), mister, sir: bârba

used to address several individuals in direct informal communication, you all, you guys: brȁćo

used to address several persons in direct informal communication, you guys, you folks: bóni

used to ask for a pause, hang on, hold on, one moment, please: sekùndu

used to ask for a pause, hold on, hang on: čȅk, čȅka

used to ask for a pause, one moment: mòmenat, mòment

used to ask for a pause, one moment, please: trenútak

used to ask for a pause, wait: stân, stȃni

used to ask musicians to play a song: ožèži

used to attract attention in direct informal communication, look, watch: glȅ

used to attract attention of a single male in informal communication: mâjstore

used to attract attention of a single person in direct informal communication: glâj

used to attract attention, look over there: kȉbī

used to attract one's attention in informal communication, hey: hȉ

used to avoid discussion on a particular subject, leave that alone, don't ask me: mánte

used to calm down a horse: dûr, dȕra

used to calm down a she-goat: tîr[1]

used to calm down one's interlocutor, cool it: oládi

used to cast spell on somebody: anatèmate

used to change the topic of conversation, well, ok or similar expression: dòbro[1], ê[2], êee[2]

used to check for the understanding on the part of one's interlocutor, Got it?: ȉkiš[1]

used to check if one's interlocutor wants something: ȍli[2], ȍš

used to check if the channel of communication is open, got it: znâš[2]

used to check if the import of the message has been captured: kȕžiš

used to clam down one's interlocutor, cool off: odmòri

used to command a cat to go away: vòštac

used to command a horse to move on, go: hȉjo, ȍhēj

used to command a horse to stop, stop: ȍhā

used to command an action, do it: jȁla, jȁlāh

used to command an animal to move on, go: ȉo

used to command an ox to move on, go: hȁjs

used to command an ox to pull back: stû

used to command an ox to stop: jô-jā

used to command an ox to turn left: čȁ[2]

used to command cattle to move on, go: hȁe

used to command cessation of an action, stop, enough: ȕjā[1]

used to command dismissal: mȁrš[1]

used to command donkeys to move on: ćȕš, ćȕše

used to command somebody to move on, go ahead: kréći

used to command to run away, run: páli

used to draw attention (usually of an attractive female): ks-ks

used to draw attention: ȁnu, čûj[1]

used to draw attention in direct informal communication, attention: pâj

used to draw attention in direct informal communication, hey: ê[1], ȅhe, ȅhēj, êj, hêj, hôj, njȍfra[2], ôj, ô-ôj, ôooj used to draw attention in direct informal communication, listen up: pȁzi

used to draw attention, look: dȉvi, ȉkele, ìkiši[2], kȉš, nȕ, nȕt, nȕti, nȕto, šȉkoi, trȁkoš, vîd, vȉdē, vȉđi, vȉđu, vîš, zȉpa žȉku, žrâk

used to draw attention, you know: znâš [1]

used to drive away a cat: pȉs [1]

used to drive away a cat, scat: šȉc, šȉca

used to drive away a crow: ȕj

used to drive away a dog, shoo: ȍš, ȍša

used to drive away a goat: kȅc [1], kȅca [1]

used to drive away a goat or a bird: kš

used to drive away a goose: kȍt

used to drive away a pig: ȕsa

used to drive away an ox: ȍjc

used to drive away cattle: kȉt [2]

used to drive away or lure a calf: ljȍk, ljȍke

used to drive away pigs: šȉke

used to drive away poultry, shoo: šȉš

used to drive away various animals: ȕš, ȕša

used to emphasize a directive: ȁ-nu

used to emphasize a directive: ȁnu, ȁnute

used to emphasize close relationship with a person from the same generation, my generation: gêro

used to emphasize one's own point, I swear to God! or similar expression: bȍgam, bȍgami, bògme, bȍgomi, bȍgumi, rȅko

used to encourage an action, go for it: mâz

used to encourage to an additional performance, encore: bȉs [1]

used to express a dangerous situation, watch out: vârda

used to express absence: nȁre, nȍaj

used to express amazement, disbelief, etc.: čúj [2]

used to express anger, hell or similar expression: bȅstraga, dȍđavola

used to express appreciation: mâšalā, mâšalāh, pȕška [1], zgȍdno

used to express appreciation, congratulate, etc.: avèrim

used to express appreciation, good for you: èjvalā, ȅvalā, ȅvalāj

used to express appreciation, way to go, good show: afȅrim

used to express approval: bùjrum

used to express approval or appreciation: áaa

used to express approval, bravo: brȁo, brȁvo, brȁvos

used to express approval, good intentions, etc., cheers: ȅškula

used to express approval, great: ȍhā

used to express approval, okay: ȉgrā [1]

used to express assurance, I swear to God!: bȍrami

used to express astonishment, amazement, etc., hey: ȁiii

used to express astonishment, disbelief, etc.: ćú [2], ćúj [2]

used to express astonishment, unbelievable: hȁos [1]

used to express astonishment, wow: ȕhā

used to express compassion, poor thing: jȁdan, jâdo [1], nèsrećo

used to express denial, impossibility, etc.: cvŕkac

used to express difference of opinion, but: ȁma

used to express different emotions ranging from approval to outrage, oh: jȁ [1]

used to express different emotions ranging from satisfaction to grief, ah, oh: ȅh

used to express disagreement: ê [1]

used to express disagreement, lack of regard, etc.: bakráči [1]

used to express disappointment: pȉh

used to express disapproval, No way: kakvbakráči

used to express disbelief: cvȑc, dâj, fóra [1], nȍkat [1]

used to express disbelief or disagreement: kȕrac [2]

used to express disbelief or distrust: zajèbāvāš

used to express disbelief or negative attitude: šípak

used to express disbelief or pain, oh: jȍh, jôj

used to express disbelief, no kidding: ìdi

used to express disbelief, no way: pàmpur [2]

used to express disbelief, oh, really: ȕf

used to express disbelief, unbelievable: svȁšta

used to express discomfort (usu. from being cold), brr: bȓ, bȓr

used to express disgust, phew: fȑr, fȕ, fȕj

used to express disgust, yuck: bljȁk

used to express disregard, lack of appreciation, etc.: zvȑc

used to express dissatisfaction: zajèbi

used to express excitement or joy, wow: i-i-ijȕ

used to express excitement or joy, yippee, whoopee: iiijȕ, ijȕ

used to express extreme disgust: fȁk [2], gûrām, ȍprēm, tvȓd [1], zbȉjēm, zbȕtām

used to express extreme disgust and to offend one's interlocutor: pȕši

used to express extreme dissatisfaction: čȕkām, govnàrija, góvno [1], mȁterinu, mȕnēm, pîzdo, šȉt [1]

used to express good intentions or wishes, good luck: bôgdaj, bôgdo

used to express gratitude, thanks: fála, hvála, vála [2]

used to express great joy, whoopee, hurrah: jȕha-hâj

used to express grief: dȁvor, dȁvori

used to express grief or sorrow: kȕku

used to express grief, despair, etc., oh, alas: àvāj

used to express grief, woe or similar expression: lèle

used to express hesitation: tȁmo-vâmo, tȓc-vȓc

used to express hesitation or uncertainty, uh: òvāj

used to express hesitation, huh: hȁ, hȅ, héee, hjȁ, hm, ȕf

used to express hesitation, I mean, you know: mȉsīm

used to express hesitation, I think, I mean, you know: mȉslīm

used to express hesitation, mmm: mmm

used to express hesitation, things like that: òvō-ònō

used to express hesitation, this and that: tȓte-mȓte, tȓt-mȓt [1]

used to express hesitation, you know: znâš [2]

used to express high satisfaction, awesome: milȉna

used to express impossibility: néjde

used to express impossibility of an event, don't even think about it: Èdipe

used to express indifference and lack of control: ȁko

used to express indifference, nothing special, no big deal: bèzē

used to express indifference, that's how it is: štȃš [2]

used to express indifference, who cares: cvȑc

used to express intimacy: máčak

used to express joy, great: ȍjā

used to express joy, hurrah: úara

used to express joy, hurray: hȕrā

used to express joy, oh yeah: đèrček

used to express joy, satisfaction, etc., yes: ȁjhāj

used to express negative attitude, shit: sránje [1]

used to express negative opinion, nonsense: Èdipe

used to express one's extreme disgust and offend one's interlocutor: pòpuši

used to express one's readiness to respond, what can I do for you: izvòli, izvòlite, izvòlte

used to express one's uncertainty and lack of control over events, God willing: ȁkobōgda

used to express pain or astonishment, ah: àj

used to express pain or grief, oh, woe: jȁo, jȁoh, jȁoj

used to express pain, disbelief, surprise, etc., ah, ouch, wow: jô [2]

used to express pain, displeasure, etc., ow, ouch: ȁoj

used to express pain, grief, despair, etc., oh, ow: ȁjāj, ȁjaō, ȁjaoh

used to express pain, grief, despair, oh, ow: ȁjōj

used to express pain, regret, etc., ah: ȁi

used to express praise or joy (usu. in religious contexts), hallelujah: alilúja

used to express praise or joy (usu. religious), hallelujah: alelúja, alȉluj

used to express public disagreement, boo: ȕā

used to express relief, huh: ȕhā

used to express remorse or to make an other give way, sorry, excuse me: izvínte

used to express resignation, ah: tȅh

used to express satisfaction: pȕška [1]

used to express satisfaction with food, mmm: mmm

used to express satisfaction, approval, etc.: bȁnja [1]

used to express satisfaction, surprise, delight, dislike, pain, etc., ah: ȁh, ȁo

used to express satisfaction, surprise, delight, dislike, pain, etc., ah, aah: a [1]

used to express satisfaction, surprise, delight, dislike, pain, etc., ah, aah: àē

used to express satisfaction, surprise, delight, dislike, pain, etc., ah, oh, ugh: ȁhā [1]

used to express sorrow or dismay, woe: bȕah

used to express strong emotions, such as excitement, impatience, grief, pain, etc.: ȉh, ȉhāj, ȉh-ȉh-ȉh, ȉhū, ȉhuhū

used to express strong emotions, such as excitement, impatience, grief, pain, etc., ah: ȉhā, ȉhāaa

used to express surprise (usu. when one remembers something), a ha, oh: a-hâ

used to express surprise or astonishment, ugh: hȕ, hûj

used to express surprise or disbelief, oh: čȕ

used to express surprise or disbelief, wow: hȍho

used to express surprise or fear, oh: jȕ, jȕf, jȕh, jȕj, jûuuu

used to express surprise or pain, oh: ȍh

used to express surprise, admiration, etc., wow: àlā [2]

used to express surprise, ah: ȁlāj [1]

used to express surprise, amazement, etc., ah: ȁoh

used to express surprise, astonishment, amazement, etc., hey: ȁi, ȁih

used to express surprise, astonishment, etc.: ȅhe-hē

used to express surprise, astonishment, etc., ah: ȁuf, ȁuh

used to express surprise, astonishment, etc., ah, wow: ȁu

used to express surprise, astonishment, etc., oh: bâ, bȁh, ȍpā

used to express surprise, astonishment, etc., oh, God: àmān, àmān-zàmān

used to express surprise, astonishment, etc., wow: ȁuuu

used to express surprise, disbelief, etc., no kidding: èki, èkši

used to express surprise, excitement, joy, etc., oh my: ȍla-ôl

used to express surprise, whoa: gêee

used to express surprise, wow: áaa

used to express surprise, wow: jèbote, ȍhō, ȍhoho, ȍhōj, ȍpalā, ȍpalāc

used to express the absence of readiness to reach an agreement, no deal: pȕkī [1]

used to express the closing time of a bar, last call: fàjronat [1]

used to express the feeling of not being threatened by one's interlocutor: cȉnci-lȉnci-dvójka-Dòrćol

used to express the hope that something will happen: dàbōgda

used to express the opinion that one has to continue the job he/she started: tȁknūto-mȁknūto

used to express the state of being shocked: šlȍg [1]

used to express the unpleasant smelling sensation: snȉfā

used to express uncertainty: béše, fôl [1], grèsli, kȁnda, kȁo, k.b.s.z [kəbəsəz], kobajági, lȉnafo [1], šȁtro [1], tȍbož, tȍbože

used to express uncertainty, God only knows: bôgznā

used to express unpleasant sense of smell, It stinks: kàndišē

used to express various emotions, such as satisfaction, surprise, delight, dislike, or pain, oh: ȕ

used to express various emotions, such as satisfaction, surprise, delight, dislike, or pain, oh, well: êee [1]

used to express willingness or approval of an event, let: nȅk

used to express wish or surprise, oh, hey: ô

used to frighten one's interlocutor, boo: dzȁdz, džȁ

used to great a group of individuals informally, hi: žívjeli

used to greet a group of individuals, hi: žíveli

used to greet a group of people informally, hi: žívili

used to greet a religious person: pòmāgābôg, pòmāgā-vi-bôg

used to greet a single female informally, hi: žívila

used to greet a single male informally, hi: žíviō

used to greet informally on arrival, ciao, hi: ćȁo, ćȁos

used to greet informally on arrival, hi: hâj [1], ȍgbo, poštovànskī, vȍzdra, zdrȁo, zdrávko, zdrȁvo

used to greet mostly in direct formal communication, hello: poštovánje

used to greet on arrival, hello, hi: mȅraba

used to heighten attention to what follows conversationally, so, well: ȅvo

used to hurry up a horse, giddyup: đȉo

used to indicate acknowledgment of message, That's right!: štȉma

used to indicate lack of control over events, God willing: ABD [ā-bê-dê]

used to indicate that the import of what was said has been grasped, uh-huh, got it: ahâ [3]

used to intensify one's own utterance, you know: pȁzi

used to introduce a verb in the present tense having the infinitive function, to: d

used to lure bees: kȍt

used to lure cats: cȉc, mȉc

used to lure chicken: pȉ, pȉh, pȉha, pȉlo, pȉ-pī

used to lure chickens: ćȗ [1], ćȗk

used to lure cows: mâ-mâ

used to lure ducks: pȁt

used to lure geese: gȕs, gȕsa

used to lure goats: ȁc, jȁc, jȁco, kȉs [1]

used to lure or command cows to go away: vȍč, vȍčke

used to lure pigeons: vȉt, vȉta

used to lure pigs: gȉc, kȉc, pȁjs, vȉcī

used to lure the queen-bee: mȁt [1]

used to lure turkeys: ćȕr, ćȕri, pȕć

used to lure turkeys or geese: bȋr, bȉri

used to maintain the channel of communication by signaling attention, uh-huh, right: ȁhā [1]

used to make a dog retrieve: ȕc

used to make a horse or ox back up, back: curȉk

used to make a vague reference to anything: ònō [2]

used to make somebody come, come over: hȍdi

used to make somebody go away: àlā [2], đȉm [1], klȉš, màdo, màgla [1], mȁkac, mȅtak [1], mètla [2], mȑš, otpúši, pìksla [1]

used to make somebody go away: bêž, cirkùliši, cȑta [1], čȕbe, fȕćkāj!, gljȁka [1], hȁ, ȉka [1], ȉkamor, kȉfele, rȉči, ȑš

used to make somebody go away, beat it: bjȁži, bjêž, brȋs [1], brȉš, brȉši, brȉś, brȉtva [1], čìstac [1], dȁlga, dvójka [2], hàjdac, kȉdāj, kidavȅla [1], kidavȅlo, kȉfeli, kȉfli, klȋs [1], mȁr [1], nòga [1], nȍkat [1], ȍdbīj, ȍdgibāj, odjèbi, Ȍtplivāj!, páli, sêvāj, sȉkter, sjȁši, šêtāj, šȉbāj, šȉbe, šȉmāj, štrǻfta, štúra [1], šumagȅle, šumangȅle, tàban [1], tȗtanj [1], tutavȅla [1]

used to make somebody go away, beat it, back off: ȍtkači, ȍtkači se

used to make somebody go away, get out: odsmr̀di

used to make somebody go away, hit the road: džáda [1], đáda [1]

used to make somebody go away, hit the road, beat it: drȕm

used to make somebody go away, scram: šȉk

used to make somebody join you, come over: ȍdi [1]

used to make somebody leave: ȁvtos

used to make somebody leave, beat it: cȉmāj

used to make somebody leave, Beat it!: cìpela [1]

used to make somebody leave, beat it, scram: àvte

used to mark the beginning of the point or purpose of conversation, Listen up, here is the deal: ovȁko

used to mark the end of a significant point: ȅto

used to offend one's interlocutor: kȍnju

used to offer a cigarette to one's interlocutor: zapáli

used to open a portion of text with one's own thoughts, I say: vȅlju

used to open telephonic conversation or maintain the channel of communication, hello: ȁlō, hȁlō

used to point to something, look: ȉkši

used to point to something, there: ȅno

used to politely address one female in direct formal communication, ma'am: gȍspoja [1]

used to prevent action: nèmōj

used to prevent actions: mȍjne, nâj [2], nèmō, nȉcaj

used to prevent children from doing something: tȉta

used to prevent one's interlocutor from speaking, shut up: pàuza

used to prevent the action of putting something in a wrong place: mòjnegadèntro

used to prevent the action of putting something in a wrong place, Don't put it where it does not belong!: mòjnegastèrmo

used to refer to a hectic or dangerous situation: dȑži-nèdāj, dȑž-nèdāj

used to refer to a situation which involves intensive bargaining, going back and forth: povúci-potégni

used to refer to danger (e.g. when something is falling from a building), watch out: čȗvāj

used to refer to something which one does not consider to be true: gȉstro [2]

used to refer to the current social and political situation (particularly to the events in the 1990s in the former Yugoslavia): òvō

used to refer to the regular state of affairs (usu. in response to the question Kako si? 'How are you'), so-so: đȅne-đȅne

used to refer to the words of others, as they say: vèlī

used to refer to unwillingness to make a transaction, no deal: pùškīn

used to respond to thanking, you are welcome: mȍlīm

used to scare birds, shoo: ȉš, ȉša

used to scare one's interlocutor, boo: bȗu

used to scare pigs and other domestic animals, shoo: ȉške

used to scare somebody (esp. young children), boo: bȁu, bȁu-bȁu

used to signal agreement, okay: bȁro [1]

used to signal another's being frightened: vȕna [1]

used to signal approval (usu. religious), amen: ámen, ámin

used to signal approval, readiness, etc., deal, agreed: dogȍvoreno

used to signal assurance: ȁle

used to signal impossibility, hardly: têško

used to signal indifference, nothing special, no big deal:

bèzvzē, bèzzē

used to signal lack of willingness to negotiate, period: kvȉt [1]

used to signal occupancy, this one's taken (e.g. a seat): bèzec

used to signal possession: ròdilo

used to signal presence: ȁre

used to signal readiness (in hide-and-seek game), we are ready: ȕjā [1]

used to signal readiness to accept what has been proposed, it's a deal: vàži

used to signal something being highly humorous: šôu [2]

used to signal that another person is frightened: zȍrt [1]

used to signal that everything is well: ròdilo

used to signal that import of message is captured, I got it: žȉmku

used to signal that import of the message has been captured: tȕdom

used to silence one's interlocutor: kȕš [1]

used to silence one's interlocutor in a specific speech act or in general, shut up, be silent about this: tȉću

used to silence one's interlocutor, cut it out: prèkini

used to silence one's interlocutor, hush: psst, pst, š-š-š

used to silence one's interlocutor, shut up: ćùtkac, ćȕt, kajâdo, kȁjdo, kênjāj, njȁjke, šȉma, šȉnati, šút [1], tišnòća

used to silence one's interlocutor, shut up: zavéži

used to silence one's interlocutor, Shut up! or similar expression: fèrmāj

used to stimulate common departure from a certain place, let's go home: demoìćȉku

used to stimulate one or more individuals to a common action, let's: hàjmo

used to stimulate one's interlocutor to do something he or she is not willing to do: čȉk [1]

used to stimulate somebody to a common action, heave-ho: hô-rȕk [1]

used to stimulate somebody to a common effort, heave: ô-rȕk

used to stimulate somebody to do something: dâj

used to stimulate somebody to pass something: dâjde

used to stimulate to a common action: àjmo

used to stop a horse, whoa: eéhaa, êhā, éja

used to stop actions, basta: bȁsta

used to stop an action, that's enough: pȉk [1], šlȕs [1]

used to sum up point, that means, so, you see: znâči

used to support important thoughts or actions by giving them a religous approval, in the name of God: bismìlāh, bismìlāj

used to take leave of a group of individuals informally, bye: žíveli, žívjeli

used to take leave of a group of people informally, bye: žívili

used to take leave of a single female informally, bye: žívila

used to take leave of a single male informally, bye: žíviō

used to take leave of someone informally: dâjna

used to take leave of someone informally, bye: bâj, ȍgbo, papâ [1], vȍzdra, zdrȁo, zdrávko, zdrȁvo

used to take leave of someone informally, bye-bye: bâj-bâj, doahtánja, doviđénce, pȁ-pâ

used to take leave of someone informally, bye-bye: poštovȁnskī

used to take leave of someone informally, bye-bye, adieu: àdijo, àdio

used to take leave of someone informally, bye-bye, adios: adȉos

used to take leave of someone informally, ciao, bye: ćȁo, ćȁos

used to take leave of someone informally, take care: hȁirala

used to take leave of someone, bye-bye: doviđénja

used to urge a horse to go ahead or go at a faster pace, giddyup: đȉ, đȉhā, đȉja, đȉjo

used to urge a horse to move on: đȁ

used to urge an ox to move on: ȁjs, ȅjs

used to urge cattle on: ćȅja

used to urge on a horse: ȁrto

used to urge one's interlocutor to approach, come here: đȅl, đȅla

used to urge somebody on: mȁrš [1]

used to urge somebody to act, do it: dȅla, ȅlā, ȅlāj

used to urge somebody to do something: àlōv

used to urge somebody to move: pohíti

used to urge somebody to move straight forward: pràvac [1]

used to urge to an action: dȅ [1], dȅd, dȅdē, dȅdēr, dȅdēra

used to warn and command hiding of some object (usu. from the police), hide it: dèken, švȁj, švêj

used up: òtrcān

used when giving something and then pulling it back in a taunting fashion: ȁc

used when jumping, hop: đȉk, đȉp, đȉpac, hȍpā, hȍpsā, ȍp [1], pȍ [1], pȍa

used when offering food, help yourself, dig in: bùjrum

used when offering something to somebody: nâj [1]

used when passing something in direct formal communication, here you go: izvòlite, izvòlte

used when passing something in direct informal communication, here you go: izvòli

used when passing something to somebody: mâj [1]

used when passing something to somebody, here: nȁ

used when passing something to somebody, here you go: bȁka

used when passing something, here: dȓž

used when pointing to or passing something: ȅto, ȅvo

used when something important, usu. dangerous or illegal, is observed, aha: ahȁ [2]

used when taking photos, cheese: tȉca [1]

used while dancing kolo (a traditional folk dance): hȍpā-cȕpā [1]

used while dancing the kolo (a traditional folk dance): hȍp-cȕp [1]

Ustasha-like (Croatian nazi): ȕstašoīdan

utilities (e.g. electricity): kȍmunālnō

vacation: bȍlovānje, férići, frȅmt, gòdišnjāk [1], gòdišnjī

vacation in the fall: jȅsenovati

vacation resort: odmorīška

vacuum: sàugati

vacuum cleaner: sīsavac

vagina: bānka, crévce [2], cvéba, čānta, čīzma, fīga,kâr-bùnār, míca [1], míndža, mòja, pèćina, pīša, pûz, pûž, rālje, rūndosava, rūnja, svòja, šljīva [1], šóder [2], šūmica

vagina with a large clitoris: kapàklija

vagina, cunt: brána, brázda, bríca [1], brūca, bùbnjača, cána, cánta, cāpi, cūca,cūpī, čkāpi, ćūća, dānfa, dlākavica, dōtka, džāmin, džùmina, đānfa, fànfulja, flônda, flôndža, flôndra, fōka, fīga, fudžijàma, fūkica, gavrànčina, glônđa, gôndža, grāba, grāha, hâl, hèvina, hōlcerica, jāma, jòčkapinj, jòčkicapinj, jòndžaminj, kāpa, karfiōl, kàrulja, kènda, klâmfa, kóka, kòza, kōža, lōkot, ljērga, mánda, Mīcika, míndža, mìndžina, mindžōsava, mīndžoslava, mìndžulja, mjēhūr, mūholōvka, mūka, njēgra, njērga, njēzga, pahùljača, pāru, pîc, píca, pìcāć, pīcalo, pìcara, pícīn, picòlīn, picóljak, picùlīn, piculìnčić, picùlīnka, picúljak, picùljān, picùljica, picúrak, pìcuša, píčak, pìčetina, pìčevina, pìčić, pīčka, pīčkica, pičúljak, pīčvajs, pićóka, pićókara, píka, pīpica, pīšica, pīškica, pìšulja, pīšura, pízda, pōtkova, ptīčica, pùpčić, pústinja, pûž, ràfūng, rájngla, ràjūng, rāka, rāna, réma, rība, rībica, rìbīć, rōklja, ròndža, rōnđa, ròzbīf, rùndulja, rūpica, slinàrkapa, slūnjavica, slūzavica, slúznica, smōkva, smřdulja, svřdla, šàjkača, šēvkalica, škèmbreg, škôljka, škrābljica, škūlja, škūljica, šljíva [2], šnāperica, šóder-grāba, šólja [1], štūka, šùbara, šūma [2], tàmbura, tórba, trākalica, trōkūt, trokùtić, vèrna, vřč, vrútak, zdāpi, zēlja, zèmlja, zévalica, zvřda, zvřnda, žèlja, žēmlja, žlūndra, žûlj

vagina, hole: rūpa [2]

vagina, jelly roll: bùhtl

vagina, love tunnel: tùnēl

vagina, muff: mūf

vagina, pussy: máca

vaginal: pícīn

vaginal deodorant: mīndžosprēj

vaginal excretion: lìkēr, sāft

valley: ūrvina

vampire: vàmpijēr

varnish: fīrnajs, fīrnajz

VCR: vīdeo

Večernji list (a daily paper from Zagreb, Croatia): Večernjâk

vegetate, barely live (socially or financially): gìljati

vegetate, veg out: životinjáriti

veil: bōšča

velvet trousers: radijâtōrke, somòtnjare

vending: pàzarnī

venereal disease department (of a hospital): ēf

venereal disease hospital: Džòrdžika, đòrđika

very: dòzlaboga, gānjc, gřdno, stràvično, strōgo, tīlī, zdrâvo, zòrli

very affluent male: buržùjčina, sòmovac

very attractive female, hot number: bòing, kāle, kàluša, sīnger, šláger [1]

very bad: jèziv, kurčèvito

very difficult situation: fōrpās [4], sôs

very difficult, screwed up: jebèno, kurčèvito

very distant part of a village: pīcodēr

very famous person, legend: lègēnda

very frequent public bus: limuzína

very funny: pìšičan, strāobālan, strášan, stràvičan, ubístven

very important or influential person, big shot: bàtina, Bôg, Bōnd, búdža, budžòvān, dása, dīrnāroš, fóra [2], fotèljēr, gàvan, glāfōr, glávonja, grògan, gúzonja, hàdžija, kapùtār, lâf [1], màrka [1], múdonja, nâjlaf, nósonja, pòmed, premijéra, tīrbonja, tītonja, zvêrka

very important, very influential: glàvnī [1], pòtkovān, skōžen

very inexpensive item or service: džabalək, džabàluk

very inexpensive merchandise: bagatèla [1]

very inexpensive, bargain: bāgatēlan, bāmbadàva, džə, džàbāk, džabalèskū, džāb-džabàluk, džāb-džàbē

very modern thing: vrīsak

very much: prâvō

very old: bībliōzan

very pleasant event: ótkid

very poor: gô ko pīštōlj

very potent male: Frézer, mjēsečina

very sad event: ótkid

very slowly: klâj-klâj

very suspicious person: tipusáner

very tall person, giant: kīkī, kìklop, vitamìndžija

very tidy, tip-top: cākum-pākum

very tight panties: francùzice

very tired, dead tired: cřkaō, cřkō

very unattractive female, real dog: garagâbor, gargâbor

very unintelligent male, complete moron: šónjca

very unintelligent person: neandertálac, rōn-tōn-tōn

very unpleasant: zàguzast

very urgent: stāni-pāni

very young female, little girl: bèretka, būbica, cvřca, dokolèničārka, frcóka, gālofaks, jagnjéšce, kèlīnka, klepètuša, klincéza, klīnče, klìndōvka, klînka, kōnj [1], nàrāndža, pìčić, pòkotče, popìšulja, rībīzla, sìnčić, skopàče, skōpak, sladúnac, sūknjica, šipàrica, šmŕca, špīca, švŕca, vajzìnče, vàjzīnka, žvákalica

Vespa (model of motorcycle): bùha, štākor

vest: kūzman

vibraphone, vibes: vībrić

victim: lāzār [2], óvca, pacijēnt, Pētar

victim of a prostitute: Pētar

village: bāšća, orìjāš [2], sìćanovo, šūma [2]

violent: glàvat, grûbor

violent behavior: hajdùčija

violent person, bully: àrambaša

violet: ljubišpíca

violin: píla

virgin (female): jānje, vìrdžīnija, virdžinijána, virdžinìjānka, zèlenā, zelenàšica

virgin: blômba, cêlka, cêvka, cìferšlus, džána, džānfer, džānferica, džànifer, đána, đānf, đānfa, đānferica, jùnfer, jūnferica, jūnferka, kònzērva, līmēnka, Màrija, neosùđīvān, nikòtaka, njũferica, opàtica, plômba

virginity: džànifer, džènifer, jùnfer, jùnferšaft, mokasína, mrâk[2]

visibly: ždrâkno

visit, pop in, stop by: sũnuti

visitor at the Opera bar in Zagreb, Croatia: opèrāš

Vjesnik daily, Zagreb, Croatia: plȁhta

Vlahov (a brand of a hard liquor sold in the former Yugoslavia): vlâhović

vodka: prȍzīrnā

voice: àvaz[1]

Volkswagen (a car make): fȍlcić, fòlcika, fȍlksić, folksvagína, kórnjača, vágen

Volkswagen (a car make), bug, beetle: bũba, vagína

volume (of sound): pȉčānje, pȉčēnje

volume of an engine: kubikáža

volume of female breast: diòptrija

volume, capacity (of a containter, etc.): litráža

vomit: pégla

vomit copiously, puke one's gut out: izbljùvati se

vomit, throw up, puke: izaláčiti se, izlazìčati se, omáciti se, rȉgati, rȉgnuti, rigolètati

vomiting, throwing up: rȉglec, rigolȅto

voracious eater: klòpāroš

voyeur: rašòmōn, rašomónac, rošòmōn, rošomónac, šmȅker

voyeurism: fȍto-safârī, rašomònisānje, rošomònisānje

wagon (train car): kèbanja

wagon: fùrnjāk

waist, belt: pantalodŕžac

wait: frùlati[2], poprȉčekati

wait for a customer (of a prostitute): pâsti[2]

wait for a long time: čámiti, čȁmuti, čekìćati, ćúčati, dréždati

wait long and in vain: cȑvati se

waiter: bȁčvār, bàrkonj, jònobarkonj, kédža, kénja[1], kéša[2], konobarȉška, kontròlōr, kotùralo, kùstos, Máto, óber, pìngvīn, Pitàgora, pòreznīk, rezánac, slúga, šȅf, tȑčkalo, tròtl

waiting for a long time: čekìćānje, ćúčānje

waitress: Bȁrica, klȉnka

walk: cȉpliti, cìpljati, cúriti, čkòjiti, čkȍriti, gàmbati, gégati, gíbati, gíbati se, gìljati, giljáviti, glàvati, gljȁti, gljàvati, gúliti, guljáviti, klȁckati, lèbditi, mravìjati, mravírati, mũvati se, múving, pȁciti, plazánac, plȁziti[1], plȁžēnje, plòviti, pročȅšljati, prošnjúrati, prozújati, sandolírānje, sandolírati, šnjúrati se, špârtati, tabànati, tabànisati, znjánje, zújati, žȉbati, žȉrati

walk: giljáviti, gréti, ȉđoš, làufati, odbȁštati, ȕ

walk aimlessly: landàrati

walk around barely dressed: svirigùzati

walk away, leave: odgíbati, odgȉljati

walk clumsily: kéljati

walk clumsily and noisily: trapàrati

walk clumsily, stumble along: tetùrati se

walk fast: gùzati, guzèljati, šnírati, štrȉkati

walk for a long time: gajgerírati, izgiljáriti, šȉpčiti, štrapacírati (se), štràpati, žȉpčiti

walk in the prison courtyard: àjncelafale

walk or drive in circles: đȉrati, đirávati

walk quickly: pȉčiti

walk silently: tàpati, tȁpkati

walk slowly, amble: giljáviti, pȅrtlovati se, rakírati, šupèljati

walker (boy who can only get his girlfriend to walk with him): šètāč

walker (person): bàzāč, lȁndri, snjùvara

walking: àutotàbanić, cìpeltrans, fûrka, gíbānje, štrâp, tabànānje

walking for a long time: štrapacírānje

walkman: vòkmen

wall painter: mȍler

wallet: bârka, buđèlār, kàtārka, kèbara, kèbera, lȉsnjāk, lovčànīk, pèkljārka, pètljārka, pètljārnik, pȍva, púla, pûle, sljàjpik, svìnjāk, šlàjpek, šlàjpik, švŕća, takùlīn, tũna[1], žȁhica

wander, roam: ȁjati, bázati, džónjati, lȍdžati, potúcati se[2], prošvŕljati, slobodáriti, smúcati se, švŕljati, zvŕjati, žùljati

wandering, roaming: bázānje, frȅnta

want, wish (in all its meanings in the form different from the standard): ćȅti, stjȅti, tȅti

warning signal: zrȁkoš

warrant: vȉjalica

Wartburg (a make of simple East German car): kȁdilāk, kȁndilāk, varborđînī, varburgînī

wash (in general): làvati

wash one's face: òlanjati, òlanjati se, oligáviti

wash oneself: mòkriti se

wash with soap: safùnjati

washed: ȕmīt

washer (on a bolt): šâjba, šàjbna

waste one's time on unimportant things, fool or mess around: cìcvariti

waste, spend: skȑcati

waste, use (e.g. oil or gas by an engine): gùtati

wasting, using (e.g. of oil or gas by an engine): gùtānje

watch chain: ùlār

watch out, be careful: mȉnfora, minìfora, polìtika[1], škȍjne, zȉpa

watch smuggler: čùkāroš

watch smuggler who pretends to be an American: Amerikánac

watch, clock: čùkāč, čùkalac, čùkalec, čũka, čukárac

watch, look, observe: fȁrkati

watching: šȁcovānje

watching television: téva

watchmaker: čũkadžija, sàjdžija

watchmaker's: čùkara

watchmaker's store: čùkārna

water: cũra, dzũra, džũra, pànija, prȍšlica, víza, zùra

water source: tòčak[2], žùborīšte

water-polo player who stays at adversaries' goal: sìdrāš

watermelon: zèlenā

weak: slȁb, tànak

weak and cowardish female, crybaby: cmȉzdravica

weak and cowardish male, crybaby: cmȉzdravac, cmizdrávko

weak and cowardish person, crybaby: cmȉzdra

weak and irresolute male, wimp: pȅško

weak and irresolute person, wimp: picopévac, pȍsrorēp

weak brandy: bŕlja, tráva, trȁvka, žljóka

weak cow: posròrepa

weak drug: šèrbet

weak female, wimp: posròrepa

weak male, wimp: bokȃčo, dupeprának, jádo [2], mȑcina, pȑna, vòda

weak ox: pȍsrorēp

weak person: frȉkulja, kostúrac, kȕnjos, metiljávko, strȋna, trȍnjavac

weak person, wimp: fȅmka, frȉk [1], razmazánko, šmȍkljos, šmȑkavac, trónja, tùnezga

weak, irresolute: metȉljav, nȁjlōn

weak, lacking physical strength: mȑljav

weak, lacking strength or excellence: blêd

weakly: tànko

wear out (make unusable through long or heavy use): iberȁisovati se, izrȁubovati, rȁubovati

weary (of a male): gȍlokūr

weary: ìspušten

wedding: mamùrluk, spróvod

wedding present: boščȁluk

wedding ring: ȁlka, manđètna, ríngla

weed (the plant): gològuza

week: cvétnica, hèfta, lȁzārka

weekend house: golùbārnīk

weeping, crying: gugùtnjava

weight (usu. body): kiláža, kȉlāžnī

weld: váriti, zȁletovati, zȁšvajsovati

welded: zȁletovān

welding: várēnje

well: brȍdo, hmm, nȅgo, tȃ [1], thȅ, thjȃ, tjȃ

well done: rȇš

well off: sfȉtīljen

well-dressed: drèsīrān, skȍckān

well-played soccer: žnírānje

werewolf: vukòdlak

Western movie: kaubójac

wham (e.g. of a door slammed shot): fȉjūk, zvȉz, zvìzgac

wham, slam: fijùkati, fijúknuti

whamming (e.g. of a door slammed shot): fijùkānje

what (in any of its Serbo-Croatian meanings used in forms different from the standard): čȃ [1], čègā [1], kȃj, šȃ [1], śȃ

what do you want: štȃš [1]

what is going on, what's up: śȃe

wheat: gȍlūbovo, pčènica, šènica

wheel remover (the tool): rȁdapcīger

wheel rim: fȅlga, fȅlna

wheeze: hrípati

wheezing: hȑp, hȑpa, hrípānje

wheezy: hȑpav

when: kȁt

where: dȅ [2], dȉ [2], đȅ

where are you going to: kȕš [2]

where to, where do you want to go: dòklēn, đȅś, kùdē

whey, water left after making cheese: sȕrutka

which (in all its Serbo-Croatian meanings in the form different from the standard one): kàkav, kàkī [2]

whiffle: vȑždati, vȑždeti

whim: kèfa, šȕs

whim, pleasure, fancy: ćȇf, ćȇjf

whip: gájtaniti, kàmdžija

whisky: dȉm [2], vȉskāč

whisper: ćȕćoriti, sašȁptati, sašaptávati, sašaptávati se, šȉštati, šȕškati, śȁnuti, ȕšnuti, zȕc [2], zȕcati, zȕckati

whistle (produce the sound): fićùkati, fȕćkati, fȕćnuti, zvijùkati, zvȉždati, zviždùkati, zviždúknuti, zvȉžđeti, zvȉžnuti

whistle (the instrument): fȕćkalica, pȉfla, zvȉška, zvìždāk [2], zvȉždalica, zvȉždalo, zvȉždāljka

whistle (the sound): fićȕk, zvȉjūk, zvijùkānje, zvìzak, zvîzd, zvȉzga, zvȉzgāj, zvȋžd, zvȉždāj, zvȉždānje, zvȉždūk, zviždùkānje, zvȉžđēnje

whistling: fićùkānje, fȕćkānje, fȕka, zvȉzgav, zvìzgljiv, zvȉždav

whistling bird: zvìždāk [1], zvȉždavac

white plum: mùdara

white-slaver, one who is engaged in white-slave trafficking: dìklāš

who (in all its Serbo-Croatian meanings in the form different from the standard one): kȕj

who (in all its Serbo-Croatian meanings in the form different from the standard): kî [2], kȍj

who knows what: kȕrac [3]

who lost money in gambling: zȁklān

whole, entire: vȁs, vȁscijēlī

whose (in any of its Serbo-Croatian meanings used in forms different from the standard): čèsov

why: šȍ, štô [1], śó

wide buttocks: sinemàskop

wide hips: Tȍd-ÂÔ

wide-eyed female: búlja [1]

wide-eyed male: búlja [2]

wider end of an egg: gùzer, šȍtka

widow: hudòvica, kordaljènica, sfȉnga, svȉnga

widower: kordàljēn

wife: glavòbolja, mànuka, màunka, prìkolica, žènče

wig: pèrikle

wild (temperament, personality, etc.): mùstang

wild grapes: mudòvolja

wild see-saw ride: trȕcke
wildcard person: džȍker
willing: hȍćan, náuman
win: hȁrati, skȉnuti
win at marbles: dúljiti
win in gambling: dȉgnuti
win in gambling or marbles game: odúljiti
win money: ožèniti se
win money from, come out ahead: ȍfuljiti
win some money in gambling: liȕlinuti
win, gain: fȍrka
windbreaker (jacket): vìndjaka, vìnd-jàkna
window: ȍkvīr, pêndžer, pèndžera, prozorȉška, prȍždraka, ždrȁkavac
window blinds: firānga
windshield: šâjba, šȍferšājba, šoferšȁjbna
wine: ardìjān, nápoj, narkóza, ȍrdija, ȍrdijān, ȍrdīn, ȍrdūj, ȍrjan, rèzna, rinfúza, rȕbvīz, rȕša, šantrê, šȍre, ȕrviz, vèritās, vìnčina, vìnčuga
wine drinker: vinȍpija
wine with juice or cola: bàmbus [1]
wine with soda: nȁmeštāj, pišóka, sirànžēr
wine with water: fȉftāč, gȅm, šprȉcer
winter: prȍšlica, víza
winter coat: àmbulja, zimárac, zìmnjāk
wise male: rȉbīzla
wiseguy, smartass: mitèlija
wish happiness: haláliti
wish, hope for: begènisati
witch (the Serbo-Croatian equivalent of bogeyman): babajága, babaróga, babarúga, mètlārka, vljéštac, vljȅštica
with: sə̏s, su [1]
with closed eyes: žmírē, žmúrkē
with respect to: ȍbzīrom
without: brez
without any duties: dȍkon
without any rush, in an elaborate manner, step-by-step (usu. in reference to telling a story): natenáne
without being able to stand it, over one's needs or capabilities: nȁzōr
without enough money, short: kràtak
without hair, hairless: ćȍsav
without teeth, toothless: kȓnjozūb [2]
witness: śèdok
witty: gèniš, gìbak
witty male, clever guy: smjȅško
wolf (the animal): bíša, vlk
wolf cubs: vȕčād
womanizer: pìčkāroš
womanizer, male who frequently changes his sexual partners: kùrvār, kùrviš
wonder, be puzzled: zȉnuti
wonderful, beautiful: đùzel

wooden barrel: kȁca
woodpecker-like: totȑkav
woods, forest: gûstā, ormànjlika, zelènika
wool comb: dȓndalo
wool sock: prìglavak
word: rȉč, rȕska, tȅkst
work (at one's job): dȉtra, svȉrka
work (usu. slowly and ineffectively): žiláviti
work against something or somebody: minírati
work as a prostitute: kamenjáriti, snàlaziti se
work as a street walker: hódati, uličáriti
work bench: bȁnk
work clumsily: petljáriti
work done outside regular working hours, moonlighting: fȕš
work hard (at manual labor): àrbajtovati, àrgatovati, dìrīnčiti, dìrīndžiti, dȓmbati, gúliti, kònjosati, kràmpati, rȉntati, rȉljati, ȑmbati, rudáriti, sèdlati, skàpati, švȉcati, zaluđívati se
work hard (usu. without being rewarded accordingly): cȓnčiti
work hard, bust one's ass: gúziti se
work hard, bust one's balls: okiláviti se
work improperly (of an engine, mechanism, etc.): trokírati
work on something: pȓčkati
work poorly: bŕljati [2], brljáviti
work quickly: pȉčiti, štrȉkati
work slowly: gùslati, petljáriti, pȉmplati, radùckati
work superficially: fušèrisati, fúšeriti
work, labor: àrbajt, bànež, bȁniti, cépati, cȕglati, dȅlati, gìljati, gnjȕriti, hljȅb, kȉčmiti, kȍp [2], kòpati, kȕcati, lavòrati, mravírati, mrljáviti, mùktiti, odvájati, pàplī, pȁpliti, pòsō, proizvòditi, rȁbota, ráditi [2], reumáriti, rȉnta, sȅlpo, stȁjkati, šljȁka, šljakánac, šljakárac, šljakáriti, šljȁkati, štrȕmfovati, vȕskati
workaholism: radoholìzam, vorkaholìzam
worker (usu. manual): bȍškāč, bȍškāć
worker: gìljāč, gȉljos, gȉljotrēs, giljòvān, kòpāč, kùlučār, rȁbotnīk, šljȁkār, šljȁkāroš, šljàkātor, šljȁker
worker who paints pedestrian crossings: zȅbromīr
worker-peasant: polùtān
worm: Indijánac
worry about: brȅnovati, rezíliti, toljàgati
worsen somebody's situation: ukòpati, zakòpati
worst: zàdnjī
worthles or despicable male, bum: píčkonja
worthless: bèzveze, bóza [2], ckȁmnī, čȁbar [3], dîvča [2], fȍrpās [2], ȉzasrān, kȑdža [3], kváran, lèvāk [2], lêvī [1], pìkzibner, pȉšānī, pȉšicav, pȉšičav, pȉšljiv, skȁmnī, trúba [2], ȕsrān
worthless clothing: pȑknci
worthless object: burànija
worthless or despicable female: dȑkadžīјka, gòvnārka, lȕftērka, pizdètina, šalabȁjzerka
worthless or despicable female, shithead: pòsranica, pòsrulja

worthless or despicable group of persons, scum: bȁgra, gȍvnād, govnàdija, govnàrija, jàlija pȍlusvijēt, šljȃm

worthless or despicable person: bânda, baràba, baràpština, bljȕcoš, drȇk[2], dȑkadžija, dȑkāroš, džàbrāk, džŕker, đȉlkoš, đȕbre, džudžovànder, džùkela, fàkīn, faràun, fȅktāroš, flènter, fùnjara[2], Fràncūz, gȃd, glúvac, gnjȉda, golánfer, gòvedo, gulámfer, hȑsuz, hȕlja, jèbivetar, jèbivjetar, jèbivljetar, jébo, jébonja, kònjina, kŕlja[1], ljȉga[2], ljȉgavac, mamojébac, marginálac, mȑljimuda, mùfljūz[1], neandertálac, ničégović, ništačȍvek, ništačȍvjek, nìštāroš, njúška, ȍloš, ȍlošār, palamùdžija, picopévac, pȉčka, pȉčkāroš, pȉs[2], pìzdār, pizdolízac, pósro, propađȍt[1], pròpalca, pròpalica, propalȉtēt, prȍtuha, prȍtuva, pùšikurac, ràjber, ȑsuz, skȍt, smrâd, smrádo, stȑvina, stȕpār, svínja, šalabàhter[2], šalabàjzer, šiljòkurac, šiljokùrān, škȑplja, šȕft, tȋp[1], tìpčina, típus, ȕštva, vàljātor, vȑtigūz, vȑtiguza, zèvzek, žȍhār

worthless or despicable person or group of persons, scum: stȍka

worthless or despicable person, asshole: gúzonjica, guzòser, gùzica, guzotrèsina

worthless or despicable person, dickhead: kurcoglávac

worthless or despicable person, shithead: govnàrčina, góvno[2], govnòćera, govnoglávac, govnogrízac, gȍvnojēd, gȍvnokljūn, gȍvnonoša, góvnonja, gȍvnovālj, gôvnović, gòvnjāk, posrògaća, pòsranīk, pȍsrogūz, posròguza, pósronja, pôsrović, séronja

worthless or despicable person, zero: nȕla

worthless or mean female, bitch: pȉčka, pizdùrina

worthless or mean male, son of a bitch: jèbigūz, pizdètina, pizdùrina

worthless trifle: sràćka, sràćkalica

worthless, low-quality merchandise, junk: ništarȍba[1]

worthless, worth shit: gȍvnen

would-be (desiring) male sexual partner: jȅbūd

wrap: skvŕčiti

wrap or band worn around body to protect kidneys from cold: bùbrežnjāk

wrap, bundle: dènjāk

wrapper, bag: cȅglja

wreck: dȑnda

wrench set: gedóre

wrest from: gràbsti, gràpsti

wrestling: méšānje

wrinkled face: harmònika

write: čȕkati, istrkèljati, istrkèljisati, našárati, šárati, škrábati, tèfteriti

write a letter of reference: šarírati

write down, jot down: ušárati

write in (fill in): ućátiti

write off (e.g. office equipment): ráshodovati

write, scribble: čȑčkati

writer: piskàralo

Yamaha (make of motorcycle): jȁmāč, jȁtnāč

yawn: cupìnati

year: gòdīšće, jȁra, kalèndār, kȕka, kȕkavica, kvȑga, lȁzārka

year in prison: kȕka

yearn for love: sevdàlisati, sèvdisati

yearning for love: sèvdāh

yelp (of a young dog): škamùtati

young: bȁlav, ćȍsav, šȕman, zèlen

young and despicable or worthless person: baràpče

young and immature female: balalàjdērka, balavànderka, bàlavica

young and immature male: balalàjder, bȁlavac, balavànder, bálo[1], bálonja

young Bosnian Muslim female: bùšturica

young boy: bráco[1], piònīr

young dandy: šiljokùrān, šiljòkurac

young donkey: ušȁće

young female with loose morals, jailbait: frȃjlica

young female, girl: cvètīć, čvárak, đèvōjka, jòčkicapinj, kìkīć, lȅš[1], nòkotče, picúrak, pičúrak, piònīrka, pȑcvoljak, pȕter, pȕterica, rȉbica

young goat, kid: kòzle

young inhabitant of the countryside: dèsinče

young lover: prvobórac

young male's penis: Srȅćko

young male, boy, kid: Bòžidār, cìpōv, múlac, plàstičār, žutokljúnac

young mare: bedèvija

young prostitute: čvárak, dáša, gùmbek

young rascal: fìrciger

young sheep: šȉljeg, šȉlježe

young snob: pȑdāč

youngster, kid: ćóso, đećárac, zelèmbāć[1]

youth: balàvurda, balavùrdija, mulàrija

Yugoslav (at present Croatian) Lexicographic Institute in Zagreb, Croatia: Lȅks, Lȅksić

Yugoslav: Jȕgić, Jȕgos, Jȕgović, jȕgovićkī

Yugoslavia: Júga, Jȕgovina

yuppie: Jȁpī

Zastava 101 (a car model): kêc[2], ljèšnjanin, stojàdin, stojàdīnka

Zastava 750 (a car model): ćȍf, fíćo

zero: kròmpīr

zig-zag: felàcati, fȅršati

zipper, fly: dùćān, mésnica, rádnja, šlȉc

zoom (loud noise): zȕm

Zrinski (a brand of Croatian brandy): Zrínjevac

Zvečevo (a brand of brandy): zvèkan